The Rou

South America

ON A BUDGET

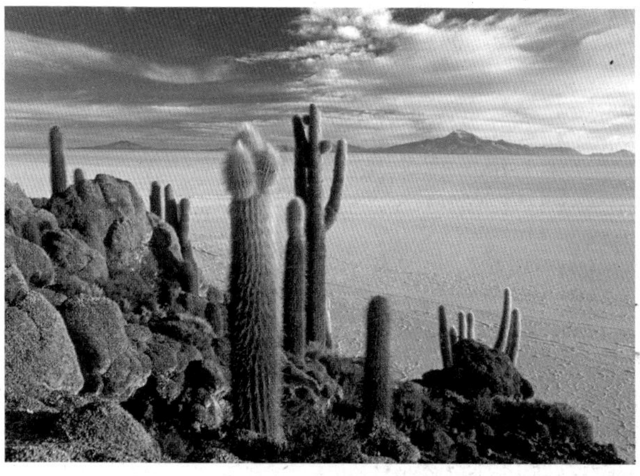

this edition written and researched by

Ismay Atkins, Katy Ball, Arthur Bovino, Martha Crowley, Lucy Cousins, Kiki Deere, Janine Israel, Anna Khmelnitski, Mike Kielty, Heather MacBrayne, Joseph Petta, Paul Smith, Ben Westwood

LONDON • DELHI • NEW YORK

www.roughguides.com

Contents

◂◂ SALAR DE UYUNI, BOLIVIA ◂ INDIGENOUS COFÁN, ECUADOR

NICARAGUA
COSTA RICA
PANAMÁ
CARIBBEAN SEA
Cartagena
Maracaibo
CARACAS
Tobago
Trinidad
Ciudad Bolívar
ATLANTIC OCEAN
VENEZUELA
GEORGETOWN
PARAMARIBO
CAYENNE
Medellín
BOGOTÁ
Gran Sabana
GUYANA
SURINAME
FRENCH GUIANA
COLOMBIA
Cali
QUITO
ECUADOR
Macapá
Equator
Galápagos Archipelago (Ecuador)
Guayaquil
Chimborazo (6310m)
Gulf of Guayaquil
Cuenca
Amazon
Manaus
Belém
Iquitos
Leticia
Tabatinga
Basin
Río Amazonas
Fortaleza
Trujillo
Huascarán (6768m)
Recife
PERU
ANDES MOUNTAINS
LIMA
BRAZIL
Cusco
Trinidad
Salvador
Illimani (6402m)
BOLIVIA
LA PAZ
BRASÍLIA
Santa Cruz
Arica
Sucre
Iquique
Potosí
Belo Horizonte
PARAGUAY
Rio de Janeiro
Antofagasta
Tropic of Capricorn

PACIFIC OCEAN
San Félix [Chile]
San Ambrosio [Chile]
Juan Fernández Islands [Chile]
CHILE
Valparaíso
SANTIAGO
Aconcagua (6959m)
Mendoza
Concepción
Valdivia
Puerto Montt
Isla de Chiloé
Corcovado Gulf
Punta Arenas
ASUNCIÓN
Tucumán
Córdoba
Rosario
BUENOS AIRES
ARGENTINA
Neuquén
PATAGONIA
Puerto Madryn
Comodoro Rivadavia
Strait of Magellan
Tierra del Fuego
Ushuaia
Cape Horn
Drake Passage
Foz do Iguaçu
Puerto Iguazú
São Paolo
Porto Alegre
Paysandú
Lagoa Mirim
URUGUAY
MONTEVIDEO
Río de la Plata
Mar del Plata
Bahía Blanca
ATLANTIC OCEAN
Falkland Islands [Islas Malvinas] [UK]
South Georgia [UK]
South Sandwich Islands [UK]
N
0
1000 km
Metres
5000
4000
2000
1000
500
200
0

Introduction to

South America

Stunning natural beauty, astonishing biodiversity, hedonistic festivals and the ruins of ancient indigenous civilizations are just a few of the attractions that make the South American continent one of the world's most mysterious, surreal and exciting destinations. It's easy to see why thousands of backpackers flock here each year in search of an unforgettable adventure. Among the many wonders the "New World" can boast are the world's largest river and rainforest, the highest waterfall, driest desert, southernmost town and longest mountain range.

The thirteen countries that comprise South America truly offer something for everyone: beach lover, adventure junky, birdwatcher and aspiring archeologist alike. Although the continent as a whole shares a common history based on its original indigenous populations, European colonization, slavery and immigration, all of its countries are fascinating for the differences within their individual borders.

Portuguese-speaking **Brazil**, the largest, most populated country in South America, shares a border with every country in the continent except Chile and Ecuador. There's metropolitan Rio de Janeiro, the exotic colonial city of Salvador, the cultural hub of São Paolo, plus the largest rainforest in the world. While adventure tourists may not flock to **Uruguay**, its relaxed capital, Montevideo, is inviting and Punta del Este's beach resorts are worth checking out, if only briefly by budget-conscious day-trippers. Travellers seeking authenticity should look no further than landlocked **Paraguay**. While not on the average itinerary, the country's Jesuit ruins and national parks offer a glimpse of a South America untrammelled by the twenty-first century.

From sophisticated Buenos Aires to wild Patagonia, rainforest to glacier, and rolling grasslands to the mighty waterfalls of Iguazú, **Argentina** is

Wildlife

South America's stunning array of **wildlife** inhabits an extreme terrain of mountains, tropical rainforests, subtropical cloudforests, deserts and sprawling fertile grasslands. The continent's enormous geographic diversity and proximity to the equator provide endless diverse and isolated habitats where new and unique species are able to evolve. Complex ecosystems such as the untamed and dense rainforest canopy of the **Amazon basin** preserve a wealth of insects, birds, reptiles and mammals. Brazil's **Pantanal** region, the world's largest wetland, and the immense plains of **Los Llanos** in Venezuela are two of the continent's best spots for wildlife-watching, with plenty of opportunities to observe extraordinary concentrations of exotic birds and mammals. The astonishing wildlife of the **Galápagos Islands** played a crucial role in the development of Charles Darwin's theories on evolution and is unsurprisingly one of the continent's biggest attractions.

one of South America's most enticing countries. No less beautiful is **Chile**, home to snowcapped volcanoes, granite towers, Patagonian icefields and the Atacama Desert. **Peru** has a dizzying range of landscapes and archeological sites, including the ancient Inca capital Cusco and the must-see citadel of Machu Picchu. Naturalists should head straight for **Ecuador**'s astounding biodiversity and the Galápagos Islands, home to some of the continent's most unique wildlife.

Away from the crowds, **Colombia** has much to offer, from the nightlife and music of Bogotá to well-preserved colonial Cartagena and Popayán. **Bolivia** is home to Salar de Uyuni, the world's biggest salt lake, the most

PARQUE NACIONAL TORRES DEL PAINE, CHILE

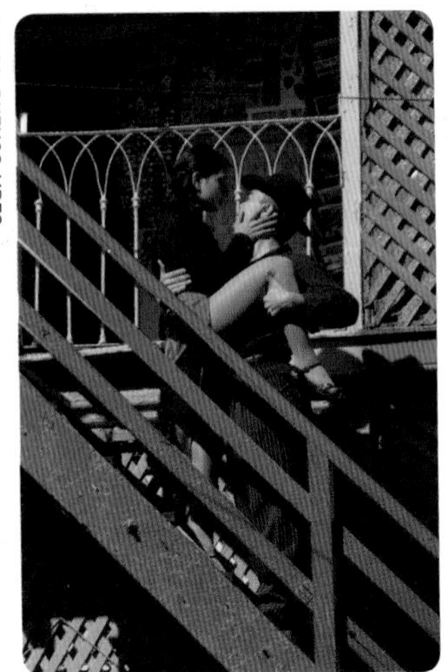
TANGO, BUENOS AIRES

dangerous road and Isla del Sol, said to be the spiritual centre of the Andean world. **Venezuela** boasts gorgeous national parks, some of South America's finest beaches and the Amazon region of Guayana, which includes Angel Falls, the world's tallest waterfall. The comparatively expensive **Guianas**, comprising the former British and Dutch colonies of Guyana and Suriname and the French overseas *département* of French Guyana, are often overlooked. However, their three vibrant capital cities, Georgetown, Paramaribo and Cayenne respectively, are home to colonial wooden architecture in picturesque decay, Dutch bars, good Amazon hiking, deserted prison islands and French cuisine.

Backpackers familiar with Europe's hostels will not find as extensive a network of cheap **lodging** as they are used to, but such accommodations are increasing and there are still plenty of options for the tight budget. South America also boasts some of the best camping and hammock-slinging spots in the world. **Travel** within the continent requires a little patience, initiative and navigating of red tape but colourful bus journeys, budget flights and ferry crossings can often make moving from place to place even more cost-effective. The bottom line is that the resourceful and

Local Food

Forget beans and rice. With more fruits than there are English names for, some of the best pasture-raised beef in the world, and coastal cities with access to excellent fish, the hungry budget traveller will not starve for lack of tasty options. English, Dutch, French, Spanish and Portuguese colonialism translates to a wealth of culinary influences. In addition to this, prominent Italian (Brazil and Argentina), Chinese (Peru and Brazil), Japanese (Brazil), and Vietnamese (French Guyana) communities have brought their palates and also left their mark. There is an overwhelming variety of inexpensive street food, and spicy peppers and sauces ensure that even the blandest offerings can pack an exciting punch. Try Bolivia's *salteñas* (street pasties), Venezuelan *arepas*, *ceviche* in Peru and *roti* in the Guianas. More adventurous eaters may find themselves up to the challenge of *cuy* (grilled guinea pig) in Ecuador, *hormigas culonas* (fried black ants) in Colombia, Guyana *pepperpot* (often made with cow's face) and piranha in the Amazon.

CAPOEIRA, BRAZIL

patient budget traveller can still count on finding great value for money. See our **Ideas** section for more can't-miss destinations, events and activities throughout South America from off-the-beaten-track ruins and eccentric markets to natural wonders and extreme fiestas. Check out our **Itineraries** to help chart the best adventures throughout the continent. Whether you follow these routes or set out on your own, our **Basics** section gives you all the practical information you will need about hostels, guesthouses, immunizations, and border crossings as well as a year planner of the best events. Each chapter within the **Guide** kicks off with a country profile explaining what not to miss, realistic costs for food and accommodation plus information about culture, getting there and away, and safety.

When to go

With about two-thirds of South America near the equator or the tropic of Capricorn, visitors to most destinations can expect a tropical or subtropical **climate** all year round. Temperatures rarely drop below 20° Celsius, while rainforest regions average maximum temperatures of about 30°. As you get further south (and don't forget the southern hemisphere reverses the seasons), you'll find stronger winters from June to August and milder summers from December to February, with the extreme south of the continent very cold between April and October. It's important to plan around the rainy season in each country, particularly when travelling in the Andes. Check the "When to go" information in the Basics section at the start of each country chapter for advice about region-specific weather.

IPANEMA BEACH, RÍO DE JANEIRO

Ideas Markets and festivals

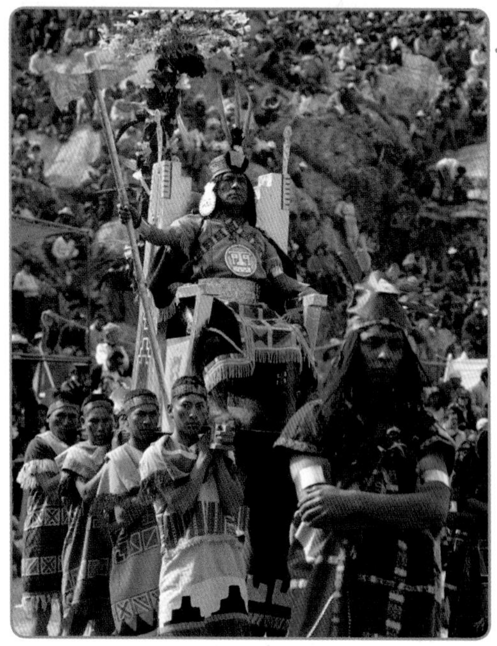

INTI RAYMI, CUSCO, PERU
Honour the sun god at Cusco's lavish and theatrical Inca festival. **See p.798**

SEMANA SANTA, BOLIVIA
Religious processions and rituals to celebrate Holy Week. **See p.189**

RÍO CARNAVAL, BRAZIL Get ready for some serious partying at this legendary bacchanalia. **See p.267**

WITCHES' MARKET, BOLIVIA Herbal remedies, curse-killers, and good luck charms abound. **See p.193**

FERIA DE MATADEROS, ARGENTINA Mingle with gauchos, snack at *parrillas* and peruse local crafts at one of Buenos Aires's most fabulous events. **See p.72**

OTAVALO CRAFTS MARKET, ECUADOR Shop for indigenous ceramics, musical instruments, and loom-woven sweaters at this colourful market. **See p.626**

Ideas Ancient sites and lost cities

EASTER ISLAND, CHILE
Explore this mysterious, remote island known for its enigmatic *moai* statues. **See p.525**

CIUDAD PERDIDA, COLOMBIA
Marvel at the ruins of this lost city of the Tayronas, only rediscovered in 1975. **See p.574**

TIWANAKU, BOLIVIA
This pre-Inca ruined city is considered by some to have been the cradle of Andean civilization. **See p.200**

MACHU PICCHU, PERU Hike the ancient Inca Trail to this precipice-surrounded, awe-inspiring citadel. **See p.836**

NAZCA LINES, PERU These unforgettable shapes and figures are one of the continent's great mysteries. **See p.852**

TILCARA, ARGENTINA A beautiful pre-Inca fortress surrounded by dramatic mountains. **See p.113**

Ideas Outdoor activities

WILDLIFE-SPOTTING, GALÁPAGOS ISLANDS The unique wildlife here inspired Darwin's theory of evolution. **See p.673**

TREKKING IN THE AMAZON BASIN Jungle trek and canoe through the largest rainforest on the planet. **See p.653**

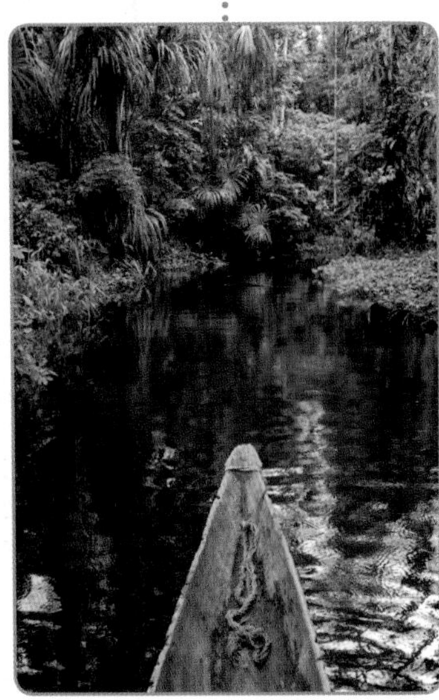

RAFTING THE IGUAÇU FALLS, BRAZIL Get soaked marvelling at these cascading waterfalls. **See p.394**

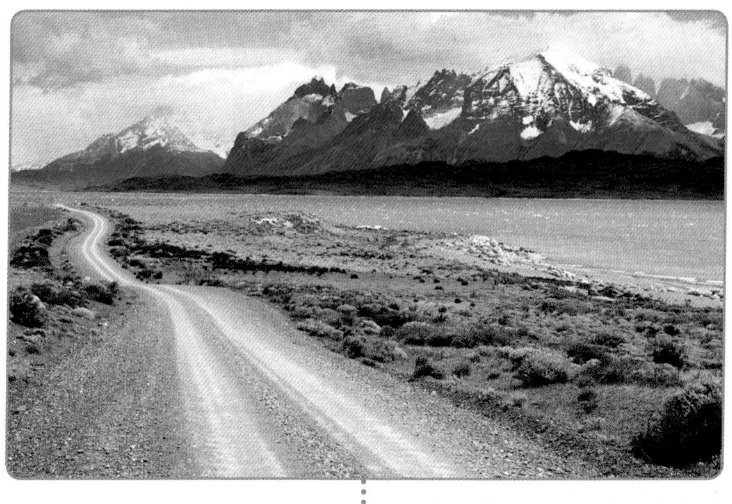

PARQUE NACIONAL TORRES DEL PAINE, CHILE Ice-walk, fly-fish, kayak and mountaineer in this wild and beautiful national park. **See p.515**

BIRD-WATCHING, PARAGUAY Spot spectacular birdlife in the wilderness of the Chaco. **See p.774**

VOLCÁN COTOPAXI, ECUADOR Midnight climb for a sunrise summit of this magnificent, active, Andean volcano. **See p.630**

ITINERARIES

ITINERARIES

South America itineraries

You can't expect to fit everything South America has to offer into one trip – or two or three or four to be fair – and we don't suggest you try. On the following pages a selection of itineraries will guide you through the different countries and regions, picking out a few of the best places and major attractions along the way. For those taking a big, extended trip around the continent you could join a few together, but remember that distances can be vast. There is, of course, much to discover off the beaten track, so if you have the time it's worth exploring smaller towns, villages and wilderness areas further afield, finding your own perfect hilltown, deserted beach or just a place you love to rest up and chill out.

SOUTHERN BRAZIL

❶ **RIO** The beaches, the samba, the towering statue of Christ the Redeemer looming over it all – Rio has every base covered to kick off your trip in style. See p.266

❷ **OURO PETRO** Towns don't come much more attractive than the cobblestone streets and colonial buildings of Ouro Petro. See p.298

❸ **BELO HORIZONTE** A big city that doesn't always feel like one, thanks to its parks and European-style layout. See p.292

❹ **BRASILIA** Come see the vision of the future, circa 1960, courtesy of Oscar Niemeyer's modernist architecture. See p.354

❺ **THE PANTANAL** If you're not going to make it out to the Galapágos during your travels, consider checking out the huge array of wildlife in this vast wetlands. See p.365

❻ **ILHA DE SANTA CATARINA** Some of the best beaches in the country can be found on the coasts near Florianopolis. See p.395

❼ **SERRA GAÚCHA** The mountain bases of Canela and Gramada serve two nearby parks with crashing falls and challenging climbs and hikes. See p.406

NORTHERN ARGENTINA AND URUGUAY

❶ **BUENOS AIRES** The most cosmopolitan of all South American cities, worthy of a few days of anyone's time. See p.66

❷ **COLONIA DEL SACRAMENTO** If you're just going to dip into Uruguay, you can't do better than the historic centre of this charming town. See p.921

❸ **ROSARIO** The perfect spot to launch yourself into the Paraná Delta. See p.92

❹ **CÓRDOBA** Wander from the colonial centre to Nuevo Córdoba, a neighbourhood chock-a-block with cool bars and restaurants in converted mansions. See p.84

❺ **MENDOZA** Undoubtedly the best stop for wine-lovers, a sophisticated city with great restaurants and hundreds of nearby *bodegas*. See p.114

❻ **CERRO ACONCAGUA** Whether you take two weeks to scale the summit or just see a bit on a day-hike, the tallest mountain in the western hemisphere will sear itself in your memory. See p.121

❼ **SALTA** Its central plaza is a lovely place to begin an evening stroll. See p.104

❽ **PARQUE NACIONAL EL REY** The lush cloudforests here hold colourful toucans, as well as other exotic flora and fauna. See p.108

❾ **IGUAZÚ FALLS** Better to see the crashing waters from the trails and catwalks on the Argentina side. See p.101

CHILE AND ARGENTINA: THE LAKE DISTRICTS AND PATAGONIA

❶ **VOLCÁN VILLARICA** Skiing, snowboarding, mountaineering – depending on the season, you can experience the smouldering volcano up close. See p.481

❷ **LAGO LLANQUIHUE** A sparkling blue lake lined with beaches and hemmed in by woods. See p.488

❸ **EASTERN CHILOE** The less-developed side of the archipelago has no major tourist sights, just some low-key villages and some great coastal hiking. See p.494

❹ **SAN MARTÍN DE LOS ANDES** A lower-key version of Bariloche: hub for getting out to the nearby lakes and Parque Lanín. See p.131

❺ **PARQUE NACIONAL NAHUEL HUAPI** Well-marked trails, plentiful campsites and huts, crystal blue lakes and much more make this the most popular Patagonian park on the Argentine side. See p.140

❻ **PENINSULA VALDES** Consider an eastern detour here to see plentiful birdlife, a sea lion colony and – if you time it right – whales on their migration route. See p.148

❼ **PERITO MORENO GLACIER** The unquestioned highlight of Parque Nacional Los Glaciares, a calving glacier that provides theatrical drama for legions of onlookers. See p.163

❽ **PARQUE NACIONAL TORRES DEL PAINE** The most famous destination on the Chilean side of Patagonia – and perhaps the best trekking in the entire region. See p.515

❾ **USHUAIA** If you've made it here you're practically at the end of the world – send a postcard, eat some seafood, ski in winter and dream of Antarctica, 1000km away. See p.165

NORTHERN CHILE AND SOUTHERN BOLIVIA

❶ **SANTIAGO** Not the most dynamic capital city, but a nice enough place to arrive, get oriented and explore some interesting museums and neighbourhoods. See p.425

❷ **VALPARAÍSO** Ride the *ascensores* (funiculars) around the hilly streets by day, then eat, drink and carouse in the gritty port area at night. See p.437

❸ **PISCO ELQUI** This charming village, with views over the Elqui valley, is the perfect place to sample a *pisco* sour. See p.451

❹ **PARQUE NACIONAL NEVADO DE TRES CRUCES** Drive by arid salt flats, spot vicuñas and guanacos and stay by a lake populated with colourful flamingoes. See p.453

❺ **SAN PEDRO DE ATACAMA** There aren't too many sights per se in this pre-Columbian settlement, but it's a perfect jumping off point for *altiplano* wilderness. See p.457

❻ **SLOW TRAIN FROM CALAMA** You could reach Bolivia more easily via Arica, but this is the methodical, scenic route, which winds up in Uyuni. See p.456

❼ **SALAR DE UYUNI** You'll have to go on a tour, but it's worth the trip to see the flat, white salt "lake", perfectly reflective in summer when covered with water. See p.222

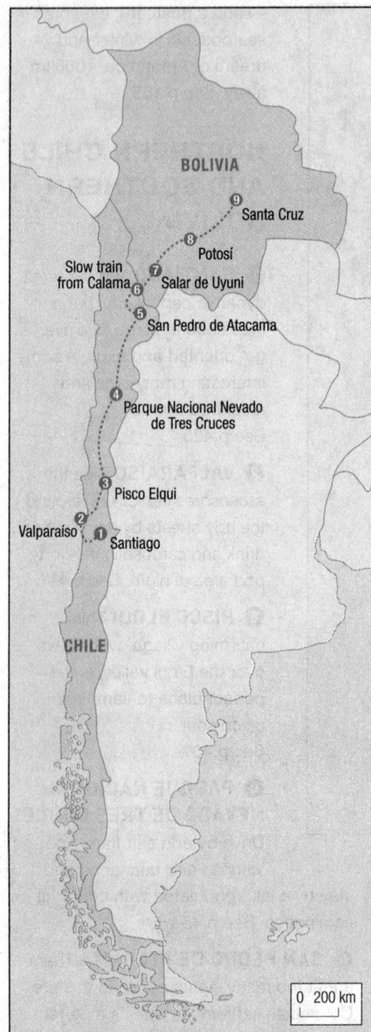

PERU AND NORTHERN BOLIVIA

❶ **LIMA** Love it or hate it, you can nevertheless find plenty to occupy you in the capital, and the proximity to the sea makes it a great place to try out *ceviche*. See p.799

❷ **HUARAZ** This lively city, nestled in a valley, affords you an approach to trekking in both the Cordillera Blanca and Cordillera Huayhuash. See p.871

❸ **INCA TRAIL TO MACHU PICCHU** You'll need to devote the better part of a week to acclimatizing and making the trek, but the lost Inca city at the end is a fantastic reward. See p.834

❹ **CUSCO** As much of a hub as Lima and closer to many of the country's highlights – though its plazas, museums, restaurants and nightlife certainly stand on their own. See p.814

❺ **LAGO TITICACA** Whether you visit the Uros islands on the Peru side or the sacred Isla del Sol in the Bolivian section, you're certain to be awed by the high-altitude lake. See p.871

❻ **LA PAZ** Now this is what an Andean capital city should be: delightfully situated high up in a canyon, full of interesting and inexpensive places to eat, drink and stay and with an undeniable energy all its own. See p.190

❼ **COCHABAMBA** Not the place to go for sightseeing, but a relaxed, unpretentious town good for soaking in the local café scene. See p.232

❽ **POTOSÍ** The colonial architecture and happening cafés are somewhat leavened by the tragic legacy of the nearby silver mines at Cerro Rico. See p.216

❾ **SANTA CRUZ** One of the rare places in Bolivia known for its excellent restaurant and club scene. See p.236

ECUADOR, COLOMBIA AND VENEZUELA

❶ **GUAYAQUIL** An alternative introduction to the country than more

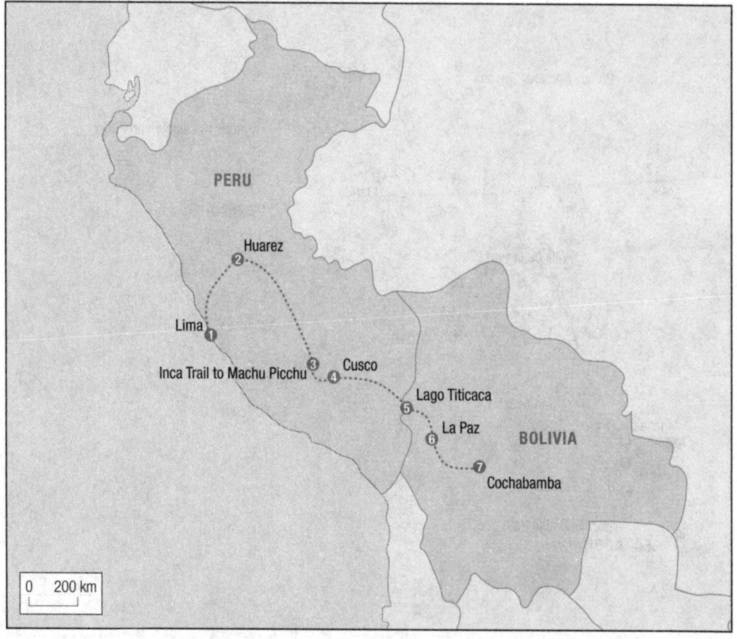

traditional Quito, where the Malecón and nearby beaches make it seem like a different land entirely. See p.661

❷ **NARIZ DEL DIABLO TRAIN RIDE** A five-hour journey starting in Riobamba and slicing its glorious way through Andes. See p.640

❸ **THE QUILOTOA LOOP** Hike for a few days around the peaceful waters of a volcanic crater lake. See p.633

❹ **QUITO** Base yourself in the old town, where plaza after plaza provides a vantage point for historic churches and narrow walkways. See p.615

❺ **MINDO** The ideal lazy resort town to base yourself in for cloudforest adventures. See p.624

❻ **OTAVALO** Few can resist the famous Saturday market the town puts on, the ultimate place to purchase a hammock or woodcarving as a keepsake. See p.626

❼ **SAN AGUSTÍN** A crazy array of monolithic statues, with a lovely mountain landscape serving as as backdrop. See p.598

❽ **CALI** This might be Colombia's most fun and freewheeling city, with plenty of salsa clubs and streetlife to balance out the sober array of museums and churches. See p.590

❾ **VILLA DE LEYVA** A thoroughly unmodern and relaxed spot to be a centre for mountain tourism north of Bogotá. See p.559

❿ **PARQUE NACIONAL TAYRONA** Beautiful beaches, lush flora and pre-Columbian ruins highlight this pristine coastal park. See p.573

⓫ **MÉRIDA** Contemplate adventures to nearby mountains, a trip to wildlife-rich Los Llanos or just enjoy the longest cable-car ride in the world in this relatively laid-back city. See p.968

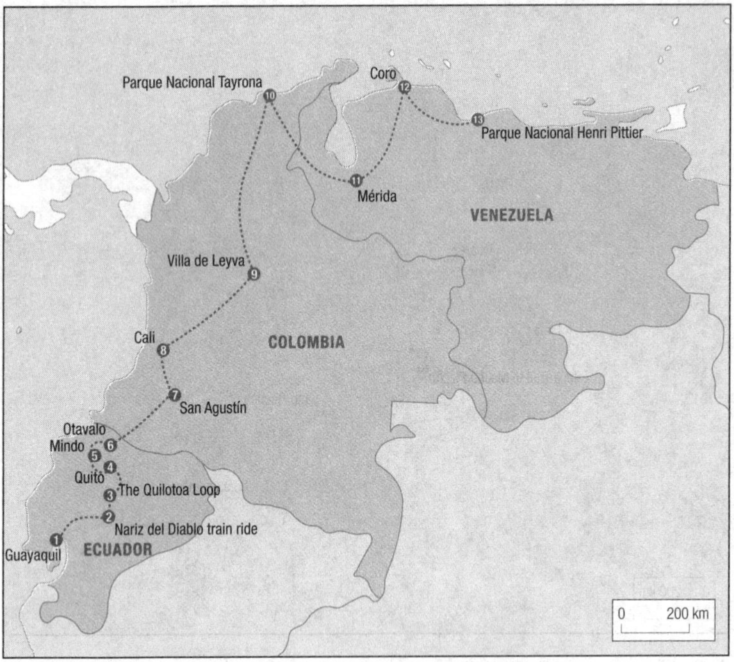

⑫ CORO The loveliest colonial town in Venezuela. See p.964

⑬ PARQUE NACIONAL HENRI PITTIER Another great mix of beaches, wildlife and walking trails, plus it's relatively near Caracas, to make your exit or travel connections an easy job. See p.958

NORTHERN BRAZIL AND THE AMAZON

❶ MORRO DE SÃO PAULO Where to base yourself for the best beaches on Tinharé island: learn how to dive, catch some surf or just relax. See p.319

❷ SALVADOR For *candomblé*, *capoiera* or Carnaval, Bahia's capital is practically the country's capital. See p.308

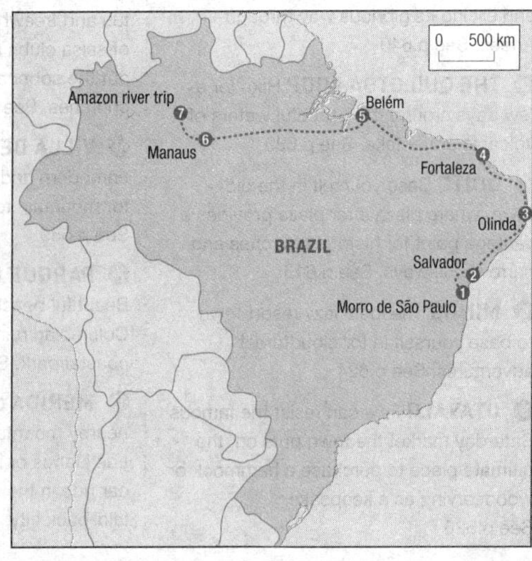

❸ **OLINDA** You won't find a prettier array of churches, plazas and houses anywhere in the north of the country. See p.325

❹ **FORTALEZA** The central market is a sure bet to buy a hammock; take it with you to Jericoara, the best beach in the area. See p.332

❺ **BELÉM** There are some good restaurants and bars, but the main reason to come is its location at the mouth of the Amazon. See p.342

❻ **MANAUS** After seeing its astounding Teatro Amazonas, grab some of the fine street food on offer and head to the lively port area. See p.347

❼ **AMAZON RIVER TRIP** Float along the Rio Negro to a jungle lodge or even just a clearing where you can string up a hammock – or head along the Amazon all the way to Iquitos in Peru. See p.352

BASICS

Basics

Getting there

The easiest way to reach northern South America is by air via the US, usually through a hub such as Houston, Atlanta or Miami, whilst further south in the continent there are direct flights from some European cities to destinations in Brazil and Argentina. The national South American airlines, such as Aerolíneas Argentinas or LanChile, provide a reasonable choice of schedules and routes. Many immigration departments in South America insist that you have an onward or return ticket to enter the country, but the application of such rules is more strict in some countries than in others.

Airfares always depend on the season, with the highest being around July, August and mid-December to mid-January; you'll get the best prices during the dry winter (May, June and late Sept) and the wet summer (Feb–April). Note also that flying on weekends – unless there are only a few flights a week – is usually more expensive.

You can often cut costs by going through a specialist flight agent – either a consolidator, who buys up blocks of tickets from the airlines and sells them at a discount, or a discount agent who, in addition to dealing with discounted flights, may also offer special student and youth fares and a range of other travel-related services such as travel insurance, rail passes, car rentals, tours and the like. Booking flights well in advance, or taking advantage of Web-only offers and airline frequent-flyer programs, can often knock a considerable amount off the price of your flight.

Another way to reduce the price of your South American travels is to book with a tour operator who can put together a package deal including flights and accommodation at a specially arranged price, and perhaps tours as well. If you are starting your flight in mainland Europe – or can get there cheaply from Ireland or the UK – it may be wise to investigate some of the charter flights offered by French airlines. A further possibility is to see if you can arrange a courier flight, although you'll need to be flying from a major city such as New York or London, will require a flexible schedule, and will preferably be travelling alone with very little luggage. In return for shepherding a parcel through customs, you can expect to get a deeply discounted ticket – maybe as little as US$250 to Rio from mainland USA. However, you'll probably be restricted in the duration of your stay.

FROM THE US AND CANADA

Most South American airlines serving North America operate flights from New York or Miami; US airlines tend to fly out of their main hubs, including Delta from Atlanta and Continental from Houston. Flying through or from Miami tends to afford you greater flexibility in travel planning and cheaper prices. There are flights to all major South American cities from at least one of the above. Direct flights from Canada are very limited: it's generally best to transfer at a US hub.

FROM THE UK AND IRELAND

If you book your flight well in advance, flying to South America from the UK can be a bargain. Generally, returning within thirty days of your departure will enable you to find a cheaper fare than if you stay in South America for two or three months. British

FLY LESS – STAY LONGER! TRAVEL AND CLIMATE CHANGE

Climate change is perhaps the single biggest issue facing our planet. It is caused by a build-up in the atmosphere of carbon dioxide and other greenhouse gases, which are emitted by many sources – including planes. Already, **flights** account for three to four percent of human-induced global warming: that figure may sound small, but it is rising year on year and threatens to counteract the progress made by reducing greenhouse emissions in other areas.

Rough Guides regard travel as a **global benefit**, and feel strongly that the advantages to developing economies are important, as are the opportunities for greater contact and awareness among peoples. But we also believe in travelling responsibly, which includes giving thought to how often we fly and what we can do to redress any harm that our trips may create.

We can travel less or simply reduce the amount we travel by air (taking fewer trips and staying longer, or taking the train if there is one); we can avoid night flights (which are more damaging); and we can make the trips we do take "climate neutral" via a carbon-offset scheme. **Offset schemes** run by climatecare.org, carbonneutral.com and others allow you to "neutralize" the greenhouse gases that you are responsible for releasing. Their websites have simple calculators that let you work out the impact of any flight – as does our own. Once that's done, you can pay to fund projects that will reduce future emissions by an equivalent amount. Please take the time to visit our website and make your trip climate-neutral, or get a copy of the *Rough Guide to Climate Change* for more detail on the subject.

www.roughguides.com/climatechange

Airways operates direct flights to both Rio de Janeiro and São Paulo in Brazil and Buenos Aires in Argentina, but fares tend to be more expensive than those of their European and South American rivals. The best value-for-money airline depends on the country you are flying to, but generally taking a flight with a European airline such as Iberia, TAP or Air France, via their main airport in Madrid, Lisbon or Paris, will be the cheapest option.

There are no direct flights from Ireland to South America. If you're trying to keep costs down, consider flying to London, or another European capital, with an economy airline such as Ryanair and making a connection there. Connecting via the US may be more straightforward, and not much more expensive, but bear in mind the hassle of passing through US immigration.

FROM AUSTRALIA AND NEW ZEALAND

Not surprisingly, the best deals to South America are offered by the major South American airlines Aerolíneas Argentinas and LanChile in conjunction with Qantas and Air New Zealand. Aerolíneas Argentinas flies from Sydney to Buenos Aires via Auckland, with connections across the continent; Qantas has code-shares with Varig and LanChile via Auckland to Santiago and beyond.

There are also plenty of flights via the US, but most are not scheduled all the way through to South America and therefore tend to offer much more time-consuming and expensive routings, as each sector has to be priced separately. Often airlines will charge more if you wish to stay in South America for longer than a month.

FROM CENTRAL AMERICA

Crossing overland from Panama into Colombia is not recommended as it entails traversing the Darién, a wild, lawless region occupied by guerrillas with a taste for kidnap and ransom. You should either fly from one of the Central American capitals – Bogotá and Caracas are the main points of entry – or else take a boat from Panama to the Caribbean coast of Colombia. There are no ferry services, but boats can be chartered in Colón and San Blás in Panama en route to Cartagena, Colombia. The journey takes four to six days.

AIRLINES, AGENTS AND OPERATORS

Online booking

www.cheapflights.com (US), www.cheapflights.co.uk (UK & Ireland), www.cheapflights.ca (Canada), www.cheapflights.com.au (Australia & New Zealand). No direct booking, but lists flights and offers from dozens of operators, with web links to most.
www.cheaptickets.com (US). Discount flight specialists.
www.expedia.com (US), www.expedia.co.uk (UK & Ireland), www.expedia.ca (Canada). Discount airfares, all-airline search engine and daily deals.
www.flyaow.com Online air travel info and reservations site.
www.gaytravel.com Gay online travel agent, concentrating mostly on accommodation but with cruises and flight offers too.
www.hotwire.com Bookings from the US only. Last-minute savings of up to forty percent on regular published fares. Travellers must be at least 18 and there are no refunds, transfers or changes allowed. Log-in required.
www.lastminute.com (UK), www.us.lastminute.com (US), www.lastminute.ie (Ireland), www.lastminute.com.au (Australia). Package holiday and flight-only deals available at short notice.
www.priceline.com (US). Name-your-own-price auction website that has deals at around forty percent off standard fares, as well as a regular flight-finder. Be sure to check the terms before bidding.
www.skyauction.com (US). Auction tickets and travel packages using a "second bid" scheme. The best strategy is to bid the maximum you're willing to pay, since if you win you'll pay just enough to beat the runner-up regardless of your maximum bid.
www.travelocity.com (US), www.travelocity.co.uk (UK & Ireland), www.travelocity.ca (Canada). Destination guides, hot web fares and deals for car rental, accommodation and lodging.
www.travelonline.co.za (SA). Discount flights and information from South Africa.
www.zuji.com.au (Australia). Now part of Travelocity (see above), with the same destination guides and deals.

Airlines

Aerolíneas Argentinas US ⓣ1-800/338 0276 or 305/648 4100, Can ⓣ1-800 688 0008, UK ⓣ0800/0969 747. Australia ⓣ02/9234 9000, NZ ⓣ09/379 3675; www.aerolineas.com.ar.
Air Canada Canada ⓣ1888/247 2262, www.aircanada.ca.
Air Europa UK ⓣ0870/240 1501, www.aireuropa.co.uk. London to Spain, Spain to Latin America.
Air France UK ⓣ0845/084 5111 or 0870/142 4343, Republic of Ireland ⓣ01/605 0383; www.airfrance.co.uk, www.airfrance.ie.
Air New Zealand Australia ⓣ13/2476, NZ ⓣ0800/737000 or 09/357 3000; www.airnz.co.nz.
Alitalia UK ⓣ0870/544 8259, www.alitalia.co.uk.

AIR PASSES AND ROUND-THE-WORLD TICKETS

If you intend to take in South America as part of a world trip, a round-the-world (**RTW**) ticket offers the greatest flexibility – and if your starting point is Australia or New Zealand, it may even be cheaper. Many international airlines are now aligned with one of two globe-spanning networks: "Star Alliance", which includes Air New Zealand, Lufthansa, SAS, Singapore Airlines, Thai, Varig and Air Canada; or "One World", which combines routes run by American, British Airways, Cathay Pacific, Iberia, LanChile and Qantas, among others. Fares depend on the time of year, your point of origin, the class you fly and the number of continents or the distance you travel, and in general only the more expensive options include South America, but they are definitely worth exploring.

If you plan to do a fair amount of travelling within South America think about buying an **airpass** with your main ticket. These passes offer substantial savings, but can be bought only outside South America when you buy an international ticket. See p.37 for more information.

American Airlines ⓣ1-800 4333 7300, ⓦwww.aa.com.

Avianca US ⓣ1-800/284-2622, ⓦwww.avianca.com; UK ⓣ0870/576 7747, ⓦwww.avianca.co.uk. Colombia, from the US and Spain.

British Airways UK ⓣ0844/493 0787, Ireland ⓣ1890/626 747; ⓦwww.britishairways.com

Caribbean Airlines UK ⓣ0870/774 7336, US & Canada ⓣ1-0800/920-4225; ⓦwww.caribbean-airlines.com. Flights to Suriname and Guyana via the Carribbean.

Continental Air Lines US ⓣ1-800/231-0856, UK ⓣ0800/028 3687, Republic of Ireland ⓣ1850 882031;ⓦwww.continental.com.

Delta Airlines US ⓣ1-800 525 3663, UK ⓣ0845/6072 6750, Ireland ⓣ1850/88 201 or 01/407 3165.

Iberia Airlines UK ⓣ0870/609 0500, Republic of Ireland ⓣ0818/46 2000; ⓦwww.iberiaairlines.co.uk.

KLM UK ⓣ08705/074074, Ireland ⓣ1850/747 400; ⓦwww.klmuk.com.

LANChile US ⓣ1-866 435 9526, UK ⓣ0800/977 6100, Australia ⓣ1800/22 1572; ⓦwww.lanchile.com.

Lloyd Aéreo Boliviano US ⓣ1-800/337-0918, ⓦwww.labairlines.com.

Northwest US ⓣ1-800/225-2525, ⓦwww.nwa.com.

Qantas Australia ⓣ13/1313, NZ ⓣ09/357 8900 or 0800 808 767; ⓦwww.qantas.com.au.

TAM UK ⓣ0118/903 4003, ⓦwww.tam.com.br. Flights from London to Brazil.

TAP Air Portugal UK ⓣ0845/601 0932, Republic of Ireland ⓣ01/814 7378; ⓦwww.tap-airportugal.co.uk

United Airlines US ⓣ1-800/538-2929, UK ⓣ0845/844 4777; ⓦwww.united.com.

Varig US ⓣ1-800/468-2744, UK ⓣ0870/120 3020, Australia ⓣ02/9244 2179, NZ ⓣ09/379 4455, ⓦwww.varigbrasil.com.

Agents and operators

The following are either student and youth specialists, or experts in South American travel.

US and Canada

Above the Clouds ⓣ1-800/233-4499 or 802/482-4848, ⓦwww.aboveclouds.com. Hiking specialists featuring trips to Patagonia.

Adventure Center ⓣ1-800/228-8747 or 510/654-1879, ⓦwww.adventurecenter.com. Hiking and "soft adventure" specialists with trips deep into most South American countries as well as the Galápagos Islands.

Backroads ⓣ1-800/462-2848 or 510/527-1555, ⓦwww.backroads.com. Cycling, hiking and multi-sport tours to Argentina, Ecuador and the Galápagos Islands, Chile and Peru.

Educational Travel Center ⓣ1-800/747-5551 or 608/256-5551, ⓦwww.edtrav.com. Student/youth discount agent.

Mountain Travel Sobek ⓣ1-888/MTSOBEK or 510/594-6000, ⓦwww.mtsobek.com. Hiking trips to Suriname, Peru, Chile, Argentina, Bolivia and Ecuador.

Nature Expeditions International ⓣ1-800/869-0639 or 954/ 693-8852, ⓦwww.naturexp.com. Varied educational adventure vacations to most of the region.

REI Adventures ⓣ1-800/622-2236, ⓦwww.rei.com/travel. Climbing, cycling, hiking, cruising, paddling and multi-sport tours to many countries in the continent.

STA Travel US ⓣ1-800/781-4040, Canada 1-888/427-5639; ⓦwww.sta-travel.com. Worldwide specialists in independent travel; also student IDs, travel insurance, car rental, rail passes, etc.

Travel Cuts Canada ⓣ1-800/667-2887, US ⓣ1-866/246-9762; ⓦwww.travelcuts.com. Canadian student-travel organization.

Worldtek Travel ⓣ1-800/243-1723, ⓦwww.worldtek.com. Discount travel agency for worldwide travel.

Wilderness Travel ⓣ1-800/368-2794 or 510/558-2488, ⓦwww.wildernesstravel.com. Adventure travel and wildlife tours throughout South America.

UK and Ireland

Apex Travel Ireland ⓣ01/241 8000, ⓦwww.apextravel.ie. Specialists in flights to all countries in South America.

Dragoman UK ⓣ01728/861133, ⓦwww.dragoman.co.uk. A range of South American overland trips, including a new line with all accommodation in hotels rather than in tents.

Journey Latin America UK ⓣ020/8622 8470, ⓦwww.journeylatinamerica.co.uk. Knowledgeable and helpful staff, good at sorting out stopovers and open-jaw flights. Also does package tours.

Kumuka Expeditions UK ⓣ0800/068 0855, ⓦwww.kumuka.co.uk. Responsible tourism, extensive overland tours and adventure packages.

Last Frontiers UK ⓣ01296/653000, ⓦwww.lastfrontiers.com. Very knowledgeable Latin America specialists with a wide range of tailor-made tours.

North South Travel ⓣ01245/608291, ⓦwww.northsouthtravel.co.uk. Friendly, competitive travel agency, offering discounted fares worldwide – profits are used to support projects in the developing world, especially the promotion of sustainable tourism.

South American Experience ⓣ0845/277 3366, ⓦwww.southamericanexperience.co.uk. Mainly a discount flight agent but also offers a range of tours, plus a very popular "soft landing package", which includes a couple of nights' accommodation and airport transfer on arrival.
STA Travel UK ⓣ020/8998 2931 or 020/8997 1378, ⓦwww.statravel.co.uk. Low-cost flights and tours for students and under-26s, though other customers welcome.
Trailfinders UK ⓣ020/7628 7628, ⓦwww.trailfinders.co.uk; Republic of Ireland ⓣ01/677 7888; ⓦwww.trailfinders.ie. One of the best-informed and most efficient agents for independent travellers.
Travel Cuts UK ⓣ020/7255 2082, ⓦwww.travelcuts.co.uk. Canadian company specializing in budget, student and youth travel, and round-the-world tickets.
Trips Worldwide ⓣ0117/311 4400, ⓦwww.tripsworldwide.co.uk. "Alternative" tailor-made holidays to Latin America include rainforests, culture, birdwatching and plenty of activities. The website lets you create your own itinerary.
usit NOW Republic of Ireland ⓣ01/602 1906, Northern Ireland ⓣ028/9032 7111; ⓦwww.usitnow.ie. Student and youth specialists for flights and overland adventure.

Australia and NZ

Adventure Associates Australia ⓣ02/8916 3000, ⓦwww.adventureassociates.com.au. Tours and cruises to South America, including the Amazon and Galápagos.
Adventure World Australia ⓣ02/8913 0755, ⓦwww.adventureworld.com.au; New Zealand ⓣ09/524 5118, ⓦwww.adventureworld.co.nz. Agent for a vast array of international adventure travel companies.
Austral Tours Australia ⓣ1800/620833 or 03/9370 6621, ⓦwww.australtours.com. Central and South American specialist covering the region from Ecuador to Easter Island and Tierra del Fuego, with special tours to Machu Picchu and the Amazon.
Australian Andean Adventures Australia ⓣ02/9299 9973, ⓦwww.andeanadventures .com .au. Trekking specialist for Argentina, Peru, Bolivia and Chile.
Budget Travel New Zealand ⓣ09/366 0061 or 0800/808040, ⓦwww.budgettravel.co.nz. Established airfare discounter.
Flight Centre Australia ⓣ02/9235 3522, ⓦwww.flightcentre.com.au; New Zealand ⓣ0800/243 544, ⓦwww.flightcentre.co.nz. Nationwide branches with competitive discounts on airfares.
Kumuka Expeditions Australia ⓣ1300/667277 or 02/9279 0491, ⓦwww.kumuka.com.au. Independent tour operator specializing in overland expeditions, as well as local and private transport tours.
Latin Link Adventure New Zealand ⓣ03/525 9945, ⓦwww.latinlink.co.nz. "Semi-independent" adventure tours to Latin America.
STA Travel Australia ⓣ134 782, ⓦwww.statravel.com.au; New Zealand ⓣ0800/474400, ⓦwww.statravel.co.nz. Fare discounts for students and under-26s, student cards and travel insurance.
Student Uni Travel Australia ⓣ02/9232 8444, ⓦwww.sut.com.au; New Zealand ⓣ09/379 4224, ⓦwww.sut.co.nz. Student/youth discounts and travel advice.
Trailfinders Australia ⓣ02/9247 7666, ⓦwww.trailfinders.com.au. Independent travel advice, good discounts on fares.

Getting around

Most South Americans travel by bus, and there is almost nowhere that you can't reach in this way. The major routes are comfortable and reliable and buses are always cost-effective transport as well. Moreover you will see more, and meet more people, both locals and fellow travellers, if you travel by bus. Remember, though, that distances between towns can be huge, and that in more remote areas such as Patagonia there are few bus and no train services. If you have a little spare cash and limited time, you may want to fly occasionally, or hire a car to explore at leisure. There are frequent flights within and between South American countries: check out the air-passes detailed on p.37, which can offer great value for money if used to the full.

BY BUS

Buses are the primary mode of transport for South Americans and are by far the cheapest – if not the most time efficient – way to see the continent. While you can technically travel all the way from the tropical north of the continent to Tierra del Fuego by bus, there are few direct international services and you will usually have to disembark at the border, cross it, then get on another bus to a large city in the new country, from where you can travel pretty much anywhere within that country. The process is repeated at most border crossings – it's not a particularly expedient way to travel, but it is by far the least expensive.

Terminals are usually situated somewhat out of town – follow the signs to the *terminal* (in Spanish-speaking countries) or the *rodoviária* (in Brazil). Levels of comfort vary, so a quick visual check in the terminal will give you an idea which company to go for. With better bus companies on long-distance routes the seating options usually include: normal seats, seats that partly recline and "cama" seats that recline fully to become beds. They are priced according to the level of comfort. Some of the cheapest companies only have one level of comfort and that can mean anything from wooden seats to springs in the backside or standing in an aisle!

BY CAR

South American roads, especially outside the major cities, are notorious for their bumpy, pothole-riddled and generally poor conditions. Most car rental companies in South America do not allow their vehicles to be driven across borders, or permit very restricted border crossing only, making independent exploring of the whole continent by car difficult.

If you are determined to go it alone and drive around South America, you will find car hire companies at all airports and in most major cities. Hotels should be able to alert you to better-value local places, but often you can get a reasonable deal by booking far enough in advance and over the Internet. Costs are high due to skyrocketing insurance rates, but the independence granted you by a car may be worth it. Be sure to check your insurance carefully for exclusions, as car theft, vandalism and general security are renowned problems in some parts of South America, especially Argentina and Brazil, and you may not be covered for these. Damage to tyres or the underside of the car may also be excluded. Rental charges vary from

EXPERIENCE
OASIS
SCANIA
the Adventure
TRIPS FROM
15 DAYS TO 15 WEEKS
Overland Expeditions
across South America
& Small Group
Adventures in Peru
OASIS
OVERLAND
www.oasisoverland.com
+44(0)1963 363400

QUALITY TRAVEL & TOURS
TO PERU, ECUADOR,
BOLIVIA, ARGENTINA, CHILE
AND BRAZIL
We have a price guarantee and the best
testimonials in the market.
INTERNATIONAL 1-817-230-4971
USA (toll-free) 1-877-269-0309
UK 44-203-002-0571
www.peruforless.com
www.argentinaforless.com
Peru for Less
BUILDING MAGICAL MEMORIES

south
america
on the
go
escorted groups and tailormade holidays
triple AAA bonded!
onthegotours.com
68 North End Road, West Kensington, London W14 9EP
020 7371 1113
Phone for our FREE colour brochure

SOUTH AMERICA
Bespoke soft
adventure trips for
the more independent
& adventurous traveller
• Cities - Rio de Janeiro,
Buenos Aires & Quito
• Wilderness, wetlands,
beaches & waterfalls
• Character hotels
• Archaeological
sites & deserts
• Galápagos
& Andes
www.sunvil.co.uk
020 8758 4774
AITO
TRUST
Sunvil
LATIN AMERICA

country to country and depend on the model of car. You will be required to present a credit card and an International Driving License or an Inter-American Driving Permit will be useful to back up your licence from back home (though rarely a legal requirement).

A certain machismo reigns here, so beware other drivers, especially at night. When driving in hilly or twisty terrain, a good rule of thumb seems to be to honk your horn before going round any corner – the locals do this with great gusto, so rest assured that no one will find you rude. South Americans drive on the right **except** in Suriname and Guyana.

BY AIR

If you plan to be doing a fair amount of travelling around Latin America, you might want to consider one of the reasonable airpasses on offer in the region. These are a godsend if you want to see as much as possible in a limited time, and – given the size of the continent – can make all the difference between arriving at your destination exhausted and frayed and arriving fresh and ready to explore.

The **All America Airpass** (ⓦwww.allairpass.com) is valid for ninety days and offers special fares throughout Latin America on more than thirty airlines. It comprises individual segment passes that combine to make a multi-sector trip up to a value of US$1800, although you can just buy one sector if you so desire. The passes are only available to travellers with a scheduled international return ticket and must be bought in the traveller's country of origin. After you have used the first sector on your pass the ticket is non-refundable. Remember that many Latin American countries charge a departure tax when leaving their airports on international flights – this tax is payable locally and is not included in the airpass price.

The **Mercosur Airpass** covers travel in and between Argentina, Brazil, Chile, Paraguay and Uruguay. Prices are calculated on a miles-flown basis, regardless of how many countries you visit. There is a maximum of two stopovers and four flight coupons for each country, and the pass is valid for a minimum of seven and a maximum of thirty days. The pass offers substantial reductions on standard air travel in the continent and is available directly from the participating airlines, VARIG, Aerolíneas Argentinas, Aerolineas del Sur and PLUNA. You can rebook to change dates (but not reroute); for more information see ⓦwww.latinamerica.co.uk/mercosur_airpass.htm. Both LAN Chile and TAM airlines also offer their own, slightly cheaper air passes for the routes that they fly.

BY TRAIN

Trains are much less frequent and efficient than South American buses, but if you have a little time to spare they provide a wonderful way to see the countryside and wildlife, as they tend to travel much more exotic routes than the more functional buses. Typically they are less expensive than the buses, but services aimed specifically at tourists, or those used mainly by tourists can be pricey. Two of the most famous and picturesque routes used by tourists are the track from Cuzco to the start of the Inca Trail in Peru and the breathtaking Serra Verde Express between Curitiba and the coast in Brazil. There are several types of train, including the fast and efficient *ferrotren*, stopping at major stations only; the average *tren rápido*; the slower *expreso*, which stops at most stations; and the super-slow and amazingly cheap *mixto*, which stops for every Tom, Dick and Harry – and their livestock too.

BY BOAT

There are several ferry and catamaran services providing travel on South America's **lakes**, especially those in Chile, Argentina, Peru and Bolivia, allowing some of the finest scenic experiences in the region. Those relevant to a single country are explored in the country chapter but there are two cross-border crossings that are particularly recommended: the Southern Lakes Crossing (see p.491) between Argentina and Chile and the Lake Titicaca Crossing (p.183) between Bolivia and Peru.

One of the finest ways to soak in South American atmosphere and get a taste for the slowed-down pace of life is to travel some of the continent's **rivers** by boat. Unfortunately, the riverboat industry is one in decline, especially on the Amazon, as increased air services have facilitated speedier transportation for the time-pressed but moneyed traveller, and cargo-only tugs have brought about the demise of several passenger-friendly services. For the time being, though, several riverboat services survive, and this is a recommended activity for anyone with the time and patience for the slow life, particularly on the narrower, less-frequented rivers. One rule of thumb is to shop around, as boats vary hugely in quality and you want to be sure that you will have a reasonably decent home for the next four to ten days. Your ticket will include hammock space and rudimentary food, but beverages are extra and will probably be expensive on board – it's best to bring your own supplies. You should also bring a hammock, rope, insect repellent, a sleeping bag (it gets cold) and aim to be on board well before departure to ensure that you don't get the hammock space right next to the toilets.

BY BICYCLE

If you're fit and hardy enough to consider cycling in South America – and it certainly is a beautiful way to see the land – there are a few common-sense rules to follow before you go. Given the nature of the terrain, a mountain bike is invariably best, unless you're planning to stick to paved roads and well-travelled routes, in which case a (good quality) touring or road bike would suffice. Bikes and bike parts tend to be of a lesser quality in South America than in other parts of the world, so it's a good idea to bring your own bicycle and to give it a thorough maintenance overhaul before you go, carry a basic repair kit and to check your machine daily when you arrive. Weather can be a problem, especially in Patagonia, where winds can reach 50mph, and be aware that bicycle theft – particularly in larger towns and cities – is common; bring a good bike lock.

Finally, remember that South American drivers can be a hazard, so try to avoid major roads and motorways if at all possible. In adventure travel centres, especially in Argentina and Chile, bikes can be hired.

HITCHHIKING

Hitchhiking is still fairly common in rural South America, and you shouldn't find it too hard to get a ride with a truck driver or another morning traveller if you're on the road early enough. Be aware, though, that an annoying sidebar to the availability of rides means that many drivers now expect to be paid for their services – it's only in the Southern Cone that hitchhiking seems to be understood to be free. Prices are usually around that of a bus fare, but if you head to the local truck park or refuelling station (most towns have one), you can ask around to get a good idea of the going rate. Hitchhiking in South America, like anywhere in the world, is a potentially perilous enterprise – travellers should be aware that they do so at their own risk. Couples and groups are safest; women should never, ever, hitchhike alone.

Accommodation

The range of accommodation available in South America – and the variety of price and quality that goes with it – is enormous and, should you be leaving on a multi-country tour, you'll find that the US$8 that buys you a night's rest in Ecuador won't even stretch to breakfast in the Southern cone or French Guiana.

Most local tourist offices will happily provide a list of available accommodation but bear in mind that establishments often have to pay to be included on these lists and that they may include little outside the main tourist hotspots. Generally, tourist boards will not recommend specific accommodation, nor will they book it for you. The Internet is a great place to look for accommodation choices in advance, as you can often check out rates, photographs of properties and rooms, and special offers and amenities before you decide on a place.

Usually there is no shortage of places to stay, but use common sense if you plan to be somewhere at the time of a local festival, such as in Rio for Carnaval. Obviously, accommodation fills up really quickly at these times, prices skyrocket and it's best to book accommodation well in advance.

While the types of lodging described below offer an overview of your options in Latin America, names, classifications and prices vary from country to country. For information regarding the nomenclature in a specific country, check the "Accommodation" section of the relevant chapter.

HOSPEDAJES, RESIDENCIAS, ALBERGUES AND PENSIONES

These categories of accommodation are all used throughout South America, and are pretty much interchangeable terms although *pensiones* (known as *pensoes* in Portuguese) and *residenciales* are officially the most basic forms of accommodation. Generally, the Andean countries are the least expensive, and you should be able to find a decent *residencial* or *pensión* for under US$8. For this price you should expect a bed and maybe a desk and chair, but little else – you will have to share a bathroom, and the water may or may not be hot, or may be hot for just a few hours a day. In Brazil, the room cost will usually include breakfast but most other places are room only. In the south of Argentina and Chile, you can expect to spend around US$40 a night – check out the quality of the local *casas familiares* (family houses where you stay with a local family in a room

BASICS ACCOMMODATION

in their house), which can be the best value for money in these areas.

HOSTALES, HOTELES, HOSTERÍAS AND HACIENDAS

Hostales tend to fill the gap between the totally basic *pensión* and the rather more classy hotel and come in many architectural shapes, sizes and forms. Usually they include private bathrooms and hot water, clean towels and maybe a television and cost from $5 to $20/night. In the southern countries, though, *hostales* may be youth hostels.

Hosterías and *haciendas* are lovely examples of South American architecture, often old, sprawling estates converted into hotels in the middle of nowhere, and are perhaps the grandest places to stay in the continent. They are often furnished in period style and offer excellent home-cooked meals, fires and hot water and maybe a swimming pool. Be aware that *hostería* can also refer to a family-style hotel complex out of town, usually an anything-but-charming experience – be sure to check which kind of *hostería* you're getting first.

CAMPING

Camping is most popular in the southern region of Latin America, particularly in the cone areas of Argentina and Chile.

It is wise to stick to official sites that are usually well equipped, with hot, running water, toilets, firepits and maybe even a laundromat. Camping is not really a popular or viable option in the northern countries, and is practically nonexistent in Colombia, French Guiana and Paraguay.

YOUTH HOSTELS

Youth hostels are not usually the cheapest or most viable option in South America, but they do exist in some areas and can be an excellent place to meet other young travellers. In the more expensive southern countries, especially Argentina and Chile, they become a more attractive option: here competition means that many of them have great facilities and offer all sorts of extras, from free Internet to party nights. Prices average around US$8 to 15 a night and most hostels are open year round, although some only open in January and February, for the South American summer. The IYHF has hostels in Argentina, Brazil, Chile, Colombia

ACCOMMODATION PRICE CODES

Throughout the guide all accommodation is coded on a scale of ❶ to ❾, which is outlined below. For places with dorms and for campsites the code indicates the cost of a bed or tent space (though these are usually quoted in local currency), for hotels and guesthouses the cheapest private double room. All codes represent high-season prices; when a price range is indicated, it means that the establishment offers a variety of services – as indicated in the listing. Note that many, but not all, establishments in South America quote prices per person rather than per room – always check this. And remember too that prices should be lower out of peak times; it's always worth asking if a better rate is available.

❶ up to US$5	❹ US$16–25	❼ US$56–70
❷ US$6–10	❺ US$26–40	❽ US$71–90
❸ US$11–15	❻ US$41–55	❾ US$90+

(Bogotá only), Peru and Uruguay. If you are planning on using hostels extensively, an official HI card will very quickly pay for itself in discounted rates.

Hostelling organizations

Argentina Hostelling International Argentina/Red Argentina de Alojamiento para Jóvenes (RAAJ), Florida 835, piso 3, Buenos Aires ⓣ011/4511-8723, ⓦwww.hostels.org.ar.

Brazil Federação Brasileira dos Albergues de Juventude (FBAJ) Río de Janeiro R da Assambleia 10, room 1211, ⓣ(21)2531-1085, ⓦwww.hostel.org.br.

Chile Asociación Chilena de Albergues Turísticos Juveniles, Hernando de Aguirre 201, Providencia, Santiago ⓣ02/233-3220, ⓔachatj@hostelling.co.cl.

Peru Asociación Peruana de Albergues Turísticos Juveniles Av Casimiro Ulloa 328, Miraflores, Lima ⓣ014/446-5488.

Hostelling International ⓦwww.hihostels.com. Membership cards and worldwide hostel booking.

Culture and etiquette

South America is a vast continent of huge contrasts and each country has its own attitude to what is acceptable socially. It is difficult to generalize about how to dress or behave, and ultimately you should take your cue from your surroundings. Try to blend in with the behaviour of the locals, behave unobtrusively and dress modestly if you are not at the beach.

CULTURAL HINTS

There are certain rules you should observe while travelling to ensure that you don't distress or offend local populations. Remember that you will be seen to be in a position of privilege (you could afford to come here, after all) and that you should **respect** rather than abuse local customs, habits and hospitality.

People generally shake hands upon introduction throughout the continent, and express pleasure at having made the acquaintance – no matter how briefly – of others. It is common to wish people you meet on the street "*Buenos días*" ("*bom dia*" in Brazil) or "*buenos tardes*" ("*boa tarde*" in Brazil). Politeness is generally a way of life in South America, and pleasantries are always exchanged before getting to any kind of business. You should also be polite to street vendors, no matter how annoyed you get with their peddling of their wares. Remember that this is their livelihood and smile, saying "*no, gracias*" or "*não, obrigado*", but if you decide to buy something, remember also to be firm – ask the price and then confirm it before proffering any cash. Dress with respect in official or religious buildings.

CRAFTS AND MARKETS

Shops and markets in South America tend to offer a wide range of beautifully crafted goods and antiques for the visitor. Prices are usually very reasonable; you can bargain in markets and outside the main tourist drags, but only do so if you really think the item is worth less than its asking price. Make sure to check that you are not purchasing objects that have been plundered from the jungle or that are made from endangered species – remember, tourism can harm as well as help.

Each country – and many regions – have their own specialities in the marketplace. As a rule of thumb, native crafts are usually of the best quality – and cheapest – when bought close to the source. Buying such items, rather than mass produced alternatives, is a good way to help local *artesania* and give something back to the communities you're visiting.

PUBLIC HOLIDAYS AND FESTIVALS

Travelling through South America entails negotiating a variety of public holidays that change from country to country. The essential ones are listed in the "Opening hours and public holidays" section of each chapter, but bear in mind that, particularly in more remote areas, some towns and villages celebrate saints' days and other local holidays that shut down businesses and make travel difficult. Check with local tourist information offices (where they exist) for more details. South Americans are not known to shy away from an excuse to celebrate, and we have included the finer festivals in the relevant chapters.

Every country in Latin America has some form of **carnival** (known in Spanish and Portuguese as *Carnaval*); the exact time varies, but the official celebrations usually take place on the days before Ash Wednesday and Lent, with the months and weeks beforehand almost as lively as excitement fills the air. There are national variations of course: in Ecuador, for instance, the festivities are most visibly represented by the water fights taking place everywhere in the country. There are a couple of locations where Carnaval has become famous internationally such as Oruro in Bolivia and Encarnación in Paraguay. The most famous Carnaval of all, however, takes place in Rio de Janeiro, Brazil. This variegated orgy lasts for weeks before and after the "official" Carnaval time and is an extravagant, heady mix of dance, sweat, drink, laughter and colour.

Work and study

Opportunities for volunteer and non-profit work abound, but be prepared to pay something towards your upkeep. If you're looking for paid work you might have a little more trouble, as almost all such efforts are likely to be illegal.

TEACHING ENGLISH

Qualified English teachers with a CELTA (Certificate in English Language Teaching to Adults), TEFL (Teaching English as a Foreign Language) or TESUL (Teaching English to Speakers of Other Languages) qualification should be able to find work, but you are strongly advised to arrange your work placement before you travel. Turning up and looking for work will likely leave you frustrated and/or violating local laws - officially you will require a work permit. The British Council (Ⓦwww.britishcouncil.org/work/job) and the TEFL website (Ⓦwww.tefl.com) each has a list of English teaching vacancies.

LANGUAGE STUDY

Latin America has long been a hugely popular destination for people wishing to brush up on their Spanish language skills: Cusco, Peru; Buenos Aires, Argentina; Sucre, Bolivia; and Quito, Ecuador seem to be the most popular destinations and a huge variety of courses and levels are available. In Brazil, most of the large cities are great locations for learning Portuguese. You can also learn indigenous languages such as Quecha in Bolivia or Guarani in Paraguay.

In general you will learn interactively, through practice and communication. Typically three types of course are on offer, a standard classroom-based course, a more active learning course through activities and excursions or the live-in option with a host family.

Language schools

Academia Latinoamericana de Español Ⓣ1-801/268-2468 (US), Ⓦwww.latinoschools.com. Spanish classes in Ecuador, Peru and Bolivia.

Amerispan PO Box 58129, Philadelphia, PA 19102 Ⓣ1-800/879-6640, Ⓦwww.amerispan.com. Spanish courses and volunteer opportunities.

Bridge Linguatec Ⓣ1-800/724-4210, Ⓦwww.bridgelinguatec.com. Spanish and Portuguese classes in Argentina, Chile and Brazil.

Don Quijote Ⓦwww.donquijote.org. High quality, internationally recognised courses offered in Argentina, Bolivia, Chile, Ecuador and Peru.

Escuela Runawasi Ⓣ00591/4424-8923, Ⓦwww.runawasi.org. Quechua and Spanish language and literature lessons in Cochabamba, Bolivia.

Master Key Ⓣ00595/985-778198. Offers unique thematic outdoor Spanish courses taught at local tourist attractions, based in Encarnación, Paraguay.

Planeta Ⓦwww.planeta.com/schoolist.html#SA. Great, frequently updated information about Spanish language schools in South America.

Simón Bolívar Spanish School Ⓣ005937/283 9959, Ⓦwww.bolivar2.com. Based in Ecuador with courses based on a study of the country.

Spanish Study Holidays Ⓣ01509/211612 (UK), Ⓦwww.spanishstudyholidays.com. Courses from one week to 9 months.

VOLUNTEERING

Volunteer opportunities are available in social, developmental, environmental and conservation work in many South American countries, though you will be expected to pay for the privilege. Working alongside local people on a worthwhile project that grabs your interest can be an unforgettable experience which enriches you and gives something back to the country you are visiting.

Volunteer organizations

While many positions are organized prior to arrival, it's also possible to pick something up on the ground through word of mouth. Notice boards in the more popular backpacker hostels are always good sources of information.

US and Canada

Amerispan PO Box 58129, Philadelphia, PA 19102 ⓣ1-800/879-6640, ⓦwww.amerispan.com. One of the best-known volunteer organizations, with opportunities throughout Latin America.
Association of American Schools in South America ⓣ305/821-0345, ⓦwww.aassa.com. Volunteer teaching work throughout Latin America.

UK and Ireland

Concordia ⓣ01273/422218, ⓦwww.concordia-iye.org.uk. Environmental, archaeological and arts projects are among some of the wide range offered by this UK company.
Global Vision International ⓣ01727/250250, ⓦwww.gvi.co.uk. Conservation projects to the Amazon.

Australia and New Zealand

Australian Volunteers International ⓣ1800/331292, ⓦwww.australianvolunteers.com. Opportunities for Australians in Colombia, Ecuador and Guyana.
Global Volunteer Network ⓣ04/569-9080, ⓦwww.volunteer.org.nz. Volunteer opportunities in community projects in several South American countries.

International

Earthwatch Institute ⓣ1-800/776-0188, ⓦwww.earthwatch.org. Long-established research company offering environmental and social volunteer programs throughout the continent.
ECOSARA ⓣ00595/71-203981, ⓦwww.faunaparaguay.com/ecosarahome.html. Biological research station in San Rafael National Park, Paraguay's most biodiverse reserve, offering a variety of packages for volunteers and would-be biologists.
RefugioBolivia ⓦwww.geocities.com/refugiobolivia, ⓔdave_gould@hotmail.com. An animal rehabilitation centre in the Inti Wara Yassi community in Bolivia. Volunteers just turn up and spend between two weeks and two months at the refuge.

Health

The potential health risks in South America read like a text-book of tropical diseases and the possibilities could easily deter nervous travellers before they even set out. However if you prepare for your trip carefully and take sensible precautions while travelling you will likely face nothing worse than a mild case of "travellers belly" as your system gets used to foreign germs and different attitudes to hygiene.

It is important to get the best health advice before you travel – prevention is always better than cure. The Centre for Disease Control (ⓦwww.cdc.gov) offers comprehensive and up to date advice on all aspects of health for travellers and is worth consulting on each of the countries you wish to visit. About ten weeks before you travel relevant **inoculations** can be arranged with your doctor or a specialized travel/tropical diseases clinic. Bring your vaccination record with you when you travel. If you are taking any prescription drugs your doctor can prescribe enough for the time you are away, and you should also take a list with you and preferably a covering letter in case of emergencies.

Good medical insurance is essential (see p.49). It is important to declare any pre-existing conditions, and also to ensure you have sufficient cover for all the extra activities you may undertake.

GENERAL PRECAUTIONS

Common illnesses such as so-called traveller's **diarrhoea** can be largely avoided by taking a few sensible precautions, such as washing your hands before eating, drinking bottled water and avoiding certain foods. Unpasteurised dairy products and all unrefrigerated food should be avoided and fruit and vegetables should be washed and peeled. If you do fall ill, the advice is to rest and replace the fluids you have lost by drinking plenty of water or an oral rehydration solution. A homemade option is 1tsp salt and 8tsps of sugar in 1 litre of water. An anti-diarrhoeal tablet can usually alleviate symptoms.

Two other common afflictions are **heat stroke** and **altitude sickness**. Gentle acclimatization is the rule of thumb in both cases, alongside avoiding dehydration by drinking plenty of bottled water and avoiding alcohol.

Pharmacies abound in every town and there is no need to bring a full first-aid kit from home. If you are travelling into jungle or rural areas, though, you might want to bring a few sensible items with you including insect repellent, painkillers, anti-diarrhoeal tablets and antiseptic cream.

BITES AND STINGS

The general advice is to use an **insect repellent** containing 35% DEET, especially in rural areas or where malaria is endemic, and to wear light clothes that cover as much of your body's surface as possible. It is wise to use a mosquito net or use a mosquito coil containing permethrin at night, especially in the cheaper hotels. A ceiling fan can also help to keep any insects at bay.

Venomous **spiders and snakes** do exist throughout the continent and bites from these, while rare, do merit seeking medical advice as soon as possible. Most responsible tour companies carry anti-venom but in the absence of this, prompt medical attention is the only answer. A photo or description of the offending species may be useful but never attempt to catch or kill it as this can provoke further bites, and don't listen to so-called local knowledge involving tourniquets, sucking venom or anything else – get yourself to a hospital.

A much more likely nuisance when visiting wilder areas are the itchy **bites** given by tiny black sand flies or the multiple and often extremely painful bites of ants and ticks. Hairy caterpillars are also capable of giving nasty stings similar to burns.

MOSQUITO-BORNE DISEASES

Malaria prevention is two-fold; in addition to avoiding mosquito bites as detailed above, travellers should be sure to take a prescription anti-malarial drug, typically chloroquine, atovanquone, doxycycline or mefloquine – consult which is best with a doctor. These should be started several weeks before you travel, and the full course must be completed. Symptoms can occur any time up to a year after travel, and so it is important to inform your doctor about your travel history.

Yellow fever is a serious disease carried by mosquitoes which, like malaria, can be avoided by vaccination and taking sensible precautions against insect bites. Vaccination against this disease is theoretically required for entry into some countries.

Dengue Fever is also mosquito-borne and the only cure is complete rest and painkillers as there is no vaccine.

INTESTINAL PROBLEMS

Other than the traveller's diarrhoea that usually lasts no more than a few days there are a number of more serious problems that you can encounter on your travels. **Cholera**, for example, is an acute infection with watery diarrhoea and vomiting; **dysentery** has similar symptoms but includes bleeding. If your diarrhoea persists a week and your symptoms includes a chill or fever or bleeding, or if you are too ill to drink, seek medical help immediately.

To help avoid problems always use bottled water, even for cleaning your teeth. Avoid buying food from street vendors and think carefully about swimming in lakes and rivers.

If bottled water isn't available there are various methods of treating water: boiling water for a minimum of five minutes is the most effective method. Filtering alongside chemical sterilization is the next best option. Pregnant women or people with thyroid problems should consult their doctors about chemical sterilization formulae.

Medical resources for travellers

Before travelling to South America travellers should seek health advice. Useful websites and major organizations are listed below:

Websites

Ⓦ wwwn.cdc.gov/travel US Department of Health and Human Services travel health and disease control department, listing precautions, diseases and preventative measures by region, as well as a summary of cruise ship sanitation levels.
Ⓦ www.fitfortravel.scot.nhs.uk British National Health Service website carrying information about travel-related diseases and how to avoid them.
Ⓦ www.istm.org The website of the International Society for Travel Medicine, with a full list of clinics specializing in international travel health.
Ⓦ www.masta-travel-health.com Comprehensive website for medical advisory services for travel abroad (see also under medical resources in the UK and Ireland).
Ⓦ www.tmvc.com.au Contains a list of all Travellers Medical and Vaccination Centres throughout Australia, New Zealand and Southeast Asia, plus general information on travel health.
Ⓦ www.travelvax.net Website detailing everything you could ever want to know about diseases and travel vaccines.
Ⓦ www.tripprep.com Travel Health Online provides an online comprehensive database of necessary vaccinations for most countries, as well as destination and medical service provider information.

US and Canada

Canadian Society for International Health 1 Nicholas St, Suite 1105, Ottawa, ON K1N 7B7 Ⓣ613/241-5785, Ⓦwww.csih.org. Distributes a free pamphlet, "Health Information for Canadian Travellers", containing an extensive list of travel health centres in Canada.
Center for Disease Control 1600 Clifton Rd NE, Atlanta, GA 30333 Ⓣ404/639-3534 or 1-800/311-3435, Ⓦwww.cdc.gov. Publishes outbreak warnings, suggested inoculations, precautions and other background information for travellers. Useful website plus International Travellers Hotline on Ⓣ1-877/FYI-TRIP.

UK and Ireland

Dun Laoghaire Medical Centre 5 Northumberland Ave, Dun Laoghaire, Co Dublin ☎01/280 6908.

Medical Advisory Service for Travellers Abroad MASTA operates a recorded 24hr Travellers' Health Line (UK ☎0906/822-4100, 60p per min; Republic of Ireland ☎01560/147000, 75c per min) and gives written information tailored to your journey by return of post (for £3.99).

Australia and New Zealand

Travellers' Medical and Vaccination Centres ⓦwww.tmvc.com.au; 27–29 Gilbert Place, Adelaide ☎08/8212 7522; 1/170 Queen St, Auckland ☎09/373 3531; 5/247 Adelaide St, Brisbane ☎07/3221 9066; 5/8–10 Hobart Place, Canberra ☎02/6257 7156; 147 Armagh St, Christchurch ☎03/379 4000; 5 Westralia St, Darwin ☎08/8981 2907; 270 Sandy Bay Rd, Sandy Bay, Hobart ☎03/6223 7577; 2/393 Little Bourke St, Melbourne ☎03/9602 5788; 5 Mill St, Perth ☎08/9321 1977, plus branch in Fremantle; 7/428 George St, Sydney ☎02/9221 7133, plus branches in Chatswood and Parramatta; Shop 15, Grand Arcade, 14–16 Willis St, Wellington ☎04/473 0991.

Travel essentials

CRIME AND PERSONAL SAFETY

South America is a continent categorized by poverty and attendant crime levels which, while much magnified by tales in the foreign news media, certainly exist. Be sure to consult the relevant "Safety and the police" section of each chapter. In general, cities are more dangerous than rural areas, although the very deserted mountain plains can harbour bandits and hungry refugees. Many of the working class *barrios* of big cities are "no go" areas for tourists, as are the marginal areas near them. One of the biggest problems in the urban parts of the region is theft, with bag snatching, handbag slitting and even armed robbery being problems in cities such as Buenos Aires, Lima, Rio, Salvador, Georgetown and Cusco. Take particular care on the street, in taxis and in restaurants. Any unsolicited approach from a stranger should be treated with the utmost suspicion, no matter how well dressed or trustworthy they may look.

In some countries, notably Guyana and Colombia, crime levels can be particularly high, and indiscriminate shootings, kidnapping and armed robberies of foreigners have been reported.

Preventative measures

There are obvious preventative measures you can take to avoid being mugged: avoid isolated and poorly lit areas, especially at night; never walk along a beach alone, or even – if you're women – in a pair. Keep a particular eye out in heavily touristed areas and watch out on public transport and at bus stations, where pickpocketing is rife. If you need to hail a taxi, get someone at your hotel to recommend one, or hail a moving one – never get into a "taxi" that just happens to be parked at the kerbside or which has two drivers. Avoid wearing expensive or flashy jewellery and watches, dress down, and keep cameras out of sight.

Car-jackings can also be a problem, particularly in certain areas of Brazil. When driving in the city, keep doors locked and windows closed, particularly at night, and be especially vigilant at traffic lights.

Drugs

Just say no! In South America drug trafficking is a huge, ugly and complicated enterprise, and large-scale dealers love to prey on lost-looking foreigners. Don't let anyone else touch your luggage, be sure to pack it yourself and don't carry anything – no matter how innocuous it may seem – for anyone else.

You will find that drugs, particularly marijuana and cocaine, are fairly ubiquitous in the region, but should be aware that they are illegal and punishments are severe. Tourists are likely to come off much worse than locals at the hands of the South American police, something of which the dealers and pushers are very aware. If you happen to be visiting a region famed for drug trafficking, stay well away from anything that looks (or smells) like trouble.

The only legal drugs on sale in South America are the leaves of coca, which are available in Bolivia and Peru. They are usually used to make *mate de coca*, a hugely popular tea in the Andes, and one that's claimed to cure altitude sickness (among other things). Some people chew the leaves as this is meant to produce a mildly intoxicating state, but the taste and texture may well convince you that you can do without the alleged high. If you want to try *mate de coca* or chewing on coca leaves, fine, but be aware that there is a possibility that you could test positive for cocaine use in the weeks following your trip.

Reporting crime

In case you are mugged or robbed, you should make sure that you have a photocopy of all your documents – passport, tickets, etc – in a safe place. Call the local police immediately and tell them what happened. It's likely that they won't do much more than take your statement, but you'll need it for insurance purposes. In some South American countries there is a special "tourist police" force, used to dealing with foreigners and hopefully able to speak English.

ELECTRICITY

The standard electrical current in most countries is 220V, 50Hz. The main exceptions are Colombia, Ecuador and Venezuela where a 110V, 50Hz current is used and Surinam where 127V is standard. Some major tourist cities also use a 110V, 50Hz current, at odds with the rest of their country, including La Paz and Potosí in Bolivia and Rio de Janeiro and São Paulo in Brazil. There is no standard plug shape in most countries and plugs in use may vary greatly, in some cases even within a building! For the most part they are flat two-pin (as in the US), but three-pin plug sockets are sometimes found and even sockets with flattened or angled pins! The South American attitude to safety may be a little more lax than you are used to, and it is not unusual to see plugs that obviously don't fit, forcibly pushed into sockets. They seem to work fine, though health and safety inspectors might have something to say about it!

ENTRY REQUIREMENTS

Country-specific advice about visas and entry requirements is given at the beginning of each chapter, where necessary. As a broad guide, citizens of the UK, Ireland, Canada, Australia and New Zealand do not need a visa for stays of up to ninety days in most South American countries. US citizens need visas for most South American countries, and all nationalities for Suriname; all countries require that your passport be valid for at least six months from your date of entry and that you have proof of onward travel. As all visa requirements, prices and processing times are subject to change, it's definitely worth double-checking with the relevant embassies or consulates.

EMBASSIES

Embassies for most major nations can be found in most capital cities, with consulates in many larger cities. Details of all the world's embassies and their contact details can be found online at Ⓦwww.embassyworld.com, and details of the relevant embassies within each country are given in the country chapters.

GAY AND LESBIAN TRAVELLERS

Rural, Catholic South America is not overly welcoming to homosexuality. Homosexual acts are even technically illegal in some countries, although this usually means simply that local gay couples tend to keep themselves to themselves and avoid flaunting their orientation in front of others. Gay and lesbian travellers would probably be safest following their example – public displays of affection between two men or two women will be frowned upon in much of the continent.

Things are generally easier in the big cities, though, and there are a couple of major destinations where anything goes. Brazil boasts most of them – Rio de Janeiro, Salvador and São Paulo providing safe and welcoming havens for any sexual orientation, as do Buenos Aires and Santiago. If you are looking for thumping night life and a very "out scene", then these cities are the best in the continent.

INSURANCE

A typical travel insurance policy provides cover for the loss of baggage, tickets and – up to a certain limit – cash or cheques, as well as cancellation or curtailment of your journey. Most of them exclude so-called dangerous sports unless an extra premium is paid: this can mean scuba-diving, whitewater rafting, windsurfing and trekking, though probably not kayaking or jeep safaris. Many policies can be chopped and changed to exclude coverage you don't need – for example, sickness and accident benefits can often be excluded or included at will. If you do take medical coverage, ascertain whether benefits will be paid as treatment proceeds or only after your return home, and whether there is a 24-hour medical emergency number. When securing baggage cover, make sure that the per-article limit – typically under US$1000 – will cover your most valuable possession. If you need to make a claim, you should keep receipts for medicines and medical treatment and, in the event you have anything stolen, you must obtain an official statement from the police.

INTERNET

Internet access is now almost ubiquitous in cities and towns across South America (though it is more restricted in the Guyanas) and only in rural areas is it difficult to come by. Connection speeds and costs vary from country to country and in some cases from area to area within a country. Ⓦwww.kropla.com is a useful website giving details of how to plug your laptop in when abroad, phone country codes around the world, and information about electrical systems in different countries.

MAIL

Post offices in cities and major towns offer a wide range of services; those in villages are much more basic, with shorter opening hours and often infuriatingly slow service. Hotels in capital cities may sell stamps and have a postbox – if you are staying in such an establishment, this can often be the most convenient way to send a letter home. Expect airmail to take at least one week to Western Europe and the USA from most destinations and occasionally longer, especially if your mail is sent from outside the country's capital. Travellers can receive mail via poste restante throughout the region, although in some countries you will be charged to pick up mail. The system is efficient enough but tends to be available only at the main post office in cities, or even only in the capital, and not in small towns and villages. Most post offices hold letters for a maximum of one month.

EXCHANGE RATES

At the time of writing exchange rates were even more volatile than usual thanks to the credit crunch (in countries whose currency is not linked to the dollar), and they will inevitably vary over the life of this edition of the Guide. However these comparative exchange rates may at least help interpret prices in the book. Equivalents for Pounds and Euros were £1 = US$1.47, and €1 = US$1.38.

Argentina (Argentine Peso; AR$) US$1 = AR$3.45
Bolivia (Boliviano; B) US$1 = B7.03
Brazil (Real; R) US$1 = R$2.47
Chile (Chilean Peso; CH$) US$1 = CH$663
Colombia (Colombian Peso; C$) US$1 = C$2305
Ecuador (US Dollar; US$)
French Guiana (Euro; €) US$1 = €0.75
Guyana (Guyanese dollar; GYD) US$1 = GYD$200
Paraguay (Guaraní; G) US$1 = G4845
Peru (Nuevo Sol; S) US$1 = S/3.12
Suriname (Suriname dollar; SRD) US$1 = SRD$2.75
Uruguay (Uruguayan Peso; UR$) US$1 = UR$24.25
Venezuela (Bolívar Fuerte; BF) US$1 = BF2.15

MAPS

Excellent maps of the continent of South America, covering the region at a scale of 1:5000000, are produced by Canada's International Travel Maps and Books (Ⓦwww.itmb.com). They also publish individual country and regional maps at various scales. Once in South America good maps can be very hard to find, and often the only source of accurate maps is the military – check at the local tourist offices for details on where to purchase them. If you'd rather be safe than sorry, buy your maps at home and bring them with you!

MONEY

ATMs are widely available in most large cities, but in smaller towns and rural areas you should not expect to rely solely on using international debit cards to access funds. Traveller's cheques are much less widely accepted than they once were: pre-paid **currency cards** are an excellent alternative, though these, too, require access to an ATM. There is still nothing as easy to use as cash, preferably US dollars, and it makes sense always to carry at least a few small denomination notes for when all else fails.

Credit card fraud is a problem in the continent, particularly in Brazil and Venezuela; be sure to keep an eye on your card, and to retain your copy of the transaction slip, along with the carbon paper. In many countries credit cards will only be accepted in the biggest hotels and shops, and banks will sometimes refuse to offer cash advances against them. Payments

PRICES

At the beginning of each country chapter you'll find a guide to "rough costs", including food, accommodation and travel. Within the chapter itself prices are quoted in local currency. Note that prices and exchange rates change all the time. We have done our best to make sure that all prices are accurate, but as tourism increases in popularity throughout the region it's likely that prices will rise incrementally, while the credit crunch has made exchange rates even more volatile than usual.

in plastic may also incur high surcharges when compared to straight cash payments. When exchanging money, you should use only authorized bureaux de change, such as banks, *cambios* and tourist facilities, rather than deal with moneychangers on the streets. For details on each country, consult the "Costs and money" section at the beginning of each chapter.

In remote and rural areas, and for shopping in local markets and stalls, **cash** is a necessity – preferably in small denominations of local currency.

It is possible to **wire money** to South America using services like Western Union (Ⓦwww.westernunion.com) and Moneygram (Ⓦwww.moneygram.com). The best advice is to consider this service before you set out, compare rates and ensure a home contact is aware of how to access the service on your behalf so that transferring money is as fast and painless as possible. It will almost always be easier and quicker than trying to have money sent to a local bank.

PHONES

With the advent of the cell phone **public phone boxes** are beginning to disappear in many South American countries, apart from in the larger cities. What you will find almost everywhere, though, are *cabinas telefónicas*, stores originally dedicated to telephone communications, but most of which have now branched out into internet access as well. Here you will have access to a phone in a private booth. You can make direct-dial international calls from most Latin American phones, apart from some of the more remote areas, where calls must be made through an operator. Where phone boxes do exist, they usually operate with cards, available from newspaper kiosks.

In general, calls are cheaper between the hours of 7pm and 5am and at weekends, although some countries in the region may start their cheap rates before or after this. See individual country chapters for details. International phone calls are, in general, expensive from South America.

Avoid calling long distance from hotels unless you have a cheap long-distance **phone card** with a free or local access number; even then check to see if the establishment charges for such calls. These are also the best way to use public phones. Generally, however, the cheapest way to call is using **Skype** or a similar service over the Internet; many Internet cafés throughout the continent offer this service.

Mobile phones

If you want to use your mobile phone abroad, you'll need to check with your phone provider whether it will work overseas, and what the call charges are. Remember that when using your phone overseas, you will almost always

YOUTH AND STUDENT DISCOUNTS

Various official and quasi-official youth/student ID cards are available and are worth the effort to obtain: they soon pay for themselves in savings. Full-time students are eligible for the International Student ID Card (ISIC, Ⓦwww.isiccard.com), which entitles the bearer to special air, rail and bus fares and discounts at museums, theatres and other attractions. For Americans, there's also a health benefit, providing up to US$3000 in emergency medical coverage and US$100 a day for sixty days in the hospital, plus a 24-hour hotline to call in the event of a medical, legal or financial emergency.

You have to be 26 or younger to qualify for the International Youth Travel Card, which carries the same benefits. Teachers qualify for the International Teacher Card, offering similar discounts. All these cards are available from student travel specialists including STA (see p.33 for addresses).

Several other travel organizations and accommodation groups also sell their own cards, good for various discounts. A university photo ID might open some doors, but is not as easily recognizable as an ISIC card.

CALLING FROM ABROAD

To phone abroad, you must first dial the international access code of the country you are calling from, then the country code of the country you are calling to, then the area code (usually without the first zero) and then the phone number. In some South American countries there may be different international access codes for different providers. See the box for details.

International access codes when dialling from:

Argentina ⓣ00
Australia ⓣ0011
Bolivia ⓣ0010 (Entel) ⓣ0011 (AES) ⓣ0012 (Teledata) ⓣ0013 (Boliviatel)
Brazil ⓣ0014 (Brasil Telecom) ⓣ0015 (Telefónica) ⓣ0021 (Embratel) ⓣ0023 (Intelig) ⓣ0031 (Telemar)
Canada ⓣ011
Chile ⓣ00
Colombia ⓣ009 (Telecom) ⓣ007 (ETB/Mundo) ⓣ005 (Orbitel)
Ecuador ⓣ00
French Guiana ⓣ00
Guyana ⓣ001
Ireland ⓣ00
New Zealand ⓣ00
Paraguay ⓣ002
Peru ⓣ00
Suriname ⓣ002
UK ⓣ00
Uruguay ⓣ00
US ⓣ011
Venezuela ⓣ00

Country codes when dialling to:

Argentina ⓣ54
Australia ⓣ61
Bolivia ⓣ591
Brazil ⓣ55
Canada ⓣ1
Chile ⓣ56
Colombia ⓣ57
Ecuador ⓣ593
French Guiana ⓣ594
Guyana ⓣ592
Ireland ⓣ353
New Zealand ⓣ64
Paraguay ⓣ595
Peru ⓣ51
Suriname ⓣ597
UK ⓣ44
Uruguay ⓣ598
US ⓣ1
Venezuela ⓣ58

be charged for calls you receive, as well as those you make. Alternatively, and assuming your phone is unlocked (most contract phones are locked so they can only be used on one network – your provider can usually unlock it for a fee), you can buy a SIM card from a local telephone company and use it in your phone. These are usually pretty cheap and your calls will be charged at a local rate.

TOURIST INFORMATION

The quantity and quality of tourist information varies from country to country, but in general, don't expect too much. While almost every city in Brazil and Argentina will have at least one, well-equipped tourist information office, they are much thinner on the ground in countries like Paraguay and the Guyanas. You should make the most of any operational office you find there. Fortunately, there is a lot of information about South America on the Web that will help you plan your trip and answer all sorts of questions about history, language and current goings-on. We've listed websites wherever pertinent throughout the guide; the following is a general list of places to begin your wanderings. For details of Internet access within the continent, see p.49.

Latin America on the Web

ⓦ **www.clarin.com** The largest Spanish-language daily newspaper in the world, printed in Buenos Aires.
ⓦ **www.buenosairesherald.com** English-language newspaper, updated weekly.
ⓦ **www.faunaparaguay.com** Massive website of information about Paraguayan wildlife with thousands

of photos and information for visitors to this often overlooked country.

www.latinnews.com Real-time newsfeed with major stories from all over South America in English.

www.latinamericanlinks.com Good site for traveller information, with links for each country in the continent.

www.narconews.com Up-to-date site dealing with the so-called Drug War and democracy in the continent.

www.zonalatina.com/Zlmusic Excellent directory of regional music links and information, covering everything from Mariachi and Sertaneja to Shakira.

www.planeta.com/south.html Excellent selection of online eco-travel and tourism resources for South America.

www.roughguides.com Not only has complete text from relevant guidebooks on the site, but links to travel journals and photos, and a catalogue to lead you to an easy place to buy the guides and maps themselves.

www.saexplorers.org The website of the South American Explorers Club, a non-profit organization with the latest research, travel and adventure information.

TRAVELLERS WITH DISABILITIES

South America is not the friendliest of destinations for travellers with disabilities and many places are downright inaccessible. As a rule, though, the more modern the society, the more likely you are to find services for physically challenged travellers – this means that while Bolivia and Paraguay are pretty impenetrable, much of inhabitable Chile and Argentina, as well as several cities in Brazil, may prove accessible.

Unfortunately, though, you may need to compromise over destination – big hotels in major cities that are very much on the tourist trail are much more likely to have facilities to cater to your needs than idyllic *cabañas* in the middle of nowhere. You might be limited as regards mobility, too, as local buses will probably prove difficult and you might need to settle for taxi services or internal flights. In any case, check with one of the agencies below before planning anything – if anyone knows how to get over inaccessibility hiccups, it is these agents.

US and Canada

Directions Unlimited 123 Green Lane, Bedford Hills, NY 10507 ⓣ914/241-1700 or 1-800/533-5343. Tour operator specializing in custom tours for people with disabilities.

UK

Access Travel 6 The Hillock, Astley, Lancashire M29 7GW ⓣ01942/888844, ⓦwww.access-travel.co.uk. Small tour operator that can arrange flights, transfers and accommodation. Personally checks out places before recommendation and can guarantee accommodation standards in many countries – for places they do not cover, they can arrange flight-only deals.

Australia

Australian Council for Rehabilitation of the Disabled PO Box 60, Curtin, ACT 2605 ⓣ02/6282 4333; 24 Cabarita Rd, Cabarita, NSW 2137 ⓣ02/9743 2699. ACROD furnishes lists of travel agencies and tour operators for people with disabilities.

WOMEN TRAVELLERS

Though violent attacks against women travellers are not very common – except in some of the particularly crime-laden cities (see p.47) – many women find that the barrage of hisses, hoots and comments in certain parts of South America comes close to spoiling their trip. It's unlikely that a woman travelling alone will leave the continent without a little harassment, some of which can be threatening and scary, most of which is just downright *pesado* (annoying). Latin American men are not renowned for their forward-thinking attitudes towards women's emancipation, and genuinely see nothing wrong with the heady sense of machismo that rules much of the continent. You may find that attitudes are less polarized in country areas.

Of course, there are measures you can take to avoid being hassled constantly. Don't go to bars or nightclubs alone, for one – this is an activity only undertaken by the most brazen prostitutes in the region, and you will be considered fair game. Don't be sarcastic or scream if approached, as the man in question may feel that you are showing him up in front of his friends and get more macho and aggressive. However, don't be afraid to seem rude; even the mildest polite response will be considered an indication of serious interest. In any event, watch how the local women behave and where they go, and never be afraid to ask for help if you feel lost or threatened.

Solo women travellers should also avoid going off to remote locations alone, and if you are going as part of an organized visit, it's always best to check the credentials of the tour company. Your safety may be in their hands, so a little asking around doesn't seem too much to ask. There are emergency numbers given in individual chapters of this book. However, if you are attacked or raped, you should contact the tourist police and your country's embassy as well as getting medical attention and going to the regular police.

Argentina

HIGHLIGHTS

IGUAZÚ FALLS: the world's largest waterfalls are framed by lush, subtropical jungle

MENDOZA: wineries and lofty peaks lie just outside this sophisticated metropolis

BUENOS AIRES: tango and football rule in this European-style capital

BARILOCHE: an outdoor adventure hub with stunning mountain vistas

GLACIAR PERITO MORENO: a frozen exhibitionist that splinters and splashes

USHUAIA: the end of the Earth and just 1000km from Antarctica

ROUGH COSTS

DAILY BUDGET Basic AR$130/ with occasional treats AR$200

DRINK Beer (300ml bottle) AR$10

FOOD *Asado* beef AR$35

CAMPING/HOSTEL/BUDGET HOTEL AR$5/30/50

TRAVEL Bus/air fare from Buenos Aires to Córdoba AR$100/300

FACT FILE

POPULATION 39.5 million

AREA 2,766,890 sq km

OFFICIAL LANGUAGE Spanish

CURRENCY Argentine peso (AR$)

CAPITAL Buenos Aires (Greater Buenos Aires population, 13 million)

TIME ZONE GMT -3 in north and east; GMT -2 in west and south; GMT -2/-1 respectively in summer

INTERNATIONAL PHONE CODE ⓣ54

Introduction

Even without the titanic wedge of Antarctica that cartographers include in its national territory, Argentina ranks as the world's eighth largest country. Stretching from the Tropic of Capricorn to the most southerly reaches of the planet's landmass, it encompasses a staggering diversity of climates and landscapes: hot and humid jungles in the northeast; bone-dry highland steppes in the northwest; through endless grasslands to windswept Patagonia and the end-of-the-world archipelago of Tierra del Fuego.

Argentina offers a variety of attractions, many of them influenced by generations of immigration from Europe. Above all, though, the extent and diversity of the country's natural scenery is staggering. Due north of the capital, Buenos Aires, stretches **El Litoral**, a region of subtropical riverine landscapes featuring the awe-inspiring **Iguazú** waterfalls. Tucked away in the northwest are the spectacular, polychrome **Quebrada de Humahuaca** gorge and the **Valles Calchaquíes**, stunningly beautiful valleys where high-altitude vineyards produce the delightfully flowery *torrontés* wine.

West and immediately south of Buenos Aires are the seemingly endless grassy plains of the **Pampas**. This is where you'll still glimpse traces of traditional **gaucho** culture, most famously celebrated in **San Antonio de Areco**. Here, too, you'll find some of the country's best *estancias*. Moving west, the **Central Sierras** loom on the horizon: within reach of **Córdoba**, the country's vibrant second city, are some of the oldest resorts on the continent. The regional capital of **Mendoza** is the country's wine capital and from here the scenic Alta Montaña route climbs steeply to the Chilean border, passing **Cerro Aconcagua**, Argentina's highest mountain and a dream challenge for mountaineers from around the world.

San Juan and La Rioja provinces are relatively uncharted territory but their star attractions are **Parque Nacional Talampaya**, with its giant red cliffs, and the nearby **Parque Provincial Ischigualasto**, usually known as Valle de la Luna on account of its intriguing, moon-like landscapes.

Argentina claims the lion's share of the wild, sparsely populated expanses of **Patagonia** and the archipelago of **Tierra del Fuego**. An almost unbroken chain of national parks here make for some of the best trekking anywhere on the planet – certainly include the savage granite peaks of the **Parque Nacional Los Glaciares** in your itinerary. For wildlife enthusiasts the **Peninsula Valdés** is also essential viewing, famous above all else as a breeding ground for Southern Right whales.

CHRONOLOGY

1516 The first Europeans reach the River Plate and clash with Querandí natives.

1535 Pedro de Mendoza founds Buenos Aires.

1609 First missions to the Guaraní established in the upper Paraná.

1806 The British storm Buenos Aires only to be expelled within a few months.

1810 The first elected junta sworn in to replace Spanish leaders.

1816 Independence is declared in the city of Tucumán.

1854 First railways built

1912 Introduction of universal male suffrage

1920s Towards the end of the decade, Argentina is the seventh richest country in the world.

ARGENTINA

INTRODUCTION

1930 Hipólito Yrigoyen overthrown in a military coup.
1943 Military coup led by Juan Domingo Perón results in ousting of constitutional government.
1946 Juan Domingo Perón elected president.
1952 Perón's wife Evita dies at the age of 33.
1955 Perón overthrown in a military coup and exiled.
1973 Perón returns and is reelected.
1974 Perón dies and power defaults to his third wife Isabelita.
1976 Videla leads military coup against Isabel Perón, marking the beginning of the "Dirty War".
1978 Argentina hosts, and wins, the World Cup.
1982 The military invades the Falkland Islands (Islas Malvinas) and is defeated by the British.
1983 Democracy is restored and radical Raúl Alfonsín is elected.
1995 Peronist Menem stands for a second term.
2001 President De la Rúa resigns in the midst of economic collapse and rioting.
2003 Néstor Kirchner is elected.
2008 His wife Cristina Fernández de Kirchner is inaugurated as the country's first elected female president.

Basics

ARRIVAL

The vast majority of visitors to Argentina arrive at Buenos Aires' **Ezeiza International Airport**, although other major cities also have flight connections to countries within South America. Fast **ferries** link Buenos Aires to the Uruguayan capital Montevideo. There are no direct international **rail** links, but a plethora of **international bus routes** link Argentina with its neighbours: Chile, Brazil, Uruguay and Paraguay.

GETTING AROUND

Distances are huge in Argentina, and you are likely to spend a considerable proportion of your budget on travel. Air travel is relatively expensive, so most people travel by bus. Car rental is useful in places, but too expensive for most budget travellers, unless they can share the cost. Extra fees are charged for drivers under 25.

By air

Argentina's most important domestic airport by far is Buenos Aires' **Aeroparque Jorge Newbery**. There are connections (with Aerolíneas Argentinas and LAN) to most provincial capitals and major tourist centres; a relatively new airline, Andes, serves Puerto Madryn and Salta. Some cut-price deals booked in advance can work out to be not much more than the bus. One of the best deals is the "Visit Argentina" **airpass** sold by Aerolíneas Argentinas and valid for domestic flights on Aerolíneas and its subsidiary, Austral. This pass must be bought abroad; it is not sold in Argentina.

Many smaller airports are not served by public transport, though some airline companies run shuttle services to connect with flights; otherwise, you're stuck with taxis.

By bus

There are hundreds of private **bus** companies, most of which concentrate on one particular region, although a few, such as TAC, operate pretty much nationwide. Most buses are modern, plush models designed for long-distance travel, and your biggest worry will be what video the driver or conductor has chosen. On longer journeys, snacks and even hot meals are served (included in the ticket price), although these vary considerably in quality. The more luxurious services are usually worth the extra money for long night-rides; some even have waiters. *Coche cama* and *pullman* services have wide, reclinable seats, and *semi-cama* services are not far behind in terms of comfort. Some companies offer a *cama completa* or *cama suite* service, which has completely reclinable seats.

Buying **tickets** is normally a simple on-the-spot matter, but you must plan in advance if travelling in peak summer season (mid-Dec to Feb), especially if you're taking a long-distance bus from Buenos Aires or any other major city to a particularly popular holiday destination.

By car

You are unlikely to want or need a **car** for your whole stay in Argentina, but you'll find one pretty indispensable if you hope to explore some of the more isolated areas of Patagonia, Tierra del Fuego, the Northwest, and Mendoza and San Juan provinces.

To rent a car, you need to be over 21 (25 with some agencies); most foreign licences are accepted for tourists. Bring your passport as well as a credit card for the deposit. Before you drive off, check that you've been given insurance, tax and ownership papers. Check too for dents and paintwork damage, and get hold of a 24-hour emergency telephone number. Also, pay close attention to the small print, most notably what you're liable for in the event of an accident: excess normally doesn't cover you for the first AR$5000 or so, and you may not be covered for windscreens, headlights, tyres and more – all vulnerable on unsurfaced roads. Look for unlimited mileage deals, as the per-kilometre charge can otherwise exceed your daily rental cost many times over given the vast distances.

By train

Argentina's **rail** network, developed with British investment from the late nineteenth century, collapsed in the 1990s with the withdrawal of government subsidies. Certain long-distance services were maintained by provincial governments, but these tend to be slower and less reliable than buses. Though you may not want to use Argentine trains as a method of getting around, however, the country's famous **tourist trains**, where the aim is simply to travel for the sheer fun of it, are a major attraction. There are two principal stars: *La Trochita*, the Old Patagonian Express from Esquel; and the *Tren a los Nubes* (due to reopen in March 2009 after three years of closure), one of the highest railways in the world, which climbs through the mountains from Salta towards the Chilean border.

ACCOMMODATION

You can often tell by a hotel's **name** what kind of place to expect: the use of the term *posada* for example usually suggests a slightly rustic feel, but generally comfortable or even luxurious. In a similar vein, *hostería* is often used for smallish, upmarket hotels – oriented towards the tourist rather than the businessman. *Hostal* is sometimes used too – but doesn't refer reliably to anything – there are youth hostels called *hostales* as well as high-rise modern hotels.

Residenciales and *hospedajes* are basically simple hotel-style accommodation. Most are reasonably clean and comfortable and a few of them stand out as some of Argentina's best budget accommodation.

A very different experience from staying in a hotel is provided by Argentina's *estancias*, as the country's large ranches are called. **Estancia** accommodation is generally luxurious, and with a lot more character than hotels of a similar price; for between US$100 and US$200 per person a day you are provided with four meals, invariably including a traditional *asado* or barbecue. At working *estancias* you will have the chance to observe or join in ranch activities such as cattle herding and branding, while almost all of them include activities such as horse riding and swimming in the price. To book *estancia* accommodation, either approach individual *estancias* directly (they're recommended throughout the text) or try one of the two specialist agencies in Buenos Aires: Comarcas, Laprida 1380 (Ⓣ011/4821-1876, Ⓦwww.comarcas.com.ar) and Estancias Argentinas, Diag. Roque Sáenz Peña 616, 9th Floor (Ⓣ011/4342-8417 Ⓦwww.estanciasargentinas.com).

Hostels and campsites

Youth hostels are known as *albergues juveniles* or *albergues de la juventud* in Argentina. Accommodation is generally in dormitories, though most places also have one or two double rooms, often excellent value. Facilities vary from next to nothing to internet access, washing machines, cable TV and patios with barbecue facilities.

There are plenty of **campsites** (*campings*), with most towns and villages having their own municipal campsite, but standards vary wildly. At the major resorts, there are usually plenty of privately owned, well-organized sites, with facilities ranging from provisions stores to volleyball courts and TV rooms. In non-touristy towns, municipal sites can be rather desolate and not particularly secure places: it's a good idea to check with locals before pitching your tent.

FOOD

You nearly always eat well in Argentina and you seldom have a bad meal; portions are always generous and the raw ingredients are of an amazingly high quality.

Traditionally, Argentine food could be summed up in a single word: **beef**. Not just any beef, but the best in the world – succulent, cherry-red, healthy meat raised on some of the greenest, most extensive pastures known to cattle. The **barbecue** or *asado* remains a national institution, but it's not the whole story.

An *asado* is prepared on a **parrilla**, and this national dish is served everywhere, at restaurants also known as *parrillas*. Usually there's a set menu, the *parrillada*, but the establishments themselves vary enormously. Traditionally, you start off by eating the offal before moving on to the choicer cuts, but you can choose to head straight for the steaks and fillets. Either way, these carnivores' delights are not for the faint-hearted. Although mustard (*mostaza*) may be available, the lightly salted meat is usually served with nothing on it, other than the traditional condiments of *chimichurri* – olive oil shaken in a bottle with salt, garlic, chilli pepper, vinegar and bayleaf – and *salsa criolla*, similar but with onion and tomato added: everyone jealously guards their secret formulae for these "magic" dressings.

Away from the *parrilla*, pizza and pasta are the mainstays of Argentine cuisine. The sheer **variety** of restaurants in the cities, however, reflects the mosaic of different communities who have migrated to Argentina over the decades: not just Italian but Spanish, Chinese, Middle Eastern, German and even Welsh. Japanese and Thai food, too, have become fashionable in Buenos Aires, where nearly every national cuisine is available. **Vegetarians** will find that there are few options on most menus, but there are staples such as *ensalada mixta*, a basic salad, or *milanesas de queso*, fried, breaded cheese, which are almost always available, and there is usually a range of pastas with meat-free sauces. In larger towns vegetarian restaurants are growing in popularity.

If you're feeling hungry during the day there are plenty of *minutas* or **snacks** to choose from. The *lomito* is a nourishing sandwich filled with a juicy slice of steak, often made with delicious *pan árabe*, while the *chivito* is made with a less tender cut. At cafés a popular snack is the *tostado*, a toasted cheese-and-ham sandwich, sometimes called a *carlitos*. *Milanesas*, in this context, refer to breaded veal escalopes in a sandwich, hamburger-style.

Excellent local-style fast food is also available in the form of *empanadas*, turnovers or pasties that come with a bewildering array of non-traditional fillings, including tuna, roquefort cheese and goat's cheese. The conventional fillings are beef, cheese and chicken. *Humitas* are made of steamed creamed sweetcorn, usually served in neat parcels made from the outer husk of corn cobs. *Tamales* are maize-flour balls, stuffed with minced beef and onion, wrapped in maize leaves and simmered. The typical main dish, *locro*, is a warming, substantial stew based on maize, with onions, beans, meat, chicken or sausage thrown in. Less common but worth trying if you see it on the menu is *guaschalocro*, similar to *locro* but based on pumpkin.

Where to eat

Argentines love **dining out**, and in Buenos Aires especially, places stay open all day and till very late: in the evening hardly any restaurant starts serving dinner before 8.30pm, and in the hotter months – and all year round in Buenos Aires – very few people turn up before 10pm. By South American standards the quality of restaurants is high. You can keep costs down by eating at the market or taking advantage of the *menú del día* or *menú ejecutivo* – good-value set meals for as little as AR$12 served primarily, but not exclusively, at lunchtime. In the evening *tenedor libre* or *diente libre* restaurants are just the place if your budget's tight. Here, you can eat as much as you like, they're usually self-service (cold and hot buffets plus grills) and the food is fresh and well prepared, if a little dull.

Cheaper hotels and more modest accommodation often skimp on **breakfast**: you'll be lucky to be given more than tea or coffee, and some bread, jam and butter, though the popular *medialunas* (small, sticky croissants) are sometimes also served. The sacred national delicacy *dulce de leche* (a type of caramel) is often provided for spreading on toast or bread, as is top-notch honey.

DRINK

Fizzy drinks (*gaseosas*) are popular with people of all ages and are often drunk to accompany a meal, in this country where fewer and fewer people drink alcohol (even if wine consumption is relatively high). All the big brand names are available, along with local brands such as *Paso de los Toros* whose fizzy grapefruit drinks (*pomelo*) are becoming increasingly popular.

Although few beans are grown in the country, good, if expensive, **coffee** is easy to come by in Argentina. In the cafés of most towns and cities you will find decent espressos, or delicious *café con leche* (milky coffee) for breakfast. Maté, the bitter national drink, is a whole world unto itself, with special rules of etiquette and ritual involved.

Argentina's **beer** is more thirst-quenching than alcoholic and mostly comes as fairly bland lager. The Quilmes brewery dominates the market with ales such as Cristal; in Mendoza, the Andes brand crops up all over the place; while Salta's own brand is also good, and a kind of stout (*cerveza negra*) can sometimes be obtained in the northwest. If you want draught beer you must ask for a *chopp*.

Argentine **wine** is excellent and reasonably priced – try the Malbec. The locally distilled *aguardientes* or firewaters are often deliciously grapey. There is no national alcoholic drink or cocktail, but a number of Italian vermouths and digestives are made in Argentina. Fernet Branca is the most popular, a demonic-looking brew the colour of molasses with a rather medicinal taste, invariably combined with cola, whose colour it matches, and consumed in huge quantities – it's generally regarded as the gaucho's favourite tipple.

CULTURE AND ETIQUETTE

Argentines are generally friendly, outgoing and incredibly welcoming to foreigners. In all but the most formal contexts, Argentines greet with one kiss on the cheek (men included), even on first meeting.

Table manners follow the Western norm and, in general, visitors are unlikely to find any huge culture shock in Argentine etiquette. Service in shops or restaurants is generally very courteous, and conversations should be started with a "buenos días" or "buenas tardes".

SPORTS AND OUTDOOR ACTIVITIES

Argentina is a highly exciting destination for outdoors enthusiasts, whether you're keen to tackle radical rock faces or prefer to appreciate the vast open spaces at a more gentle pace, hiking or on horseback. World-class fly-fishing, horseriding, trekking and rock climbing options abound, as do opportunities for whitewater rafting, skiing, ice climbing, and even – for those with sufficient stamina and preparation – expeditions onto the Southern Patagonian Icecap. The Patagonian Andes provide the focus for most of these activities, most particularly the area of the central Lake District around Bariloche and El Calafate/El Chaltén, but Mendoza and the far northwest of the country, around Salta and Jujuy, are also worth considering for their rugged mountain terrain. If you're keen on any of the above activities (bar angling, of course), ensure you have taken out appropriate insurance cover before leaving home.

Hiking and climbing

Argentina offers some truly marvellous **hiking** possibilities, and it is still possible to find areas where you can trek for days without seeing a soul. Most of the best treks are found in the national parks – especially the ones in Patagonia – but you can also find less-known but equally superb options in the lands bordering the parks. Most people head for the savage granite spires of the Fitz Roy region around El Chaltén, an area whose fame has spread so rapidly over the last ten years that it now holds a similar status to Chile's renowned Torres del Paine, not far away, and is packed in the high season (late Dec to Feb). The other principal trekking destination is the mountainous area of Nahuel Huapi National Park which lies to the south of Bariloche, centring on the Cerro Catedral massif and Cerro Tronador.

For **climbers**, the Andes offer incredible variety – from volcanoes to shale summits, from the continent's loftiest giants to some of its fiercest technical walls. You do not have to be a technical expert to reach the summit of some of these and, though you must always take preparations seriously, you can often arrange your climb close to the date through local agencies – though it's best to bring as much high-quality gear with you as you can. The climbing season is fairly short – generally

NATIONAL PARK INFORMATION

The **National Park Headquarters** at Santa Fe 690 in Buenos Aires (Mon–Fri 10am–5pm; ⓣ011/4311-0303, ⓦwww.parquesnacionales.gov.ar) has an information office with introductory leaflets on the nation's parks. A wider range of free leaflets is available at each individual park, but these are of variable quality and limited funding means that many parks give you only ones with a basic map and a brief park description. Contact the headquarters well in advance if you are interested in voluntary or scientific projects.

November to March, though December to February is the best time. The best-known, if not the most technical, challenge is South America's highest peak, **Aconcagua** (6962m), accessed from the city of Mendoza. In the far south are the Fitz Roy massif and Cerro Torre, which have few equals on the planet in terms of sheer technical difficulty and grandeur of scenery. On all of these climbs, but especially those over 4000m, you must acclimatize thoroughly, and be fully aware of the dangers of *puna* or altitude sickness.

Skiing

The main **skiing** months are July and August (late July is peak season), although in some resorts it is possible to ski from late May to early October. Snow conditions vary wildly from year to year, but you can often find excellent powder. The most prestigious resort for downhill skiing is modern Las Leñas, which offers the most challenging slopes and once hosted the World Cup; followed by the Bariloche resorts of Cerro Catedral and Cerro Otto. These are the longest-established in the country and are still perhaps the classic Patagonian ski centres, with their wonderful panoramas of the Nahuel Huapi region. For updates on conditions and resorts, check out the Andesweb website (Ⓦwww.andesweb.com).

COMMUNICATIONS

There are Correo Argentino **post offices** throughout the country, and you may also come across *locutorios* offering postal services. International post is relatively expensive and not always reliable; it is not advisable to send items of value.

Making **local phone calls** in Argentina is cheap and easy. In cities and towns, you are never far from a call centre (known as a *locutorio*). Public phones are also a common sight. They work out marginally cheaper than *locutorios*, but it's usually worth paying the extra *centavos* to have a cabin with a seat.

National calls are relatively pricey, so it's worth asking about phone cards offering cheap minutes if you are planning to make a number of calls. Reliable brands are *Habla Más* and *Direct*, which for AR$10 generally offer up to an hour of talk between landlines. Cheap **internet** cafés are everywhere in Argentina and, in all but the most remote areas, the connections are fairly fast.

ARGENTINA ON THE WEB

Ⓦ**wwww.sectur.gov.ar** The official tourist website for Argentina.

Ⓦ**www.welcomeargentina.com** Well-presented website about Argentina, containing information about accommodation, activities and detailed transport information.

Ⓦ**www.buenosaires.gov.ar** City government's site for Buenos Aires, with up-to-date details on cultural events.

Ⓦ**www.livinginargentina.com** Online magazine with articles in English about Argentine culture and travel.

Ⓦ**www.buenosairesherald.com** Buenos Aires's English-language newspaper, with national and international news updated daily.

EMERGENCIES

Argentina is one of the continent's safest countries and, as long as you take a few basic precautions, you are unlikely to encounter any problems during your stay. Indeed, you'll find many of the more rural parts of the country pretty much risk-free: people leave doors unlocked, windows open and bikes unchained. More care should be taken in large cities and some of the border towns, particularly the northeastern ones, where poverty and easily available arms and drugs make opportunistic crime a more common occurrence. Some potential pitfalls are outlined here, not to induce

EMERGENCY NUMBERS

Ambulance ⊕107
Fire ⊕100
Police ⊕101
Tourist Police ⊕0800-999-5000

paranoia but on the principle that to be forewarned is to be forearmed.

By Argentine standards, **Buenos Aires** is currently suffering something of a crime wave, and incidents of violence and armed robbery are definitely on the increase. It's sometimes difficult to know how much local anxiety is due to a genuine increase in crime and how much to middle-class paranoia but, in general, serious crime tends to affect locals more than tourists. Nevertheless, you should not take unofficial taxis and you're advised to be wary when taking a taxi from areas where serious money circulates. Though Buenos Aires doesn't really have any "no go" areas, avoid walking around the quieter neighbourhoods after dark, and stick to the touristy areas of La Boca. In the rare event of being held up at gunpoint, don't play the hero. Locals warn that this is especially the case if your mugger is a child, since they know that, as minors, they can't be jailed even if they shoot someone.

Theft from hotels is rare but, as anywhere else in the world, do not leave valuables lying round the room. Some hostels have lockers; it's worth having a padlock of your own.

Drugs are frowned upon in general. They attract far more stigma here than in most European countries, for example, and Argentine society at large draws very little in the way of a line between "acceptable" soft drugs and "unacceptable" hard drugs. You're very much advised to steer clear of buying or partaking yourself – the penalties are stiff if you get caught.

INFORMATION AND MAPS

Argentina's main **National Tourist Office** is at Santa Fe 883 in Buenos Aires (Mon–Fri 9am–5pm; ⊕011/4312-2232, ⓦwww.turismo.gov.ar) and offers maps of the country and general information about getting around. Every province maintains a *Casa de Provincia* in Buenos Aires, where you can pick up information about what there is to see or do, prior to travelling. The standard of information you'll glean from them varies wildly, often reflecting the comparative wealth of a given province.

The clearest and most accurate **map** of the whole country is the one you can get free from the national tourist office; it's called Rutas de la Argentina and has small but clear inset maps of twenty towns and cities as well as a 1:2,500,000 national map, the ideal scale for most travellers. The ACA (Automóvil Club, ⓦwww.aca.org.ar) produces individual maps for each province, which vary enormously in detail and accuracy; the regional maps or route planners the club publishes may be enough for most travellers.

MONEY AND BANKS

The **Argentine peso** is divided into one hundred centavos. In Argentina, it's represented by the dollar sign ($) but to avoid confusion we have used the symbol AR$ throughout this section. Notes come in 2, 5, 10, 20, 50 and 100 peso denominations, and 1 peso and 5, 10, 25 and 50 centavo coins are also in circulation. In Buenos Aires, guard your loose change as you will need it for the buses. Try to cash large notes in hotels and supermarkets – never in taxis – and look out for counterfeit money. Check your notes for a watermark, and that the number is printed in shiny green.

Argentina still has a relatively healthy **economy**, by South American standards, even since the crisis in early 2002, when the peso was sharply devalued. It has since settled at around 3 to the US dollar. Although the cost of basic products

STUDENT AND YOUTH DISCOUNTS

An **ISIC card** will entitle you to substantial discounts for many museums, travel and cultural events, as well as other services. See ⓦwww.isic.com.ar for details. For travel discounts, contact Asatej ⓣ011/4114-7595, ⓦwww.asatej.com.ar.

rocketed following the devaluation, the price of most services has remained surprisingly low, turning Argentina into an economical country to visit. It may still seem expensive if you arrive from Peru or Bolivia, and the far South still tends to eat up money, partly owing to the huge distances to be covered. If you are paying **cash**, especially at hotels, it's always worth trying for a discount.

ATMs (*cajeros automáticos*) are plentiful in Argentina, though you can sometimes be caught out in very remote places, especially in the northwest. Note that single withdrawals are usually limited to AR$300, three times in one day. **Traveller's cheques** are not really a viable option as fewer and fewer banks seem to accept them.

Hotels and other types of commerce, especially at the luxury end of the market, may charge foreigners in US dollars, rather than Argentine pesos, as a covert but perfectly legal way of charging more. This practice is mostly found, of course, in more touristy locations, such as Buenos Aires, Ushuaia and Bariloche.

OPENING HOURS AND HOLIDAYS

Most **shops and services** are open Monday to Friday from 9am to 7pm, and Saturday 9am to 2pm. In smaller towns they may close at some point during the day for between one and five hours – as a rule the further north you go, the longer the midday break or siesta, sometimes offset by later closing times in the evening, especially in the summer. Supermarkets seldom close during the day and are generally open much later, often until 8 or even 10pm, and on Saturday afternoons. Large shopping malls don't close before 10pm and their food and drink sections (*patios de comida*) may stay open as late as midnight. Most of them open on Sundays, too. **Banks** mostly open on weekdays only, from 10am to 3pm, while *casas de cambio* more or less follow shop hours. In the northeast, bank opening hours may be more like 7am to noon, to avoid the hot, steamy afternoons.

In addition to the national **holidays** listed below, some local anniversaries or saints' days are also public holidays when everything in a given city may close down, taking you by surprise. Festivals of all kinds, both religious and profane, celebrating local patrons such as Santa Catalina or the Virgin Mary, or showing off produce such as handicrafts, olives, goats or wine, are good excuses for much partying and pomp.

PUBLIC HOLIDAYS

January 1 New Year's Day (*Año Nuevo*)
March 25 Day of Truth and Justice
April 2 Malvinas Remembrance Day
Easter Easter Thursday and Friday are public holidays
May 1 Labour Day (*Día del Trabajo*)
May 25 May Revolution Day
June 20 Flag Day (*Día de la Bandera*)
July 9 Day of Independence (*Día de la Independencia*)
Aug 17 Remembrance of General San Martín's death (*Día del Paso a la Inmortalidad del General José de San Martín*)
Oct 12 Columbus Day (*Día de la Raza*)
Dec 8 Day of the Immaculate Virgin Mary
Dec 25 Christmas (*Navidad*)

Note that for some holidays the exact date may vary slightly from year to year.

Buenos Aires

With a huge variety of upmarket restaurants, hotels and boutiques, as well as an eclectic mix of French, English and Modern architecture, **BUENOS AIRES** is deservedly known as the Paris of the South. The influence of immigrants from all over the world, Italian and Spanish above all, can be seen in its street names, restaurants, architecture and language. It is both an essential and an attractive place to spend a few days. Sip a coffee in the famous *Café Tortoni*, visit a dark and romantic *milonga* to spy on some tango, or simply walk the streets of Recoleta watching the heavily made-up ladies in their fur-coats walking their tiny dogs on Chanel leads. If you grow weary of the people, noise and buses of the capital head out of the city to one of the nearby attractions such as the waterways of the Delta, the quiet streets of La Plata or the home of Argentina's gauchos in San Antonio de Areco.

What to see and do

The city's museums and sights of interest are well distributed between the central areas of Recoleta, Retiro, the Microcentro, Palermo and San Telmo. The historic *barrio* of San Telmo is one of the most interesting for visitors, on account of its atmospheric streets, surviving (if often faded) nineteenth-century architecture, and the weekly Sunday antiques market. The Microcentro has the greatest concentration of shops and commerce, but Palermo Viejo should also be on every visitor's itinerary for its leafy streets lined with design and fashion shops, and hip bars and restaurants.

Plaza de Mayo

The **Plaza de Mayo** has been at the heart of the best and worst moments of Argentina's history – host to ageing founding presidents, devastating military coups, the fanaticism of Evita, the dark days of the 'Dirty War', and desperate crowds after the economic crisis. It has been bombed by its own military, filled to the brink with patriots, and left deserted, guarded by the federal police, in times of uncertainty, and even now it is still the home of the **Madres de la Plaza de Mayo**. These women, whose adult children 'disappeared' during the Military Dictatorship (1976–1983), have marched in the plaza every Thursday (3.30–4pm) for over thirty years demanding information about their children's whereabouts. The huge pink building at the river end of the plaza is the **Casa Rosada** (☎011/4344-3804 for daily tours), home to the offices of the president and the executive branch of government. On the south side of the building, the **Museo de la Casa Rosada**, Hipólito Yrigoyen 219 (Mon–Fri 10am–6pm, Sun 2–6pm; free; free guided tours Mon–Fri 11am & 2pm, Sun 2pm; ☎011/4344-3802) has interesting displays on Argentina's previous presidents and the events surrounding their term in office.

At the opposite end of the plaza is the **Cabildo** which, though much altered, is one of the only examples of colonial architecture left in this part of the city. During the week there is a small crafts market and a lovely café here, as well as a **museum** of historical artefacts (Tues–Sat 10.30am–5pm, Sun 11.30am–6pm; AR$1; guided tours Sun 12.30pm & 3.30pm; AR$3; ☎011/4334-1782). The **Catedral Metropolitana** (Mon–Fri 8am–7pm, Sat & Sun 9am–7.30pm; free guided tours Mon–Sat 3.30pm; ☎011/4331-2845), close by, is a largely unattractive building, but is worth a look for its imposing columns.

Avenida de Mayo

Heading west behind the Cabildo, **Avenida de Mayo** is one of the city's most attractive streets. In the late

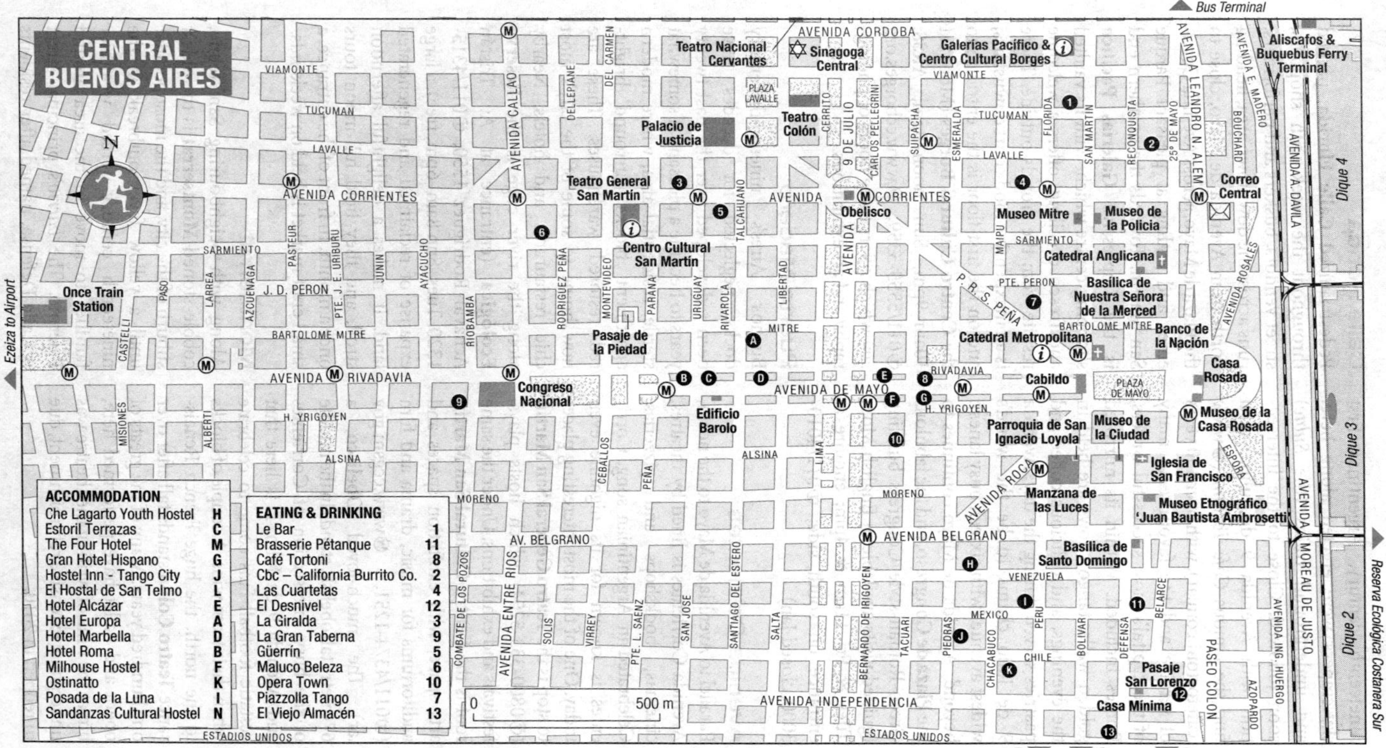

CENTRAL BUENOS AIRES
N
Bus Terminal
Ezeiza to Airport
Reserva Ecológica Costanera Sur
ACCOMMODATION
Che Lagarto Youth Hostel H
Estoril Terrazas C
The Four Hotel M
Gran Hotel Hispano G
Hostel Inn - Tango City J
El Hostal de San Telmo L
Hotel Alcázar E
Hotel Europa A
Hotel Marbella D
Hotel Roma B
Milhouse Hostel F
Ostinatto K
Posada de la Luna I
Sandanzas Cultural Hostel N
EATING & DRINKING
Le Bar 1
Brasserie Pétanque 11
Café Tortoni 8
Cbc – California Burrito Co. 2
Las Cuartetas 4
El Desnivel 12
La Giralda 3
La Gran Taberna 9
Güerrín 5
Maluco Beleza 6
Opera Town 10
Piazzolla Tango 7
El Viejo Almacén 13
0
500 m
Once Train Station
Teatro Nacional Cervantes
Sinagoga Central
Galerías Pacífico & Centro Cultural Borges
Aliscafos & Buquebus Ferry Terminal
Palacio de Justicia
Teatro Colón
Teatro General San Martín
Centro Cultural San Martín
Obelisco
Museo Mitre
Museo de la Policía
Correo Central
Catedral Anglicana
Basílica de Nuestra Señora de la Merced
Catedral Metropolitana
Banco de la Nación
Casa Rosada
Cabildo
Plaza de Mayo
Pasaje de la Piedad
Congreso Nacional
Edificio Barolo
Parroquia de San Ignacio Loyola
Museo de la Ciudad
Museo de la Casa Rosada
Iglesia de San Francisco
Manzana de las Luces
Museo Etnográfico 'Juan Bautista Ambrosetti'
Basílica de Santo Domingo
Pasaje San Lorenzo
Casa Mínima
Plaza Lavalle
Dique 4
Dique 3
Dique 2
Avenida Córdoba
Viamonte
Tucumán
Lavalle
Avenida Corrientes
Sarmiento
J. D. Perón
Bartolomé Mitre
Avenida Rivadavia
Avenida de Mayo
H. Yrigoyen
Alsina
Moreno
Av. Belgrano
Avenida Belgrano
Venezuela
México
Chile
Avenida Independencia
Estados Unidos
Avenida Callao
Avenida 9 de Julio
Avenida Leandro N. Alem
Avenida E. Madero
Avenida A. Davila
Avenida Moreau de Justo
Avenida Ing. Huergo
Paseo Colon
Azopardo
Avenida Roca
P. R. S. Peña
Avenida Entre Ríos
Combate de los Pozos

nineteenth century, Argentina's first skyscrapers were erected along here, and underground trains (the *Subte*) soon followed. Close to the intersection with Avenida 9 de Julio, you'll find the famous *Café Tortoni* (Ⓦwww.cafetortoni.com.ar), with over 150 years of service and the favourite of many of the capital's most successful writers, Borges included. Within its mirrored golden walls, tango shows are held in the evenings, and delicious coffee and pastries served during the day; Avenida 9 de Julio claims to be the world's widest avenue (with sixteen busy lanes): beyond, Avenida de Mayo continues to the **Plaza de Congreso**, and the fabulous Greco-Roman-style Congress building (guided visits available in English Mon, Tues & Fri 11am & 4pm; enquire at entrance on south side; Ⓣ011/4010-3000; closed Jan).

Avenida Corrientes

Parallel to Avenida de Mayo to the north, Avenida Corrientes is lined by theatres, cinemas, bookshops and pizzerias. Celebrated in Argentinian song, Corrientes is known for its nightlife even today. One of the most interesting places to stop is the **Teatro General San Martín** (Ⓣ0800-333-5254) which hosts plays, festivals and exhibitions. Under the same roof is the **Centro Cultural San Martín** arts space, with exhibition spaces and auditoriums for music, drama and film (Ⓣ011/4374-1251, Ⓦwww.ccgsm.gov.ar). The much-loved **Obelisco**, a 67-metre tall obelisk, stands in the middle of the busy intersection of Corrientes and Avenida 9 de Julio. It is here that ecstatic football fans come to celebrate when their team wins. A couple of blocks to the north, the huge French Renaissance **Teatro Colón** stands tall after over one hundred years. Many of the greats of opera and ballet have performed here, but at the time of writing the theatre was undergoing extensive refurbishment, due to reopen in 2010.

Calle Florida

Pedestrianized **Calle Florida**, packed throughout the week with shoppers, street vendors, buskers and performers, runs across the downtown area, heading north from Avenida de Mayo, close to the Plaza de Mayo, across Avenida Corrientes and ending at pleasant Parque San Martín. Towards the northern end is the impressive **Galerías Pacífico** shopping centre which, with its vaulted and frescoed ceiling, offers a welcome respite from the crowds outside. There is an inexpensive food court downstairs, and on the first floor is the entrance to the **Centro Cultural Borges** (Mon–Sat 10am–9pm, Sun noon–9pm; AR$8; Ⓣ011/5555-5359, Ⓦwww.ccborges.org.ar) which offers three floors of photography and art exhibitions.

Puerto Madero

Buenos Aires's nineteenth-century docks, neglected for decades, have been redeveloped over the past twenty years to become a pleasant, if somewhat sterile, residential area, where modern apartment blocks surround bright-red restored warehouses. These are now home to some of the city's most chic restaurants and hotels. Nearby along the river edge is the **Reserva Ecológica** (entrance at Av Tristán Achával Rodríguez 1550, Ⓣ011/4315-1320, Tues–Sun 8am–6pm, free), a large expanse of reclaimed and regenerated land. It makes a delightful afternoon stroll, and they hold full-moon tours once a month. In front of the entrance, a small craft market is held on weekends.

Montserrat

Along with neighbouring San Telmo, cobble-stoned **Montserrat** is the oldest suburb of the city, and the most popular until a yellow fever outbreak in the nineteenth century forced wealthier families to move to the area around Palermo. The *barrio*'s principal street is Calle Defensa, named after residents

who, trying to force back British invaders in the early 1800s, poured boiling oil from their balconies onto the attacking soldiers.

The neo-Baroque **Iglesia de San Francisco** (Wed–Sun 11am–6pm; ⓣ011/4331-0625), at the corner of Alsina and Defensa, has an intricately decorated interior that can just about be made out through the gloom. Nearby is the small **Museo de la Ciudad**, Alsina 412 (Mon–Fri 11am–7pm, Sat & Sun 3–7pm; AR$3, ⓣ011/4331-9855), which houses informative and well-presented changing exhibitions about the city. One block west of Defensa is the collection of buildings known as the **Manzana de las Luces**, (guided visits daily at 3pm, Sat & Sun also 4.30pm & 6pm; AR$5; info at Perú 272; ⓣ011/4342-9930, ⓦwww.manzanadelasluces.gov.ar) which dates back to 1662. Originally housing a Jesuit community, it has also been home to numerous official institutions throughout its history, and today you'll find the **Colegio Nacional**, an elite high school, as well as Buenos Aires' oldest church, **San Ignacio** (daily 8am–9pm; guided visits Sat & Sun 3pm; ⓣ011/4331-2458), begun in 1675.

San Telmo

San Telmo begins further south along Defensa, on the far side of Avenida Belgrano. With its myriad of antique stores and junk shops, as well as a range of busy, late-opening restaurants and bars (especially around the intersection of Chile and Defensa), it's a great place to wander. For fresh food and a variety of eclectic antiques head to the **San Telmo Food Market** (daily 8am–1pm & 3–7pm). The market takes up an entire city block, with an entrance on each side, including one on Defensa near the corner of Estados Unidos. A few blocks further, **Plaza Dorrego** is a great place to pause for a coffee under the leafy trees, at least on weekdays. On Sundays the area is taken over by the **Feria de San Pedro Telmo** (10am–5pm; buses #9, #10, #24, #28 or #86 easily picked up downtown). Vintage watches, posters, antique clothes, and jewellery are all on display at this huge open-air antiques market, enlivened by street performers and live tango acts. Another great place for antique spotting is the **Pasaje de la Defensa**, Defensa 1179, a converted mansion filled with hidden shops, cafes and workshops. Calle Defensa continues, across the busy, ugly avenues of San Juan and Juan de Garay, to **Parque Lezama**, whose green acres are home to the **Museo Histórico Nacional** (Defensa 1600, Tues–Fri 11am–5pm, Sat 3–6pm, Sun 2–6pm; AR$2; ⓣ011/4307-1182). Small and delightful, this museum was recently renovated and has an interesting permanent exhibition on Argentina's history.

La Boca

Easily accessible from Parque Lezama, the suburb of **La Boca** is known for the Caminito and as home to one of Argentina's leading football clubs, Boca Juniors, arch-rivals of the upper-class River Plate team.

The **Caminito** is a small area of brightly coloured buildings along the river, created in the 1950s by the neighbourhood's most famous artist, **Benito Quinquela Martín**. These days the Caminito is a bit of a tourist trap – there is an interesting open-air **arts and crafts fair** (daily 10.30am–6pm), street performers, and restaurants and cafes charging tourist prices – but it remains very beautiful.

A visit to the Boca Juniors' stadium, **La Bombonera** (Brandsen 805, three blocks west of Avenida Almirante Brown; ⓣ011/4362-2050), is well worthwhile even if you can't score tickets to a game. The starting point is the fascinating **Museo de la Pasión Boquense** (daily 10am–6pm; AR$20; ⓦwww.museoboquense.com), a must for football fans; guided tours of the stadium start from here (daily 11am–5pm; AR$10 extra).

La Boca can be reached by **bus** #29 from Corrientes or Plaza de Mayo, #86 from Plaza de Mayo or #53 from Constitución.

Recoleta

Immediately north of the city centre, the wide streets of the upper-class suburb of Recoleta are most famously home to the **Recoleta Cemetery**, at Avenida Quintana and Junín (daily 8am–6pm; excellent guided tours March–Nov last Sun of month at 2.30pm; free). Surrounded by café-lined streets and their designer-clad denizens, it remains immensely popular as the resting place of some of Argentina's leading celebrities, including Evita herself. A map is available at the entrance to guide you around the great monuments of dark granite, white marble and gleaming bronze.

Next door are the white walls of the second oldest church in Buenos Aires, the **Basílica de Nuestra Señora del Pilar** (daily 8am–9pm; free; ⓣ011/4803-6793). The eighteenth-century Jesuit building has been beautifully restored, and is much in demand for fashionable weddings: inside, the magnificent Baroque silver altarpiece, embellished with an Inca sun and other pre-Hispanic details, was made by craftsmen from the north of Argentina.

Next door again, the **Centro Cultural de Recoleta** (Tues–Fri 2–9pm, Sat & Sun 10am–9pm; free, AR$1 suggested; ⓣ011/4803-1040), at Junín 1930, is a fabulous art space with interesting temporary exhibitions. If by now you're in need of a coffee or a shopping fix, **Buenos Aires Design**, a shopping centre focusing on chic Argentine

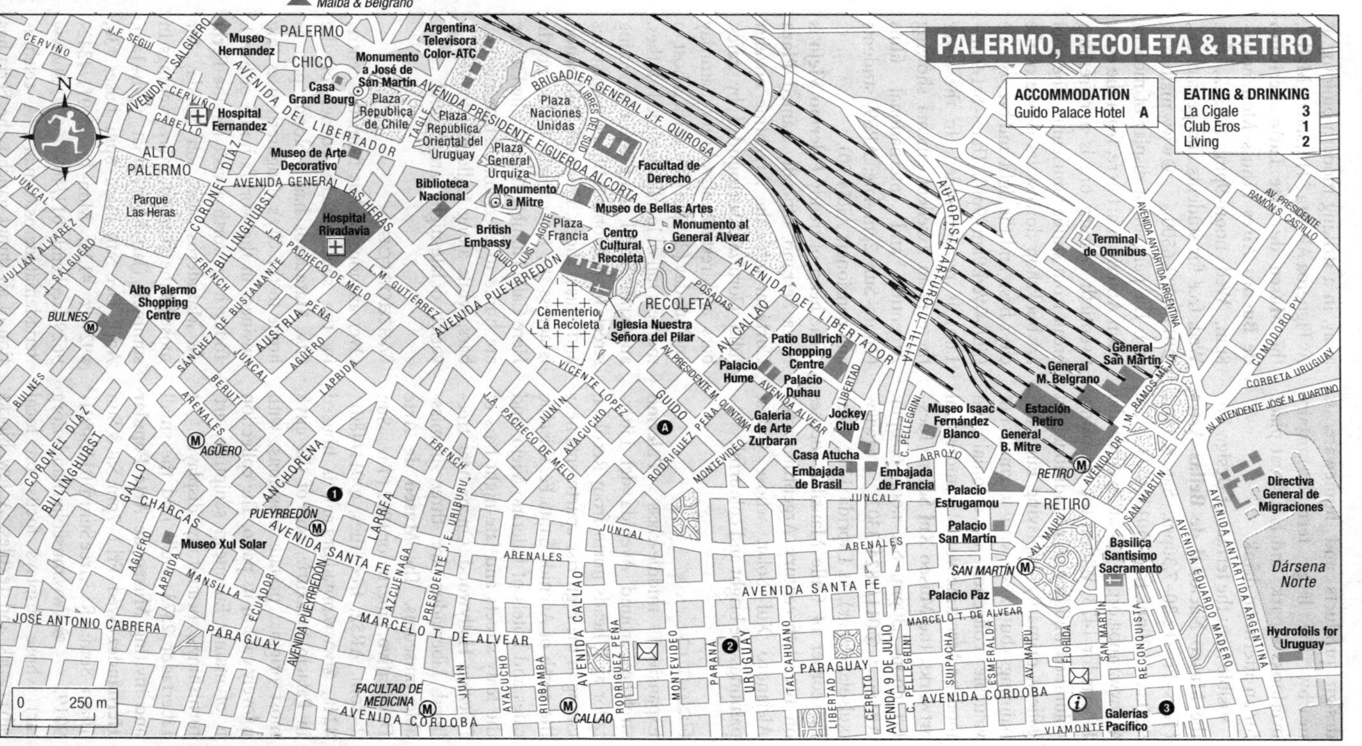
PALERMO, RECOLETA & RETIRO
ACCOMMODATION
Guido Palace Hotel A
EATING & DRINKING
La Cigale 3
Club Eros 1
Living 2
Maida & Belgrano
Museo Hernandez
PALERMO CHICO
Argentina Televisora Color-ATC
Monumento a José de San Martín
Casa Grand Bourg
Plaza Republica de Chile
Plaza Republica Oriental del Uruguay
Plaza Naciones Unidas
Plaza General Urquiza
Hospital Fernandez
ALTO PALERMO
Parque Las Heras
Museo de Arte Decorativo
Biblioteca Nacional
Monumento a Mitre
Facultad de Derecho
Museo de Bellas Artes
Hospital Rivadavia
British Embassy
Plaza Francia
Centro Cultural Recoleta
Monumento al General Alvear
Cementerio La Recoleta
Iglesia Nuestra Señora del Pilar
RECOLETA
Alto Palermo Shopping Centre
Patio Bullrich Shopping Centre
Palacio Hume
Palacio Duhau
Galeria de Arte Zurbaran
Jockey Club
Casa Atucha
Embajada de Brasil
Embajada de Francia
Museo Isaac Fernández Blanco
General B. Mitre
Estación Retiro
General M. Belgrano
General San Martín
Terminal de Omnibus
Palacio Estrugamou
Palacio San Martín
RETIRO
Basilica Santisimo Sacramento
Palacio Paz
Directiva General de Migraciones
Dársena Norte
Hydrofoils for Uruguay
Museo Xul Solar
FACULTAD DE MEDICINA
Galerías Pacífico
0 250 m

design products and homeware, is nearby. The large terrace upstairs overlooks a park, and is a great place for an afternoon drink.

Visible from the terrace of Design BA, the **Museo Nacional de Bellas Artes** (Tues–Fri 12.30–7.30pm, Sat & Sun 9.30am–7.30pm; free; ⓣ011/4803-0802, ⓦwww.mnba.org.ar) is at Avenida del Libertador 1473. Within the imposing, columned building is a traditional art gallery, primarily displaying European paintings but also with a small but valuable collection of colonial and modern Argentine work. For more local artworks, the **Museo Xul Solar** (Tues–Fri noon–7.30pm, Sat noon–6.30pm; AR$6; ⓣ011/4824-3302, ⓦwww.xulsolar.org.ar), at Laprida 1212, near the corner of Calle Mansilla, focuses on twentieth-century Argentine artist Alejandro Xul Solar, whose Cubist paintings are bright and colourful.

Palermo

Expansive, middle-class **Palermo** stretches around Avenida del Libertador as it heads north from Recoleta, taking in the high-rise apartments near the north of Avenida Santa Fe, the chic cafes and hotels of Palermo Viejo, and the leafy streets and late-night bars of Palermo Hollywood. On or near tree-lined Libertador are three unmissable museums. The **Museo de Arte Decorativo**, Libertador 1902 (Tues–Sun 2–7pm; AR$2, free Tues; ⓣ011/4801-8248, ⓦwww.mnad.org.ar), is housed in Palacio Errázuriz, one of the city's most original private mansions, with a lovely café in its patio. The collection is of mainly European sculpture, art, furnishings, beautifully displayed. At Libertador 2373 you'll find the small and inviting **Museo de Arte Popular Hernández** (Wed–Fri 1–7pm; Sat & Sun 10am–8pm; AR$3, free Sun; ⓣ011/4801-9019, ⓦwww.museohernandez.org.ar) whose displays focus on local silverwork and textiles. A few blocks away, in a striking modern building at Av Figueroa Alcorta 3415, stands **Malba**, the **Museo de Arte Latinamericano de Buenos Aires** (Thurs–Mon noon–8pm, Wed noon–9pm; AR$12, free Wed, free for students and pensioners; ⓣ011/4808-6500 ⓦwww.malba.org.ar). The permanent display of moaern Latin American art here, from the early twentieth century on, is a refreshing break from stuffier museums. The cool art bookshop downstairs is one of the city's best, and the light and breezy café (Sun–Wed 9am–9pm, Thurs–Sat 9am–1am) is recommended. In the foyer there is an excellent cinema showing Argentine and international films (Thurs–Sun 2pm–late; AR$9, students and pensioners AR$4.50).

The heart of trendy **Palermo Viejo** is Plaza Serrano, officially named **Plaza Cortázar** after the Argentine novelist Julio Cortázar, surrounded by cafes, bars and restaurants. Every Saturday and Sunday (2–9pm) the plaza is host to markets full of locally designed clothes, and craft. Stroll along the connecting streets for fashion boutiques, bookstores and music shops. **Palermo Hollywood** is across the train tracks to the north. Here Calle Humboldt and Calle Fitzroy are home to excellent restaurants and bars, while along Calle Niceto Vega a variety of late-night bars abound.

Mataderos

Over an hour by bus from the centre, in the southwestern corner of the city, **Mataderos** has a bloody past as home to the city's slaughterhouses (big business in the world's home of beef). Today it is worth a visit for the **Feria de Mataderos**, held on Sunday for most of the year, Saturday evenings in summer (Jan–March Sat 6pm–1am, April–Dec Sun 11am–8pm; buses #36, #92 & #126; Mon–Fri ⓣ011/4342-9629 weekends 011/4687-5602, ⓦwww.feriademataderos.com.ar). A celebration of all things gaucho, the Feria has stalls selling leatherwork, *maté*, gourds and silver, as well as folk music and displays of horse riding.

Arrival and information

Air All international flights arrive at **Ezeiza International Airport** (Ⓣ011/5480-6111, Ⓦwww.aa2000.com.ar), 35km (45min) west of the city centre. Tourist buses run by Manuel Tienda Léon (AR$35 one-way; Ⓣ011/4315-5115, Ⓦwww.tiendaleon.com, depart every 30min between 4am and 10.30pm and drop you at Av E Madero 1299 (at San Martín) in the Retiro area. A taxi or *remise* (radio-cab) will cost around AR$90. Buenos Aires' domestic airport is **Aeroparque Jorge Newbery** (Ⓣ011/5480-6111) on the Costanera Norte, around 6km north of the city centre. Local bus #33 runs along the Costanera past the airport and will take you to Paseo Colón, on the fringe of the *microcentro*. Alternatively, Manuel Tienda Léon (see above; AR$12) runs a minibus service for not much less than a taxi would cost.

Bus All domestic and international services arrive at **Retiro** bus terminal, at Avenida Antártida and Ramos Mejía. Taxis are plentiful and the Retiro *subte* (metro) station is just a block away, outside the adjoining train station. A variety of buses leave from outside, including #5 and #50, to Congreso, and #106 to Palermo Viejo. Take extra care around this area, as pickpockets are known to operate.

Ferries Ferry services from Uruguay (see p.210) arrive at **Terminal Dársena Norte**, Víamonte y Costanera Sur, just a few blocks from the *microcentro*.

Tourist office There are a number of *centros de informes* around the city run by the Secretaria de Turismo (Ⓣ011/4313-0187, Ⓦwww.bue.gov.ar); probably the best is at Florida 100 at Av Diagonal Roque Sáenz Peña (Mon–Fri 9am–7pm, Sat 10am–4pm). You can also pick up local (and national) information from the well-organized National Tourist Office at Santa Fe 883 (Mon–Fri 9am–5pm; Ⓣ011/4312-2232, Ⓦwww.turismo.gov.ar), which has details of the provincial tourist offices within the capital.

Train The main stations are Retiro, Constitución and Once (www.tbanet.com.ar). See p.79.

City transport

Bus Buses (Ⓦwww.locolectivos.com.ar) are one of the most useful (and cheap) ways of getting round the city – and indeed the only way of reaching many of the outlying districts. Invest in a combined **street and bus-route map**, such as Guía Lumi or Guía "T" (AR$3), both widely available from street kiosks, to work out the routes. Tickets (AR$0.90–1.40) are acquired from a machine on the bus, which gives change for coins (no notes). Many services run all night.

Subte The easiest part of the public transport system to get to grips with is the underground railway or *subte*, which serves the city centre and the north of the city from 7am to 10 or 11pm. There are six lines, plus a "premetro" system serving the far southwestern corner of the city, linking up with the *subte* at the Plaza de los Virreyes, at the end of line E. Lines A, B, D and E run from the city centre outwards, while lines C and H (still under construction) run between Retiro and Constitución, connecting them all. Tickets cost AR$0.70 and are bought from the booths at each station. If you are going to travel a lot buy a card of 10 tickets – you can share them, and it saves lining up.

Taxis The city's black-and-yellow taxis are spectacularly plentiful. The meter starts at just over AR$3.10 (charges increase at night), and you should calculate on a ride costing around AR$8 per twenty blocks. **Remises** are radio cabs or minicabs, plain cars booked through an office (and therefore preferred by some wary locals). Not particularly economical for short journeys, they're cheaper than taxis for getting to the airport and for early morning starts you may prefer to book one; try *Remises Uno* (Ⓣ011/4638-8318). Always call a Radio Taxi at night. Ask your hostel for their preferred company or try Taxi 'alo' (Ⓣ011/4855-0455).

Accommodation

Finding **accommodation** in Buenos Aires shouldn't be a problem – almost half of all the hotels in the country are to be found in the capital – but advance planning is advised, especially for high season. **Discounts** can sometimes be negotiated, particularly if you are staying for more than a few days.

Hostels

Most hostels have communal kitchens and offer free or cheap internet, breakfast and laundry.

Casa Esmeralda Honduras 5765, at Bonpland Ⓣ011/4772-2446. Small, friendly hostel with a large shady back garden and hammocks. A good place to kick back and meet people. Dorm AR$32. ❺

Che Lagarto Youth Hostel Venezuela 857, at Piedras Ⓣ011/4343-4845 Ⓦwww.chelagarto.com. Rooms are standard but the sociable atmosphere, cool bar/restaurant and lovely tree-shaded back garden make *Che* a top traveler hangout. Dorm AR$34. ❺

Estoril Terrazas Av de Mayo 1385 (1st & 6th Floors) at Uruguay ⓣ011/4372 5494. Located opposite the Palacio Barolo, one of Buenos Aires' most stunning buildings, *Estoril* has to be among the top hostels in the world. Extremely comfortable and always impeccably clean, it offers all amenities and has a roof terrace with perfect views of Av de Mayo and Congreso. Ask for the roof-top dorm. Dorm AR$39. ❻

El Hostal de San Telmo Carlos Calvo 614 and Peru ⓣ011/4300-6899, ⓦwww.elhostalde santelmo.com. Located in one of the prettiest parts of San Telmo, Buenos Aires' original hostel is cheaper than most, friendly and well kept. Dorm AR$23. ❹

Hostel Inn – Tango City Piedras 680, at Chilé ⓣ011/4300-5764, ⓦwww.hostel-inn.com. Large, fun hostel (part of a chain across Argentina) popular with party animals. A plethora of activities is organised, including *asado* nights, Spanish lessons and tango excursions. Dorm AR$36. ❻

Milhouse Hostel Hipólito Yrigoyen 959 and Bdo de Irigoyen ⓣ011/4345-9604, ⓦwww.milhouse hostel.com. A large, lively hostel in a colonial-style building with a huge range of activities on offer. *Milhouse* opened a new outpost at Av de Mayo 1249 in 2008. One of the city's most popular, so book well in advance. Full English breakfast AR$15. Dorm AR$33. ❺

Ostinatto Chile 680 and Perú ⓣ011/4362-9639, ⓦwww.ostinatto.com. Falls squarely in the category of 'hip' hostel, with cool minimalist design, spacious dorm and extremely friendly staff. Hosts free tango lessons and film viewings. Fantastic value for money. Dorm AR$28. ❺

Sandanzas Cultural Hostel Balcarce 1351 and Cochabamba ⓣ011/4300-7375, ⓦwww .sandanzas.com.ar. One of Buenos Aires' smallest hostels, set slightly off the beaten track. The common room is the setting for a variety of cosy cultural events. Dorm AR$30. ❺

Tango Backpackers Hostel Paraguay 4601, at Thames, Palermo Viejo ⓣ011/4776-6871, ⓦwww .tangobp.com. This party hostel, located next to Plaza Italia (ideal for transport links), is made up of several grand old properties. Large terrace. Dorm AR$36. ❺

Hotels and B&Bs

Hotel Alcázar Av de Mayo 935 ⓣ011/4345-0926. This old hotel with a lovely central staircase features basic rooms, all with heating, a fan and private bathroom. ❺

Casa Alfaro Gurruchaga 2155, at Paraguay, Palermo Viejo ⓣ011/4831-0517. At the higher end of the budget spectrum, *Alfaro* has 11 rooms, sparsely furnished but with plenty of colour. Attractive garden. ❺

Che Lulu Trendy Hotel Pasaje Emilio Zola 5185, at Godoy Cruz, Palermo Viejo ⓣ011/4772-0289, ⓦwww.chelulu.com. On a colourful *pasaje* in Palermo, *Che Lulu* offers a down-to-earth and homely experience. Clean, small rooms with air-con, plus a cute attic dorm. Dorm AR$65. ❺

Cypress In Costa Rica 4828 and Borges ⓣ011/4833-5834, ⓦwww.cypressin.com. Sleek B&B, with designer features and a neat location in the heart of Palermo's 'Soho'. ❼

Hotel Europa Bartolomé Mitre 1294 and Talcahuano ⓣ011/4381-9629. Immaculately maintained hotel with simple decor and comfortable rooms, all with cable TV and private bathroom. ❻

The Four Hotel Carlos Calvo 535 and Bolívar ⓣ011/4362-1729, ⓦwww.thefourhotel.com. This B&B in a traditional San Telmo house has stylish rooms, personalised service and a gorgeous terrace. Doubles AR$173. ❼

Gran Hotel Hispano Av de Mayo 861, at Tacuari ⓣ011/4345-2020, ⓦwww.hhispano.com.ar. Atmospheric old building with a beautiful central arcade, metres from the famous *Café Tortoni*. Rooms are clean if chintzy. ❻

Guido Palace Hotel Guido 1780 and Callao ⓣ011/4812-0674, ⓦwww.GuidoPalace.com.ar. An affordable, no-frills option in upmarket Recoleta, near the cemetery. ❽

Hotel Marbella Av de Mayo 1261, at Stgo del Estero ⓣ011/4383-3573, ⓦwww.hotelmarbella .com.ar. Calm, good-value lodgings in a central location. Modern rooms with cable TV and decent-sized bathrooms. Economical restaurant. ❺

Posada de la Luna Perú 565 and México ⓣ011/4343-0911, ⓦwww.posadaluna.com. Attractively decorated B&B set in a colonial townhouse between San Telmo and the Centro. Home-made bread and jam is served at breakfast on the patio. ❼

Hotel Roma Av de Mayo 1413 and Parana ⓣ011/4381-4921. Low prices and a central location are the draw at the *Roma*. Slightly noisy rooms, some with balconies looking onto Av de Mayo. ❺

Eating

Buenos Aires has a busy, increasingly diverse, restaurant scene. Many restaurants offer a good-value *menu del día* (lunchtime set menu) on weekdays, usually including a drink; this is an excellent way to sample the best of BA's restaurants at much lower prices. It is wise to book at the more popular places.

Downtown

Cbc – California Burrito Co. Lavalle 441, Centre ⓣ011/4328-3056. Busy central *burrito* joint, ideally placed for lunch on the go. White-flour *tortillas* are packed with seemingly endless combinations of fresh ingredients; portions are enormous. *Burritos* AR$18.

Las Cuartetas Av Corrientes 838, Centre ⓣ011/4326-0171. Big, brightly lit Corrientes pizzeria, opposite the Gran Rex theatre. Large pizzas from AR$25.

Freddo Buenos Aires' best ice-cream chain. *Dulce de leche* fans will be in heaven, and the passionfruit mousse flavour (*maracuyá mousse*) is superb. Branches throughout the city. Cones AR$4.50–9.

La Giralda Corrientes and Uruguay, Centre. ⓣ011/4371-3846. Brightly lit and austerely decorated Corrientes café, famous for its *chocolate con churros* (AR$13). A perennial hangout for students and intellectuals and a good place to observe the *porteño* passion for conversation.

La Gran Taberna Combate de los Pozos 95, Montserrat ⓣ011/4951-7586. A popular, bustling and down-to-earth restaurant a block from Congreso. The vast, reasonably priced menu offers a mixture of Spanish dishes, including a good selection of seafood, *porteño* staples and a sprinkling of more exotic dishes such as *ranas a la provenzal* (frogs' legs with parsley and garlic, AR$55). Many dishes are large enough to share. Mains AR$20–30.

Güerrín Av Corrientes 1368, Centre ⓣ011/4371-8141. Legendary Buenos Aires pizza parlour of the old school. Try the *faina*, a slice made with chickpea flour (AR$3.50), or share a *grande de mozzarella* (AR$27).

San Telmo and La Boca

Brasserie Pétanque Defensa 595, San Telmo ⓣ011/4342-7930. Authentic chic French-owned brasserie, serving French classics (onion soup, steak tartare, *crème brûlée*, even snails). Weekday lunch deal only AR$19.

El Desnivel Defensa 855, San Telmo ⓣ011/4300-9081. Classic San Telmo *parrilla* with accessible prices, great meat and a friendly, slightly rowdy atmosphere; popular with tourists. *Lomo* steak AR$22.

El Obrero Caffarena 64, La Boca ⓣ011/4362-9912. With Boca Juniors souvenirs on the walls and tango musicians moving from table to table at weekends, the atmosphere at the hugely popular and moderately priced *El Obrero* is as much a part of the attraction as the simple homely food (*lomo* steak AR$19, pasta dishes AR$9–13). Very popular, so prepare to line up at weekends. Closed Sun.

Parrilla 1880 Defensa 1665, San Telmo ⓣ011/4307-2746. Extremely good *parrilla* joint, right opposite Parque Lezama. Its walls are lined with photos and drawings from the restaurant's famous and mostly bohemian clients, and the very friendly owner makes sure everyone is happy. Mains AR$20–35. Closed Mon.

Palermo and surrounds

Club Eros Uriarte 1609, Palermo Viejo ⓣ011/4832-1313. Fun, noisy *cantina* at a neighbourhood sports and social club, offering Argentine standards at bargain prices. Mains AR$7–12.

La Cocina Pueyrredón 1508, Recoleta ⓣ011/4825-3171. Tiny place serving *locro* (a filling corn stew from the northeast of Argentina), *tamales* and a selection of delicious Catamarca-style *empanadas* (AR$2.80 each). Closed Sun.

La Cupertina Cabrera 5296, Palermo Viejo ⓣ011/4777-3711. Traditional Argentine dishes and excellent *empanadas* in a corner spot with gorgeous rustic décor and pastel colours. Mains AR$12–16.

Don Julio Guatemala 4699, Palermo Viejo ⓣ011/4831-9564. Excellent *parrilla* with choice cuts of meat, a good wine list and smart, efficient service. *Lomo*, fries, salad and wine will set you back AR$50–60.

Krishna Malabia 1833, Palermo Viejo ⓣ011/4833-4618. Tiny bohemian spot on the *plaza* run by the International Society for Krishna Consciousness and serving tasty vegetarian Indian food. Go for the mixed *thali* (AR$22) with a ginger lemonade (AR$10). Closed Mon.

Miranda Costa Rica 5602, Palermo Viejo ⓣ011/4771-4255. Some of the city's finest steaks are served at this airy (and fume-free), fashionable corner *parrilla* in Palermo 'Hollywood'. More expensive than your average local *parrilla* but well worth it for the slick service, chic surrounds and choice cuts. A worthy candidate for a first or last steak in Argentina. Average meal with wine AR$45.

Pura Vida Juice Bar Uriburu 1489, Recoleta ⓣ011/4806-0017. A chic snack bar serving a fantastic range of fresh shakes, lemonades and juices, with healthy optional extras such as wheatgrass, soy and linseed oil. Healthy soups (AR$7–8.50), salads (AR$10–14.50) and sandwiches (brown bread available) are also served. Heaven for the vitamin-starved traveller. Closed Sun.

Sarkis Thames 1101, Villa Crespo ⓣ011/4772-4911. Excellent tabbouleh (AR$6), *keppe crudo* (raw meat with onion – much better than it sounds;

> **TREAT YOURSELF**
>
> **Olsen**, at Gorriti 5870 in Palermo Viejo, is a fabulous upmarket Scandinavian restaurant with cutting-edge décor and superb, vodka-based cocktails. You can even treat yourself on a budget – there's an excellent daily changing lunch deal (two courses and a beer) for AR$27. Average meal with wine AR$80. Bookings required ⓣ011/4776-7677. Closed Mon.

AR$10) and falafel (AR$14) at this popular restaurant serving a fusion of Armenian, Arab and Turkish cuisine. Close to Palermo Viejo, and great value for money.

Drinking and nightlife

You'll find that Buenos Aires offers a lively nightlife every day of the week. The only exception is perhaps on Monday, when restaurants in the centre and San Telmo tend to close. Wednesday is known as 'After Office', and you'll find the city's bars and clubs packed from 6pm. Keep in mind that Buenos Aires starts – and finishes – late, so clubs don't fill up until the early hours. Check out **What's Up Buenos Aires** (ⓦwww.whatsupbuenosaires.com) for up-to-date information and articles on the city's cultural and nightlife happenings.

Bars and pubs

Bangalore Humboldt 1416, Palermo Viejo ⓣ011/4779-2621. Fine traditional pub in Palermo 'Hollywood', popular with locals, expats and tourists. Happy hour until 10pm; pints and curries served.

Le Bar Tucumán 422, Centre ⓣ011/5219-0858. A fashionable new cocktail bar in the Microcentro, with impeccable aesthetics; from the people behind Olsen restaurant.

Bar Británico Corner of Defensa and Brasil, San Telmo ⓣ011/4361-2107. Old men, bohemians and night owls while away the small hours in this traditional wood-panelled bar overlooking Parque Lezama. Open 24hr.

Centro Cultural Pachamama Argañaraz 22, between Estado de Israel and Lavalleja, Villa Crespo ⓦwww.ccpachamama.com.ar. Poetry and live music every night in a space that feels like someone's funky living room. Everyone clicks instead of claps their applause so as not to disturb the neighbours.

La Cigale 25 de Mayo 722, Centro ⓣ011/4312-8275. One of Buenos Aires' most happening bars, attracting an up-for-it crowd. Regular live music and DJs on Thurs (free). Two for the price of one Happy Hour Mon–Fri 6–10pm.

Mitos Argentinos Humberto Primo 489, San Telmo ⓣ011/4362-7810, ⓦwww.mitosargentinos.com.ar. Local rock and tango groups play Thurs–Sat. Closed Sun–Wed.

Plaza Dorrego Bar Defensa 1098, San Telmo. The most traditional of the bars around Plaza Dorrego, a sober wood-panelled place where the names of countless customers have been etched on the wooden tables and walls.

Supersoul Báez 252, Las Cañitas ⓣ011/4776-3905. Get the night started (or see it off) at this dishy, retro-themed bar in Las Cañitas.

Thelonious Club Salguero 1884, Palermo ⓣ011/4829-1562. The best of Argentine jazz every evening but Mon.

Vaca Profana Lavalle 3683, Abasto ⓣ011/4867-0934, ⓦwww.vacaprofana.com.ar. Pint-sized venue with excellent music programming (check the website for the schedule). Tapas served. Closed Jan.

Nightclubs

Amerika Gascón 1040, Villa Crespo ⓣ011/4865-4416, ⓦwww.ameri-k.com.ar. The city's biggest gay club, with three dancefloors.

Glam Cabrera 3046, Barrio Norte ⓣ011/4963-2521, ⓦwww.glambsas.com.ar. One of the city's hottest gay bar-discos. Thurs & Sat from 1am.

Living M T de Alvear 1540, Centro ⓣ011/4811-4730. Laid-back club in a rambling old building with two bars, a coffee stand and a long, narrow dance-floor that gets very packed. Plays a fun, danceable mix of funk, disco and rock music. Open from 10pm Thurs–Sat.

Maluco Beleza Sarmiento 1728, Centre ⓣ011/4372-1737. Long-running Brazilian club, playing a mix of lambada, afro, samba and reggae to a lively crowd of Brazilians and Brazilophiles. Wed & Fri–Sun.

Niceto Club Niceto Vega 5510, Palermo Viejo ⓣ011/4779-9396, ⓦwww.nicetoclub.com. One of BA's best clubs, *Niceto* has mainly electronic music at weekends, and hosts Zizek on Wed (cumbia, reggae, hip hop, reggaeton). Live gigs before 1.30am most nights.

Opera Town Alsina 940. This is the Montserrat reincarnation of former Puerto Madero club Opera Bay, insanely popular on Wed (7pm onwards) with the after-office crowd.

Podestá Super Club de Copas Armenia 1740, Palermo Viejo ⓣ011/4832 2776, ⓦwww.elpodesta.com.ar. This gritty Palermo club has an underground feel, with rock or techno on the sound system.

Roxy Club Federico Lacroze and Alvarez Thomas, Colegiales ⓦwww.theroxybsas.com.ar. The Roxy stages one of BA's longest-running club nights, the legendary Club 69 (Thurs). Hosted by besequinned transvestites, and with outrageous stage shows from 3am.

Tango shows

Tango shows are expensive (expect to pay upwards of AR$150; more with dinner), but they are the best way to see a series of top tango dancers in one evening, and most are well worth the splurge. All the following have nightly shows, and most include dinner. Prices range from around AR$50 (without food) to AR$240.

Bar Sur Estados Unidos 299, at Balcarce, San Telmo ⓣ011/4362-6086.

Café Tortoni Av de Mayo 825, Centre ⓣ011/4342-4328. Buenos Aires' most famous café, offers an affordable tango show downstairs at AR$50.

La Esquina de Carlos Gardel Carlos Gardel 3200, Abasto ⓣ011/4867-6363.

Piazzolla Tango Florida 165, Microcentro ⓣ011/4344-8200.

El Viejo Almacén Av Independencia 300, at Balcarce, San Telmo ⓣ011/4307-7388.

Cultural centres and cinema

Buenos Aires has an abundance of cultural centres. Chief among them are the **Centro Cultural Borges** (Florida and Córdoba, Centre ⓦwww.ccborges.org.ar), **Centro Cultural Ricardo Rojas** (Av Corrientes 2038, Once ⓦwww.rojas.uba.ar) and **Centro Cultural** Recoleta (Junín 1930, next to Recoleta cemetery ⓦ www.centroculturalrecoleta.org), all with stimulating programmes of exhibitions, performance, music, film and talks.

Movie-going in Buenos Aires is affordable and popular, and the standard of programming is generally excellent. Expect to see all the big international hits alongside local releases. For times and showings at all cinemas, see ⓦwww.cinesargentinos.com.ar, or a local paper. Tickets are cheaper from Mon–Wed and often during the day; student discounts are available in most cinemas. Of the multiplexes, **Village Recoleta** (Vincente López 2050, Recoleta) and **Hoyts Abasto** (in the Abasto shopping mall, Av Corrientes 3247) are the best. Hoyts Abasto also hosts Buenos Aires' Independent Film Festival in April. For art-house and local offerings, check the programme at the Malba (see p.72), the Centro Cultural Ricardo Rojas (above) and the **Cosmos cinema** (Av Corrientes 2046, Once ⓣ011/4953-5405).

Shopping

Buenos Aires offers some of the best shopping in South America, from high-end boutiques and air-conditioned malls to weekend markets and cutting-edge boutiques. Best buys include leather goods (handbags, belts, shoes), wine, home design and handicrafts (particularly handmade jewellery). Top **shopping areas** downtown include Avenida Santa Fe, Palermo Viejo and San Telmo. Note that when you buy Argentine goods totalling more than AR$70, you may be entitled to a **tax refund** at the airport. Goods must have been made in Argentina (look for the 'Industria Argentina' label) and the shop must be a Tax Free Shopping zone (look for the sticker in the window). Be sure to ask for the *factura* (form) and bring it, along with the goods leaving the country, to the desk at the airport. Make sure you have your passport with you when you shop. You'll need it anyway if you intend to pay by credit card.

Malls The city's malls house Argentina's most successful brands, as well as big international names; they open every day of the week until 10pm. Try Alto Palermo (Santa Fé and Coronel Díaz, Palermo), Galerías Pacífico (Florida and Córdoba,

MILONGAS

Milongas – regular dance clubs, usually starting with lessons (beginners welcome) – are popular with tango dancers young and old. They are a great way to try the moves for yourself and to get a feel for the tango scene for a fraction of the price of a dinner show (entrance usually costs AR$5–15). Among the city's best *milongas* are *La Viruta* (Armenia 1366, Palermo ⓣ011/4774-6357), *Salón Canning* (Scalabrini Ortiz 1331, Palermo ⓣ011/4832-6753), *La Catedral* (Sarmiento 4006, Almagro ⓣ011/4342-4794) and *Centro Cultural Torquato Tasso* (Defensa 1575, San Telmo ⓣ011/4307-6506). *Confitería Ideal* (Suipacha 384, San Nicolas ⓣ011/5265-8069), a beautiful if crumbling relic of a dancehall, also holds afternoon classes and *milongas*.

Centre) or Paseo Alcorta (Salguero 3172 and Figueroa Alcorta, Palermo Chico); the latter has a large Carrefour hypermarket downstairs. The largest of all is Unicenter (Ⓦ www.unicenter.com.ar), north of the city in the outer suburbs, full of designer shops, a cinema, and with an Imax close by. You can get there on the #60 bus from the centre, or by taxi (A$30).

Markets The city's *ferias* usually take place on weekends and are an excellent place to pick up inexpensive local handicrafts. The most extensive are: the Feria 'Hippy' next to Recoleta cemetery (Sat & Sun); Plaza Dorrego in San Telmo, spreading half a dozen blocks along Defensa (Sun); and the Feria de Mataderos (p.72; Sun). For locally made and designed clothes head to Plaza Serrano in Palermo, weekends from 3pm onwards, when the cafés surrounding the plaza are converted into indoor markets filled to the brim with affordable clothes and jewellery.

Palermo Viejo After the economic crash of the early noughties, this low-rise area became a hotbed of creative and design talent, and the streets have since filled to bursting with tiny, beautifully presented boutiques. The area is perfect for browsing but choice boutiques include: Condimentos (Honduras 4874) for comely local jewellery designs, 28 Sport (Gurruchaga 1481) for top-quality shoes for men and women, and SoldBA (Costa Rica 4656), cool T-shirt heaven.

Directory

Airlines Aerolíneas Argentinas, Perú 2 Ⓣ 011/4340-7777; Aeroperú, Av Santa Fé 840 Ⓣ 011/4311-4115; Air France, Paraguay 610, 14th Floor Ⓣ 011/4317-4747; Alitalia, Suipacha 1111, 28th Floor Ⓣ 011/4310-9910; American Airlines, Av Santa Fe 881 Ⓣ 011/4318-1111; Andes, Cordoba 755 Ⓣ 0810-777-26337; Austral, Paraná 590 y San Martín 427 Ⓣ 011/4340-7777; British Airways, Viamonte 570, 1st Floor Ⓣ 0800/222-0075; Canadian Airlines, Av Córdoba 656 Ⓣ 011/4322-3632; Cubana, Sarmiento 552, 11th Floor Ⓣ 011/4326-5291; KLM, Reconquista 559, 5th Floor Ⓣ 011/4312-1200; LAER, Maipú 935 P.B. Ⓣ 011/4311-5237; LADE, Perú 714 Ⓣ 011/4361-0853; LAN Argentina, Cerrito 866 Ⓣ 0810-9999-526; Lan Chile, Paraguay 609 Ⓣ 011/4311-5334; LAPA, Carlos Pellegrini 1075 Ⓣ 011/4819-5272; Lufthansa, Marcelo T. de Alvear 636 Ⓣ 011/4319-0600; Swiss, Av Santa Fe 846, 1st Floor Ⓣ 011/4319-0000; United Airlines, Av Madero 900, 9th Floor Torre Catalinas Plaza Ⓣ 011/4316-0777.

Bus For information about the companies travelling to your destination, call Ⓣ 011/4310-0700 or search on Ⓦ www.tebasa.com.ar.

Car rental Avis, Cerrito 1527 Ⓣ 011/ 4326-5542; Dollar, Marcelo T. Alvear 449 Ⓣ 011/4315-8800; Drivers Rent a Car, Maipú 924 Ⓣ 011/4315-8384.

Embassies and consulates Australia, Villanueva 1400 Ⓣ 011/4779 3500, Mon–Fri 8.30am–5pm; Bolivia, Av Corrientes 545, 2nd Floor Ⓣ 011/4394-1463, Mon–Fri 9.30am–5.30pm; Brazil, Carlos Pellegrini 1363, 5th Floor Ⓣ 011/4515 6500, Mon–Fri 10am–1pm; Canada, Tagle 2828 Ⓣ 011/4808-1000; Chile, San Martín 439, 9th Floor Ⓣ 011/4394-6582, Mon–Fri 9am–1pm; Ireland, Av del Libertador 1068, 6th Floor Ⓣ 011/5787-0801, 9am–1pm; New Zealand, Carlos Pellegrini 1427, 5th Floor Ⓣ 011/4328-0747, Mon–Fri 9am–1pm & 2–6pm; UK, Dr Luis Agote 2412 Ⓣ 011/4808-2200, Mon–Fri 9am–1pm; United States, Av Colombia 4300 Ⓣ 011/4514-1830 or 011/5777-4533; Uruguay, Av Las Heras 1097 Ⓣ 011/4807-3040, Mon–Fri 9.30am–5.30pm.

Exchange The centre has a host of 'casas de cambio' for foreign exchange or traveller's cheques; shop around for the best rate. Banks will also change to or from dollars.

Hospitals Private hospitals: Hospital Británico (Pedriel 74, entre Finnochietto y Caseros, Ⓣ 011/4309-6400) has English-speaking doctors and 24hr emergency care; for non-emergency visits there is also a more central location at Marcelo T de Alvear 1573 (Ⓣ 011/4812-0040). Hospital Alemán (Av Pueyrredón 1640, between Beruti and Juncal Ⓣ 011/4827-7000); emergency (enter on Beruti) and non-emergency care; English spoken. Public hospital: Hospital Juan A Fernández (Cerviño 3356, at Bulnes, Ⓣ 011/4808-2600).

Internet Internet cafés are everywhere in Buenos Aires, and many *locutorios* (phone shops) also have internet; rates are inexpensive and they tend to open late.

Laundry Laundries are plentiful and inexpensive (though not usually self-service). Expect to pay around AR$8–12 for a wash and dry.

Left luggage Retiro bus station and both the domestic and international airports have left luggage services (roughly AR$6–10 per day). Your hostel may be prepared to look after your luggage if you have a return booking. The services of South American Explorers (Ⓣ 011/430-79625, Ⓦ www.saexplorers.org) include luggage storage. Visit their clubhouse in San Telmo (Estados Unidos 577) for details.

Pharmacies Pharmacies are plentiful. Farmacity (Ⓦ www.farmacity.com.ar) has branches throughout the city, many open 24hr (for example, at Florida 474, between Corrientes and Lavalle, Centre, Ⓣ 011/4322-6559).

Police In an emergency call 101. Tourist Police, Comisaría del Turista, Av Corrientes 436, ☎011/4346-5748 or 4346-7000 ext1801/5748 or 0800-999-5000 (24hr), English spoken.
Post office Correo Central, Sarmiento 189 (Mon–Fri 10am–8pm).
Travel agents and tours Say Hueque, Viamonte 749, 6th Floor (☎011/5199-2517, Ⓦwww.sayhueque.com) is a professional tour operator covering all of Argentina (and parts of Chile). Agreste, Viamonte 1636 (☎011/4373-4442) offers adventurous trips across the country to destinations such as the Saltos de Moconá, Jujuy and the Valle de la Luna. Buenos Aires Tur, Lavalle 1444, Office 16 (☎011/4371-2304 Ⓦwww.buenosairestur.com), offers city tours of Buenos Aires, including tango shows, and visits to Tigre and nearby *estancias.* ASATEJ, Florida 835, 3rd Floor (☎011/4114-7544, Ⓦwww.asatej.com) is a young and dynamic travel agency, offering some of the cheapest flight deals in the city; student discounts available.

Moving on

Air Aerolíneas Argentinas and LAN Argentina both fly to all major cities in Argentina, usually with several services daily. Andes flies to Salta (daily Sun–Fri) and Puerto Madryn (Mon, Wed & Fri), while LADE (Perú 714 ☎011/4361-0853), the former army airline, also has cheap but infrequent flights around the country.
Bus All services arrive and depart from Retiro bus station (Terminal de Omnibus). **Domestic services** to: Bariloche (19–21hr), Córdoba (9–10hr), Mendoza (16hr), Neuquén (14–16hr), Puerto Iguazú (17hr), Puerto Madryn (20hr), Rosario (4hr), Salta (20–22hr). **International services** to: La Paz (55hr), Montevideo (8hr), Santiago de Chile (20–22hr), Sao Paulo (36hr).
Ferry The most efficient and cheapest way to get to Uruguay is by ferry. The two main companies are Colonia Express (Pedro de Mendoza 330, Dársena Sur; ☎011/4313-5100, Ⓦwww.coloniaexpress.com) and Buque Bus (Av Antartida Argentina 821; ☎011/4316-6500, Ⓦwww.buquebus.com). Prices are around AR$120 one way to Colonia, $140 to Montevideo, and depending on which boat you board it can take between 30min–3hr to reach Uruguay. Unless you are going on a weekend or public holiday you can buy your tickets an hour before the boat leaves. Otherwise book in advance online.
Train These days, the railroad is little used in Argentina as a means of long-distance travel, with the exception of services from Retiro station (Av Ramos Mejía, just to the east of Plaza San Martín) to Córdoba (Mon & Fri, 14hr, AR$25, Ferrocentral ☎011/4312-2989), Tucumán (2 weekly Mon & Fri, 25hr, AR$35, Ferrocentral), Rosario (daily at 6.43pm, 5hr, AR$33, TBA ☎0800-333-3822) and the provinces of Buenos Aires and La Pampa. Retiro is also the departure point for trains from Tigre and the northern suburbs. Trains to the Atlantic Coast and La Plata leave from Constitución; those to Mercedes and Lobos in the province of Buenos Aires and Santa Rosa from Once.

Around Buenos Aires

Argentina's most spectacular scenery can feel frustratingly far from the capital, but thankfully Buenos Aires province offers several rewarding – and easily accessible – destinations for a day-trip or more. **Tigre**, just north of Buenos Aires, is the gateway to the watery recreation of the Paraná Delta. A trip to the provincial capital, **La Plata**, is essential for natural history enthusiasts; the city's Museo de la Plata is home to an extraordinary array of megafauna skeletons. And a slice of gaucho life is the draw at **San Antonio de Areco**, where late-nineteenth-century houses and cobbled streets combine with gaucho culture to charming effect. Taking the ferry across the Río Plate to **Colonia**, in Uruguay (see p.921), also makes a great day out. Wandering around the old town's cobbled streets and eating in the sunny main plaza is a welcome relief from busy Buenos Aires.

TIGRE AND THE DELTA

An hour's train ride north of the city centre, the river port of **TIGRE** distributes the timber and fruit produced in the delta of the **Paraná River**. Originally a remote system of rivers dotted with inaccessible islands,

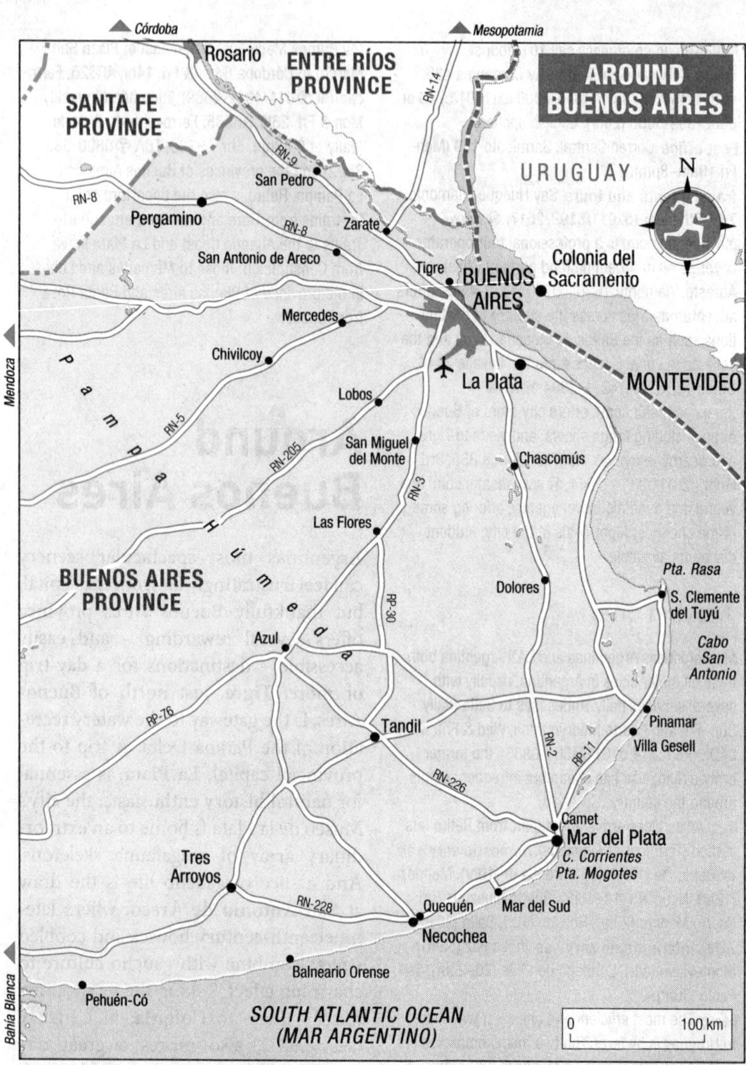

the Delta is now crowded with weekend homes and riverside restaurants.

What to see and do

The river itself is the principal attraction. To experience it, head for Tigre's **Estación Fluvial** from where inexpensive local wooden ferries leave every twenty minutes or so. Take one of these to 'Tres Bocas' (AR$11 one way) where there are two or three good restaurants and cafés with riverfront verandas, or simply enjoy a cruise. A tourist office at the Estación Fluvial can give you a map of the islands and details of the numerous boat companies serving them (among them Río Tur ☎011/4731-0280, leaving from Puerto de Frutos, and Sturla ☎011/4731-1300, from the Estación Fluvial). The town of Tigre is often forgotten by tourists plying the river, but it too has some interesting places to visit. About four blocks from the Estación Fluvial is the colourful **Puerto de Frutos** (daily 10am–6pm) where hundreds of baskets made from Delta plants, spices, wooden furniture, and handicrafts are on sale. Across the bridge you'll find the ageing but well thought-out **Museo Naval**, at Paseo Victorica 602 (Mon–Fri 8.30am–5.30pm, Sat & Sun 10.30am–6.30pm; AR$2) and if you keep walking up the river the spectacular **Tigre Club** – now the **Museo de Arte Tigre** (Wed–Fri 10am–6pm, Sat & Sun noon–7pm, AR$5) will come into view. The carefully restored early twentieth-century building gives an idea of how the other half lived, and there are great views from the terrace.

Arrival and accommodation

To get to Tigre you can either take a direct train from Retiro (Mitre line, every 10min; 1hr; AR$1.20) or take the train to Bartolomé Mitre (every 15min; AR$0.75), walk across the bridge to Maipú station, and jump on the more scenic **Tren de la Costa** (every 20min; AR$8 one-way). This train runs through the older suburbs and stations to the north of the city. Should you want to extend your visit and **stay** overnight in the Delta, try the *Marco Polo Náutico Hostel* (Paraná de las Palmas and Cruz Colorada, ⓣ 011/4728-0395, ⓦ www.marcopoloinnnautico.com; ❾), in a beautiful riverside setting with river beach and pool. They can organise hiking tours, kayaking and fishing here.

SAN ANTONIO DE ARECO

The refined pampas town of **SAN ANTONIO DE ARECO**, set on the meandering Río Areco 113km northwest of Buenos Aires, is the spiritual home of the gaucho or Argentine cowboy. A robust tourist industry has grown around the gaucho tradition: silver and leather handicraft workers peddle their wares in the town's shops, historic **estancias** (ranches) accommodate visitors in the surrounding countryside and an annual **gaucho festival** draws massive crowds every November. While bicycles rule the streets here, you'll also spot beret-clad *estancia* workers on horseback, trotting about the cobblestones.

What to see and do

The leafy town centre is laid out in grid fashion around the main square, **Plaza Ruiz de Arellano**, and is full of genteel, slightly decaying, single-storey nineteenth-century buildings, many of them painted a blushing shade of pink. On the south side of the square, the plain white **Iglesia Parroquial San Antonio de Padua** was the town's first chapel, dating from 1730. A sculpture of San Antonio graces the exterior. One block north, in a refurbished former power plant at Alsina 66, is the **Centro Cultural Usina Vieja** (Tues–Sun 11am–5pm; AR$1.50), home to the **Museo de la Ciudad**, with random everyday objects like old radios as well as temporary art exhibitions that depict life in rural Argentina. Just north of town, across the Río Areco, lies **Parque Criollo**, home to the **Museo Gauchesco Ricardo Güiraldes** (Wed–Mon 11am–5pm, guided visits Sat & Sun 12.30pm & 3.30pm; A$3). Set in a replica nineteenth-century *estancia*, the museum has a collection of gaucho art and artefacts and pays homage to the life of author Ricardo Güiraldes, whose classic novel, *Don Segundo Sombra* (1926) – set in San Antonio de Areco – served to elevate the *maté*-sucking, horse-breaking, cow-herding gaucho from rebellious outlaw to respected and romantic national icon. Demonstrations of gaucho feats are held every year in the Parque Criollo during November's week-long **Fiesta de la Tradición** festivities.

Arrival and information

Bus The bus station (ⓣ 02326/453904) is at General Paz and Av Dr Smith, a six-block walk from the town centre along Calle Segundo Sombra. There are buses to and from Buenos Aires (every 1–2hr; 2hr) and Rosario (6 daily; 4hr).

Tourist office The tourist office, which loans bicycles, is a short walk from the main square towards the river at the corner of Arellano and Zerboni (daily 8am–8pm; ⓣ02326/453165, ⓦwww.visiteareco.com).

Accommodation

While San Antonio de Areco can easily be visited on a day-trip from Buenos Aires, you might well be charmed into staying the night. Book ahead on weekends as the town is a popular weekend destination for *porteños*. Also book accommodation well in advance during the Fiesta de la Tradición in November, or contact the tourist office who can arrange homestays with families. For camping, try *Club River* (ⓣ02326/454998 or 451016), 1km west of town along Zerboni, AR$20 for two people.

Hostal de Areco Zapiola 25 ⓣ02326/456118, ⓦwww.hostaldeareco.com.ar. Centrally-located in a pink colonial building, this B&B has a nice sunny garden and offers decent doubles with private bathrooms. ❺

Eating and drinking

Many of San Antonio de Areco's restaurants and bars have been given old worldy makeovers, and their continued patronage by weathered *estancia* workers gives them an air of authenticity.

Almacén de Ramos Generales Zapiola 143 ⓣ02326/456376. Old bottles and gaucho paraphernalia line the walls of this delightful *parrilla;* the duck, rabbit and trout specials and waist-softening desserts ensure a steady stream of regulars. Mains AR$30.

Barril 900 San Martín 381. Alfresco drinking and live music lends this pub a relaxed charm.

TREAT YOURSELF

The closest *estancia* to San Antonio de Areco – and certainly the most affordable – is **La Cinacina**, a former dairy farm five blocks west of the main plaza at the end of Calle Lavalle (ⓣ02326/452045, ⓦwww.lacinacina.com.ar). It has twelve tastefully decorated rooms (some with fireplaces), a luminous communal lounge area and a good-sized swimming pool. Two people pay A$350 per night for bed and breakfast. If you don't want to sleep here, the *estancia* offers a full day of all-you-can-eat *asado*, music, carriage rides, horse-riding and a demonstration of guacho skills for AR$90, or AR$170 with transfer from Buenos Aires.

La Esquina de Marti Arellano 145 ⓣ02326/456705. Dolled up like a traditional corner store, this spacious and atmospheric plaza-side restaurant excels in fast and friendly service. *Parrilla* for two AR$49; pastas around AR$22.

La Olla de Cobre Matheu 433. Closed Tues. A small chocolate factory and sweet shop selling superb house-made *alfajores*. Sample before buying.

LA PLATA

La Plata became the capital of the province of Buenos Aires in 1880, when the city of Buenos Aires was made the Federal Capital. Close enough to make

ESTANCIAS

Reflecting Argentina's changing economic climate, many of the country's **estancias** – vast cattle and horse estates once lorded over by wealthy European settlers – are staying afloat by converting into luxury tourist accommodation. For anyone with latent cowboy or aristocratic aspirations, *estancias* offer the chance to milk cows, ride horses, go fly-fishing, play polo or simply tuck into a juicy slab of steak plucked straight off the *asado* while swanning poolside with a glass of Malbec.

Running the gamut from simple family farmhouses to pampas dude ranches to ostentatious Italianate mansions, *estancias* are a character-filled throwback to the Argentina of yesteryear. For a list of *estancias* offering accommodation in and around San Antonio de Areco, see ⓦwww.visiteareco.com. For more **information** on *estancias* in other parts of Argentina, visit ⓦwww.estanciaargentinas.com, ⓦwww.estanciastravel.com or ⓦwww.ranchweb.com.

MAR DEL PLATA

Argentina's **beaches** are somewhat overshadowed by neighbouring Uruguay's golden sands (in particular glamorous Punta del Este; see p.926). Still, a seaside outing in summer is a quintessential Argentine experience – and **Mar del Plata**, boasting some fifty kilometres of beach, is the country's number one resort. In the summer season (mid-December to March), millions of city dwellers descend on the city, generating vibrant eating, drinking and entertainment scenes (or overcrowding and overpricing, depending in your point of view).

Though Mar del Plata may have lost some of the lustre of yesteryear, glamorous glimpses can see be had in the city's restored early twentieth-century mansions (check out French-style Villa Ortiz Basualdo, now the Museo Municipal de Arte, at Av Colón 1189, and the Centro Cultural Victoria Ocampo, Matheu 1851). The renowned **International Film Festival** is held in Mar del Plata in early March, showing new Argentine and international flicks.

Nearby **Carilú** and **Mar de los Pampas** are both eco-resorts which provide a more laid-back seaside experience. Rent a house or stay in a luxury hotel and chill out for a few days.

There are numerous daily **buses** from Buenos Aires to Mar del Plata (5–6hr), or you can make the journey less comfortably by **train**, from Constitución station, or **fly** up in less than an hour.

an easy day-trip, it has a relaxed, small city feel. The geometrical design, by French architect Pedro Benoit, and grid-numbered streets, will help you get around without getting lost.

What to see and do

The most famous attractions can be found north of the city centre, next to the Zoo, in the middle of the pleasant **Paseo del Bosque**. The **Museo de la Plata** (Tues–Sun 10am–6pm; AR$12) was the first museum built in Latin America and has a wonderful collection of skeletons, stuffed animals, and fossils set in a crumbling building in the midst of the university. Though desperately in need of refurbishment, the museum is well worth visiting to see the vast whale bones and the models of prehistoric animals. From the Paseo del Bosque, avenidas 51 and 53 lead down through the historic centre to the **Plaza Moreno**. On its far side stands the colossal, Neogothic brick **Cathedral**, with an impressive marble interior of thick columns and high vaulted ceilings.

Roughly halfway between the two is **Plaza San Martín**, the lively heart of the city. On the western side, the **Centro Cultural Pasaje Dardo Rocha** (daily 9am–10pm) occupies the city's former train station, taking up an entire block between avenidas 49 and 50, 6 and 7. Behind the elegant, French- and Italian-influenced façade are housed a cinema and various exhibition spaces, including the excellent **Museo de Arte Contemporáneo Latinoamericano** (Tues–Fri 10am–8pm, Sat & Sun 2–9pm winter, 4–10pm summer; free).

Arrival and information

Buses for La Plata leave from Retiro bus station every half-hour (1hr 10min, AR$7 single). **Trains**, from Constitución station, are much slower. There's a **tourist office** inside the Pasaje Dardo Rocha cultural centre (daily 10am–8pm, ☎0221/427-1535). Many of the best places to **eat and drink** are just south of here, around the junction of avenidas 10 & 47.

Córdoba Province

CÓRDOBA PROVINCE, 700km northwest of Buenos Aires, marks Argentina's geographical bull's-eye. Serene towns dot its undulating **Central Sierras**, the second highest mountain range in Argentina after the Andes. The province is one of the country's more affordable travel destinations, a relaxed place to **learn Spanish**, go **skydiving** or just hang out for a few weeks sipping *maté* with the super-friendly Cordobeses.

Most of the action takes place in and around **Córdoba city**, which has the country's highest concentration of bars and clubs outside Buenos Aires. South of Córdoba city in the verdant **Calamuchita Valley**, towns such as **Alta Gracia** and Germanic, beer-brewing **Villa General Belgrano** have historically served as getaways for Argentina's elite. Northwest of the capital in the **Punilla Valley**, laid-back towns such as **Capilla del Monte** are growing in popularity among bohemian *porteños* looking for a clean, green city break.

CÓRDOBA

Argentina's second largest city, unpretentious **CÓRDOBA** boasts beautifully restored colonial architecture, plentiful restaurants and a legendary nightlife (best experienced when university is in session). It is a great base for exploring the province: indeed, especially during the city's stiflingly hot summers, you'll soon be lured west to the Sierras' cooler elevations.

Plaza San Martín and around

Once the bloody stage for bullfights, executions and military parades, **Plaza San Martín** was converted into a civilized public square, replete with fountains and semitropical foliage, in the 1870s.

On the square's western side, the two-storey, sixteenth-century **Cabildo** was once the city's colonial headquarters. It now accommodates the tourist office and **Museo de la Ciudad** (daily 10am–8pm; free) and hosts concerts, art exhibitions and, in summer, tango evenings (*Patio de Tango*: Fri 9pm; AR$7).

Alongside the Cabildo is the **Catedral**, the oldest in the country. Construction began in 1577 but wasn't completed for another two hundred years, rendering the cathedral something of an architectural mongrel, with a mix of Neoclassical and Baroque styles and a Romanesque dome thrown in for good measure. Note the trumpeting angels in indigenous dress gracing the clock towers.

Manzana de los Jesuitas

The seventeenth-century **Manzana de los Jesuitas** (Tues–Sun 10am–noon & 5–8pm; AR$5 guided visit), or Jesuit Block, two blocks southwest of the plaza, is Córdoba's top attraction. A testament to the missionaries who arrived hot on the heels of Córdoba's sixteenth-century colonizers, the **Templo de la Compañía de Jesús**, built in 1640, is the oldest surviving Jesuit temple in Argentina. It has a striking Cusqueño altarpiece, and its ceiling, which resembles an inverted ship, is constructed of Paraguayan cedar. Within the block are the central offices of the **Universidad Nacional de Córdoba** (which has an adjoining historical museum) and the exquisite private chapel **Capilla Doméstica** (guided visits on request).

Monasterio de Santa Teresa

Southwest of Plaza San Martín at Independencia 146, the **Iglesia Santa Teresa**, part of a working convent, contains the **Museo de Arte Religioso Juan de Tejeda**, Independencia 122 (Tues–Fri 8.30am–12.30pm, Sat & Sun 9am–12.30pm; AR$5), with perhaps the finest collection of sacred art in the country, including Jesuit artefacts and religious paintings from Cusco.

Museo de Bellas Artes Dr Genaro Pérez

The municipal art gallery, **Museo de Bellas Artes Dr Genaro Pérez**, at Av General Paz 33 (Tues–Sun 10am–1.30pm & 4.30–9pm; free), housed in a late-nineteenth-century French-style mansion, features nineteenth and twentieth-century Argentine art. The permanent collection has numerous landscape paintings from the **Escuela**

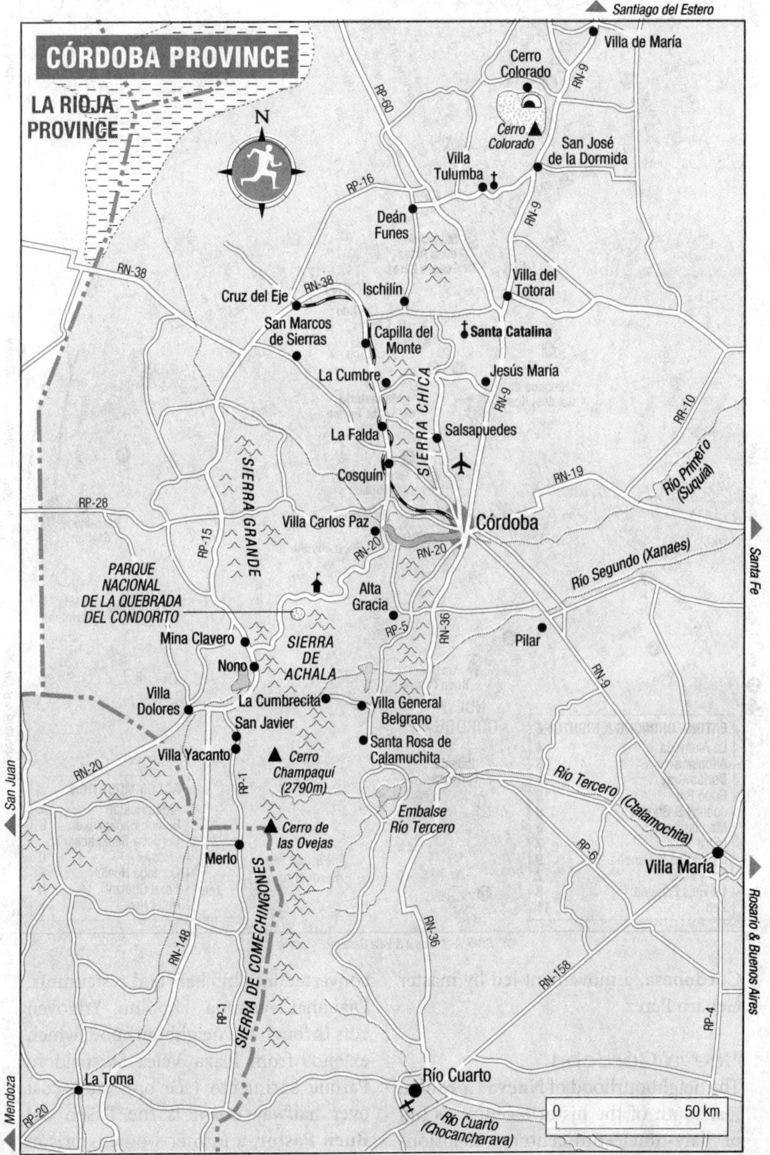

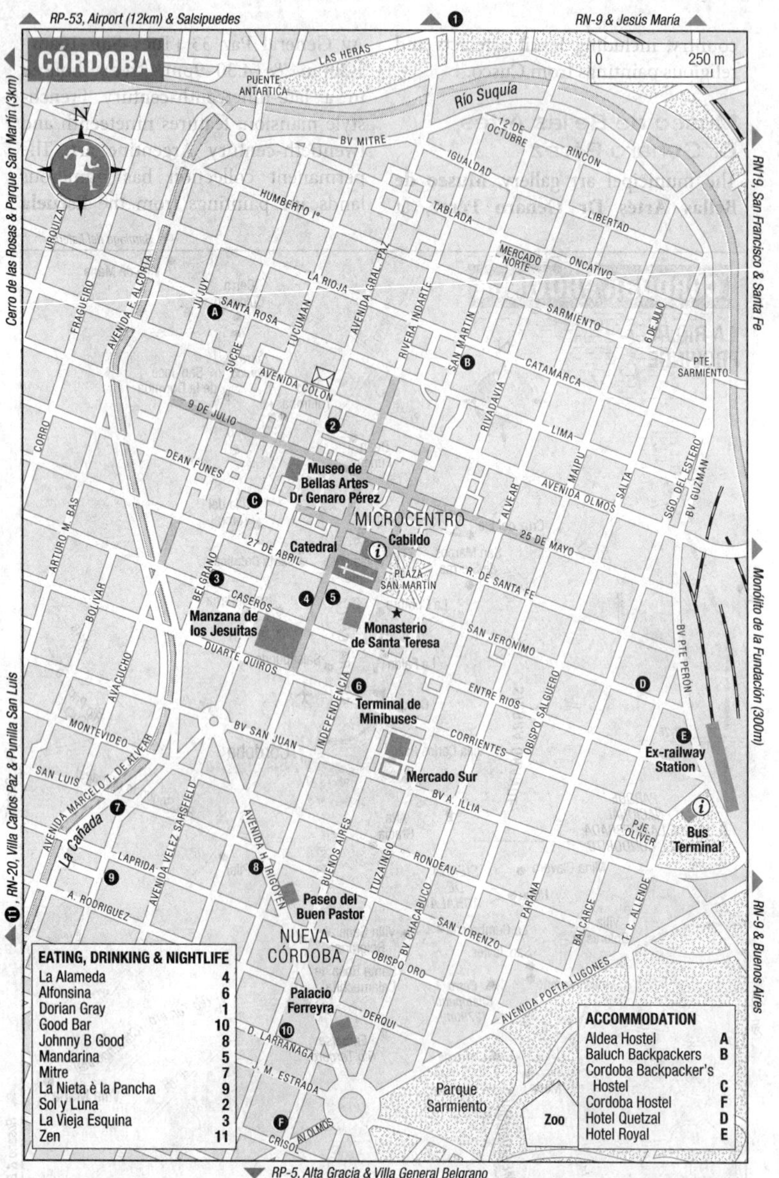

Cordobesa, a movement led by master Genaro Pérez.

Nueva Córdoba

The neighbourhood of **Nueva Córdoba**, just south of the historic centre, is full of late-nineteenth-century mansions converted into hip bars and restaurants. Diagonal Avenida Hipólito Yrigoyen cuts through the neighbourhood, which extends from Plaza Vélez Sarsfield to Parque Sarmiento (see opposite). Just over halfway down is the **Paseo del Buen Pastor**, a former women's prison

TREAT YOURSELF

Skydiving
Córdoba is the most affordable place in Argentina to jump out of an airplane. Tumbling out the door at 2500m, the bird's-eye view after twenty seconds of face-flattening freefall is of city sprawl, a patchwork of green fields and the Central sierras. The guys at CEPAC (☎0351/497-6843, Ⓦwww.cepac.com.ar) have 35 years' skydiving experience, charging AR$440 for a tandem jump and an extra AR$100 to film your fear for posterity. Paracenter (☎0351/156141501, Ⓦwww.paracenter.com.ar) also offer tandem jumps near Villa General Belgrano for a similar price.

recently converted into a culinary and cultural precinct featuring art exhibitions and free concerts. Flanked by fountains and landscaped grassy knolls, it is one of the city's most popular summertime chill-out spaces.

Museo Superior de Bellas Artes Palacio Ferreyra

An exemplary art museum, the **Museo Superior de Bellas Artes Palacio Ferreyra** (Tues–Sun 10am–8pm AR$5), at Hipólito Irigoyen and Chacabuco in Nueva Córdoba, features four floors of works in an opulent 1916 palace built in the French classical style. The top floor has rolling contemporary art exhibitions, while the basement level is devoted to photography. In between, some three hundred artists are represented, including Pablo Picasso and Argentinian artists Fernando Fader and Lino Enea Spilimbergo. A little further south is the hilltop **Parque Sarmiento**, one of the city's most popular green spaces.

Arrival and information

Air Córdoba's Aeropuerto Internacional Taravella is 13km north of downtown at Pajas Blancas. A bus runs frequently between the airport and city centre (AR$1.20). Taxis to the centre cost around AR$30.

Bus The frenetic long-distance bus station (☎0351/434-1692) is several blocks east of the centre at Blvd Perón 380. Public buses run downtown or a taxi costs AR$5. Local buses for some provincial destinations leave from the Terminal de Minibuses behind the Mercado Sur market on Boulevard Arturo Illia.

Tourist office The principal tourist office is in the Cabildo (daily 8am–8pm; ☎0351/434-1200, Ⓦwww.cordobaturismo.gov.ar) on Plaza San Martín. Far more helpful is the tourist office in the bus station (daily 7am–9pm, ☎0351/433-1987), whose friendly staff can assist with finding accommodation and provide city and provincial maps. There is also a tourist office in the airport (daily 8am–8pm; ☎0351/434-8390).

Tours Downtown **walking tours** (2hr) leave from the tourist office in the Cabildo (daily 9.30am & 4.30pm, June–Aug 9am & 4pm, in English on request; AR$20; ☎0351/434-1200). One hour thirty minute double-deckers **bus tours** are run by City Tour (Mon 4pm & 6pm, Tues & Thurs 6pm, Fri 10am, 4pm & 6pm, Sat & Sun 10am & 6pm; AR$20; ☎0351/424-6605) and depart from Plaza San Martín near the cathedral.

Accommodation

Córdoba has some of the best-value **hostels** and **hotels** in the country. There is a fully-serviced **campsite** (☎0351/433-1988; AR$8–12 per tent) 10km northwest of the centre at Av General San Martín, on the banks of the Río Suquía; take the #E1 bus from Plaza San Martín.

Hostels

All hostels listed here offer tour-booking services and include internet, breakfast and use of kitchen.

Aldea Hostel Santa Rosa 447 ☎0351/426-1312, Ⓦwww.aldeahostel.com. This bright, ambitious newcomer has space for a hundred people and is bursting with extras: two games rooms, a TV lounge, leafy patio, study room and roof terrace. Discounts for longer stays. Dorm AR$27. ❹

Baluch Backpackers San Martín 338 ☎0351/422-3977, Ⓦwww.baluchbackpackers.com. Clean and bright, this hostel has a cozy lounge area, helpful staff and hosts weekly barbecues on its roof terrace. Some rooms have a/c. Late risers might be put off by the ambient street noise. Dorm AR$28. ❹

Cordoba Backpacker's Hostel Deán Funes 285 ⓣ0351/422-0593, ⓦwww.cordobabackpackers.com.ar. A climbing wall, bar, pool table, tour desk and roof terrace with dead-on cathedral views are just some of the perks of this bustling, central hostel. Dorm AR$30; discount for HI members. ❺

Cordoba Hostel Ituzaingó 1070 ⓣ0351/468-7359, ⓦwww.cordobahostel.com.ar. In the heart of trendy Nueva Córdoba, this four-floor HI hostel offers Spanish and dance classes. Dorm AR$30. ❺

Hotels

Hotel Quetzal San Jerónimo 579 ⓣ0351/422-9106. Offers cheerful rooms with en-suite bathrooms. Steer clear of the noisy bedrooms facing the street. ❻

Hotel Royal Blvd Juan Domingo Perón 180 ⓣ0351/421-5000, ⓔroyalhotel@fibertel.com.ar. Spartan but comfortable, this is an appealing option if you want to be close to the bus station. Breakfast included. ❻

Eating

Córdoba is a real delight for winers and diners. There are **restaurants** for refined taste buds, boisterous drinking holes serving pub grub, and plenty of eat-on-the-run *empanada* joints for lining your stomach before a night out on the Fernet and Coke (Córdoba's potent signature tipple). The pick of the fashionable restaurants are in Nueva Córdoba.

La Alameda Obispo Trejo 170. Savour inexpensive Argentine staples like *empanadas* (AR$1) and *humitas* (AR$3) while sitting outside on wooden benches, or indoors where customers' poetry and art adorns the walls.

Alfonsina Duarte Quiros 66 ⓣ0351/427-2847. Antique typewriters, exposed brickwork and a jolly crowd are the hallmarks of this wildly popular restaurant that offers a taste of Argentina's northwest. Good *locro* (maize-based stew) and *empanadas*. Mains AR$12–20. Closed Sun.

Johnny B Good Av Hipólito Yrigoyen 320, Nueva Córdoba and Av Rafael Núñez 4791, Cerro de las Rosas, ⓦwww.jbgood.com. Both branches of this resto-bar are much-loved local landmarks. Attend to hunger pangs with *nachos* (AR$18) and a beer (AR$8), or on weekends, swill cocktails to live rock music at the Cerro de la Rosas location.

Mandarina Obispo Trejo 171 ⓣ0351/426-4909 This spacious, chilled-out crowd-pleaser has plenty of vegetarian options. Mediterranean and Asian mains are prepared with gourmet flair. The set lunch is good value at AR$21.

La Nieta è la Pancha Belgrano 783 ⓣ0351/468-1920. Locally sourced ingredients are imaginatively prepared at this elegant restaurant, which does flavourful chicken, goat, trout and pasta dishes at reasonable prices (mains AR$22–30). Leave room for the ice cream with peperina (a locally grown herb). On weekends there's live music on the breezy roof terrace.

Sol y Luna Av Gral Paz 278 ⓣ0351/425-1189, lunch only. Load your plate with a variety of hot and cold dishes at this vegetarian buffet with bright, hip decor. Set lunches AR$10.

La Vieja Esquina Corner of Caseroa and Belgrano. Pull up a stool at the rustic wooden bar and wash down scrumptious *empanadas* (AR$1.75) with a glass of *vino tinto* (AR$3). Closed Sun.

Drinking and nightlife

Córdoba is no wallflower when it comes to partying, with Nueva Córdoba the late-night hotspot for the young, mainstream masses. Hipsters gravitate to the revived warehouse district of El Abasto, just north of the centre, for its edgy **bars** and **night-clubs**. Further afield, in the Chateau Carreras neighbourhood, the chic **discos** *Carreras, Club F* and *Cruz* cater for an energized crowd that grooves to *cuarteto* music – a Córdoba speciality.

Dorian Gray Bv Las Heras & Roque Sáenz Peña. Bizarre decor and an alternative ambience draw an eclectic crowd who throw shapes well into the small hours to mostly electronic music. AR$4 tequila. Entry AR$15 for men, AR$10 for women. Thurs–Sat.

Good Bar Buenos Aires & Larrañaga. The surfboard out front and white leather lounges might inspire you to slip into Hawaiian-style boardshorts or a white string bikini. You'll certainly wish you had at 2am when you're sweating buckets on the basement dancefloor. All spirits AR$10.

Mitre Marcelo T de Alvear 635. Córdoba's largest disco attracts a mixed crowd of students, posers and foreigners to three floors of hedonism and electronic mayhem. AR$15 cover; beers AR$9. Thurs–Sat.

Zen Av Julio A Roca 730.. This gay-friendly club has two throbbing dancefloors and hosts kooky live shows. Fri & Sat.

Shopping

Bookshops Librería Blackpool, Deán Funes 395 (ⓣ0351/423-7172), sells novels and travel guides in English.

Markets On weekend evenings (6–9.30pm) there is an arts and crafts market at the **Paseo de las Artes** on the western edge of Nueva Córdoba, cnr Derqui & Marcelo T Alvear.

Shopping centre Nuevocentro Shopping, Duarte Quirós 1400; Sun-Thu 10am–11pm, Fri & Sat 10am–1am.

Directory

Car rental Avis, Av Colón 564/6 ⓣ0351/424-6185.
Hospital Sanatorio Allende Av Hipólito Yrigoyen & Obispo Oro ⓣ0351/426-9200.
Laundry Laveraps at Chacabuco 301, Belgrano 76 and R. Indarte 289.
Police Colón 1200.
Post office Av General Paz 201.
Spanish school Spanish Central (ⓣ0351/526-1158; ⓦwww.spanishcordoba.com.ar) at Rivadavia 85, offers private and small group classes.

Moving on

Air Internal to: Buenos Aires (12 daily; 1hr 15min); Mendoza (2 daily; 1hr 20min); Rosario (2 daily; 1hr). International to: destinations in Brazil, Chile, Panama and Uruguay. Airline offices in the city: Aerolíneas Argentinas, Av Colón 520 ⓣ0351/410-7600; Lan Chile, Figueroa Alcorta 206 ⓣ0351/475-9555; Copa (for Panama), Av Vélez Sarsfield 478 ⓣ08101/222-2672; TAM (for Brazil), Av Colón 119 ⓣⓕ0351/482-0614.
Buses to: Alta Gracia (every 15min, 1hr); Buenos Aires (hourly; 10hr); Capilla del Monte (every 30min; 3hr); Mendoza (7 daily; 9hr); San Juan (5 daily; 8hr); Rosario (6 daily; 6hr 30min); Salta (4 daily; 12hr); Villa General Belgrano (every 30min; 2hr 30min).

AROUND CÓRDOBA

The classic day-trip from Córdoba city is to the Jesuit *estancia* town of **Alta Gracia**, which attracts a steady stream of goateed Che Guevara devotees curious to see the childhood stomping ground of Latin America's favourite revolutionary. Fifty kilometres further south, quaint **Villa General Belgrano** stages the continent's largest annual beer festival, while north of the capital, the town of **Capilla del Monte** flies the flag for New Age lifestylers.

ALTA GRACIA

The pleasant colonial town of **ALTA GRACIA**, 40km south of Córdoba at the entrance of the Calamuchita Valley, was once a genteel summer refuge for *porteño* bourgeoisie. Alta Gracia continues to bask in the reflected glory of its former residents: Jesuit missionaries, the Spanish composer Manuel de Falla and the Guevara family have all left their mark here.

Plaza Manuel Solares and around

Alta Gracia came into its own after 1643 when it was chosen as the site of a Jesuit *estancia*. When the Jesuits were expelled in 1767, the *estancia* was left to the elements, only briefly re-inhabited in 1810 by Viceroy Liniers. The *estancia* buildings have been well preserved and overlook the town's main square, **Plaza Manuel Solares**. The **Iglesia Parroquial Nuestra Señora de la Merced**, dating from 1762, stands alongside the Jesuits' original living quarters, which have been converted into the UNESCO World Heritage-listed **Museo Histórico Casa del Virrey Liniers** (Jan–Feb Tues–Fri 9am–8pm, Sat & Sun 9.30am–10pm; rest of year Tues–Fri 9am–1pm & 3–7pm, Sat & Sun 9.30am–12.30pm & 3.30–6.30pm; AR$2, free on Wed; guided tours in English ⓣ03547/421303). Here, a dramatic Baroque doorway leads to a cloistered courtyard and a motley collection of furniture and religious paintings.

Ernesto "Che" Guevara house and museum

A twenty-minute walk uphill from the plaza brings you to the leafy residential neighbourhood of **Villa Carlos Pellegrini**, whose crumbling mansions once served as holiday homes and residences for moneyed socialites. The Guevara family moved within these circles after relocating from Rosario to Alta Gracia in the 1930s in the hope the fresh mountain air would alleviate the asthma plaguing their four-year-old son, **Ernesto "Che" Guevara**. The family's former home, Villa Beatriz, at Avellaneda

ARGENTINA CÓRDOBA PROVINCE

501, has been converted into the **Museo Casa de Ernesto "Che" Guevara** (Mon–Fri 9am–7pm, Sat, Sun & public holidays 9.30am–7pm, Jan & Feb open until 8pm; ⓣ03547/428579; AR$3), showcasing Che's personal effects as well as photographs charting his progression from carefree kid to swarthy teenager to sideburn-sporting revolutionary. Among the museum's highlights are video interviews with Che's childhood companions, a handwritten resignation letter to Fidel Castro and photos from a visit Castro and Hugo Chavez made to the house in 2006.

Arrival and information

Bus Buses from Córdoba (every 30min, 1hr) drop passengers at the corner of avenidas Vélez Sarsfield and Sarmiento; buses leave every 30min for Villa General Belgrano (1hr).

Car rental Rodar Rent A Car (ⓣ03547/427164 ⓦwww.autosrodar.com.ar).

Tourist office The tourist office is in the clock tower alongside the Tajamar reservoir at Luís Sáenz Peña and Calle del Molino (Mon–Fri 7am–7pm, Sat & Sun 9am–7pm, office open daily until midnight Jan & Feb; ⓣ03547/428128, ⓦwww.altagracia.gov.ar).

Accommodation and eating

If you're after some peace and quiet, Alta Gracia is just the place to spend the night. At the eastern edge of town, the *Hosteria Country El Biguá* (Ruta C45 km2; ⓣ03547/422045; AR$8 per person) offers camping and bungalows (4) in the grounds of a former *estancia*..

Alta Gracia Hostel Paraguay 218, ⓣ03547/428-810, ⓦwww.altagraciahostel.com.ar. A homely hostel five blocks from the main square. Dorm beds only, AR$28.

Morena Sarmiento 413, ⓣ03547/426365, ⓦwww.morena-ag.com.ar Closed Mon. Set in a white, neo-colonial house, this restaurant's menu runs the gamut from prawn ravioli to paella to veal in mushroom sauce. The pizzas and fish dishes are also worth a nod. Mains AR$25–$35.

VILLA GENERAL BELGRANO

The twee resort town of **VILLA GENERAL BELGRANO**, 50km south of Alta Gracia, unabashedly exploits its Germanic heritage with all kinds of kitsch. Founded by the surviving seamen of the *Graf Spee*, which sank off the coast of Uruguay in 1939, the town's main street, **Avenida Julio Roca**, comes over like an alpine theme park, with folksy German beer houses and eateries resembling Swiss chalets.

What to see and do

The best (and some might argue the only) reason to visit Villa General Belgrano is to sink steins of locally brewed beer at the annual **Oktoberfest**. Held during the second week of October in Plaza José Hernández, it is considered the continent's best celebration of this drunken German tradition. With time on your hands, you might head over to the **Museo Politemático** (Dec–Feb Sat & Sun 10am–12.30pm & 6pm–midnight, rest of year Sat & Sun 10am–6pm; AR$3; ⓣ03546/461338), housed in a mock-medieval mansion at Selva Negra 61, to see some rather average photocopied prints tracing the town's history.

The most popular day-trip from Villa General Belgrano is 30km west to the alpine-flavoured village of **La Cumbrecita** (six buses daily), where there are good opportunities for hiking, rappelling and cooling off in the Río Almbach.

Arrival and information

Bus The bus terminal is on Av Vélez Sarsfield, 10min walk northwest of the main street, although all buses make drop-offs and pick-ups in the town centre. Buses leave roughly every half-hour for Alta Gracia (1hr) and Córdoba (2hr).

Car rental Dapa Turismo, Av San Martín 20 ⓣ03546/463417; Friedrich Servicios Turísticos, Av Roca 224 ⓣ03546/461372.

Mountain bike rental Cerro Negro, Av Julio Roca 580 ⓣ03546/463142.

Tourist office The switched-on tourist office is at Av Julio Roca 168 (daily 8.30am–8.30pm; ⓣ03546/461215, ⓦwww.vgb.gov.ar).

Accommodation

Hotels in town are overpriced, while **cabañas** make a good alternative for groups of four or five. The *El Arroya* **campsite** (☎03546/463855, AR$13 per person) is five blocks south of the town centre at Nicaragua 571, and the shady *La Florida* campground (☎03546/461298, ✉laflorida@calamuchitanet.com.ar), along the RP5 east of the town centre, has lovely grounds with a swimming pool and bungalows.

Albergue El Rincón C Alexander Fleming s/n,15min walk northwest of the bus station ☎03546/461323, www.calamuchitanet.com.ar/elrincon. Set on a farm, this stellar, relaxed hostel has dorms (AR$25) and plenty of grass for pitching your tent (AR$12). Breakfasts with home-made cereal, bread and jam are AR$7.50. ❹

La Posada de Akasha Av Los Manantiales ☎03546/462440, www.elsitiodelavilla.com/akasha. A distinctive white mock-castle with twelve spotless rooms, some with bathtubs and mountain views. The water in the sparkling backyard pool looks clean enough to drink. Breakfast included. ❼

El Viejo Nogal 25 de Mayo ☎03546/463174, www.elviejonogal.viajesdelsur.com. Charming, fully-equipped *cabañas* with high wooden ceilings set around a cute pool. Massive low-season discounts. Cabins ❻–❼

Eating and drinking

Germanic fare is dished up with varying quality at the town's numerous cafes and restaurants.

Café Rissen Av Julio Roca 36. You'll want to inhale every crumb of your Black Forest gateau (AR$8.50).

Ciervo Rojo Av Julio Roca 210. Good for goulash (AR$12), *salchicha* (AR$18) and house-brewed beer.

Los Piños Av Julio Roca 73 ☎03546/461832. The cumbersome menu swerves from *wurst* to pizza (mains around AR$20), but the beer (AR$7 a glass) is what you're really here for, brewed out back in a factory with a 24,000-litre capacity. Guided brewery tours on weekends (AR$7).

Viejo Munich Av San Martín 362 ☎03546/463122, www.cervezaartesanal.com. The trout, goulash and venison mains aren't too bad, but the beer – brewed on-site – is the bomb. Free brewery tours Mon–Fri 10am & 1pm. Closed Wed March–Sept.

CAPILLA DEL MONTE

CAPILLA DEL MONTE attracts more alternative lifestylers than you can shake an incense stick at. Situated 106km north of Córdoba city, the idyllic mountain town lies at the base of **Cerro Uriturco**, which, at 1979m, is the Sierra Chica's highest peak and is claimed by many locals to possess an inexplicable magnetic pull.

Set at the confluence of two (often dry) rivers on the northern edge of the Punilla Valley, Capilla del Monte's former glory can be glimpsed in its slowly decaying nineteenth-century mansions. Perhaps drawn here by Uriturco's magnetism, artisans and New Age healers have since become the town's more conspicuous residents, and their businesses can be easily visited using the maps and listings provided by the tourist office.

What to see and do

Capilla del Monte makes a good base for outdoor adventure sports, including **horseback riding** in the surrounding countryside, **rock climbing** the strange sandstone formations around the hamlet of **Ongamira**, **hiking** to the summit of Cerro Uriturco (5km each way, or seven hours return), strolling through the multicoloured rock formations of

THE TRUTH IS OUT THERE

Capilla del Monte hosts an international **UFO convention** every November, organized by local "research" group Centro de Informes OVNI (Juan Cabus 297, ☎03548/482485; OVNI is Spanish for UFO). **Mystical tourism** is gaining in popularity, with local tour operators jumping on the extraterrestrial bandwagon by offering guided tours to sites of supposed UFO landings as well as night excursions to observe celestial happenings on remote mountaintops. You'll be in good hands with Viajes Ángel (☎03548/1563-4532), Diag. Buenos Aires 183, who do a convincing job with their range of otherworldly tours (around AR$40 for 5hr).

Los Terrones (9am–7.30pm; ⓦwww.losterrones.com, AR$10) or **paragliding** in the alluring **Aguas de Palos**.

Arrival and information

Bus The bus station is near the centre at the corner of Corrientes and Rivadavia. Empresa Sarmiento runs buses to and from Córdoba every half hour (3hr).
Tourist office Pick up a map and area information at the tourist office in the old railway station on Av Pueyrredón (Jan–Easter 8am–10pm, rest of year 8am–9pm; ⓣ03548/481903, ⓦwww.capilladelmonte.gov.ar).

Accommodation and eating

Campers are spoilt for choice in Capilla del Monte; the closest **campsite** to town is the riverside *Calabalumba* (ⓣ03546/489601), at the end of General Paz, with a range of facilities. Tent pitches AR$7; four-bed bungalows from ❸.

Hotel el Duende Azul Corner of Chubut 75 & Aristóbulo del Valle ⓣ03548/15569667, ⓦwww.cordobaserrana.com.ar/elduendeazul.htm. A guesthouse in tune with the town's hippie vibe. Frolic in the big garden or hang out in the common area overrun by pixie and elf figurines. The simple but pretty rooms have ensuites and the adorable owners arrange detox programs. ❹

Maracaibo Buenos Aires 182 ⓣ03548/482741. This unpretentious restaurant is a good all-rounder, serving fish, pasta and chicken mains (AR$12–20), as well as lots of vegetarian options; the vegetable and corn lasagne (AR$22) is mighty fine.

The Northeast

Sticky summers, *maté* tea and *chamamé* folk music characterize the sultry northeastern provinces of Entre Ríos, Corrientes, Misiones and Santa Fe, an area known as **El Litoral**. Most of the region is wedged between two awesome rivers, the Paraná and the Uruguay, which converge near Buenos Aires as the Río de la Plata. Eclipsing every other attraction in the region are the **Iguazú Falls**, the world's most spectacular waterfalls, framed by lush subtropical forest. Located in the northeastern corner of Misiones Province, the falls straddle the border with Brazil. South of **Iguazú**, the well-preserved Jesuit Mission ruins at **San Ignacio Miní** make for the region's second-biggest draw.

Further afield, in Corrientes Province, the sprawling wetlands of **Esteros del Iberá** offer prime bird- and animal-spotting opportunities. The river-hugging, siesta-loving city of **Corrientes** has some fine historic buildings, while Argentina's third-largest city, **Rosario**, in Santa Fe Province, has an attractive riverside cultural precinct and a lively weekend party atmosphere.

The star of Entre Ríos Province is the **Parque Nacional El Palmar**, with its forest of towering *yatay* palms, an easy day-trip from the resort town of **Colón**.

If you have a problem with heat and humidity, steer clear of this region between December and March, when temperatures in the far north often creep above 40°C.

ROSARIO

Super-stylish **ROSARIO** is a cleaner, greener, less daunting version of Buenos Aires. The city where Che Guevara learned to crawl is home to a handsome, academic and culturally inclined population of just over one million.

Sprawled on the banks of the **Río Paraná**, Rosario rarely passes up an opportunity to strut its assets in its riverside beaches, parks, restaurants, bars and museums. For an enjoyable day-trip, the sandy beaches of the subtropical **delta islands** lie just a short boat or kayak ride away. *Extranjeros* are still very much a novelty here, and whether you're in town to chill or to party, you'll be warmly received by the friendly locals.

Plaza 25 de Mayo and around

The tree-lined **Plaza 25 de Mayo** lies three blocks west of the river. Here at the

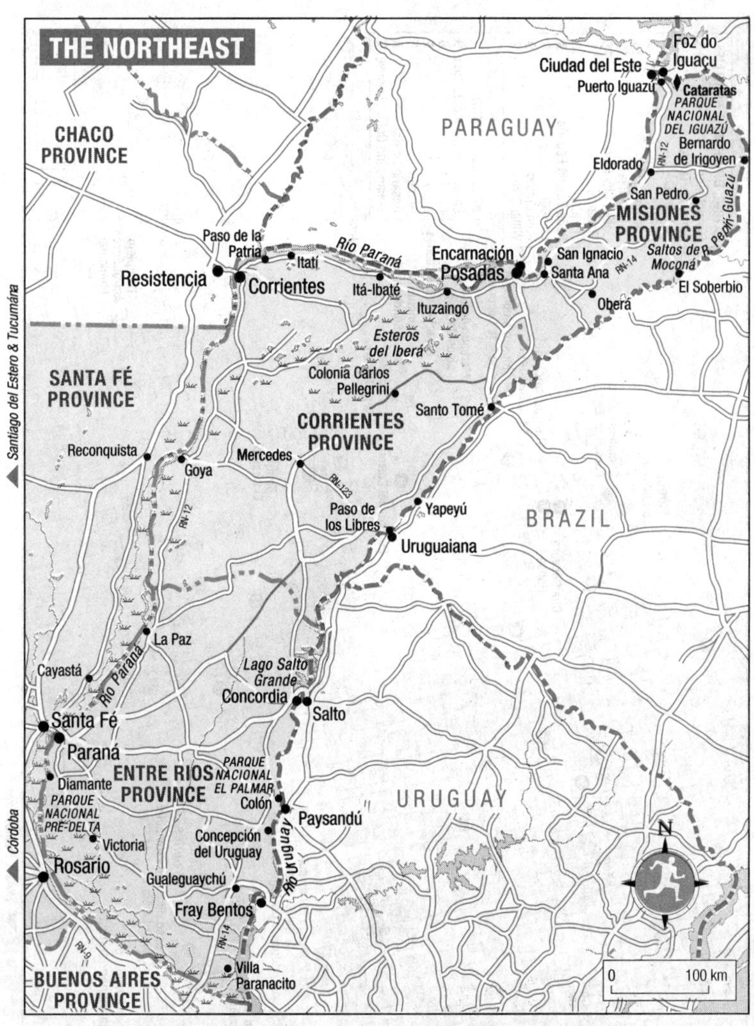

heart of the city you'll find the marble **Monumento a la Independencia** and some of the city's grandest buildings, including the late nineteenth-century **Catedral de Rosario** (daily 8am–noon & 4–9pm) with its striking Italianate marble altar. On the southern side, the **Museo Municipal de Arte Decorativo Firma y Odilio Estévez** (Wed–Fri 3–8pm, Sat & Sun 10am–8pm; AR$2; ⓣ0341/480-2547), houses the lavish art collection of the Estévez family, Galician immigrants who struck it big cultivating *maté*. Pieces include a Goya painting, a Flemish tapestry and Greek sculptures.

Monumento a la Bandera

Rising just east of the plaza, the **Monumento a la Bandera** (Monument to the Flag) is Rosario's most eye-catching landmark. A stark piece of nationalistic architecture, it marks the place where, in 1812, General Belgrano first raised the Argentinian flag. Take the

ROSARIO

Train Station, Balneario La Florida, Museo de Arte Contemporaneo, 1 & 2

Airport, RN-9, Córdoba & Santa Fe

RN-9 & Buenos Aires

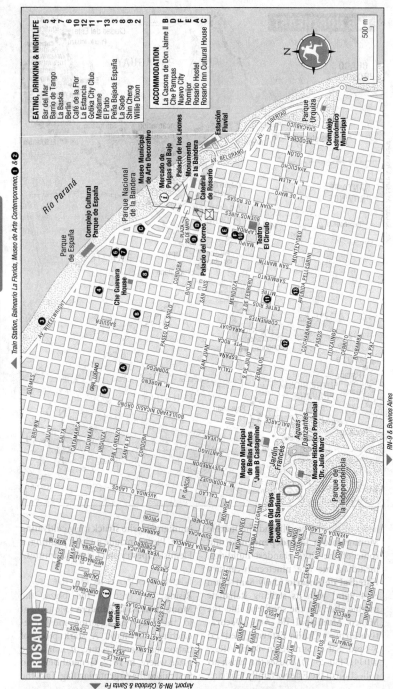

EATING, DRINKING & NIGHTLIFE	
Bar del Mar	5
Barrio de Tango	4
La Baska	7
Berlin	6
Café de la Flor	10
La Estancia	12
Gotika City Club	11
Madame	1
El Patio	13
Peña Bajada España	3
La Sede	8
Shin Cheng	9
Willie Dixon	2

ACCOMMODATION	
La Casona de Don Jaime II	B
Che Pampas	D
Nuevo City	F
Romijor	E
Rosario Hostel	A
Rosario Inn Cultural House	C

Río Paraná
Parque de España
Complejo Cultural Parque de España
Che Guevara House
Parque Nacional de la Bandera
Museo Municipal de Arte Decorativo
Mercado de Pulgas del Bajo
Palacio de los Leones
Monumento a la Bandera
Catedral de Rosario
Palacio del Correo
Plaza 25 de Mayo
Estación Fluvial
Teatro El Círculo
Bus Terminal
Museo Municipal de Bellas Artes 'Juan B Castagnino'
Newells Old Boys Football Stadium
Jardín Francés
Aguas Danzantes
Museo Histórico Provincial 'Dr. Julio Marc'
Parque de la Independencia
Parque Urquiza
Complejo Astronómico Municipal

0 500 m
N

lift up its 70-metre tower for panoramic city views (Mon 1–7pm, Tues–Sun 9am–6pm; AR$2).

Costanera

Rosario's **Costanera** (riverfront) extends for around twenty kilometres from north to south, providing plenty of green space to sunbathe or sip *maté*, as well as waterfront restaurants, bars and museums. The central **Parque Nacional de la Bandera** – a narrow strip of riverfront parkland – is the main setting for regular markets and festivals. Strolling north, the park merges with **Parque de España** and the large brick **Complejo Cultural Parque de España** (Tues–Sun 3–7pm; AR$2; ☎0341/426-0941, Ⓦwww.ccpe.org.ar), a cultural centre hosting changing modern art exhibitions. Half a kilometre north, the **Museo de Arte Contemporáneo de Rosario** (Thurs–Tues 2–8pm; ☎0341/480-4981, Ⓦwww.macromuseo.org.ar) is a kitsch temple to modern Argentine art housed inside a converted grain silo, its façade painted conspicuous pastel shades. The building as well as the views from the top floor outshine the displays, while the gallery's riverfront café, *Davis*, serves a good bite.

Most of the summer beach action happens eight kilometres north of the centre at the **Balneario La Florida** (Dec–April 8am–9pm; AR$4; bus #153). Just south of here is the Rambla Catalunya (with a free beach) and Avenida Carrasco, an upmarket restaurant, bar and club strip that is the centre of Rosario's vibrant summer nightlife.

Parque de la Independencia

The **Parque de la Independencia**, 3km southwest of Plaza 25 de Mayo, is one of Argentina's largest urban green spaces. Within its extensive grounds are a football stadium, a racetrack, a theme park, a rose garden and two museums. The **Museo Municipal de Bellas Artes Juan B Castagnino** (Wed–Mon 1–7pm; AR$; ☎0341/480-2542), Av Pellegrini 2202, has an important collection of European and Argentine fine art. West of the lake, the **Museo Histórico Provincial Dr Julio Marc** (Tues–Fri 9am–5pm, Sat & Sun 3–7pm; free; ☎0341/472-1457) is strong on religious artefacts and indigenous ceramics from across Latin America.

Che Guevara's house

Born in Rosario in 1928, **Ernesto "Che" Guevara** lived in an apartment on the corner of Entre Ríos and Urquiza until the age of two. The building is now offices and is not open to the public, but there's nothing to stop you gawking from the street. One block north and one block east, at the corner of Tucumán and Mitre, a mural of Che's intense and haggard-looking face dominates a small neighbourhood square.

Alto Delta islands

Just across the river from Rosario, the predominantly uninhabited **Alto Delta islands** are linked to the mainland by regular passenger ferries in the summer, while a weekend-only service runs in winter. **Ferries** leave from the Estación Fluvial (see p.80). Some islands have underdeveloped beaches, camping facilities and restaurants. A good way to explore the delta is by taking a **kayak excursion** (AR$120 for 7hr) with the multilingual guides at Bike Rosario (☎0341/155-713812, Ⓦwww.bikerosario.com.ar); the package includes a bicycle tour of Rosario.

Arrival and information

Air Rosario's airport (☎0341/451-1226) is 10km northwest of the centre. There are no buses to the centre; a taxi ride is around AR$25 or take a taxi to the Fisherton neighbourhood, from where buses #115, #116 and #160 run to the bus terminal.

Bus The Terminal de Omnibus Mariano Moreno is twenty blocks west of the centre, at Santa Fe and Cafferata (☎0341/437-3030). Buses #141 and #146) go to the centre.

Ferry The Estación Fluvial (Ⓣ0341/448-3737), in Parque Nacional de la Bandera, has ferries to the Delta islands. There are services year-round on weekends and a number of services daily Dec–March (AR$11 return).

Tourist office The riverside tourist office is on the corner of Av Belgrano and C Buenos Aires (daily 9am–6pm; Ⓣ0341/480-2230, Ⓦwww.rosarioturismo.com). An information kiosk in the bus terminal has city maps and hotel listings.

Train The train station (Ⓣ0800/333-3822) is 3km northwest of the centre, with slow services three times weekly to Buenos Aires.

Accommodation

Rosario has experienced a hostel boom in recent years and at weekends many fill up with party-hard *porteños*. The only time you need to book ahead is on weekends and public holidays.

Hostels

All hostels listed here have double rooms as well as dorms, kitchen facilities and offer free internet and breakfast.

Che Pampas Rioja 812 Ⓣ0341/424-5202, Ⓦwww.chepampas.com. Why can't every hostel come with a giant mirrorball, Che Guevara pop art, neon chandeliers and a red PVC throne? In the summer, you'll appreciate the a/c in the dorm rooms (AR$35). ❺

La Casona de Don Jaime II San Lorenzo 1530 Ⓣ0341/530-2020, Ⓦwww.youthhostelrosario.com.ar. A rambling HI hostel with two patios and an enormous dining area. Staff can arrange boating, kayaking and cycling excursions. Dorm AR$30. ❹

Rosario Hostel Urquiza 1911 Ⓣ0341/4404-164, Ⓦwww.rosariohostels.com.ar. Although a little on the dark side, this friendly hostel makes up for it with high ceilings, stained-glass flourishes and a patio for barbecues. Discounts for long-term stays. Dorm AR$32. ❺

Rosario Inn Cultural House Sargento Cabral 54 Ⓣ0341/421-0358, Ⓦwww.rosarioinnhostel.com.ar. With a fantastic location near the river, this light-drenched hostel has two patios to hang out in and bicycles for rent. Tango and theatre classes offered. Dorm AR$30. ❹

Hotels

Nuevo City San Juan 867 Ⓣ0341/447-1655, Ⓦwww.hotelnuevocity.com.ar. All rooms at this humble hotel have TV, a/c and private bathroom. Request one of the few rooms with external windows. Breakfast included. ❹

Romijor Laprida 1050 Ⓣ0341/421-7276. Cheap and cheerful with parking facilities to boot, this ageing hotel could do with a makeover. Still, as long as you score a bed that doesn't sag, it's good value, and there are single rooms with private bathrooms too. Breakfast in the adjoining bar included. ❺

Eating

The bulk of Rosario's **restaurants** are clustered along Avenida Pellegrini, although in summer you'll want to take advantage of the waterfront aspect and pull up an outdoor chair at one of the fine restaurants along the Costanera.

Cafés and restaurants

La Baska Tucumán 1118 Ⓣ0341/411-1110. The *empanadas* here are piping-hot, and come with a huge range of heavenly fillings including prawns, tuna, mushrooms and Roquefort cheese. AR$1.70 per *empanada*.

La Estancia Av Pellegrini at Paraguay Ⓣ0341/440-7373. Rosario's most popular restaurant is an old-fashioned place with a vast menu. The emphasis is on – you guessed it – beef, and it's fun to watch the impeccably suited waiters rush around with exotic cuts of sizzling cow. Mains around AR$25.

El Patio Above La Gallega supermarket, Pellegrini 1194. A self-service diner where you can load your plate with healthy salads, barbecued meat and a range of desserts for under AR$10.

Peña Bajada España Av Italia at España Ⓣ0341/426-1168. Popular fish restaurant with a tranquil wooden terrace overlooking the river. Access is by elevator. Barbecued fish feasts from AR$22.

La Sede Entre Rios 599 Ⓣ0341/425-4071. This atmospheric bar-cum-café is a good bet for a morning caffeine fix, a hearty lunch, a relaxed evening drink or a weekend theatre performance. For a snack try the tapas (AR$9) or a small pizza (AR$10).

Shin Cheng Rioja 954. Fresh, scrumptious and cheap Asian-vegetarian buffet (AR$12.50 per kilo). At lunchtime it's packed with suits salivating into their steamed asparagus and soya steaks.

Drinking and nightlife

Rosario's sophisticated **bars**, swinging **clubs**, aesthetically-pleasing populace and 24/7 party attitude all combine to lure *porteños* on weekend trips. In summer, the clubs and bars in the riverfront Estación Fluvial attract a modish crowd, with *Taura* the most happening place to let loose. Summer fun also transfers to Rambla Catalunya, a waterfront avenue in the city's north.

Bar del Mar Balcarce and Tucumán. A resto-bar with an aquatic theme and colourful mosaics; good for people-watching before painting the town red. Beers AR$8.

Barrio de Tango Calle Corrientes 152 ☎0341/447-4225, 🌐www.sentimientotango.com.ar. This cavernous bar and dancehall has an old-worldy vibe and is an ideal place to take your first tango steps. A range of ages share the dancefloor; tango classes daily from 8.30pm (AR$10).

Berlin Pje Zabala 1128, between the 300 block of Mitre and Sarmiento. Regular events and a steady flow of German beer (AR$8) keep locals coming back to this trendy bar.

Café de la Flor Mendoza 862 ☎0341/441-2727, 🌐www.cafedelaflor.com.ar. Live music, DJs and pizza fuel the boisterous alternative crowd at this cavernous joint. Thurs–Sun.

Gotika City Club Mitre 1539, 🌐www.gotikacityclub.com.ar. Spacious, gay-friendly club in a converted church; come here when you have some serious energy to burn. Hosts regular shows. AR$10 entrance. Fri & Sat.

Madame Brown 3126. This is *the* club for party animals – a mainstream disco with three dancefloors blaring cumbia, reggaeton, electronica and rock. Over 25s only. AR$10 entrance. Fri & Sat.

Willie Dixon Suipacha and Guemes. Rock out at this live music venue that hosts quality Argentinian acts: a disco follows the band. AR$10 entrance for disco only. Thurs–Sat.

Shopping

Bookshops Ameghino Bookshops, Corrientes 868 ☎0341/447-1147, stocks English-language books.

Markets The **Mercado de Pulgas del Bajo** flea market is on every Sat & Sun afternoon in the Parque Nacional de la Bandera near Av Belgrano 500. Stalls sell handmade crafts, used books and antiques.

Directory

Bike & kayak tours Bike Rosario, Zeballos 327, ☎0341/155-713812, 🌐www.bikerosario.com.ar.

Car rental Avis, Mendoza 3167 ☎0341/435-2299.

Laundry Lavandería VIP, Maipú 654 ☎0341/426-1237.

Post office Buenos Aires and Córdoba on Plaza 25 de Mayo.

Spanish school Punto Spanish, Level 5, San Luis 1486 ☎0341/424-0035, 🌐www.puntospanish.com. Group and one-on-one Spanish classes for reasonable rates.

Moving on

Air Internal to: Buenos Aires (5 daily; 45min); Córdoba (2 daily; 1hr). International to: Punta del Este in Uruguay. Flights with Aerolíneas Argentinas (☎0810/222-86527) and Sol Lineas Aéreas (☎0810/444-4765, 🌐www.sol.com.ar).

Bus to: Buenos Aires (every 30min; 4hr); Córdoba (40 daily; 6hr 30min); Corrientes (7 daily; 10–12hr); Montevideo in Uruguay (1 daily; 9hr); Puerto Iguazú (3 daily; 19hr); Salta (6 daily; 16hr).

Train to: Buenos Aires (2 weekly; 7hr).

PARQUE NACIONAL EL PALMAR

Only after ranching, farming and forestry had pushed the graceful *yatay* palm to the brink of extinction did it find salvation in the **PARQUE NACIONAL EL PALMAR**. The

CROSSING FROM COLÓN INTO URUGUAY

COLÓN, on the Río Uruguay 320km north of Buenos Aires, makes an inviting base for visiting the **Parque Nacional El Palmar**, 50km to the north. Colón is also a prime gateway to Uruguay, and is linked to the city of Paysandú, 16km southeast, by the Puente Internacional General Artigas. It is eight kilometres from Colón to the Uruguayan border (immigration office open 24hr a day), a further eight kilometres to Paysandú: approximately four buses daily make the journey. Colón's bus terminal is on the corner of Paysandú and 9 de Julio. There are frequent services to Concordia (9 daily; 2hr 15min), passing Parque Nacional El Palmar (see above), and plenty of connections to Buenos Aires (14 daily; 5hr 30min). Colón's helpful tourist office is in the port area on the corner of Avenida Costanera and Gouchón (Mon–Fri 6am–8pm, Sat & Sun 8am–8pm; ☎03447/421-233, 🌐www.colon.gov.ar).

85-square kilometre park, on the banks of the Río Uruguay, lies fifty kilometres north of Colón at km199 on the RN14, and is a stark reminder of how large chunks of Entre Ríos Province, Uruguay and southern Brazil once looked.

Many of the **palms**, which can grow up to eighteen metres high, are over three hundred years old. Trails wind through the park, past palm savannas, streams and riverside beaches. Sunset is the perfect time to pull out the camera, when the palms look stunning silhouetted against a technicolor sky.

El Palmar's creation in 1966 also did wonders for the habitat of local subtropical **wildlife**, including capybaras, vizcachas, monitor lizards, raccoons and the venomous *yarará* pit viper. Parakeets, egrets, *ñandúes* and storks are some of the bird species that can be spotted here. To get to the park, catch any Concordia-bound bus from Colón (9 daily; 30min) along the RN14 to the entrance (where you pay AR$12 entry). From here it's a ten-kilometre walk, drive or hitchhike to the visitor centre and adjacent **Los Loros campground** (ⓣ03447/423378; AR$4 per tent, plus AR$6 per person), serviced by showers and a basic store. If you'd prefer to spend the night **in Colón**, the *Amarello Hotel* at Calle Urquiza 865 (ⓣ03447/424063, ⓦwww.colonentrerios.com.ar/amarello; ④) has plain rooms in a range of sizes, all with private bathrooms.

CORRIENTES

Subtropical **CORRIENTES** languishes in the humidity on a curve in the Río Paraná. One of the northeast's oldest cities (it was founded in 1588), Corrientes doesn't offer much in the way of conventional attractions, but its compact historic centre, elegantly crumbling buildings and shady riverside Costanera makes it an ideal place for a leg stretch between long bus rides.

What to see and do

Corrientes' historic core fans out in grid fashion from the shady main square, **Plaza 25 de Mayo**. The square is framed by some of the city's most important nineteenth-century buildings, including the pink Italianate **Casa de Gobierno** and the plain **Iglesia de Nuestra Señora de la Merced** (daily 8am–noon & 5–8pm). On the plaza's northeast corner, the **Museo de Artesanía** (daily 8am–1pm & 3–9pm) and craft workshops (same hours), showcases regional basketwork, leather and ceramics within a whitewashed colonial residence.

One block south of the main square is Corrientes' 2.5km riverside avenue, the **Avenida Costanera General San Martín**, flanked by pretty jacaranda and native *lapacho* trees. It is the favoured haunt of fishermen, *maté* and *tereré* sippers, joggers, mosquitoes, daydreamers and courting couples. Locals flock to its promenades on summer evenings after emerging refreshed from siestas. There are a few small riverside **beaches** here, but make sure there's a lifeguard around (summer only) before taking the plunge as the river's currents are notoriously strong.

FEEELING HOT, HOT, HOT!

Despite the oppressive heat that strikes in summer, the city manages to muster up heroic levels of energy for the annual, Brazilian-style **Carnaval Correntino** (ⓣ03783/422116, ⓦwww.carnavalescorrentinos.com), which takes place mid-January to early February in the open-air Corsódromo at Avenida Centenario 2800. Alternatively, if you're in town over the second weekend in December, check out the **Festival del Chamamé** (ⓣ03783/425938, ⓦwww.corrienteschamame.com), a knees-up celebration of regional folk dancing and music.

Arrival and information

Air Corrientes' airport (☎03783/458340) is 10km northeast of the city centre. Aerolineas Argentinas (☎03783/458339) flies twice daily to Buenos Aires and four times weekly to Asunción in Paraguay. Free shuttle services can take you from the airport to the centre.

Bus The bus terminal (☎03783/449435) is 4km southeast of the city centre. Local buses run frequently between the terminal and the centre. A taxi will set you back around AR$9. There are direct bus services to: Buenos Aires (6 daily; 12hr), Posadas (9 daily; 5hr; change here for more regular services to Puerto Iguazú); Puerto Iguazú (1 daily; 10hr and Rosario (3 daily; 10hr).

Tourist office The provincial tourist office (☎03783/427200, ⓦwww.corrientesturistica.gov.ar; Mon–Fri 7am–1pm & 3–9pm) is at 25 de Mayo 1330, and there is also a municipal tourist office where the Costanera meets Pellegrini (☎03783/474702; daily 7am–9pm).

ESTEROS DEL IBERÁ

A vast area of marshy swampland, the Esteros del Iberá comprise a series of lagoons, rivers, marshes and floating islands, much of which is protected in the **RESERVA NATURAL DEL IBERÁ**. The islands are created by a build-up of soil on top of a mat of intertwined water lilies and other plants; these in turn choke the flow of water, creating what is in effect a vast, slow-flowing river, draining eventually into the Río Paraná. The wetlands make up nearly fifteen percent of Corrientes province – spreading annually in the rainy season and gradually contracting until the rains come again. With the protection of the natural reserve, the area's wildlife is thriving, and there's an extraordinary variety: some three hundred species of birds, many brilliantly coloured; forty species of mammals, including capybara, marsh and pampas deer, otters and howler monkeys; and many fish, amphibians and reptiles, including caymans. Take a trip out onto the water, and you can enjoy remarkably close encounters with many of them.

What to see and do

Access to the reserve is from the tranquil village of **COLONIA CARLOS PELLEGRINI**, on the banks of the Laguna del Iberá. At the approach to the village, immediately before the rickety wooden bridge that is the only way in, former poachers staff the Centro de Interpretación, the reserve's **visitor centre**, with useful information as well as a fascinating photo display. A nearby forest trail is a good place to spot (and hear) howler monkeys. Trips to the wetlands can be arranged in the village, and are highly recommended – without a guide it is hard to get your bearings, and you'll miss much of the wildlife. A variety of **tours** are on offer, by boat (you'll be poled through the marshier sections, where a motor is useless), on foot or on horseback; there are also moonlit night-time tours to see the nocturnal species. The fifty-three square-kilometre Laguna del Iberá is covered in water lilies, especially the yellow-and-purple *aguapé*, and its floating islands teem with an extraordinarily rich microcosm of bird and aquatic life. Birds include storks, cormorants, egrets, ducks and other waterfowl, while around the edges of the lake lives the *chajá* (horned screamer), a large grey bird with a startling patch of red around the eyes, one of the region's signature species, as well as snakes (including the alarming yellow anaconda) and caymans. The capybara, the world's largest rodent, makes an unlikely swimmer, but in fact spends most of its time in the water – listen out for the splash as it enters.

Arrival and information

Colonia Carlos Pellegrini lies 120km from the village of **Mercedes**, a bus journey of around three hours in good conditions, though rain can slow progress on the mostly unpaved RP40 (departures Mon–Sat at noon; AR$30 one-way). Mercedes has a helpful tourist office (daily 8am–noon & 4–8pm;

☎03773/420100), and you can also arrange private 4WD transfers from here, through your accommodation in Colonia Carlos. Access is also possible from Posadas, to the northwest, but this is still slower, and frequently impassable in the wet (3 buses weekly with *Nordestur*, 5–6hr; AR$90 one-way; ☎03722/445588). There's very little to Colonia Carlos, a grid of sandy streets around the Plaza San Martín, and very few facilities – bring enough cash to cover your entire stay.

Accommodation

The best accommodation in the village is provided by a handful of gorgeous *posadas*: they also provide food (often on a full-board basis) and organise tours.

Don Justino Hostel ☎03773/499415, ⓔibertatours@hotmail.com. Good quality budget accommodation option with both private rooms and dorms. Rooms have a/c and prices include breakfast and towels. Dorm AR$37. ❹

Posada Ypa Sapukai ☎03773/420155, ⓦwww.iberaturismo.com.ar. The most affordable of the *posadas*, a charming, friendly, lakeside place with a small pool, lookout tower, impeccable rooms and beautiful garden. AR$100 per person per day full-board, excursions AR$60.

SAN IGNACIO

The riverside town of **SAN IGNACIO** is home to one of the major sights of northern Argentina. There's little clue of that in the centre, though, where this is just another hot, sleepy town. If you time the buses right you can visit San Ignacio Miní and move on the same day, but there are a couple of other attractions should you be staying longer. The main street south will lead you past the **Casa de Horacio Quiroga** (daily 8am–6.30pm; AR$5; ☎03752/470124), a museum to the Uruguayan-born Argentine writer of Gothic short stories, who made his home here in the early twentieth century. The same road continues to **Puerto Nuevo** on the Río Parana, a couple of kilometres away, where a sandy beach offers wonderful views across the river to Paraguay. With a bit more time you could also head to the **Parque Provincial Teyú Cuaré**, some 10km south of the village on a good, unpaved road. Here there are camping facilities and you can seek out the **Peñón Reina Victoria**, a rockface said to resemble Queen Victoria's profile.

San Ignacio Miní

SAN IGNACIO MINÍ (daily 7am–7pm; AR$12; ticket valid for 15 days) was one of many Jesuit missions set up throughout Spanish America to convert the native population to Christianity. Originally established further north in what is now Brazil, the missionaries gradually moved south to avoid attack from Portuguese *bandeirantes* (piratical slave traders), eventually settling here in 1696. The mission became a thriving small town, inhabited by the local Guaraní people, but, following the suppression of the Jesuits, was abandoned in the early nineteenth century. Rediscovered around a hundred years ago, the ruins are now among the best preserved of their kind in Latin America, a UNESCO World Heritage Site with some spectacular Baroque architecture. At the entrance, at the northeastern end of the village, an excellent **Centro de Interpretación Regional** looks at the life of the mission and its Guaraní inhabitants. Rows of simple *viviendas*, stone-built, single-storey living quarters which once housed Guaraní families, lead down to a grassy Plaza de Armas, overlooked by the **church** that dominates the site. The roof and most of the interior have long since crumbled away, but much of the magnificent façade, designed by the Italian architect Brazanelli, still stands and many fine details can be made out. Twin columns rise either side of the doorway, and the walls are decorated with exuberant bas-relief sculpture executed by Guaraní craftsmen.

Arrival and information

There's no bus station as such in San Ignacio, but all buses drop off at the western end of the main, east–west avenue, Sarmiento. Departures for Puerto Iguazú (4–5hr; AR$25) and Posadas (1hr; AR$5) are approximately hourly, all day. A small **Centro de Informes** can be found at the corner of Av Sarmiento and RN12, at the entrance to town. Ask here, or at the ruins' entrance, about sound and light shows, held most evenings at San Ignacio Miní.

Accommodation and eating

There's not a great deal of quality when it comes to food, but for budget **eats**, try one of the pizzerias and snack bars near the ruins. There is a decent supermarket on San Martín, between Avenida Sarmiento and Belgrano.

Hospedaje El Descanso Pellegrini 270, towards the outskirts of the village around ten blocks south of the bus terminal ⓣ03752/470207. Smart little bungalows with private bathrooms but no a/c; breakfast AR$3. ❸

Hotel Residencial Doka Alberdi 518 ⓣ03752/470131, ⓔrecidoka@yahoo.com.ar. Rooms with a/c, TV, en-suite bathrooms and small kitchens, right next to the ruins. ❹

Residencial San Ignacio San Martín 823, corner Sarmiento ⓣ03752/470047. The largest hotel in town is located right in the centre. Comfortable and modern rooms with TV and a/c. Internet and phone on site. Great value and walking distance to ruins. ❹

IGUAZÚ FALLS

Around 275 individual cascades, the highest with a drop of over 80m, make up the stunning **Iguazú Falls** (*Cataratas de Iguazú*, or simply *las cataratas*). Strung out along the rim of a horseshoe-shaped cliff 2.7km long, their thunderous roaring can be heard from miles away while the mist thrown up rises 30-metre high in a series of dazzling rainbows. In the Guaraní language Iguazú means 'great water', but clearly the Guaraní are not given to overstatement, for there's little doubt that these are the most spectacular falls in the world: only the Victoria Falls in Africa can compare in terms of size, but here the shape of the natural fault that created the falls means that you can stand with the water crashing almost all around you.

This section of the Río Iguazú makes up the border between Brazil and Argentina and the subtropical forests that surround the falls are protected on both sides: by the **Parque Nacional Iguazú** in Argentina, and the **Parque Nacional do Iguaçu** over the border (see p.394). These parks are packed with exotic wildlife, and even on the busy catwalks and paths that skirt the edges of the falls you've a good chance of seeing much of it. Orchids and serpentine creepers adorn the trees, among which flit vast, bright butterflies. You may also see toucans overhead and – if you're lucky – shy capuchin monkeys. Look out too for the swallow-like *vencejo*, a remarkable small bird, endemic to the area, that makes its nest behind the curtains of water.

The Parque Nacional Iguazú

Thanks to an extensive system of trails and catwalks that lead around, above and below the falls, the Argentine side offers much the best experience of Iguazú. Everything lies within the **Parque Nacional Iguazú** (daily Oct–Feb 9am–7pm, March–Sept 9am–6pm; AR$60; ⓦwww.iguazuargentina.com), whose entrance lies 18km southeast of Puerto Iguazú along RN12. The visitor centre here can provide a map of the park and various handy leaflets. It's also the departure point of the **Tren de la Selva**, an 'ecological', natural-gas-fuelled train. This leaves every 30 minutes (last at 4pm, 4.30pm in summer) for Cataratas Station, which gives access to the walking trails, and then on to the Garganta del Diablo walkway.

Several well-signposted trails (most wheelchair-accessible) take you along a series of catwalks and paths to the park's highlights. The **Paseo Superior**, a short trail which takes you along the top of the first few waterfalls, makes a good introduction. For more drama, and a much wetter experience, the **Paseo Inferior** winds down through the forest before

taking you to within metres of some of the smaller falls. At the bottom of this trail, a regular free boat service leaves for **Isla San Martín**, a rocky island in the middle of the river. The same jetty is also the departure point for more thrills-oriented boat rides, such as those offered by Iguazú Jungle Explorer (ⓣ03757/421600, ⓦwww.iguazujunglexplorer.com; from AR$75). At the heart of the falls, the truly unforgettable **Garganta del Diablo** (The Devil's Throat) is a powerhouse display of natural forces in which 1800 cubic metres of water per second hurtles over a semicircle of rock into the misty river canyon below. The one-kilometre catwalk takes you to a small viewing platform within just a few metres of the staggering, sheer drop of water.

Puerto Iguazú

PUERTO IGUAZÚ is an inevitable stop if you're visiting the falls on a budget, a perfectly pleasant town with

CROSSING INTO BRAZIL

To make your trip to Iguazú complete you should really visit the **Brazilian side** (see p.394), where the view is more panoramic, and the photography opportunities are excellent. There are no direct buses from Puerto Iguazú to the falls on the Brazilian side – you will need to take one of the regular international buses marked 'Brasil' from the main street or bus station (AR$4), which will drop you at the border for immigration formalities. From the border pick up another bus towards Foz, changing to yet another for the falls themselves. If time is short, it is well worth considering sharing a taxi (approximately AR$100 return). Change some Brazilian cash before you go, for bus fares and the like, and bear in mind that, from October to March, Brazil is one hour ahead of Argentina.

all the facilities you need, if a little dull. On the western edge of town, the **Hito Tres Fronteras** is an obelisk overlooking the rivers Iguazú and Parana at the point where they meet and form the three-way border between Argentina, Brazil and Paraguay. From here, 'El Práctico' buses to the National Park run every half-hour (7am–7.15pm; AR$4 each way); you can also pick them up at intervals all the way along the main street, Avenida Victoria Aguirre.

Arrival and information

Air The airport is 25km southeast of Puerto Iguazú (ⓣ03757/422013). Buses meet flights and run to the bus terminal (ⓣ03757/422962; AR$8 one-way).

Bus Station All national and international bus services leave from the bus terminal on Av Córdoba, at Av Misiones. There are a number of private information booths and travel agents to be found here.

National Park office Av Victoria Aguirre 66 ⓣ03757/420722. Tues–Sun 8am–5pm winter, 8am–6pm summer.

Tourist office Av Victoria Aguirre 311 ⓣ03757/420800. Mon–Fri 7am–9pm, Sat & Sun 8am–noon & 4–8pm.

Accommodation

There are a number of big resort hotels near the falls, but budget travellers head for Puerto Iguazú, where there are plenty of good options. In high season, July and around Easter, reservations are recommended.

Hotel Lilian Fray Luis Beltrán 183 ⓣ03757/420968, ⓔhotellilian@yahoo.com.ar. One of the slickest of the budget options, offering spotless modern rooms with good bathrooms. ❺

Marcopolo Inn ⓣ0375/421823, ⓦwww.hostel-inn.com. Recently refurbished HI hostel with six-bed dorms and double rooms. There's a pool, free linternet and wi-fi, large kitchen, and breakfast is included. Dorm AR$32. ❺

Noelia Residencial Fray Luis Beltrán 119, between Moreno and Belgrano ⓣ03757/420729, ⓔresidenciafamiliarnoelia@yahoo.com.ar. Excellent value, family-run hotel not far from the bus station, with a/c, private baths and a lovely patio where breakfast is served. ❹

Viejo Americano RN12, 5km from town towards the national park ⓣ03757/420190, ⓦwww.viejoamericano.com.ar. Excellent campsite out of town with beautiful verdant grounds and a large pool. AR$15 per person. *Cabañas* also available ❼

Eating and drinking

With a few exceptions, restaurants in Iguazú serve bland and touristy fare. At the Falls there are several cafes, but the food is expensive and uninspiring, so consider packing a picnic.

Gallo Negro Av Victoria Aguirre at Curupi ⓣ03757/422165. Probably the best in town, a good-looking ranch-style *parrilla* on the main street, with outdoor seating on a verandah. Cover charge of AR$8 per person includes unlimited access to the inviting salad bar. Mains AR$25–50. Daily 11.30am–late.

Parrilla El Quincho Del Tío Querido Bonpland 110 ⓣ03757/420151. Good local *parrilla*. Mains AR$20–50.

La Rueda Córdoba 28 ⓣ03757/422531. Pleasant restaurant where fish is a speciality, with outdoor seating. Mains AR$20–52.

Terra Av Misiones 125. Bar/restaurant with an arty feel serving decent salads, stir-fries and strong *caipirinhas* (AR$8). Mains AR$12–22.

The northwest

Argentina's northwest is an area of deserts, red earth and white-washed colonial churches, punctuated with pockets of cloudforest and lush green jungle. The pretty and inviting city of Salta is known for its well-preserved colonial architecture and makes a great base for visiting the wonderful natural formations of the **Quebrada del Toro** and **Quebrada de Cafayate**, as well as the stylish wine-producing villages of the **Valles Calchaquíes**, such as **Cafayate**. To the north of Salta loom three jungle-clad **cloudforests – El Rey** above all is worth a visit – along with the busy market town of **San Salvador de Jujuy** with its palm trees and wild Andean feel. Heading further north, the seven-coloured **Quebrada de Humahuaca ravine** can be seen from the small mud brick towns of **Tilcara** and **Humahuaca**.

SALTA

SALTA is one of Argentina's most elegant provincial capitals, with leafy plazas, well-preserved colonial architecture and, thanks to the altitude, a pleasantly balmy climate. Throughout the city, and in its hotels, restaurants and museums, there's a strong emphasis on the culture of the Andes, and you'll notice that even the food is spicier than that in the south of the country. Specific attractions include the cable-car ride to the top of Cerro San Bernardo, for fabulous views over the city, a peach-coloured Neoclassical church and wonderful *peñas* that mix spicy food and Andean music. Salta is a great jumping-off point for the high passes of the **Quebrada del Toro** – ideally viewed from the **Tren a las Nubes** (though this may be closed) – and for the **Valles Calchaquíes**, where you can stay overnight amongst the vineyards of **Cafayate**. A less-visited option is the cloudforest national park of **El Rey**, to the east.

What to see and do

The verdant **Plaza 9 de Julio** lies at the heart of Salta, with scenic cafes nestled under its arches – in the evening the whole place is lit up, and half of Salta seems to descend on the square for an evening stroll. This is the place to start your exploration.

Plaza 9 de Julio

On the southern side of the leafy plaza, the whitewashed **Cabildo** houses the **Museo Histórico del Norte** (Tues–Sat 9.30am–1.30pm & 3.30–8.30pm, Sun 9.30am–1pm; AR$2), which displays an eclectic array of artefacts from horse-drawn carriages to everyday objects. The balcony here offers a great view over the goings-on in the square. Facing the museum is the peach-coloured Neoclassical **Cathedral**, built in 1882, with some interesting frescoes inside. Every night at around 6pm, the Cathedral and the plaza light up, and most *Salteñas* take their evening stroll. Just east of the plaza, Calle Caseros leads to two more interesting churches. The ox-blood coloured **Iglesia y Convento San Francisco**, designed by architect Luigi Giorgi, is one of the most impressive religious buildings in the country. Its exuberance makes a fascinating contrast with the white-washed walls of the **Convento San Bernardo**, a lesson in simplicity and tranquillity in design.

Museums

A new and controversial addition to the area is MAAM, the **Museo de Arqueología de Alta Montaña** (Tues–Sun 9am–1pm & 4–9pm; AR$15; ⓦwww.maam.org.ar). Here the mummified remains of several high-mountain child sacrifices are on display, even though many locals believe the perfectly

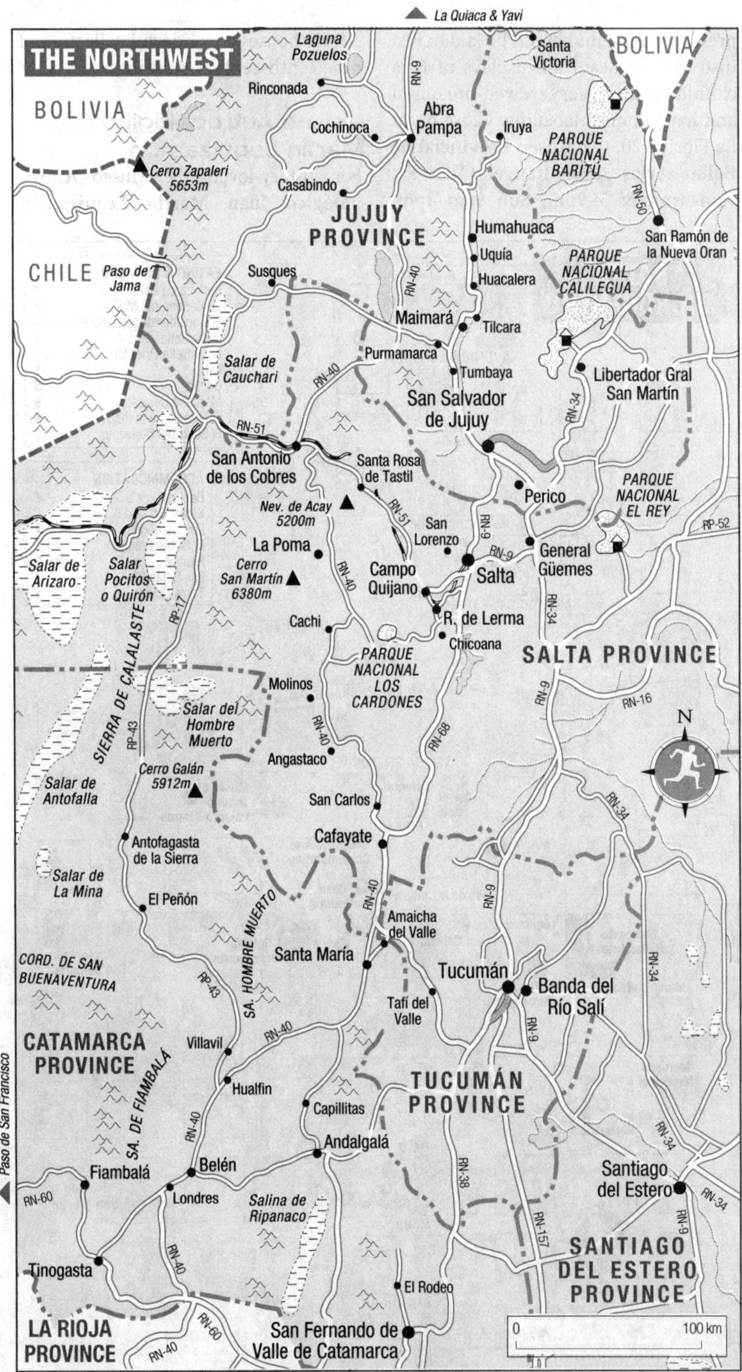
THE NORTHWEST
La Quiaca & Yavi
Laguna Pozuelos
Rinconada
BOLIVIA
Santa Victoria
Abra Pampa
Cochinoca
Iruya
PARQUE NACIONAL BARITÚ
Cerro Zapaleri 5653m
Casabindo
JUJUY PROVINCE
Humahuaca
Uquía
Huacalera
San Ramón de la Nueva Oran
PARQUE NACIONAL CALILEGUA
CHILE
Paso de Jama
Susques
Maimará
Tilcara
Purmamarca
Tumbaya
Salar de Cauchari
Libertador Gral San Martín
San Salvador de Jujuy
San Antonio de los Cobres
Santa Rosa de Tastil
Perico
PARQUE NACIONAL EL REY
Nev. de Acay 5200m
San Lorenzo
La Poma
General Güemes
Salta
Campo Quijano
Salar de Arizaro
Salar Pocitos o Quirón
Cerro San Martín 6380m
R. de Lerma
Cachi
Chicoana
SALTA PROVINCE
PARQUE NACIONAL LOS CARDONES
Molinos
SIERRA DE CALALASTE
Salar del Hombre Muerto
Angastaco
Cerro Galán 5912m
Salar de Antofalla
San Carlos
Cafayate
Antofagasta de la Sierra
Salar de La Mina
El Peñón
Amaicha del Valle
SA. HOMBRE MUERTO
CORD. DE SAN BUENAVENTURA
Santa María
Tucumán
Banda del Río Salí
Tafí del Valle
CATAMARCA PROVINCE
Villavil
SA. DE FIAMBALÁ
Hualfin
TUCUMÁN PROVINCE
Capillitas
Andalgalá
Paso de San Francisco
Fiambalá
Belén
Santiago del Estero
Londres
Salina de Ripanaco
Tinogasta
SANTIAGO DEL ESTERO PROVINCE
El Rodeo
LA RIOJA PROVINCE
San Fernando de Valle de Catamarca
0
100 km
N
RN-9
RN-40
RN-50
RN-34
RN-51
RP-52
RP-17
RN-68
RN-16
RP-43
RN-38
RN-157
RN-60

preserved remains should be laid to rest instead. The beautiful displays of Inca clothing and jewellery are well-organised and have English labelling. Close by, at La Florida 20, the **Museo Provincial de Bellas Artes Arías Rengel** (Tues–Sat 9am–1pm & 5–9pm, Sun 9am–1pm; AR$2) houses a wonderful collection of nineteenth-century paintings.

Museo Antropológico Juan Martín Leguizamón

For history-lovers the **Museo Antropológico Juan Martín Leguizamón**

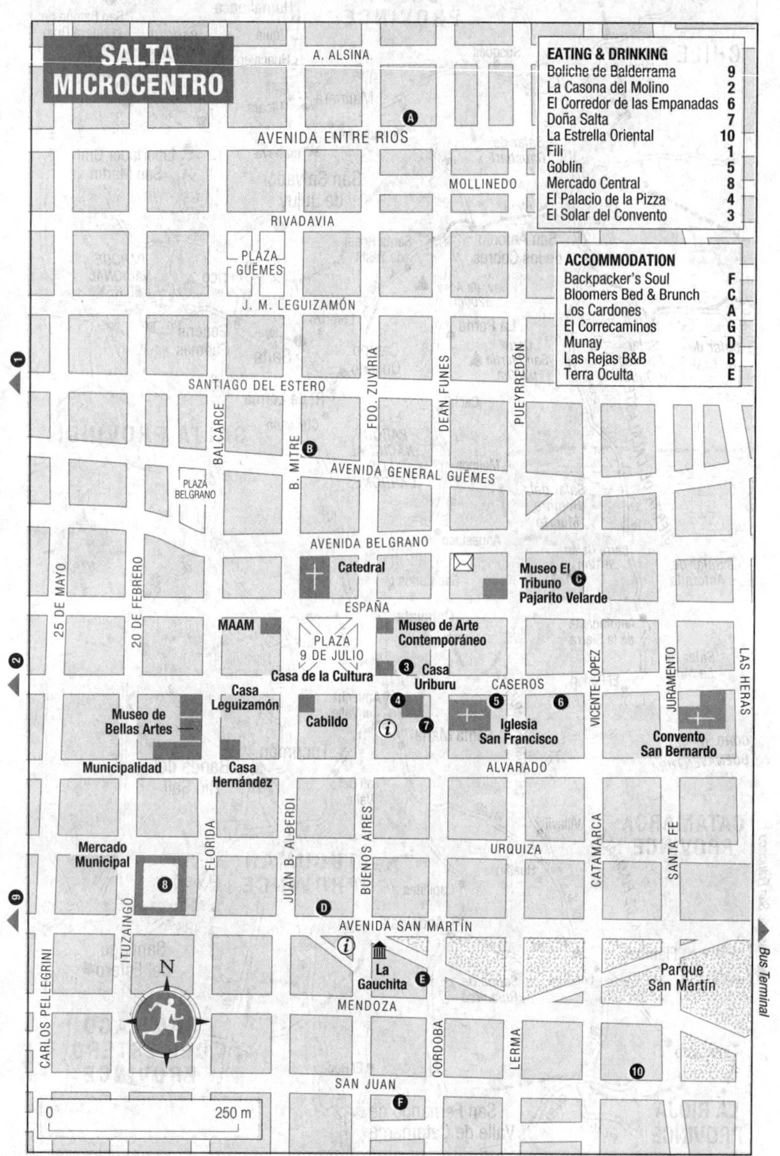

(Mon–Fri 8am–1pm & 2–6pm, Sun 10am–1pm; AR$3), at Ejército del Norte and Polo Sur, has a modern, accessible collection of pre-Hispanic arteifacts, as well as an exhibition of high-altitude burials. Behind the museum, a steep path leads you up **Cerro San Bernardo** (1458m; 45min), or you can take the easy option and hop on the **teleférico**, or cable car (daily 10am–7.30pm; AR$12 each way, AR$6 for children), from Avenida Hipólito Yrigoyen, between Urquiza and Avenida San Martín, at the eastern end of Parque San Martín. At the top are lush, well-manicured gardens, and a small café with the best views in Salta.

Arrival and information

Air Salta's airport (☎0387/424-2904) is 10km southwest of the city centre. Airbus (☎0387/1568-32897; AR$12) runs between the airport and central Salta or a taxi will cost AR$32.

Bus All buses arrive at the sleek new bus terminal (☎0387/401-1143) eight blocks east of the main plaza along Parque San Martín. It has luggage storage, cafes, chemists and bakeries but no internet.

Train Bus #5 links the bus terminal with the train station, at Ameghino 690, via Plaza 9 de Julio. The only trains that serve Salta are the tourist *Tren a las Nubes* (see p.108; currently under repairs), and infrequent goods and passenger trains to the Chilean border.

Accommodation

There are plenty of budget accommodation options in Salta, and all are within walking distance of the bus terminal and the central plaza.

Hostels

Backpacker's Soul San Juan 413 ☎0387/431-6476 Ⓦwww.backpackerssalta.com. One of three HI-affiliated hostels in town. Clean, crowded and a little noisy. Dorm AR$24.

Los Cardones Av Entre Rios 454 ☎0387/431-4026 Ⓦwww.loscardones.todowebsalta.com.ar. A little out of the centre but close to lots of bars and restaurants this hostel has five courtyards, hammocks, board games and friendly welcome, and private rooms with shared or en-suite bathrooms as well as dorm beds. Dorm AR$24. ❹

El Correcaminos Vicente Lopéz 353 ☎0387/422-0731, Ⓦwww.saltahostel.com. Basic rooms and clean bathrooms in this lively hostel with a small garden to enjoy. Dorm AR$21.

Terra Oculta Córdoba 361 ☎0387/421-8769 Ⓦwww.terraoculta.com. Set over four floors, this vacuous hostel has dorms of various sizes, a rooftop bar and table-tennis. Dorm AR$25.

Hotels

Bloomers Bed & Brunch Vicente Lopéz 129 ☎0387/422-7449 Ⓦwww.bloomers-salta.com.ar. Five beautifully decorated rooms, with private bathrooms and a spectacular breakfast which changes from day to day. ❻

Munay San Martín 656 ☎0387/422-4936, Ⓦwww.munayhotel.com.ar. Good quality budget hotel, with basic but clean rooms with private bathrooms. Breakfast included. ❺

Las Rejas B&B General Güemes 569 ☎0387/421-5971, Ⓦwww.lasrejashostel.com.ar. Family-owned and run, with comfortable doubles and English-speaking staff. ❺

Eating, drinking and nightlife

Salta has a good range of budget eating options, ranging from simple snack bars where you can enjoy delicious *empanadas* to atmospheric cafés and lively *peñas*.

Restaurants

El Corredor de las *Empanadas* Corner of Zuriria and Necochea. Pleasant outdoor patio serving northwestern treats. Try the famous *empanadas*, *humitas* and *tamales* (AR$2).

Doña Salta Córdoba 46. Don't be put off by the tacky sign and staff uniforms, this is one of Salta's best restaurants for northwestern fare. *Empanadas* from AR$1.80.

La Estrella Oriental San Juan 137. Middle Eastern food that makes a nice change from *empanadas*. Try the hummus and lamb kebabs, followed by *baklawa*. Mains AR$18–24.

Mercado Central La Florida and San Martín. Good for lunch, with a range of inexpensive food stalls.

El Palacio de la Pizza Caseros 427. Great pizzas (AR$18) and *empanadas* (AR$2).

El Solar del Convento Caseros 444 ☎0387/421-5124. Stylish décor, attentive service and quality food. Salta's top restaurant, without a doubt. Mains AR$28–36.

Bars, cafés and peñas

Boliche de Balderrama San Martín 1126 ☎0387/421-1542. Popular *Peña* with local music, and sometimes dancing while you eat.

Ask beforehand if there is a charge for the entertainment.

La Casona del Molino Luis Burela and Caseros 2500 ⓣ0387/434-2835. Wonderful old building which has great local snacks including *empanadas*, *locro*, *guaschalocro*, *tamales*, *humitas*, as well as sangria and live music.

Fili Corner of Güemes and Sarmiento 29. Best ice cream in town.

Goblin Caseros 445. Handy for the plaza: chicken burgers and Shepherd's Pie accompanied by a great range of home-brewed beers.

Directory

Airlines Aerolíneas Argentinas at the airport (ⓣ0387/424-1185) and at Caseros 475 (ⓣ0387/431-1331); Lloyd Aéreo Boliviano at the airport (ⓣ0387/424-1181) and at Deán Funes 29 (ⓣ0387/431-9388); Lapa at the airport (ⓣ0387/424-2333) and at Buenos Aires 24 (ⓣ0387/431-7080); Southern Winds, Caseros 434 (ⓣ0387/421-0808).

Car rental Rent a Truck, Buenos Aires 1 ⓣ0387/431-0740.

Post office Deán Funes 170.

Travel agents Ricardo Clark Expediciones, Caseros 121 ⓣ0387/421-5390, ⓦwww.clarkexpediciones.com; MoviTrack Safaris, Buenos Aires 68 ⓣ0387/431-6749, ⓦwww.movitrack.com.ar; Marina Turismo, Buenos Aires 1 ⓣ0387/431-0740, ⓦwww.salnet.com.ar/marinaturismo; Norte Trekking, Los Juncos 173 ⓣ0387/439-6957, ⓔfede@nortetrekking.com; Martín Pekarek, España 45, Chicoana ⓣ0387/490-7009, ⓔMartinpek@impsat1.com.ar; Salta Rafting, Ruta 47, Km 34, Cabra Corral ⓣ0387/156-856-085, ⓦwww.saltarafting.com.

LA QUEBRADA DEL TORO

There are several ways to experience the dramatic, ever-changing scenery of the **Quebrada del Toro** gorge and its surrounding towns; you can rent a car, take an organized tour or hop on the **Tren a los Nubes**. Sadly the train, a fabulous if expensive experience, is out of action for refurbishment until at least 2010, and as the journey is much more enjoyable if someone else is doing the work, you are currently best off on a **tour**. Leaving early from Salta and the Lerma valley, you start to ascend the multi-coloured gorge of the Río El Toro, deceptively tranquil most of the year, though it can be torrential in spring. The road follows the rail tracks most of the way, allowing you to experience this exceptional engineering achievement (there are 21 tunnels and more than 13 viaducts, the highlight of them the 64-metre high, 224-metre long **Polvorilla Viaduct**, almost at the top of the line). Along the way there are various stops and photo opportunities, usually including the town of **Santa Rosa de Tastil**, the pre-Incan site of **Tastil** and the small mining town of **San Antonio de los Cobres** where the local artists sell their jewellery, clothing and toys by the train station. See the Salta listings (above) for tour operators.

PARQUE NACIONAL EL REY

The spectacular cloudforests of the **PARQUE NACIONAL EL REY** (9am–dusk; free) lie just under 200km from Salta. Set in a natural, half-moon shaped amphitheatre, locked in by the curving **Crestón del Gallo** ridge to the northwest, and the higher crest of the **Serranía del Piquete** (1700m) to the east, El Rey features an upland enclave covered in lush green vegetation, with high year-round humidity and precipitation but with very distinct seasons – very wet in summer, dry (or at least not so wet) in winter. The park is frequently covered in a low-lying mist, the signature feature of cloudforests, protecting the plants and animals beneath it. El Rey is particularly good for bird watching: the giant **toucan** is the park's symbol, and it is easily seen, while at least 150 other bird species also live here. There are also large mammals, including jaguar and howler monkeys, though these are rarely spotted.

There is just one access road to the park (the RP20), and if visiting independently it is advisable that you check in with the **Guardaparques** at the park entrance before you set off. They can advise you of the status of the rivers you'll need to cross to access the park. Should you want to stay overnight, the only option is to **camp** in the central clearing, in the middle of the park. The easiest way to discover the park is on an **organized trip** from Salta (see "Listings", opposite).

VALLES CALCHAQUÍES

To the south of Salta lie the stunning **VALLES CALCHAQUÍES**, the valleys of the Río Calchaquí, a series of fertile valleys fed by snowmelt from the Andes. Here you'll find some of the highest vineyards in the world. You can hire your own car from Salta to explore the area, which would give you the opportunity to hike through some of the wonderful cactus forests of the **Cuesta del Obispo** in the **Parque Nacional Los Cardones**, or the little towns of **Cachi** and **Cafayate** are easily accessible by bus. There are also tours from both Cafayate and Salta.

CACHI

CACHI lies around 160km southwest of Salta, along an incredibly scenic route with mountainous views across lush valleys. Cachi is small and still quite undiscovered, but what it lacks in services, it makes up in scenery and location. The permanently snow-covered **Nevado del Cachi** (6380m), 15km to the west, looms ominously over life here.

What to see and do

Truth is, there's not a great deal to detain you in Cachi other than the tranquil and picturesque nature of the place itself. A small Plaza Mayor, shaded by palms and orange trees, marks the centre of town and on the north side you'll find the well-restored **Iglesia San José**. Its bright white exterior gives way to an interior made almost entirely, from pews to confessional, of porous cactus wood. Not far away, the **Museo Arqueológico Pío Pablo Díaz** (daily 8am–6pm; AR$1) displays local archeological finds in an attractive building with a wonderful patio. The museum is in need of updating, but still an interesting place to visit. For the more energetic, a hiking track to the west of the village, which will lead you to **Cachi Adentro** (6km) where you'll have wonderful views of the surrounding landscape and may be lucky to see the endless fields of drying paprika which line the route from March to May each year.

Arrival

Buses from Salta (and local buses from nearby villages) drop off at the main square. From there all services are within walking distance. There are frequent onward services to Cafayate (2hr 30min), Salta (2hr) and local destinations.

Accommodation

There are relatively few places to stay in Cachi itself, and most budget travellers looking for a bed head on to Cafayate.

Hostería ACA Sol del Valle J.M. Castilla (at the top of the hill) ☎03868/491105, www.soldelvalle.com.ar. A lovely, if pricey, option, whose modern rooms offer views over the valley. ❼

Municipal Camping Av Automóvil Club Argentina (at the end) ☎03868/491053. Basic clean camping, with cabins on offer. Pool and shaded areas. AR$4 per person.

Hotel Nevado de Cachi Ruiz de los Llanos ☎03868/491004. Right next to the bus stop on the plaza, this small family-run hotel is a good budget option. ❹

Eating and drinking

ACA Sol del Valle J.M. Castilla. The hotel restaurant serves local fare, as well as modern options. The setting is wonderful, and the staff are friendly. Mains AR$20–28.

El Jagüel Av General Güemes (☎03868/491135). Delicious locally-made *locro* (AR$4) and *empanadas* (AR$2).

AROUND CACHI

The 157km drive from Cachi to Cafayate takes you through some of the region's most spectacular scenery, and some delightful little towns. A short stop in **MOLINOS** (60km from Cachi) is recommended, to view the local crafts, see the picturesque adobe houses, and check out a fabulous church, the eighteenth-century **Iglesia de San Pedro Nolasco.** Beyond **ANGASTACO**, the red sandstone **Quebrada de las Flechas** gorge is filled with dangerous looking arrow-head formations. Shortly afterwards the road passes through **El Ventisquero**, the "wind-tunnel", and the natural stone walls of **El Cañón**, over 20-metre-high.

CAFAYATE

The largest town in the region, and the main tourist base, is **CAFAYATE**. Set amid apparently endless vineyards, it makes a perfect place to hole up for a few days while exploring the surrounding area on horseback or sipping the local wines at nearby *bodegas*. The town is lively, and filled with inviting plazas and popular restaurants.

What to see and do

Cafayate is another town where there's really not a great deal to do – the pleasure lies in getting out into the countryside and exploring the vineyards and *bodegas*. A couple of museums will fill a few hours, however. The **Museo Arqueológico** (daily 11am–8pm; donation admission; ⓣ03868/421054), at the corner of Colón and Calchaquí, is the private collection of late collector Rodolfo Bravo. On display alongside archeological relics are local ceramics, and everyday items from the colonial period. For wine-history lovers, the **Museo de la Vid y el Vino** on Avenida General Güemes (Mon–Fri 10am–1pm & 5–8pm; AR$2; ⓣ03868/21125) is an interesting introduction to wine-making in the area and shows, through old machinery, the improvements and developments made to local viticulture in recent times.

Arrival and information

Bus Buses from Salta and nearby villages use the small terminal on Belgrano, east of the plaza, though some will drop you off at your destination as you pass through town. Ask the driver. Buses from Tucumán arrive at the terminal on Güemes Norte and Alvarado.

Tourist information A kiosk on the plaza (Mon–Fri 9am–8pm, Sat & Sun 7am–1pm & 3–9pm) dispenses information about where to stay, what to do and where to rent bikes or hire horses. Look for the helpful hand-drawn map of the wineries.

Tour operators Turismo Cordillerano, Camila Quintana de Niño 59 (ⓣ03868/422137), offers trekking, and excursions to the Valle Calchaquí. Puna Turismo, San Martín 82 (ⓣ03868/421808), can arrange horse rides, trekking, 4WD tours, winery tours and mountain-bike adventures.

Accommodation

The recent boom in tourism has brought a range of budget accommodation options. All are within walking distance of the plaza, and can advise on winery visits.

Hostel Ruta 40 Güermes Sur 178 ⓣ03868/421689, ⓦwww.hostel-ruta40.com. The newest and most lively hostel in town, with clean dorms (AR$30), and small doubles. HI discount. ❸

WINERY VISITS

There are some world-class wineries around Cafayate and most offer **tours** in English and Spanish with a tasting afterwards. Taking a tour is a great way to see which wines you prefer, and to appreciate the whole process. Two of the most popular are Bodega Etchart on RN40 (ⓣ03868/421529, daily 9am–5pm) and Bodega La Rosa on RN68 (ⓣ03868/421201, Mon–Fri 8am–12.30pm & 1.30–7pm). Both are within walking or cycling distance, and offer free tours. Ask at the information centre on the small plaza in Cafayate for a winery map of the area.

Rusty K Hostal Rivadavia 281 ⓣ03868/422031, ⓔrustyhostal@gmail.com. Central, friendly hostel with a pleasant garden to relax in. Dorm AR$30. ❸

Hostal de Valle San Martín 243 ⓣ03868/421039, ⓦwww.nortevirtual.com. Large, light spacious rooms, set around a luscious patio. Ask for a room upstairs. ❺

Eating and drinking

Restaurants and cafes surround the main plaza, where in summer you can join crowds of locals strolling through the city at dusk with an ice cream.

Baco Güemes Norte and Rivadavia. Simple decor and friendly staff make this corner restaurant popular, as do its pizzas (AR$24), trout (AR$30) and local wines.

Carreta de Don Olegario Güemes Sur 20 and Quintana de Niño on the east side of the plaza. popular for its well-priced set menus. Mains AR$18–28.

Heladería Miranda Av Güemes, half a block north of the plaza. Gourmet ice creams in exotic flavours; try the wine sorbets.

El Rincón del Amigo San Martín 25. Set on the plaza, this basic restaurant has cheap lunch specials (AR$15).

Moving on

Bus To Salta (3–4 daily; 5hr); Tucumán (3 daily; 6–8hr.

SAN SALVADOR DE JUJUY

Generally playing second fiddle to its prettier cousin Salta, **SAN SALVADOR DE JUJUY** (known as Jujuy) lies ninety kilometres to the north in the province of Jujuy. Although it is the highest provincial capital in the country, at 1260m above sea level, Jujuy is set in a lush pocket of humidity and greenery. It's a busy place, with a frantic, market feel, where crumbling colonial buildings are juxtaposed with neon signs. Most travellers pass through for just one night on their way to the surrounding attractions, and they're probably right – there are some great restaurants here, but only a few sights. The real lure is out of town, above all to the north in the spectacular colours of the **Quebrada de Humahuaca** and the small towns of **Tilcara** and **Humahuaca**.

TREAT YOURSELF

Termas de Reyes
Just 19km west of Jujuy are the thermal hot springs of the **Termas de Reyes** and the **Hotel Termas de Reyes** (ⓣ0388/392-2522, ⓦwww.termasdereyes.com; ❽). Sinking into a hot mineral spa bath, or relaxing with a mineral mud mask, is just the way to shake off a long bus ride. There are fourteen private thermal baths for three people, with stunning panoramic views, as well as two saunas. Try the 30-minute deep-tissue massage (AR$60), or a revitalizing facial (AR$45). The #14 public bus runs to Termas four times a day from the main bus terminal and takes just under 20 minutes.

What to see and do

If you have time to kill in Jujuy, head to the lively **Plaza General Belgrano**, east of the city centre. This large, green open space is generally crowded with young locals, checking out the craftsmen and market sellers who set up stalls here. Across town the late eighteenth-century **Catedral** (Mon–Fri 7.30am–1pm & 5–9pm, Sat & Sun 8am–noon & 5–9pm) makes up for a plain façade by having a wonderfully decorative interior, above all a spectacular pulpit decorated by local artists over two hundred years ago. This has a rival in the intricate pulpit of the nearby **Iglesia San Francisco**, whose tiny human figures, columns and scenes are thought to have been carved in Bolivia.

Arrival and information

Air Jujuy's airport (ⓣ0388/491-1102), 30km southeast of the city, is serviced by TEA Turismo who run a shuttle service to and from the city centre (AR$8; ⓣ0388/423-6270). Taxi fare is around AR$30.

Bus The ugly bus terminal (Ⓣ0388/422-6299), at Iguazú and Av Dorrego, just south of the centre across the Río Chico, serves all local, regional and national destinations, and also offers services to Chile and Bolivia.
Tourist Information Dirección Provincial de Turismo, Belgrano and Gorriti (Mon–Fri 7am–9pm, Sat & Sun 8am–9pm; Ⓣ0388/422-1325, Ⓦwww.jujuy.gov.ar/turismo).

Accommodation

Club Hostel San Martín 155 Ⓣ0388/423-7565, Ⓦwww.hihostels.com. Busy, lively hostel with a small pool, within walking distance of the bus terminal and the centre. Dorm AR$21.
Hostal Casa de Barro Otero 294 Ⓣ0388/422-9578, Ⓦwww.casadebarro.com.ar. Wonderful and welcoming, with clean spacious bedrooms, and a pleasant common area. ❹
Hostal Los Colorados Lavalle 46 Ⓣ0388/424-3382, Ⓦwww.loscoloradosshjujuy.com.ar. New and slightly clinical, this hostel is in the commercial centre of the city. Basic bathrooms. Dorm AR$22.
Munay Tierra de Colores Alvear 1230 Ⓣ0388/422-8435, Ⓦwww.munayhotel.com.ar. Just north of the centre, this friendly small hotel has clean, rather dark rooms with private bathrooms. ❺
Yok Wahi La Madrid 168 Ⓣ0388/422-9608, Ⓦwww.yokwahi.com. Friendly, central and basic with comfortable dorms (AR$30) and one double (❹). Great breakfast.

Eating and drinking

La Candelaria Alvear 1346. West of the city, this *Parrilla* is a local institution, and a must for any meat-lover. Large steak AR$28.
Madre Tierra Belgrano 619. Fresh salads (AR$12), juices and vegetarian fare. Closed Sun.
Zorba Belgrano 802. Large, two-storey restaurant serving Greek food, as well as local favourites. Mains AR$22.

Directory

Airlines Aerolíneas Argentinas, Belgrano 1053 Ⓣ0388/422-7198. Andes Airlines, España 478 Ⓣ0387/437-3514.
Car rental Sudamerics, Belgrano 601 Ⓣ0388/422-9034, Ⓦwww.sudamerics.com.
Post office La Madrid and Independencia.
Travel agents Noroeste, San Martín 155 Ⓣ0388/423-7565, Ⓦwww.noroestevirtual.com.ar. A budget, youth travel agency attached to *Club Hostel*. Tour Andino, S Perez 355 Ⓣ0388/424-2303, Ⓦwww.tourandino.com.ar. Adventure breaks including sand boarding, parasailing and trekking among others.

Moving on

Air Flights from Salta 2–3 times daily to Buenos Aires (2hr 30min), Tucumán (40min) and Cordoba (1hr 30min).
Bus to: Buenos Aires (3 daily; 20hr); Cordoba (3 daily; 12–13hr); Tucumán (6 daily; 5hr); Jujuy (hourly; 2hr); Cafayate (4 daily, 4hr).

QUEBRADA DE HUMAHUACA

The scintillating, multi-coloured **QUEBRADA DE HUMAHUACA** gorge stretches 125km north of Jujuy, past the exclusive resort of **Purmamarca** and up through the towns of **Maimará** and **Tilcara**, with its pre-Columbian archeological site, all the way to the busy village of **Humahuaca**. From there you can carry on to reach the border crossing with Bolivia at **La Quaica**, nearly 2000m higher and 150km further on. The region is popular with Argentine holidaymakers, who come to stay in the many swish spas and resorts, to hike and take in the extraordinary mountain scenery.

Maimará and Purmamarca

Heading north, the first substantial settlement you reach along RN9 is the dusty but popular **PURMAMARCA** at km61. Something of a resort town, due the number of luxury hotels which have sprung up in recent years, Purmamarca has a fantastic seventeenth-century church, the **Iglesia Santa Rosa de Lima**, at its heart. It is faithfully maintained and is still in use today. The views of the **Cerro de los Siete Colores** (the Hill of Seven Colours) from here are breathtaking. Known for its extraordinary cemetery, **MAIMARÁ,** 75km from Jujuy, is a small hamlet surrounded by fabulously coloured hills. The cemetery is an eclectic mixture of tombs in all shapes and sizes, statues, flowers and a jumble of walls. It is an interesting photo stop.

Tilcara

The busy tourist town of **TILCARA** is a favourite with Argentine holidaymakers for its fantastic restaurants, affordable hotels and above all the pre-Incan **pukará** or fortress (daily 9am–6pm; AR$5, free Tues). Discovered in 1903 and heavily reconstructed in the 1950s, the site enjoys a wonderful, commanding location, covered in giant cacti. To get here, follow the signposted trail from the centre of town over the bridge across the Río Huasamayo. Keep your entrance ticket for admission to the **Museo Arqueológico** (daily 9am–7pm; AR$2, free Tues), on the south side of the square in a beautiful colonial house. The well-presented collection includes a mummy from San Pedro de Atacama.

Humahuaca

Humahuaca is the main tourist town in the Quebrada, a small, attractive place, originally founded in 1591. A myriad of shops, restaurants and craft stalls stand all around the leafy plaza. On the east side, the tiny **Iglesia de la Candelaria**, constructed in 1631 and rebuilt in the nineteenth century, has some interesting artworks. The cool, high-ceilinged interior offers a refreshing change from the dry heat outside. Beside the church, steps lead up to the base of the **Monumento a la Independencia**, a masculine and dramatic sculpture. There are awesome views from here, pocked by amazing human-size cacti.

Arrival and information

Bus Buses leave every hour from Jujuy and run up the Quebrada to Purmamarca (1hr), Tilcara (1hr 30min–2hr) and Humahuaca (3hr), dropping off locals at farms and houses along the way. Only certain companies go all the way to La Quiaca – look for El Quiaqueño, Panamericano and Balut. Both Tilcara and Humahuaca have a central bus terminal that offers luggage storage, at other towns you will be dropped of at the main plaza.

Tourist Offices The region's best tourist office is in Ticara, at Belgrano 590 (☎0388/495-5720, daily 8am–noon and 1–9pm). It has lists of accommodation throughout the region, and free maps. Otherwise there is a small tourist office in Humahuaca (Mon–Fri 9–6pm), in the white colonial *cabildo* building on the plaza. A small donation is required for maps.

Tour Operators Tilcara Tours, Bustamente 159 in Jujuy (☎0388/422-6113), organise good guided tours into the Quebrada de Humahuaca.

Accommodation

The best budget accommodation is found in Tilcara and Humahuaca, although campgrounds can be found in nearly every town in the valley.

Tilcara

Malka San Martín (at the top of the hill) ☎0388/495-5197, Ⓦwww.malkahostel.com.ar. A strenuous uphill walk, this hostel has comfortable cabañas for up to six people, great value if travelling in a group, as well as dorms. HI discounts. Dorm AR$40. *Cabaña* 9

Tilcara Hostel Bolívar 166 ☎0388/495-5105, Ⓦwww.tilcarahostel.com. A 10min walk from the bus station, this new hostel has clean dorms (AR$33) and a few doubles. 5

Humahuaca

Hostal Humahuaca Buenos Aires 447 ☎03887/421064 Ⓦwww.humahuacahostal.com.ar. Located just off the main plaza, this small hostel has slightly dark but cool dorm rooms set around a bright patio. Dorm AR$35. 5

Posada el Sol Barrio Medalla Milagrosa (across the river) ☎0388/421-1466, Ⓦwww.posadaelsol.com.ar. Follow the signs from the bus station to this small rustic house on the outskirts of town. Small, comfortable dorms (AR$36) and doubles in peaceful surroundings. HI discounts. 5

Eating and drinking

Tilcara

Pucará Padilla (at the top of the hill). This restaurant on the way to the ruins offers new ways of preparing traditional food. Desserts are particularly good. Mains AR$18–24.

Humahuaca

El Portillo Tucumán 69. Serves traditional food including llama meat, quinoa and Andean potatoes in a rustic environment. Mains AR$12.

Mendoza and San Juan

The vast midwestern provinces of **Mendoza** and **San Juan** are sparsely-populated, sun-fried playgrounds for lovers of mountains and vineyards. The highest peaks outside the Himalayas rise to the west, capped by the formidable **Cerro Aconcagua**, whose icy volcanic summit punctures the sky at nearly 7000 metres, an irresistible magnet for experienced climbers.

Further south down the Andean cordillera is the see-and-be-seen resort of **Las Leñas**, whose powdery slopes deliver some of the best skiing in South America.

Come summer, snowmelt rushes down the mountains, swelling rivers and creating ideal **whitewater rafting** conditions, especially along the Cañon de Atuel near the small city of **San Rafael**. At the foothills of the mountains, the same sunshine that pummels the region's inhospitable, parched desertscapes also feeds its celebrated grapevines. Wine buffs will feel right at home in the eminently liveable city of **Mendoza**, the region's urban hub, which offers easy access to Argentina's best *bodegas*.

North of here, the provincial capital of **San Juan** and the village of **Valle Fértil** act as good bases for two of the country's most striking UNESCO World Heritage-listed parks: the bizarrely-shaped rock formations of **Ischigualasto** (also known as Valle de la Luna), and just over the border in the province of La Rioja, the wide-bottomed canyon, pre-Columbian petroglyphs and rich wildlife of **Talampaya.**

For more arresting scenery, the tumbleweed town of **Malargüe** is within easy reach of the cave network of **Caverna de las Brujas** and **La Payunia**, where guanacos roam across lava-strewn pampas.

MENDOZA

The sophisticated metropolis of **MENDOZA**, with a population of around a million, has the country's best wineries on its doorstep. Set in a valley less than 100km east of the Andes' loftiest snow-covered mountains, Mendoza's spread-out downtown area is characterized by elegant, fountain-filled plazas and wide avenues shaded by giant sycamore trees. Irrigation channels run along the city's gutters, delivering snowmelt from the Andes and giving life to the city's abundant green spaces. An earthquake in 1861 laid waste to Mendoza's former colonial glories, but the modern, low-rise city that rose in its wake – awash in petroleum and bodega money –is certainly no eyesore. *Mendocinos* know how to enjoy the good life, and along with taking their siestas seriously (many businesses close between 1pm and 4pm), they enjoy wining and dining at the city's exemplary restaurants or partaking in alfresco drinking along the spacious sidewalks.

Mendoza makes an ideal base for exploring some of Argentina's undisputed highlights. Hundreds of *bodegas*, offering wine-tasting tours, lie within easy reach of downtown, while **tour operators** run a range of whitewater rafting, horseback-riding, paragliding and skydiving excursions, and those peaks looming on the horizon offer skiing in winter and world-class mountain climbing in summer.

What to see and do

At the junction of the city's two principal thoroughfares – Avenida Sarmiento and Avenida Mitre – the spacious **Plaza Independencia** is the physical and cultural heart of Mendoza. Fountains and sycamore trees create an ideal space for chilling out or, over summer, taking in one of the regular outdoor concerts. One block east and south of here, **Plaza**

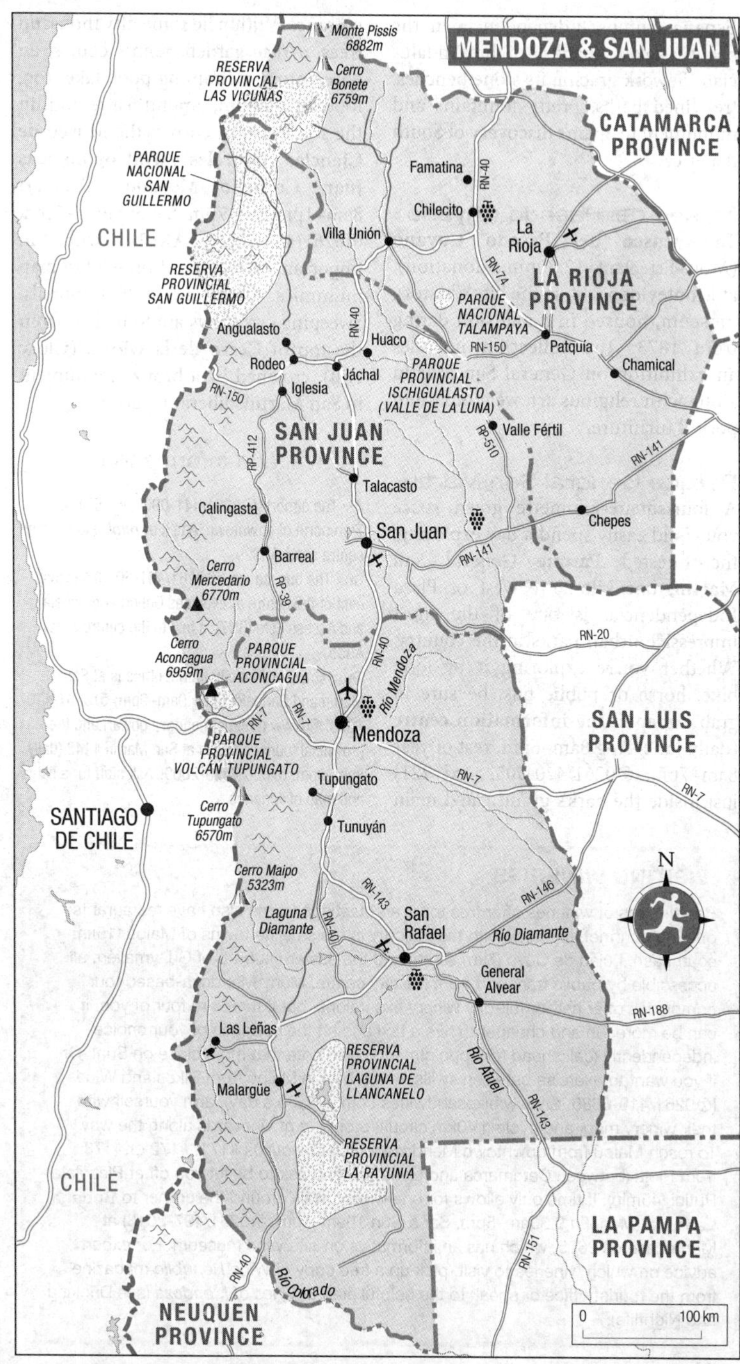
MENDOZA & SAN JUAN
Monte Pissis 6882m
Cerro Bonete 6759m
RESERVA PROVINCIAL LAS VICUÑAS
CATAMARCA PROVINCE
PARQUE NACIONAL SAN GUILLERMO
Famatina
RN-40
Chilecito
CHILE
Villa Unión
La Rioja
RESERVA PROVINCIAL SAN GUILLERMO
RN-74
LA RIOJA PROVINCE
PARQUE NACIONAL TALAMPAYA
Angualasto
Huaco
Patquía
RN-150
Rodeo
Jáchal
PARQUE PROVINCIAL ISCHIGUALASTO (VALLE DE LA LUNA)
Chamical
Iglesia
RN-150
Valle Fértil
RP-510
SAN JUAN PROVINCE
RP-412
RN-141
Talacasto
Calingasta
Chepes
San Juan
Barreal
RN-141
Cerro Mercedario 6770m
RP-39
Cerro Aconcagua 6959m
PARQUE PROVINCIAL ACONCAGUA
RN-40
Río Mendoza
RN-20
RN-7
Mendoza
SAN LUIS PROVINCE
PARQUE PROVINCIAL VOLCÁN TUPUNGATO
Tupungato
RN-7
SANTIAGO DE CHILE
Cerro Tupungato 6570m
Tunuyán
Cerro Maipo 5323m
RN-143
RN-146
Laguna Diamante
San Rafael
Río Diamante
RN-40
General Alvear
RN-188
Las Leñas
RESERVA PROVINCIAL LAGUNA DE LLANCANELO
Río Atuel
Malargüe
RN-143
RESERVA PROVINCIAL LA PAYUNIA
CHILE
LA PAMPA PROVINCE
RN-151
RN-40
Río Colorado
NEUQUEN PROVINCE
0
100 km
N

España trumps Independencia in the beauty stakes, thanks to the Andalucian tilework gracing its stone benches, tree-lined paths, pretty fountains and monument to Spain's discovery of South America.

Museo del Pasado Cuyano

The **Museo del Pasado Cuyano** (Mon–Fri 9am–12.30pm; donation), at Montevideo 544, is the city's history museum, housed in a mansion dating from 1873. The collection includes an exhibition on General San Martín along with religious art, weaponry and period furniture.

Parque General San Martín

A four-square-kilometre green space you could easily spend a day exploring, the forested **Parque General San Martín**, one kilometre west of Plaza Independencia, is one of the most impressive urban parks in the country. Whether you're exploring it by foot, bike, horse or public bus, be sure to grab a map at the **information centre** (daily June–Aug 8am–6pm, rest of year 8am–7pm; ⓣ0261/420-5052, ext 221) just inside the park's grand gated main entrance. Within lie some fifty thousand trees, a rose garden, tennis courts, an observatory, swimming pool, lake, zoo, football stadium, amphitheatre and, in the southeastern corner, the **Museo de Ciencias Naturales y Antropológicas Juan Cornelio Moyano** (Tues–Fri 8am–1pm & 2–7pm, Sat & Sun 3–7pm; ⓣ0261/428-7666, AR$2), with an important collection of pre-Columbian mummies, fossils and stuffed animals. Sweeping city views are to be had from the top of **Cerro de la Gloria** (Glory Hill), crowned by a bronze monument to San Martín's liberating army.

Arrival and information

Air The airport (ⓣ0261/441-0900, ext 521) is 7km north of downtown. A taxi or *remise* to the city centre costs AR$20.

Bus The bus station (ⓣ0261/431-5000) lies just east of the centre at avenidas Gobernador Videla and Acceso Este (RN7); a taxi to the centre costs AR$5.

Tourist office The city tourist office is at San Martín and Garibaldi (daily 9am–9pm; ⓣ0261/420-1333, ⓦwww.turismo.mendoza.gov.ar) and the provincial tourist office is at San Martín 1143 (daily 8am–9pm; ⓣ0261/420-2800). Ask staff for a list and map of wineries.

VISITING WINERIES

Barrel-loads of wineries offer free tours and tastings (some also have restaurants offering gourmet lunches), with the majority in the satellite towns of Maipú (15km southeast), Luján de Cuyo (7km south) and the eastern suburb of Guaymallén, all accessible by public transport from the city centre. Many Mendoza-based tour companies offer half-or full-day winery excursions, but if there are four of you, it can be more fun and cheaper to hire a taxi and hit the bodegas of your choice independently (call ahead for appointments; also note that most close on Sun). Or if you want to exercise between swills, rent a bike in Maipú from Bikes and Wines (ⓣ0261/410-6686, ⓦwww.bikesandwines.com, AR$35 a day), arm yourself with their winery map, and cycle a 40km circuit, stopping at vineyards along the way. To reach Maipú from downtown Mendoza, catch *colectivos* #171, #172 or #173 from Rioja (between Catamarca and Garibaldi) and ask to be let you off at Plazoleta Rutini (45min). If time only allows for one winery, walk around the corner to **Bodega La Rural** (Mon–Fri 9.30am–5pm, Sat & Sun 10am–1pm, ⓣ0261/497-2013) at Montecaseros 2625, which has an informative on-site wine museum. For expert advice on which wineries to visit, pick up a free copy of *Wine Republic* magazine from the tourist office or speak to the helpful staff at *Vines of Mendoza* (see Drinking and Nightlife).

Accommodation

Mendoza has a wide range of accommodation within walking distance of the microcentre. Book well in advance if travelling in early March as the city packs out for the *Fiesta de la Vendimia* wine festival. Mendoza also has dozens of outstanding **backpacker hostels**, the best of which have gardens and swimming pools and fill up fast; all listed here include breakfast, kitchen, internet and tour-booking services. **Campers** will find a shady spot to pitch their tents at *El Suizo* on Av Champagnat in El Challao, 6km northwest (ⓣ0261/444-1991, ⓦwww.campingsuizo.com.ar; AR$15 per person), with a swimming pool, restaurant and outdoor cinema. Bus #115 runs there from the corner of Av Alem and San Martín.

Hostels

Hostel Alamo Necochea 740 ⓣ0261/429-5565, ⓦwww.hostelalamo.com.ar. On a quiet residential street, this yellow mansion is a real score for those looking for a sociable but respectful backpackers. The massive supermarket opposite will delight self-caterers, as will the hostel's glassed-in dining area with a Zen-like garden outlook. Dorm AR$40. ❺

Hostel Campo Base Mitre 946 ⓣ0261/429-0707, ⓦwww.campobase.com.ar. Although the dorms (AR$33 or AR$28 with HI card) are a bit cramped, this well-located hostel is a hit with party people and Aconcagua climbers (treks are organized through the affiliated tour company). ❹–❺

Hostel Independencia Mitre 1237 ⓣ0261/423-1806, ⓦwww.hostelindependencia.com.ar. Boisterous party hostel in a gorgeous mansion. The location and common areas are among the best in the city; the bathrooms, sadly, are not. If you're sensitive to noise, alcohol or fun, take your business elsewhere. Dorm AR$34. ❹

Hostel Lao Rioja 771 ⓣ0261/438-0454, ⓦwww.laohostel.com. The most inviting of the city's hostels, this English-run backpackers is often full. Chilled-out but buzzing, it has plenty of common space, travel photography gracing its walls, a large garden with a pool and hammocks, a roof terrace, wi-fi and very clean dorm rooms (AR$42). Wine flows on the house when the owner is feeling generous. ❺

Winca's Hostel Sarmiento 717 ⓣ0261/425-3804, ⓦwww.wincashostel.com.ar. This well-appointed hostel set in a large peach-coloured house has a chef's-quality kitchen and big backyard with swimming pool. The dorms (AR$35) however, are small and dark. The owners have another hostel at San Lorenzo 19 and fully-furnished apartments for rent – a good option for couples or long-term stayers. ❺

Hotels

Confluencia Hostal Av España 1512 ⓣ0261/429-0430, ⓦwww.hostalconfluencia.com.ar. Perfect for couples who want more privacy and sophistication than a hostel, this modern boutique hotel offers spacious doubles (and quadruples) with wooden floorboards and private bathrooms. There's a TV lounge and large roof terrace with mountain views. Breakfast included. ❺

Quinta Rufino Rufino Ortega 142 ⓣ0261/420-4696 ⓦwww.quintarufino.com.ar. A bed and breakfast offering large, classy rooms in a converted villa. It's a short stroll to the city's bar strip. Breakfast included. ❺

Eating

Mendoza has some exceptional restaurants, many specializing in local produce, Pacific seafood and regional wine.

Anna Bistro Juan B Justo 161 ⓣ0261/425-1818. Cocktail-sucking diners lounge outside on white leather couches amid fragrant foliage and romantic lighting at this top-notch French-run restaurant. The eclectic menu features standouts like seafood pasta (AR$24). Set lunches are good value. Closed Mon.

Azafrán Sarmiento 765 ⓣ0261/429-4200. From venison ravioli to Patagonian deer, the dining experience at this lauded restaurant is pure gourmet. A rummage in the wine cellar will pull up 450 vintages from 80 different vineyards. Mains around AR$35. Closed Sun

Govinda's San Martín 453, bus ride or AR$7 taxi from centre ⓣ0261/424-3799. Simply the best vegetarian restaurant in the city; load up your plate with lovingly-prepared dishes from the gigantic buffet (AR$18 per kilo). Closed Sun dinner.

La Marchigiana Patricias Mendocinas 1550 ⓣ0261/423-0751. This airy, family affair is the city's best Italian restaurant. Start with a mixed salad, move on to the cannelloni (AR$18) and top it off with to-die-for tiramisu (AR$9).

Mercado Central Las Heras between España & Patricias Mendocinas. Stock up on fresh fruit, veggies and meat at this indoor market; fast-food restaurants also do the likes of fish and chips for around AR$10.

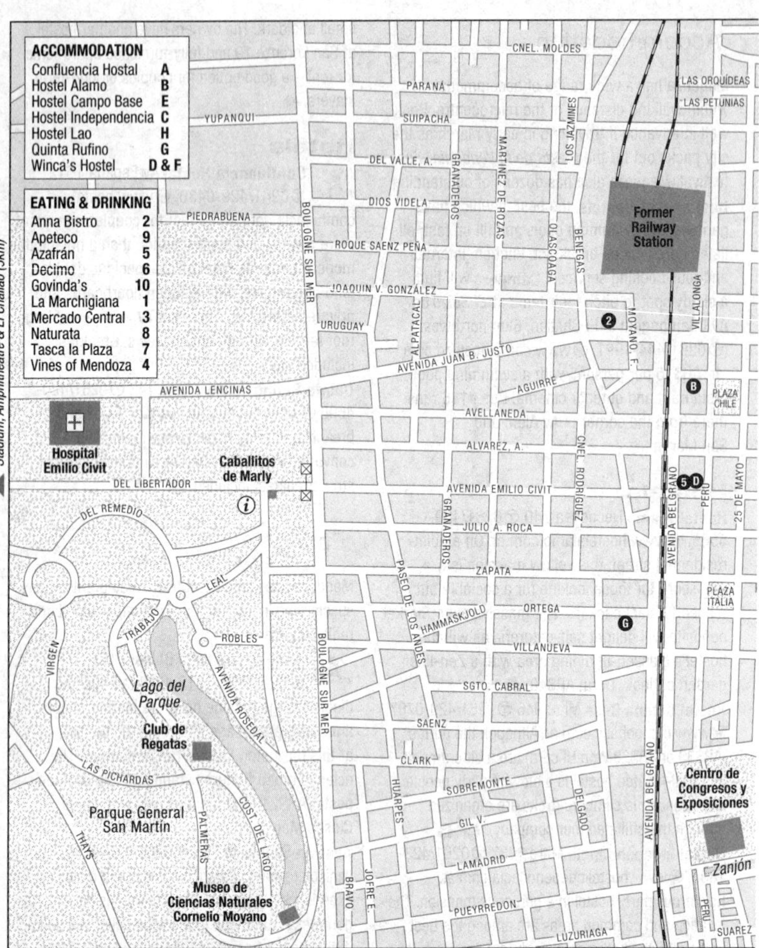

Naturata Don Bosco 73 ☎0261/420-3087. Wholesome vegetarian buffet in light and airy surrounds on a leafy residential street (AR$18 all-you-can-eat or AR$20 per kilo). Closed Sun.

Tasca la Plaza Montevideo 117 ☎0261/420-0603. Flickering candles set off the wooden floorboards, bright red walls and funky Mendocino art at the city's coolest tapas bar and restaurant where you can swill a *mojito* (AR$9) with your grilled king prawns (AR$18).

Drinking and nightlife

Mendoza's bar scene is concentrated along trendy **Aristides Villanueva** where on summer evenings, sidewalk tables fill with drinkers. The best **nightclubs** are in outlying neighbourhoods like El Challao to the northwest, Las Heras to the north, and Chacras de Coria to the south. Women generally get in free, and while *Mendocinos* like to party late, keep in mind a city law stipulates that last entry is at 2.30am.

Apeteco San Juan and Barraquero, Free entry until 11pm, then AR$20 for men. A sophisticated crowd packs into this sleek, cavernous club on weekends. Following the midnight live music set, punters lose their cool on the dancefloor to a mixed soundtrack of electronica, rock, reggaeton and salsa. Open Wed–Sat.

Decimo Garibaldi 7, 10th floor of Edificio Gómez ⓣ0261/434-0135. Yuppie wine bar and restaurant par excellence. Set on the top floor of a downtown apartment block, it offers a winning combination of city and mountain views along with a hundred Argentinian wines to wrap your palate around (small bottles from AR$15). Put on your gladrags and live the high life.

Vines of Mendoza Espejo 567 ⓣ0261/438-1031, ⓦwww.vinesofmendoza.com. A swanky wine-tasting room with more than sixty wines from regional boutique *bodegas*. Let the English-speaking staff talk you through a tasting session (from AR$45) or nurse a glass of *vino tinto* in the wisteria-shaded courtyard. Daily 3–10pm.

Directory

Car rental Alamo Nacional Rent, Pvo de la Reta 928 ⓣ0261/429-3111; Avis, Pvo de la Reta 914 ⓣ0261/429-6403; Hertz, Espejo 415 ⓣ0261/423-0225; Via Rent a Car, San Juan 931 ⓣ0261/429-0876.

Laundry Lavandería Necochea, 25 de Mayo 1357.

Post office San Martín and Colón.

Shopping There is a **handicraft market** on Plaza Independencia every weekend. The upscale Mendoza Plaza **shopping mall** (ⓦwww.mendozaplazashopping.com), at Av Acceso Este 3280 in Guaymallén, to the east of the city centre, has around 200 shops and restaurants and a cinema.

TREAT YOURSELF

Winery lunches

Try to make time (and room in the budget) for a trip out of town for a gourmet lunch among the vineyards at a nearby **bodega**: ask at the tourist office or pick up the *Vines of Mendoza* magazine for further listings). The restaurant at *Ruca Malen* (Ruta Nacional 7km 1059, Luján de Cuyo; take a bus to Luján and then a taxi ($A20); ⓣ0261/410-6214, ⓦwww.bodegarucamalen.com; lunch daily) looks out on to vineyards and mountains, and lunch is a belly-busting five-course degustation (AR$110), with each delectable plate – from roasted eggplant in plum sauce to *dulce de leche* mousse – perfectly paired with *bodega* wine. *La Bourgogne* (Roque Sáenz Peña 3531, Vistalba, Luján de Cuyo, taxi from Luján AR$15; ⓣ0261/498-9400, ⓦwww.carlospulentawines.com; closed Sun & Mon) is attached to the Vistalba winery (producing since 2002) and prepares French cuisine using regional and seasonal produce. Dishes like veal in mushroom sauce (AR$66) and quince tart with lavender ice cream ($25) go down a treat with a bottle of vino (AR$50–AR$650). Reserve in advance and ask for a table by the window with cordillera and vineyard views.

Spanish school Intercultural, Rep de Siria 241 (ⓣ0261/429-0269, ⓦwww.spanishcourses.com.ar), offers one-week group crash courses.

Tour operators Argentina Rafting, Potrerillos ⓣ02624/482037, ⓦwww.argentinarafting.com, run **whitewater rafting** trips down the class III-IV rapids of the Mendoza River; Aymara, 9 de Julio 1023 ⓣ0261/420-2064, ⓦwww.aymara.com.ar, specialize in guided **Aconcagua treks**; Bikes and Wines, Urquiza 1601, Maipu ⓣ0261/410-6686, ⓦwww.bikesandwines.com, organize **bicycle tours** to wineries. Campo Base, Peatonal Sarmiento 229 ⓣ0261/425-5511, ⓦwww.campobase.com.ar, offer **adventure excursions** that combine trekking, mountain-biking and rappelling in one action-packed day; El Rincón de los Oscuros, Av Los Cóndores, Potrerillos ⓣ02624/48-3030, ⓦwww.elrincondelososcuros.com, are **horseriding** specialists; Fly Excursions, ⓣ0261/426-2115, ⓦwww.i-mendoza.com.ar, run tandem **paragliding** flights off 1700m-high Cerro Arco.

Moving on

Air to: Buenos Aires (4 daily; 1hr 50min); Córdoba (2 daily; 1hr 20min); Santiago de Chile (2 daily; 40min). Airlines with offices in town include Aerolíneas Argentinas, Paseo Sarmiento 82 ⓣ0261/420-4101; Air New Zealand, Espejo 183 ⓣ0261/423-4683; American Airlines, Av España 943 ⓣ0261/425-9078; Avianca, Espejo 183 ⓣ0261/438-1643; Iberia, Rivadavia 180 ⓣ0261/429-5608; LanChile, Rivadavia 138 ⓣ0261/425-7900; Lufthansa, 9 de Julio 928 ⓣ0261/429-6287; Varig, Rivadavia 209 ⓣ0261/429-5898.

Bus to: Bariloche (two daily; 18hr); Buenos Aires (around 40 daily; 17hr); Córdoba (hourly; 10hr); Salta (9 daily; 19hr); San Juan (hourly; 2hr 30min); San Rafael (hourly; 3hr 15min); Santiago de Chile (12 daily, 7hr).

ALTA MONTAÑA

The cathedral-like peaks of the Parque Provincial Aconcagua lie just three hours west of Mendoza, easily visited on a popular one-day-trip dubbed the **ALTA MONTAÑA ROUTE**. Leaving behind verdant vineyards and climbing into barren hills, this scenic excursion takes the RN7 (the highway to Santiago de Chile), following the former Trans-Andean railway and the Río Mendoza into the spectacular Uspallata valley where Brad Pitt filmed *Seven Years in Tibet*. From the crossroads village of Uspallata (105km west of Mendoza), it's a further 65km to **LOS PENITENTES**, a winter ski resort with 28 pistes (ⓣ0261/428-3601, ⓦwww.penitentes.com), and in summer, a base for Aconcagua climbers (see opposite). Some 6km west of Los Penitentes lies one of the area's most photographed landmarks, the **PUENTE DEL INCA**, a natural stone bridge traversing the Río de las Cuevas at 2700m. Beneath it, thermal waters seep among the ruins of an abandoned 1940s spa resort. The route passes Parque Provincial Aconcagua and ends at the Chilean border where a statue of **Cristo Redentor** (Christ the Redeemer) commemorates the 1902 peace pact between historic enemies.

Parque Provincial Aconcagua

At 6959m, **CERRO ACONCAGUA** – "the roof of the Americas" – lords it over the 710-square-kilometre Parque Provincial Aconcagua. The highest mountain in both the western and the southern hemispheres, Aconcagua's faces are ringed by five glistening glaciers. In 1985, the discovery of an Inca **mummy** at 5300m on Aconcagua's southwest face lent further weight to the theory that the Incas worshipped the mountain and offered it human sacrifices.

Nowadays, Inca worshippers have been replaced by ardent mountain climbers, who ascend in droves throughout summer. Only the most experienced attempt the **climb** without a professional guide. Taking into account acclimatization time, it should take at least thirteen days to reach the summit. There are three possible routes – south, west or east – with the least difficult being the western route leaving from the Plaza de Mulas (4230m). For **route details** and advice on what to take, see ⓦwww.aconcagua.mendoza.gov.ar. Easier **day hikes** are also possible in the park as well as multi-day treks to base camps and mountain *refugios*.

ARGENTINE WINE

Argentina is the world's fifth-largest producer of wine, and more than three-quarters of the stuff flows out of **Mendoza**. Enjoying around three hundred days of sunshine a year and a prime position at the foothills of the Andes, Mendoza's high-altitude vineyards are now producing premium vintages on a par with Chile's. The idyllic desert climate (cool nights, little rain and low humidity) works especially well for reds: **Malbec** – brought over from Bordeaux – is Argentina's star grape, producing rich fruity flavours that go down superbly well with the ubiquitous steak.

Arrival and information

Bus Expresso Uspallata operates four buses daily from Mendoza to the base camps at Los Horcones and Punta de Vacas.

Tourist office and permits To trek or climb in the Parque Provincial Aconcagua between mid-Nov and mid-March, you need to obtain a permit (bring your passport) from the **Dirección de Recursos Naturales Renovables** (Mon–Fri 8am–6pm, Sun & Sun 9am–1pm; ⓣ0261/425-8751), at San Martín 1143, 2nd floor, in Mendoza. Foreign trekkers pay AR$150–330 to hike in the park (price depends on number of days in park and time of year). From Feb 21–March 15 & Nov 15–Nov 30 the fee to climb the mountain is AR$500; this rises to AR$1000 Dec 1–Dec 14 & Feb 1–Feb 20; and AR$1500 Dec 15–Jan 31. The rest of the year snow cover makes the climb extremely dangerous, the fee is AR$1500–2000 and climbers must apply for a special permit.

Accommodation

For accommodation at or near the base camps, there are options at Puente del Inca (where many people spend a couple of days acclimatizing), Las Cuevas and Los Penitentes. On the mountain trail, it is possible to overnight on day two at the *Refugio Plaza de Mulas* (ⓣ0261/421-4330, ⓦwww.refugioplazademulas.com.ar; dorm bed from AR$75, private room ❼) where there are hot showers and cooked meals.

Hostel Campo Base Penitentes Los Penitentes ⓣ0261/425-5511, ⓦwww.penitentes.com.ar. This lively, 28-bed hostel, with well-equipped kitchen, is a jumping-off point for organized ski trips in the winter and Aconcagua climbs in the summer. Prices halve Oct–May. Dorm AR$60 including breakfast and dinner (June–Sept only); prices halve off season.

La Vieja Estación Puente del Inca ⊕0261/452-1103. A hostel with large dorm rooms and communal bathrooms offering a variety of adventure excursions. The restaurant and bar will warm the cockles. Dorm AR$25.

Directory

Mule hire Mules can carry around 60kg, but demand is high and prices around US$150 for the first mule from Puente del Inca to Plaza de Mulas. If you're in a group, prices drop if you hire several mules. Fernando Grajales Expeditions and Aconcagua Trek (below) can make the arrangements.

Tours Due to the mountain's unpredictable weather (storms claim lives every year), climbers are advised to go on organized trips with experienced local guides. Mendoza-based operators that specialize in Aconcagua trips include Aconcagua Trek at Barcala 484 (⊕0261/429-5007, ⓦwww.aconcaguatrek.com); Aymara at 9 de Julio 1023 (⊕0261/420-2064, ⓦwww.aymara.com.ar); Campo Base at Peatonal Sarmiento 229 (⊕0261/425-5511, ⓦwww.campobase.com.ar); Fernando Grajales Expeditions (⊕0261/428-3157, ⓦwww.grajales.net); and Inka Expediciones at Juan B Justo 242 (⊕0261/425-0871, ⓦwww.aconcagua.org.ar).

SAN RAFAEL AND AROUND

In the heart of wine country, the laid-back city of **SAN RAFAEL,** 230km south of the provincial capital, likes to think of itself as a smaller, friendlier version of Mendoza. Home to just over one hudred thousand people, San Rafael's wide, flat streets are filled with cyclists and its leafy plazas are squeaky clean. The city itself offers few distractions, and boredom will probably set in once you've become acquainted with the main square, **Plaza San Martín**, and visited the **Museo de Historia Natural** (daily 8am–1pm & 2.30–7pm; AR$1), on Isla Diamante, 6km south of the centre, where the pre-Columbian displays include ceramics from Ecuador and a mummified child dating from 40 AD.

There are however, worthwhile sights just beyond the city itself in the San Rafael department, including six hundred square kilometres of vineyards and around eighty *bodegas*. Most of the wineries are small, family-run affairs; the tourist office has a list of those open to the public. For **whitewater rafting** enthusiasts, the **Cañon del Atuel**, a short journey to the southwest, is one of the top destinations in the country for riding the rapids. For adventurous and slightly morbid types, San Rafael-based tour operator Risco Viajes (Av Hipólito Yrigoyen 284; ⊕02627/436439, ⓦwww.riscoviajes.com), offers three-day combined **trekking and horse-riding trips** for US$360 to the air crash site on the Argentine-Chilean border where members of a Uruguayan rugby team famously survived subzero Andean conditions by eating snow and their friends' corpses. The harrowing episode was made into the 1993 movie *Alive*.

Arrival and information

Air San Rafael's airport is 5km west of downtown, with daily flights to and from Buenos Aires. There are buses to the centre (AR$1) or a taxi costs around AR$10.

Bus The centrally-located bus terminal is at Coronel Suárez, between calles Almafuerte and Avellaneda. There are connections to Buenos Aires (4 daily; 13hr); Las Leñas (June–Sept 1 daily, Dec–Feb 3 weekly on Tues, Thurs & Sat; 2hr 40min); Malargüe (3 daily; 2hr 30min); Mendoza (hourly 3hr 15min).

Tourist office The friendly tourist office is on the corner of avenidas Hipólito Yrigoyen and Balloffet (daily 8am–9pm; ⊕02627/424217, ⓦwww.sanrafaelturismo.gov.ar).

Accommodation

San Rafael's accommodation options lack the range and quality found in Mendoza. If you're **camping**, make for the shady *Camping El Parador* on Isla Río Diamante, 6km south of downtown (AR$6 per tent).

Hotel Rex Hipólito Yrigoyen 56 ⓣ02627/422177, ⓦwww.rexhotel.com.ar. This bright, modern hotel on the main drag has spotless rooms arranged around a quiet courtyard. Cable TV, breakfast and parking included. ❺

Tierrasoles Hostel Alsina 245 ⓣ02627/433449, ⓦwww.tierrasoles.com.ar. A family-run HI hostel offering modest dorms, a simple breakfast and cheap internet. You have to be a contortionist to use the toilets though. Dorm AR$30. ❹

Trotamundos Hostel Barcala 300 ⓣ02627/432-795, ⓦwww.trotamundoshostel.com.ar. A new, funky hostel with an open-plan kitchen and comfortable dorms (AR$35). ❺

Eating and drinking

San Rafael springs to life post-siesta, when locals pack the restaurants, bars, nightclubs and ice-cream parlours along Hipólito Yrigoyen.

La Fusta Hipólito Yrigoyen 538. The best *parrilla* in the city, where you can tuck into a juicy steak (AR$21) and quaff local wine without breaking the bank.

Jockey Club Belgrano 330 ⓣ02627/487007. Upscale and with an old-worldy feel, this much-loved restaurant does reliable, filling mains. Set lunch AR$33.

Lorenzo Hipólito Irigoyen 1850, Thurs–Sat. The dancefloor at this popular bar is often shaking, thanks to a mixed soundtrack of rock, retro and electronica. On steamy nights, the drinking spills into the garden. Occasional live music.

Tienda del Sol Hipólito Yrigoyen 1663. A hip, modern restaurant with outdoor tables, serving imaginative beef, chicken and fish mains (around AR$25) along with a wide range of regional wines.

LAS LEÑAS

Some 180km southwest of San Rafael and 445km south of Mendoza, the exclusive ski resort of **LAS LEÑAS** is to winter what Uruguay's Punta del Este is to summer – a chic party playground for *porteño* socialites. Between June and September (snow permitting), they flock here on week-long packages. Beyond the pressing of flesh and *après-ski* glamour, Las Leñas' setting is exquisite. The resort, which sits at 2240m, has the dramatic Cerro Las Leñas (4351m) towering over its 29 runs and thirteen lifts. Pistes range in difficulty from nursery slopes to hair-raising black runs, with night-time and cross-country skiing also possible.

In summer, Las Leñas transforms into an outdoor action hub, offering horse-riding, whitewater rafting, trekking, climbing, rappelling, 4WD tours, mountain biking, summer skiing and even high-altitude lake scuba-diving.

Arrival and information

Bus During the ski season there are daily buses from Mendoza (7hr), Malargüe (1hr 30min) and San Rafael (2hr 40min). Regular direct buses also run from Buenos Aires (14hr, book through the central tourist office).

Lift ticket office Mid-June to late Sept 7.30am–5pm; ⓣ02627/471100, ⓦwww.laslenas.com. Daily lift ticket prices range seasonally from AR$99 to $AR152.

Tourist office The resort's office for booking ski packages and accommodation is in Buenos Aires at Bartolomé Mitre 401, 4th floor (Mon–Fri 9am–6pm; ⓣ011/4819-6000, ⓦwww.laslenas.com).

Accommodation

Las Leñas accommodation needs to be booked through the resort's central Buenos Aires office (see above). Low-priced lodging is non-existent. If you are in a group, the most affordable places are the self-catering **apartments** known as "dormy houses": *Laquir*, *Lihuén*, *Milla* and *Payén* cost around AR$500 per night and accommodate up to five people. The closest **hostel** to Las Leñas is *Jose Hostel* (ⓣ02627/1560-0962, ⓔjosehostel@yahoo.com), 18km away in Los Molles. The ski patroller owner runs a tight ship, with two large dorm rooms, a kitchen, wine bar, fireplace, TV lounge, book exchange and wi-fi. Prices are AR$85 per night including transport to and from Las Leñas; AR$51 without the transfer.

Eating and drinking

Innsbruck A log cabin *confitería* in the ski village where you can buy expensive fast food (a steak is AR$35) to enjoy over a beer from a terrace with piste views.

El Refugio In the central Pirámide building. ⓣ02627/471100 ext 1134. Dip into cheese fondue

(AR$80) at this pricey French restaurant. Reservations necessary.

UFO Point The pizzas touching down on plates has earned this restaurant a devoted following, but at around AR$60, it's not cheap. At night, it turns into a club where folks break loose to electronic music.

MALARGÜE

Set at the arid base of the Andes, 186km southwest of San Rafael, **MALARGÜE** is a small, nondescript town that's a jumping-off point for some of Argentina's most remarkable scenery. In winter its *raison d'être* is as an affordable base **for skiing** at the resort of Las Leñas (see p.123), while in summer the surrounding landscape offers ample opportunities for hiking, horseriding, fishing and whitewater rafting. Worthwhile day-trips from town are to the underground limestone caves of **Caverna de las Brujas** (73km southwest), the volcanic wonderland of **La Payunia** (208km south), and to **Laguna Llancanelo** (60km southeast), a high-altitude lagoon speckled pink with flamingos.

What to see and do

Malargüe's flat, compact centre is easy to get your head around: the wide main drag is the RN40, known in town as **Avenida San Martín**. Here you'll find the tourist office, shops and the main square, **Plaza General San Martín**. Just south of the tourist office, the landscaped greenery of **Parque del Ayer** ("Park of Yesteryear") is filled with sculptures and native trees. Opposite, you can take a free guided tour at the **Observatorio Pierre Auger** (Mon–Fri 5–6pm; ⓣ02627/471562, ⓦwww.auger.org.ar), an astrophysics centre that studies cosmic rays.

Arrival and information

Bus Malargüe's bus terminal (ⓣ02627/470690) is at Esquibel Aldao and Fray Luis Beltrán, four blocks south and two west of Plaza San Martín.

Tourist office The tourist office (daily 8am–10pm; ⓣ02627/471659, ⓦwww.malargue.gov.ar) is on the RN40 four blocks north of the plaza.

Tour operators Many local companies run tours to La Payunia, Laguna Llancanelo and Caverna de las Brujas, as well as horseriding and other adventure activities. Check out Karen Travel at San Martín 1056 (ⓣ02627/470342, ⓦwww.karentravel.com.ar), where you can also hire 4WDs.

Accommodation

Malargüe has plenty of affordable places to stay, including a handful of well-run hostels, all of which have kitchens and free breakfast, and arrange excursions in the area. If you're travelling in a group, a cost-effective option is a fully-equipped *cabaña* (ask for a list at the tourist office). Prices rise significantly during the winter when Malargüe becomes a popular base for skiing at Las Leñas. Some Malargüe hotels offer fifty percent discounts on Las Leñas ski lift tickets if you stay in town (again, ask for a list at the tourist office). In summer there is a **campsite** conveniently located at *Camping Polideportivo* at Capdeval and Esquibal Aldao (ⓣ02627/470691; AR$10).

Cabañas Newen Mapu Av Roca and Villa del Milagro ⓣ02627/472318, ⓦwww.newenmapu.com. Buy yourself some space with a two-storey *cabaña* (sleeps six) complete with cable TV, full kitchen, fireplace and mountain views. Prices halve in the low season. *Cabaña* ❼

Ecohostel Colonia Pehuenche I, Finca N. 65, 5km south of town (free transfer from the Choique Turismo Alternativo office at San Martín and Rodríguez) ⓣ02627/1540-2439, ⓦwww.hostelmalargue.net. There's some serious star-gazing and R&R to be had at this rustic hostel set on an organic farm. Home-made meals and horse-riding excursions offered. Dorm AR$36 (HI discount offered). B&B ❺

Hostel La Caverna Cte Rodríguez 445, ⓣ02627/472569, ⓦwww.lacavernahostel.com.ar. Run by an enthusiastic young local, this hostel has a spacious common area and plenty of dorm beds. The self-catering apartment out back is ideal for groups. Free laundry and internet. Dorm AR$40. ❻

Hostel Nord Patagonia Fray Inalicán 52 ⓣ02627/472-276, ⓦwww.nordpatagonia.com.ar. A centrally located backpackers with intimate if spartan dorm rooms with private bathrooms. There's a fireplace, lounge and kitchen. Dorm AR$45. ❺

Eating and drinking

El Bodega de Maria Rufino Ortega at General Villegas. Trout and pizza get all the attention at this rustic-style restaurant. Set lunch AR$25.

Cuyam-Co 8km west of Malargüe in El Dique. Catch your own meal and have it cooked to perfection at this trout farm. AR$32 for full menu and AR$10 for fishing.

Hotel Río Grande RN40 Norte ⓣ02627/471589. The restaurant in this upmarket hotel serves decent steaks (AR$16), pastas (AR$12–22) and trout ($A25).

Moving on

Bus Mendoza (3 daily; 5hr); San Rafael (3 daily; 2hr 30min); Las Leñas (one daily during ski season; 1hr 30min).

AROUND MALARGÜE

The **CAVERNA DE LAS BRUJAS** ("Witches Cave") is an otherworldly limestone cave filled with incredible rock formations, including **stalactites and stalagmites** with rather suggestive names ("Virgin's Chamber", anyone?). The cave, located 73km southwest of Malargüe and 8km along a dirt road off the RN40, is within a provincial park and is staffed by *guardaparques*. Guided visits (AR$20) are the only way to see the cave and numbers are restricted to nine at a time. The **temperature** inside the grotto can be 20°C lower than outside, so be sure to wrap up.

Continuing along the RN40, you'll reach the entrance to **LA PAYUNIA** at El Zampal. This expansive, visually arresting, wildlife-rich reserve spans 4500 square kilometres. Flaxen grasslands, black lava flows and eight hundred threatening-looking volcanoes (the highest concentration of volcanic cones in the world) provide a starkly wild backdrop for the guanaco, puma and condor that call it home. The best way to see La Payunia is on a full-day-trip from Malargüe that takes in the Caverna de las Brujas along the way. If you want to visit the cave independently, you must first make an appointment and **register** with Malargüe's tourist office.

SAN JUAN

Sun-soaked **SAN JUAN** is a modern, low-rise provincial capital. In 1944, one of South America's most powerful earthquakes (8.5 on the Richter scale) razed the city, killing more than ten thousand people. Essentially a poorer, smaller, less attractive version of its southerly neighbour Mendoza, San Juan is unlikely to capture your imagination. It does however makes a convenient base for sampling the fruits of nearby wineries as well as for excursions to some of Argentina's most iconic natural wonders – the sculptural desert landscapes of **Parque Provincial Ischigualasto** and the surreal rock formations of **Parque Nacional Talampaya**.

Try to avoid visiting in the summer, when *Sanjuaninos* cope with the midday heat by taking long, sluggish siestas.

What to see and do

The leafy Plaza 25 de Mayo, flanked by a couple of inviting cafés, marks the city centre. On its northwestern side, the modern cathedral's fifty-metre brick campanile is a nod to St Mark's in Venice. If the mood takes, climb the **bell tower** (daily 9am–1pm & 5–8pm; AR$1) for great city and countryside vistas. Not far away at Sarmiento 21 Sur, opposite the tourist office, is the whitewashed childhood home of former Argentine president **Domingo Faustino Sarmiento** (1811–88), now a museum (Tues–Fri 9am–1.30pm & 5–9.30pm, Mon & Sat 8.30am–1.30pm; AR$3; guided tours half-hourly). Although damaged in the 1944 earthquake, the house has been lovingly restored and displays belongings and paraphernalia from Sarmiento's eventful life. More ancient history is represented at the **Museo de Ciencias Naturales** (daily 9am–1pm; AR$3; ⓣ0264/421-6774), in the former train station at avenidas España and Maipú, the final resting place of the skeleton of the carnivorous **dinosaur**, Herrerasaurus, excavated in the Parque Provincial Ischigualasto (see p.127). And finally, if all that has left your mouth dry, the historic **Bodega Graffigna** (Tues–Fri 9am–1pm, Sat 9am–8pm, Sun 10am–2pm; free; ⓣ0264/421-4227), at Colón 1342 Norte, houses the **Museo de Vino Santiago Graffigna** wine museum, and perhaps more importantly a wine bar where you can quench your thirst and sample provincial vintages.

Arrival and information

Air Las Chacritas airport (ⓣ0264/425-4133) is 12km east of the city centre. A taxi downtown costs around AR$15.

Bus The bus station (ⓣ0264/422-1604), at Estados Unidos 492 Sur, is eight blocks east of Plaza 25 de Mayo.

Tourist office The tourist office at Sarmiento 24 Sur has good city and provincial information (Mon–Fri 7.30am–8.30pm , Sat & Sun 9am–8.30pm; ⓣ0264/421-0004; ⓦwww.turismo.sanjuan.gov.ar).

Accommodation

Economical accommodation is of a reasonable standard in San Juan. A convenient campsite is *Camping Don Bosco* (ⓣ0264/425-3663, AR$5 per person), 3km east on RN20, with hot showers and a swimming pool. Catch bus #19 from the centre.

Colpa Hostel-Apart 25 de Mayo 554 Este ⓣ0264/422-5704, ⓦwww.colpahostelsanjuan.com.ar. The spotless rooms in this stylish hostel-cum-apartment complex have first-rate beds and – hallelujah – a/c. It's AR$50 per person, whether you're sharing or alone. Includes breakfast, two kitchens, swimming pool and TV room. ❺

Hotel Jardín Petit 25 de Mayo 345 Este ⓣ0264/42-11825. A welcoming hotel with cozy, plain rooms and an inviting patio. Breakfast included. ❻

San Juan Hostel Av Cordoba 317 Este ⓣ0264/4201-835, ⓦwww.sanjuanhostel.com. Helpful staff and a comfortable common area, as well as low prices, make up for the depressing dorms and basic bathrooms at this backpackers pad. Includes breakfast and internet. Dorm AR$28. ❹

Zonda Hostel C Caseros 486 Sur ⓣ0264/420-1009 ⓦwww.zondahostel.com.ar. Conveniently located four blocks from the bus station, this 35-bed HI hostel boasts a TV room, patio, kitchen, free internet and breakfast. Dorm AR$30. ❹

Eating and drinking

San Juan has a wide selection of places to refuel, including a vegetarian restaurant that could convert the staunchest of carnivores.

Antonio Gómez Supermercado, General Acha and Córdoba. The heaving paellas (AR$25) draw the lunchtime crowd at this Spanish-centric market stall. Lunch only.

A Sanchez Rivadavia 55 Oeste. The city's classiest restaurant serves beautifully prepared salmon (AR$39) and beef (AR$31) with a fine selection of local wines. After the meal, browse the adjoining book and music shop.

Freud Café Plaza 25 de Mayo. A swanky café-bar overlooking the main plaza where you can people-watch in a/c comfort over a sandwich (AR$9–19) and Irish coffee (AR$10).

El Ricón de Nápoli Rivadavia 175 Oeste. Noisy and cheerful fast-service restaurant whipping up pizza, pasta, burgers and plenty of grilled *carne* (mains AR$8–20).

Soychú Av José Ignacio de la Roza 223 Oeste. Slip into something elasticized before gorging yourself on one of the continent's best vegetarian all-you-can-eat-buffets (AR$17). Don't pass up a freshly-squeezed juice. Closed Sun dinner.

Directory

Car rental Renta Auto, San Martín 1593 Oeste ⓣ0264/423-3620.

Laundry Laverap, Rivadavia 498 Oeste.

Post office Av José Ignacio de la Roza 259 Este.

Tour operators Companies offering Ischigualasto and Talampaya excursions include Algarrobo, Sarmiento 62 Sur (ⓣ0264/427-2487, ⓦwww.algarroboturismo.com.ar), and Triassic Tour, Hipólito Yrigoyen 294 Sur (0264/421-9528, ⓦwww.grupohuaco.com.ar).

Moving on

Air to: Buenos Aires (daily; 1hr 50min).
Bus to: Buenos Aires (10 daily; 16hr); Córdoba (5 daily; 8hr); Mendoza (hourly; 2hr 30min); San Rafael (2 daily; 5hr 30min); Valle Fértil (3 daily; 4hr). Most long-distance buses, including two daily services to Santiago de Chile, require a change in Mendoza.

DAY-TRIPS FROM SAN JUAN

The neighbouring UNESCO World Heritage-listed parks of **Ischigualasto** (better known as Valle de la Luna) and **Talampaya** lie in the provinces of San Juan and La Rioja respectively. The former is known for its otherwordly rock formations, the latter its red sandstone cliffs. Both can be visited on day-trips from San Juan, but the sleepy village of **San Agustín de Valle Fértil**, 250km northeast, is a much closer base. Some **tour operators** pack both parks into one day-long excursion, stopping off at Talampaya in the morning when the wind is low and the light best illuminates the red in the sandstone, before taking in Ischigualasto in the mid-to-late afternoon.

San Agustín de Valle Fértil

Set in a valley carved out by the Río San Juan and surrounded by olive groves and sheep pasture, **SAN AGUSTÍN DE VALLE FÉRTIL** is something of a verdant oasis in an otherwise desert province. Valle Fértil is also ideally located for visiting both Talampaya and Ischigualasto.

Arrival and information

Bus The bus terminal is at Mitre and Entre Rios; there are three daily services from San Juan (4hr) and three weekly from La Rioja (4hr).
Tourist office The super-friendly tourist office (daily 7am–1pm & 2–10pm, ⓣ02646/420104, ⓔischigualasto@sanjuan.gov.ar) is at Plaza San Agustín and can advise on tours and transport to the parks as well as bicycle and horseriding excursions to view pre-Hispanic petroglyphs in the nearby mountains.

Accommodation

Valle Fértil has plenty of cheap, if not terribly appealing, places to sleep. **Campers** can try the central *Camping Valle Fértil* (ⓣ02646/420015), a shady establishment on Rivadavia (AR$10 per tent).
Campo Base Valle de la Luna Tucamán between San Luis and Libertador ⓣ02646/420063, ⓦwww.hostelvalledelaluna.com.ar. The only bona-fide backpacker hostel in town, this modest place has a kitchen, TV lounge, free breakfast and tour advice. Dorm AR$22 (discount for HI members).
Hostería Valle Fértil Rivadavia 5400 ⓣ02646/420015, ⓦwww.alkazarhotel.com.ar. The village's most inviting accommodation, thanks to its setting on a breezy hillside overlooking the Dique San Agustín reservoir. Some of the small, modern rooms have lake views. There's a restaurant, and guests can use the swimming pool in the hosteria's *cabaña* complex down the hill. 7
Pension Doña Zoila Mendoza between Rivadavia & Laprida ⓣ02646/420308. This budget pension has bare-bones rooms and shared bathrooms set around a peaceful, grapevine-shaded courtyard. 3

Eating

La Cocina de Zulma North side of the plaza. Tuck into pesto pasta served with steak for a bargain AR$15.
La Florida South side of the plaza. Above-average Argentine fare (mains AR$15–20) and very attentive service.

Parque Provincial Ischigualasto

Sculptured by more than two million years of erosion, wind and water, the **PARQUE PROVINCIAL ISCHIGUALASTO**, otherwise known as the Valle de la Luna (Moon Valley), is San Juan's most visited attraction. Set in a desert valley between two mountain ranges some 80km north of Valle Fértil, it is considered one of the most significant **dinosaur graveyards** on the planet. Skeletons dating from the Triassic era around two hundred million years ago have been unearthed here. Given its size (150 sq km), you need a vehicle to explore the park properly; rangers accompany visitors in convoy on a bumpy 45-kilometre circuit of the park's highlights (two-to-three hours), imparting explanations of its paleontological history, photogenic moonscapes and precarious sandstone rock formations. The southern section of the circuit resembles the arid lunar landscapes of Cappadocia in Turkey, with surreally-shaped rock formations dubbed El Submarino (the submarine), El Esfinge (the sphinx) and Cancha de Bolas (bowling alley); while further north on the circuit lie stark white fields strewn with petrified tree trunks. If you're lucky, you might catch a glimpse of some of the park's inhabitants, which include hares, red foxes, armadillos, lizards, guanacos, snakes and condors.

Arrival and information

Bus The easiest way to visit the park is on an organized tour. For those coming independently, Empresa Vallecito buses from San Juan to La Rioja run on Mon, Wed & Fri and pass the Los Baldecitos checkpoint, a 5km walk to the park entrance, where the park authorities hire out vehicles.

Park information The park entrance, where there's a helpful *guardaparque* post, is along a signposted road off the RP510 at Los Baldecitos. Entrance (daily April–Sept 9am–4pm, Oct–March 8am–5pm) is AR$35 per person and includes a guided tour or, for non-Spanish speakers, a self-guided mp3 tour in English. An extra AR$15 buys you a range of special tours, including two-hour guided bicycle excursions, full-moon night tours and three-hour treks to the top of Cerro Morado (1748m) with tremendous views of the park.

Accommodation

Campers can pitch their tents for AR$3 next to the park visitors' centre where there is also a bathroom and small café. Most people spend the night in nearby Valle Fértil (see p.127) and get a transfer to the park with one of the village's tour operators.

Parque Nacional Talampaya

Familiar from regular appearances on posters promoting Argentinian tourism, the smooth sandstone cliffs and surreal rock formations of **PARQUE NACIONAL TALAMPAYA** are far more eye-boggling in real life. The centrepiece of the 215-square-kilometre park is a 220-million-year-old **canyon**, with 180-metre-high rust-red sandstone cliffs rising on either side, rendering everything in between puny and insignificant. At the centre of the canyon, armadillos and grey foxes scurry among groves of cacti and native trees in a lush **jardín botánico**. Elsewhere, erosion has carved out towering columns and gravity-defying **rock formations** where condors and eagles have found nesting sites.

Other park highlights include a series of pre-Hispanic **petroglyphs and pictographs** etched onto gigantic rock faces. Thought to be around a thousand years old, the etchings depict llamas, pumas, hunters, stepped pyramids and phallic symbols.

Arrival and information

Talampaya lies 93km northeast of Ischigualasto and around 190km from Valle Fírtil, but the closest urban centre to the park is actually Villa Unión, an entirely forgettable town in La Rioja Province, 55km away along the RP26.

Bus Organized tours from San Juan, Valle Fértil, La Rioja or Villa Unión are the easiest ways to visit the park. Otherwise, buses from Villa Unión to La Rioja and Valle Fértil can drop you off on the main road.

Park information The *guardería* (daily April–Sept 9am–4pm, Oct–March 8am–5pm; AR$20; ☎03825/470397) is staffed year-round. Private vehicle are not allowed inside; official guides with their own trucks offer excursions (2hr 30min AR$45 per person; 4hr 30min AR$60).

Accommodation and eating

There is a basic, windswept campsite next to the *guardería*; it can get brutally cold at night. A small shop here sells snacks and simple meals.

The Lake District

The Argentine **LAKE DISTRICT** in northern Patagonia is an unspoiled region of azure glacial lakes, pristine rivers, snow-clad mountains, extinct volcanoes and verdant alpine forests. Dominated until the late nineteenth century by the indigenous Mapuche people, the Lake District is now Argentina's top year-round vacation destination – the place to go for hiking, camping, fishing, watersports, biking, climbing and skiing.

A series of spectacular national parks run down the region's serrated Andean spine, providing easy access to wilderness. The most northern of Patagonia's national parks is **Parque Nacional Lanín** in Neuquén Province, accessible from both the sleepy fishing town of **Junín de los Andes** or its fashionable neighbour **San Martín de los Andes**. Heading south, the dazzling 110km route between **San Martín de los Andes** and the upmarket village of **Villa La Angostura** affords roadside vistas of snow-capped peaks reflected in picture-perfect lakes as well as the first glimpse of the gigantic **Parque Nacional Nahuel Huapi**. The route continues south to the lakeside party town of **Bariloche**, the region's transport hub and base for hiking in **Nahuel Huapi** in summer, skiing in winter and gorging on chocolate and locally-brewed beer all year round. Further south, in the province of Chubut, the dusty town of **Esquel** is within day-trip distance of the **Parque Nacional Los Alerces**, a dramatic wilderness area of lakes, rivers, glaciers and thousand-year-old **alerce** trees.

PARQUE NACIONAL LANÍN

The perfect snow-clad cone of extinct Volcán Lanín, which dominates the skyline from hundreds of kilometres away, rises 3776m at the centre of its namesake **PARQUE NACIONAL LANÍN**. Home to dozens of Mapuche communities, Lanín sits on the Chilean border, spanning 4120 square kilometres of varied Andean terrain. Fishing enthusiasts flock to its glacial lakes and gushing rivers, campers pitch their homes lakeside at free or Mapuche-run campgrounds, while trekkers take advantage of the park's hiking trails or attempt the ascent of Volcán Lanín. Endangered pudú, a native deer, are preyed upon by elusive puma, while Andean condors soar above. Forests of monkey-puzzle trees (also known as araucaria or *pehuén)* are common in the north to middle section of the park between Ñorquinco and Huechulafquen lakes. Perfect volcano views can be enjoyed from **Lago Huechulafquen** (entrance AR$20 Dec–March), 22km northwest of Junín de los Andes, where there are good hiking, fishing and boating opportunities and a handful of *hosterías* and campgrounds. Lanín's southern sector is best explored from **San Martín de los Andes** (p.131), set on the eastern shores of the park's **Lago Lácar**, or on the first part of the Seven Lakes Route (see box, p.134). Optimal visiting months are from October to mid-May, when there are tours available from Junín.

JUNÍN DE LOS ANDES

Argentina's self-proclaimed trout capital, the pint-sized town of **JUNÍN DE LOS ANDES** is picturesquely set on the banks of Río Chimehuín. Junín is also well-positioned for excursions to the **Parque Nacional Lanín** (see above), in particular the area around **Lago Huechulafquen**, 22 kilomtres northwest

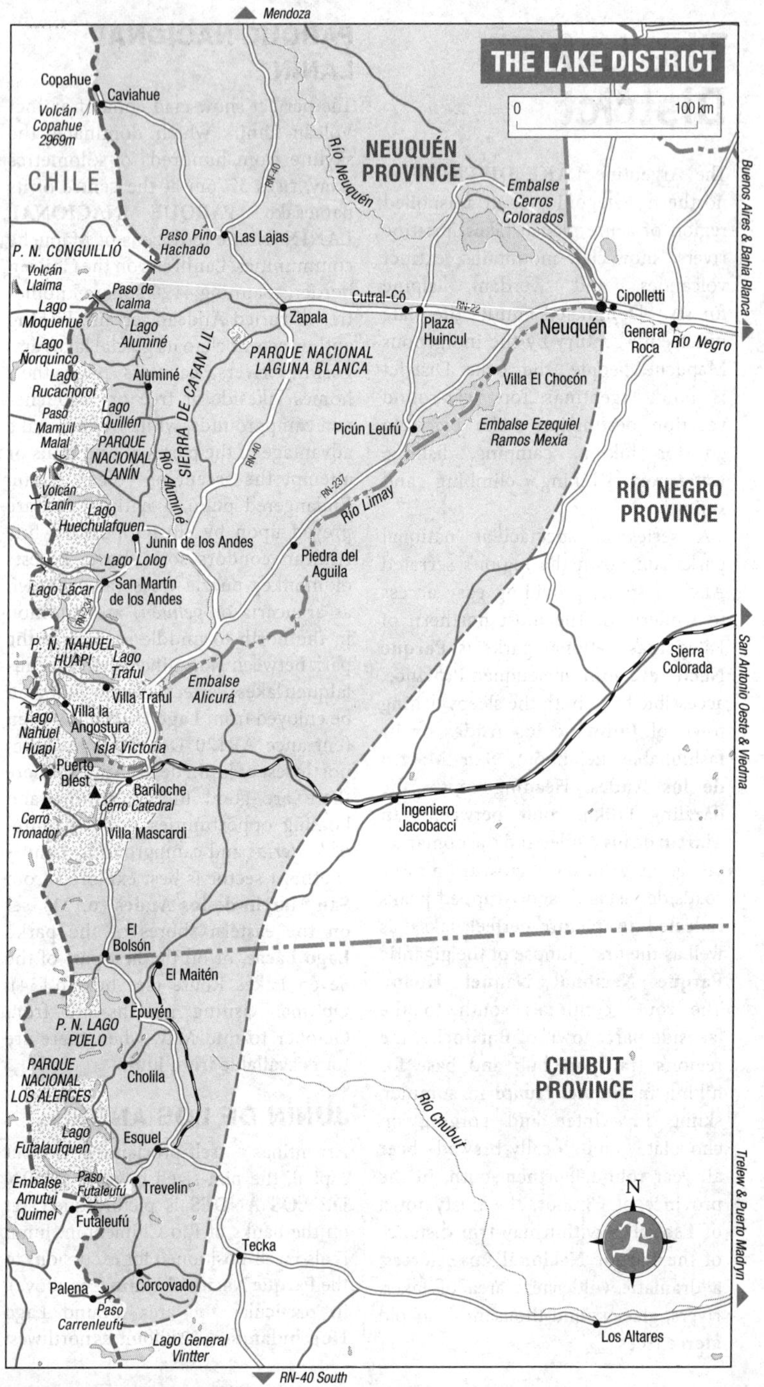
THE LAKE DISTRICT
0
100 km
Mendoza
RN-40 South
Buenos Aires & Bahía Blanca
San Antonio Oeste & Viedma
Trelew & Puerto Madryn
CHILE
NEUQUÉN PROVINCE
RÍO NEGRO PROVINCE
CHUBUT PROVINCE
Copahue
Caviahue
Volcán Copahue 2969m
Río Neuquén
RN-40
Embalse Cerros Colorados
Paso Pino Hachado
Las Lajas
P. N. CONGUILLIÓ
Volcán Llaima
Paso de Icalma
Lago Moquehue
Zapala
Cutral-Có
Plaza Huincul
RN-22
Cipolletti
Neuquén
General Roca
Río Negro
Lago Aluminé
Lago Ñorquinco
PARQUE NACIONAL LAGUNA BLANCA
SIERRA DE CATAN LIL
Lago Rucachoroi
Aluminé
Villa El Chocón
Paso Mamuil Malal
Lago Quillén
PARQUE NACIONAL LANÍN
Río Aluminé
Picún Leufú
Embalse Ezequiel Ramos Mexía
Volcán Lanín
Lago Huechulafquen
RN-237
Río Limay
Junín de los Andes
Piedra del Aguila
Lago Lolog
Lago Lácar
San Martín de los Andes
RN-234
P. N. NAHUEL HUAPI
Lago Traful
Villa Traful
Embalse Alicurá
Villa la Angostura
Lago Nahuel Huapi
Isla Victoria
Puerto Blest
Bariloche
Cerro Catedral
Cerro Tronador
Villa Mascardi
Sierra Colorada
Ingeniero Jacobacci
El Bolsón
El Maitén
Epuyén
P. N. LAGO PUELO
PARQUE NACIONAL LOS ALERCES
Cholila
Río Chubut
Lago Futalaufquen
Esquel
Embalse Amutui Quimei
Paso Futaleufú
Trevelin
Futaleufú
Tecka
Palena
Corcovado
Paso Carrenleufú
Lago General Vintter
Los Altares
N

of town along a rough road. Tour operators in town offer excursions.

For something to do in town, take a stroll around the **Vía Christi** sculpture project (Ⓦwww.viachristi.com.ar), which starts at the base of Cerro de la Cruz, fifteen-minutes' walk west of Plaza San Martín at the end of Avenida Antártida Argentina. A path winds through a pine-forested hillside dotted with sculptures and mosaics depicting the Stations of the Cross, which fuse Catholic with Mapuche symbolism.

Arrival and information

Air Chapelco airport (Ⓣ02972/428388) is 19km south of town. A *remise* to the centre costs around AR$40.
Bus The bus station is three blocks from Plaza San Martín at Olavarría and F.S. Martín, with services to Neuquén (2 daily, 6hr), San Martín de los Andes (9 daily, 1hr) and Pucón in Chile (1 daily, 4hr). Empreza Castelli runs buses to Lago Huechulafquen in Parque Nacional Lanín (Jan to mid-March 4 daily, 1hr 30min; rest of year one daily Tues, Fri & Sun only).
Tourist office The tourist office is opposite Plaza San Martín at Padre Milanesio and Coronel Suárez (daily April–Nov 8am–9pm: Dec–March 8am–10pm; Ⓣ02972/491160, Ⓦwww.junindelosandes.gov.ar). Fishing licences can be purchased here (AR$50 a day or AR$300 a season Nov–March). Next door is the helpful **Parque Nacional Lanín information office** (Dec–March daily 8am–10pm, rest of year Mon–Fri 8am–5pm; Ⓣ02972/492748, Ⓔpnljunin@fronteradigital.net.ar).

Accommodation

Hotel prices hit Andean peaks in the summer, when advance bookings are recommended. The pretty *La Isla* **campsite** (Ⓣ02972/492029, AR$10 per person) is within easy reach of the main plaza, on an island at the eastern end of Gines Ponte, and has hot showers and a shady, riverside setting.
Albergue Tromen Lonquimay 195 Ⓣ02972/491498, Ⓔtromen@fronteradigital.net.ar. A characterless but serviceable budget option with a variety of dorm rooms and doubles scattered around a large house. The bottom floor has a TV room and kitchen. Dorm AR$24. ④
La Casa de Marita y Aldo 25 de Mayo 371 Ⓣ02972/491042, Ⓔcasademaritayaldo@hotmail.com. A cozy stone cottage half a block from the river with two five-bed dorm rooms and a well-equipped kitchen. The house out back with rickety floorboards and drooping beds is not half as nice. The owners rent out large rubber dinghies (AR$40 for two hours) for leisurely river floats. Dorm AR$25.
Hostería Chimehuin Coronel Suárez and 25 de Mayo Ⓣ02972/491132, Ⓦwww.interpatagonia.com/hosteriachimehuin. The rooms in this great-value bed and breakfast have picture windows that look out onto a landscaped garden. ⑦

Eating

There are few restaurants in town, so Junín de los Andes might be just the place to stock up on fresh produce and go wild in the kitchen.
Ruca Hueney Padre Milanesio and Coronel Suárez Ⓣ02972/491113. With that crystal clear river flowing just a few blocks away, you'd be *loco* not to order the trout (AR$30); failing that, they also make a reasonable stab at Middle Eastern cuisine and do set lunches for AR$20.

SAN MARTÍN DE LOS ANDES

Pleasant but pricey, **SAN MARTÍN DE LOS ANDES** is a smaller version of neighbouring Bariloche, albeit without the gobsmacking vistas, high-rise hotels or packs of party-hard students. Alpine-style chalets, boutique chocolate shops and gourmet restaurants line the holiday town's impeccably clean streets. San Martín is set on the shores of **Lago Lácar**, in a peaceful valley wedged between two forested mountains, with the southern sector of the verdant Parque Nacional Lanín on its doorstep. The lake offers great summer splashing, while hiking and biking trails lead off to lakeside viewpoints. Pleasure boats depart from the pier for excursions to Paso Hua-Hum near the Chilean border and to the bay of Quila Quina on Lácar's southern shore.

What to see and do

The **Museo de los Primeros Pobladores** (Tues–Sat 1.30–8.30pm, Sat & Sun 3–8pm; AR$1), on the main plaza, puts the area in a historical context and displays Mapuche art and pre-Columbian arteifacts. If you're here in winter (June–Oct) and wondering where all the people are, your answer may lie 19 kilomtres south on the slopes of **Cerro Chapelco** (☎02972/427845, Ⓦwww.cerrochapelco.com; one-day ski pass AR$133), where there are 29 ski runs, a snowboard park and night skiing. San Martín is also the northern starting or finishing point for the **Ruta de Los Siete Lagos** (see box, p.134).

Arrival and information

Air Chapelco airport (☎02972/428388) is 25km from town, with minibus connections to the centre (AR$15).

Bus The bus terminal is on General Villegas between Juez del Valle and Coronel Diaz.

Car rental Avis (☎02972/411141), Coronel Pérez.

Tourist office The helpful tourist office is on Plaza San Martín (daily 8am–9pm; Jan & Feb 8am–10pm; ☎02972/427347, Ⓦwww.sanMartíndelosandes.gov.ar). For trekking and camping maps as well as general park information, head to the **Intendencia del Parque Nacional Lanín**, on the corner of Perito Moreno and Eduardo Elordi (Mon–Fri 8am–3pm, ☎02972/427233, Ⓦwww.parquenacionallanin.gov.ar).

Accommodation

San Martín's prices reflect its popularity with Argentina's upper crust. Advance reservations are necessary during the height of summer and in the ski season when prices can double. Backpackers can choose from a handful of good hostels, although prices are somewhat inflated. There are

three **campsites**, with the pick of the pitches the Curruhuinca Mapuche community-run *Camping Lolen* (AR$15 per person), beautifully positioned on the lake at Playa Catritre 4km southwest of town.

Hostel La Colorada Av Koessler 1614 ⓣ02972/411041, ⓦwww.lacoloradahostel.com.ar. The newest hostel in town has certainly made a splash with its bright red paint-job, crackling fireplace, big backyard and to-drool-for kitchen. Some of the dorm rooms (AR$45) have private bathrooms. Breakfast included. ❺

Hostería Laura Misionero Mascardi 632 ⓣ02972/427271, ⓔhosterialaura@smandes.com.ar. There's plenty of charm and comfort to the simple little rooms in this unassuming, wooden house. Breakfast included. ❻

Puma Hostel Fosberry 535 ⓣ02972/422443, ⓦwww.pumahostel.com.ar. A serviceable enough hostel with plenty of backpacker buzz, three double rooms, dorm beds (AR$45), kitchen and laundry. Discounts for HI members. Includes breakfast. ❺

Secuoya Hostel Rivadavia 411 ⓣ02972/424485, ⓦwww.hostelsecuoya.com.ar. The welcoming staff, tranquil vibe, spotless kitchen and wooden floorboards make this superb little hostel feel more like a guesthouse. The doubles are a bit pokey, but the three-bed dorm rooms (AR$60) are a treat. Internet included. ❻

Eating and drinking

Dining out is an expensive pastime in San Martín, but generally worth every peso.

Downtown Matias Calderón and Coronel Diaz ⓣ02972/421699, Jan & Feb Tues–Sun, rest of year Wed–Sat. So this is where all the nocturnal action is – a cool, two-storey Irish pub and restaurant that shakes its drunken groove thing well into the small hours to whatever the DJ's spinning. It's up a long, bumpy driveway, so take a cab if you're wearing heels. A Guinness is AR$12.

Hipócrates Belgrano 1057 ⓣ02972/411284.. Gluten-intolerant vegans rejoice, because this classy little wholefood restaurant, set above a natural health shop, is just your cup of herbal tea. Along with wok-fried vegetables and *miso* soup, the eclectic menu includes non-veggie options such as sushi, fried calamari, grilled salmon and deer in white wine sauce. Mains AR$20–30.

Pizza Cala San Martín 1129 ⓣ02972/422511. When you're hankering for pizza (AR$18), you can't beat this local favourite. Attend to your carbs-induced thirst with a litre of beer (AR$7).

Pura Vida Villegas 745 ⓣ02972/429302. A restaurant vegetarians and carnivores can actually agree on, with cheesy vegetarian moussaka alongside trout and chicken dishes. Mains AR$20–30.

TREAT YOURSELF

Avataras (Teniente Ramayón 765 ⓣ02972/427104) use locally-sourced ingredients with more skill and imagination than anyone else in town, their finely-tuned global menu taking its inspiration from Asia, North Africa and the Mediterranean (mains AR$50–90). If you haven't got the budget or the threads for the main restaurant, the intimate pub out back serves inexpensive Tex Mex dishes (AR$10–30), cheese fondue (AR$80 for two), and stocks seventy brands of beer. Closed Sun.

Moving on

Air to: Buenos Aires (daily during ski season; 2hr).
Bus to: Bariloche (5 daily; 3hr 30min); Junín de los Andes (9 daily; 1hr); Villa La Angostura (2-4 daily; 2hr 30min).

VILLA LA ANGOSTURA

A hit with well-heeled Argentinians, **VILLA LA ANGOSTURA** is a lovely little village spread loosely along the northern shores of Lago Nahuel Huapi. It makes a tranquil alternative to buzzing Bariloche and is the obvious place to overnight before taking a stroll in the unique woodlands of Parque Nacional Los Arrayanes. Most of the village's shops and restaurants are in the commercial area known as **El Cruce**, spread along the RN231 (Av Arrayanes as it passes through town), a squeaky-clean main street with twee log-cabin buildings. The pretty lakeside settlement of **La Villa** is three-kilometres downhill from here along Boulevard Nahuel Huapi, where you'll find the port and entrance to Parque Nacional Los Arrayanes.

Ten kilometres northeast of town, **Cerro Bayo** (ⓣ02944/494189, ⓦwww.cerrobayoweb.com) is a lovely small

RUTA DE LOS SIETE LAGOS

The Ruta de los Siete Lagos (Seven Lakes Route) is one of South America's most picturesque drives. It winds for 110kilometres between San Martín de Los Andes and Villa La Angostura along the RN234, traversing the dense alpine forests, snow-capped Andean peaks, brilliant blue lakes, trout-stuffed rivers and plunging waterfalls of two magnificent Patagonian national parks – Lanín and Nahuel Huapi. Seven principal photogenic alpine lakes are visible or accessible from the roadside. From north to south they are: Machónico, Falkner, Villarino, Escondido, Correntoso, Espejo and Nahuel Huapi. You can spend the night en route at numerous free and serviced lakeside campsites as well as at *refugios* and lodges. The first half of the road is paved, while the final stretch, between Lago Villarino and Lago Espejo, is a bumpy dirt track, with vehicles spewing up walls of blinding dust in their wake. After rainfall, the road becomes a muddy mess. Despite obvious hazards from rip-roaring cars and buses, the route is also extremely popular with cyclists.

ski resort in winter, catering for **hiking and mountain biking** in the summer. Villa La Angostura is also the southern starting (or ending) point for the scenic Ruta de Los Siete Lagos (see above), which heads north to San Martín de los Andes.

Parque Nacional Los Arrayanes

A mini-park nestled within the mammoth Parque Nacional Nahuel Huapi (see p.140), **PARQUE NACIONAL LOS ARRAYANES** (daylight hours, last entry 2pm; AR$20) lies at the tip of **Península Quetrihué**, which dips into **Lago Nahuel Huapi** from Villa La Angostura. The diminutive park (just over seventeen square kilometres) shelters the **Bosque de los Arrayanes**, the world's most significant stand of rare *arrayán* myrtle woodland. Some of the trees here are more than 650 years old. The myrtle's corkscrew-like trunks, terracotta-coloured bark and white flowers are a stunning contrast to a blue sky or shimmering lake. To reach the Bosque, follow the undulating trail (12km one-way) from the park entrance to the end of the peninsula. Cycling is allowed on the trail and bikes can be rented in El Cruce. Hikers should allow for a five-to-six-hour round-trip and bear in mind the last entry to the park is at 2pm. Tourist boats for the Bosque leave from the Puerto Angostura jetty at **Bahía Mansa**, on the peninsula's eastern bay in La Villa. Organized boat tours also run out of Bariloche.

Arrival and information

Bus The bus station is at Av Siete Lagos 35 (☎02944/494961).

Tourist office Pick up a map or organize accommodation at the tourist office (Dec–Feb daily 8am–10pm, rest of year 8.30am–8.30pm; ☎02944/494124, Ⓦwww.villalaangostura.gov.ar), across the road from the bus terminal at Av Siete Lagos 90.

Accommodation

As a shameless tourist town, Villa La Angostura is luxury accommodation central, with the most exclusive hotels hugging the lakeshore. Increasingly, budget travellers are being well catered for too, with a couple of excellent hostels. The closest **campsite** to downtown is *Camping Unquehué* (☎02944/494103), half a kilometre west of the bus station on Av Siete Lagos, with pitches for AR$22 per person.

Hostel La Angostura Barbagelata 157 ☎02944/494834, Ⓦwww.hostellaangostura.com.ar It's a short uphill walk west of Plaza San Martín to this enormous white house fronted by windchimes. The comfortable dorms have ensuites (AR$45) and the front room is a huge chill-out space, with pool table, TV lounge and kitchen. Breakfast and wi-fi is included and there are bikes for rent and discounts for HI members. ❻

Hotel Angostura Blvd Nahuel Huapii 1911, La Villa ⓣ02944/494224, ⓦwww.hotelangostura.com. Splash out on lakeside accommodation at this traditional-style hotel with cozy rooms. There are also separate, fully-equipped bungalows, a restaurant and a private beach. ❼

Italian Hostel Los Maquis 215 ⓣ02944/494376, ⓦwww.italianhoste.com.ar. Closed April–Oct. Two blocks south of the main street, this lovely hostel has spacious dorms (AR$40) as well as doubles and triples set in a large wooden-beam house with plenty of communal nooks and crannies. Extras include wi-fi, breakfast, bike rental, backyard hammocks, herb garden and well-equipped kitchen with a recycling system. ❺

Eating

Many restaurants in town are of the upmarket variety, although it's not impossible to eat on the cheap.

La Encantada Belvedere 69 ⓣ02944/495436. Lamb casserole (AR$40), woodfire pizzas (AR$24–45) and plenty of cuts from the *parrilla* do the rounds in this local favourite. Closed Sun night and Mon.

Gran Nevada AvLos Arrayanes 102. An unpretentious local eatery serving heaving portions of pasta, pizza, trout and predictable Argentinian staples at rock-bottom prices (mains AR$11–15).

Moving on

Bus to: Bariloche (hourly, 1hr); San Martín de los Andes (2–4 daily, 2hr 30min).

TREAT YOURSELF

Serving food fit for royalty (literally – the owner's sister is Princess Máxima of Holland), **Tinto Bistro**'s bold fusion menu is well-versed in the ways of the world. Vegetarians can enjoy the Asian stir-fry (AR$39), while the Patagonian lamb marinated in red wine (AR$57) is a tasty meaty feast. A wine list of more than 150 vintages seals the deal. Nahuel Huapi 31 ⓣ02944/494924, closed Sun.

BARILOCHE

Set on the southeastern shores of sparkling Lago Nahuel Huapi and framed by dramatic snow-capped Andean peaks, **BARILOCHE** has its breathtaking setting to thank for its status as one of Argentina's top holiday destinations. Known in full as San Carlos de Bariloche, the town is unabashedly touristy. And while garish souvenir stores, tour agencies, high-rise hotels and chocolate shops do their best to distract passers-by, it is the lake that remains Bariloche's real attention-grabber. At its best when the sun is reflecting off a placid, cobalt-blue surface, the lake can rapidly transform into a tempestuous sea, lashing icy wind through the streets, sending every warm-blooded being indoors to huddle around a pot of cheese fondue.

Bariloche's forte is as an **outdoor adventure** hub. The town's proximity to the lakes, mountains, forests and rivers of Parque Nacional Nahuel Huapi makes it one of the top spots in the country for whitewater rafting, kayaking, paragliding, mountain biking, trekking and climbing. Come winter, the fun shifts to the nearby pistes of Cerro Catedral (see p.140). Plenty of people also come to Bariloche simply to kick up their heels, including, every **January and February**, busloads of overexcited final year secondary school students. To avoid the crowds, come in **spring or autumn**.

What to see and do

Bariloche's heart is its **Centro Cívico**, a spacious plaza with splendid lake views dominated by an equestrian statue of a defeated-looking General Roca. Forming a horseshoe around the square are a set of attractive, mid-twentieth-century public buildings constructed of local timber and green-grey stone, a collaboration between Ernesto de Estrada and famed Argentinian architect Alejandro Bustillo, whose work can be

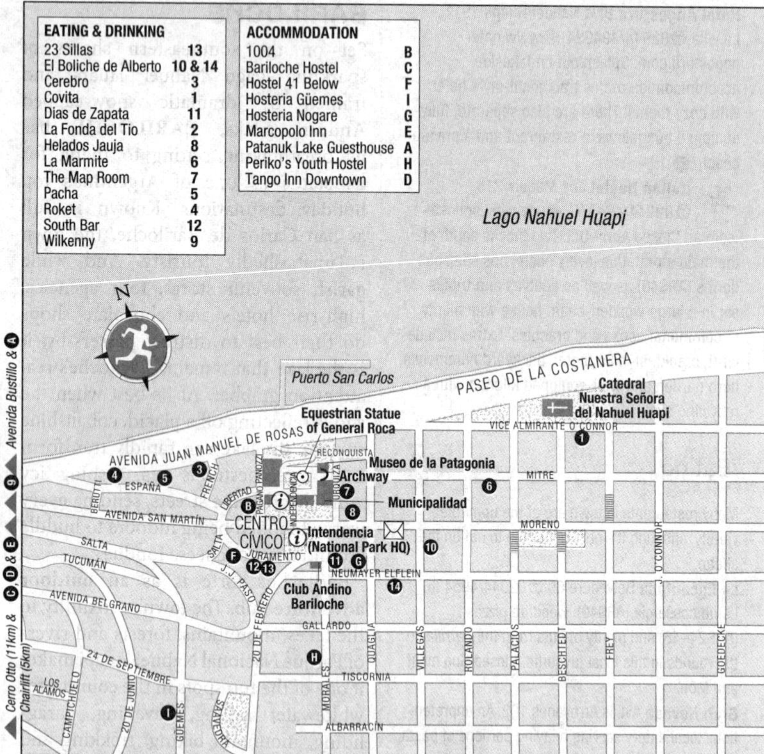

appreciated throughout much of the Lake District. Within these buildings is the **Museo de la Patagonia** (Mon–Fri 10am–12.30pm & 2–7pm, Sat 10am–5pm, closed Sun; AR$3), which does an exemplary job of tracing the area's Mapuche and European history. Bariloche's main drag, **Calle Mitre**, runs east of the plaza.

In the height of summer, you might be tempted to dip a toe beneath the lake's frosty surface; the most popular **beach** is rocky Playa Bonita, 8km west of town (buses #10, #20, #21 or #22), or for a warmer and more secluded dip, head 13km southeast to Villa Los Coihues on Lago Gutiérrez (buses #41 or #50).

For the most camera-battery-depleting 360-degree **views** in the region, catch a local bus (#10, #20 or #22) west of Bariloche to Avenida Bustillo Km 18 and take the chairlift (AR$20) or poorly marked trail (thirty minutes' steep walk) to the lookout at **Cerro Campanario**. Grab a beverage in the café and spend an hour or two drinking in the scenery.

Arrival and information

Air The airport (☎02944/426162 or 405016) lies 14km east of the centre. Local bus #72 runs into town every couple of hours; a taxi or *remise* will set you back around AR$25.

Bus and train The bus terminal (☎02944/432860) and train station (☎02944/423172) lie next to each other, a couple of kilometres east of the centre. Local buses #10, #20 and #21 run into town along C Moreno; a taxi to the Centro Cívico costs around AR$11.

Club Andino Bariloche 20 de Febrero 30 ☎02944/527966, Ⓔinfo@activepatagonia.com.ar; Dec–Feb 9am–9pm, rest of year 9am–1pm &

4.30–8.30pm. Sells maps and has information on hikes and *refugios* in Parque Nacional Nahuel Huapi. Also arranges minibus transfers to Pampa Linda, the trailhead for the hike to Refugio Otto Meiling and Ventisquero Negro (Black Glacier).

Intendencia del Parque Nacional Nahuel Huapi Av San Martín 24 Mon–Fri 9am–3pm, Sat & Sun 9am–6pm; ⓣ02944/423111, ⓦwww.nahuelhuapi.gov.ar. Pick up official national park pamphlets here.

Tourist office The busy tourist office (Mon–Fri 8am–9pm; ⓣ02944/429850, ⓦwww.bariloche.gov.ar) is in the Centro Cívico.

Accommodation

Bariloche's accommodation is among the most expensive in Argentina. Bookings are essential in the high season (mid-Dec to Feb and July–Aug). In January and February, the town's high-rise budget hotels are packed with rowdy school-leavers. Many of the cabins and hotels that lie west of town along Avenida Bustillo offer great lake views and are a quieter alternative to staying in town. In recent years, dozens of excellent backpacker hostels have mushroomed in the city centre, all which have kitchens, internet and tour-booking services, although their double rooms are generally overpriced. The closest campground to town is the forested *La Selva Negra*, Av Bustillo Km 2.95 (ⓣ02944/441013; AR$20 per person), with good facilities.

Hostels

1004 San Martín 127 ⓣ02944/432228, ⓦwww.penthouse1004.com.ar. Swan around this penthouse hostel on the tenth floor of an apartment block and gawp at panoramic mountain and lake vistas. Travellers hang out in the mellow living room, or watch the sunset – *vino* in hand – from the balcony. The dorms (AR$40) need a style revamp but are perfectly clean. Breakfast and internet included. ❻

Bariloche Hostel Salta 528 ⓣ02944/425460, ⓦwww.barilochehostel.com.ar. With killer lake views, polished wooden floorboards and slick modern bathrooms, this intimate hostel is a real gem. Dorm beds are AR$40 or treat yourself to one of their luxurious double rooms. Price includes breakfast. 6

Hostel 41 Below Juramento 94 ⓣ02944/436433, ⓦwww.hostel41below.com. A chilled, Kiwi-owned hostel with 24 beds, friendly staff and quality music grooving in its common area. Most dorms (AR$45) and doubles have partial lake views. The owner also rents rooms in luxury apartments (7), a good option for couples. 6

Marcopolo Inn Salta 422 ⓣ02944/400105, ⓦwww.marcopoloinn.com.ar. This seventy-bed hostel scores brownie points for its free dinners and tasteful travel photography on the walls. All dorms (AR$55) and doubles have en suites and some enjoy lake views. Hook up with other travellers in the bar,over a game of pool or in the TV room. Breakfast included. Discounts for HI members. 6

Periko's Youth Hostel Morales 555 ⓣ02944/522326, ⓦwww.perikos.com Recharge at this earthy log cabin with a big backyard swinging with hammocks. The four- and six-bed dorms (AR$40) have ensuites and there are four bright doubles. Includes breakfast. 6

Tango Inn Downtown Salta 514 ⓣ02944/400004, ⓦwww.tangoinn.com A four-storey mega-hostel with stupendous lake views and a Jacuzzi. Those in the comfortable dorms (AR$55) can settle for en suites, big breakfasts and lounge with wide-screen TV. Discounts for HI members. 6

Hotels

Hostería Güemes Güemes 715 ⓣ02944/424785. Some of the rooms at this welcoming guesthouse have private bathrooms and you can cozy up by the living room fire. Breakfast included. 6

Hostería Nogare Elflein 58 ⓣ02944/422438, ⓦwww.hosterianogare.com.ar A welcoming, central budget hotel, with five pleasant blue-and-white rooms with cable TV. Internet is included as is a hearty breakfast. 5

Patanuk Lake Guesthouse Juan Manuel de Rosas 585 ⓣ02944/434991, ⓦwww.patanuk.com Right on the lake, this new guesthouse has its own private pebble beach, a bar, and Spanish owners who'll go the extra mile. The spacious six-bed dorms (AR$50) enjoy gorgeous views and the doubles have private bathrooms. Breakfast included and bicycles for rent. 7

Eating

Between its decadent chocolate shops and first-rate restaurants, expect to leave Bariloche carrying a few extra pounds.

23 Sillas 20 de Febrero. Healthy, scrumptious *and* vegetarian-friendly, this intimate café does good omelettes, crêpes, salads, whole-wheat sandwiches and quiches. The freshly squeezed juices (AR$9) are the perfect antidote to the night before. Good book exchange too. Breakfast and lunch only.

El Boliche de Alberto Elflein 158 (ⓣ02944/434568), Villegas 347 (ⓣ02944/431433) and Bustillo 8800 (ⓣ02944/462285); ⓦwww.elbolichedealberto.com. Make a glutton of yourself at a branch of the town's best *parrilla*. An artery-clogging *bife de chorizo* is AR$30.

Covita Vice Alte O'Connor 511 ⓣ02944/421708. A vegetarian-friendly restaurant that does gourmet versions of Asian staples like sushi (AR$19), Pad Thai (AR$18) and fish curries (AR$28). Closed Mon.

Dias de Zapata Morales 362 ⓣ02944/423128. This colourful Mexican-owned Mexican restaurant serves mains (AR$25–30) as delicious as they are generous. Arrive before 9pm for cheap cocktails and to skip the queues.

La Fonda del Tío Mitre 1330 ⓣ02944/435011. Packed to the fluorescent-lit rafters with ravenous locals, this unpretentious, economical diner does outstanding versions of Argentinian staples (beef, *milanesas* and pastas). The set meal is a steal at AR$18.

Helados Jauja Moreno 18. In a country hardly lacking in superb ice-creameries, this gem still manages to stand out a mile. The range of berry and *dulce de leche* flavours are heavenly. AR$4 for a small cone.

La Marmite Mitre 329 ⓣ02944/423685. An old-fashioned joint that's a bit of a wallet-sapper, but pulls in crowds for its cheese fondue (AR$60 for two). Closed Sun lunch.

Drinking and nightclubs

Exhaustion after a day on the slopes/rapids/trails leaves many travellers tucked into bed by 10pm, but those with more energy can enjoy any number of knees-up **bars** and **after-midnight** action in the three lakeside discos *Cerebro* (Av Juan Manuel de Rosas 406), *Roket* (Av Juan Manuel de Rosas 424) and *Pacha* (España 415).

The Map Room Urquiza 248 ⓣ02944/456856. Adorned with maps from around the world, this dimly-lit gastropub does a mean salad, super sandwiches and hearty American breakfasts. Pints are AR$10. Closed Sun.

South Bar Juramento 30 ⓣ02944/522001. Locals and tourists alike pack this down-to-earth Irish bar to chew the fat and swill AR$8 pints. If the mood takes, the tables are moved aside for a bit of late-night dancing.

Wilkenny San Martín 435 ⓣ02944-424444. A meat-market Irish bar with a big dancefloor that gets very lively in the small hours. Regular live music and extortionate drink prices (AR$14 for a pint of beer).

Shopping

Bookshops Cultura Librería, Elflein 74, stocks some English language books.
Chocolate shops C Mitre has numerous chocolate shops (some the size of supermarkets) selling row upon mouthwatering row of gourmet chocolate. Mamuschka, Mitre 216 (ⓣ02944/423-294, ⓦwww.mamuschka.com), usually has plenty of samples on the counter.
Markets The bustling Feria de Artesanos is held daily behind the Centro Cívico on Urquiza between Mitre and Moreno, and sells locally made crafts.

Directory

Car rental Avis, San Martín 162 (ⓣ02944/431648, ⓦwww.andesrentacar.com.ar); Budget, Mitre 717 (ⓣ02944/422482, ⓦwww.budgetbariloche.com.ar).
Hospital Moreno 601 ⓣ02944/426100.
Police Centro Cívico ⓣ02944/422772.
Post office Moreno 175.
Spanish school ECELA, Pasaje Gutiérrez 843 (ⓣ02944/428935, ⓦwww.ecela.com), offers private and group classes (max six people).
Tour operators Aguas Blancas, Morales 564 (ⓣ02944/432799, ⓦwww.aguasblancas.com.ar), run rafting excursions; Bike Cordillera at Av Bustillo Km 18.6 (ⓣ02944/524828) rent bicycles; Overland Patagonia (ⓣ02944/456327, ⓦwww.overlandpatagonia.com) offer a range of backpacker-friendly excursions, including a four-day Ruta 40 trip to El Calafate. Turisur, Mitre 219 (ⓣ02944/426-109, ⓦwww.bariloche.com/turisur) specialise in boat trips; Pura Vida (ⓣ02944/400327) offer kayaking trips on the lake.

Moving on

Air to: Buenos Aires (6-8 daily; 2hr); El Calafate (daily; 1hr 45min); Esquel (2-3 weekly; 30min); Mar de Plata (1 weekly; 35min). There are also seasonal flights to Córdoba, Mendoza, Puerto Madryn and Trelew as well as direct international flights to a number of cities in Brazil and Chile. Airlines with offices in town include Aerolíneas Argentinas, Mitre 185 (ⓣ02944/433304, ⓦwww.aerolineasargentinas.com); LAN, Mitre 534 (ⓣ02944/427755, ⓦwww.lanchile.com); and LADE, Villegas 480 (ⓣ02944/423562, ⓦwww.lade.com.ar).
Boat Catedral Turismo, Palacios 263 (ⓣ02944/425444, ⓦwww.crucedelagos.com), organize boat crossings from Bariloche to Puerto Montt in Chile (see p.491; Sept–April; 12hr; US$170). The scenic journey, known as the Cruce Internacional de los Lagos (Three Lakes Crossing) cruises lagos Huapi, Frieas and Todos Los Santos with the overland segments traversed by bus. Optional overnight stops at Puerto Blest and Peulla.
Bus to: Buenos Aires (8 daily; 20hr); El Bolsón (14 daily; 2hr); El Calafate (4 weekly; 34hr); Esquel (15 daily; 4hr 30min); Mendoza (2 daily, 18hr); Puerto Madryn (2 daily; 12hr); Puerto Montt in Chile (2 daily; 6hr) with onward connections to Santiago de Chile; San Martín de Los Andes (5 daily; 3hr 30min) and Villa La Angostura (hourly; 1hr 30min).
Train The Tren Patagónico (ⓣ02944/422450, ⓦwww.trenpatagonico.com.ar) runs twice weekly from Bariloche to Viedma (18hr).

DAY-TRIPS FROM BARILOCHE

Being Argentina's outdoor adventure capital, most day-trips from Bariloche involve conquering – or at least ogling – the mountains, rivers and lakes on its doorstep. Outside the winter months, when **skiing** at **Cerro Catedral** reigns supreme, the most popular excursions are cycling or driving the scenic **Circuito Chico** route (see p.140), **whitewater rafting** on the class III-IV Río Manson some 80km southwest of Bariloche, and hiking in **Parque Nacional Nahuel Huapi** (see p.140). Local tour outfitters also offer kayaking, kitesurfing, windsurfing, scuba diving, horseriding, canyoning, rock climbing, mountain-biking, parapenting, scenic flights, bus tours on the Ruta de Los Siete Lagos (see box, p.134) and boating trips. Meanwhile, shopaholics and beer-lovers will find their spiritual home 123km south of Bariloche in the alternative lifestyle town of **El Bolsón**, where the outstanding **feria artesanal** (every Tues, Thurs and Sat), sells locally crafted wares and food. Afterwards, sample a pint of the local brew at **Cervecería El Bolsón**, RN258 Km 124 (Ⓣ02944/492595, Ⓦwww.cervezaselbolson.com), or stay on in the valley for exemplary hiking in the surrounding mountains.

Circuito Chico

The **CIRCUITO CHICO**, a 65km road circuit heading west of Bariloche along the shores of Lago Nahuel Huapi, is an essential day excursion. It can be explored by bike (5–7hr), hire car, mini-bus tour (4hr) or by catching a public bus and jumping on and off wherever you fancy. The first photo stop en route is the luxurious, mountain-framed **Llao Llao Hotel** at Km 25 along Avenida Bustillo (Ⓣ02944/448530, Ⓦwww.llaollao.com; ⑨), an alpine-style creation by architect Alejandro Bustillo. Non-guests can feast on pastries at the hotel's decadent afternoon tea (4–7.30pm; AR$75).

Just after the turn-off for the *Llao Llao* is **Puerto Pañuelo** where boats leave for leisure trips to Puerto Blest, Isla Victoria and the Parque Nacional Los Arrayanes (see p.134). Beyond here the traffic dissipates and the circuit follows an undulating road flanked by thick forest. The scenery is superb, with worthwhile stops at **Villa Tacul**, **Lago Escondido**, **Bahia López** and **Punto Panorámico**, the latter offering the most recognized postcard shot of the region. For a detour, the pretty Swiss village of **Colonia Suiza** offers an enjoyable opportunity for a lunch or afternoon tea break. **Cycling** the circuit allows the flexibility to leave the main road and ride along forested trails to hidden beaches and lakes. As traffic is heavy along the first 20km stretch west of Bariloche, it is best to take a bus (#10, #20 or #22) from downtown to Av Bustillo Km 18.6, where Bike Cordillera (Ⓣ02944/524828) rent bicycles for AR$45 a day. To see the circuit by **public bus**, take #20 along the lakeshore for *Llao Llao* and Puerto Pañuelo or #10 inland for Colonia Suiza. In summer, #11 does the entire circuit.

Cerro Catedral

Named for a summit (2405m) that resembles the spires of a Gothic cathedral, **CERRO CATEDRAL** (Ⓣ02944/409000, Ⓦwww.catedralaltapatagonia.com; mid-June to Oct) is one of South America's top ski resorts, offering bedazzling lake and cordillera views, more than fifty runs, forty lifts and descents of up to nine-kilometres-long. The village of **Villa Catedral**, just twenty kilometres south of Bariloche, lies at the base of the mountain and has hotels, restaurants and ski hire shops. When the snow melts, Cerro Catedral stays open for trekking and a cable car and chairlift provide access to **Refugio Lynch** (1870m; AR$40 dorm bed per night) from where trails lead to *Refugio San Martín* or *Refugio Frey*. Mountain biking, rappelling and horseriding are other popular summertime activities on the mountain. Buses marked "Catedral" leave from Moreno 470 in Bariloche.

PARQUE NACIONAL NAHUEL HUAPI

Spanning a whopping 7050 square kilometres, the magnificent **PARQUE NACIONAL NAHUEL HUAPI** (Ⓦwww.nahuelhuapi.gov.ar) is deservedly Argentinian Patagonia's most visited national park. It incorporates the tourist towns of Villa La Angostura and Bariloche, and takes in **Lago Nahuel Huapi**, a 557-square-kilometre sapphire-blue glacial lake flanked by forest-quilted slopes and garnished with islands and peninsulas. In the park's wild heart lie forests of cypress and beech trees, crystal-clear rivers, cascading waterfalls, lupin-filled meadows, ancient craggy glaciers and formidable snow-capped summits. Nahuel Huapi's crown is **Cerro Tronador**, an extinct volcano whose three icy peaks (around 3500m)

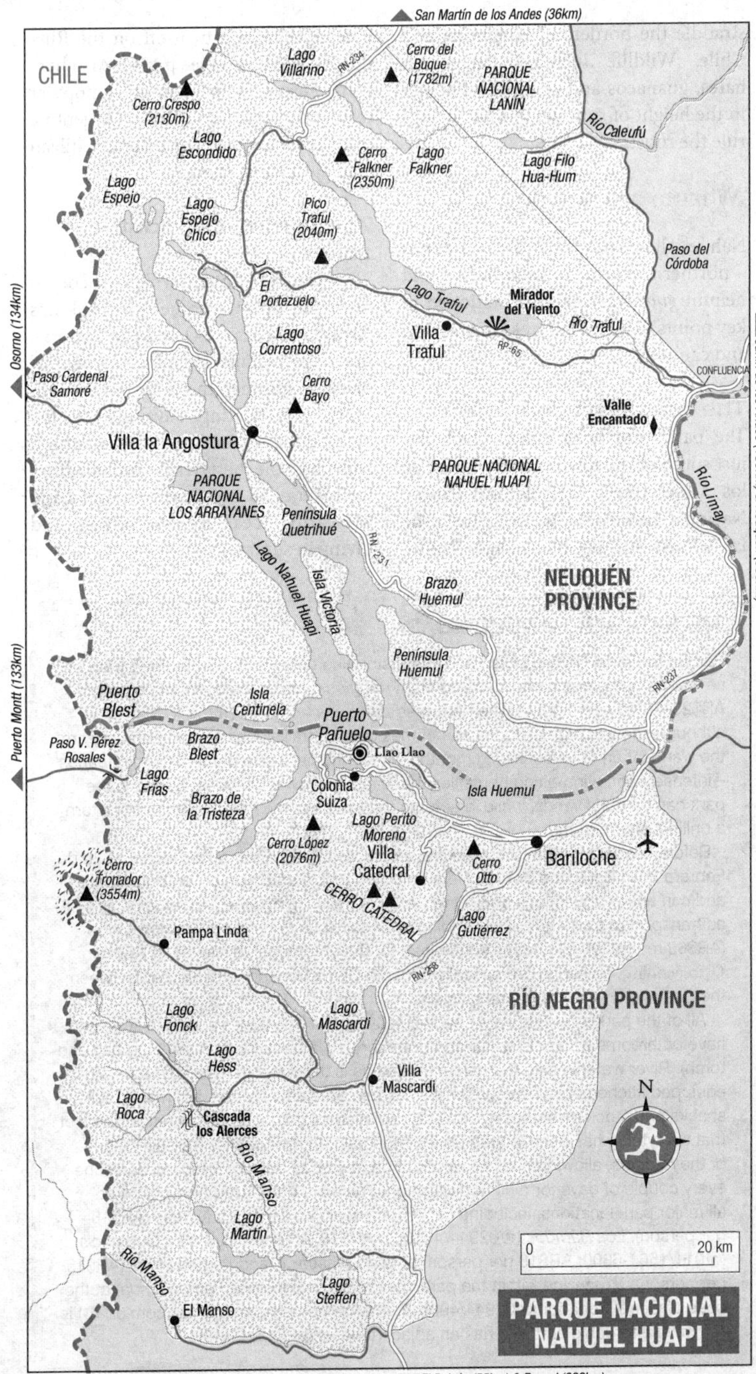
San Martín de los Andes (36km)
CHILE
Lago Villarino
RN-234
Cerro del Buque (1782m)
PARQUE NACIONAL LANÍN
Cerro Crespo (2130m)
Río Caleufú
Lago Escondido
Cerro Falkner (2350m)
Lago Falkner
Lago Filo Hua-Hum
Lago Espejo
Lago Espejo Chico
Pico Traful (2040m)
Paso del Córdoba
El Portezuelo
Lago Traful
Mirador del Viento
Villa Traful
Río Traful
Osorno (134km)
Lago Correntoso
RP-65
CONFLUENCIA
Paso Cardenal Samoré
Cerro Bayo
Valle Encantado
Villa la Angostura
PARQUE NACIONAL NAHUEL HUAPI
PARQUE NACIONAL LOS ARRAYANES
Península Quetrihué
Río Limay
RN-231
Lago Nahuel Huapi
Isla Victoria
Brazo Huemul
NEUQUÉN PROVINCE
Junín de los Andes (130km) & Neuquén (350km)
Península Huemul
Puerto Montt (133km)
Puerto Blest
Isla Centinela
RN-237
Puerto Pañuelo
Paso V. Pérez Rosales
Brazo Blest
Llao Llao
Lago Frías
Colonia Suiza
Isla Huemul
Brazo de la Tristeza
Lago Perito Moreno
Cerro López (2076m)
Villa Catedral
Cerro Otto
Bariloche
Cerro Tronador (3554m)
CERRO CATEDRAL
Lago Gutiérrez
Pampa Linda
RN-258
RÍO NEGRO PROVINCE
Lago Fonck
Lago Mascardi
Lago Hess
Villa Mascardi
N
Lago Roca
Cascada los Alerces
Río Manso
Lago Martín
0
20 km
Río Manso
Lago Steffen
El Manso
PARQUE NACIONAL NAHUEL HUAPI
El Bolsón (55km) & Esquel (222km)

straddle the borders of Argentina and Chile. Wildlife includes Patagonian hares, guanacos and condors, although in the height of summer, human beings rule the roost.

What to see and do

Nahuel Huapi has three distinct **zones** – northern, central and southern – and helpful *guardaparques* are stationed at key points to advise on trekking, fishing and camping.

The northern zone

The park's **northern zone**, which lies just south of the town of San Martín de los Andes (see p.131), adjoins Parque Nacional Lanín (see p.129). This zone is defined by sky-blue Lago Traful, accessible from a turn-off on the Ruta de los Siete Lagos (see p.134). Also here is the Paso Cardenal Samoré, a popular overland pass into Chile (Argentine immigration open 8am–8pm; Chilean side open 8am–7pm).

The central and southern zones

The **central zone**, which incorporates the pretty Parque Nacional Los Arrayanes (see p.134) and Isla Victoria, has Lago Nahuel Huapi as its centrepiece. In summer, this zone buzzes with tourists on boating, kayaking, cycling and hiking excursions. The southern zone has the best trails and facilities for hikers and is focused around **Lago Mascardi**, ideal for swimming and diving in summer.

TREKKING IN NAHUEL HUAPI

Parque Nacional Nahuel Huapi has an outstanding network of well-marked trails as well as numerous campsites and eight *refugios* (basic staffed mountain huts, AR$25–30) to overnight in. The **hiking season** runs from December to March, although snow at high altitudes sometimes cuts off trails. January and February are the warmest and busiest hiking months, although this is also prime time for *tábanos* – intensely annoying biting horseflies that infest the lower altitudes. Spring in the park can be quite windy, while in autumn the leaves of the *ñire* and *lenga* trees turn a brilliant shade of red.

Before heading for the hills, trekkers should visit **Club Andino Bariloche**, at 20 de Febrero 30 in Bariloche (p.135). Here, knowledgeable staff give out trekking maps and can answer questions about the status of trails, campsites and *refugios* as well as transport to trailheads. Club Andino offer daily bus transfers to **Pampa Linda** (AR$60 return), 90 kilometres southwest, for the unforgettable hike to **Refugio Otto Meiling**, cowering dramatically beneath Cerro Tronador and nestled between the Castaño Overa and Alerce glaciers.

All of the park's **refugios** are spectacularly sited in the park's southern zone and have bathrooms with cold water and dormitory-style beds (bring a sleeping bag and torch). River water is safe to drink untreated as is the water from *refugio* taps. Fully equipped kitchens can be used for a small fee. Staff also prepare hot meals, sell snacks and stock an impressive selection of alcohol, although prices reflect the fact that everything has been lugged up the mountain on their backs. Trails link many of the *refugios*, allowing hikers to embark on multi-day treks or return to Bariloche every couple of days for a hit of civilization. There are authorized **campsites** at all major park locations, including *Lago Roca* near Cascada Los Alerces (AR$18 per person), *Los Rápidos* (T 02944/461861; AR$18 per person) and *La Querencia* (T 011/1561-6300; AR$18 per person) at Lago Mascardi, and *Pampa Linda* (AR$15 per person). **Hosterías** within the park are expensive; *Hostería Pampa Linda*, at the base of Cerro Tronador (T 02944/490517, W www.hosteriapampalinda.com.ar; 8) is the most affordable and also has an adjacent basic *refugio* (4).

ESQUEL

Cowboys and urban sophisticates should feel equally at home in **ESQUEL**, the main town in northern Chubut province. Some 340km south of Bariloche, Esquel means "bog" in the Mapuche language, a name which says nothing of the town's arresting mountainous backdrop. Although Esquel is often relegated to a snack-and-snooze stop en route to Bariloche or Chile, the town makes a perfect base for the lush **Parque Nacional Los Alerces** and for riding the historic **Old Patagonian Express** steam train. Other local drawcards include the Welsh settlement of **Trevelin**, 23km south, and in winter, the ski resort of **La Hoya** (Ⓣ02945/451315), 13km northeast, where there are 22 kilometres of runs, plenty of off-piste skiing and a season that often extends into early October.

Arrival and information

Air Esquel's airport is 21km east of town; Urielito offer airport minibus transfers (Ⓣ02945/155-0830; AR$12).

Bus The bus terminal (Ⓣ02945/451584) lies eight blocks from the town centre on the corner of A.P. Justo and Av Alvear, the main street.

Club Andino Esquel Staff at the Club Andino office at Pellegrini 757 (Mon–Fri 5am–9pm; Ⓣ02945/453248) can provide information on hiking and camping in Parque Nacional Los Alerces.

Tourist office The tourist office is at Av Alvear and Sarmiento (Jan & Feb 7am–11pm, March–Dec 8am–10pm; Ⓣ02945/451927, Ⓦwww.esquel.gov.ar).

Train The *La Trochita* train station (see box, p.134) is at Roggero and Brun.

Accommodation

Esquel has plenty of budget accommodation and there's usually no need to book ahead.

Campers will love *El Hogar de Mochilero* (Ⓣ02945/452166), two blocks northwest of the centre at Roca 1028, with an endearing white statue of a backpacker out front. You can set up your tent (AR$10) in the big leafy garden or crash out in one of the beds in the rustic dormitory (AR$15). There's also a kitchen and common area.

Casa del Pueblo San Martín 661 Ⓣ02945/450581, Ⓦwww.epaadventure.com.ar. This colourful HI hostel has a big kitchen and a garden that lends itself to late-night jam sessions. The dorms (AR$35) are modest and the shared toilets cramped. ❺

Lago Verde Volta 1081 Ⓣ02945/452251, Ⓦwww.patagonia-verde.com.ar. A quiet family home with small but clean rooms and a cute garden. ❹

Planeta Hostel Av Alvear 2833 Ⓣ02945/456846, Ⓦwww.planetahostel.com. A hostel with delightful owners, wacky artistic touches, an indoor climbing wall and a bright little kitchen. The dorm beds (AR$35) are just what the chiropractor ordered and there's one tiny double room. Internet and breakfast included. ❹

Eating and drinking

La Barra Sarmiento 638 Ⓣ02945/454321. The best *parrilla* in town, serving big juicy slabs of *lomo* in a relaxed setting (try their home-made mayonnaise). Mains around AR$15.

Fitzroya Pizza Rivadavia 1048 Ⓣ02945/450512. Cheesy pizzas loaded with creative toppings such as broccoli, salmon and trout (AR$18–24) are delivered piping hot by effervescent staff.

Moe Bar Rivadavia 873. Cocktails and good music are the orders of the night at this boisterous drinking hole with half a yellow car protruding from its entrance. Tend to your hunger pangs with one of their tasty pizzas (AR$15–24).

La Tour D'Argent San Martín 1063 Ⓣ02945/454612. Pastas and chicken dishes are some of the filling staples on the well-priced tourist menu; or tuck into fancier *à la carte* options, such as trout with a variety of appetizing sauces (AR$35). Closed Tues.

Moving on

Air to: Bariloche (2–3 weekly; 30min); Buenos Aires (1 daily Mon–Sat; 3hr); and occasional services to Puerto Madryn.

Bus to: Bariloche (15 daily; 4hr 30min); Comodoro Rivadavia (5 daily; 9hr); El Bolsón (15 daily; 2hr 30min); El Calafate (1 daily; 29hr); El Chaltén (1 daily; 26hr); Futaleufú in Chile (Jan & Feb 2 daily 3 times a week; rest of year 2 daily twice a week; 2hr); Mendoza (2 daily: 24hr).

THE OLD PATAGONIAN EXPRESS

Puffing and chugging its way across the arid Andean foothills at around 30kph, the **Old Patagonian Express** is both a museum on wheels and a classic South American train journey. Affectionately known as "*La Trochita*" ("narrow gauge" in Spanish), the locomotive's tracks are a mere 75cm wide. The historic steam train opened in 1945 and did its time transporting wool from *estancias* to markets as well as providing a lifeline for locals living in isolated, windswept communities. Immortalized in Paul Theroux's 1979 train travel novel *The Old Patagonian Express*, La Trochita these days is little more than a tourist train and the scaling back of the line in recent years has rendered the trip a rather twee, toy-train type experience. Passengers pile into antique wooden coaches for half-day tours from Esquel to Nahuel Pan, 22km away (Jan–mid-Feb Mon–Sat 10am & 2pm; rest of Feb Mon–Sat 10am; March & April Tues & Fri 10am; May–Dec Wed 10am; 3hr; AR$50; further information on ⓣ02945/451403, ⓦwww.latrochita.org.ar). Peering out the window, you might spot guanacos, rheas and hares.

As an **alternative route**, *La Trochita* also chuffs the 38km between El Maitén and Norquinco (Jan–March Tues & Fri 11am; Wed, Thurs & Sat 3pm, ⓣ02945/495190), lurching past the *Estancia Leleque*, owned by Italian clothing mogul Benetton. El Maitén is 130km northeast of Esquel and can be reached three times weekly by a bus.

Occasionally, the train makes the 165km journey all the way from Esquel to El Maitén, where there is a museum and railway workshops.

PARQUE NACIONAL LOS ALERCES

PARQUE NACIONAL LOS ALERCES, 40 kilometres west of Esquel, encompasses 2,630 square kilometres of gorgeous, glacial-carved Andean landscape. Although far less visited than Parque Nacional Nahuel Huapi to the north, its network of richly coloured lakes and pristine rivers makes it a prime destination for anglers, while more than a hundred kilometres of hiking trails through verdant forest attract summer hikers and campers.

The *alerce* (or Patagonian cypress) that grows here numbers itself among the oldest living tree species on the planet, with some examples surviving for as long as three thousand years. Sizewise, they're almost comparable to the grand sequoias of California, growing up to seventy metres tall and four metres wide.

What to see and do

Though the *alerce* gives the park its name, the flora is wildly varied: **Valdivian temperate rainforest** thrives in its luxuriant western zone near the Chilean border, which is deluged by around 3000mm of annual rainfall. Elsewhere, incense cedar, bamboo-like *caña colihue*, *arrayán*, *coihue*, *lenga* and southern beech thrive. Most visitors gravitate towards the park's user-friendly and photogenic **northeast sector** where there is a network of four dazzling lakes – **Rivadavia**, **Verde**, **Menéndez** and **Futalaufquen**. The emerald-hued Lago Verde is often the first port of call for day-trekkers and campers. Spilling over from Lago Verde is the **Río Arrayanes**, crossed by a suspension bridge that marks the start of an easy hour-long interpretive loop walk.

One main dusty, bumpy road (the RP71) runs through Los Alerces. Public transport is scarce outside peak season, so a vehicle is recommended;

otherwise, hikers need to walk along the road between trails, enduring clouds of body-coating dust from passing cars and trucks. Some hikes, including the trek to the summit of Cerro Alto El Dedal (1916m), require registration with a *guardaparque* first. The most popular day excursion is the **boat** trip leaving from either Puerto Limonao (3km north of the *Intendencia*) or Puerto Chucao (halfway around the Lago Verde/Río Arrayanes loop trail), crossing Lago Menéndez to visit **El Abuelo** (The Grandfather), a 57m-high *alerce* estimated to be more than 2600 years old. Tours with English-speaking guides can be booked through tour operators in Esquel.

Arrival and information

Park entrance is AR$20. The **Intendencia** (open daily 8am–1pm; ⓣ02945/471020) is at **Villa Futalaufquen**, a village with a smattering of shops, public telephones, eateries and accommodation options. A **museum** and **visitors' centre** here (daily Jan–Easter 8am–9pm, Easter–Nov 9am–4pm; ⓣ02945/471015) can provide information on camping, park accommodation, hiking and fishing (and sells fishing permits). The RP71 is the main road through the park and is usually accessible year-round, although occasionally blocked by snow in winter. Peak season is January and February, when Transportes Esquel (ⓣ02945/453529, AR$9 one-way) runs buses to the park three times daily; it takes three bumpy hours to reach Lago Verde. Autumn colours illuminate the park in March and April, while in the spring (Oct and Nov) the winds can be treacherous. Fishing season is from mid-November to Easter.

CROSSING INTO CHILE

Esquel is well-placed for crossing into Chilean Patagonia, with several buses weekly making the two-hour trip to the settlement of Futaleufú, where there is excellent whitewater rafting on its namesake river. A bus leaves Esquel (travelling south via Trevelin) twice daily three times a week in January and February, and twice daily two times a week the rest of the year. At the Chilean border (immigration open Jan & Feb 8am–9pm, rest of year 8am–8pm), passengers transfer to a minibus for the final 10km leg to Futaleufú.

Accommodation

A number of *cabañas*, *hosterías* and campsites lie within the park, including pricey **lodges** that cater for anglers. *Hostería Futalaufquen* (ⓣ02945/471008; ⑥; closed Easter–Sept) is a granite-and-log Bustillo creation, 4km north of the *Intendencia* on the western shores of Lago Futalaufquen. There are a dozen free **campsites** with no facilities at all, three basic campsites with cold-water bathrooms (AR$10) and five organized campgrounds (AR$14-25) with hot water, gas and electricity. The closest campsite to Villa Futalaufquen is *Los Maitenes* (ⓣ02945/471006; AR$16), 400m from the *Intendencia*. Other organized campsites are at Lago Futalaufquen, Bahía Rosales, Lago Verde and Lago Rivadavia.

Patagonia

Lonely, windswept and studded with glaciers, **PATAGONIA** conjures up an undeniable mystique, a place where pioneers, outlaws, writers and naturalists have long come in search of open space and wild adventure. And while Argentina's southernmost chunk is now an established destination for the summer tourist hordes, you'll hardly care. Whether standing on a beach watching orcas feast on baby elephant seals or strapped into crampons on the Southern Patagonian Icecap, you'll find Patagonia still has its mojo.

For those short on time, domestic flights offer a way to hop between Patagonia's key attractions, but to truly appreciate the region's vastness, it is best to travel overland – by bus, 4WD or bicycle. After hundreds of kilometres of desolate steppe, nothing quite bedazzles like the sight of serrated

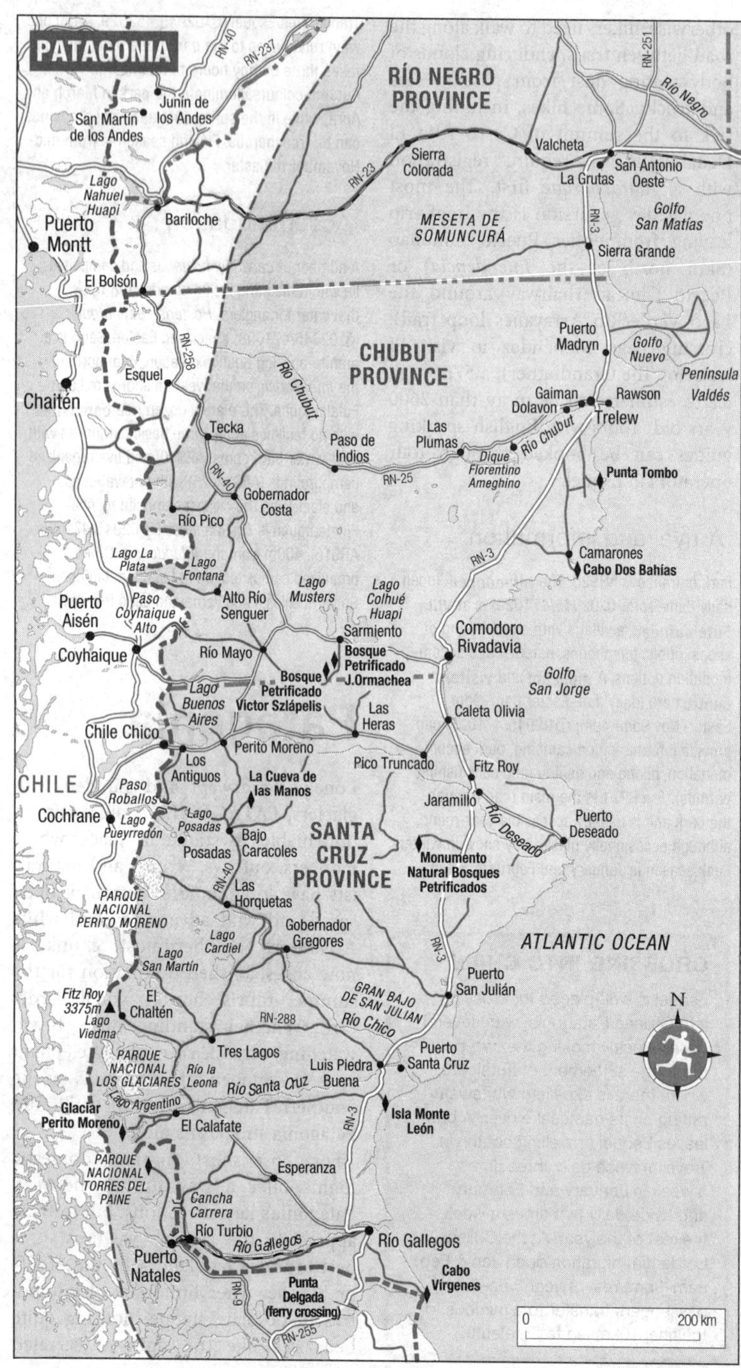
PATAGONIA
RÍO NEGRO PROVINCE
CHUBUT PROVINCE
SANTA CRUZ PROVINCE
CHILE
ATLANTIC OCEAN
MESETA DE SOMUNCURÁ
Junín de los Andes
San Martín de los Andes
Lago Nahuel Huapi
Bariloche
Puerto Montt
El Bolsón
Esquel
Chaitén
Tecka
Paso de Indios
Las Plumas
Gobernador Costa
Río Pico
Lago La Plata
Lago Fontana
Alto Río Senguer
Lago Musters
Lago Colhué Huapi
Sarmiento
Puerto Aisén
Paso Coyhaique Alto
Coyhaique
Río Mayo
Bosque Petrificado J.Ormachea
Bosque Petrificado Victor Szlápelis
Lago Buenos Aires
Las Heras
Chile Chico
Los Antiguos
Perito Moreno
Pico Truncado
La Cueva de las Manos
Paso Roballos
Cochrane
Lago Pueyrredón
Lago Posadas
Posadas
Bajo Caracoles
Las Horquetas
PARQUE NACIONAL PERITO MORENO
Lago Cardiel
Gobernador Gregores
Lago San Martín
Fitz Roy 3375m
El Chaltén
Lago Viedma
Tres Lagos
PARQUE NACIONAL LOS GLACIARES
Río la Leona
Río Santa Cruz
Lago Argentino
Glaciar Perito Moreno
El Calafate
PARQUE NACIONAL TORRES DEL PAINE
Esperanza
Cancha Carrera
Río Turbio
Río Gallegos
Puerto Natales
Punta Delgada (ferry crossing)
Cabo Vírgenes
Sierra Colorada
Valcheta
San Antonio Oeste
La Grutas
Río Negro
Golfo San Matías
Sierra Grande
Puerto Madryn
Golfo Nuevo
Península Valdés
Gaiman
Dolavon
Rawson
Trelew
Río Chubut
Dique Florentino Ameghino
Punta Tombo
Camarones
Cabo Dos Bahías
Comodoro Rivadavia
Golfo San Jorge
Caleta Olivia
Fitz Roy
Jaramillo
Río Deseado
Puerto Deseado
Monumento Natural Bosques Petrificados
Puerto San Julián
GRAN BAJO DE SAN JULIAN
Río Chico
Puerto Santa Cruz
Luis Piedra Buena
Isla Monte León
RN-40
RN-237
RN-23
RN-251
RN-3
RN-258
RN-25
RN-288
RN-9
RN-255
N
0
200 km

ESTANCIAS EN PATAGONIA

Patagonia's empty steppe is speckled with isolated *estancias*, many of which open their doors to visitors. While most cater for high-end tourists, others are more modest and allow camping in their grounds. Good examples include *Estancia Telken* (see p.153), near Perito Moreno, *Estancia La Quinta*, 5km south of El Chaltén (see p.158), and *Estancia Menelik* (p.154). Contact Estancias de Santa Cruz in Buenos Aires (Viamonte 920, 5th floor, office H; ⓣ011/5237-4043, ⓦwww.estanciasdesantacruz.com) for bookings and a comprehensive list of *estancias* in Patagonia.

Andean peaks rising up on the horizon like a Gothic mirage.

Two main arteries traverse Patagonia. The RN40, a bone-rattling, mostly unpaved road, parallels the Andes and links some of Patagonia's major sights: the ten thousand-year-old rock art of the **Cueva de las Manos Pintadas,** the Fitz Roy sector of **Parque Nacional Los Glaciares** around the village of El Chaltén, and the **Perito Moreno** and **Upsala** glaciers in the park's southern sector, both easy day-trips from El Calafate. To the east, the RN3 loosely traces the Atlantic seaboard, passing the town of **Puerto Madryn**, a launching pad for the marine wildlife-rich shores of **Península Valdés**, before heading south to the Welsh heartland of **Trelew**, a short jump to the continent's largest penguin colony at **Punto Tombo**. December to February are the warmest months to visit Patagonia, but to avoid the crowds, inflated prices and high winds, March and April are better. Tourism all but grinds to a halt come winter.

PUERTO MADRYN AND PENÍNSULA VALDÉS

Having spent hours travelling through the barren bleakness of the Pampas, you may wonder why you bothered when you first hit **PUERTO MADRYN**. A breezy, sprawling, seaside city of around 76,000 residents clinging to the barren coast of northern Patagonia, it has no obvious tourist attractions. However, its proximity to one of the world's most prolific nature reserves – the **Reserva Faunísta Península Valdés**, seventeen kilometres to the north – makes it an essential stop. Spread over 3600 square kilometres, the Peninsula Valdés is home to a dizzying array of birds and marine life. More than a million Magellanic penguins live here, along with 75 colonies of seas and sea lions, and over two thousand dolphins. Topping even that is a breeding colony of over two thousand southern right whales that can be observed directly from the beach of **Puerto Pirámides**, the only town on the peninsula.

Puerto Madryn itself is easy to get around on foot, and has some fine restaurants overlooking the beach as well as good-value hostels and budget hotels. In addition to tours to the peninsula, it also makes a convenient base from which to explore the nearby Welsh towns of Trelew and Gaiman, with their Welsh teahouses and leafy plazas.

EcoCentro

Located high on the cliffs overlooking the ocean, the **Ecocentro**, Julio Verne 3784 (daily Oct–Dec 3–8pm, Jan & Feb 5–9pm, rest of year Wed–Sun 3–7pm; AR$25; ⓦwww.ecocentro.org.ar, ⓣ02965/457470), promotes research into and conservation of marine life and is a fantastic place to learn a little more about the animals and geography of the area. The three-level building, with stunning views

from the reading room at the top, has permanent interactive exhibitions on Patagonian ecosystems and southern right whales, as well as a changing art exhibition. Just outside the entrance is the skeleton of a whale which stranded itself in 2001. To get here either take a brisk, forty minute walk along the coast to the south of the city or a taxi from the centre of town (AR$10). For more on the local ecosystem, you can also visit the not-quite-so-modern **Museo Provincial de Ciencias Naturales Y Oceanográphico**, back in town at D. Garcia and Menéndez (Mon–Fri 9am–1pm & 3–7pm, Sat & Sun 3–7pm; ☎02965/451139; AR$3), which has nine small rooms with interesting displays including preserved animals, and the complete skeletons of many marine mammals.

Península Valdés

PENINSULA VALDÉS is brimming with life: birds hover in the strong wind, dolphins surf the waves, sea lions bark aggressively. With vast distances between viewing areas and no public transport, much the easiest way to appreciate the place is on a day-trip from Puerto Madryn. You could also rent a car to visit independently, which can be good value if you are travelling in a group, but note that all the roads are dirt tracks and can be a challenge if it has been raining. Either way you'll want to stop in Puerto Pirámides, where you can board a boat to visit the nearby sea lion colony and, in season, see frolicking whales up close. It's an unforgettable experience.

Organized minibus **tours** (10–12 hours, bring lunch and warm clothes) all have much the same itinerary, with minor variations according to the season and weather. First stop, a short drive out of town, is to pay the entrance fee and visit the **information centre**, followed by an impressive lookout over the **Isla de los Pájaros** (Bird Island). Next, across the isthmus on the peninsula proper, you'll stop off in the small resort town of **PUERTO PIRÁMIDES**, where sea-lion- and whale-watching boat trips are offered. In season you can see whales swimming just offshore while you sip coffee in one of the cafés at the end of the beach. From here you head north to **Punto Norte**, at the far tip of the peninsula, to see fat and fuzzy sea lions, elephant seals and penguins sunbathing on the beach; sometimes orcas make an appearance as well. You'll also see penguins up close at **Caleta Valdés**, followed by more elephant seals and dolphins at **Punta Delgada**.

The best tours leave Puerto Madryn early in the morning and cost around AR$150 not including the optional boat trip (AR$80) nor the park entrance (AR$40). Marine life is present all throughout the year but some viewing stations close from Easter to June; optimal viewing is between September and February, but whales can be seen from June to December. A local bus runs a few times a week from the bus station in Puerto Madryn to Puerto Pirámides (AR$7.50), returning the same afternoon; handy if you want to stay out here, but not much use for visiting the peninsula. Check with the tourist office in Puerto Madryn for up-to-date timetables.

TREAT YOURSELF

Like the idea of waking up to the sight of whales at play from your luxury king-size bed? An ocean-facing room at **Las Restingas**, Primera Baja al Mar (☎02965-495101, Ⓦwww.lasrestingas.com, ⑨), on the beach at Puerto Pirámides, could be just the thing. Quadruple rooms offer a cheaper option for groups, and the hotel also has an attractive beachfront restaurant (open to non-guests) serving delicious seafood, with mains starting at AR$28, as well as a heated pool and gym, all with stunning beach views.

Arrival and information

Air Puerto Madryn's airport, Aeropuerto El Tehuelche (☎02965/451909) is 5km west of town. Flamenco tour (☎02965/455505; AR$8) runs into town or a taxi to the centre costs AR$16.. You can also fly into nearby Trelew airport (☎02965/428021), an hour away, which has more scheduled flights. A taxi from there is around AR$90.

Bus The bus terminal is on avenidas Avila and Independencia, four blocks from the centre of town and close to most accommodation.

Tourist office The large tourist office is on Av Roca 223, along the coastal boulevard (daily 8am–10pm; ☎02965/456067, Ⓦwww.madryn.gov.ar/turismo).

Tours

The following companies all do good tours out to **Península Valdés**: Tito Bottazzi, Mitre 80 (☎02965/474110); El Gualicho, Marcos A Zar 480 (☎02965/454163, Ⓦwww.elgualicho.com.ar); Alora Viaggio, Roca 27 (☎02965/455106, Ⓦwww.aloraviaggio.com). For **scuba diving** and **snorkelling** in the area consult Scuba Duba, Brown 893 (☎02965/452699) or Lobo Larsen, Roca 885 (☎02965/470277, Ⓦwww.lobolarsen.com) – a company that offers diving with sea lions.

Accommodation

Most accommodation is close to the centre of town and within walking distance of the bus terminal. It is much cheaper to stay in Puerto Madryn than inside the nature reserve at Puerto Pirámides, but if you prefer the latter, consider one of two good options; *Cabañas del Mar*, Av de las Ballenas, (☎02965/495049, Ⓦwww.piramides.net, ⑨), or *La Nube del Angel*, Segunda Baja (☎02965/495070, Ⓦwww.lanubedelangel.com.ar, ⑨). Both have comfortable cabins for 2 to 6 people, which can be good value for a group. For camping, the best option is the municipal camping site behind the beach in Puerto Pirámides (☎02965/495084), or *Camping El Golfito*, Camino a Loberia Punta Loma not far out of Puerto Madryn (☎02965/454544; from AR$8.50 per person).

Hostels

All hostels listed here include breakfast, internet and use of kitchen. Prices drop greatly outside the January to March high season.

El Gualicho Marcos A Zar 480, ☎02965/454163, www.elgualichohostel.com.ar. The best hostel in town. Warm, cosy six-bed dorms with private bathrooms, plus a large lively common area with wi-fi and a pleasant garden. Excursions organized. Dorm AR$35. 7

Posada del Catalejo Mitre 446 ☎02965/475224, www.posadadelcatalejo.com.ar. Popular bed & breakfast-type hostel close to the beach and the town centre. Large rooms with crisp white sheets, and a lovely homely feel; wi-fi too. Dorms AR$35. Comfortable doubles, some ensuite. 5–6

El Retorno Bartolomé Mitre 798 ☎02965/4506044, www.elretornohostel.com.ar. A welcoming hostel with slightly dated décor. Small dorms with 4–8 beds (AR$35), as well as en suite doubles with TV and comfy mattresses. Free pickup from bus terminal if prearranged. 5

La Tosca Sarmiento 437 ☎02965/456133, www.latoscahostel.com. Located six blocks from the bus station, this hostel may not be the prettiest, but it's clean, friendly and close to the beach. The helpful staff will pick you up from the bus station on request. Dorm AR$35. 5

Hostel Viajeros Gobernador Maíz 545 ☎02965/456457, www.hostelviajeros.com. A little out of the centre and with worn furnishings, but offering a warm welcome and a little garden to relax in. Basic doubles and twins and even more basic but cheap dorms (AR$35) with private bathroom and TV. 5

Hotels

Hotel Bahia Nueva Av Roca 67 ☎02965/451677, www.bahianueva.com.ar. Overlooking the boulevard and the beach, this is a reliable central choice. The rooms are large, and bright, and the buffet breakfast is well presented and delicious. 7

Hotel J & S 9 de Julio 57 ☎02965/476074. Budget hotel with basic but clean doubles, one block from the beach. Good choice if you want something somewhat modern, with private bathroom, but don't want to spend too much. Discounts for longer stays. 6

Hotel El Muelle Viejo Av Hipólito Yrigoyen 38, ☎02965/4711284, www.muelleviejo.com. Pleasant, modern, wood-floored rooms with views of the ocean. Common areas and reception are a little old-fashioned but the staff are welcoming. There's parking in back. 6

Eating and drinking

Ambigú Roca and Roque Sáenz Peña ☎02965/472541. Don't be put off – *Ambigú* looks more exclusive from the outside than it actually is. Try the yummy pizzas (AR$23) or home-made pastas (AR$22). Open late.

Los Colonos Roca and A. Storni ☎02965-458486. Located in the hull of a large wooden ship on the main street, this place is just plain fun. Their speciality is seafood; oven-baked fish goes for around AR$35.

De Miga 9 de Julio 160 ☎02965/475620. Inexpensive café serving overstuffed sandwiches (AR$12) and large pizzas (AR$19). Popular with locals.

Vernardino Blvd Brown 860 ☎02965/474289. Wonderful beach views from this modern restaurant set right off the boulevard. Best at lunch: try the fresh salads (AR$15) or the salted calamari (AR$22).

Vesta Punta Cuervas ☎02965/1566-3927. Although this restaurant is also open for dinner (from 9pm), the best time to come here is at sunset as the restaurant is located at the end of the beach near the Ecocentro, a 40min walk from the centre. Sipping drinks on their terrace watching the sun sink is just perfect.Try the wonderful calamari (AR$26).

Nightlife

La Frontera 9 de Julio 254. Electronica music and visiting DJs. It's only open on the weekends, and don't even think about going before 2am.

Margaruta Roque Sáenz Peña 15 ☎02965/470885. Come here after 11pm to enjoy some good music and and rub shoulders with the locals. Also serves expensive but good quality bar meals.

La Oveja Negra Hipólito Yrigoyen 144. Relaxed pub with a studenty atmosphere, live music and snack food.

Directory

Airlines Aerolíneas Argentinas, Roca 427 ☎02965/451998; Andes, Roca 624 ☎02965/452355; LADE, Roca 119 ☎02965/451256.

Banks and Exchange Banco Galicia, Mitre 25 ☎02965/452323 (Mon–Fri 9am–3pm) changes money and has an ATM. Thaler, corner of Av Roca and Sarmiento ☎02965/455858 (daily 10am–6pm) is a friendly *casa de cambio*.
Car rental Wild Skies Rent a Car, Hipólito Yrigoyen 144 ☎02965/15676233, Ⓦwww.wildskies.com.ar.
Internet Cyber Internet Arnet, Marcos A Zar 125, ☎02965/473232.
Post Office Gobernador Maíz 293.

Moving on

Air Flights from Puerto Madryn 2–3 times weekly to Buenos Aires (2hr), Comodoro Rivadavia (1hr) and Viedma (45min). Trelew airport, an hour away, is served by more frequent flights.
Bus to: Buenos Aires (1 daily; 18hr); Bariloche (2 a week, 14–15hr); Comodoro Rivadavia (2–3 daily; 8hr); Viedma (2 daily; 5–6hr); Rio Gallegos (1 daily, 16hr); Trelew (8 daily; 1hr).

DAY-TRIPS FROM PUERTO MADRYN

Puerto Madryn was originally founded and settled in 1865 by 153 Welsh families who bravely battled with the frigid weather and the arid land. Despite all odds the town survived and more settlers arrived, enabling the fledging community to expand to the southeast, founding **Trelew** (pronounced trey-le-oo) and **Gaiman**. Both are easily reached by local bus from **Puerto Madryn**, making them an interesting combined day-trip. A little further afield, the penguin colony at Punto Tumbo provides an interesting counterpoint to the sealife at Península Valdés.

Trelew and Gaimain

TRELEW doesn't offer a huge amount in the way of sights, but a visit to one of its two great museums is well worth it. The **Museo Regional Pueblo de Lewis** (Mon–Fri 8am–8pm, Sat & Sun 5–8pm; AR$3), at the corner of Lewis Jones 9100 and Fontana, has fascinating displays on Welsh settlement in the area. Nearby, the highly acclaimed **Museo Paleontológico Egidio Feruglio** (Mon–Fri 10am–6pm, Sat & Sun 10am–8pm; Ⓦwww.mef.org.ar; AR$15), at Fontana 140, houses one of the country's most important paleontological collections; excellent guided tours in English, German and Italian (free on request) can lead you through the exhibits.

From Trelew it is a quick twelve-minute bus ride to **GAIMAN**. Much smaller and prettier than its busy neighbour, Gaiman's claim to fame is its **Welsh Teas**, so renowned that even Princess Diana came to enjoy one in 1995. Served at around 3pm every day in decidedly lovely cottage gardens and restaurants with floral tablecloths, they consist of freshly-brewed tea, home-made cakes and jams, scones, toast and the famous *Torta Negra* (traditional Welsh fruitcake). For around AR$35, you won't go hungry.

Arrival and information

Air Trelew airport (☎02965/428021) is only 15min from the centre of town. A taxi to the centre will cost AR$10, and AR$15 to Gaiman.
Bus Buses from Puerto Madryn to Trelew (Linea 28 de Julio) leave every 15–20min, take an hour and are AR$7.50 each way. The bus from Trelew to Gaiman (AR$3.50) leaves every 15min; it will drop you off at the edge of the main plaza.
Tourist office Mitre 387, Trelew ☎0285420139, Ⓦwww.trelew.gov.ar.

Accommodation and eating

Plas y Coed: Casa de Té on the main square, Gaiman ☎02965/491133. Serves a wonderful afternoon tea with home-made cakes, tarts, fresh tea and scones. They also offer rooms with private bathrooms and a lovely living area. ❻
Ty Gwyn 9 de Julio 147, Gaiman ☎02965/491009. Has a cottage-style dining area serving large portions of freshly baked bread, locally made jams and wonderful cakes. If you can't pull yourself away, stay the night in one of their simple but comfortable rooms. ❼

Punto Tumbo

Around four hours south of Puerto Madryn, the **Reserva Provincial Punta Tumbo** (Aug–April, AR$30 park entrance), home to the largest penguin nesting site on the continent, makes a perfect spot to get up close with the creatures. Aside from the million or so Magellanic penguins wandering the area – so curious and numerous you may have to step around them on the path – you'll be treated to a vast variety of birds from rock cormorants to kelp gulls flying overhead. The reserve can be visited independently by car or on a long day's tour from Puerto Madryn. These usually include stops in Trelew and Gaiman on the way home for around AR$150, plus another AR$75 to take an optional boat cruise.

RUTA 40

RN 40 runs from top to bottom of Argentina, following the line of the Andes all the way to the far south from the border with Bolivia in the north. It covers five thousand kilometres and eleven provinces, crosses eighteen important rivers on 236 bridges, and connects thirteen great lakes and salt flats, twenty national parks and hundreds of communities. In recent years the section between **El Calafate** and **Bariloche**, two burgeoning tourist towns, centres for outdoor activity in Patagonia and the Lake District respectively, has become increasingly popular with backpackers. If you don't travel between them via Ruta 40, you'll need to catch a bus all the way to the coast, and then back. This is classic Patagonian landscape: miles of flat grassland, with hundreds of cattle roaming freely, interrupted by only the occasional village or *estancia*. There's little to see along the way apart from the stunning deserted grassland landscape itself. However, the ancient **cave paintings** near the unattractive town of Perito Moreno almost justify the journey on their own, while the leafy oasis of nearby **Los Antiguos** makes a great place to break the trip. With transport of your own, you can also visit the wonderful and isolated **Parque Nacional Perito Moreno**, just off the route along route 37.

TRAVELLING RUTA 40

The **best time to travel** Ruta 40 from El Calafate to Bariloche is between October and April. Outside of these months, buses are less frequent and accommodation can be hard to find. The Cueva de los Manos can only be visited from December to February.

Several companies offer **bus services** between El Calafate and Bariloche, via Los Antiguos. Well-established **Chalten Travel** (Ⓦwww.chaltentravel.com) have offices in El Calafate, El Chaltén, Los Antiguos and Bariloche, but only operate in the summer months (Dec–April). For cheaper, all-year-round transport try **Taqsa** (Ⓦwww.taqsa.com.ar), who run basic services (no food served) between El Calafate and Bariloche and will stop off at Los Antiguos and Perito Moreno. If you have more time and money, plus a sense of adventure, the best way of all to see the region is to rent a **car**. Distances are huge, the road is mainly gravel and fuel stops are few and far between, but a car gives you the freedom to stop and look around. Two places to break for fuel are Bajo Caracoles, 128km south of Los Antiguos, and Gobernador Gregores, 437 kilometres north. Neither offers anything in the way of attractions, but they are essential for petrol and food. There is little in the way of budget **accommodation** along the route (especially as the windy, hard plains make camping virtually impossible), but there are a few welcoming *estancias* where you can try the local produce, and learn from the farmers about their way of life. For general **information** on Ruta 40 see Ⓦwww.ruta40.net (in Spanish) or Ⓦwww.patagonia-argentina.com (in English); there's an excellent tourist office in Los Antiguos.

LOS ANTIGUOS

A sixteen-hour bus ride from El Calafate brings you to the small, oasis-like town of **Los Antiguos**, a little under halfway to Bariloche. Set on the banks of deep blue **Lago Buenos Aires** (after Lake Titicaca in Bolivia, the second biggest in South America) and sheltering from the winds in the lee of the Andes, Los Antiguos comes as a welcome break from the endless grassy plains and is a great base from which to visit the Cueva de los Manos. The wealth of luxuriant vegetation and the wonderful river-front adds to the attraction. The town sports the title of "National Cherry Capital" and books out in January for the **Fiesta Nacional de la Cereza** (the National Cherry Festival). A worthwhile afternoon can be spent visiting the nearby cherry farms: ask at the Tourist office for details.

Arrival and information

Bus There is no bus terminal in Los Antiguos – buses stop along the main street.

Tourist office Av 11 de Julio 446 ⓣ02963/491 261 ⓦwww.losantiguos.gov.ar. They can recommend tour operators and local guides for the trip to Cueva de los Manos.

Tour operators Patagonia Emotions, Cruz del Sur 137 (ⓣ011/15628-42177) can arrange tours to the caves, as can the helpful Turismo Toscas Bayas, 11 de Julio 797 (ⓣ02963/491016). Chalten Travel are at Lago Buenos Aires 537 (ⓣ0297/1541-31836).

Accommodation

Albergue Padilla San Martín 44 ⓣ02963/491140. One of the least expensive options in town, with large dorm rooms and space for camping. Dorm A$21, camping AR$8 per person.

Albergue y Bungalows Sol de Mayo 11 de Julio 133a ⓣ02963/491232. Central and friendly, this hostel offers basic rooms and clean bathrooms. Dorm A$24.

Hotel Argentino 11 de Julio 850 ⓣ02963/491132. Central hotel with comfortable rooms. They also can arrange local tours such as fishing, and visits to the Cueva de los Manos. ❻

Camping Municipal Two kilometres from the centre ⓣ02963/491265. Lovely campsite with hot showers and *cabañas* for up to four people. Camping from AR$8. *Cabañas* ❺

Eating and drinking

Along the main street of Los Antiguos, Avenida 11 de Julio, you'll find many food options, bakeries and takeaway food stores.

El Negro 'B' Parrilla 11 de Julio 571 ⓣ02963/491358. This is a popular *parrilla*, also serving fish and pasta. Mains from AR$18.

Pizza Uno 11 de Julio 895 ⓣ02963/491471. Offers a delivery service, and fast, delicious pizzas and *empanadas*. A large pizza costs AR$12.

CUEVA DE LOS MANOS

The **Cueva de los Manos** is an astounding cave displaying 9300-year-old cave paintings depicting guanacos, abstract figures and hundreds upon hundreds of hand stencils made by ancient local inhabitants. The cave is easily accessible from the unattractive town of **Perito Moreno**, but Los Antiguos makes a far more pleasant base from which to take one of the organised day tours. Expect to pay around AR$150 for a six-to eight-hour tour including entrance fees.

Accommodation

Estancia Telken RN 40 ⓣ02963/432079, ⓦwww.estanciasdesantacruz.com. Located on the road to the cave, this working sheep ranch provides nicely decorated doubles, with home-cooked meals included. Also camping (AR$18). Open Sept–Apr. ❾

Estancia Los Toldos RN40 ⓣ02963/432856, ⓦwww.estanciasdesantacruz.com. The caves are actually located inside this *Estancia*'s perimeters. There are dorm rooms available (AS$50) as well as comfortable doubles. Open Nov–Apr. ❽

PARQUE NACIONAL PERITO MORENO

Created in 1937, the **Parque Nacional Perito Moreno** covers over 11,500 square kilometres of windy Patagonian steppe and stunning high-mountain landscapes. Located just off Ruta 40 towards the town of Gobernador Gregores, the park is hard to get to unless you have your own transport, and you may find yourself alone amongst the abundant wildlife, which includes guanacos, flamingoes and condors. There are several enjoyable short hikes (self-guided) which are not too challenging. You'll need to register with the Park Officials at the park entrance before you set off (daily 8am–10pm; Ⓦwww.parquesnacionales.gov.ar).

Accommodation

There are four basic camping grounds within the park but there are no services and no fires permitted. Otherwise the two *estancias* which border the park provide comfortable accommodation.

Estancia Menelik RN37 Ⓣ011/ 5371-5555 Ⓦwww.estanciasdesantacruz.com. Located just outside the park, and offering pleasant doubles in a 1920s homestead, with all meals included in the rate. The old shearing shed has been renovated and offers dorm accommodation (AR$60). Activities include horseriding excursions into the park. Open Nov–Apr. ⑧

La Oriental Ⓣ02962/452235, Ⓦwww.estanciasdesantacruz.com. Only 1km from the tranquil Lago Belgrano, this *estancia* offers simple doubles (all meals included) as well as camping (AR$20), and organises many activities within the park such as horseriding and birdwatching. Open Nov–Mar. ⑦

EL CHALTÉN

Argentina's self-proclaimed "national trekking capital", the rapidly growing village of **EL CHALTÉN**, lies within the boundaries of the Parque Nacional Los Glaciares, 217 kilometres northwest of El Calafate. It enjoys a stupendous setting, at the confluence of two pristine rivers with the granite spires of Cerro Fitz Roy (3405m) and Cerro Torre (3102m) protruding like vampire fangs on the horizon. El Chaltén means "smoking mountain", a name given to Cerro Fitz Roy by the Tehuelche, who probably mistook the wisps of cloud around its summit for volcanic activity.

El Chaltén is Argentina's youngest village, created in 1985 to counter Chile's claims to the territory. Since then it has experienced a tourist boom, with tent-toters, hikers and rockclimbers descending in droves every summer. Buildings seem to be in perpetual bloom along the dusty streets, making the otherwise pretty village feel like a giant construction site. San Martín, the main street, boasts a smattering of restaurants, supermarkets and hostels, but there is no bank or ATM and few businesses accept credit cards, so bring plenty of cash.

High season is January and February. In spring the winds are fierce; March is the best month to visit, with fewer tourists and less wind. Most businesses close between Easter and mid-October.

PARQUE NACIONAL LOS GLACIARES

The **PARQUE NACIONAL LOS GLACIARES** hugs the eastern slopes of the Andes, extending for 170km along the border with Chile. A UNESCO World Heritage Site, nearly half of the park's six thousand square kilometres consist of virtually inaccessible continental ice fields. Elsewhere, thirteen glaciers sweep down from craggy mountains into two turquoise lakes – Argentino and Viedma – while dry Patagonian steppe and sub-Antarctic forests of *ñire* and *lenga* trees provide exceptional trekking country and a home for endangered *huemul* deer, red fox and puma. The park's northern section can be reached from the village of **El Chaltén**, where the jagged jaws of the **Fitz Roy Massif** dominate a skyline as dramatic as anything in Torres del Paine in Chile. Tremendous glaciers, including the show-stopping **Glaciar Perito Moreno**, highlight the park's southern sector, within easy reach of the resort town of **El Calafate**. For details on the park offices and where to stay and eat when in the area, see listings for nearby bases El Chaltén (see above) and El Calafate (p.159).

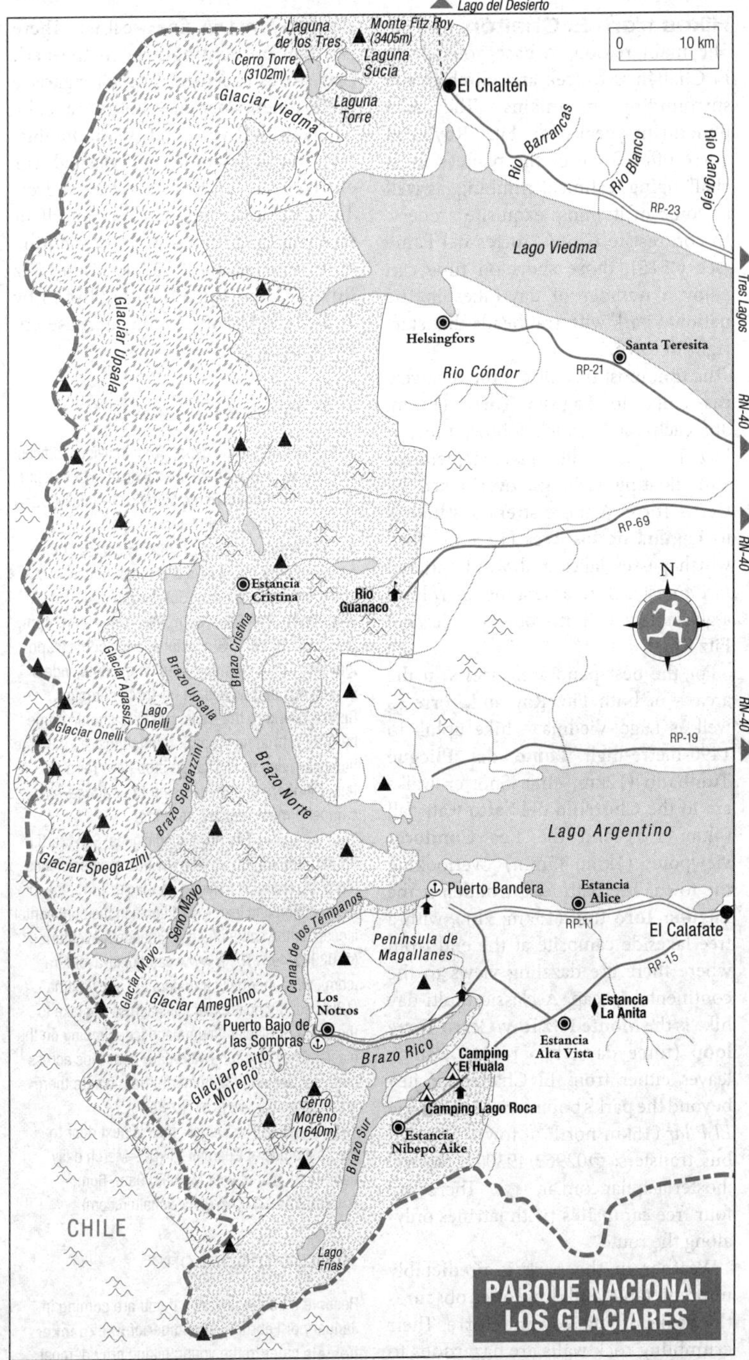

PARQUE NACIONAL
LOS GLACIARES
Lago del Desierto
Laguna de los Tres
Monte Fitz Roy (3405m)
Cerro Torre (3102m)
Laguna Sucia
El Chaltén
Laguna Torre
Glaciar Viedma
Río Barrancas
Río Blanco
Río Cangrejo
RP-23
Lago Viedma
Tres Lagos
Helsingfors
Santa Teresita
Río Cóndor
RP-21
RN-40
RP-69
Glaciar Upsala
Estancia Cristina
Río Guanaco
Brazo Cristina
Brazo Upsala
Glaciar Agassiz
Lago Onelli
Glaciar Onelli
Brazo Spegazzini
Brazo Norte
RP-19
Lago Argentino
Glaciar Spegazzini
Seno Mayo
Canal de los Témpanos
Puerto Bandera
Estancia Alice
RP-11
El Calafate
Península de Magallanes
RP-15
Glaciar Mayo
Glaciar Ameghino
Los Notros
Estancia La Anita
Puerto Bajo de las Sombras
Estancia Alta Vista
Brazo Rico
Camping El Huala
Glaciar Perito Moreno
Cerro Moreno (1640m)
Camping Lago Roca
Estancia Nibepo Aike
Brazo Sur
CHILE
Lago Frías
N
0
10 km

ARGENTINA

PATAGONIA

Hikes from El Chaltén

The main reason to base yourself in El Chaltén is to trek and climb in the surrounding mountains. The sky-puncturing peaks of Fitz Roy and Torre offer some of the planet's most challenging technical climbing, as well as some of its most exquisite scenery. In contrast to Chile's Torres del Paine (see p.515), those short on time can enjoy a number of day-hikes in the national park with trailheads that start right in town.

The trail most travelled is the relatively easy hike to **Laguna Torre** (11km; 3hr each way), which follows the Río Fitz Roy to a silty lake resplendent with floating icebergs, overlooked by Cerro Torre. A more strenuous hike is to **Laguna de los Tres** (12.5km; 4hr), which passes lakes and wind-battered *ñire* forest before ascending sharply to a glacial lake with in-your-face views of Fitz Roy.

For the best panoramic views in the area – of both Fitz Roy and Torre as well as Lago Viedma – hike uphill to 1490-metre-high **Lomo del Pliegue Tumbado** (12km; 4hr). Shorter walks are to the **Chorrillo del Salto** waterfall (4km; 1hr) and the **Los Condores** viewpoint (1km; 45min) overlooking the town. The path least trodden is the **Laguna Toro** trail (15km; 7hr), with a free lakeside campsite at the end from where there are dazzling views to the continental icecap. A classic multi-day hike is the **Monte Fitz Roy/Cerro Torre loop** (three days, two nights), which leaves either from El Chaltén or just beyond the park's boundaries at *Hostería El Pilar* (15km north of town, frequent bus transfers; Ⓣ02962/493002, Ⓦwww.hosteriaelpilar.com.ar, ⑨). There are four free **campsites** (with latrines only) along the route.

Weather in the park is predictably unpredictable, and cloud often obscures the peaks of Fitz Roy and Torre. Their crumbling rock walls are hazardous to climbers even in fine weather. There is a ban on lighting fires in the park (gas stoves excepted) and all cigarette butts, toilet paper and rubbish must be taken away. River water is still potable, and nothing should be washed (or excreted) in or near a water source. The park office produces an excellent **free trekking map**, but for something more detailed, the 1:50,000 Monte Fitz Roy & Cerro Torre map published by Zagier and Urruty can be purchased in El Chaltén.

Arrival and information

Bus Buses arrive and depart from individual offices in the town centre. There are services to El Calafate (8 daily; 3hr 30min); Perito Moreno (1–2 daily; 13hr) and Bariloche (1–2 daily; 30hr).

Parque Nacional Los Glaciares office The excellent park office is in a wooden house at the entrance to town (Oct–March daily 9am–6pm, April 9am–5pm, May–Sept 9am–4pm; Ⓣ02862/493004, Ⓔseccionallagoviedma@apn.gov.ar), with free maps, wildlife exhibits, video screenings and advice on no-trace camping. Before taking to the trails, trekkers should come here for a briefing on park regulations; all daytime buses arriving in El Chaltén stop here for a pep talk. Climbers and those using the *Laguna Toro* campsite must register here first.

Tour agencies Fitz Roy Expediciones, San Martín 56 (Ⓣ02962/493017, Ⓦwww.fitzroyexpediciones.com.ar), organize trekking on Glaciar Torre, teach ice-climbing and lead expeditions on the continental icecap. In the same office is Patagonia Aventura (Ⓣ02962/493110, Ⓦwww.patagonia-aventura.com), who offer daily transfers to Lago Viedma (18km south), boat excursions across the lake to the snout of Glaciar Viedma and ice-climbing on the glacier. They also run twice-daily boat trips across Lago del Desierto (37km north) from where there are spectacular views of Fitz Roy.

Tourist office The tourist office is next door to the post office at Güemes 21 (Oct–March daily 8am–9pm, rest of year Mon–Fri 9am–6pm; Ⓣ02962/493270, Ⓦwww.elchalten.com).

Accommodation

Reserve a bed in advance if you are coming in January or February. A number of **backpacker hostels** cater to the young hiking crowd: most

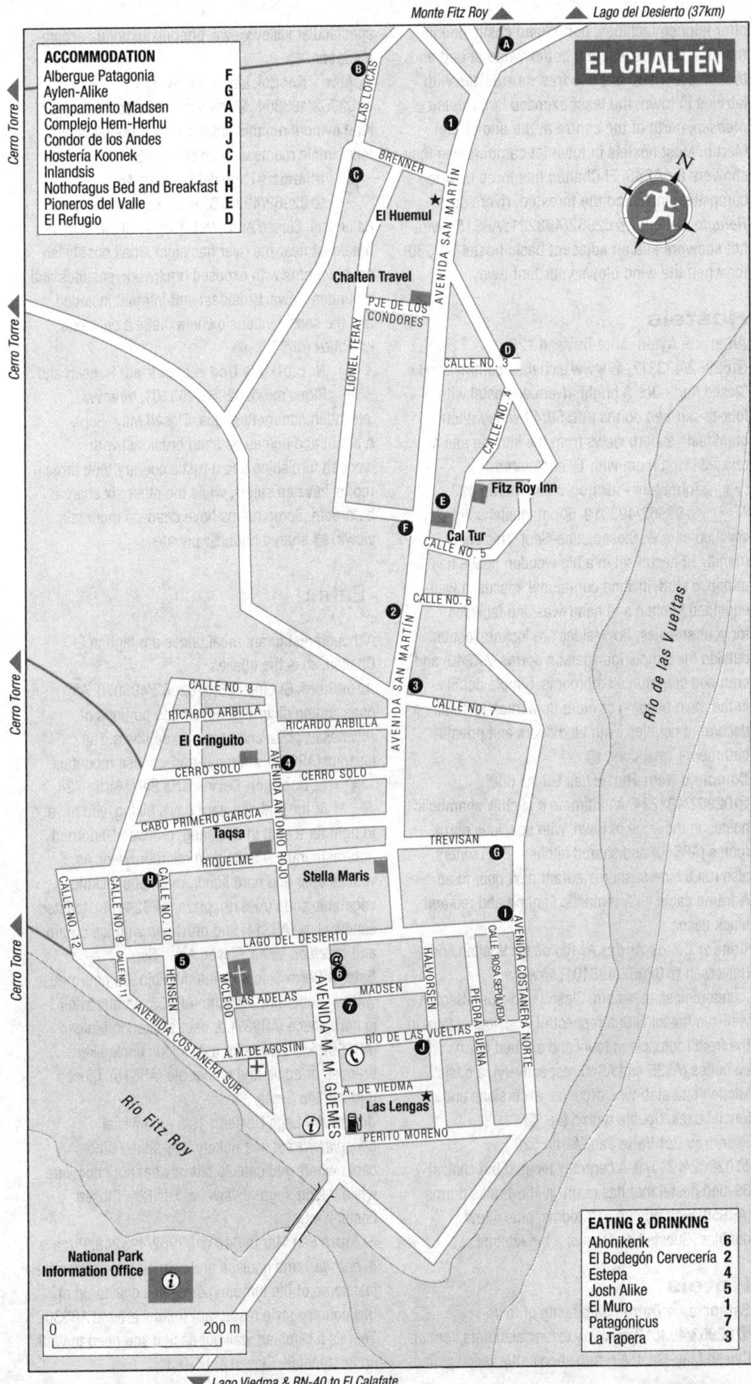
EL CHALTÉN
Monte Fitz Roy
Lago del Desierto (37km)
Cerro Torre
Cerro Torre
Cerro Torre
Cerro Torre
Lago Viedma & RN-40 to El Calafate
ACCOMMODATION
Albergue Patagonia F
Aylen-Alike G
Campamento Madsen A
Complejo Hem-Herhu B
Condor de los Andes J
Hostería Koonek C
Inlandsis I
Nothofagus Bed and Breakfast H
Pioneros del Valle E
El Refugio D
EATING & DRINKING
Ahonikenk 6
El Bodegón Cervecería 2
Estepa 4
Josh Alike 5
El Muro 1
Patagónicus 7
La Tapera 3
LAS LOICAS
BRENNER
AVENIDA SAN MARTÍN
El Huemul
Chalten Travel
PJE DE LOS CÓNDORES
LIONEL TERAY
CALLE NO. 3
CALLE NO. 4
Fitz Roy Inn
Cal Tur
CALLE NO. 5
CALLE NO. 6
CALLE NO. 7
CALLE NO. 8
RICARDO ARBILLA
El Gringuito
CERRO SOLO
AVENIDA ANTONIO ROJO
CABO PRIMERO GARCIA
Taqsa
RIQUELME
Stella Maris
TREVISAN
CALLE NO. 12
CALLE NO. 9
CALLE NO. 10
CALLE NO. 11
LAGO DEL DESIERTO
HENSEN
MCLEOD
LAS ADELAS
MADSEN
HALVORSEN
CALLE ROSA SEPÚLVEDA
PIEDRA BUENA
AVENIDA COSTANERA NORTE
AVENIDA COSTANERA SUR
A. M. DE AGOSTINI
RÍO DE LAS VUELTAS
AVENIDA M. M. GÜEMES
A. DE VIEDMA
Las Lengas
PERITO MORENO
Río Fitz Roy
Río de las Vueltas
National Park Information Office
0
200 m

offer kitchen facilities, dorms and costly double rooms – couples will find better value at bed and breakfasts. There are two free **campsites** with latrines in town; the least exposed is *Camping Madsen*, north of the centre at the end of San Martín. Most hostels in town let campers use their showers for AR$5. El Chaltén has three private campsites, including the forested, riverside *El Refugio*, Calle 3 (ⓣ02962/493221; AR$15), with hot showers and an adjacent basic hostel (AR$30) for when the wind blows your tent away.

Hostels

Albergue Aylen-Aike Trevisan 125 ⓣ02962/493317, ⓦwww.elchalten.com/aylenaike. Closed April–Oct. A bright, riverside hostel with four-to-ten-bed dorms (AR$50/40 with/without breakfast), superb views from the kitchen and a relaxed living room with TV and stereo.

Albergue Patagonia San Martín 493 ⓣ02962/493019, ⓔpatagoniahostel@yahoo.com.ar. Closed June-Sept. This cozy, friendly HI hostel set in a big wooden house has attentive staff, inviting communal spaces, a well-equipped kitchen and hand-washing facilities for your smellies. Downsides are lockers located outside the simple four-person dorms (AR$40) and cramped communal bathrooms. Simple doubles in the main building or more upmarket, tastefully decorated doubles, with tiled floors and private bathrooms, next door. 5

Complejo Hem-Herhu Las Loicas 600 ⓣ02962/493224. An intimate if slightly shambolic hostel on the edge of town, with spacious dorm rooms (AR$40) and shared kitchen. The owners also run a cute sushi restaurant next door in an A-frame cabin with romantic lighting and red and black décor.

Condor de los Andes Av Río de las Vueltas and Halvorsen ⓣ02962/493101, ⓦwww.condordelosandes.com. Closed mid-April–Sept. A well-run hostel with a respectful vibe, lots of light in the front room, clean four- and six-bed dorms with en suites (A$35 and A$40 respectively), a basic kitchen and staff who organize excursions and lunch boxes. Double rooms too. 6

Pioneros del Valle San Martín 520 ⓣ02962/493079. A centrally located but clinical 69-bed hostel that has cram-in-the-bunks dorms (AR$50) with private bathrooms, plus a few doubles. Guests have use of a big kitchen. 6

Hotels

Estancia La Quinta 5km south of town ⓣ02962/493012, ⓦwww.estancialaquinta.com.ar. Closed May–Sept. A refurbished cattle ranch with spectacular valley views, offering luxurious accommodation. 9

Hostería Koonek Lionel Terray 415 ⓣ02962/493304, ⓦwww.hosteriakoonek.com.ar. Kind owners run this small bed and breakfast with four simple rooms with en suites. 6

Inlandsis Lago del Desierto 480 ⓣ02962/493276, ⓦwww.elchalten.com/inlandsis. Closed April–Oct. This boutique bed and breakfast near the river has eight small but stylish double rooms with exposed brickwork, ensuites and mountain views. Breakfast and internet included, and the conscientious owners make a delicious lunchbox (AR$22). 6

Nothofagus Bed & Breakfast Hensen and Riquelme ⓣ02962/493101, ⓦwww.elchalten.com/nothofagus. Closed May–Sept. A bright and homey bed and breakfast with wooden furnishing and a rustic country feel; three rooms have en suites, while the other six share a bathroom. Some rooms have dead-on mountain views. 5 shared bath, 6 private.

Eating

Although restaurant meal prices are high in El Chaltén, so is the quality.

Ahonikenk Güemes 23 ⓣ02962/493070. An unassuming diner that does huge portions of *milanesas*, pizza and home-made pasta. The lasagna (AR$22) is a meat-and-cheese mountain.

El Bodegón Cervecería San Martín 724. At the end of a hard day's hiking, you have to fight for a seat in this snug, driftwood-adorned pub/restaurant with its own microbrewery. As well as beer and hard liquor, the menu includes vegetable soup (AR$12), pizza (AR$24–38), toasted sandwiches (AR$14) and brownies with ice cream and *dulce de leche*. Closed April–Sept.

Estepa Cerro Solo and Antonio Rojo. Go gourmet with an aubergine lasagne (AR$35), lamb ravioli in herb sauce (AR$37) or beef soaked in Malbec (AR$50). Save room for a delicious finale like tiramisu or apple and ginger pie (AR$15). Closed mid-April to Sept.

Josh Aike Lago Desierto 104. A convivial *chocolateria* set in a rickety two-storey timber cabin where you can sip bittersweet hot chocolate while taking in great views of Fitz Roy. Closed Easter–Oct.

El Muro San Martín 948 ⓣ02962/493248. Pizza *a la parrilla*, lamb goulash and salmon *sorrentinos* are just some of the tempting creations dished up at this country-style restaurant (mains around AR$30). There's a climbing wall out back if you need to work up an appetite. Closed April–Oct.

HIKE, BIKE AND SAIL INTO CHILE

From El Chaltén, it is possible to cross to **Villa O'Higgins** in Chile (see p.505) by undertaking an adventurous two-day-trip by boat and foot (or bicycle). Start by catching a bus from El Chaltén and heading 37km north to the southern end of Lago del Desierto. The lake's northern shore can be reached either by **scenic boat ride** or by **hiking** (5hr) along its eastern shore to a free campsite. After overnighting at the campsite, get up early the next morning, grab an exit stamp from the Argentine police and hike or cycle (be prepared to carry your bike part of the way along a muddy single-track forest trail) over the pass **into Chile** (approx 16km, allow for a full day and bring plenty of supplies). Horses can be hired from Lago del Desierto to help with the luggage burden (AR$60). The trail ends at Lago O'Higgins where you go through the Chilean passport-stamping ritual. It is possible to camp and buy meals here at the lakeside hamlet and *estancia* of *Candelario Mancilla*. A boat crosses the lake to the hamlet of Villa O'Higgins (summer only, Wed & Sat 5.30pm; 5hr), the final settlement on Chile's stunning 1000km-plus Carretera Austral. Ask at El Chaltén's tourist office for updated boat times, prices and general information on this increasingly popular route. Note the border crossing is only open November to March.

Patagónicus Güemes and Madsen. The best pizza in town (AR$13–39) is served to hungry diners at big wooden tables. Closed April–Sept.

La Tapera San Martín 249 ⓣ02962/493138. When the menu is recited in person by the gregarious chef, you know you're in for food prepared with passion. House staples include tapas plates, lamb and lentil stew and vegetable crêpes. Soup and a main course is AR$38. Closed mid-April to Oct.

EL CALAFATE

If global warning were suddenly to lay waste to Glaciar Perito Moreno, **EL CALAFATE** would promptly fizzle out in its wake. The brazen tourist town, whose population has exploded from six thousand residents in 2001 to more than 22,000 in 2008, exists primarily to absorb the huge number of visitors who come to gawk and walk on one of the world's natural wonders. Luckily, Perito Moreno is the only glacier in the nearby Parque Nacional Los Glaciares to show no signs of receding, leaving El Calafate to sprawl confidently outwards along its dusty dirt roads. New hotels are going up all the time, vying for views of snow-clad Andean peaks and the milky-blue 1600-square-kilometre **Lago Argentino** (Argentina's largest lake) on which the town sits. Avenida Libertador is the main drag, filled with restaurants, bars, supermarkets, chocolate shops, *heladerías*, banks, tour agencies, souvenir stores and an eyesore of a casino. Visitor season reaches its crowded peak in January and February.

What to see and do

There are few attractions in El Calafate itself, although the **Centro de Interpretación Histórica**, Av Brown and Bonarelli (daily 10am–8pm; ⓣ02902/492799; AR$17), does a decent job of recounting the area's natural and cultural history in Spanish and English, and screens a video showing some of Perito Moreno's more dramatic antics. A bird reserve lies just north of town (head along Calle Ezequel Bustillo) at **Laguna Nimez** (9am–9pm; AR$2), where there are exotic waterfowl such as Chilean flamingoes and black-necked swans. And finally, although not as well preserved as the rock art at Cueva de las Manos (see p.153), the 4000-to-7000-year-old cave and cliff paintings at **Punta Walichu** (daily

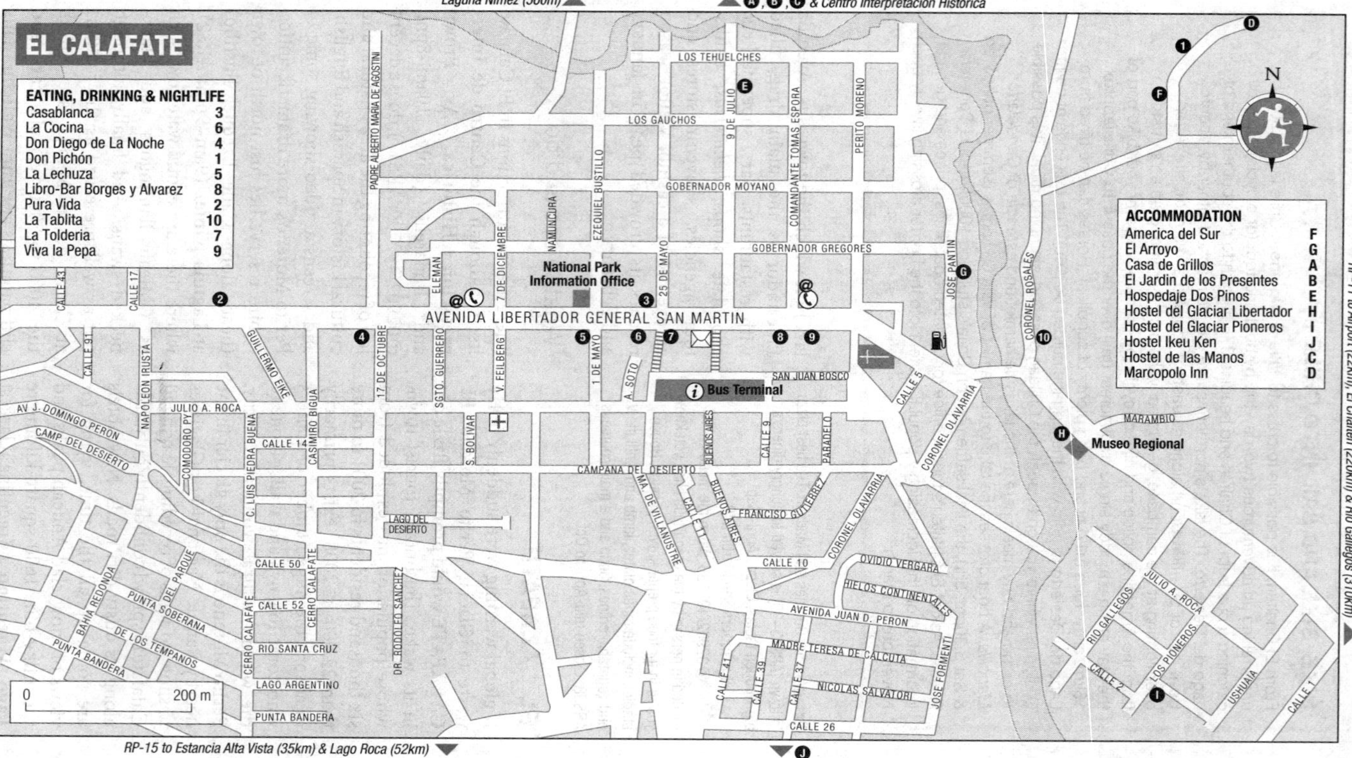
EL CALAFATE
EATING, DRINKING & NIGHTLIFE
Casablanca 3
La Cocina 6
Don Diego de La Noche 4
Don Pichón 1
La Lechuza 5
Libro-Bar Borges y Alvarez 8
Pura Vida 2
La Tablita 10
La Toldería 7
Viva la Pepa 9
ACCOMMODATION
America del Sur F
El Arroyo G
Casa de Grillos A
El Jardin de los Presentes B
Hospedaje Dos Pinos E
Hostel del Glaciar Libertador H
Hostel del Glaciar Pioneros I
Hostel Ikeu Ken J
Hostel de las Manos C
Marcopolo Inn D
Laguna Nimez (500m)
A, B, C & Centro Interpretacion Historica
RP-11 to Airport (22km), El Chaltén (220km) & Río Gallegos (310km)
RP-15 to Estancia Alta Vista (35km) & Lago Roca (52km)
J
RP-11 to Puerto Bandera (47km) & Glaciar Perito Moreno (80km)
National Park Information Office
Bus Terminal
Museo Regional
AVENIDA LIBERTADOR GENERAL SAN MARTIN
LOS TEHUELCHES
LOS GAUCHOS
GOBERNADOR MOYANO
GOBERNADOR GREGORES
PADRE ALBERTO MARIA DE AGOSTINI
EZEQUIEL BUSTILLO
NAMUNCURA
9 DE JULIO
COMANDANTE TOMAS ESPORA
PERITO MORENO
7 DE DICIEMBRE
ELEMAN
25 DE MAYO
JOSE PANTIN
CORONEL ROSALES
CALLE 43
CALLE 17
CALLE 91
NAPOLEON IRUSTA
GUILLERMO EIKE
17 DE OCTUBRE
SGTO. GUERRERO
V. FEILBERG
1 DE MAYO
A. SOTO
SAN JUAN BOSCO
CALLE 5
CORONEL OLAVARRIA
MARAMBIO
AV J. DOMINGO PERON
CAMP. DEL DESIERTO
JULIO A. ROCA
COMODORO PY
C. LUIS PIEDRA BUENA
CALLE 14
CASIMIRO BIGUA
S. BOLIVAR
BUENOS AIRES
CALLE 9
PARADELO
CAMPANA DEL DESIERTO
MA. DE VILLANUSTRE
CALLE 11
FRANCISCO GUTIERREZ
LAGO DEL DESIERTO
CALLE 50
CERRO CALAFATE
CALLE 52
RIO SANTA CRUZ
LAGO ARGENTINO
PUNTA BANDERA
DR. RODOLFO SANCHEZ
DEL PARQUE
BAHIA REDONDA
PUNTA SOBERANA
DE LOS TEMPANOS
CALLE 10
OVIDIO VERGARA
HIELOS CONTINENTALES
AVENIDA JUAN D. PERON
MADRE TERESA DE CALCUTA
NICOLAS SALVATORI
JOSE FORMENTI
CALLE 41
CALLE 39
CALLE 37
CALLE 26
RIO GALLEGOS
JULIO A. ROCA
LOS PIONEROS
CALLE 2
USHUAIA
CALLE 1
N
0 200 m

guided tours at 10.30am, 12.30pm, 3.30pm & 6.30pm; ⓣ02902/497003; AR$49), 7km east of town on the shores of Lago Argentino, are worth visiting. They depict animals, people and human hands. Morresi Viajes, Av Libertador 1341, run excursions with bilingual guides (fantastic value at AR$50, including transfer and entrance; ⓣ02902/492276).

Arrival and information

Air El Calafate's airport (ⓣ02902/491220) is 23km east of downtown. The Aerobus (ⓣ02902/494355; AR$18) runs into town or a taxi to the centre costs AR$50.

Bus The bus terminal is at Av Julio A Roca, one block up the staircase from Av Libertador, the main street.

Parque Nacional Los Glaciares office The national park office at Av Libertador 1302 has maps, sells fishing licenses and has updated information on park campsites (Mon–Fri 8am–7pm, Sat & Sun 9.30am–7pm; ⓣ02902/491005).

Tourist office The tourist office is in the bus terminal (daily: April–Sept 8am–9pm, Oct–March 8am–10pm; ⓣ02902/491090, ⓦwww.elcalafate.gov.ar).

Accommodation

Reserve in advance for January and February. Outside high season (November to Easter) the town's inflated prices come down a notch.

For **camping** in the centre, try the well-serviced, riverside *El Arroyo* at José Pantín s/n (ⓣ02902/492233; AR$14). Inside the park, 50 kilometres from town, the tranquil *Lago Roca* (ⓣ02902/499500, ⓦwww.losglaciares.com/campinglagoroca; AR$16), beside the lake of the same name, has showers, a restaurant, bicycle hire and telephones.

Hostels

There are many backpacker hostels in town, although their double rooms tend to be pricey for what you get. All hostels listed here include breakfast, internet and use of kitchen.

America del Sur Puerto Deseado 153 ⓣ02902/493525, ⓦwww.americahostel.com.ar. In-floor heating, uninterrupted lake views, an airy common area and cool staff make this modern hostel one of the best. Dorms (AR$40) have private bathrooms. ❻

Hostel del Glaciar Libertador Av Libertador 587, ⓣ02902/491792, ⓦwww.glaciar.com. A newer and pricier version of its sister HI-affiliated hostel *Glaciar Pioneros*, this enormous wooden house sleeps more than a hundred, has spotless dorms (AR$49) with private bathrooms and beautiful bright double, though it suffers from understaffing and can feel impersonal. Free breakfast for those in doubles only, otherwise it's an extra AR$15. ❽

Hostel del Glaciar Pioneros Los Pioneros 255 ⓣ02902/491243, ⓦwww.glaciar.com. There are pros and cons to this 92-bed HI hostel. The four-bed dorm rooms (AR$42) are cramped and you have to hire cutlery to use the kitchen, but some of the newer double rooms have been tastefully furnished with private bathrooms and the on-site restaurant does hearty home-style cooking. ❻

Hostel Ikeu Ken FM Pontoriero 171 ⓣ02902/495175, ⓦwww.patagoniaikeuken.com.ar. An intimate but lively hilltop hostel with a balcony that enjoys the afternoon sun and lake vistas. Dorms (AR$45) and bathrooms are pretty ordinary, although the two adjacent fully equipped *cabañas*, with kitchens and private bathrooms, are highly sought after. Smoking permitted indoors. *Cabañas* ❼

Hostel de Las Manos Egidio Feruglio 59 ⓣ02902/492996, ⓦwww.hosteldelasmanos.com.ar. Somewhere between a hostel and a guest-house, this light-drenched house on a quiet street has immaculate private rooms (sleeping two-to-four people) and less salubrious dorms (AR$35) with shared bathrooms. ❺–❻

Marcopolo Inn Calle 405, No. 82 ⓣ02902/493899, ⓦwww.marcopoloinncalafate.com. Its pool table, bar area and inexpensive dinners attract a young, raucous crowd. The clean, modern dorms (AR$40) have en suites but can be overheated. ❼

Hotels

Casa de Grillos Los Condores 1215 ⓣ02902/491160, ⓦwww.casadegrillos.com.ar. A peaceful bed and breakfast in a two-storey family home with four colourful, themed rooms (some with private bathroom), a comfy living area, free internet and all-day tea and coffee. ❻

Hospedaje Dos Pinos 9 de Julio 358 ⓣ02902/491271, ⓦwww.losglaciares.com/losdospinos. An ambitious, impersonal holiday complex that sleeps 200, offers camping (AR$15), rudimentary dormitories with no bedding (AR$25), basic doubles (❺) and modern doubles with private bathrooms (❻). Guests can use the communal kitchen. Breakfasts AR$7.

El Jardin de los Presentes Guido Bonarelli 72 ☎02902/491518, ⓦwww.lospresentes.com.ar. You couldn't ask for warmer hospitality or better value than this spotless, family-run bed and breakfast. The large doubles have television, private bathrooms and partial lake views, while the roomy, fully equipped two-storey *cabañas* are excellent value, sleeping up to five. ❺

Eating and drinking

Casablanca Av Libertador 1202 ☎02902/491402. Pizzas (AR$24–40), burgers, sandwiches and artisanal beer nourish a relaxed crowd at this two-storey resto-bar. Plenty of vegetarian options.

La Cocina Av Libertador 1245 ☎02902/491758. Closed Tues. The town's best Italian restaurant, with mains such as aubergine ravioli with creamy mushroom and onion sauce (AR$39) and a huge range of Patagonian and Mendozan wines. For dessert, you won't be able to resist the ice cream dribbled with hot *dulce de leche*, nor should you try.

Don Pichón Puerto Deseado 242 ☎02902/492577. Tuck into lamb in Calafate sauce (AR$38) or mushroom risotto (AR$24) while taking in panoramic views of town from the wrap-around windows. An extensive wine list completes this fine-dining experience. Closed all day Mon and Tues for lunch.

La Lechuza Av Libertador 1301 ☎02902/491610. Wood-fired pizzas and *empanadas* that are lip-smacking and easy on the wallet. Choose from imaginative pizza toppings such as lamb, salmon and sheep's cheese. Mains AR$20–40.

Libro-Bar Borges y Alvarez Av Libertador 1015 ☎02902/491464. Eclectic literary bar-cum-café serving aged Scotch whiskies (up to AR$120 a shot), yummy cakes (AR$14), gourmet coffee and savoury snacks in a laid-back, first-floor setting overlooking the main street.

Pura Vida Av Libertador 1876 ☎02902/493356. Easily the town's best restaurant, where delectable stuffed pumpkin, lamb stew and aubergine pie and just some of the hearty warmers that accompany an upbeat Latin soundtrack.The service is first-rate and cushions and wooden furnishings create a cozy ambience. Mains AR$30–35. Closed Wed & Sun lunch.

La Tablita Colonel Rosales 28 ☎02902/491065. *Muy buena carne* (from AR$45) is plucked straight off the fiery *asador* and served with panache by the English-speaking staff.

Viva la Pepa Emilio Amado 833 ☎02902/491880. Specializes in crêpes with all kinds of delicious savoury and sweet fillings (AR$30–40). The sandwiches are divine too.

Nightlife

Don Diego de La Noche Av Libertador 1603. Live music and a rocking dancefloor; locals tend to arrive around 3am after the tourists have gone to bed.

La Toldería Av Libertador 1177. Those with energy to burn and the opposite sex on their mind flock here for pub grub, live music and a let-it-all-hang-out dancefloor that on weekends throbs until sunrise with electronica, rock and pop. Closed Mon.

Directory

Airlines Airlines with offices in town include Aerolíneas Argentinas, 9 de Julio 57 ☎02902/492814; LADE, Julio A Roca 1004 ☎02902/491262, and LAN Argentina, Av Libertador 960 ☎02902/492155.

Car rental Localiza Rent a Car, Av Libertador 687 (☎02902/491398, ⓦwww.localiza.com); On Rent a Car, Av Libertador 1831 (☎02902/493788, ⓦwww.onrentacar.com.ar); Servi Car 4WD, Av Libertador 698 (☎02902/492301, ⓦwww.servicar4x4.com.ar).

Laundry El Lavadero, 25 de Mayo 43 (☎02902/492182).

Police Av Libertador 835 (☎02902/491824).

Post office Av Libertador 1133

Tour operators Hielo & Aventura, Av Libertador 935 (☎02902/492205, ⓦwww.hieloyaventura.com) offer ice-trekking trips and boat excursions to see Glaciar Perito Moreno; Fernandez Campbell, Av Libertador 867 (☎02902/491155, ⓦwww.fernandezcampbell.com) run Upsala and Perito Moreno boat excursions; *Hostel del Glaciar Los Pioneros* (see p.161) offer recommended day tours to the glacier that are popular with backpackers.

Moving on

Air Flights leave El Calafate daily for Bariloche (2hr); Buenos Aires (3hr); Trelew (1hr 30min); Ushuaia (1hr 10min); and sporadic services to Comodoro Rivadavia, Puerto Madryn, Río Gallegos and Río Grande.

Bus to: Bariloche (1–2 daily; 34hr); El Chaltén (8 daily; 3hr 30min); Perito Moreno (daily in summer; 13hr); Río Gallegos (4 daily; 4hr).

VISITING PERITO MORENO

The **entrance fee** for the Perito Moreno section of the park is AR$40 (payable at the entrance, 30km before the glacier), although some people avoid the charge by sneaking in outside the park's opening hours (8am–8pm).

Most tour operators in El Calafate (see below) offer **day excursions** to the glacier starting from AR$175; many include a catamaran cruise and around three hours to roam the boardwalks. To visit independently, **buses** leave from El Calafate's terminal three times daily (AR$60 return). You could also hire a taxi (AR$250 including three hours' wait at the glacier) or rent a car (roughly AR$190 a day), taking either the less-travelled gravel RP15 past historic *estancias*, or the less scenic but paved RP11. One-hour **catamaran excursions** to see Perito Moreno's southern face leave from Puerto Bajo de las Sombras, 6km from the boardwalks with Hielo & Aventura (minibus shuttle from boardwalk; hourly 10.30am–3.30pm; AR$38); to see the northern face, catamarans leave from Canal de los Témpanos, just 1km from the boardwalks with Fernandez Campbell (hourly 10.30am–4.30pm; AR$38). For a close-up view of Perito Moreno's crevasses and lagoons, Hielo & Aventura offer ice-trekking trips (wearing crampons) on its surface from AR$310.

DAY-TRIPS FROM EL CALAFATE

Make sure your camera is charge, and you are well wrapped up, to visit the stunning glaciers around El Calafate.

Glaciar Perito Moreno

wSome two kilometres of **boardwalks** and terraces on the Península de Magallanes allow visitors to view Perito Moreno from different heights and angles, and to get within 150 metres of its face. Aim to spend at least two hours at the boardwalks, taking photos from every conceivable angle. To avoid the crowds, arrive early in the morning or late in the afternoon when the glacier is also at its most active.

Upsala and other glaciers

Although receding fast, **GLACIAR UPSALA** remains the longest glacier in the park and indeed in South America. The same height as Perito Moreno, Upsala is twice as long, seven kilometres wide and known for carving huge translucent, blue-tinged icebergs that bob around Lago Argentino like surreal smooth art sculptures. Located 45km west of El Calafate, Upsala is accessible by **catamaran excursion** along Lago Argentino's northern arm (boats leave from Puerto Bandera). All-day tours, which also take in the Spegazzini, Onelli, Bolados and Agassiz glaciers, are run by Fernandez Campbell (AR$269, plus AR$40 park entrance). Boats are generally packed to the max with other camera-wielders, but this excursion is well worthwhile: the closest thing to experiencing Antarctica without actually going there.

RÍO GALLEGOS

Grim and windy **RÍO GALLEGOS** is an inevitable stop for travellers heading south to Ushuaia, north towards Puerto Madryn or west to El Calafate or Chile. The capital of Santa Cruz province, the city lies on the banks of the estuary of the Río Gallegos, a river whose giant, thrashing sea-going brown trout lure **fly-fishing** enthusiasts from around the world.

What to see and do

Río Gallegos' city centre has a couple of worthwhile museums and some nicely restored historic buildings. In an early settler home dating from 1890, on Albedí at Elcano, the **Museo de los Pioneros**, (daily 10am–7.30pm; free;

☎02966/437763), is decked out with period furniture and old photographs. Better still, the **Complejo Cultural Santa Cruz**, at Ramón y Cajal (Mon–Fri 10am–7pm, Sat & Sun 11am–7pm; free; ☎02966/426427), offers rolling contemporary art exhibitions, a motley collection of stuffed regional fauna and artefacts from the indigenous Tehuelche. If live animals interest you more, consider a tour with a local operator to the **penguin colony** at Cabo Vírgenes, a nesting site for around 180,000 Magellanic penguins, 140km southeast of the city; trips are on offer between October and March.

Arrival and information

Air Río Gallegos' airport is 7km west of downtown. There are no buses to the centre, and taxis cost AR$15.

Bus The bus station (☎02966/442585) is 2km west of town at the corner of Av Eva Perón and the RN3. A taxi to the centre costs AR$12; bus #A runs downtown.

Tourist office There is a **provincial** tourist office (late-Sept–Easter 9am–9pm, rest of the year Mon–Fri 9am–6pm; ☎02966/438725, Ⓦwww.epatagonia.gov.ar) at Av Roca 863 and a **municipal** office (Mon–Fri 8am–4pm; ☎02966/436920, Ⓦwww.turismo.mrg.gov.ar) at Av Roca 1587. There is also an office at the bus station (Sept–Easter daily 7am–9pm, rest of year 8am–8pm; ☎02966/442159).

Accommodation

Accommodation is generally expensive, of poor quality and fills up quickly. The closest **campsite** is *ATSA*, half a kilometre southwest of the bus terminal at Asturias and Yugoslavia (☎02966/442310; AR$10).

Hospedaje Elcira Pje Zuccarino 431 ☎02966/429856. Handy for the bus station, this neat guesthouse is popular with Argentines and has dorm rooms (AR$30), one double and a big kitchen and TV area. ❺

Hotel Colonial Urquiza 212 and Rivadavia ☎02966/422329, Ⓔines_frey@hotmail.com. A hospitable *dueña* runs this rambling old house, in which lurk a hotchpotch of basic rooms with shared bathrooms. Dorm AR$50. ❺

Hotel Sehuén Rawson 160 ☎02966/425683, Ⓦwww.hotelsehuen.com. Boasts 34 tidy, spacious rooms (some triples and quadruples) all with TV and en suite. Breakfast included. ❻

Sleepers Inn Hostel Federico Sphur 78 ☎02966/444359, Ⓦwww.sleepersinn.blogspot.com. The most inviting budget option in town, this bright, white and scrupulously clean hostel has doubles and small dorms (AR$50) with no lockers and shared bathrooms. ❺

Eating and drinking

When boredom hits (and it's only a matter of time), you can always fall back on wining and dining, two things Río Gallegos does surprisingly well.

Club Británico Roca 935. Río Gallegos' dwindling populace of British descent prop up the bar, while

CROSSING INTO CHILE AND TIERRA DEL FUEGO

Reaching Tierra del Fuego from the Argentine mainland requires travelling through Chilean territory. The journey, which takes the better part of a day and involves crossing two borders as well as the Magellan Straits, can feel like a time-wasting exercise in theatrical passport-stamping between two frosty neighbours. The **Chilean border crossing** (no fresh vegetables, fruit or meat allowed) is 68km south of Río Gallegos at Monte Aymond. Once in Chile, a road heads for **Punta Arenas** (see p.507) and **Puerto Natales** (see p.511). If your destination is Argentine Tierra del Fuego, turn left onto the RN257 at Kimiri Aike, 48 kilomtres from the border. Follow this road to Primera Angostura, where a **car ferry** takes twenty minutes to cross the narrowest section of the Magellan Straits (8.30am–11pm, every 45min; vehicles US$24; Ⓦwww.tabsa.cl). If you're headed to Río Grande and Ushuaia (see opposite), the road travels through part of Chilean Tierra del Fuego until reaching San Sebastián, the island's first Argentine settlement.

An alternative route to Puerto Natales from Río Gallegos is to head 260km west along the RN-40 to the coal mining town of Río Turbio; the Chilean border crossing (open 24hr) is 35km south at Paso Casas Viejas/La Laurita.

the adjoining restaurant serves a hearty range of beef, lamb, fish and pasta dishes (mains around AR$37).

Laguanacazul Gob Lista and Sarmiento ⓣ02966/444144. This tastefully decorated waterfront restaurant serves haute cuisine using mostly locally-sourced ingredients: thick, grilled Patagonian lamb with Malbec and vegetarian options like aubergine lasagne. Mains AR$32–40.

Puesto Molino Av Roca 854 ⓣ02966/429836 A cavernous pizzeria and *parrillada* with a big woodfire oven, rustic wood and straw furnishings and forty-odd Argentine wines on offer. Mains AR$20–35.

Directory

Airlines Aerolineas Argentínas, San Martín 545 ⓣ0810/2228-6527; LADE, Fagnano 53 ⓣ02966/42231; LAN, Marcelino Alvarez 246 ⓣ0810/999-9526.

Currency exchange Thaler, San Martín 484 (ⓣ0296/436052).

Internet @, Av Roca 1426; otherwise, numerous *locutorios* in town offer internet services.

Post office San Martín at Av Roca.

Tours Maca Tobiano, Roca 988 (ⓣ02966/422466, ⓦwww.macatobiano.com), run day-trips to Cabo Vírgenes from AR$150.

Moving on

Air daily flights to: Buenos Aires (3hr); Comodoro Ridavavia (1hr 15min); El Calafate (50min) and Ushuaia (55min) and two weekly to Río Grande (1hr 15min).

Bus to: Comodoro Rivadavia (12 daily; 10–12hr); El Calafate (4–5 daily; 4hr); Puerto Madryn (7 daily; 18–19hr); Río Grande (2 daily; 9–10hr); Ushuaia (2 daily; 12hr) and in Chile Punta Arenas (2 daily; 3hr 30min); Puerto Natales (2 weekly; 4hr).

Tierra del Fuego

A rugged and isolated archipelago at the extreme southern tip of the continent, **TIERRA DEL FUEGO** ("Land of Fire") marks the finish line for South America. Here the Andes range tapers into the chilly southern oceans, deciduous forests and Ice Age glaciers lie a stone's throw from a wildlife-rich shoreline, penguins and sea lions huddle on rocky islets, salmon and trout thrash about in the rivers and sheep graze on arid windswept plains.

The archipelago is shared with historic hostility by Argentina and Chile, and only about a third of Isla Grande (the main island and the largest in South America) belongs to Argentina. This includes **Ushuaia**, however, the region's top destination. Claiming to be the planet's most southerly city, it's a jumping-off point for the lakes and mountains of **Parque Nacional Tierra del Fuego**, as well as historic **estancias**, boat trips on the **Beagle Channel**, downhill and cross-country skiing in the winter, and cruises to **Antarctica** in summer.

To the north, a stop in the unattractive town of **Río Grande** may be a necessary evil if you are travelling to or from the Argentinian mainland; though it's a destination in its own right for fly fishermen in hot pursuit of **brown trout**.

High season is from December to February, when days are longest and warmest. Spring (Oct to mid-Nov) is beautiful and lush, but even windier than normal. Autumn (late-March to April) is arguably the best time to visit, when the countryside is lit up in warm shades of red and orange. But Ushuaia's growing status as a wintersports playground ensures the "uttermost part of the earth" is now a year-round destination.

USHUAIA

USHUAIA is the end of the world as we know it. But aside from some conspicuous casinos and strip joints, there's nothing fire and brimstone here. Quite the contrary: the world's southernmost city is cold, damp and disarmingly pretty, set on a bay on the wildlife-rich

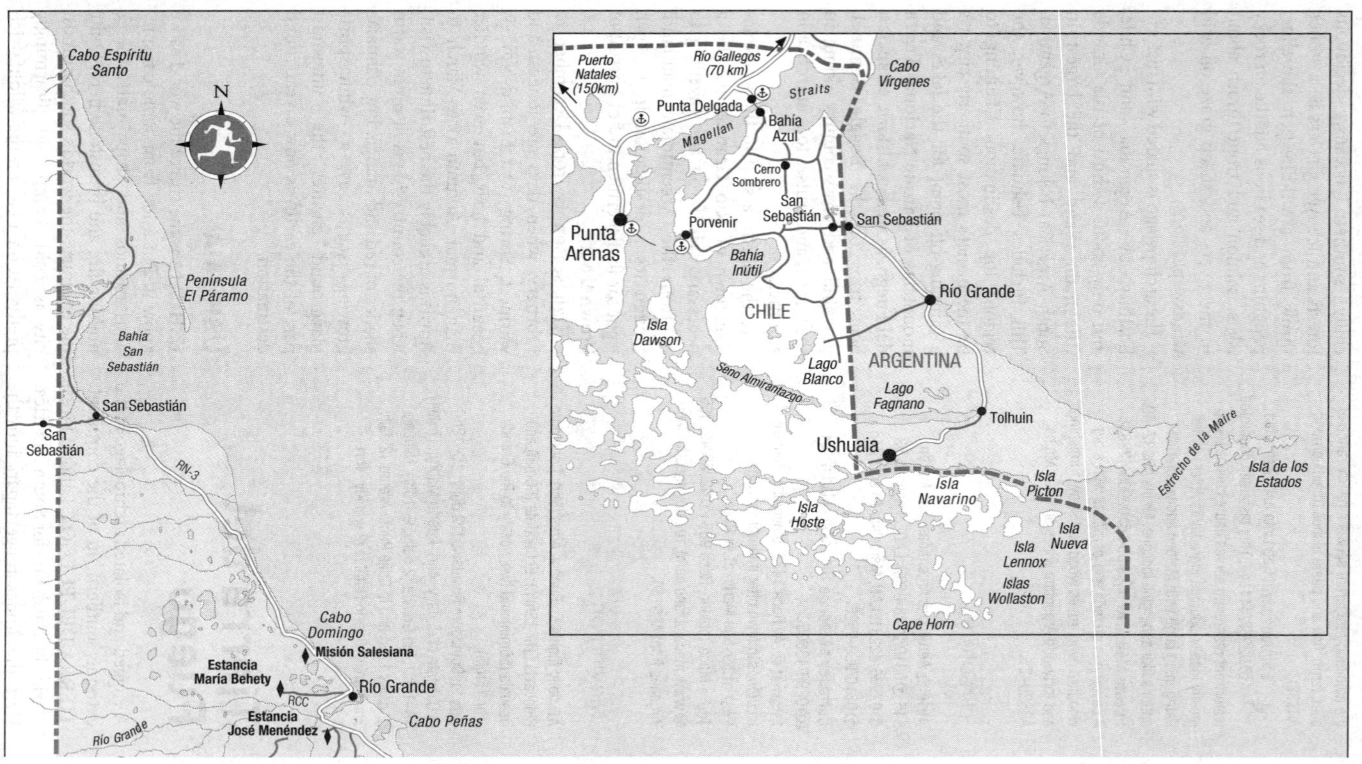
Cabo Espíritu Santo
N
Península El Páramo
Bahía San Sebastián
San Sebastián
San Sebastián
RN-3
Cabo Domingo
Misión Salesiana
Estancia María Behety
RCC
Río Grande
Estancia José Menéndez
Cabo Peñas
Río Grande
Puerto Natales (150km)
Río Gallegos (70 km)
Straits
Magellan
Cabo Vírgenes
Punta Delgada
Bahía Azul
Cerro Sombrero
San Sebastián
San Sebastián
Punta Arenas
Porvenir
Bahía Inútil
Río Grande
CHILE
Isla Dawson
ARGENTINA
Lago Blanco
Seno Almirantazgo
Lago Fagnano
Tolhuin
Ushuaia
Estrecho de la Maire
Isla de los Estados
Isla Navarino
Isla Picton
Isla Hoste
Isla Nueva
Isla Lennox
Islas Wollaston
Cape Horn

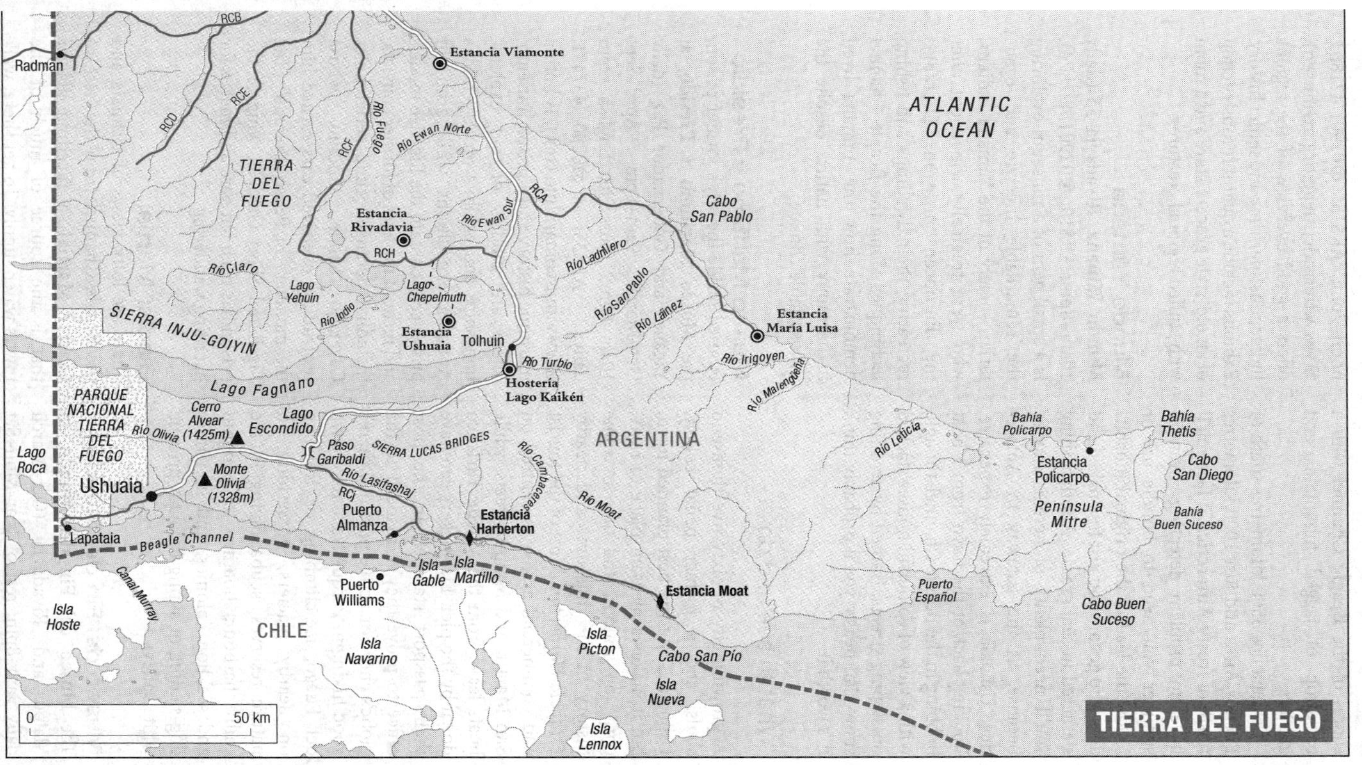
TIERRA DEL FUEGO
ATLANTIC OCEAN
Radman
RCB
RCD
RCE
RCF
Estancia Viamonte
Río Fuego
Río Ewan Norte
TIERRA DEL FUEGO
RCA
Cabo San Pablo
Estancia Rivadavia
Río Ewan Sur
RCH
Río Claro
Lago Yehuin
Río Indio
Lago Chepelmuth
Estancia Ushuaia
Tolhuin
Río Ladrillero
Río San Pablo
Río Láinez
Estancia María Luisa
SIERRA INJU-GOIYIN
Río Turbio
Hostería Lago Kaikén
Río Irigoyen
Río Malengueña
Lago Fagnano
PARQUE NACIONAL TIERRA DEL FUEGO
Cerro Alvear (1425m)
Lago Escondido
Río Olivia
Paso Garibaldi
SIERRA LUCAS BRIDGES
ARGENTINA
Río Cambaceres
Río Leticia
Bahía Policarpo
Bahía Thetis
Lago Roca
Monte Olivia (1328m)
Río Lasifashaj
Río Moat
Estancia Policarpo
Cabo San Diego
Ushuaia
RCj
Puerto Almanza
Estancia Harberton
Península Mitre
Bahía Buen Suceso
Lapataia
Beagle Channel
Isla Gable
Isla Martillo
Estancia Moat
Puerto Español
Canal Murray
Puerto Williams
Cabo Buen Suceso
Isla Hoste
CHILE
Isla Navarino
Isla Picton
Cabo San Pío
Isla Nueva
Isla Lennox
0
50 km

shores of the **Beagle Channel** with a backdrop of jagged mountains and glaciers.

Ushuaia lies 3500 kilometres south of Buenos Aires and just 1000 kilometres north of frosty **Antarctica**, a fact you'll have no problem detecting. Even in summer you need to bundle up, or follow the lead of the original inhabitants who got around just fine naked and slathered in seal grease. Another thing you'll need plenty of here is money because, as the gateway to Antarctica, Ushuaia is extremely expensive. Looking back at the town from a boat bobbing in the Beagle Channel, though, with a view of colourful houses stacked on sloping streets, framed by arresting snow-clad peaks, you'll probably think it 's worth it.

What to see and do

A growing city of sixty-five thousand souls, and a former penal colony, Ushuaia is not the best planned town, but it makes a pleasant place to relax, gorge on seafood and take in some history in the museums and nearby *Estancia Harberton*. Most of the tourist and commercial action is centred on **San Martín** and **Maipú** streets, while boats leave from the Muelle Turístico down by the pier. List-tickers can have their passport stamped in the post office to prove they've made it to the globe's end. For active pursuits, there's good hiking in Parque Nacional Tierra del Fuego, ice-climbing or trekking on nearby glaciers, horseriding in nature reserves, scuba diving in the chilly harbour, boating to penguin and sea lion colonies, and in winter dog-sleding or skiing through pristine white valleys.

Museo del Fin del Mundo

The **Museo del Fin del Mundo**, at Maipú and Rivadavia (Oct–March daily 9am–8pm, rest of year Mon–Sat noon–7pm; AR$15; ⓣ02901/421863, ⓦwww.tierradelfuego.org.ar/museo), offers a good overview of the region's indigenous, maritime and settler history. Exhibits include a quaint reconstruction of an old-style grocery store and a room with stuffed regional creatures.

Mundo Yámana

Mundo Yámana, Rivadavia 56 (daily 10am–8pm; AR$10; ⓣ02901/422874), is a small gem of a museum exploring the remarkable lifestyle and egalitarian society of the Yámana Indians, who were tragically wiped out after the European invasion. Dioramas recreating their dwellings and fishing techniques along the Beagle Channel demonstrate how the Yámana lived in harmony with nature despite the inhospitable climate.

Museo Marítimo y Presidio

Housed inside the city's former prison, the **Museo Marítimo y Presido**, at Yaganes and Gobernador Paz (daily Oct–March 9am–8pm, April–Sept 10am–8pm, tours in English 2pm daily; AR$35; ⓣ02901/437481, ⓦwww.museomaritimo.com), is both a maritime history and a prison museum. There are models of old exploration ships and exhibits on Argentina's Antarctic expeditions, while grim old prison cells contain the life-size models and recount the lives of former convicts, including deranged child serial killer Cayetano Santos Godino, whose protruding, oversized ears earned him the moniker "El Petiso Orejudo" (The Big-Eared Short Guy). A wing of the prison has been left bare and makes for haunting wandering.

Glaciar Martial

There are lofty views of Ushuaia and the Beagle Channel from the base of **Glaciar Martial**, a receding glacier that is the source of much of the town's water supply. To get there, walk

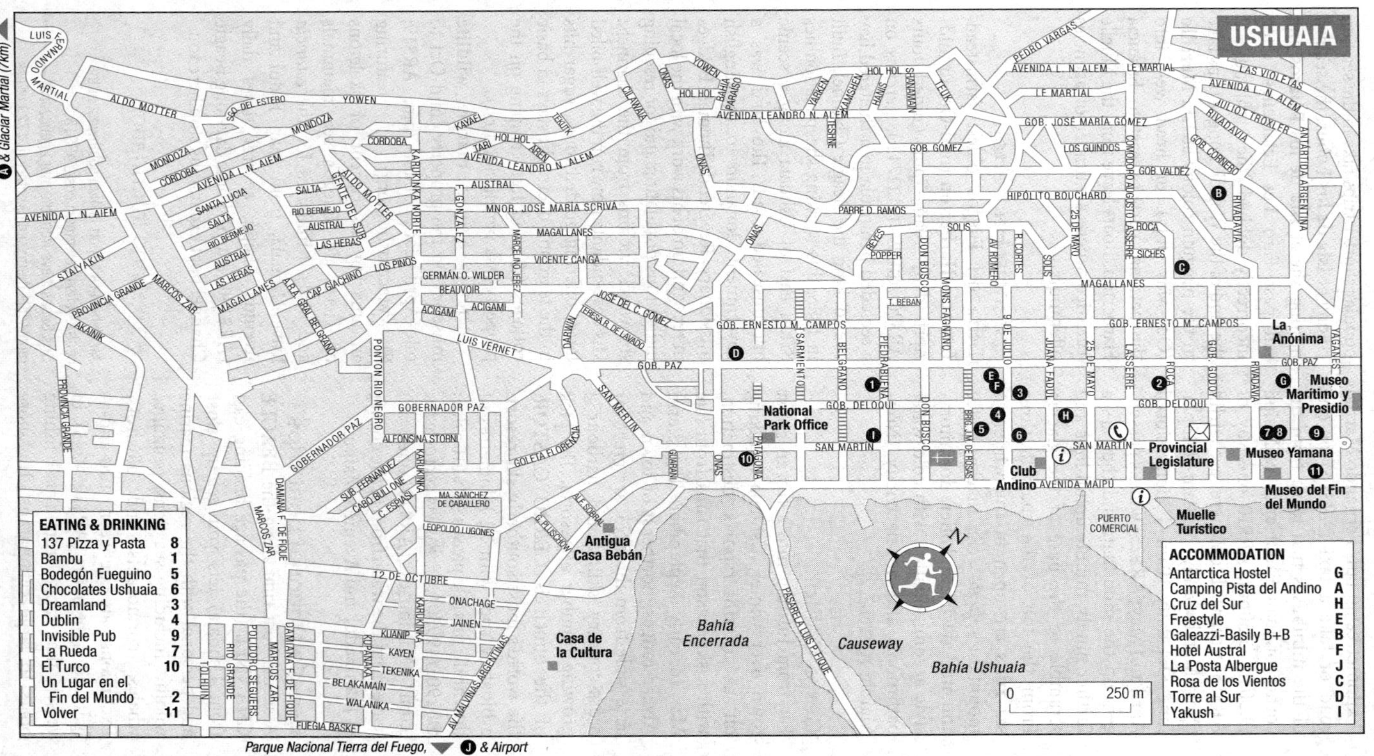
USHUAIA
A & Glaciar Martial (7km)
Parque Nacional Tierra del Fuego, J & Airport
EATING & DRINKING
137 Pizza y Pasta 8
Bambu 1
Bodegón Fueguino 5
Chocolates Ushuaia 6
Dreamland 3
Dublin 4
Invisible Pub 9
La Rueda 7
El Turco 10
Un Lugar en el Fin del Mundo 2
Volver 11
ACCOMMODATION
Antarctica Hostel G
Camping Pista del Andino A
Cruz del Sur H
Freestyle E
Galeazzi-Basily B+B B
Hotel Austral F
La Posta Albergue J
Rosa de los Vientos C
Torre al Sur D
Yakush I
0 250 m
N
La Anónima
Museo Marítimo y Presidio
Museo Yamana
Museo del Fin del Mundo
Provincial Legislature
Club Andino
National Park Office
Antigua Casa Bebán
Casa de la Cultura
Muelle Turístico
PUERTO COMERCIAL
Bahía Encerrada
Causeway
Bahía Ushuaia
AVENIDA MAIPÚ
SAN MARTÍN
GOB. DELOQUI
GOB. PAZ
GOB. ERNESTO M. CAMPOS
MAGALLANES
AVENIDA LEANDRO N. ALEM
AVENIDA L. N. ALEM
PASARELA LUIS P. FIQUE
AV. MALVINAS ARGENTINAS
LUIS FERNANDO MARTIAL
ALDO MOTTER
YOWEN
LUIS VERNET
PONTON RIO NEGRO
KARUKINKA NORTE
12 DE OCTUBRE
HIPÓLITO BOUCHARD
COMODORO AUGUSTO LASSERRE
MNOR. JOSÉ MARÍA SCRIVA
YAGANES
RIVADAVIA
GOB. GODOY
ROCA
LASSERRE
25 DE MAYO
JUANA FADUL
9 DE JULIO
AV. ROMERO
BRIG. J.M. DE ROSAS
MONS FAGNANO
DON BOSCO
PIEDRABUENA
BELGRANO
SARMIENTO
PATAGONIA
ONAS
GUARANI

7 kilometres up Luis Fernando Martial road or take a taxi (AR$16) or one of the minibuses that leave from the corner of Juan Fadúl and Av Maipú (9.30am–5.30pm; AR$10 one-way or AR$15 return). From here, a chairlift (Nov–March daily 9.30am–4.45pm, June–Oct daily 10am–4.30pm, closed April and May; AR$25) whisks passengers up the mountain and then it's a further ninety-minute uphill hike and scramble to the base of the glacier. From the top of the chairlift, three **ski runs** are open in the winter. A mountain *refugio* sells snacks, coffee and mulled wine and offers dormitory-style accommodation with cold-water bathrooms and no electricity (Nov–March; AR$60).

Cerro Castor

Far from turning into a frozen ghost town over winter, Ushuaia is taking off as a **wintersports** destination, with a ski season that runs from late May to early September. The Sierra Alvear ranges, northeast of town and accessible from the RN3, are great for cross-country skiing and harbour a growing number of resorts. The pick of the bunch is **CERRO CASTOR**, the world's most southerly **ski resort**, a blustery spot with 22 kilometres of downhill runs (ski passes AR$110 a day; ⓣ02901/499301, ⓦwww.cerrocastor.com). Minibuses (AR$20 one-way) leave from the waterfront at the corner of Juan Fadul and Avenida Maipú.

Beagle Channel boat trips

A scenic boat ride along the **BEAGLE CHANNEL** (the passage heading east from Ushuaia) lets you get up close and personal with the region's marine wildlife, including sea lions, penguins, whales, cormorants and albatross. Excursions are between two-and-a-half and eight hours (AR$125–245), in vessels that range from small fishing boats to large catamarans. The more popular shorter trips take in the sea lion colony at **Isla de los Lobos**, the seabird nesting site at **Isla de los Pájaros** and sail past Faro **Les Eclaireurs**, often incorrectly dubbed "the Lighthouse at the End of the World". Longer trips take in the penguin colony at **Isla Martillo** (Oct–May only), or head west into the national park or east to Estancia Harberton. Boats leave from the Muelle Turístico where a number of agencies offer tours.

Estancia Harberton

Tierra del Fuego's oldest farmstead, **Estancia Harberton** (mid-Oct to mid-April daily 10am–7pm; guided tours AR$20; ⓣ02901/422742;), perches on a secluded peninsula in a sheltered bay overlooking the Beagle Channel. Built in 1886, this working sheep station lies 85km east of Ushuaia along a scenic but unsealed road. The land was a government donation to the English missionary Reverend Thomas Bridges in recognition of his work with the local indigenous population and for rescuing shipwreck victims from the channels. His descendants now run the well-oiled farm, offering guided tours, sugar hits in the tearoom, overnight stays in basic cottages (❾) and free camping on the property (ask permission first).

There is also a **marine wildlife museum** on the property (mid-Oct to mid-April daily 10am–7pm; AR$19; ⓦwww.acatushun.org), featuring an amazing assortment of skeletons of Tierra del Fuego's sea mammals and birds. Minibuses for the *estancia* leave Ushuaia, from Juan Fadúl and Avenida Maipú, several times daily (AR$150 return). Some day-long Beagle Channel boat excursions stop here too.

Arrival and information

Air Ushuaia's airport is 4km southwest of the centre. A taxi downtown costs AR$15.

Bus Buses leave from the tour agency that represents them; see directory (p.172) or ask at the tourist office where to buy tickets for your destination.

Fishing licenses To purchase a fishing license, head to the Club Caza y Pesca at the corner of Maipú and 9 de Julio (Mon–Fri 9am–5pm, ⓣ02901/423168). Licenses are also available at the National Park office.

Parque Nacional Tierra del Fuego office Av San Martín 1395 (Mon–Fri 9am–4pm; ⓣ02901/421315, ⓦwww.parquesnacionales.gov.ar).

Tourist office The tourist office is at Av San Martín 674 (Mon–Fri 8am–6pm; Sat & Sun 9am–6pm; ⓣ02901/432001, ⓦwww.e-ushuaia.com). Register here if you plan to go hiking as many area trails are poorly marked. There are also tourist offices at the Muelle Turístico (Mon–Fri 8am–10pm, Sat & Sun 9am–8pm; ⓣ02901/437666) and at the airport, open to coincide with flight arrivals (ⓣ02901/423970).

Accommodation

In summer, book accommodation in advance, and be prepared for high prices. The closest **campsite** to town is *Camping Pista del Andino*, 3km uphill at Alem 2873 (ⓣ02901/435890, ⓦwww.lapistadelandino.com.ar; AR$15 per person), with bay views and good facilities, including a kitchen and bike rental. They offer free pick-up from town.

Hostels

For the budget traveller, a number of excellent hostels offer good services and plenty of *buena onda* (good vibes). All have kitchens, free breakfast and internet. **Antarctica Hostel** Calle Antartida Argentina 270 ⓣ02901/435774, ⓦwww.antarcticahostel.com.ar. This sociable hostel has a light-drenched lounge area, enticing aromas wafting from its kitchen and a downstairs bar that pegs things up a notch at night. The plain upstairs dormitories (AR$40) are a bit of a hike from the downstairs bathrooms. ❻

Cruz del Sur Deloqui 636 ⓣ02901/434099, ⓦwww.xdelsur.com.ar. A slightly shambolic hostel with a central location and helpful Canadian-Italian owners. The dorms (AR$40) are a bit cramped and the showers temperamental.

Freestyle Gobernador Paz 866 ⓣ02901/432874, ⓦwww.ushuaiafreestyle.com. Promoting itself as a "five-star hostel", this backpacker's favourite certainly looks more like a hotel; only the young party crowd and top-floor communal lounge with pool table and pumping stereo suggest otherwise. Dorms (AR$40) are clean and spacious while private doubles have bathtubs. ❻

La Posta Albergue Perón Sur 864 ⓣ02901/444650, ⓦwww.laposta-ush.com.ar. Too bad it's so far from town (25min walk), because this sparkling new hostel ticks every other box: two kitchens, free laundry, free local calls, well-scrubbed dorm rooms (beds AR$40) and staff who will bend over backwards. ❺

Torre al Sur Gobernador Paz 1437 ⓣ02901/430745, ⓦwww.torrealsur.com.ar. A rickety wooden blue-and-white mansion that's not the most salubrious hostel you'll ever clap eyes on, but the doubles are the cheapest in town and the top-floor dormitory (AR$36, discount with HI card) gives you 360-degree mountain, harbour and city views. AR$70. ❹

Yakush Piedrabuena 118, ⓣ02901/435807, ⓦwww.hostelyakush.com.ar. Spacious and modern yet move-right-in-cozy, this central hostel, which overlooks the main drag, has a piano and owners who know their stuff. The dorms (AR$40) are roomy enough to spread out in, and one of the doubles has an en suite with bathtub. ❺

Hotels

All hotels listed here include breakfast and internet. **Hotel Austral** 9 de Julio 250 ⓣ02901/422223, ⓦwww.hotel-austral.com.ar. A modern, one-star-hotel with well-appointed rooms that look out onto a glassed-in hallway. Very central and clean. ❽

Galeazzi-Basily B&B Gobernador Valedéz 323 ⓣ02901/423213, ⓦwww.avesdelsur.com.ar. Run by hospitable English- and French-speaking owners, this large family house on a quiet residential street has small, simple rooms with shared bathroom, use of kitchen, and hot drinks and persistent cake offers all day. T he self-contained *cabañas* in the backyard offer more privacy and sleep up to four. Room ❻ *Cabaña* ❼

Rosa de los Vientos Roca 533 ⓣ02901/430078, ⓦwww.hrosadelosvientos.com.ar. A good option for couples, the ten tastefully furnished rooms at this modern B&B include spotless en suites, fridge, TV, hair dryer, coffee maker and free-standing mirrors. Some look out onto a shady garden. ❽

Eating

Cheap restaurants are thin on the ground in Ushuaia. Seafood is king here, especially the tasty *centolla* (king crab); *cordero* (lamb) is another local speciality.

137 Pizza y Pasta San Martín 137 ☎02901/435005. The crowds speak for themselves at this busy restaurant. If you're not excited by pizza (from AR$39) or pasta (from AR$38), you'll warm to the lamb and lentil stew (AR$22).

Bambu Piedrabueno 276 ☎02901/437028. You don't often see "vegetarian", "cheap" and "Ushuaia" in the same sentence, but this Asian take-away buffet fits the bill (large portions under AR$10).

Bodegón Fueguino San Martín 895, ☎02901/431972. Park yourself down on a sheepskin-draped wooden bench and order what this restaurant does best – succulent roast lamb, marinated in a choice of twelve sauces (AR$29–37). Closed Mon.

Chocolates Ushuaia San Martín 783. Sometimes you have to travel to the end of the Earth for the world's best hot chocolate.

Un Lugar en el Fin del Mundo Roca 258 ☎02901/434441. This humble restaurant offers good value (for Ushuaia) as well as warm service and hearty fare. Everything – down to the heart-shaped mashed potatoes – is served with love. Mains range from pepper steak (AR$32) to paella ($69 for two).

La Rueda San Martín and Rivadavia ☎02901/436540. If your tastebuds are turned on by the sight of a big open fire pit filled with freshly slaughtered, slow-roasting beasts, you'll adore this all-you-can-eat *parrilla* (AR$46).

El Turco San Martín 1440 ☎02901/424711. Typical Argentine fare (*milanesas*, pastas and pizza) at reasonable prices, scoffed by ravenous locals (mains around AR$30).

Volver Av Maipú 37 ☎02901/423977. For everything fishy and one heck of a realistic Che Guevara statue, take your appetite to this harbourfront institution. While waiting for your food (mains AR$40–90) greet the king crab in the fish tank or get an eyeful of the eclectic knick-knacks tacked to the wall. Nov–Easter closed Sun lunch, rest of year closed Mon.

Drinking and nightlife

Dreamland 9 de Julio and Deoqui ☎02901/421246, ⓦwww.dreamlandushuaia.com.ar. This funky bar with posh white couches, an artsy vibe and mood lighting, pulses to electronic music when it's not hosting live music or tango nights. Beers (AR$8) and cocktails (AR$15) are served until late.

Dublin 9 de Julio 168. The best of the Ushuaia Irish bars that battle it out for the dubious crown of "world's most southerly Irish pub". Wooden furnishings and a musty smell provide the perfect backdrop for sinking a bottle of Guinness (AR$12) with a plate of *picadas*.

Invisible Pub San Martín 19 ☎02901/435255. Rock on night or day at this cavernous pub, which screens music DVDs and stages live bands. Beer (AR$8) and burgers (AR$18) are the nutritional staples.

Directory

Airlines Aerolíneas Argentinas, Maipú and 9 de Julio ☎02901/421218; LADE, San Martín 542 No. 5 ☎02901/421123. LAN flies here between Oct and March and sells tickets through local agent Rumbo Sur, San Martín 350 (☎02901/422441).

Bus companies Lider to Río Grande, Gob Paz 921 (☎02901/436421); Marga y Taqsa to Río Gallegos and Río Grande, Godoy 41 (☎02901/435453); Montiel to Río Grande, Deloqui 110 (☎02901/421366); Pacheco for connections from Río Grande to Punta Arenas, San Martín 1267 (☎02901/437073); Tecni Austral for Comodoro Rivadavia, Puerto Natales, Punta Arenas, Río Gallegos and Río Grande, Roca 157 (☎02901/431408).

Car rental Crossing Patagonia, Maipú 857 (☎02901/435475, ⓦwww.crossingpatagonia.com).

Currency exchange Thaler, Av San Martín 209 (☎02901/421911).

Post office San Martín and Godoy.

Spanish school Finis Terrae Spanish School, Rosas 475 (☎02901/433871, ⓦwww.spanishpatagonia.com).

Tour operators All Patagonia, Juan Fadul 60 (☎02901/433622, ⓦwww.allpatagonia.com) run Antarctic expeditions, scenic flights and nature and sailing excursions; Rumbo Sur, San Martín 350 (☎02901/422275, ⓦwww.rumbosur.com.ar) organise Antarctica cruises, Beagle Channel boat trips as well as a range of excursions in and around Ushuaia; Ushuaia Divers (☎02901/444701, ⓦwww.ushuaiadivers.com.ar) operate diving trips in the Beagle Channel to see shipwrecks, sea lions and king crabs.

Moving on

Air to: Buenos Aires (8 daily; 3hr 30min); El Calafate (8 daily; 1hr 10min); Río Gallegos (daily; 55min); sporadic services to Puerto Madryn (2hr) and Trelew (2hr) and international connections to Punta Arenas and Santiago de Chile.

Bus to: El Calafate (Mon–Sat once daily; 18hr); Puerto Natales (4 weekly; 16hr); Punta Arenas (daily except Tues; 12hr); Río Gallegos (1–2 daily; 13hr); Río Grande (12–16 daily; 3.5-4hr).

PARQUE NACIONAL TIERRA DEL FUEGO

Wet and wild **PARQUE NACIONAL TIERRA DEL FUEGO**, 12km west of Ushuaia, stretches from the Beagle Channel in the south to the border with Chile in the west. Encompassing 630 square kilometres of mountains, waterfalls, glaciers, lakes, rivers, valleys, sub-Antarctic forest and peat bog, most of the park is closed to the public, with less than thirty kilometres of accessible trails. With a couple of days up your sleeve, you could tackle all the short treks in the park. The most popular trail is the **Senda Costera** (approx 11km, 3hr 30min), which follows the shoreline through coastal forest of deciduous beech trees, affording spectacular views of the Beagle Channel, passing grass-covered mounds that were former campsites of the indigenous Yámana and offering birdwatchers prime opportunities for spotting Magellanic woodpeckers, cormorants, gulls and oystercatchers. For the park's best views, trudge to the top of 970-metre-high **Cerro Guanaco** (8km return, 4hr). Another popular trail, **Senda Hito XXIV** (5km; 90min), is a level path tracing the shores of Lago Roca and ending at a small obelisk that marks the border with Chile (it is illegal to continue beyond here). Guanacos, Patagonian grey foxes, Fuegian foxes, Southern river otters and some ninety bird species are among the park's fauna, while introduced Canadian beavers and European rabbits also run amok, wreaking environmental havoc.

Arrival and information

By bus The easiest way to reach the park without your own transport is with the buses that leave

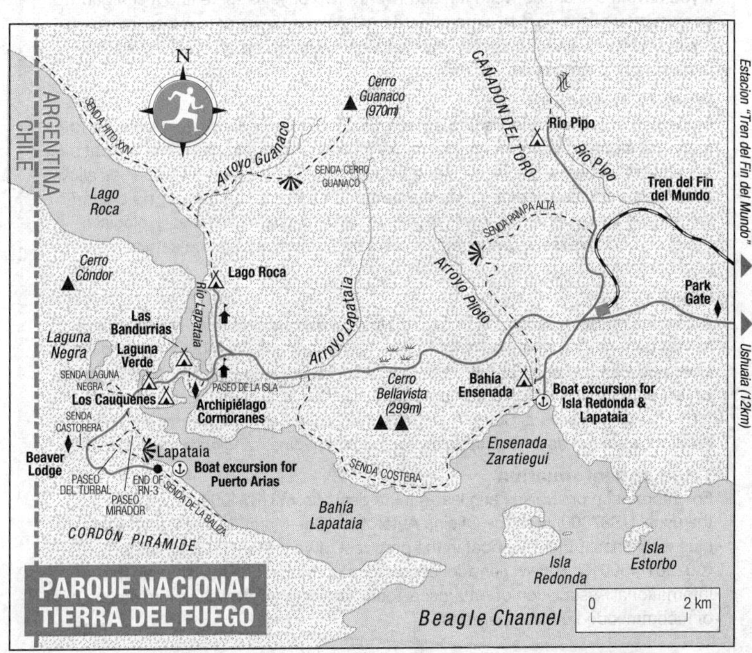

Ushuaia from the corner of Juan Fadul and Av Maipú (AR$35 return).

By train El Tren del Fin del Mundo (AR$70 return or AR$65 one-way; ⓣ02901/431600, ⓦwww.trendelfindelmundo.com.ar) runs to the park on the world's most southerly (and possibly slowest) steam train, along tracks originally laid by prisoners for transporting wood. Trains leave three times daily in the summer from the Fin del Mundo station, 8km west of Ushuaia.

Entrance fee AR$30, to be paid at the office at the park entrance.

What to bring As elsewhere in the region, weather in the park is four seasons in one day, so pack sunscreen, waterproofs and warm clothes.

Accommodation

There are four rudimentary free **campsites** plus one serviced campground at Lago Roca. This has hot showers, a restaurant and a lakeside setting (ⓣ02901/433313; AR$12). Alongside the Lago Roca campground is a **refugio** with dormitory-style accommodation (AR$35).

RÍO GRANDE

Trout fishing aside, the only reason to be in dreary, gusty **RÍO GRANDE** is to change buses or to use the airport if all flights servicing Ushuaia, 230 kilometres southwest, are booked. Built on its namesake river, Río Grande consists of grid after grid of flat urban sprawl, its colourful houses the city's only aesthetic saving grace. Sheep and oil are the economic staples, while the **Monumento a la Trucha** – a giant trout statue on the RN-3 – references why high-rolling anglers are drawn to the nearby rivers. For something to do in town, the **Museo Municipal Virginia Choquintel**, Alberdi 555 (Mon–Fri 9am–5pm, Sat 3–7pm;

SPLURGE: ANTARCTICA

You've come this far south, so what's another thousand kilometres? Well, at least US$4000 and a stomach-churning journey across the stormy Drake Passage. Still, if you have the cash, between ten and twenty-two days to spare and a charged-up camera, you might want to jump aboard one of the cruisers or icebreakers sailing south from Ushuaia to the great white continent. Ushuaia is after all, the world's closest port to Antarctica.

What to see and do

More than forty thousand visitors a year make the journey south from Ushuaia to marvel at elephant seals, penguins, minke whales and albatrosses, and to float past translucent icebergs, glacial cliffs and fields of virgin snow. Some companies allow passengers to disembark the ship, walk around and camp on the ice, zip around icebergs in zodiac boats or kayak alongside wildlife. Naturalists and geologists travel on board vessels, giving regular talks on Antarctica's unique natural environment.

When to go

Antarctica cruise season runs from mid-November to mid-March. The best time to visit depends on what you want to see: November has the most snow and ice coverage, January and February see baby penguins taking their first clumsy steps, while February and March are prime whale-spotting season. Longer Antarctica trips also take in several South Atlantic islands. Summer coastal temperatures in Antarctica are not as inhospitable as you might imagine, ranging from -5°C to 5°C.

Tours and information

For information on cruises and last-minute deals (from US$4000, down from the usual US$7000), visit the Oficina Antarctica (Oct–March Mon–Fri 9am–6pm, plus weekends if there's a boat in the port, rest of year Mon–Fri 9am–5pm; ⓣ02901/430015, ⓦwww.tierradelfuego.org.ar) at Maipú 505 in Ushuaia. The International Association of Antarctica Tour Operators (ⓦwww.iaato.org) keeps a list of recommended cruise operators.

free; ⓣ02964/430647), has exhibits on the region's indigenous and pioneering history.

Arrival and information

Air Río Grande's airport (ⓣ02964/431340) lies 5km west of town and is serviced by Aerolíneas Argentinas and LADE flights. A taxi to the centre costs AR$12.
Bus There is no bus terminal. Buses arrive and leave from company offices; ask for directions at the tourist office.
Fishing licenses Pick up a fishing license at the Asociación de Pesca con Mosca, Montilla 1040 (Mon–Fri 10.30am–1.30pm & 4–8pm, Sat 10.30am–2pm; ⓣ02964/1545-8048).
Tourist office The friendly tourist office is at Plaza Almirante Brown, Rosales 350 (Mon–Fri 9am–5pm; ⓣ02964/431324, ⓦwww.riogrande.gov.ar).

Accommodation

Most hotels are fishing for wealthy anglers, leaving budget travellers bereft of options. If you want to brave the relentless wind, there is a wooded riverside **campsite** about ten blocks from downtown at O'Higgins and Montilla (ⓣ02964/420536, ⓔnauticorg@speedy.com.ar; AR$8).

Albergue Hotel Argentino San Martín 64 ⓣ02964/422546. The only hostel in town, this run-down old house has a big kitchen, a nice communal space, basic shared rooms, piping hot showers and free internet. The relaxed *dueña* is a bundle of warmth and fun. Dorm AR$40. ❹
Noal Hospedaje Obligado 557 ⓣ02964/427516. Offering great value, this ten-room hotel has plain, spotless rooms with comfortable beds and TV. Some singles, and some with private bathrooms. ❺

Eating and drinking

Epa!!! Bar-café Rosales 445. Dolled up in shocking shades of purple and yellow, this pub-cum-diner does fruit juices, cocktails, gourmet coffees and a set menu (chicken and rice, drink and dessert) for AR$20. A beer is AR$10.
Hotel Ibarra Restaurante Rosales 357 ⓣ02964/426935. A sandwich-and-coffee bar during the day and fancy restaurant come night, with an imaginative selection of mains (around AR$30) ranging from king crab ravioli to grilled sea bass.

Moving on

Bus To Punta Arenas in Chile (3 weekly; 8hr), Río Gallegos (2 daily; 9–10hr) and Ushuaia (roughly every 40min; 3–4hr).

Bolivia

HIGHLIGHTS ✪

PARQUE NACIONAL MADIDI: this pristine rainforest protects remarkable diversity

CORDILLERA REAL: these dramatic Andean peaks are a paradise for mountaineers

ISLA DEL SOL: the spiritual centre of the Andean world

LA PAZ TO COROICO: perilous yet spectacular highway

CERRO RICO: an unforgettable glimpse of the working conditions endured by miners

SALAR DE UYUNI: the world's biggest salt lake– a truly surreal experience

ROUGH COSTS

DAILY BUDGET Basic $15/with the occasional treat $30

DRINK Paceña beer $1

FOOD *Chairo* (potato soup) $1.50

HOSTEL/BUDGET HOTEL $6–11

TRAVEL Bus: La Paz-Copacabana (155km) $2.80

FACT FILE

POPULATION 9.1 million

AREA 1,098,581 sq km

LANGUAGE Spanish (also more than thirty indigenous languages)

RELIGION Roman Catholicism

CURRENCY Boliviano, aka Peso

CAPITAL La Paz

INTERNATIONAL PHONE CODE ⊕591

Timezone GMT – 4hr

Introduction

Surrounded by Brazil, Paraguay, Argentina, Chile and Peru, Bolivia lies at the heart of South America. Stretching from the majestic icebound peaks and bleak high-altitude deserts of the Andes to the exuberant rainforests and vast savannas of the Amazon basin, it embraces an astonishing range of landscapes and climates, and encompasses everything outsiders find most exotic and mysterious about the continent.

Three centuries of Spanish colonial rule have certainly left their mark, most obviously in some of the finest colonial architecture on the continent. Yet the European influence is essentially a thin veneer overlying indigenous cultural traditions that stretch back long before the Conquest: while Spanish is the language of business and government, more than thirty indigenous languages are still spoken.

The country is dominated by the mighty **Andes**, which march through the west of the country along two parallel chains. In the north and east, they give way to the tropical rainforests and grasslands of the **Amazon and Eastern Lowlands**; in the southeast to the dry thornbrush and scrub of the **Chaco**. Underdevelopment and a lack of tourism have actually been blessings in disguise for the extraordinary biodiversity these landscapes support; owing to it's remoteness, Bolivia remains one of South America's least-visited countries, despite it's myriad attractions.

Most visitors spend a few days in the fascinating city of **La Paz**, which combines a dramatic high-altitude setting with a compelling intermingling of traditional indigenous and modern urban cultures. Close by is the magical **Lago Titicaca**, which serves as a good base for trekking, climbing or mountain biking in the **Cordillera Real**, a magnificent range of high Andean peaks. Just north of La Paz, the Andes plunge precipitously down into the Amazon basin through the deep valleys of the **Yungas**, a region of dramatic scenery and sudden transformations in climate and vegetation. The best base for visiting the Bolivian Amazon further north is **Rurrenabaque**, but more adventurous travellers can head east via the **Reserva de la Biosfera del Beni** – the start of exciting trips north along the **Río Mamoré** towards Brazil.

South of La Paz, the southern **Altiplano** – the bleak, high plateau that stretches between the Andes – has historically

WHEN TO VISIT

Climate varies much more as a result of altitude and topography than it does between different seasons. Winter (May–Oct), is the **dry season**, and in many ways the best time to visit Bolivia, with sunny, trekking-friendly highland days and slightly (but pleasantly) lower temperatures in the generally hot and humid **lowlands**. While highland temperatures hover in the mid-teens most of the year (albeit with chilly winter nights), the summer **rainy season** (Nov–March), can see lowland temperatures reach 31°C. Rain affects the condition of roads throughout the country, especially in the Amazon, where river transport takes over from often impassable overland routes. The parched Altiplano and mountainsides nevertheless briefly transform into lush grassland, as wild flowers proliferate and the earth comes to life.

been home to most of Bolivia's population as well as it's foremost attractions: **Potosí**, which merit's a visit for colonial architecture and the opportunity to experience underground life in the mines of **Cerro Rico**; and Uyuni, the jumping-off point for expeditions into the astonishing landscapes of the **Salar de Uyuni** and the **Reserva de Fauna Andina Eduardo Avaroa**, a remote region of high-altitude deserts and half-frozen, mineral-stained lakes. Also well worth visiting are the towns of **Sucre**, with it's fine colonial architecture and charming atmosphere, and **Santa Cruz**, a brash, modern and lively tropical metropolis – and a good base for exploring the diverse attractions of the Eastern Lowlands, including the rainforests of the **Parque Nacional Amboró** and the immaculately restored Jesuit missions of **Chiquitos**.

CHRONOLOGY

1000BC Founding of Tiwanaku on the shores of Lago Titicaca, centre of a colonial empire comprising much of modern Bolivia, southern Peru, northeast Argentina and northern Chile.

c.1000AD Tiwanaku dramatically collapses, most likely as a result of a prolonged drought.

Eleventh–fifteenth centuries The Aymara take control of the Altiplano, maintaining a more localised culture and religion.

Mid-fifteenth century The Aymara are incorporated into the Inca Empire, albeit with a limited degree of autonomy.

1532 Francisco Pizarro leads his Spanish conquistadors to a swift and unlikely defeat of the Inca army in Cajamarca, (Bajo) Peru.

1538 Pizarro sends Spanish troops south to aid the Aymaran Colla as they battle both the remnants of an Inca rebellion and their Aymara rivals the Lupaca, establishing Spanish control of the territory known as Alto Peru.

1545 The continent's richest deposit of silver, Cerro Rico, is discovered, giving birth to the mining city of Potosí.

1548 La Paz is founded in the northern altiplano as a transit point between Potosí and Lima.

1558 La Plata (later Sucre) is confirmed as the capital of Alto Peru.

1574 Cochabamba and Tarija are founded as bread baskets for the mines of Potosí.

1561 Santa Cruz is established by conquistadors from Asunción, though it remains geographically isolated for the following three and half centuries.

1570s Viceroy Francisco Toledo precipitates Potosí's silver boom – and subsequent economic growth in Europe – by reinstating the Inca system of forced labour, the *mita*.

1691 San Javier is founded as the first of the Chiquitos Jesuit missions.

1767 The Spanish crown expels the Jesuit order from the Americas.

1780–82 The last major indigenous uprising, the Great Rebellion, is led by combined Inca-Aymara army of Túpacs Amaru and Katari.

1809 La Paz becomes the first capital in the Americas to declare independence from Spain.

1810–17 A succession of Argentine armies – supported by local guerrillas – attempt to drive the Spanish from Alto Peru.

1824 The last Spanish army is destroyed at the battle of Ayacucho in (Bajo) Peru.

1825 The newly liberated Alto Peru rejects a union with either (Bajo) Peru or Argentina, and adopts a declaration of independence, naming it'self Bolivia after Venezuelan independence hero, Simón Bolívar.

1825–29 Bolívar's general, Antonio José de Sucre, serves as Bolivia's first president, his reformist policies including stripping the Catholic Church of most of it's wealth.

1879 Chile begins the War of the Pacific by occupying the entire Bolivian coastline and invading Peru.

1899 The Federal Revolution consolidates power of the new tin-mining barons and createsa new administrative capital in La Paz.

1904 Bolivia finally cedes it's coastline to Chile, in addition to losing the Acre to Brazil.

1932–35 The Chaco War with Paraguay ends in stalemate and huge loss of life, precipitating a shift towards radical politics.

1952 The National Revolution sees armed civilians defeat the army in La Paz and the ascension to power of the MNR, followed by the introduction of universal suffrage, mine nationalisation and wholescale agrarian reform.

1964 A resurgent army led by General René Barrientos seizes power, beginning eighteen years of military dicatatorship.

1967 Having previously formed a pact with the *campesinos*, Barrientos ensures the failure of Che Guevara's guerrilla campaign. Aided by CIA advisors, the Bolivian military crush the campaign and execute Guevara in the hamlet of La Higuera.

1970s General Hugo Banzer heads a brutal military regime, coinciding with an unprecedented period of

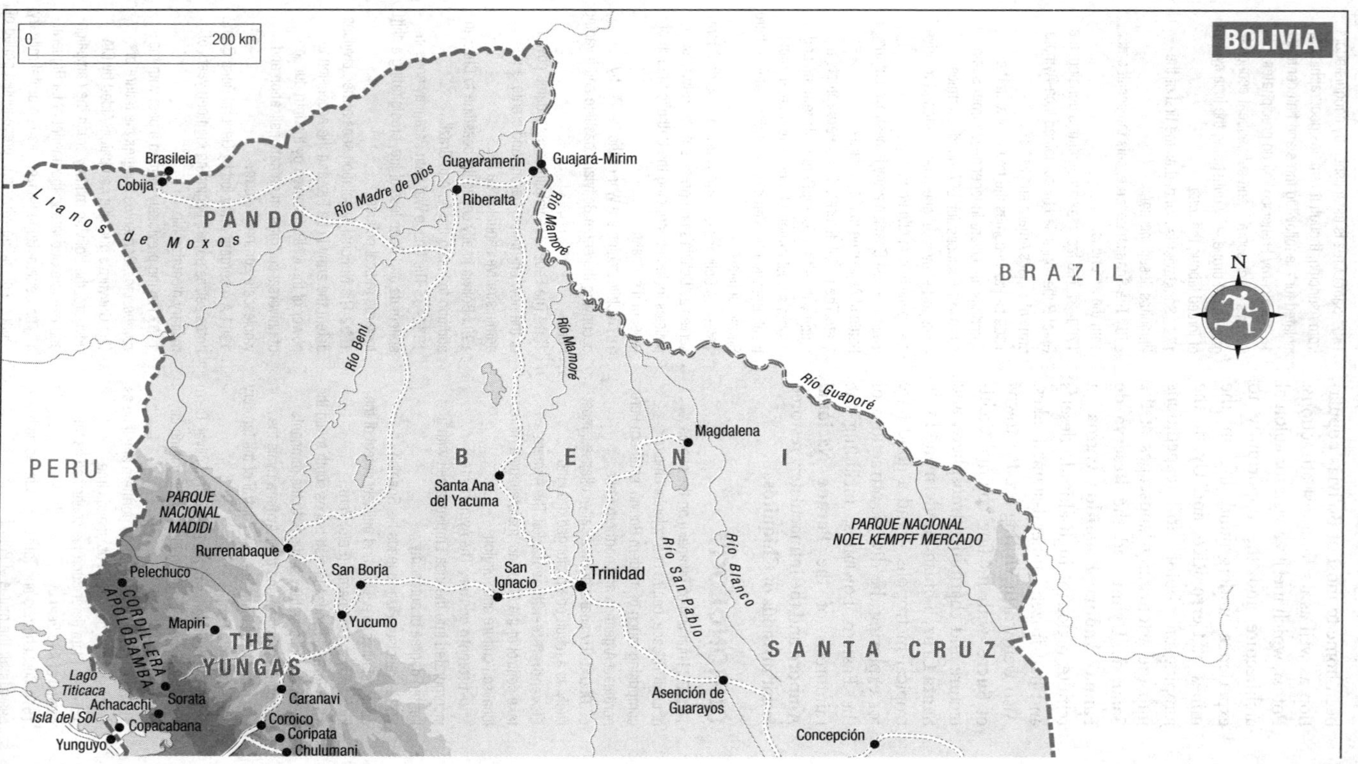
BOLIVIA
0
200 km
N
BRAZIL
PERU
PANDO
BENI
SANTA CRUZ
THE YUNGAS
Llanos de Moxos
CORDILLERA APOLOBAMBA
PARQUE NACIONAL MADIDI
PARQUE NACIONAL NOEL KEMPFF MERCADO
Río Madre de Dios
Río Beni
Río Mamoré
Río Guaporé
Río San Pablo
Río Blanco
Lago Titicaca
Isla del Sol
Brasileia
Cobija
Guayaramerín
Guajará-Mirim
Riberalta
Santa Ana del Yacuma
Magdalena
Rurrenabaque
San Borja
San Ignacio
Trinidad
Yucumo
Pelechuco
Mapiri
Sorata
Achacachi
Copacabana
Yunguyo
Caranavi
Coroico
Coripata
Chulumani
Asención de Guarayos
Concepción

Tiwanaku
LA PAZ
Illimani 6439m
CORDILLERA REAL
CHAPARE
San Javier
San Ignacio de Velasco
Santa Ana
San Rafael
San Miguel
San Matías
San Ramón
Buena Vista
Cochambamba
Patacamaya
ALTIPLANO
Quillacollo
Totora
CORDILLERA ORIENTAL
Quimone
Oruro
Santa Cruz
Volcán Sajama
CORDILLERA OCCIDENTAL
Samaipata
San José de Chiquitos
Aiquile
Vallegrande
Lagó Poopó
Chállapata
Puerto Suárez
Sucre
CHACO
Corumbá
Tarabuco
Salar de Coipasa
Potosí
Camiri
Salar de Uyuni
Uyuni
CHUQUISACA
Avaroa
Villamontes
Volcán Ollagüe
Tupiza
PARAGUAY
Tarija
Villazón
Yacuiba
Laguna Colorada
CHILE
Laguna Verde
ARGENTINA
Metres
4000
3000
2000
1000
500
0

economic growth and the emergence of Santa Cruz as the nation's second biggest city.

1980–81 The most brutal and corrupt regime in modern Bolivian history is led by General Luis Garcia Meza, backed by drug barons, Italian fascists and even Nazi war criminals including Klaus Barbie.

1983 The country returns to democratic rule with Hernán Siles as president.

1985 Bolivia plunges into a recession as the bottom falls out of the tin market, and the economic vacuum is filled by the production and export of cocaine, with much of the drug profit's reinvested in Santa Cruz.

1993 US-raised millionaire mining entrepreneur Goni Sánchez de Lozada begins his first term as president with sweeping privatisation.

Late 1990s US-backed coca eradication policies provoke widespread resistance, led by indigenous activist Evo Morales.

2000 Cochabamba witnesses a popular uprising, the Water War, after the city utility is sold into foreign ownership.

2003 After having narrowly beaten Morales to the presidency the previous year, Goni provokes massive protests over plans to export natural gas via Chile, resulting in eighty deaths and his subsequent flight into US exile.

2005 Evo Morales is elected as Bolivia's first indigenous president with an absolute majority and a programme of nationalisation and agrarian reform.

2006 The Morales administratiom completes it's nationalisation of the gas sector.

2007 Clashes in Cochabamba between Morales supporters and pro-autonomists leave two dead.

April 2008 The Santa Cruz-based right wing launches it's proposed statutes for provincial autonomy.

August 2008 Evo Morales wins 67 percent of the vote in a recall referendum.

September 2008 Morales declares a state of emergency in the northern province of Pando after thirty *campesinos* are massacred, reportedly on the orders of pro-autonomy prefect Leopoldo Fernández; Bolivia expels US ambassador amid allegations of pro-autonomy agitation.

October 2008 Congress approves content of a new constitution giving greater rights to the indigenous majority.

November 2008 Morales suspends US Drug Enforcement programme, accusing agents of espionage. In retaliation, the US adds Bolivia to it's drugs blacklist and suspends trade preferences. Morales hails the election of Barack Obama and expresses the wish for closer relations with the US administration.

Basics

ARRIVAL

Bolivia isn't the easiest country to fly to. The only direct services are from Miami in the US and from neighbouring South American countries, the most frequent connections being from São Paulo in Brazil, Buenos Aires in Argentina and Lima in Peru. In Bolivia it'self there are only two international airports: El Alto in La Paz (see p.195) and Viru Viru in Santa Cruz (see p.238), the former with the distinction of being the highest in the world. Once you're in Bolivia, flying is actually a relatively cheap and convenient way to get around, especially in the rainy season when many roads are impassable. Bolivia has land borders with Argentina, Brazil, Chile, Peru and Paraguay, with full details of the main border crossings given in accounts of relevant departure points.

From Argentina

The principal border crossing is from La Quiaca in Argentina to Villazón in the southern Altiplano (see box, p.223), with regular bus and train connections on to the desert town of Tupiza. There's also a crossing between Pocitos in Argentina and Yacuiba in the Chaco (see p.243), from where it's possible to travel by bus or train to Santa Cruz.

From Brazil

The busiest crossing is the rail border at Quijarro (see p.239), near the Brazilian city of Corumbá, where the Bolivian Pantanal meets it's more famous Brazilian counterpart. From Quijarro, it's a full day's train journey on to Santa Cruz. There are also a couple of borders in Amazonia, from Guajará-Mirim (transit point Porto Velho) by boat across the Rio Mamoré to Guayaramerín, from where there are regular onward flights; and from Brasiléia (transit point Rio Branco), to Cobija, the capital of Pando province (see p.249).

From Chile

There are three trans-Andean routes which cross from Chile, the most popular being the road up from Arica on the coast to Tambo Quemado (see p.213), and on to La Paz. A less frequent but more exhilarating alternative is the twice weekly train from Calama to Uyuni via the Bolivian border post of Avaroa (see p.223). Even more adventurous is the remote border crossing of Laguna Verde, at the southern edge of Reserva Eduardo Avaroa, accessible via organised tours from the Chilean town of San Pedro de Atacama.

From Peru

The most widely used land border of all is the Yunguyo-Kasani crossing at the southern tip of Lago Titicaca near Copacabana, easily accessible from Puno in southern Peru. Less busy but just as easy to get to from Puno is the crossing at Desaguadero, with regular onward transport to La Paz.

From Paraguay

For the adventurous only, the trans-chaco border between Bolivia and Paraguay (see p.243) is navigable only in the dry season, during which the route – all the way from Asunción to Santa Cruz – is served by an endurance-testing two-to-three day bus journey.

VISAS

Many visitors to Bolivia – including citizens of the United Kingdom and most European countries – don't need a visa. However, new rules implemented in 2007 mean that citizens of the **United States** are now **required** to obtain a visa, at a cost of $100 per person; they're valid for five years and allow visitors to enter Bolivia three times a year, with a maximum of ninety days per year spent in the country. US citizens will also need a passport valid for the next six months, with at least one blank page, as well as proof that they have the necessary funds to leave the country (such as a photocopy of your credit card). A passport photo is also required, as is proof of onward travel (a copy of a hotel reservation will usually do the trick). You can obtain an application form for the visa at the airport or border, or download one from Ⓦwww.bolivia-usa.org.

For other nationalities, the situation does change periodically, so always **check** with your local embassy or consulate a month or two before travelling. On arrival, you'll be issued with a **tourist card** (*tarjeta de turismo*) valid for thirty or ninety days, depending on your nationality. Before entry, check the number of days you're allowed to stay and make sure the border officials give you the stamp with the maximum amount of days your nationality allows you; if they give you less than the maximum, you can request it on the spot (though there's no guarantee you'll get it) or go to the Immigration office in La Paz or the nearest city to your border crossing and receive another stamp.

GETTING AROUND

Bolivia's topography, size and lack of basic infrastructure mean that getting around is often a challenge, especially in the rainy season. However, buses are very cheap and numerous, and even flying within the country is very affordable, with **flights** costing around $70 each way.

Air

La Paz, Santa Cruz, Sucre and Cochabamba are all connected by **daily flights** ($40–100), and there are also frequent services to Tarija, Trinidad, Rurrenabaque and a number of remote towns in the Amazon and the eastern lowlands. There is currently one main commercial carrier, AeroSur (Ⓦwww.aerosur.com), as well as a smaller internal, lowland operator, Amaszonas (Ⓦwww.amaszonas.com). The former flagship airline, Lloyd Aéreo Boliviano, is still to resume a full service after falling into financial difficulties in 2007, with the Morales administration, at the time of writing, reportedly working on setting up a new flag carrier. **The Bolivian air force** also operates passenger services under it's commercial arm Transportes Aereo Militar (TAM; Ⓣ02/212-1582), particularly to the further flung corners of the country. Busier routes should be booked at least several days in advance. Flights are often cancelled or delayed, especially in the Amazon, where the weather can be a problem.

Bus

Bolivia's **buses** are run by a variety of private companies and ply all the main routes in the country. Due to poor road conditions, journey times are unpredictable, and you should always be prepared for major delays, especially in the rainy season. When travelling in the highlands, always bring warm clothing and a blanket or sleeping bag, as journeys can get bitterly cold.

Train

The sole Andean operator, FCA (Empresa Ferroviaria Andina; Ⓦwww.fca.co.bo), runs two passenger lines – *Expresso del Sur* and *Wara Wara del Sur* – from Oruro south across the Altiplano via Uyuni and Tupiza to Villazón on the Argentine border. A separate company, Ferroviaria Oriental, runs two lines in the lowlands: one from Santa Cruz east to the Brazilian border at Quijaro; the other from Santa Cruz south to Yacuiba in the Chaco, on the Argentine border.

Boat

Although Bolivia is a landlocked country, there are still several regions – particularly Lago Titicaca and the Amazon – where water is still the best way of getting around. There are two main forms of **river transport** in the Bolivian Amazon: dugout canoes, powered by outboard motors, are used to visit protected areas such as the Parque Nacional Madidi; alternatively, more economic but less comfortable cargo boats ply the Río Mamoré, between Trinidad and Guayaramerín on the Brazilian frontier, and the Río Ichilo, between Trinidad and Puerto Villaroel in the Chapare.

Car rental

If you're short on time or want to get to some really out-of-the-way destinations, **renting a car** is a possibility, though it's often easier and not much more expensive to hire a taxi or *camioneta* to drive you around for a day or longer.

Outside towns, most roads are unpaved and in very poor condition, so **four-wheel drive** (4WD) is essential. Petrol stations are few and far between and breakdown services even scarcer, so you should fill your tank whenever you can. Speed limit's are irregularly posted. Virtually none of the major international **car rental companies** are represented in Bolivia, but you'll find local rental companies in all the major cities: see the relevant listings section in each city account for details. Generally, you'll pay a flat fee of US$25–40 per day, plus about US50¢ extra for each kilometre you drive; 4WDs cost about double. You'll need to be over 25 to rent a car, and to leave a major credit card or large cash deposit as security; you'll also require some kind of insurance.

ACCOMMODATION

While **accommodation** in Bolivia is generally good-value, the standard is not particularly high, especially in smaller towns. Room rates vary according to season, rising during the May to September high tourist season and on weekends in popular resort towns, and doubling or tripling during major fiestas.

Budget travellers will almost always be able to find a double room, often with a private bathroom, in a clean and reasonably comfortable hotel for around **US$10–15**. There are also usually at least one or two places that can offer **dorm beds** at a low price. Even in the coldest highland cities, heating is usually non-existent; in the lowlands, heat, rather than cold, is often a problem, though all but the cheapest rooms are equipped with a fan. Whatever climactic zone you're in though, all but the cheapest places usually have **hot water**, although the reliability and effectiveness of water-heating systems varies considerably. Most common are the individual electric heaters that you'll find attached to the tops of showers; don't touch the apparatus while the water is running unless you want an electric shock. Remember, the less water, the warmer it will be – it requires a delicate balance to get right.

Camping

With few designated campsites and an abundance of inexpensive accommodation, few travellers **camp** in Bolivia unless exploring the country's wilderness areas. Outside cities and towns, you can camp almost everywhere, usually for free; make sure you ask for permission from the nearest house first; local villages may ask for a small fee of a few dollars. In some **national parks** you'll also find shelters where you can stay for a minimal charge.

FOOD AND DRINK

The style of eating and drinking varies considerably between Bolivia's three main geographical regions – the Altiplano, the highland valleys and the tropical lowlands – differences that reflect the different produce commonly available in each region and the different cultural traditions of their inhabitants. Each region has *comidas típicas* (traditional dishes).

All larger towns in Bolivia have a fair selection of **restaurants**; almost all offer enormously filling good-value set lunches, or *almuerzos*, usually costing between US$1 and US$3, while many offer a set dinner, or *cena*, in the evening and also have a range of à la carte main dishes (*platos extras*), rarely costing more than US$3–4. For US$5 you should expect a very good meal in more upmarket restaurants, while about US$10 will get you most dishes even in the best restaurants in La Paz or Santa Cruz.

Eating

While Altiplano cuisine is dominated by the humble **potato**, often served in hearty soups (llama and mutton are also common), the valley regions cook with **corn**, often used as the basis for thick soups known as *laguas* or boiled on the cob and served with fresh white cheese – a classic combination known as *choclo con queso*. Meat and chicken are often cooked in spicy sauces known as *picantes:* a valley mainstay is *pique a lo macho*, a massive plate of chopped beef and sausage fried together with potatoes, onions, tomatoes and chillies. In the tropical lowlands, **plantains** and **yucca** take the place of potatoes; beef is also plentiful - the lowlands are cattle-ranching regions, so beef is of good quality and relatively cheap.

Although Bolivia is obviously not the place to come for seafood, fish features regularly on menus, especially the succulent *trucha* (trout) and *pejerrey* (kingfish) around Lago Titicaca and the juicy white river fish known as *surubí* and *pucú* in the lowlands. Ordinary restaurants rarely offer much in the way of vegetarian food, although you can almost always find eggs and potatoes of some description (usually fried), as well as the ubiquitous potato soup, often cooked without meat. The situation changes a great deal in cities and in popular travellers' haunts, where a cosmopolitan selection of vegetarian dishes, salads and pancakes is widely available, and wholly vegetarian restaurants are becoming increasingly common.

The most popular snack throughout Bolivia is the **salteña**, a pasty filled with a spicy, juicy stew of meat or chicken with chopped vegetables, olives and hard-boiled egg, usually sold from street stalls and eaten in the mid-morning accompanied by a cold drink and a spoonful or two of chilli sauce if desired.

Drinking

Mineral water is fairly widely available in large plastic bottles – a good thing, as it's best not to drink tap water. The delicious variety of tropical fruit's grown in Bolivia are available as juices from market stalls throughout the country, and **freshly squeezed orange and grapefruit juice** is also sold on the streets from handcarts for about US$0.20 a glass. **Tea and coffee** are available almost everywhere, as well as *mates*, or herbal teas – *mate de coca* is the best known and a good remedy for altitude sickness, but many others are usually available.

Locally produced alcoholic drinks are widely available in Bolivia, and drinking is a serious pastime. Beer is available almost everywhere - Paceña, produced in La Paz, is the most popular and widely available, followed by Huari, made by the same company but with a slightly saltier taste. Although not widely consumed, Bolivia also produces a growing variety of exceptional high-altitude – and highly underrated – **wines** (*vinos*), mostly from the Tarija Valley; the best labels are Campos de Solana, Concepción and Kohlberg. While production is still a fraction of neighbouring Argentina and Chile, Bolivia's wines deserve – and may yet attract – as equally high a profile.

One of the problems the industry has faced is that much cultivation is dedicated to muscat grapes, which, rather than fine reds, are used to a produce a white grape brandy called *singani*, the beverage most Bolivians turn to when they really want to get drunk. It's usually mixed with Sprite or Seven-Up, a fast-acting combination known as *chufflay*. Finally, no visit to the Cochabamba is complete without a taste of *chicha cochabambina*, a thick, mildly alcoholic yeasty-flavoured beer made of fermented maize and considered sacred by the Incas.

SPORTS AND OUTDOOR ACTIVITIES

Dominated by the dramatic high mountain scenery of the Andes, Bolivia is ideal for **trekking** and **climbing**; whether you want to stroll for half a day, take a hardcore hike for two weeks over high passes down into remote Amazonian valleys, or climb one of the hundred peaks over 5000m, it's all possible. The best season is between May and September, while the most pleasant and reliable weather is between June and August.

The easiest way to go trekking or climbing is with a tour operator. There are dozens of these in La Paz (see box opposite) and in several other cities, with treks costing between US$20 and $40 per person per day, depending on what's included and how many people are in the group. Things are much cheaper if you have your own equipment, organize the logistics yourself, and simply hire a guide. In rural towns and villages you can usually find locals who know all the trails and will act as a guide for a relatively small fee (on treks of more than one day you'll also need to provide them with food and possibly a tent).

ORGANIZED TOURS

Amboro Tours (based in Santa Cruz but can organise tours by phone or email) C Pari 81, Santa Cruz ⓣ03/339-0600 ⓦwww.amborotours.com. Recommended agency specialising in trips to national parks within the Amazon, including Jesuit Missions tours and the Ché Guevara route. They also organise excursions from La Paz to Lake Titicaca.
America Tours ground-floor office 9, Edificio Avenida, Av 16 de Julio 1490 ⓣ02/237-4204, ⓦwww.america-ecotours.com. Efficient and reliable travel agency: they're the main booking agent for Chalalán Ecolodge in Parque Nacional Madidi, and are a good place to book internal flights, as well as trips to the Pampas del Yacuma and the Salar de Uyuni.
Bolivian Journeys Sagárnaga 363 ⓣ02/235-7848, ⓦwww.bolivianjourneys.org. Highly regarded mountaineering specialists, offering well organised and professionally equipped expeditions into the Cordillera Real.
Crillon Tours Av Camacho 1223 ⓣ02/233-7533, ⓦwww.titicaca.com. Eco-friendly agency who work together with local communities to provide cultural immersion experiences. Offer a variety of tours throughout Bolivia, including pricey hydrofoil cruises on Lake Titcaca.
Downhill Madness Sagárnaga 339 ⓣ02/239-1810; also Av 16 de Julio 1490 ⓣ02/231-8375, ⓦwww.madnessbolivia.com. A recommended agency for cycling the 'world's most dangerous road', with top-of-the-range Rocky Mountain bikes, a good safety record and English-speaking guides.
Fremen Av 6 de Agosto, Edif. V Centenario ⓣ02/240-8200, ⓦwww.andes-amazonia.com. La Paz branch of the excellent and highly respected Cochabamba-based agency offering a wide range of excellent tailor-made tours throughout Bolivia, including river trips on the Río Mamoré on their own luxury floating hotel, the *Reina de Enín*.
Gravity Assisted Mountain Biking Ground-floor office 10, Edificio Avenida, Av 16 de Julio 1490 ⓣ02/231-3849, ⓦwww.gravitybolivia.com. The original and possibly still the best downhill mountain-bike operator, offering daily trips to Coroico or the Zongo Valley with excellent US-made bikes and experienced and enthusiastic English-speaking guides.

Bolivia is likewise home to some of the finest **mountain bike** routes in the world, and travelling by bike is one of the best ways to experience the Andes. Over the last decade a number of tour companies in La Paz have set up downhill mountain biking trips; the most popular route by far is down the road from La Paz to Coroico in the Yungas (see p.209), a stunning 3500m descent that many travellers rate as one of the highlights of South America, and a route which up until recently was still officially the **world's most dangerous road.** While you don't need any previous mountain-biking experience to do this ride, and it's easy to organize as a day-trip from La Paz, bear in mind that several bikers have been killed on this route in the past, and though the most dangerous stretch was bypassed in 2007, some vehicles still use it.

COMMUNICATIONS

Airmail (*por avión*) to Europe and North America tends to take between one and two weeks to arrive; mail to the rest of the world outside the Americas and Europe takes longer. Letters cost about US$1 to Europe, a little less to the US and Canada, and about US$1.20 to Australia and New Zealand. For a small extra charge, you can send letters certified (*certificado*), which is more reliable, but even then it's not a good idea to send anything you can't afford to lose.

There are **ENTEL** phone centres in all cities and most towns, where you can make local, national and international calls. While there a few coin-operated **telephone booths** in the street, most use **pre-paid cards.** These are widely available at street stalls, which are often sited next to booths, and come in denominations of 10, 20 and 50 Bolivianos. If you're dialling long-distance within Bolivia, you'll need the respective area code, which for La Paz, Oruro and Potosí is ⓣ02; for Beni, Pando and Santa Cruz ⓣ03; and for Cochabamba, Chuquisaca and Tarija ⓣ04.

Calling internationally, the cheapest option is via an Internet phone or Skype service, which will cost no more than the standard surfing rate (about US$0.40–0.80 an hour, though this can double in remote areas where competition is thin on the ground). **Internet cafés** themselves are ubiquitous in all but the most remote corners of Bolivia. The speed of machines and servers usually isn't very fast, but with a little patience you'll get a connection eventually.

SAFETY

In recent years, Bolivia's crime levels have risen partly in response to the country's worsening economic situation. If you apply **common sense precautions**, however, there's no need to be paranoid: the vast majority of crime against tourists is opportunistic theft, and **violence is rare**. An increasingly common method of theft is through the use of **fake police officers** and **fake taxi drivers**. Fake policemen may approach you on the street and ask to search you or see your documents (before making off with them) or may ask you to go with them in a taxi to the 'police-station'. Be aware that real policeman would never do this, so on no account ever hand over your documents or valuables and never accompany a stranger in a taxi.

Alternatively, **fake taxi drivers** or even minibus drivers pick up unsuspecting passengers before either stopping in a deserted part of town where they and/or their associates rob the victims, or, in even worse scenarios, kidnap and seriously assault the victims to force them to reveal their PIN numbers. Always check the ID of any taxi you get in to and only ever use official taxis; better still, whenever possible ask your hotel to order one for you. Unless you're using a collective taxi, never let the taxi stop to pick up other passengers; if this happens, get out.

Another common means of theft is the 'spitting' or 'mustard' trick. You may be spat on or have a substance such as mustard spilt on you; a 'helpful passerby' will stop you, point out the offending substance and attempt to clean it off you (whilst their partner in crime quickly relieves you of your valuables). If this happens to you, don't stop and walk on as quickly as possible before stopping to clean yourself up.

Political upheaval is pretty much a regular feature of everyday life in Bolivia, both in terms of **street protests** and **road blockades**. While traditionally these have been focused on the Altiplano and organised by radical Aymara, recent months have seen an upsurge in – increasingly violent – protests and attacks by right wing pro-autonomists in the Amazon and Eastern Lowlands. Keep an eye on the current political situation and avoid areas where demonstrations are planned.

EMERGENCY NUMBERS

Police ⓣ110
Ambulance ⓣ118
Directory assistance ⓣ104

INFORMATION AND MAPS

Most major cities have a regional **tourism office**, either run by the city municipality or by the departmental prefecture. Local Bolivian tour operators are generally a good source

BOLIVIA ON THE WEB

www.boliviaweb.com Links to related web pages and general background information on subjects such as Bolivian art, history and food.

www.enjoybolivia.com A user-friendly site with information on Bolivia's main cities and regions.

www.gosouthamerica.about.com/od/bolivia/Bolivia.htm An excellent resource with a wide range of information and articles about Bolivia.

of information, and many are happy to answer queries, often in English, though obviously their main aim is to sell you one of their tours.

It's worth buying a good map of the country to take with you, as these are rarely available in Bolivia it'self. The best general map of Bolivia is the Travel Map of Bolivia (1:2,200,000), produced by O'Brien Cartographics; it can be purchased online from www.saexplorers .org or www.boliviaweb.com.

MONEY AND BANKS

The Bolivian currency is the **boliviano**, sometimes referred to as the peso. It's usually written "Bs." and is subdivided into 100 centavos. Notes come in denominations of 10, 20, 50, 100 and 200 bolivianos; coins in denominations of 1, 2 and 5 bolivianos, and of 5, 10, 20 and 50 centavos. Because of the likelihood of devaluation, however, prices in this chapter are quoted in US dollars. At the time of writing the **exchange rate** was roughly Bs7.09 = US$1. US dollars can be changed at banks, hotels or shops and by street moneychangers almost everywhere in the country, and are a good way of carrying emergency back-up funds. The easiest way to access funds in cities and larger towns is byusing plastic; Visa and MasterCard are most widely accepted. Banks in all major cities and larger towns are connected to the nationwide Enlace network of **ATMs**. In rural areas and smaller towns, it's important to carry plenty of cash as plastic and traveller's cheques are fairly useless.

OPENING HOURS AND HOLIDAYS

Public offices in Bolivia have adopted a new system, *horario continuo*, whereby they work Monday to Friday straight through from 8.30am to 4pm without closing for lunch.

Banks' opening hours are generally Monday to Friday from 8.30am to noon and 2.30pm to 6pm; some bank branches are also open on Saturdays from 9am until noon. ENTEL **telephone** offices usually open daily from around 8am to 8pm, sometimes later.

Bolivians welcome any excuse for a party, and the country enjoys a huge number of national, regional and local **fiestas**, which are taken very seriously, often involving lengthy preparation and substantial expense.

February/March Carnaval, celebrated throughout the country in the week before Lent. The Oruro Carnaval (see p.214) is the most famous, but Santa Cruz, Sucre and Tarija also stage massive fiestas.

March/April Semana Santa (Easter) is celebrated with religious processions throughout Bolivia. Good Friday is a public holiday.

May 1 Labour Day (movable public holiday).

May/June Corpus Christi (public holiday). La Paz stages the Señor del Gran Poder, it's biggest and most colourful folkloric dance parade.

July 16 Virgen del Carmen. Processions and dances in honour of the Virgen del Carmen, the patron saint of many towns and villages across Bolivia.

August 6 Independence Day (public holiday). Parades and parties throughout the country, notably in Copacabana.

November 1–2 All Saints and Day of the Dead (public holiday).

December 25 Christmas Day (public holiday).

La Paz

Few cities have a setting as spectacular as **LA PAZ,** founded in 1548 as La Ciudad de Nuestra Señora de la Paz – the City of Our Lady of Peace – and now the political and commercial hub of Bolivia. Home to over a million people, and sited at over 3500m above sea level, the sprawling city lies in a narrow, bowl-like canyon, it's centre cradling a cluster of church spires and office blocks themselves dwarfed by the magnificent icebound peak of **Mount Illimani** rising imperiously to the southeast. On either side, the steep slopes of the valley are covered by the ramshackle homes of the city's poorer inhabitants, which cling precariously to even the harshest gradients. From the lip of the canyon, the satellite city of **El Alto** sprawls in all directions across the Altiplano, a dirt-poor yet dynamic locus of urban Aymara culture and protest. The fact that it's grid-locked main streets control access to La Paz below has often been exploited by the Aymara in recent years, with roadblocks used for political leverage.

What to see and do

There are still some fine colonial palaces, and churches in the centre, with the two main plazas, Murillo and **San Francisco**, bisected by the frantic thoroughfare of Av Marisca Santa Cruz and it's continuation, Av 16 de Julio, collectively knows as **El Prado**. While tiny, congested pavements and nose-to-tail traffic often present a challenge just to stay on your feet, most visitors are nevertheless enthralled by the energy of La Paz's **street life** and the blazing colour of it's indigenous population; once you're used to it, it's easier to explore what is really a very compact city. Though in general the architecture is rather drab and functional, and most of the colonial buildings which do survive are in a poor state of repair, their crumbling facades and dilapidated balconies obscured by tangled phone lines and electric cables, there's at least one street, **Calle Jaén**, where you can get a sense of how La Paz used to look. Most of the city's museum's are also conventiently situated here. To the west of the Prado, lung-busting lanes sweep up to the travellers' enclave of **Calle Sagárnaga** and the Aymara bustle of **Mercado Buenos Aires** beyond. To the south lies the wealthy suburb of **Sopocachi**, the preserve of the city's nightlife and eating scenes. Whatever direction you head in, the far horizon is ever dominated by the majestic, snow-covered, 6,439-metre peak of Illimani.

Plaza Murillo

Though it remains the epicentre of Bolivia's political life, the Plaza Murillo – the main square of the colonial city centre – has an endearingly provincial feel, busy with people feeding pigeons and eating ice cream in the shade.

On the south side of the plaza stand two great symbols of political and spiritual power in Bolivia, the **Cathedral** – which, with it's rather plain facade and relatively unadorned interior is fairly unremarkable - and the **Palacio Presidencial** (Presidential Palace), with it's yellow facade, thin, elegant columns and ceremonial guards in red nineteenth-century uniforms; it's not open to the public however. On the east side of the plaza is the **Palacio Legislativo**, the seat of the Bolivian parliament, built in a similar Neoclassical style in the early twentieth century.

On the southwest corner of the plaza on Calle Socabaya, the Palacio de Los Condes de Arana, one of La Paz's finest surviving colonial palaces, houses the Museo Nacional de Arte (Tues–Sat 9.30am–12.30pm & 3–7pm, Sun 9.30am–12.30pm; $1.40). The palace it'self is a magnificent example of Baroque architecture, with a grand

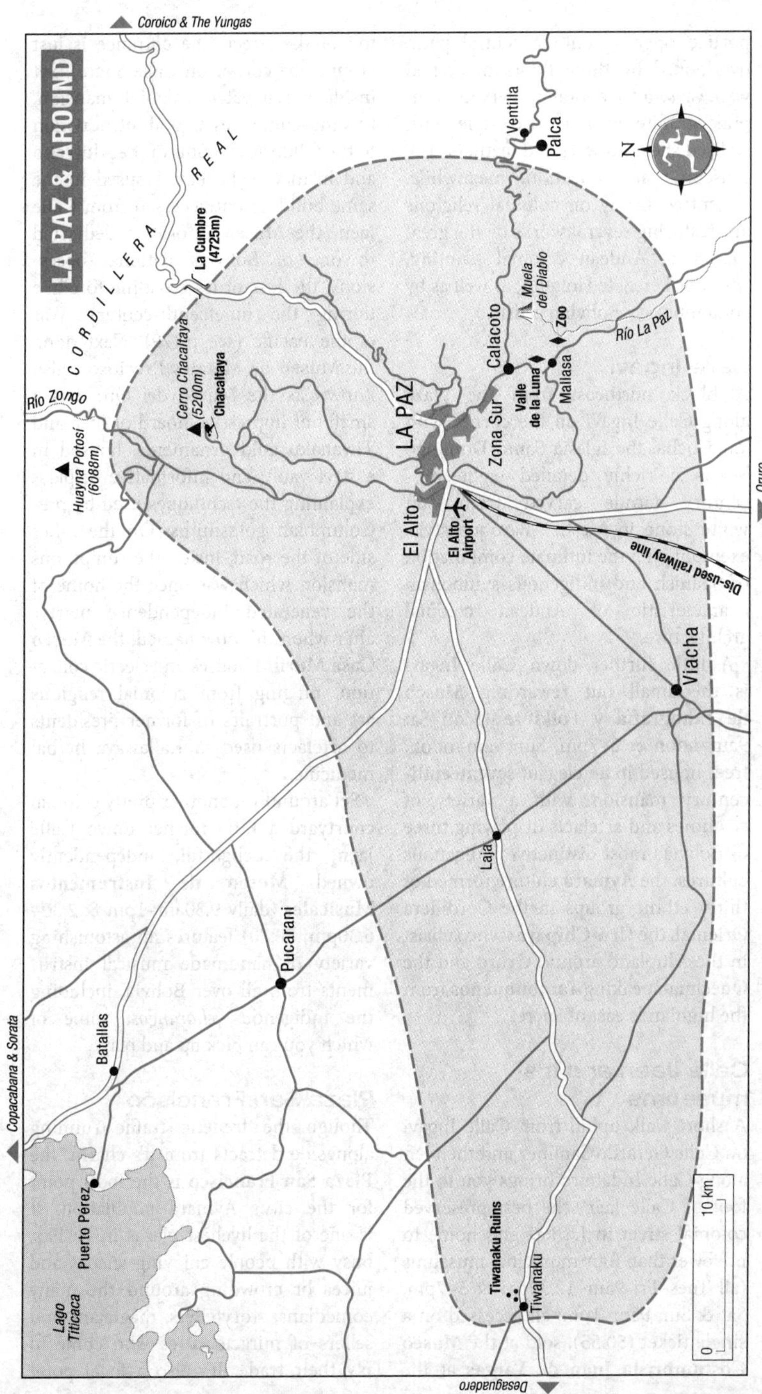
LA PAZ & AROUND
Copacabana & Sorata
Coroico & The Yungas
Desaguadero
Oruro
Lago Titicaca
Puerto Pérez
Batallas
Pucarani
Tiwanaku Ruins
Tiwanaku
Laja
Viacha
Dis-used railway line
El Alto
El Alto Airport
LA PAZ
Zona Sur
Calacoto
Valle de la Luna
Mallasa
Zoo
Muela del Diablo
Río La Paz
Ventilla
Palca
Huayna Potosí (6088m)
Río Zongo
CORDILLERA REAL
Cerro Chacaltaya (5200m)
Chacaltaya
La Cumbre (4725m)
N
0
10 km

portico opening onto a central patio overlooked by three floors of arched walkways, all elaborately carved from pink granite in a rococo style with stylised shells, flowers and feathers. The museum's art collection, meanwhile, is centred firmly on colonial religious art, featuring several works by the great master of Andean colonial painting, Melchor Pérez de Holguín, as well as by contemporary Bolivian artists.

Calle Ingavi

A block northeast from the plaza along Calle Ingavi on the corner with Yanacocha, the Iglesia Santo Domingo boasts a richly detailed eighteenth-century facade carved from soft white stone in Mestizo-Baroque style, exemplifiying the intimate combination of Spanish and indigenous symbolism characteristic of Andean colonial architecture.

A little further down Calle Ingavi is the small but rewarding **Museo de Etnografía y Folklore** (Mon–Sat 9am–noon & 3–7pm, Sun 9am–noon; free) housed in an elegant seventeenth-century mansion, with a variety of costumes and artefacts displaying three of Bolivia's most distinctive indigenous cultures: the **Aymara** culture formed of thirty ethnic groups in the Cordillera Oriental, the **Uru-Chipayas** who subsist in the Altiplano around Oruro and the Quechua-speaking **Tarabuqueños** from the highlands east of Sucre.

Calle Jaén and it's museums

A short walk uphill from Calle Ingavi on Calle Gerardo Sanjinez and then left along Calle Indaburo brings you to the foot of Calle Jaén, the best preserved colonial street in La Paz and home to no fewer than four municipal museums (all Tues–Fri 9am–12.30pm & 3–7pm, Sat & Sun 9am–1pm; all accessed on a single ticket ($0.55), sold at the **Museo Costumbrista Juan de Vargas** at the top of the street (the entrance is just around the corner on Calle Sucre). Set inside a renovated colonial mansion, this museum gives a good introduction to the folkloric customs of the Altiplano and history of La Paz. Housed in the same building but accessed from Calle Jaén, the **Museo Litoral** is dedicated to one of Bolivia's national obsessions: the loss of it's coastline to Chile during the nineteenth-century War of the Pacific (see p.179). Next door, the **Museo de Metales Preciosos**, also known as the Museo del Oro, has a small but impressive hoard of Inca and Tiwanaku gold ornaments, housed in a steel vault, and informative displays explaining the techniques used by pre-Columbian goldsmiths. On the other side of the road, inside the sumptuous mansion which was once the home of the venerated independence martyr after whom it's now named, the **Museo Casa Murillo** houses an eclectic collection, ranging from colonial religious art and portrait's of former presidents to artefacts used in Kallawaya herbal medicine.

Set around yet another pretty colonial courtyard a little further down Calle Jaén, the delightful, independently owned **Museo de Instrumentos Musicales** (daily 9.30am–1pm & 2.30–6.30pm; $0.70) features an astonishing variety of handmade musical instruments from all over Bolivia, including the indigenous *charangos*, some of which you can pick up and play.

Plaza San Francisco

Though the frenetic traffic running alongside detracts from it's charm, the **Plaza San Francisco** is the focal point for the city's Aymara population. It is one of the liveliest plazas in La Paz, busy with people enjoying snacks and juices or crowding around the many comedians, storytellers, magicians and sellers of miracle cures who come to ply their trade. It's also a focal point for political protest, most of which is peaceful, as well as noisy and colourful, although larger demonstrations can sometimes turn violent, and protesting miners are wont to ignite the odd stick of dynamite. On the south side of the plaza stands the **Iglesia de San Francisco**, the most beautiful colonial church in La Paz, first constructed in 1549 and rebuilt in the mid-seventeenth century. The richly decorated facade is a classic example of the Mestizo-Baroque style, showing clear indigenous influence, with carved anthropomorphic figures reminiscent of pre-Columbian sculpture as well as more common birds and intertwined floral designs. Attached to the church is the recently opened **Centro Cultural-Museo San Francisco** (Mon–Sat 9am–6pm; Ⓦ http://ofmsanfranciscolapaz.org/CentroCultural-MuseoSanFrancisco/informaciones.html; $2.80, students and children $2.10; price includes guided tour), which is well worth a visit. The museum is housed in a beautiful, newly renovated Franciscan monastery (part of which is which is inhabited still) and has a large collection of seventeenth-century Franciscan art and furniture.

Calle Sagárnaga and around

To the left of the Iglesia San Francisco, **Calle Sagárnaga**, La Paz's main tourist street, is crowded with hotels, tour agencies, restaurants, handicraft shops and stalls. Sometimes referred to rather dismissively as "Gringo Alley", the street has catered to travellers' needs since colonial times. It's also the gateway to the main Aymara neighbourhoods of La Paz, with it's narrow, winding and at times almost vertical streets filled with lively markets that make it one of the most vibrant and distinctive parts of the city. The Mercado de Hechicería – or Witches' Market – up Sagárnaga on Calle Linares – offers a fascinating window on the usually secretive world of Aymara mysticism and herbal medicine, it's stalls laden with a colourful cornucopia of ritual and medicinal items, ranging from herbal cures for minor ailments like rheumatism or stomach pain to incense, coloured sweets, protective talismans and dried llama foetuses. The area abounds with great photo opportunities, but remember to ask permission; buying a memento will make vendors more receptive to your camera-snapping.

Museo de la Coca

Also on Calle Linares, a block south of Sagárnaga, is the small but excellent **Museo de la Coca** (daily 10am–7pm; Ⓦ www.cocamuseum.com; $1.40), dedicated to the small green leaf that is both the central religious and cultural sacrament of the Andes and the raw material for the manufacture of cocaine. The museum gives a good overview of the history, chemistry, cultivation and uses of this most controversial of plants.

The Mercado Buenos Aires

Three blocks further up Sagárnaga, a right turn along Calle Max Paredes takes you into the heart of the **Mercado Buenos Aires**, also known as the Huyustus. This vast open-air market sprawling over some thirty city blocks is where La Paz's Aymara conduct their daily business; street after street is lined with stalls piled high with sacks of sweet-smelling coca leaf, mounds of brightly coloured tropical fruit, enormous heaps of potatoes and piles of silver-scaled fish; there's also smuggled stereos and televisions, and endless racks of the latest imitation designer clothes. In the last week of January, the area, as well as most of the rest of the city, is taken over by stalls selling all manner of miniature items during the **Feria de Alasitas**, which is centred on representations of Ekeko, the diminutive mustachioed household god of abundance.

Museo Tambo Quirquincho

Just northwest of Plaza San Francisco, **Plaza Alonso de Mendoza** is a pleasant square named after the founder of La Paz, whose statue stands at it's centre. On the southern side of the square on Calle Evaristo Valle, the **Museo Tambo Quirquincho** (Tues–Fri 9.30am–12.30pm & 3–7pm, Sat & Sun 10am–1pm; $0.15) is one of the most varied and interesting in La Paz, with an eclectic collection focusing on the city's culture and history, with exhibit's including an extensive collection of grotesque yet beautiful folkloric masks; several rooms full of quaint old photos of La Paz, and a room dedicated to the city's quintessential icon, the **chola**. This is the vernacular term for the ubiquitous Aymara women dressed in voluminous skirts and bowler hats who dominate much of the day-to-day business in the city's endless markets.

Plaza Sucre and the San Pedro Prison

Two blocks southwest of the Prado along Calle Colombia, **Plaza Sucre** lies at the centre of San Pedro, one of the city's oldest suburbs. Also known as the **Plaza San Pedro**, the square's tranquil and well-tended gardens surround a statue of Bolivia's first president, and are popular with portrait photographers with ancient box-cameras. On the southeast side of the square rises the formidable bulk of the **Cárcel de San Pedro**, one of La Paz's most infamous attractions, albeit one which is currently barred to tourists. Basically a prison with no guards, San Pedro is essentially controlled by the prisoners, who work to pay for cells: those with money can live quite well in luxurious accommodation complete with cellphones and satellite television, while those without any income sleep in the corridors and struggle to survive on the meagre official rations.

The interior is like a microcosm of Bolivian society – there are shops, restaurants, billiard halls, and even crèches – the prisoners' families often live with them. Although San Pedro was officially closed to travellers at the time of writing, it is worth trying, as people have been known to get in even during these "blackout" periods, and there's also talk of reopening the place to visitors. If you do manage to get through, though, be aware of the risks involved, and the fact that you'll almost certainly be offered drugs.

Sopocachi, Miraflores and around

South of Plaza San Francisco, the busy, tree-lined Prado ends at the Plaza del Estudiante, to the south of which lies the relatively wealthy suburb of **Sopocachi**, home to some of the city's best restaurants and a lively nightlife centred around the parallel Avenues 6 de Agosto and 20 de Octubre. Shortly before the Prado ends at Plaza del Estudiante, a left turn down the steps and two blocks along Calle Tiahuanaco brings you to the **Museo Nacional de Arqueología** (Mon–Fri 9am–12.30pm & 3–7pm, Sat 9am–noon; Ⓦwww.bolivian.com/arqueologia/; $1.40), also known as Museo Tiahuanaco. Set inside a bizarre Neo-Tiwanaku building, it houses a reasonable collection of textiles, ceramics and stone sculptures from the Inca and Tiwanaku cultures, though the exhibit's are poorly explained.

The **Museo de Textiles Andinos,** Plaza Benito Juarez 488 (Mon–Sat 9.30am–noon & 3–6.30pm, Sun 10am–12.30pm; $2.10) in the student suburb of Miraflores, northeast of the Prado, is a must-see for textile lovers. Set in a beautifully kept house, the museum boasts an interesting display of textiles from all over the Bolivian Andes. The museum's gift shop sells products made by Quechuan women, who receive ninety percent of the profit's.

Arrival

By Air International and domestic flights arrive at the small El Alto airport (flight information on ⓣ02/281-0240), on the rim of the Altiplano about 11km from La Paz and at over 4000m above sea level. The easiest way into town from here is by taxi; they wait right outside the terminal and the half-hour ride should cost $6–7. Alternatively, Cotranstur run shuttle minibuses (*micros*) down into the city and the length of the Prado to Plaza Isabella La Católica ($0.55 per person; every 10min). Internal flights with the military airline TAM arrive at the military airport (ⓣ02/284-1884), alongside the commercial airport on Avenida Juan Pablo II in El Alto. Taxis wait here for passengers, but the shuttle bus does not; to get down to La Paz by public transport you'll need to catch any *micro* heading west along Avenida Juan Pablo II to La Ceja, the district on the edge of the Altiplano above La Paz, and change there.

By Bus Buses from southern and eastern Bolivia and international buses arrive at the Terminal Terrestre on Plaza Antofagasta, about 1km northeast of Plaza San Francisco. From here, it's a short taxi ride ($0.90) or a twenty-minute walk down Avenida Montes to the main accommodation areas in the city centre. Buses from Copacabana, Tiwanaku, Sorata and Charazani arrive in the cemetery district, high up on the west side of the city. Plenty of *micros* head down to the city centre from here, but it's a pretty chaotic part of town, so it's a good idea to take a taxi ($0.85) - but be careful to choose an official one. Buses from Coroico and Chulumani in the Yungas, and from Rurrenabaque and the Beni, arrive in the Villa Fátima district, in the far northeast of the city. The different companies all have offices around the intersection of Avenida de las Américas and Calle Yanacachi. Again, plenty of *micros* head down to the city centre from here, but a taxi ($0.85) is quicker, easier and more secure.

Information

Tourist information There's a small tourist information office (Mon–Fri 8.30am–noon & 2.30–7pm; Sat & Sun 9.30am–1pm ⓣ02/237-1044) on Plaza del Estudiante at the end of the Prado, which has plenty of information on La Paz and the surrounding area. The helpful staff usually includes one English-speaker, and they sell good city and regional maps and offer flyers for most of the main tour agencies, which are the best places to go for information on the rest of the country. **Tourist police** Edificio Olimpio, Plaza Tejada Sorzano, opposite the stadium in Miraflores (open 24hr, ⓣ02/222-5016). This is the place to report thefts for insurance claims.

City transport

Buses, *micros* and trufis There are two main forms of public transport in La Paz: city buses and privately owned minibuses, known as *micros*. Though quicker and more numerous than the big buses, *micros* can be incredibly cramped and their routes very confusing. The names of the *micros*' destinations are written on signs inside the windscreen and bellowed incessantly by the driver's assistants so it's usually enough to wait by any major intersection until you hear the name of your destination shouted out. Your third option is a *trufi* – basically a car operating as a *micro* with a maximum of four passengers and following fixed routes. *Trufis* charge a flat rate of about $0.25 in the city centre and *micros* about $0.20; city buses cost slightly less.

Taxis Unlicensed taxis charge about $0.55 per passenger for journeys anywhere in the centre of town – there are no meters so it's best to agree on the fare at the beginning of the journey. The more reliable, marked radio taxis charge a flat rate of about $0.80 for anywhere in the city centre regardless of the number of passengers.

Accommodation

There's plenty of budget accommodation in La Paz, though things get busier and pricier in the peak tourist season from June to August. Most places to stay are in the city centre within a few blocks of Plaza San Francisco, close to or in the midst of the colourful market district and within walking distance of most of the city's main attractions.

Near the bus station

Adventure Brew Hostel Av Montes 533 ⓣ02/246-1614, ⓦwww.theadventurebrewhostel.com. One of the nicest backpackers' hostels, the *Adventure Brew* is housed in a refurbished, five-storey building very close to (and within walking distance) of the bus station. It's become so popular that they've acquired an annexe, a less comfortable but more relaxed and cheaper option set in a colonial building five minutes down the road. There are both dorms and private rooms, both of which come with free breakfast and internet, an array of DVDs to watch and a free beer for every guest each day, served in the lovely bar – along with a nightly dinner – overlooking the city. Dorm $7, Double $20

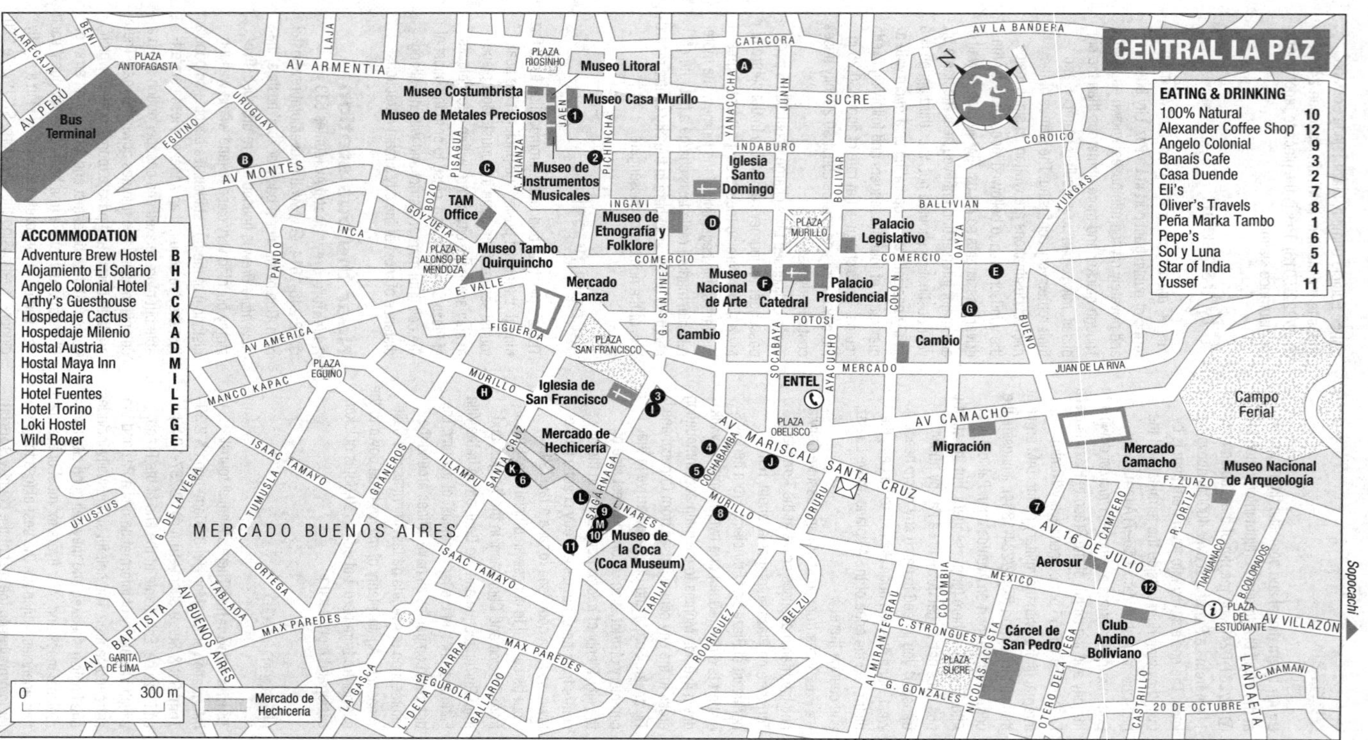
CENTRAL LA PAZ
EATING & DRINKING
100% Natural 10
Alexander Coffee Shop 12
Angelo Colonial 9
Banais Cafe 3
Casa Duende 2
Eli's 7
Oliver's Travels 8
Peña Marka Tambo 1
Pepe's 6
Sol y Luna 5
Star of India 4
Yussef 11
ACCOMMODATION
Adventure Brew Hostel B
Alojamiento El Solario H
Angelo Colonial Hotel J
Arthy's Guesthouse C
Hospedaje Cactus K
Hospedaje Milenio A
Hostal Austria D
Hostal Maya Inn M
Hostal Naira I
Hotel Fuentes L
Hotel Torino F
Loki Hostel G
Wild Rover E
El Alto & Airport
Cemetery District
Sopocachi
Bus Terminal
Museo Litoral
Museo Costumbrista
Museo Casa Murillo
Museo de Metales Preciosos
Museo de Instrumentos Musicales
Iglesia Santo Domingo
TAM Office
Museo de Etnografía y Folklore
Palacio Legislativo
Museo Tambo Quirquincho
Mercado Lanza
Museo Nacional de Arte
Catedral
Palacio Presidencial
Cambio
ENTEL
Iglesia de San Francisco
Mercado de Hechicería
Museo de la Coca (Coca Museum)
Migración
Campo Ferial
Mercado Camacho
Museo Nacional de Arqueología
Aerosur
Cárcel de San Pedro
Club Andino Boliviano
MERCADO BUENOS AIRES
PLAZA ANTOFAGASTA
PLAZA RIOSINHO
PLAZA MURILLO
PLAZA ALONSO DE MENDOZA
PLAZA SAN FRANCISCO
PLAZA EGUINO
PLAZA OBELISCO
PLAZA SUCRE
PLAZA DEL ESTUDIANTE
GARITA DE LIMA
AV ARMENTIA
AV MONTES
AV PERÚ
AV AMÉRICA
AV MARISCAL SANTA CRUZ
AV CAMACHO
AV 16 DE JULIO
AV VILLAZÓN
AV LA BANDERA
AV BUENOS AIRES
AV BAPTISTA
SUCRE
COMERCIO
MERCADO
INGAVI
BALLIVIAN
0 300 m
Mercado de Hechicería

Arthy's Guesthouse Av Montes 693 ⓣ02/228-1439, ⓔarthyshouse@gmail.com, ⓦwww.arthyshouse.tripod.com. Very pleasant hostel situated halfway between the bus station and Plaza San Francisco, and suitable for those looking for peace, quiet and comfort (but not partying - there's a midnight curfew). Rooms are simple but decent, and there's a lovely lounge with leather sofas, cable TV, games and a fire for when it's particularly cold. Guests can make use of the good kitchen, and it's wise to book in advance. No breakfast. $19.60

Plaza Murillo and East of the Prado

Hospedaje Milenio Yanacocha 860 ⓣ02/228-1263, ⓔhospedajemilenio@hotmail.com. It's a bit of a climb to this hostel - it's 3 steep blocks up from Plaza Murillo - but for those looking for pleasant, quiet and good-value accommodation, it's worth the effort. Staff are friendly, rooms are comfortable (those at the front are significantly lighter) and there's a communal area with cable TV and book exchange. Breakfast (not included), tourist info and laundry services are available. $7.50

Hostal Austria Yanacocha 531 ⓣ02/240-8540, ⓔhotelaustria@acelerate.com, ⓦwww.hostelaustria.wf. This place is not very well sign-posted - but keep looking, it's there! Popular with young backpackers, it's a cosy, friendly place with clean rooms, kitchen and internet facilities and a comfortable communal area with sofas and cable TV. There's no breakfast, however. $8.40

Hotel Torino Socabaya 457 ⓣ02/240-6003. A former backpackers' favourite, this hotel's maze of simple rooms are often empty but it's cheap and central (just off Plaza Murillo), showers are hot and rooms are set around an elegant colonial courtyard (the restaurant in the courtyard can get rather noisy however). The reception area has cable TV, a chess game or two and a small book exchange. $8.40

Loki Hostel Loayza 420 ⓣ02/211-9042, ⓔinfo@lokihostel.com, ⓦwww.lokihostel.com. Not as charming as it's Cusco partner - guests have complained of bad showers and a less than sociable atmosphere - Loki is nevertheless still extremely popular and reservations are recommended. Housed in a huge colonial mansion, facilities are good - decent mattresses, free breakfast, dinner served every night in the pleasant bar, and a roof terrace that at the time of writing was still being completed. It's a good place to meet people, but not a good option for those looking for a quiet place to stay. Online booking available. Dorm $5–7.

Wild Rover Comercio 1476 ⓣ02/211-6903, ⓦwww.wildroverhostel.com. Very popular backpackers' option, this place has barely been open a year but is already gaining a reputation as a bit of a party hostel. It's very new, light and clean, with a comfy TV room, decent bar with pool tables and food served all day. Staff speak English and there's free internet and breakfast, though the dorms (there are no private rooms) are a bit pokey. There have, however, been negative reports of rude staff, theft and excessive drug use, so beware. Dorm $5.60–$6.30.

Calle Sagárnaga and West of the Prado

Alojamiento El Solario Murillo 776 ⓣ02/236-7963, ⓔelsolariohotel@yahoo.com. Popular budget option, close to Plaza San Francisco, with welcoming staff and a friendly atmosphere. There's use of a kitchen, communal area and free internet. It's basic but clean and comfortable. Dorm $2.80, Double $8.40

Angelo Colonial Hotel Av Mariscal Santa Cruz 1058 ⓣ02/212-5067, ⓔhostalangelocolonial@yahoo.com. Good, very central option, with friendly staff and clean rooms, each with shared bath and kitchen facilities. Rooms are interestingly furnished (including huge iron beds, some of which look more comfortable than others); those at the front are lighter and have balconies, but overlook the noisy Prado. Internet access available. $11.90

Hospedaje Cactus Jiminéz 818 ⓣ02/245-1421, ⓔhostal_cactus@hotmail.com. Popular with backpackers, this hostel is a basic but friendly and good-value place, with a good location on a quiet road just off the main tourist street. Guests can make use of a kitchen (but no living room), a small terrace, book exchange and internet (not included). $7.50

Hotel Fuentes Linares 988 ⓣ02/233-4145, ⓦwww.hotelfuentesbolivia.com. Unlike so many

TREAT YOURSELF

Hostal Naira Sagárnaga 161 ⓣ02/235-5645; ⓦwww.hostalnaira.com. It's nowhere near five-star, but if you're looking for a bit more comfort and privacy than the standard budget backpackers' place, *Hostal Naira* is highly recommended for it's very central location and good, clean rooms with cable and private bath. Rooms are carpeted and heated (bliss for cold La Paz nights) and a good breakfast is included. $35

hotels, *Fuentes* delivers on almost as much as it's plush exterior promises. For the price (24hr hot water, free internet and continental breakfast are included) , you'll struggle to find as neat, bright and comfortable a stack of rooms anywhere in La Paz. $22

Hostal Maya Inn Sagárnaga 339 ⓣ02/231-1970, ⓔmayahost_in@hotmail.com. Large, very central place with decent, clean rooms (some are dark; ask for one with an outside window). Continental breakfast is included. Rooms with private bath come with cable TV. There's internet (not included) and laundry facilities. $15.40

Eating

La Paz has an excellent range of restaurants, cafés and street stalls to suit pretty much all tastes and budgets – from traditional eateries that dish up local meat-based delicacies to the more exotic ethnic restaurants and tourist-orientated spots with international menus. For those whose stomachs have adjusted to basic local food, the cheapest places to eat are the city's markets, where you can get entire meals for less than $1. Street food is another good low-cost option: the ubiquitous *salteñas* and *tucumanes* – delicious pastries filled with meat or chicken with vegetables – make excellent mid-morning snacks, especially if washed down by the freshly squeezed orange and grapefruit juice which is sold from wheeled stalls all over the city.

Cafés

100% Natural Sagárnaga 345. Largely vegetarian health-food joint big on fruit juices, soya and the like.

Alexander Coffee Shop Av 16 de Julio 1832, C Potosí 1091, C Montenegro in Zona Sur and El Alto airport. Very fashionable but expensive chain café with several locations in the city, serving extremely good coffee, and fantastic home-made cakes and cookies, though the main dishes are not so recommended.

Banais Café Sagárnaga 161. Adjacent to *Hostal Naira* (see p.197), this pleasant, colourful café, popular with travellers, boasts heavenly breakfasts, with huge bowls of muesli, cereal and fruit, as well as decent crêpes, salads and sandwiches.

Pepe's Jiménez 894, just off Linares between Sagárnaga and Santa Cruz. Friendly little place with colourful décor and a winning menu of sandwiches, omelettes, crêpes and great organic coffee. Box lunches also available. Often closed Sun.

Restaurants

Angelo Colonial Linares 922, just off Sagárnaga. Popular, characterful hangout set around a colonial courtyard and imaginatively decorated with all manner of antiques. Food can be hit and miss, but it's a lovely place to have a meal, especially in the evenings when there's a cosy, romantic feel.

Eli's El Prado with Bueno. Cosy, 1950s-style film-themed corner bistro in business since 1942, with a great selection of cakes and pastries and an extensive good-value menu of delicious American staples such as burgers and Philly cheese steaks.

La Comédie Pasaje Medinacelli 2234 ⓣ02/242-3561, Beautifully décorated French restaurant with excellent dishes, including steaks, *carpaccio* and pasta. Highly recommended.

Nuevo Hong Kong Belisario Salinas 355, between 6 de Agosto and 20 de Octubre, Sopocachi. Excellent-value Chinese food; for a special treat, try the platters with shiitake mushrooms, bamboo shoots and other Asian delicacies.

Oliver's Travels Murillo 1014. Cosy, central and very popular gringo pub complete with sofas, big screen TVs, comfort food (think bangers and mash, pies, huge breakfasts etc), and a busy crowd in the evenings. There's also a very good (if fairly pricey) book exchange. Service is slow, however, and the English owner, though friendly, can be rather unprofessional.

The Star of India C Cochabamba 170 ⓣ02/211-4409. Frequently recommended for it's good curry. Delivery available.

Vienna Zuazo 1905 ⓣ02/244-1660. Impressive restaurant boasting exquisite Austrian cuisine and immaculate service, but still surprisingly good-value with main dishes from just $4.

Wagamama Pasaje Pinilla 2557, just off Av Arce ⓣ02/243-4911. Upmarket and authentic Japanese restaurant with a varied menu including sublime sushi and sashimi; it's not particularly cheap however. Closed Mon.

Yussef Sagánaga 380 (upstairs). Simple, small restaurant with highly recommended, good-value Arab and vegetarian food.

TREAT YOURSELF

Chalet La Suisse Muñoz Reyes 1710, Calacoto; ⓣ02/279-3160; ⓦwww.chaletlasuisse.com. It's not particularly Bolivian, but the impressive Chalet La Suisse is repeatedly cited by ex-pats as the best restaurant in town, and for good reason. Mains range between $8-12.

Drinking, nightlife and entertainment

La Paz is generally fairly quiet on weekday evenings, but explodes into life on Friday nights when much of the city's male population goes out drinking. In the city centre – and above all in the market district along Max Paredes and Avenida Buenos Aires – there are countless rough and ready *whiskerías* and karaoke bars. Going out to one of these bars is certainly a very authentic Bolivian experience, but is best avoided for women.

With one or two exceptions, the more cosmopolitan nightspots are concentrated in the suburb of Sopocachi, running the gamut from live jazz to raucous travellers' hangouts. And although La Paz's club scene isn't what it was, you can still find a busy dancefloor heaving to just about any kind of music. For more traditional entertainment, head to one of the folk music venues known as *peñas*, where – with varying degrees of authenticity – you can witness age-old Andean music and dance.

Bars and nightclubs

Casa Duende Indaburo 848. Great little bohemian hideaway favouring modern artwork and a dark, cosy atmosphere. Although a steep climb from the centre, it's a great alternative to the touristy bars around Calle Sagárnaga. Open late Thurs–Sat.

Dead Stroke Av 6 de Agosto 2460. Stylishly seedy, US-owned late-night bar and pool hall with good tables and a fair share of hustlers.

Diesel Av 20 de Octubre with Rosendo Gutiérrez. Industrial-chic style bar with an extraordinary post-apocalyptic design, complete with aircraft engines hanging from the ceiling and bathrooms straight out of a science-fiction movie.

Mongo's Hermanos Manchego 2444. The original gringo rendezvous and some may still say the best, where televised sports and decent food give way to serious drinking, live music and raucous dancing as the evening wears on. Despite super-slow service, it's hugely popular with Bolivians, travellers and expats alike, and packed on weekends. Opens at 7pm daily, until the wee hours.

Ram Jam C Presbitero Medina 2421. Spacious, interior-design conscious and hugely popular bar/club with discreet layout and an anything-goes music policy. Also serves good food, including some of La Paz's best curries.

La Salsa del Loro Rosendo Gutiérrez, just up the steps from Av 6 de Agosto. Lively salsa nightclub where serious *salseros* dance the night away to throbbing Latin beats. Open Thurs–Sat.

Sol y Luna Cochabamba with Murillo. Snug bar-café serving strong coffee and cold beer in a mellow, candlelit atmosphere. There's live music at night, pool tables, a book exchange and typical Dutch dishes (during the week it's open for lunch too).

Thelonious Jazz Bar Av 20 de Octubre 2172. The best jazz bar in town, with an intimate basement atmosphere and live music Tues–Sat. $3.50 cover charge. Closed Sun and Mon.

Cinemas

Cine 16 de Julio Av 16 de Julio 1807 ⓣ02/244-1099. Cheaper than it's Prado rival with afternoon and evening showings.

Cine Monje Campero Corner of Av 16 de Julio y Calle Bueno ⓣ02/233-3332. The most comfortable big screen cinema, again with afternoon and evening showings.

Cine Municipal 6 de Agosto Av 6 de Agosto 2284 ⓣ02/244-2629. Wonderful old Art Deco cinema bypassing Hollywood for a more engaging programme of Latin American and European film.

Peñas

Peña Marka Tambo Jaén 710 ⓣ02/228-0041. (Thurs-Sun). Perhaps the most authentic traditional music and dance show in La Paz, with an ideal setting in an old colonial mansion and one of the best-value cover charges in town ($4.20). The food, however, is mediocre. Shows start at 10pm.

Directory

Airlines For flights with the military airline TAM, it's easiest to book through a travel agent. Aerolineas Argentinas, Paseo del Prado 1616 ⓣ02/235-1711; AeroMexico, Capitán Ravelo 2101 ⓣ02/212-4475; AeroSur, Av Arce 2177 ⓣ02/244-4930; Amaszonas, Av Saavedra 1649 ⓣ02/222-0848 or 224-4705; American Airlines, Av 16 de Julio, Edif. Hermann 1440 ⓣ02/277-1970; British Airways, Ayachucho 378 ⓣ02/220-3885; Continental Airlines, Alto de la Alianza 664 ⓣ02/228-0232; Iberia, Ayacucho 378 ⓣ02/220-3869; LanChile, Av 16 de Julio 1566 ⓣ02/235-8377; Lufthansa, Av 6 de Agosto 2512 ⓣ02/243-1717; Grupo TACA, Av Montenegro 1420 ⓣ02/231-3132; Transporte Aero Militar (TAM), Av Montes 738 ⓣ02/212-1585 or 212-1582.

Banks and exchange There are plenty of banks with ATMs in the centre of town, especially on Av Camacho, and a growing number of freestanding ATMs. The best places to change cash and traveller's cheques include Money Exchange International, Mercado 990 with Yanacocha

(Mon–Fri 8.30am–12.30pm & 2.30–7pm, Sat 9am–12.30pm) and Casa de Cambios, Colon 330 between Mercado and Potosí (Mon–Fri 9.30am–noon & 2.30–4.30pm).

Car rental American, Av Camacho 1574 ⓣ02/220-2933; Dollar ⓣ02/243-0043; Imbex, Av Montes 522 ⓣ02/231-6895; Oscar Crespo Maurice, Av Simón Bolívar 1865 ⓣ02/222-0989; Localiza, at *Hotel Radisson* ⓣ02/244-1011.

Embassies and consulates Argentina, Aspiazu 497 ⓣ02/241-7737; Australia, Aspiazu 416 ⓣ02/211-5655; Brazil, Edificio Multicentro, Av Arce ⓣ02/244-0202; Canada, Plaza España with Sanjinez ⓣ02/241-5021; Colombia, Calle 9, Calacoto 7835 ⓣ02/278-4491; Chile, Calle 14, Calacoto 8024 ⓣ02/279-7331; Ecuador, Edificio Hermann, Av 16 de Julio 1440 ⓣ02/231-9739; Paraguay, Edificio Illimani, Av 6 de Agosto ⓣ02/243-3176; Peru, Edificio Alianza, Av 6 de Agosto 2190 ⓣ02/244-0631; UK, Av Arce 2732 ⓣ02/243-3424; USA, Av Arce 2780 ⓣ02/216-8222; Venezuela, Av Arce 2678 ⓣ02/243-2023.

Immigration Migración office is on Av Camacho 1433 ⓣ02/211-0960 (Mon–Fri 8.30am–4pm).

Internet access There are internet cafés all over the city and their number seems to grow by the day; most charge about $0.70 an hour. Try Punto Entel, Potosí 1110 (Mon–Sat 8am–9.30pm); MicroNet, Av Mariscal Santa Cruz 1088, Ed. Sagrados Corazones (Mon–Fri 9am–9pm); Banaís Café, Sagárnaga 161 (daily 7am–10pm); or Angelo Colonial, Linares, just off Sagárnaga (daily 9am–11pm).

Post office Correo Central, Av Mariscal Santa Cruz with Oruro (Mon–Fri 8am–8pm, Sat 8am–6pm, Sun 9am–noon).

Shopping With it's many markets, La Paz is a great place for shopping, with a wide range of *artesanía* (handicrafts) on sale from all over the country. You'll find dozens of shops and stalls along Calle Sagárnaga and the surrounding streets, selling traditional textiles, leather items, silver jewellery and talismans. Beware that most fossils sold on this street are fake.

Outdoor Equipment There are a number of outdoor equipment shops around Sagárnarga. Two recommended ones are The Base (Calle Illampu 850), and Andean Base Camp (Calle Illampu 863).

Telephones The main ENTEL office is at Ayacucho 267, just below Mercado (daily 7am–midnight). There are phone booths all over the city which accept cards available from any stall – the most expensive card costs about $7, for which you can make a short international call. Directory enquiries are on ⓣ104.

Moving on

By Air International and domestic flights depart from the small El Alto airport (ⓣ02/281-0122), up on the Altiplano, 11km or so from the centre of town. Taxis should cost around $7–8, depending on how bad the traffic is. Alternatively, regular *micros* – marked "aeropuerto" – run up and down the Prado. TAM flights leave from the nearby military airport (ⓣ02/284-1884). Between them, TAM, Aerosur (ⓦwww.aerosur.com) and Amaszonas (ⓦwww.amaszonas.com) cover most destinations with at least one or two flights daily.

By bus Most long-distance buses depart from the Terminal Terrestre on Plaza Antofogasta, near Plaza San Francisco (ⓣ02/228-5858), while buses and *micros* for the Lago Titicaca region and the north leave from the Cemetery District high up on the northwest slopes of the city. *Micros* race up here constantly from Plaza San Francisco; look for those marked "Cementerio". Buses for the Yungas and northern Amazon region leave from the Villa Fátima district high up on the northeast side of the city; regular *micros* marked "Villa Fátima" ply Avenida 6 de Agosto.

Terminal Terrestre to: Cochabamba (hourly; 7hr 30min); Oruro (every 30min, with connections to Uyuni; 3hr 30min); Potosí (every evening, with connections to Sucre, Tarija & Tupiza; 11hr). There are also daily departures to international destinations - Arica (8hr); Buenos Aires (50hr); Cusco (12hr) and Lima (27hr).

Cemetery District to: Copacabana (regular services throughout the day; 3hr 30min); Sorata (every 30min; 4hr). From **Villa Fátima** to: Chulumani (hourly; 3hr 30min) Coroico (every 30min; 3hr); Rurrenabaque (daily; 18–25hr). Also weekly services to Cobija, Guayaramerín and Riberalta in the dry season.

TIWANAKU

The most worthwhile attraction within a few hours of La Paz is the mysterious ruined city of **Tiwanaku**, Bolivia's most impressive archeological site.

Set on the Altiplano 71km west of La Paz, the ancient ruined city of **TIWANAKU** (also spelt Tiahuanaco) was declared a cultural patrimony site by UNESCO in 2000. Founded some three millennia ago, Tiwanaku became the capital of a massive empire that lasted almost a thousand years, developing into a sophisticated urban-ceremonial complex that, at it's peak, was home to some fifty thousand people. Tiwanaku remains a place of exceptional symbolic meaning for the Aymara of the Altiplano, who come here to make ceremonial offerings to the *achachilas*, the gods of the mountains. The most spectacular of these, the **Aymara New Year**, takes place each June 21 (the winter solstice), when hundreds of *yatiris* (traditional priests) congregate to watch the sun rise and celebrate with music, dancing, elaborate rituals and copious quantities of coca and alcohol.

Though the city of Tiwanaku originally covered several square kilometres, only a fraction of the site has been excavated, and the main ruins (daily 9am–5pm; $11.00) occupy a fairly small area which can easily be visited in half a day. Two museums by the entrance house many of the smaller archeological finds, as well as several large stone monoliths. The main ruins cover the area which was once the ceremonial centre of the city, a jumble of tumbled pyramids and ruined palaces and temples made from megalithic stone blocks, many weighing over a hundred tons. It requires a leap of the imagination to visualize Tiwanaku as it was at it's peak: a thriving city whose great pyramids and opulent palaces were painted in bright colours and inlaid with gold, surrounded by extensive residential areas built largely from mud brick (of which little now remains) and set amid lush green fields, rather than the harsh, arid landscape you see today.

Minibuses to Tiwanaku depart from the corner of Aliaga and Eyzaguirre in the cemetery district in La Paz (every 30min; 1hr 30min; $1.40 round-trip); on the way back they leave from the square in Tiwanaku town. You can hire a guide outside the museum to show you around the ruins for about $7, but if you want a guided tour you're better off coming with an agency from La Paz (see box, p.187); most run one-day tours to the site for about $15 to $20 per person.

Lago Titicaca, Cordillera Real and the Yungas

The region immediately around La Paz is sometimes known as "Little Bolivia", because the variety of landscapes it encompasses can seem like a microcosm of the entire country. To the northwest lies the vast, high-altitude Lago Titicaca, with it's idyllic islands, Isla del Sol and Isla de la Luna, and lakeside pilgrimage town of Copacabana. East of here is the Cordillera Real, the highest and most spectacular section of the Bolivian Andes, easily explored from La Paz, or else from the magical outpost of Sorata. Sweeping down from the Cordillera Real, the Yungas is a rugged region of rugged, forest-covered mountains, rushing rivers and humid, fertile valleys, with the humid languor of Coroico at it's heart.

LAGO TITICACA

Some 75km northwest of La Paz, **LAGO TITICACA**, an immense, sapphire-blue lake, easily the largest high-altitude body of water in the world, sit's astride the border with Peru at the northern end of the Altiplano. The area around the lake is the heartland of the Aymara, whose distinct language and culture have survived centuries of domination, first by the Incas, then by the Spanish.

Titicaca has always played a dominant role in Andean religious conceptions; The Incas, who believed the creator god Viracocha rose from it's waters to call forth the sun and moon to light up the world, also claimed their own ancestors came from here. The remains of their shrines and temples can still be seen on the Isla del Sol and the nearby

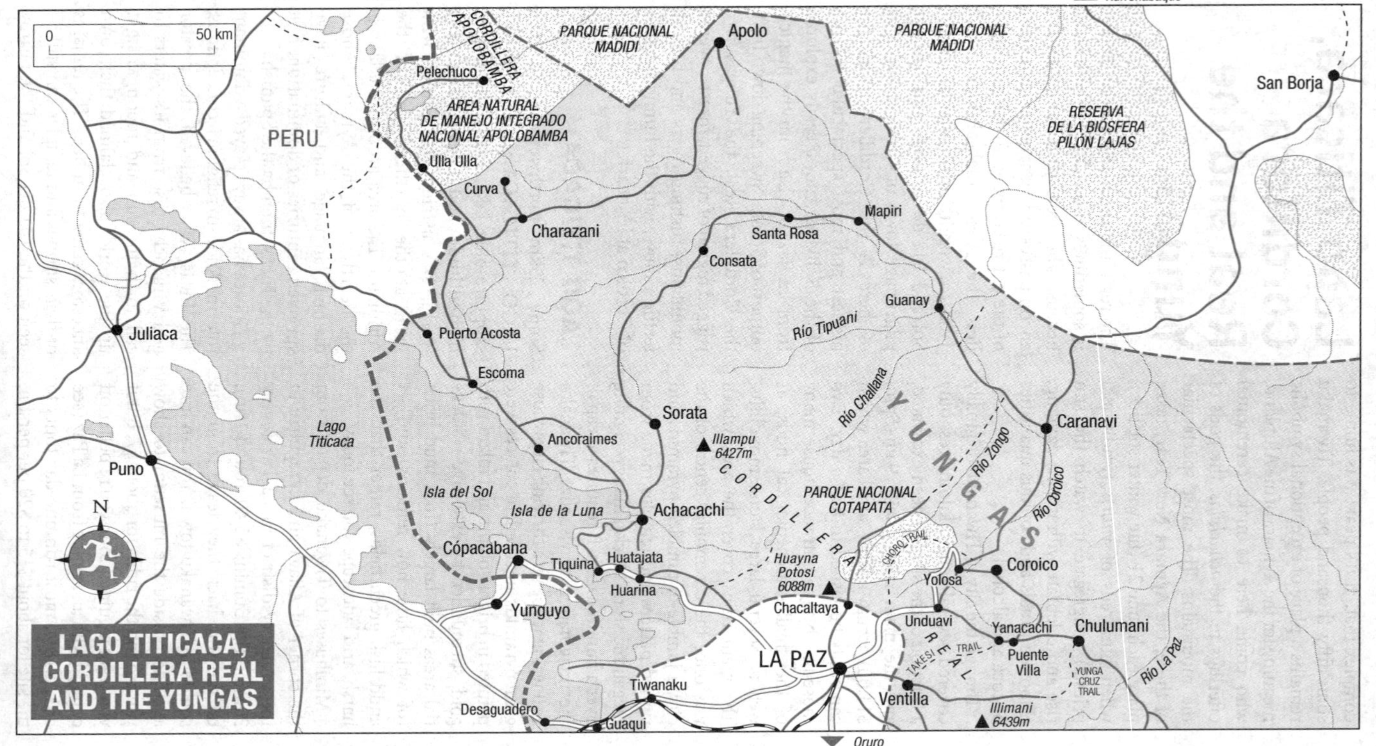
LAGO TITICACA, CORDILLERA REAL AND THE YUNGAS
0
50 km
PERU
Juliaca
Puno
N
Lago Titicaca
Isla del Sol
Isla de la Luna
Cópacabana
Yunguyo
Tiquina
Huatajata
Huarina
Desaguadero
Guaqui
Tiwanaku
LA PAZ
Oruro
Chacaltaya
Huayna Potosi 6088m
CORDILLERA REAL
Achacachi
Ancoraimes
Escoma
Puerto Acosta
Charazani
Curva
Ulla Ulla
Pelechuco
CORDILLERA APOLOBAMBA
AREA NATURAL DE MANEJO INTEGRADO NACIONAL APOLOBAMBA
PARQUE NACIONAL MADIDI
Apolo
PARQUE NACIONAL MADIDI
Rurrenabaque
RESERVA DE LA BIÓSFERA PILÓN LAJAS
San Borja
Mapiri
Santa Rosa
Consata
Sorata
Illampu 6427m
Guanay
Río Tipuani
Río Challana
YUNGAS
Río Zongo
PARQUE NACIONAL COTAPATA
CHORO TRAIL
Caranavi
Río Coroico
Coroico
Yolosa
Unduavi
TAKESI TRAIL
Yanacachi
Puente Villa
Chulumani
YUNGA CRUZ TRAIL
Río La Paz
Ventilla
Illimani 6439m

Isla de la Luna, whose serene beauty is a highlight of any visit to the lake. Nor did Lago Titicaca lose it's religious importance with the advent of Christianity: it's no coincidence that Bolivia's most important Catholic shrine can be found in Copacabana, the lakeside town closest to the Isla del Sol.

COPACABANA

The pleasant town of **COPACABANA** overlooks the deep blue waters of Lago Titicaca and is the jumping-off point for visiting Titicaca's sacred islands. It's also the most important Catholic pilgrimage site in the country, as home to Bolivia's most revered image, the Virgen de Copacabana; hordes of pilgrims descend on the city in early Febraury and early August for the two main religious fiestas.

What to see and do

The focal point of Copacabana is the imposing **Catedral** (daily 7.30am–8pm; free), also known as the "Moorish Cathedral", set on the Plaza 2 de Febrero six blocks east of the waterfront. Inside the bright, vaulted interior, a door beside the massive gold altarpiece leads upstairs to a small chapel that houses the beautiful **Virgen de Copacabana** herself. Encased in glass, the lavishly dressed statue is only taken out of the sanctuary during fiestas: locals believe moving her at any other time might trigger catastrophic floods.

Another interesting religious site is **Cerro Calvario**, the hill that rises steeply above the town to the north. It's a half-hour walk up to the top along a trail that begins beside the small church at the north end of Calle Bolívar, five or so blocks up from Plaza Sucre. The trail follows the stations of the cross up to the summit dotted with ramshackle stone altars where pilgrims light candles, burn offerings and pour alcoholic libations to ensure their prayers are heard. Though without the attractions of it's more famous namesake in Brazil (which was named in honour of the shrine here), Copacabana's **beach** is a pleasant place for a lakeside stroll and a bite to eat; if you fancy it, there are also plenty of pedal boats and kayaks to hire.

Arrival and information

Bus Buses and *micros* from La Paz and Kasani at the Peruvian border arrive and depart from just off Plaza Sucre, midway between the lake shore and the central Plaza 2 de Febrero.

Money Although there's no ATM, Prodem, on Avenida 6 de Agosto, can advance money on Visa and MasterCard for a hefty fee. To change dollars or traveller's cheques, try the Casa de Cambio Copacabana at the eastern end of Avenida 6 de Agosto.

Tourist info There's no formal tourist information office in Copacabana, but staff in the cluster of tour agencies on and around Plaza Sucre can tell you all you need to know about how to get to the islands or on to Peru.

Accommodation

Owing to it's role as a pilgrimage centre, Copacabana has an enormous number of places to stay, though they fill up fast and prices double or triple during the main fiestas.

Hostal Brisas de Titicaca 6 de Agosto ⓣ02/862-2178, ⓦwww.hostellinginternational.org. This HI hostel is right on the shore and has both dormitories ($5 per person) and private rooms, internet, laundry facilities and good views of the lake. $17

TREAT YOURSELF

Hotel La Cúpula Michel Pérez 1-3 ⓣ02/862-2029, ⓦwww.hotelcupula.com. Delightful hotel (and the nicest place to stay in Copacabana), built in neo-Moorish style on a hillside overlooking the town and lake. Rooms are light and airy, and one suite in particular affords spectacular lake views. Staff are friendly, and there's also a nice garden with hammocks, kitchen, laundry, games room and bespoke restaurant. Breakfast is included and reservations are recommended. $25

Hostal Emperador Murillo 235 ⓣ02/862-2083. Good budget option, popular with backpackers, with clean, simple rooms (with or without bath) set around a bright courtyard. Staff are friendly and full of great tourist info, and there are kitchen and laundry facilities and breakfast is available. $7

Hostal Sonia Murillo 256 ⓣ07/196-8441. Run by the same owners as the *Emperador*, this place is an equally good, friendly option, and as well as kitchen facilities there is a rooftop terrace with lovely views. $7

Eating and drinking

There's no shortage of restaurants in Copacabana, most catering to travellers and pilgrims, and some also doubling as bars and evening hangouts. There are also a number of stalls along the waterfront selling decent and cheap local *almuerzos*.

Café Bistrot Av 6 de Agosto. Pleasant café inside *Hostal Wara*, with friendly multilingual owners, book exchange, tourist info, full English breakfasts, excellent strong coffee, vegetarian food and barbecues upon request. Opens early morning and closes for siesta between 3 and 5.30 pm.

La Cúpula Inside the hotel of the same name on Michel Pérez. Cosy restaurant overlooking the lake and serving good breakfasts, fruit's and salads as well as tasty, veggie-friendly main courses ($3–5), served up in a bright room with views over the lake; great packed lunches for island trips. Closed Tues morning.

Pueblo El Viejo 6 de Agosto. Cosy cafe with good coffee; a nice place to relax.

Puerta del Sol 6 de Agosto & Bolívar. Good-value local place with Bolivian and international dishes. Also does boxed lunches. Closed Mon.

Moving on

By bus There are regular departures from Plaza Sucre to both La Paz (3hr 30min) and Puno (4hr) as well as daily departures to Cusco, generally via Puno (10hr), Arequipa (9hr) and Lima (18hr).

ISLA DEL SOL

Just off the northern tip of the Copacabana Peninsula about 12km northwest of Copacabana, the **Isla del Sol (Island of the Sun)** has been attracting pilgrims and visitors for many hundreds of years. Now a quiet rural backwater, the island was one of the most important religious sites in the Andean world in the sixteenth century, revered as the place where the sun and moon were created and where the Inca dynasty was born. Scattered with **enigmatic ancient ruins** and populated by traditional Aymara communities, Isla del Sol is an excellent place to spend some time hiking and contemplating the magnificent scenery. Measuring 9.5km long and 6.5km across at it's widest point, the Isla del Sol is the largest of the forty or so islands in Lago Titicaca, with three main settlements – Yumani, Ch'alla and Ch'allapampa. You can visit the island (along with nearby **Isla de la Luna**, see over) on a day- or even half-day trip from Copacabana, but it's really worth spending at least one night on the island to fully appreciate it's serene beauty.

What to see and do

The best way to see the Isla del Sol is to walk the length of the island from Yumani in the south to Ch'allapampa in the north, or the other way round – a four-hour hike. From the lakeshore at **Yumani**, where most boats dock, a functional Inca stairway, the **Escalera del Inca**, runs steeply up to the village through a natural amphitheatre covered by some of the finest Inca agricultural terracing on the island, irrigated by bubbling stone canals fed by a natural spring believed to have magic powers.

Two parallel paths – an inland ridgetop one that provides great views and another that runs along the island's east coast – head from Yumani in the south to Cha'llapampa at the other end of the island. About an hour and a half north of Yumani on the coastal path you reach the quiet village of Ch'alla, which sit's above a calm bay, and from where the path drops to **Playa Ch'alla**, a picturesque stretch of sand. About an hour's walk from Ch'alla is the island's northernmost settlement, **Ch'allapampa**, a pleasant and peaceful village founded by the Incas as a centre for the nearby ceremonial complexes. From here it's a forty-minute walk northwest along an easy-to-follow path to the **Chincana** (8am–6pm; $2.10), the ruined Inca complex of rambling interlinked rooms, plazas and passageways built around the sacred rock where the creator god Viracocha is believed to have created the sun and moon.

Arrival and information

By boat Full- and half-day boat tours to the Isla del Sol leave every morning from the beach at the end of Avenida Jaúregui in Copacabana – boats usually depart at around 8am for a full day ($3.40 round-trip), with further departures at around 10.30am and 1.30pm for a half day ($2 round-trip).

Tours There are numerous private boats and tour companies making the trip to the islands, including a number of upmarket packages from La Paz-based agencies.

Titicaca Tours Av 6 de Agosto, Caseta 2, Copacabana ⓣ02/862-2060; in La Paz Illampu 773; ⓣ02/246-2655; ⓔtiticacabolivia@yahoo.com.ar. Half-and whole-day tours that can include Isla de la Luna. **Crillon Tours** Av Camacho 1223 ⓣ02/233-7533, ⓦwww.titicaca.com. La Paz agency who run a variety of pricey one-and two-day tours, with accommodation at their exclusive ecolodge on Isla del Sol.

Transturin Av Arce 2678, La Paz ⓣ02/242-2222, ⓦwww.transturin.com. Luxurious one and two day catamaran cruises to the Isla del Sol, including a night in their own hotel at Chúa on the southern end of the lake.

Accommodation

Yumani is home to most of the island's accommodation, most of which offers only sporadic (and usually cold) water. There are also a couple of simple but friendly places to stay in Ch'allapampa.

None are signposted but the hostels' owners will be waiting to greet you when you get off the boat. Most places charge between $1.40–$2.80 per person per night, though accommodation is basic and water is scarce; there may only be (cold) water for a few hours or so.

Hostal Inti Wayra Near the church, Yumani ⓣ07/194-2015. A good choice, with excellent views and friendly owners. $8

Hostal Templo del Sol Right at the very top of the ridge, Yumani. Basic rooms with equally good views, as well as much-needed thick blankets for the cold nights.

Eating

Most of the hostels have basic restaurants attached serving pizza, pasta and, inevitably, freshly caught Titicaca trout upon request. There's also usually alfresco dockside catering to meet the incoming boats. Prices across the board tend to be higher than the mainland, however, largely due to transport costs and the lack of running water.

ISLA DE LA LUNA

About 8km west of the Isla del Sol, the far smaller **Isla de la Luna (Island of the Moon)** was another important pre-Columbian religious site. For much of the twentieth century, the island was used as a prison for political detainees, yet for the Incas it was a place of great spiritual importance. Known as Coati ("Queen Island"), it was associated with the moon, considered the female counterpart of the sun, and a powerful deity in her own right. The main site on the island – and one of the best-preserved Inca complexes in Bolivia – is a temple on the east coast known as **Iñak Uyu** (8am–7pm; $0.70), the "Court of Women", probably dedicated to the moon and staffed entirely by women. From the beach a series of broad Inca agricultural terraces lead up to the temple complex, a series of stone buildings with facades containing eleven massive external niches still covered in mud stucco, all around a broad central plaza.

To reach the island by boat, it takes about an hour from the Isla del Sol; some agenices will include a brief visit to Isla de la Luna with the Isla del Sol tour; if you want to stay longer, you can hire a private sail boat (for about $12) or private motor boat ($20) from Isla del Sol to take you to the island and back. It's possible to camp on the island, but ask permission and bring your own food and drinking water; another alternative is a basic *hostal* next to the ruins which can put you up for approximately $2 a night.

Moving on

By bus Regular buses leave Copacabana for La Paz from Plaza Sucre, while crossing into Peru from Copacabana is just as easy. *Micros* to the border at Kasani, fifteen minutes away, leave from Plaza Sucre every half-hour or so when full. At Kasani you can get your exit stamp at the passport control (8am–9pm) and then walk across to Peru, where *micros* and taxis wait for passengers to take them to Yunguyo, which has regular departures for Puno and on to Cusco. Alternatively you can catch one of the tourist *micros* which travel direct from Copacabana to Puno several times a day; these are run by all the companies that have an office around Plaza Sucre and, at around $3, cost just a little more than the public *micros*.

By boat It is also possible to reach Peru by crossing the lake. The best way to do this is by the bus and catamaran tours from La Paz to Puno – or vice versa – with Transturin (see p.205).

THE CORDILLERA REAL

Stretching for about 160km along the northeastern edge of the Altiplano, the **Cordillera Real** – the "Royal Range" – is the loftiest and most dramatic section of the Cordillera Oriental in Bolivia, with six peaks over 6000m high and many more over 5000m forming a jagged wall of soaring, ice-bound peaks separating the Altiplano from the tropical lowlands of the Amazon Basin. Easily accessible from La Paz, the mountains are perfect for climbing and trekking (see box opposite) – indeed, walking here is the only way to really appreciate the overwhelming splendour of

TREKKING AND CLIMBING IN THE CORDILLERA REAL

The easiest base from which to explore the Cordillera Real is **La Paz**. Many of the best and most popular treks start close to the city, including the three so-called "Inca trails" which cross the cordillera, connecting the Altiplano with the warm, forested valleys of the Yungas. Two of these ancient paved routes – the **Choro Trail** and the **Takesi Trail** – are relatively easy to follow without a guide; the third, the **Yunga Cruz Trail**, is more difficult. You can do all three of these treks, as well as many other more challenging routes, with any of the adventure tour agencies based in La Paz (see box, p.187).

The other major starting point for trekking is the small town of **Sorata**. From here, numerous trekking routes take you high up amongst the glacial peaks, while others plunge down into the remote forested valleys of the Yungas. The **Sorata Guides and Porters Association** provides trekking guides, mules and porters. Further afield, the remote and beautiful **Cordillera Apolobamba**, a separate range of the Cordillera Oriental, north of Lago Titicaca and with almost no tourist infrastructure, offers excellent trekking possibilities for the more adventurous traveller. It's unadvisable, however, to attempt these treks without a guide due to unpredictable weather conditions and the region's remoteness.

With so many high peaks, the Cordillera Real is also obviously an excellent place for **mountain climbing, for both serious and inexperienced climbers - Huayna Potosí** (6090m), near La Paz, is one of the few peaks in South America over 6000m that can be climbed by someone with no mountaineering experience (albeit with the help of a specialist agency - you should check carefully that the guide they provide is qualified and experienced and the equipment adequate).

the Andean landscape. Populated by isolated **Aymara communities** that cultivate the lower slopes and valleys and raise llamas and alpacas on the high pastures, the cordillera is a largely pristine natural environment, where the mighty **Andean condor** is still a common sight, pumas, though rarely seen, still prowl the upper reaches, and the elusive Andean spectacled bear roams the high cloudforest that fringes the mountains' upper eastern slopes.

SORATA

Set at an altitude of 2695m, **SORATA** is a placid and enchanting little town that's the most popular base for trekking and climbing in the Cordillera Real. Hemmed in on all sides by steep mountain slopes, often shrouded in clouds and with a significantly warmer climate than La Paz, it was compared by Spanish explorers to the Garden of Eden. There's not a lot to do in Sorata it'self but hang out and relax while preparing for or recovering from some hard trekking or climbing, or less strenuous walks in the surrounding countryside.

Arrival and information

By bus Buses from La Paz pull up every hour - starting at 5am until 4pm - in front of the bus company, Transportes Unificada, on the Plaza Enrique Peñaranda.

Tourist information For information and advice on trekking in the surrounding mountains, try the **Sorata Guides and Porters Association**, whose office lies opposite the *Residencial Sorata*, just off the plaza on Calle Sucre (Ⓣ02/213-6672, Ⓔguiasorata@hotmail.com). They can arrange guides for all the main trekking routes around Sorata; they also organize the hire of mules and have a limited amount of camping equipment available for rent, though don't count on what you need being available. It's also a good place to meet up with other travellers in order to split costs. **Andean Biking**, on the main plaza (Ⓣ02/712-76685, Ⓦwww.andeanbiking.com) is a good source of information on mountain biking in the region and organises English-speaking trekking and rafting trips.

Accommodation

There's a good choice of inexpensive places to stay in Sorata, as well as a couple of mid-range options with creature comforts that grow more alluring the longer you've spent climbing or trekking in the surrounding mountains.

Alojamiento Sorata On the main plaza (no phone). Very simple, with cold water showers only, but also very central - and cheap. $2.80

Altai Oasis ⓣ07/151-9856; ⓦwww.altaioasis.lobopages.com. Set by the river (follow the path that passes by the *Hostal Mirador*, take the first right down the hill and then the next right-hand turning, which steeply curves down towards the hostel), this is an absolutely exquisite place to stay, with lush, sprawling grounds, swinging hammocks and a very peaceful feel. There's also a restaurant on-site, set on a balcony with gorgeous views. Rooms are available with shared or private bath, or alternatively treat yourself to one of the cosy, thatched-roofed cabins dotted around the site (sleeping 2–5 people), complete with kitchens, living areas, and even wood-burning stoves. Rooms $9.80; cabins $15–20 per person; camping $2.80

Café Illampu Fifteen to twenty minutes' walk across the valley on the road leading to the Gruta de San Pedro. While noted for the delicious food rustled up by it's Swiss chef/owner, this is also great place to camp ($2.50 per person) - bring your own tent.

Hostal El Mirador Muñecas 400 ⓣ07/350-5453. A good-value, very popular option, 5 minutes' walk from the plaza. Rooms are basic but there's a lovely terrace with beautiful views, hot showers and a laid-back feel. $5.60

Hostal Panchita On the plaza, next to the church ⓣ02/213-4242. A welcoming, simple place with a sunny courtyard and clean rooms (though the 'hot' shower doesn't quite live up to It's name). $7

Las Piedras Villa Elisa 2 ⓣ07/191-6341. A bit further out of town, Las Piedras is a serene place with characterful rooms, balconies with deckchairs and an inviting communal area with plenty of cushions to relax on and games to play. Breakfast with home-made yoghurt and wholemeal bread is available and the German owner will make you feel at home. $7

Residencial Sorata Corner of the main plaza ⓣ02/213-6672. Set in the delightful, rambling nineteenth-century Casa Gunther, this residencial makes you feel you've stepped back in time by at least eighty years. There are delightful gardens, attractive simple rooms and a huge, wonderfully decorated drawing room. $6

Eating and drinking

While there's not a huge a range of culinary choice in town, the setting more than makes up for it. As well as the usual gringo and Bolivian standbys, you can sample some great home-made baking, and even a curry if you're feeling really homesick.

Café Illampu Fifteen to twenty minutes' walk across the valley on the road leading to the Gruta de San Pedro. Worth a visit for it's delicious breakfasts and pastries in a wonde-fully relaxing setting.

Casa Reggae One block west of *Hostal El Mirador*. A basic, outdoor bar with drinks and sandwiches in the evening and a chilled out, hippyish feel. Evenings only.

Pete's Place Plaza Enrique Peñaranda. By far the best place to eat in Sorata, Pete's Place has excellent vegetarian food (including breakfast and a different set *almuerzo* every day) and curries served in a warm and welcoming atmosphere. The ex-pat owner nips home from time to time, so it may be occasionally closed out of season.

Pizzeria Italia There are numerous pizza restaurants on the plaza; the best of an uninspiring bunch is the pizzeria attached to *Hostal Panchita*, with fairly decent and quickly turned-out pizza.

Restaurante Jalisco Plaza Enrique Peñaranda. This simple restaurant boasts a rather varied menu of Mexican and Italian food, though the local dishe, such as Milanesa de Pollo (chicken in breadcrumbs with rice and salad) are the best choice.

Moving on

By bus From both sides of the plaza, rival bus companies run services every half hour to La Paz (4hr) until 5pm.

THE YUNGAS

East of La Paz, the Cordillera Real drops precipitously into the Amazon lowlands, plunging down through a region of rugged, forest-covered mountains and deep subtropical valleys known as **THE YUNGAS**, abundant with crops of coffee, tropical fruit and coca. Three of the well-built stone roads that linked the agricultural outposts of the Yungas to the main population centres before the Spanish conquest, the so-called "Inca" trails – the **Takesi, Choro** and **Yunga Cruz trails** – are still in good condition, and make excellent three- to four-day

COCA IN THE YUNGAS

The Yungas is one of Bolivia's major coca-producing regions, a role it has played since the colonial era. Considered sweeter and better for chewing than that produced in the **Chapare** region, Yungas coca still dominates the Andean market, and remains legal for traditional use. It's worth checking on the coca-eradication situation before travelling anywhere off the beaten track in the Yungas; if an eradication campaign starts up before you arrive, strange gringos wandering around the backcountry might easily be misidentified as undercover US drug-enforcement agents. With president Morales' current attempts to have the coca leaf taken off the official narcotics list, however, the situation may become more relaxed in the near future.

hikes from La Paz. The most frequently visited Yungas town is the idyllic resort of **Coroico**, set amidst spectacular scenery and exuberant tropical vegetation. From Coroico, the road continues north towards Rurrenabaque and the Bolivian Amazon (see p.243). Alternatively, you can avoid Coroico and head to **Chulumani**, a less-touristed Yungas market town that's the centre of the equally scenic but less frequently visited **South Yungas**.

LA PAZ TO COROICO

Few highways in the world have as intimidating a reputation as the old road linking La Paz with Coroico in the north Yungas. Widely referred to as the **world's most dangerous road** (a title bestowed on it by the Inter-American Development Bank), it's a rough, narrow track chiselled out of near-vertical mountainsides that descends more than 3500m over a distance of just 64km; dozens of vehicles tumbled off it's edges every year, with fatilities often reaching the hundreds. Recently however, a new - and safer (though still slightly hair-raising) road to Coroico was built, meaning traffic on the old road is almost non-existent; instead, travelling the road – which boasts spectacular views – by **mountain bike** has fast become one of Bolivia's most popular tourist attractions, an exhilarating ride that's easy to organize as a day-trip with tour companies in La Paz, though it's not cheap - between $50 and $80 with a reputable company (see p.187 for a list of recommended agencies).

COROICO

Rightly considered one of the most beautiful spots in the Yungas, the peaceful little town of **COROICO** is perched on a steep mountain slope with panoramic views across the forest-covered Andean foothills to the icy peaks of the Cordillera Real beyond. It enjoys a warm and pleasantly humid climate, and this, combined with the dramatic scenery and good facilities, makes it an excellent place to relax and recuperate.

What to see and do

There are no sights as such in Coroico, and it's hardly surprising that most visitors spend much of their time relaxing on the peaceful **Plaza Principal**, lounging by a swimming pool, sipping a cold drink and enjoying the fantastic views. For those with a bit more energy, though, there are some pleasant walks through the surrounding countryside, with forested mountain slopes covered in a lush patchwork of coffee and coca plantations, and banana and orange groves.

Arrival and information

By bus Buses and *micros* from La Paz arrive in the newly built bus station on the southwest side of town, opposite the football pitch. If you're coming to Coroico from anywhere else, you'll have to catch a pick-up truck for the fifteen-minute ride up from the main road at Yolosa – these drop passengers off outside the Mercado Municipal, on Sagárnaga.

Tourist info German restaurant *Back-Stube*, on Calle Linares, has a wealth of tourist information about Coroico, with maps and information on activities and walks around the town.

Accommodation

For a small town Coroico has a good range of places to stay, aimed primarily at visitors from La Paz. At weekends and on public holidays everywhere gets very full and prices go up, so it's worth booking in advance. Conversely, things are pretty quiet midweek, when prices are much more reasonable.

El Cafetal Beside the hospital, about a 10min walk southeast of the town centre ⓣ07/195-4991, ⓔdanycafetal@hotmail.com. A gorgeous retreat far from the lazy bustle of town, *El Cafetal* has clean, pleasant rooms, a pool, terraces and sweeping grounds. Rooms with private bath open onto balconies with exhilarating views, and there's also a restaurant with scrummy food (see below). $5–15

Hostal Kory Linares 3501 ⓣ02/243-1234, ⓔinfo@hostalkory.com. Longstanding backpacker favourite, with plenty of small but clean rooms (with or without bath) around a series of terraces and a large, sparklingly clean swimming pool. The views across the valley are stunning. There's also a reasonable restaurant, a kitchen for guest use and laundry facilities are available. $5–15

Hostal Sol y Luna Just under 1km outside town uphill on Julio Zuazo Cuenca (beyond the *Hotel Esmeralda*; ⓣ07/156-1626, in La Paz ⓣ02/236-2099, ⓦwww.solyluna-bolivia.com). Tranquil hideaway with six delightful rustic cabins, with cooking facilities and private showers, spread out on a beautiful hillside garden, with hammocks, fire pit's, a hot bath and plunge pools. There are also several basic rooms with shared bath ($2/ 3.50 per person) in the main building, and camping space is available for $2 per person. Staff are friendly and welcoming, there's a meditation room and a small restaurant serving a variety of dishes and excellent home-grown and roasted Yungeña coffee. You can also get a wonderful shiatsu massage for $10–12.

Residencial Pando Calle Pando ⓣ07/191-6497. This is pretty basic, but rooms are set around a sweet courtyard and it's one of the cheapest places in town.

Eating and drinking

There's no lack of variety when it comes to places to eat, including everything from pizza and Mexican food to quality French cuisine, German pastries and even Swiss fondue, as well as plenty of places serving inexpensive standard Bolivian food. Nightlife tends to involve drinking beer in the town's bar-restaurants or poolside in the better hotels.

Back-Stube Linares, off the main plaza. German café-bakery serving excellent soups, snacks and sandwiches, and deliciously decadent home-made cakes. The terrace has wonderful views of the valleys below. Closed Tues.

Bamboo's Café Iturralde. Candlelit hideaway open in the evenings for reasonable Mexican staples like burritos, enchiladas and tacos at about $3.50 a plate, as well as ice-cold beers and mean margaritas. It's open late, with live music at weekends.

El Cafetal Beside the hospital, about 15min southeast of the town centre. Small French-run restaurant with panoramic views and a delicious menu of crêpes, soufflés, fish and meat dishes, as well as great coffee. Closed Tues.

Pizzeria Italia Calle Pinilla. Decent, tasty pizza.

La Senda Verde Feliz Reyes Ortiz. Set around a lovely peaceful courtyard, this café has great coffee (also available to buy) as well as home-made cookies and sandwiches. There's also a small shop with guide books, home-made jam and chutneys and crafts for sale.

Villa Bonita Calle Héroes del Chaco. Open from midday until 6pm, *Villa Bonita* boasts delicious home-made ice-cream and good Italian dishes.

TREAT YOURSELF

La Senda Verde
ⓣ07/153-2703 / ⓣ02/213-996; Situated 20min outside of Coroico (a taxi will usually charge about $5) and set next to the river in a beautiful valley, this is the kind of gorgeous hideaway you won't ever want to leave. There are sprawling, lush grounds to wander around, a swimming pool, very pretty views and an outdoor restaurant serving up tasty meals. Accommodation is in 2-4 person cabins, which are dotted around the grounds. $25 for two people, including breakfast.

Moving on

Buses and *micros* to La Paz depart from the bus station every half an hour until 6pm.

CHULUMANI

From Unduavi on the road from La Paz to the Yungas, a side road heads east off the main highway towards the provincial capital of **CHULUMANI**, a very tranquil little town set on a steep hillside overlooking a broad river valley, where life is taken at an easy pace. With it's palm-shaded plaza and steep and narrow cobbled streets, lined with neat houses with red-tiled roofs, the main attractions of Chulumani are the surrounding hamlets, splendid scenery and exuberant tropical vegetation of the countryside.

Arrival and information

By bus Buses leave from Villa Fátima in La Paz more or less every 30min (4hr) and arrive outside the bus offices on Plaza Libertad.
Money There's no ATM, but the Prodem bank, a few blocks south-west of the main plaza, can change US dollars and give cash advances on Visa and MasterCard (with a 5 percent fee).
Tourist Info There's no tourist office in Chulumani; however English-speaking Javier Sarabia, owner of the **Hostal Country House**, is a mine of information on hikes from Chulumani and also runs guided excursions and camping trips on foot or by jeep and can arrange bicycle and motorbike rental.

Accommodation

Accommodation options are rather limited in Chulumani, although there are at least a couple of decent options.

Hostal Country House 1km southeast of town, beyond the mirador (no phone). By far the best option in Chulumani, this quirky little guesthouse extends a welcoming, homely feel, with comfortable rooms (private bath and breakfast included) around a lovely garden, replete with small swimming pool. The owners are very friendly and informative, and the food is delicious. $12.60
Hostal Dion Bolívar, just off the plaza ⓣ 02/213-6070. A good budget choice with clean rooms with or without private bath. $8

Eating and drinking

The selection of places to eat in Chulumani is disappointing, and the better places are usually open only at weekends. If your budget really is tight, there are a number of places grouped around the plaza serving cheap *almuerzos*, although none look too salubrious.

Cafetería Dely's Located underneath *Hostal Dion*, and run by the same people, this is an oasis amid Chulumani's fly-blown plaza, offering burgers, fruit juices and the like in a cool, fresh interior.
Panorama Inside the hotel of the same name, a block or so north of the plaza on Murillo. The most reliable restaurant in town, serving decent set *almuerzos* and standard main courses including fresh trout.

Moving on

Buses leave for La Paz from outside the bus offices on Plaza Libertad when they're full (until 5pm). If you're looking to go from Coroico to Chulumani, or vice versa, it's generally easier (and quicker) to go back to La Paz and take a direct bus.

The Southern Altiplano

South of La Paz, the **SOUTHERN ALTIPLANO** stretches 800km to the Chilean and Argentine borders. Set at an average altitude of around 3700m, this starkly beautiful landscape is the image most frequently associated with Bolivia: a barren and treeless expanse whose arid steppes stretch to the horizon, where snowcapped mountains shimmer under deep-blue skies.

The unavoidable transport nexus of the Altiplano is the unattractive tin-mining city of **Oruro**, 230km south of La Paz, a grim monument to industrial decline that comes alive once a year during the **Carnaval**. Some 310km further southeast of Oruro is the legendary silver-mining city of **Potosí**, a city of sublime colonial architecture,

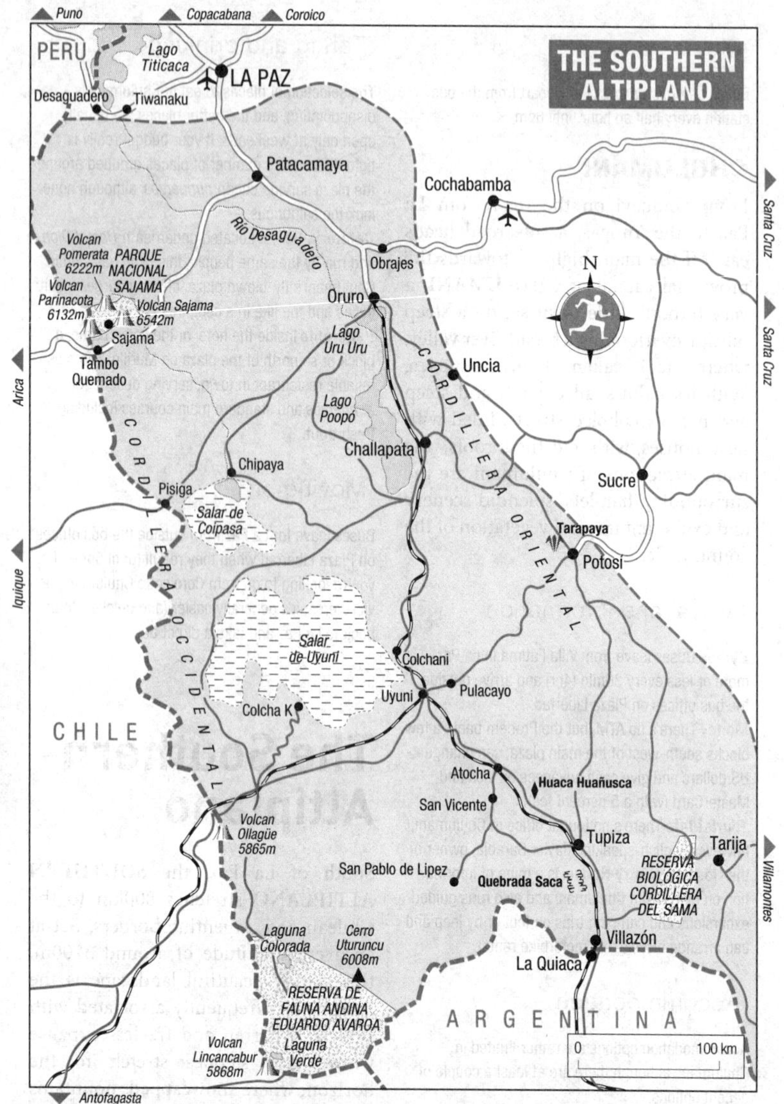

marooned at 4100m above sea level and filled with monuments to a glorious but tragic past.

The Altiplano grows more desolate still as it stretches south towards the Argentine border. From the forlorn railway town of **Uyuni**, 323km due south of Oruro by road and rail, you can venture into the dazzling white **Salar de Uyuni**, the **world's largest salt lake**. Beyond the Salar in the far southwestern corner of the country is the **Reserva de Fauna Andina Eduardo Avaroa**, a bleak-looking nature reserve of lunar landscapes and home to a surprising array of wildlife.

Southwest of Uyuni, the Altiplano changes character. The pleasant little mining town of **Tupiza** is surrounded by arid red mountains and cactus-strewn badlands eroded into deep gullies and rock pinnacles. In the far south of the country lies the provincial capital of **Tarija**, a remote yet welcoming city set in a deep and fertile valley that enjoys a much warmer climate than the Altiplano.

PARQUE NACIONAL SAJAMA

Southwest of La Paz, the road to Chile passes through a desert plain from the middle of which rises the perfect snowcapped cone of Volcán Sajama. At 6542m, Sajama is the tallest mountain in Bolivia and the centre of the country's oldest national park, the **PARQUE NACIONAL SAJAMA**. The park encompasses the entire mountain, the slopes of which support the highest forest in the world, as well as much of the surrounding desert, where pumas, rare Andean deer and the rarely seen, flightless, ostrich-like rheas. Mountain climbers are drawn by the peak's relative ease of ascension – it is only allowed between April and October, when the ice is sufficiently frozen – and the mountain's lower slopes, containing bubbling geysers and hot springs, make for excellent hiking.

The administrative centre of the park, where you can register to climb the mountain and arrange guides, mules and porters, is the village of Sajama. There are two ways to reach Sajama by public transport from La Paz. The first is to take any Oruro-bound bus as far as the crossroads town of **Patacamaya**, from where a *micro* goes directly to Sajama every day at about 1pm, returning to Patacamaya at 7am the next day. The other way of reaching the park is to get on a bus from La Paz (several daily; 3hr 30min–4hr) headed for Arica in Chile and alight at the turn-off to Sajama on the main road. Jeeps from the village usually wait there to collect passengers arriving from La Paz; it's a twelve-kilometre drive back to the village.

If you want information before the trip, contact **SERNAP** at Av Mariscal Santa Cruz, edif. Litoral no. 150 in La Paz (ⓣ02/211-1360, ⓦwww.sernap.gov.bo). On arrival in Sajama village you must register at the park office (daily 8am–noon & 2.30–7pm) and pay the $2 entrance fee. There's very basic **accommodation** in the village as well as various places serving simple and inexpensive **food**.

ORURO

Huddled on the bleak Altiplano some 230km south of La Paz, the grim mining city of **ORURO** was the economic powerhouse of Bolivia for much of the twentieth century, due to enormous mineral wealth in the surrounding mountains and tin mines established here in the late nineteenth century. Since the fall of world tin prices in

CROSSING INTO CHILE AT TAMBO QUEMADO

The **border** between Chile and Bolivia is 9km west of the turn-off to Sajama at **Tambo Quemado**. Crossing into Chile is straightforward: there's a Bolivian *migración* where you get your exit stamp, and a couple of restaurants catering mainly to truck drivers. A couple of kilometres further on from Tambo Quemado is the Chilean border post of Chungará, open daily from 8am till 9pm, where you'll have your passport stamped for entry to Chile. If you're coming from La Paz, the bus will take you all the way through to **Arica** on Chile's Pacific Coast. If you're heading to Chile from Sajama, you can get to the border on the 7am *micro* to Patacamaya (which comes to Tambo Quemado to pick up passengers), then walk across the frontier and pick up transport on the Chilean side.

1985, however, Oruro's fortunes have plummeted and more than two decades of economic decline have made it a shadow of it's former self.

What to see and do

Oruro is a cold and rather sombre place, with the melancholic air of a city forever looking back on a golden age that is unlikely to return. There's not really much reason to stop in Oruro and most travellers simply pass on through. This all changes however, celebrates it's annual Carnaval.

Carnaval

Every year in late February or early March, Oruro explodes into life, celebrating it's **Carnaval** in what is without doubt one of the most spectacular cultural events in all South America. Tens of thousands of visitors flock here to watch a sensational array of costumed dancers parading through the streets. There's always a good deal of heavy drinking and chaotic water-fighting thrown in for good measure. At the centre of the festivities are two events: the **Entrada** on the Saturday before Ash Wednesday, with a massive procession of more than fifty different troupes of costumed dancers passing through the streets, and the **Diablada**, or Dance of the Devils, led by two lavishly costumed dancers representing Lucifer and St Michael, followed by hundreds of devil dancers who leap and prance through the streets. If you're coming to Oruro at this time of year, make sure to book accommodation in advance.

Plaza 10 de Febrero and Museo Antropológico

The town's main plaza, Plaza 10 de Febrero is a pleasant square shaded by cypress trees. Five blocks west of the plaza stands the **Santuario del Socavón** (Sanctuary of the Mineshaft), home to the image of the Virgin del Socavón, the patron saint of miners, in whose honour the Carnaval celebrations are staged. The abandoned mineshaft beneath the church is now home to the **Museo Antropológico** (daily 9am–1pm & 3–6pm; $1.25) with an interesting display of equipment that explains the history of mining, as well as two fearsome-looking statues of El Tío, the devil-like figure worshipped by Bolivian miners as the king of the underworld and owner of all minerals.

Arrival and information

By bus Almost all long-distance buses pull in at the Terminal Terrestre, ten blocks northeast of the city centre on Avenida Rajka Bakovic. A taxi into town from here should cost $0.50 per person, the flat rate for journeys within the city; alternatively, take any *micro* heading south along Avenida 6 de Agosto.

By train The train station (☎02/527-4605) is a short walk east of the city centre on Avenida Galvarro (note that the ticket office is closed all day Saturday).

Money There are several banks in Oruro which change cash and traveller's cheques, and have ATMs. Try Banco Bisa, on Bolívar between Presidente Montes and La Plata, or Banco Unión, at Montecinos and Pegador. The city centre, especially on 6 de Octubre, abounds with internet cafes; try Leo Net on the corner of Pegador and Herrera or Infocomp on Bolívar between La Plata & Galvarro, inside Galería Onasis.

Tourist info The tourist office (Mon–Fri 8am–noon & 2.30–6.30pm; ☎02/525-0144), on the south side of Plaza 10 de Febrero (to the right of the cinema; it's not actually signposted, unhelpfully enough, but go up the stairs to the second floor to find the office). They can provide maps, tour guides and information on activties in and around Oruro.

Accommodation

There's a fairly good range of places **to stay** in Oruro; during Carnaval prices go up by as much as five times, and most places will only rent rooms for the entire weekend. There are several places to stay near the train station, which is handy for those catching an early morning or late-night train.

Alojamiento Copacabana Av Galvarro 6352 ☎02/525-4184. A handy option very close to the

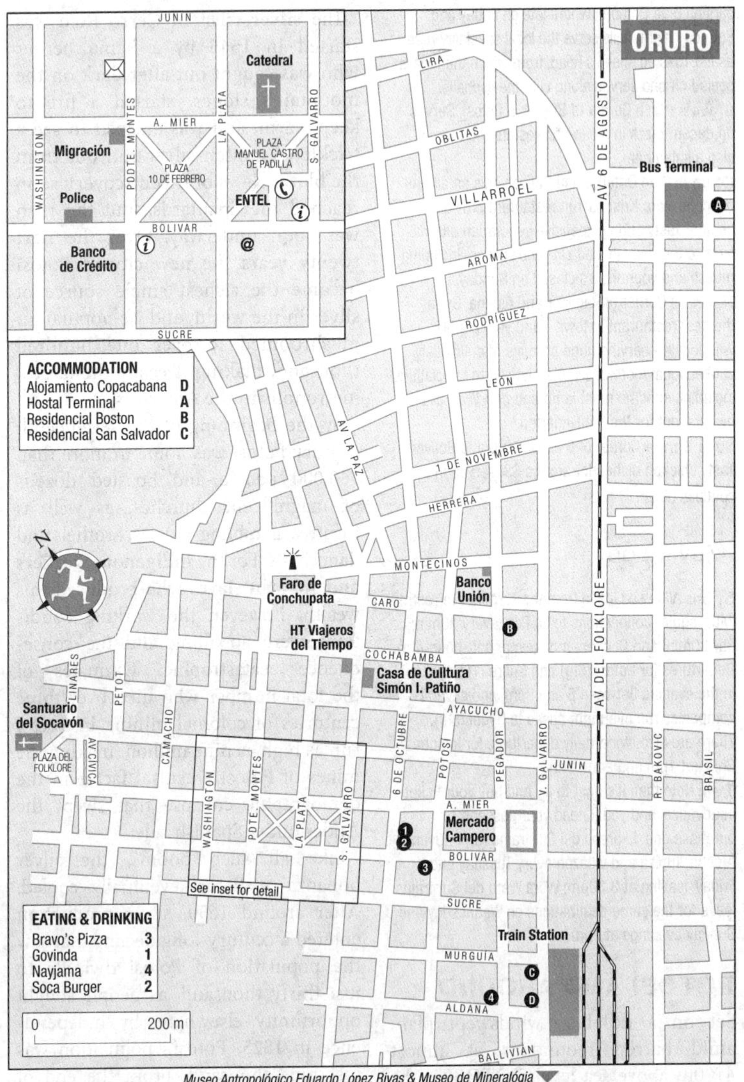

train station; rooms are well-kept, and the staff are friendly. $5

Hostal Terminal Av 21 de Enero ⓣ02/527-3431. Conveniently situated next to the bus station, this hostal has decent rooms, with or without private bath and all with cable. $9.80

Residencial Boston Pegador 1159 ⓣ02/527-4708. Pleasant hostel whose good-value rooms come with or without private bath. Staff can be less than friendly however. $10

Residencial San Salvador Av Galvarro 6325 ⓣ02/527-6771. Also near to the train station, amd basic but clean. Just a few dollars extra buys you a private bath and cable TV. $5.60

Eating and drinking

Oruro has a fairly diverse selection of places to eat, though most don't open until mid-morning. There are plenty of cheap roast-chicken restaurants and snack bars on 6 de Octubre, where late on Friday and Saturday night stalls serve the local speciality *rostro asado*, roasted sheep's head, from which the face is peeled off and served along with the eyeballs.

Bravo's Pizza Corner of Bolívar & Potosí. Serves up decent pizza in a cheerful restaurant; there's also a salad bar.

Govinda 6 de Octubre and Bolívar. This small and peaceful Hare Krishna-run restaurant provides healthy, tasty and inexpensive vegetarian alternatives to the meat-based *Orureño* cuisine, including muesli and yoghurt; it's closed on Sundays.

Nayjama Corner of Pagador and Aldana. By far the best restaurant in town - and very popular with locals - serving huge portions of deliciously cooked local food for $4–5 a plate, with specialities including sublime roast lamb and *criadillos*, prairie oysters, not for the faint-hearted.

Soca Burger Corner of 6 de Octubre and Bolívar. Tasty chicken dishes for around $3, served in a spotless diner.

Moving on

By bus All buses leave from the Terminal Terrestre, with regular connections to La Paz (every 30min; 3hr 30min) and Cochabamba (every half-hour; 4hr). Departures for Potosí (8hr) and Sucre (10hr) leave in the evening between 6 and 9pm, and several companies run overnight buses to Uyuni (8hr). There are also twice-daily departures for Iquique in Chile (at 1pm and 2am; 8hr).

Train Note than it's best to try and buy your ticket in advance, and you'll need your passport to purchase one. Expreso del Sur trains run to Uyuni, Atocha, Tupiza and Villazón every Tuesday and Friday, leaving at 3.30pm; Wara Wara del Sur trains leave for the same destinations on Wednesday and Sunday evenings at 7pm.

POTOSÍ AND AROUND

Set on a desolate, windswept plain amid barren mountains at almost 4100m above sea level, **POTOSÍ** is the highest city in the world, and at once the most fascinating and tragic place in Bolivia. Given it's remote and inhospitable location, it's difficult to see at first glance why it was ever built here at all. The answer lies in **Cerro Rico** ("Rich Mountain"), the conical peak that rises imperiously above the city to the south and was, quite simply, the richest source of silver the world had ever seen.

The **silver rush** of Cerro Rico was started in 1545 by a llama herder who was caught out after dark on the mountain's slopes, started a fire to keep warm, and was amazed to see a trickle of molten silver run out from the blaze. News of this discovery soon reached the Spaniards, and the rush was soon underway. Over the next twenty years the new city of Potosí became the richest single source of silver in the world, and it's population mushroomed to over one hundred thousand, making it easily the largest metropolis in the Americas.

By the beginning of the seventeenth century Potosí was home to more than 160,000 people and boasted dozens of magnificent churches, as well as theatres, gambling-houses, brothels and dancehalls. For the **indigenous workers and African slaves** who produced this wealth, however, the working conditions were appalling and the consequences catastrophic. Estimates of the total number who died over three centuries of colonial mining in Potosí run as high as nine million, making the mines of Potosí a central factor in the demographic collapse that swept the Andes under Spanish rule.

Like all such booms, the silver bonanza at Potosí eventually cooled. After around 1650, silver production entered a century-long decline that saw the population of Potosí dwindle to just thirty thousand, as people sought opportunity elsewhere; by independence in 1825, Potosí's population was just nine thousand. From the end of the nineteenth century Potosí came to rely more and more on the mining of **tin**, but the town never recovered from the decline of silver production, much less the crash of the tin market in the mid-1980s. Today, the city's many fine churches are all that remains of the immense wealth that once flowed from it's mines, and it's tragic history weighs heavily on the shoulders of the living.

What to see and do

Potosí's legacy reflects both the magnificence and the horror of it's colonial past. The city is a treasure-trove of colonial art and architecture, with hundreds of well-preserved buildings, including some of the finest churches in Bolivia.

Plaza 10 de Noviembre

The centre of the city is the **Plaza 10 de Noviembre**, a pleasant tree-shaded square with a small replica of the Statue of Liberty, erected in 1926 to commemorate Bolivian independence. On the north side of the square, the site of the original church (which collapsed in 1807) is now occupied by the twin-towered **Catedral**, completed in Neoclassical style in 1836. To the east of the square lies the **Plaza 6 de Agosto**, at the centre of which is a column commemorating the Battle of Ayacucho in 1824, which secured Bolivian independence early the following year.

Casa Real de la Moneda

West of the Plaza 10 de Noviembre on Calle Ayacucho stands the unmissable **Casa Real de la Moneda**, or Royal Mint (Tues-Sat 9–10.30am & 2.30–5.30pm, Sun 9–10.30am; ⓦwww.bolivian.com/cnm; $2.50). One of the most outstanding examples of colonial civil architecture in all South America, it is now home to the best museum in Bolivia. **The vast and eclectic collection** includes the original machinery used in the various stages of the minting process, some of Bolivia's finest colonial religious art, militaria, archeological artefacts and a display of coins and banknotes.

Built between 1759 and 1773, La Moneda is a truly formidable construction, built as part of a concerted effort by the Spanish crown to reform the economic and financial machinery of the empire to increase revenues. Over 7500 square metres in size, La Moneda is enclosed by stout stone walls over a metre thick with only a few barred windows looking out, giving it the appearance of a fortress. Inside, the rambling two-storey complex of about **two hundred rooms** is set around five internal courtyards, all finely built with cut stone blocks and neat brickwork. In addition to housing the heavy machinery and equipment needed to produce coins – much of which is well preserved and on display – **La Moneda** also housed troops, workers, African slaves and the senior royal officials responsible for overseeing operations. A vital nerve centre of Spanish imperial power in the Andes, it also served as a prison, treasury and near-impregnable stronghold in times of disorder.

La Torre de la Compañia

Also on Calle Ayacucho stands **La Torre de la Compañia** (Mon–Fri 8am–noon & 2–6pm; Sat & Sun 8.30am–12.30pm, 2.30–6.30pm; $1.40), a bell tower which is all that now remains of a Jesuit church originally founded in 1581. Completed in 1707 and recently restored, the grandiose tower is one of the finest eighteenth-century religious monuments in Bolivia and a sublime example of the Mestizo-Baroque style. You can climb to the top of the tower, from where there are excellent views of the city and Cerro Rico.

Convento and Museo Santa Teresa

The **Convento-Museo Santa Teresa** (Calle Ayacucho; Mon–Sat 9–11am & 2.30–5pm; Sun 9–11am, 3–5pm; $3) is a beautiful colonial church and convent worth visiting both for it's fine collection of colonial religious painting and sculpture, and for a somewhat disturbing insight into the bizarre lifestyle of nuns in the colonial era. Visits are by guided tour only, so you need to get here at least an hour before closing.

CERRO RICO

Immediately south of Potosí the near-perfect cone of **Cerro Rico** rises above the city, pockmarked with the entrances to the thousands of mines that lead deep into it's entrails. All the tour operators listed below run regular tours of the mines. Be warned, though, that this is an unpleasant and highly dangerous environment, where safety precautions are largely left to fate; anyone suffering from claustrophobia, heart or breathing problems is advised against entering. Some question the ethics of making a tourist attraction of a workplace where conditions are so appalling; however, most visitors find the experience one of the most unforgettable in Bolivia.

Tours of the mines begin with a visit to the miners' market on and around Plaza El Calvario, where you can buy coca leaves, dynamite, black-tobacco cigarettes, pure cane alcohol and fizzy soft drinks – you should take a selection of these as gifts for the miners you'll be visiting.

Arrival and information

By bus All buses (except those from Uyuni) arrive at the Terminal de Buses on Avenida Universitario. Buses from Uyuni pull in at the various bus company offices on the corner of Avenida Universitario and Sevilla. From the terminal, a taxi into the city centre costs $0.60 per person (the basic rate for journeys throughout the city), or you can catch *micro* "A" heading up Avenida Universitario, which will take you to Plaza 10 de Noviembre, the central square.

Tourist information The best place for information is the Oficina de Turismo Municipal (Mon–Fri 8am–noon & 2–6pm; Sat & Sun 8am–noon; ⓣ02/622-6408), accessible through the arch of Torre de la Compañía on Calle Ayacucho, a block west of Plaza 10 de Noviembre.

Tours operators A number of tour operators offer half-day trips to the mines of Cerro Rico, purportedly fixed at $10 per person. One of the best is Koala Tours at Ayacucho 5 (ⓣ02/622-2092, ⓔk_tours_potosi@hotmail.com), with trips run by experienced (ex-miner) multilingual guides, with a percentage of each mine tour sold going towards improving health-care facilities for the miners. For trips to the Salar de Uyuni, try Andean Salt Expeditions, on the corner of Padilles and Linares (ⓣ02/622-5175, ⓔturismo_potosi@hotmail.com), or Sin Fronteras, Bustillos 1092 (ⓣ02/622-4058, ⓦwww.organizacionsinfronteras.com).

Accommodation

With night-time temperatures often falling below zero, the main consideration when choosing where to **stay** in Potosí is warmth. A couple of places have central heating, but otherwise try to find a room that gets some sun during the day.

La Casona Chuquisasa 460 ⓣ02/623-0523, ⓔcasona@boliviahostels.com. A relaxed backpacker-friendly place set around a pleasant, brightly painted courtyard, with dorms for $3.90 per person. There are good facilities, including a kitchen, comfy living room with films shown every night, and a sunny terrace. Breakfast is included. $9

Hostal Compañía de Jesús Chuquisaca 445 ⓣ02/622-3173. Delightful converted colonial building in the centre of town with clean, snug and good-value rooms, toasty hot showers and a welcoming family atmosphere. Simple breakfast included. $11.20

Hostal Maria Victoria Chuquisaca 148 ⓣ02/622-2132. Tucked away in a pretty street, this restful old colonial house is run by friendly staff. There are gas showers, an on-site travel agency and a terrace due to be completed in early 2009. $9.80

Koala Den Junín 56 ⓣ02/622-6467, ⓣktours-potosi@hotmail.com. A travellers' favourite, this charming, amicable hostel owned and run by Koala Tours features decent dormitories ($4.90 per person) and more expensive private rooms (the double bedrooms with private bath and cable are particularly inviting and worth treating yourself for a night or two). Heating in all rooms means you won't feel the frost, while great showers, a lovely communal area, kitchen, large DVD collection, and internet and breakfast are included. $11.50

Eating and drinking

Potosí's popularity with travellers is reflected in the city's growing variety of places to eat, with more and more cafés and restaurants offering vegetarian food and travellers' favourites like pizza and pasta. The Mercado Central - on Bolívar, between Bustillos and Oruro - is your best bet for large portions of cheap local food.

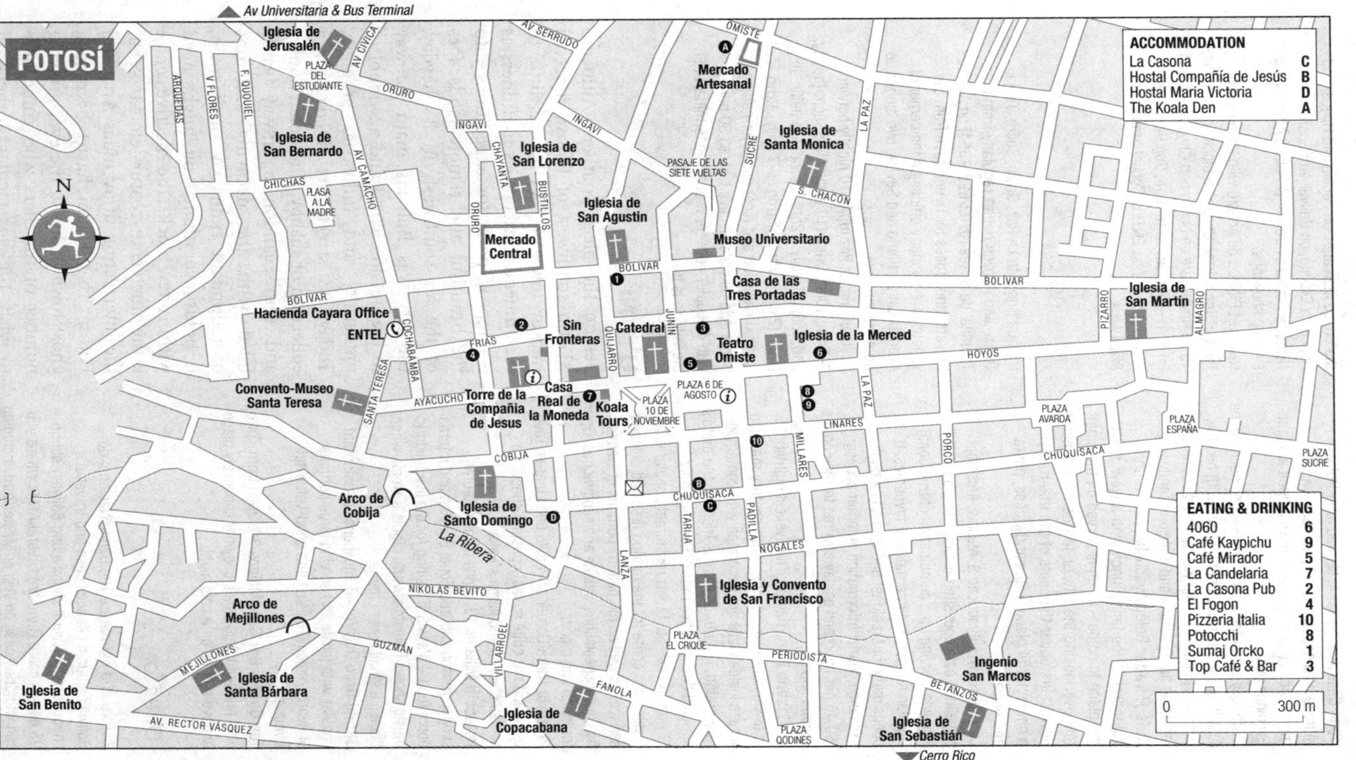
POTOSÍ
Av Universitaria & Bus Terminal
Cerro Rico
ACCOMMODATION
La Casona C
Hostal Compañía de Jesús B
Hostal Maria Victoria D
The Koala Den A
EATING & DRINKING
4060 6
Café Kaypichu 9
Café Mirador 5
La Candelaria 7
La Casona Pub 2
El Fogon 4
Pizzeria Italia 10
Potocchi 8
Sumaj Orcko 1
Top Café & Bar 3
0 300 m
N
Iglesia de Jerusalén
Plaza del Estudiante
Iglesia de San Bernardo
Plasa a la Madre
Iglesia de San Lorenzo
Mercado Central
Iglesia de San Agustin
Mercado Artesanal
Pasaje de las Siete Vueltas
Iglesia de Santa Monica
Museo Universitario
Casa de las Tres Portadas
Iglesia de San Martín
Hacienda Cayara Office
ENTEL
Sin Fronteras
Catedral
Teatro Omiste
Iglesia de la Merced
Convento-Museo Santa Teresa
Torre de la Compañia de Jesus
Casa Real de la Moneda
Koala Tours
Plaza 10 de Noviembre
Plaza 6 de Agosto
Plaza Avarda
Plaza España
Plaza Sucre
Arco de Cobija
Iglesia de Santo Domingo
La Ribera
Iglesia y Convento de San Francisco
Arco de Mejillones
Plaza El Crique
Ingenio San Marcos
Iglesia de San Benito
Iglesia de Santa Bárbara
Iglesia de Copacabana
Plaza Qodines
Iglesia de San Sebastián
Av Serrudo
Av Civica
Oruro
Ingavi
Arquedas
V Flores
F. Quouiel
Chichas
Av Camacho
Chayanta
Bustillos
Omiste
Sucre
La Paz
S. Chacon
Bolivar
Pizarro
Almagro
Frias
Cochabamba
Santa Teresa
Ayacucho
Quijarro
Junin
Hoyos
Linares
Porco
Chuquisaca
Cobija
Tarija
Padilla
Millares
Nogales
Lanza
Nikolas Bevito
Villarroel
Guzman
Mejillones
Av. Rector Vásquez
Fanola
Periodista
Betanzos

4060 Calle Ayachucho 4. Named after Potosi's altitude, this popular café / pub has a varied menu and is a good place to have a drink at night. Evenings only.

Café Kaypichu Millares 14. Follow the stairs to the first floor for this sweet, simple cafe with healthy, tasty vegetarian food, as well as meat options, including llama steaks and delicious sandwiches.

Café Mirador Belén Ayacucho, next to the cathedral. If you fancy lunch with a view, this is the place to come - lunch is served on the small roof overlooking the city, or, for the faint of heart, downstairs under the seats of the theatre. It's a characterful place, with sandwiches, pasta and pizza.

La Candelaria Ayacucho 5. Mellow, first-floor travellers' café opposite the Case Real de la Moneda, serving up a combination of traditional Bolivian recipes and international favourites. It opens early for breakfast and also has a book exchange, tourist information, internet access ($0.45 per hour) and a cosy covered terrace on the second floor.

La Casona Pub Frías 38. The liveliest nightspot in town, housed in an eighteenth-century mansion whose inside walls are decorated with contemporary graffiti. The atmosphere is friendly, and there's ice-cold beer and live music. Evenings only.

El Fogón Frías 58. Smart restaurant popular with locals, who come for the roaring fires and obliging service, as well as the healthy portions of steaks, fish, local specialities, salads and sandwiches. Open for lunch and dinner.

Pizzeria Italia Corner of Padilla and Linares. Tasty pizza and not quite so tasty pasta dishes. Also serves chicken and llama steaks.

Potocchi Millares 13. Small café-restaurant serving reasonable traditional Bolivian and international food – it's worth visiting for the live folkloric music shows it hosts several nights a week, when there's a small cover charge.

Sumaj Orco Quijarro 46. Inexpensive restaurant popular with locals and serving large portions of hearty regional cuisine and good-value set *almuerzos*.

Top Café & Bar Calle Mateos 30. Open from 7pm until midnight, this small, cosy bar is a lovely place to have a drink on a cold night.

Directory

Banks and exchange The Banco Nacional de Bolivia on Junín changes cash and traveller's cheques, and several shops along Bolívar change US dollars cash. There are several ATMs where you can withdraw cash on Visa or MasterCard, including the Banco Mercantil, on Padilla and Hoyos, and Banco de Crédito, on Bolívar and Sucre.

Cinema Corner of Bolívar & Potosí. Afternoon and evening showings.

Internet Plaza 6 de Agosto with Paseo Blvd.

Post office Correo Central, a block south of Plaza 10 de Noviembre on Lanza and Chuquisaca (Mon–Fri 8am–8pm, Sat 8am–6pm, Sun 9am–noon).

Telephone office ENTEL, Cochabamba and Plaza Arce.

Moving on

By bus Buses to La Paz, Oruro, Sucre, Tarija, Tupiza and Villazón depart regularly from the Terminal de Buses (☎02/622-7354) on Avenida Universitario. Buses for Uyuni leave from the various bus company offices on the corner of Avenida Universitario and Sevilla, two blocks up from the terminal.

Destinations: La Paz (up to 10 nightly between 7–9pm; 10hr); Oruro (10 daily; 8hr); Sucre (hourly; 3hr); Tarija (1 daily; 12hr); Tupiza (3–4 daily; 9hr); Uyuni (2 daily; 7hr); Villazón (6–7 daily; 12hr).

By taxi A quicker and nicer option for getting to Sucre is to take a collective taxi ($3.50 per person with 4 people) - drivers wait at the terminal until the vehicle is full.

UYUNI

Set on the bleak southern Altiplano 212km southwest of Potosí, the cold railway town of **UYUNI** has little to recommend it except it's usefulness as a jump-off point for expeditions into the beautiful and remote landscapes of the far southwest. In it's heyday, the city was Bolivia's main gateway to the outside world and a symbol of modernity and industrial progress. Today, it's streets are lined with a collection of shabby, tin-roofed houses and semi-abandoned railway yards filled with the decaying skeletons of redundant trains. A small town, it holds everything you might need within a few blocks; the effective centre is the nineteenth-century clocktower at the intersection of avenidas Arce and Potosí. That Uyuni hasn't become a ghost town is due to the ever-growing number of travellers who come here to visit the spectacular scenery of the **Salar de Uyuni** and the **Reserva de Fauna Andina Eduardo Avaroa**, which are usually visited together on a three-day tour from Uyuni.

Arrival and information

Bus Buses from Potosí, Oruro and Tupiza pull up in front of the various bus company offices (an area optimistically described as "the terminal"), three blocks north of the train station along the partly pedestrianized Avenida Arce.

Tourist Info The Oficina Municipal de Turismo can be found on the corner of Arce and Potosí, but it's rather erratic opening hours means you may have trouble even getting through the door. The tour agencies, all situated within a few blocks of Avenida Arce, are a better source of information, though their main aim is to sell you a trip to the Salar and the reserve (see p.222).

Train The train station is on Avenida Ferroviaria, right in the centre of town. If you're arriving on a late night train, note that most hostels will open their doors to you, no matter what time it is.

Accommodation

There's a limited range of **accommodation** in Uyuni, and most of it is fairly basic.

Hotel Avenida Av Ferroviaria 11 ⓣ02/693-2078. Conveniently located right by the train station, and highly popular with backpackers for the clean functional rooms with or without bath and good hot showers. $7

Hostal Marith Potosí 61 ⓣ02/693-2174. Further out of town, but offering comfortable rooms (and lots of blankets) around a nice courtyard. The showers, though, are far from hot. $8.40

Hostal San Salvador Av Arce ⓣ02/693-2407. Right next to the bus station, so convenient for those late-night buses. Rooms are basic and hot water is only available in the day, but it does the trick for a night. $8.40

Hotel Palacio Av Arce 7 ⓣ02/693-2259. Good-value, decent rooms and the possibility of heating and cable TV for just $1.40 extra each. $8.40

Eating and drinking

As with accommodation, the range of places to eat in Uyuni is pretty limited. The food market on Potosi and Avaroa has cheap and decent local dishes, whilst there are a fair few restaurants concentrated around the pedestrianized Plaza Arce, offering generally overpriced and gringo-oriented food.

Arco Iris Plaza Arce. Popular with travellers, with a cosy atmosphere in which to pass a chilly night.

Kactus Av Potosí. Another place with more atmosphere than appetite, *Kactus* is a reliable place for small hours socialising, with well subscribed happy hours, drinking challenges and plenty of travellers.

Minuteman Pizza In the *Toñito Hotel*, Av Ferroviaria. The best place to eat in town, with a warm, secluded ambience, great décor and arguably the best pizza in Bolivia (they're thin, crispy, and loaded with top quality ingredients). Also serves pasta dishes, creative salads and delicious muffins and pancakes. Pizza service starts at 5pm, but it's open for breakfast too.

Pizzeria Italia Plaza Arce. Invariably packed with tourists, this place trades more on it's gregarious vibe than it's food: while the pizza is tasty enough, the pasta dishes are best avoided.

Moving on

By bus Buses leave from the handful of offices on Avenida Arce.

Destinations: La Paz (1 daily; 11hr); Oruro (2–3 daily; 8hr); Potosí (4 daily; 7–8hr); Sucre (4 daily; 10hr); Tarija (1 daily; 18hr); Tupiza (1 daily; 7hr). There are also daily services to Avaroa and Calama in Chile.

Train Expreso del Sur trains leave for Atocha, Tupiza and Villazón at 10.40pm on Tuesdays and Fridays; services to Oruro leave at 12.05am on Thursdays

CROSSING INTO CHILE FROM UYUNI

There are two ways of crossing into Chile from Uyuni. Twice a week, on Wednesday and Sunday at 4am, a passenger train travels from Uyuni to **Calama** in Chile via the Bolivian border post of **Avaroa**. If you're travelling this way you'll need to get an exit stamp, $2 at the *migración* in Uyuni on Av Potosí. A more popular route into Chile is across the border at Laguna Verde in the far south of the **Reserva Eduardo Avaroa**, which can be arranged through one of the tour agencies in Uyuni; most agencies have daily departures. The officials at this border post have been known to charge small unauthorized fees for letting you cross.

and Sundays (ie Wednesday and Saturday night). Wara Wara del Sur trains leave for Atocha, Tupiza and Villazón at 2.50am on Mondays and Thursdays; the service to Oruro leaves at 1.45am on Tuesday and Friday mornings. Remember to buy your ticket in advance; you will need your passport.

SALAR DE UYUNI

One of Bolivia's most extraordinary attractions, the **Salar de Uyuni**, covering some 9000 square kilometres of the Altiplano west of Uyuni, is by far the largest salt lake in the world. The Salar is not a lake in any conventional sense of the word – though below the surface it is largely saturated by water, it's uppermost layer consists of a thick, hard crust of salt, easily capable of supporting the weight of a car. The surface is mostly covered by water between December and April, but even then it's rarely more than a metre deep, and usually much less. Driving across the perfectly flat white expanse of the Salar, with the unbroken chains of snowcapped mountains lining the far horizon, it's easy to believe you're on another planet, so harsh and inhospitable is the terrain.

RESERVA DE FAUNA ANDINA EDUARDO AVAROA

The southwesternmost corner of Bolivia is covered by the **Reserva de Fauna Andina Eduardo Avaroa**, a 7147-square-kilometre wildlife reserve, ranging between 4000m and 6000m in altitude and encompassing some of the most startling scenery in Bolivia. Like the Salar de Uyuni, the desolate landscapes of this remote region possess an otherworldly beauty, with glacial salt lakes whose icy waters are stained bright red or emerald green; snowcapped volcanic peaks; high-altitude deserts and a wide range of rare **Andean wildlife** including the world's largest population of the

VISITING THE SALAR AND THE RESERVE

Pretty much the only way to visit the **Salar de Uyuni** and **Reserva Eduardo Avaroa** is on an organized tour, which can be easily arranged from Uyuni. The standard trip (usually between $70 and $90, including food, accommodation, transport and Spanish-speaking guide) is a three-day tour by 4WD around a circuit comprising the Salar de Uyuni and **Lagunas Colorada** and **Verde** in the reserve; four-day and longer trips are also available, if you find enough people who are interested. Note that wind-chill temperatures can drop to anything from -25°C to -40°C and that you should bring sun block and sunglasses to counter the very real possibility of snow blindness, as well as a good sleeping bag and plenty of warm clothing (your agency should be able to rent you a sleeping bag).

Bear in mind that issues such as late departures, inadequate accommodation and vehicle breakdowns are problems that may occur no matter which agency you choose, but it's definitely worth paying a little more to ensure good safety conditions and good food, and to minimise the chances of the jeep you're travelling in breaking down. The cheaper agencies tend to have older cars, bad (and often cold) food and dangerous (and often drunk) drivers. The best method of choosing an agency is to talk to travellers just returned from a tour and to request a written contract detailing exactly what you are paying for; however, the following agencies have been repeatedly recommended by travellers (though may of course also be subject to changes and problems): **Cordillera Tours** Av Ferroviaria; **Monte Blanco Tours** Av Ferroviaria ⓣ02/693-3259 and **Oasis Tours** Av Arce ⓣ02/693-2308 (Oasis also offer three-day tours with a slightly different, and therefore less crowded, route)

Despite all the hassles and potential pitfalls, however, these tours are well worth the trouble.

CROSSING INTO ARGENTINA AT VILLAZÓN

The main border crossing between Bolivia and Argentina is at the dusty ramshackle frontier town of Villazón, about 92km south of Tupiza by road or rail. There's no reason to stay overnight, so you're better crossing into Argentina, which couldn't be easier. Just walk south from the plaza down to the frontier along Avenida Internacional and get an exit stamp at the Bolivian *migración* office (daily 6am–8pm), then walk across the bridge into Argentina, where immigration is open 24 hours a day. From the Argentine border town of La Quiaca there are regular buses to the city of Jujuy, from where there are connections to the rest of the country. Accommodation and food in La Quiaca are much better than in Villazón, but cost a bit more.

James flamingo, the elusive **Andean fox** and herds of **graceful vicuñas.**

TUPIZA AND AROUND

Some 200km southeast of Uyuni, the isolated mining town of **Tupiza** nestles in a narrow, fertile valley that cuts through the harsh desert landscape with it's cactus-strewn badlands, deep canyons and strangely shaped rock formations and pinnacles. The town draws visitors largely because of it's **dramatic surrounding desert landscape**, ideal for hiking, horse riding or just touring by jeep. All these activities are easily arranged in this friendly town, which features a fledgling but well-organized tourist industry.

In the late nineteenth and early twentieth centuries, Tupiza was the home of one of Bolivia's biggest mining barons, Carlos Aramayo. His mines were rich enough to attract the attention of the infamous North American gunslingers **Butch Cassidy and the Sundance Kid**, who are believed to have died in a shoot-out in the town of **San Vicente**, some 100km to the northwest.

Arrival and information

Bus The bus terminal is on Avenida Arraya, three blocks south and two blocks east of the main square, Plaza Independencia.

Train The train station is three blocks east of the main plaza on Plazuela Adolfo Torres del Carpio, just off Avenida Serrudo.

Tourist info There's no formal tourist office in the town, but the main tour operators will be able to tell you all you need to know. The Instituto Geográfico on the Plaza Independencia (next to the church) can give advice and sell maps both for trekking and of the town.

Internet There's slow internet access on the main plaza (corner of Avaroa). The post office and the ENTEL office are just west of Plaza Independencia on Plazuela Gualberto Villaroel.

Money Be warned that there are no ATMs in town, and the only way of accessing money is through cash advances on Visa or MasterCard credit cards. The two banks in town, Prodem (open Mon–Fri 8.30am–12.30pm & 2.30–6pm, Sat 9am–noon) and Banco de Crédito (9.30am–12.30pm, 2–5pm) both on the main plaza, offer cash advances on credit cards (Prodem charge a 5 percent fee; Banco Crédito charge a much more reasonable flat fee of $5.60). Several *cambios* east of the plaza on Calle Avaroa will change traveller's cheques, as well as US dollars, Argentine pesos and sometimes Peruvian soles.

Accommodation

There's only a small range of accommodation in Tupiza, all of it inexpensive and relatively simple, and aimed specifically at backpackers on limited budgets.

Hostal Valle Hermoso Av Pedro Arraya 478 ⓣ02/694-237. ⓔhostalvh@hotmail.com. dorm bed). A welcoming and helpful establishment with a cosy rooftop terrace and comfortable common room. The recently refurbished, clean and sunny dorms ($4.9o per person) and private rooms (with or without bath) are set around a small patio shaded by a giant fig tree. $11.40

Hotel Mitru Av Chicas 187 ⓣ02/694-3001; ⓔmitru@hotmail.com. A particularly pleasant place to stay is this popular hotel, mainly because of it's

ORGANIZED TOURS FROM TUPIZA

Tupiza's three tour agencies all offer broadly similar guided excursions into the desert landscapes around the town in 4WDs or on horseback, as well as longer but not terribly rewarding trips to **San Vicente,** where **Butch Cassidy and the Sundance Kid** are thought to have died. The agencies can also organize trips to the Reserva de Fauna Andina Eduardo Avaroa and the Salar de Uyuni, a four-day circuit that should cost about $100 per person in a jeep with at least four passengers. Tupiza's agencies are:

El Gran de Oro Tours Av Pedro Arroya 492 ⓣ02/694-4763, ⓔelgrandeorotours @hotmail.com.

La Torre Tours *Hotel La Torre* ⓣ02/694-2633, ⓔlatorrehotel@hotmail.com.

Tupiza Tours Av Chichas 187, inside the *Hotel Mitru* ⓣ02/694-3003, ⓦwww .tupizatours.com **Valle Hermoso Tours** Av Pedro Arraya 478, inside the *Hostal Valle Hermoso* ⓣ02/694-2370, ⓦwww.bolivia.freehosting.net.

sunny central courtyard complete with swimming pool - a perfect way to spend an afternoon. Rooms are clean, there's a games room and breakfast is included. $11.40

Hotel La Torre Av Chichas 200 ⓣ02/694-2633, ⓔlatorrehotel@yahoo.es. A friendly, family-run place with good rooms (with or without private bath and cable TV), a small sunny roof terrace and a communal lounge with cable TV. Dorm beds come in at $5.60, and a good continental breakfast is included. $12.60

Residencial El Rancho Av Pedro Arraya 86 ⓣ02/694-3116. The most decent of the real cheapies, with basic but clean and spacious rooms (with or without bath) set around a green patio; rooms upstairs are far nicer and lighter. There's also use of a simple kitchen. $5.60

Eating and drinking

There's only a small choice of places to eat and drink in Tupiza. As usual, the cheapest place for food is the market, on the first floor of the corner of calles Chichas and Florida. Local specialities include *asado de cordero* (roast lamb), usually served on weekends, and *tamales* stuffed with dehydrated llama meat – the best are to be found outside the Mercado Negro on Avenida Chichas. Nightlife is rather limited in Tupiza; if you fancy a drink, though, you can always try your luck at the town's two karaoke bars, the **Diver Centre** and **D&B Karaoke** (both on the corner of Florida and Santa Cruz).

Bella Napoli C Florida. There are numerous, similar pizza restaurants on Florida serving breakfasts, pizza and pasta dishes to gringos at gringo prices, but this is the best of the bunch, with tasty thin-crust pizzas served in an inviting atmosphere.

California Plaza Independencia. A local favourite, with cheap, filling fare, serving breakfasts, hamburgers, pizzas and a particularly appetising lasagne.

Los Helechos Avaroa. A bit more expensive but a good bet for reliable local dishes, served up in huge portions.

Moving on

By bus Buses depart from the terminal on Avenida Arraya. Cochabamba (daily at 6pm); La Paz (2 daily; 16hr); Potosí (2 daily; 8hr); Tarija (several departures between 7pm–8pm; 8hr); Uyuni (1 daily; 6hr); Villazon (4.30am, 10.30am and at hourly intervals in the afternoon; 3hr).

By train Expreso del Sur trains leave for Villazón at 4.10am Wednesday and Saturday mornings; services to Atocha, Uyuni and Oruro leave at 6.25pm on Wednesday and Saturday evenings. Wara Wara del Sur trains leave for Villazón at 9.05am on Monday and Thursday mornings, and to Atocha, Uyuni and Oruro at 7.05pm on Monday and Thursday evenings. Be sure to buy your ticket in advance.

TARIJA

In the far south of the country, the isolated city of **TARIJA** is in many ways a world apart from the rest of Bolivia. Set in a broad, fertile valley at an altitude of 1924m, Tarija is famous for it's **wine** production, and the valley's rich soils and fecund climate historically attracted large numbers of Andalucian farmers. The surrounding countryside is beautiful, particularly in the spring

(Jan–April), when the vineyards come to fruit and the whole valley blooms.

What to see and do

Though it doesn't boast much in the way of formal tourist attractions, it's a great place to hang out for a few days and relax, with a couple of petite, lazy plazas for sunny afternoons, and at least one worthwhile museum.

Plazas Luis de Fuentes and Sucre

The centre of town is the tranquil, palm-lined **Plaza Luis de Fuentes**, named after the city's founder, whose statue stands in the middle. It's a pleasant place to sit and pass an hour in the sun and watch the world go by. The small, charming **Plaza Sucre**, two blocks southeast of the main plaza, is a great place to while away an afternoon sitting in one of the many cafés and enjoying the city's laid-back and gregarious Mediterranean flavour. The plaza is also the centre of most of Tarija's nightlife.

Museo Paleontológico

A block south of the plaza on the corner of Virginio Lema and Trigo, the outstanding **Museo Paleontológico** (Mon–Fri 8am–noon & 3–6pm, Sat 9am–noon & 3–6pm; free) offers a fantastic collection of fossils from the Tarija Valley, most of which are of mammals from the Pleistocene era, between a million and 250,000 years ago, many of them from species similar to ones that still exist today, such as horses, bears and llamas.

Casa Dorada

Also worth visiting is the **Casa Dorada** (Mon–Fri 8.30am–noon & 2.30–6pm; $0.50), also known as Casa de la Cultura, on the corner of Ingavi and Trigo. Built in the nineteenth century in the Art Nouveau style by a wealthy merchant, the house has been restored and declared a national monument. You can wander through it's rooms with photo displays depicting the history of Tarija, or check out one of the many cultural events hosted here, including concerts and dance performances.

Arrival and information

By air The airport (☎04/664-3135) is on the outskirts of town a few kilometres further east along Avenida Las Américas. A taxi into the town centre from here should cost about $1, and there are also frequent *micros* from the Avenida into the centre ($0.50).

By bus The bus terminal is ten blocks or so southeast of the city centre on Avenida Las Américas; it's about twenty minutes into the city centre on foot from here, or a short taxi ride ($0.50). Alternatively, catch one of the frequent *micros* that run along Avenida Las Américas from the stop opposite the terminal. Note that after midnight until about 7am, all taxis charge a minimum of $0.90.

Tourist Info There are two tourist information offices in Tarija; the Oficina Departamental de Turismo (Mon–Fri 8am–noon & 2.30–6.30pm; ☎04/663-1000) on the Plaza Luis de Fuentes tends to be rather unfriendly and not very helpful; the Oficina Municipal de Turismo (Mon–Fri 8am–noon & 2.30–6.30pm, Sat 8am–noon; ☎04/663-3581) on the corner of Bolívar and Sucre is a much better bet; friendly staff offer a wealth of information, maps and leaftlets.

Accommodation

Tarija has a good range of accommodation, almost all in the very centre of town – the exceptions are around the bus terminal, though there's no point staying down there unless you're just passing the night before continuing your journey.

Hostal Bolívar Bolívar 256 ☎04/664-2741. Quiet, clean option set around a pretty courtyard, with reasonable rooms (all have private bath, but those with cable TV are newer and much nicer) and a communal living room. Breakfast included. $16.80

Hostal Miraflores Sucre 920 ☎04/664-3355 or 04/664-4976. Converted colonial house with a sunny central courtyard, helpful and efficient staff, and a choice between comfortable (and signifcantly more expensive) rooms with cable TV, private bath and breakfast, or small, spartan and much cheaper rooms without. $8.40

Hostal Segovia Angel Calabi, right by the bus terminal ☎04/663-2965. Friendly hostel with clean rooms, with or without bath and all with

cable TV, conveniently located right by the bus terminal $14.
Hosteria España Alejandro Corrado 546 ⓣ04/664-1790, ⓔguimediaz@yahoo.com.ar. A relaxed place popular with backpackers on a budget. It's very simple and the bathrooms could do with a clean, but there's an amiable atmosphere and the use of a kitchen. Rooms with private bath also come with cable TV. $9.80
Residencial El Rosario Ingavi 777 ⓣ04/664-3942. Friendly, sparkling clean and quiet hostel with small but decent rooms with comfortable beds, set around a courtyard. The showers are reliably hot. $9.80

Eating and drinking

Nowhere is Tarija's strong Argentine influence more evident than in it's restaurants. Good-quality grilled beef features strongly, ideally accompanied by a glass of local wine, while *Tarijeños* are also justly proud of their distinctive traditional cuisine featuring chicken and meat dishes cooked in delicious spicy sauces – try *ranga-ranga*, *saice* or *chancao de pollo*.
El Amigo Lema with Ballivián. Busy restaurant with generous portions of meat dishes and delicious salads for $2.50. Open evenings only, with folkloric shows every Fri ($2 entrance).
La Candelera Plaza Sucre. Serves good *almuerzos* for $1.80. Food is only served at lunch but it's a pleasant place to have a drink in the evening.
Chingo's Plaza Sucre. Local favourite, serving very tasty steaks served with a heap of chips and salad. They also do takeaways (ⓣ02/663-2222).
Mateos Trigo and Madrid. Superior restaurant with indoor and outdoor seating and a refined ambience, serving a superb four-course *almuerzo* ($3.50), as well as á la carte meat, fish and pasta dishes and a very good salad bar.
Taverna Gattopardo Plaza Luis de Fuentes. It may have gringo prices, but it's worth treating yourself for the delicious food (try the steak) - and great service - served in a lovely, atmospheric restaurant with seating outside on the plaza.
El Tropero Virginio Lema and Daniel Campos. Authentic Argentine steakhouse with outdoor seating serving excellent grilled beef and chicken as well as a filling *almuerzo* for $2.

Directory

Banks and exchange The Banco Nacional de Bolivia, opposite the *Hotel Gran Tarija* on Sucre, changes cash and traveller's cheques and has an ATM that takes Visa and MasterCard. There are several other ATMs in town, including one at the Banco de Santa Cruz on Trigo and Lema.
Cinema Virgina Lema 126 (corner of Plaza Sucre).
Immigration Ingavi 789 (on corner of Ballivián). Mon–Fri 8.30am–12.30pm & 2.30–6.30pm.
Internet access There are plenty of places to surf the web in the city centre; try Consultel on Plaza Sucre ($0.60 per hr).
Post office The Correo Central is on Lema, between Sucre and Trigo.
Radio taxis 4 de Julio ⓣ04/664-6555.
Telephone office The ENTEL office is on Lema and Daniel Campos.
Tour operators VTB Turismo Receptivo inside the *Hostal Carmen* at Ingavi 784 (ⓣ04/664-4341, and Viva Tours, on the corner of 15 de Abril and Delgadillo (ⓣ04/663-8325, ⓔvivatour@cosett.com.bo), both run one-day tours of the city and around the vineyards and bodegas of the Tarija Valley with experienced English-speaking guides. Sur

WINE IN THE TARIJA VALLEY

There are some worthwhile excursions close to Tarija in the warm and fertile Tarija valley, which is notable as Bolivia's prime **wine-producing region**. A visit to one of the nearby **bodegas** (wineries) to see how the wines are produced (and sample a few glasses at source) makes an excellent half-day excursion from the city. Generally, you can only visit the closest bodegas on an organized trip with a Tarija-based agency, but this can cost between $10–30pp depending on the size of the party (see directory on above). However you can independently visit the lovely **Casa Vieja** bodega, about 35km from Tarija. *Micros* marked "v" leave from the corner of Campero and Corrado every half-hour or so ($0.70) and will drop you off in the village of Concepción, from where it's a ten-minute walk from the plaza to the bodega – ask the driver or anyone in the village for directions. You can taste the wine, wander around the pretty vineyards and eat lunch in the restaurant.

Bike, Ingavi 601 (www.sur-bike.com), organises cycling tours and rents bikes and equipment.

Moving on

By Air There are regular flights to Cochabamba, La Paz and Santa Cruz, with tickets available from AeroSur, 15 de Abril 143, between Daniel Campos & Colón ☎ 04/663-0893; and TAM, Madrid and Trigo ☎ 04/664-2734.

By bus La Paz (1–2 daily between 7–8am; 24hr); Oruro (nightly; 20hr); Potosí (3–4 daily; 12hr); Tupiza (2 nightly; 10hr); Villazón (nightly, 10hr). There are also daily services to destinations in Argentina and Chile; the closest border crossing into Argentina is at Bermejo (10 daily; 7hr).

The central valleys

East of the Altiplano, the Andes march gradually down towards the eastern lowlands in a series of rugged mountain ranges, scarred with long, narrow valleys; blessed with rich alluvial soils, and midway in climate and altitude between the cold of the Altiplano and the tropical heat of the lowlands, these **CENTRAL VALLEYS** have historically been among the most fertile and habitable areas in Bolivia.

The administrative and political centre of Bolivia during Spanish rule, and still officially the capital of the republic, **Sucre** is a masterpiece of immaculately preserved colonial architecture, filled with elegant churches and mansions, and some of Bolivia's finest museums. The charms of **Cochabamba**, on the other hand, are more prosaic. Although lacking in conventional tourist attractions, it's a pleasant and interesting city nonetheless – and not only due to the lack of tourists. It is also the jumping-off point for an adventurous journey south into the **Parque Nacional Torotoro**, Bolivia's smallest national park, boasting labyrinthine limestone caves, deep canyons and waterfalls, dinosaur footprints and ancient ruins; and the Amazon basin.

East of Cochabamba, the main road to Santa Cruz passes through the **Chapare**, a beautiful region of rushing rivers and dense tropical forests, where the last foothills of the Andes plunge down into the Amazon basin. The area has become notorious in recent decades as the source of most of Bolivia's coca crop, and, with Evo Morales now refusing to co-operate with the USA's coca eradication programme, it seems that one of the great dramas of contemporary Bolivia has some way to run.

It's hardly an ideal area for travellers, then, but some areas remain safe to visit and provide a frontline insight into current events.

SUCRE AND AROUND

Set in a broad highland valley on the eastern edge of the Altiplano, **SUCRE**, declared a **UNESCO** World Heritage site in 1991, is widely considered the most sophisticated and beautiful city in Bolivia, with some of the finest Spanish colonial architecture in South America and a pleasant, spring-like climate all year round. Neon signs are banned, and a municipal regulation requires all buildings to be whitewashed once a year, maintaining the characteristic that earned Sucre another of it's many grandiose titles: "La Ciudad Blanca de Las Américas" – the White City of the Americas. It is also the administrative and market centre for a mountainous rural hinterland inhabited by the Quechua-speaking indigenous communities, particularly renowned for their beautiful weavings. These can be seen – and bought – in the city it'self or on a day-trip to **Tarabuco**, a rural town about 60km southeast of Sucre that hosts a colourful Sunday market.

Founded some time between 1538 and 1540 and initially named Chuquisaca, Sucre's official title subsequently changed to Villa de la Plata (City of Silver). After independence, it was made the capital of the new **Republic of Bolivia** and renamed **Sucre**, but the city's economic importance declined. When the seat of both congress and the presidency was moved to La Paz after the civil war between the two cities in 1899, the transfer merely confirmed long-established realities. Sucre remained the seat of the supreme court and was allowed to retain the title of official or constitutional capital, an honorary position it still holds today. This unusual state of affairs preserves Sucre's capital status and an exaggerated sense of it's own importance, while giving the feel of a provincial backwater basking in past glories.

What to see and do

Strict building codes mean most of Sucre's lavish, silver mine-funded churches and monasteries, extravagant palaces and administrative buildings have been preserved much as they were was a hundred years ago. A more unusual attraction, preserved from even further back in time, are the dinosaur foortprints of Cal Orko.

Plaza 25 de Mayo

The centre of Sucre is the spacious **Plaza 25 de Mayo**, shaded by tall palms and dotted with benches where people of all social classes pass the time of day. It's a great place to watch the world go by while having your shoes shined or enjoying a hot *salteña* (arguably Bolivia's best) and a cool glass of the orange juice sold from handcarts by ever-present street vendors.

Casa de la Libertad

On the northwest side of the square stands the simple but well-preserved colonial facade of the original seventeenth-century Jesuit University. Now known as the **Casa de La Libertad** (Mon–Sat 9.45–11.45am & 2.45–7.45pm, Sun 9.15–11.45am; guided tours in Spanish, English, French and German; $2.00), this was where the **Bolivian act of independence** was signed on August 6, 1825, and it now houses a small but very interesting museum dedicated to the birth of the republic. Inside, the original signed document proclaiming a sovereign and independent state is on display in the assembly room, as well as a gallery of portrait's of almost all Bolivia's presidents.

The Cathedral and Iglesia de San Miguel

Sucre's sixteenth-century Cathedral is also to be found on Plaza 25 de Mayo and opens on Sundays only; next door is the **Museo de la Catedral** (Mon–Fri 10am–noon & 3–5pm, Sat 10am–noon; $1.40), which has a wonderful collection of important religious relics.

Half a block northwest of Plaza 25 de Mayo along Calle Arenales, the modest whitewashed Baroque facade of the **Iglesia de San Miguel** (sporadic opening hours; best to visit during Sunday mass between 6.30 and 8pm), completed in 1621, conceals one of the most lavish church interiors in Sucre, with glorious carved Baroque altarpieces covered in gold leaf and an exquisite panelled *mudejár* ceiling of intricate interlocking geometric shapes.

Museo de Arte Indígena

Housed in an elegant colonial building on the corner of calles San Alberto and Potosí, the fascinating **Museo de Arte Indígena** (Mon–Fri 8.30am–noon & 2.30–6pm, Sat 9.30am–noon & 2.30–6pm; Ⓦwww.bolivianet.com/asur/museosp.htm; $2) is dedicated to the distinctive weavings of two local Quechua-speaking indigenous groups, the Jalq'a and the Tarabuqueños, and provides an excellent insight into a distinctly Andean artistic expression.

Museo Universitario Charcas

On the corner with Bolívar is the rambling but worthwhile **Museo Universitario Charcas** (Mon–Fri 8.30am–noon & 2.30–6pm, Sat 9am–noon & 3–6pm; $1.40), housed in a delightful seventeenth-century mansion. It is really four museums in one, combining the university's archeological, anthropological, colonial and modern art collections. Visits are by guided tour only, mostly in Spanish, and last at least an hour.

Convento-Museo La Recoleta

On the southeast side of Plaza Pedro de Anzures stands the **Convento-Museo La Recoleta** (Mon–Fri 9–11.30am & 2.30–4.30pm, Sat 3–5pm; $1.40), a tranquil Franciscan monastery that now houses an interesting little museum of colonial religious art and materials related to the missionary work of the Franciscan order in Bolivia. Visit's are by guided tour in Spanish only.

The footprints at Cal Orko

Five kilometres outside Sucre on the road to Cochabamba, the low mountain of **Cal Orko** is home to the world's largest collection of **dinosaur footprints**, discovered in 1994 by workers at a local cement works and limestone quarry. The site has been declared a national monument, and has become a major tourist attraction for it's five thousand or so prints from at least 150 different types of dinosaur that cover an area of around 30,000 square metres of near-vertical rock face; it requires a good guide and some imagination to appreciate the footprints, as they're not easy to spot at first sight. The tracks are seen from **Parque Cretacio** (Mon–Fri 10am–5pm, Sat & Sun 10am–3pm; $4.20; guides available at 10am, 12.30pm & 3pm). *Micros* 'A' and '3' take you to outside the site, however the easiest way to visit the park is to take the Dino Truck, a colourful painted pick-up which leaves Mon–Sat at 9.30am from outside the cathedral.

Arrival and information

Air The airport (☎04/645-4445) is about 8km northwest of the city; *Micros* I and F run from there into the centre of town along Avenida Siles (30min); alternatively, a taxi should cost about $3.

Bus All long-distance buses arrive and depart from the bus terminal, about 3km northwest of the town centre on Ostria Gutiérrez. From here it's a $0.50 taxi ride into the centre of town, or you can catch *Micro* A, which runs down to the Mercado Central, a block north of the main Plaza 25 de Mayo. Collective taxis arriving from Potosí will drop you off outside your hotel or anywhere else in the centre of town.

Tourist Info The main municipal tourist office (Mon–Fri 8am–noon & 2–6pm; ☎04/645-1083 or ☎04/642-7102) is on the first floor of the Casa de Cultura, a block southeast of Plaza 25 de Mayo on Calle Argentina; there's also an Oficina Universitaria de Turismo (Mon–Fri 9am–noon & 3–6pm) on Calle Estudiantes, just off the Plaza 25 de Mayo, run by enthusiastic student guides who sometimes volunteer to show you around for free, although a tip is always welcome.

Accommodation

Sucre has a pretty good range of accommodation, almost all of it conveniently located in the heart of the old city centre.

Alojamiento La Plata Ravelo 32 ☎04/645-2102. Popular budget option offering small and basic but clean rooms with shared bath around a radiant courtyard, as well as recently added (and more comfortable) rooms in the back. There's also a terrace, and the location - opposite the market - is noisy but very central. $7

Casa de Huéspedes Arce 233 ☎04/646-2087. A peaceful and friendly place to stay, with simple rooms as well as longer-stay apartments (all featuring kitchens, dining rooms and sofas) for $7 per person. Don't miss the sunlit terraces with views across the city. $9.80

Hostal Charcas Ravelo 62 ☎04/645-3972. Modern and very central establishment, with helpful, welcoming staff, abundant hot water and the obligatory sunny rooftop terrace. Rooms are scrupulously clean if rather cramped, however, and those with private bathrooms lack ventilation.

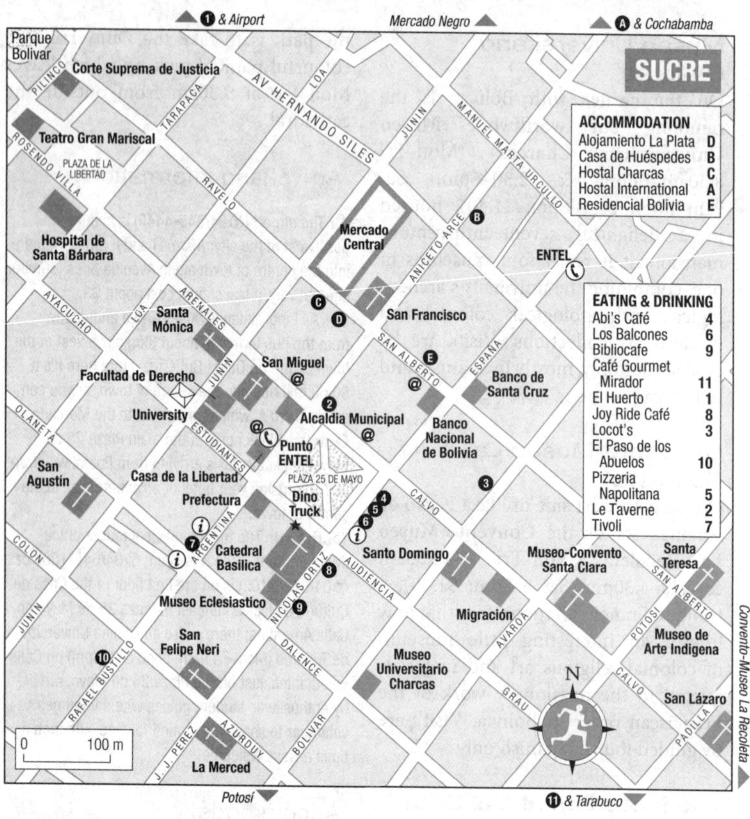

There's also a communal living room with cable TV, and breakfast is available (but not included). $11.20

Hostal International Guillermo Loayza 119 ⓣ04/644-0471, ⓔhisucre@yahoo.com. It may be a fifteen-minute walk to town, but the friendly backpackers, sociable feel and great facilities at this hostel make up for the distance. There's a good kitchen, huge garden and terrace, and the dorm rooms ($4.90 per person) are spacious and comfortable. Breakfast and internet are available but not included. $13.45

Residencial Bolivia San Alberto 42 ⓣ04/645-4346. Friendly and good-value *residencial*, with spacious, airy rooms (with or without bathroom) set around a bright courtyard with plenty of plants. A meagre breakfast is included. $11.20

Eating and drinking

Sucre is home to a good variety of restaurants where you can get everything from the spicy local cuisine to authentic French, Italian and vegetarian food at reasonable prices. The markets are great places to find cheap, filling lunches (usually about $1.50 for a two-course meal with a drink) - try the second floor of Mercado Central on Calle Zabelo and the food hall in Mercado Negro on Calle Junín. Make sure not to miss the amazing, huge fresh fruit salads in Mercado Central.

Abi's Café Plaza 25 de Mayo 32. A friendly cafe with scrumptious sandwiches, wraps and cakes.

Los Balcones Plaza 25 de Mayo. Upstairs overlooking the plaza, this smart restaurant is a lovely place to watch the world go by whilst enjoying steaks, sandwiches, as well as the huge salad bar.

Bibliocafé N. Ortíz 50. Bohemian bar-café attracting a good mix of locals and travellers from early evening until late at night with it's mellow live music and intimate atmosphere. Also serves snacks and light meals, and gets packed on weekends.

Café Gourmet Mirador Plaza de la Recoleta. A fantastic place to sit in the sun, admire the gorgeous views and feel like you're somewhere in the Mediterranean. The menu includes reasonably authentic crêpes, tapas and pasta dishes, and the hot chocolate is delicious.

El Huerto Ladislao Cabrera 86. Ask a local for the best restaurant in town, and chances are they'll direct you here. The menu features excellent meat, chicken and fish dishes cooked to both traditional Bolivian and sophisticated international recipes for about $4–5, served outdoors in a beautiful garden. It's some distance from the city centre, but well worth the taxi fare. Lunchtimes only.
Joy Ride Café N Ortíz 14. Trendy, Dutch-run bar-café and the most popular gringo spot in town for food and night-time drinking, serving tasty breakfasts, meals and snacks as well as excellent coffee, cocktails and cold beer; there's a small, charming patio upstairs. Opens at 7.30am on weekdays and 9am on weekends, until late; gets particularly busy on Friday and Saturday nights. Also the place to book one of the popular mountain biking or motorbike tours, through Joy Ride Bolivia agency on site.
Locot's Café C Bolívar 465. A very popular nightspot, famous for it's salsa, generous cocktails and mouthwatering Mexican food (also served during the day). There's an onsite agency too, which can arrange horse-riding, paragliding, and mountain and motor biking trips.
El Paso de los Abuelos Bustillos 216. The best *salteñas* in town.
Pizzeria Napolitana Plaza 25 de Mayo 30. Sucre's longest-established Italian restaurant, serving tasty pizza and pasta, home-made ice cream, strong coffee and a daily choice of six different set lunches for $2–3.
Le Taverne Arce 35. Authentic French restaurant serving classic dishes like *coq au vin, boeuf bourguignon* and rabbit for about $4, as well as excellent home-made pâté and delicious chocolate gateaux. They also put on popular French film nights ($0.70 entrance). Open evenings only, closed Sun.
Tivoli Corner of Argentina and Olaneta. Charming restaurant serving probably the best and most authentic pizza in town.

Directory

Banks and exchange Casa de Cambios Ambar, San Alberto 7, and El Arca, España 134, both change traveller's cheques and cash dollars at reasonable rates. There are also plenty of ATMs around town where you can withdraw cash on Visa or MasterCard, including those of the Banco de Santa Cruz and Banco Nacional de Bolivia, opposite each other at San Alberto with España.
Car rental Auto Cambio Chuquisaca, Av Jaime Mendoza 1106 ⓣ04/646-0984; Imbex, Serrano 165 ⓣ04/646-1222.
Cinema Cine Universal Plaza 25 de Mayo. Shows new releases. $1.40 per person.
Internet access There are internet cafés all over the city, most of which charge about $0.50 an hour: try Cyber-Station on the east side of the plaza or Café Internet Maya on Arenales 5.
Post office Correo Central, Junín with Ayacucho.
Telephone office The main ENTEL office is at España 271 with Camargo, and there are smaller Punto ENTEL offices on the northeast side of Plaza 25 de Mayo and on the corner of Ravelo with Junín, plus numerous card-operated phone booths on Plaza 25 de Mayo and at major intersections around the city.
Tour operators Candelaria Tours, Audiencia 1 ⓣ04/646-1661, ⓦwww.candelariatours.com; Joy Ride Bolivia inside the *Joy Ride Café* at Ortíz 14 ⓣ04/642-5544, ⓦwww.joyridebol.com; Locot's Aventura at *Locot's Café*, Bolívar 465 ⓣ04/691-5958; ⓦwww.locotsadventure.com and Sur Andes, Junin 855 ⓣ04/645-3212.

Moving on

By air Daily flights to La Paz and Santa Cruz. AeroSur, Arenales 31 ⓣ04/646-2141; TAM, Junín 744 ⓣ04/696-0944.
By bus Cochabamba (several daily; 12hr); La Paz (4 daily; 12hr); Oruro (2 daily; 10hr); Potosí (hourly; 3hr); Santa Cruz (5–6 daily; 15hr).
By taxi Collective taxis for Potosí cost $3.50 per person with 4 people (2hr 30min); drivers wait at the bus station until full.

TARABUCO

By far the most popular excursion from Sucre is to the small rural town of **Tarabuco**, set amid crumpled brown mountains about 60km southeast of the city. The town it'self is an unremarkable collection of red-tiled adobe houses and cobbled streets, but it's real claim to fame is the Sunday market. This is the focus for the indigenous communities of the surrounding mountains, the Tarabuqueños, who come to sell the beautiful weavings for which they're famous throughout Bolivia. The market is actually a bit of a tourist trap, but the stalls selling weavings and other handicrafts to tourists are still far outnumbered by those selling basic supplies such as dried foodstuffs,

TREAT YOURSELF

Hacienda Candelaria Owned and run by Candelaria Tours (see p.231), this seventeenth-century *hacienda* lies in the weaving village of Candelaria, amidst quiet countryside of apple orchards, lush forests and a mountainous backdrop. Visit's have to be booked with the agency, and tours range from full-day excursions from Sucre ($50–80 per person, including private transport, bilingual guide and meals) to overnight stays with activities ($80–120 per person, with basic accommodation), such as visit's to the peasants' houses and partaking in their daily activities of weaving, spinning wool, baking bread and cooking traditional foods.

agricultural tools, sandals made from tyres, big bundles of coca and pure alcohol in great steel drums.

Buses and trucks to Tarabuco from Sucre (2hr; $1) leave most mornings from Av de las Américas returning in the afternoon; however, it's much more convenient and only slightly more expensive to go in one of the **tourist buses** (they usually charge around $3 for the return trip) organized by hotels and tour agencies in Sucre. A taxi will cost about roughly $2 per person each way.

COCHABAMBA

Set at the geographical centre of Bolivia, midway between the Altiplano and the eastern lowlands, **COCHABAMBA** is one of the country's most vibrant and youthful cities and the commercial hub of the country's richest agricultural region, the Cochabamba Valley, known as the breadbasket of Bolivia. It's a friendly and unpretentious city, also known as the "City of Eternal Spring" for it's year-round sunny climate matched by the warmth and openness of it's population, and is perfect for relaxing in one of the many cafés and hideaways around Calle España.

What to see and do

Though Cochabamba isn't the place for colonial architecture, there are at least a couple of historic sights. Shopaholics will love the huge outdoor market of La Cancha, and for those with the time and inclination, there are also opportunities for exploring the understated attractions of the surrounding valleys.

Plaza 14 de Septiembre and around

The centre of Cochabamba is **Plaza 14 de Septiembre**, a placid and pleasant square with flower-filled ornamental gardens and plenty of benches where *Cochabambinos* sit under the shade of tall palm trees. A block south of the plaza on the corner of calles Aguirre and Jordán stands the extensive **Museo Archeológico** (Mon–Fri 8am–6pm; $2), which explains the evolution of pre-Hispanic culture in the Cochabamba region.

Convento de Santa Teresa

The lovely **Convento de Santa Teresa** (9am–noon, & 3–6pm, $2.80) on Ecuador and Baptista (the entrance is on Baptista, through the small café) is worth taking a look at; it consists of a beautiful building that, alongside the convent, houses a church built within a church (the original church was destroyed in the 1700s). The nuns still live on the site, though they are now housed in the complex next door.

La Cancha

The commercial heart of this market city is the south, with it's massive rambling street markets. An entire block between calles Tarata and Pulucayo is occupied by the massive covered street market known as **La Cancha** (Quechua for walled enclosure), where *campesinos* and merchants come to buy and sell their produce. Wandering through the market's sprawling labyrinth of stalls is the best way to get a feel for the vibrant commercial culture of the city and the surrounding region.

Palacio Portales

About 1km north of the city centre, with it's entrance off Avenida Posí, the **Palacio Portales** (visit's by guided tour only; Mon–Fri 3.30–6pm, Sat 10–11.30am, Sun 11–11.30am; $1.40) is the luxurious former house of the Cochabamba-born "King of Tin", Simón Patiño. Built between 1915 and 1922 in a bizarre mix of architectural styles, including French Neoclassical and mudéjar, the palace's interior is decorated with astonishing opulence. If anything, though, it's the lush, magnificent gardens (same hours; admission included with Palace entrance, or free if visiting the **gardens** only) that really impress, laid out in perfect proportion by Japanese specialists and featuring a beautiful and rare ginkgo tree.

Arrival and information

By air Cochabamba's extremely modern but underused Jorge Wilsterman airport is a few kilometres outside town; a taxi into the city centre should cost about $3; alternatively, take *micro* B, which goes up Avenida Ayacucho to Plaza 14 de Septiembre.

By bus The bus terminal is on Avenida Ayacucho just south of Avenida Aroma, from where many of the city's hotels are within easy walking distance; otherwise, a taxi to anywhere in the city centre should cost about $0.50 per person. Buses from the Chapare region east of Cochabamba arrive around the junction of Avenida Oquendo and Avenida 9 de Abril to the southeast of the city centre.

Tourist info The tourist office (Mon–Fri 8am–noon & 2.30–6.30pm, Sat 8.30am–noon; ⓣ04/451-0023; ⓦwww.cochabamba.gov.bo) is on Plaza 14 de Septiembre, and distributes free maps and leaflets on tours to the surrounding attractions.

Accommodation

Accommodation in Cochabamba reflects the nature of the city: though functional and reasonably priced, it's unexceptional and generally not aimed at tourists (the city sees few). The only time accommodation is difficult to find is in mid-August during the Fiesta de la Virgen de Urkupiña in nearby Quillacollo; it's best to book in advance during this period.

Hostal Colonial Junín N-0134 ⓣ04/422-1791. Friendly and good-value family-run place offering clean but simple rooms on two floors, overlooking a charming garden with lush tropical vegetation. All rooms have private bath and there's the option of paying $1.40 extra for cable TV. Breakfast is available but not included. $9.80

Hostal Elisa Lopéz S-0834 ⓣ04/425-4406, ⓔhelisa@supernet.com.bo. Helpful and friendly little place just a block away from the bus terminal. It's much nicer than it appears from outside, with small but clean rooms (with or without bath and cable TV) around a pleasant central garden with outdoor seating. Internet access and breakfast are available. $8.40.

Hostal Florida 25 de Mayo S-0583 ⓣ04/425-7911, ⓔfloridahostel@elatinmail.com. Justly popular backpackers' favourite halfway between the bus terminal and the city centre. The simple but clean rooms (with or without bath) are set around a sunny central courtyard, and non-inclusive breakfast is available. $9.80

Residencial Familiar Sucre 552 (between Lanza & San Martin) ⓣ04/422-7988. Set in a lovely building with rooms around a pretty courtyard, this hostel is spotless, with clean, decent rooms and plenty of character. The location is very central. $12

Eating and drinking

The best places to eat if you're on a tight budget are Cochabamba's many markets, and the choice of restaurants in the city is broad, with some very good meals available at relatively low prices. Boulevar Recolta, a modern pedestrianised strip on the right-hand turning from the roundabout before Avenida Pando, is a popular night-time place for a meal and a drink; there's an abundance of modern restaurants, bars and a few karaoke joints too.

Café Kausay 25 de Mayo with Ecuador. Sweet little cafe serving pancakes, waffles, breakfasts and aromatic coffee; you can also buy coffee from the Yungas here. Closed Sun.

La Cantonata Corner of España and Mayor Rocha. Smart Italian restaurant with great service and serving up filling pasta dishes.

Casablanca 25 de Mayo 344. Trendy Hollywood-themed bar serving cold beer, fruity cocktails and the usual fare of pizzas, pasta, breakfasts and sandwiches. There's a pile of magazines to browse through and the restaurant also hosts jazz gigs and art exhibit's. Closed Sun afternoon.

Espresso Cafe Bar Esteban Arce 340, on the corner of Plaza Principal. A bustling, characteful

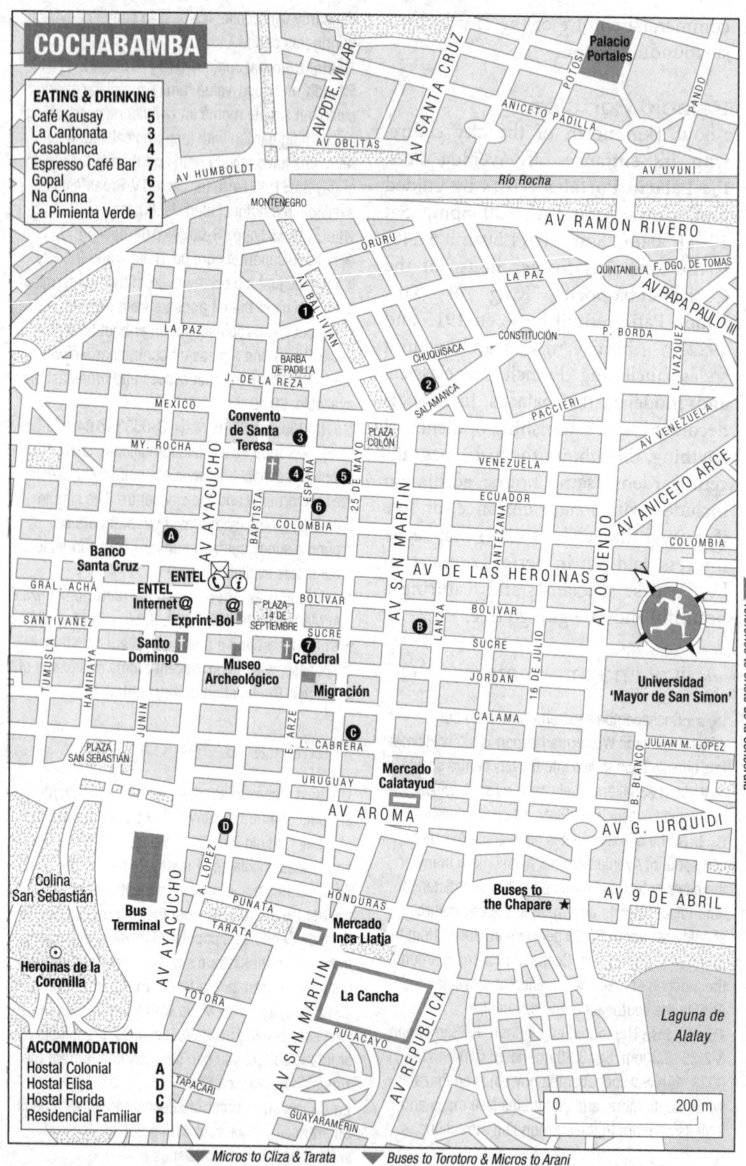

café, very popular with locals who come for the delicious coffee and variety of cakes. Closed Sun.

Na Cúnna Av Salamanca 580. If you're craving a taste of Guinness (no pints, though, sadly), this popular Irish café-bar is the place to come.

La Pimienta Verde Av Ballivían and La Paz. The wildest nightclub of the moment, popular with travellers for it's raucous atmosphere and loud music. Open Thurs–Sat only.

Directory

Banks and exchange Casa de Cambio Exprinter, on the west side of Plaza 14 de Septiembre, changes cash dollars and traveller's cheques, and there are street moneychangers at all the major intersections in the centre of town. There are also plenty of ATMs in the city centre where you can withdraw cash in dollars or bolivianos on Visa or MasterCard.

Internet access Internet cafés abound and most charge around $0.40 per hour. Some of the best with late-night hours are Black Cat, on Achá, just off the main square, Cliksmania, on España with Colombia and ENTEL on Av Ayacucho with Achá.

Outdoor equipment The Spitting Llama, España 615. A useful place which rents bikes and camping equipment and sells novels and guidebooks.

Post office Correo Central, Av Ayacucho with Av Heroínas. Mon–Fri 8am–9pm, Sun 8am–noon.

Tour operators Fremen, at Tumulsa N-0245 ⓣ04/425-9392, ⓦwww.andes-amazonia.com; Bolivia Cultura at Ecuador 342 ⓣ04/452-6028, ⓦwww.boliviacultura.com.

Moving on

By air There are daily flights to La Paz, Santa Cruz, Tarija and Trinidad. The Aerosur office is located at Av Villarroel # 105 ⓣ04/440-0912.

By bus Buses leave from the terminal on Avenida Ayacuco. La Paz (every 30min; 7hr); Oruro (every 30min; 4hr); Potosí (nightly at 8pm; 10hr); Santa Cruz (10 daily; 12hr); Sucre (several daily; 10hr); Trinidad (2 daily; 20hr).

PARQUE NACIONAL TOROTORO

Some 139km south of Cochabamba, the **PARQUE NACIONAL TOROTORO** covers just 165 square kilometres and is Bolivia's smallest national park; however, what it lacks in size it makes up for with it's powerful scenery and varied attractions – high valleys and deep canyons, ringed by low mountains whose twisted geological formations are strewn with fossils, dinosaur footprints and labyrinthine limestone cave complexes. The park's cactus and scrubby woodland supports considerable wildlife – including flocks of parakeets and the rare and beautiful red-fronted macaw. The main attractions are the limestone caves of **Umajallanta**, the beautiful, waterfall-filled **Torotoro Canyon**, and hiking expeditions to the pre-Inca ruined fortress of **Llama Chaqui**.

Torotoro's main annual celebration is the Fiesta de Tata Santiago. It is held on July 25 each year, when the *ayllus* descend on the town to drink, dance and stage Tinku fights, ritualized hand-to-hand combats. Buses (several weekly; 7hr) to Torotoro leave Cochabamba from the corner of Avenida 6 de Agosto and Avenida. Note that in the rainy season the journey takes much longer and the route can become impassable. On arrival you should head to the tourist office (daily 8am–noon & 2–5pm), on the main street of the village, where you'll need to pay the $2.50 park admission fee.

The office has basic information about the park and can find you a guide for about $7 a day for groups of up to five people (slightly more for larger groups). There's a couple of places to stay in the village, all very simple, and locals will prepare basic meals for around $1. It's also possible to visit Torotoro on a tour – which is significantly easier but obviously more expensive. Try Fremen Tours (see above).

THE CHAPARE

Northeast of Cochabamba, the main road to Santa Cruz drops down into the **CHAPARE**, a broad, rainforest-covered plain in the Upper Amazon Basin and an area of natural beauty. However, it's also Bolivia's largest provider of coca grown to make cocaine; while it's unclear how recent political developments will affect the conflict between coca farmers and Bolivian government troops on the ground, this is not the place for expeditions far off the beaten track. For all the region's troubles, however, it's worth a visit for it's natural beauty and the peaceful towns along the main Cochabamba to Santa Cruz road, which are perfectly safe to visit, unless you go during one of the sporadic road blockades by protesting *cocaleros*; these are usually announced in advance, so make sure to look through the local newspapers before your trip.

The small laid-back town of **Villa Tunari** is a good place to break a journey between Cochabamba and Santa Cruz and also to get a brief introduction to the Amazon lowlands. In Cochabamba, regular minibuses leave from the corner of Av Oquendo and Av 9 de Abril (5hr); alternatively you can take a bus heading to Santa Cruz and inform the driver you want to get off just after the Espíritu Santo Bridge. The best place to stay is *Hotel Villa Tunari*, with clean, decent rooms and hot showers ($6). The best restaurant in town is in the *Hotel Las Palmas*, on the main plaza; there are also a number of passable food stalls in the market. There's no ATM in Villa Tunari, so remember to bring cash.

A few kilometres south of Villa Tunari, some 6226 square kilometres of the forested northern slopes of the Andes are protected by the **Parque Nacional Carrasco** to the east. Plunging steeply down from high mountain peaks, the park encompasses a variety of ecosystems from high Andean grasslands and cloudforest to dense tropical rainforest and also supports a great range of wildlife, including all the major Amazonian mammals and over seven hundred species of bird.

The eastern lowlands

Stretching from the last foothills of the Andes east to Brazil and south to Paraguay and Argentina, Bolivia's **EASTERN LOWLANDS** were until recently amongst the least-known and least-developed regions in the country; however, the region has undergone astonishingly rapid development, while it's economy has grown to become the most important in the country, fuelled by oil and gas, cattle-ranching and massive agricultural development. At the centre of this economic boom is the regional capital of **Santa Cruz**, a young, lively city and the ideal base for exploring the many attractions of the surrounding area. Just an hour and a half's drive west of the city are the pristine rainforests protected by the **Parque Nacional Amboró**; the beautiful cloudforest that covers the upper regions of the park can be visited from the idyllic resort town of **Samaipata**. From Samaipata, you can also head further southwest to the town of **Vallegrande** and the nearby hamlet of **La Higuera**, where the iconic Argentine revolutionary, Ernesto "Che" Guevara, was killed in 1967. East of Santa Cruz, the railway to Brazil passes through the broad forested plains of **Chiquitos**, whose beautiful **Jesuit mission churches** bear witness to one of the most extraordinary episodes in Spanish colonial history, when a handful of priests established a semi-autonomous theocratic state in the midst of the wilderness. Finally, south of Santa Cruz, the vast and inhospitable **Chaco**, an arid wilderness of dense thorn and scrub, stretches south to Argentina and Paraguay.

SANTA CRUZ

Set among the steamy, tropical lowlands just beyond the last Andean foothills, **SANTA CRUZ** has emerged in recent decades as the economic powerhouse of Bolivia. An isolated frontier town until the middle of the twentieth century, the city has grown in the last fifty years to become the second biggest in the country, as well as the locus of Bolivia's wealthy right wing. The election of Evo Morales and his plans for constitutional reform have met with increasingly violent opposition here, culminating in the late 2008 expulsion of the US ambassador, whom Morales accused of fomenting political agitation, and a march on the city by Morales' Aymaran supporters. While you're unlikey to encounter any trouble, the situation remains unstable and it's worth keeping an eye on the media for new developments.

What to see and do

Largely because most of it is so new, Santa Cruz has little to match the colonial charm of highland cities like Sucre and Potosí, and few conventional

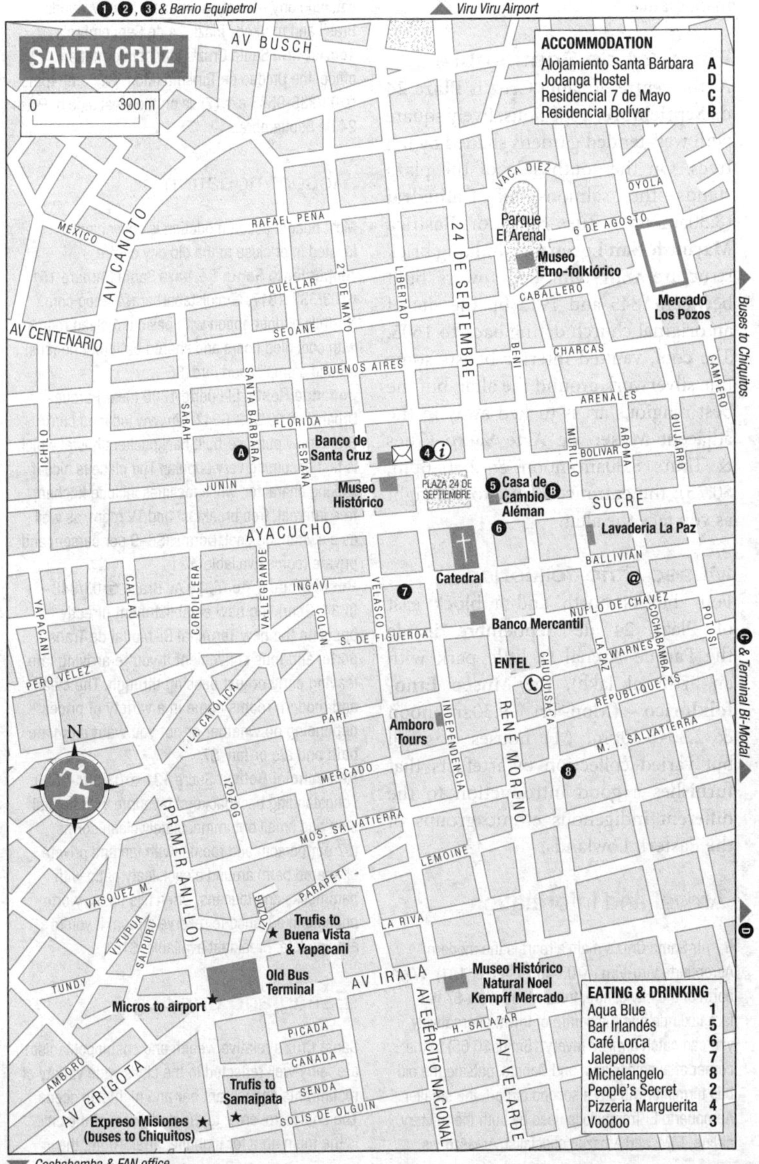

tourist sights beyond several mediocre museums and an architecturally unexciting cathedral. While some travellers find it's unapologetic modernity, commercialism and pseudo-Americanism unappealing, others enjoy it's blend of dynamism and tropical insouciance.

Plaza 24 de Septiembre

At the centre of Santa Cruz is **Plaza 24 de Septiembre**, a spacious, lively square with well-tended gardens shaded by tall trees. On the south side of the plaza stands the salmon-pink **Cathedral** (8.30am–6pm Tues–Sun), or **Basílica Mayor de San Lorenzo,** a hulking brick structure with twin bell towers built between 1845 and 1915 on the site of an original church dating back to 1605. The cool, vaulted interior boasts some fine silverwork around the altar, but the best religious art is tucked away in the adjacent **Museo de Arte Sacro** (Tues & Thurs 8.30am–noon & 2.30–6pm; $0.75); the entrance is just to the right as you face the altar.

Museo Etno-folklórico

Four blocks north and a block east of Plaza 24 de Septiembre inside the Parque Arenal (a little park with an artificial lake), the **Museo Etno-folklórico** (Mon–Fri 9.30am–noon & 2.30–5.30pm; $1) houses a small but varied collection of artefacts that furnishes a good introduction to the different indigenous ethnic groups of the Eastern Lowlands.

Arrival and information

By air Santa Cruz's main airport is the modern Aeropuerto Viru-Viru (T 03/385-2400 or 181), 17km north of the city centre, from where it's a $7 flat-fare taxi ride into the centre of town; alternatively, you can catch a *micro* (every 15min; $0.65) to the corner of avenidas Irala and Cañoto, outside the old bus terminal. The city's second airport, the smaller Aeropuerto El Trompillo is used by both the military airline, TAM, and Amazon specialist, Amaszonas.

By bus Long-distance buses and all trains arrive and depart from the recently completed Terminal Bi-Modal de Transporte, the combined bus and train terminal about 2km west of the city centre just outside the Segundo Anillo at the end of Avenida Brasil. There are always plenty of taxis outside (a trip to most city hotels will cost you about $1); otherwise, you can get into the city centre by catching any *micro* heading east along Avenida Brasil and marked "Plaza 24 de Septiembre".

Tourist Info Santa Cruz's tourist information office, the Unidad de Turismo (Mon–Fri 8am–4pm; T 03/336-9595 ext 17), is on the west side of Plaza 24 de Septiembre.

Accommodation

Most budget accommodation is conveniently located in or close to the old city centre.

Alojamiento Santa Bárbara Santa Bárbara 151 T 03/332-1817, E alojstabarbara@yahoo.com. No-frills budget option with basic but clean rooms with cool tiled floors and shared bath (but no fans) around a small courtyard. $6

Jodanga Hostel El Fuerte 1380 (near Parque Urbano) T 03/339-6542, W www.jodanga.com. Brand new purpose-built backpackers hostel which is fast becoming very popular. The place is nice if lacking character, while facilities include kitchen, free internet, free breakfast and TV room, as well as a swimming pool. Dorms ($8–9 per person) and private rooms available. $21

Residencial 7 de Mayo Av Brasil T 03/348-9634. Sparkling new establishment directly opposite the new Terminal Bi-Modal de Transporte, and thus convenient if you're arriving late, leaving early or just passing through. The clean and modern rooms come in a variety of prices depending on whether or not you want a private bath and a/c or fan. $7

Residencial Bolívar Sucre 131 T 03/334-2500. Longstanding backpackers' favourite with helpful staff and small but immaculately clean dorms ($7 per person) and rooms (with fan and private or shared bath) around a cool, leafy patio with hammocks and toucans. Often fills up, so worth phoning in advance to reserve a room if you're arriving late. Breakfast available. $15

Eating and drinking

Santa Cruz's relative wealth and cosmopolitanism are fairly well reflected in the city's wide variety of restaurants and vibrant bar and nightclub scene. The Equipetrol area, to the northwest of the city, is the main area for nightlife: after 10pm, the

TREAT YOURSELF

Michaelangelo
Chuquisaca 502. One of the finest restaurants in Bolivia offering superb, authentic Italian cuisine and immaculate service in an intimate atmosphere. It's not cheap, but an excellent place to splash out, especially if you've just hit town after a spell in the wilderness. Closed Sun.

streets are lined with revellers and cars blaring loud music. There are numerous bars and clubs; try *People's Secret*, *Aqua Blue* and, on Tuesdays nights, *Vodoo*.

Bar Irlandés Plaza 24 de Septiembre. On the firstfloor of the Bolívar shopping centre, with tables overlooking the plaza, this upmarket Irish-themed bar is a great place to enjoy a beer, cocktail or coffee while watching the world go by outside. Gets very lively with locals and travellers in the evenings, and especially on weekends.

Cafe Lorca Sucre 8. Popular cafe overlooking the plaza with fairly overpriced food; it's a good place for a drink in the evenings, however, and they hold regular art exhibitions events and live music.

La Casa del Camba Av Cristóbal de Mendoza 539. The best of the many traditional *Cruceño* restaurants on this stretch of the Segundo Anillo, and a great place to enjoy moderately priced *parillada* (barbecued meat), *majao de charque* (rice with beef jerky, fried egg and bananas) and *pacumutu* (massive shish kebab).

Jalepeños Ingavi 164. Good-value $1.80 buffet, popular with both meat-eaters and vegetarians.

Pizzeria Marguerita Plaza 24 de Septiembre. Cosy restaurant serving fantastic pizza.

Moving on

By air As well as several daily flights to Cochabamba, La Paz and Sucre, operated by Aerosur, Av Irala 616 (ⓣ03/336-4446), there are less frequent flights to further-flung lowland destinations serviced by Amaszonas (ⓣ03/357-8988) and TAM (ⓣ03/337-1999), both of whom operate out of Aeropuerto El Trompillo (see p.238).

By bus Buses depart from the Terminal Bi-Modal de Transporte. Cochabamba (2 daily; 12hr; connections to La Paz, Oruro & Uyuni); Potosí (2–3 daily; 18hr); Sucre (4–5 daily; 15hr); Trinidad (4–5 daily; 12hr). There are also daily departures to Argentinean destinations, including Buenos Aires.

Trains Trains to Quijarro, on the Brazilian border, leave at 5pm on Mondays, Wednesdays and Fridays, and at 7.30pm on Tuesdays, Thursdays and Saturday. There's also a daily service (Mon–Sat) at 1.15pm; be aware though that these are run by the cheaper – and less comfortable – Ferroviaria Oriental company. Trains can be chilly, so be sure to wrap up. From the station in Quijarro, it's a five-minute taxi ride to the border town of Corumbá ($2 per person).

Directory

Banks and exchange You can change US dollars and traveller's cheques at the Casa de Cambio Alemán (Mon–Fri 8.30am–noon & 2.30–6pm, Sat 8.30am–noon), on the east side of Plaza 24 de Septiembre, and there are plenty of banks with ATMs where you can make cash withdrawals on Visa or MasterCard – try Banco Santa Cruz on Junín or Banco Ganadero on Bolívar with Beni.

Internet access There are numerous internet cafés around the city centre, especially along Calle Murillo between Ballivián and Parque Arenal; most charge around $0.50 per hour. Try Light-Soft Internet on Junín 333, Web Boli on Ballivián 267, between La Paz and Cochabamba, or the small shop inside the Bolívar shopping complex on the main plaza.

Tour operators The following companies are all well established and have good reputations: Amboro Tours, Pari 161 ⓣ03/314-5858, ⓦwww.amborotours.com; Fremen, Beni 79; Edificio Libertador ⓣ03/333-8535, ⓦwww.andes-amazonia.com; Rosario Tours, Arenales 193 ⓣ03/336-9977, ⓔaventura@cotas.com.bo.

PARQUE NACIONAL AMBORÓ

Forty kilometres West of Santa Cruz, the **PARQUE NACIONAL AMBORÓ** covers some 4300 square kilometres of a great forest-covered spur of the Andes that juts out into the eastern plains. Amboró's steep, densely forested slopes support an astonishing biodiversity, including over 830 different types of bird and pretty much the full range of rainforest mammals, including jaguars, giant anteaters, tapirs and several species of monkey, while it's enormous range of plant and insect species is still largely unexplored.

The northern gateway to the park is the picturesque and peaceful town of **Buena Vista**, some 100km northwest of Santa Cruz along the main road to Cochabamba. There are two ways to visit the park from Buena Vista. The easiest is to go on an organized trip with one of the tour operators in town. For about $50 per person (two person minimum) they offer two-day excursions, camping overnight or staying in one of the refuges in the park ($5 per person extra), with all meals, a Spanish-speaking guide, camping equipment and transport included. They can also arrange longer trips and treks deeper into the park. Amboró Tours (Ⓣ03/932-2093, Ⓦwww.amborotours.com), opposite the church just off the plaza in Buena Vista, is the most professional outfit.

SAMAIPATA

Some 120km west of Santa Cruz, the tranquil little town of **SAMAIPATA** is enjoying growing popularity as a tourist destination amongst Bolivians and foreign travellers alike. Nestled in an idyllic valley surrounded by rugged, forest-covered mountains, it's the kind of place where many travellers arrive planning to stay a couple of days and end up staying a week or longer. Innumerable walking trails run through the surrounding countryside, the beautiful cloudforests of the Parque Nacional Amboró are within easy reach, and just 9km outside town stands one of Bolivia's most intriguing archeological sites – the mysterious, ruined pre-Hispanic ceremonial complex known as El Fuerte (see box opposite).

What to see and do

At the centre of town lies the small **Plaza Principal**, the core of the grid of tranquil streets lined with whitewashed houses under red-tiled roofs. A few blocks north on Bolívar, the small **Museo Archeológico** (Mon–Sun 9am–noon & 2–6pm; $4.50, including entrance to El Fuerte) offers a small collection of archeological finds from all over Bolivia, including beautiful Inca-carved, ceremonial *chicha*-drinking cups, Inca stone axes and mace heads and a range of pottery from various cultures.

Arrival and information

By micro Mircos leave Av Grigota in Santa Cruz for Samaipata daily at 4pm (3hr) and arrive in Samaipata in the Plaza Principal.

By taxi From Santa Cruz, shared taxis depart from the corner of Chávez Ortiz and Solis de Olguin ($3.50 per person, with four people in a taxi; 2hr 30min).

Tourist Info For information on Samaipata and the surrounding area, the best place to go is the helpful and enthusiastic English, German and Spanish-speaking Roadrunners (Ⓣ03/944-6294), next to *Cafe Latina* on Calle Bolívar. Ben Verhoef Tours (Campero 217 Ⓣ03/944-6365, Ⓦwww.benverhoeftours.com) is also a good source of information and can organise a variety of tours and actitivies, including the Ché Guevara route, Jesuit Missions tours, camping and 4WD tours.

Accommodation

There's a good range of budget accommodation in Samaipata, including a couple of tranquil out-of-town options. Note that it fills up (and prices go up) at weekends and public holidays, particularly between October and April.

Cabañas de Traudi Ⓣ03/944-6094, Ⓦwww.traudi.com. Austrian-run retreat set in picturesque grounds complete with a swimming pool and a volleyball court; the *cabañas* are fairly expensive but there are simple, cheaper rooms available. $8

Guesthouse La Víspera Ⓣ03/944-6082, Ⓦwww.lavispera.org. You can camp in this secluded hideaway, which features comfortable lodgings, idyllic location amidst orchards and terraced herb, vegetable and flower gardens, and friendly owners who will happily share their immense knowledge of the region with you, as well as organise tailor-made trips to other parts of Bolivia. $4–5 per person for camping

Hostal Andorina Calle Campero Ⓣ03/944-6333, Ⓦwww.andorinasamaipata.com. A tranquil, meditative lace to stay, with sunny patios and

EL FUERTE

Located 10km east of Samaipata, **El Fuerte** (daily 9am–5pm; $4.50) is a striking and enigmatic ancient site with a great sandstone rock at it's centre, carved with a fantastic variety of abstract and figurative designs and surrounded by the remains of more than fifty **Inca buildings**. The easiest way to reach El Fuerte is by taxi from Samaipata (about $5 one way, or $8 return with an hour's waiting time), or to join a guided tour with one of the tour agencies in town. While it's possible to walk to the ruins in about two to three hours – just follow the road out of town toward Santa Cruz for a few kilometres, then turn right up the marked side road that climbs to the site – it's a tiring and very hot walk, and it's more advisable to take a taxi to the site and just walk back, otherwise you'll probably end up too exhausted to fully appreciate the ruins.

hammock-strewn balconies, characterful rooms and dorms ($5 per person), and a homely TV room where films are shown every night. Free internet and a good breakfast is included and there's a library and book exchange. $16.80

Paola Hotel Main plaza ⓣ03/944-6093, ⓔpaolahotel_samaipata@hotmail.com. A good-value central hotel with clean rooms, hot showers, a kitchen and a large terrace with exhilarating views. Breakfast included. $7

Eating and drinking

Samaipata's status as a resort town and it's significant international community ensure a varied range of restaurants and cafés.

La Chakana Plaza Principal. A small European-run café with delicious food, including fresh salads and sticky cakes and cookies. There's also a book exchange and detailed tourist information.

La Oreja Negra Campero. A good bet for an evening drink, with fragrant coffee, vegetarian food and even a dart board. Closed Tues.

Tiaga Libre Just off the plaza on Sucre. This newly opened place boasts some wonderful local and international dishes - try the lasagne. Closed Wed.

La Vaca Loca Plaza Principal. Serves up luxurious icecream, to be devoured in it's balmy garden.

Directory

Internet Expensive internet access ($1.15 per hour) can also be found next to the *Vaca Loca* café (see above)

Money There are no banks or ATMs in Samaipata, but La Cooperativa La Merced on Calle Sucre, a block east of the plaza, will change dollars.

Telephone office The ENTEL office is on the main plaza.

Moving on

By bus Buses to Santa Cruz leave Samaipata's main plaza at 5am and 6.30am Mon–Fri, and noon and 4pm on Sundays. Buses to Sucre and Vallegrande pass by the highway, between 6.30pm and 7.30pm for Sucre, and 11.30am–12.30pm and 3.30pm–4.30pm for Vallegrande.

By taxi The easiest option of returning to Santa Cruz is to take one of the shared taxis leaving from the petrol station on the main highway (10min from the main plaza). Be aware that you may have difficulties finding one after 6pm.

VALLEGRANDE AND LA HIGUERA

West of Samaipata on the old road from Santa Cruz to Cochabamba, a side road leads to the market town of **VALLEGRANDE**. Vallegrande leapt briefly to the world's attention in 1967, when it witnessed the endgame of a doomed guerrilla campaign led by Cuban revolutionary hero, **Ernesto "Che" Guevara**. After Che was captured and executed on October 9 in the hamlet of **La Higuera**, his body was flown here and put on display in the town hospital; today, Che's grave and the hamlet of La Higuera, where his dreams of leading a continent-wide revolution ended, attract a steady trickle of pilgrims, but unless you share their veneration of the revolutionary icon, there's little reason to come here. There's a small **museum** (Mon–Fri 10am–noon, 3–5pm & 7–9pm, Sat

EAST FROM SANTA CRUZ TO THE BRAZILIAN BORDER

From Santa Cruz, the railway line runs some 680km east to the **Brazilian border** across a seemingly endless expanse of forest and tangled scrub, gradually giving way to the vast swamplands of the **Pantanal** as the border draws near. The last stop on the railway line in Bolivia is Quijarro, a dismal collection of shacks and dosshouses surrounding the station – if you're heading on to Brazil, you're better off pushing on to the border at Arroyo Concepción. If you end up having to spend the night here, the best budget option is the basic but clean *Residencial Ariane* ($6), directly opposite the station.

10am–noon; $0.80) in the municipal **Casa de Cultura** on the central Plaza 26 de Enero, which houses an unexciting collection of local archeological finds and photographs of Che.

The most comfortable place to stay is the friendly *Hostal Juanita* (☎03/942-2231; $8), the best restaurant is probably the German-run *El Mirador* (evenings only; closed Mon), which offers a daily selection of tasty beef, pork, chicken and trout dishes.

La Higuera, the hamlet where Che Guevara met his end, lies about 50km south of Vallegrande and can be reached by taxi or by lorry. It's a miserable collection of simple adobe houses with tiled roofs, and a one-room **Museo Histórico del Che** (Thurs & Sun; $1), with the atmosphere of a shrine, complete with relics including Che's machete, bullets and ammo clips.

Both Vallegrande and La Higuera can be visited on a tour; try agencies in Samaipata (p.240) or Santa Cruz (p.239).

CHIQUITOS: THE JESUIT MISSIONS

East of Santa Cruz stretches a vast, sparsely populated plain which gradually gives way to swamp as it approaches the border with Brazil. Named **CHIQUITOS** by the Spanish, this region was the scene of one of the most extraordinary episodes in Spanish colonial history. In the eighteenth century, a handful of Jesuit priests established a series of flourishing mission towns, where previously hostile indigenous Chiquitanos converted to Catholicism, adopting European agricultural techniques and building some of the most **magnificent colonial churches** in South America. This theocratic, socialist utopia ended in 1767, when the Spanish crown expelled the Jesuit's from the Americas. Six of the ten Jesuit mission churches have since been restored and are recognized as UNESCO World Heritage Sites. Their incongruous splendour in the midst of the wilderness is one of the most remarkable sights in Bolivia.

The six missions can be visited in a five to seven-day loop by road and rail from Santa Cruz. A rough road runs northeast to **San Javier** and **Concepción**, then continues to **San Ignacio** (from where the churches of **San Miguel**, **San Rafael** and **Santa Ana** can all be visited by taxi in a day). From San Ignacio, the road heads south to San José. Buses connect all these mission towns as far as San José, from where you can get the train back to Santa Cruz or continue east to the Brazilian border. Alternatively, many agenices organise tours to the missions; see the list of Santa Cruz's agencies on p.239.

THE CHACO

South of the Santa Cruz–Quijarro railway line, the tropical dry forest gradually gives way to **THE CHACO**, a vast and arid landscape that stretches beyond the **Paraguayan border**. The Chaco is one of the last great wildernesses of South America and supports plenty of wildlife, including jaguars, peccaries and deer – much of it now protected by the **Parque Nacional Kaa-Iya del Gran Chaco**, the largest protected area in all South America. The park covers over 34,000 square kilometres southeast of Santa Cruz adjacent to the Paraguayan border. There are no organized tourist facilities in the Chaco so, unless you have your own 4WD and are prepared to organize a wilderness adventure, your view of the region will be limited to what you can see from the window of a bus or train.

There are two routes through the Bolivian Chaco, both starting from Santa Cruz. The first and less taxing is the route by road or railway down the region's western edge to the towns of **Villamontes**, the biggest settlement in the Bolivian Chaco, and **Yacuiba** on the Argentine border. The second and more strenuous is along the rough **trans-Chaco road**, which split's off from the road and rail route to Yacuiba at Boyuibe, heading east to the Paraguayan border at **Hito Villazón**, from where it runs across the heart of this great wilderness to Asunción. This arduous and adventurous journey (served by daily buses from Santa Cruz) takes 24 hours in the May to September dry season, when conditions are good, and much longer after rain, when the road turns to mud.

The Amazon basin

About a third of Bolivia lies within the **AMAZON BASIN**, a vast, sparsely populated and largely untamed lowland region of swamp, savanna and tropical rainforest, which supports a bewildering diversity of plant and animal life. Roads are poor in the best of conditions and in the rainy season between November and April are often completely impassable; even in the dry season sudden downpours can quickly turn roads to quagmires.

Linked by road to Santa Cruz, the capital of the Beni is **Trinidad**, the starting point for slow boat journeys down the **Río Mamoré** to the Brazilian border or south into the **Chapare**. From Trinidad, a long and rough road heads east across the Llanos de Moxos, passing through the **Reserva del Biosfera del Beni** – an excellent place to get close to the wildlife of the savanna – before joining the main road down into the region from La Paz at Yucumo.

Just north of Yucumo, the small town of **Rurrenabaque**, on the banks of the Río Beni, is the obvious destination for anyone wanting a taste of the Amazon, given it's proximity to the pristine forests of the **Parque Nacional Madidi**, one of Bolivia's most stunning protected areas. From Rurrenabaque, the road continues north to the city of **Riberalta**, a centre for rubber and Brazil nut collection, and on to the Brazilian border and the remote, forest-covered department of **Pando**.

TRINIDAD

Close to the Río Mamoré, some 500km northwest of Santa Cruz, the city of **TRINIDAD** is the capital of the Beni and a modern commercial city dominated by a vigorous cattle-ranching culture and economy. Hot and humid, with few real attractions, Trinidad doesn't really merit a visit in it's own right. It is, however, the jumping-off point for adventurous trips to the rainforest and savanna that surround it.

What to see and do

Though most of it's buildings are modern, Trinidad maintains the classic layout of a Spanish colonial town, it's streets set out in a neat grid around a

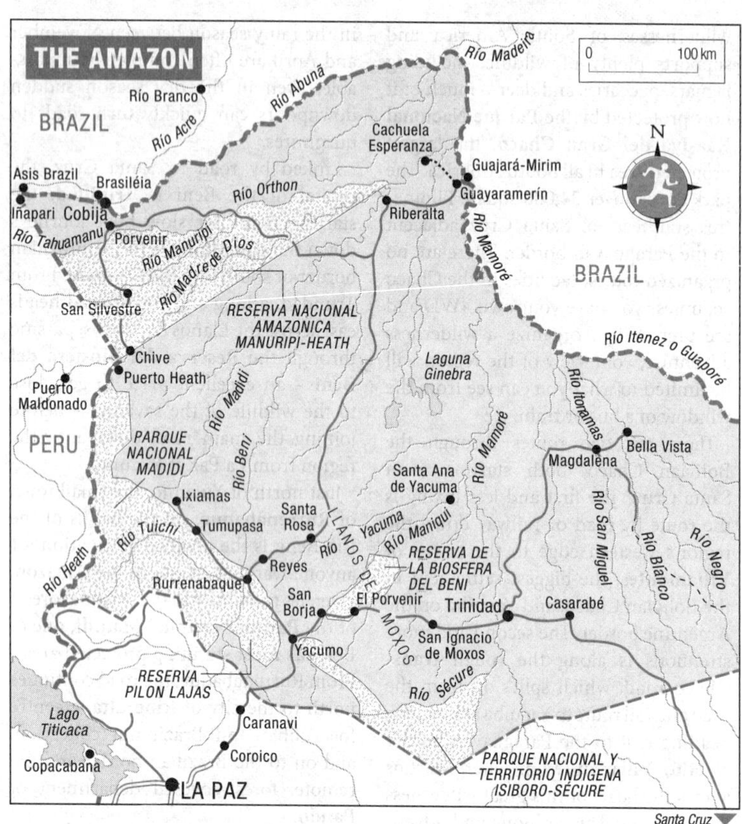

central square, the **Plaza Ballivián**. Shaded by tall trees hiding three-toed sloths and with well-maintained gardens, the plaza is the most popular hangout in town and Trinidad's only real redeeming feature. A popular place to go for the afternoon is **Puerto Varador**, about 13km out of town, where you can relax at a number of simple restaurants serving up fresh fish. Take a motortaxi to the Mercado Campesino on Av Oscar Paz Hurtado, where *micros* leave regularly for the port; it's about a half-hour journey.

Arrival and information

By air The airport is located to the northeast of town; a motorcycle taxi into the centre should cost around $1.50–2.

By boat If you are arriving by boat along the Río Mamoré from Guayaramerín to the north, or Puerto Villaroel in the Chapare to the south, you will dock at Puerto Varador, Trinidad's river port, about 13km west. Motortaxis ply the 30min route back into town.

By bus Buses from Santa Cruz, Guayaramerín and Rurrenabaque arrive at the Terminal Terrestre on Av Romulo Mendoza between calles Viador Pinto Saucedo and Beni. Buses from San Borja arrive just behind the terminal on Avenida Beni.

Tourist info There's a tourist information office (Mon–Fri 7.30am–noon) of sorts in the Prefectura building one block south from the main plaza, on the corner of Joaquín de Sierra and La Paz. The office is located behind a maze of corridors; ask anyone in the building the way and they'll probably take you there themselves. It's a simple place but they're willing to help and have maps of the town. There's also a very helpful tourist information kiosk on the corner of Busch and Cochabamaba, next to the river.

Money There are a number of ATMs in town; remember to get cash here if you're heading anywhere further into the Amazon (including ATM-less Rurrenabaque).

Accommodation

There are quite a few simple, good-value **places to stay** in Trinidad, most of them a short distance from the Plaza Ballivián.

Hostal Copacabana Villaviencio 627 ⓣ03/462-2811. Pretty basic and a bit further from the main plaza, but the upstairs rooms with private bath and balcony are spacious and pleasant, and all rooms come with cable TV. Rooms with air conditioning are also available, but cost quite a bit extra. $12.60

Hostal Palmas La Paz 365 ⓣ03/462-8601. The rooms downstairs are dark and rather dire, while those upstairs are airier and cooler. All come with fan, and there's a choice of shared or private bath with cable TV. $7

Residencial 18 de Noviembre Av 6 de Agosto with Santa Cruz, two blocks west of the plaza ⓣ03/462-1272. Basic, good-value place, with a pleasant, hammock-strewn garden and rooms with private or shared bath. $8.40

Eating

There are some pretty good restaurants on and around Plaza Ballivián. The beef in Trinidad is excellent and very good-value, while the local speciality is *pacumutu*, great chunks of meat and chicken marinated and grilled on a skewer.

La Casona Plaza Ballivián. Lively and popular place with great atmosphere and good *almuerzos* as well as steak, hamburgers and fried river fish.

Club Social 18 de Noviembre Plaza Ballivián. A vast, elegant dining hall with a rather old-fashioned feel, serving up good-value filling *almuerzos* and standard Bolivian dishes like *milanesa* and *pique macho*.

Don Pedrito Calle Manuel Maraza. Out of the centre, but worth a taxi ride for it's great variety of local river fish, served on a narrow patio underneath mango trees; try *pacu* or *surubí*.

Heladería Kivon Plaza Ballivián. Ice-cream parlour right on the plaza serving cakes, sandwiches and main dishes. The breakfasts are fairly disappointing, however.

Moving on

By air Between them, Amaszonas 18 de Noviembre 267 ⓣ03/462-2426 and TAM, corner of Bolívar & Santa Cruz ⓣ03/462-2363, cover most destinations.

By bus Santa Cruz (4–5 daily; 10hr). Services to Guayaramerín, San Borja and Rurrenabaque supposedly leave daily in the dry season; be aware that these services will usually arrive in their respective destinations hours after the predicted time, and may see you being squashed into a tiny minibus.

RESERVA DE LA BIOSFERA DEL BENI

Covering some 1350 square kilometres of savanna and rainforest to the east of the mission town of San Borja, the **RESERVA DE LA BIOSFERA DEL BENI** was one of the first protected

RAINFOREST TRIPS FROM TRINIDAD

A couple of tour operators run trips into the wilderness around Trinidad.

Turismo Moxos Avenida 6 de Agosto 114 ⓣ03/462-1141, ⓔturmoxos@sauce.ben.entelnet.bo. Organizes popular birdwatching excursions with the star attraction of spotting rare blue-bearded macaws. They also offer various one- to three-day trips into the rainforest by motorized canoe along the Río Ibare, a tributary of the Mamoré, with plenty of opportunity for seeing wildlife and visiting indigenous communities. Trips cost around $20 per person per day.

Fremen (no actual office in Trinidad but you can book by phone ⓣ03/462-2276, ⓦwww.andes-amazonia.com). Highly professional operator organising similar excursions, as well as four- to six-day cruises on the Mamoré aboard it's luxury floating hotel, the *Reina de Enín*, starting at $349 per person. They also offer more adventurous six-day camping trips into the enormous Parque Nacional y Territorio Indígena Isiboro-Sécure at $550 per person (for a group of 9); make sure you book in advance.

areas established in Bolivia. The reserve is exceptionally biodiverse, hosting some five hundred species of birds and one hundred species of mammals. Unusually for Bolivia, the reserve also has very well-organized facilities for visitors, based at the Beni Biological Station at El Porvenir, a former ranch about 100km west of San Ignacio on the road to San Borja. To reach the station take any bus or truck west from San Ignacio and ask the driver to let you off at El Porvenir. Admission to the reserve costs $5 per person and accommodation in basic but clean barrack-like rooms with shared bathrooms costs $13 per person, including three meals a day. Moving **on** from El Porvenir can be tricky: try flagging down one of the few passing vehicles; alternatively buses heading to Trindad usually pass by every morning.

RURRENABAQUE

Set on the banks of the Río Beni some 430km by road north of La Paz, the small town of **RURRENABAQUE** has recently emerged as the most popular eco-tourism destination in the Bolivian Amazon. Rurrenabaque, or "Rurre," is close to some of the best-preserved and most accessible wilderness areas in the region. These include the spectacular rainforests of the **Parque Nacional Madidi** and the **Reserva de Biosfera y Territorio Indígena Pilón Lajas**, as well as the wildlife-rich pampas along the **Río Yacuma**, all of which are easily visited with one of Rurrenabaque's numerous tour agencies.

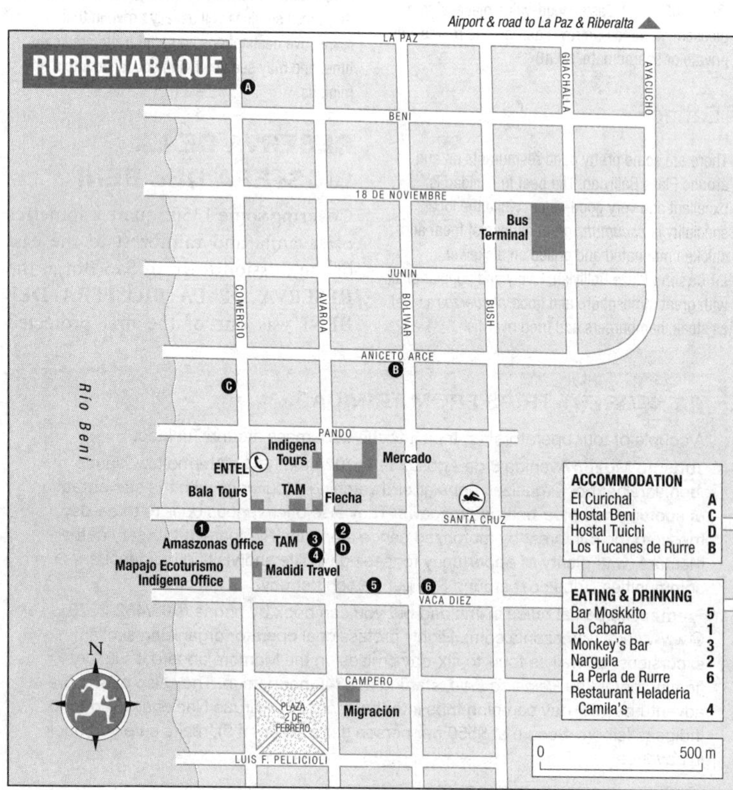

What to see and do

There's not much to see here, but it's a pleasant (if inevitably traveller-orientated) place to hang out: if you've an afternoon to spare in Rurrenabaque, head up to the **Butterfly Pool Mirador**, which boasts a lovely swimming pool with a beautiful view, a bar and restaurant, and a very friendly atmosphere. You can ask a motortaxi to take you ($0.70) and pay the $4.20 entrance fee; alternatively many of the agencies (see p.248) can organise trips, which can be easier and not necessarily more expensive.

Arrival and information

By air Due to often impassable roads, many people choose to fly to Rurrenabaque - the alternative is a nightmarish bus journey of at least 18hr (and sometimes a lot more). Both Amaszonas and TAM have daily flights to Rurrenabaque from La Paz; make sure you book ahead. Note that flights are frequently delayed or cancelled due to bad weather conditions, even in the dry season. All flights arrive at the gravel airstrip a short distance north of the town, and are met by free hotel minibuses for those with reservations, and airline shuttle buses for those without, which charge a small fee for transport to their offices in the centre of town.

By bus Buses arrive at the Terminal Terrestre, a few blocks away from the centre of town on the corner of calles Guachalla and 18 de Noviembre; you can get a motorbike taxi into the centre for about $0.50.

Money There are no ATMs in Rurrenabaque. Some tour agencies accept payment with traveller's cheques and credit cards, and there are a couple of places where you may change cheques or get advance cash on credit cards, though only for a large commission: try the Prodem bank on Comercio (9am–6pm) - they will do cash advances on Visa and MasterCard with a 5 percent fee.

Accommodation

For a small town, Rurrenabaque has an impressive number of places to stay rooms can still be difficult to find in high season (May–Aug) - book ahead.

El Curichal Comercio & Beni ⓣ03/892-2647, ⓔelcurichal@hotmail.com. Located further out of town, *El Curichal* is very quiet and has numerous hammocks in a pretty garden in which to relax and enjoy the silence. $8.40

Hostal Beni Comercio and Aniceto Arce ⓣ03/892-2408. Clean and modern rooms set around a peaceful patio with cool, tiled floors. Rooms with air-conditioning are available but they're double the price. $7

Hotel Tuichi Avaroa and Santa Cruz ⓣ03/892-2372 A popular Israeli haunt, Tuichi is a simple hostel that can get rather noisy but it is still agreeable nonetheless, with the obligatory hammocks hanging in it's garden, cheap rooms and a central location. $7

Los Tucanes de Rurre Corner of Ancieto Arce and Bolívar ⓣ03/892-2039, ⓔtucanesderurre@hotmail.com. A very popular and spacious hostel with hammocks hung around the grounds, a huge roof terrace, pool table, bar and free breakfast; the location, though (next to a karaoke bar) means it can get noisy. $9.80

Eating and drinking

A large number of restaurants have sprung up in Rurrenabaque to cater to the eco-tourism boom.

Bar Moskkito Vaca Diez. Another favourite drinking haunt with more pool tables, cocktails and the obligatory happy hour.

La Cabaña Bottom of Av Santa Cruz. Try this place for large meat and fish dishes and filling *almuerzos*, as well as great views of the river at sunset.

Monkey's Bar Avaroa (between Vaca Diez & Santa Cruz). A traveller's favourite that serves up tasty pizzas and strong cocktails; backpackers flock here in the evening for the 7–9pm happy hour, busy atmosphere and pool tables.

Narguila Corner of Santa Cruz and Avaroa. Boasts good Israeli food as well as local dishes (served in huge portions) and simply delicious juices and smoothies.

La Perla de Rurre Corner of Bolívar and Vaca Diez. This moderately priced place dishes up mouthwatering lowland river fish specialities, including the delicious *surubí a la plancha* in the house sauce, in a plant-filled patio shaded by tall mango trees.

Restaurant Heladería Camila's Av Santa Cruz with Avaroa. Popular for it's delicious ice cream, filling standard mainstays and good breakfasts.

Moving on

By air Between them, Amaszonas, Comercio between Santa Cruz and Vaca Diez (ⓣ03/892-

2472), and TAM, corner of Santa Cruz and Avaroa (☎03/892-2398) cover La Paz, Santa Cruz and most lowland destinations with regular departures.

By boat When the road is closed in the rainy season, motorized canoes occasionally carry passengers between Rurrenabaque and Guanay (6–8hr; $139–195 per boat carrying up to six people) and Riberalta (8–10 days; $42 per person), though you'll have to book in advance with one of the tour agencies.

By bus In the dry season, there are daily departures for La Paz (minimum of 18hr) and Trinidad (10–20hr), and, when possible, departures to Guayamerín and Riberalta.

THE NORTHERN AMAZON FRONTIER

From Rurrenabaque a dirt road continues north across a wide savanna-covered plain towards the remote backwater of the **NORTHERN AMAZON FRONTIER**, more than 500km away. As the road draws near to **Riberalta**, the largest city in the region, the savanna gives way to dense Amazonian rainforest. East of Riberalta, the road continues 100km to **Guayaramerín**, on the banks of the Río Mamoré, which is the main border crossing point if you're heading north into Brazil.

RIBERALTA

Set on a bluff above a great sweep of the Río Madre de Dios, sleepy, sun-baked **RIBERALTA** is the second biggest town in the Amazon lowlands, with a population of about 40,000, largely employed in the processing and export of Brazil nuts. At least twelve hours by road from Rurrenabaque when conditions are good in the dry season, there's no great reason to stop unless you're heading for Cobija (see p.249) and want to break your journey.

TOUR AGENCIES IN RURRENABAQUE

A growing number of tour agencies offer trips to the rainforest and the pampas, generally lasting three nights. Most guides only speak Spanish, but agencies can usually arrange an English-speaking interpreter for larger groups. Prices for all-inclusive trips are fixed by the local authorities at $30 per person per day for the selva, and $35 per person per day for the pampas, although agencies are still offering trips starting at $20–25 per day. Security is also an issue owing to several rape cases in recent years; avoid going on a trip alone or with freelance guides who don't hold an official licence issued by the municipal authorities.

Bala Tours Av Santa Cruz with Comercio ☎03/892-2527, ⓦwww.balatours.com. Specializes in longer five- to eight-day camping tours into Parque Nacional Madidi, as well as standard selva and pampas programmes. They're more expensive, but the jungle tours in particular are very highly recommended, and they own their own camps.

Indigena Tours Avaroa with Pando ☎03/892-2091, ⓦwww.indigenatour.com. Popular agency offering the usual three-and four-day pampas and jungle tours.

Flecha Avaroa with Santa Cruz ☎07/112-2080, ⓦwww.flechatour.lobopages.com. Popular, friendly agency offering three- to four-day tours of the pampas and rainforest, as well as longer trips into Parque Nacional Madidi.

Mapajo Ecoturismo Indígena Comercio with Vaca Diez ☎03/892-2317, ⓦwww.mapajo.com. Indigenous community-run agency specializing in five-, four- and three-night lodge-based trips into the Reserva de Biosfera y Territorio Indígena Pilón Lajas; the lodge is fully operated and owned by the Río Quiquibey communities.

Madidi Travel Comercio between Santa Cruz & Vaca Diez ☎03/892-2153, ⓦwww.madidi-travel.com. Extremely environmentally-conscious agency offering tailor-made tours. Profit's go towards conservation and community work.

Arrival and information

By air The airport is about 10min walk along Avenida Ochoa from the town centre.

By bus Buses arrive and depart from the offices of various transport companies in the centre of town around República de Brasil.

Accommodation

Hotel Lazo Calle Nicolas Salvatierra ☎03/852-2352 or ☎03/852-8326. Basic but clean place a couple of blocks from the plaza. $10

Residencial Los Reyes ☎03/852-8018. Pleasant hotel near the airport. $8

Eating and drinking

There are plenty of places to eat on the Plaza Principal.

Cabaña Tom Southeast corner of the plaza. *Tom's Cabin* does decent *almuerzos* as well as the two Beni stalwarts: beef steaks and river fish.

Club Social Nautico Parque Costanera, on the river-front. Good Bolivian food and cheap *almuerzos*; you can also cool off in the swimming pool for $1.50.

Moving on

By air Between them, Amaszonas, Chuquisaca with corner of Sucre (☎03/852-3933), and TAM cover La Paz, Santa Cruz and most lowland destinations with regular departures.

By bus There are 4–5 daily services to Guayaramerín (3hr) and, when possible, services to Rurrenabaque, Trinidad and Cobija, leaving from their respective company offices.

GUAYARAMERÍN

On the banks of the Río Mamoré some 86km east of Riberalta, **GUAYARAMERÍN** is the main crossing point on Bolivia's northern border, a modern and prosperous frontier town with a distinctly Brazilian flavour and a thriving economy based on duty-free sales. Most people only come here to cross the border.

Arrival and information

Air The airport is four blocks east of the plaza along Calle 25 de Mayo.

Bus Buses from Riberalta and beyond arrive at the Terminal de Buses, about 3km from the centre of town along Calle Beni; a motorbike taxi from here should cost about $0.50.

Tourist info The post office is on Calle Oruro, three blocks south of the plaza. The ENTEL office is on Calle Mamoré, two blocks north of the plaza.

Money The *Hotel San Carlos*, a block north and east from the Plaza on Avenida 6 de Agosto, changes traveller's cheques – the only place in town that does – and also changes dollars and Brazilian reais. There are no ATMs in town.

Accommodation and eating

The best places to eat are on and around the plaza; the two *heladerías* are good for ice cream, coffee, juices and snacks.

Hotel Santa Ana (☎03/855-3900) If you gert stuck before your border crossing, try this reasonable hotel with an inviting garden, located just east of the plaza on Avenida 25 de Mayo. $5.50

Moving on

By air Amaszonas, Avenida 25 de Mayo and corner of 16 de Julio (☎03/855-3731), and TAM, cover most destinations.

By bus Buses to Riberalta leave throughout the day (3hr); in the dry season, buses attempt the long journeys to Trinidad, Rurrenabaque, and Cobija - the success and length of the journey vary widely due to road conditions.

COBIJA AND THE PANDO

The northwesternmost tip of Bolivia is covered by the department of **THE PANDO**, a remote and sparsely populated rainforest region that until recently was accessible only by boat along the Madre de Dios, Tahuamanu and Orthon rivers, which flow into the region from Peru; today, a rough road cuts through the rainforest running from just south of Riberalta to **Cobija**.

With a population of just fifteen thousand, **COBIJA** is the smallest departmental capital in Bolivia, an isolated border town with a distinctly Brazilian flavour.

The town's busiest area is around the central plaza, close to the Río Acre, which forms the border with Brazil.

CROSSING INTO BRAZIL: GUAJARÉ-MIRIM

From the port at the bottom of Avenida Federico Roman, **regular passenger boats** (every 15min; $1; $1.65 to return) make the ten-minute crossing to Guajará-Mirim in Brazil. The Bolivian migración (Mon–Fri 8–11am & 2–6pm, Sat 8am–noon) is to the right of the port as you face the river; you should get an exit stamp here if you're continuing into Brazil but it's not necessary if you're just making a day-trip across the river. If you need a visa, the **Brazilian Consulate** (Mon–Fri 11am–3pm) is on the corner of Calles Beni and 24 de Septiembre, a block east of the plaza. Note that to enter Brazil, you need to have an international certificate of yellow fever vaccination. From Guajará-Mirim there are frequent buses to Porto Velho, from where there are connections to other destinations in Brazil.

The Bolivian **immigration office** is on the main border crossing, the international bridge over the Río Acre at the end of Avenida Internacional. Taxis from the town centre across the bridge to the federal police office (where you'll need to clear immigration) in the Brazilian town of **Brasiléia** charge a steep $10; otherwise it's a twenty-minute walk or you can take a cheaper motorbike taxi or a canoe. Be aware that you need an international **yellow-fever vaccination certificate** to enter Brazil here. If you need a visa go to the Brazilian Consulate (Mon–Fri 8.30am–1.30pm), just off the plaza on Calle Ayacucho. From Brasiléia, there are regular buses to **Río Branco**, from where you can get further onward connections.

Brazil

HIGHLIGHTS

THE AMAZON: take in lush jungle scenery and native settlements on the world's largest river

SALVADOR: watch Afro-Brazilian martial art at one of Salvador's capoeira schools

RIO DE JANEIRO: hang glide past Christ the Redeemer for a unique view of one of the world's most beautiful cities

MORRO DE SÃO PAULO: laze away days on this party beach sipping caipirinhas

IGUAÇU FALLS: straddling Argentina and Brazil, this is one of the planet's most impressive waterfalls

ROUGH COSTS

DAILY BUDGET Basic US$45/ occasional treat US$60

DRINK Skol beer (600ml bottle) R$3.40

FOOD *Pão de Queijo* R$2

HOSTEL/BUDGET HOTEL R$30/ R$100

TRAVEL From Rio to Saö Paulo by bus, $38.

FACT FILE

POPULATION 187 million

AREA 8,511,965 sq km

LANGUAGE Portuguese

CURRENCY Real (R$)

CAPITAL Brasília (population 2.3 million)

INTERNATIONAL PHONE CODE ⓣ55

Introduction

Brazil is special. You'll notice the energy soon after arriving. In typical "only in Brazil" fashion you may quickly find yourself playing foosball with the lead singer of Sepultura and dancing samba until sunrise. And yes, it's true: Brazilians are friendly, beautiful, football-crazed and they know how to party. It's a huge country (larger than the United States excluding Alaska) with all the diverse scenic and cultural variety you'd expect, from Bahian beaches to Amazonian jungles. But Brazil isn't all Club Med and Indiana Jones – it's cosmopolitan too. Rio and São Paulo are two of the world's great metropolises and eleven other cities each have over a million inhabitants.

Brazilians are one of the most **ethnically diverse** peoples in the world: in the extreme south, German and Italian immigration have left distinctive European features; São Paulo has the world's largest Japanese community outside Japan; there's a large black population concentrated in Rio and Salvador; and Indian influence is pervasive in Amazônia and the Northeastern interior.

Brazil is a land of **economic contradictions**. It has enormous natural resources, and rapid postwar industrialization made it one of the world's ten largest economies and put it among the most developed Third World nations. But this hasn't improved the lives of many of its citizens: there may be a growing middle class, but cities are still dotted with **favelas** and the contrast between rich and poor is glaring. Be prepared for requests for your leftovers.

Nowhere, however, do people know how to enjoy themselves more – most famously in the orgiastic annual four-day celebrations of **Carnaval**, but also reflected in the lively year-round nightlife you'll find almost everywhere. Brazil has the most relaxed and tolerant attitude to **sexuality**, straight and gay, of anywhere in South America. And the country's hedonism also manifests itself in a highly developed **beach culture**, superb music and dancing, and rich regional cuisines.

No, this isn't paradise, but it does feel like it sometimes.

CHRONOLOGY

At the time of first contact with Europeans there were thought to be between two and six million indigenous Indians in the region.

1500 Off course, en route to India on behalf of Portugal, Pedro Álvares Cabral lands in Bahia.

1502 Amerigo Vespucci enters Guanabara Bay and calls it Rio de Janeiro.

1533 King João III divides colony into 15 hereditary captaincies.

1549 King João unifies captaincies under governor-general Tomé de Sousa, who founds Salvador, the first capital. Portuguese settlers begin to flow in.

1555 French take possession of Rio and are finally expelled by Portuguese in 1567.

1574 Jesuits given control of converted Indians.

1624 Dutch seize and briefly hold Salvador.

1630 Dutch West India Company fleet captures Pernambuco.

1654 Brazilians, without Portuguese aid, defeat and expel the Dutch.

1695 *Bandeirantes* discover gold in Minas Gerais.

1759 Jesuits expelled by prime minister Marquis de Pombal, who grants legal rights to Indians and helps centralize Brazilian government.

1763 Capital shifted from Salvador to Rio.

1789 First rebellion against Portuguese ends in defeat when José Joaquim da Silva Xavier, known as *Tiradentes*, is executed.

1807 Napoleon I invades Portugal. Portuguese prince regent Dom João evacuates to Brazil.

1808 Dom João declares Rio temporary capital of the empire, opens harbours to commerce and abolishes restrictions on Brazilian trade and manufacturing.
1815 Brazil decreed coequal with Portugal.
1823 With Dom João (King João IV) in Portugal, his son, Dom Pedro, declares Brazil independent and crowns himself emperor.
1825 Portugal recognizes independent Brazil.
1854 Slave trade abolished, slavery continues.
1864–70 War of the Triple Alliance pits landlocked Paraguay against Argentina, Uruguay and Brazil.
1870s The beginning of subsidized Italian immigration for plantation labour.
1888 Princess Isabel, acting as regent, signs the "Golden Law" abolishing slavery.
1889 Dom Pedro II abdicates.
1894 Prudente de Morais elected first civilian president after years of unstable military rule.
1907 Brazil and Japan sign a treaty allowing Japanese immigration to Brazil.
1930 Great Depression leads to revolution. Getúlio Vargas rises to power.
1937 Vargas declares himself dictator, creates the "New State," the Estado Novo.
1944 Brazil accepts US aid in return for bases, joins Allies in WWII, and sends Expeditionary Force to fight in Italy.
1956 Juscelino Kubitschek elected president with an ambitious economic programme. Construction of Brasília begins.
1960 Brasília declared capital of Brazil.
1964 Massive population growth, disparity in wealth, economic inflation and fears of a rising proletariat leads to a military coup.
1968 The beginning of the "economic miracle." Brazil's GDP averages more than 11percent annually through 1973.
1969 General Emilio Garrastazú Médici assumes presidency. Censorship and torture are routine and thousands are driven into exile.
1983–84 Mass campaign in Rio and São Paulo for direct elections.
1985 Tancredo Neves wins electoral college vote – military rule ends.
1989 Fernando Collor de Mello is first popularly elected president in 29 years.
1994 Inflation peaks, Real introduced as new currency along with new economic plan.
2002 Liberal Luiz Inácio Lula da Silva elected on promises to curb hunger and create jobs.
2004 Corruption scandal engulfs Lula presidency.
2006 Lula re-elected; raises minimum wage by 13percent and announces new economic plan.
2007 Very large deep-water oil field discovered off southeastern Brazil.

Basics

ARRIVAL

There are direct **flights** to Rio and São Paulo from Europe, North America, Asia, Australia and New Zealand, as well as from most major cities elsewhere in South America. Brazil has a very well developed network of domestic flights, so you can easily connect straight through to your final destination. **Overland crossings** to Brazil are possible from every South American country except Chile, Ecuador and Suriname. The first two have no land borders with Brazil and Suriname, while adjacent, has no official crossing. Flights from Santiago, Quito and Paramaribo, however, depart for most major cities in Brazil. If you do decide to enter the country overland, remember that Brazil is a vast place – crossing points can be very remote from your final destination.

From Argentina

Most people crossing between Argentina and Brazil do so at the frontier at **Foz do Iguaçu** (see p.392). Another handy crossing further south is at the Argentine city of Paso de los Libres, across the border from **Uruguaiana**, 694km west of Porto Alegre. There are daily **flights** from Buenos Aires to Iguazu Falls and to Rio de Janeiro.

From Bolivia

You can reach Bolivia's southeastern border by train from the station a few kilometres out of Puerto Suárez or by hourly bus from Quijarro. From the border there's frequent transport to the *rodoviária* in **Corumbá**, where you'll find regular onward buses to Campo Grande (5–7hr), São Paulo (21hr) and Rio de Janeiro (26hr). In the north, passenger boats make the ten-minute

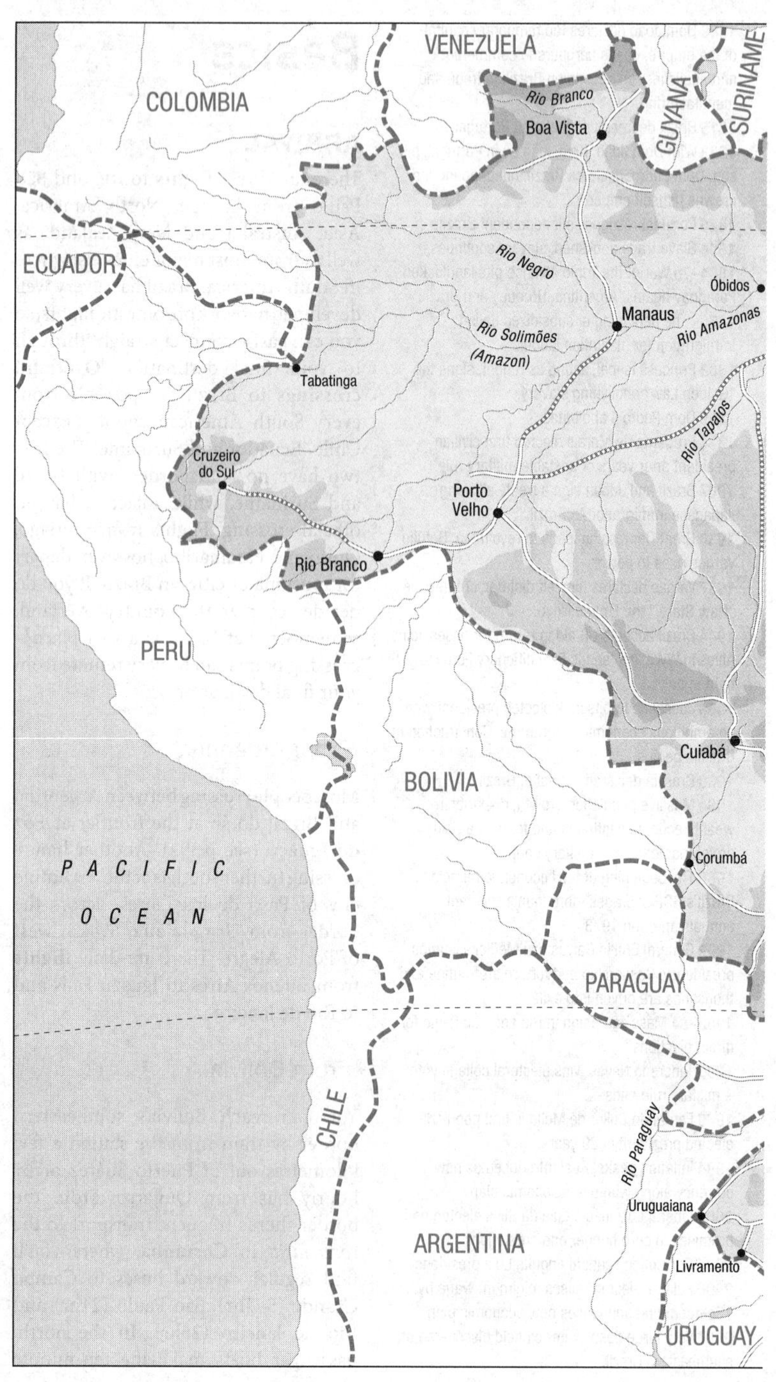
VENEZUELA
COLOMBIA
GUYANA
SURINAME
Rio Branco
Boa Vista
ECUADOR
Rio Negro
Óbidos
Manaus
Rio Amazonas
Rio Solimões
(Amazon)
Tabatinga
Rio Tapajós
Cruzeiro
do Sul
Porto
Velho
Rio Branco
PERU
Cuiabá
BOLIVIA
PACIFIC
OCEAN
Corumbá
PARAGUAY
CHILE
Rio Paraguay
Uruguaiana
ARGENTINA
Livramento
URUGUAY

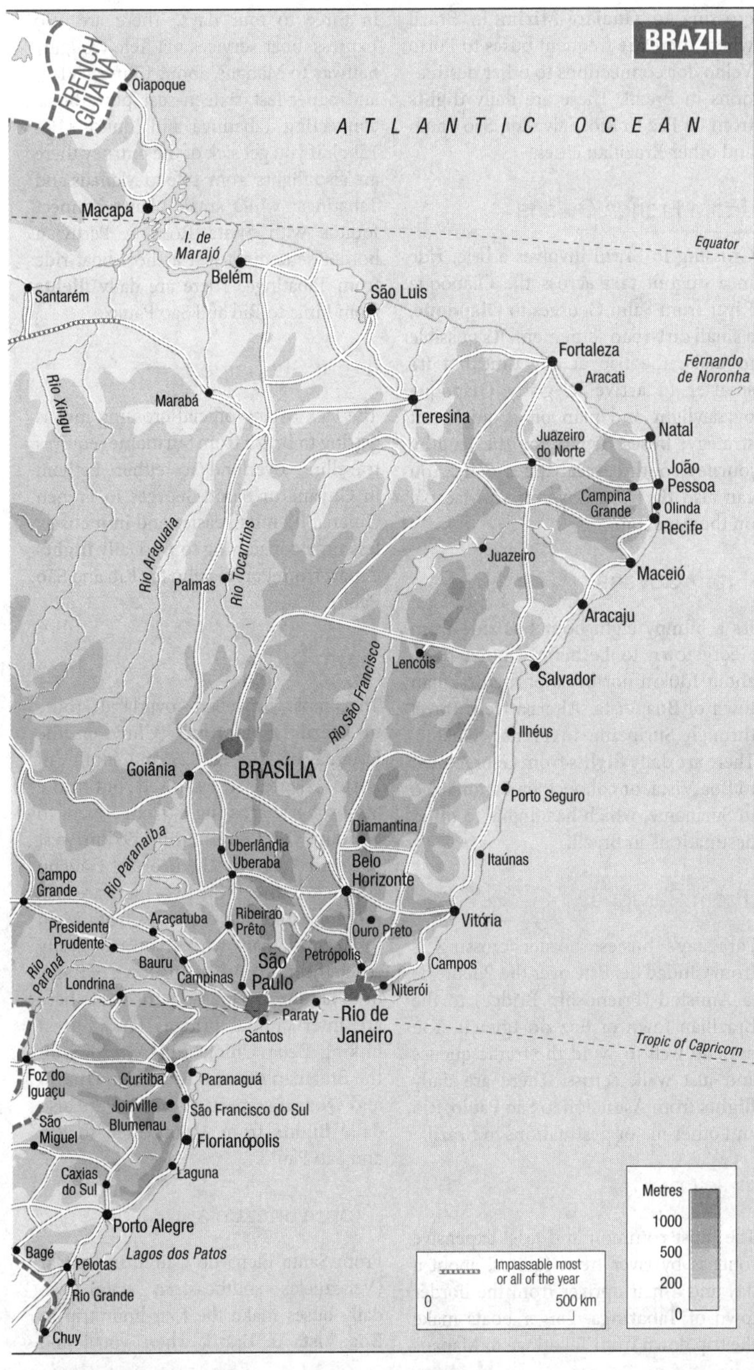
BRAZIL
ATLANTIC OCEAN
FRENCH GUIANA
Oiapoque
Macapá
I. de Marajó
Belém
Equator
Santarém
São Luis
Fortaleza
Aracati
Fernando de Noronha
Rio Xingu
Marabá
Teresina
Natal
Juazeiro do Norte
João Pessoa
Campina Grande
Olinda
Recife
Rio Araguaia
Rio Tocantins
Juazeiro
Maceió
Palmas
Aracaju
Rio São Francisco
Lençóis
Salvador
Ilhéus
Goiânia
BRASÍLIA
Porto Seguro
Rio Paranaiba
Diamantina
Uberlândia
Uberaba
Itaúnas
Campo Grande
Belo Horizonte
Presidente Prudente
Araçatuba
Ribeirao Prêto
Vitória
Ouro Preto
Rio Paraná
Bauru
Campinas
São Paulo
Petrópolis
Campos
Londrina
Niterói
Paraty
Rio de Janeiro
Santos
Tropic of Capricorn
Foz do Iguaçu
Curitiba
Paranaguá
Joinville
São Francisco do Sul
São Miguel
Blumenau
Florianópolis
Caxias do Sul
Laguna
Porto Alegre
Bagé
Lagos dos Patos
Pelotas
Rio Grande
Chuy
Impassable most or all of the year
0
500 km
Metres
1000
500
200
0

BRAZIL

BASICS

crossing to **Guajará-Mirim** in Brazil where there are frequent buses to Porto Velho, for connections to other destinations in Brazil. There are daily **flights** from La Paz to Rio, Salvador, São Paulo and other Brazilian cities.

From French Guiana

Crossing to Brazil involves a brief ride in a dugout taxi across the Oiapoque River from Saint Georges to **Oiapoque**, a small dirt-road settlement. It's possible to make the trip at any time but it's smarter to arrive in gritty Oiapoque by daylight and plan on a quick exit strategy; buses depart for the lengthy journey south several times daily. You can also **fly** from Cayenne to Macapá, on the Amazon.

From Guyana

It's a bumpy eight-hour bus ride from Georgetown to **Lethem**, a quiet place about 130km northeast of the Brazilian town of Boa Vista. Alternatively, travel through Suriname to French Guiana. There are daily **flights** from Georgetown to Boa Vista, or connect via Paramaribo in Suriname, which has flights to other destinations in Brazil.

From Paraguay

Paraguay's busiest border crossing is from Ciudad del Este over the Puente de la Amistad (Friendship Bridge) to the Brazilian town of **Foz do Iguaçu**. You may do well to avoid the traffic queues and just walk across. There are daily **flights** from Asunción to São Paulo, Rio and other major destinations in Brazil.

From Peru

The most common and least expensive route is by river from Iquitos, about a day and a half upriver from the border town of **Tabatinga**. Larger boats make the trip down from Tabatinga to Manaus in three to four days. There are also 'express' boat services via Tefé (roughly halfway to Manaus; about 13hr each leg) and super-fast sixteen-seat powerboats connecting Tabatinga and Iquitos (10–12hr). If you get sick of the journey there are also flights from Tefé to Manaus and Tabatinga, while small planes connect Iquitos with Santa Rosa, a Peruvian border settlement just a short boat ride from Tabatinga. There are daily **flights** from Lima to Rio and São Paulo.

From Suriname

The lack of any official crossing means getting to Brazil from Suriname requires travelling overland to either Lethem in Guyana or Saint Georges in French Guiana. It's much easier and immensely less time consuming to fly. Daily **flights** depart from Paramaribo for Rio and São Paulo.

From Uruguay

The most travelled overland route to Brazil is via **Chuí** (Chuy on the Uruguayan side), 527km south of Porto Alegre. A less-used but more atmospheric crossing is from Rivera to **Santana Do Livramento**, 497km west of Porto Alegre in the heart of Gaúcho country. Between the two, there are also more complicated crossings from Melo to Aceguá, from where you can easily reach the more interesting town of **Bagé**, or to **Jaguarão**. Finally, in the west, there are international bridges (and buses) linking Bella Unión and Artigas with the Brazilian towns of **Barra do Quarai** and **Quarai** respectively. There are also daily **flights** from Montevideo to Rio and São Paulo.

From Venezuela

From Santa Elena de Uairén in Bolívar (Venezuela's southeastern state) two daily buses make the four-hour trip to **Boa Vista** in Brazil, where you'll find a twelve-hour connection to Manaus. Daily **flights** connect Caracas to Brasília, Rio, São Paulo and other destinations in Brazil.

VISAS

Generally, Brazil requires **visas** based on the principle of reciprocity of treatment given to its citizens. Visitors from most European nations, including Britain and Ireland, need only a valid passport and either a return or onward ticket or evidence of funds to purchase one, to enter Brazil. You fill in an entry form on arrival and get a tourist visa allowing you to stay for ninety days. Try not to lose the receipt of this entry form; you'll need it if you plan on extending your stay. **Australian**, **American** and **Canadian** citizens need visas in advance, available from Brazilian consulates abroad; a return or onward ticket is usually a requirement. You'll also need to submit a passport photo with your visa application and pay a processing fee (AUS$49, US$130 or CAN$67 respectively).

For anything to do with entry permits and visas you deal with the **Polícia Federal**, the federal police. Every state capital has a federal police station with a visa section: ask for the *delagacia federal*. You can extend tourist permits for another ninety days if you apply at least fifteen days before expiry, but it will only be extended once; if you want to stay longer you'll have to leave Brazil and re-enter. A R$67 charge is made on tourist permit and visa extensions. If you stay past the visa date without having extended it you will be charged R$8.28 per day at the airport before you leave the country.

GETTING AROUND

Local travel in Brazil is always easy. Public transport outside the Amazon is generally by bus or plane, though there are a few passenger trains, too. However you travel, services will be crowded, plentiful and, apart from planes, cheap. Car rental is also possible, but driving in Brazil is not for the faint-hearted. Hitchhiking, over any distance, is not recommended.

By air

It's not surprising that a country Brazil's size relies heavily on air travel. **TAM** (Ⓦwww.tam.com.br), **GOL** (Ⓦwww.voegol.com.br) and **Varig** (Ⓦwww.varig.com.br) are the biggest domestic carriers. You can often find good deals for flights between far-flung cities on their websites, and if you plan on flying within Brazil at least four times within thirty days, and don't mind sticking to an itinerary, it can make sense to buy an **airpass**. These need to be purchased before you travel (you can't buy them in Brazil) the **TAM Brazil Airpass** and **Varig Brazil Airpass** each cost somewhere between US$500 and US$1200, depending on the number of flights included. A useful website with frequent cheap flights, promotions and special deals, is Ⓦwww.submarinoviagens.com.br.

The US$36 **departure tax** is usually, but not always included in the price of your ticket: there's also a tax on domestic flights of US$12–16.

By bus

Hundreds of bus companies offer services that criss-cross Brazil. **Bus travel** is a great budget option provided you have the time, although many buses are packed, roads outside cities are in poor condition and you'll want to watch your belongings. Intercity buses leave from a station called a **rodoviária**, usually built on city outskirts. Journey prices are standardized, even when more than one firm plies the same route, and thus reasonable. Long-distance buses are comfortable enough to sleep in, and have on-board toilets; they stop every few hours, but bringing water and food to last the trip is a good idea.

Leitos are luxury buses which do nocturnal runs between major cities, with fully reclining seats in curtained partitions. They cost about a third of the price of an air ticket, and should be booked days in advance. For any journey, in fact, it's best to buy your ticket at least a day in advance, from the *rodoviária* or some travel agents. An exception is the Rio–São Paulo route, where shuttle service means you can turn up without a ticket. If you cross a state line you'll get a small form with the ticket asking for your seat number (*poltrona*), ticket number (*passagem*), passport number (*identidade*) and destination (*destino*). You must fill it in and give it to the driver before you'll be let on board.

By car

Brazil has one of the highest death rates from driving-related accidents in the world. Cities are well signposted but, outside urban areas, many roads are death-traps at night: poorly lit, in bad condition and lightly policed. In addition, few road rules are obeyed, and no one ever signals. Worth avoiding at night are the **Via Dutra**, linking Rio and São Paulo, because of the huge numbers of trucks and the treacherous ascent and descent of the Serra do Mar, and the **Belém–Brasília highway**, whose potholes and uneven asphalt make it difficult enough to drive even in daylight. Avoid driving after dark in the Mato Grosso and Amazon regions too – though rare, armed roadside robberies have happened here. Service stations don't always accept international credit cards, so bring cash enough for the trip.

Renting a car is easy – Hertz, Avis and other big-name international companies operate here; and there are Brazilian alternatives such as Interlocadora, Nobre, Localiza and Unidas. Car rental offices (*locadoras*) are at every airport and in most towns.

An **international driving license** is recommended: foreign licenses are accepted for visits of up to six months but you may find it tough convincing a police officer of this. The police can be intimidating, pointing to trumped-up contraventions when they're probably angling for a bribe. If such an on-the-spot *multa*, or fine, is suggested it's your choice whether to stand your ground or pay up. Whatever you do, stay calm and bend over backwards to appear polite. If your passport is confiscated, demand to be permitted to call your consulate – there should always be a duty officer available.

By taxi

Metered **taxis** are easy to flag down and relatively inexpensive, though base fares vary from place to place. An alternative is the radiotaxi, a metered cab you can call to pick you up – generally much cheaper on airport trips and the like.

By boat

Amazon river travel is slow and basic, but fascinating. The range of boat transport in the Amazon runs from luxury tourist vessels and large three-level riverboats to smaller one- or two-level boats and covered launches operated by tour companies. Prices are generally calculated per day, and include food: as a rule, local boats are less expensive than tourist boats and launches. On longer journeys there are different classes; avoid *cabine*, sweltering cabins, and choose instead *primeiro* (first class), sleeping in a hammock on deck. *Segundo* (second class) is often hammock space in the lower deck or engine room. Bring provisions, and prepare to practise your Portuguese. The popular four- to six-day Belém–Manaus trip costs about R$220 (for *primeiro* hammock space).

ACCOMMODATION

As ever, you've a wide choice of styles of accommodation in Brazil. The cheapest, most unappealing options are **dormitórios**, small, unsavoury and sometimes even dangerous hotels near bus stations in poorer parts of town. Avoid them where possible. You are far better off in a **hostel**. There is an extensive network of **HI-affiliated hostels**, so it's worth taking out an HI membership (Ⓦwww.hihostels.com) when you arrive – it will pay for itself within a week. Prices vary but a spot in a dorm averages R$15–25. In bigger cities and resorts you'll also find other hostels, usually known as an *albergue de juventude* or *casa de estudante*. Here the cost per person is generally R$20–$30 a night. Slightly higher in price are the small, family-run hotels, called **pensão** (*pensões* in the plural) or *hotel familiar*. *Pensões* are often better in small towns than in large cities. You'll also find the **pousada**, which can just be another name for a *pensão*, but can also be a small hotel, often very luxurious in an offbeat way. In the Amazon and the Pantanal in particular, *pousadas* tend to be purpose-built **fazenda** lodges geared towards the growing eco-tourist markets and are not aimed at budget travellers.

Hotels proper run the gamut from cheap dives to ultra-luxe. The Brazilian classification star system (one to five) depends on bureaucratic requirements as much as the standard of accommodation – many perfectly good hotels don't have stars. There's a range of rooms, with significant price differences: a **quarto** is a room without a bathroom; an **apartamento** is en suite (usually with a shower – Brazilians don't use baths); an **apartamento de luxo** is normally just an *apartamento* with a fridge full of (marked-up) drinks. A **casal** is a double room, a **solteiro a** single. In a starred hotel, anything from an *apartamento* upwards would normally come with telephone, air-conditioning (*ar condicionado*) and a TV; a *ventilador* is a fan. Room **rates** vary tremendously by region and season. Generally, for R$80–R$140 a night you can stay in a reasonable mid-range hotel, with bathroom and air-conditioning. During the off-season hotels in tourist areas offer hefty discounts of around 25–35 percent.

There are a number of **campsites** in Brazil, almost all of them on the coast near the bigger beaches. They usually have basic facilities – running water and toilets, a simple restaurant – and are popular with young Argentines and Brazilians.

FOOD AND DRINK

Brazil has four main **regional cuisines**: **comida mineira**, from Minas Gerais, is based mainly on pork with imaginative vegetable use and thick bean sauces; **comida baiana** (see p.317), from Bahia, has a rich seafood base and an abundance of West African ingredients; **comida do sertão**, from the interior of the Northeast, relies on rehydrated dried or salted meat and regional fruits, beans and tubers; and **comida gaúcha** from Rio Grande do Sul, the world's most carnivorous diet, revolves around charcoal-grilling every meat imaginable.

Alongside regional restaurants, there is a **standard fare** available everywhere: steak (**bife**) or chicken (**frango**), served with *arroz e feijão* (rice and beans) and often with salad, fries and *farinha*, dried manioc (**cassava**) flour that you sprinkle over everything. *Farofa* is toasted *farinha*, and usually comes with onions and bits of bacon mixed in. **Feijoada** is the closest Brazil comes to a national dish: a stew of pork, sausage and smoked meat cooked with black beans and garlic, garnished with slices of orange. Eating it is a national ritual at weekends, when restaurants serve *feijoada* all day.

There are more **fruits** than there are English words for them. Some of the fruit is familiar – *manga* (mango), *maracujá* (passion fruit), *limão* (lime) – but most of it has only Brazilian names: *jaboticaba*, *fruta do conde*, *sapoti* and *jaca*. The most exotic fruits are Amazonian: try *bacuri*, *cupuaçu* and *açaí* (the last usually mixed with *guaraná*).

Eating cheaply

Portions are usually large and prices reasonable at the average restaurant. **Prato comercial** and **prato feito** (literally, pre-made dish) are two very budget-friendly phrases you'll see on most menus – usually rice, beans, a choice of meat and a small salad for about R$6–8. The **prato do dia**, plate of the day, is similarly a cheap but filling meal. Also economical are *lanchonetes*, where you can choose from vast buffets then pay by weight (**comida por kilo**), R$15–20 will buy you a feast here. **Rodizio** restaurants are fantastic deals – specialized restaurants (pizza, sushi, tapioca) where you pay a set fee and eat as much as you want of the endless supply of food waiters bring around. The *churrascaria*, the classic Brazilian **steakhouse**, operates similarly, with a constant supply of charcoal-grilled meat on huge spits brought to your table. These too can be a terrific budget deal providing you stay away from the ritzy ones.

Açaí na tigela (*açaí*, *guaraná* and crushed ice with sliced bananas and granola) is ubiquitous and turns a smoothie into a satisfying meal at almost any corner fruit stand at almost any time of day. You'll also find cheap and excellent **street food** like *salgados* (savoury snacks): *pão de queijo* (cheese profiteroles), *pastel* (fried pastry with meat or cheese filling) and *coxinha* (minced or shredded chicken, battered and fried) that can sate even the most voracious eaters and should be easily handled by most stomachs (conversely, beach shrimp-skewers might wisely be avoided). If it's sweets you're after you're in luck: ice cream, condensed milk puddings and *pudim*, condensed milk flan, are just a few of the treats you'll find everywhere. Street markets are good for deals on fruit that make terrifically cheap and exotic breakfasts – like a bag of *maracuja*, R$1.

Drinking

Brazil is famous for **coffee** and you'll find decent espresso in most local cafes, but Brazilians like to put sugar in *everything* and you'll draw looks if you don't follow suit (cappuccinos are loaded with chocolate). Starbucks has made inroads in ritzier neighbourhoods but there are excellent local chains in São Paulo like Supplicy and Fran's Cafe. **Tea** (*cha*) is surprisingly good. Try **cha mate**, a strong green tea with a noticeable caffeine hit, or one of the wide variety of herbal teas, most notably that made from *guaraná*. The great variety of fruit in Brazil is put to excellent use in **succos**: fruit is popped into a liquidizer with sugar and crushed ice to make a deliciously refreshing drink. Made with milk rather than water it becomes a **vitamina**.

RESSACA (HUNG OVER)? TRY ENGOV

Caipirinhas go down easily and don't strike at once, which makes getting *bêbado* (drunk) easy. If you know you're going to tie one on, do what the locals do; stop into a local *farmácia* and buy some gold packets of **Engov tablets**, a cheap, over-the-counter hangover preventative and "cure" whose ingredients, Aluminium hydroxide, caffeine, acetylsalicylic acid and pyrilamine maleate can be found in antacids, aspirin, and antihistamines. You're meant to take one before your first drink and another after the last; but, it helps the next day too, trust us.

TÔ LIGADO, MANO

In, Portuguese, "*tô ligado, mano*," means "I'm switched on, man," it means you're "down." However cool you are, or *think* you are, to truly be "with it," in Brazil you first need to understand the concept of *jeitinho*. Literally it means, 'a knack,' a 'fix,' or 'twist' but in a larger sense it means "a way," and it's how Brazil works. Can't get tickets to the football game two minutes before the match? Go to the head of the line and get creative. Bouncer giving you trouble getting into the club? Smile, joke, and get persuasive. In other words start blagging. In Brazil, there's always a way to make happen what at first glance seems impossible.

Beer is mainly of the lager type. Brazilians drink it ice-cold, mostly from 600ml bottles: ask for a *cerveja*. Draught beer is *chopp*. The regional beers of Pará and Maranhão, *Cerma* and *Cerpa*, are generally acknowledged as the best; of the nationally available brands *Skol*, *Brahma*, *Antarctica* and *Bohemia* are all popular. Despite the undoubted improvement in the quality of Brazilian **wines** in recent years, imported wines from Chile and Argentina (or Europe) remain more reliable and can sometimes even be cheaper.

As for spirits, stick to what Brazilians drink – **cachaça**, sugar-cane rum. The best way to drink it is in a **caipirinha** – *cachaça* mixed with fresh lime, sugar and crushed ice – which along with football and music is one of Brazil's great gifts to the world. It's the best cocktail you're ever likely to drink. One thing to remember when enjoying Brazil's beverages: most clubs and some bars will give you an **individual card** when you enter upon which your drinks are tabulated. Don't lose it. Even if you have paid, unless you have the receipt at the door, you will have difficulty leaving and may even have to pay again.

CULTURE AND ETIQUETTE

The official and most widely spoken language in Brazil is **Portuguese**. Educated Brazilians usually speak some English, and there are plenty of Spanish speakers, but knowing Spanish is of limited help in interpreting spoken Portuguese. You will do yourself a huge favour and likely make several new friends if you learn some Portuguese words. Even a little effort goes a long way.

On the whole, Brazilians are very friendly, open people (you'll be minded to your stop by passengers on public transportation if you ask for help). The pace differs depending on the region. In major cities things operate fairly quickly and on a schedule. Things work in the Northeast too, but in their own special way – you're better off slowing to *their* pace.

Though attitudes vary regionally, in general it is true that Brazilians are remarkably open with their **sexuality**. Brazil's reputation as a sex destination is not completely without merit – prostitution *is* legal and you'll see love motels (hourly rates) everywhere. Have fun but be careful – there are plenty of what locals call 'gringo-hunters,' Brazilians looking for foreign passports, and not every lady of the night is actually a lady (as AC Milan striker Ronaldo could attest in May, 2008). Whatever you do, use protection (a condom is a *camisinha*): about a third of the people with HIV in Latin America live in Brazil (an estimated 620,000 in 2005). And don't make too many assumptions. While known for being accepting of alternative sexualities during Carnaval, Latin machismo still applies here and Brazilians can be as bigoted against gays and lesbians as anybody.

SPORTS AND OUTDOOR ACTIVITIES

Brazilian **football** (*futebol*) is globally revered and a privilege to watch. In fact, you won't really have experienced Brazil until you've attended a match. Stadiums are spectacular sights, games enthralling, and crowds are wildly enthusiastic. The finest stadiums (*estadios*) are the temples of Brazilian football, **Maracanã** in Rio and the Art Deco **Pacaembu** in São Paulo, one of the world's most beautiful. Tickets are not expensive, ranging from R$20 to R$150 depending on whether you stand on the terraces (*geral*) or opt for stand seats (*arquibancada*) – major championship and international matches may cost more. Grounds are large and crowds usually below stadium capacity except for important matches, meaning you can usually pay at the turnstile (though there are long last-minute lines).

Regional rivalries are strong, and fans of visiting teams are seated separately from those of the home team and given different exit routes to prevent fighting. For the most part it's safe to attend – just don't wear a visiting jersey or their colours unless you're looking for trouble. In Rio, **Flamengo** and **Fluminense** have historically had the most intense rivalry in Brazilian club football and have long dominated *carioca* football. In São Paulo there is a similar rivalry between **São Paulo** and **Corinthians**. But wherever you are, and whatever game you see, Brazilian football at its best can remind you why it's known as 'the beautiful game'.

COMMUNICATIONS

Post offices – *correios* – are easily identified by their bright yellow post-boxes and signs. A foreign postage stamp costs R$1.60 for either a postcard or a letter up to 10 grams. Expect airmail letters to Europe and North America to take around a week, sometimes less. Although the postal system is generally reliable, it's better not to send valuables by mail.

Public phones are operated by phonecards (*cartão telefônico*) available at newspaper stands, street sellers' trays and some cafés. Cards come in various denominations from 10 to 100 reais: for local calls a 20 reais card should be enough; calls to the US or Europe cost about R$6.50 per minute. Before dialling, lift the phone, insert the card and listen for a dial tone.

Brazil's telephone system is privatized and different phone companies are responsible for different areas of the country. Pay phones display which company code should be used from that phone. This doesn't affect **local calls**, just dial the seven- or eight-digit number. For **long-distance** or **international calls**, however, you must first select a phone company (only two, Embratel, code 21, and Intelig, code 23, allow international calls from Brazil – one of these numbers will be an option from most phones). Insert the two-digit code between the zero and the area code or country code of the number you're calling. To call Rio, for example, from anywhere else in Brazil, dial 0+XX+21 (zero + phone company code + city code) followed by the seven-digit number; for international calls, start with two zeros, followed by the phone company code and country code.

Long-distance and international calls can also be made from a *posto telefônico*, where you are given a numbered key (*chave*) to a booth, in which you can make up to three calls. You are billed when you return the key. For international calls, ask for *chamada internacional*; a reverse-charge call is a *chamada a cobrar*. Having said all this, with the prevalence of the internet and the availability of discounted phone calls on the likes of **Skype**, it's hard to imagine why you'd want to make a national or international call any other way.

You should have no difficulty finding an **Internet cafe** anywhere in Brazil – they're sprinkled throughout major cities, and even obscure jungle towns have a/c places with web connections. Rio and São Paulo boast a number of wi-fi spots and even have free web portals in some coffee shops. Prices vary drastically – a fair rate is R$1 per half-hour.

CRIME AND SAFETY

Brazil's reputation as a rather dangerous place is not entirely undeserved, but it is often overblown, and many visitors arrive with an exaggerated idea of the perils lying in wait. **Street crime** can be a problem, especially in the evenings and late at night (the targeting of tourists is worst in Rio, Salvador and Recife), but as when travelling anywhere be sensible and aware but don't let fear grip you. Criminals are also getting more sophisticated – there has been a reported increase in the **cloning of ATM cards**, so you should check your account online often and change your pin occasionally.

Personal safety

Being a gringo attracts unwelcome attention but it also provides a measure of protection. The Brazilian police can be extremely violent, and law enforcement tends to take the form of periodic crackdowns. Therefore, criminals know that injuries to foreign tourists mean a heavy clampdown, which in turns means slim pickings for a while. So unless you resist, nothing is likely to happen to you. Still, it's shocking to have a knife or a gun pulled on you. If you *are* unlucky enough to be the victim of an **assalto**, a hold-up, remember, it's your possessions that are the targets. Don't resist: your money and anything you're carrying will be snatched, your watch yanked off, but within seconds it will all be over. Most *assaltos* happen at night, in back streets and desolate areas of cities, so stick to busy, well-lit streets, and where possible take taxis; city buses generally run late too, and are very safe for the most part (just mind your belongings when it's crowded).

Buses, beaches and hotels

Long-distance **buses** are generally pretty secure, but it pays to keep an eye on your things. Baggage compartments on long-distance bus trips are generally safe but be sure get a **baggage check** from the person loading it and keep an eye on your stuff until it goes in. Overhead racks are less safe, especially during night journeys.

On city **beaches**, never leave things unattended; any beachside bar will stow things for you. Shared **rooms** in *pousadas* and hostels usually have lockers (it's handy to have brought a combination lock) and even many cheap hotels have **safes**, *caixas*.

Police and drugs

If you are robbed or held up, it's not necessarily a good idea to go to the **police**. Except with something like a theft from a hotel room, they're unlikely to be able to do much, and reporting something will likely take hours even without the language barrier. You may have to do it for insurance purposes, when you'll need a local police report; this could take a full and very frustrating day so consider how badly you want to be reimbursed. If your passport is stolen, go to your consulate first and they'll smooth the path. If you go to the police in a city where there is a consulate, get in touch with the consulate first and take their lead.

Marijuana – *maconha* – is fairly common but be very, very careful. If the police find it on you, you will be in serious trouble. The following cannot be overstated: under no circumstances do you want to spend *any* time in a Brazilian jail. **Cocaine** is not as common as you might think as most of

EMERGENCY NUMBERS

Ambulance ☎192

Fire ☎193

Police ☎190

Tourist Police Rio ☎21/511-5112 or 511-5767; São Paulo ☎11/214-0209; Salvador ☎71/322-7155 or 322-1188

it passes through Brazil from Bolivia or Colombia for export.

MEDICAL CARE AND EMERGENCIES

Public healthcare in Brazil is not somewhere you want to go, but private medical and dental treatment *can* be of the same quality as that in the US and Europe. Anyone used to a subsidized system obviously won't think it cheap but costs are significantly less than in North America. Check directories at the end of each section for hospital information and refer to advice from your country's embassy or consulate. Standard drugs are available in *farmácias* (pharmacies) without prescriptions.

BRAZIL ON THE NET

www.brasil.gov.br Government site with information on visas, travel, and tourism in English.

www.braziltour.com The official site of the Brazilian Ministério do Turismo.

www.bbeco.org Bureau Brasil de Ecoturismo, a non-profit civil organization comprised of local and national operators working for ecotourism destinations.

www.brazilmax.com The self-described *Hip Guide to Brazil* has information in English ranging from the art scene to the Patanal.

www.virtually-brazil.com Virtual panoramic tours of attractions and hotels.

PUBLIC HOLIDAYS

January 1 New Year's Day

February/March (variable) Carnaval. The five days leading up to Ash Wednesday

March/April (variable) Good Friday

April 21 Remembrance of *Tiradentes*

May 1 Labour Day

June 11 Corpus Christi

September 7 Independence Day

October 12 Nossa Senhora Aparecida

November 2 Dia dos Finados (Day of the Dead)

November 15 Proclamation of the Republic

December 25 Christmas Day

INFORMATION AND MAPS

Considering how much Brazil has to offer its visitors one would think there would be plenty of tourist information in English, but in practice **tourist offices** across the country have closed in recent years. That said, when you do find an office, people are very friendly and helpful. Generally, the airport information offices have the best English speakers and are usually open the longest. They have decent free maps but little else in English. At the newsstands, you won't likely find *Veja* magazine itself very readable, but it does put out an annual issue highlighting bars, restaurants and clubs in major cities with pictures and addresses, helpful even if you don't read Portuguese.

OPENING HOURS AND HOLIDAYS

Basic **hours of operation** for shops and businesses are weekdays from 9am until 6pm and Saturday 9am to 1pm. **Shopping centres** are usually open 10am to 10pm and are closed Sundays. Some supermarkets in major cities stay open 24 hours. **Museums and historic**

monuments generally cost just a few reais and follow regular business hours, though many are closed on Mondays.

In addition to the public holidays listed, there are plenty of local and state holidays when you'll find everything closed.

CARNAVAL

Carnaval is by far the most important festival in Brazil and when it comes, the country comes to a halt as it gets down to some of the most serious partying in the world. The most familiar and most spectacular celebration is in **Rio** (see p.267), one of the world's great sights, televised live to the whole country. Traditionally, **Salvador**'s Carnaval (see p.318) has been less commercialized but this has been changing in recent years with bigger headliners performing. **Olinda** and its winding colonial hilltop streets make for a less frenzied Carnaval and **Fortaleza** also has a good reputation.

CARNAVAL DATES

2009 February 20–24
2010 February 12–16
2011 March 4–8
2012 February 17–21
2013 February 8–12

OTHER FESTIVALS AND CELEBRATIONS

Carnaval is Brazil's most famous and important festival but it certainly isn't the only one. Some other cool celebrations:

Reveillon New Year's Eve. Major cities along the coast try to outdo each other with fireworks. Rio is again the biggest and best.

Lavagem do Bonfim Second Thursday of January. Hundreds of women in traditional Bahian garb clean the steps of Salvador's beloved church with perfumed water (food and music follow).

Celebration of Yemanjá February 2. Devotees make offerings on beaches along the coast to celebrate the goddess of the sea. Salvador's Praia Vermelha hosts one of the largest.

São Paulo Bienal March 2010. The largest art event in Latin America (and the world's second oldest biennial) takes place in São Paulo every even year, though following controversy in 2008, you may want to check the dates.

The Passion Play Ten days leading up to Easter. Latin America's largest passion plays are enacted in Nova Jerusalem, outside Recife.

Bumba-meu-boi June 13–29. The people of São Luis re-enact the folk tale of a farmer who, having killed another farmer's ox, must resurrect it or face his own death. Costumes, dancing, *capoeira*, heckling and hilarity ensue.

São João June 13–24. The celebration of Saint John in Salvador and the Northeast is a raucous celebration with *forró* music, dancing, drinking and eating.

Pinga Festival of Paraty Third weekend in August. Local *cachaça* producers organize tastings, with performances by top Brazilian musicians.

Cirio de Nazaré Second Sunday in October. An effigy of the Virgin of Nazaré is carried across the water from Vila de Icoaraci to the port of Belém.

Oktoberfest October 10–27. German-settled Blumenau has all the beer-swilling, German food and traditional garb you'd expect. Ⓦwww.oktoberfestblumenau.com.br.

Free Jazz Festival Mid to late October. Rio and São Paulo host top national and international jazz acts.

Grand Prix November. Brazil's Interlagos circuit, a few miles from São Paulo, is one of the most atmospheric of all Grand Prix venues. Ⓦwww.gpbrasil.com.

Río de Janeiro

The citizens of **RÍO DE JANEIRO** call it the *cidade marvilhosa* – and there can't be much argument about that. It's a huge city with a stunning setting, extending along twenty kilometres of sandy coast, sandwiched between an azure sea and jungle-clad mountains. The city's unusual name has a curious history: Portuguese explorers arriving at the mouth of Guanabara Bay on 1 January, 1502 thought they had discovered the mouth of an enormous river which they named the January River or Río de Janeiro. By the time the first settlement was established and the error was realized, the name had already stuck.

Although riven by inequality, Rio has great style. Its international renown is bolstered by a series of symbols that rank as some of the greatest landmarks in the world: the **Corcovado** mountain supporting the great statue of Christ the Redeemer; the rounded incline of the **Sugarloaf mountain**, standing at the entrance to the bay; the **Maracanã stadium**, a huge draw for football fans; and the sweep of **Copacabana beach**, probably the most famous length of sand on the planet. It's a setting enhanced by the annual, frenetic sensuality of **Carnaval**, an explosive celebration which – for many people – sums up Rio and her citizens, the **cariocas**.

What to see and do

Getting around this vast metropolis is easier than you might think, and the city can easily be split into three major sectors. The **Centro Histórico** contains the last vestiges of the metropolis's colonial past, and is easily walkable in half a day. The most obvious place to start is the Praça XV de Novembro, while south of here are the lively *bairros* of **Lapa**, capital of the local samba scene, and **Glória**, home to arguably the prettiest of Rio's churches. Southwest is the unmissable bohemian *bairro* of **Santa Teresa**. The run-down **Zona Norte** is where you'll find the Maracanã

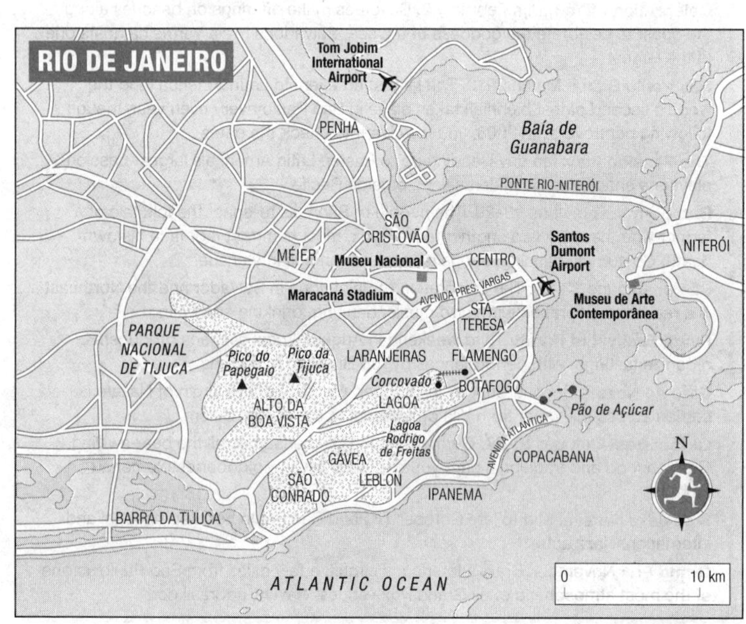

CARNAVAL

Carnaval is celebrated in all of Brazil's cities, but Rio's is the biggest and most famous of all. From the Friday before Ash Wednesday to the following Thursday, the city shuts up shop and throws itself into the world's most famous manifestation of unbridled hedonism. Rio's Carnaval ranks as the most important celebration on the Brazilian calendar, easily outstripping either Christmas or Easter. In a poverty-stricken city, it represents a moment of release, when *cariocas* can express their aspirations in music and song.

The action

Rio's street celebrations centre on the **evening processions** that fill **Avenida Rio Branco** (Metrô Largo do Carioca). The processions include rival samba schools and loudspeaker-laden floats blasting out frenetic dance music. Each neighbourhood or social club has its own **samba school**, competing in three leagues, each allowing promotion and relegation. It's a year-round occupation, with schools mobilizing thousands of supporters, choosing a theme, writing the music and learning the dances choreographed by the **carnavelesco** – the school's director. By December, rehearsals have begun and, in time for Christmas, the sambas are recorded and released to record stores.

The main procession of Division 1 schools – the **Desfile** – takes place on the Sunday and Monday nights in the purpose – built **Sambódromo** at Rua Marques de Sapuçai (Metrô Praza Onze), a concrete structure 1700m long that can accommodate ninety thousand spectators. Some schools may have fifty thousand participants, each wearing their school colours; they compete for points awarded by judges according to the presentation of their song, story, dress, dance and rhythm. Each school must parade for between 85 and 95 minutes, with the **bateria**, or percussion section, sustaining the cadence that drives the school's song and dance.

The **carros alegóricos** (decorated floats) carry the more prominent figures, among them the **porta-bandeira** ("flag bearer"), who carries the school's symbol. The bulk of the procession behind is formed by the **alas** – hundreds of costumed individuals, each linked to a part of the school's theme.

The **parade** of schools starts at 7.30pm, with eight schools parading on each of the two nights, and goes on till noon the following day. Two stands in the Sambódromo (7 & 9) are reserved for foreign visitors and **tickets** cost over US$80 per night. Other sections of the Sambódromo cost US$5–30 and the seating options are: the high stands (*arquibancadas*), the lower stands (*geral*) and the prestigious ringside seats (*cadeiras de pista*). Most people don't turn up until 11pm, by which time the show is well under way. **Tickets**, available from Riotur (see p.279) and Banco do Brasil, need to be booked well in advance.

and the Museu Nacional. It's the **Zona Sul**, or southern sector, however, where you're likely to spend most of your time, with its legendary beaches, Corcovado and Sugarloaf Mountain.

Praça XV de Novembro

Praça XV de Novembro (Metrô Uruguaiana) was once the hub of Rio's social and political life, taking its name from the day in 1899 when Marechal Deodoro de Fonseca proclaimed the Republic of Brazil. On the south side of the square is the imposing **Paço Imperial** (Tues–Sun noon–6.30pm; free). It was here in 1808 that the Portuguese monarch, Dom João VI, established his court in Brazil, and the building continued to be used for royal receptions and special occasions: on May 13, 1888, Princess Isabel proclaimed the end of slavery in Brazil here. The **Arco de Telles** was constructed on the site of the old *pelourinho* (pillory) in around 1755 and links the Travessa do Comércio to the Rua Ouvidor. These days it is an enclave

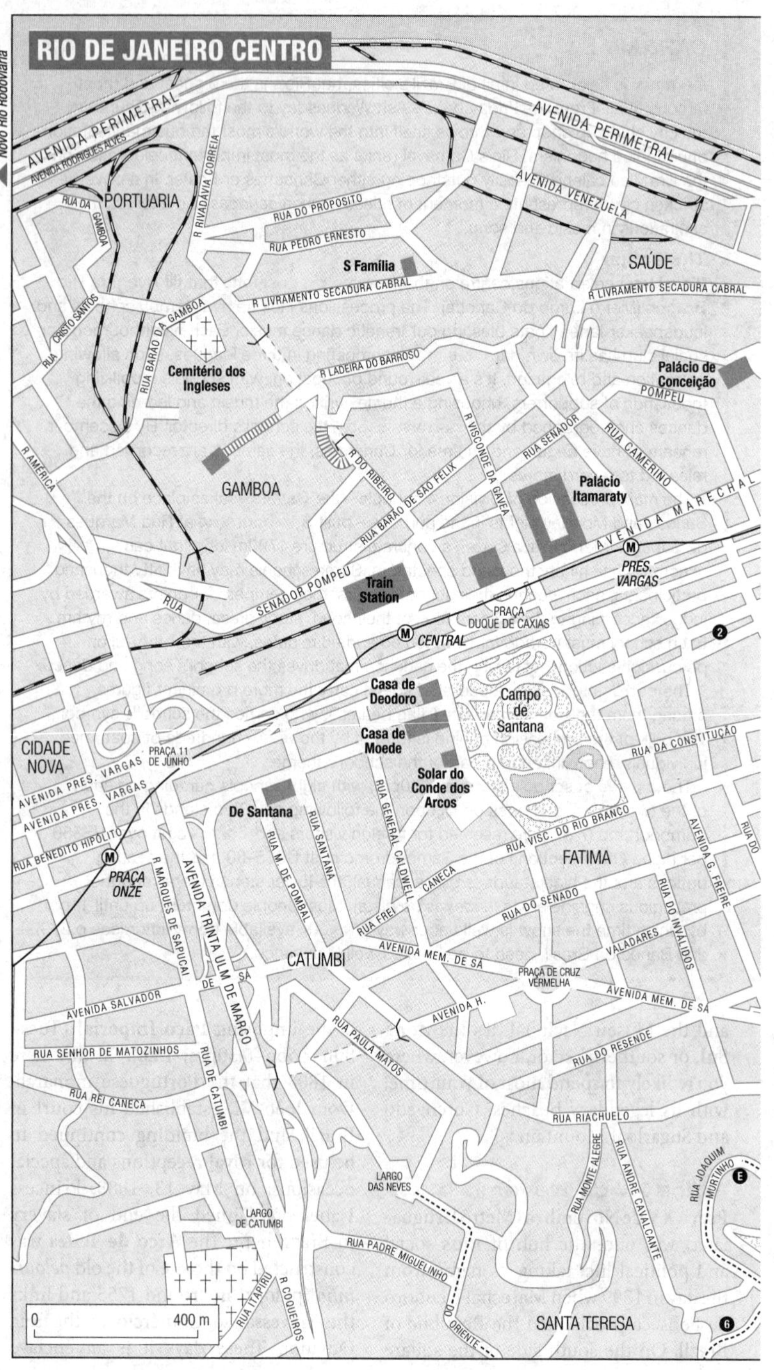
RIO DE JANEIRO CENTRO
Novo Rio Rodoviária
AVENIDA PERIMETRAL
AVENIDA RODRIGUES ALVES
PORTUARIA
RUA DA GAMBOA
R RIVADAVIA CORREIA
RUA DO PROPOSITO
RUA PEDRO ERNESTO
AVENIDA VENEZUELA
SAÚDE
S Família
R LIVRAMENTO SECADURA CABRAL
RUA CRISTO SANTOS
RUA BARÃO DA GAMBOA
Cemitério dos Ingleses
R LADEIRA DO BARROSO
Palácio de Conceição
POMPEU
R AMERICA
GAMBOA
R DO RIBEIRO
RUA BARÃO DE SÃO FELIX
R VISCONDE DA GAVEA
RUA SENADOR
RUA CAMERINO
Palácio Itamaraty
AVENIDA MARECHAL
PRES. VARGAS
RUA SENADOR POMPEU
Train Station
PRAÇA DUQUE DE CAXIAS
CENTRAL
Casa de Deodoro
Campo de Santana
Casa de Moede
CIDADE NOVA
PRAÇA 11 DE JUNHO
AVENIDA PRES. VARGAS
RUA DA CONSTITUÇÃO
Solar do Conde dos Arcos
De Santana
RUA BENEDITO HIPÓLITO
PRAÇA ONZE
R MARQUES DE SAPUCAÍ
AVENIDA TRINTA ULM DE MARCO
RUA M. DE POMBAL
RUA SANTANA
RUA GENERAL CALDWELL
RUA VISC. DO RIO BRANCO
FATIMA
RUA FREI CANECA
RUA DO SENADO
RUA DO INVÁLIDOS
AVENIDA G. FREIRE
RUA DO
AVENIDA MEM. DE SÁ
VALADARES
CATUMBI
PRAÇA DE CRUZ VERMELHA
AVENIDA SALVADOR
DE SÁ
AVENIDA H.
RUA PAULA MATOS
RUA SENHOR DE MATOZINHOS
RUA DE CATUMBI
RUA DO RESENDE
RUA REI CANECA
RUA RIACHUELO
RUA MONTE ALEGRE
RUA ANDRE CAVALCANTE
RUA JOAQUIM MURTINHO
LARGO DAS NEVES
LARGO DE CATUMBI
RUA PADRE MIGUELINHO
RUA ITAPIRU
R COQUEIROS
DO ORIENTE
SANTA TERESA
0
400 m

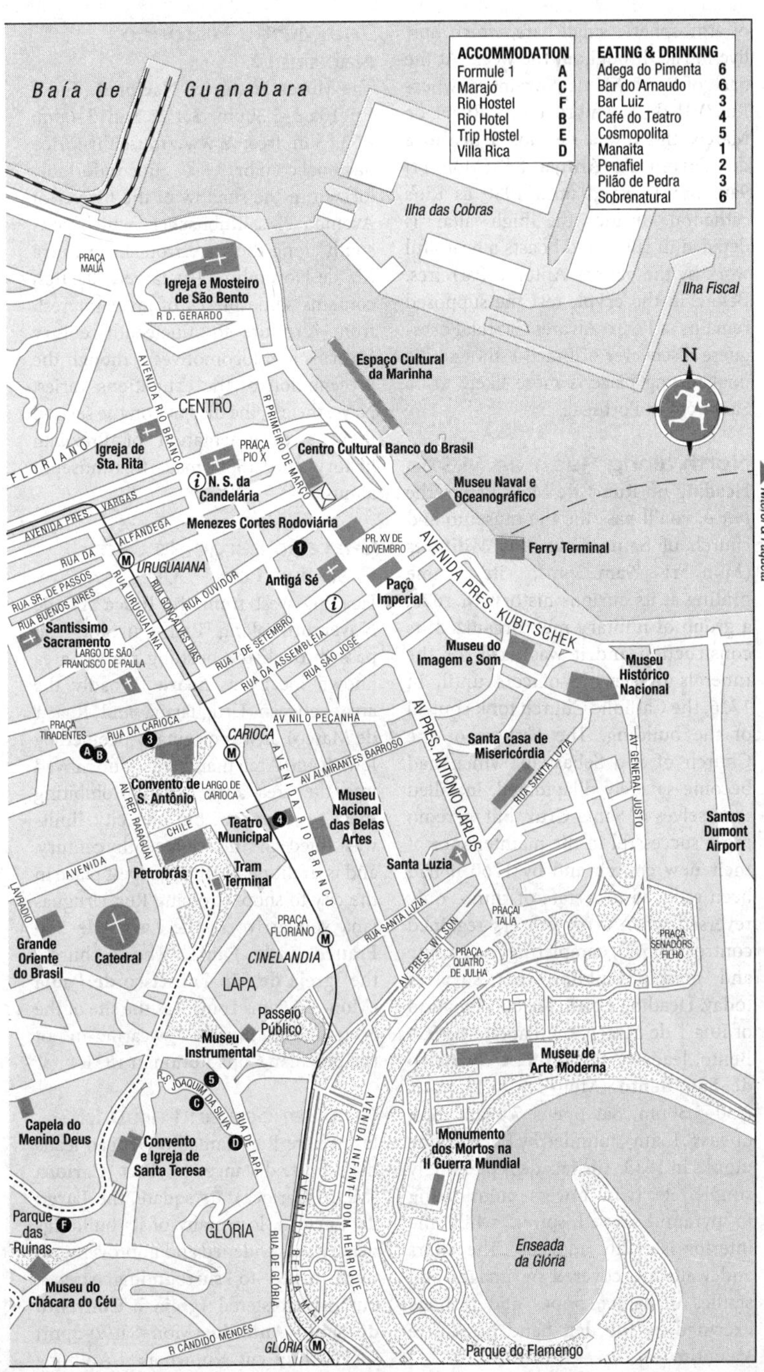

Baía de Guanabara
ACCOMMODATION
Formule 1 A
Marajó C
Rio Hostel F
Rio Hotel B
Trip Hostel E
Villa Rica D
EATING & DRINKING
Adega do Pimenta 6
Bar do Arnaudo 6
Bar Luiz 3
Café do Teatro 4
Cosmopolita 5
Manaita 1
Penafiel 2
Pilão de Pedra 3
Sobrenatural 6
Ilha das Cobras
Ilha Fiscal
N
Niterói & Paquetá
PRAÇA MAUÁ
Igreja e Mosteiro de São Bento
R D. GERARDO
Espaço Cultural da Marinha
AVENIDA RIO BRANCO
R PRIMEIRO DE MARÇO
CENTRO
FLORIANO
Igreja de Sta. Rita
PRAÇA PIO X
Centro Cultural Banco do Brasil
N. S. da Candelária
Museu Naval e Oceanográfico
AVENIDA PRES. VARGAS
ALFANDEGA
Menezes Cortes Rodoviária
PR. XV DE NOVEMBRO
Ferry Terminal
RUA DA
URUGUAIANA
RUA SR. DE PASSOS
RUA BUENOS AIRES
RUA URUGUAIANA
RUA GONÇALVES DIAS
RUA OUVIDOR
Antigá Sé
Paço Imperial
AVENIDA PRES. KUBITSCHEK
Santissimo Sacramento
LARGO DE SÃO FRANCISCO DE PAULA
RUA 7 DE SETEMBRO
RUA DA ASSEMBLÉIA
RUA SÃO JOSÉ
Museu do Imagem e Som
Museu Histórico Nacional
AV NILO PEÇANHA
PRAÇA TIRADENTES
RUA DA CARIOCA
CARIOCA
AV ALMIRANTES BARROSO
AV PRES. ANTÔNIO CARLOS
Santa Casa de Misericórdia
AV GENERAL JUSTO
RUA SANTA LUZIA
Convento de S. Antônio
LARGO DE CARIOCA
AV. REP. PARAGUAI
Museu Nacional das Belas Artes
Teatro Municipal
CHILE
Santos Dumont Airport
AVENIDA
Petrobrás
Tram Terminal
Santa Luzia
LAVRADIO
PRAÇA FLORIANO
PRAÇA I TALIA
Grande Oriente do Brasil
Catedral
CINELANDIA
RUA SANTA LUZIA
AV PRES. WILSON
PRAÇA QUATRO DE JULHA
PRAÇA SENADORS. FILHO
LAPA
Passeio Público
Museu Instrumental
Museu de Arte Moderna
R. S. JOAQUIM DA SILVA
RUA DE LAPA
Capela do Menino Deus
Convento e Igreja de Santa Teresa
AVENIDA INFANTE DOM HENRIQUE
Monumento dos Mortos na II Guerra Mundial
Parque das Ruinas
GLÓRIA
RUA DE GLÓRIA
AVENIDA BEIRA MAR
Enseada da Glória
Museu do Chácara do Céu
R CÂNDIDO MENDES
GLÓRIA
Parque do Flamengo

of atmospheric small bars, which host live music throughout the week. At the back of Praça XV de Novembro, where Rua VII de Setembro meets Rua I de Março, the **Igreja de Nossa Senhora do Carmo da Antigá Sé** (Mon–Fri 9am–5pm) served until 1980 as Rio's cathedral. Inside, the high altar is detailed in silver and boasts a beautiful work by the painter Antônio Parreires. Below, in the **crypt**, rest the supposed remains of Pedro Alvares Cabral, Portuguese discoverer of Brazil – though his final resting place is more likely to be Santarém in Portugal.

North along Rua 1 de Março

Heading up **Rua 1 de Março** from the *praça*, you'll pass the the museum and church of **Santa Cruz dos Militares** (Mon–Fri 9am–3pm), its name hinting at its curious history. In 1628, a group of military men organized its construction and it was used for the funerals of serving officers until, in 1716, the Catholic Church took control of the building. The Fathers of the Church of São Sebastião, which had become severely dilapidated, installed themselves in Santa Cruz, but were no more successful in the maintenance of their new church and by 1760 it had been reduced to a state of ruin – only reversed when army officers regained control in 1780, completing the granite and marble building that survives today. Heading north, the continuation of Rua 1 de Março, the Ladeira de São Bento, leads to the **Igreja e Mosteiro de São Bento** (Mon–Fri 8–11am & 2.30–5.30pm, Sat opens 7.15am, Sun opens 8.15am), founded by Benedictine monks in 1633. The facade is pleasingly simple, its twin towers culminating in pyramid-shaped spires, while the interior is richly adorned. The altars and walls are covered by images and statues of saints, popes and bishops executed by the deft hand of Mestre Valentim.

The Museu Histórico Nacional

The **Museu Histórico Nacional** (Tues–Fri 10am–5.30pm, Sat & Sun 2–6pm; R$3; Sun free; Ⓦwww.museuhistoriconacional.com.br) is uncomfortably located in the shadow of the flyover of Avenida Pres. Kubitschek, which runs south along the waterfront from Praça XV de Novembro. The large collection contains some pieces of great interest, from furniture to nineteenth-century firearms and locomotives – though the presentation of the exhibitions varies. Nevertheless, the displays on the second floor, a documentation of Brazilian history since 1500, make this museum a must.

Saara to Largo de São Francisco de Paula

Heading west from the **Praça XV de Novembro** along Rua Ouvidor you pass through the bustling market area known locally as **Saara** (broadly the area between Uruguaiana and Rua 1 de Março). It was originally peopled by Jewish and Arab merchants, who moved into the area after a ban prohibiting their residence within the city limits was lifted in the eighteenth century, and is traditionally the cheapest place in the city to shop. Crossing Rua Uruguaiana you arrive at the **Largo de São Francisco de Paula**, whose church, the **Igreja de São Francisco de Paula** (Mon–Fri 9am–1pm) was the site of the Mass celebrating the "swearing-in" of the Brazilian Constitution in 1831.

Rua Carioca and around

From here Rua Ramalho Ortigão leads the short distance to **Rua Carioca** (Metrô Carioca). Its square, the **Largo da Carioca**, lost many of its buildings when it was widened and improvements were made to surrounding streets, but the cloistered **Igreja e Convento de Santo Antônio** (Mon–Sat 2–5pm) survived the cut. Known as St Anthony of the Rich (to differentiate from St Anthony of the Poor, located elsewhere in the city), it's Rio's oldest church, built between 1608 and 1620.

Nova Catedral

Behind the Largo da Carioca, the unmistakeable form of the **Nova Catedral** (daily 7am–5.30pm) rises up like some futuristic teepee. Built between 1964 and 1976, it's an impressive piece of modern architecture, resembling the blunt-topped Mayan pyramids of Mexico. The cathedral is 83m high with a diameter of 104m and has a capacity of twenty-five thousand people. Inside, it feels vast, its remarkable sense of space enhanced by the absence of supporting columns. The most striking features are the four huge stained-glass windows, each measuring 20m by 60m. From outside, you'll be able to see the **Aqueduto da Carioca**, which carries trams up to Santa Teresa and the ugly Cubist-style **headquarters of Petrobrás**, the state oil company.

Cinelândia: Praça Floriano

Towards the southern end of Avenida Rio Branco, the dead-straight boulevard that cuts through the centre from north to south, you reach the area known as **Cinelândia** (Metrô Cinelândia), named for the long-gone 1930s movie houses that once peppered the streets here. The main point of interest is the impressive **Praça Floriano**. In the centre of the square is a bust of **Getúlio Vargas**, still anonymously decorated with flowers on the anniversary of the ex-dictator's birthday, March 19. At the northern end, the **Teatro Municipal** was modelled on the Paris Opera Garnier – all granite, marble and bronze, with a foyer decorated in Louis XV-style white and gold. Across the road, the **Museu Nacional das Belas Artes** (Tues–Fri 10am–6pm, Sat & Sun 2–6pm; R$5; Sun free) is a grandiose construction imitating the Louvre in Paris. The European collection includes Boudin, Tournay and Franz Post amongst many others, but it's the **Brazilian collection** that is of most interest, containing works by most of the Brazilian masters. The last building of note on the Praça Floriano is the **Biblioteca Nacional** (Mon–Fri 9am–8pm, Sat 9am–3pm), whose stairway was decorated by some of the most important artistic names of the nineteenth century, including Modesto Brocas, Eliseu Visconti, Rodolfo Amoedo and Henrique Bernadelli.

Lapa

Immediately to the south of here is *bairro* **Lapa**, a gracefully decaying neighbourhood and the beating heart of Rio's **samba scene** (see box, p.272). South along Avenida Rio Branco, it's a short walk to the **Passeio Público** park (daily 7.30am–9pm). Opened in 1783 and now a little past its best, this green oasis still possesses a faded charm – much like the rest of the neighbourhood. Beneath the shade of the trees stand busts of famous figures from the city's history, many by Mestre Valentim de Fonseca, Brazil's most important late eighteenth-century sculptor, who also figures in bust form. Besides the proliferation of samba clubs, Lapa's most recognizable feature is the eighteenth-century aqueduct known as the **Arcos de Lapa**. Built to a Roman design and consisting of 42 wide arches, in its heyday it carried water from the Rio Carioca to the thirsty citizens of the city. Today it forms part of the **tramline** running from near the Nova Catedral to *bairro* Santa Teresa.

Santa Teresa

Further west, **Santa Teresa** is a leafy *bairro* of labyrinthine, cobbled streets and steps (*ladeiras*), clinging to a hillside with stupendous views of the city and bay below. Atmospheric but slightly dishevelled early nineteenth-century mansions and walled gardens line the streets, while the resident community

SAMBA – THE SOUND OF RIO

The *bairro* of Lapa is the undisputed capital of **samba**, but you can get a flavour of Rio's quintessential sound from any number of samba **clubs** dotted around the city. These days they churn out standard tourist shows, with well-practiced performers turning out their routines to crowds of foreigners each night. Things get a bit more serious during the rehearsals for Carnaval (Sept–Jan), however, when the emphasis is on perfecting routines for the major event of the year. The main clubs are listed below with their traditional colours.

For a more authentic samba experience and an overwhelmingly local crowd, head to **Lapa** where the Avenida Mem de Sá and surrounding streets are lined with samba bars offering the real deal. Especially recommended are *Carioca da Gama* (Mon–Sat from 6pm) at Av Mem de Sá 79, and *Bar Semente* at Rua Joaquim Silva 138. Despite Lapa's vibrancy and obvious appeal, it's not safe to walk around at night here; take a taxi after dark. If you feel uncomfortable going alone, contact Rio Hiking (ⓣ21/9721-0594, ⓦwww.riohiking.com.br) who run Rio **nightlife tours** (R$170 per person, excluding drinks).

Beija-Flor Rua Pracinha Wallace Paes Leme 1652, Nilopolis ⓣ21/2253-2860, ⓦwww.beija-flor.com.br. Founded 1948; blue and white. Carnaval champions 2008.

Mangueira Rua Visconde de Niterói 1072, Mangueira ⓣ21/2567-4637, ⓦwww.mangueira.com.br. Founded 1928; green and pink.

MoÁidade Independente de Padre Miguel Rua Cel. Tamarindo 38, Padre Miguel ⓣ21/3332-5823. Founded 1952; green and white.

Portela Rua Clara Nunes 81, Madureira ⓣ21/3390-0471. Founded 1923; blue and white.

Salgueiro Rua Silva Telles 104, Tijuca ⓣ21/2238-5564, ⓦwww.salgueiro.com.br. Founded 1953; red and white.

enjoys something of a bohemian reputation. Santa Teresa is widely regarded as Rio's main artistic centre: twice a year (the last weekends in May and November) about a hundred artists open their studios, offering the public an opportunity to buy or simply to look.

Undoubtedly the most picturesque way to get to Santa Teresa is by taking the **tram**. From the Historic Centre, the line crosses the Arcos de Lapa and affords glorious panoramic views of Guanabara Bay as it climbs. En route you'll pass the *Bar do Arnaudo* (see p.281) on the right, a traditional meeting-place of artists and intellectuals. From the bar, it's an enjoyable ten-minute walk downhill to one of Rio's better museums, the **Museu Chácara do Céu** (Wed–Mon 1–5pm; ⓦwww.museuscastromaya.com.br/chacara.htm; R$2), Rua Murtinho Nobre 93, in a Modernist stone building set in its own grounds. It holds a good, eclectic collection of twentieth-century Brazilian and European art, with regularly changing displays. A pathway links the museum to the **Parque das Ruínas** (Wed–Fri & Sat 10am–10pm, Sun 10am–5pm), an attractive public garden containing the ruins of a mansion that was once home to a Brazilian heiress with her own clique of artists and intellectuals. Following her death the mansion fell into disrepair, but reopened as a cultural centre in the 1990s, housing temporary art exhibitions and evening concerts.

Glória

Southernmost of the central *bairros*, **Glória** has one major attraction that is so easily visited that it's well worth making the effort to do so. Atop the Morro da Glória, opposite the Glória Metrô station, is the eighteenth-century **Igreja de Nossa Senhora da Glória**

do Outeiro (Tues–Fri 9am–noon & 1–5pm, Sat & Sun 9am–noon). Notable for its innovative octagonal ground plan and domed roof, the latter decked with striking seventeenth-century blue-and-white *azulejos* and nineteenth-century marble masonry, this architectural gem is arguably the prettiest church in the city.

Zona Norte

Despite being somewhat run-down and largely ignored by visitors, the **Zona Norte** has a few attractions that make it worth exploring, and is easily reached from the centre: change lines at Estácio for Metrô Linha 2, which runs to the Zona Norte. Fans of the "beautiful game" may want to make the pilgrimage to the **Maracaná football stadium**, while for the more culturally-minded there's the **Museu Nacional**, one of the country's most important scientific institutions, set on a small hill in the attractive gardens of the **Quinta da Boa Vista**.

Maracaná

Football fans will not want to miss the opportunity to visit the **Maracaná** (Metrô Maracaná) – arguably the world's most famous football stadium and steeped in soccer history. With a capacity of 110,000, this monumental arena hosted the World Cup final in 1950 when, much to the disappointment of the hosts, the home nation ended up on the wrong end of a 2–1 defeat to Uruguay. Few fans realise that the real name of the stadium is actually **Estadio Mario Filho**, and that *Maracaná* is a nickname derived from the Brazilian word for a macaw and given to a nearby river. But it's not just football that earns the stadium its place in the record books. In 1991 former Beatle Paul McCartney played to a crowd of 180,000 people here, the highest ever concert attendance. If your visit doesn't coincide with a match, the stadium can still be visited – by expensive guided **tour** only (Mon–Sat 8am–5pm; R$20). Entry for stadium tours is via a side gate, not through the main entrance.

Quinta da Boa Vista

The area covered by the **Quinta da Boa Vista** (daily 5am–6pm; Metrô São Cristóvão) was once incorporated in a *sesmaria* – colonial plot of land – held by the Society of Jesus in the sixteenth and seventeenth centuries. In 1808 it became a country seat of the Portuguese royal family. The park, with its wide open expanses of greenery, tree-lined avenues, lakes, sports areas and games tables, is an excellent place for a stroll, though it can get very crowded at weekends. Looking out from a hilltop in the centre of the park is the imposing Neoclassical **Museu Nacional** (Tues–Sun 10am–4pm; Ⓦ www.museunacional.ufrj.br; R$3). Its **archeological section** deals with the human history of Latin America; in the Brazilian room, exhibits of Tupi-Guarani and Marajó ceramics lead on to the indigenous **ethnographical section**, uniting pieces collected from the numerous tribes that once populated Brazil. A display dedicated to Brazilian folklore has the emphasis on the Afro-Brazilian cults that are still prominent in modern society.

ZONA SUL

The **Zona Sul** is the principal attraction for most visitors to Rio, in no small part because of the 90km of sandy **beaches** that line its shores. The city's identity is perhaps more closely linked to the beach lifestyle than any other on earth, and the sands provide the focal point of the social lives of all of the city's six million inhabitants. The most famous of Rio's beaches are along the southern coast of the city, principally **Copacabana** and **Ipanema**, both of which have been immortalized in song, though these days **Leblon** is challenging them as the place for the beautiful people to be seen. The eastern *bairro* of **Catete** holds

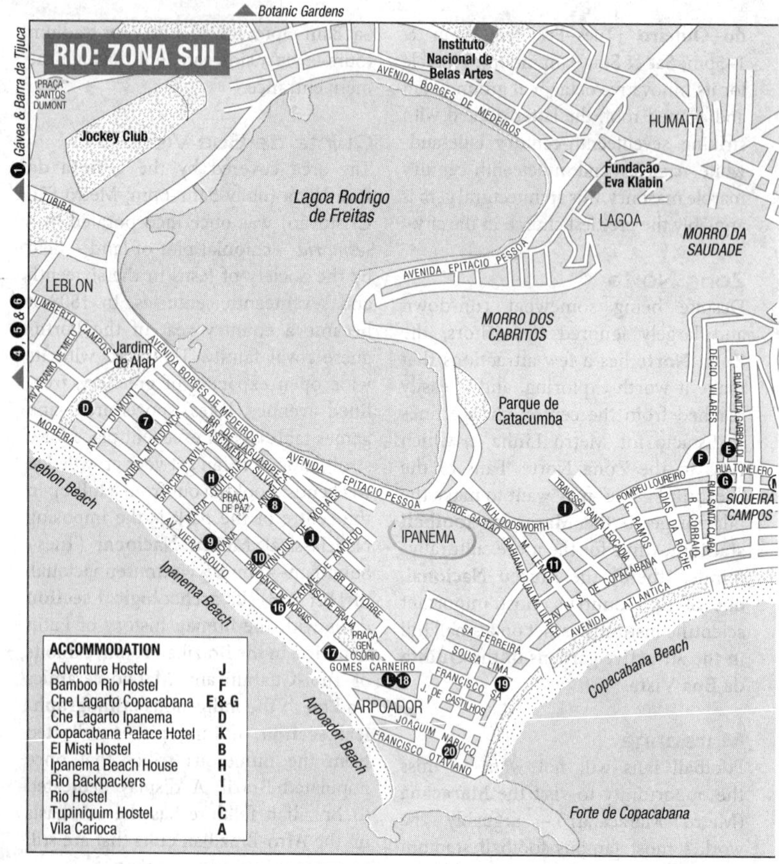

some interesting museums, whilst **Flamengo** also has its beaches, whose proximity to the centre means you may find yourself using them more than you expect. Sandwiched between here and the southern beaches are **Botafogo**, with a series of cultural attractions, and the peninsula of **Urca**, home to one of Rio's most instantly recognizable landmarks, **Sugarloaf Mountain**. Away from the coast, the area around **Lagoa** is the haunt of the rich and famous, while the **Jardím Botânico** nurtures as much real, wild forest as it does potted plants. One sight that nobody visiting Rio will want to miss is **Corcovado**, topped by the **Christ the Redeemer statue**, a powerful symbol recognizable the world over which provides heart-stoppingly glorious views over the *cidade marvilhosa*. The statue stands within the leafy expanse of the **Parque Nacional da Tijuca**.

Catete

At Rua do Catete 153, adjacent to the **Catete** Metrô station, the Palácio do Catete houses the **Museu da República** (Tues, Thurs & Fri noon–5pm, Wed 2–5pm, Sat & Sun 2–6pm; R$6; Wed free; ⓦwww.museudarepublica.org.br). The displays begin with the period of the establishment of the first Republic in 1888, though it's the opulent marble and stained glass of the building itself that make a visit so worthwhile.

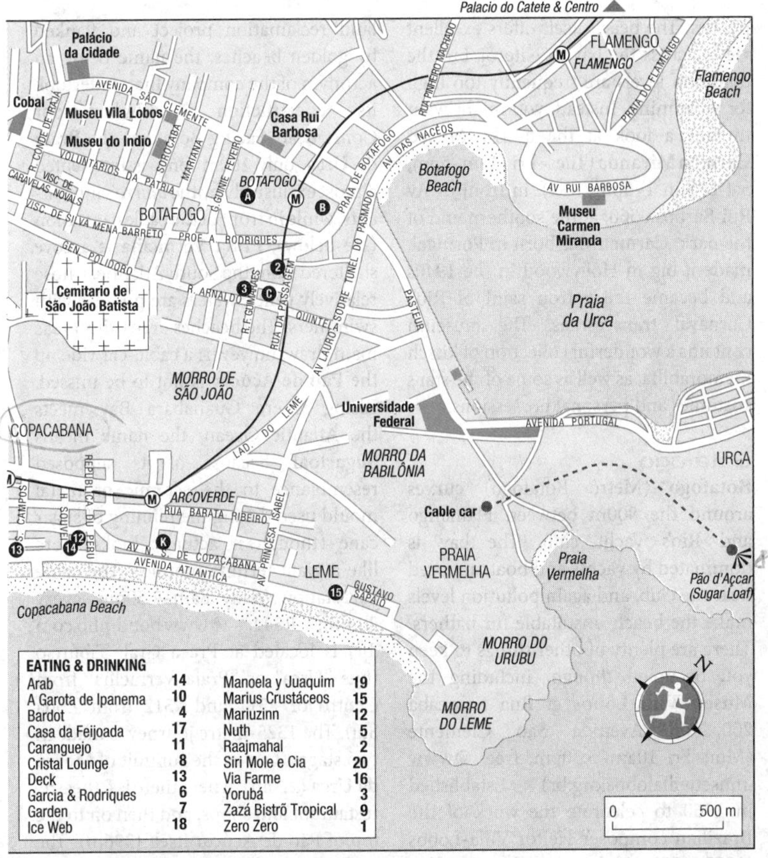

Divided between two buildings, one also inside the grounds of the Palácio do Catete, the other in an adjacent house, the **Museu de Folclore Edison Carneiro** (Tues–Fri 11am–6pm, Sat & Sun 3–6pm; R$3) is a fascinating folkloric collection that unites pieces from all over Brazil – leatherwork, musical instruments, ceramics, toys, Afro-Brazilian cult paraphernalia, photographs and votive offerings.

Flamengo

Busy during the day, the tree-lined streets of **Flamengo** are also lively after dark with residents eating in the local restaurants. There's a pleasant atmosphere in this part of town and it's tranquil enough to encourage sitting out on the pavement at the bars, beneath the palm trees. The closest **beach** to the city centre is here (Metrô Largo do Machado), and although not the best in Rio, its proximity to the centre and cheap accommodation makes it the most convenient for budget travellers. Skirting the beach as far as Botafogo Bay is the **Parque do Flamengo**. The biggest land reclamation project in Brazil, it was designed by the great Brazilian landscape architect and gardener, Roberto Burle Marx, and completed in 1960. The park comprises 1.2 square kilometres of prime seafront, popular with local residents who use it mostly for sports – there are countless tennis courts (9am–11pm) and football pitches. The beach itself offers excellent views across the bay to Niterói, but the pollution levels are frequently too high for swimming. Instead, you might want to take a look at the quirky **Museu Carmen Miranda** (Tues–Fri 11am–5pm, Sat & Sun 1–5pm; R$3), in front of Av Rui Barbosa 560, at the southern end of the park. Carmen was born in Portugal, made it big in Hollywood in the 1940s and became the patron saint of Rio's Carnaval transvestites. The museum contains a wonderful collection of kitsch memorabilia, as well as some of the star's costumes and personal possessions.

Botafogo

Botafogo (Metrô Botafogo) curves around the 800m between Flamengo and Rio's yacht club. The bay is dominated by yachts and boats moored near the club, and again pollution levels make the beach unsuitable for bathers. There are plenty of other things to keep you occupied though, including the **Museu Villa-Lobos** at Rua Sorocaba 200, off Avenida São Clemente (Mon–Fri 10am–5.30pm; free; ⓦwww.museuvillalobos.org.br). Established in 1960 to celebrate the work of the Brazilian composer Heitor Villa-Lobos (1887–1959), it's largely a display of his personal possessions and original music scores. Botafogo's other museum, the **Museu do Índio** (Tues–Fri 9am–5.30pm, Sat & Sun 1–5pm; R$3, Sun free; ⓦwww.museudoindio.org.br), lies in the next street along, at Rua das Palmeiras 55. Housed in an old colonial building, the museum boasts a broad and interesting collection, containing utensils, musical instruments, tribal costumes and ritual devices from many of Brazil's dwindling indigenous peoples, as well as an extensive library on the subject.

Urca and Sugarloaf Mountain

The small, wealthy *bairro* of **URCA** stands on a promontory formed by a land reclamation project and flanked by golden beaches, the name being an acronym of the company that undertook its construction – Urbanizador Construção. Facing Botafogo, the **Praia da Urca**, only 100m long, is frequented almost exclusively by the *bairro*'s inhabitants, while in front of the cable car station (see below), **Praia Vermelha** is a cove sheltered from the South Atlantic, whose relatively gentle waters are popular with swimmers. The beaches aren't this area's main draw, however: a cable-car ride up the **Pão de Açúcar** is not to be missed. Rising where Guanabara Bay meets the Atlantic Ocean, the name means **Sugarloaf**, because of its supposed resemblance to the ceramic or metal mould used during the refining of sugar cane (though it actually looks more like a giant termite mound). The **cable car** station (daily 8am–7.50pm; every 20min; R$44; ⓦwww.bondinho.com.br) is located at Praça Gral. Tibúrcio (bus "Urca" or "Praia Vermelha" from Centro or #511 and #512 from Zona Sul). The 1325-metre journey is made in two stages, first to the summit of **Morro da Urca** (220m), where there is a theatre, restaurant and shops, and then on to the top of Pão de Açúcar itself (396m). The cable cars have glass walls, and once on top the view is as glorious as you could imagine. Facing inland, you can see right over the city; look towards the cable car terminal, and to the left you'll see the sweep of Copacabana and Ipanema. Try to avoid the busiest times of day, between 10am and 3pm.

18-21

Copacabana and Leme

Leme and **Copacabana** are different stretches of the same 4km beach. The **Praia do Leme** extends for a kilometre, between the Morro do Leme and Avenida Princesa Isabel, by the *Meridien Hotel*, where the security on the beach in front means it is a safe place to park your towel. From here, the **Praia de Copacabana** runs a further 3km to the military-owned **Forte de Copacabana**. Immortalized in song by Barry Manilow, the beach is amazing, right down to its over-the-top mosaic pavements, designed by Burle Marx to mimic rolling waves. The seafront is backed by a line of prestigious, high-rise hotels and luxury apartments that have sprung up since the 1940s, while a steady stream of noisy traffic clogs the two-lane **Avenida Atlântica**. Copacabana was originally an isolated area, cut off from the city by mountains, until 1892 when the Túnel Velho link with **Botafogo** was inaugurated. The open sea and strong waves soon attracted surfers, but its reputation did not grow until the *Copacabana Palace Hotel*, one of Rio's finest, opened its doors in 1923. A steady stream of famous guests made the beach the place to be seen and alerted enterprising souls to the commercial potential of the area. The area of beach in front of the hotel is now Copacabana's gay section. It's worth bearing in mind that a strong undercurrent at Copacabana means that it is dangerous even for strong swimmers – don't do anything the locals don't do. Another problem is theft: take only the money and clothes that you will need.

Arpoador, Ipanema and Leblon

On the other side of the point from Forte de Copacabana, the lively waters off the **Arpoador** are popular with families and the elderly as the ocean here is slightly calmer than at Ipanema. The name means "harpooner" in Portuguese, in reference to the whalers who used to gather here to hunt the whales that came to breed in the warm waters. From here, as far as the unkempt and balding greenery of the **Jardim de Alah**, a couple of kilometres away, you're in **Ipanema**; thereafter lies **Leblon**. More laid-back than Copacabana, the beaches here are stupendous, and aside from a few stalls selling fresh coconuts there's not much in the way of bars and restaurants. As with Copacabana, Ipanema's beach is unofficially divided according to the particular interests of beach users. The stretch of sand east from Rua Farme de Amoedo to Rua Teixeira de Melo is where gay men are concentrated, while posto 9 is where artists and intellectuals gather. On Sunday, the seafront roads – Avenida Vieira Souto in Ipanema, Avenida Delfim Moreira in Leblon – are closed to traffic, and given over to strollers, skateboarders and rollerbladers. Since the 1960s, Ipanema has developed a reputation as a fashion centre, purveying the very best names in fine threads. Try to visit on a Friday to take in the large **food and flower market** on the Praça de Paz.

Gávea

North of Leblon is **Gávea**, home of the **Jockey Club**, on the shores of Lagoa

THE GIRL FROM IPANEMA

One of the classic bossa nova songs, **The Girl from Ipanema** achieved worldwide success in the 1960s. Written in 1962 by Antonio Carlos Jobim with lyrics by Vinicius de Moraes, it was inspired by fifteen year-old local girl Heloisa Paez Pinto who would pass each morning on her way to the beach in front of the **Veloso Bar** where the composers were regulars. These days the original bar has been renamed *A Garota de Ipanema* (the Portuguese title of the song) and can be found at Rua Vinicius de Moraes 49 (see p.281) – changed from Rua Montenegro in honour of the lyricist. The popularity of the song led to the formation of a local chain of bars, so there's a sprinkling of *A Garota de Ipanemas* around the city, as well as a theme park of the same name at Arpoador. Heloisa posed as a *Playboy* playmate in 1987 and 2003 – at the age of 58 – and now runs a chain of fashion stores (one next door to the bar, at Rua Vinicius de Moraes 53). No prizes for guessing the name.

(see below). **Races** take place four times a week, throughout the year (Mon 6.30–11.30pm, Fri 4–9.30pm, Sat & Sun 2–8pm; shorts not allowed). On alternate weekends throughout the year, part of the club is taken over by an arts and crafts market, the **Babilônia Feira Hype** (2–11pm; R$3). Apart from the clothes, jewellery and handicrafts on sale, there are food stalls and music and dance performances. Any bus marked "via Jóquei" will get you here; get off at Praça Santos Dumont at the end of Rua Jardim Botânico. About 3km northwest of the Jockey Club, at Rua Marquês de São Vicente 476, is the **Instituto Moreira Salles** (Tues–Sun 1–8pm; ⓣ21/3284-7400, ⓦwww.ims.com.br; free), one of Rio's most beautiful cultural centres. Completed in 1951, the house is stunningly beautiful – one of the finest examples of Modernist domestic architecture in Brazil – and the gardens, landscaped by Roberto Burle Marx, are attractive too.

Lagoa and Jardim Botânico

Inland from Ipanema's plush beaches is the Lagoa Rodrigo de Freitas, always referred to simply as **Lagoa**. A lagoon linked to the ocean by a narrow canal that passes through Ipanema's Jardim de Alah, Lagoa is fringed by apartment buildings, where Rio's richest, most status-conscious inhabitants live. On Sundays, the 7.5km perimeter pathway that surrounds the lagoon comes alive with strollers, rollerbladers, joggers and cyclists. Summer evenings are especially popular, with food stalls, live music and *forró* dancing on the west side of the lagoon in the Parque dos Patins (Skaters' Park). To the northwest of the Lagoa lies **Jardim Botânico** *bairro*, whose **Parque Lage** (daily 8am–5pm; ⓦwww.eavparquelage.org.br), designed by the English landscape gardener John Tyndale in the early 1840s, consists of fifty hectares of forest, with a labyrinthine network of paths and seven small lakes. A little further along the Rua Jardim Botânico, at no.1008, is the **Jardim Botânico** itself (daily 8am–5pm; ⓦwww.jbrj.gov.br; R$4), half of it natural jungle, the other half laid out in impressive avenues lined with immense imperial palms that date from the garden's inauguration in 1808. A number of sculptures are dotted throughout the garden, notably the Greek mythology-inspired *Ninfa do Eco* and *Caçador Narciso* (1783) by Mestre Valentim, the first two metal sculptures cast in Brazil.

Corcovado and Christ the Redeemer

The unmistakable **statue of Cristo Redentor**, gazing across the bay from the **CORCOVADO** ("hunchback") hill with arms outstretched in welcome, or as if preparing for a dive into the waters below, is synonymous with Río de Janeiro. The immense statue – 30m high and weighing over 1000 metric tons – was scheduled for completion in 1922 as part of Brazil's centenary independence celebrations. In fact, it wasn't finished until nine years later. In clear weather, it's every bit as awe-inspiring as you'd imagine: the journey up to the statue is a stunning experience by day, and even more breathtaking by night. Keep an eye on the weather, however: what ought to be one of Rio's highlights can turn into a great disappointment if the Corcovado is hidden by cloud. By day the whole of Rio and Guanabara Bay is laid out magnificently before you; after dark, the flickering city lights of this vast metropolis create a stunning visual effect far more impressive than any artificial light show, enhanced by your position at Jesus's feet. The easiest way to reach the statue is by the **Corcovado cog train** (daily every 30min 8.30am–6.30pm; ⓦwww.corcovado.com.br; R$55 return), which leaves from the station at Rua Cosme Velho 513 (take a bus marked "Cosme

Velho" from the centre). It proceeds slowly upwards, chugging through lush forest as it enters the **Parque Nacional da Tijuca** (see below), giving frustratingly brief glimpses of the view that awaits you at the top. Cars (including taxis) can only go as far as **Paineiras**, about halfway up the mountain, at which point you must switch to a shuttle bus or the train. Walking is not to be recommended: besides the fact that it's an extremely long and steep climb, there are frequent reports of robberies along the trail.

Parque Nacional da Tijuca

The mountains running southwest from the Corcovado are covered with exuberant forest, representing the periphery of the 120-square-kilometre **Parque Nacional da Tijuca** (daily 7am–9pm; ⓣ21/2492-2252; free). The park offers sixteen walking trails and some excellent views of Rio, and makes an appealing retreat from the city for a few hours. The park's trails are steep and not for the unfit, but if you have the energy for an all-day climb, you can trek all the way to the **Pico do Papagaio** (975m) or **Pico da Tijuca** (1021m) – peaks in the far north of the forest, above the popular picnic spot known as **Bom Retiro**.

Arrival

Air Rio de Janeiro is serve[illegible] central Santos Dumont (ⓣ[illegible] regional flights, and Gale[illegible] (ⓣ21/3398-5050), 15k[illegible] Frequent buses link the [illegible] and city centre – there's no nee[illegible] over-priced taxis.

Bus Buses arrive at the Novo Rio *rodoviária* (ⓣ21/3213-1800), 3km north of the centre at Av Francisco Bicalho. The central Menezes Cortes *rodoviária* on Rua São José (ⓣ21/2533-8819) handles services from some in-state towns, as well as buses to and from the suburbs and Zona Sul.

Information and tour operators

Tourist information Riotur's main office is next to the Igreja Candelaria on Praça Pio X at the northern end of Av 1 de Março (Mon–Fri 9am–6pm; ⓣ21/2004-0020). Alô Rio is an English-speaking telephone information service (daily 8am–8pm; ⓣ0800/282-2007).

Tours Favela Tours run responsible, community-approved trips to Favela Roçinha (ⓣ21/3322-2727, ⓦwww.favelatour.com.br). Heli Rio offers helicopter trips over the city for a bird's-eye view of the attractions (ⓣ21/2437-9064, ⓦwww.helirio.com.br). Rio Hiking offers a variety of hiking trips around the city and state, as well as nightlife tours and adventure sports (ⓣ21/9721-0594, ⓦwww.riohiking.com.br).

PARK PRACTICALITIES

There is no convenient public transport to the park, which is most easily visited if you have your own car or by taxi. Alternatively, take the Metrô to Saens Peña at the end of Linha 1 and jump any bus marked "Barrio de Tijuca", asking to be let off at **Alta de Boa Vista** – a short distance from one of the seven park entrances. An easier, if more expensive option is to join a **tour** run by Rio Hiking (ⓣ21/9721-0594, ⓦwww.riohiking.com.br), who organize hikes for small groups. For a bird's-eye view take a tandem **hang-glider** flight from the Pedra Bonita ramp on the western edge of the park. The most experienced and reliable operator, Just Fly (ⓣ21/2268-0565; ⓦwww.justfly.com.br; R$240), offers daily flights (10am–3pm) when weather permits. The price includes pick-up and drop-off from your hotel.

None of the **park entrances** are particularly conveniently located. One approach is via the Cosme Velho *bairro*, near the **Entrada dos Caboclos**, following Estrada Heitor da Silva Costa; another is on Rua Leão Pacheco, which runs up the side of the Jardim Botânico (off Rua Jardim Botânico) to the **Entrada dos Macacos** and on to the **Vista Chinesa** from where there's a marvellous view of Guanabara Bay and the Zona Sul.

transport

Buses are frequent and run till midnight. umbers and destinations are clearly marked on the front of buses. Get on at the back and pay the seated conductor.

Ferries The 30min crossings from the ferry terminal at Praça XV de Novembro to Niterói (see p.284) are very frequent and cost from R$2. Transtur (☎21/2533-4343) operates hydrofoils to Niterói every 15min from 6.35am to 9pm; the journey takes 10min.

Metrô Rio's Metrô runs Mon–Sat 5am–midnight, Sun 7am–11pm. Tickets are sold as singles (*ida*; R$2.60), returns (*duplo*; R$5.20) or ten-journey carnets (*dez*; R$26).

Taxis Rio's taxis come in two varieties: yellow with a blue stripe which cruise the streets; or the larger, more comfortable radio cabs, white and with a red and yellow stripe, which you order by phone. Both have meters and you should insist that they are activated. Taxis from the *rodoviária* have a fixed price; pick up a ticket at the booth.

Trams Rio's last remaining electric trams, the *bondes* (pronounced "bonjis"), climb from near Largo de Carioca, across the eighteenth-century Aqueduto da Carioca, to the suburb of Santa Teresa and on to Dois Irmãos. Two lines run every 15min between 5am and midnight; tickets cost R$0.60

Accommodation

Rio is by no means cheap, and during Carnaval (when you should book well in advance) you can expect to pay way over the odds for even the most basic rooms. That said, a proliferation of **youth hostels** have opened up in recent years, catering to an increasingly large crowd of budget travellers looking for an alternative to the pricey hotels. If you're looking for a more authentic *carioca* experience, get in touch with *Cama e Café* (Mon–Fri 9am–5pm, Sat & Sun 9am–4pm; ☎21/2225-4336, ⓦwww.camaecafe.com). Located inside the Cine Santa at Largo dos Guimarães, Santa Teresa, they can provide details of rooms with local families, and cater for all budgets.

Centro, Lapa and Santa Teresa

There is little in the way of accommodation in the historic centre itself – you're better off heading to the nearby *bairros* of Lapa and Santa Teresa where there's a good selection of well-located and affordable hotels.

Formule I Rua Silva Jardim, Centro ☎21/3511-8500, ⓦwww.formule1.com.br. Opposite the *Rio Hotel* (see below), but a world away in terms of service and facilities – and in price. ⑤

Marajó Rua São Joaquim da Silva 99, Lapa ☎21/2224-4134. Excellent choice for budget travellers not keen on the hostel scene. Modern facilities, clean, spacious rooms and friendly service in a vibrant area of town – though it can be a little noisy at times. ④

Rio Hostel Rua Joaquim Murtinho 361, Santa Teresa ☎21/3852-0827, ⓦwww.riohostel.com. Not to be confused with the central *Rio Hotel* (below), this is a cool backpacker hangout for bohemian types, with a pool and a great bar serving *caipirinhas* until dawn. For every seven nights, you get one night free. Dorm R$37. ⑤

Rio Hotel Rua Silva Jardim 3, Centro ☎21/2282-1213. Crusty, peeling and just on the acceptable side of basic, this is a very central choice for hardcore budget travellers, within spitting distance of the major attractions of the area. Don't be fooled by the attractive facade – the rooms are sadly neglected. ④

Trip Hostel Rua Joaquim Murtinho 514, Santa Teresa ☎21/2507-0916, ⓦwww.triphostel.com. The second youth hostel on this street, *Trip Hostel* is located in an atmospheric nineteenth-century building with a terrace, set in wooded surroundings in the heart of the Santa Teresa arts district. The *bondinho* tram line passes right in front of the hostel. ⑤

Villa Rica Rua Conde de Lages 2, Lapa ☎21/2232-2983, ⓦwww.hotelvillarica.com.br. One of the more upmarket options in this area, with well-equipped rooms with free wi-fi access. ⑤

Botafogo

The options in Botafogo are well located for both the centre and the southern beaches and benefit from being in quiet, safe neighbourhoods.

El Misti Hostel Rua Praiado Botafogo 462 ☎21/2226-0991, ⓦwww.elmistihostel.com. Close to the Botafogo Metrô station and convenient for the beach, this hostel offers a variety of clean dorms and double rooms – the more people that fit into the dorms the lower the cost. Great breakfasts too. Dorm R$29. ⑥

Tupiniquim Hostel Rua Sao Manuel 19 ☎21/3826-0522, ⓦwww.tupiniquimhostel.com.br. Billed as an alternative hostel for alternative people, there's no denying the facilities offered at this place, which range from broadband internet and a pool table to a bar and BBQ terrace. Great value, but fills fast. Dorm R$28–35. ⑤

Vila Carioca Rua Estacio Coimbra 84 ☎21/2535-3224, ⓦwww.vilacarioca.com.br. Small and friendly hostel with neat, balconied dorm rooms and a patio for chilling out. There's internet access too, and adventure excursions with reliable operators can be booked here. Dorm R$35. ❻

Copacabana

Accommodation is expensive in Copacabana, but easy access to some of the world's best beaches might make it worth those extra few *reais*.

Bamboo Rio Hostel Rua Lacerda Coutinho 45 ⓣ21/2236-1117, ⓦwwwbamboorio.com. Three blocks from the beach in a quiet, leafy suburb, *Bamboo Rio* is a new hostel with refreshingly colourful, a/c rooms, a good pool (though not exactly the spa they like to call it) and a pleasant garden with wild monkeys. Great value, considering the facilities. Dorm R$30–39. ❻

Che Lagarto Youth Hostel Rua Anita Garibaldi 87 ⓣ21/2256-2778 & Rua Santa Clara 305 ⓣ21/2257-3133, ⓦwww.chelagarto.com. Two branches of this, the most established chain of youth hostels in Rio, are in Copacabana, with a third in Ipanema (see below). Standard hostelling stuff. Dorm R$36–40. ❻

Rio Backpackers Travessa Santa Leocádia 38 ⓣ21/2236-3803, ⓦwww.riobackpackers.com.br. One of the cheaper hostels in the area, but that's not to say it doesn't have all the facilities you'd expect from a top-class hostel. Some rooms are a little cramped, but given the price and location there's no room for complaints. Dorm R$30. ❺

Ipanema

Accommodation is even more expensive in Ipanema than in Copacabana, but there are plenty of hostels to choose from if you can't stand the thought of public transport eating into your sunbathing time.

Adventure Hostel Rua Vinicius de Moraes 174 ⓣ21/3813-2726, ⓦwww.adventurehostel.com.br. Don't let the name put you off: this is a well-maintained HI hostel and whilst they don't have many beds, the rooms are spacious. Dorm R$45.

Che Lagarto Youth Hostel Rua Paul Redfearn 48 ⓣ21/2512-8076, ⓦwww.chelagarto.com. In the same chain and along the same lines as the Copacabana hostels (see above). More expensive though, and can get noisy with the bouncing *Bar Code Pub* on the ground floor. Dorm R$43. ❻

Ipanema Beach House Rua Barão da Torre 485 ⓣ21/3202-2693, ⓦwww.ipanemahouse.com. Despite the word "beach" figuring in the name, it's actually three blocks back from the waterfront, but this is a friendly and welcoming hostel with a laid-back atmosphere and hippy-chic rooms. Dorm R$45. ❼

Rio Hostel Rua Canning 18 ⓣ21/2287-2928, ⓦwww.riohostel.com. Another branch of this backpackers' favourite (see opposite). Dorm R$37. ❺

Eating and drinking

As you might expect, Rio offers a huge variety of exotic cuisines to discerning diners. In general, eating out is pricey, especially in Copacabana, Ipanema and anywhere with a sea view.

Centro and Lapa

Bar Luiz Rua Carioca 39, Centro. This manic, but essentially run-of-the-mill, restaurant and bar, serving German-style food and ice-cold *chopp*, was founded in 1887 and is considered quite an institution. Still a popular meeting place for journalists and intellectuals. Try the *bolinhos de bacalao* (R$25). Closed Sun.

Café do Teatro Praça Floriano, Centro. Richly adorned with Assyrian-inspired mosaics, this café inside the Teatro Municipal is a decent place to take a break from sightseeing. Mon–Fri 11am–4pm.

Cosmopolita Travessa do Mosqueira 4, Lapa. An excellent Portuguese restaurant established in 1926 with a loyal, rather bohemian, clientele. Fish dishes are the firm favourites here. Try *lulas con arroz e broccolis* (squid with rice and broccoli; R$33.90). Closed Sun.

Manaita Rua de Ouvidor. Japanese *rodizio*, with buffet sushi (R$42) or more expensive à la carte options in faux-Japanese surroundings. Closed Sun.

Penafiel Rua Senhor dos Passos 121. Superb – and inexpensive – Portuguese dishes have been served here since 1912. Fish dishes and stews (such as bean, tongue and tripe) are the speciality. Lunch only; closed Sat & Sun.

Pilão de Pedra Rua Carioca 53. Just up from *Bar Luiz*, this place is hugely popular with office workers who take advantage of the extensive buffet of eighty different dishes for cheap eats. Buffet R$12.90 per kg.

Santa Teresa

Adega do Pimenta Rua Almirante Alexandrino 296. Moderately priced German cooking – most people go for the sausage and sauerkraut, but the duck with red cabbage is excellent. From R$25 for a dish. Closed Mon.

Bar do Arnaudo Rua Almirante Alexandrino 316. An excellent mid-priced place to sample traditional food from Brazil's northeast, such as *carne do sol* (sun-dried meat), *macaxeira* (sweet cassava) and *pirão de bode* (goat meat soup). Closed Mon all day Sat & Sun from 8pm .

Sobrenatural Rua Almirante Alexandrino 432. Basically a fish restaurant, where the highlights are the *moquecas* and the catch of the day. With deliberately rustic decor, this is an inviting place for a leisurely meal. Closed Mon.

Flamengo and Botafogo

Huasi Rua Barão do Flamengo 35D, Flamengo. If you won't get to Peru this is a chance to try their unusual cuisine. It's a novel experience, but there is no guinea-pig on the menu. Try *quinhua com mani*, a creamy vegetarian dish with peanuts (R$23).

Lamas Rua Marquês de Abrantes 18, Flamengo. This 130-year-old restaurant serves well-prepared Brazilian food (the *Oswaldo Aranha* steak, pan fried with lots of garlic, is a popular choice) to artist and journalist types. Always busy, with a vibrant atmosphere, *Lamas* is a good example of middle-class *carioca* tradition, and highly recommended. Open until 4am.

Majórica Rua Senador Vergueiro 11–15, Flamengo. A long-established, better-than-average place for a meaty feast – the *picanha especial* (special rump steak) is the favourite. If you're not in the mood for beef, try the excellent grilled trout (R$22).

Raajmahal Rua Gral. Polidoro 29, Botafogo, ⓣ21/2541-1117, ⓦwww.raajmahal.com.br. One of the city's very few Indian restaurants, decked out with silks, statues, lamps and low-set tables. The menu appears expensive but prices are for two and portions are more than ample. Dishes from R$70.

Yorubá Rua Arnaldo Quintela 94, Botafogo ⓣ21/2541-9387. Friendly restaurant serving up moderately priced Bahian cooking with strong African influences in an attractive setting. Service is slow, but the *bobó* (a dish based on *mandioca* purée), *moquecas* and other Bahian specialities are well worth the wait. Sun lunch only, closed Mon & Tues; .

Copacabana

Arab Av Atlântica 1936. One of the very few good restaurants on Av Atlântica, this is a reasonably priced Lebanese restaurant where you can opt for a cold beer and snack on the terrace or a full meal inside (the *por kilo* lunch is excellent value). Though the menu is rather heavy on meat dishes, vegetarians won't go hungry.

Caranguejo Rua Barata Ribeiro 771, corner of Rua Xavier da Silveira. Excellent, inexpensive seafood – especially the *caranguejo* (crab, from R$30) – served in an utterly unpretentious environment packed with locals and tourists alike. Closed Mon.

Deck Av Atlântica 2316, corner of Rua Siqueira Campos. This always-busy restaurant serves an all-you-can-eat Brazilian buffet for just R$10 per person. There are also à la carte choices including the delicious *rodizio de galeto* (mouthwatering thyme-and-garlic chicken with polenta fried in palm oil) and all-you-can-eat pasta for R$10. Closes 5pm.

Manoela y Juaquim Av Atlântica. Fun menu of seafood and meat on the beachfront (though the wrong side of the avenue). Very reasonably priced for the area, and outdoor tables allow you to soak up Copacabana's unique atmosphere. Give the bizarrely-named yucca and shredded-beef jerk balls a try for R$12.50.

Siri Mole e Cia Rua Francisco Otaviano 50 ⓣ21/2267-0894. A rarity in Rio: an excellent Bahian restaurant, serving beautifully presented dishes (many of them spicy) in an upmarket, yet comfortable, setting. Inside, the restaurant is quite formal, but there are also a few tables outside where you can munch on *acarajé* and other Bahian snacks. Mon 6pm–midnight, Tues–Sun noon–midnight.

Ipanema, Leblon and Leme

A Garota de Ipanema Rua Vinicius de Moraes 49, Ipanema, ⓦwww.garotaipanema.com.br. More of interest for its historical value as the bar frequented by the composers of "The Girl from Ipanema" (see box, p.277), it has capitalized on the success of the song. Famed for its ice-cold beers, but the food's not bad either – though obviously not cheap. Try the *peixe a Garota* (R$35).

Casa da Feijoada Rua Prudente de Morais 10, Ipanema. *Feijoada*, traditionally served only on Sat, is available seven days a week here, along with other classic, moderately priced and extremely filling Brazilian dishes, from R$20.

Garcia & Rodriques Av Ataulfo de Paiva 1251, Leblon. A foodie's paradise: although the French restaurant is unimaginative and stuffy, there's also an excellent bistro, wine shop, ice-cream parlour, bakery and deli. This is one of the few places in Rio where you can buy good bread and there's an excellent choice of take-out salads and other prepared meals. Dishes from R$30. Open Sun–Fri 8am–midnight, Sat 8am–1am.

Garden Rua Visconde de Pirajá 631, Ipanema. A small restaurant that tries hard to be posh, located where Ipanema becomes Leblon. Try the trout stuffed with salmon (R$29.50). Closed Mon.

Ice Web Rua Visconde de Pirajá 37, Ipanema. An ice-cream parlour and internet café hybrid, with ice cream at R$4.60 per kg.

Marius Crustáceos Av Atlântica 290, Leme ⓣ21/2543-6363. The place to come for oysters, crabs, crayfish, prawns and other seafood. The menu is varied, though Italian-Brazilian cuisine dominates and there is a pricey all-you-can-eat seafood option for R$115.

Via Farme Rua Farme de Amoedo 47, Ipanema. Good Italian food – especially the pizzas and seafood. Choose from a/c dining upstairs or open-air downstairs. Not cheap, but reasonable for the area and one of a number of restaurants on this block. Try *ravioli alla caprese* for R$21.

Zazá Bistrô Tropical Rua Joana Angelica 40, Ipanema. Unique, kitsch, South Asian bistro where there's always something different going on. Downstairs is relatively traditional, upstairs is all cushions, rugs and low Moroccan tables where you are invited to kick off your shoes, lay back and enjoy the food. There are inventive cocktails and tropical fruit juices too.

Clubs

Rio's vibrant personality is reflected in its nightlife and there's a lively **club** scene, largely located in the Zona Sul. Most clubs play a mix of English-language dance, techno and rock, interspersed with Brazil's own unique musical styles including samba and MPB (*Música Popular Brasileira*). Most places don't really get going until close to midnight, but continue on until sunrise. An entry fee of R$10–20 (more at weekends) is usually charged.

Bardot Rua Dias Ferreira 247, Leblón ⓣ21/2247-8220. Small, New York-style club with a great atmosphere for a slightly more mature crowd.

Cristal Lounge Rua Barão de Torre 334, Ipanema ⓣ21/2247-8220, ⓦwww.cristallounge.com.br. New, chic and stylish, this club has three floors, with a huge dancefloor on the first. The funk and hip-hop bias guarantees a packed dancefloor. Over-21s only.

Mariuzinn Av Copacabana 435, Copacabana. Copacabana's oldest and most established disco, and still one of the hottest nightspots in the area. A casual affair, attracting an alternative crowd, with Wed nights set aside for sensual *lambada,* with single *cariocas* looking to end their night as a couple.

Nuth Av Armando Lombardi 999, Barra da Tijuca. On the outskirts of the city, this is one of the most popular clubs in Rio and one of the few places you should aim to get to early – the queues are huge and it's packed throughout the week, even on Sun. Mon are for over-40s; the rest of the week it's taken over by the beach crowd.

Zero Zero Av Padre Leonel Franca 240, Gávea ⓣ21/2540-8041. One of the city's trendiest clubs, frequented by a rich and trendy crowd. Some of Brazil's top DJs play an eclectic mix of music with the emphasis on drum'n'bass. Over-25s only.

Gay and lesbian nightlife

Rio's gay nightlife is perhaps surprisingly discreet, and clubbers of all persuasions tend to share the same venues. Most of the action is around the beaches of the Zona Sul, especially on Rua Farme de Amoedo in Ipanema, but also popular is Sul Rua Visconde Silva in Botafogo, which is lined with numerous gay and lesbian cafés, bars and restaurants. Gay Kiosk Rainbow on Avenida Atlântica, at the junction with Rua Siqueira Campos, is a summer-time information point for gay visitors – ask about circuit parties, usually held in Centro. For up-to-date information on the scene check out ⓦwww.riogaylife.com and http://riogayguide.com.

Bofetada Rua Farme de Amoedo 87, Ipanema. The post-beach gay crowd heads to this bar and restaurant to wind down and gear up for the night's frivolities. One of several gay-friendly options on this street.

Le Boy Rua Raul Pompéia 102, Copacabana ⓣ21/2513-4993, ⓦwww.leboy.com.br. Well-established and hugely popular gay nightclub with a vast interior with dancefloors, drag shows and much more besides. Particularly lively on Sun nights. Closed Mon.

Cine Ideal Rua Carioca 64, Centro ⓣ21/2221-1984. This trendy gay club in a former cinema has an open-air terrace and mezzanine, making it ideally suited to Rio's steamy summer nights. Fri & Sat only.

Dama de Ferro Rua Vinicius de Moraes 288, Ipanema ⓣ21/2247-2330. On two floors, with a gallery, lounge and nightclub forming an unlikely ensemble. Closed Mon & Tues.

Foxfobox Rua Siquiera Campos 140-22a, Copacabana. Located in a converted basement, this trendy small club plays underground (literally), techno and alternative music to an animated crowd. Closed Mon–Wed.

Moving on

By air Aeroporto Santos-Dumont handles flights to Sao Paulo and other nearby regional cities. The international airport is Aeroporto Galeão (or Aeroporto António Carlos Jobim). Destinations include: Asunción (3 daily; 3hr); Brasilia (hourly; 2hr); Buenos Aires (12 daily; 3–4hr); London (7 daily; 13–15hr); Madrid (6 daily; 11hr); Miami (12 daily; 8–10hr); Paris (4 daily; 11–14hr); Porto Alegre (hourly, 2–3hr); Santiago (12 daily; 5–8hr).

By bus Local buses #127 and #128 link Copacabana, Centro and Ipanema with the *rodoviária*, while #172 connects it with Botafogo, Gloria and Flamengo. Inter-city services fill up fast, so it's wise to book a couple of days in advance if you don't want to be disappointed. Rio is linked by bus to almost every major city in Brazil and neighbouring countries including: Belo Horizonte (hourly; 7hr), Florianópolis (8 daily; 18hr), Foz do Iguassu (5 daily; 22hr), Porto Alegre (8 daily; 26hr), São Paulo (every 15min; 6hr).

Directory

Banks and exchange Main bank branches are concentrated in Av Rio Branco in Centro and Av N.S. de Copacabana in Copacabana.
Car rental Avis, Av Princesa Isabel 150, Copacabana ⓣ21/2542-3392; Hertz, Av Princesa Isabel 334, Copacabana ⓣ21/2275-3245 & 800/701-7300; Localiza-National, Av Princesa Isabel 214, Copacabana ⓣ800/99-2000. Prices start at about $40 per day and you'll need a credit card to rent the car.
Consulates Argentina, Praia de Botafogo 228, Botafogo ⓣ21/2553-1646; Australia, Rua Rio Branco 1, Centro ⓣ21/2518-3351; Canada, Rua Lauro Müller 116, Botafogo ⓣ21/2542-9297; UK, Praia do Flamengo 284, 2nd floor, Flamengo ⓣ21/2553-9600; US, Av Presidente Wilson 147, Centro ⓣ21/2292-7117.
Hospitals English-speakers should try a private clinic such as Sorocaba Clinic, Rua Sorocaba 464, Botafogo (ⓣ21/2286-0022) or Centro Médico Ipanema, Rua Anibal Mendonça 135, Ipanema (ⓣ21/2239-4647). For non-emergencies, Rio Health Collective has a free phone-in service (ⓣ21/3325-9300, ext 44) providing details of doctors who speak foreign languages.
Police Emergency number ⓣ190. The beach areas have police posts at regular intervals. The efficient, English-speaking Tourist Police are at Av Afrânio de Melo Franco (opposite the Teatro Casa Grande), Leblon (ⓣ21/3399-7170).
Post office Central branch on Rua 1 de Março (Mon–Fri 8am–noon & 2pm–6pm and Sat 8am–1pm).
Shopping As one of the trendiest cities in South America, Rio is replete with high-class shopping malls and designer stores. Budget shoppers however should head to **Saara** (see p.270) where quality goods are available at reasonable prices. One of the best and certainly amongst the most charismatic **markets** in the city is the Hippie Fair, held every Sun at Praça General Osório in Ipanema, where souvenirs, street shows and typical foods could easily take up a full day of your time. For traditional handicrafts check out Brasil & Cia, Rua Maria Quitéria in Ipanema.

Río de Janeiro state

The draw of its glorious capital city is often so strong for travellers that the urge to dash through the state to get there can be difficult to resist. However, Rio state holds enough attractions to more than reward the visitor willing to devote the time to explore it. Either side of Rio lie two idyllic sections of coast: the **Costa do Sol** to the east, beyond almost suburban **Niterói**, and to the south the unspoilt **Costa Verde**. Both are dotted with charming resort towns and blessed with dreamy stretches of deserted beach. On the Costa Verde the town of **Paraty** is one of the region's best-kept secrets, while **Ilha Grande**'s verdant forests create a stunning setting for sunbathers. The Costa do Sol's main resort is the trendy and increasingly commercial town of **Búzios**, popular with the rich and famous but less of a draw for budget travellers. Inland, the state becomes suddenly mountainous, the forested peaks of the **Serra dos Orgãos** rising suddenly, at times cloaked in a mist that enhances the feeling of heading into the unknown. Gateways to this region include the historic towns of **Teresópolis** and **Petrópolis**, both with a distinctly cooler and more humid climate than the coast. Lovers of the great outdoors will not want to miss the state's two famous national parks, **Serra dos Orgãos** and, in the far west, **Itatiaia**. The TurisRio **state tourist office** is at Mexico 125 in Rio (Mon–Fri 9am–6pm; ⓣ21/2544-7992; ⓦwww.turisrio.rj.gov.br).

NITERÓI

Cariocas have a tendency to sneer at **NITERÓI**, typically commenting that the best thing about the city is the view back across Guanabara Bay to Rio. On a clear day, the views are undeniably gorgeous – but Niterói's appeal doesn't stop there.

What to see and do

The Oscar Niemeyer-designed **Museu de Arte Contemporânea**, or MAC (Tues–Sun 10am–5pm; R$4; ⓦwww.macniteroi.com.br) is Niterói's biggest draw. Opened in 1996, and located just south of the centre on a promontory by the Praia da Boa Viagem, the spaceship-like building offers 360-degree views of Niterói and across the bay to Rio. MAC boasts a worthy, though hardly exciting, permanent display of Brazilian art from the 1950s to the 1990s, and also hosts temporary exhibitions, but the real work of art is the building itself, which even hardened critics of Niemeyer find it difficult to dismiss. The curved lines of the building are simply beautiful, and the views of the headland, nearby beaches and Guanabara Bay as you walk around inside it breath-taking. The town's largest beach is the **Praia de Icaraí**.

Arrival and information

Bus #999 from the Menezes Cortes bus terminal runs to Niterói.

Car You arrive in Niterói via the 14km of the Ponte Costa e Silva, the Rio–Niterói bridge.

Ferry An atmospheric way to get to Niterói is via ferry or hydrofoil (see p.280). Although MAC is just 1.5km from the ferry terminal, take a taxi, as tourists have been robbed along the route.

Tourist office Estrada Leopoldo Froes 773 (ⓦwww.neltur.com.br, ⓣ0800/202-7755).

Eating

While you're unlikely to feel the need to stay in Niterói, you may want to eat something during your visit. Though the restaurants don't rival Rio for their cosmopolitan flavour, they're generally easier on the pocket.

Legau Pizzeria Rua Profesor Otacílio 118. Reasonably priced pizzas at this cheerful and central pizzeria. Plenty of special offers, with family-size pizzas cheaper Tues–Thurs (R$20).

Miksi Rua Nóbrega 264. *Miksi* means mixture in Esperanto, a reference to the diversity on offer: from pizzas and burgers, to contemporary dishes and even sushi. Closed Mon.

COSTA DO SOL

The **Costa do Sol** to the east of Ni... is an area of gorgeous white beach... peppered with a string of low-key resort towns. The coast is dominated by three large **lakes** – Maricá, Saquerema and Araruama – separated from the ocean by long, narrow stretches of white sandy beach, and each with an eponymous town.

BUZIOS

The most famous resort on this stretch, "discovered" by Bridget Bardot in 1964 and nicknamed "Brazil's St Tropez", is Armação dos Búzios, or **BÚZIOS** as it's more commonly known. A former whaling town, it's now cashing in on the tourist market. Bardot described the sea here as "foaming like blue champagne" and the seafront promenade, the **Orla Bardot**, now bears a statue of her in homage to her role in making the town what it is today. From December to February the population swells from 20,000 to 150,000, and boats that once ferried the catch back to shore now take pleasure-seekers island-hopping and scuba diving. If a crowded resort full of high-spending beautiful people is your thing then you're sure to fall for Búzios; if not, give it a miss – at least during the high season.

Arrival and information

Bus Direct buses from Rio run at least five times a day, arriving at the *rodoviária* on Estrada da Usina Velha.

Tourist information There is no tourist office, but you can get information by calling ⓣ0800/229-999 (ⓦwww.buzios.com.br). Try also ⓦwww.buziosonline.com.br.

Accommodation

Meu Sonho Av José Bento Ribeiro Dantas 1289, Ossos ⓣ22/2623-0902, ⓦwww.meusonho-buzios.8k.com. The best budget option in town and just a block from the beach, this *pousada* has clean, basic rooms and a plunge pool. ❻

…cus Beach Hotel …22, Praia de João … ⓣ22/2623-6221; …scucusbeach.com … gorgeous …each with a small … wonderful sea views. It's a welcoming, British-owned and -run *pousada* with a good-sized pool in a flower-filled garden, and the area's best snorkelling beach is just seconds away.

Morombo Av José Bento Ribeiro Dantas 1242, Armação ⓣ22/2623-1532. An extremely hospitable Argentine owner, good rooms and an attractive terrace combine to make the *Morombo*, on the waterfront road leading to Ossos, an appealing place to stay. ❸

Eating and drinking

Restaurants are, predictably, expensive, the trendiest places being located along Rua das Pedras; cheaper options include the *barracas* selling grilled fish on the beaches and the numerous pizza places in outlying parts of Búzios.

Bananaland Rua Manoel Turíbio de Farias 50. On a street parallel to Rua das Pedras, this is the best *por kilo* (R$15 per kilo) restaurant in Búzios, and one of the cheapest for a good meal. Outstanding buffet of salads and hot dishes.

Chez Michou Crêperie Rua das Pedras 90, ⓦwww.chezmichou.com.br. Belgian-owned, this has long been the most popular hangout in Búzios, thanks to its open-air bar, cheap drinks and authentic crêpes. Open until dawn, when it serves breakfast to the patrons pouring out of the nearby *Fashion Café*.

Sawasdee Av José Bento Ribeiro Dantas 422, ⓦwww.sawasdee.com.br. Excellent, spicy Thai food, with mainly vegetarian and seafood dishes at reasonable prices (meals from R$20).

THE COSTA VERDE

One of Brazil's truly beautiful landscapes, the **Costa Verde** is billed by the state tourist office as the area "where the Atlantic Forest meets the sea". Although the construction of the **Rio–Santos BR-101 Highway** has made the region more accessible for visitors, the downside is that it has also opened the doors to commercial exploitation. The fate of this 280-kilometre stretch of lush vegetation, rolling hills and tropical beaches hangs in the balance between rational development and ecological destruction, and so far the signs augur badly. Enjoy your trip; you may be amongst the last to have the privilege of visiting the beaches of **Ilha Grande** or the colonial architecture of **Paraty**.

ILHA GRANDE

The island of **ILHA GRANDE** comprises 193sq km of mountainous jungle, historic ruins and beautiful beaches, excellent for some scenic tropical rambling. The entire island, lying about 150km southwest of Rio, is a state park with limits on building development and a ban on motor vehicles.

What to see and do

Ilha Grande offers lots of beautiful **walks** along well-maintained and fairly well-signposted trails. As you approach the low-lying, whitewashed colonial port of **VILA DO ABRAÃO**, the mountains rise dramatically from the sea, and in the distance there's the curiously shaped summit of **Bico do Papagaio** ("Parrot's Beak"), which rises to a height of 980m. There's little to see in Abraão itself, but it's a pleasant base from which to explore the rest of the island. A half-hour walk along the coast west from Abraão are the ruins of the **Antigo Presídio**, a former prison for political prisoners that was dynamited in the early 1960s. Among the ruins, you'll find the *cafofo*, the containment centre where prisoners who had failed in escape attempts were immersed in freezing water. Avoid straying from the path anywhere on the island: besides the risk of getting lost, there are rumours of booby traps primed to fire bullets at escaped prisoners. Just fifteen minutes inland from Abraão, overgrown with vegetation, stands the **Antigo Aqueduto**, which used to channel the island's water supply. There's a fine view of the aqueduct from the **Pedra Mirante**, a hill near the centre of the island and, close by, a waterfall provides the opportunity to cool off. For the most part the **beaches** – Aventureiro, Lopes Mendes, Canto, Júlia and Morcegoare to name a few – are wild, unspoilt and most easily reached by boat.

Arrival and information

Bus From Rio's *rodoviária*, buses leave the city by the Zona Norte and follow the BR-101 to Itacuruçá and beyond.
Car From Rio, drive through the Zona Sul by way of Barra de Tijuca, to Barra de Guaratiba.
Ferry Get to the ferry ports by bus or car, as described above. Boats (Ⓦwww.barcas-sa.com.br) run from Mangaratiba, leaving at 8am and returning at 5.30pm, and from Angra dos Reis, at 3.15pm Mon–Fri and 1.30pm at weekends, with return services at 10am every day. Tickets cost R$5.90 (double at weekends) and the journey takes about an hour.
Tourist information There is a tourist office in Angra dos Reis at Av Ayrton Senna (Ⓣ24/3365-5186), but no official office on the island itself, though most *pousadas* offer assistance. Online try Ⓦwww.ilhagrande.org.

Accommodation

Most of the best choices are around Vila do Abraão where there are quite a few **pousadas**, generally simple but fairly expensive. Reservations are essential in the high season, especially at weekends, but prices may be halved in the off-season. If you prefer to **camp**, *Camping Peixoto* (Ⓦwww.campingdopeixoto.com.br; R$15 per person) is the best of the island's campsites.
Che Lagarto Praia do Canto Ⓣ21/3361-9669. Much like the members of the same chain in Rio (see 281), this is a well-organized hostel with breakfast served on a glorious wooden sun deck overlooking the sea. Dorm R$38. ❻
Oásis Praia do Canto Ⓣ24/3361-5549. Cosy, friendly and one of the nicest *pousadas* on the island. Rooms are unpretentious and simply furnished and the *pousada* is peacefully located on the far end of the beach, a 10min walk from the jetty. ❺
Pousada do Holandês Rua do Assembléia Ⓣ24/3361-5034. Always popular, this trendy youth hostel is behind the beach next to the Assembléia de Deus. Accommodation in dorms or lovely chalets in lush gardens. Dorm R$35. chalets ❼
Pousada Tropicana Rua da Praia 28 Ⓣ24/3361-5047; Ⓦwww.ilha-grande.net. French-owned and one of the oldest *pousadas* on the island. There's a good restaurant and the staff here are extremely helpful and will help you arrange tourist activities. ❼

Eating

There are some decent **restaurants** on the island, and as you might expect fish and seafood figure heavily on many menus.
Rei do Moqueca Rua da Praia. Reasonably priced seafood – try the garlic prawns for R$20.
Tropicana Rua da Praia. The restaurant of the *Pousada Tropicana*, serving an interesting menu of French dishes with a Brazilian twist, with outdoor tables in a verdant garden.

Directory

Banks and exchange Bring plenty of cash: there's no ATM, nowhere to change money or traveller's cheques and few places accept credit cards.
Scuba diving The Elite Dive Center (Ⓣ24/3361-5501; Ⓦwww.elitedivecenter.com.br) is the only PADI-registered dive centre on the island.

PARATY AND AROUND

PARATY, 236km from Rio along the BR-101, is the Costa Verde's main attraction, and rightly so. Inhabited since 1650, Paraty remains much as it was in its heyday as a staging post for the eighteenth-century trade in Brazilian gold. Today, UNESCO considers the city one of the world's most important examples of Portuguese colonial architecture, and it has been named a national monument. Besides the town's charmingly relaxed atmosphere, the main draws are its **churches** and, of course, the local **beaches**.

What to see and do

One of Brazil's first planned urban projects, Paraty's centre is a warren of narrow, pedestrianized cobbled streets bordered by houses built around quaint courtyards. The cobbles of the streets are arranged in channels to drain off storm water and allow the sea to enter and wash the streets at high tides and full moon.

Churches

Paraty's **churches** traditionally each served a different sector of the population. **Nossa Senhora dos Remédios** (daily 9am–5pm) on the Praça da Matriz is the town's most imposing building. Although the original church was built on the site in 1668, the current construction dates from 1873 (with building having begun 84 years earlier). Along Rua do Comércio is the smallest church, the **Igreja do Rosário** (Mon–Fri 9am–noon), once used by the slaves, whilst at the southern edge of the town, the Portuguese Baroque **Igreja de Santa Rita** (Wed–Sun 10am–noon & 2–5pm) dates from 1722. The oldest and most architecturally significant of the town's churches, it now houses the **Museu de Arte Sacra de Paraty** (Tues–Sun 8am–6pm; R$1.50).

Beaches and islands

From the **Praia do Pontal**, across the Perequê-Açu river from town, and from the **port quay**, boats leave for the **beaches** of Parati-Mirim, Iririguaçu – known for its waterfalls – Lula and Conceição. In fact, there are 65 islands and about two hundred beaches to choose from – ask around for the current favourites. Hotels and travel agents sell tickets for trips out to the islands, typically at a cost of around R$20 per person, leaving Paraty at noon, stopping at three or four islands, giving time for a swim, and returning at 6pm. Some 21km south of Paraty and reached by a steep but well-maintained winding road is the village of **Trinidade** (7 daily buses; 45min). Sandwiched between the ocean and Serra do Mar, Trinidade has reached its physical limits of growth and is crammed with tourists in the peak summer season. The main beach is nice enough, but crossing the rocky outcrops brings you to **Praia Brava** and **Praia do Meio**, arguably some of the most perfect mainland beaches on this stretch of coast, and completely unspoilt by tourism.

Arrival and information

Bus The *rodoviária* is about half a kilometre from the old town on Rua Jango de Padúa; turn right out of the bus station and walk straight ahead.
Tourist office On the corner of Av Roberto Silveira and Praça Macedo Soares (daily 9am–9pm; ⓣ24/3371-1222; ⓦwww.pmparaty.rj.gov.br).

Accommodation

Pousada da Matriz Rua da Matriz ⓣ24/3371-1610. Small, basic, but clean rooms in one of the cheapest *pousadas* in the old town. ❹
Pousada Tropical Rua Waldemar Mathias 38 ⓣ24/3371-2020. A cheap option next to the *rodoviária*, located in a quiet suburb, ideal if you arrive late or are leaving early – but not so handy for the beaches. Rooms are simple but comfortable. ❹
Solar dos Gerânios Praça da Matriz ⓣ24/3371-1550. Beautiful Swiss-owned and run *pousada* filled with rustic furniture and curios. The rooms are spartan but impeccably kept; most have a balcony and all are en suite. Superb value (prices remain much the same throughout the year) and rightly popular: reservations are always advised – request a room overlooking the beautiful *praça*. ❺

Eating, drinking and entertainment

Banana da Terra Rua Dr Samuel Costa 198 ⓣ24/3371-1725, ⓦwww.bananadaterra.com. Paraty's most interesting restaurant, using local ingredients (most notably bananas) in its regional cooking. The grilled fish with garlic-herb butter and banana is delicious (R$30), as are the wonderful desserts. Evenings only except Fri, Sat & Sun, when lunch is also served; closed Tues.
Beija Flor Rua Dr Pereira. A Lebanese-Portuguese café in a quiet corner of the historic centre – a good place for a cold beer or *caipirinha* and some savoury snacks. Open from 4pm; closed Wed.

Café Paraty Rua do Comércio 353 ⓦwww.cafeparaty.com.br. From a regular restaurant serving seafood and Portuguese dishes, nightly live music after 10pm helps convert the *Café Paraty* into one of the town's liveliest spots. There's a cover charge (R$3) if you just come to drink and listen to the music.

Sabor da Terra Av Roberto Silveira 180. The inexpensive *Sabor da Terra* is Paraty's best *por kilo* (R$15/kilo) restaurant, offering a wide variety of hot and cold dishes, including excellent seafood. The restaurant even has its own fishing boats, guaranteeing a fresh meal.

INLAND

The mountainous wooded landscape and relatively cool climate of the state's interior make a refreshing change from the coastal heat. Immediately to the north of Rio, high in the mountains, lie the imperial city of **Petrópolis** and the stunningly set **Teresópolis**, gateway to the magnificent **Parque Nacional Serra dos Orgãos.** In the far west lies another breathtaking protected area, the **Parque Nacional Itatiaia.**

PETRÓPOLIS

Some 66km to the north of Rio, high in the mountains, stands the imperial city of **PETRÓPOLIS**, so named because in the nineteenth century Pedro II had a summer palace built here, rapidly making the place a popular retreat for Brazilian aristocracy. En route the scenery is dramatic, climbing among forested slopes that suddenly give way to ravines and gullies, while clouds shroud the surrounding peaks. You can easily tour Petrópolis in a day – its cultural attractions and stunning setting make it well worth the trip.

What to see and do

The **Museu Imperial** on Avenida VII de Setembro (Tues–Sun & holidays 11am–6pm; R$8; ⓦwww.museuimperial.govbr) is a fine structure, set in beautifully maintained gardens. Upon entry, you're given felt overshoes with which to slide around the polished floors of this royal residence, and inside there's everything from Dom Pedro II's crown to the regal commode. The cathedral of **São Pedro de Alcântara** (Tues–Sun 8am–noon and 2–6pm) blends with the surrounding architecture, but is much more recent than its neo-Gothic style suggests – it was finished in 1939. Inside lie the tombs of Dom Pedro himself and several royal personages. Perhaps the town's most recognizable building is the **Palacio de Cristal** (Tues–Sun 9am–6.30pm) on Rua Alfedo Pachá, essentially a greenhouse erected for the local horticultural society in 1879.

Arrival and information

Bus Buses leave Rio for Petrópolis every 15min (sit on the left side of the bus for best views), arriving at the *rodoviária* on Rua Dr Porciúncula.

Tourist office At the entrance to town at Quitandinha on Av Ayrton Senna (Mon–Fri 8am–6pm, Sat 8am–7pm, Sun 8am–5pm; ⓣ800/241-516).

Accommodation

There are some reasonable mid-range **hotels** in town, as well as some very classy places housed in former colonial mansions.

Bragança Rua Raul de Leon 109 ⓣ24/2242-0434. Located in a former mansion behind the cathedral, this hotel maintains some of the residence's former style. ❼

Casablanca Imperial Rua de Imperatriz 286 ⓣ24/2242-6662, ⓦwww.casablancahotel.com.br. Next to the Museu Imperial, this classy hotel has an institutionalized feel to it. There's a nice pool and rooms are colonial in style. ❽

Comércio Rua Dr Porciúncula 55. One of the cheapest options in town, though by no means a bargain. Rooms without bathroom are cheapest. ❹–❺

Pousada Monte Imperial Rua José Alencar 27 ⓣ24/2237-1664; ⓦwww.pousadamonteimperial.com.br. On a hilltop and with the air of a country inn rather than a city hotel, this is one of the nicer *pousadas* in town, though this is reflected in the price. Rooms are small but appealing, and there's a pleasant garden with a pool, too. Only drawback is that it's quite a walk from the town's main attractions. ❼

Pousada 14 Bis Rua Buenos Aires 192 ⓣ24/2231-0946, ⓦwww.pousada14bis.com.br. A themed *pousada* based on the life of the inventor Santos Dumont. Rooms are nothing flashy, but are decorated in attractive colonial style. ❻

Eating

Restaurants are surprisingly lacklustre in Petrópolis, most of the best being some distance from town.

Armazem Rua Visconde de Itaboraí 646. Welcoming bar-restaurant with live music most nights and a varied menu of meat and fish that will suit most tastes. Try *camarão com catupiry* (prawns with catupiry cheese; R$19.90).

Arte Temporada Rua Ipiranga 716 ⓣ24/2237-2133. In the converted stable of a beautiful nineteenth-century mansion. Offerings include Brazilian specialities made with local produce, such as trout, and good salads. Wed–Sun lunchtime, Fri & Sat also dinner.

Braganca Rua Raul de Leon 109. In the hotel of the same name. This is a decent, moderately-priced Portuguese restaurant.

Rink Marowil Praca Rui Barbosa 27. Cheap *por kilo* restaurant (R$15/kilo). The food is nothing to write home about, but you'll struggle to find better value for money in town.

TERESÓPOLIS

TERESÓPOLIS is, at 871m, officially the highest city in the state of Rio. There is not a great deal to do around town, and the main reason for heading up here is for access to the nearby **Parque Nacional Serra dos Orgãos** (see below). The Brazilian national football team uses the area for high-altitude training prior to matches against Andean countries, at which times the town is gripped by football fever. They allow access to their training ground at **Granja Comary** (check with the tourist office for details).

Arrival and information

Bus Buses run hourly from Rio and every 90min from Petropolis, arriving at the *rodoviária* on Rua 1 de Maio.

Tourist office Av Rotariana (daily 8am–7pm; ⓣ21/2642-1737; ⓦwww.teresopolis.rj.gov.br). Information about visiting the National Park.

Accommodation

If you are planning on visiting the national park you will probably want to base yourself in Teresópolis, where there are a few reasonably priced accommodation options.

Pousada Villa Tiroleza Rua da Mariana 144 ⓣ21/2742-7337. Handsome, chalet-style building and rustic wooden interior make this hotel excellent value for money. There's a sauna too. ❺

Recanto do Lord Rua Luiza Pereira Soares ⓣ21/2742-5586; ⓦwww.teresopolishostel.com.br. A HI hostel, some distance from the centre of town but well worth the trek for the *reais* that you'll save. Great service, with dorms and double rooms, and a glorious view over town from the terrace. Dorm R$15. ❹

Eating

Big Lanches Av Feliciano Sodré 1108 ⓣ21/2643-2490. Self-service lunch place using local produce and one of the cheaper places to fill yourself up in Teresópolis without taking the junk food route. A meal will cost around R$15.

Cheiro do Mato Rua Delfim Moreira ⓣ21/ 2742-1899. This vegetarian restaurant has a diverse menu that will satisfy even the staunchest of carnivores; a reasonably priced, healthy option that will keep you off the fried foods, at least for one meal (from R$15).

PARQUE NACIONAL SERRA DOS ORGÃOS

The **Parque Nacional Serra dos Orgãos** is breathtakingly beautiful and refreshingly easy to visit. Dominated in its lower reaches by lush Atlantic forest, the bare mountain peaks that emerge from the trees create a stunning effect against the backdrop of a clear blue sky. It is these peaks that give the park its name, the rocks reminding the early Portuguese explorers of the pipes of cathedral organs.

What to see and do

There are a number of **walking trails** in the park, most of them short, easily accessible and suitable for people who like their hiking easy, but be aware that most include some uphill walking.

Many of the park's most recognizable landmarks are visible on the horizon from Teresópolis. The most famous of all is the **Dedo de Deus** (Finger of God) – a bare, rocky pinnacle that points skyward – whilst arguably more picturesque is the **Cachoeira Véu da Noiva** waterfall. The longest and most challenging trail is the **Pedra do Sino** (Stone Bell), starting some distance from the park entrance, passing the bell-shaped rock formation (at 2263m the park's highest point) and emerging some 30km further on close to the town of Petrópolis (see p.289) – a guide is strongly recommended.

PARQUE NACIONAL DO ITATIAIA

On the border with Minais Gerais, 167km west of Rio, the **Parque Nacional do Itatiaia** takes its unusual name from an Indian word meaning "rocks with sharp edges". Holding the distinction of being Brazil's first national park (1937) it's incredibly varied, from dense Atlantic forest in the foothills, through to treeless, grassy summits. The park's loftiest peak, **Agulhas-Negras**, is the second highest in Brazil, at 2789m.

What to see and do

There's no shortage of **walking trails** here, as well as a couple of two-day walks for serious hikers. The better, but more difficult, of the two is the **Jeep Trail**, which scales the valle
reaches the peak of Ag
second is the **Tres P**
but care should still l
becomes narrow an
A **guide** is recomm
(available from ho
and essential for the Jeep Trail, fo
you should seek prior permission from the IBAMA office at the park entrance. Itatiaia is also a popular **birdwatching** destination thanks to its varied terrain and flora: highland species present in the park include the Itatiaia Spinetail, a small, brownish, skulking bird that occurs only in this range of mountains.

PARK PRACTICALITIES

Teresópolis is located right at the edge of the park, the **entrance** being just to the south of town (head towards the Dedo de Deus). The **park office** at the entrance (daily 8am–5pm) rents out camping equipment and can provide information on reliable local **guides**. There is a R$3 entrance charge to the park, increasing to R$8 if you wish to walk the Pedra do Sino trail.

Arrival and information

Access to the park is via the town of Itatiaia – buses between Rio and São Paulo pass through. Local buses (R$1.90, 30min) run from the footbridge in Itatiaia, a short walk from the *rodoviária*, to the park visitors' centre.

Accommodation

Staying in the town of Itatiaia is cheaper, but it is a 30min bus ride from the park entrance. Within the park are several pricier options.

Simon Rodavia Br-485 km12, PN Itatiaia (☎24/3352-1122). A huge hotel within the park boundaries, this is the most convenient place to stay if you are thinking of hiking the park's trails: the Tres Picos trail begins just behind the hotel. Comfortable but by no means cheap. Some rooms have attractive views out over the valleys. ⑦

Pousada Isa Five hundred metres from the *rodoviária*, Itatiaia; no phone. Turn right out of the bus station and look for the *Pousada* sign. A basic, if not particularly attractive, option for budget travellers, including a half-decent breakfast. ④

Minas Gerais

Following the discovery of gold in 1693, explorers flocked to **Minas Gerais** to exploit its abundant natural resources, later discovered to include diamonds and other gemstones. For nearly a hundred

years the region was by far the wealthiest in Brazil, as its mines (the state's name means, simply, 'general mines') poured out riches. But as the gold reserves became exhausted so Minas Gerais declined, and by the mid-nineteenth century it was again a backwater. Today there are still minerals extracted from the hills, but only more workaday metals like iron. Left behind by the boom, however, are a series of startlingly beautiful towns filled with glorious churches encrusted in gold, built in the over-the-top local version of Baroque architecture, *Barroco Mineiro*. Many have magnificent statues and decoration by local artists. And all of this is set in an area of stunning natural mountain beauty, where many of the towns are connected by restored historic steam trains.

BELO HORIZONTE

Founded at the beginning of the eighteenth century by *bandeirantes* in search of gold and gemstones, **BELO HORIZONTE**, capital of Minas Gerais, nestles between the beautiful hills of the Serra do Curral which gave the city its name. The third-largest city in Brazil may at first appear daunting, but this cosmopolitan metropolis has preserved the welcoming hospitality of Minas, and is home to an eclectic mix of architectural styles, from the modern Niemeyer building to beautiful parks which retain a European feel, their layout having been inspired by the beautiful gardens of the Palace of Versailles. Give the city a chance and you will soon be enchanted by its hidden treasures. Thanks to its proximity to the *Cidades*

Históricas, Belo Horizonte also serves as an excellent base to explore the surrounding areas.

What to see and do

For all its size, the centre of Belo Horizonte is fairly easy to explore on foot. Heading south from the *rodoviária*, walk to Praça Raul Soares and then take Rua dos Guajajaras where you can visit the bustling **Mercado Central** (Mon–Sat 7am–6pm, Sun 7am–1pm), with more than four hundred stalls and restaurants selling a variety of products from cheese to local bamboo artefacts. It is a great spot to observe local life as you sip a beer and munch on a typical *mineiro* dish. From here, head to Avenida Afonso Pena where you can stroll around the beautiful **Parque Municipal** (Tues–Sun 6am–6pm). Inspired by the Parisian *Belle Époque* parks, its pleasant shaded walkways, artificial lakes and greenery – including two thousand species of trees – are especially busy on Sunday afternoons. If you are in town on a Sunday morning, don't miss the **Arts & Crafts Fair** on Avenida Afonso Pena, the largest open-air fair in Latin America, with three thousand stalls selling a myriad of artefacts. Heading further south you will reach the **Praça da Libertade** with its famous **Niemeyer building,** designed by renowned Brazilian modern architect Oscar Niemeyer, before reaching the **Palacio do Governo**. Finish your day around **Praça Savassi**, where you can sip a *caipirinha* in one of the many trendy bars in the area.

Pampulha

Set around an artificial lake, the smart, modernist neighbourhood of Pampulha north of the city centre contains some architectural gems, many of them designed by the greats of modern Brazilian architecture, including Oscar Niemeyer. The **Museu de Arte de Pampulha** (Tues–Sun 9am–9pm; R$6), on a peninsula in the lake, is one of the finest, home to permanent art collections and exhibitions. Designed by Niemeyer and influenced by Le Corbusier, the building is a work of art in itself and was originally designed to be a casino, before becoming a museum in 1957. Reach it on bus #2215A, B or C from Avenida Paraná between Rua Tamoios and Rua Carijós; it takes almost an hour to get to Pampulha. Also in Pampulha, **the Igreja de São Francisco de Assis** (Tues–Sat 9am–5pm, Sun 9am–1pm; R$2) is among the finest works of Niemeyer and artist Candido Portinari, who created the beautiful *azulejo* tiles and panels.

Mangabeiras

In the highest part of the Mangabeiras neighbourhood, south of the centre, the **Praça do Papa** has commanding views of the entire city. The monument in the square pays homage to Pope John Paul II who held a mass here in 1980. Bus #4103 from Avenida Afonso Pena between Avenida Amazonas and Rua Tamóios will get you up here. Stay on the same bus to continue to the mountainous edge of the city, where the vast **Parque das Mangabeiras** (Tues–Sun 8am–6pm) makes a pleasant spot for a relaxing Sunday afternoon walk. A nature reserve, the park supports capuchin monkeys as well as squirrels and other wildlife.

Museu Histórico Abílio Barreto

In the swanky Savassi neighbourhood, the **Museu Histórico Abílio Barreto** (Tues–Sun 10am–5pm, Thurs till 9pm; free) is set within a beautiful colonial mansion, the sole remnant of the small village of Curral del Rey. It is home to some interesting photographs, objects, furniture, sculptures and documents of the time.

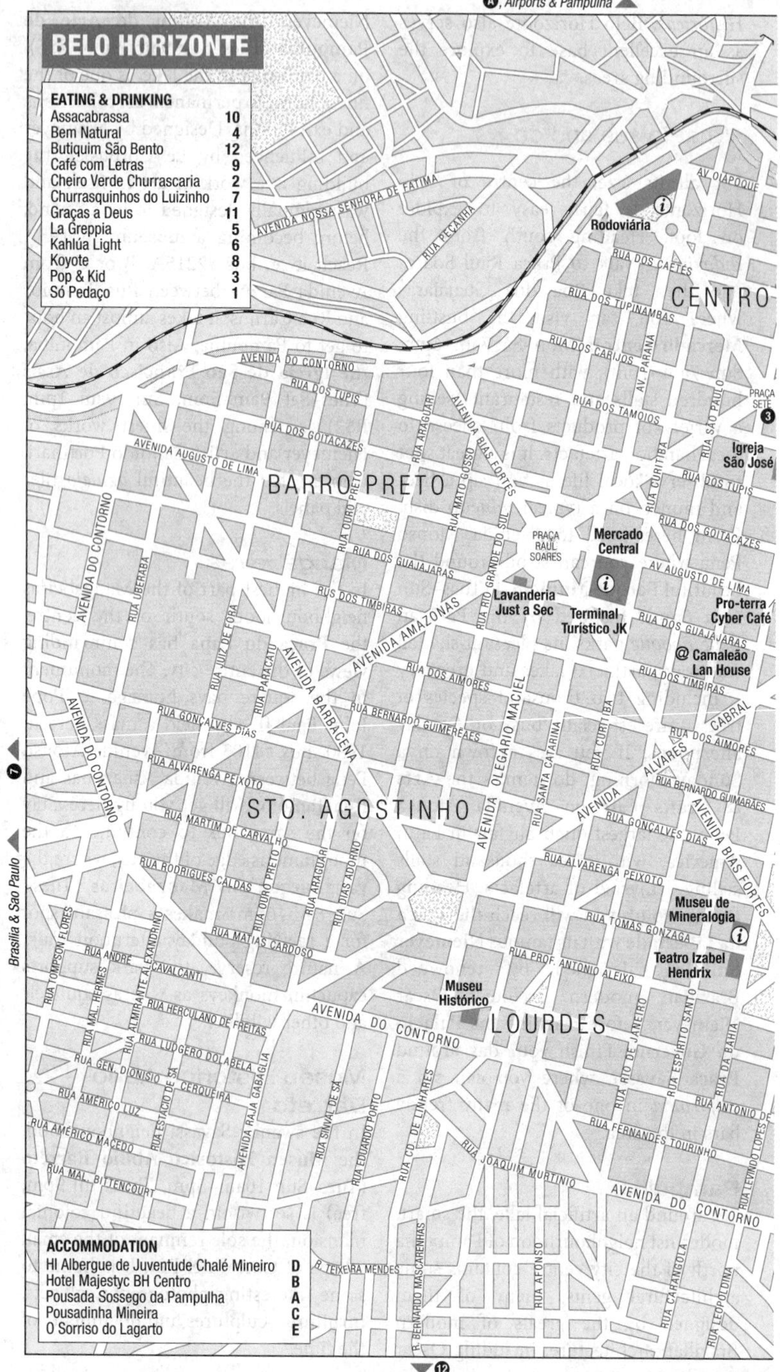

A, Airports & Pampulha
BELO HORIZONTE
EATING & DRINKING
Assacabrassa 10
Bem Natural 4
Butiquim São Bento 12
Café com Letras 9
Cheiro Verde Churrascaria 2
Churrasquinhos do Luizinho 7
Graças a Deus 11
La Greppia 5
Kahlúa Light 6
Koyote 8
Pop & Kid 3
Só Pedaço 1
ACCOMMODATION
HI Albergue de Juventude Chalé Mineiro D
Hotel Majestyc BH Centro B
Pousada Sossego da Pampulha A
Pousadinha Mineira C
O Sorriso do Lagarto E
CENTRO
BARRO PRETO
STO. AGOSTINHO
LOURDES
Rodoviária
Praça Sete
Igreja São José
Praça Raul Soares
Mercado Central
Lavanderia Just a Sec
Terminal Turístico JK
Pro-terra Cyber Café
Camaleão Lan House
Museu de Mineralogia
Teatro Izabel Hendrix
Museu Histórico
Avenida Nossa Senhora de Fatima
Rua Pecanha
Av. Oiapoque
Rua dos Caetés
Rua dos Tupinambas
Rua dos Carijos
Av. Paraná
Avenida do Contorno
Rua dos Tupis
Rua dos Tamoios
Rua São Paulo
Rua dos Goitacazes
Avenida Augusto de Lima
Rua Araguari
Avenida Bias Fortes
Rua Mato Gosso
Rua Curitiba
Rua Ouro Preto
Rua dos Guajajaras
Rua Rio Grande do Sul
Rus dos Timbiras
Avenida Amazonas
Rua Uberaba
Rua Juiz de Fora
Rua Paracatu
Avenida Barbacena
Rua dos Aimores
Rua Bernardo Guimerães
Avenida Olegario Maciel
Rua Santa Catarina
Avenida Alvares Cabral
Rua Gonçalves Dias
Rua Alvarenga Peixoto
Rua Martim de Carvalho
Rua Rodrigues Caldas
Rua Dias Adorno
Rua Tomas Gonzaga
Rua Matias Cardoso
Rua Prof. Antonio Aleixo
Rua Tompson Flores
Rua André Cavalcanti
Rua Almirante Alexandrino
Rua Mal. Hermes
Rua Herculano de Freitas
Rua Ludgero Dolabela
Rua Gen. Dionisio Cerqueira
Rua Estácio de Sá
Rua Américo Luz
Rua Américo Macedo
Avenida Raja Gabaglia
Rua Sinval de Sá
Rua Eduardo Porto
Rua Cd. de Linhares
Rua Joaquim Murtinio
Rua Rio de Janeiro
Rua Espírito Santo
Rua da Bahia
Rua Antonio de
Rua Fernandes Tourinho
Rua Levindo Lopes
Rua Mal. Bittencourt
R. Teixeira Mendes
R. Bernardo Mascarenhas
Rua Afonso
Rua Carangola
Rua Leopoldina
Brasília & São Paulo

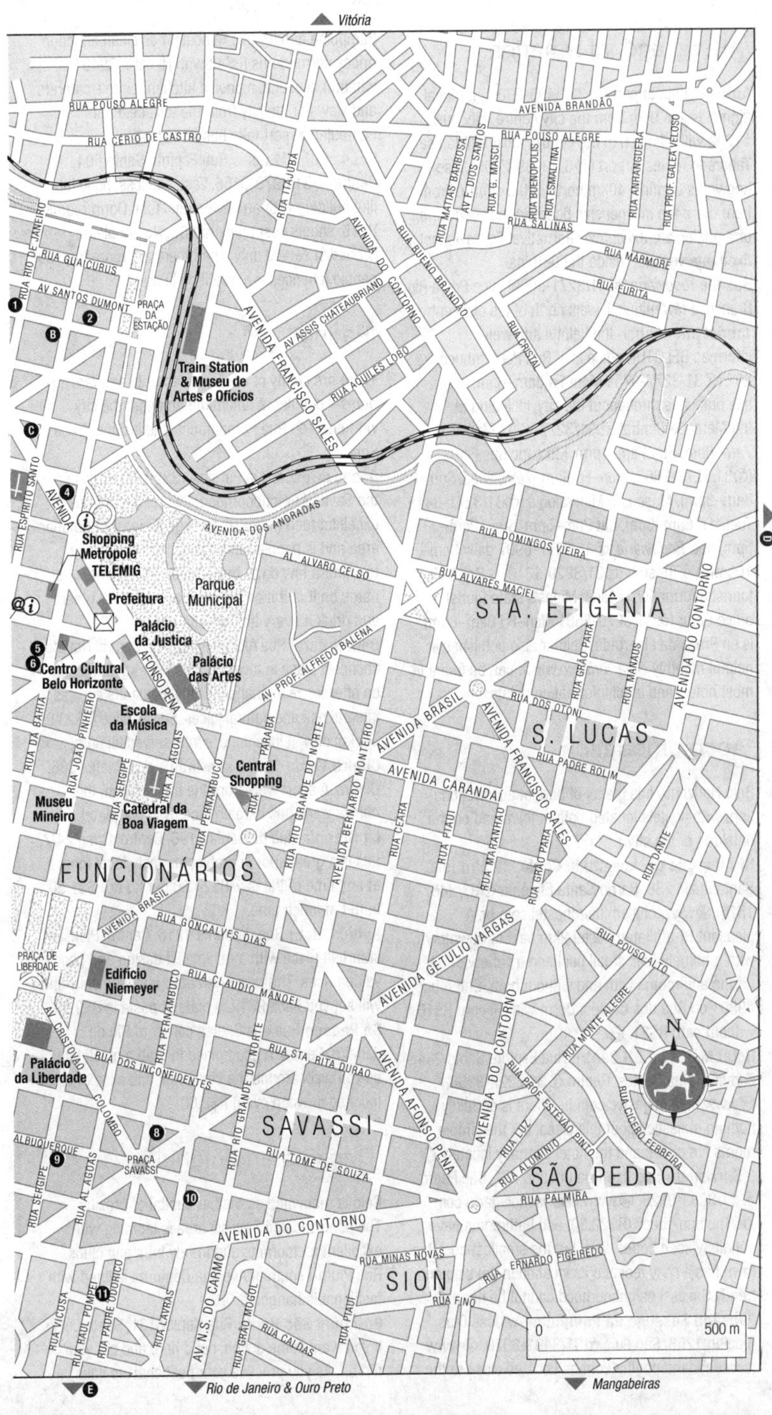
Vitória
RUA POUSO ALEGRE
RUA CÉRIO DE CASTRO
AVENIDA BRANDÃO
RUA POUSO ALEGRE
RUA SALINAS
RUA MÁRMORE
RUA EURITA
RUA CRISTAL
RUA ITAJUBÁ
AVENIDA DO CONTORNO
RUA BUENO BRANDÃO
RUA MATIAS BARBOSA
AV F. DIOS SANTOS
RUA G. MASCI
RUA BUENÓPOLIS
RUA ESMALTINA
RUA ANHANGUERA
RUA PROF. GALEA VELOSO
RUA RIO DE JANEIRO
RUA GUAICURUS
AV SANTOS DUMONT
PRAÇA DA ESTAÇÃO
Train Station & Museu de Artes e Ofícios
AVENIDA FRANCISCO SALES
AV ASSIS CHATEAUBRIAND
RUA AQUILES LOBO
RUA ESPÍRITO SANTO
AVENIDA
AVENIDA DOS ANDRADAS
Shopping Metrópole
TELEMIG
Prefeitura
Parque Municipal
AL. ALVARO CELSO
RUA DOMINGOS VIEIRA
RUA ALVARES MACIEL
STA. EFIGÊNIA
Palácio da Justica
Centro Cultural Belo Horizonte
AFONSO PENA
Palácio das Artes
AV. PROF. ALFREDO BALENA
Escola da Música
RUA DA BAHIA
RUA JOÃO PINHEIRO
RUA AL. AGOAS
RUA SERGIPE
AVENIDA BRASIL
AVENIDA FRANCISCO SALES
RUA DOS OTONI
S. LUCAS
RUA GRÃO PARÁ
RUA MANAUS
AVENIDA DO CONTORNO
RUA PADRE BOLIM
Central Shopping
RUA PARAÍBA
RUA RIO GRANDE DO NORTE
AVENIDA BERNARDO MONTEIRO
AVENIDA CARANDAÍ
RUA PERNAMBUCO
Museu Mineiro
Catedral da Boa Viagem
RUA CEARÁ
RUA PIAUÍ
RUA MARANHÃO
RUA GRÃO PARÁ
RUA DANTE
FUNCIONÁRIOS
AVENIDA BRASIL
RUA GONÇALVES DIAS
AVENIDA GETÚLIO VARGAS
RUA POUSO ALTO
PRAÇA DE LIBERDADE
Edifício Niemeyer
RUA CLAUDIO MANOEL
RUA PERNAMBUCO
AV CRISTOVÃO
COLOMBO
Palácio da Liberdade
RUA DOS INCONFIDENTES
RUA STA. RITA DURÃO
AVENIDA AFONSO PENA
AVENIDA DO CONTORNO
RUA MONTE ALEGRE
RUA PROF. ESTEVÃO PINTO
RUA CICERO FERREIRA
N
ALBUQUERQUE
PRAÇA SAVASSI
SAVASSI
RUA TOMÉ DE SOUZA
RUA RIO GRANDE DO NORTE
RUA LUZ
RUA ALUMÍNIO
SÃO PEDRO
RUA PALMIRA
RUA SERGIPE
RUA AL. AGOAS
AVENIDA DO CONTORNO
RUA MINAS NOVAS
RUA ERNARDO FIGEIREDO
SION
RUA FINO
RUA VIÇOSA
RUA RAUL POMPÉIA
RUA PADRE ODORICO
RUA LAVRAS
AV. N.S. DO CARMO
RUA GRÃO MOGOL
RUA CALDAS
RUA PIAUÍ
0
500 m
Rio de Janeiro & Ouro Preto
Mangabeiras

Arrival and information

Air Pampulha airport (☎31/3490-2001), for local flights, is just 9km from the city centre; city bus #1202 will take you to the centre. Most flights use Tancredo Neves airport (☎31/3689-2700), also known as Confins, 40km north of the centre. From here there are inexpensive buses to the *rodoviária*, or a pricier, a/c *executivo* alternative. For taxis, get a fixed rate voucher inside the terminal.

Bus the *rodoviária* (☎31/3271-3000) is on Praça Rio Branco, a few minutes' walk north of the city centre.

Tourist Information the helpful and well-informed BELOTUR office is at Rua Pernambuco 282 (☎31/3277-9754 Mon–Fri 8am–6pm). It has branches throughout the city, including at the Mercado Central (☎31/3277-4691 Mon–Sat 7am–6pm, Sun 7am–1pm), Mercado das Flores (☎31/3277-7666, Mon–Fri 8am–7pm, Sat & Sun 8am–3pm), Museu de Mineralogia (☎31/3271-3415 Tues–Fri 8am–5pm, Sat 9am–5pm, Sun 10am–5pm) and *Rodoviária* (☎31/3277-6907 daily 8am–10pm). Alô Turismo (☎31/3220-1310) is Belotur's tourist information hotline. Minas's state tourist office Setur (☎31/3270-8501 Mon–Fri 8am–6pm) is on Praça da Libertade. Belotur also publishes a helpful monthly *Guia Turístico* which can be found in most hotels and at all information points.

Accommodation

Belo Horizonte has plenty of budget accommodation, with hostels located both in town and on the outskirts of the city.

HI Albergue de Juventude Chalé Mineiro Rua Santa Luzia 288, Barrio Santa Efigênia ☎31/3467-1576, Ⓦwww.chalemineirohostel.com.br. A pleasant HI-affiliated hostel 2km east of downtown, with a homely feel, small pool and a variety of dorms and rooms with and without bath. Catch bus #9801 on Rua dos Caetés. Dorm with HI card R$16, without card R$21. ❸

Hotel Majestyc BH Centro Rua Espíritu Santo 284, corner of Rua Caetés, Centro ☎31/3222-3390, Ⓦwww.hotelmajestyc.com.br. There is certainly nothing majestic about this place, but the simple rooms are cheap and the hotel centrally located. ❸

O Sorriso do Lagarto Rua Cristina 791, São Pedro, ☎31/3283-9325, Ⓦwww.osorrisodolagarto.com.br. The bunk beds (R$22.50) and bathrooms have definitely seen better days, but the smallest hostel in town has a cosy feel and its location in the safe and trendy Savassi neighbourhood cannot be beat. ❸

Pousada Sossego da Pampulha Av José Dias Bicalho 1258, São Luis ☎31/3491-8020, Ⓦwww.sossegodapampulha.com.br. Located close to the Pampulha airport, this HI hostel has clean although pricey dorm rooms (R$43 with HI card, R$49 without), a sauna, a pool, a kitchen for self-caterers and views of the city from the terrace. From Pampulha airport take bus #5401. ❺

Pousadinha Mineira Rua Espíritu Santo 604, Centro ☎31/3273-8156. Vast, soulless, hospital-like building with an institutional feel. Dorm rooms R$16, sheets cost an extra R$5. No doubles. Breakfast served only when there are more than 50 people (chances are, you'll go hungry).

Eating

There are plenty of cheap restaurants and *lanchonetes* – popular at lunchtime amongst the city workers – on Rua Pernambuco and around Praça Sete.

Assacabrassa Rua Paraiba 1332B, Savassi. In the Savassi neighbourhood, this restaurant has excellent food (R$24.90 per kg), a pleasant outdoor area and is popular amongst locals. If you're in town for a few days, buy a bottle of JD, write your name on it, put it on the shelf amongst the others and drink it every time you go back.

Bem Natural Rua Afonso Pena 941, Centro. Not the cheapest place in town (R$23.90 per kg) but plenty on offer for vegetarians; healthy foodstuffs such as integral rice and natural juices. Self-service (R$23.90 per kg) only at lunchtime, soups served till 6pm.

Cheiro Verde Churrascaria Rua dos Caetés 236, Centro. A short walk from the train station, this *churrascaria* has bargain food (R$6 per plate).

La Greppia Rua da Bahia 1196, Centro. Open 24/7, this is a great spot to grab some tasty local food at any time of the day. R$24.90 per kg or R$21.50 buffet at lunch time.

Kahlúa Light Rua da Bahia 1216, Centro. Pleasant smartish place with a minimalist design and good-value prices. The *prato executivo* changes daily and will set you back R$12, a plate of pasta is R$9.90.

Só Pedaço Rua dos Caetés corner of Rio do Janeiro, Centro. A good place to grab a quick bite as you walk around the city. Drink and slice of pizza (cooked in wood oven) R$2.60.

Drinking and nightlife

Belo is renowned as the bar capital of Brazil. The sophisticated Savassi area is teeming with excellent restaurants and trendy bars and clubs. Rua Pium-í south of Avenida Contorno is lined with fashionable hangouts.

Butiquim São Bento Rua Kepler 131, Santa Lúcia. If you want some action, head here and get your flirt on. As you practise your best chat-up lines, sip on an excellent cocktail (try the *caipirinhas*) to lubricate your chat box. Or try one of the twenty-eight kinds of beer on offer. Closed Mon.

Café com Letras Rua Antônio de Albuquerque 781, Savassi. Books cover the walls of this trendy bar with a little patio out back. Good selection of cocktails (Rum & Coke R$5.50)

Churrasquinhos do Luizinho Rua Turquesa 327, in the Prado district. Packed on Thurs, sometimes with more than 500 people, *Luizinho's* serves delicious *espetos* (R$2.50) – owner Luiz says the secret lies in the sauce, a recipe of his mother's. Free shot of *cachaça* with your *espetinho* on Mon. Strangely enough it's closed on weekends.

Graças a Deus Rua Padre Odorico 68, São Pedro. Little colourful house from the outside but darker lighting inside, with wooden tables and chilled beats setting the mood. Mean *caipivodkas*.

Koyote Rua Tomé de Souza 912, Savassi. Young crowd, fun atmosphere and a pleasant spot for an evening drink in the Savassi district, with tables spilling out onto the street. Closed Mon.

Pop & Kid Rua do Janeiro 661, Centro. *The* place for *chopp* fanatics – the bar was recognised by the *Real Academia do Chopp* (yes, it exists!) for the quality of its draught beer. Live MPB music daily at 6.30pm.

Directory

Airlines Aerolíneas Argentinas, Rua Tupis 204, sala 209, Centro ☎31/3224-7466; Air Canada, Av Prudente de Morais 135, sala 211, Cidade Jardim ☎31/3344-8355; American Airlines, Av Bernardo Monteiro 1539, Funcionários ☎31/3238-7200; Delta Air Lines, Av Cristóvão Colombo 519, sala 1002, Savassi ☎31/3284-7558; Gol, call centre ☎0300/1152121; TAP-Air Portugal, Rua Timbiras 1200, sala 311, Funcionários ☎31/3213-1611; TAM, Rua Marília de Dirceu 162, Lourdes ☎31/3115-1050 and at Confins Airport ☎31/3689-2234; United Airlines, toll free ☎0800/162323.

Banks and exchange There are plenty of banks downtown on Av João Pinheiro between Rua dos Timbiras and Av Afonso Pena.

Car rental Hertz, at the airports and Av Prof. Magalhães Penido 101, Pampulha district ☎31/3492-1919; Alpina Serviços Automotivos, Rua dos Timbiras 2229 ☎31/3291-6111; Localiza, at the airports and Av Bernardo Monteiro 1567 ☎31/3247-7956; Locar-alpha, Av Santa Rosa 100 ☎31/3491-3833.

Consulates Argentina, Rua Ceará 1566, 6th floor, Funcionários ☎31/3047-5490; Paraguay, Rua Guandaus 60, apt. 102, Santa Lúcia ☎31/3344-6349; UK, Rua Cláudio Manoel 26, Funcionários ☎31/3225-0950; Uruguay, Av do Contorno 6777, Santo Antônio, ☎31/3296-7527.

Health matters For an ambulance, phone ☎192. Pronto Socorro do Hospital João XXIII, Av Alfredo Balena 400, Santa Efigênia (☎31/3239-9200).

Internet Camaleão Lan House, Rua São Paulo 1409 (Mon–Fri 8.30am–7pm, Sat till 1pm; R$2.50 per head) is a bit of a squeeze; Pro-Terra Cyber Café, Av Augusto de Lima 134 (Mon–Fri 8am–11pm, Sat 9am–11pm, Sun 2–11pm) has fast connections and Skype.

Laundry Lavanderia Just a Sec, Rua dos Guajajaras 1268, Centro (Mon–Fri 8am–6pm, Sat 8am–1pm). Wash your own clothes (R$16 per load) or have them washed (R$20 per load).

Police ☎190. For visa or tourist permit extension, go to the Polícia Federal at Rua Nascimento Gurgel 30, Gutierrez ☎31/3330-5200.

Post office The main post office is at Av Afonso Pena 1270 (Mon–Fri 8am–5pm).

Taxis Coomotaxi ☎31/3419-2020 or 0800/392020; Coopertáxi/BH ☎31/3421-2424 & 0800/9792424.

Moving on

Air Numerous domestic and international flights depart from Pampulha and Confins airports. Regular airport buses leave from the *rodoviária*. For Pampulha airport first bus daily 4.15am, last bus Mon–Fri 11.15pm, Sat 11.45pm, Sun 11.30pm. For Confins first bus Mon–Sat 4.30am, Sun 4.40am; last bus Mon–Fri 10.40pm, Sat 10.30pm, Sun 10.10pm.

Bus There are regular buses to most cities in the country, including Diamantina (6 daily; 5hr; R$55), Foz do Iguaçú (daily at 8am; 21hr; R$197), Salvador (daily at 6pm and 7pm; 24hr; R$169), São João del Rei (8 daily; 4hr; R$35).

Train The train station (☎31/3273-5976) serves just one route, to Vitória, with a daily 7.30am departure.

THE CIDADES HISTÓRICAS

Minas Gerais's **CIDADES HISTÓRICAS** started life as mining camps, as rough and basic as imagination can make them. But the wealth of the surrounding mountains soon transformed them, and today they are considered to be amongst the most beautiful cities in the Americas, with cobbled streets and alleyways, gilded Baroque churches and beautifully preserved colonial buildings surrounded by breathtaking rugged landscapes. **Ouro Preto** and **Diaman-**

...th UNESCO World Heritage ...**ão del Rei** and **Tiradentes** ...ss impressive. And all are ...to easily get to grips with.

OURO PRETO

Founded at the end of the seventeenth century, **OURO PRETO**, or 'Black Gold', is one of the prettiest towns in Brazil. Built on a hill in the Serra do Espinhaço, the former capital of Minas Gerais is home to some of the finest Baroque architecture in the country and was the birthplace of renowned sculptor **Aleijandinho**. The town was also the focal point of the **Inconfidência Mineira**, a failed attempt in 1789 to break from the colony and form a Brazilian republic. People flock to Ouro Preto from all over Brazil for **Semana Santa**, with its grand processions and plays of Christ in open-air theatres. **Carnaval** also attracts large crowds so book in advance at both these times. The city also hosts a number of enjoyable festivals, including the **Festival do Jazz** in September, the **Festival do Cinema Brasileiro** in mid-June and the **Festival das Letras**, a literary event, at the beginning of November.

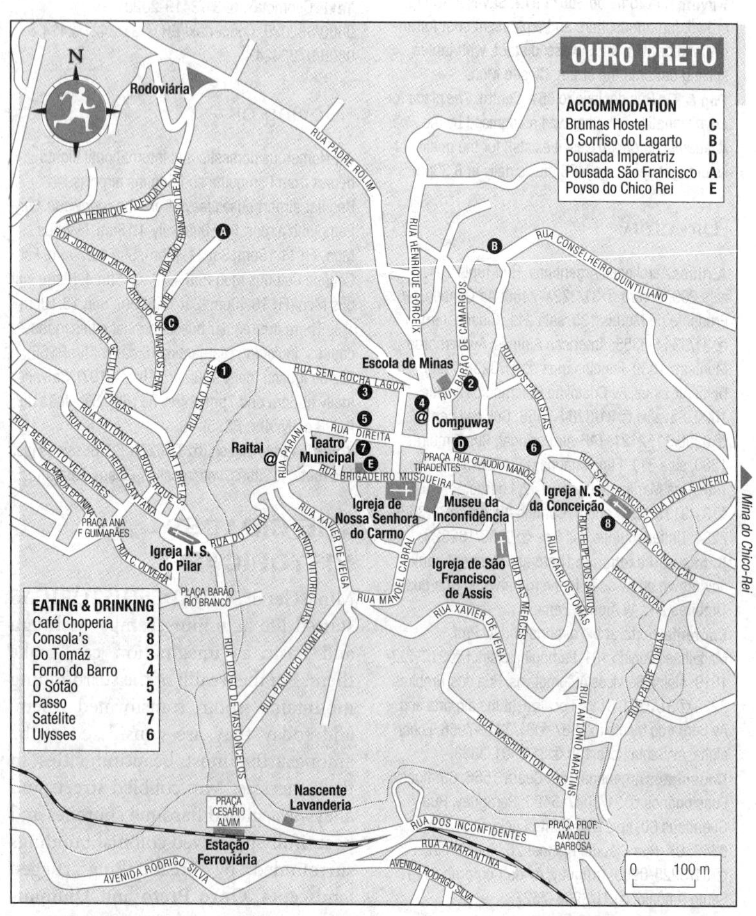

What to see and do

A single omnibus ticket includes all the major sites: the Museu Aleijandinho, the Igreja N. Senhora das Mercês e Perdões and the Igreja de São Francisco de Assis.

Praça Tiradentes

The Praça Tiradentes lies right at the heart of Ouro Preto, in easy reach of all the major sights, and with several right on the square. The **Museu da Inconfidência** (Tues–Sun noon–5pm; R$2), inside the Paço Municipal, has plenty of local history, including the tomb of Tiradentes, leader of the failed rebellion. You'll also find documents on the *Inconfidência Mineira*, torture instruments, Indo-Portuguese images and statuettes, and numerous other interesting objects of everyday eighteenth-century life. On the opposite side of the square, inside the vast **Escola de Minas**, the **Museu de Ciência e Técnica da Escola de Minas** (Tues–Sun noon–5pm; R$2) houses a large geological and mineralogical collection, including gemstones from all over the world. There is also an **astronomical observatory** within the museum (Sat 8–10pm).

Teatro Municipal

A couple of minutes' walk west of the square is the beautiful **Teatro Municipal** (Mon–Fri 9am–5.30pm, Sat & Sun 10am–5pm; R$2), worth a look for the magnificent interior. According to the Guinness Book of Records, this is the oldest theatre in Brazil, inaugurated on June 6, 1770. Details of performances can be found here or at the tourist office.

Two churches, and Aleijandinho

Arguably the most beautiful church in Ouro Preto, the **Igreja de São Francisco de Assis** (Tues–Sun 8.30am–noon & 12.30–5pm; R$6), east of Praça Tiradentes, is also one of the most important works of Aleijandinho (see below). The exterior was entirely sculpted by the great master himself and the ceilings decorated by his partner Athayde. The **Museu Aleijandinho** (Tues–Sun 8.30am–noon & 1.30–5pm), containing many more beautiful works by the renowned sculptor, is in the **Igreja Matriz de N.S. da Conceição** (Tues–Sat 8.30am–noon & 1.30–5pm, Sun noon–5pm, R$6). Designed by his father, the church also houses Aleijandinho's tomb.

Igreja Matriz N.S. do Pilar

Across town from here, the early eighteenth-century **Igreja Matriz N.S. do Pilar** (Tues–Sun 9–10.45am & noon–4.45pm; R$4) is the most opulent church in Minas Gerais, as well as one of the oldest in town. Over-the-top even

ALEIJANDINHO

Antônio Francisco Lisboa (1738–1814) was the son of the Portuguese architect Manoel Lisboa; his mother was almost certainly a slave. The most important sculptor of the colonial period, he was incredibly prodigious, turning out scores of works throughout Minas Gerais. What makes this more remarkable is not just that he was self-taught, but that from his mid-thirties he suffered the effects of a degenerative disease which led to a loss of movement in his legs and hands, eventually forcing him to sculpt using tools tied to his body (the name **Aleijandinho** derives from 'aleijado', meaning 'wounded'). At this point in his life, he developed a personal style of profound originality. His works reflect his Christian spirituality and abound in most of the *cidades históricas*, in particular in Ouro Preto. To learn more about this extraordinary figure, visit the Museu Aleijandinho.

by Baroque standards, it's said to be the second richest in Brazil, with 434kg of gold and silver used in its decoration.

Mina do Chico-Rei

On the outskirts of town, at Rua Dom Silvério 108, is the **Mina do Chico-Rei** (daily 8am–5pm; R$10). The abandoned mine has claustrophobic tunnels to explore, and gives a good sense of the scale of the local mining operations. This was only a small mine. It is also an interesting place to learn more about Chico-Rei ('Little King') himself, a legendary figure said to have been an enslaved African king who bought himself and his people out of slavery, and became fabulously wealthy.

Parque Estadual do Itacolomi

A twenty-minute bus journey outside of town (numerous local buses pass), the **Parque Estadual do Itacolomi** (Tues–Sun 8am–5pm, last entry 3.30pm; R$6) is a great place to spend a day immersed in nature, with well-organised trails ranging in length for one-and-a-half to sixteen kilometres. If you have your own tent and are feeling adventurous, you can also **camp** here (R$12 during the week, R$15 on weekends).

Arrival and information

Bus The *rodoviária* (☎31/3559-3225) is on Rua Padre Rolim 661, a few minutes' walk northwest of the city centre. Buses arriving from Mariana will pass via Praça Tiradentes – get off here if you're staying in the centre of town.

Tourist information The helpful and well-informed Centro Cultural Turístico is at Praça Tiradentes 4 (daily 8.15am–7pm).

Train The train station (☎31/3551-7705) is south of town on Praça Cesário Alvim 102.

Accommodation

Ouro Preto is very popular in high season and on weekends, when reservations are always a good idea. Mid-week and off-season, you should expect substantial discounts.

TREAT YOURSELF

Pouso do Chico Rei, Rua Brigadeiro Musqueira 90, Centro ☎31/3551-1274, Ⓦwww.pousodochicorei.com.br. Wooden floorboards give this *pousada* a rustic touch and the inviting living-room upstairs with a grandfather clock adds to the homely feel. All rooms are individually furnished and most have commanding views of the Carmo Church. Breakfast is served in the dining room, home to a number of antique relics and a cosy fireplace. ❺

Brumas Hostel Rua Padre José Marcos Pena 68 ☎31/3551-2944, Ⓦwww.brumashostel.com.br. This HI hostel (dorms R$25 for members, R$30 for non-members) has clean rooms and a pleasant communal living area with couches, books and a stereo. Kitchen for self-caterers and laundry service available. ❸ with card, ❹ without.

O Sorriso do Lagarto Rua Conseheiro Quintiliano 271 ☎31/3551-4811, Ⓦwww.osorrisodolagarto.com.br. At 150m from Praça Tiradentes, this hostel has big clean dorms (R$35), brightly decorated rooms and a kitchen for guests' use. Owner Washington speaks English. ❸

Pousada Imperatriz Rua Cláudio Manoel 23 ☎31/3551-5435 or 6932. Spacious simple rooms (all doubles with private bath) and excellent rates for single travellers (R$25). Fantastic value given its prime location just off Praça Tiradentes. ❸

Pousada São Francisco Rua Padre José Marcos Pena 202 ☎31/3551-3456, Ⓦwww.pousadasaofranciscodepaula.com.br. Extremely spartan dorms, but friendly management and doubles a lot more pleasant, those on the top floor definitely worth spending the extra R$10 for. Breakfast is served on a little balcony with commanding views of town. Dorms from R$25. ❹

Templo Zen Pico de Raios in the São Sebastião district ☎31/3551-6102, Ⓔpicoderaios@yahoo.com.br. A Buddhist retreat up in the hills overlooking Ouro Preto with rooms decorated in light, peaceful Zen-like colours. A number of alternative therapies such as yoga, acupuncture and reiki are on offer. Get bus to Morro São Sebastião from the *rodoviária*. R$50 per day including food.

Eating

You won't go hungry in Ouro Preto – there are scores of excellent *mineira* and international food places for every budget.

Consola's Rua da Conceiçao 18, behind the Matriz N.S. da Conceiçao.. A variety of food from cutlets (R$9) to pizzas (R$10); try the excellent (huge) *tutú a mineira* (R$24 for two people). Closed Tues.

Do Tomáz Rua Senado Rocha Lagoa 75. Very simple place with walls bruised with dirt and paint wearing off, but the lunch dish changes daily and the price hits the spot at R$5.50.

Forno do Barro Praça Tiradentes 54. Excellent range of *mineira* specialities kept warm on the stove; lunch & dinner buffet R$12.

Passo Rua São José 54 ⓣ31/3552-3716. Very popular amongst students and buzzing most weekend evenings for a pre-dinner drink on the terrace, this place has excellent pizzas (R$15) and a very pleasant atmosphere. Call for pizza delivery.

Satélite Rua Direita 97. Good place to grab a snack (try the *batatas recheadas* for R$7); also busy in the evenings, with locals sipping on beer (R$2) and *caipirinhas* (R$3.50).

Ulysses Rua Bernardo Vasconcelos 25. Family-run place with very reasonable lunches served on a little terrace for a bargain R$5. You can see the eponymous owner at work in the little kitchen at the back. Closed Mon.

Drinking and nightlife

Most of the action is centred on Rua Direita (aka Rua Conde de Bobadella), where crowds of students spill out of bars and restaurants, aggregating and chatting on the street.

Café Choperia Real Rua Barão de Camargo 8. A few freaky psychedelic paintings decorate the walls of this popular joint, where tables spill onto the cobbled street, perfect for a drink on a warm evening (*chopp* R$2.50). Live Bossanova-style music every night from 8pm. Food also served (*prato executivo* R$10.90).

O Sótão Rua Direita 124. Fun, colourful paintings decorate this student-friendly place with straw lights. Live chilled Bossanova-style music sets the mood from 8pm. Closed Mon.

Directory

Banks and exchange There are plenty of banks wih ATMs in town, mainly on Rua São José. There is also a Bradesco at Praça Tiradentes 32. HSBC, Rua São José 201. changes traveller's cheques.

Internet Compuway, Praça Tiradentes 52 (Mon–Fri 8am–9pm, Sat till 6pm; R$4 per head) has broadband internet and Skype; Raitai, Rua Paraná 100 (Mon–Fri 9am–10pm, Sat & Sun till 9pm; R$3 per head)) also has Skype.

Laundry There are no laundry places in the historic centre of town. Nacente Lavanderia, Rua dos Inconfidentes 5 (ⓣ31/3551-5070; Mon–Fri 8am–5pm, Sat 8am–noon) will pick up and drop off your washing. R$4 per kg.

Shopping The *Feria do Artesanato* on Praça Largo do Coimbra sells a variety of local artefacts made from soapstone.

Moving on

Bus There are regular buses to Mariana (every 30min) which you can catch either at the *rodoviária* or at the bus stop north of Praça Tiradentes.

Also to: Belo Horizonte (10 daily 6am–8pm, extra services on Sun; 1hr 45min; R$17); Brasilia (daily at 7.30pm; 11hr 30min; R$105); Rio (daily at 10pm; 7hr; R$60); São João del Rei (daily at 6am, 6.30pm & 7.20pm; 4hr; R$42)

Train The historic *Trem da Vale* steam train runs between Mariana and Ouro Preto on Fri, Sat & Sun, leaving Ouro Preto at 11am and 7pm and leaving Mariana at 9am and 2pm (one hour; R$18 one way, R$30 return).

MINA DA PASSAGEM

On the road between Ouro Preto and Mariana, not far from the latter, the **Mina da Passagem** (Mon & Tues 9am–5pm, Wed–Sun 9am–5.30pm; R$24; ⓦwww.minasdapassagem.com.br) is one of the oldest deep-shaft gold mines in the region, as well as one of the richest. From the discovery of reserves here at the beginning of the eighteenth century to its closure in 1985, approximately 35 tons of gold were extracted from the mine. Today it is worth visiting as much for the roller-coaster journey down into the tunnels as for what the mine itself has to offer. The tour begins in a rickety cart that wobbles down the irregular tracks, taking you 120m below ground. En route you pass caverns where as many as three thousand slaves daily sweated blood and tears at the rock face. You will then be shown around on foot and can take a refreshing dip in a little lagoon of spectacularly clear water. Any local Transcotta bus going between Ouro Preto and Mariana will drop you at the mine.

MARIANA

A half-hour bus ride from Ouro Preto, lovely **MARIANA**, founded in 1696 and named after King Dom João V's wife Maria Ana de Austria, is home to two of Minas's most elegant town squares and a beautifully preserved colonial centre. The town can be visited as a day-trip from Ouro Preto, but it's also a great place to stay the night should you wish to escape the hordes of Brazilian tourists in Ouro Preto.

What to see and do

Once a more important town than Ouro Preto, and home to the first governors of the state, Mariana today is no more than a small town. Which means no one is too far from the centre. Head first to the impressive, elaborate **Catedral de N.S. da Assunção** (Tues–Sun 7am–7pm) on Praça Cláudio Manoel. The church was designed by Aleijandinho's father and contains many carvings by the man himself; in addition the *tapa o vento* door, painted by Athayde, is considered by many to be the most beautiful in South America. Further riches include 365kg of gold and a beautiful German organ with 1039 flutes and a keyboard made of elephants' teeth. **Organ concerts** are held on Friday at 11am and Sunday at 12.15pm. Not far away, at Rua Frei Durão 49, the former bishop's palace now houses the **Museu Arquidiocesano de Arte Sacra** (Mon–Fri 8.30am–noon & 1.30–5pm, Sat & Sun 8.30am–2pm; R$5). Among the many treasures in this lovely building, principally religious objects, are more paintings by Athayde and Aleijandinho sculptures. Two more stunning Baroque churches stand on the **Praça Minas Gerais**: the **Igreja de São Francisco de Assis** (daily 8am–5pm), with more Aleijandinho carving, is the final resting place of Athayde; the relative restraint of the **Igreja do Carmo** (daily 9am–4pm) makes an interesting contrast.

Arrival and information

Bus The local Transcotta buses from Ouro Preto will drop you off at Praça Tancredo Neves, pretty much at the heart of town. The *rodoviária* (☎31/3557-1215) is a couple of km from the centre of town – if you don't want to walk grab a local bus coming from Ouro Preto.

Tourist Information The Terminal Turístico (daily 9am–5pm; ☎31/3557-1158) is on Praça Tancredo Neves. There is also a Centro de Atenção ao Turismo (daily 8am–5pm) at Rua Direita 91–93.

Train The station for the steam train from Ouro Preto is right by the *rodoviária*.

Accommodation

Mariana boasts a number of good cheap places to stay, including a newly opened hostel.

Hotel Central Rua Frei Durão 8 ☎31/3557-1630 or 4316. The hotel is set in a beautiful colonial building, but with sixty rooms it has a strangely soulless feel. Excellent rates nonetheless and perfect location. ❸

Hotel Faisca Rua Antônio Olinto 48A ☎31/3557-1206 or 1765. Thirty-five spotless rooms, some with TV and private bath, 2min walk from the *rodoviária*. ❹

Mariana Hostel Rua Mestre Vicente 41 ☎31/3557-1435, Ⓦwww.marianahostel.com.br. HI-affiliated hostel with sparkling rooms and bathrooms, a communal area and breakfast and internet facilities available. Dorms R$25 for members, R$32 for non-members. ❹

Eating

Mariana has some excellent value *mineira* food – for dessert, treat yourself to a self-service selection of per kg ice cream and toppings at Sorvetes Lagoinha on Praça Gomes Freire.

Cozinha Real Rua Antônio Olinto 34. Next door to the Hotel Faisca, this place has a good range of *mineira* food (buffet R$9, lunch R$14.90), friendly staff and live music Fri & Sat from 9.30pm. Closed Mon.

Gaveteiros Praça Cláudio Manoel 26, opposite the cathedral. Painted in white, bright green and salmon pink, this simple restaurant with equally bright-green table cloths has pizzas for R$10 and self-service at lunchtime (R$15.90 per kg).

Rancho Praça Gomes Freire 108. Set on the beautiful *praça*, *Rancho* has excellent local cuisine kept warm on a wooden stove. Lunchtime buffet R$15, pizzas (R$18), soups (R$4) and tapas (R$6) available at dinner time. Closed Mon.

Moving on

Bus There are regular Transcotta buses to Ouro Preto (30min that leave from Praça Tancredo Neves.

Train The *Trem da Vale* connects Mariana with Ouro Preto (see p.298)

SÃO JOÃO DEL REI

Named in honour of Dom João V, king of Portugal, **SÃO JOÃO DEL REI** was one of the first settlements in the region, dating back to the end of the seventeenth century. Today the modern city has an eclectic mix of architectural styles, from imposing Baroque churches to postwar apartment blocks; it's one of the few gold towns to have found a thriving place in the modern world. Try to be in town on a Friday, Saturday or Sunday to get a ride on the nineteenth-century *Maria Fumaça* **steam train** to nearby Tiradentes.

What to see and do

As you make your way through this modern *cidade histórica*, colonial buildings will catch you unawares: **Rua Santo Antônio** in particular has preserved many of the characteristics of colonial times, while the beautiful Igreja do São Francisco de Assis should not be missed.

Igreja de São Francisco de Assis

By far the most impressive and important of the city's churches, the Baroque **Igreja de São Francisco de Assis** (daily 8am–5pm; R$1) on Praça Frei Orlando gives onto a beautiful square lined with palm trees. A vast barn of a place with carvings by Aleijandinho and his pupils, it also has a graveyard out back where President Tancredo Neves is buried. One of the most revered of modern Brazilian politicians, he is widely credited with masterminding the return to democracy in the 1980s.

Teatro Municipal

The **Teatro Municipal** (Mon–Fri 8–11am and 1–5pm; R$10; fifty percent off if you pick up a flyer from the tourist office) reopened in 2003 after a major refurbishment. The wonderful building promotes tours of its facilities for one hour every third Sunday of the month at 10am. There are also regular performances and concerts – go to the tourist office for more information on current shows.

Three museums

Three small museums round out São João's sights. The **Railway Museum**, at the station (Tues–Sun 9–11am and 1–5pm; R$1, free with a train ticket), has some interesting facts on the origins of the *Maria Fumaça* and houses valuable relics such as the first engine that ever ran on the railway track. The **Brazilian Expeditionary Force Museum** or Museu F.E.B. (Mon–Fri 8am–noon & 1–6pm; Sat & Sun 8–11am & 1.30–4pm; R$1), a couple of minutes' walk east of here, tells the story of the country's involvement in World War II, including uniforms used in combat, radios, photographs, weapons, banknotes and a Nazi flag and arm strap. Finally, the **Museu Regional** (Tues–Fri noon–5.30pm; Sat & Sun 8am–1pm; R$1), on Rua Marechal Deodoro, has a rich collection of historical and artistic objects from furniture to paintings, housed in a beautifully restored mansion.

Arrival and information

Bus The *rodoviária* (☎32/3373-4700) is about 1.5km northeast of town. If you don't want to walk into town take a local bus (10min; R$1.70) and get off at Av Tancredo Neves – turn left at the main entrance and get the bus in front of the Drogaria Americana. Alternatively, get a moto taxi from Cooperativo Moto Taxi (ⓣ31/3371-6389), which costs about R$3.

Tourist information The tourist office (Mon–Fri 8am–6pm ⓣ32/3372-7388 or 8711, ⓔcultura@saojoaodelrei.mg.gov.br) is in a little hut by the river at Av Tiradentes 136. Check locally, though, as it is due to move..

Train The train station is in the centre of town on Av Hermílio Alves. The *Maria Fumaça* train leaves São João for Tiradentes on Fri, Sat and Sun at 10am and 3pm, and returns from Tiradentes at 1pm and 5pm.

Accommodation

There are plenty of cheap hotels in São João, though quality is generally higher in nearby Tiradentes.

Aparecida Hotel Praça Dr Antonio Viegas 13 ⓣ32/3371-2540. Garishly-decorated foyer with an extraordinary mix of dark versus light colours and a fish tank with more kitsch religious bric à brac in it than fish. Clean smallish rooms all with TV. ❷

Hotel Brasil Av Tancredo Neves 395 ⓣ32/3371-2804. Facing the river, this is one of the biggest hotels in town, with fifty simple but clean rooms. ❷

Pouso Acochegante Rua Marechal Bittencourt 61 ⓣ32/3371-2637. Kitsch collectables pervade this private home, but the price cannot be beat and the rooms are clean, although small. ❷

Eating

Given the size of the town, the choice of cheap restaurants is surprisingly limited.

911 Rua Getúlio Vargas. Excellent *mineira* food all kept warm on a stove; buffet for a bargain R$8.

Chico da Roça Av Presidente Tancredo Neves 523. Simply decorated place conveniently located just across the river from the train station. Pizzas R$12; filet with fries R$25.

Restaurante Villeiros Rua Padre José Maria Xavier 132. A homely, comfy restaurant with knick-knacks scattered around. Typical *mineira* food from R$35 for two people.

Drinking and nightlife

There are plenty of late-opening bars, although most get busy only at weekends.

Bar do Zotti Av Tiradentes 801. Pleasant atmosphere within a stone, brick and wood setting; busy on weekends.

Pantanal Rua Getúlio Vargas. A popular joint to have an evening drink close to the Igreja do N.S. do Carmo.

Directory

Banks and exchange Most banks are on Av Tancredo Neves, where you will find Mercantil do Brasil, Itaú and Caixa, all with ATMs.

Internet World Game Internet, Rua Ministro Gabriel Passos 281 (daily 9am–10pm; R$2 p/h).

Post office Av Tiradentes 500 (Mon–Fri 9am–5pm, Sat 9am–noon).

Shopping The *Feria do Artesanato*, held every Sunon Av Presidente Tancredo Neves, sells local crafts.

Moving on

Bus To get to the *rodoviária* from town get the bus in front of the train station. Buses leave for Ouro Preto (daily 3am and 6pm, 4hr, R$40). São Paulo (8 daily between 8.40am and 11.05pm, 7hr 30min, R$59); Rio (Mon–Fri 8am, 2pm & 11.59pm, Sat 6am & 2pm, Sun 10am, 4 pm and 11.59pm, 5hr 30min, R$53) and Belo Horizonte (8 daily between 6am and 7pm with extra services on Sun, 3hr 30min, R$32).

TIRADENTES

With its quaint historic houses, cobblestone streets and horse-drawn carriages, **TIRADENTES** at first appears like something out of a movie set. Surrounded by mountains, the charming town is better appreciated during the week, as Brazilian tourists swarm in on weekends for a romantic break or to shop at one of the many little boutiques in town.

What to see and do

Despite being described as a *cidade histórico*, modern Tiradentes is little more than a village, which at least ensures that everything is easily found.The chief landmark, pretty much at the highest point in town, is the **Igreja Matriz de Santo Antônio** (daily 9am–5pm; R$3). Among the largest and most gold-laden of Minas Gerais's Baroque churches, it also features some of Aleijandinho's last work. Nearby, at Rua Padre Toledo 190 in the former home of one of the heroes of the *Inconfidência Mineira*, the **Museu Padre Toledo** (Tues–Sun 9am–5pm; R$3) has period furnishings and art, documents dating back to the eighteenth century, and the original slave quarters preserved out back. Some of the slaves may have worshipped at the small **Igreja da N.S. do Rosário dos Pretos** (Tues–Sun 10am–5pm; R$2), down the hill, which was built by and for slaves in 1708. There are a number of images of black saints in the chapel.

Arrival and information

Bus The *rodoviária* is in the centre of town off Rua Gabriel Passos.

Tourist information The Secretária de Turismo is on the main square at Rua Resende Costa 71 (daily 9am–5pm; ⓣ32/3355-1212, ⓦwww.tiradente.mg.gov.br). Alternatively, Estrada Real Turismo, Rua dos Inconfidentes 218B (daily 8am–7pm; ⓣ32/3355-1187 or 9959-5598) has useful tourist information and maps. They can also organize tours to the surrounding areas.

Train The train station is about 700m southeast of the main square.

Accommodation

Tiradentes caters primarily for the well-to-do and even the budget options are relatively expensive. Prices can double on national holidays, so try visiting midweek when many *pousadas* offer substantial discounts.

Pousada Arco-Iris Rua Frederico Ozanan 340 ⓣ32/3355-1167, ⓦwww.arcoiristiradentesmg.com.br. Right by the *Pousada da Bia*, this place has clean spacious rooms with private bath, a big back garden and a little pool. Free internet. ❹

Pousada da Bia Rua Frederico Ozanan 330 ⓣ32/3355-1173, ⓦwww.pousadadabia.com.br. Set in a beautiful plot of land with a little herb garden and pool at the back, you can't go wrong with the *Pousada da Bia*. ❹

Eating

Divino Sabor Rua Gabriel Passos 300. Popular place with some tables outside – buffet for R$16 or R$23.90 per kg. Closed Mon.

Empório Maria Monteiro Largo de Ô 15. Tucked away on a little street off Rua Gabriel Passos, perfect to have a coffee or snack (mini pizzas R$7, soup R$8.50) in the little courtyard or at one of the tables on the street.

Mandalun Largo das Forras 88. Although the menu may at first seem expensive, there are some cheap international options among the selection of Lebanese food, such as hamburgers (R$3.30), sandwiches (R$9) and pizzas (R$13.50).

Sabor de Minas Rua Gabriel Passos 62. Typical *mineira* food and an excellent value *prato especial* for R$8.50. Closed Wed.

Drinking and nightlife

Most bars are centred around Largo das Forras, an area which gets pretty busy most nights.

Confidências Mineiras Rua Ministro Gabriel Passos 26. Warm candlelit place with an infinite range of *cachaças* to choose from.

Sapore d'Italia Largo das Forras. Popular for an evening drink on the terrace overlooking the beautiful square.

Directory

Banks and exchange Bradesco Bank and Itaú, both with ATMs, are on a little alley to the left off Rua Gabriel Passos.

Internet Game Mania Lan House, Rua dos Incônfidentes (daily 9am–10.30pm; R$2.60 per head)).

Post office Rua Resende Costa 73 (Mon–Fri 9am–5pm).

Moving on

Bus Buses leave regularly for São João del Rei (30min; R$2). There is a bus to Belo Horizonte leaving at 7am on Mon only.

Train The *Maria Fumaça* departs for São João on Fri, Sat and Sun at 1pm and 5pm.

DIAMANTINA

Beautiful **DIAMANTINA**, six hours by bus from Belo Horizonte, is the most isolated of the historic towns. Nestled in the heart of the Serra do Espinhaço, it is surrounded by breathtakingly wild and desolate landscape. Named after the abundant diamond reserves that were first exploited in 1729, the town is rich in history, traditions and architecture and was designated a UNESCO World Heritage Site in 1999.

What to see and do

Diamantina's narrow streets are set on some exceptionally steep hills. Fortunately, almost everything of interest is tightly packed into the central area close to the main Cathedral square, the Praça Conselheiro Mota.

Museu do Diamante

The **Museu do Diamante** (Tues–Sat noon–5pm, Sun 9am–noon) is right on the square at Rua Direita 14. It's an enjoyable place to visit, bringing the colonial period vividly to life through an extraordinary variety of exhibits. They include real gold, real and fake diamonds, mining paraphernalia and reproductions of paintings depicting slaves at work. There are also a number of swords, pistols, guns and torture instruments used on slaves.

Mercado Velho and Casa da Glória

The **Mercado Velho** on Praça Barão de Guaicuí, just below the Cathedral Square, is exceptional structure, worth visiting for the building alone. The wooden arches inspired Niemeyer's design for the exterior of the Presidential Palace in Brasilia. The market itself is held only on weekends. Another place arguably more worthwhile for the building than its contents is the eighteenth-century **Casa da Glória** at Rua da Glória 298 (Tues–Sun 8am–6pm), inspired by Venetian structures. This former residence of diamond supervisors, see of the first bishops of Diamantina and subsequently a school, is now part of the Centre of Geology and contains a collection of maps, gemstones and minerals.

Igreja de N.S. Senhora do Carmo

The **Igreja de N.S. Senhora do Carmo** on Rua do Carmo (Tues–Sat 8am–noon and 2–6pm, Sun 8am–noon), built between 1760 and 1765, is probably the most worthwhile of Diamantina's churches, with an exceptionally rich interior. This includes an organ built locally in 1782 on which Lobo de Mesquita, considered the best composer of religious music of the Americas, performed many of his own works.

Arrival and information

Bus The *rodoviária* is on a steep hill, about 10min walk above the centre of town (triple that if going back and walking uphill). A taxi into town (or more importantly back up the hill from town) will cost you around R$8.

Tourist information Centro de Atendimento ao Turista, Praça JK 23 (Mon–Sat 9am–6pm, Sun 9am–2pm; ⓣ38/3531-8060, ⓔcatdiamantinaturismo@yahoo.com.br).

Accommodation

Diamantina has just one – newly opened – hostel; other than that, you won't find much in the way of budget accommodation.

Diamantina Hostel Rua do Bicame 988 ⓣ38/3531-5021 or 3531-2003, ⓦwww.diamantinahostel.com.br. HI-affiliated hostel with spotless dorms and rooms, 5min from the *rodoviária* and a 10min (uphill) walk from town. Dorms R$25 with card, R$32 without. ❸

Hotel JK Largo Dom João 135 ⓣ38/3531-8715, ⓔhotel_jk@yahoo.com.br. Set in an ugly 1960s building opposite the *rodoviária*, this is the cheapest option in town, with basic but cheap rooms. Midweek discounts. ❷

Pousada dos Cristais Rua Jogo da Bola 53 ⓣ38/3531-2897, ⓦwww.diamantinanet.com.br/pousadadoscristais. Lovely *pousada* with well-decorated spacious rooms and a pleasant patio, with commanding views of the surrounding landscape, where breakfast is served. ❹

Eating and drinking

There are a few good cheap options in town that serve tasty *mineira* dishes. Nightlife is concentrated on the little bars on Rua Direita and Rua da Quitanda.

Café A Baiúca Rua da Quintanda 13. Little place with tables spilling on the square, perfect to watch life go by as you sip a *chopp* (R$2.50) and munch on a snack (*caldo de feijão* R$5, sandwiches R$3.50) or a heartier meal (*carne de sol com mandioca* R$16).

Grupiara Rua Campos Carvalho. As you walk through the lovely old doors that conjure up images of the town at its height, the garish green, white and orange painted walls come as a bit of a surprise. Good food, though: R$15.90 per kg for lunch, pastas R$14, filet R$10.
HS Alimentacão Rua da Quitanda 57. The cheapest place in town for tasty per kg (R$10.90) food.

Listings

Banks and exchange Banco do Brazil, Praça Conselheiro Matta 23, and Banco Bradesco, Praça Barão de Guaicú 119, both have ATMs.
Internet Padaria Central, Praça Joaquim Costa 34 (Mon–Sat 6am–9pm and Sun 6am–1pm; R$2 per head)), is a cyber-bakery with a good internet connection.
Post office Praça Monsenhor Neves 59A.

Moving on

Bus Buses for Belo Horizonte leave at 1am, 6am, 10.45am, noon, 3.30pm and 6pm daily.

The Northeast

THE NORTHEAST (Nordeste) of Brazil covers an immense area and features a variety of climates and scenery, from the dense equatorial forests of western Maranhão, only 200km from the mouth of the Amazon, to the parched interior of Bahia, some 2000km to the south. It comprises all or part of the nine states of Maranhão, Piauí, Ceará, Rio Grande do Norte, Paraíba, Pernambuco, Alagoas, Sergipe and Bahia, which altogether form roughly a fifth of Brazil's land area and have a combined population of 36 million.

Notorious for its poverty within Brazil, it has been described as the largest concentration of poor people in the Americas. Yet it's also one of the most rewarding areas of Brazil to visit, with a special identity and culture nurtured by fierce regional loyalties, shared by rich and poor alike. The Northeast has the largest concentration of black people in Brazil, most of whom live on or near the coast, concentrated around Salvador and Recife, where African influences are very obvious – in the cusine, music and religion. In the *sertão* (the semi-arid region inland, though, Portuguese and Indian influences predominate in popular culture and racial ancestry. As far as specific attractions go, the region offers more than two thousand kilometres of practically unbroken beach, much of it just as you imagine tropical beaches to be: white sands, blue sea, palm trees. Colonial heritage survives in the Baroque churches and cobbled streets of Salvador and Olinda. Salvador and Recife have populations of around two million each but inland, the smaller bustling market towns of the *agreste* (a narrow hilly zone between the *sertão* and the coastal Mata Altântica) and the enormous jagged landscapes of the *sertão* more than repay the journeys. Getting around the Northeast is straightforward thanks to the region's extensive bus network. However, even the main highways get bumpy at times and minor roads can be precarious, especially during the rainy season. Generally, the rains come to Maranhão in February, in Piauí and Ceará in March, and points east in April, lasting about three months. That said, Maranhão can be wet even in the dry season, and Salvador's skies are liable to give you a soaking any time of year.

BAHIA

Bahia has over 1200kms of fabulous coastline, long hours of sunshine and an average temperature around 27 degrees centigrade. Cruise ships frequently visit the three most historic port towns: Salvador, Ilhéus and Porto Seguro. Not just the largest city in Bahia state, but the oldest and most historic city in Brazil, **Salvador** has some of the finest colonial architecture in Latin America. It was the national capital for more than two centuries, before Rio took the title

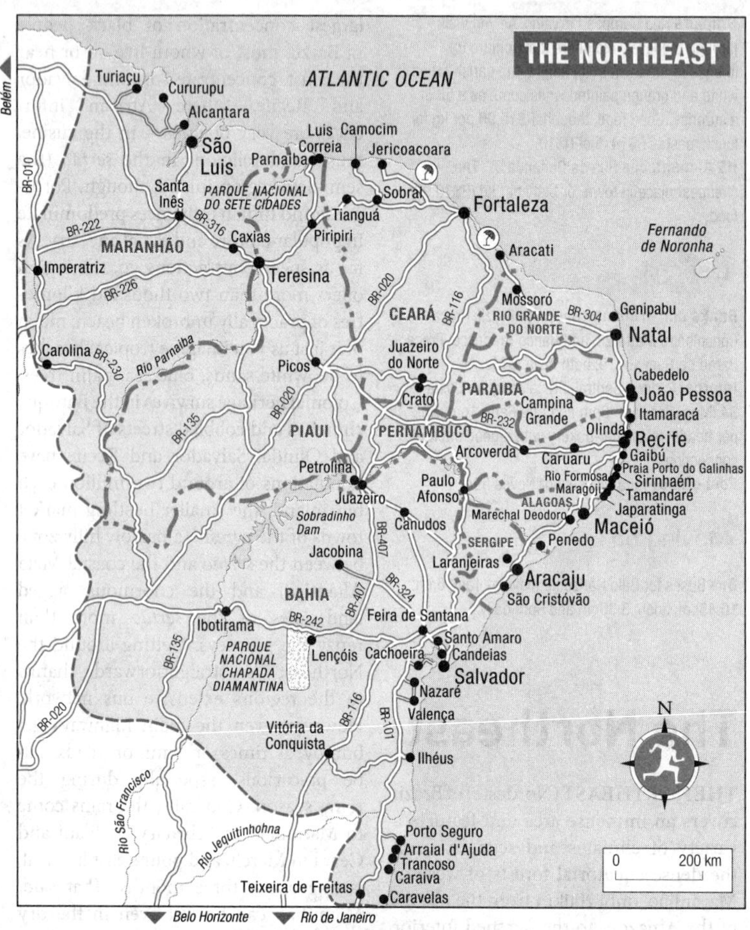

in 1763. The countryside changes to the south, with mangrove swamps and fast-developing island resorts around the town of **Valença**, before reverting to a spectacular coastline typical of the Northeast. Inland, the Bahian **sertão** is massive, a desert-like land which supports a few interesting frontier towns.

SALVADOR

Dramatically set at the mouth of the enormous bay of Todos os Santos, its old city atop a cliff, peninsular **SALVADOR** has an extraordinary energy. Its foundation in 1549 marked the beginning of Brazil's permanent occupation by the Portuguese. It wasn't an easy birth: the Caeté Indians killed and ate both the first governor and bishop before they were eventually subdued. Then, in 1624, the Dutch destroyed the Portuguese fleet in the bay and took the town by storm, only to be forced out within a year by a joint Spanish and Portuguese fleet.

These days there's a strange feeling to the old town – the number of tourist shops makes it feel a little like a Brazilian

SALVADOR ON THE WEB

Ⓦ**www.emtursa.ba.gov.br** The local tourism site is thorough, with excellent links, event schedules, information on culture, cuisine, museums, ideas on what to do, where to go and a list of every hostel and hotel in town.

Ⓦ**vejabrasil.abril.uol.com.br/Salvador** Great for pictures of and information about bars and restaurants, in Portuguese only.

Ⓦ**www.visiteabahia.com.br** For information on *candomblé*, art galleries and museums. There is an English version of the site translated by Google.

colonial Disneyland. This is Brazil, however, so the crowds of tourists also attract entrepreneurs, anglers and dregs who are bound to ensure your stay, however long, is interesting and eventful.

If you tire of the city, go down to the pier and grab a boat for the choppy ride over to **Morro de São Paulo**, an island with beautiful beaches just two hours away. Here, with a beachside room in a *pousada*, you'll lie in your hammock and wonder why you'd ever go home.

What to see and do

Salvador is built around the craggy, fifty-metre-high bluff that dominates the eastern side of the bay, and splits the central area into upper and lower sections. The heart of the old city, **Cidade Alta** (upper city, or simply Centro), is strung along its top – this is the administrative, cultural and heavily touristed centre of the city where you'll find most of the bars, restaurants, hostels and *pousadas*. This cliff-top area is linked to the more earthy financial and commercial district, **Cidade Baixa** (lower city), by precipitous streets, a funicular railway and the towering Art Deco liftshaft of the **Carlos Lacerda elevator** (open 24x7; R$0.05), t largest landmark. Stretching d cliff and along the coast are l forts, expensive hotels: **Barr** quieter neighbourhood where you will find more restaurants and *pousadas*.

Praça Municipal

Praça Municipal, **Cidade Alta**'s main square overlooking Cidade Baixa, is the place to begin exploring. Dominating the *praça* is the **Palácio do Rio Branco**, the old governor's palace, burnt down and rebuilt during the Dutch wars. Regal, plaster eagles were added by nineteenth-century restorers, who turned a plain colonial mansion into an imposing palace. The fine interior is a blend of Rococo plasterwork, polished wooden floors, painted walls and ceilings. There's also a museum, the **Memorial dos Governadores** (Mon 2–6pm, Tues–Fri 10am–noon & 2–6pm; free), with colonial pieces, less interesting than the building itself. Also facing the square is the **Câmara Municipal**, the seventeenth-century city hall.

Rua da Misericórdia

To the east, Rua Chile becomes Rua da Misericórdia where you'll find the **Museu da Misericórdia** (Mon–Sat 10am–5pm; Sun 1–5pm). For R$5 you get a tour in English of this seventeenth-century former hospital: the main room, the Salão Nobre, has 170 square metres of painted wood ceilings and walls covered with pretty Portuguese tiles. There are wonderfully photogenic views of the city, too.

Praça da Sé

Rua da Misericórdia leads into the **Praça da Sé**, the heart of Cidade Alta, where the *executivo* buses terminate. Here you've entered the **Pelourinho** or Pelô, the historic district, now home to some of the city's finest colonial mansions though less than twenty years ago it was

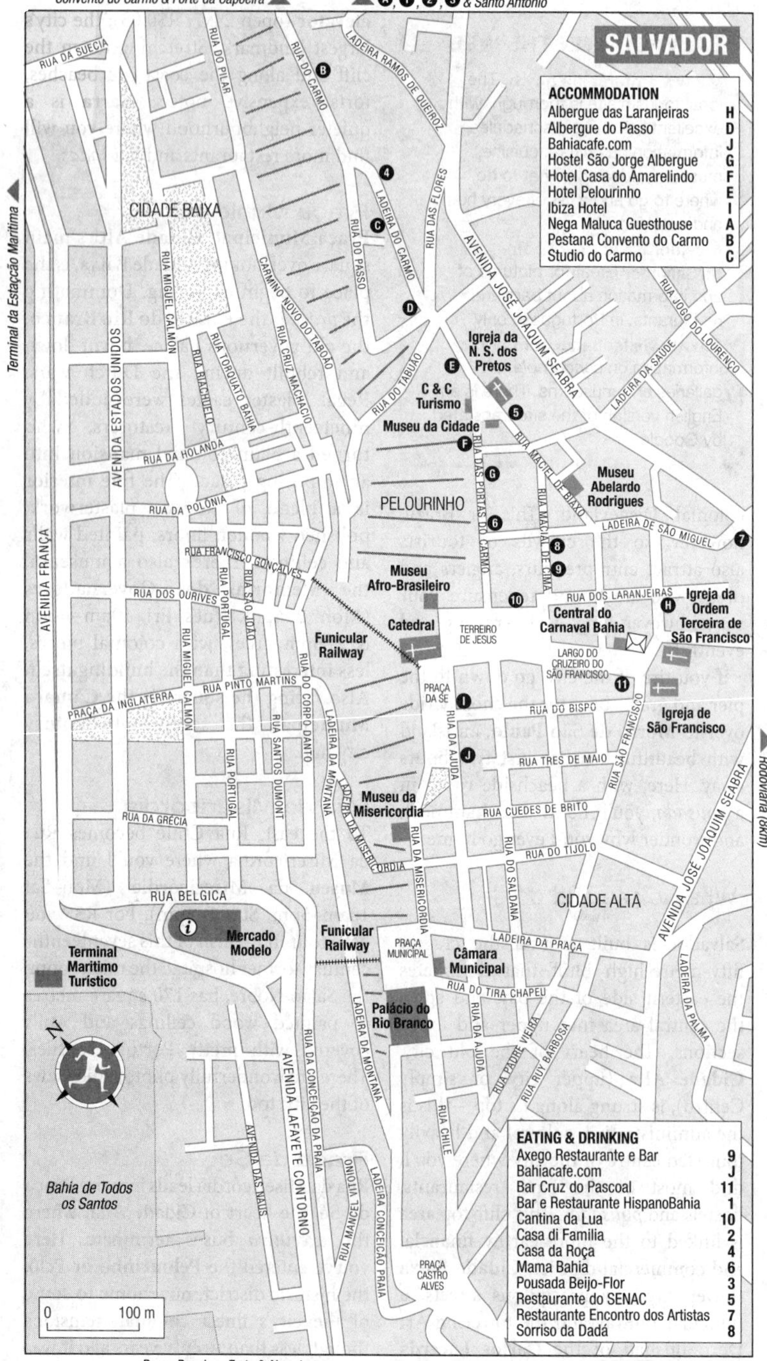

SALVADOR
ACCOMMODATION
Albergue das Laranjeiras H
Albergue do Passo D
Bahiacafe.com J
Hostel São Jorge Albergue G
Hotel Casa do Amarelindo F
Hotel Pelourinho E
Ibiza Hotel I
Nega Maluca Guesthouse A
Pestana Convento do Carmo B
Studio do Carmo C
EATING & DRINKING
Axego Restaurante e Bar 9
Bahiacafe.com J
Bar Cruz do Pascoal 11
Bar e Restaurante HispanoBahia 1
Cantina da Lua 10
Casa di Familia 2
Casa da Roça 4
Mama Bahia 6
Pousada Beijo-Flor 3
Restaurante do SENAC 5
Restaurante Encontro dos Artistas 7
Sorriso da Dadá 8
Convento do Carmo & Forte da Capoeira
A, 1, 2, 3 & Santo Antônio
Terminal da Estaçcão Maritima
Rodoviaria (8km)
Barra, Beaches, Forts & Airports
Museu da Arts Sacra
CIDADE BAIXA
PELOURINHO
CIDADE ALTA
Igreja da N. S. dos Pretos
C & C Turismo
Museu da Cidade
Museu Abelardo Rodrigues
Museu Afro-Brasileiro
Catedral
Funicular Railway
TERREIRO DE JESUS
Central do Carnaval Bahia
LARGO DO CRUZEIRO DO SÃO FRANCISCO
Igreja da Ordem Terceira de São Francisco
Igreja de São Francisco
PRAÇA DA SÉ
Museu da Misericordia
Mercado Modelo
Terminal Maritimo Turístico
PRAÇA MUNICIPAL
Câmara Municipal
Palácio do Rio Branco
PRAÇA CASTRO ALVES
Bahia de Todos os Santos
0 100 m
RUA DA SUECIA
RUA DO PILAR
RUA DO CARMO
LADEIRA RAMOS DE QUEIROZ
LADEIRA DO CARMO
RUA DO PASSO
RUA DAS FLORES
AVENIDA JOSÉ JOAQUIM SEABRA
RUA JOGO DO LOURENÇO
LADEIRA DA SAÚDE
RUA MIGUEL CALMON
AVENIDA ESTADOS UNIDOS
RUA TORQUATO BAHIA
RUA RIACHUELO
CARMINO NOVO DO TABOÃO
RUA CRUZ MACHACIO
RUA DO TABUÃO
RUA DAS PORTAS DO CARMO
RUA MACIEL DE BAIXO
RUA MACIAL DE CIMA
LADEIRA DE SÃO MIGUEL
RUA DA HOLANDA
RUA DA POLÔNIA
AVENIDA FRANÇA
RUA FRANCISCO GONÇALVES
RUA DOS OURIVES
RUA PORTUGAL
RUA SÃO JOÃO
RUA DOS LARANJEIRAS
RUA PINTO MARTINS
PRAÇA DA INGLATERRA
RUA DO CORPO SANTO
LADEIRA DA MONTANA
RUA SANTOS DUMONT
RUA DO BISPO
RUA DA AJUDA
RUA TRES DE MAIO
RUA SÃO FRANCISCO
RUA CUEDES DE BRITO
RUA DA GRÉCIA
LADEIRA DA MISERICORDIA
RUA DA MISERICORDIA
RUA DO SALDANA
RUA DO TIJOLO
RUA BELGICA
LADEIRA DA PRAÇA
LADEIRA DA PALMA
RUA DO TIRA CHAPEU
RUA PADRE VIEIRA
RUA RUY BARBOSA
RUA CHILE
RUA DA CONCEIÇÃO DA PRAIA
AVENIDA LAFAYETE CONTORNO
AVENIDA DAS NAUS
RUA MANCEL VITÓRIO
LADEIRA CONCEIÇÃO PRAIA

IMPORTANT DATES IN SALVADOR

Lavagem do Bonfim (second Thursday in January). The washing of the church steps by *baianas* in traditional dress is followed by food, music and dancing.
Pescadores do Rio Vermelho (February 2). A celebration of *Yemanjá*, the *candomblé* goddess of the sea, with a procession carrying offerings to her to the sound of Afro-Brazilian music.
Carnaval (week preceding Lent).
Festa de Santo Antônio (June 13). The main celebration of the patron saint of matrimony is held at Largo de Santo Antônio.
Dia de São João (June 24). The biggest holiday in Bahia outside Carnaval celebrates Saint John with *forró*, straw hats and traditional food.

decaying and run-down. Ahead of you is the plain **Catedral Basílica** (Mon–Sat 8–11.30am & 2–5.30pm), which was once the chapel of the largest Jesuit seminary outside Rome. The interior is one of the city's most beautiful, particularly the panelled ceiling of carved and gilded wood, which gives the church a light, airy feel – an effective antidote to the overwrought Rococo altar and side chapels. To the left of the altar is the tomb of **Mem de Sá**, third viceroy of Brazil (1556 – 1570), the most effective of Brazil's colonial governors; it was he who supervised the first phase of building in Salvador, in the process destroying the Caeté Indians. Check out the restored sacristy – portraits of Jesuit luminaries, set in the walls and ceiling, gaze down intimidatingly on intruders. In front of the Cathedral, at the heart of the Pelo, is a wide plaza known as **Terreiro de Jesus**.

Museu Afro-Brasileiro

Next to the cathedral stands one of the best museums in the city, the **Museu Afro-Brasileiro** (Mon–Fri 9am–5pm; R$5) which houses different collections, recording and celebrating the black contribution to Brazilian culture. There are displays about *candomblé* (popular religion), *capoeira* (the balletic martial art the slaves developed, see p.319), weaving, music and Carnaval. Highlights include the gallery of large photographs of *candomblé* leaders, some dating from the nineteenth century, most in full regalia and exuding pride and authority; and the famous carved panels by Carybé. The basement, containing the **Museu Arqueológico e Etnológico**, is largely given over to fossils and artefacts from ancient burial sites and incorporates the only surviving part of the old Jesuit college, a section of the cellars, in the arched brickwork at the far end. It was from here that the conversion of the Brazilian Indians was organized.

São Francisco

Terreiro de Jesus has more than its fair share of churches; there are two more fine sixteenth-century examples on the square. But outshining them, on nearby **Largo do Cruzeiro de São Francisco**, are the superb carved stone facades of two ornate Baroque buildings in a single, large complex dedicated to St Francis: the **Igreja de São Francisco** and the **Igreja da Ordem Terceira de São Francisco** (Mon–Fri 8–11:30am & 1–5pm). Of the two, the latter has the edge, covered with a wild profusion of saints, virgins, angels and abstract patterns. Remarkably, the facade was hidden for 150 years until, in 1936, a painter knocked off a chunk of plaster by mistake and revealed the original frontage, Brazil's only example of high-relief facade carved in ashlar (square-cut stones). It took nine years of careful chipping before the façade's original glory was restored, but today the whole church is one of the city's most beautiful buildings. Its **reliquary**, or *ossuário*, is extraordinary, redecorated in the 1940s in Art Deco style. From here, there's a door to a pleasant garden in back.

To reach the centre of the complex go via the Igreja de São Francisco; the entrance is by a door to the right of the main doors. The cloister in this church is decorated with one of Brazil's finest single pieces of *azulejo* – running the entire length of the cloister, this **tiled wall** depicts the marriage of the son of the king of Portugal to an Austrian princess. The realism of the incidental detail in the street scenes is remarkable: beggars and cripples display their wounds, dogs skulk, children play in the gutter; and the panoramic view of Lisbon is an important historical record of how the city looked before the calamitous earthquake of 1755.

Largo do Pelourinho

The beautiful, cobbled **Largo do Pelourinho**, down narrow Rua Alfredo de Brito beside the Museu Afro-Brasileiro, has changed little since the eighteenth century. Lined with solid colonial mansions, it's topped by the Asian-looking towers of the **Igreja da Nossa Senhora dos Pretos** (Mon–Fri 8am–noon & 1–6pm, Sat 9am–1pm, Sun 9am–noon), built by and for slaves and still with a largely black congregation. Across from here is the **Fundação Casa da Cultura Jorge Amado** (Mon–Sat 10am–6pm; free), a museum given over to the life and work of the hugely popular novelist, who doesn't number modesty among his virtues; you can have fun spotting his rich and famous friends in the collection of photographs.

More Pelourinho museums

Next door, inside an attractive Pelourinho mansion, is the **Museu da Cidade** (Mon & Wed–Sat 9.30am–6.30pm, Sun 9am–1pm; free). Among the rather tired exhibits are models of *candomblé* deities, mannequins in Carnaval costumes from years past and the personal belongings of the greatest Bahian poet, Castro Alves. There are also fascinating photographs from the early twentieth century and paintings and sculptures by young

GET YOUR FITA ON

You'll see coloured ribbons reading *Lembraça do Senhor do Bonfim da Bahia* everywhere, often with someone trying to give them to you as a 'gift.' Here's the deal, they're called **fitas** (ribbons) and the phrase roughly means 'Remembrance of Our Lord of a Good End.' Originating in the early nineteenth century, these *fitas* were originally worn around the neck after miraculous cures. Traditionally they were silk and 47cm long (the length of the right arm of an altar statue of Jesus); nowadays they're made of nylon and act as talismans rather than giving thanks for past cures.

Superstitions surrounding *fitas* are many and varied. Everyone agrees, though, that you're not meant to buy your own (hence the 'gift' pitch; you get one for yourself free, plus ten for your friends and family that you pay for) and that someone else is meant to tie it in three knots on your left wrist. Each knot gets you one wish. The catch? The wishes only come true when the *fita* breaks – naturally. If you purposefully break it, not only will your wishes go ungranted but you'll also have bad luck. Usually they break after three months or so, but they have been known to last a year.

Some say *fitas* identify you as a tourist, but you're just as likely to be identified without the bracelet, and having bought one once at least you can fend off all the other vendors. If you are going to make the commitment, the Igreja do Bonfim is the authentic place to buy.

city artists, some startlingly good, some pretty dire.

Another Pelourinho museum worth a look is the **Museu Abelardo Rodrigues** (Tues–Fri 1–6pm, weekends 1–7pm; R$1, free Thurs), at Rua Gregório de Matos 45, which has a good collection of Catholic art from the sixteenth century onwards, well displayed in a restored seventeenth-century mansion.

Igreja Bonfim

Salvador has enough churches to spend an entire week visiting but if you only have time for one more, make it the miraculous **Igreja do Nosso Senhor do Bonfim** (Tues–Sun 6.30am–noon & 2–6pm; free). If you have a prayer to make or a wish to fulfil, whether for a cure from illness or a promotion at work, this is the place to come (see box opposite). Inside, to the right of the nave, you'll find the antechamber to the **Museu dos Ex-Votos do Senhor do Bonfim** (Tues–Sat 9am–noon & 2–5pm; R$2). This is lined with heart-wrenching photos of supplicants, written pleas for divine aid and thanks for wishes fulfilled. Hanging from the ceiling are a hundred body parts – arms, heads and organs made of plastic and wood, offerings from the hopeful and thankful. The museum upstairs has less macabre, but often more valuable, offerings. Salvador's most beloved church is a thirty-minute bus ride from the centre ('Bonfim' from the bottom of the Lacerda elevator), or take a taxi.

Mercado Modelo

Cidade Baixa has few sights, but it is well worth the effort to get to the **Mercado Modelo** (Mon–Sat 9am–7pm; Sun 9am–2pm). You'll find it across the street from the bottom of the Lacerda elevator, behind a row of outdoor handicraft stalls. It's full of Bahian handicrafts, trinkets and beachwear – great for gifts and souvenirs.

Three forts

The circular, sandstone **Forte de Nossa Senhora do Pópulo e São Marcelo** (Forte do Mar), out in the harbour, was constructed around 1650 to protect Salvador from potential invasion. It can be visited only by prior arrangement (ⓣ71/3495-8359).

SALVADOR'S BEACHES

Getting to the beaches around Salvador involves taking a taxi or a **bus**. The "Via Orla" bus runs from Praça da Sé south along Avenida Oceanida and much of the nearby coast to many of the beaches below.

Praia do Porto da Barra The closest swimming beach to historic Salvador is calm and narrow, just a short bus ride away.

Praia do Farol da Barra Windswept palms and thatched huts punctuate this small, rocky beach near the lighthouse.

Praia de Ondina About 10km from the old city, with natural pools just offshore.

Praia do Rio Vermelho This beach is the starting point for the February's annual Yemanjá procession.

Praia Amaralina The strong wind and big waves make this a good beach for surfing and kiteboarding.

Jardim de Alá Wider than the closer beaches and currently one of Salvador's most popular, it's usually covered by umbrellas. About 8km from downtown.

Praia de Itapã One of the most scenic beaches mainly because of the tall, lilting palm trees.

Aldeia Hippie Arembepe, about 50km from Salvador. Aldeia Hippie beach was made famous by Mick Jagger and friends in the 1960s.

Three other forts are rather easier to visit. The first, way above Pelourinho in Santo Antonio, is the **Forte Santo Antônio Além do Carmo**, which is now the home to several Capoeira schools, which have rechristened it **Forte da Capoeira**. There are terrific views of the city from here. On the way up you pass the impressive stairs up to the **Igreja do Santíssimo Sacramento do Passo**. The church is something of a local movie star, having featured in the first Brazilian film to win an award at the Cannes film festival, "O Pagador de Promessa" (The Promise, 1962).

Another fort worth visiting is the **Forte de Santo Antônio da Barra**, past the beach at **Praia do Porto da Barra** (good street food here), at the end of the peninsula. Site of South America's first lighthouse, it now houses the **Museu Náutico da Bahia** (Tues–Sun 8.30am–7pm; R$6). The views and the room of 25 ships-in-bottles by Manecha Brandão are worth the entrance fee by themselves, but you'll also find recovered archeological treasures from coastal shipwrecks.

Arrival and information

Air Aeroporto Internacional Dep. Luís Eduardo Magalhães (☎71/3204-1010) is 20km northeast of the city, connected to the centre by an hourly shuttle express bus service to Praça da Sé (45min to 1hr 30min depending on traffic, last at 10pm; R$4) via the beach districts and Campo Grande. If you're relying on this to catch your plane bear in mind that the word 'schedule,' in Bahia is a relative term. During the week the public "Aeroporto" bus leaves Praça da Sé every 15min (weekends every 40min, starting at 7.40am; R$4) and travels along Av Oceânica. A taxi to the centre will set you back around R$80.

Bus The *rodoviária* (☎71/3460-8300) is 8km east of the centre. To get to the Cidade Alta take a taxi (about R$20) or catch the *executivo* bus from the Iguatemi shopping centre across the busy road. The bus costs R$4–6 and makes a stately progress through the beach districts of Pituba and Rio Vermelho before dropping you off at the Praça da Sé.

Tourist Office The state tourist agency, Bahiatursa (Ⓦwww.bahiatursa.ba.gov.br), runs several **tourist information booths**, most of which have English-speakers. The most helpful are at the airport (daily 7.30am–11pm; ☎71/3204-1244), and the main office in Pelourinho, at Rua João de Deus 1, corner of Rua de Langeiras (☎71/3321-2463). Branches also at: *rodoviária* (daily 7.30am–9pm; ☎71/3450-3871); Centro de Convenções da Bahia, Jardim Armação (Mon–Fri 8.30am–6pm; ☎71/3370-8494); Instituto Mauá Praça Azevedo Fernandes 01, Porto da Barra (Mon–Sat 9am–6pm, Sun 9am–1.30pm; ☎71/3264-4671); Mercado Modelo (Mon–Sat 9am–7pm, Sun 9am–noon; ☎71/3241-0242); SAC Shopping Barra, Av Centenário 299 (Mon–Fri 9am–7pm, Sat 9am–2pm; ☎71/3264-4566); Shopping Iguatemi, Av Tancredo Neves 148, Pituba (Mon–Fri 9am–11pm, Sat 9am–2pm; ☎71/480-5511). Another source of information is the **tourist hotline**, "Disque Turismo" – call ☎0800/716-622 and you should find an English-speaker at the other end. Look out too for the *Veja* 'best of' guide to Salvador (Portuguese only) which has excellent listings.

City transport

Buses There are three **local bus terminals**, and the bus system is efficient, cheap (R$2) and easy to use, running till midnight daily. To reach the centre, any bus with "Sé", "C. Grande" or "Lapa" on the route card will do. Air-conditioned **frescãos** run most of the same routes and usually cost R$4–6.

Taxis Taxis are metered and plentiful; recommended at night although most museums, churches and historic buildings are concentrated within walking distance of each other in Cidade Alta. An average trip between Pelô and Barra will cost R$20. Alôtaxi ☎71/3388-4411; LigueTaxi ☎71/3357-7777.

Accommodation

Salvador is the second most popular tourist destination in Brazil and consequently full of hotels. Unless you want to stay near a beach (in which case you'll want to choose Barra over expensive and distant Ondina), the best area to head for is **Cidade Alta**, not least because of the spectacular view across the island-studded bay. While *pousada* prices generally stay within reason be aware that during Carnaval all bets are off, while out of season good discounts may be on offer.

Pelourinho

Albergue das Laranjeiras Rua da Ordem Terceira 13 ☎71/3321-1366, Ⓦwww.laranjeirashostel.com.br. This is the HI hostel in Pelô's centre where

TREAT YOURSELF

Some of the more expensive places to stay are so cool they're worth seeing or having a drink at even if you can't afford to stay the night.

Grande Hotel da Barra Av Sete de Setembro 3564, Porto da Barra ⓣ71/2106-8600, ⓦwww.grandehoteldabarra.com.br. Nothing special about the rooms, but if you get one with a balcony the view will blow you away. Just 75 steps from the stairs to the beach. ❻

Hotel Casa do Amarelindo Rua das Portas do Carmo 6, Pelourinho ⓣ71/3266-8550, ⓦwww.casadoamarelindo.com. This boutique hotel with a rooftop pool in a meticulously renovated building is pricey but rooms lack for nothing. Modern furniture, chic accoutrements and details like double-glazed windows to give revellers respite from Carnaval. ❼

Pestana Convento do Carmo Rua do Carmo 1, Pelourinho ⓣ71/3327-8400, ⓦwww.pestana.com. On a hilltop above central Pelourinho, this hotel in a former sixteenth-century convent is truly beautiful. Forget the modern conveniences you'll have to cut your trip short to pay for (a gym, spa, LCD TVs, etc), the breezy 'lobby' is colonnaded, lined with fine-tiled murals and marvellous old floors. Stop by just to see it. ❾

the hip kids hang. It's almost chic, as good as Europe's best with laundry, a lobby crêperie and even bunks that manage to be cool. HI discounts offered. Dorm R$35. ❹

Albergue do Passo Rua do Passo 3 ⓣ71/326-1951, ⓦwww.passoyouthhostel.com.br. Another good Pelourinho hostel in an attractive building; variety of rooms with showers, some with a/c and TV, plus good breakfasts and a communal room with cable TV. Dorm R$34. ❹

Bahiacafe.com Praça da Sé 20 ⓣ71/322-1266. You can't beat the location, it has the best coffee in town and the rooms are modern with bright colours. ❹

Ibiza Hotel Rua do Bispo 6–8, Praça da Sé ⓣ71/3322-6929. The beds, in strange tiled structures, still sag somehow, the TV & fan controls are in your headboard but you get a budget view of Praça da Sé in all its glory. ❹

Hotel Pelourinho Rua das Portas do Carmo 20 ⓣ71/3322-3939, ⓦwww.hotelpelourinho.com. Soulless but near the churches and with helpful information about *candomblé* ceremonies. ❹

Hostel São Jorge Albergue Rua das Portas do Carmo 25, 1st Floor ⓣ71/3266-709, ⓦwww.saojorgehostel.com. Walk through a display of T-shirts and upstairs to a little hostel. Dorms have wooden beds and funky sheets; breakfast included with room rate. Dorm R$30. ❸

Nega Maluca Guesthouse Rua dos Marchantes 15, Santo Antonio ⓣ71/3242-9249, ⓦwww.negamaluca.com. A backpackers' paradise: access to a washing machine, hookahs, free internet, a balcony with hammocks and temporary pets (two cats and a dog live there). Dorm R$26. ❹

Studio do Carmo Ladeira do Carmo 17, Pelourinho, ⓦwww.studiodocarmo.com.br, ⓣ71/3326-2426. Proper, colourful rooms in a lovely renovated colonial house. Breakfast is included and there's kitchen access. ❺

Santo Antonio

Casa di Familia Rua Direita do Santo Antonio 22 ⓣ71/3241-4321. The owner of this no-frills *pousada*, Nalva, doesn't bother having a sign and the fluorescent-lit rooms are the barest of bare, but there's access to two kitchens and a roof with one of Salvador's most spectacular views, perfect with a beer before crashing. Dorm R$15. ❷

Pousada Beijo-Flor Rua Direita de Santo Antonio 259 ⓣ71/3241-7085, ⓦwww.beijaflorpousada.com.br. Seven impressively renovated rooms in a quiet, upscale *pousada* near the Forte da Capoeira, some with a/c and lovely terraces with sea views. ❺–❻

Barra and the beaches

Albergue do Porto Rua Barão de Sergy 197, Barra ⓣ71/3264-6600, ⓦwww.alberguedoporto.com.br. A gated, bright-yellow HI hostel, blocks from the beach with sea breezes floating through open windows. A beautiful pool table and funky chill areas lock it in as a good place to stay, even if the staff is too-cool-for-school. HI discounts. Dorm R$35. ❹

Ambar Pousada Rua Afonso Celso 485, Barra ⓣ71/3264-6956, ⓦwww.ambarpousada.com.br. A friendly *pousada* close to Praia do Porto da Barra. Basic, clean, cosy rooms on two storeys set around a pleasant courtyard with a renowned free breakfast. Dorm R$38. ❹

Pousada Manga Rosa Rua Cesar Zama 60, Porto da Barra ⓣ71/267-4266, ⓦwww.mangarosa.com. More bed and breakfast than *pousada*, but either way the wooden floors, baby blue colouring and location a block from the ocean make this a great place to stay. ⑤

Pousada Noa Noa Sete de Setembro 4295, Farol da Barra ⓣ71/3264-1148, ⓦwww.pousadanoanoa.com. Right across from the ocean: the spacious rooms inside this upscale *pousada* are just as colourful as its bright orange exterior. ⑤

Camping

Camping Ecológico Stella Mares Itapuã, in front of Itapuã beach ⓣ71/3374-0102. City-run site about 30min from downtown; it has shower and restaurant facilities and space for motorhomes as well as campers. R$12 per person, or R$22 to rent a tent.

Eating

Eating out is a pleasure in Salvador. There's a huge range of restaurants and the local cuisine (*comida baiana*) is deservedly famous so you really can't go wrong. Street food is fabulous too. While Pelourinho has a growing number of stylish, expensive places, it's still relatively easy to eat well for less than R$20 (albeit easier to spend twice that).

Restaurants

Axego Restaurante e Bar Rua João de Deus 1, 1st Floor, Pelourinho ⓣ71/3242-7481. Tiled colonial building with seafood dishes for two just R$40 and desserts just R$3.

Bar e Restaurante HispanoBahia Rua do Carmo 68, Santo Antonio ⓣ71/3241-0325. Black-lit yet somehow still unpretentious and no-frills, *HispanoBahia* does per kilo meals for R$18.90 as well as snacks for less than R$5. Try the *bobo de camarão* (shrimp in coconut and yucca purée) for R$40.

Cantina da Lua Rua das Portos do Carmo on Largo Terreiro de Jesus ⓣ71/3322-4041, ⓦwww.cantinadalua.com.br. This standby on the square is a little jaded but still does Bahian standards well, until the wee hours. They also have an affordable self-service, R$24.90/kilo.

Casa da Roça Ladeira do Carmo 27, Pelourinho/Santo Antonio ⓣ71/3241-8580. Lively pizzeria that also does pastas, often accompanied by live music.

Mama Bahia Rua das Portos do Carmo 21, Pelourinho ⓣ71/3322-4397. An enjoyable corner restaurant good for a bottle of cheap wine and some Bahian standards; choose carefully and you'll get a feast for just R$30.

Restaurante do SENAC Av Tancredo Neves 1109, Pelourinho ⓣ71/3273-9785. The municipal restaurant school in a restored mansion looks expensive from outside, but it's good-value: there's a buffet of forty labelled Bahian dishes and more than twelve desserts – pay per kilo during the week; prices are slightly higher at weekends. Open daily 11.30am–3.30pm, Mon–Sat 6:30–10pm.

Restaurante Encontro dos Artistas Rua Francisco Muniz Barreto (Antigas Laranjeiras) 15–34, Pelourinho ⓣ71/3242-7783. Down a quiet street away from the craziness. Indoor and outdoor seating and a terrific *moqueca* and *vatapá* R$32.

Sorriso da Dadá Rua Frei Vicente 5, Pelourinho ⓣ71/3321-9642. Locals still rave about the local Bahian cuisine here, despite gradually smaller portions and higher prices.

Cafés, Bakeries, self-catering and street food

Bahiacafe.com Praça da Sé 20 ⓣ71/322-1266. The best coffee in town is at Salvador's best internet café in this hotel 'lobby.'

CRIME AND SAFETY

Salvador has more problems with **robberies** and **muggings** than anywhere else in the Northeast save Recife. The buildings in tourist-heavy Pelourinho have video cameras perched on them and the area is heavily policed until late at night. It's safe, but you'll definitely feel you're being observed by scallywags and ne'er-do-wells so **precautions** are in order. Don't wander down ill-lit side streets at night unless you are within sight of a policeman and don't use the Lacerda elevator after early evening. Avoid walking up and down the winding connecting roads between the Cidade Alta and Cidade Baixa, and be careful about using city buses on Sundays when few people are around; the *executivo* bus is a safer option. Give the Avenida do Contorno – the seafront road that runs north from the harbour past the *Solar do Unhão* restaurant – a miss too; it's dangerous even in daylight when gangs lie in wait for tourists who don't know better. If you want to go to the restaurant, or the Museu de Arte Moderna nearby, take a taxi. Lastly, the area between Praça da Sé and Praça Campo Grande, while busy by day, is ominous at night. If you're in Pelourinho late at night and need to get back to a hostel in Barra, take a taxi.

COMIDA BAIANA

The secret to Bahian cooking is twofold: a rich seafood base, and traditional West African **ingredients** such as palm oil, nuts, coconut and hot peppers. Many ingredients and dishes have African names: most famous of all is *vatapá*, a bright yellow porridge of palm oil, coconut, shrimp and garlic, which looks vaguely unappetizing but is delicious. Other dishes to look out for are *moqueca*, seafood cooked in the inevitable palm-oil based sauce; *caruru*, with many of the same ingredients as *vatapá* but with the addition of loads of okra; and *acarajé*, deep-fried bean cake stuffed with *vatapá*, salad and (optional) hot pepper. Bahian cuisine also has good **desserts**, less stickily sweet than elsewhere: *quindim* is a delicious cake of coconut flavoured with vanilla, often with a prune at the centre.

Some of the best food is also the cheapest – even gourmets could do much worse than start with the street *baianas*, women in traditional white dress. Don't be scared of *pimenta*, the tasty hot pepper sauce whose punch locals tend to exaggerate. The *baianas* serve *quindim*, *vatapá*, slabs of maize pudding wrapped in banana leaves, fried bananas dusted with icing sugar, and fried sticks of sweet batter covered with sugar and cinnamon – all gorgeous.

Internet do F@rol Av Sete de Setembro 42, Barra. Snacks and burgers, coffee and beer along with cheap internet (R$2.50 per hr), across the street from the beach in an open-air café.

Drinking and nightlife

Salvador's most distinctive **nightlife** is to be found in Pelourinho. The Rua das Laranjeiras, Cruzeiro de São Francisco and Rua Castro Rabelo all have lively bars where you can sit outside and watch human drama unfold. Wherever you choose you won't be far from undoubtedly the biggest attraction of the area, **live music**. Instead of being connected to a single style – as Rio is to samba and Recife is to *frevo* – Salvador has spawned several and claims to have become the creative centre of Brazilian music. Some of the best music comes from organized cultural groups who have clubhouses and an *afoxé* – Salvador's Africanized version of a *bloco* – or two for Carnaval. They are overwhelmingly black, a lot of their music is political and in the weeks leading up to Carnaval, their *afoxés* have public rehearsals around the clubhouses – the music is superb.

Fun as it is, it should be noted that Pelourinho is heavily touristed so prices are a little higher and it attracts the hangers-on, beggars and prostitutes you'd expect. Quieter and less touristy but just as fun are the bars on the edge of Pelourinho and up-and-coming Santo Antônio, just up Ladeira do Carmo. There are some really cool local spots here you should check out.

Bar Cruz do Pasquel Rua Joaquim Tavora 2, Santo Antonio. A true local hangout. Walk right past the yellow patio furniture outside and behind the bar like you own the place and you'll be rewarded by a secret patio and a great view. Try the *carne de sol* with a Skol.

Hotel Casa do Amarelindo Rua das Portas do Carmo 6, Pelourinho/Santo Antonio. You can visit the pristine rooftop bar even if you're not staying at the hotel – something most locals haven't caught onto yet. The bar's view is spectacular, especially as the sun sets, and the *cajú caipirinha* deliciously deadly. Just be careful going back down the spiral staircase.

Shopping

Instituto de Artesanato Visconde de Mauá Praça Azevedo Fernandes 02, Porto da Barra (☎71/3116-6110, ⓦ www.maua.ba.gov.br). Founded by the government to promote regional artists, you'll find carving, ceramics and hammocks at fixed prices among other handicrafts here.

Mercado Modelo Praça Visconde de Cayru 250 ☎71/3241-2893. Handicraft market in Cidade Baixa.

Shopping Barra Av Centenário 2992 ☎71/2108-8222; Mon–Fri 9am–10pm; Sun noon–9pm. Mall handy for the Barra beaches.

Directory

Aeroclube Plaza Show Av Otávio Mangabeira 6000 (☎71/3462-8000). An open-air mall near the airport with bowling, cinemas, go-karting as well as bars and restaurants. Take the bus marked 'Praia de Flamengo'.

Airlines Air France Rua Portugal 17, Ed. Regente Feijó, Cidade Baixa ☎71/351-6631; GOL

CARNAVAL

Although, as everywhere, increasingly commercialized, **Carnaval** in Salvador remains at heart a street event of mass participation. Even if you're not going to be in town for the main event you can still get a taste of what's to come. From December onwards Carnaval groups hold **public rehearsals** and dances city-wide, in the Largo do Pelourinho, the Teatro Miguel Santana on Rua Gregório de Matos, on Rua Chile, and near the fort of Santo Antônio Além do Carmo. These rehearsals get very crowded, so be careful with your belongings.

Carnaval is a pretty accepting atmosphere but it's worth bearing in mind that all-black *blocos* may be black culture groups who won't appreciate being joined by non-black Brazilians, let alone gringos; be sensitive or ask before leaping in.

Information about Carnaval is published in special supplements in the local papers. Bahiatursa and EMTURSA offices have schedules, route maps, and sometimes sell tickets for the Campo Grande grandstands. For *blocos* reservations, information and all the Carnaval gear you could possibly imagine, visit the conveniently located **Central do Carnaval Bahia**, Largo São Francisco 12 (ⓣ71/3321-0219, ⓦwww.centraldocarnaval.com.br).

ⓣ0300/7892121; LANchile ⓣ71/3241-1401; Lufthansa, Av Tancredo Neves 805, Sala 601, Iguatemi ⓣ71/341-5100; TAP Air Portugal, Av Tancredo Neves 1632 ⓣ71/3113-2600; TAM, Av Tancredo Neves 3343 ⓣ71/3273-6700; Varig, Rua Carlos Gomes 6, Cidade Alta ⓣ71/343-3100.

Banks and Exchange You'll find plenty of ATM's in Salvador but banks aren't concentrated in any one place. If you fly in try the Confidence Câmbio and Banco do Brasil at the international airport otherwise there is a Citibank on Rua Marquês de Leão 71 in Barra.

Car Rental Aerocar, Rua Fonte do Boi 26, Loja 2, Rio Vermelho (ⓣ71/3335-1110); Hertz, Aeroporto Internacional de Salvador (ⓣ71/3377-6554); Localiza, Av Oceânica 3057, Ondina (ⓣ71/3332-1999); Unidas, Aeroporto Internacional de Salvador (ⓣ71/3204-1175) and Av Oceânica 3097, Ondina (ⓣ71/3247-2121).

Embassies and Consulates Netherlands, Largo do Carmo 4, Room 101, Bairro Santo Antonio ⓣ71/3241-3001; US, Av Tancredo Neves, 1632, Room 1401, Salvador Trade Center, Torre Sul, Caminho das Árvores, ⓣ71/3113-2090.

Football Esporte Clube Bahia, Av Otávio Mangabeira, Boca do Rio (ⓣ71/3461-3433, ⓦwww.eusoubahia.com); Esporte Clube Vitória, Estrada Velha do Aeroporto Pau da Lima (ⓣ71/3393-3929, ⓦwww.ecvitoria.com.br).

Hospitals Hospital Aliança, Av Juracy Magalhães Jr 2096, Rio Vermelho (ⓣ71/2108-5600); Hospital São RafaeL, Av São Rafael 2152, São Marcos (ⓣ71/3281-6111).

Internet Bahiacafe.com, Praça da Sé 20 (R$4 per hr); Internet Café.com, Rua João de Deus 02, 1st Floor, Pelourinho; Internet do F@rol, Av Sete de Setembro 42, Barra (R$2.50 per hr).

Laundries Branches of O Casal at: Av Sete de Setembro 2721, Barra (ⓣ71/3267-1189); Rua César Zama 20, Loja 01 (ⓣ71/264-9320); Av Presidente Vargas 2400, Loja 46 ⓣ71/203-8209.

Left luggage Malubag at the airport (ⓣ71/3204-1150, 24hr). Small/large lockers: R$7/9 per day.

Pharmacies Farmácia Sant'ana, Largo Porto da Barra & Rua Barão de Sergy, Barra.

Post office Largo do Cruzeiro de São Francisco 20, Pelourinho (Mon–Fri 8am–6pm).

Tour operators Backpackers, Rua Cézar Zama 180, Barra (ⓣ71/3264-2024, ⓦwww.backpackerstour.com.br) are helpful for travel arrangements; C & C Turismo, Largo do Pelourinho (ⓣ71/3326-6969, ⓦwww.cecturismobahia.com.br) can arrange visits to *candomblé* ceremonies; Salvador Bus (ⓣ71/3356-6425, ⓦwww.salvadorbus.com.br) operate double-decker buses that do various city-tours, with tickets available at hotels and travel agencies; Visao Turismo, Aeroporto Internacional Dep. Luís Eduardo Magalhães (ⓣ71/3251-8000, ⓦwww.visaotur.com.br) can help you book budget flights at the airport.

Moving on

Air The usual suspects, GOL, TAM and Varig, all have more than five flights a day to Fortaleza, Rio, São Paulo, and Recife and several a day to other destinations throughout Brazil. TAM and other international carriers have direct flights to Miami, Buenos Aires and Lima.

CAPOEIRA

Capoeira began in Angola as a ritual fight to gain the nuptial rights of women when they reached puberty. It has evolved into a graceful, semi-balletic art form somewhere between fighting and dancing. It's usually accompanied by the characteristic rhythmic twang of the *berimbau*, and takes the form of a pair of dancers/fighters leaping and whirling in stylized "combat" – which, with younger *capoeiristas*, occasionally slips into a genuine fight when blows land accidentally and tempers fly. There are regular displays on Terreiro de Jesus and near the entrances to the Mercado Modelo in Cidade Baixa, largely for the benefit of tourists and their financial contributions but still interesting. The best *capoeira*, though, can be found in the *academias de capoeira*, organized schools with classes you can watch for free:

Associação de Capoeira Mestre Bimba Rua das Laranjeiras 1, Terreiro de Jesus, 1st Floor. Probably the most famous *academia*, it sometimes has classes open to tourists.

Academia de João Pequeno de Pastinha Largo Santo Antônio, Forte Santo Antônio ⓣ71/3323-0708. If you want a *really* cool Capoeira experience get out of Pelourinho and up to the Forte Santo Antônio, just a short walk up the hill. Inside the renovated white fort are several schools of Capoeira where the setting may contribute to making you feel more like a Jedi knight or Shaolin monk in training. You can watch, or if you want to join in, classes (R$20 each; R$70 for a month) last three hours (Mon, Wed, & Fri, 9am, 4pm, 7.30pm).

Bus Buses leave for all parts of the country from Terminal Rodoviária Armando Viana de Castro, Av ACM 4362, Pituba (ⓣ71/3460-8300).

MORRO DE SÃO PAULO

The island of **Tinharé**, about 75km southwest of Salvador, is home to the world famous beaches at **MORRO DE SÃO PAULO**, where there's *always* a great atmosphere, with reggae bars, hippy dives, divers, surfers and terrific seafood restaurants. With no roads on the island (people use wheelbarrows to transport things along the sandy paths), it's still relatively peaceful and undeveloped, though at the weekends, especially between December and March, vast crowds descend.

What to see and do

The island itself is quite large, around 30km by an average of 8km. At the northwest end there's the main settlement and resort of Morro de São Paulo, while at the diagonally opposite end sits the much smaller and less developed fishing village of **Garapua**. There are four main beaches on the populated corner of the island (known simply as First, Second, Third and Fourth beaches), all linked by paths. The small settlement of Morro de São Paulo sits on a hill between the port and the first of the four beaches, **Primeira Praia**.

You won't have finished paying your R$6.50 **Taxa de Turismo** before being besieged by locals offering to be your "guide." They're tenacious but there's one easy way to shake them if you've worn your bathing suit – from the port, follow the coastal path (clockwise if you were circling the island) up the hill, past the *pousadas* and the health clinic, to the lighthouse. Behind it to the right you'll find an old, semi-ruined fortification and a view of Primeira Praia as well as your escape route: the **Tiroleza Zipline** (daily 10am–5.30pm; ⓦwww.tiroleza.com.br). It's 70m high, about 350m long, and you can pay R$25 to ride down superman-style, or seated, from below the rusting canon jutting out over the ocean. The 25-second ride ends with a splash in the water about 25 metres off the beach. Of course, you can just as easily, if less dramatically, walk to the beach in five minutes from the pier.

Arrival and information

You can reach Tinharé by air or sea. It's obviously much quicker to fly, but it's also far more expensive.

Air Aero Star flies thrice daily to and from the island (8am, 12.30pm & 3.30pm out, 8.40am, 1pm & 4.10pm return; R$180 each way; ⓣ71/3377-4406, ⓦwww.aerostar.com.br). Check online for special promotions. Adey Táxi Aéreo also has three flights there and back (8.30am, 12.30pm and 3.30pm out, 9.15am, 1.15pm & 4.15pm return; R$170, each way; ⓣ71/3204-1393).

Boat All boats are priced the same (R$60 each way) and leave daily from Salvador's Terminal Turistico Maritimo, the blue building at water's edge behind the Mercado. Buy tickets a half-hour in advance. Lancha Ilha Bela (ⓣ71/9195-6744) departs 8.30am, returns 3pm; Catamará Farol do Morro (ⓣ71/3326-7674) departs 7am, returns 5.30pm; Catamará Biônica de Tinharé (ⓣ71/3326-7674) departs 9am & 2pm, returns 11.30am and 3pm.

Tourist office The tourist information office (ⓣ75/3652-1083, ⓦwww.morrosp.com.br) is at Marcos e Ana, just as you enter the island from the top of the port steps. They're friendly, speak English and give excellent advice about food and lodging. A good **website** for the history of the island and information about *pousadas*, restaurants and nightlife is ⓦwww.morrodesaopaulo.com.br.

Accommodation

It sometimes feels as though there are more *pousadas* than people on the island, a feeling only reinforced on arrival by the number of people trying to persuade you to follow them to the 'best' place to stay. As long as you're not carrying too much stuff, take some time to walk down at least to beach three. There are plenty of reasonably priced places here where, for R$40–60, you can find a room literally on the beach, with a hammock where you can listen to the waves crash all night. Others have beach-level bar/pool combinations where you can watch the preening, posing and lazing all around you (*Pousadas Palmeiro*, *Da Torre*, *Porto dos Milagres*, *Pousada* and *Villa Das Pedras* all have these kinds of charms). Certainly don't jump at the first thing, *Pousada Natureza* (ⓦwww.hotelnatureza.com, ⓣ75/483-1361) unless you're looking to splash out (starting from R$590 per night).

Eating and drinking

Food-wise, the island offers everything from crêpes and sushi to pizza, fruit, sandwiches and Bahian specialities. It's not necessarily all gourmet, but it's pretty hard to go wrong. There is one way to really go right, and that's *Bar e Restaurante Piscina* (ⓣ75/3652-1461) a weather-beaten wooden structure directly on the fourth beach. The *mariscada* here, an incredibly delicious fish stew big enough for two people to share (R$70), is worth the trip to Morro de São Paulo on its own. Nightlife? Well, with all the beach bars, *pousadas*, and supermarkets with fruit juice steeped *cachaça* for R$6, let's just say *it* will find *you*.

PERNAMBUCO

Recife, capital of the state of **Pernambuco**, wasn't founded by the Portu-

ISLAND ACTIVITIES

Diving enthusiasts or anyone wishing to learn scuba can contact Companhia do Mergulho, Primeira Praia (ⓣ75/3652-1200, ⓦwww.ciadomergulho.com.br). They go out in fast boats by day and night to clear-water areas around the island.

Horseback rides They don't have zebras but it's possible to ride along the beach playing Sheena by calling ⓣ75/3652-1070.

Surfing amateurs looking for instruction can call MSP Surf School (ⓣ75/3652-1642).

guese: when they arrived in the 1530s, they settled just to the north, building the beautiful colonial town of **Olinda** and turning most of the surrounding land over to sugar. A century later, the Dutch, under Maurice of Nassau, took Olinda and burned it down, choosing to build a new capital, Recife, on swampy land to the south, where there was the fine natural harbour that Olinda had lacked. The Dutch, playing to their strengths, drained and reclaimed the low-lying land, and the main evidence of the Dutch presence today is not so much their few surviving churches and forts dotted up and down the coast, as the reclaimed land on which the core of Recife is built.

RECIFE

RECIFE, the Northeast's second-largest city, appears rather dull at first, but it's lent a colonial grace and elegance by **OLINDA**, 6km to the north and considered part of the same conurbation. Recife itself has long since burst its colonial boundaries – much of the centre is now given over to uninspired modern skyscrapers and office buildings. But there are a few quiet squares, where an inordinate number of impressive churches lie cheek by jowl with the uglier urban sprawl of the past thirty years.

North of the centre are some pleasant leafy suburbs, dotted with museums and parks, and to the south is the modern beachside district of **Boa Viagem**. For all the beaches, it's surprising how few restaurants and bars you'll find along them; Olinda's sea road has a handful, Boa Viagem, fewer. It will be a long walk, perhaps to Rio, before you see these establishments with any frequency.

Whether swimming in the water or wandering around Recife and Olinda, be careful – sharks are known to patrol these waters and Recife is one of Brazil's most violent cities, an unsurprising statistic given the immediately obvious disparity of wealth and stark poverty, and the large number of homeless people on the streets. This is also a place where you'll be happy to have brought your mosquito net.

What to see and do

Modern Recife sprawls onto the mainland, but the heart of the city is three small **islands**, **Santo Antônio**, **Boa Vista** and **Recife** proper, connected with each other and the mainland by more than two dozen bridges over the rivers Beberibe and Capibaribe. From South to North you have the Boa Viagem district, then Santo Antônio situated between Recife on the East and Boa Vista on the West. Where Boa Vista stretches North leaving Santo Antônio (Centro) behind, is Olinda.

Recife Island

There's not *that* much to see on Recife island proper but this one-time rundown part of the city now has some bars and restaurants and is a pleasant place during the day to walk around. One of the few sites is the **Sinagoga Kahal Zur Israel**, Rua do Bom Jesus 197 (☎81/3224-2128), said to be the first synagogue built in the whole of the Americas, in 1637. On the Eastern side of the island in the

RECIFE AND OLINDA ONLINE

Ⓦwww.olindaarteemtodaparte.com.br Official site with pictures and listings of everything Olinda.

Ⓦwww.pernambuco.com Portuguese site helpful for extensive listings, addresses and opening hours.

Ⓦwww.recife.info An excellent, thorough site with information on everything from shopping to Carnaval.

Ⓦvejabrasil.abril.com.br/recife *Veja* magazine's listings of all things food and drink are in Portuguese but still helpful.

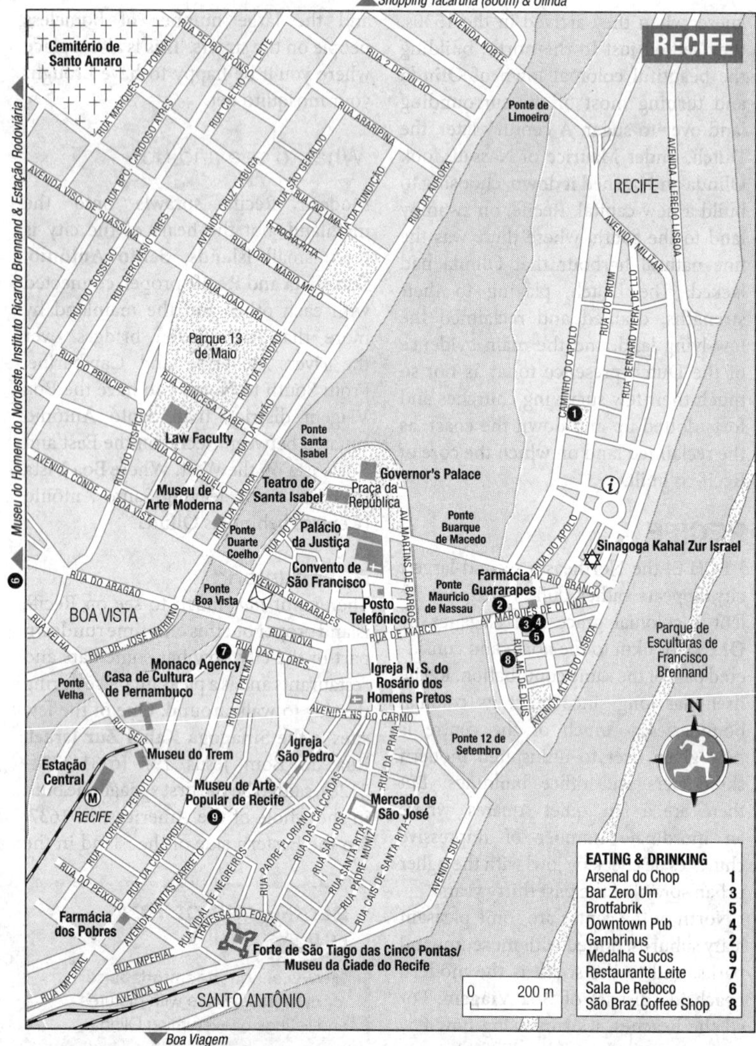

square just off Avenida Alfredo Lisboa, is the **Marco Zero**, the bronze sign from which all distances in Pernambuco are measured. It's at the pier here that you can hire a rowboat (R$4 one-way) to take you across the water to the **Parque de Esculturas de Francisco Brennand** where you can see the extremely phallic statues up close. From here you can walk along the reef all the way to Boa Viagem should you wish, although depending on the weather you may have to dash through some dodgy bits where waves crash dramatically over the reef and there's a *favela* at the end you'll have to pass by.

Santo Antônio Island

The broad **Avenida Dantas Barreto** forms the spine of the central island of **Santo Antônio**. In southern Brazil, similar avenues are lined with skyscrapers. Here, although some have sprouted in the financial district, the centre generally is on a human scale, with crowded, narrow lanes lined with shops opening directly onto the streets. Dantas Barreto, the main thoroughfare, ends in the fine **Praça da República**, lined with majestic palms and surrounded by Recife's grandest public buildings – an ornate theatre and the governor's palace, which contains some beautiful stained-glass windows (free guided tours Thurs, Fri & Sun 10am, arrive a half-hour in advance).

Santo Antônio do Convento de São Francisco

Perhaps the most enticing of the central buildings is the seventeenth-century Franciscan complex known as the **Santo Antônio do Convento de São Francisco**, on Rua do Imperador (Mon–Fri 8–11.30am & 2–5pm, Sat 2–5pm; R$2),– a combination of church, convent and museum. Waiting outside are the poor and ailing but inside is a cool, quiet haven. Built around a beautiful, small cloister, the museum has some strange but delicately painted statues of saints (one either legless or a midget) and other artwork rescued from demolished or crumbling local churches. The highlight is the **Capela Dourada** (Golden Chapel), a rather vulgar demonstration of colonial prosperity. Finished in 1697, the Rococo chapel has the usual wall-to-ceiling-to-wall ornamentation, except that everything is covered with gold leaf. Before leaving check out the bizarre crucifixion and ponder whether Jesus really needs a wig.

Pátio de São Pedro

Just off the Avenida Dantas Barreto, the **Catedral de São Pedro** (Mon–Fri 8–11am & 2–4pm, Sat 8–10am) is on the Pátio de São Pedro. The impressive facade is dominated by a statue of St Peter that was donated to the church in 1980 by a master sculptor from the ceramics centre of Tracunhaém in the interior. Inside there's some exquisite woodcarving and a *trompe l'oeil* ceiling. Another corner of the Pátio is home to the **Museu de Arte Popular de Recife** (Mon–Fri 8am–5pm; free), which has some interesting exhibits, including pottery and wooden sculpture. If you've missed the opening hours, content yourself with the exterior views, best seen with a cold beer from one of the several bars which set up tables in the square outside. The whole of the Pátio has been beautifully restored, which lends it a charm of its own.

Recife is probably the best big Brazilian city to find **artesanato**, and the area around São Pedro is the place to look for it. If you shop around, even tight budgets can manage great bargains. Stalls are everywhere, but they coagulate into a bustling complex of winding streets, lined with beautiful but dilapidated early nineteenth-century tenements, beginning on the Pátio de São Pedro. The streets are choked with people and goods, all converging on the market proper, the **Mercado de São José**, an excellent place for *artesanato*.

Museu da Cidade

Determined culture vultures can make the hop from here to Recife's most central museum, the **Museu da Cidade** (Tues–Fri 9am–6pm, Sat & Sun 1–5pm; R$1), in the star-shaped Forte das Cinco Pontas, off the western end of Avenida Dantas Barreto. Built in 1630 by the Dutch, the fort was the last place they surrendered upon expulsion in 1654. The fort itself is far more interesting than its museum, which is dedicated to the city's history, with old engravings and photographs.

Casa da Cultura

Opposite the Estação Central, in Rua Floriano Peixoto, the forbidding **Casa da Cultura de Pernambuco** (Mon–Fri 9am–7pm, Sat & Sun 10am–3pm; free) was once the city's prison and is now an essential stop for visitors. It's cunningly designed, with three wings radiating out from a central point, so that a single warder could keep an eye on all nine corridors. The whole complex has been turned into an arts and crafts centre, the cells converted into little boutiques and one or two places for refreshment. The goods here are high quality, but prices are also a lot higher than elsewhere in the city, so go to look not to buy. The Casa da Cultura is also the best place to get information on cultural events in the city, providing a monthly *Agenda Cultural* with listings of plays, films and other entertainment.

More museums

The **Museu de Arte Moderna** (Tues–Sun noon–6pm; R$1), just over the river from Santo Antônio at Rua da Aurora 265 in Boa Vista, displays prestigious changing exhibitions of mainly Brazilian modern artists, many amongst Pernambuco's best. The **Museu do Homem do Nordeste** (Tues, Wed & Fri 11am–5pm, Thurs 8am–5pm, Sat & Sun 1–5pm; R$4) was assembled by anthropologists and is one of Brazil's great museums and a terrific introduction to the Northeast's history and culture. It's a fair way from central Recife in Casa Forte at Av 17 de Agosto 2187. Take the "Dois Irmãos" bus from the post office or from Parque 13 de Maio, at the bottom of Rua do Hospício; there are two "Dois Irmãos" services, "via Barbosa" is the one to get, a pleasant half-hour drive through leafy northern suburbs. The museum is hard to spot, on the left, so ask the driver or conductor where to get off.

Instituto Ricardo Brennand

More of an adventure but probably Recife's coolest attraction (more interesting than visiting yet another church), especially after a few days dealing with Recife's rush hour, is the **Instituto Ricardo Brennand** (Tues–Sun 1pm–5pm, R$5) an impressive estate which belonged to one of three brothers who inherited a tile and ceramic factory. Another of the brothers, Francisco Brennand, was driven to become a famous ceramics artist and his very phallic art graces the reef across from Recife island. The Instituto is impressive right from the entrance, a long road colonnaded on either side with palm trees. There's an air-conditioned art gallery and a small castle, the ultimate bachelor pad, with working drawbridge inside which are suits of armour, Swiss-army knives with more functions than you can count and a room full of nudes and knives. Take the bus "EDU Caxangá," on Avenida Domingos Ferreira and take it to the end of the line. Continue on foot to the end of the road, make a right onto Rua Isaac Buril. The institute is at the end of the road on the left.

Boa Viagem

Regular buses make it easy to get down to **BOA VIAGEM** and the beach, an enormous skyscraper-lined arc of sand that constitutes the longest stretch of urbanized seafront in Brazil. Recife, too, was once studded with beaches, but they were swallowed up by industrial development, leaving only Boa Viagem within the city's limits – though there are others not that far away to the north and south. Much of Boa Viagem is only four blocks deep, so it's easy to find your way. Inland are hotels and new construction of soulless apartment complexes as well as a smattering of restaurants, clubs and malls.

The **beach**, packed at weekends, deserted during the week, is longer and (claim locals) better than Copacabana, with warm natural rock pools to wallow in just offshore when the tide is out. It's also rather narrow, and more dominated by concrete than most in the Northeast. Pavilions punctuate the sidewalk along the noisy road, selling fresh coconut

water, beers, pre-mixed *batidas* (rum cocktails), *açaí*, pineapples, watermelon, ice creams, straw hats and suntan lotion. The usual **cautions** apply about not taking valuables to the beach or leaving things unattended. There have also been a small number of shark attacks over the years, but they usually involve surfers far offshore.

Olinda

OLINDA is, quite simply, one of the largest and most beautiful complexes of **colonial architecture** in Brazil: a maze of cobbled streets, hills crowned with brilliant white churches, pastel-coloured houses, Baroque fountains and graceful squares. Not surprisingly, in 1982 it was designated a cultural heritage site by UNESCO. Founded in 1535, the old city is spread across several small hills looking back towards Recife, but it belongs to a different world. It's here that many of the larger city's artists, musicians and liberal professionals live, and it's also the centre of Recife's gay scene. Olinda is most renowned, though, for its **Carnaval**, famous throughout Brazil. This attracts visitors from all over the country, as well as sizeable contingents from Europe, to see more than 480 huge, artistically created puppets among the celebrations.

A city in its own right, Olinda is far larger than it first appears. The old colonial centre is built on the hills, slightly back from the sea, but arching along the seafront and spreading inland behind the old town is a modern Brazilian city of over 300,000 people known as **Novo Olinda**, the usual bland collection of suburbs and main commercial drags. Like Recife, Novo Olinda has a growing reputation for robberies, but colonial Olinda is safe enough. Despite its size, Olinda is effectively a neighbourhood of Recife: a high proportion of its residents commute to the city so **transport links** are good, with buses leaving every few minutes.

Alto da Sé

Olinda's hills are steep, so don't try to do too much too quickly. A good spot to have a drink and plan your attack is the **Alto da Sé**, the highest square in the town, not least because of the stunning view of Recife's skyscrapers shimmering in the distance, framed in the foreground by Olinda's church towers, gardens and palm trees. There's always an arts and crafts **market** here during the day, busiest in the late afternoon; there's plenty of good stuff, but tourists have driven prices up, and there's little here you can't get cheaper in Recife or the interior.

The **Igreja da Sé**, on the *praça*, is bland and austere inside – more of a museum than a living church – but is worth a look if only to see the eighteenth-century sedan chair and large wooden sculptures in the small room at the northeast wing. It's also notable for being at the highest point in the region's landscape, making it visible from all the other churches for miles around. This viewing patio at the back right-hand side of the church offers a particularly beautiful view of the city.

Olinda's churches

Olinda's **churches** are not quite as old as they look. The Dutch burnt them all down, except one, in 1630; they built none of their own, and left the Portuguese to restore them during the following centuries. There are now eighteen churches dating from the seventeenth and eighteenth centuries, seemingly tucked around every corner. Very few have set opening times, but they're usually open during weekday mornings, and even when they're closed you can knock and ask for the *vigia*, the watchman.

If you have time to see only one it should be the **Convento Franciscano** (Mon–Fri 8–11.30am & 2.30–5pm, Sat 8am–5.30pm), tucked away on Rua São Francisco. Built in 1585, the complex of convent, chapel and church has been restored to its former glory; particular highlights are the tiled cloister depicting the lives of Jesus and St Francis of Asissi, and the sacristy's beautiful Baroque furniture carved from jacaranda wood. Behind the convent there's a patio with grand panoramas across the ocean.

Among other churches, the **Igreja da Misericórdia**, right at the top of an exhaustingly steep hill, has a fine altar and rear walls covered in blue *azulejo*, while the **Mosteiro de Sâo Bento** (Mon–Fri 8am–noon & 2–6pm, Sat 8am–noon, Sun 10am–5pm), across town, looks quite wonderful from the outside with palm trees swaying in the courtyard, though the interior is less striking.

Olinda's museums

There's a good sampling of religious art on display in the **Museu de Arte Sacra de Pernambuco** (Mon–Fri 9am–12.45pm; R$1), in the seventeenth-century bishop's palace by the Alto da Sé, while modern art is on display in the **Museu de Arte Contemporânea**, on Rua 13 de Maio next to the market (Mon–Fri 9am–2.30pm; free). The latter is a fine eighteenth-century building that was once used as a jail by the Inquisition, though the exhibits themselves are a bit disappointing. Much more interesting is the **Museu do Mamulengo** (Tues–Fri 9am–5pm, Sat & Sun 10am–6pm; free) at Rua de Sâo Bento 344 Amparo 59, which houses an excellent collection of traditional puppets.

Arrival and information

Air The Aeroporto Internacional dos Guararapes is only 11km from the city centre, at the far end of Boa Viagem. You can buy a voucher for an airport taxi from COOPSETA (☎81/3464-4153, ISIC members get a 10 percent discount) before going outside. Taxis to Boa Viagem cost about $18, to Santo Antônio about $30, to Olinda, R$51. The Aeroporto bus from right outside drives through Boa Viagem and drops you in the centre (R$2.60).

Bus The *rodoviária* (☎81/3452-2824) is about 14km from the centre. From here the **Metrô** (R$1.30; ☎81/2102-8500, ⓦwww.metrorec.com.br), an overground rail link, whisks you through various *favelas* to the old train station in the centre, Estação Central ("Recife"). From here to your hotel, whether in Santo Antônio, Boa Viagem or Olinda, it's best to take a taxi – Recife is confusing even after a few days.

Tourist Office The state tourist office, EMPETUR (ⓦwww2.setur.pe.gov.br), runs several information posts, some of which have good English-speakers – most have helpful, free maps and event calendars: the offices at the airport (24hr, ☎81/3232-3594) and in Olinda (Rua Prudente de Morais 472; Mon–Fri 8am–6pm, Sat & Sun 9am–7pm) are best. Branches also at the *rodoviária* (☎81/3452-1892) and Recife (Rua da Guia and Travessa do Bom Jesus; daily 9am–10pm; ☎81/3232-2942). Make sure to pick up the monthly cultural pamphlet, *What's On – Acontece Em Recife e Olinda*) as well as the free maps of the greater Recife area and of Olinda.

City transport

Bus Most city buses originate and terminate on the central island of Santo Antônio, on Av Dantas Barreto, either side of the Pracinha do Diário (aka Praça da Independência). They range in price from R$1.60 to R$3. To get from the city centre to Boa Viagem, take buses marked "Aeroporto," "Iguatemi," or "Boa Viagem," or catch the more comfortable *frescão* marked "Aeroporto", from outside the offices of the *Diário de Pernambuco*, on the Pracinha do Diário; it goes every 20min and costs R$2.50. To get to Olinda, walk south down Av Dantas Barreto from the Pracinha do Diário to the last of the series of bus stops, and catch the "Casa Caiada" bus. Buses follow the seafront road; get off in the Praça do Carmo, just by Olinda's main post office, from where it's a 2min walk up into the old city

Taxi The bus system is so thorough and comparatively cheap that it rarely makes sense to take a taxi. If you do choose to use them, they're metered and straightforward, though the cost can add up: from central Recife to Olinda should cost around R$20 and will take about 15min.

Accommodation

Although the run-down town centre is the cheapest place to stay, we don't really recommend it. You're far better off in Boa Viagem, where the beach compensates for the steep prices, or in Olinda, where costs are more reasonable and there's plenty to see, though not much of a beach (with what there is being along Novo Olinda). As ever, if you want to visit during Carnaval, you'll need to book months in advance.

Boa Viagem

Albergue da Juventude Maracatus do Recife Rua Maria Carolina185 ⓣ81/3326-1221. Bare but functional dorm rooms in a safe setting,with swimming pool and free breakfast. R$30.

Boa Viagem Praia Av Boa Viagem 5576 ⓣ81/3462-6454, ⓦwww.boaviagempraia.com.br, . This is a proper hotel, if one with barely any personality, right across from Praia Boa Viagem. R$154/170.

Hotel Aconchego Félix de Brito e Melo 382 ⓣ81/3464-2960, ⓦwww.hotelaconchego.com.br. This small and comfortable hotel has a swimming pool and good restaurant open 24hr. ❺

Onda Mar Hotel Rua Ernesto de Paula Santos 284 ⓣ81/2128-4848, ⓦwww.ondamar.com.br. Modern rooms with laundry, room service and an in-house pizzeria. ❺

Pousada Casuarinas Rua Antônio Pedro Figueiredo 151 ⓣ81/3325-4708, ⓦwww.pousadacasuarinas.com.br. Wireless internet, pool and laundry just 200m from Praia Boa Viagem. Single rates available too. ❹

Recife Monte Hotel Rua dos Navegantes 363 ⓣ81/2121-0909, ⓦwww.recifemontehotel.com.br. A glorified apartment building with all mod cons and the claim to fame that Chico Buarque and Charles Aznavour once stayed here. ❹

TREAT YOURSELF

Hotel Jangadeiro Av Boa Viagem 3114, Boa Viagem ⓣ81/3086-5950, ⓦwww.jangadeirohotel.com.br. A high-rise with sea views, and all the basics you would expect (a/c, Internet, safes and pool) along with its own restaurant. ❻

Hotel Sete Colinas Ladeira de São Francisco 307, Olinda ⓣ81/3493-7766, ⓦwww.hotel7colinas.com.br. Fabulous hotel in the centre of Olinda, set in beautiful gardens with modern sculptures and a fine swimming pool. There's a range of rooms, suites and luxury apartments, and a good restaurant too. ❼

Pousada dos Quatro Cantos Rua Prudente de Morais 441, Olinda ⓣ81/3429-0220, ⓦwww.pousada4cantos.com.br. This leafy, walled-in *pousada* with rooms and suites arranged around a courtyard is a little pricey but is Olinda's most regal. ❺

Olinda

Hotel Albergue de Olinda Rua do Sol 233, Carmo ⓣ81/3439-1592,ⓦwww.albergue deolinda.com.br. Gated behind this dusty bus route is a nice hostel with a pool, hammocks and a small but decent free breakfast. Just mind the mosquitoes. Dorm R$30.

Hotel Pousada São Francisco Rua do Sol 127 ⓣ81/3429-2109, ⓦwww.pousadasaofrancisco.com.br. It's a hotel, no, it's a *pousada*. Okay, with room service, a pool, laundry and a/c rooms it's more of a hotel but rates are less than most hotels offering similar facilities. ❺

Pousada Alto Astral Rua 13 de Maio 305 ⓣ81/3439-3453. Funky, no-frills *pousada* with mazelike corridors and a pool. Ask for a balcony room. Singles too and a choice of fan or a/c. ❸–❹

Pousada do Amparo Rua do Amparo 199 ⓣ81/3439-1749, ⓦwww.pousadadoamparo.com.br. Quality place combining excellent rooms, an art gallery and a restaurant in a colonial mansion; sauna and pool, too. ❻

Pousada d'Olinda Praça Conselheiro João Alfredo 178 ⓣ81/3493-6011, ⓦwww.pousadadolinda.com.br. Friendly atmosphere with a pool and a quiet garden for sunbathing. Breakfast included. ❺

Pousada Marin dos Caetes Av Segismundo Gonçalves 732, Carmo ⓣ81/3429-1532 Charming. hostel with colourful dorms and private chambers. ⓦwww.pousadamarindoscaetes.com.br. ❹

Pousada Peter Rua do Amparo 215 ⓣ81/3439-2171, ⓦwww.pousadapeter.com.br. Located among other art galleries, this is a comfortable gallery-cum-lodging situated in a colonial-style building. ❹

Eating and drinking

After dealing with the brutal sun, relentless traffic, indecipherable buses and shark-infested waters, you may need some good food to soothe the soul. Luckily, you're in the right place. In general, eating is cheapest in Santo Antônio, more expensive in Recife Island and Boa Viagem, with Olinda in between. If

RECIFENSE CUISINE

Local cuisine revolves around **fish** and **shellfish**. Try *carangueijo mole*, crabs cooked in a spicy sauce until shells and legs are soft and edible, which solves the problem of digging out the meat; small crabs called *guaiamum*; and *agulhas fritas*, fried needle fish.

you want to eat for less than R$20, try the *comida por kilo* places along the Olinda seafront and in Novo Olinda. For a bit more, you can eat far better in the old town. Best and least expensive of all, though, is to join the crowds drinking and eating serious street food at the Alto da Sé. These charcoal-fired delights can't be recommended too highly; try *acarajé*, from women sitting next to sizzling wok-like pots – bean-curd cakes, fried in palm oil, slit, and filled with salad, dried shrimps and *vatapá*.

Olinda

Banana Split Gelados e Calientes Praça do Carmo, Loja 5-D. Yes, you can get the namesake dessert but the real draw is the lovingly made *açaí na tigela*. R$8.

Bar Guaiamum Av Ministro Marcos Freire 1023, Novo Olinda ⓣ81/3429-3383. Nurse a few beers while prying meat out of a plateful of steamed crabs, right across the street from the sea wall. R$30.

Blues Bar-Comedoria e Pizzeria Rua do Bonfim 66 ⓣ81/3429-8272. *Gratinados* are the house speciality but they also serve 24 different types of pizza. The place is moderately priced, often with authentic blues.

Creperia Praça João Alfredo 168 ⓣ81/3429-2935. Serves great salads as well as 46 different kinds of the obvious.

Oficina do Sabor Rua do Amparo 335 ⓣ81/3429-3331, ⓦwww.oficinadosabor.com. High up in Olinda is a sunset view of the city that goes perfectly with *jerimum recheado con camarão e lagostini ao molho de maracuja e arroz de coco*, pumpkin stuffed with shrimp and lobster served with a cream of passion fruit and rice covered with toasted coconut. Wow. Expensive, but worth it. R$66.

Sargação Av Sigismundo Gonçalves 716, ⓣ81/3439-2040. This sandwich shop at the base of Olinda's old town is open until late.

Trattoria Don Francesco Rua Prudente de Morais 358 ⓣ3429-3852. Cute little Italian restaurant that makes a hearty lasagne and has the *limoncello* in reserve. R$25.

Santo Antônio

Restaurante Leite Praça Joaquim Nabuco 147, close to the *Hotel Quatro de Outubro* ⓣ81/3224-7977. This classy restaurant serves good local dishes in a very stylish nineteenth-century interior.

Recife Antigo

Brotfabrik Rua da Moeda 87 ⓣ81/3224-2496. Excellent coffee, *salgados*, pastries, custards and bread as the constant queue attests.

Gambrinus Av Marquês de Olinda 263 ⓣ81/3224-0466. Established in 1930, this is said to be one of the oldest bars in the city. You can get huge portions of local dishes here, for less than R$15. Daily 8am–7pm.

Medalha Sucos Av Dantas Barreto 900. Juices and sandwiches as well as self-service for R$13/kg.

São Braz Coffee Shop Rua da Alfandega 35, Shopping Paço Alfândega, ⓦwww.saobraz.com.br. Recife's best espresso is served in a/c comfort at this busy café.

Boa Viagem Restaurants

Bargaço Av Boa Viagem 670 ⓣ81/3465-1847. It's a little expensive but this branch of the excellent seafood chain is across the street from the beach and it doesn't disappoint with its spicier Bahian dishes.

CRIME AND SAFETY

Recife has a bad reputation throughout Brazil. Everyone has a story about how they were followed, harassed, mugged or intimidated. It's enough to send even seasoned travellers rushing back to their hostels at sundown for fear of turning into flak-jacket-wearing Cinderellas.

While it's true that crime rates are high, many of the stories are just that – stories. Take the usual **precautions** and you should stay safe: be discreet, don't wear fancy watches and jewellery, know where you're going, travel with a friend, take taxis or public transportation at night, stick to populated, well-lit areas and be wary of open, free drinks. **CIA-Tur**, the Tourist Police, patrol areas of the city that tourists normally visit like Olinda and are on emergency call should you need them (ⓣ190, ⓦwww.ciatur.pe.gov.br).

Boi Preto Grill Av Boa Viagem 97, Pina ☎81/3466-6334, www.grupoboipreto.com.br. Gorgeous restaurant with a splendid buffet including mussels and sushi along with all you can eat quality *churrascaria* for R$40.

La Cuisine Av Boa Viagem 560, Pina ☎81/3327-4073. Fancy palm-café seating and white tablecloth fine dining, but despite appearances you can get a meal for R$30. Standard dishes including salads, steaks and fish.

Ponteio Grill Av Boa Viagem 4824 ☎81/3326-2386. One of the few beachside restaurants, this busy *churrascaria*is popular for quality *Rodizio* (R$19.90) and its separate buffet outside called **Sushi Beach** where you can stuff yourself with good sushi (R$25.90) while listening to waves crash in the dark.

Drinking and nightlife

Recife's nightlife is pretty spread out and, as eveywhere in Brazil, doesn't even think of getting going till after 10pm. **Recife Island** in the city centre is an increasingly lively place: there are all kinds of bars here, including quiet places where middle-aged professionals discuss daily events, but the scene is mainly young. There's also some action in **Boa Viagem**, where bars open and close with bewildering speed. The liveliest area here is around Praça de Boa Viagem, quite a long way down the beach from the city centre, near the junction of Avenida Boa Viagem and Rua Bavão de Souza Leão. There's fun to be had in Olinda, too, but it's not quite as frenetic. The variety of music and dances is enormous, and Recife has its own frenetic carnival music, the **frevo**, as well as the *forró* you'll find all over the Northeast.

Recife

Arsenal do Chopp Praça Artur Oscar 59 ☎81/3224-6259. A great place to sit outside watching the afternoon go by over a *chopp*, a tasty *salgado* or coconut shrimp.

Bar Zero Um Rua Vigário Tenório 199 ☎81/3224-4405. This place has live music on Fri & Sat.

Downtown Pub Rua Vigário Tenório 105 ☎81/3424-6317, www.downtownpub.com.br. Not exactly a London pub, but it does have fried snacks, long-neck beers and live music and it *is* downtown.

Sala De Reboco Rua Gregório Júnior 264 ☎81/3228-7052, www.saladereboco.com.br. *Forró* dance club downtown is popular with the locals and is a good place to get an idea of the Recife scene.

Olinda

Bar Aritana Praça João Pessoa. This chilled, plastic-patio-chair bar seems relaxed, yet it goes late into the night with some steady music keeping the beat.

Ximxim da Baiana Avenida Sigismundo Gonçalves 742. A local bar on a busy road with a constant soundtrack of reggae music.

Boa Viagem

Bar do Deca Rua José Maria de Miranda 140 ☎81/3465-9656. They must be doing something right here because they've been serving gizzards and *caipirinhas* to locals for four decades. Open noon–3am, closed Sun.

Nox Av Engenheiro Domingos Ferreira 2422 ☎81/3326-8836, www.clubnox.com.br. This electronic dance club really turns on when it finally gets going, with street food vendors setting up outside. One of the best places for dancing in the city. Thurs–Sat 10pm–6am.

Restaurante e Bar 75 Av Cons Aguiar 75, Pina ☎81/3467-7995. Live music most Fri & Sat nights at this restaurant/bar with old photographs.

Entertainment

For a taste of strongly regional music of all types it's worth checking out an **espaço cultural** or two. The *Espaço Nodaloshi*, at Estrada dos Remédios 1891 in Madalena (☎81/3228-3511), frequently brings together large numbers of musicians from all over Pernambuco, generally starting the shows around 10pm or later. The *Espaço Cultural Alberto Cunha Melo*, at Rua Leila Félix Karan 15 in Bongi (☎81/3228-6846), runs similar live music shows.

Parque Carvalheira Rua Manoel Didier 53, Imbiribeira ☎81/3081-8130, www.carvalheira.com.br (Mon–Fri 9am–5pm). It's the *cachaça* (sugar-cane spirit) tasting at the *cachaça* museums here that makes visiting them so much fun.

Shopping

Feira de Artesanato (daily noon–6pm) & **Mercado das Artes** (daily, noon–8pm), Praça do Carmo. This massive market takes over the Av Afonso Pena bordering the Parque Municipal.

Mercado Eufrasio Barbosa Av Sigismundo Gonçalves, Varadouro (☎81/3439-2911). Large crafts market in a former candy factory (Mon–Sat 9am–6pm).

Mercado da Ribeira Rua Bernardo Vieira de Melo ☎81/3493-9708 (daily 9am–6:30pm).

Shopping Paço Alfândega Rua Alfândega 35 ☎81/3419-7500 (Mon–Sat 10am–10pm; Sun noon–8pm). Chic, refurbished former customs building on Recife island. No cinemas.

Shopping Recife Rua Pe. Carapuceiro 777, Boa Viagem ⓣ81/3464-6000 (Mon–Sat 10am–10pm; Sun noon–8pm). Large, suburban shopping mall with multiplex.

Shopping Tacaruna Av Governador Aguamenon Magalhães 153, Santo Amaro ⓣ81/3412-6000 (Mon–Sat 9am–10pm; Sun noon–8pm). Has cinemas.

Directory

Airlines American Airlines, Av Cons Aguiar 1472, Boa Viagem (ⓣ81/3326-2640); GOL, Aeroporto Internacional dos Guararapes, (ⓣ0300-115-2121); TAM, Av Cons Aguiar, 1360 Loja 1 (ⓣ81/3327-8313); TAP Air Portugal, Rua Conselheiro Aguiar 1472, Loja 9, Boa Viagem (ⓣ81/3341-0654); United Airlines, Av Gov Agamenon Magalhães 2656, Torreão (ⓣ81/2119-8666); Varig, Aeroporto Internacional Guararapes (ⓣ81/4003-7000).

Banks and exchange Câmbio Europa Shopping Tacaruna ⓣ81/3301-7051. There are plenty of banks with ATMs in Boa Viagem and Recife including HSBC.

Car rentals The usual suspects are at the airport and local auto rentals are throughout the city: Avis, Aeroporto Internacional Dos Guararapes (ⓣ81/3322-4016); Unidas, Aeroporto Internacional Dos Guararapes, (ⓣ81/3461-4661).

Embassies and consulates Netherlands, Av Cons Aguiar 1472, Sala 142, Boa Viagem (ⓣ81/3465-6704); UK, Av Conselheiro Aguiar 2941, 3rd floor (ⓣ81/3465-0230); US, Rua Goncalves Maia 163, Boa Vista ⓣ81/3416-3050.

Hospital Real Hospital Português de Beneficência em Pernambuco-Posto Avançado, Av Cons Aguiar 147, Boa Viagem (ⓣ81/3301-3411).

Internet NGS Internet & Services, branches at Shopping Recife (ⓣ81/3464-6449), Shopping Tacaruna (ⓣ3421-6721) and Shopping Paço Alãdega (ⓣ81/3424-8923); Olinda@Net, Rua do Sol 116, Carmo (ⓣ81/3429-6581; R$1.99 per hr).

Laundries Vivaz Lavanderia, Av Cons Aguiar 2775, Boa Viagem (ⓣ81/3466-3755).

Pharmacies Farmácia Bicentenária, Rua S Miguel 277, Novo Olinda (ⓣ81/3429-2148); Farmácia dos Pobres, Av Dantas Barreto 498, Santo Antônio (ⓣ81/3301-8206); Farmácia Guararapes, Av Marq Olinda 150, Recife (ⓣ81/3224-3994); Farmácia Pague Menos-Boa Viagem 24 Horas, Av Cons Aguiar 4635, Boa Viagem (ⓣ81/3301-4209).

Post office Av Guararapes 250, Santo Antônio, ⓣ81/3425-3644 (Mon–Fri 9am–5pm); Av Dantas Barretto 1090, Santo Antônio; Av Dr Joaquim Nabuco, 2445, Olinda ⓣ81/3439-7740.

Tour Operators Martur, Recife Palace Hotel, Av Boa Viagem, 4070, Loja 04, Boa Viagem (ⓣ81/3465-7778, ⓦwww.martur.com.br) organise flights, cruises and trips to Fernando de Noronha; Victor Tur, Av Sigismundo Gonçalves 732, Carmo, Olinda (ⓣ81/3429-1532, ⓦwww.pousadamarindoscaetes.com.br) is an agency run out of the *Pousada Marin dos Caetes* that arranges bus and air tickets and car rentals, as well as city and beach tours.

Moving on

Air TAM, Varig and Gol connect Recife with the rest of the country and TAM, TAP Air Portugal and United have connecting flights to Europe and the States.

Bus Long-distance buses leave Recife for Fortaleza, three buses daily, R$107 (12hr); João Pessoa, 11 buses daily, R$19 (2hr), Maceió, eight buses daily, R$20 (4hr); Natal 10 buses daily, R$44 (4hr 30min); Salvador, once daily, R$115 (12hr); among other destinations, several times daily. Tickets can be bought on the phone and delivered (if your Portuguese is good and you don't mind some anticipation) by calling Disk Rodoviária ⓣ81/3452-3990. For current rates and routes check Penha (ⓦnspenha.locaweb.com.b); Progresso (ⓦwww.autoviacaoprogresso.com.br), Guanabara (ⓦwww.expressoguanabara.com.br), and São Geraldo (ⓦwww.saogeraldo.com.br).

FERNANDO DE NORONHA

Recife is one of the main launch points for this beautiful archipelago 545km off the coast of Pernambuco. It has pristine beachesandisenvironmentallyprotected so it's absolutely terrific for scuba diving. The water is clear for more than 30m in many places, with turtles, dolphins and a wide range of fish species to observe. Since 1988 much of the archipelago has been protected as a marine national park to maintain its ecological wonders (it's also the breeding territory for many tropical Atlantic birds). The main island is **Ilha de Fernando de Noronha** which has plenty of its own gorgeous beaches. While you can no longer swim with the dolphins, you're likely to see quite a few should you visit, though you'll have to wake up early – they enter the bay every day between 5am and 6am.

It's not cheap to get here (R$988, two daily flights from Recife with Varig and TRIP) and you're also charged the **TPA tax** (Taxa de Preservação, R$34.48, daily) which goes towards protecting the archipelago, but if you're into this kind of thing, it can be quite an experience. For more information, including restaurants and places to stay check, the government-run website, Ⓦwww.noronha.pe.gov.br.

FORTALEZA

FORTALEZA may be the "Rio of the Northeast," but let's not mince words: the fact that it's on the coast and surrounded by beaches are only theoretical resemblances. More than two million people live here, but outside the immediate downtown it feels sleepier. If you're looking for hordes of beautiful beach-goers and a dramatic natural setting stick to the original – this is no Rio.

Portuguese settlers who arrived here in 1603 were defeated initially by Indians, who ate the first bishop, and then by the Dutch, who drove the Portuguese out in 1637. It was well into the eighteenth century before the Indians were finally overwhelmed and the Portuguese securely established. In 1816, they built the Fortaleza de Nossa Senhora da Assunção on the site of an earlier Dutch fortress. The city prospered in the **nineteenth century** as the port to a hinterland where ranching had rapidly expanded. Since then it has been the commercial centre of the northern half of the Northeast.

More recently, Fortaleza has been pouring resources into expanding its tourist trade, developing the city centre and attracting gleaming luxury hotels. The resulting small, refurbished "colonial centre," the appealing beach-bars and waterfront eateries, and the laid-back, congenial locals all make it a pleasant place to visit, but ultimately they're not enough to make it a destination in its own right. Instead, it's a place to break your journey up the coast and a base for daytrips to the celebrated **beaches**: Cumbuco, Jericoacoara, Canoa Quebrada, Morro Branco, Lagoinha and Iguape.

What to see and do

You can do Fortaleza in a day, and culturally, much of what there is to see can be seen before noon. The nerve centre of the city is its largest square, **Praça José de Alencar**, four blocks inland from the train station. While not the most visually attractive of Brazilian city centres it's never boring: the downtown streets are crowded with shops, and hawkers colonize the pavements and plazas, so that much of the centre seems like one giant market. In the late afternoon and early evening, crowds here attract *capoeira* groups, street sellers and especially *repentistas*. These street poets gather audiences with skill and wit, improvising verses about onlookers, passing a hat for you to show your appreciation. If you refuse, or give what they consider too little, the stream of innuendo and insults is unmistakable, even if you don't understand a word of Portuguese.

Teatro José de Alencar

On the square you'll also find the one truly impressive building in the city, the beautiful **Teatro José de Alencar**, named after the great nineteenth-century novelist and poet, a native of the city. The fine tropical Edwardian exterior is in fact only an elegant facade, which leads into an open courtyard and the main body of the theatre. This is built in ornate and beautifully worked cast-iron sections, brought over complete from Scotland and reassembled in 1910. In 1991 it was superbly restored and is now a key venue for theatrical performances and concerts.

Centro de Turismo

Overlooking the sea at the bottom of Rua Senador Pompeu is the gritty

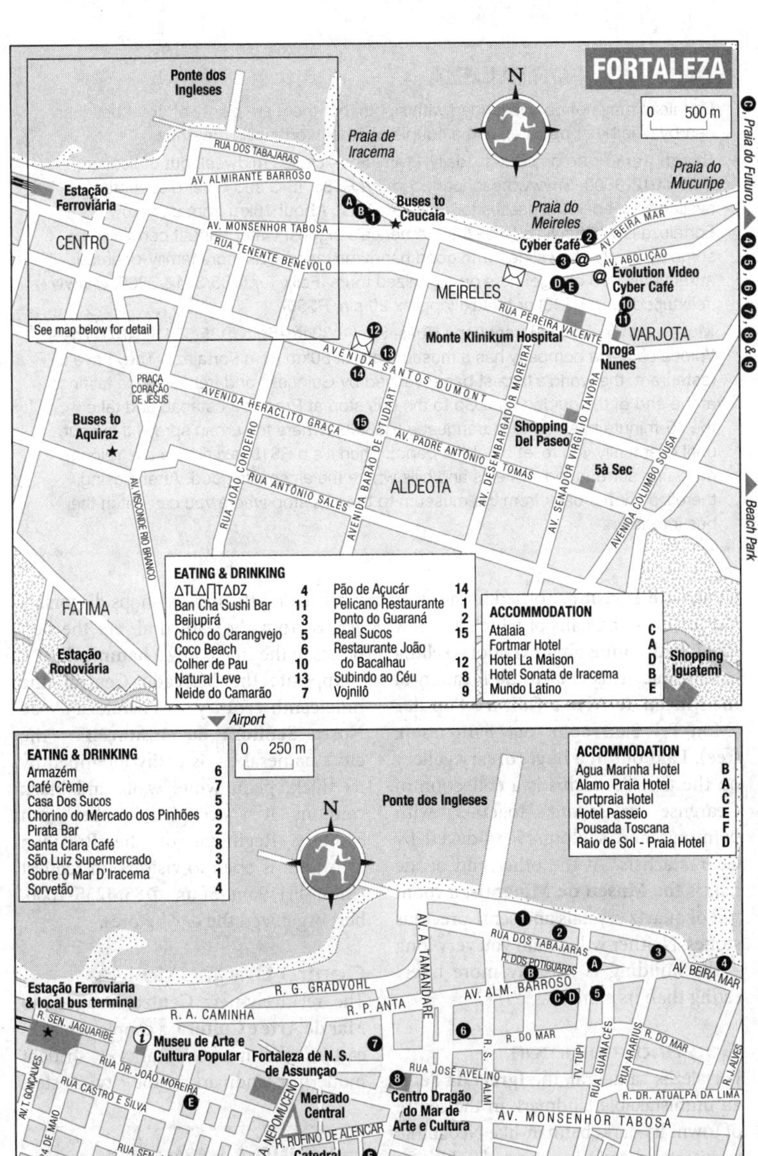
FORTALEZA
N
0 500 m
Ponte dos Ingleses
Praia de Iracema
Praia do Meireles
Praia do Mucuripe
C, Praia do Futuro, 4, 5, 6, 7, 8 & 9
Estação Ferroviária
CENTRO
Rua dos Tabajaras
Av. Almirante Barroso
Av. Monsenhor Tabosa
Rua Tenente Benevolo
Buses to Caucaia
Cyber Café
Evolution Video Cyber Café
Av. Beira Mar
Av. Abolição
MEIRELES
Rua Pereira Valente
VARJOTA
Monte Klinikum Hospital
Droga Nunes
See map below for detail
Avenida Santos Dumont
Avenida Heraclito Graça
Praça Coração de Jesus
Buses to Aquiraz
Av. Padre Antônio Tomas
Shopping Del Paseo
5à Sec
Rua Antônio Sales
ALDEOTA
Rua João Cordeiro
Avenida Barão de Studart
Av. Desembargador Moreira
Av. Senador Virgilio Tavora
Avenida Columbo Sousa
Av. Visconde Rio Branco
Beach Park
FATIMA
Estação Rodoviária
Shopping Iguatemi
Airport
EATING & DRINKING
ΔTLΔ∏TΔDZ 4
Ban Cha Sushi Bar 11
Beijupirá 3
Chico do Carangvejo 5
Coco Beach 6
Colher de Pau 10
Natural Leve 13
Neide do Camarão 7
Pão de Açucár 14
Pelicano Restaurante 1
Ponto do Guaraná 2
Real Sucos 15
Restaurante João do Bacalhau 12
Subindo ao Céu 8
Vojnilô 9
ACCOMMODATION
Atalaia C
Fortmar Hotel A
Hotel La Maison D
Hotel Sonata de Iracema B
Mundo Latino E
0 250 m
EATING & DRINKING
Armazém 6
Café Crème 7
Casa Dos Sucos 5
Chorino do Mercado dos Pinhões 9
Pirata Bar 2
Santa Clara Café 8
São Luiz Supermercado 3
Sobre O Mar D'Iracema 1
Sorvetão 4
ACCOMMODATION
Agua Marinha Hotel B
Alamo Praia Hotel A
Fortpraia Hotel C
Hotel Passeio E
Pousada Toscana F
Raio de Sol - Praia Hotel D
Ponte dos Ingleses
Rua dos Tabajaras
R. dos Potiguaras
Av. Beira Mar
Av. Alm. Barroso
Av. A. Tamandare
R. G. Gradvohl
R. A. Caminha
R. P. Anta
Estação Ferroviaria & local bus terminal
R. Sen. Jaguaribe
Museu de Arte e Cultura Popular
Fortaleza de N. S. de Assunçao
Rua Dr. João Moreira
Rua Castro e Silva
Mercado Central
Av. A. Nepomuceno
R. Rufino de Alencar
Rua José Avelino
Centro Dragão do Mar de Arte e Cultura
R. do Mar
Tv. Tupi
Rua Guanacés
Rua Ararius
R. J. Alves
R. Dr. Atualpa da Lima
Av. Monsenhor Tabosa
Catedral
Rua Sen. Alencar
R. São Paulo
Praça José de Alencar
Av. T. Gonçalves
Rua 24 de Maio
Rua Guilherme Rocha
Bank
R. Gov. Sampaio
R. S. José
R. V. Saboia
São Luis Cinema
R. Liberato Barroso
Rua Barão do Rio Branco
Rua Major Facundo
Rua Floriano Peixoto
Rua General Bezerril
R. Sena Madureira
R. Pedro Borges
Rua Coronel Feraz
Rua 25 do Março
Av. Dom Manuel
Rua Tenente Benevolo
Rua Pereira Filgueiras
Rua Rodrigues Júnior
Rua Dom Joaquim
R. P. Climério
R. Dep. Moreira
Rua Costa Barros
Rua Dona Leopoldina
Av. Santos Dumont
Rua Franklin Tavora
R. Gen. Sampaio
R. Sen. Pompeu
R. Pedro Pereira
R. Pedro Primeiro
Rua Pinto
Rua Nogueira Acioli
Rua Gonçalves Ledo
Rua João Cordeiro
Rua Algusto
Rua Idelfonso Albano

AROUND FORTALEZA

Fortaleza may not be overloaded with sights, but there are plenty of great beaches nearby (see box opposite), and a couple of other worthwhile day-trips.

Beach Park Porto des Dunas (daily 11am–5pm, closes midweek out of season; ⓣ85/4012-3000, ⓦwww.beachpark.com.br; R$85, ISIC and other discounts available, good-value passes for multiple visits). About 16km from downtown Fortaleza is what claims to be Latin America's biggest water park. It certainly has some seriously hairy slides with good hangtime, as well as more family-oriented attractions. You can get here on organized tours (Felix Tur ⓣ85/3242-7200, ⓦwww.felixtur.com.br; R$20) or by taxi (approx 20min, R$50).

Museu da Cachaça Maranguape (Tues–Sun, 8:30am–5pm ⓣ85/3341-0407). The Ypióca *cachaça* company has a museum about 30km from Fortaleza. They have a restaurant, the world's largest barrel verified by Guinness and free *cachaça* tastings at the end of the guided tour. Go to the bus stop at Praça da Estação and take the 45-minute bus ride to Maranguape (R$3.00), where the urban sprawl thins out until eventually you're let off at the depot. Then it's a R$15 taxi ride to the Ypióca museum, surrounded by fields and hills where the air smells good. After closing, there's a shuttle back from the museum to the bus stop where you can catch the bus into town.

Centro de Turismo, housed in the city's old prison – the halls of which are now filled with uninspired vendors selling bric-à-brac. This is also the location of the **Museu de Arte e Cultura Popular** (Mon–Fri 8am–6pm, Sat 8am–noon; free). Laid out in a huge, dreary gallery on the first floor, this is a collection of Cearense *artesanato*, together with paintings and sculptures produced by Ceará's artists. At the other end of the hall is the **Museu de Minerais**, a room full of quartz crystals and semi-precious stones. Neither will detain you very long – the building is actually more interesting than its exhibits.

God and mammon

Fortaleza's cathedral, the **Igreja da Sé**, is an unmistakable landmark in the centre of town. Its dark, batman-like Neogothic architectural style is almost shocking at first, and striking rather than beautiful. Megalithic flying buttresses lift the weird building from the ground, all black and grey with age and city grime. Next to it, on Rua Conde d'Eu, the **Mercado Central** dominates the skyline: a huge complex resembling a parking garage crowded with hundreds of small stores. The market, and the nearby shops diagonally across from the cathedral, are the best places in the city to buy a **hammock**.

Opposite the Mercado Central, the nineteenth-century **Fortaleza de Nossa Senhora da Assunção** – the city's namesake – is easily identified by its thick, plain white walls and black cannons. It is occupied by the Tenth Military Regiment of the Brazilian army, but is open to visitors on request (Mon–Fri 9am–5pm; ⓣ85/3255-1600, best organized the day before).

Centro Dragão do Mar

The relatively-new **Centro Dragão do Mar de Arte e Cultura**, a couple of blocks east of the market, marks a strident modernist landmark in the city; its steel

BUYING A HAMMOCK

If you're going to use a hammock on your travels, purchase it with care. Cloth ones are the most comfortable, but are heavier, bulkier and take longer than nylon ones to dry out if they get wet. Nylon is less comfy in the heat, but more convenient, much lighter and more durable.

and glass curves blend surprisingly well with the brightly-coloured, attractive old terraced buildings over and around which it is built. Within the complex, there's a small, shiny-domed planetarium, cinemas, an auditorium and a couple of museums. There's also a bookshop, toilets and, in the tower that supports the covered walkway between the two main sections of the Centro, a small but very good, perpetually packed coffee bar, the *Torre do Café*. At night the square below is Fortaleza's most vibrant nightlife spot.

The beaches

About a ten-minute walk from Centro Dragão toward the water is **Ponte dos Ingleses**, "The Bridge of the Englishmen". Actually a pier, built in 1920 and restored in 1994, it's a lively spot in the late afternoon when people gather to look out on the view of the city or watch young men dive off, climb up and nimbly dance back across to dive off again. Dolphins are said to play in the water nearby, while the surrounding area is good for bars and *forró* dancing clubs that come alive at night.

The main city beaches begin steps away with **Praia de Iracema**. Although there are a few bars and restaurants overlooking the sands, this is a pretty dull stretch, with only the occasional beach-football game until you reach **Praia do Meireles** and **Praia do Mucuripe** (the beach nearer to the industrial peninsula with the windmills). Here the beaches are spotted with palm trees and restaurants. Sadly, the water off all these beaches is badly **polluted**, and you are advised not to go in. If you want to swim, head for Praia do Futuro (see below).

In the evening it's a different story, as the seafront promenade behind these beaches comes alive. At Iracema white plastic tables are commandeered by vendors selling local handicrafts. Further down, Meireles is livelier still, as people

OUT-OF-TOWN BEACHES

The state of Ceará has plenty more beach adventures on offer if you are prepared to travel a bit further. All can be reached on tours or by regular buses from the *rodoviária*: departure times and prices vary so you'll want to shop around for the best rates. The closer ones make an easy day-trip, but if you want to stay longer check the quoted websites for places to stay. Felix Tur (Ⓣ85/3242-7200, Ⓦwww.felixtur.com.br) has transport to all of those below.

Canoa Quebrada (Ⓦwww.canoa-quebrada.es). Dramatic cliffs, dune-buggy rides, and no shortage of nightlife on this popular beach 181 km from Fortaleza. Day-trips with Felix Tur depart at 7:30am and return at 4pm (R$35). There are also public buses from the *rodoviária* for much the same price (5 daily, 3hr 30min).

Cumbuco 35km from Fortaleza. Action-packed beach with activities including horseback riding, sailing, jet-skiing and kayaking. Regular buses leave from Av Beira Mar at the *Grand Marquis Hotel* across from Mucuripe Beach (Vitória Ⓣ85/3342-1148; $R4.10 one way) and there are also day-trips with Felix Tur (R$20).

Jericocoara (Ⓦwww.jeri-brazil.org). Probably Ceará's most famous beach, with fine white sands and high dunes, especially popular with wind- and kite-surfers. The second half of the trip is by 4WD, and it can take up to seven hours for the 312km trip. Rendenção Transporte & Turismo (Ⓣ85/3256-2728,Ⓦwww.redencaoonline.com.br) have departures from the *rodoviária* at 10:30am and 6:30pm daily (R$35.50; downtown pick-up approx one hour earlier), and Felix Tur also run 4WDs.

Lagoinha This small fishing village about 100km from Fortaleza has palm trees, small waterfalls and some decent places to eat. Felix Tur departs at 8am, returns 4pm (R$30).

Morro Branco About 85km from Fortaleza, Morro Branco's beaches are backed by maze-like cliffs of multi-coloured sand. Felix Tur departs at 8am, returns 4pm (R$30).

FORTALEZA ONLINE

www.dragaodomar.org.br The centre's official site has information about events there as well as a complete list of its restaurants and bars.

www.vejabrasil.abril.uol.com.br/fortaleza In Portuguese only, but full of excellent restaurant and bar listings.

turn out to stroll or rollerblade down the boulevard, which has replaced the city's squares as the favoured meeting place. It comes alive at night with joggers, thronging crowds of friends, families browsing for restaurants, revellers, sex tourists and street-sellers with everything from sunglasses to cashew nuts.

Praia do Futuro

For **swimming**, the further away from the centre, the better. That means heading over to **Praia do Futuro**. Getting there will involve taking a bus marked either "Praia do Futuro" or "Caça e Pesca" from Avenida da Abolição, a taxi or at least a forty-five minute walk along the seafront through an industrial and *favela* neighbourhood (you certainly won't want to walk through this at night and you should note the taxi numbers below for your return). Once there, though, the beaches are worth it: wide, lined with restaurants and bars, and seeming to stretch as far as you can see.

Arrival, information and tours

Air Aeroporto Internacional Pinto Martins (85/3477-1200) is about 8km from downtown Fortaleza. To use public transportation first take the "404 Aeroporto bem Fica" (R$1.60) bus to the corner of Av de Maio and Av dos Expedicionários. Then transfer to bus 011 Circular 1 (R$1.60) downtown. The buses run all night but the names change after 11pm. Alternatively, the 15min taxi-ride which costs about R$33.

Bus Rodoviária São Tomé, Av Borges de Melo 1630, 85/3256-2100. The bus station is about 16km from Praia Iracema. To get into town, take bus #78 "Siqueira Mucuripe," from in front of Telemar across from the station on Av Borges de Melo. You can disembark at Meireles or Mucuripe beaches where you can either walk or transfer to a "Circular 1" bus to Iracema beach.

Tourist Office Inexplicably, the SETUR office at the Centro do Turismo (www.setur.ce.gov.br) is permanently closed. At the time of writing there were three tourist information booths, one at the airport (24hr), one in the Mercado Central and the best, run by FORTUR, the municipal tourist organization downtown at **Praça do Ferreira** (8am–6pm; 85/3252-1444) where they also have the best city maps. While the people working the booths are genial, few speak much English.

Tour operators Ernanitur, Av Senador Vigílio Távora, 205-2nd Floor, Sala A, Meireles (85/3533-5333, www.ernanitur.com.br), organize tours of the area and beaches; Felix Tur, Av Oswaldo Cruz 1, sala 706, Meireles (85/3242-7200, www.felixtur.com.br), has good day-trips to beaches and attractions.

City transport

Bus Fortaleza has plenty of local buses, R$1.60. Useful routes that take you to the main beaches and back to the city centre are marked "Grande Circular", "Caça e Pesca", "Mucuripe" and "P. Futuro". Two buses, the "Circular 1" and "Circular 2", run services that cover Fortaleza's outskirts and centre respectively.

Taxi These are metered, start at R$2.96 and are parked along Praia do Meireles. Expect to pay over R$18 to get anywhere in town. For taxis on-call try Cooperativa Radio Táxi 85/3254-5744 or Disque Táxi at 85/3287-7222.

Accommodation

The budget hotels, as ever, tend to be in the centre, which hums busily during the day but empties at night – you're better off staying elsewhere. The more expensive ones are primarily at Meireles with a few *pousadas* sprinkled in at Iracema. Wherever you sleep, remember, it gets hot – air-conditioning is desirable, a fan essential.

Praia de Iracema

Agua Marinha Hotel Av Almirante Barroso 701 85/3219-0303 www.aguamarinhahotel.com.br. There's not much personality at this red and

CRIME AND SAFETY

Fortaleza is heavily policed and feels much safer than many other Brazilian cities, though the usual basic precautions are still in order. By day the beaches are fine (though you should look out for **shark warnings**) but the area between Praia Meireles and Praia do Futuro is dodgy at any time and should *not* be walked by night. Fine during the day, downtown is deserted and unnerving at night. On Sunday wandering around there by yourself isn't bright either. Centro Dragão and the area around the Pirata Bar are well populated at night but draw brazen panhandlers.

white hotel but there is a pool and internet and the well-equipped rooms have safes. 5

Alamo Praia Hotel Av Almirante Barroso 885 ⓣ85/3219-7979, ⓦwww.alamohotel.com.br. A little stuffy inside but handy for the beach and the nightlife. 4

Atalaia Av Beira Mar 814 ⓣ85/3219-0755, ⓦwww.atalaiahostel.com.br. This HI-hostel operates two locations, one across from the beginning of Iracema beach, about a 10min walk from Centro Dragão, the other a block away. Most beds are in dorms with noisy fans. Dorm R$32. 4

Fortmar Hotel Av Beira Mar 1160 ⓣ85/219-5363, ⓦwww.fortmar.com.br. A proper, reasonably-priced hotel just across the street from the beach with its own small pool. 4

Fortpraia Hotel Av Almirante Barroso 714 ⓣ85/3219-6677, ⓦwww.fortpraia.com.br. Sunny rooms with comfortable beds, a/c, small fridges and safes. 4

Hotel Sonata de Iracema Av Beira Mar 848 ⓣ85/4006-1600 ⓦwww.sonatadeiracema.com.br. This very sharp, new hotel with wireless internet has a lobby-restaurant and great people-watching patio seating. 5

Raio de Sol Praia Hotel Av Almirante Barroso 772 ⓣ85/3219-0077, ⓔraiodesol@secrel.com.br. Great location just blocks from Praia Iracema, Ponte dos Ingleses and Centro Dragão, with low beds in a/c rooms, and a pool. 4

The city centre

Hotel Passeio Rua Joao Moreira 221 ⓣ85/3226-9640, ⓦnuke.hotelpasseio.com. More hostel than hotel, with small dorms as well as private rooms with fan or a/c. The shady park across the street is pleasant but the nearby bars are a little noisy and the area gets trafficked by prostitutes at night. Dorm R$40. 4

Pousada Toscana Rua Rufino de Alenar 272 ⓣ85/3088-4011, ⓦwww.pousadatoscana.com.br. Close to the central market and the Centro Dragão, this very clean and well-run hostel is located in an attractive, modest-sized house; rooms are bright and airy, beds comfortable. Dorm R$25. 3

Praia Meireles

Hotel La Maison Av Desembarador Moreira 201 ⓣ85/3242-7017, ⓦwww.hotellamaison.com.br. Thirteen-room *pousada* based in a tastefully converted family house just a few blocks from the beach; the rooms are pleasant and have air-conditioning, TVs and telephone. French and English spoken; parking spaces available. 4

Mundo Latino Rua Ana Bilhar 507 ⓣ85/3242-8778, ⓦwww.mundolatino.com.br. This bright yellow *pousada* blocks from the beach certainly isn't shy and the tiled rooms, though bare, are clean and comfy. 4

Eating

The best food options are scattered across the city. Downtown, Praça do Ferreira offers a few per kilo *lanchonetes*, and Iracema has a smattering of good restaurants, while the Centro Dragão do Mar has at least seven sidewalk cafés overflowing with people having fun. The beach areas are better, though: Meireles and Mucuripe each have beach huts offering some of the best deals on seafood, while Praia do Futuro is slightly pricier, but with even better seafood options: everyone comes here on Thursdays to eat *caranguejo* (crab). Varjota, not far inland from Mucuripe, also has a couple of excellent places.

Downtown

Café Crème Rua Dragão do Mar 92 ⓣ85/3219-7821. *Rodizío* place with all-you-can-eat pizza for R$9.90, and R$4.90 whiskies, right in the centre of Dragão's nightlife.

Neide do Camarão Av da Abolição 4772, ⓣ85/3248-2680. You buy your shrimp at the door (small, medium, large), choose how you want it prepared, hand it to the waiter, then eat the crispy shrimp, shell and all, washed down with ice cold beer. Local, authentic, awesome.

Self LeScale Rua Guilherme Rocha 48 ⓣ85/3226-8802; Rua Senador Pompeu 856, Shopping Central, 1st Floor; Rua Floriano Peixoto 589

ⓣ85/3253-1976. Three branches of a chain where the vast buffet has over 60 salads and meat dishes at R$22.90 per kilo.

Iracema and Meireles

Casa Dos Sucos Av Almirante Barroso 780, Praia Iracema ⓣ85/3219-5439. A small, family-run juice and sandwich shop serving a refreshing *açaí na tigela.*

Pelicano Restaurante Av Beira Mar 914, Praia de Iracema ⓣ85/3219-1726. Beachside restaurant specializing in grilled seafood. Try the octopus or garlic fried shrimp.

Sobre O Mar D'Iracema Rua dos Tremenbés 02, Praia de Iracema ⓣ85/3219-7999. This two-storey restaurant overlooking the Ponte dos Ingleses is a great place for a sunset seafood meal.

Varjota

Ban Cha Sushi Bar Rua Frederico Borges 368 ⓣ85/3267-7327, ⓦwww.restaurantefogaoalenha.com.br. Excellent sushi place: lunchtime prices are R$27.90 per kg or buffet for R$25; in the evening R$31.90 per kg or R$29 for the buffet.

Colher de Pau Rua Frederico Borges 204 ⓣ85/3267-3773. A popular, family-run restaurant serves up local Cearense cuisine at reasonable prices and plates you can share with a friend.

TREAT YOURSELF

Beijupirá Av Beira Mar 1680, Praia de Iracema ⓣ85/3248-8811, ⓦwww.beijupirafortaleza.com.br. You can't beat the ambience at this chic, arch-filled, candle-lit beachside restaurant with the pond out front. The creative menu changes monthly and features seafood with interesting ingredients.

Restaurante João do Bacalhau Rua República do Líbano 1073, Centro ⓣ85/3267-3029. Cod is the house speciality of this open-kitchen where one plate can usually satisfy two people.

Vojnilô Rua Frederico Borges 409, Varjota ⓣ85/3267-3081. The doors to this Mediterranean-style grill-house are opened for you by guys in tuxes. Class. Try the ribs, baked lobster and mashed potatoes served with fried cashew nuts.

Praia do Futuro

ΔTLΔΠTΔDZ Av Zezé Diogo 558 ⓣ85/3249-4606. This polished tiki bar with the inexplicable pseudo-Greek motif has plenty of R$30 fish options, plus grilled lobster for R$90 or crabs in bunches of three for R$8.99.

Chico do Caranguejo Av Zezé Diogo 4930 ⓣ85/3262-0108. A chilled crab-house which sells *caranguejo* for just R$3/crab, has live music and even a small playground for kids.

Coco Beach Av Zezé Diogo 6421 ⓣ85/3249-9858. Plenty of R$20 pasta options, hamburgers, sandwiches and fish. Massages on offer too.

Cafés, bakeries, self-catering and street food

Natural Leve Rua Costa Barros 2000 ⓣ85/3224-4422. Good juices, sandwiches and milkshakes at hard-to-beat prices: *açaí* R$4.50; cheeseburger and fries R$3.30.

Pão de Açucár Av Bezerra Menezes 571, Centro ⓣ85/3433-6444; Av Dep Oswaldo Studart 600, Fátima ⓣ85/3452-5370; ⓦwww.paodeacucar.com.br. This quality grocery has several locations in Fortaleza.

Ponto do Guaraná Av Beira Mar 3127-A, Meireles ⓣ85/3086-5650. When the heat really starts to get to you, this *açaí* pavilion just steps from the beach feels like a godsend.

Real Sucos Heráclito Graça 1709 ⓣ85/3244-3923; Shopping Aldeota ⓣ85/3458-1104; Shopping Benfica ⓣ85/3281-4029. Excellent juices and *açaí* with lots of sandwich options; the *cajú* juice is especially good.

Santa Clara Café Rua Dragão do Mar 81, Centro Dragão do Mar ⓣ85/3219-6900. The best coffee in town. Try the rich, delicious *chocolate grande*; it's more warm chocolate pudding than hot chocolate.

São Luiz Supermercado Av Beira Mar 693, Praia de Iracema. This supermarket is small but it's conveniently located near the *Pousada Atalaia*.

Sorvetão Av Beira Mar 762, Praia de Iracema. The sixty flavours of ice cream change with the seasons, even if it feels like the weather never does. Try the café, *doche de leite* or *cajú*.

Drinking and nightlife

Fortaleza is justly famous for its **forró**. There's no better way to see what Cearenses do to have fun than to spend a night in a *dancetaria*. One of the busiest nightspot areas is the streets around the Ponte dos Ingleses. Most *dancetarias* open at 10pm, but they don't really get going until about midnight. Other nightlife is mainly out by the beaches: Meireles appeals to a broad cross-section of the local and tourist populations, whereas Iracema is slightly younger.

Armazém Av Almirante Barroso 444, Praia de Iracema ⓣ85/3219-4322. This *forró* nightclub near the Centro Dragão complex draws onlookers sitting at the cafés. Inside, the lights flash, music pumps and the dancing goes on until late. Wed, Fri & Sat 10pm–4am.

Chorino do Mercado dos Pinhões between ruas Nogueira Acioly and Gonçalves Ledo ⓣ85/3251-1299. A French iron market pavilion, inaugurated in 1897 and now a terrific place to visit in the evenings. The sides of the building are open and there's live music inside. Sit outside one of the surrounding bars, order some beer and soak it all up.

Pirata Bar Rua dos Tabajaras 325 ⓣ85/4011-6161, ⓦwww.pirata.com.br. This easily accessible nightclub has live music (Tues–Sat) ranging from rock and pop to *forró* (with accordions). Later the acclaimed Banda do Pirata often takes the audience through a medley of *axe, salsa, baiao, pagode* and *zouk*. Pirata does what they call "the craziest Monday in the world," a party with a free *sopão da madrugada* 'dawn soup' served at 3am to re-energize the party until it ends at dawn.

Subindo ao Céu Av Zezé Diogo 5461, Praia do Futuro ⓣ85/265-1059. A popular venue on Tues nights. Cover R$10.

Directory

Airlines GOL ⓦwww.voegol.com.br; TACV, Av D Luis 880, Aldeota (ⓣ85/3266-1755); TAM, Av Santos Dumond 2626 ⓣ85/3133-9222; TAP Air Portugal, Av D Luís, 500 A s 909, Aldeota ⓣ85/3458-1540; Varig, Aeroporto Internacional Pinto Martins ⓣ85/3392-1078.

Banks and exchange Câmbio Brasil Turismo, Aeroporto Internacional Pinto Martins (diagonally across from Café Com Pão at the end of the terminal). There are a fair number of ATMs near the beaches and hotels with several HSBC loacations near Iracema, Meireles and Mucuripe: Rua Rosário, 199, Centro; Av Mons Tabosa, 1200, Meireles; Av Santos Dumont, 3581, Aldeota.

Car rental Lokar, Av Beira Mar 720, Praia de Iracema (ⓣ85/3218-6768, ⓦwww.lokarentacar.com.br); Maresia Rent a Car, Av Monsenhor Tabosa 1001, Loja 11, Praia de Iracema (ⓣ85/3219-8000, ⓦwww.maresiarentacar.com.br); Localiza Rent A Car, Av da Abolição 2236, Meireles (ⓣ85/3248-2900).

Cinema All the malls listed below have cinemas; check out also São Luis Cinema-SESC Cultural Centre, Rua Major Facundo 500 (ⓣ85/3253-3332).

Embassies and consulates Netherlands, Avenida Dom Luiz 880, sala 707/708 Edificio Top Center (ⓣ85/3268-2700); UK, British Honorary Consulate, Rua Leonardo Mota 501, Meireles (ⓣ85/242-0888); US, Torre Santos Dumont, Avenida Santos Dumont 2828, Suite 708, Aldeota (ⓣ85/486-1306).

Hospital Monte Klinikum Hospital, Rua República do Libano 747 ⓣ85/4012-0012, ⓦwww.monteklinikum.com.br.

Internet Evolution Vídeo Cyber Café, Av da Abolição 3230, Meireles (ⓣ85/3242-9833); Cyber Café, Av da Abolição 2655, Meireles (ⓣ85/3242-5422).

Laundry 5 à Sec, Rua Cel Juca 470, Aldeota ⓣ85/3267-5034.

Left luggage Lockers are at the airport outside by the taxis and cost R$25 per day.

Pharmacies Farmácia Santa Branca, Av da Universidade 3089, Benefica ⓣ85/3223-0000; Droga Nunes, Av Sen Virgílio Távora 597, Meireles ⓣ85/3433-1818.

Post office Rua Br Aracati 909, Aldeota ⓣ85/3221-2960; Av Mons Tabosa 1561, Meireles ⓣ85/3248-1544 (Mon–Fri 8am–5pm, Sat 8am–noon).

Shopping The Mercado Central at Av Alberto Nepomuceno 199 is the place for *artesanato* (and almost eveything else).

The following are modern malls with all you could desire, including multiplex cinemas:

Shopping Del Paseo Av Santo Dumont 3131, Aldeota (ⓦwww.shoppingdelpaseo.com.br).

Shopping Aldeota Av D Luis 500, Aldeota, (ⓦwww.shoppingaldeota.com.br).

Shopping Benfica Av Carapinima 2200, Benefica (ⓦwww.shoppingbenfica.com.br).

ShoppingIguatemi Av Washington Soares 85, Guararapes (ⓦwww.iguatemifortaleza.com.br).

Moving on

Air TAM flies several times a day to *São* Paulo, Rio and Recife. TACV flies to Praia and Sal once a day. TAP Air Portugal flies to Lisbon once daily and Gol and Varig fly to other points within Brazil.

Bus There are departures from the *rodoviária* to almost all parts of the Northeast, as well as Rio and São Paulo. Fortaleza to Canoa Quebrada, five buses daily, R$18 (3hr 30min); Jericoacoara, two buses daily, R$35 (6hr); João Pessoa, two buses daily, R$90-150 (11hr); Natal, eight buses daily, R$70-130 (8hr); Recife, three buses daily, R$107 (12hr); Rio, once daily except Sundays, R$315 (46hr); Salvador, one bus (Mon, Wed, Fri & Sat) R$145 (20hr).

Guanabara Express (ⓦwww.expressoguanabara.com.br) operates routes to several Northeast states; **Viação Nordeste**, (ⓦwww.viacaonordeste.com.br) go to Natal; **Redencão** (ⓦwww.redencaoonline.com.br) to Brasilia. For Rio and São Paulo try São Geraldo (ⓦwww.saogeraldo.com.br), Itapemirim (ⓦwww.itapemirim.com.br) or Nossa Senhora da Penha (ⓦnspenha.locaweb.com.br).

The Amazon

The Amazon is a vast forest – the largest on the planet – and a giant river system, covering over half of Brazil and a large portion of South America. The forest extends into Venezuela, Colombia, Peru and Bolivia, where the river itself begins life among thousands of different headwaters. In Brazil only the stretch below Manaus, where the waters of the **Rio Solimões** and the **Rio Negro** meet, is actually known as

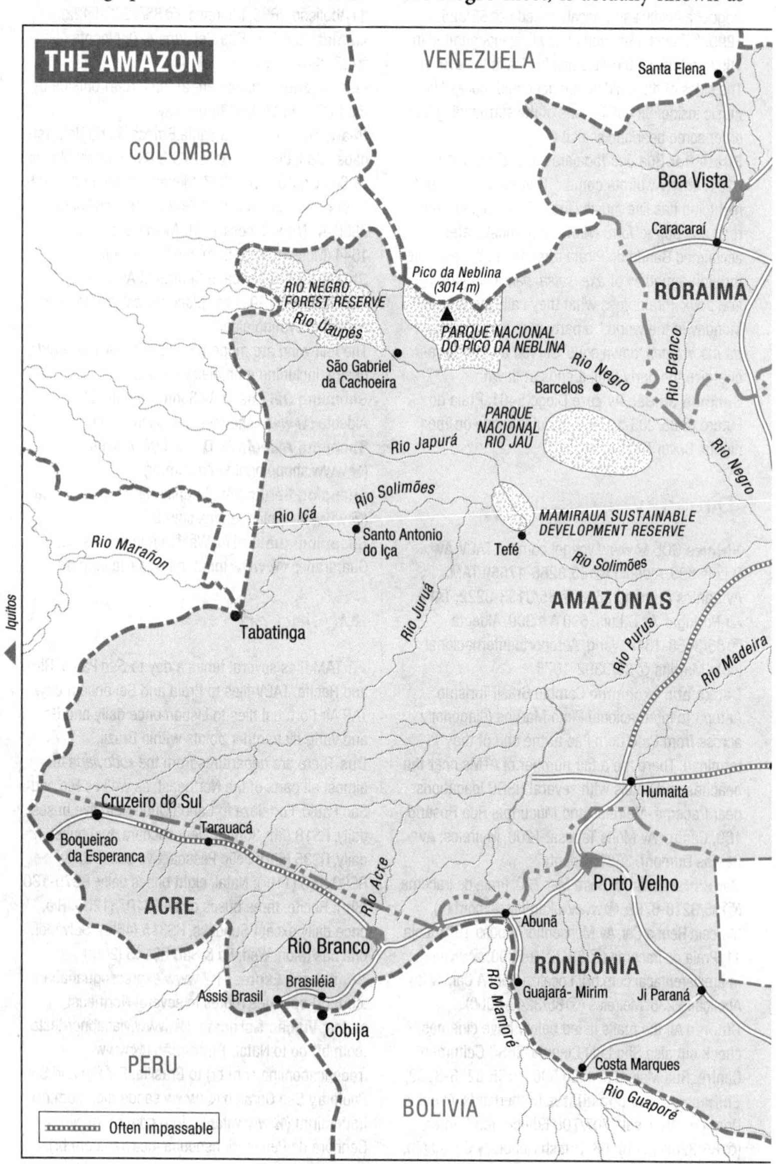

the **Rio Amazonas**. The daily flow of the river is said to be enough to supply a city the size of New York with water for nearly ten years, and its power is such that the muddy Amazon waters stain the Atlantic a silty brown for over 200km out to sea.

EASTERN AMAZÔNIA

Politically divided between the states of Pará and Amapá, the **Eastern Amazon** is essentially a vast area of forest and savanna plains centred on the final seven hundred miles or so of the giant river's

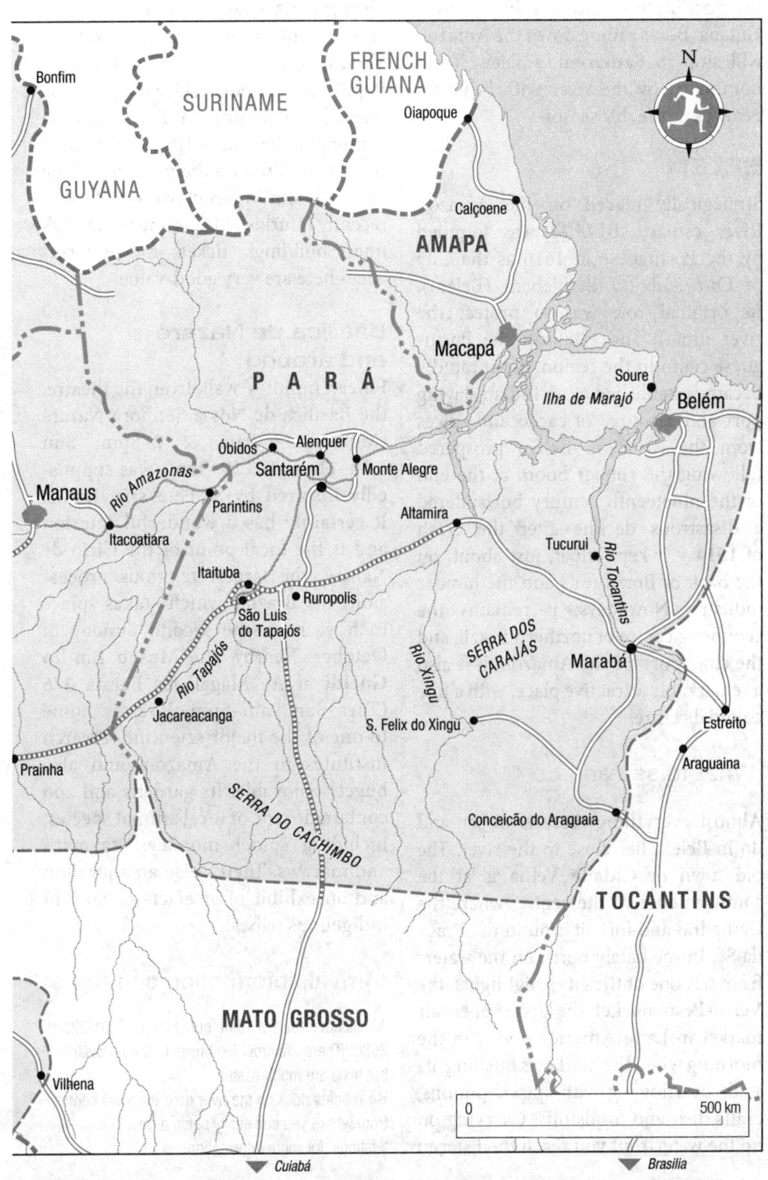

course. **Belém**, an Atlantic port near the mouth of the estuary, overlooks the river and the vast **Ilha do Marajó**, the largest island surrounded by freshwater in the world. **Amapá**, in the north-eastern corner of the Brazilian Amazon, is a poor and little-visited area offering the possibility of crossing into French Guiana. Boats sailing down the Amazon will stop in **Santarém**, a sleepy town dominated by the river with beautiful beaches in the dry season.

BELÉM

Strategically placed on the Amazon River estuary, **BELÉM** was founded by the Portuguese in 1616 as the City of Our Lady of Bethlehem (Belém). Its original role was to protect the river mouth and establish the Portuguese claim to the region, but it rapidly became established as an Indian slaving port and a source of cacao and spices from the Amazon. Belém prospered following the rubber boom at the end of the nineteenth century but suffered a disastrous decline after the crash of 1914 – it kept afloat, just about, on the back of Brazil nuts and the lumber industry. Nowadays, it remains the economic centre of northern Brazil, and the chief port for the Amazon. It is also a remarkably attractive place, with a fine colonial centre.

What to see and do

Almost everything there is to see and do in Belém lies close to the river. The old town or **Cidade Velha** is at the southern edge of the centre, where the Cathedral and fort sit around the Praça da Sé. Immediately north on the waterfront lies one of the city's highlights, the **Ver-o-Peso market**, the largest open-air market in Latin America – visit in the morning when the market is bustling, its stalls overflowing with spices, potions, crafts, fish and foodstuffs. Carrying on up the waterfront you reach the Estação das Docas cultural centre (Mon–Thurs 10am–midnight, Fri–Sun 10am–3am) where some (rather pricey) *artesanato* stalls compete with numerous restaurants, cafés and exhibition spaces in a refurbished warehouse area.

Praça da Republica

Heading inland up Avenida Presidente Vargas, you reach the shady Praça da República, a popular place to stroll. The magnificent **Teatro da Paz** (Tues–Fri 9am–5pm, Sat 9am–1pm; R$4) faces the square. Built on the proceeds of the rubber boom in Neoclassical style, and recently refurbished, it is one of the city's finest buildings; tickets for performances here are very good-value.

Basílica de Nazaré and around

Fifteen minutes' walk from the theatre, the Basílica de Nossa Senhora Nazaré (Mon–Sat 6–9am & 2–8pm, Sun 6.30–11am & 3.30–9pm) was supposedly inspired by St Peter's in Rome. It certainly has a wonderful interior, and is the focal point of the Cirio de Nazaré, the largest religious procession in Brazil, which takes place each year on the second Sunday of October. Nearby, the **Museu Emílio Goeldi** at Av Magalhães Barata 376 (Tues–Sun 9am–5pm; R$2) is home to one of the major scientific research institutes in the Amazon, and also hugely enjoyable. Its gardens and zoo contain dozens of local animal species, including spider monkeys, caymans and macaws. There's also an aquarium and an exhibit of artefacts of ancient indigenous tribes.

Arrival, information and tours

Air Belém airport is 15km out of town (☎91/3233-3986). There are crowded buses to the *rodoviária*, but taxis are much easier.

Boat boats dock on the river near the town centre, from where you can easily catch a taxi. See 'Listings' for more information.

Bus Belém's *rodoviária* is situated some 2km from the centre on Av Gov. José Malcher; any bus from the stops opposite the entrance to the *rodoviária* will take you downtown. If you want Praça da República, catch the #316 or #904, or take one with "P. Vargas" on its route card; for the port area take the #318.

Tourist Information Belémtur are at Av Gov. José Malcher 257 (Mon–Fri 8am–6pm; ⓣ91/3283-4850, ⓦwww.belem.pa.gov.br); the Paratur offices are by the Praça Maestro Waldemar Henrique (previously Praça Kennedy; Mon–Fri 8am–6pm; ⓣ091/3212-0669, ⓦwww.paratur.pa.gov.br). There is also a tourist information point (daily 8am–10pm; ⓣ91/3210-6268) at the airport, although information can be limited depending on who assists you. Maps and town guides can be bought cheaply from the newspaper stands on Av Presidente Vargas or in the shop inside the foyer of the *Belém Hilton*.

Tour operators Eco Travel, in the *Amazônia Hostel* (ⓣ91/4008-4800, ⓦwww.ecotravel.tur.br) organize trips to the Ilha do Marajó, Ilha do Algodoal and Santarém. They also offer jungle trips (R$120 per day) and city tours. Valeverde Turismo, in the Estaçao das Docas (ⓣ91/3212-3388, ⓦwww.valeverdeturismo.com.br) organize good-value river tours around Belém. Amazon Star Turismo, Rua Henrique Gurjão 236 (ⓣ91/3241-8624, ⓦwww.amazonstar.com.br) is an excellent French-run agency specializing in eco-tours, including visits to Cotijuba, Icoaraçi, Mosqueiro island and Ilha de Marajó.

Accommodation

Amazônia Hostel Av Gov. José Malcher 592 ⓣ91/4008-4800, ⓦwww.amazoniahostel.com.br. This spacious (rather pricey) YHA-affiliated hostel has beautiful *acapu* and *pau-amarelo* floors, a kitchen, wi-fi and a/c in all dorms; unfortunately the chairs in the lounge don't scream comfort. Substantial discounts with HI card. Dorm R$38. ❺

Hotel Amazônia Rua Ó de Almeida 548 ⓣ91/3222-8456, ⓦwww.amazoniahostel.com. Part of this hotel/hostel was home to a museum and most artefacts were taken to what is now the Museu de Arte Sacra. Ask for room 1 or for the rooms upstairs as these are much brighter. Dorm R$18. ❹

Hotel Fortaleza Travessa Frutuoso Guimaraes 276 ⓣ91/3212-1055. Pleasantly colourful, safe family-run place with lovely wooden floors in a colonial building in a bustling backstreet of the colonial centre; the price, quite simply, cannot be beat. Dorm R$10. ❸

Eating

Belém boasts plenty of excellent cheap restaurants, which have especially good deals at lunchtime. You can also eat cheaply – a soup is about R$2 – at the restaurants within the Lider Supermarket on Av Visconde de Souza Franco (R$25 per kg) which is open 24/7.

Albatroz Av Nazaré 194, corner of Dr Moraes. A bustling place with excellent food and tables lined outside. R$18 per kg.

Boteco da Nina Travessa Rui Barbosa 946. Small local restaurant with some tables outside, run by smiley and friendly Katia. Always packed at lunch which is not surprising: R$5 for a meat *prato* of the day, R$6 for fish. Dinner only served if food is left after lunch. Closed Sun.

Koma Bem Rua 28 de Setembro 143. Large canteen-like restaurant with murals trying to decorate the walls. Very good food nonetheless, for R$20 per kg. Lunchtime only, closed Sun.

Lá em Casa in the Estação das Docas. Not the cheapest place in town, but certainly the best for local grub, with a deserved reputation in the city for its local cuisine.

Drinking and nightlife

There are many bars along Av Visconde de Souza Franco (Doca).

Bar do Parque Praça da República. The oldest bar in town has 24hr drinking and is a good place to watch Belém streetlife go by. Watch your wallet when walking around the square.

Café Imaginario Travessa Quintino Bocaiúva 1086, corner of Rua Boaventura da Silva. Renowned nationwide for its *pizza de jambu*, *Café Imaginario* attracts an arty crowd of painters, journalists and music lovers. Colourful walls and a fun atmosphere, with live jazz and blues Tues–Sun from 10.30pm.

Directory

Airlines Taba, Av Dr. Feitas 1191, office at the airport ⓣ91/3257-4000; TAM, Av Assis de Vasconcelos 265 ⓣ91/212-2166; Tavaj ⓣ91/3210-6257; Transbrasil, Av Presidente Vargas 780 ⓣ91/3212-6977; Varig, Av Presidente Vargas 768 ⓣ91/3210-6262.

Banks and exchange Banco da Amazônia, Banco do Brasil and HSBC are all on Av Presidente Vargas.

Car hire Dallas, Trav. Quintino Bocaiúva 1273 ⓣ91/3213-2237; Hertz at the airport

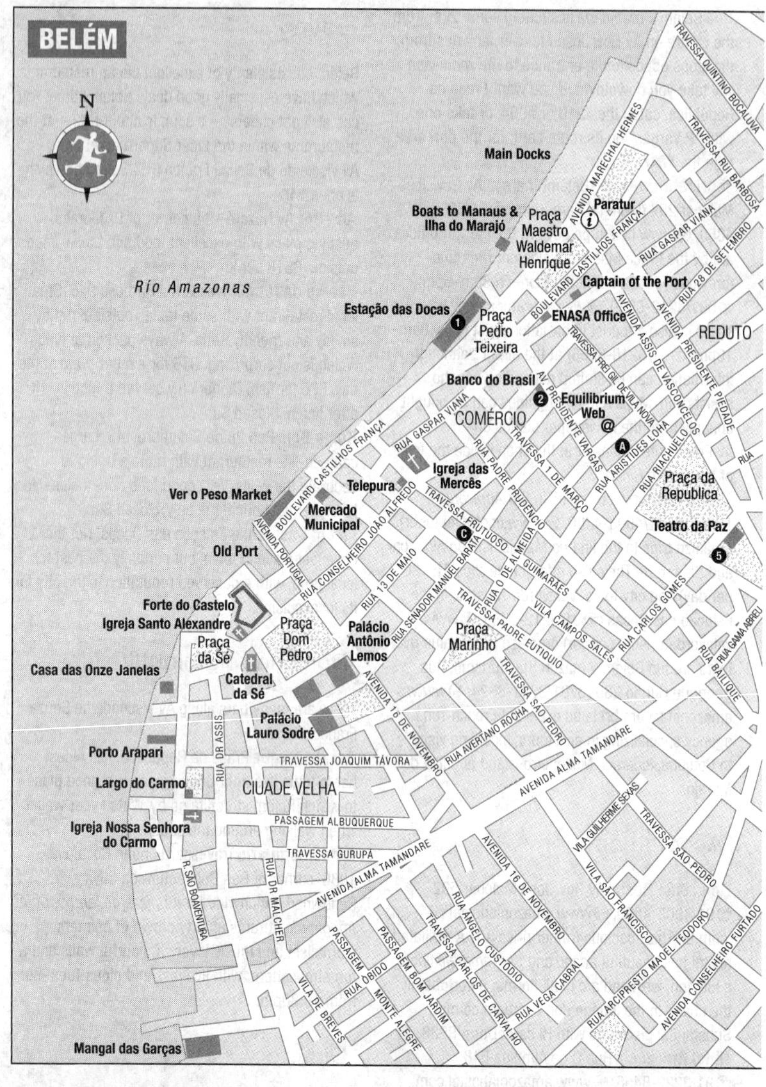

☎91/3210-6440 or 3257-0177; Localiza, at the airport (☎0800/979-2000) and at Av Gov. José Malcher 1365 ☎91/3212 2700; Unidas, at tha airport (☎91/3257-2300) and at Av Almirante Barroso 986-A ☎91/3226-8888.

Hospital Hospital Guadalupe, Rua Arcipreste Manoel Teodoro 734 (☎91/4005-9877 or 9820).

Internet Equilibrium Web, Rua Ó de Almeida 533 (Mon–Sat 8am–8pm; R$2.50 per hr) has flat-screen computers, excellent broadband connection and Skype; A.S. Net, Travessa Frutuoso Guimaraes 276 (in the same building as *Hotel Fortaleza*; Mon–Sat 8am–9pm, Sun 2–9pm; R$2 per hr)) also has Skype.

Post office The central post office (Mon–Fri 9am–5pm) is an impressive building at Av Presidente Vargas 498. However, as this is frequently crowded, it's often quicker to walk to the small post office at Av Nazaré 319, three blocks beyond the Praça da República.

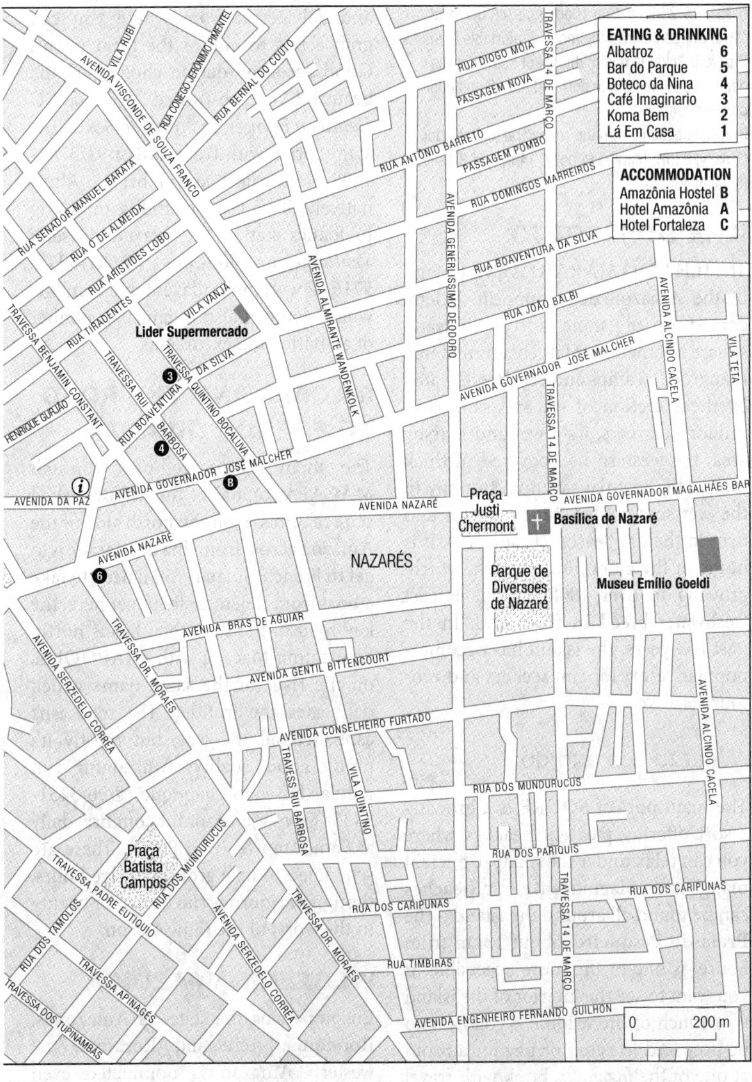

Shopping Belém is one of the best places in the world to buy hammocks (essential if you go upriver) – the best place is at the Ver-o-Peso market, where you can also buy beautiful local crafts. There is a Lider Supermarket on Av Visconde de Souza Franco.

Taxi Cooperdoca ⓣ091/3241-3555 or 3099; Amazônia Rádio Táxi ⓣ091/3253-0345 or 3274 4393.

Telephones There are a number of cheap calling places on Av Presidente Vargas between Rua Riachuelo and Travessa Ó de Almeida.

Moving on

Air There are daily flights from Belém to most major Brazilian cities, including Boa Vista and Manaus. There are also several flights a week to Cayenne, French Guiana, and Paramaribo, Suriname, with connections to Gerogetown, Guyana.

Boats Boats leave Belém for Santarém and Manaus Tues, Wed & Fri at 6pm; for Macapá on Wed & Sat at 10am; for Ilha do Marajó Mon–Sat

6.30am & 2.30pm, Sun 10am. Amazon Star and Navio Rondonia have the most comfortable boats. Buy your ticket in one of the ticket booths in the departure lounge at the port and not off someone on the street.

Bus Connections from the *rodoviária* to: Salvador (1 daily; 33hr); Marabá (4 daily; 14hr) and Brasília (5 daily; 36hr).

ILHA DO MARAJÓ

The **ILHA DO MARAJÓ** is a vast island in the Amazon delta opposite Belém, consisting of some forty thousand square kilometres of largely uninhabited mangrove swamps and beaches. Created by the accretion of silt and sand over millions of years, it's a wet and marshy area, the western half covered in thick jungle, the east flat savanna, swampy in the wet season (Jan–June), brown and firm in the dry season (June–Dec). It is home of the giant *pirarucu* fish, which, growing to over 180kg, is the largest freshwater breed in the world. In the past few years, the island has become a popular resort for sun seekers and eco-tourists alike.

What to see and do

The main port of **SOURE** is a growing resort offering pleasant beaches where you can relax under the shade of ancient mango trees. Magnificent empty **beaches** can be found all around the island – the **Praia do Pesqueiro**, about 13km from Soure, is one of the more accessible. If you want to see the interior of the island – or much of the wildlife – you have to be prepared to camp or pay for a room at one of the *fazendas*: book with travel agents in Belém or take your chance on arrival. **JOANES**, with another tremendous beach, is much quieter.

Island practicalities

Boats leave Belém Mondy to Saturday 6.30am and 2.30pm, Sunday 10am (3hr; R$12.22); they dock at **Porto Camará**, about 25km from Soure and Salvaterra, from where you can grab a bus to any of the local towns. Good **accommodation** choices are the beautiful French-owned *Pousada O Canto do Francês*, in Soure on Sexta Rua at the corner with Travessa 8 (Ⓣ91/3741-1298, Ⓔthcarliez@ig.com.br; ❹). Alternatively, if you are planning on going to Joanes stay at the relaxed *Pousada Ventania do Rio-Mar* (Ⓣ091/9992-5716, Ⓦwww.pousadaventania.com; ❺) where you can also organize a number of activities and excursions.

MACAPÁ AND THE ROAD TO FRENCH GUIANA

The main reason to pass through **MACAPÁ**, capital of the impoverished state of Amapá, on the north side of the Amazon across from Ilha do Marajó, is to get to French Guiana. You'll need to take a boat from Belém or fly to get here: the key road in the state then heads north, connecting Macapá with **OIAPOQUE**, on the river of the same name which delineates the frontier. The road isn't asphalted all the way, but mostly it's pretty good quality; Amazontur run regular buses to Oiapoque (Ⓣ96/3251-3435 Ⓦwww.amazontur.com.br; daily at 9am, 1pm & 7pm; R$52). These are scheduled to take around twelve hours, though the journey can be nearer twenty in the worst of the rainy season.

WESTERN AMAZÔNIA

Encompassing the states of **Amazonas**, **Rondônia**, **Acre** and **Roraima**, the western Amazon is dominated even more than the east by the Amazon and Solimões rivers and their tributaries. To the north, the forest is centred on the Negro and Branco rivers, before phasing into the wooded savannas of Roraima. To the south, the Madeira, Purús and Juruá rivers meander through the forests from the prime rubber region of Acre and the recently colonized state of Rondônia. The hub of this area is **Manaus**, more or less

ENTERING FRENCH GUIANA

If you are not a citizen of a European Union country, the USA or Canada, you will need a **visa** to enter French Guiana. There is a French consulate in Macapá at the *Pousada Ekinox*, Rua Jovina Dinoa 1693 (☎96/3223-7554), though it's better to arrange visas before you leave home. Buy **Euros** at the Casa Francesa Turismo either in Belém (at the airport or at Travessa Padre Prudencio 40) or in Macapá (Rua Binga Uchoa 236); you can get them in Oiapoque but the rates are worse, and you can't depend on changing either Brazilian currency or US dollars for euros in Saint-Georges-de-l'Oyapok.

Dug-out taxis are the usual means of transport between Oiapoque and **Saint-Georges-de-l'Oyapok** (see p.741), about ten minutes downriver. Brazilian **exit stamps** can be obtained from the Polícia Federal at the southern road entrance into Oiapoque; on the other side you have to check in with the *gendarmes* in Saint-Georges.

Most travellers, in fact, cross the border the easy way – by **flying** from Macapá to the capital at Cayenne (TAF Airlines, from around $200). Once you're across the border you'll probably want to fly from the border settlement of Saint-Georges to Cayenne in any case – or else catch a boat – since overland transport is atrocious.

at the junction of three great rivers – the Solimões/Amazonas, the Negro and the Madeira – which between them support the world's greatest surviving forest.

MANAUS

MANAUS is the capital of Amazonas, a tropical forest state covering around one-and-a-half million square kilometres. Manaus isn't actually on the Amazon at all, but lies on the Rio Negro, six kilometres from the point where that river meets the Solimões to form (as far as Brazilians are concerned) the Rio Amazonas. Arriving in Manaus may at first seem overwhelming given its two million inhabitants, noise and confusion, but you will soon discover some of the city's pluses.

It is certainly an extraordinary place – a city in the midst of the jungle, consciously designed to show the mastery of man over nature. Towards the end of the nineteenth century, at the height of the rubber boom, architects were summoned from Europe to redesign the city which rapidly acquired a Western feel – broad Parisian-style avenues were laid down, interspersed with Italian piazzas centred on splendid fountains. Innovative Manaus was one of the first cities to have electricity, trolley buses and sewage systems. However, this heyday lasted barely thirty years, and by 1914 the rubber market was collapsing fast, preserving the glories of the past in aspic. Today, largely thanks to the Free Trade Zone, the *Zona Franca*, created in 1967, Manaus is thriving again: an aggressive commercial and industrial centre for an enormous region – the Hong Kong of the Amazon.

What to see and do

To start with the real flavour of Manaus, head for the riverfront and the **docks**, a constant throng of chaotic activity to set against the serenity of the moored ships as they bob gently up and down. During the day there's no problem wandering around the area, and it's easy enough to find out which boats are going where just by asking around. At night, however, the port is best avoided: many of the river men carry guns.

Customs house and market

Known locally as the Alfândega, the **Customs House** (Mon–Fri 8am–1pm) stands overlooking the floating docks. Erected in 1906, the building was shipped

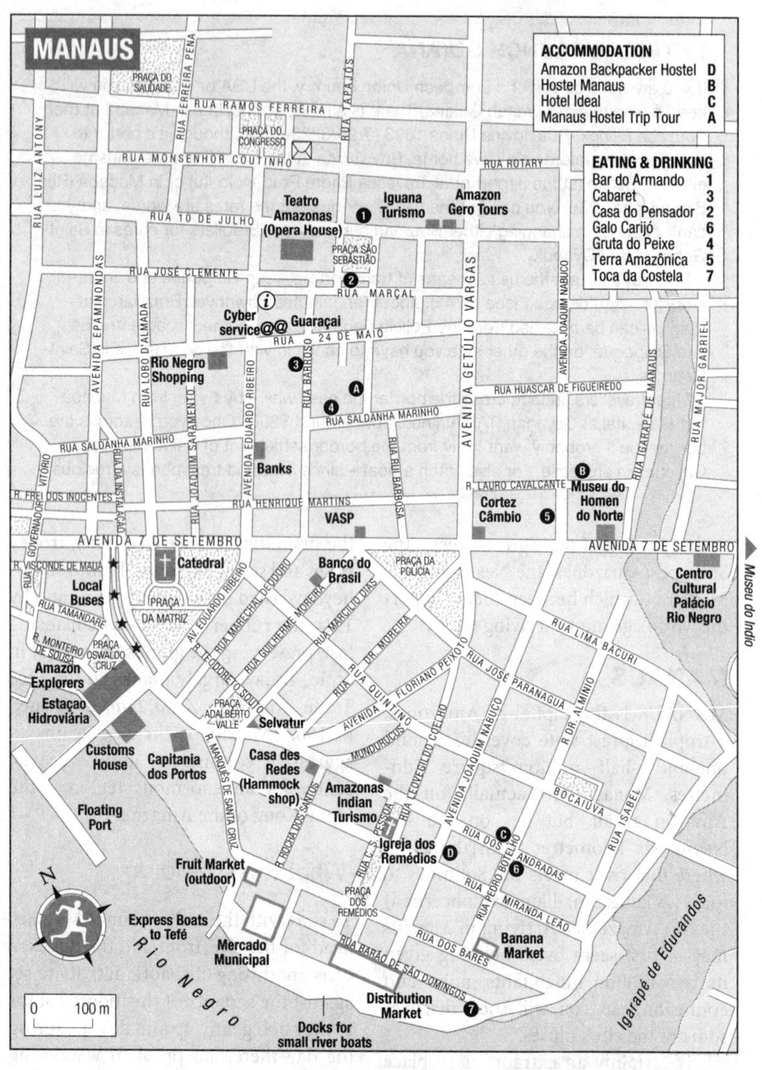

over from Britain in prefabricated blocks. The tower here once acted as a lighthouse guiding vessels in at night. The floating docks, too, were built by a British company, at the beginning of the twentieth century. To cope with the river rising over a 14m range, the concrete pier is supported on pontoons which rise and fall to allow even the largest ships to dock all year round. Across the main road from the port is the **Praça Terreira Araña**, where there are several craft stalls selling indigenous Amazon tribal *artesanato*, leather sandals and jungle souvenirs. The main **market**, the Mercado Municipal Adolfo Lisboa, is further round the riverfront. It is best visited early in the morning when freshly-caught fish of all sizes are laid out on display; by afternoon, most merchants have closed shop.

Teatro Amazonas

By far the most famous building in Manaus is the sumptuous **Teatro Amazonas** or Opera House (Mon–Sat 8am–5pm; R$10 including guided tour; ⓣ92/3622-2420), immortalized in Werner Herzog's movie *Fitzcarraldo*. Inaugurated in 1896, it's the most extreme example of Manaus's rubber boom: built with materials brought from Europe and entirely decorated by European artists. The Opera House hosts regular concerts, including in April the **Festa da Manaus**, initiated in 1997 to celebrate thirty years of the Zona Franca.

The wavy black and white mosaic designs of the **Praça São Sebastião**, in front of the Teatro, are home to the "Monument to the Opening of the Ports", a marble and granite creation with four ships that represent four continents – America, Europe, Africa and Asia/Australasia – and children who symbolize the people of those continents. The black and white wavy mosaics themselves symbolize the meeting of the waters of the Rio Solimões and the Rio Negro. The beautiful little **Igreja de São Sebastião**, on the *praça*, was built in 1888; like many other churches in Brazil it has only one tower, the result of a nineteenth-century tax payable by churches with two towers.

Museu do Índio

The excellent **Museu do Índio**, at Rua Duque de Caxias 356 (Mon–Fri 9am–noon & 2–4pm, Sat 9am–noon; R$5), lies a little way east of the centre off Avenida Sete de Setembro. Run by the Salesian Sisters, who have long-established missions along the Rio Negro, especially with the Tukano tribe, it features excellent, carefully presented exhibits ranging from sacred ritual masks and inter-village communication drums to fine ceramics, superb palm-frond weavings and even replicas of Indian dwellings.

The meeting of the waters

The most popular and most widely touted day-trip from Manaus is to the **meeting of the waters**, some 10km downstream, where the Rio Negro and the Rio Solimões meet to form the Rio Amazonas. For several kilometres beyond the point where they join, the waters of the two rivers continue to flow separately, the muddy yellow of the Solimões contrasting sharply with the black of the Rio Negro, which is much warmer, and more acidic. The are dozens of tours (R$90 upwards; see the operators in Listings on p.351), but if you want to do this under your own steam, take the "Vila Burity" **bus** (#713) from Praça da Matriz to the end of the line, from where there is a free half-hourly government ferry over the river, passing the meeting of the waters.

Parque Ecológico Janauary

Most tours to the meeting of the waters stop in at the **Parque Ecológico do Janauary**, an ecological park some 7km from Manaus on one of the main local tributaries of the Rio Negro. Usually you'll be transferred to smaller motorized canoes to explore its creeks (*igarapés*), flooded forest lands (*igapós*) and abundant vegetation. One of the highlights of the area is the abundance of *Victoria Amazonica*, the extraordinary giant floating lily for which Manaus is famous, reaching a diameter of two metres.

Praia Ponta Negra

At weekends, the river beach at **Praia Ponta Negra**, about 13km northwest of Manaus, is packed with locals. It's an enjoyable place to go for a swim, with plenty of bars and restaurants serving freshly cooked river-fish nearby. The bus to Ponta Negra (#120) leaves every half-hour; catch it by the cathedral on Praça da Matriz.

JUNGLE TRIPS FROM MANAUS

The amount and nature of the **wildlife** you get to see on a standard **jungle tour** depends mainly on how far away from Manaus you go and how long you can devote to the trip. Birds like macaws, *jabarus* and toucans can generally be spotted, and you might see alligators, snakes and a few species of monkey on a three-day trip. For a reasonable chance of glimpsing wild deer, tapirs, armadillos or wild cats then a more adventurous trip of a week or more is required. On any trip, make sure that you'll get some time in the smaller channels in a canoe, as the sound of a motor is a sure way of scaring every living thing out of sight. The Rio Negro region has water with high acidity because of the geology of its main sources in the Guyana Shield. Because of the acid water, it tends to have fewer mosquitoes which is an obvious bonus; but it also tends to have less abundant wildlife than some of the lakes and channels around the Rio Solimões. Plenty of tours combine both the Solimões and Negro rivers in their itineraries.

Tour itineraries

The **one-day river trip**, usually costing around R$130 per person, generally includes an inspection of the famous meeting of the waters, some 10km downriver from Manaus (see p.347). The other most popular jungle river trips tend to be the **three- to five-day expeditions**. If you want to sleep in the forest, either in a lodge, riverboat or, for the more adventurous (and perhaps those with a low budget), swinging in a hammock outside in a small jungle clearing, it really is worth taking as many days as you can to get as far away from Manaus as possible. The usual price for guided tours, including accommodation and food, should be between R$85 and R$200 a day per person (no matter the sales pitch). As well as the itinerary, check that you're getting what you need in terms of security, health and safety, food, sleeping arrangements, guide quality and transfers.

The most commonly operated tours are three-day-trips combining both the **Rio Negro** and **Rio Solimões**, although some trips only cover the former, as it is more accessible from Manaus. Four-day-trips should ideally also include the **Anavilhanas Archipelago** on the Rio Negro, the second-largest freshwater archipelago in the world with around four hundred isles, as well as a good day's walk through the jungle. On the Solimões, some of the three- to five-day options include trips to Lago Mamori or Manacapuru.

If you want to forgo organized tours entirely and travel independently, **milk boats** are a very inexpensive way of getting about on the rivers around Manaus. The best place to look for these is down on Flutuante Três Estrelas, one of the wooden wharves behind the distribution market, further along the river edge from the Hidroviária at the back of the Mercado Municipal.

Arrival and information

Air The airport (Aeroporto de Eduardo Gomes; ☎92/3652-1210 or 1212) is on Av Santos Dumont, 17km north of town. It is served by bus #306 (first bus 5.30am, last bus 11.30pm; 40min); alternatively, take a taxi (around R$50). Many tour operators will offer airport pickup if you're booked with them; and Antonio Gomes (☎92/9961-8314) also offers airport pickup (R$40 for four passengers).

Boat Boats dock right in the heart of the city, either by the Mercado Municipal or a short way along in the floating port. If you're arriving from Peru or Colombia, don't forget to have your passport stamped at the Customs House, if you haven't already done so in Tabatinga.

Bus The *rodoviária* (☎92/3642-5805) is 7km north of the centre; numerous buses pass nearby heading into the centre (including #300, #301, #306, #500, #580 and #640), or taxis cost around R$25.

Tourist Information The tourist office is close to the back of the Opera House at Av Eduardo Ribeira 666 (Mon–Fri 8am–6pm, Sat 8am–1pm); it has helpful, friendly staff who can supply town maps and informative brochures. There is also a tourist office at the airport, which should be open to meet most flights (☎92/3652-1120).

Accommodation

There is plenty of affordable accommodation in Manaus, including three hostels. Make sure you avoid the dodgy *Hotel Dona Joana*.

Amazon Backpacker Hostel Av Joaquim Nabuco 204 ⓣ92/3622-1395, ⓔportokar@vivax.com.br. Set in an old building that could do with some restoration, this converted house has two dorm rooms, one double room and a little terrace with two sunbeds. The dorms (R$17) have a/c. Miserable staff included. ❹

Hostel Manaus Rua Lauro Cavalcante 231 ⓣ92/3233-4545, ⓦwww.hostelmanaus.com. Aussie-owned HI-affiliated hostel with firm comfortable dorm beds with lockers (some with a/c), lovely views of the Palácio Rio Negro from the breakfast table and an eccentric and eclectic

JUNGLE TOUR OPERATORS AND LODGES

There are scores of different **jungle tour companies** in Manaus offering very similar services and the competition is intense. Tourists regularly get hassled by touts all over town, and the sales patter is unrelenting. Your best bet is to shop around, talk to other tourists who have already been on trips and to be wary of parting with wads of cash before you know exactly what you'll be getting in return. Better still is to book through one of the more established outfits, with the security of an office and, ideally, registration with EMBRATUR as an operator.

Amazon Antonio Jungle Tours Rua Lauro Cavalcante 231, in the *Hostel Manaus* (ⓣ92/3233-4545, mobile ⓣ92/9961-8314, ⓦwww.antonio-jungletours.com). Owned and run by smiley Antonio who was born and bred in the forest, Amazon Antonio Jungle Tours offers a variety of trips – stay with local families in floating houses to the south of Manaus, sleep on a boat (cabins or hammocks) along the Rio Negro or stay four hours northeast of the capital in Antonio's beautiful eco-lodge (go to the *mirador* to soak in the surrounding view as you swing in a hammock) followed by a night or more in the jungle. Tour guides are all native and couldn't be friendlier. Day-trips to the meeting of the waters (R$135 per person) are also offered. If you're around in September, October or November make sure you go night fishing with the locals.

Amazonas Indian Turismo Rua dos Andradas 311 (ⓣ92/3633-5578, mobile ⓣ92/9198-3575, ⓔamazonasindia@hotmail.com). Owned and run by a lovely native Indian family who want to share their culture and knowledge of survival techniques in the jungle. Individually customized trips can include overnight stays at indigenous people's homes on the Rio Tarumá or sleeping in the forest. Most explore the Rio Urubú or the Rio Tarumá. R$165 per day, discounts for groups of four or more.

Iguana Turismo Rua 10 de Julho 667, in the *Hotel 10 de Julho* (ⓣ92/3633-6507, mobile ⓣ92/96150480, ⓦwww.amazonbrasil.com.br. Tours include the Meeting of the Waters, visiting the Reserva Mamiraua, the Rio Negro, Lago Mamorí, the protected area of Lago Juma and city tours of Manaus. Iguana also offers customized and survival tours in the jungle. Sleep in hammocks or dorms (both R$150 per day) or in a private room (R$180 per day) at the lodge. Discounts for groups of eight or more.

Amazon Gero Tours Rua 10 de Julho 679, by the *Hotel 10 de Julho* (ⓣ92/3232-4755, mobile ⓣ92/9983-6273, ⓦwww.amazongerotours.com). An independent, reliable and pleasant guide, Geraldo Neto Mesquita speaks some English. A wide range of tours are available, including boat and canoe trips, jungle hiking and visits to native people, with accommodation in hammocks at the lodge (R$150 per day or R$200 for a private room), overnight in the bush or at local family houses. Mainly visits the Mamori and Juma areas.

Amazon Explorers Rua Marquês de Santa Cruz 25, Terminal Hidroviária at the Port ⓣ92/3232-3052, mobile ⓣ92/9112-6333, ⓦwww.amazonexplorers.com.br. Well established company that organizes city tours, very good-value overnight stays in the jungle (R$85 per day) and river trips.

bunch of staff. Laundry service, wireless internet, TV lounge and kitchen. Can also organize tours. HI discounts offered. Dorm R$22. ❹

Hotel Ideal Rua dos Andradas 491 ⓣ92/3622-0038, ⓦwww.geocities.com/hotelidealmanaus. Not so ideal (other than the bargain price), as rooms are dark with no ventilation – most give onto the interior corridor – ask for rooms 101, 201 or 301 which have a balcony and views over the Rio Negro. They also organize tours. ❸

Manaus Hostel Trip Tour Rua Costa Azevedo 63 ⓣ92/3231-2139, ⓦwww.manaushostel.com.br. Pleasant hostel with clean rooms and bathrooms, a little TV area and a kitchen for guests. Dorms R$20 with fan, R$30 with a/c. ❺

Eating

There is plenty of cheap **street food** everywhere, especially around the docks, the Mercado Municipal and in busy downtown locations like the Praça da Matriz, where a plate of rice and beans with a skewer of freshly grilled meat or fish costs about R$5. One traditional dish you should definitely try here is **tacacá** – a soup that consists essentially of yellow manioc root juice in a hot, spicy dried-shrimp sauce. It's often mixed and served in traditional gourd bowls, *cuias*, and is usually sold in the late afternoons by *tacacazeiras*.

Galo Carijó Rua dos Andradas 536. Excellent place for fresh fish at bargain prices given its superb quality. *Jaraqui* R$8, or try the *pirarucu* (R$23 for two people), the largest freshwater scaled fish in the world. Closed Sun.

Gruta do Peixe Rua Saldinha Marinho 609. A fish-lover's paradise in a candle-lit, cave-like den which keeps cool thanks to its location. R$17.90 per kg. Closed Sun.

Terra Amazônica Av Joaquim Nabuco 887. Colombian owned and family run, this no-frills place has a bargain *prato* (R$5) that changes daily and Peruvian and Colombian food that can be cooked upon request. Always crowded at lunchtime. Live music Fri 5–11pm. Closed Sun.

Toca da Costela Rua Barão de São Domingos 268. Only open at lunchtime and always packed, this is a great location, right by the banana market, from which to watch the daily mayhem. R$12.99 per kg.

Drinking and nightlife

There are some good bars in the centre of town, but if you really want to get immersed in Manaus nightlife, the bulk of the action is on Estrada do Turismo, northwest of the city (taxi for four R$35), where bars line the Avenue. Alternatively, try Praça Caranguejo (taxi R$23), also home to many bars and restaurants.

Bar do Armando Rua 10 de Julho 593. Nothing to get excited about during the day but very pleasant and packed at night, with tables outside looking onto the square and the Opera House. Closed Sun.

Cabaret Rua Barroso 293. In a converted mansion with a modern feel, this nightclub plays electronica, and attracts a similar trendy crowd to *Botequim Bar* a few doors down.

Casa do Pensador Rua José Clementes 632. A perfect spot, along with the *African House* next door, to enjoy the warm evenings as you join the locals over a beer at one of the wooden tables outside. Food is also served (R$14.90 for a filling *pensador a cavalo*).

Moving on

Air Numerous domestic and international flights depart from Manaus's Eduardo Gomes Airport.

Bus EUCATUR buses depart Manaus for Boa Vista daily at 6pm, 7pm, 8pm, 10pm & midnight (12hr, R$90, ⓣ92/3648-1493); the first continues to Porto La Cruz in Venezuela (32hr, R$190). All tourists going **to Venezuela** must have a yellow fever vaccination card to buy their tickets – you can get the injection and card at the *rodoviária* or at the main floating harbour for free.

Boats There are regular passenger boat services to **Belém**, **Santarém** and all ports along the Amazon; along the Rio Solimões to **Tabatinga**; and up the Rio Madeira to **Porto Velho**. Less frequent services go up the Rio Negro to **São Gabriel da Cachoeira** and up the Rio Branco to **Caracaraí**.

Directory

Airlines Varig, Rua Marcílio Dias 284 ⓣ92/3083-4501; TAM, at the airport ⓣ92/3652-1300; Gol, at the airport ⓣ92/3652-1634; Rico, Av Eduardo Ribeiro 620 ⓣ92/3633-5166; Tavaj, at the airport ⓣ92/3652-1214; Copa, Av Eduardo Ribeiro ⓣ92/3622-1750; TAF, Av Santos Dumont s/n ⓣ92/3652-1355.

Banks and exchange There are several banks on Av Eduardo Ribeiro, just a block or two down the street from the SEC Tourist Information offices.

Car rental Avis, Rua Major Gabriel 1721 ⓣ92/3234-4440 and at the airport ⓣ92/3652-1579; Interlocadora, Rua Duque de Caxias 750 ⓣ92/3234-5840; Hertz, Av Eduardo Ribeiro 664 ⓣ92/3663-3363; Le Mans, at the airport ⓣ92/3652-1560 or toll free 0800/905100.

Consulates Chile, Rua Marquês de Caravelas, casa 08, Parque das Laranjeiras ⓣ92/3236-6888; UK,

RIVERBOAT PRACTICALITIES

Tickets for the regular services can be bought from the ticket windows inside the port building off Praça da Matriz, next to where the boat departure list is posted. Before buying your ticket, ask for a **pass** (*papel do permissão*), which allows you into the docks (you'll need your passport, too) where the bigger, long-distance riverboats are moored; here you can have a look at the boats before deciding which you want to travel on. It's sensible to buy tickets in advance, for which you can often get a reasonable discount, and always to get on your boat at least two hours before it's due to depart to secure a decent berth. Standard boats from Manaus to Belém can **cost** anything from R$120 to R$170 and take three to five days, often stopping off in Santarém. Smaller boats with no regular schedules, and those serving local settlements up the Rio Negro, are found to the east of the Mercado Municipal. They usually display signs with their destinations marked up. For a fast boat to Tefé, it's best to take the Expreso Barcos service (13hr; $40) from the Hidroviária near the Mercado Municipal.

Rua Poraquê 240 ⓣ92/6132-1819; Ecuador, Rua 06, Conj. Jardim Belo Horizonte Casa 16, Parque 10 ⓣ92/3236-6108; Venezuela, Rua Rio Jutaí 839 Vieiralves ⓣ92/3233-6006.

FUNAI Praça Terreiro Araña. This is where you'll need to get (rarely given) authorization to visit any Indian reserves.

Health matters For tropical complaints the best is the Instituto de Medicina Tropical, Avenida Pedro Teixeira 25 ⓣ92/3238-1711 or 6485. The Drogueria Nossa Senhora de Nazaré, 7 de Setembro 1333, is a well-stocked pharmacy.

Internet LAN House, Av Joaquim Nabuco 648 (daily 8am–10pm; R$1.50p/h), is air-conditioned and has Skype; Guaraçai 359 (daily 6am–6pm; R$2 per hr); Cyber Service, Rua 24 de Mayo 245 (Mon–Fri 8am–7pm, Sat 10am–2pm; R$2 per hr)) has Skype.

Police ⓣ190.

Post office The main one, with a reliable poste restante service (first floor), is just off the Praça da Matriz on Rua Marechal Deodoro at the corner with Rua Teodoreto Souto (Mon–Fri 9am–5pm, Sat 8am–noon).

Shopping *Artesanato* is available from the Museu do Índio (p.276) and several shops around the square in front of the Teatro Amazonas. The best selection (and the most fun way to shop) is at the Sunday morning **street market** that appears out of nowhere in the broad Avenida Eduardo Ribeira, behind the Teatro Amazonas. Indian crafts are also sold at the Mercado Municipal and *artesanato* (including hand-made jewellery) at the stalls on **Praça Terreira Araña**. Interesting *macumba* and *umbanda* items, such as incense, candles, figurines and bongos, can be found at Cabana São Jorge at Rua da Instalação 36 and at Cabana Pomba Gira on Rocha dos Santos 92, corner of Rua Miranda. A good hammock shop is Casa des Redes on Rua dos Andradas.

Taxis Amazonas Rádio Taxi ⓣ0800/280 8228 or 92/3658-5888; Cidade Nova Rádio Táxi ⓣ0800/726 6700 or 92/2125-6700; Tocantins ⓣ92/3656-1330.

Telephones National and international calls can be made with phonecards in public booths around the city; most internet cafés in town have Skype.

THE RIO SOLIMÕES: CROSSING TO PERU AND COLOMBIA

The stretch of river upstream from Manaus, as far as the pivotal frontier with **Peru** and **Colombia** at Tabatinga, is known to Brazilians as the **Rio Solimões**. Once into Peru it again becomes the Rio Amazonas. Although many Brazilian maps show it as the Rio Marañón on the Peru side, Peruvians don't call it this until the river forks into the Marañón and Ucayali headwaters, quite some distance beyond Iquitos.

From Manaus to **Iquitos** in Peru (see p.893), the river remains navigable by large ocean-going boats, though few travel this way any more. Since the collapse of the rubber market and the emergence of air travel, the river is left to smaller, more locally oriented riverboats. Many travellers do come this way, however; and, although some complain about the food and many get upset stomachs (especially on the Peruvian leg), it can be a really pleasant

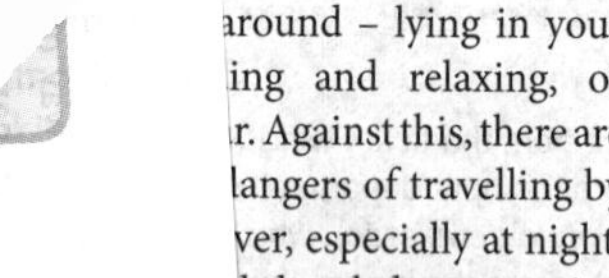

around – lying in your ing and relaxing, or r. Against this, there are langers of travelling by ver, especially at night. ly break down, causing nany captains seem to take great pleasure in overloading their vessels with both cargo and passengers. In spite of the discomforts, however, the river journey remains popular; and it's unarguably an experience that will stick in the memory.

The river journey is also, of course, by far the cheapest way of travelling between Brazil and Peru. There are reasonable facilities for visitors in the border town of **TABATINGA**, though most people prefer to stay in the adjacent Colombian town of **Leticia** (see p.603). All boats have to stop at one of these ports, and most will terminate at the border whichever direction they've come from. If you want to break the journey, you can do so at **TEFÉ**, around halfway; but the main reason to call here is to visit the **Mamiraua Sustainable Development Reserve**, an accessible, beautiful and wild area of rainforest upstream from the town. An alternative reason for stopping here might be if you really can't face the boat journey any longer: there are several flights a week from Tefé to Manaus and Tabatinga. There's also an express boat service (13hr; US$40) connecting Tefé with Manaus.

River practicalities

The boat trip **from Manaus to Tabatinga** – five to eight days upstream – costs around R$160 inclusive of food (though bring some treats, as the fare on board, though good, does get a bit monotonous). The downstream journey, which is often very crowded, takes three to four days and costs upwards of R$115. Five large boats currently ply this section of the river regularly, all pretty similar and with good facilities (toilets with paper, showers, mineral water and enough food). Smaller boats also occasionally do the trip, but more often terminate at Tefé, from where other small boats continue. On the other side of the border, the boat trip **to Iquitos from Tabatinga** costs around US$30–50 and takes three or four days, sometimes more, rarely less. Coming downstream from Iquitos to Tabatinga (US$20–30) gives you one-and-a-half days on the river. Again, it's advisable to take your own food and water – all normal supplies can be bought in Tabatinga. There are also super-fast sixteen-seat powerboats connecting Tabatinga and Leticia with Iquitos. They cost upwards of US$50 and take ten to twelve hours. Small planes also connect Iquitos with Santa Rosa, an insignificant Peruvian border settlement just a short boat ride over the river from Tabatinga and Leticia; there is at least one flight a week operated by the Peruvian airline TANS.

Brasília

In the savanna-like *cerrado* of the Brazilian highlands, almost 1000km northwest of Rio, is **BRASÍLIA,** the largest and most fascinating of the world's "planned cities". Declared the national capital in 1960 and a UNESCO World Heritage Site in 1995, the futuristic city was the vision of **Juscelino Kubitschek**, who realized his election promise to build it if elected president in 1956. Designed by **Oscar Niemeyer**, South America's most able student of Le Corbusier, it is located in its own federal zone – Brasília D.F. (Distrito Federal) – in the centre of Goiás state.

Intended for a population of half a million by 2000, today the city is Brazil's fastest growing, with almost two-and-a-half million inhabitants. At first glance the gleaming government buildings and excellent roads give you the impression this is the modern heart of a new world superpower. Look closer and you'll see cracks in the concrete structures; drive ten minutes in any direction and you'll hit miles of low-income housing for commuters from the *cidades satellites* (poorer satellite cities).

This is a city of diplomats, students, government workers and the people who serve them. Prices can be high. Still there are beautiful sunsets, two or three days' worth of things to see, and exuberant bars and restaurants with good food frequented by students on either side of the city-centre.

What to see and do

Brasília's layout was designed to resemble an airplane (some say a bird, others a bow and arrow). At its centre is a sloped, grassy plain and two central traffic arteries, the **Eixo Monumental** (north/south) and the **Eixo Rodoviário** or **Eixão** (east/west), which neatly divide the centre into sectors: administrative, shopping, banking, commercial, and embassy. These are the treeless (and thus shadeless) though walkable parts of Brasília with much of what there is to see. North and south of the centre are self-contained **residential areas** – each with its own shopping, facilities, restaurants and nightlife.

Esplanada dos Ministérios

The heart of Brasília, and its raison d'être, is the government complex known as the **Esplanada dos Ministérios**, focused on the iconic 28-storey twin towers of the **Congresso Nacional**, the Congress building (the nose of the plane or the bird's "beak"). The buildings here, designed by **Niemeyer**, can all be seen in half a day for free and are regarded as among the world's finest modernist buildings. The white marble, water pools, reflecting glass and flying buttresses on the presidential palace and Supreme Court lend the buildings an elegance made more impressive at night by floodlighting. A taxi or bus ride around the Esplanada in the evening before the commuter traffic, when the buildings glow like Chinese lanterns, is a must.

Praça dos Três Poderes

At the complex's centre is the **Praça dos Três Poderes** (Plaza of the Three Powers), representing the Congress, judiciary and presidency. Two large "bowls" on each side of the Congresso Nacional house the **Senate** Chamber (the smaller, inverted one) and the **House of Representatives**. Guided tours depart every half-hour on weekdays, hourly at weekends. Some guides speak English and there is a strict dress code – trousers, shirt and shoes for men, smart casual for women (Senate tours Mon–Fri 1.30–5.30pm, Sat & Sun 10am–2pm; ⓣ61/311-2149; House of Representatives tours Mon–Fri 1–5pm, Sat & Sun 9am–2pm; ⓣ61/318-5092).

> **BRASÍLIA ONLINE**
>
> ⓦ**www.aboutBrasilia.com** Facts and information along with city satellite maps.
>
> ⓦ**www.Brasiliaconvention.com.br** This site run by the non-profit Brasília e Região Convention & Visitors Bureau, has an event calendar, and English information about hotels, attractions and restaurants.
>
> ⓦ**www.funarte.gov.br** Event schedule.
>
> ⓦ**www.infoBrasilia.com.br** Pictures, history and information in English.
>
> ⓦ**vejabrasil.abril.com.br/Brasilia** Online listings of *Veja magazine's* selection of the best restaurants, bars and nightlife. Portuguese only.

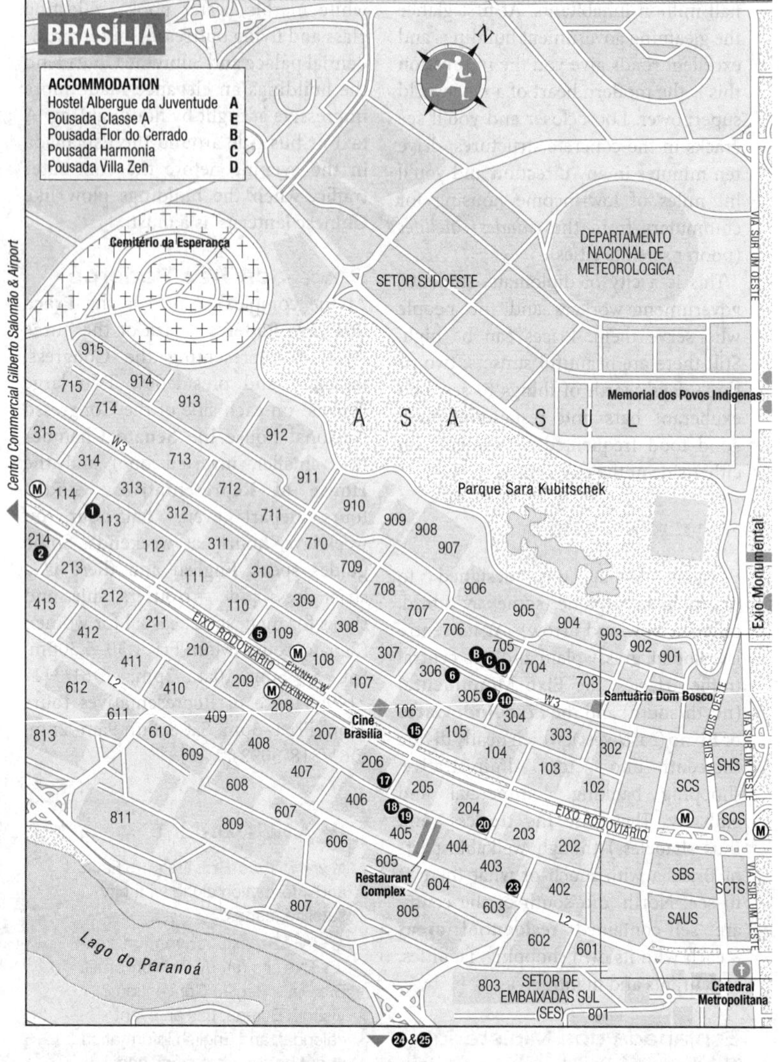

Also worth a quick peek at the edge of the *praça* near the Avenida das Naçoes, is the nearby **Panteão da Pátria Tancredo Neves** (daily, 9am–6pm, free) dedicated to ten Brazilian national heroes featuring murals and painted glass.

Justice and foreign policy

The **Palácio da Justiça** (Mon–Fri 10am–noon & 3–5pm; dress code as above) is beside the Congresso building, on the northern side of the Esplanada dos Ministerios. The building's concrete facade was covered with fancy – and, to many, elitist – marble tiles by the military government during the dictatorship. With the return to democracy the tiles were removed, baring the concrete waterfalls between the pillars, but the water has long been shut off; the

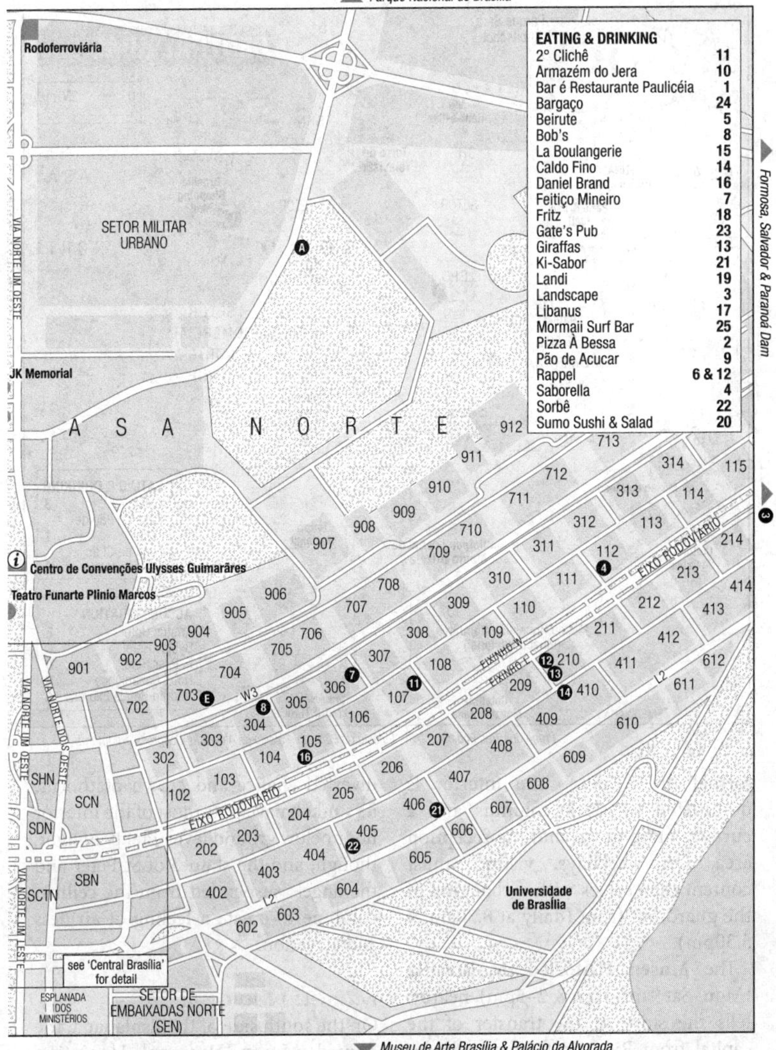

pools were breeding grounds for dengue mosquitoes.

More worthwhile is the **Palácio Itamarati**, the vast Foreign Office structure (Mon–Fri 2–4.30pm, Sat & Sun 10am–3.30pm, no guided tours, restricted visiting areas, dress code as above; ⓣ61/411-6159). Combining modern and classical styles, it's built around elegant courtyards, gardens and sculptures, including Bruno Giorgi's stunning marble *Meteor*. Inside its airiness and space, set off by modern art and wall-hangings, is breathtaking.

The president's office

Behind the Congresso Nacional, on the northern side, the **Palácio do Planalto** houses the president's office (guided tours Sun 9.30am–1.30pm;

formal dress code). The interior is dominated by sleek columns and a curving ramp down into the reception area. On weekdays, visitors must content themselves with a changing of the guard out front (daily at 8.30am & 5.30pm).

The **Museu Histórico de Brasília** (Mon–Sat 9am–1pm & 2–5pm), nearby, tells the story of the transfer of the capital from Rio and features a large-scale model of the city.

The cathedral

Between the ministries and the downtown *rodoviária*, and within walking distance of either, the striking **Catedral Metropolitana Nossa Senhora Aparecida** (daily 7am–6.30pm; no shorts allowed) marks the spot where the city was inaugurated in 1960. Built in the form of an inverted chalice and crown of thorns, its sunken nave puts most of the interior floor below ground level. Plenty of light, though, and the statues of St Peter and the angels suspended from the ceiling, combine to create a feeling of airiness and elevation.

Museu Nacional

On the south side of the Esplanada, the domed **Museu Nacional** Honestino Guimãres Tues–Sun 9am–6.30pm, free), with its suspended curved walkway, looks more like a crashed, white Saturn half-submerged in concrete than a museum but it houses art exhibits and is a welcome shelter from the sun.

Teatro Nacional

Heading up towards the *rodoviária*, on the northern side of the Eixo

Monumental, you'll reach the **Teatro Nacional**. Built in the form of an Aztec temple, it's a largely glass-covered pyramid angled to allow light into the lobby, where there are often art exhibitions. Inside are three halls: Martins Pena, Villa-Lobos (the largest) and the smaller Alberto Nepomuceno. Most productions are in Portuguese, but the venues are also used for **concerts** – Brasília has a symphony orchestra, and pop stars play here.

Torre de Televisão

The landmark TV Tower, the **Torre de Televisão**, would make a good place to start your city exploration. The viewing platform (Tues–Sun 9am–9pm) atop the 218-metre-high tower is great for putting Brasília into perspective, and there's no better spot to watch the sunset. Lower down, above the concrete supports, the **Museu Nacional das Gemas** (Tues–Fri 3–8.30pm, Sat & Sun 10.30am–6.30pm; $1) is actually little more than a glorified and expensive gem shop. On weekends the base of tower is popular for its craft market. The tower is on Eixo Monumental, easily reached on foot or by bus (#131 from the *rodoviária*).

JK Memorial

For the **Juscelino Kubitschek (JK) Memorial** (Tues–Sun 9am–5.45pm; $2), further out on the Eixo Monumental, you'll need to take the bus – dozens head up in this direction. Here, a Soviet-like statue of Brasília's founder stands inside a giant question mark, pointing towards the heart of government. The museum below has some of JK's personal mementoes, reproduces his library and study and features a display of the

CRACKING THE ADDRESS CODES

While initially confusing, Brasília's logical address system does eventually make finding places easier than in cities with named streets. For example: SQN 210, Bloco B – 503, means *superquadra* north no. 210, building B, apartment 503. The superquadra number (210) is the location, the first digit the direction east or west of the Eixo Rodoviário, with odd numbers to the west, even numbers to the east, the numbers increasing as you get further from the centre. The final two digits give the distance north or south of the Eixo Monumental. The logic also applies to roads: even numbers apply east of the Eixão, odd to the west with a letter in front indicating the side of the Eixão it runs, L for east (*leste*), W for West. Some other helpful terms:

Asa Norte/Asa Sul The city's two "wings" (*asas*), north and south.

CLN/CLS or **SCLN/SCLS** *Comércio Local Norte/Sul*. Shopping blocks interspersed throughout the residential *superquadras* of Asa Norte and Asa Sul.

EQN/EQS *Entrequadras Norte/Sul*. The area between quadras at Eixinhos' edge.

SBN/SBS *Setor Bancário Norte/Sul*. Two bank districts, either side of Eixo Monumental.

SCN/SCS *Setor Comercial Norte/Sul*. Two commercial office areas set back from the shopping centres.

SDN/SDS *Setor de Diversões Norte/Sul*. Two shopping centres (*conjuntos*) on either side of Eixo Monumental.

SEN/SES *Setor de Embaixadas Norte/Sul*. The embassy areas east of the bank sectors.

SHIN/SHIS *Setor de Habitações Individuais Norte/Sul*. Two peninsulas jutting into Lago Paranoá.

SQN/SQS or **SHCN/SHCS** *Superquadras Norte/Sul*. Individual *superquadras* in the residential wings, Asa Norte and Asa Sul.

COST-CUTTING TIP

It's easy to burn cash on taxis because Brasília is only really walkable in the centre or for short distances between (deceptively long) *quadras*. Further out in the city's wings, though, you'll be rewarded by better, cheaper food and lodging and friendlier people. After you've seen the centre, pick an area with several restaurants and bars, take a bus there and walk between *quadras*.

construction of the city. JK himself lies in state in a black marble sarcophagus, backlit by purple, violet and orange lights – only a sound system piping in "The Age of Aquarius" is missing.

Memorial dos Povos Indígenas

Across the road from the JK Memorial is another Niemeyer building, the **Memorial dos Povos Indígenas** (Tues–Fri 10am–4pm; free), which houses one of the best collections of indigenous art in Brazil, much of it from the surrounding *planalto* and made by the indigenous groups who inhabit the headwaters of the Xingú River. Highlights are the ceramic pots of the Warao, the Xingú's ceramic specialists, beautifully adorned with figures of birds and animals, and vivid, delicate featherwork. The gallery itself is set in a long, downward curve around a circular courtyard, the smoked glass set against Niemeyer's trademark brilliant white exterior. Run by the chronically hard-up state government, the museum's opening hours are largely theoretical. If you arrive and find the main entrance at the top of the ramp shut, go to the right of the ramp at ground level and bang hard on the large metal door. It's worth it.

Palácio da Alvorada

To complete your Niemeyer tour take a short taxi or bus ride to the president's official residence, the **Palácio da Alvorada**, about 3km away by the banks of Lake Paranoá (bus #104 from stand 13 of Platform A at the *rodoviária*). Some consider this building, with its brilliant white exterior nestled behind an emerald green lawn and carefully sculpted gardens, to be Niemeyer's most beautiful – note the distinctive slender buttresses and blue-tinted glass. If you go by taxi, make sure it waits for you.

Don Bosco and New Age Brasília

Brasília attracts cults and New Agers of all sorts. One of the prime reasons for this is that in 1883 the Italian priest **Don Bosco**, founder of the Salesians and later canonised, foresaw the appearance of a "great civilization," here between "Parallels 15° and 20° South." Even if the doors of perception thing isn't for you, you should check out the **Don Bosco Sanctuary**, W-3 South, Bloco 702 (Mon–Sat 7am–7pm). Built to honour the saint, it's worth visiting for the atmosphere created by brilliant blue floor-to-ceiling stained glass.

Arrival and information

Air Aeroporto Internacional de Brasília – Presidente Juscelino Kubitschek is about 12km south of the city. Bus #102 runs from the airport to the

CRIME AND SAFETY

You'll feel pretty safe walking the streets by day, but at night the central area, with its strikingly lit Niemeyer buildings, is mostly deserted, so take care. Walking between *quadras* at night is fine but stay alert when crossing large, open, semi-lit grassy tracts between *quadras*. Remember, there are few if any traffic lights outside the centre and crossing main roads, north to south requires either entering the dodgy tunnels underneath or playing human "Frogger." Lastly, take care in the *rodioviária* and when using public transport at rush hour.

ESCAPING THE CITY

If you sicken of all the concrete, the **Sarah Kubitschek National Park**, sprawling southwest of the TV Tower, has ponds and walking trails for a quick and easy escape from the hustle. There are more parks and gardens on the outskirts of the city, and some wilder natural attractions a little further out will probably require renting a car. Entrance to most places is free, but occasional R$3 fees are charged.

Botanical Garden Setor de Manões Dom Bosco, Module 12 (entrance by QI-23 of South Lake) ⓣ61/366-3007. About two square kilometres of gardens with more than one hundred species of native herbs, a 9km taxi-ride southwest of the city centre. Tues–Sun 8.30am–5.30pm, free.

Brasília Nacional Park EPIA Highway, North Exit ⓣ61/465-2016. Trails and two swimming pools with running mineral water, about 6km northwest of the city centre. Take bus #128 from the *rodoviária*. Daily 8am–4pm, free.

Chapada Imperial ⓣ61/9984-4437, ⓦwww.chapadaimperial.com.br. Locals rave about spending weekends camping at this park, which has walking trails and more than thirty natural waterfalls. It's about 50km from the city so renting a car is your best bet.

Jardim Zoológico de Brasília Avenida das Naceos, South Exit, Via L4 Sul ⓣ61/245-5003, ⓦwww.zoo.df.gov.br. The zoo has more than 250 species of birds, reptiles and mammals. Tues–Sun 9am–5pm, R$2. To get here, take one of the buses running along Avenida das Nações.

Olhos d'Água Park Asa Norte, entrance by Bloco 414 ⓣ61/340-3777. Trails and playgrounds at this park within the residential wing. Daily 6am–7pm, free. Take one of the buses running along Eixo Rodovíaria Norte to Blobo 213 and walk one block to the park.

Pontão Lago Sul The beautiful people come to this lakeside area to eat, drink and be seen. They've got the right idea. Walk along the lake and check out the JK Bridge, a series of arcs. There's no bus so you'll have to take a taxi but a line of waiting cabs are there for your return.

downtown *rodoviária*, hourly (R$3.50). A taxi from the airport to the hotel sector costs about R$42. Going *to* the airport it is cheaper to call Rádio Táxi Brasília (24hr) ⓣ61/3323-3030, which gives a 30 percent discount.

Bus Long-distance buses arrive at the *rodoferroviária* (where there's no longer a train station), at the tail of the Eixo Monumental. From here bus #131 runs down the Eixo to the city-centre *rodoviária*.

Tourist Office At the time of writing there were few helpful, conveniently located tourist information booths; new offices are planned but locations have not been set. At the airport the firstfloor office is far more helpful than that on the ground floor, and should have free maps. Brasíliatur (ⓣ61/3322-6611, ⓦwww.Brasiliatur.com.br), the official tourism board, has a second-floor office north of the TV Tower in the Centro de Convenções Ulysses Guimarães. They are friendly, helpful and have free maps. At magazine stands you can pick up *Veja's* annual issue on Brasília (R$9.90), highlighting the best restaurants, bars and nightlife (in Portuguese); some have the rarer *Brasília Tourist Guide*, (R$6) an amateur information booklet that manages to be fairly informative.

City transport

Buses City buses are based at the downtown *rodoviária*. Useful services include the #131, up Eixo Monumental past the TV Tower and JK Memorial to the *rodoferroviária*, and #108 and #104 which run frequently past the Museo Nacional, Cathedral, Ministries, Praça dos Tres Poderes, Congresso Nacional, Palacio do Planalto, and the Supremo Tribunal Federal. Tickets cost R$3.50 on the bus.

Car Lúcio Costa didn't seem to design the city's layout with stoplights in mind; the incredible rush hour traffic and getting the hang of roundabouts and tunnels may make renting a car more trouble than it's worth. If you do drive, take care, there are speed cameras everywhere.

Subway Unless you're planning on going to one of the satellite cities (Guará I, Águas Claras,

CLAIMING THE RIGHT OF WAY

Brasília has many cars, few traffic lights, and an endless number of roundabouts. At most road crossings you'll see a yellow sign on the asphalt near the curb depicting an outstretched hand with the words, "*Dê sinal de vida*," a prompt to claim right of way. If you see approaching cars a fair distance away do as the locals do and raise your hand with authority. As long as you don't do it at the last second drivers are well trained to cede the road to you. Trying this elsewhere in Brazil may be your last act.

Samambaia, Taguatinga or Ceilándia) the subway (R$2) is only useful for getting to the end of Asa Sul. Starting from the *rodoviária* there are currently four city stops: Central, Galeria, 108 Sul and 114 Sul; 102 Sul, 104 Sul, and 106 Sul are under construction.

Taxis Taxis are metered, fares start at R$3.30, and they can be flagged down on major thoroughfares, or found at monuments and at taxi stands on the corners of most residential *quadras*. Expect to pay R$15–20 for quick trips and R$30 wing to wing.

Accommodation

The centrally located hostels you'll find everywhere else in Brazil must be making up for the lack of them in the capital. Hotels in the hotel sectors are with few exceptions aimed at diplomats and expense accounts, though many do offer huge discounts at weekends. In general, the taller the hotel, the more expensive, so go for the squat, ugly ones. Given that none of the interesting restaurants or nightlife are nearby you're better off heading for the reasonably priced, perfectly acceptable *pousadas* south of the *rodoviária*.

Hotels

Aristus Hotel SHN Quadra 2, Bloco O ⓣ61/3328-8675, ⓦwww.aristushotel.com.br. Small, clean rooms with awkwardly mounted TVs, 1970s design and paintings of boats in the hallways. ❼

Byblos Hotel SHN Quadra 03, Lote 3 ⓣ61/3326-1570, ⓔbybloshote@terra.com.br. The shelves are a little dusty but the sheets are clean. Ask for the ground-floor room with the enclosed balcony. ❻

Hotel Casablanca SHN Quadra 03, Bloco A, Asa Norte ⓣ61/3328-8586, ⓦwww.casablancaBrasilia.com.br. Their rooms are perfectly acceptable even if the selection of room art is a little weird – sad Charlie Chaplin and waterfalls? ❼

Naoum Hoteis Express SHS Quadra 03, Bloco J ⓣ61/3212-4545, ⓦwww.naoumhotels.com.br. A very good deal, proving that low-rise is the way to go: friendly staff, luxurious rooms, breakfast included. ❽

El Pilar Hotel Setor Hoteleiro Norte 03, Lote F ⓣ61/3328-5915, ⓦwww.elpilar.com.br. These stiff beds in overpriced stucco rooms with fans are sadly one of the better deals in the sector. ❺

Hostels, pousadas and pensões

Hostel Albergue da Juventude SRPN Quadra 2, Lt. 2, Camping de Brasília ⓣ61/3343-0531, ⓔhibsb@opendf.com.br. This HI-hostel is a pain to get to and is even farther from the nightlife than the hotel sector but it's of decent quality. You'll need bus #143. ❺

Pousada Classe A SCLRN 703, Bloco H, Entrada 56 ⓣ61/3327-3339, ⓦwww.hvpousadas.com.br. The cleanest, most decent *pousada* in *asa norte*, just off the W3. Yellow-curtained rooms are crisp if bare. ❺

Pousada Flor do Cerrado Av W3 Sul, Quadra 705, Bloco M, Casa 67 ⓣ61/3242-6990. The red-and-white tiled front won't titillate your inner designer but rooms are clean, it's very secure and in high demand. ❹

Pousada Harmonia W3 Sul, Quadra 705, Bloco A, Casa 3 ⓣ61/3443-6527. This corner *pousada* has good vibes and its own attached barbershop as well as a gated parking spot: rooms have cots, fans and candelabras. ❹

Pousada Villa Zen Av W3 Sul, Quadra 705, Bloco G, Casa 51 ⓣ61/3443-2548, ⓦwww.pousadavillazen.com.br. Feels the most like a hostel of any of the *pousadas*. With wireless, internet and breakfast included. ❹

Eating

A combination of the government, the university and diplomats supports one of the densest concentrations of good restaurants in Brazil, though they tend to get pricey. People hang out in bars until 10pm before heading out to eat. There are pockets of restaurants everywhere in the *quadras* but *asa sul* is particularly popular, peppered with places ranging from Mexican and Chinese to Italian or Fondue; good areas are around 206/205, 204/203 and 405/404. Most places here close on Monday night, not Sunday.

Restaurants and cafés

Armazém do Jera SCLS 304 Bloco D Loja 02 ⓣ61/ 3223-3332. Great people-watching sidewalk patio; you can't beat a beer in the shade of its beautifully manicured, parasol-shaped tree. ❹

Bar é Restaurante Paulicéia CLS 113, Bloco A, Loja 20 ⓣ61/3245-3031. A cheap, local dive excellent for cheap *picanha*, salty snacks and ice-cold beer as smoke from charring meats wafts over the patio. Patrons range from old men with forests of chest hair to students and office workers. ❸

Bob's Sep/Norte Quadra 504, Bloco D Loja 50, Asa Norte, and numerous other locations including the airport. Definitely skip the burgers but do *not* miss the shakes, especially the thick, delicious *ovomaltine*; it's special. ❷

Daniel Brand 104 Norte, Bloco A, Loja 26, Asa Norte ⓣ61/3326-1135. Patisserie/teahouse serving Brasília's best quiche. Great for coffee, cake, late weekend breakfast or afternoon tea as well. ❸

Feitiço Mineiro CLN 306, Bloco B, Lojas 45/51 ⓣ61/3272-3032. Even without the live music at weekends this place would be worth patronizing for the food; a buffet of *comida mineira*, heavy on the pork, bean sauce and sausages, served the traditional way on a wood-fired stove. ❹

Fritz SCLS 404, Bloco D, Loja 35 ⓣ61/3226-8033. The German food is good and cheap, if a little heavy, at this corner restaurant. ❹

TREAT YOURSELF

Bargaço SHIS QL 10, Pontão Sul ⓣ61/364-6091, ⓦwww.restaurantebargaco.com.br. Brasília's best seafood restaurant, complete with palm trees. Try the *camarão na moranga*, shrimp baked in pumpkin with a pumpkin crème fraiche *catupiry* sauce (R$70). ❼

Fogo de Chão Churrascaria SHS Quadra 5, Bloco E ⓣ61/3322-4666. White tablecloth *churrascaria* with seven rotating spits in the front entrance and a terrific salad buffet (don't fill up on it too soon). ❽

Sumo Sushi & Salad SHC/SUL, Comercial Local, Quadra 204, Bloco B, Loja 28, Asa Sul ⓣ61/3323-1115. You'll have to splurge for the buffet in the chic upstairs but if you want all-you-can-eat sushi (including strawberry and chocolate sushi) this is the place. ❺

Giraffas 209 Norte ⓣ61/3273-9676, 210 Sul ⓣ61/3443-6900, and over a dozen other locations. Everyone makes fun of this local institution, but they do so between bites of the cheap rice, beans, meat and salad, especially late at night when everything else is closed. Delivery service too. ❷

Ki-Sabor SHCN 406, Bloco E, Lojas 20/30/34 ⓣ61/3036-8525. Popular student self-service with patio-seating has salads, *feijoada* and grilled meats as well as free thimblefuls of coffee, *caipirinhas*, *doce de leite* and *leite caramelado* (caramel & cinnamon). ❷

Libanus CLS 206, Bloco C, Loja 36 ⓣ61/3597-7575. Perennially crowded spot serving up excellent-value, hearty Lebanese food. A young and humming scene at night. ❹

Pizza À Bessa CLS 214, Bloco C, Loja 40 ⓣ61/3345-5252. This excellent pizza *rodizio* serves 40 different slices including dessert pizza. It's all you can eat for R$18 so you can try each kind if you dare – we only made it to 25.

Cafés, bakeries, self-catering and street food

La Boulangerie 106 Sul, Bloco A, Loja 3 ⓣ61/3244-1394. The bread at this relatively new bakery is quickly garnering local acclaim. ❶

Caldo Fino SQN b/n 409/410, Bloco B. Awesome soup nightly under an open tent that workers put up and take down each night. Try the *abóbora com gorgonzola* (pumpkin and gorgonzola) or the *verde* (potato, leek & sausage). ❶

Casa Do Pão De Queijo Brasília Shopping ⓣ61/3327-2888. Branch of a chain with decent coffee, *salgados* and the addictive namesake cheese puffs, plus a/c and shade. ❷

Feira de Artesanato TV Tower Base. Saturdays and Sundays this area bursts into life, becoming a paradise of cheap food and street food standards from tapioca rolls, sugarcane juice and *pastels* to full buffets. ❷

Landi 405 Sul ⓣ61/9970-1507. Hot dogs are taken to a new level here, with fresh bread and toppings including tomato, corn and *catupiry* (like a liquid cream cheese). ❶

Pão de Açúcar EQS 304/305, s/n ⓣ61/3224-8835. A branch of one of Brazil's major supermarket chains; you'll find several others around the city and they usually have ATMs just inside the entrance.

Rappel CLN 210, Bloco B, Loja 73 ⓣ61/3272-2426 or CLS 306, Bloco B, Loja 10 ⓣ61/3244-2426. Very respectable coffee and a good selection of sweets, *salgados* and *gelado* (ice cream). A nice place to start the day.

Saborella 112 Norte, Bloco C, Lojas 38/48 ⓣ61/3340-4894. Exquisite *gelado*. You'll want to taste several before deciding on just one or two; try the *pistache*.

Sorbê CLN 405, Bloco C, Loja 41 ⓣ61/3447-4158 or CLSW 103, Bloco A, Loja 74, Sudoeste ⓣ61/3967-6727. Artesanal *sorveteria* that has exotic fruit sorbets and unusual, enticing flavours like tapioca, toasted coconut, *canastra* and *queijo*.

Drinking and nightlife

Brasília has plenty of nightlife, but to find it you're going to have to get out of downtown and check out either wing. Remember, the university is in Asa Norte.

20 Clichê CLN 107, Bloco C, Loja 57 ⓣ61/3274-3032. 300 different kinds of *cachaça* line the walls of this *cachaçeria*. Terrific on Sat when drinks are half-price.

Beirute SCLS 109, Bloco A, Lojas 02/04 ⓣ61/3244-1717. You'll have to wait for a table at this long-time favourite open-air café, but it has the best *kibe* in Brasília. If you're feeling adventurous try the infamous, if dangerous, drink called the "Green Devil."

Calaf Edificio Empire Centre, Quadra 2, Bloco S ⓣ61/3325-7408. Electronic, bossa, 70's funk, and contemporary Brazilian and American music. This is *the* place in Brasília on Mon; it's the club the students go to find someone to kiss, and *Veja* named it best place to flirt.

Gate's Pub 403 Sul, Bloco B, Loja 34 ⓣ61/3225-4576. This dank Irish bar has two stages and is bigger inside than it seems at first. On Fri & Sat nights it's *the* venue for live music.

Landscape SHIN CA 07, Bloco F1, Loja 33 ⓣ61/3468-4678. House music (Fri & Sat nights) at this two-storey hilltop dance club in the north lake district. It's a bit of a trek (by taxi) but the small dancefloor and bar are hopping.

Mormaii Surf Bar Pontão Lago Sul ⓣ61/3248-1265. The food is decent if pricey, but the point here is to grab a cocktail on a weekend night and scope the scene.

Entertainment

There are lots of top-quality cultural events at the performance spaces listed below (see ⓦwww.funarte.gov.br) and more than fifteen cinemas show films in their native tongue with Portuguese subtitles.

Culture

Centro Cultural Banco do Brasil Setor de Clubes Sul, Bloco 4 ⓣ61/310-7087.

Espaço Cultural 508 Sul – Renato Russo ⓣ61/3443-1559.

Teatro Funarte Plino Marcos Eixo Monumental Setor de Divulgação Cultural, Lote II ⓣ61/3322-2076.

Teatro Nacional Setor Cultural Norte, S s/n ⓣ61/3325-6239. Free performances once a week but days alternate so call.

Cinemas

Prices vary: Mon half-off, city-wide, R$9; Tue R$15; Wed R$12; Fri–Sun & holidays R$18.

Aeroporto Internacional de Brasília - Presidente Juscelino Kubitschek Films on four screens when your flight is delayed.

Cine Brasília EQS 106/107, Asa Sul ⓣ61/3244-1660, ⓦwww.sc.df.gov.br. Independent cinema.

Cinemark Pier 21, SCES, Trecho 2, Conjunto 32 ⓣ61/3223-7506. Brazilian, international and big budget Hollywood flicks.

Pátio Brasil Setor Comercial Sul, Quadra 7 – Bloco A, 3 P. L. 20N ⓣ61/3225-1595

Shopping

Brazilians love to shop and whether you're looking for joke T-shirts and comics at the "alternative" shopping mall or *capim dourado*, golden grass jewellery, you can find plenty of places to join them.

Brasília Shopping Setor Comercial Norte, Quadra 05 ⓣ61/2109-2122. Centrally located mall with a food court just a short walk from the TV Tower. Mon–Sat 10am–10pm.

Conic Opposite Conjunto, parallel and adjacent to the *rodoviária*. This 'alternative' shopping mall should be avoided at night.

Conjunto Nacional Opposite Conic parallel and adjacent to the *rodoviária*. Not as flashy as Brasília Shopping but more pleasant and upmarket than Conic.

Feira de Artesanato The market at the base of the TV Tower has stalls selling clothes and crafts, from hammocks to meticulously pin-pricked dried leaves and *copim dourado*. Stalls and food stands are open every day but are only at full strength at weekends from 8am – 6pm.

Pier 21 Setor de Clubes Esportivo Sul, Tr.02, Conjunto 32 ⓣ61/3223-2100. You'll need to take a taxi to this lakeside mall with cinemas and several upscale restaurants. Daily 11am–11pm.

Directory

Airlines Air Canada, SCN, Quadra 2, Bloco D, s/n, s 1019 ⓣ61/3328-9203; Air France, SHS Quadra 1, Bloco A, s/n Loja 39 ⓣ61/3223-4152; Alitalia,

SHS, Galeria Hotel Nacional, Loja 36/37 ☎61/321-5266; American Airlines, SCS Quadra 4, Bloco A, s/n s 401 ☎61/3321-3322; British Airways, SHS, Galeria Hotel Nacional, Loja 18 ☎61/226-4164; GOL, SHIS, Quadra 7, s/n, Bloco E ☎61/3364-9272 and at the airport; Lan Chile, SCS, Quadra 8, Bloco B-60, Ed. Venâcio ☎61/3226-0318; Lufthansa, SHS Quadra 1, Bloco A, s/n, Loja 1 ☎61/3223-8202; TAM, SHS, Quadra 1, Bloco A, Loja 21/49, Sh/SU ☎61/3701-3800 and at the airport; Varig, Camara dos Deputados-Anexo 4, Praça Tres Poderes ☎61/3216-9934 and at the airport ☎61/3364-9121.

Banks and exchange You'll find plenty of ATMs in malls and supermarkets but prepare for some trial and error as many machines don't take foreign cards. There is a centrally located Citibank branch across from the Brasilia Shopping Mall. Confidence Cambio, Aeroporto Juscelino Kubitschek, Departures, Ground Floor, and at Pátio Brasil Shopping, 1st Floor, Loja 202, Asa Sul.

Car rentals Airport branches include: Avis (☎61/3365-2782); Hertz (☎61/3365-4425); Interlocadora (☎61/3365-3656); Locadora (☎61/3327-4792); and Unidas (☎61/3365-2955).

Embassies and consulates Australia, SES Quadra 801, Conjunto K, Lote 7 ☎61/3226-3111; Canada, SES, Av das Nações, Quadra 803, Lote 16 ☎61/3424-5400; Ireland, SHIS QL 12, Conjunto 05, Casa 09, Lago Sul ☎61/3248-8800; Netherlands, SES, Quadra 801, Lote 05 ☎61/3961-3200; South Africa, Av das Nações, Lote 6 ☎61/3312-9500; Suriname, Quadra 9, Conjunto 8, Lote 24 ☎61/2483-3595; UK, Setor de Embaixadas Sul, Quadra 801, Conjunto K ☎61/3329-2300; US, Av das Nações Quadra 801, Lote 03 ☎61/3312-7000.

Hospitals Ambulance service is to the nearest hospital, of which there are several. Hospital de Base do Distrito Federal, SMHS 101, Bloco A ☎61/3325-5050 (Emergency 24hr).

Internet Most shopping malls have internet cafés. Good ones include: Neon Lights Cyber Café, Pátio Brasil Shopping 2nd floor (☎61/322-8060; R$8 per hr); Mediacyber Internet, Brasília Shopping, 1st Subsolo Gl, Lojas 34/43, Asa Norte (R$8 per hr); Cyber Office, Aeroporto Juscelino Kubitschek, 2nd floor (R$13 per hr).

Laundries You're unlikely to find self-service laundries (even students have cheap maids) but there are *lavanderias* in most residential *quadras*, which will wash your clothes for around R$5 per item. Try the ubiquitous 5 à Sec, CLS 309 BL D, s/n Loja 35 ☎61/3242-2190.

Left Luggage The airport has lockers and baggage storage open 24hr (R$7 per day).

Pharmacies They're easy to find – try Drogaria Santa Maria in the centrally located *rodoviária*.

Post office Two main post offices: SHS 2 Bloco B, Asa Sul ☎61/3325-1782 (Mon–Fri 9am–5pm); SDN CNB Bloco A, 2nd Loja 2010 ☎61/3328-6383 (Mon–Fri 9.30am–10pm, Sat 9am–9pm). There's also one at the airport and in most shopping malls, try Pátio Brasil, SCS Quadra 7, Bloco A, Loja 2P, 3rd floor, Asa Sul.

Moving on

Air TAM, Gol and Varig all serve Brasília, with direct flights to most state capitals and frequent flights to São Paulo and Rio.

Bus Several long-distance bus companies have coaches that leave Brasília's *rodoferroviária* for major destinations across the country. It's a long journey to almost anywhere. All the following have at least one bus daily: Belém, 36hr; Recife, 48hr; Rio, 20hr; Salvador, 26hr; São Paulo, 16hr.

The Pantanal

An open, seasonally-inundated wetland larger than France, extending deep into the states of Mato Grosso and Mato Grosso do Sul, **THE PANTANAL** is one of the best places in Brazil for watching wildlife. The word Pantanal is derived from the Brazilian word *pantano* (meaning marsh) reflecting its general appearance, but originally it was the site of a giant, prehistoric, inland sea. Today, with an area of 195,000 square kilometres it represents the world's largest wetland and is one of the most ecologically important habitats in Brazil.

Travelling alone in the Pantanal is difficult and the easiest way to experience it is by taking an economical **organized tour** or, if your budget stretches far enough, spending a night or two at a *fazenda*-**lodge** (called **pousadas** in the north). The *fazenda*-lodges are generally reached by jeep; those deeper in the interior require access by boat or plane. At least one night in the interior is essential if you want to see animals;

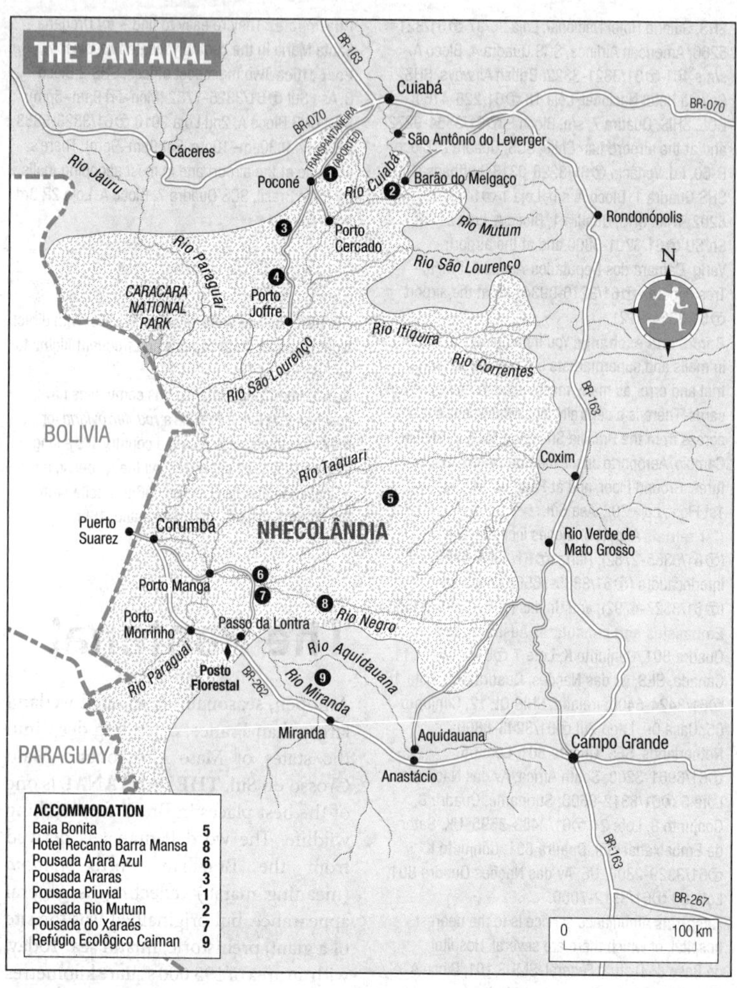

three- or four-day excursions will greatly increase your chances of seeing the more elusive species. The cheapest, but least comfortable way of visiting the Pantanal is to catch a ride on a local cargo boat (take a hammock and mosquito repellent). These inevitably take longer than expected and obviously there is no guide to tell you what you are seeing. Most tours enter the Pantanal by road and spend a couple of days exploring in canoes, small motorboats or on horseback from a land base.

There are three main entry points to the Pantanal, one in the north, one in the west and one in the east. Arriving from Bolivia, the most obvious initial target is **Corumbá**. There's lots of accommodation here and no end of agencies and operators running trips into the wetland. Other routes into the wetland are from **Campo Grande** in the east or **Cuiabá**, to the north, through settlements like **Porto Jofre** and **Cáceres**. The **best time** to explore the Pantanal is towards the end of the rainy season, around April, when your chances of spotting wildlife are high. Renting a car is not recommended unless you hire a local guide who knows the area well to accompany you – you will need a 4WD.

CORUMBÁ

CORUMBÁ was founded as a military outpost in 1778 and rose to prominence due to its strategic location on the Paraguay river. Located in the western Pantanal, today it dedicates itself to the more peaceful pursuits of ranching, mining and eco-tourism. Of the three main Pantanal towns, **Corumbá** is best placed for getting right into the Pantanal by bus or jeep, and has a welter of guides and agencies to choose from, as well as boats for hire. Oddly enough the town is more accessible from Bolivia than from Brazil. The town is not safe at night, so you do need to take care and avoid walking the streets after 10pm.

Arrival and information

By bus Corumbá is a border town with the Bolivian town of Puerto Quijarro on the other side of the frontier. Bolivian customs formalities take place at the office a short distance from the frontier. An hourly bus (3R) runs from the border to the *rodoviária* (ⓣ67/3231-2033), five blocks north of the centre at Rua Porto Carrera. There are regular buses to Campo Grande (5–7hr) some continuing on to Sao Paulo (21hr) and Rio de Janeiro (26hr).

Customs The Brazilian customs point is also here so do not forget to get your entry stamp. Note that the office is open for only a few hours each day, so if you intend to leave Brazil get your exit stamp the day before you cross.

Tourist information There is a tourist information office (ⓣ67/3231-7336; ⓦwww.corumba.com.br) at Rua Manuel Cavassa 275 on the waterfront.

Accommodation

Hotels in Corumbá vary considerably but their sheer quantity means you should have no problem finding a room. Out of season, especially January

TOUR OPERATORS

Organized tours inevitably include at least some water-based transport and a guide who can tell you what you see. Numerous tour companies are based out of the main access towns Corumbá, Campo Grande and Cuiabá.

Corumbá

Aguas do Pantanal Av Afonso Pena 367, Miranda ⓣ067/3242-1242, ⓦwww.aguasdopantanal.com.br. This company owns and runs several *pousadas* around Miranda, Passo do Lontra and Porto Morrinho on the Rio Paraguai.

Campo Grande

Ecological Expeditions Rua Joaquim Nabuco 185 ⓣ067/3042-0508, ⓔecoexpeditionsbr@hotmail.com, ⓦwww.pantanaltrekking.com. Supported by Hostelling International this is the cheapest option for going deep into the Pantanal though the cheaper tours include mainly camping facilities.

Open Door Rua do Barao do Rio Branco.ⓣ67/3321-8303, ⓦwww.opendoortur.com.br. Offers a wide range of activities and packages and e-mail responses are rapid.

Pantanal Express Av Afonso Pena 2081 ⓣ067/382-5333, ⓦwww.pantanalexpress.com.br. Agents for some of the more upmarket tour operators and *fazenda* experiences.

Cuiabá

Anaconda Av Isaac Póvoas 606 ⓣ065/3028-5990, ⓦwww.anacondapantanal.com.br. Short but well-organized and comfortable tours in the Pantanal and elsewhere in the Brazilian wilderness.

Modus Vivendí Av Isaac Póvoas ⓣ65/6324-0091, ⓦwww.modusvivenditour.com.br. The leading Cuiabá tour operator and most popular with Brazilians. Uses a/c eco-friendly hotels and local Cuiabán guides.

to Easter, there are heavy discounts and prices can be bargained even lower. The clutch of cheap lodgings around Rua Delamare tend to be popular with backpackers.

Hotel Angola Rua Antônio Maria Coelho 124 ⓣ67/3231-7233. Safe, perfectly reasonable, and cheapest of the bunch around Rua Delamare in low season. ❶

Hotel Beatriz Rua Porto Carrero 896 ⓣ67/3231-7441. Facing the *rodoviária*, very cheap and pretty basic, but useful if you arrive late at night by bus and can't face the 2km hike into town. ❷

Hotel Beira Rio Rua Manoel Cavassa 109 ⓣ67/3231-2554, ⓕ67/3231-3313. One of the more characterful hotels right by the shore, with cheerful management. Its best rooms overlook the river and the Pantanal, and there are boats for guests' use. ❺

Hotel Laura Vicuña Rua Cuiabá 775 ⓣ67/3231-5874, ⓕ67/3231-2663. A peaceful place, very neat and tidy in traditional fashion. All rooms have phone and TV. ❹–❺

Hotel Nelly Rua Delamare 902 ⓣ67/3231-6001, ⓕ67/3231-7396. Long a favourite haunt for budget travellers and kids from Rio and São Paulo, and excellent value, if a little dank. Rooms with TV cost more. ❷

Eating and drinking

There's no shortage of restaurants in Corumbá. There are plenty of cheap snack bars throughout town, especially on Rua Delamare west of the Praça da República, serving good set meals for less than R$5. Being a swamp city, fish is the main local delicacy, with *pacu* and *pintado* among the favoured species. There's a huge choice of inexpensive meat and fish in vast portions from *Galpão*, Rua 13 de Junho 797 at the corner of Rua Antônio Maria Coelho. For pizza freaks, there's *Fiorella Pizza*, on the eastern corner of Praça da República and Rua Delamare. As for **bars**, you'll find these all over town. The more relaxed bars are those down on the riverfront – where you can usually get a game of pool with your drink.

Directory

Airlines TAM (ⓣ67/3231-7099) and Pantanal Linhas Aéreas (ⓣ67/3231-1818).

Banks and exchange There's a host of banks including HSBC, some with ATMs, on Rua Delamare west of Praça da República.

Car rental Localiza is at Rua Frei Mariano 51 (ⓣ67/3231-6379); Unidas, Rua Drei Mariano

PANTANAL WILDLIFE

First-time visitors to the Pantanal will be struck by the sheer quantity of animals that populate the region, allowing for some great photo opportunities. Undoubtedly the most visible inhabitants of the region are the waterbirds, vast flocks of egrets, cormorants and ibises flush in the wake of your boat as you cruise the channels and provide an unforgettable spectacle. The most spectacular of the region's waterbirds is the immense Jabiru, a prehistoric-looking snow-white stork as tall as a man and the symbol of the Pantanal. Another species that will undoubtedly catch your eye is the Spectacled Caiman (*jacare*) a South American alligator with regional populations estimated at over ten million! The mammal you'll see most of is the Capybara, a rodent resembling a huge guinea-pig that feeds in herds on the lush plant life, but you will need a bit more luck to see the rare Marsh Deer or the endangered Giant Armadillo. Listen out for the squeaky calls of the Giant Otter, a species that inhabits the more isolated parts of the Pantanal, but which is often overcome by its own curiosity when approached by a boat-load of tourists. Jaguar and Puma are present in the area but are active mainly at night; you will need a huge dose of luck to see either, and you shouldn't count on seeing Maned Wolf or Bush Dog either. Lowland Tapir, looking something like a cross between a horse and a short-nosed elephant, are sometimes seen bathing in streams. You will likely be serenaded each morning by the far-carrying song of the Black Howler Monkey, often observed lying prone on thick branches, whilst the gallery forests are the preserve of the Black Spider Monkey, considerably more svelte and active as they swing acrobatically through the trees. Birdwatchers will be on the look-out for Hyacinth Macaws, the species with the gargantuan bill used to crack open palm nuts on which they feed almost exclusively. Sadly this large, bright blue parrot is now severely endangered as a result of illegal capture for the pet trade – the species fetches upwards of $10,000 on the black market.

633 (Mon–Sat 8am–6pm; ⓣ67/3231-3124), has reliable cars that can be taken out of Brazil, but must be returned to Corumbá. Both charge R$90 a day upwards.

Consulates Bolivia, Rua Antônio Maria Coelho 852 ⓣ67/3231-5605; Paraguay, Rua Cuiabá ⓣ67/231-4803.

Health Clinica Samec ⓣ67/3231-3308.

Post office The main post office is at Rua Delamare 708, opposite the church on Praça da República.

Moving on

Air TAM (ⓣ67/3231-7099) and Pantanal Linhas Aéreas (ⓣ67/3231-1818) fly regularly from Corumbá to Campo Grande, and from there to other destinations.

Bus Daily buses depart from the *rodoviária* (ⓣ67/3231-2033) on Rua Porto Carrero to Campo Grande (5–7hr) some continuing on to Sao Paulo (21hr) and Rio de Janeiro (26hr).

CAMPO GRANDE

Capital of Mato Grosso do Sul, **CAMPO GRANDE** is the most popular gateway into the Pantanal on account of its excellent transport links with the rest of Brazil, plethora of tour companies and good facilities for visitors. Though it was only founded in 1877 its growth has been rapid, and today it is a large city with some 800,000 inhabitants.

Arrival

By air Campo Grande has an international airport, the Aeroporto Antonio João (ⓣ67/3368-6000) at Av Duque de Caixas.

By bus Buses arrive at the *rodoviária* at Rua Joaquim Nabuco (ⓣ67/3383-1678). There are regular services from most major cities including Foz do Iguassu, Rio de Janeiro and Brasília.

Tourist information There is a tourist information office (ⓣ67/3318-6060) at the airport. The very helpful Morada dos Bais tourist office is at Av Noroeste 5140, on the corner with Av Afonso Pena (Tues–Sat 8am–7pm, Sun 9am–noon; ⓣ67/3324-5830 and 3382-9244).

Accommodation

There are reasonable budget choices around the junction of Rua Barão do Rio Branco and Rua Allan Kardek, one street west of the *rodoviária*.

TREAT YOURSELF

Hotel Metropolitan Av Ernesto Geisel 5100 ⓣ67/3324-4688. A central location and well-kitted out with TV and mini-bar. A good place to relax after a long journey. ❼

Anache Rua Cândido Mariano Rondon 1396 ⓣ67/3383-2841. A no-frills option with shared bathrooms and fans rather than a/c, but clean and safe, and in a good central location, with friendly service. ❸

Campo Grande Hostel Rua Joaquim Nabuco 185 ⓣ67/3321-0505. Conveniently located opposite the bus station, this HI hostel offers economical accommodation if you just intend to spend a night in the city before heading into the Pantanal. Rooms for 1–6 people and if you book in advance they'll even meet you at the bus station or airport. ❸

Rocha Hotel Rua Barão do Rio Branco 343 ⓣ67/3325-6874, ⓔajcampogrande@hotmail.com. Near the bus station and offering a little more comfort than the *Nosso Novo*, with parking facilities in front and adequate rooms that include a/c, TV and breakfast. ❺

Santo Antônio Av Calógeras 1813 ⓣ67/3324-4552. Very central, with a very blue painted exterior, the *Santo Antônio is* excellent value with private baths and a pleasant breakfast room; basic but stylish. ❺

Eating and drinking

Eating out is an important part of the local lifestyle and this is reflected in the diversity of restaurants. There are scores of *lanchonetes*, especially around the *rodoviária* and east along Rua Dom Aquino,

Cantina Romana Rua da Paz 237 ⓣ67/3324-9777. Wonderful Italian food, good atmosphere, fine wines and a/c; very fair prices.

Casa Colonial Av Afonso Pena 3997 ⓣ67/3383-3207 or 3042-3207. Primarily a *churrascaria*, this place serves excellent Brazilian *rodizio*, where you can eat meat until you drop. Expensive, but the décor is refined, quite spacious and pleasant.

Casa do Peixe Rua João Rosa Pires 1030 ⓣ67/3382-7121. Very popular spot for delicious regional dishes, with fish as the main speciality, and often with live music at weekends. Exceptional value and excellent service. Closed Sun evening.

FAZENDA-LODGES

Most of the *fazenda*-lodges are located east and northeast of Corumbá, and also on either side of the Rio Cuiabá in the north. With few exceptions these lodges cost between US$120–200 a night per person; prices always include various activities, including trips by boat or jeep, horse riding, guided walks or fishing expeditions, as well as meals. Prices are generally more reasonable in the northern Pantanal (accessible from Cuiabá) than in the south (Corumbá, Miranda and Aquidauana). The most popular *fazenda*-lodges are those in Nhecolândia, roughly the area between the rios Negro and Taquari east of town. These benefit from a well-established dirt access road, the MS-184/MS-228, which loops off from the main BR-262 highway 300km from Campo Grande near Passo do Lontra (it's well signposted), and crosses through a large section of wetland before rejoining the same road some 10km before Corumbá.

Accessible from Corumbá:

Baia Bonita Rodovia Bonito/Guia Lopes de Laguna Km7 ⓣ67/225-1193, ⓦwwwbaiabonita.com.br. An eco-friendly reserve and research centre with full and half-day activities for you to mix and match..

Pousada Arara Azul Rio Negrinho ⓣ67/389-9910, ⓦwww.pousadaararaazul.com.br. Close to the Rio Negro in Nhecolândia 38km up the MS-184 past Passo do Lontra, this *pousada* offers all the comforts you could want, plus access to some of the more spectacular species of wildlife. Camping allowed, too ($10 a night).

Pousada do Xaraés 130km from Corumbá, transfers by boat or road arranged on your behalf ⓦwww.xaraes.com.br. Situated in one of the most beautiful regions of the Pantanal.

Accessible from Campo Grande:

Recanto Barra Mansa Lodge ⓣ67/3325-6807, ⓦwww.hotelbarramansa.com.br. This is one of the best of the working ranches, in a beautiful setting with room for sixteen guests. The facilities are excellent, and fishermen, birdwatchers and photographers are expertly catered for.

Refúgio Ecolôgico Caiman Rio Aquidauana. The main Reservation Centre is in São Paulo ⓣ11/3706-1808, though you can reserve directly (ⓣ067/3242-1450), ⓦwww.caiman.com.br. This award-winning lodge is located some 240km west of Campo Grande, 36km north of Miranda, and covers over 530 square kilometres. Full board, all activities and bilingual guide services are included in the daily rate.

Accessible from northern Pantanal:

Pousada Araras Eco Lodge Offices at Cuiabá airport and Av Ponce de Arruda 670, Várzea Grande ⓣ065/3682-2800, ⓦwww.araraslodge.com.br. At km132 of the Transpantaneira, this long-established *pousada* is more atmospheric than most of the more modern *pousadas*, with a pool, as well as boats and horses, but it's likely to be full in high season. Free stays are offered to biology students with regional experience who can act as guides.

Pousada Piuvial 100km from Cuiabá, ⓦwww.pantanaltours.com.br. Twelve guest rooms with air conditioning and private bathrooms. Hiking, boat trips and piranha fishing from a pontoon.

Pousada Rio Mutum Baía de Siá Mariana bay near the Rio Mutum. Book through Ladatco Tours ⓦwww.ladatco.com. Transfers, programme and meals included in price. Don't forget to try the piranha soup.

Don Leon Av Afonso Pena 1901 ⓣ67/3384-6520. A popular *churrascaria* and pizzeria, with scores of tables, fast friendly service and the added bonus of live music some evenings.

Fruta Nativa Rua Barão do Rio Branco 1097. This busy lunchtime snack bar serves light and inexpensive meals, including chips and chicken, outside at the yellow tables. Next door there's an unnamed

Porto Jofre

After 145km, having crossed around a hundred wooden bridges in varying stages of dilapidation, the track eventually arrives at **PORTO JOFRE**, literally the end of the road. This is as far as the Transpantaneira route has got – or ever looks like getting, thanks to technical problems and the sound advice of ecological pressure groups. As far as **accommodation in town** goes, the *Hotel Porto Jofre* (Ⓣ065/3637-1593; ❼; closed Nov–Feb; Ⓦwww.portojofre.com.br) has the monopoly and therefore charges through the nose. If you have a hammock or a tent, it's usually all right to sleep outside somewhere, but check with someone in authority first (ask at the port) and don't leave your valuables unattended.

From Porto Jofre, there are irregular cargo **boats** to Corumbá (about twice a month), normally carrying soya or cattle from Cáceres, and the journey takes between two and five days, depending on whether the boats sail through the night. It's also possible to arrange a day or two-day excursion up the Piquiri and Cuiabá rivers from Porto Jofre.

São Paulo

SAO PAOLO – or 'Sampa', as the locals know it – doesn't have Rio's natural setting or international reputation as a party town. In fact it's Brazil's workhorse, home to a staggering half of the country's industrial output. But what Brazil's largest city lacks in beach and leisure culture it more than makes up for in other ways, with a cultural scene that is by far the country's most vibrant, and all the urban buzz and modern grandeur that you would expect from the world's third-largest metropolis. With more than 150 theatres and performance spaces, more than 250 cinemas, and no fewer than ninety museums, São Paulo is Brazil's New York, and there are echoes of that city everywhere: in Avenida Paulista, it has South America's Park Avenue, in the Edifício Martinelli, its Empire State Building. São Paulo too, is a city of immigrants, with a heritage of Italian and Japanese immigration – it has the largest Japanese population outside Japan – which also means it's a much better place to eat than Rio. Sao Paolo's denizens, known as *Paulistanos*, have a bit of a chip on their shoulder about their more illustrious rival, and the city inevitably lives in Rio's shadow to some extent. But somehow São Paulo manages its underdog status well, with the average *Paulistano* friendlier and a lot less snooty than your average *Carioca*. If you're someone who gets a thrill out of buzzing streets, weave-walking at rush-hour, and discovering the hottest bar, club or restaurant, then you'll love Sao Paolo – a city of both pure grit and cosmopolitan savoir-faire.

What to see and do

São Paulo is a vast city but the neighbourhoods it divides into make it significantly easier to get a handle on it. The centre focuses on **Praca da Sé** and **Praca da República** – two big squares separated by the wide stretch of **Vale do Anhangabaú**. The area around the Praca da Sé is the oldest part of town, while immediately to the northwest is the financial district of the **Triângulo**. North of here, **Luz** is the centre's red-light district, though it's now well on the way to a big clean-up; **Bela Vista** and **Liberdade**, to the south, are immigrant neighbourhoods, home to a sizeable chunk of Sao Paolo's Italian and Japanese immigrants respectively. West of here, **Jardins** is an upscale suburb on the far side of the commercial artery of **Avenida Paulista**.

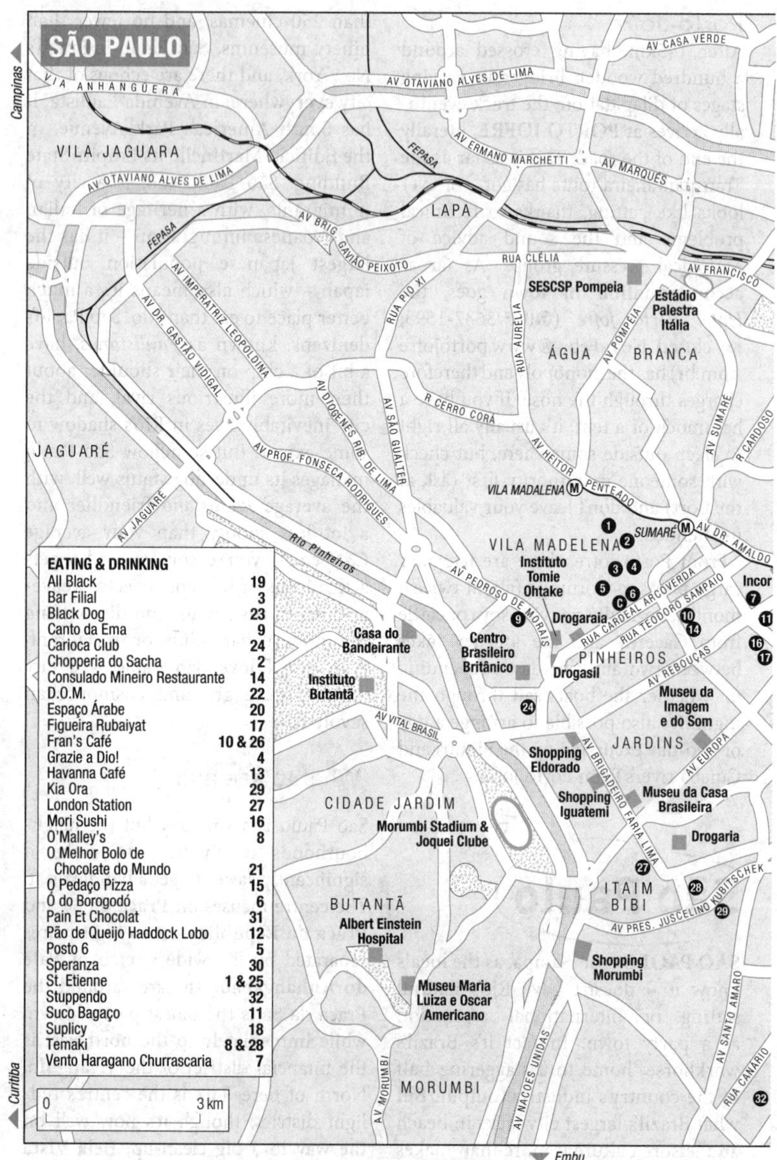

Centro

The heart of the old part of São Paolo is **Praça da Sé,** a busy, palm-tree lined square dominated by the large but unremarkable neo-Gothic **Catedral Metropolitana**, completed in 1954. On the opposite side of the square, along Rua Boa Vista, is the white-washed **Pátio do Colégio**, a replica of the chapel and college founded in 1554 by the Jesuit mission. The **Museu Padre Anchieta on** Largo Pateo do Colégio 2

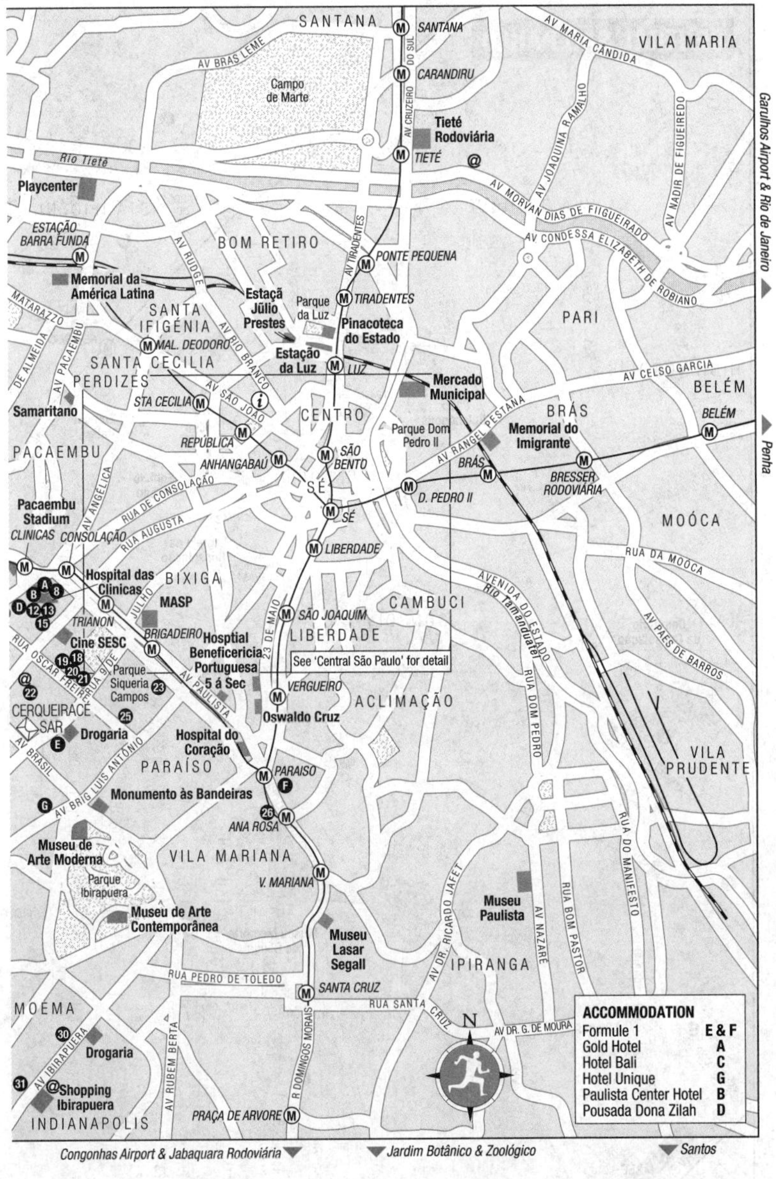

(Tues–Sun 9am–5pm, R$5) has a few boring rooms with early seventeenth-century relics; you'd be better off spending the admission on a coffee at its lovely patio café out the back. Around the corner, an eighteenth-century manor house, the **Solar da Marquesa de Santos**, at Rua Roberto Simonsen 136, houses another museum, São Paolo's **Museu da Cidade** (Tues–Sun 9am–5pm, free), which has a few displays telling the story of the city, while a short

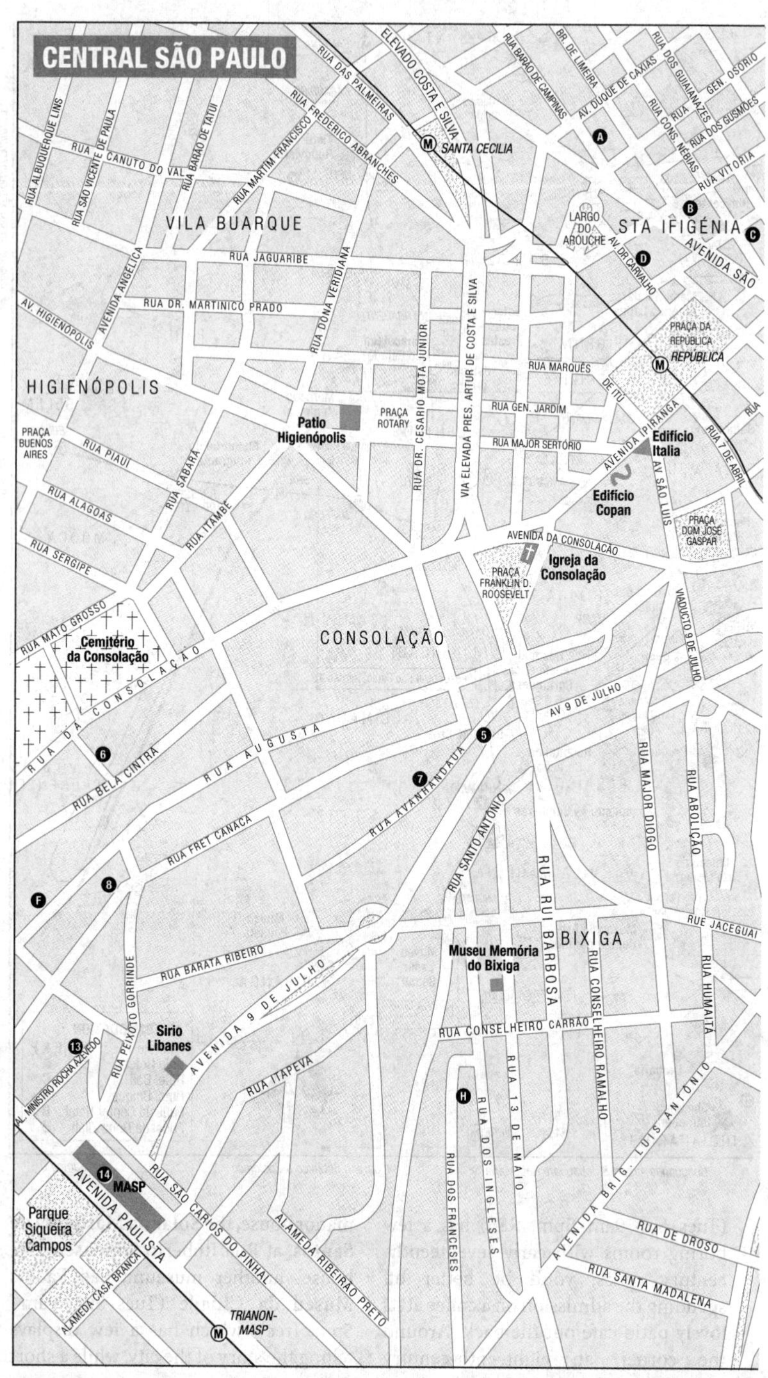
CENTRAL SÃO PAULO
VILA BUARQUE
HIGIENÓPOLIS
CONSOLAÇÃO
STA IFIGÉNIA
BIXIGA
SANTA CECILIA
REPÚBLICA
TRIANON-MASP
LARGO DO AROUCHE
PRAÇA DA REPÚBLICA
PRAÇA ROTARY
PRAÇA BUENOS AIRES
PRAÇA DOM JOSÉ GASPAR
PRAÇA FRANKLIN D. ROOSEVELT
Patio Higienópolis
Edifício Italia
Edifício Copan
Igreja da Consolação
Cemitério da Consolação
Museu Memória do Bixiga
Sirio Libanes
MASP
Parque Siqueira Campos
ELEVADO COSTA E SILVA
VIA ELEVADA PRES. ARTUR DE COSTA E SILVA
RUA DAS PALMEIRAS
RUA FREDERICO ABRANCHES
RUA MARTIM FRANCISCO
RUA BARÃO DE TATUÍ
RUA CANUTO DO VAL
RUA SÃO VICENTE DE PAULA
RUA ALBUQUERQUE LINS
RUA BARÃO DE CAMPINAS
BR. DE LIMEIRA
AV. DUQUE DE CAXIAS
RUA DOS GUAIANAZES
RUA CONS. NÉBIAS
RUA GEN. OSÓRIO
RUA DOS GUSMÕES
RUA VITÓRIA
AV. DR CARVALHO
AVENIDA SÃO
RUA JAGUARIBE
AVENIDA ANGÉLICA
RUA DR. MARTINICO PRADO
AV. HIGIENÓPOLIS
RUA DONA VERIDIANA
RUA DR. CESARIO MOTA JUNIOR
RUA MARQUÊS DE ITU
RUA GEN. JARDIM
RUA MAJOR SERTÓRIO
AVENIDA IPIRANGA
RUA 7 DE ABRIL
AV SÃO LUIS
AVENIDA DA CONSOLAÇÃO
RUA PIAUI
RUA SABARÁ
RUA ALAGOAS
RUA ITAMBÉ
RUA SERGIPE
RUA MATO GROSSO
RUA DA CONSOLAÇÃO
VIADUCTO 9 DE JULHO
AV 9 DE JULHO
RUA AUGUSTA
RUA BELA CINTRA
RUA AVANHANDAUA
RUA SANTO ANTÔNIO
RUA MAJOR DIOGO
RUA ABOLIÇÃO
RUA FREI CANECA
RUA RUI BARBOSA
RUE JACEGUAI
RUA BARATA RIBEIRO
RUA PEIXOTO GORRINDE
AVENIDA 9 DE JULHO
RUA CONSELHEIRO CARRÃO
RUA CONSELHEIRO RAMALHO
RUA HUMAITÁ
AL. MINISTRO ROCHA AZEVEDO
RUA ITAPEVA
RUA 13 DE MAIO
RUA DOS INGLESES
RUA DOS FRANCESES
AVENIDA BRIG. LUIS ANTONIO
RUA DE DROSO
RUA SANTA MADALENA
AVENIDA PAULISTA
RUA SÃO CARLOS DO PINHAL
ALAMEDA RIBEIRÃO PRETO
ALAMEDA CASA BRANCA
A
B
C
D
F
H
5
6
7
8
13
14

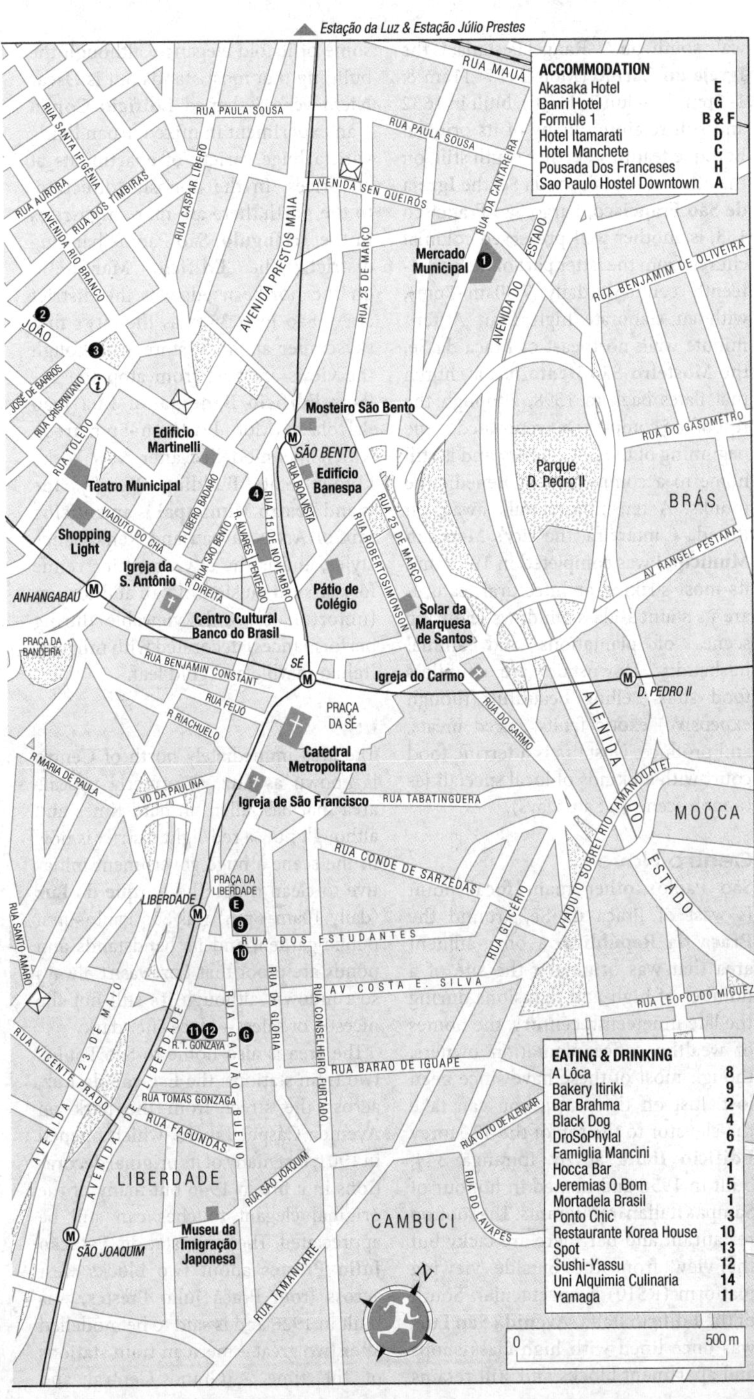
Estação da Luz & Estação Júlio Prestes
ACCOMMODATION
Akasaka Hotel E
Banri Hotel G
Formule 1 B & F
Hotel Itamarati D
Hotel Manchete C
Pousada Dos Franceses H
Sao Paulo Hostel Downtown A
EATING & DRINKING
A Lôca 8
Bakery Itiriki 9
Bar Brahma 2
Black Dog 4
DroSoPhylal 6
Famiglia Mancini 7
Hocca Bar 1
Jeremias O Bom 5
Mortadela Brasil 1
Ponto Chic 3
Restaurante Korea House 10
Spot 13
Sushi-Yassu 12
Uni Alquimia Culinaria 14
Yamaga 11
Mercado Municipal
Mosteiro São Bento
SÃO BENTO
Edifício Martinelli
Edifício Banespa
Teatro Municipal
Shopping Light
Igreja da S. Antônio
ANHANGABAU
Centro Cultural Banco do Brasil
Pátio de Colégio
Solar da Marquesa de Santos
Parque D. Pedro II
BRÁS
Igreja do Carmo
D. PEDRO II
SÉ
PRAÇA DA SÉ
Catedral Metropolitana
Igreja de São Francisco
PRAÇA DA BANDEIRA
MOÓCA
PRAÇA DA LIBERDADE
LIBERDADE
LIBERDADE
CAMBUCI
Museu da Imigração Japonesa
SÃO JOAQUIM
RUA MAUÁ
RUA PAULA SOUSA
RUA SANTA IFIGÊNIA
RUA AURORA
RUA DOS TIMBIRAS
AVENIDA RIO BRANCO
RUA CASPAR LIBERO
AVENIDA PRESTOS MAIA
AVENIDA SEN QUEIRÓS
RUA 25 DE MARÇO
RUA DA CANTAREIRA
AVENIDA DO ESTADO
RUA BENJAMIM DE OLIVEIRA
JOÃO
JOSÉ DE BARROS
RUA CRISPINIANO
RUA TOLEDO
VIADUTO DO CHÁ
R LIBERO BADARÓ
RUA SÃO BENTO
R. ALVARES PENTEADO
RUA 15 DE NOVEMBRO
RUA BOA VISTA
RUA ROBERTOSIMONSON
RUA DO GASOMETRO
AV RANGEL PESTANA
R DIREITA
RUA BENJAMIN CONSTANT
RUA FEIJÓ
R RIACHUELO
RUA DO CARMO
AVENIDA DO ESTADO
R MARIA DE PAULA
VD DA PAULINA
RUA TABATINGUERA
VIADUTO SOBRE RIO TAMANDUATEI
RUA CONDE DE SARZEDAS
RUA GLICERIO
RUA DOS ESTUDANTES
RUA SANTO AMARO
AV COSTA E. SILVA
RUA LEOPOLDO MIGUEZ
RUA DA GLORIA
RUA CONSELHEIRO FURTADO
RUA GALVÃO BUENO
RUA 23 DE MAIO
R. T. GONZAYA
RUA BARAO DE IGUAPE
RUA VICENTE PRADO
RUA TOMÁS GONZAGA
RUA FAGUNDAS
AVENIDA DA LIBERDADE
AVENIDA
RUA OTTO DE ALENCAR
RUA DO LAVAPES
RUA SÃO JOAQUIM
RUA TAMANDARE
N
0
500 m

BRAZIL

SÃO PAULO

walk south, on Av Rangel Pestana, is the **Igreja do Carmo** (Mon–Fri 7–11am & 1–5pm, Sat–Sun 7–11am), built in 1632 and still retaining many of its original Baroque features.Further south still, on the other side of Praca da Sé, the **Igreja de São Francisco**, Largo São Francisco 133, is another well-preserved colonial church from the latter part of the seventeenth century (daily 7.30am–7pm), with an elaborate high altar. A ten-minute walk northeast of Praça da Sé, the **Mosteiro São Bento** has a church that dates back to 1598, although the rest of the complex was renovated at the beginning of the last century and is still home to a community of Benedictine monks. A ten-minute walk away, on Rua da Cantareira, the city's **Mercado Municipal** was completed in 1933, and its most striking architectural features are its stained-glass windows featuring scenes of plantations and animal husbandry. Downstairs are countless food stalls selling beautiful (though expensive) exotic fruits, cured meats, and produce. Upstairs is a terrific food court with all kinds of local specialities (a mob scene on Saturdays).

Centro Novo

São Paolo's other main focal point is west of Praça da Sé, around the **Praça da República**, a once-affluent area that was originally the site of a number of high-end mansions during the late nineteenth century, the homes of wealthy coffee plantation owners, though most of these have since been lost. Just off the *praça*, you can take the elevator to the top of the 42-storey **Edifício Italia** at Av Ipiranga 344, built in 1956 and named in honour of Sampa's Italian immigrants. The rooftop restaurant and bar there are tacky but the view from the outside viewing platform (R$10) is spectacular. South of the Edificio Italia, **Avenida São Luis** was once lined with high-class shops and apartment blocks and still retains some of its old elegance, although the building that most stands out is Oscar Niemeyer's S-shaped **Edifício Copan** – an experiment in mixed urban living with a huge variety of apartments at all prices. In the opposite direction, to the north,there are more high-rises in the **Triângulo**, São Paolo's banking district. The **Edifício Martinelli**, on the northern edge of the district at Av São Joao 35, was the city's first skyscraper at thirty storeys, although the views are best from atop the 36-floor **Edifício Banespa**, at Rua João Bricola 24 (Mon–Fri 10am–5pm; free), which was modelled after New York's Empire State Building. Nearby, the grand **Teatro Municipal** is an enticing mix of Art Nouveau and Renaissance styles, and is the city's premier venue for classical music, with an auditorium (unfortunately only viewable during performances) decorated with mirrors, Italian marble and gold leaf.

Luz

The area immediately north of Centro is known as **Luz**, a formerly upscale area that has fallen on hard times and although now a red-light district is now in the scene a huge government initiative to clean it up. The **Parque da Luz** (daily 10am–6pm) was São Paulo's first public garden, and its bandstands and ponds are proof that Luz wasn't always so rundown, although it's still not the nicest – or safest – place after dark.

The area is also home to São Paulo's two train stations: the **Estação da Luz**, across the street from the park on Avenida Cásper Líbero, which opened in 1901, lost many of its original decorations in a fire in 1946 but many of the original elegant touches can still be appreciated. The other station, **Estação Júlio Prestes** about two blocks west across from Praça Júlio Prestes, was built in 1926 and is said to be modelled after two great American train stations of the time – Grand Central and

Pennsylvania Stations in New York. Sadly it's only used for suburban train services these days, but the Great Hall was transformed in the 1990s into **Sala São Paulo**, a 1500-seat concert hall in which the Orquestra Sinfônica do Estado de São Paulo now performs. Nearby, on Avenida Tiradentes, adjacent to the park, is the **Pinacoteca do Estado**, Av Tiradentes 141 (Tues–Sun 10am–6pm), which houses nineteenth-and twentieth-century Brazilian art, including works by Di Cavalcanti, Larsar Segall, Cândido Portinari and Almeida Junior.

Liberdade and Bixiga (Bela Vista)

South of Centro, **Liberdade** is the home of São Paulo's large Japanese community, with streets lined on either side with overhanging red lampposts. You'll find good traditional Japanese food here on the streets off **Praça da Liberdade** (site of a good Sunday market), as well as lots of Chinese, Korean and Vietnamese eateries and stores. There is even a **Museu da Imigração Japonesa** at Rua São Joaquim 381 (Wed–Sun 1.30–5.30pm, R$5), which documents the contributions Japanese immigrants have made in Brazil in the hudred years since they first started arriving to work on the coffee plantations. The neighbourhood immediately west of here, the Italian enclave of Bixiga or **Bela Vista**, is also a good place to eat, with great restaurants, bars, clubs and hotels, especially on Rua 13 de Maio and the streets branching off it, and really comes to life at night. By day, the **Museu Memória do Bixiga** at Rua dos Ingleses 118 (Wed–Sun 2–5pm, R$5) gives the lowdown on the Italian community here in a traditional early twentieth-century house.

Avenida Paulista

Still further southwest, **Avenida Paulista** is central São Paulo's third major focal point, a three-kilometre stretch that in the early 1900s was lined with Art Nouveau mansions owned by coffee barons. The avenue was redeveloped in the 1960s, and is now lined with skyscrapers, many topped by TV antenna towers dramatically lit by different colours at night, but the **Casas das Rosas**, at Av Paulista 35, gives some sense of what the avenue once looked like, a French-style mansion set in a walled garden that's a huge contrast to the steel and glass buildings around. It's now a state-run museum that hosts small art exhibits. The other building that stands out is the **Museu de Arte de São Paulo** or **MASP** at Av Paulista 1578 (Tues, Wed, Fri–Sun 11am–6pm, closed Mon; R$15, Thurs 11am–8pm, free), which stands on four red stilts floating above the ground, allowing you a view of the city behind it. The galleries upstairs contain one of Latin America's largest collection of Western art while the basement below has a very enjoyable and reasonable buffet.

Jardins

Separated from Bela Vista by Avenida Paulista is **Jardins**, one of São Paulo's most expensive and fashionable neighbourhoods, modelled in 1915 according to the principles of the British Garden City movement, with cool, leafy streets leading down the hill away from the hectic pace of Av Paulista. Actually a compendium of three smaller neighbourhoods, Jardim America, Jardim Europa and Jardim Paulista, it's home to swanky villas and condos, and is a great place for an afternoon stroll, with a number of São Paulo's best food and drink options, and some pretty expensive shopping on **Rua Oscar** and **Rua Augusta**.

Vila Madalena, Pinheiros, Itaim Bibi

West of Jardins, the *bairro* of **Vila Madalena** is also chock-a-block with nightlife and restaurants, though with a younger, trendier feel than nearby Jardins. South of Vila Madalena, **Pinheiros** and further south, **Itaim Bibi** are chic neighbourhoods with galleries, bars and more good restaurants. **Avenida Brig. Faria Lima** is the main drag here, home to the **Museu Brasileiro da Escultura**, Av Europa 218 (Tues–Sun 10am–7pm), temporary home to travelling exhibits of Brazilian artists and sculptors. Cutting through Pinheiros is Rua Teodoro Sampaio, a street lined with music stores some of which have live, free music performances, usually on weekends. Worth driving over nearby (especially when dramatically-lit at night) is the unusual, 138m tall, cable-stayed **Octavio Frias de Oliveira bridge** which connects Marginal Pinheiros to Jornalista Roberto Marinho Avenue. Separate roadways pass under a giant 'X' going in opposite directions. Opened in May 2008, it's sure to quickly become a postcard image.

Butantã and Morumbi

Further west of Pinheiros near the **Cidade Universitária** Butantã and Morumbi are a bit of a pain to get to but you'll find the **Casa do Bandeirante**, a preserved, whitewashed adobe homestead from the time of the *bandeirantes*. The Instituto Butantan's **Museu Biológico** at Av Vital Brasil 1500 (Wed–Sun 9am–4.30pm) will titillate snake-lovers – it houses rattlesnakes, boas and anacondas among others.

Moema

South of Jardins and sandwiched between Itaim-Bibi and Vila Mariana, **Moema** is a rich district with some really good eateries, although its main feature is the **Parque do Ibirapuera** (daily 5am–midnight), opened in 1954 to celebrate the four-hundredth anniversary of the founding of São Paulo. Outside its main north entrance, the **Monumento às Bandeiras** is a 1953 sculpture by Victor Brecheret that celebrates a *bandeirante* expedition, while inside there are a number of museums. Of these, the best is the **Museu de Arte Contemporânea** (Tues–Fri 10am–6pm, Sat & Sun 10am–4pm), with regularly rotated works by twentieth-century European and Brazilian artists. There's also the **Museu de Arte Moderna** (Tues–Sun & holidays, 10am–6pm, R$5.50; Sunday free), a smaller museum which mostly has temporary exhibits of Brazilian artists, and the **Museu Afro-Brasil** in the northern part of the park at Pavilhão Manoel da Nóbrega, Avenida Pedro Álvares Cabral, Gate 10 (daily 10am–5pm), which has exhibitions related to African Brazilians.

Vila Mariana and Ipiranga

East of the park is the **Museu Lasar Segall**, Rua Berta 111 (Tues–Sat 2–7pm, Sun 2–6pm; free), which houses the work of the Latvian-born, naturalized-Brazilian painter who was originally a member of the German Expressionist movement. Further east, in Ipiranga, is the impressive **Museu do Ipiranga** (aka Museu Paulista) at the intersection of avenidas Dom Pedro and Nazareth, with paintings and furniture that once belonged to the Brazilian royal family (Tues–Sun 9am–5pm, R$4, free 1st & 3rd Sun of each month). The park the museum stands in was the place where Brazilian independence was declared in 1822.

Arrival and information

By air São Paolo has two airports, Congonhas, which is literally *in* the city, and Guarulhos, about 25km from downtown. From Congonhas taxis downtown cost about R$50; from Guarulhos a taxi into the city will cost you about R$100. An airport bus service (Ⓦwww.emtu.sp.gov.br) runs the following routes to and from Guarulhos (R$28): Paulista/Augusta hotel circuit (almost hourly, 6.10am–11.10pm); Praça da República (almost every half-hour all day, reduced service early morning); Itaim Bibi/Faria Lima (almost hourly, 6.10am–11.10pm); Tietê (almost hourly, 24hr); Barra Funda (almost hourly, 5.45am–10.15pm); Congonhas (almost every half-hour).

By bus Inter-city buses arrive at one of four *rodoviárias*, all of which are on the metro. The main terminal is the vast Tiete, north of the centre, were you'll arrive from all major Brazilian cities and on international services. To the south there's Jabaquara, Barra Funda and Bresser, each of which serves lesser places to the south of São Paolo.

Tourist information There's a tourist information office at the Tietê Rodoviária is at both Congonhas and Guarulhos but they're not very helpful and you're probably better off either just buying a *Mapa Turistico* (R$14.99) at the Laselva Bookstore or heading to the central information booth at Av São João 473, Centro, near Praça da República (Mon–Fri 6am–10pm, Sun 8am–8pm), where they're friendly and have excellent pamphlets and many free maps.

City transport

The city is huge but manageable in terms of getting around. Still – and this can't be emphasized enough – wherever you plan to be at 7pm, get there at 5pm or at least be on your way by then: once rush hour hits, above ground or below, the city seizes up.

Buses A dozen private companies make up Sampa's public transportation and navigating the more than 1500 bus routes can be complicated if you don't speak Portuguese. But at R$2.30 per trip it's a cheap way to get around. You can load up a *bilhete único*, wave it near a bus card reader and ride on up to four buses within two hours and pay only one fare (on Sun and holidays, up to 8 buses with a single fare). The card can be used on any bus – local, intercity, regional and the subway. Buses run from 4am–midnight.

Subway São Paolo's subway system consists of three lines: Linha Azul (blue, north-south) from Tucuruvi to Jabaquara, Linha Vermelha (red, east-west) from Barra Funda to Corinthians-Itapuera, and Linha Verde (green, east-west) under Av Paulista from Ana Rosa to Vila Metró. A one-trip ticket costs R$2.40. If you buy a *Cartão Fidelidade,* you get 20 trips for R$44 (saving R$0.30 per trip). Trains run from 5am–midnight. Buses and trains run from the end of most subway lines.

Taxis Taxis are metered and start at R$3.50. You can also call the following cab companies: Coopertaxi ⓣ11/6195-6000, Ligue Táxi ⓣ11/3866-3030, Especial Rádio Taxi ⓣ11/3146-4000.

Tours Turis Metrô run free three-hour city tours (Sat & Sun 9am & 2pm, with some English), which depart from the Anhangabaú and Trianon-MASP stops that rely on the metro for transportation – your only expense; ⓦwww.metro.sp.gov.br. If you want someone else to do the work for you check out City Tour São Paulo (ⓣ11/5182-397) whosea/c bus city tours and historic, shopping, culinary and night walking tours start at R$35; ⓦwww.circuitosaopaulo.com.br.

Accommodation

Finding budget hotels in São Paulo isn't difficult but some of the cheapest places to stay are in the seedier parts of town, so cabbing it back to your hotel or hostel isn't a bad idea after dark.

Hostels, pousadas and pensões

Pousada Dona Zilah Alameda Franca 1621, Jardim Paulista ⓣ11/3062-1444, ⓦwww.zilah.com. The rooms here are on a par with a good hotel, although so are the prices. ❽

Pousada Dos Franceses Rua dos Franceses 100, Bela Vista ⓣ11/3288-1592, ⓦwww.pousadadosfranceses.com.br. Just a few blocks from Av Paulista, this gated *pousada* has fresh, blue rooms, and feels like a proper European youth hostel. Dorm beds start at ❸, double rooms around ❺

São Paulo Hostel Downtown Rua Barão de Campinas 94, Centro ⓣ11/3333-0844, ⓦwww.hostel.com.br. The area is grimy but this HI-hostel is quite safe, with a friendly desk staff and 120 beds in dorms and separate rooms. ❸

TREAT YOURSELF

There are more than 15 Mercure Hotels in São Paulo. They'd normally be outside the price-range of most budget-travellers but Mercure offers a promotion called, "Diária Cultural," that brings a night of relative luxury within reach. If you buy a ticket to a cultural event (cinema, theatre or museum) you can use it to get a room for one night for up to two people during the weekend at a discounted rate of R$129 (plus tax) including breakfast. ⓦwww.mercure.com.br/mercure/pt/promo_diariacultural.asp

Hotels

Akasaka Hotel Praça da Liberdade 149 ⓣ11/3207-1500, ⓦwww.akasakahotel.com.br. The name has changed (formerly *Osaka*) but this Japanese business hotel's location is still great. ❺

Banri Hotel Rua Galvão Bueno 209, Liberdade ⓣ11/3207-8877. There may be cracking plaster in the hallways but this is one hotel where the rooms are better than the public spaces – recently renovated and almost stylish! ❺

Formule 1 Rua Vergueiro 1571 ⓣ5085-5699 ⓦwww.hotelformule1.com. The Jardins branch of this chain, right by the Paraiso metro station, is a good-value but the last word in characterless. There are three other locations around the city. ❺

Gold Hotel Alameda Jaú 2008, Jardins ⓣ11/3085-0805, ⓦwww.hotelgold.com.br. This place on a noisy corner two blocks from Paulista at Jardins' edge has some serious personality, with décor that's Greek diner meets kitsch Taj Majal via Suzy Wong and the funky red rooms with doors with room service openings ❺

Hotel Bali Rua Fradique Coutinho 740, Pinheiros ⓣ11/3812-8270, ⓦwww.hotelbali.com.br. The mirrors behind the beds make you wonder if it's not a "love motel" at first, but it stands up to scrutiny ❹–❺

Hotel Itamarati Av Dr. Vieira de Carvalho 150, Centro Novo ⓣ11/3474-4133, ⓦwww.hotel itamarati.com.br. The area is a little noisy and the formica furniture won't make you feel warm and fuzzy, but it's clean and breakfast is included. ❺–❻

Hotel Manchete Av São João 1124, Centro Novo ⓣ11/3337-1323. It's a bit noisy and lacking in character but there are small balconies and the price is hard to beat. ❸–❹

Paulista Center Hotel Rua da Consolação 2567, Consolação ⓣ11/3062-0733, ⓦwww.paulista centerhotel.com.br. A crisp business hotel with free wi-fi, conveniently located near to Pão da Açúcar. ❻

TREAT YOURSELF

Hotel Unique Av Brigadeiro Luis Antônio 4700, Jardim Paulista ⓣ11/3055-4710, ⓦwww.hotelunique.com.br. This hotel's portal-windows make it look like a watermelon but it sure ain't the pits inside – chic and luxurious from the ground floor lobby all the way up to the rooftop bar. ❾

Eating

São Paolo hosts a wide range of good-value eateries, street food and even decent fast food, but this is the city you'll want to splurge in at least once. Self-caterers should take advantage of street fairs, and the pricier though excellent quality Mercado Municipal (don't neglect the upstairs food court). Even if you're not going to splash out you should have a small plate or a drink at one of Rua Avanhandava's six restaurants, where a palpable buzz spills into the street. Barflies should keep in mind that most bars and pubs also have very high-quality food, particularly in Vila Madalena.

Bakeries, fast-food and street food

Bakery Itiriki Rua dos Estudantes 24, Liberdade ⓣ11/3277-4939. Brazilian and Japanese pastries and savoury snacks, with upstairs seating.

Black Dog Rua Alameda Joaquim Eugênio de Lima 612 ⓣ11/3578-1110; Rua Líbero Badaró 456 ⓣ11/3101-4284 (more than 10 locations, ⓦwww.blackdog.com.br). The pressed hot dogs here, filled with oozing *catupiry* cheese and other strange fillings, are perfect after-drinks food but they taste really good sober too.

Pão de Queijo Haddock Lobo Rua Haddock Lobo 1408, Jardins ⓣ11/3088-3087. There's a reason Jardins' rich set crowd this cramped counter: oven-fresh *pão de queijo* and Brazil's best *coxinha*.

Suco Bagaço Rua Haddock Lobo 1485, Jardins ⓦwww.sucobagaco.com.br. Get your *açaí* (or other frozen fruit) fix or grab a quiche and a salad for just R$7.90.

Coffee, dessert, snacks

Fran's Cafe Praça Benedito Calixto 191 ⓣ11/3083-5351; Rua Cubatão 1111, Vila Mariana, Jardins ⓣ11/5579-3641; ⓦwww.franscorp.com.br. Excellent coffee, and free wi-fi access.

Havanna Café Rua Bela Cintra 1829 ⓣ11/3082-5722. Excellent coffee and free internet and wi-fi at this airy café perfect for lounging around and reading the paper. Try the *empanadas* or foil-wrapped *alfajor* cookies.

O Melhor Bolo de Chocolate do Mundo Rua Oscar Freire 125, Jardins ⓣ11/3061-2172. Its name ('the world's best chocolate cake') gives it away – and after tasting their creations here, modelled on those of a renowned Lisbon bakery, you may well agree.

Stuppendo Rua Canário 1321, Moema ⓣ11/5093-2967. A great place for top-notch ice cream, with flavours galore rivalling Italy's best.

Suplicy Alameda Lorena 1430 ⓣ11/3061-0195. Perhaps the city's best cup of coffee, served in five different locations around the city.

Brazilian

Consulado Mineiro Restaurante Praça Benedito Calixto 74, Jardins ⓣ11/3064-3882. Great Brazilian food from the Minas Gerais region at this crowded and popular choice in the Jardins/Pinheiros area. Not too expensive either.

Figueira Rubaiyat Rua Haddock Lobo 1738 ⓣ11/3063-3888. Built around a massive, golden-lit, 130-year-old majestic fig tree, this place serves the city's best steak, *feijoada* and Brazilian specialities. Not exactly cheap, but good for a splurge.

Hocca Bar Mercado Municipal, Rua da Cantareira 306, Centro. The legendary *bacalhau* pasties here are not the cheapest in town but are well worth the extra money – as is the equally enticing *mortadella* sandwich.

Mortadela Brasil Mercado Municipal, Centro ⓣ11/3311-0024. The staff says they make an average of 1500 of these huge sandwiches each Sat. Try one (R$14) and you'll see why.

Pain et Chocolat Rua Canário 1301, Moema ⓣ11/5094-0550. The cosy backroom is a great breakfast spot but they also do a good all-you-can-eat soup buffet for R$26.

Ponto Chic Largo do Paissandu 27, Centro Novo ⓣ11/3222-6528. Established in 1922, this low-key sandwich shop is home to the scrumptious Bauru sandwich (roast beef, four cheeses with tomato and pickle on a French baguette), as well as lots of other meaty goodies. Three other locations around town.

TREAT YOURSELF

D.O.M. Rua Barão de Capanema 549 ⓣ11/3088-0761, ⓦwww.domrestaurante.com.br. One of Brazil's best restaurants starring celebrated chef Alex Atala. If you are going, there's no other way to do it than by working your way through the tasting menu.

Spot Al. Ministro Rocha Azevedo 72, Bela Vista ⓣ11/3284-7500. Food's not the point, you dress sharp and go to experience the scene and rub shoulders with *novella*-stars.

Uni Alquimia Culinaria MASP, Av Paulista 1578, ⓣ11/3253-2829. This basement buffet is not the typical museum cafeteria. For R$24 you can endlessly sample the more than sixty types of salad hot dishes and desserts.

Vento Haragano Churrascaria Av Rebouças 1001, Jardins, ⓣ11/3083-4265, ⓦwww.ventoharagano.com.br. The place to come if you want to eat meat, with high-quality cuts and an extensive buffet, including sushi, salads and the best hearts of palm you're likely to ever have. Not cheap, but a good place to come if you're hungry.

Italian

Famiglia Mancini Rua Avanhandava 81, Bela Vista ⓣ11/3256-4320. Great lasagne and other pasta dishes, and nice antipasti as a warm-up.

O Pedaço Pizza Rua Augusta 1463, Consolação ⓣ11/3285-2117; Rua Augusta 2931 ⓣ11/3891-2431; Rua J Floriano 313 ⓣ11/3071-2525. Decent pizza by the slice until 5am at this citywide chain.

Speranza Av Sabiá, 786, Moema ⓣ11/5051-1229, ⓦwww.speranza.com.br. This labyrinthine pizza-house with balcony seating has been open since 1958, and makes a decent stab at replicating genuine Neapolitan pizza.

Japanese and Korean

Korea House Rua Galvão Bueno 43, Liberdade ⓣ11/3208-3052. One of São Paolo's few Korean restaurants, with great Korean soups for R$18 and barbecue for R$30 – a nice haven from the busy street downstairs.

Mori Sushi Rua da Consolação, Jardins, 3610 ⓣ11/3898-2977. This chic, very popular, high-end restaurant recently expanded next door so you won't have to wait as long to eat the elegant sushi rolls.

Sushi-Yassu Rua Tomas Gonzaga 98, Liberdade ⓣ11/3209-6622; Rua Manoel da Nóbrega 199/209 ⓣ11/3288-2966, ⓦwww.sushiyassu.com.br. Great sushi, sashimi and other Japanese dishes, in a very traditional environment.

Temaki Rua Iguatemi 265 Itaim, ⓣ11/3168-5202; Rua da Consolação 3113 ⓣ11/3088-3719, Jardins. Fast-food sushi handrolls, R$7 each, from several locations around town.

Yamaga Rua Thoaz Gonzaga 66, Liberdade ⓣ11/3275-1790. Lunch specials bring the price of this good quality sushi-place down to R$15 for a full plate of sashimi.

Middle Eastern

Espaço Árabe Rua Oscar Freire 168, Jardins ⓣ11/3081-1824. This large and welcoming restaurant does great, tasty chargrilled chicken and steak kebabs, hummus and other excellent Middle Eastern fare – a cut above the better-known *Habibs*.

Nightlife and entertainment

São Paolo's nightlife is fantastic, and a good enough reason alone for visiting the city. Vila Madalena (corners of Morato Coelho and Aspicquelta) and Pinheiros are the bohemian/student nightlife hotspots; Bela Vista has good live music, while Jardins is the upscale choice, popular with those long in years or deep in the pockets. Pick up copies of *Em Cartaz* (monthly) and *Guia da Folha* (every Fri) at the tourist office or shell out R$2.50 for *Divirta-Se* (weekly) at a newsstand – ⓦ divirta-se .correioweb.com.br. All three are in Portuguese but they contain music, theatre, dance and film listings which you should be able to follow well enough.

Bars

Bar Brahma Av São João, 677, Centro ⓣ11/3333-3030. Yellow-vested waiters serve good food and beer at the bar where Caetano Veloso is supposed to have written his song, "Sampa." Live music upstairs daily. Try the *carneseca acedboulada*.

Bar Filial Rua Fidalga, 254, Vila Madalena ⓣ11/3813-9226. Order a *caipirinha vermelha* from a bowtie-wearing waiter at this busy chequered-floor bar.

DroSoPhyla! Rua Pedro Taques 80, Consolação ⓣ11/3120-5535. The strange art and bizarre décor contribute to making this funky bar a popular spot, but the good food and drink are what bring people back.

Jeremias O Bom Rua Avanhandava 37, Bela Vista, ⓣ11/3255-4120. This dark bar has a great atmosphere and live piano music.

London Station Rua Tabapuã 1439, Itaim Bibi ⓣ11/3368-8300. Chic bar/lounge with DJs and live music. You may want to wear that collared shirt or little black dress you brought. Cover R$15–25. R$2.50 beers during happy hour.

Posto 6 Rua Aspicquelta. This big corner bar is one of the four mammoth standbys in Vila Madalena. Get some chop with your *picanha* and cook it at your table.

SKYE Av Brigadeiro Luis Antônio 4700, Jardim Paulista ⓣ11/3055-4700. This is the place to *start* your night, on the 'watermelon hotel's' roof (*Hotel Unique*) sipping a cocktail along with the beautiful people and a 360-degree view of the skyline.

St. Etienne Al. Joaquim Eug. de Lima 1417, Jardins ⓣ11/3885-0691; Rua Harmonia 699, Vila Madalena ⓣ11/3819-2578. A busy, unpretentious bar with sidewalk-seating, good sandwiches and a R$15 soup buffet.

Clubs

A Lôca Rua Frei Caneca 916, Consolação ⓣ11/3159-8889, ⓦwww.aloca.com.br. Crazy-busy, this place gets crammed with people (gay & straight) looking to dance to techno, house and electronica. There's a second bar upstairs but it is sometimes reserved for VIPs. Cover varies.

Carioca Club Rua Cardeal Arcoverde 2899, Pinheiros ⓣ11/3813-8598. Great dance hall with live samba and friendly people not averse to showing newcomers the ropes. Cover R$25.

Canto da Ema Av Brig. Faria Lima 364, Pinheiros ⓣ11/3813-4708, ⓦwww.cantodaema.com.br. You can hear the *Forró* outside despite the airlock entrance. Inside, it's all *forró* dancing fun and *cachaça*. Cover women R$7, men R$10.

Grazie a Dio! Rua Girassol 67, Pinheiros ⓣ11/3031-6568, ⓦwww.grazieadio.com.br. Buckets of beer and live music at this popular venue. For food, there's a decent restaurant at the back and good street hot dogs outside. Cover varies.

Ó do Borogodó Rua Horácio Lane 21. This is the real Brazil, a gritty, authentic samba bar where everybody dances with everybody. R$20 cover.

Pubs

All Black Rua Oscar Freire 163, Jardins ⓣ11/3088-7990, ⓦwww.allblack.com.br. São Paulo's best Irish pub if you're dying for a Guinness.

Chopperia do Sacha Rua Harmonia 472, Vila Madalena ⓣ11/3813-5734. There's a great buzz at this stucco-and-brick Brazilian beer hall with football on the big screen and good plates that average R$18.

Kia Ora Rua Dr. Eduardo de Souza Aranha 377, Itaim Bibi ⓣ11/3846-8300, ⓦwww.kiaora.com.br. A little bit of 'down-under' in Brazil, the spacious, wooden bar here has a pool table and regular live music (though covers can be pricey).

O'Malley's Alameda Itú 1529, Jardins ⓣ11/3086-0780, ⓦwww.omalleysbar.net. This cavernous Tudor-style Irish pub has a great happy hour (6–8pm), with a free bread and cold cuts buffet, free wi-fi, and live music with pool and darts to boot.

Directory

Airlines Aerolíneas Argentinas, Al Santos, 2441 ⓣ11/3214-4233; British Airways, Al Santos, 745 ⓣ11/4004-4440; Continental, Av Brg Faria Lima

1795 ☎11/3812-7535; GOL, Rua Prof Heloisa Carneiro 21 ☎11/5034-1127; Lan Chile, Rua da Consolação 247 ☎11/2121-9000; TAM, Av Jurandir 856 ☎11/5587-3243; United, Av Paulista 777 ☎11/3145-4200; Varig, Rua da Consolação 368, Consolação ☎11/4003-7000; Qantas, Al Santos 745, Cerqueira César ☎11/3145-8181.

Banks and exchange There are *cambios* at the airports and sprinkled throughout the city: Banco do Brasil, Rua São Bento 465, Centro. The HSBC, Av Brigadeiro Faria Lima 3064 and Citibank, Av Paulista 1111 are just a few of the international ATMs you'll easily find.

Car rentals Hertz Seven locations in São Paulo (Ⓦwww.hertz.com.br) including Congonhas (☎11/5542-7244) and Guarulhos (☎11/6445-2801); Rua Da Consolação 431 ☎11/3258-9384. Starting at R$54 per day. Localiza Seventeen locations in São Paulo (Ⓦwww.localiza.com) including Congonhas (☎11/3617-3939) and Guarulhos (☎0800-979-2000). Starting at R$85 per day. Movida Rent a Car Six locations (Ⓦwww.movida.com.br) including Guarulhos ☎11/6445-4638; Congonhas ☎11/5094-5900; Rua da Consolação 271, Centro ☎11/3255-6870. Starting at R$84 per day.

Crime and safety Like any big city, São Paulo has issues with crime. For the most part, the most dangerous areas are on the city's outskirts in its *favelas*. Downtown, at night the red-light district around Luz should be avoided and you should be on alert if you're staying around Praça da República – it gets seedy after dark.

Embassies and consulates Australia, Alameda Santos 700, 9th floor, Unit 92 Edifício Trianon Corporate ☎11/2112-6200; Canada, Av das Nações Unidas 12901, CENU Torre Norte, 16th Floor ☎11/5509-4321; Germany, Av Brigadeiro Faria Lima 2092, 12th Floor, Jardim Paulistano ☎11/3097-6644; India, Av Paulista 925, 7th Floor ☎11/3171-0340; Netherlands, Av Brigadeiro Faria Lima 1779, 3rd Floor, Jardins ☎11/3811-3300; South Africa, Av Paulista 1754, 12th Floor ☎11/3285-0433; US, Rua Henri Dunant 700, Chácara Santo Antonio ☎11/5186-7000.

Football Estádio Morumbi Butantã. Home of the São Paulo Futebol Clube. Estádio Pacaembu, Praça Charles Millar, Consolação. Home to Corinthians. Estádio Parque Itália Rua Turiaçu, Barra Funda. Home to Palmeiras.

Hospitals São Paulo is served by several hospitals: Albert Einstein, Av Albert Einstein 627 ☎11/3747-1233; Beneficência Portuguesa, Rua Maestro Cardim 769 ☎11/3253-5022; Hospital das Clínicas, Av Dr. Enéas Carvalho de Aguiar 255 ☎11/3887-6611; Hospital do Coração, Rua Des. Eliseu Guilherme 123 ☎11/3887-6611; Incor, Av Dr. Enéas Carvalho de Aguiar 44 ☎11/3069-5000; Oswaldo Cruz, Rua João Julião 331 ☎11/3549-0000; Samaritano, Rua Conselheiro Brotero 1486 ☎11/3821-5300; Sirio-Libanês, Rua Adma Jafet 91 ☎11/3155-0200.

Internet Cyber Coffee & Book,Travessa Casalbuono, 120, Shopping Center Norte ☎11/6222-2132; Av Reboucas 3970, Shopping Eldorado ☎11/870-2892; Av Ibirapuera 3103, Moema ☎11/5561-0575; Cyberlan, Rua Augusta 2346 ☎11/3511-2580.

Laundries Sprinkled throughout São Paulo: Lavesec Lavanderia Praça Julio Mequita 13, Sta. Efigênia ☎11/3223-3883 & Av Castro Alves 437, Aclimação ☎11/3277-8014 (small washer/dryer R$11, large R$22) as well as the ubiquitous 5 à Sec, Rua José Maria Lisboa, 1079 ☎11/3083-4624; Brigadeiro Luis Antonio 2013, Loja 4 ☎11/3287-2166, Ⓦwww.5asec.com.br.

Left luggage Guarulhos and Congonhas have small and large lockers open 24hr per day in the Arrivals area operated by Malex do Brasil, R$19/28 per day.

Pharmacies Drogaraia, Rua Pamplona 1274, Jardins; Rua Teodoro Sampaio 2324, Pinheiros; Rua João Cachoeira 732, Itaim; Av Moema 370, Moema; Drogasil, Av Brigadeiro Faria Lima 767, Jardins; Av Prof. Alfonso Bovero 1185, Pompéia.

Post offices Praça Correio at the corner of Av São João (Mon–Fri 8am–10pm); Av Brigadeiro Luis Antonio 996, Bela Vista ☎11/3112-0046 (Mon–Fri, 9am–5pm); Rua Florencio de Abreu 591, Centro ☎11/3227-9529 (Mon–Fri 9am–5pm); Rua Estados Unidos 1434, Jardim America ☎11/3083-1575. For a complete list visit: Ⓦwww.correios.com.br.

Moving on

Air Regional and domestic flights leave for throughout the country from Congonhas. Most international flights leave from Guaralhos.

Bus Buses leave from Rodoviária Tietê to points throughout Brazil and to neighbouring countries.

The South

The southern states of Brazil – Paraná, Santa Catarina and Rio Grande do Sul – are generally considered to be the most developed in the country and show little of the obvious poverty found elsewhere. The smallest of Brazil's regions, the South maintains an

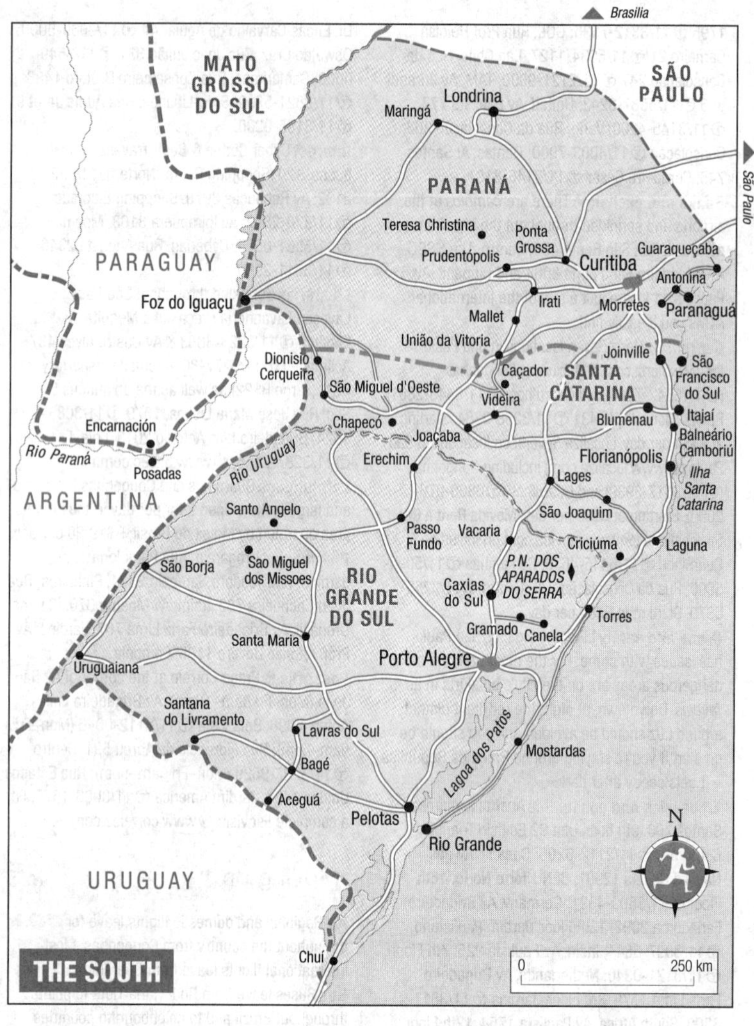

THE SOUTH

economic influence completely out of proportion to its size, largely the result of an agrarian structure that is based on highly efficient small and medium-sized units and an economically over-active population that produces a per capita output considerably higher than the national average.

There's a lot in the South to appeal to the tourist. The **coast** has a sub tropical climate that in the summer (Nov–March) offers welcome respite from the oppressive heat of the Brazilian cities. Much of the Paranaense coast is still unspoilt by the ravages of mass tourism, and development is virtually forbidden on the beautiful islands of the **Bay of Paranaguá** – the most frequently visited being the gorgeous **Ilha do Mel**. By way of contrast, tourists have encroached along Santa Catarina's coast, but development has been restrained, and resorts such as most of those on the **Ilha de Santa Catarina** around **Florianópolis** remain small and in tune with the region's natural beauty.

Despite the attractions of the coast, the spectacular Iguaçu Falls are deservedly the South's most visited attraction, the powerful waters set against a background of unspoiled rainforest. The rest of the interior is less frequently visited. Much of it is mountainous, the home of people whose way of life seems to have altered little since the arrival of the first Europeans. The highland areas and the grasslands of southern Rio Grande do Sul are largely given over to vast cattle ranches, where latter-day *Gaúchos* keep alive many of the skills of their forebears, whilst to the north the remnants of the Jesuit missions pay homage to their brief but productive occupation of the area.

PARANÁ

PARANÁ is the northernmost of Brazil's southern states and one of the wealthiest in the country. Unless you're heading straight for **Foz do Iguaçu** and the **Iguaçu** waterfalls, **Curitiba** is the best base. Transport services fan out in all directions from the state capital, where there's plenty to keep you occupied between excursions. The **Bay of Paranaguá** can be visited as a day-trip from Curitiba, but the bay's islands, such as the **Ilha do Mel**, could easily take up a week or more of your time.

CURITIBA

Founded in 1693 as a gold-mining camp, **CURITIBA** was of little importance until 1853 when it was made capital of Paraná. Since then, the city's population has risen steadily from a few thousand to 1.5 million; its inhabitants are largely descendants of Polish, German, Italian and other immigrants. On average, *curitibanos* enjoy Brazil's highest standard of living and the city boasts facilities that are the envy of other parts of the country. Its eco-friendly design, abundant with green spaces, is a model that many urban planners would like to emulate.

What to see and do

Most of Curitiba's main attractions can be visited relatively in a day or so on foot. However, if you have limited time, take the Linha Turismo **bus tour** which departs from Praça Tiradentes (Tues–Sun every 30min 9am–5.30pm; R$16). Stopping at 25 attractions around the city centre and suburbs, it takes 2 hours 30 minutes to complete the full circuit. Tickets allow passengers five hop-on hop-off stops.

Rua das Flores

The **Rua das Flores** – a pedestrianized precinct section of the Rua XV de Novembro, lined with graceful, pastel-coloured early twentieth-century buildings – is the centre's main late afternoon and early evening meeting point. Few of the surrounding streets are especially attractive, but the former city hall, at **Praça José Borges** across from the flower market, is well worth a look.

Praça Tiradentes and the historic quarter

A couple of blocks north from Rua das Flores is **Praça Tiradentes**, the site where the city was founded and home to the Neo-Gothic **Catedral Metropolitana**. From here a pedestrian tunnel leads to Curitiba's **historic quarter**, an area of impeccably preserved eighteenth- and nineteenth-century buildings of Portuguese and central European design, all with preservation orders. The **Igreja da Ordem**, on Largo da Ordem, dates from 1737 and is the city's oldest surviving building, dominating the historic quarter. Plain outside, the church is also simple within, its only decoration being typically Portuguese blue and white tiling and late Baroque altars. The church contains the **Museu**

de Arte Sacra (Tues–Fri 9am–noon & 1–6pm, Sat & Sun 9am–2pm; free), with relics gathered from Curitiba's churches. Opposite is the mid-eighteenth-century **Casa Romário Martins**, Curitiba's oldest surviving house, now the site of a cultural foundation and exhibition centre for regional artists. A short distance uphill from here, on the same road, the **Igreja Nossa Senhora do Rosário** was built by and for Curitiba's slave population in 1737, though it was completely reconstructed in the 1930s. Further uphill, the **Museu Paranaense** on the neglected Praça João Cândido (Tues–Fri 9am–noon & 2–6pm, Sat & Sun 10am–4pm; R$3) contains work by Paranaense artists who have documented the changing local landscape over time.

On Sundays (9am–2pm) the **Feira de Artesanato** takes over the Largo da Ordem and adjacent Praça Garibaldi, with stalls selling local and regional handicrafts – look out, too, for Polish and Ukrainian items, including simple embroideries and intricately painted eggs.

Modern Curitiba

Some of Curitiba's more unusual and impressive attractions are more modern and easily accessible by foot from the centre. Brazil's largest and most futuristic museum is the **Museo Oscar Niemeyer** (Tues–Sun 10am–6pm; R$4), about three kilometres to the north of Curitiba's old town, on Rua Marechal Hermes. Designed by the architect after whom it was named, its most notable feature resembles a giant eye. This bizarre surrealist building houses modernist exhibits, including many works by Niemeyer himself. While in the area check out the **Bosque João Paulo II**, a memorial garden dedicated to Polish settlers; it was opened by Pope John Paul II in 1980. You could also head out to the **Jardím Botânico** (daily 8am–6pm; R$5) on the eastern edge of town at Rua Ostoja Roguski. Packed with native plants, it centres on the immense **greenhouse**, adopted as one of the symbols of the city. West of the *rodoferroviária* along Avenida Sete de Setembro is the **Shopping Estacão**, the city's former railway station now converted into an atmospheric mall incorporating the small **Museu Ferroviária** which houses relics fom Paraná's railway era as well as temporary exhibits (daily 8am–10pm; free).

Arrival and information

By air The ultramodern airport (T 41/3381-1153) is about 30min from the city centre. Taxis from the airport to the centre charge about R$20; there is also a bus service.

By bus The main bus (T 41/3320-3121) and train (T 041/323-4008) stations – the *rodoferroviária* – are next to one another in the southeast of town, about ten blocks from the city centre.

Tourist information There's a year-round tourist information booth at the *rodoferroviária* (Mon–Sat 8am–6pm; T 41/3352-8000, W www.viaje.curitiba.pr.govbr).

City transport

Curitiba is small enough to be able to **walk** to most places within the city centre. **City buses** stop at the strange glass boarding tubes you see dotted around town. Pay at the turnstile on entering the tube, not on the bus.

Accommodation

There are numerous cheap and secure hotels near the *rodoferroviária*. Places in the city centre are within walking distance of most attractions and are generally excellent value.

Elo Hotel Universidade Rua Amintas de Barros 383 T 41/3028-9400, W www.hoteiselo.com.br. Modern, rather characterless hotel with a pool, next to the university's main administrative building. Rooms are clean and comfortable and the staff are very helpful. 6

Grand Hotel Itamaraty Av Presidente Afonso Camargo 279 T 41/3362-2022, W www.hotelitamaratycwb.com.br. Directly opposite the *rodoferroviária*, this retro hotel offers a range of rooms for every budget – though in reality the difference lies more in the price than the facilities! Rates includes room service and use of a small gym. Also a decent restaurant on site. ❺

Nikko Rua Barão do Rio Branco 546 ⓣ41/2105-1808, ⓦwww.hotelnikko.com.br. Modern hotel set behind a pretty nineteenth-century facade. The small rooms are simply and attractively furnished, with mineral water supplying the bath and shower, and there's a Japanese-style garden, a tiny swimming pool and a sushi bar. ❻

Plaza Rua Luiz Xavier 24 ⓣ41/3888-0900. A good affordable choice, more for its excellent location at the end of the Rua de las Flores than for its minimalist rooms. ❺

Rheno Pedro Ivo 538 ⓣ41/3224-0412. A clean and perfectly acceptable budget option with modern, no-frills rooms and tiled bathrooms. Easily the best of the numerous cheap options on this street – some of the others charge by the hour! ❹

Roma Hostel Rua Barão de Rio Branco 805 ⓣ41/3224-2117, ⓦwww.hostelroma.com.br. A block from the Shopping Estacão, midway between the *rodoferroviária* and the centre, this is a standard HI hostel with dorms and some private rooms and an attractive garden. ❷

Eating and drinking

Curitiba's prosperity and its inhabitants' diverse ethnic origins have given rise to a good range of restaurants, with the most interesting centred in the historic centre. For the cheapest eats check out the food court in Shopping Estacão.

Mein Schatz Rua Jaime Reis 18. Next door to the Igreja do Rosário, offering a variable and affordable menu of German and Brazilian dishes in quasi-Bavarian surroundings. Mains from R$20.

No Kafé Fest Rua Duque de Caxias 4. On an alley next to the Igreja do Rosário, *No Kafé Fest* offers an excellent and reasonably priced *por kilo* lunchtime buffet of hot and cold dishes (R$20). A German-style high tea is served in the afternoon in a very pleasant building shared with an art gallery.

Oriente Arabe Rua Kellers 95, corner of Praça Garibaldi. Excellent, reasonably priced Arabic food, with main meals starting from R$15 and a variety of picking options from R$5. If you want to try a bit of everything go for the lunchtime *rodízio* of hot (R$23.50) and cold (R$19) dishes.

Schwarzwald Rua Claudino dos Santos 63. Excellent German food served with cold beer – a popular evening student meeting point in the Largo da Ordem. Daily 5pm to late.

TREAT YOURSELF

Durski Rua Jaime Reis 254. Curitiba's only Ukrainian restaurant, located in a renovated house in the heart of the historic centre looking onto Largo da Ordem. The food (including Polish and Brazilian dishes) is attractively presented and very tasty, but not for those on a tight budget. Try the Rissoto de Frutos do Mar for R$59. Closed Sun evening.

Directory

Airlines Aerolíneas Argentinas ⓣ41/3232-9012; Gol ⓣ41/3381-1744; TAM ⓣ41/3323-5201.

Banks and exchange Main offices of banks are concentrated at the Praça Osório end of Rua das Flores.

Car rental All have offices at the airport. Avis ⓣ41/3381-1370; Hertz ⓣ41/3269-8000; Localiza ⓣ41/3253-0330; Unidas ⓣ41/3332-1080; Yes ⓣ41/3366-2525.

Consulates Argentina, Rua Benjamin Constant 67, 15th floor ⓣ41/3222-0799; Paraguay, Rua Gen. Osório 400 ⓣ41/3322-9226; UK, Rua Presidente Faria 51, 2nd floor ⓣ41/3232-2912.

Hospitals In emergencies use the Nossa Senhora das Graças hospital at Rua Alcides Munhoz 433 which has a 24hr hotline ⓣ41/3240-6555.

Internet Widely available throughout the city. A convenient internet café near the *rodoviária* is on Av Presidente Afonso Camargo, next to the *Grand Hotel Itamaraty*.

Laundry Auto Serviço Gama at Rua Tibagi 576 near the intersection with Rua Nilo Cairo is a good central option.

Post office The main offices are next door to each other at Rua XV de Novembro 700, by Praça Santos Andrade.

Moving on

By air Curitiba's airport has frequent flights to all major cities in Brazil and international flights to Uruguay and Argentina. Buses to the airport from the centre leave about every hour from outside the *Hotel Presidente* on Rua Westphalen by Praça Rui Barbosa.

By bus Buses run to Foz do Iguaçu (8 daily; 10hr), Paranaguá (hourly; 1hr 30min), São Paulo (hourly; 7hr), Rio de Janeiro (5 daily; 12hr), Florianópolis (8 daily; 5hr) and other major Brazilian cities.

SERRA VERDE EXPRESS

The Serra Verde Express (☎41/3323-4007; www.serraverdeexpress.com.br) is one of the most scenic train rides in Brazil, winding around mountainsides, slipping through tunnels and traversing one of the largest Atlantic Forest reserves in the country. It is undoubtedly the most atmospheric way to travel between Curitiba and Paranaguá (for the Ilha do Mel); make sure to sit on the left-hand side of the train for the best views (or on the right if you're not good with heights!). The complete five-hour run to Paranaguá departs only on Sundays, leaving Curitiba at 8.15am and returning at 2pm; during the rest of the week the service goes only as far as Morretes. A variety of tickets are available, with coach class from R$22 return (one-way is more expensive) through to luxury class at R$190. Cheaper tickets should be booked several days in advance as they are limited and sell out quickly.

By train The only remaining passenger train from Curitiba is the Serra Verde Express (see below), which runs from the *rodoferroviária* to Morretes and Paranaguá.

PARANAGUÁ

Brazil's second most important port for exports, **PARANAGUÁ**, 91km east of Curitiba, has lost much of its former character, though the pastel-coloured buildings along the waterfront retain a certain charm. It was founded in 1585, making it one of Brazil's oldest cities, but only recently have measures been undertaken to preserve its colonial buildings.

What to see and do

The appeal of Paranaguá lies in wandering around the cobbled streets and absorbing the faded colonial atmosphere of the town. Almost everything worth seeing is concentrated along **Rua XV de Novembro** a block inland from the waterfront. At the corner of Avenida Arthur de Abreu is the **Teatro da Ordem**, housed in the very pretty former **Igreja São Francisco das Chagras**, a small and simple church built in 1741 and still containing its Baroque altars. Further along is the **Mercado Municipal do Café**, an early twentieth-century building that used to serve as the city's coffee market. Today the Art Nouveau structure contains handicraft stalls and simple restaurants serving excellent, very cheap seafood. Just beyond the market, Paranaguá's most imposing building, the fortress-like **Colégio dos Jesuítas**, overlooks the Praça do Junho. Construction of the college began in 1698, sixteen years after the Jesuits were invited by Paranaguá's citizens to establish a school for their sons. Because it lacked a royal permit, however, the authorities promptly halted work on the college until 1738, when one was at last granted and building recommenced. In 1755 the college finally opened, only to close four years later with the Jesuits' expulsion from Brazil. Today it is home to the **Museu de Arqueologia e Etnologia** (Tues–Fri 9.30am–noon & 1–6pm, Sat & Sun noon–6pm; R$2). Exhibits concentrate on prehistoric archeology, indigenous culture and popular art, and the poor old Jesuits don't even get a mention. Three blocks inland from here is the town's oldest church, **Igreja Nossa Senhora do Rosário**, dating from 1578 (daily 8am–6pm; free).

Arrival and information

By bus Buses arrive at the *rodoviária* in the southwest of town on the waterfront.

By train The train station is three blocks from the waterfront on Av Arthur de Abreu.

Tourist information There's a useful summer-only information office (☎41/3425-4542) in the Estacão

Nautica on Rua Gral. Carneiro, a departure point for ferries to the bay islands (see opposite).

Accommodation

There is no real reason to hang around in Paranaguá but should you need to, you can choose from a cluster of reasonably priced **hotels** within walking distance of the major transport terminals.

Camboa Rua João Estevão ⓣ41/3423-2121, ⓦwww.hotelcamboa.com.br. A few blocks west of the *rodoviária*, this is the best hotel in town with large, well-equipped rooms and a pool. ❻

Hostel Continente Rua Gral. Carneiro 500 ⓣ41/3423-3224, ⓦwww.hostelcontinente.com.br. Handy HI hostel in front of the Estacão Nautica. Standard dorms and doubles with reductions for HI members. ❺

Serra do Mar Rua XV de Novembro 588 ⓣ41/3422-8907. Don't be put off by the rather dozy service at this hotel, a block behind the Praça do Junho. It represents excellent value for money with modern rooms and spacious bathrooms. ❹

Eating

Cheap seafood and the local speciality, *barreado* (stew baked in clay vessels), are the order of the day at most restaurants There are some excellent inexpensive seafood places in the Mercado Municipal do Café, though they are open at lunchtimes only.

Casa do Barreado Rua Antonio da Cruz 9. The best place to try the local *barreado*; the lunchtime buffet of Brazilian dishes (R$15) is also good.

Lar do Ma Praça do Junho. Next to the Colégio dos Jesuítas, this place offers a reasonably priced Chinese lunch buffet (R$14.50) as well as à la carte seafood in the evenings.

Moving on

Hourly buses run daily to Curitiba and, on Sundays only, the Serra Verde Express departs from the *ferroviária* at 2pm and arrives in Curitiba 5hr later. Ferry services depart from the Estacão Nautica to the bay islands, with seven daily ferries to the Ilha do Mel in summer (2hr; R$20; service reduced in winter).

ILHA DO MEL

Famed for its golden beaches and tranquil setting, the idyllic **ILHA DO MEL** in the Bay of Paranaguá is a hit with backpackers looking to enjoy the simpler things in life. It's an unusually shaped island, to say the least. Its bulbous northern half, an Atlantic forest ecological station, is joined to the slender south by a bridge of land where the lively main town **Nova Brasilia** is located. The island's other major settlement, **Encantadas**, near the southwest corner, has the atmosphere of a sleepy fishing village. It's little more than 12km from north to south, but given the relief of the island most walks hug the coast. Bear in mind that there are no cars, no public transport and no shops on the island and electricity for only a short period each day – so come prepared.

What to see and do

Praia do Farol is the closest beach to Nova Brasilia, curving a wide arc around the northeastern part of the island. It's a four-kilometre walk north along these sands to the Portuguese fort **Fortaleza** which once guarded the bay from invaders. Encantadas' nearest beach is **Praia de Fora**. The entire stretch of coastline along the southeast side between Praia de For a and Praia do Farol is dotted with enchanting coves, rocky promontories and small waterfalls. The rocks are slippy here, so care should be taken, and the three-hour walk along the beach from Praia de Fora as far as Fortaleza should only be attempted at low tide or you risk being stranded. The southern tip of the island, known as **Ponta Encantada**, is where you will find the **Gruta das Encantadas** (Enchanted Cave), focal point for a number of local legends.

Arrival and information

By boat In summer seven daily ferries (2hr; R$20) link Ilha do Mel with Paranaguá. You can also catch the bus from Paranaguá to Ponto do Sul, from where boats leave every 30min from the beach to the island from 8am–7pm (20–40min). There are fewer boats to the island in winter.

Tourist information There is a tourist information booth at the dock in Nova Brasilia (open daily 7.30am–8pm in summer.

Accommodation and eating

If you plan to visit in the height of summer, it's best to arrive during the week and as early as possible in the morning as **accommodation** is scarce. The island is always filled to capacity over New Year and Carnaval when reservations are essential and are accepted only for minimum stays of four or five nights. Typically the food served at the *pousadas* represents the best value if you are looking for somewhere to eat.

A Ilha Verde Hotel Pousada Praia das Encantadas ⓣ41/3426-9036, ⓦwww.ailhaverde.com.br. The only real hotel on the island. Staff will meet you in Encantadas and carry your belongings to the hotel with prior notice. ❼

Caraguatá Pousada Praia das Encantadas ⓣ41/3426-9097, ⓦwww.caraguata-ilhadomel .com.br. Full of character with spacious rooms, some with balconies offering glorious sea views. ❻

Pousadinha Praia do Farol ⓣ41/3426-8026, ⓦwww.pousadinha.com.br. Popular backpacker hangout with leafy gardens and relaxing hammocks for chilling out. Rooms are simple but good-value and multilingual staff can assist with booking activities. Rooms with shared bathroom are half the price of others. ❻

Pousada das Palmas Praia do Farol ⓣ41/3426-9006, ⓦwww.pousadadaspalmas.com.br. Less than 100m from the dock, this wood cabin-style *pousada* is a good bet if you arrive tired, and includes an ample breakfast to get you started in the morning. ❻

FOZ DO IGUAÇU

A standard stop on the backpacker trail, the city of **FOZ DO IGUAÇU** is the Brazilian gateway to the magnificent **Iguaçu Falls**, one of the world's greatest natural wonders, which lie 20km south. Much larger than its Argentinian counterpart **Puerto Iguazu** (see p.102), it makes a better base for exploring the falls, with the advantage of good restaurants and lively nightlife.

What to see and do

Foz do Iguaçu is a modern city, with no real sights of its own, but there are a couple of attractions on the road to the falls that are worth checking out. The **Parque das Aves** (daily 8.30am–6pm; R$18; ⓦwww.parquedasaves.com.br) maintains both small breeding aviaries and enormous walk-through aviaries in dramatic forested surroundings. There's also a large walk-through butterfly cage – butterflies are bred throughout the year and released when mature. All the butterflies and eighty percent of the eight hundred bird species are Brazilian, many endemic to the Atlantic forest. Across the road is the **Parque Acuatico Cataratas** (Tues–Fri 8am–6pm, Sat & Sun 8am–7pm; R$10) which maintains a series of thermally heated pools with the water springing directly from the underground Guaraní aquifer, the largest natural freshwater source in the Americas. It features a series of giant slides, children's pools and, for when your hunger gets the better of you, a decent grill restaurant.

Arrival, information and tours

Air The airport (ⓣ45/3521-4200), 16km outside town on the road to the falls, is served by flights from Curitiba, São Paulo, Rio de Janeiro, Brasília, Salvador and Belém. A taxi into town costs around R$30.

Bus The *rodoviária* (ⓣ45/522-3633) is on the northern outskirts of town; buses #105, #115 and #145 marked "Rodoviária" can take you to the local bus terminal on Av Juscelino Kubitschek in the city centre; taxis cost around R$8.

Tour operators Martin Travel, Rua Jorge Sanways 835 ⓣ45/3523-4959, is a reliable local travel agency that specializes in eco-tourism and puts together groups to go canoeing or mountain biking along forest trails. Macuco Safari ⓦwww .macucosafari.com.br offers a guided forest safari and a boat trip into the Devil's Throat (see p.395) among its varied programmes.

Tourist information There are **tourist offices** at the airport (daily 7am–11pm) and at the *rodoviária* (daily 6.30am–8.30pm), and in the local bus terminal in town (daily 7am–7pm). For information by phone, call the Foz tourist office, Teletur, on ⓣ0800/3521-1455 (7am–11pm).

Accommodation

When choosing **where to stay** your main decision is whether to pick a central option or to go for a place closer to the falls. Central options have the advantage of proximity to good restaurants and bars, while those closer to the falls cut down your travelling time and include a number of excellent hostels. There's a great **campsite** run by the *Camping Club do Brazil* (☎45/529-8064; R$12per person) at km17 on the road to the falls; facilities include a laundry area and a clean swimming pool), and the experience of sleeping surrounded by jungle.

Central

Continental Inn Av Paraná 1089 ☎45/3523-5000, Ⓦwww.continentalinn.com.br. Decent value for a centrally located and high-quality – if somewhat anonymous – hotel. The well-equipped rooms are spacious, breakfasts are ample, the staff are efficient and there's a good pool. 9

Paudimar Centro Rua Antonio Rapeso 820 ☎45/3028-5503. Run by the same people as the *Paudimar* (see below), this gives you the same great service and facilities in a central location, and free internet. 2

Pousada Evelina Navarrete Rua Kalichewski 171 ☎45/3574-3817. Extremely friendly place with a youth hostel atmosphere that mainly attracts foreign backpackers. Rooms are simple but spotless, breakfasts are adequate, there's internet access and multilingual Evelina goes out of her way to be helpful. Well located for buses to the falls. 5

Pousada El Shaddai Rua Engenheiro Rebouças 306 ☎45/3024-4493, Ⓦwww.pousadaelshaddai.com.br. A good, central, hostel-type establishment; rates include a sumptuous Brazilian buffet breakfast. The multilingual staff, pool, internet access and on-site travel agency all help make your stay comfortable. 5

San Remo Rua Xavier da Silva 563 ☎45/3523-1619. Though the spartan rooms could do with an upgrade, this economical hotel is within a couple of blocks of the local bus terminal and the Avenida Brasil. Trips to the falls and surrounding attractions can be arranged if you prefer not to go it alone. 5

Road to the Falls

Paudimar Av das Cataratas km12.5 ☎45/3529-6061, Ⓦwww.paudimarfalls.com.br. The favourite with backpackers, this excellent HI establishment has superb facilities. Cabins (each with a private bathroom) sleep five to eight people and there are family rooms. The extensive grounds include a swimming pool and bar. Kitchen facilities are available, and they also serve evening meals. The hostel organizes daily trips to the Argentine side of the falls. 2 per person

> **TREAT YOURSELF**
>
> **Tropical das Cataratas Eco Resort** Parque Nacional do Iguaçu ☎45/2102-7000 or 0800/701-2670, Ⓦwww.hoteldascataratas.com.br. The only hotel within the Brazilian national park, discreetly located just out of sight from the falls. The rooms are comfortable with colonial-style furnishings. Even if you can't afford to stay here, you should take a wander around the grounds or eat in the restaurant (see p.394). Reservations are usually required; but check the website for special offers. 9

Eating and drinking

Whilst it's no gastronomic paradise, Foz do Iguaçu is a good place to eat cheaply, with a proliferation of buffet-style *por kilo* restaurants.

La Bella Pizza Rua Xavier da Silva. The best of several pizza *rodízios* on this block, where you can gorge yourself on endless servings of pizza for just R$10. An added attraction are the "sweet pizzas", including white chocolate and caramelized banana flavours.

Churrascaria Bianco Rua Quintino Bocaiúva 839. Excellent quality all-you-can-eat meals for R$15 per person make this popular with visitors and locals alike.

Clube Maringá Porto Meira ☎45/3527-3472; reservations advised on Sun. Justly popular among locals for its superb *rodízio de peixe* lunch and stunning views of the Iguaçu river. Apart from a selection of local freshwater fish, there's an excellent salad bar and you can pay a little extra for some of the freshest sashimi you're likely to come across. Expect to pay R$15-30 per person. Take the "Porto Meira" bus and ask for directions, or a taxi (R$10).

O Capitão Rua Jorge Shimelpfeng & Almirante Barroso. One of a series of lively bars on this stretch, this is a particularly popular nightspot with the local youth on account of its loud music, extensive cocktail menu and affordable pizzas. Outdoor tables fill quickly so arrive early in summer if you want to sit outside. Cocktails from R$8.

Recanto Gaúcho Av das Cataratas, km15, near the Brazilian park entrance ⓣ45/3572-2358. A favourite Sun outing for locals: the atmosphere's lively, the meat's excellent and cheap (R$15 for all you can eat) and the owner (who dresses in full *gaúcho* regalia) is a real character. Turn up soon after 11am; food is served until 3pm. It's advisable to phone ahead. Closed Dec & Jan.

Trigo & Cia Rua Almirante Barroso 1750. Adjoining the *Hotel Internacional Foz*, this busy café serves tasty savoury snacks, good coffee and the best cakes in Foz.

Tropical das Cataratas Parque Nacional do Iguaçu. The only hotel restaurant worth trying. In peak season they offer an excellent buffet lunch of typical Brazilian dishes for R$20.

Directory

Airlines TAM ⓣ45/3521-4241; Gol ⓣ45/3521-4230.

Banks and exchange Dollars (cash or traveller's cheques) can be easily changed in travel agents and banks along Avenida Brasil; the banks have ATMs.

Car rental Avis ⓣ45/3529-6160, Localiza ⓣ45/3529-6300 and Yes ⓣ45/3522-2956 are all represented at the airport. Driving between Foz do Iguaçu and Puerto Iguazú in Argentina needs no special documentation. Crossing to Paraguay or going further afield in Argentina than the falls requires paperwork and costs extra.

Consulates Argentina, Eduardo Bianchi 26 ⓣ45/3574-2969; Paraguay, Rua Marechal Deodoro 901 ⓣ45/3523-2898.

Hospital Ministro Costa Cavalcanti ⓣ45/3576-8000 is a good private hospital. Ambulance ⓣ193.

Police Tourist police ⓣ45/3523-3036.

Post office Praça Getúlio Vargas near Rua Barão do Rio Branco (Mon–Fri 9am–5pm).

Taxi Coopertaxi Cataratas ⓣ0800 643-7878.

Moving on

Air Buses marked "Aeroporto Parque Nacional" leave the local terminal on Av Juscelino Kubitschek every 20min from 5.30am to 7pm, and then hourly until midnight (45min; R$2), passing via the airport on the way to the falls. Flights serve all the major Brazilian cities.

Buses Campo Grande (1 daily; 15hr), Curitiba (8 daily; 10hr), Florianópolis (1 daily; 16hr), Porto Alegre (5 daily; 16hr), Rio de Janeiro (4 daily; 23hr), São Paulo (2 daily; 17hr).

International buses leave every 15min from the *rodoviária* via the local bus terminal bound for Ciudad del Este in **Paraguay** (R$2.90), which is 7km northwest of Foz do Iguaçu. You need to disembark at the Brazilian customs for your exit stamps – the bus will not wait but your ticket is valid for the next one. You will then cross the Friendship Bridge to the Paraguayan customs where you will again be asked to disembark. Buses for Puerto Iguazu (40min; R$5) in Argentina leave every 30min from the *rodoviária*; you don't need entry and exit stamps if you are returning the same day.

Taxis from central Foz to Ciudad del Este cost R$30. A taxi to Puerto Iguazu will set you back R$50.

THE IGUAÇU FALLS

The **Iguaçu Falls** are, unquestionably, one of the world's great natural phenomena and form the centrepiece of the vast bi-national reserve **Iguaçu National Park**. First designated in 1936, the park was declared a UNESCO World Heritage Site fifty years later, a long time coming given that the falls were discovered as early as 1542 by the Spanish explorer Alvar Nuñez Cabeza de Vaca. To describe their beauty and power is a tall order, but for starters cast out any ideas that Iguaçu is some kind of Niagara Falls transplanted south of the equator – compared with Iguaçu, Niagara is a ripple. The falls are formed by the Rio Iguaçu, which has its source near Curitiba. Starting at an altitude of 1300m, the river snakes westward, picking up tributaries and increasing in size and power during its 1200-kilometre journey. About 15km before joining the Rio Paraná, the Iguaçu broadens out, then plunges precipitously over an eighty-metre-high cliff in 275 separate falls that extend nearly 3km across the river. To properly experience the falls it is essential to visit both sides. The Brazilian side gives the best overall view and allows you to fully appreciate the scale of the show; the Argentinian side gets you up close and personal to the major individual falls (see 101).

What to see and do

At its best in the early morning, a 1.5km cliffside trail runs alongside the falls, offering breathtaking photo opportunities. A stairway leads down from the bus stop to the start of the trail. The path ends by coming perilously close to the ferocious "Garganta do Diablo" (Devil's Throat), the most impressive of the individual falls. Depending on the force of the river, you could be in for a real soaking, so if you have a camera be sure to carry a plastic bag. From here, you can either walk back up the path or take the elevator to the top of the cliff and the road leading to the hotel. You'll undoubtedly come across coatis on the trails (though raccoon-like they are not raccoons, whatever the local guides may say) – don't be fooled by their cute and comical appearance, these little creatures are accomplished food thieves with long claws and sharp teeth. Every fifteen minutes the **Helisul helicopter** (Ⓣ45/3529-7327, Ⓦwww.helisul.com) takes off just outside the park entrance, offering eight-minute flights over the falls for US$80, or a 35-minute flight over the falls and the Itaipú Dam, the world's largest hydroelectricity scheme, for US$700 (minimum 4 people). The Argentines refuse to allow the helicopter to fly over their side of the falls as they do not wish to disturb the wildlife.

Arrival and information

The falls are mindblowing whatever the season, but they are always more spectacular following a heavy rainstorm. Weekends and Easter are best avoided if you don't want to share your experience with hordes of Brazilian and Argentinian holidaymakers. Buses from Foz do Iguaçu terminate at the entrance to the falls. It costs R$20.50 to enter, after which a shuttle bus will deliver you to the trails.

SANTA CATARINA

The colonization of the state of **SANTA CATARINA** took place relatively late, and it was not until the mid-eighteenth century that immigrants from the Azores began to form the first settlements along the coast. Gradually cattle herders from Rio Grande do Sul spread into the higher reaches of the mountainous interior, and European immigrants and their descendants made new homes for themselves in the fertile river valleys. Today, small communities on the **island of Santa Catarina**, and elsewhere on the coast, continue a way of life that has not changed markedly over the generations. However for the tourist the great appeal of the region lies in its subtropical climate and stunning beaches, set against a verdant, mountainous backdrop that makes it one of the most atmospheric holiday destinations in Brazil. Santa Catarina's **state tourist board** is based in the capital Florianópolis at Rua Felipe Schmidt on the 8th floor of Edificio ARS (Ⓣ0800/664-6300; Ⓦwww.guiasantacatarina.com.br or Ⓦwww.santacatarinatour.com)

ILHA SANTA CATARINA

The **island of SANTA CATARINA** is noted throughout Brazil for gorgeous scenery, attractive fishing villages and the city of **Florianópolis**, the small and prosperous state capital, half of which lies on the mainland and the other half on Santa Catarina Island.The climate is ideal, rarely cold in winter and with a summer heat tempered by refreshing South Atlantic breezes. Joined to the mainland by two suspension bridges (the longest, British-designed, open only to cyclists and pedestrians), the island retains a natural beauty that even some questionable developments in the capital itself have failed to diminish. An entire fifty percent of the island has been placed under a permanent national preservation order, ensuring that its timeless appeal will survive at least for the foreseeable future.

NEW YEARS

Florianópolis

FLORIANÓPOLIS was founded in 1700 and settled fifty years later by immigrants from the Azores. Since then, it has gradually developed from a sleepy provincial backwater into a lively state capital. With the construction of the bridges linking the island with the mainland, Florianópolis as a port has all but died, and today it thrives as an administrative, commercial and tourist centre. Land reclamation for a multi-lane highway and new bus terminals may have eliminated the character of the old seafront, but the late nineteenth-century pastel-coloured, stuccoed buildings of the old town still have a whiff of old-world appeal. Though few people visit Ilha Santa Catarina for the express purpose of seeing the capital, it is a pleasant enough place to walk around and makes a good base for exploring the rest of the island.

What to see and do

On the former waterfront, you'll find two ochre-coloured buildings: the **Mercado Público** (Mon–Fri 8am–9pm & Sat 8am–4pm), which contain some excellent bars and small restaurants, and the **Alfândega** (Mon–Fri 8am–7pm), a former customs house which has been converted for use as a crafts market. Most sights of interest, however, are centred on the lushly vegetated square, the **Praça XV de Novembro**, at the centre of which is the enormous, gnarled **"Centenary Fig" tree**. According to legend, walking three times around the tree will guarantee you fame and fortune. On one side of the square is the **Palácio Cruz e Souza**, an imposing pink building built between 1770 and 1780 as the seat of provincial government – it houses the **Museu Histórico de Santa Catarina** (Tues–Fri 10am–6pm, Sat & Sun 10am–4pm; free) whose nineteenth-century interior is more engaging than its collection of military memorabilia. The **Catedral Metropolitana**, overlooking the square, is disappointingly modern; the only church in the city centre dating back to the colonial era is the mid-eighteenth-century **Igreja de Nossa Senhora do Rosário**, best approached by a flight of steep steps from Rua Marechal Guilherme two blocks north of the Praça.

Arrival and information

By air The airport (☎48/3331-4000), 12km south of the city, is reached by taxi (30R) or "Aeroporto" buses (R$2).

By bus Buses arrive at the *rodoviária* (☎48/3224-2777) at the foot of the road bridge that links the island to the mainland. Cross the dual carriageway and it's a short walk to the centre and the local bus terminal which serves buses to the rest of the island (R$2.50). Faster yellow minibuses (R$4.50), serving the northern beaches only, depart from the Mercado Público.

Tourist information There's a tourist information kiosk (Dec–March Mon–Sat 7am–10pm, Sun 8am–7pm; April–Nov Mon–Sat 8am–6pm; ☎48/3223-7796, ⓦwww.guiafloripa.com.br) at the *rodoviária*.

Accommodation

Most tourists choose to stay at the beaches and resorts around the island (see below), but staying in Florianópolis itself has the benefit of direct bus services to all parts of the island. It's not cheap, though, and accommodation is snapped up quickly in high season

Central Sumaré Rua Felipe Schmidt 423 ☎48/3222-5359. The cheapest of the central hotels, in a secure area of town. The minimal rooms are nothing to write home about, but will do if you'd rather spend your money on enjoying yourself than your digs. Rooms with shared bathroom are cheapest. ❺

Florianópolis Palace Rua Artista Bittencourt 2 ☎48/3222-9633. The most luxurious hotel in the city centre, with excellent facilities and a minibus service to its private beach at Canasvieras. ❽

Floripa Hostel Rua Duarte Schutell 227 ☎48/3225-3781, ⓦwww.floripahostel.com.br. Everything you would expect from an HI hostel, though as in the rest of town you'll find yourself paying more than elsewhere. It fills rapidly in summer, so get here early. 3–4

Valerim Center Rua Felipe Schmidt 554 ⓣ48/3225-1100, ⓦwww.hotelvalerim.com.br. The largest of the mid-range hotels, with perfectly comfortable rooms (some of which sleep up to six people), all with a/c, TV and minibar. 6

Eating and drinking

Getting a snack in Florianópolis is no problem, but getting a decent feed sometimes can be, and many of the better restaurants are some way from the centre along Avenida Beira Norte (take bus #134 from the local bus terminal). Whatever you choose to eat, be prepared to pay a little more than you would for an equivalent meal elsewhere in Brazil.

Botequim Floripa Av Rio Branco 632. Pub-style beer house with a lively happy hour and cold beer on tap.

Box 32 Mercado Público. Seafood specialist and meeting place of the local glitterati who come to suck oysters and munch prawns. That said, it's not as expensive as you might fear, with a decent plate of garlic prawns setting you back R$20.

Mini Kalzone Rua Felipe Schmidt. If you're hungry, broke and in a hurry, *Mini Kalzone* is the answer to your prayers. Top notch, bite-sized fold-over pizzas come with a wide variety of meat and vegetarian fillings. For a good healthy bet try the *Joaquina*: spinach, ricotta and parmesan in a wholemeal casing, for R$3.

Miyoshi Av Rubens de Arruda Ramos 1068 ⓣ48/3225-5050. The best Japanese and Chinese cuisine on the island, with a decent-value lunch buffet and more expensive evening à la carte dishes (from 25R). There's another branch at Lagoa (see p.398), which is open lunchtimes only.

Scuna Bar Rua Forte Santana 405. A somewhat refined drinking place in the shadow of the road bridge that links the island to the mainland. Live music and a dancefloor – though this is not the place for you if you are looking for an all-night rave.

Tropical Sucos Rua Pedro Ivo & Conseihero Mafra. There's nothing fancy about this juice joint, but it's a decent central place to fill up on the home-made food and Brazilian dishes which make up their lunch buffet (R$12.90). And the fruit juices are excellent.

Vida Natural Rua Visconde de Ouro Preto 62. Vegetarian buffet for R$12 for who those who like their food to be predominantly green. Mon–Sat lunch only.

Directory

Airlines Aerolíneas Argentinas ⓣ48/3224-7835; Gol ⓣ48/3331-4128.

Banks and exchange Banks are located on Rua Felipe Schmidt and by Praça XV de Novembro.

Boat trips Scuna Sul (ⓣ48/3225-1806, ⓦwww.scunasul.com.br) offer boat trips around the island.

Car rental Avis, Rua Silva Jardim 495 ⓣ48/3225-7777; Hertz, Rua Bocaiuva 2125 ⓣ48/3224-9955; Localiza, Rua Henrique Valgas 112A ⓣ48/3225-5558; Unidas ⓣ48/3236-0607; YES ⓣ048/3284-4656. Advance reservations recommended in summer.

Consulates Argentina, Av Rio Branco 387 ⓣ48/3024-3036; Uruguay, Rua Walter de Bona Castelon 559 ⓣ48/3222-3718.

Internet Quantum.com at Rua Alvaro de Carvalho at the corner with Felipe Schmidt has a decent, cheap connection (R$3 per hour; daily 10am–10pm).

Pharmacies Farmacia Bela Vista, Rua Tenente Silveira 110. For homeopathic remedies Farmacia Homeopática Jaqueline, Rua Felipe Schmidt 413.

Post office The main post office is on Praça XV de Novembro (Mon–Fri 9am–5pm, Sat 8am–noon).

Moving on

By air Daily flights to São Paulo and Porto Alegre with onward connections.

By bus Inter-city buses depart from the *rodoviária*. Curitiba (hourly; 5hr), Porto Alegre (8 daily; 7hr), Foz do Iguaçu (5 daily; 14hr), São Paulo (6 daily; 12hr).

The rest of the island

The island's best beaches are found on the **north** and **west** coasts and with 42 beaches around the island to choose from, even the most crowded are rarely unbearably so. Though anywhere on the island can be reached by bus within an hour or so from Florianópolis, **renting a car** (see "Listings" above) is a good idea if you have limited time, allowing you to explore the island more thoroughly.

Canasvieras

The island's built-up **north coast** offers safe swimming in calm, warm seas and is popular with families. The long, gently curving bay of **Canasvieras** is the most crowded of the northern resorts, largely geared towards Argentine families who own or rent houses near the beach. By walking away from the concentration of bars at the centre of the beach, towards the east and **Ponta das Canas**, it's usually possible to find a relatively quiet spot. Unless you're renting a house for a week or more (agencies abound), finding **accommodation** is difficult, as the unappealing hotels are usually booked solid throughout the summer. That said there is a *Floripa Hostel* here (Ⓣ48/3266-2036; ❸–❹) run very much along the same lines as the one in the city. For **campers**, *Camping Canasvieras* is at Rua Mario Lacombe 179 (Ⓣ48/3266-0457; ❷). The local **restaurants** mostly offer the same menu of prawn dishes, pizza and hamburgers. If you fancy learning how to scuba dive Aquanauta Mergulho Ⓣ48/3266-1137 offers PADI scuba courses for all levels.

Lagoa da Conceição

A large saltwater lagoon in the centre of the island, **Lagoa da Conceição** is popular for swimming, canoeing and windsurfing. **Centro da Lagoa**, a bustling little town at the southern end of the lagoon, is both an attractive and convenient place to stay: there are good bus services from here into Florianópolis and to the east coast beaches, and the main road is lined with restaurants and bars. This is arguably the liveliest nightspot on the island during the summer and at weekends throughout the year, with restaurants always crowded and people overflowing into the street from the bars. The lagoon's beaches are close by; cross the small bridge on the road leaving Centro da Lagoa and it's a ten-minute walk. For **accommodation** you can't go far wrong with the *Backpackers Sharehouse* at 29 Barra de Lagoa (Ⓣ48/3232-7606, Ⓦwww.backpackersfloripa.com; ❹), an Aussie-run backpackers' hostel with a great atmosphere that will even lend you surfboards and beach gear for free. Rather more spartan is the *Pousada do Grego* at Rua Antônio da Silveira 58 (Ⓣ048/3232-0734; ❺). The largest place in Lagoa is the *Hotel Samuka*, Travessa Pedro Manuel Fernandes 96, at the intersection with Avenida Das Rendeiras (Ⓣ48/232-5024, Ⓦwww.samukahotel.com.br; ❼); it has a rather institutional feel but might have room when other places are fully booked. There is a decent **campsite** at Jornalista Manuel de Menezes 3292 (Ⓣ48/3232-5934; ❷).

East coast beaches

The beaches of the east coast are accessed via the bus terminal in Rio Tavares, south of Lagoa da Conceição. **PRAIA MOLE** (a few kilometres from Centro da Lagoa) is particularly beautiful, slightly hidden beyond sand dunes and beneath low-lying cliffs. Mole is extremely popular with young people but, rather surprisingly, commercial activity has remained low-key, probably because there's a deep drop-off right at the water's edge. Approached by a road passing between gigantic dunes, the next beach heading south is at **JOAQUINA**, attracting serious surfers. The water's cold, however, and the sea rough, only really suitable for strong swimmers. If you have the energy, climb to the top of the dunes where you'll be rewarded with the most spectacular views in all directions. If looking to **stay** in this area, try the excellent *Pousada Mirante do Campeche* at Rua das Gaviotas 776 (Ⓣ48/3389-2123; ❻), which offers double rooms and small apartments just 150m from the beach.

West coast beaches

The principal places of interest on the **west coast** are **Santo Antônio de Lisboa** to the north of Florianópolis and **Ribeirão da Ilha** to the south. The island's oldest and least spoilt settlements – their houses almost all painted white with dark blue sash windows, in typical Azorean style – both villages have a simple colonial church. Fishing, rather than catering to the needs of tourists, remains the principal activity, and the waters offshore from Santo Antônio are used to farm mussels and oysters, considered the best on the island Because the beaches are small and face the mainland, tourism has remained low-key. The few visitors here are tend to be on day–trips, staying just long enough to sample oysters at a local bar. **Accommodation** is limited, your best hope being in Santo Antônio: the *Pousada Mar de Dentro* (ⓣ48/3235-1521; ❻) has a lovely setting and a tiny pool, right on the beach. In the heart of Ribeirão da Ilha, try the simple *Pousada do Museu* (ⓣ48/3237-8148; ⓦwww.pousadadomuseu.com.br; ❼) which has some rooms with glorious sea views and a decent restaurant.

THE NORTH COAST TO SÃO FRANCISCO DO SUL

Santa Catarina's coastal highway (the BR-101) north of mainland Florianópolis is an experience in itself during the Brazilian summer. The bumper-to-bumper traffic moves at terrifying speeds, and wrecked cars litter the highway. Fortunately, much of the BR-101 passes alongside absolutely stunning beaches, some of which have remained totally devoid of buildings and people, so at least you can distract yourself by admiring the view. The two main stopping points along this stretch will attract you for two very different reasons. **Balneario Camboriu** is a lively beach resort popular with a youthful party crowd, whilst the more refined **Ilha de São Francisco** is steeped in history and considerably more tranquil.

Balneário Camboriú

If you are travelling in search of the Santa Catarina party scene, look no further than **BALNEÁRIO CAMBORIÚ**, an effervescent resort town 80km north of Florianópolis with a distinctly hedonistic approach to life. A popular summer destination with young Paraguayans, Brazilians and Argentinians, the town is packed out during the peak season, guaranteeing fun in the sun for those who prefer the lighter side of life.

What to see and do

Camboriú has something of a Mediterranean holiday resort feel to it, with its high-rise buildings and pedestrian streets peddling souvenirs, and walking around town you could be forgiven for thinking that you were on the Portuguese Algarve. That said, the place is not without its charms, not least its seven-kilometre-long **Praia Central**, offering safe swimming and golden sand. **Praia do Pinho** on the other side of the peninsula west of town is the site of Brazil's first nudist beach if you are adventurous enough to go for an all-over tan. Camboriú even has its own 33m-high Rio-style Christ statue, the **Cristo Luz**, illuminated at night and casting a faint greenish glow over the town. On summer evenings the park at the foot of the statue is the site of concerts, theatre and poetry recitals. The forested hillside in the south of town is a nature reserve, the **Parque Unipraias** (ⓦwww.unipraias.com.br; R$28) You can reach it via a cable car (9.30am–6pm) that passes through three stations, the first an **ecological park**, the second an **adventure park** and the third, the summit, offering glorious views over the town, beaches and out to sea. Buses between the Cristo Luz and Parque Unipraias run along the seafront **Avenida Atlantica** every thirty minutes in summer.

Arrival and information

By bus Camboriú is served by buses (every 15min; 2hr) from the state capital; they arrive at the *rodoviária* (ⓣ47/3367-2901) on Av Santa Catarina on the edge of town close to the highway.

Tourist information There is a tourist information office at Rua 2950 771 (ⓣ0800/647-8122, ⓦwww.guiacamboriu.com.br).

Accommodation

You'd be wise to book ahead in the peak season when block bookings take up the majority of the more affordable **hotels**. That said there is always the possibility of reductions if you ask around during late afternoon, with hotels desperate to be full to capacity. If you're in a group ask at the tourist office about renting a house, it's cheaper than you might think.

Hostel Rezende Rua 3100 780 ⓣ47/3361-1008. Standard HI hostel a few blocks back from the beach. It's decent value for money, and dorms are small and uncrowded, with just four beds each. ❸–❺

Marambaia Av Atlantica 300 ⓣ47/3361-1008. Shaped like a football stadium, this bizarre but classy hotel has pride of place on the beach. When the sea is a bit choppy you can enjoy no fewer than three pools, one indoors in case of inclement weather. ❼

Pousada Villa Germania Rua 1021 322 ⓣ47/3363-3147, ⓦwww.pousadavillagermania.com.br. Attractive *pousada* with simple but elegant rooms each with a balcony, in a quiet area of town. Rates include a sumptuous breakfast buffet. ❺

Pousada Camboriú Village Rua 1536 26 ⓣ47/3367-5052. Billed as a *pousada*, essentially these are apartments with 1, 2 or 3 bedrooms, kitchen and internet access. Good-value if you are part of a small group or want to save a bit of money by self-catering, though it's quite a walk from the beach. ❻

Eating

In addition to the proliferation of fast-food joints and *lanchonetes* that you might expect in a town populated by twenty-somethings, there are also some excellent restaurants around if you look hard enough, with seafood platters featuring heavily on most menus.

Alibabá Av Atlantica, corner of Rua 4500, Barra Sul. Arabic dishes in an Arabic setting.

Guacacole Av Beira Rio 1122, Barra Sul. Charismatic Mexican restaurant with live music, mariachis and "tequileros" who are only too happy to wet your whistle. Cultural attractions every Tues night spice up the already spicy food. Mains from R$20.

O Pharol Av Atlantica 5900. Upmarket seafood restaurant, well worth the extra reais. The seafood platter (R$40) is immense, and everything – prawns, lobster, oysters and anything else that tickles your fancy – tastes good.

Nightlife

Camboriú has a vibrant **nightlife** aimed mainly at a young crowd who seek loud music, bare flesh and lots of dancing. Most places are on or around the Av Atlantica, especially at the southern end, the Barra Sul, where you'll find a huge array of beach bars and discos. Things don't start to get lively until well after midnight and the action continues until after the sun comes up.

Baturité Divine Av Atlantica 5900, Barra Sul. One of Camboriú's largest and most established discos, *Baturité* has indoor and outdoor dancefloors, playing a mixture of pop and dance music. Doors open 9pm.

Cachaçaria Uai Av Atlantica 2334. Bar-style hangout on the beach specializing in *caipirinha*, the Brazilian carnival cocktail made with *cachaça* and crushed lemons.

Djunn Music Place Rua 4500, Barra Sul. Featuring visiting DJs and live music, this is a plush nightclub with table service and a bouncing dancefloor. Not cheap, but always full. Cover charge R$15.

Mein Beer Av Atlantica 4450, Barra Sul. Popular drinkers' hangout and a good place to start the evening off, with cold beers served in a beachfront location.

THE ILHA DE SÃO FRANCISCO

Just beyond Camboriú at the town of Itajaí, the highway gradually turns inland towards Joinville. Some 45km east of here is the **ILHA DE SÃO FRANCISCO**, a low-lying island separated from the mainland by a narrow strait spanned by a causeway. As Joinville's port and the site of a major Petrobras oil refinery, it might be reasonable to assume that São Francisco should be avoided, but this isn't the case. Both the port and refinery keep a discreet distance from the main town, **São Francisco do Sul**, and the beaches blend perfectly with the slightly dilapidated colonial setting.

São Francisco do Sul

Though the island was first visited by French sailors as early as 1504, it was not until the middle of the following century that the town of **SÃO FRANCISCO DO SUL** was established. One of the oldest settlements in the state, it is also one of the very few places in Santa Catarina with a well-preserved historic centre.

What to see and do

Dominating the city's skyline is the **Igreja Matriz**, the main church, originally built in 1669 by Indian slaves, but completely reconstructed in 1926. The **Museu Nacional do Mar** on Rua Babitonga in the historic centre (Ⓦwww.museunacionaldomar.com.br, Tues–Fri 10am–6pm, Sat & Sun 10am–7pm; R$3) has a maritime collection with an emphasis on southern Brazil and its people. The prettiest beaches, **Paulos** and **Ingleses**, are also the nearest to town, just a couple of kilometres to the east. Both are small, and have trees to provide shade. Surprisingly few people take advantage of the protected sea which is ideal for weak swimmers. On the east coast, **Praia de Ubatuba** 16km from the centre, and the adjoining **Praia de Enseada**, 20km from town, offer enough surf for you to have fun but not enough to be dangerous. A ten-minute walk across the peninsula from the eastern end of Enseada leads to **Praia da Saúdade** (or just Prainha), where the waves are suitable for only the most macho surfers.

Arrival

The *rodoviária* is inconveniently located few kilometres outside of town; you'll need to catch a local bus to the market in the town centre. Buses to the beaches at Enseada and Ubatuba leave from the market, with the last services in both directions departing at about 9.30pm.

Accommodation, eating and nightlife

Most of the island's visitors bypass the town altogether and head straight for the beaches to the east, so, even in midsummer, there's rarely any difficulty in finding a central hotel with room. Quite comfortable, and with sea views, is the *Hotel Kontiki* (Ⓣ47/3444-2232; ④) at Rua Babitonga 33, near the market; if you want a pool, there's the relatively luxurious *Hotel Zibamba* (Ⓣ47/3444-2020; ⑤) at Rua Fernando Dias 27. **Eating** out holds no great excitement, with the *Hotel Zibamba*'s restaurant the best of a generally poor bunch. **Enseada** boasts a lively nightlife. If you are looking to stay here *Pousada Farol da Ilha* just behind the beach on Rua Maceió 1156 (Ⓣ47/3449-1802, Ⓦwww.pousadafaroldailha.tur.br, ⑤) is as good a bet as any. If you are just looking for a good time then check out *Canoas Bar* and the predictably named *Surf Bar* on Av Brasil for some beach-bum hedonism.

Moving on

By bus There are hourly connections from the **rodoviária** to Joinville (20mins) and daily services to São Paulo (9hr) and Curitiba (2hr).

RIO GRANDE DO SUL

Famed for its "Gaúcho" lifestyle, the state of **RIO GRANDE DO SUL**, bordering Argentina and Uruguay, is for many people their first or last experience of Brazil. In the eighteenth century, the pioneering settlers of largely European origin forged a strong regional identity based around farming, fishing and of course cattle-ranching, and today "Gaúcho" is the nickname given to all inhabitants of the state, whatever their origins. Beef continues to play a major part in the lifestyle – the *churrasqueria* (beef grills) being the focal points of social interactions. The **road and bus network** is excellent and it's easy to zip through the state without stopping. However, Rio Grande do Sul is as Brazilian as Bahia or Rio and it would be foolish to ignore the place. The capital, **Porto Alegre**, is southern Brazil's commercial centre and the state's transportation hub. For a more traditional taste of Rio Grande do Sul, visit the **Serra Gaúcha**, a range a couple of hours north of Porto Alegre, populated with the descendants of German and Italian immigrants. The mountain towns of **Gramado** and **Canela** are full of alpine charm and make good bases for visiting the nearby **Parque Nacional dos Aparados da Serra** and **Parque Estadual do Caracol**, two of the region's most stunning natural attractions. To the west are the **Jesuit Missions**, accessed via the town of **São Miguel do Missoes**, which are far less visited than the *reducciones* of Argentina and Paraguay. For information on tourism in the state see ⓦwww.turismo.rs.gov.br.

PORTO ALEGRE

The capital of Rio Grande do Sul, **PORTO ALEGRE** lies on the eastern bank of the Rio Guaiba, at the point where five rivers converge to form the **Lagoa dos Patos**, a giant freshwater lagoon navigable by even the largest of ships. Founded in 1755 as a Portuguese garrison to guard against Spanish encroachment into this part of the empire, Porto Alegre developed into Brazil's leading commercial centre south of São Paulo when it became the port for the export of beef. Despite an attractive core, Porto Alegre gives the impression of a hard-working industrial city, grinding out a living. Apart from a few nice, if not very historical, buildings there isn't much to hold your attention, unless your visit coincides with one of the main **festivals**: Semana Farroupilha (Sept 13–20) features traditional local folk dancing and singing, while the highlight of Festa de Nossa Senhora dos Navegantes (Feb 2) is a procession of fishing boats.

What to see and do

The city centre is a little run down but everything worth seeing is within an easy walk, and a half-day or so is enough to visit most places of interest. If you prefer your surroundings a little more upmarket, then head out to the plush modern suburb of Moinhos de Vento where the in-crowd gather after dark.

Mercado Público and around

The golden-coloured **Mercado Público** (Mon–Sat 9am–5pm) stands at the heart of the lower town, located alongside Praça Rui Barbosa and Praça XV de Novembro. A replica of Lisbon's Mercado da Figueira, this imposing building contains an absorbing mix of stalls selling household goods, food and regional handicrafts. Much of the maze of streets around the market is pedestrianized. Next to the market is the ochre **Palácio Municipal**, the old *prefeitura*, built in Neoclassical style between 1898 and 1901, its impressive proportions an indication of civic pride and self-confidence during the period when Porto Alegre was developing into an important city. East of here along Rua Sete de Setembro is the pleasantly verdant **Praça de Alfândega**, home of the **Museu de Arte do Rio Grande do Sul** (daily 8am–6pm; free). You can spend an hour or so here, including a visit to the grand **Memorial Rio Grande do Sul** next door (Wed–Sat 10am–8pm), which houses pictorial exhibitions on the history of the state.

Praça da Matriz

If you walk uphill from the Praça de Alfândega along Rua General Chaves, you will come to the **Praça da Matriz**. Porto Alegre's oldest buildings are concentrated here, though they have been so heavily altered over the last few centuries that few retain their original character. The **Palácio Piratini** (the state governor's residence) dates from only 1909, while, across from it, the **Teatro São Pedro** was inaugurated in 1858. Surprisingly, its Portuguese Baroque appearance has remained largely unmolested, and the theatre is an important venue for local and visiting companies. The **Consulado Italiano** (Italian consulate) is an impressive colonial mansion and its prominent position, on the east side of the *praça* (no. 134), is a symbol of the important role Italians maintained in Porto Alegre and elsewhere in Rio Grande do Sul.

Along the waterfront

There are two cultural centres along Porto Alegre's waterfront that are worth a quick look. The **Casa de Cultura Mário Quintana**, Rua dos Andradas 736 (Tues–Fri 9am–9pm, Sat & Sun noon–9pm) was a hotel until 1980; the poet Mário Quintana was a long-time resident. Pride of place is given to his room, which is maintained in the state it was in when he lived here At the western tip of the peninsula, housed in a converted 1920s power plant, the **Centro Cultural Usina do Gasômetro** hosts frequent exhibitions, recitals and shows.

Outside the centre

Those wanting to escape the oppressive heat of the city should head to the **Jardim Botánico** (Wed–Sun 8am–5pm; free), large enough to justify having a whole suburb named after it. More than 1500 native plant species are represented here, in four hectares of gardens that also support a seed bank and research centre. If animals are more your thing, head for the excellent **zoo** 24km outside of town along the BR116 (Tues–Sun 8.30am–5pm; R$4).

Arrival, information and tours

Air The airport (☎51/3358-2000) meets flights from all major national destinations and nearby capitals. A taxi from the airport to the centre costs about R$20, or you can take the metro (6am–10pm, R$1.70), which joins the airport, *rodoviária* and Mercado Público on its single line.

Boat tours Two-hour excursions on the Rio Guaiba leave from the tour-boat berth (Doca Turística) on Avenida Mauá, near the train station. Schedules vary, so check with the tourist office. There are also boat excursions on the Rio Guaiba from the Usina do Gasômetro (see above).

Bus The *rodoviária* (☎51/3210-0101) is in the northeast of town, within walking distance of the centre; after dark it's safer, and easier, to ride the metro to the Mercado Público.

Taxi Porto Alegre is developing a reputation for street crime to rival the worst of Brazilian cities, so try to avoid walking around after dark, and call a taxi (☎51/3221-9371).

Tourist information There are tourist information offices at the *rodoviária* (daily 8.30am–6pm; ☎51/3212-3464), airport (daily 7.30am–11.45pm; ☎51/3358-2047), Usina do Gasômetro (Tues–Sun 9am–9pm) and Mercado Público (Mon–Sat 9am–7pm).

Accommodation

Most hotels are scattered around the city centre, but distances are small and it's possible to walk to most places – though you should take a cab after dark.

Elevado Av Farrapos 63 ☎51/3224-5250, ⓦwww.hotelelevado.com.br. This friendly hotel offers excellent value for homely, and well-equipped, if slightly small rooms. ❺

Lancaster Travessa Acelino de Carvalho 67 ☎51/3224-4737, ⓦwww.hotel-lancaster-poa.com.br. Located in one of the liveliest commercial areas of downtown Porto Alegre, this modern 2-star hotel is set behind an imposing 1940s facade. The rooms are small but well equipped, and offer decent value. ❻

Minuano Av Farrapos 31 ☎51/3226-3062, ⓦwww.minuanohotel.com.br. Despite the ugly high-rise building in which they are housed, rooms here are pleasant and surprisingly modern, and the sound-proof windows ensure a good night's sleep regardless of the traffic on the busy avenue outside. ❺

Plaza São Rafael Av Alberto Bins 514 ☎51/3220-7000, ⓦwww.plazahoteis.com.br. All the features you'd expect in the city's best downtown hotel, including an efficient business centre. Rates are sometimes heavily discounted, especially at weekends, and include an evening meal in the hotel's reasonable, though hardly exciting, restaurant. Ask for a room overlooking the river. ❾

Terminal-Tur Largo Vespasiano Júlio Veppo 125 ☎51/3061-0447. Box-like in every respect, both architecturally and in room design, this is a secure option right next to the *rodoviária*, ideal if you are planning an early escape. ❺

Eating and drinking

Getting a meal in Porto Alegre is not as easy as you might expect; budget travellers should head directly for one of the many malls where you can eat quickly, cheaply and with a variety of choice.

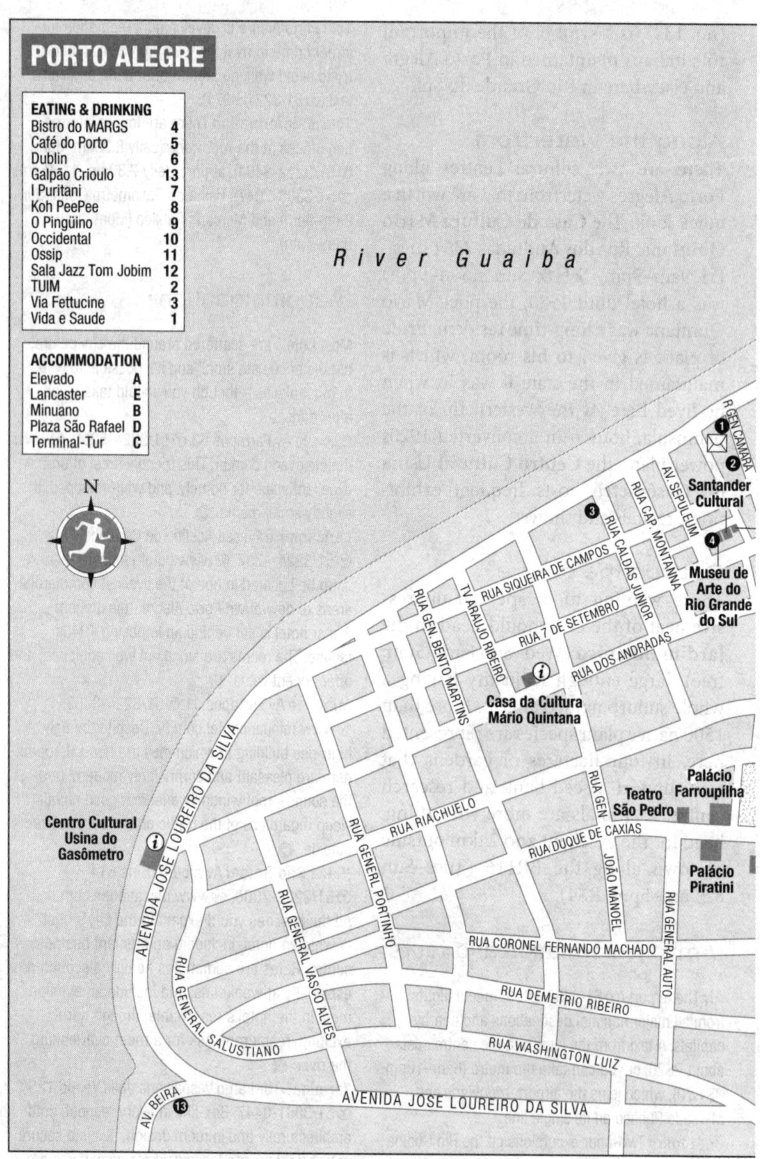

The historic centre is almost bereft of restaurants, and with very few exceptions the best places to eat are out in the plusher suburbs such as Moinhos de Vento – a taxi ride away.

Bistô do MARGS Praça da Alfândega. In the Museu de Arte do Rio Grande do Sul and with tables on the *praça* itself, this is one of the few restaurants in the area. Food is simple – pastas, steak, and salads – but pretty good, with mains starting from R$20. Tues–Sun 11am–10pm.

Café do Porto Rua Padre Chagas 293. Excellent light meals, sandwiches, wine and cakes are served in this pleasant Moinhos do Vento café; there are plenty of similar places to choose from in the area. Try the roast beef and artichoke wrap for R$18.

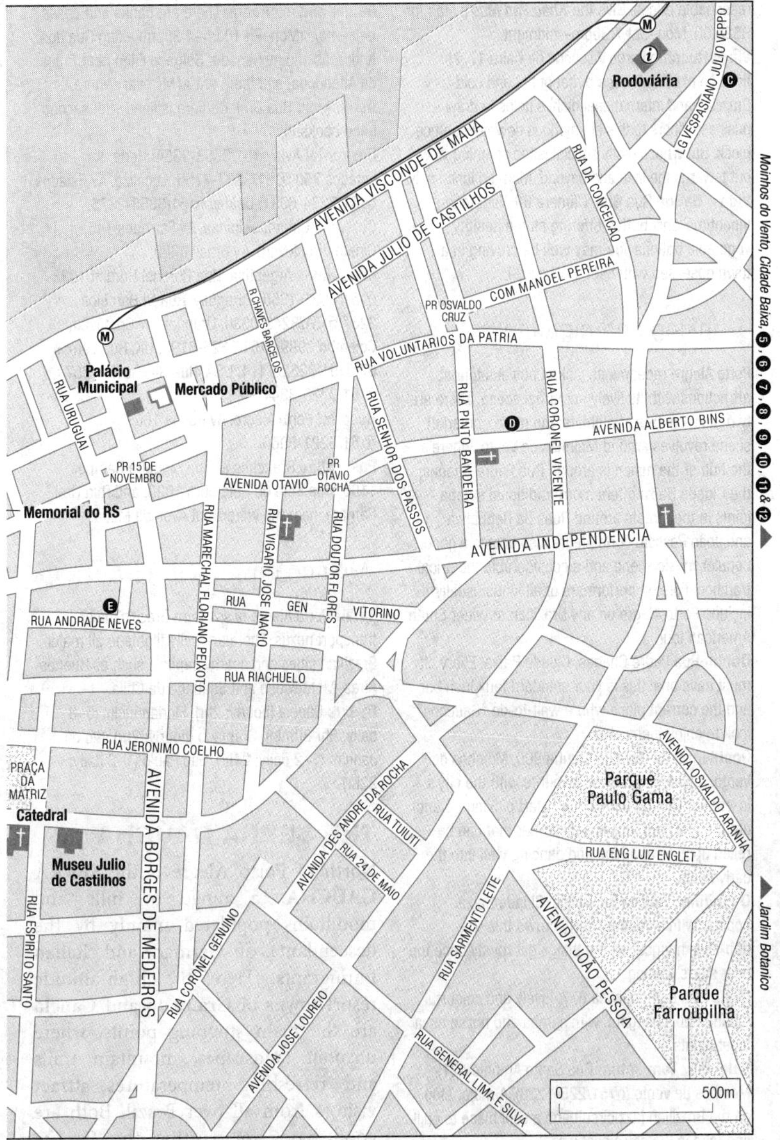

Galpão Crioulo Parque da Harmonia ☎51/3326-8194. An excellent, very reasonably priced city-centre *churrasqueria* offering a bewildering selection of meats in its *rodízio*, along with 20 different types of salad. In the evenings there's *gaúcho* music and dance performances. From R$13 per person.

I Puritani Rua Hilário Ribeiro 208. A rather plush bistro in Moinhos de Vento serving a mix of French-, Italian- and Brazilian-influenced dishes such as artichoke risotto, wild boar in an apricot sauce and passion fruit mousse served with a *jabuticaba coulis*.

Koh Pee Pee Rua Schiller 83, Moinhos de Vento. A brave – and rather successful – attempt to introduce Thai food to Porto Alegre. A good assortment of dishes, pleasant surroundings and reasonable prices. Give the *Khao Pad Moo* a stab for R$26.60. Mon–Sat 7.30pm–midnight.

Via Fettuccine Largo Visconde de Cairú 17, 7th floor. An excellent-value buffet of hot and cold Brazilian and international dishes helps to draw business diners to this anonymous downtown office block. But what's really special is the stunning view out towards the lake and beyond. Mon–Fri lunch only.

Vida e Saude Rua Gral. Câmara 60. Vegetarian, lunchtime-only buffet, offering all the healthy vegetable options you may well be craving in a town obsessed with beef. Buffet R$9.

Drinking and nightlife

Porto Alegre redeems its lack of obvious tourist attractions with its lively nocturnal scene. There are two main centres of nightlife: the more upmarket scene revolves around Moinhos de Vento, where the hub of the action is around Rua Padre Chagas; the Cidade Baixa offers more traditional samba joints in the streets around Ruas da República and João Pessoa. Porto Alegre also boasts a good popular music scene and a considerable theatrical tradition. Foreign performers of all kinds usually include Porto Alegre on any Brazilian or wider South American tour.

Dublin Rua Padre Chagas, Cidade Baixa. Every city must have one: this is your standard faux Irish bar and the current place where well-to-do "Gaúchos" look to enjoy themselves.

Occidental Av Osvaldo Aranha 960, Moinhos de Vento. A well-established favourite with the city's in-crowd. Though things don't start picking up until around midnight, this is a disco-bar that can be relied upon for drinking and dancing well into the early hours.

O Pingüino Rua da República, Cidade Baixa. Popular with a youthful party crowd this is a pub-style hangout where things get rowdy once the beer starts flowing.

Ossip Rua da República 677. Lively and colourful Cidade Baixa hangout, with samba and bossa nova most nights.

Sala Jazz Tom Jobim Rua Santo Antônio 421, Moinhos de Vento (☎51/225-1229). A major stop on the Brazilian jazz circuit and a cool place to chill and take in the city's best jazz.

TUIM Rua General Camara, just off Praça de Alfândega. A pocket-sized pub ideal for a cool, quiet beer.

Directory

Airlines Aerolíneas Argentinas ☎51/3221-3300; Gol ☎0800/701-2131; TAM ☎51/3323-3200.

Banks and exchange There are banks and *casas de câmbio* (Mon–Fri 10am–4.30pm) along Rua dos Andradas and Av Senador Salgado Filho near Praça da Alfândega, and there are ATMs everywhere.

Bookshops Rua Gral. Câmara is lined with second-hand bookshops.

Car rental Avis ☎51/3358-2354; Hertz, Av Estados 750 ☎51/3337-7755; Localiza, Av Estados ☎51/3374-6331; Unidas ☎51/3358-2375.

Cinemas Cinemas Unidaa, Av Farrapos 146; Cinema Boulevard, Av Brasil 4320.

Consulates Argentina, Rua Coronel Bordini 1033 ☎51/3321-1360; Paraguay, Rua Di Barcelos 2237 ☎51/3249-0530; Uruguay, Av Cristóvão Colombo 2999 ☎51/3325-6193; UK, Rua Lemos 57 ☎51/3232-1414; USA, Rua Riachuelo 1257 ☎51/3226-3344.

Hospital Porto Alegre, Av Rocha 100 ☎51/3221-6066.

Post office Branches at Rua Siqueira Campos 1100; Rua Sete de Setembro 1020; and Rua Gral. Câmara, near the waterfront Avenida Mauá.

Moving on

By air Porto Alegre is southern Brazil's major transport nexus. There are daily flights to all major Brazilian cities and nearby capitals such as Buenos Aires, Montevideo and Santiago de Chile.

By bus Canela (hourly; 2hr), Florianópolis (5–8 daily; 6hr 30min), Gramado (hourly; 2hr), Rio de Janeiro (1–2 daily; 24hr), São Paulo (1–2 daily; 22hr).

THE SERRA GAÚCHA

North of Porto Alegre is the **SERRA GAÚCHA**, a range of hills and mountains populated mainly by the descendants of German and Italian immigrants. Here the high-altitude resort towns of **Gramado** and **Canela** are the main stopping points, where unspoilt landscapes, mountain trails and refreshing temperatures attract visitors from all over Brazil. Both are good bases for visiting the **Parque Estadual do Caracol** and the **Parque Nacional dos Aparados da Serra**, two of the highlights of the Serra Gaúcha.

GRAMADO

Some 130km north of Porto Alegre, **GRAMADO** is Brazil's best-known mountain resort. At 825m you're unlikely to suffer from altitude sickness, but Gramado is high enough to be refreshingly cool in summer and positively chilly in winter. Architecturally, Gramado tries hard to appear Swiss, with "alpine" chalets and flower-filled window boxes the norm. It's a mere affectation, though, since hardly any of the inhabitants are of Swiss origin – and only a small minority is of German extraction. The most pleasant time to visit the area is in spring (Oct & Nov) when the parks, gardens and roadsides are full of flowers.

What to see and do

For most visitors, Gramado's appeal lies mainly in its clear mountain air and generally relaxed way of life – something that inhabitants of Brazil's major cities rarely get to enjoy. There really isn't much to do in town, but a stroll around the large and very pretty flower-filled **Parque Knorr** (daily 9am–6pm), and the secluded **Lago Negro**, surrounded by attractive woodland, are welcome respites from urban stress. The surrounding region is magnificent, and the **Vale do Quilombo**, settled in the nineteenth century by German and Italian farmers, is especially verdant. Although just 6km from town, it's a difficult trek and you'll need a good map to identify the incredibly steep unpaved approach road, Linha 28. Due to the incline, much of the original forest cover has survived intact and can be best appreciated at the **Refugio Família Sperry** where you'll be guided (R$12) along forest trails, past waterfalls, by the English-speaking owner who is a font of knowledge on the local flora. A neighbouring family-owned vineyard, the **Quinta dos Conte**, can also be visited. Arrangements to visit both should be made in advance and together by calling the Refugio Família Sperry ⓣ54/3504-1649. Roads in the mountainous areas around Gramado are unpaved and can be treacherous after rain, so **guided tours** are a safe bet – ask at the tourist office for recommendations.

Arrival and information

Bus Hourly buses from Porto Alegre arrive at the *rodoviária* (ⓣ54/3286-1302) on Av Borges de Medeiros, a couple of minutes' walk south from the town centre.

Tourist information The **tourist office** (Mon–Thurs 9am–6pm, Fri–Sun 9am–8pm; ⓣ54/3286-1475, ⓦwww.gramado.rs.gov.br) is on Av Borges de Medeiros at no. 1674.

Accommodation

Accommodation is expensive and you should book ahead during peak periods. Outside busy times many hotels offer discounts during the week.

Dinda Rua Augusto Zatti 160 ⓣ54/3286-2810, ⓦwww.pousadadoviajante.com.br. One of the town's cheapest options, this is a perfectly acceptable central bet with modest rooms and friendly service. ❺

Hostel Viajante Av Das Hortências 3880 ⓣ54/3282-2017, ⓦwww.pousadadoviajante.com.br. About 1.5km outside town on the road to Canela, this HI hostel is decent value with dorm rooms (24R) and some doubles. ❺

Eating

Gramado has some reasonably good restaurants, but again expect to pay through the nose for anything resembling a good meal.

La Caceria Av Borges de Medeiros 3166. An interesting but expensive restaurant in the classy *Hotel Casa da Montanha*, specializing in game dishes with unusual tropical fruit sauces that complement the often strong-tasting meat. Thurs–Sun evenings only.

TREAT YOURSELF

Estalagem St. Hubertus Rua da Carriere 974 ⓣ54/3286-1237, ⓦwww.sthubertus.com. Set on the shores of Lago Negro, this is a refined, luxury hotel named after a saint who swapped his pretentious lifestyle for a religious existence after coming face to face with a talking deer. ❾

Tarantino Ristorante Av das Hortênsias 1522, by Praça Major Nicoleti. Fairly authentic and very reasonably priced northern Italian dishes.

CANELA

Marginally cheaper than Gramado, but arranged very much along the same lines, **CANELA** (which means "cinnamon"), 8km further east, is another mountain retreat popular with holidaying Brazilians. The town originally grew as a centre for the local logging industry, but today its main source of income is from the streams of tourists who come to exploit the natural resources of the region in a rather different way. Better located for visits to the nearby national parks than Gramado, it's preferred by many people as a base for exploring the surroundings.

Arrival and information

Bus Canela is served by hourly return buses from Porto Alegre – a spectacular journey winding around forested mountainsides and snaking through valleys – sit on the left-hand side of the bus for the best views. Buses arrive at the *rodoviária* (Ⓣ52/3282-1375), a short walk from the centre.

Tourist information The tourist office, at Lagoa de Fama (Ⓣ52/3282-2200, Ⓦwww.canelaturismo.com.br) in the town centre, can put you in touch with a host of tour companies arranging adventure-style trips to the national parks; buses to Parque Estadual do Caracol also run from here.

Accommodation

Accommodation can be hard to come by during peak periods, when you should book ahead. Though it's cheaper than Gramado, it is not cheap per se, and the town can be easily visited on a day-trip from Porto Alegre.

Hostel Viajante Rua Ernesto Urbani 132 Ⓣ54/3282-2017, Ⓦwww.pousadadoviajante.com.br. Right next to the *rodoviária* and under the same ownership as the hostel of the same name in Gramado, this is the best budget choice, with economical dorms and neat and tidy doubles – perfect for travellers winding down after a hard day's bungee jumping. ❺

Pousada Canela Rua Ernesto Dorneles 333 Ⓣ54/3282-8410, Ⓦwww.pousadacanela.com.br. Architecturally interesting and supremely comfortable, this pleasant mid-range hostel is excellent value for money and well-located a block from the main square. Some rooms have balconies. ❽

Eating

You can forget about finding cheap eats in Canela but there are some interesting restaurants around town that make it worth investing the extra few Reais.

Churrascaria Espelho Gaúcho Rua Danton Corrêa and Baden Powell 50. Meat, meat and more meat. In fact all the meat you can eat for a one-off R$15.

Toca da Bruxa Praça da Matriz 25 Ⓣ54/3282-9750. A thematic pizza house served in a witch's den! A series of savoury and sweet pizzas with haunting names such as the "Furiosa" and the "Venenosa", the latter with a healthy serving of chilli peppers! Pizzas from R$20.

PARQUE ESTADUAL DO CARACOL

Just 7km outside Canela, the highlight of the **PARQUE ESTADUAL DO CARACOL** is the spectacular 131-metre-high **Cascata do Caracol** waterfall that gives the park its name. The water cascades down over basaltic rock formations and forms a natural feature of stunning beauty. For the best views of the waterfall take the nerve-jangling **cable car** (Ⓣ52/3504-1405, Ⓦwww.canelateleferico.com.br; R$14). More accessible than other nearby reserves, Caracol is a popular weekend destination and has big appeal for adrenalin junkies who perform all manner of adventure activities as they search for their next rush. While here don't forget to climb the **Observatorio Ecológico** (Ⓦwww.observatorioecologico.com.br), which will give you a bird's-eye view over the tree-tops.

Arrival and information

Buses run from the tourist office in Canela to the park entrance (daily 9am–6pm; R$5) every two hours daily except Monday. The admission fee (R$4) should be paid at the excellent visitors centre

(☎52/3278-3035; daily 8.30am–5.30pm). Here you will find details about walking trails and adventure activities such as rock-climbing, rappelling and bungee jumping. A number of tour companies in Canela can arrange guided visits and adventure tours to the park. Ask in the tourist office for details.

PARQUE NACIONAL DOS APARADOS DA SERRA

The dominant physical feature of south central Brazil is a **highland plateau**, the "Planalto", the result of layer upon layer of ocean sediment piling up and the consequent rock formations being lifted to form the Brazilian Shield. Around 150 million years ago, lava slowly poured onto the surface of the shield, developing into a thick layer of basalt rock. At the edge of the plateau, cracks puncture the basalt and it is around the largest of these that the **Parque Nacional dos Aparados da Serra** (Wed–Sun 9am–5pm; R$4), 100km east of Canela, was created.

Approaching the park from any direction, you pass through rugged cattle pasture, occasionally interrupted by the distinctive umbrella-like *araucaria* pine trees and solitary farm buildings. As the dirt road enters the park itself, forest patches appear, suddenly and dramatically interrupted by a canyon of breathtaking proportions, **Itaimbezinho**. Some 5.8km in length, between 600m and 2000m wide and 720m deep, Itaimbezinho is a dizzying sight. The canyon and its immediate surroundings have two distinct climates and support very different types of vegetation. On the higher levels, with relatively little rainfall, but with fog banks moving in from the nearby Atlantic Ocean, vegetation is typical of a cloudforest, while on the canyon's floor a mass of subtropical plants flourishes.

Three trails are open to visitors, the most difficult of which is the **Trilha de Rio do Boi** (8hr) – an option for experienced hikers that must only be attempted with a guide. It involves a 5m vertical descent of a rock face by rope and a complete descent to the rocky river in the canyon floor. Rather easier is the **Trilha do Vértice** (1.4km), which affords views of Itaimbezinho and the two spectacular waterfalls **Véu da Noiva** and **Andorhinas**. If this isn't challenging enough for you try the **Trilha do Cotovelo** (6.3km) which runs along the rim of the canyon and provides some glorious photo opportunities.

WHEN TO VISIT

The Parque Nacional dos Aparados da Serra can be visited throughout the year, but is at its best during spring (Oct and Nov) when the blooming flowers create a spectacular effect. In the winter (June through Aug), it can get very cold, though visibility is often excellent. Summers are warm, but heavy rainfall sometimes makes the roads and trails impassable and fog and low-level cloud often completely obscure what should be spectacular views. Avoid April, May and September, the months with the most sustained rain.

Arrival and information

If you don't have your own transport, visiting can be complicated and it is worth bearing in mind that trying to visit the park on your own is much more difficult and barely cheaper than doing it with a **guided tour**. If you intend to make the trip in your own vehicle it is imperative that you call ☎54/3251-1230 for up-to-date information on local road conditions. Only 1000 visitors are permitted to enter the park each day, so it's advisable to phone the **visitors' centre** (☎54/3251-1262) in advance to reserve a place. To get to the park on **public transport**, take a bus from Gramado or Canela to **São Francisco de Paula**, 69km from the park's entrance. From São Francisco you need to take another bus northeast to **Cambará do Sul** and ask to be let off at the entrance to the park. From here it's a further 15km to Itaimbezinho. Buses occasionally run between São Francisco or Cambará and Praia Grande (which has a couple of basic hotels, one on the main square and the other at the *rodoviária*), on the Santa Catarina side of the state line. These will drop you just 3km from Itaimbezinho but you'll need to walk the difference – there is no bus service to the canyon. Camping is prohibited in the park, though there is a **visitors' centre** (☎54/3251-1262) and a **snack bar**.

JESUIT MISSION LANDS: SANTO ANGELO

Though less well known than those in Argentina and Paraguay, Rio Grande do Sul is home to no fewer then seven **Jesuit Missions** in an excellent state of preservation. Unfortunately, because of their isolated location and difficulties of access, very few foreign tourists ever make it out to visit them – which is not to say that it is not worth making the effort to do so. The best place to base yourself is the town of **SANTO ANGELO** in the northwest of the state, where there is a cluster of accommodation options around Praça Rio Branco – the cheapest being *Hotel Comercio* (☎55/3312-2542; R$45). Eight daily buses run from Porto Alegre to Santo Angelo (7hr 30min).

The most accessible of the missions is **SÃO MIGUEL ARCANJO** (Ⓦwww.missoesturismo.com.br), declared a UNESCO World Heritage Site and the best of the Brazilian ruins. Guided tours are available, and a nightly light show brings the story of the Jesuits to life. Four daily buses run the 53km southwest from Santo Angelo to São Miguel. Next to the ruins is an excellent themed hostel, *Missões Hostel* (☎55/3381-1202, Ⓦwww.pousadatematica.com.br; R$45) which has dorm rooms (R$35 per person) as well as doubles and a relaxing pool. For more information on the Jesuits.

GAÚCHO COUNTRY: LAVRAS DO SUL AND BAGÉ

If you want to witness the everyday working life of the pampas close up, head to **LAVRAS DO SUL**, 324km southwest of Porto Alegre. Dedicated to raising cattle, horses and sheep, the town has nothing to obviously mark it out from countless others in the region, other than its local **fazenda** owners who have started taking guests, turning part of either the main house or their outhouses into *pousadas*. On arrival at a *fazenda*, you first have to show whether you can handle a horse. If you can't, you're quickly coached to develop some basic equestrian skills. Guests then join the *fazenda*'s workers in their day-to-day duties minding the livestock around the property. There are natural pools and streams for cooling off on hot summer days, while the extremely comfortable *fazenda* buildings all have open fires for the frequently bitterly cold winter evenings. Visits to *fazendas* are arranged through Lavras do Sul's tourist office at Rua Dr Pires Porto 351 (☎51/3282-1239, Ⓦwww.lavrasdosul.famurs.com.br). **Reservations** are essential as the *fazendas* only have room for between six and eight guests each and will need some notice if you need collecting from the rodoviária in town.

Arrival

Bus Buses arrive at the **rodoviária** (☎055/3282-1777) near the town centre at Dr João Luchsinger Bulcão 514. Three daily services connect the town with Porto Alegre (6hr).

Bagé

BAGÉ, 374km west of Porto Alegre, is first and foremost a cattle and commercial centre, rather than a tourist town, but unlike most of the other towns in the area it possesses a certain rural charm that makes it worth a visit if you are passing through the region.

What to see and do

Like all towns in the *campanha* (countryside), Bagé has its own lively events, which attract people from the surrounding cattle ranches. The most important **festival**, held in January in odd-numbered years, is the **Semana Crioula Internacional**, but the Semana de Bagé (a folklore festival held annually from July 10–17), or even the Exposição (first half of Oct), will give you a taste of the *campanha*. For an understanding of the region's history, a visit to the **Museu Diogo de Souza**, Av Guilayn 5759 (Tues–Fri 8.30–11.30am & 1.30–5.30pm, Sat & Sun 1.30–5.30pm; R$2), is a must. Also worth visiting is the **Museu da Gravura Brasileira** at Rua Coronel Azambuja 18 (Mon–Fri 1.30–7.30pm, Sat 1.30–6pm; closed Jan; R$2.50), which has a collection of eight hundred mainly Brazilian engravings. Rio Grande do Sul has a long tradition of this art form and some of the most important artists worked in Bagé.

Arrival, information and accommodation

Accommodation Hotels are plentiful, with the clean and friendly *Mini*, Av Sete de Setembro, near Praça General Osório (no phone; ❹), the centre's cheapest. If you want something more refined, there's the *Hotel Fenícia* at Rua Juvêncio Lemos 45 (Ⓣ53/3242-8222; ❺), while the best, largest and oldest hotel in town, dating from 1850, is the *Obinotel*, at Av Sete de Setembro 901 (Ⓣ53/3242-8211; ❺).

Bus Buses arrive at the *rodoviária* (Ⓣ53/3242-8122) outside the town centre at Rua Dr. Freitas 146.

Tourist office Bagé's tourist office at Praça Silveira Martins (Mon–Fri 9–11.30am & 2–6pm, Sat 9am–noon) has details of local festivals and other events.

Moving on

By bus There are five daily buses to Porto Alegre (4hr).

CROSSING THE BORDER TO URUGUAY

There are three major border crossings to Uruguay in Rio Grande do Sul. By far the most travelled route is via **CHUÍ** (or "Chuy" on the Uruguayan side, see p.932), 527 kilometres south of Porto Alegre. **Buses** entering and leaving Brazil stop at an immigration office a short distance from town for customs formalities. The Uruguayan immigration post is 3km outside town – you'll either have to walk or take a taxi. **SANTANA DO LIVRAMENTO**, 497km west of Porto Alegre in the heart of Gaúcho country, is a less-used but more atmospheric crossing point into Uruguay. There's no duty-free here, just *gaúcho* memorabilia and *erva mate*. If you are really interested in the *gaúcho* lifestyle, check out the possibility of visiting or staying at a local *fazenda* with the local tourist office on Rua Tamandaré (Mon–Sat 7am–1pm & 3–6pm, Sun 3–8pm; Ⓣ55/3243-6060, Ⓦwww.santanadolivramento.rs.gov.br). Before leaving Livramento and Rivera, you'll need a Brazilian exit (or entry) passport stamp from the Polícia Federal, Rua Uruguai 1177, near the central park, and a stamp from Uruguay's Dirección Nacional de Migración, Calle Suarez 516 (three blocks from Plaza General José Artigas, Rivera's main square). If you have any problems, head for the Uruguayan consulate at Av Tamandaré 2110 (Ⓣ55/3242-1416). The third, and most complicated, border crossing is at **ACEGUÁ** (to Melo in Uruguay). You'll need to have your passport stamped in the town of **Bagé** (see opposite), 60km north of the frontier; the Policia Federal are located in Aceguá at Rua Barão do Trunfo 1572, a few blocks north of the Praça General Osório. Aceguá is little more than a conglomeration of buildings, so make sure you check your onward journey connections before you arrive as you don't want to get stuck here. Change money in Uruguayan *casas de cambio*, as the rates here are generally better than those offered in Brazil.

CROSSING THE BORDER TO ARGENTINA: URUGUAIANA

Most people heading to Argentina from Brazil cross the frontier at Foz do Iguaçu (see p.392), but if you find yourself in the south of the country, **URUGUAIANA,** 694km west of Porto Alegre, is by far the most convenient crossing to Argentina – with Paso de los Libres on the other side. There is little reason to hang around more than the time required to complete the customs formalities, unless of course you are here during one of the local festivals – check dates at the **tourist office** on Praça Barão do Rio Branco (Mon–Sat 8.30am–6pm; ⊕55/3414-4181, ⊛www.uruguaiana.rs.gov.br). Customs formalities take place at either end of the 1400-metre-long road bridge across the Rio Uruguai. Accommodation and restaurant options are both better on the Argentinian side of the border. The Argentinian consulate is at Rua Santana 2496 (⊕55/3412-1925).

Chile

HIGHLIGHTS

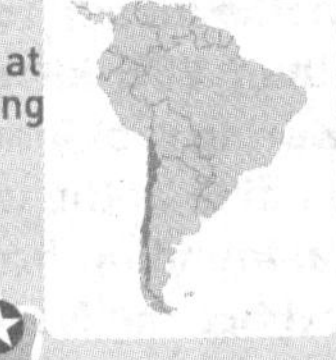

IQUIQUE: take to the skies at this top paragliding spots

SAN PEDRO DE ATACAMA: explore fascinating desert landscapes and surf the sand dunes

THE ELQUI VALLEY: laid-back villages, *pisco* tasting and incomparable stargazing

VALPARAÍSO: fantastic nightlife and bohemian culture characterize this colourful city

PUCÓN: backpacker central for volcano climbing, whitewater rafting and relaxing hot springs

PARQUE NACIONAL TORRES DEL PAINE: unbeatable hiking opportunities amidst majestic scenery

ISLA NAVARINO: tackle a challenging hike at the true "end of the world"

ROUGH COSTS

DAILY BUDGET CH$25,000

DRINK Pisco Sour CH$1500

FOOD *Pastel de choclo* CH$3500

CAMPING/HOSTEL/BUDGET HOTEL CH$4000/6000/10,000–15,000

FACT FILE

POPULATION 16.5 million

AREA 576,950 sq km

OFFICIAL LANGUAGE Spanish

INDIGENOUS LANGUAGES Aymará, Huilliche, Kawéscar, Mapudungun, Quechua, Rapanui and Yámana

CURRENCY Chilean Peso (CH$)

CAPITAL Santiago (population: 5.4 million)

TIME ZONE GMT -4; GMT -3 from second Sunday in October to second Sunday in March

INTERNATIONAL PHONE CODE ⓣ56

Introduction

From the crystalline lakes, frigid fjords and glaciers in the south to the majestic altiplano and the world's driest desert – the Atacama – in the north, Chile is perhaps the most geographically diverse and fascinating country in Latin America. Long and thin, Chile stretches along the Pacific coast for over 4300 kilometres, yet is nowhere more than 285 kilometres wide. Separated from Argentina by the towering rock-and-ice crest of the Andes, the country encompasses nine of the world's eleven climatic zones and is home to an astounding array of animal and plant life. Thanks to a position where the Nazca and South American tectonic plates collide, and along the Pacific "ring of fire", Chile can also boast over two hundred active volcanoes and is highly prone to earthquakes. With pristine wilderness on a grander scale than anything in Europe or North America, Chile poses its visitors one overwhelming dilemma: which part to explore first?

If you want to experience the whole of Chile in all its diversity you'll need to come prepared for both extreme cold and extreme heat. The **Lake District**, **Patagonia** and **Tierra del Fuego** are best explored from October through April, since the Chilean winter effectively shuts down much of the south and transport can be very limited. **Norte Grande**, **Norte Chico**, Middle Chile and the Pacific island territories, however, can be accessed year-round.

Today, in spite of its troubled past, Chile is among the most politically and economically stable of all Latin American countries. The tainted memory of the Pinochet dictatorship is gradually fading, and a popular socialist government now leads the country. Women have more rights than ever and steps are being taken to remedy the injustices suffered by Chile's indigenous population. While there is still a great disparity between rich cities and marginalized rural areas, for the most part Chile is westernized and affluent, an easy country to navigate.

CHRONOLOGY

Pre-European contact Vast swathes of Chilean territory are under Inca rule.

1520 Ferdinand Magellan is the first European to sail through what is now the Magellan Strait.

1536 Expedition from Peru to Chile by conquistador Diego de Almagro and his four hundred men ends in death for most of the party.

1541 Pedro de Valdivia, a lieutenant of Francisco Pizarro, founds Santiago de Chile; a feudal system in which Spanish landowners enslave the Indian population is established.

1808 Napoleon invades Spain and replaces Spanish king Ferdinand VII with his own brother.

1810 The *criollo* elite of Santiago de Chile decide that Chile will be self-governed until the Spanish king is restored to the throne.

1817 Bernardo O'Higgins defeats Spanish royalists in the Battle of Chacabuco with the help of Argentine general José San Martín, as part of the movement to liberate South America from colonial rule.

1818 Full independence won from Spain. O'Higgins signs the Chilean Declaration of Independence.

1829 Wealthy elite seizes power with dictator Diego Portales at the helm.

1832–1860s Mineral deposits found in the north of the country, stimulating economic growth.

1879–1883 Chilean troops occupy the Bolivian port of Antofagasta, precipitating the War of the Pacific against Bolivia and Peru.

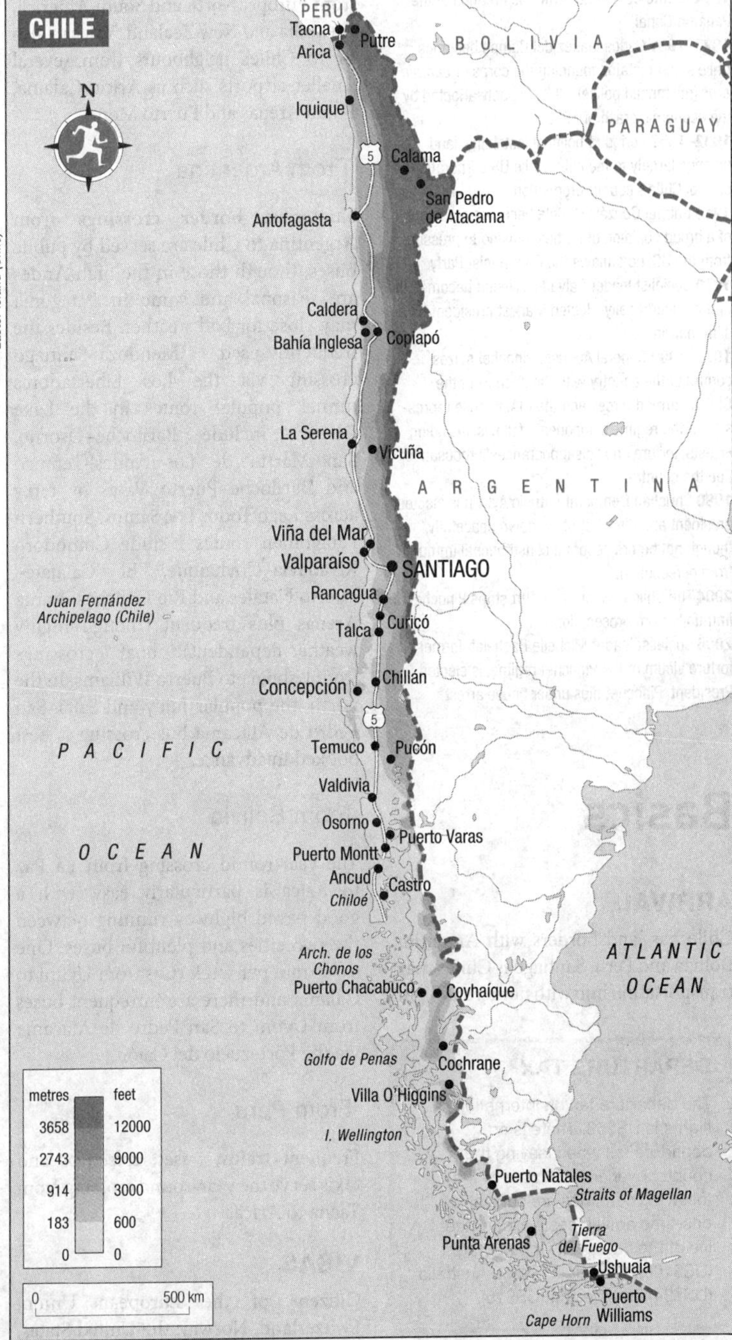
CHILE
N
PERU
Tacna
Putre
Arica
BOLIVIA
Iquique
PARAGUAY
Calama
San Pedro de Atacama
Antofagasta
Easter Island (Chile)
Caldera
Copiapó
Bahía Inglesa
La Serena
Vicuña
ARGENTINA
Viña del Mar
Valparaíso
SANTIAGO
Rancagua
Juan Fernández Archipelago (Chile)
Curicó
Talca
Chillán
Concepción
PACIFIC
Temuco
Pucón
Valdivia
Osorno
Puerto Varas
OCEAN
Puerto Montt
Ancud
Castro
Chiloé
Arch. de los Chonos
ATLANTIC OCEAN
Puerto Chacabuco
Coyhaíque
Golfo de Penas
Cochrane
Villa O'Higgins
I. Wellington
metres
feet
3658
12000
2743
9000
914
3000
183
600
0
0
Puerto Natales
Straits of Magellan
Tierra del Fuego
Punta Arenas
Ushuaia
Puerto Williams
Cape Horn
0
500 km

1914 Nitrate boom ends with the creation of the Panama Canal.
1927–1931 Carlos Ibáñez del Campo becomes Chile's first dictator, founding the corps of *carabineros* (militarized police); Chile is badly affected by the economic crash of 1929.
1932–1952 Period of political instability: land belongs largely to the elite, while US corporations control Chile's copper production.
1946 Gabriel González Videla becomes president of a broad coalition of parties; bowing to pressure from the US, he outlaws the Communist Party.
1970 Socialist leader Salvador Allende becomes the first democratically-elected Marxist president by a slim margin.
1973–1989 General Augusto Pinochet seizes control of the country with the support of the Chilean armed forces and the CIA. Intense repression of the regime's opponents follows, including arrests, torture and "disappearances"; thousands flee the country.
1990 Christian Democrat Patricio Aylwin is elected president and Pinochet steps down peacefully, though not before securing constitutional immunity from persecution.
2004 The Chilean Supreme Court strips Pinochet of immunity from prosecution.
2006 Socialist leader Michelle Bachelet, former torture victim of the Pinochet regime, is elected President. Pinochet dies under house arrest.

Basics

ARRIVAL

Chile has land borders with Argentina, Bolivia and Peru. Santiago is Chile's main transportation hub with numerous flights from Europe, North and South America, Australia and New Zealand. You can also fly to Chile's neighbours from several smaller airports such as Arica, Calama, Punta Arenas and Puerto Montt.

DEPARTURE TAX

The departure tax on international flights is US$56. There is no departure tax when leaving the country overland. Citizens of the following countries are subject to one-time arrival fees, valid for the life of the passport: United States (US$100); Canada (US$55); Australia (US$34) and Mexico (US$15).

From Argentina

Numerous **border crossings** from Argentina to Chile are served by public buses, though those in the high Andes are seasonal and some in Patagonia may close for bad weather. Besides the frequently-used Mendoza–Santiago crossing via the Los Libertadores tunnel, popular routes in the Lake District include Bariloche–Osorno, San Martín de Los Andes–Temuco and Bariloche–Puerto Varas by ferry across Lago Todos Los Santos. Southern Patagonian routes include Comodoro Rivadavia–Coyhaique, El Calafate–Puerto Natales and Río Gallegos–Punta Arenas plus frequent (though highly weather-dependent) boat crossings from Ushuaia to Puerto Williams. In the north, the popular Jujuy and Salta–San Pedro de Atacama bus crossing is best booked in advance.

From Bolivia

The year-round crossing from La Paz to Arica is particularly easy, with a good paved highway running between the two cities and plentiful buses. One slow train per week runs from Uyuni to Calama and there are infrequent buses from Uyuni to San Pedro de Atacama via the Portezuelo del Cajón.

From Peru

Frequent trains, buses, *colectivos* and taxis serve the year-round crossing from Tacna to Arica.

VISAS

Citizens of the European Union, Switzerland, Norway, the United States,

Canada, Mexico, Israel, South Africa, Australia and New Zealand do not require **visas**. Tourists are routinely granted 90-day entry permits and must surrender their tourist cards upon departure. In theory, visitors can be asked to produce an onward ticket and proof of sufficient funds, though that rarely happens. 90-day visa extensions can be granted by the Departamento de Extranjería, Moneda 1342, Santiago Centro (ⓣ2/672-5320) at a cost of US$100, although it may be cheaper and easier simply to cross the border into a neighbouring country and back again. If you lose your tourist card, you can get a replacement from the Policía Internacional, General Borgoño 1052, Independencia, Santiago (ⓣ2/737-1292).

GETTING AROUND

The majority of the population in Chile travels by bus, and it's such a reliable and inexpensive option that you'll probably do the same. However, domestic flights are handy for covering long distances in a hurry.

By plane

Several airlines offer frequent and reasonably priced flights within Chile. You'll often find better fares by booking locally, rather than in advance from home. **LAN** (ⓣ600/526-2000 in Chile, ⓣ866/435-9526 in the USA, ⓦwww.lan.com) is probably the best, with efficient online booking, last-minute discounts and a good-value **"South America Air Pass"**. Punta Arenas-based **Aerovías DAP** (ⓣ61/616100, ⓦwww.aeroviasdap.cl) flies to various destinations in Chilean and Argentine Patagonia and Tierra del Fuego, as well as the Falkland Islands; it's best to book tickets directly at the airline offices as their website is inefficient. **Sky Airline** (ⓣ600/600-2828, ⓦwww.skyairline.cl) competes with LAN price-wise, with daily flights between Chile's major cities. Finally, Spanish-owned **Aerolíneas del Sur** (ⓣ800/710-300, ⓦwww.aerolineasdelsur.cl) offers daily Santiago–Punta Arenas flights, as well as flights to Iquique, Antofagasta, Calama and Puerto Montt.

By bus

Bus travel is popular, affordable, and convenient. The level of comfort depends on how much you are prepared to pay for your ticket, with the *cama* buses being the plushest, their seats reclining almost horizontally. South of Puerto Montt, and especially during the peak months, demand outstrips supply, so it is important to book your outward bus journey in advance if you are on a tight schedule. Bus tickets are valid only for specified buses, and the major bus companies, such as Tur Bus and Pullman, require you to buy tickets in advance. If crossing **international** borders by bus, remember that it's prohibited to transport animal and plant matter to neighbouring countries.

PACHAMAMA BY BUS

This hop-on, hop-off bus service is especially tailored for independent travellers and designed to cover the most scenic spots in the Lake District and the Atacama Desert. You purchase a pass for the number of days you wish to travel, and you can stay at any of the given stops for as long as you want. You are responsible for booking your own accommodation, which the guides can assist with. There are weekly departures on both routes; check the website for exact dates. To book a pass, contact the Santiago office at least 48 hours in advance: Agustinas 2113, Barrio Brasil, Metro República (ⓣ2/688-8018, ⓦwww.pachamamabybus.com).

Smaller **local buses** and minibuses (*micros*) connect city centres with outlying neighbourhoods and smaller towns with villages. In some parts of Chile, especially in the north, *colectivos* (shared taxis with fixed fares) provide a faster and only slightly pricier service between towns than local buses.

By car

Car rental is costly (US$25–40 per day) and complicated, with expensive insurance due to the varying condition of the dirt roads; carrying spare tyres, a jack, extra petrol and plenty of drinking water is essential for driving around more remote parts of Chile; punctures are frequent. Since public transport is perfectly adequate in most parts of the country, the only place where it may make sense to rent a four-wheel-drive vehicle is on Easter Island. To rent a car, you need to be over 21 years old; take your passport as ID, and have a national driver's licence and major credit card on hand.

By bicycle

Cycling can be a good way of getting to the more remote national parks, some of which are inaccessible by public transport. It's a good idea to carry spare parts, although bike repair shops are found in most medium-sized towns. While in the south of Chile **drinking water** can typically be acquired from streams, in the northern half of the country, it is highly advisable to carry your own, and essential if cycling anywhere in the arid Atacama region. There are few cycle lanes and for the most part, cyclists share the road with motorists, though traffic outside cities tends to be light. Stray dogs can also be a nuisance in populated areas.

By ferry

South of Puerto Montt, where Chile breaks up into a plethora of islands and fjords, you will have to take a **ferry**, either to continue along the Carretera Austral or to work your way down to Southern Patagonia. Travelling south by boat is more expensive than going by bus, but it allows you access to some of the remotest and most beautiful parts of Chile. Popular routes include Puerto Montt to Puerto Natales, Puerto Montt to Chacabuco and Chacabuco to Laguna San Rafael.

Hitching

Hitchhiking is popular in Chile and widely practised by locals, especially in rural areas. While it's never an entirely safe method of travel, Chile is the safest country in Latin America to hitch, although it's always best to do so at least in pairs.

ACCOMMODATION

Chile has a wide range of **budget accommodation**, often great quality, occasionally not so great. Prices are highest during the peak season from December through February, when Chileans go on summer holiday; in shoulder seasons, they generally drop by around twenty percent. Many lodgings in the south of Chile close down during the winter months, so check ahead.

Residenciales, cabañas and refugios

Residenciales are the most commonly-available budget lodgings, found in both large cities and villages. Typically they consist of furnished rooms in someone's home, often with breakfast included; not surprisingly, the quality varies enormously. **Cabañas** are usually found in well-visited spots, particularly by the ocean. They tend to come with a fully-equipped kitchen, bathroom and bedrooms, and can be a great option for those travelling in groups. **Refugios** are cheap (except those in Torres del Paine National Park), bare-bones lodgings found in national parks, usually consisting of several bunk beds in a wooden hut; most have clean bedding, showers and flushable toilets; some require you to bring your own sleeping bag. Many *refugios* stay open year-round, but if you are planning on wilderness trekking, or on travelling in the south of Chile in the winter, try to arrange lodgings with the local **Conaf** office (Chile's national forestry service) in advance.

Hostels and camping

There is an increasing number of **youth hostels** around Chile, especially in well-visited cities and popular outdoor destinations. New places are often advertised by word of mouth or with brochures disseminated by fellow travellers from one hostel to another; some groups of independent hostels compile booklets of good hostels in Chile, and these are worth picking up. Good starting points for finding backpacker-oriented accommodation are Ⓦwww.hostelworld.com, www.hostelscentral.com and www .hostels.com. Also see Ⓦwww.hihostels .com for a comprehensive list of official HI-affiliated hostels worldwide which offer discounts to its members. Note that in some widely-visited places, such as Pucón and San Pedro de Atacama, a *hostal* may not necessarily mean a bona fide youth hostel – in many cases they simply turn out to be family homes.

Chile has marvellous opportunities for **camping**, with a proliferation of both fully-equipped campsites (which can be somewhat pricey) and beautiful wilderness spots. There is ample free camping on empty beaches, although in most national parks you should only camp in designated spots. *Campings y Rutas Chile*, published only in Spanish by Turistel, and updated annually, has an extensive, though not entirely complete, list of campsites around Chile.

COUCHSURFING

Couchsurfing is becoming more and more popular, especially with young budget travellers. Taking advantage of the free web-based hospitality service, Ⓦwww.couchsurfing.com, and staying in a local's home is an excellent way to immerse yourself in Chilean culture. After creating a profile on the site, you can search for hosts offering fellow travellers a free place to stay, with lodgings being particularly plentiful in Santiago and Valparaiso. When picking a host, look for the number of positive ratings and their rate of response to emails.

FOOD

Food in Chile can seem somewhat bland as, despite the abundance of fresh produce, few spices are used; exceptions are *pebre* (a spicy salsa served with bread) and *ají chileno*, served with barbecued meat. *Almuerzo* (**lunch**) is the main meal of the day, typically made up of three courses; at lunchtime most restaurants offer a good value fixed-price *menú del día*. *Desayuno* (**breakfast**) consists of *café con leche* and the ubiquitous pockmarked bread with butter and jam. *La comida* (**dinner**), served late, generally means lighter fare.

Chicken and beef are the commonest **meats**, the latter often served boiled or grilled with a fried egg on top (*lomo a la pobre*) or as part of a *parillada* (mixed grill). When in Patagonia, do not miss the *asador patagónico*, spit-roasted *cordero* (lamb) and *jibalí* (wild boar) steaks, while llama and alpaca steaks and stew are a staple of *altiplano* cuisine in the north of Chile. Both the island of Chiloé and Easter Island serve up *curanto*, an elaborately-prepared dish of meat and seafood.

There is a fantastic range of **fish and seafood**, and some of the best meals are to be had in informal little *marisquerías* attached to produce markets. Fish are typically served *frito* (battered and deep-fried), or *a la plancha* (grilled) with

STUDENT AND YOUTH DISCOUNTS

ISIC International Student or Youth cards can get you reduced air fares to Chile with travel agencies such as STA Travel. Some museums offer reduced student rates. It may also be possible to get **reduced bus fares** with certain bus companies; enquire in advance. Having a Hostelling International (HI) card is very worthwhile, since you can get member discounts in a network of hostels around Chile.

different sauces. Alternatively, try the *ceviche* – raw fish marinated in lemon juice with cilantro. Excellent seafood dishes include *machas a la parmesana*, baked razor clams covered with parmesan cheese, *chupe de locos*, creamy abalone casserole topped with breadcrumbs, and *paila marina*, seafood soup.

Excellent **fruit and vegetables** are abundant in most parts of Chile, barring Patagonia and Tierra del Fuego. The north of the country grows exotic delights like scaly green *chirimoya* (custard apple), *papaya*, *tuna* (cactus fruit) and melon-like *pepino dulce*. Easter Island cuisine incorporates Polynesian tubers such as the *camote* (sweet potato).

DRINK

Tap water is generally drinkable all over Chile, with the exception of the Atacama. Santiago tap water may upset some stomachs unaccustomed to the high mineral content. **Mineral water** is inexpensive and comes in two varieties: *sin gas* (still) and *con gas* (carbonated). *Gaseosas* or *bebidas* (**soft drinks**) are plentiful and very popular. Freshly-squeezed *jugos* (**fruit juices**) are abundant, especially in the fertile region of Middle Chile; beware that most Chileans like their juice sweetened, so if you don't want a half-juice, half-sugar concoction, ask for it *sin azúcar* (without sugar). *Licuados* are fruit smoothies mixed with water or *leche* (milk). *Mote con huesillo* – a drink made from boiled, dried apricots – is especially popular in Middle Chile.

It can be difficult to find real **coffee** (*café de grano*) in smaller towns, as Nescafe seems to be the drink of choice. In the Lake District and Patagonia, due to the proximity to Argentine culture, you are likely to encounter *yerba mate*, an antioxidant-rich, energizing herb drunk from a gourd through a metal straw.

Chile has several generic lager **beers** including Escudo, Cristal and Austral; the best beers are found in microbreweries, with Kunstmann being the pick of the bunch. Chileans start most meals with a pisco sour, a refreshing aperitif made from *pisco* (grape brandy) mixed with lemon jiuice, sugar syrup and sometimes a beaten egg white.

Chilean **wine**, renowned worldwide, features on many restaurant menus, though Chileans themselves seem to prefer beer. Wine tourism is also on the rise, with the Rutas del Vino (Wine Routes) in the Maule and Colchagua valleys giving visitors easy access to both the process of wine-making and the sampling of many different varieties.

CULTURE AND ETIQUETTE

Chilean city lifestyle, superficially at least, has more similarities with Europe than with neighbouring Bolivia. When eating out, a ten-percent **tip** in restaurants is normal and appreciated. Bargaining is not common and rarely done, even in marketplaces.

Chileans are family and **child-oriented**, and young people tend to live with their parents until they get married. The predominant religion is **Catholicism**, though the Church is not as influential as it used to be and Chile recently legalized divorce. Machismo is not as prevalent here as in other parts of Latin America; women are very much respected and a lone woman travelling around the country is not likely to encounter any trouble. While homosexuality is still frowned upon, it is tolerated, and there is a thriving gay scene in larger cities.

There is a **large income gap** between urban residents and the rural population, the marginalized indigenous tribes in particular. That said, native languages are making a comeback, and Chile's sizeable Mapuche population has been making successful claims to some of their ancestral lands.

Chileans are very **sociable** people and will go out of their way to greet you in the street if they know you. If going out with Chileans or invited to a Chilean home, it's polite to arrive half an hour after the agreed time. When it comes to topics of conversation, Pinochet's rule is still very much a divisive subject, so unless you wish to be drawn into a heated discussion, steer clear.

SPORTS AND OUTDOOR ACTIVITIES

Spectator sports

While Chile is not quite in the same league when it comes to **football** as Argentina or Brazil, the game is taken very seriously and attending a live match in Santiago (CH$10,000–15,000) is very worthwhile for the atmosphere alone. Amongst the Mapuche, the popular sport of *palín* resembles field hockey, though it's played barefoot and the games are preceded with a shaman-led ceremony.

Every year, over three hundred **rodeos** are staged during the September–May season in Middle Chile and Aisén in particular. Evolved from the rural *huaso* (cowboy) culture, the rodeo is a spectacle worth going out of your way for.

La cueca, Chile's national dance, is also firmly rooted in *huaso* culture; it re-enacts the courting ritual between a rooster and a hen. Men and women clad in traditional outfits dance largely to guitar-led ballads, though the tempo and the instruments vary from region to region.

Watersports

The mighty rivers of the Lake District and in Patagonia offer excellent **whitewater rafting** and **kayaking**, with Río Trancura, Río Petrohué and Río Futaleufú offering level V challenges. Futaleufú in particular is hailed as one of the top whitewater runs in the world.

Sea kayakers can choose between multi-day paddling in the frigid Patagonian fjords to shorter trips to small islands off the coast of Chiloé and wildlife viewing on Isla Damas near La Serena.

Surfers head to Chile's top spot, Pichilemu, just south of Santiago, though there are excellent **surfing** and **windsurfing** opportunities all along the coast north of the capital, around Iquique in particular, and year-round swells on Easter Island.

In the northern half of the country, lack of rain makes for good visibility and abundant marine life for **divers** and **snorkelers,** while Easter Island and the Juan Fernandez Archipelago both have world-class dive spots.

Hiking, cycling and the mountains

Hiking in the **Torres del Paine National Park**, on Isla Navarino or anywhere in the south is limited to the summer, spring and autumn, but the rest of Chile can be visited at any time of year. There are twenty-five *Rutas Patrimoniales* (Ⓦwww.bienes.gob.cl/rutas/) covering the whole of Chile as part of a government initiative to preserve and develop land that has natural and historical value. These can all be explored on foot, by bike or on horseback. Another ambitious project, *Senderos de Chile* (Ⓦwww.senderodechile.cl), due to be completed in 2010, consists of thirty-five trail sections intended to span the whole of Chile, including its Pacific islands. Once completed, it will become the longest trekking route in the world.

Ice climbers will find excellent **climbing routes** in the Central and Patagonian Andes from November through March, with plenty of accessible glaciers, while the granite towers of Torres del Paine rank among the world's most challenging rock climbs. Middle Chile and the Lake District, however, have the greatest variety of climbing and mountaineering spots.

Along with Argentina, Chile boasts world-class powder snow, with some of the best **skiing** spots found in easy reach of Santiago (see p.436). The Lake District's Villarica-Pucón and Osorno give you the opportunity to whizz down the slopes of volcanoes.

Spectacular **biking terrain** can be found from Norte Grande to Tierra del Fuego, though you will need a sturdy mountain bike to cope with the potholed trails. While the best time to cycle around much of Chile is between October and March, Norte Chico and Norte Grande can be explored year-round, though altitude is often a consideration, especially if you're planning on exploring Parque Nacional Lauca. Norte Chico offers easy and enjoyable coastal rides, while the Lake District and Chiloé have the greatest variety of cycling routes, and the Carretera Austral is a challenging undertaking that rewards with amazing scenery.

COMMUNICATIONS

Overseas mail sent from any part of Chile via **Correos de Chile**, Chile's postal service, generally takes two or three weeks to reach its destination, while FedEx and DHL provide express courier services. Important shipping to Chile is best sent via registered mail. The larger post offices have a *lista de correos* (alphabetical list) for collecting *poste restante* (general delivery); since Chileans generally have two surnames, a foreigner's middle initial might mistakenly be filed as the first letter of the surname.

Chile has about ten different telecoms operators, and in order to make an **international call**, you dial the three-digit carrier code of the telecom, followed by 0, then the country code and finally the phone number itself. Most local numbers consist of six or seven digits, preceded by the city/area code; if dialing from the same area, drop the city or area code and dial the six or seven digits directly. Mobile phone numbers start with 07, 08 or 09, followed by seven digits; drop the 0 when calling mobile-to-mobile. To call a different area code you would dial the carrier code, followed by the area code, followed by the number. Calls abroad from the numerous *centros de llamadas* to most European countries and North America cost around CH$100/min, although prices vary from area to area. Setting up a Skype account is cheap and convenient, as many internet cafés in Chile are Skype-equipped; a Skype call to Europe or the US costs around CH$10/min. Alternatively, getting a Chilean SIM card for an "unlocked" mobile phone costs around CH$5000, and all incoming calls are free.

CARRIER CODES

Entel 123
Telefónica 188
Telefónica del Sur 121
Telefónica Manquehue 122
Telmex 171
VTR 111

EMERGENCY NUMBERS

Air rescue ⓣ138 (for mountaineering accidents)
Ambulance ⓣ131
Coast Guard ⓣ137
Fire ⓣ132
Investigaciónes ⓣ134 (for serious crimes)
Police ⓣ133

CHILE ON THE NET

Ⓦ**www.sernatur.cl** the official website of Chile's government-run tourist board, has facts about regional attractions, places to stay and restaurants.

Ⓦ**www.conaf.cl** offers information on Chile's protected natural areas (in Spanish only).

Ⓦ**www.turismochile.cl** gives descriptions of regional attractions (mostly in Spanish).

Ⓦ**www.conadi.cl** is a site for indigenous affairs (Spanish only).

Ⓦ**www.gaychile.com** gives up-to-date information on gay nightlife and more.

Ⓦ**www.transantiago.cl**, **www.metrosantiago.cl** and **www.efe.cl** offer the latest on transportation.

Ⓦ**www.dibam.cl** gives thorough information on cultural attractions and museums.

Internet is widely available across Chile. Most towns and villages have broadband-equipped **internet cafés**, at a cost of around CH$500 per hr, although on Isla Navarino and Easter Island it is considerably pricier.

EMERGENCIES

The risk of **violent crime** in Chile is very low; in larger cities pickpocketing and petty thievery are minor concerns, but assaults are practically unknown. There is little corruption among Chile's police, and the sort of highway robberies that blight neighbouring countries are very rare.

There are no compulsory **vaccinations** for Chile, though there have been reported incidents of mosquito-borne **dengue fever** on Easter Island; use insect repellent. Hantavirus, caused by inhaling or ingesting rat droppings, is uncommon but deadly. When staying in rural buildings that could potentially have rodents, air them out thoroughly and do not sleep on the floor. Chile has two **spiders** whose bite is venomous and potentially dangerous, especially for old people, children and people with health problems: the Black Widow and the Funnelweb. Black Widows are outdoor spiders – small and black with distinctive red hourglass marking, and found in parts of Torres del Paine National Park, among other areas. Funnelwebs live in dusty corners of buildings and are an unremarkable brown in colour. Both spiders will bite only if cornered.

INFORMATION AND MAPS

Official **Sernatur** tourist offices (Servicio Nacionál de Turismo, Ⓦwww.sernatur.cl) are found in all the major cities and towns. They produce a plethora of brochures on local attractions, accommodation and outdoor activities, though some are better-stocked than others.

For information on Chile's natural attractions, as well as maps and up-to-date trekking conditions in a specific area, you should head to the local **Conaf** office (Corporación Nacionál Forestál, Ⓦwww.conaf.cl), again found in most towns. Some Conaf offices sell the complete guide to Chile's National Parks, Reserves and Monuments, which has plenty of factual information, although the maps of the parks are not very helpful. For up-to-date **maps of national parks**, seek out the Copec National Park guide, sold in petrol stations in conjunction with their Chile road guide, which includes helpful city maps.

JLM Cartografía maps are found in most bookshops; they cover both cities and trekking routes in Chile and tend to be accurate and helpful. The Instituto Geográfico Militar (Ⓦwww.igm.cl) produces detailed topographic maps of the entire country, but they can be pricey. **TurisTel guidebooks** (Ⓦwww.turistel.cl), published by Telefónica Chile, are an excellent source of information on the country (in Spanish); they come in three volumes, covering the south, middle Chile and Santiago, and the north, updated annually. TurisTel also produces a series of bilingual area-specific guides to major attractions, such as Pucón, Chiloé and Torres del Paine; these are also updated annually and sold in many bookshops.

MONEY AND BANKS

The **peso** is the basic unit of Chilean currency, and it comes in 1000, 5000, 10,000 and rare 20,000 denomination notes, and 10, 20, 50, 100 and 500 peso coins. It is usually represented with the $ sign, not to be confused with $US. Very few places will accept US dollars or other foreign currencies. Chile is fairly expensive compared to its Latin American counterparts (besides Brazil), with prices comparable to those in North America and Europe.

There are numerous **banks** and **ATMs** in large and medium-sized cities; Banco de Chile and Santander are good bets for withdrawing cash with debit cards. **Credit cards** can also be widely used to pay for purchases, especially in larger towns; however budget lodgings and eateries rarely accept them. Some smaller towns (and Easter Island) only have a Banco Estado ATM, which accepts just Cirrus and MasterCard. Wherever you go, it's wise to carry enough cash to cover a few days, and in smaller towns to carry plenty of loose change. Santiago and some of the more visited destinations have *casas de cambio* which can change traveller's cheques and foreign currencies at a reasonable rate.

OPENING HOURS AND HOLIDAYS

On weekdays, most services and shops tend to be open from 9am to 1pm, then between 3pm and 6 or 7pm; Saturday hours are usually 10 or 11am to 2pm. In smaller towns, restaurants are often closed in the afternoon, between the lunchtime hours of 1 to 3pm and the dinnertime hours of 8 to 11pm. Banks have shorter opening hours, typically closing at 2pm on weekdays, while post offices do not break for a siesta and close around 1pm on Saturdays. Monday is a day off for most museums, which are open on Sundays instead, often with free entry. Shops and services are closed during national holidays, local festivals and on local and national election days.

PUBLIC HOLIDAYS

January 1 New Year's Day (*Año Nuevo*)

Easter, late March to late April (Semana Santa) with national holidays on Good Friday, Holy Saturday and Easter Sunday

May 1 Labour Day (*Día del Trabajo*)

May 21 Navy Day (*Día de las Glorias Navales*) marking Chile's naval victory at Iquique during the War of the Pacific

June 29 St Peter and St Paul (*San Pedro y San Pablo*)

July 16 Our Lady of Mount Carmel (*Solemnidad de la Virgen del Carmen, Reina y Patrona de Chile*)

August 15 Assumption of the Virgin Mary (*Asunción de la Virgen*)

September 17 If it falls on a Monday, an extension of Independence celebrations.

September 18 National Independence Day (*Fiestas Patrias*) celebrates Chile's proclamation of independence from Spain in 1810

September 19 Armed Forces Day (*Día del Ejército*)

September 20 If it falls on a Friday, an extension of Independence celebrations

October 12 Columbus Day (*Día del Descubrimiento de Dos Mundos*) celebrates the European discovery of the Americas

November 1 All Saints' Day (*Día de Todos los Santos*)

December 8 Immaculate Conception (*Inmaculada Concepción*)

December 25 Christmas Day (*Navidad*)

Santiago

While not a destination in itself, **SANTIAGO** is an easy city to arrive in and a pleasant place to spend a day or two. Home to over a quarter of Chile's population, the capital is a mix of elegant colonial buildings and multistorey, concrete constructions, all set in a "bowl" surrounded by snow-streaked mountains, with smog that infamously hangs over the city for much of the year. Public transport is excellent and Santiago's compact centre is easy to navigate on foot.

Plaza de Armas

Pedro de Valdivia, the city's founder, intended the lush tree-studded **Plaza de Armas** to be the epicentre of Chile, surrounding it with splendid colonial architecture. The oldest building on the west side of the plaza is the **Catedral Metropolitana** (1748), its neoclassical facade designed by the Italian architect Joaquín Toesca. To the north is the **Palacio de la Real Audiencia** (1804), housing the Museo Histórico Nacional and the **Correo Central**. A lively gathering point since the mid-1800s, the plaza's flower gardens and the fountain in the centre honouring Simón Bolívar attract a multitude of chess players, lovers, buskers, vagrants, stray dogs, soap-box preachers, strolling families and giggling children, making the square an ideal place to linger on a bench and people-watch.

Mercado Central and La Vega

Three blocks north of the Plaza de Armas, by the south bank of Río Mapocho, lies the lively **Mercado Central** (daily 6am–4pm), a mass of stalls spilling over with wondrous fish and seafood, dotted with busy little *marisquerías* whose delicious smells draw crowds of customers at lunchtime. All of this is gathered inside an elaborate metal structure prefabricated in Birmingham, England, and erected in Santiago in 1868. Cross the Río Mapocho and you reach **La Vega**, an enormous roofed market surrounded by outdoor stalls, selling all kinds of fresh produce, with fruit and vegetables at rock bottom prices. La Vega is full of local character, giving you a glimpse of "real" Santiago, fragrant, pungent and chaotic; it is also the best place in town to grab a giant fruit smoothie.

Museo Chileno de Arte Precolombino

A block east from the southwest corner of the Plaza de Armas along Compañía, at Bandera 361, is the excellent **Museo Chileno de Arte Precolombino** (Mon 10am–2pm, Tues–Sun 10am–6pm; CH$3000, Sundays and students free; free guided tours Tues–Fri at 5pm; ⓦwww.museoprecolombino.cl), housed in the elegant late colonial Real Casa de Aduana (Royal Customs House, 1807). The unparalleled collection of pre-Columbian artefacts spans a time period of around ten thousand years and covers the whole of Latin America, from Mexico down to the south of Chile. Over 1500 examples of pottery, finely woven textiles and jewellery are on display, including permanent collections from the Andes, Mesoamerica, the Amazon and the Caribbean, as well as outstanding temporary exhibitions.

La Moneda

Stroll south down Bandera for two blocks, then a block east along Agustinas to reach the large **Plaza de la Constitución**, facing the restored **Palacio de la Moneda**. La Moneda is the presidential palace and site of the dramatic siege that brought Pinochet to power on September 11, 1973, and led to the death of President Salvador Allende. A wide, squat neoclassical construction, originally built to house the Royal Mint, the palace stages an elaborate changing

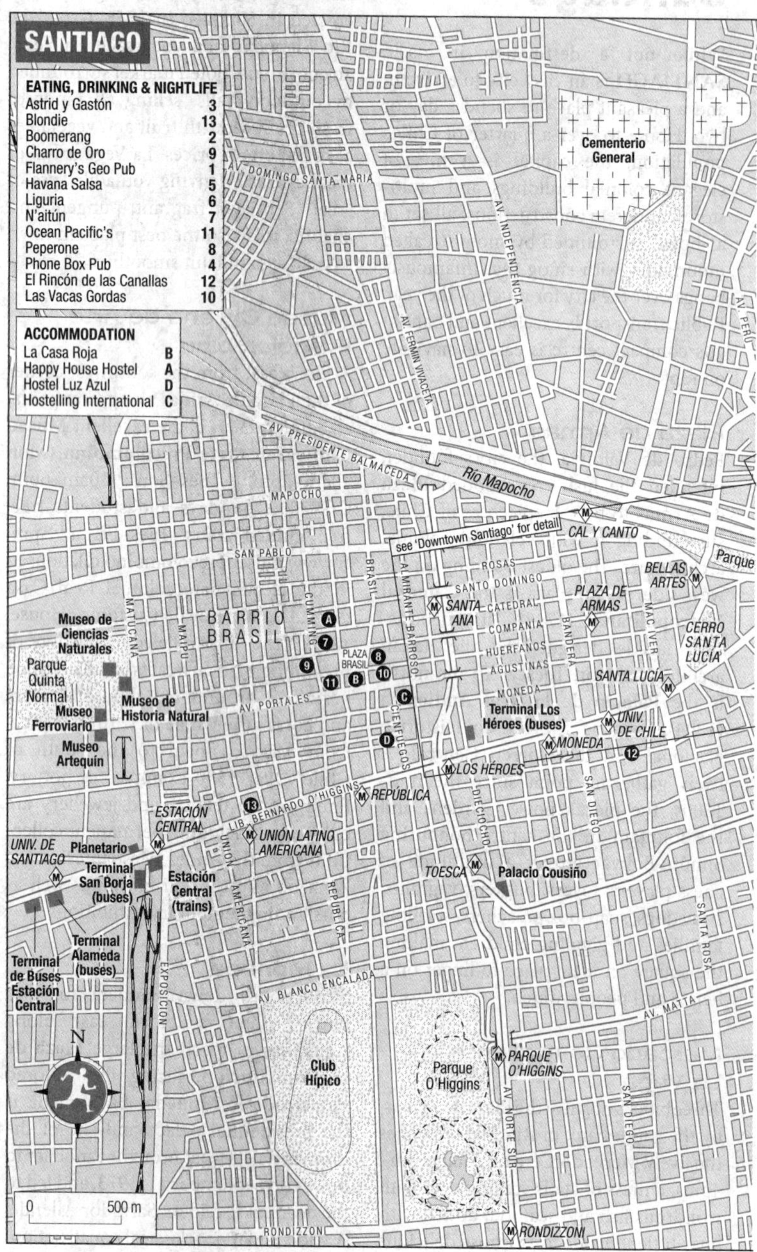
SANTIAGO
EATING, DRINKING & NIGHTLIFE
Astrid y Gastón 3
Blondie 13
Boomerang 2
Charro de Oro 9
Flannery's Geo Pub 1
Havana Salsa 5
Liguria 6
N'aitún 7
Ocean Pacific's 11
Peperone 8
Phone Box Pub 4
El Rincón de las Canallas 12
Las Vacas Gordas 10
ACCOMMODATION
La Casa Roja B
Happy House Hostel A
Hostel Luz Azul D
Hostelling International C
Cementerio General
AV. DOMINGO SANTA MARÍA
AV. INDEPENDENCIA
AV. FERMIN VIVACETA
AV. PERÚ
AV. PRESIDENTE BALMACEDA
Río Mapocho
MAPOCHO
see 'Downtown Santiago' for detail
CAL Y CANTO
Parque
SAN PABLO
ROSAS
SANTO DOMINGO
CATEDRAL
COMPAÑÍA
HUÉRFANOS
AGUSTINAS
MONEDA
BELLAS ARTES
PLAZA DE ARMAS
CERRO SANTA LUCÍA
SANTA LUCÍA
SANTA ANA
BRASIL
CUMMING
ALMIRANTE BARROSO
BANDERA
MAC IVER
BARRIO BRASIL
PLAZA BRASIL
MATUCANA
MAIPÚ
Museo de Ciencias Naturales
Parque Quinta Normal
Museo de Historia Natural
Museo Ferroviario
Museo Artequín
AV. PORTALES
CIENFUEGOS
Terminal Los Héroes (buses)
UNIV. DE CHILE
MONEDA
LOS HÉROES
REPÚBLICA
LIB. BERNARDO O'HIGGINS
DIECIOCHO
SAN DIEGO
ESTACIÓN CENTRAL
UNIÓN LATINO AMERICANA
UNIV. DE SANTIAGO
Planetario
Terminal San Borja (buses)
Estación Central (trains)
UNIÓN AMERICANA
REPÚBLICA
TOESCA
Palacio Cousiño
SANTA ROSA
Terminal Alameda (buses)
Terminal de Buses Estación Central
EXPOSICIÓN
AV. BLANCO ENCALADA
AV. MATTA
N
Club Hípico
Parque O'Higgins
PARQUE O'HIGGINS
AV. NORTE SUR
SAN DIEGO
0
500 m
RONDIZZONI
RONDIZZONI

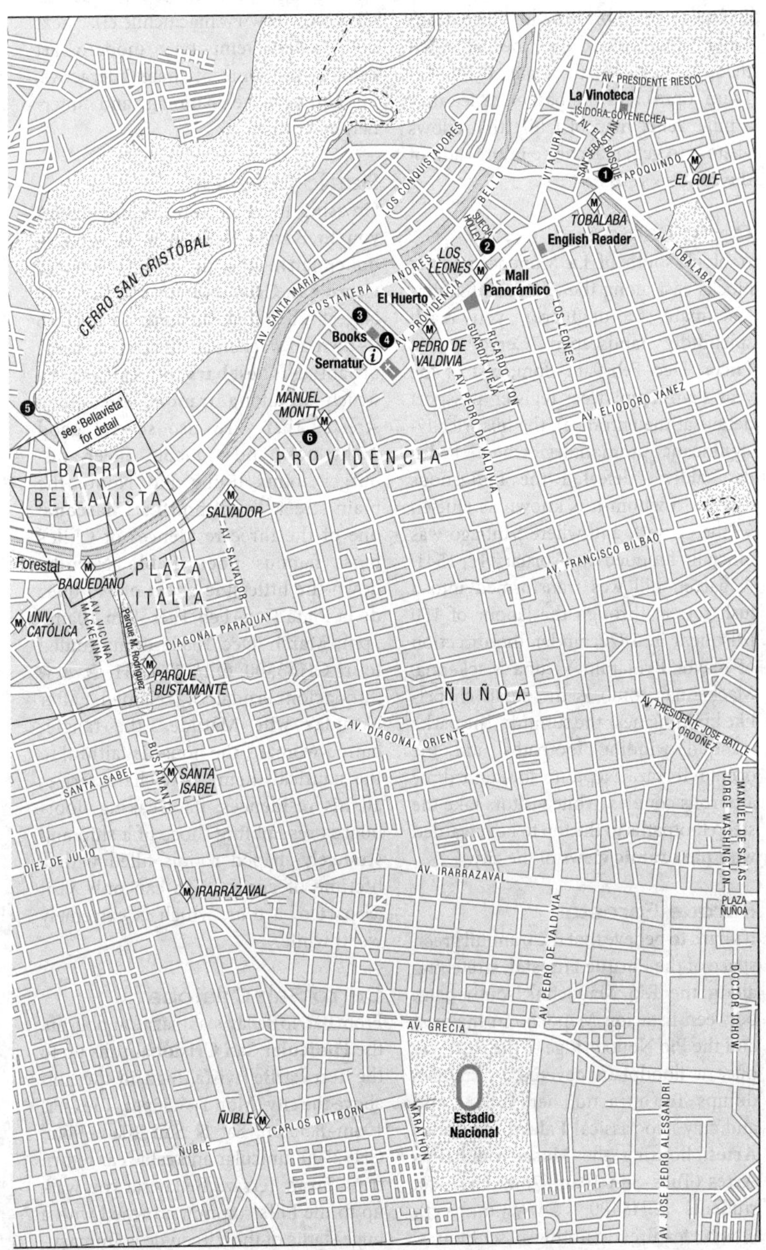
CERRO SAN CRISTÓBAL
La Vinoteca
AV. PRESIDENTE RIESCO
ISIDORA GOYENECHEA
AV. EL BOSQUE
SAN SEBASTIÁN
VITACURA
APOQUINDO
EL GOLF
TOBALABA
AV. TOBALABA
English Reader
SUECIA
HOLLEY
BELLO
LOS CONQUISTADORES
LOS LEONES
Mall
Panorámico
El Huerto
AV. PROVIDENCIA
ANDRES
COSTANERA
AV. SANTA MARIA
Books
Sernatur
PEDRO DE VALDIVIA
RICARDO LYON
GUARDIA VIEJA
AV. PEDRO DE VALDIVIA
MANUEL MONTT
AV. ELIODORO YANEZ
see 'Bellavista' for detail
BARRIO BELLAVISTA
PROVIDENCIA
SALVADOR
AV. SALVADOR
AV. FRANCISCO BILBAO
Forestal
BAQUEDANO
PLAZA ITALIA
UNIV. CATÓLICA
AV. VICUÑA MACKENNA
Parque M. Rodríguez
DIAGONAL PARAGUAY
PARQUE BUSTAMANTE
ÑUÑOA
AV. PRESIDENTE JOSÉ BATLLE Y ORDOÑEZ
AV. DIAGONAL ORIENTE
BUSTAMANTE
SANTA ISABEL
JORGE WASHINGTON
MANUEL DE SALAS
DIEZ DE JULIO
AV. IRARRAZAVAL
IRARRÁZAVAL
PLAZA ÑUÑOA
AV. PEDRO DE VALDIVIA
DOCTOR JOHOW
AV. GRECIA
Estadio Nacional
MARATHON
ÑUBLE
CARLOS DITTBORN
AV. JOSE PEDRO ALESSANDRI

of the guard every other day at 10am, featuring white-jacketed officers, cavalry and an inspired brass band. The palace's inner courtyards can be accessed through the North Gate (Mon–Fri 10am–6pm) and the basement features a huge relief map of Chile that allows visitors to get an accurate impression of the country's size.

Cerro Santa Lucía

A block south of La Moneda, and six blocks east along the Alameda (Santiago's main thoroughfare), you reach splendidly landscaped **Cerro Santa Lucía** (Dec–Feb 9am–8pm; rest of the year 9am–7pm; free; register passport details at the entrance), the historically-significant promontory where Pedro de Valdivia defeated the indigenous forces (to whom it is known as Huelén – "the curse"), and where Santiago was officially founded on February 12, 1541. A barren hill was transformed into a lush retreat through the labour of 150 prisoners in 1872, under the direction of mayor Benjamín Vicuña Mackenna. Mackenna's tomb is the small chapel-like building near the summit. The park's tranquil winding footpaths and the ornate Terraza Neptuno fountain draw amorous couples, while visitors take the steep footpaths to the top to be rewarded with **panoramic views** of the city.

Parque Forestal

It's hard to believe that the tranquil green space of the **Parque Forestal**, stretching along the Río Mapocho's south bank between Estación Mapocho in the west and the Pío Nono bridge to the east, was once a floodplain covered in rubbish dumps. Top attraction here is the grand and airy neoclassical **Palacio de Bellas Artes**, housing the **Museo de Bellas Artes** (Tues–Sun 10am–7pm; CH$600, students CH$400; Ⓦwww.mnba.cl), which features paintings, sculptures, prints and drawings by predominantly Chilean artists. The **Museo de Arte Contemporáneo** (Tues–Sat 11am–7pm, Sun 11am–6pm; CH$600, students CH$400; Ⓦwww.mac.uchile.cl), next door, offers temporary modern art exhibitions, some of them interactive, by cutting-edge national and international artists.

Barrio Bellavista

Crossing the Pío Nono bridge brings you to **Barrio Bellavista**, the trendy bohemian neighbourhood at the foot of **Cerro San Cristóbal**, the city's second largest hill. Bellavista really comes into its own on weekends; it's home to some of Santiago's best **bars** and **restaurants**, which sit along tranquil, tree-lined streets. There are also several good nightclubs and raucous beer-and-burger joints lining Pío Nono, the main street. You'll find **La Chascona**, one of the three residences of Chile's most famous poet, **Pablo Neruda**, down the little side-street of Márquez de la Plata (Jan–Feb Tues–Sun 10am–7pm; March–Dec 10am–6pm; guided tours CH$3500; Ⓣ2/777-8741, Ⓦwww.fundacionneruda.cl). Named after Neruda's wife Matilde, "the tangle-haired woman", the house is faithful to the nautical theme that characterizes all his residences, its creaking floorboards resembling those of a ship and strangely-shaped rooms filled with a lifetime of curios. You can only visit as part of a tour, which is extremely worthwhile.

Cerro San Cristóbal

From Barrio Bellavista's Plaza Caupolicán, the **Funicular San Cristóbal** runs up to the Terraza Bellavista, high in the hills above the city (Mon 1–8.30pm, Tues–Fri 10am–8.30pm, Sat & Sun 10am–9pm; CH$2500 funicular and cable car return trip). From Terraza Bellavista you walk up to the hill's summit, crowned with a huge statue of the Virgen de la Immaculada Concepción and offering excellent views of the city, though the outlying

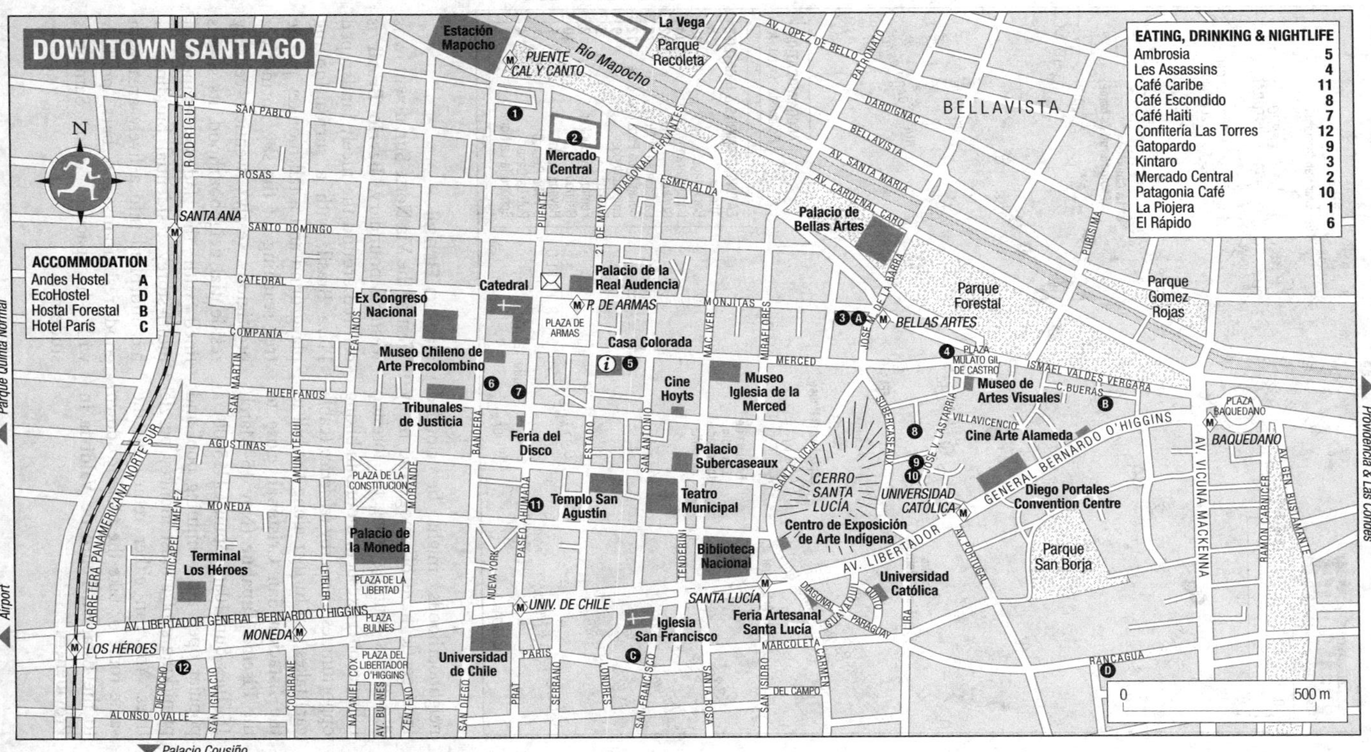
DOWNTOWN SANTIAGO
ACCOMMODATION
Andes Hostel A
EcoHostel D
Hostal Forestal B
Hotel París C
EATING, DRINKING & NIGHTLIFE
Ambrosia 5
Les Assassins 4
Café Caribe 11
Café Escondido 8
Café Haiti 7
Confitería Las Torres 12
Gatopardo 9
Kintaro 3
Mercado Central 2
Patagonia Café 10
La Piojera 1
El Rápido 6
N
0
500 m
Providencia & Las Condes
Parque Quinta Normal
Airport
Palacio Cousiño
Estación Mapocho
PUENTE CAL Y CANTO
Río Mapocho
La Vega
Parque Recoleta
BELLAVISTA
Mercado Central
Palacio de Bellas Artes
Parque Forestal
Parque Gomez Rojas
Catedral
Palacio de la Real Audencia
P. DE ARMAS
PLAZA DE ARMAS
Ex Congreso Nacional
Museo Chileno de Arte Precolombino
Casa Colorada
Cine Hoyts
Museo Iglesia de la Merced
BELLAS ARTES
PLAZA MULATO GIL DE CASTRO
Museo de Artes Visuales
PLAZA BAQUEDANO
BAQUEDANO
Tribunales de Justicia
Feria del Disco
Palacio Subercaseaux
CERRO SANTA LUCÍA
UNIVERSIDAD CATÓLICA
Cine Arte Alameda
Diego Portales Convention Centre
Templo San Agustín
Teatro Municipal
Centro de Exposición de Arte Indígena
Parque San Borja
PLAZA DE LA CONSTITUCIÓN
Palacio de la Moneda
Biblioteca Nacional
Universidad Católica
Terminal Los Héroes
PLAZA DE LA LIBERTAD
UNIV. DE CHILE
SANTA LUCÍA
Iglesia San Francisco
Feria Artesanal Santa Lucía
PLAZA BULNES
MONEDA
LOS HÉROES
PLAZA DEL LIBERTADOR O'HIGGINS
Universidad de Chile
SANTA ANA
AV. LOPEZ DE BELLO
PATRONATO
DARDIGNAC
BELLAVISTA
AV. SANTA MARIA
AV. CARDENAL CARO
PURISIMA
SAN PABLO
RODRIGUEZ
ROSAS
SANTO DOMINGO
CATEDRAL
COMPAÑIA
HUERFANOS
AGUSTINAS
MONEDA
DIAGONAL CERVANTES
ESMERALDA
PUENTE
21 DE MAYO
MONJITAS
MERCED
TEATINOS
SAN MARTIN
AMUNATEGUI
MORANDE
BANDERA
ESTADO
SAN ANTONIO
MAC IVER
MIRAFLORES
JOSE M. DE LA BARRA
ISMAEL VALDES VERGARA
C. BUERAS
VILLAVICENCIO
JOSE V. LASTARRIA
SUBERCASEAUX
SANTA LUCIA
AV. VICUNA MACKENNA
RAMON CARNICER
AV. GEN. BUSTAMANTE
GENERAL BERNARDO O'HIGGINS
AV. LIBERTADOR
AV. PORTUGAL
LIRA
QUITO
PARAGUAY
GUAYAQUIL
DIAGONAL
CARRETERA PANAMERICANA NORTE SUR
TUCAPEL JIMENEZ
LETELLER
NUEVA YORK
PASEO AHUMADA
TENDERINI
AV. LIBERTADOR GENERAL BERNARDO O'HIGGINS
PARIS
MARCOLETA
CARMEN
RANCAGUA
DIECIOCHO
SAN IGNACIO
ALONSO OVALLE
COCHRANE
NATANIEL COX
AV. BULNES
ZENTENO
SAN DIEGO
PRAT
SERRANO
LONDRES
SAN FRANCISCO
SANTA ROSA
SAN ISIDRO
DEL CAMPO

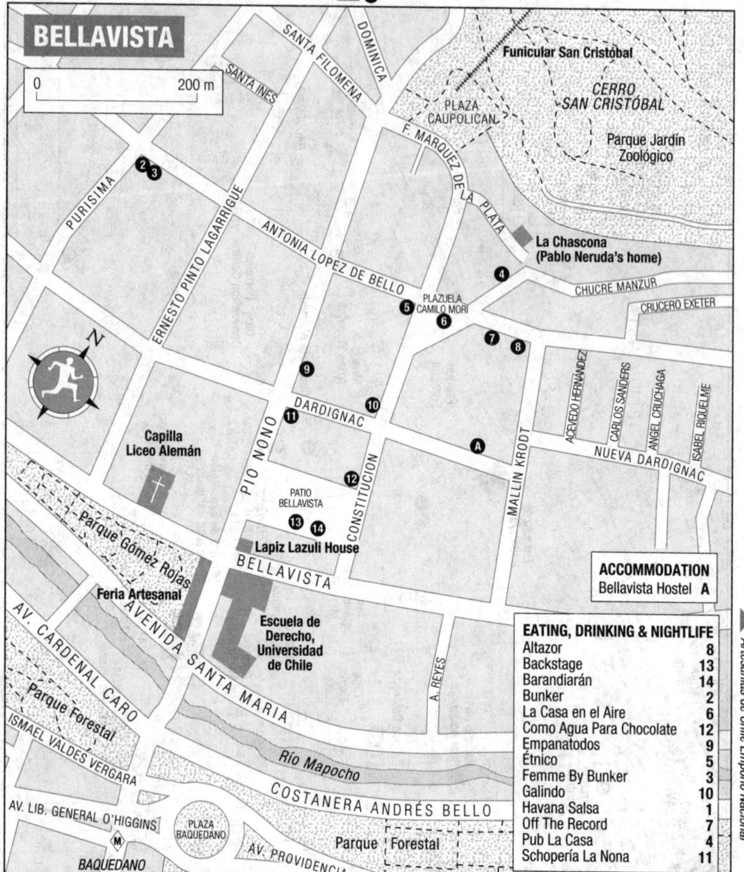

neighbourhoods might be clouded in a gentle haze of smog. The many dirt tracks running along the forested hillsides offer excellent mountain biking opportunities. A nearby *teleférico* (cable car) takes you further along the hill to the **Estación San Cristóbal**, close to the **Piscina Tupahue** (Nov 15–March 15 Tues–Sun 10am–6pm; CH$5000) a popular open air swimming pool and picnicking spot amidst monkey puzzle trees. You can either return by the same route or take the *teleférico* down to the **Estación Pedro de Valdivia** in Providencia.

Barrio Brasil

West of the Vía Norte Sur, downtown's western boundary, **Barrio Brasil** is centred around the nicely landscaped Plaza Brasil, with a surreal-looking playground and a tall monkey puzzle tree reaching for the sky. Formerly a prestigious, early twentieth-century residential neighbourhood, its streets lined with the faded elegance of multi-storey residential buildings, it has morphed into a lively area with good restaurants and bars, popular with backpackers and Santiago's students.

Ñuñoa

Southeast of central Santiago, the laid-back neighbourhood of **Ñuñoa**, with the attractive **Plaza Ñuñoa** at its heart, is overlooked by many visitors to the city, though it has a **lively nightlife** due to the proximity of two university campuses. Football fans also flock here to watch the matches at the **Estadio Nacional**, at Av Grecia 2001. The stadium has a grim past – it was once used by Pinochet as a torture centre and prison.

Arrival and information

Airport Aeropuerto Arturo Merino Benítez (Ⓣ 2/690-1900, Ⓦ www.aeropuertosantiago.cl), half an hour from the city centre, has useful facilities including ATMs, currency exchange, tourist information kiosk and mobile phone rentals. The blue Centropuerto bus (daily 6am–10.30pm; CH$1600 one-way), just outside the terminal doors, is the cheapest way to get to the city centre and stops at the Los Héroes metro station. Tur Bus has transfers to the Terminal Alameda (daily, every 30min 6.30am–9pm; CH$1700), while TransVip (Ⓣ 2/677-3000) and Tur Transfer (Ⓣ 2/677-3600) charge CH$5000 to drop you off at your destination.

Buses International buses arrive at either the Terminal Buses Estación Central (Ⓣ 2/376-1755), at Alameda 3850, near the Universidad de Santiago metro station, or at the Terminal Alameda next door, at Alameda 3750, served by Pullman and Tur Bus (Ⓣ 2/270-7424). The two terminals have ATMs, snack shops and luggage storage, as well as easy access to public transport along Alameda. Buses from northern and central Chile use Terminal San Borja (Ⓣ 2/776-0645), at San Borja 184, near the Estación Central metro station, while the smaller Terminal Los Héroes (Ⓣ 2/420-0099), at Tucapel Jiménez 21, near the Los Heroés metro station, serves a variety of destinations in both northern and southern Chile.

Conaf has an office at Av Bulnes 291 (Mon–Fri 9am–1pm & 2–4.30pm; Ⓣ 2/390-0282, Ⓦ www.conaf.cl) which provides information on national parks and reserves, as well as some pamphlets and inexpensive maps.

Tourist offices The main Sernatur office is at Av Providencia 1550, near the Manuel Montt metro station, east of the city centre (Mon–Fri 9am–5.45pm, Sat 9am–2pm; Ⓣ 2/731-8300, Ⓦ www.sernatur.cl). It provides maps of the city and is well-stocked with brochures on the surrounding area. An Oficina de Turismo inside the Casa Colorada, at Merced 860 (Ⓣ 2/632-7783), half a block east of the Plaza de Armas, has friendly and helpful staff offering information on downtown attractions. For entertainment listings, check Friday's "Recitales" page in *El Mercurio* or in *La Tercera* (Santiago's main newspapers).

Trains Estación Central, at Alameda 3322 (Ⓣ 2/376-8500, Ⓦ www.efe.clis), is served by TerraSur trains from various destinations in Middle Chile.

City transport

Buses Fleets of gleaming new white-and-green **"TransSantiago"** buses run around the city. To use them, you need to purchase a **"BIP" transit card**, sold in most metro ticket booths, which you can then add credit to (at the same booths). Bus destinations are posted on window signs and at marked stops; a standard fare is CH$380. "BIP" cards can be used on the metro as well.

Colectivos Slightly pricier than buses, *colectivos* have their destinations displayed on their roofs and carry passengers on fixed itineraries, reaching their destination slightly quicker than regular transport, though you need to know where you are going; useful for destinations outside the city centre.

Metro Metro (Mon–Sat 6.30am–10.30pm, Sun 8am–10.30pm) is the quickest way to get around the city, with just five lines that are easy to navigate, though it gets rather cramped during rush hour. Buy tickets from the ticket booths inside the stations; they are valid for any length of journey. The orange *unitario* ticket is valid at rush hours (7.15am–9am & 6–7:30pm CH$420); the rest of the time you use green *unitario rebajado* stubs (CH$360). Buy as many tickets as you anticipate using to avoid having to stand in line each time you travel.

Accommodation

There are a number of accommodation options in Santiago to suit budget travellers although really cheap places are scarce. Good inexpensive lodgings can mostly be found in the city centre and Barrio Brasil.

Central Santiago

Andes Hostel Monjitas 506, Metro Bellas Artes Ⓣ 2/633-1976, Ⓦ www.andeshostel.com. Excellent, centrally-located hostel popular with younger travellers, with modern decor, spotless, bright dorms complete with individual lockers and a whole range of facilities – guest kitchen, lounge with pool table and cable TV, free internet, laundry service and a fully-stocked bar. Dorm CH$8000–8500. 5

EcoHostel General Jofré 349B, Metro Universidad Católica ⓣ2/222-6833, ⓦwww.ecohostel.cl. With its clean and spacious dorms, chilled-out common areas and fully-equipped guest kitchen, this hostel and its environment-friendly ethic attracts mostly younger travellers. Lockers, internet, good breakfast and knowledgeable bilingual staff are a big plus. Dorm CH$8000.

Hostal Forestal Coronel Santiago Bueras 120, Metro Baquedano ⓣ2/638-1347, ⓦwww.hostalforestal.cl. Perpetually popular, *Hostal Forestal* throws impromptu barbecues and the friendly bilingual staff can advise on sightseeing. Luggage storage, outdoor patio, guest kitchen and lounge with cable TV are some of the perks, but the lone single room is very basic, rather noisy and overpriced for what it is. Dorm CH$7000-12,000. 5

Hotel París París 813, Metro Universidad de Chile ⓣ2/664-0921, ⓔcarbott@latinmail.com. Atmospheric, centrally-located budget hotel with a newer annexe featuring comfortable rooms and spotless bathrooms, with cheaper rooms to suit backpackers. Continental breakfast CH$1500 extra. 4

Bellavista

The Bellavista Hostel Dardignac 184, Metro Bellavista ⓣ2/732-8737, ⓦwww.bellavistahostel.com. It's easy to see why this hostel is extremely popular with younger travellers – a stone's throw from some of Santiago's best eating and nightlife, it's cosy, colourful, run by a helpful bilingual staff and has all the standard backpacker conveniences. 6

Barrio Brasil

La Casa Roja Agustinas 2113, Metro Los Héroes ⓣ2/696-4241, ⓦwww.lacasaroja.cl. Sprawling Aussie-owned, converted mansion firmly established as backpacker party central, with spacious dorms and rooms, complete with jacuzzi and poolside barbecues; large common areas, free internet, kitchen, on-site travel agency and Spanish language school make this a top budget choice, though not a place to catch up on your sleep. Dorm CH$6500. 4

Happy House Hostel Catedral 2207, Metro Cumming ⓣ2/688-4849, ⓦwww.happyhousehostel.cl. Travellers are made to feel really welcome at this beautifully-decorated, spacious guesthouse, with large rooms, attractive common areas, pool table, guest kitchen and bar, and a sauna alongside the rooftop patio. Breakfast and internet included. Dorm CH$11,500. 6

Hostel Luz Azul Santa Mónica 1924, Metro Los Héroes ⓣ2/696-4856, ⓦwww.luzazulhostel.com. Brand-new hostel with a bright, appealing interior, laid-back atmosphere and helpful staff, as well as impromptu barbecues on the upstairs patio, kitchen privileges, free Internet, wi-fi and Playstation 2 use. Dorm CH$7000–9000. 5

Hostelling International Cienfuegos 151, Metro Los Heroés ⓣ2/671-8532, ⓦwww.hisantiago.cl. Large, professionally-run, three-storey hostel with clean dorms, plush bunk beds, spacious dining room and bonuses including on-site travel agency, internet and wi-fi, book exchange, breakfast and laundry service. Dorm CH$6500–8500. 5

Eating

Santiago has a proliferation of restaurants. Most are concentrated in Downtown, Bellavista and Providencia, with some good options, popular with backpackers and students, in Barrio Brasil.

Downtown

Ambrosia Merced 838. Trendy little eatery serving up a selection of well-executed Peruvian, Italian and French dishes; those wanting a light meal can indulge in one of their fresh salads. Mains CH$5000; salads CH$3000.

Les Assassins Merced 297B, near the corner of Lastarria. Long-established favourite serving excellent French dishes, packed with loyal customers at lunchtimes and on weekends. Closed Sun. Lunch menu CH$5000.

Gatopardo Lastarria 192, Metro Universidad Católica. Excellent Chilean and Mediterranean cuisine, good value at lunchtimes, served in

TRAITORS' CORNER

For an unusual eating experience, seek out "Traitors' Corner". Not the easiest place to find, as it deliberately doesn't advertise itself, *El Rincón de las Canallas*, at San Diego 379B, Metro Universidad de Chile, was once a secret meeting place for the opposition during Pinochet's dictatorship and now, as then, entry requires the password. When asked, "Quién vive, canalla?", respond, "Chile libre, canalla."

TREAT YOURSELF

Astrid y Gastón Antonio Bellet 201, Metro Pedro de Valdivia ☎2/650-9125. Flawless fusion cuisine with Peruvian, Spanish, French and Japanese influences by Lima's famous chef, Gaston Acurio. The tuna steak (CH$12,000) borders on divine. Reservations required.

an attractive interior. The stuffed *calamari* are particularly tasty. Closed Sun. Fixed price lunch CH$5000.

Kintaro Monjitas 460. Tasty and authentic sushi, along with *teriyaki* and *udon* dishes, all at very reasonable prices. Closed Sun. Fixed price lunch CH$5000.

Mercado Central Bordered by Paseo Puente, Vergara, 21 de Mayo and San Pablo. The best place for large portions of inexpensive fish and seafood, the fish market's bustling eateries offer such delights as sea bass in seafood sauce (CH$4500), and *machas a la Parmesana* (CH$3500); *Rincón Marino* is a popular spot. Lunch only.

Patagonia Café Lastarría 96. Well-prepared Patagonian-style lamb and other meats served within a cosy, rough-hewn wood interior; the weekend buffet brunch is a bargain, as is the fixed-price lunch menu CH$5000.

El Rápido Bandera 371. Established *empanadería* serving perfectly-prepared *empanadas* and sandwiches; a snack counter rather than a restaurant. CH$1500.

Bellavista and Providencia

Backstage Patio Bellavista. Half bar, half decent pizzeria, popular *Backstage* has an open-air patio, perfect for enjoying live jazz on Sat nights. Pizza CH$4500.

Barandiarán Patio Bellavista. Spicy and flavourful Peruvian concoctions, including superb *ceviche* and sea bass dishes; the pisco sours stand out, too. Ceviche CH$4500.

TREAT YOURSELF

Etnico on Constitución at López de Bello. Trendy restaurant and bar drawing a hip younger crowd and offering dishes with Japanese and Vietnamese influences; the tempura and stir-fries are excellent and the bar is perpetually lively. Mains CH$4000–7000. Open late; closed Sun.

Como Agua Para Chocolate Constitución 88. The dishes have a Mexican-Caribbean flavour at this cosy, welcoming restaurant; the grilled fish is beautifully prepared and the extensive dessert menu extremely tempting. Mains CH$5000.

Empanatodos Pío Nono 153. Bustling takeaway doing brisk business, turning out 31 types of delicious *empanadas*. CH$1500.

Galindo on Constitución at Dardignac. Perpetually packed spot serving traditional Chilean food, such as hearty *pastel de choclo*, *cazuela* and *lomo a la pobre*, along with beers until late, even on weekdays. If sitting outside, you *will* be entertained by street musicians. *Cazuela* CH$3500.

El Huerto Orrego Luco 54, Metro Pedro de Valdivia. An excellent choice for a wide variety of lovingly-prepared vegetarian dishes, such as hearty *burritos*. *La Huerta* café next door offers sandwiches and breakfasts accompanied with freshly-baked bread. Stir-fries CH$4000.

Liguria Av Providencia 1373, Metro Manuel Montt. Large portions of Chilean and Italian dishes are on offer in this ever-popular bar-bistro, as well as large sandwiches and good salads. Mains CH$4000.

Off The Record Antonia López de Bello 155. Cosy wood-panelled pub serving delicious meat, fish and pasta dishes, and allegedly frequented by President Bachelet. Pasta CH$5000.

Schopería La Nona on Pío Nono at Darginac. Drawing a younger crowd, this informal eatery offers cheap beers, hamburgers and *completos* (hot dogs) accompanied by heavy rock. Burger CH$2500.

Barrio Brasil

Charro de Oro Av Ricardo Cumming 342A. Spicy and inexpensive Mexican tacos and burritos served here. Tacos CH$1500. Open until 3am Fri & Sat; closed Sun.

Ocean Pacific's Av Ricardo Cumming 221. One of the few restaurants open on Sun, serving consistently good fish dishes (though not the cheapest), including an excellent salmon platter for two. Check out the puffer fish decorations. Mains CH$5000–7000.

Peperone Huérfanos 1934. Excellent *empanadería* dishing out baked *empanadas* with myriad fillings, including scallops. CH$1500.

Las Vacas Gordas Cienfuegos 280. Probably the best restaurant for carnivores in the city, with steaks grilled to perfection at very reasonable prices. Extremely popular, especially on weekends. Veal medallions with pancetta CH$4500. Closed Sun night.

Drinking, nightlife and entertainment

Santiago is not a 24-hour party town, and compared to other Latin capitals can seem rather tame. However, Thursdays, Fridays and Saturdays are lively, with crowds pouring into the streets and bars of the nightlife *zonas*.

Downtown

Café Escondido Rosal Interior 346, Metro Bellas Artes. If you want cheap beer and bar snacks in a less-than-raucous environment, this intimate bar is the perfect spot. Open until 2am Mon–Sat.

Cine Arte Alameda Alameda 139, Metro Baquedano. An arts cinema showing independent and avant-garde films.

Cine Hoyts Huérfanos 735. Multiplex cinema showing the latest releases; English-language films tend to be subtitled.

La Piojera Aillavilú 1030, Metro Plaza de Armas. Carve your name into the wooden tables at this rough-and-ready bar with a loyal clientele, and knock back a *terremoto* (earthquake) – a powerful wine and ice cream mix. Drinks CH$1700.

Teatro Municipal Agustinas 749, Metro Universidad de Chile ⓣ 2/463-1000, ⓦ www.municipal.cl. You can find the best of Chile's classical music inside this magnificent historical building. Special productions take place throughout the year; check the website for more details.

Bellavista and Providencia

Altazor Antonia López de Bello 189. Popular bar packed on weekends, often featuring live folk music and blues. Cover CH$1000.

Boomerang Holley 2285. Lively Australian-run watering hole with nightly drink specials, popular with foreign travellers and locals alike.

Bunker Bombero Núñez 159, Metro Baquedano. Giant dancefloor with varied alternative music events and a devoted young following. Cover CH$5000.

La Casa en el Aire Antonia López de Bello 125 ⓦ www.casaenelarie.cl. Inviting candle-lit venue offering poetry reading, contemporary theatre performances, film screenings and folk music; check the website for listings.

Femme By Bunker Next door to *Bunker*, this is its lesbian branch.

Flannery's Geo Pub Encomenderos 83, Metro Tobalaba, Providencia. Extremely popular with expats, this pub has authentic Irish charm and a welcoming staff. While the exotic cocktails are not their strong suit, this is a great spot for a beer and surprisingly tasty *fajitas*.

Havana Salsa Dominica 142 ⓦ www.havanasalsa.cl. If you want to shake your hips to some salsa beats, this is the place. Open until 5am Fri & Sat. Cover and Cuban-style buffet dinner CH$8000.

Phone Box Pub Av Providencia 1670, Providencia. Relaxed and lively pub, popular with expats, offers a wide selection of beers, including the delectable Kunstmann.

Pub La Casa Chucre Manzur 9. Popular with a younger crowd, this bar and dancefloor features music ranging from hip hop and reggaeton to electronica; there are also live bands on occasion. Open from 11pm until late Thurs–Sat.

COFFEE WITH LEGS

In downtown Santiago you may encounter the strange phenomenon of *café con piernas*, or "coffee with legs" – cafés where besuited businessmen are served coffee by skimpily-clad waitresses. *Café Caribe*, at Ahumada 120, and *Café Haiti*, at Ahumada 336, are both tamer examples of the genre. At the raunchier cafés, customers are offered more than just coffee.

Barrio Brasil

Blondie Alameda 2879, Metro Unión Latino-americana ⓦ www.blondie.cl. Large and popular four-floor dance club featuring techno, goth, indie and other musical styles, depending on the night, as well as occasional live music. Admission CH$3000.

Confitería Las Torres Alameda 1570, Metro Los Héroes. Elegant, nineteenth-century building hosting spellbinding live tango shows on weekends to accompany the expertly cooked traditional Chilean dishes.

N'aitún Av Ricardo Cumming 453, Barrio Brasil. An activist bookshop since the 1970s features gritty folk music, attracting bohemian types.

Shopping

Artesanías de Chile Av Bellavista 357 ⓦ www.artesaniasdechile.cl. High-quality crafts from Chile's indigenous communities, including Aymará textiles, Mapuche silverwork and wood carvings. There is also a small outlet within Patio Bellavista (see opposite).

Books Av Providencia 1652. good selection of English-language books, to exchange or to buy.
Centro de Exposición de Arte Indígena Alameda 499, Centro. Alongside Cerro Santa Lucía, this *feria artesanal* stocks some excellent Mapuche, Rapanui and Aymará crafts. Mon–Sat 10am–6pm.
Emporio Nacional Av Bellavista 360 ⓦwww.emporionacional.cl. Gourmets flock to this food heaven for speciality food products from all over the country, including jams, smoked meats and salmon.
English Reader Av Los Leones 116. Bookshop offering a wide range of new and used English-language titles.
Feria Artesanal Santa Lucía, Cerro Santa Lucía. Large crafts market stocking both indigenous crafts, tie-dyed clothing and T-shirts featuring the Chilean flag. Mon–Sat 10am–7pm.
Feria del Disco Ahumada 286. A large branch of the ubiquitous music store stocking a wide variety of Chilean music as well as international rock and pop.
Lapiz Lazuli House Bellavista 14, Barrio Bellavista. One of the better places to buy the expertly-crafted lapis lazuli jewellery that Chile is famous for.
Patio Bellavista Between Constitución and Pío Nono, Barrio Bellavista ⓦwww.patiobellavista.cl. Open-air space with a concentration of gift shops selling high-quality crafts and clothing, postcards, jewellery and home-made honey. A bookshop by the Constitución entrance stocks a plethora of guidebooks and maps.
La Vinoteca Av Isidora Goyenechea 2966 ⓦwww.lavinoteca.cl. If you're looking for some of Chile's best wines to take home with you, the knowledgeable staff here can help locate some of the rarer vintages, and will even wrap up a case so that you can check it in at the airport.

Directory

Airlines Aerolíneas Argentinas, Roger de Flor 2921, Las Condes ⓣ2/210-9300; Air Canada, Andres Bello 2687, 16th floor, Las Condes ⓣ2/337-0022; Air France, Américo Vespucio Sur 100, Oficina 202, Las Condes ⓣ2/290-9330; Air New Zealand, Av 11 de Septiembre 1881, Oficina 713, Providencia ⓣ2/376-9039; American Airlines, Huérfanos 1199 ⓣ2/679-0000; British Airways, Don Carlos 2929, Oficina 1105, Las Condes ⓣ2/330-8600; Iberia, Bandera 206, 8th floor ⓣ2/870-1010; LanChile, Huérfanos 926, ⓣ2/526-3000; Lloyd Aero Boliviano, Moneda 1170 ⓣ2/688-8680; Lufthansa, Av El Bosque Norte 500, 16th floor, Las Condes ⓣ2/630-1655; Qantas, Isidora Goyenechea 2934, Oficina 301, Las Condes ⓣ2/232-9562; Swissair, Av Barros Errázuriz 1954, Oficina 810 ⓣ2/940-2090.
Banks, cambios and ATMs There are plenty of ATMs downtown, especially along Huérfanos, Agustinas, Bandera, Moneda and Av Alameda, as well as at the large bus terminals. Banks are open Mon through Fri from 9am to 2pm. There are several exchange houses on Agustinas, between Ahumada and Bandera, which give a reasonable rate on foreign currencies and traveller's cheques; (Mon–Fri 9am–2pm & 4–6pm, Sat 9am–2pm).
Embassies and consulates Argentina, Vicuña Mackenna 41 (ⓣ2/582-2606); Australia, Isidora Goyenechea 3621 (ⓣ2/550-3500, ⓦwww.chile.embassy.gov.au); Bolivia, Av Santa María 2796, Providencia (ⓣ2/232-8180); Brazil, MacIver 225, 15th floor (ⓣ2/425-9230); Canada, Nueva Tajamar 481, 12th floor (ⓣ2/362-9660); Germany, Las Hualtatas 5677, Vitacura (ⓣ2/463-2500);

SANTIAGO TOUR OPERATORS

Attractions around Santiago include wineries, thermal baths, the outdoor enthusiast paradise of the mountainous Cajón del Maipo valley and more.

Fueginos ⓣ2/737-3251 or 9/162-4707, ⓦwww.fueguinos.cl. Full-day nature tours around Santiago; destinations include the Cajón del Maipo valley, Parque Nacional La Campana and the San Francisco glacier. CH$35,000 per person includes transportation, meals and entry to national parks. English and French spoken.
Monteagudo Aventura ⓣ2/346-9069, ⓦwww.monteagudoaventura.cl. Experienced outfit running full-day horse-riding and white-water rafting trips in the Cajón del Maipo, as well as treks to the San Francisco and Morado glaciers and night excursions to the Colina thermal baths; prices vary from CH$40,000–60,000 depending on the trip.
Rockside Expediciones Moneda 2570 ⓣ2/861-1947 or 9/895-8599. If you're after adrenalin-filled activities, this recommended operator can organize the outdoor adventure for you, including rafting, kayaking, rock climbing and mountain biking in the Cajón del Maipo.
Santiago Adventures Guardia Vieja 255, oficina 403, Providencia ⓣ2/244-2750, ⓦwww.santiagoadventures.com. Established operator running trips to wineries around Santiago, as well as city tours and outdoor adventures in the Cajón del Maipo.

Israel, San Sebastian 2812, 5th floor, Las Condes (ⓣ2/750-0500); New Zealand, Av El Golf 99, Oficina 703 (ⓣ2/290-9800, ⓦwww.nzembassy.com/chile); Peru, Padre Mariano 10, Oficina 703, Providencia (ⓣ2/235-4600); Switzerland, Américo Vespucio Sur 100, 14th floor, Las Condes (ⓣ2/263-4211); UK, Av El Bosque Norte 125 (ⓣ2/370-4100); US, Av Andrés Bello 2800 (ⓣ2/232-2600, ⓦwww.usembassy.cl).

Emergencies Ambulance ⓣ131; fire department (*bomberos*) ⓣ132; police (*carabineros*) ⓣ133.

Hospitals Clínica Indisa Santa María, Av Santa María 1810 (ⓣ2/362-5555); Clínica Las Condes, La Fontecilla 441 (ⓣ2/210-4000); Clínica Universidad Católica, Lira 40, downtown (ⓣ2/633-4122), Clínica Alemana, Av Vitacura 5951, Vitacura (ⓣ2/212-9700).

Internet access There are a large number of internet cafés scattered around Santiago; most youth hostels also offer free internet use. Try also Café.com, at Alameda 143, or Ciber Librería Internacional, at Merced 324 (ⓣ2/638-6245).

Language schools Bridge Linguatec Language Center, at Los Leones 439, Providencia (ⓣ2/233-4356 or 800/724-4216 in the US, ⓦwww.bridgelinguatec.com) offers intensive immersion Spanish courses, group tutorials and private lessons. Instituto Chileno-Suizo de Idioma, at José Victorino Lastarria 93, 2nd floor (ⓣ2/638-5414 ⓦwww.chilenosuizo.tie.cl) combines Spanish language courses of varying intensity with homestays, city tours and introduction to Chilean culture.

Laundry Try Lavandería Autoservicio, at Monjitas 507, or Lavanderia Lolos, at Moneda 2296, Barrio Brasil.

Pharmacies There are plenty of Farmacias Ahumada and Cruz Verde pharmacies all over Santiago; Farmacia Ahumada, at Av El Bosque 164, is open 24hr.

Post offices Correo Central, Plaza de Armas 559 (Mon–Fri 8.30am–7pm, Sat 8.30am–1pm). Other branches are at Moneda 1155, near Morandé; Local 17, Exposición 57 Paseo Estación; and Av 11 de Septiembre 2092.

Telephone centres There are numerous *centros de llamados* run either by Entel, whose largest branch is at Morandé, between Huérfanos and Compañía, or by Telefónica CTC Chile, located inside metro stations, such as Universidad de Chile and Moneda, and on the streets.

Moving on

Bus to: Arica (several daily; 28hr; CH$42,000); Chillán (several daily; 6hr; CH$11,000); Copiapó (several daily; 10hr; CH$17,000); Iquique (several

SKIING NEAR SANTIAGO

It's easy to arrange day-trips from Santiago to experience some world-class powder snow. The ski season lasts from mid-June to early October. All resorts rent ski equipment and clothing, and day passes cost CH$20,000–35,000. At the upper end of the Cajón del Maipo valley, east of Santiago, three large ski resorts are clustered in the Tres Valles area: El Colorado, La Parva and Valle Nevado. All three can be accessed from Farellones, a village at the foot of Cerro Colorado (3333m). Portillo is set on the banks of the stunning Laguna del Inca on the Argentine border, a two-hour drive from Santiago. Ski Van (ⓣ2/192672) has daily departures to both El Colorado and La Parva; Ski Total, Avenida Apoquindo 4900 (ⓣ2/466881) departs for Valle Nevado from the Omnium building daily from 7.30am. Manzur Expediciones (ⓣ2/777-4284) departs for Tres Valles (Wed, Sat & Sun at 8.30am) and Portillo (Wed, Sat & Sun at 7.30am), from Plaza Italia, Metro Baquedano.

El Colorado ⓦwww.elcolorado.cl. The resort boasts nineteen chairlifts and 22 runs, most of intermediate level, between elevations of 2430m and 3333m.

La Parva ⓦwww.skilaparva.cl. The resort's Cerro Franciscano (3608m) and Cerro La Falsa Parva offer 30 runs for skiers of all abilities, with some excellent long advanced runs, as well as extensive backcountry skiing and heliskiing.

Portillo ⓦwww.skiportillo.com. Chile's most exclusive resort boasts 23 runs that cater to intermediates and experts alike between altitudes of 2590m and 3322m, along with ample backcountry terrain and heli-skiing opportunities.

Valle Nevado ⓦwww.vallenevado.com. With the best skiing conditions in Tres Valles and geared towards foreign visitors, this luxury resort has a good mixture of advanced and intermediate runs, as well as a snowboard park and half-pipe along with extraordinary terrain for heli-skiing.

daily; 24hr; CH$35,000); La Serena (7hr; several daily; CH$10,000); Pucón (12hr; CH$22,000); Puerto Montt (several daily; 13hr; CH$25,000); Valparaíso or Viña del Mar (1hr 45min; CH$3500). Terminal Buses Estación Central has international departures to various South American countries including Argentina (Buenos Aires, Mendoza), Brazil (Saõ Paulo, Río de Janeiro) and Peru (Lima, Cuzco, Tacna, Arequipa).
Plane: LAN, Aerolíneas del Sur and Sky Airline have multiple daily flights to all major Chilean destinations. Lassa and Aerolíneas ATA fly to the San Fernández Archipelago both from the international airport and the Aeródromo Tobalaba.
Train to: Chillán (7 daily; 4hr 30min; CH$10,500); Concepción (3 daily; 6hr 30min; CH$12,500); Curicó (2hr; CH$6000); Rancagua (7 daily: 1hr; CH$4300); Talca (7 daily; 3hr; CH$6500); all served by TerraSur (Ⓦ www.efe.cl). A slower Metrotrén has hourly departures to Rancagua (7am–10pm; CH$1300).

Valparaíso and Viña del Mar

Draped in a crescent shape around the Bahía de Valparaíso, **VALPARAÍSO** is Chile's principal port and naval base, and also perhaps the country's liveliest and most vibrant city. The **nightlife** and eating scene here upstage both Santiago and the nearby beach resort of **VIÑA DEL MAR**. Viña's attractions are wide, white beaches surrounded by expensive high-rise apartments, casinos and pricey, touristy restaurants. There's none of the character that distinguishes Valparaíso; the good news is that since they're so close together, it's easy enough to stay in Valparaíso and visit Viña's beaches for the day.

VALPARAÍSO

As an important stopover for ships rounding Cape Horn en route to the Pacific coast, **VALPARAÍSO** came into its own during the California gold rush. This gritty and colourful UNESCO World Heritage Site is effectively split into two halves – the flat part, **El Plan**, comprises the busy port area, home to an extensive nightlife quarter, as well as the shopping and adminstrative districts, all linked by traffic-choked narrow streets. By contrast, colourful houses cling to the residential **cerros** (hills) surrounding the city, linked to El Plan by numerous **funiculars.**

Barrio Puerto

El Plan consists of long east-west streets, crossed by shorter north-south streets leading into the hills, and is divided into two halves, with **Barrio Puerto** located northwest of **Cerro Concepción**. Its centrepiece, the pedestrianized **Plaza Sotomayor**, is lined with a mixture of modern concrete blocks and grand, early twentith-century buildings, and is home to the **Primera Zona Naval**, the country's naval headquarters. At the port end of the plaza, near the Metrotrén Estación Puerto, is **Muelle Prat**, the passenger pier currently undergoing extensive renovation. West of the pier, the five-block portside stretch of Avenida Errázuriz and parallel Blanco make up Valparaíso's principal nightlife district, with **Mercado Puerto** and its plethora of fishy eateries at the northwest corner. A couple of blocks south of the market is the elegant **Iglesia Matriz del Salvador**, built in 1842, while the **Plaza Aduana** and Ascensor Artillería (see box, p.441) lie two blocks west.

El Almendral

El Almendral, east of Cerro Concepción, is the commercial half of the city; starting at the small **Plaza Aníbal Pinto**, it is bordered by the port, Avenida Colón to the south and Avenida Argentina to the east. The southern end of **Subida Ecuador**, lined with bars, comes raucously to life late at night. From here Calle Condell leads east into Pedro Montt and past Parque Italia to **Plaza O'Higgins** – home to a huge antiques market on weekends and doubling as a live music venue – before

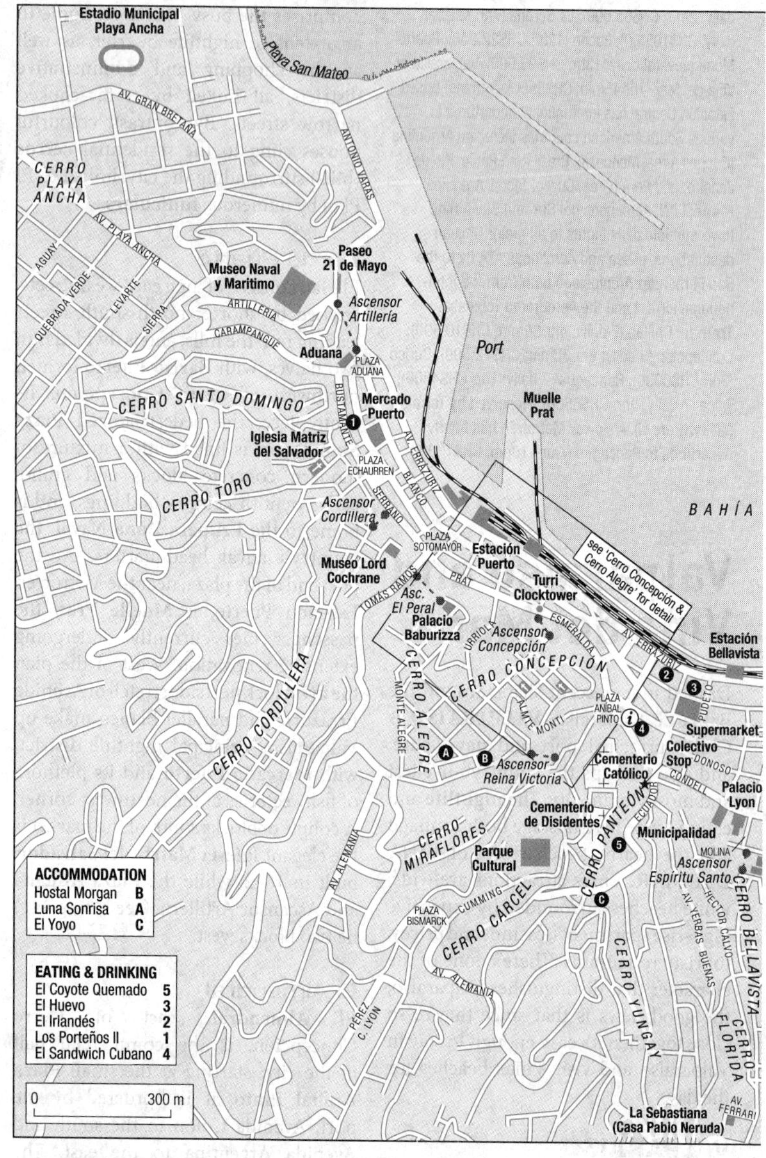

culminating in the north-south Avenida Argentina. The long and narrow **Plaza Rodomiro** runs through the centre of the avenue, drawing weekend shoppers with its flea market. Across the intersection from the square lies the main **Terminal Rodoviario**, with the monolithic **Congreso National** building directly opposite it.

The hills

Without a doubt, Valparaíso's biggest attraction is its **hills**. Few pastimes are as enjoyable as meandering up and

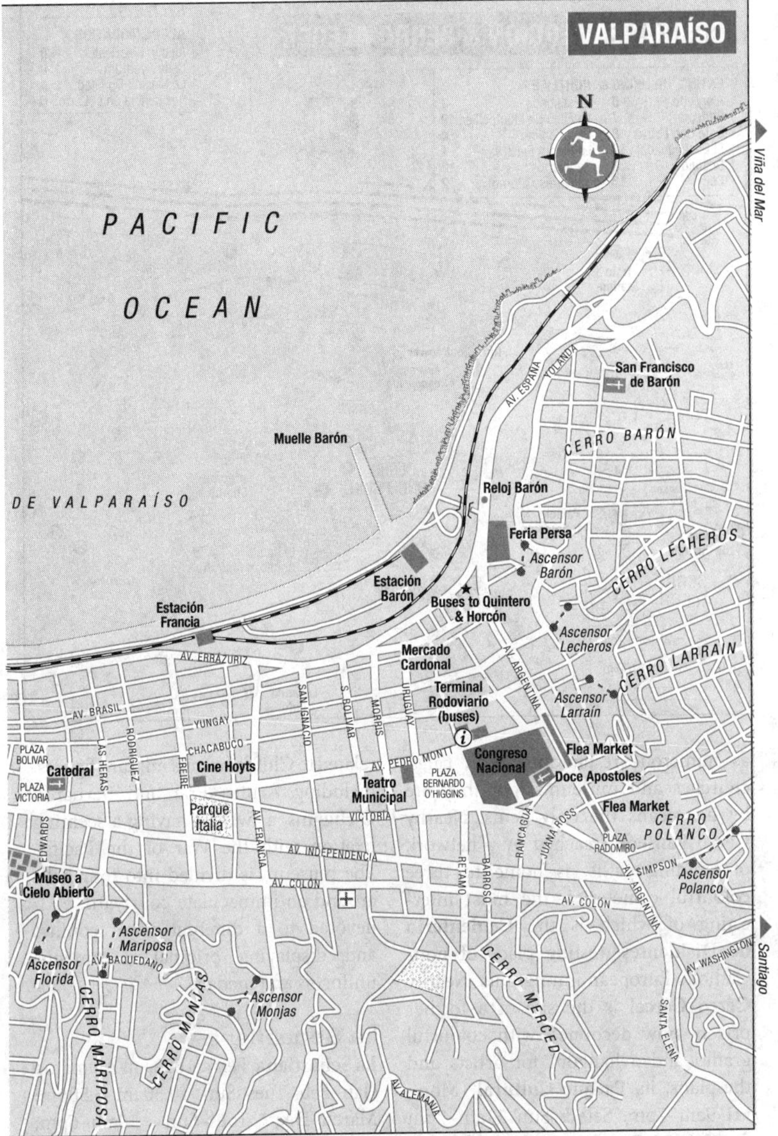

down the area's winding, narrow streets, or riding its antique funiculars. Visitors can stop to marvel at the impressive views of the city from a multitude of **miradores** (viewpoints), or duck into little shops and cafés to admire the colourful **murals** – a striking example of the city's bohemian culture. It is easy to see how Valparaíso has produced more writers, artists and poets than any other Chilean city. **Cerro Concepción** and **Cerro Alegre** are the best known of the hills and have the highest concentration of quality accommodation, as well

as numerous restaurants, bars, cafés, churches and museums, but they are by no means the only gems. Nearby **Cerro Panteón**, reached by a network of winding paths, is home to three colourful cemeteries, the most interesting of which is the **Cementerio de Disidentes**, resting place of non-Catholic European immigrants. Nearby **Cerro Cárcel** is the site of a former prison, now decorated with colourful graffiti and a hangout for artists and thespians, its **Parque Cultural** (Mon–Fri 9am–7pm, Sat & Sun 11am–7pm ⓣ322/258567) sometimes hosting outdoor theatre performances.

Museo Naval y Marítimo

Up on **Cerro Artilería**, the naval **museum** (Paseo 21 de Mayo s/n, Tues–Sun 10am–5.30pm; CH$1000) houses an in-depth collection of artefacts related to Chile's famous military figures, including Arturo Prat and Bernardo O'Higgins, as well as having a seeming fixation with the War of the Pacific. The museum is divided into four halls around an immaculate courtyard, each devoted to a different naval conflict and displaying original documents, uniforms and medals.

La Sebastiana

La Sebastiana, Ferrari 692, off Alemania (Jan–Feb Tues–Sun 10.30am–6.50pm; March–Dec Tues–Sun 10am–6pm; CH$3000; ⓣ322/256606, ⓦwww.lasebastiana-neruda.cl) was the least lived-in of the poet **Pablo Neruda**'s three residences, but it offers incredibly picturesque views of the city and the interior design reflects the poet's quirky tastes. Like his other homes, the five-storey house has a nautical

LOS ASCENSORES DE VALPARAÍSO

Once numbering thirty-three and now down to just over a dozen, Valparaíso's *ascensores*, or funiculars, were built between 1883 and 1916. As well as being one of the city's enduring attractions, they remain an essential way of getting about. Most run daily from 7am to 11pm and cost between CH$100 and CH$250. Here are the top five, listed from east to west:

Ascensor Barón At the top of this funicular, Mirador Diego Portales gives you a panoramic view of the city from its easternmost point, taking in the port and the hillside homes towards the west. Best visited at sunset, its entrance is tucked away behind the **Feria Persa Barón** flea market.

Ascensor Polanco The only *ascensor* that is an actual elevator, Polanco is reached through a long underground tunnel from Calle Simpson, off Avenida Argentina. It rises vertically through the yellow tower to a *mirador* offering excellent views of the port.

Ascensor Espíritu Santo The nearest funicular to La Sebastiana, it is also the best approach to Cerro Bellavista and the extremely worthwhile open-air **Museo al Cielo Abierto**, brightly decorated with abstract murals painted by students of Universidad Católica's Instituto de Arte in the early 1970s.

Ascensor Concepción (also known as Ascensor Turri) The city's **oldest funicular**, built in 1883 and originally steam-powered, is one of the most popular. It climbs up to Paseo Gervasoni on Cerro Concepción, a delightful residential area and the start of many walking tours that cover Cerro Alegre as well. The lower entrance is opposite the **Relój Turri** clock tower.

Ascensor Artilería Extremely popular with visitors, this funicular rivals Ascensor Barón for views, running from Plaza Aduana up to **Cerro Playa Ancha**, and offering a beautiful panoramic view of the city and coastline, with Viña del Mar in the distance. The Museo Naval Marítimo (see opposite) is nearby.

theme and is crammed with random knick-knacks that Neruda picked up on his travels; unlike the others, you can explore this one without a guide. The vista from his bedroom window is nothing short of spectacular. Though sacked by the military after Pinochet's 1973 coup, the house has been restored by the Fundación Neruda and opened to the public in 1992. To get here, take a short ride on *colectivo* no. 39 (CH$450), or catch the bus, Verde "D" from Plaza Ecuador (CH$350).

Arrival and information

Buses Long-distance buses arrive at the Terminal Rodoviario, Pedro Montt 2800 (ⓣ322/216568), a 20min walk from Cerro Alegre and Cerro Concepción. There are snack shops, an ATM and luggage storage inside.

Tourist office There are two tourist information kiosks in the city. One is in the centre of Plaza Aníbal Pinto (Mon–Fri 10am–2pm & 3.30–5.30pm, Sat & Sun 10.30am–5.30pm; ⓣ322/939365, ⓦwww.ciudaddevalparaiso.cl). The other is a kiosk at the bus terminal (daily 8.30am–5.30pm). Fundación Valparaíso, at Héctor Calvo 205, Cerro Bellavista (ⓣ322/593156, ⓦwww.fundacionvalparaiso.cl) runs various restoration projects around the city; its "Bicentennial Heritage Trail" guide is full of curious trivia about the city. The foundation has even placed arrows around the city to mark their suggested walking tour.

Train Frequent trains from Viña del Mar stop at the stations along the waterfront. Barón is the closest station to Terminal Rodoviario, while Bellavista and Puerto are the handiest for Cerro Alegre and Cerro Concepción.

City transport

Buses, colectivos and micros Frequent transport of all sorts runs to and from Viña del Mar; look for "Viña" displayed in the window. In El Plan, buses labelled "Aduana" run west towards the centre along Pedro Montt while "P. Montt" buses run back to the bus station; fares range between CH$300–600.

Metrotrén Fast, frequent, air-conditioned commuter trains run to Viña del Mar and beyond from the stations along the harbour (6.30am–11pm); you have to make a one-off purchase of a swipe card (CH$650) on top of the fares.

Trams Antique German trams offer limited but cheap service around El Plan; just look for the rails (CH$300).

Accommodation

Álecon FineHostel Abtao 684, Cerro Concepción ⓣ322/491164, ⓦwww.alecon.cl. Wonderfully friendly family-run guesthouse with airy single rooms, doubles, triples and quads; excellent breakfast and internet are included and the hostel offers a free Spanish language course to long-term guests. ⑤

Casa Aventura Pasaje Gálvez, Cerro Alegre ⓣ322/755963, ⓦwww.casaventura.cl. Hostel with friendly and knowledgeable staff, spotless dorms, a sunny lounge, kitchen privileges and internet; popular with backpackers. Dorm CH$7000. ⑤

Hostal Luna Sonrisa Templeman 833, Cerro Alegre ⓣ322/734117, ⓦwww.lunasonrisa.cl. Professional hostel run by Footprint Guide author, drawing a younger crowd; fully-equipped kitchen, tranquil lounge with book exchange and large rooms with tall ceilings in a central location make it a top choice. Dorm CH$7000. ⑤

Hostal Morgan Capilla 784, Cerro Alegre ⓣ322/114931, ⓦwww.hostalmorgan.cl. This luxurious bright-yellow B&B has spotless rooms for up to four people with down comforters, a roof terrace, internet, wi-fi, breakfast included and a congenial hostess. ⑥

La Maison Du Filou Papudo 579, Cerro Concepción ⓣ322/124681 or 9/8762-0456, ⓦwww.lamaisondufilou.overblog.com. Colourful double and twin rooms with high ceilings and wonderful views; kitchen privileges, laundry service, book exchange, wi-fi and breakfast included. French and a smattering of English spoken. ④–⑤

Residencia en el Cerro Pasaje Pierre Loti 51, Cerro Concepción ⓣ322/495298. A large, wonderfully friendly, family house; good breakfast, internet, and cosy rooms with fantastic views. Dorm CH$6000. ④

El Yoyo Av Ecuador 355 ⓣ322/591087. This roomy hostel has energetic and helpful staff, 24hr reception, common area with a TV, occasional barbecues, guest kitchen and breakfast. The only drawbacks are the lack of towels and that the mattresses could be more comfortable; it's more of a party hostel. Dorm CH$6500. ④

Eating

Alegretto Pilcomayo 529, Cerro Concepción. Complete with an entertaining vintage jukebox, this Italian spot serves good pizza and excellent gnocchi. Medium pizza CH$5000.

Café Con Letras Almirante Montt 316, Cerro Alegre. A popular artsy café with quirky decor and a book exchange; serves a good range of real coffee, too. Espresso CH$1500.

El Desayunador Almirante Montt 399, Cerro Alegre. If all-day breakfast tickles your fancy, this informal eatery offers generous servings from 9am onwards. Breakfast platter CH$4500.

Destajo Cumming 55. Takeaway offering excellent *empanadas* with myriad meat, fish and vegetable fillings – perfect for a late-night snack. Open all evenings except Sun. *Empanada* CH$1000–1500.

Epif C Dr. Grossi 268, Cerro Concepción. A great little restaurant run by a young Chilean-American couple, with plenty of choices for vegetarians and vegans: the *gazpacho* and veggie burgers are particularly good. Thurs–Sat open 7pm–late; Sun 1–4pm. Dishes CH$3000–5000.

Le Filou de Montpellier Almirante Montt 382, Cerro Alegre. Consistently imaginative meat and fish dishes are served at this well-established and popular French spot. Fixed-price lunch menus are particularly good value (CH$4500). Closed Mon.

Los Porteños II on Matriz at Cochrane. Specializing in fresh fish and seafood, this cheerful eatery is an extension of the equally popular *Los Porteños* across the street. *Paila marina* CH$3500.

L'Escapade Almirante Montt 51, Cerro Alegre. A popular bar in the evenings, this lively spot also offers excellent fresh fruit juices; the melted Gruyère cheese mix with large dipping croutons is excellent (CH$4000). Closed Mon; Fri–Sun open until 2am.

Samsara Almirante Montt 427, Cerro Alegre. Seamless service and presentation distinguish this intimate Thai restaurant. The fish dishes, in particular, are flavourful. Three-course fixed-price meal CH$10,000–12,000.

TREAT YOURSELF

Pasta e Vino Templeman 352 ⓣ322/496187. Hands down, the best Italian restaurant in the city and perhaps even in all of Chile; each dish is lovingly prepared and the flavours are faultless. Reservations are essential. Pasta dishes CH$6000–9000.

El Sandwich Cubano O'Higgins 1221. Small and very popular lunchtime stop serving excellent-value plates of tasty *ropa vieja* (beef dish) with *moros y cristianos* (rice and beans). CH$2500.

Drinking and entertainment

Bitácora Cumming 68. A popular bar that is also a cultural centre and gathering place for local artists and thespians; open late.
Cine Hoyts Pedro Montt 2111. A five-screen cinema showing the latest blockbuster releases.
El Coyote Quemado Subida Equador 144. Dark two-tiered bar playing heavy rock and packed with a younger crowd. Rum and coke CH$600.
El Huevo Blanco 1386. Huge five-level nightclub with different music on each one, packing a student crowd. Entry CH$3000.
El Irlandés Blanco 1279. A fairly raucous Irish pub run by an actual Irishman offering a large selection of beers (CH$1200–2000); imported beers are pricier.
La Piedra Felíz Errázuriz 1054. An excellent catch-all dance club and bar featuring DJs in the subterranean lounge, a salsa room, a tango room and occasional live rock.
Valparaíso Eterno Señoret 150, 2nd floor. Besides offering reasonably-priced meals and beers, this joint has heaps of personality; some Sat nights a singer-songwriter belts out Communist tunes.

Directory

Banks, cambios and ATMs Prat has a number of banks, ATMs and *cambios*; Banco de Chile, at Condell 1481, also has an ATM and there is a *cambio* on Plaza Sotomayor which offers a decent exchange rate.
Festivals Valparaíso hosts spectacular *Año Nuevo* (New Year) celebrations, drawing thousands of Chileans. Fundación de la Ciudad commemorates the city's founding on April 17, 1791. The Festival Cinematográfico de Valparaíso (Valparaíso Film Festival) takes place in Aug.
Hospital Hospital Carlos van Buren, at San Ignacio 725, has modern facilities (ⓣ322/204000).
Internet access There are several internet cafés on Cerro Concepción and Cerro Alegre; most hostels have access as well.
Language courses Escuela Español Interactivo, at Pasaje Gálvez 25 (ⓦwww.interactivespanish.cl), offers Spanish courses at beginner and intermediate levels. *Álecon Hostel* offers free Spanish courses to guests staying longer than one week.
Laundry Lavanda Café, at Pedro Montt 454, combines laundry and excellent coffees.

PABLO NERUDA

Neftalí Ricardo Reyes Basoalto, better known as **Pablo Neruda** (1904–73), is Chile's most famous poet. A flamboyant and eccentric literary figure, he held a diplomatic post, as well as being actively involved in Chilean politics. Famous for his provocative and often sentimental poetry, Neruda was awarded the Nobel Prize for Literature in 1971.

Post office Prat 856 on Plaza Sotomayor (Mon–Fri 9am–6pm).

Moving on

Bus to: Arica (5 daily; 24hr; CH$35,000); Iquique (5 daily; 24hr; CH$30,000); Isla Negra (daily; 1hr 30min; CH$2500); La Serena (5 daily; 7hr; CH$10,000); Puerto Montt (6 daily; 16hr; CH$30,000); Santiago (several daily; 1hr 45min; CH$3500).
Metrotrén to: Viña del Mar (frequent departures 6:30am–11pm; 15min; CH$280–620).

VIÑA DEL MAR

Though only fifteen minutes from Valparaíso by public transport, **VIÑA DEL MAR** could hardly be more different from its grittier neighbour. Purpose-built in the late nineteenth century as a weekend getaway for wealthy Santiago and Valparaíso residents, it draws thousands of local holidaymakers during the summer and on weekends. Viña makes for an enjoyable day-trip to the beach, and is especially worth a visit during its February **music festival**. The city is split in two by the broad, none-too-clean **Marga Marga** estuary, with a largely residential area to the south and the beaches in the northern half. **Avenida San Martín**, parallel to the beach, and the side streets off it feature numerous dining and nightlife options. At the heart of Viña lies the large, shady **Plaza Vergara** – a popular spot with the occasional busker or *capoeira* demonstration and horse-drawn carriages parked around it. Several blocks of **Avenida Valparaíso**, Viña's main thoroughfare running from the square's southeast corner, have been turned into a pleasant pedestrian mall with a number of shops and **eateries**.

The beaches

Playa Caleta Abarca lies in a sandy cove south of **Castillo Wulff**, an impressive castle-like structure built on a rocky outcrop at the mouth of the estuary by a Valparaíso businessman in 1906. Located next to the large **Reloj de Flores (flower clock)**, the beach draws a lively picnicking crowd on weekends. Just north of the estuary, Avenida Perú runs parallel to the sea, past the brash **Casino Viña del Mar**. Beyond you will find an almost unbroken line of sandy beaches, backed by high-rise apartment buildings, stretching all the way to the smaller resort of **Reñaca**, which itself has more good beaches and nightlife.

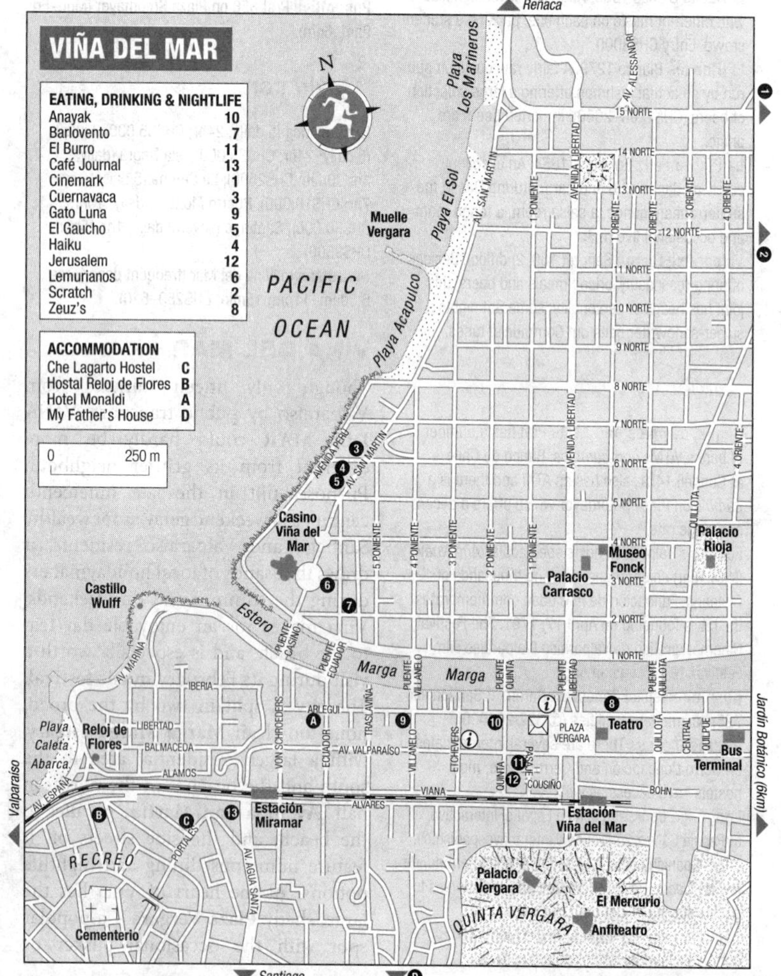

Quinta Vergara

The one spot besides the beaches where you might want to spend some time in **Viña del Mar** is the lovely **Quinta Vergara** park (Dec–Feb 7am–7pm daily; rest of the year 7am–6pm; closed on rainy days), whose manicured grounds are home to a vast array of exotic imported plants. It is located a couple of blocks south of Plaza Vergara behind the Metrotrén Estación Viña, with the futuristic-looking **Anfiteatro**, home to the annual music festival, as its centrepiece.

Arrival and information

Buses Long-distance buses pull up at Terminal Rodoviario (ⓣ322/752000), at Avenida Valparaíso 1055; it has a tourist information booth and an ATM.

Metrotrén The commuter train from Valparaíso stops at Estación Miramar, Estación Viña del Mar and Estación Hospital along Alvares; Miramar is the closest station to the beaches.

Tourist office The main tourist information office is inside the Municipalidad building on the north side of Plaza Vergara (Mon–Fri 9am–7pm, Sat & Sun 10am–8pm; ⓣ322/269330, ⓦwww.visitevinadelmar.cl).

Accommodation

Che Lagarto Hostel Diego Portales 131 ⓣ322/625759, ⓦwww.chelagarto.com. Though the bilingual staff are not particularly helpful, the hostel has clean dorms, kitchen use, communal lounge, free internet and wi-fi and nightly activities for the guests. Hostelling International members get a discount. Dorm CH$7000. ❺

Hostal Reloj de Flores Los Baños 7 ⓣ322/485242, ⓦwww.hostalrelojdefloresbb.com. This popular and welcoming family-run guesthouse has a good location a block from the beach, comfortable single, double and triple rooms (some en-suite), guest kitchen, free internet, cable TV in the rooms and a good breakfast. Dorm CH$12,000. ❺

Hotel Monaldi Arlegui 172 ⓣ322/881484, ⓦwww.hotelmonaldi.cl. The hostel part of this attractive budget hotel features clean and spacious rooms for up to four people, shared bathrooms and kitchen privileges. ❺

My Father's House Gregorio Marañón 1210 ⓣ322/616136, ⓦwww.myfathershouse.cl. The best budget choice in Viña, with spacious, quiet single, double and triple rooms, swimming pool, internet and gracious owners. The only drawback is the distance from the centre of town; catch *colectivo* "31", "82" or "131". ❻

Eating

Anayak Quinta 134. A good, unpretentious spot for breakfast and real coffee. Coffee CH$1400.

Barlovento 2 Norte 195. Trendy minimalist decor, good salads, wraps and appetizer platters draw a younger crowd. Great spot for a cocktail, too. Wraps CH$4000.

Cuernavaca San Martín 501. Bustling, noisy and popular Mexican spot serving up generous portions of *enchiladas* and *burritos*. Mains CH$3500.

El Gaucho San Martín 435. The ideal place to satisfy your carnivorous cravings, this Argentine-style steakhouse serves succulent steaks, chorizo and sweetbreads, among other offerings. Steak CH$6500.

Haiku 6 Norte 96. Hole-in-the-wall offering excellent Japanese dishes; the sushi is fresh and well-presented and the tuna tempura is truly delicious. Sushi platter for two CH$8000.

Jerusalem Quinta 259. Tasty Middle Eastern cuisine dispensed by this tiny food counter; the falafel is excellent (CH$2500).

Lemurianos 3 Norte 60. Refined Italian cuisine and excellent service beckon at this small restaurant and wine bar; the pasta dishes are well-executed and good value. Mains CH$4500.

Drinking and entertainment

El Burro Pasaje Cousiño 12 D, off Av Valparaíso. Dark and atmospheric pub-disco popular with local youth and foreigners alike; very busy on weekends.

Café Journal Agua Santa 2. Thriving university student haunt, complete with pub grub and regular live music.

Cinemark 15 Norte 961, Local 224. Multiplex cinema showing the latest releases.

Gato Luna Arlegui 396. Local bar with a good atmosphere; live Latin jazz and dancing at weekends.

Scratch Quillota 898, at the end of Bonn St. Established favourite on the disco scene, perpetually packed on Frid and Sat nights; nothing happens before midnight.

Zeuz's Arlegui 829 ⓦwww.zeuzs.cl. Large and popular gay disco, complete with entertaining drag queen shows and strippers.

Directory

Banks, cambios and ATMs Numerous banks, most with ATMs and *cambios*, are found along Av Arlegui.
Festivals The two-week long Feria del Libro, held in Jan, attracts important literary figures and hosts live readings. The extremely popular, week-long Festival de la Canción is held either in the second or third week of Feb, drawing top Latino and international artists. Acclaimed Festival Cine Viña del Mar film festival happens every second or third week of Oct (ⓦwww.festivalcinevinadelmar.cl).
Hospital Hospital Gustavo Fricke is on Álvarez at Simón Bolívar (ⓣ322/675067); for emergencies call ⓣ322/652328.
Internet access and telephone centre There are several internet cafés and telephone centres along Valparaíso.
Post office Plaza Latorre 32, near the municipal tourist office.

Moving on

Bus to: Arica (5 daily; 24hr; CH$35,000); Isla Negra (daily; 1hr 30min; CH$2500); Iquique (5 daily; 24hr; CH$30,000); La Serena (5 daily; 7hr; CH$10,000); Osorno (6 daily; 14hr; CH$27,000); Puerto Montt (6 daily; 16hr; CH$30,000); Santiago (several daily; 1hr 45min; CH$3700).
Metrotrén to: Valparaíso (numerous daily 6.30am–11pm; 15min; CH$260–620).

ISLA NEGRA

The seaside village of **ISLA NEGRA** (which, incidentally, is not an island), an hour and a half south of Valparaíso by bus, was the site of Pablo Neruda's favourite and most permanent home. The **Casa Museo Pablo Neruda**, at Calle Poeta Neruda s/n (March–Nov Tues–Sun 10am–2pm & 3–6pm; Dec–Feb Tues–Sun 10am–8pm; CH$3500 including tour in English; ⓣ35/461284, ⓦwww.fundacionneruda.org), lies down a wooded trail by the sea, a short walk from the main road. Larger than his other two homes, Isla Negra is fascinating for the sheer amount of **exotic objects** that Neruda accumulated here, and the amount of thought that went into every aspect of the design – from the arrangement of wooden ships' figureheads in the living room, to the positioning of blue glass bottles along the seaward side of the house. The poet's exotic collection of objects includes African wooden carvings, ships in bottles, a gigantic *moai kavakava* (a statue from Easter Island, see p.525) and an amazing array of seashells, housed in a purpose-built room that Neruda designed but never completed. A strong **nautical theme** runs throughout; there is even a small boat out on the terrace so that the poet could be "a sailor on land". Reservations are essential in the summer.

Norte Chico

LA SERENA

LA SERENA, 474 kilometres north of Santiago, was founded in 1544. During the seventeenth century it was the target of multple raids by the French and English, including the pirate Francis Drake. Today the city has surpassed Viña del Mar as Chile's prime **beach resort**. The palm-tree studded Plaza de Armas is La Serena's centrepiece, with **Iglesia Catedral** (1844) on the east side. Banks line the square's south side and Municipalidad buildings border the north, while **Casa Gonzáles Videla**, a former president's residency, now a museum, is located next door to the **Sernatur** office along the west side. One block west of the square lies the large, green and somewhat scruffy open space of Parque Pedro de Valdivia, with the tranquil and beautifully-sculpted Japanese-style **Jardín El Corazón** (daily 10am–6pm; CH$1000) at its south end. From this end of the park it is a half-hour walk west along busy Avenida Francisco de Aguirre to the lighthouse, from where a series of **beaches** stretch south. Heading east from the square, Calle Prat is lined

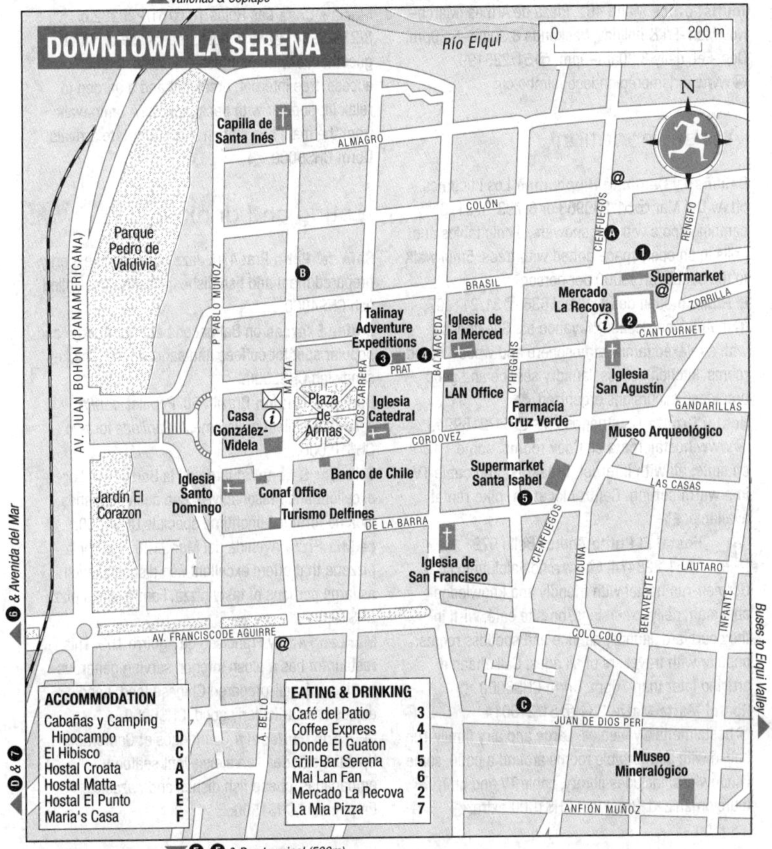

with eateries and leads you straight to the **Mercado La Recova**, the city's principal crafts market with a lively eating area upstairs. The **Museo Arqueológico** (Tues–Fri 9.30am–5.50pm, Sat 10am–1pm & 4–7pm, Sun 10am–1pm; CH$1000, Sun free, ticket is also valid for Museo Gonzáles Videla), a block south of the market along Cienfuegos, displays elaborate Diaguita ceramics, as well as a 2.5-metre *moai* statue from Easter Island and lapis lazuli jewellery.

The beaches

Between La Serena and the town of Coquimbo, a **cycle lane** runs beside a dozen or so wide, sandy beaches lined with pricey condominiums, hotels and restaurants; an easy and enjoyable day-trip. Bikes are available for rent in the city centre at Camawi Bike, Vicente Zorilla 990 (☎51/227939). While quite crowded in the summer, you have the beaches pretty much to yourself for the rest of the year. Most are suitable for swimming and windsurfing, although Playa Cuatro Esquinas is known to have strong **rip currents**.

Arrival and information

Airport Aeropuerto La Florida is 5km east of town along Ruta 41; catch a taxi or *micro* to the centre (CH$1000–2500).

Buses Main bus terminal is located at the corner of Amunátegui and Avenida El Santo, a 20min walk south of the centre.

Tourist office Matta 461, Plaza de Armas (March–Nov Mon–Fri & holiday weekends 8.30am–5.30pm; Dec–Feb daily 8.30am–9pm; ⓣ51/225199, ⓦwww.turismoregiondecoquimbo.cl).

Accommodation

Cabañas y Camping Hipocampo Los Lucumos, off Av Del Mar ⓣ51/230968 or 8/793-3761. Sixty camping spots with hot showers, picnic tables and grills in an open space dotted with trees. 5min walk to the beach. CH$3000 per person.

El Hibisco Juan de Dios Pení 636 ⓣ51/211407, ⓔmauricioberrios2002@yahoo.es. Guesthouse with a relaxed family atmosphere and wood-floored rooms, kitchen access, laundry service and good breakfast; excursions organized. ④

Hostal Croata Cienfuegos 248 ⓣ51/216994, ⓦwww.hostalcroata.cl. Cosy rooms, some en suite, all with internet, breakfast and cable TV, in a warm setting. Central location; bike rental available. ④

Hostal El Punto Andres Bello 979 ⓣ51/228474, ⓦwww.hostalelpunto.cl. German-run hostel with friendly and knowledgeable staff, daily excursions, on-site café, wi-fi in the courtyard, laundry service and spotless rooms; popular with travellers of all ages. Call ahead if arriving later than 10pm. Dorm CH$6000. ④

Hostal Matta Matta 234 ⓣ51/210014 ⓔhostalmatta@yahoo.es. Large and airy family-run house with comfortable rooms around a patio, some windowless; includes library, cable TV and grill; tours organized. Breakfast CH$1000 extra. ④

Maria's Casa Las Rojas 18 ⓣ51/229282 or 8/218-9984, ⓦwww.hostalmariacasa.cl. Small guesthouse with an effusive hostess, kitchen access, free internet, breakfast and a garden to relax in; popular with backpackers. A 3min walk from the main bus station – good for late arrivals. Dorm CH$6000. ④

Eating and drinking

Café del Patio Prat 470. Jazz bar serving expertly-prepared meat and fish dishes; closed Sun. Grilled fish CH$4000.

Coffee Express on Balmaceda at Prat. A large and popular spot for coffees and sandwiches. Chicken sandwich CH$2500.

Donde El Guaton Brazil 750. Popular *parilla* serving excellent grilled meat. *Parillada* for two CH$10,000.

Grill-Bar Serena Eduardo de la Barra 614. For excellent and reasonably-priced seafood dishes, look no further. Lunchtime specials CH$4000.

La Mia Pizza Avenida del Mar 2100. Seafront pizzeria that offers excellent fish dishes as well as large portions of tasty pizza. Family-sized pizza CH$10,000.

Mai Lan Fan Av Francisco de Aguirre 109. This restaurant has a plush interior, serving generous portions of well-prepared Chinese food; noodle dishes are particularly good. CH$6000.

Mercado La Recova Cienfuegos at Canternet. Upstairs eateries serve excellent seafood empanadas, cheap fish dishes and *cazuela*. Empanadas CH$1500.

TOUR OPERATORS

From La Serena, a number of tour companies run excursions in the surrounding area. Popular tours of the Elqui Valley include *pisco*-tasting (around CH$20,000), stargazing at the Observatorio Mamalluca (CH$12,000) and penguin-watching at Isla Damas (CH$30,000).

Daniel Russ ⓣ9/9291-8105, ⓦwww.jeeptour-laserena.cl. One experienced and extremely knowledgeable man (with a jeep) runs standard excursions for small groups, as well as trips to Paso Agua Negra (CH$50,000) and tailor-made outings. German and English spoken.

Elqui Total Parcela 17 Sector Titón Km 27 ⓣ51/198-1186 or 9/219-7872, ⓦwww.elquitotal.cl. Stables 20km outside La Serena offering varied horse-riding trips, including one at night (CH$25,000).

Kayak Australis ⓣ2/650-8264, ⓦwww.kayakaustralis.com. Specializes in multi-day sea-kayak trips around Chile, including one to Isla Damas.

Talinay Adventure Expeditions Prat 470 Local 22 ⓣ51/218658. Horseriding, diving, sea kayaking and multi-day trekking and volcano-climbing expeditions, as well as visits to the Campana and La Silla observatories.

Turismo Delfines Matta 591A ⓣ51/223624, ⓦwww.turismoaventuradelfines.cl. Established operator specializing in bilingual guided trips to Isla Damas.

Moving on

Bus to: Antofagasta (8 daily; 13hr; CH$22,000); Arica (7 daily; 23hr; CH$34,000); Copiapó (8 daily; 5hr; CH$10,000); Iquique (7 daily; 19hr; CH$24,000); San Pedro de Atacama (1 direct Tur Bus overnight; 17hr; CH$24,000); Santiago (7hr; 8 daily; CH$14,000); Valparaíso (6 daily; 6hr 30min; CH$14,000); **Via Elqui** serves: Pisco Elqui (6 daily; 2hr; CH$2500); Vicuña (8 daily; 1hr; CH$1500); 24hr Elqui Valley pass CH$4500.
Colectivos to: Coquimbo (frequent daily departures from Av Francisco de Aguirre, between Los Carrera and Balmaceda; CH$700); Elqui Valley (several departures daily from Domeyko in the centre; CH$1500).
Plane to: Antofagasta (1 daily); Copiapó (1 daily); Iquique (1 daily); Santiago (4–5 daily).

COQUIMBO

A fifteen-minute *colectivo* ride south from La Serena lies its rougher, livelier twin – Coquimbo, the region's main port. With colourful houses clustered along a hill and the prominent 93-metre **Cruz del Tercer Milenio** looming atop Cerro El Vigía, offering 360-degree views of the La Serena-Coquimbo area, Coquimbo is also home to the **Centro Cultural Mohammed VI**. This striking 36-metre monument on top of Cerro Dominante has a fifteen-storey minaret. Its construction by Moroccan craftsmen was funded by the king of Morocco, for the benefit of Coquimbo's Lebanese Muslim community. The beautifully-restored historical district of **Barrio Inglés** comprises several lively plazas, and has a far more exciting **eating** and **nightlife scene** than La Serena. *De Costa a Costa*, Aldunate 502, has excellent three-course lunch specials featuring fresh fish and seafood (CH$4000), while nearby *London House*, Argandoña 350, offers four-course lunches in a plush imperial setting (CH$6000). Down by the seafront, the bustling and fragrant **Caleta Pescadores** sells fresh **fish** and exquisite seafood *empanadas*.

Coquimbo's only real drawback is the lack of **budget accommodation**. One exception is the HI-affiliated *Hostal Nomade*, at Calle Regimento Coquimbo

STARGAZING IN CHILE

With an average of 360 cloudless nights per year, northern Chile has some of the clearest skies in the world, so it's little wonder that it's home to some of the world's most **powerful telescopes**. Largest to date is the forthcoming E.L.T. (Extremely Large Telescope), though this in turn will be dwarfed when the imaginatively-named O.W.L. (OverWhelmingly Large), with a hundred-metre mirror, opens further north in the Atacama Desert. The larger observatories allow public visits **free of charge** during the day, allowing you to view the equipment, though not to use it.

To date, there are only three places in Chile that have nocturnal stargazing facilities expressly for tourists: **Cerro Mamalluca** (see p.450) and Cerro Collowara in the Elqui Valley, and **Cielo Austral** (see p.459) near San Pedro de Atacama.

Following is the pick of the big Elqui observatories – there is no public transport other than organised tours, and you need to reserve in advance.

Cerro Paranal 126km south of Antofagasta, the observatory sports four VLTs (Very Large Telescopes), each with an 8m mirror. Antofagasta-based Desértica Expediciones arranges full-day-trips, including lunch (CH$25,000; ⓣ55/282522). Open for visits the last two weekends of every month except Dec; 2–4pm. To reserve, contact ⓣ55/435335; ⓦwww.eso.org.
La Silla 147km northeast of La Serena, and home to 14 telescopes (Sept–June Sat at 1:30pm). Reserve with the Santiago office at ⓣ2/285006; ⓦwww.eso.org.
Cerro Tololo 70km east of Serena, this I nter-American observatory features an impressive 8.1m Gemini telescope, whose identical twin is currently being built in Hawaii (Sat 9am–noon & 1–4pm). The observatory's office is at Colina El Pino s/n (ⓣ51/205200, ⓦctio .noao.edu).

5 (☎51/315665 or 9/369-5885, ⓦwww.hostalnomade.cl; dorms CH$6–8000, ❹–❺), housed in the large and rambling former residence of the French ambassador. It offers friendly and informative staff, large rooms with exceptionally high ceilings, internet and kitchen facilities and other backpacker conveniences.

ELQUI VALLEY

The fertile greenery along the bottom of the tranquil **ELQUI VALLEY** contrasts greatly with the sandy sides of the valley, its slopes a spectrum of red, green and gold due to the mineral-rich soil. The ribbon of the highway, lined with pink peppercorn trees, runs along the valley floor, past vineyards and grapes drying on canvas sheets by the roadside. Ruta 41 runs inland to Vicuña before splitting into two; the east branch continues on to Pisco Elqui, with a nearby dirt road leading into the **Río Cochiguaz canyon**, a hippie-ish New Age community known for frequent UFO sightings. The west branch climbs steeply to the top of the highest pass between Chile and Argentina – **Paso del Agua Negra** – at an altitude of 4779 metres. Open only from November to March, its sole inhabitants are migrant goat herders and otherworldly snow sculptures known as *penitentes* (penitent monks), shaped by the fierce sun and wind. Tours of the valley typically take in the giant dam and man-made **Lago Puklara**, popular with windsurfers and kitesurfers, the historical village of Vicuña, the laid-back community of Pisco Elqui and a *pisco*-tasting distillery before finishing with stargazing at the Observatorio Mamalluca.

Vicuña

Sleepy **Vicuña** makes a convenient stopover for those exploring the Elqui Valley. Formerly home to Nobel Prize-winner **Gabriela Mistrál**, it has a **museum** at Gabriela Mistrál 759 (Jan–Feb Mon–Sat 10am–7pm, Sun 10am–6pm; March–Dec Mon–Fri 10am–1pm & 2.30–6.30pm, Sat & Sun 10am–1pm) dedicated to her. **Planta Capel** (Dec–Feb daily and public holidays 10am–6pm; rest of the year daily 10am–12.30pm & 2.30–6pm; ☎51/411251, ⓦwww.piscocapel.cl), the valley's largest **pisco distillery**, lies just south of town, and has half-hourly bilingual tours tracking the Muscatel grape's journey from the vine to the pisco bottle, culminating in a small free sample at the end. Vicuña's sleeping options include *Hostal Rita Klampt*, Condell 433 (☎51/419611, ⓔrita_klampt@yahoo.es), where you are fussed over by the effusive German hostess and the excellent breakfast includes home-made jam. Alternatively, head to the newly-refurbished *Hostal Valle Hermoso*, Gabriela Mistrál 706 (☎51/411206) – a family-run, colonial-style house with small, clean rooms, some windowless. *Halley*, at Gabriela Mistrál 404, is Vicuña's best eating option, serving inexpensive roast *cabrito* (baby goat) in a rather formal setting; its fast food branch on the east side of the plaza, *Halley Pronto*, dishes out delicious *empanadas*. Alternatively, take a *colectivo* to the village of Villaseca, where *Restaurant Solar de Villaseca*, Punta Arenas s/n (closed Mon), cooks all its dishes in solar ovens – for obvious reasons, daylight hours only!

Observatorio Cerro Mamalluca

The **Observatorio Cerro Mamalluca** is located nine kilometres northeast of Vicuña. Compared to those in other observatories in the area, its thirty-centimetre telescope is tiny, but still offers magnification of 150 times – sufficient to look closely at the craters on the **moon** and to view **nebulas**, **star clusters** and **Saturn**. There are two tours offered: "Basic Astronomy" and "Andean Cosmovision", looking at the night sky as seen by the pre-Columbian inhabitants of the area. There are four two-hourly tours of each type in the summer (CH$3500); "Basic Astronomy" commences at 8.30pm, while "Andean Cosmovision" kicks off at 9.15pm; in the winter there are only three tours nightly, starting at 6.30pm and 7.15pm, respectively. Shuttles to and from the observatory (CH$1500 return) depart from the Cerro Mamalluca office in Vicuña (Gabriela Mistrál 260; Mon–Sat 9am–10pm, Sun 10am–10pm; ⓣ51/411352, ⓦwww.mamalluca.org), half an hour before the tour starts. Reserve tickets in advance, especially in the peak months from December through February.

Arrival and information

Buses The main terminal is one block south of the square, on O'Higgins at Prat (ⓣ51/411348).

Colectivos from La Serena stop across the street from the main bus terminal.

Tourist office Inside the Torre Bauer, San Martín s/n (daily 8.30am–5.30pm; ⓣ51/209125, ⓔluis_hernan_vigorena@latinmail.com).

PISCO ELQUI

PISCO ELQUI, a green and laid-back village, boasts a beautiful hillside setting alongside the Río Clara, with unparalleled views of the Elqui valley. The shaded **Plaza de Armas**, with its brightly-painted Gothic church, hosts the **Mercado Artesanal** in the summer. A block away, the **Solar de Pisco Tres Erres**, Chile's oldest pisco distillery, offers free guided tours, complete with tastings (Jan–Feb daily 11am–1.30pm & 2.30–8pm; March–Dec daily 10am–12.30pm & 2.30–6pm). **Los Nichos** (March–Oct daily 10am–1pm & 2–6pm; Nov–Dec daily 11am–7pm; free tours) is an old-fashioned distillery 3km south of Pisco Elqui, and worth visiting to see pisco processed by hand.

El Tesoro de Elqui, on Prat s/n (ⓣ51/451069, ⓦwww.tesoro-elqui.cl), has cosy adobe dorms and **rooms** – one with a skylight for stargazing – and the food is excellent. The owners can help organize kite- and windsurfing on Lago Puklara. *Hostal Triskel*, Baquedano s/n (ⓣ9/4198-8680, ⓦwww.hostaltriskel.cl), another good spot, has uniquely-decorated rooms, decent breakfast and can arrange hiking, biking and horse riding. *Alcohuaz Expediciones* (Prat s/n ⓣ51/451168 ⓦwww.caballo-elqui.cl) run by a genuine *huaso* (Chilean cowboy) offers excellent horse-riding trips in the area. Just up from the church, *El Ranchito de Don René* serves Chilean classics, such as *pastel de choclo*, on a shaded patio, while *Los Jugos*, on the square, offers delicious fruit juices and large portions of pizza.

PISCO

Pisco, the clear, brandy-like drink derived from **Muscatel grapes**, is Chile's national drink and a constant source of **dispute** between Chile and Peru. The climatic conditions in the Elqui Valley are ideal for growing the sweet grapes; furthermore, only distilleries in Chile's Regions III and IV have the right to call their distilled drink *pisco*. Peru claims that *pisco* originates from the Peruvian port of the same name, and some historical records demonstrate that the drink has been consumed in that area since the Spaniards introduced vineyards in the early 1600s. Chileans claim that they have also been producing *pisco* for centuries, that their *pisco* is of better quality and that it plays a greater role in Chilean society. In both Chile and Peru, *pisco* is normally consumed in a **pisco sour** – a mix of *pisco*, lemon juice, sugar syrup, egg white, crushed ice and a drop of angostura bitters. It goes down deceptively smoothly, but packs a real punch.

Arrival and information

Buses Via Elqui buses stop in front of the Plaza de Armas.
Tourist office Information on the area is available at the internet café Migrantes, at Prat 280 (Tue–Sun 9am–2pm & 4–11pm; ⓣ51/451-1917, ⓦwww.turismomigrantes.cl).

RESERVA NACIONAL PINGÜINO DE HUMBOLDT

This remarkable **marine wildlife reserve**, 110 kilometres north of La Serena, comprises three islands jutting from the cold Pacific waters: Isla Chañaral, Isla Choros and Isla Damas. There is a Conaf-run Centro de Información Ambiental (Mon–Thurs, Sat & Sun 8.30am–5.30pm, Fri 8.30am–4.30pm) at Caleta de Choros, the small fishing community closest to the islands, with informative displays on local flora and fauna. Boats depart from Caleta de Choros to sail along the steep jagged coastline of Isla Choros, home to *chundungos* (sea otters), a noisy colony of **sea lions**, the **Humboldt penguin**, four species of cormorants, clamouring **Peruvian boobies** and countless seagulls. You get close enough to see the wildlife in great detail and on the way to the island, pods of curious **bottle-nosed dolphins** often frolic around the boat; it's also possible to spot humpback, blue and killer **whales**. On the way back, visitors are allowed a short ramble on sandy Isla Damas, whose pristine beaches are home to a smaller penguin population. There are opportunities for wild **camping** in the summer; reserve in advance at the Conaf office in La Serena, or email ⓔcarolina.pasten@conaf.cl. Be sure to give names, dates (the maximum stay is three days and two nights) and the number of campers (CH$12,000/site for up to six people). Bring all necessary supplies, including water.

COPIAPÓ

The prosperous mining town of **COPIAPÓ**, 333 kilometres north of La Serena, was founded in 1744 and benefited greatly from the **silver boom** of the 1830s. Today, Copiapó still makes its living from mining, nowadays for **copper**. At the heart of Copiapó is the large **Plaza Prat**, dotted with pepper trees; handicraft stalls line the plaza's east side, facing the mall. The Neoclassical **Iglesia Catedral Nuestra Señora de Rosario** graces the southwest corner, while half a block from the northwest corner of the square, at the corner of Colipí and Rodriguez, is the extremely worthwhile **Museo Mineralógico** (Mon–Fri 10am–1.30pm & 3.30–7pm, Sat 10am–1.30pm; CH$500), with an impressive mineral collection including copper, silver ore, part of a meteorite which landed in the Atacama Desert and massive chunks of semi-precious stones, such as malachite, onyx, jasper and amethyst. Budget **accommodation** is not particularly exciting, although *Residencial Chañarcillo*, a block from the Tur Bus bus station at Chañarcillo 741 (ⓣ52/238872), makes a convenient stopover, with dark but tidy rooms and friendly owners. Alternatively *Residencial Ben Bow*, Rodriguez 541 (ⓣ52/238872), has clean, no-frills rooms around a narrow courtyard. *Bavaria*, at Chacabuco 487, is a reliable choice for meaty dishes, while *Cactus*, at Atacama 260, serves large plates of *fajitas*, rice and beans and other Mexican staples; there are also several large, well-stocked supermarkets in the city centre.

Arrival and information

Airport Aeropuerto Desierto de Atacama is 45km west of the city; take Transfer Casther (CH$4500) to Copiapó or a *colectivo* (CH$2000) to Caldera.
Buses Tur Bus terminal is at Freire and Colipí; Terminal Torreblanca, with numerous carriers, directly opposite. Pullman bus terminal is a block south, at Colipí 109; buses Casther and Recabarren,

from Caldera, stop just east of the Hiper Lider supermarket, at Buena Esperanza 552.

Conaf Juan Martínez 55 (Mon–Fri 8.30am–5.30pm; ⓣ52/237042, ⓔatacama@conaf.cl). Good source of information on Nevado de Tres Cruces and Pan de Azúcar.

Tourist office Los Carrera 691 (Dec–Feb Mon–Fri 8.30am–7pm, Sat 10am–2pm; ⓣ52/231510, ⓔinfoatacama@sernatur.cl). Helpful staff, but not very well stocked.

AROUND COPIAPÓ

The landscape surrounding Copiapó is astonishingly varied, with the salt flats of the **Parque Nacional de Tres Cruces**, mesmerising **Laguna Verde**, active volcano Ojos de Salado and to the west, the fine white sands of **Bahía Inglesa**.

Parque Nacional Nevado de Tres Cruces

Remote and ruggedly beautiful **Parque Nacional Nevado de Tres Cruces** is located east of Copiapó via Ruta 31, which winds through the mercilessly desolate desert landscape, occasionally enlivened by a splash of gold or green or pink, courtesy of the minerals in the soil. The road climbs steeply before reaching the **Salar de Maricunga** – a great field of white crystals on the edge of the park, dotted with emerald-coloured salt pools – and continuing on towards **Paso San Francisco** on the Argentine border. The park consists of two separate parts: the larger, 49,000-hectare **Laguna Santa Rosa** sector, 146 kilometres east of Copiapó, at an altitude of 3700 metres, comprises half of the salt flat and the namesake lake with roaming herds of **vicuñas** and **guanacos** feeding on the abundant grasslands. The pale blue lagoon, dotted with flamingoes and giant coots, is set against a backdrop of snow-streaked volcanoes, including the grand **Nevado Tres Cruces** (6749m). On the west side of the lake is a small and very rustic Conaf-run refugio, consisting of bare floorspace, basic cooking facilities and a privy out back. Cutting across a vast expanse of parched brown land, dotted with hardy yellow altiplano plants, you reach 12,000-hectare **Laguna del Negro Francisco** sector, around 85 kilometres south. In summer it becomes a sea of pink and beige thanks to the presence of eight thousand or so Andean, Chilean and James **flamingoes** that migrate here from neighbouring Argentina, Bolivia and Peru. On the west side of the lake, Conaf's *Refugio Laguna del Negro Francisco* has beds, hot showers and kitchen facilities; make reservations with Copiapó's Conaf office.

COPIAPÓ TOUR OPERATORS

Since the area's national parks are difficult to get to without a sturdy vehicle of your own, it is easier to go as part of a tour. Day-trip prices are typically around CH$45,000 per person to the Parque Nacional Pan de Azúcar and CH$60,000 to Parque Nacional Nevado Tres Cruces, including lunch and entrance fees.

Atacama Chile Maipú 580B ⓣ52/211191, ⓦwww.atacamachile.com. Reputable bilingual company running separate day-trips to Laguna Santa Rosa and Laguna Verde, as well as four-wheel-drive, dirt-biking and sandboarding trips in the Atacama Desert and diving excursions off the coast.

Atacama Expeditions Infante 661 ⓣ52/223640 or 9/891-8212, ⓦwww.atacamaexpeditions.com. Standard and tailor-made tours of the area for small groups offered by the extremely knowledgeable local guide, Ovidio Rodríguez; includes both Laguna Verde and Laguna Santa Rosa in a day-trip to Nevado Tres Cruces. Spanish only.

Aventurismo Colipí 484, Local B-212 ⓣ52/235430, ⓦwww.aventurismo.cl. Mountaineering outfit specializing in multi-day ascents of the volcanoes Ojos de Salado, Nevado Tres Cruces and Llullaillaco (Nov 1–March 31).

Laguna Verde and Volcán Ojos de Salado

The magnificent spectacle of the misnamed **LAGUNA VERDE** lies 65 kilometres beyond Laguna Santa Rosa, at a whopping altitude of 4325 metres (14,190ft). The first flash of its brilliant turquoise waters, around a bend in the road, is breathtaking. On the lake's salty white shore are some rustic and relaxing **hot springs** inside a little wooden shack; it's also possible to camp here. You must bring all necessary supplies with you, including water, and remember that night-time temperatures drop well below freezing. Beyond the lake loom three volcanoes, including the second-highest peak in Latin America – **OJOS DE SALADO**. At an elevation of 6887 metres, it trails just behind Argentina's 6962-metre Aconcagua, the tallest mountain in the Americas. It is also the world's highest active volcano, with recent eruptions in 1937 and 1956.

Caldera

The towns of **CALDERA** and Bahía Inglesa, 75 kilometres west of Copiapó, are both popular **beach resorts** famous for their large, delicious **scallops**. Caldera itself is an unremarkable little town, though the Gothic **Iglesia San Vicente** (1862) on the pretty Plaza Condell is worth a look. Pedestrian **Gana**, lined with craft stalls in the summer, makes for a nice stroll between the square and the waterfront **Costanera** (pier) – home to the oldest railway station in Chile, dating back to 1850, now a museum and events centre. The pier is the best place to sample inexpensive seafood *empanadas* and other fishy delights. Caldera's main beach, small seaweed-tinted Copiapina, is not the best in the area; for crystal-clear turquoise waters and long stretches of fine white sand, head to nearby Bahía Inglesa, seven kilometres south, either by *colectivo* or the cycle path parallel to the road.

Bahía Inglesa

BAHÍA INGLESA is immensely popular with locals in the summer, and it's easy to see why: the laid-back atmosphere, the proximity of the ocean and an abundance of cheap seafood *empanadas* sold by vendors along the seafront entice you to linger longer. There are several small and **sheltered beaches** along the main Avenida El Morro, with the wide crescent of **Playa Las Machas** stretching into the distance. **Accommodation** tends to be overpriced, though prices drop outside peak season. *Camping Bahía Inglesa*, off Playa Las Machas (☎52/315424; CH$19,000 per site for up to six people), is an excellent place to **camp**, with hot water showers, bathrooms, picnic tables and cooking facilities; otherwise, *Domo Chango Chile*, Av El Morro 619 on the waterfront (☎52/316168, Ⓦwww.changochile.cl), has bizarre but comfortable tent-like dome rooms (private or shared; CH$12,000 per person) and an excellent restaurant specializing in **seafood**.

Arrival and information

Buses Copiapó-bound Casther and Recabarren buses stop at Ossa Varas 710 (every half hr; 1hr; CH$1500). *Colectivos* to Copiapó leave from Cifuentes, just south of Ossa Varas.

Tourist office On Plaza de Armas (daily 9am–2pm & 4–7pm; ☎52/316076, Ⓦwww.caldera.cl).

PARQUE NACIONAL PAN DE AZÚCAR

Parque Nacional Pan de Azúcar entices visitors with its spectacular coastal desert landscape, which alternates between steep cliffs, studded with a multitude of cactus species, and pristine white beaches. A dirt road runs along the coast past Playa Blanca and Playa Los Piqueros to **CALETA PAN DE AZÚCAR,** a small fishing village inside the park. **Isla Pan de Azúcar**, home to **Humboldt penguins**,

sea lions, sea otters and a wealth of marine birds, lies a short distance offshore. Although landing on the island is forbidden, fishing boats get visitors close enough to see (and smell) the wildlife at close quarters. A nine-kilometre trail runs north from the village to the **Mirador Pan de Azúcar**, a lookout point offering staggering panoramic views of the coastline. A dirt road heading north from the village toward Ruta 5 has a fifteen-kilometre trail branching off to the west that leads you through the arid landscape to Las Lomitas, an **outlook point** often visited by inquisitive **desert foxes** and shrouded in rolling *camanchaca* (sea mist), the main water source for all the coastal vegetation. **Camping** is available on the nearby Cerro Soldado, at Playa Los Piqueros and at Caleta Pan de Azúcar (☎52/213404); it costs CH$10,000 per site for up to six people and includes twenty litres of drinking water, picnic tables, hot showers and WC use. Groups of four to six people may prefer to rent beachside *cabañas* complete with kitchen facilities (❻). For food, try the eateries in the village, which cook the day's fresh catch.

Arrival and information

Boats Fishing boats run to Isla Pan de Azúcar year-round (Dec–Feb 9am–7pm; Mar–Nov 9am–6pm; CH$50,000 for up to ten people).

Buses There are no public buses to the park, though northbound buses from Copiapó can drop you off in Chañaral, the nearest town. Turismo Chango (☎52/480484) runs two daily buses from opposite the Municipalidad in Chañaral in the summer at 8.30am and 3pm (CH$3000). Be warned: departures are not always as scheduled. Taxis cost CH$10,000 each way; worth it for a group. Alternatively, take a day-trip tour from Copiapó (see p.452).

Tourist information Conaf's Centro de Información Ambiental (daily 8.30am–12.30pm & 2–6pm) is opposite Playa Piqueros and has maps and information on the park, as well as a display of local cacti. The park fee of CH$3000 is payable here; no fee is charged if entering the park from the east.

Norte Grande

ANTOFAGASTA

ANTOFAGASTA is the biggest city in northern Chile; a busy industrialized port and major transportation hub, it has few attractions to detain travellers, though it's a good place to stock up on necessities. Antofagasta's compact centre boasts the surprisingly lovely **Plaza Colón**, the apparent British influence accentuated by its centrepiece, the Torre Reloj, a small-scale Big Ben replica. To the north, three blocks of Arturo Prat are pedestrianized and feature shops and cafes, while three blocks south along Matta is a large pedestrian square presided over by the impressive pink, grey and cream **Mercado Central**, with its wafting smells of fish and cooking food. A block east of the square, along Bolívar, lies the handsome green railway station dating from 1885 to 1887.

At the port end of this street you'll find the oldest building in the city, the former **Aduana**, now housing the **Museo Regional** (Tues–Fri 9am–5pm, Sat & Sun 11am–4pm; CH$600), with exhibitions on regional natural history, archeology and the War of the Pacific and an outstanding mummified babies exhibit. The waterfront's wooden piers are currently undergoing extensive renovation; it stretches north towards a shopping mall with a multi-screen cinema. *Colectivos* (CH$400) run along Matta to the often-crowded Balneario Municipal, and further south to the Balneario El Huáscar and Caleta Coloso. These are Antofagasta's better beaches, lined with eateries, bars and discos, though not really suitable for swimming.

La Portada

Much featured on postcards, the natural monument of **La Portada**, fifteen kilometres north of Antofagasta, makes quite an impression. A giant rock eroded into a natural arch over the course of three million years, it juts out of the churning ocean, with seagulls and *jotes* (turkey buzzards) circling overhead, and is well worth the trip out. To get there, take a ten-minute ride on a Mejillones-bound bus (CH$1000) and ask to be dropped off at the junction, from where it is a half-hour walk towards the ocean.

Arrival and information

Airport Twenty-five kilometres north of the city on Ruta 1; the Aerobús shuttle will drop you off at your destination (CH$4000). Alternatively, take a bus into the city centre (CH$700).

Buses Tur Bus terminal is on the corner of Latorre and Bolívar. Pullman buses are across Latorre from Tur Bus, and local buses to Mejillones nearby. Both Tur Bus and Pullman have luggage storage and snacks for sale.

Tourist office Prat 384, on Plaza Colón (Mon–Fri 8.30am–5.30pm; ⓣ55/451818, ⓔinfoantofagasta@sernatur.cl); helpful staff provide city maps and information on local attractions.

Accommodation, eating and drinking

Bavaria Latorre 2618. Two-tiered grill-caféteria, the latter serving inexpensive fast food, and the former specializing in tasty *parilladas* and German-style meat-and-vegetable dishes. Lunch special CH$3500.

Casa El Mosaico C-18 El Huáscar ⓣ9/938-0743, ⓦwww.chilegreentours.com. Newly-opened hostel near Balneario el Huáscar run by the helpful Marcelo and Loreto who organize sandboarding, paragliding and diving with sea lions, amongst other trips; includes breakfast and internet. Laundry serrvice is available. Dorm CH$7000. ❹

Mercado Central Matta, between Maipú and Uribe. Besides fresh produce, the market's eateries cook up fishy delights for a reasonable price. *El Sureño* comes recommended. Grilled fish CH$3000.

Natura Gourmet Av Gabriela Mistral 032. Popular vegetarian restaurant serving filling dishes and fresh fruit juices. Fixed lunch CH$3000.

Residencial El Cobre Arturo Prat 749 ⓣ55/225162. Centrally-located no-frills rooms with a shared bathroom. ❷

Wally's Pub Antonino Toro 982. A cosy pub with a chilled-out ambience serving exotic international food and a wide range of drinks, including imported beers. Beer CH$1500.

Moving on

Bus to: Arica (6 daily; 10hr; CH$12,000); Calama (several daily; 3hr; CH$3000); Copiapó (8 daily; 7hr; CH$13,000); Iquique (6 daily; 6hr; CH$8000); La Serena (8 daily; 12hr; CH$15,000); San Pedro de Atacama (several daily; 5hr; CH$5000); Santiago (10 daily; 18hr; CH$20,000).

Plane to: Arica (once daily); Calama (twice daily); Iquique (once daily); Santiago (several daily).

CALAMA

The busy city of **CALAMA**, at the heart of the Atacama **copper mining** industry, is a convenient transportation hub and an almost inevitable stop for travellers heading to San Pedro de Atacama. A slow, cold and frequently late train departs from Calama's Estación de Ferrocarril, on Balmaceda 1777 (ⓣ55/348900), for Uyuni, Bolivia, every Wednesday at 10pm, taking 23 hours to reach its destination and subject to delays at the border; bring a three-season sleeping bag. There is no central bus terminal, and **bus companies** are either clustered near the train station to the east of the city centre, or lie to the north of it. Tur Bus has frequent departures to all big destinations in the north of Chile, as well as Santiago, leaving from its terminal on the corner of Granderso and Montt (ⓣ55/316699); Pullman Bus, with similar services, departs from Mall Calama at Balmaceda 3242. Buses Atacama 2000, Abaroa 2106 (ⓣ55/314757), and Buses Frontera, Antofagasta 2041 (ⓣ55/318543), have multiple daily departures to San Pedro de Atacama, while Frontera also runs twice-weekly to the village of Ollagüe on the Bolivian border, from where it's possible to get an ongoing connection to Uyuni. Géminis, at Antofagasta 2239 (ⓣ55/341993), and Pullman have Tuesday, Friday and Sunday morning departures for Salta and Jujuy between them. From Aeropuerto El Loa (ⓣ55/342348) there are multiple daily flights to Santiago and Antofagasta, and a daily flight to Copiapó.

SAN PEDRO DE ATACAMA AND AROUND

SAN PEDRO DE ATACAMA, a little oasis town of single-storey adobe houses and unpaved streets, is situated 75 kilometres east of Calama, the nearest city. No other northern destination can compete with the sheer number of natural attractions: the stunning *altiplano* scenery in the surrounding area draws scores of travellers year-round; nearby volcanoes, sand dunes, geysers and lagoons will keep any nature lover busy. One of the oldest settlements in Chile, San Pedro was originally a stop on a pre-Columbian trade route between the highland and coastal communities; in 1547, the Spanish established their first mission here and subjugated the locals. The town later became an important rest stop for cattle drives from Salta, Argentina, when the nitrate industry took off in Chile and fresh meat was needed for the workers. Despite being somewhat crowded during the peak season, San Pedro retains a friendly and relaxed vibe, and has an excellent assortment of budget accommodation and facilities for visitors, as well as the widest range of cuisine north of Santiago. Centre of town is the cheery little **Plaza de Armas**, framed by *algarrobo* and pink peppercorn trees. The whitewashed **Iglesia de San Pedro** (1641) stands on the west side of the square, while most eateries and other services are found along nearby Caracoles.

Museo Arqueológico Gustavo Le Paige

The intriguing **Museo Arqueológico Gustavo Le Paige** (Jan–Feb daily

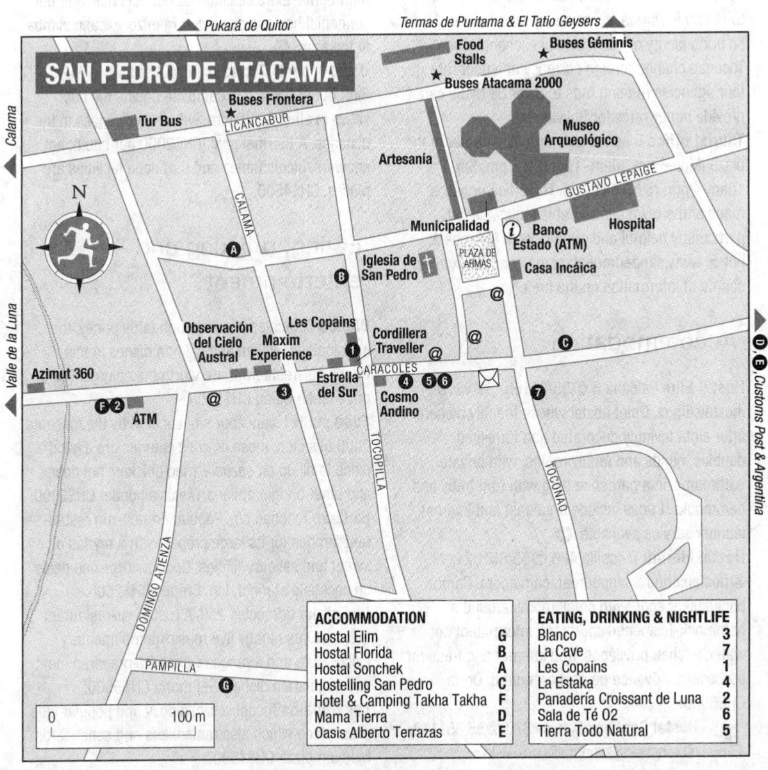

10am–1pm & 3–7pm; March–Dec Mon–Fri 9am–noon & 2–6pm, Sat & Sun 10am–noon & 2–6pm; CH$2000), located northeast of the square, is well worth a visit, though it no longer displays its famous prehistoric mummy exhibit. Founded by a Belgian Jesuit, after whom it is named, it is home to over 380,000 clearly labelled pre-Columbian artefacts, perfectly preserved in the dry desert air, including ceramics, gold work and a wide range of tablets and straws for the ritual inhalation of hallucinogenic cacti.

Arrival and information

Buses Tur Bus terminal (Ⓣ55/851549) is at the corner of Domingo Atienza and Licancábur; Buses Frontera, Buses Atacama 2000, Buses Gemini and Pullman stop further east on Licancábur.
Money San Pedro has two ATMs; the one on Gustavo Le Paige, opposite the museum, does not take Visa, while the other, on Caracoles next to *Hostal Puritama*, is frequently out of order, so bring plenty of cash. Money exchanges on Toconao change foreign currency at a poor rate; tour agencies running trips to Salar de Uyuni can provide better rates for Bolivianos.
Tourist office Toconao s/n, northeast corner of the plaza (Mon–Fri 9.30am–1pm & 3–7pm, Sat 10am–2pm; Ⓣ55/541420). The office provides maps of the town centre but is otherwise not particularly helpful and often closed. Also check out Ⓦwww.sanpedrodeatacama.com, an excellent source of information on the area.

Accommodation

Hostal Elim Palpana 6 Ⓣ55/851567, Ⓦwww.hostalelim.cl. Quiet hostel whose friendly owners offer eight lovingly decorated and furnished doubles, quads and family rooms, with private bathrooms, in a garden setting with fruit trees and hammocks. Prices include breakfast and internet; laundry service available. ❻
Hostal Florida Tocopilla 406 Ⓣ55/851021, Ⓔhostalflorida@sanpedroatacama.com. Central backpacker spot, with small rooms around a hammock-festooned courtyard, intermittent hot water, kitchen privileges, free internet and frequent barbecues. Advance payment required. Dorm CH$6000.
Hostal Sonchek Calama 370 Ⓣ55/851112, Ⓔsoncheksp@hotmail.com. With a welcoming and helpful English- and French-speaking hostess, this extremely popular and conveniently located hostel has cosy rooms, kitchen use, courtyard with hammocks, laundry service and an excellent café next door. Dorm CH$6000. ❹
Hostelling San Pedro Caracoles 360 Ⓣ55/851426, Ⓦwww.hostellingatacama.com. Bustling Hostelling International branch with member discounts, three-tiered bunk beds in dorms (CH$8000), clean singles and doubles, a shaded courtyard, free internet and breakfast. It also organizes a plethora of tours in the area and rents bikes and sandboards. ❺
Hotel & Camping Takha Takha Caracoles 101 Ⓣ55/851038, Ⓦwww.takhatakha.cl. Camping sites in a shaded area and clean rooms, with private or shared bathrooms, set in a tranquil oasis of vegetation. Popular with travellers of all ages, there's also a good café on the premises. ❺–❼
Mama Tierra Pachamama 615 Ⓣ55/851418, Ⓔhostalmamatierra@sanpedroatacama.com. Popular with backpackers and a 5min walk from the centre, this tidy hostel offers dorms (CH$8000), singles and doubles with private or shared bathrooms. Extras include laundry service, and the congenial hostess can help organize volcano climbs in the area. ❺
Oasis Alberto Terrazas Pozo 3 Ⓣ55/851042. 3km out of town, this campsite boasts the best views in all of San Pedro, with the volcanoes in the distance. A thermal pool (CH$2000 per adult), hot showers, picnic tables and barbecue facilities are pluses. CH$4500.

Eating, drinking and entertainment

Blanco Caracoles s/n. Although fairly pricey, the imaginative chicken and salmon dishes in this trendy bar-restaurant are worth the splurge. Fixed-price lunch menu CH$5500.
Food stalls Licancábur s/n. Located by the Atacama 2000 bus stop, these no-frills eateries are a good place to fill up on *cazuela*, fried chicken, hot dogs and other budget options. Meals all under CH$2000.
La Cave Toconao s/n. Popular French-run restaurant famous for its large crêpes with a myriad of sweet and savoury fillings. Good two-for-one deals on cocktails at night, too. Crêpes CH$2500.
La Estaka Caracoles 259. A rustic bar-restaurant that features nightly live music, complimentary pisco sours and a range of expertly-prepared meat and vegetarian dishes. Set menu CH$5500.
Les Copains Tocopilla s/n. A cosy and popular little pizza place which also rents bikes and sandboards. Medium pizza CH$4500.

SAN PEDRO TOUR OPERATORS

Choosing a reputable **tour operator** in San Pedro can be difficult, but at least the intense competition keeps prices fairly stable. Expect to pay around CH$25,000 for a tour of the *altiplano* lagoons and villages, CH$5000 to visit Valle de la Luna, CH$15,000 to visit El Tatio geysers and CH$10,000 for a three-hour sandboarding trip (including an instructor and board rental); trip prices normally exclude entrance fees. The following are reliable:

Azimut 360 Caracoles 195 ⓣ55/851469 ⓦwww.azimut.cl. Multi-day treks, camping and volcano ascents in the area are offered by this long-standing Santiago-based outfit.
Cosmo Andino Caracoles s/n ⓣ55/851069, ⓦwww.cosmoandino-expediciones.cl. Established and reliable bilingual operator running standard trips to El Tatio geysers, Valle de la Luna and the *altiplano* villages.
Estrella del Sur Caracoles 238 ⓣ9/8516-6032. One of the better operators offering all-inclusive three-day trips across the Salar de Uyuni.
Maxim Experience Caracoles 174C ⓣ55/851952, ⓔmaximexperience@hotmail.com. Sandboarding and trips to Ojos de Salado, among others.
Observación del Cielo Austral Caracoles 166 ⓣ55/851935, ⓦwww.spaceobs.com. French astronomer Alain Maury brings the night sky to life during the tours at his home in the desert, where he has set up several powerful telescopes (nightly 7.30pm & 9.30pm; 2hr 30min; CH$12,000 per person). Funny and engaging, he will show you nebulas and planets up close and personal, and also explains how to stargaze solo. Tours are conducted in English, French and Spanish. Warm clothes are essential.

Panadería Croissant de Luna Caracoles 101B. This small bakery has a wide range of white and wholegrain breads, croissants and delectable vegetable empanadas; open late. Croissants CH$800.
Sala de Té 02 Caracoles 295B. Unpretentious eatery serving excellent quiches alongside standard fast food, as well as devilishly good chocolate cake and a range of teas. Quiche, salad and drink CH$2000.
Tierra Todo Natural Caracoles 46. Fantastic daily set menus, which always include imaginative vegetarian dishes. Evening service can be slow. Fixed-price menu CH$5500.

Moving on

Bus to: Antofagasta (6 daily; 5hr; CH$6000); Arica (1 daily; 14hr; CH$14,000); Calama (6 daily; 1hr 45min; CH$2000); Santiago (1 daily; 22hr; CH$35,000). **Frontera del Norte** to: Socaire (1 daily at 7.30pm; 2hr; CH$2000); Toconao (4 daily; 1hr 30min; CH$1500). **Buses Gemini** to: Salta and Jujuy (Tues, Fri & Sun 7am & 11am; 14hr; CH$17,000).

DAY-TRIPS FROM SAN PEDRO

Beyond San Pedro, the scenery is dramatic, dominated by large volcanic peaks, **Valle de la Luna**'s magnificent lunar landscape, the famous **El Tatio geysers**, Chile's largest salt flat **Salar de Atacama** and dazzling lagoons.

Valle de la Luna

Most people come here at sundown with one of a plethora of tour groups, but the lunar landscape of **Valle de la Luna** (Moon Valley), at the heart of the Cordillera del Sal, is equally impressive at **sunrise**, when the first rays of sunlight turn the surrounding jagged red peaks various shades of pink and gold. Though the effect is even more intense at **sunset**, at dawn there are far fewer spectators, and after making your way up the giant sand dune along a marked trail, you can walk up the crest of the dune for a better vantage point. If cycling the fourteen kilometres to the valley, go west along Caracoles out of town, turn left at the end and carry straight on; plenty of water, sunscreen and a torch are essential.

Valle de la Muerte

The easiest attraction to cycle to – only three kilometres from San Pedro – the

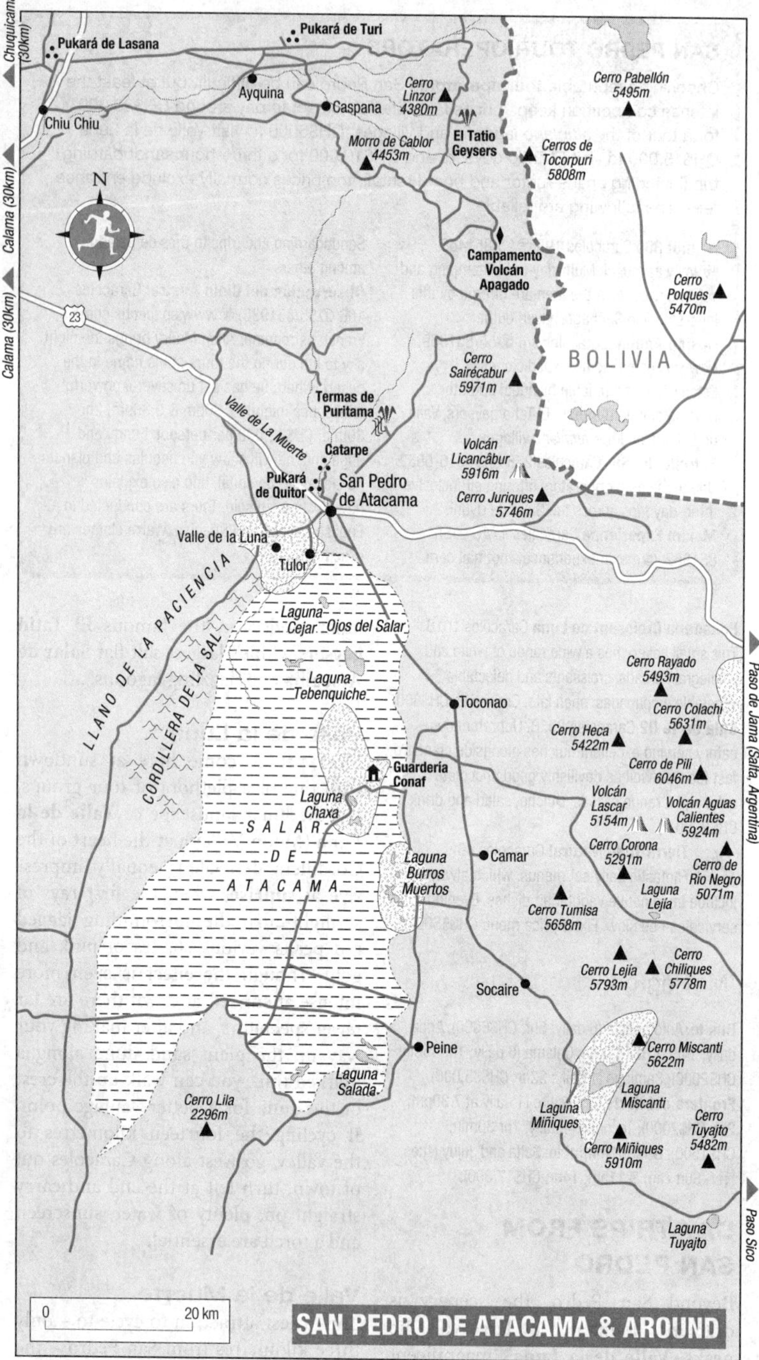
Chuquicamata (30km)
Pukará de Turi
Pukará de Lasana
Ayquina
Caspana
Chiu Chiu
Cerro Linzor 4380m
Cerro Pabellón 5495m
El Tatio Geysers
Morro de Cablor 4453m
Cerros de Tocorpuri 5808m
Calama (30km)
N
Campamento Volcán Apagado
Cerro Polques 5470m
Calama (30km)
23
BOLIVIA
Cerro Sairécabur 5971m
Termas de Puritama
Valle de La Muerte
Catarpe
Volcán Licancábur 5916m
Pukará de Quitor
San Pedro de Atacama
Cerro Juriques 5746m
Valle de la Luna
Tulor
LLANO DE LA PACIENCIA
CORDILLERA DE LA SAL
Laguna Cejar
Ojos del Salar
Laguna Tebenquiche
Toconao
Cerro Rayado 5493m
Cerro Colachi 5631m
Cerro Heca 5422m
Cerro de Pili 6046m
Paso de Jama (Salta, Argentina)
Guardería Conaf
Laguna Chaxa
Volcán Lascar 5154m
Volcán Aguas Calientes 5924m
SALAR DE ATACAMA
Laguna Burros Muertos
Camar
Cerro Corona 5291m
Cerro de Río Negro 5071m
Laguna Lejía
Cerro Tumisa 5658m
Cerro Lejía 5793m
Cerro Chiliques 5778m
Socaire
Peine
Cerro Miscanti 5622m
Laguna Salada
Laguna Miscanti
Cerro Lila 2296m
Laguna Miñiques
Cerro Tuyajto 5482m
Cerro Miñiques 5910m
Paso Sico
Laguna Tuyajto
0
20 km
SAN PEDRO DE ATACAMA & AROUND

Valle de la Muerte, with its narrow gorges, peculiar **red rock formations** and 150-metre high **sand dunes** is also a prime **sandboarding** destination, with scores of enthusiasts whizzing down the slopes in the early mornings and late afternoons. The rest of the time an exquisite silence reigns over the still sand and rocks, and you can often enjoy the views of the snow-peaked volcanoes in the distance entirely undisturbed.

Salar de Atacama

The edge of Chile's largest salt flat, the **Salar de Atacama**, lies ten kilometres away; it may disappoint those expecting a sparkling white field, but still makes an unforgettable spectacle. A jagged white crust, resembling dead coral, created by water flowing down from the mountains, stretches as far as the eye can see. Several shallow lakes dot the Salar, including **Laguna Chaxa**, made bright by the resident Andean, Chilean and James flamingoes, which spend up to fourteen hours a day feeding on tiny saltwater shrimp. Entry CH$1000.

El Tatio geysers

The **El Tatio geysers**, ninety kilometres north of town, are a morning attraction, with tours (CH$3500) setting off at 4am in order to reach them by sunrise, when the fumaroles that spew steam and the jets of scalding water that shoot up from the geysers are at their most impressive. At dawn, there is a surreal quality to the plateau: dark shadowy figures move through the mist and the sunlight glints on patches of white ground frost. When walking around, stick to marked paths, since the ground crust can be very fragile – breaking it might result in a plunge into near-boiling water. The temperature here, at the world's highest geothermal field (4320 metres), is often below freezing, so warm clothes are essential. A soak in the nearby thermal pool is a must.

Lagunas Miscanti and Miñiques

These two *altiplano* lagoons (entry CH$2500) lie 134 kilometres from town, at an elevation of around 4200 metres. Visitors here are left breathless not just by the altitude, but also by the first sight of the huge shimmering pools of deep blue, ringed with white ribbons of salt. There's abundant bird and animal life as well, and it is possible to see both flamingoes and the inquisitive *zorro culpeo*, a type of **fox** that often approaches the area's picnic site to look for scraps.

Ojos del Salar

The "eyes" of the **Ojos del Salar** salt flat are two small and almost perfectly round cold-water pools, set in the middle of a vast arid plain just outside San Pedro. A standard tour stops first by the saltwater Laguna Cejar (CH$2000), where the **salt** content is so high that you float merrily on the surface, followed by a dip in the Ojos for the brave. The last stop is **Laguna Tebenquiche**, situated on the gleaming white salt flat – a must-see for those not taking a trip to the Salar de Uyuni in Bolivia. As the sun sets, the distant volcanoes turn pink, and there is a bluish glow to the salt flat, crisscrossed with surreal patterns.

Toconao and Socaire villages

Toconao, 38 kilometres from San Pedro, is a small village with houses built entirely of volcanic *liparita* stone, nestled in an idyllic spot surrounded by sandy hills. A cool stream runs through the valley and the surrounding fertile soil supports lush vegetation, including fig, pear and quince trees, as well as a hallucinogenic type of cactus. The site has been inhabited since 11,000 BC; its present population of around seven hundred villagers make traditional crafts. It is possible to stay in several rustic *hospedajes* here, and there are delicious *humitas* (corn paste wrapped in corn leaves) for sale. Further afield, a hundred kilometres away, **Socaire** is another village of pre-Hispanic origin, with pretty stone houses, a church with a thatched roof and a fabulous view of the Salar de Atacama.

IQUIQUE

The approach to the busy coastal city of **IQUIQUE** is unforgettable, especially if coming from the east. The highway along the plateau suddenly gives way to a spectacular six-hundred-metre drop, looking down onto the giant Cerro Dragón sand dune which in turn towers over the city. At sunset, the dune and the surrounding cliffs turn various shades of pink and red, giving the city an almost unearthly feel. Almost 500 kilometres north of Antofagasta, Iquique prospered in the nitrate era, between 1890 and 1920. Most of the grand old buildings in the city's historical centre date back to that heyday. When the nitrate boom collapsed, Iquique recovered with the advent of the fishmeal industry. The town's biggest draws nowadays are its beaches, though the huge **duty-free** Zona Franca, or "Zofri", in an industrial area to the north of the city, also draws locals and visitors alike. The city is also one of the top destinations in Latin America for paragliders.

Plaza Prat

At the heart of Iquique's historic centre lies **Plaza Prat**, lined with banks and restaurants, with the tall white **Torre Reloj**, the city's symbol, built in 1877, as centrepiece. On the south side of the

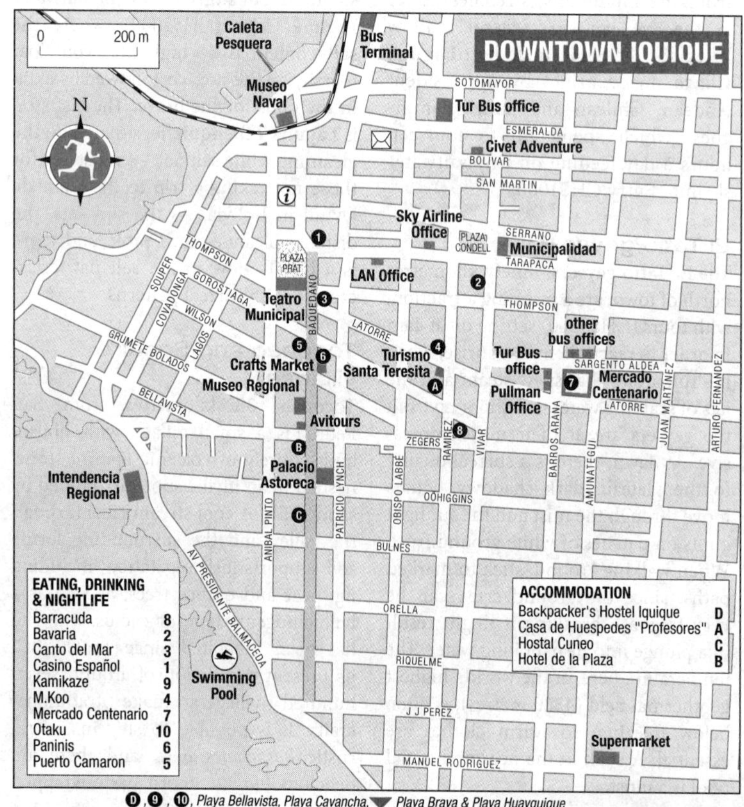

square stands the Neoclassical **Teatro Municipal** (Mon–Sun 10am–7.30pm), which used to host European opera singers during the nitrate era. The **Casino Español**, a 1904 Moorish-style wooden building with an opulent interior, graces the northeast corner of the square and is worth a visit both for the interior decorations and the delicious pisco sours.

Calle Baquedano

Heading south from Plaza Prat towards Playa Bellavista, quiet pedestrianized Calle Baquedano, with its elevated boardwalks, is strikingly different from the modern parts of Iquique. It is lined with Georgian-style wooden buildings, with a few restaurants, eateries and guesthouses thrown in, and has a faded colonial feel about it; at the north end of the street sits a restored antique tram. The **Museo Regional**, at no. 951 (Mon–Fri 9am–5.30pm, Sat & Sun 10am–5pm; voluntary donation), is home to a number of curious pre-Columbian artefacts, the most impressive of which are the Chinchorro mummies and skulls, deliberately deformed by having bandages wrapped tightly around them. The natural history section features a sea lion embryo pickled in formalehyde and an informative exhibition on nitrate extraction in the area, along with a scale model of the ghost town of Humberstone.

The beaches

Centrally located **Playa Cavancha**, sheltered in a bay alongside the busy main thoroughfare of Avenida Arturo Prat, is particularly popular with sunbathers and boogie-boarders and is safe for swimming. The boardwalk, which winds along the beach amidst the palm trees and giant cacti, is always teeming with bikers, rollerbladers and scores of sun worshippers; in the evenings a relaxed atmosphere prevails. At the north end of Playa Cavancha lies rocky **Playa Bellavista**, with several good surf breaks, while the large stretch of **Playa Brava**, lined by fun fairs and themed restaurants, is south of the Peninsula de Cavancha, and is a popular landing spot for paragliders. The less crowded **Playa Huayquique** is located to the very south of the city; it also boasts good waves for surfers and can be reached by *colectivos* from the centre.

TREAT YOURSELF

Few things compare to the sheer rush of running off the cliff at Alto Hospicio on the plateau above Iquique. Once the butterflies settle, you find yourself soaring gently with white-headed eagles and fellow gliders, as tiny houses with minute turquoise swimming pools, oceanside high-rises, beaches and the giant sand dune of Cerro Dragón spread out beneath you. **Paragliding** feels entirely different from flying in an airplane, as there is no turbulence, and the views from above are nothing short of incredible. You fly in tandem with an **experienced instructor**, who guides you through the entire procedure, from takeoff to landing. Altazor Sky Sports (Ⓣ57/380110, Ⓦwww.altazor.cl) and Iqairus (Ⓣ57/383006 or 9/8768-7732, Ⓦwww.vuelolibre.cl) are both established certified operators with excellent reputations who offer paragliding courses as well as tandem flights. Flights typically cost CH$25,000 for half an hour; transport to and from the paragliding site is included.

Arrival and information

Airport Aeropuerto Diego Arecena lies 41km south of Iquique; Aerotransfer drops you off at your door for CH$3500.

Buses The main terminal is inconveniently located at the north end of Patricio Lynch; numerous *colectivos* run to the city centre (CH$1500) and some bus companies pick up passengers at their central offices around Mercado Centenario. The brand new Tur Bus terminal is slightly more central, at the corner of Esmeralda and Ramírez.

Tourist office Aníbal Pinto 436 (March 16–Dec 14 Mon–Thurs 9am–5pm, Fri 9am–4.30pm; Dec

15–March 15 Mon–Sat 9am–8pm, Sun 9am–2pm; ⓣ57/419241, ⓔinfoiquique@sernatur.cl). Staff can advise on city attractions and provide maps of the city.

Accommodation

Backpacker's Hostel Iquique Amunategui 2075 ⓣ57/320223, ⓦwww.hosteliquique.cl. With helpful English-speaking staff who help organize trips in the area, a friendly atmosphere and a superb beachside location, this hostel remains a firm backpacker favourite. Kitchen facilities, free internet and frequent barbecues are part of the draw. Dorm CH$5500. ❹

Casa de Huéspedes "Profesores" Ramirez 839 ⓣ57/314475, ⓔinostrozafloresltda@gmail.com. Newly refurbished guesthouse with spotless rooms, internet and wi-fi, laundry service, bike rental, a tour agency and extremely friendly hosts. Popular with travellers of all ages, although the dorm is a little cramped. Dorm CH$5000. ❺

Hostal Cuneo Baquedano 1175 ⓣ57/428654, ⓔhostalcuneo@hotmail.com. Cosy, quiet and conveniently located family-run *residencial*, with tidy rooms for up to four and dorms, many with cable TV, some en suite; breakfast included. ❹

Hotel de la Plaza Baquedano 1025 ⓣ57/419339. Quiet rooms (some rather small) with up to four beds, with cable TV and private bathrooms, around a pleasant courtyard. ❺

Eating

Bavaria Vivar 647. Dependable option for decent grilled meats, tasty *parilladas* for two and German-style sausage, sauerkraut and potato meals. Set lunch CH$3500.

Canto del Mar Baquedano at Thompson. Popular and bustling restaurant on the Plaza, serving filling meat and fish options and good daily specials. Grilled fish CH$4000.

Mercado Centenario Barros Arana, between Latorre and Sargento Aldea. This market is *the* place for fresh produce and generous helpings of fish and seafood for lunch; *Sureña II* and *La Picada* are very popular. Fish with side dish CH$3000.

M.Koo Latorre 596. An excellent central spot for takeaway *pastel de choclo* and *humitas*, as well as tasty *empanadas* and *chumbeques* (local sweet biscuits). *Empanada* CH$1500.

Otaku Av Arturo Prat 2089, ⓣ57/542850. Small but excellent and reasonably-priced sushi restaurant with takeaway on Playa Brava; open late. Six California rolls CH$2500.

Paninis Baquedano s/n, opposite *Puerto Camarón*. Tiny café in front of the Fería Artesanal, good for morning coffee, fresh juices and croissants. Juice CH$1200.

Puerto Camaron on Baquedano at Gorostiaga. Brightly-painted restaurant with outdoor seating, a fish net suspended above the tables and excellent seafood *empanadas* as well as cheap set menus. Two *empanadas* with drink CH$2500.

Drinking and entertainment

Barracuda Gorostiaga 601 at Ramírez. Chilled-out pub extremely popular with locals and visitors alike, with decent drinks specials, good snacks, international cuisine and excellent service. Beers CH$1200.

Casino Español Plaza Prat 584. The food here is pricey, but it's worth a visit for some of the best pisco sours in Chile. Pisco sour CH$2000.

BOXIQUIQUE TOUR OPERATORS

Apart from sandboarding trips to Cerro Dragón, and surfing all along Iquique's coast, the area around the city has a wealth of attractions on offer, including trips to the **ghost town** of Humberstone (CH$15,000), the Gigante de Atacama geoglyph, the **hot springs** of Mamiña and the Pica oasis (CH$20,000), the burial site of an Inca princess at the village of La Tirana (CH$15,000) and the sobering mass graves from the Pinochet era at the tiny settlement of Pisaqua (CH$20,000). The following operators are recommended:

Avitours Baquedano 997 ⓣ57/473775, ⓦwww.avitours.cl. Day-trips to the local hot springs, geoglyphs and ghost towns as well as longer excursions to Parque Nacional Volcán Isluga and multi-day trips to Parque Nacional Lauca and Reserva Las Vicuñas, finishing either in Arica or Iquique.

Civet Adventure Bolívar 684 ⓣ57/428483. Customized four-wheel-drive and biking trips to *altiplano* destinations.

Turismo Santa Teresita Ramírez 839 ⓣ57/314475 or 9/465-3259. Arranges paragliding sessions and runs day-trips to the hot springs, Pisagua, La Tirana and other regional attractions.

Kamikaze Bajo Molle km 7 ⓦwww.kamikaze.cl. Lively party-till-morning disco popular with locals and backpackers, featuring various live artists and DJs.

Moving on

Bus to: Arica (10 daily; 4hr; CH$4000); Calama (4 daily; 6hr; CH$10,000); Copiapó (6 daily; 15hr; CH$16,000); La Serena (6 daily; 18hr; CH$20,000); San Pedro de Atacama (1 daily; 8hr; CH$12,500); Santiago (8 daily; 24hr; CH$30,000).
Plane to: Arica (3 daily); La Paz (4 weekly); Santiago (4 daily).

AROUND IQUIQUE

The nitrate pampas inland from Iquique are dotted with **ghost towns** left over from the area's mining heyday, with the biggest and best-preserved example being **Humberstone** (daily: March–Nov 9am–6pm; Dec–Feb 9am–7pm; CH$1000), 45 kilometres to the east. Established in the middle of parched desert land in 1862 under the misnomer La Palma, it was renamed in 1933 in the honour of its British manager, James Humberstone. Squalid and partially-wrecked worker barracks contrast sharply with the faded glamour of the theatre and the well-maintained church – both the theatre and church are regularly leased for private functions. Workers here, mostly Chilean but some foreign, earned a pittance by putting in long hours in a hot and dangerous environment; they were paid in tokens which could only be exchanged for goods at the company store; worker strikes requesting better conditions were brutally quashed. Besides the giant warehouses housing dusty black machinery and the disused railroad tracks, which formerly carried nitrate to the coast, another object of interest is the empty swimming pool built out of a ship's hull, located in the back of the town's hotel ruin. A nearby *mirador* offers a bird's-eye view of the town.

ARICA

ARICA, Chile's northernmost city, 316 kilometres north of Iquique, was the principal **port** exporting silver from Bolivia's Potosí mines until 1776. Under Peruvian rule up to the 1880s, the city became part of Chile after the **War of the Pacific**. Trade has been an important part of Arica's economy throughout its existence, although now the sprawling city benefits greatly from tourism, with foreign visitors flocking to its pleasant sandy beaches in the summer.

El Morro

The city is dominated by the towering cliff of **El Morro**, with a steep path leading up to the top from the southern end of Calle Colón. From the clifftop, which is home to a number of turkey vultures and a giant Jesus statue that lights up at night, you can enjoy a magnificent panoramic view of the entire city. Also up here, with cannon stationed outside, is the **Museo Histórico y de Armas** (daily 8am–8pm; CH$600) with displays of weaponry, uniforms and other artefacts from the War of the Pacific.

The city centre

Below El Morro is the large, palm-tree-lined **Plaza Vicuña Mackenna**, and alongside that lies Avenida Máximo Lira, the main coastal road. On the east side is the attractive **Plaza Colón**, decorated with pink flowers and ornate fountains. The plaza is home to one of Arica's most celebrated buildings, the gothic **Iglesia de San Marcos**, designed by Gustave Eiffel (of Eiffel Tower fame), made entirely out of iron and shipped over from France in 1876. Eiffel was also responsible for the grand 1874 **Ex-Aduana** building nearby, alongside the Parque General Baquedano. This now houses the Casa de Cultura, regularly hosting art and photo exhibitions. The main throughfare, **21 de Mayo**, heads east from here before becoming a pedestrian strip, lined with restaurants and banks. To the west is the bustling

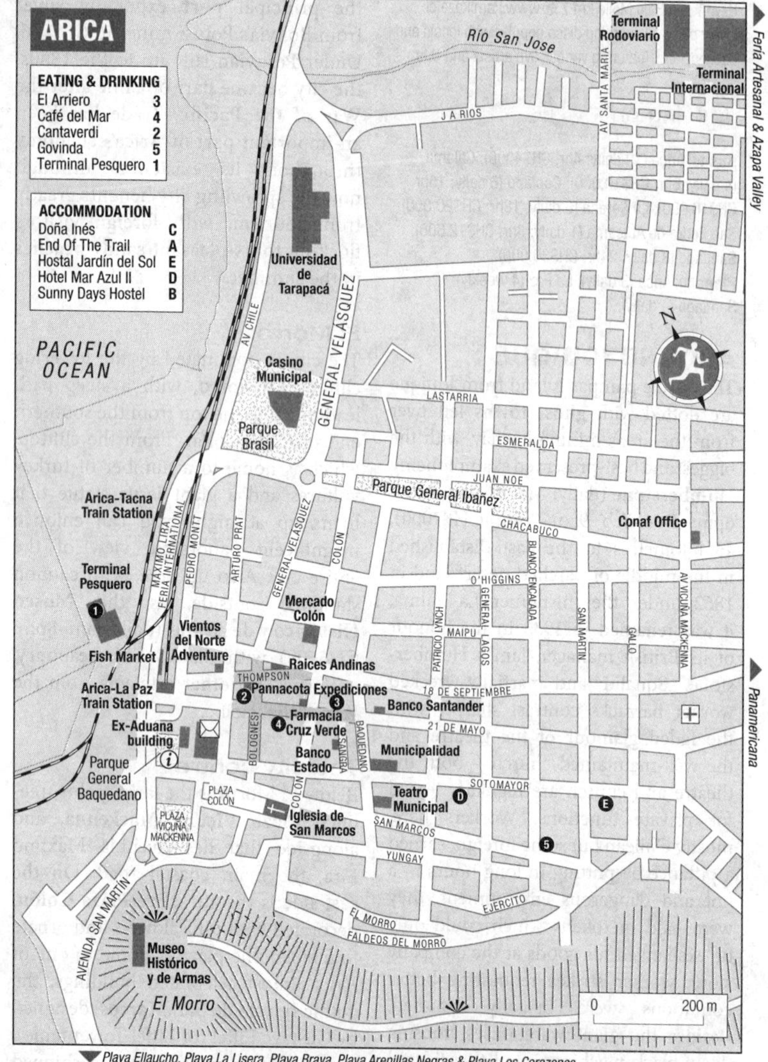

Terminal Pesquero, where sea lions compete with pelicans for scraps from the dockside fish stalls.

The beaches

North of the centre and west of the bus terminals lies the popular **Playa Chinchorro**, which is ideal for swimming, sunbathing and body-boarding. The city's northernmost beach, Playa Las Machas, is not suitable for swimming due to the strong undertow but has some good surf breaks; it's also possible to camp here for free. A twenty-minute walk south of the centre will bring you to the sandy **Playa El Laucho** and **Playa La Lisera**, both popular with sun worshippers and good for swimming, followed by the pretty

Playa Brava and the dark-sand **Playa Arenillas Negras** with rougher waves. Finally, **Playa Los Corazones**, a beautiful expanse of clean sand flanked by cliffs, is located eight kilometres south of town. The southern beaches can be reached by *colectivo*, though these tend to run only during the summer season.

Museo Arqueológico

The excellent **Museo Arqueológico** (Jan–Feb daily 9am–8pm; March–Dec 10am–6pm; CH$2000) lies twelve kilometres from Arica in the green **Azapa Valley**. The museum traces the history of the valley's inhabitants, from the earliest hunter-gatherers, via a remarkably thorough collection of regional pre-Hispanic artefacts. Most impressive of these are the four elaborately-prepared **Chinchorro mummies** – a male, a female and two young children, their flesh preserved by the valley's aridity. They are believed to be around seven thousand years old, making them by far the oldest mummies in the world. To get there, catch one of the yellow *colectivos* labelled "Azapa" which run along Avenida Diego Portales past the bus terminals.

Arrival and information

Airport Aeropuerto Internacional Chacalluta is eighteen kilometres north of Arica; a radio taxi downtown costs around CH$2500 (shared) or CH$5500 (single).

Conaf Av Vicuña Mackenna 820 (Mon–Fri 8.30am–5.15pm; ⓣ58/201200, ⓦwww.chilesat.net/conaf-tarapaca). Staff provide information on, and maps of, local national parks; reserve beds at regional Conaf *refugios* here.

Buses Terminal Rodovario, at Diego Portales 948, is the main stop for local arrivals, plus a few international; inside there are cash machines and snack kiosks. Terminal Internacional is immediately adjacent, with arrivals from La Paz and numerous *micros* and *colectivos* crossing the border from Tacna, Peru.

Tourist office San Marcos 101 (March–Nov Mon–Fri 8.30am–5.20pm, Dec–Feb daily 8.30am–7pm; ⓣ58/252054, ⓔinfoarica@sernatur.cl). Helpful staff provide maps of town and a plethora of brochures on local attractions.

Train The Arica–Tacna train station is located at Máximo Lira 889, on the northwest edge of the city centre.

Accommodation

Doña Inés Manuel Rojas 2864 ⓣ58/248108, ⓔhiarica@hostelling.cl. The inconvenient location of this hostel is compensated for by the owner's hospitality and knowledge. Free internet, bike rental, cosy common room with TV and flexible breakfast times, as well as a wall for graffiti artists, make this a top choice. Dorm CH$5500. ❹

End of the Trail Esteban Alvarado 117 ⓣ58/314316 or 9/7786-3972, ⓦwww.endofthetrail-arica.cl. A congenial American owner runs this brand-new hostel with comfortable, quiet rooms around an indoor courtyard, amazing showers and a specially-designed roof that keeps the house cool. Breakfast included. Dorm CH$7000. ❹

Hostal Jardín del Sol Sotomayor 848 ⓣ58/232795, ⓦwww.hostaljardindelsol.cl. Central hostel run by a very helpful and welcoming couple who organize all manner of outdoor activities for guests; most rooms are en suite; shares arranged. Kitchen, lounge, wi-fi, cable TV, bicycle rent and laundry service are some of the bonuses. Breakfast included. ❺

Hotel Mar Azul II Sotomayor 540 ⓣ58/233653. Centrally-located hotel has little character but offers clean en-suite rooms with cable TV at a bargain. Be aware that the owner "discourages" competition by offering commissions to taxi drivers. ❹

Sunny Days Hostel Tomas Aravena 161 ⓣ58/241038, ⓦwww.sunny-days-arica.cl. Extremely friendly and knowledgeable Kiwi-Chilean hosts preside over travellers of all ages in this custom-built hostel. Free internet, excellent breakfast, kitchen and lounge facilities and a relaxed communal atmosphere all add to its appeal. Dorm CH$7000. ❹

Eating and drinking

Café del Mar 21 de Mayo 260. Popular restaurant with a bargain *menú del día*, plus large salads and good quiches. Quiche CH$2500.

Cantaverdi Bolognesi 453. Attractive, much frequented pub with a pleasant buzz, serving snacks and pizzas along with a wide range of drinks. Beers CH$1000.

El Arriero 21 de Mayo 385. Atmospheric steakhouse with fantastic grilled meat and expertly-prepared fish dishes; slightly pricier than the competition. Grilled fish CH$4500.

Fish market Avenida Máximo Lira at Calle 21 de Mayo. Excellent place to pick up some inexpensive sea bass *ceviche*. *Ceviche* CH$1000.
Govinda Blanco Encalada 200. Top vegetarian lunch option, with fresh organic produce used to create imaginative dishes. Set three-course lunch CH$2500.
Terminal Pesquero Off Avenida Máximo Lira, across from entrance to Calle 21 de Mayo. Several no-frills oceanside eateries here cook up hearty portions of inexpensive fish dishes; *Mata Rangi*, in particular, stands out. Set lunch CH$2500.

Moving on

Bus to: Antofagasta (6 daily; 10hr; CH$12,000); Calama (several daily; 9hr, CH$10,000); Copiapó (several daily; 16hr; CH$22,000); Iquique (frequent daily departures; 4hr; CH$5500); La Paz (4–5 daily, morning departures; 7hr, CH$8000); La Serena (several daily; 19hr; CH$30,000); San Pedro de Atacama (1 overnight; 11hr; CH$12,000); Santiago (4–6 daily; 28hr; CH$40,000).
Buses Gemini to: Salta and Jujuy, Argentina (Mon, Thurs & Sat at 10pm; 25hr; CH$37,000).
Buses Zambrano to: Arequipa (daily 8am; 12hr; CH$15,000), Cusco (daily 10am; 20hr; CH$25,000) and Lima (daily at noon; 20hr; CH$25,000).
Colectivos to: Tacna, Peru depart frequently from Terminal Internacional (CH$2500).
Plane to: Iquique (several departures daily); La Paz (5 departures weekly); Santiago (several departures daily).
Train to: Tacna (Mon–Sat at 9.30am and 7pm; 1hr; CH$1800).

PUTRE

The highland village of **PUTRE** sits at an altitude of 3500 metres and provides an ideal acclimatization point for venturing into the Parque Nacional Lauca. Populated by the indigenous Aymará people, Putre consists of basic stone houses centred around a square. The square's main church, originally built in 1670, was restored in 1871 after being destroyed by an earthquake. The **tourist office** (Mon–Thurs 8am–1pm & 2.30–7pm, Fri 8am–2pm), on the south side of the square, is not well stocked, and the only bank, in the square's southeast corner, does not accept Visa. There are few sleeping options – *Hostal Pachamama*, Lord Cochrane s/n (☎58/228564, ❸), is the top choice, with rustic yet cosy **rooms** in a colonial-style house and knowledgeable owners. Next best is *Residencial Cali*, Baquedano 399 (☎9/282-1152, ❸), whose rooms are dark and basic, though clean, for the same price. Dining options include *Kuchu Marka*, on Baquedano, which serves tasty alpaca stew, and *Cantaverdi*, on the east side of the square, serving large, inexpensive meals, often accompanied by a football game on TV. Buses La Paloma (☎58/222710) depart daily from Arica to Putre at 6.30am, and return to Arica from in front of Putre's *Hotel Kukuli* at 1.30pm (CH$2700).

TOUR OPERATORS

A number of tour companies offer trips into the national parks outside Arica. The standard three- to four-day trip takes in Parque Nacional Lauca, Reserva Nacional Las Vicuñas, Salar de Surire and Parque Nacional Volcán Isluga, with overnight stops in the *altiplano* villages of Putre and Colchane. Most tours either return to Arica or drop passengers off in Iquique. Normally, a minimum of two people is required per tour and a three-day all-inclusive package costs around CH$165,000, or less, depending on the number of participants.

Parinacota Expediciones Thompson at Bolognesi ☎58/256227, ⓦwww.parinacotaexpediciones.cl. Experienced bilingual guides running two- to four-day tours.
Raices Andinas Thompson 21 ☎58/233305, ⓦwww.raicesandinas.com. Tour operator with close links to the local Aymará communities, running standard trips as well as promoting eco-tourism and Aymará culture.
Vientos del Norte Adventure Prat at Thompson ☎58/231331 or 9/897-50186, ⓦwww.vientosdelnorteadventure.cl. Knowledgeable, bilingual guide offering trips to Bolivia and Peru as well as the standard circuit.

ALTITUDE SICKNESS

Known here as *puna* or *soroche*, altitude sickness affects roughly a quarter of all travellers who venture above the altitude of about 2500 metres, regardless of age or fitness, though people with respiratory problems tend to suffer more. It is rarely life-threatening, though dangerous for people suffering from hypothermia. Symptoms include vertigo, headaches, nausea, shortness of breath, lethargy and insomnia. Keeping properly hydrated and taking Aspirin can alleviate some of the symptoms; **mate de coca** (tea brewed from coca leaves) is also widely believed to help. Avoid alcohol consumption, over-eating and over-exertion; if symptoms persist, try to move to a lower elevation. The best way to avoid altitude sickness is to acclimatize gradually by breaking up your journey to higher regions into segments.

PARQUE NACIONAL LAUCA

From Putre, Ruta 11 leads up onto the *altiplano* to the **PARQUE NACIONAL LAUCA**, 4300 metres above sea level.

Las Cuevas

The Conaf-run **Las Cuevas** *refugio* is located nine kilometres into the park, and the nature trail near it is the best place to see **viscachas**, the long-tailed, rabbit-like relatives of chinchillas, as they use their powerful hind legs to leap from boulder to boulder. The well-watered *bofedal* (alluvial depression) here provides permanent grazing for herds of vicuñas, the wild relatives of llamas and alpacas, which are also commonly seen. In addition, you'll find numerous examples of the *llareta* plant, which takes three hundred years to grow to full size; the plant looks like a pile of oddly-shaped green cushions but is actually rock-hard. The local Aymará break up the dead plants with picks for use as firewood. Just off the *refugio*'s nature trail are some rustic thermal baths.

Parinacota

The **Conaf** headquarters (daily 9am–12.30pm & 1–5.30pm) are located in the tiny Aymará village of **PARINACOTA**, nineteen kilometres east of the Las Cuevas *refugio*. Parinacota is worth a stop for its cheerful, whitewashed little church, reconstructed in 1789, and for the stalls opposite, selling colourful local **artesanía**. Besides a fetching bell tower with a tiny doorway, the church has murals depicting scenes of Jesus being borne to the cross by soldiers resembling Spanish conquistadors, as well as sinners burning in hell. A small wooden table is tethered to the wall to the left of the altar; legend has is it that the table wandered around the village, causing the death of a man by stopping in front of his house – the chain prevents the table from escaping again. Ask around for the guardian of the key to the church. There are two weekly **buses** to Parinacota from Arica's International Bus Terminal (Tues & Fri at 11.30am, returning the following day; ⓣ58/222710) and it may be possible to rent a very basic room from a villager.

Lago Chungará

Eighteen kilometres east of Parinacota, at a breathtaking altitude of 4600m, lies the grand **LAGO CHUNGARÁ**. With its brilliant blue waters perfectly reflecting the towering snow-capped cone of **Volcán Parinacota** (6350m), this is undoubtedly one of the highlights of the national park. The roadside **Conaf refugio** here has six basic beds (CH$6000 per person), kitchen facilities and three **camping** spaces (CH$5500 per site). There is a short lakeside **nature trail**, which provides a good vantage point for viewing the giant coots, flamingoes and Andean geese that nest here.

RESERVA NACIONAL LAS VICUÑAS AND SALAR DE SURIRE

A southbound turnoff from Ruta 11 by Lago Chungará heads through the 209,131-hectare **RESERVA NACIONAL LAS VICUÑAS** towards the Salar de Surire salt lake. The Reserva is made up of seemingly endless marshes and green steppes, with herds of **vicuñas** seen grazing in the distance. At an altitude of 4295 metres, the enormous, dirty-white **SALAR DE SURIRE** is home to up to ten thousand **flamingoes** – mostly Chilean, but with a smattering of James and Andean species. Surire means "place of the rhea" in Aymará, and it's also possible to catch glimpses here of these swift, ostrich-like birds. On the southeast side of the salt flat, the **Termas de Polloquere**, several hot thermal pools amidst a small geyser field, are a good spot to soak and pamper yourself using the mud at the bottom of the pools.

PARQUE NACIONAL VOLCÁN ISLUGA

Further south, the dirt track drifts eastwards, passing by large herds of **llamas** and their shorter and hairier **alpaca** cousins, as well as tiny, seemingly-deserted Aymará hamlets. All these are overshadowed by the towering **VOLCÁN ISLUGA** (5218m), from which the park takes its name. The little village of **Enquelga** is home to a small Conaf-run **refugio** with five beds and hot showers (CH$6000 per person), as well as a free campsite (1km east of town) with Conaf-maintained shelters alongside a stream and some hot springs. One warm pool here, against the impressive backdrop of the volcano, is large enough for swimming. Just outside the park, the small farming settlement of **COLCHANE**, surrounded by fields of bright red quinoa and *kiwicha* (a highly nutritious local staple), has several basic guesthouses providing simple home-cooked food.

Middle Chile

RANCAGUA

RANCAGUA is a busy agricultural city that lies 87 kilometres south of Santiago. The best time for a day-trip here is either in April, to witness the **National Rodeo Championships**, or the last weekend in March, during the **Fiesta Huasa**, a three-day celebration of cowboy culture held in the main square, involving traditional food and wine. Alternatively, if coming in November, try to catch the **Encuentro Internacional Criollo**, a demonstration of spectacular horse-breaking and lassoing skills on the part of expert riders from all over Latin America. The best way to get to Rancagua is to take the **Metrotrén** from Santiago; turn one block left out of the station and then turn right into Avenida Brasil. Brasil becomes the pedestrianized Independencia, lined with banks and **eateries**, before arriving at the uniquely-designed **Plaza de Héroes**.

Arrival and information

Buses The new Terminal O'Higgins, hub for long-distance destinations, lies northeast of town, just off Ruta 5. Tur Bus, at O'Carrol 1175 (☎72/241117), has a more convenient, central location.

Tourist office The helpful Sernatur office at Germán Riesco 277, 1st floor (Dec–Feb Mon–Fri 8.30am–5.15pm, Sat 9am–1pm; rest of the year Mon–Fri 8.30am–5.15pm ☎72/230413, Ⓦwww.turismoregiondeohiggins.cl), can provide plenty of information on the city and its festivals.

Train The hourly Metrotrén from Santiago and the faster EFE train to Concepción stop at the Estación Rancagua (☎72/225239), on Av Estación, between O'Carrol and Carrera Pinto, at the western edge of downtown.

SAN FERNANDO AND THE COLCHAGUA VALLEY

The busy agricultural service centre of **SAN FERNANDO**, 55 kilometres south of Rancagua along the Panamericana highway, is a forgettable transportation hub, with multiple long-distance services leaving from the Terminal de Buses (Ⓣ72/713912) on Avenida Manso de Velasco at Calle Rancagua, and frequent trains passing through the Estación San Fernando, Quereche-guas s/n, serving various Middle Chile destinations. It is also the gateway to the renowned **Colchagua Valley Ruta de Vino**, though for that it's better to be based at the heart of the action, in nearby Santa Cruz.

SANTA CRUZ

Thirty-seven kilometres southwest of San Fernando, the attractive little town of **SANTA CRUZ** lies at the heart of the fertile Colchagua Valley, home to Chile's best-organized *Ruta de Vino*; the hot climate here has proved to be perfect for growing carmenère, cabernet, malbec and syrah grapes. The ideal time to visit is during the first weekend in March, when the **Fiesta de La Vendimia del Valle de Colchagua** (grape harvest festival) is held, allowing you to sample the best wines and the region's typical dishes. The heart of Santa Cruz is the gorgeous **Plaza de Armas**, dotted with araucarias, conifers and palm trees, with an ornate fountain at its centre and drinking fountains around its periphery. Within a couple of blocks of the plaza are numerous eateries and *hospedajes*.

Museo de Colchagua

The excellent, privately-run **Museo de Colchagua**, at Errázuriz 145 (Dec–Feb Tues–Sun 10am–7pm; rest of the year 10am–6pm; CH$3000, students CH$1000; Ⓦwww.museocolchagua.cl), displays the unmatched private collection of Carlos Cardoen, which includes pre-Columbian artefacts from around Latin America, conquistador weaponry, exquisite gold work, Mapuche weavings, a collection of antique carriages and much more. Cardoen himself is a highly controversial figure: still wanted by the FBI for allegedly selling weapons to Iraq in the 1980s, the former arms dealer has transformed himself into a successful businessman and philanthropist with extensive interests in wine and tourism.

Arrival and information

Buses Terminal Municipal is on Casanova, four blocks southwest of the Plaza de Armas.

Tourist office There is a small Sernatur office inside the little, white clock tower on the plaza (Mon–Fri 10am–1pm & 3–6pm, Sat 10am–2pm), which has limited information on the town. The Ruta de Vino headquarters on the east side of the plaza (Mon–Fri 9am–6.30pm, Sat & Sun 10am–6.30pm; Ⓣ72/823199, Ⓦwww.rutadelvino.cl) is an excellent source of information on the Valle Colchagua (see box, p.472).

Accommodation

Hotel Alcázar Besoain 285 Ⓣ72/822465. Guesthouse a couple of blocks northwest of the plaza, with a friendly proprietress and passable rooms, though some are rather small. Breakfast included. ❸

Hostal Santa Cruz Carvacho 40 Ⓣ72/822046, Ⓔhostalsantacruz@terra.cl. Spacious and clean rooms in a friendly *hospedaje* on a busy street, which can be noisy during the day. Breakfast included. ❹

Residencial Plaza Plaza de Armas 306 Ⓣ72/822456. Centrally-located guesthouse whose rather dark but clean rooms circle a lush green courtyard. Breakfast included. ❸

Eating and drinking

Bar Pizzeria Chaman *Hotel Santa Cruz Plaza*, Plaza de Armas 286. Besides expertly-prepared pizza, the menu at this spot, located inside the town's classiest hotel, features a good selection of reasonably-priced tapas. Mains CH$5500.

Licanray Plaza de Armas 130-A. Informal eatery and bar serving up hot dogs, meat dishes and tasty *empanadas*, as well as cold beers. Mains CH$3000.
Sushi Plaza Santa Cruz General del Canto 5. Friendly service and very palatable sushi and teriyaki dishes, though some items on the menu may be unavailable. Mains CH$4500.

Moving on

Buses to: Pichilemu (several daily; 2hr; CH$2700); San Fernando (daily every 30min until 7:30pm; 40min; CH$600); Santiago (numerous daily; 2hr 30min; CH$3500).

PICHILEMU

The drive to the surfing magnet of **PICHILEMU**, ninety kilometres west of Santa Cruz, is particularly scenic. The road meanders past sun-drenched vineyards before snaking in and out of patches of pine forest. "Pichi", as it's known, was originally planned as an upmarket vacation spot by the local land baron Agustín Ross Edwards, though in recent years it's become ever more popular with a motley crew of **surfers** and local beach bums. A spread-out town, Pichilemu has numerous **guesthouses** and **eateries** concentrated along the east-west Avenida Ortúzar, and the north-south Aníbal Pinto, a couple of blocks from the sea.

Playa Las Terrazas

Avenida Costanera Cardenal Caro runs alongside the black sand expanse of **Playa Las Terrazas**, Pichilemu's principal beach. Good for both sunbathers and surfers, it has a cluster of eateries and **surf schools** concentrated towards its southern end, at the rocky promontory of La Puntilla. Steps lead up to the meticulously landscaped **Parque Ross**, dotted with palm trees and boasting an excellent view of the coast.

Punta de Lobos

Chile's most famous wave, **Punta de Lobos**, where the **National Surfing Championships** are held every summer, can be found 6km south of downtown Pichilemu; to get there, take a *colectivo* along Jorge Errázuriz (CH$600), or cycle down Comercio until you reach the turnoff towards the coast and make your way to the end of the jutting, cactus-studded headland.

RUTA DEL VINO DE COLCHAGUA

The Colchagua Valley has some of the best **red wines** in the world, not to mention the best-organized **wine route** in Chile. There are **fourteen wineries** in all, including both large, modern producers and small-scale, traditional bodegas; many of them can be visited on a drop-by basis or at short notice. The Ruta del Vino headquarters in Santa Cruz organizes full-day and half-day tours that commence at 10.30am, taking in two or three wineries, along with lunch and a visit to either the beautiful seventeenth-century **Hacienda del Huique**, or the Museo de Colchagua. Rates depend on the number of people and type of tour; a half-day tour without lunch will cost around CH$27,000, while full-day tours start at CH$60,000. Another enjoyable way to do the Ruta de Vino is aboard the leisurely **Santa Cruz Wine Train** (from CH$22,000 per person; ⓣ2/470-7403, ⓦwww.trendelvino.cl), a steam engine that leaves San Fernando at 10:30am every Saturday. Excellent wineries include:

Viña Casa Silva Hijuela Norte s/n Angostura, Km 132, Ruta 5, San Fernando ⓣ72/710204, ⓦwww.casasilva.cl. Award-winning winery set in a colonial-style hacienda, using modern technology to produce carmenère, as well as the less common viognier, sauvignon gris and shiraz.
Viña Laura Hartwig Camino Barreales s/n ⓣ72/823179, ⓦwww.laurahartwig.cl. Small, family-owned, boutique winery producing only reserve-quality wines; the owners directly oversee each stage of production.
Viña Viu Manent Carretera del Vino km 37 ⓣ72/858751, ⓦwww.viumanent.cl. Family-owned winery famous for its excellent reds, especially Malbec, offering horse-drawn carriage tours as part of its attraction.

At the tip of the promontory, intrepid surfers descend via a steep dirt path before swimming across the short churning stretch of water to **Las Tetas**, the distinctive sea stacks, and catching the powerful, consistent left break just beyond.

Arrival and information

Buses The main Terminal Municipal is located at Millaco and Los Alerces, though unless you're staying in Pichi's southeastern quarter it's more convenient to disembark at a bus stop on Angel Gaete.

Tourist office There is a helpful tourist information booth on Angel Gaete, between Montt and Rodríguez (Mon–Fri 8am–1pm & 2.30–7pm; Ⓦwww.pichilemu.cl), which gives out maps of town and can help with accommodation.

Accommodation

Buena Vista Cabañas Cerro La Cruz Ⓣ72/842488 or 7/808-4964, Ⓦwww.343sur.com. Eco-friendly, wi-fi-equipped *cabañas* with great sea views, 15min walk from the main bus terminal, run by a friendly English owner who can help you organize surfing lessons. Call upon arrival for free pickup or to get the exact directions. ❹

Los Dos Soles Miramar 66 Ⓣ72/841546, Ⓔgazzachile@yahoo.com. Australian-run surfer hostel right by the beach, with basic dorms and private rooms and a laid-back ambience. Dorm CH$5000. ❹

Hostal Bahía Av Ortúzar 262 Ⓣ72/842272. Friendly guesthouse with a fish motif and large, somewhat dusty en-suite rooms with cable TV, all around a plant-lined common area. Breakfast included. ❸

Hotel Chile España Av Ortúzar 255 Ⓣ72/841270, Ⓦwww.chileespana.cl. Popular with surfers, this central guesthouse has clean and comfortable rooms with breakfast included. ❸

Eating, drinking and nightlife

100% Pizza Aníbal Pinto, between Aguirre & Acevedo. Takeaway featuring tasty *empanadas al horno* (oven-baked) and a wide variety of pizza. *Empanada* CH$1500.

El Balaustro Av Ortúzar 289. Conveniently-located, two-tiered pub which serves excellent lunchtime specials, both meat and fish, and has nightly drinks deals. Mains CH$4500.

Disco 127 Av Angel Gaete s/n. Pounding venue that acts as a magnet for Pichilemu's youth and surfing population. Doesn't kick off until after midnight.

Waitara Av Costanera 1039 Ⓣ72/843026, Ⓦwww.waitara.cl. The restaurant here is more appealing than the *cabañas* – its lunchtime menu features tasty and well-cooked fish dishes. Mains CH$4000.

Moving on

Bus to: Santiago (hourly departures daily 4.30am–6.40pm with Buses Cruz Mar and Buses Nilahue, stopping in Santa Cruz, San Fernando and Rancagua; CH$7000). Buy your ticket at the bus offices on Angel Gaete at Aníbal Pinto, and catch them at the bus stop on Santa María, four blocks northeast.

CURICÓ

The garden city of **CURICÓ**, 54km south of San Fernando along the Panamericana highway, makes for a good brief stop if you want to visit the nearby wineries or the Reserva Nacional Radal Siete Tazas. The **Plaza de Armas** is shaded by a variety of native trees, with several modern sculptures to add character. The **Vinícola Miguel Torres** (daily autumn and winter 10am–5pm, spring and summer 10am–7pm; CH$5000; Ⓣ75/564100, Ⓦwww.migueltorres.cl), a Spanish-owned vineyard just south of Curicó, is a good

SURF'S UP!

Budding surfers wanting to get in on the action can hone their skills with the help of several surfing schools:

Infernillo Surf Ⓣ9/711-1202. Experienced surfing instructor charges CH$10,000 per lesson (2hr 30min), which includes board and wetsuit rental.

Manzana 54 Surf School Ⓣ9/574-5984, Ⓦwww.manzana54.cl. Professional surf school and equipment rental offering lessons for CH$12,000 (3hr), all equipment included. Board rental alone is CH$10,000 for a half-day, CH$15,000 for a full day.

spot for a drop-in visit, with an informative video on wine production followed by sampling the many wines available; there is also an excellent restaurant on-site. Molina-bound *colectivos* can drop you off very near the entrance. *Hotel Prat*, Peña 427 (☎75/311069, ❸), is a good place for an overnight stay, with clean and comfortable rooms around a courtyard, complete with free internet access and cable TV, while *Pronto Plato*, Carmen 792, serves up well-executed and reasonably-priced Chilean dishes (mains CH$4500).

Arrival and information

Buses Most long-distance carriers arrive at the Terminal de Buses Rurales, on Montt and O'Higgins.

Tourist office Sernatur has a small and not particularly helpful office at the Edificio Servicios Públicos on the east side of the plaza (summer Mon–Fri 9am–1.30pm; no tel).

Train Station for services between Concepcion and Temuco is at Maipú 657 (☎75/310028).

RESERVA NACIONAL RADAL SIETE TAZAS

Seventy-three kilometres southeast of Curicó, the **RESERVA NACIONAL RADAL SIETE TAZAS** (April–Nov 8.30am–6pm; Dec–March 8.30am–8pm; CH$2000) is named after an astonishing natural phenomenon where the crystalline Río Claro has carved the basalt rockface into a series of "cups", interconnected by seven **waterfalls**, plummeting from high above. Though the waterfall run is a favourite of expert **kayakers** during the spring snowmelt, the reserve otherwise gets few visitors outside the summer holidays and weekends.

From the **Conaf Administration**, a short trail runs through a lush forest to a **mirador** overlooking the "teacups". Longer hikes to Cerro El Fraile and Valle del Indio are also possible. Of several campsites, the large *Camping Los Robles* (CH$12,000/site; ☎71/228029) at Parque Inglés is the pick, with hot showers, toilets, picnic tables and fire pits in an attractive spot, surrounded by native forest and within walking distance of several waterfalls; the site at Radal tends to be rather dirty during peak season.

TREAT YOURSELF

The best place to stay in the area by far is the **Casa Chueca**, Camino Las Rastras s/n (☎71/197-0096 or 9/419-0625, Ⓦwww.trekkingchile.com; dorm CH$8000, ❻). Located on the banks of the Río Lircay, a short distance out of Talca, this German-Austrian-run guesthouse is a tranquil retreat with comfortable and uniquely-decorated rooms for one to three people, delicious, home-cooked, mainly vegetarian meals and a swimming pool set amidst its lush gardens. Franz Schubert, its knowledgeable owner, also runs excellent guided excursions into the little-visited and underappreciated protected areas nearby.

To get here, take a "Taxutal A" bus from the bus stop at the southeast corner of the main bus terminal to the end of the route; if possible, call the guesthouse beforehand so that they can pick you up. Otherwise, follow the dirt road from Taxutal for about twenty minutes.

Arrival and information

Buses Public buses run year-round from Curicó to Radal, at the western tip of the park, via the village of Molina, along a poorly maintained dirt track (Mon–Sat 5.30pm; CH$2000). In summer, Buses Radal 7 Tazas runs to Parque Inglés (mid-Dec–Feb, 8 services Mon–Sat 10am–8pm; 6 on Sun, 7.45am–9pm).

Conaf Conaf Administration is located in the western Parque Inglés Sector, where the park fee is collected. There are talks on the flora and fauna at the Centro de Información on Sat

TALCA

The agricultural city of **TALCA** has few attractions, but makes an ideal base for exploring the nearby **Valle del Maule** and its **Ruta de Vino**. The city's streets are on a numbered grid, making it very easy to navigate. Most of the commercial activity revolves around the **Plaza de Armas**, dominated by the cathedral, between 1 Norte, 1 Sur, 1 Poniente and 1 Oriente. **Banks** and **pharmacies** line 1 Sur, and there are numerous inexpensive **eateries** and *completo* stands within a couple of blocks of the square. It is worth checking out the **Museo O'Higgiano**, at 1 Norte 875, to see if it has reopened after renovation. Here the national hero Bernardo O'Higgins spent his childhood and signed the Declaration of Independence in 1818; there's an impressive collection of Chilean art.

Frequent *colectivos* go east along 1 Sur in the direction of the **train and bus stations**. Two blocks west of the plaza, *Hostal del Río*, 1 Sur 411 (ⓣ71/510218, ⓦwww.hostaldelrio.cl, ❺), and its neighbour, *Hostal De Puente*, 1 Sur 407 (ⓣ71/220930 ⓦwww.hostaldelpuente.cl, ❺), provide comparable **accommodation** – comfortable rooms with cable TV in a friendly family environment. *Rubén Tapia*, 2 Oriente 1339, is one of the better eating options; the reasonably-priced, imaginative dishes here display Thai and French influences, among others (mains CH$4500).

Arrival and information

Buses Most long-distance and local buses arrive at the Terminal Rodoviario at 2 Sur 1920 (ⓣ71/243270), ten blocks east of the Plaza de Armas; the Tur Bus terminal (ⓣ71/265715) is one block south, at 3 Sur 1940.

Conaf The helpful office, at 2 Poniente and 3 Sur (ⓣ71/228029), has information on the Reserva Nacional Altos de Lircay and Radal Siete Tazas.

Tourist office The well-stocked and helpful Sernatur office is found in the Municipalidad building, on the east side of Plaza de Armas, at 1 Oriente 1150 (Mon–Fri 8.30am–5.30pm; ⓣ71/233669, ⓔinfomaule@sernatur.cl).

Train The station (ⓣ71/226254) is at 11 Oriente 1100; there is no luggage storage.

Moving on

Bus to: Chillán (numerous daily; 2hr; CH$3000), Puerto Montt (several daily; 10hr; CH$18,000); Santiago (several daily; 3hr 30min; CH$5500); Temuco (numerous daily; 6hr; CH$10,000).

Train to: Chillán (7 daily; 2hr 20min; CH$6000); Curicó (7 daily; 45min; CH$4000); San Fernando (7 daily; 1hr 10min; CH$5500); Santiago (7 daily; 3hr; CH$6500). A slow scenic train runs twice daily, at 7.30am and 4.30pm, to the beach town of Constitución (2hr 50min; CH$1400).

RUTA DEL VINO DEL MAULE

Valle Maule is rapidly developing a **Ruta del Vino** involving fifteen **wineries**, the majority of which require reservations to visit. The Ruta del Vino del Maule headquarters, at Villa Cultural Huiquilemu, km 7 Camino San Clemente, Talca (Mon–Fri 8.30am–1pm & 2.30–6.30pm, Sat & Sun noon–6pm; closed weekends in winter; ⓣ71/246460, ⓦwww.valledelmaule.cl) can help to arrange full-day and half-day visits to the nearby wineries. Good ones include:

Viña Casa Donoso Fundo La Oriental, Camino a Palmira km 3.5, Talca ⓣ71/341400, ⓦwww.casadonoso.com. Beautiful, traditionally-run vineyard that produces fine wines for export, including merlot, chardonnay and carmenère.

Viña Gillmore Camino a Constitución km 20, San Javier ⓣ73/197-5539, ⓦwww.gillmore.cl. A boutique winery producing cabernet franc, carignan, malbec, syrah, carmenère and merlot that doubles as a luxury agro-tourism resort, complete with a "winotherapy" spa.

Viña Hugo Casanova Fundo Viña Purísima, Camino Las Rastras km 8 ⓣ71/266540, ⓦwww.hugocasanova.cl. Family-run four-generation winery with attractive colonial buildings that turns out cabernet sauvignon, merlot, carmenère, sauvignon blanc and chardonnay.

CHILLÁN

CHILLÁN lies 150 kilometres south of Talca in the middle of the green **Itata Valley**. A nondescript town rebuilt time and time again after earthquake damage and Mapuche attacks, Chillán is famous as the birthplace of Chile's national hero and founding father, Bernardo O'Higgins. It also boasts an excellent market, overflowing with an abundance of fresh produce and authentic Mapuche handicrafts. The centre of town is the **Plaza Bernardo O'Higgins**, featuring a towering thirty-six-metre cross commemorating the thirty thousand victims of the 1939 earthquake that largely destroyed the city. **Escuela Mexico**, a school built with Mexico's donations in the wake of the earthquake, draws visitors with its frescoes, painted by the famous **Mexican muralists** David Alfaro Siqueiros and Xavier Guerrero. They depict famous figures from Latin American history. A good place to **spend the night** is *Hostal Canadá*, Av Libertad 269 (Ⓣ42/234515, ❸); its welcoming hostess presides over spotless rooms with cable TV. **Eating** options include the excellent, vegetarian *Arcoiris*, Roble 525, which specializes in delicious juices, crêpes and salads (mains CH$4000). Inexpensive, traditional Chilean dishes, such as *pastel de choclo* and *completos*, are served at the multitude of *cocinerías* at the **Mercado Municipal**, bordered by Roble, Riquelme, Prat and 5 de Abril.

Arrival and information

Buses Most long-distance buses arrive at the Terminal María Teresa at Av O'Higgins 10 (Ⓣ42/272149), though some still use the grotty Terminal de Buses Interregionales, Constitución 1 (Ⓣ42/221014). Buses from local destinations, such as the Valle Las Trancas, arrive at the rural bus terminal at the market.

Tourist office The helpful and well-stocked Sernatur office is located at 18 de Septiembre 455 (Dec–Feb Mon–Fri 8.30am–7pm, Sat & Sun 10am–2pm; rest of the year Mon–Fri 8.30am–1pm & 3–6pm; Ⓣ42/223272).

Train Seven train services daily from Concepción to Santiago pass through the station at Av Brasil s/n (Ⓣ42/222267).

AROUND CHILLÁN

One of the biggest attractions of the area is the hot springs resort of **Termas de Chillán** (Ⓣ2/557-8112, Ⓦwww.termaschillan.cl), which in the winter becomes a bona fide **ski resort** with 29 runs, most of intermediate level. There is also ample **off-piste terrain**, ideal for **snowboarders**, who are not allowed on some of the resort's runs. During the summer, hiking, horse riding and downhill biking, in the valley overlooked by the looming **Volcán Chillán** (3212m), are all popular activities. The majority of holidaymakers stay at the cheaper lodgings in the nearby **Valle Las Trancas**, which offers a scattering of *hospedajes*, campsites and restaurants, surrounded by immense mountains. Good digs here include *HI Las Trancas*, km 73.5 (Ⓣ42/243211, Ⓔhilastrancas@hostelling.cl; dorm CH$8000), its cosy rooms and on-site bar popular with younger travellers, and the brand-new *Chill'In*, km 72.1 (Ⓣ42/247075, dorm CH$8000), with its own pizzeria, attractive rooms and Skype-equipped free internet. **Public transport** to the resort is scarce during the shoulder seasons (March–May and Sept–Nov), though regular Rem Bus (Ⓣ42/229377) services go to Valle Las Trancas between 7.50am and 7.20pm from Chillán's rural bus terminal; the last bus departs Las Trancas at 9pm.

CONCEPCIÓN

CONCEPCIÓN is Chile's second-largest city, a bustling sprawl some 112 kilometres southwest of Chillán. Founded in 1550 by Pedro de Valdivia, the city was the administrative and military capital of colonial Chile, and as such, constantly threatened by the indigenous Mapuche. After a successful indigenous uprising regained control of the land south of the Río Biobío, the city became the headquarters for the Ejército de la Frontera, the Spanish garrison. Wrecked by the massive earthquakes of 1730 and 1751, Concepción was moved to its present location on the north bank of the Biobío, and is now a thriving industrial centre with a large student population.

The Town

The heart of Concepción's walkable city centre, lined with a mixture of elegant old buildings and modern concrete blocks, is the carefully landscaped **Plaza de la Independencia**. Partially pedestrianized Barros Arana, the main thoroughfare, has shops and eateries, while at the western end lies the lively **Barrio Estación**, whose trendy bars and restaurants are centred around **Plaza España**, across Calle Prat from the new **train station**. A four-block walk south from the Plaza de la Independencia along Aníbal Pinto brings you to the long green stretch of **Parque Ecuador**, popular with joggers. Three blocks west, the **Galería de la Historia** (Mon 3–6pm, Tues–Fri 10am–1.30pm & 3–6.30pm, Sat & Sun 3–7pm; free), at the corner of Lamas and Lincoyán, showcases the region's turbulent history through a series of interactive dioramas, with voice-overs dramatizing the scenes. There's also a large collection of ornate silver maté gourds.

Casa del Arte

Three blocks south of the Plaza de la Independencia, you can catch a *colectivo* eastwards to the **Casa del Arte** (Tues–Fri 10am–6pm, Sat 11am–5pm, Sun 11am–2pm; free), on the corner of **Plaza Perú**. The highlight of this museum, with its modest collection of Chilean art and its captivating modern art exhibitions in the basement, is the giant **mural**, *La Presencia de América Latina*, by Mexican muralist Jorge Gonzáles Camarena. Latin America – its conquest, its cultural and agricultural wealth – is captured in a series of densely-packed images oriented around the main figure of an *indígena* (a native woman). Interwoven throughout are colourful ribbons representing every Latin American flag and numerous national symbols.

Arrival and information

Airport Aeropuerto Internacional Carriel Sur (☎412/732000) is 5km northwest of downtown; a door-to-door airport service is available (CH$5000; ☎412/239371).

Buses Most long-distance buses arrive at the Terminal de Buses Collao, Tegualda 860 (☎412/749000), from where numerous local buses run downtown (CH$300).

Tourist office The Sernatur office is at Aníbal Pinto 460 (Mon–Fri 8.30am–1pm & 3–6pm; ☎412/741337, Ⓦwww.descubrebiobio.cl) and has plenty of information on the Biobío region.

Train Estación Concepción (☎412/227777) is located across Prat from Barros Arana.

Accommodation

Hostal Barros Arana Barros Arana 521 ☎412/254207. Centrally-located, quiet guest-house; clean rooms come with cable TV, private bath and breakfast. ❺

Hostal Cervantes O'Higgins 825 Local 24-A ☎412/730640. Compact rooms with cable TV, some rather dark, in a cul-de-sac off Barros Arana. ❺

Hostal Don Matías Colo Colo 155 ☎412/256846. An attractive B&B with friendly service, large rooms, some with private bathrooms, and a good breakfast. ❹

Eating, drinking and nightlife

30 y Tantos Prat 402. One of the liveliest watering holes in Barrio Estación, serving a wide range of drinks and 21 varieties of delicious, artery-clogging, fried *empanadas* (CH$1500).

Barrabirra Plaza España. To catch the latest match and knock back a beer, try this popular bar with nightly drink specials. Beers CH$1200.

Chung Hwa Barros Arana 262. Large and popular *chifa* (Chinese-Peruvian restaurant), cooking up a wide selection of substantial meat, seafood and noodle dishes. Mains CH$6000.

Hiper Lider Prat at Freire. Massive supermarket with an excellent selection of fresh produce, as well as rare Thai and Chinese cooking ingredients.

Mercado Central Rengo, between Maipú and Freire. The informal *cocinerías* here are a good spot for inexpensive Chilean standards, such as *cazuela* (CH$2500).

Il Padrino Barros Arana at Plaza España. Bustling Italian restaurant and bar, serving generous portions of pasta and pizza. Mains CH$5000.

Verde Que Te Quiero Verde Colo Colo 174. An excellent choice for vegetarians, with a tasty and healthy range of dishes, including vegetable lasagne and delicious fruit juice combinations. Closed Sun. Mains CH$4500.

Directory

Banks, cambios and ATMs Numerous banks with ATMs on Barros Arana and O'Higgins; Afex, at Barros Arana 565, Local 7, changes foreign currencies.

Hospital Hospital Regional is at San Martín and Av Roosevelt (☎412/237445).

Internet access There are several internet cafés around Concepción's centre; Fonossa Internet, at the corner of Freire and Lincoyán, has broadband and Skype-enabled computers.

Laundry Try Laverap, Caupolicán 334.

Pharmacy Numerous pharmacies can be found along Barros Arana.

Post office O'Higgins 799.

Telephone centres Entel, Barros Arana 541, Local 2, is the best phone centre.

Moving on

Bus to: Angol (several daily; 2hr; CH$3500), Chillán (numerous daily; 1hr 30min; CH$3000); Los Ángeles (numerous daily; 1hr 30min; CH$3000); Santiago (several daily; 7hr; CH$20,000); Talca (several daily; 4hr; CH$5500).

Plane to: Puerto Montt and Temuca (several weekly flights) and Santiago (3–4 daily) with LAN (☎412/248824) and Sky Airline (☎412/218941).

Train Daily depatures at 8am, noon & 4pm to: Chillán (2hr; CH$2000); Curicó (4hr 30min; CH$9000); San Fernando (5hr 30min; CH$11,000); Santiago (6hr 30min; CH$12,500); Talca (3hr 45min; CH$8000).

ANGOL

ANGOL, a frontier town razed to the ground half a dozen times during the "pacification of Araucanía" – the frequent skirmishes between European settlers and the Mapuche – is the last settlement of any size before reaching Temuco in the Lake District and an inevitable stop if you want to visit the Parque Nacional Nahuelbuta. There is little to do in the town itself, though the meticulously landscaped **Plaza de Armas** is rather attractive, with the four marble sculptures by its fountain representing Europe, America, Africa and Asia. For an **overnight stay**, try the *Residencial Olimpia*, northwest of the plaza at Caupolicán 625 (☎45/711162, ④); the clean rooms with shared bath are a good bargain. Food-wise, *Lomitón*, at Lautaro 146, offers decent sandwiches and *completos*.

Arrival and information

Buses Terminal Rodoviario (☎45/711854), serving long-distance destinations, is at Oscar Bonilla 428, east of the river. Terminal Rural (☎45/712021), at Ilabaca 422, serves local destinations.

Conaf The office at Prat 191, 2nd floor (☎45/712191), has up-to-date information on Parque Nacional Nahuelbuta.

Tourist office Oficina Municipal de Turismo, Av O'Higgins s/n (Mon–Fri 8.30am–5.30pm; ☎45/20157), provides helpful information on the area.

PARQUE NACIONAL NAHUELBUTA

High in the Cordillera de Nahuelbuta, 35 kilometres west of Angol, lies the remote sixty-eight-square-kilometre **PARQUE NACIONAL NAHUELBUTA** (daily Jan–Feb 8.30am–8pm; March–Dec 8.30am–6pm; CH$4000). The park is 1600 metres at its highest point and benefits from coastal rainfall, creating a **rare ecosystem** that sustains both *coigüe* and *lenga* trees, common to temperate coastal areas, and the *araucaria* trees of the mountains. The area is a haven for **diverse wildlife**, including *pudú* (pygmy deer), Chilote fox and puma, not to mention many species of birds. From the park administration at Pehuenco, five kilometres from the park entrance, a dirt trail snakes its way through monkey

next door to the tourist office, is considered to be the best Mapuche craft market in the region.

Arrival and information

Buses A block south of Avenida Pedro de Valdivia, several **bus terminals** face each other across Anfíon Muñoz. Buses JAC run to Pucón, as well as the attractive lakeside villages of Licán Ray and Coñaripe; Tur Bus offers frequent services to Santiago and Temuco; and Buses San Martín and Igi Llaima serve Argentinian destinations, such as San Martín de Los Andes.
Tourist Office The helpful tourist office, at Avenida Pedro de Valdivia 1070 (daily 9am–10pm in the summer; ⓣ45/415057, ⓦwww.villarrica.com), has maps of the town and brochures on attractions and accommodation.

Accommodation, eating and drinking

Hostería Hue-quimey Valentín Letelier 1030 (ⓣ45/411462, ⓔhue_quimey@yahoo.com). Quiet and spacious doubles with lake view and cable TV. ⑤
El Rey De Marisco Letelier 1030. If good, reasonably-priced seafood is what you're after, then this unassuming restaurant is a good choice.
La Torre Suiza Bilbao 969 (ⓣ45/411213, ⓦwww.torresuiza.com). A haven for outdoor lovers, complete with a book exchange, kitchen privileges, bike rental, good breakfast and tons of helpful advice. Dorm/double CH$6000–8000. ④–⑤
The Travellers Letelier 753. A top spot for coffee or meals of any description – the eclectic menu features dishes from all over the world, including a great Thai curry (CH$5500).

PUCÓN

On a clear day, you will be greeted by the awe-inspiring sight of the **Volcán Villarrica** smouldering in the distance long before the bus pulls into **PUCÓN**, 25 kilometres east of Villarrica. This small mountain town, awash with the smells of wood smoke and grilled meat, has firmly established itself as a top backpacker destination in the last decade. Each November–April season brings scores of hikers, climbers, whitewater enthusiasts and mountain bikers looking to climb the volcano, brave the **rapids** on the Río Trancura, or explore the nearby Parque Nacional Huerquehue. A day outdoors is usually followed by eating, drinking and partying in the town's restaurants and bars, or by a soak in the nearby **thermal springs**. Pucón's wide, tree-lined streets are arranged in a compact grid, and most **tour companies**, supermarkets, outdoor clothing outlets, **banks** and **bars** are located along bustling **Avenida O'Higgins**, which bisects the town. O'Higgins ends by **La Poza**, a black-sand beach on the dazzling blue Lago Villarrica. If you follow Calle Lincoyán to its northern end, you will reach **Playa Grande**, with a multitude of *pedalos*, jet skis and rowing boats for rent. **Restaurants** are scattered throughout the centre, with many found on Fresia and Lincoyán, and you are never more than a couple of blocks from a hostel.

Volcán Villarrica

The volcano is undoubtedly Pucón's biggest attraction, with tourists flocking to climb its peak; in the winter it becomes a **ski and snowboard** destination for the daring. To do the climb, unless you have mountaineering experience, you have to go with a guide; guides will provide all the necessary equipment. It is a fairly challenging five-hour ascent, starting at the chairlift at the base of the volcano, with much of the walking done on snow. If the chairlift (CH$5000) is running, it cuts an hour off the climb. At the top, by the lip of the smoking crater, you'll be rewarded with **unparalleled views** across the Lake District, with Lago Villarrica, Lago Caburga and distant volcanos stretching out before you. The sulphuric fumes, though, mean you can't linger long over the spectacle. Check the weather forecast before embarking on the climb, as many tour companies take groups out even in cloudy weather, only to turn back halfway.

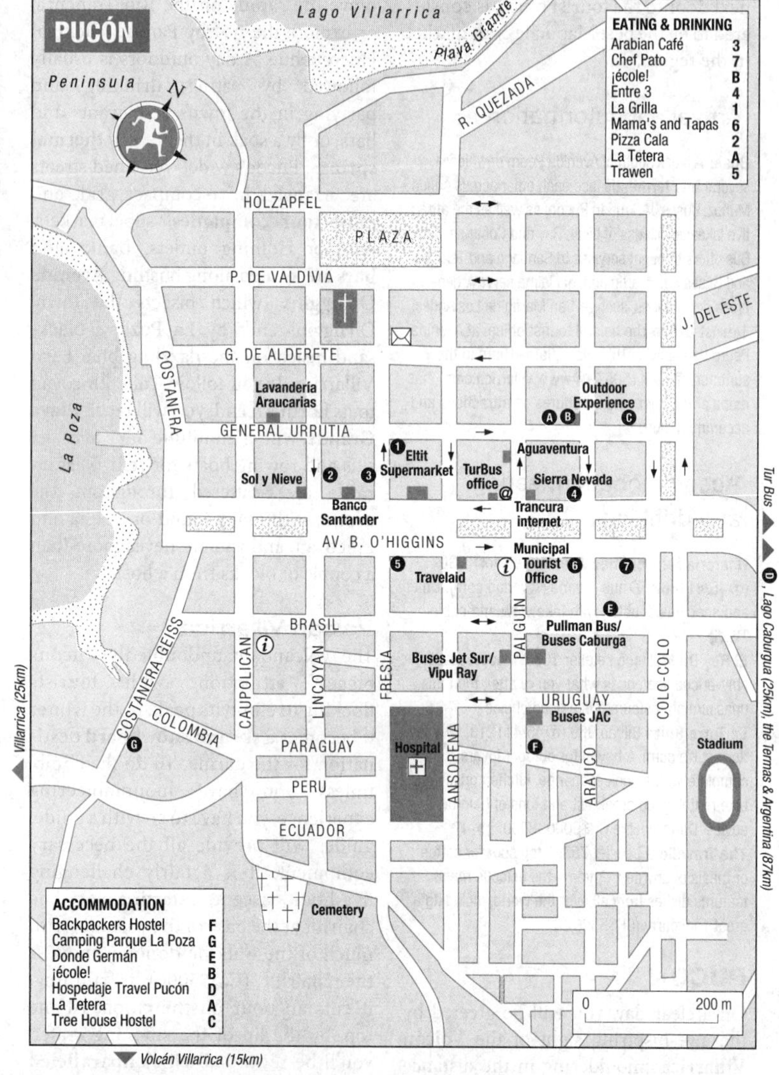

Other outdoor activities

The nearby **Río Trancura** offers a popular class III run on the lower part of the river, with the more challenging class VI, upper Trancura run made up almost entirely of drop pools; some operators allow you to combine the two. The loop to **Ojos del Caburgua** makes an excellent day-trip for **bikers**; follow the paved road out of town towards Caburgua, cross the bridge over the Río Liucura, then take a left along the dirt road by the "El Cristo" cross, eighteen kilometres away. The signposted dirt trail winds past the Ojos de Caburgua swimming holes as well as some waterfalls along the Río Liucura before emerging at the Pasarela Quelhue (hanging bridge) eight kilometres later, and just two kilometres from the paved road back to Pucón.

Arrival and information

Airport There's a small airport on the outskirts of town.

Buses The three main long-distance carriers have separate terminals: Buses JAC, Palguín 605 (Ⓣ45/443693); Pullman Bus, Palguín 575; Tur Bus, O'Higgins 910 (Ⓣ45/443328).

Tourist office The Oficina de Turismo Municipal is on the corner of O'Higgins and Palguín (March–Nov daily 8.30am–8pm; Dec–Feb daily 8.30am–10pm; Ⓣ45/293002, Ⓦwww.pucononline.cl). The helpful staff speak some English and dish out a plethora of brochures on local attractions.

Travelaid Ansorena 425, Local 4 Ⓣ45/444040, Ⓦwww.travelaid.cl. Knowledgeable Swiss-run travel agency that sells guidebooks and maps of Chile, and can help you book passage on the Navimag tour boat (see box, p.484). English and German spoken.

Accommodation

Backpackers Hostel Palguín 695 Ⓣ45/441417, Ⓦwww.backpackerspucon.com. This friendly hostel provides clean (though somewhat dark) dorms and private rooms with or without bathrooms, as well as free internet and on-site laundry service. They also have their own tour company and offer a variety of excursions, including canopy tours, whitewater rafting and volcano climbs. Breakfast included. Dorm CH$7000. ❹

Camping Parque La Poza Costanera Roberto Geis 769 Ⓣ45/441435. Large, shaded campsite near the lake with hot showers and cooking facilities, popular with overland expeditions, cycling tourists and backpackers. CH$10,000 per site.

Donde Germán Brasil 640 Ⓣ45/442444 Ⓦwww.dondegerman.cl. The welcoming owners offer cosy rooms with rustic wooden decor, an inviting common area that serves as a gathering point for travellers, wi-fi, internet and kitchen privileges, as well as an outdoor terrace to relax on. Two night minimum stay required. ❺

¡école! Urrutia 592 Ⓣ45/441675 Ⓦwww.ecole.cl. Very popular guesthouse with an excellent restaurant, spotless comfortable rooms and bunk beds (bring your own sleeping bag), catering to an international crowd. The knowledgeable owners organize trips to the nearby Santuario Cañi, as part of the conservation project they are involved in. Dorm CH$6000. ❹–❺.

Hospedaje Travel Pucón Blanco Encalada 190 Ⓣ45/444093, Ⓔpucontravel@terra.cl. Quiet, Swiss-run guesthouse near the Tur Bus terminal offering large, clean rooms with kitchen privileges; breakfast is CH$2500 extra. Massages on offer (CH$15,000–20,000) for sore and weary hikers. Dorm CH$7000. ❺

La Tetera General Urrutia 580 Ⓣ45/441462, Ⓦwww.tetera.cl. Small, professionally-run guesthouse with cosy rooms, some en-suite. A good book exchange, bright common area and helpful owners who can arrange excursions into the area are all pluses, not to mention the best breakfast around. ❺

Tree House Hostel Urrutia 660 Ⓣ45/444679, Ⓦwww.treehousechile.cl. Run by a congenial and extremely knowledgeable bilingual couple who can help organize all manner of outdoor activities, including visits to the nearby Mapuche communities, this hostel has clean, cosy rooms with good beds, guest kitchen and wi-fi. Relax in the garden hammocks, join in on an impromptu barbecue or try one of the owner's herbal teas. Dorm CH$8000. ❺

Eating and drinking

Arabian Café Fresia 354. Authentic Middle-Eastern restaurant offering falafel, tasty stuffed vegetables and nicely-grilled kebabs. Stuffed aubergines CH$4500.

Chef Pato Av O'Higgins 619A. Reasonably-priced and well-cooked Chilean food, as well as decent pasta and pizza. Pasta dishes CH$4000.

¡école! Urrutia 592. Good helpings of consistently delicious vegetarian fare. Try the sublime vegetable lasagne, or the yellow Thai salmon curry with home-made multi-grain bread. Mains CH$5000.

Entre 3 O'Higgins at Arauco. Lively bar popular with local mountain guides has a rooftop patio and the cheapest drinks in Pucón. Beer CH$1200.

La Grilla Fresia 243. Sate all your carnivorous cravings here. While not the cheapest, *La Grilla* is definitely a cut above the rest when it comes to grilled meat; the chef's specials are excellent. Steak CH$6000.

Mama's and Tapas Av O'Higgins 587. An established watering hole featuring some spectacularly bad music but enticing a large clientele with their nightly drinks specials.

Pizza Cala Lincoyán 361. Arguably the best pizzeria in town, specializing in sizeable portions of thin-crust pizza. Relaxed ambience and good music to boot. Pizza CH$4500.

La Tetera Urrutia 580. Excellent breakfasts and a wide selection of teas, accompanied by fresh pastries. Teas CH$1500.

PUCÓN TOUR OPERATORS

A visitor to Pucón is usually struck dumb by the sheer variety of tour operators. Since the activities on offer are not without an element of risk, it's important to use a reliable operator. We don't recommend Trancura, the largest agency.

Aguaventura Palguín 336 ⓣ45/444246, ⓦwww.aguaventura.com. Experienced French outfit offering volcano ascents, rafting trips, canyoning and snowboarding.
Centro de Turismo Huepil ⓣ9/643-2673. Ranch run by a wonderful couple who organize everything from day-trips into Parque Nacional Villarrica (around CH$35,000) to multi-day horse-riding treks of the Lake District (CH$55,000 per day; all inclusive).
Outdoor Experience Urrutia 952-B ⓣ45/442809, ⓔinfo@outdoorexperience.org. Seasoned duo specializing in small-group volcano ascents, as well as climbing and rappelling trips and excursions to the Santuario Cañi forest reserve.
Paredon Andes Expeditions ⓣ45/444663, ⓦwww.paredonexpeditions.com. A small team of expert trekking and mountaineering guides lead small group ascents up Volcán Villarrica and other Lake District volcanoes, and also offer tailor-made excursions around Chile. English and French spoken.
Sol y Nieve Av O'Higgins at Lincoyán ⓣ45/463860, ⓦwww.chile-travel.com/solnieve.htm. Long-standing and reliable operator, running safe and enjoyable rafting trips and excursions up Volcán Villarrica.

Trawen Av O'Higgins 311. Imaginative and inexpensive menu of healthy, eclectic dishes. The whole-wheat *empanadas* with Antarctic krill are excellent (CH$3000).

Directory

Banks, cambios and ATMs There are several banks with ATMs along the right-hand side of Av O'Higgins, towards the end closest to the lake.
Bike rental Several outfits on O'Higgins rent mountain bikes for around CH$8000 per day.
Hospital Hospital San Francisco, Uruguay 325 (ⓣ45/441177).
Internet access Numerous outfits along O'Higgins: Trancura (O'Higgins at Palguín) has several Skype-equipped computers and offers the cheapest rates (CH$500 per hr).
Laundry Many hostels offer laundry service at an extra cost. Otherwise, try Lavandería Araucarias on General Urrutia 108, Local 4.
Post office Fresia 183.

Moving on

Bus to: Puerto Montt (several daily; 5hr; CH$7500); San Martín de Los Andes (one daily; 5hr; CH$13,000); Santiago (several daily; 11hr; CH$22,000); Temuco (numerous daily; 1hr; CH$1300); Valdivia (6 daily; 3hr; CH$5300); Villarrica (numerous daily; 45min; CH$1000).
Plane to: Santiago (Dec–Feb twice-weekly) with LANExpress, General Urrutia 102 (ⓣ45/443514).

PARQUE NACIONAL HUERQUEHUE

Though small compared to neighbouring national parks, the 125-square-kilometre **PARQUE NACIONAL HUERQUEHUE** (daily 8.30am–6pm; CH$3500) has much to offer, including densely forested **precordillera** (foothills) crossed by clear streams, waterfalls and several beautiful **lakes**, the largest of which – Tinquilco, Chico, Toro and Verde – are accessed via the **Sendero Los Lagos** trail, making for excellent day hikes. Thirty kilometres northeast of Pucón, the park is easily reached by public transport (CH$3200); Buses JAC run five daily services to the park during peak season (8.30am–7pm), while Buses Caburgua offer three (8.20am–5.05pm). From the Conaf *guardería* at the entrance, a clearly signposted trail runs past Lago Tinquilco to the beginning of the Sendero Los Lagos. The excellent *Refugio Tinquilco* (ⓣ9/539-2728, ⓦwww.tinquilco.cl, ❺), a fifteen-minute walk from the Conaf *guardería*, is an airy wooden guesthouse in a beautiful streamside location offering cosy bunks (CH$8000) and double rooms, home-cooked meals, sauna and even a book exchange.

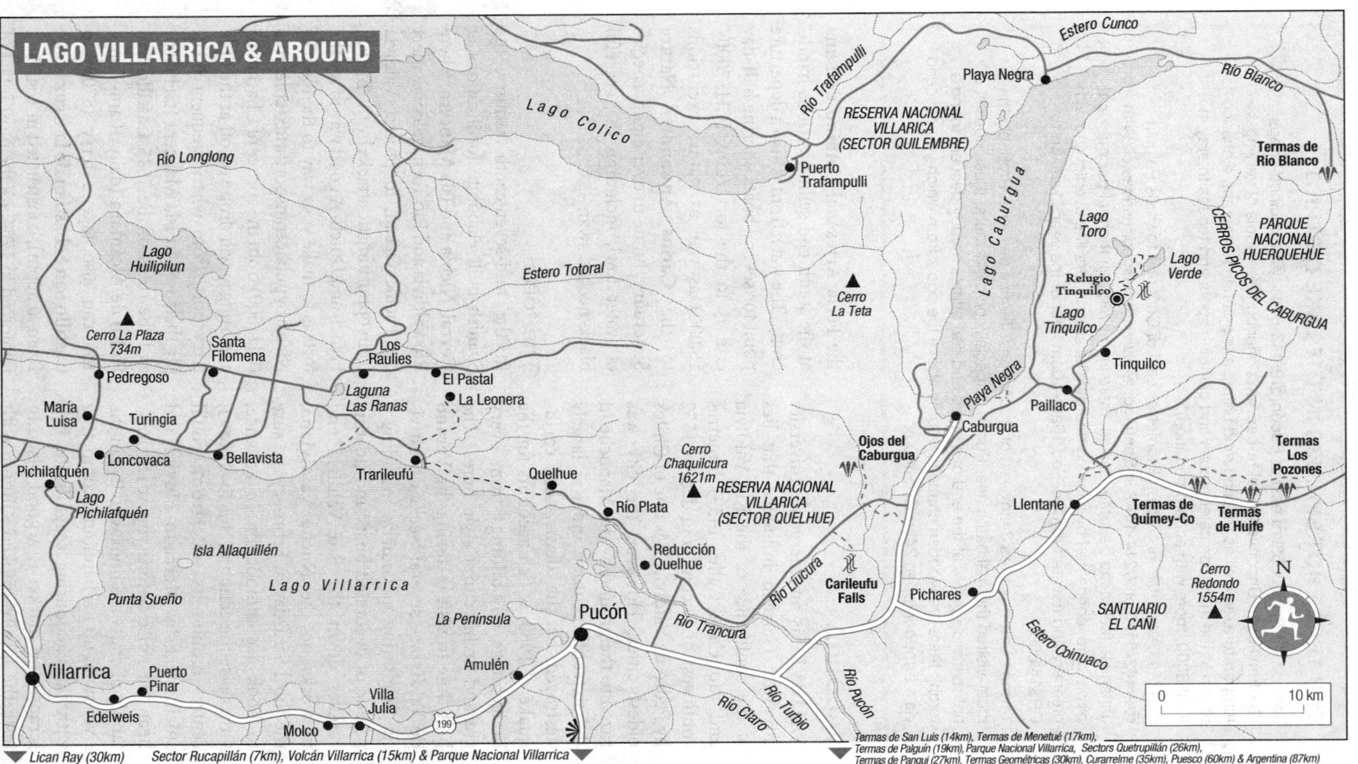
LAGO VILLARRICA & AROUND
Lago Colico
Río Trafampulli
Estero Cunco
Playa Negra
Río Blanco
RESERVA NACIONAL VILLARICA (SECTOR QUILEMBRE)
Termas de Río Blanco
Río Longlong
Puerto Trafampulli
Lago Caburgua
Lago Toro
PARQUE NACIONAL HUERQUEHUE
CERROS PICOS DEL CABURGUA
Lago Verde
Lago Huilipilun
Estero Totoral
Relugio Tinquilco
Cerro La Teta
Lago Tinquilco
Cerro La Plaza 734m
Santa Filomena
Los Raulies
Tinquilco
Pedregoso
Laguna Las Ranas
El Pastal
La Leonera
Playa Negra
Paillaco
María Luisa
Turingia
Caburgua
Ojos del Caburgua
Termas Los Pozones
Loncovaca
Bellavista
Trarileufú
Cerro Chaquilcura 1621m
Pichilafquen
Quelhue
RESERVA NACIONAL VILLARICA (SECTOR QUELHUE)
Llentane
Termas de Quimey-Co
Termas de Huife
Lago Pichilafquén
Río Plata
Isla Allaquillén
Reducción Quelhue
Río Líucura
Carileufu Falls
Cerro Redondo 1554m
N
Lago Villarrica
Pichares
Punta Sueño
Pucón
La Península
Río Trancura
SANTUARIO EL CAÑI
Estero Coinuaco
Villarrica
Puerto Pinar
Amulén
Villa Julia
Río Pucón
Río Turbio
0
10 km
Edelweis
Molco
199
Río Claro
Temuco (82km)
Valdivia (104km)
Lican Ray (30km)
Sector Rucapillán (7km), Volcán Villarrica (15km) & Parque Nacional Villarrica
Termas de San Luis (14km), Termas de Menetué (17km), Termas de Palguín (19km), Parque Nacional Villarrica, Sectors Quetrupillán (26km), Termas de Panqui (27km), Termas Geométricas (30km), Curarrelme (35km), Puesco (60km) & Argentina (87km)

TOP THREE HOT SPRINGS IN THE LAKE DISTRICT

Termas de Panqui 58km east of Pucón ⓣ9/443-6741, ⓔpanquihotsprings@hotmail.com. Unconventional **hot springs** offering three pools of varying temperature, as well as relaxing mud baths, a vegetarian restaurant, a chance to join in the full moon celebrations and camping spots and tepees to stay in (CH$6000; more with accommodation).

Termas Geométricas Sixteen kilometres east of Coñaripe towards Palguín ⓣ9/442-5420 or 2/214-1147 in Santiago, ⓦwww.termasgeometricas.cl. With a Japanese feel to the beautiful design, there are seventeen thermal **geometrical pools** here, connected by winding boardwalks around a ravine overflowing with greenery and a waterfall (Dec–Feb 10am–10pm; rest of the year 11am–8pm; CH$14,000).

Termas Los Pozones 34km east of Pucón, past Termas de Huife. Probably the most-visited thermal baths near Pucón, especially on night tours, these consist of hot **riverside pools** at the end of a steep and sometimes muddy descent (bring a torch); there are wooden changing rooms above the pools from which you descend via a trapdoor (open 24hr; CH$6000).

VALDIVIA

VALDIVIA is an energetic university city with German influence that lies at the confluence of the Río Valdivia and Río Calle Calle, 145 kilometres southwest of Pucón. Founded in 1552 by Pedro de Valdivia, it is one of Chile's oldest cities. However, the city was razed to the ground by the Mapuche in the sixteenth century and was largely destroyed by the devastating earthquake of 1960, which accounts for the hodgepodge of buildings from every era and architectural style here. The best time to visit is during the **Verano de Valdivia** – several weeks of festivities beginning in January, including a parade of decorated boats and floating candles down the Río Valdivia and fireworks on the **Noche Valdiviana**, the third Saturday in February; be sure to book accommodation in advance. Otherwise the action in this lively town centres around its **waterfront**; you'll smell the fishy **Mercado Fluvial** and hear the noise before you reach it. A family of crafty sea lions who live in the river swim up for handouts, competing with the clamouring seagulls for fish scraps. The market is a good place to taste the locally-smoked salmon, with the **Feria Artesanal Camino de Luna** at the south end selling various handicrafts. The waterfront is also a departure point for several boats offering half-day cruises to the fort ruins (CH$7000–15,000) as well as nature excursions to the **Carlos Anwandter Nature Sanctuary**, home to over eighty species of water fowl, including the graceful black-necked swan.

The forts

In the mid-seventeenth century, the Spanish built elaborate fortifications at **Corral**, **Niebla** and **Isla Mancera**, where Río Valdivia and Río Tornagaleones meet the Pacific Ocean, to protect Valdivia from opportunistic attacks by the British, French and Dutch. A good way to see the forts is to make your way to the town of Niebla by public transport; a taxi **colectivo** (CH$600) from the corner of Chacabuco and Yungay will drop you off at the little ferry port, from where frequent boats ply their way to Isla Mancera (CH$500) and the ruins of the 1645 **Castillo San Pedro de Alcántara** (daily 10am–7pm). You can also take a ferry ($700) to **Castillo San Sebastián de la Cruz** (daily 10am–6.30pm), constructed in 1645 and reinforced in 1764; it's the most intact of all the forts, and a short walk from the pier in Corral. The ferry trips give you plenty of opportunity to enjoy the views of the brightly-coloured houses clustered along the green hillsides. To reach **Fuerte Niebla**, which comprises the original 1645 battlements and the **Museo de Sitio Fuerte Niebla** (Tues–Sun 10am–5.30pm), ask the *colectivo* driver to be drop you off further up the road through Niebla. Entry to each of the fort ruins costs CH$600, and Fuerte Niebla is free on Wednesdays.

Arrival and information

Airport Aeropuerto Pinchoy lies 32km northeast of the city; a Transfer Valdivia minibus into town will set you back CH$3000 (ⓣ63/225533).
Buses The main Terminal de Buses (ⓣ63/212212) is located at Anfión Muñoz 360, by Río Calle Calle.
Conaf Helpful office at Ismael Valdés 431 (Mon–Fri 9am–1pm & 3–5pm; ⓣ63/245200, ⓔelke.huss@conaf.cl).
Tourist office There is a well-stocked and helpful Sernatur office at Prat 555, on the waterfront (Mon–Thurs 8.30am–5.30pm, Fri 8.30am–4.30pm; ⓣ63/342300, ⓦwww.valdiviachile.cl).

Accommodation

Airesbuenos Hostel García Reyes 550 ⓣ63/22202, ⓔairesbuenoshostel@gmail.com. Well-run HI-affiliated hostel, bustling with younger travellers, with bright, cheery dorms at their new central location, complete with internet, TV lounge and guest kitchen, as well as friendly staff on hand to help and advise. Dorm CH$7000. ❺
Hostal Arrayan Pérez Rosales 852 ⓣ63/527058 or 8/549-7727, ⓔmacarenapaz26@yahoo.es. Exceptionally welcoming atmosphere, clean rooms for up to four guests with kitchen privileges, all in a rambling, centrally-located house. ❹
Hostal Totem Carlos Anwandter 425 ⓣ63/292849, ⓦwww.turismototem.cl. Quiet guesthouse with clean, spacious, en-suite single to quad rooms; cable TV, internet access, wi-fi and breakfast are included. ❹–❺

Eating and drinking

Bacarana Arauco 379. Student hangout that delivers hearty sandwiches and local brew at low prices. Sandwiches CH$3000.
Cervecería Kunstmann 950 Ruta T-350 ⓣ63/292969, ⓦwww.laserveceria.cl. Come hungry, as this restaurant-brewery serves monster portions of meat, sauerkraut, and potatoes to accompany its range of beers; try the honey-tinted Miel or the darker Torobayo, and finish off with tasty beer ice cream. To get here, take any bus or *colectivo* bound for Niebla from the corner of Yungay and Chacabuco. Mains CH$5000; beers CH$1500.
Guacamole Esmeralda 693. Somewhat gaudy Tex-Mex joint, though the enormous portions more than make up for the decor. Mains CH$4500.
Plaza de los Ríos Arauco 561. Large central shopping mall with a popular and extensive food court featuring typical fast food branches such as *Schopdog*, which specialises in hot dog *combos*. Meals CH$3000.
El Rey de Marisco Chacabuco at Prat, across the street from the Mercado Fluvial. A homely restaurant popular with locals, offering expertly-prepared fresh fish and seafood. *Congrio a la plancha* CH$4500.
La Última Frontera Pérez Rosales 787. Casual café decorated with local artwork, serving excellent sandwiches and tasty crêpes with a variety of fillings (including vegetarian options) late into the evenings; wash them down with fresh fruit juice or a Kunstmann beer. Crêpes CH$3500.
Único Arauco, next door to *Plaza de los Ríos*. A huge and well-stocked supermarket; a must-stop for self-catering travellers.

Moving on

Bus to: Bariloche (several daily; 8hr; CH$13,000); Osorno (several daily; 1hr 30min; CH$2200); Pucón (several daily; 2hr; CH$3200); Puerto Montt (numerous daily; 3hr; CH$3700); Santiago (several daily; 11hr; CH$14,000); Temuco (several daily; 2hr; CH$3000).
Plane to: Concepción (once daily); Puerto Montt (once weekly); Santiago (twice daily); all flighs on LANExpress.

OSORNO AND AROUND

OSORNO is a bustling city 107 kilometres south of Valdivia whose main industries are agriculture and forestry; for travellers it's primarily a busy **transport hub**, acting as a gateway to the **Parque Nacional Puyehue** and Argentina's Lake District. The two bus terminals are within a block of each other, three blocks from the **Plaza de Armas**, the heart of the city. The helpful **Sernatur office** (Mon–Fri 8.30am–1pm & 2.30–5.30pm; ⓣ64/237575) is located at O'Higgins 667, on the ground floor of the Gobernación building at the west side of the plaza; they can advise on accommodation. **Conaf**, at Martínez de Rosas 430 (Mon–Thurs 9.30am–1pm & 2.30–5.30pm, Fri 9.30am–1pm & 2.30–4:30pm; ⓣ64/234393), provides basic information on the Parque Nacional Puyehue, as well as rudimentary maps of the park. If you have to stay overnight, *Villa Eduviges*, Eduviges 856 (ⓣ64/235023, ⓦwww.hoteleduviges.cl; ❺–❻), is a good option for groups, providing friendly service, a wide variety of clean rooms with cable TV, breakfast in a cheerful dining room and wi-fi, while *Residencial Bilbao*, Bilbao 1019 (ⓣ64/262200; ❹–❺), has slightly cheaper and smaller rooms. Osorno's cuisine displays strong German influence; fill up on cheap and hearty portions of sausages, potatoes and sauerkraut at *Bavaria*, O'Higgins 743. Also worth trying are the freshly-baked **empanadas** from the hole-in-the-wall eateries in front of the **Mercado Municipal**, or the fresh seafood in the market's busy *marisquerías*. The main **Terminal de Buses**, Avenida Errázuriz 1400 (ⓣ64/234149), has frequent daily services to Bariloche, Argentina, Santiago and destinations in southern Chile, while the **Terminal de Buses Rurales**, behind the Mercado Municipal at Avenida Errázuriz 1300 (ⓣ64/232073), serves local destinations.

LAGO LLANQUIHUE

Sixty-five kilometres south of Osorno, on the east side of the Panamericana highway, you are greeted with the dazzling sight of **LAGO LLANQUIHUE**, the second-largest lake in Chile, its shimmering blue waters framed by thick forest, with the peaks of volcanoes visible in the distance. The lake draws local and foreign visitors alike to its appealing **beaches**, the best found in the lakeside town of **Frutillar** (ⓦwww.frutillar.cl). People also come for the ample natural attractions around the bustling little town of **Puerto Varas**, and to experience the laid-back lifestyle of lakeside villages such as **PUERTO OCTAY** (ⓦwww.puertooctay.cl). Puerto Octay's Swiss-Chilean-run *Hostal Zapato Amarillo* (ⓣ64/210787, ⓦwww.zapatoamarillo.com; dorm CH$9000, ❻), just north of the village, is a huge budget-traveller draw in itself, providing a welcoming place to stay amidst stunning scenery. The owners can arrange Volcán Osorno climbs, visits to the nearby hot springs and various hikes in the surrounding area; they also rent bikes and canoes.

PUERTO VARAS

PUERTO VARAS, on the southern shore of pristine Lago Llanquihue, is a popular backpacker haunt with unparalleled sunset views of the two nearby volcanoes, Osorno and Calbuco, and attractive Germanic colonial architecture. Rivalling Pucón in terms of nearby **outdoor attractions**, Puerto Varas does not feel too crowded despite its popularity with travellers, and makes an excellent base for volcano-climbing, whitewater rafting, kayaking and cycling; it also serves as a popular stopover on the way to Patagonia. Though this charming little town is fairly spread out, most services, hostels and restaurants are located within a couple of blocks of the little Plaza de Armas.

Arrival and information

Buses There is no central bus station. Cruz del Sur (ⓣ65/236969) stops at San Francisco 1317, a few blocks south of the centre, and has an office at Walker Martínez 239; Tas Choapa and Andesmar stop at Walker Martínez 320 (ⓣ65/233831); Tur Bus and Intersur stop at San

Pedro 210 (☎65/233787); Buses JAC and Cóndor Bus stop at Walker Martínez 227 (☎65/237225). Minibuses to Petrohue stop in front of *Don Jorge* on Walker Martínez, and frequent minibuses to Puerto Montt stop in front of a shopping gallery on Del Salvador, between San Pedro and Santa Rosa.

Tourist office The Casa del Turista is found at the foot of a pier, on Av Costanera (daily Feb–Nov 9am–1.30pm & 3–7pm; Dec–March 9am–10pm; ☎65/237956, Ⓦwww.puertovaras.org); helpful staff provide maps of town and a plethora of leaflets.

Accommodation

Casa Azul Manzanal 66 ☎65/232904, Ⓦwww.casaazul.net. Firm backpacker favourite run by a German-Chilean couple with comfortable rooms, kitchen privileges and an excellent breakfast that includes muesli and home-made bread (CH$2500 extra). Dorm CH$7500. ❹

Casa Margouya Santa Rosa 318 ☎65/511648, Ⓦwww.margouya.com. Lively and friendly hostel with guest kitchen, comfortable lounge area and shared facilities; bathroom queues are the only drawback. Dorm CH$7500. ❹

Compass Del Sur B&B Klenner 467 ☎65/232044, Ⓦwww.compassdelsur.cl. Large wooden guesthouse popular with a mix of travellers, with airy dorms and rooms, communal breakfast (muesli, eggs and real coffee; CH$1000 extra), internet, kitchen use and laundry service. The helpful staff are happy to organize all manner of outdoor activities. Dorm CH$8000. ❹

Hospedaje Ellenhaus Martínez 239 (☎65/233577, Ⓦwww.ellenhaus.cl). Cosy rooms and dorms, all small but immaculately clean. Kitchen privileges included. Dorm CH$6000. ❹

Hostel Patiperros Mirador 135 ☎65/235050, Ⓦwww.jardinsa.cl. HI-affiliated hostel with clean and bright dorms. Amenities include a guest kitchen, free internet, a large dining area, laundry service and luggage lockers. Dorm CH$7500.

Eating and drinking

Club Alemán San José 415. Superior German fare at this excellent restaurant includes duck, goose, and pork chops with ubiquitous sauerkraut; the sandwiches are ample. Mains/sandwiches CH$5000/2500.

Don Jorge San Bernardo 240. An unpretentious place popular with locals, with an emphasis on fish dishes. You can't go wrong with the *congrio* (conger eel) prepared in several different ways. Mains CH$4000.

Donde El Gordito San Bernardo 560, inside the market. Busy and popular little eatery serving large portions of inexpensive seafood. Try the *paila marina* CH$3500.

El Barómetro Walker Martínez 584. A pub and restaurant offering well-executed Chilean dishes as well as a wide range of beers, including Kunstmann. Open late. Mains CH$4500.

Las Brisas Del Salvador at San Bernardo. Large, well-stocked supermarket where you can pick up pizza and *empanadas* from the hot food counter as well as the usual groceries.

Mediterráneo Santa Rosa 068. If you're after large portions of pasta and exquisitely-prepared fish, try this Chilean-Mediterranean fusion restaurant with great views of the lake and attentive service. Thai-style pasta with abalone CH$7000.

Pim's Pub San Francisco 712. Watering hole popular with both locals and visitors, with good bar snacks and Tex-Mex offerings, though the latter are somewhat overpriced. Try the *enchiladas* (CH$4000).

TREAT YOURSELF

Imperial 605 Puerto Varas's standout restaurant, whose German chef consistently works wonders with local fish, seafood and meat. Roast pork loin CH$10,000.

Directory

Banks, cambios and ATMs There are several banks with ATMs downtown, including the reliable Banco de Chile, at Del Salvador 201. You can change foreign currency at Afex, San Pedro 410.

Hospital Centro Médico Puerto Varas is located at Walker Martínez 576.

Internet access and telephone Most hostels offer free internet use; otherwise, there are several call centres with internet connections around the town centre.

Post office San José 242.

Moving on

Bus to: Bariloche (one or two morning departures daily; 8hr; CH$18,000); Frutillar/Puerto Octay (numerous daily; 1hr; CH$1000); Petrohué (numerous daily; 45min; CH$800); Puerto Montt (numerous daily; 30min; CH$700); Santiago (several daily; 14hr; CH$30,000).

PUERTO VARAS TOUR OPERATORS

The area around Puerto Varas offers a variety of outdoor adventures, from challenging climbs up the nearby volcanoes Osorno and Calbuco to rafting on the turbulent turquoise waters of the Río Petrohué and exploring the surrounding wilderness on horseback. Here are several reputable operators.

Aquamotion Expediciones San Pedro 422 ⓣ65/232747, ⓦwww.aquamotion.cl. Experienced, professional operator arranging volcano climbs, rafting, horse riding and more.

Ko'Kayak Ensenada km 40 ⓣ2/584-8171 or 9/310-5272, ⓔinfo@kokayak.com. Excellent outfit specializing in rafting trips down Río Petrohué with fun-loving bilingual guides and an emphasis on safety.

Pachamagua ⓣ9/208-3660, ⓦwww.pachamagua.com. A reliable and professional canyoning specialist arranging all-day, adrenalin-filled excursions.

Puelo Adventure San Pedro 311 ⓣ9/799-1920, ⓦwww.pueloadventure.cl. Reputable operator offering multi-day bike tours in the Lake District and Chiloé, as well as kayaking in the Chilean fjords, multi-day hikes and horse-riding excursions.

Yak Expediciones ⓣ65/234409 or 9/299-6487, ⓦwww.yakexpediciones.cl. Long-standing operator running multi-day sea-kayaking adventures in Patagonia and beyond.

PUERTO MONTT

PUERTO MONTT is beautifully situated on the **Seno de Reloncavi** (Strait of Reloncavi), at the end of the Panamericana highway, with snow-capped mountains clearly visible beyond the sound. Though not, perhaps, deserving its "Muerto Montt" moniker, Puerto Montt is a large, busy city with traffic-choked streets and shopping malls. It's a place to stock up on provisions and equipment on the way to Patagonia and a major **transport hub** with connections to all parts of Chile, but little else. Puerto Montt stretches along the bay, with Avenida Diego Portales running east along the seafront towards the **Plaza de Armas** – the centre of town, surrounded by **bars** and **eateries**. West of the main bus terminal, Avenida Costanera takes you to the busy **passenger port** with a **Feria Artesanal** (craft stalls) and the Angelmó fishing district. There are a number of **guesthouses** in the residential area uphill from the passenger port, with a few more budget options scattered around the Plaza de Armas.

TREAT YOURSELF

Puerto Varas lies on the well-beaten path between Puerto Montt and Bariloche in Argentina. If you're Argentina-bound, a **lake crossing** that allows you to experience the beauty of Chile's oldest national park – **Parque Nacional Vicente Pérez Rosales** – is an excellent alternative to a long bus journey. Starting out at 8am, you are first driven along the banks of Lago Llanquihue to **Petrohué**, whose waterfalls are much-admired, before boarding the ferry that takes you across **Lago Todos Los Santos**, a spectacular expanse of clear blue-green. As you sail along the densely-forested shores, skirting lovely Isla Margarita, the volcanoes Osorno (2660m) and Puntiagudo (2190m) loom to the north, with the majestic Tronador (3491m) to the east. After going through **Chilean customs** at Peulla, you then cross the Argentine border at **Paso Pérez Rosales**, and get stamped in at tiny Puerto Frías. At this point you'll board the ferry again for the short crossing of Laguna Frias, then transfer by bus to your final nautical leg of the journey, a boat across the stunningly beautiful **Lago Nahuel Huapi**, arriving at your destination around midnight. At CH$170,000, crossing by lake is significantly pricier than a bus journey, but it's worth it. The route is very popular, so book in advance with **Turismo Peulla** (☎65/437127, Ⓦwww.turismopeulla.cl), especially during the peak season.

Arrival and information

Airport Aeropuerto El Tepual (☎65/252019) is located 16km west of the city along the Panamericana; Buses ETM (☎65/256253; CH$1700) meet flights and drop you off at the main bus terminal.

Buses Both long-distance and local buses arrive at the large Terminal de Buses (☎65/294533), Av Portales s/n on the waterfront, a 20min coastal walk from the city centre. The bus station has ATMs, snack shop and luggage storage.

Ferry The Terminal de Transbordadores lies at Av Angelmó 2187, several blocks west of the main bus terminal; Navimag (☎65/432300, Ⓦwww.navimag.com) and Naviera Austral (☎65/270400, Ⓦwww.navieraaustral.cl) ferries have offices here.

Tourist office There is a small tourist information kiosk by the main bus terminal and a well-stocked and helpful Sernatur office on the Plaza de Armas, on Varas at San Martín (April–Nov Mon–Fri 9am–1pm & 2.30–7pm, Sat & Sun 9am–1pm; Dec–March daily 9am–9pm; ☎65/261823).

Accommodation, eating and drinking

Angelmó Av Angelmó, to the west of the ferry terminal. A lively fish market sells fresh produce, as well as locally smoked salmon, while the nearby two-storey Angelmó cluster of cheap *marisquerías* serves super-fresh fish and seafood dishes – an ideal place to try *chupe de locos* (CH$5000) or *curanto* (CH$4000); *Señorita Teresa* (Local 14) is an excellent choice.

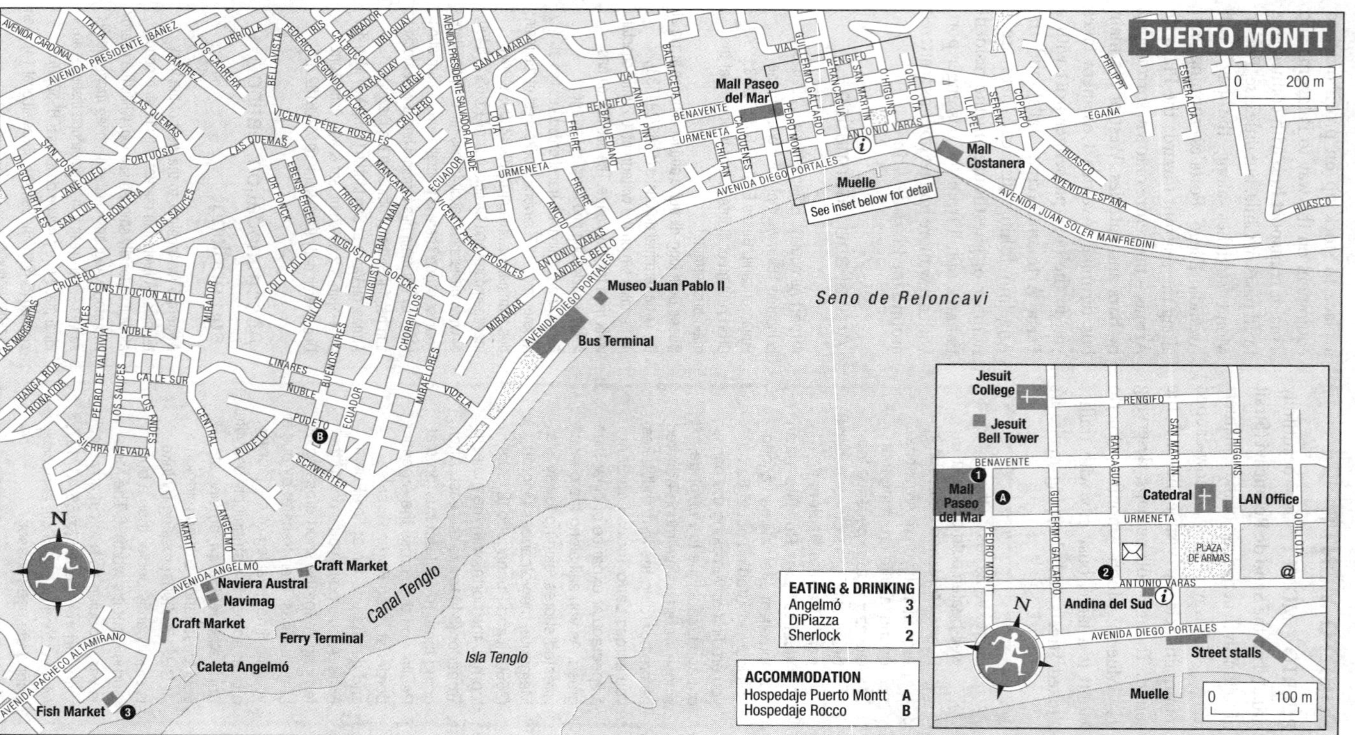
PUERTO MONTT
0 200 m
Mall Paseo del Mar
Mall Costanera
Muelle
See inset below for detail
Seno de Reloncavi
Museo Juan Pablo II
Bus Terminal
Craft Market
Naviera Austral
Navimag
Craft Market
Ferry Terminal
Canal Tenglo
Isla Tenglo
Caleta Angelmó
Fish Market
AVENIDA DIEGO PORTALES
AVENIDA ANGELMÓ
AVENIDA JUAN SOLER MANFREDINI
AVENIDA ESPAÑA
AVENIDA PRESIDENTE SALVADOR ALLENDE
AVENIDA PRESIDENTE IBAÑEZ
AVENIDA CARDONAL
AVENIDA PACHECO ALTAMIRANO
URMENETA
BENAVENTE
RENGIFO
VIAL
QUILLOTA
O'HIGGINS
SAN MARTÍN
RANCAGUA
GUILLERMO GALLARDO
PEDRO MONTT
ANTONIO VARAS
ILLAPEL
SERENA
COPIAPÓ
EGAÑA
ESMERALDA
PHILIPPI
HUASCO
CAUQUENES
CHILLÁN
BALMACEDA
ANÍBAL PINTO
BAQUEDANO
FREIRE
LOTA
ANCUD
ANDRÉS BELLO
MIRAMAR
SANTA MARÍA
VICENTE PÉREZ ROSALES
ECUADOR
CRUCERO
EL VERGEL
PARAGUAY
URUGUAY
MIRADOR
CALBUCO
IRIS
FEDERICO SEGUNDO DE ECKERS
BELLAVISTA
URRIOLA
LOS CARRERA
RAMÍREZ
ITALIA
LAS QUEMAS
FORTUOSO
SAN JOSÉ
JANEQUEO
SAN LUIS
FRONTERA
LOS SAUCES
DIEGO PORTALES
DR FONCK
EBENSPERGER
TRIGAL
MANCANAL
AUGUSTO TRAUTMAN
AUGUSTO GOECKE
CHORRILLOS
MIRAFLORES
VIDELA
COLO COLO
CHILOÉ
BUENOS AIRES
LINARES
ÑUBLE
PUDETO
SCHWERTER
CENTRAL
MARTÍ
ANGELMÓ
CONSTITUCIÓN ALTO
YATES
PEDRO DE VALDIVIA
CALLE SUR
LOS ANDES
SIERRA NEVADA
TRONADOR
HANGA ROA
LAS MARGARITAS
N
EATING & DRINKING
Angelmó 3
DiPiazza 1
Sherlock 2
ACCOMMODATION
Hospedaje Puerto Montt A
Hospedaje Rocco B
Jesuit College
Jesuit Bell Tower
Catedral
LAN Office
PLAZA DE ARMAS
Andina del Sud
Street stalls
0 100 m

DiPiazza Montt 181. Unpretentious restaurant offering good thin-crust pizza as well as less-than-inspiring pasta dishes. Pizza CH$4000.

Hospedaje Puerto Montt Montt 180 ⓣ65/252276. Central guesthouse with friendly owners; though downstairs rooms are a bit cramped, the generous breakfast is a bonus. ④

Hospedaje Rocco Pudeto 233 ⓣ65/272897 ⓦwww.hospedajerocco.cl. Another good backpacker choice, just five blocks from the Navimag ferry, offering clean dorms and rooms with breakfast and internet included, kitchen privileges, laundry service and camping equipment rental. Dorm CH$8000. ⑤

Sherlock Varas 542. The best pub in town, perpetually popular with locals, serving excellent Chilean food, good sandwiches and a wide range of beers in a dark, cosy setting. Mains/sandwiches CH$4000/2500.

Directory

Banks, cambios and ATMs There is an ATM at the main bus terminal and several banks with ATMs along Urmeneta and Gallardo downtown. La Moneda de Oro, inside the main bus terminal, is a reasonable currency exchange; also try Trans Afex, at Portales 516.

Hospital Hospital de la Seguridad, at Panamericana 400 (ⓣ65/25733), and Hospital Base, Seminario s/n (ⓣ65/261100).

Internet access and telephone Try Entel, on Pedro Montt at Urmeneta, or New-Cyber Café, at San Martin 230.

Pharmacy There are numerous pharmacies along Urmeneta and inside the malls.

Post office Rancagua 126.

Shopping There are two large, central shopping malls – the towering Mall Paseo Costanera by the pier, good for outdoor and camping gear, and Mall Paseo del Mar, bordered by Urmeneta and Pedro Montt.

Moving on

Bus to: Ancúd (numerous daily; 2hr 30min; CH$1700); Bariloche, Argentina (several daily, morning departures; 6hr; CH$18,000); Castro (numerous daily; 3hr 30min; CH$5500); Puerto Varas (numerous daily; 30min; CH$700); Punta Arenas (several daily; 28hr; CH$40,000); Santiago (numerous daily; 14hr; CH$30,000).

Ferry: Navimag has departures to Puerto Chacabuco (Fri at 10pm; 24hr; CH$38,000 and upwards) and Puerto Natales (Monday at 2pm departures; 4 days, 3 nights; CH$260,000 upwards).

Plane Daily flights to Santiago, Punta Arenas, Balmaceda (Coyhaique) and Temuco with LANExpress, O'Higgins 167 (ⓣ65/253315, ⓦwww.lan.com), and Sky Airline, Benavente 405, Local 4 (ⓣ65/437555, ⓦwww.skyairline.cl).

NAVIMAG: THE GOOD, THE BAD AND THE JUST PLAIN HIDEOUS

The Navimag trip from Puerto Montt to Puerto Natales can be the most incredible introduction to Patagonia a traveller experiences, or it can be a journey from hell. Lasting four days and three nights, the trip takes you through pristine and deserted waterways, past uninhabited islands and Chile's largest **glacier**, the Piu XI, with frequent sightings of marine life. It passes by **Puerto Edén**, the last remaining settlement of the **Kawéscar** people, before sailing into the cold and little-explored fjords of the south, finally docking in Puerto Natales on the Seno Última Esperanza. If you're lucky with the weather, you will not want to leave the deck for the duration of the trip, except to take part in a raucous game of bingo on the last night with a crowd of new friends. The flipside is a cruise entirely shrouded in mist and fog, topped with a sleepless night as the ship navigates the turbulent waters of the **open ocean**, followed by the equally sick-inducing waves of the **Golfo de Penas**, while you spend your trip stuck in the bar or the dining room, watching *Shrek III* with people you will have grown mightily tired of by the end of the trip. Either way, it's an **unforgettable experience**, and you will most likely find yourself running into fellow Navimag travellers all over Patagonia for weeks afterwards.

"C" is the cheapest category of cabin: you get a room divided into several lots of four bunks, each bunk equipped with curtains, its own light and a large luggage locker. Bathroom facilities are shared; bring your own towel. The food is basic, but the staff are extremely helpful. Book your passage several weeks in advance during the peak months of January and February.

Chiloé

As the ferry ploughs through the grey waters of the Canal de Chacao that separates the **CHILOÉ** archipelago from the mainland, an island appears out of the fog. One of many inhabited **islands** that make up the archipelago, **Isla Grande de Chiloé** is the second-largest island in South America, covered with a patchwork of forests and fields, with traditional villages nestling in sheltered inlets. Its residents still largely make a living from fishing and farming, as they have done for centuries. Chiloé draws visitors with the accessibility of its two main towns, **Ancúd** and **Castro**. The rich and diverse food, wild and remote national parks sheltering wildlife unique to the island, and wealth of architecturally unique eighteenth- and nineteenth-century wooden **churches** are also major attractions. Originally populated by the Huilliche (southern Mapuche) Indians, most of whom died from a smallpox epidemic shortly after European contact, Chiloé was colonized by the Spanish as early as 1567. Scores of refugees fled the fierce Mapuche on the mainland to the island, and Chiloe's very **distinct culture** evolved in relative isolation, resulting in a diverse and rich mythology that permeates people's lives to this day.

ANCÚD

A spread-out small town on Chiloé's northern coast, built on a hilly site with excellent views of the Canal de Chacao and the Golfo de Quetalmahue, **ANCÚD** is the island's largest settlement and a pleasant place to linger. Its importance as a Spanish fortification was highlighted when it became the royalists' last stronghold, holding out against hostile forces for a decade after Chile's declaration of independence in 1818. Ancúd is bordered by the white-sand **Playa Gruesa** to the north and much of the action centres around the lively little **Plaza de Armas**, where there

MYTH AND BLACK MAGIC

Chiloé's distinctive mythology is populated with colourful characters. Here are a few that you might encounter.

La Pincoya A beautiful mermaid who lives in the sea, to whom fishermen attribute a good catch.

El Trauco A repulsive little troll with an insatiable appetite for young virgins, whose gaze has an irresistible power over women, blamed for unexplained pregnancies on the island.

El Basilisco A cross between a serpent and a rooster, he steals into people's houses at night to suck the phlegm from his victims' throats and lungs, after which they inexplicably sicken and die unless the house is burnt down.

La Cueva de Quicaví The legendary witches' cave located on Chiloé's eastern coast, reportedly containing a book of spells given to the Chilote *brujos* (male witches) by a Spanish warlock; the Spanish Inquisition and countless others have searched for the cave in vain.

El Invunche The hideously deformed guardian of the witches' cave, raised on cats' milk and human flesh stolen from graveyards, who terrorizes anyone who catches a glimpse of him.

El Caleuche A ghost ship used to transport the witches that appears out of the sea mist. It helps those who are on good terms with the *brujos*, but sometimes entices new crew members; those beckoned turn into mere shadows of themselves, leaving their homes forever, with a sack of gold left behind as payment for taking them.

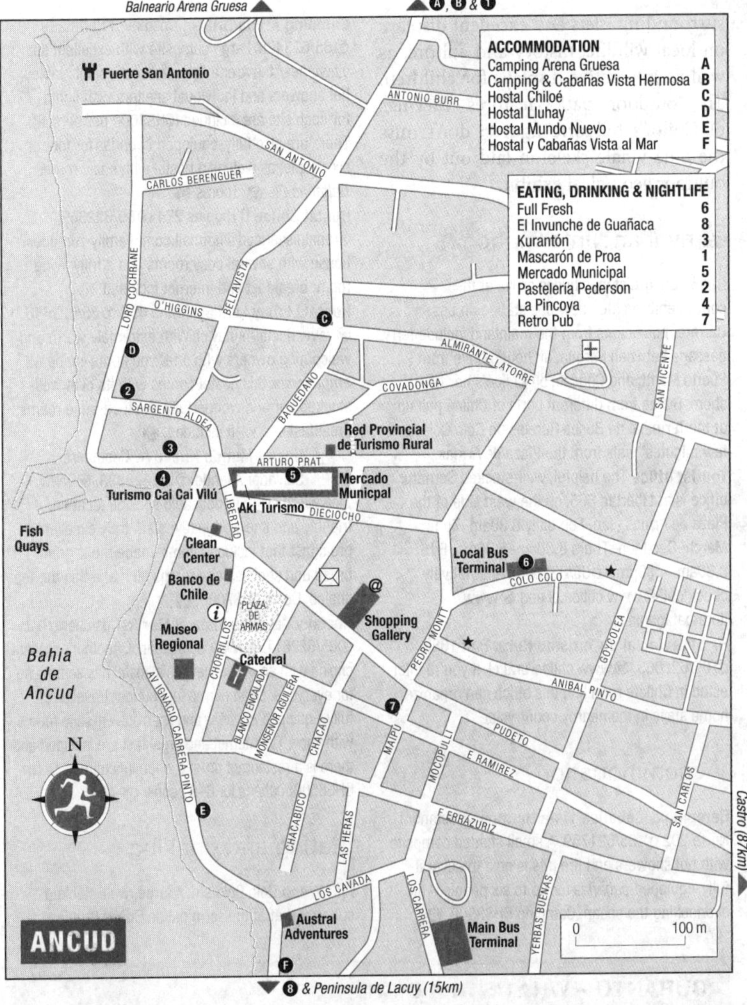

are crafts and book stalls in the summer and locals chill out in the evenings. There are numerous bustling *marisquerías* at the Mercado Municipal, a block north, with craft stalls inside and **tour agencies** offering penguin-watching trips out front. **Guesthouses** and restaurants are mainly located close to the main square or along Avenida Costanera, which runs along the town's western side, its attractive **promenade** dotted with modern sculptures. Costanera culminates in a busy fishing port at its northern end, beyond which Cochrane leads north to the ruins of **Fuerte de San Antonio** (1770), on a promontory overlooking the harbour.

Museo Regional

In the southwest corner of the Plaza de Armas, the well-organized **Museo Azul de las Islas de Chiloé** (Jan–Feb Mon–Sun 10.30am–7pm; March–Dec Mon–Fri 9.30am–12.30pm & 2.30–5.30pm, Sat, Sun & holidays 10am–2pm; CH$700) features a relief map of Chiloé and the surrounding islets and excellent displays on local wildlife, history and culture, as well as interactive displays for children. The outdoor patio features carvings of Chiloé's folkloric figures; don't miss the blue whale skeleton laid out by the outdoor geological exhibit.

Arrival and information

Buses Long-distance buses arrive at the conveniently located new bus station on Los Carrera; bus tickets from the mainland include ferry passage between Pargua, an hour's drive from Puerto Montt, and Chacao, on Chiloé's northern shore. Buses from different parts of Chiloé pull up at the Terminal de Buses Rurales on Colo Colo, a few minutes' walk from the Plaza de Armas.

Tourist office The helpful, well-stocked Sernatur office is at Libertad 665, on the west side of the Plaza de Armas (Jan–Feb daily 8.30am–7pm; March–Dec Mon–Thurs 8.30am–5.30pm, Fri 8.30am–4.30pm; ⓣ65/622800). Alternatively, check out ⓦwww.chiloe.cl and ⓦwww.interpatagonia.cl.

Red Provincial de Turismo Rural Prat 168B ⓣ65/625003, ⓦwww.chiloerural.cl. If you're interested in Chilote rural life, this office can organize home stays in the nearby countryside.

Accommodation

Camping & Cabañas Vista Hermosa Costanera Norte 292 ⓣ 65/621759. A small shaded campsite with hot showers and fire pits is next to several fully-equipped *cabañas* for up to six people – all overlooking the ocean. Camping CH$3500. ❻

Camping Arena Gruesa Costanera Norte 290 ⓣ65/623428. Large campsite with excellent sea views near the Arena Gruesa beach; picnic tables, hot showers and individual shelters with lights for each site are included (CH$3000 per person). There are also fully-equipped *cabañas* for four or six people, as well as a hostel with basic rooms. *Cabañas* ❻–❼; rooms ❺.

Hostal Chiloé O'Higgins 274 ⓣ65/622869, ⓔanaluisaancud@hotmail.com. Family-run guesthouse with several cosy rooms and a frilly living room; breakfast and internet included. ❺

Hostal Lluhay Lord Cochrane 458 ⓣ65/622656, ⓦwww.hostal-lluhay.cl. With extremely warm and welcoming owners who offer you home-made *empanadas*, this hostel comes with its own well-stocked bar and wonderfully plush en-suite rooms; breakfast and wi-fi included. ❺

Hostal Mundo Nuevo Av Costanera Salvador Allende ⓣ65/628383, ⓦwww.newworld.cl. An impeccable seaside location, friendly and knowledgeable staff, truly excellent breakfast that includes home-made multi-grain bread and spotless airy rooms all make this the top choice. Dorm CH$7000. ❹

Hostal y Cabañas Vista al Mar Av Costanera 918 ⓣ65/622617, ⓦwww.vistaalmar.cl. Another excellent choice with an ocean view, this hostel has something for everyone: clean dorms for younger travellers, fully-equipped *cabañas* and spacious en-suite rooms with cable TV; internet and breakfast are included and there is a restaurant on-site, open lunchtimes. Dorm CH$8500; *cabaña* for 6–8 people ❸–❺

Eating and drinking

Full Fresh Colo Colo s/n. A large, well-stocked supermarket at the Terminal de Buses Rurales.

CURANTO – WHAT'S IN A DISH?

It has only recently been acknowledged that people of Polynesian origin once visited mainland Chile – the DNA of a Polynesian chicken was found on Mapuche land. Chiloe's signature dish, *curanto*, however, has been prepared for several centuries using cooking methods very similar to those used in Polynesia. First, extremely hot rocks are placed at the bottom of an earthen pit; then, a layer of shellfish is added, followed by chunks of meat, *longanisa* (sausage), potatoes, *chapaleles* and *milcaos* (potato dumplings). The pit is then covered with *nalca* (Chilean wild rhubarb) leaves and as the shellfish cooks, the shells spring open, releasing their juices onto the hot rocks, steaming the rest of the ingredients. Traditional *curanto* (*curanto en hoyo*) is slow-cooked in the ground for a day or two, but since traditional cooking methods are only used in the countryside, you will probably end up sampling *curanto en olla*, oven-baked in cast iron pots. The dish comes with hot broth that you pour over it when it begins to cool down.

El Invunche de Guañaca Twelve kilometres west of Ancúd, along the coast ⓣ9/019-0571 or 9/427-7798, ⓦwww.invunchedeguanaca.com. Highly recommended restaurant within cycling distance of Ancúd, where excellent *curanto en hoyo* is combined with stunning views of the coast. Call ahead to reserve.
Kurantón Prat 94. The best place in town to try *curanto en olla*, as well as super-fresh fish dishes, in an elegant setting, surrounded by black-and-white photos of a bygone era. *Curanto* CH$4500.
Mascarón de Proa Baquedano s/n, in *Cabañas Las Golondrinas*. An unpretentious spot to the north of town, this restaurant cooks up ample servings of solid fish dishes. Mains CH$5000.
Mercado Municipal The no-frills eateries at the market tend to be packed at lunchtime, all serving a variety of inexpensive fish and seafood dishes; *Sanchoin*, in particular, is a long-standing favourite. Mains CH$3000–4000.
Pastelería Pederson Lord Cochrane 470. This pastry house serves a range of excellent cakes and tarts – the raspberry cheesecake is particularly tasty. Those without a sweet tooth can still enjoy the great sea view while sipping a real coffee. Cakes CH$1500.
La Pincoya Prat 61. Opposite *Kurantón*, *La Pincoya* overlooks the fish harbour and serves excellent *carapacho* (crab casserole), *curanto* and delicious *cancato* (steamed salmon stuffed with sausage, cheese and tomatoes). *Cancato* CH$5500.
Retro Pub Maipú 615. Those in danger of overdosing on *curanto* can tuck into decent pizza and pretty good Mexican dishes at this lively pub. Mains CH$4500.

Directory

Banks, cambios and ATMs There is a bank with an ATM in the northwest corner of the Plaza de Armas.
Hospital Almirante Latorre 301 (ⓣ65/622356).
Internet access and telephone There are several internet cafés that also serve as call centres along Pudeto; try Entel, at no. 219.
Laundry Clean Center, Pudeto 45, offers standard laundry service.
Shopping The Feria Rural y Artesanal at the Mercado Municipal has a number of stalls selling woollen goods and wood carvings, as well as home-distilled liqueurs in various garish colours.

Moving on

Bus to: Castro (several daily; 1hr; CH$1500); Chonchi (4 daily; 2hr; CH$2200); Puerto Montt (numerous daily; 2hr 30min; CH$4300); Quellón (4 daily; 2hr 30min; CH$3200); Santiago (4 daily in the afternoon; 16hr; CH$24,000).

AROUND ANCÚD

The three islands off the western coast of Chiloé, 27 kilometres southwest of Ancúd, are breeding grounds for both Magellanic and Humboldt penguins. Several tour agencies offer half-day tours of the **penguin colony** (CH$7000), which take you along a dirt road through picturesque, hilly country and along the rugged coastline to the little fishing village of **Puñihuil**. From Puñihuil, it's a half-hour round trip to the offshore islands, where you are likely to catch sight of sea lions and sea otters, as well as the penguins and a wealth of seabirds. Don't miss the incredible *empanadas de locos* at the far end of the beach. Though there are no regular scheduled trips as yet, a large pod of **blue whales** has been spotted in Chiloé's coastal waters, and local fishermen occasionally take groups of visitors in search of the magnificent

ANCÚD TOUR OPERATORS

Aki Turismo Mercado Municipal Patio Externo ⓣ65/545253 or 65/547181, ⓦwww.akiturismochiloe.cl. Established outfit running twice-daily tours to the Pinguinera Puñihuil (see above); reserve a day ahead and you will be picked up from your hostel.
Austral Adventures Av Ignacio Carrera Pinto 904 ⓣ65/625977, ⓦwww.austral-adventures.com. A reputable outfit run by an extremely knowledgeable American-Peruvian couple, specializing in multi-day tours of Patagonian fjords and the Chiloé archipelago aboard the "Cahuela"; sea-kayaking and land tours of Chiloé are also on offer.

mammals; ask around. For more information on the blue whales, check out ⓦwww.ballenaazul.org.

Eastern Chiloé

If Chiloé's towns are too "modern" for you, the eastern coast, just north of Castro, is the place to witness **traditional village life**. Here you can wander around the Sunday market in coastal **Dalcahue**, watching fishermen from outlying islands unload their produce, take a ferry to the elongated Isla Quinchao to see the island's **oldest church** in Achao or travel up the coast to Tenaún to enjoy some spectacular coastal hiking. Look for the legendary **witches' cave** near tiny Quicaví, near the village of Quemchi (see box, p.494), or spend several days camping and **sea kayaking** between Isla Mechuque and the Islas Chauques. Buses JM have daily departures for Quemchi and Quicaví from Ancúd's Terminal de Buses Rurales (one daily; 12.45pm; CH$1200) and there's a once-daily Cruz del Sur journey to Dalcahue from the main terminal (6.05pm; CH$1500); there are more frequent departures from Castro.

CASTRO

The third oldest continuously-inhabited city in Chile, **CASTRO** was founded in 1567 on the Fiordo de Castro and survived a number of calamities through the centuries – from being pillaged by English and Dutch pirates to the great earthquake of 1960, which largely destroyed it. These days it's the bustling capital of Chiloé.

The Town

A large **Plaza de Armas** surrounded by bars and restaurants is Castro's focal point; in summer, outdoor musical events are staged here. The peachy-pink Neogothic **Iglesia San Francisco** (1911), one of Chiloé's fabled wooden churches, stands on the northeast corner of the plaza. The **Museo Regional** (Jan–Feb Mon–Sat 9.30am–7pm, Sun 10.30am–1pm; March–Dec Mon–Fri 9.30am–1pm & 3–6pm Sat 9:30am–1pm; free) is found on Esmeralda, just half a block south of the plaza, and features a collection of black-and-white photos of the 1960 earthquake and its devastation. Two blocks from the plaza, steeply downhill, lies the Lillo, the coastal road featuring a number of **seafood restaurants**, with the large **Feria Artesanal** by the water selling all sorts of woollen goodies and other crafts.

Palafitos

Though deemed unsanitary by some locals, Chiloé's famous **palafitos** are still found at several locations around Castro. Perched precariously on stilts above the water, these brightly-painted, shingled, traditional wooden dwellings are an unforgettable sight. The most impressive examples are found at the north end of town, where they are perfectly reflected in the mini-lake by the roadside. More *palafitos* are found slightly south along the same Avenida Pedro Montt, while others are used as restaurants at the southern end of town, by the Feria Artesanal. A final batch can be seen from the western end of Lillo, across the Río Bamboa.

Arrival and information

Buses Long-distance buses use the main bus terminal, at San Martín 486, a block north of the Plaza de Armas. Buses from other parts of Chiloé arrive at the Terminal de Buses Rurales, two blocks north of the main terminal, at San Martín 667.

Conaf Gamboa 424 ⓣ65/532501, ⓔmparedes@conaf.cl. A good source of information on the Parque Nacional Chiloé (Mon–Fri 8.30am–5pm).

Red Provincial de Turismo Rural Portales 494 ⓣ65/639960, ⓦwww.chiloerural.cl. Has useful information on the area's rural tourism for those interested in experiencing traditional Chilote life.

Tourist office There is a large new tourist information centre (Mon–Sat 8.30am–12.30pm & 2.30–6pm; ⓣ65/633760) on the Plaza de Armas, with plenty of information on the area (though you have to know what to ask for, since it's all behind

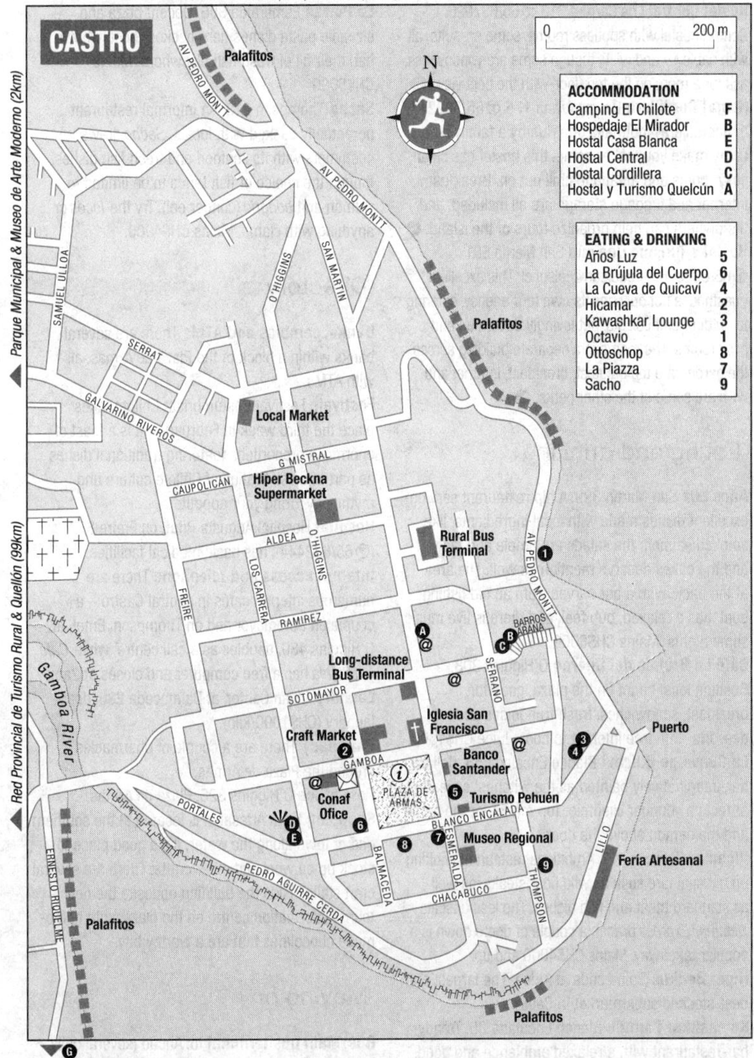

the counter) and scale models of Chiloé's famous wooden churches.

Accommodation

Camping El Chilote 5km south of Castro ☎65/636537, ✉andez8@123mail.cl. Large campsite with a panoramic view of Castro and plenty of shade, 100m from the beach; each site (CH$10,000) has its own picnic table and fire pit; price includes hot showers. There is a café on-site and it's possible to arrange horseriding and boat trips; tents and bicycles are also available for rent.

Hospedaje El Mirador Barros Arana 127 ☎65/633795 or 9/579-6793, ✉maboly@yahoo.com. The best choice of guesthouse on this pedestrian street, with immaculate rooms and a friendly proprietress; breakfast is included. ❸ upwards.

Hostal Casa Blanca Los Carrera 308 ☎65/632726. Singles are on the small side, while doubles are spacious with en-suite bathrooms; wi-fi and breakfast included. ❺

Hostal Central Los Carrera 316 ⓣ65/637026. Central hostel with spotless rooms, some en-suite, all with cable TV and wi-fi, though some are windowless; ask for a room on the top floor, with the best view. ⑤
Hostal Cordillera Barros Arana 175 ⓣ65/532247, ⓔhcordillera@hotmail.com. Run by a family who really make you feel at home, this hostel has clean, cosy rooms and a patio to chill out on. Breakfast, internet and luggage storage are all included, and the owners can help organize tours of the island. ④
Hostal y Turismo Quelcún San Martín 581 ⓣ65/632396, ⓔquelcun@telsur.cl. This excellent guesthouse not only has its own tour agency, catering to outdoor enthusiasts, but lovingly decorated and cosy rooms. The rooms in a separate building across the garden are the quietest; breakfast, internet and wi-fi are some of the other perks. ⑤

Eating and drinking

Años Luz San Martín 399. A hip restaurant serving excellent dishes made with local ingredients, like smoked salmon; the salads are ample and tasty, and the cakes deserve mention as well. The area at the back, with a bar carved from an old fishing boat, has a relaxed, pub feel, and there is live music some nights. Mains CH$6000.
Café La Brújula del Cuerpo O'Higgins 308. Bustling local haunt on the plaza, good for breakfast, sandwiches, fresh fruit juices and desserts, with free internet to boot. Juice CH$1500.
La Cueva de Quicaví Blanco Encalada 55. Cellar bar, imaginatively painted as the witches' cave, that attracts a younger clientele. Top marks for the name and the demon above the door.
Hicamar Gamboa 413. Ambitious restaurant cooking up unusual fare such as wild boar steaks, as well as standard meat and fish dishes. The less upscale *Hicamar Express* branch a couple of doors down is a popular takeaway. Mains CH$4000 and up.
Hiper Beckna Balmaceda at Aldea. The largest and best-stocked supermarket in Castro.
Kawashkar Lounge Blanco Encalada 35. Trendy bar-restaurant with a relaxed ambience and good beats, extensive cocktail list and plenty of tasty vegetarian options, including crêpes with sweet and savoury fillings and large sandwiches. Crêpes CH$3500.
Octavio Pedro Montt 261. With exemplary service, excellent location right over the water and a simple but expertly-executed menu, this is the best place in Castro for *curanto en olla*. *Curanto* CH$4500.
Ottoschop Blanco 356. Dark, cosy and popular with a younger crowd, this bar serves a good selection of beers, including Kunstmann. Beers CH$1200.
La Piazza Esmeralda 306. Decent pizza and sizeable pasta dishes here beckon those who've had their fill of fresh fish elsewhere. Mains CH$5000.
Sacho Thompson 213. An informal restaurant perpetually packed with locals, *Sacho* draws customers with its seafood and fresh fish dishes, though the choice of fish tends to be limited to salmon and *congrio* (conger eel). Try the *locos* or anything with clams. Mains CH$4000.

Directory

Banks, cambios and ATMs There are several banks within a block of the Plaza de Armas, all with ATMs.
Festivals Festival Costumbrista Chilote takes place the third week in February – it is a feast of enormous proportions featuring traditional dishes as part of a celebration of Chilote culture and mythology. Bring your appetite.
Hospital Hospital Augusta Rifat, on Freire 852 (ⓣ65/632444), has basic medical facilities.
Internet access and telephone There are numerous internet cafés in central Castro – a couple on Sotomayor and on Thompson. Entel, at O'Higgins 480, doubles as a call centre, while *Café la Brújula* has a free computer and closes at 2am.
Laundry Clean Center, at Balmaceda 230, does laundry (CH$1000/kilo).
Pharmacy There are a couple of pharmacies around the Plaza de Armas.
Post office O'Higgins 326, Plaza de Armas.
Shopping Feria Artesanal is located at the southern end of town along the water; it's a good place to stock up on wool and other crafts. There are several craft stalls inside the building opposite the new tourist information centre on the plaza, with home-made chocolates that are a worthy buy.

Moving on

Bus: Main bus terminal to: Ancúd (several daily; 1hr; CH$1500); Puerto Montt (several daily; 5hr; CH$5500); Santiago (4 daily; 18hr; CH$28,000).
Rural bus terminal to: Chonchi (several daily; 30min; CH$350); Cucao (6 daily; 1hr; CH$700); Quellón (numerous daily; 2hr; CH$700).

PARQUE NACIONAL CHILOÉ

On the island's western coast, the **PARQUE NACIONAL DE CHILOÉ** comprises vast areas of native evergreen

CASTRO TOUR OPERATORS

Altué Expeditions Dalcahue ☎9/419-6809, 🌐www.seakayakchile.com. Find this excellent outfit at their kayak centre in Dalcahue; they offer multi-day trips around the Chiloé archipelago, as well as multi-activity combination trips in the Lake District and Patagonia.

Turismo Pehuén Blanco Encalada 299 ☎65/635254, 🌐www.turismopehuen.cl. Organizes city tours, summer boat trips to the uninhabited islets off the east coast and other excursions.

Turismo Quelcún San Martín 581 ☎65/632396. Runs sea-kayaking tours as well as excursions to Parque Nacional de Chiloé and sightseeing trips to the smaller islands on the east coast.

forest, covering the slopes and valleys of the **Cordillera de Piuchen**, as well as wide deserted beaches and long stretches of **rugged coastline**, home to dozens of seabird species, penguins and sea lions. The dense vegetation hides the elusive *pudú* (pygmy deer) and the shy Chilote fox. The park is divided into three sectors – the southern **Sector Anay** is the most visited by local and foreign outdoors enthusiasts, while Sector Abtao, at the north end of the park, and the remote Sector Chepu, southwest of Ancúd, are both difficult to access. To reach Sector Anay, take a bus to the tumbledown village of **Cucao** from Castro's rural bus terminal (six daily in peak season; 1hr; CH$1000). Pay the park entrance fee at **Chanquín** (daily 9am–7pm; CH$2000), across the river from the village, where Conaf's **Centro de Visitantes** has displays on local fauna, flora and the local Huilliche communities, and provides visitors with a detailed map of the park. **Camping Chanquín** (☎9/644-2489), 200m beyond the visitor centre, has twenty sites with running water, hot showers, toilets and fire pits, and there are several **guesthouses** of varying quality in Cucao itself. Wild camping is free on the beach and along the trails. Though you can pick up some supplies at Cucao and buy fresh catch from the fishermen, you'll need adequate food to explore the park. There are some attractive **short walks** from the visitors' centre – the 750-metre Sendero El Tepual winds its way through humid, slippery *tepú* woods, and the Sendero Dunas de Cucao switches between patches of dense vegetation and sand dunes, before arriving at a white beach. An enjoyable **twenty-kilometre trail** runs to the Conaf refugio *Cole Cole*, alternating between stretches of beach and forest, with dramatic views of the coastline, pounded by the fierce Pacific surf. Another two hours' walk brings you to the refugio *Anay*, with a chunk of largely unexplored wilderness beyond.

PARQUE TANTAUCO

At the very south of Chiloé lies the remote private reserve of **PARQUE TANTAUCO**, at least double the size of Parque Nacional Chiloé and completely uninhabited apart from the fishing hamlet of **Inio** on the southern coast. Though its infrastructure is currently being developed, it is possible to take the one weekly boat from the southeastern port of Quellón to Inio (CH$15,000) and stay at a campsite, equipped with hot showers, toilets, picnic tables and fire pits (CH$5000; ☎65/698-0066), located near a pretty river that you can swim in. There are extensive beaches near Inio, protected from the rough waters of the Gulf of Corcovado by small offshore islands. A total of seven trails, three of which lead from Inio into the forested wilderness, make for good hikes. The most developed trail leads northwest to the attractive Chaiguaco and Chaiguata lagoons, the latter with a well-equipped campsite alongside it. Besides the ample hiking terrain, the numerous coastal inlets are ideal for kayaking. For more information on the park, contact the Oficina de Parque Tantauco in Quellón, at Av La Paz 68 (☎65/685064, Ⓦwww.parquetantauco.cl). Bring all necessary supplies with you, including a sturdy tent and waterproof gear.

Northern Patagonia: Aisén

Though Patagonia as a region is difficult to define, it is generally agreed that the province of **AISÉN** comprises its northern half. Aisén is the wildest, least populated and least visited of all of Chile's provinces. The dirt-and-gravel track of the **Carretera Austral**, or "Southern Highway", stretches for 1240 kilometres down from Puerto Montt to tiny **Villa O'Higgins**, interrupted in places by various bodies of water and supplemented by short ferry rides. The only town of any size is **Coyhaique**, a good base for exploring the surrounding area and for taking a boat excursion to the awe-inspiring **San Rafael Glacier**. Planning ahead is key: Aisén is best explored in the peak season of December through February, and transport tends to be scarce at other times of year. In peak season, book ahead whenever possible and be prepared for any contingency, as travel is susceptible to changes in the weather. Meanwhile, the future of the area around Chaitén is uncertain. With the town's population recently evacuated due to the unforeseen **volcanic eruption**; the area is currently out of bounds.

COYHAIQUE

The town of **COYHAIQUE**, 634 kilometres south of Puerto Montt, is nestled in the shadow of the great slab of Cerro Macay, at the confluence of the Simpson and Coyhaique rivers. It is the region's capital and a welcome pocket of civilization compared to the smaller hamlets and villages along the Carretera Austral. The **transportation hub** for the entire area, Coyhaique has departures to destinations up and down the Carretera Austral, as well as neighbouring Argentina. The heart of the city is the hexagonal **Plaza de Armas**, which resembles a wheel with ten spokes stretching out in various directions, making navigation a little confusing. The plaza offers wi-fi access, and there are outdoor concerts here in the summer. Most places to eat and drink are to be found within a few blocks of the plaza, and the small **Feria de Artesanos**, between Dussen and Horn, on the plaza's western side, sells regional handicrafts. The **Monumento de Ovejero**, three blocks up Condell and one block east along the main thoroughfare of Avenida Baquedano, immortalizes the region's pastoral roots in the form of a sculpture of a mounted sheep farmer herding his flock. Across the street, the small **Museo Regional de la Patagonia** (Mon–Fri 8.30am–6pm; CH$400) has displays on the region's history, mineralogy and flora and fauna, featuring stuffed wildlife and a worthwhile collection of historical photographs, including some of the workmen who built the Carretera Austral highway, commissioned by Pinochet.

Arrival and information

Airport Aeropuerto de Balmaceda, 55km south of town, serves LAN flights from Santiago, Punta Arenas, Puerto Montt and Temuco; the flights are met by minibuses that do door-to-door drop-offs (CH$7000–8000). Aeródromo Teniente Vidal, 7km out of town, has charter flights from Villa O'Higgins, Cochrane and Chile Chico.

Buses The main Terminal de Buses, on the corner of Lautaro and Magallanes, is used by Buses Queulat (☎67/242626), Buses Daniela (☎67/231701), Interlagos (☎67/240840), Queilén Bus (☎67/240760), Buses Don Carlos

(Ⓣ67/232981), Bus Sur (Ⓣ67/258261) and Buses São Paolo (Ⓣ67/255726) among others. Some carriers also have separate bus stops in other parts of town.

Conaf There are two offices south of downtown, one at Ogana 1060 (Mon–Fri 8.30am–5.30pm; Ⓣ67/212109) and another at Los Coigües s/n (Mon–Fri 8.30am–5.30pm; Ⓣ67/212125), offering information on the Laguna San Rafael Glacier as well as rudimentary maps of Paque Nacional Queulat.

Ferry Navimag ferries from Puerto Montt arrive at Puerto Chacabuco's Terminal de Transbordadores, 82km from Coyhaique and served by frequent buses.

Tourist office The well-stocked and helpful Sernatur office at Bulnes 35, just off the Plaza de Armas (Jan–Feb Mon–Fri 8.30am–8.30pm, Sat & Sun 11am–6pm; March–Dec Mon–Fri 8.30am–5.30pm; Ⓣ67/231752, Ⓦwww.patagoniachile.cl), dishes out detailed maps of town and is able to advise on accommodation and travel in the area.

Accommodation

HI Albergue Las Salamandras Carretera Teniente Vidal, km 1.5, towards the airport Ⓣ67/211865, Ⓦwww.salamandras.cl. The owners of this large, attractive lodge assist with planning your outdoor adventures. Comfortable rooms and fully-equipped *cabañas* come complete with breakfast, laundry service, use of a kitchen, a TV loft and ample common spaces. Dorm CH$8000. ❺

Hospedaje María Ester Lautaro 544 Ⓣ67/233023. Quiet, spotless rooms in a friendly environment; breakfast included. CH$5500. ❸

Hospedaje Natti Almirante Simpson 417 Ⓣ67/231047. Friendly guesthouse with clean rooms, though some have windows into the corridor, with a separate guest kitchen and eating area, space for a couple of tents and a handy laundry service next door. ❸

Hostal Bon Ignacio Serrano 91 Ⓣ67/231189. Friendly hostess presides over a variety of cosy rooms; breakfast included. ❺

Ogana Pasaje 8 s/n, off Av Ogana. Small campsite in an orchard, complete with indoor cooking facilities and hot showers, though the latter could be cleaner. CH$3500.

Eating and drinking

Café Ricer Horn 48. For well-cooked Patagonian specialities (such as barbecued lamb), as well as giant sandwiches and good vegetarian options, try this popular café-restaurant, a firm favourite with locals and foreigners alike. Mains CH$4500.

Club Sandwich 21 de Mayo 473. A 24hr sandwich and burger joint conveniently located in the town centre. Sandwiches CH$3000.

La Fiorentina Prat 230. An Italian restaurant, well-liked by locals, offering a large choice of pizzas and tasty pasta dishes; the two-course lunch menu is a good deal. Mains CH$4500.

La Olla Prat 176. Tiny old-fashioned restaurant with exceptionally friendly owners. The short menu is full of well-executed Chilean classics, such as *congrio frito* (fried conger eel) and *estofado de cordero* (lamb stew); Sunday is paella day. Mains CH$5000.

Piel Roja Moraleda 495. An excellent spot for a beer and snack, this lively pub with a quirky interior serves up good burgers and *quesadillas*. Strut your stuff on the dancefloor of the adjacent disco (bar and disco open until 4am). Beers CH$1200.

Supermarket on Cochrane at Lautaro. Large and well-stocked supermarket several blocks from the town centre.

> **TREAT YOURSELF**
>
> **El Reloj** Baquedano 828. The service is attentive and the salmon carpaccio divine, in this elegant upscale restaurant. Pisco sours are expertly prepared. Mains CH$6000.

Directory

Airlines LAN, Moraleda 401 (Ⓣ67/231188), Sky Airline, Prat 203 (Ⓣ67/240825), Transporte Aéreo Don Carlos, Subteniente Cruz 63 (Ⓣ67/231981).

Banks, cambios and ATMs Banco de Chile, Condell 184, and several others within a couple of blocks of the plaza, have ATMs.

Ferry The Navimag office is at Paseo Horn 47-D (Ⓣ67/223306).

Hospital Jorge Ibar 168 (Ⓣ67/219100).

Internet access/telephone centre *Café Ricer* has free wi-fi access and there are several Skype-equipped internet cafés along Paseo Horn.

Pharmacy There are a couple of pharmacies at the crossroads of Bilbao, Prat and Paseo Horn.

Post office Cochrane 226.

Moving on

Bus to: Cochrane (1 daily at 9:30am; 10hr; CH$17,000); Perito Moreno via Chile Chico (Tues, Thurs & Sat; 8hr; CH$15,000); Puerto Chacabuco

(several daily; 1hr; CH$1700); Puerto Montt via Argentina (1 daily; 15hr; CH$38,000); Punta Arenas via Argentina (Tues 4pm; 20hr; CH$42,000).
Ferry: Navimag has three weekly departures to Puerto Montt: Mon at 6pm, Thurs at 2am and Sat at 10am; C berths, high season/low season CH$38,000/30,000; check ⓦwww.navimag.cl for updated timetables.
Plane: Daily flights to Puerto Montt and Santiago with LAN and Sky Airline, and weekly flights to Punta Arenas. Transporte Aéreo Don Carlos has weekly charter flights to Cochrane and Villa O'Higgins, though its safety record leaves something to be desired.

PUERTO CHACABUCO

The port and **ferry terminal** of **PUERTO CHACABUCO** lies 82 kilometres west of Coyhaique, and sixteen kilometres south of Puerto Aisén, a bustling port until the 1960s, when its harbour silted up and forced the port to redirect its maritime traffic to its neighbour. While the road to the two ports cuts through the stupendous scenery of the **Reserva Nacional Río Simpson**, there is little to see in the towns themselves. Furthermore, in Puerto Chacabuco you are pursued by the smell of fishmeal from the large processing plants. If you're planning on taking a trip to **Laguna San Rafael**, however, you have little choice but to spend a night or two here due to the early departure and late arrival of the catamaran. *Residencial El Puerto*, at O'Higgins 80 (ⓣ67/351147, ❸), has adequate rooms with shared bathroom and breakfast.

PARQUE NACIONAL QUEULAT

A five-hour drive north of Coyhaique lies the little-explored **PARQUE NACIONAL QUEULAT** (daily April–Nov 8.30am–5.30pm, Dec–March 8.30am–7pm; CH$3000). The park's crowning feature is the stunning **Ventisquero Colgante**, or "hanging glacier", a frozen blue-white mass spilling over a rock face, while a mighty **waterfall** fed by the melting ice roars into the Laguna

TREAT YOURSELF

Laguna San Rafael, 200km southeast of Coyhaique and part of the enormous namesake national park, is only accessible by **boat** or **plane**. If you only see one glacier in Latin America, make it this one. Though retreating year by year – it is estimated that it will completely disappear in the next twenty years or so – it remains immensely impressive. An ocean inlet at the end of the long narrow inner passage of **Estero Elefantes**, accessed via the tight squeeze of the Río Témpanos ("Iceberg River"), Laguna San Rafael is bordered by the hills of the Península de Taitao to the west, while Monte San Valentín looms to the east. As you sail through the fjords past the silent, densely forested shores, you catch numerous glimpses of marine wildlife. Nearing the impossibly huge glacier, over 4km in width and 60m in height, the boat dodges massive bobbing icebergs, some the size of small houses. From time to time you'll hear a loud "crack" as another massive slab of blue ice calves from the glacier face, temporarily disturbing the still waters. Most boat trips allow the passengers to get close to the glacier in inflatable **Zodiacs**, and one of the trip's highlights is drinking whisky on the rocks – using the millennia-old ice, of course.
Patagonia Express (ⓣ67/351208 or 351196, or 2/225-6489 in Santiago, ⓦwww.patagonia-connection.com) runs high-speed catamaran day-trips from Puerto Chacabuco to the glacier (Dec–Feb Fri 9am–10pm; CH$170,000); the trips are extremely popular and need to be booked several weeks in advance. If travelling with a group, a cheaper and just as spectacular option is to take a three-hour return **charter flight**, disembarking near the glacier (CH$590,000 for up to to five people). Aerohein, at Baquedano 500 (ⓣ67/252177), and Empresas Don Carlos, at Subteniente Cruz 63 (ⓣ67/231981), both in Coyhaique, offer similar deals.

Los Tempanos below. You can stay at a partially shaded **campsite** (CH$10,000 per site of up to six people, ⓣ67/314250) by the park *guardería*, complete with a hot shower, toilets, picnic tables and running water. Two trails run from the park entrance – a two-kilometre trail to the *mirador* overlooking the hanging glacier, and a hopelessly overgrown path on which you may catch sight of the elusive *pudú* (pygmy deer). There is no public transport to the park besides the occasional day tour by Buses Queulat in the summer; you can ask any north-bound bus to drop you off at the park entrance, though it can be difficult to hitch a lift onwards.

SOUTH OF COYHAIQUE

From Coyhaique, the Carretera Austral runs south, interrupted by the dark blue Lago General Carrera, then passes the attractive village of Puerto Río Tranquilo, on the lake's north shore, and the popular cyclist and fly-fisherman stop of **Puerto Bertrand**, alongside the nearby Lago Bertrand. Fifty kilometres south, the only settlement of any size on the remaining chunk of the road is **Cochrane**, where you are likely to have to stop overnight, as buses in Northern Patagonia run only during daylight hours. *Residencial Cero a Cero*, at Lago Brown 464 (❸), is a wonderfully cosy, family-run guesthouse that serves good breakfast, while *Café Ñirrantal*, on the corner of Avenida O'Higgins and Esmeralda, a block south of the Plaza de Armas, whips up excellent vegetarian crêpes and meat dishes. Beyond Cochrane, the paved road becomes a dirt-and-gravel track that makes its way through a dense carpet of evergreens and giant wild rhubarb plants. After around two hours, a track splits off to the west, leading you to the picturesque hamlet of **Caleta Tortél**, where a few houses on stilts sit at the mouth of Río Baker and there is fishing-boat access to both the Northern and Southern Patagonian ice fields. Continuing south to the last stop of Villa O'Higgins, the Carretera Austral narrows to a single lane, ribboning its way around hairpin bends as the terrain becomes even hillier, with sheer drops on the side of the track revealing spectacular vistas of glacial rivers cutting through endless forest, and distant mountains shrouded in mist.

VILLA O'HIGGINS

Until 1999, **VILLA O'HIGGINS**, a cluster of wooden houses huddled against a sheer mountain face, was reachable only by a small prop plane from Coyhaique or by boat from Argentina. Once here, there are two choices: turn back or cross the lake into Argentina. It truly feels like the end of the road. You are likely to linger longer than intended, partly because of the scarcity of public transport, and partly to enjoy the relaxed pace of life, small-town hospitality and the hiking and horse-riding opportunities the rugged scenery provides. The town is built on a simple grid, with the Carretera Austral runing along the western side all the way down to the boat landing on **Lago O'Higgins**, several kilometres away. The **Plaza de Armas**, featuring the tourist information office and a bust of **Bernardo O'Higgins**, is at the heart of town, with the local **library and internet centre** at its northeast corner. A footpath off Calle Lago Cisnes runs through Parque Cerro Santiago up to a *mirador* that offers an excellent view of the village; from there, the path continues on towards the ice "tongue" of the **Ventisquero Mosco**, the nearest hanging glacier, though the trail is sometimes impassable. There are no banks in town, so bring plenty of cash with you.

Arrival and information

Airport The Aeródromo, for charter flights from Coyhaique and Cochrane, is on the west side of town.

Buses The bus from Cochrane stops in front of the small Supermercado San Gabriel on Lago O'Higgins.

Ferry The ferry that collects passengers from the Argentine side of Lago O'Higgins docks at the Bahía Bahamóndez, seven kilometres east of town; a private minibus charges CH$1500 per person to Villa O'Higgins.

Tourist office The youthful staff at the small tourist office on the plaza (Mon–Fri 9am–5.30pm; no tel, ⓦwww.villaohiggins.com) are very helpful and provide plenty of information on the town and the surrounding area. Hielo Sur (ⓣ67/431821 ⓦwww.hielosur.com), on a nameless side street off the west end of Calle Mosco, has up-to-date timetables for the Lago O'Higgins crossing (CH$20,000) as well as day-trips to the Ventisquero O'Higgins and Ventisquero Chico (CH$25,000).

Accommodation, eating and drinking

There are several guesthouses and campsites in and around the village, with most *hospedajes* offering full board at extra cost.

Camping Los Ñires Carretera Austral s/n. Just south of *Hostal Runín*, this spacious, tree-lined campsite has indoor cooking facilities and hot showers, though the ground can be muddy. CH$2500.

Entre Patagones Carretera Austral s/n. Excellent family-run restaurant, busy after 8pm, serving tasty Patagonian favourites such as *asadór patagónico* (spit-roasted lamb) and hearty *cazuela* in a homely environment. To reach it, follow Carretera Austral to the north end of town. Dinner CH$5500.

Hospedaje Patagonia Río Pascua 191 ⓣ67/431818. A comfortable, family-run choice by the plaza, with clean rooms and shared bathroom. Breakfast CH$1500 extra; lunch or dinner CH$3500. ❸

Hospedaje La Cascada Lago Salto at Río Mosco s/n ⓣ67/431833. Another good budget accommodation choice; ample servings of delicious home-cooked food and its own bakery are bonuses. ❸

Hostal Runín Loto 5, Predio Angelita ⓣ67/431870. Tranquil and popular guesthouse with welcoming rooms, hot showers and tasty home cooking. It may be possible to camp outside. Breakfast/dinner CH$3500/6500. ❺

Moving on

Bus Buses Los Ñadis run two weekly trips to Cochrane (Tues & Fri at 10am; 7hr; CH$10,000);

TO CROSS OR NOT TO CROSS?

The crossing between Villa O'Higgins and Argentina's El Chaltén is remote and challenging, yet more and more hardy travellers are prepared to take on the lake crossing, followed by a strenuous hike over the border. The sixty-passenger *Quetru* leaves Bahía Bahamóndez at 8.30am (Dec Wed & Sat; Jan–Feb Mon, Wed & Sat; CH$20,000) and arrives at the hamlet of **Candelario Mancilla** at around 11am. Here there are no-frills accommodations (CH$6000) and **camping spots** (CH$2000 per tent) and you will get your passport stamped by **Chilean border control**. Beyond, a wide gravel track runs slightly uphill through patches of woodland to the international border; on the way, you will have to either ford the shallow, glacial **Río Obstáculo**, or cross it on some rickety planks. Beyond the border, the 7.5-kilometre stretch of trail to the **Argentine Gendarmería** on the banks of the **Laguna del Desierto** becomes a narrow, muddy footpath snaking its way through hilly forest and scrubland; cyclists have to push and sometimes carry their bikes. After being stamped into Argentina, you can either pitch a tent at *Camping Laguna del Desierto* (CH$2000), catch the *Viedma* motor launch across the lake (daily at 1.30pm, 4.45pm & 6.30pm; 30–45min; CH$8000, bicycles CH$4000 extra) or hike the remaining 15km (5hr) along a thickly forested path on the left side of the lake, emerging at the *guardería* by the pier on the south side. Minibuses to **El Chaltén** meet the arriving boats, the last one leaving for town at 7.45pm (CH$5000). While it is possible to complete the border crossing in a day, boat schedules are weather-dependent; pack enough food for several days. To book a guide and packhorses (CH$15,000 per packhorse), and for up-to-date information on the trek, visit the helpful website, ⓦwww.villaohiggins.com.

buy tickets in advance from the Supermercado San Gabriel, as the bus is usually full.
Plane Transportes Aéreos Don Carlos has charter flights to Coyhaique on Mondays and Thursdays (CH$35,000); confirm the departure time at the office on Lago O'Higgins.
Ferry see box opposite.

Southern Patagonia

Enormous glaciers calving icebergs the size of houses, pristine fjords and dozens of islands make up the otherworldy vistas of Magallanes province, or **SOUTHERN PATAGONIA**. Add in forbidding craggy peaks, impossibly blue glacial lakes, a wealth of wildlife and the sheer size and majesty of the internationally-renowned **Torres del Paine** national park, and it's easy to see why Patagonia captures the imagination of travellers and explorers. Sparsely-inhabited, the region is buffeted by storms from the Pacific and subject to a powerful wind, known as the "escoba de Díos" ("God's broom"), that is capable of snapping large trees in two; winters are exceptionally harsh. Cut off from the rest of Chile by the giant Campo de Hielo Sur (Patagonian Ice Fields) to the northeast, the locals have a strong camaraderie with their counterparts across the Andes; many consider themselves to be Patagonians first, Chileans or Argentines second.

PUNTA ARENAS

On the shores of the turbulent Magellan Strait, 241 kilometres southeast of Puerto Natales, **PUNTA ARENAS** is Patagonia's largest and southernmost city. Originally a remote military garrison know to British sailors as "Sandy Point", the city provided a convenient stopover for ships heading to California during the gold rush of 1849, and then grew in size and importance with the introduction of sheep from the Falkland Islands to the Patagonian plains. Punta Arenas emerged as a wool empire, drawing migrant workers from Croatia, Italy, Spain and Britain, among others, and evolved into a thriving port. Following the decline of the wool economy after World War II, the city benefited from the discovery of petroleum in Tierra del Fuego in the 1940s, and now makes its living from a combination of petroleum production, commercial fishing and tourism. The city centre is compact and easy to navigate, its streets laid out in a grid, and most services and conveniences lie within a few blocks of the main square.

Plaza Muñoz Gamero

The heart of the city is this tranquil, shady square lined with lofty Monterrey cypresses and craft stalls, hosting occasional live music. In the centre stands a fierce-looking statue of **Ferdinand Magellan**, donated by wool magnate José Menéndez in 1920 to commemorate the four-hundred-year anniversary of the explorer's voyage. A statue of a **Tehuelche Indian**, symbolizing Patagonia, sits at the foot of the monument; it is believed that if you touch or kiss his big toe, you will one day return to Punta Arenas. Around the square you can also see a number of ornate mansions and edifices, dating back to its wool-producing heyday.

Mirador Cerro La Cruz

A five-block walk along Calle Fagnano from the southeast corner of the square brings you to some steep steps leading up to the *mirador*, offering an excellent view of the brightly-coloured, galvanized metal rooftops of Punta Arenas and the deep blue Magellan Strait beyond. Nearby, at España 959, stands a red brick tower with gothic windows – **Castillo Milward** (Milward's Castle), the house which formerly belonged to the eccentric explorer Charley Milward, relative of the writer Bruce Chatwin and described in his travel memoir *In Patagonia*.

Casa Braun-Menéndez

Casa Braun-Menéndez, the former family residence of the marriage that united the two wealthiest and most influential families in Punta Arenas, is located half a block northeast of the plaza, at Magallanes 949, and is divided between perfectly preserved living quarters and the **Museo Regional Magallanes** (May–Oct daily 10.30am–2pm; Nov–April Mon–Fri 10.30am–5pm, Sat & Sun 10.30am–2pm; CH$1000, free on Sun and holidays). The museum, housed in the back rooms, features pioneer articles, historical photos and bilingual displays on the maritime and farming history of the region, as well as the region's **native tribes** – the Kawéscar (Alacalúf) and the Selk'nam (Ona). Ironically, the displays fail to point out that the destruction of the native tribes' traditional lifestyle owes much to the wool barons' pursuit of wealth.

Museo Naval y Marítimo

Two blocks east of the plaza, at Pedro Montt 981, lies the small and entertaining **Museo Naval y Marítimo** (Mar–Nov Mon–Fri 9.30am–12.30pm, Sat & Sun 3–6pm; Dec–Feb Mon–Sat 9.30am–5pm; CH$1000), with a focus on Punta Arenas's naval history and exploration of the southern oceans. The ground floor features a multitude of scale models of famous ships, including Sir Ernest Shackleton's "Endurance", while the first floor is decked out as a ship, complete with nautical equipment and interactive displays.

Museo Salesiano Maggiorino Borgatello

Located seven blocks north of the plaza, at Av Bulnes 336, **Museo Salesiano Maggiorino Borgatello** (Tues–Sun 10.30am–12.30pm & 3–6pm; CH$1500) is very much worth a visit to get a sense of local flora, fauna and geology, with a plethora of stuffed, pickled and pinned examples on the ground floor. One room is entirely devoted to a life-size replica of the **Cave of Hands**. The original, decorated with 11,000-year old rock paintings, is found near the small settlement of Chile Chico, off the Carretera Austral. There are several rooms displaying Kawéscar Indian artefacts, including hunting tools and garments, as well as a fascinating collection of black-and-white photographs documenting native cultures, taken by Alberto D'Agostini, an early missionary.

Cementerio Municipal

A stroll through the darkly impressive **Cementerio Municipal** (daily 7.30am–10pm; free), further out along Avenida Bulnes, gives you insight into the city's cultural diversity and social hierarchy. In this large **necropolis**, the English and Spanish names of the gentry, elaborately engraved on immense marble tombs, mingle with the Croatian names of immigrant labourers, etched on more modest grave spaces the size of lockers, all hiding amidst immaculately sculpted cypresses. A monument depicting a **Selk'nam Indian** is festooned with necklaces; people often make wishes to the statue, and plaques surrounding it convey the gratitude of those whose wishes were granted.

Arrival and information

Airport Aeropuerto Presidente Ibáñez is 20km out of town. Flights are met by Buses Transfer Austral (CH$3500 door-to-door, ☎61/229613) and Buses Pacheco (CH$2000 to their terminus at Colón 900, ☎61/225527). Transfers to Puerto Natales meet flights arriving during daytime hours.

Buses There is no central bus station, though the Central de Pasajeros, on av Colón and Magallanes (☎61/245811), sells tickets for all companies.

Buses Pacheco, Av Colón 900 (☎61/242174); Buses Fernández, Armanda Sanhueza 745 (☎61/242313, www.busefernandez.com); Bus Sur, José Menéndez 552 (☎61/614224); Buses Transfer Austral, Pedro Montt 966 (☎61/229613); Buses Tecni Austral, Lautaro Navarro 975 (☎61/222078); and Buses Ghisoni, Lautaro Navarro 971 (☎61/223205).

Conaf Av Bulnes 309, 4th floor (Mon–Fri 8.30am–5pm; ☎61/238581, www.conaf.cl). Information on the region's national parks.

Ferry Ferries from Puerto Williams and Porvenir arrive at the Terminal Tres Puntes on the north side of town; frequent *colectivos* (CH$600) shuttle between the docks and the city centre.

Tourist office Tourist information kiosk on the east side of Plaza Muñoz Gamero (Mon–Thurs 8am–5.30pm, Fri 8am–4.30pm; ☎61/200610), and a helpful and well-stocked Sernatur office at Navarro 999, at Pedro Montt (Mon–Fri 8.15am–7pm, Sat & Sun 10am–6pm; ☎61/241330 or 61/225385, wwww.sernatur.cl).

Accommodation

Backpackers' Paradise Ignacio Carrera Pinto 1022 ☎61/240104, backpackersparadise@hotmail.com. Run by an effusive hostess and perpetually popular with younger travellers, this hostel offers cheap bunks in two large, open-plan rooms. Laundry service, free hot drinks, secure luggage storage, kitchen facilities, internet access and bike rentals are among the extras. Dorm CH$5000.

Hospedaje Independencia Av Independencia 374 ☎61/227572, www.chileaustral.com/independencia/. Friendly young owners have camping spaces in their front yard and rent camping equipment; they also organize tours of the area. Dorms and rooms are small but warm and comfortable; breakfast is included and kitchen facilities and internet are available. Camping/dorm/room CH$3000/5500. ❸

Hostal Al Fin Del Mundo O'Higgins 1026, ☎61/710185, www.alfindelmundo.cl. Clean rooms of various sizes and a dorm (with beds rather than bunks) in a central location; free breakfast, free internet and wi-fi, kitchen use, pool tables, book exchange and a comfy lounge with massive flat-screen TV and extensive DVD collection are all on offer. ❺

Hostal Blue House Balmaceda 545 ☎61/227006, crigar73@hotmail.com. This hostel really stands out by providing an excellent organizational service, allowing you to book all your tours, onward bus tickets and even pick your bus seat; buses pick you up from in front of the hostel. Clean dorms, kitchen and lounge area, and internet as well. Dorm CH$5000.

Hostal Casa Azul Chiloé 263. Contact details and services as above. Newly opened branch of the *Blue House*, a block away, featuring clean and cosy singles and doubles with its own guest kitchen. ❹

Hostal Fitz Roy Lautaro Navarro 850 ☎61/240430, www.hostalfitzroy.com. Run by a knowledgeable Torres del Paine guide, this hostel has warm, comfortable dorms and rooms; kitchen privileges and an excellent breakfast, including home-made bread, are bonuses. There is also a self-contained *cabaña* out back. Dorm CH$7000. ❺

Eating, drinking and entertainment

Abu-Gosch supermarket Bories, between Pinto and Mejicana. A good stop for self-catering travellers, this well-stocked supermarket has a hot food and salad counter as well as good fresh fruit and vegetables.

Brocolino O'Higgins 1055. Hands down the best restaurant in town, and possibly in all of Patagonia, serving imaginative and consistently outstanding meat and seafood dishes as well as sumptuous deserts. Mains CH$5000–7000.

Café Montt Pedro Montt 976. A book exchange and wi-fi are on offer in this cosy coffee shop, as well as a good selection of teas and coffees. Coffee CH$1200.

La Marmita Plaza Sampaio 678. Homely, friendly restaurant serving a good variety of Chilean dishes made from organic produce, as well as a number of vegetarian options. Mains CH$4000–6000.

El Mercado Mejicana 617, 2nd floor. This unpretentious eatery is a good place for large helpings of local seafood at reasonable prices. The garlic squid and the *centolla* (king crab) are excellent. Mains CH$5000.

O Sole Mio O'Higgins 974. An Italian restaurant decorated with classic movie posters, serving tasty pastas, gnocchi and other fare. Mains CH$4500.

Olijoe Pub Errázuriz 970. A cosy and atmospheric pub with reasonably-priced drinks and good snacks; music can be a little loud. Beers CH$1500.

Pub 1900 Bories at Colón. Good for people-watching, this pub comes into its own in the evenings. Beers CH$1200.

Santino Colón 657. Lively and popular pub offering typical Chilean fare, such as *lomo a la pobre*, as well as good sandwiches. Mains CH$4000.

Tenedor Libre Bories, between Pinto and Mejicana, next door to the Abu-Gosch supermarket. An all-you-can-eat buffet with a reasonable selection of meat, seafood and Chinese dishes, as well as salads and desserts. CH$4500.

Directory

Airlines LAN/LanExpress, Lautaro Navarro 999 (☎61/241100, ⓦwww.lan.com); Sky Airline, Roca 935 (☎61/710645, ⓦwww.skyairline.cl); Aerovías DAP, O'Higgins at Menéndez (☎61/616100, ⓦwww.aeroviasdap.cl); Aerolíneas del Sur, Pedro Montt 969 (☎61/221020).

Banks, cambios and ATMs There are numerous banks and ATMs located around the Plaza Muñoz Gomero. Scott Cambios (closed Sun), Av Colón at Magallanes, is a good currency exchange.

Hospital Hospital de las FF. AA. Cirujano Guzmán (☎61/207500) is at Av Manuel Bulnes and Guillermos; Clínica Magallanes, Av Bulnes 1448 (☎61/211527).

Internet and phone Try *Hostal Calafate*, Magallanes 922, which has an excellent phone centre and internet café (daily 9am–11pm; CH$600 per hr); or nearby *E-Green*, at Nogueira 1179 (Mon–Sat 9am–9pm; CH$600).

Laundry Autoservicio Lavasol, O'Higgins 969, or Lavandería Antártica, Jorge Montt 664.

Pharmacy There are several well-stocked pharmacies along Bories.

Post office Bories 911.

Shopping Zona Franca, the massive duty-free shopping area 4km north of the city centre, is a good place to stock up on camping gear and electronics. Most *colectivos* heading north along Av Bulnes pass by, though be careful about catching the correct one back to the city centre. Disembark just before the Sanchez and Sanchez warehouse.

Moving on

Bus to: Puerto Montt (4 daily; 30–34hr; CH$45,000); Puerto Natales (several daily with Buses Pacheco, Fernández and Bus Sur; 3hr; CH$3500); Ushuaia (several daily with Buses Ghisoni, Buses Pacheco and Buses Tecni Austral; 12–14hr; CH$10,000); Río Gallegos (several daily with Buses Pacheco and Buses Ghisoni; 4hr; CH$6500).

Ferry Transbordadora Austral Broom, Av Bulnes 5075 (☎61/218100, ⓦwww.tabsa.cl) operates the ferry *Cruz Australis* to Puerto Williams on Wed from Sept–May; CH$105,000 for a berth; CH$90,000 for a Pullman seat. The journey takes approximately 34hr and departure times are subject to weather conditions.

Plane Daily flights to Santiago and frequent flights to other parts of Chile with LAN and Sky Airline. Aerolíneas del Sur flies to Santiago and Ushuaia, and Aerovías DAP has frequent flights to Puerto Williams and Porvenir, as well as twice-weekly flights to Ushuaia.

AROUND PUNTA ARENAS

In the middle of the stormy Magellan Strait lies **Isla Magdalena** – the largest Magellanic **penguin colony** in all of Chile, with an estimated 100,000 nesting birds residing on a one-kilometre-square cliff by the historical lighthouse. The monogamous birds spend the September to March breeding season here, living in burrows in the ground. The female lays two eggs in October, with both parents taking turns looking after the chicks

PUNTA ARENAS TOUR OPERATORS

Turismo Aónikenk Magallanes 619 ☎61/221982, ⓦwww.aonikenk.com. Multi-day hiking excursions in southern Patagonia and Tierra del Fuego; trips to the penguin colonies are also offered.

Turismo Pali Aike Navarro 1125 ☎61/233301 or 61/615750, ⓦwww.turismopaliaike.com. A variety of nature-watching trips, including daily trips to Isla Magdalena, and Seno Otway and Estancia Lolita safari, as well as full-day canopy trips, transfers to the nearby Reserva Nacional Magallanes and excursions to the historical Fuerte Bulnes.

Turismo Yámana Errázuriz 932 ☎61/710567, ⓦwww.turismoyamana.cl. Intrepid single- and multi-day kayaking trips on and around the Strait of Magellan, taking in seal and penguin colonies, as well as multi-day trekking and riding excursions in Tierra del Fuego.

once they've hatched in December, while the other fishes for food. In early February you'll find the grown chicks huddled near the sea, as large as their parents but still growing the adult feathers necessary for swimming. The best time to visit the colony is January, when the population is at its largest; though you have to stick to the designated walking routes, the penguins don't fear humans and will come close to you. You can visit with the large ferry *Melinka*, run by **Turismo Comapa** (Magallanes 990 ☎61/200200, Dec Tues, Thurs and Sat 4pm, with around 90 minutes on the island; CH$20,000), or on **Turismo Pali Aike**'s smaller boat, which carries a dozen passengers at most and spends more time on the island (see box opposite; Dec–Feb daily 7am and 5pm, though the latter is often cancelled due to high winds; CH$32,000). This tour also takes in the smaller **Isla Marta**, home to a large sea lion colony that uses nearby Isla Magdalena as its local takeaway.

Pingüinera Seno Otway

If you can't make the boat trip to Isla Magdalena, then don't miss the land-based excursion to the colony of **Seno Otway**. Hosting around eight thousand Magellanic penguins at its peak, the breeding site is fenced off and visitors are obliged to stick to the wooden boardwalk that runs between the penguin burrows, with several elevated wooden platforms. While not as up-close-and-personal as Isla Magdalena, you still get excellent views of the penguins, especially at the viewpoint by the beach, where you can watch them frolic in the frigid waves just a few metres away. Several tour operators run half-day tours (CH$2000 entry charge not included) to the Seno Otway site, seventy kilometres northwest of Punta Arenas, which is best visited in the mornings.

PUERTO NATALES

The young town of **PUERTO NATALES** is situated in relative isolation on the **Seno Última Esperanza** ("Last Hope Sound"). Officially founded in 1911, it was used primarily as a port for exporting wool and beef from the nearby Puerto Prat cattle *estancia*, built by German explorer **Hermann Eberhard** in 1893. Though the export trade has since declined, the town's proximity to one of the continent's most popular national parks – Torres del Paine – as well as Argentina's Parque Nacional Los Glaciares, combined with daily buses to various Chilean and Argentine cities and a popular Navimag cruise from Puerto Montt, has led to a tourist boom that has firmly established Puerto Natales as one of Patagonia's top destinations for outdoor enthusiasts.

Faced with a motley collection of tin and wooden houses, a visitor's first impression of Puerto Natales is invariably coloured by the weather. On a clear day, Seno Última Esperanza, bordering the town's west side, is a remarkably vivid, tranquil blue, with magnificent views of the snow-capped **Cordillera Sarmiento** and **Campo de Hielo Sur** visible across the bay. Bad weather can be very bad indeed.

The Town

The town is built on a grid pattern and very easy to navigate. It is centred around the **Plaza de Armas**, with a multitude of guesthouses, restaurants and services located along nearby streets, and its main commercial thoroughfares are north-south Baquedano and east-west Bulnes. The plaza is overlooked by the colonial church – **Iglesia Parroquial María Auxiliadora**, and has an old **locomotive engine** formerly used in the Puerto Bories abattoir as its centrepiece, an evening magnet for lovers and drunken teenagers.

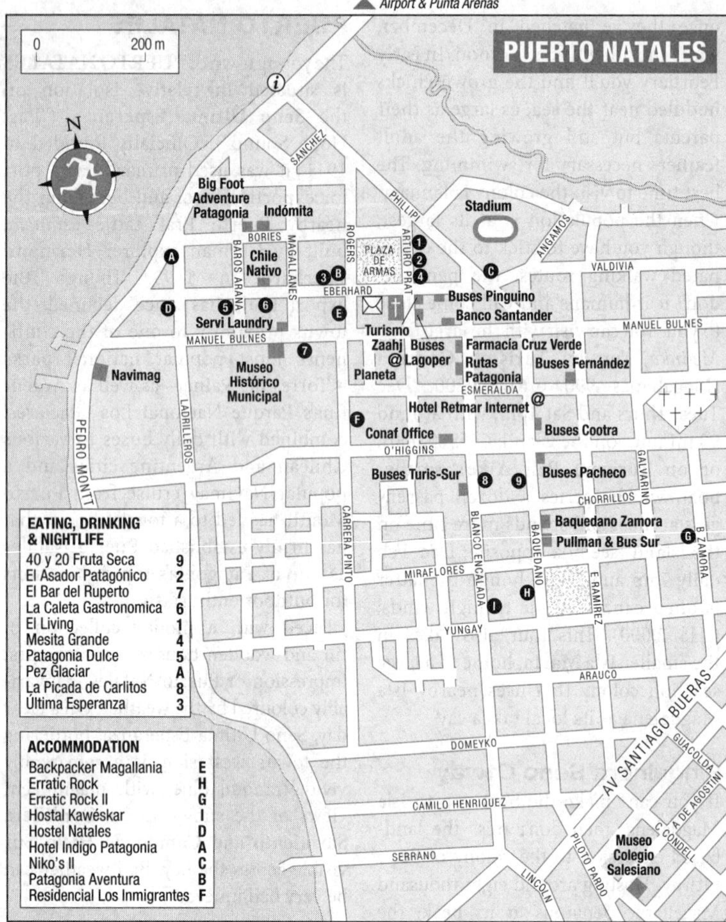

Museo Histórico Municipal

The worthwhile little **Museo Histórico** at Bulnes 285 (Mon–Fri 8.30am–1pm & 3–8pm, Sat & Sun 2.30–6pm; CH$1000), less than two blocks from the plaza, has attractive bilingual exhibits on the region's **native tribes**, illustrated with black-and-white photos of Aónikenk and Kawéscar Indians, as well as on European settlement and natural history, including the story of the Milodon's cave. A room is dedicated to Hermann Eberhard, the intrepid German explorer responsible for early settlement in the region; his collapsible boat that turns into a suitcase is a fascinating exhibit.

Arrival and information

Airport The tiny airport, with just one daily flight from El Calafate, Argentina, is a 5min drive from town.

Buses Puerto Natales has no central bus station: Buses Fernández, Ramirez 399 (Ⓣ61/424313); Bus Sur, Baquedano 688 (Ⓣ61/614224 Ⓦwww.bus-sur.cl); Buses Pacheco, Bulnes 518 (Ⓣ61/229613 Ⓦwww.busespacheco.com); Cootra, Baquedano 456 (Ⓣ61/412785); Buses Lagoper, Prat 234 A (Ⓣ61/415700); Turismo Zaahj, Prat 236 (Ⓣ61/412260);

Buses Turis-Sur, Blanco Encalada 555 (☎61/411202); Buses Pinguino, Eberhard 555 (☎61/411111).

Conaf O'Higgins 534 (Mon–Fri 8.30am–5pm; ☎61/411438, Ⓦwww.conaf.cl), is not particularly well-stocked; tour operators are a better bet for information on the national parks.

Ferry The Navimag ferry docks at the pier five blocks west of the Plaza de Armas.

Tourist office Sernatur is at Pedro Montt 19, on the shore of the Seno Última Esperanza (Mon–Fri 8.15am–7pm, Sat & Sun 10am–1pm & 3–6pm; ☎61/412125, Ⓦwww.sernatur.cl), with very helpful staff. "Black Sheep", a monthly freebie widely available around town, contains entertaining articles and lots of useful information about the surrounding area.

Accommodation

Backpacker Magallania Tomás Rogers 255 ☎61/414950, Ⓦwww.chileaustral.com/magallania. Drawing a younger crowd, this relaxed central hostel offers clean, spacious dorms, breakfast, kitchen privileges and a common room with TV. Camping/dorm CH$3000/5000. ❹

Erratic Rock Baquedano 719 ☎61/410335 Ⓦwww.erraticrock.com. Firm backpacker favourite with all-you-can-stuff American breakfast, informative daily talks on Torres del Paine, good book exchange, equipment rental and multi-day treks to Cabo Froward and other destinations. Dorm CH$6000-9000. ❹

Erratic Rock II Zamora 732 Contact details as above. Spillover from the original *Erratic Rock* with cheaper basic rooms; bring own sleeping bag. ❸

Hostal Kawéskar Encalada 754 ☎61/414553. Incredibly laid-back backpacker haunt, run by the knowledgeable Omar. Kitchen privileges and lockers are included; it's possible to camp out back and Omar helps to organise your stay. Dorm CH$5000. ❸

Hostel Natales Ladrilleros 209 ☎61/410081, Ⓦwww.hostelnatales.cl. Spacious, light and beautifully-decorated hostel with a tranquil lounge with fountain, numerous computers with broadband, comfy dorm beds, rooms for up to four, an adjoining travel gear shop and helpful staff. Ample breakfast CH$2000 extra; some dorms only have a window into the lounge. Dorm CH$12,000. ❼

Niko's II Philippi 528 ☎61/413543, Ⓦwww.nikostwoadventure.com. A friendly hostel with cosy rooms, communal breakfast, café with internet and mostly younger guests. ❺

Patagonia Adventure Tomás Rogers 179 ☎61/415636, Ⓦwww.apatagonia.com. Brightly-decorated central hostel run by young owners; a good breakfast is included and other bonuses include internet, a camping gear outlet next door, and the hostel's own adventure outfit for kayaking enthusiasts. Dorm CH$6000. ❹

Residencial Los Inmigrantes Carrera Pinto 480 ☎61/413482. A good choice for outdoor enthusiasts; the congenial owner – a former guide – is a treasure trove of information on Torres del Paine; kitchen privileges included. Dorm CH$5000.

Eating, drinking and entertainment

40 y 20 Fruta Seca Baquedano 443. The place to stock up on a bewildering array of dried fruit and nuts for the forthcoming hike. Dried mango is especially good. CH$400/hundred grams.

El Asador Patagónico Prat 158. An excellent restaurant catering primarily to carnivores and specializing in *asador patagónico* – spit-roasted lamb. Mains CH$6000.

El Bar del Ruperto Bulnes 310. Popular bar with loud music and pool tables, drawing a younger backpacking crowd – a good spot for a post-hike beer. Beers CH$1200.

La Caleta Gastronómica Eberhard 261. A moderately-priced restaurant specializing in fish and seafood, with generous portions and attentive service. Fish dishes CH$4500.

El Living Prat 156. Not just an excellent vegetarian restaurant, with changing daily specials, but also the town's most popular café/lounge, playing chilled-out tunes, and featuring the best book exchange in town. Smoothies, sandwiches and salads stand out, and the

TREAT YOURSELF

Returning from Torres del Paine National Park, muscles aching from days of roughing it in tents and from pushing yourself to make the steep ascents, unwind at the **spa** of Puerto Natales' top hotel – the *Hotel Indigo Patagonia* at Ladrilleros 105 (☎61/413609, Ⓦwww.indigopatagonia.com). The hotel's spa extends its services to non-guests and boasts extensive pampering facilities as well as unparalleled views of the Seno Última Esperanza from one of its rooftop pools.

proprietress makes excellent cakes, too; the only drawback is that it seems to close too early! Daily specials CH$3500.

Mesita Grande Prat 196. Truly excellent pizzeria with a communal feel, where customers sit around the two wide wooden tables, tucking into generous portions of thin-crust pizza and sumptuous desserts. Pizza CH$5000.

Patagonia Dulce Arana 233. Those with a sweet tooth shouldn't miss out on the home-made chocolates and ice cream in this little gingerbread house-like café. Try the calafate berry ice cream CH$1500.

Pez Glaciar Ladrilleros 105. A trendy bar-restaurant in Puerto Natales' ritziest hotel, serving reasonably-priced and well-prepared dishes and excellent pisco sours in relaxed surroundings overlooking Last Hope Sound; great for watching the sunset. *Ceviche* CH$4500.

La Picada de Carlitos Encalada 444. Ever popular and perpetually packed eatery with an extensive menu featuring large portions of meat, pasta and fish, as well as big sandwiches. Open late. Sandwiches CH$3000.

Última Esperanza Eberhard 354. Come early to get seats in this extremely popular restaurant which serves some of the tastiest fish and seafood in southern Chile. Mains CH$5000.

Directory

Airlines Aerovías DAP, O'Higgins 891 (☎61/223340, Ⓦwww.aeroviasdap.cl).

Banks, cambios and ATMs Banco Santander, on Blanco Encalada at Bulnes, and Banco de Chile, at Bulnes 544, both have ATMs. Cambios Sur, at Eberhard 385, gives reasonable exchange rates.

Camping equipment Rent camping gear at Patagonia Adeventure, Tomás Rogers 179; Sendero Aventura, Bulnes 322B; or at *Café & Books Patagonia*, Blanco Encalada 226 A. Buy camping essentials at La Madera, Prat 297, or at the Survival Outdoor Store, Baquedano 622.

Hospital Hospital Puerto Natales, at the corner of Pinto and O'Higgins, handles basic medical emergencies, but the facilities in Punta Arenas are far better.

Internet and phone Telephone centres tend to be expensive, so it's better to use Skype at one of the many Skype-equipped internet cafés. *Hotel Reymar*, Esmeralda at Baquedano, has fast broadband; *Planeta*, on Bulnes between Pinto and Prat, doubles as a café and call centre.

Laundry ServiLaundry, Bulnes 513.

Pharmacy Farmacía Cruz Verde, Bulnes at Blanco Encalada.

Post office Eberhard 429.

Moving on

Bus to: El Calafate (daily morning departures during high season; 5hr 30min; CH$10,000), with Turismo Zaahj, Cootra and Bus Sur; Punta Arenas (several daily; 3hr; CH$4000), with Bus Sur, Buses Pacheco and Buses Fernandez; Torres del Paine (daily at 7.30am & 2.30pm; 2hr; CH$3500), with Bus Sur, Buses Fortaleza and Buses JBA; Ushuaia (Tue & Fri at 7am; 14hr CH$20,000) with Bus Sur.

Plane to: El Calafate (daily departures with Aerovías DAP).

Ferry: The Navimag ferry MV *Magallanes* (Bulnes 533, ☎61/414300, Ⓦwww.navimag.cl) departs for Puerto Montt weekly on Fri mornings; passengers board on Thurs night and sleep aboard the ferry. Prices for the four-day cruise vary depending on the type of cabin, and start from around CH$160,000 (see box, p.493); book a couple of weeks in advance in summer.

PUERTO NATALES TOUR OPERATORS

Baquedano Zamora Baquedano 534 ☎61/613530 or 61/613532, Ⓦwww.baquedanozamora.com. Horse-trekking trips of varying length in Torres del Paine National Park.

Big Foot Adventure Patagonia Bories 206 ☎61/414611, Ⓦwww.bigfootpatagonia.com. Mountaineering, climbing, multi-day kayaking trips on the Río Serrano and ice hikes on Glacier Grey – organize in advance.

Chile Nativo Eberhard 230 ☎61/411835, Ⓦwww.chilenativo.com. Youthful operator offering birdwatching trips, as well as multi-day horse-trekking and hiking tours of the region.

Indómita Bories 206 ☎61/414525, Ⓦwww.indomitapatagonia.com. One of the best operators for mountaineering, climbing and ice hiking.

Rutas Patagonia Blanco Encalada 353 ☎61/415855, Ⓦwww.rutaspatagonia.cl. Up-and-coming outfit offering ice hiking and kayaking trips in Torres del Paine National Park.

PARQUE NACIONAL TORRES DEL PAINE

Your first glimpse of the Paine Massif, the mountain range at the heart of the **PARQUE NACIONAL TORRES DEL PAINE**, comes some 112 kilometres northwest of Puerto Natales, after an interminable stretch of brown scrubland, enlivened only by a few **ñandú** (small ostriches). The park teases you with glimpses of the sheer granite towers of **Las Torres**, to the east, and the multicoloured **Los Cuernos**, to the west, dominating the startling emerald-green waters of **Laguna Amarga** at the park entrance. Rich in wildlife, the park offers incomparable opportunities for backcountry hiking, as well as animal spotting. There are also more challenging scrambles to the park's *miradores* and a host of other outdoor activities – from ice trekking on the Glacier Grey to birdwatching to horseriding in the outlying hills.

Hiking: the "W"

Though Torres del Paine offers myriad hiking trails, the most popular is undoubtedly the **"W"**, a four- to five-day hike that takes in the park's highlights: the massive Glacier Grey, steep Valle Francés, and finally, the *mirador* Las Torres. Though the majority of travellers hike the "W" from east to west, tackling the steepest ascent first, it makes more sense to go from west to east, especially if carrying camping gear, as you will have eaten most of your provisions by the time you approach the challenging *mirador*, and will have grown used to the rigours of the hike.

Lago Pehoé

If you stay on the bus at Laguna Amarga (see Arrival and information, p.512), the track winds its way through green hilly terrain covered in *coirón* bunch grasses and dotted with thorny bushes. You are likely to catch glimpses of the **guanacos** – wild relatives of llamas – that dwell here in large numbers. Pumas also live in the park, though there's little chance of seeing one, as well as foxes, the elusive *huermul* deer and condors. The bus stops at the northern tip of **Lago Pehoé**, a short distance from the tiny catamaran pier. From here you can take a fifteen-minute walk uphill to **Salto Grande**, a spectacular thundering waterfall, fed by melting glacial waters, with views of Los Cuernos in the distance. From the waterfall it's an easy hour's walk along the lakeside to the Mirador Nordenskjöld **viewpoint**, offering a spectacular vista of the Cuernos del Paine, reflected in the icy blue waters of Lago Nordenskjöld. Back at the pier, set out on the "W" by taking the Hielos Patagónicos catamaran (see p.520) to the *Paine Grande Lodge* and campground.

Glacier Grey

From *Hostería Pehoé*, a clearly marked trail runs north through the scrubland, partially shaded by clusters of *ñire*, until a gentle ascent brings you to the east shore of a small lagoon before ducking into a *lenga* forest, criss-crossed with narrow, icy streams. During this leg of the hike you don't have to worry about carrying enough water, as you can periodically top up with some of the cleanest drinking water on earth. The trail meanders before emerging at the **Quebrada de los Vientos** ("Windy Gorge"), an hour or so into the hike, where your first glimpse of **Glacier Grey** stops you in your tracks. For the next couple of hours, you walk across exposed terrain, mesmerized by the pale water of Lago Grey and its house-sized chunks of blue ice. The glacier peeks from behind the dark rock of **La Isla Nunatak** on the lake's far side. The trail then descends steeply through the silent *lenga* woods, almost doubling back on itself and crossing a wooden bridge over a gushing torrent, before emerging on the lakeshore. Ten

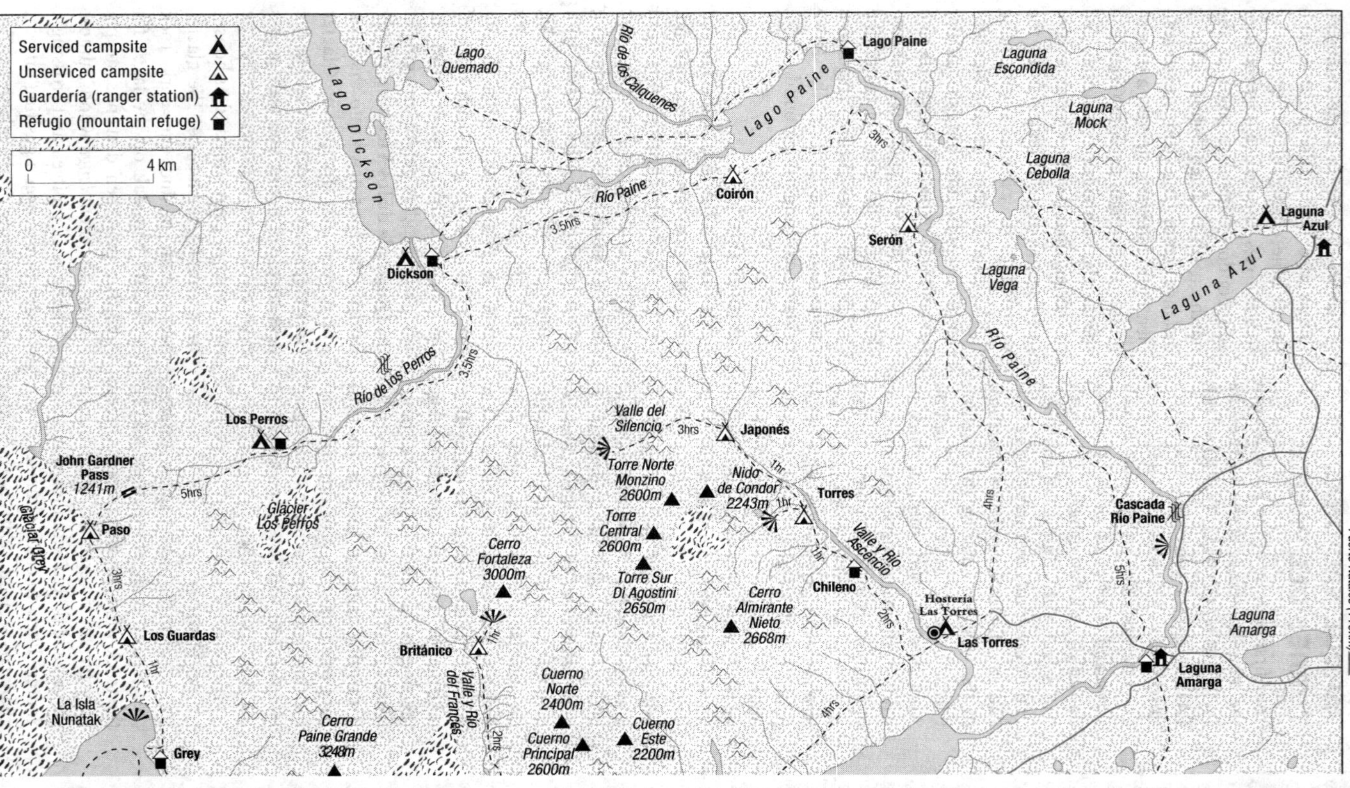
Serviced campsite
Unserviced campsite
Guardería (ranger station)
Refugio (mountain refuge)
0
4 km
Lago Dickson
Lago Quemado
Río de los Calquenes
Lago Paine
Lago Paine
Laguna Escondida
Laguna Mock
Laguna Cebolla
Laguna Azul
Laguna Azul
Laguna Vega
Río Paine
Río Paine
Coirón
Serón
Dickson
3.5hrs
3hrs
Río de los Perros
3.5hrs
Los Perros
Valle del Silencio
3hrs
Japonés
1hr
Torres
Torre Norte Monzino 2600m
Nido de Condor 2243m
1hr
Torre Central 2600m
Torre Sur Di Agostini 2650m
Valle y Río Ascencio
Chileno
1hr
2hrs
Hostería Las Torres
Las Torres
4hrs
4hrs
5hrs
Cascada Río Paine
Laguna Amarga
Laguna Amarga
Puerto Natales (116km)
John Gardner Pass 1241m
5hrs
Glaciar Los Perros
Glaciar Grey
Paso
3hrs
Los Guardas
1hr
La Isla Nunatak
Grey
Cerro Fortaleza 3000m
Cerro Almirante Nieto 2668m
Británico
1hr
Valle y Río del Francés
2hrs
Cerro Paine Grande 3248m
Cuerno Norte 2400m
Cuerno Principal 2600m
Cuerno Este 2200m

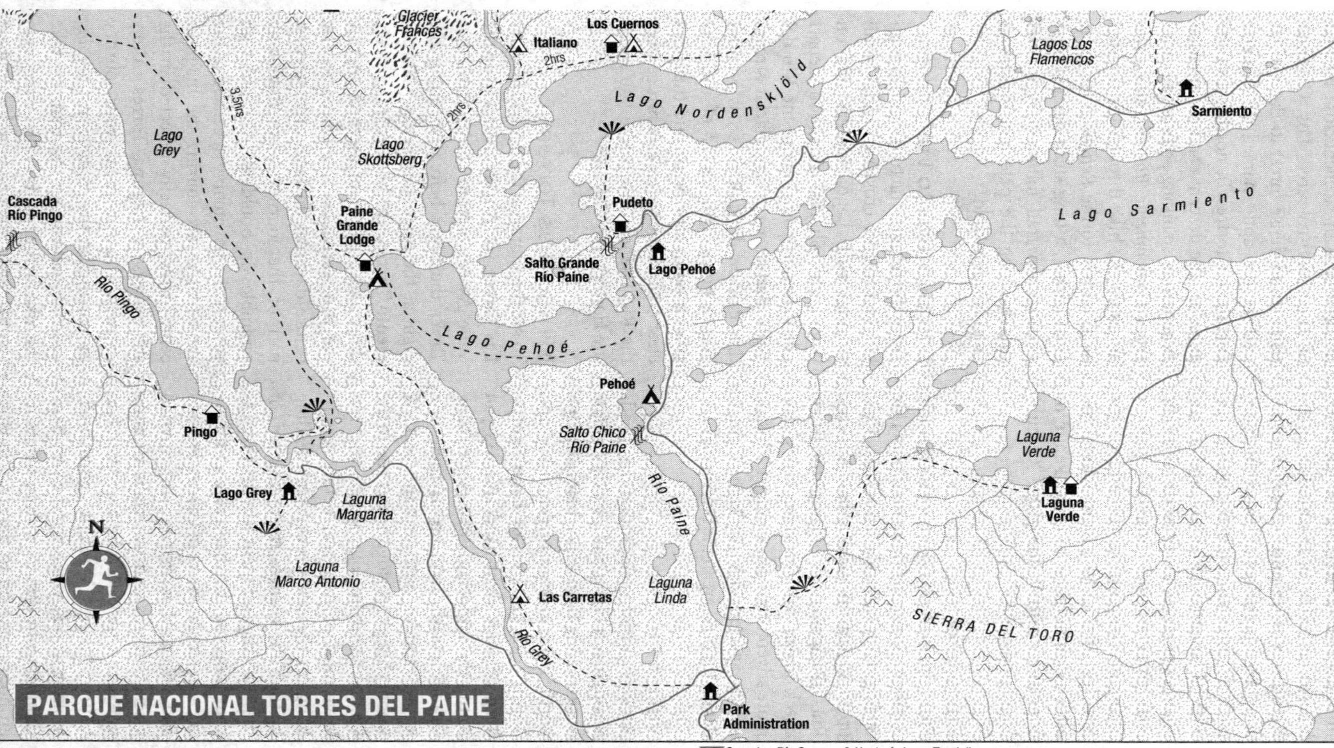
PARQUE NACIONAL TORRES DEL PAINE
Puerto Natales (116km)
Refugio Zapata
Camping Río Serrano & Hostería Lago Tyndall
Glaciar Francés
Los Cuernos
Italiano
2hrs
Lagos Los Flamencos
Sarmiento
3.5hrs
Lago Grey
Lago Skottsberg
2hrs
Lago Nordenskjöld
Lago Sarmiento
Cascada Río Pingo
Paine Grande Lodge
Pudeto
Salto Grande Río Paine
Lago Pehoé
Río Pingo
Lago Pehoé
Pehoé
Pingo
Salto Chico Río Paine
Laguna Verde
Lago Grey
Laguna Margarita
Río Paine
Laguna Verde
N
Laguna Marco Antonio
Las Carretas
Laguna Linda
SIERRA DEL TORO
Río Grey
Park Administration

minutes before arriving at a shaded lakeside clearing accommodating the **Refugio y Camping Grey**, another short trail branches off from the main path, leading you to a rocky outcrop with a spectacular close-up of the glacier's gigantic ice crystals. The hike lasts three or four hours; *Refugio y Camping Grey* marks the end of the first leg of the "W", from where you either double back to Lago Pehoé or continue north if doing the "Circuit" (see opposite).

Lago Grey

From the *Hostería Lago Grey* it's possible to take a spectacular three-hour **boat ride** up Lago Grey to the glacier, or kayak right up to it, past the massive blue icebergs. Rutas Patagonia can organise the latter; check ahead for departure times. The more adventurous can arrange ice hiking on the glacier with Big Foot. Contact details for both are in the box on p.514.

Valle Francés

A two-hour long, eastbound trail heads through scrubland and prickly *calafate* bushes along Lago Pehoé before leading north along a series of gentle ups and downs with glimpses of **Lago Skottsberg** on your right-hand side. As you round the imposing, 3050-metre Paine Grande massif, look up, as there is a known condor nest near the peak. A wobbly hanging bridge brings you to the *Campamento Italiano*, where you can leave most of your gear before scrambling up the steep rocky path leading up the **Valle Francés**, the middle part of the "W". The turbulent **Río del Francés** churns on your left-hand side and there are spectacular views of Glacier Francés and Glacier Los Perros, with myriad glacial streams and waterfalls running down the rock face below. After two hours hiking through enchanted-looking woods, you reach the very basic *Campamento Británico*, from where it's an hour's hike up to the steep lookout that gives you an excellent close-up view of the multi-coloured Los Cuernos, rising from dense forest to the east, as well as the aptly named 2800-metre **Fortaleza** ("fortress"), northeast of the *mirador*. The descent can be somewhat treacherous, so hiking poles are a bonus. From *Campamento Italiano*, allow two hours for the hike through the forested backcountry to the *Refugio y Camping Los Cuernos*; a long steep descent on a scree-strewn trail followed by a brief stretch along the pale blue waters of Lago Nordenskjöld.

Los Cuernos to Las Torres

From the refugio, the trail runs through hilly scrubland, crossing several small streams, with Lago Nordenskjöld on your right. Shortly after you depart Los Cuernos, you come to the **Río del Valle Bader**, a rushing glacial stream that can be difficult to cross without hiking poles. This sector of the hike takes around four hours and there is a clear track which crosses a bridge over the Río Asencio just before you reach the *Hostería Las Torres*.

Mirador Las Torres

To see the sunrise at the famous *mirador* **Las Torres**, some make their way up the Valle Ascencio from the *Hostería Las Torres* the night before, spending the night at the basic, unserviced **Campamento Torres**. The hike itself is a steep, three-and-a-half-hour ascent alongside the **Río Ascencio**. You'll need to rise before daybreak to tackle the steepest part of the journey – an hour-long scramble up boulders – in order to witness the bewitching spectacle of the sun's first rays colouring the magnificent Torres, perfectly reflected in the still waters of **Laguna Torres**. Alternatively, you can break your journey by staying at the *Refugio y Camping Chileno*, halfway up the trail. Or take the hike further up the Valle Ascencio to *Campamento Japonés*, used by climbers tackling the Torres, then up another steep yet spectacular climb along the aptly-named **Valle del Silencio** to a less-visited *mirador*. The "W" ends with a short trek or minibus ride from *Hostería Las Torres* back to Laguna Amarga and the park entrance.

The "Circuit"

The "Circuit" is an extended version of the "W" (see p.515), a the seven- to ten-day hike that leads you around the back of the Torres, giving you respite from the inevitable crowds during peak season, and offering unique glimpses of the park, which you may be able to experience in complete solitude. You can follow the trail directly from **Laguna Amarga**, from where it's a straightforward five-hour hike along Río Paine to *Camping Serón*, and another three hours to *Campamento Coirón*, just west of Lago Paine. Or you can pick up the trail from the *Hostería Las Torres*, cutting across the base of Mount Paine. A three-hour stretch from Coirón brings you to the shores of **Lago Dickson**, where you can spend the night at the *Refugio y Camping Dickson*, or press on southwards along the **Río de Los Perros**, crossing the bridge over the Río Cabeza de Indio and passing the beautiful Salto Los Perros on your right, before reaching *Camping Los Perros* on the far side of a small lagoon, three or four hours later. A challenging crossing of the rocky **John Garner Pass** takes five hours, leading you to *Campamento Paso* alongside the impossibly massive Glacier Grey. You rejoin the "W" after a four-hour hike along the glacier, passing *Campamento Los Guardas* just an hour from the *Refugio y Camping Grey*. Since there is only one *refugio* along the Circuit, you will have to stop at unserviced campsites most of the way, bringing food and camping supplies with you.

Arrival and information

Buses Buses from Puerto Natales stop at the Laguna Amarga park administration building, the only terrestrial entrance to the park; there is a small grocery store and café nearby. Some buses drop you off at Lago Pehoé at no extra charge if you wish to tackle the "W" from the west. Minibus transfers (CH$2000) meet the Puerto Natales buses and run to *Refugio y Camping Las Torres*, the popular starting point of the "W" on the eastern side.

Conaf The Conaf *guardería* at Laguna Amarga has information on the park's fauna and flora, as well as basic trekking maps, though it's best to bring a detailed JLM map of your own if you're planning to hike off the beaten track. You must register and pay your CH$15,000 entrance fee here. Ranger stations at Portería Lago Sarmiento, Guardería Laguna Azul, Guardería Lago Grey and Guardería Lago Verde also have basic information on the park. The Conaf-run Centro de Informaciones Ecológicas (Dec–Feb daily 8:30am–8pm;

REFUGIOS IN TORRES DEL PAINE

Most of the park's **refugios** are open only from September to May, as winter weather makes them inaccessible. Some belong to Conaf, while others are run by Andescape (Eberhard 599 ⓣ61/412592, ⓦwww.andescape.cl), or Fantástico Sur (Magallanes 960 ⓣ61/710050, ⓦwww.lastorres.com), both in Puerto Natales. Conaf-run *refugios* tend to be rather basic, with bare bunk beds and a wood-burning stove, while those that are privately-run rent bedding and offer pricey hot meals (around CH$4500 for breakfast, CH$7000 for lunch and CH$9000 for dinner). Though it is widely suggested that you book your *refugio* space in advance, especially in the peak season from December through February, prohibitive prices mean that many hikers opt for camping instead, so it's often possible to turn up and get a bed. There are several unserviced campsites in the park, which are free of charge and consist of a clearing with a fire pit; these include *Campamento Los Guardas*, *Campamento Paso*, *Campamento Coirón*, *Campamento Las Carretas*, *Campamento Británico* and *Campamento Torres*. Wild camping inside the park is not permitted.

Ⓣ61/691931 Ⓔptpaine@conaf.cl) at the Lago del Toro Park Administration building has extensive displays on the park fauna and flora.

Ferry A Hielos Patagónicos catamaran (Ⓣ61/411438; CH$11,000 one way, CH$17,000 return) crosses Lago Pehoé at 9.30am, noon and 6pm (Nov 1–Mar 15); noon & 6pm (Mar 16–Mar 31 & Oct 16–Oct 31); or noon only (Oct 1–Oct 15 & Apr 1–Apr 15); there is no service the rest of the year.

Accommodation, eating and drinking

Campamento Italiano Free campsite consisting of a few shaded tent spaces on uneven ground at the foot of Valle Francés; bathrooms, showers and small shelter available; no phone.

Camping Laguna Azul Ⓣ61/411157 (Conaf). This campsite has a scenic location and the price includes firewood and fire pits; there is also a *guardería* on-site. CH$12,000 for up to six people.

Campamento Los Perros (Andescape). Halfway between the John Garner pass and the *refugio Dickson*, this campsite comes equipped with hot showers, food shop and equipment rental; meals have to be reserved in advance. CH$3000.

Campamento Pehoé (Conaf). Small campsite on a peninsula on Lago Pehoé; hot showers, toilets and firewood included; CH$12,000 site for up to six people; no phone.

Campamento Serón Ⓣ61/710050 (Conaf). Partially-shaded campsite on the Circuit beside the Río Paine; hot showers, toilets and a *guardería* on-site. CH$3500 per person; CH$12,000 site for up to six people; CH$3000 to picnic.

Refugio y Campamento Chileno (Fantástico Sur). A popular stop halfway along the Valle Ascencio, this *refugio* has friendly staff and offers kitchen privileges after certain hours as well as hot meals; CH$20,000 per person. Camping CH$3500.

Refugio y Campamento Dickson (Andescape). On the shore of Lago Dickson, this *refugio* offers hot showers, hot meals and equipment rental; CH$18,000 per person, without sleeping bag. Camping CH$3000.

Refugio y Campamento Grey (Andescape). A small popular *refugio* a stone's throw from Glacier Grey; book meals in advance. Campsite includes hot showers and a small on-site grocery store. CH$20,000, camping CH$3000.

Refugio y Campamento Los Cuernos (Fantástico Sur). A cosy *refugio* serving excellent meals, with kitchen privileges after 10pm; campers share bathroom facilities with *refugio* guests. Camping spots are sheltered amongst vegetation. CH$20,000, camping CH$3500.

Refugio y Campamento Los Torres (Fantástico Sur). Near the entrance to the park and the *Hostería Las Torres*, this *refugio* is split between two buildings and has comfortable bunks as well as palatable food. Camping spots have hot showers, picnic tables and fire pits. More upmarket eating can be found at the excellent restaurant at nearby *Hostería Las Torres*. CH$20,000, camping CH$3500.

Refugio y Campamento Paine Grande (Andescape). The campground, where you can rent gear, has an indoor cooking area, hot showers and bathrooms. The popular *refugio* has great views of Lago Pehoé, as well as a small grocery store, café-bar and restaurant, though the food is decidedly uninspiring. CH$20,000, camping CH$3500.

Tierra del Fuego

TIERRA DEL FUEGO, the most remote of Chile's land territories, was named "Land of Fire" by Fernando Magellan, who sailed through the strait that now bears his name, and saw a multitude of cooking fires lit by the native Indians, hunter-gatherers who made this inhospitable terrain their home. Prior to the creation of the Panama Canal, the frigid waters around Cape Horn – buffeted by ferocious winds and the largest ship graveyard in the Americas – formed a link in the perilous yet lucrative trade route from Europe to the west coast of the Americas. Tierra del Fuego's Isla Grande is split between Chile and Argentina; the Chilean half features the nondescript town of **Porvenir**, settled by a mixture of Chilote and Croatian immigrants in the late nineteenth century, as well as a number of remote sheep-rearing *estancias*. The Argentine half boasts the lively town of **Ushuaia**, the base for Antarctic voyages. The region's biggest natural draw is southern Tierra del Fuego – a scattering of rocky islands, separated by labyrinthine fjords, home to the craggy Darwin Range and the southernmost permanently inhabited town in the world – Isla Navarino's **Puerto Williams**.

PUERTO WILLIAMS

Although Argentine Ushuaia, on the north side of the Beagle Channel, loudly proclaims its **"end of the world"** status, that title rightfully belongs to **PUERTO WILLIAMS**. Home to just over two thousand people, the windblown town has a desolate quality to it even in the height of the brief summer; the streets appear deserted and few businesses open after 4pm. The weather is prone to rapid change and the contrast of leaden skies and sunshine, plus the occasional onslaught of ferocious wind, remind you that you are very much at the mercy of the elements. In contrast to the weather, the people of Puerto Williams are exceptionally warm and welcoming; you get a real sense of a close-knit community, brought together by isolation from the rest of Chile. The isolation is occasionally broken by the arrival of an Antarctica-bound ship of researchers, or European hikers looking to tackle the arduous Dientes de Navarino hiking circuit.

The Town

Most **businesses** are concentrated in the **Centro Comercial**, by the Plaza O'Higgins, with a few **guesthouses** scattered around the nearby streets and several small **supermarkets** along Piloto Pardo. Parallel Yelcho leads west to the colourful, wind-blown **cemetery**, uphill from the seaside Avenida Costanera, with the Beagle Channel beyond. Avenida Costanera takes you past a cluster of beached fishing boats and the rusted hulk of a half-sunken barge loaded with *centolla* traps, towards the indigenous community of **Villa Ukika**. In the other direction, it leads you towards the **airport** and the *Club Naval de Yates Micalvi*, past the **Mirador Plaza Costanera**, the bright-red pier leading up to the channel's cold blue waters, from which you get a wonderful view of the town against a backdrop of forest-covered mountain peaks beyond.

Museo Martín Gusinde

This professional **museum**, at Aragay 1 (Mon–Fri 9am–1pm & 2.30–7pm, Sat & Sun 2–6pm; donations), is named after a clergyman and anthropologist who spent a great deal of time among the native tribes of Tierra del Fuego. Located on the west side of town, it features informative and well-laid-out displays on the native Kawéscar, Selk'nam and Yámana Indians, complete with a replica of a Selk'nam ritual hut, as well as exhibits on local geology, flora and fauna.

THE YÁMANA, THE SELK'NAM AND THE KAWÉSCAR

The unforgiving lands of Tierra del Fuego and Isla Navarino were originally home to three tribes, the Yámana (Yahgan), the Selk'nam (Ona) and the Kawéscar (Alacalúf), all of whom lived along the coast and subsisted on a diet of fish, shellfish and marine animals. Though dismissed by European explorers as savages (Charles Darwin famously commented that the "Canoe Indians" were "among the most abject and miserable creatures I ever saw"), and now largely culturally extinct, the tribes had complex rituals. The Selk'nam, for example, performed a sophisticated male initiation ceremony, the Hain, during which young male initiates, or *kloketens*, confronted and unmasked malevolent spirits they had been taught to fear since their youth, emerging as *maars* (adults). Father Martín Gusinde was present at the last **Hain ceremony** in 1923, and managed to capture the event in a series of remarkable photographs, copies of which circulate as postcards today.

Arrival and information

Airport The tiny airport receiving Aerovías DAP flights from Punta Arenas and chartered flights from Ushuaia lies a short distance from Puerto Williams; flights are met by local minivans that double as taxis.
Boat The Transbordadora Austral Broom (Ⓦwww.tabsa.cl) ferry arrives at Puerto Williams on Fri nights in the summer. Speedboats from Ushuaia dock at tiny Puerto Navarino, on the eastern end of the island, where visitors have to check in with Chilean immigration authorities; minibus transfers take passengers to their *residenciales* in Puerto Williams, an hour's drive across the island.
Tourist office The booth that provides tourist information, including photocopied maps of the Dientes de Navarino Circuit, and sells vintage postcards, is located at the main entrance to the Centro Comercial, and is perpetually closed. Go to the nearby yellow bakery and ask the proprietress to open it.

Accommodation

Hostal Bella Vista Teniente Muñoz 118 Ⓣ61/621010, Ⓦwww.victory-cruises.com. A new hostel with incredible views of the Beagle Channel, run by an American-Chilean family. Warm rooms, some en-suite, with laundry service, wi-fi and discounts at the internet café and the minimart. Sailing trips to Cape Horn and Antarctica on their yacht "S/V *Victory*" are on offer. ❻
Hostal Coirón Ricardo Maragaño 168 Ⓣ61/621227, Ⓔhostalcoiron@tie.cl. Knowledgeable and helpful young owner runs a friendly hostel popular with backpackers, with a dorm, a couple of en-suite twin rooms, kitchen use and intermittent internet. Dorm CH$6000. ❸
Hostal Patagonia Yelcho 230 Ⓣ61/621294, Ⓔpedroortiz@chilesat.net. Owned by the proprietor of *Club Naval de Yates Micalvi*, this guesthouse has several clean and cosy singles and doubles, and the owners cook up traditional Chilean food: full board CH$8,000 extra. ❸
Residencial Pusaki Piloto Pardo 222 Ⓣ61/621116, Ⓔpattypusaki@yahoo.es. Another backpacker favourite run by an extremely hospitable family, this hostel has warm, cosy rooms with shared bath as well as a common lounge and kitchen. ❷

Eating and drinking

Café Ángelus Centro Comercial Norte 151. A popular place day and night for a beer, with a range of alcoholic coffees, cakes and decent sandwiches and pasta. The friendly proprietress is a good source of local information and speaks fluent English and French. Pasta CH$3500; coffee CH$1000.
Club Naval de Yates Micalvi Seno Lauta Costanera s/n. The former Navy ship is a nightly gathering point for travellers, local sailors and Antarctic explorers; open late. Beers CH$1000.
Dientes de Navarino Centro Comercial Sur 14. A popular eatery serving hamburgers, pizza or whatever's in the kitchen at the time. Pizza CH$3500.
Hostal Patagonia Yelcho 230. The owner, a former sailor, can rustle up some home cooking, be it chicken, *centolla* or beaver. Lunch menu CH$5000.
Residencial Pusaki Piloto Pardo 222. Even if you're not a guest here, give the owner a couple of hours' warning and try some of her delicious home cooking at dinnertime; *centolla* night is the best. CH$4500.
Simón y Simón Piloto Pardo, opposite *Hostal Pusaki*. Of all the little supermarkets in town, this is the best-stocked; open until 10pm nightly.

Directory

Airlines Aerovías DAP is at Centro Comercial Sur 151 (Mon–Sat 4pm–9pm; Ⓣ61/621114).
Banks, cambios and ATMs There is just one bank and ATM on the island, Banco de Chile, located down a narrow passageway from the Centro Comercial towards the seafront. They exchange US dollars ($100 minimum) but not traveller's cheques.
Hospital and pharmacy The hospital and pharmacy are located behind the Capitanía de Puerto.
Internet access The internet café by the yellow bakery in the Centro Comercial has several slow and expensive computers (Mon–Sat 9am–10pm); entrance through grocery store. Cape Horn Cyber Net Café, at Teniente Muñoz 118, has newer computers, though still slow (daily 9am–10pm).
Post office Centro Comercial Sur, next to Aerovías DAP (Mon–Fri 9:30am–noon & 3pm–7pm, Sat 9.30am–1pm).
Telephone centres There are two phone centres in the Centro Comercial: CTC and EntelChile. Calls abroad are expensive.

Moving on

Boat: Servicios Marítimos y Turisticos, at Costanera 436 (Ⓣ61/621015 Ⓦwww.tabsa.cl), sells tickets for the *Bahía Azul*, the Transbordadora Austral Broom ferry that sails to Punta Arenas (Sept–May every Sat night; CH$105,000

ISLA NAVARINO TOUR OPERATORS

Outdoor activities on and around Isla Navarino tend to be on the expensive side and not for the faint-hearted, but if you've had fantasies about yachting in the frigid waters of the extreme south, or tackling some of the most challenging hiking in Latin America, several experienced tour operators in Puerto Williams can help you realize your dream.

Sea & Ice & Mountains Adventures Unlimited Austral 74 ⓣ61/621227, ⓦwww.simltd.com. Intrepid German-Venezuelan operator organizing hiking and horseriding on Isla Navarino and Cordillera Darwin, as well as sea-kayaking trips and multi-day yacht excursions around Cape Horn and even to Antarctica.

Shila Turismo Aventura Atamu Tekena s/n ⓣ61/621366 or 9/123-3179, ⓔturismoshila@gmail.com. Luis and family run hiking trips around Isla Navarino and fishing excursions to Lago Windhond, Lago Navarino and Laguna Rojas; they also rent outdoor gear.

Wulaia Expediciones ⓣ9/870-0112. Boat trips around the Beagle Channel, Murray Channel and to the remote and beautiful Wulaia Bay.

for a berth; CH$90,000 for a Pullman seat). The journey takes approximately 34hr and departure times are subject to weather conditions. Reserve the trip in advance as it is often booked up, especially from Dec through Feb. *Ushuaia Boating*, at Gobernador Godoy 190, Ushuaia, has multiple weekly speedboats to and from Puerto Navarino (CH$105,000 return; ⓣ+54/2901-436-193, ⓔushuaiaboating@argentina.com.ar); book several days in advance. The crossing of the Beagle Channel takes 30min and can be a memorable experience in windy weather; the boats do not sail in extreme conditions, so be prepared to spend an extra day or two on Isla Navarino. It may also be possible to hitch a ride on a private yacht; speak either to the Gobernación Maritima (ⓣ61/621090) or enquire at the *Club de Yates Micalvi*.

Plane Aerovías DAP, Centro Comercial Sur 151 (ⓣ61/621051, ⓦwww.aeroviasdap.cl), has flights to Punta Arenas (Nov–March daily; April–Oct thrice-weekly); reserve several weeks in advance if flying between Dec and Feb. One-way CH$67,000; return CH$105,000; luggage restriction 10–15kg.

AROUND PUERTO WILLIAMS

Most travellers come to Puerto Williams to complete the challenging seventy-kilometre **Los Dientes de Navarino Circuit** – a strenuous four- to seven-day hike in the Isla Navarino wilderness. Follow Vía Uno west out of town; the trail starts behind the statue of the Virgin Mary in a grassy clearing. The road leads uphill up to a waterfall and reservoir, from where a marked trail climbs steadily through the *coigüe* and *ñire* forest. It is a two-hour ascent to **Cerro Banderas**, a *mirador* with a wonderful view of the town, the Beagle Channel and the nearby mountains; a climb that is definitely worthwhile even if you're not thinking of doing the circuit. The rest of the trail is not well marked, and leads you past the starkly beautiful **Laguna El Salto**, then crosses a fairly steep pass to **Laguna de los Dientes**. Continue west past Lagunas Escondido, Hermosa and Matrillo before reaching the particularly steep and treacherous descent of **Arroyo Virginia**; beware of loose rocks. The trail officially finishes behind the **Centolla Factory**, from where you can follow the main road back to Puerto Williams. Before setting out, ensure you have plentiful food and water supplies, sunscreen and warm and waterproof outdoor gear; be prepared for inclement weather – it can snow even in summer – and inform people in town of your plans before leaving.

Ukika

A twenty-minute coastal walk east along Costanera Ukika brings you to the hamlet of **Villa Ukika**, home to the last remaining descendants of the Yámana people, and to the last elderly Yámana speaker, **Christina Calderón**, though there is some talk of a language revival amongst younger members of the tribe. The only object of note here is the replica of a traditional Yámana dwelling – the **Kipa-Akar** (House of Woman) – which is uninhabited. The hut can be unlocked and viewed on request, and there are handicrafts for sale, including reed baskets and miniature canoes. From Villa Ukika, the road runs south-east through the dense forest for 26 kilometres before ending at **Puerto Toro**, a tiny fishing post frequented by *centolla* fishermen. Beyond lies the cold expanse of the Atlantic Ocean, the treacherous Cape Horn, and Antarctica – the final frontier.

The Pacific Islands

Chile boasts two of the world's most unique and isolated island territories, the **Juan Fernández Archipelago** and **Easter Island**. These **PACIFIC ISLANDS** are both UNESCO protected sites. Although similar in size, Easter Island, once home to a remote civilization, receives thousands of visitors per year, while **Isla Robinson Crusoe**, part of the Juan Fernández Archipelago, remains one of the least-visited and most tranquil parts of Chile. Far away and expensive to reach, the islands reward those who venture forth with archeological riches and an incredible wealth of plant and animal life.

THE JUAN FERNÁNDEZ ARCHIPELAGO

Consisting of three ruggedly steep islands rising from the ocean, the **JUAN FERNÁNDEZ ARCHIPELAGO** lies 667km west of the Chilean mainland and boasts a population of less than seven hundred people. Its only inhabited island, **Isla Robinson Crusoe**, is named after Daniel Defoe's classic novel, inspired by the Scotsman Alexander Selkirk, who spent over four years on this island in complete isolation, from 1704 to 1709. Most of the island is within the **Parque Nacional Archipiélago Juan Fernández**, a UNESCO World Biosphere Reserve since 1977; there are plenty of natural attractions within hiking distance of its only town **SAN JUAN BAUTISTA**, founded in 1950. San Juan Bautista has a number of good (though not cheap) **guest-houses**, most of which feature the local speciality of rock lobster on their menus. They include *Residencial Barón de Rodt*, La Póvora s/n (Ⓣ322/751109, Ⓔbaronderodt@yahoo.es; ❹) and *Residencial Mirador de Selkirk*, at El Castillo 251 (Ⓣ322/751028, Ⓔmfernandeziana@hotmail.com; ❺). There are **camping** spots at *Camping Los Cañones*, Vicente Gonzáles s/n, though the facilities are decidedly basic and the showers lack hot water, and basic Conaf **refugios** at Puerto Vaquería and Puerto Francés. The Conaf-run **Caseta de Informaciones,** Larraín Alcalde s/n (Mon–Fri 8.45am–12.30pm & 2–5.30pm, Sat & Sun 8.30am–noon & 2–5.30pm), dishes out maps of the town and the national park, while the Centro de Información Ambiental Eduardo Paredes, Vicente Gonzáles s/n (daily 8.30am–12.45pm & 2–6pm; extended hours in summer; Ⓣ322/751004) provides information on the park, and has displays on its fauna and flora.

What to see and do

A narrow trail leading from San Juan Bautista through dense vegetation snakes to the **Mirador de Selkirk**, the island's famous scenic point, where the castaway tried to attract passing ships with smoke signals. The trail then leads to the large **fur seal colony** at Bahía Tierras Blancas, near the airfield.

Alternative hikes include the spectacular and strenuous trail to **El Camote**, a *mirador* on Cerro El Yunque, the island's steep 915-metre peak, and a short westbound trail to **Puerto Inglés**, a clearing featuring a replica of Selkirk's shelter. Hiring a **launch** at San Juan Bautista allows you to see sites inaccessible on foot, though it can be an expensive option.

Arrival and information

Flights There are frequent seven-seater flights from Santiago with either Lassa, Av Larraín 7941, La Reina (Ⓣ2/273-5209 or 2/273-1458, Ⓔlassa@terra.cl), or Aerolíneas ATA, Av 11 de Septiembre 2155, Oficina 1107, Providencia (Ⓣ2/234-3389 Ⓦwww.aerolineasata.cl); the average cost is US$600–700 return trip.

Ships The more adventurous may wish to contact either the shipping company Naviera del Sur, Blanco 1623, Oficina 602, in Valparaíso (Ⓣ322/594304, Ⓦwww.navieradelsur.cl), regarding its monthly voyages to San Juan Bautista, or the naval supply ships at the Comando de Transporte, Primera Zona Naval, Plaza Sotomayor 592, in Valparaíso (Ⓣ322/506354), as they sometimes take passengers for around CH$20,000 a day.

Banks Bring plenty of cash in small denominations as the island does not have banks or financial facilities.

Tour operator While you can explore much of the national park by yourself, local guides are required for some of the most challenging hikes; Endémica Expediciones (Ⓣ322/751077 or 322/751023, Ⓦwww.endemica.com) organizes hikes, sea-kayaking and diving trips around the island.

Moving on

Boat Naviera del Sur's freighter *Navarino* sails monthly from San Juan Bautista to Valparaíso but since passenger spaces are very limited, reservations are imperative. Naval supply vessels are even less frequent, so plan your journey carefully.

Plane to: Santiago; Lassa and Aerolíneas ATA take off from the small airstrip on the west side of the island; the motor launch from San Juan Bautista is included in the price. Be flexible with your plans, as inclement weather can delay flights.

EASTER ISLAND

The most remote island on earth, over two thousand kilometres from the nearest inhabited part of the world, **EASTER ISLAND** entices visitors with the enduring mystery of its **lost culture**. A remarkable civilization arose here, far from outside influence on an island only 163 square kilometres in extent. It apparently declined rapidly and had all-but disappeared by the time Europeans first arrived here, its monuments in pieces. Originally known as "Te Pito O Te Henua", or "the navel of the world", due to its isolation, and now called "Rapa Nui" by its inhabitants (*Pascuenses*), the island is home to a culture and people with strong Polynesian roots and a language of their own (Rapanui), which sets it well apart from mainland Chile. Archeological mysteries aside, the island has much to offer: year-round warm weather, excellent diving and surfing conditions and plenty of scope for leisurely exploration of the more out-of-the-way attractions, both on foot and on horseback. Welcoming people, excellent food and a laid-back atmosphere seal the deal.

Hanga Roa

The island's only settlement and home to around four thousand people, **HANGA ROA** is a dusty village spread out along the Pacific coast. At night there is limited street lighting and the sky, lit with endless stars, is spectacular. North–south Atamu Tekena is the main road, lined with small **supermarkets**, cafés and **tour agencies**. Most of the action is centred around the pier, Caleta Hanga Roa, overlooked by **Ahu Tautira**, the only *moai* site in the town proper. Restaurants and eateries spread from here along oceanside Policarpo Toro and east–west Te Pito O Te Henua, which takes you past the small Plaza Policarpo Toro before ending at the Iglesia Hanga Roa – a Catholic **church** lavishly decorated

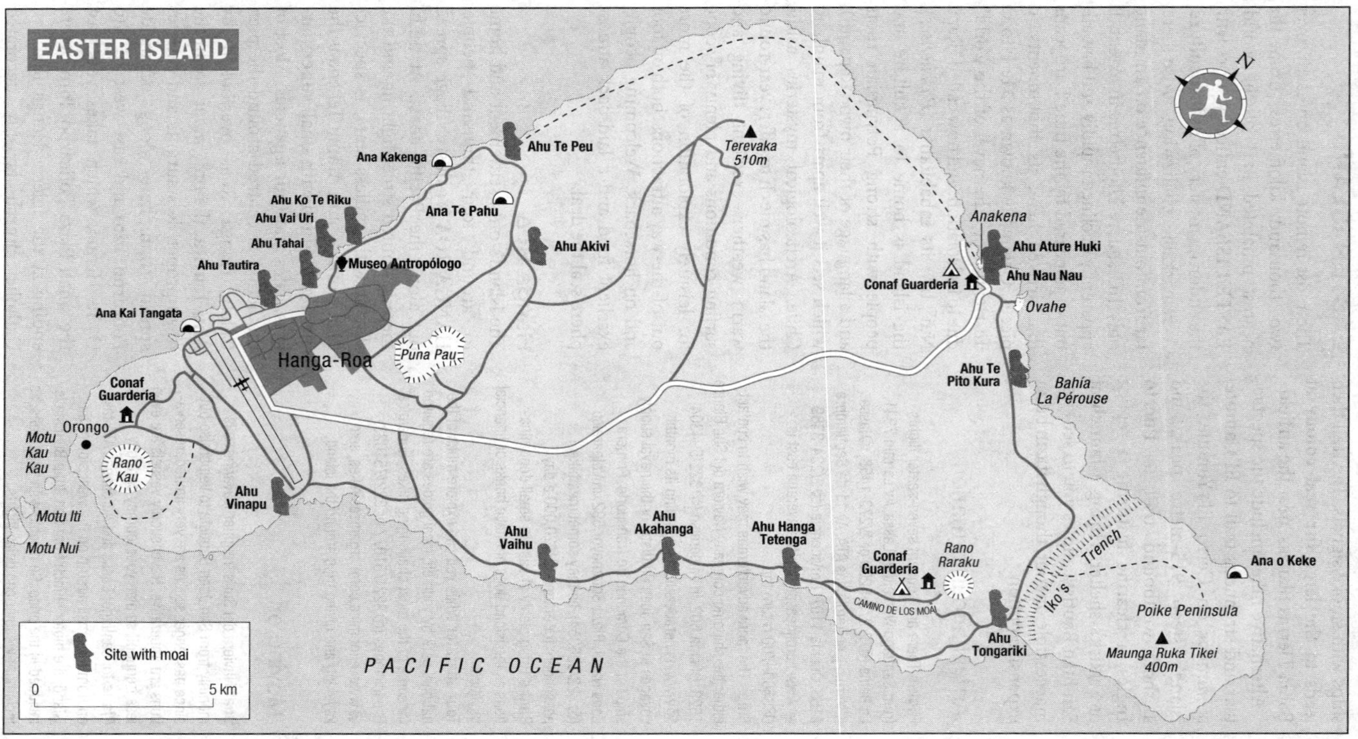
EASTER ISLAND
N
Ahu Te Peu
Ana Kakenga
Terevaka
510m
Ana Te Pahu
Ahu Ko Te Riku
Ahu Vai Uri
Ahu Tahai
Ahu Akivi
Ahu Tautira
Museo Antropólogo
Anakena
Ahu Ature Huki
Conaf Guardería
Ahu Nau Nau
Ovahe
Ana Kai Tangata
Hanga-Roa
Puna Pau
Ahu Te
Pito Kura
Bahía
La Pérouse
Conaf
Guardería
Orongo
Motu
Kau
Kau
Rano
Kau
Ahu
Vinapu
Motu Iti
Motu Nui
Ahu
Vaihu
Ahu
Akahanga
Ahu Hanga
Tetenga
Conaf
Guardería
Rano
Raraku
Camino de los Moai
Iko's
Trench
Ana o Keke
Poike Peninsula
Ahu
Tongariki
Maunga Ruka Tikei
400m
Site with moai
0
5 km
PACIFIC OCEAN

A BRIEF HISTORY OF EASTER ISLAND

500–800 AD Easter Island is settled by King Hotu Matu'a and his extended family, who come from either the Pitcairn Islands, or the Cook or Marquesas Islands in Polynesia. The island is divided between mata (tribes), each led by a male descendant of the original king.

800–1600 Population grows to an estimated 20,000. Island culture evolves into a complex multi-tiered society and flourishes; *ahu* (ceremonial platforms) are built and *moai* (stone statues) are erected all over the island.

1600–1722 Natural resources are depleted and deforestation takes its toll. Two warring factions form: the Ko Tu'u Aro, who rule the island's western half, and the Hotu Iti, who populate its eastern half. *Moai* construction stops, the population declines and the Birdman cult develops.

1722 Dutch admiral Jacob Roggeveen lands and names the island after the day of his arrival – Easter Sunday.

1770 The expedition of Felipe Gonzáles de Haedo claims Easter Island for King Carlos III of Spain.

1774 Captain James Cook visits; he finds the *moai* in ruins and the population bedraggled.

1862 Nearly one thousand islanders are kidnapped to work as slaves in the guano mines of the Chincha Islands off the coast of Peru, including the island's king and all the priestly elite able to read the *rongorongo* tablets. Later, one hundred islanders are shipped back to Easter Island; the final fifteen survivors of this voyage infect the islanders with smallpox and the population is reduced to a few hundred.

1870 The island is purchased for a pittance by Frenchman Jean Baptiste Dutroux-Bornier, who wages war on missionaries. Most islanders agree to be shipped to Tahiti.

1888–1953 Easter Island is leased to the Compañía Explotadora de la Isla de Pascua, a subsidiary of the sheep-rearing Scottish-owned Williamson, Balfour and Company. Villagers are confined to Hanga Roa.

1953 Company's lease is revoked; Easter Island comes under the control of the Chilean Navy.

1967 Mataveri Airport is built. Islanders are given full rights as Chilean citizens.

1967–present day The island undergoes material improvement and the Rapanui language is no longer suppressed. Disputes with the Chilean government over ancestral land rights, however, continue.

with elaborate wood carvings. Just south of the pier and opposite the tourist office lies tiny **Playa Pea**, a rock pool safe for swimming, cordoned off from the stretch of ocean popular with surfers and body boarders. Avenida Policarpo Toro heads north, past the Hanga Roa **cemetery** with its colourful crosses, to three main sites. First is **Ahu Tahai**, with a single large *moai*, then **Ahu Vai Uri**, with five standing *moai* in various states of repair, and finally the much-photographed **Ahu Ko Te Riku**, a single *moai* with a *pukao* (topknot) and intact, pensive-looking coral eyes. Also in this direction, amid gentle hills dotted with numerous *hare paenga* (boat-shaped foundations of traditional houses), lies the **anthropological museum** (see below). To the south, Policarpo Toro heads towards the extinct Rano Kau volcano.

Museo Antropológico Padre Sebastían Englert

Off the coastal road just north of Ahu Tahai, this excellent **museum** (Tues–Fri 9am–12.30pm & 2–5.30pm, Sat

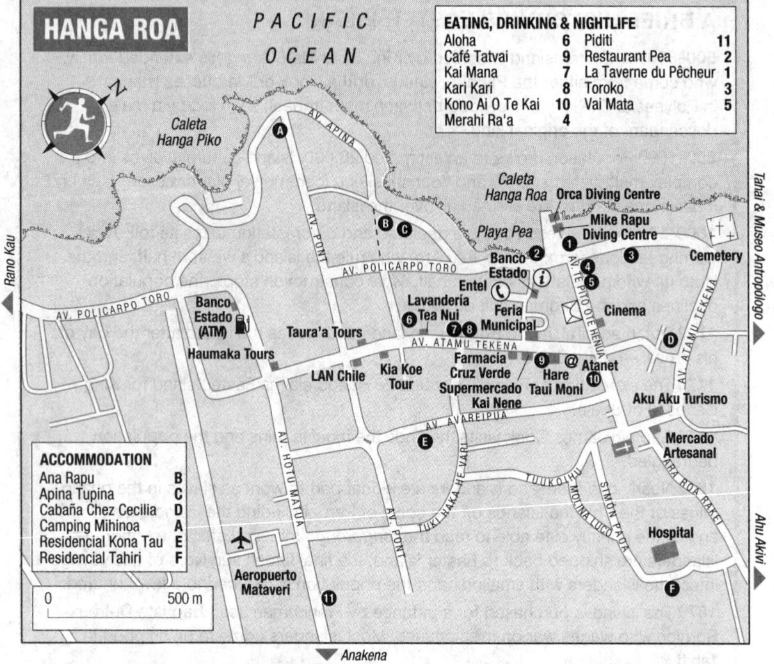

& Sun 9.30am–12.30pm; CH$1500; ⓣ322/551020, ⓦwww.museorapanui.cl), is not to be missed, as it gives a thorough and informative introduction to the island's geography, history, society, **Birdman cult** and the origins and significance of the *moai*, though it does not cover recent Easter Island history or the impact of Chilean rule on the island. The well-labelled displays are in Spanish, with English language handouts, and include a rare female *moai*, replica *rongorongo* tablets and a wooden carving of a *moai kavakava*, a gaunt figure, believed to represent the spirits of dead ancestors.

RONGORONGO – A MYSTERY REMAINS

Though no original examples remain on Easter Island, a number of wooden tablets in museums around the world bear examples of **rongorongo**, a system of glyphs in the shape of animals, plants and people, which appears to be a form of writing or proto-script. *Rongorongo* script is thus one of only four written languages in the world that developed completely independently of outside influence. Tablets are traditionally made from *toromiro* wood, though some that have recently been discovered appear to be made of Pacific rosewood, which has Eastern Polynesian origins.

The *rongorongo* tablets were first mentioned in the nineteenth-century accounts of French missionary **Eugene Eyraud**, and their purpose remains unclear. In 1864, a few islanders claimed to be able to read the script, but it seems that only a small priestly elite was literate and that the knowledge perished with the elite during the slave raids and smallpox epidemic of the early 1860s. The script remains undeciphered to this day.

THE RISE AND FALL OF THE MOAI OF EASTER ISLAND

The giant stone statues, around 887 of which litter the island, are a unique symbol of a lost civilization, whose existence raises many questions. Why were they made? By whom? How were they transported around the island and erected, without machinery? Why was their construction suddenly abandoned?

Believed to be representations of ancestors, the statues range from two to ten metres in height, with an average weight of twelve tons. The majority of the *moai* share a similar appearance: elongated features and limbs, prominent noses, heavy brows and rounded bellies. Most are male, and some wear *pukao*, carved of red stone in a separate quarry. All *moai* once had coral-and-rock eyes, though now the only intact example is Ahu Ko Te Riku.

Carved from the slopes of the Rano Raraku quarry, the *moai* were buried upright in earthen pits so that the sculptors could shape their facial features with basalt *toki*, and then lowered down the volcano's slopes, presumably using ropes. Most archeologists believe that to transport them to the coastal *ahu* (platforms) the islanders used wooden rollers or sledges – a practice which resulted in deforestation – and that once at the foot of the *ahu*, the *moai* were lifted into place using wooden levers. All *moai*, apart from those at Ahu Akivi, were positioned around the coast facing inland, so as to direct their *mana* (life energy) towards their creators and to bless them with plentiful food and other bounties.

It is known that at the height of Easter Island's civilization (800–1500 AD), the tiny island supported a large and complex multi-tiered society, with a ruling class who worshipped Make-Make, the creator, and oversaw the construction of these statues. A phenomenal amount of energy must have gone into their creation and transportation, ultimately depleting the island's resources and causing acute food shortages. Full-scale warfare erupted when farmers and fishermen couldn't or wouldn't support the *moai*-carving workforce any longer. The carving ceased and the *moai* were toppled from their pedestals.

Rano Kau crater and Orongo ceremonial village

South of Hanga Roa, a dirt road climbs steeply past a *mirador* offering an excellent panoramic view of the town and island, to one of the most awe-inspiring spots on the island – the giant crater of the extinct **Rano Kau volcano**. The dull waters of the volcano's reed-choked lake contrast sharply with the brilliant blue of the Pacific, visible where a great chunk of the crater wall is missing. Just before you reach **Orongo ceremonial village**, on the edge of the crater, a path disappears into the lush vegetation; it is possible to follow this around the crater as a leisurely day's walk, but bring plenty of water. At the **Conaf** ranger station at the village entrance (sometimes closed) you pay the CH$5000 entry fee to **Parque Nacional Rapa Nui**, which comprises much of the island, valid for the duration of your stay. The Orongo site of the Birdman cult consists of 53 restored houses, made of horizontally overlapping flat stone slabs, with tiny doorways to crawl through, hugging the side of the cliff. A winding labelled footpath leads past them to the edge of Rano Kau, where a cluster of basalt rocks depicting the half-bird, half-human Birdman, as well as Make-Make, the creator, overlook a sheer drop with the islets Motu Kao Kao, Motu Iti and Motu Nui jutting out of the azure waters below.

The southern coast

Heading east out of Hanga Roa, Hotu Matu'a leads you towards the **southern coast**. A right turn at the end, followed by an almost immediate left by the fuel

THE CULT OF THE BIRDMAN

The Birdman cult venerating the creator Make-Make flourished in the eighteenth and nineteenth centuries, up until the 1860s. An important element of the religion was a brutal and dangerous **competition** staged each year to pick the Tangata Manu, or **Birdman**. Contestants would send their representatives, or *hopu*, on a swim through shark-infested waters to the *motu* (islets) off the coast; the *hopu* would often attempt to stab their rivals on the way. Once on the *motu* the competitors would wait for days to retrieve the first Manutara (a type of seabird) egg of the season; the winner communicated his victory to those waiting in Orongo. The chosen Birdman then spent the year in complete seclusion, either in one of the houses in the Orongo village or in Anakena, attended to only by a priest, while his family enjoyed an elevated social status.

storage tanks, takes you to **Vinapu**, an important site consisting of three *ahus* (stone platforms) with a number of broken *moai* scattered around. The *ahus* are made of overlapping stone slabs, seemingly similar in construction to those built by the Inca in Cusco, Peru, leading some archeologists to believe that Easter Island culture has Latin American roots. Continuing east along this coast you reach **Ahu Vaihu**, with its eight toppled *moai* and their scattered *pukao*, reclaimed from the ocean in 1986. Up the road, the large **Ahu Akahanga** is widely believed to be the burial place of Hotu Matu'a, the first king of the island. The site features a dozen *moai*, lying face down, with petroglyphs carved into one of the platforms. There are also the remains of a village, consisting of *hare paenga* outlines, as well as a number of *pukao*. Another three kilometres east, the almost utterly ruined **Ahu Hanga Tetenga** consists of two toppled and shattered *moai*. Beyond, the road forks, the northern branch looping inland toward Rano Raraku, while the east-bound branch continues to **Ahu Tongariki**, one of the island's most enduring and awe-inspiring images. Consisting of fifteen *moai*, one significantly taller than the rest and another sporting a topknot, the island's largest *ahu* was destroyed by a tsunami in 1960, all its statues having toppled long before. They were rebuilt by the Japanese company Tadano between 1992 and 1995.

Rano Raraku

Just inland of Ahu Tongariki lies the unforgettable spectacle of **Rano Raraku** – site of the gigantic **quarry** where all of Easter Island's *moai* were chiselled out of the tuff, or compressed volcanic ash, that makes up the sides of the crater. From the Conaf ranger station, with a eucalyptus-shaded campground and various souvenir stalls, a dirt path leads up to the volcano's slopes, littered with dozens of completed *moai*, abandoned on the way to their *ahus*. The right branch meanders between the giant statues, buried in the ground up to their necks, their heads mournfully looking out to sea. You pass *moai* in various stages of completion, including the largest one ever carved, **El Gigante**, measuring 21 metres tall and four metres wide, its back still joined to the stone from which it was carved. The east end of the path culminates in the kneeling, round-headed **Moai Tukuturi**, the only one of its kind, discovered by Thor Heyerdahl's expedition in 1955. To the west, the trail winds its way up between wild guava trees into the crater itself, with several dirt paths running through knee-high shrubbery alongside the large reed-strewn, freshwater lake. If you follow the trails all the way up to the crater's eastern rim (avoid treading on the toppled *moai* right at the top), you are rewarded with unparalleled views of the bay and Ahu Tongariki in the distance.

Ovahe Beach

This small, sheltered **beach** is located off a dirt road just before Anakena Beach, on the other side of the Maunga Puha hillock. Backed by tall cliffs, its pristine sands are very popular with locals who come here to picnic, swim and snorkel. It's best earlier in the day, before the cliff blocks the afternoon sun.

Anakena Beach

Easter Island's largest and most popular beach is found on the northeast side of the island, and can be reached directly by the paved, cross-island road. A white-sand beach dotted with coconut trees, it has picnic tables and fire pits, public toilets and showers, as well as food stands offering drinks and snacks, so if you're camping at the Conaf-run campground, you won't need to bring all your food with you. The beach is also home to the largest *hare paenga* on the island and is believed to have been the landing point for the legendary King Hotu Matu'a. To the east stands the large, squat *moai* on **Ahu Ature Huki**, re-erected by Thor Heyerdahl's expedition of 1955 with the help of some islanders, while nearby stand the seven *moai* of **Ahu Nau Nau**, four sporting *pukaos* and two badly-damaged, the re-erection of which was overseen by Easter Island archeologist Sergio Rapu in 1979.

Northern coast and the inner loop

Heading up the coast from the north end of Hanga Roa, a dirt-and-gravel road takes you past **Ana Kakenga**, or Caverna Dos Ventanas – a cave set in the cliff with a spectacular view of the coast. Look for two offshore **islets**, Motu Ko Hepko and Motu Tautara; the cave is directly opposite them, with a cairn indicating the location. Bring a torch if you wish to explore. Further along, at the site of Ahu Tepeu, the road turns inland while a path carries on up to a copse of trees. The inland road leads you along fenced-off pasture land to **Ana Te Pahu** on your right-hand side – one of many underground **lava caves** on the island, used as a garden to cultivate sweet potatoes, *taro* and other tropical plants due to its moisture and fertile soil. Further along, at the south-western base of **Maunga Terevaka**, the island's highest point (507m), lies **Ahu Akivi**, with seven intact *moai*, unusually looking out to sea. As the road heads south to link up with the island's main thoroughfare, a dirt track to the west takes you to **Puna Pau**, the quarry where the *pukao* were carved.

Arrival and information

Airport Aeropuerto Mataveri (Ⓣ 322/100277) is located on Hotu Matu'a, southeast of Hanga Roa; most *residenciales* provide free transfers. Flights to Easter Island tend to be in the region of US$700–900, unless you buy your ticket very much in advance and also in conjunction with a long-distance LAN flight.

Boat Naval supply boats from Valparaíso dock at Caleta Hanga Piko, the cargo harbour south of Hanga Roa's centre.

Conaf Rano Kau s/n, south of Hanga Roa (Mon–Fri 8.30am–6pm; Ⓣ 322/100236, Ⓦ www.conaf.cl), stocks the excellent brochure "Archeological Field Guide, Rapa Nui National Park". You can also make reservations for Conaf-run campgrounds here. Conaf ranger stations are found at Rano Raraku, Anakena Beach and Orongo ceremonial village.

Tourist office Policarpo Toro at Tu'u Maheke (Mon–Fri 8.30am–1.30pm & 2.30–5.30pm; Ⓣ 322/100255). Helpful staff provide detailed information on the island's attractions and can help you organize camping, activities such as horse-riding and vehicle rental; some English and French spoken. There is a tourist information booth at the airport providing brochures on the island.

Accommodation

Ana Rapu Apina Iti s/n Ⓣ 322/100540, Ⓦ www.anarapu.cl. Airy rooms, some en-suite, in a very popular guesthouse set amidst lush vegetation, presided over by a knowledgeable hostess. Includes kitchen privileges and good breakfast; camping is possible and horseriding can be arranged. Camping CH$7000. ❺

Apina Tupina Policarpo Toro s/n ⓣ322/100763, ⓦwww.apinatupuna.com. Oceanside *residencial* with bright rooms, decorated with the owner's own artwork, popular with younger travellers. Breakfast and fully-equipped kitchen included; camping allowed. Camping CH$7500. ❹

Cabaña Chez Cecilia Atamu Tekena s/n ⓣ322/100499, ⓦwww.rapanuichezcecilia.com. Cosy en-suite rooms are offered here, along with fully-equipped, six-person *cabañas* and garden camping; rates include breakfast, and dinner can also be arranged. Good for organizing multi-lingual guided tours of the island as well as diving excursions. Camping CH$5000. ❻

Camping Mihinoa Pont s/n ⓣ322/551593, ⓦwww.mihinoa.com. Large campsite with an excellent ocean view, run by a friendly family. Showers, kitchen facilities, dining room, internet access and car, scooter and bike rental; lack of shade is the only drawback. Adjoining guesthouse has basic, clean rooms and a five-bed dorm; it's also possible to rent tents (CH$5000). Camping/dorm CH$4000/7000. ❺

Conaf campsites at Rano Raraku and on Anakena Beach; equipped with showers, fire pits and picnic tables. Reserve at the Conaf office or tourist office.

Residencial Kona Tau Avareipua s/n ⓣ322/100321, www.hostelz.com/hostel/44363-Kona-Tau, ⓔhieasterisland@hostelling.cl. HI-affiliated hostel in a large family home with a friendly atmosphere, with sixteen comfortable dorm beds, as well as basic en-suite rooms set in a mango-strewn garden; large breakfast a bonus. Dorm CH$7500. ❸

Residencial Tahiri Ara Roa Rakei s/n ⓣ322/100570, ⓔkontutty@hotmail.com. Bungalow run by a congenial owner, featuring bright and spotless rooms and a lush garden; breakfast is included and traditional *curanto* meals can be arranged. ❻–❼

Eating, drinking and entertainment

Aloha Atamu Tekena s/n, at S. Englert. Trendy bar-restaurant serving excellent (though pricey) fish dishes; a good spot for a beer and snacks, such as Japanese *gyoza* dumplings. Evening service can be leisurely. Fish dishes CH$6000.

Café Tatvai Atamu Tekena s/n. Small, informal spot serving sandwiches and fresh fruit juices. Sandwich CH$3500.

Kai Mana Atamu Tekena s/n, opposite Tuki Haka He Vari. Ignore the unexceptional pizza on the menu and go for the succulent fish dishes. Leisurely service. Grilled fish CH$7000.

Kari Kari Atamu Tekena s/n, opposite Tuku Haka He Vari. Extremely entertaining and worthwhile dance-and-music show, featuring talented young dancers and musicians in elaborate costumes. Be warned that there is usually some audience participation. Three shows a week. Entry CH$10,000.

Kono Ai O Te Kai Plaza Policarpo Toro. Handy takeaway spot serving hot dogs, pizza and excellent *empanadas* in the evenings. *Empanada* CH$2000.

Merahi Ra'a Te Pito O Te Henua s/n. This is *the* place for large servings of expertly-prepared fish and the local speciality of *rape rape* (spiny lobster), as well as melt-in-your-mouth tuna *ceviche*. *Ceviche* CH$7000; *rape rape* CH$25,000.

Piditi Av Hotu Matua s/n, by the airport. Smaller club that gets packed with an older crowd on weekends; action kicks off after midnight. Open until 6am.

Restaurant Pea Policarpo Toro s/n, next to Playa Pea. The delicious seafood *empanadas* and other fishy offerings are complemented by the view of the surfing action. *Empanada* CH$1500.

Supermercado Kai Nene Atamu Tekena s/n, opposite Tu'u Maheke.The biggest and best-stocked supermarket in Hanga Roa.

Toroko Av Policarpo Toro s/n, near the cemetery. Popular disco with a mellow atmosphere that seems to draw all the young islanders on a Sat night.

Vai Mata Te Pito O Te Henua s/n. Inexpensive eatery serving sandwiches and light meals. Sandwich CH$3000.

Directory

Airlines LAN, Atamu Tekena s/n, at Av Pont (ⓣ322/100279).

Banks, cambios and ATMs There is only one bank on the island, Banco Estado, Tu'u Maheke

TREAT YOURSELF

La Taverne du Pêcheur, Te Pito O Te Henua s/n. Hanga Roa's most expensive restaurant serves large platters of well-cooked fish with sides of sweet potato, taro and other island tubers. The chocolate cake is excellent, too. Fish platter CH$10,000; cake CH$5000.

s/n (Mon–Fri 9am–1pm), with an adjoining ATM which only accepts Cirrus network cards. You can also change dollars or, with difficulty, get a cash advance on other credit and debit cards. Another Banco Estado ATM can be found at the gas station, at the west end of Av Hotu Matu'a. Hare Tani Moni, towards the north end of Av Atamu Tekena, changes foreign currency at poor rates. Many establishments accept US dollars and credit cards.

Car, scooter and bicycle rental Vehicles and bikes are rented by numerous agencies and private individuals; car rental costs are typically around CH$35,000 per 12hr, while bikes go for CH$8000/24hr. Most agencies and bike rentals are found along Av Atamu Tekena; Oceanic Rent a Car and Kia Koe Tour rent hardy 4WDs. There is no insurance on the island.

Festivals Tapatai Rapa Nui, a ten-day cultural celebration in mid-Feb, involving traditional dance and music, statue-carving competitions, canoe races and more, is the most popular time to visit Easter Island. Semana Santa (Easter week) has lively celebrations at Hanga Roa's Iglesia Parroquial de la Santa Cruz. The Ceremonia Culto al Sol is a feast that takes place on June 21 for the winter solstice, and Día de la Lengua Rapanui, a celebration of the Rapanui language, is held in late Nov

Hospital Hospital Hanga Roa on Simón Paoa s/n (☎322/100183), southeast of the church, has basic medical facilities.

Internet and phone Internet cafés in Hanga Roa tend to be expensive, charging upwards of CH$2000 per hr. At@net on Akamu Tekena s/n (Mon–Sat 9am–10pm, Sun 10am–10pm), doubles as a call centre and is somewhat cheaper than the competition. When dialling a Rapa Nui number, all local numbers are preceded by a "2", making them seven-digit numbers.

Laundry Lavandería Tea Nui, on Akamu Tekena s/n, opposite the *Banana Pub* (Mon–Sat 10am–1.30pm & 4–8pm).

Pharmacy Farmacía Cruz Verde, Akamu Tekena s/n, opposite Tu'u Maheke (Mon–Sat 9am–1pm & 4.30–8pm).

Post office Te Pito O Te Henua s/n (Mon–Fri 9am–1pm & 2.30–6pm).

Shopping There are two crafts markets in town: Feria Municipal, Tu'u Maheke at Atamu Tekena, and Mercado Artesanal, Tu'u Koihu at Ara Roa Rakei. Local crafts, and wood carvings in particular, tend to be expensive; a cheaper option is to seek out the local jail (off Manutara, behind the airport), as local craftsmen sometimes outsource to inmates.

Surfing and diving Surfing schools Hakangaru and Makohe, near Playa Pea, offer lessons to beginners,

EASTER ISLAND TOUR OPERATORS

There is a proliferation of tour operators in Hanga Roa, and touring the archeological sites with a knowledgeable guide, especially if you have limited time on Easter Island, can be very worthwhile. If you are not thrilled at the idea of being cooped up in a van, horseriding can be an excellent way of seeing the sites instead. A full-day car tour costs around CH$20,000, while a day's horseriding can set you back CH$38,000 or so.

Aku Aku Turismo Av Tu'u Koihu s/n ☎322/100770, Ⓦwww.akuakuturismo.cl. Established outfit offering standard guided tours of the island's sites.

Cabalgatas Pantu ☎322/100577 Ⓦwww.pantupikerauri.cl. Reputable operator offering half- and full-day horseback tours of the west and north coasts, including the ascent of Maunga Terevaka, the island's highest point. Includes grilled fish cooked in the traditional Rapa Nui manner, or *curanto*, seafood and meat slow-cooked in an earth oven.

Haumaka Archaeological Tours Puku Rangi Uka s/n ☎322/100274, Ⓦwww.haumakatours.com. Guided tours of the island's archeological sites in English, French and German, as well as horseriding tours and diving trips. They can also organize traditional Rapa Nui meals, including *curanto*.

Kia Koe Tour Atamu Tekena s/n ☎322/100852, Ⓦwww.kiakoetour.cl. Bilingual archeological tours of the island.

Piti Pont ☎322/100664 or 9/574-0582. Renowned guide running various horseriding trips around the island.

Taura'a Tours Atamu Tekena s/n ☎322/100463. Excellent operator offering full-day, small-group tours of the south coast, including Anakena Beach as well as the principal sites, or the west coast, incorporating the inland *moai* site of Ahu Akivi. English and French spoken; tailor-made tours possible.

and Hare Orca, next to the Orca Diving Centre, rents surf- and boogie boards (CH$10,000/7000). The established and reputable Orca Diving Centre on the Caleta Hanga Roa (Ⓣ322/550877 or 322/550375, Ⓦwww.seemorca.cl) and Mike Rapu Diving Centre next door (Ⓣ322/551055, Ⓦwww.mikerapu.cl) both offer a range of dives (CH$30,000–40,000).

Moving on

Boat to: Valparaíso; quarterly naval boats, returning from the island, may accept paying passengers for around CH$18,000 per day; the journey takes seven to ten days and the facilities are very basic. Contact the Comando de Transporte at the Primera Zona Naval, at Plaza Sotomayor 592, in Valparaíso (Ⓣ322/506354), for details.

Plane LAN (Ⓣ322/100279) is the only airline with commercial flights to Easter Island, with flights to Santiago every day except Mon; two on Wed, and two weekly flights, on Wed and Sun to Papeete, Tahiti. Flights to Santiago are often full, so book well in advance. Some travellers have complained that due to overbooking, they have been bumped off their return flight, so it may be worthwhile to confirm flights at Hanga Roa's LAN office or check in for the afternoon flight in the morning.

Colombia

HIGHLIGHTS

PARQUE NACIONAL TAYRONA: a paradise of white sandy beaches, falling coconuts and the sounds of howler monkeys at night

CARTAGENA'S OLD CITY: visit Spain's most enduring architectural legacy in Latin America

LA ZONA CAFETERA: stay on an authentic coffee plantation and indulge in caffeine-propelled activities

BOGOTÁ: see one of Latin America's largest collections of art at the Donación Botero museum

CALI: take partying seriously in the country's salsa capital

SAN AGUSTÍN: ponder the mystery behind the Parque Arqueológico's seven-metre statues

ROUGH COSTS

DAILY BUDGET Basic US$35/With lo-fi frills US$70

DRINK Aguardiente (big bottle to share) US$10–15

FOOD *Pargo frito con arroz con coco* (fried snapper with coconut rice) US$6

HOSTEL/BUDGET HOTEL US$15/25

TRAVEL Bogotá to Cartagena (663km): 18–19hr by bus, US$75

FACT FILE

POPULATION 44.1 million

AREA 1,141,748 sq km

LANGUAGES Spanish (official), plus various indigenous languages

CURRENCY Colombian peso (C$ or COP)

CAPITAL Bogotá, DC (Distrito Capital; population: 8.6 million)

INTERNATIONAL PHONE CODE ⓣ57

TIME ZONE GMT -5hr

Introduction

Home to a rich history, stunning scenery and some of the continent's most welcoming and sophisticated people, Colombia should be a natural draw for travellers to South America. Its reputation, however, often overshadows these assets – namely, the country's drug trade and the four-decade-long civil war, both of which create a threat of violence that hangs over many aspects of Colombian life. That said, the country is safer than it has been in decades, with the only armed personnel you're likely to encounter being the surprisingly friendly young army officers that man frequent checkpoints on main roads.

In an area roughly one-and-a-half times the size of France, Colombia – the only country in South America to border both the Pacific and the Caribbean – offers every ecosystem imaginable, from the Amazon rainforest near Leticia to the snowcapped mountains of the Sierra Nevada de Santa Marta.

Cosmopolitan **Bogotá** is, like most capitals, a busy commercial centre, one with a vibrant cultural scene and festive nightlife, as well as one of the most extensive and thoughtfully designed urban bike networks in the world.

The two other major cities, **Medellín** to the north and **Cali** to the south, are also lively but less overwhelming. Better still are the small towns scattered throughout the country that could turn out to be the highlight of your visit. **Popayán**, for example, just south of Cali, is famed for its raucous Semana Santa (Easter week) celebrations.

Most visitors make time – and rightfully so – to head north to the Caribbean for the sun. Just a stone's throw away from the beach, the walled city of **Cartagena** is the biggest Spanish colonial port in South America. A few hours east, the less-scenic **Santa Marta** is near **Parque Nacional Tayrona**, whose beachcombing is unrivalled. Santa Marta is also the base for a six-day trek to the archeological ruins of **La Ciudad Perdida**, the Lost City, an experience as overwhelming as being in Peru's Macchu Pichu (and far less visited).

Heading north from Bogotá through the Andes makes an appealing route, via the many picturesque towns on the way to **Bucaramanga**. Quaint colonial villages like **Villa de Leyva**, each with a lovely church in the town square, give way to more tropical, river-fed bastions of adventure tourism such as **San Gil**.

WHEN TO VISIT

Colombia's proximity to the Equator keeps regional **temperatures** stable throughout the year, around 24°C (75°F) along the coast and 7–17°C (45–63°F) as you move higher inland. Instead, seasons do vary in response to **rainfall**. In the Andean region there are two dry and two wet seasons per year, the driest months being December through March and then July and August. In low-lying areas, especially southern Colombia, rainfall is more constant but showers never last very long. The Amazon climate is uniformly wet the entire year. Depending on how you feel about planning ahead and crowds, the most intense tourist season, with the highest prices, is Semana Santa (Easter Week), in spring, the week before Easter.

In the southeast corner of the country, Colombia's stake of the Amazon, centred on the charming backwater town of **Leticia**, may not be as well-known as Peru's or Brazil's but it's just as lush and far more peaceful. The southwest, near Popayán, boasts some wonderful scenery perfect for hiking, as well as the enigmatic archeological ruins of **San Agustín** and **Tierradentro**.

Colombia's coffee-growing region, the **Zona Cafetera** of the central highlands near Medellín, is up-and-coming, offering walks in the foothills where the bean is grown, accommodation in authentic *fincas* and such activities as horseback riding and trekking.

CHRONOLOGY

1200 BC–1525 Indigenous cultures – including the Tayrona, Calimas, Sinú, Muisca, Pastos, Nariño, Tierradentro and San Agustín – live scattered across the country's narrow valleys and isolated cloudforests.
1525 Rodrigo de Bastides establishes the first Spanish settlement in Santa Marta, kicking off the hunt for El Dorado.
1533 The Spanish gain control of Cartagena.
1538 Spanish conquistador Gonzalo Jiménez de Quesada wrests power (and staggering amounts of gold and emeralds) from the native Chibchas and founds Santa Fe de Bogotá, now known simply as Bogotá, the nation's capital.
1717 The Spanish consolidate their colonial holdings, creating the viceroyalty of Nueva Granada from the land now occupied by the independent nations of Colombia, Ecuador, Panama and Venezuela.
1819 Simon de Bolívar overthrows Spanish rule and founds Gran Colombia, comprised of Colombia, Ecuador, Venezuela and Panama. He becomes its first President, thus fulfilling his desire for a united, independent South America.
1830 Political tensions and disputes over territory lead to the secession of Venezuela and Ecuador.
1853 Colombia adopts a constitution that includes a prohibition against slavery.
1886 New Granada is renamed Colombia, after Christopher Columbus, as a nod at the region's then-status as the New World.
1902 End of The War of a Thousand Days, the bloody three-year-long civil war born of escalated antagonism between the Conservative and Liberal political parties.
1903 With the support of the US Navy, Panama secedes from Colombia.
1948 The assassination of the working class's greatest advocate, Bogotá's populist mayor, Jorge Eliécer Gaitán, begins the massive rioting known as *El Bogotazo* which catalyzes a decade of partisan bloodletting, *La Violencia*, leaving 300,000 dead.
1953 A military coup by General Rojas Pinilo restores order.
1954 The group that would develop into Communist-linked Fuerzas Armadas Revolucionarios Colombianos (FARC) forms.
1957 Liberals and Conservatives form the Frente Nacional coalition, by which power alternated with every presidential election.
1965 Leftist National Liberation Army (ELN) and Maoist People's Liberation Army (EPL) are founded.
1984 The government intensifies efforts to do away with drug cartels, as violence by narco-trafficker death squads and left-wing terrorists escalates.
1985 Members of radical leftist guerrilla group Movimiento 19 de Abril (M-19) take over the Palace of Justice, killing eleven judges and nearly a hundred civilians.
1986 Pope John Paul II visits Colombia. A grandiose cathedral is built in preparation in Chiquinquirá.
1989 President Cesar Gaviria is elected on anti-drug platform in the wake of the murders of both the UP (Patriotic Union) and Liberal Party candidates.
1993 Drug kingpin Pablo Escobar is shot dead evading arrest.
1999 Plan Colombia, which took aim at the country's drug problem with great backing from the US, is launched.
2002 Álvaro Uribe Vélez elected president on a platform of law and order.
2008 The US and Venezuela assist in a government-orchestrated operation that frees high-profile kidnapping victims. French-Colombian Presidential candidate Ingrid Betancourt, held hostage for six years, and fifteen other captives are liberated.

Basics

ARRIVAL

Nestled smack in the middle of the country some 2800m above sea level, Bogotá is the best entry point to the country for visitors arriving **by air**.

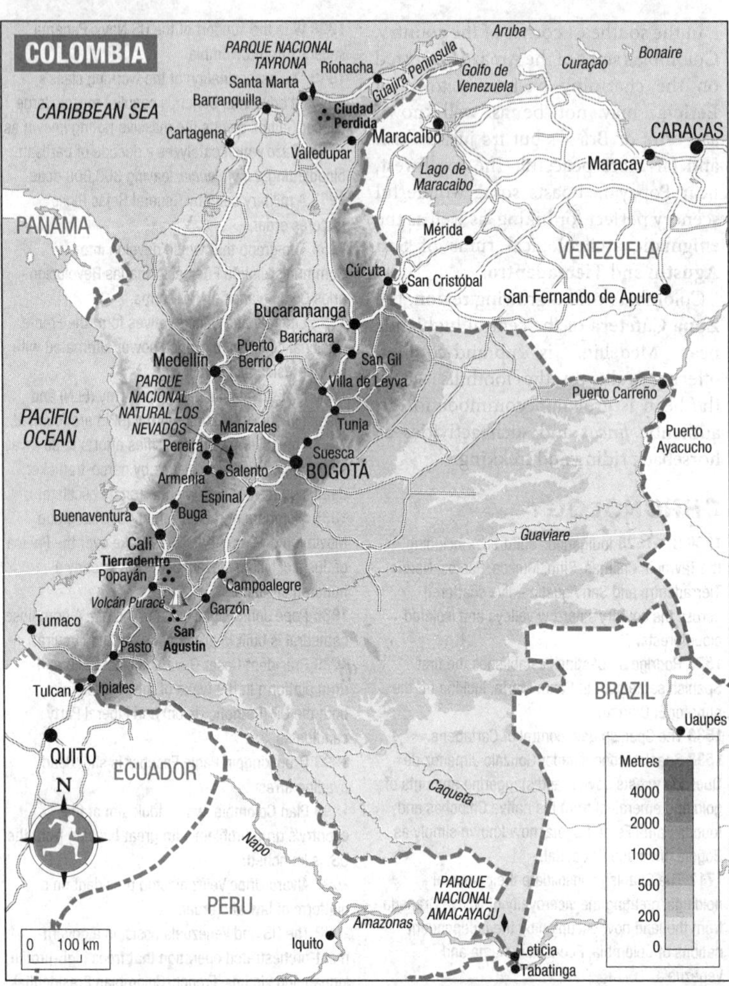

Iberia Airlines offers direct service from London and other European cities to Bogotá, and airlines such as British Airways and Air France cover the route, albeit with stopovers. Round-trip fares start around £600/US$1075. You might find cheaper flights that connect via Miami, though remember the US requires all those touching down on American soil to pass through customs, which can be time-consuming.

From the US, the competition among carriers is more intense and service more frequent, with daily flights from Miami starting around US$400. It's also possible to fly from Miami directly to Santa Marta, Cartagena and Medellín. In South America, Avianca also flies to Buenos Aires, Caracas, Guayaquil, Lima, Mexico City, Panama City, Quito, Río de Janeiro, Santiago (Chile) and São Paulo.

Overland

There are two official overland **border crossings** to and from neighbouring countries, one with Ecuador (Ipiales–Tulcán) and another with Venezuela (Cúcuta–San Antonio), both of which are open daily and don't charge taxes for entry into the country. The Venezuelan overland crossing can be dangerous. One bus company (Ormeño) covers several international routes to and from Bogotá, including Quito (US$100), Caracas (US$95) and Lima (US$150). In general, though, it's cheaper to take buses at the border and travel on more frequent national lines.

Another crossing between Venezuela and Colombia (Maico–Maracaibo) does exist. Buses here pass through the remote Guajira Peninsula between Maracaibo, Venezuela's second-largest city, and Colombian coastal cities like Santa Marta and Cartagena. It's best to travel during daylight hours as robberies have been reported. From the Amazon region it's also possible to cross to or from Colombia into Brazil and Peru by taking a ferry from Leticia. If you're travelling from Colombia and plan to return, be sure to have your passport stamped at Leticia's airport before departing.

VISAS

A passport and onward ticket (though this is checked only patchily) are the sole entry requirements for nationals of English-speaking countries.

Upon arrival, you'll normally either be ushered straight through if you're staying for less than two months or be given a **sixty-day tourist visa**, though it's possible to request up to ninety days if you have proof that you plan to stay that long. For those staying less than sixty days, no visa is issued. Once in the country, you can stay a maximum of ninety days continuously and 180 days in any single calendar year. Thirty-day **extensions** cost US$35 and can be obtained at any DAS (Departamento Administrativo de Seguridad) immigration office in Colombia. A passport photo with a white background is also required.

Airport **taxes** are sometimes assessed for international flights and vary between US$23–35. If you stay sixty days or more a tax will certainly be levied upon your departure.

GETTING AROUND

As in most aspects of daily life, Colombians prioritize **security** over price and comfort when considering their travel options; you should do the same. One golden rule is to avoid travel at night (especially given the scenery you'd be missing) or on rural roads whose security status you aren't sure of. As well, use air travel whenever possible.

By bus

Learning how to travel **by bus** in Colombia is an art perfected only over time and not really necessary for short visits. The wide range of options in comfort and quality is compounded by the size and diversity of the country, making lengthy how-tos an unwieldy proposition. Suffice to say, it's a good idea to shop around at different companies' kiosks within larger stations and place your chips based on your personal priorities. Generally, the Pullman or *lujo* categories denote larger, long-distance buses with reclining seats, air conditioning, toilets, cheesy music videos and possibly snacks for sale from a cooler. Service is usually direct and the ride comfortable, though prices tend to be higher and service less frequent. Some recommended companies are Berlinas, Expreso Bolívariano, Copetran and Flota Magdalena.

For shorter trips, you're better off sacrificing comfort and price for speed by buying a ticket on a *buesta*, *colectivo* or any similarly sized minibus or minivan that departs on demand. Within this category prices and quality fluctuate but at a minimum are the same price as Pullman service. Velotax and Taxiverde are two companies with a nationwide presence and a reputation for modern vehicles.

By car

Renting a **car** is a decent option for short distances, especially touring small towns around Bogotá, where the roads are generally safe. However, for the most part the risks of getting lost on a country road and stuck in unsafe surroundings aren't worth the risk. Several international chains operate in Bogotá and other major cities and tend to offer the same prices, starting at US$40 a day for unlimited mileage. If you are driving, be prepared for frequent roadblocks by police and the military, who are primarily there to keep the roads safe and free of guerrillas. Although the sight of young men, some still teenagers, with machine guns can be intimidating, most are friendly and more interested in making sure you're not involved in running guns than trying to squeeze small bribes out of you for imagined road violations. Driving with a foreign licence is allowed, though it's highly advisable to have an international driver's licence handy to avoid harassment.

By plane

There are three domestic commercial airlines: Avianca, serving more than twenty cities, AeroRepública, the second largest, and Aires. Avianca offers a **five-stop airpass** called Discover Colombia for travel within the country over a thirty-day period. Prices start at US$200 for three flight coupons when bought in combination with an international ticket on Avianca, nearly double in conjunction with another carrier. Although theoretically a good deal, the cumbersome restrictions and high penalties charged for changes make it worthwhile only if you plan to keep a rigid itinerary. A US$30 fee (and $30 more if your change puts you in a higher fare class) is assessed per itinerary change. Plus, some popular destinations like San Andrés and Cartagena cost US$50 extra.

Booking in advance doesn't guarantee a low fare (except during Semana Santa) so keeping your schedule open is a viable option. A one-way fare between Santa Marta and Bogotá purchased a day – or a month – in advance costs about US$220 (in high season). When travelling by plane, be sure to arrive at the airport well in advance as vigilant security controls can extend check-in times.

ACCOMMODATION

Accommodation ranges considerably, but given the country's relative prosperity you'll be pleasantly surprised at the bargains available. **Backpacker hostels** start around US$7 per person a night, and more comfortable but still modest lodgings will rarely cost you more than US$50 for a room for two, often with a private bathroom and breakfast included. Even in Cartagena and Santa Marta, just about the only parts of Colombia that survive on tourism, there are an increasing amount of **mid-range options** amid the rundown joints and plethora of overpriced high-rise hotels, though that middle strata remains the most elusive of the three.

They're the most desirable, too, since most offer Western comforts such as air conditioning, decent mattresses, private bathrooms, internet access, towels and breakfast. Often you'll find such hotels with enthusiastically decorated public gathering spaces fitted with hammocks, brightly patterned sofas, wicker furniture and perhaps a small pool. Hostels will naturally be on the more Spartan side, though they are often the best places to find out about local attractions, as well as explore them; some rent bicycles, even horses. And many do have private rooms available, as well as internet access. Camping is an option in more rural areas, and can be an affordable, fun way to meet locals (lots of high school and college students camp). Be aware that many campsites don't rent tents, so it's best to bring your own if you plan to camp regularly.

In the coffee-growing region, you can stay on one of the stately *fincas*, coffee-growing plantations that have barely changed over the decades. Though these farms range from tiny to sleek, modernized operations, the majority are small estates that offer comfortable accommodation for a moderate price (US$10–30 person). Meals prepared from locally grown food as well as numerous outdoor activities, like farm tours and horseback riding, are often included or available.

FOOD AND DRINK

Whether it's a platter full of starch or a suckling pig stuffed with rice, Colombian **food** is anything but light. Not even the heat of the coast seems to infringe on the country's obsession with fried foods.

The carbo-loading begins with breakfast, which usually consists of *huevos pericos*, scrambled eggs with onion and tomatoes, accompanied by a fried maize pancake known as an *arepa* or a *tamale* stuffed with chopped pork, rice, potatoes and anything else under the sun.

The most important meal of the day is the midday *almuerzo* or *comida corriente*, consisting of soup, a main course and dessert. Dinners, after 6pm, are somewhat lighter but also consist of chicken or meat.

In Bogotá and other major cities there's a high supply of fashionable restaurants of the same quality you'd expect in any major European or US city but at a fraction of the price. Bogotá also offers an excellent array of Western and international cuisine, especially Arabic foods.

Local specialities

Traditionally each region in Colombia had its own local speciality, though now many are available across the country. One of the most widespread is the *bandeja paisa*, which consists of a cafeteria-sized tray filled to the brim with ground beef, *chorizo* sausage, beans (*frijoles*), rice, fried banana (*plátano*), a fried egg, avocado and fried pork. You can usually find one served at inexpensive **market stalls** known as *fondas*, or at restaurants catering to local palates.

In rural areas, vegetarians will be hard-pressed for entrees, but medium and large cities cook up a decent spread of vegetarian dishes, with savoury crêpes and pastas being the most regular menu items. Many restaurants also whip up excellent *cremas*, which are simple pureed vegetable soups and usually don't contain dairy.

One of the tastiest Colombian dishes is *ajiaco*, a thick chicken stew replete with vegetables, maize, three types of potato, cream, capers and sometimes avocado. Despite its peppery-sounding name (*aji* is Spanish for chilli peppers), it's a surprisingly mild dish, ideally suited for the high Andean climate around Bogotá. *Mazamorra* is a similar meat and vegetable soup but with beans and corn flour. Both are often served with a *patacón*, a mashed and heavily salted cake of fried *plátano*. Don't leave Colombia without trying one.

The most sophisticated of the regional specialities, not for the fainthearted, is called *hormigas culonas*, which consists of fried black ants and comes from Bucaramanga and the Santander area. In Cali and southern Colombia, grilled guinea pig, known as *cuy* or *curí*, is popular. On the coast, fish – especially shellfish and whitefish, like *pargo* (snapper) – is more common and often served with aromatic *arroz con coco*, rice with coconut. Rotisserie chicken is also widely consumed.

TROPICAL FRUIT

Dotting the country's streets are vendors who will happily blend drinks for you from the juicy bounty in their baskets. Some of the varieties below are especially good with milk, some tastier with the standard ice and sugar. Contamination concerns are largely unfounded, as the water used in the fruit drinks comes from a bag: filtered water packaged in thin plastic instead of a bottle.

Corozo A round, maroon-skinned fruit, not unlike a cranberry in tartness and robust flavour. A building block of a bracing breakfast.

Cuyabaná A pulpy, yellow fruit that tastes like a milder guava, with a refreshing touch of grapefruit. Perfect antidote to humid afternoons.

Lulo Resembling a vivid yellow persimmon, this tangy fruit ranks among the most popular with Colombians. Perfectly balanced sweet and tartness make for a delicious taste.

Mora Close cousin of the blackberry.

Níspero Also known as *zapote*, this combination of pear and and papaya is intensely rich and musky, and goes great with milk.

Sandía A sunnier term for watermelon.

Tomate de árbol Literally, "tree tomato," this orange-red fruit blurs the line between fruit and vegetable, being sharp and only faintly sweet. A common breakfast juice.

Zapote Though resembling a wrinkly sweet potato, this luscious orange fruit's uncanny resemblance to sherbet is confirmed by the tendency of some locals to freeze its pulp to eat as dessert.

Drinking

For a country that produces some of the world's finest grinds, **coffee** is of a remarkably poor quality in most places other than speciality cafés. In any case, the only thing Colombians have adopted from the art of espresso making is the *demitasse* cup, from which they drink heavily sugared, watered-down black coffee known as *tinto*. Colombians also consume large amounts of herbal infusions, called **aromáticas**, made from plants like *yerbabuena* (mint) and *manzanilla* (camomile). A good combatant against altitude sickness is *agua de panela*, hot water with unrefined sugar.

If there's one item you'll pine for when you've returned home it's Colombia's exotic variety of **fresh fruit juices**, found especially on the coast at as little as 25 cents a glass. Many are completely foreign to western palates and lack English translations. Worth trying are *guanábana*, *lulo*, mango, *fraijoa*, *maracuyá*, *mora* and *guayaba*.

While **beer** is reasonably good – and sometimes cheaper than water – and inexpensive in Colombia (try light, fizzy lagers like Dorado, Club and Aguila), the locally produced wine tends to be of the boxed variety. Far more popular among locals is the anise-flavoured *aguardiente*, pure grain alcohol, and rum (called *ron*), both of which are drunk straight-up. Each *departamento* akes pride in its particular variant of the former, most commonly referred to as *guaro* (GWAR-ooh). Brave souls won't want to pass up any offer to try *chicha*, a frothy moonshine found in rural areas made with the fermenting enzyme found in saliva.

CULTURE AND ETIQUETTE

As in much of South America, family plays a central, guiding role in the lives of Colombians of all socioeconomic levels. You'll find Colombians to be quite courteous; when visiting someone's home, it is customary to bring a small gift, such as chocolates or flowers.

When it comes to **table manners**, common-sense rules apply: no elbows on the table, be free with compliments regarding the food and eat with decorum. Westerners will note that sincerity in expression, often expressed via good eye contact, is valued more highly than the typical steady stream of pleases and thank yous.

Tipping about ten percent at mid-range restaurants is the norm, though some Colombians don't tip at all. As a general rule of thumb, the nicer the establishment, the greater the tip expected (topping out at about fifteen percent), though check to see if the tip has already been included, as is sometimes done at more touristy cafés and restaurants. For reasonably short taxi trips, US$0.50 is adequate. The best way to show your appreciation can be to take the driver's phone number and call him when next you need a ride.

The **machismo** often ascribed to Latin American culture is largely absent from Colombia, and there is some flexibility – and contradiction – in views toward gender and sexual orientation. Young straight men tote traditionally woven bags across their chests, but *marica* (poof) is among the most common insults. Gay clubs catering largely to men are common, especially in bigger towns like Bogotá and Santa Marta. Otherwise, the country's Catholic roots run quite deep and are apparent in sexual attitudes among both men and women.

There is a good deal of variety regarding formality of dress, with skin-tight leggings and shoulder-baring tank tops as ubiquitous as more elegant daywear. If you feel good in what you're wearing, you're not likely to turn heads for the wrong reasons.

SPORTS, OUTDOORS AND OCEAN ACTIVITIES

Adventurers might hyperventilate when they discover Colombia. From almost every vantage point in Colombia

LOCAL SLANG

Colombians take much joy in their particular style of linguistic acrobatics and slang. Using typical words and phrases is sure to get you a smile – perhaps of the incredulous variety. Keep in mind that, like most Spanish speakers, Colombians freely convert verbs to nouns and vice-versa, so take each word as a fluid concept to be tailored to your communicational wants. A Spanish language primer can be found on p.1008.

Un camello (n), **Camellar** (v) work, or working. A good way to refer to a particularly trying task.

La/Una chimba (adj) Used to describe a situation or thing that is wonderful. Roughly synonymous with the youthful American usage of "awesome." Variations include: "Qué chimba!" (Right on!/Nice!).

Chucha (n.) Body odour. A crass but still usable term.

Elegante (adj.): "Cool," loosely. Used to describe the subset of cool things – or happenings – that's particularly classy, well-executed or, well, elegant. Think soccer passes or a good outfit. *Chevere, bacán* are other words for "cool".

Paila (adj) "That really sucks." Used in response to a comment or situation that's aggressively bad or heavy.

Perico (n) Cocaine.

Al pelo (adj.) Common response to a question like "How was your day?" that means "Good!" or "Perfect!" Another common way to express the same sentiment is by saying *Todo bien* ("It's all good").

COLOMBIA ON THE NET

Ⓦ **www.turismocolombia.com** Colombia's official tourism site, with plenty of photos, good background and some practical information.

Ⓦ **www.colombia.com** A mega-portal with links to the most popular Colombian websites.

Ⓦ **www.poorbuthappy.com** Expat website with answers to all the questions you were afraid to ask and forums for travellers to exchange recommendations.

Ⓦ **www.vivatravelguides.com/south-america/colombia/** The best of the online travel guides

Ⓦ **www.eltiempo.com** Colombia's newspaper of record (in Spanish).

Ⓦ **www.colombiahotels.travel** Focuses on geographical features and cultural history as much as hotels.

Ⓦ **www.hosteltrail.com/colombia** Budget accommodations and local attractions.

there's a snowcapped peak to climb, an untamed river to ride or some sunken coral reef to explore. Though many of the country's most impressive cliffs and shorelines are off-limits because of the ongoing civil war, the areas open to the public should provide more than enough adventure to satisfy even the most hardened adrenaline addict.

Football is the national sport and Colombians have a reputation as being some of South America's most skilled if untidy players. Going to see any of the big teams play in Bogotá, Medellín or Cali is an unforgettable experience.

The mountainous land here is made for rugged **cycling**. After coffee and drugs, cyclists are probably Colombia's best-known export, and Santiago Botero, a consistent top-ten finisher in the Tour de France, is a national hero even though he now trains in Spain because of repeated kidnapping threats.

Among the most popular activities for adventure travellers is **scuba diving**. Colombia's waters may not be the most impressive place in the world to learn, but they might be around the cheapest. All along its three thousand kilometres of coastline, but especially near Santa Marta and the Caribbean islands, operators offer week-long PADI certification courses for under US$260. Snorkelling and sailing are two other popular waterborne activities.

There is a bracing concentration of Class II–IV rapids thanks to the many rivers in the *departamento* of Santander – three intersect near San Gil – that are gaining attention from **river-rafting** enthusiasts (see p.562).

COMMUNICATIONS

Sending a postcard or a **letter** abroad can be done for about US$1 from almost anywhere in the country, using Colombia's Correos de Colombia. Standard service isn't reliable, however, and packages or important documents should be sent *certificado* (certified mail) or through one of the international couriers available in major cities.

Local phone calls cost around five cents, and phonecards are commonly sold at local kiosks in denominations of as little as US$1. **Long-distance calls** are best made using the cell phone of someone selling their minutes piecemeal, a widespread practice that's delightfully Colombian in its rogue capitalism. Look for any sign – and they are often scrawled crazily in marker on a piece of cardboard in front of an unlikely doorway – including the word "minutos." The person you speak with will be happy to lend you their cell phone for about $0.50 a minute. A more formal and less ubiquitous alternative is to visit one of the call centres called *telecentros* – you can choose between Orbitel (code 05), ETB (07) and Telecom (09) before dialling the country code or national area code (*indicitavo*) followed by the local number.

Cybercafés can be found even in small towns, though fast **internet connections** are only available in big cities. Rates start around US$2 per hour.

CRIME AND SAFETY

There's an undeniable basis for being cautious about a trip to Latin America's fourth largest nation. As the US Department of State pointed out in 2008, "while security in Colombia has improved significantly in recent years, violence by narco-terrorist groups continues to affect some rural areas and cities." Still, stepped-up efforts by the government have struck major blows to the country's major rebel groups, FARC (Fuerzas Armadas Revolucioanrios Colombianos) and ELN (Ejército Liberación Nacional), though the government has been criticized for using techniques as dirty as those employed by the rebels and not cracking down hard enough on the ultra-conservative paramilitary groups.

Statistics on the country can be quite sobering, despite vast improvements: the per-capita murder rate is five times higher in Colombia than in North America, higher still when compared to Western Europe. On top of typical **street crime**, there's the additional threat posed by guerrillas, vigilante right-wing paramilitary groups and narcotraffickers. As with most politically volatile countries, the traveller would be wise to take care with whom they talk to, and about what – it's no surprise Colombia ranks in the top ten in Robert Young Pelton's *The World's Most Dangerous Places*.

THE URIBE GOVERNMENT

The election in 2002 of **Álvaro Uribe** on a law-and-order platform has rekindled hopes that the government may yet put an end to the cycle of violence. The Colombian government has turned to the US for help in tipping the military balance in their favour in the hopes of negotiating a settlement from a position of strength. Under **Plan Colombia**, launched in 1999 but intensified under Uribe, the US has committed US$1.6 billion in foreign aid, most of it to the military, to root out illegal drug trafficking and the guerrilla protectors that allow it to blossom.

Uribe's strategy has proved immensely popular, both at home with war-weary Colombians and with the US.

Plan Colombia, intended to eradicate the growing of **coca**, is one element of Colombia's own efforts to quash guerrilla groups like the FARC and ELN. Thanks in part to government efforts to woo guerrillas back to society with a well-advertised "reinsertion" program, these groups are weaker than they've been in twenty years. The string of international incidents that resulted in the deaths of the FARC's two top leaders in 2008 and the brilliantly staged and well-publicized liberation of former Presidential candidate Ingrid Betancourt have also done a great deal to weaken the spirit as much as the size of rebel organizations.

At the same time, the high cost of fighting the war is sapping scarce resources from the government coffers and forcing Uribe to adopt some unpopular economic belt tightening.

It's the collateral damage wreaked by the clash between the right-wing paramilitaries and the left-wing rebels – criminals both – that has created the most ongoing devastation in the lives of average Colombians. The farmers and rural peoples caught in the crossfire have been forced from their homes in such numbers that only Sudan has more internally displaced people. It remains to be seen how long Uribe can retain popular faith in his leadership without inciting his backers to take an even more heavy-handed, unilateral approach.

Things are at least moving in the right direction. **Kidnappings** have declined a dramatic eighty percent from their peak of 3572 in 2000. And while it's a small reassurance, most tourists have not been targeted specifically by any of the actors in the country's civil war; both the FARC and ELN are incredibly sensitive to bad press. Certain areas should be avoided altogether, including the *departamentos* of Chocó, Meta, Caqueta, Putumayo and Arauca. **Rural areas only** (cities are fine) of Antioquia, Cauca, Nariño, Magdalena, and Norte de Santander were also considered potentially dangerous at press time. Most guerrilla activity is confined to rural areas near the border with Panama and Venezuela, as well as the low-lying *Llanos* dominating the country's eastern half. If you are crossing into Venezuela by land, take care, and minimize your time in Cúcuta. Though all major Colombian cities have achieved marked reductions in crime, Cali, in the southwest, has had the most modest dip. Heading too far off the beaten path poses additional risks – be sure to stay abreast of current events and consult local authorities to assess the safety of any planned excursion. For up-to-date travel advice check ⓦwww.travel.state.gov/colombia or ⓦwww.fco.gov.uk.

Note, too, that drug-related violence has all but disappeared. Rather than be caught in the crossfire of rival gangs, the only contact you're likely to have with Colombia's drug war is if your hotel room is raided by police or during a random interrogation before boarding your plane home. To protect yourself, don't transport any sealed packages for your new Colombian friends. Common sense and standard procedures for avoiding theft apply.

MEDICAL CARE AND EMERGENCIES

All major cities have **hospitals** and offer medical services. In the case of serious health issues, you may be transferred to a larger hospital with more specialized doctors and facilities. Simply dial 1-2-3 on any phone for all health and security concerns. You will be connected to the National Police who will ask a few basic questions before dispatching help. For less time-sensitive issues, contacting your country's embassy for help is advised.

MONEY AND BANKS

Colombia's national currency is the **peso (COP)**, divided into 100 centavos. You'll find in circulation coins of 50, 100, 200, 500 and 1000 pesos and notes of 1000, 2000, 5000 10,000, 20,000 and 50,000 pesos. As elsewhere in Latin America, changing large bills can be problematic.

The easiest way to obtain cash is through **ATM machines**, which you'll find pretty much everywhere. Check with your bank regarding fees for withdrawing funds abroad, which can be anywhere from two to fifteen percent. For exchanging dollars or other currencies, *casas de cambio* offer similar rates, have more flexible hours and provide quicker service than most banks. Traveller's cheques can also be exchanged at *casas de cambios* and banks – though sometimes only in the morning – but are generally frowned upon by most businesses other than hotels. Changing money on the street is not recommended. A byproduct of Colombia's burgeoning drug trade is the glut of illegally laundered dollars circulating in the country, a phenomenon that has lowered the demand for cash dollars. You're likely to get a **better exchange rate** paying with a credit card than you are exchanging dollars.

With the drop in the value of the US dollar, Colombia's prices are not much below those of a mid-sized American city though British travellers and those using the Euro will find prices relatively inexpensive by Western European standards. Your **largest expense** is likely to be transportation, as Colombia is a big country. Still, there's stiff competition in road transport and most bus ticket prices can be negotiated down easily. Rising fuel costs worldwide have caused a surge in the price of domestic airfares, though they remain enticing given how many of the country's main routes take upwards of eighteen hours.

Food isn't notably inexpensive outside of Cartagena and Bogotá, but you can save if your stomach can withstand the *comida corriente* served at cheaper restaurants. A typical meal costs no more than US$4, but for lighter, healthier meals expect to pay more. For a standard meal, modest lodging and sightseeing, it's possible to survive on less than US$35 a day.

INFORMATION AND MAPS

Colombia's **official tourist board** has been contracted out to the privately owned El Fondo de Promoción Turística. Despite the significant rise in tourism to Colombia in the past five or six years, the Fondo's sole office in Bogotá, at Cra 16A No. 78–55, office 604 (Ⓣ1/611-4330, Ⓦwww.turismocolombia.com), focuses more on promoting Colombia abroad than it does assisting travellers inside the country. Still, the staff is helpful, and visitors who show up during weekday office hours will be rewarded with plentiful brochures and a free copy of an English-language guidebook and road atlas. Almost every town boasts a tourist office, though their relative merit varies.

There are a good number of quality **roadmaps** available. The *Auto Guia,* updated annually, and available in bookstores for US$14, has detailed departmental maps with hotels and attractions listed. The best guidebook available (Spanish only) is the annually updated *Guía de Rutas*, which costs about US$15 and can be found in tourism offices in larger cities. The book is divided up into potential road-trip routes, but offers extensive local listings despite the uniformly gushing prose.

CALENDAR OF PUBLIC HOLIDAYS

Note that when holidays do not fall on a Monday, the public holiday is often moved to the following Monday.

January 1 New Year's Day
January 6 Día de Reyes
March 21 St Joseph's Day
March or April Easter
May 1 Labour Day
May 9 Ascension Day
May 30 Corpus Christi
June 29 Saint Peter and Saint Paul
July 20 Independence Day
August 7 Battle of Boyacá
August 15 Assumption
October 12 Columbus's arrival in the New World
November 1 All Saints' Day
November 11 Independence of Cartagena
December 8 Immaculate Conception
December 25 Christmas

OPENING HOURS AND FIESTAS

Most shops open early at 8am until 6pm Monday through Friday. Many businesses also often open Saturday until mid-afternoon. Outside Bogotá it's common for businesses to close at noon for a two- or three-hour siesta. Commercial hours in cities in warmer areas such as Cali often get started and end earlier. Government offices often follow the same pattern. Banks tend to open around 9am and close at 4pm, though *casas de cambio* stay open later.

Barranquilla's two-week long Carnaval, second in importance in Latin America after Río's, kicks off in the last half of February.

Bogotá and around

At first glance Colombia's capital, **SANTA FÉ DE BOGOTÁ**, looks as drab and unwelcoming as any other ringed-in Andean capital. Name your urban ill – poverty, gridlock traffic, crime and choking smog – this overcrowded city of 7.5 million suffers from it in excess. But within the otherwise grim snapshot of modern-day Latin America lie some of the continent's most impressive examples of colonial architecture and art, and a cultural scene among the most vibrant in South America.

Situated on the **Sabana de Bogotá**, Colombia's highest plateau at 2600m, the city was founded on August 6, 1538 by Gonzalo Jiménez de Quesada in what was a former citadel belonging to the Muisca king **Bacatá**, for whom the city's name is derived. It served as the capital of the new Viceroyalty of Nueva Granada in 1740 and, after Independence, remained the seat of authority of the Gran Colombia confederation then of Colombia proper.

Despite its political influence, Bogotá was long neglected. Scarce transport links with the rest of the country kept the population down throughout the early republic era, and as late as the 1940s the city had just 300,000 inhabitants. The balance tipped in the 1940s and 50s with the advent of civil war and the mass exodus of peasant families from the war-torn countryside. Industrialization was a further magnet.

Today, Bogotá is South America's fourth largest city as well as one of its most modern and cosmopolitan. Apart from Buenos Aires, there may be no other place on the continent with such a wide variety of gourmet restaurants and chic, all-night clubs. Moreover, because so few visitors come to Bogotá, residents go out of their way to be hospitable – even though within Colombia, *cachacos*, as residents of Bogotá are known, have somewhat of a reputation for being cold, uptight and arrogant.

What to see and do

The city's historic centre, **La Candelaria**, full of colourfully painted colonial residences, occupies an area that begins at Plaza de Bolívar and stretches northward to Avenida Jiménez de Quesada and is bordered by Carrera 10 to the west and the mountains to the east. **Downtown Bogotá** is the waning commercial centre, with several museums and office buildings, while **North Bogotá**, a catchall term for the wealthier neighbourhoods at the north of the centre, offers stylish shopping districts and gourmet ghettos.

Plaza de Bolívar

The heart of La Candelaria is **Plaza de Bolívar**, between calles 10 and 11 and carreras 7 and 8, the site of a number of monumental buildings and disparate architectural styles spanning more than four centuries. The district is renowned for its churches (see box, p.550), few more historic than Bogotá's **Catedral**,

> **A WORD ON GETTING AROUND**
>
> Getting around Bogotá – and all Colombian cities for that matter – is facilitated by a foolproof **numbering system**, derived from the original Spanish grid layout, that makes finding an address virtually arithmetic. The names of the streets indicate their direction: **calles** run at right angles to the hills, from east to west, while **carreras** run from north to south. Addresses are a function of both with the prefix indicating the cross street. For example, the address Cra 73 No. 12–20 can be found on Carrera 73 between calles 12 and 13.

bordering the concrete plaza, completed in 1823. Its opulent gold-laced interior is a tribute to the Baroque religious art popular during the colonial era. To the cathedral's left stands the Neoclassical **Capital**. While its imposing colonnaded stone facade is impressive, the interior is now strictly off limits to tourists because of security concerns – Congress meets here. On the plaza's north side, the modern **Palacio de Justicia** was reconstructed in 1999 after

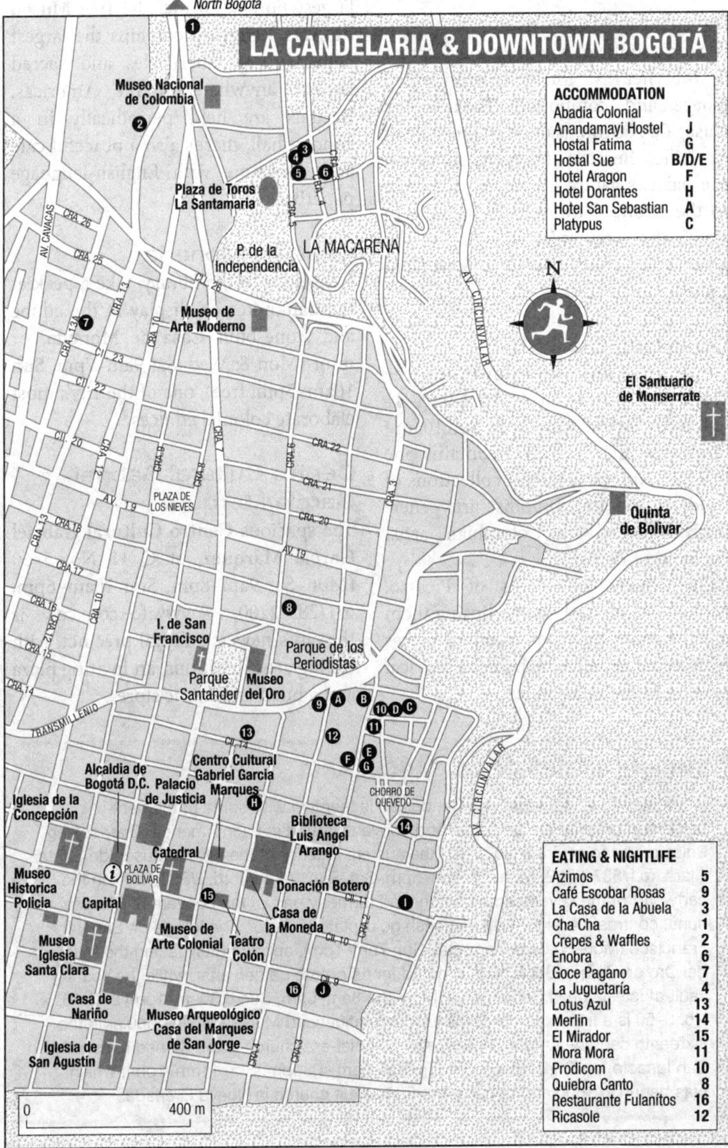

the original was damaged during the Army's much-criticized storming of the building in 1985, in response to the M19 guerrilla group taking it over. More than a hundred people, including twelve Supreme Court justices, were killed in the raid.

Palacio (or Casa) de Nariño

A block south of the plaza on Carrera 8 the heavily fortified presidential palace and compound, **Palacio (or Casa) de Nariño**, is done in the style of Versailles. Because of security concerns, the palace's gaudy interior is not open to the public. However, it's possible to watch the ceremonial changing of the guard three times a week at 5pm from the adjacent streets.

Donación Botero

Housed in a fine colonial mansion, the **Donación Botero** at C 11 No. 4–41 (Mon & Wed–Sat 9am–7pm, Sun 10am–5pm; free; ⓣ1/343-1212) contains one of Latin America's largest collections of modern and Impressionist art, generously donated by Colombian artist Fernando Botero.

On display are works of Picasso, Monet, Renoir and Dali; eclipsing them are the more than one hundred pieces by Botero himself, which offer a satirical take on human plumpness.

Biblioteca Luis Angel Arango

In front of the Donación Botero stands the thoroughly modern **Biblioteca Luis Angel Arango** (Mon–Sat 8am–8pm, Sun 8am–4pm; ⓣ1/343-1212, ⓦwww.lablaa.org), reputedly South America's largest library. Inside, the free **Museo de Arte Religioso** contains the largest collection of tabernacles and sacred goblets anywhere in the Americas. Recitals are held periodically in a concert hall; there's also a peaceful café and bookstore with English-language paperbacks.

Casa de Moneda

Next door to the library, take a peek at the banknotes on display at the adobe and stone-built **Casa de Moneda**, or mint (Mon & Wed–Sat 9am–7pm, Sun 10am–5pm; free), one of the city's most elaborate colonial edifices.

Centro Cultural Gabriel García Márquez

The spacious **Centro Cultural Gabriel García Márquez**, at C 11 No. 5–60 (Mon–Sat 9am–8pm, Sun 10am–6pm; ⓣ1/283-2200, ⓦwww.fce.com.co), is the city's newest cultural precinct, with rolling art exhibitions, an inviting plaza and a book and music store.

THE CHURCHES OF LA CANDELARIA

In addition to its cathedral, La Candelaria is teeming with some of the best-preserved colonial-era churches and convents found in Latin America. Overlooking Palacio Nariño at Cra 8 No. 8–91, the austere exterior of the Iglesia Museo de Santa Clara (ⓣ1/337-6762; Mon–Fri 9am–5pm, Sat–Sun 10am–4pm; US$1), built in the early part of the seventeenth century and formerly part of the convent of Clarissa nuns, contrasts sharply with its garish gold-plated interior. The Iglesia de San Francisco (Mon–Fri 6am–7pm, Sat–Sun 7am–1pm), appropriately facing the Museo del Oro on Parque Santander, is noted for its ornate golden altar, while the soaring vault at Iglesia de la Concepción (Mon–Sat 8am–6pm, Sun 6.30am–1pm) at C 10 No. 9–50 is a fine example of the Moorish-influenced Mudéjar style popular in the sixteenth century. Another noteworthy colonial-era church is the domed Iglesia de San Ignacio, on C 10 No. 6–35 (Mon–Sat, 9am–4.30pm, Sun 11am–1pm), which was begun in 1605 and became the first Jesuit church in Nueva Grenada.

Museo Arqueológico

For an overview of pre-Columbian cultures visit the **Museo Arqueológico**, Cra 6 No. 7–43 (Tues–Fri 8.30am–5pm, Sat 9.30am–5pm, Sun 10am–4pm; US$1.70; ⓣ1/243-0465, ⓦwww.museoarqueologico.com), which is housed in a restored colonial townhouse.

Museo de Arte Colonial

The impressive **Museo de Arte Colonial** (Tues–Fri 9am–5pm, Sat & Sun 10am–4pm; ⓣ1/341-6017; US$1.70), Cra 6 No. 9–77, has some three thousand items on display, including fine colonial-era paintings, sculptures and furniture.

Museo Histórico Policía

The **Museo Histórica Policía**, C 9 No. 9–27 (Tues–Sun 8am–5pm; ⓣ1/233-5911), features the uniforms and weaponry of Colombia's crime-fighters. The entire basement is given over to a display on the notorious 499-day police hunt for murderous drug lord Pablo Escobar; English-speaking police offer free guided tours.

Plazoleta del Chorro de Quedevo

Nowhere is La Candelaria's grittier, bohemian side better captured than on the streets surrounding the **Plazoleta del Chorro de Quevedo**, at C 13 and Cra 2. Scholars say the tiny plaza was the site of the first Spanish settlement, though the tiled-roof colonial chapel on the southwest corner was built much later.

Monserrate

Perched above La Candelaria is the rocky outcrop known as **Cerro de Monserrate**, an obvious landmark. The hilltop, crowned by **El Santuario de Monserrate** church, offers spectacular views back down on the city. It is easily reached by frequent *teleférico* cable car (Mon–Sat noon–midnight, Sun 6am–6pm; US$7 return, $4 Sun) or by funicular railway (Mon–Sat 7.45am–11.45pm, Sun 6.30am–4.30pm; ⓣ1/284-5700, US$7 return, $4 on Sun) up the road from the Quinta de Bolívar (see below). Alternatively it's an hour-and-a-half trek along a stoned path that begins at the base of the hill and leads to the summit 600 metres above. If you go on foot, leave all but essentials at the hotel as tourists are frequently robbed here. The **safest time** to go is Sunday, when you'll be accompanied by thousands of pilgrims hoping for miracles from the church's dark-skinned Christ. Atop are snack bars and a few pricey **restaurants**, including the French-inspired *Casa San Isidro* (ⓣ1/281-9309, mains around US$29).

Casa Museo Quinta de Bolívar

At the foot of Monserrate is the **Casa Museo Quinta de Bolívar** (Tues–Fri 9am–4.30pm, Sat & Sun 10am–3.30pm; US$1.70; ⓣ1/284-6819, ⓦwww.quintaBolívar.gov.co), a spacious colonial mansion where Simón Bolívar lived from 1820–1829. The informative museum retells the story of Bolívar's final, desperate days in power before being banished by his political rivals. One object you won't find among the plethora of "El Libertador" paraphernalia is the sword he used to free the continent from four centuries of Spanish rule. It was stolen in 1974 from the collection containing his bedpan, military medals and billiard table in what is the now legendary debut of urban guerrilla group **M-19**. When they handed in its arsenal in 1991, the sword was quickly shuttled into the vaults of the Banco República for fear of another embarrassing burglary.

Museo del Oro

On the northeast corner of **Parque de Santander**, at Cra 6 and C 16, is the must-see **Museo del Oro**, or Gold

Museum (Tues–Sat 9am–4.30pm, Sun 10am–4.30pm; US$3; ⓣ1/343-2221, ⓦwww.banrep.gov.co/museo). Most of Colombia's gold was hauled away by its Spanish plunderers, but the leftover scraps were still sizeable enough to assemble the world's largest collection of auriferous ornaments, some 35,000 pieces strong, not all of which are on exhibition. A maze of informative displays on Colombia's indigenous cultures culminates in the Salón Dorado, where eight thousand gold objects dazzle in an otherwise pitch-dark bank vault brought to life by Andean pipe music and moody jungle sounds. Self-guided audio tours in English are available for a fee.

Museo Nacional de Colombia

As exhaustive as the Museo de Oro, the **Museo Nacional de Colombia**, Cra 7 at C 28 (Tues–Sat 10am–6pm, Sun 10am–5pm; US$1.60; ⓣ1/334-8366, ⓦwww.museonacional.gov.co), provides a detailed look at the country's tumultuous history. The converted jailhouse's most impressive exhibits relate to the conquest and the origins of the beguiling El Dorado myth that so obsessed Europe. The second floor houses an extensive collection of paintings by modern Colombian artists, including Fernando Botero.

Museo de Arte Moderno

The **Museo de Arte Moderno**, C 24 at Cra 6 (Tues–Sat 10am–6pm & Sun noon–5pm; US$0.50; ⓣ1/286-0466, ⓦwww.mambogota.com), contains six rooms of contemporary Colombian art, the largest collection in the country; there's also a *cinemeteca* here that projects art films.

Plaza de Toros La Santamaría

The **Plaza de Toros La Santamaría** on Carrera 6, two blocks north of the Museo de Arte Moderno, is the Moorish-style bullring where the Temporadas Taurinas take place each January and February with the enthusiastic support of well-heeled *cachacos*. If the blood-spattered spectacle seems repugnant, you can join the loud protesters that gather beyond the police barricades before each "match". Tours of the complex are given on weekdays (9.30am–12.30pm & 2–5pm, ⓣ1/334-1482).

North Bogotá

North of Calle 60, the museums peter out and are replaced by leafy neighbourhoods peppered with gourmet restaurants, lively bars and modern shopping malls. An exception is the cobblestoned *barrio* of **Usaquen**, which was a small village before being swallowed up by the capital's expansion. On weekends the central plaza hosts the **Mercado de las Pulgas** antiques fair. To get to Usaquen, catch a bus heading north along Carrera 7.

Arrival

By air Most international flights land at El Dorado International Airport, 14km northwest of the city centre, though some use Puente Aéreo domestic terminal, a kilometre away. A taxi downtown costs about US$10 – be sure to buy a ticket at one of the authorized stands instead of arranging directly with the driver, who's likely to charge you more. Bus rides into town cost less than US$1 and can take about an hour. Just beyond the baggage claim in El Dorado there's a city-run tourist stand that can supply you with brochures and advice on buses.

By bus The mammoth-sized long-distance bus terminal, Terminal de Transportes (ⓣ1/428-2424, ⓦwww.terminaldetransportes.gov.co), is on the southwest edge of Bogotá near Av Boyacá (C 72) between El Dorado (Av 26) and Av Centenario (C 13). It's divided into four hubs, serving destinations north, south, east or west of the city. To the centre, a taxi costs about US$7.50. You can also get into town by hailing any *buseta* from Cra 10 or *micro* along Cra 7, marked "Terminal".

Information and tours

National park information For up-to-date safety information on Colombia's 51 national parks and protected areas, visit the eco-tourism office of Unidad de Parques Nacionales at Cra 10 No. 20–30 fourth floor (ⓣ1/243-3095, ⓦwww.parquesnacionales.gov.co).

Publications Be sure to pick up a copy of *Plan B*, a monthly publication listing cultural events, restaurants, theatres and the like. On Fri, Bogotá's leading newspaper, *El Tiempo*, publishes a weekend entertainment guide.

Tourist information Bogotá's tourist bureau produces helpful guides, many in English, to the city's main churches, museums and other historical attractions. There are small informational stands at the airport and bus station and an excellent and centrally located one on the southwest corner of Plaza Bolívar (Mon–Sat 8am–6pm, Sun 10am–4pm; ⓣ1/283-7115) at Cra 8 No. 10–65. The main office of the Instituto Distrital de Cultura y Turismo (Mon–Fri 8am–5pm; ⓣ1/245-6328, ⓦwww.bogotaturismo.gov.co) is inside the vast public recreation space Parque Nacional Olaya Herrera at Cra 5, No. 36–21, first floor, but they are not overly helpful.

Tour operators Ecoguías, Cra 7 No. 57–39 office 501 (call first for appointment) ⓣ1/212-1423 or 347-5736, ⓦwww.ecoguias.com; Sal Si Puedes, Cra 7 No. 17-01 office 739 ⓣ1/283-3765, ⓦwww.salsipuedes.org.

City transport

Most sightseeing can be done **on foot**, as the bulk of Bogotá's tourist attractions are in or near one neighbourhood: La Candelaria.

By bus For moving around the city your best public transport option is the clean and efficient Trans-Milenio (5am–11pm), an electrically driven bus system that costs US$0.75 no matter the journey. The most popular line follows Av Caracas from La Candelaria all the way to the city's northern edge, El Portal del Norte.

Crowded and more confusing to the uninitiated, but covering a wider range of routes, are gas-guzzling *busetas*, which charge around US$0.50 per ride. Take note that Carrera 7 is closed off to southbound traffic every Sun so that the street can be enjoyed by pedestrians, joggers, cyclists and rollerbladers.

By taxi Taxis in Bogotá are relatively inexpensive, with a trip across the city costing about US$10. They are yellow, all have meters and levy a small surcharge at night; be sure to check the fare table before paying as some drivers overcharge. At night, it's better to use a radio taxi; when you call, the dispatcher will give you a confirmation number that you must verify with the driver. Try Radio Taxi ⓣ1/288-8888, Taxi Real ⓣ1/333-3333 or Taxi Express ⓣ1/411-1111.

Accommodation

Inexpensive options and backpacker hostels are concentrated in La Candelaria.

Hostels

Anandamayi Hostel C9 No. 2-81, La Candelaria ⓣ1/341-7208, ⓦwww.anandamayihostel.com. This hostel is pure Zen, set in a restored colonial house around two flower-filled, hammock-strung courtyards. Rustic dormitories (US$12) come with lockers, and shared bathrooms have spacious stone showers. At night, guests huddle around the woodfire stove in the communal kitchen before nipping off to bed with hot water bottles. Includes internet and wi-fi. ❻

Bogotá B&B-Hostel C 32 No. 15-63, Barrio Teusaquillo ⓣ1/323-2428, ⓦwww.bogotabyb.com. Attractive large doubles and bright dorms greet weary travellers to this twenty-person hostel set in a charming two-storey home. The common area has hammocks, a fireplace and book exchange, and guests can contribute to the kitchen wall graffiti. Free internet and local calls. ❸–❺

El Cafecito Cra 6 No.34-70, La Merced ⓣ1/285-8308, ⓦwww.cafecito.net. Set in an old English-style mansion on a residential street just north of the centre, the dorm and private rooms upstairs are chilly, while beds are lumpy and showers have erratic hot water. Downstairs is an excellent bar and restaurant serving mostly vegetarian food. ❸–❺

Hostal Fatima C 14 No. 2-24, La Candelaria ⓣ1/281-6389, ⓦwww.hostalfatima.com. Popular with a young party crowd, this 31-bed hostel is superbly arranged around a luminous courtyard. The large chill-out space, TV lounge, games room, inviting kitchen and free internet compensates for otherwise cramped shared rooms (US$11). ❺

Hostal Sue Cra 3 No. 14-18, La Candelaria ⓣ1/341-2647, ⓦwww.suecandelaria.com. This well-maintained hostel with a party vibe has just about everything a backpacker could want: neat dorms, three doubles with TV, bean-bag-stacked TV lounge, landscaped courtyard, kitchen, free coffee, laundry service, ping-pong table and four computers. Has two other locations in La Candelaria at C 16 No.2-55, ⓣ1/334-8894 and at Cra 3 No. 15-97 ⓣ1/284-2348. ❷–❹

Platypus C 16 No. 2–43, La Candelaria ☎1/352-0127 or 341-3104, ⓦwww.platypusbogota.com. An institution, mostly because English–German speaking owner German warmly shares knowledge accumulated from extensive travels. Comfortable shared and private rooms with kitchen facilities. ❷–❹

Hotels

Hotel Aragon Cra 3 No. 14–13, La Candelaria ☎1/342-5239 or 284-8325. Cheap, clean and popular with young travellers. Their double rooms have shared bathrooms. ❹

Hotel Dorantes C 13 No. 5–07, La Candelaria ☎1/334-6640, ⓦwww.hoteldorantes.com. A crumbling old hotel with basic but airy doubles with TV and en suite. Some rooms have stupendous views of Monserrate. ❺

Hotel San Sebastián Av Jiménez No. 3–97, La Candelaria ☎1/243-8937. The double rooms at this well-priced hotel are more like large suites, complete with lounge area, private bathroom, TV and kitchenette. Rooms do get nippy at night. Includes wi-fi. ❺

Eating

While the traditional highlander diet consists of vegetables and starch, middle-class *cachacos* prefer the same cosmopolitan cuisine as their counterparts in London or New York. Bogotá has four main restaurant zones; from south to north they are: touristy La Candelaria; yuppie La Macarena (Cra 4 between calles 23 & 28); gay-friendly Chapinero also called the "G-Zone" (between calles 58 & 72 and carreras 3 & 7); and upmarket Zona Rosa (concentrated in the "T Zone" at C 82 and Cra 12).

TREAT YOURSELF

Of all the elegantly revamped colonial houses in La Candelaria, **Abadia Colonial** at C 11 No. 2-32 (☎1/341-1884, ⓦwww.abadiacolonial.com; ❾), is the pick of the pack. Twelve immaculate rooms with wooden floors, colourful bedspreads, wicker furniture, safe box, telephone, TV and modern bathrooms are arranged around three serene patios and a garden. And you only have to saunter upstairs to their romantic Italian restaurant. Wi-fi and breakfast complete the package.

Cafés, markets and light meals

Ázimos Cra 5 No. 26A–64, La Macarena ☎1/342-5296 A bakery-cum-gourmet deli that's a much-loved local hole in the wall. Salivate over the fig and caramel strudel (US$1).

Crêpes & Waffles Cra 10 No. 27–91 and Cra 12 No. 83–40 in the Zona Rosa as well as 25 other city outlets. A hugely popular chain restaurant that fulfils every savoury and sweet craving with its huge variety of crêpes (US$5) and waffles (US$2.50). Its ice cream is also worth trying (US$2). Closed Sun.

Mora Mora Cra 3 No. 15–98, La Candelaria ☎1/400-8466 A funky juice and sandwich bar that's ideal for breakfast and people-watching. Closed Sun.

Paloquemao C 19 & Cra 24. For the largest and most bustling Latin market in the city, head to this wholesale fruit and vegetable market.

Plaza de los Nieves C 19 & 20 between Cra 8 & 9, Downtown Bogotá. A covered outdoor market with several colourful mom and pop stalls serving inexpensive but filling *comida corriente* and fresh fruit juices.

Ricasole Cra 4 No. 14–83, La Candelaria ☎1/910-4707. This fast-service pizza joint in the heart of the historic centre is open late and does cheap and filling vegetarian slices (US$1).

Restaurants

La Casa de la Abuela C 27 No. 4–75 ☎1/243-0831, La Macarena. This simple diner serves Bogotá's best – and cheapest – *ajiaco* (a chicken stew blended with maize, potatoes, avocado and capers), but only on Fri (US$4). Lunch only; closed Sun.

El Corral Gourmet C 81 No. 13–05 in Atlantis Shopping Centre, Zona Rosa, North Bogotá ☎1/530-7309. Judging from its chain-eatery decor there's nothing to distinguish *El Corral* from *TGI Friday's* or any other American after-work bar. But after you try its beefy burgers (around US$8) you'll know why it's so popular.

Enobra Cra 4 No. 26A–37, La Macarena ☎1/284-0310. A trendy restaurant with a moody vibe, industrial minimalist decor and an adventurous contemporary menu. Mains around US$8.

La Jugueteria C 27 No.4A–03, La Macarena ☎1/341-1188. Decked out like a children's fairground on acid – complete with distortion mirrors, carousel horses and plastic dolls dangling from the ceiling – this restaurant serves plenty of fun with its barbecued meat. Best stay off the alcohol if you score the spinning table. Mains US$13–16. Closed Sun & Mon.

Lotus Azul Cra 5 No. 14–00, La Candelaria ⓣ1/334-2346. A Hare Krishna-run vegetarian café that does a roaring trade in three-course lunches for US$3. Relax in the upstairs cushioned area. Closed Sun.

Merlin Cra 2 No. 12–84, La Candelaria ⓣ1/284-9707. The house speciality of this candle-lit poets' café and restaurant, a quaintly refurbished colonial residence, is anything concocted with mushrooms. Mains US$7–15.

El Mirador Cra 5 No.10–72, La Candelaria ⓣ1/336-2066 On the top floor of the lavish *Hotel de la Opera*, overlooking the red-tiled roofs of the historic centre, this is the perfect spot for a long, decadent lunch. Start with the *ajiaco* soup, move onto a seafood main (US$17) and top it off with a mango mousse (US$4).

Museo del Tequila Cra 13 No. 86–18, Zona Rosa, North Botoga ⓣ1/256-6614; closed Sun dinner and Mon. A mariachi band entertains tequila-lubricated diners who tuck into authentic Mexican fare (mains around US$16). Wall cabinets are jammed with some 1600 bottles of tequila. Closed Sun.

Prodicom C 15A & Cra 3, La Candelaria ⓣ1/337-4325. This no-frills workers' co-op serves inexpensive, nutritious breakfasts (US$2–3) and typical mains (US$5–6).

Restaurante Fulanitos Cra 3 No. 8–61, La Candelaria ⓣ/352-0173. Typical Valle del Cauca fare is served in an atmospheric old colonial house with sensational old city views. Delightful service too. Mains US$10–12.

Wok Cra 13 No. 82–74, Zona Rosa, North Bogotá ⓣ1/218-9040. Trendy, but moderately priced sushi bar popular with the young and beautiful. All-white modern decor and electronic music add to the cosmopolitan appeal. There's also a branch located at Parque de 93. Mains US$7–13.

TREAT YOURSELF

Colombia's party central is a destination in itself. On weekends, more than a thousand people pay top dollar for the privilege of dining (US$30 for three courses) and dancing salsa in **Andrés Carne de Res**, at C 3 No. 11A–56 in the suburb of Chia (ⓣ1/863-7880, ⓦwww.andrescarne deres.com), a rustic *rancho* decorated with eccentric knick-knacks rescued from a junkyard. The long schlep by taxi (40min; US$22 one-way) is well worth the effort and the US$10 cover. A closer version is due to open in the city centre mid-2009.

Drinking and nightlife

Rumbear, literally to dance the rumba, is how *cachacos* refer to a night's partying, which invariably involves heavy doses of dancing. Bars and discos in La Candelaria attract a somewhat bohemian crowd and are very lively until 3am, when they shut down. Their fluorescent-lit counterparts in the Zona Rosa in North Bogotá around Calle 83 and Carrera 13, appealing to the city's beautiful people, get around the early curfew by declaring themselves social clubs. One-time membership dues (which substitute for cover charges) can be paid at the doors.

Blues C 86A No. 13–30 Zona Rosa, North Bogotá. Attracting a young gay crowd, this intimate club has red vinyl couches, a courtyard with a raging woodfire and flamboyant bar staff. All you can drink Fri & Sat (cover US$9). Thurs–Sat.

Café Escobar Rosas C 4 No.15–01, La Candelaria. The infectious funk music spun at this pea-sized former pharmacy makes it nearly impossible not to dance and intermingle with locals. US$7 cover, though that does get converted to a drinks voucher.

Cha Cha Cra 7 No. 31–16, 41st floor of the former Hilton Hotel ⓣ1/350-5074, ⓦwww.elchacha.com. The hippest club in Bogotá where, if you can take your eyes off the gorgeous people or indeed yourself in the mirrored hallways, you'll be treated to sensational views of Bogotá. Leather couches, chandeliers, an outdoor terrace and bass-heavy electronica set the scene for nights that end when day breaks. Hosts a monthly Sunday gay night (see ⓦwww.myspace.com/simgaybogota). Cover US$12. Thurs–Sat.

Goce Pagano Cra 13A No. 23–97, Downtown. Less is more in this legendary watering hole, which boasts a barebones dancefloor and Bogotá's largest rack of golden-era salsa LPs. Sapient owner Gustavo is a throwback to the era when the revolution was fought listening to salsa; you won't soon forget your visit. No cover. Take a taxi as the area is unsafe at night. Thurs–Sat only.

Gótica Cra 14 No. 82–50 Zona Rosa, North Bogotá ⓣ1/616-9720, ⓦwww.clubgotica.com. Hitting its peak well after 2am, this three-storey club attracts international DJs and a mixed crowd. Cover US$12. Wed–Sat.

Invitro C 59 No. 6–38. Popular with locals, this aquamarine-lit lounge changes moods with the hour, from quiet cocktail bar early on to late-night dance joint embracing diverse musical styles.

Shows locally produced short films on Tues & Wed nights.

The Irish Pub Cra 12A No. 83–48, Zona Rosa, North Bogotá. Gringo expats and yuppie Colombians sink pints of Murphys (US$5.50) and hoe into fish and chips (US$8.50) at this lively, upmarket Irish bar.

Quiebra Canto Cra 5 No. 17–76, Downtown ⓣ1/243-1630, ⓦwww.quiebracanto.com. Salsa like it was meant to be – hot and sticky. Its two dancefloors fill up on Wed for funk night. Cover US$5.

Theatron C 58 No. 10–42, Chapinero ⓣ1/249-2029, ⓦwww.theatrondepelicula.com. A slick, neon-lit wonderland, this colossal gay club is spread over three floors and six rooms. Hosts flashy live shows. Cover US$12. Thurs–Sat (Thurs & Fri men only).

Directory

Airline offices (domestic) Aires, Cra 7 No. 26–20 level 28 ⓣ1/294-0300, ⓦwww.aires.aero; AeroRepública, Av El Dorado Entrada 1 Interior 20 ⓣ1/320-9090, ⓦwww.aerorepublica.com.co; Avianca, C21 No. 13–23 Loc 6 ⓣ1/401-3434, ⓦwww.avianca.com; Satena, Cra 7 No. 33–24 ⓣ1/423-8500, ⓦwww.satena.com.

Banks and exchange ATMs are available throughout the city. Several currency exchanges, charging 2–3 percent commission, can be found near the Museo de Oro, at most shopping centres, hotels and the city's airports.

Car rental Most car rental agencies have offices at the airport. Hertz, Cra 11 No.75–19 (ⓣ1/327-6700, www.hertz.com), is a good bet, costing about US$70 a day for unlimited mileage. Or try Dollar, C 90 No. 11A-09 (ⓣ1/413-5533, ⓦwww.dollar.com).

Embassies Australia, Cra 16 No. 86A–05 ⓣ1/636-5247; Brazil, C 93 No. 14–20, 8th floor ⓣ1-218-0800; Canada, Cra 7 No. 115–33, 14th floor ⓣ1/657-9800; Ecuador, C 67 No. 7–35 ⓣ1/317-5328; Peru, C 80 No. 6–50 ⓣ1/257-0505; UK, Cra 9 No. 76–49, 9th floor ⓣ1/326-8300; US, Cra 45 No. 24B-27 ⓣ1/315-1566; Venezuela, Cra 13 No. 87–51 ⓣ1/640-1213.

Immigration For visa extensions (they cost around US$33) visit the DAS (Departamento Administrativo de Seguridad) at their Dirección de Extranjería office C 100 No. 11B–27 (Mon–Fri 8am–5pm). You can apply for a one-month visa extension in DAS offices in most Colombian cities.

If for some reason your hostel or hotel doesn't have internet access (frequently free), there are plenty of cafés across the city that do, charging roughly US$0.50–1 per hr.

Medical Dial 123 for an ambulance in a medical emergency. Clínica Marly at C 50 No. 9–67 ⓣ1/343-6600 is a modern medical facility accustomed to attending foreigners.

Police Headquarters of the tourist police is at Cra 13 No. 26–62 ⓣ1/337-4413 (daily 8am–6pm). In an emergency dial ⓣ112 from any phone.

Moving on

By air Multiple flights daily to Bucaramanga (1hr); Cali (1hr); Cartagena (1hr 20min); Leticia (1hr 50min); Manizales (50min); Medellín (40min); Pasto (1hr 30min); Pereira (50min); Popayán (1hr 15min); San Andres (2hr); Santa Marta (1hr 30min). International direct flights to: Buenos Aires, Caracas, Guayaquil, Lima, Rio de Janeiro, Santiago, São Paulo.

By bus Cali (hourly; 10hr); Cartagena (14 daily; 19hr); Manizales (10 daily; 18hr); Medellín (hourly; 10hr); Pasto (8 daily; 21hr); Pereira (hourly; 8hr); Popayán (7 daily; 13hr); San Agustin (11 daily; 12hr); Santa Marta (11 daily; 16hr); Villa de Leyva (4 daily; 4hr). International buses to: Buenos Aires (4 weekly; 7 days); Caracas (2 weekly; 28hr); Lima (4 weekly; 3 days); Santiago (4 weekly; 5 days); Quito (4 weekly; 32hr).

DAY-TRIPS FROM BOGOTÁ

The **Zipaquirá** salt cathedral – one of Colombia's most impressive man-made wonders – as well as the up-and-coming adventure sports town of **Suesca**, are both within easy day-trip distance of the capital.

The salt cathedral of Zipaquirá

High on the list for anyone staying more than a few days in Bogotá is a visit to the magnificent salt cathedral of **Zipaquirá** (Tues–Sat 9am–5pm, Sun 10am–4pm; US$6, Wed half price; ⓣ1/852-9890, ⓦwww.catedraldesal.gov.co), some fifty kilometres north of the city. Inaugurated in 1995 to great fanfare – having replaced an earlier one that closed for risk of collapse – the cathedral lies completely underground, topped by a huge mountain that was mined by local Indians even before the Spaniards started salting away its hidden treasures in the seventeenth century. As you descend 180m into the earth, you'll pass **fourteen chapels** built entirely of salt that glow like marble in the soft light. The main nave is a sublime feat of modern engineering, complete with the world's largest subterranean cross and a baptism carved from a natural waterfall of stalagmites. Above ground, there's a museum (same hours as cathedral) explaining the history of salt extraction. Mass is held on Sundays at 1pm. Informative tours are available in English and included in the entrance fee. From Bogotá take the TransMilenio to the Portal del Norte station at the end of the #2 or #3 line and from here a *buseta* (US$2) to Zipaquirá. From the centre of Zipaquirá, it's a short cab ride or fifteen-minute walk to the entrance.

Suesca

Some 70km north of Bogotá, the small town of **SUESCA** is fast becoming one of Colombia's top rock-climbing destinations. Mountain bikers, trekkers, paragliders, white-water rafters, cavers and horse riders can also flex their muscles here, but it is the sandstone cliffs on the town's doorstep that steal the show, offering traditional and sport rock-climbing with more than six hundred routes including multi-pitch. The majority of the rock-climbing and adventure sports outfitters are located at the entrance to the rocks, a fifteen-minute walk from the town centre. Try Vamonos Pa'l Monte (US$30 for a half-day, $50 for a full; ⓣ1/274-4649, ⓦwww.escaladaencolombia.com). A further fifteen minutes on is the *El Vivac Hostal*, Autopista Norte (ⓣ1/284-5313, ⓦwww.hostalelvivac.com; ❺), a cozy place to overnight and recharge, with a communal kitchen, fireplace and good mattresses in the shared rooms (US$10). Campers can pitch out back. To get to Suesca from Bogotá, take the TransMilenio to the northern terminus at Portal del Norte and then jump on one of the regular buses for Suesca (40min).

North of Bogotá

Just a few kilometres from Bogotá, the smog and busy streets quickly give way to a rolling spread of resplendent piedmonts and rustic farming hamlets. The Central Andean departments of Boyacá, Cundimarca and Santander mark the geographical heart of the country. First inhabited centuries ago by the gold-worshipping Muisca Indians, these mountainous highlands played a pivotal role in forging Colombia's national identity. Near **Tunja**, one of Colombia's oldest cities, stands the bridge where Bolívar defeated the Spanish army in 1819, clearing the way for independence. An hour northwest by bus from Tunja is one of Colombia's best-preserved colonial towns, sleepy **Villa de Leyva**, whose cobblestone streets and refined B&Bs help maintain the city's aristocratic air. Beyond the reaches of the weekend Bogotá crowd, tiny **Barichara** offers an even more genteel atmosphere, just a steep 22km from the burgeoning adventure town of **San Gil.** Further north, the thoroughly modern city of **Bucaramanga** makes a pleasant enough midway point if you're heading to the coast. On the border with Venezuela lies **Cúcuta**, generally regarded as severly lacking in charm, where the tripartite federation of Gran Colombia comprised of Ecuador, Venezuela, and modern-day Colombia was born in 1821. All these destinations are easily accessed **by bus**.

TUNJA

Capital of the Boyacá department, **TUNJA's** historic centre is one of the foremost preserves of the country's colonial heritage, though once you've gotten beyond that, it doesn't feel much different from a functional mid-sized city. The city was founded in 1539 on the ruins of the ancient Muisca capital of Hunza, and it makes a worthwhile few hours' detour for anyone visiting the more popular Villa de Leyva. It is also the most convenient base from which to visit **El Puente de Boyacá** (see below).

What to see and do

The majority of the sights are gathered around **Plaza de Bolívar**, including the **Casa del Fundador Suárez Rendón** (Wed–Sun 8.30am–12.30pm & 2–6pm; free to walk the grounds, US$1 for upstairs museum), home of the town's founder. Dating from 1540, it was built in the Moorish Mudéjar style and contains some colonial artwork, as well as the local tourism office. At Calle 20 and Cererra 8, the 1590 **Casa de Don Juan de Vargas** (daily 8am–noon & 1–6pm) stands out for its eighteenth-century interior frescoes and its garden, which suggests an Andalusian landscape.

Like much of the town's architecture, Plaza Bolívar 's **Catedral**, built in 1569, contains Islamic motifs. More ornate are the **Santo Domingo** and **Santa Clara** churches; the former, on Calle 11 between carreras 19 and 20, is known for its Rosario Chapel, which exhibits religious paintings and woodwork by Gregorio Vázquez de Arce y Ceballos. The latter, on Carrerra 7 and Calle 19, was the first convent in the region and is now a religious museum.

El Puente de Boyacá

About 16km south of Tunja on the main road back to Bogotá is a reconstructed colonial-era bridge, **El Puente de Boyacá,** commemorating the Battle of Boyacá of August 7, 1819, which cleared the way for Bolívar and his freedom fighters to march triumphantly into Bogotá. The trickling river's trivial girth lends a new perspective to the popular myth of Bolívar's bravery – perhaps during the battle it formed a more substantial natural barrier. There's a monument to El Libertador here as well as a restaurant and small museum. *Busetas* leave from Tunja's conveniently located bus terminal every half-hour.

Information

Calle 19, on the southern border of Plaza de Bolívar, is the drag for internet access, ATMs, and places to stay. You'll find the main **Culture & Tourism office** within the Casa del Fundador Suárez Rendón, on the west side of Plaza de Bolívar.

Accommodation

Hotel Lux C 19 No. 10–78 ⓣ8/742-5736. A charming old colonial home converted into an inn with nine rooms, most of which are doubles. Special touches include hand-carved beds and a small café in the foyer downstairs. Rooms with private bath ❹

Saboy C 19 No. 10–40 ⓣ8/742-3492. Family-run spot that offers Spartan rooms and a central skylight. Shared bath ❶, private bath ❷

Eating

Roma Cra 9 No. 20–69. Pasta-focused vegetarian restaurant, with dishes starting at US$4. Lunch and dinner.

Moving on

By bus The city's bus terminal is a quick walk southeast from Plaza Bolívar. Buses north to Bucaramanga, the main jumping-off point for the trips to the Caribbean Coast, leave about every hour (US$20, 6–7hr). You can get off in San Gil (US$12, 4hr 30min) to head on to Barichara (see p.561). Small buses – some direct, some not – to Villa de Leyva leave every 15min (US$4, 45min) until about 7pm.

VILLA DE LEYVA AND AROUND

Just four hours by bus from Bogotá and an hour from Tunja, tucked against the foot of spectacular mountains, scenic **VILLA DE LEYVA** is the hub of tourism in the high Andes heartland. Whether you're hunting for fossils, checking out the countryside on horseback or just sitting around the four-hundred-year-old plaza drinking sangria, the town's untroubled ambience blankets everything.

Founded in 1572, the town is a showcase of colonial architecture and was declared a national monument in 1954; it also draws those looking to visit the many nearby natural attractions. Posh *cachacos,* native *Bogotanos*, typically descend in droves on weekends, though during the rest of the week, it's a relatively peaceful place.

What to see and do

Villa de Leyva looks and feels immaculately preserved, right down to hand-painted tiles prohibiting horseback riding and car traffic along the main plaza.

Plaza Mayor and around

The impressive **Plaza Mayor** is one of the largest in Colombia, completely paved over in large cobblestones and centred on a stone well. Dominating the plaza is the huge stone portal of the seventeenth-century **Catedral**, rebuilt after an 1845 earthquake. Directly in front across the plaza, the **Casa-Museo Luis Alberto Acuña** (daily 9am–6pm; US$1) houses sculptures and large murals by the early avant-garde twentieth-century artist it is named after. Facing the simple church is one of Colombia's largest religious art museums, the **Monasterio de las**

Carmelitas (Sat, Sun & holidays only, 10am–1pm & 3–5pm; $1), containing large numbers of wooden icons from the Church's early years of proselytizing in the New World.

A few blocks east, at Carrera 8 and Calle 15, the **Casa de Antonio Ricaurte** (Wed–Fri 9am–noon & 2–5pm, Sat–Sun 9am–1pm & 2–6pm, $0.75) was home to a national hero who fought for Bolívar. Operated by the Colombian armed forces since 1970, the house contains military objects pertaining to one of the country's most noteworthy patriots.

West of the city

El Fósil (daily 9am–5pm; $1.50) is a decidedly low-key museum featuring the fossilized remains of a Kronosaurus, a prehistoric marine lizard found by a *campesino* here in 1977. The 12.8 metre-long lizard, whose head exceeds that of North America's Tyrannosaurus Rex, is one of only two in the world excavated in its entirety. Two kilometres further along the road from El Fósil, you'll find **El Infiernito**, a Muisca observatory made famous in tourist photos because of its large, phallic stone monoliths. Tiny **Ráquira** makes a good stop only if you're looking to buy some crafts – hammocks, jewellery and terra cotta pottery spill from storefronts onto its single main street. At the nearby **Ostrich Farm**, you can see these elegantly grizzled creatures strut and even sample a bird burger, though it's not cheap.

North of the city

The arid desert highlands surrounding Villa de Leyva attract trekkers, but 120 million years ago the huge flood plain would have been better suited to scuba diving. The ocean waters have since retreated, and in their wake they've left the country's largest repository of **fossils**. What has been discovered is on display at the well-maintained **Museo Paleontológico**, a kilometre north of town along Carrera 9 (Tues–Sat 9am–noon & 2–5pm, Sun 9am–3pm; US$1). Fifteen kilometres north lies **El Santuario de Iguaque**, a large nature reserve with excellent hiking named for the park's most sacred lake, believed by the native Muiscas to be the birthplace of humanity. To get here, head on the road to Arcabuco, 12km northeast out of town, where a visitor centre offers basic accommodation, a camping area and food. The entrance fee for the reserve is a steep US$14 for foreigners. Take one of the buses that leave four times a day for Arcabuco and let the driver know where you're headed.

LOCAL FIESTAS

The city plays host to two spectacular festivals during the year. The larger is the **Festival of Lights** (Dec 6–8), a fireworks extravaganza that gathers the best of the region's pyrotechnicians, while the popular **Kite Festival** (Aug) sees the country's finest kite-flyers compete in a variety of categories as spectators shout encouragement.

Arrival and information

By bus The bus stop is a short walk southwest from the city centre, towards the road to Tunja.

Tourist information The tourist office at Cra 9 No. 13–04 is helpful in pointing out what's going on. The nearby headquarters of Colombian Highlands, Cra 9 No. 11–02 (daily 9am–noon & 1–8pm; ☎8/732-1379), is an excellent first stop to pick up information on a variety of outdoor excursions and on local transportation. There are many ATMs located around the perimeter of central Plaza Mayor.

Transport and tours

Chiva **bus tours** will take you on one of four routes. The most popular includes visits to tiny Ráquira well known for its quality pottery and craft shops the museum of El Fósil, the Ostrich Farm (Granja de Avestruz), and El Infiernito, all west of the city. You can also hire a **taxi** for the day to drive you site to site, travel by **horseback** or

walk, though the latter is often on winding, paved roads, and can be dangerous. Youth hostel and tour operator **Colombian Highlands** (see above) offers a staggering variety of outdoor and historical excursions from horseback riding through the surrounding countryside's verdant hills to abseiling (rappelling) down waterfalls (prices range from US$18–36). Ten percent discounts are extended to those who stay in their fiendishly located digs just outside town: don't go without directions.

Accommodation

Villa de Leyva has a wide range of quality hotels, many of them former colonial residences. Various campsites with basic bathrooms make the best true budget sleeping options, though many (catering to young *Bogotános* arriving by car) are BYO tent. Discounts of up to thirty percent are often available during the week; book early for weekends and holidays.

Bahia Olivo Av Perimetral (near C 8) No. 10–40 ⓣ8/732 0935, ⓦwww.hotelbahiaolivo.com. A small fountain and outdoor space with their namesake olive tree add atmosphere to this simple, clean option. All rooms with private bath. ❻

Hospedería La Roca (off Plaza Mayor) ⓣ8/732-0331. Drawing a friendly crowd of travellers and with a great location at the main square, this spot is very popular with backpackers. ❺

Marqués de San Luis Cra 13 No. 8–58 Av Perimetral ⓣ8/732-0710. This ranch-style hotel ranks among the least expensive offering both a pool and breakfast. Modestly sized rooms, spacious grounds, four blocks from the main square. All rooms with bath. ❼

Posada de Los Angeles Cra 10 No. 13-94 ⓣ8/732-0562. Elegant, cozy two-storey hotel, which makes a mean breakfast, served in their outdoor courtyard and included in the price of the stay: baked eggs layered with oregano, tomatoes and cheese. Room decor is carefully chosen, and many beds are topped with crisp, white mosquito lining that is more ornamental than functional. Cash only. ❼

Zona de Camping Corner of Calle 10 and Carrera 10. Offers no-frills camping, with a wall set up around a large patch of grass. Males and females are supposed to sleep in separate sections. US$5 per person, with showers and bathroom.

Eating and drinking

Stiff competition among quality restaurants means that even backpackers can eat like gourmands. The greatest density of restaurants lies in the vicinity of the intersection of Calle 11 and Carrera 9. Although Villa de Leyva attracts large numbers of visitors on weekends, weeknights can be a bit subdued; a few pubs with live guitar music are always open around the main plaza. After dark join the exuberant crowds that throng Plaza Mayor. Fire-eaters and other local characters are on-hand on weekends to help make the night pleasantly surreal.

Casa Quintero on the southern corner of the Plaza Mayor. Something of an indoor mall, full of small shops and restaurants. In addition to the tasty Lebanese offerings of *Zarina* and the pseudo-health food of *Eqqus*, inside you'll find *El Pote*, one of the town's most bohemian bars, complete with eucalyptus-heaped floors.

Pasteleria Francesa C 10, between Carrera 9 and Carrera 8. A homey breakfast spot with simple, fresh breakfast pastries and good coffee. Closed Tues & Wed.

Portales Off Plaza Mayor, on C 13 at Cra 9. An upscale pizza joint at heart, supplemented by various pastas. It's more affordable than the well-appointed outdoor seating and attentive wait staff would seem to indicate.

Restaurante Azteca 4–37, Cra 9, between C 10 and C 11. Catering to every imaginable sub-section of the tourist trade with Mexican food and pizza as well as traditional Colombian dishes, this low-key spot has great prices and a pleasant storybook atmosphere.

Sazón & Sabor next to *Plaza Mayor* hotel on Cra 10. This candlelit, late-night pub features low-key guitar music.

Moving on

By bus The two main bus companies are Reina and Libertadores. Six buses a day (3 on Sun and holidays) leave for Bogotá (US$9, 4–5hr) between 5am and 5pm. To continue north to San Gil and Barichara, or further on to Bucaramanga and Cúcuta, you typically must first take a bus south to Tunja (US$3, 45min, leaving every 15min) or to closer Chinquinquira (Colombia's religious capital) and transfer.

BARICHARA

With its undulating stone-slab roads, clay-tiled *tejas* roofs draped in bougainvillea blossoms and single-storey adobe homes, the sedate alpine hamlet of **BARICHARA** looks like it probably hasn't changed much in its 250 years.

So well-kept is the town that it was declared a national monument in 1978. Barichara is also considerably less crowded than similarly picturesque Villa de Leyva, making it an ideal resting spot for weary travellers on the way to Venezuela. Indeed, the town's name comes from an Indian word, *Barachala*, meaning "a good place to rest". Check out the striking **Catedral de la Inmaculada Concepeión** on the Parque Central, which stands on fluted sandstone columns.

One of the most appealing places to **stay the night is** *Hostal Aposentos* C 6 No. 6–40 (☎7/726-7294; ❼ sleeps three), a fittingly named hotel on the main plaza offering "princess quarters." Polished beams and high ceilings augment the fairytale feel conjured by large, sliding wooden window panels that let in the warm mountain breeze.

Keep in mind that most **restaurants** are only open on weekends, and that the big meal in Colombia is lunch, with fast food or soup being the main dinner offerings. Pizza at the main square is a reliable alternative. *Plenilunio Café*, C 6 No. 7–74, serves upscale Italian in its homey environs (mains start at US$7), but prepare for a wait.

Buses leave every half-hour for San Gil (30–45min, US$2.50).

SAN GIL

Drawing an increasing number of adventure seekers and travellers looking for a less-trammelled destination, compact **SAN GIL** provides enough in the way of activities and grubby charm to justify a jaunt north, or at least a stop-over en route from Colombia's interior to the Caribbean coast.

What to see and do

The main attraction in town is **Parque Gallineral** (8am–6pm), whose sylvan, riverside grounds can be enjoyed in an hour, or savoured for an entire day. The nightlife goes on late here, driven by raucous gatherings in the main plaza.

The other worthwhile draws also involve the outdoors. You can go **whitewater rafting** on one of the three nearby rivers; a day-trip down Class IV/V (depends on the season) Río Suarez will run you about US$65 with the well-accredited guides at **Colombia Rafting Excursions**. That said, the government was looking to consolidate all operators to standardize pricing at the time of writing, so for the future there may be one go-to outfitter for such trips. The **waterfalls** at Juan Curí, reached by bus, are also a favourite, as is a spelunking trip into the **Cueva de Indio**: visitors hop a zip line into the cave and end their journey with a leap into the waters below (US$14). You can book most excursions through your hostel. For some rock scrambling at river mostly just known to locals, hop a bus to **Pescadarito**, 25 minutes north in the town of **Curiti**. You can also pitch a tent for the night.

Arrival, city transport and moving on

By bus The bus terminal is 2km southwest of town, with both city buses and taxis available. Buses to Bogotá leave frequently (6–8hr). Buses between Bucaramanga and San Gil leave every 30min (2hr 30min).

By taxi Though regular buses service all sites of interest, you can also rent a taxi for a whole day for relatively little (around US$17).

Accommodation

Carrera 11, the street that runs parallel to the river on the north, is the hotbed of cheap beds. Some of the newer hotels can be found on Calle 10.

Hotel Victoria Cra 11 No. 10-40 ☎7/724-2347 or 724-5955, ⓔHvictoria1040@yahoo.es or fora30m@yahoo.es. Rooms at this well-located hotel represent a step up from the town's low-budget options, with private bath, TV, and a/c in each. Prices can double in high season. Be sure to confirm your reservation: they're not the best at keeping them. ❹

Macondo Guesthouse C 12 No. 7-26 ⓣ7/724-4463. Shaun Carter, the Australian owner and operator of this ramshackle nook a few blocks from the main plaza, helps book activities and tours. All bathrooms are shared. Dorm beds ❷, doubles ❸

BUCARAMANGA

Founded in 1622, **BUCARAMANGA** has shed much of its colonial heritage and evolved into one of Colombia's largest, most modern cities. There's little to detain visitors, but the capital of Santander *departamento* makes a convenient stopover point for anyone travelling to the coast of Venezuela. If you're lucky enough to make it here during Easter Week, be sure to try the local delicacy – *hormigas culonas*, or fried ants, which are available in local markets and food stalls along main highways into town.

For a short while in 1828, Simon Bolívar (El Libertador) lived in the **Casa de Bolívar**, C 37 No. 12–15 (Mon–Fri 8am–noon & 2–6pm, Sat 8am–noon; US$1.50), which now contains a small historical museum and research centre. It's near **Parque Garcia Rovira**, the city's administrative centre, on Calle 37 between carreras 12 and 13. Across the street another colonial mansion houses the **Casa de la Cultura** (Mon–Fri 8am–noon, 2–6pm, Sat 8am–noon; US$1.50), with a museum on regional handicrafts. Catching any *buseta* heading to Floridablanca (45min, US$1), a neighbourhood to the northeast, will take you near the **Jardín Botánico Eloy Valenzuela** (daily 8am–5pm; US$2), where the Río Frío runs through the verdant gardens.

Arrival

By air Palonegro International Airport lies about 30km southwest of the downtown area. A taxi to the downtown area can be negotiated for as little as US$12.

By bus The Terminal de Transportes is about 5km southwest of the city, and is accessible by city bus or taxi. A night journey (most leave between 7 and 10pm) can be preferable for longer-haul trips if you're willing to forgo the beautiful scenery. Bring a blanket or keep out a sweatshirt as the buses get chilly.

Accommodation

There's a shortage of clean, safe budget options in town. Steer clear of the Parque Centenario neighbourhood near Calle 31 and Carrera 17–24. Calle 34 offers some upper mid-range options in the Carrera 20s, also near the city's concentration of discos. Since the city's a popular stop-over point for long-haul bus rides, meeting up with trustworthy fellow travellers to share a room can be the safest option; it can also help you afford hotels with amenities like a pool or free breakfast. Another option is to take a bus to the teensy Girón, 9km southwest (US$5 by taxi, 15min), an engaging mix of colonial and hip.

La Hormiga Cra 17 C No. 55–56 ⓣ7/644-9010. An affordable, clean hotel with restaurant, bar and swimming pool. ❺

Hotel Guane C 34 No. 22–72 ⓣ7/634-7014. A five-floor hotel offering all the comforts its marble lobby implies: saunas, a swimming pool with a restaurant and bar alongside, and a buffet breakfast. Affordable multi-room suites are a good value for larger groups if you don't mind thin mattresses. ❼

Las Nieves C 30 No. 25–71, Girón ⓣ7/681-0144, ⓦhotellasnievesgiron.com. Simple rooms, all with private bath, overlooking the pretty main plaza. ❺

Eating and drinking

Strip clubs have taken over much of the once-fashionable Zona Rosa. The nightlife scene has shifted to the nearby Cabecera district, with Carrera 33 holding the top clubs.

La Calle C.C. Cabecera Et IV L-505 ⓣ7/ 643 0835. Located atop one of the city's malls, this local favourite has great views of the city and, more important, a happening scene of youthful types who keep the party going past 3am on weekends.

Govindas Cra 20 34–65. This fast-food vegetarian bakery and restaurant serves a *prix-fixe* lunch for about US$4 during lunch, though various á la carte items are on offer from breakfast to sundown.

Mi Pais Cra 34 52–07 ⓣ7/647 8021. A lively, somewhat traditional club spinning mostly Colombian music like merengue, salsa and *vallenato* for a young crowd.

Pizzeria Asturias *Hotel Asturias*, Cra 22 35–01. This pizza joint serves a wide variety of tasty pies loaded with more toppings than you can shake a stick at. Steer clear of menu items sporting maraschino cherries or pineapple and opt for unfamiliar seafood options if craving something new.

El Viejo Chiflas Cra 33 at C 34. *Comida típica* at low prices. Open 24hr.

Moving on

By air Bogotá (US$160–180, 1hr).

By bus Bus companies Berlinas and Copetran offer the most comfortable and frequent trips. To Bogotá (US$38; 8–9hr); Santa Marta (US$46; 9hr); Cartagena (US$56; 13–16hr, often via Barranquilla).

CROSSING INTO VENEZUELA: CÚCUTA

The only reason to visit **CÚCUTA**, capital of Norte de Santander department, is if you're heading by land to Venezuela, as the city offers precious few attractions and the outlying area has been the focus of intense guerrilla and paramilitary activity in recent years. Tensions between Venezuela's vehemently anti-US head of state, Hugo Chávez, and Colombia, which has close, if problematic, ties to the United States, present another reason for minimizing time here.

Following a March 2008 international incident kicked up when the Colombian army killed a high-ranking FARC member in Ecuador, Chavez briefly closed the border between the countries in retaliation for what he saw as a right-wing government acting unchecked by international law.

If you do spend time in the city, take a peek inside the ornate Neoclassical **Palacio de la Gobernación**, the department's main administrative building on Avenida 5 between calles 13 and 14, and the **Casa de la Cultura**, at C 13 No. 3–67, which contains a museum recounting the city's history. Just eight kilometres south is the small colonial town of **Villa del Rosario**, where a municipal park houses the ruins of the temple where Gran Colombia's independence was declared in 1821.

BORDER CROSSING

The border is open 24 hours a day, though it can become unexpectedly backed up or closed at short notice. Visitors should exercise utmost caution as muggings are not uncommon on both sides of the border. At the time of writing, Americans, Canadians and Europeans don't need to purchase visas for surface travel, but make sure all is in order with your passport to ensure a smooth passage through the various checkpoints. For the most up-to-date information, contact the **Venezuelan consulate** (Mon–Fri 8am–noon; ⓣ7/579 1954 or 579 1951, ⓔweconsul@col1.telecom.com.co) at Avenida Camilo Daza in Zona Industrial. Entering into Venezuela from Cúcuta, the first town you reach is San Antonio, but it's advisable to take the bus directly to the larger **San Cristóbal** if you want to make connections to **Caracas** (see p.945).

Several basic *residencias* are situated along Avenida 7, though the area can be somewhat dangerous at night. *Imperial*, Av 7 No. 6–28 (ⓣ7/572-3321; ❸–❹), is one option, catering mainly to working-class Venezuelans crossing into Colombia for business; there's a 24-hour restaurant on site. Comparatively upmarket, *Amaruc*, Av 5 No. 9–73 (ⓣ7/571-7625; ❻), has 48 rooms, each with a/c and cable. Breakfast is included.

Cartagena and the Caribbean

Ever since Rodrigo de Bastidas became the first European to set foot on Colombian soil in Santa Marta in 1525, there's been a long history of foreigner fascination with the country's Caribbean coastline, and hundreds of thousands – Colombian vacationers chief among them – follow in his footsteps annually. Indeed, if it weren't for Colombia's reputation for violence **Cartagena** would be even more of a tourist gold mine than it already is. In addition to hot weather and cool breezes, there are the splendours from the town's past as the main conduit for the Spanish crown's imperial plundering. For its extensive fortifications and colonial legacy, the walled city was declared a UNESCO World Heritage Site in 1984.

The 1600-kilometre coast holds a wider variety of things to see and do than anywhere else in the country. There are the dense jungles of the **Darien Gap** on the border with Panama and the arid salt plains of the **Guajira Peninsula**. If it's a tropical paradise you're after, try the white, jungle-fringed beaches of **Tayrona National Park** near Santa Marta. The translucent waters around **Santa Marta** and the nearby fishing village of **Taganga** number among the most inexpensive places in the world to learn to scuba dive. Inland, the most mesmerizing part about the six-day trek to the archeological ruins of **Ciudad Perdida** is the chance to cross paths with the coca-chewing Kogis.

CARTAGENA DE INDIAS AND AROUND

Without a doubt one of the Caribbean's most beautiful cities, **CARTAGENA DE INDIAS** offers all-night partying, colonial architecture, gourmet dining and beachcombing. Cartagena literally embodies Colombia's Caribbean coast, with many of the city's colourful, weathered buildings using coral from the surrounding sea's reefs as their primary construction material.

Founded in 1533, Cartagena was one of the first Spanish cities in the New World and served as the main port through which the continent's riches were salted away to the mother country. Not surprisingly, the city proved an appetizing target for English pirates prowling the Caribbean, and it suffered several dreadful sieges in the sixteenth century, the most infamous led by Sir Francis Drake in 1586, during which he held the town hostage for more than a hundred days. After "the Dragon" withdrew, the Spaniards began constructing the elaborate network of fortifications that are now the city's hallmark.

Little of the city's aristocratic ways remain, though its attractiveness does. **San Diego**, home to a good number of mid-priced hostals and hotels, offers a more mellow, though still lively, version of the pricey, pretty **Old City**. Grittier **Getsemaní**, in pockets of which shirtless men play dominoes and *cumbia* music blasts from open plazas, marks the most authentic entry point to workaday local life, despite lacking some of the architectural grandeur of the other two. The most raucous nightlife and nearly all budget accommodation are found here.

You can take in the city in one long pan by strolling the eleven kilometres of stone ramparts that encircle it, though it's best to avoid this at night.

What to see and do

Bursting with history and generally aglow with Caribbean langour, Cartagena's walled **Old City** is where the bulk of the sightseeing is. Expect to get lost – as if the labyrinth of narrow, winding streets isn't disorienting enough, each block bears a different name. As such, the city's many **plazas** can guide you, acting not only as convenient landmarks but as distinct social hangouts. Take a shady afternoon break on a polished wood bench or enjoy people-watching while sipping an Aguila come evening.

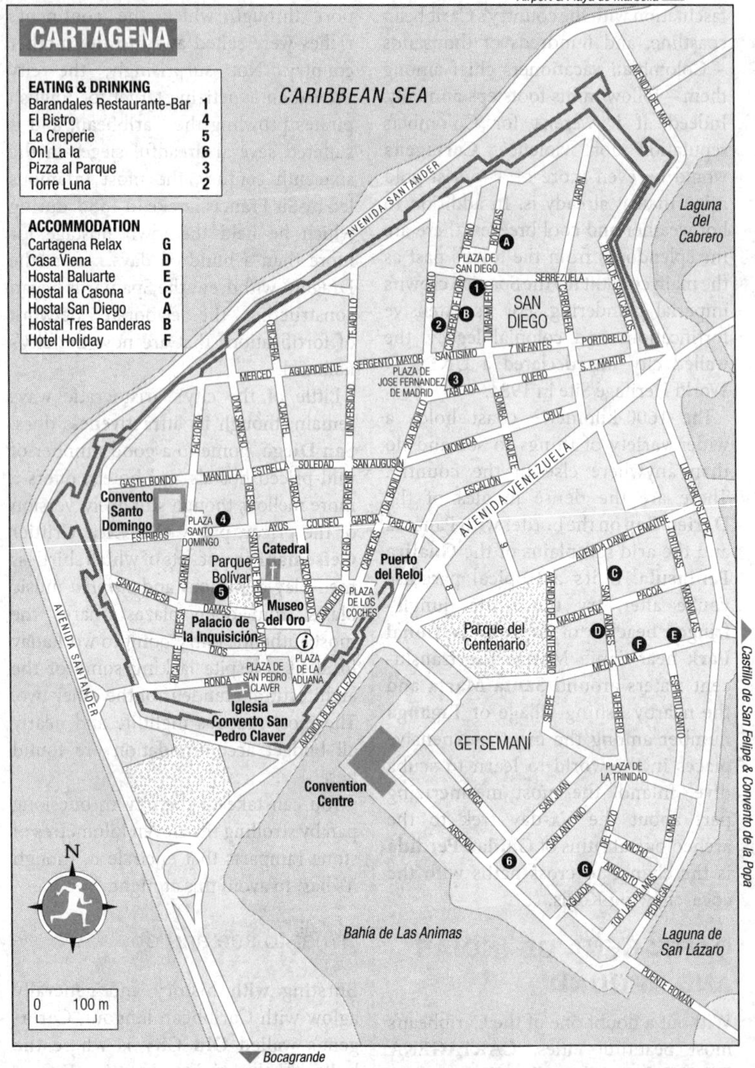

Plaza de los Coches and around

The city's main entranceway is the triple-arched **Puerta del Reloj**, which gives way to the **Plaza de los Coches**, a former slave-trading square. Today, it's the area where horse-drawn carriages can be hired at night for romantic tours around the city and the stage for a variety of street performances. Equally entertaining are the no-nonsense vendors at the covered **Portal de los Dulces**, who adeptly pluck bite-size sweets out of a sea of huge glass jars at your choosing. In the evening, several bars open up above the arcade.

Plaza de la Aduana and around

A half-block south of the Puerta del Reloj is the **Plaza de la Aduana**, the administrative centre during the colonial era, with a statue of Columbus in the centre.

A few steps in the same direction and you'll bump into the imposing **Iglesia Convento San Pedro Claver** (daily 8am–5pm), on the quiet plaza of the same name. Built by Jesuits in 1603, it's where Spanish-born priest Pedro Claver lived and died, in 1654, before his canonization some two centuries later. Called the "slave of the slaves" for his door-to-door fundraising on behalf of the city's slaves, the ascetic monk's skull and bones are guarded in a glass coffin at the church's altar. The well-preserved church has a religious art museum, where you can plop down on the same throne Pope John Paul II sat in during his 1986 visit to Cartagena.

Plaza de Bolívar and around

A popular meeting place for locals is the flower-filled **Plaza de Bolívar**, perhaps the most opulent in town. On its west side stands the **Palacio de la Inquisición**, a block-long example of late-colonial architecture, the city's finest remnant of the era. It was completed in 1776 and is believed to be the site where at least eight husand people were sentenced to death. Scenes from the 2009 movie adaptation of García Márquez's *Love and Other Demons* were shot at the torture museum within. To the right of the Palacio, the **Museo de Oro** (Tue–Fri 10am–1pm & 3–7pm, Sat 10am–1pm, 2–5pm, Sun 11–4pm; free) specializes in ornaments hailing from the Sinú culture and is well worth seeing if you don't have time to visit the Gold Museum in Bogotá. On the northeast corner of the plaza is the **Catedral**, whose construction began in 1575, was almost derailed by cannon fire in 1586 by Drake, and not completed until 1612. Mass is still said regularly in keeping with Colombia's strong Catholic heritage and can be quite moving to hear.

Plaza de Santo Domingo

Head a block west past a series of nicely preserved balustrades to the lively **Plaza de Santo Domingo**. The **Iglesia y Convento de Santa Domingo**, with Botero's satirical sculpture *La Gorda* as de facto sentinel, constitutes the plaza's main draw. Completed in 1579, the fortress-like structure's austere interior belies its status as Cartagena's oldest church. On the Baroque altar there's a Christ carved from the sixteenth century.

East of the Old City

For a bird's-eye view of Cartagena, take a short cab ride (US$2) up to the **Convento de la Popa** (Mon–Fri 8.30am–5.30pm; US$3), just outside the city's walls. Don't walk: the area around it is unsafe. The restored whitewashed chapel, built in 1608, is clearly visible from almost anywhere in the city. In addition to offering spectacular panoramic views of the city, photos of Pope John Paul II's 1986 visit to Cartagena are also on display in the small chapel. On February 2, when the city celebrates the day of its patron saint, the **Virgin of Candelaria**, protector against pirates and the plague, a candle-lit procession of pilgrims storms the hill.

The fortresses

More than a single, uniform wall, Cartagena is surrounded by a series of impressive fortresses, most of which are still standing. The largest and most important was **Castillo de San Felipe de Barajas** (daily 8am–6pm, US$6; bring student ID for a discount), a towering stone fort just east of the walled city along Avenida Pedro de Heredia. Built between 1656 and 1798 with plans from a Dutch engineer, the castle is an ideal spot from which to watch the sunset or tour the maze of underground tunnels connecting the various areas of the fort.

The utter lack of informational placards in and around the castle has to do with keeping the freelance tour-guide industry afloat, so if you'd like detailed information on the various cannons, passageways and the architectural strategy at work, you may want to hire one of the guides (Spanish or English).

Most of Cartagena's other remaining defences, most of them nearer to the sea than San Felipe, were built much later, during the dawning of the Spanish Empire in the late eighteenth century. Visible on excursions to Islas del Rosario (see below), the **Fuerte de San Fernando** on Tierrabomba Island was built to seal off Bocachica, which, after a sandbar blocked Bocagrande in 1640, was the only access to the city's harbour. As part of the complex engineering feat, a heavy bronze chain was dangled across the entrance, beneath the water, to the restored **Fuerte San José** on Barú Island.

Bocagrande

A quick cab ride (US$3.50) or more colourful city bus jaunt (US$1.25) south of the Old City is **Bocagrande**, Cartagena's modern sector, a thin isthmus dotted with high-rise hotels and timeshare apartments catering to Colombian vacationers. Other than its overcrowded and dirty beach, the closest one to the Old City, there's little reason to visit.

Nearby beaches

For a peaceful tan, take a bus or cab north along the coast to **Marbella**, or further to the local favourite beach near **Las Américas Beach Resort**, which is also good for swimming.

Boat trips

At least fifty minutes (the bigger the boat, the faster the trip) out to sea from Cartagena lies an archipelago of small coral islands known as the **Islas del Rosario**, sunk in transparent turquoise waters. In total there are over forty islands, many of them private islets barely large enough for a bungalow. Not technically part of the chain, **Playa Blanca**, on Barú island, is one of the more popular beach spots.

For day-trips by boat, all of which depart in the morning, you can either book through your ho(s)tel or head straight to the **Muelle Turística**, the wharf across from the Convention Center, and approach anyone with a clipboard. Thirty-four dollars will get you a round-trip boat ride to Playa Blanca with about twenty others, plus a messy, tasty lunch of fried fish, *patacones* (smashed, fried plantains), rice, and salad. Snorkelling costs about US$12 extra, and entrance to the open-water aquarium that's a stop on some trips (ask ahead) is US$8. A US$6 park fee is extracted from all those leaving from the port since the entire island area is protected by the **Corales del Rosario National Park**.

Some boats stop at **Fuerte de San Fernando** (where it's too polluted to swim) on **Tierrabomba Island** and offer brief stops at other nearby islands, so be sure to clarify the itinerary before handing over cash or hopping aboard. At all beaches, islanders offering beaded jewellery and massages are tough to rebuff, but the water is crystal-blue and the beaches clean.

Arrival and information

By air Cartagena's Rafael Nuñez International Airport is 10min by taxi (US$5) or a slightly longer bus ride (US$2) from the city centre.

By bus The city's large bus terminal is some 45min away by bus from the city centre; a taxi will set you back US$11.

Tourist information Proturismo (☎5/665-1843 or ☎5/655-0277) is located at the Muelle Turística and is dedicated primarily to selling excursions to the outlying beaches.

City transport

It's barely a stretch to say that all touristic areas are within walking distance, so getting around **by foot** is the favoured mode of transport – at least by day.

That said, the streams of available cabs make a **taxi** trip to nearby beaches, or the other end of town after a long night out, a snap. Taxis are also available at night, especially around Getsemaní. Local city **buses** aren't as inexpensive as their peeling paint exteriors and tricked-out destination placards would indicate (US$1.50 for most one-way trips).

Accommodation

Finding comfortable accommodation at an affordable price is easier than you might think. Handsome San Diego offers many nicely outfitted mid-range options, while Getsemaní, a short walk from the Old City, holds the lion's share of cheap hostels along Calle Media Luna. Prices during the summer high season from December to February usually surge thirty to fifty percent.

San Diego

Hostal San Diego C de las Bóvedas 39–120 ⓣ5/660-1433. Medium-sized and modern, with a/c in all rooms and a delicious breakfast, this is among the best deals near the centre. Paintings of intriguingly misshapen figures intended to conjure Botero's voluptuous style adorn the walls. ❽

Hostal Tres Banderas C Cochera del Hobo 38–66 ⓣ5/660-0160. A small B&B a block from Plaza San Diego features quiet rooms with a/c. Its lovely patio has caged parakeets and a cooling fountain. ❽

Getsemaní

Cartagena Relax C del Pozo, 20–105, ⓣ5/664 1117, ⓦwww.cartagenarelax.com. Unique among economical options for having a hammock-lined pool. Breakfast, included in the price, is served around a large kitchen table. Includes a French-leaning book exchange and a/c in all rooms. Located on a colourful, lived-in street. ❼

Casa Viena C San Andres 30–53 ⓣ5/664 6242. Your typical shabby backpacker paradise. The potential to meet up with other travellers and some of the cheapest shared rooms in town would steer you here, plus free coffee and internet. ❷–❹

Hostal Baluarte C Media Luna No. 10–81 ⓣ5/664-2208. One of the more airy and upmarket options in the area, housed in a colonial building. The atmosphere is pleasant, and terracotta-tiled floors contrast nicely with the white-laquered external staircase. The 24 well-kept rooms in this quiet, family-run hostel all come with a/c and private bath. ❹

Hostal La Casona C Tripita y Media, 31–32 (at Cra 10) ⓣ5/639-5644. Rooms in this bric-à-brac-filled hostel are on the small side, but the private bathrooms, plant-filled courtyard and price make it a stellar deal, especially given it's the closest spot in the neighbourhood to the Old City. ❹–❺

Hotel Holiday C Media Luna 10–47 ⓣ5/664-0948. Seventeen modest, clean rooms ring a breezy outdoor patio at this popular hostel, known for its friendly, social traveller scene. ❹

TREAT YOURSELF

One of the best ways to experience the Islas del Rosario is to stay put at a beachside hotel as the flotilla of *lanchas* motors day-visitors back to the mainland. Because of the remoteness of the islands, most bookings are all-inclusive, and you can add-on activities like canoe trips through mangrove-forested lagoons, snorkelling over coral reefs, kayaking and sport-fishing. Options include **Hotel Isla de Pirata** (ⓣ5/665 2952, ⓔreservas@hotelislapirata.com; US$180 for 2 people, with food, transport and basic tours included) and **San Pedro de Majaguaa** (ⓣ5/664 6070, ⓦwww.hotelmajagua.com; ❾). **Hotel Tres Banderas** does quality accommodation at the same reasonable rates as their Cartagena location (see opposite).

Eating

Among Cartagena's greatest charms is its array of fine restaurants – nowhere else in Colombia is the urge to splurge so intense, if partially because inexpensive options are so few and far between. For cash-conscious dining, consider grabbing some pizza then taking a seat in the nearest plaza for prime people-watching. Alternatively, you can hit up street vendors for everything from hot dogs and hamburgers to griddle-cooked corn *arepas* served with meat or egg on top.

Barandales Restaurante-Bar C de Tumbamuertos No. 38–85, Piso 2. This second-storey restaurant boasts outdoor tables on a wooden balcony overlooking the Plaza de San Diego. The ubiquitous *patacón* – a plantain smashed to resemble a patty and then fried – is served with all manner of toppings, pizza-like, rounding out a menu of chicken dishes and entree salads, starting at US$5.

El Bistro C de Ayos No. 4–42/46, the Old City. German-owned bistro and bakery, serving a

French-leaning set menu of soup and an entrée; a fantastic deal at US$5.

La Creperie No. 31–110 Plaza de Bolívar. A variety of crêpes sweet and savoury, plus meat and fish dishes and pastas, at reasonable prices for the plaza. Mains US$8–13.

Oh! la la Cafe Restaurant 2 Callejón Vargas, aka Cra 9a, off C 25. Colombian/French couple Carolina and Gilles serve fresh, innovative food that reflects their respective cultural backgrounds, including outstanding soups and robust meat dishes, plus vegetarian options. The candy-coloured decor is modern yet homey, and the bathroom's sliding mirror door covered in wonderfully mad scrawl. Easily the most exciting affordable meal in the city. Mains US$6.50–11. Closed Sun.

Pizza al Parque San Diego, Plaza de Jose Fernández de Madrid. People flock here after dark for tasty, inexpensive pizza and to check each other out. Enjoy your dinner sitting on the stone planters off the picturesque plaza directly across the street.

Drinking and nightlife

When the hot sun sinks into the ocean Cartagena gets its second wind. A concentration of tourist bars and dance clubs above the Portal de los Dulces overlook the Plaza de los Coches. Depending on business and the season, most will charge a small cover. Locals tend to gather at the cheaper but no less rowdy clubs in Getsemaní along Calle del Arsenal. Another option for a night out is a *chiva* ride – essentially a party bus in an old-fashioned, luridly decorated trolley that takes you on a late-night city tour fuelled by rum or red wine, fried regional finger foods, and *vallenato* music. *Chivas* depart at 8–8.30pm from Bocagrande locations such as *Hotel Capilla del Mar*, Cra 1 No. 8–12 (☎5/665-1140; rides around US$25, return at midnight).

Antigua Bar Plaza de los Coches, the Old City. Each of this modern nightclub's four floors plays a different music – salsa, disco or merengue. Fills up on weekends.

El Bodeguita del Medio C Santo Domingo 33–81 (across from the *Hard Rock Café*, right off the Plaza de la Aduana, against the city wall). These outdoor tables are the place to chill out and order a beer between the city wall and the Plaza de los Coches. Pounding Cuban music from the comparatively tiny indoor portion of the café reaches the tables outside.

Cafeteria de la Mantilla Provides an authentic – and affordable – alternative to the crowded cafés off Plaza de Santo Domingo, around the corner. Grab a cold drink or fried snack while taking in one of the *fútbol* matches that are so popular you'd think the city had but one TV channel on offer.

Mr Babilla Av del Arsenal No. 8B–137, Getsemaní. It's impossible not to dance in this club, where the party usually extends until dawn.

Quiebra Canto Cra 8B No. 25–10, Getsemaní. A local mainstay where old-school salsa mixes with endless shot glasses of locally distilled *ron*. The second-floor balcony offers a great view of Puerta del Reloj and the Old City.

Tu Candela Above the Portal de los Dulces, Old City. Cartagena's wildest and most popular salsa club is frequented by tourists and Colombian jetsetters, who dance the night away packed tightly in this second-floor club.

TREAT YOURSELF

Slip into one of the artisanal wooden chairs at **Torre Luna**, San Diego, C del Curato de Santo Toribio No 38-34, right off Plaza de Jose Fernández de Madrid, while Mass is being said at the church across the street and you can enjoy some live music with your meal.

This fine-dining restaurant serves freshly home-made meat, fish and vegetarian dishes all worth the wait. Their unusual pesto is a standout, with peanuts and spinach supplementing the traditional basil and olive oil. Entrees US$10 and up.

Directory

Banks and exchange Several banks with 24hr ATMs and *casas de cambio* are on the Plaza de la Aduana and adjoining streets as well as along Av San Martín in Bocagrande.

Car rental There's a concentration of rental agencies at the airport and along Av San Martín in Bocagrande. Upscale hotels in the Old City also have representatives in their foyers.

Embassies and consulates Canada: Cra 3 No. 8–129 ☎5/665-5838; United States: Centro, Cra 3 No. 36-37 at C de la Factoría ☎5/660 0415.

Immigration For visa extensions DAS has an office in Calle Gastelbondo near the Ramparts. Otherwise dial ☎153 for any immigration-related emergencies.

Medical Hospital Bocagrande ☎5/665-5270 on C 5 and Cra 6.

Police Dial ☎112 for the Policía Nacional.

Taxis Easy to flag around the Old City and beyond.

Moving on

By air One-way flights to Bogotá are typically US$225 and up (80min).
By bus To Santa Marta (4.30am–6pm every hour). Non-stop buses are US$20 and take 3hr while buses making stops cost US$14 and take 4hr. To Bogotá (US$75, every hour, 7.30am–6pm, 18hr). To Medellín (US$60, 6.30am–6.30pm, 12hr).

DAY-TRIP FROM CARTAGENA: BARRANQUILLA

Despite being Colombia's fourth largest city and main port, **BARRANQUILLA**, on the mouth of the Río Magdalena, about three hours by bus from Cartagena, would be all but overlooked if it were not for its annual **Carnaval** (Ⓦ www.carnavaldebarranquilla.com). For four days at the start of each March, this miserably hot, industrial city drapes itself in a salmagundi of vibrant colours, playful costumes and pulsating music – salsa, *cumbia*, *vallenato* and African drumming. Preparations begin much earlier, in mid-January, with the public reading of a municipal diktat ordering residents to have fun. Once the festivities begin, the town converts into one huge street party, kicked off by traditional parades like the "Battle of the Flowers" and "Dance of the Caiman". Parallel to the festivities, the city-sponsored gay Carnaval, though less publicized, is equally bacchanalian. Although barely known outside Latin America, Barranquilla's festivities are second only to Rio's Carnaval in size.

Be sure to arrange **accommodation** well in advance if you visit during Carnaval.

SANTA MARTA AND AROUND

Although Colombia's oldest city, founded in 1525, **SANTA MARTA**'s colonial heritage was all but swept away at the hands of English and Dutch pirates. The result is a friendly, understated beach city geared to middle-class Colombians on holiday. The simple pleasures predominate: purchasing a snack from one of the many itinerant vendors peddling cigarettes, candies and super-sweet *tinto* (brewed coffee) served in tiny plastic cups; entering the fray in the indoor and outdoor markets to find jerseys of a favourite *fútbol* team, and so on.

Not far away are some of Colombia's most placid beaches, particularly **Parque Nacional Tayrona**, Colombia's premier Caribbean paradise. The lovably tacky **Rodadero** resort area four kilometres south of the city offers clean, placid beaches in the off season and is swarming with families in the high season. Close by but a world away, the quiet fishing village of **Taganga** contains unpaved dirt streets and a small bay clustered with equally petite wooden boats. Santa Marta also acts as the hub for organizing hikes to the ruins of **Ciudad Perdida**.

What to see and do

Although better known for drawing sun worshippers, Santa Marta does boast a few worthwhile museums. A striking building with wooden garrets underneath a pitched tile roof, the well-maintained **Casa de la Aduana** (Customs House), on the corner of C 14 and Cra 2, is the city's oldest building, dating from 1531. Simon Bolívar stayed here briefly, and his body lay in state in an upstairs gallery after his death. On its ground floor, the **Museo Antropológico y Etnológico** (Mon–Fri 8am–noon & 2–6pm; free) has extensive displays on ancient Tayrona culture and its modern-day descendants – the Kogis, Arhuacos and Arsarios. An oversized replica of Ciudad Perdida provides a valuable introduction for anyone planning to visit the ruins.

The sun-bleached **Catedral**, at Cra 4 and C 17, is the oldest church in Colombia but has received successive facelifts. The current structure, with its bulky bell tower and stone portico, dates mostly from the seventeenth century. Bolívar's remains were kept here until 1842, when they were sent off to his native Venezuela.

An obligatory stop for history buffs is the **Quinta de San Pedro Alejandrino** (daily 9.30am–4.30pm; US$6), the sugar plantation five kilometres south of town where Bolívar spent his last agonizing days. The hacienda's peaceful grounds and exotic gardens are worth a visit, but the displays are more an exercise in Libertador fetishism – an Italian marble toilet bowl, military badges, a lock of hair – than they are biographical. Guided tours (in Spanish) are included in the price of admission. There's also a contemporary art museum on the premises. Buses leaving the waterfront main drag (Cra 1) for the Mamatoco suburb will drop you off at the Quinta if you ask the driver (US$0.50).

El Rodadero

While boasting no historical attractions **Rodadero**, four kilometres south of Santa Marta, draws visitors to its palm-lined boardwalk and smooth beaches. An invasion of high-rise apartments and tacky tourist shops has rubbed away Rodadero's exclusivity of late, yet it remains the cleanest and safest place to swim near Santa Marta. In the evening, it's also popular with clubbers. Local buses from Santa Marta cost US$0.75, and a taxi will set you back about US$3.50.

Accommodation

The majority of inexpensive lodging choices centred on Calle 10C – sit just a few blocks from the sea, and are in easy walking distance of the historic downtown area and the discos. In January and February, prices can double and reservations are recommended.

Casa Familiar C 10C No. 2–14 ⓣ5/421-1697. The cleanest and best serviced of the backpacker dens. Rooms have private bath, and the fourth-floor terrace affords views of harbour. The proprietors of the hotel can organize excursions, including trips to Ciudad Perdida. ❹

Hotel Miramar C 10C No. 1C–59 ⓣ5/421-4756. By far Santa Marta's cheapest hotel – just a few bucks to hang a hammock – the *Miramar* often gets overcrowded with dazed hippies hanging out on the patio. But its charm lies in its sordid atmosphere, and it has good tourist info. ❶–❷

Hotel Nueva Granada C 12, No. 3–17 ⓣ5/421-0685 or 421 1337. The vibe is simultaneously chic and homey in the central courtyard, onto which each modest room faces. Watching the stars from the small pool provides a great end to a night out. Hot breakfast and 30min internet use included. ❺–❻

Hostel Sun City C 18 No. 3-28 5/421-1925, ⓦwww.sahlmann.net. A pleasant alternative to the backpacker-filled C 10C. The bright decor is chintzy, but welcoming and clean enough, and a half-hour of internet time comes included. ❹

Eating

There are a substantial number of bustling restaurants lining Carrera 1, the city's main thoroughfare, which runs parallel to the beach. Carrera 1 is not unlike Miami's Lincoln Road: an oceanside parade of restaurants with outdoor seating, except with more street dogs and local colour.

Cesar Cra 2 (near C 17), Rodadero. A gritty, urban beach version of a beer garden right off the main road offering pizza and fast food. Just pretend you're at a continuous open-air party. You'll be hard-pressed to find items over US$5.

Merkabar C 10C 2–11. If you can ignore the food-encrusted tablecloths, you'll be rewarded with tasty, straightforward Colombian dishes at unbeatable prices. The various *cremas* on the menu – pureed soups not containing actual cream – are especially good. Mains from US$4.

Ricky's Cra 1 17–05 ⓣ5/421-1564. The gargantuan portions are the draw at this self-dubbed purveyor of Chinese-cum-international cuisine; one dish easily feeds two. Numerous outdoor tables and frequent live music help compensate for inconsistent food. Crêpes US$11, Chinese mains from US$8.

Nightlife

The fun, youthful scene melts into Colombian-dominated nightlife once the sun goes down. Be prepared to dance to reggae remixes, traditional offerings like *chumpeta* and 1990s international hits at clubs in both Santa Marta proper, Rodadero and nearby Taganga.

La Escollera C 5 No. 4–107. The pioneer of Rodadero's nightclub scene, this giant-sized disco plays salsa music, sometimes featuring live acts.

El Garaje C 8 at Cra 3, Taganga. The frisson sparked by the mix of locals and foreigners that fill the place and the low, tropical lighting make this place taxi-worthy even if you're staying in Santa Marta. A raised, palm-fringed *palapa* acts as a dancefloor while club classics, traditional Colombian music and reggae rotate through. Wed–Sat.

La Puerta C 17, No. 2–29. Colombians and foreign travellers in their twenties and thirties frequent this jam-packed, sexy club. Salsa, electronica, and American club hits will have you sweating on the narrow dancefloor that snakes into one of the club's many nooks and crannies. Cool off on the outdoor patio in back if the crowd gets to be too much, as it does on weekends.

Moving on

By air Taking a taxi 16km to the airport costs $13–17. One-way flights to Bogotá and to Medellín go for about US$125.

By bus Brasilia and Berlinas are two of the biggest coastal bus companies (the latter with an especially comfortable and modern fleet). To Bogotá (US$66, hourly 2–8pm, 4–16hr); to Bucaramanga (US$45, 3 daily, 9–10hr); to Cartagena (US$14/$20, 5am–8pm, 45min). Buses between Taganga and Santa Marta run about every 15min 5am–10pm and cost US$2.50. Taxis are US$3.50-4.50.

PARQUE NACIONAL TAYRONA

Colombia's most unspoilt tropical area, **TAYRONA**, a 45-minute drive east of Santa Marta, is around 45 times the size of New York's Central Park. It's a wilderness of jungle-fringed beaches, archeological ruins and lush forest with maddeningly elusive howling spider monkeys and falling coconuts. Silhouettes of swaying palm trees set against sunsets complete the cinematic image. The laid-back attitude of the place makes it feel like a paradisiacal summer camp.

The park gets its name from the Tayrona Indians, one of South America's greatest pre-Columbian civilizations. This area was a major trading centre for the Tayrona, as many as one million of whom inhabited it at one point. However, with the arrival of the Spanish, their peaceful existence came to an end. The Spanish governor ordered their annihilation in 1599 on the trumped-up charges that the Tayrona men practised sodomy; the brutal massacre that followed forced the remaining Tayronas to seek refuge high into the Sierra Nevada de Santa Marta, whose foothills flank the park to the south. Rising from sea level, these snowcapped sierras reach their apex just 42km from the coast, at the 5775-metre **Cristóbal Colón**, Colombia's tallest peak.

Pueblito

A clear and physically demanding uphill path leading from Cabo San Juan brings you to the archeological site of **Pueblito**, a former Tayrona village with a large number of terrace dwellings, sometimes called a mini-Ciudad Perdida. Although it's possible to complete an Arrecifes–Cabo San Juan–Pueblito circuit in one long, strenuous day, the trip is better made as part of a multi-day stay in the park. From Pueblito, you can also hike two hours through the jungle back down to the road and catch a bus back to Santa Marta from that park exit point instead of traversing your original route back to Cabo San Juan, but you may be better off hiring a guide for this less trafficked hike out, which has no signage and is quite taxing.

Beaches

Besides the archeo-anthropologically rich Pueblito, Tayrona's beaches and the prehistoric-feeling jungle that edges them are the irrefutable stars of the park. **Arrecifes**, though having a gorgeous sea-green layer cake of waves, has notoriously lethal riptides; more than two hundred overconfident tourists have drowned there over the years. The nearest swimming beach, **La Piscina**, is a fifteen-minute walk.

Wander another thirty minutes to reach **Cabo San Juan**, a tranquil swimming beach with hammock-strung gazebo peached atop a rocky outcropping. Further into the park you'll stumble onto an endless variety of beaches studded with hulking rocks, the first being a **nudist beach** that's followed by a beach with pretty decent waves for body surfing about ten minutes on. There's not much to do but hike, eat, drink and sleep, but don't be surprised if the place grows on you in a way that makes getting on with the rest of your journey oddly tough.

Arrival and information

By bus You'll likely come from Santa Marta, where buses (US$3 one-way) leave the market every half-hour for El Zaino, 35km away; they'll gladly drop you off at the Tayrona Park entrance, where your passport will be checked, and entrance fee (US$14 foreigners, $5 Colombian nationals) collected. From here, you'll take one of the many taxis and jeeps that regularly traverse the 4km to the entrance proper for US$2, or walk if you enjoy hikes on paved roads.

Park information It's possible to buy a map and a Coca-Cola at the visitors' centre at Canaveral (8am–6pm) before beginning the 45min walk through alternating patches of forest to the crowded Arrecifes Beach, the first in a string of gorgeous beaches. At the park entrance, you may be asked for your Yellow Fever vaccination, so best to be immunized (though the checking is haphazard and the actual danger of infection debatable). You can do so in a large Colombian city if you haven't had one back home; it takes ten days for the vaccine to take effect. Be sure to bring plentiful cash as only one restaurant and set of accommodations accept credit cards.

Accommodation and eating

The two beaches offering accommodation are Arrecifes and Cabo San Juan; both offer the option of renting tents, *cabañas* suitable for medium to large groups and hammocks.

Arrecifes The greatest variety of accommodation is in Arrecifes, with upscale tourism company Aviatur running a hammock/camping/*cabaña* (❷, ❹ and ❾ respectively) operation alongside a more bare-bones operation renting *cabañas* (❺) and tents (❹) for slightly lower prices. Aviatur's tasty, well-priced restaurant is here, the only one in the park that accepts credit cards. It looks more expensive than other dining options, but don't be intimidated: the food is consistently top-notch and costs only slightly more than the competing restaurant and the restaurant in Cabo San Juan.

Cabo San Juan The downside to the hammocks (❷ on beach, ❸ in gazebo) at Cabo San Juan is that they offer no mosquito netting – and it can get quite chilly at night. Seek out the information hut next door to the restaurant, the only real building in sight.

CIUDAD PERDIDA

CIUDAD PERDIDA, the 'Lost City' of the Tayronas, ranks among South America's most magical spots. More than a lost city, it's a lost world. Although its archeological ruins are less spectacular than those found at Machu Picchu, thanks to its geographic isolation the once-teeming city perched high in the Sierra Nevada de Santa Marta effortlessly preserves all the natural allure that the overrun Inca capital lost years ago to tourism. While steadily climbing the sierra's luxuriant foothills, you'll get a chance to bathe under idyllic waterfalls, visit inhabited indigenous villages and marvel at the swarms of monarch butterflies and abundant jungle wildlife.

Built sometime after 500 AD, the Tayrona capital is less than fifty kilometres southeast of Santa Marta. It wasn't discovered until 1975 when a few of the more than ten thousand *guaqueros*, or tomb raiders, from Santa Marta chanced upon it while scavenging for antiquities. Perched atop a steep slope 1300-metres-high in the vast jungle, the site consists of more than a thousand circular **terraces** – with more still being uncovered – that once served as foundations for Tayrona homes. Running throughout the city and down to the Buritaca river valley is a complex network of paved footpaths and steep, stone steps – over 1350 if you're counting – purportedly added later to obstruct the advance of Spanish horsemen.

THE KOGI INDIANS

Although now uninhabited, Ciudad Perdida is in many respects a living monument. It's surrounded by villages of **Kogi Indians**, who call the revered site Teyuna. By far the biggest highlight of any visit is the chance to interact with the Kogis as they drift on and off the main trail you'll traverse as part of a tour. As it comprises only a fraction of the wilderness they call home, they are increasingly less present on this popular tourist trail. The men are recognizable by their long, ragged hair, cream-coloured smocks and trusty *poporo*, the saliva-coated gourd holding the lime that activates the coca leaves they constantly chew. About nine thousnd Kogis are believed to inhabit the Sierra Nevada.

When flower power was in full bloom in the US in the 1970s, the Sierra Nevada became a major marijuana factory, and an estimated seventy percent of its native forests were burned to clear the way for untold amounts of the lucrative Santa Marta Gold strand. As the forest's prime inhabitants, the Kogis suffered dearly from the arrival of so many fast-buck farmers, one of the reasons why they're so skeptical of the outside world. Although some Kogis are friendly, and a few even speak Spanish, you'd be begging for a machete whip if you take a picture without their permission. To make quick friends, present them with some seashells, which they grind to extract the lime for their *poporos*.

Hiking practicalities

While the hills around Ciudad Perdida are considered safe by Colombian standards, it's easy to lose the trail, so go with either of the two companies that mount excursions, **Turcol** and **Sierra Tours.** You can book tours through any hostel or hotel, or middle-man operators you encounter on the streets of Santa Marta, the most reputable being **Magic Tour** (Ⓣ5/421-9432, Ⓦwww.hosteltrail.com/magictour). Prices for the six-day-long hike (a slightly shorter trip can be arranged) start around US$265 and include all meals, hammock lodging at farmhouses, the entrance fee to the ruins and transportation to and from the trailhead. The hike can be done all year round, though during the wet months from May to November the trail can get quite muddy. In any case, expect to get and stay wet any time of the year.

TAGANGA

Although no longer as pristine as it used to be, **TAGANGA** retains much of the spirit of the quiet fishing village it was before being absorbed in recent years by Santa Marta's expansion. Only fifteen minutes from Santa Marta by frequent public buses along the boardwalk on Carrera 1C, Taganga offers a wholly different vibe. Built on the side of a mountain, the town has an uncanny Mediterranean feel, with incongruously pleasant unpaved dirt streets. For budget travellers, it's an ideal base for exploring the surrounding area's attractions, though you'll need to backtrack to Santa Marta for most excursions.

What to see and do

One of the cheapest spots in the world for **scuba** certification, both PADI and NAUI, Taganga has sprouted so many new dive shops in recent years that the prices and services offered by each are quite competitive. A 4 to 6 day certification course costs about US$260 and often includes basic accommodation options, English or Spanish-speaking dive masters, and six dives (four open-water, two pool). Conveniently, Lost City treks and a whole manner of adventure travel options are on offer, too, at bigger shops on the main drag, along the beach. Many travellers report excellent experiences with Octopus Dive Center, C 15 1B–14 (Ⓣ5/421 9332).

Everything else here is pretty much water-related too. Fishermen troll an easy alternate access route to Tayrona National Park's southern beaches, the most popular being the crystalline waters of **Bahia Concha**, about an hour away by boat. At least US$55, this is a good excursion for a small group rather than an individual. Accessible by boat and foot is the much closer **Playa Grande**, which is modestly sized, heavily touristed and a bit pebbly, but still has the makings for a day of sun and sand. Keep in mind that Taganga's main beach is awash in small crafts, many available for hire, and not fit for swimming.

Accommodation

In catering to the budget traveller, most hostels in the town offer some kind of kitchen facilities.

Casa de Felipe Cra 5A No. 19–13 ⓣ5/421-9101, ⓦwww.lacasadefelipe.com. Three blocks uphill from the beach, the rustic rooms at this long-time backpacker fave come with (slow) internet service and a basic kitchen. A continental breakfast is included with all rooms except dorms (US$3, if desired). ❷–❺

Divanga B&B C 12 No. 4–07 ⓣ5/421-9092. This French-run hostel boasts a small pool lined with hammocks, an upstairs bar, and a distinct party vibe. Rooms are small and can be noisy but the proximity to *El Garaje* (see p.573), low rates, and frequent cookouts enjoyed on their pair of picnic benches create an appealing sense of community. ❺

Hotel Bahía Taganga C 4 No. 1B–35, Camino Playa Grande ⓣ5/421-9049, ⓦwww.hotelbahiataganga.com. Easily the town's most prettily kept and romantic hotel. Vivid-hued flowers flank white terrace steps that run along the rocky hill abutting the beach. Its hillside location makes for spectacular sunset views. ❻

Pelikan Hostal Cra 2 No. 17–04 ⓣ5/421-9057. Comfy pleather couches greet you upon entering this character-drenched spot, a favourite hang-out of salty locals and even saltier ex-pats. A shared kitchen and cozy hammock out front sweeten the deal. ❹

Eating

For dining, you need look no further than the road gently curving with the line of the shore, which is chock-full of restaurants specializing in seafood. **Bitácora Restaurante-Bar**, across from the bay, serves a very veggie-laden signature salad, as well as carefully prepared meat and chicken dishes that complement locally caught *pargo* (snapper). The Tiki-tinged atmosphere permeates the indoor and outdoor seating. Mains US$7–12.

RIOHACHA

Founded in 1539 by German explorer Nicolás de Federmán, **RIOHACHA** is the capital of the little-explored Guajira Peninsula, an arid spit that juts into the Caribbean to form the northern tip of South America. The city itself offers few attractions other than its fine white beaches, but makes a comfortable base from which to explore the surrounding badlands.

Guajira Peninsula's hostile, desert climate has kept it largely isolated since colonial times. As a result it's one of those special places where independent travellers can still feel as if they're leaving fresh tracks. Some 240- kilometres-long and no more than fifty- kilometres-wide, the barren peninsula is empty except for the semi-nomadic Wayúu, or Guajiro, Indians – and drug smugglers. The infinite number of sheltered coves from which drugs leave for the US has earned Guajira Peninsula the reputation of being Colombia's contraband capital. Most illicit activity, however, is kept hidden, and, as in any frontier area, the absence of the law doesn't pose any risks so long as you don't seek out trouble.

Twice-daily **buses** make the three-hour trip along the northern coast from Riohacha to Manaure, where traditionally dressed Wayúu extract salt manually and pile it in mounds against a stark white background. Otherwise, the beautifully remote **Cabo de la Vela** is famous for its large flamingo population and long sunsets, while at the peninsula's northern tip, six hours from Riohacha, the **Parque Nacional La Macuira** is home to an elfin cloudforest that rises five hundred metres straight up like a lush, island habitat amid the otherwise scorching desert. The heat and lack of good roads can make travelling in La Guajira hazardous so you'll probably want to contract a **tour agency** in Riohacha.

If you do make it here and plan to stay, *Gimaura*, C 7 Av La Playa (☎5/427-4587; ⑧), is a peaceful if somewhat decadent resort on the beach just a short walk from downtown. It has a pool and allows camping.

Tierra Paisa

Nominally a slang term to describe anyone from the region of Antioquio, **paisas** are alternately the butt of jokes and the object of envy for many Colombians. What makes them stand out is their rugged individualism and reputation for industriousness. Their fame dates back to the early nineteenth century, when they cleared Colombia's hinterland for farming in exchange for the government's carrot of free land. The rapid progress over the next century earned the mostly European colonists a reputation for hard work, exaggerated frugality and an unequalled skill at turning a profit from any enterprise, legal or otherwise. Perhaps the biggest *paisa* contribution to Colombia is its role in the spread of coffee.

The heart of *paisa* country is the burgeoning metropolis of **Medellín**, which has made a remarkable turnaround since its days as Colombia's murder capital in the early 1990s. The picturesque coffee-growing *fincas* near the modern cities of **Manizales** and **Pereira** were almost all established by *paisa* homesteaders. With the collapse in international coffee prices in the early 1990s, many growers have since opened their estates to tourists, who during harvest time can partake in the picking process. The so-called **Zona Cafetera**, or "Coffee Zone", is Colombia's newest and fastest growing tourist attraction. The zone is also the base for exploring one of Colombia's most postcard-perfect national parks, the **Parque Nacional Natural Los Nevados**.

COFFEE AND COCAINE

It's hard to say which of Colombia's two cash crops garners more international attention, the white or the black one. One thing is for certain: whether or not it contains the seal of approval of Juan Valdez or Pablo Escobar, both are synonymous with quality. The country's first bumper crop was **coffee**. Colombia is the world's leading producer of mild Arabica coffee and the third-largest overall coffee producer in the world, claiming ten percent share of the world's market (behind Vietnam and Brazil). High temperatures, heavy rainfall and a cool evening breeze make Colombia the bean's ideal habitat.

Cocaine was perceived as an innocuous stimulant until the twentieth century. Two US presidents, several European monarchs, even a pope were early addicts (and vocal advocates) of Vin Tonique Mariani, a nineteenth-century liqueur made from coca extract. The "real thing" Coca-Cola initially pushed on its customers was cocaine. For Sigmund Freud, a spoonful of coke each day was the cure for depression. As supplier of eighty percent of the world's cocaine, Colombia is responsible for an estimated US$4 billion each year, the equivalent of a sixth of its legal exports. Plan Colombia – a drug eradication programme involving aerial spraying of coca crops and a crackdown on insurgency groups that control the trade – kicked off in 1999 with multi-billion dollar backing from the United States. However, it has yet to make a dent in the world cocaine market, and in 2007, coca cultivation in Colombia actually rose by 27 percent.

MEDELLÍN

It's hard to think of a city – apart perhaps from Baghdad – more in need of a public relations makeover than **MEDELLÍN**. When turf wars between rival **drug gangs** became public in the 1980s and 1990s, Colombia's second largest city was rampaged by teenage hitmen, called *sicarios*, who, for as little as US$30, could be hired to settle old scores. The bloodthirst earned Medellín the world's highest murder rate.

But when cocaine kingpin **Pablo Escobar** was snuffed out in 1993, Medellín began to bury its sordid past. These days, while poverty is still prevalent in the crowded slums sloping around the city, and parts of the centre are unsafe to walk around at night, Medellín is overall the safest big city in Colombia. The increasing number of travellers who come here find an inviting, modern city with one of the country's best climates – year-round temperatures average 24°C. The ugly flipside to Medellín's ascendancy on the backpacker circuit has been a rise in sex tourism.

Dramatically perched 1538 metres high in the Central Cordillera overlooking the Aburrá Valley, the city was founded in 1675, purportedly by so-called "New Christian" Jews escaping the Spanish Inquisition. Today's descendants of these immigrant roots, **paisas**, as residents of the Antoquia department are known, are renowned for their rigid work ethic, and the country's most famous *paisa*, Colombian President Alvaro Uribe, is routinely satirized for his 5 am cabinet meetings. Medellín came into its own at the start of the twentieth century, when the coffee boom spurred industrialization. The city's organized layout and architecture mostly dates from that period.

Pablo Escobar's grave

Much to the displeasure of the well-intentioned tourist board, the former stomping grounds of **Pablo Escobar** – his homes, the modern buildings he built, the country-club mountain jail he was ambushed at – are becoming a minor draw for curious visitors. The former godfather of the Medellín cartel is still very much venerated for his extensive philanthropy by the city's poorer residents, who've even named a *barrio* after him. To make your own pilgrimage, visit his austere gravestone at the **Jardines Montenegro cemetery** near the Itaguí metro station.

Basílica Nuestra Señora de la Candelaria

A few churches from the late colonial era survive. The most important is the **Basílica Nuestra Señora de la Candelaria**, whose Baroque interior dates from 1776. The whitewashed, flat-naved chapel, which overlooks the centrally located **Parque Berrío**, was Medellín's cathedral until 1931.

Catedral Metropolitana

The current cathedral is the fanciful **Catedral Metropolitana**, four blocks away from Basílica de la Candelaria, along a pedestrian walkway, at **Plaza Bolívar.** The fortress-like structure was constructed between 1875 and 1931 and claims to be the largest church in the world built entirely of bricks – 1.2 million, if you're counting. A large **handicraft fair** is held on the first Saturday of every month in the plaza.

Museo de Antioquia

Medellín is the birthplace of sculptor and painter **Fernando Botero**, known for his satirical representation of all things fat – oranges, priests, even Mona Lisa. Although Medellín residents felt miffed by Botero's donation of his extensive European art collection to a Bogotá museum (see Donación Botero, p.550), the largest collection of his works is housed in the modern **Museo de Antioquia** at

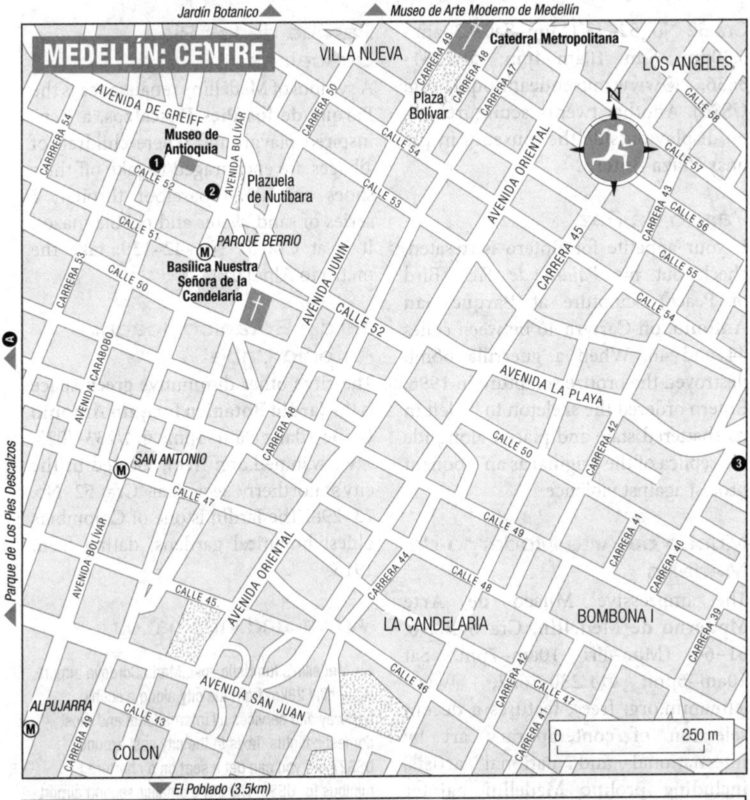

Jardín Botanico
Museo de Arte Moderno de Medellín

MEDELLÍN: CENTRE

VILLA NUEVA
Catedral Metropolitana
LOS ANGELES
Plaza Bolívar
Museo de Antioquia
Plazuela de Nutibara
PARQUE BERRIO
Basílica Nuestra Señora de la Candelaria
SAN ANTONIO
LA CANDELARIA
BOMBONA I
ALPUJARRA
COLON
AVENIDA DE GREIFF
AVENIDA BOLÍVAR
AVENIDA JUNIN
AVENIDA ORIENTAL
AVENIDA LA PLAYA
AVENIDA CARABOBO
AVENIDA SAN JUAN
CARRERA 54
CARRERA 53
CARRERA 50
CARRERA 49
CARRERA 48
CARRERA 47
CARRERA 45
CARRERA 44
CARRERA 43
CARRERA 42
CARRERA 41
CARRERA 40
CARRERA 39
CALLE 58
CALLE 57
CALLE 56
CALLE 55
CALLE 54
CALLE 53
CALLE 52
CALLE 51
CALLE 50
CALLE 49
CALLE 48
CALLE 47
CALLE 46
CALLE 45
CALLE 43
Parque de Los Pies Descalzos
0 250 m
El Poblado (3.5km)

ACCOMMODATION				EATING & DRINKING							
Black Sheep Hostel	B	Palm Tree Hostal	A	Al Rojo	9	Blue	4	Il Forno	12	Sandwich Qbano	6
Casa Kiwi	D	Pit Stop	C	Azur Café	2	Café Botero	1	Le Bon Café	10	Sushi to go	7
Global	E	Provenza Hostal	G	Berlin	5	Exfanfarria	3	Oz	11	Thaico	8
Hostel Tamarindo	F										

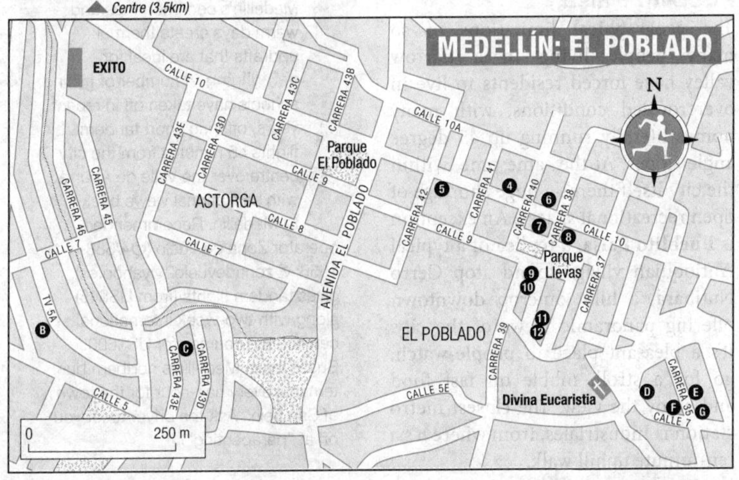

COLOMBIA

TIERRA PAISA

Cra 52 No. 52–43 (Mon–Sat 9.30am–5.30pm, Sun 10am–4pm; ⓣ4/251-3636, ⓦwww.museodeantioquia.org; US$5). Another twenty sculptures are on display outside the museum in the busy **Plaza Botero.**

Pájaro de Paz

If your appetite for Botero isn't sated, check out his *Pájaro de Paz* (Bird of Peace) sculpture at **Parque San Antonio**, on Carrera 46 between calles 44 and 46. When a guerrilla bomb destroyed the bronze sculpture in 1996, Botero ordered the skeleton to be left in its shattered state and placed alongside it a replica of the original as an eloquent protest against violence.

Museo de Arte Moderno de Medellín

The impressive **Museo de Arte Moderno de Medellín**, Cra 64B No. 51–64 (Mon–Fri 10am–7pm, Sat 10am–5pm; ⓣ4/230-2622, ⓦwww.elmamm.org; free), features a decent selection of contemporary art by international and national artists, including prolific Medellín painter Débora Arango. Take the metro to the Suramericana stop.

Pueblito Paisa

The geographical limitations of so many people living in a narrow valley have forced residents to live in overcrowded conditions, with many homes literally running up 45 degree angle slopes. At the same time, within the city itself there's a huge shortage of open recreational spaces. An exception is **Pueblito Paisa**, a replica of a typical Antioquian village found atop Cerro Nutibara, a hilly outcrop downtown offering panoramic views of the city. It's a pleasant place to people-watch, go for a stroll, nibble on fast food and enjoy the view. The closest metro station is Industriales, from where it's a ten-minute uphill walk.

Parque de los Pies Descalzos

A symbol of Medellín's renaissance is the **Parque de los Pies Descalzos**, a Zen-inspired playground where children of all ages are encouraged to take off their shoes and tread barefoot through a series of sand, water and pebble mazes. It is at Cra 57 No. 42–139; take the metro to Alpujarra.

Jardín Botánico Joaquín Antonio Uribe

The city's other diminutive green space is the **Jardín Botánico Joaquín Antonio Uribe** (daily 9am–5pm; ⓣ4/233-7025, ⓦwww.jbmed.org; free), located in the city's northern sector at Cra 52 No. 73–298. The Jardín is one of Colombia's oldest botanical gardens, dating from 1913.

Arrival and information

Air Medellín's futuristic José María Córdova airport lies a hilly 28km from the city along a scenic highway and services all international and most domestic flights. Taxis to the city cost around US$27 but you can get a seat on a chartered minibus for US$6. The city's smaller second airport is Olaya Herrera, located beside the southern bus terminal; taxis to El Poblado are US$2.

TREAT YOURSELF

Medellín's cool mornings and warm days create thermal updrafts that are ideal for **paragliding**. A number of gliding schools have taken off in recent years, offering short tandem flights 45 minutes from the city centre over the Valle de Aburrá with sensational views back to Medellín. Recommended operator Zona de Vuelo (ⓣ4/388-1556; ⓔzonadevuelo2@yahoo.es) gives tandem flights (from US$45) along with two-week international certification courses for US$600. Buses leave Medellín's northern bus terminal every half-hour for the town of San Felix. Ask the driver to let you off at "parapenting".

Bus Depending on which part of the country you're arriving from, long-distance buses arrive either at the Terminal del Norte or Terminal del Sur, both almost equidistant from the centre. A taxi from the northern terminal to El Poblado, where most of the hostels are, costs about US$5.50, but it is cheaper and quite easy to get the metro. A taxi from the southern terminal to El Poblado is US$2.

Tourist information There are information stands at both airports as well as at Pueblito Paisa (Mon–Wed noon–6pm; Thurs–Sun 10am–8pm; ⓣ4/235-8370). The main tourist office (Mon–Sat 8am–midday & 2–5pm; ⓣ4/232-4022) is tucked away in the Palacio de Exposiciones, C 41 No. 55–35, a long (and ultimately worthless) hike from the centre.

City transport and tours

By foot, taxi, metro and bus Most sightseeing in the centre can be done on foot. Taxis are cheap and plentiful (try Tax Individual ⓣ4/331-1111 or Coodetaxi ⓣ4/311-7777). Better yet is the city's excellent metro system (US$0.80), among the cleanest and most efficient in the world; included in the price of a metro ride are cable cars that leave from both the Acevedo and San Javier metro stations, carrying passengers high above the city for remarkable views. The safety and efficiency of the metro has rendered buses mostly redundant; at US$0.70 a ride they're a cheap – though not recommended – option after the metro closes at 11pm.

City tours For an overview of the city, Turisbus (ⓣ4/371-5054, ⓦwww.seditrans.com) hits all the main sights, allowing you to jump on and off throughout the day (US$7). Eco Rutas (ⓣ312/269-5647, ⓦwww.ecorutascolombia.com), operated by anthropologist Pablo Aristizábal (who speaks English, French and German), runs city tours as well as two-day cultural and trekking excursions to off-the-beaten-track pre-Hispanic archeological sites 60km southwest of Medellín, culminating in an ascent of the 800-metre-high Cerro Tusa, an extinct volcano and sacred indigenous site.

Accommodation

Like any big city, **hotels** in Medellín come in many different varieties. Inexpensive, if rundown, lodging tends to be located in the centre, which becomes a ghost town and therefore dangerous at night. Most of the hostels and more modern hotels can be found closer to the nighttime action in El Poblado and Patio Bonito.

Hostels

Black Sheep Hostel Transversal 5A No. 45–133, Patio Bonito ⓣ4/311-1589, ⓦwww.blacksheepmedellin.com. This sociable backpacker's pad has all bases covered, including Spanish classes, high-pressure showers and weekly barbecues. The affable Kiwi owner has travelled extensively in Colombia and is happy to share his knowledge. ❷–❹

Casa Kiwi Cra 36 No. 7–10 ⓣ4/268-2668, ⓦwww.casakiwi.net. Owned by a motorcycle-loving American, this excellent 50-bed hostel has clean dorms, DVD room, pool table, kitchen, bicycles for rent, laundry service, wi-fi and an adjoining luxury wing with fancy doubles, some en suite. ❷–❹

Hostal Tamarindo C7 No. 35–36 ⓣ4/268-9828, ⓔhostaltamarindo@gmail.com. Tranquil hostel run by a warm Colombian-American and her dog Ramona, with kitchen, DVD lounge, wi-fi, internet, laundry service and tattoo parlour. ❷–❺

Palm Tree Hostal Cra 67 No. 48D–63 ⓣ4/260-2805, ⓦwww.palmtreemedellin.com. Comfortable, quiet youth hostel with internet, cable TV and guest kitchen. Private or shared rooms are available. Three blocks from Suramericana metro stop. ❷–❹

Pit Stop Cra 43e No. 5-110, Patio Bonito ⓣ4/352-1176, ⓦwww.pitstophostel.com. The party place in Medellín, this 70-bed (and growing) Irish-owned hostel is more like a self-contained luxury resort, complete with marble floors, sports bar, basketball court, restaurant, swimming pool, steam room and DVD lounge with plasma TV. One of the dorms even has a Jacuzzi in its private bathroom. ❷–❺

Hotels

Global Cra 35 No. 7–58 ⓣ4/311-5418, ⓦwww.globalhostelcolombia.com. Slick and modern, this eight-room boutique hotel has doubles with big beds, en suite, TV and minibar. Guests have access to a kitchen. ❼

Provenza Hostal Cra 35 No. 7–2, El Poblado ⓣ4/326-5600, ⓔprovenzahostal@gmail.com. Another boutique hotel, with small but light-drenched doubles with ensuite, TV and fridge. Includes breakfast, wi-fi and internet. ❼

Eating

Paisa cuisine, among Colombia's most distinctive, is heavy on the *frijoles* (black beans), grilled meat, plantains and rice. Perhaps no dish is more characteristic of the region than the *bandeja paisa*, a large bowl filled with ground beef, *chorizo* sausage, *frijoles*, rice, fried green bananas, a fried egg, avocado and fried pork. The city's trendiest restaurants are around the leafy Parque Lleras in El Poblado, also known as the Zona Rosa.

Azur Café Cra 51 No. 52–03 ⓣ4/251-3633. Located within the ornate Palacio de la Cultura, built in 1925, they feature cafeteria-style lunches for around US$5 in a shaded outdoor plaza. Closed Sat & Sun.

Le Bon Cafe C 9 No. 39–09. Excellent pastries and 32 types of coffee are on offer at this El Poblado café, which has several other locations throughout the city.

Café Botero Cra 52 No. 52-43 inside Museo de Antoquia ⓣ4/513-2901. Excellent salads and international cuisine, popular with a business lunch crowd. Mains around US$9.

Exfanfarria Cra 40 No. 50B–32 ⓣ4/217-2605. This high-ceilinged and wooden-floor bohemian poet's café and underground theatre serves cheap beer (US$1.20).

Il Forno C 12 Sur No. 51B–29 ⓣ4/361-3900. A modern, open-air Italian eatery and El Poblado institution with plenty of mood lighting and satisfying pizza, pasta and salads. Mains US$6–10.

Sandwich Qbano C 10, No. 38–32 ⓣ4/312-1975. Giant, cheesy grilled sandwiches for under US$6 go down a treat the morning after a late night.

Sushi To Go C 9A No. 38–26 local 108 ⓣ4/268-2951. For a taste of raw fish, try this spacious sushi restaurant. Plenty of Asian noodle and rice dishes too. Plates up to US$11.

Thaico C 9A No. 37–40 ⓣ4/311-5639. Overlooking Parque Lleras, this restaurant is full of *paisas* eating appetizing (if slightly inauthentic) Thai food and getting steadily drunk on three-for-one cocktails. Mains around US$14.

Drinking and nightlife

A Zona Rosa of bars and clubs – most of them catering to a young clientele – are in El Poblado. For the best clubs though (*Mangos* and *Vinacuré*), you'll have to take a taxi to the suburbs.

Berlin C 10 No. 41–65 ⓣ4/266-2905. Laid-back drinking hole with quirky wall art and an indie rock soundtrack ideal for nursing a beer, shooting some pool or playing cards with friends.

Blue C 10 and Cra 41. Giant speakers pump hard electro beats to a student and backpacker-centric crowd who wave along to flashing green laser lights. Cover US$5.50. Thurs–Sat.

Carnival C 80 Sur No. 50–61 ⓣ4/262-9166. Open late (until 8am), this electronic club hosts international DJs and is packed with wired revellers who don't want the party to end. Cover US$11. Thurs–Sat.

Mangos Cra 42 No. 67A–151. Hipsters, narco-traffickers and "prepagos" all rub shoulders at Medellín's most notorious club. The live shows alone are worth the cover charge (US$9–23 depending on the night).

Oz Cra 38, No. 8–8 ⓣ4/311-5781. There's plenty of eye candy at this fun, satin-draped club that attracts a young, yuppie crowd. Cocktails US$9, cover $7. Thurs–Sun.

Vinacuré Cra 50 No. 100D Sur-7, Caldas ⓣ4/278-1633. A hedonistic temple to kitsch featuring raucous live shows, gender-bending staff, cheesy pop music and eye-boggling wall art. Cover US$6.

Moving on

By air International: Caracas (daily); Lima (daily); Quito (1–2 daily). Domestic: Barranquilla (14 daily; 1hr 45min); Bogotá (31 daily; 50min); Bucaramanga (5 daily; 50min); Cali (2 daily; 50min); Cartagena (3 daily; 1hr 20min); Manizales (2 daily; 30min); Monteria (6 daily; 50min); Pereira (7 daily; 35min); San Andrés (1 daily; 1hr 50min); Quibdó (6 daily; 35min).

By bus Bogotá (every 30min; 9hr); Cali (50 daily; 8–9hr); Buenaventura (2 daily; 10hr); Cartagena (14 daily; 13hr); Guatapé (every 30min; 2hr); Ipiales (5 daily; 20hr); Magangue for Mompos (2 daily; 10hr); Manizales (hourly; 5hr); Pasto (5 daily; 18hr); Pereira (more than 50 daily; 5–6hr); Popayán (3–4 daily; 10hr); Santa Fe de Antioquia (every 30min; 1hr 30min); Santa Marta (12 daily; 15hr); Tolu (14 daily; 10hr); Turbo (hourly; 10hr).

DAY-TRIPS FROM MEDELLÍN

A few nearby parks make good if not absolutely essential stops within range of Medellín; the attractions around the lake Embalse del Peñol come close to qualifying.

Parque Ecológical Piedras Blancas

The **Parque Ecológical Piedras Blancas** (daily 8am–6pm; ⓣ4/262-0592), 26km east of the city, serves as the lungs of Medellín. Set at the cool height of 2500metre, much of this nature reserve has been reforested with native species, attracting butterflies and birds such as the brilliant blue soledad and toucanet. Well-preserved pre-Columbian stone trails constructed between 100 BC and 700 AD weave through the park, while there is a new butterfly gallery and a slick **insect museum** close to the official entrance. Camping is permitted (US$4) and a basic **hotel** offers beds and three meals for US$28 per person. To get to the park, board a bus from the corner of Ayacucho and Córdoba in the city centre (leaves every 30min) to the village of Santa Elena (30min) where another bus runs every half-hour to the park. The metro cable car that leaves from Acevedo is currently being extended for another four kilometres to connect the city to the park. Eco Rutas (see tours p.581) offers full-day park tours with a multilingual anthropologist guide.

Parque de las Aguas

One of Latin America's largest water parks, **Parque de las Aguas** (Tues–Sun 9am–5pm; ⓣ4/467-5000; US$4), km23 Autopista Norte, Barbosa, is a fun place to cool off. There are ten high-speed waterslides, a wave pool and a slow-flowing river for riding tubes. To get here take the metro to Niquia station (the last stop) and then jump on one of the frequent buses to the park.

Piedra del Peñol and Guatapé

Bearing a freakish resemblance to Rio de Janeiro's Sugar Loaf Mountain, **Piedra del Peñol**, or simply "the rock", rises spectacularly from the edge of Embalse del Peñol, an artificial lake some 70km east of Medellín. Locals might wax that the 200m granite and quartz monolith is a meteorite. Whatever geological or intergalactic anomaly brought it here, it's well worth climbing the 649 stone steps to the rock's peak for phenomenal 360-degree views of emerald green peninsulas jutting into the azure Embalse del Peñol – a hydroelectric dam that submerged the original town of El Peñol in the 1970s.

There are a handful of restaurants and tourist stalls at the base of the rock, but better to walk or take a jeep (US$1 per person) to the delightful lakeside village of **Guatapé**, 3km away, full of eateries serving trout fresh from the lake. The palm-lined main square, Plaza Simón Bolívar, is well-preserved, with its crowning glory the Iglesia La Inmaculada Concepción; throughout the town you'll find colourful colonial houses adorned with intricate artistic motifs. A few blocks away by the lake, you can opt for one-hour cruises, boat hire or zip-line rides. If you want to **stay the night**, the scrubbed-to-a-pulp *Hospedaje Familiar*, Cra 27 No. 31–58 (ⓣ4/861-0574; ❹), has twenty simple rooms with TV and private bathroom. The best places to eat, on lakefront Avenida Malecón (also known as Calle 32), include *Vaso é Leche*, C 32 No. 26–35, where you'll get filling trout mains for US$4.50. **Buses** leave for Guatapé roughly every half-hour from Medellín's northern bus terminal (2hr). Ask the driver to let you off at "La Piedra".

MANIZALES AND AROUND

Founded in 1849 by migrating *paisas*, **MANIZALES** developed in the late nineteenth century with the growth of the coffee industry. One legacy is the numerous Neoclassical buildings from the era found in the city centre, which has been declared a national monument. The high-mountain city (altitude 2150m) of 386,000 people sits at the base of the snowcapped Nevado del Ruiz volcano (see p.585), which occasionally on a clear day can be seen burping vapour from the bridge in front of the Teatro Los Fundadores. The town owes its hilly topography – most streets are steep and windy – to the fact that the earth below it is geologically volatile, and earthquakes occur with some frequency. This capital of Caldas department is a university town – there are seven in all here – and the large student population gives the city a festive air that other large cities in the region lack. The party comes to a head in the first weeks of January during the **Feria de Manizales**, when there are colourful parades, a beauty pageant in search of a new Coffee Queen and bloody bullfights staged in the Plaza de Toros (C8 and Cra 27). Manizales makes an ideal base for exploring the surrounding **coffee farms** and the **Parque Nacional Natural Los Nevados**.

Plaza de Bolívar

While the bulk of your stay in the Manizales area will be spent outside the city, there are a few buildings worth checking out around the **Plaza de Bolívar**, on Cra 21 and C 22. Linger on the north side of the square and appreciate the Romanesque facade of the departmental government building, the **Palacio de la Gobernación**, which was built in 1925. Opposite it stands the Gothic-style **Catedral**, built entirely of reinforced concrete in 1928.

Monumento a Los Colonizadores

In the northwest suburb of Chipre, on a high bluff at the end of Avenida 12 de Octubre, the **Monumento a Los Colonizadores** is a 25-tonne bronze sculpture reliving the trials and triumphs of the Antioquian mule drivers who founded the city. It's the city's best viewpoint and on a clear day you can see seven *departamentos* and three mountain ranges.

Estación del Cable Aéreo

In the well-manicured Cable neighbourhood, you'll find the **Estación del Cable Aéreo**, the well-conserved end station for the 73-kilometre, suspended funicular (once the world's longest), which linked Manizales with the Magdalena River port of Honda (and hence the Atlantic Ocean) from 1910 to 1961. This incredible monument to *paisa* ingenuity, with a little help from migrant Australian engineers, can be found at Carrera 23 (also called Av Santander) and Calle 65.

Jardín Botánico

A short stroll down the hill from El Cable on the campus of the Universidad de Caldas, the **Jardín Botánico**, C 65 No. 26–10 (Mon–Fri 8am–5pm, Sat 8am–2pm; free; ⓣ6/878-1588), offers a peaceful place to walk among orchid gardens, Andean forests and endangered native tree species.

Arrival and information

Air Manizales' La Nubia airport is 8km southeast of downtown. A taxi to the centre costs US$4 or you can jump on the frequent buses for US$0.60.

Bus The bus terminal (ⓣ6/874-5451) is at Av 19 between carreras 14 and 17. It is a short walk or taxi ride to the main square, and a long US$3.50 ride to El Cable.

Tourist information There is a tourist office at Cra 21 No. 22–23 (Mon–Fri 8am–noon & 2–6pm; ⓣ6/884-9280) at the back entrance of the Palacio de la Gobernación (Mon–Fri 7.30am–noon & 2–6.30pm; ⓣ6/884-6211), which is good for city maps but not much else. There's another tourist office at Parque Benjamin López on the corner of Cra 22 and C 31 (Mon–Sat 8am–noon & 2–6pm, Sun 8am–noon & 2–4pm; ⓣ6/873-3901).

Accommodation

Hotel California C 19 No. 16–37 ⓣ6/8847-720, ⓔltg71@hotmail.com. A no-frills, cheap and clean hotel, right in front of the bus terminal for a quick getaway when the thrill is gone. Includes cable TV. ❹

Mountain House C 66 No. 23B–137 ⓣ6/887-4736, ⓦwww.mountainhousemanizales.com. On a quiet suburban street just two blocks from the lively Zona Rosa, this lively backpacker's hostel has comfortable dorms, a cozy TV room stocked with DVDs, free breakfast, kitchen, a backyard, internet and laundry service and helpful staff. ❷–❹

Eating, drinking and nightlife

The city centre clears out at night and most eating and drinking is done in the suburbs. The liveliest area, popular with students, is between calles 60 and 75 along Cra 23, the Zona Rosa, where you'll find the best selection of restaurants, pubs and discotheques.

101 Perros C 51 No. 22A–07. This nondescript hot dog and hamburger stand makes some of the best patties anywhere in Colombia (US$3.40). Open late.

Las Cuatro Estaciones C 65 No. 23a–32 ☎6/886-0676. A stylish Italian restaurant that does a fine trade in tomato soup, tasty pizzas (up to US$16), cheese-smothered steak (US$13) and vegetarian-friendly pastas (up to US$10).

Manimez Cra 21 No. 20–18 ☎6/883-0299. Handy for the main plaza, this health food store and bakery does a US$3 vegetarian set lunch including soup and main course. Closed Sun.

Roho Torre Casa Luker on Cra 23 and C 64. Good Thai cuisine (for Colombia at least) in a modern, chic setting, at moderate prices. Mains US$8–11.

Santelmo Cra 23B No. 64–80 ☎6/885-8200. Heaving with students who down cocktails (US$5.50) and jugs of sangria (US$15) and dance the night away between the tables. Serves carb-centric food to soak up the booze. Wed–Sat.

PARQUE NACIONAL NATURAL LOS NEVADOS

Indisputably one of the crown jewels in Colombia's national parks system, the 583 square-kilometre **PARQUE NACIONAL NATURAL LOS NEVADOS** (US$13 entrance fee), forty kilometres southeast of Manizales, protects some of the last surviving snowcapped peaks in the tropics. In total, there are five volcanoes – three of them are covered in snow year-round – the tallest being the 5321-metre **Nevado del Ruiz**. The majority of the peaks are now dormant, but Nevado del Ruiz remains an active threat, having killed 22,000 people and buried the now extinct town of Armero when it erupted in 1985. Sadly, though, for a park whose name, Nevado, implies perpetual snow, global warming has lifted the snow line to almost 5000 metres on most peaks. The best months to visit are January and February – clear days make for the best views of the volcanic peaks. March, July, August and December can also be ideal, while the rest of the year sees a fair amount of rain.

What to see and do

The park's **northern sector** is the more touristy and is easily accessible from Manizales. Though it's of little compensation, because of the severe melt, it's now possible for even moderately fit armchair adventurers to reach Nevado del Ruiz's summit in a long day's journey from Manizales. Although not technically difficult – with good weather you can climb in regular hiking shoes – a **guide** is required to navigate the confusing path and assist in the event of altitude sickness. Your easiest option is to contact Ecosistemas (☎6/880-8300) at Cra 21 No. 23–21 Local 108, which runs a ten-hour trip from Manizales for around US$55, including transport, breakfast, lunch, park entrance, the ascent of Ruiz and a visit to the thermal baths at the park's entrance.

The dramatic **southern end**, where a dense wax palm tree forest slowly metamorphoses into *páramo* near the cobalt-blue **Laguna del Otún** (3950m), can only be accessed on foot. Reaching Laguna del Otún from Manizales involves an initial four-hour drive, taking in park highlights such as the extinct Olleta crater, Laguna Verde and Hacienda Potosí, before culminating in a two-hour trek to the trout-stuffed lagoon (fishing permitted). You can also approach from either the Valle de Cocora in Salento (see p.590) or a 18km uphill hike from the *Refugio La Pastora* in Parque Ucumarí near Pereira (see p.588). In the past there has been guerrilla activity on these routes, so check conditions before setting out.

Accommodation and information

Visitors with time will want to spend at least a couple of nights inside the park exploring the boggy *páramo* landscape, an important freshwater reserve dominating the high massifs. There is

STAYING ON A COFFEE FARM

Coffee is the planet's heaviest traded commodity after oil, with prices such that Colombian coffee farmers have been riding a lucrative wave. Back in the early 1990s, however, when the price of coffee was plummeting, some of Colombia's 300,000-plus growers began to look to tourism to supplement their incomes. Instead of harvesting rich berries, hundreds of **coffee fincas** in the Zona Cafetera now exploit their heritage to curious tourists.

Fincas range from traditional estates still attended by their owner to deceptively modern rural hotels where the only coffee you'll find comes served with breakfast. Scenically, the farms look out on lush slopes, overgrown with the shiny-leaved coffee shrubs and interspersed with banana plants and bamboo-like *guadua* forests. Many will also arrange horseback riding and walks. Indeed, for those with a more flexible budget, *fincas* make an ideal base to explore the region's many attractions.

To locate the best *fincas* for your needs, ask other travellers or a trusted travel agency like Ecoguías in Bogotá (see p.553). You can also enquire at the local tourist offices in Manizales or Pereira (see p.583 & p.586).

Recommended fincas

Finca El Ocaso Vereda de Palestina Km 4, 15min by jeep from Salento ⓣ310/451-7194. Offers guided tours of a 24-hectare riverside coffee farm (daily 6am–6pm) and overnight stays with breakfast in a colonial-style farmhouse. Some beds are in shared rooms and guests can use the communal kitchen. ❷–❹

Hacienda Guayabal Cra 3 No. 15–72 Chinchin, (30min by bus from Manizales or Pereira to Chinchiná and then 3km by taxi or bus to the farm) ⓣ6/840-1463, ⓦwww.haciendaguayabal.com. Runs tours of their postcard-perfect coffee farm (US$8.50). Guests can stay in the main house (❻ per person), including tour, three meals and use of swimming pool. There are also cheaper *cabañas* with a kitchen. ❸–❺

La Pequeña Granja de Mamá Lulú Take a taxi (US$4) or Jeep Willys (US$1.50, three daily) to Vereda Palermo from the village of Quimbaya, 31km south of Pereira, ⓣ6/752-1260 or 311/389-4646, ⓔgranjaluluquimbaya@yahoo.es. Although it no longer grows coffee, this is a model ecological farm and guest lodge, where everything from animal manure to rainwater is recycled. Owned by a family of *campesinos*, Mamá Lulú and her children warmly receive tourists in a guesthouse built entirely of *guadua*. Organic meals are served. For non-guests, a guided tour of the tiny farm patch costs US$3.50. ❺

camping (US$5 per person) at *Chalet Arenales del Ruiz* (4500m) at the base of Ruiz. There's also a campsite (US$5) and upscale **hotel** (❻ per person, with two meals) at El Cisne, the base for exploring the park's less-visited interior, including the hidden mountain pond Laguna Verde and the cloud-covered Nevado de Santa Isabel. For further information, a map and good logistical advice on camping or hiking, call the **park office** (Mon–Fri 8am–noon & 2pm–6pm; ⓣ6/886-4703 or 6/886-8367) at Cra 19A No. 76A–04.

Moving on

By air Bogotá (12 daily; 50min); Medellín (2 daily; 30min).

By bus Bogotá (hourly; 8hr); Cali (hourly; 5hr); Medellín (hourly; 5hr); Pereira (every 15min; 1hr 20min).

PEREIRA

Just 56km south of Manizales, **PEREIRA** (1480m) makes an equally suitable base for exploring the Zona Cafetera. The region's largest city, with 429,000 inhabitants, it shares Manizales' history as a centre for the coffee industry but lacks its sister city's youthful energy. Its historic centre has been repeatedly destroyed by earthquakes, the most recent striking in 1999. However, it's closer to many of the region's coffee *fincas*, thermal springs and the Parque Nacional del Café.

Pereira's **Plaza de Bolívar** is unique among the uniformly named central plazas of Colombia for its modern sculpture of the El Libertador nude on horseback, a controversial pose when it was unveiled in 1963 but now a beloved city symbol. Also on the plaza is the town's magnificent **Catedral**, built in 1875. Otherwise nondescript from the outside, the single-nave interior is supported by an elaborate latticework of twelve thousand wooden beams forming a spider's web-like canopy.

Arrival and information

By air Pereira's airport (☎6/314-2688) is 5km west of the city centre. A taxi downtown costs US$4 or you can jump on one of the frequent buses for US$0.60.
By bus The bus terminal lies 1.5km south of the city centre at C 17 No. 19. A taxi downtown is US$2 or a bus costs US$0.60.
Tourist information The helpful tourist office (Mon–Thurs 7.30am–noon & 2–6pm, Fri 8am–noon & 2–6pm, ☎6/335-1676; ⓦwww.pereira.gov.co), is on the corner of C 17 and Cra 10 on the first floor of the Centro Cultural Lucy Tejada.

Accommodation

Pereira's accommodation is fairly uninspiring, with few options for budget travellers. If you can swing it, it's worth staying at one of the converted *fincas*, many of them former coffee plantations, between 5 and 35km from the city. Most have swimming pools, offer meals and are accessible by bus from Pereira; prices range US$37–68 per person per night. Tourist agency TurisCafe (Mon–Fri 8am–noon & 2–6pm, Sat 9am–noon; ☎6/325-4157, ⓦwww.turiscafe.net), C 19 No. 5–48 office 901 in CC Novacentro, can organize stays.
Hotel Cataluña C 19 No. 8-61 ☎6/335-4527. Close to Plaza de Bolívar, this hotel has large, spartan rooms (some with external windows) with hospital-style beds, telephone, TV and private bath. Breakfast included. ❺
Los Tunjos Cra 4A No. 20–23 ☎6/335-4710, ⓔhotelostunjos@hotmail.com. Offers clean but pokey rooms with TV, fridge and private bathroom; most rooms have internal windows. Includes breakfast, internet and small gym. ❺

Eating and drinking

G&G Cra 8 No. 19–17 Offers buffet-style food and a good salad bar and is open 24hr. Lasagne is US$3.50 and steak US$4.50.
Le Gascon at Cra 7A bis No. 18B–09 ☎6/335-0866. An outdoor French bistro and café on the pedestrian walkway near Plaza de Bolívar. Does a filling set lunch for US$4.50. Closed Sat night and Sun.
El Mesón Español C 14 Cra 25-57 ☎6/321-5636. This Spanish restaurant is Pereira's top eatery; bring an appetite and order the paella (US$12.50). Closed Sun.
Restaurante Vegetariano El Champiñon C 22 No. 7–24 ☎6/335-0187. Standard vegetarian set lunches for around US$3. Lunch only, closed Sun.

Moving on

By air Bogotá (8 daily; 50min); Cali (4 daily; 30min); Medellín (5 daily; 35min).
By bus Armenia (every 10min; 50min); Bogotá (hourly; 9hr); Cali (hourly; 3hr 30min); Manizales (every 15min; 1hr 20min); Medellín (hourly; 5hr 30min); (Salento (5 daily, hourly on weekends; 50min).

DAY-TRIPS FROM PEREIRA

Pereira itself is not a place you'll spend a lot of time; if you do base yourself here, you'll likely be striking out on numerous ventures to the nearby hot springs, hiking trails and the like.

Termales San Vicente

The lavishly landscaped **Termales San Vicente** (daily 8am–1am; US$10; ☎6/333-6157; ⓦwww.sanvicente.com.co), 35km northeast of Pereira via the town of Santa Rosa de Cabal, features a selection of steaming medicinal thermal pools scattered across some five square kilometres of cloudforest, river, waterfalls and luxuriant countryside. At 2330m, it gets pretty chilly up here, so it helps that the average pool temperature is 38°C. A variety of spa treatments are also offered, including massage (US$20) and mud therapy (US$8.50). If you want to **spend the night** at the springs, the most cost-effective option is camping (US$25 including entrance fee and breakfast). Further up the accommodation ladder are *cabañas* (❽) or for the height of romantic luxury, honeymoon-worthy cottages with private thermal pools (⑨). The easiest way to get to San Vincente is with one of the direct **daily buses** that leave at 8.30am from the thermal springs' office in Pereira, Cra 13, No. 15–62, returning at 5pm. The price, including entrance, transport and lunch, is US$27. Spa treatments are extra.

Parque Nacional del Café

Some 30km southwest of Pereira, Juan Valdez meets Disney World at the **PARQUE NACIONAL DEL CAFÉ** (Wed–Sun 9am–6pm; admission from US$10; ⓣ6/741-7417, ⓦwww.parquenacionaldelcafe.com). The park occupies a former coffee *finca* whose main house has been barely touched. During the two-hour interpretative walk through the park's manicured grounds, you'll pass a wide range of exotic coffee shrubs, a Quimbaya Indian cemetery, a model *paisa* village – even a roller-coaster. As in any theme park, kitsch comes first – witness the singing orchid show – but beyond the frivolity, there's a well-organized museum that retraces the history of coffee, its marketing and its importance in Colombia's development.

To **get here**, take a bus from Pereira or Salento to Armenia. From there, take a bus to Montenegro where you can grab a seat on any Willys Jeep marked "Parque". Some buses from Armenia also pass the park – ask the driver to drop you at the entrance.

Parque Ucumarí

The lush and wild **Parque Ucumarí** (ⓣ6/325-4781), 24km southeast of Pereira, forms a seamless biological corridor with the western side of Parque Nacional Los Nevados. The 42-square-kilometre reserve acts as a refuge for the endangered Andean spectacled bear as well as tapir, deer and puma. Around two hundred bird species have been spotted here, including condors, eagles and hummingbirds. A steep 18km trail leads from the reserve's Andean tropical forest to the *páramo* landscape of the little-visited southern sector of Parque Nacional Los Nevados before culminating at Laguna del Otún. Due to the poor condition of the trail, a guide is ideal.

Transporte Florida, C 12 No. 9–40, operates two *chivas* daily (7am and noon; more on weekends) from Pereira to **El Cedral**, the entrance to the park. It's then a 6km walk to the *Refugio La Pastora* (altitude 2400m), where you can overnight (US$7 per person) or camp (US$3) and also buy meals. From here it's a breathtaking six-hour uphill hike to Laguna del Otún in Los Nevados, where most trekkers spend a chilly night camped just beneath the snow line. Pereira-based **tour operator** Eco Montaña (ⓣ6/333-5181 or 6/333-9879) at Cra 14 No. 11–93, offers three-day tours with English-speaking guides for US$75 per person. The route can also be done in two days on horseback.

SALENTO

In the heart of coffee country, the quaint hamlet of **SALENTO** is one of the region's earliest settlements, and its slow development has barely altered the original lifestyle or buildings of the *paisa* journeymen who settled here in 1842. Rural workers clad in cowboy hats and *ruanas*, the name for Colombian ponchos, are a common sight. The colourful, one-storey homes of thick adobe and clay-tile roofs that surround the plaza are as authentic as it gets. Although an afternoon visit is worthwhile, one could easily spend a few relaxing days here taking in Salento's unpretentious charms and hiking in the Valle de Cocora or use it as a base to explore the rest of the Zona Cafetera. Salento is a popular weekend destination for Colombians, and on Saturdays and Sundays the main plaza hosts a food and handicrafts fair catering to the day-trippers. During the rest of the week, though, the town is as sleepy as ever. Salento's annual fiesta falls in the first week of January when the town kicks up its heels for a week of horse processions, mock bullfighting and folk dancing.

The main street, Carrera 6, also known as Calle Real, is full of handicraft stalls and restaurants. From the top of the street, steps lead to **Alto de la Cruz**, a hilltop mirador offering unbeatable vistas of the Valle de Cocora and, on a clear day, the peaks of snow-clad volcanoes.

Arrival and information

By bus Buses arrive and depart from Salento's main plaza. There are services to Armenia (every 30min; 1hr) and Pereira (4 daily; 50min). Jeep Willys (3 daily; 20min) run between Salento and Cocora.

Tourist information There is a tourist information office (daily 9am–noon & 2–5pm) at Alto de la Cruz, a 10min climb up the stairs at the end of Cra 6. The English-speaking staff at *Plantation House* (see accommodation below) are very knowledgeable about the area.

Accommodation

Salento has some peaceful B&Bs, and backpackers will find one of Colombia's prettiest and most chilled-out hostels.

Hospedaje Las Palmas C 6, No. 3–02, ⓣ6/759-3065. The six simple rooms in this cute green and yellow house have TV and most have private bathrooms. The interior is a little on the dark side, but the roof terrace, economical price and kitchen make up for that. ❹

Plantation House C 7 No.1–04 ⓣ6/759-4303, ⓦwww.theplantationhousesalento.com. A charming old colonial house set on a picturesque coffee plantation, this British/Colombian-run hostel is the perfect place to recharge and meet fellow travellers. An adjacent building accommodates guests when the main house is full. Amenities include internet and wi-fi, book exchange, laundry service, use of kitchen and free coffee. Dorms (❷) are plain and some doubles rooms have ensuites. ❹

Eating and drinking

Fresh trout is on the menu in all the town's restaurants and is usually served with big crunchy *patacones* (fried plantains).

Barroco Cra 6 No. 2–51 ⓣ6/759-3636. Low-key Latin grooves, casually slung hammocks and eclectic art set the scene for this relaxed bar-cum-restaurant with great coffee and even better baked trout. Service is slow, but it's a beautiful place to wait. Mains US$5–13.

La Fonda de Los Arrieros Cra 6, No. 6–02 ⓣ6/759-3466. This plaza-side restaurant does a divine *trucha criolla a la plancha* (trout topped with onion and tomato) served with a gigantic *patacón* (US$8).

Rincon de Lucy Cra 6 No. 4–02. A whiz in the kitchen, Lucy serves the best set lunches in town. For US$3 you get juice, soup with banana, main course and dessert. Closed for dinner.

Sueña de Fresas C 5 next to the church. Literally "strawberry dreams", this plaza-side café serves locally grown strawberries with lashings of whipped cream (US$2).

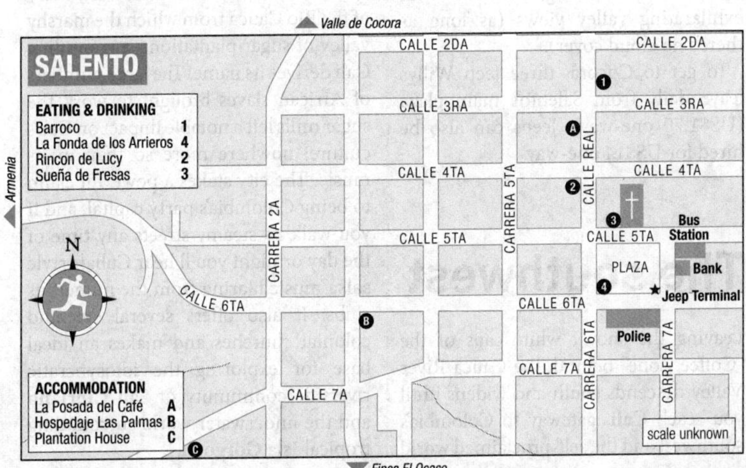

Day-trip from Salento: Valle de Cocora

Salento sits atop the **Valle de Cocora,** which contains a thick forest of the skyscraper wax palm, Colombia's national plant that grows up to 60m high. The valley, which offers picturesque hikes, is easily explored in a day-trip from Salento. The hamlet of Cocora, with a handful of restaurants, small shops and hotels, lies 11km east of Salento. From Cocora a well-trodden path leads into misty, pristine cloud-forest, scattered with the remains of pre-Columbian tombs and dwellings. Orchids, bromeliads and heliconias are just some of the species thriving in this high-altitude jungle, which ranges from 2000 to 3010m. Spectacled bear, native deer and puma, along with hundreds of bird species, including toucans, eagles, motmots, woodpeckers and owls, call the cloudforest home. A **five-to-six-hour loop walk** starts from the blue gate in Cocora, passing a trout farm and, a couple of kilometres on, the Reserva Acaime (entrance US$1.15), home to eighteen species of hummingbirds. The trail crosses nine rickety wooden Indiana Jones-style bridges over the Río Quindío before culminating at a mountaintop viewing platform with exhilarating valley views (as long as there's no cloud cover).

To get to Cocora, three Jeep Willys leave daily from Salento's main plaza (US$1.70 one-way). Jeeps can also be hired for US$14 one-way.

The southwest

Leaving the snowy white caps of the "Coffee Zone" behind, the Cauca River Valley descends south and widens until you reach **Cali**, gateway to Colombia's southwest and the self-proclaimed world capital of salsa music. Further south, the Panamerican Highway stretches past steamy fields of sugar cane to the serene, colonial town of **Popayán**, Colombia's *joya blanca*, or white jewel, known for its blindingly white Rococo colonial architecture. The hilly, multihued scenery behind Popayán is some of Colombia's finest, and the hippies who flock here say it's also endowed with an otherworldly aura emanating from the enigmatic stone monoliths, twice the size of humans, found at the archeological sites of Tierradentro and San Agustín. Heading further south from the overlooked town of **Pasto**, you ascend a ridge dominated by volcanoes all the way to Ecuador.

CALI

Colombia's third largest city, with a population of 2.3 million, **CALI** was founded in 1536 but only shed its provincial backwater status in the early 1900s, when the profits brought in by its sugar plantations prompted industrialization. Today it's one of Colombia's most prosperous cities, in part because of its central role in the drug trade since the dismantling of the rival Medellín cartel in the early 1990s.

The low-lying and extremely hot city (with temperatures routinely surpassing 40°C) saddles the **Río Cali**, a tributary of the Río Cauca from which the marshy valley of sugar plantations surrounding Cali derives its name. The large numbers of African slaves brought to work the sugar mills left a notable impact on Cali's culture, nowhere more so than in its music. The city stakes a powerful claim to being Colombia's party capital, and if you walk its steamy streets any time of the day or night you'll hear Cuban-style **salsa** music blaring from the numerous clubs. It also offers several splendid colonial churches and makes an ideal base for exploring the idiosyncratic riverside community of **San Cipriano** and the underwater world surrounding tropical **Isla Gorgona**.

Plaza de Caycedo and around

The city's centre is **Plaza de Caycedo**, which has a statue of independence hero Joaquín de Caycedo y Cuero in the middle. On the plaza's south end is the nineteenth-century **Catedral San Pedro**, with its elaborate stained-glass windows. Walk north along Calle 12 and you'll run into the Río Cali. On your right, at Carrera 1 and Calle 13, the Gothic-style is the **Iglesia de la Ermita** with its tall spires and powder-blue facade.

Iglesia de la Merced

The oldest church in the city is the **Iglesia de la Merced**, on the corner of Carrera 4 and Calle 7, built from adobe and stone shortly after the city's founding. In the adjoining former convent is the **Museo Arqueológico la Merced** (Tues–Sat 9am–1pm & 2–6pm, Sun 10am–4pm; ⓣ2/889-3434; US$2.25), with displays of pre-Columbian pottery including funerary urns and religious objects unearthed throughout central and southern Colombia. Across the road, the **Museo de Arte Colonial y Religioso**

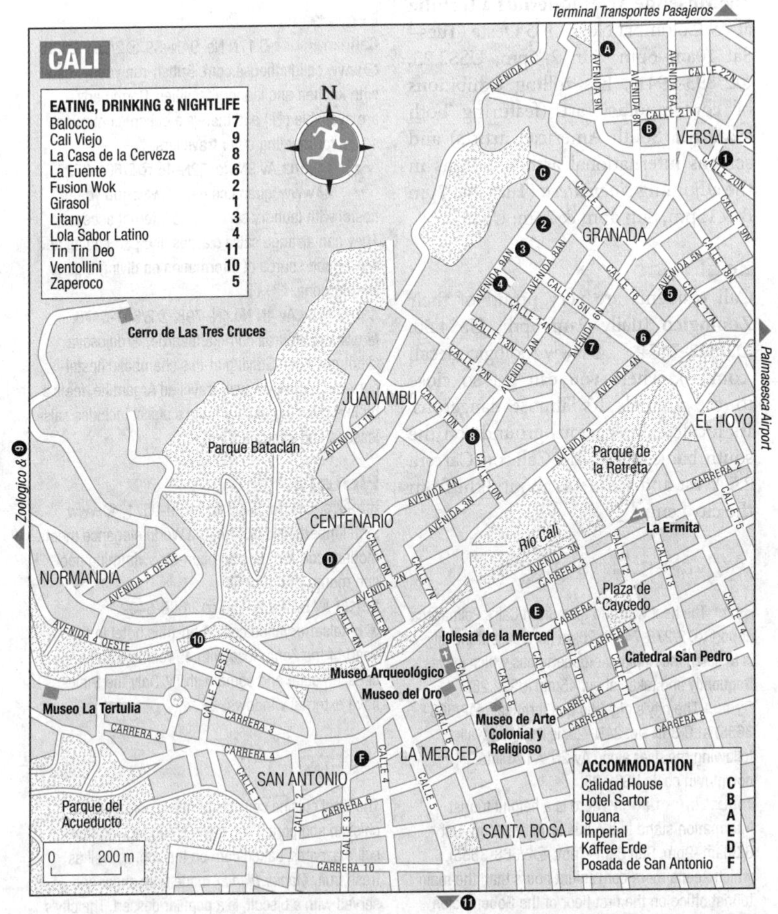

(daily 9am–4.30pm & 2–6pm; ⓣ2/881-8643) features an extensive collection of New World religious relics.

Museo del Oro

Cali's small **Museo del Oro**, in the Banco de la República building at C7 No. 4–69 (Tues–Fri 9am–5pm, Sat 10am–5pm; ⓣ2/684-7754, ⓦwww.banrep.org/museo), has a collection of gold and ceramics from the Calima culture from the region northwest of Cali.

Museo de Arte Moderno La Tertulia

The **Museo de Arte Moderno La Tertulia** at Av Colombia No. 5–105 Oeste (Tues–Sat 10am–6pm, Sun 2–6pm; US$2.25; ⓣ2/893-2941), has rolling exhibitions of contemporary art (featuring both local and South American artists) and screens international arthouse films in the adjoining *cinemateca* (Tues–Sat 7pm & 9.15pm, Sun 4pm & 7pm; US$3).

Zoológico

Cali residents are very proud of their **Zoológico** (daily 9am–5pm; US$4.50; ⓣ2/892-7474, ⓦwww.zoologicodecali.com.co), where you can get so close to the animals it's almost dangerous. It's located on spacious grounds on the south bank of the Río Cali, on Carrera 2A West and Calle 14, about 3km from the city centre.

Arrival and information

By air The best way into town from Cali's Palmaseca airport (ⓣ2/275-7414), 20km northeast of the city, is to catch the Rápido Aeropuerto bus which leaves frequently and takes about 45min (US$2.25).

By bus The city's gigantic bus terminal (ⓣ2/668-3655) at C 30N No. 2AN–29, is a 30min walk following the river along Av 2N. A taxi into downtown costs US$2.25.

Tourist information There is a helpful tourist information stand in the bus terminal (Mon–Sat 6.30am–9pm, Sun 8am–7pm; ⓣ2/668-3655), which keeps more convenient hours than the main tourist office on the first floor of the Gobernación del Valle del Cauca building on the corner of C 4 and Cra 5 (Mon–Fri 8am–noon & 1.30–4.30pm; ⓣ2/620-0064).

City transport

Most local sightseeing can be done on foot; **buses** in the centre cost (US$0.80). At night, however, be sure to call a **taxi**. Try Taxi Libre ⓣ2/444-4444 or Taxi Libre Aeropuerto ⓣ2/555-5555.

Accommodation

Most of Cali's backpacker hostels are concentrated around the Granada neighbourhood with good access to nightlife on Avenida 6N and the restaurants around Avenida 8N.

Hostels

Calidad House C 17N No. 9AN–39 ⓣ2/661-2338, ⓦwww.calidadhouse.com. British-run youth hostel with kitchen and laundry facilities. Dorm beds are available (❷) and there's a decent communal space for meeting other travellers. ❹

Iguana Av 9N No. 22N-46 ⓣ2/661-3522, ⓦwww.iguana.com.co. Swiss-run youth hostel with laundry service and internet access. They can arrange salsa classes and paragliding and are a good source of information on diving trips to Isla Gorgona. ❷–❹

KaffeeErde Av 4N No.4N–79B ⓣ2/661-5475, ⓦwww.hosteltrail.com/kaffeeerde, ⓔdojoseva@hotmail.com. Staying at this shambolic hostel-cum-café, run by a well-travelled Argentine, feels a bit like crashing at your mate's place. Includes salsa lessons and internet. ❷–❹

Hotels

Imperial C 9 No. 3–93 ⓣ2/889-9571, ⓦwww.hotelimperialdecali.com. Old World elegance meets modern comfort; has an open-air swimming pool and rooms with a/c. ❻

Sartor Av 8N No.20–50 ⓣ2/668-6482, ⓔhotelsartoryahoo.com. A no-frills hotel in the heart of the Zona Rosa with 49 rooms with lumpy beds, en suite and some with TV. Only the triples have external windows. ❺

Eating

The local cuisine consists of heavy portions of chicken and pork. Food stalls around town often sell *mazorcas*, baked corn on the cob, as well as fresh fruit. *Manjar blanco*, made from sugar and served with a biscuit, is a popular dessert. The city's gourmet zone is concentrated around avenidas 8N,

9AN and 9N in Granada, where there are oodles of chic restaurants dishing up fusion and ethnic cuisine.

Balocco Av 7N No.14–06 ☎2/661-2896. Don't be put off by the fluorescent lights and diner-style decor. This long-standing Italian restaurant does scrumptious home-made pastas (US$6–10) and to-die-for tiramisu (US$3).

Cali Viejo Parque El Bosque near the Zoológico ☎2/893-4927, Ⓦwww.restaurantecaliviejo.com. Fine restaurant with lovely flowered garden. Specializes in local Cauca Valley cuisine. Mains up to US$16. Closed Sun night.

Fusion Wok Av 9AN No. 15A–30 ☎2/661-0302. Asian food that's not overly authentic, but with minimalist Japanese decor and staff dressed like they're about to pull karate moves, it at least looks the part. The menu ranges from sushi plates (US$10) to Pad Thai (US$8–11).

Girasol Av 5BN No. 20N–30 ☎2/661-2423. Serves tasty vegetarian set lunches for US$3. Lunch only; closed Sun.

Litany C 15AN No. 9N–35 ☎2/661-3736. A Lebanese restaurant that's the real deal, serving mouth-watering *tabouli*, falafel, vine leaves, *tahini* and hummus. Vegetarian plates for US$11. Closed Fri & Sun night.

Lola Sabor Latino C 14N No.9–28 ☎2/667-5656. Seafood is the forte at this funky Nuevo Latino restaurant with tropical kitsch decor. Sample the fried red snapper with passionfruit sauce and green plantain (US$16) and request the "lover's corner" if you're feeling amorous. Closed Sun.

Ventollini Av 4W No.1–152 ☎2/892-1311. A large riverside establishment where you can fill up on crêpes, sandwiches and wraps (mains US$9–13) or just cool off at the ice-cream counter (US$3 small cone).

Drinking and nightlife

Much of the late-night action is just beyond the city limits, in suburbs like Menga and Juanchito, the latter home to the city's liveliest *salatecas*. Most don't charge admission, but drinks are generally ordered by the bottle, with a bottle of rum around US$30. The clubs around Avenida 6N rarely have cover charges and get started early in the afternoon, but really pullulate with revellers on the weekends.

Agapito Vía Cavasa Km 2, Juanchito. An institution for salsa fanatics of all ages where, even if you can't hold your own on the dancefloor, you should at least dress like you can.

La Casa de la Cerveza Av 8N No. 10N–18 Ⓦwww.casadelacerveza.com.co. Serving cheap beer in boot-size glasses, this rustic pub has an excellent ambience for kicking off any night. If you're still here after 10pm, you'll find up to 300 people crowding the dancefloor. Cocktails from US$5.

Changó Vía Cavasa Km 2, Juanchito Ⓦwww.chango.com.co. Named after the African god of virility and leisure, *Changó* overlooks the Río Cauca at the entrance to Juanchito. It features two dancefloors and a relaxed environment. Beers from US$2.20.

La Fuente Av 4N No.15–39. Beer-swilling, salsa-dancing students spill out into the sultry night from this grungy but oh-so-hip hole in the wall. The beer is cheap, the atmosphere super-friendly, and by the end of the night, everyone is dancing on the footpath. Thurs–Sat.

Tin Tin Deo C 5 No. 38–71 ☎2/557-4534, Ⓦwww.tintindeocali.com. A fun and unpretentious salsa temple where couples, students and groups of friends strut salacious moves while singing along to the music. Entrance is US$6 for women and US$8 for men. Thurs–Sat 10pm–2am.

Zaperoco Av 5N No.16N–42 ☎2/661-2040, Ⓦwww.zaperocobar.com. Photos of salsa stars plaster the walls of this club popular with a 30-something crowd. Things really sizzle after midnight. Bottles of rum from US$36; beers from US$2.80. Thurs–Sat.

Moving on

By air Bogotá (23 daily; 50min); Cartagena (1 daily; 1hr 25min); Ipiales (4 weekly; 50min); Medellín (5 daily; 40min); Pereira (4 daily; 30min); Pasto (2 daily; 1hr); San Andrés (2 daily; 2hr).

By bus Armenia (every 30min; 3hr); Bogotá (hourly; 8hr); Manizales (hourly; 5–6hr); Pasto (hourly; 9hr); Pereira (hourly, 3hr 30min); Popayán (every 10min; 3hr).

DAY-TRIPS FROM CALI

Once you've had your fill of fun in Cali, you can visit a few sights that give some cultural context to the area.

El Paraíso

A number of historic sugarcane plantations that have been converted into museums lie just north of Cali and make for a pleasant day excursion. The most famous is **El Paraíso** (Tues–Sun 9am–4.30pm; ☎2/514-6848; US$2), the colonial hacienda that served as the backdrop for Jorge Isaacs's *María*, considered the apogee of nineteenth-century Latin American literary romanticism. The well-maintained house is decorated as it would have been when

Isaacs lived here, with bedpans, candlestick chandeliers and a working aqueduct that delivers water throughout the estate. More impressive is its location, on a gentle slope halfway between a verdant mountain chain rising directly from the backyard and an immense spread of sugarcane fields. To get to El Paraíso take any bus from Cali north that passes El Cerrito (40km away) and ask the driver to let you off at Amaime, just before El Cerrito, from where you can share a taxi to the estate for US$1. Alternatively, on Sundays, *busetas* shuttle picnickers every two hours between El Paraíso and Palmira, 18km from Cali.

San Cipriano

Set in the sweltering tropical jungle 128km northwest of Cali and just inland from the Pacific port city of Buenaventura, the straggly riverside community of **San Cipriano** makes for an adventurous day or overnight excursion. The crystalline river here provides plentiful secluded cooling-off opportunities, but it is the unique journey to the 300-strong community of African slave descendants that has made San Cipriano such an alluring travel destination. There are no roads into San Cipriano, just a forest-flanked railway line linking the community with the town of Córdoba, 6km away. Nowadays the railway sees very little train action, so to bring visitors to their community from Córdoba, inventive locals have attached motorcycle-powered wooden carts to the tracks. The carts leave when they are full of people (US$4.50 return).

San Cipriano lies at the confluence of the Escalarete and San Cipriano rivers and there are nine sites for safe river swimming spread over three kilometres. Follow the only road out of the settlement (the river will be on your right); well-signed tracks positioned every few hundred metres lead down to the river. Some 7km of nature trails branch off into the surrounding forest. A number of **restaurants** serve meals and many also offer basic **accommodation**. If you do plan to spend the night here bring a mosquito net as there is malaria. The rooms at *Posada Don José* (☎311/318-9831; ❸) are among the cleanest in town and come with fans and mosquito nets and shared cold water bathrooms. To reach

TREAT YOURSELF

Before 1984, the volcanic and mountainous **Isla Gorgona**, 55km northeast of the mainland, was Colombia's least desirable high-security prison. Twenty-five years on, the 44 square-kilometre tropical island is a national park and the country's most exclusive travel destination, offering scuba diving, deserted palm-fringed beaches and lush jungle crawling with capuchin monkey, sloth and twenty varieties of snake, seven of them poisonous. Marine life includes white-tip, black-tip, silky and whale sharks, while humpback whales and dolphins make seasonal visits.

All permits, tours and accommodation must be booked through Aviatur, and prices are not cheap. The most economical way to visit the island is with one of Aviatur's all-inclusive package tours. Four-night packages start from US$427 and include boat transfer to the island, a guide, all meals, accommodation and snorkelling. A four-night diving-focused trip which includes transport in live-aboard dive boats from Buenaventura, two nights' accommodation on the island and two on a boat, plus meals, guide and six scuba dives costs US$677. Theoretically you can reach the island independently by taking one of the daily cargo boats from Buenaventura (10–12hr) or by lancha from Guapí, but then fixed island accommodation fees start at an extortionate US$627 per person per night. For bookings and information contact Aviatur, Av 6N No.37BN–94 in Cali (☎2/664-5050, ⓦwww.aviatur.com).

San Cipriano, catch any Buenaventura bus from Cali's bus terminal and ask to be let out in Córdoba (2hr). Walk down the hill (10min) to the train tracks from where carts leave roughly every hour.

POPAYÁN

Although less illustrious than Cartagena, Colombia's other open-air colonial museum, **POPAYÁN**, has little reason to envy its more celebrated rival. Founded in 1537 by Sebastián de Belálcazar on his march northward from Quito, the town was a powerful counterweight to Bogotá's dominance during the colonial era and a bastion of Spanish loyalty during the wars of independence. Unlike Cartagena, which saw its influence wane after independence, Popayán's aristocrats remained very active in politics, and no fewer than eleven presidents have emerged from their ranks.

Civic pride runs high in Popayán. When a disastrous earthquake destroyed most of the historic centre in 1983 residents banded together to rebuild, and the result is one of the most attractive cities in Colombia, with cobblestone streets and whitewashed mansions that in many ways look better and more uniformly conserved than before the quake. In addition to its architectural splendour, the city of 243,000 is uniquely tranquil and traditional for a city of its size. Not a single traffic light pervades the quiet centre, which still comes to a complete standstill during the midday siesta. During Easter week the city is cordoned off to make way for thousands of parading worshippers brandishing candles and colourful flowers. Popayán's Semana Santa celebrations are the second largest in the world, after Seville in Spain.

What to see and do

The best way to appreciate Popayán's Rococo riches is to aimlessly wander the streets radiating from Parque Caldas.

The cathedral and other historic churches

There are so many **churches** in Popayán that it's almost impossible not to run into one every two or three blocks. The whitewashed **Catedral** overlooks **Parque Caldas**, the town's main square. Although the biggest and most frequently used, architecturally it's the least important having been built around 1900 on the site where two earlier structures stood. Four blocks east, on Calle 5 and Carrera 2, the city's

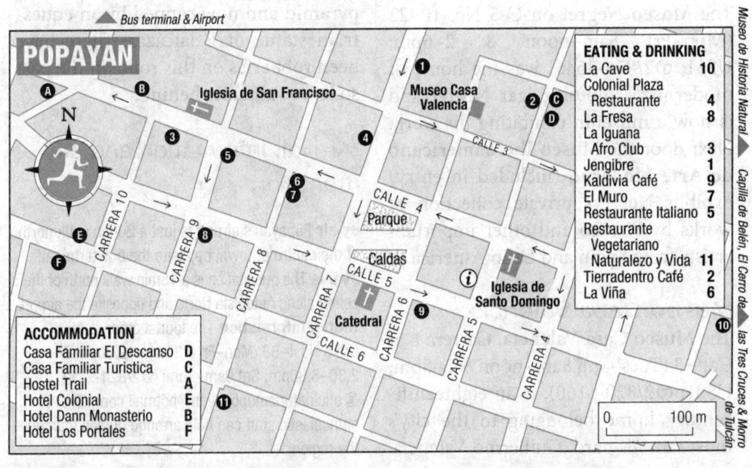

oldest standing church, **La Ermita**, features an austere single-naved chapel comprised of wooden ribbing and a golden altar dating from 1564. Three blocks away, on Calle 4 and Carrera 5, the **Iglesia de Santo Domingo**'s Baroque stone portal is an excellent example of Spanish New World architecture. Equally ornate is the staircased pulpit of **Iglesia de San Francisco**, situated on a quiet plaza on Calle 4 and Carrera 9, where several of Popayán's patrician families are buried.

Museo Mosquera

Several colonial homes have been donated to the government and converted into museums, offering a rare glimpse into the salon society of the colonial and early independence era. One of the best maintained is the **Museo Mosquera** on C 3 No. 5–14 (Mon–Fri 8am–noon & 2–6pm; US$1; ⓣ2/824-0683), which was the childhood residence of Tomás Cipriano de Mosquera, four times Colombia's president. There's a room dedicated to General Carlos Albán, who died a hero resisting Panama's secession from Colombia.

Museo Negret and Museo Iberoamericano de Arte Moderno

The **Museo Negret** on C 5 No. 10–23 (Mon–Fri 8am–noon & 2–6pm; US$1; ⓣ2/824-4546) was the home of modernist sculptor Edgar Negret and is now a museum exhibiting his work. Next door the **Museo Iberoamericano de Arte Moderno** (included in entry) exhibits Negret's private collection of works by Picasso and other important artists from Spain and Latin America.

Museo Casa Valencia

The **Museo Casa Valencia**, Carrera 6 at Calle 3 (Tues–Sun 8am–noon & 2–5pm; US$1; ⓣ2/820-6160), is an eighteenth-century home belonging to the city's most famous bard, Guillermo Valencia. The well-conserved, two-storey mansion contains a vast collection of colonial paintings and furniture as well as the burial remains of the poet's son, Colombian President Guillermo León Valencia.

Museo de Historia Natural

A few blocks east of the historic centre, the three-storey **Museo de Historia Natural**, Cra 2 No. 1A–25 (Tues–Sun 9am–noon & 2–5pm; US$1.70; ⓣ2/820-1952), has a good collection of stuffed animals and birds – many endemic to Colombia, although the insect display might prompt you to buy a one-way ticket out of the country. There is also a modest display of pre-Columbian artefacts from Tierradentro and San Agustin.

Capilla de Belén, El Cerro de las Tres Cruces and Morro de Tulcán

For a scenic two-hour leg stretch that offers tremendous views over Popayán and the surrounding verdant countryside, walk to the eastern end of Calle 4 and follow the steep cobbled path up to the **Capilla de Belén**. From here, a path continues to the hilltop **El Cerro de las Tres Cruces** and on to **Cerro el Morro**, once the site of a pre-Columbian pyramid and now capped by an equestrian statue of Belalcázar. There have been robberies on this route in the past so leave valuables behind.

Arrival, information and city transport

By air Popayán's airport is just a 20min walk north of the centre of town, opposite the bus terminal.

By bus The bus station is a 15min walk north of the centre along Autopista Norte and opposite the airport.

Tourist information The tourist office is at Cra 5 No.4–68 (Mon–Fri 8.30am–12.30pm & 2.30–6.30pm; Sat 9am–1pm; ⓣ2/824-2251, ⓔoficinaturismopopayan@hotmail.com). The enthusiastic staff can help arrange guided tours in the region.

Accommodation

Popayán boasts a plethora of colonial residences tastefully converted into hotels and small B&Bs, many of which are ridiculously inexpensive.

Casa Familiar El Descanso Cra 5 No. 2–41 ⓣ2/822-4787. The very clean but small rooms here look out onto a luminous lounge shared with the family. ⑤

Casa Familiar Turística Cra 5 No. 2–11 ⓣ2/824-4853. Set on a quiet street, the friendly owner of this nice colonial house has shared rooms (②) with bath. Popular with backpackers. ④

Hostel Trail Cra 11, No. 4–16 ⓣ314/696-0805, ⓦwww.hosteltrail.com. This nineteen-bed backpacker's hostel (dorms US$8) is one of the best in the country, thanks to its affable Scottish owners whose contagious enthusiasm for Popayán often translates into taking guests out for fun guided strolls. Cheap internet and wi-fi. Has a DVD room and kitchen. ④

Hotel Colonial C 5 No.10–94 ⓣ2/831-7848, ⓔhotelcolonial@hotmail.es. A comfortable budget option with clean and bright double rooms with private bath and cable TV. Includes free local calls. ④

Hotel Los Portales C 5 No. 10–125 ⓣ2/821-0139, ⓔlosportaleshotel@yahoo.com. A great value, this spotless and characterful colonial hotel has large rooms with fancy bedspreads, cable TV and private bathrooms, nicely set around three pretty patios. ⑤

Eating, drinking and nightlife

Popayán is renownrd for its quality restaurants and dedication to traditional cuisine of which potatoes, corn, rice, chicken and pork are the main ingredients. Nightlife is sedate: the historic centre boasts several appealing spots ideal for settling in with a book, meeting locals and soaking up the town's heritage.

La Cave C 4 No. 2–07 ⓣ316/753-7670. A candlelit bistro started by two Frenchmen, *La Cave* serves sumptuous sandwiches during the day and affordable, freshly prepared cuisine like crêpes and herb chicken (US$4.50–8) at night.

Chiva Rumbera ⓣ314/614-5739. Every Thurs & Fri night the La Patoja *chiva* (a colourfully painted traditional Colombian bus) cruises Popayán's streets, blaring Latin standards and picking up revellers with dry throats and itchy feet. If you don't fancy dancing, park yourself on one of the *chiva*'s bar stools and watch the city roll by. US$3 to board the bus.

Colonial Plaza Restaurante C 3 No. 7–35. This nondescript eatery in the Plaza Colonial food hall serves outstanding and filling *patacones* topped with meat, vegetables and melted cheese (US$3–5).

La Fresa C 5 No. 8–89. A basic diner that does decadently delicious *empanadas de pipián*, a regional speciality of deep-fried *empanada* stuffed with crushed peanuts and potato and served with peanut sauce (US$0.10 each). Closed Sun.

La Iguana Afro Club C 4 No. 9–67. Knowledgeable owner Diego Velásquez spins records from his extensive Latin Jazz and 1970s salsa collection in this low-key, rustic pub.

Jengibre Cra 7 No. 2–71 ⓣ314/612-8527. A snug little restaurant with low ceilings that serves good lunch menus for US$4 and an appealing selection of trout, lamb, beef and pasta dishes. Mains US$7. Closed Sun night.

Kaldivia Café C 5 No. 5–63. This inviting café does gourmet grinds, by the cup or in bulk, in decorative, airtight pouches that make excellent gifts.

El Muro Cra 8 No.4–11. A lunchtime crowd flock to this dimly lit, ten-table vegetarian restaurant for its four-course set meal (US$2.50). Lunch only; closed Sun.

Restaurante Italiano C 4 No. 8–83 ⓣ2/824-0607. This Swiss-owned pizzeria serves good pasta as well as fondue and more exotic European dishes. Set menus are US$4.

Restaurante Vegetariano Naturalezo y Vida Cra 8 No. 7–19 ⓣ2/822-1118. A place where malnourished vegetarians can go three meals a day for scrumptious, four-course vitamin hits (US$2). Closed Sun.

Tierradentro Cafe Cra 5 No 1–78 ⓣ2/820-9535. A late-night, candlelit refuge for caffeine addicts, serving more than fifty types of

TREAT YOURSELF

A converted Franciscan monastery, the palatial, whitewashed **Hotel Dann Monasterio**, C 4 No.10–14 (ⓣ2/824-2191, ⓦwww.hotelesdann.com; ⑨), offers the chance to live it up in affordable five-star splendour. The 47 bedrooms, arranged around a generous courtyard, are lavishly adorned with antique furnishings, candelabras, LCD TV and ensuite with bathtub. A restaurant, terrace, landscaped garden, swimming pool, outdoor gymnasium and sauna complete the picture.

gourmet coffees, many spiked with shots of liquor. The hot chocolate is particularly smooth.

La Viña C 4 No. 7–79. Does a good breakfast complemented by fresh fruit juices. Otherwise serves fast but good Colombian dishes at economical prices. Mains US$6–12.

Moving on

By bus Bogotá (7 daily; 13hr); Cali (every 10min; 3hr); Pasto (hourly; 6hr); San Agustín (7 daily; 6-8hr); Silvia (hourly; 1hr 30min); Tierradentro (1 daily; 4hr 30min).

DAY-TRIPS FROM POPAYÁN

Don't miss the chance for a local market day in the highlands or the ascent to an active volcano in Parque Nacional Natural Puracé.

Silvia

Well worth a detour is the rural village of **Silvia**, 60km northeast of Popayán, which fills up with Guambiano Indians in colourful blue and fuchsia dress every Tuesday for market day. They live in the mountain villages above Silvia, including Guambia and Pueblito. Buses (US$3) leave for Silvia regularly from Popayán's bus terminal. The scenery during the one-and-a-half-hour ride is breathtaking. Once here, it's possible to hire horses (US$3 per hour) and ride up to Guambia (1hr) where the Guambiano cook up fried trout, plucked fresh from nearby trout farms.

Parque Nacional Natural Puracé

The high-altitude **Parque Nacional Natural Puracé**, 58km east of Popayán (daily 8am–5pm; US$8), encompasses 860 square kilometres of fuming volcanoes, snow-capped mountains, boiling sulphurous springs, milky waterfalls, deep canyons, trout-stuffed lagoons and multicoloured grasslands. The park's literal high point is **Volcán Puracé** (4700m), which last blew its top in 1956. It is a lung-straining four-hour climb to the steaming crater where, on a clear day, there are sensational views of Cadena Volcánica de Los Coconucos – a chain of forty volcanoes. Six buses daily leave Popayán for the park entrance at El Cruce de San Juan (2hr). For those wanting to make an early ascent of the volcano, it is possible to **overnight** in the park in basic *cabañas* (☎2/823-1279; ❸ per person) or camp (US$5.50), which includes use of a bathroom with hot showers.

Thermal springs at Coconuco

The village of **Coconuco**, 26km from Popoyán, is a short hop to two rudimentary outdoor thermal baths. The better maintained of the two is **Termales Agua Tibia** (daily 8am–6pm; ☎2/824-1161; US$3), 5km southwest of Coconuco on the road to San Agustín. Set at the base of a steep-sided valley, the nicely landscaped complex has three lukewarm pools, a waterslide and a basic mud pool rich in rejuvenating minerals. Facilities are scant and there is no place to lock up valuables. The bus to and from San Agustín can drop you outside on request.

The indigenous-run **Agua Hirviendos** (Tues–Sun 24hr, US$1.70), 3km east of Coconuco, is less picturesque than Agua Tibia but its sulphur-reeking pools are far toastier, with temperatures around 38ºC. The on-site waterfall is a refreshing shock to the system. The baths are a thirty-minute walk from Coconuco and there are also regular buses.

SAN AGUSTÍN AND PARQUE ARQUEOLÓGICO

The thoroughly laid-back little town of **SAN AGUSTÍN**, 140 kilometres southeast of Popayán, has everything a hippie could want – awesome landscape, cryptic ruins and bargain-basement prices. If that's not enough, there's also the San Isidro mushroom, a powerful hallucinogenic that grows especially well in the surrounding area's perennially green pastures. But even if you're not part of the rainbow culture there's still plenty to discover here. The town, with a population of around thirty thousand, is home to one of the continent's most important archeological sites. Some 3300 years ago the jagged landscape around the town was inhabited by masons whose singular legacy is the hundreds of monumental stone statues comparable in size and detail to the more famous Moai statues found on Chile's Easter Island.

Much mystery still surrounds the civilization that built the monoliths, though the surreal imagery of sex-crazed monkeys, serpent-headed humans and other disturbing zoomorphic glyphs suggests that San Isidro may have already been working its magic when the statues were first created. What is known is that the priestly culture disappeared before the Spanish arrived, probably at the hands of the Inca, whose empire stretched into southern Colombia. The statues weren't discovered until the middle of the eighteenth century.

It's a good seven-hour journey from Popayán via the small town of Coconuco along a mostly unpaved road, but the beautiful scenery more or less redeems the bumpy ride. For those going on to Bogotá, or coming from the capital, it makes sense to exit San Agustín via the paved road to Neiva rather than backtrack to Popayán.

Parque Arqueológico

The nearest archeological sites are 2.5km west of San Agustín in the **Parque Arqueológico** (daily 8am–4pm; US$4), declared a UNESCO World Heritage Site in 1995. The park contains over a hundred statues – some as tall as seven metres – the largest concentration of statues in the area. Many of them are left as they were found, and others, like the ones in the sector of the park known as the **Bosque de las Estatuas**, are rearranged and linked by an interpretative trail. There's also a museum in the park that displays Indian earthenware. To tour the park you'll need at least two hours and if you don't want to spend up to US$20 for a guide you could buy an English-language guidebook for about US$8.

Other statue sites and activities

Hundreds more statues are littered across the colourful hillside on either side of the Río Magdalena, the source of which can be visited in a strenuous five-day hike. For most visitors, walking, horse-riding or motorcycling through the steep, unspoiled landscape is more impressive than the ruins themselves. The numerous trails could keep you busy for more than a week but the most popular destinations, all which are within a day's return hike from town, are **El Tablón**, **La Chaquira**, **La Pelota** and **El Purutal**. While none of these requires a guide, it is advisable to walk in groups or with a guide when visiting **El Tablón** and **La Chaquira** as there have been robberies on this route in the past. **Alto de los Idolos** (daily 8am–4pm; US$4 entrance fee) is the area's second most important archeological site after the Parque Arqueológico, and is home to the region's tallest statue, measuring seven metres high. It can be reached via a three-hour hike from San Agustín or by driving to San José de Isnos, 30km along the road to Popayán and another 5km along a side road. If you do venture into the hills bring along rain gear and good boots as the weather near San Agustín often changes throughout the day. If you hire a guide – don't worry, they'll find you first – be sure they're accredited by the **tourism office** and not overcharging. If in doubt, check with rates at your hotel, as they can usually arrange cheaper packages. Aside

archeological attractions, **whitewater rafting** and **kayaking** are also taking off in San Agustín thanks to ready access to the Class II–IV Río Magdalena. Magdalena Rafting (ⓣ311/271-4788; ⓦwww.magdalenarafting.com) offers excursions.

Arrival and information

By bus Buses arrive and depart in the centre of town near the corner of C3 and Cra 11 where there is a cluster of bus company offices. Buses coming from Popayán usually drop off passengers at El Cruce de San Agustín, 5km before the town, where it is necessary to transfer to a taxi (taxis pass regularly). Buses to Popayán will only come into San Agustín if at least three people have reserved tickets the day before; otherwise take a taxi to El Cruce and flag down a passing bus.

Tourist information San Agustín's relaxed tourist office (Mon–Fri 7.30am–noon & 2–6pm; ⓣ8/837-3062 ext 15) is inside the town hall at C3 and C12. When the office shuts, the police station opposite, at C 3 No. 11–56, functions as an information centre (Mon–Fri 6pm–10pm, Sat & Sun 8am–noon & 2–10pm).

Accommodation

There is an abundance of budget accommodation in San Agustín, with some beautiful backpacker-friendly guesthouses just out of town on stunning blocks of land.

La Casa de Francois One kilometre along Via El Tablón ⓣ8/837-3847, ⓦwww.hosteltrail.com/lacasadefrancois. The French owner of this colourful shack on a bluff overlooking the city is so laid-back he's horizontal most of the time. Offers cheap lodging, communal kitchen and an easy-going, sociable environment, making it popular with backpackers. Home-made bread and free coffee too. ❷

Casa de Nelly Via la Estrella 1.5km along Av 2, ⓣ8/837-3221. A 20min walk from the centre of town along a poorly lit dirt track, this is a peaceful and attractive lodge ideal for canoodling couples looking for privacy. ❸

Finca Ecológica El Maco One kilometre along the road to the Parque Arquológico and then 1km up a rough road ⓣ8/837-3437, ⓦwww.elmaco.ch. Set on a luxuriant hillside a good hike from the centre, this Swiss-run guesthouse has four *cabañas* scattered across an organic farm. There are dorms (❷) and spots for camping (US$3.50) and use of a guest kitchen. The on-site restaurant is open to the public (reserve first) and does a vegetarian Thai green curry worth schlepping up the hill for (US$6). ❹

Hospedaje El Jardin Cra 11 No. 4–10 ⓣ8/837-3455, ⓦwww.hosteltrail.com/eljardin. Cheap and cheerful, this old colonial house has basic rooms with droopy beds (some en suite) set around an inviting courtyard. The bubbly *dueña* plies her guests with coffee. ❸

Hostal Ítaca Cra 13 No. 6–78 ⓣ8/837-9910. This centrally located hostel has been built with natural materials such as *guadua* and stone and dolled up with plenty of artsy flourishes. There's a well-equipped kitchen, a common room with hammocks and the Colombian owners are cleaning machines. Dorm ❷, doubles ❹

Eating

Since many of the hotels in San Agustín offer kitchen facilities for guests, you might want to stock up on produce at the town's Monday fruit and vegetable market and cook for yourself. If you're eating out, there are plenty of affordable options too.

Brahama On C 5 No. 15–11. Serves *comida típica* (US$2.20 for set two-course meal) as well as vegetarian options. Is also good for breakfast and pancakes (US$2).

Donde Richard One kilometre along the road to the Parque Arquológico at C 5 No. 23–45 ⓣ312/432-6399. The town's top restaurant does carnivore-friendly fare such as barbecued pork, chicken, beef and fish (mains US$7.50). Good selection of Chilean and Argentinian wine.

Pizza Mania Cra 13, No. 3–43. "What the customer wants the customer gets" is the philosophy of the gregarious French, German, English and Spanish-speaking owner of this cute pizza restaurant. Slices US$1.30 and giant pizzas US$13.50. Closed Tues.

Surabhi C 5, No.14–09. Great for hearty meals; primarily trout, lamb and meat mains with a side helping of fries, rice and salad (from US$6).

Moving on

By bus Bogotá (5 daily; 10–12hr); Pitalito (frequent; 45min); Popayán (at least 5 daily; 7hr). Getting to Tierradentro from San Agustín takes at least 7hr and involves two bus transfers; the first transfer is at Pitalito, then at La Plata (after 4–5hr). From La Plata it's 2hr 30min to El Cruce de San Andrés, then a 20min walk to the museum in Tierradentro.

TIERRADENTRO

After San Agustín, **Tierradentro** is Colombia's most treasured archeological complex. Its hallmarks are a hundred-odd circular burial caverns – some as deep as seven metres – decorated with elaborate geometric iconography. Monumental statues have also been found here, indicating a cultural influence from San Agustín, yet, like the latter, little is known about the Tierradentro civilization other than that it flourished around 1000 AD.

No large population centres have been discovered, lending credence to the belief that the original inhabitants belonged to a dispersed group of loosely related farmers. The tomb dwellers' modern descendants are the **Paez Indians**, twenty-five thousand of whom live in the surrounding hillside. During the colonial era, the Paez were known as a ruthless warrior tribe, and they remained free of Spanish subjugation well into the seventeenth century.

What to see and do

Tierradentro means "Inner Land", an appropriate nickname to describe the rugged countryside of narrow valley and jagged summits. **Hikes** to outlying Indian villages, cascading waterfalls and high altitude *paramos* could easily keep walkers busy for more than a week.

Most visitors stay in **San Andrés de Pisimbalá**, 4km from El Cruce de San Andrés, which is on the main Popayán–La Plata road. The tiny village is within walking distance of most burial sites. It has a picturesque thatched-roof chapel that dates from the seventeenth-century mission. Start your visit at the **Tierradentro Museum** (daily 8am–5pm; US$1.50), halfway on the road to El Cruce, which contains pottery urns and other ossuary artefacts. There's also information on the Paez and a useful model of the surrounding region. Your ticket to the museum is valid for entry into the archeological park, which contains one statue site (El Tablón) and four **cave sites** – Segovia, El Duende,

TATACOA DESERT

The surreal **Tatacoa Desert** makes for a compelling detour en route from Bogotá to San Agustín or Tierradentro. Measuring 300 square kilometres, Tatacoa's arid topography – complete with cracked earth, giant cacti, orange and grey soil and towering red rock sculptures – is all the more astonishing because it lies just 37km northeast of Neiva, a city encircled by fertile coffee plantations. Scorpions, spiders, snakes, lizards, weasels and eagles have all found a home in Tatacoa, while fossils indicate the area was an ancient stomping ground for monkeys, turtles, armadillos and giant sloth. Some of the fossils are on display at the paleontology museum on the main plaza in the village of Villavieja, 4km from the desert. An observatory, a few shops and some simple cabins are Tatacoa's only nods to tourism infrastructure; campers can pitch where they choose beneath the desert's starry sky. Villavieja has a few basic hotels and restaurants; one option is *Hotel y Restaurante La Casona*, C 3 No. 3–60 (Ⓣ8/879-7635, Ⓔhotellacasonavillavieja@yahoo.es; ❸), which has modest doubles with private bathrooms. A number of locals offer guided desert tours by car, mototaxi or horseback, although it is possible to reach some of the highlights on foot. Villavieja is an hour by bus from Neiva which in turn is 8hr by bus from Bogotá and 4hr 30min from San Agustín on the main Bogotá to San Agustín road. The best time to explore the desert is early morning before the heat becomes intolerable (temperatures frequently reach 43°C).

Alto de San Andrés and El Aguacate – spread across a sublime landscape. Be sure to bring your own torch when exploring the tombs, as most are unlit.

Arrival, accommodation and eating

Tierradentro is 113km from Popayán along a rough mountain road. There is one direct **bus** daily (5–6hr) from Popayán and an additional four daily that pass El Cruce de San Andrés from where it's a 4km walk to San Andrés de Pisimbalá where most of the hostels are.

As in San Agustín, the **accommodation** in Tierradentro is cheap. *Hospedaje Lucerna* (❷), next to the museum near the park entrance, has basic rooms and temperamental showers and is run by a charming elderly couple who are generous with coffee and allow camping out back (❶). Uphill from here, 100m past the church on the right is the rundown *Hotel Los Lagos* (☎311/454-0195; ❸), set in a blue and white colonial house. The best **restaurant** is *La Portada*, with set lunch menus for US$2.50.

PASTO

Capital of Nariño *departamento* and home to some 384,000 residents, **PASTO** is the commercial hub of southern Colombia. Although the surrounding foothills of the Galeras Volcano are attractive, the bustling town is devoid of major sights and likely to be visited only in passing on the way to Ecuador, 88km further south along the Panamerican Highway. The southern stretch of the highway between Pasto and Popayán has been unsafe in the past; to err on the side of caution, avoid travelling overland at night.

Founded in 1537 by Sebastían de Belalcázar on his march from Quito, Pasto sided with Spain during the wars of independence and later tried to fuse with Ecuador when Bolívar's Nueva Granada confederation split up in 1830. Successive earthquakes have destroyed most of Pasto's colonial architecture but a few churches still recall its past glory.

Each year in early January, the politically incorrect **Carnaval de Blancos y Negros** presents one of Colombia's most traditional celebrations. The festival's racist roots date from the colonial period when, once a year, slaves would paint themselves white and their masters, in approval, would parade the next day in blackface.

What to see and do

The **Cristo Rey** at Calle 20 and Carrera 24, noted for its stained-glass windows and beautiful paintings, is the best-preserved church in town. The pulpit at the city's oldest church, **San Juan Bautista**, on Calle 18 and Carrera 25 – the city's principal plaza – was built in the Arabesque Mudéjar style. The **Museo de Oro**, C 19 No. 21–27 (Tues–Sat 10am–5pm; free, ☎2/721-9108), exhibits art from the region'spre-Columbian cultures.

Pasto is known for its handicrafts, especially the *barniz de pasto*, a china-like finish to decorate wooden objects. Examples can be bought at the **Mercado de Bomboná**, an artisan market on Calle 14 and Carrera 27.

CROSSING INTO ECUADOR

The Colombian town of **Ipiales**, a two-hour bus ride from Pasto, is 2km from the **Rumichaca Bridge**, where there are Colombian and Ecuadorian border control offices on either side. From the bridge it's another two kilometres to the town of Tulcán in Ecuador (see p.629). There are money changers on both sides of the border on and close to the bridge. You will need to change transport at the border and also cross the border on foot. From Ipiales, you can catch a taxi (US$2) or a *colectivo* to the border. The heavily crossed border is open 6am to 9pm.

SANTUARIO DE LAS LAJAS

Set on a stone bridge straddling a canyon over the raging Río Guáitara, the neo-Gothic **Santuario de Las Lajas** (daily 6am–6pm) is arguably the most dramatically situated cathedral on the continent. Located 7km southeast of Ipiales, Las Lajas owes its spectacular setting to an apparent sighting of the Virgin Mary in a rockface above the river. Every Easter, miracle-seeking pilgrims from Colombia and Ecuador converge on the cathedral. Taxis (US$3 one way) leave for Las Lajas from Ipiales' bus station. Otherwise *colectivos* leave from the town centre near the corner of Carrera 6 and Calle 4.

Arrival and information

By air Pasto's airport (☎2/732-8013) is 27km north of the city. There are no buses to downtown and taxis cost US$5.
By bus The bus terminal (☎2/730-9200) lies 2km south of downtown at C 18 No. 16D–50. A taxi to the centre costs US$2, otherwise buses #1, 6, 9, 15 run to the centre (US$0.50).
Tourist information The obliging tourist office is at Calle 18 No. 25–25 (Mon–Fri 7am–noon, 2–6pm, Sat–Sun 8am–noon, 2–6pm; ☎2/723- 4962; Ⓦwww.emprendecaminoconoceanarino.com).

Accommodation

Don Saul C 17 No. 23–52 ☎2/723-0618. Live it up in this swanky hotel with comfortable rooms, gym, sauna and restaurant. ⑧
Koala Inn C 18 No. 22–37 ☎2/722-1101. Just two blocks from the main square, a typical backpackers' hostel with fifteen private rooms (some with cable TV) arranged around a central courtyard. ④

Moving on

By bus Frequent departures for Ipiales (2hr), Popayán (6hr) and Cali (9hr).

Amazonia

Although Colombia's portion of the Amazon River basin occupies a third of its total territory, it remains only loosely integrated with the rest of the country. The region's staggering biodiversity – more than six thousand bird and animal species – is safeguarded in a half-dozen national parks. However, owing to the boggy terrain and thick forest, which makes road building impossible, only one, **Parque Nacional Amacayacú**, is at all accessible from the port city of **Leticia**, where most tourism is concentrated. Despite the fact that the region's difficult topography and isolation make travelling expensive, one silver lining is that it's not riddled like other areas by political violence. You'd be hard-pressed to find a safer "safe hole" than Leticia in Colombia.

LETICIA AND AROUND

A stone's throw from Brazil and Peru, the end-of-the-world settlement of **LETICIA** is a superb, if until recently overlooked, gateway to the Amazon. With 35,000 residents, it's the largest and most modern of Colombia's Amazon colonies, but still barely a shadow of the river's two other, rapidly growing tourist centres, Iquitos in Peru and Manaus in Brazil. The pint-sized town was settled by Peruvians in the mid-nineteenth century but passed into Colombian hands when the region's irregular border was redrawn in the 1930s to quell a series of skirmishes between Colombia, Peru and Brazil sparked by the rubber boom. Despite past tensions, relations with their neighbours couldn't be better today. The town has all but fused with the Brazilian port of **Tabatinga**, 4km down the road, for which no entry visa is required.

Carved, as it were, from the otherwise impenetrable jungle, here you don't need

CROSSING INTO BRAZIL AND PERU

There are regular **flights** to Manaus from the Brazilian town of Tabatinga, just across the border. Minibuses leaving Leticia for the Tabatinga airport cost US$2. Although flights occasionally operate to **Iquitos** (see p.893) and **Lima** (see p.799), don't count on that as a sure thing. Your only way to cross into Peru is by **river cruise** on the Amazon. Speedboats to Iquitos leave daily for about US$55. For a more adventurous, if somewhat primitive, experience you can hang a hammock on the deck of one of the slow barges (about US$25) that follow the same route in three days. Food is provided, but be sure to bring water and plenty of insect repellent. Several boats of varying standards also leave Tabatinga for **Manaus** (see p.347), a journey of no more than four days. Even if you leave Colombia overland you'll have to go to the airport in Leticia to have your passport stamped.

to venture very far to experience the region's wildlife. Indeed, the town's main plaza, **Parque Santander**, is a symphony of sound and colour, especially when exotic parrots flock here at sunset.

Arrival and accommodation

Leticia is landlocked and the only way to and fro, if you haven't reached overland from Brazil or Peru, is by air; direct flights between Leticia and Bogotá are available on Aero República. Several small **hotels** and *residencias* catering to tourists offer reasonable lodging in Leticia.

Anaconda Cra 11 No. 7–34 ⓣ8/27119. This full-service resort hotel – the most upscale in town – offers creature comforts like pool, cable TV, restaurant and terrace. It also runs jungle tours. ❺

Hostel Mahatu C 9–69 at Cra 7 ⓣ8/351265, ⓔinfo@mahatu.com. Simple, colourful space with four rooms, a small kitchen, free internet and bicycle rental catering to backpackers. They offer tourist info and book jungle excursions in conjunction with SelvaAventura. ❷–❹

PARQUE NACIONAL AMACAYACÚ

Most visitors to Letitica will want to take a jungle tour two hours up the Amazon by boat to **PARQUE NACIONAL AMACAYACÚ** (entrance fee US$10), a 2930-square kilometre preserve created in 1975. The park, only a small part of which is open to the public, is home to some five hundred bird species and 150 mammals, including pink river dolphins and the world's smallest monkey, the *tití leoncito*. Tours of the park are led by indigenous guides from the **Ticuna** tribe still living in virtual isolation in the park's interior. The highlight is a walk on a rope bridge built above the forest canopy from which you can see the virgin jungle stretch off into the horizon. You can also visit several indigenous settlements to buy handicrafts made before your eyes by the villagers. **Boats** to the park can be hired along the riverfront in Leticia (US$15). A restaurant and affordable lodging in beds or hammocks are available. Be sure to bring cash, as there are no places to get money.

Ecuador

HIGHLIGHTS

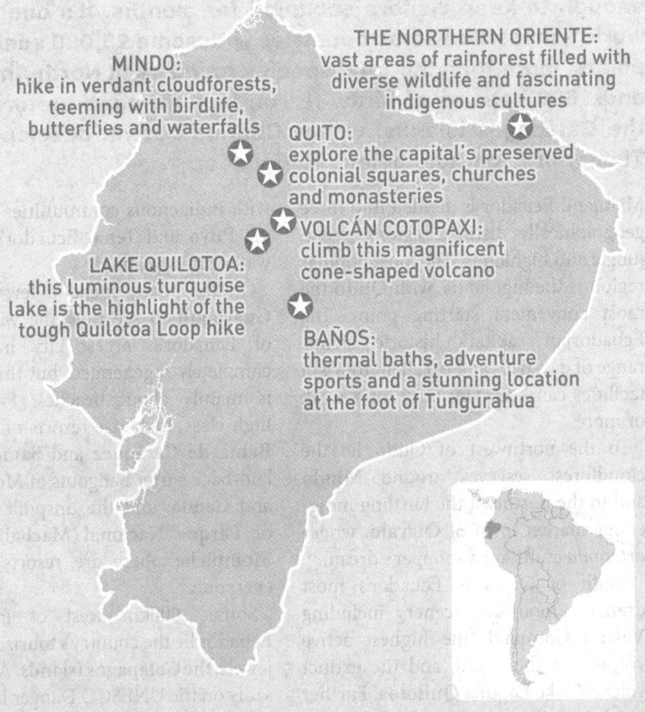

MINDO: hike in verdant cloudforests, teeming with birdlife, butterflies and waterfalls

THE NORTHERN ORIENTE: vast areas of rainforest filled with diverse wildlife and fascinating indigenous cultures

QUITO: explore the capital's preserved colonial squares, churches and monasteries

VOLCÁN COTOPAXI: climb this magnificent cone-shaped volcano

LAKE QUILOTOA: this luminous turquoise lake is the highlight of the tough Quilotoa Loop hike

BAÑOS: thermal baths, adventure sports and a stunning location at the foot of Tungurahua

ROUGH COSTS

DAILY BUDGET Basic US$20/ occasional treat US$30–40

DRINK Cerveza Pilsener US$1

FOOD Set menu two-course lunch US$2

HOSTEL/BUDGET HOTEL US$5–10

TRAVEL Quito to Baños: 4hr, US$5

FACT FILE

POPULATION 13.9 million

AREA 283,000 sq km

LANGUAGE Spanish

CURRENCY US dollar

CAPITAL Quito (population: 1,400,000)

INTERNATIONAL PHONE CODE ☎593

TIME ZONE GMT -5hr

Introduction

In Ecuador it's possible to wake up on the Pacific coast, drive through the snow-capped Andes and reach the edge of the Amazon jungle by sundown. Although Ecuador is only slightly larger than the UK, its wildly different terrains have more than enough to keep visitors occupied for months. It's one of the world's most biodiverse countries with some 25,000 species of plants, more than the total species found in all North America, and 1600 species of birds. It's entirely fitting, therefore, that the Galápagos Islands, where Charles Darwin developed his Theory of Evolution, belong to Ecuador.

Mainland Ecuador is divided into three geographically distinct regions: coast, jungle and highlands. The most popular region is the highlands, with **Quito** the most convenient starting point. The Ecuadorian capital's historic sights, range of day-trips and excellent tourism facilities can keep you busy for a week or more.

To the northwest of Quito lie the cloudforest reserves around **Mindo** and to the northeast the bustling indigenous market town of **Otavalo**, whose *artesanía* crafts are a shopper's dream.

South of Quito is Ecuador's most dramatic mountain scenery including **Volcán Cotopaxi**, the highest active volcano in the world, and the extinct volcanic lake **Laguna Quilotoa**. Further south is the popular spa town of **Baños** and **Riobamba**, the most convenient base to explore Ecuador's highest mountain, **Chimborazo** (6310m), and the **Nariz del Diablo** train ride. Heading south into the Southern Highlands you'll find Ecuador's best-preserved Inca ruins, **Ingapirca**, its beautiful third city **Cuenca** and towards the Peruvian border the relaxing "Valley of Longevity", **Vilcabamba.**

In the Oriente, excursions deep into unforgettable wildernesses of primary jungle can be arranged via the unsightly oil towns of **Lago Agrio** and **Coca**, while shorter trips and stays with indigenous communities are best via **Puyo** and **Tena**, Ecuador's white-water rafting capital.

On the coast, spend a few days in **Guayaquil** to see how the waterfront of Ecuador's largest city has been completely regenerated, but this region is mainly about beaches. From the high-class, high-rise resorts of **Salinas, Bahía de Caráquez** and **Same** to the laid-back surfer hangouts of **Montañita** and **Canoa**, and the unspoilt beaches of **Parque Nacional Machalilla** and **Mompiche**, there are resorts to suit everyone.

Some 1000km west of mainland Ecuador lie the country's tourism crown jewels, **the Galápagos Islands**. Although sadly on the UNESCO Danger List, they remain among the world's top destinations for watching wildlife.

CHRONOLOGY

4000 BC The first evidence of human population in Ecuador is the Valdivia culture on the Santa Elena Peninsula.

1460 AD Tupac Yupanqui leads the first Inca invasion of Ecuador.

1495 Tupac's son Huayna Capac conquers Ecuador and establishes centres in Quito and Ingapirca.

1526 Civil War erupts between Huayna Capac's sons Huascar and Atahualpa, who eventually wins.

1532 Spaniard Francisco Pizarro arrives in Ecuador, captures and executes Atahualpa the following year, completing the conquest by 1535, giving rise to the wealthy Audiencia de Quito.

1541 Francisco de Orellana journeys down the Amazon, reaching the Atlantic.
1820 On October 9, Guayaquil declares independence, supported by Venezuelan Simón Bolívar.
1822 On May 24, Quito wins its independence at the Battle of Pichincha. Ecuador becomes fully independent in 1830.
1861 Conservative Gabriel Garcia Moreno seizes power, quashes rebellions and makes Catholicism a prerequisite for all citizens. He is assassinated on the streets of Quito in 1875.
1895 Liberal Eloy Alfaro becomes president and introduces sweeping reforms ending the connection between church and state and legalising divorce. He is assassinated in 1912 by angry conservatives.
1941 Peru invades Ecuador and forces through a treaty giving Peru a 200,000 square km section of Ecuadorian jungle.
1967 Oil is discovered in the Ecuadorian Oriente, prompting an oil boom in the 1970s.
1979 Left-winger Jaime Roldós is elected President, bringing to an end a long period of military rule. He dies in a mysterious plane crash two years later.
1996 Self-styled *loco* (crazy) Abdalá Bucharam wins the presidency but is ousted by Congress a few months later for 'mental incapacity' and goes into exile in Panama.
1998 President Jamil Mahuad and Peruvian President Fujimori sign a peace treaty, which finally ends the long-running border dispute.
2000 The sucre plummets from 6000 to 25,000 to the dollar in less than a year. President Mahuad is ousted in a coup but his successor Gustavo Noboa presses ahead with a radical dollarisation plan.
2001 In November, Ecuador qualifies for the FIFA Football World Cup for the first time in its history, sparking wild national celebrations.

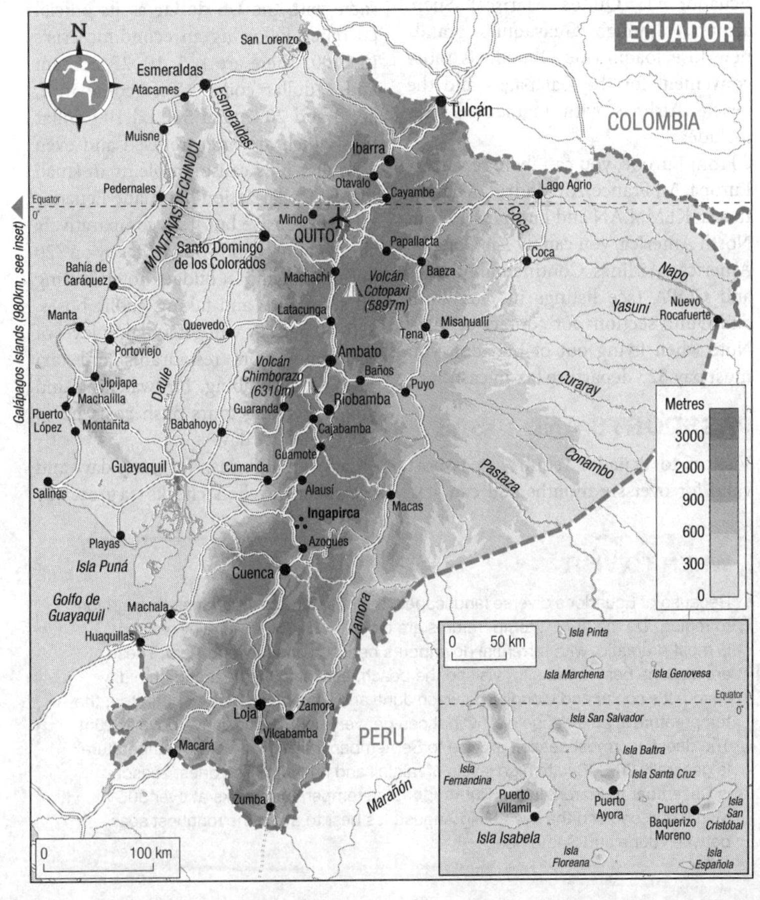

2002 Former coup leader Lucio Gutiérrez wins the Presidency but is removed after two years after attempting to increase his presidential powers.
2007 Rafael Correa, a friend of Venezuelan President Hugo Chavez, becomes Ecuador's seventh President in ten years. He promises to stamp out corruption, engages in a war of words with the rich classes and replaces Congress with a newly elected Assembly.

Basics

ARRIVAL

Arriving by **air**, most travellers enter Ecuador via Quito's Mariscal Sucre airport, although Guayaquil's brand-new José Joaquín de Olmedo is more convenient for the Galápagos and the beach. Airlines with regular services include:

From Europe, you can fly here via Air Europa, Air France, Air Madrid, Avianca, Iberia, KLM, LAN and Lufthansa. From North America, you can fly Air Canada, American Airlines, Continental Airlines and COPA (see listings in Guayaquil and Quito sections for contact details). Note when flying out of Ecuador, you must pay $25 departure tax in cash.

PASSPORTS AND VISAS

Visitors to Ecuador require a passport valid for over six months and can stay for up to ninety days on an automatic 12-X tourist visa. You will receive a T3 tourist card to be kept with your passport until you leave. It is possible to get an extension to a maximum of 180 days but this requires going to the immigration office on the day the visa expires and is at the discretion of officials. If the visa does expire, you are liable for a hefty $200 fine. Officially you should bring proof of sufficient funds to support yourself and a return ticket or proof of onward travel, although this is rarely demanded in practice.

MONEY AND BANKS

Ecuador replaced the plummeting *sucre* with the **US dollar** as its official currency following an economic crisis in 2000. There are 1, 5, 10, 25, 50 cent and 1 dollar coins. Notes come in 1, 5, 10 and 20. Avoid 50 and 100 dollar bills which are often refused and even 20 dollar bills cause problems in small towns. Dollarization has made Ecuador more expensive but it's a comparatively cheap country and you can get by on $20 per day staying in budget hotels, eating off set menus and taking public buses. $30–40 per day will get a higher level of accommodation, restaurants and taxi rides. The climbing, birdwatching and jungle-trekking tours push costs up to $35 to $80 per day.

Carry enough cash for a few days and use dollar travellers' checks – a great way

WHEN TO VISIT

Because of Ecuador's diverse landscapes, the best time to visit varies from region to region. On the **coast**, temperatures are typically 25-35C. The rainy season is most dramatic, with torrential downpours between January and April. These are also the best months for visiting the beach, escaping the heat and humidity inland. It's cooler and cloudier between June and December. In the **highlands**, the temperature is an average of 15C but can get very cold, particularly above 2500m. The driest, warmest season is June to September. In the **Oriente** the temperature Is generally 20-30C with high levels of rainfall and humidity. The driest season is December to March. In the **Galápagos**, the temperature peaks at over 30C in March and cools to the low 20s in August. It's best to avoid the roughest seas between June and September.

of safeguarding funds because they are refundable if lost or stolen. A credit card is useful as backup. Off the beaten track, change enough money to last you as you may have problems changing travellers' checks. Visa, MasterCard, Cirrus and Maestro are most commonly accepted at ATMs. In larger agencies, you can pay for tours with a credit card but it's normal to be charged 5 to10 percent extra. Note that rates of exchange for currencies outside South America (eg British pounds) are often poor so bring cash and traveller's checks in US dollars wherever possible.

INFORMATION AND MAPS

There are Ministry of Tourism iTur offices (Ⓦwww.vivecuador.com) in provincial capitals and the main tourist centres, supplying maps, lists of hotels and restaurants and information on sightseeing. Some are better than others.

An excellent source of information is **South American Explorers** (Ⓣ02/222-5228, Jorge Washington 311 and Leonidas Plaza, www.saexplorers.org), a member-supported nonprofit organization providing the latest general and tourist information. Membership is $50/$80 (individual/couple), which entitles you to use the clubhouses in Quito, Lima and Cusco, with access to detailed country information, trip reports, maps, a library, bag storage and book exchange. Nonmembers can purchase a wide range of useful information sheets.

El Instituto Geográfico Militar in Quito, at Senierges and Paz y Miño, sells topographical maps for just $2 and a giant map of Quito $8 (bring your passport or ID). The best internationally available general map of Ecuador is the 1:1,000,000 International Travel Maps Ecuador map (530 W Broadway, Vancouver, BC V5Z 1E9, Canada, Ⓦwww.itmb.com). There are also maps of the Galápagos Islands and Quito available.

CROSSING TO AND FROM BORDERING COUNTRIES

Peru overland

Arriving by bus from Peru you come via iTumbes and Huaquillas. It's also possible to cross via Macará (see p.649 for further information).

Colombia overland

Travelling to and from Colombia overland is only possible via Tulcán in the northern highlands. The border region has a troubled history and many travelers choose to fly to Cali from Tulcán (national Ecuadorian airline TAME Ⓣ02/2397-7100, Ⓦwww.tame.com.ec offers this route).

GETTING AROUND

Ecuador's inexpensive and generally reliable **buses** are the country's most useful and preferred form of public transport, trundling along just about everywhere there's a road. The **Panamericana** (Panamerican Highway) forms the backbone of the country's road network, linking all major highland towns and cities.

By bus

The best way to see and get around Ecuador is by **bus**. Public buses are very cheap – typically about $1 per hour of travel. But quality varies considerably so it's worth checking out the bus you're going to travel on before purchasing a ticket. The variable quality of the roads, particularly in the rainy season, is another problem and often results in delays. However travellers are rewarded for their patience with spectacular views and a more intimate experience of Ecuador and its people. If you're lucky the stereo will be pumping out a pulsating salsa soundtrack to your journey, if you're unlucky there'll be a horrendous macho action movie ruining the trip. For longer bus rides at peak weekend and holiday period, buy your ticket in advance.

By car

Hiring a car is possible but not recommended because of the expense and Ecuador's poor roads, and, frankly, crazy drivers. It costs an average $300–500 per week, depending on the size of vehicle, with an alarming excess of $1000 in case of damage.

By air

It's tempting for those either pushed for time or weary of long bus rides to **fly**. TAME (Ⓣ02/2397-7100, Ⓦwww.tame.com.ec) offers reasonably priced flights from Quito to Coca, Cuenca, Esmeraldas, Galápagos, Guayaquil, Lago Agrio, Loja, Machala, Manta, Porto Viejo and Tulcán. There are also flights from Guayaquil to Cuenca and Loja. Prices start at about $60 one-way. Icaro (Ⓣ02/244-8626/ 02/245-0928) and Aerogal (Ⓣ02/294-2800) both serve Quito, Guayaquil and Cuenca and are often marginally cheaper than TAME.

ACCOMMODATION

Ecuador has a wide variety of **accommodation**, from dirt-cheap rickety shacks to a large supply of comfortable mid-range hotels and then a big jump in price up to the luxury options. You can pay as little as $3–5 per person for a basic dormitory in a cheap *pensión*, *residencial* or *hostal*. The mid-range is where Ecuador is the best value: in most destinations $20–30 will get you a good-sized double room in a *hotel* or *hostería* with comfortable beds, private bathroom, hot water and cable TV. In the $50–100 range, you can stay at a glitzy international city hotel, a colonial *hacienda* or a secluded jungle lodge. Cities such as Quito, Guayaquil and Cuenca are slightly more expensive but competition keeps the prices reasonable. On the coast, air conditioning often costs a bit extra, and budget places sometimes have no hot water, although the climate renders it unnecessary. Consider bringing your own mosquito net if you plan to spend a lot of time in the jungle or the coast during the rainy season. Bear in mind that deep in the jungle, budget options are often hard to find so expect to pay more (usually as part of an all-inclusive tour price).

Camping is not widely available but possible in some areas, but you must usually bring your own gear unless you book a tour which includes camping in the itinerary.

FOOD

There's a lot more to Ecuadorian cuisine than roasted guinea pig. Rice and beans are the staple and don't be surprised to be served rice with everything (even with pasta or potatoes). Budget travellers can take advantage of the cheap set menu *almuerzos* (lunches) and *meriendas* (dinners), which typically serve a soup, main course and drink for $1.50–2.50. *Sopa* (soup), *caldo* (broth) and *seco* (stew) are also healthy, cheap and tasty ways to stay full. Try *locro de papa*, a blend of cheese, pasta and potato or *chupe de pescado*, a thick fish and vegetable soup. *Caldo de pata* (pig's foot soup) is for the more adventurous. For main course, *seco de pollo*, a chicken stew made with coriander and *lomo salteado* (salted beef steak) are dependable options. The famous *cuy* (guinea pig) and *hornado* (giant pigs) are sights to behold, roasted whole on a spit.

On the Ecuadorian coast, the seafood is among the best in the world. *Ceviche*, a cold spicy seafood dish marinated with lemon and onion, is excellent, as is *encebollado*, a fish and onion soup, which is often eaten to stave off a hangover. It would be difficult to find a better fresh white fish than *corvina a la plancha* (steamed sea bass). Note though that shellfish is a common cause of illness among tourists so always eat in clean, popular places and be especially careful in the highlands and Oriente, where the shellfish has been transported further.

Snacks which come in handy throughout the country are *empanadas* (meat or cheese-filled pastries), *tortillas de verde* (fried mashed green bananas) or *de yucca* (a local root vegetable) and delicious *humitas* (mashed corn with cheese steamed wrapped in its leaves).

DRINK

Always buy bottled water and never drink from the tap. It's best to avoid ice in cheaper places as it's sometimes made from tap water. Ecuador's abundant tropical fruits mean that the fresh *jugos* (juices) and *batidos* (milkshakes) are great options for breakfast. As well as pineapple, melon, papaya and banana, try some unusual fruits such as *naranjilla* (a sour orange) or *tomate de arbol* (a sweet tomato). Coca-Cola, Sprite and Fanta are everywhere, while coffee is of variable quality, annoying in a country which produces so much. The most common beers are the good quality local Pilsener and slightly more expensive Club Verde, but if you're a beer connoisseur you'll be disappointed. Whisky, rum and the local firewater *Agua Ardiente* are cheap and strong enough to give you a stonking hangover if you overindulge. *Chicha*, made from fermented corn, yucca or potato, is widely drunk by the indigenous people, especially in the jungle. If you don't try it, don't worry – you won't be missing much.

COMMUNICATIONS

The **postal** system in Ecuador is very unreliable so your postcard may reach its destination after many weeks, if at all. Receiving mail is even worse because of the lengthy and often costly process of clearing customs. If you need to send or receive something, particularly if it's valuable, use an international courier service such as DHL or Fedex, although bear in mind there is usually a minimum charge of $50.

Ecuador's **phone** system is getting slowly better and international calls are far cheaper than they used to be. There are countless phone offices, most commonly Andinatel, in cities and even smaller towns. These are generally the cheapest and easiest places for conventional calls, particularly useful if you want to call hotels or tour operators. There are also cellular public phones (mainly Porta and Bell South), which use prepaid phone cards available at shops or kiosks.

Calling North America costs as little as $0.10–0.20 per minute and Europe $0.30–40 per minute, although there is usually a connection charge.

The **internet** is of course the cheapest and easiest way to keep in touch. You're never far frominternet cafes in tourist towns and even remote places have a connection somewhere. Expect to be charged $0.50–1 per hour, although prices can be higher in the back of beyond.

Writing a travel blog is a great way to let those back home know where you are and what you're doing. They're easy to set up – Ⓦwww.bloggers.com and Ⓦwww.travelblog.org are popular.

HEALTH

Vaccinations which are strongly recommended include Typhoid, Hepatitis A and Yellow Fever. Others to consider are Hepatitis B and Rabies. Malaria is present in the Oriente and on the northern coast. Wear long sleeves, light-coloured clothes and use repellent to minimize bites. The best anti-malarial medication is Malarone, which must be taken daily. Avoid Lariam/Mefloquine which can have serious side effects. Dengue fever is spread by day-biting mosquitoes mainly during the rainy season and is becoming more of a problem in urban areas on the coast. There is no vaccine so seek medical help as soon as possible.

You would be unlucky to catch a disease in Ecuador, and the most common problem is the dreaded travellers diarrhoea. You can minimize the risks by avoiding food from street and bus vendors and eating in clean restaurants. Tap water, ice, salad, ice cream, unpeeled fruit and seafood are common culprits. Eat plenty of carbohydrates, drink plenty of fluids and pack oral rehydration salts and Imodium just in case.

Another common problem is altitude sickness. It's not to be taken lightly – at best you will feel lousy, but at worst, particularly on treks, it can be dangerous. At altitudes over 2000m (which includes Quito, Cuenca and much of the highlands), take things easy for a day or so, don't overexert yourself and avoid alcohol.

SAFETY AND POLICE

Sneak theft is the most common crime travelling around Ecuador. In Quito, in particular, tourists are targeted by expert pickpockets. Be vigilant in crowded areas and on public transport, keep your money out of sight and be wary of strangers engaging you in conversation on the street as this is a common diversionary tactic. Don't carry large amounts of cash - it's asking for trouble.

Armed robbery is less common but it does happen. Danger spots in Quito include the Mariscal hotel district, parts of the Old Town, the walk up to El Panecillo (take a taxi) and Parque Carolina. Avoid walking alone at night and take taxis (but not unmarked cabs). In Guayaquil, be extra vigilant at night, particularly in the downtown area. Esmeraldas and Atacames also have problems with theft and robbery. Avoid arriving at Esmeraldas bus station at night if possible. Drug smuggling and Colombian guerrilla activity in the northern border areas have made areas of Sucumbíos (capital Lago Agrio), Carchi (capital Tulcán) and Esmeraldas (capital Esmeraldas) provinces unsafe. On the southern border, the Cordillera del Cóndor, southeast of Zamora, contains landmines from the conflicts with Peru.

By law you must carry identification – for foreigners this means your passport. If you can't produce identification, you may be detained by the police.

Carrying drugs in Ecuador may end you up in jail – for up to fifteen years. Avoid any contact with drug dealers. Foreigners are vulnerable to set-ups and bailing you out is an easy way for corrupt police officials to make some serious money.

OPENING HOURS AND HOLIDAYS

Most shops and public offices are open Monday to Saturday from 9am to 5pm or 6pm, although smaller family-owned businesses will open and close at the owner's discretion and lunch hours are often extended.

Banks open between 8am and 9am Monday to Friday and close between 2pm and 4pm. Some extend hours to 6pm but it's preferable to go before 2pm. Telephone call centres are generally open 8am to 10pm. Restaurant and bar opening hours vary widely. Museums are usually open at weekends and closed Mondays. On Sundays and some public holidays you may often find yourself in a ghost town with everything closed.

Most national holidays mark famous historical events as well as the standard Catholic festivals. Ecuadorians love to party with lots of food, drink and late nights, so it's a great experience for travellers to get involved. Most of the following are national holidays although some are only celebrated in certain areas of the country. Note that the government habitually changes the dates of national holidays, often to tag them onto the weekend.

PUBLIC HOLIDAYS

January 1 New Year's Day (*Año Nuevo*). This is recovery day with millions nursing hangovers.
January 6 Epiphany (*Reyes Magos*). Celebrated mainly in the highlands.
February/March Carnival (*Carnaval* – literally 'goodbye to meat'). The week before Lent is Ecuador's biggest party. Usually Monday and Tuesday are holidays. The beaches are packed and in the highlands Ambato and Guaranda are famous for their celebrations. Don't be surprised to get wet as throwing water is an essential part of the fun.
March/April Holy Week (*Semana Santa*). The big processions in Quito are on Good Friday, which is a Public Holiday.
May 1 Labour Day (*Día del Trabajo*).
May 24 Battle of Pichincha (*La Batalla del Pichincha*). Celebrating the decisive battle for independence in 1822 (highlands only).
July 24 Birthday of Simón Bolívar, the man who dreamed of a united South America and helped to liberate Ecuador.
August 10 Quito Independence Day (*Día de la independencia*).
October 9 Independence of Guayaquil (Guayaquil only).
October 12 Columbus Day (*Día de la Raza*).
November 2 All Souls' Day or Day of the Dead (*Día de los Muertos*).
November 3 Independence of Cuenca (Cuenca only).
December 6 Foundation of Quito. Bullfights are the order of the day (Quito only).
December 25 Christmas Day (*Navidad*). Most Ecuadorians celebrate Christmas on Christmas Eve night and relax on Christmas Day.
December 31 New Year's Eve (*Nochevieja*), *Años viejos*. Rivals Carnival as the country's biggest party. Locals burn effigies of well-known characters – everyone from the President to Homer Simpson. Note that safe use of fireworks is conspicuously absent.

CULTURE AND ETIQUETTE

One of the best aspects of Ecuador is the friendly, hospitable, fun-loving people. Ecuador's population of nearly fourteen million is divided almost equally between the coast and highlands. Most of the population, 65 percent, are *mestizo* (mixed race), 25 percent are indigenous, 5 percent Afro-Ecuadorian, with power still concentrated mainly in the hands of the 5 percent white minority. While many of the Indians hold on to the traditional customs and dress, the mainstream population aspire to dress like Americans in blue jeans and designer labels. This aspiration coupled with successive economic crises has led to nearly two million emigrants in recent years, mainly to the US and Europe. Most Ecuadorians have a close friend or relative living abroad and this is particularly hard on the family unit, which is extremely important in Ecuador. Children usually live with their parents until marriage. Around 90 percent of Ecuadorians are Roman Catholic, although evangelical Christianity is increasing rapidly, particularly among the richer classes. However, many young people are far from conservative.

Rivalry between the mountains and coast, particularly between Quito and Guayaquil, is fierce. *Costeños* consider *Serranos* (mountain people) to be conservative, uptight and two-faced and they resent paying taxes to Quito. *Serranos* call *Costeños* 'monos' (monkeys) and consider them rude, uncultured, immoral gossips. The rivalry ranges from friendly banter to deep-rooted resentment so it can be a touchy subject.

Football (soccer to North Americans) is undisputedly the number one sport in Ecuador and watching a local match at one of the larger stadiums in Quito and Guayaquil is an unforgettable experience. If there is a national team match or a *clásico* (local derby) between Quito or Guayaquil teams, the cities grind to a halt because everyone's glued to the television.

OUTDOOR ACTIVITIES

You'll never be stuck for something to do in Ecuador. The problem is more likely to be fitting in some relaxation time in between jungle treks, hikes, climbs and rafting.

Hiking and climbing

The highlands' wide open spaces offer the widest range of **hiking** options – the Quilotoa Loop, Parque Nacional Cotopaxi, Mindo cloudforest, the hills around Baños, Parque Nacional Cajas and Vilcabamba are just a few that stand out. On the coast, Parque Nacional Machalilla and Cordillera Chongón near Montañita also offer good hiking, although the heat can be a problem.

The best opportunities for **climbing** are Cotopaxi and Chimborazo, although ensure you are fully fit, properly acclimatised and travelling with a qualified guide before attempting these summits.

Watersports

For watersports including **rafting** and **kayaking**, Tena and Baños are the best bases with a wide variety of trips on fast-flowing rapids and gentler tributaries to suit all levels. For **surfing**, head to the beach resorts of Montañita, which holds a famous surfing competition around Carnival and Canoa, a quieter option.

Scuba-diving and **snorkelling** opportunities are limited on the mainland. Parque Nacional Machalilla has a few reputable operators but the best place by far is the Galápagos Islands, whose amazing marine life makes it one of the world's top destinations for diving and snorkelling.

For **birdwatching**, it's hard to beat the cloudforests of Mindo which have more than four hundred species as well as 250 species of butterflies. The tiny hummingbirds are a particular highlight, most commonly seen in the cloudforests and the jungles of the Oriente. The Andean condor is a rare but unforgettable sight, occasionally seen in Parque Nacional Cotopaxi and other areas of the highlands.

For other **wildlife watching**, you're unlikely to see many wild mammals on the coast or in the mountains, but the Oriente offers great opportunities to watch sloths, otters, cayman, tapir and many species of monkeys. The Galápagos is of course unbeatable for close encounters with wildlife.

Quito

At a dizzying elevation of 2850m, Quito is the second highest capital city in the world after Bolivia's La Paz. Its location could not be more dramatic with the active Volcán Pichincha, which covered the city in ash in 1999, looming to the west and Valle de los Chillos descending east towards the Amazon basin. If the altitude doesn't leave you breathless then the architecture surely will. Founded by the Spanish in 1534, Quito rapidly became a major colonial centre and its churches, monasteries, cobbled streets and wide plazas have been beautifully preserved.

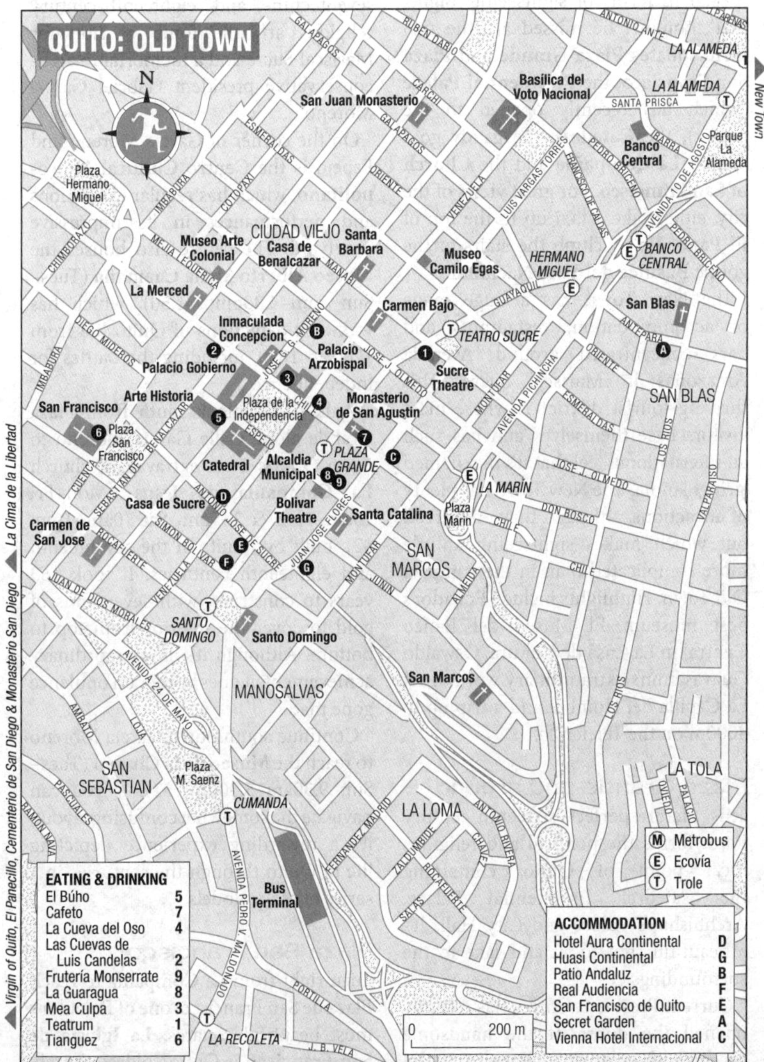

The warmest, driest time is June to September, but the rest of the year can be very chilly with frequent rain showers in the afternoons.

What to see and do

Although most visitors stay in the New Town, the **Old Town**, also known as "El Centro Histórico", is what makes Quito special in terms of sightseeing. Sights that shouldn't be missed are the two main squares **Plaza Grande** and **Plaza San Francisco**, the **Presidential Palace** (which has recently opened to the public), the **Catedral**, the gaudy gold church **La Compañia** and the **Church of San Francisco**. For great views of the city, either take a taxi up to the top of **El Panecillo** or climb the stairs of the gothic **Basílica del Voto Nacional**.

The **New Town** has a huge range of accommodation, restaurants and bars concentrated around Avenida Amazonas in Mariscal Sucre. This thriving tourist district is where most visitors base themselves and has such an international feel that it's nicknamed 'gringolandia'. The New Town has plenty of attractions, although they are spread out which makes sightseeing a little more complicated than in the compact Old Town. Highlights include Ecuador's best museum El Museo del Banco Central in La Casa de Cultura, Oswaldo Guayasamín's extraordinary work of art La Capilla del Hombre and a trip up to 4000m on the Teleférico.

Plaza Grande and around

This picture-perfect sixteenth-century Plaza forms the political and religious focal point of Quito, containing the Catedral, Presidential Palace, Archbishop's Palace and City Hall. It's a beautiful spot to sit and take in the surroundings.

Current President Correa has recently opened the doors of the handsome seventeenth-century **Palacio del Gobierno** to the public (10am–5pm Tues–Sun; free). Visitors can only enter on one of the guided tours (there are five per day), but it's worth the wait.

On the other side of the square is the **Catedral** which is entered through the museum (entrance on Venezuela, 9.30am–4pm Mon–Fri, 10am–4pm Saturday; $1.50, Sunday services free). There's an impressive collection of seventeenth- and eighteenth-century religious art, the tomb of liberator Mariscal Sucre and a memorial to arch-conservative president Gabriel Garcia Moreno.

On the corner of García Moreno and Espejo is the **Centro Cultural Metropolitano**, which has regular exhibitions and performances in its impressive courtyard. The centre also houses the **Museo Alberto Mena Caamaña** (Tues–Sun 9am–4.30pm; $1.50), which has waxwork depictions of Quito life from 1700 to 1830, including the battles for independence.

Walk half a block south from Plaza Grande along Calle García Moreno to reach Quito's most extravagant church **La Compañía de Jesús** (Mon–Fri 10am–1pm & 2–5pm, Sat 10am–1pm; $2), built by Jesuits in the seventeenth and eighteenth centuries. It took 163 years to construct, with seven tons of gold to cover the interior from top to bottom. Although it's an extraordinary achievement, it does border on opulence gone mad.

Continue south down García Moreno to reach the **Museo de la Ciudad** (Tues–Sun 9.30am–5.30pm; $2). If you can navigate the somewhat confusing layout, it's a rewarding experience depicting life in Quito through the centuries in a series of scale models.

Plaza San Francisco

Turn right from La Compañía to reach Plaza de San Francisco, one of Ecuador's most beautiful squares. **La Iglesia de San Francisco** is Quito's oldest church, constructed in the sixteenth century and its twin bell tower is one of the city's most famous sights. At the time of writing the church was being restored, but is open to the public at restricted times in the early morning and early evening. Behind the impressive facade of the church and monastery on the northwest side is the largest religious complex in South America.

The Museo de San Francisco is housed among the cloisters of the complex and has an impressive collection of religious sculptures, paintings and furniture. Through the museum, you can enter the choral room of the church with a statue of the "dancing virgin" and depictions of planets revolving around the sun on the ceiling.

Plaza Santo Domingo and La Ronda

Walk east along Simón Bolívar down to Quito's third impressive square, Plaza Santo Domingo, dominated by the sixteenth-century **Iglesia Santo Domingo**. Walk further down Guayaquil to reach the narrow alley of **La Ronda** (Ⓦwww.callelaronda.com), one of Quito's oldest streets. This working class neighbourhood used to be a dangerous area but has been completely renovated. The result is a pleasant walkway of tiny art galleries, bakeries and traditional cafés.

El Panecillo

Old Quito's skyline is dominated by the 40-metre-high statue of **the Virgin of Quito** high up on the hill known as El Panecillo ("little bread loaf") to the southwest. It's not safe to walk up the hill so take a taxi (about $3 single from the Old Town or $8 round-trip including waiting time). There are regular buses at weekends between El Panecillo and Mitad del Mundo. From the top, the view over the city is spectacular and the close-up of the statue with a chained dragon at her feet is equally impressive. Although she's nicknamed "la Bailarina" (the dancing virgin), she's actually preparing to take flight. You can climb up the statue for $1.

Basílica del Voto Nacional

Walk uphill northeast on Calle Venezuela from Plaza Grande to admire the gothic grandeur of the **Basílica del Voto Nacional** (open daily 9am–5pm; $2). Construction has taken place over the past century, beginning in 1892. Instead of gargoyles, the church has iguanas and Galápagos tortoises protruding from its sides. Climbing the steep stairs and ladders up the115-metre towers is an unnerving experience so take the lift part of the way up if you're afraid of heights. The views across the city are fantastic.

La Casa de La Cultura

Next to the Parque El Ejido, the large oval building of La Casa de la Cultura (Patria between 6 de Diciembre and 12 de Octubre, Ⓣ02/222-3392, Ⓦwww.cce.org.ec) has the appearance of a convention centre. Within the complex are cinemas, theatres, auditoriums and, of most interest to tourists, the **Museo del Banco Central** (Tues–Fri 9am–5pm, Sat & Sun 10am–4pm; $2). This is arguably Ecuador's best museum with an astonishing collection of pre-Columbian ceramics and artefacts as well as colonial, republican and modern art. The museum is divided into four rooms: archeology, colonial art, contemporary art and the Gold Room, which displays the majestic Inca sun-mask which is the symbol of the Banco Central.

Museo Fundación Guayasamín and the Capilla del Hombre

Oswaldo Guayasamín is Ecuador's most famous contemporary artist and Quito's Bellavista district, where he used to reside, houses two collections of his art. The **Museo Fundación Guayasamín**

(Jose Bosmediano 543, Mon–Fri 9.30am–6pm, closed weekends; $3) has a large collection of the artist's work as well as his enormous collection of pre-colombian ceramics and colonial religious art. A further ten-minute walk up the hill is the extraordinary **Capilla del Hombre** or "Chapel of Man", one of South America's most important works of art. This was Guayasamín's last great project, initiated in his last years and not fully completed until after his death in 1999. From the museum you can walk up to the garden of Guayasamín and see where his ashes are buried under the "Tree of Life". Just up from the Capilla del Hombre is the **Parque Metropolitano**, Quito's largest park with forested trails, picnic areas and sweeping views. There are occasional buses up to Bellavista but it's best to take a taxi ($2).

Parque Carolina

The best place to relax in Quito's New Town is Parque Carolina. This is where locals come to enjoy themselves, playing sports on the grass and eating from the food stalls. The park contains a beautiful set of **Botanical Gardens** (Tues–Sun 9am–4.30pm; $2), which showcases Ecuador's huge biodiversity with a vast array of plant and tree species, including more than five hundred orchid species in greenhouses. Next door, the **Museo de Ciencias Naturales** (8.30am–4.30pm Mon–Fri; $2) has a huge collection of dead insects and arachnids. The park also contains **The Vivarium** (Tues–Sun 9.30am–5.30pm) with more than forty species of reptiles including caiman, frogs, turtles and a variety of poisonous snakes. The highlights are the six-metre-long python and the boa constrictor which you are invited to hold and have a photo taken ($3).

The Teleférico

Quito's most dizzying tourist attraction is the **Teleférico** (Mon–Thurs 9am–7pm, Fri–Sun 9am–9pm; $4 or $7 express line), a cable-car ride high above the city. There's a rather tacky theme park with discos, bars and handicraft stores at the entrance but the main attraction is the 15-minute ride up to a height of 4100m, from where the views are spectacular on a clear day. At the top you can take in the views, relax in the café or tackle the half-hour hike to Ruca Pichincha, 3km away. Bring warm clothes and take care overexerting yourself at this altitude if you've just arrived in Quito. It can get very busy on weekends so come early. Teleférico shuttles run from Rio Coca y 6 Diciembre (Ecovía) and Estación Norte (Trole).

Arrival

By air Aeropuerto Internacional Mariscal Sucre (ⓣ 02/294-4900), serving national and international flights, is about 6km north of the New Town. The airport has a *casa de cambio* in the international terminal and there are several ATMs in the wall outside. **Taxis** outside the arrivals gate charge around $4–5 to the New Town (about $1 more at night), or pay a slightly higher fixed fare at the taxi desk in the airport just beyond customs. For **public buses** to the New Town, walk to Av 10 de Agosto about 150m from the terminal entrance, from where regular buses travel along Amazonas to the Mariscal hotel district.

By bus Quito's main bus terminal, the Terminal Terrestre de Cumandá at Av Maldonado is situated in an unpleasant district just south of the Old Town. Take care arriving at night. There's an information desk (Mon–Fri 8.30am–5.30pm), an ATM and plenty of taxis. Ensure you only use a marked cab as there are plenty of unsavoury characters hanging around. A taxi to Mariscal should be only $2–3. Just up the hill is the Cumandá trolley stop but beware of pickpockets on crowded trolleys.

Maps and information

Tourism office The **Ministerio de Turismo** ⓦ www.quito.com.ec, ⓦ www.experiencequito.com) has several offices in the city with glossy brochures, maps of Quito and general information on the rest of Ecuador. In the Old Town (Mon–Fri 9am–8pm, Sat 10am–8pm, Sun 10am–4pm, 02/257-0786, ⓔ infotur-ch@quito-turismo.com) the office in the Palacio Municipal on Plaza Grande

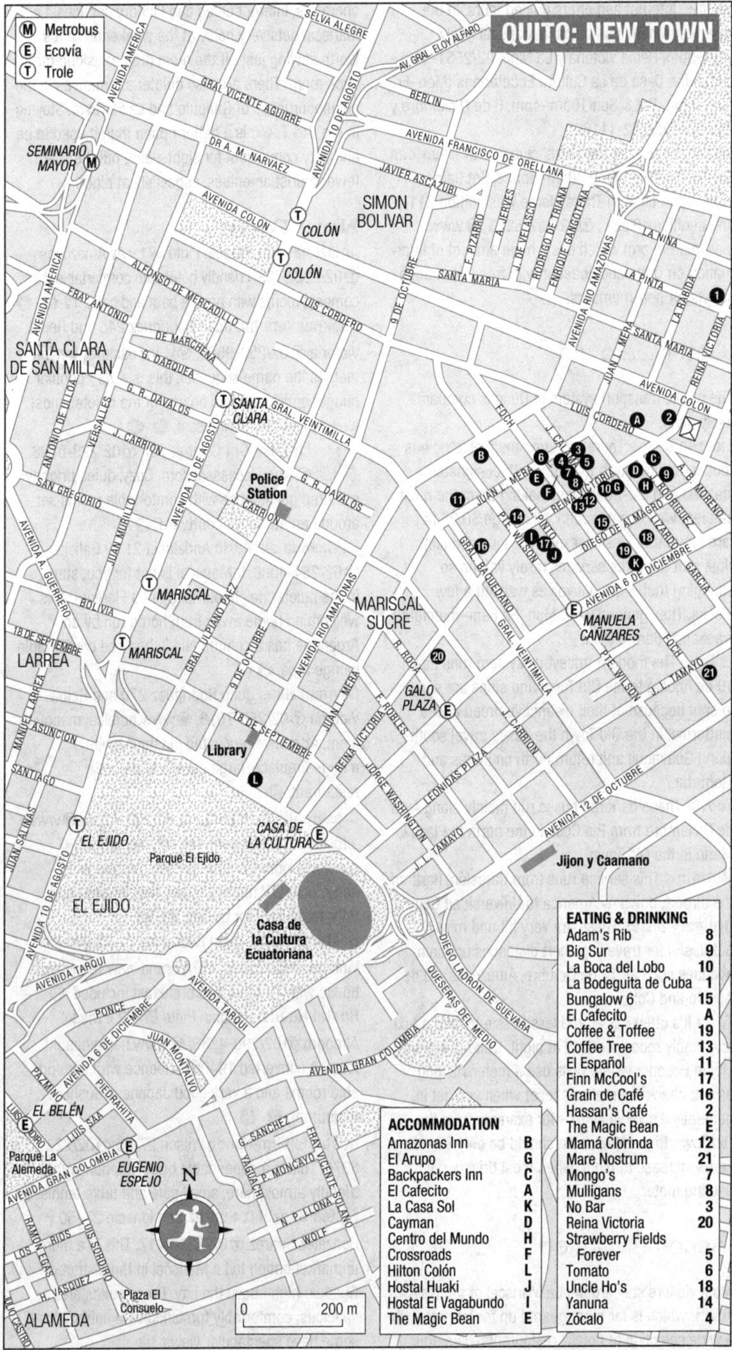
QUITO: NEW TOWN
Metrobus
Ecovía
Trole
SEMINARIO MAYOR
SIMON BOLIVAR
COLÓN
SANTA CLARA DE SAN MILLAN
SANTA CLARA
Police Station
MARISCAL
MARISCAL SUCRE
LARREA
MANUELA CAÑIZARES
GALO PLAZA
Library
CASA DE LA CULTURA
Parque El Ejido
EL EJIDO
Casa de la Cultura Ecuatoriana
Jijon y Caamano
EL BELÉN
Parque La Alemeda
EUGENIO ESPEJO
Plaza El Consuelo
ALAMEDA
N
0
200 m
SELVA ALEGRE
AV. GRAL. ELOY ALFARO
AVENIDA AMERICA
GRAL VICENTE AGUIRRE
AVENIDA 10 DE AGOSTO
BERLIN
AVENIDA FRANCISCO DE ORELLANA
DR A. M. NARVAEZ
JAVIER ASCAZUBI
AVENIDA COLON
F. PIZARRO
A. JERVES
J. DE VELASCO
RODRIGO DE TRIANA
ENRIQUE GANGOTENA
LA NINA
SANTA MARIA
9 DE OCTUBRE
AVENIDA RIO AMAZONAS
LA PINTA
LA RABIDA
ALFONSO DE MERCADILLO
FRAY ANTONIO
LUIS CORDERO
DE MARCHENA
G. DARQUEA
G. R. DAVALOS
GRAL. VEINTIMILLA
J. CARRION
ANTONIO DE ULLOA
VERSALLES
JUAN L. MERA
REINA VICTORIA
FOCH
J. CALAMA
SAN GREGORIO
JUAN MURILLO
P. DE WILSON
J. PINTO
DIEGO DE ALMAGRO
A. R. MORENO
RODRIGUEZ
LIZARDO
GARCIA
AVENIDA 6 DE DICIEMBRE
GRAL. BAQUEDANO
AVENIDA A. GUERRERO
BOLIVIA
18 DE SEPTIEMBRE
GRAL ULPIANO PAEZ
R. ROCA
E. ROBLES
J. L. TAMAYO
MANUEL LARREA
ASUNCION
SANTIAGO
JUAN SALINAS
JORGE WASHINGTON
LEONIDAS PLAZA
AVENIDA 12 DE OCTUBRE
DIEGO LADRON DE GUEVARA
QUESERAS DEL MEDIO
AVENIDA TARQUI
PONCE
JUAN MONTALVO
AVENIDA GRAN COLOMBIA
PAZMINO
PIEDRAHITA
LUIS SAA
LUIS DE...
G. SANCHEZ
YAGUACHI
P. MONCAYO
FRAY VICENTE SOLANO
N. P. LLONA
T. WOLF
RAMON EGAS
LOS RIOS
LUIS SODIRO
H. VASQUEZ
ACCOMMODATION
Amazonas Inn B
El Arupo G
Backpackers Inn C
El Cafecito A
La Casa Sol K
Cayman D
Centro del Mundo H
Crossroads F
Hilton Colón L
Hostal Huaki J
Hostal El Vagabundo I
The Magic Bean E
EATING & DRINKING
Adam's Rib 8
Big Sur 9
La Boca del Lobo 10
La Bodeguita de Cuba 1
Bungalow 6 15
El Cafecito A
Coffee & Toffee 19
Coffee Tree 13
El Español 11
Finn McCool's 17
Grain de Café 16
Hassan's Café 2
The Magic Bean E
Mamá Clorinda 12
Mare Nostrum 21
Mongo's 7
Mulligans 8
No Bar 3
Reina Victoria 20
Strawberry Fields Forever 5
Tomato 6
Uncle Ho's 18
Yanuna 14
Zócalo 4

has free internet and offers guided tours. In the New Town there's an office in Mariscal (daily 9am–5pm, Reina Victoria y La Nina, 02/2551-566) and in the Casa de La Cultura Ecuatoriana (Mon–Fri 9am–5pm, Sat & Sun 10am–4pm, 6 de Diciembre y Patria, ⓣ02/222-1116).

Also check out the travellers' club **South American Explorers** (Mon–Fri 9.30am–5pm & Sat 9am–noon, open till 8pm Thurs; Jorge Washington 311 and Leonidas Plaza , ⓣ02/222-5228, ⓦwww.saexplorers.org) which has a huge amount of information on Quito and Ecuador with free information sheets for non-members.

Getting around

The public transport system in Quito is comparatively good.

Electric Buses There are three main electric bus routes running north to south, with designated stations and car-free lanes, making them the most efficient way to get around. All charge $0.25 flat fare (bought at kiosks or machines in advance). Note that the three services rarely link up so changing routes often involves walking a few blocks. They generally run Mon–Fri 6am–midnight, weekends 6am–10pm.

El Trole The modern trolleybus system runs down 10 de Agosto to the Old Town and stops are easy to spot because of their distinctive green raised platforms. In the Old Town the buses travel south along Guayaquil and return north on Flores and Montufar.

Ecovía These dark red buses run mainly along Av 6 de Diciembre from Río Coca in the north to Plaza la Marín in the Old Town.

Metrobus This service runs from Carcelén, north of the airport, down Av América to Universidad Central.

Ordinary buses These are very hit and miss but useful for travelling short distances up main avenues such as 12 de Octubre, Amazonas, 10 de Agosto and Colón.

Taxis It's often easier and less hassle to take a taxi and highly recommended at night. Quito is the only city in Ecuador where taxis use a meter. As long as you check the meter is reset when you get in, generally it's very cheap – for example from the Old Town to the New Town should be only $2–3. Fares increase at night, when most drivers don't use the meter.

Accommodation

Most visitors stay around La Mariscal of the **New Town**, which is far more geared up for tourists with a wide selection of hotels, restaurants, bars, tour operators, internet cafes and laundry services. La Mariscal gets very noisy at the weekends so it's worth staying just off the main drag or asking for a back room. There are also quieter alternatives in the neighbourhoods of Guapulo and La Floresta. Staying in the **Old Town** is a better option than it used to be and very convenient for sightseeing but there are fewer tourist amenities, especially at night.

New Town

Amazonas Inn Joaquín Pinto 471 y Av Amazonas ⓣ02/222 5723. Friendly hotel with comfortable if compact rooms with private bath and cable TV. ❺–❻

Backpackers Inn Juan Rodríguez 245 and Reina Victoria ⓣ02/250-9669, ⓦwww.backpackersinn.net. As the name suggests, this is a very popular budget option situated on one of the quieter, most pleasant streets in Mariscal. ❷–❹

La Casa Sol Calama 127 ⓣ02/223-0798, ⓦwww.lacasasol.com. Cozy, quiet, brightly coloured guesthouse with comfortable rooms set around an attractive courtyard. ❺

La Casona de Mario Andalucia 213 y Galicia ⓣ02/254-4036. If Mariscal is not for you, stay in the quieter neighbourhood of La Floresta. This welcoming home away from home run by an Argentine has a communal kitchen and comfortable lounge area. ❹

Cayman Hotel Juan Rodríguez 270 and Reina Victoria ⓣ02/256-7616, ⓦwww.hotelcaymanquito.com. Attractive renovated old house with a huge fireplace, large garden and good restaurant. ❻

Crossroads Foch E5-23 ⓣ02/223-4735, ⓦwww.crossroadshostal.com. Friendly hostel with spacious rooms, a large garden, terrace with hammocks, TV room, kitchen, free internet and 24hr restaurant for guests. ❷–❹

Hostal El Arupo Juan Rodriguez E7-22 y Reina Victoria ⓣ02/255-7543. A brand-new renovated house with TV room and breakfast included. ❺

Hostal Huaukí Joaquín Pinto E7-82 y Diego Almagro ⓣ02/290-4286, ⓦwww.hostalhuauki.com. A converted 1940s residence with comfortable rooms and a very good Japanese Sushi restaurant. ❷–❺

Hostal El Vagabundo Wilson E7-45 ⓣ02/222-6376. This is a dependable budget option with a friendly atmosphere, small café and table tennis. ❹

Suites González Suarez San Ignacio 27–50 y González Suarez ⓣ02/222-4417. This is a more upmarket option to La Mariscal in the district of Guapulo high above the city. These suites are spacious, comfortably furnished with cable TV and some have spectacular views. ❼

Old Town

Hotel Catedral Mejia 638 y Benalcazar ☎02/258-3119. Basic hotel for those on a tight budget with private bath and TV. ❸

Hotel Auca Continental Sucre OE-414 y Venezuela ☎02/295-4799. Clean no-frills option with firm beds, private bath and TV. ❹

Hotel La Real Audiencia Bolívar 220 y Guayaquil, ☎02/295-0590, www.realaudiencia.com. Try this for a more upmarket Old Town option with stylish rooms, black and white photography and fabulous view of Plaza Santo Domingo from the restaurant (open to non-guests). ❻

Hotel San Francisco de Quito Sucre 217 and Guayaquil ☎02/228-7758, www.sanfranciscodequito.com.ec. Probably the best Old Town mid-range option with pleasant rooms set around a beautiful courtyard, a fountain, rooftop patio and good views of the Old Town. ❺

Secret Garden Calle Antepara E4-60 y Los Rios, www.secretgardenquito.com. Hidden away southeast of the Historic Centre in a listed building, this is a great budget hostal set on five floors with a rooftop terrace serving big breakfasts. Basic but always bustling with backpackers. There's also a Spanish school and tour operator. ❷–❹

Eating

Quito boasts easily the best selection of international restaurants in Ecuador – everything from Asian to Middle Eastern and Mediterranean. Most are found in the New Town with Old Town eating options rather restricted. Expect to pay more than in the rest of the country though. For those on a budget, fill yourself up at lunch, as most of the restaurants offer great-value lunch specials for $2–4.

Big Sur Juan Rodriguez 228, New Town. Eat alfresco in this new restaurant's garden terrace. Choose from an imaginative menu of mainly chicken and meat dishes. Live jazz every Thurs. Mains $6–8. There are rooms upstairs.

La Bodeguita de Cuba Reina Victoria N26-105, New Town ☎02/254-2476. Tasty Cuban specialities with live Cuban music on Thurs nights, when drinking and dancing continues well into the early hours. Mains $4–5.

TREAT YOURSELF

La Boca del Lobo Calama 284 y Reina Victoria, New Town. With a brightly coloured glass-encased patio, flamboyant décor and an eclectic Mediterranean menu, this is a place to indulge. Mains $8–12.

El Cafecito Luis Cordero 1124, New Town. Cozy café with great coffee, homemade cakes, crêpes and vegetarian meals.

Coffee and toffee Calama y Diego Almagro, New Town. Start the day with breakfast or the evening with cocktails lounging on armchairs and using the free internet in this relaxed café.

Frutería Montserrate Espejo Oe2-12, Old Town. The perfect place to take a break from sightseeing with an extravagant helping of fruit salad and ice cream ($2–3). Cheap *almuerzos* and sandwiches also available.

El Guaragua Espejo Oe2–40, Old Town. Appealing little restaurant just down from Plaza Grande. Ecuadorian specialities and filling set lunches ($2–4).

The Magic Bean Foch E5-08, New Town. Hugely popular café with a small garden where you can sit out until late. Great breakfasts, pancakes and fresh juices.

Mama Clorindas Reina Victoria 1144 ☎02/254-4362, New Town. Well-prepared but comparatively pricey Ecuadorian specialities. Try half a guinea pig (*cuy*) for $9. Mains $5–7.

Mongo's Grill Calama, New Town. This hugely popular Mongolian barbecue has a great atmosphere, offering sizzling meat and vegetable dishes such as chicken teriyaki and lamb in spicy yogurt, all cooked in front of you. Excellent-value buffet $6.

Tomato Juan León Mera y Calama, New Town. A great place for pizza ($5–7) and pasta. The *calzone* is particularly good.

Uncle Ho's Calama 166-E8-29, New Town. New Vietnamese restaurant run by a friendly Irish guy serving delicious Asian food. The Beef Medallions are delicious. Mains $5–7.

Yanuna Wilson y Reina Victoria, New Town. An assault on the eyes as well as the taste buds with wacky décor including ceramics, carvings and indigenous art, serving a wide range of international food, including Asian and Middle Eastern ($3–5).

Drinking and nightlife

Mariscal in the New Town has a vibrant nightlife scene and gets packed on weekends. The most happening area is along José Calama and Foch between avenidas Amazonas, Juan León Mera and Reina Victoria. Bars are busy from 8pm onwards with the clubs filling up towards midnight and things wind down by 3am. Remember to take a taxi at night. The place is completely dead and feels more dangerous on Sundays, when the entire police force seems to take the day off.

Bungalow 6 Calama y Diego Almagro. A mixture of locals and tourists flock to enjoy the great atmosphere and dance to latin and pop classics in this bar/disco (entrance $4 including one drink).

El Pobre Diablo Isabel La Católica and Galavis. A Quito institution with a Bohemian atmosphere, cocktails, a good restaurant and live music.

Finn McCool's Pinto 251 y Reina Victoria. A friendly Irish pub with darts, table football and a roaring log fire.

La Reina Victoria Reina Victoria 530 and Roca. Just like walking into an English pub with dart board, open fire and the obligatory fish and chips on the menu.

No Bar Calama 380. Raucous Mariscal disco with a large dancefloor pumping out latin and pop tunes. Absolutely packed on weekends (entrance $5 including one drink).

Seseribó Edificio El Girón, Veintimilla and 12 de Octubre. A Quito institution and the best place to dance salsa and meringue. Or just stand back and watch the experts. Thurs nights are particularly good.

Strawberry Fields Forever Calama E5-23. A world away from *No-Bar* next door, this tiny rock bar, brimming with Beatles memorabilia, is a good place to escape the disco craziness.

Zócalo corner of Reina Victoria and Calama. This Mexican restaurant has live music most nights and is a popular place to start the evening.

Directory

Airlines Air France 12 de Octubre y Cordero ⓣ02/222-4818,ⓦ www.airfrance.com; American Airlines, Amazonas y Robles ⓣ02/299-5000, ⓦwww.aa.com; Avianca, 6 de Diciembre y 18 de Septiembre ⓣ02/330-2202; Continental Airlines, World Trade Centre, 12 de Octubre and Luis Cordero ⓣ02/255-7290; Iberia, Amazonas 239 and Jorge Washington ⓣ02/256-6009; Icaro, Palora 124 and Amazonas ⓣ02/244-8626/ 02/245-0928; KLM, 12 de Octubre and A Lincoln, Torre 1492 ⓣ02/298-6859; LanChile, Pasaje Río Guayas and Amazonas ⓣ02/299-2300; Lufthansa, 18 de Septiembre and Reina Victoria ⓣ02/250-8396; Tame, Amazonas and Colón ⓣ02/397-7100.

Banks and exchange There are plenty of banks on and around Av Amazonas in the New Town but fewer in the Old Town. They are generally open from Mon–Fri 8.30am–4pm and Sat mornings. Try Banco de Guayaquil on Reina Victoria and Colón or Banco del Pacífico, on 12 de Octubre y Cordero.

Car rental Many reputable international companies have offices outside the international terminal of the airport, including Avis ⓣ02/244-0270 and Hertz ⓣ02/225-4258.

Embassies and consulates Argentina, Amazonas 21–147 and Roca, ⓣ02/250-1106; Bolivia, Eloy Alfaro 2432 and Fernando Ayarza ⓣ02/244-6652; Brazil, Amazonas 1429 and Colón, Edificio España ⓣ02/256-3086; Canada, 6 de Diciembre 2816 and Paul Rivet, Edificio Josueth González ⓣ02/250-6162; Chile, Juan Pablo Sanz 3617 and Amazonas ⓣ02/224-9403; Colombia, Colón 1133 and Amazonas, Edificio Arista ⓣ02/222-2486; Ireland, Antonio de Ulloa 2651 and Rumipamba ⓣ02/245-1577; Peru, República de El Salvador 495 and Irlanda ⓣ02/246-8411; UK, Naciones Unidas and República de El Salvador, Edificio Citiplaza, 14th floor ⓣ02/297-0801, ⓦwww.britembquito.org.ec; US, 12 de Octubre and Patria ⓣ02/256-2890, ⓦwww.usembassy.org.ec; Venezuela, Cabildo 115 and Quito Tenis ⓣ02/226-8635.

Emergencies 911, police 101, fire 102, ambulance 131.

Hospitals Hospital Metropolitano, Av Mariana de Jesús and Av Occidental ⓣ02/226-1520, emergency and ambulance ⓣ02/226-5020.

Internet facilities Quito's New Town is full of internet cafes, charging about $0.70–$1 per hour. Friendly, comfortable places include Papaya Net (Calama y JL Mera, ⓣ02/255-6574) and Sambo.net (JL Mera and J Pinto, ⓣ02/290-1315).

Police La Policía de Turismo (Reina Victoria and Roca ⓣ02/254-3983).

Post offices The most convenient office for La Mariscal is on the corner of Reina Victoria and Colón (ⓣ02/250-8890) Mon–Fri 8am–7pm, Sat & Sun 8am–noon.

Taxis Reliable 24hr services include Central Radio Taxis ⓣ02/250-0600 and Teletaxi ⓣ02/222-2222.

Telephones Andinatel (ⓦwww.andinatel.com) has its main office on Eloy Alfaro near 9 de Octubre and plenty of branches around the city. In Mariscal there are offices in JL Mera and Reina Victoria near Calama. You can also buy Porta and Bell South phonecards at most larger shops.

Tour operators Alta Montaña (Jorge Washington 8-20 ⓣ02/252-4422), climbing and trekking tours. Biking Dutchman (Foch 714 and Juan León Mera ⓣ02/256-8323, ⓦwww.biking-dutchman.com), a wide range of biking tours. Ecuadorian Alpine Institute, (Ramírez Dávalos 136 and Amazonas ⓣ02/256-5465, ⓦwww.volcanoclimbing.com), top-class climbing tours and climbing school. Enchanted Expeditions (De las Alondras N45-102 y Los Lirios ⓣ02/334-0525, ⓦwww.enchantedexpeditions.com), wide range of top-class tours to mountains, jungle and Galápagos. Gulliver (JL Mera and

Calama ⓣ02/252-9297, ⓦwww.gulliver.com.ec), huge range of well-priced tours including climbing, trekking, cycling, horseriding, jungle and Galápagos cruises. Safari Tours (ⓣ02/255-2505, Foch and Cordero E4-132, ⓦwww.safari.com.ec) wide range of climbing, hiking, birdwatching, jungle and Galápagos tours. Sierra Nevada Expeditions (J Pinto and Cordero E4-150 ⓣ02/255-3658, ⓦwww.hotelsierranevada.com) climbing and river rafting specialist. Yacu Amu (Foch 746 and Juan León Mera ⓣ02/290-4054, ⓦwww.yacuamu.com) the longest-established whitewater rafting and kayaking specialist in Ecuador.

DAY-TRIPS FROM QUITO

There's a huge amount of interesting destinations which can be reached on a day-trip from Quito – Otavalo, Mindo and Cotopaxi are all less than three hours from the city.

Mitad del Mundo

The most popular day-trip is up to the **Mitad del Mundo** (The Middle of the World, 9am–6pm daily; $2) on the Equator, 22km to the north. There are various buildings in the complex, notably Francia where you learn of French scientist Charles-Marie de la Condamine's measurements in 1736 which proved the location of the Equator. But the centrepiece is the 30m-high **monument** ($3 to go inside), topped by a brass globe. Climb to the top and then descend the stairs through the **Ethnographic Museum,** which has fascinating displays of Ecuador's richly varied indigenous populations. **The Plaza** is a pleasant place to relax and have lunch. At weekends there are regular music and dance performances.

Although everybody wants to get the photo straddling the Equator in front of the monument, bear in mind that this is not the real Equator, which actually lies approximately 300m along the main road east of the complex at the **Museo Solar Inti Ñan** (9.30am–5.30pm; $3). This is definitely worth visiting, particularly to see the fun experiments performed to prove you are standing on the Equator – for example, water rushing down a plug in the opposite direction on either side. There's also an interesting exhibition of indigenous housing and, bizarrely, a step-by-step guide on how to make a shrunken head. To get to Mitad del Mundo, take the Metrobus north to Cotocollao and then a green marked Mitad del Mundo **bus** ($0.50). The trip takes about an hour.

Papallacta

About 65km (two hours) from Quito the road leading to Lago Agrio and Tena passes through the quiet highland town of **Papallacta**, probably the best thermal baths in Ecuador. The entrance to **Las Termas de Papallacta** (7am–10pm, $7) is situated about a mile before the village. From here it's a 20-minute walk up a dirt road so consider taking a taxi from town or from your hotel if you're staying overnight. The complex is very impressive with some 25 baths of different temperatures up to a scalding 60 degrees. You can cool off with an exhilarating plunge into the river next to the complex. On clear days there are great views over the town and snowcapped Volcán Artisana. Note that at an elevation of 3300m, it can get very cold out of the baths so bring warm clothes. *Termas de Papallacta* (ⓣ02/250-4787, ⓦwww.termaspapallacta.com; from $110), a spa hotel next to the complex, is a luxurious option to stay the night with comfortable rooms and spacious cabins, private Jacuzzi and free use of the baths. A great budget option at the junction with the road to the baths is the friendly *Choza de Don Wilson* (ⓣ06/232-0627; $24 including breakast) with decent rooms, great views over the village and a good restaurant serving a $4 set menu to beat off the chills. Trout is a speciality.

The Northern Highlands and Western Andean slopes

To the north of Quito lie two dramatically different regions. To the northwest are verdant **cloudforests**, teeming with birdlife. The small town of **Mindo** is the best base to explore the forest's huge biodiversity and indulge in some adrenalin-pumping adventure sports. To the northeast, magnificent Andean scenery populated by proud indigenous cultures extends up to the Colombian border. Passing the snow-capped **Volcán Cayambe**, the most popular destination is **Otavalo**, whose colourful Saturday market is one of the largest in South America and heaven for lovers of indigenous handicrafts and clothing. Some 30km to the north are the stately squares of La Ciudad Blanca, **Ibarra**, the largest city in the region and an important transport hub. North of Ibarra is the road less-travelled and mainly visited by those crossing into Colombia via **Tulcán**.

MINDO

Snuggled in a cloudforest at a pleasant elevation of 1200m, **Mindo** is a truly idyllic destination. Whether you want to watch for some of the four hundred species of birds and 250 species of butterfly, swing above the forest canopy on ziplines, plunge down the rivers on rubber tubes or simply gaze at the wonderful waterfalls, there's something for everyone here. The cool climate means that this is a far more comfortable region to explore pristine forest than the Oriente. Tourism has developed relatively slowly in Mindo so you can usually avoid the crowds in this endearingly sleepy town, although weekends get busy with day-trippers from Quito.

Mariposas de Mindo

The town is surrounded by the Bosque Protector Mindo-Nambillo cloudforest but most of the accessible areas are due south. The dirt road leading out

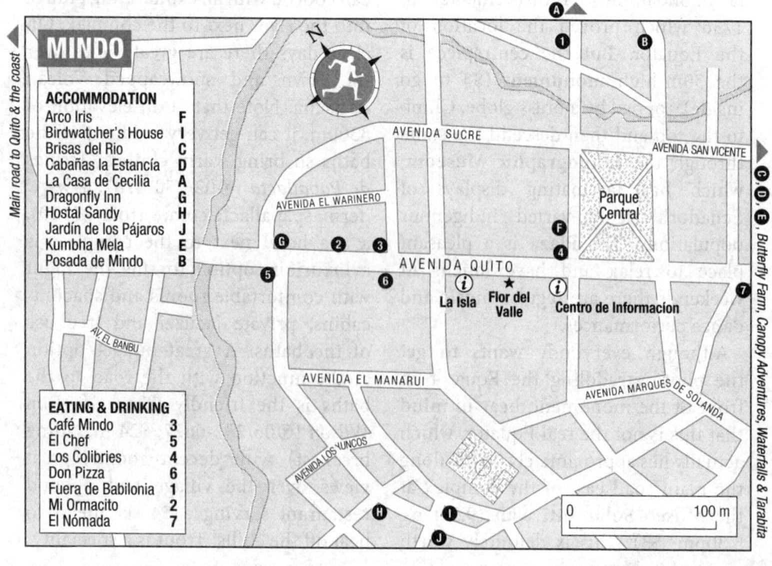

of town forks after about 1km. To the left is the butterfly farm **Mariposas de Mindo** (ⓦwww.mariposasdemindo.com, 9am–6.30pm; $3) which breeds 25 species, including the Brown Owl Eye and the Peleides Blue Morpho with a wingspan of 20cm. The guide shows the lifecycle from eggs to caterpillars, pupae to butterfly. Come in the early morning and you may be lucky enough to see them hatch.

Mindo canopy adventure

Take a right where the road forks and this will lead you up to **Mindo Canopy Adventure** (ⓣ0854 28758, ⓦwww.mindocanopy.com; $15). Adrenalin lovers can get their fix by zinging along cables high above the forest. The thirteen lines range from 20m to 400m in length. Go solo or be accompanied by a guide. It's great fun – try adopting the 'Superman' pose with arms outstretched. The lines and harnesses are designed and tested by experts so they're very safe.

About 1km up the hill is a more relaxed way to travel across the treetops. **La Tarabita** cable car cruises 150m above a river basin. On the other side are trails leading to seven waterfalls. The paths are confusing in places but you can't really get lost as there is only one exit. The entire circuit takes two hours and is muddy so bring boots, but it's worth it to get deep inside the dense, well-preserved cloudforest. You can hire a guide for $25 per day to gain a better insight. Guides with specialist knowledge of birds cost $35 per day.

Other adventure sports

For adventure sports lovers, there's plenty to keep you occupied in Mindo. As an unusual alternative to rafting you can tumble down the river rapids in an inflatable **tube** ($5 for a couple of hours including transport). **Canyoning** is also available ($10 for a half-day). Recommended tour operators, who can organise all of the above, include La Isla Mindo (ⓣ02/390-0481) and Mindo Bird, both on the main Avenida Quito.

Arrival and information

By bus From Quito's Ofelia bus station, Cooperativa Flor de Valle (ⓣ02/252-7495) goes to Mindo at 8am and 3.45pm Mon–Fri, returning at 6am and 2pm. On Sat, there are buses leaving Quito at 7.40am, 8.20, 9.20am and 4pm and leaving Mindo at 7.40am, 8.20, 9.20am, 1.45pm and 5pm. On Sun buses from Quito 6.30am, 2pm, 3.30pm and 5pm, returning 6.30am, 2pm, 3pm and 5pm. Tickets cost $2.50 and the journey takes just under two hours. Take the Metrobus north to Ofelia but allow yourself an hour as it is a long distance from the centre.

Getting around A taxi will cost $5–7 from the New Town. Mindo is easy to get around because it's a small compact town but be aware that streets are very poorly signposted so you may need to ask directions for specific hotels. Most of the attractions in the cloudforest are a 1–2 hour walk away, there are taxis available in the centre of town for $5–10 depending on the number of people and how far into the reserve you want to go. At weekends taxis are easier to find, whereas during the week it can get very quiet, particularly in the afternoons.

Accommodation

Mindo has a wide selection of accommodation and while there are some good hotels in town, it's a more enjoyable and authentic experience to stay in one of the lodges on the edge of town, surrounded by cloudforest. Going south out of town towards the waterfalls and Tarabita, there is a good selection of cabins.

Arco Iris Quito and 9 de Octubre, ⓣ02/390-0405. This is a dependable option with comfortable rooms and a central location on the main square in town. ❹

The Birdwatcher's House Los Colibres, ⓣ02/390-0412. On the western edge of town, this homely place stands out for the stunning photography in the rooms, humming birds in the gardens and outdoor Jacuzzi. ❹

Cabañas la Estancia ⓣ098/783272, 02/390-0500. Cross the rickety bridge to these spacious cabins are set in landscaped gardens with outdoor restaurant, a swimming pool and even a waterslide. ❸

Casa de Cecilia End of 9 de Octubre, ⓣ0933/45393. On the eastern edge of town, these great value rustic cabins stand on the banks of a roaring river. ❸

Jardin de los Pajaros Los Colibres, ⓣ0917/56688. Well-presented hotel with carpeted rooms, and a balcony lounge with hammocks and outdoor swimming pool. ❹

Kumbha Mela ⓣ094/051675. Deeper into the forest you'll find a selection of cabins and rooms nestled in extensive gardens. There's a good restaurant, swimming pool and even a private lagoon. ❺

Posada de Mindo End of Vicente Aguirre, ⓣ02/390-0499. For a bit more comfort, try these new spotless cabins with a good restaurant attached. ❺

Eating

There are plenty of restaurants on the main street in the centre of town. *El Chef* is one of the best places in town and usually full at lunchtime. The set lunch ($2) is outstanding value. To treat yourself try the speciality *Lomo a la Piedra* (barbecued steak served with fries and salad). Fuera de Babilonia on 9 de Octubre bills itself as an alternative bar with assorted Indian artefacts on the walls, misshapen tables, a wide-ranging menu and live music at weekends.

OTAVALO

If you love wandering around markets and picking up *artesano* bargains, then Otavalo is your town. The famous **Saturday market** (from 7am) is easily the best of its kind in Ecuador and possibly in South America, spreading out across the town from the Plaza de Ponchos. Here you can find a wide range of handicrafts, clothing, hammocks, weavings, carvings, jewellery, ceramics and even oddities such as fake shrunken heads. The *Otavaleño* traders are very friendly and will greet you as 'amigo', inviting you to their stalls. Of course, behind the smiles, they're very savvy salespeople and foreigners habitually get offered inflated prices. Take your time gauging the prices and then knock them down by a few dollars, but bear in mind that while this is all part of the fun, the extra dollar means a lot more to the locals that it does to you. During the week the town is quieter but the market is open and still offers a better range of artesan wares than in other tourist towns. There is so much to buy that shopoholics should consider leaving a trip to Otavalo until late in their trip to avoid carting their purchases around the country. Outside the market, the **Museo de Tejidos el Obraje** (Mon-Sat 9am–1pm and 3–5pm, $2) is worth a visit for its demonstrations of textile production.

Otavalo's surroundings are also impressive – the town is nestled between the extinct volcanic peaks of Imbabura and Cotacachi, looming on opposite ends of town. Some 4km out of town is the **Parque Condor** (ⓣ02/292-4429, 9.30am–5pm Tues–Sun, $2.50) which rehabilitates owls, eagles, falcons and the famous condor. There are regular flying demonstrations. On the way to the park is El Lechero, a tree revered by locals for its healing powers, and a pleasant walk for pleasant views over Otavalo.

Arrival and information

By Bus Buses to Otavalo leave Quito's main Cumanda terminal every half hour or so ($2). Improved roads mean that the journey is only 2hr 30min and therefore easily done as a day-trip from Quito. There are also regular services from Ibarra (35min, $0.50). The bus station is on Atahualpa and Neptali Ordoñez, a couple of blocks northeast of the central Plaza de Ponchos market. Otavalo is small and compact enough to walk around but a taxi across town costs just $1 and is recommended at night.

Tourism information For information and maps, try the Cámara de Turismo office (Quiroga y Modesto Jaramillo, ⓣ06/292-7230; Mon–Fri 8.30am–12.30pm & 2–5.30pm).

Accommodation

Otavalo has a lot of hotels for such a small town, most of which are empty during the week but fill up at weekends (consider booking ahead for Friday or Saturday night).

Hostal Doña Esther Montalvo 4-44, ⓣ06/292-0739, ⓦwww.otavalohotel.com. Owned by a Dutch family, this small colonial-style hotel has friendly service, a verdant courtyard and a great restaurant with Mediterranean specialities. ❺

Hostal Rincón Viajera Roca 11-07, ⓣ06/292-1741. This is a hospitable option for budget travellers with artwork on the walls, a TV lounge with fireplace, rooftop terrace and restaurant. ❹

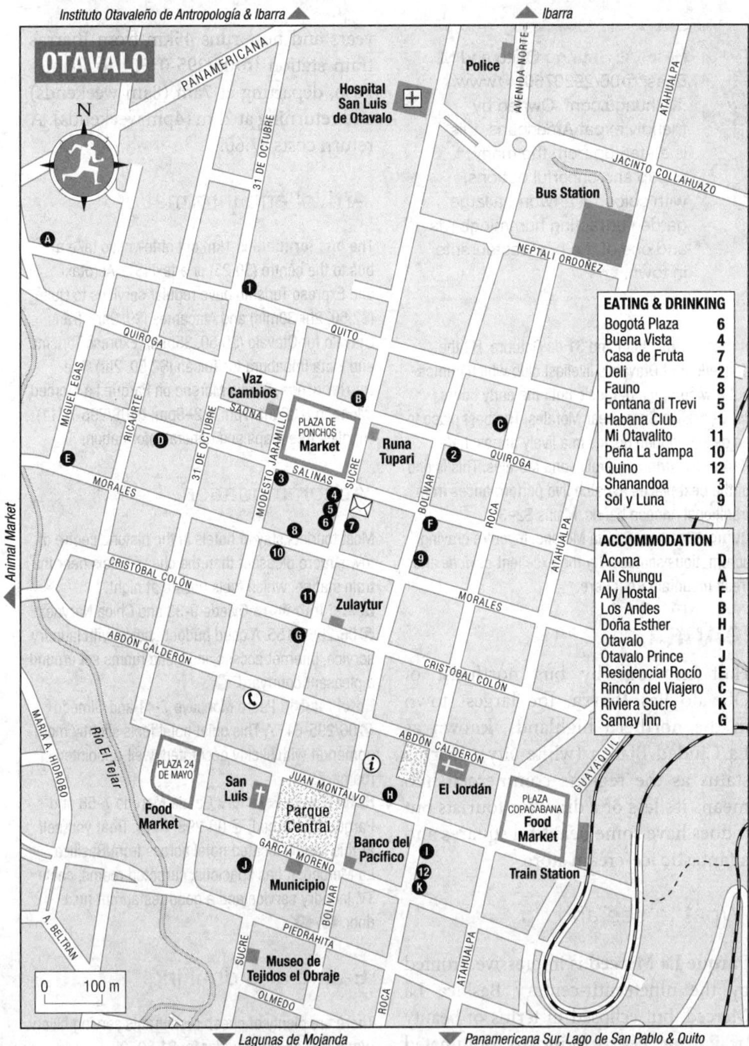

Samay Inn Sucre and Colon ⓣ06/292-1826. Although its central location means it can be noisy, there's hot water, comfortable beds, cable TV and the balconies are good for people-watching. ④

Eating

Otavalo has plenty of restaurants so after browsing in the market, take some time to browse the menus. After dinner, check out live Andean music at Otavalo's *peñas*, particularly on Friday and Saturday nights.

Buena Vista Plaza de Ponchos and Salinas. From the balcony you can observe the market from afar and choose from a wide-ranging menu. The brownies are a speciality.

Casa de Arte Da Pinto Colón 410, between Bolívar and Sucre. A good place for a drink with creative décor and a Bohemian atmosphere.

Casa de Frutas Sucre between Salinas and Morales. For vegetarian dishes served in a fragrant courtyard garden, try this endearing little place.

Fontana di Trevi Sucre near Salinas. Look no further for the best Italian food in town.

> **TREAT YOURSELF**
>
> **Hotel Ali Shungu** Quito and M Egas, ⓣ06/2920750, ⓦwww.alishungu.com. Owned by friendly expat Americans, this is a step up from the many cheap and cheerful options, with colourful artwork, a large garden attracting hummingbirds and one of the best restaurants in town. ❻

Habana Club Quito and 31 de Octubre. Hit the dancefloor at Otavalo's liveliest club which pumps out a wide range of music until the early hours.
Mi Otavalito Sucre near Morales. The best place to enjoy Ecuadorian dishes in a lively atmosphere.
Peña La Jampa Jaramillo and Morales. This is one of the best places to catch live performances from traditional Andean bands. Mains $2–3.
Quino Roca near García Moreno. If you're craving scrumptious seafood, try the excellent *ceviche* and fresh mountain trout here.

IBARRA

Half an hour by bus northeast of Otavalo lies **Ibarra**, the largest town in the northern highlands, known as La Ciudad Blanca (white city). Ibarra's status as the region's commercial hub means it's less of a draw for tourists but it does have some beautiful squares and a fantastic ice-cream store.

What to see and do

Parque La Merced is impressive, fronted by the nineteenth-century Basilica La Merced, but eclipsed in terms of beauty by **Parque Pedro Moncayo**, dominated by the baroque-influenced **cathedral** adorned with a golden altar and portraits of the disciples by Rafael Troya, one of Ecuador's greatest artists, born in Ibarra in 1845. The **Museo Banco Central**, a block to the south on Sucre and Oviedo (Mon–Fri 8.30am–1.30pm & 2.30–4.30pm, $0.50), has an exhibition of national and local archaeology from prehistory to Inca times. A **train service** used to run all the way to San Lorenzo on the north coast but it's been defunct for years and now runs 45km from Ibarra's train station (ⓣ06/295-0390) to Primer Paso, departing at 7am (8am weekends) and returning at 2pm (4pm weekends). A return costs $7.60.

Arrival and information

The **bus terminal** is 1km out of town, so take a bus to the centre ($0.25) or a taxi ($1). Aerotaxi and Expreso Turismo have regular services to Quito ($2.50, 2hr 30min) and Atacames ($9, 9hr); Trans Otavalo for Otavalo ($0.50, 35min); Expreso Turismo and Flota Imbabura for Tulcán ($2.50, 2hr). The **tourist office**, García Moreno on Parque La Merced (Mon–Fri 8.30am–1pm & 2–5pm; ⓣ06/295-5711) supplies free maps and general information.

Accommodation

Most tourists stay at hotels in the historic centre of town, more pleasant than the cheap hotels near the train station, which feels unsafe at night.
Hostal Imbabura Oviedo 9-33 and Chica Narváez ⓣ06/295-0155. A good budget choice with laundry service, internet access and clean rooms set around a pleasant courtyard. ❸
Hotel Madrid Pedro Moncayo 7-41 and Olmedo ⓣ06/295-6177. This quiet hotel feels slightly more upmarket with slickly décorated, well-appointed rooms. ❹
Hotel Nueva Estancia Garcia Moreno 7-58 and Parque La Merced, ⓣ06/295-1444. Treat yourself at this ideally located hotel across from Basílica La Merced. It has spacious, carpeted rooms, cable TV, laundry service and a good restaurant next door. ❺–❻

Eating and drinking

There are plenty of cheap restaurants serving filling *almuerzos* and *meriendas* for $1.50–2.
Antojitos de mi Tierra Plaza de la Ibarreñidad. Traditional Ecuadorian dishes and tasty snacks such as *humitas* and *quimbolitos*.
Cafe Arte Salinas 5-43 and Oviedo. A wide variety of international food in a vibrant setting with live music at weekends.
Donde El Argentino Plaza de la Ibarreñidad. A good option for steaks and barbecued meats.
El Horno Rocafuerte and Flores. Great pizza cooked in a clay oven.
Heladería Rosalía Suárez Corner of Oviedo and Olmedo. Ibarra is famous for its sorbet and this is the best place to try it.

CROSSING INTO COLOMBIA

Seven kilometres east of Tulcán, the **Rumichaca Bridge** marks the busy **Colombian border**, open daily 6am–10pm. To cross the border, obtain an **exit stamp** from Ecuadorian customs, in the *Migración* building, and an **entry stamp** from the Colombians on the other side of the bridge. Tourist entry stamps for both Colombia and Ecuador are valid for 90 days. Arriving from Colombia, the Ecuadorians will also give you up to 90 days and a tourist card, which you retain until you leave the country. **Buses to the border** leave from Parque Isidro Ayora (15min; $0.80), while a taxi costs about $4. From the border, **Ipiales** is the nearest town with decent hotels, 3km away. Buses cost $0.50, while taxis are around $2. Official **moneychangers** abound on the border, but check the calculations before handing money over.

TULCÁN

The border between Ecuador and Colombia is a problematic region and the only recommended place to cross is via **Tulcán**. Don't wander out of town and take care at night. There's little reason to stay here very long and, with Otavalo and Ibarra only three hours south of the border by bus, staying in Tulcán overnight is unnecessary. If you do decide to linger however, don't miss the town cemetery near the Parque Ayora, whose **topiary gardens** boast trimmed bushes and hedges sculpted into pre-Columbian figures, animals and geometric shapes.

Arrival and information

There are regular **buses** to Ibarra ($2.50, 2hr 30min) and Quito ($5, 5hr). The bus terminal on Bolívar is 1.5km from the centre so take a taxi (about $1). The Cámara de Turismo office (Mon–Fri 9am–12.30pm and 2.30–6pm; ⓣ06/298-6606) is on Bolívar and Ayacucho. The **Colombian Consulate** is on Bolívar and Junín (ⓣ06/298-0559, Mon–Fri 8am–1pm & 2–3pm). To **exchange** dollars, you should get a slightly better rate in Tulcan than at the border so try the official moneychangers on Plaza de la Independencia, where there are also ATMs.

There are plenty of **hotels**. *Hotel San Francisco* (Bolívar near Atahualpa, ⓣ06/298-0760, $9) is a good budget option with decent rooms, hot water and cable TV. If you want to treat yourself, try *Hotel Sara Espindola* (Sucre and Ayacucho, ⓣ06/298-6209; $50), which has a sauna, steam room, disco, restaurant, free internet and laundry service.

There are several decent **restaurants** close to the main plaza. *Mama Rosita* (Sucre at Chimborazo) offers Ecuadorian staples for under $2. Try *El Patio* (Bolívar near 10 de Agosto) for large portions of Colombian specialities such as *Bandeja Paiso* (pork, sausage, egg, fried bananas, avocado, beans and rice).

The Central Highlands

South of Quito is where you'll find Ecuador's most dramatic Andean scenery as the Panamericana winds its way between two parallel mountain chains. Eight of Ecuador's ten highest peaks are found here so it's unsurprising that nineteenth-century German explorer Alexander von Humboldt named the region "the Avenue of the Volcanoes". On the eastern side, the most popular peak to visit (and climb if you're fit enough) is **Cotopaxi** (5897m), its majesty dominating the surrounding valley. To the southwest lies the turquoise luminescence of **Lake Quilotoa**, arguably Ecuador's

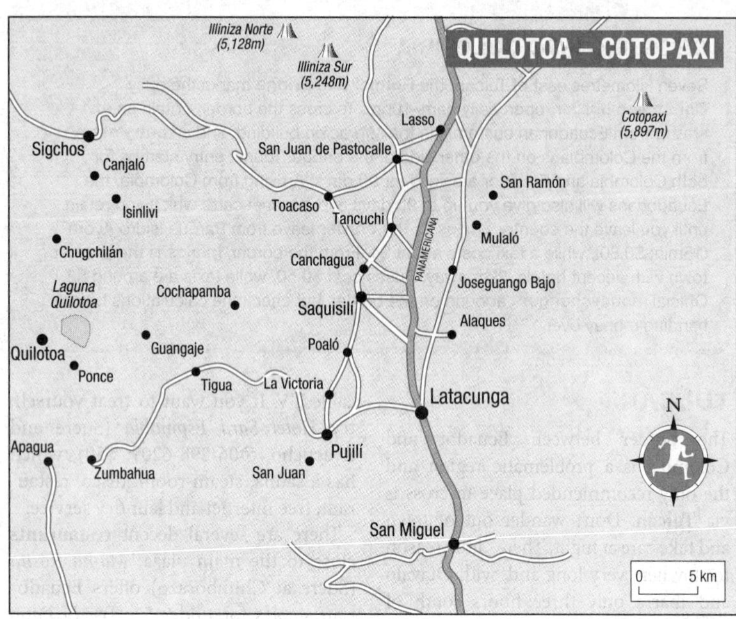

most stunning sight. The region's principal towns **Latacunga, Ambato** and **Riobamba** all sit at an altitude of around 2800m and provide convenient bases to explore from. The little town of **Baños**, with its ideal climate, beautiful setting, thermal baths and abundant adventure sports is a highlight of the region for many travellers. Nearby **Volcán Tungurahua** is still erupting at the time of writing and has become an attraction in itself. South of Riobamba, the hair-raising **Nariz del Diablo train ride** remains popular, although riding on the roof is no longer permitted due to safety concerns.

PARQUE NACIONAL COTOPAXI

About 60km south of Quito, the cone-shaped **Volcán Cotopaxi** (5897m) is everybody's idea of a picture-perfect volcano, its symmetrical cone-shaped peak dominating the surrounding valley. But Cotopaxi's beauty belies its destructive heritage – it has erupted on more than ten occasions since 1742, destroying nearby Latacunga several times. Luckily for the local inhabitants, it has been quiet since 1904, although still officially active with plumes of smoke visible only to climbers who reach the crater. As well as being Ecuador's most photogenic volcano, Parque Nacional Cotopaxi (open 8am–5pm, $10) is also Ecuador's most visited park. The volcano offers a spectacular climb but for a more relaxed experience, the surrounding 33,000 hectares of verdant *páramo* (Andean grasslands) offer great opportunities for trekking and cycling plus wonderful close-up views of the volcano. Inhabitants of the park include deer, rabbits, foxes, pumas and some ninety species of birds, among them the elusive Andean condor.

Tours

Most people take a guided tour from Quito, Latacunga, Riobamba or even Baños. A one-day tour costs $50, visiting the museum, Limpiopungo Lake, the mountain refuge and involves several hours of hiking and cycling. A two-day climbing tour costs about $160 and the more recommended three-day tour about $200. Recommended tour operators in Latacunga include Volcán Route (2 de Mayo y Guayaquil, ⓣ03/281-2452; ⓔvolcanroute@hotmail.com). In Quito, try Gulliver (ⓣ02/252-9297, ⓦwww.gulliver.com.ec; JL Mera and Calama).

Arrival and information

To enter the park without a guided tour, take a **bus** between Quito and Latacunga along the Panamericana to the village of Lasso and hire a pick-up truck which will charge about $25 per group to go up to the parking area below the refuge ($40 round-trip).

There are several interesting **accommodation** options near the national park. A good budget option is *Cuello de Luna* (ⓣ099/700 330, ⓦwww.cuellodeluna.com; ❸–❺) just 2km from the main park entrance. A brand new option is *Secret Garden Cotopaxi*, (ⓣ088/519 435, ⓦwww.secretgardencotopaxi.com; ❹–❺) in the foothills of Pasochoa, near the village of Pedregal, overlooking the national park. The price includes three meals, snacks, drinks and use of mountain bikes. For more comfort in a historic setting, try *Hosteria la Cienega* (ⓣ03/271-9052, 02/254-9126; ❽) a 400-year-old *hacienda*, 2km from Lasso, with period furnishing and an excellent restaurant.

LATACUNGA AND AROUND

Some 30km south of Cotopaxi National Park, **Latacunga** doesn't look very inviting from the highway, but venture towards the centre of town and you'll find quaint cobbled streets and a charming centre bustling with friendly people. There's not a huge amount to do, but the town serves as the best base to explore **Quilotoa** (see p.633) and **Cotopaxi** with some good local tour operators and decent accommodation.

What to see and do

The town has been rebuilt in colonial style after being destroyed several times by Cotopaxi's devastating eruptions, the most recent in 1877. The main square

CLIMBING COTOPAXI

Climbing Cotopaxi can be done with little technical mountaineering experience. However, this is not a challenge to be taken lightly. You must be in good physical shape, strong, fully acclimatized and travel with a qualified guide, preferably certified by ASEGUIM (Asociación Ecuatoriana de Guías de Montaña). The importance of proper acclimatization cannot be stressed enough. If you're pushed for time and feeling bold, it's all too tempting to get up in the morning and think: "let's climb a volcano today". Some unscrupulous guides will have no hesitation in taking your money and going straight up to the high-altitude refuge. But above 3000 metres you need to move slowly up in altitude over a few days. A couple of days in Quito (2800m) is not enough to immediately tackle Cotopaxi (5897m). Lake Quilotoa (3800m) is good preparation and a three-day climbing tour of Cotopaxi is far more recommended than the two-day tour. From the José Rivas refuge at 4800m, it's six to eight very strenuous hours to the top, negotiating snow, ice and several crevices. The views of Ecuador's other major peaks are truly breathtaking, as is the view down into the steaming crater. The descent takes three to four hours. December to April are usually the best times to climb Cotopaxi, when the snow is hardest, but it can be climbed year-round.

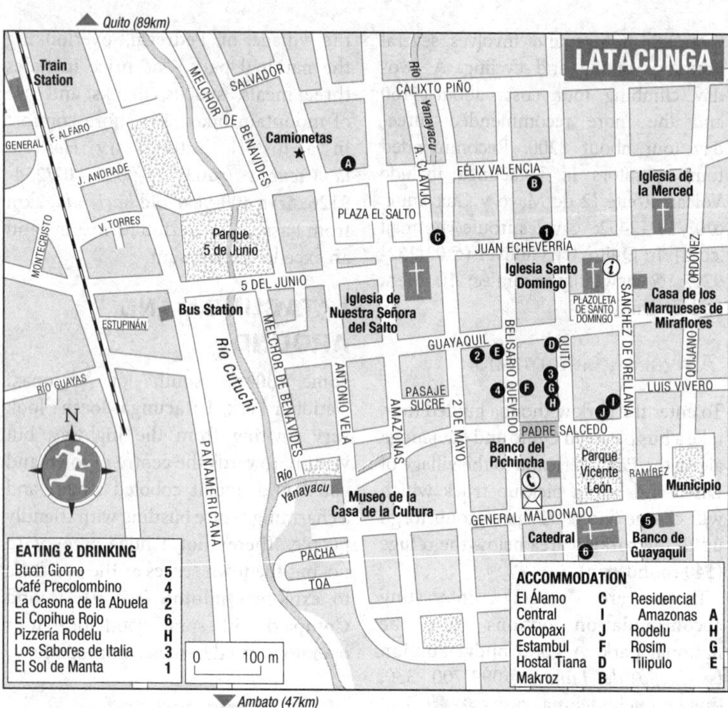

Parque Vicente León forms the town's focal point, flanked by the Catedral and stately Municipio. A few blocks to the west next to the river Cutuchi is the **Museo de la Casa de la Cultura** (corner of Vela and Salcedo, Tues–Fri 8am–noon & 2–6pm; $0.50), which has a small ethnography and art museum. A 20-minute bus ride north-west takes you to **Saquisilí** which has a large morning market on Thursdays. In late September (exact date varies so check), Latacunga parties hard for **La Fiesta de la Mama Negra** with a parade of colourful costumed characters culminating in the arrival of the Mama Negra, a man dressed up as a black woman in honour of the liberation of African slaves in the nineteenth century.

Arrival and information

Latacunga's bus station is on the Panamericana, five blocks west of town. If Latacunga is not the final destination of your bus, you may be dropped off 400m further west (taxi to the centre $1 or walk over the Av 5 de Junio bridge).

Latacunga has a cluster of good **hotels** in the centre of town. A popular new option for backpackers is the friendly *Hostal Tiana* (Guayaquil 5-32 y Quito, ⓣ03/281-0147, ⓦwww.hostaltiana.com; ④), a converted nineteenth-century *hacienda* set around a relaxing courtyard café. For more comfort, try *Hotel Central* (ⓣ02/280-2912; Orellana at Salcedo; ④) with private bathroom, cable TV and a great view of the main square. A quieter option is *Hotel Rosim* (ⓣ03/280-2172, Quito 16-49; ④), and for something more upmarket, try *Hotel Rodelu* (ⓣ03/280-0956, ⓦwww.rodelu.com.ec; ⑤) with wood panelling, indigenous motifs on the walls, free internet and an excellent restaurant downstairs.

Other **restaurants** worth a visit are the pretty *El Copihue Rojo* (Quito 14-38, mains $6) tucked away behind the cathedral which does great grilled meats and *Pizzeria Bon Giorno* (corner of Orellana and Maldonado $4–5) has great lasagna and large pizzas to share.

LAKE QUILOTOA AND THE QUILOTOA LOOP

The luminous turquoise water of the 800-year-old volcanic crater lake **Laguna Quilotoa** is one of Ecuador's most awe-inspiring sights. On a clear day the sky's reflection in the lake is jaw-droppingly beautiful. You can visit from Latacunga on a day-trip but it's better to at least stay overnight or spend a couple of days hiking parts of the **Quilotoa Loop**.

What to see and do

The first town of note is **Tigua** (3500m), famous for its indigenous arts and handicrafts. Another 30km along the road is **Zumbahua**, a small village that gets rather boisterous at the weekend with its busy Saturday market and accompanying merriment. A further 14km north is the sleepy little village of **Quilotoa** (3800m), perched above the famous lake. You pay $1 to enter the village which allows you unlimited access to the lake. There are two main walks to appreciate the beauty of Laguna Quilotoa. Hike down into the crater to the waterside in about 40 minutes (over an hour to come back up or a donkey ride costs $5). The water's high sulphurous content makes it unsuitable for swimming but there are canoes for hire ($2.50). There is also basic cabin accommodation available if you want to spend the night ($8 per person). For a longer walk and to appreciate the lake from all angles, allow four hours to walk around the perimeter.

Getting around

The biggest problem in this region is getting around because public transportation is infrequent and often full. During the rainy season, bus routes are sometimes cancelled and roads impassable. It is strongly advised that you don't attempt parts of the loop alone because of the remoteness of the region. From Latacunga you can take the daily **bus** to Quilotoa at midday (2hr). If you miss the bus to Quilotoa, there are more frequent services to Zumbahua, from where you can hire a taxi to Quilotoa ($5 per person).

Accommodation

Quilotoa has a few **accommodation** options run by friendly indigenous people. The best is *Hostal Cabanas Quilotoa* (Ⓣ092/125962; ❹ including breakfast and dinner) owned by local artist Humberto Latacunga. The hostal has comfortable rooms, hot showers and wood burners (it gets very cold at night). All hostals provide two meals but another option is a new restaurant (name unconfirmed at the time of writing) opposite Princesa Toa overlooking the lake.

Tours

If you're travelling alone or want to see Quilotoa without the inconvenience of relying on public transport, take a **guided tour** from Latacunga. A one-day tour to the lake costs $40, two days taking in Zumbaggua, Quilotoa and Chuhchilán costs $120. Three days to do the entire loop costs $160. Recommended tour operators include Volcan Route (2 de Mayo y Guayaquil, Ⓣ03/2812452; volcanroute@hotmail.com), Tova Expeditions (Guayaquil 5-38 y Quito, Ⓣ03/281-1333) and Tierra Zero (Padre Salcedo y Quito, Ⓣ03/280-4327). All these operators also offer hiking and climbing tours to Cotopaxi.

Trips to Chugchilán

When the road is open, you can continue by **bus** (leaving Quilotoa at 2.30pm daily) to **Chugchilán**. The dramatic scenery makes this a five-hour popular hike but don't attempt it alone and do not set off after 1pm. There are a few good places to **stay** in Chugchilán. For cheap and cheerful go to the basic *Hostal Cloudforest* (Ⓣ03/281-4808; ❹) or more comfortable *Mama Hilda* (Ⓣ03/281-4814; ❺ including breakfast) To treat yourself, stay at the award-winning eco-lodge *The Black Sheep Inn* (Ⓣ03/281-4587, Ⓦwww.blacksheepinn.com; ❻–❽ including two meals) with spacious rooms and delicious food.

Book in advance. Getting back from Chugchilán is not easy. If you don't want to hike it or splash out on a **taxi**, you have to get a bus at the ungodly hour of 3am back to Latacunga via Sigchos.

AMBATO

Some 47km south of Latacunga, most tourists merely pass through Ambato en route to Baños or Riobamba. There's little to hold your interest for more than a few hours and the downtown area suffers from traffic problems, which somewhat ruins the experience of wandering around what is, in parts, a beautiful city.

What to see and do

Of most interest on the **Parque Juan Montalvo** is the Casa de Montalvo (Mon–Fri 9am–noon & 2–6pm, Sat 10am–1pm; $1), the former residence of Ambato's most famous literary son. A noted liberal, he was forced into exile by arch-conservative president Gabriel García Moreno in 1869. The house has an interesting collection of photos, manuscripts, clothing and a huge lifesize portrait. Rather unnervingly, Juan Montalvo's body is on display in the mausoleum. His face is covered by a death mask but his decayed fingers are visible. On the other side of the park is the city's huge but ugly modern cathedral, rebuilt after the devastating 1949 earthquake. The interior is more impressive with huge bronze statues of Mary and Jesus and fabulous acoustics during mass. On Parque Cevallos the **Museo de Ciencias Naturales** (Mon–Fri 8.30am–12.30pm & 2.30–5.30pm; Sat 9am–5pm; $2) houses stuffed birds, mammals and reptiles, including a rather grisly display of freak animals such as six-legged lambs. Escape the city's bustle by visiting **La Quinta de Juan León Mera** (Av Los Capulies; 9.30am–5.30pm, Wed–Sun; $1), just 2km from the centre (a half-hour walk or $1 taxi ride). Wander through the gardens and relax on the banks of the river.

Arrival and information

Ambato's bus station is 2km north of the centre. Taxis cost $1.50 or catch a local bus. Ambato is hardly brimming with good hotels but *Hotel Cevallos* (corner of Av Cevallos 05-76 y Montalvo, ☎03/242-2009; ❺) and *Hotel Pirámide Inn* (Av Cevallos y Mariano Egüez, ☎03/242-1920; ❹) have well-appointed rooms with hot water, private bathroom and cable TV.

Eating and drinking

For restaurants, try the little *Café la Catedral* in a small mall opposite the cathedral entrance for good-value lunches. Check out *La Fornace* (Av Cevallos 17–28) for excellent pizza, *Parrilladas El Gaucho* (Bolívar and Quito) for grills and *El Álamo Chalet* (Cevallos and Montalvo) for traditional Ecuadorian fare.

BAÑOS

Locals call it 'un pedacito de cielo' (a little piece of heaven) and this is no exaggeration because **Baños** is as close as you can get in Ecuador to a perfect destination. If you're only in Ecuador for a short time, this is one place that is not to be missed. With an ideally warm climate at 1820m above sea level, a stunning location set in a verdant valley surrounded by steep hills, an excellent choice of hotels and restaurants, thriving nightlife (at least at weekends), great walking and adventure sports, plus of course the thermal baths that give the town its name – don't surprised if you end up spending longer than planned here. Be aware that Baños is only 8km from the active **Volcán Tungurahua** which was erupting at the time of writing. Luckily, the crater is on the opposite side to the town and Baños has been relatively unaffected. (for further information see p.630).

What to see and do

In town, don't miss the **Basílica de Nuestra Señora de Agua Santa** on

the main Ambato street. This massive church is dedicated to the Virgin Mary, who is credited with several miracles, including saving the town from Tungurahua's eruption in 1773. It's spectacular when lit up at night, dominating the town's skyline. Inside the church are 10 huge paintings depicting the Virgin saving the town and its citizens from various calamities. Next to the church is a charming Spanish courtyard, where visitors are free to wander around. Upstairs is a small **museum** (open daily 8am–5pm, $0.50) with an impressive collection of the Virgin's processional clothes, religious art and a somewhat bizarre collection of stuffed animals.

The thermal baths

The thermal baths, which give Baños its name, are the main attraction for many visitors. There are four sets of public baths around the town and many of the better hotels have their own, although they don't draw on volcanic spring water. The most popular baths are the **Piscinas de la Virgen** (4.30am–5pm & 6–10pm; $1.60 daytime, $2 at night) at the foot of a small waterfall at the eastern end of Avenida Martínez. The cloudy yellow waters don't look immediately appealing but they are high in minerals and make for a very relaxing soak. Next to the changing rooms you can see where the boiling waters emerge from the rock-face. There are three pools – freezing cold, warm and hot (just a little too hot to linger for more than a few minutes). The baths get very busy at weekends so it's best to go either early morning or early evening to avoid the crowds.

THE ROAD FROM BAÑOS TO PUYO

One of Ecuador's most beautiful routes, the road from Baños to Puyo drops nearly 1000m following the Río Pastaza down from lush Andean foothills, through cloudforest to the edges of the tropical jungle. It's best admired from the saddle of a bike, which can be hired from any agency in Baños for $5 per day, including helmet, map and repair kit. Leaving Baños you cross the Agoyan hydroelectric project and it's about 40 minutes until you reach the impressive **Manto de La Novia** (Bride's Veil) waterfall. You can take the *tarabita* cable car ($2) 500m across the river gorge for a closer look. A 25-minute ride then brings you to the village of Río Verde, where you can lock your bike and hike 15 minutes downhill to see the even more spectacular **Pailón del Diablo** (Devil's Cauldron) waterfall. View it from a rickety suspension bridge or pay 50 cents to get a closer look from the lookout balcony. Cycling half an hour uphill from Río Verde, you reach **Machay**. From here hike a 2.5km trail into the cloudforest past eight waterfalls, the most beautiful of which is Manantial del Dorado. From Machay, it's downhill to **Río Negro** where the surroundings begin to feel truly tropical with bromeliads, giant tree ferns and colourful orchids. Start early if you want to cover the entire 61km but the route is far more scenic than the end destination of **Puyo**, a rather ugly jungle town. Most people hop on a bus back to Baños from Río Verde or Río Negro.

Piscinas El Salado

About 2km out of town Piscinas El Salado used to boast five pools ranging from 16–42 degrees with the water visibly bubbling up from underground. These baths are quieter most of the week but also get busy at weekends. Note that this area was affected by Tungurahua's eruptions and in August 2008 the complex was destroyed by a landslide. At the time of writing it is unclear whether the site is safe enough to rebuild. Please check with the Municipal tourist office on the east side of the Parque Central for up-to-date information.

AROUND BAÑOS

The best way to take in the town's stunning setting is to **walk to Bellavista**, high above the town. It's a steep 40-minute climb up a rocky, often muddy path but you're rewarded with spectacular panoramic views over Baños and the Pastaza valley leading down to the Oriente. The cross at Bellavista is lit up at night giving the illusion that it sits in the middle of the night sky. There are a couple of cafes at the top selling light lunches and drinks. If you're feeling energetic, the path continues uphill for a further hour to the small village of **Runtun;** you can then loop around to the other side of Baños, passing the statue of La Virgen del Agua Santa and back to town. The entire walk takes about four hours. You can **hire horses** to see this route ($12 for 2hr, $22 for 4hr, including guide).

Arrival and information

By bus Baños's bus terminal is a few blocks north of the main square surrounded by stalls selling *Jugo de Caña* (sugar cane juice). There are regular buses to Puyo. For most other destinations including Quito, Riobamba and Guayaquil, it's usually easier to change at Ambato, although there are occasional direct services. The direct road to Riobamba was closed at the time of writing due to Tungurahua's eruptions.

Getting around Baños is so compact that you can walk everywhere. A taxi across town will cost just $1 if you're laden with luggage.

Tourist information You can purchase guidebooks and pick up free maps at the municipal tourist office (Mon–Fri 8am–12.30pm & 2–5.30pm; Haflants near Rocafuerte, ⓣ03/274-0483) on the east side of Parque Central.

ACTIVITIES AND TOURS

Adventure sports are popular in the Pastaza valley between Baños and Puyo. **Rafting** is particularly good. A half-day on the class 3 part of the Rio Pastaza costs $30 including transport, equipment, licensed guide and lunch. A half-day on the faster class 4 part of the river costs $45. Other adrenalin-filled activities include **Bridge Jumping** (rather like bungy except you swing like a pendulum) for $10–15 as well as zipping across the valley on **canopy lines** ($3–6). You can also hire *Cuadrones* buggies and motorbikes for about $8 per hour ($20 for 3hr).

Most of the **tour operators** in Baños offer the above activities but some are more experienced than others. Geotours (Ambato and Thomas Haflants, ⓣ03/274-1344) have been in the business for more than 15 years and are highly recommended. Other agencies to try include Expediciones Pailontravel (12 de Diciembre y Montalvo, ⓣ03/274-0899) and Wonderful Ecuador (Maldonado and Oriente, ⓣ03/274-1580).

Jungle tours can be arranged with several tour operators in Baños, including Geotours and Wonderful Ecuador (see above). You can book tours to many of the jungle destinations including Coca and Lago Agrio but these tours generally go through Quito so you may be better off booking there. For a shorter, more accessible jungle experience, there are good trips via Puyo. For more information on jungle trips, see the chapter on the Oriente (see p.649).

Baños has many skilled professionals and you can get all types of **massage** treatments here from soothing aromatherapy to reflexology, deep tissue treatments and physiotherapy. Most charge around $20 for an hour's massage and $15 for a facial. Stay in Touch (ⓣ03/274-0973, Pasaje Ibarra y Montalvo) is particularly good, as is Martha Quishpi at *Hostal Casa Real* (see below).

Accommodation

Baños has a great choice of accommodation for such a small town. The best hotels are to the south of the centre.

Hospedaje Santa Cruz ⓣ03/274-0648, 16 de Diciembre. A funky little place with simple but colourfully decorated rooms. ❸

Hostal Casa Real ⓣ03/274-0215, Montalvo y Pasaje Ibarra. This is an excellent-value mid-range option close to the waterfall. Rooms have murals of wildlife and the massages are among the best in town. ❹

Hostal Eden ⓣ03/274-0616, 12 de Noviembre. This hostel has decent rooms equipped with cable TV facing a pleasant garden courtyard. There's an economical restaurant next door. ❸

TREAT YOURSELF

Hostería Monte Selva ⓣ03/2740566, Haflants, ⓦwww.hosteriamonteselva.com. This is the best place to stay in town with comfortable cabins snuggled below the hillside, swimming pool, games room and an excellent spa with Turkish baths, jacuzzi and sauna. ❼

Hostal Plantas y Blanco ⓣ03/274-0044, Martínez near 12 de Diciembre. This backpackers' institution is a great place to swap stories with kindred spirits. There's a rooftop terrace, sunloungers, kitchen, Turkish baths, free internet and compact but clean rooms. ❸–❹

Hostal Posada del Arte ⓣ03/274-0083, Pasaje Ibarra, ⓦwww.posadadelarte.com. A truly special place containing a feast of South American art. The plushly decorated rooms have fireplaces with chimneys to keep you warm. The Hostal also owns the delightful *Casa del Abuelo* up the road which has a free art exhibition but rather basic rooms for the price. ❺

Hostal Rosita ⓣ03/274-0396,16 de Diciembre near Martínez. This is a good-value budget option with free internet. There are also two larger apartments for longer stays. ❸

Hotel Palace ⓣ03/274-0470, Montalvo 20-03. A stone's throw from Piscina de la Virgen, the hotel has its own spa free to guests ($5 for non-guests) with sauna, pool, jacuzzi, hydromassage and Turkish baths. ❻

Eating

Baños has many fantastic **restaurants** and offers some of the best international cuisine outside Quito.

Most of the finest are situated away from the main street. The town is also paradise for those with a sweet tooth, famous for its dozens of stalls selling *membrillo* (a gelatinous red block made with fruit) and *milcocha*, chewy sugar cane bars which you can watch being made, swung over wooden pegs. Outside the market on Ambato, there's also the memorable sight of *cuy* (guinea pigs) being roasted on a spit.

La Abuela Café Ambato near 16 de Diciembre. Much of the restaurants on the main street are uninspiring but this is one of the best options with a wide-ranging menu and a balcony to watch the world go by. Mains $4.

Café Good ⓣ03/274-0592, 16 de Diciembre. Specialises in vegetarian and Asian food. The Hindu curry is particularly good. Mains $3–7.

Café Hood ⓣ03/274-0537, Maldonado near Parque Central. An eccentric little café, run by Italians, specialising in Mexican and Italian food but the Thai and Indian dishes are also good.

El Chozón de la Molienda ⓣ03/274-1816, Montalvo y Pasaje Ibarra. Enjoy excellent barbecued dishes such as *lomo volcánico* (steak in ginger sauce) served in a thatched hut set in a large garden. Mains $5–7.

El Jardín 16 de Diciembre, $5). A popular place to eat alfresco in the leafy garden with a wide selection of dishes and an economical set menu. Mains $4.

Quilombo ⓣ03/274-2880, Montalvo y 12 de Noviembre. A quirky, humorous place set in a wooden cabin decked out with eclectic decor, from hammocks to horseshoes and even a broken bicycle. The menu comes on cubes in little bags and the barbecued steaks and chicken dishes are cooked to perfection. Mains $6–8.

Swiss Bistro ⓣ094/004-019, Martínez y Alfaro. The new sensation in town with cow skins on the walls and even cow-patterned lamp shades that place you in the heart of the Swiss Alps. The cheese and meat fondues are fabulous, rounded off by stewed pears in red wine for dessert. Mains $6–8.

Nightlife

Nightlife in Baños has improved in recent years. Although it's still rather sleepy during the week, it can get busy at weekends, particularly on Saturday night. Most of the best places are situated on the stretch of Alfaro north of Ambato. Start the evening off with some rock classics at either *Bar Mocambo* or *Jack Rock*, which is decked out with music memorabilia. As midnight approaches, make for *Volcán Peña* bar which plays mainly latin music or *Leprechaun Bar*, which is more popular with backpackers and has a dancefloor and a roaring bonfire in the back garden. To catch some traditional *folklórica* music, go to *Peña Ananitay* (16 de Diciembre and Espejo).

VOLCÁN TUNGURAHUA

The aptly-named Tungurahua, which means 'throat of fire', has a troubled relationship with Baños. The volcano supplies the hot springs that make the town so famous and popular but its eruptions have caused regular alerts in recent years. The volcano awoke from years of dormancy in October 1999 with a spectacular eruption which covered Baños in ash. However, because the crater is on the opposite side, the town escaped any further damage. There have been subsequent eruptions in August 2006 and February 2008. *Bañenos* have been living in Tungurahua's shadow for centuries and nobody in town seems particularly worried about the volcano but it's important to check on its current state of activity before visiting the town, either from the national press or from South American Explorers in Quito (see p.609). For more detailed information check the Instituto Geofísico's Spanish website ⓦwww.igepn.edu.ec or the Smithsonian Institute's English site ⓦwww.volcano.si.edu. When Tungurahua is erupting, it becomes a star attraction. The best views of the volcano are from the town of Runtun above Bellavista (see "Around Baños" p.636). Most agencies in town will take you at night for $3 but chances are, you'll see very little.

Riobamba and around

The main draw of Riobamba is that it's the starting point for the dramatic **Nariz del Diablo** (Devil's Nose) train ride, but this traditional town's nineteenth-century architecture and wide avenues

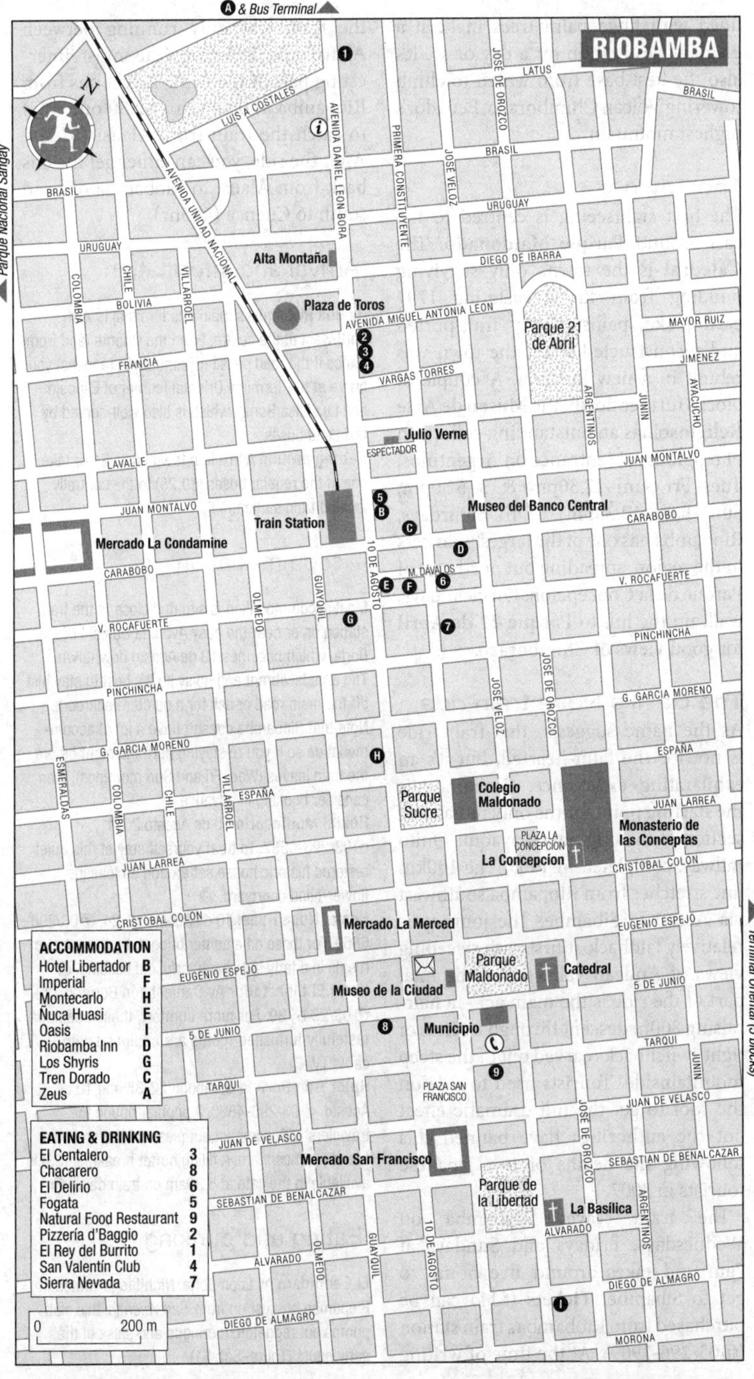

RIOBAMBA
A & Bus Terminal
Parque Nacional Sangay
Terminal Oriental (5 blocks)
ACCOMMODATION
Hotel Libertador B
Imperial F
Montecarlo H
Ñuca Huasi E
Oasis I
Riobamba Inn D
Los Shyris G
Tren Dorado C
Zeus A
EATING & DRINKING
El Centalero 3
Chacarero 8
El Delirio 6
Fogata 5
Natural Food Restaurant 9
Pizzería d'Baggio 2
El Rey del Burrito 1
San Valentín Club 4
Sierra Nevada 7
0 200 m
Alta Montaña
Plaza de Toros
Julio Verne
Train Station
Museo del Banco Central
Mercado La Condamine
Parque 21 de Abril
Parque Sucre
Colegio Maldonado
Plaza La Concepción
La Concepción
Monasterio de las Conceptas
Mercado La Merced
Museo de la Ciudad
Parque Maldonado
Catedral
Municipio
Plaza San Francisco
Mercado San Francisco
Parque de la Libertad
La Basílica
Luis A Costales
Avenida Unidad Nacional
Avenida Daniel Leon Bora
Primera Constituyente
José Veloz
José de Orozco
Latus
Brasil
Uruguay
Diego de Ibarra
Avenida Miguel Antonia Leon
Mayor Ruiz
Jimenez
Vargas Torres
Espectador
Argentinos
Junin
Ayacucho
Juan Montalvo
Carabobo
M. Dávalos
V. Rocafuerte
Pinchincha
G. Garcia Moreno
España
Juan Larrea
Cristobal Colon
Eugenio Espejo
5 de Junio
Tarqui
Juan de Velasco
Sebastian de Benalcazar
Alvarado
Diego de Almagro
Morona
Bolivia
Francia
Lavalle
Colombia
Chile
Villarroel
Esmeraldas
Olmedo
Guayaquil
10 de Agosto

lined with huge palm trees make it a pleasant destination for a day or so. It's also the best base from which to climb towering Volcán Chimborazo, Ecuador's highest mountain.

The Town

The best sightseeing is centred to the east around **Parque Maldonado**. The **Catedral** is the town's only surviving building from the devastating 1797 earthquake, painstakingly transported and reconstructed when the town was rebuilt in a new location. A couple of blocks further north, the **Museo de Arte Religioso** has an outstanding collection of religious art (entrance on Argentinos, Tues–Fri 9am–12.30pm & 3–6.30pm, Sun 9am–12.30pm). On Saturdays, Riobamba has one of the largest **markets** in the region, spreading out northeast of Parque de la Concepción. On clear days, walk up the hill to **Parque 21 de Abril** for good views of Chimborazo.

The Devil's Nose train ride

As the name suggests, this train ride is not for the faint-hearted, but it's an exhilarating experience. Riobamba is the starting point for the only remaining section of the original Guayaquil-Quito railway, completed in 1905. The 100km line stretches from Riobamba southwest via Alausi to Sibambe. The journey is relatively laidback at first with sweeping views of Andean valleys. But the final part of the ride is the main act – a hair-raising 800m descent through a series of tight switchbacks carved out of the steep mountainside. Tourists used to ride on the roof to get the full dramatic effect but the authorities have banned this following the deaths of two Japanese tourists in 2007.

The train leaves Riobamba on Wednesdays, Fridays and Sundays at 7am and takes around five hours to get to Sibambe. **Tickets** ($11) can be purchased from Riobamba's train station (☎03/296-1909). At the time of writing the train was only running between Alausi and Sibambe (the most interesting part of the trip). Take a bus from Riobamba at 6am (2hr; $2.50 one way) to catch the train from Alausi ($7.50). After the ride, you can either get the bus back from Alausi to Riobamba or head south to Cuenca (4–5hr).

Arrival and information

By bus Riobamba's main bus terminal is 2km northwest of the centre. From the Oriente (and from Baños if the road passing Tungurahua reopens) you arrive at the Terminal Oriental (corner of Espoejo and Luz Elisa Borja), which is also well-served by taxis and buses.

Getting around A taxi into town costs $1 or take one of the regular buses ($0.25) to the centrally located train station.

Accommodation

Most accommodation is situated close to the train station on or near the busy Avenida Daniel León Borja, which becomes 10 de Agosto downtown. The area is vibrant and noisy so it's best to stay just off the main road or ask for a quieter backroom. Note that Riobamba doesn't have a lot of accommodation so if you're staying here the night before the train leaves (Wed, Fri and Sun mornings), then consider booking in advance.

Hostal Montecarlo 10 de Agosto 25-41, ☎03/296-0557. To treat yourself stay at this quiet restored historic house set around a pleasant flower-filled courtyard. ❺

Hostal Ñuca Huasi 10 de Agosto 10-24, ☎03/296-6669. For those on a tighter budget, try these basic rooms in a tatty but characterful old building. ❸

Hotel El Libertador Av Daniel León Borja 29-22, ☎03/294-739. For more comfort, these spacious, tastefully furnished rooms are equipped with cable TV. ❹

Hotel Tren Dorado Carabobo 22-35 and 10 de Agosto, ☎03/296-4890. A popular option for travellers with compact but pleasant rooms and a friendly atmosphere. A filling buffet breakfast ($3) is available in the café at 5.30am on train days. ❹

Eating and drinking

El Centadero Av León Borja. Nightlife is limited in Riobamba but just up from *San Valentín*, this club pumps out reggeton, meringue and salsa til the early hours (Thurs–Sat; $1).

El Delirio Primera Constituyente 28-16, ⓣ03/296-6441. This traditional colonial house is the perfect place for a romantic meal. Book in advance. Mains $6–8.
Pizzeria d'Baggio Av Leon Borja 33-24, ⓣ03/296-1832. Unbeatable for sumptuous pizzas handmade in front of you.
San Valentín Av Leon Borja and Torres, ⓣ03/296-3137. For something cheap and cheerful, try the Tex Mex and varied fast food served in an informal atmosphere.
Sierra Nevada Primera Constituyente 27-38, ⓣ03/295-1542. An excellent value eatery offering imaginative seafood and meat dishes. Mains $5.

VOLCÁN CHIMBORAZO

Just 30km northwest of Riobamba, the extinct **Volcán Chimborazo** looms large. At 6310m, it's Ecuador's highest peak and is the furthest point from the centre of the Earth due to the Equatorial ridge. The mountain has good roads so is easily visited on tours from Riobamba. On a day-trip you can walk up from the lower refuge (4800m) to the second refuge (5000m) but bear in mind the climb in altitude from Riobamba could leave you suffering badly. For experienced mountaineers planning to tackle the summit, there are several good tour operators in Riobamba charging approximately $200 for a two-day tour. Recommended operators include: Alta Montaña, Av Daniel León Borja and Diego Ibarra (ⓣ03/294-2215, ⓔaventurag@ch.pro.ec) and Andes Trek, Colón 22-25 and 10 de Agosto (ⓣ03/294-0964, ⓦwww.andes-trek.com).

The Southern Highlands

South of Riobamba, the majestic mountains of the Central Highlands fade from view to be replaced by undulating green hills. The tourist hub of the region is **Cuenca**, Ecuador's third largest city and possibly its most beautiful. The city's colonial architecture and idyllic location on the banks of the rushing river Tomebamba make it an enchanting place to stay for a few days. Cuenca is also the best base to explore **Ingapirca**, Ecuador's only major Inca ruins, as well as the rugged moors and lakes of **Parque Nacional El Cajas**.

South of Cuenca, distances between towns lengthen and the climate warms up. The historic plazas and award-winning parks of the provincial capital of **Loja** are worth a visit before heading to the relaxing backpacker favourite of **Vilcabamba**, nicknamed the "Valley of Longevity". Recharge your batteries and take advantage of great hiking and horse-riding trails in the surrounding hills.

To get further off the beaten track, explore the diverse scenery of **Parque Nacional Podocarpus,** which descends dramatically from Andean *páramo* to the lush tropical forests on the edge of the Oriente. The quieter border crossing to Peru via **Macará** is preferable to the coastal crossing via Huaquillas.

INGAPIRCA

Between Riobamba and Cuenca lies the site of Ingapirca (daily 8am–6pm; $6 including guide), Ecuador's only major Inca ruins. Those who've already visited Peru may be disappointed by this comparatively modest site. However, it is worth the visit, in particular to see the Inca empire's sole remaining sun temple. The site's strategic position is also impressive, at a height of over 3200m with panoramic views over the surrounding countryside.

Ingapirca was built at the end of the fifteenth century by Huayna Capac on top of the ruins of a Cañari city. The stone of the Cañari moon temple, which the Inca preserved from its earlier construction, is still visible. Sadly, now much of the site is little more than stone foundations and it takes imagination and a guided tour to bring it to life.

What to see and do

Points of interest include the **calendar stone** and sacrificial site, but the highlight is the well-preserved **Temple of the Sun,** constructed with more than three thousand intricately carved blocks. It's entertaining to stand in the sentry posts of the temple and hear your whispers reverberate through the walls. Just outside the complex is a small **museum** (included in the entrance fee), which houses a small collection of Cañari and Inca ceramics, sculptures, tools and a skeleton found at the site.

Arrival

To **get to** Ingapirca, take a Transportes Cañar bus from Cuenca's bus terminal (departing 9am and 1pm, returning 1pm and 4pm except weekends when there are no afternoon buses; 2hr; $2.50).

Accommodation

To stay overnight, treat yourself at *Posada Ingapirca* (Ⓣ07/282-7401; ❼), a beautiful converted farmhouse overlooking the ruins, adorned with indigenous art and with a decent restaurant. For very basic rooms and a friendly atmosphere, stay at *Hostal Inti Huasi* (Ⓣ07/229-0767; ❸) in Ingapirca village, 5min from the site. Bring warm clothes as it gets cold at night.

CUENCA

Cuenca is Ecuador's third largest city with a population of more than 400,000, but it doesn't feel that way, retaining the atmosphere of a traditional old Andean town. Cuenca is far more relaxing to explore than Quito or Guayaquil. The cobbled streets, charming squares, colonial architecture and magnificent **Catedral** make the historic centre a delight to wander around and it's no surprise that it was declared a **UNESCO World Heritage Site** in 1996.

Prior to the Spanish conquest, the Incas founded the city of **Tomebamba** here in the late fifteenth century, one of the most important cities in the Inca empire. But the city was destroyed shortly afterwards by the civil war between brothers Atahualpa and Huascar. The Spanish founded Cuenca in 1557 and little remains of the city's Inca past, although ruins of Tomebamba have been excavated behind the **Museo del Banco Central** (see opposite). Note that most museums and restaurants are closed on Sundays, which makes it a good day to take a trip outside the city to **Cajas, Ingapirca** or **Baños.**

The historic city centre

The focal point of Cuenca's centre is **Parque Calderón**, an elegant square filled with flowerbeds and palm trees, dominated by the towering eighteenth century **Catedral Nueva**. The interior is relatively bare except for the stunning gold-leaf altar and the massive sky-blue domes are best viewed from the side or rear. To the left of the cathedral entrance, along Calle Sucre on the Plazoleta del Carmen, in front of the small church of El Carmen de la Asunción, is a daily flower market. Turn left along Padre Aguirre to reach the ramshackle clothes market on **Plaza San Francisco** and the slightly battered **Iglesia San Francisco**. Five blocks to the west is the seventeenth century **Iglesia San Sebastián** on a quiet square of the same name. Opposite is the **Museo de Arte Moderno** (Mon–Fri 9am–1pm and 3–6.30pm, Sat 9am–1pm; free), which houses temporary exhibitions of national and Latin American modern art.

Along the Río Tomebamba

After exploring the historic centre, head south to the riverside. Along the aptly-named Calle Larga, there are several interesting museums. The **Museo Remigio Crespo Toral** (Mon–Fri 8.30am–1pm & 3–6pm, Sat 10am–noon; free) has an interesting collection of pre-Columbian ceramics as well as colonial and modern art in a beautifully restored nineteenth-century house. A couple of blocks further

east, the **Museo de las Culturas Aborígenes** (Mon–Fri 8.30am–6pm, Sat 9am–1pm; $2) has an enormous collection of pre-Hispanic artefacts – from Stone Age tools to Inca ceramics. Calle Larga has three staircases, the largest of which is **La Escalinata,** leading down to the banks of the river, which is very pleasant to stroll along. To the east is the landmark **Puente Roto** (Broken Bridge), the remaining third of a bridge which once spanned the river. Rejoin Calle Larga and walk up the hill past a modest set of Inca ruins to the **Museo del Banco Central**.

Museo del Banco Central Pumapungo and archeological site

Museo Pumapungo (Calle Larga near Huayna Capac, ☏07/283-1255, Mon–Fri 9am–6pm, Sat 9am–1pm; $3) is easily Cuenca's best museum and well worth the 20-minute walk east of the centre (taxi $1.50). The museum is spread out across three floors and includes a large collection of colonial art, an archeology room and an exhibition of indigenous costumes and masks. But the highlight is the excellent **ethnographic** exhibition of Ecuador's diverse indigenous cultures with animated dioramas, reconstructed dwellings and a stunning display of five *tsantsas* (shrunken heads) from the Shuar culture in the Southern Oriente. Entrance includes access to the **Pumapungo archeological site** behind the museum. This is where the most important buildings of the Inca city of Tomebamba were located, although mainly foundations remain. Below the ruins is a beautiful set of extensive landscaped gardens and a bird rescue centre with parrots, hawks and a magnificent black-chested eagle.

Mirador de Turi

For the best views over Cuenca, take a taxi ($2.50 each way) to the **Mirador de Turi**, a lookout point on a hill 4km south of the centre. The views are particularly good on the occasional evenings when the churches are lit up.

Arrival and information

By air and bus Cuenca's airport and bus terminal are both located 2km northeast of the centre. There are daily flights to Quito and Guayaquil from Icaro (Av España 11-14 ⓣ07/280-2700) and Tame (Av Florencia Astudillo ⓣ07/288-9581, ⓦwww.tame.com.ec). There are regular buses to Quito (10hr, $10), Guayaquil (4–5hr, $6), Ambato (7hr, $7), Riobamba (6hr, $6) and Loja ($7, 5hr).

By taxi Taxis cost about $2 or buses run on Av España to the northern edge of the centre.

Tourist information Go to the iTur office on the main square (Mariscal Sucre ⓣ07/282-1035; ⓦwww.cuenca.gov.ec), which has friendly staff providing maps and regional information.

Tour operators

The following tour operators offer tours to Ingapirca, Cajas and a wide range of itineraries in Ecuador: Expediciones Apullacta, Gran Colombia 11-02 and General Torres, ⓣ07/283-7815, ⓦwww.apullacta.com. Metropolitan Touring, Mariscal Sucre 6-62 and Hermano Miguel, ⓣ07/283-1463, 07/283-1185, ⓦwww.metropolitan-touring.com. Río Arriba Expeditions, Hermano Miguel 7-14 and Córdova, ⓣ07/283-0116 or 07/284-0031. Terra Diversa Travel and Adventure, Hermano Miguel 5-42 and Honorato Vásquez, ⓣ07/282-3782, ⓦwww.terradiversa.com.

TREAT YOURSELF

Hotel Victoria Calle Larga 6-93 y Borrero ⓣ07/282-7401. Splash out on one of Cuenca's finest hotels and stay in a beautifully restored colonial building overlooking extensive gardens. Most of the spacious, elegantly furnished rooms have views of the river. ❽

Accommodation

Cuenca has a wide range of accommodation with a wealth of hotels in charming colonial buildings. The best area to stay is south of the centre on the north bank of the river. Consider booking ahead at weekends and particularly on national holidays when accommodation fills up quickly.

La Casa Cuencana Hermano Miguel 4-36 ⓣ07/282-6009. With terracotta walls adorned with artwork and a friendly family atmosphere, these simple rooms with private bathrooms are excellent value for the price. ❷

Hostal Casa del Barranco Calle Larga 8-41 y Cordero ⓣ07/283-9763. Many of the hotels on Calle Larga come at a premium but this historic house displaying paintings by local artists is a great-value mid-range option. Includes breakfast. ❺

Hostal Colonial Gran Colombia 10-13 y Padre Aguirre ⓣ07/2841-644. Comfortable mid-range rooms in an 18th-century house set around a small courtyard. Includes breakfast. ❺

Hotel El Capitolio Hermano Miguel 4-19 ⓣ07/282 4446. Opposite *La Casa Cuencana*, this is an equally good budget option offering decent basic rooms with shared bathroom in a quiet, homely ambience. ❸

Hotel Milan Córdova 9-89 y Padre Aguirre 07/283 1104. Centrally located hotel offering bland but well-appointed rooms and helpful staff. Great views over Plaza de San Francisco from the top-floor café. Includes breakfast. ❹

Hostal Monarca Borrero 5-47 y Honorato Vasquez ⓣ07/283-6462. Loud, bright décor but this quiet family hostal has excellent-value budget accommodation with shared bathroom. ❸

Eating and nightlife

The sweetness of *Cuencanos*' temperaments extends to their palates. You're never far from a stall or bakery selling a wide range of cakes and confectionery, including the ubiquitous *membrillo* (a gelatinous red block made with fruit). Along with Baños in the Central Highlands, Cuenca has the best choice of **restaurants** outside Quito, offering diverse international and local cuisine. **Nightlife** gets going close to midnight Thurs–Sat with a good selection of bars and discos staying open until the early hours, mostly south of downtown and along Calle Larga. Note that many bars and restaurants are closed on Sun.

Cacao y Canela Jaramillo y Borrero. Snug little café serving a huge selection of hot chocolate drinks ($2–3) – rum, cinnamon, almonds and

> **TREAT YOURSELF**
>
> **El Jordan** Calle Larga 6-111 y Borrero, ⓦwww.eljordanrestaurante.com. Middle Eastern specialities such as Moussaka with Falafel served attentively in a formal setting with French and Moorish decor. Perfect for a romantic meal. Mains $6–8. Closed Sundays.

mozzarella are just a few of the flavours available. Great cakes and snacks too. Closed Sun.

Café Austria Benigno Malo 5-95 and Juan Jaramillo. Tasty Central European specialities such as Roulade and Goulasch plus tasty cakes and ice creams for dessert. Mains $5–6.

Café Eucalyptus Gran Colombia and Benigno Malo. Lively fun café-bar with a diverse tapas menu, draught beer, couches to lounge on and live music Wed–Sat. Mains $5–6. Closed Sun.

Los Capulies Córdova y Borrero. Well-priced Ecuadorian specialities such as *Seco de Chivo* (goat stew) and *Chuleta* (pork chops) served in a pleasant enclosed courtyard. Mains $3–5. Closed Sun.

Moliendo Café Honorato Vásquez 6-24. Huge selection of cheap Colombian *arepas* (corn tortillas) and filling *almuerzos* ($2–4). Closed Sun.

Monday Blue Calle Larga y Cordero. Funky little bar with walls covered in art and eclectic memorabilia, serving cheap Mexican and Italian food. Closed Sun.

Pio Pio Borrero entre Córdova y Jaramillo. Cheap fried chicken and fast food. Mains $2–3.

Raymipamba Benigno Malo and Bolívar, Parque Calderón. Bustling café under the colonnaded arches of the New Cathedral, offering large portions of filling Ecuadorian staples. Mains $3–5.

Tal Cual Calle Larga 7-57. This popular bar pulls in the crowds at weekends when it turns into a lively disco, playing mainly salsa and merengue. Closed Sun & Mon.

Wunderbar Escalinata, off Calle Larga. Popular German-owned place in a large red-brick building with a small garden nestled above the river. The bar is lively in the evenings with occasional live music.

BAÑOS

The ideal way to relax after a few days' sightseeing is to visit the small town of Baños, 15 minutes southwest of Cuenca. The mineral content of the baths is debatable and the town certainly doesn't rival its namesake in the Central Highlands (see p.634), but it's still worth the trip. There are two sets of baths: the *Balneario Durán* (Av Ricardo Durán) has two warm pools ($2.50), while there are more upmarket facilities up the road at the *Hostería Durán* (Av Ricardo Durán, ⓣ07/289-2485; ❼). Use of the warm pool (36 degrees) and steam rooms costs $5.50. Massages are available for $25 per hour. A taxi from Cuenca costs about $4, or catch the bus ($0.25) from the corner of Vega Muñoz and Padre Aguirre or the corner of Av 12 de Abril and Av Fray Vicente Solano just south of the river.

PARQUE NACIONAL EL CAJAS

Just 30km northwest of Cuenca, the enormous Parque Nacional El Cajas (daily 6am–5pm; $10) spans nearly 300 sq km of spectacular moor-like *páramo*. With more than two hundred lakes shining beneath rugged hillsides, this is one of Ecuador's most compelling wildernesses, offering great hiking and trout fishing opportunities. However, the wind, rain and fog can often make visits uncomfortable so come prepared with rainproof gear, snacks, warm clothing and walking boots. Most of the park lies above 4000m so also ensure you are properly acclimatized before you tackle any long hikes. It's best to visit the park with a Cuenca-based tour operator, costing about $40 per person (see opposite). To get here independently, take a Cooperativa Alianza bus from the terminal (1hr, $2) and walk to the Laguna Toreador refuge station where you can get maps and information on popular hiking trails. The station also has a few beds, or you can camp in the recreation area for about $5 per person, although bear in mind it gets very cold.

LOJA

South of Cuenca, there is little to catch the visitor's attention until you reach the city of Loja, some 200km away. Loja is

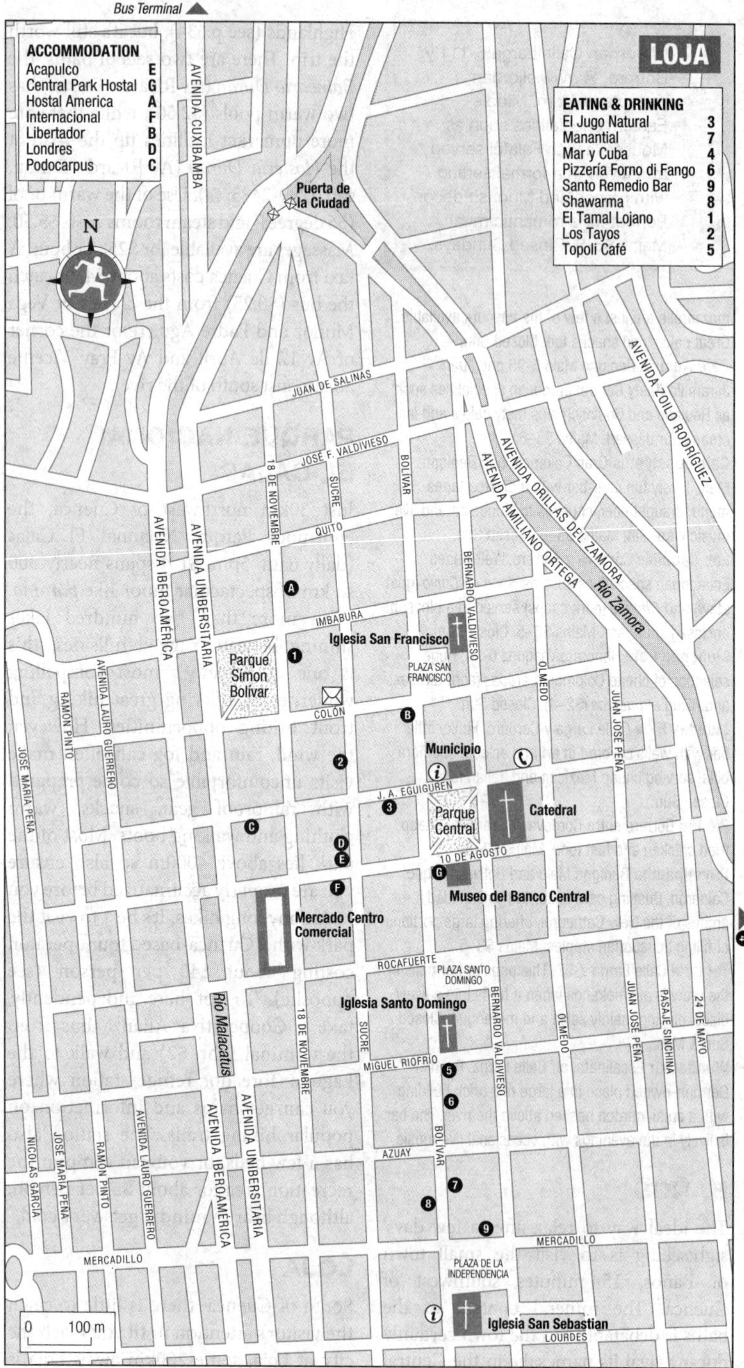
Bus Terminal
LOJA
ACCOMMODATION
Acapulco E
Central Park Hostal G
Hostal America A
Internacional F
Libertador B
Londres D
Podocarpus C
EATING & DRINKING
El Jugo Natural 3
Manantial 7
Mar y Cuba 4
Pizzería Forno di Fango 6
Santo Remedio Bar 9
Shawarma 8
El Tamal Lojano 1
Los Tayos 2
Topoli Café 5
N
Puerta de la Ciudad
AVENIDA CUXIBAMBA
AVENIDA ZOILO RODRÍGUEZ
JUAN DE SALINAS
JOSÉ F. VALDIVIESO
18 DE NOVIEMBRE
SUCRE
BOLÍVAR
AVENIDA ORILLAS DEL ZAMORA
AVENIDA AMILIANO ORTEGA
Río Zamora
QUITO
AVENIDA IBEROAMÉRICA
AVENIDA UNIBERSITARIA
IMBABURA
Iglesia San Francisco
BERNARDO VALDIVIESO
PLAZA SAN FRANCISCO
OLMEDO
JUAN JOSÉ PEÑA
Parque Símon Bolívar
COLÓN
AVENIDA LAURO GUERRERO
RAMÓN PINTO
JOSÉ MARÍA PEÑA
Municipio
J. A. EGUIGUREN
Parque Central
Catedral
10 DE AGOSTO
Museo del Banco Central
Mercado Centro Comercial
ROCAFUERTE
PLAZA SANTO DOMINGO
PASAJE SINCHINA
24 DE MAYO
Iglesia Santo Domingo
Río Malacatus
MIGUEL RIOFRÍO
AZUAY
NICOLÁS GARCÍA
MERCADILLO
PLAZA DE LA INDEPENDENCIA
Iglesia San Sebastian
LOURDES
0 100 m

one of Ecuador's oldest cities, founded in 1548, with an historic centre, thriving music scene and spectacular parks. Begin at the **Parque Central**, dominated by the towering green and white **Catedral**. On the south side, the **Museo del Banco Central** (Mon–Fri 9am–1pm & 2–4.30pm; $0.40) has a small collection of pre-Columbian ceramics and religious art. Walk south on Bolívar, passing the beautiful **Iglesia Santo Domingo**, which houses more than one hundred oil paintings. A couple of blocks further on is arguably the highlight of Loja's centre, the **Plaza de la Independencia** (also known as Plaza San Sebastián), lined by refurbished brightly coloured colonial buildings. On the southwest corner is the **Iglesia San Sebastián**, which is packed to the rafters at mass. The focal point of the square is an impressive clock tower with stone depictions at the base of the battles for Ecuador's independence. After seeing Loja's historic old town, the best thing to do is visit the parks, easily reachable with a short taxi ride ($2). The best option is the 90-hectare **Parque Universitario de Educación Ambiental y Recreación** (PUEAR, daily 9am–4pm; $1), which has good trails up through the forest and impressive views over Loja and the surrounding valley. Across the road is the **Jardín Botánico Reynaldo Espinosa** (Mon–Fri 9am–4pm, Sat & Sun 1–6pm; $0.60) which has more than two hundred species of orchids from southern Ecuador.

Arrival and information

Flights from Quito and Guayaquil arrive at the **Aeropuerto La Toma**, 33km west in the town of Catamayo. A shared taxi (about $5 per person) is the only way to get there. Loja's **bus terminal** is 2km north of the centre on Avenida Cuxibamba, with plenty of taxis ($1) and buses to the centre.

Loja has plenty of good-value **hotels**. The best low-budget option is *Hostal Londres* (Sucre 07-51, ☎07/256-1936; ❷) with small adequate rooms and shared bathrooms. *Hotel Metropolitan* (18 de Noviembre 06-31, ☎07/257-0007; ❹) has larger rooms with cable TV and private bath. *Central Park Hostal* (10 de Agosto y Bolívar, ☎07/256-1103; ❺) is of a better standard and an ideal location on the Parque Central. *Hotel Libertador* (Colon 14-30, ☎07/2560779 $60/double including breakfast) is the best option to treat yourself with plush decoration, a pool sauna and steam bath.

Loja also has some good **restaurants**. For tasty snacks such as *humitas, tamales* and *empanadas*, try *El Tamal Lojano* (18 de Noviembre; $1–2). *Manantial* on Bolívar just off the Plaza de la Independencia serves good Ecuadorian staples ($2–4). Opposite you can get Arabic food served on floor cushions at *Shawarma* ($2–3). *Forno di Fango* (Bolívar y Azuay) serves great pizza and pasta dishes ($5).

Nightlife is limited in Loja but at weekends the bars get busy later on. Try *Santo Remedio* bar on Plaza de la Independencia with delightful décor themed on the seven deadly sins.

VILCABAMBA

Vilcabamba has been attracting travellers for years in search of relaxation and the apparent secret to a long, healthy life. Although reports of locals living to 140 years of age are wildly exaggerated, there seems to be something in the water in the famous 'Valley of Longevity'. Backpackers, hikers and hippies flock here to enjoy the region's perfect climate, spectacular scenery and friendly people. The town itself is not brimming with tourist attractions; the main draw is in the surroundings which offer great **hiking** and **horse-riding** opportunities. At the end of the day there are plenty of places to pamper yourself with a relaxing massage.

Vilcabamba has also long been associated with the hallucinogenic San Pedro

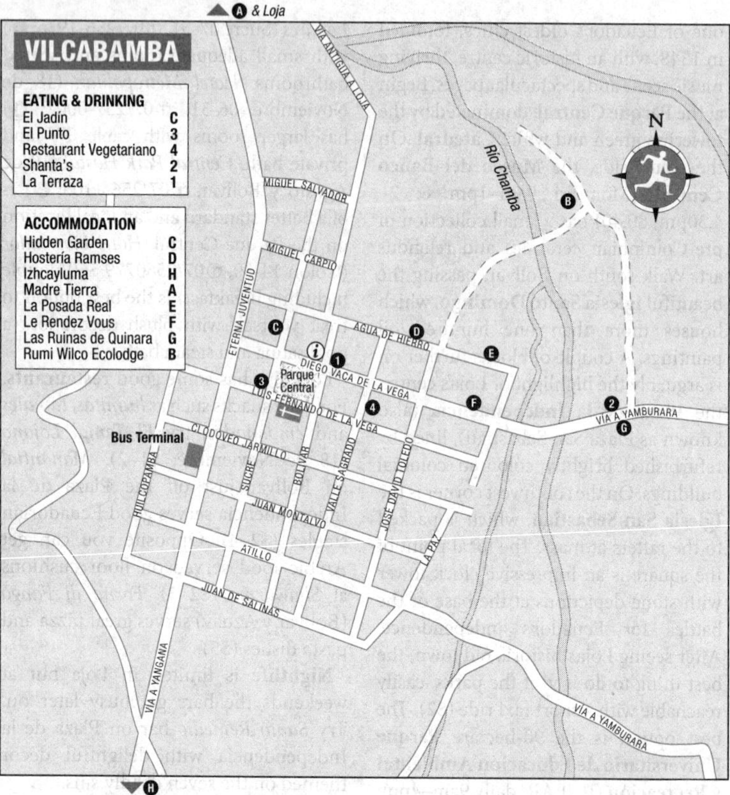

cactus, which grows in this region. Be warned that San Pedro is illegal and local police have been dealing more severely with anyone found taking it.

What to see and do

There are plenty of hiking trails around Vilcabamba to keep you busy for a few days. Perhaps the most impressive is up to the jagged **Cerro Mandango**. Walk south of town along Avenida Eterna Juventud to find the trail entrance ($1.50). It's a steep 45-minute climb up to the first peak and then a rather unnerving trek across the very narrow ridgeline to the second peak. You can then loop around descending slowly back towards town. The entire walk is about four hours. To shorten it simply retrace your steps back down from the first peak.

Many hotels have excellent **massage** facilities attached but two great-value options in town are Piedad Masajes (Calle Agua de Hierro y La Paz, ⓣ09/179-4292) and Karina at Massage Beauty Care (Diego Vaca de Vega y Bolívar, ⓣ07/264-0359). Both charge just $10 per hour.

Northeast of town is the small Rumi-Wilco Nature Reserve ($2 donation) which has a self-guided trail system. To hire **horses**, contact Caballos Gavilán (ⓣ07/264-0281, Sucre y Diego Vaca) run by a friendly New Zealander. Half-day/full-day tours with guide cost $20/30. A two-day tour including overnight stay in a cloudforest cabin and a day in nearby **Podocarpus National Park** costs $80.

Arrival and information

By bus Buses run to and from Loja every half an hour from the corner of Av de la Eterna Juventud and C Jaramillo.

By taxi Pick-up trucks act as taxis and charge $1–1.50 to most of the accommodation in and around Vilcabamba.

Tourist information The tourist office, on the northeast corner of Parque Central (open daily 8am–1pm and 3–6pm, ⓣ07/264-0090), provides maps and information on hikes and excursions around Vilcabamba.

Accommodation

Expect to pay a little more for accommodation in Vilcabamba than in other parts of Ecuador unless you want to stay at one of the town's grubbiest dives.

Hostal Jardín Escondido (Sucre y Diego de Vaca, ⓣ07/264-0281) has simple but spacious rooms around a garden with lemon trees, a small pool and jacuzzi. The hotel's Mexican restaurant is excellent. ❹

Hostal Las Margaritas (Sucre y C Jaramillo, ⓣ07/264-005) is another good option with a homely atmosphere and cable TV. ❹

Izhcayluma ⓣ07/264-0095, ⓦwww.izhcayluma.com). This *hostal* has been welcoming visitors to Vilcabamba for years. About 2km south of town, this friendly German-owned *Hostería* has rustic cabins, free mountain bikes, buffet breakfasts and one of the best views in town. The staff has painstakingly mapped out several trails around Vilcabamba for keen hikers. Don't miss the Bavarian Stroganoff or the German Weissbier in the fantastic restaurant. ❷–❺

Madre Tierra (ⓣ07/2640269, ⓦwww.madretierra1.com). For a little luxury, stay at this award-winning spa hotel 1km north of town. Enjoy the view from the balcony of your comfortable cabin and take advantage of the huge range of spa treatments on offer. ❽ including breakfast and dinner.

Le Rendez-Vous (Diego Vaca de Vega, T09/219-1180), east of the town centre has good-value, cosy rooms with hammocks on the terrace overlooking the garden. ❹

Eating

Many hotels have good **restaurants** attached (see above).

La Terraza (on the northeast corner of Parque Central). This restaurant serves good *almuerzos* as well as tasty Mexican, Italian and Chinese dishes ($3–4).

CROSSING INTO PERU

If you're in the southern sierra, it's much better to cross to Peru via **Macará**, 190km southeast of Loja, than go down to the coast and cross via frenetic Huaquillas. A bus service operated by Cooperativa Loja (ⓣ07/257-9014) travels to Piura in Peru via Macará (eight hours, $8), daily from Loja at 7am, 1pm and 11pm. Buy tickets in advance if possible. The company has offices in Loja bus terminal and next to Vilcabamba's bus terminal. From Vilcabamba take a bus to Loja and change. In Macará the bus stops at the 24-hour *Migración* office where you get your exit stamp. You then walk across the bridge which forms the border to get your entry stamp on the other side and then get back on the bus.

Restaurant Vegetariano (Valle Sagrado) is another dependable option, offering a selection of curries, tarts, pasta and soups ($3–4).

Shantas Going east out of town on Diego Vaca de la Vega, the spot offers a wide selection of dishes, including trout and frog's legs ($4–6). The more adventurous can try the snake juice ($2), made from pickled coral snake, sugar cane and *aguardiente*.

The Oriente

East of Quito, the Andes drop dramatically and snow-capped mountains give way to verdant swathes of tropical rainforest stretching some 250km to the Colombian and Peruvian borders. Ecuador's chunk of the Amazon basin, known as the Oriente ("The East"), constitutes almost half of the country's territory, although only five percent of the population lives here in ramshackle towns and remote indigenous communities.

The Northern Oriente offers the most spectacular opportunities for visitors to encounter a bewildering array of flora and fauna in primary rainforest. The highlights are the two huge protected areas **Parque Nacional Yasuní** and the **Reserva Faunística Cuyabeno**. Unfortunately, reaching these unforgettable wildernesses usually involves travelling through the decidedly forgettable hubs of **Lago Agrio** or **Coca**. The contrast between these ugly oil towns and the natural beauty beyond them exemplifies the struggle between industry and conservation in the region, which has been ongoing since the discovery of oil in the 1970s.

For those with limited time or who are seeking a more accessible experience, the more pleasant towns of **Tena** and **Puyo** are surrounded by secondary rainforest with opportunities to stay with **indigenous communities**. These tours are recommended, not least because they provide locals with regular income and help to preserve the communities and their territory. The higher elevation of these towns means that **whitewater rafting** and **kayaking** are popular activities in the river rapids tumbling down towards the Amazon basin.

Tour operators

It's easiest to book your tour in Quito. The New Town, particularly around Mariscal Sucre, has scores of tour operators and travel agencies offering tours to the main jungle destinations. The following are recommended:

Dracaena J Pinto E4-453 y Amazonas ⓣ 02/254-6590, ⓦ www.theamazondracaena.com. Offers tours of Cuyabeno, staying at *Nicky Amazon Lodge* 5 days $230.

Kem Pery Tours Pinto 539 and Amazonas ⓣ 02/222-6583, ⓦ www.kempery.com. Offers trips to the Huaorani reserve staying in *Bataburo Lodge*. 4 days $285, plus $20 donation to the Huaorani. Trips also available on the 'Flotel' boat *Jungle Discovery* in Cuyabeno, 4 days $420.

Neotropic Turis J Pinto E4-340 near Amazonas and Wilson ⓣ 02/252-121. 4 day tours, staying in *Cuyabeno Lodge* from $200.

JUNGLE BASICS

If you dream of striking out on your own and hacking through dense jungle like a modern-day explorer, dream on. Unguided travel is strongly discouraged by the Ecuadorian government and certainly not advisable, considering how inhospitable and inaccessible parts of the Oriente remain. **Guided tours** are the best option and are relatively cheap, costing $30-50 per person per day. Prices rise if you stay in a more luxurious lodge or on an air-conditioned river cruiser but bear in mind that some discomfort is part of the jungle experience. Always check that your guide has a **permit** from the Ministry of Tourism. Generally the larger the number of people in your group, the lower the price will be. Tour operators regularly advertise tours leaving imminently with last-minute spaces. Solo travellers usually have to share a cabin or pay a higher rate for a separate room.

Tours range from two to eight days. For tours around Puyo and Tena, a couple of days will give you an insight into life in the Oriente. If you are travelling deep into the jungle, more than four days is recommended, considering that nearly two days will be spent travelling.

The best place to organise a jungle tour is definitely Quito, while Baños, Puyo and Tena have plenty of operators running regular tours. Booking locally is more difficult in Coca and Lago Agrio (although you may be lucky) so it's better to make arrangements prior to arrival.

You must prepare thoroughly and pack the **essentials** before heading into the jungle. Be sure to take plenty of insect repellent, long sleeves, trousers, waterproofs, a torch and boots. A first-aid kit is also advisable, although the guide will carry one. See p.611 for information on anti-malarials and yellow fever vaccinations. You must carry your original **passport**, as copies are not sufficient at military checkpoints.

THE ROAD TO LAGO AGRIO

The bus ride from Quito to Lago Agrio (8hr, $8) is long and arduous and you might consider flying, at least on the journey out, to avoid a night in Lago Agrio (from $60 one way with Tame, Ⓦwww.tame.com.ec). If you take the bus, it makes sense to break the journey up with visits to **Papallacta** (see 623) and **San Rafael Falls**, Ecuador's largest waterfalls. These are located three hours after Baeza, 2.5km along a trail from the main road (ask the bus driver). You should allow yourself about 90 minutes to walk down and back.

Nuevo Mundo Expeditions Av Coruña N26-207 and Orellana Ⓣ02/250-9431, Ⓦwww.nuevomundotravel.com. Operates the *Manatee Amazon Explorer*, a comfortable river cruiser with a/c cabins for thirty people. Tours along Napo river including the Yasuní reserve. 45 days $507-665.

Rainforestur Ⓣ02/223-9822, Ⓦwww.rainforestur.com, Amazonas 410 y Robles. Wide range of jungle tours throughout the Oriente via Lago Agrio, Coca, Puyo and Tena.

Tropic Ecological Adventures Av República 307 and Almagro, Edif Taurus Ⓣ02/222-5907 or 223-4594, Ⓦwww.tropiceco.com. Tours and eco-tourism projects throughout the Oriente. Four days in Yasuni from $510 in *Sani Lodge*. Four days in *Huaorani Lodge* $480 (not including flights from Puyo). Indigenous community stays available.

LAGO AGRIO

Lago Agrio, also known as Nueva Loja, was used by Texaco in the 1960s as a base for oil exploration in the Ecuadorian Oriente and takes its name (meaning Sour Lake) from the company's original headquarters in Texas. In many ways the town epitomises the power struggle between oil companies keen to get their hands on the 'black gold' underneath the jungle and tour operators keen to preserve the once pristine forests of the **Cuyabeno Reserve**. Add to this the infiltration of Colombian FARC guerrillas from the border just 21km to the north and it's a **dangerous area**. If you are staying over in Lago Agrio, do not wander from the centre of town and take care at night.

Arrival and information

The **bus station** is 2km northeast and the **airport** 4km east. Take a **taxi** to the town centre ($2) unless your tour operator has arranged a transfer. Most of the hotels, restaurants and tourist agencies are located along the Avenida Quito.

Accommodation and eating

Hotel D'Mario (Ⓣ06/283-0172; ❺) is a popular option and has a bar, cable TV, swimming pool, air conditioning and free internet. *Hotel Gran Colombia* (Av Quito 265 Ⓣ06/283-1032; ❹) has decent rooms with fans (a/c extra) and cable TV. You're better off eating in either of these two hotels' **restaurants** rather than wandering around town.

Tour operators

There are a few Lago Agrio-based **tour operators** but most tours are organised from Quito. Lago Agrio is not a nice place to hang around waiting for a tour to start so it's preferable to make prior arrangements. Recommended local operators include Pioneer Tours (Barrio Colinas Petroleras y Amazonas Ⓣ06/283-1845), run by Galo Sevilla, who has more than 20 years' guiding experience. Five days costs $200 staying in *Cabañas Payaguaje*. Magic River Tours (18 de Diciembre, C Primera and Pacayacu Ⓣ06/283-1003, Quito Ⓣ02/262-9303 Ⓦwww.magicrivertours.com) is a German-owned company specialising in canoe trips in the Cuyabeno reserve. Five days $295, 8 days $580. To find out more about staying with the indigenous Cofán community which lives 25km east of Lago Agrio, contact the **Fundación para la Sobrevivencia del Pueblo Cofán** via the Quito office (Mariano Cardenal N74-153 y Joaquín Mancheno Ⓣ02/247-0946, Ⓦwww.cofan.org).

RESERVA FAUNÍSTICA CUYABENO

This beautiful reserve (admission $20) of unique flooded rainforest spreads out over more than 6000 square kilometres east of Lago Agrio, extending to the Peruvian border. It contains an astonishing biodiversity of plants, trees, mammals and aquatic wildlife. Meandering down the Rio Aguarico, a tributary of the Amazon, through huge areas of inundated forest and passing countless lagoons, is an unforgettable experience. Pink freshwater dolphins, white and black caiman, giant otters and many species of monkeys are commonly seen, while the famous anaconda and jaguar will likely prove elusive. The borders of the reserve were expanded in the early 1990s, partly in response to the damaging activities of oil companies in the region. Sadly, areas of Cuyabeno have been badly polluted but vocal indigenous protest has improved the situation and there remain areas of largely unspoilt jungle to explore. The remoteness of this region means that you need to be on a guided tour.

COCA

The capital of Orellana province has grown rapidly since the 1970s into an ugly oil town. Similar to Lago Agrio, there's little to tempt you to stay longer than is necessary. Coca is, however, the last major town on the Río Napo, the gateway to the enormous **Parque Nacional Yasuní** and also emerging as a route over the border to Peru via **Nuevo Rocafuerte**.

Arrival and information

By bus Coca's bus terminal is 500m north of town but most bus companies have offices in the centre of town. Trans Baños (Napo and Bolívar) offers the best services to Quito ($10, 8–10hr) while El Dorado and Transportes Jumandy at the terminal go to Tena ($6, 6hr).

By taxi White pick-up truck taxis will take you around town from about $1.

By air Tame (☎06/288-1078) and Icaro (☎06/288-0997) both operate two or three flights daily from Quito to Coca (from $60 single), which is tempting to avoid the grueling bus ride. The airport is 2km north of town (taxi $1).

By boat Coop de Transportes Fluviales Orellana (☎06/2880087) operates boat services to Nuevo Rocafuerte ($15, 8hr) on Mon and Thurs, departing at 7.30am. Book the day before.

Accommodation

For **accommodation**, *Hotel San Fermin* ($20–28) is a comfortable mid-range choice with spacious rooms, private bathroom, cable TV. Or choose from rustic cabins and upscale hotel rooms at *Hotel El Auca* (Napo y Rocafuerte ☎06/288-0127; ❹–❻), one of the best options in town and popular with tour groups with a good restaurant. Coca has plenty of cheap **restaurants**. *Ocaso* (Eloy Alfaro and Napo) is economical and popular for Ecuadorian staples. *Parrilladas Argentinas* (Cuenca and Inés) is the best place in town for steaks. After dinner, have a drink with fellow jungle-seekers at the *Emerald Forest Blues Bar* (Espejo and Napo). Similar to Lago Agrio, it can be

CROSSING INTO PERU: NUEVO ROCAFUERTE

For adventurers wanting to emulate Francisco de Orellana and float deeper down the Río Napo into the Amazon Basin, improved relations between Ecuador and Peru in the past decade have made it easier to cross the border via Nuevo Rocafuerte. There are even plans afoot to make the trip possible all the way to Brazil's Atlantic coast, although it remains to be seen if and when this will happen. This is not a trip for those who like comfort, some eight hours downstream from Coca. Boats leave Coca at 7.30am Monday and Thursday ($15 one-way), usually stopping off at Pañacocha. From Nuevo Rocafuerte to Coca there are usually departures Wednesday and Sunday. Come prepared with adequate supplies of food, water purification tablets and insect repellent. In Nuevo Rocafuerte there are a few very basic, cheap places to stay but nowhere good enough to linger long. From Nuevo Rocafuerte you receive an **exit stamp** and boats cross the border to Pantoja, where you get an **entry stamp**. Pantoja also has a small amount of basic accommodation. Boats leave to Iquitos only once a month, a trip which takes six long days.

difficult to find **tour operators** locally in Coca, as most are organized from Quito. It's recommended that you book in advance. Try Tropic Ecological Adventures or Kem Pery (see Quito-based tour operators, p.650).

PARQUE NACIONAL YASUNÍ

Yasuní ($20) is one of Ecuador's last great wildernesses and the country's largest mainland national park. The terrain of nearly 10,000 square kilometers ranges from upland tropical forest to seasonally flooded forest, marshes, swamps, lakes and rivers. This region was untouched by the last Ice Age and has staggering biodiversity – more than five hundred species of birds and more than 60 percent of Ecuador's mammals including rarer species such as jaguars, harpy eagles, pumas and tapirs. UNESCO declared it an International Biosphere Reserve in 1979 but unfortunately this didn't prevent oil exploration. The construction of a road, Vía Maxus, through the park and pollution from irresponsible oil companies has damaged areas of the park. However, large sections remain unscathed and Yasuní still offers the best opportunities in Ecuador to experience pristine rainforest. Most tours coming through Coca will include a visit to the park.

TENA AND AROUND

Tena is the most pleasant town in the northern Oriente to be based for a few days. Rather than being merely a gateway to the jungle, it's a destination in itself with a slightly cooler climate, good hotels and restaurants and an impressive setting on the river surrounded by lush forest. Aside from wandering around the laidback centre and relaxing in a riverside restaurant, the main attraction in the town itself is **Parque Amazónico La Isla** (daily 8.30am–5pm; $2), just south of the main pedestrian bridge.

JUNGLE TOURS

The following operators offer jungle tours in addition to rafting and kayaking. Most tours are all-inclusive of transport, accommodation, food and guides.

Agency Limoncocha (Sangay 533, ⓣ06/288-7583) is based in the *hostal* of the same name (see below) and offers 1–4 day jungle tours at $35–45 per day.

Amarongachi Tours (15 de Noviembre, ⓣ06/288-6372, ⓦwww.amarongachi.com) offers tours staying in *Cabañas Amarongachi* or, preferably, *Cabañas Shangri-La*, perched 100m above the Napo River commanding wonderful views. From $45 per day.

RICANCIE (Av El Chofer y Cuenca, ⓣ06/288-8479, ⓦhttp://ricancie.nativeweb.org) co-ordinates 10 indigenous community eco-tourism projects in the upper Napo region. Tours cost around $45 per person per day.

Sacharicsina Tours (Montesdeoca 110 and Pano ⓣ06/288-6839) is run by a local Quechua family and offers jungle tours in *cabañas* on the Río Illoculín, southwest of Tena. $40–50 per day.

This 27-hectare park has several self-guided forested trails, diverse plants and wildlife including tapir, toucan, a rather fierce ostrich and various species of monkeys who will jump on your back and follow you around with some persistence.

Arrival and information

The **bus terminal** is 1km south of the centre. A **taxi** anywhere in town costs $1. Tena is divided by the river of the same name and the best places to stay and eat are located close to the riverfront.

Accommodation

La Casa del Abuelo Sucre 432 ⓣ06/288-8926. This excellent mid-range choice is as cosy and

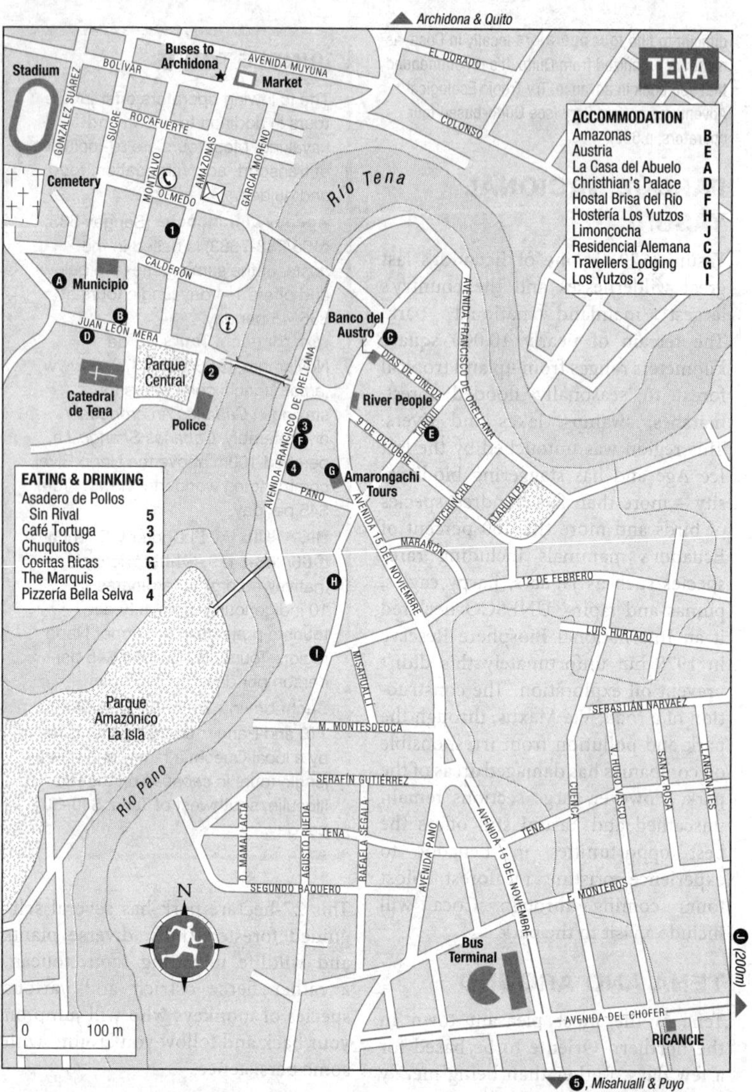

homely as the name suggests (grandfather's house) with well-furnished rooms, high ceilings and a pleasant rooftop terrace. ❹

Hostal Limoncocha ⓣ06/288-7583. A popular backpacker option is this German-run *hostal* on the southeast edge of town with a travel agency, guest kitchen and free internet (20min walk from centre). ❷

Hostal Travellers Lodging Av 15 de Noviembre 438 and 9 de Octubre, ⓣ06/288-7102; $11. Budget travellers will feel right at home here. The good-quality rooms are excellent value for the price, with hot water, private bathroom and cable TV. The reputable Amarongachi travel agency is attached. River views cost extra. ❸

Hostal Los Yutzos Agusto Rueda 190 y 15 de Noviembre ⓣ06/288-6717 or 288-6769. The riverside location and spacious, tastefully decorated rooms make this the best place in town. Lounge on the balcony overlooking the river or relax in the verdant gardens. ❺

RAFTING AND KAYAKING

As well as offering plenty of jungle tours, Tena is also the best place in Ecuador for **whitewater rafting** and **kayaking** on the countless tributaries surrounded by spectacular jungle scenery. There are plenty of tour operators in town but ensure you book with an experienced, well-equipped operator, ideally accredited by AGAR. The most famous stretches of river are the Jondachi and Jatunyacu or Upper Napo (both class 3) and the wilder Misahuallí and Hollin (class 4). Recommended local operators include the British-run River People (15 de Noviembre and 9 de Octubre, ⓣ06/288-8349, ⓦwww.riverpeopleraftingecuador.com) and Yacu Amu (Tarqui 230, ⓣ06/288-6727 or Quito ⓣ02/290-4054, ⓦwww.raftingecuador.com). Day trips are $50–$80. Longer trips with overnight accommodation are available.

Eating

Tena has plenty of good restaurants. As with much of the Oriente, food is solid if unspectacular.

Chuquitos off Parque Central. An excellent riverside position, with a wide-ranging menu and attentive service. The fish is particularly good. Mains $5.

Cositas Ricas Av 15 de Noviembre and 9 de Octubre. This cheap, cheerful place serves tasty Ecuadorian staples and is a good option for lunch. Mains $2–4.

The Marquis Grille Amazonas and Olmedo. The ideal choice to treat yourself and one of Tena's few upmarket restaurants. The steak and trout are specialities. Mains $8.

PUYO AND AROUND

If you're arriving from Baños or even Tena, Puyo will at first sight be a disappointment. It's rather an ugly commercial town with little to offer beyond being the starting point for a jungle tour. Most worth visiting is the **Jardín Botánico Las Orquídeas** (daily 8am–6pm, ⓣ03/288-4855; $5 book in advance), 3km southeast of town (take a taxi for $1). These botanical gardens, set amongst lush hills boast more than two hundred species of native Amazonian orchids. Also worth visiting is **Parque Pedagógico Etno-Botánico Omaere** (daily 8am–6pm; $3), a ten-minute walk north from the city centre, which has guided tours along forested paths past indigenous dwellings.

The **bus station** is 1km west of the centre, a 15-minute walk or $1 by taxi.

Accommodation and eating

Accommodation in the centre of Puyo is decidedly ordinary. *Hostal Araucano*, on Ceslao Marín 576 y 27 de Febrero (ⓣ03/288-5686; ❸) is a cosy but basic budget option while *Hotel Puyo* (ⓣ03/288-4497; ❹) is a step up with cable TV and a good restaurant *La Casa de Cangrejo* attached. For more comfort and a more pleasant setting, stay north of the centre. Towards Parque Omaere, *El Jardín* (ⓣ03/288-6101, ⓦwww.eljardin.pastaza.net; ❺) is a rustic wooden house set behind a large garden and boasts an award-winning restaurant. Puyo can't compete with nearby Baños in terms of its **restaurants** but there are a few good ones. *El Jardín* (see above, mains from $5) is probably the best in the area with specialities including *Pollo Ishpingo* (chicken with cinammon). In town there are plenty of cheap places. Try *Chifa Ken Wah* on Atahualpa for Chinese, or *El Toro Asado* on Atahualpa for barbecued meat dishes including *Guanta* (a type of Amazonian rodent) for the more adventurous.

Tour operators

Most travellers book from Quito or Baños but there are a few good **tour operators** in Puyo offering tours to communities close to town. Other communities such as the Huaorani are only reachable by light aircraft from the Shell airport 10km west of town. These tours are more expensive. Papangu (27 de Febrero and Sucre, ⓣ03/288-3875) is an indigenous-run agency offering tours to nearby Quechua communities and further afield to Sarayacu and Río Curaray (travel by light aircraft). $45–60 per day not including flights. Amazonía (Atahualpa y 9 de Octubre, ⓣ03/288-3219) offers a range of tours close to Puyo from $35–50 per day. Further information about Huaorani communities can be obtained from the political body ONHAE (ⓣ03/288-6148).

The northern coast and lowlands

The lush, green vegetation that provides the backdrop for Ecuador's northern coast gives it the edge over the south in terms of beauty. As with all of Ecuador's coastline, the contrast is stark between the jam-packed craziness of high season (Jan–April, July–Aug and national holidays) and the eerie quiet of low season. But the region has **beach resorts** to suit all tastes, whether you're seeking all-night parties or a beach to yourself. The Afro-Ecuadorians that make up a large part of the population of **Esmeraldas** province in the far north give the region a very different cultural feel to the rest of the country. You'll find the locals exuberant, extrovert and talkative, which can make a refreshing change from the mountains.

The main route from the Sierra descends dramatically via **Santo Domingo de los Colorados**, an unattractive transport hub. Avoid **Esmeraldas** town and head south to a string of beach resorts. **Atacames** is by far the busiest and most popular, great if you're looking for party central. Further down the coast the fishing village of **Súa** and the island of **Muisne** offer quieter beach options for budget travellers, while the beautiful beach at **Mompiche** is emerging as a popular spot. Moving further south into the province of **Manabi**, head to **Canoa**, a haven for surfers and sunseekers alike and one of the country's most pleasant resorts to stay for a few days. Nearby the elegant resort of **Bahía de Caráquez** juts out dramatically on a slim peninsula and offers easy access to mangroves and tropical dry forest. Further south is Ecuador's second largest port **Manta**, a bustling city with its own beaches. Note that in Esmeraldas province **malaria** is present, though comparatively rare, so cover up and use plenty of repellent, especially during the rainy season (Dec–May).

SANTO DOMINGO DE LOS COLORADOS

This transport hub is the most convenient route from the Sierra to the coast. From here you can head north to Esmeraldas and Pedernales or south to Bahía de Caráquez, Manta and Guayaquil. Parts of town are dangerous so take care arriving at night. Try to begin your journey as early as possible so that an overnight stop becomes unnecessary because Santo Domingo has little to offer. The bus terminal is 1.5km north of the town centre (take a taxi for $1 or a public bus). If you are stuck here, **accommodation** is unimpressive. Opposite the bus terminal *Hotel Sheraton* (☎02/275-1988, Av Calazacón 111; ❸) is a decent option with clean rooms, hot water, cable TV and fans. In town, *Hotel Diana Real* (☎02/275-1380, corner 29 de Mayo y Loja; $18) has much the same facilities and a restaurant attached. For **eating**, the upmarket *Gran Hotel Santo Domingo* has a good restaurant or try *La Tonga* (Rio Toachi y Galápagos) or *Chifa Happy* (Tulcan 117) for Chinese.

ESMERALDAS

Esmeraldas is the north coast's most important industrial town with oil pumped in for refining and cash crops shipped out for export. Little of the wealth stays here so it's a very poor town and one of Ecuador's most **dangerous**, particularly on the Malecón Maldonado. You're advised either to take a direct bus to the beach resorts or time your journey to arrive in Esmeraldas before nightfall so that you have time to change and avoid an overnight stay.

Bus services run by Transportes La Costeñita and Transportes del Pacífico depart regularly to the beach resorts of Atacames, Súa and Same from Malecón Maldonado (6.30am–8pm). The **airport**, served by flights from Quito, is 25km east of town and the only way to get there is by taxi ($18, but $25 will get you direct to Atacames instead). If you really must stay over in Esmeraldas, find **accommodation** at *Hostal Miraflores* (ⓣ06/272-3077, Bolívar 6-04; ❷) near the Central Plaza with small rooms, mosquito nets and shared bathrooms. For more comfort, stay in the more pleasant suburb of Las Palmas, 3km north of the centre. *Hotel Cayapas* (ⓣ06/272-1318, Av Kennedy 401; $50) has comfortable rooms with TV and hot water plus a good restaurant. You're best off **eating** in one of the hotels in Las Palmas. There are plenty of cheap eateries downtown but take care after dark.

ATACAMES AND AROUND

Atacames is the busiest, brashest beach resort on the north coast and, along with Salinas, the most popular in Ecuador. Most of the hotels, restaurants and bars are situated on the thin peninsula, which forms the **Malecón**. The long sandy beach is lined with bamboo bars serving up fruit shakes by day and cocktails by night. During the week it's relatively quiet and a bit depressing with staff desperately trying to lure you into their empty bars, but at the weekends and on national holidays Atacames turns into a heaving party town. Boom boxes pump out ear-splittingly loud salsa and reggeton, while bars are packed with revellers dancing and drinking until dawn. If you love all-night parties, then come here for the weekend, but if you're seeking a tranquil

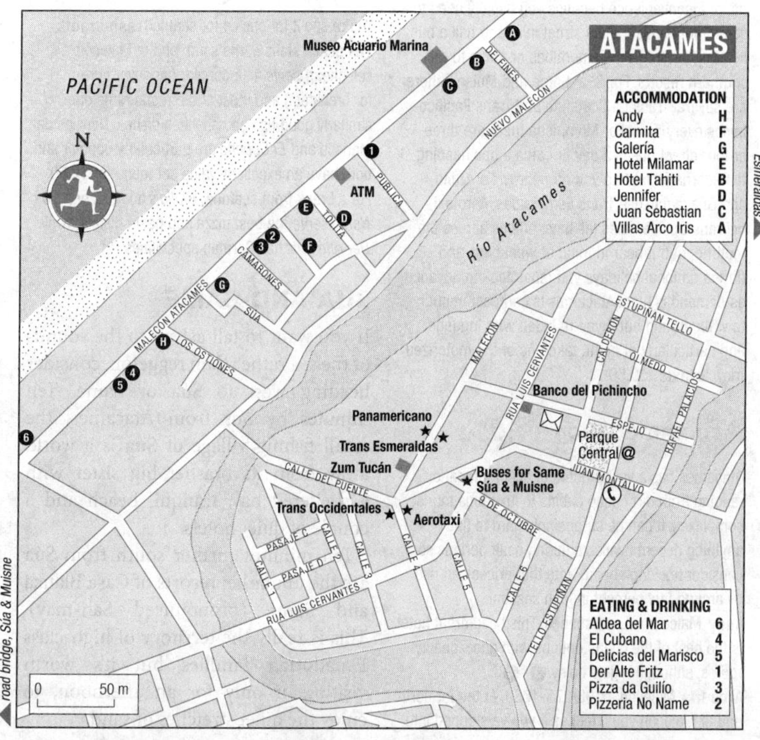

couple of days by the ocean, head to Súa or Mompiche along the coast. There are a few interesting excursions, including boat trips to nearby Isla Encantada ($3) which has abundant birdlife. Between June and September, you can watch humpback whales off the coast. These can be organised through *Le Castell Hotel* (Malecón, T06/273-1442).

The town of Atacames is inland over the bridge but it's a dusty unpleasant place which only necessitates a visit if you need a bank or internet café. Note that tourists, particularly women, get hassled more here than in the southern resorts. **Muggings** have also been reported so avoid taking valuables onto the beach, stay off it at night, take taxis and stay in well-lit areas.

Arrival and information

Atacames has no central **bus** terminal which is a minor inconvenience because you usually need to stand on the dusty main street inland to hail a bus heading to and from Esmeraldas or down to the southern resorts. For Súa, Same and Muisne, there are several Trans La Costeñita and Trans Pacífico buses every hour. For Mompiche there are three or four direct buses a day or catch a bus heading to Pedernales to drop you off nearby. For Quito and Guayaquil, use Trans Esmeraldas, Aerotaxi or Trans Occidentales (all have offices across the footbridge) but bear in mind at weekends and during national holidays you must book in advance as demand is high. Atacames is compact enough to walk around but if you're laden with luggage and particularly at night, take one of the motorized tricycle **taxis** ($0.50).

Accommodation

Atacames has a vast amount of accommodation ranging from dirt cheap cabins to luxurious tourist complexes. It can be surprisingly hard to find anything decent available during peak periods so consider booking ahead. Note that prices can rise by around fifty percent in high season.

Andy Malecón y Los Ostiones. This beachfront hotel is the best of the cheap options with good-quality rooms, although it gets noisy. 3–4

Arco Iris Malecón, T06/273-1069. At the far north end of Malecón you'll feel as if you've stepped into the Oriente, lazing on a hammock in rustic cabins tucked away in verdant gardens. 5–6

Hostal Carmita Las Taguas y Malecón, T06/273-1784. For a quieter stay just off the front, this *hostal* is good value with cable TV and a/c. 4

Hotel Aldea Mar Av Las Acacias, T06/273-1676. With bright comfortable rooms, many with sea view, air conditioning, hot water and a small pool, this is excellent value and its location at the south end of Malecón means you can actually get some sleep. 4–5

TREAT YOURSELF

Juan Sebastián Malecón, T06/273-1049, Wwww.hoteljuansebastian.com. Splash out on the pick of the top-range hotels at the northern end of town and enjoy the large pool, sauna, Turkish baths and comfortable cabins. 6

Eating

You're spoilt for choice for seafood **restaurants**. The beach stalls at the south end of Malecón sell cheap *ceviche* (a popular hangover cure for breakfast) and most of the restaurants offer similarly good fish and shellfish dishes. Delicias del Marisco and *El Cubano* are particularly popular and both have an excellent-value set menu for $2.50. For a break from seafood, *Giulio's* and *Pizzeria No Name* serve the best pizza and pasta dishes, while *Der Alte Fritz* has German specialities.

SÚA AND SAME

If you want to fall asleep to the sounds of the sea rather than reggeton, consider heading west to Súa or Same. Ten minutes by bus from Atacames, the small fishing village of **Súa** is a world away from its brasher big sister with a sheltered bay, tranquil beach and a couple of quiet hotels.

Ten minutes further south from Súa are the upmarket resorts of Casa Blanca and **Same** (pronounced Sah-may). This is really the territory of high-class Ecuadorian families but it's worth visiting, if only for an afternoon, to enjoy the quiet stretches of sand.

Accommodation and eating

Your best bet for **accommodation** is *Hotel Chagra Ramos* (☎06/273-1006; $16-20), which has decent cabins with balconies perched on a hill overlooking the beach on the north side of town. *Las Buganvillas Hotel* (☎06/273-1008; $16–20) on the Malecón also has comfortable rooms set facing a pretty courtyard with small swimming pool. For **restaurants**, there are plenty of options serving great seafood, including *Kikes* and *Malibu* on Malecón.

TONCHIGÜE

About 3km further south is the more reasonably-priced village of **Tonchigüe**. To stay **overnight**, try the German-run *El Acantilado* (☎06/273-3466, Ⓦwww.hosteriaelacantilado.com; doubles $45–75), which has rustic suites and cabins with hammocks, hot water, sea views and a small pool.

MUISNE

Nearly 50km down the coast from Atacames, the poor island of Muisne offers an off-the-beaten-track experience. At first sight it's a run-down place with dilapidated buildings just off the mainland from the town of El Relleno. The highlight is the tranquil 2km beach on the other side of the island. There have been thefts reported recently so take care with valuables. There are regular **bus** services from Atacames (1hr 30min; $1.50). A good budget **accommodation** option is the beachfront *Hostal Playa Paraiso* (☎06/248-0192; $10–15).

MOMPICHE

The tiny little village of Mompiche is home to one of the most beautiful beaches in Ecuador. This combined with great surfing conditions have increased its popularity recently, albeit at a reassuringly slow pace. The town has limited **accommodation** options and is booked up during busy periods. The best place is *Gabeal* (☎09/969-6543; ❸) located up the beach to the right. This eco-lodge has 25 rooms in bamboo cabins with private bathroom. Other options located on the main street in front of the beach are *Hostal Oga* and *Hostal Tu Regreso* (no phone; ❸–❹) offering basic rooms with private bath and fan. You can get your seafood fill at any of the **restaurants** on the beachfront. There are a few **buses** daily from Esmeraldas via Atacames. If you miss one, either take a bus to Muisne and change at El Salto or take a bus to Pedernales and ask the driver to drop you off at the entrance to Mompiche. From there, you can either hitch a ride or sweat it on a half-hour walk.

CANOA AND AROUND

Canoa is to those who know Ecuador well rather like the Montañita of ten years ago – a quiet fishing village, which has developed into a laidback resort by virtue of its beautiful beach and great surfing conditions (particularly Dec–May). It's a dramatic setting with wave after wave crashing upon long stretches of sand flanked by steep cliffs. At present, it just might be Ecuador's best beach resort for budget travellers without the overblown weekend craziness of Atacames or Montañita. Let's hope it stays that way.

An interesting excursion from Canoa is **Río Muchacho Organic Farm**, where you can see sustainable farming in practice and learn about the culture of the *Montubia* (coastal farmers). There are also guided hikes, horseriding and birdwatching. Guacamayo Bahiatours offers all-inclusive tours (1 day: $25, 3 days $100) and has offices in Bahía de Caráquez (Bolívar 902, ☎05/269-1412) and Canoa (☎091-479849).

Buses between Pedernales and San Vicente come through Canoa's main street every half hour or so.

Accommodation

Most of Canoa's **accommodation** is in the budget category and **camping** is also popular. The best of the cheap options are at the south end of the beach.

Coco Loco ⓣ09/544-7260. Basic but decent rooms in a large thatched bamboo house with fans, hammocks on the balconies, a kitchen for guest use and a friendly atmosphere. ❸–❹

Hotel Bambú ⓣ08/926-5225. At the north end of the beach is Canoa's most happening hotel. Rooms are small but the vibrant atmosphere and beautiful beachfront gardens make up for it. The restaurant is worth visiting even if you don't stay. Camping available ($3 per person) and surfboards for hire. ❸–❺

La Posada del Daniel Javier Santos, ⓣ09/750-8825. Walk inland, next to the park to find a set of decent cabins, a pleasant bar area and small swimming pool. ❹

La Vista Hotel beachfront next to *Coco Loco*, ⓣ08/647-0222. For a bit more comfort, this beachfront hotel offers more comfortable, airy rooms, all with sea view, private bathroom and breakfast included. ❹–❺

Eating, drinking and nightlife

For **eating** out, the two seafood restaurants *Costa Azul* and *Jixsy* opposite each other at the beach are dependable options, or try *Brisas del Mar* walking south along the beachfront. For international cuisine, go to *Shamrock* owned by a friendly Irish guy, to get your fill of Mexican, Italian, Chinese and fast food. There's a sports bar downstairs with cocktails from $2.50. Canoa is quiet for **nightlife** during the week but at the weekends things get going at *Coco's Bar* on the main street.

BAHÍA DE CARÁQUEZ AND AROUND

The most dramatic location of Ecuador's coastal resorts, Bahía de Caráquez sits on a slim sand peninsula jutting out from the mouth of the river Chone into the Pacific Ocean. The city, known simply as Bahía to locals, also has a troubled history, having endured two disasters in the late 1990s. The 1998 El Niño rains washed away roads and triggered massive landslides before an earthquake in August of the same year destroyed more than two hundred buildings and left twenty people dead. But the city recovered and introduced a wide-ranging environmental programme, converting itself into an 'eco-city' with recycling, sustainable development and reforestation. The result is that, unlike many of Ecuador's resorts, which have well-kept Malecóns backed by dirty, shabby streets, Bahía is comparatively clean and a pleasant place to stroll around.

The **Museo Bahía de Caráquez** (Tues–Sat 10am–5pm, Sun 11am–3pm; $1) has a small collection of pre-Columbian artefacts, and the **Mirador La Cruz,** a large cross above the south end of town, offers good views over the city and surrounding bay. Some 15km south of town is the **Chirije archeological site,** which has countless ancient artefacts such as ceramics and burial sites dating from 500 BC. The site can be visited through Bahía Dolphin Tours (Bolívar 100405/2692097). Inland from Bahía, the river Chone has some excellent unspoilt mangroves which are inhabited by abundant birdlife, including a colony of frigate birds to rival those found in the Galápagos. A half-day tour with Guacamayo Bahiatours (Bolívar 902, ⓣ05/269-1412) costs $25 per person.

Arrival and information

Buses arrive and leave from the south end of Malecón. There are regular services to Portoviejo, Manta and Guayaquil and 4 per day to Quito (or travel via Pedernales). It's a short walk to the passenger ferry dock, which has regular **boats** speeding across the bay to San Vicente, from where you can continue north up the coast. There are plenty of **tricycle taxis** to get around town (most fares $0.50–$1).

Accommodation and eating

Accommodation fills up quickly during high season (Dec–April) and on national vacations. At the budget end, try *Bahía Bed and Breakfast* (ⓣ05/269-0146, Ascazubi 322; ❷–❸) overlooking the passenger ferry dock. For something smarter, head to the northwest of town. La Herradura (ⓣ05/269-0446, Bolívar 202; ❹–❺) has comfortable rooms in a charming old Spanish house and a good restaurant attached. *Hotel La Piedra* (ⓣ05/269-0780, Av Circunvalación Virgilio Ratti; ❼) has large rooms, a pool and spectacular ocean views.

The best **places to eat** tend to be near the docks. Try the string of cheap restaurants on the pier near the ferry dock. Other Malecón options include *El Capitán*, *La Chozita* or *Puerto Amistad* for something more upscale.

MANTA

Manta is a thriving commercial centre and Ecuador's second largest port after Guayaquil. The city is also used as an American air base which, while bringing further riches into the town, has also been blamed for drawing Ecuador into the drug war with Colombia. At the time of writing President Rafael Correa has controversially vowed to close the base. Although Manta is a popular resort with locals, it doesn't have a huge amount to offer foreign tourists. There are better beaches elsewhere and the areas of the city with budget accommodation are **dangerous** at night. You're better off heading south to Machalilla National Park or north to Bahía de Caráquez and Canoa. The main beach **Playa Murciélago**, north of the centre, is the city's main beach, packed with restaurants and snack bars along the Malecón Escénico. Note the beach can be dangerous for swimming with a strong undertow. To the east of town past the fishing boat harbour is **Playa Tarqui**, with calmer waters but it's a run-down and dangerous area.

Arrival and information

The **bus** station in front of the fishing boat harbour on C 7 and Av 8 has regular services to Bahía de Caráquez, Portoviejo, Puerto López, Montañita as well as hourly departures to Guayaquil and Quito and occasional services up the coast to Esmeraldas.

Accommodation, eating and nightlife

For **accommodation**, you are stuck between overpriced hotels in the northwest district and cheaper options in the rundown Tarqui district. In Tarqui, a good budget option is *Hotel El Inca* (Ⓣ05/262-0440,Calle 105 y Malecón de Tarqui; ❹).
For more comfort, try *Hotel Las Gaviotas* (Ⓣ05/262-0140, Malecón de Tarqui 1109; ❻) with hot water, a/c, phones and a pool. There are plenty of cheap seafood **restaurants** on the beaches and the best Chinese is at *Hotel Lun Fun* (Ⓣ05/262-2966, C 2; doubles $67 including breakfast). For **nightlife**, head inland from Playa Murciélago to Flavio Reyes street, which is lined with bars and discos.

Guayaquil

Ecuador's coast feels like a separate country compared to the sierra and, with regionalist feelings burning strongly, many *costeños* wish it was. While Quito is Ecuador's cultural capital, **Guayaquil** is the country's largest city and its economic powerhouse, handling most of Ecuador's imports and exports. Previously there was little to attract tourists to Guayaquil and the heat, dirt and danger were reasons enough to stay away. But the city has undergone quite a facelift in the past decade and the waterfront and city centre have enough to keep visitors occupied for a couple of days.

For those arriving from the mountains, the contrast is striking between Quito's cool colonial charms and Guayaquil's hot, humid, vivacity. *Guayaquileños* (or *Guayacos*) are fiercely proud of their city and finally they have a centre that is worth showing off. In the past decade, successive mayors León Febrés Cordero and the hugely popular incumbent Jaime Nebot have brought about an impressive transformation. Guayaquil's 3km-long **Malecón** and the renovated artistic district of **Las Peñas** are great achievements. Add to this a reorganised public transport system, a new airport, new museums and policed pedestrianised zones, it's no wonder that Guayaquil has won a United Nations award for development. But be aware that the **heat,**

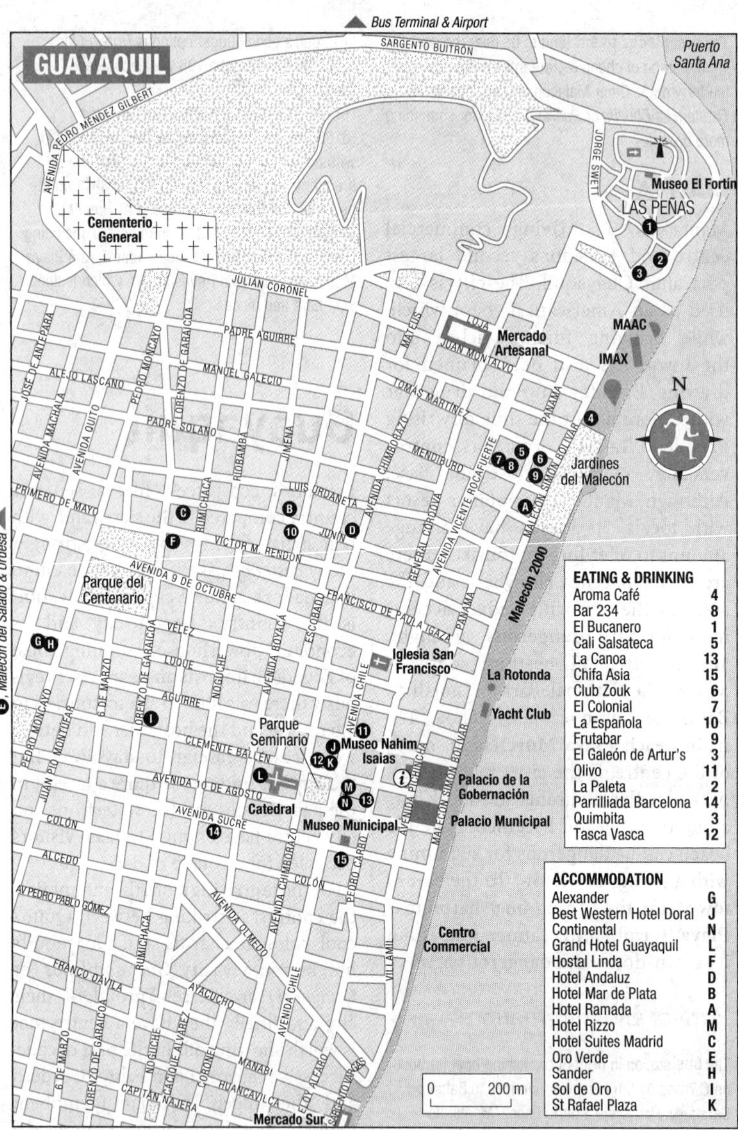

as well as pollution from heavy traffic, can make sightseeing an uncomfortable experience. Weekends are the best time to explore when most of the citizens seem to head for the beach. Outside the centre, Guayaquil is far from picturesque and the city remains dangerous in places, particularly at night.

Malecón

To anyone who knew Guayaquil's dirty, depressing waterfront ten years ago, Malecón 2000 (or Malecón Bolívar) is an extraordinary achievement. The multimillion-dollar project was begun by Mayor León Febrés Cordero in the late 1990s and continued by his successor Jaime Nebot. This 3km public space is easily the highlight of the city – enclosed, pedestrianised and patrolled by security guards so safety is not a problem.

La Plaza Cívica

The best point to enter Malecón is **La Plaza Cívica** at the end of 9 de Octubre. Here you're greeted by the impressive sight of **La Rotonda**, a statue of South America's liberators, José de San Martín and Simón Bolívar, shaking hands in front of a semi-circle of marble columns. The monument is stunning when lit up at night and it's fun for two people to whisper into the pillars at opposite ends and hear the voices carry.

Walking south from La Rotonda, you'll pass four towers dedicated to the four elements, which are also lookout towers. Past the plush Guayaquil Yacht Club is the 23-metre Moorish Clock Tower, constructed in 1931. Just south of the Clock Tower, the *Henry Morgan* is docked, a replica of a seventeenth-century pirate ship. A one-hour trip on the river costs $5 (afternoons and evenings only, late-night trips at weekends). Beyond this is a series of blandly commercial shopping malls with cut-price clothing stores, which are an ideal place to escape the heat and gaze out on the river over a coffee and *humita*. On the other side is an outdoor food court with a series of good-quality, cheap restaurants offering fast food, traditional Ecuadorian specialities and great seafood (lunches $2–5).

Plaza Olmedo

Keep walking to reach Plaza Olmedo, with its contemplative monument of José Joaquín de Olmedo (1780–1847), the first mayor of Guayaquil and a key figure in the struggle for independence. The southern end of Malecón reaches La Plaza de la Integración with the transparent glass and iron structure of the Mercado Sur and an artesans' market, smaller than its counterpart at the north end. From here you can cross the road and enter the bustling Bahía black market.

Botanical gardens

Walking north from La Rotonda you come to a large children's play area, packed with families at weekends. Further on is a stunning set of botanical gardens with more than three hundred species of coastal vegetation. The gardens are divided into four zones: ornamental trees, humid forest, palms and coniferous. There are two plazas: the Precolumbian Plaza, with Manteña balsa wood and palm trees, and the Neoclassic Plaza, with its bronze fountain and marble floor surrounded by lanterns. Pick your way through verdant vegetation and young lovers seeking solitude in the shade to emerge at the lagoon. Above the gardens is a set of 32 transparent panels with the names of some 48,000 citizens who contributed to the Malecón project.

Museo Guayaquil en La Historia

At the north end of Malecón is a new IMAX theatre, the first of its kind in South America and the best place in the city to watch movies with a 180-degree screen. Below the cinema is Museo Guayaquil en La Historia (open 10am–6.30pm daily; $2.50), which condenses a compact history of the city, from pre-history through to the present day, into 14 dioramas. Unlike many of the city's museums, the entire tour is available in English.

Museo Antropológico y de Arte Contemporáneo

The north end of Malecón culminates in the spacious new Museo Antropológico y de Arte Contemporáneo (MAAC) (Ⓦwww.museomaac.com Tues–Sat 10am–6pm, Sun 10am–4pm; $1.50, Sun free), which has an exhibition on "10,000 years of ancient Ecuador" as well as an enormous collection of pre-Columbian ceramics and an extensive modern art exhibition. A couple of blocks inland along Calle Loja is the huge, enclosed Mercado Artesanal, which has a wide selection of traditional handicrafts and indigenous clothing. Prices are slightly higher than in the Sierra and of course haggling is obligatory.

Malecón del Salado

At the opposite end of 9 de Octubre (a 20-minute walk or short taxi ride), is the recently completed **Malecón del Salado**, next to the Estero Salado, a tributary of the river Guayas. Citizens used to bathe here in the nineteenth century and while the river is too dirty nowadays, the green banks make this a picturesque place for a stroll. Walk onto the bridges, which tower over 9 de Octubre, for great views of the river, take a boat trip or simply relax in one of the riverside seafood restaurants.

LAS PEÑAS

Rising above the north end of Malecón is the colourful artistic district of **Las Peñas**. This formerly dangerous, rundown area has been completely revamped and now foreign and locals flock here to enjoy the atmosphere, especially at weekends. Up to the right is the historic, cobbled street of Numa Pompillo Llona, named after the *Guayaco* who wrote Ecuador's rousing national anthem. There are several galleries as well as the Asociación Cultural Las Peñas (10am–4pm daily).

The street leads from old to new, reaching **Puerto Santa Ana**, the city's latest grand project. At the time of writing it was incomplete but is planned to be an extensive marina with waterfront shops, restaurants and luxury apartments, due to be completed by 2012.

Cerro Santa Ana

For spectacular views of Guayaquil and the surrounding area, climb the 444 steps up Las Peñas to **Cerro Santa Ana**. Due to the heat, the walk is best done in the early morning or late afternoon. En route, there's a wide selection of craft shops, restaurants, cafes and bars. At the top of the hill in the Plaza de Honores is a new colonial-style chapel and the **Lighthouse** (admission free) based on Guayaquil's first, built in 1841. There's also the open-air **Museo El Fortín del Santa Ana,** which holds the foundations of the Fortress of San Carlos. The fortress, which defended the city from pirates, has the original cannons and replicas of Spanish galleons. But the highlight is the sweeping panoramic view – to the north lies the intersection of the rivers Daule and Babahoyo with the Guayas and to the south downtown Guayaquil and, across the river, the protected reserve of Santay Island.

Parque Seminario and the Catedral

Three blocks behind the grand Palacio Municipal is the small Parque Seminario, also known as Parque Bolívar or, more aptly, Parque de las Iguanas. This is the city's most beautiful park, where you can enjoy the unique experience of observing dozens of urban iguanas which descend from the trees to rest in the sun. The iguanas are unconcerned by people, but don't attempt to touch them. There's also a small pool filled with turtles. At the centre of the park is an imposing monument of liberator Simón Bolívar on horseback. The huge white Neo-Gothic **Catedral** towers over the west side of the square. Originally dating from 1547, it has been destroyed by fire several times and was reconstructed in 1948.

Museo Municipal

One block southwest from the park is the **Museo Municipal** (Sucre and Chile, Tues–Sat 9am–5pm; free). This is the oldest museum in Ecuador and still the city's best. The Pre-Hispanic room has fossils, including the tooth of a mastodon, dating back ten thousand years, as well as sculptures from Ecuador's oldest known civilization the Valdivia and a huge Manteña funeral urn. Other highlights include a model of colonial Guayaquil and original cannons and muskets from the colonial era. Upstairs is a room of portraits of Ecuadorian presidents, nicknamed "room of thieves" by more cynical citizens, plus a small exhibition of contemporary art. There are five shrunken heads on display in a closed room upstairs, which can only be viewed on a guided tour. Free tours in English are regularly available and recommended because the museum has no English information otherwise.

Parque Histórico Guayaquil

Situated across the bridge in the wealthy district of Entre Rios, the **Parque Histórico** (Wed–Sun 9am–4.30pm; $3 or $4.50 Sun; ⓦwww.parquehistorico.com) is well worth the trip out of town. The park is divided into three zones. Created out of the natural mangroves on the banks of the Daule, the **wildlife zone** provides a snapshot of the Ecuadorian jungle with deer, tapir, monkeys, sloths, ocelotes, tortoises, parrots, toucans and caimans. The smells of the jungle are even recreated with fermenting termite mounds. The **traditions zone** depicts the rural way of life with *haciendas*, "peasant" houses, crops of cacao, banana, coffee and rice. At weekends, boisterous shows entertain with music and comedy. In the **urban architecture zone** some of Guayaquil's late nineteenth-century buildings have been reproduced including the house of renowned local doctor Julián Coronel and la Capilla del Hospicio del Corazón de Jesús, a nineteenth-century church, rebuilt with original wood and stained-glass windows. The colonial-styled *Café 1900* is the perfect place to relax and gaze out over the river. There are occasional buses to Entre Ríos from the bus terminal but it's probably easier to get a taxi from downtown ($4–5).

Arrival and information

By bus Arriving in Guayaquil is a more pleasant experience than it used to be. The citizens are justifiably proud of the brand-new bus terminal, about 6km north of downtown, with its food courts and spacious shopping malls.

By air Guayaquil's award-winning new José Joaquín de Olmedo airport is Ecuador's only other international airport outside Quito, about 5km north of downtown. There are regular flights to and from Quito with Tame and Icaro (see listings p.667) as well as the Galápagos, Cuenca and Loja. The airport is well-served with money changers and ATM machines.

Metrovia ($0.25, ⓣ04/214-0453). You could take a chance with the hordes of ramshackle public buses but it's better to use the new Metrovia modelled on Quito's system. It runs from Terminal Rio Daule opposite the bus station through downtown to the south. Get off at La Catedral stop for the main tourist sights downtown.

Taxis There are plenty of taxis but none of them uses a meter so negotiate the price first. You should pay $3–4 to the centre from the terminal and $4–5 from the airport. Avoid unmarked cabs. Short taxi rides around donwtown should cost about $2, negotiated in advance.

Tourist information The Dirección Municipal de Turismo office at Pedro Icaza 203 (Mon–Fri 9am–5pm; ⓣ04/259 9100, ⓦwww.visitaguayaquil.com) has friendly staff and up-to-date maps and brochures.

Accommodation

Guayaquil has plenty of hotels but is still not well geared up for the backpacker market. Many of the budget hotels are of a very poor standard in unappealing areas, while the top-end hotels charge very high rates for foreigners. It's best to stay near to **Parque Bolivar** or **Parque Centenario**. The centre can get very noisy so consider asking for a back room or a higher floor. It doesn't really make sense to stay in the suburbs because there are few tourist sights.

Hotel Andaluz Baquerizo Moreno y Junín ⓣ04/230-5796. Bright, breezy hotel with comfortable well-presented rooms, artwork and a lounge area with leather sofas. ❺

Hostal Linda Lorenzo de Garaicoa 809 ⓣ04/256-2495. Brand-new hotel overlooking Parque Centenario with marble floors and plush, newly-furnished rooms. ❺

Hotel Mar de Plata Junín 718 y Boyacá ⓣ04/230-7610. Many of Guayaquil's budget hotels border on intolerable but this is a good deal with basic but clean rooms equipped with a/c, cable TV and private bathrooms. ❹

Hotel Oro Verde 9 de Octubre y García Moreno ⓣ04/232-7999. The city's best hotel with 250 rooms, gym, sauna, pool, casino and three top-notch restaurants. ❾

Hotel Plaza St Rafael Chile 414 ⓣ04/232-7140. Smallish but comfortable rooms with a/c, cable TV and hot water, next to Parque Bolívar. ❺

Hotel Ramada Malecón ⓣ04/256-5555. Enjoy great views of the waterfront and some pampering in the pool, sauna and steam room of this upmarket hotel. ❾

Hotel Rizzo Clemente Ballén y Chile ⓣ04/232-5210. Well-appointed rooms, some with small balconies, ideally situated next to Parque Bolívar. ❺

Hotel Suites Madrid Quisquis ⓣ04/230-7804. Not the best location but certainly the best-value mid-range hotel in the city with colourful decor, patterned bedspreads, spacious rooms, a feast of artwork covering the walls and friendly service. ❺

Eating

Guayaquil has a wide range of restaurants spread around the city. Downtown, most places are either cheap and very basic, serving *almuerzos* and *meriendas* for $1.50–2, or else attached to hotels and rather overpriced. **Las Peñas** is the most pleasant area to eat close to the centre with a cluster of endearing traditional eateries. An alternative is to take a taxi ($2–3) up to the fashionable neighbourhood of **Urdesa**, where there is a wide range of restaurants along the main street Victor Emilio Estrada.

Aroma Café Jardines del Malecón 2000. The best place to eat on Malecón with a wide selection of Ecuadorian specialities served in the cool, shaded atmosphere of the botanical gardens. Mains $5–8.

Frutabar Malecón y Martinez. Surfboards, tropical murals and a huge selection of *batidos* (fruit shakes) make this the perfect repose after a hard morning's sightseeing.

La Española Junín y Boyaca. Excellent bakery with a wide selection of delicious cakes, pastries, sandwiches and big breakfasts.

La Fondue Hotel Oro Verde, 9 de Octubre and García Moreno. The Ideal place to blow your budget with sumptuous Swiss fondues cooked to perfection. Mains $13–20.

El Hornero Estrada 906, Urdesa. Delicious pizzas baked in a large clay oven. Portions from $2.

Manantial Estrada 520, Urdesa. Large, popular café with benches, serving a wide range of Ecuadorian specialities and pitchers of beer.

La Parillada del ñato Estrada and Laureles, Urdesa. Treat yourself to a huge plate of barbecued meats in this enormously popular Urdesa institution.

Tasca Vasca Ballén 422 Parque Bolívar. Beautifully laid-out Spanish restaurant in a cosy cellar-like ambience with waiters wearing traditional dress. Choose from a large menu of tapas and Spanish specialities. Mains $6–10.

Nightlife

Guayaquileños love to party so it's no surprise that the city has great nightlife to rival Quito. **Las Peñas** has a wide selection of café-bars and Urdesa is also a good place for a few drinks after dinner. To hit the dancefloor, go to the **Zona Rosa**, between downtown and Las Peñas, centred around Rocafuerte and Pánama. Most discos open at 10pm and close around 4am. There is usually a minimum consumption charge of $10, which includes entrance.

Bar 234 Imbabura y Rocafuerte, Zona Rosa. If you've had enough of reggeton, head to this popular rock bar.

El Bucanero La Escalinata, Las Peñas. Just one of many welcoming, traditional bars mid-way up the steps to Cerro Santa Ana. It gets raucous later on.

El Colonial Rocafuerte y Imbabura, Zona Rosa. A traditional *Peñas* bar with Ecuadorian specialities and live music at weekends.

Cali Salsateca Pánama y Imbabura, Zona Rosa. Dance the night away to the best salsa and merengue in this loud steamy club.

Chappus Estrada, Urdesa. A Guayaquil institution. Have a few drinks on the wooden balcony or hit the dancefloor – one of the few in Urdesa.

El Galeón de Artur's La Escalinata, Las Peñas. With its maritime decor and live music at weekends, this is a good place for a drink and a light meal.

El Jardín de Salsa Av Las Américas (near the airport). Swivel those hips or just stand back and watch the experts on one of the biggest dancefloors in Ecuador.

Liverpool Av Las Monjas 402, Urdesa. Bright, vibrant café-bar packed with Beatles memorabilia. Live music Tues–Sat.

La Paleta Numa Pompillo Llona, Las Peñas. One of the city's most aesthetically pleasing watering holes with a Bohemian atmosphere, cosy nooks and crannies and bars on two floors.

Quimbita Galeria La Escalinata, Las Peñas. At the bottom of the steps, this art gallery doubles as a café-bar and is a relaxing place to start the evening with live folk music at weekends.

Zouk Pánama and Imbabura, Zona Rosa. Loud disco playing mainly reggeton and electronic latin music.

Directory

Airlines American Airlines, Edificio San Francisco 300, Córdova 1021 and 9 de Octubre ⓣ04/256-4111; airport ⓣ04/228-2082; Continental, Edificio Banco La Previsora, 9 de Octubre 100 and Malecón ⓣ04/256-7241; airport ⓣ04/228-7311; Copa, 9 de Octubre and Malecón, Edificio Banco La Previsora ⓣ04/230-3227, airport ⓣ04/228-6336; Iberia, 9 de Octubre 101 and Malecón ⓣ04/232-9558; airport ⓣ04/228-4151; Icaro, Av 10 de Agosto y Malecón ⓣ04/251-0070, airport ⓣ04/390-5060; KLM, airport ⓣ04/216-9070; Tame, Edificio Gran Pasaje, 9 de Octubre 424 ⓣ04/2310-305; airport ⓣ04/228-2062.
Banks and exchange The most convenient downtown banks are Banco del Pacífico on Pedro Carbo and Icaza, and on 9 de Octubre and Ejército; Banco de Guayaquil is on Rendón and Pánama.
Consulates Australia, San Roque and Av Francisco de Orellana, Ciudadela Kennedy Norte ⓣ04/268-0823; Canada, Edificio Nobis Executive Centre, 702 Av Joaquin Orranita y Av Juan Tanca Marengo ⓣ04/256-3580; UK, General Córdova 623 and Padre Solano ⓣ04/256-0400; US, 9 de Octubre and García Moreno ⓣ04/232-3570.
Hospital Clínica Kennedy on Av del Periodista, Kennedy 04/228-6963.
Post office The main office is on Pedro Carbo and Ballén, just off the Parque Bolívar.
Telephone office There are Pacifictel offices all over the city.
Travel agents Carlson Wagonlit Travel, 4th floor, Edificio El Fortín, Padre Aguirre 104 and Malecón ⓣ04/231-1800; Ecoventura ⓣ04/220-7177, Miraflores Av Central 300A, ⓦwww.ecoventura.com; Metropolitan Touring, Artarazana Calle 11A NE103 ⓣ04/228-6565, ⓦwww.metropolitan-touring.com.

The south coast beaches

At weekends, *Guayacos* flee the city's heat in droves and head west to the cooler Pacific beaches of the self-styled **Ruta del Sol**. It gets very crowded on the roads and on the most popular beaches in the peak season between Christmas and Easter, when the weather is hottest. In low season (May–Nov), it's cooler and quieter, verging on depressing at times. Along the E-40 highway **Playas** is the closest significant resort to Guayaquil. It's a shabby little place but very popular with locals for day-trips.

In the newly-created province of **Santa Elena**, the beach resort of Salinas is the playground of wealthy *Guayacos*. It has a beautiful waterfront but is overpriced and unpleasantly crowded in high season. Backpackers tend to go north to the hippy surfer hangout of **Montañita**, whose laidback vibes and beach parties tempt many to stay for weeks.

Further north is the beautiful province of Manabí which contains Ecuador's only protected coastal area, **Parque Nacional Machalilla**. The backdrop of dense, tropical dry forest makes this arguably the country's most beautiful stretch of coastline. The port of Puerto López is the most convenient base to explore the park as well as Isla de la Plata, billed as the "poor man's Galápagos" because of its abundant birdlife, including frigates, boobies and pelicans. **Whalewatching** is another highlight between June and September.

SALINAS

Most budget travellers head to Montañita and avoid overpriced Salinas, the resort preferred by affluent *Guayacos*. On arrival, it looks like a wannabe Miami Beach with high-rise apartment blocks and expensive yachts in the harbour. But it's worth stopping here, at least for a day-trip, to walk along the attractive waterfront and swim in the calm waters. The resort has plenty of great restaurants and nightlife if you want to party with rich kids. West of the Malecón is a second beach, **Chipipe**, quieter and more pleasant with a plaza, church and park. For the big kids, there's a new water park with slides and pools (adults $6).

Arrival

CLP **buses** run regularly from Guayaquil ($3.30, every 30min) and have improved dramatically in quality recently, many equipped with a/c, TV and seatbelts. Change at Santa Elena for Montañita. Leaving Salinas is a bit more complicated. Get a bus from Calle Enriquez (one block in from the front) to Libertad ($0.25) and buses run to Guayaquil and Montañita ($1.50) from there.

Accommodation

Remember to always book **hotels** ahead in high season, particularly at weekends and on national holidays, because Salinas gets extremely busy. Hotels on the waterfront come at a premium, while inland from the waterfront, Salinas is surprisingly ugly.

Cocos Malecón y Fidón Tomala, ☎04/277-2609. The most economical of the options on the waterfront with sea views, a restaurant, bar, disco and games room. ❺

Hostal Las Palmeras Enriquez Gallo and Rumiñahui ☎04/277-0031. This hotel offers the best value with decent rooms but a rather uninspiring view. ❺

Hotel Francisco Enríquez and Rumiñahui, ☎04/277-4106. A dependable mid-range option with a/c rooms and a small pool. ❻

Oro del Mar ☎04/277-1334. Budget travellers will find this the most economical choice, but like most of the cheap accommodation in Salinas, it's a bit shabby. ❹

Eating

You're spoilt for choice on where to eat, particularly seafood. Note that you should avoid the seafood stalls, nicknamed "Cevichelandia", on Calle 17 and Enriquez, as sanitation is a problem. Salinas's nightlife hots up at weekends, particularly in high season when you can take your pick from a cluster of discos on the waterfront.

Amazon Malecón ☎277-3671. A wide variety of international cuisine in a rustic ambience. Mains $6–10.

Holmurguesa (☎277-1868). Great value homemade burgers for just $2.

Oh Mar Malecón. One of the best places on Malecón to enjoy freshly caught seafood. Mains $5–10.

LA RUTA DEL SOL

Travelling north up the "Ruta del Sol", the barren flat scrubland, which provides a rather depressing backdrop to Salinas and Playas, gives way to the green undulating hills of Cordillera Chongón. The verdant surroundings combined with excellent surfing conditions have made this region very popular. However, owing to the often dangerous tides further north, it's worth stopping on the way at some of the calmer stretches. **Punta Blanca** and **Punta 7** are two great beaches for swimming, just past Ballenita, a five-minute walk from the highway. The sheltered bay of **Ayangue** is another option, although it's a longer 2km walk from the highway. Check out the spectacular views from the *Cumbres de Ayangue* hotel, perched on the rocks above the town, although staying there is very overpriced for what you get (☎04/291-6040; $60).

MANGLARALTO AND DOS MANGAS

Just south of Montañita is the little fishing village of Manglaralto. The pace is very slow and in low season it's almost deserted. The sea is too dangerous for swimming but the *estero* where the river Manglaralto flows into the Pacific is a safe bathing place. There are only three decent hotels in the town – *Hostal Manglaralto* (☎04/290-1369, $10) which offers comfortable rooms some with a sea view; the slightly cheaper *Sunset Hostel* (☎04/244-0797, $8) has hammocks but an uninspiring view; *Kamala Hostería* (☎04/242-3754; from $5 per person) is the most interesting option and popular with travellers with a selection of individual cabins set on the beach. There's a bar, restaurant, swimming pool and dive school. A few kilometres from Manglaralto, **Dos Mangas** is the best base to explore the beautiful green hills of the Cordillera Chongón. Trucks from the main coast road head to Dos Mangas every hour ($0.25) and from there you can hire guides and horses. The park entrance fee is $1.

MONTAÑITA

You'll probably either love or hate Montañita. The core surfing contingent has been joined in recent years by hippies and partygoers, making it the coast's most happening resort for budget travellers. Many people like it so much they stay for months, while others get out after a couple of excessive nights. If you like to party all night, this is the place to be, but if you're seeking a relaxing beach break, then go elsewhere. Surfers can enjoy rideable breaks most of the year, frequently 2–3m on good days. It's not the best place to learn but there are plenty of experienced teachers. There's a renowned international surf competition around Carnival (Feb/March). Sweet Surf on the main street offers surfboard rentals for $15 per day ($4 per hr) and two-hour lessons for $12. There are also tours available, ranging from day-trips to a week-long surf tour of the coast.

Arrival

Comfortable CLP **buses** leave Guayaquil at 5am, 1pm and 5pm ($5, 4hr). If you can't catch one of these, there are several buses to Salinas every hour. Ask the driver to drop you at Santa Elena to catch a connection (daytime only).

Accommodation

Montañita has a huge amount of accommodation and where you stay depends mainly on how much sleep you want to get. It seems that almost every building in town has a restaurant, bar or shop downstairs and rooms for rent upstairs but quality is decidedly variable. The centre is very noisy and at weekends the partying continues until after dawn. The south end of town is cheapest while the north end is quieter with the best quality mid-range accommodation.

Casa del Sol ⓣ04/290-1302, ⓦwww.casasol.com. Further north towards the point is this laidback surfer hangout with charming rooms, a great restaurant and bar area. ❹

El Centro de Mundo ⓣ0972/82831. Look no further for cheap, basic rooms in this three-storey, wooden beachfront building. ❷

Charos Malecón entre 15 de Mayo y Rocafuerte, ⓣ04/206-0044, ⓦwww.charoshostal.com. Right on the beachfront with more comfortable rooms, a bar, restaurant and a small pool. ❺

Hostal South Point 15 de Mayo, ⓣ04/206-0020. At the south end is this rustic wooden hostal that wouldn't be out of place in the jungle with basic rooms but a friendly atmosphere. ❹

Paradise South ⓣ04/290-1185, ⓦwww.paradisesouthec.com. For something quieter and more upmarket, go north of town to enjoy the comfortable thatched cottages and large lawns of this tranquil, welcoming place. ❸

Tiki Limbo ⓣ04/254-0607, 09/367-7086; ⓦwww.tikilimbo.com. This backpackers' favourite has a vibrant atmosphere, bright colours, bamboo beds and an imaginative restaurant serving Asian and vegetarian food. ❸

Eating and drinking

There are scores of good restaurants in the centre of town but bear in mind that service can be slow in busy periods so bring a book and patience. Montañita throws quite a party at weekends, particularly in high season (Dec–April). Most bars on the main street offer two-for-one happy hours on cocktails ($3) but take it slow until things get going towards midnight.

Cañagrill. This is the town's busiest disco with two dancefloors playing a mix of electronic and latin music. It gets packed in the early hours and the partying continues until after dawn (entrance $5 at weekends).

The Funky Monkey As the name suggests, this is a fun bar to start the evening and watch the Montañita nightlife get going.

Hola Ola Big breakfasts in the morning and a wide range of cocktails in the evening – what more could you want?

Karukera A good option for breakfast with a wide selection of crêpes.

Machu Picchu For something different, this place specialises in Peruvian food and also does good seafood. Mains $6–10.

OLÓN

This tranquil village on the other side of the point is beginning to develop as a quiet alternative to Montañita with a long beach and a few good hotels and restaurants. The sea is not really surfable but just about swimmable. Stay at *Quimbita* (ⓣ04/278-0204, $12), a charming, colourful hotel with a permanent art exhibition by the owner. *Hostería N&J* (☎04/239-0643; $25 with breakfast) on the beachfront is another friendly place. Enjoy seafood specialities at one of the wooden huts at the beach ($3–4).

PUERTO LÓPEZ AND AROUND

Heading north from Montañita, cross into the province of Manabí. This is probably the most beautiful stretch of Ecuador's coastline so if you prefer peace to partying and wildlife watching to people watching, this is the place to come. Pass a succession of fishing villages – Ayampe, Las Tunas, Puerto Rico (see below) and Salango – on the way to the hub of Puerto López, which has a beautiful beach set in a sheltered bay surrounded by green hills. The Malecón is pleasant enough with a selection of appealing restaurants and tiny beach bars but the rest of town is rather rough round the edges with dusty streets, abandoned buildings and stray dogs. Tourism has been slower to develop here than in other resorts, which is why some people prefer it. For most visitors, Puerto López is not a destination in itself but the best base from which to explore **Parque Nacional Machalilla** and **Isla de la Plata**.

Arrival

Buses to Puerto López run along the coast road to La Libertad in the south (every 30min, 3hr) and Manta in the north (hourly, 2hr), as well as north to Jipijapa inland (every 30min, 1hr 30min) which is the best route to Guayaquil. Reina del Camino (☎05/230-0207) offers comfortable secure services to and from Quito at 8am and 8pm ($12, 10hr). Buses drop passengers on the main road, General Córdova, by the church from where it's a short walk to the waterfront or you can take a tricicycle taxi for $0.50 or mototaxi for longer journeys.

Accommodation

Puerto López has plenty of cheap and mid-range accommodation though quality is variable.

Sol Inn Juan Montalvo y Eloy Alfaro, ☎05/230-0248. The basic, wooden cabins and the laidback vibe are ideal for those on a tight budget.

Hostal Isla los Islotes (Malecón y General Córdoba, ☎05/230-0108; $20). A good mid-range choice on the Malecón, with well-presented rooms, hot water and cable TV. ❸

Hotel Pacifico ☎05/262-6250. Further along the Malecón, this upmarket hotel has a beautiful recreation area with swimming pool. Seaviews and a/c extra. ❹

Hosteria Mandala ☎05/230-0181. North of town is this very popular travellers' option with beachfront cabins set in beautiful gardens, plus a games room, small library and a good restaurant. ❺

Eating

Restaurant Carmita Stands out from the cluster of restaurants along the Malecón with a great selection of seafood in a polished setting. Mains from $5.

Spondylus Further up, this is a cheaper option, although avoid eating the oyster which gave the restaurant its name because it's endangered. Mains $2–3.

Patacón Pisa'o General Córdoba. For something different, try Colombian specialities such as *Arepas* at this friendly little place. Mains $3–5.

SOUTH OF PUERTO LÓPEZ

Although Puerto López is the most popular base to explore Machalilla, some of the smaller villages have excellent accommodation and are just as convenient. Perhaps the best alternative is further south in the village of **Puerto Rico**. A very popular hotel is the unique wooden, boat-shaped *La Barquita* (☎04/278-0051, ⓦwww.labarquita-ec.com; $24). Most of the beach cabins have sea views and private bathroom. *Hostería Alandaluz* (☎04/2780-690, ⓦwww.alandaluzhosteria.com; $28–60) is an award-winning eco-resort with a great location in front of the beach, enclosed by a garden, orchard and bamboo forest. For those on a budget, there are more basic rooms and camping available.

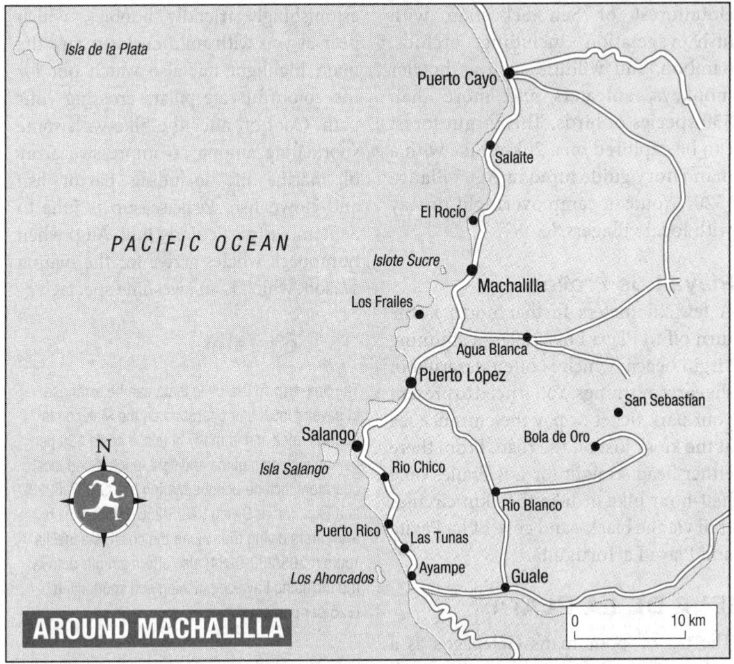

PARQUE NACIONAL MACHALILLA

Ecuador's only coastal national park was set up in 1979 to preserve the rapidly disappearing tropical dry forest which once stretched north all the way to Costa Rica. It's a dramatic setting with thickly forested hills crowned by candelabra cacti, dropping down to pristine, peaceful beaches. The park headquarters (open 8am–5pm) is based in Puerto López, opposite the market, just off the main road running through town. This is where you pay your entrance fee valid for five days. Mainland only is $12, Isla de la Plata only $15 and a combined ticket $20.

What to see and do

The best place to explore the park's dry forest is **Agua Blanca**, a village inhabited by some 280 indigenous people and an important archeological site of the Manteño culture that lived here from 800 to 1500 AD. Getting to Agua Blanca involves either taking a bus north from Puerto López and then walking the unpleasant 5km trail up a dirt track, or hiring a mototaxi for $5 one-way, $10 return. The museum houses an interesting collection of sculptures, funeral urns and, rather bizarrely, pickled snakes. A guided tour ($5) includes museum entry followed by a two-hour walk through the forest. Highlights include the towering Ceibos, Barbasco and the fragrant Palo Santo trees whose wood is burnt as incense and to repel mosquitoes. Take in the spectacular views up to San Sebastián before a refreshing soak in a pungent but relaxing Sulphur pool, considered sacred by the local indigenous people.

San Sebastián

The landscape rises to 800m inland where the dry forest turns into the cloudforest of San Sebastián with lush vegetation including orchids, bamboo, and wildlife such as howler monkeys, anteaters and more than 350 species of birds. This virgin forest can be explored on a 20km hike with a mandatory guide hired in Agua Blanca ($20). You can camp overnight or stay with local villagers.

Playa Los Frailes

A few kilometers further north is the turn off to Playa Los Frailes, a stunning virgin beach, which is often deserted in the early mornings. You'll need to present your park ticket or pay the entrance fee at the kiosk just off the road. From there either head straight for Los Frailes on a half-hour hike or take the 4km circular trail via the black-sand cove of La Payita and Playa La Tortiguita.

ISLA DE LA PLATA

The tag of 'poor man's Galápagos' is a rather unfair comparison for this small island 37km from Puerto López. Don't visit the island as a substitute for the world-famous archipelago as it will inevitably come up short, but Isla de la Plata is worth a day-trip to see its abundant bird life and, in the summer months, the whale-watching is excellent.

The island is home to numerous blue-footed boobies, masked boobies and frigate birds and these are the species most frequently on view. There are also red-footed boobies and waved albatrosses, most commonly seen April to October. The island has a small colony of sealions but it's rare to see them.

What to see and do

From the landing point in Bahía Drake, there are two circular footpaths around the island, the 3.5km Sendero Machete and the 5km Sendero Punta Escaleras. The hikes are about three hours and there's no shade so bring sunscreen and a hat. The close encounters with the astonishingly friendly boobies, which peer at you with mild curiosity, are the main highlight but also watch out for the colourful caterpillars crossing your path. Cool off after the hike with some snorkelling among an impressive array of marine life including parrot fish and clown fish. Peak season is June to September (particularly July–Aug) when humpback whales arrive for the mating season, which is an awesome spectacle.

Tour operators

The **day-trip** to Isla de la Plata can be arranged at several local tour operators on the Malecón in Puerto López and in many hotels. It costs $30 per person including guide and light lunch. Good local operators include Bosque Marino (☎09/337-6223), and Exploramar Diving (☎05/256-3905), which also offers diving trips along the coast. Machalilla Tours (☎05/230-0234) also offers a multi-activity trip including kayaking, fishing and snorkelling ($25 per person).

South of Guayaquil and the Peruvian border

The only significant coastal town between Guayaquil and the Peruvian border is **Machala**, which prides itself on being Ecuador's 'banana capital'. But apart from the commercial World Banana Festival at the end of September, there's not much reason to stop here on the way to Peru, particularly because Guayaquil and Cuenca are both within five hours of the border by bus. But if you need a place to stay, consider *Hotel Inés*, (Juan Montalvo 1509 (☎07/293-2301; $20), or *Oro Hotel*, at Sucre and Juan Montalvo (☎07/293-7569; $35 including breakfast); both have good

CROSSING INTO PERU

Crossing the border is an annoying and fraught business but you need to ensure you do it right, as falling foul of immigration laws in South America could be serious. If you don't get the correct stamps on your passport, you're in big trouble. Keep your wits about you, a close eye on your belongings and try to avoid changing money here as the rates are bad. The border crossing is a bridge over the Río Zarumilla, but before crossing the border you need to get the **exit stamp** from the **Ecuadorian immigration office** (open 24hr, ☎07/299-6755), inconveniently located 3km north. If you're coming along the road from Machala, ask the driver to stop here, otherwise take a taxi ($1.50). From here take a bus or taxi to the bridge, which must be crossed on foot, then get your passport checked by Peruvian officials on the other side. Note that the **entry stamp** is usually obtained at the main **Peruvian immigration office** at **Zarumilla** a couple of kilometres away ($1 by mototaxi). There are regular direct buses to Tumbes, Piura, Trujillo or Lima. A taxi to Tumbes costs $5-7.

quality rooms with air conditioning and cable TV. Good restaurants include the economical *Don Angelo* (9 de Mayo and Rocafuerte) serving filling local dishes or the more upmarket *Mesón Hispano* (Av Las Palmeras and Sucre) with a wide range of meat and seafood dishes cooked in front of you.

HUAQUILLAS

Some 75km south of Machala is the grubby border town of Huaquillas, the most popular crossing point between Ecuador and Peru. Spend the minimum amount of time possible here but if you arrive at night, *Hotel Vanessa* (1 de Mayo 323 and Hualtaco, ☎07/2996263; $22), and the *Grand Hotel Hernancor* next door (☎07/2995467; $22) offer decent rooms with bathroom, air conditioning and cable TV. *La Habana* (T. Córdovez and Santa Rosa), serves cheap seafood and meat, as well as filling breakfasts and lunches.

Arrival and information

For those arriving in Ecuador, **buses** from Huaquillas leave from depots a few blocks from the international bridge. Co-op CIFA (Santa Rosa and Machala) has several buses an hour to Machala ($1.50, 1hr), the closest city. But better to head straight to Guayaquil ($4.50, 4hr 30min) with either CIFA, or more comfortable Ecuatoriano Pullman (T. Córdovez) or Rutas Orenses (R. Gómez). Panamericana (T. Córdovez and Santa Rosa) has six comfortable buses daily to Quito ($10, 12hr). For Cuenca ($5, 5hr) use Trans Azuay, (T. Córdovez and Santa Rosa), which has eight daily buses. If you intend to go to Loja, it's better to cross from Peru at Macará.

The Galápagos Islands

Charles Darwin developed his revolutionary theory of evolution after travelling to the Galápagos in the 1830s, and it's no exaggeration that the wildlife of these enchanting islands has changed the way we human beings view ourselves.

When visiting the Galápagos, you may find yourself wishing we had evolved with eyes in the back of our heads, such is the fabulous array of mammals and marine life on offer. From giant tortoises to marine iguanas, sea lions to sharks and blue-footed boobies to magnificent frigate birds, it's hard to know which way to turn. Unique is an overused word but it certainly applies to these unworldly volcanic islands, some 600 miles west of the Ecuadorian coast.

WHAT IT COSTS

If you decide to go, there's no escaping the fact that the cost of visiting the Galápagos is extremely high. While $2000 will last for months on the Ecuadorian mainland, you won't get much change out of it for a week of the Galápagos on a boat tour. At the time of writing, the government is considering doubling the park entrance fee from $100–200 and even banning tours shorter than eight days, policies intended to push prices up further and deter tourists from visiting.

Nowhere else on earth can you view wild mammals and birds that are utterly unconcerned by human presence, the legacy of there being no natural predators on the islands.

However, human presence has done huge damage to the Galápagos' fragile ecosystem and the islands are no longer the ecological paradise they used to be. High levels of immigration from the Ecuadorian mainland, the introduction of invasive species such as livestock and pets, as well as uncontrolled overfishing have all contributed to the deterioration of the islands. Tourism has been particularly damaging with visitor numbers more than trebling in the past fifteen years to a clearly unsustainable level of over 160,000 in 2007. The Galápagos were placed on the UNESCO Danger List in April 2007 and the government has taken steps to deport illegal immigrants and increased patrols to prevent illegal fishing. But the number of tourists – and the number of larger cruise ships – continues to rise to the point where it is becoming a moral issue whether you should visit the islands at all.

THE ISLANDS

Although there are flights to San Cristóbal, most visitors arrive on the tiny island of Baltra, just north of **Santa Cruz**. This is the Galápagos' most developed island with the archipelago's largest town, **Puerto Ayora**, the tourism hub and starting point for many cruises. Here you can find the widest selection of hotels and restaurants. About 20 minutes' walk east of town is the headquarters of the **Charles Darwin Research Station** (ⓦwww.darwinfoundation.org), which contains an information centre and a museum.

But the highlight is the walk-in **giant tortoise enclosure** where you can meet the Galápagos giants face-to-face. Conservationists have worked to preserve these amazing creatures for more than thirty years and the research station has 11 different sub-species including the famous Lonesome George, the only survivor of the Pinta island sub-species.

Turtle Bay

About 3km southwest of Puerto Ayora is Turtle Bay, with a beautiful beach ideal for swimming and snorkelling. Off the north coast of Santa Cruz is the tiny island of **Seymour Norte**, which offers great opportunities to watch magnificent frigate birds. The males inflate their red chests to the size of a basketball when in search of a mate. There are also the endearingly curious blue-footed boobies. Sea lions and iguanas are commonly seen here too. Off the east coast of Santa Cruz are the two tiny islands of **Plazas**, which are home to a large sea lion colony. There is a 1km trail around the cliffs on South Plaza which offers good views of birdlife including pelicans and frigate birds.

WHEN TO VISIT

The conditions are best between December and April, although this is also high season, particularly Christmas, Carnival and Easter. After May, the weather becomes cooler and the sea rougher, particularly in August and September.

Santa Fé

Southeast of Puerto Ayora, the island of Santa Fé has great snorkelling and opportunities to see white-tipped reef sharks, marine iguanas, sea lions and stingrays. There are trails through a forest of ten-metre-high *Opuntia* cacti where land iguanas are commonly seen.

Isla Santiago

Northwest of Santa Cruz are the blackened lava fields of Isla Santiago, also known as San Salvador. The highlight is the tiny island of **Bartolomé**, just off the east coast which contains the Galápagos' most famous landmark. **Pinnacle Rock** rises 114m above the island and commands spectacular views over two horseshoe shaped beaches and Santiago's Sullivan Bay. There is fantastic snorkelling below and opportunities to see the Galápagos penguins and marine turtles. On the southeastern tip of Santiago, the waters around the volcanic cone of **Sombrero Chino** (Chinese Hat) are also excellent for snorkelling.

Around San Cristóbal

On the eastern side of the archipelago, San Cristóbal is the administrative centre of the islands. **Puerto Baquerizo Moreno** is the capital and beginning to rival Puerto Ayora as a tourism hub. The Centro de Interpretación is an interesting place to learn about the islands' history. Other highlights include El Junco Lagoon, one of the few freshwater lakes in the islands with abundant birdlfe. Isla Lobos off the north coast has the largest sea lion colony in the area.

Isabela

Isabela is by far the largest island in the Galápagos and the most dramatic because of its recent volcanic activity. There are six intermittently active volcanoes, many of which can be explored, including the massive crater of Sierra Negra. Cerro Azul erupted in May 2008 although damage to the island's large population of giant tortoises was limited. Many of the island's best landing sites are on the west side, making them inaccessible to any but the longer tours. Highlights include penguins, flightless cormorants, whales and dolphins.

West of Isabela is the equally volcanic **Fernandina**, the highlight of which is the huge population of marine iguanas sunning themselves on the rocks of Punta Espinoza. There are also trails through the recently formed lava fields.

Floreana

The southern island of Floreana is famous for its Punta Cormorant, an excellent spot for snorkelling and spotting sea lions, turtles and sting rays, and the nearby Devil's Crown, a half-submerged volcanic cone with diverse bird and marine life.

Española

Española is the southernmost island and not on many itineraries but well worth visiting. As well as an abundance of sea lions, iguanas and boobies, there is a waved albatross colony and opportunities to see the rare Hood mockingbird and the finches made famous by Charles Darwin's studies.

Genovesa

The northern island of Genovesa is seldom visited but has fabulous birdlfe including enormous colonies of blue and red-footed boobies, frigate birds and storm petrels.

Arrival and information

Return **flights** to San Cristóbal or Baltra cost about $350 from Guayaquil and $400 from Quito with TAME (Quito ⓣ 02/397-7100, Guayaquil ⓣ 04/231-0305). Icaro and Aerogal also offer flights from Quito and Guayaquil (see listings for each city). Censo holders pay substantially less - about $110–150. For further information about the islands, contact the Galápagos National Park (ⓣ 05/252-6511, ⓦ www.Galápagospark.org).

Getting around

Most people get around on organised boat tours but you can get around independently if you have time on your hands.

By air The small **airline** EMETEBE (Guayaquil ⓣ04/229-2492, Santa Cruz ⓣ05/252-6177, San Cristóbal ⓣ05/252-0615, Isabela ⓣ05/252-9255) flies between San Cristóbal, Baltra and Isabela several times per week. Prices from $100 one-way, $170 return.

By ferry Ingala (ⓣ05/252-6151) operates regular services from Santa Cruz to San Cristobal. There are less frequent services to Isabela and Floreana. Prices from about $50 one way.

By boat There are many levels of boats available to tour the Galápagos, from the small basic vessels to luxury cruise ships. 5-day tours enable you to explore the islands close to Santa Cruz while 8-day tours include islands further afield such as Isabela and Floreana. Single cabin supplements are usually very high. Prices are for f5 days and 8 days based on two sharing. **Economy class** boats cost around $800–1000. Boats have tiny bunk beds, shared bathrooms, uninspiring food and Class 1 guides with a low level of training. **Tourist class** boats cost $900–1200 and are slightly bigger with better facilities and Class 2 guides with a higher level of knowledge and English language skills. **Tourist-superior** boats cost $1200–1500 and have more comfortable cabins, better food and Class 2 guides. **First-class** or **luxury yachts** cost $2000-3000, can travel faster and have a decentlevel of comfort, a/c, high-quality food and Class 3 guides, the highest level of accreditation. The most expensive level are the **luxury cruise ships** which cost over $3000.

Accommodation

If you're on a tight budget or suffer badly from seasickness, it may be preferable to stay in a hotel and book day-trips locally rather than stay on one of the basic, economy boats. You'll avoid seasickness and save money, although the downside is being restricted to day-trips relatively close by. Most of the cheap accommodation is in **Puerto Ayora**, although San Cristóbal also has some cheap hotels. Book in advance in high season. For relatively basic rooms with hot water, fans and TV, try *Hotel Salinas* (Av Bolívar Naveda ⓣ05/252-6107; ❺) or *Lirio del Mar* (Av Bolívar Naveda ⓣ05/252-6212; ❺); *Hotel Sir Francis Drake* (Av Padre Julio Herrera, ⓣ05/252-6221; ❺) has a/c. For more comfortable mid-range rooms, try *Estrella del Mar* (ⓣ05/252-6427; ❼) or *Hotel Ninfa* (ⓣ05/252-6127; ❽), which has a small swimming pool and bar. There are plenty of high-class luxury hotels on the Galápagos charging over $150 per night, but you're better off booking these through an agent.

Tour operators

In Quito Etnotur (Cordero 1313 y JL Mera, ⓣ02/256-4565); Galasam (Amazonas 1354 y Cordero, ⓣ02/250-7079, ⓦwww.galasam.com.ec); Kem Pery Tours (Pinto 539 and Amazonas ⓣ02/2226583, ⓦwww.kempery.com); Metropolitan Touring (Av Amazonas N20-39 near 18 de Septiembre, ⓣ02/250-6650 or 02/298 8200, ⓦwww.metropolitan-touring.com); Ninfa Tour (Av Amazonas n24-66 y J Pinto ⓣ02/222-3124); Nuevo Mundo Expeditions Av Coruña N26-207 and Orellana ⓣ02/2509 431, ⓦwww.nuevomundotravel.com; Parir (General Baquedano near JL Mera, ⓣ02/222-0892); Safari Tours (ⓣ02/255-2505, Foch and Cordero E4-132, ⓦwww.safari.com.ec); Scuba Iguana (Av Amazonas 1004 y Wilson, ⓣ02/290-6666, ⓦwww.scubaiguana.com).

In Guayaquil Centro Viajero (Baquerizo Moreno 1119 y 9 de Octubre, ⓣ04/230-1283); Ecoventura (Miraflores Av Central 300A, ⓣ04/220-7177, ⓦwww.ecoventura.com); Dreamkapture Travel (Alborada 12ª Etapa, Av Benjamin Carrion y Av Francisco de Orellana, ⓣ04/224 2909, ⓦwww.dreamkapture.com); Galápagos Sub-Aqua (Orellana 211 y Panamá, ⓣ04/230-5514); Galasam (9 de Octubre 424, ⓣ04/230 4488, ⓦwww.galasam.com.ec); Metropolitan Touring (Artarazana Calle 11A NE103 ⓣ04/2286-565, ⓦwww.metropolitan-touring.com); Ninfa Tour (Córdova 646 y Urdaneta, ⓣ04/230 0182).

In the Galápagos Galapatour (Av Rodriguez Lara y Genovesa, ⓣ05/252-6088); Metropolitan Touring (Finch Bay Hotel, ⓣ05/252-6297, ⓦwww.metropolitan-touring.com); Moonrise Travel (Av Charles Darwin, ⓣ05/252-6348); We are the Champions Tours (Av Charles Darwin, ⓣ05/252-6951, ⓦwww.wearethechampionstours.com).

The Guianas

HIGHLIGHTS

KAIETEUR FALLS: Stand on the dramatic promontory in front of the world's highest single-drop waterall

GALIBI NATURE RESERVE: visit this important turtle nesting beach and witness hordes of olive ridleys laying their eggs

ILES DU SALUT: spot monkeys and peacocks at these former French prison islands

PLAGES LES HATTES: observe egg-laying leatherback turtles on this easily accessible beach

BROWNSBERG NATURE RESERVE: enjoy a hike and spot wildlife in Suriname's forest-covered interior

RUPUNUNI SAVANNA: feel like a cowboy as you help round up the herd on the Rupununi ranches

ROUGH COSTS

BASIC DAILY BUDGET G: Basic G$8,200; S: S$125; FG: US$100

DRINK G: Banks beer G$220; S: Parbo beer S$10; FG: Ti' Punch US$9.50

FOOD G: G$600; S: *Saoto soep* S$8; FG: Croque-Monsieur US$2.30

HOSTEL/BUDGET HOTEL G: G$5,000/10,000; S: S$60/130; FG: US$47/63

TRAVEL G: Georgetown–Bartica, bus & water taxi (2hr), G$1,200; S: Paramaribo-Albina, taxi (2hr), S$40; FG: Cayenne–Saint-Georges-de-L'Oyapok taxi (2hr), US$32

G = Guyana S = Suriname FG = French Guiana

FACT FILE

POPULATION G: 769,095; S: 470,784; FG: 210,000

AREA G: 214,970 sq km; S: 163,270 sq km; FG: 91,000 sq km

OFFICIAL LANGUAGES G: English; S: Dutch; FG: French

CURRENCY G: Guyanese dollar (G$); S: Suriname dollar (S$); FG: Euro (€)

CAPITAL G: Georgetown; S:Paramaribo; FG: Cayenne

INTERNATIONAL PHONE CODE G: ⓣ592; S: ⓣ597; FG: ⓣ594

TIME ZONE GMT -3hr

Introduction

The GUIANAS, which comprise the independent nations of Guyana and Suriname and the French overseas *département* of French Guiana, are in some ways very un-South American. The official languages in the three countries are English (Guyana), Dutch (Suriname) and French (French Guiana) as opposed to Spanish, the continent's lingua franca, the result of the historical legacy of English, Dutch and French colonizers. This legacy has spawned an ethnically diverse population, with indigenous peoples, descendants of European colonizers and the slaves who manned their plantations, East Indians, Indonesians, Southeast Asian refugees and Haitians present across the region. The region's linguistic and ethnic diversity gives travelling in the Guianas a rather Caribbean feel, especially in the low-lying alluvial plain along the Atlantic Coast where most of the population lives.

Tucked between Brazil's Amazonian region and the continent's northeast coast the Guianas are as lush and verdant a place as you will find in South America. Between eighty and ninety percent of the area is covered by dense tropical forests, and rivers run through it in abundance (indeed, the Indian word *guiana* means "land of water"). Jaguars, pumas, caimans, iguanas, ocelots, tapirs and other diverse wildlife thrive in this environment, making the Guianas an excellent destination on any sort of eco-tourist itinerary you might have – it's not likely to be the cities that lure you here.

With its mostly muddy beaches and murky waters (the result of silt deposits from the mouths of the region's many rivers), the Guianas' main attraction is their stunning interior of **pristine rainforest.** Although eco-tourism in this part of the world does not come cheaply, it's well worth trying to sample the nature either by staying at a **jungle lodge** or taking a **river trip**; you will

WHEN TO VISIT

Temperatures in the Guianas vary little from one country to another and from one month to the next: generally 20°C to 33°C, with a mean temperature of around 26°C (slightly hotter in the interior owing to the absence of the cooling coastal trade winds). This makes deciding when to plan a trip much more dependent on the vagaries of the dry and wet seasons. While the nature is undeniably lush and verdant during the **wet season**, road travel can be extremely difficult (if not impossible) along the many unsealed roads that govern land access to the interior. The big rains fall in French Guiana from mid-April to the end of June and, although drier in comparison, from April or May to around August in Guyana and Suriname. November to January or February can also be wet, but the rains are light compared with the periods mentioned above. Therefore, late winter and early spring are the optimum times for a visit – the more so because this is when the various **carnival** celebrations take place.

have missed the region's finest asset if you don't. Aside from the rainforeSt the greatest natural wonder comes in the form of majestic **Kaieteur Falls**, made all the more dramatic by its isolated location in a tree-covered mountain range in southwestern Guyana. Eco-tourism also holds sway along the coaSt where **Shell Beach** (Guyana), **Galibi Beach** (Suriname) and **Plage Les Hattes** (French Guiana) are three of the best sites in the world to observe various species of sea turtle laying their eggs. Visitors entering Guyana from Brazil should definitely take a day or two to explore the **Rupununi Savanna**: vast tracts of flatlands dotted with cowboy ranches and easy-to-spot wildlife.

While the towns take a backseat to nature in the Guianas, the capital cities, **Georgetown** (Guyana), Paramaribo (Suriname) and Cayenne (French Guiana) are charming, if somewhat dilapidated, architectural gems, worth exploring for a day or two. Of the three, **Paramaribo** is most comfortable and best preserved, while sleepy **Cayenne**, with little in the way of budget accommodation, will probably not detain you long.

Perhaps the most unexpected thing in this land of rivers, trees, and chirping, slithering and screeching creatures is the **Centre Spatial Guyanais** at Kourou in French Guiana, where rocket-launch towers, silos and high-tech machinery help to send satellites into orbit from a clearing in the jungle.

Basics

ARRIVAL

While overland travel between the three countries is relatively straightforward, the Guianas are not the easiest – or the cheapest – region to reach in South America. The main international gateways are Georgetown (Guyana), Paramaribo (Suriname) and Cayenne (French Guiana). See "Arrival" sections of each country for details.

North American travellers will find the widest choice and best deals on flights to Georgetown, and those combining travel to the Guianas with visits to the Caribbean should consider BWIA's Caribbean airpass (US$450), which includes Georgetown among its other destinations. The pass lasts for thirty days; you have to plan your itinerary at the time of booking, start in one of the airline's Caribbean destinations and not visit any place more than once (unless making a connection).

Visitors from Europe will find it easier to get to Suriname and French Guiana. Suriname's national carrier, Surinam Airways or SLM, has four direct flights a week to Paramaribo from Amsterdam, while French Guiana is linked to Paris by two or three flights daily on Air France, either directly or via the other overseas *départements* of Martinique and Guadeloupe.

Within South America, you can fly to the Guianas from Caracas, Venezuela (a useful option given that the border between Guyana and Venezuela is closed owing to a longstanding border dispute between the two countries), and Belém, Brazil. Flights also operate between Georgetown, Paramaribo and Cayenne. BWIA and Surinam Airways are the main carriers.

Travellers arriving overland from Brazil can enter Guyana at the town of Lethem, about 130km northeast of the Brazilian town of Boa Vista, or by crossing the Oyapok River to Saint-Georges-de-l'Oyapok in French Guiana (there is no border crossing between Brazil and Suriname). You can then continue by public transport to Georgetown and Cayenne respectively.

GETTING AROUND

Borders between the Guianas are marked by imposing rivers, and crossing involves taking infrequent ferries. From Guyana to Suriname, cross the Corentyne River from Moleson Creek to South Drain near Nieuw Nickerie (see p.715); from Suriname to French Guiana, you will need to cross the Maroni River from Albina to Saint-Laurent-du-Maroni (see p.735).

For details on negotiating your way around each country, see the relevant "Getting around" section.

ACCOMMODATION

In Guyana and Suriname, accommodation in the main towns will normally consist of hotels and guesthouses, the difference between the two often being ambiguous. The former are generally larger and pricier, while the latter are sometimes in private homes and can be quite basic. No matter how luxurious or lamentable your lodgings, almost all rooms will come equipped with running water, mosquito nets and fans.

There are a number of resorts in Guyana – several of them on islands in the Essequibo River and in the interior not far from Georgetown – and tourist ranches in the Rupununi Savanna. Suriname also has several resorts around Paramaribo, primarily along the Suriname River, and lodges in the nature parks and reserves. Staying at these types of accommodation will usually be on an all-inclusive basis, and bookings are best made through tour operators, who will also arrange transfers; these are tricky if attempted independently.

Accommodation in French Guiana is tailored to business people and package tourists, and somewhat limited in extent and variety. The few budget options are hopeless dives – and not cheap for travellers used to prices elsewhere in South America. The ever-so-French *gîte* (inexpensive lodgings typically in a rural setting) is available, though more commonly referred to as *carbets*; makeshift wooden huts on the beach or in the forest with hammocks slung to the rafters and adjacent ablution blocks. While it may only cost €10 or so for hammock space (sometimes hammock rental is extra), note that few are conveniently located, and the expense of getting to them will probably negate any savings made on sleeping costs.

OPENING HOURS AND HOLIDAYS

General opening hours don't differ too much across the three countries. In Guyana, banks are usually open Monday to Friday 8am to 2pm, with an additional couple of hours Friday 3 to 5pm. This, at least is the rule; some branches, particularly those outside Georgetown, could be closed during the week and open at weekends. Opening hours

CALENDAR OF PUBLIC HOLIDAYS

January 1 New Year's Day
February 23 (Guyana) Republic Day
February but varies, (French Guiana) Ash Wednesday
March/April Good Friday, Easter Monday
May 1 Labour Day
May 5 (Guyana) Indian Heritage Day
May 29 (French Guiana) Ascension Day
June 9 (French Guiana) Whit Monday
June 10 (French Guiana) Slavery Day
July 1 (Suriname) National Union Day
July 7 (Guyana) Caribbean Day
July 14 (French Guiana) National Day
August 4 (Guyana) Freedom Day
November 11 (French Guiana) Armistice Day
November 25 (Suriname) Independence Day
December 25 Christmas Day

for government offices are Monday to Thursday 8am to noon and 1 to 4.30pm, Friday 8am to noon and 1 to 3.30pm; and for shops and other businesses, Monday to Friday 8am to 4pm, Saturday 8am to noon. In Suriname, banks are open Monday to Friday 9am to 2pm; government offices Monday to Thursday 7am to 3pm, Friday 7am to 2.30pm; and shops and businesses Monday to Friday 9am to 4.30pm, Saturday 9am to 1pm, although almost all close for at least a couple of hours' siesta in the afternoons. Apart from those in Paramaribo, it often seems that they never reopen. Meanwhile, in French Guiana most shops and businesses are open Monday to Saturday 9am to noon and 4 to 7pm. Supermarkets usually stay open until later in the evenings (around 9.30pm) and sometimes do business Sunday 9am to12.30pm. You may find that the mainly Chinese-owned convenience stores or *libre service* stay open during the afternoon siesta period.

INFORMATION AND MAPS

International Travel Maps, 530 W. Broadway, Vancouver, BC Can V5Z 1E9 (ⓣ604/879-3621, ⓦwww.itmb.com) produces a convenient Guianas map (CANS$12) including Suriname and French Guyana in about as much detail as you will need. If you're not planning ahead, the best (and often only) free city plan to be found in Georgetown is produced by **Advertising & Marketing Services Ltd**, ⓣ592/225-5383, and can be found at the **Tourism Hospitality Association**, and tour operators like **Wilderness Explorers**, Cara Suites, 176 Middle St ⓣ592/227-7698.

Guyana

GUYANA, *(guy-ana)* is known both as the "Land of Six Peoples," and the "Land of Many Waters," a meaning derived from its Amerindian name and the diverse population; a legacy of colonial rule, plenty of rivers and awe-inspiring waterfalls back up these names. Rum-drinking, cricket-loving Guyana is the only English-speaking country in South America and at first glance has rather more in common with the Caribbean than the rest of the continent. Indeed, **Georgetown**, the capital city of the Guianas' largest and most populous country, offers wooden architecture and a cosmopolitan mix of black, white, East Indian and Asian faces, a cultural diversity typical of Caribbean countries. The first giveaway, though, occurs when you stroll along

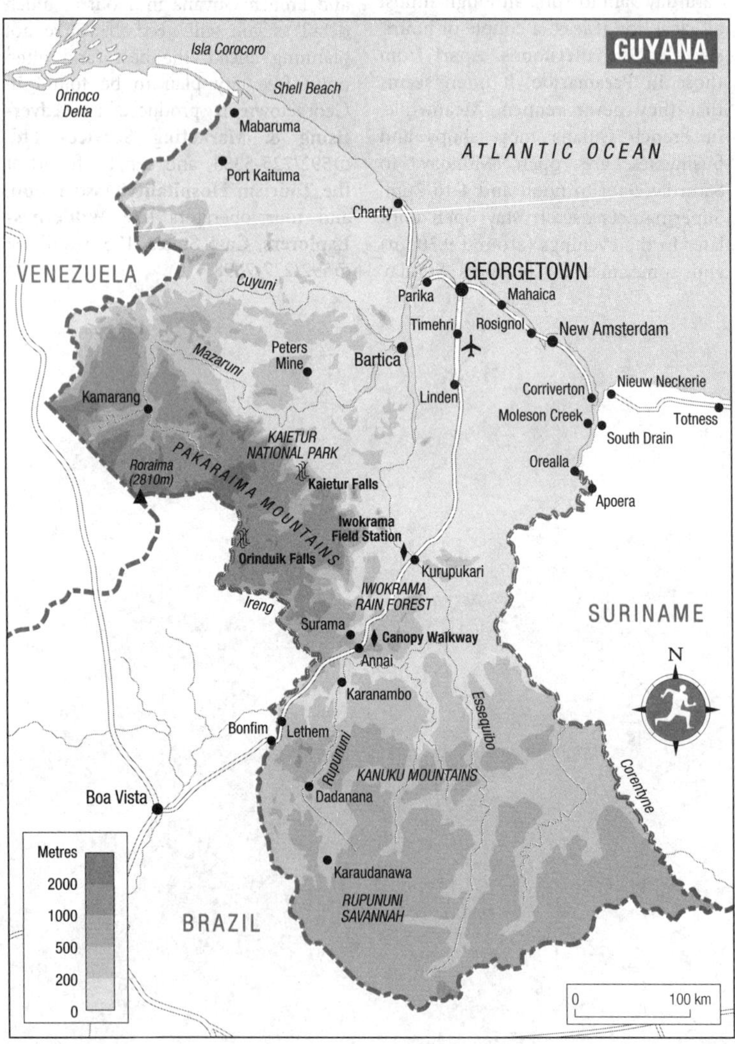

Georgetown's sea wall and see a muddy stretch of beach and a murky brown sea where white sand and emerald waters should be sparkling under the sun's rays – this is no tropical paradise.

And that's just fine because if you're visiting Guyana, it won't be for Georgetown or the rice paddies and sugar plantations along the coastal belt where most of the country's population lives, but for the majesty of the natural attractions in the interior where the vibe is unmistakably Amazonian. In fact, if you're looking for the best city in the Guianas, move on to Paramaribo, Suriname. But Guyana's vast expanse of tropical rainforest is a hiker's dream and contains one of the tallest most powerful waterfalls in the world, **Kaieteur Falls**, as well as the **Iwokrama Rainforest** where the sustainable use of the forest for eco-tourism is a priority. At the edge of the jungle in the far south of the country, the **Rupununi Savanna** offers a flat landscape, contrasting with the several highland regions in the interior, where you can stay at working ranches, play cowboy and stare at birds, caimans and giant river otters for days.

CHRONOLOGY

Before the Europeans arrived, the Warrau, Arawak and Carib tribes inhabited the highlands.

1498 Christopher Columbus first lays claim to the area for Spain.

1580 Dutch build settlements and trading posts around this time and import slaves from Africa over the next century to work the sugarcane plantations.

1763 Slave revolt led by Guyana's national hero, Cuffy.

1796 Dutch lose de facto control of colony to the British.

1814 British formally purchase Essequibo, Demerara and Berbice.

1831 Britain unites its territories as the colony of British Guiana.

1834 Slavery is abolished. Thousands of indentured labourers (mostly from India but also from China and Portugal) are brought to Guyana to work the sugarcane plantations.

1917 Practice of importing indentured labourers is terminated.

1950 The People's Progressive Party (PPP) is established, Guyana's first modern political party.

1953 PPP wins majority in first popular elections allowed by the colonial government; Dr Cheddi Jagan becomes leader of the house and minister of agriculture.

1953 British suspend constitution and send troops fearing Jagan and the PPP are planning to establish Guyana as a communist state.

1957 Elections permitted, Jagan's PPP wins.

1961 Jagan and PPP win again, Jagan becomes first premier of British Guiana.

1964 Forbes Burnham becomes prime minister; his time in power is seen as increasingly autocratic, elections are considered fraudulent abroad and human rights and civil liberties are suppressed.

1966 Guyana achieves independence.

1970 Guyana becomes a republic.

1971 Guyana becomes a member of Caricom.

1979 Jesuit priest and journalist Bernard Drake is assassinated. A year later, distinguished historian and WPA Party leader Walter Rodney is also killed. Burnham's agents are suspected to be responsible for the killings.

1980 Guyana gets a new constitution and Burnham becomes executive president.

1985 Burnham dies, Prime Minister Hugh Desmond Hoyte becomes president and is formally elected that year.

1992 First Guyanese election widely recognized as free and fair since 1964.

1992 Cheddi Jagan accedes to the presidency.

1997 Jagan dies, Prime Minister Samuel Hinds replaces him until Jagan's widow, Janet Jagan, is elected president later that year.

1999 Janet Jagan resigns due to ill health and is succeeded by Bharrat Jagdeo.

2001 Jagdeo is formally elected president.

2004 From December to January 2005 Guyana gets more than 60 inches of rainfall resulting in severe flooding and US$465 million in damages.

2006 Jagdeo re-elected in the first non-violent elections held in more than 20 years.

2007 Guyana's largest donor, the Inter-American Development Bank, forgives more than US$450 million in debt.

ARRIVAL

Guyana's only international airport, **Cheddi Jagan**, an hour south of Georgetown, receives direct flights from Barbados, New York, and Trinidad. Transguyana Airways has one-way flights to interior hamlets and jungle clearings via **Ogle Aerodrome**,

Georgetown's domestic airport, seven kilometres east of the capital, one-way for about G$15,000 (☎592/222-2525, ⓦwww.transguyana.com). Planes are small (sometimes only eight-seats).

It is an eleven-hour **bus** ride from Lethem and the Brazilian border to Georgetown. From Paramaribo, Suriname, it is a six-hour bus ride to the Moleson Creek **ferry** crossing (one per day, allow two hours) and another four-hour bus ride to Georgetown. If you are renting a car be sure it's 4WD.

GETTING AROUND

There are few, if any places to rent **cycles**; however, a few stores like China Trading Shopping Centre (32 Robb St) sell them relatively cheaply (G$12,000). **Minibuses** at Stabroek Market leave for all destinations by road except for Lethem.

ACCOMMODATION

There are no HI-affiliated hostels in Guyana and you should be careful when looking at anything too cheap (often inexpensive 'hotels' also rent rooms by the hour attracting the "women of the night," and their clientele, and they're often not even up to the standards of Brazilian love motels. Georgetown features several reasonably priced guesthouses where G$5000 will get you a mosquito net and a clean bed. Aside from one in Bartica you may do better by staying in one of the few designated hotels in smaller towns.

There are plenty of options in Georgetown where G$7000 may even land you wi-fi and usually at least one clean, reasonably priced hotel. In smaller towns, though, rarely do they go beyond bare accommodation and hardly ever breakfast.

FOOD

Curries, cassava and coconut milk reign over **Guyanese cuisine**. Chicken and beef are fried **Creole-style**, curried with East Indian spices or flavoured with ginger, and other Chinese ingredients. Rice is ubiquitous, boiled with beans (usually black-eye beans), okra and perhaps some other meat to make a traditional Creole one-pot *cook-up*, or fried in the Chinese style with shrimp, sausage and vegetables. Other staples include *chow mein*, *roti* and *puri*, the last two being fried pancakes used to mop up and envelope curries; *puri* containing a thin layer of spiced split peas within.

The lasting Amerindian contribution to Guyanese cuisine is *pepperpot*, a blood-red meat stew served with bread or rice and usually featuring cow's heel and face. Made with cassava juice or *casareep*, *pepperpot* is a breakfast and Christmas dish. *Tomapot*, found only in Amerindian communities, is a variant of *pepperpot* that uses fresh *casareep* as opposed to the recycled stuff in *pepperpot*. The *Georgetown Club* (a member's club) in Georgetown has apparently had a pot of *casareep*, known for its preservative properties, on the go for over a hundred years.

Locals consider **wild meat** a delicacy and more adventurous eaters will find deer, iguana, wild pig, manicou (opossum) and labba or agouti (jungle rat). Locals like to tell foreigners that if they eat labba and drink creek water they will return to Guyana. That said, drinking creek water, blackened by rotting vegetation, might just prevent you from leaving in the first place.

DRINK

The locally brewed **Banks Beer** does the job and cheaply (G$220) but the drink that you should be ashamed to miss is the El Dorado Special Reserve fifteen-year-old **rum**. Brewed by Demerara Distillers (G$10 distillery tours finish with tastings and a complimentary bottle of the 5-year, no slouch itself), the rum has won competitions and international acclaim, and mixing anything with it is a travesty – it should be sipped straight up with an ice cube if anything.

GUYANA ON THE NET

www.guyana-tourism.com Food, festivals and good accommodation details including pictures of the nicer rooms.

www.guyanalive.com Forums, festival info, up-to-date event listings, videos and articles about the local scene.

www.guyana.org News, government links, recipes, proverbs, you name it.

www.lanic.utexas.edu/la/sa/guyana Links to everything to do with the country.

www.sdnp.org.gy/gallery/travel_guyana/index.htm Features specific information on various places in Guyana's ten regions.

Familiar soft drinks are sold everywhere, along with regional offerings such as the multi-flavoured Busta (from Trinidad and Tobago) and Guyana's very own, I-Cee. While tap water is drinkable fragile stomachs might prefer **bottled waters** like Diamond Mineral or Tropical Mist.

CULTURE AND ETIQUETTE

While the coast of Guyana has a Caribbean vibe, it is in the smaller towns outside Georgetown and in the interior where you will find a more laid-back sensibility. In the capital men are paid to shepherd riders to waiting minibuses and merchants at Stabroek market are loud and aggressively pursue customers (read: they will touch you) shaking fists at each other one minute then sharing a beer the next. **Flirting** and sexual harassment can be intense and members of both sexes make persistent, loud kissing noises toward the objects of their affection. The three major **religions** are Christianity (57 percent), Hinduism (28 percent and Islam (7 percent, mostly Sunni). **Tipping** 10 percent for good service is the norm but make sure to check the bill for service charges which are often already added.

SPORTS AND OUTDOOR ACTIVITIES

The country may be located in South America where **football** rules, but nobody told the Guyanese, who by far favour **cricket** (children play it with makeshift bats in Independence Square and in Bourda road islands alike). It is a passion that led to the construction of the Guyana National Stadium in Providence, which was built with funding by India in time for the Cricket World Cup in 2007 (the legacy of which is still controversial for some) and *Buddy's International Hotel* a short drive from Georgetown. After **football**, young Guyanese follow **basketball**, which you will also see being played on the court in Independence Square even after the lights go out. **Cycling** in the city and **horse riding** in the Rupununi savanna are more practical matters than sport.

COMMUNICATIONS

Sending letters and postcards from Guyana is cheap (G$80–160) and almost timely but post offices outside Georgetown are harder to find. For urgent deliveries, try **private mailing**

PRESS, TV AND RADIO

Newspapers *Guyana Chronicle* (government-owned daily), *Kaieteur News* and *Stabroek News* (both private dailies)

TV One public broadcast station and two private stations that relay US satellite service

AM Radio 560, Voice of Guyana; 760 Radio Roraima

FM Radio 100.1, Radio Roraima; 102.5, Voice of Guyana

companies in the capital like FedEx, through Camex Ltd, 125 C. Barrack St (☎592/227-6976) or UPS, 210 Camp Street (☎592/271-853). **Phone calls** – local, national and international – can be made with cards issued by the Guyana Telephone and Telegraph Company which can be purchased at most stores, pharmacies or any GT&T or Digicel business center office. **Internet cafés** charging G$150–$300/hour are present in most towns as are Internet calling centres, usually G$40–80/min.

CRIME AND SAFETY

Armed attacks by criminals in early 2008 did little to diminish the reputation of **Georgetown** and its neighbouring communities as the Wild West of the Guianas. Attacks east of Georgetown in **Buxton** and **Lusignan**, and west in **Bartica** (a peaceful, riverside town foreigners are 'relocated' *to*) resulted respectively in the deaths of two Guyanese Defense Force soldiers, a direct attack on the Guyanese Police Force Headquarters in Georgetown near the US embassy and the killing of 21 civilians. There are no reports of foreigners being targeted so as common sense dictates, avoid displaying your wealth for everyone to see and take taxis after dark. For the most part, the Guyanese are honest welcoming people (particularly so in the interior). Know that crime levels are high, seek local advice about where *not* to go and use your common sense about visiting troubled areas (Buxton) and walking on Georgetown's many sparsely lit streets after dark.

STUDENT AND YOUTH DISCOUNTS

You will be hard-pressed to find any discounts for any demographic, student, youth, senior and otherwise.

EMERGENCY NUMBERS

911 is the general emergency number for the police.

912 is the number for the fire service.

913 is the number for public ambulance services.

EMERGENCIES

St. Joseph's Mercy Hospital 130–132 Parade St (☎592/227-2072) is recommended by the US embassy.

Georgetown Public Hospital New Market St ☎592/227-8232. The largest busiest hospital in Georgetown.

MONEY AND BANKS

The unit of **currency** is the Guyanese dollar (G$), which comes in 20, 50, 100, 500, and 1000 notes and 1, 5, and 10 coins. It is not uncommon to see people walking around with stacks of rubber-banded 1000 notes.

Banks are usually open Mon–Fri 8am–2pm and are closed weekends; street currency exchanges often offer better exchange rates. While major credit cards are accepted by tour operators and in some restaurants and hotels, they are mostly useless elsewhere and cash advances are only possible at Scotiabank. ATMs in Georgetown often have ten-minute lines, do not accept foreign credit cards and are even sparser outside town so carry a little extra cash for the interior and places like Moleson Creek. At the time of writing, US$1=G$200, €1=G$285, £1=G$306. Prices throughout this guide are given in Guyana dollars.

Georgetown

The magnificent wooden, colonial buildings are creaking with neglect, crime rates are high, and in view of

GEORGETOWN's forgotten parks, gardens and tree-lined promenades, the epithet, "Garden City of the Caribbean," is somewhat misleading. Set on the east bank of the Demerara estuary, the capital is a grid-city designed largely by the Dutch in the eighteenth century, and is easily the country's largest. Known as Stabroek under the Dutch, it was renamed Georgetown by the British in 1812 after George III. For all its problems there is definitely a charm and appeal to the wild flowers, dirty creeks, *roti* stands and sidewalk mango-vendors. The sheer hustle, sweat and energy of **Stabroek market**, the soul of the city, is enough to inspire a respect for Georgetown and its plucky 150,000 inhabitants.

What to see and do

Georgetown is made up of various districts, bounded to the north by the seawall, which keeps the Atlantic Ocean at bay (the city is seven feet below sea level) and to the west by the Demerara River. Along the seawall from west to east is a sleepy residential stretch including **Kingston, Thomaslands**, and **Kitty** and **Subryanville.** The physical centre of the city from the river, west to east consists of **Cummingsburg, Alberttown, Queenstown, Newton, Bel Air Park** and **Campbellville**, the last representing the bulk of the city's nightlife. The southwestern quarter along the river is the true city-centre: **Robbstown, Lacytown**, and **Stabroek.** East of Stabroek is **Bourda**, home to **Merriman's Mall**, a smaller market than Stabroek but not less lively.

The southern part of town

Stabroek Market, the city's heart, on and around Water Street, is dominated by its postcard picture four-faced, non-functioning clock tower. The market is the focal point for Georgetown's merchants, gadabouts, stray dogs, shoppers, buses, moneychangers, beggars and pickpockets. You can find anything from canned mackerel and rat poison to gold necklaces and wooden handicrafts. Police, both armed and unarmed, patrol throughout the day but it gets less safe at twilight and at night visitors should use taxis to and from its restaurants.

North of the market between Water Street and the Avenue of the Republic is the **National Museum** (Mon–Fri 9am–5pm, Sat 9am–noon; free) which houses little of interest beyond what it claims is the world's rarest postage stamp and shelter from the afternoon heat. East on Church Street by the roundabout is Georgetown's other postcard building, the impressive **St. George's Cathedral**, which at 143 feet is said to be the world's tallest free-standing wooden structure (don't miss the beams inside).

On Brickdam, east of the market is the well-kept **Parliament Building** and the **High Court** (1887), both imposing nineteenth-century colonial structures and the rather dour **Cathedral of the Immaculate Conception**. In the Bourda, for several blocks between North Road and Church Street is **Merriman's Mall**, a colourful shantytown filled with fruit, vegetable and coconut vendors. Near the eastern end of North Road is the **Georgetown Cricket Club**, past which on Vlissengen Road you will find the **Botanical Gardens**. The green space is a nice break from the frenzy of Stabroek and the highlight of the sad animals at the distressed **Guyana Zoo** (daily 7.30am–5.30pm; G$100) are its manatees that you can get close enough to pet. South on Vlissengen is the **National Art Gallery** (Mon–Fri 10am–5pm, Sat 2–6pm; free) featuring Amerindian art and sculpture, and the **1763 Monument**, a not altogether flattering tribute to Cuffy, an African slave who led an unsuccessful slave rebellion in 1763.

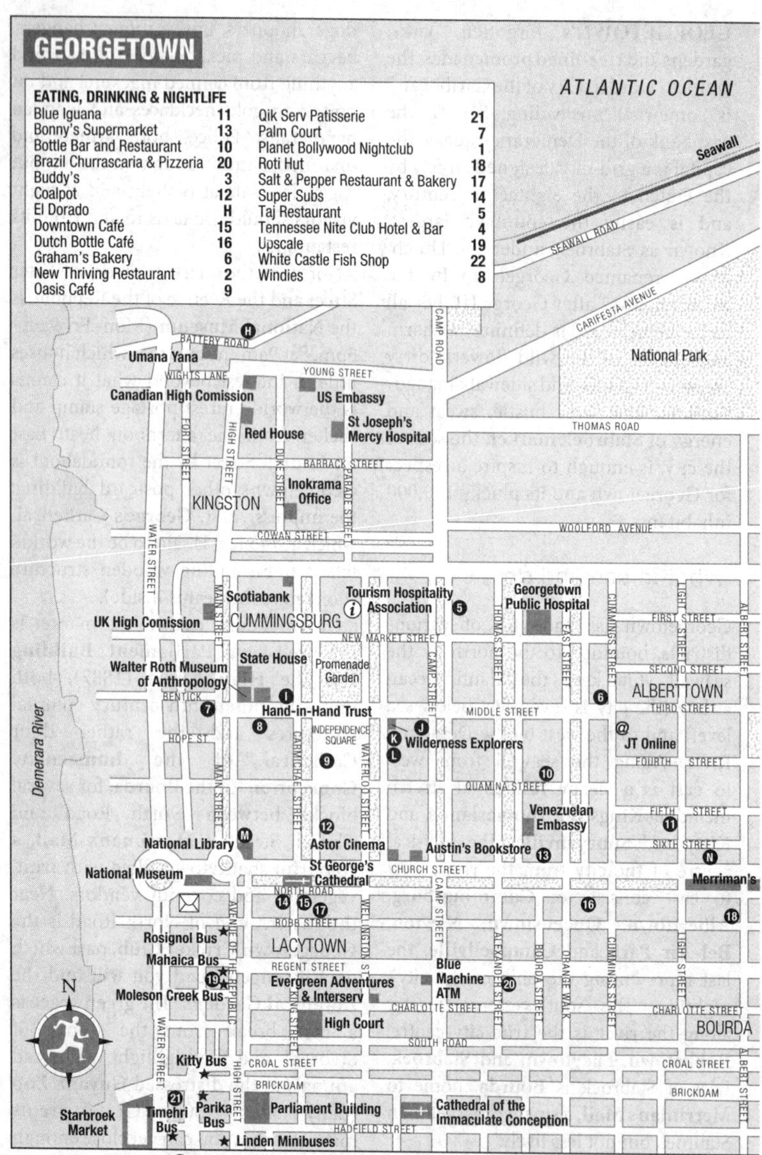

Central Georgetown

Most sites are in the western part of the city on or around Main Street with its grassy, tree-lined central walkway. At the beginning of Main Street is the **National Library** funded by American philanthropist Andrew Carnegie. Two blocks north on Main Street is the **Walter Roth Museum of Anthropology** (Mon–Thurs 8am–4.30pm, Fri 8am–3.30pm; free) worth a look for its Amerindian artefacts (often closes early), and just past

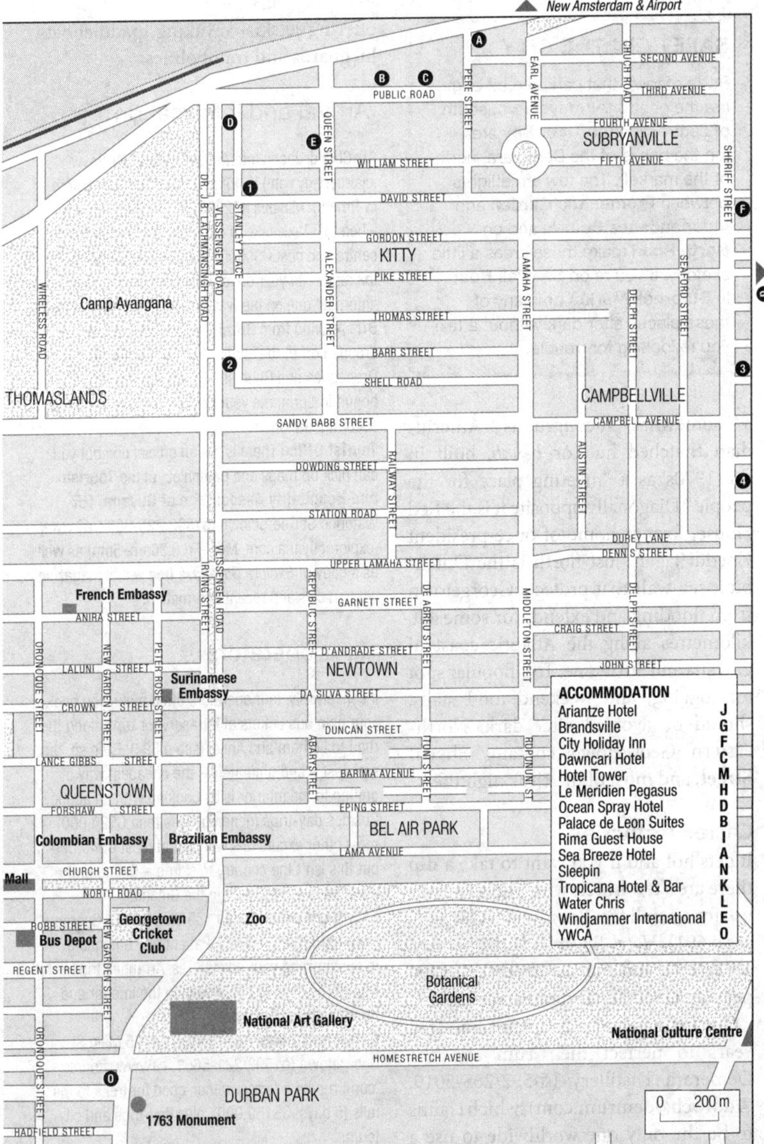

the museum, the **State House**, the presidential residence. A block to the east is the **Promenade Garden**, with benches, flowers, bandstand and tributary statue to Mahatma Gandhi. Opposite the garden is **Independence Square**, a large grass field and blacktop court usually filled with impromptu cricket and basketball games.

The northern part of town

Main Street turns into High Street at the end of which are the **Umana Yana**,

SAFETY IN THE CITY

Parts of town that can be a bit edgy are the ghetto, **Albouystown**, south of centre, and the **Tiger Bay** area (on the banks of the Demerara, north of the market). The few streetlights between **Promenade Garden** and **Independence Square** and on **North Road** make those areas a little sketchy. If you're on **Seawall Road**, in **Stabroek Market** or in any of these places after dark without a taxi you're looking for trouble.

a somewhat incongruous Amerindian thatched hut, or *benab*, built in the 1970s as a "meeting place for the people." Diagonally opposite it is the Red House, former home of once-president Cheddi Jagan. Just north is the Dutch-built **sea wall** that protects Georgetown from flooding and extends for some 450 kilometres along the Atlantic coast of Guyana and Suriname. This popular spot for jogging, and weekend food stalls, should be avoided after dark. Northeastern Georgetown contains **Sheriff Street**, and most of the city's nightlife.

Other activities

It gets hot and if you want to take a **dip** there are a few **hotels** with pools you can use for a small fee: *Brandsville* (G$1,000, see p.691), *Hotel Tower* (G$1160 per day, see p.692), and the *Sea Breeze* (G$1200 per day, G$6000 per month, see p.692).

Guyana has had a couple of hundred years to perfect their rum and the Demerara Distillery (T 592/265-5019, E ddlweb@demrum.com), which claims to be the only one worldwide to use a wooden Coffey still in the production process, demonstrates this. A **distillery tour** (G$200) including a free bottle of their 5-year rum is definitely worth the ten-minute minibus ride.

Splashmin's Fun Park and Resort, 48 High Street, Werk-en-Rust (T 592/223-7301), is a man-made black-water lake offering jetskis, kayaking, paddleboats, lifeguards and trampolines.

Arrival and information

Air Cheddi Jagan International Airport (W www.cjairport-gy.com) is 40km south of the city centre in Timehri. Minibus #42 (G$260, 1–2hrs) departs when full. Taxis take about an hour to reach the city centre and cost G$5000. There are no *cambios* at the airport so your driver may offer to stop at an 'informal' one on the way or take you to one in town.

Bus Arriving from Brazil via Lethem you are dropped off at the 'station' on the corner of Oronoques and Robb sts. On minibus journeys begun in Suriname your driver will leave you at your accommodation.

Tourist Office There is not an official one but you can pick up maps and pamphlets at the **Tourism and Hospitality Association of Guyana**, 157 Waterloo St Georgetown (T 592/225-0807, W www.exploreguyana.com, Mon–Fri 8.30am–5pm) as well as a copy of *Explore Guyana*, a free yearly magazine with articles and recent information.

Tour operators

Inconceivably, tour operators often make you book your own bus tickets at Intraserv for trips along the road to Lethem and Annai (see p.694). Even so, the simplest – and ultimately – the cheapest way of getting to the interior is by booking with an agency. Besides day-trips (generally less than G$20,000) most other excursions will cost at least G$40,000 but this isn't the country to skimp – the natural attractions are the best in the Guianas.

Evergreen Adventures 159 Charlotte St Georgetown (T 592/226-0605). Patient and amenable to customizing your adventures. Arranges trips from three days to two weeks to the interior and throughout the Guianas.

Rainforest Tours *Hotel Tower*, 74–75 Main St Georgetown (T 592/231-5661, W www.rftours.com) run by a former miner, good for treks to the falls (5 days, G$159,000), plus day-trips and city tours.

Shell Beach Adventures *Le Meridien Pegasus*, Georgetown (T 592/225-4483, W www.sbadventures.com), for turtles at Shell Beach (seasonal, Mar–Aug).

Wilderness Explorers *Cara Suites*, 176 Middle St Georgetown (T 592/227-7698, W www.wildernessexplorers.com) all the basics and good for trips to Kaieteur Falls and the interior but staff become obtuse if you want to stray from the script.

City transport

Buses Complicated routes, frequent stops, colourful driving, reggae-blasting, and very intimate, but rarely above G$100 within town – hail once for the experience.
Taxis Taxis are unmetered, everywhere, on constant lookout for passengers and are the cheapest in the Guianas; take advantage of them. Fares rarely top G$300.

Accommodation

There are plenty of decent hotels at varying prices in central Georgetown even though many are a little worn and seem held together by duct tape and sheer will. The hotels in **Kitty**, the quiet, northeastern part of town, are remote from Stabroek but nearby the bars on Sheriff Street. Kitty is fine on foot by day but at night you'll want to take a cab home. Don't rely on email for reservations.

Hostels and guesthouses

Rima Guest House 92 Middle St ⓣ592/225-7401, ⓔrima@networksgy.com. The secure, budget, family-run, self-proclaimed "cleanest guesthouse in town," doesn't lie. Drawbacks: thin walls, cold water and sparse rooms not en suite. Room #10 has free wi-fi. ❹–❺
Sleepin Compact, fresh and comfortable en suite rooms with wi-fi (the more expensive have a/c). Two locations: 151 Church St ⓣ592/231-7667, ⓔreservations@sleepinguesthouse.com and 24 Brickdam ⓣ592/227-3452, ⓔstay@sleepininternationalhotel.com. ❹–❻
Tropicana Hotel & Bar 177 Waterloo St ⓣ592/225-1176. Staff barely seem to understand you or each other but the central location (overlooks Independence Square), Brazilian lunch buffet, and mosquito nets are good draws. ❹
YWCA 106 Brickdam St ⓣ592/226-5610. The hostel welcomes both men and women to its dorm beds and private rooms. ❹–❺

Hotels

Ariantze Hotel 176 Middle St ⓣ592/227-2011, ⓔariantze@networksgy.com. The rooms are thread-worn but have TV and the concierge takes credit cards (5 percent fee). Breakfast and nearby pool access included. Good hotel lunch café. ❼–❽
Brandsville 88–90 Pike St ⓣ592/227-1133, ⓔbrandsville@gol.net.gy. New, secure, clean, wi-fi, a/c, pool, bar, restaurant, coffee maker, even hot water and an alarm clock. ❽
City Holiday Inn 314 Sheriff St ⓣ592/903-0175, ⓔcityholiday@yahoo.com. There's little 'exotic' about this place despite the sign's claim but rooms do have a/c, ceiling fans, hot/cold water and are near the nightlife. Ask for a room with a balcony. No affiliation. ❺–❼
Hotel Tower 74–75 Main St ⓣ592/903-0175, ⓔinfo@hoteltowerguyana.com. Tiles, walls and furniture have all seen better days but the oldest and second largest hotel in Georgetown is comfortable and just minutes by foot from most central attractions. ❽–❾

FERRIES/WATER TAXIS

Vreed en Hoop (from Georgetown) River, behind clock tower, 15 minutes, G$80
Bartica (from Parika) Beach, left of loading dock, 1 hour G$1800
Rosignol (to New Amsterdam) 15 minutes, G$600

MINIBUSES FROM GEORGETOWN

Kitty Route #40, Croal Street, in front of Demico House, G$60
Linden Route #43, Corner of Hadfield & High, behind Parliament Building, G$500
Mahaica (Ogle Aerodrome) Route #44, Avenue of Republic & Regent, in front of Digicel, 20 minutes, G$240
Moleson Creek (Suriname Border) Route #63, Avenue of Republic & Commerce, in front of Western Union, 3 hour, G$2000
Parika (for Bartica) Route #32, Brickdam, behind Parliament Building, 1 hour, G$400
Rosignol (for New Amsterdam) Route #50, Avenue of Republic & Robb, 1 hour 30 minutes, G$700
Timehri (Cheddi Jagan Airport) Route #42, opposite clock tower, 1 hour 30 minutes, G$340

Water Chris 184 Waterloo St ⓣ592/226-5257, ⓔwaterchris@mail.com. Good location, friendly cleaning staff, quirky lobby art, and en-suite rooms, with a/c, hot/cold and hotpots. ❺–❼

Kitty Hotels

Dawncari Hotel 42 Public Rd ⓣ592/227-3571. Tiled floors, verandas, TV and a/c near the sea wall. ❻

Ocean Spray Hotel Stanley Place ⓣ592/903-0175, ⓔreservations@oceanspray.co.gy. Sparkling new, spotless, wi-fi, a/c, hot/cold water, ocean-view communal balconies. Suite with kitchen and two beds good for sharing with travel buddies. ❹–❽

Palace de Leon Suites 32 Public Rd ⓣ592/223-7328, ⓔpalacedeleon2000@yahoo.com. G$5000. A bit dingy but open-air hallways, a/c, lively staff, and serviceable basics do the trick especially if you're sharing the cost with friends. ❹–❻

Sea Breeze Hotel 8 Pere St ⓣ592/225-0542, ⓔsabiah_83@yahoo.com. This secure hotel overlooks the ocean, has a pool and is said to be the former Russian embassy. ❼–❾

Windjammer International 27 Queen St ⓣ592/227-7478, ⓔinfo@windjammergy.com. Café is reasonably priced (breakfaSt $600–$1000), singles are expensive (though nice enough) and small rooms in the back are more like New York closets but cheap. ❺–❾

Resorts

If you're looking to get away from the Stabroek hustle and want to splash out a bit at a resort there are really two options.

TREAT YOURSELF

Le Pegasus Meridien Seawall Rd ⓣ592/225-2853 is the only business hotel of a truly international standard in Georgetown but if you're tired of mosquito nets and thin mattresses and you do decide to treat yourself here the place to do it is at the **Cara Lodge**, 294 Quamina St ⓣ592/225-5301, ⓔcaralodge@carahotels.com. If the breezy white tablecloth restaurant doesn't send you back to visions of the "Grand Tour," the 1840s pedigree wooden floors and mango tree in the courtyard may still rescue your sense of romance. Climatized rooms are spacious and you almost forget the third world. This is living. ❾

Timberhead Rainforest Resort offers wooden lodges overlooking savanna land bordering Pokerero Creek 8 miles from Cheddi Jagan in an Amerindian reserve, near the village Santa Mission, with activities like birdwatching, fishing, and badminton, jungle walks canoeing. Travellers with a taste for comfort and might also enjoy **Arrowpoint Nature Resort's** (located near Santa Mission) jungle trails cleared for mountain-biking.

Arrowpoint Nature Resort c/o Roraima Airways, R 8 Eping Ave ⓣ592/225-9648, ⓦwww.awpt.roraimaairways.com.

Timberhead Rainforest Resort 8–10 Providence ⓣ597/233-5108, ⓦwww.timberheadguyana.com/index.htm

Eating

Head to the enclosed part of Stabroek Market for cheap, tasty curry and *roti* lunches at the many **cook shops**.

Cafés and fast food

Bonny's Supermarket 302 Church St. Not quite your local grocery but it has cups of noodles and some imported items.

Downtown Café Corner, Church & Ave Republic. Friendly, pink café, serves saltfish and bake, chicken chow mein, *roti*, iced coffee drinks, brownies and custard. Breakfast all day.

Graham's Bakery 345 Cummings St ⓣ592/225-7417. Tennis rolls, bread and Georgetown's best *salara* (coconut swirl sweet bun, G$140).

Oasis Cafe 125 Carmichael St ⓣ592/226-9916, ⓦwww.oasiscafegy.com. Seemingly hamster-wheel powered wi-fi but good milkshakes, pastries, lunch buffet and one of Georgetown's few decent cups of coffee make it a favourite for expats and locals.

Qik Serv Patisserie Demico House, Brickdam, Stabroek ⓣ592/225-7400. Pinwheels, chesters, mac 'n' cheese squares, soft-serve, sweet buns and cheddar pastries make this Stabroek standout a good spot for a tasty snack.

Roti Hut Lot 18 North Rd ⓣ592/227-3802. Best *roti* in town, period. Try the curried, shredded chicken with sweet pumpkin and chickpea. *Roti* & water, $695.

Salt & Pepper Restaurant & Bakery Four locations, Stabroek, Vreed-en-Hoop; Regent & Robb sts. Pastries, bread and Creole food.

Super Subs Corner of North & King. Six-inch ($595) or foot-long (G$1190) All sausage products are chicken-based.

White Castle Fish Shop 21 Hadfield St ☎592/227-5469. Watch kids play cricket in the median while gaffing a Banks beer and putting away fish and chips on the outdoor patio.

Restaurants

Bottle Bar and Restaurant *Cara Lodge*, ☎592/225-5301. Breezy, open dining room serves up paté, crab cakes, pepperpot, Beef Wellington, gingersnap pork and a decent burger.

Brazil Churrascaria & Pizzeria 208 Alexander St ☎592/225-6037. The pizza crust is sub-par but tasty-charred steak, chicken and sausage come until you say stop.

Coalpot 125 Carmichael St ☎592/225-8556. New location, same well-balanced Guyanese fare with a great twilight balcony-view of the cathedral. Entree & drink, G$680.

El Dorado *Le Meridien Pegasus* ☎592/225-2856. Georgetown's swankiest restaurant serves *confit de canard*, beef tenderloin and other gourmet dinners.

Dutch Bottle Café 10 North Rd ☎592/231-6561. Salads, roast beef sandwich, cow heel soup, curry prawns, pepper steak and tiramisu. Free *caipirinhaon* Fri night. Mains, G$1000–G$3000.

New Thriving Restaurant 165 Barr St ☎592/226-6348. Between this and *Buddy's* for Georgetown's best Chinese regardless of the Seiko hype (122 Regent, convenient only if you're waiting for the Lethem bus).

Taj Restaurant 228 Camp St ☎592/223-1630. Quiet, second-floor Indian restaurant with balcony and decent lamb curry.

Upscale 32–33 Regent St ☎592/225-4721. It's not as chic as advertised but varied cocktails, a reasonable menu from coconut prawns to chow mein, and poetry (Tues) and comedy events a storey above Stabroek's fray make it worthwhile.

Drinking and nightlife

Georgetown's party spirit bumps and grinds especially at the **bars** and **clubs** along Sheriff Street, the city's most famous place for nightlife. Weekends are the liveliest but the laser-lights and smoke machines don't really strobe and fume until midnight.

Blue Iguana 71 Fifth St ☎592/223-6266. This bar has two quarter-operated pool tables (there's a girl who operates them) and a dance club that's only open on Fri & Sat.

Buddy's 137 Sheriff St ☎592/231-7260. It's a laser-lit nightclub pumping East Indian beats. It's a 13-table pool hall. It's a Chinese restaurant. The only thing this multi-storey, balconied, Georgetown institution doesn't have is hotel rooms but it has its own taxi service to return you to yours. Club admission is G$600 for men.

Planet Bollywood Nightclub Corner of Vlissengen & David sts ☎592/223-6416. Cosier than Buddy's but Indian dance tracks don't kick it any less fiercely.

Palm Court 35 Main St ☎592/225-7938. Centrally located bar and restaurant, with palm-surrounded outdoor café seating. *Palm* pumps out the tunes down Main and Middle until the wee hours of the morning.

Tennessee Nite Club Hotel & Bar Sheriff St. There's a sign outside this 'authentic' joint with a list of banned personalities and prices for rooms rented by the hour. Consider yourself warned.

Windies 91 Middle St ☎592/231-3624. Watch cricket on the big screen, in the a/c while eating a club sandwich and downing a drink. Bring your laptop to surf with free wi-fi, or laze away the night on the guarded patio while expats party upstairs.

Entertainment

Astor Cinema 189 Waterloo St corner of Church. Daylight seeps through the slats of this wooden cinema that has been playing flicks since 1940 (in original English).

Karma Bowling Alley 371–371 East Industrial Site, Rumsveldt ☎592/227-2787. "Lime" your hours away drinking cold beverages, playing air jockey, pool, and of course, bowling.

National Cultural Centre Corner of Mandela & Homestretch Ave ☎592/226-2161. This auditorium seats about 2000 and features performances, plays and poetry readings with Indian, African, Caribbean, European and North American backgrounds with some regularity. Your best bet to find out what is going on is to stop by the centre.

Shopping

Arts and crafts You can find high-quality hammocks woven by the Makushi Weavers Society, as well as beaded jewellery and *casareep* (a cassava sauce used in native dishes) at Hibiscus Plaza in front of the post office. Here and along the grass-lined median on Main Styou will find local artists selling wood sculptures. On Sun mornings in Parika there is an arts and crafts market.

Designer stores Haute couture is not really Georgetown's strongest suit, but Regent St is a good place to shop around for local fashions.
Shopping centres You can find hammocks, beaded jewellery and *matapis* (cassava juice extractors) at Hibiscus Plaza in front of the post office. On Sun mornings in Parika there is a market displaying furniture, handicrafts and produce.

Directory

Embassies and Consulates Australia, 18 Herbert St Port of Spain, Trinidad ⓣ868/628-0695; Brazil, 308 Church St ⓣ592/225-7970; Canada, Young & High sts ⓣ592/227-2081; Colombia, 306 Church & Rose sts ⓣ592/227-1410; France, Honorary Consulate, 46 First St ⓣ592/227/5435; Netherlands, 61 Ave of the Republic ⓣ592/227-4085; Suriname, 171 Peter Rose & Crown sts ⓣ592/267-844, ⓔsurnemb@gol.net.gy (consular section MWF 8am–noon, visa issued next day consular section open, US$100 bills NOT accepted; UK, 44 Main St ⓣ592/226-5881; US, 100 Young & Duke Sts, ⓣ592/226-2614, Venezuela, 296 Thomas St ⓣ592/226-1543.
Exchange The best rates are on the street, otherwise, there are plenty of *cambios* in town, among others: Hand-In-Hand Trust 62–63 Middle St ⓣ592/226-9781; Swiss House Cambio, 25A Water St.
Hospitals Public ambulances will take patients to Georgetown Public Hospital, New Market St ⓣ592/227-8204.
Internet Plaza Internet Café, 245 Sheriff St $200 per hr; JT Online Internet Café, 28 Cummings St $200 per hr; Netsurf.com Cyber Café, 60 Croal St $200 per hr; The Net Library, 113 Regent Rd, $200 per hr; free wi-fi at Windies and Oasis.
Laundries There are no laundromats but many hotels will wash your clothes for a fee.

RENTING A CAR

There are several places to rent a car in Georgetown. Because the roads outside of town are mostly unpaved and potholed you will want to get 4WD if possible. Make sure you check the car thoroughly.

Compass Auto Rental 301 Church ⓣ592/227-6021.

Sleepin Car Rental, 151 Church St ⓣ592/231-7667.

Left Luggage Leaving it with your hotel is the safest bet.
Pharmacies There are several sprinkled throughout town, like Medi-care Pharmacy, 18 Hinck St (ⓣ592/225-9369) but as supplies may be limited hospital pharmacies may be the best alternative: St. Joseph's Mercy Hospital, 130–132 Parade St ⓣ592/227-2072; Davis Memorial Hospital, 121 Durban Backlands Lodge ⓣ592/227-2041.
Post office on North Rd at the northern end of the market.

Moving on

Air Both **American** and **Caribbean Airlines** link Guyana to the Caribbean islands, **North America** and beyond via Trinidad, Miami and New York. There is a **$4000 departure tax**. There are flights once-daily to **Boa Vista, Brazil** (Mon, Wed & Fri, 1hr 30min), and **Paramaribo, Suriname** (Mon Thurs & Fri; 2hr via **Meta Airlines** (ⓦvoemeta.com) and **Paramaribo** via **Blue Wing Airlines** (Tues, Thus & Sat, ⓦbluewingairlines.com).
For domestic and interior flights: **Roraima Airways** (ⓦwww.roraimaairways.com) and **Trans Guyana Airways** (ⓦwww.transguyana.com).
Bus Intraserv buses serve the interior and the Brazilian border. Ticketing office, 159 Charlotte ⓣ592/226-0605. They do not accept credit cards but Evergreen Adventures (see p.690), the tourist agency upstairs, will process the transaction for a fee. There are several **minibuses to Suriname** that will pick you up so you do not have to go to Stabroek at 4am: Brian Mini Bus Service, Georgetown to Paramaribo via Moleson Creek ⓣ592/218-4460, ⓣ597/89-00-08-43 (Suriname to Georgetown); Bobby, 185 'B' Pike St ⓣ592/226/8668; P&A Ice Cream Parlor & Transportaiont Service, 75 Church St ⓣ592/225-5058.

West to Venezuela

There is no legal border crossing to Venezuela but that does not mean there is nothing west along Guyana's coast. The nearest site meriting attention is the sleepy mining town, **Bartica**, two hours of bus and boat travel from Georgetown. More obvious is **Shell Beach** in the extreme northwest the best place in Guyana to observe egg-laying turtles. The beach is accessible from the town of **Mabaruma** reachable only by flying or taking the ferry from Georgetown.

BARTICA

One of the country's oldest settlements, situated on the confluence of the **Essequibo**, **Mazaruni** and **Cuyuni** rivers, there's not much to Bartica beyond First Avenue but it remains an important hinterland mining town. Bartica's population, a gritty mix of gold and diamond miners and lumberjacks, is rough and raucous (witness the preponderance of bars) but very friendly.

What to see and do

Apart from strolling down First Ave and Fourth St (shopping arcade), soaking up the laid-back atmosphere, and sipping some rum at *Kool Breeze*, Bartica's dock-side bar, there is not much to do in Bartica. Most things to see are on and around the **Essequibo** and **Mazaruni** rivers and the town is best used as a point to meet up with your guide (below) and a base from which to explore the surrounding area.

All that remains of **Kyk-Over-Al** (See-Over-All), the seventeenth-century Dutch-built fort on one of the 365 islands in the Essequibo, is an arch. After defeat by the English in 1676, the Dutch moved from the fort to a site on the banks of the Mazaruni River, now occupied by **Mazaruni Prison** on the outskirts of Bartica.

Upstream, on the banks of the Mazaruni, **Marshall Falls** is a reasonably pleasant waterfall (G$1000 entrance fee; G$6000 overnight in hammocks with meals) where despite the wine-coloured water (the result of leaves and mineral deposits) there is good year-round swimming.

For all things Bartica-tour related, **Bhagwandas Balkarran** is your man (Lot 2, Triangle St ⓣ592/455-2544, 621-0469, ⓔsilkyshomia@hotmail.com). He runs a guesthouse (see below) and gives **guided tours** in his boat for G$28,000 (seating six) with overnight camping and machete night fishing by torch.

If you are in need of internet access head to Cyber Dragon, Lot 55 First Ave, ⓣ597/455-2298, the town's only cyber-point. In case of emergency, Bartica Hospital, ⓣ592/455-2339.

Arrival and information

Getting to Bartica involves catching minibus #32 (G$400) across the Demerara River's pontoon bridge and an hour-long spine-bruising wooden-speedboat ride which you catch at the pier where the boats load up bananas and other cargo. The bus will drop you off on a busy, dusty road about 300m from the water's edge. Follow the bustle and keep left of the pier to the beach where the boats are waiting. The best way to move on from Bartica is to reverse your steps and head back to Georgetown.

Accommodation

D'Factor Interior Guesthouse Lot 2 Triangle St ⓣ592/455-2544. On the river in a cul de sac at the end of First Ave, Bhagwandas' (see above) rooms are clean, fresh, well furnished and have mosquito nets. The balcony is for everyone; the nicer rooms are downstairs. ❹

New Modern Hotel 9 First Ave, ⓣ592/455-2301. Wood-walled rooms with ceiling fans, TV and standing fans. ❹–❻

Platinum Inn Lot 7 First Ave (ⓣ592/455-3041, ⓔplatinum_inn@hotmail.com). The small rooms are reasonably priced. Free internet. ❺

Relax Inn Hotel 6870 First Ave G$3000. Bearable self-contained rooms with a/c but the lively courtyard downstairs may make your stay a little less than relaxing. ❸–❻

Zen's Plaza 43 Second Ave ⓣ592/455-2441. Rooms that smell like Chlorox with noisy fans with and without a/c but there's a small kitchen that serves up Creole snacks and a bar on the veranda. ❹–❺

Eating

There's not much variety to the food in Bartica but you can find, *roti*, pastries and even soft-serve ice cream along **First Ave**, and in the arcade. There are

BENNY'S MOBILE SNACKETTE

Bartica residents claim to have the best *salara* in Guyana and look forward to Benny's 4pm walk down **First Ave**, pushing his cart full of the coconut-swirled sweetbread. If you don't catch him before he reaches the arcade there may not be any left for you to make your own call.

also fruit stands on First at the opposite end from *D'Factor* and a small supermarket.

Hong Kong Chinese Restaurant Corner of 1st & Fourth St ⓣ592/455-2217. Try the Hong Kong fried rice (a half-order is enough for one person).

J&D Spicy Corner & Hangout Bar First Ave ⓣ592/455-3179. Creole repertoire ranging from okra and chicken to beef curry, black-eye cook-up and labba stew at low, low prices.

Morocco Cafeteria 14 First Ave ⓣ592/455-2946. There's little that's Moroccan about this green shack but it's a popular spot with Creole specialities that change daily.

Drinking and nightlife

At night, reggae and Caribbean beats flood onto First Avenue, from the now-glowing open-air cafés and welcoming bars you might not have given a second glance during the day.

Kool Breeze Ferry Dock. Bar is a box of liquor and an ice cooler but there aren't many tourists and it's a great place for a sundowner.

Micky's Hangout Lot 4, First Ave ⓣ592/455-2495. This baby-blue brick building has a bar, TV and the best pool table in town.

MABARUMA

The main reason for making the one-hour flight from Georgetown is to visit the nearby turtle-nesting site at **Shell Beach** but the town of **MABARUMA**, situated on a hill overlooking the rainforest and the Kaituma River is a pleasant enough place to rest your weary feet. Mabaruma is the administrative centre of Region 1, and around ninety percent Amerindian. Mabaruma's river port, **Kumaka**, takes about a day to get to by ferry from Georgetown.

What to see and do

Shell Beach extends from the mouth of the **Pomeroon River** to the Venezuelan border (160 km) but the most interesting parts are the dozen or so seashell-comprised beaches a short boat-ride from Mabaruma. From around March to August four species of **turtle** – leatherback, green, Olive Ridley and hawksbill – come to these beaches at night to lay their eggs. During the day, there is good **birdwatching**, for corri-corris, scarlet ibises, egrets, herons and the occasional flamingo.

The **Guyana Marine Turtle Conservation Society** (ⓦwww.gmtcs.org) has a field station at **Almond Beach**, where there is basic accommodation in tents. The simplest way to arrange a visit is to organize it all with a tour operator such as Shell Beach Adventures (see p.690).

If you're intent on going it alone look in Kumaka for a boat to take you to Shell Beach and back. You might be lucky and find transport carrying provisions upriver to the beach communities; otherwise, count on paying at least G$35,000 return to charter your own boat.

Arrival and information

You must fly or take the boat to get here from Georgetown. Transguyana Airways flies four times weekly (Mon, Wed, Fri & Sat, G$15,000 one-way, G$28,000 return) and the ferry *Kimbia* leaves Georgetown fortnightly on Wed at 1pm, taking roughly 24hr to reach Kumaka. The ferry-return to Georgetown is on Sat and leaves at 6am. Fares, departure times and days are subject to change.

Accommodation and eating

There are few options food-wise apart from some snackettes in Kumaka. You can get boxes of chicken and fried rice at Broomes Shop, located 400 metres before *Broomes Guest House* (see opposite). Rooms fill up quickly with civil servants in Mabaruma, so it is wise to make a reservation and bring provisions.

JONESTOWN MASSACRE

The chilling events of November 18, 1978, when over nine hundred members of a sect died in an apparent mass suicide in a jungle clearing in northwestern Guyana, about 80km southwest of Mabaruma, have been the subject of many books and theories. It is undisputed that in 1974, **Reverend Jim Jones**, the leader of a sect called **The People's Temple**, chose Guyana to establish a self-sufficient community of about 1100 based on utopian socialist ideals. He humbly named it Jonestown. Referring to an unnamed enemy that would come to destroy Jonestown, he told his flock that "revolutionary suicide" was the only way to combat this threat. When Congressman Leo Ryan and a party of journalists and concerned family members visited Jonestown in November 1978 to investigate alleged human rights abuses, the enemy had apparently arrived. Ryan was shot and killed at Port Kaituma airstrip as he tried to leave, while back at Jonestown the men, women and children of The People's Temple drank poison. A total of 913 people died in the suicide, although a Guyanese coroner's report suggested that as many as seven hundred of the victims were forcibly killed. Nowadays the Jonestown site is covered by forest, and there is no monument or other reminder of its existence.

Broomes Guest House Halfway between town centre and Kumaka ⓣ 592/777-5118. Pleasant self-contained rooms in this hotel perched on one of the main hills. East-facing rooms have balconies with views of the Kumaka stelling (waterfront) and the Arouaca River. ❹

Government Guest House Town centre, ⓣ 592/777-5091. Eight basic but comfortable rooms. ❺

South to Brazil

The potholed, dirt road from Georgetown to the Brazilian border crossing in the southwest of the country traverses pristine rainforests and wide-open plains. Guyana's most famous attraction, the dramatically isolated **Kaieteur Falls**, lies southwest of Georgetown, deep in the interior – you will have to either fly or trek through the forest for a few days. The other places most worth exploring before crossing into Brazil at **Lethem** are the **Iwokrama RainforeSt** a good example of the country's efforts to promote sustainable eco-tourism, and the **Rupununi Savanna**, an area of wooded hills and dry grassland strewn with cattle ranches and providing excellent possibilities for bird and animal spotting.

KAIETEUR FALLS

At 226 metres tall, **KAIETEUR FALLS**, the centrepiece of the ancient Pakaraima mountain range in southwestern Guyana, is almost five times the height of Niagara. It stands in a cavernous gorge surrounded by the forests of the **Kaieteur National Park**, which encompasses an area of eight square kilometres around the falls. Contrary to many claims you will hear in Guyana, Kaieteur is not the highest single-drop waterfall (Angel Falls is, at 807m, in Venezuela). In fact according to the world waterfall database, Kaieteur is only the 122nd tallest. It is one of the top five most powerful waterfalls in the world and is also rated one of the most visually impressive. Regardless of its place in the record books, its isolation and trickle of visitors (about two planeloads a week) give it an aura not found at many of the world's other great waterfalls.

The high chance of spotting **wildlife**, including the brilliant orange cock-of-the-rock bird and thumb-sized golden frogs that reside in giant bromeliads and produce a toxin 160,000-times more potent than cocaine, is an additional reason for forking out the money to visit Kaieteur.

Costs and tours

Seeing Kaieteur Falls does not come cheap. Day-trips from Georgetown, including the flight from Ogle, park entrance fees and lunch, start at G$33,600. For an additional G$9170 or so you can take another twenty-minute flight to **Orinduik Falls**, a series of mini-falls and pools on the Ireng River bordering Brazil, ideal for swimming. The best time to visit Kaieteur is in the wet season when the falls are at their widest (while high, they are relatively narrow when compared with the likes of Niagara, Iguaçu, Angel and other well-known waterfalls). The problem here is that planes often have trouble landing on the airstrip owing to mist. Most tour operators in Georgetown offer Kaieteur trips (see p.690).

While flying in will give you a panoramic view of the falls, Kaieteur Gorge and the Pakaraima Mountains, trekking there is the more rewarding experience – provided you have the time and money. Rainforest Tours, Hotel Tower, 74–75 Main St Georgetown (Ⓣ592/227-5632, Ⓦwww.rainforesttoursgy.com), offers five-day **overland tours** to Kaieteur, which involve driving to the Potaro River and continuing by boat and on foot to the falls, sleeping at basic campsites en route. At Kaieteur itself, there is a **guesthouse** with hammocks – but no running water – for G$1000 a night. It is just down the path from the entrance to the park where you will most likely have arrived with a guide by biplane. Be sure to bring your own food.

IWOKRAMA RAINFOREST AND AROUND

The pristine, 400-square kilometre **IWOKRAMA RAINFOREST** is home to 474 bird species, 130 different mammals, 420 types of fish and 132 species of reptile – subjects of the ongoing scientific research at the field station and the basis of Iwokrama's other main activity: eco-tourism. The road south of Georgetown to Iwokrama passes through **Linden**, Guyana's second largest town with little of interest for visitors. The unsealed road gets increasingly bumpier as it nears the **Essequibo River crossing** (G$9000 for 4WD vehicles; G$25,000 for trucks; when driving yourself, you only pay if you are coming from Georgetown, since prices are for a return), roughly 160km south.

Rainforest field station

A short way downriver is the **Iwokrama Rainforest Field Station** (reservations through Iwokrama International Centre, 77 High St Ⓣ592/225-1504), the focal point of an ambitious, internationally funded project to promote sustainable development of the rainforest. Tourists staying at the field station share lodgings and meals with biologists, botanists and other researchers engaged in projects aimed at conserving and developing the forest in a sustainable way for economic and social ends. The eco-tourism side of things involves nature walks, nocturnal caiman spotting and visits to a nearby Amerindian village, all conducted by knowledgeable, well-trained guides.

Canopy walkway

Don't miss the opportunity to visit the rainforest's other tourist attraction, the **Canopy Walkway** (G$3600, not at the Field Station). A short hike from the **Atta Rainforest Camp** (Ⓣ592/227-7698, Ⓔinfo@iwokramacanopywalkway.com) about one kilometre off the road to Lethem, and about a 45-minute drive south from the Essequibo River. This 140-metre network of aluminium suspension bridges in the treetops has four observation platforms, the highest of which is some thirty metres above the forest floor, an excellent vantage point to spot birds, monkeys and various fauna on the forest floor. The bridges wobble, but are very solid and have high ropes to hang on to; even so, vertigo sufferers might find the experience challenging.

An overnight stay at the canopy including three meals, the canopy user fee and a trained guide will set you back G$18,000.

Surama

A few kilometres further south is the turn-off for **Surama Village** at the southern end of the Iwokrama Rainforest. A small Amerindian settlement of some 226 people, it rests on a patch of savanna land in the forest. Of all the native villages in Guyana, Surama has been one of the most proactive in preparing for the arrival of tourists: there are individual guesthouses (an overnight stay with meals and guided hikes starts at about G$26,000) and local guides conduct nature walks and mountain hikes. One of the most popular excursions is a night spent on the banks of the nearby **Burro River**, where you can enjoy (and be kept awake by) the sounds of the forest.

RUPUNUNI SAVANNA

Travel in the **RUPUNUNI SAVANNA** is expensive without your own car but it provides a welcome break from the typical rainforest-and-river experience offered throughout the Guianas. A few kilometres further south of the turn-off for Surama village, the dense, surrounding vegetation suddenly disappears as you enter the flatlands that stretch across the whole of southern Guyana (about one-third of the whole country). Here, you'll find cowboys working vast cattle ranches, which you can visit and work at. These ranches constitute the lifeblood of the small Amerindian settlements – **Annai**, **Karanambo** and **Dadanawa** – that have formed around them.

The wildlife becomes much easier to spot during boat trips on the nearby Rupununi River than under the forest canopy. The highlight for many visitors are the **giant river otters**, the rehabilitation of which is close to the heart of Karanambo Ranch's owner, Diane McTurk (note that during the wet season, *kaboura* flies, sandflies and mosquitoes can be a problem in this part of the savanna and in general, driving becomes difficult, if not impossible, as much of the savanna is under several metres of water.)

Arrival and information

It is easy to get to the savanna's main settlements such as Annai, Lethem and Karanambo by **air** from Georgetown. Transguyana Airways have flights to all three for G$21,000 one way, G$39,000 return. If you then want to fly from one point to another within the savanna you must pay an additional G$21,000 for a confirmed seat. Standby tickets are possible assuming there is space on the flight and the plane is scheduled to stop at your desired destination (Lethem is always a scheduled stop but landings at Annai and Karanambo are by request only). **Land transfers** by 4WD prearranged by tour operators can be more expensive than flying. Typical one-way prices for Lethem-Annai, Annai-Karanambo and Annai-Iwokrama can cost you G$27,000 and up while a trip between Annai and Surama starts at G$9,000. Aside from the infrequent **bus** between Lethem and Georgetown, there are no passenger services in the savanna. Villagers are usually amenable to driving you for a little less.

PERMITS FOR AMERINDIAN VILLAGE VISITS

In Guyana, a **permit** may be necessary should you wish to visit an Amerindian village and if you are on an organized excursion, the tour operator will have done all of the necessary paperwork. Independent travellers, however, should contact the Ministry of Amerindian Affairs in Georgetown (☎592/226-5167) to find out whether or not a permit is required.

Accommodation and eating

Visitors can stay at the **cattle ranches**, which have incorporated a range of activities for the eco-tourist into the day-to-day operation of running a ranch. These activities have the feel of being complementary to – rather than the purpose for – the ranch, so when you accompany a *vacqueiro*, or cowboy, to round up cattle, you really feel more like a fly-on-the-saddle than a tourist being taken for a (horse) ride.

Dadanawa c/o Wilderness Explorers ⓣ592/227-7698, ⓦwww.wilderness-explorers.com/dadanawa. This is the largest and most isolated – and therefore the most difficult to access – ranch in the country, a 3hr drive southeast of Lethem and the Kanuku Mountains in the tiny settlement of Dadanawa. ⑨

Karanambo c/o Wilderness Explorers, Annai, ⓣ592/227-7698, ⓦwww.wilderness-explorers.com/karanambu.htm. The largest ranch in the North Rupununi and the first to offer nature-based tourism in the region. Accommodation is in five twin-bedded *cabañas* with verandas, hammocks and a bewildering selection of toiletries, creams and repellents. ⑨

Rock View Lodge Annai, ⓦwww.rockviewlodge.com or c/o Evergreen Adventures, (see p.690). The only ranch accessible by public transport, *Rock View* is a short way from the Lethem-Georgetown road. The lodge has comfortable, self-contained rooms, one of the few swimming pools outside Georgetown and excellent food. It provides comprehensive bird lists and maps of the local area for birders and trekkers and is also the logical base from which to explore the other attractions of the North Rupununi such as Karanambo, Surama, and Iwokrama. ⑦–⑨

LETHEM

Apart from an airstrip and one or two administrative buildings and hotels, there is not much to detain you in this relaxing Guyanese town on the Brazilian border, unless you are breaking your journey either on your way to or from Boa Vista in Brazil.

Those wanting to get a **vehicle to Georgetown** should contact Peter (ⓣ592/772-2033), who operates 4WD passenger services more or less daily, from the blue and white building at the turn-off before the roundabout in the town centre. The daily departure is scheduled for 10pm, and his friendly mother will let you sleep for free in hammocks until the vehicle is ready to leAve The trip to Georgetown takes around eleven hours and starts at G$10,000.

Accommodation and eating

Kanuku View Restaurant and Snackette Next to the roundabout. Both hotels offer meals but this snackette next to the roundabout boasts a menu of Chinese, Indian and Brazilian specialities (rice is guaranteed at all times.)

Savannah Inn ⓣ592/772-2035. Comfortable, self-contained a/c rooms and cabins with televisions. The hotel even has its own restaurant and bar. ⑤–⑥

Takatu Guest House ⓣ592/772-2034. Friendly staff, clean rooms, with a patio and garden for barbecues. ⑤

CROSSING INTO BRAZIL

Lethem is separated from the Brazilian town of Bonfim by the Takutu River. The official crossing is about 1.5 kilometres north of Lethem (pick-ups from the airstrip to the crossing G$300), although Guyanese **immigration formalities** should be completed either at the airstrip, when there are flights, or at the Lethem immigration office in a nondescript house in a residential part of town – ask at the Chinese restaurant at the first turning on the left when entering town from the river crossing for directions. Dug-outs transport foot passengers across the river (G$200), while a pontoon carries vehicles. You can get your passport stamped on the Brazilian side of the border before making your way to Bonfim, from where you can get buses to Boa Vista. **Moneychangers** on the Lethem side of the river will change Guyanese dollars for Brazilian reals and vice-versa (US dollars are harder to sell); make sure that you have enough reals to get you to Bonfim, if not Boa Vista.

East to Suriname

Take the cliché, 'time is money,' to heart. Making the trip to Paramaribo from Georgetown by land is easily arranged through **Brian Mini Bus Service, Bobby Taxi Bus Service** and **P&A Ice Cream Parlor & Transportation Service** (see p.694), G$9,000 (includes the G$3,000 one-way Moleson Creek ferry ticket). It's an ungodly wake-up time but there is only one ferry each way a day and you will need to wake up that early to make the 10am crossing. The buses above will pick you up at your hotel so you can avoid the barely-lit walk to the sketchy Berbice carpark. All told, the journey can take until 8pm which makes the 7am, G$33,200 flight (Tues, Thurs & Sat) very attractive. The trip between capitals *can* be broken up with a stop in **Corriverton, New Amsterdam** or Suriname's **Nieuwe Nickerie** but you would be better off just getting yourself to Paramaribo as quickly as possible where the food, lodging and nightlife far surpasses anything you will have found in Georgetown.

VISAS FOR SURINAME

Suriname is the most bureaucratic country in the Guianas – only nationals of Brazil, Chile, Ecuador, Gambia, Hong Kong, Israel, Japan, Malaysia, Philippines, Singapore, South Korea, Switzerland and CARICOM countries can enter without a visa. Overland travellers can obtain visas for Suriname in Cayenne, French Guiana (see p.729) and Georgetown, Guyana (see p.694). The consular section only accepts visa applications Monday, Wednesdays and Fridays, from 8am to noon. They will ask you to return on the next day the consular section is open but can be persuaded with a smile to process it the same day. For **US citizens** a multiple-entry visa costs US$100 (good for five years, US$100 bills not accepted as anti-counterfeiting measure). For travellers from other countries a multiple-entry visa costs US$45. Note: the embassy only accepts US$.

NEW AMSTERDAM

While hardly a highlight of Guyana, the compact town of **NEW AMSTERDAM**, just over a hundred kilometres from Georgetown, is certainly a better place to rest your head than rowdy Corriverton. An important port town for the export of bauxite, New Amsterdam's points of interest are limited to a rather sad-looking wooden church at the end of Main Street, a municipal park and some grand old wooden buildings around the market on Strand Street.

Arrival and information

Getting to New Amsterdam (often referred to as "Berbice" by **minibus** drivers) from Georgetown is simple: take a #50 bus to Rosignol (1hr 30min; G$500), then cross the Berbice River by ferry to New Amsterdam (roughly every half-hour; G$40). Minibuses to Corriverton (1hr 10min; G$400) and the Suriname ferry at Moleson Creek (1hr 30min; G$500) leave from the road leading to the New Amsterdam ferry stelling.

Accommodation

Hotel Astor 7 Strand St ⓣ592/333-3578, In an attractive wooden building with a veranda 100 metres or so from the ferry stelling. ❹–❺

Parkway Hotel 4 Main St ⓣ592/333/3928, Self-contained rooms with fan and TV. ❺–❻

Eating

Caribbean Cuisine The most upscale and expensive restaurant in the region serves local and international cuisines about two kilometres out of New Amsterdam on the road to Corriverton.

Lim Kang 12 Chapel St ⓣ333-2755. Large portions of sweet-and-sour pork and fried rice are served up while Indian music plays in the background.

Jokwesan's 7 Charlotte St ☎333-2464. The place to go for Creole cook-up and *channa*.

CORRIVERTON

From New Amsterdam, the road continues to run parallel to the Atlantic coaSt bending evermore southward towards its terminus at the mouth of the Corentyne River. Before reaching **CORRIVERTON** (actually comprised of Springlands and Skeldon), facing Suriname across the river, you will pass the Guyana Sugar Corporation at Albion, which – for now at least – is the largest sugar estate in the country. The main reason for coming here, however, is the cricket ground on the estate that plays host to international matches. About ten kilometres before Corriverton, No. 63 Beach in Village 63 is arguably Guyana's most popular beach despite that it's a muddy stretch of coast more suited to cricket than sunbathing.

Accommodation and eating

Mahogany Hotel 50 Public Rd, Village 78 ☎592/339-2289. The best choice by virtue of its pleasant, compact, clean rooms and veranda overlooking the Corentyne River. ④–⑤

The Train next to the Shell Service Station. A popular place to eat a curry and *roti* breakfast before crossing the border.

Suriname

SURINAME (pronounced *Suranama*), one of South America's smallest nations, shares certain traits in common with its Caribbean neighbours. Like its Guyanese cousin it has the palm trees without the crystal-clear water beaches and feels unlike much of the rest of the continent on which it is situated. Suriname only gained independence from the Dutch in 1975 and the vestiges of colonialism, not least of which are the language, many Dutch tourists and some attractive wooden architecture in the capital, **Paramaribo**, make Suriname a quirky place to include on a pan-South American trip.

For serious eco-tourists, meanwhile, the fact that nearly thirteen percent of the country's land surface area is under official environmental protection has led to the creation of a number of nature parks and reserves offering good opportunities for hiking and observing wildlife. **Brownsberg Nature Park** is the most easily accessible from Paramaribo; the **Central Suriname Nature Reserve** is one of the largest of its kind in the world; and Olive Ridley turtles can be seen laying their eggs in **Galibi Nature Reserve**.

CHRONOLOGY

Suriname's earliest inhabitants are thought to be the Surinen Indians after whom the country is named.

1498 Columbus sights Surinamese coast.

1499 Alonso de Ojeda discovers northern coast of South America.

1593 Spain explores Suriname.

1602 Dutch begin to settle the land.

1651 England establishes first permanent settlement.

1667 Becomes Dutch Guiana with the Treaty of Breja, a formal exchange with the British for Nieuw Amsterdam (now New York).

1853 Chinese plantation labourers begin arriving.

1863 Abolition of slavery.

1873 Labourers from India begin to arrive.

1890 Indonesian labourers mostly from Java begin to arrive.

1916 Discovery of bauxite deposits leads ALCOA to begin investments in the country.

1949 First elections based on universal suffrage held.

1954 Netherlands grants colony autonomy in the running of its internal affairs.

1975 Nov. 25 Suriname wins independence.

1980 Military coup led by Sergeant Major Dési Boutersi topples government.

1982 Fifteen prominent leaders of re-democratization movement executed.

1986 Surinamese Liberation Army, a group constisting mainly of Bush Negroes, attacks economic targets in the interior.

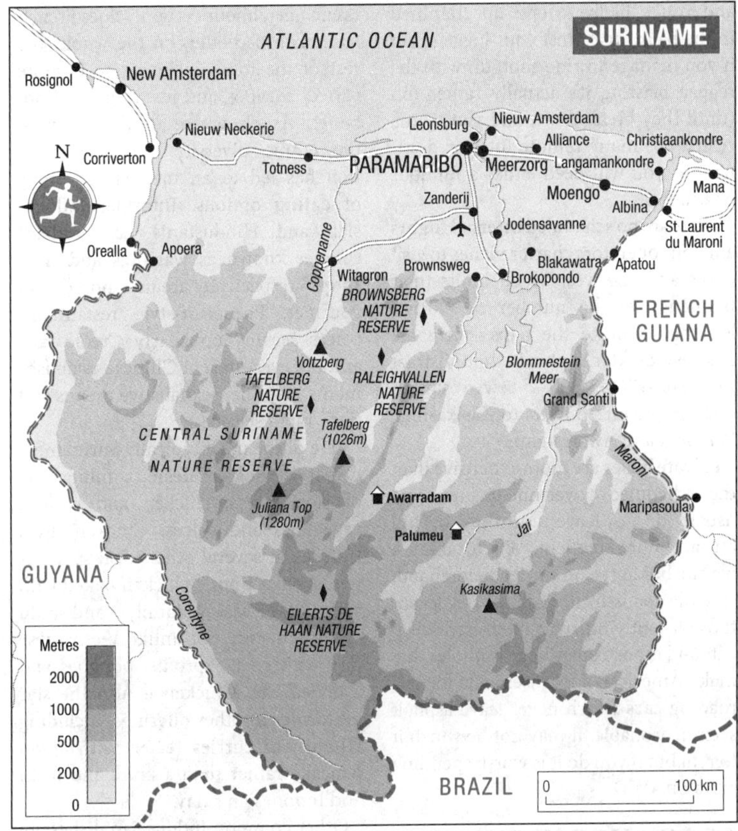

1987 Civilian government installed with new constitution for Republic of Suriname.
1990 Military overthrows civilian government.
1991 Under international pressure Bouterse holds elections. The New Front, a coalition of parties, wins and Ronald Venetiaan is elected president.
1992 Peace accord signed between new government and the Bush Negro insurgency.
1996 National Democratic Party (founded by Bouterse in the early 1990s) wins election.
2000 Venetiaan and the New Front coalition regains presidency with promises of fixing the economy.
2006 Venetiaan reelected.

ARRIVAL

Johan Adolf Pengel International Airport (also known as Zanderij), an hour south of Paramaribo, receives direct flights from Amsterdam; Belem, Brazil; Port of Spain and Tobago; Curacao and Cayenne. **Zorg en Hoop**, Suriname's airport for internal flights, is in a southeastern suburb of Paramaribo.

From Georgetown, Guyana, it is a four-hour **bus** ride to the Moleson Creek **ferry** crossing (one per day, allow two hours) followed by a six-hour bus ride from South Drain to Georgetown. As in Guyana you cannot take **rental cars** over the border.

GETTING AROUND

Learn to love the minibuses that are the number one means of travel both between the capital and smaller cities near the coast and to Parbo's different neighbourhoods. Sure they're crowded and you're likely to end up crammed in the back up against your luggage but if you manage to ride shotgun with the reggae blasting it's actually rather fun (until they break down and you're in a rush). For many remote interior destinations you will need either a minibus or a flight.

There are no scheduled **internal flights** and tour operators charter planes to visit parks and reserves, which limits their frequency to the number of tourists looking to make the trips. Suriname Airways, Dokter Sophie Redmondstraat 219 ⓣ597/432-700, ⓦwww.slm.nr, does fly organized tours to Kasikasima, Palumeu and Awarradam.

Private buses are more expensive than the scheduled government ones and usually do not leave until they are full but are more frequent. When taking a private bus agree on the fee beforehand.

While roads in the capital are decent those in outlying areas often have deep ruts and monstrously huge potholes that make American advertisements for off-roading **cars** which never leave asphalt seem reasonable. It may not be worth it to rent but if you do it is worth spending extra on 4WD.

ACCOMMODATION

There are plenty of options to suit almost any budget in Suriname. **Hostels** provide the cleanest most fun budget-options in the Guianas and the only two *true* hostels (always abuzz with young people and a good vibe) in all three countries.

There are plenty of **midrange** hotels and guesthouses in Parbo and a few in Nieuw Nickerie but do not count on creature comfort elsewhere, especially Albina where you are better off crossing into French Guiana to spend the night.

FOOD

Some would have you believe the food in French Guiana is better than that in Suriname – don't buy it. While its French neighbour certainly does French *haute cuisine* better, on the whole, the rest of the food in Suriname is more varied, cheaper, and just as good if not better. As elsewhere in the Guianas, the ethnic diversity of the population has led to an interesting variety of **eating** options. Informal Indonesian and Hindustani (East Indian) eateries known as **warungs** and "**roti shops**" respectively are juxtaposed with gourmet, European-style restaurants, places serving up hearty Creole fare, and the ever-present Chinese establishments with their exhaustive menus and ultra-rapid service.

One of the most typically Surinamese dishes is **moksie alesie**, a filling mix of rice, beans, chicken and various vegetables and spices. Chicken (**kip**) features in several other local specialities, such as **pom** – chicken baked with a root of the cassava family – and **saoto** – chicken soup not unlike Vietnamese phô with bean sprouts, potatoes and a boiled egg. Chicken is also the star performer in other offerings, including Hindustani curries (eaten with a *roti* pancake rather than a knife and fork) and Indonesian **satay**.

Other common Indonesian dishes are **bami** and **nassie goreng** – fried noodles and fried rice respectively. **Pindasoep** and **petjil** are two tasty peanut soups, the former made with **tom-tom** (plantain noodles), the latter with vegetables. While no one is about to put the cuisine of the Netherlands at the head of the class, traditional Dutch favourites like **bitterbollen** (minced meat, broth and flour rolled, breaded and fried), **berehap** (meatball and onion ring fried and smothered with peanut sauce), **poffertjes** (small pancakes served with powdered sugar), and **pannekoeken** (pancakes) are plentiful. **Patat** (Dutch french fries) may not have quite the reputation of their Belgian neighbour but they certainly are crispy, tasty and easy to find.

DRINK

Local **rum** does not rival Guyana's 15-year El Dorado but both Boerga and Black Cat hold their own (the latter better mixed with cola or coconut water). While **beer** – both imported and local brands such as Parbo – spirits, soft drinks and bottled water are widely available, **dawet**, a local concoction of coconut milk and lemongrass, is worth a try. Good coffee and espresso can be found at several cafés and restaurants. Generally, the tap **water** in Suriname is safe to drink, especially in Paramaribo, although it is better to ask locals first in outlying areas.

CULTURE AND ETIQUETTE

With so many different ethnic groupings, Surinamese **culture** is a patchwork of different influences, each ethnic group preserving its own cultural traditions in isolation from the rest; even in public spheres such as politics racial allegiances die hard. Even so, the Surinamese are proud of their diversity. Thirty-seven percent of the population is Hindustani (the local term to describe East Indians), thirty-one percent is Creole (people of African or mixed European and African origins), fifteen percent is Javanese, ten percent Bush Negro and the remainder Amerindian, Chinese, Portuguese and Jewish. **Religious practice** is similarly diverse: Hindu 27.4 percent; Protestant 25.2 percent; Roman Catholic 22.8 percent; Muslim 19.6 percent; indigenous beliefs 5 percent.

The official **language** in Suriname is **Dutch** and that famous Dutch acceptance can certainly be found in the general population. But English is readily spoken in the capital and in reality Dutch is a second tongue for most Surinamese. Hindustani and Sranan Tongo (Surinamese Creole) are the first languages of more than 60 percent of the population, while other ethnicities have clung to their own linguistic traditions. Several *maroon* languages, the principal of which are Saramaccan and Aukan, as well as Javanese and Amerindian languages such as Carib are also spoken.

It is customary to leave 10 percent for good service. When **tipping** at a hotel, make sure a service charge has not already been added.

SPORTS AND OUTDOOR ACTIVITIES

The Surinamese are not cricket-crazy like the Guyanese; here, instead, **football** fields are prevalent. Most good footballers leave to play in the Dutch professional leagues thus becoming ineligible to play for their national team.

Though not a conventional sport, but still very competitive, **bird-singing contests** are held on Onafhankelijkheidsplein in front of the presidential palace on Sunday mornings. Picolets and twatwas are persuaded to sing in turns with the winning bird earning the payout for its owner.

COMMUNICATIONS

Surpost (Kerkplein 1 ⓣ597/477-524, ⓦwww.surpost.com), a block away from RBTT can be hectic but its service is reliable if slow and airmail rates for

SURINAME ON THE NET

ⓦwww.suriname-tourism.org The Suriname Tourism Foundation promotes tourism in Suriname. Its office in Paramaribo is very friendly and helpful.

ⓦwww.stinasu.com Do not travel to a park or preserve without first touching base with Stinasu, which manages them.

ⓦwww.parbo.com Devoted to the capital, the site offers information on culture, climate and hotels.

ⓦwww.surinam.net Current affairs and Suriname-related message boards.

PRESS, TV AND RADIO

All Surinamese newspapers and television and radio stations are in Dutch.

Newspapers The main daily is De Ware Tijd (www.dwt.net), where you can sometimes read the news.

Radio Radio 10 (88.1FM) and Radio Paramaribo (89.7FM) are the principal stations – both have news bulletins in English. Radio ABC (104.1).

Television ABC, Apintie and SRS also show programmes and sports events, like basketball games, in English.

postcards are S$2.60 or less to anywhere in the world.

Public **telephone booths** in Suriname do not accept coins so you are going to have to buy a **phonecard** issued by Telesur in denominations of US$3, 5 and 10, sold at shops and street stands everywhere. Telesur cards work with PIN numbers and can be used to make local, national and international calls. **Internet cafes** are common in Paramaribo (about S$4 per hr), but much less so elsewhere.

CRIME AND SAFETY

Locals are proud of saying that tourists can walk from one end of the city to the other at night without incident. While there are not many reports of criminal incidents within **Paramaribo** near the major tourist hotels, visitors may be seen as targets of opportunity and should stay alert. Travel to the interior is usually without issue but there is not a major police presence outside the capital. **Moengo** should be avoided and there is no reason to stay in **Albina** longer than to get off the bus and onto a boat across the river to French Guiana (see p.720).

EMERGENCY NUMBERS

115 the general emergency number for the police.

110 for the fire service.

113 for public ambulance services.

EMERGENCIES

Medical care is limited as is the small ambulance fleet but the **Academisch Ziekenhuis** (www.azp.sr, 597/442-222, Flustraat) has an emergency room and general practitioners who speak English.

INFORMATION AND MAPS

Paramaribo is the easiest city in the three Guianas to find maps. The **tourist office** at Waterkant 1 at the end of Gravens Straat has two types of city **maps** and is overflowing with pamphlets in Dutch and English providing information about banks, health, restaurants, transportation, nightlife and day-trips. Larger, laminated maps can be found at the tourist office next to *Zeelandia Suites* near the *'T Vat* bar (see p.712).

MONEY AND BANKS

The unit of **currency** is the Suriname dollar (S$), which comes in 5, 10, 20, 50 and 100 notes and 1, 5, 10, 25, 100 and 250 cent coins. Rates are often given in Euros.

Banks are usually open Mon–Fri 7am–2pm and street **currency exchanges** often offer better exchange rates. Major **credit cards** are accepted by most tour operators and in many restaurants and hotels in Paramaribo, but **cash advances** are only possible at RBTT Bank

STUDENT AND YOUTH DISCOUNTS

Check out the Suriname section of the ISIC website (www.istc.org) for the latest offers on accommodation, bikes, mopeds and restaurant specials.

(Kerkplein 1 ☎597/471-555). **ATMs** in Paramaribo do not accept foreign credit cards and are sparse outside town so carry a little extra **cash** for the interior, river crossings and South Drain. At the time of writing, US$1 = S$2.75, €1 = S$3.82, £1 = S$4.12. Prices throughout this guide are given in Suriname dollars.

Paramaribo

Sure, there's traffic and urban sprawl, but this Guiana capital has much more to offer than either Georgetown or Cayenne. Like Georgetown, much of the colonial architecture has been in a state of disrepair for quite some time but the Surinamese are actually *doing* something to prevent the loss of their heritage. Many of the buildings on **Waterkant** and **Mr Lim A Postraat** have already been rehabilitated, making a sunset walk along the river practically romantic. And while things at the market and in the shopping district get messy, there are people paid to pick it all up at the end of the business day – even the gutters and dirt paths get raked clean in many of the touristed areas. Less ominous and safer than Georgetown, **Parbo** (as locals call it) has great food, the best budget accommodation in the Guianas and a buzzing nightlife with casinos to boot.

Onafhankelijkheidsplein

Most of the worthwhile things to see in Parbo are around Onafhankelijkheidsplein, the well-manicured green, which attracts locals, musicians and bird-singing competitions. A **statue** of a very portly Johan Adolf Pengal, the former president of Suriname, is overlooked by the dramatically-lit **Presidential Palace** and other attractive state buildings. Behind the palace is the **Palmentuin**, an impressive park full of lofty, breeze-swayed, palm trees (avoid at night). East just past the Palmentuin on Kleine Waterstraat is the main tourist area filled with hotels, bars and restaurants, all seemingly centred around the patio bar, **'T Vat**.

North of the green

North of the green on Gravenstraat is the colourful **St Peter and Paul's Cathedral**. Made entirely of wood and almost as large as St George's Cathedral in Georgetown (see p.687), it is finally undergoing a restoration.

South of the green

South of the green, on the river, are a cluster of tree-shaded paths and well-preserved old buildings including **Fort Zeelandia** which houses the **Suriname Foundation Museum** (Tues–Fri 9am–2pm, Sun 10am–2pm; $8; free guided tours Sun 11am & 12.30pm). While the dusty exhibits related to Surinamese history are uninspired, the fort has a café and a good view of the **Suriname River**. **Mr Lim A Postraat** has several preserved colonial buildings, and contains the **Numismatic Museum of the Central Bank of Suriname**, at no. 7 (Mon–Fri 8am–2pm; free), for those interested in Surinamese coins and banknotes dating from the seventeenth century.

Rehabilitated colonial buildings can be found on the streets between Onafhankelijkheidsplein and Kerkplein. The best buildings were built after the fires of 1821 and 1832 along Waterkant, where ships used to load and unload cargo.

West of the green

West of Onafhankelijkheidsplein on Waterkant along the river are ever-open **food stalls**. A few blocks further is the vast covered, bustling two-storey **central market** where you can find clothes, fruit, vegetables, pastries and fake watches.

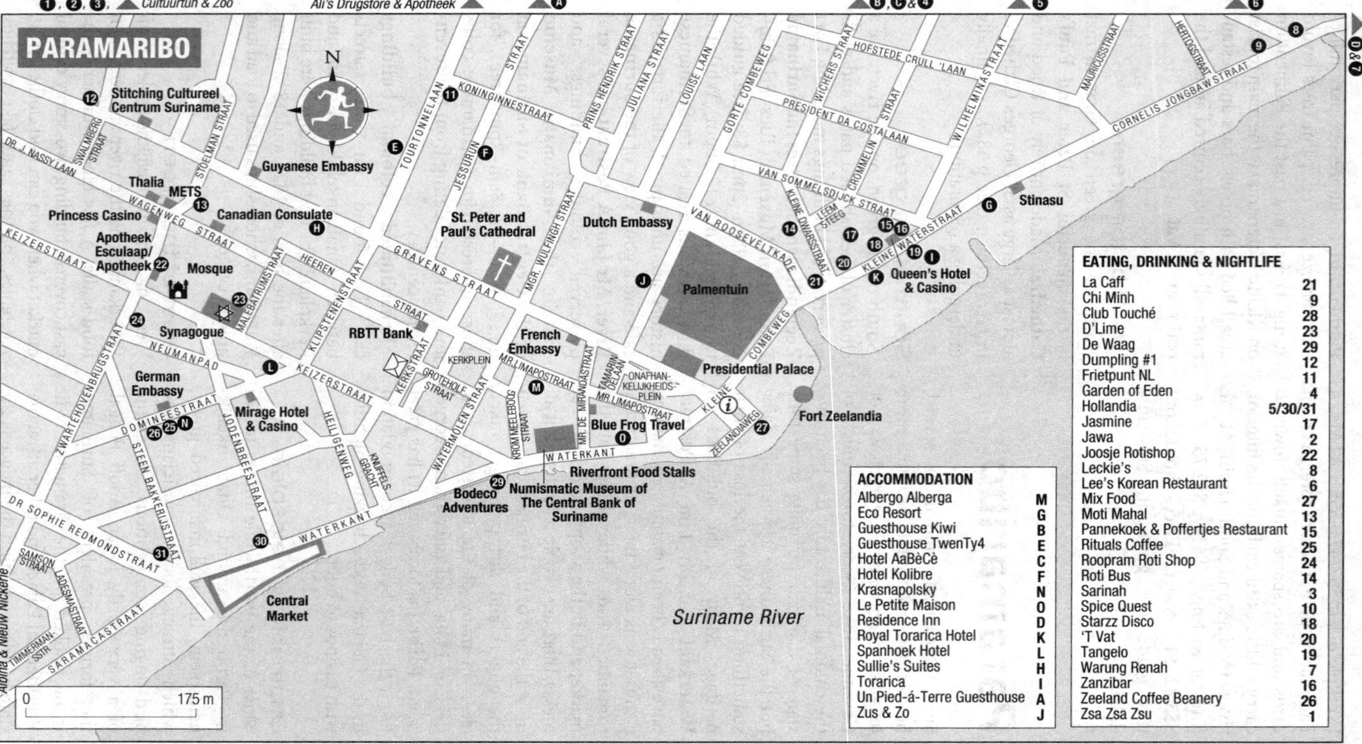

ACCOMMODATION	
Albergo Alberga	M
Eco Resort	G
Guesthouse Kiwi	B
Guesthouse TwenTy4	E
Hotel AaBèCè	C
Hotel Kolibre	F
Krasnapolsky	N
Le Petite Maison	O
Residence Inn	D
Royal Torarica Hotel	K
Spanhoek Hotel	L
Sullie's Suites	H
Torarica	I
Un Pied-á-Terre Guesthouse	A
Zus & Zo	J

EATING, DRINKING & NIGHTLIFE	
La Caff	21
Chi Minh	9
Club Touché	28
D'Lime	23
De Waag	29
Dumpling #1	12
Frietpunt NL	11
Garden of Eden	4
Hollandia	5/30/31
Jasmine	17
Jawa	2
Joosje Rotishop	22
Leckie's	8
Lee's Korean Restaurant	6
Mix Food	27
Moti Mahal	13
Pannekoek & Poffertjes Restaurant	15
Rituals Coffee	25
Roopram Roti Shop	24
Roti Bus	14
Sarinah	3
Spice Quest	10
Starzz Disco	18
'T Vat	20
Tangelo	19
Warung Renah	7
Zanzibar	16
Zeeland Coffee Beanery	26
Zsa Zsa Zsu	1

Past the market is downtown Parbo, full of casinos, gold and jewellery stores, shopping malls, and heavy traffic ;the only significant buildings are side-by-side on **Keizerstraat**, a **mosque** and a **synagogue**, with the temple to American capitalism, *McDonald's* just a block away.

Arrival and information

Air Taxis to Paramaribo from Johan Adolf Pengel International Airport (Zanderij) an hour south of Paramaribo cost about S$140. From Zorg en Hoop, the domestic airport, taxis take30min and cost about S$50 to reach the city centre.

Bus Buses to or from the Guyana river crossing will pick you up and drop you off at your hotel (S$200). Minibuses to Albina (S$7.50) for the crossing into French Guyana can be found in the large lot on Heiligenweg.

Ferry The new Paramaribo-Meerzog bridge has made the narrow wooden boats (S$2) along the river past the foodstands on Waterkant superfluous and there's really no reason to venture to the other side.

Tourist Office Waterkant 1 (Mon–Fri 9am–3.30pm, ⓣ597/410-809) will provide you free maps (one with a walking tour), leaflets by subject, and information on tours, restaurants, and anything you could possibly want to know. Don't forget to pick up a copy of *Destination Guide*.

Tour operators

The natural attractions do not come cheaply (count on S$340–425 per day. While it is possible to get to Brownsberg by STINASU bus on your own and to organize local guides to take you on boat day-trips in the areas surrounding Parbo you'll have to go through a tour operator if you plan on going anywhere else in the interior.

TAXIS

They're unmetered but there's no dearth of drivers you can have at your beck and call. Fares start at about S$10 and increase the farther you get from the centre of town. Ask at your hotel for their recommendations.

Djo's Taxi ⓣ597/471-048
Kleine Min Garage ⓣ597/474-826
Roepi's Taxi ⓣ597/491-100
Romeo's Taxi ⓣ597/492-956
Tourtonne Taxi ⓣ597/475-734
Torarica Taxi ⓣ597/479-977

Blue Frog Travel Mr Dr J C de Mirandastraat 8 ⓣ597/420-808, ⓦwww.etostravel.info. Day-trips and overnight tours to Brownsberg, 4WD adventures, and visits to river rapids.

Bodeco Adventures Waterkant 5, Paramaribo ⓣ597/474-515, ⓦwww.bodeco.sr. All the basics plus dolphin and manatee tours, and visits to local ceramicists and hammock-braiders.

METS Dr J F Nassylaan 2, Paramaribo ⓣ597/477-088, ⓦwww.surinamevacations.com. Operates jungle lodges in the far south and sells tours to points of interest from Jodensavanne and resorts to Bush Negro villages.

STINASU Cornelis Jongbawstreet 14, Paramaribo ⓣ597/476-597, ⓦwww.stinasu.com. Can arrange transport, accommodation and tours to Brownsberg, Raleighvallen and Galibi.

City transport

This is a foot-friendly city. Bus schedules are often organized around the last filled seat so you are better off walking or renting a **bicycle** for the

BUSES FROM PARAMARIBO

Albina (for French Guiana river crossing) minibuses leave from the Central Market, Waterkant 5hr, S$7.50 (use taxi, 2hr, S$40).

Brownsweg (for Brownsberg Nature Park) Saramacastraat, at Ladesmastraat, before 9am, S$12.

Nieuw Nickerie Dr Sophie Redmondstraat, opposite *Hotel Ambassador*, 3hr 30min, S$100 minibus, S$16 state-run bus.

South Drain (for Guyana border crossing) Dr. Sophie Redmondstraat, opposite *Hotel Ambassador*, one a day at 5–6am, S$200, call Bobby Taxi Bus Service ⓣ597/892-8133.

Zanderij (for Johan Pengel International Airport) Knuffelsgracht, 1–1hr 30min, S$4 minibus.

CRIME AND SAFETY

Avoid the **Palmentuin** (Palm Garden area behind the presidential palace) after dark; it is an unlit area popular for sex, drugs and the homeless. Similarly, the residential area **east** of **Van Sommelsdijick Straat** is the domain of drug-pushers and its intersection with **Kleine Dwarsstraat** is a popular place for pimps and prostitutes. While there is safety in numbers at the sidewalk food-stands on the riverbank along the **Waterkaant**, it too gets sketchy as the night progresses. Travellers venturing beyond these cafés on foot are looking for trouble.

day (Cardy Adventures & Bike Rental, Cornelis Jongbawstraat 31 ⓣ597/422-518, S$15 per day).

Buses There are no available timetables but there are bus stops along major roads. Unscheduled **minibuses** leave from the carpark just past *De Waag Restaurant* on Waterkant and a little further along in the carpark on the right at Heiligenweg. For more information call NVB ⓣ597/473-591 or PLO ⓣ597/410-922 but don't be shy about flagging.

Taxis While not the cheapest in the Guianas, taxis are still a good deal and should be taken advantage of for visiting *warungs* and several of Paramaribo's other good restaurants in outlying areas of the city. They are unmetered but journeys within the confines of the city rarely amount to more than S$16. Agree a fare with your driver in advance.

Accommodation

Most of the wide-ranging accommodation options are found either in the busy, gritty, **downtown area** or the holiday resort-like strip of hotels and restaurants **east of Onafhankelijkheidsplein**. You will find hot water at most budget and midrange options but not at any of the hostels or guesthouses. A comprehensive list of **guesthouses** can be found at ⓦwww1.sr.net/~t100956/accommodations.htm.

Hostels and Guesthouses

Hotel AaBèCè Mahonylaan 55 ⓣ597/422-960, ⓔaabece@sr.net. Removed from the tourist area on a quiet street, the rooms are clean and unrefined but very secure. 5–6

Albergo Alberga Mr Lim A Postraat 13B, ⓣ597/520-050, ⓦguesthousealberoalberga.com. Clean, bright, self-contained rooms in a lovely nineteenth-century wooden house with veranda and swimming pool on an aesthetically pleasing street not far from the *'T Vat* area. 4

Guesthouse Kiwi Two locations: Mahonyland 88a, ⓣ597/421-373; Mahonyland 84, ⓣ597/410-744, ⓦwww.guesthousekiwi.com. Behind the black faux-marble front of either location on the same block are sharp, bright rooms with access to the kitchen. 4–5

Guesthouse TwenTy4 Jessurunstraat 24, ⓣ597/420-751 ⓔinfo@crozrootz.com. This new hostel offers clean, bare rooms with fans and sinks. Good breakfast (S$15), reasonably-priced snacks, a covered veranda, friendly staff and a lively bar open until 11pm. 3

Hotel Kolibre Jessurunstraat 9 ⓣ597/891-9051, ⓔinfo@guesthouse-kolibrie@.com. The owners (who unreasonably refuse you wi-fi-access) claim the house was once owned by the son of former coup-leader, Dési Bouterse. This would explain the property size and high walls. Clean rooms but pricey even with the pool. See all apartments before choosing. 6–7

Un Pied-À-Terre Guesthouse Costerstraat 59, ⓣ597/470-488, ⓔfabyayo@sr.net. The basement apartments in this romantic colonial are damp but upstairs, breezy rooms have four-post beds draped with mosquito nets, and hanging a hammock in the garden is the cheapest option in town, just blocks from the action. 3–6

Zus & Zo Grote combéweg 13a ⓣ597/520-905, ⓔzusensosuriname@gmail.com. The rooms in this Swiss-family Robinson-style hostel, the sequel to *Guesthouse TwenTy4*, are basic and not self-contained but the hip downstairs café with good coffee, free wi-fi, wonderful staff, more than 25 varied tours, bicycle rental, and great location (facing the Palmentuin) make this Paramaribo's best budget option. 4–5

Hotels

Eco Resort Cornelis Jongbawstraat 16 ⓣ597/425-522, ⓦecores.com. Slightly smaller rooms than its sister hotel *Torarica*, but just as comfortable and cheaper with access to *Torarica's* pool and other facilities. Free airport transfer and same annoying check-in time. 8–9

Krasnapolsky Domineestraat 39 ⓣ597/475-050, ⓔreservations@krasnapolsky.sr.com. Large, six-storied, 84-room business hotel in the centre of downtown has a third-floor pool, and excellent buffet breakfasts (included in rates) with uninspired but functional rooms. 9

Mirage Hotel & Casino Domineestraat 11 ⓣ597/473-380, ⓦpashagaming.com. This

TREAT YOURSELF

You have been extensively travelling in the Guianas. You are caked with red soil from Amazon adventures, you are tired of sleeping in hammocks and being squashed into minibuses. You want terry cloth, dry, perfectly climate-controlled rooms, pillowtop mattresses and impeccable furnishings. You want the four-star pampering that comes with the fourth star. There's no ambivalence, you want the **Royal Torarica Hotel**. This is the most luxurious hotel in the Guianas. You also must really need spoiling to stay here as rooms cost more than most locals probably make in a month.

Kleine Waterstraat 10 ⓣ597/473-500, ⓔinfo@royaltorarica.com. ⑨

downtown hotel has surprisingly nice rooms with hardwood floors at a reasonable price. Breakfast included. ⑦

La Petite Maison Waterkant 4 ⓣ597/475-466, ⓔinfo@hotellapetitemaison.com. Comfortable bed and breakfast in a two-storey restored mansion facing the Suriname River. Ask for a room facing the river and open the curtains for sunset. ⑦–⑧

Residence Inn Anton Dragtenweg 7 ⓣ597/472-387, ⓔresinpbo@sr.net. Sweet-smelling, spacious, a/c cabana-rooms. There's a swimming pool and bar all slightly removed from the noise of the '*T Vat* area. ⑧–⑨

Spanhoek Hotel Domineestraat 2-4, ⓣ597/477-888, ⓔreservation@spanhoekhotel.com. Downtown, classy, designer wood-finished rooms in this boutique hotel are nicer than *Torarica's* but without its other perks. ⑨

Sullie's Suites Gravenstraat 53 ⓣ597/520-522, ⓔsulliessuites@sr.com. Rooms are superbly-equipped (kitchen with toaster and microwave, video recorder and CD player) but damp, tacky and fluorescently-lit. The most expensive room has a full-size Jacuzzi next to the bed. ⑥–⑦

Torarica Mr L J Rietbergplein 1 ⓣ597/471-500, ⓔinfo@torarica.com. At this price the stale rooms and poor service should be extravagant enough to make you forget the cigarette smoke-filled lobby. Tourists still flock for live music, tennis courts, sauna, poolside bar and Jacuzzi despite the incomprehensible 5pm check-in time. Free airport transfer. ⑨

Eating

There are several restaurants in and immediately around **'T Vat**, the favourite hangout for Dutch tourists (mostly because of the patio seating and central location). Paramaribo has even more options downtown and even on the periphery of the city. At least once during your stay take a taxi to the neighbourhood of **Blauwgrond** (past *Residence Inn*) to eat at one of the many **warungs** (Javanese restaurants) found in abundance here. There are also several worthy **food stands** by the Suriname River that are good for late night snacks – try Uncle Ré, which specializes in Creole food or the amusing, Chung Kee's Ken Tucky Fried Chicken.

Cafés and bakeries

Frietpunt NL Tourtonnelaan 48. From *bitterbollen* to *broodje kroket*, burger to berehap, this is the place for Dutch snacks, including *frites oorlog* ("fries at war," with various sauces together).

Hollandia Local bakery chain with several locations (Wilhelminastraat, Waterkant). Their popular pizza-bread runs out by 2pm.

Leckie's Mahonylaan 66b ⓣ597/474-237. This former butcher now churns out great burgers and Dutch *krokets*. Try the namesake burger: two all-beef patties with the works.

TREAT YOURSELF

If you are the kind of person who scrimps on lodging in order to spend on good food there are a few good places to start spending in Parbo.

D'Lime Malebatrumstraat 1–7 ⓣ597/470-533. Chic downtown lounge serves fancy cocktails, and a menu ranging from smoked fish and spicy pasta to steak and duck.

Garden of Eden Virolastraat 61 ⓣ597/499-448. You'll need a taxi but the tranquil outdoor setting, quality Thai curries and on-point service are well worth the trip.

Spice Quest Nassylaan 107 ⓣ597/520-747. Parbo's most upscale restaurant does decent haute cuisine from amuse-bouches and paté to confit and lobster tail. Reserve day-ahead for their sushi menu. Try a shot of the house-steeped ginger rum.

Mix Food Zeelandiaweg 1 ☎597/420-688. Generous, rice-heavy portions of Creole and Indonesian food, including the Surinamese dish *moksi alesie*, served at tables next to the Suriname River removed from the traffic.

Rituals Coffee Next door to *Zeeland*, you can substitute the first word of this café's name, squint and swear it's *Starbucks*. Decent bagel sandwiches and panini made to order.

Tangelo Mr Rietbergplein 1. Serves light fare along with desserts, coffee and cocktails on a terrace perched across nearly across from *'T Vat*.

'T Vat Kleine Waterstraat 1A. Popular Dutch hangout known for its *satays* and shady sidewalk terrace which sometimes features live music and shows. Portions are small and the waiters are more concerned with each other than you.

Zeeland Coffee Beanery Domineestraat 39. Outdoor seating at this corner cafe is a good place to sip espresso and observe the strip.

Restaurants

Chi Minh Cornelis Jongbawstraat 83 ☎597/412-155. *Chi Minh* has a vast menu and an ornate a/c dining room with takeaway at street level. Try the spicy shrimp.

De Waag Waterkant 5 ☎597/426-994. If you are determined to eat Italian food in Suriname this beautiful open-air, riverside café is the place to do it.

Dumpling #1 Nassylaan 12 ☎597/477-904. This breezy, candlelit, unpretentious Chinese restaurant on tree-lined, peaceful Nassylaan has great ambience, quick service and good food. Locals flock for the king crab legs.

Jasmine Kleine Dwarsstraat 85 boven ☎597/473-558. Enjoy the chicken *jalfrezi* and an order of fried banana with spicy peanut sauce at a balcony table overlooking the *'T Vat* crowd.

Jawa Kasaboloweg br 7 ☎597/492-714. Two *minutes* past *Sarinah* is *Jawa*, another upscale *warung* with a bigger dining room and a takeaway counter that also sells Surinamese Oldies CDs.

Lee's Korean Restaurant Mahonylaan 12–14 ☎597/479-834. Private screened rooms and excellent spicy garlic prawns, reasonably priced.

Pannekoek & Poffertjes Restaurant van Sommeldijckstraat 11 ☎597/422-914. Dutch pancakes and crêpes, sweet and savoury, served with a vast list of preserves, fruits and jams.

Sarinah Verlengde Gemenelandsweg 187 ☎597/430-661. This Javanese café on Parbo's outskirts which serves staples from *saoto* (chicken soup) and *rijstaffel* (rice table) to *loempia* (spring roll) and you'll find plenty of other tourists here too.

ROTI

Roti is a staple of the Guianas; you can find everywhere throughout the day and it appeals to carnivores and vegetarians alike. Here are Parbo's best:

Joosje Rotishop Three locations: Zwartenhovenbrugstraat 9; Grote Combeweg; Johannes Mungrastraat. Each of its three locations serves piping hot *roti* with curried chicken, beef, lamb or duck.

Moti Mahal Wagenwegstraat 56–58 ☎597/474-367. Lowkey *roti* shop with a proper dining room as well as a takeaway counter.

Roopram Roti Shop Three locations: Grote Hofstraat 4, Watermolenstraat 37, Zwartenhovenbrugstraat 23. All three cavernous locations quickly serve large, tasty portions of *roti* and *puri* with all the fixings in somewhat antiseptic though popular environs (fried chicken upstairs).

Roti Bus Kleine Dwarsstraat 17. The engine is gone but Pamela and Jerrel churn out tasty *roti* from the kitchen at the back of this clean, white schoolbus (with cognac!).

Warung Renah J S Greenstraat 106 ☎597/450-987. This covered, open-air authentic local standby is quick and does everything from *satay* to *dawat*.

Drinking and nightlife

La Caff Kleine Dwarsstraat 27. The fact that it's small and packed only further encourages the grinding and when it really gets going, the mess spills out onto the patio seating while the owner watches with a young lady on his knee.

Club Touché Dr Sophie Redmondstraat, at A L Waaldijkstraat (Fri & Sat). One of the older clubs in Parbo but still a good place to go for a weekend boogie.

Starzz Disco Kleinewaterstraat 5–7 (Wed–Sat 10pm–3am). Centrally located nightclub is right on the strip next to *'T Vat* with an open balcony for watching the action on the street below.

Zanzibar Sommelsdijkstraat 1. This alcoholic outpost has a lively, open-air bar, outdoor seating and also serves food.

Zsa Zsa Zsu J Pengelstraat. You'll need to take a cab to his new addition to the club scene but it's where the beautiful people go to enjoy the multiple dance areas, varying music styles, bar and restaurant, while dressed to the nines (cover S$12.50)

Entertainment

Locals match pirated DVDs of the latest releases and while there are plans to build a cinema, the only current one you'll find here is the adult variety.
Pro-Ice Kleine Dwarstraat 3, ⓣ597/476-277). Snacks, ice cream, drinks, foojsball, music and pool in the heart of the *'T Vat* area.

Live music and theatre

Check page 4 of *De Ware Tijd* newspaper for the 'Cultuuragenda,' which lists the week's cultural events. There are several annual festivals in Paramaribo depending on the time of year (see ensuing websites) and you can call ahead at the theatres below which occasionally house live performances.

Festivals

Salsuri Festival ⓦwww.salsuri.com. Salsa and zouk dance performances.
Suriname Jazz Festival ⓦwww.surinamejazzfestival.com. Annual event since 2002.

Theatres

NAKS Thomsonstraat 8 ⓣ597/499-033.
Stichting Cultureel Centrum Suriname (Suriname Cultural Centre), Gravenstreet 112–114 ⓣ597/472-369
Thalia Dr J F Nassylaan 4 ⓣ597/472-812.
Unique Fred Derbystraat 23–25 ⓣ597/471-006.

Shopping

It's not quite El Dorado but some locals call Maagdenstraat between Steenbakkerijstraat and Heiligenweg "Gold Street" because it is lined with small **jewellery and gold stores** where reasonable prices can be had and haggling is not unheard of. If you're looking for flip-flops, Indian knick-nacks or cheap knock-offs try **Steenbakkerijstraat**, while the stores on and along **Domineestraat** are good for Amerindian, Javanese and maroon **handicrafts**, most often wood carvings.

On Sunday morning from 7am–2pm there is a Chinese **flea market** on Tourtonnelaan past Koningiinnestraat where you can buy produce, handicrafts and birds (if you want to enter the bird-singing contest on the Onafhankelijkheidsplein).

Directory

Airlines Blue Wing Airlines Doekhieweg 3 ⓣ597/434-393; Caribbean Airlines,

CASINOS

There are plenty of casinos in Parbo where you can take on the house. Here are a few of the nicer places to try your luck.
Ambassador Hotel & Casino Dr S Redmondstraat 66–68. Restaurant, 84 gaming machines and 18 table games.
Golden Truly Hotel & Casino Jozef Israelstraat 43. Over 130 gaming machines and 19 table games (blackjack, poker, roulette).
Mirage Hotel & Casino Domineestraat 11. Slots, poker, roulette and sports betting.
Princess Casino Wagenweg Straasse 81. Over 370 gaming machines and 15 table games in what many claim are Parbo's best surroundings.
Queen's Hotel & Casino Kleine Waterstraat 15. Gaming at over 50 machines and six tables (roulette, blackjack and poker) just a block away from 'T Vat. Free drinks and snacks for players.
Royal Inn Hotel & Casino Steenbakkerijstraat 6–12. Slots, roulette, poker, blackjack and bingo.
Torarica Hotel Casino Mr. Rietbergplein 1. Small space packs in 160 gaming machines and four table games (blackjack, poker, roulette).

Wagenwegstraat 36 ⓣ597/340-035; Gum Air, Doekleweg 3 ⓣ597/498-760; Hi-Jet, Doekhieweg oost 1 ⓣ597/432-577; KLM, Hofstraat 1 ⓣ597/411-811; Martinair, Burenstraat 4ª ⓣ597/471-767; SLM, Coppenamestraat 136, Paramaribo ⓣ597/465-531; Surinam Airways, Dr Sophie Redmondstraat 219 ⓣ597/434-723.

Bookstore Vaco Press Domineestraat 26.

Embassies and Consulates Australia, 18 Herbert St Port of Spain, Trinidad ⓣ868/628-0695; Brazil, Maratakastraat 2 ⓣ597/400-200; Canada, Young & High sts Georgetown ⓣ592/227-2081 Guyana; France, Gravenstraat 5–7 ⓣ597/476-455; Guyana, Gravenstraat 82 ⓣ597/475-209 (Mon–Fri 7.30–1pm; visa issued in 1–2 days); Mexico, Algico Plaza, 91-93 St. Vincent St Trinidad, ⓣ868/627-7047; Netherlands, Mr Dr J C de Mirandastraat 10 ⓣ597/477-211; UK, Van't Hogerhuysstraat 9–11 ⓣ597/402-558; US, Dr Sophie Redmondstraat 129, ⓣ597/477-900; Venezuela, Gravenstraat 23–25 ⓣ597/475-501.

Exchange There are many *cambios* about town – here are a few central ones: Multi Track Exchange, Wilhelminastraat 35 and Kleine Waterstraat 11; Trade Exchange, Waterkant 78; Surora, Mahonylaan 41; Moneyline, Domineestraat 35c.

Hospitals Public ambulances will take patients to Academisch Ziekenhuis (ⓣ597/442-222, Flustraat).

Internet The Browser, Hi de Vriestraat 13; Cybershop, Kerkplein 1; I Walk In, Domineestraat 27; Carib Walkin, Heerestraat 22.

Laundries There are no laundromats but most hotels will do your laundry for a fee.

Left luggage Leaving it at your hotel is best.

Pharmacies Ali's Drugstore & Apotheek, Tourtonnelaan 127; Apotheek Esculaap, Zwartenhovenbrugstraat 11; Apotheek Farmsur, Kwattaweg 402; Apotheek Wong, Heck Aronstraat 88.

Post office Kerkplein 1 ⓣ597/477-524.

DAY-TRIPS FROM PARAMARIBO

A lot of these trips are more easily accomplished if you have your own transport or join an organized **tour** (see p.709).

Fort Nieuw Amsterdam

Visits to eighteenth century Fort Nieuw Amsterdam from Parbo can be done in a day but may better be broken up by staying in the town of Leonsburg, eight kilometres northeast of Paramaribo on the Suriname River. Organized tours cost around S$275–315. There is a museum with a limited selection of exhibits in the fortress on the other side of the river, as well as several colonial plantations in the area, including the one at Marienburg, the oldest sugarcane plantation in Suriname.

Should you wish to **stay** over in Leonsburg *Hotel Stardust* ⑥ (Condorstraat 1 ⓣ597/451-544, ⓦwww.hotelstardust.com) has more than 135 rooms, a swimming pool, tennis court, fitness centre and even a miniature-golf course.

Jodensavanne and around

Seventy kilometres south of Paramaribo on the east bank of the Suriname River is **Jodensavanne** (ⓦwww.jodensavanne.sr.org), named after the Jews who settled in this savanna area in around 1650. The surrounding forest at times seems barely to be kept at bay and

> **CAR RENTALS**
>
> There are many places to rent a car in Parbo but you'll need to leave a US$500 credit card deposit and you'll want to get 4WD because if you're planning on venturing out of town you'll find some roads challenging even with it. Here are a few companies:
>
> **Avis** Kristalstraat 1 ⓣ597/551-158. Compact S$148, 4WD S$239 per day.
>
> **Budget** Kristalstraat 1 ⓣ597/457-363.
>
> **Enterprize** Fred Derby Straat 60 ⓣ597/473-494. Compact S$182, 4WD S$300 per day.
>
> **Europcar** Kleine Waterstraat 1a ⓣ597/424-631. Compact S$132, 4WD S$236 per day
>
> **Hertz** van't Hogerhuysstraat 23 ⓣ597/400-409. Compact S$96, 4WD S$250 per day.
>
> **Hotel Zeelandia** Kleine Waterstraat 1a ⓣ597/424-631. Compact S$131, 4WD S$235 per day.

little remains of the rest of the village but have a look at the ruins of the **synagogue** – said to be the oldest in the Americas – and the graveyard. There is a small museum to give you a sense of its historical importance.

BLAKAWATRA is a recreation resort about five kilometres east of Jodensavanne where if you please, you can splash about in the dark, mineral-rich waters of the creek.

COLACREEK, about five kilometres from the international airport, is a recreation resort in a savanna (reservations through METS, Dr J F Nassylaan 2, Paramaribo ⓣ597/477-088, ⓦwww.surinamevacations.com) that's busy on the weekends by virtue of its proximity (50km) to Paramaribo. The daily **entrance fee** for access to the resort's basic waterslides, paddleboats and rope ladder walkways is S$10, overnight **accommodation** costs from S$35 in an open-air cabin for hanging a hammock to S$275 in a self-catering cabin with water and electricity (bring bed linens).

Moving on

Air KLM and Martinair fly non-stop to Amsterdam and Air France flies to Cayenne, French Guiana. Surinam Airways, Martinair and Caribbean Airlines link Suriname to the Caribbean islands, with Caribbean also flying from Port of Spain, Trinidad, to North America (Miami, New York and beyond) and Coastal Travel flying to Trinidad and Curacao. Caribbean Airlines and Surinam Airways also fly to Caracas, Venezuela. The departure tax is about S$55 and is usually figured into the price of your ticket. Meta Airlines (ⓦvoemeta.com) flies to Belém (Mon, Thurs & Fri 2hr) and Boa Vista, (Mon, Wed & Fri) Brazil as well as Georgetown, Guyana (Mon, Wed & Fri 2hr) and Blue Wing Airlines (ⓦbluewingairlines.com).

By air There are **no scheduled internal flights** in Suriname; tour operators charter planes to visit the parks and reserves in the interior, making flights dependent on having a minimum number of people for a tour. You can **charter your own planes** from SLM, and Gum Air (ⓦwww.gumair.com), or **helicopter** from Hi-Jet.

By bus There are no formal bus companies that run scheduled trips to either Guyana or French Guiyana. For travel to Guyana the easiest way to travel is to prearrange your trip through Bobby Minibus ⓣ597/498-583 which will pick you up at your hotel at 4am to make the one 10am ferry crossing. Minibuses leave Parbo for Nieuw Nickerie from 3hr 30min, $10. To travel to Guyana from Nickerie, see next box. For French Guiyana take the bus from Parbo to Albina (5hr, $7.50) or much more effective, a taxi (2hr, $40) and cross the Maroni river by dugout (to St. Laurent de Maroni, €3 or ferry €2–5) with connecting buses to Kouru and Cayenne (€25 & €35).

West to Guyana

The drive along the coastal belt **west of Paramaribo** is a scenic one, even if there are few reasons to stop en route. Around 140 kilometres from Paramaribo, the road passes through **Totness**, once a Scottish settlement, as it continues towards the district of Nickerie, where salt ponds, Dutch-style *polders* (land reclaimed from water) and, most notably, rice paddies start to appear. **Nieuw Nickerie** is the largest town in these parts – and the second largest in the country – and the obvious place to break your journey to Guyana. The ferry crossing the Corentyne River into Guyana is at **South Drain** (where crossing is about all there is to do) about an hour's drive southwest of Nieuw Nickerie on an unsealed and potholed track.

NIEUW NICKERIE

If you have just arrived on the ferry from Guyana and your first taste of Suriname is **NIEUW NICKERIE**, the country's second largest town, you will not see the type of compact, lively town that predominates in Guyana. A sprawling place with an ill-defined centre and an atmosphere which is at times sleepy, at others completely comatose, Nieuw Nickerie is 237 kilometres west of Paramaribo along

TRAVEL TO PARAMARIBO

Minibuses to Parbo leave when full from the parking lot next to the market (3hr 30min, S$30, depending on the size). Two **state-run buses** make the trip daily, at 6am and 1pm (S$10). It is difficult to find buses going anywhere after 1pm. In this case, a taxi to Parbo will cost about S$200.

a good stretch of paved road and about an hour's drive north from the ferry stelling at South Drain. The best thing to do in Nieuw Nickerie is leave town and spend the day at **Bigi pan**, a mangrove-ridden stretch of swampy coast with excellent birdwatching. Day-trips can be organized at *Residence Inn*.

Accommodation

Hotel Ameerali Maynardstraat 32–36 ⓣ597/231-212. These a/c rooms are clean but not all of them have hot and cold water so check before agreeing to a room. The hotel also has a bar and a restaurant that serves up fried rice, chow mein and *satay*. ❺–❻
Concorde Hotel Wilhelminastraat 3 ⓣ597/232-345. This worn but clean budget hotel does the trick if you don't mind sharing a bathroom and having a fan instead of a/c. The food at the restaurant downstairs is the best in town. ❸–❹
Hotel De President 104 Gouvernerstraat ⓣ597/231-848. The walls are thin, the beds rickety and the place needs a good scrub. Only stay here if you absolutely must. ❸
Residence Inn R P Bharosstraat 84 ⓣ597/210-950, ⓦwww.resinn.com. The most expensive hotel in Nickerie has comfortable, a/c rooms, hot and cold water and a terrace in front for drinks. ❻–❼
Hotel River Breeze G G Meimastraat 34 ⓣ597/212-111. Basic, clean, self-contained, a/c rooms that look like a basement finished in the 70s. ❺
Pak Hap Hotel Emmastraat 9 ⓣ597/212-381, ⓦwww.pakhap.com. Clean sheets, roof terrace, steps away from the market and breakfast is included. ❹–❻

Eating

In the morning you can find fresh fruit, vegetables, cakes, little pastries and small *roti* stands in the **market**. Otherwise, dining options are spread out and limited so if you get in late and you see something that appeals to you that's still open (see *Restaurant Melissa's*, below), tuck in, you're not likely to miss out terribly if you don't go exploring.
Café de Smuller St Jozefstraat 12 ⓣ597/232-098. This tiny hole in the wall has burgers, fries and *bitterbollen* along with other Dutch snacks.
De Palm *Residence Inn* ⓣ597/232-345. Not high dining but this busy hotel restaurant does basic meat and fish dishes adequately.
KowLoon Restaurant Corner of Sawnstraat & Oostkanaalstraat. There are several Chinese restaurants in town but this one appears to be the cleanest and does the standards decently including chop suey and wonton soup.
Restaurant Melissa's *Hotel Concord 2000* ⓣ597/232-345. Many of the chairs don't match but the phone rings off the hook for takeaway orders at this Indonesian restaurant. Try the *saoto soep* – now that's a good stock.
Okopibamboesie Grill Cafe Hoek G G Maynard-straat & Tak Adamsonstraat ⓣ597/212-111. You may have trouble saying the name three times fast but the fruit platters and Brazilian BBQ chicken are easy choices.
P & G Rotishop A K Doerga Sawhstraat 95. *Roti*, curried accompaniments, beer and soft drinks on the second floor of the Doerga Mall.

RESORTS

Arapahu Island ⓦwww.mytropicalgemtours.com. Four days of sportfishing, hiking and birdwatching at this island in the Corantijn River for S$1853.
Bergendal Resort ⓣ597/471-150, ⓣwww.bergendalresort.com. An hour and a half drive from Paramaribo this resort, has 45 lodges, and 24 square kilometres of jungle and river adventure including ziplines through jungle canopies. Independent access to the ziplines costs $50.
Kabalero This resort offers 3–8 day tours (starting at S$1523) in the mid-west region of Suriname offering birdwatching, mountain climbing, hiking and sportfishing.

TRAVEL TO GUYANA

Getting to Guyana involves crossing the Corantijn River on the one ferry-crossing (S$45) a day (10am) at **South Drain**, an hour west of Nickerie, where you will have to go through customs. Note that there is no *cambio* or ATM at South Drain so bring Euros or US$, preferably the latter, to exchange for Guyanese dollars at Moleson Creek. To **get there** you must leave Nickerie by minibus at 8am (S$20). It is best to reserve your place on the bus the day before through your hotel. Once you arrive at **Moleson Creek, Guyana**, you will have to go through customs again and get your passport stamped before taking one of the waiting buses to Georgetown (G$2045).

Note that there is also no *cambio* at Moleson Creek. Undoubtedly, someone there will be looking to exchange your money for local currency and street exchange rates are often better than official ones anyway.

Drinking and nightlife

De Tropen Bar In the *Residence Inn*. A pleasant enough place to have a drink outdoors on the streetside terrace with Dutch tourists and to watch the scooters buzz by.

Roshnie Casino Corner of Barrosstraat and Wilhelminastraat. There are more than twenty slot machines and one gaming table at this largely empty casino where you can pretty much take on the house all by yourself.

Viking Club A K Doerga Sawhstraat 87. This small bar has a pool table and is the best alternative to *De Tropen*.

Directory

Banks Surinammsche Bank, Landingstraat 3 ☎597/231-381, gives cash advances on MasterCard. RBTT, Gouverneurstraat 79.

Exchange Eurora Exchange, West Kanalstraat.

Hospital Nickerie Medical Centre, A K Doerga Sawhstraat 80, ☎597/210-700.

Internet Telesur Office, St Kanalstraat 3

Pharmacy Apotheek Fung, Gouverneursstraat 104.

South to the interior

You will not have seen the real Suriname until you venture south of Paramaribo into the interior. The country's natural riches are easy to reach either by day-trips (see "Day-trips From Paramaribo", p.714) or by visiting **Brownsberg Nature Park.** However, seeing the more isolated areas such as **Raleighvallen** in the sprawling **Central Suriname Nature Reserve** and a few **privately owned resorts** in the far south of the country will take more time and money. Although still on the tourist circuit, these resorts are as far away from civilization as you can get without crash-landing in the middle of the Amazon Rainforest.

BROWNSBERG NATURE PARK

About 130 kilometres south of Paramaribo on the 500-metre high Mazaroni Plateau, **BROWNSBERG NATURE PARK** (S$15) is the only protected area in Suriname that can be easily visited from Paramaribo using public transport. STINASU operates a lodge on the plateau (from S$30–41 per person to camp), and maintains several hiking trails to the impressive waterfalls, which, given the unpredictability involved in spotting much of the wildlife, constitute the park's main attractions. Among the **animals** you might run into on a lucky day are howler and spider monkeys, deer, agouti and birds such as woodpeckers, macaws and parrots. There are also fine views from your elevated position on the plateau of the rainforest and **Van Blommestein Lake**, created to provide electricity for the Alcoa aluminium industry.

The simplest way to visit Brownsberg is on an **all-inclusive tour** arranged by STINASU (S$205 for the day, S$412 overnight). Even if you choose to go it alone, you will still have to rely on STINASU (Cornelis Jongbawstreet 14, Parbo ⓣ597/476-597) for certain things – accommodation at the lodge, for instance, should be paid for at the STINASU office in Paramaribo before you leAve **Public transport** runs as far south as Brownsweg, the generic name for seven villages some thirteen kilometres from the plateau, with buses leaving from Paramaribo (see box, p.707) before 9am. Once in Brownsweg, you can arrange for a STINASU bus to pick you up (S$21 return). Getting to Brownsberg by public transport is fine provided you are planning to spend the night; day-trippers; however, will not be able to get back to Paramaribo in the same day if relying on the buses.

THE CENTRAL SURINAME NATURE RESERVE

Created in 1998 by amalgamating the nature reserves of Raleighvallen, Tafelberg and Eilerts de Haan, the **CENTRAL SURINAME NATURE RESERVE** occupies a 16,000 square kilmetres of southwestern Suriname, some nine percent of the country's total surface area. Most tourist trips are to **Raleighvallen**, where STINASU has a lodge located on Foengoe Island on the upper Coppename River (from S$192 per person or S$41 to camp). Other than bathing in the river (the island has the odd sandy beach), the main thing to do is hike to and up the **Voltzberg**, a 375-metre granite mountain affording good views of the surrounding forest canopy. It takes about three hours to get to the base of the mountain (where there is a jungle camp with hammocks); it is another 240 metres or so to the summit. The Voltzberg is a good place to see the world's largest-known species of cock-of-the-rock.

STINASU runs **four-day tours** to Raleighvallen for S$1523, whereby you fly one way (50min from Paramaribo) and travel overland the other. The overland journey involves a five-hour drive to a *maroon* village called Witagron and then a three-hour boat trip up the Coppename River to Foengoe Island. There is an entrance fee of S$41 to visit Raleighvallen; note that having a guide is obligatory.

East to French Guiana

It only takes two hours to cover the 141 kilometres between Paramaribo and **Albina**, the last town in Suriname before crossing into French Guiana. You could, however, conceivably dally longer exploring the stretch of coast parallel to which the road to Albina runs, the location of the country's two coastal nature reserves: the wild and little-explored **Wia-Wia Nature Reserve**, access to which is from **Matapica Beach** and **Galibi Nature Reserve** with its population of nesting turtles and nearby Amerindian villages of **Christiaankondre** and **Langamankondre**. Make sure you leave Parbo with **US dollars** as there are not many ATMs outside the capital and banks in French Guiana can be tempermental about accepting foreign cards; US$ are often easier to exchange in French Guiana than Surinamese dollars.

WIA-WIA NATURE RESERVE

Although geographically close to Paramaribo, **WIA-WIA NATURE RESERVE**, which occupies 360 square kilometres of coast halfway between the Surinamese capital and the French Guiana border, is perhaps the least visited of the country's protected areas. Indeed, the reserve itself has no tourist facilities and will be of most interest to researchers.

Matapica Beach is just west of Wia-Wia, at the end of a channel that links it to the Commewijne River, where turtles come to lay their eggs. Unfortunately, STINASU no longer provides overnight tours to visitors and the STINASU camp is now unavailable. Travellers who do venture out this way are going to have to drive to Leonsberg and arrange for a boat to take them to Margaretta and then on to Matapica, taking care to mind the tide, which is only high enough for boats to get through the channel twice a day.

GALIBI NATURE RESERVE

Situated in the northeastern corner of Suriname at the mouth of the Maroni River, the 40 square kilometres **GALIBI NATURE RESERVE** (S$15) is one of the Guianas' most famous nesting areas for **sea turtles**. Unlike Shell Beach in Guyana (see p.696) and Plage Les Hattes in French Guiana (see p.738), where leatherbacks predominate, Galibi Beach is the most important nesting area in the western Atlantic region for the much smaller Olive Ridley. Leatherbacks, greens and, to a much lesser extent, hawksbills are also present. The **nesting season** is generally from March–July. The **peak time** for Olive Ridleys is mid-May to the end of July, leatherbacks April to June, greens April to May and hawksbills May to July.

Accommodation

The STINASU-run lodge (S$137 per room sleeping up to four people) is on the beach itself. The alternative is to base yourself in the Amerindian villages of Christiaankondre and Langamankondre on the banks of the Maroni Estuary and walk the few hours to Galibi Beach. As Amerindian villages go, these are relatively large (approximately 750 inhabitants) and used to having tourists pop in on them en route to Galibi (visits to the villages are included in most Galibi tours offered by tour operators). Indeed, so comfortable are the villagers with foreigners that they organize and host the annual Galibi Beach Festival in September, where you can listen to

CROSSING INTO FRENCH GUIANA

There's nothing to do in **ALBINA**, the poor brother of Saint-Laurent-du-Maroni across the Maroni River in French Guiana but get your passport stamped and hightail it out of this sketchy town. It's easy to cross the border by ferry or motorized dug-out but first you'll need to get your passport stamped at the **immigration office** (7am–6pm).

Facing the river, turn right and walk past the market. Follow the road to the right for about 500 metres and the immigration office will be on your left in front of the pier for the official ferry. Don't forget to do this. Many travellers report having had problems when either trying to leave or re-enter Suriname because they have failed to get this stamp.

The **official ferry** (from Albina, Mon & Tues, Thurs & Fri 8am, 10am, 3pm & 5.30pm; Weds 7.30am & 5.30pm; Sat 8.30am & 9.30am; Sun 4pm & 5.30pm; $10-20, one-way, depending on your negotiation skills; with a car, $120) but unless you have a car there's no reason to take it (rental companies don't allow their cars to cross the border!). The **motorized canoes** take about fifteen minutes to cross the river and cost $10.

If you absolutely must **spend the night**, you can find rooms at the *Guesthouse Albina Breeze 4* (also known as the Hotel Wong So, Poeloegoedoeweg 8 ⓣ597/034-2120. The rooms are small but clean and breezy and the owner friendly. Have someone drive you if it's after dark.

traditional and not-so-traditional music and witness the election of Miss Galibi.

Overnight tours

Overnight tours to Galibi, whether organized by STINASU (S$631) or other tour operators, will top S$550. Travellers can do the trip independently – costing at least as much as an organized tour – by going by taxi from Paramaribo to Albina (2hr, S$40), then finding a boat to take you down the Maroni River to Galibi. If you are lucky, you may find a boat carrying provisions that might be prepared to take you for a negotiated fee. Of course, you will then have to find another vessel for the return to Albina. Chartering a boat specially for the purpose of carrying you to Galibi is obviously going to be more expensive. The owner of *The Creek Guesthouse* in Albina has various contacts.

French Guiana

Until about sixty years ago, **FRENCH GUIANA**'s muggy, oppressive climate, malaria-ridden forests and inhospitable terrain were considered an ideal way to punish criminals and social misfits of Mother France. The prisons were then abandoned to monkeys and wildlife, but in the 1960s it was noticed that the country was an excellent place to launch satellites into orbit, and the European Space Agency duly cleared a patch of jungle and built a space centre. Now, as the number of rocket launches dwindles, French Guiana may need to find a new niche - and why shouldn't this be tourism? The French *département d'outre-mer* already attracts a considerable number of visitors from metropolitan France, the majority interested in taking a look at the **space centre at Kourou**, many visiting family members and friends working there, and the infamous penal colony on the isolated but beautiful **Iles du Salut.** Both attractions are within easy access of the *département*'s capital **Cayenne**, where mosquitoes, expensive lodgings, and a distinct lack of things to do will probably not detain you long. If you find yourself in Cayenne and you're wondering where the reasonable accommodation and heaving nightlife are you're in the wrong place—head west to Paramaribo.

Most likely if you're in this part of South America you will be looking for eco-tourism not frozen margaritas. And if you've been travelling long throughout the Guianas the smooth, French-paved roads will probably have you thinking it's a shame there's not more to see along them. Pirogue trips along **rivers** such as the Maroni, Approuague and Oyapok and treks in the **Amazonian interior** are popular, but the eco-highlight remains **Plage Les Hattes**, one of the finest places in the world to observe huge leatherback turtles laying their eggs on the beach. Nature-loving French speakers travelling through South America will have found a pleasant spot for fish soup and the odd eco-adventure but those who do not speak the language may find getting around outside Cayenne where transportation options are pathetic fairly challenging.

CHRONOLOGY

10,000 BC Original inhabitants are thought to have been either the Arawak Indians or Amerindians. Later Karibs move into territory.

1496 AD Discovered by the Spanish.

1604 Settled by the French.

1624 French merchants from Rouen open a trading centre in Sinnamary.

1643 Cayenne founded.

1664 Dutch occupy Cayenne.

1667 Territory officially awarded to France under the Treaty of Breda. All inhabitants become French citizens.

1676 Dutch expelled.

1763-1765 France looks to bolster it's presence in the Americas after the loss of Canada. Of about 15,000 immigrants sent to develop the region as part of the Kourou Expedition, around 10,000 die of yellow fever and typhoid.

1815 Congress of Vienna reconfirms territory as French after 200 years of alternating between Britain, France, Netherlands and Portugal.

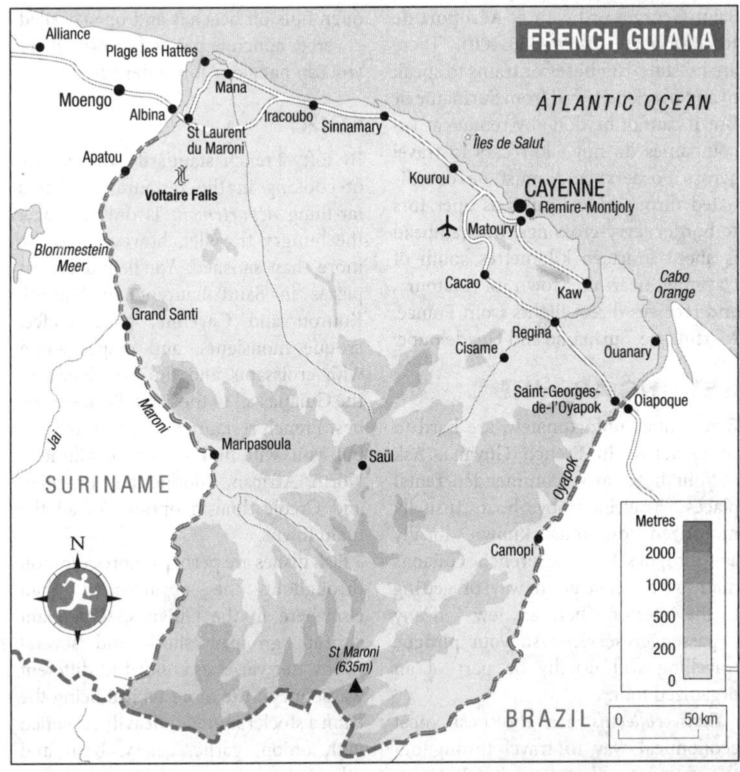

1848 Slavery is abolished. The colony's fragile plantation economy begins to collapse. The region is soon repurposed as a penal colony.

1852 Region is repurposed as a penal colony. Until its abolition as a penal colony some 70,000 French convicts served their time here, some in the notorious Iles du Salut.

1894 Alfred Dreyfus is condemned to Ile du Diable.

1946 French Guiana becomes an overseas *département* of France.

1947 Penal colony abolished.

1964 European Space Agency establishes a rocket-launching base in Kourou from which to launch communications satellites.

1974 French Guiana becomes a region with its own Conseil Régional, enjoying a certain amount of autonomy in social and economic matters.

1975 Plan Vert, implemented to improve production of agricultural and forestry products.

1977 Hmong refugees from Laos establish communities in Cacao and Javouhey.

1980 Several bomb attacks by extremist groups prompt the French government to devolve more power over local affairs to the Conseil Régional.

1996 Rioting and looting break out after a boycott of classes by secondary school pupils demanding improved conditions.

1997 Independence leader Jean-Victor Castor arrested by police leading to civil violence in Cayenne. After negotiations the *département* obtains a vice-chancellorship.

2000 Riots occur in Cayenne following an organized march calling for greater autonomy.

2001 Local officials publish a series of proposals, including a request that the territory be given legislative authority on issues concering French Guiana alone.

2008 On his first trip to the department President Sarkozy dedicates 1,000 troops to combat the growing immigration problem.

ARRIVAL

You will most likely be arriving via one of three ways: overland from Suriname via Saint Laurent du Maroni or Brazil via

Saint-Georges or by air at **Aéroport de Rochambeau** (☎594/350-300). There are no state-run buses or trains to speak of and overland travel from Suriname or Brazil cannot be done by rental car (as companies do not allow cars to travel across borders) and must be coordinated through local minibus operators to border ferry-crossings. Rochambeau is about fourteen kilometres south of Cayenne near the town of Matoury, and receives direct flights from France, Martinique, Suriname and Guadeloupe.

GETTING AROUND

Bike rentals unfortunately, are hard to come across in French Guyana. Ask at your hotel for recommended rental places. Travelling by boat (usually motorized dug-outs known locally as "pirogues") along French Guiana's many rivers is a good way of getting to the interior. There are few – if any – passenger services, so your pirogue travelling will usually be part of an organized tour.

Taxis collectifs are the best most economical way to travel throughout the country (see box opposite). In towns throughout French Guiana taxis are hard to find, especially in Kourou (and sorely needed) but can be organized at hotels for travel from one town to another; rates, depending on the time of day you wish to travel, can be cutthroat. In Cayenne taxis are metered, but unnecessary since the city is small enough to do completely on foot.

ACCOMMODATION

There are no HI-affiliated hostels in French Guiana and really no such thing as a budget option. Rooms in general are very expensive with little recourse for the traveller. Perhaps nowhere else in the Guianas should you most consider buying a hammock – they are cheap, often sold by street vendors, at local markets and in general stores (similarly mosquito nets) and there are sometimes open huts on beaches and open-walled covered, concrete patios in town where you can hang one for under €10.

FOOD

By lofty French standards, the quality of cooking in the restaurants of this far-flung *département* is only average; the hungry traveller, however, will be more than satisfied. You'll find decent pizzas in Saint Laurent du Maroni, Kourou and Cayenne, good coffee, croque monsieurs, and crêpes along with croissants and the best bread in the Guianas all in the capital's cafés. The best French restaurants are in Cayenne, but you will find plenty of Chinese, North African, Indonesian, Brazilian and Creole dine-in options in all the main towns.

Fish dishes are perhaps more common throughout the *département* than elsewhere in the Guianas, with giant shrimp, grouper, shark and several freshwater varieties cooked in different ways, one of the more typical being the *blaff*: a stock (*bouillon*) heavily seasoned with onion, garlic, celery, basil and other spices.

Another popular stock, used only at Easter and the Pentecost is *bouillon d'awara*, made from the fruit of the *awara* palm tree and cooked with chicken, shrimp, crab and various vegetables. *Fricassée* and *colombo* are typical Creole stews, the latter with a strong curry taste. While you *can* find reasonably priced meals and tasty snacks from street vendors, on the whole you'll be paying more for what you get than elsewhere in the Guianas.

DRINK

The authentic drink here is the beloved French **apéritif**, the *ti' punch (petit* or little *punch)*: lime, sugarcane syrup and rum – *sans* ice and downed in one (the bottles are often left for you to mix to your taste and for a second pour). There is a better selection of **wines** in French

TAXIS COLLECTIFS FROM CAYENNE

Public Transport consists of **taxis collectifs,** minibuses, which leave when full from main towns along the coastal road. **Fares** are up to ten times more expensive than in Suriname and Guyana, very frustrating given that you still have to wait (at times for hours) before there are enough people to leave. Also note that *taxis collectifs* do not go – at least with regularity – to many places of interest such as Cacao, Kaw and Plages Les Hattes. You can catch the following minibuses opposite Canal Laussat on Ave de la Liberté.

Kourou 1hr; €10

Matoury (Rochambeau) 20min; €2

Montjoly 15min; €1.52

Regina (for St-Georges-de-l'Oyapok, you will be left at the river jetty) 2hr; €23

Remire 20min; €1.83

Saint-George-de-l'Oyapock 2hr; €20

St Laurent du Maroni (Suriname border) 3hr; €40

Guiana than you will find in most of the rest of South America, and every now and then you will stumble across a café that would not look out of place in Montmartre, serving short, sharp espressos and shots of *pastis*. The tap water is generally safe to drink, although most visitors guzzle bottled water (as they do in metropolitan France).

CULTURE AND ETIQUETTE

Amerindian tribes and ethnic blacks maintain their own **cultural traditions,** as do other groups – notably the immigrant population of Laotians in towns such as Cacao and Javouhey. However, the majority of the population is **Creole**, descendants of seventeenth century African slaves since mixed with their African, European and Native American countrymen. A mixed-Creole culture is dominant in the metropolitan areas. This is typified by **carnival** (see p.725), when much of the population dresses up in colourful costumes and performs dances with French, African and East Indian overtones. While there have been calls for independence over the past twenty years, French subsidization has made the standard of living one of the highest in South America and for most of the population, France is *their* nation.

The official and most widely spoken **language** in French Guiana is obviously French. A significant proportion of the population also speaks a French-based patois or Creole, with Chinese, Bush Negro (*neg maron*) and Amerindian languages spoken in certain areas.

SPORTS AND OUTDOOR ACTIVITIES

Observing football is the main pursuit here with water sports and fishing being favourite activities. You'll also find

PRESS, TV AND RADIO

Newspapers The main daily newspaper is the French *La Presse de la Guyane* – there is no English daily.

Television French television is beamed by satellite to most homes in French Guiana: ACG, Canal + Guyane et Canal Satelliite, France 0, Tele Guyane, and Tempo.

Radio The principle FM radio stations (all in French) include: France Inter (102 in Cayenne, 104 in Kourou), Gabriel FM (92.5), Nostalgie (99.3), NRJ (97.3), Radio Loisir (100.6), RFI (98.7), RFO (92.2), RTM (102.5)

many serious cyclists, dressed in full gear, enjoying the finely paved roads in the suburbs of Cayenne.

COMMUNICATIONS

The postal system is integrated with that of metropolitan France, which makes deliveries to Europe quick and cheap. There is at least one **post office** (La Poste) in each town, and some have ATM machines that accept major international credit cards (though not American Express). Public **telephone** booths do not take coins, but cards issued by France Telecom are OK for making local calls. However, they are not good value for calling abroad, and it is better to buy phone cards that work with PIN numbers. These cards are usually available from convenience stores (*libre service*).

Internet cafés are generally harder to find in French Guyana than in Guyana or Suriname but common enough in Cayenne (around €3 per hr).

CRIME AND SAFETY

The French military check **passports** at armed checkpoints along major roads and there is a notable police presence in Cayenne and Kourou, which makes the cities feel safer than the rest of the Guianas. That said, consulate warnings do report a sharp rise in serious crimes in Kourou and St-Laurent-du-Maroni.

EMERGENCY NUMBERS

17 general emergency number for the police.
18 fire service.
15 public ambulance services.

While most travellers' visits will be trouble-free, you should use common sense, avoid isolated areas (beaches included), try not to walk alone and mind your valuables.

EMERGENCIES

Medical care is available at the **Centre Hospitalier de Cayenne Andrée Rosemon** (☎594/395-050, 3 Avenue des Flamboyants, Ⓦwww.cg-cayenne.com) but the best hospital in the country is said to be the **Centre Médico Chirurgical de Kourou** (☎594/327-676, Avenue des Iles.)

INFORMATION AND MAPS

You may have to write the tourist information yourself in Guyana but it flows freely in French Guiana, albeit mostly in French. In **Cayenne**, try the Comité du Tourisme de la Guyane and the Office de Tourisme for brochures and maps. Elsewhere in the *département*, you will normally find either a **tourist office** or a *syndicat d'initiative* with relevant local information. Most of the documentation

FRENCH GUIANA ON THE NET

Unsurprisingly, most websites are in French. If you don't understand the language you can still glean information about hours and locations.
Ⓦ**www.tourisme-guyane.com** Guide to recreation, tour agencies and information about life in French Guyana run by the Comité du Tourisme de la Guyane with a tab that translates the site into English.
Ⓦ**laguyane.free.fr** Offers general information – including in-depth coverage of the space centre at Kourou (in French).
Ⓦ**www.outremer.com/GF/Guyindex** One of the better resources for French-speaking visitors with good tourist and background information (in French).
Ⓦ**www.terresdeguyane.fr/guyane** News, politics, history, nature and some helpful links (in French).

is in French, and the English-speaking skills of the staff are generally quite limited.

COSTS AND MONEY

If you are arriving in French Guiana from Suriname or Brazil, brace yourself, or more specifically, your wallet. Perhaps nowhere else in South America will your **credit card** be as useful as it will be in French Guiana. The currency of French Guiana is, as in metropolitan France, the **euro** (€) and costs here are at least as expensive as there. The food served in the restaurants is generally good but it's not Parisian good and the expensive and limited accommodation and lack of good transportation (especially within Kourou) can make travelling expenses vexing for the budget traveller.

Luckily, you can pay for most goods and services with plastic, and **ATM** machines at the major banks and the post office (La Poste) occasionally accept Visa, MasterCard, Eurocard (but rarely American Express), but can be temperamental about American ATM cards and banks do not always have foreign exchange facilities (in Cayenne you will have to go to a *bureau de change* to exchange dollars, pounds sterling, other major currencies and traveller's cheques for euros).

CARNIVAL

The major festival in French Guiana is **carnival**, which lasts from the first week in January to Ash Wednesday, the last five days of which feature street parades. On Saturday nights during carnival you can witness at certain dance clubs the tradition of Touloulou, when the women or Touloulou, heavily disguised and wearing masks, are given the sole, non-reciprocal right to ask the men to dance; guys are not allowed to refuse.

If you are just travelling overland from Suriname through to Brazil, expect to pay over US$90 in public transportation costs. Independent, budget-conscious travellers who are able to split costs with travel companions should budget on around €55 a day each for food and lodging – double this if you plan to be on the move each day and visit every museum and tourist trap.

Cayenne

French Guiana is not blessed by a wealth of beautiful towns, and **CAYENNE** is perhaps the best of a rather average bunch. The administrative capital of the *département* is compact, easy to walk around and the sleepiest of all three Guiana capitals. Still, there is an attractive central *place*, several good spots from which to gaze out over the Atlantic Ocean, a busy, colourful market and some decent beaches a few kilometres south of town. However, all of this can be seen in a day or two, after which Cayenne loses its lustre. The capital is enjoyable in small doses, and should be treated as a base for excursions into the interior, not as an end in itself.

There's not much in the way of **beaches** in Cayenne although there is one good place to watch the ocean sunset, **Place des Amandiers** (officially, Place Auguste-Horth).

What to see and do

The view of Cayenne and the ocean from the hill at the end of Rue de Rémire west of the Place des Palmistes is the best place to establish your bearings. At the top of the hill (owned by the Ministry of Defence, but not subject to any great security) are the remains of **Fort Céperou**, the first building to

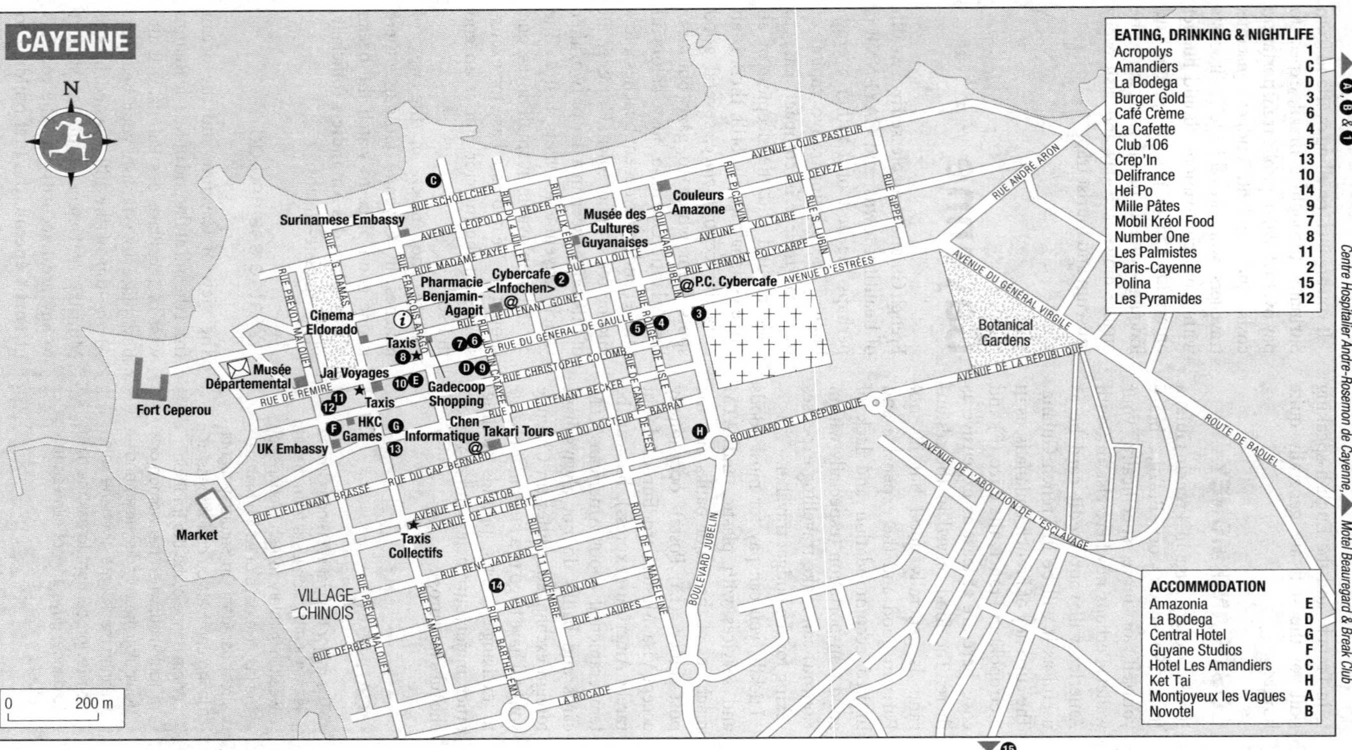
CAYENNE
N
EATING, DRINKING & NIGHTLIFE
Acropolys 1
Amandiers C
La Bodega D
Burger Gold 3
Café Crème 6
La Cafette 4
Club 106 5
Crep'In 13
Delifrance 10
Hei Po 14
Mille Pâtes 9
Mobil Kréol Food 7
Number One 8
Les Palmistes 11
Paris-Cayenne 2
Polina 15
Les Pyramides 12
ACCOMMODATION
Amazonia E
La Bodega D
Central Hotel G
Guyane Studios F
Hotel Les Amandiers C
Ket Tai H
Montjoyeux les Vagues A
Novotel B
A, B & 1
Centre Hospitalier Andre-Rosemon de Cayenne, Motel Beauregard & Break Club
15
Surinamese Embassy
Musée des Cultures Guyanaises
Couleurs Amazone
Cybercafe <Infochen>
Pharmacie Benjamin-Agapit
P.C. Cybercafe
Cinema Eldorado
Taxis
Musée Départemental
Jal Voyages
Gadecoop Shopping
Fort Ceperou
HKC Games
Chen Informatique
Takari Tours
UK Embassy
Market
Taxis Collectifs
VILLAGE CHINOIS
Botanical Gardens
RUE SCHOELCHER
AVENUE LEOPOLD HEDER
RUE MADAME PAYEE
RUE LALLOUETTE
RUE VERMONT POLYCARPE
AVENUE VOLTAIRE
RUE DEVEZE
AVENUE LOUIS PASTEUR
RUE ANDRÉ ARON
AVENUE D'ESTRÉES
AVENUE DU GÉNÉRAL VIRGILE
AVENUE DE LA RÉPUBLIQUE
ROUTE DE BADUEL
BOULEVARD DE LA RÉPUBLIQUE
AVENUE DE L'ABOLITION DE L'ESCLAVAGE
RUE LIEUTENANT GOINET
RUE DU GÉNÉRAL DE GAULLE
RUE CHRISTOPHE COLOMB
RUE DU LIEUTENANT BECKER
RUE DU DOCTEUR BARRAT
RUE DU CAP BERNARD
RUE LIEUTENANT BRASSÉ
AVENUE ELIE CASTOR
AVENUE DE LA LIBERTÉ
RUE RENÉ JADFARD
AVENUE RONJON
RUE J. JAURES
RUE DERBES
LA ROCADE
RUE DE REMIRE
RUE PREVOT MALOUET
RUE G. DAMAS
RUE FRANÇOIS ARAGO
RUE JUSTIN CATAYEE
RUE DU 4 JUILLET
RUE FÉLIX EBOUÉ
BOULEVARD JUBELIN
RUE PICHEVIN
RUE S. LUBIN
RUE GIPPET
RUE ROUGET DE LISLE
RUE DE CANAL DE L'EST
ROUTE DE LA MADELEINE
RUE DU 11 NOVEMBRE
RUE R. BARTHELEMY
RUE P. AMUSANT
0 200 m

appear in Cayenne after the Compagnie de Rouen purchased the hill from an Indian chief named Céperou in 1643. Descending the hill, you will pass the Jesuit-built **Hôtel de la Préfecture** and the **Fontaine de Montrard**, a popular place for the homeless to take an afternoon bath, before arriving at **Place des Palmistes**. It is not as beautiful as Parbo's Palmentuin but this three hectares of green space covered sparsely with palms imported from the Approuage region, one of the rare places in French Guiana where they grow, is where much of Cayenne's limited activity is centred: a few banks, tourist T-shirt shops, a cinema, taxis, Internet, the tourist office, a café and at night, mobile snackcarts are all on or around the *place*.

Musée Départemental

Next to the *place* is the library and **Musée Départemental**, 1 Ave du Général de Gaulle (Mon–Fri 8am–1.30pm & 3–6pm; Sat 8am–noon, 3–6pm; €2), with its exhibits highlighting the cultural and natural riches of the *département*, including paintings by local artists and an impressive butterfly collection.

Fruit and vegetable market

From the museum turn onto Rue E Prevot, make a right onto Avenue Monnerville and follow the road to the **fruit and vegetable market** (open Wed, Fri & Sat mornings), a lively place where most of the fruits and vegetables on sale come from the Laotian farmers in Cacao (see p.738). Under the covered market you can find local handicrafts, different rum punches and delicious Vietnamese phô soup.

Musée des Cultures Guyanaises

There are two other places of some note in Cayenne. In the northeast part of town, the **Musée des Cultures Guyanaises** (78 Rue Madame-Payé, Mon & Tue 8am–12:45pm & 3–5.45pm; Wed 8am–12.15pm; Thurs & Fri, 8am–12.15pm & 3–5.45pm; Sat 8am–11.45am; closed Sun, €2) houses Amerindian artefacts and information. Further east past the cemetery, the somewhat paltry **Botanical Gardens** (Blvd de la République; free).

Arrival and information

Air The cheapest option (€2) into Cayenne is a *taxi collectif* from nearby Aéroport de Rochambeau (about 16km) but if you can't find one or don't want to wait for one to fill up you'll have to take a proper taxi which will cost more than €25. Going to the airport it is much cheaper to take a *taxi collectif* to Matoury and there is almost always one waiting opposite Canal Laussat on Ave de la Liberté.

Tourist Office Comité du Tourisme de La Guyane, (Mon–Fri 8am–1pm, 3-6pm; Sat 8am–noon, ⓦ594/296-500, ⓦwww.tourisme-guyane.com) has hotel fliers, bus schedules and tour agency pamphlets but you will have to press for a map that they keep sequestered under the desk.

City transport

Buses SMTC runs local buses on five limited lines to Rémire-Montjoly (€1.10). Most of them leave from Place du Coq opposite the market.

Taxis They're metered, start at €2.10 and are usually on the corner of Rue Molé and Rue de Rémire across the street from the Place des Palmistes. Expect to pay over €6 to get anywhere in town.

CRIME AND SAFETY

You should not have much of a problem in Cayenne—although outlying areas can be somewhat desolate most of the city is safe by day. At night, avoid the city fringe, the market and the area south called the Village Chinois. While both the Place des Palmistes and the bars and snack carts by the cemetery across town are both well-populated at night, they are the territory of the homeless and druggies after nightfall and the stretch between the two areas is dark, deserted and can be sketchy if you're solo.

Accommodation

Amandiers Place Auguste-Horth ⓣ594/289-728, ⓔarmand877@hotmail.com. *Amandiers* is friendly, has a good restaurant, is set in one of the best places in Cayenne to watch a sunset, and has agreeable rooms with a/c. ❾

Amazonia 28 Ave du Général de Gaulle ⓣ594/310-000, ⓦwww.amazonia-hotel.com. Reliable, if unspectacular accommodation at this Best Western hotel in the town centre. The small swimming pool is the major selling point. ❾

La Bodega 42 Avedu Général de Gaulle ⓣ594/302-513, ⓦwww.labodega.fr. If the beer keg puddles in the hall en route to your room perturb you have another *ti' punch* at the downstairs bar and go to bed knowing the orange, non-self-contained *chambres* are the only budget options in Cayenne. Cold showers wash it all away in the morning anyway. No phone reservations. ❻–❼

Central Hotel Corner of Rues Molé & Becker ⓣ594/256-565, ⓔcentralhotel@orange.fr. Charming as a 70s Chinese dormitory, still it's only 100 metres from Place des Palmistes and the comfortable rooms have a/c and even mini-bars. ❽

Guyane Studios Between Rues Molé et C. Colombe ⓣ594/282-929, ⓔdalmazir.pierre @orange.fr. Furnished apartments with a/c just blocks from Place des Palmistes. ❽

Ket Tai 72 Blvd Jubelin ⓣ594/289-797, ⓔg.chang@orange.fr. The sheets are crisp in these white, non-smoking, self-contained, concrete rooms on the edge of town but it smells like stale cigarettes and the walls are stained with god-only-knows what. ❻–❼

Montjoyeux Les Vagues Chemin Grant ⓣ594/302-020. An inconvenient 5km away from Cayenne with a reputation for unfriendly staff, but these a/c rooms have kitchens, wi-fi and sea views. They'd better for the price. ❾

Novotel Route de Montabo ⓣ594/303-888, ⓔh0677@accor-hotels.com. While not cheap, the good facilities, comfortable rooms and lush, tropical setting 3km from the city centre, make this an attractive option considering the alternatives. ❾

Eating

Note that most restaurants are **closed** on Sundays.

Cafés and street food

Burger Gold Corner of Jubelin & Ave du Général de Gaulle. The fact that it's a mobile cart on a corner next to a cemetery doesn't seem to bother locals who line up until late for sloppy sandwiches and burgers with all the fixings.

Café Crème 44 Rue J Catayée. A great place to start the day off with a café, croissant or croque-monsieur on sidewalk tables and the service is surprisingly friendly.

Delifrance 26 Ave du Général de Gaulle. Parisians snicker but they all queue up here at breakfast for a café and *pain au chocolat*.

Mobil Kréol Food 27 Ave de Gaulle. Sure it's a kitchen in a van but it has a small, cheap, tasty menu featuring fried plantains, chicken, pork and casseroles.

Restaurants

Amandiers Place Auguste-Horth ⓣ594/289-728. This popular restaurant has a breezy outdoor terrace café near the coast and a large menu if rather unspectacular service. While there's no ocean view it's a good place (outside the hotel) for people-watching. Try the fish dishes.

La Cafette 120 Ave du Général de Gaulle ⓣ594/307-392. On the east side of town this is a good late night, low-key, sophisticated (for Cayenne) restaurant-café which serves *moules frites*, *salade nicoise* and has a fine selection of whiskies.

Crep'In 5 Rue Lieutenant Becker ⓣ594/302-806. This busy creperie has salads and fresh juices as well as crêpes with endless combinations of sweet and savoury fillings, among them the exemplary curried chicken crepe.

Hei Po 13 Rue Réné-Barthélemy, ⓣ594/303-959. This hole in the wall is said to have Cayenne's best dim sum and the weekend local Chinese crowd seems to back up the claim.

Mille Pâtes 52 Rue Justine Catayee, ⓣ594/289-180. Busy pizzeria with a/c is a favourite of off-duty gendarmes and serves up good thin-crust pizza with plenty of topping options if a little light on the sauce. Calzones and pasta round out the fare. Karaoke, Thurs nights.

Les Palmistes 12 Ave du Général de Gaulle ⓣ594/300-050. On Place des Palmistes in one of Cayenne's most famous buildings, this nineteenth-century bourgeois house contains a chic wooden-beamed dining room and outdoor café and a menu featuring foie gras, duck, steak frites and smoked chicken.

Paris-Cayenne 59 Rue Lalouette. One of Cayenne's most prestigious, longstanding and expensive restaurants, this is the place to splurge on such dishes as atipa ravioli with ginger or salmon with sea urchin coral, rounded off by passion fruit tart with mango coulis.

Les Pyramides Corner of Rues Christophe Colomb & Malouet ⓣ594/379-579. Couscous, tagines, hummus and good pastries at this Mediterranean bistro.

Drinking and nightlife

Acropolys Route de Cabassou ☎594/319-781. This incongruously Greek-facaded nightclub 3km from central Cayenne plays a variety of music including disco, techno, salsa and zouk and has smoke machines and the works along with a €16 cover.

La Bodega 42 Ave du Général de Gaulle, ☎594/302-513. This bar with sidewalk seating where tourists, journalists and the people of the night rub shoulders glows brightly.

Club 106 106 Ave du Général de Gaulle, ☎594/300-106. Air-conditioned discotheque that plays reggae, salsa and zouk and advertises cabaret, karaoke and erotic shows.

Number One 7 Ave du Général de Gaulle ☎594/309-001. This two-floor discotheque with a dancefloor and bar on each plays techno, salsa and meringue and is largely the domain of the young and off-duty gendarmes looking for love.

Entertainment

Entertainment at night in Cayenne can consist mostly of sipping '*ti punch* 'til the wee hours but there are other options. If you understand French you can catch a flick on one of the two screens at **Cinema El Dorado** off the Place des Palmistes, 21 Rue Léon-Gontrand-Damas ☎594/301-314 (tickets are €7).

If you prefer to get off your duff you can head for either the two pool tables behind the magazine racks in the family-run **HKC Games**, 60 Rue Christophe Colombe, or shoot some stick over a pie and a few drinks at the **Pizza Game Center**, 45 Ave du Général de Gaulle (no credit cards).

Shopping

Most of the shopping in Cayenne is centred around pirated CDs, cheap jeans, as well as knockoff shoes and clothing. You can also find Amerindian handicrafts though not as many as in Suriname and Guyana. Try **Ram's Shopping Centre**, 36 Steenbakkerijstraat or **Gadecoop** (31 Rue Arago).

Directory

Airlines Air Caraibes, Centre Commercial de Katoury, Route de la Rocade ☎594/29-36-36 and at Aéroport Rochambeau ☎594/83-58-35; Air France, 17–19 Rue Lalouette, ☎594/299-700. Air Guyane Express, at Rochambeau Airport ☎594/350-300.

Embassies and Consulates Australia, 18 Herbert St Port of Spain, Trinidad, ☎868/628-0695; Brazil, 444 Chemin Saint-Antoine ☎594/296-010; Canada, Young ¶High sts Guyana ☎592/227-2081, Netherlands, Mr Dr J C de Mirandastraat 10 ☎594/477-211; Suriname, 3 Ave Leopord Heder ☎594/282-160; UK, Honorary British Consul, 16 Ave Président Gaston-Monnerville ☎311-034; US, Dr Sophie Redmondstraat 129, Suriname ☎597/477-900.

Exchange You cannot change money at the banks but there is a *bureau de change* at Rochambeau and two in town (right next to one another): Change Caraïbes, 64 Ave de Général-de-Gaulle; Guyane Change, 63 Ave du Général-de-Gaulle.

TOUR OPERATORS

Virtually the only way of getting off the beaten track and out into nature is to join an excursion run by a **tour operator**. As in Guyana and Suriname, the natural attractions do not come cheaply.

Couleurs Amazone, 2bis Ave Pasteur ☎594/287-000, Ⓦwww.couleursamazone.fr. Its young, dynamic owners make a conscious effort to appeal to similar customers. Their most challenging trip involves being air-dropped by helicopter into a remote part of the jungle and trekking for six days back to civilization.

Guyanespace Voyages, 39 Ave Hector-Berlioz ☎594/223-101, Ⓦwww.guyanespace.com. Tours of up to 14 days including a range of activities from river excursions to guided visits to the the Centre Spatiale in Kourou.

JAL Voyages, 26 Ave du Général-de-Gaulle ☎594/316-820, Ⓦwww.jal-voyages.com. This agency specializes in bird-watching river trips to Kaw and on the Maroni River aboard floating *carbets*.

Takari Tour, 8 Rue du Capitaine-Bernard, ☎594/311-960, Ⓦwww.takaritour.gf. Specializing in river tours, Takari leads overnight expeditions on the Maroni, the Oyapok and even white-water rafting on La Mana.

Hospitals The limited ambulance service takes patients to Centre Hospitalier Andre-Rosemon de Cayenne (☎594/395-238/253/050) 3 Ave des Flamboyants.
Internet Cybercafe, 27 Ave du Général-de-Gaulle; Chen Informatique, 6 Rue du Capitaine-Bernard; P.C. Cybercafe 27 Blvd Jubelin.
Laundries There are no laundromats but most hotels will do your laundry for a fee.
Pharmacies Pharmacie Benjamin-Agapit, 23 Ave de Général-de-Gaulle ☎594/30-25-03; Pharmacie Billery, 3494 Route Montabo ☎594/25-60-30; Pharmacie de Cayenne, Rue 14 et 22 Juin 1962 ☎594/28-70-88.
Post office Just off Place des Palmistes opposite Hotel de la Préfecture (Mon–Fri, 7.30am–1.30pm, Sat 7.30–11.45am).

DAY-TRIPS FROM CAYENNE

There are a couple of outlying areas of Cayenne that are worth checking out. Unless you do not mind wasting a lot of time eschew public transportation – rent a car or, in view of how expensive accommodation is in Cayenne, you may as well relocate yourself temporarily to one of the **hotels** in the area where you are spending the day. Most often they will be around the same price and the setting will be much more enjoyable.

Rémire-Montjoly is actually two separate sprawling towns that spread into each other near the coast just outside of Cayenne. The area alternates between unattractive strip-malls, asphalt roundabouts before turning a few kilometres south of Cayenne into deserted coastline (save the occasional kite-surfer) with sparse roadside eateries but some of the best opportunities for sunbathing and swimming in French Guiana. Like the rest of the Guianas, the ocean water is not clear but the beaches themselves, dotted with palm trees and giving slightly to stiff breezes, are often quite picturesque. **Plage Montjoly** in Rémire-Montjoly is the longest stretch of beach in these parts: a pleasant-enough spot spoiled slightly by stiff breezes and constant rumours of shark-infested waters. *Taxis collectifs* go to Rémire-Montjoly from opposite Canal Laussat in Cayenne. None of the hotels are particularly easy to find and everything is pretty spread out but you're not here to be in the thick of it, are you?

Everywhere is someone's somewhere, and **Montsinéry Tonnégrande** about 40km southwest of Cayenne, fits the bill – it has two things to offer: the peace a remote place gives you to collect your thoughts and the nearby **Réserve Animalière Macourienne** (along the Montsinéry River), home to spider monkeys, anteaters, jaguars and tapirs

CAR RENTALS

Cayenne, St-Laurent-du-Maroni and St. Georges de l'Oyapok are negotiable on foot but Kourou is a sprawling city and travelling to any of these places and the beaches in Rémire-Montjoly is expensive. If you don't have gobs of cash or a car, you would do well to find a friend with either or keep the *ti' punch* coming at *La Bodega*. Many of the agencies have offices in both Cayenne and at Rochambeau airport (Hertz has an agency in St Laurent and Kourou as well).

ACL 44 Blvd Jubelin ☎594/30-47-56
ADA Lot 26, ZA Galmot ☎594/25-05-73
Aria 28 Blvd Jubelin ☎594/31-31-32
Auto Guyane 454 Route de Montabo ☎594/35-07-60
Avis 58 Blvd Jubelin ☎594/30-25-22
Europcar ZI Collery Ouest ☎594/35-62-69
Hertz ZI Collery ☎594/29-69-30
Sixt 11 Rue du Capitaine Bernard ☎594/29-80-42

alike. The reserve's main attraction is the feeding of caimans (crocodilian reptiles).

Accommodation

Mme Cécile Thebault Rémire-Montjoly, 2 Lotissement Amarillys, PK 7, 5 Route de Monjoly ⓣ594/381-820, ⓔcecile.thebault@orange.fr. Only rentable by the week but if you're here that long, given the limited options, taking one of these two a/c rooms with a kitchenette makes sense. ❺

Motel Beauregard Rémire-Montjoly, 2 Route de Rémire ⓣ594/354-100, ⓔcriccrac@orange.fr. All rooms are comfortable with a/c but you should take one of palm-surrounded *cabanas*. As a hotel guest you have discounted access to the nearby *Break Club* which has a gym, tennis courts, swimming pool and bowling. ❽

Motel du Lac Rémire-Montjoly, Chemin Poupon ⓣ594/380-800, ⓔmoteldulac@opensurf.net. Ten minutes from Rochambeau, five from Cayenne, these 32 a/c rooms are in a quiet, residential area steps away from a pool surrounded by more palm trees. ❽

Residence Siloe Rémire-Montjoly, Villa Douglas, PK 7, Route de Montjoly ⓣ594/382-207, ⓔcontact@residencesiloe.com. No one would describe these seven self-contained rooms as luxurious but they have access to a kitchen and do the trick near a beach, butcher, baker and supermarket. ❻

Villa Le Verger Montsinéry Tonnégrande, 12 Domaine Les Champs Virgile ⓣ594/388-605, ⓦwww.villaleverger.com. Two a/c rooms one with a double bed and the other sleeping four people. Both have access to a pool. ❼

Eating

L'Auberge Du Lotus Montsinéry Tonnégrande, PK2, 5 Rue Tonnegrande ⓣ594/315-008. Nothing fancy in these parts but this little *carbet* serves up decent Vietnamese specialities.

La Belle Amédée Rémire-Montjoly, Place Auguste-Horth ⓣ594/289-728. This chic restaurant in a colonial-style building just across from the beach would be perfect if you just had an unobstructed view of the ocean but the food including decent, though expensive sushi does not disappoint.

Break Club Rémire-Montjoly, PK 9, 2 Route de Rémire ⓣ594/354-100. Cafeteria and snacks surrounded by bowling, billiards, swimming pool, arcade games and mini-golf.

Le Cric-Crac Rémire-Montjoly, PK 9, 2 Route de Rémire ⓣ594/354-100. Heaping portions of uncomplicated local cuisine with fish as a central player.

Mille Pates Rémire-Montjoly, 1 Lot Colline, ⓣ594/382-903. Sure it's a chain restaurant but the pizza and pasta are actually pretty decent, especially if you haven't had either in a while.

Moving on

Air Air France flies direct to Paris, Fort de France, Martinique and Paramaribo, Suriname. Caraibes Air also flies to Fort de France as well as Pointe-á-Pitre, Guadeloupe. Air Guyane Express flies to the interior (Maripasoula and Saul).

Bus SMTC buses have limited service in Cayenne and extend into outlying areas like Matoury and Rémire-Montjoly's beaches €1.10 (one way). You can take minibuses to almost anywhere along the coast.

West to Suriname

If much of French Guiana's eco-style tourism takes place to the south of Cayenne, the *département*'s most visited attractions are strung along the coast between Cayenne and the border with Suriname. Prime among these is the **Centre Spatial Guyanais** in **Kourou**, the focal point of the European space programme, and **Iles du Salut**, home during the nineteenth century to the most notorious convict settlements. The road (RN1) continues west to the turtle-nesting beach at **Plage Les Hattes**. Continuing along RN1, you will arrive eventually at **Saint-Laurent-du-Maroni**, the last town in French Guiana before crossing the Maroni River into Suriname.

KOUROU

Kourou, roughly in the middle of French Guiana's coast between Suriname and Brazil, was not designed with tourists in mind. It is a hopelessly sprawling place with no defined centre, difficult to get

ON THE ROAD

A bona fide road near the coast stretches across the *département*. From its westernmost town, Saint-Laurent-du-Maroni, to Cayenne the road is called RN1 and from Cayenne to its easternmost outpost, Saint-Georges, the road is called RN2. Keep your passport with you as there are occasional armed checkpoints where gendarmes will ask to see it.

around on foot with no public transportation to speak of. **Accommodation** is more limited than in Cayenne with the benefit of being just as expensive. The best **places to eat** are in Le Vieux Bourg (the old village), along Avenue du Général de Gaulle—considering how difficult it is to get around these places double as convenient watering holes.

The majority of the 20,000-strong population have something to do with the **Centre Spatial Guyanais**, and most visitors come for the **rockets** or because it is the access point for **Iles du Salut**. That said, budget travellers with an eye for hammock-hanging will find a beach-*carbet* that wows, sunrise and sunset.

Be warned that the areas surrounding **Lac Bois Diable** and **Lac du Bois Chaudat** are mosquito-ridden and if you plan to arrive late, reserve a room in advance and make sure you have euros—not many people speak English and getting either without the other will be difficult, and extremely so on foot. Minibus drivers will take you directly to your hotel and often know residents who will put tourists up in their homes for a fee.

Centre Spatial Guyanais

It's not set up for tourism like the Kennedy Space Center, but the sight of the **Centre Spatial Guyanais**'s rocket launch towers surrounded by tropical forest is like something out of a Bond film, making a visit both surreal *and* educational. The CSG occupies a total area of 850 square kilometres and has sent over five hudred rockets (most carrying satellites) into orbit since *Véronique* blasted off on April 9, 1968. Three-hour **guided tours** of the CSG (Mon–Thurs 7.45am & 12.45pm, Fri 7.45am; compulsory reservations by phone ⓣ594/326-123, ⓔvisites.csg@orange.fr; must be over eight years of age; ID required; free) include a film charting the history of the centre and a visit to the Jupiter Control Centre.

TROIS, DEUX, UN, DÉCOLLAGE!

At the time of writing the Ariane 5 was the active launcher. Unless you have very lucky timing you'll have to do a little prep-work to actually see a launch as they only happen about once every two months. The launch site is fifteen kilometres up the road (no public transport) from the welcome centre.

After the drama of the countdown and ignition, the rocket gives off enough light that you can watch a launch almost anywhere in Kouru and the Carapa site, just before the CSG welcome centre, is free for anyone to use. Still, try to get invited to one of the official outdoor observation sites where the view is even more impressive (though initially silent until the sound reaches you). The Toucan, Kikiwi, Colibri and Agami sites are between 4.5 and 6.5 km from the launch pad (you must be over sixteen), and the Ibis site is 12 km away (no one under eight). To get an invitation, write including your full name, age (must be over sixteen) and contact details to: CNES, Centre Spatial Guyanais, Relations Publiques, BP 726, 97387 Kourou Cedex. Lift-offs can be hard to predict so check the website ⓦwww.csg-spatial.tm.fr for updates and contact the agency in advance. For more information try ⓣ594/334-200 or ⓔcsg-accueil@cnes.fr.

MAKE FRIENDS, WILL TRAVEL

Cayenne, St Laurent and especially Kourou are places where the lack of affordable accommodation would make having a friend to 'visit' very helpful. There are a few sites that can provide you with these new friends with sometimes less than a few days' notice.

www.travelbuddy.com Online community of travellers, and would-be explorers looking for travel partners and citizens of the world who often offer to put up weary tourists.

www.couchsurfing.com A network connecting travellers with locals who offer accommodation and insight.

A résumé of the CSG and space exploration in general is available at the **Musée de l'Espace** (Mon–Fri 8am–6pm, Sat 2–6pm; €6.10; if attending a guided tour of the CSG Mon–Sat, €3.80; ⓣ0594/33-53-84) next to the CSG welcome centre about four kilometres from central Kourou and reachable by bus.

Accommodation

Association Taliko Hang your hammock on a beach under a *carbet* built by local Amerindian villagers. It's the cheapest way to stay in town. Just mind your things. ❷

Ballahou 1–3 Rue Amet-Martial ⓣ594/32-97-78. Not far from the beach but with a reception open only from noon to 2 and 6–8pm it's somewhat service-challenged. ❻–❼

Le Gros Bec 56 Rue du Docteur-Floch ⓣ594/32-91-91, ⓔhotel.legrosbec@orange.fr. Expensive but a good location for an early catamaran departure to the Iles du Salut from the nearby jetty. All rooms have a kitchen and a mezzanine with an additional double bed. ❽–❾

Hotel des Roches Pointe des Roches ⓣ594/32-00-66, ⓔsmirakoff@hoteldesroches.com. Benefits from its attractive, coastal location next to Kourou's most popular beach, Plage des Roches. The most expensive rooms have views of the sea – and some, Iles du Salut. ❾

Mercure Ariatel Ave St Exupéry ⓣ594/32-89-00. Bungalow-style suites at the northern edge of town on Lac du Bois Diable with access to a gym, ping-pong, tennis courts, a pool and access to bicycles. ❾

Mme Renold 1 Rue Jules Séraaphin ⓣ594/32-08-95. Two clean, reasonably priced, secure, self-contained, rooms with a/c just a few blocks from the eateries along Ave du Général de Gaulle make this the only budget option in this sprawling, unnavigable town unless you want to hang a hammock on the beach. ❷

Eating and drinking

Le Baraka 37 Ave du Général de Gaulle ⓣ594/32-33-23. Another lively Bourg restaurant, this inviting, Christmas-light lit spot serves Moroccan tagine-fare.

Le Créolia Ave des Roches, next to Hotel des Roches ⓣ594/32-00-66. Grilled shark fillet and *magret de canard* in a pleasant beachfront setting.

Cupuacu 27 Ave du Général de Gaulle ⓣ594/42-37-52. Colourful Brazilian *churrascaria* in Le Vieux Bourg with charming owners offers *feijoada, vatapa* and other such dishes.

Latina Café *Mercure Atlantis Hotel* ⓣ594/32-13-00. French Creole, Surinamese and Brazilian cuisines as well as an excellent club sandwich (ask for specially because it is not on the menu).

N'Jifa 21 Ave du Général de Gaulle ⓣ594/32-87-01. Little Creole eatery in Le Vieux Bourg that serves up hearty cook-up and fish dishes.

Le Relais Du Bourg 77 Ave du Générale de Gaulle. Popular sports bar with a pool table and projection television with satellite hookup.

Directory

Banks BFC, Place Jeanne-d'Arc, BNP, Ave des Roches; BRED, 85 Ave Gaston-Monnerville; La Poste, 4 Ave des Frères-Kennedy.

Hospital Centre Médico Chirugical de Kourou Ave des Iles ⓣ594/32-76-76, ⓦcmc-kourou.croix-rouge.fr/.

Internet Webcom, CV 14, Simarouba

Pharmacies Pharmacie du Bourg, Ave Thomas Guidigio ⓣ594/32-13-66; Pharmacie Colibri, Quartier Simarouba ⓣ594/32-14-00.

Post 4 Ave des Frères-Kennedy.

Tourist Office Point Information Tourisme, 30 Ave du Général de Gaulle (ⓣ594/32-25-40), dispenses tourist information on the CSG, Iles due Salut and other attractions in the Kourou area.

Moving on

By taxi Getting to Kourou by *taxi collectif* from either Cayenne or Saint-Laurent is easy (see p.723), leaving is not. There is no central place where taxis *collectifs* depart, let alone any fixed times (try early morning). A good place to wait for them is at the bus stand opposite the Gendarmerie in Place de l'Europe. It's best to call the companies directly on ⓣ594/326-093 or ⓣ594/322-800 to arrange a ride (hotels can help with this). Tropic Alizés, which ferries passengers to Iles du Salut also has a Cayenne/Kourou transfer for €15. Hitchhiking is a realistic option, especially to Cayenne where traffic is regular.

ILES DU SALUT

The **ILES DU SALUT** (Salvation Islands) fifteen kilometres north of Kourou, are three islands (**Ile Royale**, **Ile Saint-Joseph** and **Ile du Diable**) infamous for their use as a penal colony from 1852 to 1953. Unlike the Guiane coastline, the islands are surrounded by clear blue water, and the vegetation is green and lush. Popularized by the book entitled *Papillon* – and later the Steve McQueen film of the same name – in which former prisoner Henri Charrière recounts the horrors of life in the colony and his various attempts at escape (which finally succeeded), the islands have become a major tourist attraction leading to the somewhat incongruous presence of an upscale **hotel**, *Auberge des Iles du Salut* on Ile Royale ❽–❾ (ⓣ32-11-00, ⓦwww.ilesdusalut.com) where you can get comfortable rooms (or pay €10 to hang a hammock) and good meals (excellent fish soup and *rouille*).

What to see and do

A rather contradictory aspect of the Iles du Salut given their gruesome past is their natural beauty. The island's "prisoners" are jungle rats and monkeys who blissfully ravage mangoes dangling from the local trees and seek better ways to crack open fallen coconuts.

Ile Royale, the main island and the one most visited now by tourists was used for administration and housing common law criminals. **Ile Saint-Joseph** was where the "incorrigible" convicts and those who tried to escape were sent. While Ile Royale has been restored, the ruins of the penal colony on Ile

GETTING TO THE ISLAND

There are two ways to get to the island, the noisy, daily ferry or more enjoyable, a catamaran-ride. Either way you need to make reservations. Except for boats belonging to Tropic Alizés, the companies leave from the **appontement des pecheurs** (fisherman's jetty) at the end of Avenue du Général de Gaulle.

Ferry (1hr each way, €35, ⓣ594/32-09-95) Departs for Ile Royale at 7.50am. The return from Ile Royale leaves at 5pm.

Private Yacht Several companies offer one- or two-day tours (€39 and €65 respectively, children under half-price) and include visits to Ile Royale and Ile Saint-Joseph. On the two-day tour you usually end up spending the night on Saint-Joseph's small beach. Just be certain to be at the island pier a half hour before you are told as boats often depart early for Kourou.

Albatros (ⓣ594/32-16-12, ⓔhalliercatherine@orange.fr)

La Hulotte (ⓣ594/32-33-81, ⓔlahulotte@terresdeguyane.fr)

Royal Ti'Punch (ⓣ594/32-09-95) Your trip back to town is accompanied by the beverage for which the company is named.

Tropic Alizés (ⓣ594/25-10-10, ⓔtropic.alizes@orange.fr) Departs from Club Nautique de Kourou at the Pointe de Roches.

GETTING TO AND LEAVING SAINT LAURENT

The official **ferry** to and from Albina will cost you €2-5 depending on your negotiation skills. The small benefit to taking the ferry is that you arrive at the pier where customs will stamp your passport. Motorized dug-outs (15mins, €3) come and go when you are ready but are a fifteen-minute walk from customs. **Taxis collectifs** will be waiting where dug-outs from Suriname arrive – and at the ferry terminal – to take passengers to Kourou (2hr; €25) and Cayenne (3hr; €35). Unless there is a wave of arrivals from Suriname, these vehicles can take some hours to fill up. With this in mind, hitchhiking becomes an increasingly attractive – and feasible – option.

You can also **rent a car:**

ADA 14 rue Hector Rivierez ⓣ594/27-94-82

Hertz 3 rue de la Zone Industrielle ⓣ594/34-19-81

Saint-Joseph are overgrown with vegetation and arguably offer a more authentic and atmospheric experience. These days there is nothing to stop you slinging a **hammock** or **camping** anywhere on Ile Royale and Ile Saint-Joseph, but note that once you take the boat over there you're stuck until the return trip to the island later in the afternoon.

The virtually inaccessible **Ile du Diable** is off-limits to tourists and was once reserved for political prisoners, most famously Alfred Dreyfus, who was arrested for passing military secrets to the Germans but was later cleared.

The islands are not for adventure junkies—while you can sign up for a guided tour of Ile Royale (in French) at the Auberge or check out the quaint museum, most of the rest of your stay will consist of wandering the island's paths and observing the incredibly unintimidated wildlife. Although you can purchase basic supplies at the hotel, bring your own food and water if you are considering the camping option.

SAINT-LAURENT-DU-MARONI

Now one of French Guiana's larger towns with a population of around twenty thousand, **SAINT-LAURENT-DU-MARONI** on the east bank of the Maroni River some 260 kilometres from Cayenne is quiet and down at heel. If you have just arrived from Suriname you will be relieved, this is no Albina. Still, St Laurent was originally conceived as an agricultural penal colony, where convicts were put to cultivating bananas and sugarcane, and managing forests, and there is not much here. Note that the few nice (and expensive) accommodations are not near the pier and are often booked well ahead.

What to see and do

First things first: if you have taken one of the wooden speedboats across the river from Suriname you'll have to hoof it about 400 metres down Ave Hector Rivierez to the official ferry crossing to get your passport stamped (same if you're preparing to leave *for* Suriname).

Camp de la Transportation

The town's highlight is the old Camp de la Transportation (guided tours Mon–Sat 8am, 9.30am, 11am, 3pm & 4.30pm, Sun & public holidays 9.30am & 11am July–Aug also 3pm & 4.30pm; €5) on a bend in the Maroni River. You can walk round the grounds and check out the permanent exhibition of photos in the camp's former kitchen for free, but tours of the detention cells (in French) and other installations put everything into its chilling context and should

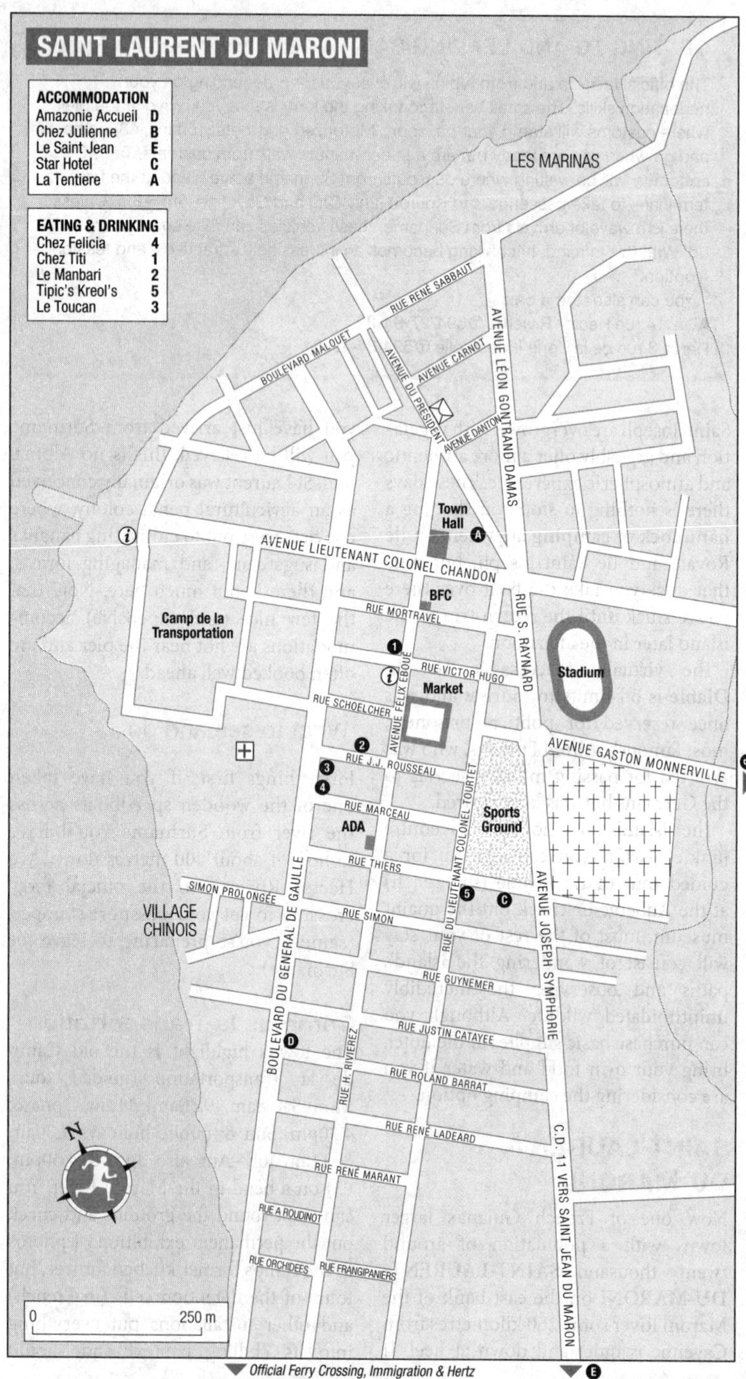

SAINT LAURENT DU MARONI
ACCOMMODATION
Amazonie Accueil D
Chez Julienne B
Le Saint Jean E
Star Hotel C
La Tentiere A
EATING & DRINKING
Chez Felicia 4
Chez Titi 1
Le Manbari 2
Tipic's Kreol's 5
Le Toucan 3
LES MARINAS
RUE RENÉ SABBAUT
BOULEVARD MALOUET
AVENUE CARNOT
AVENUE DU PRESIDENT
AVENUE DANTON
AVENUE LÉON GONTRAND DAMAS
Town Hall
AVENUE LIEUTENANT COLONEL CHANDON
BFC
RUE MORTRAVEL
Camp de la Transportation
RUE S. RAYNARD
RUE VICTOR HUGO
Market
Stadium
RUE SCHOELCHER
AVENUE FELIX EBOUÉ
AVENUE GASTON MONNERVILLE
RUE J.J. ROUSSEAU
RUE MARCEAU
ADA
Sports Ground
RUE DU LIEUTENANT COLONEL TOURTET
RUE THIERS
SIMON PROLONGÉE
VILLAGE CHINOIS
RUE SIMON
AVENUE JOSEPH SYMPHORIE
RUE GUYNEMER
BOULEVARD DU GENERAL DE GAULLE
RUE JUSTIN CATAYEE
RUE H. RIVIEREZ
RUE ROLAND BARRAT
RUE RENÉ LADEARD
C.D. 11 VERS SAINT JEAN DU MARON
RUE RENÉ MARANT
RUE A ROUDINOT
RUE ORCHIDEES
RUE FRANGIPANIERS
0
250 m
Official Ferry Crossing, Immigration & Hertz

THE GUIANAS

FRENCH GUIANA

not be missed. Buy tickets for the tour at the **Office du Tourisme** (Mon–Fri 7.30am–6pm, Sat 7.45am–12.45pm & 2.45–5.45pm, Sun 9am–1pm; ⓣ594/342-398), which also provides plenty of documentation (also in French) on the history of the camp and Saint-Laurent-du-Maroni, as well as details of excursions up the Maroni River (see below).

Accommodation

Amazonie Accueil 3 rue R Barrat ⓣ594/34-41-78, ⓔam-ac@antilladoo.com. Guarded *carbet* will provide you with a hammock and mosquito net. ❸
Chez Julienne Rue Gaston Monnerville ⓣ594/34-11-53. Six basic rooms with all the modern conveniences just a few blocks out of town past the cemetery and football field opposite a shantytown. ❻
Le Relais des Trois Lacs 19–21 Domaine du Lac Bleu ⓣ594/34-05-05, ⓔer3lacs@nplus.gf. St Laurent's most picturesque hotel is three kilometres from the centre of town in an attractive lake and forest setting with a huge swimming pool. All 23 have a/c and satellite TV. ❽–❾
Le Saint Jean 3 Chemin du Parc ⓣ594/34-14-22).This *carbet* near the Maroni river has slots for 12 hammocks and does not provide them nor do they have mosquito nets but there is a terrace and bathroom for less than €10. ❸
Star Hotel 109 Rue Thiers ⓣ594/34-10-84. The fact that these ugly, bare, tiled, a/c rooms cost the same as *La Tentiaire* is ludicrous but you'll be grateful in a pinch. ❼
La Tentiaire 12 Rue Roosevelt ⓣ594/34-26-00, ⓔtentiaire@orange.fr. Colourful, climatized rooms in a secure building with access to a pool. The staff doesn't need to be friendly to keep business so they're not. ❼–❾

Eating

Chez Felicia 23 Ave du Général de Gaulle ⓣ594/34-30-87. A small, bustling place with open-shuttered windows that serves *fricassée* and other Creole dishes.
Chez Titi 18 Ave Félix Éboué, ⓣ594/34-29-00. Open-air pizzeria has two outdoor tables and decent food but the service is laughable. The corner bakery attached to the restaurant is the place to go for your morning croissant (although the coffee is an automatic dispenser).
Le Mambari 13 Rue Jean-Jacques Rousseau, ⓣ594/34-35-90. You can eat *moules frites* or pizza before or after a game of billiards or foosball.
Tipic Kreol's Between rues Tourtet & Thiers, ⓣ594/34-09-83. This neon-lit bar has a pool table and terrace where you can get Creole dishes and grilled and smoked local fish like *jamais-gouté* and *d'acoupa.*
Le Toucan 17 Blvd du Général de Gaulle, ⓣ594/27-82-50. Has salads and daily menus for €13–16.

Directory

Banks BFC, 11 Ave Felix Eboué (exchange also).
Hospital Centre Hospitalier de l'Ouest Guyanais Franck Joly, 16 Blvd du Général du Gaulle ⓣ594/348-888.

MARONI RIVER

Most tour operators in French Guiana (see box, p.729) offer **pirogue river trips**. The attractions – compared to the Approuage or Oyapok – are the relatively large Amerindian and Bush Negro populations on both sides of the river. Excursions focus more on village visits than wildlife spotting.

Operators also offer day-trips for those who just want to take in an "authentic" village, with dance performance and local crafts. Try Maroni Club, 1 Esplanade Laurent Baudin next to the Office du Tourisme (ⓣ594/34-73-73).

Another way to go is to make your own way to the Bush Negro village of Apatou, about seventy kilometres upriver. A pirogue leaves daily (€15, one way) from the Glacière in Saint Laurent at 11am, arriving in Apatou at around 2pm. The return is the following morning at 7am next to the riverbank in the village centre. You can sleep in a room at *Mawina Chouti* ⓣ694/44-27-72 for €20 or €10 (including hammock rental). Forty-two kilometres east of Apatou are the Voltaire Falls, with nearby facilities for picnics and lodging – l'Auberge des *Chutes Voltaire*, Route de Paul Isnard (closed Tue–Wed; at least €11 per person for a hammock).

CROSSING INTO SURINAME

The quickest and easiest way to cross the Maroni River to **Albina** (see p.719) in Suriname is by taking a motorized dug-out (€3) from the end of rue Ho-Kong-You in the Village Chinois, not forgetting to get your passport stamped at the **immigration office** (6am–7pm) at the ferry terminal about 500 metres south from where the dug-outs leave. There is no real reason to wait for the **ferry**, unless of course you have a car. Sailing times from Saint-Laurent-du-Maroni are as follows: Mon–Tues & Thurs–Fri 7am, 9am, 2pm & 5pm; Wed 7am & 5pm; Sat 8am & 9am; Sun 3.30pm & 5pm. The one-way fare is €2–5 depending on your negotiation skills for a foot passenger, €27 with a car.

There is a **cambio** at the ferry terminal in Albina (see p.719) which gives good rates when buying Suriname dollars with euros and US dollars. Indeed, these rates are better than you will get in Paramaribo.

Internet Infocenter, 16 Rue Victor Hugo.
Post Blvd du Général du Gaulle, has ATMs that accept Visa and MasterCard.
Tourist Office Office du Tourisme 1 Esplanade Laurent Baudin ⓣ594/342-398.

PLAGE LES HATTES

From roughly April to July, **PLAGE LES HATTES**, at the mouth of the Maroni River a few kilometres from the Suriname border, is French Guiana's best place to view **leatherback turtles** laying their eggs. Said to be the world's largest turtle, leatherbacks can grow up to two metres in length and weigh almost 900kg. During the peak of egg laying, it is estimated that more than two hundred of these giant, grunting, shell-less turtles crawl up onto the beach each night. Compared with Galibi Beach in Suriname (see p.719) and Shell Beach in Guyana (see p.696), Plage Les Hattes is relatively accessible, lying a mere four kilometres from Awala-Yalimapo.

Accommodation and eating

There is an abundance of **accommodation** in the vicinity – unusually for French Guiana, much of it is quite affordable. In Awala-Yalimapo, at **Chez Judith et Denis** ❺, Ave Paul Henri (ⓣ594/34-24-38 or 26-33-27), you can rent a hammock 100 metres from the beach (breakfast included); or rent a hammock under a *carbet* at **Yalimale** ❹ (ⓣ594/34-34-32), whose restaurant serves Amerindian specialities. If you're looking for something a bit more enclosed try one of the three basic rooms at **Soeurs de Saint-Joseph de Cluny** ❺, 1 Rue Bourguignon (ⓣ594/34-82-70).
The **eating** options in Awala-Yalimapo basically boil down to the Creole–Amerindian although there are a few alternatives like **Le Buffalo**, 36 Rue A.M. Javaouhey (ⓣ594/34-80-36) which serves French dishes adapted from local produce and eaten in a cowboy-themed dining room.

South to Brazil

The settlements in the southern part of the *département* are few and far between compared with the relatively populous north coast and tourism here is mainly nature-oriented. Interesting side-trips can be made to the Hmong (Laotian) village of **Cacao** and the *marais* or swamp of **Kaw**. At the end of the paved section of RN2, **Régina** is the departure point for excursions on the **Approuague River**, but the road continues on the opposite bank of the river as an unsealed track all the way to **Saint-Georges-de-l'Oyapok** on the Brazilian border.

CACAO

A once-abandoned little town along the River Comté, about 75km southwest of Cayenne, **CACAO** was resettled in 1977 by refugees from Laos that no other town in French Guiana wanted. Since then, this small Hmong community (less than fifteen hundred inhabitants, most of whom are fruit and vegetable farmers) has become the fruit and vegetable basket of the *département*.

What to see and do

There is a picturesque local market on Sunday mornings where you can find good produce, soups and papaya salads, as well as arts and handicrafts. The **Association Le Planeur Bleu** (Ⓣ594/270-034, €3), has a small museum some of whose exhibits are living: rare butterflies and spiders are a treat for those who aren't squeamish about insects.

Arrival

You may have trouble finding an inexpensive way to get to Cacao. *Taxis collectifs* do leave occasionally from Cayenne but not daily and without regularity. Local guidebooks recommend intrepid travellers ask for a ride from farmers selling their produce on market days. If you are **driving**, the turn-off for Cacao from RN2 is about forty kilometres before the small town of Régina on the north bank of the Approuague River. More conventionally, Jal, Takari and Couleurs Amazone (p.729) offer organized tours to the town.

Accommodation and eating

Auberge Des Orpailleurs PK 62, Route de Régina, Ⓣ594/270-622, Ⓦwww.aubergedesorpailleurs.com. This *gîte* (French guesthouse) on RN2 near the turn-off has six no-frills rooms, a restaurant and lets you hang a hammock for less than €6. ❷–❻

Chez By Et Daniel 111 Bourg de Cacao Ⓣ594/270-998, closed Tue & Wed. The best Laotian restaurant in Cacao serves pork steamed in a banana leaf and chicken with Laotian caramel lunches on a shady terrace in a little flower garden. five percent discount on your tab if you show your ticket from the Planeur Bleu museum.

Quimbe Kio Ⓣ594/270-122, Ⓦwww.quimbeki.com. You can hang a hammock here for a few euros in a *carbet* on a wooded hill next to the village. ❶

ROURA

Roura is a picturesque town nestled on the banks of the Orapu River, its church spire poking out through the trees. The drive here along a sixty kilometre stretch of road winding its way up and across the heavily forested Kaw hills is surely one of the most scenic in the Guianas. To get here, just past Matoury, instead of continuing along RN2 towards Régina, take the turn-off on the left, which leads eventually to Kaw. You can get **tourist information** at the Syndicat d'Initiative de Roura (Ⓣ594/311-104).

Accommodation

La Créola Village Dacca, 2km from the centre Ⓣ594/28-07-15. Two rooms with air conditioning and hot water as well as bungalows for up to six people, and hammock space or €4. There is also a restaurant which serves Creole food. ❺–❼

KAW

Located on an island in the middle of an Everglades-style swamp known as Marais de Kaw, some fifty kilometres past Roura, **Kaw** itself is not the main reason for coming out this far. Marais de Kaw covers about one thousand square kilometres, and the surrounding hills complete with mists during the wet season make for some stunning vistas. This is an excellent place to observe many species of water birds including buzzards and flamingos, and organized tours make a great deal of the after-dark pirogue trips to spot black caiman (rarer than red caiman). You can **spend the night** on a floating *carbet* in the middle of the swamp. Surprisingly, mosquitoes are not a problem on the swamp itself; there are more on the banks and in the hills around it. There are enough hammocks in town for more than twenty people, although half this number is preferable if the swamp's serenity is not to be completely shattered by screaming kids and disgruntled Parisian tourists. JAL Voyages (see opposite) specializes in one-day and overnight trips.

Accommodation

Gîte Communal ⓣ594/270-465. In the heart of the village, for less than €6 euros you can hang a hammock in a space that fits about 15 people with access to two sinks, showers and toilets. ❷

Gîte Tropico ⓣ594/280-179. At the left of the church, less than €10 will get you a slot to hang your hammock. Breakfast is served for another €6. ❷

Restaurant Gingembre Shop ⓣ594/27-04-65. Meals average €14, breakfasts €5 at this restaurant that can arrange hammock lodging as well as nature hikes.

REGINA

About 122km from Cayenne, **Régina** may mislead you at first glance. Do not be confused by the numerous Renaults, Peugeots and Citroens often seen parked next to its small river jetty – there is nothing to the town itself – the cars belong to tourists who are there to join **pirogue trips** up the **Approuague River**. A good number of these tourists have booked a **stay** at *Cisame* (ⓣ594/270-122), arguably the area's main attraction a one hour thirty minute journey upriver – make bookings through Couleurs Amazone (see p.729). Probably French Guiana's most comfortable jungle camp, *Cisame* has good sanitary facilities, constant electricity, tasty meals and offers activities like river swims, gold-panning and informative guided (in French) nature walks. If you are continuing on to Saint-Georges-de-l'Oyapok and the Brazilian border, you can take a *taxi collectif* (1hr 30min) for €17. There is usually one minibus a day back to Cayenne, €23.

The Amazon: Maripasoula and Saül

The remoteness of Maripasoula and Saül, the two main settlements in French Guiana's Amazon Rainforest interior, has been promoted by the tour operators to such an extent that both of them have ceased to become particularly off-the-beaten-track destinations. OK, so getting to them will involve flying or spending several days on the river (and sometimes on foot), but once there you will likely be surrounded by fellow tourists and the odd local inhabitant trying a little too hard to be as authentic as the brochures promised. This said, being this far into the Amazon while still having a reasonably comfortable place to lay your head is good recompense for the company.

MARIPASOULA, nearly 300 kilometres up the Maroni River, is the logical starting or finishing point for pirogue trips (for more on the Maroni River, see box, p.738). The towns are small but they do offer some nightlife. Upon your return from your nature-commune be sure to check out one of the local dancehalls which initially tend to resemble private parties (just follow your ears!). **SAÜL**, an old gold-mining town a hundred and fifty kilometres from Cayenne, in the geographical centre of the *département*, is the base for exploring the ninety kilometres of marked jungle trails.

Arrival

The only ways into Maripasoula and Saül are either by **plane** or a combination of river-travel and hiking (sensibly through one of the tour operators below). If you decide to fly you will have to book a flight through Air Guyane Express (ⓣ594/350-300), which has **flights** to both Maripasoula and Saül from Cayenne: to

TOURS TO THE INTERIOR

Tour operators (see p.729) offer trips of varying lengths for the intrepid adventurer interested in pirogue-ing and hiking their way to their destinations.

Couleurs Amazone Six-to-seven hour pirogue trips to Amerindian villages along the Maroni River for four days, €500.

JAL Voyages Five-day river trips with nights spent in hammocks sheltered by *carbets* for €530.

Maroni Tours John Dimpai, Village de Saint-Jean (☎594/34-11-75) Seven-to-ten-day trips with visits to Amerindian villages costing from €335 to €430.

Maripasoula twice a day Monday, Wednesday, Saturday, and three times daily the rest of the week (one-way, €80; return €151); to Saül twice a day Tuesday and Thursday, once daily on remaining days (one-way, €65; return €120).

Accommodation

Visit the *mairies* (town halls) in Maripasoula and Saül for further information on accommodation.

Maripasoula Guesthouses

Hotel Chez Dede 18 rue Leonard Domerger, ☎594/37-22-63. Fourteen rooms with fans for €20 or a place to hang a hammock for €5. ❷–❺

Hotel Poti Soula ☎594/37-25-82. Seven rooms starting from €22 or a place to hang a hammock (not provided) €7. ❷–❺

Saut Sonnelle Crique Inini ☎594/31-49-45. Hammock *carbet* with mosquito nets and showers about 30min from Maripasoula. ❺–❾

Le Terminus Poti Soula ☎594/37-21-84. Little, self-contained rooms with terraces are €50 otherwise you can hang a hammock for €9. ❸–❼

Tolenga Lodge Crique Inini ☎594/37-12-35. Individual bungalows for €80. ❾

Saül Guesthouses

Les Carbets du Bord Ⓔlescarbetsdubord@orange.fr. Individual bungalows for €10 gets you one of twelve spots to hang your hammock and breakfast. ❸

Chez Lulu ☎594/31-42-47, Ⓔtimanelucien@msn.com. Large or small bungalows fitting 2–4 people for hanging hammocks equipped with bathrooms starting at €35. ❻

Gîte Communal For €13 you can actually get a bed in this guesthouse in the centre of town. ❹

SAINT-GEORGES-DE-L'OYAPOK

SAINT-GEORGES-DE-L'OYAPOK, is the last town (and quite a small one at that) in French Guiana before crossing the Oyapok River to Brazil. Apart from excursions on the river organized by tour operators, there is not a great deal to do but get your passport stamped and hightail it into Brazil. If you do feel like sticking round for a while, check out the **Saut Maripa** rapids, the longest in French Guiana, about thirty minutes upstream past the Brazilian town of Oiapoque. Oyapock Evasion (☎594/37-02-59 or 694/41-60-01) can organize day-trips from €44 and JAL Voyages (see opposite) has five-day-trips for €395. You might also consider staying in Oiapoque where hotel rooms are cheaper (though give yourself some time to check them out as some of them are of much higher quality than others). Eating options are almost exclusively limited to the

CROSSING INTO BRAZIL

Taxi collectifs from Régina will drop you on the eastern edge of town where boats cross the Oyapok River to Oiapoque in Brazil (15min; €8). The **immigration office** can also be found here. Once in Brazil you should go to the **Federal Police** to get your passport stamped. With the river on your right, follow the main street until you see a road to your left with a church in its middle. The Federal Police can be found on the right side of this road past the church. **Moneychangers** operate on the Brazilian side of the river, but not in Saint-Georges.

hotel restaurants and meat grilled on skewers by street vendors.

Accommodation

Hotel-Restaurant Caz Calé rue E Elfort ☎594/37-00-13. Fifteen small rooms some with a/c a few blocks off the main square. The place does do food but you're better off eating on the main square. ❼

Chez Modestine ☎594/37-08-84. The doors in this hotel on the main square are a little flimsy but the rooms with a/c themselves are clean, self-contained and the best in town with a very decent restaurant café downstairs. The hotel can also arrange for you to sleep in hammocks (€5 per person) on Ilet Sophia 30min upstream. ❾

Ilha do Sol On the river itself the small islet facing Saint-Georges has hammocks for negotiable prices. Have one of the boatmen take you over. ❹

FRENCH GUIANA THE GUIANAS

Paraguay

HIGHLIGHTS

THE CHACO: spot abundant wildlife in this vast wilderness

THE ITAIPÚ HYDRO-ELECTRIC PROJECT: the world's second biggest dam–an extraordinary feat of engineering design

ASUNCIÓN: visit Paraguay's most famous monument, the Panteón de los Héroes

SAN RAFAEL PARQUE NACIONAL: this leafy paradise, Paraguay's most biodiverse reserve, is a must-see for nature lovers

ENCARNACIÓN: glimpse Jesuit life at nearby missions or party at the vibrant February Carnaval

ROUGH COSTS

DAILY BUDGET basic US$20 occasional treat US$35

DRINK 1 litre Pilsen Beer US$1.50

FOOD *chipa* US$0.25, *asado completo* US$10

HOSTEL/BUDGET HOTEL US$6–10/ US$15–25

TRAVEL Asunción–Encarnación (365km): bus US$13

FACT FILE

POPULATION 6.1 million (2007)

AREA 406,750 sq km

LANGUAGE Guaraní and Castellano (Spanish)

CURRENCY Guaraní (G)

CAPITAL Asunción (population of Greater Asunción: 1.6million)

TIME ZONE GMT -4hr

INTERNATIONAL PHONE CODE ☎595

ELECTRICAL CURRENT 220v

Introduction

Paraguay is billed by the tourist board as the "Heart of South America", but perhaps "South America's forgotten corner" is more appropriate. Despite being one of the most traditional countries on the continent and the only one with an indigenous tongue as its official language (Guaraní), Paraguay is far too often passed over by travellers rushing from one twelve-hour bus journey to another in search of the next "mega attraction". Those people that do make it to Paraguay will find themselves pleasantly surprised by this deeply cultural society with a host of under-promoted natural attractions, a fascinating and bloodthirsty history and a real feeling of being "off the beaten track".

A country of extremes, Paraguay combines the scorching, arid wilderness of the **Chaco** – remarkably one of the best places in South America to see large mammals – with the wet and humid **Atlantic forests** of eastern Paraguay; the rampant commercialism of **Ciudad del Este** with the muted, backwater feel of colonial towns like **Concepción** and **Pilar**; and the austere seriousness of central **Asunción** with the unabashed hedonism of **Encarnación** during February's **Carnival**. Paraguay is part owner of the second largest hydroelectric dam in the world – **Itaipú**, home to a superbly-preserved series of **Jesuit ruins** and, thanks to its extraordinary biodiversity and varied natural habitats, one of the continent's fasting growing **eco-tourism** destinations. Tourism in Paraguay is still in its infancy so this is not the place for pampered travellers, but if you crave a sense of adventure and a real, uncommercialized South American experience, then Paraguay is your spot.

CHRONOLOGY

1537 The Spanish found the city of Nuestra Señora de Asunción.

1609 The Jesuit missionaries arrive with the aim to convert indigenous tribes.

1767 The Jesuits are expelled from Paraguay by King Carlos III of Spain.

1811 Paraguay declares its independence from Spain in a bloodless revolution.

1814 Dr José Gáspar Rodriguéz de Francia is chosen as the first president and takes Paraguay into a period of isolation and industrialization.

1816 Francia declares himself "El Supremo" – dictator for life, becoming progressively more arbitrary through his reign, suppressing the church and oppressing the population.

1844 Francia is succeeded by Carlos Antonio López and Paraguay enters its period of greatest prosperity, becoming the most prosperous country on the fledgling continent.

1862 Mariscal Carlos Antonio López takes over as president from his ailing father, who leaves him with the deathbed advice that the pen is mightier than the sword.

1865–1870 Mariscal López launches Paraguay into the disastrous War of the Triple Alliance against Brazil, Argentina and Uruguay, the end of which saw the country lose much of its territory and the male population decimated.

1871 Paraguay initiates a period of inward migration, selling huge areas of the country for low prices to foreign settlers in an effort to stimulate economic growth.

1902 The first Mennonites arrive in Paraguay, part of a campaign to colonize the Chaco.

1932–37 Though the Bolivian army had been encroaching on the Chaco for many years, rumours of undiscovered oil reserves provoke a violent reaction from the Paraguayan government and the start of the Chaco War, with both sides secretly funded by international oil companies.

1954 After a prolonged period of weak government with 22 presidents in 31 years, General Alfredo

Stroessner seizes power and goes on to become the longest lasting dictator in South American history, holding power for 34 years.
1989 Stroessner is driven into exile and Paraguay declares itself a Republic. The coup leader General Andrés Rodriguez begins liberalization measures.
1993 The first democratic elections are held, won by the quasi-liberal Colorados, effectively returning Stroessner's political party to power. Their unpopular reforms lead to a general strike the following year.
1998 General Lino César Oviedo is chosen as the Colorado candidate, but is imprisoned shortly afterwards for his role in an attempted coup two years earlier. He is succeeded by Raúl Cubas Grau who causes a constitutional crisis by freeing General Oviedo within a week of assuming power. The supreme court impeaches Cubas – who flees into exile – and sends Oviedo back to prison.
2003 Nicanor Duarte-Frutos is elected president promising to put an end to corruption. In fact his period in office is dogged by allegations of extreme corruption and, mirroring Francia, he unsuccessfully attempts to change the constitution implemented after the departure of Stroessner which forbirds any president from serving more than one term in office.
2007 General Lino César Oviedo is released from prison and announces his intention to stand for election as an independent candidate. Liberal candidate Archbishop Fernando Lugo also puts himself forward for election as the Colorado party deteriorates through political infighting.
2008 Blanca Ovelar, sister-in-law of outgoing President Nicanor Duarte-Frutos is chosen as the Colorado Party Presidential candidate despite allegations of electoral fraud from within her own party.
2008 Fernando Lugo is elected as the new president of Paraguay with a clear majority, ending 61 years of Colorado party rule, the longest reign by any one political party anywhere on earth.

PARAGUAY INTRODUCTION

Basics

ARRIVAL

A **passport** valid for six months after entry is required by all nationals, except residents of Argentina or Brazil who can use their national identity documents for brief entry. Australian, Canadian, and US citizens are required to have an **entry visa** that must be obtained prior to travelling; other Western European, UK and Japanese citizens do not (see Ⓦwww.columbusguides.com for a full list of countries not requiring visas).

If **arriving by land** be aware that buses frequently cross the border without stopping at the customs post. It is your responsibility to get exit stamps from Bolivia, Brazil and Argentina upon departure and to obtain the required entry stamp when entering Paraguay or you risk a substantial fine – inform your driver that you need your stamps and take your bags with you to passport control as the bus won't wait. At the major entry points Posadas-Encarnación and Foz do Iguazu-Ciudad del Este, the customs formalities are performed at either end of the respective international bridges. The buses will not always wait for you but the ticket will be valid for the next service. The entry stamp usually entitles you to a ninety-day stay in Paraguay and this can be renewed once without cost. You should make sure that you have a Yellow Fever Certificate before entering Paraguay – it is occasionally asked for. There is a US$25 departure tax payable on leaving the country by air.

Paraguay is an extremely hot country for most of the year. Eastern Paraguay (Orient) can be very humid, while western Paraguay (Chaco) is dry. The **hottest time of year** is from November through to February when daytime temperatures can peak around 45ºC and high atmospheric pressure makes just walking along the street a tough task. Winter (June–Aug) is pleasantly warm during the day (around 20–25ºC), generally sunny and dry but frequently cool at night with the occasional morning frost. There is no real rainy season, but from September to November spectacular electric storms become more frequent and travelling off-road can be more difficult. The climate is governed by the prevailing winds, *viento sur* (southerly winds) bringing cooler temperatures from Patagonia and *viento norte* (*northern winds*) bringing hotter weather from the tropics.

GETTING AROUND

Travelling around Paraguay is, like in much of South America, generally cheap and easy. There are currently no passenger train services in Paraguay so travellers are best off using buses to get around.

Air

Though most visitors arrive in Paraguay crossing by land from neighbouring Brazil or Argentina, those arriving on international flights will land at Pettirossi International Airport 15km northeast of the centre (Ⓣ021/645444) in Luque, a satellite town of Asunción. The only **airlines** operating in and out of Paraguay at the time of writing are TAM (Ⓣ021/645500, Ⓦwww.tam.com.py) and Aerosur (Ⓣ021/614743, Ⓦwww.aerosur.com), though they subcontract for other airlines for services from Santiago de Chile, São Paulo and Buenos Aires. Many visitors travelling with TAM have reported that their flight times have been changed at the last minute and that they were advised only by email, so you should confirm your flight 24 hours in advance. Note that due to union rules taxi fares departing from the airport are extremely high (around 100,000G to central Asunción – if you arrive by day you may be better walking to the avenue outside the airport and flagging down a passing city taxi.

Bus

The easiest and cheapest way to get around in Paraguay is by **bus** and there are frequent and affordable services daily between each of the major cities. Visiting areas away from the major cities is more difficult and when they exist, bus services that serve such routes are uncomfortable.

Unsurprisingly, Asunción is the country's major transport hub and at the central bus terminal, at Argentina y Fernando de la Mora (☎021/551740), a large number of companies compete for business along the various routes, ensuring that outside of the holiday seasons there is no need to book tickets in advance. The quality of service provided by the different companies varies greatly – in general you pay for what you get. During the hot summer months a bus service with air-conditioning will make travelling a more pleasant experience and is worth the extra few guaranies. An information kiosk on the ground floor of the bus terminal should be your first stop if you are overwhelmed by the number of bus companies to choose from.

City buses are cheap and have a set fare (2200G) regardless of how far you go. It is worth mastering the initially bewildering routes; if you plan to spend in any time in Asunción, it will save you a fortune in taxi fares. City bus services tail off around 10pm. Taxis are reasonably priced but only take taxis from marked taxi ranks and insist that the meter is switched on or you risk being overcharged. Within Asunción you should not need to pay more than 50,000G for a long journey and 20,000G for a trip within the centre. In smaller towns such as Encarnación and Ciudad del Este maximum fares for city journeys should be around 20,000G.

Car

Hiring a **car** is possible only in Asunción or Ciudad del Este and a 4WD is required for the dirt roads that criss-cross the country away from the main national Ruta system – many roads become impassable after rain. Car hire is expensive (plan on around 450,000G per day for a 4WD) and there is a charge for extra kilometres, making it difficult to see more remote areas of the country cheaply. On the other hand petrol costs are low (a little over 4500G a litre for unleaded). An **International Driving Permit** is required to hire a car and you should have your headlights switched on at all times, even during the day. If you plan on going deeper into the Chaco than the Mennonite colonies in the Central Chaco, you are highly-recommended to take a guided tour (see p.778) – though things have improved in recent years many tourists still come to grief annually by embarking on poorly-planned journeys in an effort to save a little money. Even on the Ruta Trans Chaco (which is now fully paved), once past the Mennonite colonies there is nowhere to stay, few places to refuel and nowhere to buy food. Heading off the Ruta Trans Chaco on your own is strongly discouraged. There are no commercial train services; the train that departs from Asunción to Aregua is a tourist attraction not a public service (see p.755).

ACCOMMODATION

On the whole **accommodation** in Paraguay represents excellent value for your money, though away from major population centres it can be difficult to find and occasionally falls short of expectations. It is not usually necessary to book in advance, although it is a must in Caacupé during the weeks surrounding the feast of the Día del Virgen (Dec 8), during the Carnival in Encarnación (Feb) and in the Mennonite Colonies during the Trans-Chaco Rally (Sep–Oct). Prices are correspondingly higher during these events.

All but the very cheapest of hotel rooms are en-suite and in most places, it is possible to get a decent double room for as little as 100,000G, usually with TV and breakfast – lower than that and you sacrifice certain comforts. Budget travellers should have no problem finding a good deal, and should not necessarily be scared off by very cheap rooms – though it pays to ask to see the room before handing over any cash. Many very cheap hotels also rent rooms by the hour, so it is up to you to decide whether or not it is worth going a bit more upmarket. There are no **youth hostels** in Paraguay and campsites are few and far between. Do not expect to camp in rural areas; the vast majority of the land is in private hands and if you do not have the permission of the landowner you risk being accused of trespassing.

FOOD

At first glance **Paraguayan cuisine** may appear to consist entirely of ubiquitous junk food joints selling hamburgers, *milanesas* and pizza. However explore a little bit and you'll uncover a number of excellent restaurants hidden away, at least in the major cities. The mainstay of the Paraguayan diet is the **asado** – essentially remarkably cheap grilled meat. The best cuts are *tapa de cuadril*, *corte Americano* and *colita de cuadril*. If you don't like to chew too hard avoid *costillas* (ribs). *Vacio* is extremely tasty at its best, but at its worst is like boot leather – ask for a decent piece. Those with a weak stomach should avoid *mondongo* (tripe), *lengua* (tongue), *chinchulín* (small intestine) and *tripa gorda* (large intestine) – though the adventurous will find they are surprisingly tasty. *Morcilla* is black pudding and *chorizo* is sausage – but no relation to Spanish chorizo. *Pollo asado* (grilled chicken) is often sold on roadside grills and makes a cheap and filling meal, and don't forget to try *corazoncitos* (chicken hearts). *Asado* and everything else is almost always accompanied by *mandioca* (manioc), the staple food plant. Fish is generally expensive and at least twice the price of beef, *surubí* being the most frequently available. For a cheap, tasty snack *empanadas* (pasties) are widely available and there is almost always somebody on hand willing to sell you *chipa* (cheese bread made with manioc flour) – it is best when hot and the southern town of Coronel Bogado is renowned nationally as the "capital of chipa". Oddly, *chipa* in Asunción is frequently disappointing, so don't let it put you off trying it elsewhere. *Sopa Paraguaya* is corn bread, not soup. Other traditional Paraguayan foods are hard to come by and rarely sold in restaurants. Ask around for unmarked eating houses which local people always know about but tourists always miss. Here you will be able to try home-cooked Paraguayan fare such as *Bori-bori* (soup with corn balls), *guiso de arroz* (a sort of Paraguayan paella), *so'o apu'á* (meat ball soup) and *so'o yo* (soup with mince meat and egg) amongst others.

Paraguayan **desserts** include the sandwich spreads *dulce de leche* and *dulce de guayaba*, as well as *dulce de batata con queso paraguayo* (a candied sweet potato accompanied with cheese).

DRINK

Undoubtedly the most widely consumed drink is **tereré**, ice-cold *yerba mate*, a herbal tea that is surprisingly refreshing and addictive –

served hot it is called *mate*. Paraguayans are not averse to experimenting with their *yerba mate* in the search for new flavours, and locals will even drink it mixed with fruit juice (*tereré Ruso*) or milk with dessicated coconut (*tereré dulce*). Look out for street vendors with baskets of "*yu-yos*" –native plants with **medicinal** properties. Whether you have a hangover, want to lose weight or just drink something refreshing, let the vendor know your ailment and then stick the resulting plant mix in your *tereré* to enjoy the benefits they claim to provide. *Mosto* is a sickly sweet juice made from sugar cane, while *caña* is a distilled alcoholic spirit from the same source. **Local beers** *Pilsen* and *Baviera* are both good. *Chopp* is a generic term for draft beer although beer is more widely available in returnable litre bottles.

CULTURE AND ETIQUETTE

Paraguay is generally an informal and laid-back country. Men greet each other with a shake of the hand and women are greeted with a fake kiss on each cheek (unless they first offer you their hand). The main **religion** is Roman Catholicism. As in many Latin American countries, there is a typically macho attitude to women, and females travelling alone may be seen as "fair game", and should be careful to avoid any behaviour or clothing that may be misconstrued as "leading" or "flirty" – especially away from the major cities. Though there is a more liberal attitude amongst younger generations it is not considered normal or appropriate for respectable women to be drunk in public places. Men wishing to talk to a Paraguayan woman should take care that she is not already accompanied. Even if your intentions are perfectly innocent it may be considered disrespectful to approach her instead of her escort. Especially in rural areas it is quite common for Paraguayan men to have several families but to react angrily towards a woman with similarly liberal ideas. If faced with any problems, especially men under the influence of alcohol, be polite but firm and avoid becoming embroiled in conversation or argument. If you wish to take a photo of somebody it is courteous to ask their permission and do not offer payment if it is not asked for.

Tipping is not expected but is always appreciated. A tip of 2000G is appropriate for a snack or ordinary meal.

SPORTS AND OUTDOOR ACTIVITIES

Like most South American countries, **soccer**, or *fútbol*, is the main sporting obsession and the headquarters of the Latin American Football Federation is located in Luque in the outskirts of Asunción (ⓣ021/645781; Autopista Aeropuerto Internaciónal y Leonismo Luqueño). Matches are played on Sundays and the two biggest clubs are Olimpia at Mariscal Francisco S López 1499 (ⓣ021/200680) and Cerro Porteño at Cerro León and Pedro Juan Caballero (ⓣ021/371022). **Tickets** to see games are bought at the stadium upon entry. **Volleyball** is also a popular sport, at least to play, teams taking frequent breaks between plays to sup on a *tereré*. The Chaco is home to the **Trans-Chaco Rally** – usually held in September or October – one of the most demanding motor races on earth.

Fishing is becoming increasingly popular, with *surubí* and *pacu* popular game species. Undoubtedly the biggest prize for any angler in Paraguay though is the *dorado* of the rapids of the Ríos Paraguay, Paranà and Tebicuary, a monster fish of up to 30kg (68 pounds) – but now increasingly rare. A permit is required for fishing obtainable from SEAM (Av Madame Lynch 3500 ⓣ021 614687, ⓦwww.paraguaysilvestre.org.py).

Eco-tourism is a growing industry in Paraguay, a country blessed with large unspoilt areas of natural habitats. Despite its aridity, the Chaco is one of the best places in South America to see large mammals such as jaguar, tapir and puma, and the Paraguayan Pantanal region – whilst difficult to get to – is truly unspoilt and lacks the commercial aspect of its Brazilian counterpart. The Atlantic Forests of eastern Paraguay are officially the most threatened natural habitat on the planet and count on an endemic birdlife that is attractive to many birdwatchers, whilst the *cerrado* grasslands of northern Paraguay and Brazil have been declared to be the world's fastest disappearing habitat – though large tracts of virgin *cerrado* still remain in Paraguay. This habitat is home to the ghostly white-winged nightjar, a bird known from only three places on earth, two of which are in Paraguay. However, independent travel to areas of natural interest is difficult or impossible, frequently requires a 4WD vehicle and advanced permission; in many areas all supplies will also need to be taken with you. With this in mind, guided tours are your best bet, such as those provided by FAUNA Paraguay Ⓦwww.faunaparaguay.com.

COMMUNICATIONS

Postal services are unreliable, and important mail should always be sent *certificado* (registered) despite the slightly higher cost, or else by international courier. Telephone services are provided by COPACO, and there are numerous *cabinas telefónicas* in the major cities. Directory enquiries can be reached by dialling 112. These days most people keep in touch with **mobile phones**; chips with the local mobile phone companies *Tigo* and *Personal* can be purchased very cheaply with free credit to fit into your own phone. **Internet access** is ubiquitous in the major cities and is very cheap (around 4000G per hour), with generally good connections. The most popular **newspapers** (*diarios*) are the tabloids *Crónica* and *Popular*, both written in a mixture of Spanish and Guaraní and typically sensationalist in their approach to reporting. For a more serious read try *ABC* or *Ultima Hora*.

CRIME AND SAFETY

Paraguay is generally a safe country to visit, and with so few tourists around they are not deliberately targeted by thieves. The border area in Ciudad del Este is occasionally considered **unsafe** and you should take a taxi if you have all your belongings with you. The usual precautions regarding personal safety and the safety of belongings should be taken, and it is unwise to wander alone after dark in unpopulated areas of the capital. Though crime against tourists is rare do not expect the **police** to offer more assistance than the taking of your statement for insurance purposes.

Do not use street **money changers**; though most are honest some are not and employ a variety of tricks to make the money they give you seem like more than it is. One of their classic tricks is to miss a 0 off the end whilst performing the calculation in front of you – easily missed when you are dealing with hundreds of thousands of Guaraníes. If you have no other choice but to use a street changer make sure you know the exchange rate in advance and ask him to count the money into your hand. Further afield, the vast, largely unpopulated wilderness of the Chaco is an extremely desolate and hostile environment, and you should not go off the beaten track without a local guide and/or substantial preparation and supplies. The High Chaco, north of the Mennonite Colonies, is particularly harsh, and every year expeditions north to the Bolivian border come to grief because of insufficient planning.

SHOPPING

The market areas of border towns Encarnación (see p.765) and Ciudad del Este (p.760) are a shopper's paradise where anything from clothes to electronics and duty-free goods can be purchased at knockdown prices – largely because of the contraband origin of many of the goods! A number of American-style shopping malls can be found in Asunción, and though prices tend to be higher than elsewhere in the country, the goods are of guaranteed quality.

Items in some shops (especially in border towns) may lack **price tags** and to avoid overcharging, it is advisable to compare prices before buying or, if you feel up to it, to negotiate a better price, especially if buying in bulk.

As tourism is limited in Paraguay, there are few shops aimed directly at tourists. Perhaps the most typically Paraguayan souvenirs are Ñanduti lace (see p.758), *guampa* and *bombilla* for drinking *tereré* (see p.748) and Guaraní wood-carved animals, all of which are freely available throughout the country, with prices slightly higher in the capital.

INFORMATION, WEBSITES AND MAPS

Paraguay is slowly catching on to the potential benefits of **tourism** and a recent makeover of the tourist office in Asunción at Palma y Alberdi (Ⓣ021/494110) has turned it into a useful source of information. It is worth visiting as this is likely to be the last functional tourist office that you will come across.

Permits, required to visit many of the **national parks**, are available from the government ministry SEAM (Av Madame Lynch 3500 Ⓣ021 614687, Ⓦ www.paraguaysilvestre.org.py) – these will be arranged for you if you take organized tours.

Good national and local **maps** are available from the Servicio Geográfico Militar in Asunción at Artigas 920. FAUNA Paraguay (Ⓦwww.faunaparaguay.com) provides an extraordinary amount of information in English about the country's wildlife and natural habits, including accurate lists and image galleries of the majority of the species that occur here.

MONEY AND BANKS

The **Guaraní** has proved itself to be one of the more stable regional currencies in recent years, despite a history of devaluation and high inflation. Though prices have risen sharply during that same period, Paraguay remains one of the cheaper countries in South America, and prices are noticeably lower than in neighbouring Argentina and Brazil. Notes are issued in denominations of 1000, 5000, 10,000, 20,000, 50,000 and 100,000. Coins are in short supply but come in denominations of 50, 100, 500 and 1000. It is almost impossible to change the Guaraní outside Paraguay, and you should attempt to get rid of any spare currency before crossing the border. **Credit cards** are not widely accepted outside the capital and incur a charge of five to ten percent – plan on paying cash wherever you go. **ATMs** are widely available in the cities and most accept foreign cards such as Visa and MasterCard, though an administration charge of 20–30,000G is made for the use of some machines when withdrawing money. **Traveller's cheques** can be troublesome and some banks refuse to cash them if you cannot produce a bill of sale. Banks are typically open Monday to Friday from 8am to 3pm and closed at weekends, though ATMs can be used at any time.

OPENING HOURS AND HOLIDAYS

Opening hours are generally from 8am until 6pm from Monday to Friday, with half day closing on Saturday and all day closing Sunday. Many businesses observe a "*siesta*" from noon to 2pm. In addition to the national holidays listed below, some local anniversaries or saints' days are also public holidays when everything in a given town may close down, taking you by surprise.

January 1 New Year's Day (Año Nuevo)
February 3 San Blas Day, Patron Saint of Paraguay (Día de San Blas)
March 1 Death of Mariscal Francisco Solano López (Cerró Corà)
March/April Easter and Holy Week (Pascua y Semana Santa)
May 1 Day of the Worker (Día del Trabajador)
May 15 Independence Day (Día de la Independencia Patria)
June 12 Commemoration of the end of the Chaco War (Paz del Chaco)
August 15 Founding of Asunción (Fundación de Asunción)
August 25 Victory in the Battle of Boquerón (Victoria del Boquerón)
December 8 Immaculate Conception (Día del Virgen)
December 25 Christmas Day (Navidad)

ASUNCIÓN

Less oppressive than other South American capital cities, **ASUNCIÓN** sits astride a broad bay on the Rio Paraguay. Once the historic centre of government for the Spanish colonies of Rio de la Plata, the city declined in importance with the founding of Buenos Aires, while the impenetrable Chaco prevented it from becoming the envisioned gateway to the riches of Peru. The centre of the city is based on a grid square system, a leftover from the days of the paranoid despot **Dr Francia** who, convinced of plots to kill him, declared that the buildings had to be short enough that he could see who was on the roof while riding his horse, and at that every street corner he should be able to see in all four directions so that would-be assassins would have nowhere to hide. The destruction of colonial buildings that didn't fit with this vision robbed Asunción of some architectural gems.

What to see and do

Modern Asunción is a strange city; with a decaying historical centre and modern, trendy suburbs, the city encapsulates the extremes and contrasts that visitors will find throughout Paraguay. The old colonial centre is weirdly deserted at weekends when office workers retire to their suburban homes, but provides enough cultural attractions to fill a day or two of wandering. The action is centred in the area around the **Plaza Uruguaya** and **Plaza de los Héroes,** as

well as the **Waterfront**. Those seeking more tranquil surroundings will find solace in the numerous green spaces that surround the city. The best of the city's **restaurants** have now relocated to the suburbs, especially in the area around the monstrous **Shopping del Sol complex**, but central Asunción is still the best base to look for cheap accommodation and nightlife.

The Waterfront and Plaza de la Independencia

El Paraguayo Independiente, and its continuations, Avenidas República and Mariscal Francisco S. López, run along **THE WATERFRONT**. At the western end, set among highly manicured gardens, is the stunning, marble president's residence, the **Palacio de Gobierno** (Palacio López). The building was completed in 1892 to a design based on the Palace of Versailles. Across the street is the **Manzana de la Rivera** (daily 8am–6pm; free), a series of restored houses dating from 1750 some of which house small museums. One block east, Avenida República begins to branch north to the **Plaza de la Independencia**. Marked largely by balding lawns, it is dominated by the ageing, pink **Cabildo** (Mon–Fri 7am–3pm; free), the former seat of government. Constructed by Carlos Antonio López in 1844 it now houses the **Museo del Congreso Nacional**. On the southeastern corner of the plaza stands the Neoclassical **Catedral**, a rather disappointing structure which fails to capture the imagination. The western side houses the **Casa de la Cultura** (Mon–Fri 9am–3pm; free), a former Jesuit College. A few blocks south of here, along 14 de Mayo, the 1772 **Casa de la Independencia** (Tues–Fri 7am–noon & 2–6pm, Sat & Sun 7am–noon; free) is one of the oldest and most important buildings in the country. It was here that the architects of Paraguayan independence met to discuss their plans. Today it houses a museum with period artefacts from the time of the declaration of independence.

Plaza de los Héroes and around

The **PLAZA DE LOS HÉROES** is a huge and verdant square encompassing four blocks. The square itself is immense and filled with *lapacho* trees that bloom a dramatic pink in July and August. A lively and vibrant place, and frequent concert venue, it attracts tourists and pedlars alike.

In the northwest corner of Plaza de los Héroes, the **Panteón de los Héroes** (daily 8am–6pm; free) is Paraguay's most instantly recognizable monument. This great domed memorial to Paraguayan héroes was begun in 1863, but not completed until 1937 and the end of the Chaco War. Permanently guarded by foot soldiers, it suffers somewhat from the close proximity to the surrounding modern buildings, which make it difficult to view and photograph from the outside. The Panteón contains the remains of former presidents Carlos Antonio López and his son Mariscal Francisco Solano López as well as Chaco War hero Mariscal Estigarribia. Towards the end of the War of the Triple Alliance (1865–70), when the male population had been severely depleted, children as young as twelve years old were routinely drafted. Their deaths are marked by **La Tumba de los Soldaditos Desconocidos** (the tomb of the unknown child soldiers). The interior of the Panteón is like a mini-cathedral, with statues and busts adorning the walls, while the tombs are viewed from a raised balcony in the centre of the building.

West of here, you'll find the busy commercial and shopping street of **Calle Palma**, where high-street shops and boutiques rub shoulders with street traders peddling counterfeit wares at apparently bargain prices.

Plaza Uruguaya and around

Another two blocks east is the leafy but rather charmless **PLAZA URUGUAYA**. With patchy lawns and prostitutes touting their wares freely among the palms, it can be a little intimidating after dark, but the surrounding streets boast some excellent restaurants and hotels. On the northern edge is the **Estación de Ferrocarril**, the city's railway station, defunct in terms of public transport but now serving as an exhibition centre; there are occasional recitals of classical music held here at weekends. There is still one train in operation, albeit departing from another train station adjacent to the Jardín Botánico (see below): though it no longer functions as a passenger service, the old steam engine *Sapucai* has now been put into service as a **tourist train**, heading out to the town of Areguá (see p.758) every second Sunday (☎021/447848; 100,000G). This thoroughly enjoyable journey not only transports you to another place, but also to another time, with ticket collectors in period dress and a hilarious show with actors doubling as mock passengers who contravene nineteenth-century rules and regulations and have to be reprimanded.

Two blocks west of the Plaza Uruguaya along Mariscal Estigarribia is the **Museo de Bellas Artes** (Tues–Fri 8am–6pm, Sat & Sun 8am–noon; free). Minor works by Tintoretto and Courbet, as well as numerous pieces by Paraguayan artists including Pablo Alburno and Juan Samudio, figure in this large collection of fine arts, though some of the displays are rather disappointing.

Outside the city centre

The **Cementerio de la Recoleta,** 3km east of the centre along Avenida Mariscal Francisco S. López, is an atmospheric and attractive cemetery of ornate tombs and mausoleums, far less morbid than you may imagine. Perhaps the most distinguished occupant is **Eliza Lynch**, the Irish mistress of Mariscal Francisco Solano López, who gained notoriety for her lavish lifestyle while the people starved. She is buried near to the tomb of their baby daughter.

Winding its way northeast from the centre around the bay, Avenida General Artigas arrives at the **Jardín Botánico** (daily 7am–darkness; 5000G; bus #24 or 35 from Cerro Corá). Once the López family estate, today the gardens are open to the public. Set around the banks of the river, there are suggested walks through the trees and a small, if rather distressing zoo of native wildlife. The **Museo de Historia Natural** (Mon–Sat 8am–6pm, Sun 8am–1pm; free) inside the Jardín Botánico houses an unkempt collection of natural history displays housed in the colonial-style former home of Carlos Antonio López; the nearby house of his son, Francisco Solano López, is an altogether grander affair housing the **Museo Indigenista** (same hours; free).

East of the centre, the **Museo del Barro** (Thu–Fri 3.30–8pm; 8000G), three blocks from Shopping del Sol at Grabadores del Cabichui, is jam-packed with a host of fascinating bits and pieces, both historical and contemporary, which give an alternative look at Paraguayan life and culture. Continuing along Avenida Aviadores del Chaco towards the airport you pass **Parque Ñu Guazu** on the left-hand side, a tranquil park with attractive lakes and excellent walking opportunities – an oasis within the city. "**La Expo Rural**", an annual agricultural exhibition, is held every July at the nearby Parque Mariano Roque Alonso. Not nearly as dull as it sounds, it is a great opportunity to try traditional Paraguayan foods, see more breeds of farm animal than you ever knew existed, watch gauchos in action and take advantage of the generosity of the countless companies plugging their wares by picking up a few freebies.

TREAT YOURSELF

If you are the sort of person who can never make your mind up when confronted with a menu, then head for **Paulista Grill** on Av San Martín and Av Mariscal López (☎021 611501). For 60,000G a head you can take your pick from what must be amongst the world's most well-stocked buffets featuring everything from salads to seafood, while waiters will attend to your meaty needs by bringing skewers of the finest cuts to your table.

Arrival and information

By air The international airport, Silvio Pettirossi (☎021/645444), is 15km northeast of the city along Av España and its continuation Aviadores del Chaco.

By bus The two-tiered intercity bus terminal (☎021/551740) at Argentina and Fernando de la Mora lies in the south of the city. A taxi from the terminal to the centre will cost around 40,000G.

Tourist information An excellent tourist office (☎021/491230; daily 7am–7pm) at De la Palma 468 and Juan Bautista Alberdi is packed with information for visitors – make the most of it, it will be one of the last functioning *turismos* that you will come across in Paraguay.

City transport

Buses While the centre of the city is compact and easily walkable, city buses stop at all street corners, and while you may be initially overwhelmed by the sheer number of them, it won't take you long to work out those that are of most use to you. Destinations are advertised on the front of the buses and there is a flat fare of 2200G for most journeys. Buses #28 and 31 run along Oliva/Cerro Corá to the bus terminal.

Taxis A journey within the centre shouldn't come to more than about 20,000G ; there are ranks at the main plazas.

Accommodation

Accommodation in Asunción is generally good and though prices are higher than elsewhere in Paraguay they are still very affordable. The best areas for cheap, central accommodation are in the streets around the two main plazas, de los Héroes and Uruguaya, in the north of the city, and are also ideally located for the main sights.

Miami Mexico 449 and 25 de Mayo, just off Plaza Uruguaya ☎021/444950. One of the cheapest places in central Asunción, and an acceptable, central hotel for those on a tight budget. The rooms are sparsely furnished and some of the bathrooms could do with retiling, but at least they have a/c. 100,000G

Plaza Dr. Eligio Ayala and Paraguarí ☎021/444196. A well-established hotel with slightly-dated but fully-equipped rooms, an excellent buffet breakfast and a great location overlooking Plaza Uruguaya, next to the old railway station. 150,000G

Portal del Sol Av Dennis Roa 1455 and Sta Teresa ☎021/609395, ⓦwww.hotelportaldelsol.com. Handy for the Shopping del Sol and the Museo del Barro, this is an excellent 4-star hotel with 3-star prices, boasting stone-clad rooms, a pleasant courtyard with waterfall and pool, and free internet access for guests. 220,000G

Preciado Dr. Félix de Azara 840 ☎021/447661. Located three blocks southeast of Plaza Uruguaya, the *Preciado* is handily placed for the city's best nightlife without ever getting noisy. Modern and spotless, and run by a friendly, helpful staff, it offers rooms with cable TV, a/c and marble bathrooms. The price also includes an excellent buffet breakfast and use of a swimming pool. 150,000G

Quinta Ykuá Satí Evacio Perinciollo, off Av Aviadores del Chaco ☎021/601230, ⓦwww.quintaykuasati.com.py. Set in leafy gardens (hyperbolically described as a nature reserve) in a quiet suburb close to the airport, the *Quinta* offers an ideal mix of comfort, affordability and tranquillity. It is some way from the centre and the food isn't the best, but you are in walking distance of the Shopping del Sol and its extensive culinary options. 140,000G

Eating

If you are looking for a cheap, filling feed, the food in shopping malls (see shopping) can often be surprisingly good and they offer a wide range of choices. The top floor of Shopping Excelsior in the centre has a particularly good selection of eateries, as does the enormous Shopping del Sol where you can find everything from Mexican, Italian and Chinese food through to Burger King and an *Empanada* specialist. For cheap eats and *comida tipica*, head out to Avenida Francisco Acuña de Figueroa, known locally as La Quinta Avenida, which is lined with enough possibilities to satisfy even the fussiest of eaters – though it's a taxi ride from the centre.

Almicar Estados Unidos 1734 and Quinta Avenida. Serving fast food with a Paraguayan flavour, *Almicar* is the place to head for if you want to sample cheap, affordable portions of *comida típica*. Try the *Pajaguá Mascada* (translated from Guaraní it means "what the dog chewed"), a delicious meat pattie that comes in at 5000G.

Bolsi Estrella and Juan Batista Alberdi. With its range of pastries and snacks, *Bolsi* is a diner-style hangout that is a great place for breakfasts from 10,000G.

Lido Bar Av José Felix Mariscal Estigarribia and Chile. Located right in front of the Panteón de los Héroes, the *Lido Bar* is a popular meeting place for *Asuncenos*. It has a café-style interior and the menu includes some typical dishes, including *Sopa Paraguaya* 6,000G.

Pancholo's Palma and 14 de Mayo. Good, affordable junk food in pleasantly a/c surroundings – a great place to refuel after a hard day's sightseeing in the city centre. Pick from pizza, burgers or hot dogs and swill them down with an ice-cold *chopp*. Pizzas start at around 25,000G, burgers 5,000G.

Rodizio Palma 591 and 14 de Mayo. Brazilian-style buffet – price is dependent on weight so you pay for what you eat. Grill, salad bar, pasta and pizzas make this a very popular choice among those wanting as much as possible for as little as possible. 35,000G per kilo.

La Vida Verde Palma and 15 de Agosto. Lime-green walls hammer home the eco-friendly message of this vegetarian Chinese buffet. Interesting meat-free *empanadas* and *comida por kilo* makes it a great place to detox if you have been overdoing the *asados*. 24,000G per kilo.

Drinking and nightlife

Asunción has a thriving nightlife, especially on weekends. Things only really get going around midnight but a recent change in municipal law means that alcohol is no longer served after 2am. In the centre, the blocks east of Plaza Uruguaya are where most of the action is. For more upmarket options head out to Paseo Carmelitas off Avenida España where there are a number of places to party. With the exception of those on Paseo Carmelitas, the great majority of nightspots do not open on Mondays.

Asunción Rock Mariscal Estigarribia and Tacuary. Wacky rock hang-out, packed with revellers at weekends. What with the ample dancefloor and bustling bars, you'll hardly notice the unusual choice of décor, which includes a car apparently crashing out of a wall.

Boehemia Legión Civil Extranjero and Av España. Trendy and yes, you guessed it, bohemian hangout in Barrio Manorá. Offers a wide cocktail menu and live alternative music most nights.

Britania Pub Cerro Corá and Tacuary. Ever popular with travellers and locals alike, *Britania* serves English pub grub and beer to a cosmopolitan crowd and even has its own brand of beer. Unlike most Asunción nightspots it's busy on week nights and the action starts earlier than elsewhere. While there's also a pleasant outdoor courtyard and bar, the indoor seating is limited – a problem if it rains.

Café Literario Av Mariscal José Felix Estigarribia and México. A laid-back café-bar in a former convent, this is a chilled place to enjoy a quiet drink whilst reading a book during the day, though things liven up after the sun goes down.

Flow Manzana T and Av Mariscal Francisco S López. All pub-style atmosphere and pop music blaring from over-sized speakers, *Flow* is popular with a younger crowd on account of its cheap beer and delicious pizzas.

Kilkenny Paseo Carmelitas and Av España. Every city must have one, and this is a typical faux-Irish bar with drunken revelry guaranteed. In keeping with its trendy surroundings, though, the prices are higher than in central Asunción.

Shopping

Arts and crafts Try the tourist office on De la Palma or Folklore at Palma and Iturbe.

Shopping malls Asunción has a series of US-style malls where you can buy everything you can imagine. Shopping del Sol, Av Aviadores del Chaco, is the largest shopping mall in the country, even including its own cinema. Alternatively, try Shopping Excelsior, Nuestra Señora de la Asunción and Manduvirá.

Directory

Airlines TAM, Oliva 761 and Ayolas ⓣ021/646010, ⓦwww.tam.com.py; Aerosur, Senador Long 856 and Av España ⓣ021/614743, ⓦwww.aerosur.com.

Banks Lloyds TSB is at Palma and Juán O'Leary and has an ATM. Palma is full of *casas de cambio*; shop around for the best rates.

Bookshops A series of bookshops are on the Plaza Uruguaya. The shop, Books, in the Shopping del Sol sells a variety of English-language titles.

Bus companies The following bus companies all operate out of the main bus terminal and are listed here in alphabetical order with their major route destinations – Buenos Aires (BA), Ciudad del Este (CDE), Concepción (CON), Encarnación (ENC), Filadelfia (FIL), Pedro Juan Caballero (PJC), Villarrica (VIL): Alborada, ENC; Carreta del Amambay, PJC, CON; La Concepcionera, CON; El Tigre, FIL; Flecha de Oro, ENC; Guareña, VIL; Golondrina, PJC, CON, FIL; La Encarnacena (☎021/551745), BA, ENC; La Ovetense (☎021/551737), CON, PJC; La Santaníana, CON; Libertador, PJC; NASA (☎021/551731), CON, PJC, FIL; Nuestra Señora de Asunción (☎021/298100), ENC; Pycasu, ENC, CDE; Rápido Caaguazu, CDE; San Luis, CDE; RYSA (☎021/551601), ENC, CDE, PJC; San Juan, ENC; Yacyreta (☎021/551725), CDE, ENC, BA.

Car Rental Renta Car, Aeropuerto Internacional Silvio Pettirossi ☎021/646083, www.rentacar.com.py.

Embassies and consulates Argentina, Av España and Perú ☎021/212320; Brazil, Gral Díaz 521 3rd floor ☎021/444088; Canada, Prof. Ramirez y J. de Salazar ☎021/227207; Germany, Av Venezuela 241 ☎021/214009; Spain, Yegros 437 6th floor ☎021/490686; UK, Av Boggiani 5848 ☎021/612611; USA Mariscal Francisco S. López 1776 ☎021/213715.

Internet Countless options all around the city, with several along Palma.

Pharmacy Catedral, on the Plaza de Armas at Palma and Independencia Nacional.

Post office Central branch at Juan Bautista Alberdi and Presidente Franco.

Tour Companies DTP, Gral. Bruguez 353 and 25 de Mayo ☎021/221816, www.dtp.com.py.

Moving on

By bus At the bus terminal a plethora of companies (see listings, above) run regular services across the country from the upper tier, while the lower tier (*subsuelo*) serves shorter journeys to Lago Ypacaraí and surrounding area (see below).

Destinations: Buenos Aires (8 daily; 21hr); Ciudad del Este (hourly; 4hr 30min); Concepción (hourly; 7hr); Encarnación (hourly; 5hr 30min); Filadelfia/Loma Plata (2–4 daily; 8hr); Pilar (13 daily; 5hr);

DAY TRIPS FROM ASUNCIÓN: THE CENTRAL CIRCUIT

Respite from the urban jungle of Asunción is easier than you might imagine, and just a short distance from the city limits the pace of life slows to a more typically Paraguayan tempo. The lushness of the area is immediately striking, the greenness of the vegetation contrasting with the brick-red clay soils to create a textbook image of fertile South America, which the smoky streets of the capital may have pushed to the back of your mind. Ruta 2 heads east out of Asunción passing the cool waters of **Lago Ypacaraí** and its surrounding resort towns. Known locally as the **Central Circuit**, this takes in a series of small towns famed for their crafts and laid-back atmosphere, and all of which are are easily visited on public transport in a day trip from Asunción.

Lago Ypacaraí

LAGO YPACARAÍ, 30km east of Asunción, is a popular watersports and beach resort. Around its shores are a series of small towns warranting a brief visit and reached by buses departing from the platforms on the ground floor of the Asunción terminal. Straddling the *ruta* east of Asunción, **ITAGUÁ** (platforms 31–35) is a picturesque town and the home of *ñandutí* (spiderweb) lace, fine early examples of which can be seen at the **Museo San Rafael** (daily 8am–6pm; free). Visit in July to catch the annual Festival de Ñandutí. Three blocks east of the plaza is the **Mercado Municipal**, where you can buy quality lace.

Areguá

A pleasant town located among the cool hills above the lake, 7km north of Ruta 2 at Km 20, **AREGUÁ** (multiple operators) is noted for its ceramics, and is the choice destination for Asunción day-trippers; it becomes crowded from December to February. Should you wish to stay, *Hotel Ozli*, Av Mariscal Estigarribia (☎0291/432380; 70,000G) is a decent bet. Hourly buses leave from Asunción, but a more enjoyable way to get here is on the tourist train (see p.755).

San Bernardino

From Areguá boat trips run at weekends in summer (☎021/311949) to the shady village of **SAN BERNARDINO** (platform 36) on the eastern shore of the lake. Favoured by Asunción's mega-rich, prices are have higher than elsewhere, but the surrounding mix of valleys and wooded slopes make for some fantastic walking. The cheapest place to stay is *Hotel Balneario*, Nuestra Señora de la Asunción and Yegros (☎0512/232252; 150,000G).

Caacupé

CAACUPÉ (Empresa Villa Serrana), 54km east of Asunción, is the country's main religious centre, transformed into a focus of pilgrimage on December 8 – the **Día de la Virgen**. Candlelit processions lead a statue of the sacred virgin through the town streets, while celebrations involve fireworks and bottle dancers. The prelude to the celebration is a period of prayer in the glorious copper-domed **Basílica de Nuestra Señora de los Milagros**. Most of what you will want to see is contained in or around the cobbled plaza, said to hold 300,000 worshippers on feast days. Prices are unsurprisingly higher in early December and it is essential to book ahead. *Hotel Katy María*, Dr Pino y Eligio Ayala (☎0511/242860; 180,000G), is a decent choice and has a good restaurant.

EAST OF ASUNCIÓN

Beyond the Central Circuit, Ruta 2 continues east on to the crossroads of **Coronel Oviedo**. A major transport centre and meeting point of four main *rutas*, it is depressingly bereft of interest and not somewhere to be stranded. North of here is the gorgeous **Laguna Blanca**, a perfect place to get away from it all, while to the south along Ruta 8 lies the well-kept town of **Villarrica**, and east along Ruta 7 is the consumer-driven mayhem of **Ciudad del Este** – crossing point for Brazil and the Iguazú Falls. In this same general area eco-tourists will want to seek out the **Itaipú Reserves** and the world-famous **Mbaracayú Forest Reserve**

LAGUNA BLANCA

Paraguay's only true lake, crystal clear **LAGUNA BLANCA** is named for its white sandy substrate visible even in the deepest parts of the lake. Completely unspoilt (the water is clean enough to drink) it is one of Paraguay's best kept secrets, its comparative isolation meaning that few people make it out here to enjoy the white sand beaches and paradisiacal surroundings. Horses and kayaks are available for rent, or else keep yourself busy by sunbathing, swimming in the tepid waters of the lake or walking in the stunning natural surroundings. For animal lovers Laguna Blanca has its own special appeal, with over 25 square kilometres of pristine *cerrado* habitat – the native South American grasslands – surrounding the lake. Though for much of the year *cerrado* vegetation can appear brown and lifeless, it springs to life during the **rainy season** (September to November) with plants rapidly coming into bloom, trees fruiting and a patchwork of colours dotting the landscape, lending it a beauty almost unrivalled in nature. Given its unique *cerrado* avifauna, Laguna Blanca is also a must for **birdwatchers**, being home to the only population of the rare Lesser Nothura (a small partridge-like bird) to be found outside of Brazil and one of only three known global populations of the endangered White-winged Nightjar – one of the world's rarest birds. In fact no fewer than twelve globally-threatened bird species can be found in this comparatively small area. Maned wolves are also present here, as are other large mammals such as puma and Collared peccary – your best chances of seeing them are by taking a night drive.

Arrival and information

By bus Take any bus from Asunción to San Pedro or Pedro Juan Caballero and get off at the town of Santa Rosa del Aguaray. From here, a local bus (several daily) to Santa Barbara passes in front of the entrance to the property. The journey may take 6–8hr by public transport and an early start is recommended. Your visit must be arranged in advance with Malvina Duarte, owner of *Estancia Laguna Blanca*, itself one of several properties that abut the lake, but the only one open to tourists. (ⓣ021/424760; ⓦwww.lagunablanca.com.py).

By Car Malvina Duarte (see above) can arrange transport to the area for a negotiable price. Alternatively you can make your own way to the *estancia* by hiring a 4WD vehicle (see p.750), a mode of transport which will also greatly enhance your chances of seeing wildife in the *cerrado*.

Tours Guided eco-tours are available through the Encarnación-based FAUNA Paraguay ⓦwww.faunaparaguay.com.

Accommodation and eating

Accommodation (150,000G per person) is only available in the ranch house on the shores of the lake – the price includes food during your stay; vegetarians can be catered for with advance notice. Camping is also possible but you will need to bring your own food.

CIUDAD DEL ESTE

Commercial, tacky, frequently intimidating and occasionally sordid, **CIUDAD DEL ESTE** is a shock to the system for many entering Paraguay for the first time – you may be forgiven for considering turning round and heading straight back to Brazil again. Founded in 1957 as Puerto Presidente Stroessner (the city dropped the link to the hated dictator almost as soon as he fell from power), it grew rapidly as the centre of control for the **Itaipú damming project**. Capitalizing on its position on the Brazilian border, the town provides cheap **duty-free** – and frequently contraband – goods to a public hungry for bargains. Growth has slowed since the completion of the dam and in recent years customs have tightened the net on the *contrabandistas*, but Ciudad del Este remains one of the best places on the continent for purchasing cheap **electronic goods**. Though the city suburbs are pleasant enough, its relative modernity means that Ciudad del Este has little in the way of sights of it own. The surrounding area, however, contains some of Paraguay's biggest attractions.

Arrival and information

By bus The bus terminal (ⓣ061/510421) is some way south of the centre on Chaco Boreal y Capitán del Puerto, adjacent to the Club 3 de Febrero soccer stadium. Regular services run west to the capital and south to Encarnación. For visits to the Iguazú Falls local buses (6000G) run to Foz do Iguaçu and Puerto Iguazú every quarter of an hour from the bus terminal – don't forget to get your exit and entrance stamps on crossing the respective frontiers. The airport, 30km west of town on Ruta 7, has irregular flights to Asunción, as well as nearby destinations in Brazil and Argentina, but suffers from frequent unexplained cancellations

Tourist information The tourist office (ⓣ061/511626; daily 7am–7pm) is in the Edificio Libano on Coronel Franco and Pampliega. It can provide a map of the city as well as information regarding day-trips to the Itaipú Dam and other nearby attractions.

Accommodation

Accommodation in Ciudad del Este is surprisingly affordable. A cluster of good hotels line Emilio Fernández, two blocks north of the *ruta* near the bridge.

Austria Emilio Fernandez ⓣ061/500883, ⓦwww.hotelaustriarestaurante.com. Excellent rooms with TV, minibar and a spacious terrace with majestic views out over the river. German is spoken here, and the price includes a breakfast so mammoth it has to be seen to be believed. 150,000G

Caribe Emilio Fernández ⓣ061/512460. If you're looking to go back to basics to save a few guaranies then this is the hotel for you. Cheap and cheerful with shady, sparsely-furnished rooms offset by a sun-trap courtyard. 80,000G

Munich Emilio Fernández and Capitán Miranda ⓣ061/500347. Neat, tidy and efficient, *Munich* offers excellent value and spacious rooms, as well as secure parking should you be travelling with your own vehicle. 160,000G

Eating

Some of the best places to eat are outside the Microcentro in the more attractive suburbs, especially along Avenida del Lago. The city boasts a proliferation of excellent Asian restaurants and a number of gems offering *comida típica*. For cheap filling food check out the food courts in any supermarket.

Al Carbón Av Teniente Armada, 100m from bus terminal. The biggest burgers you will ever see in your life, the gargantuan Extrema is big enough for two. Great place to refuel while you are waiting for a bus. Hamburguesa Extrema 20,000G.

Austria Emilio Fernandez ⓣ061/500883. You could do a lot worse than eating at *Hotel Austria*, whose astonishingly cheap menu consists largely of Austrian and German specialities. Mains from 20,000G.

Faraone y Heladería Mitai Av Rogelio Benítez, in front of the Municipalidad. Actually two establishments under the same management, *Faraone* is an Italian á la carte restaurant with one of the best reputations in the city. Not cheap by Paraguayan standards, but eminently affordable by northern hemisphere prices. The adjacent ice-cream parlour is exquisite and just what the doctor ordered in the midday sun. Mains from 30,000G.

Gauchito Grill Av del Lago. If you haven't had enough *asado* yet, this carnivore's paradise should be your next stop. Huge slabs of meat cooked on charcoal grills. The tables overlooking an attractive lake replete with waterbirds will add to your enjoyment. An asado *completo* for two people comes in at 60,000G.

Las Delicias Carlos Antonio López and Oscar Rivas. It doesn't look like much from the outside, but with home-made specials on weekdays it's a great place to sample exactly the kind of typical – and cheap – Paraguayan food that can be so hard to find elsewhere, dishes like *Vori vori* (corn ball soup) for 14,000G. Menu changes daily.

Nightlife

The Microcentro can be a little seedy at night and so you are best taking a taxi out to the suburbs if you are looking to party hard.

Cerca del Río Choperia Av del Casino and 11 de Septiembre. This has a terrace with fantastic views of the Paraná river and international bridge, and is a good place to drown your sorrows if you lose at the Gran Casino opposite.

Inside Bar One of a series of lively nightspots along the winding Av del Lago.

Shopping

Not for nothing is Ciudad del Este known as the "Supermarket of South America", and just about everything you can think of can be purchased here at prices well below market rates, Shoppers will not stray far from the ugly Microcentro, a maze of shops and stalls on either side of the main *ruta*, near the border with Brazil. It is here that the bulk of the bargains are to be found, but

CROSSING TO BRAZIL AND ARGENTINA

The Puente de la Amistad (Friendship Bridge) at the eastern end of the Microcentro marks the border with the Brazilian town of **Foz do Iguaçu**. Immigration formalities take place at either end of the bridge. This is Paraguay's busiest border crossing, and there are frequently huge queues of traffic waiting to cross in either direction. A local bus (every 15min; 6,000G) runs from the bus terminal to the terminal in "Foz", as it's known locally. In many cases crossing on foot is quicker, but be sure to obtain all necessary entrance and exit stamps – it is not true that you do not need them if you are just visiting the waterfalls. Traffic police do not help matters by putting pressure on pedestrians to speed up their crossing, occasionally directing them away from the customs checkpoint. There is now also a local (yellow) bus (every 15min; 6,000G) run by El Práctico to **Puerto Iguazú** in Argentina also leaving from the bus terminal. This is an easier border crossing, but again be sure your paperwork is in order.

the area also attracts petty thieves like bees to a honey-pot – do not carry valuables with you. Electronics, alcohol and perfumes provide the best deals, but beware of substandard goods passed off as genuine and do not be afraid to haggle or barter; it is expected. Compare prices before completing any transaction and ask for the product to be tested; not all dealers are honest.

Directory

Banks Banco do Brasil at Nanawa 107 and Monseñor Rodríguez, Interbanco at Av San Blas 122 and Patricio Colmán.
Car hire Avis office at the airport ⊕061/504770.
Cinema Cinecenter Zuni in Shopping Zuni, Av San Blas 122 and Patricio Colmán.
Hospital Fundación Tesai on Av Caballero behind the bus terminal.
Post office Alejo Garcia and Centro Democrático (Mon–Fri 7am–6pm, Sat 7am–noon).

Moving on

By bus Destinations: Asunción (hourly; 4hr 30min); Encarnación (hourly, 4hr 30min); Foz do Iguaçu (every 15min, 1hr); Puerto Iguazú (every 15min, 1hr).
By taxi Taxis (⊕061/510660) are a relatively inexpensive and convenient way of making day-trips.

AROUND CIUDAD DEL ESTE

The number one reason for staying in Ciudad del Este is to visit the **Itaipú Hydroelectric Project**. Though now relegated to the second largest dam in the world, it is still an extraordinary engineering feat. The Itaipú Dam company oversees the management of eight **small nature reserves** in the area immediately north of Ciudad del Este. Representing the last refuges of the once extensive Alto Paraná Atlantic Forest, most of which was washed away by the dam-related flooding, these reserves harbour important populations of endangered wildlife including jaguar, bush dog and marsh deer. None, though, are as famous as **Mbaracayú Forest Reserve**, listed by the WWF as one of the hundred most important natural areas on the planet, and home to hundreds of bird species. If Iguazú has given you a taste for waterfalls, meanwhile, **Salto de Monday** (pronounced Mon-da-oo) 10km south of the city is also well worth a visit. At 80m high, they are a stunning natural feature, though they suffer from being so close to their more famous and spectacular neighbours across the border. A return taxi ride from the centre costs 60,000G.

Itaipú Hydroelectric Project

Sited 20km north of the city on the hyperbolically-named Hernandarias Supercarretera (taxi 40,000G one way or 60,000G return, or take bus marked "Hernandarias" from the terminal), Itaipú was once referred to as one of the seven wonders of the modern world. With a maximum height of 195m and generating up to 75,000GWh of energy per year, it's still something to behold. Visits are by guided tour only (Mon–Sat 8am, 9.30am, 1.30pm, 2pm and 3pm, Sun mornings 8am and 9.30am only; free, although a passport is required) and last about an hour and a half. The highlight of the trip is undoubtedly the opportunity to see the inside of the dam and the colossal one-kilometre long machine room. It's not all good news though; the building of the dam (with the first of four phases of construction beginning in 1975, it was finally completed in 1991) was dogged with corruption scandals, missing money and considerable ecological damage. Much of the unexplored Atlantic Forest in the surrounding area was flooded, and the Sete Quedas, a set of waterfalls comparable to those at Iguazú, were also lost. As a result, the project's backers were forced to invest heavily in ecological damage limitation projects including relocation of wildlife, replanting of forests and habitat enrichment schemes (see Itaipú reserves below). This entailed the setting-up of the **Flora and Fauna Itaipú Binacional** (ⓣ061/599-8652; 9am–5pm; free) a few kilometres south of the dam's entrance. An excellent zoo by South American standards, it was set up to house animals rescued from the flooding including a rare black jaguar and a breeding colony of Bush dogs. It also contains well-maintained **natural history** and **archaeological museums**.

Itaipú Reserves

The most accessible of the reserves is **Refugio Tati Yupi**, 26km north of Ciudad del Este. It has become popular with weekend visitors from the city and is best visited during the week if you actually want to see animals. If you are serious about wildlife a better bet is **Itabó**, some 100km from the city, approximately a third of which is dirt road. With an area of 130 sq km this is one of the larger reserves and is one of the last strongholds of the endangered Vinaceous-breasted Amazon parrot. The largest reserve is **Limoy** (157 sq km), 165km from Ciudad del Este. However it suffers from problems with access and the facilities are much more basic than at Itabó. **Refugio Mbaracayú**, 226km from the city, is not to be confused with the much more famous and spectacular Mbaracayú Forest Reserve (see below) though the two are close to each other – the names are taken from the nearby Cordillera Mbaracayú, a series of rolling hills marking the border with Brazil.

You will need your own vehicle to get the most out of the Itaipú reserves and prior permission from the **Flora and Fauna Itaipú Binacional** (see above). You will have to sign a form that you present on arrival and it may take a day or two to process your permissions, so plan in advance. If you wish to stay, basic accommodation is available free of charge, but you will have to bring and prepare your own food. Alternatively the reserves can be visited on a day-trip from Ciudad del Este, though you will not be allowed to enter before 7.30am and must leave before 10pm if you are not staying the night. For short guided day-trips in Spanish only contact Nelson Pérez of the Itaipú company (ⓔguajaki@gmail.com).

Mbaracayù Forest Reserve

MBARACAYÚ FOREST RESERVE remains a model for conservation in Paraguay, consisting of a patchwork of Atlantic Forest and *cerrado* habitat, criss-crossed by snaking streams and containing viable populations of large mammals such as jaguars and tapirs. Over four hundred **bird species** have been recorded here and from September to February the earsplitting call of Paraguay's national bird, the Bare-throated bellbird, rings out across the forest canopy. Other highly **endangered bird species** that may be seen here include the prehistoric-looking Black-fronted Piping-guan and the Woody Woodpecker lookalike Helmeted woodpecker.

Prior to travelling you should arrange your visit with the Fundación Moisés Bertoni (Prócer Carlos Argüello 208 ⓣ021/608740, ⓦwww.mbertoni.org.py), who will provide you with the paperwork necessary for **entry into the reserve** and instructions on how to get there. **Accommodation** (150,000G per person) is available at the Jejui-Mi base camp where there are a couple of double rooms and some dorms, all with shared bathroom and a well-equipped kitchen. The reserve can be accessed with difficulty by public transport – you will need to take an Empresa Paraguarí bus to the town of **Ygatimi** where you should arrange to be picked up by FMB forest guards to take you to the reserve. Whether you have your own vehicle or not, you will need to bring all your own food and drink for your stay.

SOUTH OF ASUNCIÓN

The main road south of the capital is Ruta 1, following a rather convoluted route to the attractive border city of **Encarnación**. Along the way it passes a number of small towns, some with colourful histories, though none except **Villa Florida** is worthy of more than a passing visit. Ruta 1 meets Ruta 4 at **San Ignacio de Misiones**, the latter running west to the colonial town of **Pilar**. The south of the country, particularly the area around **Encarnación**, is the heart of the Jesuit mission lands, with several sites of historic and archeological importance to explore, notably the *reducciones* at **Jesús** and **Trinidad**. Animal lovers will not want to miss **Parque Nacional San Rafael**, the country's most biodiverse reserve.

ALONG RUTA 1

Several towns line the road to Encarnación from Asunción, which if you have your own vehicle, are worth a brief stop without warranting a stay. The attractive citrus-growing town of **YAGUARÓN** is the first real point of interest south of the capital. Founded in 1539, it is noted for the church of **San Buenaventura**, which dates from a time when the town was at the centre of the Franciscan missions. Although heavily reconstructed, parts of the original building still remain, including sections of the facade and some interior pillars and walls. The **Museo del Doctor Francia** (Mon–Fri 7am–11am & 2–5pm; free) commemorates the life of the Paraguayan dictator known as "El Supremo" with a series of portraits depicting his life. Fifteen kilometres further south at Km 63 is **PARAGUARÍ**, site of a church notable for its two free-standing bell towers, while a few kilometres northeast of here is the historically important town of **PIRIBEBUY**. Capital of the country briefly during the War of the Triple Alliance, it played a pivotal role in the conflict. Then, as now, it was a small, largely rural, farming town, but its stand in 1869 against the invading Brazilians with an army consisting largely of children will live long in the nation's memory. The **Museo Histórico Comandante Pedro Juan Caballero** (Tues–Fri 8am–noon & 1–6pm; 3000G), at Estigarribia and Yegros, details much of this history, although many of the displays are in need of a revamp. At the small town of **Carapeguá** a road branches off east to the **PARQUE NACIONAL YBYCUÍ.** A favourite weekend break site for *Asuncenos*, it gives a relatively tame introduction to the more impressive Atlantic Forest sites of eastern Paraguay.

Villa Florida

Located where Ruta 1 crosses a bend in the Río Tebicuary, **Villa Florida** is the closest that Paraguay comes to a beach resort. When the river is not in flood it is flanked by glorious white sand beaches, a favourite with sunseekers, fishermen and townies looking for a break from the trials and tribulations of the working week. Besides the beach lifestyle there is not much else to do here, unless you visit during Easter week when the nation's youth gather to hold impromptu all-night beach raves. Year after year the gutter press runs stories about the degradation of the Paraguayan youth whilst simultaneously dedicating pages and pages to full colour spreads of this so-called "depravity" – the photographers paying particularly close attention to scantily-clad females.

Cheap if unspectacular accommodation is available at *Hotel La Misionera* (Ⓣ083/240215; 70,000G) near the beach, but a better option if you are in a group is to rent a house (around 100,000G) along the riverfront – ask around. For food you can get a half-decent feed at the *Parador* next to the bridge. There's a pleasant garden out back with nice river views.

PILAR

A delightful colonial town with a slightly Wild West feel, **PILAR** bills itself as "The City of Birds" and a series of fifty statues of native species are dotted around the town. In truth Pilar is perhaps more better nationally as the city of textiles, a huge factory on the riverfront providing most of the town's populace with an income. Whilst in Pilar it is worth paying a visit to **IBIS** (Mon–Sat 8am–6pm; free but contributions welcome) at Mariscal Estigarribia 335, the entomological branch of the Universidad Nacional de Pilar. IBIS is involved in insect studies and has set up an open-air butterfly house packed with native plants which attract myriad species of colourful Lepidoptera, as well as being home to an impressive collection of mounted specimens. IBIS publishes a small tourist guide to the bird statues around the city (for birdwatchers who don't like their birds to move) and is also in the process of locating a similar series of butterfly statues in an effort to make Pilar "The City of Birds *and* Butterflies".

Arrival

By bus Buses arrive at the small terminal (☎086/32315) in the north of town on Avda Irala and Tacuary.

Accommodation

Accommodation is thin on the ground in Pilar with the few options available typically basic but eminently affordable.

IBIS Mariscal Estigarribia 335 (no phone). Basic accommodation. 30,000G per person

Liza Aparthotel Tacuary and Antequera ☎086/32944. Modern mini-apartments representing excellent value for those looking to self-cater. 120,000G

Eating

Pilar is not a town for gourmet diners, with most eating options consisting of greasy burger joints or pizza houses. If you are looking for something more filling your options are limited.

Comedor Velazco Alberzoni and Teniente René Rios. The place to come for a decent meal, wtih a variable and affordable menu.

Moving on

By bus There are direct buses between Pilar and Asunción (5 daily; 4hr 30min), but access to and from Encarnación (3 daily; 6hr) is more difficult – you will have a lengthy wait at San Ignacio de Misiones for a connection. Don't despair, it will give you time to visit the nearby ruins.

ENCARNACIÓN

The "Pearl of the South", **ENCARNACIÓN** is Paraguay's wealthiest city outside of the capital and boasts a laid-back modernity that makes it instantly likeable. Founded in 1615 by Beato Roque González under the overly-verbose title of Nuestra Señora de la Encarnación de Itapúa, today – despite a population of only just over seventy thousand – Encarnación qualifies as the third largest city in Paraguay. San Roque had long been considered the Patron Saint of Encarnación, even before he was officially beatified in 1988, becoming Paraguay's first official saint in the process. The city's other famous son was the less than saintly dictator Alfredo Stroessner, born here in 1912. His former residence (now a neurological hospital) is near the bus station at Carlos Antonio López and Jorge Memmel.

What to see and do

Encarnación can be broadly split into two, the modern Zona Alta and the decaying old port area the Zona Baja, much of which is due to be flooded by the Yacyretá dam in 2010. Currently it is populated by a vast open-air market

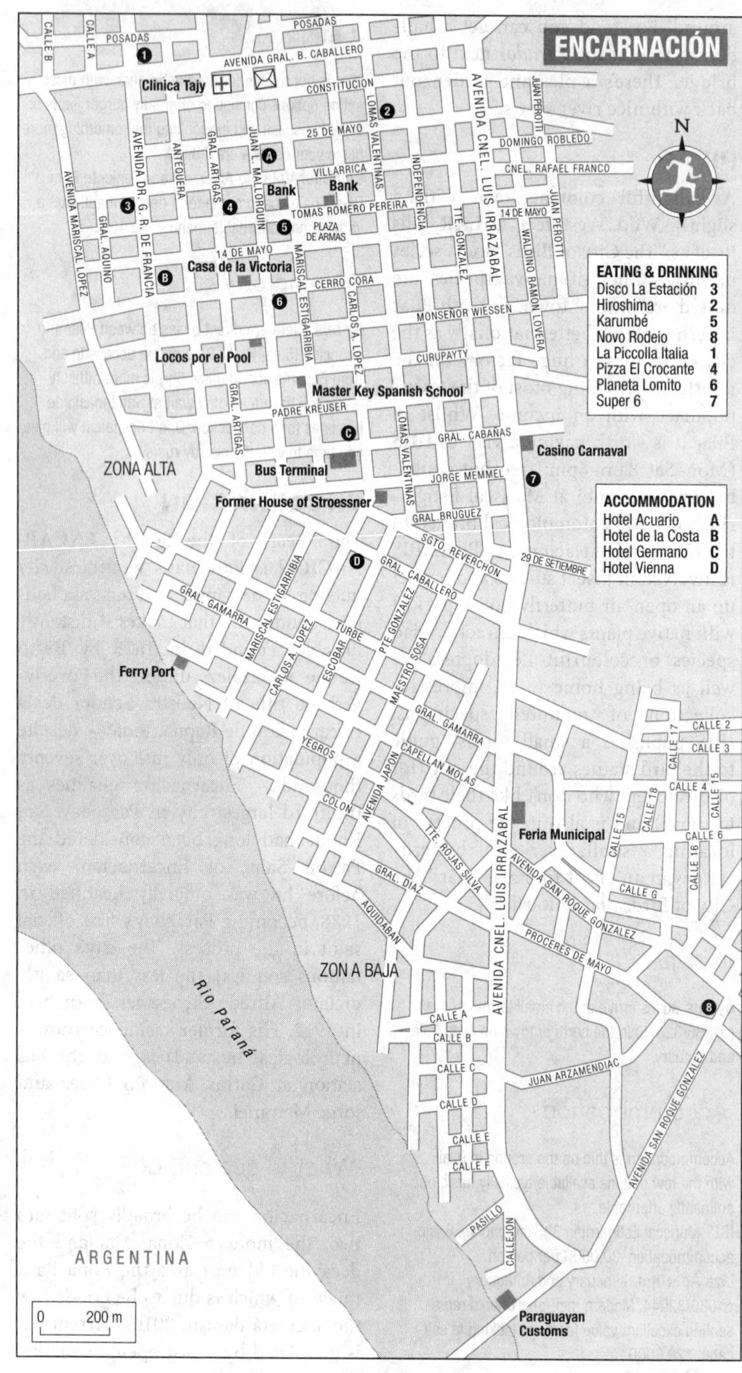
ENCARNACIÓN
EATING & DRINKING
Disco La Estación 3
Hiroshima 2
Karumbé 5
Novo Rodeio 8
La Piccolla Italia 1
Pizza El Crocante 4
Planeta Lomito 6
Super 6 7
ACCOMMODATION
Hotel Acuario A
Hotel de la Costa B
Hotel Germano C
Hotel Vienna D
Clinica Tajy
Bank
Bank
Casa de la Victoria
Locos por el Pool
Master Key Spanish School
Bus Terminal
Former House of Stroessner
Casino Carnaval
Ferry Port
Feria Municipal
Paraguayan Customs
ZONA ALTA
ZON A BAJA
Rio Paraná
ARGENTINA
PLAZA DE ARMAS
0 200 m

CARNAVAL

For most Paraguayans Encarnación is synonymous with **Carnaval,** a spectacular celebration transforming the city into a whirlpool of frivolity during the first three weekends of February. Things begin to hot up during the week with bands of children roaming the streets armed with spray-snow and water balloons, looking to make a fool out of the unwary, but the main events are the weekend *corsos* (parades) along the Avenida Francia. The *corso* is opened by the *Rey Momo*, an elected local fat-man whose job it is to set the mood and whip the crowd into a frenzy. Each neighbourhood of the city is represented by its *comparza,* a group of dancers, performers and hangers-on, who compete to impress the *jurado* (judges) with the outrageousness of their costumes, the animation of their dancing and overall fluidity of the spectacle. The action begins around 9pm each night and lasts through to the early hours, but tickets, sold at the entrance on Avenida Francia, (20–50,000G) sell out rapidly and you'll need to get there early to claim a good seat.

with some remarkable deals to be had if you shop around. Though many visitors use Encarnación as little more than a base to visit the Jesuit ruins, the city rewards those willing to spend a few days to get to know it better and is at its best during the February Carnaval, which draws thousands of visitors from across the continent for four weekends of rampant hedonism.

Centre of life in the Zona Alta is the **Plaza de Armas**, a spacious and attractive tree-lined square split into several "gardens" that pay homage to the various immigrant groups in the city. Two blocks further towards the river, the **Casa de la Victoria** at General Artigas and Cerro Corá, (Mon–Fri 8–11.30am & 2–5pm; free) is a small but interesting museum of artefacts from the Chaco War, with the emphasis on the contribution by local soldiers. The **first railway line in South America** ran between Asunción and Encarnación, and incredibly one of the first trains to use it, the *Carlos Antonio López*, is still in active service. Today it is a goods train and the best place to see it is in front of the **Feria Municipal** on Avenida Coronel Luis Irrazábal.

Arrival and information

By bus Most visitors arrive at the bus station conveniently situated where the Zona Alta meets the Zona Baja at General Cabañas y Mariscal Estigarribia – from here it's uphill six blocks to the Plaza de Armas (the town centre), downhill three blocks to the bargains. If crossing from Argentina you will arrive at the San Roque González International Bridge in the south of the city.

Tourist Information There is a tourist information office at the customs point here, but it is rarely open.

City transport

Taxis Bordered on three sides by broad avenues, central Encarnación is of an easily walkable size and it shouldn't take you more than half an hour to cross from one side to the other, though if it's hot you may prefer to take a taxi. There is a taxi rank at the bus terminal and another at the Plaza de Armas or you can call a radio taxi (☎071/202420). No journey within the city should cost more than 20,000G, slightly more to get to the frontier with Argentina.

Accommodation

Book ahead during Carnaval when prices rise considerably. Avoid the hotels around the bus terminal (except *Germano*) and those along Tómas Romero Pereira in the centre. The former attract an undesirable clientele, the latter have serious noise issues at weekends.

Hotel Acuario Juan L Mallorquín and Villarrica ☎071/202676. Central, secure and offering good value for money, this hotel makes up for its characterless rooms with friendly service and an Olympic-size indoor swimming pool hidden behind a door. 110,000G

TREAT YOURSELF

Five-star comfort at Paraguayan prices, the **Encarnación Resort Hotel** on Ruta 1 Km 361 (☎071/207267, ⓦwww.encarnacionresorthotel.com.py) gives you the perfect opportunity to get a taste of how the other half lives. Sauna, gym, pool, games room, tennis courts and two football pitches are at your disposal, whilst the price of the luxury suite is eminently accessible at 450,000G.

Hotel de la Costa Av Francia and Cerro Corá ☎071/200590. If you are looking to splash out without breaking the bank this is your best bet. There's an outdoor pool, pleasant gardens and a distinctly affordable luxury suite (300,000G) complete with Jacuzzi and breakfast in bed. Great views across the river to Argentina will soon get even better, with the Yacyretá Dam flooding due to land this hotel right on the coast. 180,000G

Hotel Germano General Cabañas and Mariscal Estigarribia ☎071/203346. Conveniently located right in front of the bus station, this is the city's best-value budget option. It is basic, but with en-suite bath and ceiling fan, it's a good place to get your head down for the night if you've an early bus to catch in the morning. 70,000G

Hotel Vienna General Pedro Juan Caballero 658, ☎071/203486. Cheap as chips, but dodgy décor and a location in a distinctly uninteresting part of town mean this hotel is best left to those on a tight budget. 60,000G

Eating

There is surprisingly good eating to be had in Encarnación if you look for it, the multi-cultural population offering up a smorgasbord of different eating options as well as the traditional *asados* and fast food.

Hiroshima 25 de Mayo and Lomas Valentinas ☎071/203505. The more authentic of the city's two excellent Japanese restaurants, this is your chance to sample sushi Paraguayan-style. Mains around 15–20,000G

Karumbé Mariscal Estigarribia and Tomás Romero Pereira ☎071/201147. Named after the traditional yellow horse-drawn carts, a uniquely *Encarnaceno* form of transport that you are likely to see around town, *Karumbé* offers a diverse menu including fish dishes – try the grilled *surubí*. If you're not hungry just chug a beer on the outdoor tables and watch the world go by. Mains in the range 18–35,000G.

Novo Rodeio Av San Roque González, near the international bridge ☎071/204691. Brazilian-style all-you-can-eat grill and buffet. Try to resist the allure of the succulent barbecued meats roasting over hot coals on the *parrilla* and give your arteries a rest by sampling some of the huge variety of innovative salads on offer. Price per person around 29,000G.

La Piccola Italia Ruta 1 and Posadas, ☎071/202344. Faux Mediterranean surroundings and a cheery Paraguayan/Italian host at this popular trattoria. Pig out on huge portions of quasi-authentic pizza and pasta – one plate is easily enough for two. Mains are in the 12-15,000G backet.

Pizza El Crocante Tomás Romero Pereira and General Artigas. This place doesn't look like much, but these are some of the best and cheapest pizzas in Paraguay. Pizza for two comes in at 18,000G.

Planeta Lomito Juan L Mallorquín and Cerro Corá. Junk food at its best; this place is open until the early hours of the morning and is a popular twilight meeting place for weekend revellers winding down after a night out. Make sure you give the *Lomito Arabe* a try. Mains in the range 5–10,000G.

Super 6 Av Coronel Luis Irrazábal. Yes, it is a supermarket, but at lunchtimes you'll struggle to find better value anywhere in the world. You pay by weight, so a kilogram of steak will cost you exactly the same price as a kilogram of lettuce leaves. Mains around 25,000G per kg.

Drinking and nightlife

Encarnación suffers from an ephemeral **nightlife** in which bars open and close with alarming regularity – ask around for the latest hot spot. On warm evenings the local youth gather around the Plaza de la Ciudad on Avenida Francia with coolboxes full of beers and loud music pumping from their car stereos. This is also the site of Carnaval when, during the entire month of February, all the festivity takes place in the streets.

La Estación Avenida Francia. Among a cluster of drinking options on this street (including a couple of discos), *La Estación* is the most-established, although opens only for private parties with tickets sold in the street outside.

Entertainment

Frequent open-air events and concerts are held at the Plaza de Armas, especially during the summer months – ask around for the latest information.

Casino Carnaval Avenida Coronel Luis Irrazábal. Live music every night, and open 24hr.

Locos por el Pool Monseñor Wiessen and Juan L Mallorquín. A decent pool hall open daily until the early hours of the morning.

Directory

Banks Amambay and Interbanco on the Plaza de Armas both have ATMs.

Emergencies Fire and Ambulance ⓣ132; Police ⓣ911.

Hospital Best private hospital is Clínica Tajy at General Artigas y Constitución.

Internet Countless options around town. Pya'e where Tomás Romero Pereira meets the Plaza has a particularly good connection.

Post office Central branch opposite the Sanatorio Itapúa on Juan L Mallorquín and Constitución.

Spanish school Master Key Institute, Galería San Jorge, Mariscal Estigarribia y Curupayty ⓣ0985 778198, runs unique and professional open-air Spanish courses for all levels, with nearby tourist attractions replacing the classroom, and a five-day course coming in at 750,000G; pre-booking essential.

Tour companies FAUNA Paraguay, ⓦwww.faunaparaguay.com. Paraguay's only professional, expert-led eco-tours, based out of Encarnación.

Moving on

By bus An International Bus between the bus terminal in Posadas, Argentina, and Encarnación runs along Juan L Mallorquín one block west from the Plaza de Armas every 15min (5am–11pm; 5000G). Don't forget to get off the bus at both ends of the bridge for customs formalities. The bus won't wait for you to get your stamps, but your ticket remains valid for the next service. Destinations: Asunción (hourly; 5hr 30min); Ciudad del Este (6 daily; 4hr 30min); Posadas (every 15min; 1hr).

By ferry Ferries leave for the hour-long crossing to Posadas (5000G) every 15min (8am–5.45pm) from the dock at Juan L Mallorquín and Capellan Molas in the Zona Baja. Customs formalities are completed before boarding and on disembarking.

AROUND ENCARNACIÓN

The area immediately around Encarnación is home to some interesting attractions and the city is a perfect base from which to explore them. As the heartland of the **Jesuit Missions**, southern Paraguay is home to some of the best preserved Jesuit ruins (*reducciones*), considered to be of cultural as well as historical value. The most famous of these are **Jesús** and **Trinidad**, and both are relatively easy to visit on a day-trip. If your interests are more ecological then it's worth taking the short journey to **Hotel Tirol**, one of

SANCTUARIO DE ITACUA

Many *Encarnacenos* mark Paraguay's main religious festival, Día de la Virgen (Dec 8), with an overnight eight-kilometre pilgrimage to the **Sanctuario de Itacua**. According to legend a Guaraní man fleeing from pursuers arrived at the site and found a piece of wood in the shape of the Virgin Mary. She duly answered his prayers that his life be spared and the "miracle" was marked by the site's conversion into a centre of pilgrimage. Thousands of pilgrims arrive for early morning prayers in the impressive new chapel, and pass the rest of the day enjoying the pleasant forested surroundings, cooking up *asados* on the lawns, and swimming in the river. The original chapel is the wooden hut adjacent to the main church, whilst the Virgin herself sits in a grotto looking out across the Rio Paraná.

To **get there** with your own vehicle follow the signposts from the roundabout on the Avenida San Roque González in Encarnación, crossing the railway line and following the rough dirt road directly to the church, or take bus Linea 4 marked Itacua (every 15min from Carlos Antonio López and Villarrica a block north of the Plaza de Armas; 2200G).

the last patches of Atlantic Forest in the immediate area and an oasis for native wildlife retreating from Departamento Itapúa's expanding agricultural frontier. The country's largest remaining block of humid Atlantic Forest, however, is **SAN RAFAEL NATIONAL PARK**, the most biodiverse area in Paraguay, and as such its most important protected area. Despite concern over the reserve's future (see opposite), it remains for the moment one of the most beautiful and easily-accessible natural areas in Paraguay,

Hotel Tirol

Twenty kilometres east of Encarnación, just past the town of Capitán Miranda, is **Hotel Tirol** (Ⓣ071/202388, Ⓦwww.hoteltirol.com.py, 250,000G). This Belgian-owned monolith is perched on the edge of a forested valley and has something of a monasterial feel to it. The imposing hotel buildings are built from local stone, a deliberate constructional quirk which ensures that rooms remain cool even during the fierce Paraguayan summer. The hotel is a favourite with the King of Spain and members of the Paraguayan gentry. It counts on 0.2 sq km of atmospheric Atlantic Forest in its grounds, home to a troop of capuchin monkeys and some 190 species of birds, including various species of toucans and hummingbirds. If walking in the wilderness isn't your thing, then relax around one of the four swimming pools or enjoy the majestic view of the forest canopy from the hotel bar. Staying the night is surprisingly affordable and the price includes three abundant meals – you should book ahead between November and February. Even if you don't stay at the hotel you can use the pools and walk around the forest for a minimal fee (10,000G), perhaps combining a visit with a trip to the Trinidad ruins (see opposite) a little further along Ruta 6. If you don't have your own vehicle, all buses heading between Encarnación and Ciudad del Este pass the hotel entrance, or alternatively take local bus line 1y2 Capitán Miranda (2200G), which passes every fifteen minutes along General Artigas in Encarnación, terminating 100m from the hotel entrance.

Jesuit Ruins

The arrival in 1609 of the **Jesuit missionaries** from the order of the Company of Jesus, sparked the beginning of one of the most daring social experiments of its time. Establishing a cultural, social and political order of its own, the company invited the native Guaraní peoples to join them and attempted to create a written vocabulary of the Guaraní tongue for the first time. Although the natives weren't accorded equal rights, they were trained in agricultural methods and a select few were given a classical education. The colonies, which totalled thirty missions in the eighteenth century (fourteen in Paraguay and sixteen in what today is Argentina), thrived until King Carlos III of Spain expelled the Jesuits in 1767, leaving their grand building projects to decay gracefully.

The most impressive of the Paraguayan Missions are **Trinidad** and **Jesús**, and both are easily visited on a day-trip from Encarnación. **Trinidad** (daily 7am–7pm, 5000G), 28km east of Encarnación, is located on the main *ruta* to Ciudad del Este and any bus (5000G) between the two cities passes right in front – get off at the slightly out-of-place power station, on your right when heading east. A hilltop settlement and UNESCO World Cultural Heritage Site, the partially restored church (which is for the most part roofless) will immediately capture your attention, filled as it is with fantastically ornate stone carvings of religious figurines. These have survived well despite their exposure to the frequently harsh climate, while the pulpit and font are also worth checking out. The stone-paved turn-off to **Jesús** is signposted a few hundred metres further along Ruta 6 from Trinidad, and runs 13km to the site (same times and price), but isn't served by public transport. For two years, three thousand natives worked on the construction of the vast church here, which was left incomplete when the Jesuits were expelled. Besides the church (itself a bit bare, with only walls and columns surviving), however, there is little to see here and Trinidad is both more accessible and more impressive if your time is limited. Bilingual guides are available for both sites and are worth the investment, as there is a distinct lack of other information for visitors.

PARQUE NACIONAL SAN RAFAEL

Though designated as a "National Park" in 1992, all of the land within Paraguay's most biodiverse reserve still remains in private hands, creating a conflict of interest between landowners, conservationists and indigenous groups in the area, each of which have legitimate claims to the tenure. A government promise to buy out the landowners has not been acted upon due to a perpetual "lack of funds", and the goodwill of many of the affected is now unsurprisingly beginning to run out. The landowners insist that if the money cannot be found to compensate them, they should be allowed to use their land to generate their own income. The long-term conservation of San Rafael is as a result far from secure and it has fallen to local NGOs such as Pro Cosara – whom you should inform of any visit in advance – to ensure the implementation of environmental law in the area (see Ⓦhttp://procosara.org/index_en for more information). That said, San Rafael remains one of the true highlights of Paraguay, where nature abounds against a spectacularly verdant backdrop. Some 414 species of birds occur here, including a great many species endemic to the Atlantic Forest biome. You might expect to see trogons, toucans, tanagers, tinamous and hummingbirds during walks in the forest, and large mammals such as jaguar and tapir are still present in the area.

Arrival and information

By bus San Rafael is easy to reach on public transport. A bumpy bus run by Empresa Pastoreo departs daily from Encarnación at 8am and 11.30am. Ask the driver to drop you off at the town of Ynambú where, if you've notified Pro Cosara (see below), you will be met by a 4WD vehicle to take you to the reserve.

Accommodation

Pro Cosara/ECOSARA Estación Ecológica de San Rafael Ⓣ0768295046, Ⓦwww.faunaparaguay.com/ecosarahome.html. Besides offering a bed for the night for tourists (call Christine Hostettler in advance on the number above to reserve your bed), this place also offers reduced-rate volunteerships for conservation-minded travellers, internships for biology students and positions for professional researchers, with a permanent scientific research team involved in ongoing biological studies and inventory work. 150,000G per person

Moving on

Buses from Ynambú back to Encarnación leave at 5am and 1pm every day except Sunday. You'll need to arrange your transport to Ynambú with Pro Cosara the day before you wish to leave.

NORTH OF ASUNCIÓN

Crossing the Río Paraguay, the main route north from the capital is Ruta 1, via the town of **Villa Hayes**. Named after the otherwise forgettable US president Rutherford B Hayes – whose decision to support Paraguay's bid to keep the Chaco after the War of the Triple Alliance was influential in moderating Argentine claims – the town is peppered with monuments to him. From here it is a long and uneventful journey to the crossroads of **Pozo Colorado** at the gateway to the Chaco. Ruta 9 – the "Trans-Chaco" – continues north to **Filadelfia** and the **Mennonite colonies**, while the dramatic and beautiful Ruta 5 heads east through glorious countryside in which wildlife abounds. The main towns along here are **Concepción** on the Río Paraguay and **Pedro Juan Caballero** on the border with Brazil. The only reason to visit the latter is as a base for visiting the nearby **Cerro Corá National Park** – it is not recommended that you try to cross to Brazil here, as the border is a well-known smuggling route. North of Concepción the little town of **Valle Mí** has reinvented itself as a centre for eco-tourism and river trips on the Rio Apa.

CONCEPCIÓN

A pretty port town on the eastern bank of the Río Paraguay, **CONCEPCIÓN** is the main trading centre in the north of the country. More recently it has become popular with tourists as a centre for uncomfortable but picturesque river trips along the Río Paraguay.

What to see and do

The town is bisected north to south by **Avenida Agustín Pinedo**, its central reservation filled with a mixed bag of industrial and agricultural machinery – the **Museo al Aire Libre**. Two blocks east of here along Don Bosco is the **Mercado Municipal**, a dingy warren of tiny, cramped stalls selling all manner of merchandise. Most of the interest lies to the west of the Avenida, centred on the balding **Plaza Libertad**. An eclectic, almost Venetian-style **Catedral** (access after 5pm) overlooks the plaza, and adjacent to it is the **Museo Diocesano** (Mon–Sat 7.30–11.30am; free), packed with religious paraphernalia. Two blocks east of here along Estigarribia is a series of charming **mansion houses** that now operate as municipal buildings. A pastel blue mansion dating from 1898 houses the Intendencia (council headquarters), while the delightful honey-coloured **Mansión Otaño** (1940) houses the public works department. On the western outskirts of town, the strange, pyramidal **Monumento al Indio** commemorates the indigenous population, while the unnecessarily steep **bridge** over the Río Paraguay, 9km southwest, provides exceptional views along the river's course. Perhaps the main reason for visiting Concepción is to take a **river cruise** along the Río Paraguay to the Paraguayan Pantanal (see p.778).

Arrival and information

Banks Banks are a problem, as no ATMs accept foreign cards – be sure to take all the cash you need with you.

By bus Buses arrive at the terminal on Garal, eight blocks north of the town centre. There is no functional tourist office and no map of the town, but the centre is small and you'll soon know your way around.

Accommodation

The best place to look for accommodation is along Franco, west of Avenida Pinedo, which is well-located for both the port and the town centre. **Victoria** Franco and Pedro Caballero ⓣ03312/42256. A handsome old whitewashed building with spacious communal areas, and cable TV, breakfast and air conditioning all included. There's also dormitory accommodation at a slightly cheaper rate (55,000G per person). 140, 000G.

Center Franco and Yegros ⓣ03312/42360. A real cheap option if rather unappealing on account of spartan furniture and lumpy beds. Discounts on fan-only rooms. 60,000G

Francés Franco and Carlos Antonio López ⓣ03312/42383. The best bet in town, with a great pool and buffet breakfast worthy of the price alone. 130,000G

Eating

Places to eat are limited, with no end of chicken grills and burger joints.

Toninho y Jandri Mariscal Estigarribia and Iturbe, in front of the plaza. A excellent Brazilian-style *churrasquería*, and probably your best bet .although good, filling food can also be had at the **Francès** (Franco and Carlos Antonio López). Restaurant under the hotel of the same name, where chicken dominates the menu.

Moving on

By bus Hourly buses leave from the terminal for Asunción (7hr) and Pedro Juan Caballero (4hr).
By ferry A number of ferry services leaving from the port area run along the Río Paraguay to Fuerte Olimpo and Bahía Negra in the Paraguayan Pantanal. Schedules change regularly and you are advised to check latest departure times with the tourist office in Asunción (see p.756). Boats are uncomfortable, beds little more than hammocks and you would do well to take your own food with you – prices can often be negotiated on board.

CERRO CORÁ NATIONAL PARK

Parque Nacional Cerro Corá lies 35km west of the border town of **Pedro Juan Caballero**. This 220 sq km park was the site of Paraguay's final defeat in the War of the Triple Alliance and the place where Francisco Solano López finally met his end – it is of historical importance as well as intense natural beauty. The site of **López's death** is marked by a monument set above a small wooded brook, at one end of a long line of busts of the war leaders, while at the opposite end is an abstract **monument to the war dead** featuring commemorative plaques from groups as diverse as the Uruguayan Rotary Club and Brazilian Air Force.

There is an administrative office with a small museum (free) and information centre where you can ask about **camping** – all buses between Concepción and Pedro Juan Caballero pass the park entrance. If you have your own vehicle it may be easier to commute from Pedro Juan Caballero. *Eiruzú* at Mariscal López y Estigarribia (☎0336/272435; 200,000G) is as good an option as any if you wish to stay here. Now rather dated, but clearly once very grand, its 1970s furniture and décor make you feel like you are stuck in a time warp. There is a small pool and the price includes breakfast at the excellent restaurant below.

VALLE MÍ

The small town of **Valle Mí** has reinvented itself as a centre for eco-tourism on the Ríos Apa and Aquidaban. Though the atmosphere is somewhat affected by the giant cement plant, the town's major employer and one of the country's most unusual tourist attractions, the river beaches and river cruises make it well worth a visit. There are also a series of *cerros* and caves in the area which can be visited on a guided tour, offering opportunities for adventure tourism such as rappelling and rock-climbing.

Arrival and information

By boat Getting to Valle Mí is a problem; by far the most reliable, if not the most comfortable, way to arrive is by boat from Concepción – there are 11am departures on Tues & Thurs and the entire trip takes about 30hr. You should book in advance if you want a cabin.
By bus Alternatively, two buses leave daily for Valle Mí from the terminal in Concepción at 5.30 & 6am, a bumpy journey along a rutted dirt road that takes seven hours in good conditions.
By car To attempt the same journey in your own transport, a 4WD is essential, though even then bear in mind that the road becomes impassable with rain.
Tourist information Information about the town and the options available to visitors are available through the excellent web page http://ciudadValleMi.tripod.com/.

Accommodation and tours

Accommodation is basic and the limited options are all much of a muchness in terms of price and the basic facilities that they provide.
El Prado Near the port ☎0351/230545. Arguably the best option, which at least has nice river views. 100,000G

THE MENNONITE COLONIES

The **Mennonites** first arrived in Paraguay in 1926, having purchased a large area of the central Chaco which today constitutes the Mennonite colonies. They arrived in the Río Paraguay port of Puerto Casado where they were received with much pomp and ceremony by the then president of the Republic Dr Eligio Ayala, who had campaigned hard to bring them to Paraguay with the aim of settling the Chaco. The following year they began their overland migration to the lands that they had bought with the promise of a better life awaiting them. Their first encounters with the dry Chaco summer came as a huge shock and of the 1700 or so initial colonists, a large percentage fell victim to the heat, lack of water and disease in the early years. Those that remained suffered enormously as they tried to establish themselves in one of the harshest environments on earth. Against all odds the Mennonites have succeeded in becoming the major providers of dairy produce in the country, their beef is recognised as amongst the best on the continent and their settlements operate with a clinical efficiency that belies their isolated location.

Valle Mí Tour Río Apa y 13 de Junio, in the municipalidad building ⓣ0351 230764. This operator offers a variety of affordable packages to all the local sights, including a tour of the cement factory, as well as organizing all hotel bookings and travel arrangements. Open Mon–Fri 7am–1pm.

Moving on

By boat Boats to and from Concepcíon (heading to Fuerte Olimpo and the Pantanal) pass through Valle Mí at least twice a week but progress is slow and you should take all your food and water with you. Check at the port for the latest schedules.

By bus Two daily buses run to Concepción in fair weather only, taking about 7hr.

THE CHACO

The Chaco's reputation as a hot, dusty, thorny hell is only partially true. In fact it consists of two distinct and very different eco-systems. The first 300km or so of the **Ruta Trans-Chaco** – the colloquial name for the single long, straight highway which traverses the region, officially known as Ruta 9 – passes through the **Humid Chaco**, a flat, seasonally-flooded palm savanna that teems with waterbirds at certain times of year, offering superb opportunities to spot spectacular species such as jabiru stork, roseate spoonbill and giant wood rail on waterside pools. The Mennonite colonies of the **Central Chaco** mark the transition zone from Humid to **Dry Chaco** habitat. Far from the desert wasteland that many people imagine, true Dry Chaco is in fact a dense, stunted and thorny forest environment, characterized by high temperatures and frequent hot winds. Though the Chaco makes up over sixty percent of the territory of Paraguay it is home to less than three percent of the population. If you want to see more of the Chaco than just the Mennonite colonies (see above), you are strongly advised to take a guided tour or else hire a 4WD vehicle in Asunción and ensure you have enough fuel, food and water for several days. Note that while the Trans-Chaco is now paved along almost its entire length, the tarmac runs out at around Km 647 to be replaced by an increasingly pot-holed dust road that is navigable only by 4WD in favourable weather. The crossing point to Bolivia is not actually on the Trans-Chaco at all, but on the newly paved Picada 108 that branches off west at the small settlement of La Patria (see box, p.776). It goes without saying that it's a long, hot drive, although there are a couple of places en-route to rest up: **Pirahú** (no phone; 130,000G), Km 250, as well as providing a bed for the night, is nationally famous for its delicious and inventive *empanadas*, while at Km 283, **Buffalo Bill's** (☎0981/832411; 150,000G) offers good accommodation, bordered by an artificial lake jam-packed with wild caiman.

CRUCE LOS PIONEROS AND FORTÍN BOQUERÓN

The last place on the Trans-Chaco where you can guarantee that you will be able to refuel, sleep in a hotel – **Hotel Los Pioneros** (☎04914/32170; 100,000G), which at least has air-conditioning – and have a half-decent meal is at the crossroads outpost of **Cruce Los Pioneros** – make the most of it, but be aware that this is all you *can* do here; it's not a town, or even a village, as such.

Even if you don't need to avail yourself of the facilities, though, it's worth stopping here for a look at **Fortín Boquerón**, accessible via a turn-off on the left just as you reach Cruce Los Pioneros; the site is signposted along the way. Another Chaco War battleground, Fortín Boquerón is particularly worth a visit for its excellent museum (Tue–Sat 8am–6pm; 5000G), featuring munitions and cannons from the conflict, as well as a poignant display of photographs and writings by the combatants. A small cemetery and remains of trenches will also capture your attention, but most interesting is the hollowed-out *palo borracho* (bottle tree), used as a sniper's nest by the Paraguayan army to pick off the advancing Bolivians. Though it looks for all the world like a woodpecker hole from the front, from the rear the tree is completely open with a cramped sitting area that was occupied by the sniper. Remarkably, despite missing most of its innards, the tree is still alive and well and continues to grow.

THE MENNONITE COLONIES

The Mennonite colonies (see box, opposite) are most easily accessed via the turn-offs at **Cruce Los Pioneros** (see above) and, 50km or so further on, **Cruce Loma Plata**. There are three colonies in all, each with its own administrative capital – Menno (capital **Loma Plata**) and Fernheim (capital **Filadelfia**) are the largest and most easily reached from Asunción. Unless you are a motor-racing fanatic, the area is best avoided during September when it becomes gripped with **Trans-Chaco Rally** fever. Billed as one of the toughest motorized events on earth, it is accompanied by a considerable hike in hotel prices and you will have to book well in advance if you want a room. For more information see ⓦwww.transchacorally.com.py.

FILADELFIA

FILADELFIA is the Chaco's most highly populated settlement, and its innate "Germanness" is somewhat surprising given its dry and dusty location. The perfect lawns and well-trimmed hedges may seem out of place in the harsh climate, but neatly symbolise the triumph over adversity of the original settlers.

What to see and do

Most of the action centres around the dual-laned **Avenida Hindenburg**, which bisects the town. From a tourist point of view there is relatively little to keep you occupied and the main interest lies in absorbing the colonial lifestyle of the people, built largely around dairy farming and cooperation with native populations. The **Unger Museum** (Mon–Fri 9–11.30am and 2–5pm; free) on Avenida Hindenburg is worth a brief visit. Jakob Unger was a collector of animal specimens in the

CROSSING TO BOLIVIA

At the small town of **La Patria**, a fully-paved road (formerly Picada 108) now branches off the Trans-Chaco to the border crossing of **Fortín Infante Rivarola**. There is a small guard post here which does not have exit stamps (you should attempt to either get them prior to travelling or in the small settlement of Mariscal Estigarribia en-route) and the Bolivian side of the border remains unpaved and unattended. This border point is extremely isolated and a popular smuggling route so you are not advised to attempt to cross the border here by yourself. Nevertheless, international buses (1–3 daily; 30hr) do run between Asunción and Santa Cruz in Bolivia with companies Yacyretá, Pycasu and Ester Turismo.

Chaco from 1950 to 1975 and the fruits of his labours are housed on the second floor. The ground floor is given over to artefacts dating from the time of the colonization – the wooden building itself, known as the Casa de la Colonia, was the original headquarters of the colony. Filadelfia is the "base camp" of Trebol, one of the country's major dairy producers, and their gigantic factory is on the avenue of the same name.

Arrival and information

By bus In the absence of a bus terminal, buses arrive and depart from their own offices along Chaco Boreal, off Hindenburg.

Money There is only one ATM in Filadelfia at Interbanco in the Portal del Chaco development. Although it accepts foreign cards, you are strongly advised to bring enough money for your stay with you.

Accommodation and eating

Filadelfia offers some surprisingly good accommodation with the two mentioned the pick of the bunch. There are no restaurants in Filadelfia so you will have to eat at one of the hotel restaurants where buffet lunches are the norm.

Florida Hindenburg 984, opposite the Unger Museum ⓣ0491/432151. Attractively laid out with a great pool and garden, the hotel has a range of rooms: at the higher end are spacious rooms with cable TV and minibar, while the cheapest consist of little more than four walls and a bed. Its restaurant is also excellent. 60,000–150,000G

Safari Industrial 149E, around the corner from *Florida* ⓣ0491/432218. A plusher option, and attractive, if slightly retro, with rooms boasting cable TV and a/c. 180,000G

Moving on

There is no public transport in the Mennonite colonies except for the bus companies that connect the towns with Asunción. Most services from Filadelfia pass through Loma Plata en route to the capital. Taxis are non-existent and there is nowhere to hire a car. Visiting on a guided tour or hiring a car in Asunción gives you much greater flexibility for further exploration.

By bus There are several daily services south to Asunción, all via Pozo Colorado, where it is possible to change for buses to Concepción. Unless you enjoy a leisurely bus ride be sure to take a direct service, as indirect services are extremely slow.

LOMA PLATA

The oldest of the Mennonite towns, **LOMA PLATA** is arranged along a similar pattern to Filadelfia, with a neat grid square system of side streets arranged around a dusty central avenue. Loma Plata's main tourist attraction is the **Museo de Historia Mennonita** (daily 7am–noon & 2–6pm; free) on the main avenue. Though small, it is a fascinating documentation of the trials and tribulations that faced the original settlers and the challenges that they had to overcome. Buses from Asunción to Filadelfia pass through Loma Plata en route. One of the best places to stay is at the *Loma Plata Inn* (ⓣ0492/253235; 150,000G), which also has a good buffet restaurant, *Chaco Grill*.

FORTÍN TOLEDO

At Km 475 a rough road runs 9km south to **FORTÍN TOLEDO**. An important

Chaco war site with a combatants' cemetery and well-preserved vestiges of trenches, it is perhaps more often visited for the Peccary breeding project **PROYECTO TAGUÁ.** The principal objective of the project – overseen by San Diego Zoo – is the reproduction and reintroduction of the Chaco peccary (*taguá*), a pig-like animal that was known only from fossil remains until its remarkable discovery alive and well in the Paraguayan Chaco in 1976. Today all three known species are bred here, the *taguá* being the largest and shiest species, and the other two being the bad-tempered white-lipped (*tañykati*) and the mild-mannered collared (*kure'i*). Check out the aggressive threat displays of the male white-lipped – releasing a foul-smelling fluid before dashing towards the observer and gnashing the enormous jaws together to produce a blood-curdling, bone-crushing sound that makes you glad they are behind bars. The project has been a huge success and large numbers of all species are maintained at the site. Launched in 1985 with just three animals, by 2007 more than 250 *taguá* had been released into the wild, representing an important percentage of the known population of this threatened species. No public transport passes Fortín Toledo, so you will need your own vehicle. The site is well-signposted off the Trans-Chaco.

CENTRAL CHACO LAGOONS

Correctly known as the Cuenca del Upper Yacaré Sur lagoons, the **CENTRAL CHACO LAGOONS**, as they are more commonly called, are a series of unpredictable and temporary saline lakes east of the Mennonite colonies. Because of their importance for migrating water-birds they have been declared an "Important Bird Area" or IBA. The amount of water around depends greatly on the amount of rainfall in previous months and lagoons may be dry for several years before suddenly filling with water again in favourable conditions. In winter they are occupied by ducks and flocks of Chilean flamingos, whilst during the southbound migration for Nearctic water-birds (Sept – Dec) they are dominated by huge flocks of sandpipers and plovers. Probably the best place to base yourself is **Laguna Capitán** (☎0991/650101; 60,000G per person), actually a Mennonite holiday resort, where there is comfortable shared accommodation with air-conditioning and food on offer – though you should arrange this in advance with the owners. The gardens here are packed with birdlife and grey brocket deer, armadillos and capybara are common in the surroundings. The best place to see the flamingos is **Reserva Privada Campo María** which plays host to as many as one thousand individuals, as well as other spectacular birds such as *coscoroba* swan and mammals like tapir and peccary. Generally speaking Campo María is the last of the lagoons in the surroundings to dry out. There is a 10,000G per person entry fee payable at the house at the entrance to the reserve.

PARQUE NACIONAL TENIENTE ENCISO AND MÉDANOS DEL CHACO

In the highest part of the High Chaco, almost at the Bolivian border, **TENIENTE AGRIPINO ENCISO NATIONAL PARK** (Enciso for short) is the most accessible of the Chaco protected areas. This impenetrable reserve consists almost entirely of dense Chaco forest, a dry, stunted and spiny vegetation-type typical of the area. The park was established to protect a series of trenches dating from the Chaco War and to conserve a healthy population of Chaco peccary (*taguá*).

TREAT YOURSELF

Really getting off the beaten track is harder than ever these days, but visiting the Paraguayan Pantanal you can guarantee that your only companions will be the wildlife that you came to see! FAUNA Paraguay (Ⓦwww.faunaparaguay.com) offer all-inclusive, made-to-measure tours to the remotest areas of the country with professional expert eco-guides who can tell you everything you want to know about every bird, beast, butterfly or "*bicho*" that you encounter along the way.

The species is regularly seen in the area along with puma, tapir and a host of Chaco endemic bird species including Black-legged Seriema, Chaco Owl and the turkey-like *Chaco chachalaca*. Your best chance of seeing mammals is on night-walks with a torch – stake out the waterhole and salt-lick just after dark to increase your chances of bumping into the more spectacular species. A series of walking trails are well-maintained and allow for hiking, but the frequent hot, dry winds can seriously impede your chances of seeing wildlife during the day. The best time of year to visit is during winter (May to September) when temperatures are lower, summer temperatures frequently reaching 50ºC. It is only another 65km along the Ruta Trans-Chaco to **MÉDANOS DEL CHACO NATIONAL PARK**, a more open habitat-type and home to the last lowland herd of the llama-like guanaco. However, beyond Enciso the Trans-Chaco deteriorates into a series of "talcales" (dust baths) which are only occasionally passable by a 4WD vehicle. It is not recommended that you attempt this journey unless accompanied by a professional guide or somebody with local knowledge. Note also that there are no accommodation or visitor facilities at Médanos del Chaco, and that whether travelling alone or by public transport to the vicinity, you will need to take all food and drink with you – there is nowhere to buy supplies.

Arrival and tours

By bus NASA runs buses (2 daily, 16hr) from the Asunción bus terminal to Nueva Asunción, that pass in front of the visitors centre at Enciso, but it's a long and uncomfortable journey.

By car If hiring a car, a 4WD vehicle is absolutely necessary as the tarmac runs out some 22km before the reserve.

Tours Guided eco-tours are available through FAUNA Paraguay Ⓦwww.faunaparaguay.com.

Accommodation

SEAM Av Madame Lynch 3500, Asunción ⓣ021/614687, Ⓦwww.paraguaysilvestre.org.py. Despite its isolated location on the Ruta Trans-Chaco at approximately Km 664, Enciso counts on excellent visitor facilities, with running water, 24hr electricity, a passable kitchen and even a/c in some rooms (100,000G per room sleeping 4). Your visit must, however, be co-ordinated in advance via the above contact details.

PARAGUAYAN PANTANAL

The **Paraguayan Pantanal**, on the other side of the Río Paraguay from its Brazilian neighbour, is rarely visited by tourists. Getting there can be expensive, accommodation is thin on the ground and it can be reached only by boat or aeroplane for more than half of the year. On the plus side it lacks the commercialism of the Brazilian Pantanal, the wildlife is, if anything, more abundant, and the chances of having your experience adversely affected by hordes of other tourists are nil. The two main **entry points** into the Pantanal are the small towns of **Fuerte**

Olimpo and **Bahía Negra**, but to get the most out of your visit it is worth taking a private tour.

FUERTE OLIMPO AND BAHÍA NEGRA

The gateway to the Pantanal, **FUERTE OLIMPO** is an attractive, if somewhat run-down old town, giving the impression of an abandoned military outpost. The old Spanish **fort** that gives the town its name dates from 1537 and looks out over the Río Paraguay, here a conglomeration of marshy islands penetrated by a meandering series of windy channels. The town's other major architectural treasure is the three-towered **Catedral Morada de Dios** – though it is most impressive from the outside. Despite the colonial charms of the town itself the two main reasons for visiting are eco-tourism and fishing. Boats can be hired with a driver for 300,000G per half-day, but petrol is in short supply and it is a good idea to bring your own and pay a reduced fee. Capybara and caiman abound along the river channels, whilst howler monkeys sing each morning from the forested *cerros* around the town. Game fisherman will be tempted by the opportunity to snare monster *pacu* and *surubí*, but restrictions exist on how many fish you are allowed to take home. Even more remote than Fuerte Olimpo, **BAHÍA NEGRA** is a small town located almost at the junction of the Ríos Paraguay and Negro. It is Paraguay's last population centre before the triple-frontier with Bolivia and Brazil some 20km further north. The only reason to head up here is for eco-tourism, and animals abound – everything from giant anteaters and giant otters to tapir and jaguar, while huge numbers of wading birds gather along the waterways. Three kilometres south of town, the Puerto Diana indigenous community sells authentic arts and crafts for reasonable rates. The cacique will be able to arrange for you to witness a traditional dance ceremony (450,000G) if you give advance notice, the performance consisting of twenty people in tribal dress and lasting a total of two hours. Boat trips organised locally cost 200,000G per half-day but you must bring your own petrol – they are a must if you want to see wildlife. There are no restaurants or petrol stations in Bahía Negra so you should take all your supplies with you.

Arrival and information

Access to the Paraguayan Pantanal is troublesome, with no reliable public transport to speak of.

By air It is possible to fly to both Fuerte Olimpo (2hr) and Bahía Negra (3hr) with pilot Juan Carlos Zavala (☎0971/201540). Four passengers fit in the plane and it costs US$300 per hour.

By car Road access is only via the Mennonite colonies of the Central Chaco and is a two-day trip from Asunción – do not attempt the trip without a 4WD vehicle, and if there is any hint of rain there is a real risk of being stranded for several days. Avoid making the journey during the wettest time of year (Sept–April) unless you have to, and do not attempt it alone. The last chance to buy petrol is at Loma Plata – you should make sure that you take enough with you to get where you want to go and back again.

By ferry A ferry leaves Concepción once a week on Wedfor Bahía Negra, stopping at Fuerte Olimpo. The entire trip takes three days and it is an uncomfortable but extremely picturesque ride.

Information When calling the Pantanal by phone you will need to communicate first with the operator on 010 and he will attempt to put you through – sometimes with limited success.

Accommodation

Accommodation is in short supply in both towns, although there is at least one decent option in each. Advance booking is essential.

Fundación Hombre y Naturaleza Bahía Negra Task operator for Marcelo Bobadilla in Bahía Negra. Basic accommodation in a rustic wooden building on the waterfront at the southern entrance to town. 50,000G per person.

Puerta del Pantanal Fuerte Olimpo Task operator for Fuerte Olimpo 117. Basic at best, if welcoming, with great river views, and your meals are caught that same morning. The price includes meals and the management can also assist with arranging river trips. 70,000G per person.

Moving on

Moving on from the Paraguayan Pantanal basically involves going back by the same route you came in. If you wish to fly you should arrange your return journey at the same time as your outward flight or before leaving an area with a reliable phone connection. The ferry to Concepcíon departs on Saturdays from Bahía Negra.

PARQUE NACIONAL RIO NEGRO

Paraguay's most northerly national park, **Río Negro** consists of 160 sq km of pristine Pantanal wetland across the river from neighbouring Bolivia and an hour or so boat ride west of Bahía Negra. This is a paradise for water-birds with huge flocks of herons, storks, ducks and cormorants scattering in the wake of your boat, and the spectacle alone is worth the trip. The riverbanks here are populated with large numbers of caiman and capybara and, if you're lucky, you might catch a glimpse of the elusive marsh deer. Boat trips into the park are arranged in Bahía Negra through *Fundación Hombre y Naturaleza* (see p.779), and these will take you past the *tres fronteras* area where Brazil, Bolivia and Paraguay meet, separated by rivers. The park takes its name from the Río Negro, so-called because of its high tannin and silt load which gives the water the appearance of cold tea. The area where the dark waters of the Río Negro meet the clear-watered Río Paraguay creates a spectacular optical effect. Expensive accommodation is available inside the park at *Fortín Patría* but they will only accept groups and you need to book ahead, Ⓦwww.fortinpatrialodge.com Ⓣ021/446189).

Alternatively, Asunción-based Birdlife International partner *Guyra Paraguay* offer no-frills accommodation at their *Tres Gigantes Lodge* with packages including transport from Asunción or Bahía Negra (Ⓣ021/223567; $80 per person not including transport).

Peru

HIGHLIGHTS ★

PACAYA SAMIRIA NATIONAL RESERVE: remote and stunningly beautiful virgin rainforest

HUARAZ: trek the stunning snow-capped peaks of the Andes

MACHU PICCHU: walk the Inca Trail to these awe-inspiring Inca ruins, surrounded by cloudforest

NAZCA LINES: dazzling geometric figures and animal designs, inexplicably etched into the desert

COLCA CANYON: a look into the depths of this canyon for a breathtaking view of circling condors below

ROUGH COSTS

DAILY BUDGET Basic US$15/ occasional treat US$30

DRINK Cristal Beer US$1–2

FOOD Lunchtime Menu US$1–3

HOTEL/BUDGET HOTEL US$4–9

TRAVEL Tumbes–Lima: 18hr, US$20–40, Lima–Tacna: 20hr, US$20-40

FACT FILE

POPULATION 27 million

AREA 1,285,215 sq km

LANGUAGE Spanish

CURRENCY Nuevo Sol

CAPITAL Lima (population: 8,15,000)

TIME ZONE GMT -5hr

INTERNATIONAL PHONE CODE ☎51

Introduction

Peru is the most varied and exciting of all the South American nations, with a combination of mountains, Inca relics, immense desert coastline and vast tracts of tropical rainforest. Dividing these contrasting environments, the Andes, with its chain of breathtaking peaks, over seven thousand metres high and four hundred kilometres wide in places, ripple the entire length of the nation. So distinct are these regions that it is very difficult to generalize about the country, but one thing for sure is that Peru offers a unique opportunity to experience an incredibly wide range of spectacular scenery, a wealth of heritage, and a vibrant living culture.

In the more rural parts of Peru, native life has changed little in the last four centuries. However, "progress" is gradually transforming much of Peru already the cities wear a distinctly Western aspect, and roads and tracks now connect almost every corner of the Republic with the industrial *urbanizaciones* that dominate the few fertile valleys along the coast. Only the Amazon jungle–nearly two-thirds of Peru's landmass but with a mere fraction of its population – remains beyond modernization's reach, and even here oil and lumber companies, cattle ranchers cocaine producers and settlers are taking an increasing toll.

Always an exciting place to visit, Peru can sometimes appear frantic on the surface; however, the laid-back calmness of the Peruvian temperament continues to underpin life even in the cities.

CHRONOLOGY

c.40,000–15,000 BC The first Peruvians, descendants of nomadic tribes, cross into the Americas from Asia during the last ice age. Many of the tribes make their way south, through Central America, and down along the Andes, into the Amazon, and the Peruvian and Ecuadorian coast, while others find their niches en route.

c.20,000–15,000 BC Human occupation in the Ayacucho Valley.

WHEN TO VISIT

The best time to visit Peru will depend upon which areas of the country you intend to visit, and what activities you plan on doing. **The coast** tends to be mostly dry year-round, but (especially Lima) sits under a blanket of fog from April to November each year, so those looking for some sunshine on the coast will be best advised to visit from December to March.

In the **Andes** the seasons are more clearly marked, with heavy rains from December to March and a relatively dry period from June to September, which, although it can be cold at night, is certainly the best time for trekking and most outward-bound activities. A similar pattern dominates much of the jungle, though rainfall here is heavier and more frequent, and it's hot and humid all year round. In the lowland rainforest areas around Iquitos water levels are higher between December and January, which offers distinct advantages for spotting wildlife and access by canoe to remote creeks.

Those wishing to avoid the crowds will prefer to visit between September and April, as from May to August many popular tourist attractions are packed with tour groups.

12,000 BC Stone blades and knives for hunting develop in the Chillon Valley (just above modern Lima).
5,000 BC First cultivation of seeds and tubers; the coast becomes more arid and occupants use riverbeds for agriculture.
2,600 BC The complex civilisation at the site of Caral begins to develop, lasting for an estimated 500 years. It grows into a major trading and administrative centre housing thousands of people before being inexplicably abandoned, perhaps owing to a lack of water.
1,500 BC–200 AD The formative Era. Agriculture and village life become established, and many isolated regions come into contact with each other mainly because of the widespread dispersal of the Chavín Cult. Remarkable in that the cult spread without the use of military force; the cult was based on a conceptualization of nature spirits and an all-powerful feline creator god, who was responsible for a ubiquity of temples and pyramids.
200–1100 AD The Classical Era. A diverse period, and one marked by intense development in almost every field including the emergence of numerous distinct cultures, both on the coast and in the sierra. The best documented are the Moche and Nazca cultures as well as the Tiahuanuco, all forebears of the better-known Incas.
1200 The Inca Empire begins to emerge; originally a tribe of around forty thousand, the Incas gradually take over each of the separate coastal empires.
1438 Pachacuti becomes ruler of the Inca Empire and begins a great era of expansion. Within three decades, Pachacuti consolidates his power over the entire sierra region from Cajamarca to Titicaca, defeating all main imperial rivals except for the Chimu. At the same time the capital at Cusco Is spectacularly developed, with the evacuation and destruction of all villages within a 10km radius, a massive programme of agricultural terracing, and the construction of unrivalled palaces and temples.
1500 At the end of the fifteenth century the Inca Empire Is thriving, vital as any civilization before or since. Its politico–religious authority Is finely tuned, extracting what it needed from its millions of subjects and giving what Is necessary to maintain the status quo—be it brute force, protection or food. At this point in history, the Inca Empire Is probably the largest in the world even though it had neither horse nor wheel technology. The empire Is over 5500km long, stretching from southern Colombia right down to northern Chile, with Inca highways covering distances of around 30,000km in all.
1527 Civil War breaks out between two heirs to the Inca throne: Atahualpa and Huascar.
1532 Francisco Pizarro (who had stumbled upon and named the Pacific Ocean about two decades earlier) leads a small band of Spaniards, totalling less than 170 men to the Inca city of Cajamarca to meet the leader of what they were rapidly realizing was a mighty empire. Although ridiculously outnumbered, the Spaniards have the advantages of surprise, steel, cannon and, above all, mounted cavalry. The day after their arrival, in what at first appears to be a lunatic endeavour, Pizarro and his men massacre thousands of Inca warriors and capture the Inca ruler Atahualpa. The decisive battle Is over in a matter of hours. It's likely that European-introduced smallpox, which had been ravaging the area for years, plays a factor in Spain's easy victory.
1535–1821 Spanish Rule. Despite the evangelistic zeal of the Spanish, religion changes little for the majority of the native population. In return for the salvation of their souls the native population Is expected to surrender their bodies to the Spanish. The most feared form of service Is the *mita de minas* – forced work in the mines where millions of Indians are literally worked to death. Two major rebellions against Spanish rule are initially successful but eventually repressed, in 1571 and later in 1781.
1535 The foundation of Lima begins with a multilayered process of satellite dependency that continues even today. The fat of the land (originally mostly gold and other treasures) Is sucked in from regions all over Peru, processed in Lima, and sent on from there to Spain. Meanwhile Peruvian society is transformed by the growth of new generations: Creoles, descendants of Spaniards born in Peru, and mestizos, of mixed Spanish and native blood, create a new class structure. In the coastal valleys where populations had been decimated by European diseases, slaves are imported from Africa. There are over fifteen hundred black slaves in Lima alone by 1554.
1821 San Martín declares Peruvian Independence, on July 28.
1845 Ramon Castilla assumes the presidency, and the country begins to exploit one of Peru's major resources, ßguano (birdshit) fertilizer.
1872 During the elections, an attempted military coup Is spontaneously crushed by a civilian mob, and Peru's first civilian president – the laissez-faire capitalist Manuel Pardo – assumes power.
1879 The War of the Pacific with Chile begins. Lasting over four years, the war is basically a battle for the rich nitrate deposits located in Bolivian territory. Victorious on land and at sea, Chilean

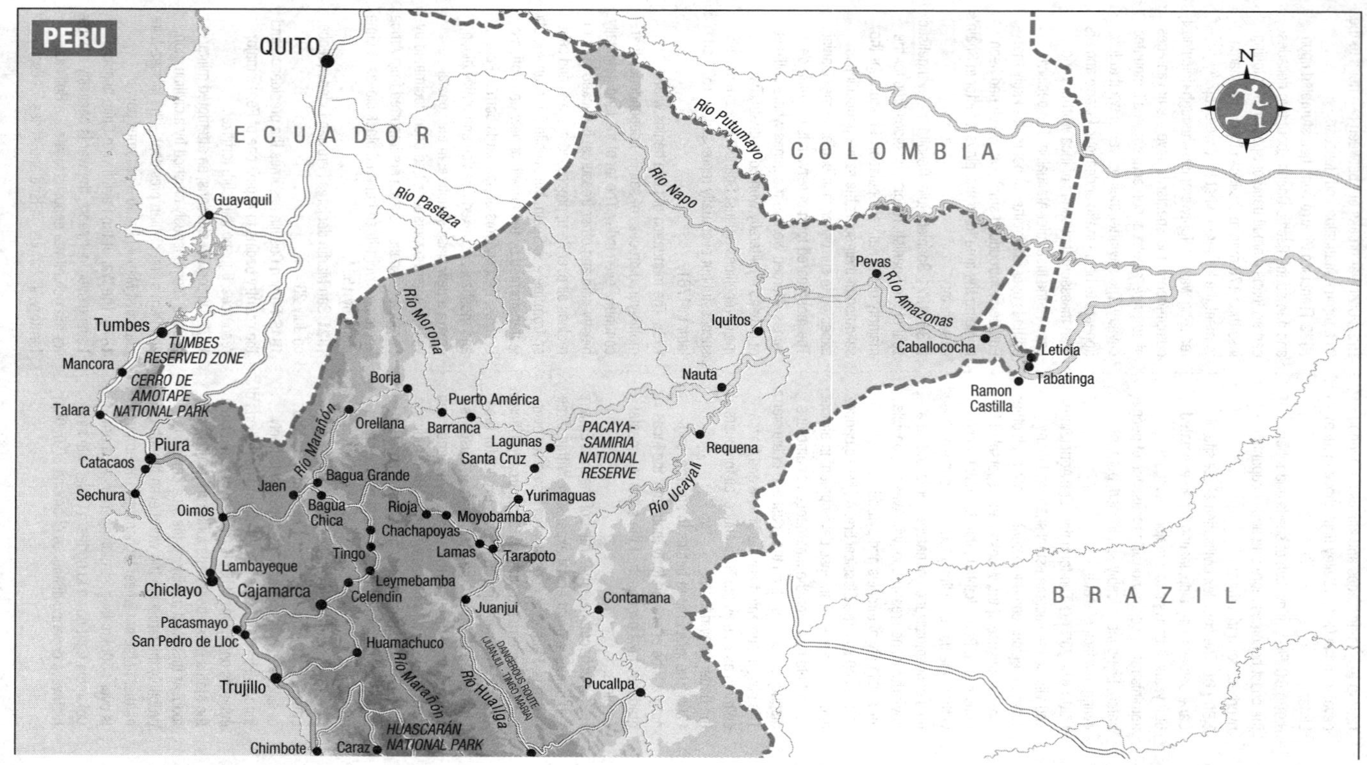
PERU
QUITO
ECUADOR
COLOMBIA
BRAZIL
N
Guayaquil
Río Pastaza
Río Putumayo
Río Napo
Río Morona
Río Amazonas
Río Marañón
Río Ucayali
Río Huallga
Tumbes
TUMBES RESERVED ZONE
Mancora
CERRO DE AMOTAPE NATIONAL PARK
Talara
Piura
Catacaos
Sechura
Oimos
Jaen
Bagua Grande
Bagua Chica
Borja
Orellana
Barranca
Puerto América
Lagunas
Santa Cruz
PACAYA-SAMIRIA NATIONAL RESERVE
Yurimaguas
Rioja
Moyobamba
Chachapoyas
Tingo
Lamas
Tarapoto
Lambayeque
Chiclayo
Cajamarca
Leymebamba
Celendín
Juanjui
Pacasmayo
San Pedro de Lloc
Huamachuco
Trujillo
Chimbote
Caraz
HUASCARÁN NATIONAL PARK
DANGEROUS ROUTE (JUANJUI - TINGO MARIA)
Contamana
Pucallpa
Iquitos
Nauta
Requena
Pevas
Caballococha
Leticia
Tabatinga
Ramon Castilla

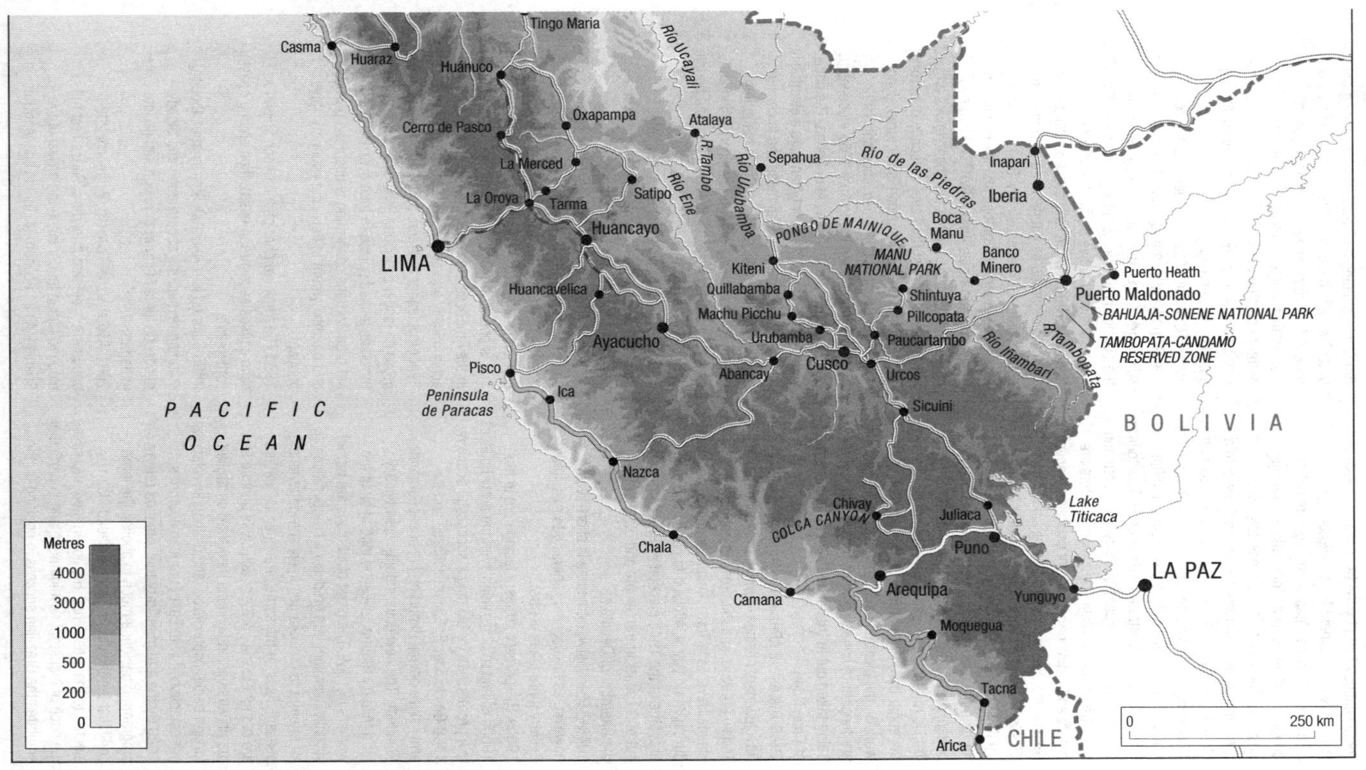
Tingo Maria
Casma
Huaraz
Huánuco
Río Ucayali
Oxapampa
Atalaya
Cerro de Pasco
R. Tambo
Río Urubamba
Sepahua
Río de las Piedras
Inapari
Iberia
La Merced
Satipo
Río Ene
La Oroya
Tarma
Huancayo
PONGO DE MAINIQUE
Boca
Manu
MANU
NATIONAL PARK
Banco
Minero
LIMA
Kiteni
Puerto Heath
Puerto Maldonado
BAHUAJA-SONENE NATIONAL PARK
Huancavelica
Quillabamba
Shintuya
Machu Picchu
Pillcopata
Ayacucho
Urubamba
Paucartambo
Río Iñambari
R. Tambopata
TAMBOPATA-CANDAMO
RESERVED ZONE
Cusco
Pisco
Abancay
Urcos
Peninsula
de Paracas
Ica
PACIFIC
OCEAN
Sicuini
BOLIVIA
Nazca
Chivay
COLCA CANYON
Juliaca
Lake
Titicaca
Metres
4000
3000
1000
500
200
0
Chala
Puno
LA PAZ
Arequipa
Camana
Yunguyo
Moquegua
Tacna
0
250 km
Arica
CHILE

forces occupy Lima by the beginning of 1881 and the Peruvian president flees to Europe.

1883 Peru "lay helpless under the boots of its conquerors" and only a diplomatic rescue seems possible. The Treaty of Anco, possibly Peru's greatest national humiliation, brings the war to a close in October 1883. Peru Is forced to accept the cloistering of an independent Bolivia high up in the Andes, with no land link to the Pacific, and the even harder loss of the nitrate fields to Chile. The country seems in ruins: the guano virtually exhausted and the nitrates lost to Chile, the nation's coffers are empty and a new generation of caudillos prepare to resume the power struggle all over again.

1930s The worldwide Depression of the early 1930s hits Peru particularly badly and demand for its main exports (oil, silver, sugar, cotton and coffee) drastically falls off. Finally, in 1932, the Trujillo middle class lead a violent uprising against the sugar barons and the primitive conditions of work on the plantations. Nearly five thousand lives are thought to have been lost, many of the rebels being taken out in trucks and shot among the ruins of Chan Chan.

1945 The rise of APRA – the American Popular Revolutionary Alliance – which has instigated the Trujillo uprising, and the growing popularity of its leader, Haya de la Torre, keeps the nation occupied during World War II. Allowed to participate for the first time in the 1945 elections, APRA controls 18 out of 29 seats in the Senate and 53 out of 84 in the Chamber of Deputies.

1948–1956 Postwar euphoria Is short-lived, however, as the economy spirals into ruin, and a military junta takes control.

1960s The primary problem facing Peru in the 1960s is land reform, which even the army believes Is a prerequisite for building a successful economy.

1968 On October 3, General Velasco and the army seize power, deporting President Fernando Belaunde. The new government, revolutionary for a military regime, gives the land back to the workers in 1969. The great plantations are turned virtually overnight into producer's co-operatives, in an attempt to create a genuinely self-determining peasant class. At the same time guerrilla leaders are brought to trial, political activity Is banned in the universities, indigenous banks are controlled, foreign banks nationalized, and diplomatic relations are established with East European countries.

1980 By the end of military rule, the land reform programme has done much to abolish the large capitalist landholding system. Belaúnde Is re-elected to the presidency. His government increases the pace of industrial development, and in particular emulates the Brazilian success in opening up the Amazon – building new roads and exploiting the untold wealth in oil, minerals, timber and agriculture. But inflation continues as an apparently insuperable problem, and Belaúnde fares little better in coming to terms with either the parliamentary Marxists of the United Left or the escalating guerrilla movement.

1980–1992 The Maoist Sendero Luminoso (the Shining Path), founded in 1970 and led by **Abimael Guzman**, persistently discounts the possibility of change through the ballot box. Sendero Is very active during the late 1980s and early 1990s, when they carry out attacks on anything regarded as interference with the self-determination of the peasantry. By 1985, new urban-based terrorist groups like the Movimiento Revolucionario Tupac Amaru (**MRTA**) begin to make their presence felt in the shantytowns around Lima. The country suffers over a decade of terrorist attacks, until Abimael Guzman Is captured along with other Sendero Luminoso leaders in 1992.

1985 Belaúnde loses in the April 1985 elections to an APRA government led by Alan Garcia. The once young and popular President Alan Garcia eventually gets himself into a financial mess and Is chased by the Peruvian judiciary from Colombia to Peru, having been accused of high-level corruption and stealing possibly millions of dollars from the people of Peru.

1990 Elections prove to be a turning point for Peru, the real surprise coming in the guise of a young college professor of Japanese descent, Alberto Fujimori, who just barely beats renowned author Mario Vargas Llosa. Fujimori manages to turn the nation around and gains international confidence in Peru, reflected in a stock exchange that is one of the fastest growing and most active in the Americas. However, the real turning point, economically and politically, Is the capture of Sendero's leader Guzman. Soon, the international press no longer describes Peru as a country where terrorists looked poised to take over. Despite many aid organizations confirming widespread poverty and unemployment in Peru, the economy stays buoyant.

1998 The freak weather phenomenon known as El Niño causes widespread destruction among coastal settlements.

2000 Fujimori is re-elected. Shortly after, though, stunning revelations of corruption and bloody misdeeds force Fujimori to resign and go into exile in Japan.

2001 **Alejandro Toledo**, Fujimori's 2000 opponent, Is elected president: Peru's first full-blooded Indian leader since the arrival of the Spanish. As an economist, Toledo concentrates on strengthening Peru's position in the international stock exchange, and makes strategic trade alliances.

2006 Back from exile, Alan García representing APRA is stunningly re-elected as president. The only other two contenders being the violently nationalist Ollanta Humala and the conservative Lourdes Flores; García Is left representing a middle-ground, socialist line, and Is the favoured option despite the mistakes made during his first presidency.

Basics

ARRIVAL

Peru has land borders with Chile, Ecuador, Bolivia, Brazil and Colombia. While the borders with Chile, Ecuador and Bolivia are easily negotiated, the borders with Brazil and Colombia are deep in the jungle and not easily reached. Lima is a major transport hub with international flights from the USA and Europe; there are also good connections from Lima to other South American countries. International flights within South America tend to be expensive, while national flights within Peru average around $60 to any destination. Save money by crossing borders by land and only flying within Peru.

> There is a $32 departure tax payable at Lima airport when flying to an international destination. For national flights the fee from Lima is $7, and similar fees apply from regional airports in Peru. Only cash payments are accepted.

Major operators include Lan Ⓦwww.lan.com and Taca Ⓦwww.taca.com, also American Airlines from the US, Iberia from Europe via Madrid, and KLM from Europe via Amsterdam. Local airlines struggle to compete with Lan. Currently there is only Star Peru, Ⓦwww.starperu.com and LC Busre, Ⓦwww.lcbusre.com. Aerocondor, Tans, and Wayra Peru have all gone out of business.

VISAS

In August 2008 a new Immigration law was passed concerning foreign tourists in Peru. EU, US, Canadian, Australian and New Zealand citizens can now all stay in Peru as tourists for up to 183 days without a visa. For

LAND AND SEA ROUTES TO PERU

From Chile

The Arica-Tacna border in the far south of Peru causes few problems for travellers. Taxi colectivos run regularly across the border and the driver will help with border formalities for a small tip. See p.864.

From Ecuador

There are three border crossings open between Ecuador and Peru. The most commonly used is the Tumbes-Machala crossing on the coast; the other two options are further inland where roads are not so good and personal safety is a consideration. Direct buses run from major destinations in each country, stopping at the Peruvian and Ecuadorian Immigration offices en route. See p.889 for more information.

From Bolivia

The southern cities of Puno, Cusco and Arequipa are easily reached overland from Bolivia. There are two crossings:Yungayo from Copacabana on Lake Titicaca, and Desaguadero from La Paz. Regular buses run direct to Puno (and some to Cusco) from both destinations. The Bolivian airline Aerosur began direct flights from La Paz to Cusco in April 2008.

other nationalities, check with the local Peruvian Embassy. If you are planning to stay a long time in Peru, make sure to ask for the maximum time allowance when entering the country, as it is no longer possible to extend tourist visas. However, the situation does change periodically, so always check with the local Peruvian Embassy some weeks before departure.

All nationalities need a **tourist or embarkation card** (*tarjeta de embarque*) to enter Peru, which is issued at the frontier or on the plane before landing in Lima. In theory you have to show an outbound ticket (by air or bus) before you'll be given a card, but this isn't always checked. For your own safety and freedom of movement, keep a copy of the tourist card and your passport on you at all times – particularly when travelling away from the main towns. It is very important that you keep your original tourist card safe since you will be asked to return it to immigration officials when leaving the country. Fines are applicable if you lose your card.

GETTING AROUND

With the distances in Peru being so vast, many Peruvians and travellers are increasingly **flying** to their destinations, as all Peruvian cities are within a two-hour flight from Lima. Most budget travellers get around the country by bus, as these go just about everywhere and are extremely good value. On some routes there is also a rail service, which makes a change from the monotony of long bus rides, despite being considerably slower and more expensive than the equivalent bus journey.

By bus

Peru's privately operated buses offer remarkably low fares. Long-distance bus service costs from around US$1.50 per hour on the coastal highway, and is even cheaper elsewhere. The condition of the buses ranges from the efficient and relatively luxurious Cruz del Sur and Ormeño fleets to the scruffy old ex-US schoolbuses used on local runs throughout the country. If you don't want to miss the scenery, you can hop relatively easily between the smaller towns, which usually works out to be not much more expensive. Cruz del Sur (Ⓦwww.cruzdelsur.com.pe) and Ormeño (Ⓦwww.grupo-ormeno.com.pe) both have good websites with timetables and ticket purchase option (credit cards accepted).

At least one bus depot or stop can be found in the centre of any town. Peru is investing in a series of terminal *terrestres* (bus stations), or *terrapuertos*, centralizing the departure and arrival of the manifold operators, but it's always a good idea to doublecheck where the bus is leaving from, since in some cities, bus offices are in different locations from the bus terminal. For intercity rides, it's best to buy tickets in advance direct from the bus company offices; for local trips, you can buy tickets on the bus itself. On long-distance trips, try to avoid getting seats right over the jarring wheels, especially if the bus is tackling mountain or jungle roads.

By taxi, mototaxi and colectivo

Taxis can be found anywhere at any time in almost every town. Any car can become a taxi simply by sticking a taxi sign up in the front window; a lot of people, especially in Lima, take advantage of this to supplement their income. However in recent years this has led to an increase in crime, particularly kidnappings, and serious efforts have been made to regulate taxi firms and drivers. Wherever possible call a radio taxi from a recommended company; you can get phone numbers for local companies from information offices, hotels, agencies and embassies.

A radio taxi will cost an extra $0.30. Whenever you get into a taxi, always fix the price in advance since few of them have meters, even the really professional firms. Relatively short journeys in Lima generally cost around US$2, but it's cheaper elsewhere. Minicabs and airport taxis tend to cost more. Taxi drivers in Peru do not expect tips.

In many rural towns, you'll find small cars and motorcycle rickshaws – known variously as mototaxis or motokars – all competing for customers. The latter are always cheaper if slightly more dangerous and not that comfortable, especially if there are more than two of you or if you've got a lot of luggage. Expect to pay less than 5 soles for a ride within a town.

Colectivos (shared taxis) are a very useful way of getting around that's peculiar to Peru. They connect all the coastal towns, and many of the larger centres in the mountains, and tend to be faster than the bus, though often charge twice as much. Most *colectivo* cars manage to squeeze in about six people plus the driver and can be found in the centre of a town or at major stopping-places along the main roads. *Colectivo* minibuses, also known as *combis*, can squeeze in twice as many people, or often more. They cost on average 10 soles per person, per hour travelled.

In the cities, particularly in Lima, *colectivos* (especially *combis*) have an appalling reputation for safety. They frequently crash, turn over and knock down pedestrians. Equally dangerous is the fact that the driver is in such a hurry that he does not always wait for you to get in.

By train

Peru's spectacular train journeys are in themselves a major attraction, and you should aim to take at least one long-distance train during your trip. Peru Rail runs passenger services inland from Puno on Lake Titicaca north to Cusco, from where another line heads down the magnificent Urubamba Valley as far as Machu Picchu (see p.836). The trains move slowly, and are often much bumpier than buses. However, trains generally allow ample time to observe what's going on outside, and are quite comfortable. In recent years Peru Rail has completely segregated services into Local trains which are only available to locals with ID, and tourist trains which are priced in US dollars, making the train a much more expensive option than the bus. The Cusco–Puno line costs $143 at time of writing, and a bus costs $10. Wherever possible tickets should be bought in advance by at least a day, and about a week on the Cusco–Machu Picchu route.

By air

You can reach some places in the jungle more easily by plane, as land and river routes will take much longer and eventually cost as much as a plane ticket, although offer a much more spectacular journey. Peru is so vast that the odd flight can save a lot of time. Tickets can be bought from travel agents or airline offices in all major towns. The most popular routes, such as Lima–Cusco, cost upwards of US$60 and usually need to be booked at least a few days in advance (more during the run-up to and including major fiestas).

Flights are often cancelled or delayed, and sometimes they leave earlier than scheduled – especially in the jungle where the weather can be a problem, so it is important to reconfirm your flight 48 hours before departure. If a passenger hasn't shown up twenty minutes before the flight, the company can give the seat to someone on the waiting list.

All the Peruvian domestic airlines offering flight passes went bust in the late 1990s, and airline companies in Peru are still in a state of flux. New companies arrive regularly and either cannot compete with the dominating Chilean company LAN, or are shut down for poor safety standards and poorly maintained aircraft. Check with your travel agent before travelling.

By car

Cars can be very handy for reaching remote destinations or sites, though not for exploring Lima.

If you bring a car into Peru that is not registered there, you will need to show (and keep with you at all times) a *libreta de pago por la aduana* (proof of customs payment), normally provided by the relevant automobile association of the country you are coming from. Spare parts, particularly tyres, will have to be carried as will a tent, emergency water and food. The chance of theft is quite high – the vehicle, your baggage and accessories are all vulnerable when parked.

Renting a car costs much the same as in Europe and North America. The major rental firms all have offices in Lima, but outside the capital you'll generally find only local companies are represented. You may find it more convenient to reserve a car in advance from your own country – expect to pay around US$35 per day, or US$200 per week, for the smallest car. In the jungle it's usually possible to hire motorbikes or mopeds by the hour or by the day; this is a good way of getting to know a town or to be able to shoot off into the jungle for a day.

International driving licences are generally valid for thirty days in Peru, after which a permit is required from the Touring y Automóvil Club del Peru, Trinidad Morán 698, Lince, Lima (Ⓣ01/211-9977, Ⓦwww.touringperu.com.pe).

What few traffic signals there are are either completely ignored or obeyed at the drivers' "discretion". The pace is fast and roads everywhere are in bad shape: only the Panamerican Highway, running down the coast, and a few short stretches inland, are paved.

By boat

There are no coastal boat services in Peru, but in many areas – on Lake Titicaca and especially in the jungle regions – water is the obvious means of getting around. From Puno, on Lake Titicaca, there are currently no regular services to Bolivia, but there are plenty of smaller boats that will take visitors out to the various islands in the lake for around US$10 per person.

In the jungle areas motorized canoes come in two basic forms: those with a large outboard motor and those with a Briggs and Stratton *peque-peque* engine. The outboard is faster and more manoeuvrable, but it costs a lot more to run. Though hitching is possible, it is more practical to hire a canoe along with its guide or driver for a few days. This means searching around in the port and negotiating, but you can often get a *peque-peque* canoe from around US$40–50 per day, which will invariably work out cheaper than taking an organized tour, as well as giving you the choice of guide and companions. Obviously, the more people you can get together, the cheaper it will be per person.

ACCOMMODATION

Peru has the typical range of Latin American accommodation, from top-class international hotels to tiny rooms at the back of someone's house for a couple of dollars a night. Virtually all upmarket accommodation will call itself a hotel or, in the countryside regions, a posada. In the jungle, tambo lodges can be anything from quite luxurious to an open-sided, palm-thatched hut with space for slinging a hammock. Technically, something that calls itself a pension or *residencial* ought to specialize in longer-term accommodation, and while they may well offer discounts for stays of a week or more, they are just as geared up for short stays.

Hotels

The cheaper hotels are generally old – sometimes beautifully so, converted from colonial mansions with rooms grouped around a courtyard – and tend to be within a few blocks of a town's central plaza, general market, or bus or train station. At the low end of the scale, which can be fairly basic with shared rooms and a communal bathroom, you can usually find a bed for between US$5 and US$10, and occasionally even less. For a few dollars more you can find a good, clean single or double room with private bath in a mid-range hotel, generally for somewhere between US$15 and US$45. A little haggling is often worth a try, and if you find one room too pricey, another, perhaps identical, can often be found for less: the phrase "*Tiene un cuarto más barato?*" ("Do you have a cheaper room?") is useful.

Note that all three-star and above hotels in Peru charge nineteen percent tax and often ten percent service on top of this, although foreigners are exempt from paying tax; if you let the hotel take a copy of your passport when you check in, the tax will not be added to your bill.

One point of caution – it's not advisable to pay tour or travel agents in one city for accommodation required in the next town. By all means ask agents to make reservations but do not ask them to send payments; it is always simpler and safer to do that yourself.

Hostels and camping

There are currently 19 HI-affiliated youth hostels spread throughout Peru (Ⓦ www.hihostels.com/dba/country-PE.en.htm). This is not the standardized institution found in Europe, but is relatively cheap and reliable; expect to pay US$5–12 for a bed, perhaps slightly more in Lima. All hostels are theoretically open 24 hours a day and most have cheap cafeterias attached. There are also many non-HI-affiliated hostels throughout the country, specifically in the most popular tourist areas of Lima, Cusco, Arequipa and Mancora, which cater specifically for backpackers and offer beds in huge mixed dorms and an extensive range of other services, such as bar/restaurants, internet access, storage facilities, TV or DVD room and use of a shared kitchen. While these are great for meeting people and if you intend to use the services, they are often not the cheapest option if you are travelling with other people as dorm beds cost from $10-$15, the same price as a room for two at a budget hotel.

Camping is possible all over Peru, and it's rarely difficult to find space for a tent in areas far away from cities. In towns and cities you may find yourself being charged the same amount to put up a tent in the grounds of a hostel as you would be charged for a room. Organized campsites are gradually being established on the outskirts of popular tourist destinations; however, these are still few and far between. Outside urban areas, however, it is a different story; some of the country's most fantastic places are well off the beaten track and with a tent – or a hammock – it's possible to go all over without worrying if you'll make it to a hostel. If you are setting up camp anywhere near a village or settlement however small, always ask permission or advice from the nearest farm or house first. Apart from a few restricted areas, Peru's enormous sandy coastline is open territory, the real problem not being so much where to camp as how to get there; some of the most stunning areas are very remote. The same can be said of both the mountains and the jungle – camp anywhere, but ask first, if you can find anyone to ask.

FOOD AND DRINK

Depending on the very different ingredients available locally, food is essentially a *mestizo* creation, combining indigenous Indian cooking with four hundred years of European – mostly Spanish – influence. Along the coast, not surprisingly, fish is the speciality. *Ceviche* is the classic Peruvian seafood dish and has been eaten by locals for over two thousand years. It consists of fish, shrimp, scallops or squid, or a mixture of all four, marinated in lime juice and chilli peppers, then served "raw" with corn, sweet potato and onions. *Ceviche de lenguado* (soul fish) and *ceviche de corvina* (sea bass) are among the most common, but there are plenty of other fish and a wide range of seafoods served on most menus.

Mountain food is more basic – a staple of potatoes and rice with the meat stretched as far as it will go. One speciality is the *Pachamanca,* a roast prepared mainly in the mountains but also on the coast by digging a large hole, filling it with stones and lighting a fire over them, then using the hot stones to cook a wide variety of tasty meats and vegetables.

In the jungle, bananas and plantains figure highly, along with *yuca* (a manioc rather like a yam), rice and plenty of fish. There is meat as well, mostly chicken supplemented occasionally by game – deer, wild pig or even monkey. Beware of eating turtle or other endangered species in the jungle, that all too often still find their way onto tourist menus.

Guinea pig (*cuy*) is the traditional dish most associated with Peru, and indeed, you can find it in many parts of the country, and especially in the mountain regions, where it is likely to be roasted in an oven and served with chips. In the past twenty years, however, the wave of North American interests in the country has made fast food very commonplace, and hamburgers, as well as the ubiquitous pizza, have been adopted with enthusiasm and are now more readily available than the traditional guinea pig.

Where to eat

All larger towns in Peru have a fair choice of restaurants, most of which offer a varied menu. Among them there's usually a few *chifa* (Chinese) places, and nowadays a fair number of vegetarian restaurants too. Often places will offer *almuerzo*, or set lunch, from morning through to lunchtime and sometimes *cena* in the evening. Ranging in price from US$1 to US$3, these most commonly consist of three courses: soup, a main dish and a hot drink or small dessert (often rice pudding) to follow.

Drinks

Beers, wines and spirits are served in almost every bar, café, restaurant or corner shop at any time of day. There is a deposit on taking glass beer and soda bottles out and you will often see people hanging out in the corner shop while they finish their drink, to return the bottle immediately and avoid paying the deposit. Plastic soda bottles are causing serious litter problems throughout the country, so try to use the refillable glass bottles when possible.

Most Peruvian beer – except for *cerveza malta* (black malt beer) – is bottled lager almost exclusively brewed to five percent, and extremely good. In Lima the two main beers are *Cristal* and *Pilsen*. You can get three 620ml bottles for just over US$3 in local places, or a 330ml bottle in a tourist restaurant for an average of US$2. *Cuzqueña* (from Cusco) is one of the best and by far the most popular at the moment, but not universally available; you won't find it on the coast in Trujillo, for example, where they drink *Trujillana*, nor are you likely to encounter it in every bar in Arequipa where, not surprisingly, they prefer to drink *Arequipeña* beer. Fruit juices (*jugos*), most commonly papaya or orange, are prepared fresh in most places, and you can get coffee and a wide variety of herb and leaf teas almost anywhere. Surprisingly, for a good coffee-growing country, the coffee served in cafés and restaurants leaves much to be desired, commonly prepared from either *café pasado* (previously percolated coffee mixed with hot water to serve) or simple powdered Nescafé.

Peru has been producing wine for over four hundred years, but it tends to be very sweet and almost like sherry. Among the better ones are *Vista Alegre* (*tipo familiar*) and *Tacama Gran Vino Blanco Reserva Especial*, both produced in the Ica area and ranging from US$5 to US$20 per bottle.

As for spirits, Peru's main claim to fame is Pisco. This is a white grape brandy with a unique, powerful and very palatable flavour – the closest equivalent elsewhere is probably tequila. The jungle regions produce *cashassa*, a sugarcane rum also called *aguardiente*, which has a distinctive taste and is occasionally mixed with different herbs, some medicinal. While it goes down easily, it's incredibly strong stuff and leaves you with a very sore head the next morning.

In the more touristy areas, many bars and restaurants will offer happy hours and sometimes free drinks; be aware that these are made from the cheapest available barely refined alcohol.

CULTURE AND ETIQUETTE

Due to the huge variety of geological conditions found within Peruvian territory, culture and traditions vary greatly between regions. On the whole, coastal people tend to be more outgoing and vivacious, while the mountain people of Quechua descent are more reserved and humble. The jungle is still home to many indigenous groups who keep their ancestral traditions and way of life.

One of the most common things travellers do that unwittingly offends local people is to take their picture without asking. In many highland and jungle regions, people use their traditional dress and can often look quite stunning as they go about their daily business. Think twice before taking photographs of these people. At main tourist sites people work as "models" and stand around offering to pose for pictures for $0.30.

Particularly in the highlands there is a strong culture of exchange, meaning that if you receive something, you are expected to give in return. This can be as simple as giving someone coca leaves in exchange for directions on a trail, a simple "thank you" may leave people feeling hard done by. Similarly, if you give someone a gift, you will most likely be given one in return, even if it is boiled potatoes.

Tipping is another issue which can cause confussion in Peru. There is no culture of tipping in Peru and local people will usually only "tip" when the person offering a service is not receiving any payment, for example, someone who helps you with your bags at the airport; they will not tip on top of something they are paying for such as a meal in a restaurant or a night in a hotel. That said, people have become accustomed to tourists leaving tips, so in a restaurant or hotel aimed at tourists, a tip of 10-15 percent is expected. Likewise, some unscrupulous travel agencies pay their guides very low wages, expecting them to receive generous tips. As always tipping is optional and a personal decision.

SPORTS AND OUTDOOR ACTIVITIES

Few of the world's countries can offer anything remotely as varied, rugged, colourful and stunningly beautiful as

Peru when it comes to exploring the wilderness.

Hiking

Hiking – whether in the desert, mountains or jungle – can be an enormously rewarding experience, but you should go properly equipped and bear in mind a few of the potential hazards. Never stray too far without food and water, something warm and something waterproof to wear. The weather is renowned for its dramatic changeability, especially in the mountains, where there is always the additional danger of *soroche*, or altitude sickness (see p.820).

In the mountains it's often a good idea to hire a pack animal to carry your gear. Mules can be hired from upwards of US$8 per day, and they normally come with an *arriero*, a muleteer who knows the route but is not a guide. It is also possible to hire mules or horses for riding but this costs a little more. With an *arriero* or guide and beast of burden it's quite simple to reach even the most remote valleys, ruins and mountain passes, travelling in much the same way as Pizarro and his men over four hundred years ago.

Mountain biking

In Peru, cycling is a major national sport, as well as one of the most ubiquitous forms of transport available to all classes in towns and rural areas virtually everywhere. Consequently, there are bike shops and bicycle repairs workshops in all major cities and larger towns. Perhaps more importantly, a number of tour companies offer guided cycling tours which can be an excellent way to see the best of Peru. Huaraz and Cusco are both popular destinations for bikers.

For mountain-biking tours from Cusco, try Ecotrek Peru (Ⓦwww.ecotrekperu.com) and Amazonas Explorer (Ⓦwww.amazonas-explorer.com).

White-water rafting and kayaking

Again, Peru is hard to beat for these adventurous activities. The rivers around Cusco and the Colca canyon, as well as Huaraz and, nearer to Lima, at Lunahuana can be exciting and demanding, though there are also sections ideal for beginners.

Cusco is one of the top white-water rafting and kayaking centres in South America, with easy access to a whole range of river grades, from 2, 3, 4 and 5 on the Río Urubamba (shifting up grades in the rainy season) to the most dangerous white-water on the Río Apurimac, only safe for rafting during the dry season. On the Vilcanota, some 90km south of Cusco, at Chukikahuana there's a 5km section of river which offers exhilarating rafting year round, and between December and April offers a constant level 5 (this is the highest level for commercial rafting, so be extremely careful about which company you go with; unscrupulous companies will take passengers when water levels are too high to be safe; see p.822 for recommended operators). One of the most amazing trips from Cusco goes right down into the Amazon Basin on the Tambopata River.

COMMUNICATIONS

Communictions in Peru have improved dramatically with the widespread availability of Internet cafés. The phone service, too, has improved in the last seven years since being taken over by the Spanish company Telefónica. Postal services are slow but quite acceptable for normal letters and postcards.

You can have mail sent to you *poste restante*, care of any main post office (Correo Central) and, on the whole, the system tends to work quite smoothly. Have letters addressed: full name (last name in capitals), Poste Restante, Lista de Correos, Correo Central, city or

PERU ON THE NET

Peru is surprisingly switched on to electronic communications, with Internet cafés in all towns of any size and in many small, out-of-the-way places. Some of the best websites devoted to Peru are the excellent

www.andeantravelweb.com/peru This site links to a whole range of travel-related features and listings;

www.perulinks.com, which has English pages on a range of Peruvian topics like art, entertainment, and travel.

www.virtualperu.net Peruvian geography, history and people with satellite photos, maps and other information can be found here. The I-Peru website listed overleaf is also very helpful.

town, Peru. To pick up mail, you'll need your passport. The South American Explorers' Club (see box, p.797) offers members a postal address service.

With a little patience you can make international calls from just about any town in the country. All Peruvian towns have a Telefónica del Peru or Locutorio Telefónico office, which offers an operator service; give the receptionist your destination number and they will allocate you to a numbered phone booth when your call is put through (you pay afterwards); or, just dial direct from the booth. These offices also take phones cards (see below). In Lima, the central Telefónica del Peru office (see "Listings", p.814) is often crowded, so a better option is to phone from your hotel or from the street telephone kiosks.

All phone kiosks are operated by coins or *tarjetas telefónicas* – phone cards – which are available in a variety of denominations, and *nuevo sol* coins. You can buy cards at *farmacias* (corner shops) or on the street from cigarette stalls in the centres of most towns and cities. 147 cards are good for local and national calls, while Hola Peru offers good rates for international calls; both are available in values ranging from 3 to 50 soles.

If you need to contact the international operator, dial ⓣ108. Collect calls are known either simply as *collect* or *al cobro revertido* and are fairly straightforward. Calls are cheaper at night. Most shops, restaurants or corner shops in Peru have a phone available for public use, which you can use for calls within Peru only.

Peru has good Internet connections, with cybercafés and Internet cabins in the most unlikely of small towns. Lima and Cusco have abundant Internet facilities, closely followed by Arequipa, Huaraz, Puno, Iquitos and Trujillo; beyond that it gets a little patchy, but the odd public access office or café does exist and many hotels now offer access too. The general rate is 50¢ an hour, though thirty- and fifteen-minute options are often available.

CRIME AND SAFETY

While pickpockets are remarkably ingenious in Peru, this country no longer deserves such a poor reputation when compared with Venezuela, Colombia and even Ecuador or Brazil. As far as violent attacks go, you're probably safer in Peru than in New York, Sydney or London; nevertheless muggings do happen in certain parts of Lima (such as in the Centro main shopping areas and also in the parks of Miraflores), Cusco, Arequipa and, to a lesser extent, Trujillo. And as for terrorism – as the South American Explorers' Club once described it – "the visitor, when considering his safety, would be better off concentrating on how to avoid being run over in the crazed Lima traffic".

The dangers of robberies cannot be over emphasized, though the situation does seem to have improved since the dark days of the late 1980s. Although you don't need to be in a permanent state of paranoia and constant watchfulness in busy public situations, common sense and general alertness are still recommended.

A few simple precautions, however, can make life a lot easier. The most important is to keep your ticket, passport (and tourist card), money and traveller's cheques on your person at all times (under your pillow while sleeping and on your person when washing in communal hotel bathrooms). Money belts or leg pouches are a good idea for traveller's cheques and tickets, or a holder for your passport and money can be hung either under a shirt, or from a belt under trousers or skirts.

Terrorism is much less of a problem in Peru these days than it was in the 1980s and 1990s. You can get up-to-date information on the situation in each region from the South American Explorers' Club (see box opposite), Peruvian embassies abroad or your embassy in Lima.

Most of your contact with the police will, with any luck, be at frontiers and *controls*. Depending on your personal appearance and the prevailing political climate the police at these posts (*Guardia Nacional* and *Aduanas*) may want to search your luggage. This happens rarely, but when it does the search can be very thorough. Occasionally, you may have to get off buses and register documents at the police *controls* that regulate the traffic of goods and people from one *departamento* of Peru to another. Always stop, and be scrupulously polite – even if it seems that they're trying to make things difficult for you.

In general the police rarely bother travellers but there are certain sore points. The possession of (let alone trafficking in) either soft or hard drugs (basically grass or cocaine) is considered an extremely serious offence in Peru – usually leading to at least a ten-year jail sentence. There are many foreigners languishing in Peruvian jails after being charged with possession, some of whom have been waiting two years for a trial – there is no bail for serious charges.

If you find yourself in a tight spot, don't make a statement before seeing someone from your embassy, and don't say anything without the services of a reliable translator. It's not unusual to be given the opportunity to pay a bribe to the police (or any other official for that matter), even if you've done nothing wrong.

MEDICAL CARE AND EMERGENCIES

If you're unlucky enough to have anything stolen, your first port of call should be the tourist police (*policia de turismo*), from whom you should get a written report. Bear in mind that the police in popular tourist spots, such as Cusco, have become much stricter about investigating reported thefts, after a spate of false claims by dishonest tourists. This means that genuine victims may be grilled more severely than expected, and the police may even come and search your hotel room for the "stolen" items. For emergency services, call ⓣ105.

In most cities there are private clinics (*clínica*) with better medical facilities than general hospitals, and if given the choice in a medical emergency, opt for a *clínica*. The EsSalud national hospitals have undergone drastic improvements in the last few years, and although they are supposed to be for Peruvians who pay into an insurance scheme with them, they can take independent patients (who pay a higher price). Even in relatively small villages there is a *posta médica* where you can get basic medical attention and help arriving at a larger medical facility. The South American Explorers' Clubs in Lima and Cusco as well as I-Peru offices can provide you with a list of recommended doctors and clinics.

EXPLORERS' CLUB

The nonprofit **South American Explorers' Club** is your best bet for getting relevant, up-to-date information both before you leave home and when you arrive in Lima (membership starts at US$60 a year). It has clubhouses in Lima (see p.809) and Cusco (Ⓣ084/245-484), and a main office in the US at 126 Indian Creek Rd, Ithaca, NY 14850 (Ⓣ607/277-0488, Ⓦwww.saexplorers.org). The Club offers a variety of **maps** as well as brochures.

INFORMATION AND MAPS

The government I-Peru offices present in every large city are very useful for information and advice, as well as free local maps and leaflets (Ⓦwww.peru.info/e_ftoiperueng.asp). Look out for English-language publications such as newspapers and magazines, which you can often pick up for free from tourist establishments. Among them, the *Peru Guide* booklet, available free from hotels and travel agencies in most major cities, has a few good city maps and gives recommendations for hotels and restaurants plus other useful information for Lima, Arequipa, Cusco, Huaraz, Chiclayo, Ica/Nazca/Paracas and Iquitos.

MONEY AND BANKS

Although more under control since the 1980s, devaluation is a regular occurrence, leading to two major currency switches in the past couple of decades. The current Peruvian currency, the nuevo sol, whose symbol is S/, is still simply called a "Sol" on the streets and has so far remained relatively steady against the US dollar.

Despite being closely tied to the US dollar, the value of the nuevo sol still varies from day to day, so prices throughout this section are quoted in US dollars, against which costs have so far remained relatively stable.

Banks and ATMs are easily found in all major cities. The Global Net network accepts all major credit cards and ATMs are even present in some small towns; see their website for their useful ATM locator (Ⓦwww.globalnet.com.pe). Another thing to remember when using any ATM is that contrary to in Europe, the money is dispensed before the card is returned. Make sure you remember to wait to get your card back before stashing away your cash and leaving the machine.

OPENING HOURS AND HOLIDAYS

Most services in Peru open Monday to Saturday 9am to 6pm, although some are open until around 1pm and then close for a long lunch and reopen 4 to 8pm. Most shops are open from around 9am to 9pm. Many are open on Sunday as well, if for more limited hours. Peru's more important ancient sites and ruins usually have opening hours that coincide with daylight – from around 7am until 5pm or 6pm daily.

Peruvians love any excuse for a celebration and the country enjoys a huge number of religious ceremonies,

PUBLIC HOLIDAYS

January 1 New Year's Day.
March/April Easter Semana Santa (Holy Week). Superb processions all over Peru (the best are in Cusco and Ayacucho). Maundy Thursday and Good Friday are national holidays, Easter Monday is not.
May 1 Labour Day
July 28–29 National Independence Day. Public holiday with military and school processions.
October 8 Battle of Angamos
November 1-2 Day of the Dead, and All Souls' Day
December 25 Christmas Day.

festivals and local events. Carnival time (generally late Feb) is especially lively almost everywhere in the country, with fiestas held every Sunday – a wholesale licence to throw water at everyone and generally go crazy. It's worth noting that most hotel prices go up significantly at fiesta times and bus and air transport should be booked well in advance.

FESTIVALS

Peru is a country rich with culture and traditions, and on any given day there is town or village celebrating their anniversary or similar occasion. Most festivals consist of processions, usually with live music and dancing, and a proud usage of traditional dress. They can be quite spectacular events and small towns will become completely booked up, transport services stop running or prices double, and often most people will stop work and celebrate (usually by drinking) for a few days either side of the festival. Below are some of the major festivals celebrated throughout the country:

February Carnival. Wildly celebrated immediately prior to Lent, throughout the whole country.

February 2 Virgen de la Candelaria. Celebrated in the most spectacular way in Puno (known as the Folklore Capital of the country) with a week of colourful processions and dancing.

May Qoyllor Riti. One of the most breathtaking festivals in Peru, thousands of people make the overnight pilgrimage up to a shrine located on a glacier just outside of Cusco - Apu Ausangate.

June 24 Inti Raymi is Cusco's main Inca festival.

July 16 Virgen del Carmen. Celebrated in style in the town of Paucartambo, on the road between Cusco and Manu Biosphere Reserve. Dancers come from surrounding villages in traditional dress for the celebration which lasts several days. There is a smaller celebration in the Sacred Valley town of Pisac.

August 13–19 Arequipa Week. Processions, firework displays, plenty of folklore dancing and craft markets.

August 30 Santa Rosa de Lima. The city of Lima stops for the day to worship their patron saint – Santa Rosa.

September end of the month Spring Festival. Trujillo festival involving dancing, especially the local Marinera dance.

October 18–28 Lord of Miracles. Festival featuring large and solemn processions (the main ones take place on October 18, 19 and 28).

Lima

Once one of the most beautiful cities in Spanish America, Peru's sprawling capital Lima is now home to more than eight million people, over half of whom live in relative poverty without decent water, sewerage or electricity. This is not to say you can't enjoy the place, but it's important to be aware of the realities faced by the majority of the city's inhabitants.

Francisco Pizarro founded **Spanish Lima**, "City of the Kings", in 1535, only two years after the invasion. By the 1550s, the town had grown up around a large plaza with wide streets leading through a fine collection of mansions, all elegantly adorned by wooden terraces and well-stocked shops run by wealthy merchants. Since the very beginning, Spanish Lima has always looked out, away from the Andes, towards the Pacific, as though seeking contact with the world beyond.

Lima rapidly developed into the capital of a Spanish viceroyalty including Ecuador, Bolivia and Chile. By 1610 its population had reached a manageable 26,000 and the town's centre was crowded with stalls selling silks and furniture from as far as China. In the nineteenth century Lima expanded far into the east and south, creating poor suburbs, while above the beaches, at Miraflores and Barranco, the wealthy developed new enclaves. An early twentieth-century renovation programme modernized the city and boosted the city's explosive population growth. Lima's 300,000 inhabitants of 1930 became 3.5 million by the mid-1970s and many of its current eight million are rural peasants who escaped the theatre of civil war that raked many highland regions between the early 1980s and 1993.

There is still a certain elegance to the old **colonial centre**, and the city hosts a string of excellent and important **museums**, but sadly central areas struggle with pollution and constant traffic-jams. However, many areas have been considerably cleaned up in recent years through concerted efforts on the part of local goverments, and there are many clean and pleasant parks and walkways to be found in the suburbs of **Miraflores**, **Barranco**, San Isidro and San Miguel. With its numerous facilities and firm footing as a transport and communications hub, Lima makes a good base from which to explore Peru and furnishes a good introduction to the county.

What to see and do

Laid out across a wide, flat alluvial plain, Lima fans out in long, straight streets from its heart, Central Lima. The old town focuses on the colonial Plaza Mayor and the more modern Plaza San Martín, which are separated by some five blocks of the Jirón de la Unión, Central Lima's main shopping street.

From Central Lima, the city's main avenues stretch out into the sprawling suburbs. The two principal routes are **Avenida Colonial**, heading out to the harbour area around the suburb of **Callao** and the airport, and, at right angles to this, the broad, tree-lined **Avenida Arequipa**, extending to the old beach resort of **Barranco**. Some 7 or 8km down Avenida Arequipa, the suburb of **Miraflores** is the modern, commercial heart of Lima, where most of the city's businesses have moved during the last thirty years.

Central Lima

Since its foundation, Lima has spread steadily out from the Plaza Mayor – virtually all of the Río Rimac's alluvial soil has now been built on and even the sand dunes beyond are rapidly filling up with migrant settlers. When Pizarro arrived here, he found a valley dominated by some four hundred temples and palaces, most of them pre-Inca, well spread out to either side

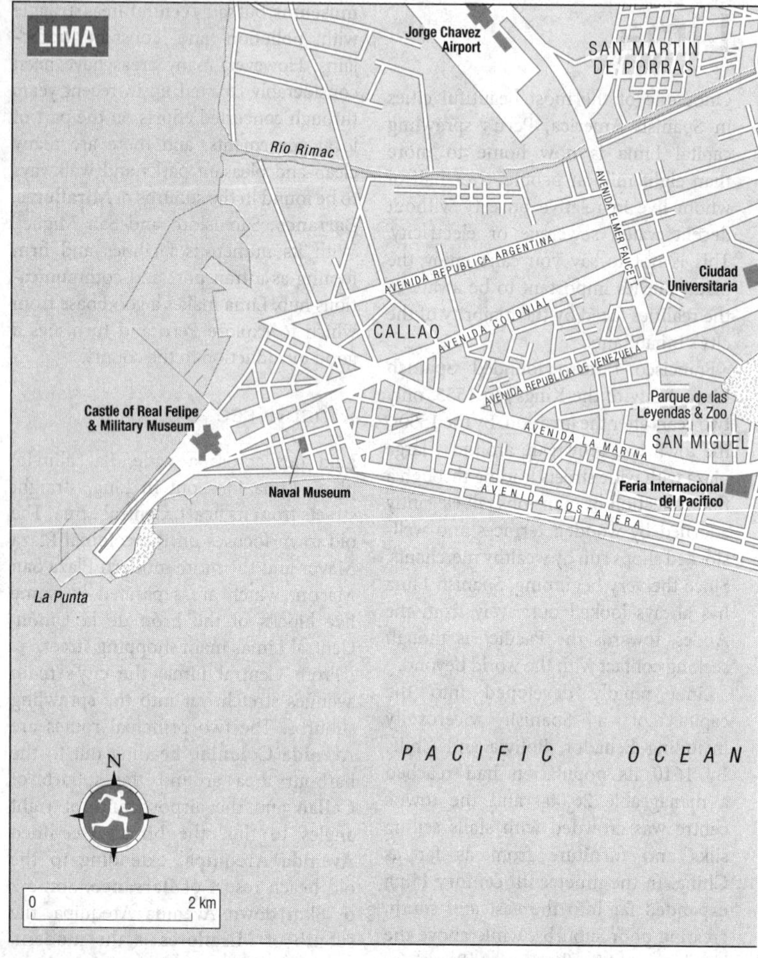

of the river. The conquistador founded Lima on the site of an existing palace belonging to Tauri Chusko, the local chief who had little choice but to give up his residence and move away.

The Plaza Mayor

Today the heart of the old town is around the Plaza Mayor or Plaza de Armas, as it is often referred to. There are no remains of any Indian heritage in or around the square; standing on the site of Tauri Chusko's palace is the relatively modern Palacio del Gobierno, while the cathedral occupies the site of an Inca temple once dedicated to the Puma deity, and the Municipal Building lies on what was originally an Inca envoy's mansion. The Palacio del Gobierno – also known as the Presidential Palace – was Pizarro's house long before the present building was built in 1938. It was here that he spent the last few years of his life, until his assassination in 1541. The changing of the guard takes place outside the palace (Mon–Sat starts 11.45am) which is fun to watch and listen to the soldiers play in their brass band.

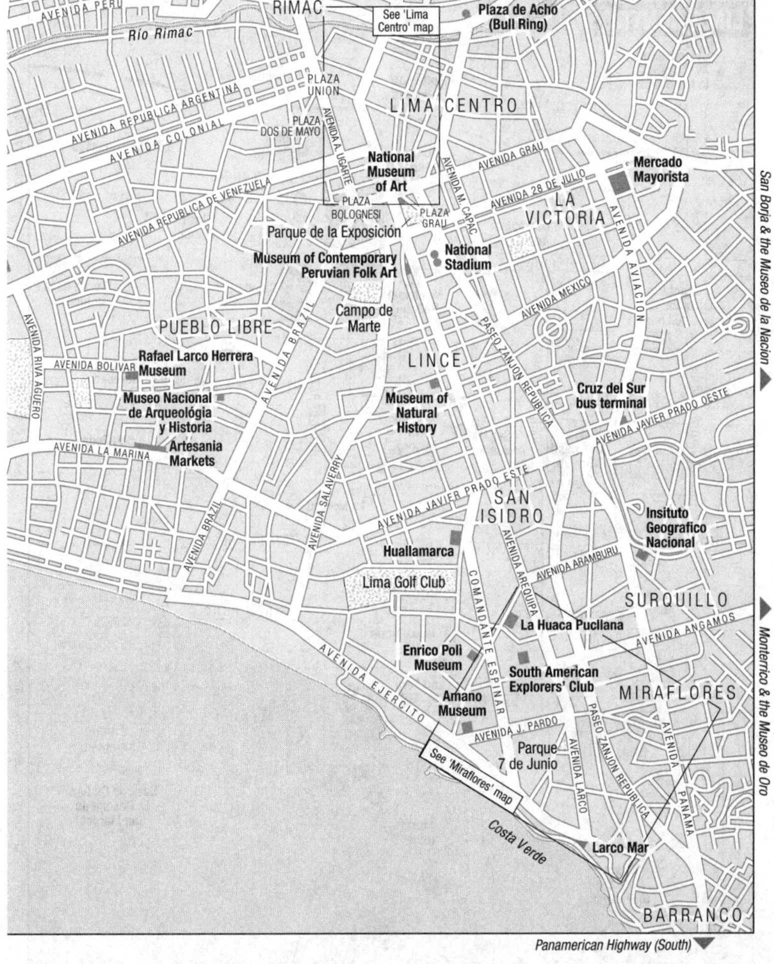

On the eastern corner of the plaza stands the squat and austere Renaissance-style **Cathedral** (Mon–Fri 9am–5pm, Sat 10am–1pm). It is primarily of interest for its **Museum of Religious Art and Treasures** (same hours as Cathedral; US$2), which contains seventeenth- and eighteenth-century paintings and a collection of human remains thought to be Pizarro's body. Although gloomy, the interior retains some of its appealing Churrigueresque (highly elaborate Baroque) decor.

San Francisco Catacombs

Jirón Ancash leads away from the Palacio del Gobierno towards one of Lima's most attractive churches, San Francisco ☎01/427-1381 (daily 9.30am–5.30pm; US$1.80). A large seventeenth-century construction with an engaging stone facade and towers, San Francisco's vaults and columns are elaborately decorated with Mudéjar (or Moorish-style) plaster relief. It's a majestic building that has withstood the passage of time and the devastation of successive earth tremors. The

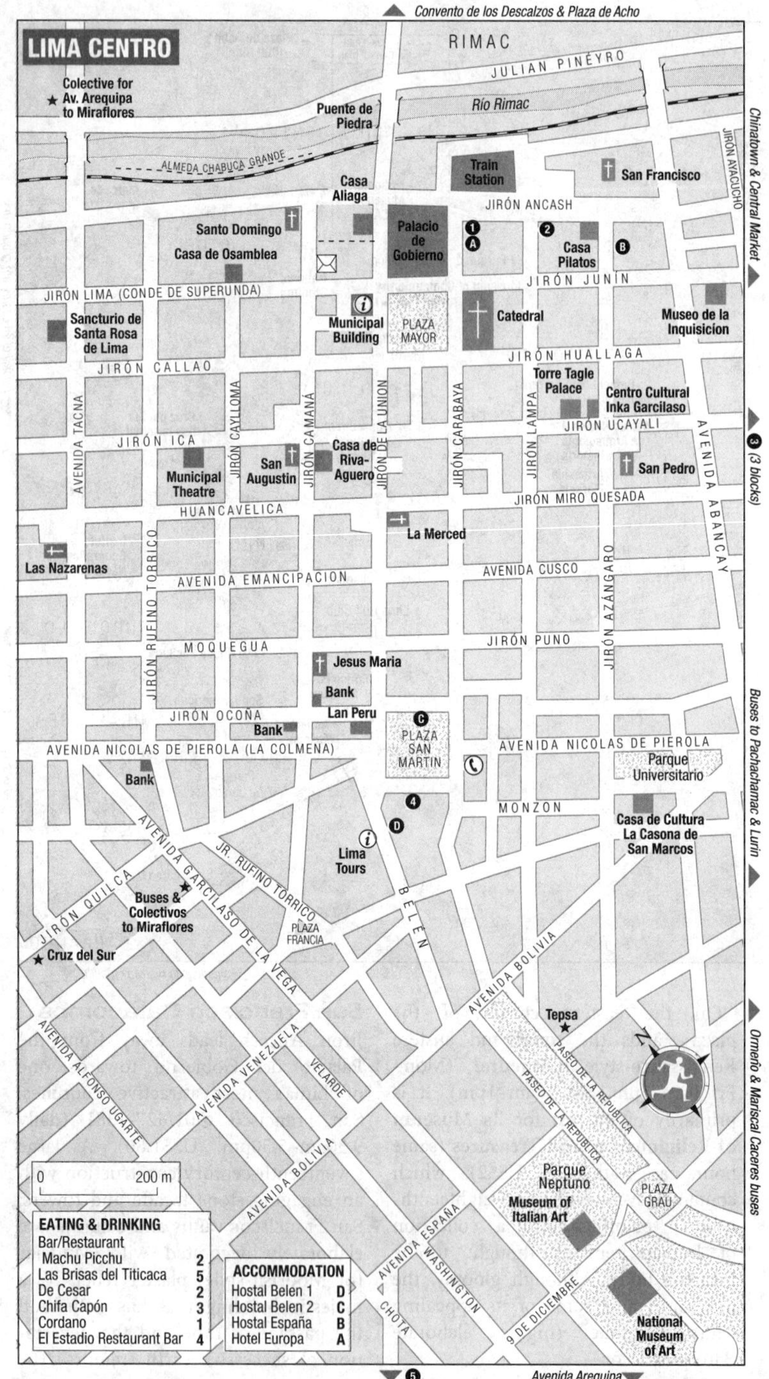
LIMA CENTRO
Convento de los Descalzos & Plaza de Acho
RIMAC
JULIAN PINÉYRO
Río Rimac
Colective for Av. Arequipa to Miraflores
Puente de Piedra
ALMEDA CHABUCA GRANDE
Casa Aliaga
Train Station
San Francisco
JIRÓN AYACUCHO
Chinatown & Central Market
JIRÓN ANCASH
Santo Domingo
Casa de Osamblea
Palacio de Gobierno
Casa Pilatos
JIRÓN JUNÍN
JIRÓN LIMA (CONDE DE SUPERUNDA)
Sancturio de Santa Rosa de Lima
Municipal Building
PLAZA MAYOR
Catedral
Museo de la Inquisicion
JIRÓN HUALLAGA
JIRÓN CALLAO
Torre Tagle Palace
Centro Cultural Inka Garcilaso
JIRÓN UCAYALI
AVENIDA TACNA
JIRÓN CAYLLOMA
JIRÓN CAMANÁ
JIRÓN DE LA UNION
JIRÓN CARABAYA
JIRÓN LAMPA
AVENIDA ABANCAY
JIRÓN ICA
Municipal Theatre
San Augustin
Casa de Riva-Aguero
San Pedro
(3 blocks)
HUANCAVELICA
JIRÓN MIRO QUESADA
La Merced
Las Nazarenas
JIRÓN RUFINO TORRICO
AVENIDA EMANCIPACION
AVENIDA CUSCO
JIRÓN AZÁNGARO
MOQUEGUA
JIRÓN PUNO
Jesus Maria
Bank
Lan Peru
JIRÓN OCOÑA
Bank
PLAZA SAN MARTIN
AVENIDA NICOLAS DE PIEROLA (LA COLMENA)
AVENIDA NICOLAS DE PIEROLA
Parque Universitario
Bank
MONZON
Casa de Cultura La Casona de San Marcos
Buses to Pachachamac & Lurin
AVENIDA GARCILASO DE LA VEGA
JR. RUFINO TORRICO
Lima Tours
BELEN
JIRÓN QUILCA
Buses & Colectivos to Miraflores
PLAZA FRANCIA
Cruz del Sur
AVENIDA BOLIVIA
Tepsa
PASEO DE LA REPUBLICA
PASEO DE LA REPUBLICA
Ormeño & Mariscal Caceres buses
AVENIDA ALFONSO UGARTE
AVENIDA VENEZUELA
VELARDE
AVENIDA BOLIVIA
Parque Neptuno
Museum of Italian Art
PLAZA GRAU
AVENIDA ESPAÑA
WASHINGTON
9 DE DICIEMBRE
CHOTA
National Museum of Art
0
200 m
EATING & DRINKING
Bar/Restaurant
Machu Picchu 2
Las Brisas del Titicaca 5
De Cesar 2
Chifa Capón 3
Cordano 1
El Estadio Restaurant Bar 4
ACCOMMODATION
Hostal Belen 1 D
Hostal Belen 2 C
Hostal España B
Hotel Europa A
Avenida Arequipa

San Francisco Monastery also contains a superb library and a room of paintings by (or finished by) Pieter Paul Rubens, Jordaens and Van Dyck. You can take a forty-minute guided tour of the monastery and its Catacombs Museum (daily 9.30am–5pm; US$1.80), both of which are worth a visit. The museum is inside the church's vast crypts, only discovered in 1951 and containing the skulls and bones of some seventy thousand people.

Museum of the Inquisition

A couple of blocks south, the Museo de La Inquisición, Jr Junin 548 ⓣ01/311-7777 x2910 ⓦwww.congreso.gob.pe/museo.htm (daily 9am–5pm; free but by guided tour only), faces out onto Plaza Bolívar near the Congress building. Behind a facade of Greek-style columns, the museum contains the original tribunal room with its beautifully carved mahogany ceiling. This was the headquarters of the Inquisition for the whole of Spanish-dominated America from 1570 until 1820 and, beneath the building, you can look round the dungeons and torture chambers, which contain a few gory, life-sized human models.

Chinatown

The few blocks behind the museum and Avenida Abancay are taken over by the **central market** and **Chinatown**. Perhaps one of the most fascinating sectors of Lima Centro, Chinatown is now swamped by the large and colourful (if also smelly and rife with pickpockets) daily market. An ornate Chinese gateway, crossing over Jirón Huallaya, marks the site of Lima's best and cheapest *chifa* (Chinese) restaurants.

San Pedro and Torre Tagle Palace

Heading from Chinatown back towards the Plaza Mayor along Ucayali, at number 451 you'll pass **San Pedro** (Mon–Sat 9.30–11.30am & 5–6pm; free) on the corner of Jirón Azángaro. Built by the Jesuits in 1636 and occupied by them until their expulsion in 1767, this richly decorated colonial church dripping with art treasures is worth a look around. Just over the road, you'll find the spectacular **Torre Tagle Palace**, at Ucayali 358 ⓣ01/311-2400, pride and joy of the old city. Now the home of Peru's Ministry for Foreign Affairs and recognizable by the security forces with machine guns on the roof and top veranda, Torre Tagle is a superb, beautifully maintained mansion built in the 1730s. Visit by prior arrangement only.

District of Rimac

Heading north from the Plaza Mayor along Jirón de la Unión, you pass the Casa Aliaga, at no. 224 ⓣ01/427-7736 (daily 9.30am–4pm), an unusual mansion, reputed to be the oldest in South America, and occupied by the same family since 1535. It's one of the most elaborate mansions in the country, with sumptuous reception rooms full of Louis XIV mirrors, furniture and doors. It is now a popular venue for cultural events.

Continuing up Jirón de la Unión, it's a short walk to the **Puente de Piedra**, the stone bridge that arches over the Río Rimac – usually no more than a miserable trickle – behind the Palacio del Gobierno. Initially a wooden construction, today's bridge was built in the seventeenth century to link the centre of town and the district of San Lazaro, known these days as **Rimac**, or Bajo El Puente ("below the bridge"). This zone was first populated in the sixteenth century by African slaves, newly imported and awaiting purchase by big plantation owners; a few years later, Rimac was plagued by outbreaks of leprosy. Although these days its status is much improved, Rimac is still one of the most run-down areas of Lima and can be quite an aggressive place at night.

Rimac is also home to the **Plaza de Acho**, on Hualgayoc 332, Lima's most important bullring, which also houses the **Museo Taurino de Acho**, or Bullfight Museum ⓣ01/482-3360 (Mon–Fri 9am–4.30pm, Sun by arrangement only; US$2), containing some original Goya engravings, several interesting paintings and a few relics of bullfighting contests. At the far end of the Alameda a fine 1592 Franciscan monastery, **El Convento de los Descalzos** (Wed-Mon 10am–1pm & 2–6pm; ⓣ01/481-0441; US$2, usually including a forty-minute guided tour), houses a collection of colonial and Republican paintings from Peru and Ecuador. Its Chapel of El Carmen possesses a beautiful Baroque gold-leaf altar.

Santa Rosa de Lima and Las Nazarenas

Two interesting sanctuaries can be found on the western edge of old Lima, along Avenida Tacna. The Sanctuario de Santa Rosa de Lima (daily 9am–12.30pm & 3–5.30pm; free), on the first block of Tacna, is a fairly plain church named in honour of the first saint canonized in the Americas. The construction of Avenida Tacna destroyed a section of the already small seventeenth-century church, but in the patio next door you can visit the fascinating Museo Etnográfico, containing crafts, tools, jewellery and weapons from jungle tribes, plus some photographs of early missionaries.

At the junction of Avenida Tacna and Huancavelica, the church of **Las Nazarenas** (daily 6am–noon & 4–8.30pm; free) is again small and outwardly undistinguished but it has an interesting history. After the severe 1655 earthquake, a mural of the crucifixion, painted by an Angolan slave on the wall of his hut, was apparently the only object left standing in the district. Its survival was deemed a miracle – the cause of popular processions ever since – and it was on this site that the church was founded. The widespread and popular processions for the Lord of Miracles, to save Lima from another earthquake, take place every autumn (Oct 18, 19, 28 & Nov 1), based around a silver litter which carries the original mural. Purple is the colour of the procession and many women in Lima wear it for the entire month.

Jirón de la Unión

The stretch between the Plaza Mayor and Plaza San Martín is the largest area of old Lima, although it is now the main shopping drag with everything from designer brands to thrift stores. Worth a quick look here is the church of San Augustín (daily 8.30am–noon & 3.30–5.30pm; free), founded in 1592 and located on the corner of Ica and Camana. Although severely damaged by earthquakes (only the small side chapel can be visited nowadays), the church retains a glorious facade, one of the most complicated examples of Churrigueresque architecture in Peru.

Perhaps the most noted of all religious buildings in Lima is the Iglesia de La Merced (daily 8am–noon & 4–8pm; free), just two blocks from the Plaza Mayor on the corner of Jirón de la Unión and Jirón Miro Quesada. Built on the site where the first Latin mass in Lima was celebrated, the original church was demolished in 1628 to make way for the present building. Its most elegant feature, a beautiful colonial facade, has been adapted and rebuilt several times – as have the broad columns of the nave – to protect the church against tremors. But by far the most lasting impression is made by the Cross of the Venerable Padre Urraca, whose silver staff is smothered by hundreds of kisses every hour and witness to the fervent prayers of a constantly shifting congregation.

Plaza San Martín and around

The Plaza San Martín is a grand, large square with fountains at its centre which is virtually always busy by day, with traffic tooting its way around the square, and buskers, mime artists and soapbox politicos attracting small circles of interested faces. The Plaza San Martín has seen most of Lima's political rallies in the last century and one sometimes still sees rioting office workers and attendant police with water cannons and tear gas.

The wide Avenida Nicolás de Pierola (also known as La Colmena) leads off the plaza, west towards the **Plaza Dos de Mayo**, which sits on the site of an old gate dividing Lima from the road to Callao and hosts a great street market where some fascinating bargains can be found. Built to commemorate the repulse of the Spanish fleet in 1866 (Spain's last attempt to regain a foothold in South America), the plaza is probably one of the most polluted spots in Lima and is markedly busier, dirtier and less friendly than Plaza San Martín. East of Plaza San Martín, Avenida Nicolás de Pierola runs towards the **Parque Universitario**, site of South America's first university, San Marcos. Nowadays, the park itself is base for *colectivo* companies and street hawkers, and is almost permanently engulfed in crowds of cars and rushing pedestrians.

Art Museum and Italian art museum

South of Plaza San Martín, Jirón Belén leads down to the Paseo de la República and the shady Parque Neptuno, home to the pleasant Museo de Arte Italiano, Paseo de la República 250 (Mon–Fri 10am–5pm; ⓣ01/423-9932; US$1). Located inside an unusual Renaissance building, the museum exhibits contemporary Peruvian art as well as reproductions of the Italian masters and offers a very welcome respite from the hectic modern Lima outside. Just south of here at Paseo Colón 125 is the Museo de Arte (Thurs–Tues 10am–5pm; ⓣ01/423-4732, ⓦwww.museodearte.org.pe; US$2), housed in the former International Exhibition Palace built in 1868. It contains interesting, small collections of colonial art and many fine crafts from pre-Columbian times, and also hosts frequent temporary exhibitions of modern photography and other art forms, as well as lectures and film screenings.

Miraflores

Miraflores, with its streets lined with cafés and flashy shops, is the major focus of Lima's action and nightlife, as far as most of the capital's residents are concerned. Although still connected to Lima Centro by the long-established Avenida Arequipa, another road – Paseo de la República (also known as the Via Expressa) – now provides the suburb with an alternative approach. The fastest way to get here is by yellow bus marked "Via Expressa" from Avenida Abancay to Benavides bridge.

Huaca Pucllana

Once there, make for the Huaca Pucllana (ⓣ01/445-8695; Wed–Mon 9am–5pm; US$2), a vast pre-Inca adobe mound which continues to dwarf most of the houses around and has a small site museum, craft shop and restaurant. It's just a two-minute walk from Avenida Arequipa, on the right as you come from Lima Centro at block 44. One of a large number of *huacas* – sacred places – and palaces that formerly stretched across this part of the valley, little is known about the Pucllana, though it seems likely that it was originally named after a pre-Inca chief of the area.

Parque Kennedy and Larco Mar

The suburb's central area focuses on the attractive, almost triangular **Parque Kennedy** (or Parque 7 de Junio) at the end of the Avenida Arequipa, which has a good craft and antiques market set up in stalls every evening (6–10pm). The streets around the park are filled

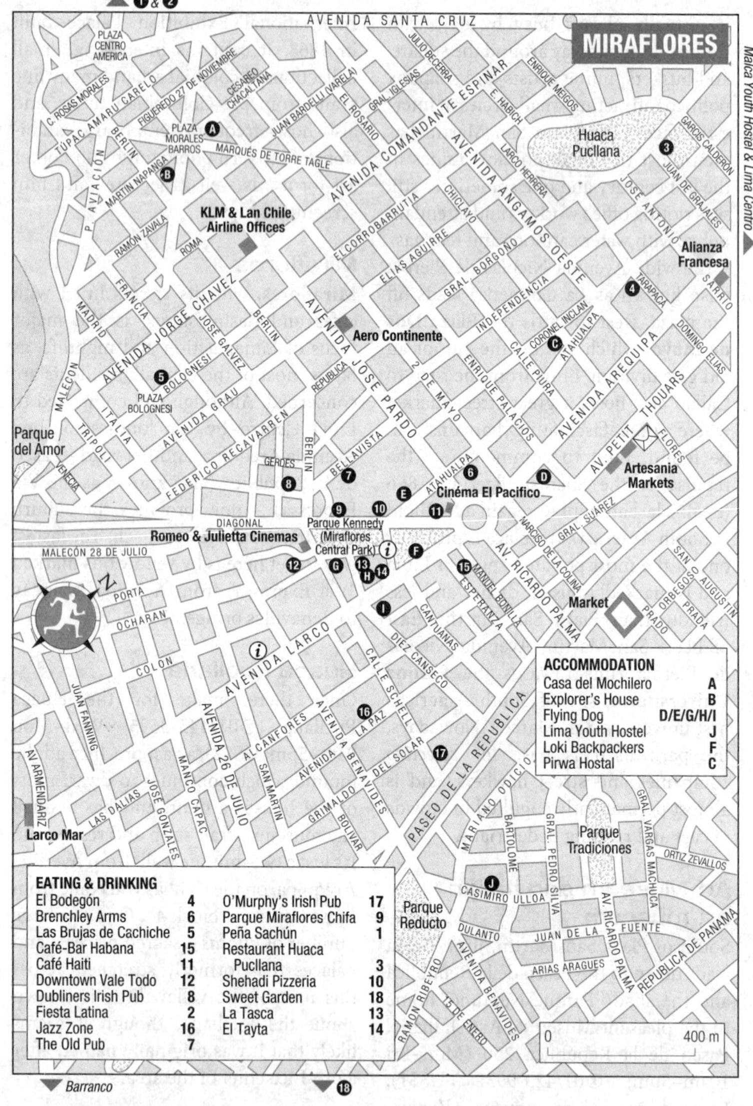

with flashy cafés and bars and crowded with shoppers, flower-sellers and young men washing cars. **Larco Mar**, the popular, flash clifftop development at the bottom of Avenida Larco, which has done an excellent job of integrating the park with what was previously a rather desolate point, is home to several flashy shops, decent bars, ice-cream parlours, eating establishments, cinemas and nightclubs.

Mansions and Museums

Miraflores' only important mansion open to the public is the Casa de Ricardo Palma, at General Suarez 189 (Mon–Fri 9.15am–12.45pm & 2.30–4.45pm; US$2), where Palma, probably Peru's greatest historian, lived for most of his life. There are two museums worth visiting: the Enrico Poli Museum, Lord Cochrane 466 (hours by appointment; ⓣ01/422-2437; US$10 per person for a minimum of five), contains some of the finest pre-Inca archeological treasures in Lima, including ceramics, gold and silver. The private Amano Museum, on C Retiro 160, off block 11 of Angamos Oeste (Mon–Fri, hours by appointment; ⓣ01/441-2909; entry by donation), also merits a visit for its fabulous exhibition of Chancay weavings, as well as bountiful ceramics.

Barranco

Barranco, a quieter place than Miraflores, is easily reached by taking any bus or *colectivo* along Diagonal. Overlooking the ocean, and scattered with old mansions as well as fascinating smaller homes, this was the capital's seaside resort during the nineteenth century and is now a kind of *limeño* Left Bank, with young artists and intellectuals taking over many of the older properties. There's little to see specifically, though you may want to take a look at the clifftop remains of a funicular rail-line, which used to carry aristocratic families from the summer resort down to the beach; there's also a pleasant, well-kept municipal park, where you can while away the afternoon beneath the trees. Worth a browse is the Museum of Electricity, Pedro Osma 105 (daily 9am–5pm; free), which displays a wide range of early electrical appliances and generating techniques. Otherwise the main joy of Barranco is its bars, clubs and cafés clustered around the small but attractive Plaza Municipal de Barranco, which buzz with frenetic energy after dark while retaining much of the area's original charm and character.

Callao

Still the country's main commercial harbour, and one of the most modern ports in South America, **Callao** lies about 14km west of Lima Centro. It's easily reached on bus #25 from Plaza San Martín, which runs all the way there – and beyond to La Punta – or by taking buses (marked "La Punta") from Avenida Arequipa west along either Avenida Angamos or Avenida Javier Prado. The suburb is none too alluring a place – its slum zones, infamous for prostitution and gangland assassins, are considered virtually no-go areas for the city's middle classes – but if you're unworried by such associations, you will find some of the best *ceviche* restaurants anywhere in the continent, as well as beautiful views from La Punta.

Further along, away from the rougher quarters and dominating the entire peninsula, you can see the great **Castillo del Real Felipe** (Mon–Fri 9am–2pm), on the Plaza Independencia. Built after the devastating earthquake of 1764, which washed ships ashore and killed nearly the entire population of Callao, this is a superb example of the military architecture of its age, designed in the shape of a pentagon. The fort's grandeur is marred only by a number of storehouses, built during the late nineteenth century when it was used as a customs house. Inside, the **Military Museum** (Mon–Fri 9.30am–4pm; free) houses a fairly complete collection of eighteenth- and nineteenth-century arms and has various rooms dedicated to Peruvian war heroes. Also in Callao is the **Naval Museum**, Av Jorge Chavez 121, off Plaza Grau (Mon–Fri 9am–2pm; free), displaying the usual military paraphernalia, uniforms, paintings, photographs and replica ships.

San Borja and the Museo de la Nación

The Museo de la Nación, Javier Prado Este 2465 in the suburb of San Borja (Tues–Sun 9am–5pm; US$1, US$3 extra for exhibitions; ⓣ01/476-9878), is Lima's largest modern museum

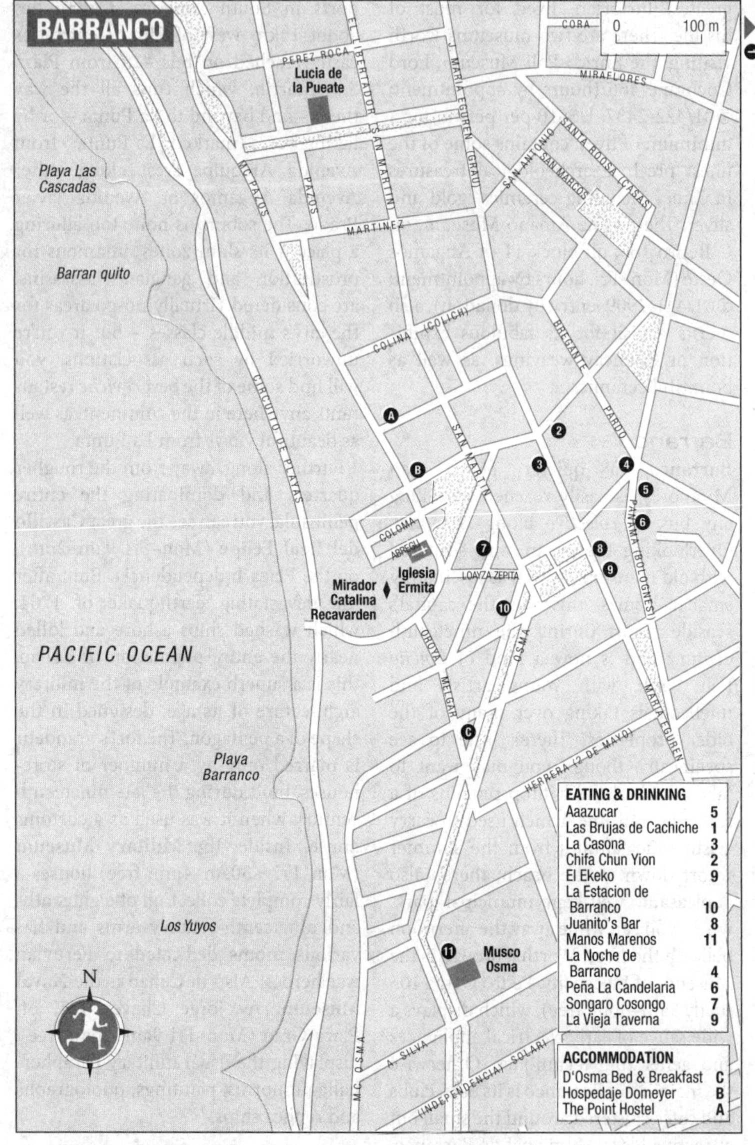

and contains permanent exhibitions covering most of the important aspects of Peruvian archeology, art and culture; there's also a café (daily 10am–6pm). If you see only one museum in Peru, it should be this one. The exhibits, displayed mainly in vast salons, include a range of traditional, regional peasant costumes from around the country and life-sized and miniature models depicting life in pre-Conquest times. The museum can be visited by taking a *colectivo* along Avenida Javier Prado east from Avenida Arequipa; after ten to fifteen minutes you'll see the vast, concrete building on the left.

Arrival

By air From Jorge Chavez Airport, 7km northwest of the city centre, the quickest way to get into the city is by taxi, which will take around 45 minutes to Lima Centro or downtown Miraflores. There is a secure taxi company which has desks just outside the baggage claim areas for national and international arrivals, before the main arrivals halls. "Taxi Green" has licensed drivers and set prices to different parts of the city – pay at the desk and you will be assigned a driver. They charge US$8-$15 for different parts of the city. A much cheaper option is to hail a cab from outside, however this is much less secure, and not worth the risk if you are arriving with luggage. There is currently no tourist bus serving the airport. Local combis are a cheap way to get around when you know the city, but theft is rife and again, when you arrive with your luggage they are probably not the best idea.

By bus If you arrive in Lima by bus, you'll probably come in at one of the terminals either in the district of La Victoria if it is a cheaper bus company, or on Avenida Javier Prado if it is a larger and more expensive company. For full details of Lima bus companies and their terminals, see "Listings", p.813. Whichever terminal you arrive at, your best bet is to hail the first decent-looking taxi you see and fix a price – about US$3 to anywhere in the central area, or US$5 for anywhere else in Lima.

By car Driving into the city is only for the adventurous, as the roads are highly congested, only principal routes are clearly signed, and local driving practices may leave you wondering if you entered a Formula 1 race by mistake.

Information

Tourist information Tourist information offices in Lima are plentiful. I-Peru offers free maps and informative leaflets for Lima and throughout the country as well as help when tourists experience problems. They have desks in the national and international departure and arrivals halls at Lima airport (open daily, 24hours ⓣ01/574-8000), as well as an office in San Isidro (Jorge Basadre 610, ⓣ01/421-1627, ⓔiperulima@promperu.gob.pe), and in Miraflores (Larcomar, stand 14 in the food court, daily 11am–noon, 1pm–8pm ⓣ01/4459400). The South American Explorers' Club, at C Piura 135, Miraflores (Mon–Fri 9.30am–5pm, Sat 9.30am–1pm; ⓣ01/445-3306, ⓔlimaclub@saexplorers.org, ⓦwww.saexplorers.org), has good information, including maps, listings and travel reports, available to its members. Look out for the free monthly magazine "Vida Lima" available from I-Peru offices, South American Explorers and hundreds of hotels and restaurants which lists cultural events taking place that month as well as useful information for tourists. If you are planning to stay longer in Lima, consider buying the "Lima Survival Kit" available from South American Explorers which has all the information you could possibly need from where to buy antiques to the best dentists in town. City tours are offered by several companies; see the listings section on p.814 for more info.

City transport

Buses Almost every corner of this huge city is linked by a regular **municipal bus service**, with flat-rate tickets (around 15¢) bought from the driver as you board. In tandem with these public buses are the much more ubiquitous, privately owned **microbuses**, some older and some smaller than others, more colourful and equally crowded, but again with flat rates (25¢).

Colectivos Quickest of all Lima transport, **combi colectivos** race from one street corner to another along all the major arterial city roads. Colectivos dash dangerously fast (frequently crashing), and speeding off before their passengers have got both feet into the vehicle; wave one down from the corner of any major street and pay the flat fare (around 20¢) to the driver or fare collector. You can catch colectivos or buses to most parts of the city from Avenida Abancay; for routes and destinations covered in this chapter you'll find the number or suburb name (written on the front of all buses).

Taxis **Taxis** can be hailed on any street, and cost US$2–4 to most central parts of the city; try CMV (ⓣ01/422-4838), or Tata Taxis (ⓣ01/274-5151). Always agree on a price beforehand. If you want to rent a car to take out of the city (the city's anarchic driving is best avoided), see "Listings" p.814.

Accommodation

Accommodation choices will be largely dictated by area as there are good budget and mid-range options throughout the city. **Central Lima** offers accommodation within walking distance of some of the most important religious and historical buildings in the city as well as museums and quaint cafés. Traditionally the artisan's quarter, **Barranco** offers a bohemian atmosphere close to the sea, with regular food and handicrafts fairs held in the charismatic square. The most popular district for tourists is still **Miraflores**, with bright lights and American fast-food joints on every corner; you could be in any cosmopolitan city in the world. There are no **campsites**, official or otherwise.

Central Lima

Hostal España Jr Azángaro 105 ⓣ01/428-5546, ⓦ www.hotelespanaperu.com. Popular and centrally located, *Hostal España* is very secure and has a dormitory, plus rooms with or without private bath, internet connection, book exchange and its own tour operator service, all based around a nice courtyard and rooftop patio. Worth visiting just for the stunning colonial building filled with antique oil paintings, marble statues and trailing pot plants. ❸–❹

Hostal Belen With two locations at Jr de la Union 1049 ⓣ01/427-8995 (all rooms with shared bath), and Plaza San Martín ⓣ01/4277391 (all rooms with private bath), Hostal Belen is one of the best-value budget options (definitely the best for single rooms) in Central Lima. Both buildings are well-maintained colonial gems with restaurants serving bargain lunches to guests and passers by. ❸

Hotel Europa Jr Ancash 376 ⓣ01/427-3351. Centrally located opposite the San Francisco church, with a lovely courtyard, the building itself is run-down and more or less clean. Most rooms with shared bath. ❸

Miraflores

Casa del Mochilero Jr Cesareo Chacaltana 130a, 2nd floor, Miraflores ⓣ01/444-9089, ⓔpilaryv@hotmail.com. Close to block 10 of José Pardo, this safe place is remarkably good, with hot water, cable TV and kitchen facilities. It's not right at the centre of Miraflores's action, but it's close enough. ❸–❹

Lima Youth Hostel Casimiro Ulloa 328, Miraflores ⓣ01/446-5488, ⓦwww.limahostell.com.pe. Unbeatable hostel located just over the Paseo de la República highway from Miraflores in the peaceful suburb of San Antonia. Beautiful clean dorm and private rooms, very secure, in a large house with TV room, well-equipped and clean shared kitchen, garden area and small pool. Not a party hostel, this is backpacking for grown-ups. ❺

Flying Dog Hostels The Flying Dog empire continues to expand in Miraflores with no less than four locations: Backpackers on Diez Canseco, Bed and Breakfast on Calle Lima, Hostel on Olaya and Long stays on Pershing ⓦwww.flyingdogperu.com. All locations offer cheap accommodation, kitchen use, TV room, storage service and internet access, as well as being hugely popular and therefore a great place to meet people. They also run the small and trendy Tasca Bar on Diez Canseco. ❹

Pirwa Hostel Coronel Inclan 494 ⓣ01/445-2811 ⓦwww.pirwahostelsperu.com. Clean dorm rooms with shared bath with loads of the services backpackers love: safe storage, TV room, 24hr kitchen use, hot water, free internet, laundry, terrace and garden. ❹

Loki Backpackers Avenida Larco 189, ⓣ01/242-4350 ⓦwww.lokihostel.com. This chain of hostels started in Cusco by backpackers is rapidly expanding and gaining a reputation as the place to party. With dorm rooms, hot water and standard backpacker facilities, Loki also has a bar on the top floor, good information, regular parties and events. Great if you want to meet people, not so good if you want to sleep. ❹–❺

Explorer's House Av Alfredo Leon 158 ⓣ01/241-5002 ⓦwww.geocities.com/explorers_house. Out of the centre of Miraflores but close to the beach, Explorer's House is a good old-fashioned backpackers with a family atmosphere and comfy if well-used beds. Dorm and private rooms with hot water, and a roof-top terrace, and there is a small kitchen for guests to use. Book ahead as it is small and popular. ❹

Barranco

D'Osma Bed & Breakfast Av Pedro de Osma 240 ⓣ01/251-4178. Small bed and breakfast with just four rooms, all comfortable with private bath and cable TV. Homely and friendly atmosphere. ❺

The Point Malecón Junin 300 ⓣ01/247-7997, ⓦwww.thepointhostels.com. Has large, medium or small dorms to choose from as well as private rooms. With lots of facilities including internet, TV room, and kitchen, as well as the on-site "Pointless Bar", a great place to meet other travellers and have a good time. ❹

Domeyer Calle Domeyer 296 ⓣ01/247-1413. Small, homely hostel with kitchen use and monthly rates. ❺

Eating

Predictably, Lima boasts some of the best **restaurants** in the country, serving not only traditional Peruvian dishes, but cuisines from all over the world. Seafood is particularly good here, with **ceviche** – raw fish or seafood marinated in lime juice and served with onions, chillis, sweet corn and sweet potatoes – being the speciality. Many of the more upmarket restaurants fill up very quickly, so it is advisable to reserve in advance; where this is the case we have included the phone number.

Central Lima

Chifa Capon Ucayali 774. An excellent and traditional Chinese restaurant, the best of many in this block of Chinatown, close to the centre. It offers a range of authentic *chifa* dishes, but doesn't stay open very late. Soup and main course 7–15 soles.

Cordano Jr Ancash 202, Lima Centro ⓣ01/427-0181. Beside the Palacio del Gobierno in Central Lima this is one of the city's last surviving traditional bar-restaurants, open since 1905. It is easy to imagine that the décor has not changed much since then. Old-fashioned service and very reasonably priced drinks make this a great place to stop for a rest while visiting sites. Sit back and feel yourself slip back in time. Mon–Sat 8am–11pm. Mains 15–20 soles.

De Cesar Ancash 300, ⓣ01/428-8740. Great little café-cum-restaurant and bar right in the heart of old Lima; food is fine and cheap, service friendly, decor pleasant and the range of breakfasts quite endless. Mains 15–25 soles.

Bar/Restaurant Machu Picchu Ancash 312. A busy place opposite San Francisco church in Lima Centro, serving inexpensive snacks and cheap lunchtime menus for around US$2. Daily 8am–10pm.

El Estadio Restaurant Bar Nicholas de Pierola 926, ⓣ01/428-8866, ⓦwww.estadio.com.pe. On the Plaza San Martín, this sports bar is a football fan's dream, with the walls on several floors covered in murals and paraphernalia. You can also share a table with life-size busts of several football heroes. The food is not the cheapest, main dishes costing around US$10, but is good and portions are large. There is a nightclub in the basement which regularly holds special events with live bands and a small cover charge to pay.

Miraflores

El Bodegón Tarapaca 197-199, ⓣ01/445-6222. Relatively new café/bar/restaurant with a charming arty atmosphere. Each table comes equipped with drawing paper and crayons in case you should feel artisticaly inspired while waiting for your food to arrive. Mon–Sat noon–11pm. Mains average 20 soles.

Café Haiti Diagonal 160, ⓣ01/4450539. A Miraflores tradition, Café Haiti is still the most popular meeting place for middle-class limeños, based by the Cinema El Pacifico in the heart of Miraflores with streetside tables spilling out towards Parque Kennedy. Excellent snacks and drinks but mains are relatively expensive at around s/.25 a plate. A great place to have a coffee and watch the world go by. Daily 8am–midnight.

TREAT YOURSELF

Restaurant Huaca Pucllana Gral. Borgoño, block 8, Miraflores ⓣ01/445-4042. Chic upmarket restaurant serving delicious modern and international versions of traditional Peruvian dishes. Beautiful setting in the evenings and you can sit right next to the softly lit Huaca Pucllana and sip on a cocktail. Mon–Sat 12.30pm–midnight, Sun 12.30–4pm. Mains 35–50 soles.

Parque Miraflores Chifa Calle Juan Figari 117 ⓣ01/241-7060 (also for take away). On the corner of Parque Kennedy this vast hall serves up huge portions of tasty Chifa plus soup for less than US$3. There are also comfy sofas where you can enjoy a jasmine tea while digesting or waiting for takeaway.

Shehadi Pizzeria Diagonal 220 ⓣ01/444-0630. Also on Parque Kennedy this pizzeria is renowned for great service, delicious food and a trendy atmosphere in the evenings. Go at lunchtime for a US$3 menu of well prepared local food. Mains 20–30 soles.

Sweet Garden Av 28 de Julio 1301. The best place for home baked cakes and sweets, breads, coffee and breakfasts. Daily 8am–11.30pm. Cake 1.50 soles.

Tai-i Vegetarian Av Petit Thouars 5232 ⓣ01/444-0641. Great value vegetarian set lunches for s/.5, with takeaway and delivery service.

Barranco

Las Brujas de Cachiche Av Bolognesi 460, ⓣ01/447-1883. An interestingly conceived, top-class restaurant and bar, which serves conventional Peruvian dishes as well as a range of pre-Columbian meals using only ingredients available more than one thousand years ago. Very trendy and expensive, its theme is traditional Peruvian healing and magic. Mains 25–40 soles.

Chifa Chun Yion C Union 126, ⓣ01/477-0550. An excellent, cheap and very busy Chinese restaurant, quite traditional with some private booths in the back room. Soup and mains 8–12 soles.

Songoro Cosongo Ayacucho 281, ⓣ01/247-4730. Traditional very friendly restaurant offering some of the best seafood and Creole dishes around at very reasonable prices. They also often have live music and special events. Daily 12.30–5pm & 7–11pm. Mains 8–15 soles.

La Vieja Taberna Av Grau 268, Barranco ⓣ01/247-3741. A fascinating, historic place built in 1903 and the venue where the political party APRA was created. It's very stylish, with views over the Barranco plaza and often has music weekend evenings. Particularly good for tasty traditional *limeño* cuisine. Mains 25–30 soles.

Drinking and nightlife

The daily *El Comercio* provides good **information** about music events and its Friday edition carries a comprehensive supplement guide to Lima's nightlife, which is easy to understand, even if your Spanish is limited. Also see "Vida Lima", a free magazine with events listings in English and Spanish. The suburb of **Barranco** is now the trendiest and liveliest place to hang out, especially "The Boulevard" where touts compete fiercely for business offering very cheap drinks to entice you in. Similarly in **Miraflores** – "Pizza Street" (Calle San Ramón) is lined with popular pizza restaurants with very cheap beer and outside seating.

Live music and dance

All forms of **Peruvian music** can be found in Lima, some of them, like salsa and Peruvian black music, better here than anywhere else in the country. Even Andean folk music is close to its best here (though Puno, Cusco and Arequipa are all contenders). As far as the **live music scene** goes, the great variety of traditional and hybrid sounds is one of the most enduring reasons for visiting the capital. Things are at their liveliest on Friday and Saturday nights, particularly among the folk group *peñas* and local **discotecas** (usually dedicated to all-night salsa and other Latin beat dancing). Most places charge around US$10 entrance fee, which sometimes includes a drink.

Aazucar Av Bolognesi 296, Barranco, ⓣ01/247-5678. Colourful and lively afro-latino/caribbean music and dance shows with the chance to get up on stage and shake your thing with the best of them. Fri & Sat from 9.30pm only, entrance fee varies depending on shows.

Las Brisas del Titicaca Jr Wakulski 168, Central Lima, ⓣ01/332-1901. Famous for its folkloric shows and relaexed atmosphere, they serve lunch and dinner. Shows are on Tues–Sat starting at 9pm. Entrance from 26–52 soles per person.

La Estación de Barranco Av Pedro de Osma 112, Barranco, ⓣ01/247-0344. Just across the road from the suburb's main plaza, this established *peña* regularly varies its flavour between folklore, *criolla* and even Latin jazz at times; it has a very good atmosphere most Fri & Sat.

La Candelaria Av Bolognesi 292, Barranco, ⓣ01/247-1314. Impressive costumes and choreography and plenty of audience participation, this is one of Barranco's most popular *peñas*. Shows on Fri & Sat only starting at 9.30pm. Entrance is 25 soles per person and includes a pisco sour.

Manos Morenas Av Pedro de Osma 409, Barranco. This club usually hosts *criolla* gigs, often with big names like Eva Ayllon and internationally renowned dance groups such as Peru Negro; excellent food and shows, though the atmosphere can be a little constrained.

Peña Sachún Av del Ejército 657, Miraflores ⓣ01/441-0123. Very lively and popular tourist restaurant with a good reputation for live folklore music and *criolla* dancing at weekends, usually till at least 2am.

Latino music and Jazz clubs

Fiesta Latina Federico Villareal 259, Miraflores. A lively place to get a feel for popular salsa music. Thurs–Sat 10pm–2am.

La Casona de Barranco Av Grau 329, Barranco. Very popular club with Lima's trendy under-40s and has particularly good live jazz most weekends.

El Ekeko Av Grau 266, by the municipal plaza in Barranco. Often has Latin jazz at weekends, though also hosts Peruvian Andean and coastal music, as well as Cuban music and sometimes tango.

El Tayta & El Yaya Av Larco 421–437(second floor), Miraflores ⓣ01/444-1640, ⓦwww.eltayta.com. Live rock music every night as well as lots of drinks specials.

Jazz Zone Av La Paz 646, Pasaje El Suche, Miraflores. Open Mon–Sat from 8pm with live music (usually jazz) every night by local and international groups. Entrance fee varies depending on the show.

Bars and clubs

Lima boasts a wide range of exciting **clubs**, with the vast majority of its popular **bars** and discos to be found in either **Barranco** or **Miraflores**. Lima has a fun and rapidly growing gay and lesbian scene, see ⓦwww.gayperu.com for current information about what's on at bars and clubs around the capital.

Brenchley Arms Atahualpa 174, Miraflores. Small pub with a real old-England feel and beer on tap. With a strict doorman outside and expensive food and drink, this place is more popular with expat regulars than with young *Limeños*.

Café-Bar Habana Calle Manuel Bonilla 107, Miraflores. Chilled-out cuban bar with a huge range of cocktails (average US$5 each), small selection of over-priced Cuban snacks and sandwiches. Worth a look for the cultural ambiance and adjoining art gallery.

Downtown Vale Todo Pasaje Los Pinos 160, Miraflores. Lima's most happening gay and lesbian club complete with drag show. Wed–Sun nights from 10.30pm.

Dubliners Irish Pub Berlin 333, Miraflores. Fun and friendly Irish pub with happy hour drinks and special events for any excuse.

Juanito's Av Grau 687, Barranco. Probably the most traditional of the area's bars; facing onto the Parque Municipal, it is small and basic and offers an excellent taste of Peru as it used to be. Also offers cheap sandwiches and bar snacks.

La Noche Av Bolognesi 307, El Boulevard, Barranco, www.lanoche.com.pe. Right at the top end of the Boulevard, this club gets really packed at weekends. Small entry fee when there's live music and free jazz sessions on Mon evening. Fine decor, arguably the top nightspot in the neighbourhood and one of the best places for meeting people.

O'Murphy's Irish Pub C Shell 627, Miraflores. Mon–Fri from noon until close, Sat and Sun from 6pm until close. it's a spacious, but dark and dingy place with reasonably priced beer, pool tables and a dart board. Hosts rock concerts and shows major international sporting events on a big screen.

The Old Pub San Ramón 295, Miraflores. The most authentic of the English-style pubs in Lima; it's actually run by an Englishman, and also plays good music. Easy to find just a block or two from the park, at the far end of San Ramón (also known as pizza-street).

La Tasca Diez Canseco, Miraflores. Run by the Flying Dog backpackers this is a tiny but very popular bar with snacks for sale.

Shopping

All types of Peruvian **artesanía** are available in Lima, including woollen goods, crafts and gemstones. Some of the best in Peru are on Avenida Petit Thouars, which is home to a handful of markets between Avenida Ricardo Palma and Avenida Angamos, all well within walking distance of Miraflores centre. Artesania Gran Chimu, Av Petit Thouars 5495, has a wide range of jewellery and carved wooden items, as does Mercado Artesanal, Av Petit Thouars 5321. More places selling *artesania* are listed below.

Slightly cheaper are the *artesanía* **markets** on blocks 9 and 10 of Avenida La Marina in Pueblo Libre and the good craft and antique market, which takes place every evening (6–9pm) in the Miraflores Park between Diagonal and Avenida Larco. In Lima Centro the Artesanía Santo Domingo, at Jr Conde de Superunda 221–223, houses a range of suppliers to suit all budgets, in a little square pavement area just a stone's throw from the Correo central; it is good for beads, threads and other *artesanía* components or completed items.

For **clothing**, Polvos Azules (Av Paseo de le República, 2 blocks from Plaza Grau), and Gamarra (Prolongación Gamarra, La Victoria) are huge shopping centres/markets where you can pick up very cheap branded clothing and footwear. Both areas can be dangerous and are rife with pickpockets so take only the money you want to spend and try to visit early in the morning.

Directory

Airlines Aero Condor, Av Pardo 562, Miraflores ⓣ01/614-6014, ⓦwww.aerocondor.com.pe; Aeroparacas, ⓣ01/271-6941 or 273-0507, ⓦwww.aeroparacas.com (only for Nazca Lines flights); Lan, Av Jose Pardo 513, Miraflores ⓣ01/213-8200 or 213-8300; TACA Peru, Av Pardo 811 Miraflores, ⓣ01/511-8222, ⓦwww.taca.com; L C Busre, Calle Los Tulipanes 218, Urb. San Eugenio, Lince, ⓣ01/619-1313, ⓦwww.lcbusre.com; Star Peru, Av Comandante Espinar 331, Miraflores, ⓣ01/705-9000, ⓦwww.starperu.com.

Airport Lima airport applies a flat US$30 departure tax on international flights, paid on departure at the airport. For domestic flights the departure tax is around US$6. The airport boasts lots of shops, cafés, internet facilities, a post office and a rather expensive left luggage deposit in the international departure area (info at ⓦwww.lap.com).

Banks Banco de la Nación, Av Pardo 201, Miraflores and Abancay 491, Central Lima; BBVA Banco Continental, Av Pardo 791, Miraflores and Jr. Ucayali 735, Central Lima; Scotiabank, Av Comandande Espinar 809, Miraflores and Ucayali 750, Central Lima.

Bus companies There are several large companies which cover national and international destinations and have their own terminals, sometimes more than one, main terminals are listed here; always check which terminal your bus will leave from when buying your ticket. For nationwide destinations try: Cial Av República de Panama (ⓣ01/265-8121, ⓦwww.expresocial.com); Cruz del Sur, Av Javier Prado Este 1109 (ⓣ01/311-5050, ⓦwww.cruzdelsur.com.pe); Linea, Av José Gálvez 999 (ⓣ01/424-0836 or 332-6063); Movil Tours, Paseo de la República 749 (ⓣ01/332-9000, ⓦwww.moviltours.com.pe): Tepsa, Javier Prado Este 1091 (ⓣ01/470-6666, ⓦwww.tepsa.com.pe)

Car rental Budget, offices where you can reserve and pick up vehicles at the airport, in Miraflores and in San Isidro (Ⓦwww.budgetperu.com); Dollar, Av Canuarias 341, Miraflores Ⓣ01/444-3050; Europcar, Calle Los Eucaliptos 590, shop 11, San Isidro (Ⓣ01/222-1010, Ⓦwww.europcarperu.com; National, Calle Costanera 1380, San Miguel (Ⓣ01/5787720) and at the Airport (Ⓣ01/517-2555, Ⓦwww.nationalcar.com.pe); Avis, Av Javier Prado Este 5233, La Molina (Ⓣ01/434-1111, Ⓦwww.avisperusur.com)

Embassies and consulates Australia, Av Victor Belaúnde 147, Via Principal 155, building 3 of 1301 San Isidro Ⓣ01/222-8281; Bolivia, Los Castaños 235, San Isidro Ⓣ01/440-2095; Brazil, Av Jose Pardo 850, Miraflores Ⓣ01/512-0830; Canada, C Libertad 130, Miraflores Ⓣ01/242-4050; Chile, Javier Prado Oeste 790, San Isidro Ⓣ01/221-2080 or 221-2081; Ecuador, Las Palmeras 356, San Isidro Ⓣ01/440-9941; Ireland, Angamos Este 340, Miraflores Ⓣ01/446-3878; UK, Torre Parque Mar, Av Larco 1301, 22nd floor, Miraflores Ⓣ01/617-3000; US, Av La Encalada, block 17, Surco Ⓣ01/434-3000.

Exchange Central Lima, Miraflores, Barranco and San Isidro all have several *casas de cambio*. Money changers on the streets will often give a slightly better rate but will try all sorts of tricks, from doctored calculators to fake money. Often the best way to change money in Lima is by buying things in supermarkets with large notes and asking them to change the whole bill – they usually give the best rates.

Internet services are readily available throughout the capital, with several 24hr places in Miraflores and Barranco.

Police Tourist Police are at the Museo de La Nación, Javier Prado Este 2465, 5th Foor Ⓣ01/225-8699.

Postal services The main post office is at Pasaje Piura, Jirón Lima, block 1 near the Plaza Mayor, with other branches on Av Nicolás de Pierola, opposite the Hotel Crillon and, in Miraflores, at Petit Thouars 5201, a block from the corner of Angamos.

Telephones Phone kiosks are found all around the city. In Lima Centro the main Telefónica del Peru office is near the corner of Wiese and Carabaya 933, on Plaza San Martín.

Travel agents and tour operators Fertur Peru, Jr Junin 211, Lima Centro Ⓣ01/427-1958, Ⓦwww.fertur-travel.com; Lima Tours, Belén 1040, near Plaza San Martín Ⓣ01/619-6900, Ⓦwww.limatours.com.pe; Lima Vision, Jr Chiclayo 444, Miraflores Ⓣ01/447-0482 or 447-5323, Ⓦwww.limavision.com, which does a variety of city tours and visits, including Pachacamac and Lima museums.

Visas Migraciones, corner of Prolongación Av España 734 and Jr Huaraz, Breña, Ⓣ01/433-0731.

Cusco and around

Known to the Incas as the "navel of the world", modern **CUSCO** is an exciting and colourful city, built by the Spanish on the solid remains of Inca temples and palaces. Enclosed between high hills and dominated in equal degree by the imposing ceremonial centre and fortress of **Sacsayhuaman** and the nearby white Christ figure, it's one of South America's biggest tourist destinations, with its thriving culture, substantial Inca ruins and architectural treasures from the colonial era attracting visitors from every corner of the world. Yet despite its massive pull, this welcoming city remains relatively unspoiled, its whitewashed streets and red-tiled roofs home to a wealth of traditional culture, lively nightlife and a seemingly endless variety of museums, walks and tours.

Once you've acclimatized – and the altitude here, averaging 3500m, has to be treated with respect – there are dozens of enticing destinations within easy reach. For most people the **Sacred Valley** of the Río Urubamba is the obvious first choice, with the citadel of **Machu Picchu** as the ultimate goal, and with hordes of other ruins – **Pisac** and **Ollantaytambo** in particular – amid glorious Andean panoramas on the way. The mountainous region around Cusco boasts some of the country's finest trekking, and beyond the **Inca Trail** to Machu Picchu are hundreds of lesser-known, virtually unbeaten paths into the mountains, including the **Salcantay** and **Ausungate** treks, which begin less just a couple of hours northwest and a bus ride south of Cusco respectively. Further afield you can explore the lowland **Amazon rainforest** in Madre de Dios, such as the Tambopata and Candamo

WHEN TO VISIT

The **best time to visit** the area around Cusco is during the dry season (May–Sept), when it's warm with clear skies during the day but relatively cold at night. During the wet season (Oct–April) it rarely rains every day or all week, but when it does, downpours are heavy.

Reserved Zone, or the slightly nearer Manu Biosphere Reverve, among the most accessible and bio-diverse wildernesses on Earth.

Some history

Although actually inhabited first by the Killki between 700 and 800 AD, legend has it that Cusco was founded by **Manco Capac** and his sister **Mama Occlo** about four centuries later. Over the next two hundred years, the **Cusco Valley** was home to the Inca tribe, one of many localized warlike groups then dominating the Peruvian *sierra*. A series of chiefs led the tribe after Manco Capac, but it wasn't until **Pachacuti** assumed power in 1438 that Cusco became the centre of an expanding empire. Of all the Inca rulers, only **Atahualpa**, the last, never actually resided in Cusco, and even he was en route there when the *conquistadores* captured him at Cajamarca. In his place, **Francisco Pizarro** reached the native capital on November 15, 1533, after holding Atahualpa to ransom, then killing him anyway. The Spaniards were astonished: the city's beauty surpassed anything they had seen before in the New World, the stonework was better than any in Spain and precious metals were used in a sacred context throughout the city. As usual, they lost no time in plundering its fantastic wealth.

Today Cusco possesses an identity above and beyond the legacy left in the andesite stones carved by the Incas. Like its renowned art, Cusco is dark, yet vibrantly coloured. It's a politically active, left-of-centre city where street demonstrations organized by teachers, lecturers, miners or some other beleagured profession are commonplace.

What to see and do

The city divides into several distinct zones based around various squares, temples and churches, with the **Plaza de Armas** at the heart of it all.

The broad **Avenida Sol** runs southeast from the corner of the plaza by the university and Iglesia de la Compañía towards the Inca sun temple at **Koricancha**, Huanchaq train station and on to the airport in the south. Running southwest from the top of Avenida Sol, Calle Mantas leads uphill past **Plaza San Francisco** and the Iglesia de Santa Clara, then on towards the Central Market and San Pedro train station. Just one block west of the central plaza lies **Plaza Regocijo** and from the northeast corner of Plaza de Armas, Calle Triunfo leads uphill through some classic Inca stone-walled alleys towards the artisan *barrio* of **San Blas**, passing near **Plaza Nazarenas**, northeast of the centre. Calle Plateros heads northwest from Plaza de Armas, leading to Calle Saphi and Calle Suecia, both of which run uphill through quaint streets and on towards **Sacsayhuaman Fortress** above the city.

Each of these zones is within easy walking distance of the Plaza de Armas and their main features can be covered easily in half a day, allowing for a little extra time for browsing in the bars and shops en route. As you wander around, you'll notice how many of the important Spanish buildings were constructed on top of Inca palaces and temples, often incorporating the exquisitely constructed walls and doorways into the lower parts of churches and colonial structures.

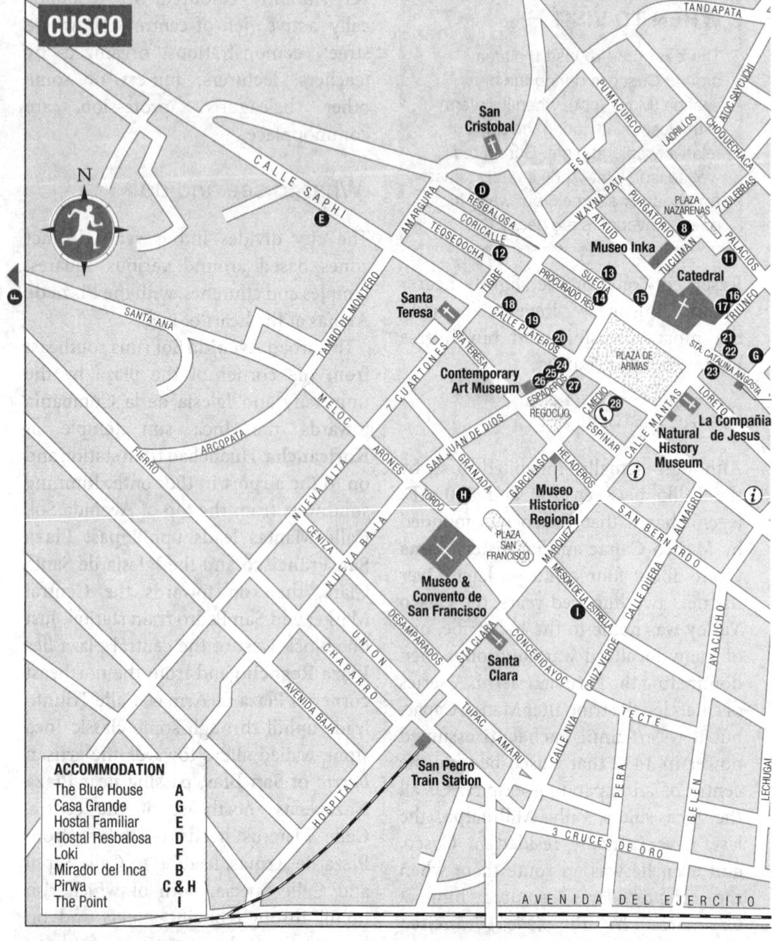

Plaza de Armas

Cusco's ancient and modern centre, the **Plaza de Armas**, corresponds roughly to the ceremonial *Huacaypata*, the Incas' ancient central plaza, and is the obvious place to get your bearings. With the unmistakable ruined fortress of **Sacsayhuaman** towering above, you can always find your way back to the plaza simply by locating Sacsayhuaman, or, at night, the illuminated white figure of Christ that stands beside the fortress on the horizon. The plaza is always busy, its northern and western sides filled with shops and restaurants. The **Portal de Panes** is a covered cloister pavement hosting processions of boys trying hard to sell postcards, and waiters and waitresses competing for customers, trying to drag passing tourists into their particular dive.

Cathedral

The plaza's exposed northeastern edge is dominated by the squat **Catedral**, (Mon–Sat 10am–6pm, Sun 2–6pm; entry by Cusco Tourist Ticket, see box, p.821), which sits solidly on the

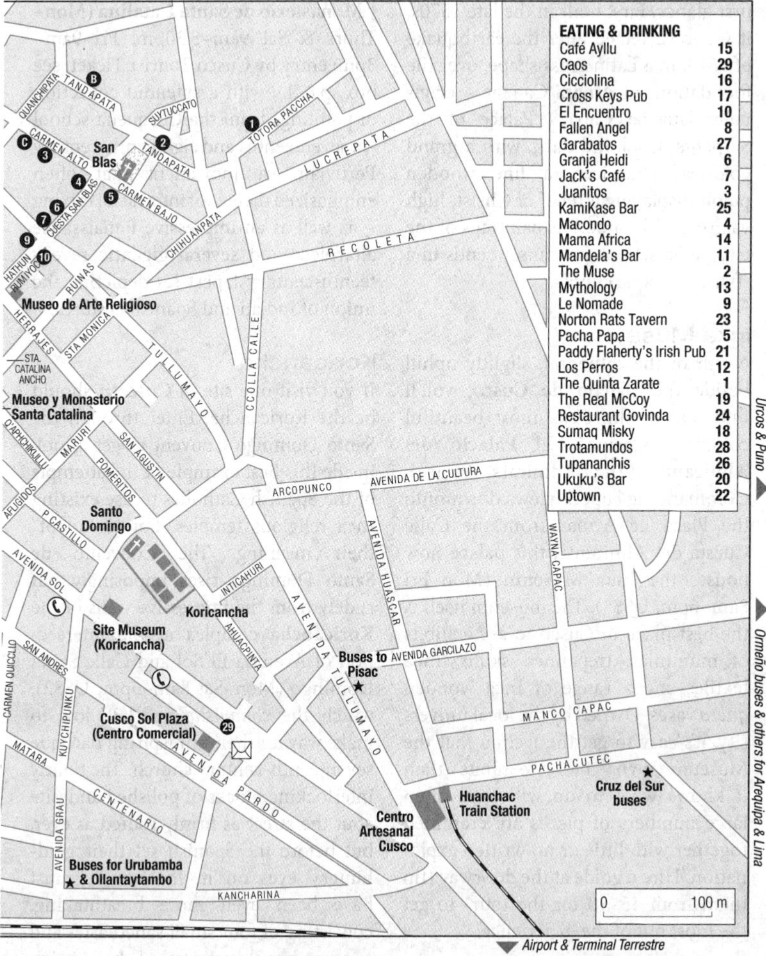

foundations of the Inca Wiracocha's palace. Its massive lines look fortress-like in comparison with the delicate form of the nearby Iglesia de la Compañía de Jesús, with its impressive pair of belfries, which sits at the southeastern end of the plaza. Check out the cathedral's finely carved granite altar and huge canvas depicting the terrible 1650 earthquake, before moving into the main cathedral to see an intricately carved Plateresque pulpit and beautiful, cedar-wood seats, as well as a neoclassical high altar made entirely of finely beaten embossed silver.

Ten smaller chapels surround the nave, including the **Chapel of the Immaculate Conception** and the **Chapel of El Señor de los Temblores** (The Lord of Earthquakes), the latter housing a 26-kilo crucifix made of solid gold and encrusted with precious stones.

Iglesia de la Compañía de Jesús

Looking downhill from the centre of the plaza, the **Iglesia de la Compañía de Jesús** dominates the skyline, and is often confused with the cathedral on first glance. First built in the late 1570s, it was resurrected after the earthquake of 1650, in a Latin cross shape, over the foundations of Amara Cancha – originally Huayna Capac's Palace of the Serpents. Cool and dark, with a grand gold-leaf altarpiece, a fine wooden pulpit displaying a relief of Christ, high vaulting and numerous paintings of the Cusqueña school, its transept ends in a stylish Baroque cupola.

Inka Museum

North of the cathedral, slightly uphill beside the **Balcón de Cusco**, you'll find one of the city's most beautiful colonial mansions, **El Palacio del Almirante** (The Admiral's Palace). Commanding superb views down onto the Plaza de Armas from the Calle Cuesta del Almirante, this palace now houses the **Inka Museum** (Mon–Fri 8am–6pm; US$3). The museum itself is the best place in Cusco to see exhibits of mummies, trepanned skulls, Inca textiles and a range of Inca wooden *quero* vases. Owned by the local university, it's easy to get the feeling that the Museum owns more exhibits than it knows what to do with and often large numbers of pieces are crammed together with little or no written explanation. Hire a guide at the doorway (tip them from $5–10 for the tour) to get the most out of the experience.

Santa Catalina Convent

Leading away from the Plaza de Armas, Callejón Loreto separates La Compañía from the tall, stone walls of the ancient **Acclahuasi**, or Temple of the Sun Virgins, where the Sun Virgins used to make *chicha* beer for the Lord Inca. Today, the Acclahuasi building is occupied by the **Convent of Santa Catalina**, built in 1610, with its small but grand side entrance half a short block down Calle Arequipa; just under thirty sisters still live and worship here. Inside the convent is the **Museo de Arte y Monasterio de Santa Catalina** (Mon–Thurs & Sat 9am–5.30pm, Fri 9am–3pm; entry by Cusco Tourist Ticket, see box, p.821), with a splendid collection of paintings from the Cusqueña school – a seventeenth- and eighteenth-century Peruvian art movement that often emphasized themes of interracial mixing – as well as an impressive Renaissance altarpiece and several gigantic seventeenth-century tapestries depicting the union of Indian and Spanish cultures.

Koricancha

If you visit one site in Cusco it should be the Koricancha. Enter through the Santo Domingo Convent to get a look inside this best example of the attempts of the Spanish Catholics to use existing Inca religious temples, but to "adapt" their meaning. The Convento de Santo Domingo rises imposingly but rudely from the impressive walls of the **Koricancha** complex at the intersection of Avenida El Sol and Calle Santa Domingo (Mon–Sat 8am–5pm; US$2), which the *conquistadores* laid low to make way for their uninspiring Baroque seventeenth-century church. The tightly interlocking blocks of polished andesite abut the street as firmly rooted as ever, but before the Spanish set their gold-hungry eyes on it, the temple must have been even more breathtaking, consisting of four small sanctuaries and a larger temple set around the existing courtyard, which was encircled by a cornice of gold (Koricancha means "golden enclosure"). Some of the inner walls, too, were hung with beaten sheets of gold. Below the temple was an artificial garden in which everything was made of gold or silver and encrusted with precious jewels, from llamas and shepherds to the tiniest details of clumps of earth and weeds, including snails and butterflies. Unsurprisingly, none of this survived the arrival of the Spanish.

To reach the **Koricancha Site Museum** (daily 9.30am–6pm; entry by

Cusco Tourist Ticket, see box, p.821), or Museo Arqueológico de Qorikancha, it's a three-minute walk downhill from the complex reception to the underground museum entrance on block 3 of Avenida Sol. There are five rooms here, each containing a number of archeological pieces. On your way round, take a moment to admire the Koricancha from the outside as the Inca stone foundations are clearly visible, holding up the colonial convent.

La Merced

Five minutes' walk southwest, along Calle Mantas from the Plaza de Armas, brings you to the **Iglesia y Convento de La Merced** (daily 8am–noon & 2–5pm; 50¢), sitting peacefully amid the bustle of one of Cusco's more interesting quarters. Founded in 1536 by Brother Sebastián de Trujillo y Castañeda, it was rebuilt some 25 years after the 1650 earthquake in a rich combination of Baroque and Renaissance styles by such artisans as the native master builders Alonso Casay and Francisco Monya. The facade is exceptional and the roof is endowed with an unusual Baroque spire, while inside there's a beautiful star-studded ceiling, a finely carved chair and a huge silver cross, which is adored and kissed by a shuffling crowd. Its highlight, however, is a breathtaking 1720s **monstrance** standing a metre high and crafted by Spanish jeweller Juan de Olmos, using over 600 pearls, more than 1500 diamonds and upwards of 22kg of solid gold. The monastery also possesses a fine collection of Cusqueña school paintings, particularly in the cloisters and vestry, but it is the exceptional beauty of the white-stone cloister here that really catches the eye.

Plaza San Francisco

Continue on another block and you'll come to the **Plaza San Francisco**, which comes alive on a Sunday with food stalls selling traditional favourites, street performers and crowds of locals out to enjoy the sunshine. The square's southwestern side is dominated by the simply decorated **Museo y Convento de San Francisco** (Mon–Sat 9am–5.30pm; 30¢), founded in 1645 and completed in 1652 and incorporating two facades and a tower. Inside, two large cloisters boast some of the better colonial paintings by such local masters as Diego Quispe Tito, Marcos Zapata and Juan Espinosa de los Monteros, who was responsible for the massive oil canvas measuring some 12m by 9m. There's also an unusual candelabra made out of human bones.

San Pedro Market

Stop in to the **San Pedro Market** (daily 8am–5pm) to enjoy a freshly squeezed juice, stock up on fresh foods for a trek, or just to watch the world go by. Altough it is principally a food market, there are several stalls selling traditional costumes (these ladies can also repair clothing). At the top end, a few interesting herb stalls can be found, as well as magic kiosks displaying everything from lucky charms to jungle medicines.

Around Plaza Regocijo

Only a block southwest of the Plaza de Armas, the **Plaza Regocijo**, a pleasant garden square sheltering a statue of Bolognesi, was originally the Inca *cusipata*, an area cleared for dancing and festivities beside the Incas' ancient central plaza. Regocijo is dominated on its northwestern side by an attractively arched municipal building housing the Contemporary Art Museum, with a traditional Inca rainbow flag flying from its roof. Opposite this is the *Hotel Cusco*, formerly the grand, state-run *Hotel de Turistas*, while on the southwest corner of the plaza lies an impressive mansion where more Inca stones mingle with colonial construction, home to the Museo Histórico Regional y Casa Garcilaso. Leading off from the top of Regocijo, **Calle Santa Teresa** is home to the House of the Pumas and leads to the Iglesia de Santa Teresa.

Museo Histórico Regional y Casa Garcilaso

Once the residence of a prolific half-Inca, half-Spanish poet and author, the **Museo Histórico Regional y Casa Garcilaso** (Mon–Sat 9am–5.30pm; entry by Cusco Tourist Ticket, see box, p.821) is home to significant regional archeological finds and much of Cusco's historic art. Fascinating **pre-Inca** ceramics from all over Peru are displayed, plus a Nasca mummy in a foetal position and with typically long (1.5m) hair, embalming herbs and unctures, black ceramics with incised designs from the early Cusco culture (1000–200 BC), and a number of **Inca** artefacts such as bolas, maces, architects' plumb lines and square water dishes for finding horizontal levels on buildings. The museum also displays gold bracelets discovered at Machu Picchu in 1995, some gold and silver llamas found in 1996 in the Plaza de Armas when reconstructing the central fountain, and golden pumas and figurines from Sacsayhuaman. From the **colonial** era there are some weavings, wooden *quero* drinking vessels and dancing masks.

The main exhibition rooms upstairs house mainly period furniture and a multitude of Cusqueña paintings, which cross the range from the rather dull (religious adorations) to the more spectacular (like the famous eighteenth-century *Jacob's Ladder*). As you progress through the works you'll notice the rapid intrusion of cannons, gunpowder and violence throughout the 1700s, something which was reflected in Cusco art as a microcosm of what happened across the colonial world.

Plaza Nazarenas

Calle Córdoba del Tucuman runs northeast from Plaza de Armas along the northern edge of the cathedral, past the Museo Inka (see p.818) and up to the small, quiet **Plaza Nazarenas**. At the top of this square, the **Larco Museum of Pre-Columbian Art** housed in the **Casa Cabrera** (daily 9am–11pm; US$8) has an open courtyard featuring one of Cusco's finest restaurants and exhibition rooms displaying some of the most impressive pieces of pre-Columbian art in the country. With top-class lighting and information, it is Cusco's only international standard museum. The building was once part of Cancha Inka, a busy Inca urban centre prior to the Spanish Conquest; it was occupied by Jerónimo Luis de Cabrera, mayor of Cusco, in the seventeenth century.

On the northeastern side of Plaza Nazarenas, the ancient, subtly ornate **Chapel of San Antonio Abad** was originally connected to a religious school before becoming part of the university in the seventeenth century. It's not open to the public, but you can usually look around the courtyard of the **Nazarenas Convent**, virtually next door and home to the plush *Hotel Monasterio*.

San Blas

Just around the corner you come to the narrow alley of **Hathun Rumiyoq**, the most famous Inca passageway of

MOUNTAIN SICKNESS

Soroche, or mountain sickness, is a reality for most people arriving in Cusco by plane from sea level. It's vital to take it easy, not eating or drinking much on arrival, even sleeping a whole day just to assist acclimatization. Coca tea is a good local remedy. After three days at this height most people have adjusted sufficiently to tackle moderate hikes at similar or lesser altitudes. Anyone considering tackling the major mountains around Cusco will need time to adjust again to their higher base camps. *Soroche* needs to be treated with respect.

all. Within its impressive walls lies the celebrated Inca **stone**, perhaps best known through its representation on bottles of Cusqueña beer. The twelve-cornered block fits perfectly into the lower wall of the Inca Roca's old imperial palace, and you will have no trouble finding it as it is guarded by an "Inca" in costume and plenty of young boys who will point it out to you and ask for a *propina* "tip" in return.

Walking up the Cuesta de San Blas, which continues from the far end of Hathun Rumiyoq, you come to the tiny **Chapel of San Blas** (Mon–Wed, Fri–Sun 10–11.30am & daily 2–5.30pm; entry by Boleto Integral, see box, below). The highlight here is an incredibly intricate pulpit, carved from a block of cedar wood in a complicated Churrigueresque style; its detail includes a cherub, a sun-disc, faces and bunches of grapes. Outside, along Calle Plazoleta (also called Suytuccato), there are a few art workshops and galleries, the most notable of which is Galeria Olave, at no. 651. The **Museo de Cerámica**, Carmen Alto 133, is worth checking out for its pottery, while on the *plazoleta* is the quaint **Museo Taller Hilario Mendivil**, containing a number of Cusqueña paintings, some interesting murals and religious icons. The Plazoleta de San Blas hosts a Saturday handicrafts market, and is full most days of the week of lingering artisans hoping to sell their handmade jewellery to passing tourists.

Arrival

By air Cusco airport (☎084/222611 for information) is 4km south of the city centre. You can either take a taxi from outside the arrivals hall (US$2–3 to the city centre), or a *colectivo combi* (frequent departures), from outside the airport car park, which goes to Plaza San Francisco via Avenida Sol and Plaza de Armas.

By train If you're coming in from Puno by train, you'll arrive at the Huanchac station in the southeast of the city. From here you can hail a taxi on the street outside (around US$1 to the centre), catch the airport *colectivo* mentioned above, or walk the eight or nine blocks up a gentle hill to the Plaza de Armas.

By bus Apart from Cruz del Sur, which has its own independent depot at Avenida Pachacutec, a few blocks east of Huanchac railway station and Avenida Sol, interregional and international buses arrive and depart from the rather scruffy Terminal Terrestre, southeast of the centre, close to the Pachacutec monument and roundabout (*ovalo*). Taxis from here to the city centre cost US$1–2, or you can walk to the Pachacutec *ovalo* and catch a *colectivo* uphill to either the Plaza San Francisco or the Plaza de Armas; otherwise, it's about a half-hour walk. Regional buses from the Sicuani, Urcos and Paucartambo areas stop around blocks 15 and 16 of Avenida de la Cultura, from where it's a bit of a hike, so you'll almost certainly want to take a taxi (US$1–2) or bus or *combi colectivo* (30¢) to the centre. For the Sacred Valley, Av Grau 525 (opposite Calle Pavitos) for Urubamba via Chincheros and two daily direct buses to Ollantaytambo, and Av Tullumayo 207 for Calca via Pisac, and Calle Puputi for Pisac only.

Information

Tourist information The main tourist office, operated by the Dirección Regional de Industria y Turismo (DRIT) at Mantas 117-A (Mon–Fri 8am–7pm,

THE CUSCO TOURIST TICKET AND BOLETO INTEGRAL

The **Cusco Tourist Ticket** (US$45 for ten days, students with ISIC card US$23) is a vital purchase for most visitors. The only key to entry for sixteen of the city and region's main attractions, it includes useful maps plus opening times. It's available from all of the sites on the ticket, or from the issuing OFEC offices at Av Sol 103, office 106 (☎084/227037 Ⓦwww.boletoturisticocusco.com). The tourist ticket no longer includes any of the city's religious buildings which have their own similar **Boleto Integral** which covers the Cathedral, San Blas Church, Archbishop's Palace and Iglesia de la Compañía. The ticket costs $13 for adults and can be purchased at any of the places on it.

Sat 8am–2.30pm; ⓣ084/222032) is a short block from the Plaza de Armas and operates a kiosk at the airport and the Terminal Terrestre. The downtown office is well staffed, spacious and offers a friendly service with sound advice on where to go and how to get there as well as maps and brochures. **I-Peru** has a desk in the arrivals hall at the airport (ⓣ084/237364) and at Av El Sol 103 (daily 8.30am–7.30pm; ⓣ084/252974), and has free maps and brochures about the area. For independent recommendations, information and good trekking maps try **South American Explorers' Club,** Choquechaca 188, bell 4 (Mon–Fri 9.30am–5pm, Sat 9.30am–1pm ⓣ084/245484, ⓦwww.saexplorers.org). The Andean Travel Web (ⓦwww.andeantravelweb.com) also has up to date information about events and festivities in the Cusco area.

Tours

The Cusco area is an adrenaline junkie's paradise with a huge range of adventure sports on offer. As well as trekking expeditions (see below), there is world-class river rafting on the Apurimac River, climbing and canyoning in the Sacred Valley, mountain biking trails, horse-riding, paragliding and bungee jumping to keep your heart rate up.

Action Valley Located in Poroy, with an office at Santa Teresa 325, Cusco ⓣ084/240835 ⓦwww.actionvalleycusco.com. Offers bungee jumping, slingshot, climbing wall and abseiling, zip-line and paint-balling in a small valley just outside of Cusco.

Andina Travel Plazoleta Santa Catalina 219, Cusco ⓣ084/251892 ⓦwww.andinatravel.com.

TOURS IN AND AROUND CUSCO

Tours in and around Cusco range from a half-day city tour to an expedition by light aircraft or a full-on adventure down to the Amazon. **Prices** range from US$20 to over US$100 a day, and service and facilities vary considerably, so check exactly what's provided, whether insurance is included and whether the guide speaks English. The main agents are strung along three sides of the Plaza de Armas, along Portal de Panes, Portal de Confiturias and Portal Comercio, up Procuradores and along the calles Plateros and Saphi and, although prices vary, many are selling places on the same tours and treks, so always hunt around.

Standard tours around the city, Sacred Valley and to Machu Picchu range from a basic bus service with fixed stops and little in the way of a guide, to luxury packages including guide, food and hotel transfers. The two to four-day **Inca Trail** is the most popular of the **mountain treks**, with five hundred people setting off on the trail every day; many agencies offer trips with guides, equipment and fixed itineraries; but it's important to remember that entry to the Inca Trail is restricted and requires tourists to travel with a guide or tour as well as to be registered with the Unidad de Gestión (your tour company does this) at least thirty days before departure (in practice it is usually necessary to reserve a place four to six months in advance). In selecting the right Inca Trail tour option it's a good idea to check with at least two or three of those listed before deciding which to go with; prices vary considerably between US$250 & US$600 and although a higher price doesn't always reflect genuine added value, usually the better and more responsible companies will have higher expenses to cover (for better food, equipment, fair wages etc). Check exactly what's provided: train tickets (which class), quality of tent, roll mat, sleeping bag, porter to carry rucksack and sleeping bag, bus down from ruins, exactly which meals, transport to start.

Other **popular hikes** are around the snowcapped mountains of Salcantay (6264m) to the north and Ausangate (6372m) to the south, a more remote trek, which needs at least a week plus guides and mules. (See p.844 for more info about these and other alternative Inca trails). Less adventurous **walks** or **horse rides** are possible to Qenko, Tambo Machay, Puca Pucara and Chacan, in the hills above Cusco and in the nearby Sacred Valley. You can also rent out **mountain bikes** for trips to the Sacred Valley and around, and some outfits arrange guided tours. Many **jungle trip** operators are based in Cusco, and those that also cover the immediate Cusco area are listed on above.

A well- established tour operator who specialise in trekking and are always opening up new and exciting alternative routes.

Apumayo C Garcilaso 265, Oficina 3, Cusco ⓣ084/246018, ⓔapumayo@terra.com.pe. Specialised in rafting trips, Apumayo is an expert operator also offering trekking in the Sacred Valley region, mountain biking around Cusco and the Sacred Valley, historic and archeological tours, tours for disabled people (with wheelchair support for visiting major sites) and horse riding.

Big Foot C Triunfo 392, Cusco ⓣ084/238568 ⓦwww.bigfootcusco.com. Specialists in climbing and mountaineering trips.

Chaska ⓦwww.chaskatours.com. With a bias towards eco-tourism Chaska run responsible treks around the Cusco area.

Eco Trek Peru Canchipata 560, San Blas, Cusco ⓣ084/247286 ⓦwww.ecotrekperu.com. Experienced and professional mountain bikers, offering trips into the Sacred Valley and around.

Enigma Clorinda Mato de Turner 100, Urb Magisterial, Cusco ⓣ084/222155 ⓦwww.enigmaperu.com. More expensive than some other operators, Enigma offers high quality trekking trips in the Cusco area as well as countrywide itineraries.

Explorandes Av Garcilazo 316-A, Wanchaq ⓣ084/238380, ⓦwww.explorandes.com or San Fernando 320, Miraflores, Lima ⓣ01/4450532. A long-established company with a range of tours, including the Inca Trail and to Cordillera Vilcanota.

Llama Path San Juan de Dios 250, Cusco ⓣ084/240822 ⓦwww.llamapath.com. One of the newer trekking operators in town, Llama Path has quickly established itself as a more affordable, high quality, responsible tour operator. Look out for their porters on the Inca Trail with their flashy bright red equipment.

Mayuc Portal Confiturias 211, Cusco ⓣ084/232666, ⓦwww.mayuc.com. Highly reliable outfit with the experience to organize any tour or trek of your choice, from an extended Inca Trail to visiting the Tambopata-Candamo area. White-water rafting is their speciality with standard scheduled 3 day/2 night Apurimac expeditions throughout the rafting season (May–Oct) – the cheapest of the reliable rafting operators.

Perol Chico Urubamba, Sacred Valley ⓣ084/213386 ⓦwww.perolchico.com. Recommended stables with well cared for horses. Riding trips around the Sacred Valley from half day excursions to nearby ruins, to 2 week expeditions.

Peru Treks & Adventures C Garcilaso 265, Interior patio, 2nd floor, Cusco ⓣ084/505863 ⓦwww.perutreks.com. Highly recommended operator for Inca trail and treks around the Cusco region. Very involved in social projects helping isolated communities.

Q'ente Choquechaca 229, Cusco ⓣ233722 ⓦwww.qente.com. Adventure travel company specializing in Alternative treks as well as the Inca Trail.

Wayki Trek Procuradores 351, Cusco ⓣ084/224092 ⓦwww.waykitrek.net. Professional company offering some off the beaten trail treks, also offers a "wayki option" on the Inca Trail whereby groups spend the night in a porter community prior to starting the trail. Wayki trek also supports many social projects in the area.

United Mice C Plateros 351, Cusco, ⓣ084/221139 ⓦwww.unitedmice.com. One of the original Inca Trail operators, the owner of this company started out as a porter on the trail. Professional service and good English-speaking guides.

Viento Sur Urubamba, Sacred Valley, ⓣ084/201620 ⓦwww.aventurasvientosur.com. Paragliding trips in the Sacred Valley, from a one-day tandem flight to a full 8 day paragliding course, as well as equipment rental to qualified pilots.

City transport

Walking Cusco's centre is small enough to walk around.

Taxis Taxis can be waved down on any street, particularly on the Plaza de Armas, Avenida Sol and around the market end of Plaza San Francisco; rides within Cusco cost under US$1 or US$2–3 for trips to the suburbs or up to Sacsayhuaman and Q'enko (some *taxistas* may prefer to charge US$5 and wait for you, in which case give them half in advance and the remainder at the end of the journey).

Buses and colectivos The city bus and *colectivo* networks are incredibly complicated, though cheap and fast once you learn your way around, and charge US$0.20 per person. For 3 or more people traveling together it's cheaper to take a taxi.

Accommodation

Much of the city's budget **accommodation** is in the zone to the north of the Plaza de Armas along calles Plateros, Procuradores and Saphi, but there are relatively inexpensive and reasonable mid-range hostels and hotels in most corners of the city. Calles Procuradores and Plateros are particularly noisy at night; more peaceful locations, though slightly pricier, are further up Calle Saphi, around Plaza Regocijo, towards San Blas and, if you are prepared to walk a little, along Choquechaca and Tandapata, further up the hill from the centre.

The Blue House Kiskapata 291, San Blas, ⓣ084/242407 ⓦwww.thebluehouse.info. Long and short term rooms with shared or private bath. There is a shared kitchen and DVD room, with additional services such as laundry and full-board option at an extra cost. Run by a friendly family. Singles and doubles with big windows, and 2 patios with great views over the city. Relatively high up in San Blas, the Blue House is only accessible on foot (and is at the top of a long flight of stairs). ❷

Casa Grande Santa Catalina Ancha 353 (ⓣ084/264156). Just around the corner from the Plaza de Armas, this slightly run down but friendly hostel is a good choice. 24hr hot water, safe luggage storage and single, double and triple rooms with private or shared bathrooms. ❸–❹

Hostal Resbalosa Resbalosa 494 (ⓣ084/224839, ⓔhostalresbalosa@hotmail.com). Up a steep, slightly slippery street (*resbalosa* is Spanish for slippery) from the Plaza de Armas, Resbalosa is a friendly, clean and popular place to stay. Great views over the city from the terrace, but can only be reached on foot. ❷–❸

Hostal Familiar C Saphi 661 ⓣ084/239353. Quiet, safe and one of Cusco's best budget options (it's best to reserve in advance). Rooms are spartan but cool, clean and nicely furnished, with or without private bath (in which case showers are communal) and there's usually hot water in the mornings. ❸–❹

Loki Cuesta Santa Ana 601, ⓣ084/243705, ⓦwww.lokihostel.com. The first of the Loki chain to open, this is the original party hostel. With a bar and travel agency on site, dorm beds and private rooms, shared kitchen and free internet, this is a great place to meet people and have a good time; its not so great if you want a quiet night's sleep. ❺

Mirador del Inca Tandapata 160 (ⓣ084/261384, ⓔmiradordelinca@latinmail.com). Very quiet and with great views of Cusco from its San Blas perch. Some rooms feature Inca stone walls which although very atmospheric can make the rooms feel cold and a bit dungeon like. Ask if any of the higher up rooms are free. ❷–❸

Pirwa Plaza San Francisco 360 and Carmen Alto 283, ⓦwww.pirwahostelscusco.com. A slightly more sedate backpacker option, Pirwa has 70 dorm beds in the San Fransisco location, and more private rooms at the Carmen Alto hostel. Both have kitchen and internet access, as well as laundry service and backpack storage. ❹

The Point Mesón de la Estrella 172 ⓣ084/252266, ⓦwww.thepointhostels.com, Another favourite for backpackers who like to party, The Point often hosts parties with international DJs. Other services include onsite bar and restaurant, free internet, kitchen, and laundry service. ❸

Eating

Cusco **restaurants** range from cheap and cheerful to top quality fine dining establishments. Many serve international cuisine but the *quintas*, basic local eating houses, serve mostly traditional **Peruvian fare**, full of spice and character in a typical Cusco ambience. Generally speaking trout is plentiful, reasonably priced and usually excellent, and roast guinea pig (*cuy*) can usually be ordered, but **pizza** seems to lead in the local popularity stakes. The more central **cafés and restaurants** accommodate most tastes, serving anything from a toasted cheese sandwich to authentic Andean or *criolla* dishes (a Peruvian form of Creole).

Café Ayllu Portal de Carnes 208, Plaza de Armas. Serves one of the best breakfasts in Peru, including fruit, yogurt and toasted sandwiches, though it's not cheap. Centrally located with downstairs views across the plaza, it's Cusco's most traditional meeting place and the service is fast. Breakfast 15 soles.

El Encuentro Santa Catalina 384 and Choquechaca 136. These two joints serve up an impressingly imaginative range of strictly vegetarian fare, as well as very cheap lunch and dinner menus with fresh salad buffet (5 soles).

Restaurant Govinda Espaderos 128. The original vegetarian eating house in Cusco, serving simple healthy food which is generally adequate; the fruit and yogurt breakfasts are very good and the set lunches excellent value. If you get the chance, eat upstairs where there's more atmosphere and more room. Mains 12–15 soles.

Granja Heidi Cuesta San Blas 525 ⓣ084/238383. A huge healthy selection of breakfasts with lots of homemade dairy products. Main courses are around 25 soles in the evening, but go at lunchtime and snap up a 18 soles three-course menu of delicious wholefood dishes.

Jack's Cafe Choquechaca 509. Probably the most popular place with Gringos in Cusco, expect to queue for up to an hour outside Jack's Café in high season. The food is definitely worth the wait – with a menu packed full of breakfast and sandwich options as well as great coffee and juices, it's just like home – or maybe better! Mains 15 soles.

Juanitos Carmen Alto 227. This may not look like much from the outside, but this tiny sandwich joint serves the best sandwiches in Cusco. Everything is freshly cooked to order with your choice of garnishes and sauces and the finished sandwiches are so big that they need a small electric saw to cut them in half for you. Sandwich 8 soles.

Macondo Cuesta San Blas 571 ☎084/229415. A gay-friendly restaurant with wacky decor and serving some of the best nouveau Andean and Amazonian cuisine you'll find anywhere; try the *yuquitas* stuffed with *chimbivalcano* cheese, the vegetarian curry or the Alpaca mignon *a la parmesana*. Best in evenings when it's a good idea to book in advance, but serves meals, a menu and sandwiches during the day. Mains 15–25 soles. If you like this place, try the more extravagant and expensive **Fallen Angel** on Plaza Nazarenas. Mains 30–50 soles.

Pacha Papa Plaza San Blas 120. A great, comparatively inexpensive restaurant set around an attractive courtyard, serving a range of hard-to-find Andean dishes, from a *gulash de alpaca* to the highly nutritious *sopa de quinoa*. Reservations recommended. Mains 20–40 soles.

The Quinta Zarate Totora Paccha 763. Excellent traditional food and atmosphere, close to the San Blas plaza – just climb the steps to the right of the fountain, turn right and keep going until you get to the end of the road, it's right there on the left hand side. You can also take a taxi as most drivers will know it. Mains 18–25 soles.

The Real McCoy Plateros 326, second floor. Very authentic British themed and owned restaurant serving pie and mash, full roast dinners and great breakfast buffets with an "all you can eat" option. Also a good place to drink as they have happy hour specials every night. Mains 14–27 soles.

Sumaq Misky Plateros 111, second floor. A great place to try some innovative takes on traditional Andean food – try the curried guinea pig! A large comfortable atmosphere and a huge open kitchen so that you can marvel at the chefs as they prepare your food. Not the cheapest but great value for the quality and quantity of food. Mains 16–34 soles.

Trotamundos Portal de Comercio 177 (2nd floor), Plaza de Armas. Has great coffee and sandwiches, with balconies overlooking the Plaza de Armas. Also try their chocolate *turrón*. Sandwich 12 soles.

TREAT YOURSELF

As Cusco has become more cosmopolitan in recent years, several excellent restaurants have opened around the centre. Experiment with some of Cusco's finest cuisine at **Cicciolina**, Calle Triunfo 393, 2nd floor, an Italian restaurant which also has tapas and an extensive wine list (mains from $15-$20), or at the sumptuously decorated **Tupananchis**, Plazoleta Espinar 180-184, featuring a daring Novo-Andean menu as well as old classics including great steaks (mains $18-$25).

Drinking and nightlife

Apart from Lima, no Peruvian town has as varied a **nightlife** as Cusco. The corner of Plaza de Armas, where Calle Plateros begins, is a hive of activity until the early hours, even during the week. Most nightspots in the city are simply **bars** with a dancefloor and sometimes a stage, but their styles vary enormously, from Andean folk joints with panpipe music through to reggae or jazz joints and more conventional **clubs**. Most places are within staggering distance of each other, and sampling them is an important part of any stay in Cusco. Many open around 9pm and keep going until 2 or 3am, so it shouldn't be too difficult to manage.

Pubs and bars

The Cross Keys Pub Calle Triunfo 350, second floor. One of the hubs of Cusco's nightlife, this classic English pub has recently moved location from its traditional spot on the Plaza de Armas. Bar food is available and there are often English-language newspapers and magazines.

Mandela's Bar Palacio 121, 3rd floor (above an alpaca shop). Huge bar with cozy corners for couples, lot of cocktails and a heated outdoor rooftop terrace, so you can sit back and sip while watching the stars (without freezing to death).

The Muse Bar Café Art Gallery Tandapata 682. On the terrace above the Plazoleta San Blas. It has a cosy atmosphere, good drinks and food all day with tables outside; also plays live music from 10-ish most weekends and sometimes during the week.

Le Nomade Choquechaca 207 (2nd floor). Trendy French-run café bar with live music most nights. Also a variety of flavoured rums and different wines, and hookah pipes to smoke.

Norton Rats Tavern Santa Catalina Angosta 116, second floor, Plaza de Armas. Best known as a drinking establishment, it serves special jungle cocktails, is spacious, plays rock, blues, jazz and Latin music and features a pool table and dartboard and cable TV for sports. There's also a café serving great hamburgers.

Paddy Flaherty's Irish Pub Triunfo 124. Just off the Plaza de Armas, this pub is a great place to meet people and drink real Guinness. They also have good food in huge portions.

Los Perros Teqsecocha 436. Billing itself as "the original couch bar", *Los Perros* is a trendy hang-out where travellers snack, drink and play board games or read magazines.

Clubs and dance bars

Many of the clubs around the Plaza de Armas will offer free entrance passes and free drinks tokens to you as you walk around the Plaza. Be aware that the free drinks are made from the cheapest alcohol available and often ice made from tap water – one night of free drinks is unlikely to kill you, but often medical bills after the event will end up being more costly than just buying drinks from a reputable bar.

Caos The only swanky nightclub in Cusco, *Caos* charges a US$10 cover to get in, but plays a good variety of international music and has a great atmosphere.

Garabatos Espaderos, second floor The most popular place among Cusco's over 30 crowd to go dancing. With a huge variety of cocktails to keep you busy, straddle one of the saddle-style bar stools, sit back and watch some serious salsa as couples fight for space on the dancefloor to show off their moves. Live salsa and Creole bands at the weekends.

KamiKase Bar Portal Cabildo 274, Plaza Regocijo. One of Cusco's best-established nightspots, with modern Andean rock-art decor and basic furnishings. Drinks are quite cheap, though when it hosts live music (most weekends), there's usually a small entrance fee, but it's worthwhile if you're into rock and Andean folk. Live music usually starts around 10pm.

Mama Africa Portal de Harinas 191, second floor, Plaza de Armas. A popular sweaty spot to grind away among young locals and tourists.
Daily 9pm–6am. Often shows videos in the afternoons and sometimes offers dance classes in salsa and samba.

Mythology Portal de Carnes 298, second floor, Plaza de Armas. Popular hang-out for backpackers and local guides, cheap drinks and a good mix of music with films in the afternoons. Also has a restaurant and comfy seating areas.

Ukuku's Bar C Plateros 316, down the alley and upstairs. A highly popular venue with one of the best atmospheres in Cusco, thronging with energetic revellers most nights by around 11pm, when the live music gets going. There's a small dancefloor and a long bar, with music ranging from live Andean folk with panpipes, drums and *charangos* (small Andean stringed instruments) to trance.

Uptown Plaza de Armas on the corner of Santa Catalina Angosta, second floor above Gatos Market. This club is always pumping and packed full of tourists and locals. They play films in the afternoons and have free salsa classes every night at 9pm, often with over-friendly instructors.

Shopping

The main concentration of touristy *artesanía* and jewellery **shops** is in the streets around the Plaza de Armas and up Triunfo, though Calle San Agustín (first right off Triunfo as you head towards San Blas), has slightly cheaper but decent shops with leather and alpaca work. You'll find shops selling photographic film, postcards and books in the same zone. It's worth heading off the beaten track to find other outlets hidden in the backstreets, and even in the smarter shops it's quite acceptable to bargain a little. In the markets and at street stalls you can often get up to twenty percent off. Try the artisans' centre at the junction of Avenida Tullumayo and Avenida Pachacutec for some real bargains.

Directory

Airlines Aero Condor, Santa Catalina Ancha 315 ⓣ084/246349; Lan Peru, Av El Sol 627-B ⓣ084/255552; Star Peru, Av El Sol 679, office 1 ⓣ084/234060, TACA Peru, Av El Sol 602-B ⓣ084/249921. Most companies have daily flights to Lima for about $70 one way. Departure tax is around US$10 for international departures, US$4 for domestic flights.

Banks and exchange Interbank, Av El Sol 380 (also has ATM at airport and a small branch in the Plaza de Armas) is good for traveller's cheques, cash exchange and credit card extraction and has an ATM compatible with MasterCard, Visa, Cirrus and Amex Mon–Fri 9am–6pm, Sat 9am–12.30pm; Banco de Crédito, Av El Sol 189 has a handy booth with ATM machines with 24 hour security. For faster service and better rates than banks, try LAC Dollar (Av El Sol 150; Mon–Sat 9am–7pm), one of the better and more central money changing offices; street *cambistas* can be found on blocks 2 and 3 of Av Sol, around the main banks, but as usual take great care here.

Bus companies Interregional and international buses depart from Terminal Terrestre, Sector Molino Pampa, right side Río Huatanay, in the district of

Santiago ⓣ084/224471; except for those run by Cruz del Sur, which leave from Av Pachacutec 510 ⓣ084/248255. Comfortable direct buses run from Cusco to Puno, Arequipa, Nazca and Lima. At the Terminal Terrestre there is an embarkation tax of 30¢, which you pay before getting on. Recommended operators for all national destinations include: CIVA ⓣ084/249961 or 229762; Cruz del Sur ⓣ084/221909 or 248255; and Ormeño ⓣ084/227501.

Camping equipment There are an overwhelming number of stores and agencies renting out tents, sleeping bags, sleeping mats, stoves, gas, cooking equipment etc especially around the Plaza de Armas, Calle del Medio and Calle Plateros. Try Mañay Wasy at 341 Plateros (ⓣ084/234632); and X-Treme Tourbulencia at 358 Plateros (ⓣ084/222405). For equipment repair Edson Zuñiga is best; find him at Mercado Rosaspata, Jirón Abel Landeo P-1 (ⓣ084/232815, ⓔedsonzuniga@hotmail.com).

Car hire AVIS Rent a Car, Av El Sol 808 (ⓣ084/248800, ⓦwww.avis.com.pe); National Car Rental, book through their website ⓦwww.nationalcar.com.pe and arrange to pick up the car at Cusco airport.

Consulates UK, Calle Umberto Vidal Unda G-5, Urbanización Magisterial segunda étapa ⓣ084/226671; US, contact the Instituto de Cultura Peruana Norte Americana, Av Tullumayo 125 ⓣ084/224112.

Post office The main office is at Av Sol 800 ⓣ084/224212.

Taxis Alo Cusco ⓣ084/222222; Llama taxi ⓣ084/222000.

Telephones There are countless internet and telephone cabins around the centre of Cusco, offering cheap local, national and international calls.

Tourist police C Saphi 510 ⓣ084/249654.

Train tickets The Huanchac Station ticket office (Mon–Fri 7am–5pm, Sat & Sun 7am–noon; ⓣ084/581414, ⓦwww.perurail.com) sells train tickets to Puno and Machu Picchu (although Machu Picchu trains depart from the San Pedro Station, opposite the market). For Machu Picchu it's best to buy a week in advance, whether you want to take a train leaving from Cusco or from Ollantaytambo.

Travel agents America Tour, Portal de Harinas 175 ⓣ084/227208, ⓦwww.americatours.org mostly books and sells air tickets; Condor Travel, Calle Saphi 848 ⓣ084/225961, ⓦwww.condortravel.com.pe get good deals on air tickets and also arrange tours all over the country; Milla Turismo, Av Pardo 689 ⓣ084/231710, ⓦwww.millaturismo.com will organize travel arrangements, tours, study tours and cultural tourist-related activities.

Visas Migraciones, Av Sol 620 (Mon–Fri 8am–1pm and 2–4.30pm; ⓣ084/224741).

INCA SITES OUTSIDE CUSCO

The megalithic fortress of **Sacsayhuaman**, which looks down from high above the city onto the red-tiled roofs of Cusco, is the closest and most impressive of several historic sites scattered around the Cusco hills, but there are four other major Inca sites. Not much more than a stone's throw beyond Sacsayhuaman lies the great *huaca* of **Qenko**. A few kilometres further on, at what almost certainly formed the outer limits of the Incas' home estate, you come to the small, fortified hunting lodge of **Puca Pucara** and the nearby stunning imperial baths of **Tambo Machay**.

All these sites are an energetic day's **walk** from Cusco, but you'll probably want to devote a whole day to Sacsayhuaman and leave the other sites until you're more adjusted to the rarefied air. If you'd rather start from the top and work your way downhill, it's possible to take one of the regular **buses** to Pisac leaving from Av Tullumayo or Calle Puputi every twenty minutes throughout the day. Ask to be dropped off at the highest of the sites, Tambo Machay, from where it's an easy two-hour walk back into the centre of Cusco, or at Qenko, which is closer to Sacsayhuaman and the city. Alternatively, you can take a **horseback tour** incorporating most of these sites, though you will have to get to Sacsayhuaman or Qenko first (a US$3–4 taxi ride from the centre of Cusco).

Sacsayhuaman

Although it looks relatively close to central Cusco, it's quite a steep forty-minute, two-kilometre climb up to the ruins of Sacsayhuaman from the Plaza de Armas. The simplest route is up Calle Suecia, then first right (up a few steps) and along the narrow cobbled street of Huaynapata until it meets the even narrower lane of Pumacurco going steeply up (left) to a small café-bar with a balcony commanding superb views over the city; here the lane meets the road coming up from Calle Saphi, via the **Iglesia de San Cristobal**, a fine adobe church next to the even more impressive ruined walls of Kolkampata, the palace of the expansionist emperor Manco Capac, a good diversion to take on your way back down. It's only another ten minutes from the café, following the signposted steps all the way up to the ruins.

Because **SACSAYHUAMAN** (daily 7am–5.30pm; entry by Cusco Tourist Ticket, see box, p.821) was protected by such a steep approach from the town, it only needed defensive walls on one side, and three massive, parallel walls zigzag together for some 600m. Little of the inner structures remain, yet these enormous ramparts stand 20m high, quite unperturbed by past battles, earthquakes and the passage of time. The strength of the mortar-less stonework – one block weighs more than three hundred tonnes – is matched by the brilliance of its design: the zigzags, casting shadows in the afternoon sun, not only look like jagged cat's teeth, but also expose the flanks of any attackers trying to clamber up.

It was the Emperor Pachacuti who began work on Sacsayhuaman in the 1440s, although it took nearly a century of creative work to finish it. The chronicler Cieza de León, writing in the 1550s, estimated that some twenty thousand men had been involved in its construction: four thousand cutting blocks from quarries, six thousand dragging them on rollers to the site, and another ten thousand working on finishing and fitting them into position. According to legend, some three thousand lives were lost while dragging one huge stone.

Originally, the inner "fort" was covered in buildings, a maze of tiny streets dominated by three major towers. In front of the main defensive walls, a flat expanse of grassy ground – the esplanade – divides the fortress from a large outcrop of volcanic diorite. Intricately carved in places and scarred with deep glacial striations, this rock, called the **Rodadero** ("sliding place"), was the site of an Inca throne and, most likely, ceremonial gatherings at fiesta times. Today the most colourful time to be at this site is during the **Inti Raymi festival** in June held here annually at the summer solstice. However, throughout the year, you may stumble across various **sun ceremonies** being performed by mystics from the region.

Qenko

An easy twenty-minute walk from Sacsayhuaman, the large limestone outcrop of **QENKO** (daily 7am–5.30pm; entry by Cusco Tourist Ticket, see box, p.821) was another important Inca *huaca*. Head towards the Cusco–Pisac road along a track from the warden's hut on the northeastern edge of Sacsayhuaman, and Qenko is just over the other side of the main road; the route is straightforward but poorly signposted.

This great stone, carved with a complex pattern of steps, seats, geometric reliefs and puma designs, illustrates the critical role of the Rock Cult in the realm of Inca cosmological beliefs, and the surrounding foothills are dotted with carved rocks and elaborate stone terraces. The name of the temple derives from the Quechua word *quenqo* meaning "labyrinth" or "zigzag" and refers to the patterns laboriously carved into the upper, western edge of the stone. At an annual festival priests would pour *chicha* or sacrificial llama blood into a bowl at the serpent-like top of the main zigzag channel; if it flowed out through the left-hand bifurcation, this was a bad omen for the fertility of the year to come. If, on the other hand, it continued the full length of the zigzag and poured onto the rocks below, this was a good omen.

Puca Pucara

Although a relatively small ruin, **PUCA PUCARA** (daily 7am–5.30pm; entry by Cusco Tourist Ticket, see box, p.821), meaning "Red Fort", is around 11km from the city, impressively situated overlooking the Cusco Valley and right beside the main Cusco–Pisac road. Between one- and two-hour cross-country walk, uphill from Sacsayhuaman and Qenko (longer if you keep to the sinuous main road), this area is dotted with cut rocks. The zone was well populated in Inca days, and many of these may have been worked to obtain stones for building. Although in many ways reminiscent of a small European castle, Puca Pucara is more likely to have been a hunting lodge, or out of town lodgings (a *tambo*, as the Incas would have called this) for the emperor than simply a defensive position. Thought to have been built by the Emperor Pachacuti, it commands views towards glaciers to the south of the Cusco Valley.

Tambo Machay

TAMBO MACHAY (daily 7am–5.30pm; entry by Cusco Tourist Ticket, see box, p.821), less than fifteen minutes' walk away along a signposted track that leads off the main road just beyond Puca Pucara, is one of the more impressive Inca baths, or temple of the waters, evidently a place for ritual as well as physical cleansing and purification. Situated at a spring near the Incas' hunting lodge, its main construction lies in a sheltered gully where some superb Inca masonry again emphasizes the Inca fascination with, and adoration of, water.

The ruins basically consist of three tiered platforms. The top one holds four trapezoidal niches that may have been used as seats, but have been suggested to represent the four cardinal directions; on the next level, underground water emerges directly from a hole at the base of the stonework, and from here cascades down to the bottom platform, creating a cold shower just about high enough for an Inca to stand under. On this platform the spring water splits into two channels, both pouring the last metre down to ground level. Clearly a site for ritual bathing, the quality of the stonework suggests that its use was restricted to the higher nobility, who perhaps used the baths only on ceremonial occasions.

Tipon

On the road leading east out of Cusco towards Sicuani, the town of Tipon is famous for its oven-roasted *cuy* (guinea pig), however it has a lot more to offer. From the town, it is a steep hour and a half climb (or twenty-minute taxi ride if you are lucky enough to find the town's taxi), to the ruins. They are well worth the visit. Tipon (daily 7am–5.30pm; entry by Cusco Tourist Ticket, see box, p.821) is a large structure made up of several terraces and is one of the only working examples of Inca irrigation systems, with fountains and water channels covering the area. Disputes rage among historians over whether the site was an agricultural centre, or a water temple, but either way, it is an impressive site. To get here take a bus to Sicuani which leaves from block 15 of Av La Cultura and ask the driver to let you out at Tipon. To get back, head to the main road and squeeze onto a passing bus.

Pikillaqta

One of the few well preserved pre-Inca sites in the area, Pikillaqta (daily 7am–5.30pm; entry by Cusco Tourist Ticket, see box, p.821), literally means "city of the fleas" and was built by the Wari culture. It is the earliest example in the region of two-storey buildings and many fine miniature sculptures in turquoise were discovered here (currently on exhibit at the Inka Museum in Cusco, see p.818). It is worth taking a guided tour here since it is a huge site and it's easy to miss the good bits if you are wondering around on your own. Entrance is by the tourist ticket, see p.821. You can easily visit this site together with Tipon in a day-trip from Cusco, otherwise, instructions to get there are the same as for Tipon.

Sacred Valley and Machu Picchu

The **SACRED VALLEY OF THE INCAS** traces its winding, astonishingly beautiful course to the northwest of Cusco. As a river valley it starts much further upstream to the south and also flows on right down into the jungle to merge with the other major headwaters of the Amazon, but the section known as the Sacred Valley lies just between Pisac and Ollantaytambo. Standing guard over the two extremes of the Sacred Valley road, the ancient **Inca citadels** of Pisac and Ollantaytambo hang high above the stunning Río Vilcanota-Urubamba and are among the most evocative ruins in Peru.

The Sacred Valley is developing a reputation as a spiritual and meditative centre, and is also rapidly adapting to high-end tourism, with large luxurious hotel resorts appearing from renovated haciendas around all the small villages. **Pisac** itself is a small traditional Andean town just 30km from Cusco, close to the end of the Río Vilcanota's wild run from Urcos. Further downstream is the largest town in the Sacred Valley, **Urubamba**, which boasts a wide range of tourist facilities, although it lacks the charm of Pisac or Ollantaytambo. At the far end of the Sacred Valley, the magnificent ancient town of **Ollantaytambo** is overlooked by the great temple-fortress clinging to the sheer cliffs beside it.

Beyond Ollantaytambo the route becomes too tortuous for any road to follow, the valley closes in around the rail tracks, and the Río Urubamba begins to race and twist below **Machu Picchu** itself, the most famous ruin in South America and a place that – no matter how jaded you are or how commercial it seems – is never a disappointment.

Getting to the Sacred Valley from Cusco

The classic way to arrive at Machu Picchu is to do the two- or four-day **hike** along the stirring Inca Trail, which can only be done through a licensed tour operator and must be booked months in advance due to tight control limiting the number of people allowed on the trail at any one time (see p.835).

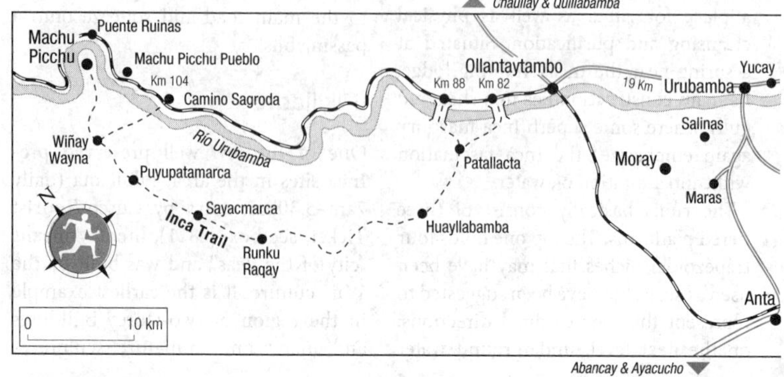

By bus Buses for Urubamba and Ollantaytambo via Chinchero leave from Av Grau 525, every 20min throughout the day from 5am to 7pm. Most services only go as far as Urubamba (1hr 30min – US$1.50), from the bus terminal in Urubamba there are regular *combis* to Ollantaytambo. A faster and more hair-raising option than the bus are the taxi *colectivos* – station wagons in which up to 8 passengers are crammed. These leave from the corner of Av Grau with Calle Pavitos (opposite the bus terminal) and charge $2.15 for the one-hour ride. Once in the valley, there are frequent *combis* who will pick you up from any point along the road.
Buses for Pisac and Calca via Tambo Machay leave from Tullumayo 207 every 15 minutes throughout the day from 5am to 7pm (or when full). Buses return from the same small plaza where they drop you off in Pisac throughout the day. Since the service starts in Calca buses are often standing room only by the time they get to Pisac, especially after 4pm on Sundays. From Ollantaytambo, afternoon buses to Cusco (US$2) leave regularly from the small yard just outside the railway station, often coinciding with the train timetable. In the mornings they mostly depart from Ollantaytambo's main plaza.
By car By road, you can follow the Sacred Valley only as far as Ollantaytambo, from where it cuts across the hills to Chaullay, just beyond Machu Picchu.
By train the train also connects Cusco with Ollantaytambo as well as Machu Picchu and recently a new piece of line has been reopened from Urubamba. The train trip from Cusco all the way to Machu Picchu is almost as spectacular as walking the Inca Trail. There are three tourist classes, each departing Cusco at least once a day with the cheapest "backpacker" class costing US$96 for the return trip. You can also take the train from Ollantaytambo which costs US$62 – US$86 for the return trip. All the Cusco departures for Machu Picchu leave from San Pedro station. For either route it is essential to buy your ticket in advance from the PeruRail office at Huanchac Station, Avenida Pachacutec ⓣ084/238722, ⓦwww.perurail.com.

PISAC

A vital Inca road once snaked its way up the canyon that enters the Sacred Valley at **PISAC**, and the ruined citadel which sits at the entrance to the gorge controlled a route connecting the Inca Empire with Paucartambo, on the borders of the eastern jungle. Nowadays, less than an hour by bus from Cusco, the village is best known for its good Tuesday, Thursday and Sunday **market**, held on the town's main square, the Plaza Constitución, where you can buy a huge array of traditional handicrafts, jewellery and art. The main local **fiesta** – Virgen del Carmen (July 16–18) – is a good alternative to the simultaneous but more remote and raucous Paucartambo festival of the same name, with processions, music, dance groups, the usual fire-cracking celebrations, and food stalls around the plaza.

What to see and do

It takes roughly two hours to climb directly to the **citadel** (daily 7am–6pm); entry by Cusco Tourist Ticket, see box, p.821), heading up through the agricultural terraces still in use at the back of Plaza Constitución. A

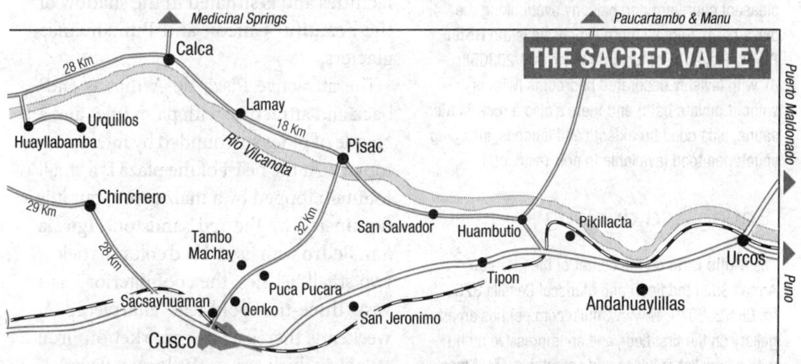

better option is to take a taxi *colectivo* to the top of the ruins (20 min, US$5) and then walk back down, visiting all four archaeological complexes on the way. Set high above a valley floor patchworked by patterned fields and rimmed by centuries of terracing amid giant landslides, the stonework and panoramas at the citadel are magnificent. On a large natural balcony, a semicircle of buildings is gracefully positioned under row upon row of fine stone terraces thought to represent a partridge's wing (*pisac* meaning "partridge"). In the upper sector of the ruins, the main **Temple of the Sun** is the equal of anything at Machu Picchu and more than repays the exertions of the steep climb. Reached by many of the dozens of paths that crisscross their way up through the citadel, it's poised in a flattish saddle on a great spur protruding north–south into the Sacred Valley and was built around an outcrop of volcanic rock, its peak carved into a "hitching post" for the sun. Above the temple lie still more ruins, largely unexcavated, and among the higher crevices and rocky overhangs several ancient burial sites are hidden.

Accommodation

In Pisac there are several good budget hotels, as well as decent restaurants. The hotel and restaurant **Samana Wasi** on the Plaza de Armas 509 (Ⓣ084/203018) has a decent restaurant with a pleasant courtyard and balcony overlooking the plaza (3–4). Slightly more expensive is the **Hotel Pisac**, Plaza Constitución 333 (Ⓣ084/203058; 4), with lavishly decorated bedrooms (with or without private bath) and there's also a rock-heated sauna, plus good breakfasts and lunches, including vegetarian food (available to non-residents).

Eating and drinking

The **Mullu Café** on the corner of the Plaza de Armas 352 (2nd floor) and Mariscal Castilla 375 (Ⓣ084/203073, Ⓦwww.mullu.com.pe) has an art gallery on the first floor, and an impressive menu with a long list of juices and smoothies. Most meals cost $2–3. German-owned **Ulrike's Café** also on the Plaza de Armas 828 (Ⓣ084/203195, Ⓔulrikes-cafe@yahoo.com) is a pleasant place to hang out featuring a book exchange and films. The filling daily menu costs $5. The cheesecake is a must. For more traditional fare try the **Restaurant Valle Sagrado Pisaq** on Av Amazonas 116 (Ⓣ084/203009) which is very popular with locals and is famous for its trout dishes. The daily threecourse menu here will set you back $4. Pisac is also famous for its "empanadas", usually something like a Cornish pasty, but in Pisac more like a bread roll baked with a tomato, cheese, onion and oregano filling. Visit the Colonial earth oven of **Santa Lucia** on the corner of the Plaza de Armas between Calle Puno and Pardo 619. Each one costs $0.35.

TREAT YOURSELF

Slightly out of town on the road towards the ruins, the **Hotel Royal Inka** (Ⓦwww.royalinkahotel.com/hpisac.html; Dbl $80/night) is a plush hotel in a beautiful setting, with "High-altitude training centre" comprising of an Olympic size pool in a glass dome, tennis courts and gardens. There is also camping for US$5 per person.

URUBAMBA AND AROUND

URUBAMBA lies about 80km from Cusco via Pisac or around 60km via Chinchero. Although it has little in the way of obvious historic interest, the town is well endowed with tourist facilities and is situated in the shadow of the beautiful Chicon and Pumahuanca glaciers.

The attractive Plaza de Armas is laid-back and attractive, with palm trees and a couple of pines surrounded by interesting topiary. At the heart of the plaza is a small fountain topped by a maize corn, but it is dominated by the red sandstone **Iglesia San Pedro** with its stacked columns below two small belfries; the cool interior has a vast three-tier gold-leaf altarpiece. At weekends there's a large **market** on Jirón Palacio, which serves the local villages.

What to see and do

Because of its good facilities and position, Urubamba makes an ideal base from which to explore the mountains and lower hills around the Sacred Valley, which are filled with sites. The eastern side of the valley is formed by the **Cordillera Urubamba**, a range of snowcapped peaks dominated by the summits of Chicon and Veronica. Many of the ravines can be hiked, and on the trek up from the town you'll have stupendous views of Chicon. **Moray**, a stunning Inca site, part agricultural centre part ceremonial, lies about 6km north of Maras village on the Chinchero side of the river, within a two- to three-hour walk from Urubamba. Make a circuit to include the spectacular Maras salt flats.

Arrival and information

By bus Regular buses connect Urubamba with Cusco, Pisac, Calca and Ollantaytambo. Buses for Ollantaytambo, Cusco and Chinchero leave regularly from Terminal Terrestre, on the main road.

Accommodation

The basic but friendly **Hostal Urubamba**, Jr Bolognesi 605 (Ⓣ 084/201400) lies behind the police station, one and a half blocks from the Plaza de Armas (❸). 5 kms outside Urubamba is the idyllic **Las Chullpas Guesthouse** (Ⓣ084/9695030, Ⓔchullpas7@hotmail.com) with great views of the Andes, information on local treks and vegetarian cuisine. ❹

Eating and drinking

There is a good selection of budget places to eat in Urubamba. **The Muse Too** on Calle Comercio 347, Plaza de Armas (Ⓣ084/984 791850, Ⓔthemusecusco@yahoo.com) is a relaxed bar with a range of food and drinks and live music in the evenings. A gringo favourite, they often hold pub quizzes. (Mains s/.15–20) For good home-made pasta try **Restaurant Pizzonay**, Mariscal Castilla # 205 (Ⓣ084/201611), mains cost from $5 to $12. Probably the most popular restaurant in Urubamba among local people is **La Chepita**. Found on Av Primero de Mayo, Plazoleta Pintacha (Ⓣ084/201387), *La Chepita* offers good-quality traditional food and truly enormous portions. Mains average 15 soles.

OLLANTAYTAMBO

On the approach to **OLLANTAYTAMBO** from Urubamba, the river runs smoothly between a series of fine Inca terraces that gradually diminish in size as the slopes get steeper and rockier. Just before the town, the rail tracks reappear and the road climbs a small hill into the ancient plaza. Built as an Inca administrative centre rather than a town, it's hard not to be impressed by the foundations that abound in the backstreets radiating up from the plaza, especially in Calle Medio. Laid out in the form of a maize corncob – and one of the few surviving examples of an Inca grid system – the plan can be seen from vantage points high above it, especially from the hill opposite the fortress.

What to see and do

The main focuses of activity in town are the main **plaza**, the heart of civic life and the scene of traditional folk dancing during festive occasions, the Inca fortress and the train station. The useful **Ollantaytambo Heritage Trail** helps you find most of the important sites with a series of blue plaques around town. Close to the central plaza there's the recently refurbished **CATCCO Museum** (Ⓣ084/204024, Ⓦwww.catcco.org), a small but very interesting museum containing interpretative exhibits in Spanish and English about local history, culture, archeology and natural history. It also has a ceramic workshop and you can buy some good pottery here.

Downhill from the plaza, just across the Río Patacancha, is the old Inca **Plaza Mañya Raquy**, dominated by the fortress. There are a few *artesanía* shops and stalls in here, plus the town's attractive church, the Templo Santiago Apóstal, built in 1620 with its almost

Inca-style stone belfry containing two great bells supported on an ancient timber. The church's front entrance is surrounded by simple yet attractive and stylized *mestizo* floral relief painted in red and cream. Climbing up through the **fortress** (daily 7am–5.30pm; entrance by Cusco Tourist Ticket, see box, p.821), the solid stone terraces, jammed against the natural contours of the cliff, remain frighteningly impressive.

High up over the other side of the Río Patacancha, behind the town, are rows of **ruined buildings** originally thought to have been prisons but now believed to have been granaries. To the front of these it's quite easy to make out a gigantic, rather grumpy-looking profile of a face carved out of the rock, possibly an **Inca sculpture** of Wiracochan, the mythical messenger from Wiracocha, the major creator god of the Incas.

Arrival and information

By train The train station is a few hundred metres down the track to the left just before the town's traditional little church, which itself is surrounded by *artesanía* shops; by road, you'll arrive at the main plaza.
Tourist Information Tourist information can be obtained from the CATCCO Museum, or call ⓣ084/204024. The telephone and post offices are on the main plaza. Ollantaytambo is something of a centre for river rafting, with a Rafting Adventure office on the main plaza. The river around Ollantaytambo is class 2–3 in dry season and 3–4 in the rainy period (Nov–March).

Accommodation

There are several budget **hotels** to choose from in Ollantaytambo. The hospitable **Hostal La Ñusta**, on Carretera Ocobamba (ⓣ084/204035; ❹), has simple rooms and a patio offering excellent views across to the mountains. The owner also rents out horses at US$10 a day (Pumamarca is reachable in about 2hr). Similar, but slightly more comfortable, there's **Chaska Wasi** (ⓣ084/203061, ⓔchaskawasihostal@hotmail.com), on Calle del Medio some two blocks from the plaza; breakfast is available and it's nicely furnished. With great views from the rooftop terrace, it can however be quite noisy. ❸–❹

TREAT YOURSELF

The attractive **El Albergue Ollantaytambo**, (ⓣ084/204014; ❽), is right next to the river and the train station at the bottom end of town, quiet and peaceful with a beautiful garden often filled with hummingbirds. The hotel has spacious and well decorated rooms, 24-hour hot water, a sauna and room service. (Reservations are necessary year round.)

Eating and drinking

For a decent **meal**, it's hard to beat the wholefoods heaven **Hearts Café** (ⓣ084/204078, ⓦwww.heartscafe.org) on the main plaza – serving home-made local and gringo favourites, proceeds fund several childrens' projects in the Sacred Valley Mains cost from 12–16 soles. The newly opened **Cactus** tapas bar is just around the corner off the main plaza, serving a range of meals and drinks and is open late. Mains 10–20 soles. *El Albergue* (see above), also has excellent food although it is more expensive. Mains 20–35 soles.

THE INCA TRAIL

The world-famous **Inca Trail** is set in the **Sanctuario Histórico de Machu Picchu**, an area of over 32,000 hectares set apart by the Peruvian state for the protection of its flora, fauna and natural beauty. Acting as a bio-corridor between the Cusco Andes, the Sacred Valley and the lowland Amazon forest, the National Sanctuary of Machu Picchu possesses over 370 species of birds, 47 mammals and over seven hundred butterfly species. Specialities include the cock-of-the-rock (*rupicola peruviana*) known as *tunkis* here, spectacled bear (*tremarctos ornatus*) and condor (*vultur gryphus*).

Although just one of a multitude of paths across remote areas of the Andes, what makes the Inca Trail so popular is the fabulous treasure of **Machu Picchu** at the end. Consider the **season** when booking your Inca Trail. The dry season runs approximately from May to October – expect blistering sun during the daytime and sub-zero temperatures at night. During the rainy season of November to April the temperature is more constant but, naturally, the path is more muddy and can be slippery, and afternoon thunderstorms are the norm. The trail is closed for restoration during the entire month of February. Year round the Inca Trail is a pretty cosmopolitan stretch of mountainside, with travellers from all over the globe converging on Machu Picchu the hard way

In recent years, due to the growing popularity of the Inca Trail, the sanctuary authority, the Unidad de Gestión del Sanctuario Histórico de Machu Picchu, has imposed a **limit of up to 500 people a day** on the Inca Trail, and they must be accompanied by a registered tour operator. By law, permits must be purchased thirty days before departure on the trail with the name and passport number of each trekker. In practice however, it is usually necessary to book four to six months in advance to make sure you get a space on the trail. Currently permits cost around US$100 per person, including entrance to Machu Picchu – this permit should always be included in the price of your trek. Always carefully research the **tour company** (see p.822) that you choose, and make sure you check the precise details of exactly what you are paying for and what is not included in the price. Typically, sleeping bags, breakfast on the first day and lunch and dinner on the last day, as well as tips for the porters and your guide, are not included. It is important to organize all this by email well in advance. As far as **preparations** go, the most important thing is to acclimatize, preferably allowing at least three days in Cusco if you've flown straight from sea level.

THE TWO-DAY INCA TRAIL

The **Two-Day Inca Trail**, a truncated Inca Trail, starts at Km104 of the Panamerican Highway, 8km from Machu Picchu. The footbridge here leads to a steep climb (3–4hr) past Chachabamba to reach Wiñay Wayna (see p.836), where you join the remainder of the Inca Trail.

Setting off and Day One

You will usually leave Cusco very early in the morning (around 5am) to drive to Ollantaytambo (where you can buy a recycled walking stick) and have breakfast. The trail begins at **Chilca**, where you will cross the Urubamba River – the first checkpoint on the trail. You will pass several villages where local people will attempt to sell you *chicha* (traditional corn beer) which although your guides will gulp it down, is alcoholic and made from fermented maize and may not be the best at the start of a four-day trek for unhardened stomachs. The first day consists of a fairly gentle climb with most groups taking just four hours to reach the first night's **campsite** at **Huayllabamba**.

Day Two

The next morning is the toughest part of the walk – an approximately five hour climb to the Abra Huarmihuañusca, **Dead woman's pass** (4200m) and the highest point on the trail.

The views from the pass itself are stupendous, but if you're tempted to hang around savouring them, it's a good idea to sit well out of the cutting wind (many a trekker has caught a bad chill here). From here the trail drops steeply down, sticking to the left of the stream into the Pacamayo Valley where, by the river, most groups will spend their second night in the attractive **campsite.**

Day Three

This morning starts with another, much shorter climb up a winding, tiring track towards the **second pass** – Abra de

Runkuracay – just above the interesting circular ruins of the same name. About an hour beyond the second pass, a flight of stone steps leads up to the Inca ruins of **Sayacmarca**. From Sayacmarca you make your way gently down into increasingly dense cloud forest where delicate orchids and other exotic flora begin to appear among the trees. By the time you get to the **third pass** (which, compared with the previous two, has very little incline) you're following a fine, smoothly worn flagstone path where at one point an astonishing tunnel, carved through solid rock by the Incas, lets you sidetrack an otherwise impossible climb. The trail winds down to the impressive ruin of **Puyupatamarca** – "Town Above the Clouds" – where there are five small stone baths and in the wet season constant fresh running water. Pause to admire the stunning views across the Urubamba valley and, in the other direction, towards the snowcaps of Salcantay (Wild Mountain).

It's a very rough, two-three hour descent along a non-Inca track to the next ruin, a citadel almost as impressive as Machu Picchu, **Wiñay Wayna** – "Forever Young" – where most groups will spend their third night. There is basic **accommodation** here and a large restaurant/bar area where you can treat your group and porters to a round of drinks. Most groups will **camp** outside the structure, but still enjoy the hot showers.

Wiñay Wayna was a companion site for Machu Picchu, just two hours' walk away. Comprising only two major groups of architectural structures – a lower and an upper sector – its most visible features are stone baths with apparently as many as nineteen springs feeding them all set amidst several layers of fine Inca terracing. Nearby there's also a small waterfall created by streams coming down from the heights of Puyupatamarca. As it's used today, Wiñay Wayna was probably used as a washing, cleansing and resting point for travellers before their arrival at the grand Machu Picchu citadel.

Day Four

To reach Machu Picchu for sunrise the next day most groups start walking around 4am with flashlights until it gets light at around 6am. A well-marked track from Wiñay Wayna takes a right fork for about two more hours through sumptuous vegetated slopes to **Intipunku**, (the Sun Gate) for your first sight of Machu Picchu – a stupendous moment, however exhausted you might be.

MACHU PICCHU

The most dramatic and enchanting of the Inca citadels lies suspended on an extravagantly terraced saddle between two prominent peaks. The beautiful stone architecture is enhanced by the Incas' exploitation of local 250 million-year-old rocks of grey-white granite with a high content of quartz, silica and feldspar among other minerals. **MACHU PICCHU** (daily 6am–5pm; US$40) is one of the greatest of all South American tourist attractions, set against a vast, scenic backdrop of dark-green forested mountains that spike up from the deep valleys of the Urubamba and its tributaries. The distant glacial summits are dwarfed only by the huge sky.

With many legends and theories surrounding the position of Machu Picchu, most archeologists agree that the sacred geography and astronomy of the site were auspicious factors in helping the Inca emperor Pachacuti decide where to build this citadel here at 2492m. The name "Machu Picchu" means simply Old or Ancient Mountain. It's thought that agricultural influences as well as geo-sacred indicators prevailed and that the site secured a decent supply of sacred coca and maize for the Inca nobles and priests in

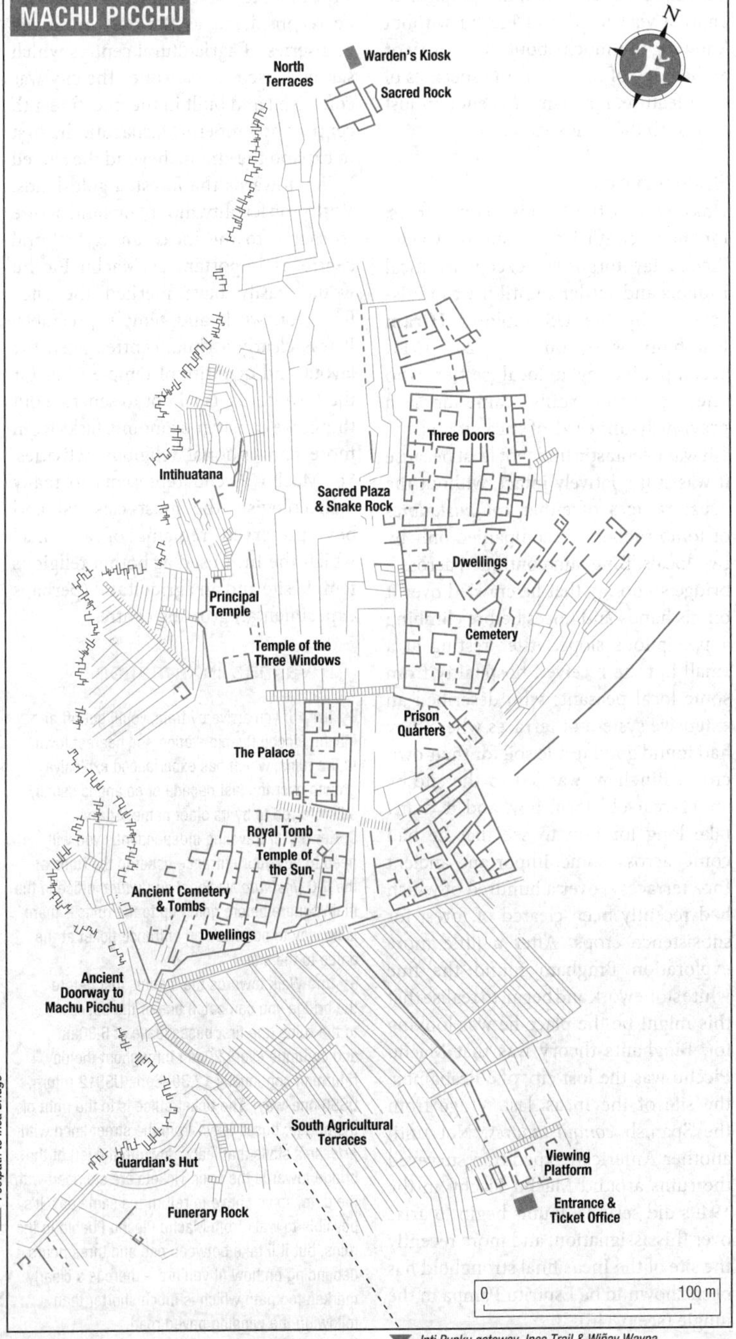
Footpath to Huayna Picchu & the Temple of the Moon
MACHU PICCHU
Warden's Kiosk
North Terraces
Sacred Rock
Three Doors
Intihuatana
Sacred Plaza & Snake Rock
Dwellings
Principal Temple
Cemetery
Temple of the Three Windows
Prison Quarters
The Palace
Royal Tomb
Temple of the Sun
Ancient Cemetery & Tombs
Dwellings
Ancient Doorway to Machu Picchu
South Agricultural Terraces
Footpath to Inca Bridge
Guardian's Hut
Viewing Platform
Entrance & Ticket Office
Funerary Rock
0
100 m
Inti Punku gateway, Inca Trail & Wiñay Wayna

Cusco. However, it is quite possible to enjoy a visit to Machu Picchu without knowing too much about the history or archeology of the site or the specifics of each feature; for many it is enough just to absorb the atmosphere.

Some history

Unknown to the Spanish conquerors, for many centuries the site of Machu Picchu lay forgotten, except by local Indians and settlers, until it was rediscovered by the US explorer **Hiram Bingham** who, on July 24, 1911, accompanied by a local settler who knew of some ruins, came upon a previously unheard-of Inca citadel.

It was a fantastic find, not least because it was still relatively intact, without the usual ravages of either *conquistadores* or tomb robbers. Accompanied only by two locals, Bingham continued across a bridge so dodgy that he crawled over it on his hands and knees before climbing a precipitous slope. After resting at a small hut, he received hospitality from some local peasants who described an extensive system of terraces where they had found good fertile soil for their own crops. Bingham was led to the site by an 11-year-old local boy, and it didn't take long for him to see that he had come across some important ancient Inca terraces – over a hundred of which had recently been cleared of forest for subsistence crops. After a little more exploration Bingham found the fine white stonework and began to realise that this might be the place he was looking for. Bingham's theory was that Machu Picchu was the lost city of Vilcabamba, the site of the Incas' last refuge from the Spanish *conquistadores*. Not until another American expedition surveyed the ruins around Machu Picchu in the 1940s did serious doubts begin to arise over this assignation, and more recently the site of the Inca's final stronghold has been shown to be Espíritu Pampa in the jungle (see p.846).

Meanwhile, Machu Picchu began to be reconsidered as the best preserved of a series of agricultural centres which served Cusco in its prime. The city was conceived and built in the mid-fifteenth century by Emperor Pachacuti, the first to expand the empire beyond the Sacred Valley towards the forested gold-lands. With crop fertility, mountains and nature so sacred to the Incas, an agricultural centre as important as Machu Picchu would easily have merited the site's fine stonework and temple precincts. It was clearly a ritual centre, given the layout and quantity of temples; but for the Inca it was usual not to separate out things we consider economic tasks from more conventional religious activities. So, Machu Picchu represents to many archaeologists the most classical and best preserved remains of a citadel which the Inca used as both a religious temple site and an agricultural (perhaps experimental) growing centre.

Arrival and information

By train If you arrive by train, you'll get off at Machu Picchu Pueblo station, the nearest town to the ruins, which has experienced explosive growth over the last decade or so and is usually still referred to by its older name, **Aguas Calientes**. If traveling independently you will need to buy your entrance ticket to the ruins at the INC (*Instituto Nacional de Cultura*) office in the main square before going up to the ruins – there is no way to purchase an entrance ticket at the gates to the site.

By bus Walk towards the station, just before the bridge you can catch one of the buses to the ruins (the first buses leave at 5.30am and continue every 20min throughout the day, returning continually 12.30–6pm; US$12 return, US$6 one-way). The ticket office is to the right of the bridge; buses leave from the street lined with *artesanía* stalls that leads down to the left of the bridge towards the river. Tickets are stamped with the date, so you have to return the same day. It's possible to walk from Machu Picchu Pueblo to the ruins, but it'll take between one and three hours, depending on how fit you are – there is a clearly marked footpath which is much shorter than following the winding paved road.

TRAIN JOURNEY TO MACHU PICCHU

The new, improved service offered by PeruRail between Cusco and Machu Picchu – one of the finest mountain train journeys in the world – enhances the thrill of riding tracks through such fantastic scenery even further by offering very good service and comfortable, well-kept carriages.

Rumbling out of **Cusco** around 6am, the wagons zigzag their way through the back streets, where little houses cling to the steep valley slopes. It takes a while to rise out of the teacup-like valley, but once it attains the high plateau above, the train rolls through fields and past highland villages before eventually dropping rapidly down into the Urubamba Valley using several major track switchbacks, which means you get to see some of the same scenery twice. It reaches the Sacred Valley floor just before getting into **Ollantaytambo**, where from the windows you can already see scores of impressively terraced fields and, in the distance, more Inca temple and storehouse constructions. The train continues down the valley, stopping briefly at Km88, where the Inca Trail starts, then following the Urubamba river as the valley gets tighter (that's why there's no road!) and the mountain more and more forested as well as steeper and seemingly taller. The end of the line these days is usually the new station at **Machu Picchu Pueblo** (also known as Aguas Calientes), a busy little town crowded into the valley just a short bus ride from the ruins themselves.

Camping The local campsite (US$5, collected every morning), is just over the Río Urubamba on the railway side of the bridge (**Puente Ruinas**), from where the buses start their climb up to the ruins of Machu Picchu. Too expensive for most travellers, the *Machu Picchu Sanctuary Lodge* hotel (Ⓣ084/241777, Ⓦwww.orient-express.com; ⑧) is located right at the entrance to the ruins. Most travellers stay at Machu Picchu Pueblo (see p.841). Next to the entrance to the ruins there's a **left-luggage office** (no backpacks or camping equipment are allowed inside, price per item is 3 soles, no time limit), toilets, a shop and very expensive café, where you can also hire a guide (approximately 100 soles for a one-hour tour, per group) and buy a **map**.

What to see and do

Though it would take a lot to detract from Machu Picchu's incredible beauty and unsurpassed location, it is a zealously supervised place, with the site guards frequently blowing whistles at visitors who have deviated from one of the main pathways. The best way to enjoy the ruins – and avoid the guards' ire – is to hire a guide, or to follow the marked trails.

Though more than 1000m lower than Cusco, Machu Picchu seems much higher, constructed as it is on dizzying slopes overlooking a U-curve in the Río Urubamba. More than a hundred flights of steep stone steps interconnect its palaces, temples, storehouses and terraces, and the outstanding views command not only the valley below in both directions but also extend to the snowy peaks around Salcantay. Wherever you stand in the ruins, spectacular terraces (some of which are once again being cultivated) can be seen slicing across ridiculously steep cliffs, transforming mountains into suspended gardens.

Temple of the Sun

Entering the main ruins, you cross over a dry moat. The first site of major interest is the **Temple of the Sun**, also known as the *Torreón*, a wonderful, semicircular, walled, tower-like temple displaying some of Machu Picchu's finest stonework. Its carved steps and smoothly joined stone blocks fit neatly into the existing relief of a natural boulder, which served as some kind of altar and also marks the entrance to a small cave. A window off this temple provides views of both the June solstice sunrise and the constellation of the Pleiades, which rises from here over the nearby peak of Huayna Picchu. The Pleiades are still a very important astronomical Andean symbol relating to crop fertility; locals use the constellation as a kind of annual signpost in the agricultural calendar giving information about when to plant crops and when the rains will come. Below the Temple of the Sun is a cave known as the **Royal Tomb**, despite the fact that neither graves nor human remains have ever been found there. In fact, it probably represented access to the spiritual heart of the mountains, like the cave at the Temple of the Moon (see opposite).

Retracing your steps 20m or so back from the Temple of the Sun and following a flight of stone stairs directly uphill, then left along the track towards Intipunku (see p.904), brings you to a path on the right, which climbs up to the thatched **guardian's hut**. This hut is associated with a modestly carved rock known as the **funerary rock** and a nearby graveyard where Bingham found evidence of many burials, some of which were obviously royal.

The Sacred Plaza

Back down in the centre of the site, the next major Inca construction after the Temple of the Sun is the **Three-Windowed Temple**; part of the complex based around the **Sacred Plaza**, and arguably the most enthralling sector of the ruins. Dominating the south-eastern edge of the plaza, the attractive Three-Windowed Temple has unusually large windows looking east towards the mountains beyond the Urubamba river valley. From here it's a short stroll to the **Principal Temple**, so-called because of the fine stonework of its three high main walls, the most easterly of which looks onto the Sacred Plaza. Unusually (as most ancient temples in the Americas face east), the main opening of this temple faces south, and white sand, often thought to represent the ocean, has been found on the temple floor, suggesting that it may have been allied symbolically to the Río Urubamba, water and the sea.

Intihuatana

A minute or so uphill from here along an elaborately carved stone stairway brings you to one of the jewels of the site, the **Intihuatana**, also known as the "hitching post of the sun". This fascinating carved rock, built on a rise above the Sacred Plaza, is similar to those created by the Inca in all their important ritual centres, but is one of the very few not to have been discovered and destroyed by the *conquistadores*. This unique and very beautiful survivor, set in a tower-like position, overlooks the Sacred Plaza, the Río Urubamba and the sacred peak of Huayna Picchu. Intihuatana's base is said to have been carved in the shape of a map of the Inca Empire, though few archeologists agree with this. Its main purpose was as an astro-agricultural clock for viewing the complex interrelationships between the movements of the stars and constellations. It is also thought by some to be a symbolic representation of the spirit of the mountain on which Machu Picchu was built – by all accounts a very powerful spot both in terms of sacred geography and its astrological function. The Intihuatana appears to be aligned with four important mountains. The snowcapped mountain range of La Veronica lies directly to the east, with the sun rising behind its main summit during the equinoxes; directly south, though not actually visible from here, sits the father of all mountains in this part of Peru, Salcantay, only a few days' walk away; to the west, the sun sets behind the important peak of Pumasillo during the December solstice; while due north stands the majestic peak of Huayna Picchu.

Sacred Rock

Following the steps down from the Intihuatana and passing through the Sacred Plaza towards the northern terraces brings you in a few minutes to the **Sacred Rock**, below the access point to Huayna Picchu. A great lozenge of granite sticking out of the earth like a sculptured wall, little is known for sure about the Sacred Rock, but its outline is strikingly similar to the Inca's sacred mountain of Putukusi, which towers to the east.

Huayna Picchu

The prominent peak of **Huayna Picchu** juts out over the Urubamba Valley at the northern end of the Machu Picchu site, and is easily scaled by anyone reasonably energetic and with no vertigo issues. The record for this vigorous and rewarding climb is 22 minutes, but most people take about an hour. Access to this sacred mountain, (daily 7am–1pm; maximum four hundred people per day) is controlled by a guardian from his kiosk just behind the Sacred Rock. From the summit, there's an awe-inspiring panorama and it's a great place from which to get an overview of the ruins suspended between the mountains among stupendous forested Andean scenery.

Temple of the Moon

About two-thirds of the way back down, another little track leads to the right and down to the stunning **Temple of the Moon**, hidden in a grotto hanging magically above the Río Urubamba, some 400m beneath the pinnacle of Huayna Picchu. Not many visitors make it this far and it's probably wise to have a guide (and if you've already walked up Huayna Picchu, you might want to save this for another day because it's another 45min each way at least). The guardian by the Sacred Rock will often take people for a small fee (around US$1 per person, provided there are two or more). Once you do get there, you'll be rewarded by some of the best stonework in the entire site, the level of craftmanship hinting at the site's importance to the Inca. The temple's name comes from the fact that it is often lit up by the moonlight, but some archeologists believe the temple was most likely dedicated to the spirit of the mountain. The main sector of the temple is in the mouth of a natural cave, where there are five niches set into an elaborate white granite stone wall. There's usually evidence – small piles of maize, coca leaves and tobacco – that people are still making offerings at these niches. In the centre of the cave there's a rock carved like a throne, beside which are five cut steps leading into the darker recesses, where you can see more carved rocks and stone walls, nowadays at least inaccessible to humans. Immediately to the front of the cave is a small plaza with another cut stone throne and an altar. Outside, steps either side of the massive boulder lead above the cave, from where you can see a broad, stone-walled room running along one side of the cave-boulder. There are more buildings and beautiful little stone sanctuaries just down a flight of steps from this part of the complex.

Intipunku

If you don't have the time or energy to climb Huayna Picchu or visit the Temple of the Moon, simply head back to the guardian's hut on the other side of the site and take the path below it, which climbs gently for thirty minutes or so, up to **Intipunku**, the main entrance to Machu Picchu from the Inca Trail. This offers an incredible view over the entire site with the unmistakable shape of Huayna Picchu in the background.

MACHU PICCHU PUEBLO (AGUAS CALIENTES)

Many people who want to spend more than just a day at Machu Picchu base themselves at the settlement of

MACHU PICCHU PUEBLO (previously known as Aguas Calientes), which is connected to the ruins by bus and has good accommodation, restaurants and shops. Its warm, humid climate and surrounding landscape of towering mountains covered in cloud forest make it a welcome change to Cusco.

By now, Machu Picchu Pueblo's explosive growth has reached the limits of the valley; there's very little flat land that hasn't been built on or covered in concrete. Not surprisingly, this boomtown has a lively, bustling feel and enough restaurants and bars to satisfy a small army.

What to see and do

The town's main attraction (apart from Machu Picchu itself) is the natural **thermal bath** (daily 5am–8.30pm; 10 soles), which is particularly welcome after a few days on the Inca Trail or a hot afternoon up at Machu Picchu. You can find several communal baths of varying temperatures right at the end of the main drag of Pachacutec, around 750m uphill from the town's small plaza.

There is also a recently restored **trail** (90min each way) up the sacred mountain of Putukusi, starting just outside of the town, a couple of hundred yards down on the left if you follow the railway track towards the ruins. The walk offers stupendous views of the town and across to Machu Picchu, but watch out for the small poisonous snakes reported to live on this mountain. It is also not for the faint-hearted as the trail is very steep in parts (some sections have been replaced by ladders) and it is very narrow.

Arrival and nformation

By train You are most likely to arrive in Machu Picchu Pueblo by train, see box, p.839.

Tourist information For information, i-Peru (☎084/211104; daily 9am–1pm & 2–8pm) has an office right next to the INC office (daily 5am–10pm) where you have to buy your entrance ticket to Machu Picchu, just off the main plaza on the first block of Pachacutec. I-Peru has informative leaflets about the area and photocopied maps. The INC office have colour maps of the site of Machu Picchu with major points of interest marked on. You can pick one up in town or at the entrance to Machu Picchu.

Accommodation

Although there is an overwhelming choice of **places to stay** in Machu Picchu Pueblo, there can be a lot of competition for lodgings during the high season (June–Sept), when large groups of travellers often turn up and take over entire hotels. Coming to town on an early train will give you some increased choice in where to stay, but for the better places try and book at least a week or two, if not months, in advance. **Camping** is also possible at a safe and secure site with evening campfires, just 10min walk from Machu Picchu Pueblo at *Campamento Intiwasi*, Las Orchideas M-23 (US$5 per tent); contact via Rikuni Tours, (see listings section) or ask in the *Café Internet Restaurant* for details). The other camping option is the *consejo*-run site (see p.839).

Gringo Bill's Colla Raymi 104 (on the plaza) ⓣ084/211046, ⓦwww.gringobills.com. The original backpackers favourite featuring money-changing, laundry, lunch packs, ample hot water, a relaxed environment, breakfasts included, grilled meats in the evening, rooms with interesting décor, and a book exchange. Although it has gone more upmarket in recent years with one luxury suite with built-in Jacuzzi, it is still an Aguas Calientes insitution. ❽–❾

Hostal Chaska Alameda Turistica Hnos Ayar ⓣ084/251216, ⓔchaska_machupicchu@hotmail.com. Basic but friendly and clean accommodation. Rooms have private bath. Located close to the artisan market on the same side of the river as the train station. ❹

Hostal Quilla ⓣ084/211009, ⓔmariquilla6@hotmail.com. A very friendly hostel offering breakfasts and good tourist information. Rooms have private bath. ❺

Hostal El Tumi Corner of Pachacutec and Tupac Amaru Inca Yupanqui ⓣ084/229627. Clean-ish basic hostel offering rooms with shared or private baths. ❸

Hostal Yakumama Av Inka Roca (just off the 3rd block of Pachacutec) ⓣ084/211185, ⓔalfreyaku@hotmail.com. Newly built in May 2008, this is the best of the budget options, with spacious rooms with private bath and simple but pleasant décor. ❸

Rupa Wasi Ecolodge Calle Huanacaure 180 ⓣ084/221101, ⓦwww.rupawasi.net. Located two blocks from the main plaza away from most of the tourist services, Rupa Wasi is a calm oasis. Run by enthusiastic young conservationists, the hotel is comfy, friendly and eco-conscious. Extra activities such as cooking lessons and treks to nearby sites can be arranged. ❽–❾

Eating and drinking

As well as the **foodstalls** specializing in excellent herb teas and fruit juices, which can be found near the little market by the police station, just over the tracks, there are plenty of **restaurants** in Machu Picchu Pueblo. This is one of the few places in Peru where prices quoted often do not include the 19 percent tax, so check before ordering if tax is included or if it will be added to your bill.

Restaurant Aiko, Imperio de los Incas 153 (ⓣ084/211001), is one of the closest restaurants to the Machu Picchu end of the tracks in the pueblo. It features good service in a cool interior and dishes out reasonably priced meals including trout, soups, pastas and burgers, with a Japanese influence. Mains 12–18 soles.

Anyes (first floor) and **Amaru** (second floor) On the plaza, fight fiercely for tourist business and often offer four drinks for the price of one in a bid to win the tourists over. The atmosphere is better upstairs in Amaru, but quality of food and drinks is similar in both places. Mains 10–18 soles.

El Indio Feliz, Lloque Yupanqui Lote 4m-12 (ⓣ084/211090), serves exceptional three- or four-course meals of French and local cuisines at remarkably inexpensive prices; try to reserve a table as far in advance as possible. Mains 25–40 soles.

Restaurant El Manu, on Pachacutec, has a nice jungle-themed open dining area (sometimes doubling up as a dance space, quite lively at night), and specializes in trout and pizzas. Mains 10–18 soles.

Govinda at Pachacutec 20, near the top end on the left, offers a proper vegetarian meal. Mains average 15 soles.

Café Internet Restaurant On the other side of the railway tracks, has fast access and a good, friendly service for coffees, omelettes, pizzas, trout, spaghetti; this place is also a contact for the campsite *Inti Wasi*, less than 10min walk from here. Mains 8–16 soles.

Restaurant Pizzeria Pachamama, at Imperio de los Incas 143 (ⓣ084/211141), opposite the small market, specializes in pizzas, pancakes, breakfasts and *lomo* steak in mushroom sauce. Mains average 15 soles.

For **drinking**, head to the top end of Pachacutec towards the entrance to the Thermal Springs, where there are several bars offering all-day happy hours and very cheap drinks. Among them are **Tezao** with comfy sofas, chess and darts, and **El Taita** which has a huge selection of cocktails and a TV where you can watch DVDs. **Wasicha Pub,** Calle Lloque Yupanqui, Lote 2, M-12 (ⓣ084/211157), is the town's loudest, hottest nightspot, with a vibrant dancefloor, a good bar and a spacious restaurant attached.

Directory

Exchange & ATM Banco de Crédito, Av Los Incas opposite the train station. ATM accepts all major cards but does sometimes run out of money.
INC Instituto Nacional de Cultura offices, responsible for management of the Nacional sanctuary of Machu Picchu (and entrance ticket sales) is on the first block of Av Pachacutec, in the main Plaza de Armas.
Internet services Café Internet Restaurant, corner of Av Imperios de los Incas next to the old railway station; decent service plus cakes, snacks and drinks 6.30am–10pm; K-Fe Internet, Av Pachacutec 145; good connection and offers transferral of photos from your memory card to CD.
Police Av Imperio de los Incas, next to the small market just down from the old railway station (ⓣ084/211178).
Post office On the railway tracks, right-hand side, towards Pueblo Hotel.
Telephones Centro Telefónica, Av Imperio de los Incas 132 (ⓣ084/211091). The post office (see above) also has a public phone.
Tour operators Rikuni Tours, Imperio de los Incas 119 (ⓣ084/211036 or 084/211151, ⓔrikuni@mixmail.com or rikunis@yahoo.com.ai). They offer a wide range of local outings, including Machu Picchu by night, the Temple of the Moon, Chaskapata ruins, Wiñay Wayna and Chacabamba ruins. You can also book tours through many operators based in Cusco, see p.822.

ALTERNATIVE INCA TRAILS

In recent years, as permits to walk the famous Inca Trail become scarcer and more expensive, many tour operators and inquisitive individuals have been exploring alternative Inca Trails, which offer stunning scenery to rival that of the Inca Trail as well as ecological biodiversity and in some cases, archeological sites larger than Machu Picchu itself. There are five principal trails which have become established as "Alternative Inca Trails", although only one (Salcantay) takes you close to the site of Machu Picchu. At the time of writing all of these trails can still be done independently, although it may be necessary to purchase a permit prior to setting off from the INC office in Cusco, and plans are afoot to enforce stricter regulations on some trails. For up to date information about requirements to walk the trails see the South American Explorers website (ⓦwww.saexplorers.org).

Salcantay

The most popular of the alternatives, with over one hundred people per day setting off on the trail during the 2007 high season, Salcantay takes you as far as the hydroelectric plant or to the town of La Playa depending which route you choose, from where it is a short bus and train ride to Machu Picchu Pueblo. Beginning in Mollepata, the first day is a gentle climb through winding cloud forest trails to Soraypampa. On the second day there is a steep climb up to the only high pass on the trail (4,700m), at the foot of the Salcantay glacier; the landscape here is sparse and dry with very little plantlife. From the pass you descend into cloud forest where you can appreciate stunning views of the verdant canyon below as well as many species of orchid and hummingbirds along the narrow trail. The second night's camp is usually at Colcapampa. On the third day it is approximately a five-hour walk to the jungle town of La Playa where is it possible to take transport all the way to Machu Picchu Pueblo. Alternatively, you can climb the steep valley wall to the site of Llactapata, and then descend on the other side to the hydroelectric plant from where there are regular trains to Machu Picchu Pueblo.

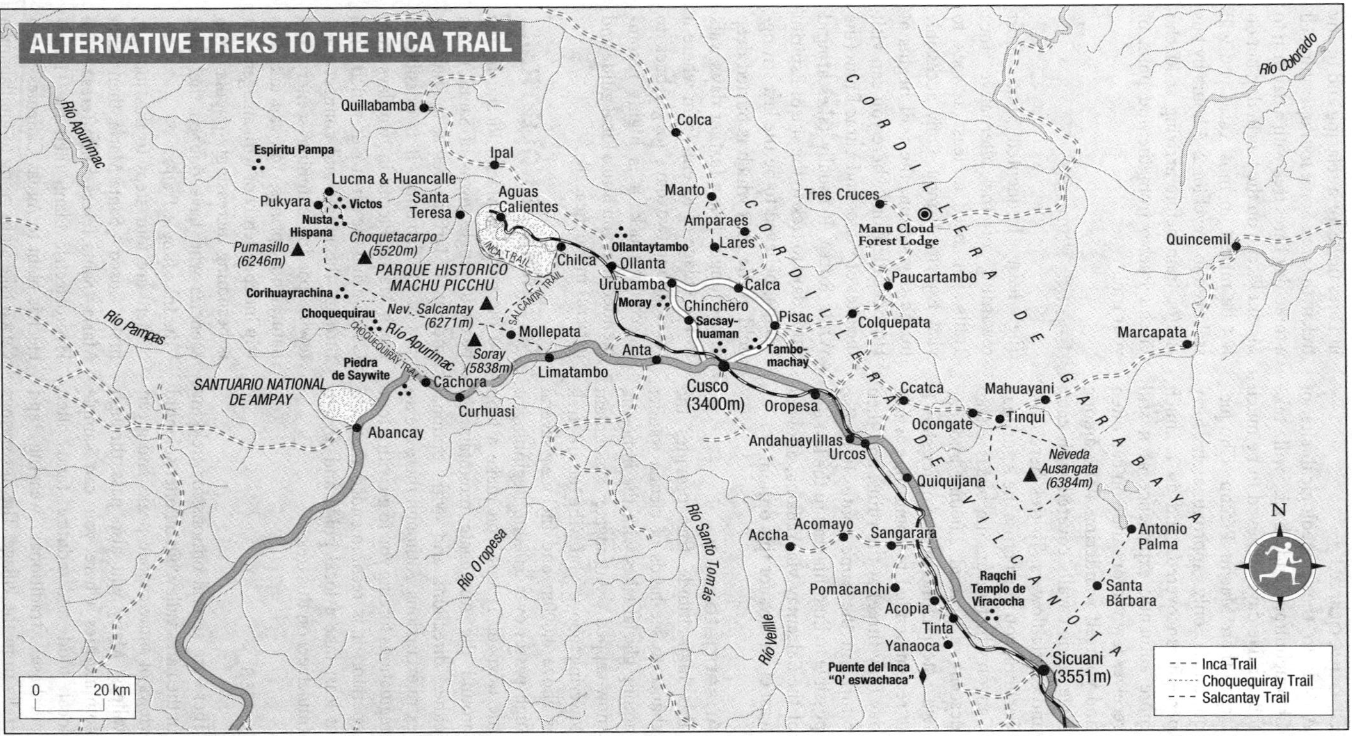
ALTERNATIVE TREKS TO THE INCA TRAIL
CORDILLERA DE VILCANOTA
CORDILLERA DE GARABAYA
CORDILLERA
Quillabamba
Espíritu Pampa
Ipal
Lucma & Huancalle
Pukyara
Victos
Nusta Hispana
Santa Teresa
Aguas Calientes
Pumasillo (6246m)
Choquetacarpo (5520m)
PARQUE HISTORICO MACHU PICCHU
INCA TRAIL
SALCANTAY TRAIL
CHOQUEQUIRAY TRAIL
Corihuayrachina
Choquequirau
Nev. Salcantay (6271m)
Mollepata
Soray (5838m)
Río Apurímac
Río Pampas
Piedra de Saywite
Cachora
Curhuasi
SANTUARIO NATIONAL DE AMPAY
Abancay
Limatambo
Colca
Manto
Amparaes
Lares
Ollantaytambo
Ollanta
Chilca
Urubamba
Moray
Chinchero
Calca
Sacsay-huaman
Pisac
Tambo-machay
Anta
Cusco (3400m)
Oropesa
Tres Cruces
Manu Cloud Forest Lodge
Paucartambo
Colquepata
Ccatca
Ocongate
Mahuayani
Tinqui
Neveda Ausangata (6384m)
Andahuaylillas
Urcos
Quiquijana
Accha
Acomayo
Sangarara
Pomacanchi
Acopia
Tinta
Yanaoca
Raqchi Templo de Viracocha
Puente del Inca "Q' eswachaca"
Sicuani (3551m)
Antonio Palma
Santa Bárbara
Quincemil
Marcapata
Río Colorado
Río Oropesa
Río Santo Tomás
Río Velille
N
Inca Trail
Choquequiray Trail
Salcantay Trail
0
20 km

Choquequirau

A trek to the archeological site of Choquequirau and back will take four or five days. Believed to be much larger than Machu Picchu, Choquequirau is only approximately forty percent uncovered, and is a much more authentic experience as it still receives few visitors and you can often find yourself wandering alone among huge ruined walls covered with cacti and exotic flowers. To trek here from Cachora, you must cross the Apurimac Canyon which means day one is a steep descent of around 2,000m, and day two a steep climb up the other side. It is recommended to spend one whole day (day three) at the ruins, and then return on the same route. It is also possible to link this trail to the last day of the Salcantay via Yanama, allow at least eight days for this option.

Ausangate

This high-altitude trek provides the chance to see herds of vicuña wander among glacial lakes with the imposing snow-capped Ausangate mountain towering above you. The entire trek is above 4,000m and includes several high passes over 5,000m. Beginning at the town of Tinqui, you make a loop around the Ausangate mountain, in either direction, and with optional extra excursions. Although there are no regulations forcing you to go with a tour operator, it is recommended that you at least take a local guide and *arriero* (muleteer) on this trek.

Lares

There are several options for trekking in the Lares valley, but all offer splendid views of snow-capped peaks and green valleys. Many will also pass through communities where you can sample local food and admire (and often purchase) traditional weaving and crafts from the village. The hot springs in Lares make for a relaxing end to any trek in the area. Some tour operators sell a three-day Lares trek with a day-trip to Machu Picchu on the fourth day, but do not be misled, in most cases you will still need to travel for 2–5 hours by bus and/or train before arriving at Machu Picchu Pueblo from the end point of your trail.

Espíritu Pampa

The least frequented but most rewarding of the alternative Inca Trails, you need at least a week to visit Espíritu Pampa. Only accessible in the dry season, the trail begins at Huancacalle from where you can visit the sites of Vitcos and Yurac Rumi (the White Rock). It usually takes around three days to trek to the site of Espiritu Pampa, believed to be the last stronghold of the Inca which is buried deep in the jungle. It is a further day's walk to the village of Kiteni, from where it takes about two days to get back to Cusco by truck. It is highly recommended that you hire a local guide and *arrieros* in Huancacalle.

THE INKA JUNGLE TRAIL

To the north of Machu Picchu lie the peaceful jungle towns of Santa Teresa and Santa María as well as the bustling city of Quillabamba. It is possible to reach Machu Picchu in two days from Cusco using the dirt roads which wind through the jungle and connect these towns, passing stunning scenery and natural hot springs. You can take this trip independently or with an agency; it is becoming increasingly popular with agencies who have dubbed the route "The Inka Jungle Trail".

There are four steps to this journey, firstly Cusco – Santa María, then Santa María – Santa Teresa, Santa Teresa to the Hydroelectric Plant, then the Hydroelectric plant to Aguas Calientes. From Cusco take a bus going to Quillabamba

– Turismo Ampay (☎084/245734) leaves from the Santiago Terminal in Cusco three times a day. You can either take the bus all the way to Quillabamba, or get off at the small town of Santa María, at the road junction which leads to Santa Teresa.

Santa María

It takes approximately seven hours to get to Santa María, and eight hours to get to Quillabamba (US$8). If you go all the way to Quillabamba, you have a good chance of getting a **bus** to Santa María or possibly Santa Teresa direct – buses leave from the main bus terminal where you arrive. You can also take a **taxi colectivo** from Cusco to Quillabamba, which leave when full from outside the Almudena Cemetery in Cusco. They take approximately five hours to Santa María and cost US$13. There are several basic **hostels** in Santa María which cost around US$5 per person – just ask around in town.

Santa Teresa

From Santa María, hop on a passing *combi* or bus coming from Quillabamba going towards Santa Teresa (2hr 30min, US$3). It is also possible to take a **private car** if necessary (up to US$20). You can also walk between the two towns on a track which follows the river, however taking a guide is recommended as it is easy to lose your way here; it takes seven to eight hours to walk. If walking you will pass the hot springs at Colcalmayo (entrance US$3), where it is possible to rent towels and buy drinks, but no food, and camp for US$3 per tent. If you take transport to Santa Teresa you can take a local bus to the hot springs which leave after 4pm. In Santa Teresa there are basic **hostels** for US$5–6 per person, *Hotel Auqui* is recommended.

From Santa Teresa *combis* and shared taxis make the trip to the Hydroelectric plant on demand to meet the trains for Aguas Calientes. The schedule at the time of writing was two daily trains leaving at 8.20am and 4.20pm, the one-hour ride cost US$9 – due to the rise in popularity of this route, it is likely that Peru Rail will increase passenger services on this route, as well as prices – call the Huanchaq Station in Cusco for up to date information ☎084/238722 (note that this service does not appear on the Peru Rail website).

Nazca and The South Coast

The south has been populated as long as anywhere in Peru – for at least nine thousand years in some places – but until the twentieth century no one guessed the existence of this arid region's unique cultures, whose enigmatic remains, particularly along the coast, show signs of a sophisticated civilization. With the discovery and subsequent study, beginning in 1901, of ancient sites throughout the coastal zone, it now seems clear that this was home to at least three major cultures: the **Paracas** (500 BC–400 AD), the influential **Nazca** (500–800 AD) and finally, contemporaneous with the Chimu of northern Peru and the Cuismancu around Lima, the **Ica Culture**, or **Chincha Empire**, overrun by and absorbed into Pachacutec's mushrooming Inca Empire around the beginning of the fifteenth century.

The area has a lot to offer the modern traveller: the enigmatic and mysterious **Nazca Lines**, the **Paracas National Reserve** and wildlife haven of the **Ballestas Islands** where sea lions abound, as well as the tranquil oasis of **Huacachina**, which has become a popular stop on the gringo trail around Peru due to the deveopment of

dune-buggying and **sand boarding** trips on the immense dunes that surround it.

PISCO, PARACAS RESERVE AND BALLESTAS ISLANDS

The town of **PISCO** itself has little to offer the visitor, as it is largely industrial and the smell of the fish-meal factories often overpowers the town. However it makes a great jumping-off point for visiting the nearby **PARACAS RESERVE** and **BALLESTAS ISLANDS,** and does offer some decent accommodation options. Approximately four hours from Lima, Pisco is a popular stop for travellers en route to Nazca, Arequipa, and other Southern destinations.

Pisco was the town to suffer most damage as a result of the **earthquake**

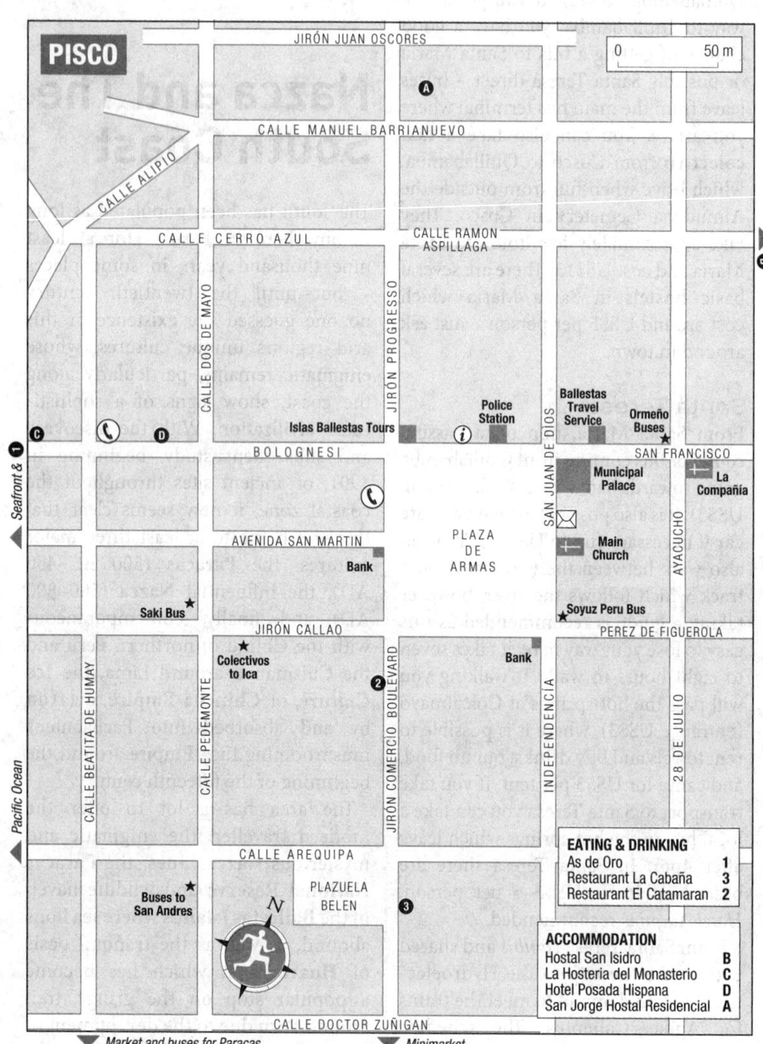

on **August 15, 2007**, which shook the entire south of Peru. At least half of all buildings were destroyed leaving the city looking like a war zone, however those in the tourist industry were quick to rebuild, and reopen businesses with the structurally sound parts while other sections remain under construction. More than ever, tourist dollars will be appreciated in Pisco over the next few years, and many NGOs continue to work in the area.

What to see and do

Most people will only stay in Pisco long enough to take **tours** out to the nearby attractions of the **Paracas Reserve** and the **Ballestas Islands**. Despite its industrial nature, the centre of Pisco has a fairly relaxed atmosphere and people spend their evenings strolling around the **Main Plaza** and nearby **Jirón Comercio**, where street sellers set up stalls selling everything from home-made sweets to secondhand electrical goods, music pumps out of streetside cafes and street entertainers are quickly engulfed by eager audiences.

The Paracas Reserve

Founded in 1975, the Paracas National Reserve covers an area of approximately 335,000 hectares; with a large area of ocean within its boundaries, it also includes beaches, stunning cliffs and islands. The reserve is Peru's principal centre for marine conservation and is home to dolphins, whales and sea lions, as well as many birds including pelicans, flamingos, penguins and cormorants. The name Paracas comes from the Quechua "raining sand", and the area is constantly battered by strong winds and sandstorms. Not discouraged by the harsh climate, the area has been inhabited for around nine thousand years, most noteably by the pre-Inca culture known as the Paracas.

After the 2007 earthquake, the Paracas Reserve was closed for several months while new routes were opened. The rock formation known as "La Catedral" collapsed. Agencies resumed tours as

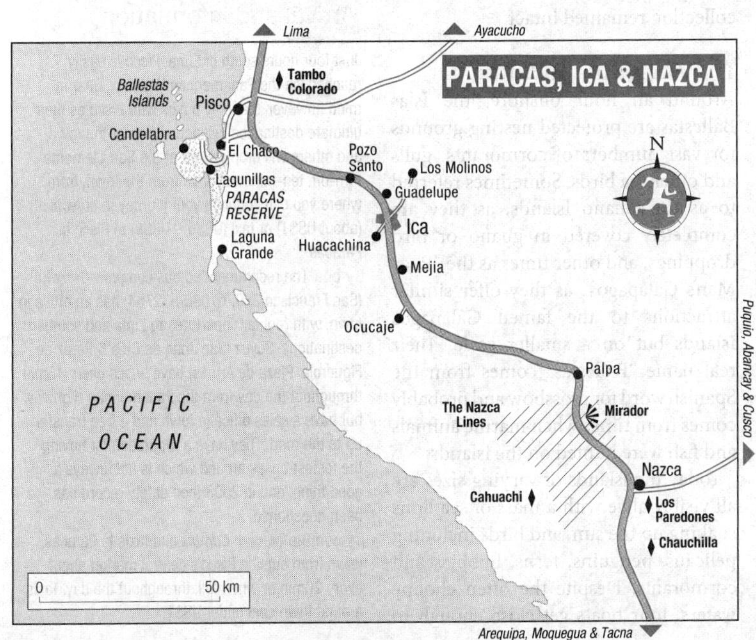

TOURS TO PARACAS RESERVE AND BALLESTAS ISLANDS

There are several local tour operators running standard half-day speedboat tours to the Ballestas Islands, leaving Pisco early in the morning and returning around lunchtime. Many people choose to go on to do an afternoon tour of the Paracas National Reserve with the same operator, making a whole day-trip. Each half-day-trip costs $8-$10; it is best to buy tickets the day before, as trips leave at around 7am and you can arrange to be picked up at your hotel if you already have tickets. Most of these companies also organize tours to other nearby attractions, such as Tambo Colorado, adobe ruins believed to have been built by the Chinca culture and then adapted and used by the Inca. Within Pisco try **Paracas Overland**, San Francisco 111 (ⓣ056/533855), or alternatively **Peru Adventures Tours**, no office in Pisco (ⓦwww.peruadventurestours.com).

soon as possible and cycling, camping and dune-buggying trips are all possible. See above for operators.

Julio C Tello Museum (Tues–Sun 9am–5pm; $3) is located within the Reserve at Km 27, between the two major Paracas archeological sites – Cerro Colorado and Cabeza Largas. It contains artifacts from the Paracas culture including mummies, trepanned skulls and ceramics. Although the museum suffered some structural damage in the 2007 earthquake, the collection remained intact.

The Ballestas Islands

Around an hour offshore, the Islas Ballestas are protected nesting grounds for vast numbers of cormorants, gulls and other sea birds. Sometimes referred to as the Guano Islands, as they are completely covered in guano or bird droppings, and other times as the "Poor Man's Galapagos" as they offer similar attractions to the famed Galapagos Islands but on a smaller scale. Their real name "Ballestas" comes from the Spanish word for crossbow and probably comes from times when marine animals and fish were hunted on the islands.

Today the islands of varying sizes are all visibly alive with a mass of sea lions soaking up the sun, and birds including pelicans, penguins, terns, boobies and cormorants. Despite the often choppy waters, tour boats get close enough to see the animals on the rocks; it is also often possible to see sea lions swimming around the boats.

If you take a **tour** from Pisco, transport from the town to the docks will be provided. To get there independently take a **bus** from the market in Pisco to San Andres, and from there, on to El Chaco where **boats** leave for the Ballestas Islands. Alternatively a taxi from Pisco to El Chaco costs around $5.

Arrival and information

Just four hours south of Lima, Pisco is easily reached via the Panamerican Highway. Bear in mind however, that only buses with Pisco as their ultimate destination will actually enter the town, and others will drop you off at the San Clemente turn-off, ten-minutes' drive from the town, from where you can continue your journey in *colectivo* (about US$1) or taxi (US$5 – US$8) to Pisco or Paracas.

By bus The recommended bus company **Ormeño** (San Francisco 259; ⓣ056/532764) has an office in town, with regular departures to Lima and southern destinations. Soyuz (San Juan de Dios & Perez de Figuerola, Plaza de Armas) have buses every 15min throughout the day from the Panamerican Highway, but have a sales office in town and a free transfer up to the road. They have a reputation for having the fastest buses around which is not always a good thing, and in 2008 their safety record has been questioned.

By combis or taxi *Combis* and taxis to Paracas leave from outside Pisco's central market about every 20min or when full, throughout the day. Taxis around town cost under US$1.

Accommodation

Sadly many previously popular hotels were partially or completely destroyed in the 2007 earthquake; the following however, remain open or have re-opened having been restored.

Hostal El Amigo Balneario Chaco, Paracas ⓣ056/545042. Basic but clean accommodation in Paracas. ❸–❹

Hostal San Isidro San Clemente 103, Pisco ⓣ056/536471, ⓦwww.sanisidrohostal.com. Affordable two-star hostel offering room service, café bar & pizzeria, flight confirmations and money exchange. All rooms except dorms have private bathrooms with hot water, and cable TV. Doubles US$28/night, dorm beds ❷

La Hosteria del Monasterio Av Bolognesi 326, Pisco ⓣ056/531383. This *hosteria* is the sister hotel of *Posada Hispana*. Hot water, cable TV, breakfast included in price. Also has a terrace. ❺

Hotel Posada Hispana Bolognesi 222, Pisco ⓣ056/536363, ⓦwww.posadahispana.com. All rooms have cable TV and private bath with hot water. On-site *Café La Posada* offers good set lunches for $3. There is also a rooftop terrace where BBQs are often held. ❺.

San Jorge Hotel Residencial Jr Barrio Nuevo 133, Pisco ⓣ056/532885, ⓦwww.hotelsanjorgeresidencial.com. Clean and modern in a new location, *San Jorge Hotel* offers security boxes, laundry service, phone & fax, internet, money exchange, cable TV, cafeteria and room service; all rooms have private bath with hot water. ❺

Eating and drinking

There are many fine restaurants in Pisco and Paracas, where you can enjoy good and very fresh seafood, especially along the sea-front in Paracas.

As de Oro Av San Martín 472, Pisco; ⓣ056/532010. Fairly expensive but worth it for the delicious seafood. Hosted a lively disco pre-earthquake, which will be reopening at some point during 2008. Mains 25–40 soles.

Brisa Marina block 2, lote 5, El Chaco, Paracas; ⓣ056/545125. Not put off by losing their kitchen in the tsunami, Brisa Marina quickly reopened and continues to serve up some of the best seafood in town. Mains average 15 soles.

Restaurant La Cabaña Comercio 211, Pisco. Serves the usual seafood dishes as well as other Peruvian favourites. Mains 15–20 soles.

Restaurant El Catamaran Comercio 166 (Boulevard), Pisco. Good for vegetarian food and pizzas. Mains 12–17 soles.

Jhonny & Jennifer Malecón El Chaco, Paracas. Consistently good and well priced food. Popular with tour groups. (Mains average s/.15)

ICA AND HUACACHINA

The city of **ICA** lies 50km inland, in a fertile valley surrounded by impressive sand dunes. The city suffered considerable damage in the 2007 earthquake with several buildings completely destroyed and almost one entire side of the Plaza de Armas (Calles Lima and Callao), which housed several agencies and restaurants, was destroyed. In the city itself, the **Museo Regional** warrants a visit, and the surrounding area offers **vineyard tours** with plenty of wine-tasting opportunities.

The nearby small desert oasis town of **HUACACHINA** has become a very popular destination for travellers in recent years, due to its tranquil setting and opportunities for adventure sports, in particular **sandboarding** and **dune-buggying.**

What to see and do

Ica's busy streets do not lend themselves to leisurely strolls (go to Huacachina for a more relaxed atmosphere), however it is easy to get around using the ubiquitous *tico* taxis who will take you anywhere in the city for around $1.

Museo Regional de Ica

The Museo Regional (Jirón Ayabaca, block 8; Mon–Fri, 8am–7pm & Sat–Sun, 9am–6pm; Adults $4, Children $0.40, Students $0.80) is one of the best in Peru housing important Nasca, Ica and Paracas cultural artifacts.

Bodega and Vineyard Tours

Ica's main tourist attraction and principal industry is the many bodegas and vineyards nearby, which can be visited on organised tours from the city, and usually involve a look around the vineyard followed by wine tasting and the chance to buy. The following vineyards produce wines and piscos which are famed throughout Peru, and several are also exported: Bodega Ocucaje (www.hotelocucaje.com), Bodega Vista Alegre, and Bodega Tacama (www.tacama.com). Organise a trip through your hotel, or an agency around the Plaza de Armas.

Arrival and Information

Ica is a major destination on the Panamerican Highway and is easily reached in approximately 5hr from Lima, 2hr 30 minutes from Nazca, and 12hr from Arequipa.

By bus There are several companies with frequent departures of different classes of bus throughout the day. Recommended among them are Ormeño (056/215600) and Cruz del Sur (056/223333). Bear in mind that Ormeño is the only major bus company with direct buses to the town of Pisco. To get from Ica to Huacachina you can take one of the **orange buses** which leave every 15min or so from outside the Santuario de Luren on Jirón Lima.

By taxi A faster and easier option is to take a private or *colectivo* (shared) taxi, expect to pay around US$2 for a private taxi, and less than US$1 for a squashed seat in a shared taxi.

THE NAZCA LINES

One of the great mysteries of South America, the **NAZCA LINES** are a series of animal figures and geometric shapes, none of them repeated and some up to 200m in length, drawn across some five hundred square kilometres of the bleak, stony Pampa de San José. Each one, even such sophisticated motifs as a spider monkey or a hummingbird, is executed in a single continuous line, most created by clearing away the brush and hard stones of the plain to reveal the fine dust beneath. They were probably a kind of agricultural calendar to help regulate the planting and harvesting of crops, while perhaps at the same time some of the straight lines served as ancient sacred paths connecting *huacas*, or power spots. Regardless of why they were made, the Lines are among the strangest and most unforgettable sights in the country.

If you don't want to fly over the lines you can see them at Km420 of the Panamerican Highway, where a tall metal **viewing tower** (or *mirador*; 50¢) has been built above the plain. Unless you've got the time to climb up onto one of the hills behind, or take a **flight** over the Lines (see box below), this is the best view you'll get.

Arrival and information

Roughly halfway between Lima and Arequipa, Nazca is easily reached by frequent bus, *colectivo*, or even by small **plane** from Lima with Aero Condor (see box below for details); *colectivos* link the airstrip with *jiróns* Bolognesi and Grau in town.

By bus Cruz del Sur buses drop off opposite the Alegria Tours office, C Lima 168; Lima–Arequipa service and Ormeño buses arrive at Avenida de Los

FLYING OVER THE NAZCA LINES

A pricey but spectacular way of seeing the Lines is to **fly** over them. Flights leave from Nazca airstrip, about 3km south of Nazca, and cost US$40–75 per person depending on the season, the size of the group, and how long you want to spend buzzing around – they can last from ten minutes to a couple of hours. Early morning flights are recommended as it is not so windy, meaning a smoother flight. Also those who suffer from motion sickness may want to skip breakfast as it is not unlike being on a rollercoaster when the small plane zips around the sky. The usual package costs between US$50 and US$80, lasting from 30–45min. **Flight operators** include **Aero Ica**, at Nazca Airport 056/522434, www.aeroica.net, or via the *Hotel la Maison Suisse* (056/522434) in Nazca; **Aeroparacas**, 056/522688, www.aeroparacas.com; **Alas Peruanas**, Jr Lima 168 (056/522444, www.alasperuanas.com).

Incas 112 several times weekly; most other buses stop around the start of Jirón Lima, by the *ovalo* on Avenida Los Incas. Buses leave every hour for the Nazca airstrip, from the corner of Grau with Jirón Bolognesi, and are normally marked *B-Vista Alegre* although if you book your flight over the lines through an agency in Nazca, transport to the airstrip will be provided.

By colectivos and taxis *Colectivos* to and from Ica arrive at and leave close to the presently closed *Hotel Montecarlo*, Jr Callao 123, on the corner of Av Los Incas and Micaelo Bastidas; those from Vista Alegre leave from the corner of Bolognesi and Grau. Most people use the noisy, beeping little *tico* taxis or **motorcycle-rickshaws**, which can be hailed anywhere and compete to take you in or around town cheaply – you shouldn't pay more than US$2 for any destination in town.

Tourist information For information the best places are Nazca Trails, Bolognesi 550, on the Plaza de Armas (Ⓣ056/522858, Ⓦwww.nascalinesperu.com), or Alegria Tours, C Lima 168 (Ⓣ056/522444, Ⓦwww.nazcaperu.com).

Accommodation

Finding a **hotel** in Nazca is simple enough, with an enormous choice for such a small town; most places are along Jr Lima or within a few blocks of the Plaza de Armas.

Friends House Juan Matta 712 Ⓣ056/523630, Ⓔelmochilero_1000@hotmail.com. A cozy and friendly backpacker haunt with tiny shared kitchen and front sitting room with TV and DVDs. ❸

Hostal Alegria Jr Lima 166 Ⓣ056/522702, Ⓦwww.hotelalegria.net. Popular with travellers, it has rooms with or without private bath set around an attractive garden, as well as a number of newer, plusher chalet-style rooms with fans and bath. It also has a café that serves delicious and good value set lunches, and their travel agency can arrange tours and bus connections to Lima or Arequipa. Camping is sometimes allowed. ❺

Nazca Lines Hotel Jr Bolognesi Ⓣ034/522293. Luxurious, with its own well-kept pool and an excellent restaurant. If you can't afford to stay here, you'll be happy to know that non-residents can also use the pool for approximately US$5 a day – well worth it in the heat. ❾

Hostal Via Morburg Jr Jose María Mejia 108 Ⓣ056/522142 Ⓔhotelviamorburg@yahoo.es. A modern, secure place in a quiet part of town, the hostel offers comfortable rooms with private bath, reliable hot water, and a small pool. ❸

Hotel Don Agucho Av Paredones, at corner with Av San Carlos 100 Ⓣ034/522048, Ⓔdonagucho@hotmail.com. One of the nicest options in and around Nazca, this hacienda-style place has comfortable rooms, with bath and TV, based around cactus-filled passages. There's also a pool and a bar-restaurant; breakfast included in price. ❺

Eating and drinking

Eating in Nazca offers more variety than you might imagine given the town's small size. What little **nightlife** exists is mainly based around **restaurants** and **bars**, particularly on Jirón Lima, Plaza de Armas and Jirón Bolognesi.

Restaurant La Encantada Jr Callao 592 Ⓣ034/522930. Excellent *criolla* food in a nice atmosphere, though pricey. Mains 18–35 soles.

Restaurant El Huarango C Arica 602 Ⓣ034/521287. The finest restaurant in Nazca, with a solid reputation among the locals, it has a rooftop patio and a great ambience. The delicious food is very well priced. Mains 14–40 soles.

Restaurant La Kañada Jr Lima 160 Ⓣ034/522917. Nice decor and a pleasant atmosphere, often full of gringos eating their great seafood; also offers internet access. Mains average 15 soles.

La Taberna Jr Lima 321 Ⓣ034/521411. Serves a good selection of local and international dishes, plus a variety of drinks; its walls are covered with graffiti scrawled over the years by passing groups of travellers. Lively most evenings until midnight. Mains 12–20 soles.

NAZCA AND AROUND

The colonial town of **NAZCA** spreads along the margin of a small coastal valley. Although the river is invariably dry, Nazca's valley remains green and fertile through the continued application of an Inca subterranean aqueduct. It's a small town – slightly at odds with its appearance on maps – but an interesting and enjoyable place to stay. Indeed, these days it has become a major attraction, boasting, in addition to the Lines, the excellent **Museo Antoni/Centro Italiano Archaeologico**, adobe

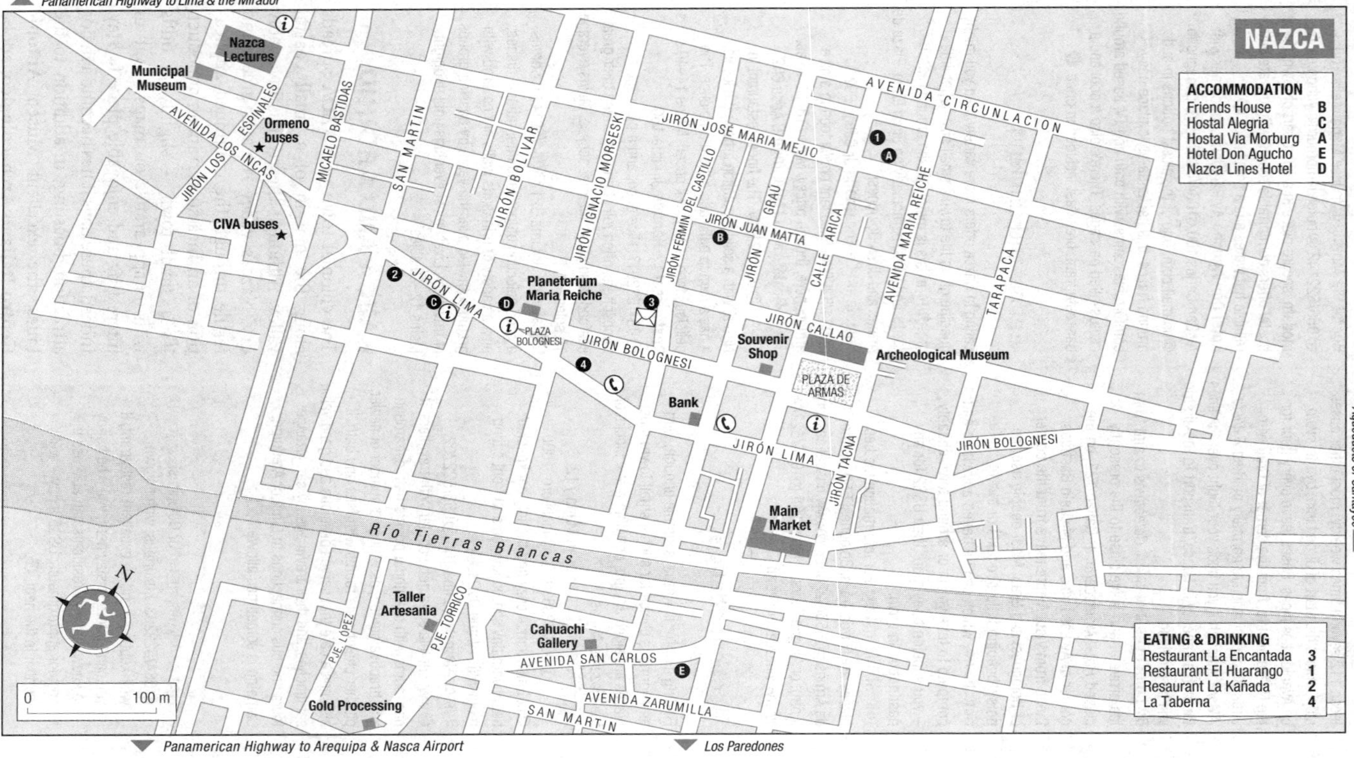
NAZCA
ACCOMMODATION
Friends House B
Hostal Alegria C
Hostal Via Morburg A
Hotel Don Agucho E
Nazca Lines Hotel D
EATING & DRINKING
Restaurant La Encantada 3
Restaurant El Huarango 1
Resaurant La Kañada 2
La Taberna 4
Panamerican Highway to Lima & the Mirador
Panamerican Highway to Arequipa & Nasca Airport
Los Paredones
Aqueducts of Cantayoc
Nazca Lectures
Municipal Museum
Ormeno buses
CIVA buses
Planeterium Maria Reiche
Souvenir Shop
Archeological Museum
PLAZA DE ARMAS
PLAZA BOLOGNESI
Bank
Main Market
Taller Artesania
Cahuachi Gallery
Gold Processing
Río Tierras Blancas
AVENIDA CIRCUNLACION
JIRÓN JOSÉ MARIA MEJIO
JIRÓN JUAN MATTA
JIRÓN CALLAO
JIRÓN BOLOGNESI
JIRÓN LIMA
JIRÓN TACNA
AVENIDA MARIA REICHE
TARAPACA
CALLE ARICA
JIRÓN GRAU
JIRÓN FERMIN DEL CASTILLO
JIRÓN IGNACIO MORSESKI
JIRÓN BOLIVAR
SAN MARTIN
MICAELO BASTIDAS
ESPINALES
AVENIDA LOS INCAS
JIRÓN LOS
AVENIDA SAN CARLOS
AVENIDA ZARUMILLA
PJE. TORRICO
PJE. LOPEZ
0 100 m
N

Inca ruins of **Paredones** only a couple of kilometres to the south, the **Casa Museo María Reiche** about 1km beyond the *mirador*, with access to several of the Nazca desert's animal figures, and two or three important **archeological sites** within an easy day's range.

What to see and do

As you come into town, Jr **Bolognesi**, the main street, leads straight into the **Plaza de Armas** where there are a few restaurants, bars and a couple of hotels.

Museo Didattico Antonini

If you continue straight across the plaza and head along Avenida de La Cultura you soon come to the new town museum – the fascinating **Museo Didattico Antonini**, an Italian Pre-Columbian Archeological Research and Study Centre, Av de la Cultura 600 (ⓣ056/523444, ⓦhttp://digilander.libero.it/MDAntonin; daily 9am–7pm). Opened in 1999, the museum stretches for six long blocks from the Plaza de Armas along Bolognesi and presents excellent interpretative exhibits covering the evolution of Nazca culture, a good audiovisual show and scale model reconstructions of local remains such as the Templo del Escalonado at Cahuachi. The museum complex extends to almost a hectare and includes an archeological park that contains the *bisambra* aqueduct (fed by the Bisambra reservoir higher up the valley) and some burial reconstructions.

South of Plaza de Armas

Heading along Calle Arica from the Plaza de Armas, south, the town's **main market**, offering the usual food and electronic goods, is based in a ramshackle collection of huts and stalls, on the left just before the river bridge on Calle Arica. The **Taller Artesanía**, Pasaje Torrico 240, in Barrio San Carlos, a short walk south of the plaza over the bridge, is worth a visit for its wonderful ceramics; if a few people turn up at the same time, they'll demonstrate the process of ceramic-making from moulding to polishing. San Carlos suburb also boasts the **Taller de Cerámica Juan Jose**, at Pasaje Lopez 400, and a **gold processing** operation, both located on the right-hand side about 500m down the Avenida San Carlos from the market bridge. Don't be put off by the fact that they're in someone's back garden – it's fascinating to watch them grind rocks into powder and then extract gold dust from it.

María Reiche Planetarium

For those with a particular interest in the Nazca Lines, or those who need a quick explanation before taking a flight over them the next day, a trip to the **María Reiche Planetarium** in the *Nazca Lines Hotel* (Bolognesi, showings daily at 6.45pm; $8) is a good idea.

TOURS AROUND NAZCA

Some well-established companies arrange **tours** to the major sites around Nazca, all offering similar trips to Los Paredones, Cantalloc, Cahuachi, Chauchilla and the Lines. Tours around Chauchilla Cemetery last two and a half hours for about US$10 a person; a trip to the viewing tower and the Casa Museo María Reiche also takes two and a half hours and costs around US$10. Tours out to the ruined temple complex in the desert at Cahuachi (see above) last four hours and cost in the region of US$50 for a party of four or five; these need to be arranged in advance. The best **tour operators** are Nazca Trails, Bolognesi 550, Plaza de Armas (ⓣ056/522858, ⓦwww.nazcatrails.com); Alegria Tours, C Lima 168 (ⓣ056/522444, ⓦwww.nazcaperu.com) and Andean Tempo, Ignacio Morsecky 126 (ⓣ056/522379, ⓔandeantempo@hotmail.com)

ICA AND HUACACHINA TOURS

Most hotels in Huacachina rent out sandboards and can book you onto a dune-buggying tour. Budget-minded travellers will want to hire a board and go it alone, but bear in mind that it soon gets very tiring dragging a board up a sand dune in the scorching sun, when the sand is so hot that it burns your feet. Irresponsible dune-buggy drivers are also a danger to the lone boarder. Make sure you book your trip with a responsible agency such as the following:

Desert Adventure a Huacachina-based tour company (☎056/228458, ⓦwww.desertadventure.net), who bill themselves as offering a 101 percent Adrenaline Experience, run the standard half-day dune-buggy tours of the dunes around Huacachina, with sandboarding included. They also run 2-day trips with a night spent camping in the desert.

Huacachina Tours (Av Angostura 355, L47, Ica; ☎056/256582, ⓦwww.huacachinatours.com). Based in Ica, Huacachina Tours is a professional outfit running trips in the surrounding area, including city tours of Ica.

ARCHAEOLOGICAL SITES AROUND NAZCA

Chauchilla and **Cahuachi**, after the Lines the most important sites associated with the Nazca culture, are both difficult to reach by public transport, and unless your energy and interest are pretty unlimited you'll want to take an organized tour.

Roughly 30km south of Nazca along the Panamerican Highway, then out along a dirt road beside the Poroma riverbed, **Chauchilla Cemetery** certainly rewards the effort it takes to visit. Once you reach the atmospheric site, you realize how considerable a civilization the riverbanks must have maintained in the time of the Nazca culture. Scattered about the dusty ground are literally thousands of graves, which have been cleaned up in recent years and organized for visitors. There is a clear walkway from which you must not stray, and open graves have roofs built over them to save the mummies, skulls, skeletons, broken pieces of pottery, bits of shroud fabric and lengths of braided hair, from the desert sun. It is an impressive experience, no less because of the curator's decision to arrange the mummies into positions to represent their daily lives. Further up the track, near Trancas, there's a small ceremonial **temple** – Huaca del Loro – and beyond this at Los Incas you can find Quemazon **petroglyphs**. These last two are not usually included in the standard tour, but if you hire your own guide you can negotiate with him to take you there – expect to pay US$5 extra.

HUACACHINA

The once peaceful oasis of Huacachina, nestled among huge sand dunes and boasting a lake with curative properties, has recently been overrun with travellers, eager for adrenaline-packed adventures, and enjoying all-night parties around dimly lit pools.

Accommodation, eating and drinking

There are several backpacker **hotels** all with lively poolside party scenes, as well as some tranquil resorts. All hostels and hotels have

TREAT YOURSELF

Hosteria Suiza Malecón de Huacachina 264, ☎056/238762, ⓦwww.hostesuiza.com. Quiet and tranquil resort-style hotel with pool and well kept gardens. Price includes internet access, rooms with private bath with hot water and an American breakfast. ❻

on-site resturants and bars, and there are also a few restaurants on the waterfront. Drinking and nightlife revolves around the various hostels with pool-side bars that have parties most nights.

La Casa de Arena Perotti ⓣ056/215439 ⓔcasadearena@hotmail.com. The original party hostel in Huacachina regularly hosts all-night BBQs at the pool-side bar. Not a good place if you want to sleep. ❷–❸

El Huacachinero Perotti ⓣ056/217435 ⓦwww.elhuacachinero.com. Popular with backpackers, this place has a small pool and garden with outside bar. Dbl US$25-$30/night, dorm bed $8/night. They also organize dune-buggy rides at 10am and 4pm daily for US$13 per person.

Hostal Rocha Perotti ⓣ056/229987 ⓔkikerocha@hotmail.com. Backpacker hotel with garden with the obligatory pool-side bar. Slightly more low-key than Casa de Arena, but still has a happening party scene. ❷

Arequipa and Colca Canyon

The country's second biggest and arguably, after Cusco, most attractive city, **AREQUIPA** nestles among volcanoes some 2400m above sea level. An elegant yet modern city, with a relatively wealthy population of over three-quarters of a million, it maintains a rather aloof attitude towards the rest of Peru. Some proud townsfolk even sport Arequipeñan passports claiming that Arequipa is so different from the rest of Peru, it couldn't possibly be part of the same country. With **El Misti**, the once snow-capped 5821-metre dormant volcano poised above, the place does have a rather legendary sort of appearance.

Some history

Arequipa has some very specific historical connotations for Peruvians. Developing late as a provincial capital, and until 1870 connected only by mule track with the rest of Peru, it has acquired a reputation as *the* centre of **right-wing political power**: while populist movements have tended to emerge around Trujillo in the north, Arequipa has traditionally represented the solid interests of the oligarchy. Arequipa typifies the social extremes of Peru more than any other of its major cities, with a huge increase in recent years in the number of street beggars, despite the tastefully ostentatious architecture and generally well-heeled appearance of most townsfolk.

The spectacular countryside around Arequipa rewards a few days' exploration, with some exciting and adventurous possibilities for trips. Around 200km to the north of the city is the **Colca Canyon**, one of Peru's major attractions, second only to Machu Picchu and developing fast as a trekking and canoeing destination (best in the dry season, May–Sept). Called the "Valley of Marvels" by the Peruvian novelist Marío Vargas Llosa, it is nearly twice the size of Arizona's Grand Canyon and one of the country's most extraordinary natural sights. Around 120km west of Arequipa, you can see the amazing petroglyphs of **Toro Muerto**, perhaps continuing on to hike amid the craters and cones of the **Valley of the Volcanos**.

WHEN TO VISIT

One of the best times to visit is around August 15, when there's a **festival** celebrating the city's foundation, with processions, music and poetry. There's also a folklore festival in the first week of July.

What to see and do

Arequipa's deeply ingrained architectural beauty comes mainly from the colonial period, characterized here by white *sillar* stone and arched interior ceilings. In general, the style is stark and almost clinical, except where baroque

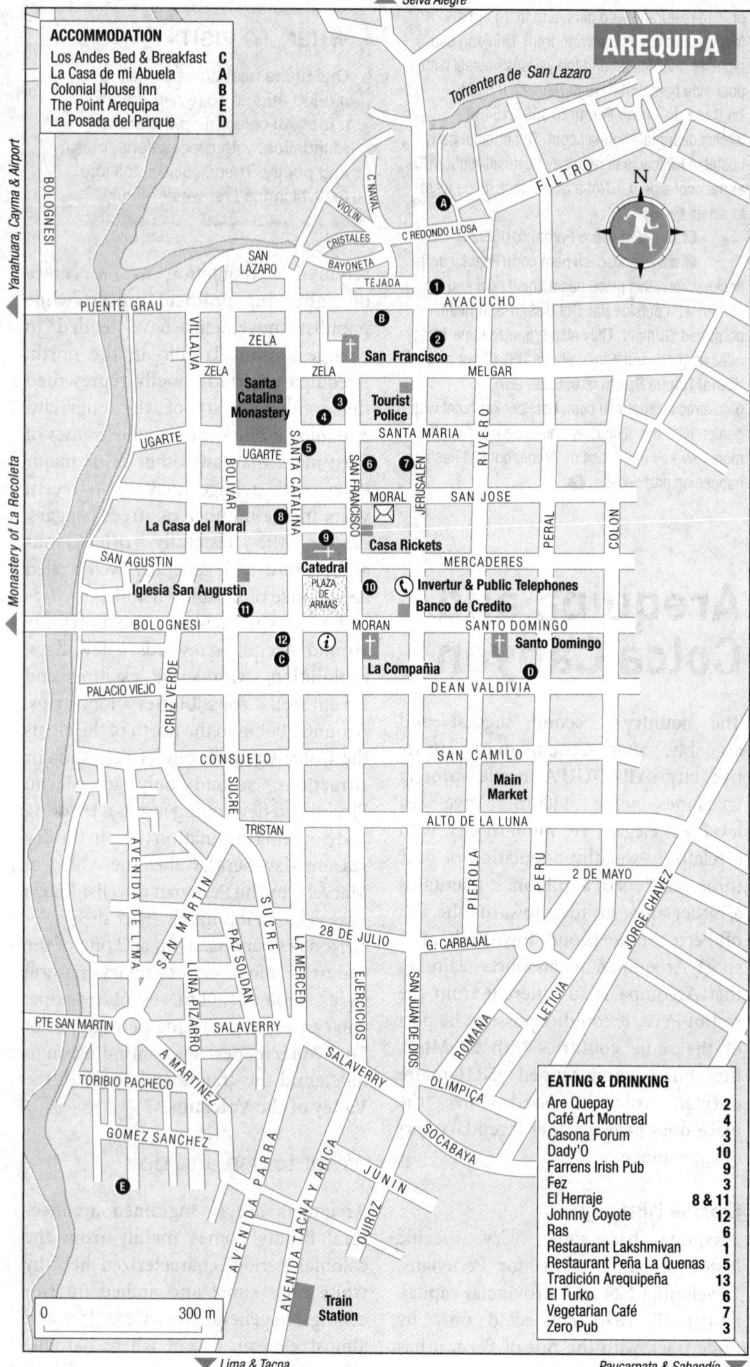
AREQUIPA
ACCOMMODATION
Los Andes Bed & Breakfast C
La Casa de mi Abuela A
Colonial House Inn B
The Point Arequipa E
La Posada del Parque D
EATING & DRINKING
Are Quepay 2
Café Art Montreal 4
Casona Forum 3
Dady'O 10
Farrens Irish Pub 9
Fez 3
El Herraje 8 & 11
Johnny Coyote 12
Ras 6
Restaurant Lakshmivan 1
Restaurant Peña La Quenas 5
Tradición Arequipeña 13
El Turko 6
Vegetarian Café 7
Zero Pub 3
Selva Alegre
Yanahuara, Cayma & Airport
Monastery of La Recoleta
Lima & Tacna
Paucarpata & Sabandía
Torrentera de San Lazaro
FILTRO
N
San Francisco
Santa Catalina Monastery
Tourist Police
La Casa del Moral
Casa Rickets
Catedral
PLAZA DE ARMAS
Invertur & Public Telephones
Banco de Credito
Iglesia San Augustin
La Compañia
Santo Domingo
Main Market
Train Station
BOLOGNESI
C NAVAL
VIOLIN
CRISTALES
BAYONETA
C REDONDO LLOSA
SAN LAZARO
TEJADA
AYACUCHO
PUENTE GRAU
VILLALVA
ZELA
MELGAR
UGARTE
SANTA MARIA
SANTA CATALINA
BOLIVAR
SAN FRANCISCO
JERUSALEN
RIVERO
MORAL
SAN JOSE
PERAL
COLON
SAN AGUSTIN
MERCADERES
MORAN
SANTO DOMINGO
PALACIO VIEJO
CRUZ VERDE
DEAN VALDIVIA
SAN CAMILO
CONSUELO
SUCRE
TRISTAN
ALTO DE LA LUNA
AVENIDA DE LIMA
SAN MARTIN
PIEROLA
PERU
2 DE MAYO
JORGE CHAVEZ
28 DE JULIO
G. CARBAJAL
PAZ SOLDAN
LA MERCED
EJERCICIOS
SAN JUAN DE DIOS
LETICIA
ROMAÑA
LUNA PIZARRO
PTE SAN MARTIN
SALAVERRY
A MARTINEZ
OLIMPICA
TORIBIO PACHECO
SOCABAYA
GOMEZ SANCHEZ
AVENIDA PARRA
AVENIDA TACNA Y ARICA
JUNIN
QUIROZ
0 300 m

and *mestizo* influences combine, as seen on many of the fine sixteenth- to eighteenth-century facades. Of the huge number of religious buildings spread about the old colonial centre, the **Monastery of Santa Catalina** is the most outstanding and beautiful. However, within a few blocks of the colonial **Plaza de Armas** are half a dozen churches well deserving of a brief visit, and a couple of superb old mansions. Arequipa has a cosmopolitan feel and there are plenty of swanky cafes where you can sit and watch the world go by while sightseeing. Further out, but still within walking distance, you can visit the attractive suburbs of **San Lazaro**, **Cayma** and **Yanahuara**, the latter being particularly renowned for its dramatic views of the valley with the volcanos, notably El Misti, patiently watching the city from high above.

The Plaza de Armas and Cathedral

The **Plaza de Armas**, one of South America's grandest, and the focus of social activity in the early evenings, comprises a particularly striking array of colonial architecture, dotted with palms, flowers and gardens. At its heart sits a bronze fountain, topped by an angel fondly known as *turututu* because of the trumpet it carries, but it's the arcades and elegant white facade of the seventeenth-century **Cathedral** (open for worship Mon–Sat 7.30–11.30am & 4.30–7.30pm; free, or for guided tours 11.30am–4.30pm; entrance for tours is through a large wooden door on Pasaje el Catedral, and on Sun for worship 7am–1.30pm & 5–7pm) that grab your attention, even drawing your sight away from El Misti towering behind. There are two bronze medallions in the facade symbolizing the Peruvian–Bolivian confederation, and the whole thing looks particularly beautiful when lit up in the evenings.

La Compañía

On the southeast corner of the plaza, opposite side from the cathedral, and rather more exciting architecturally, is the elaborate **La Compañía** (Mon–Fri 9am–12.30pm & 3–6pm, Sat 11.30am–12.30pm, Sun 9am–12.30pm & 5–6pm; free), with its extraordinary zigzagging *sillar* stone doorway. Built over the last decades of the seventeenth century, the magnificently sculpted doorway, with a locally inspired Mestizo-baroque relief, is curiously two-dimensional, using shadow only to outline the figures of the frieze. Inside, by the main altar hangs a *Virgin and Child* by Bernardo Bitto, which arrived from Italy in 1575. In what used to be the sacristy (now the Chapel of San Ignacio), the polychrome cupola depicts jungle imagery alongside warriors, angels and the Evangelists. You can also enter the fine **Jesuit Cloisters,** superbly carved back in the early eighteenth century. In the first cloister the fine squared pillars support white stone arches and are covered with intricate reliefs showing more angels, local fruits and vegetables, seashells and stylized puma heads. The second cloister is, in contrast, rather austere.

Santo Domingo

Santo Domingo (Mon–Fri 6.45am–noon & 3–7.45pm, Sat 6.45–9am & 3–7.45pm, Sun 5.30am–1pm; free), two blocks east of La Compañía, was built in the seventeenth century but was badly damaged by earthquakes in 1958 and 1960. It was originally built in 1553 by Gaspar Vaez, the first master architect to arrive in Arequipa, though most of what you see today started in 1650 and was finished in 1698, while the towers were constructed after the 1960 quake. It has been well restored, however, and on the main door you can make out an interesting example of Arequipa's *mestizo* craftsmanship – an Indian face amid a bunch of grapes, fine leaves and even cacti.

Santa Catalina Monastery

Just two blocks north of the Plaza de Armas, the vast protective walls of **Santa Catalina Monastery** (Santa Catalina 301 Ⓦwww.santacatalina.org.pe; daily 9am–5pm, last entrance at 4pm, Tues and Thurs 7–9pm; US$10; guides are optional at around US$3) housed almost two hundred secluded nuns and three hundred servants until it opened to the public in 1970. The most important and prestigious religious building in Peru, its enormous complex of rooms, cloisters and tiny plazas takes a good hour or two to wander around. Some thirty nuns still live here today, spanning between 18 and 90 years of age, but they're restricted to the quarter bordered by calles Bolívar and Zela, worshipping in the main chapel only outside visiting hours.

Originally the concept of Gaspar Vae in 1570, though only granted official licence five years later, it was funded by the Viceroy Toledo and the wealthy María de Guzmán, who later entered the convent with one of her sisters and donated all her riches to the community. The most striking feature of the architecture is its predominantly Mudéjar style, adapted by the Spanish from the Moors, but which rarely found its way into their colonial buildings. The quality of the design is emphasized and harmonized by a superb interplay between the strong sunlight, white stone and brilliant colours in the ceilings and in the deep blue sky above the maze of narrow interior streets. You notice this at once as you enter, filing left along the first corridor to a high vaulted room with a ceiling of opaque *huamanga* stone imported from the Ayacucho valley. Beside here are the **locutorios** – little cells where on holy days the nuns could talk, unseen, to visitors.

The **Novices Cloisters**, beyond, are built in solid *sillar*-block columns, their antique wall paintings depicting the various qualities to which the devotees were expected to aspire and the Litanies of the Rosary. Off to the right, the **Orange Tree Cloister**, painted a beautiful blue with birds and flowers over the vaulted arches, is surrounded by a series of paintings showing the soul evolving from a state of sin to the achievement of God's grace. In one of the side rooms, dead nuns were mourned, before being interred within the monastic confines.

Calle Toledo

A new convent, where the nuns now live, is on the right off Calle Córdoba. **Calle Toledo**, a long, very narrow street which is the oldest part of the monastery and connects the main dwelling areas with the *lavandería*, or communal washing sector, is brought to life with permanently flowering geraniums. There are several rooms off here worth exploring, including small chapels, prayer rooms and a kitchen. The **lavandería** itself, perhaps more than any other area, offers a captivating insight into what life must have been like for the closeted nuns; open to the skies and city sounds yet bounded by high walls, there are twenty halved earthenware jars alongside a water channel. It also has a swimming pool with sunken steps and a papaya tree in the lovely garden.

There is also a small coffee shop serving drinks and snacks in one of the sunny courtyards within the monastery.

Monastery of La Recoleta

Over the Río Chili is the large Franciscan **Monastery of La Recoleta** (Ⓣ054/270996 Ⓔconvento-la-recoleta@terra.com.pe; Mon–Sat 9am–noon & 3–5pm; US$2), standing conspicuously on its own on Callejón de la Recoleta, Ronda Recoleta 117, just ten- to fifteen-minutes' walk east of the Plaza de Armas. Founded in 1648 by the venerable Father Pedro de Mendoza and designed by Father Pedro de Peñaloza, the stunning major and minor cloisters were built in 1861; in 1869 it was converted to an Apostolic Mission school administered by the Barefoot Franciscans. With many interesting and bizarre exhibits, it is worth making the effort to find this little-visited gem of a museum. When you visit you will be asked to go around turning the lights on and off as you pass through each exhibit. There is an impressive library on the second floor housing many antique books, which are only used by researchers with special permission from the Father. You can visit the library for fifteen minutes, at 45 minutes past the hour during museum opening times.

The museum houses a collection of art and ceramics made by pre-Inca cultures, including the Chancay, local to the Arequipa area and notable as one of the few pre-Inca cultures with no representations of warriors or any kind of violent scenes in their ceramics, only colour and beauty.

The Amazonian section of the museum is a must-see; one room houses clothing and jewellery collected by the Franciscan monks on their early missions into the Amazon, as well as photographs of their first encounters with the "natives". The second room displays stuffed birds and animals from the Amazon in a somewhat gruesome fashion, as well as hunting equipment.

Museo Santuarios Andinos de la Universidad Católica de Santa María

Often referred to as the "Juanita" or "Ice Princess" museum, after its most famous exhibit, the immaculately preserved mummy of a 12-14 year old girl sacrificed to the Apu Ampato around five hundred years ago, the **Museo Santuarios Andinos** is easy to find just off the plaza at Calle La Merced 110 (Ⓣ054/215013 Ⓦwww.ucsm.edu.pe/santury; Mon–Sat 9am–6pm, Sun 9am–3pm; US$6). The price includes a guided tour of approximately one hour (the guide expects a tip, too) as well as a short video. Juanita is actually one of several mummies at the museum, which is well worth a visit even if Juanita herself is not on display (she takes a couple of months a year off for restoration).

The suburbs: San Lazaro and Yanahuara

The oldest quarter of Arequipa – the first place the Spaniards settled in this valley – is the *barrio* **San Lazaro**, an uncharacteristic zone of tiny, curving streets stretching around the hillside at the top end of Calle Jerusalén, all an easy stroll from the plaza. If you feel like a walk, and some good views of El Misti, you can follow the streambed from here to Puente Grau – a superb vantage point. From here, a longer stroll takes you across to the west bank of the Chili, along Avenida Ejército and out to suburbs of Yanahuara (1–2km) and Cayma (3–4km), quite distinct villages until the railway boom of the late nineteenth century, which brought peasant migrants to Arequipa from as far away as Cusco. Both are built up now, though they still command stunning views across the valley, above all from their **churches**. There are also one or two fine **restaurants** in these sectors, particularly Yanahuara. Buses and *colectivos* to these areas leave from avenidas Ayacucho and Puente Grau.

The municipal plaza at **Yanahuara** possesses a **viewing point** (*mirador*), the view of the city which, with Misti framed behind by the *mirador*'s white stone arches, has been made famous by postcards. Buses and *colectivos* to Yanahuara's *mirador* can be caught from the corner of Grau with Santa Catalina (near the *Hostal Santa Catalina*), or it's a fifteen-minute walk from Puente Grau, between blocks 2 and 3 of Avenida Ejército. The small **Iglesia Yanahuara** on the tranquil main plaza dates to the middle of the eighteenth century, and its baroque facade, with a stone relief of the

TOURS, TREKKING AND CLIMBING IN AREQUIPA AND AROUND

Taking a guided tour is the easiest and fastest way to see the area. All operators tend to offer similar packages. Most companies offer one- to three-day-trips out to the **Colca Canyon** for US$20–80 (sometimes with *very* early morning starts) or to the petroglyphs at **Toro Muerto** for US$20–40. Trips to the **Valley of the Volcanos** are only offered by a few companies. Specialist adventure activities, eg rafting in the Colca Canyon, mountaineering or serious trekking, can cost anything from US$55 up to US$350 for a three- to six-day outing. Competition between companies is high, so check out all the options and determine exactly what you're getting.

Campamento Base and Colca Trek Jerusalén 401b ⓣ054/206217, ⓦwwwcolcatrek.com.pe. An excellent tour, trek, climbing, mountain biking and canoeing company that specializes in customized tours permitting a mix of the above. Also sell maps and have equipment rental for independent trekkers.

Cusipata Expeditions Jerusalén 408 ⓣ054/203966, ⓦwww.cusipata.com. Specialists in rafting trips with short trips to the Chili River, and up to six day-trips on the Colca River; also they lead yearly Cotahuasi Canyon expeditions and regular kayaking courses.

Giardino Agencia de Viajes Jerusalén 606a ⓣ054/241206 or 226416, ⓦwww.giardinotours.com. A well-organized outfit that gives excellent two-day tours to Colca, trekking and climbing trips, plus the usual city and countryside trips.

Pablo Tour Jerusalen 400 ⓣ054/203737, ⓦwww.pablotour.com. Well established, family-run business with good 2-and 3-day Colca Canyon trips.

Peru Adventures Tours Jerusalén 410 ⓣ054/221658, ⓦwww.peruadventurestours.com. Downhill mountain biking with 4wd support in surrounding area, and trips into the Colca Canyon.

Santa Catalina Tours Santa Catalina 223 ⓣ054/284292, ⓔsantacatalina@rh.com.pe. City tours, local and Colca Canyon trips, plus ascents up El Misti and occasional rafting on the Río Chili, all at reasonable prices. Good, reliable guides.

tree of life incorporating angels, flowers, saints, lions and hidden Indian faces, is particularly fine.

Arrival and information

Arequipa is the hub of most journeys in the southern half of Peru and is generally an almost unavoidable stopping-off point between Lima and the Titicaca, Cusco and Tacna regions.

By bus Most long-distance buses arrive at the modern, concrete **Terminal Terrestre** bus station or at the newer **Terrapuerto**, next door, around 4km from the centre of town; a taxi to the Plaza de Armas should cost no more than US$2.

By plane Flights land at Arequipa airport, 7km northwest of the town. Many of the more upmarket hotels provide a free transfer from the airport in a shared shuttle bus. If you don't have reservations or are not staying at a place which includes this service, the only other option is to take a taxi – $5 into the centre of town.

Tourist information is available from three official **i-Peru Promperu offices**, at Portal de La Municipalidad 110, Plaza de Armas (Mon–Sat 8.30am–7.30pm, Sun 8.30am–4pm; ⓣ054/223265, ⓔiperuarequipa@promperu.gob.pe); Casona Santa Catalina, Calle Santa Catalina 210 (Mon–Sun 9am–7pm; ⓣ054/221227 ⓔiperuarequipacasona@promperu.gob.pe); Rodriquez Ballón Airport, Arrivals Hall (open when there are flights coming in ⓣ054/444564, ⓔiperuarequipaapto@promperu.gob.pe. At any of these offices you will find helpful staff, free maps of the city and information on sights and cultural events as well as recommendations for tour companies, hotels and restaurants.

Tourist police The Tourist Police, Jerusalén 315 (ⓣ054/201258), are very helpful with maps and information, and are available 24hr a day in case of emergency. The **Terminal Terrestre** also has a kiosk with details of hotels and tour companies, and sometimes maps. For information on **guided tours** of the city and the surrounding area, see the box opposite. If you want a **taxi** it's easy to hail one anywhere in the city; rides within the centre cost about 80¢.

Accommodation

Arequipa has a good selection of accommodation in all price ranges, with most of the better options mainly within a few blocks of the Plaza de Armas or along Calle Jerusalén.

La Casa de mi Abuela Jerusalén 606 ⓣ054/241206, ⓔlperezwi@ucsm.edu.pe. Innovative family-run hostel, combining elegance and comfort. Rooms are set in a variety of environments around lovely gardens; there are spacious colonial quarters, chalets, family apartments and a fine swimming pool. It's very secure, has a good library and an excellent *cafetería*. Reserve well in advance during high season. ❻

Colonial House Inn Puente Grau 114 ⓣ054/223533, ⓔcolonialhouseinn@ hotmail.com. Pleasant location with a pretty covered courtyard, electric heated showers, private bathrooms and access to TV and internet facilities. There is also a laundry service and book exchange. Well worth it, not least for the nice rooftop breakfast option. The owners are very friendly and can organize airport transfers. ❸

Los Andes Bed & Breakfast La Merced 123 ⓣ054/330015, ⓦwww.losandesbb.com. A great-value budget stay popular with long-stay travellers and volunteers. It is clean and well decorated, with two large TV rooms for guests to use filled with comfy sofas, use of kitchen, free internet for guests, breakfast included. ❹

La Posada del Parque Dean Valdivia 238a ⓣ054/212275 ⓦwww.posadadelparque.com. Spacious hostel with large bright comfortable rooms, good showers, 24hr hot water, rooms with private or shared bath. Large rooftop terrace with great views over the city. Living area with cable TV and DVD collection for guests to use. Wireless internet connection and luggage storeroom available. Breakfast is not included but can be bought for $2 per person if you fancy sitting on the sunny terrace for breakfast. Marlons Travel Agency (run by the same family) can book transport and tours and provide tourist information. Dorm rooms, doubles and triples available. ❹

The Point Arequipa Av Lima 515, Vallecito ⓣ054/286 920 ⓦwww.thepointhostels.com/arequipa. Part of the infamous *The Point* chain of party hostels popular with backpackers throughout Peru, the Arequipa branch is no different. With an in-house bar, cable TV and DVDs, weekly BBQs, free internet, full restaurant, laundry and Spanish classes, *The Point* is set up for backpackers. Slightly out of the centre it is a 15min walk or 5min taxi ride from the Plaza de Armas. ❹

Eating

Arequipa boasts all sorts of **restaurants** dotted about the town serving a wide variety of foods, but is particularly famous for a dish called *ocopa*, a cold appetizer made with potatoes, eggs, olives and a fairly spicy yellow chilli sauce. As it's not too far from the Pacific, the town's better restaurants are also renowned for their excellent fresh seafood. **Picanterías** – traditional Peruvian eating houses serving spicy seafood – are particularly well established here. Many restaurants have bars and live music in the evenings, and most bars and clubs also serve food.

Ary Quepay Jerusalén 502. A large restaurant space serving local food, such as alpaca steaks, as well as international dishes, vegetarian options and fine pisco sours; frequently busy at night, service is good and there is a festive atmosphere, with live folk music most nights. Mains 20–25 soles.

Fez/El Turko San Francisco 229/ San Francisco 216. Two middle-Eastern restaurants run by the same owners (who also run the more expensive *Ras* at San Francisco 227), dishing up delicious kebabs, falafel and sandwiches until late (also takeaway). Kebabs 8 soles, mains 12–20 soles.

El Herraje With two restaurants at Santa Catalina 128 and Bolognesi 127 (ⓣ054/284345 & ⓣ054/225780 respectively), this Argentine grill serves unbelievably large steaks and other BBQ grilled meats at tiny prices – it's hard to beat the menus here for good value, and all meals include unlimited visits to the salad bar. Mains 8–20 soles.

Johnny Coyote Corner of Calle Merced & Puente Bolognesi 103, just off the Plaza de Armas. American style fast-food restaurant with good quality hamburgers. Burger combo 15 soles.

Restaurant Lakshmivan Jerusalén 408 (ⓣ054/228768, ⓔlakshminatur9@hotmail.com, open Mon–Sun 8am–9.30pm). A very popular vegetarian café with breakfast, lunch and dinner menus, at the back of a small patio. They also-sell a range of healthfood products, yogurts and wholemeal bread. Often plays classical music and has a pleasant ambience. Mains average 15 soles.

Tradición Arequipeña Av Dolores 111 ⓣ054/426467 ⓦwww.tradicion-arequipena.com. Opened in 1991 and situated several blocks east of the city centre, this is probably the best *picanteria* restaurant in town. It has a pleasant garden, covered and indoor spaces and is usually bustling with locals enjoying the extremely fresh and tasty food. It is about a 10min cab ride from the Plaza de Armas. Mains 18–30 soles.

Vegetarian Café Moral 205. A very small but excellent and inexpensive Asian vegetarian restaurant that offers set lunch menus at giveaway prices. They also have cheap á la carte options and vegetarian versions of typical foods using meat substitutes such as soya and tofu. Mains average 8 soles.

Drinking and nightlife

Café Art Montreal Ugarte 210 ⓣ054/206652 ⓔlecafeartmontreal@hotmail.com. Although open for breakfasts and lunches, this attractive cafe set around a fine stone courtyard really comes to life at night (happy hour every night from 5pm–11pm; live music Thurs, Fri, Sat; Wed is ladies night) when excellent foods are served up to live local rock and Latino ballad bands. This is a *peña* but certainly isn't folkloric. The cocktails here are very interesting (happy hour 2 drinks for s/.15–20).

Casona Forum San Francisco 317 ⓣ054/202697 ⓦwww.forumrockcafe.com ⓦwww.zeropub-pool.com. This three-storey complex houses some of Arequipa's best night spots: the funky Retro pub is open from 6pm, Zero Pub & Pool opens at 6.30pm, Terrasse lounge restaurant opens at 6.30pm, offering a combo of comfortable lounge seating, fine dining, stunning views of the city through 360 degree windows, plus karaoke as the night wears on (Mains s/.25–40). The jewel in the crown of this complex is hidden in the basement: Forum disco opens at 10pm and is the place to see and be seen among young *Arequipeños*, with a lively tropical décor including palm trees, pools and a large artificial waterfall and live music at the weekends.

Farrens Irish Pub Pasaje el Catedral 107 ⓣ054/238465. Authentic and friendly Irish pub with outside seating (perfect for an afternoon drink in the sunshine), pool tables, Guinness and happy hour every night from 6pm–10pm (Mains average s/.15).

Restaurant Peña Las Quenas Santa Catalina 302 ⓣ054/281115. One of the better and larger venues in town, dishes out authentic Andean music, food and good pisco sours; music most weekends and also during the week from June–Sept. Closed on Sun, but open all other days from 10am for breakfast (Mains s/.20–25).

Dady´o Portal de Flores 112, Plaza de Armas. Open Thurs, Fri Sat at 10pm, with live music, karaoke and dangerously cheap drinks, a popular spot for weekend revelries. (2 x rum & coke for s/.8).

Directory

Airlines Aerocondor, Portal San Agustin 145, Plaza de Armas ⓣ054/608686; Lan, Santa Catalina 118-C; Star Peru, Santa Catalina 105-A ⓣ054/221896.

Banks and exchange Banco de la Nación, Rivero 107; Banco de Crédito, San Juan de Dios 123; BBVA Banco Continental, San Francisco 108; Interbank, Mercaderes 217; Scotiabank, Mercaderes 410. There are many exchange places on the Plaza de Armas and on San Juan de Dios.

Bus Leaving from the Terrapuerto for destinations including Cusco, Lima and Nazca are Cruz del Sur (ⓣ054/427375), Oltursa (ⓣ054/423152), and Cial (ⓣ054/430505).

Post office Calle Moral 118.

CROSSING INTO CHILE

The **border with Chile** (daily 9am–10pm) is about 40km south of Tacna. Regular buses and *colectivos* to **Arica** (see p.465) leave from the modern bus terminal on Hipolito Unanue in Tacna; the taxi *colectivos* are a particularly quick and easy way to cross the border. There are also daily trains which depart from the station, on Calle Coronel Albarracín, see ⓦwww.perurail.com for details of the services. If you take the train you have to visit the Passport and Immigration Police, on Plaza de Armas, and the Chilean Consulate, Presbitero Andia, just off Coronel Albarracín, beforehand. You will already have cleared Peruvian customs control on your way into Tacna, along the Panamerican Highway.

Coming back into Peru from Arica is as simple as getting there. *Colectivos* run throughout the day and there are regular trains. Night travellers, however, might be required to have a *salvoconducto militar* (safe-conduct card), particularly in times of tension between the two countries. If you intend to travel at night, check first with the tourist office in Arica, C Prat 305, on the second floor.

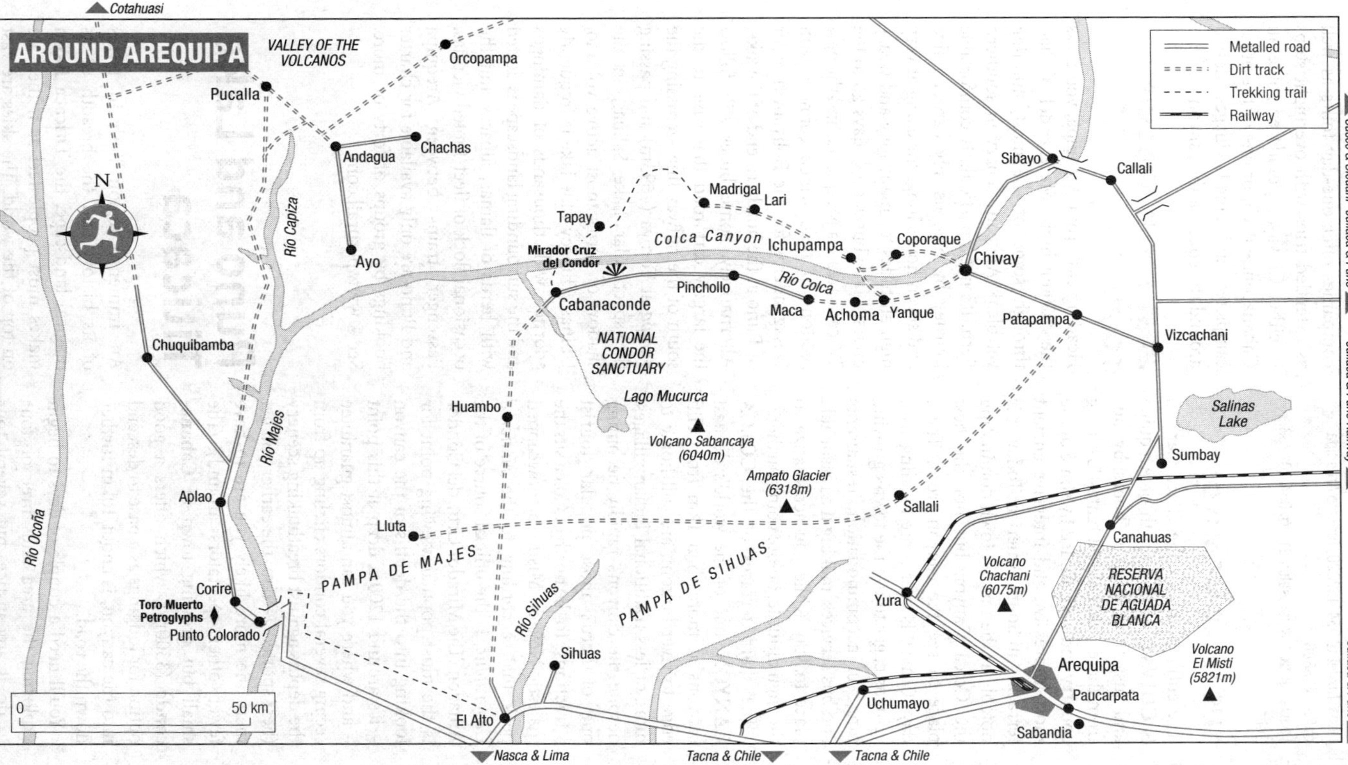
AROUND AREQUIPA
VALLEY OF THE VOLCANOS
Cotahuasi
Orcopampa
Pucalla
Andagua
Chachas
Ayo
Río Capiza
Chuquibamba
Río Majes
Aplao
Río Ocoña
Corire
Toro Muerto Petroglyphs
Punto Colorado
0
50 km
Madrigal
Lari
Tapay
Colca Canyon
Ichupampa
Coporaque
Mirador Cruz del Condor
Cabanaconde
Pinchollo
Río Colca
Maca
Achoma
Yanque
Chivay
Sibayo
Callali
Patapampa
Vizcachani
NATIONAL CONDOR SANCTUARY
Lago Mucurca
Volcano Sabancaya (6040m)
Ampato Glacier (6318m)
Huambo
Sallali
Lluta
PAMPA DE MAJES
PAMPA DE SIHUAS
Río Sihuas
Sihuas
El Alto
Salinas Lake
Sumbay
Canahuas
RESERVA NACIONAL DE AGUADA BLANCA
Volcano Chachani (6075m)
Yura
Arequipa
Volcano El Misti (5821m)
Paucarpata
Sabandia
Uchumayo
Metalled road
Dirt track
Trekking trail
Railway
Cusco & Sicuani
Juliaca & Puno
Juliaca & Puno Railway
Juliaca & Puno
Nasca & Lima
Tacna & Chile
Tacna & Chile

Taxis Taxitel ⓣ054/452020, Turismo Arequipa ⓣ054/458888.
Tourist police C Jerusalén 315 ⓣ054/201258, 24hr.

THE COLCA CANYON

The entry point for the Colca Canyon is **CHIVAY**, 150km north of Arequipa and just three to four hours by bus from there, set amongst fantastic hiking country and surrounded by some of the most impressive and intensive ancient terracing in South America. Today, it is notable as the market town dominating the Colca Canyon but not the best place to see the canyon from. These days Chivay is ever more bustling with gringos eager to use the town's growing range of accommodation, restaurants and bus services, making it a reasonable place to stay while you acclimatize to the high altitude, before going further.

The sharp terraces of the **COLCA CANYON**, one of the world's deepest canyons at more than 1km from cliff edge to river bottom, are still home to more or less traditional Indian villages, despite the canyon's rapidly becoming one of Peru's most popular tourist attractions. To the north of Colca sits the majestic Nevado Mismi, a snowcapped peak that, according to the *National Geographic*, is the official source of the Amazon. The Mirador Cruz del Condor is the most popular viewing point for looking into the depths of the canyon – it's around 1200m deep at this point – and where you can almost guarantee seeing several condors circling up from the depths against breathtaking scenery (best spotted 7–9am, the earlier you get there the more likely you are to have fewer other spectators around). The small but growing town of **Cabanaconde** (3300m), which offers a good option for lodgings as a base to descend into the canyon, is about 10km further down the road.

You'll need a couple of days to begin exploring the area and three or four to do it any justice, but several tour companies offer one-day tours as well as extended trips with overnight stops in either Chivay, a *posada* en route, in Cabanaconde itself, or one of the other campsites and small villages dotted around the edges of the canyon.

EAST FROM AREQUIPA TO PUNO

Heading east from Arequipa, you cross the 4500m-high Meseta del Collao through some of the most stunning yet bleak Andean scenery in southern Peru. It's not a particularly comfortable journey by bus, usually between five and seven hours long, travelling at very high altitudes for many long and weary hours. Many buses these days go to the Titicaca area via Moquegua and the new sections of road which connect with Desaguaderos for the Bolivian frontier or Puno at the northern end of the lake. Alternatively, some buses still follow the largely dirt road that runs to the south of the railway line – crossing the *pampa* at Toroya (4693m) and passing the spectacular Lake Salinas, in the shadow of Peru's most active volcano, Ubinas. This icy-blue lake is frequently adorned with thousands of flamingos and the surrounding landscape is dotted with herds of llamas, alpacas and the occasional flock of fleet-footed vicuñas. Passenger trains between Arequipa and Puno are only available for charter bookings by groups of forty or more. See ⓦwww.perurail.com.

Puno and Lake Titicaca

An immense region both in terms of its history and the breadth of its magical landscape, the **Titicaca Basin** makes most people feel as if they are on top of the world. The skies are vast

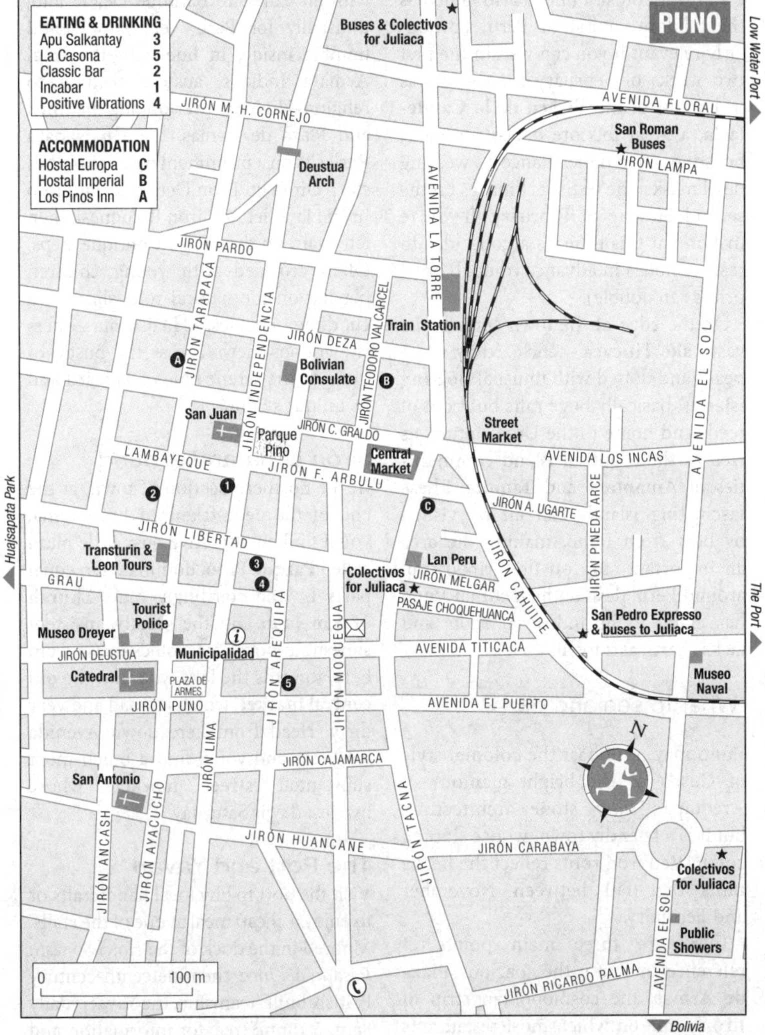

and the horizons appear to blend away below you. With a dry, cold climate – frequently falling below freezing in the winter nights of July and August – **Puno** is a breathless place (at 3870m above sea level), with a burning daytime sun in stark contrast to the icy evenings.

The town is immensely rich in traditions and has a fascinating ancient history with several stone *chullpas* nearby. The first Spanish settlement at Puno sprang up around a silver mine discovered by the infamous Salcedo brothers in 1657, a camp that forged such a wild and violent reputation that the Lima viceroy moved in with soldiers to crush and finally execute the Salcedos before things got too out of hand. At the same time – in 1668 – he created Puno as the capital of the region and from then on it developed into Lake Titicaca's main port and an important town on the silver trail from Potosi. Puno is also famed as the folklore capital of Peru, particularly relevant if you can visit in the first two weeks of February for the fiestas in honour of the **Virgen de la Candelaria**, a great folklore dance spectacle, boasting incredible dancers wearing devil masks; the festival climaxes on the second Sunday of February. If you're in Puno at this time it's a good idea to reserve hotels in advance (though hotel prices can double).

On the edge of the town spreads the vast **Lake Titicaca** – enclosed by white peaks and dotted with unusual **floating islands**, basically huge rafts built out of reeds and home to the Uros culture, as well as the beautiful island communities of **Amantani** and **Taquile**. These fascinating islands can all be visited by boat from Puno, making the area an important stop on the gringo trail around Peru, despite the fact that Puno has clung to its industrial roots and lacks charm as a town.

What to see and do

Puno may not boast the colonial style of Cusco or the bright glamour of Arequipa's *sillar* stone architecture, but it is a friendly town, whose sloping corrugated iron roofs reflect the heavy rains that fall between November and February.

There are three main points of reference in Puno: the spacious **Plaza de Armas**, the cosmopolitan strip of **Jirón Lima** on which most restaurants and bars can be found, and the bustling **Port** area with artisan stalls and local restaurants galore, as well as the restored steamship **Yavari**.

The Plaza de Armas and around

The seventeenth-century **Catedral** on the Plaza de Armas (Mon–Fri & Sun: 8am–noon, 3–6pm, Sat: 8am–noon, 3–7pm; free) is surprisingly large with an exquisite Baroque facade and, unusually for Peru, very simple and humble inside, in line with the local Aymara Indians' austere attitude to religion. High up, overlooking the town and Plaza de Armas, the **Huajsapata Park** sits on a prominent hill, a short but steep climb up Jirón Deustua, right into Jirón Llave, left up Jirón Bolognesi, then left again up the Pasaje Contique steps. Often crowded with young children playing on the natural rock-slides and cuddling couples, Huajsapata offers stupendous views across the bustle of Puno to the serene blue of Titicaca and its unique skyline.

Jirón Lima and around

In the northern section of town, at the end of the pedestrianized Jirón Lima, you'll find an attractive busy little plaza called **Parque Pino**, dominated in equal parts by the startlingly blue **Church of San Juan** and the scruffy, insistent shoeshine boys. Two blocks east from here, towards the lake, you find the **old central market**, which is small and very dirty. Head from here down Avenida los Incas and you'll find a much more substantial **street market**, whose liveliest day is Saturday.

The Port and Yavari

Visit the port to buy local handicrafts or to enjoy a cheap meal at one of the stalls. Moored in the dock of the *Hotel Sonesta Posada del Inca*, the nineteenth-century British-built steamship, the **Yavari** (daily 8am–5.15pm; free; for information and tours call ⓣ051/369329, ⓦwww.yavari.org) provides a fascinating insight into maritime life on Lake Titicaca over a hundred years ago and the military and entrepreneurial mindset of Peru in those days. The 2,766 pieces of the ship were transported from the Peruvian coast on the backs of mules and llamas, to be reconstructed on Lake Titicaca. The *Yavari* started life as a Peruvian navy gunship complete with bulletproof

TOURS AROUND PUNO

The streets of Puno are full of touts selling guided tours and trips, but don't be swayed, always go to a respected, established **tour company**; see the directory on p.870. There are four main local tours on offer in Puno, all of which will reward you with abundant bird and animal life, immense landscapes and genuine living traditions. The trip to the ancient burial towers or *chullpas* at **Sillustani** normally involves a three- or four-hour tour by minibus and costs US$7–10 depending on whether or not entrance and guide costs are included. Most other tours involve a combination of visits to the nearby **Uros Floating Islands** (half-day tour; US$5–10) and **Taquile and the Uros Islands** (full day from US$17, or from US$29 overnight). The best way to see the lake and experience life on Titicaca is to take a two-day tour, which stops at the Uros Islands then goes to Amantani, where you spend the night, and then visit Taquile on the second day. Most agencies can organize this tour staying with a local family on Amantani.

windows, but ended up delivering the mail around the lake. It has been much restored in recent years but the Yavari Project is still working towards getting the ship fully functional again to offer trips around the lake.

Arrival and Information

If you arrive in **Puno** from sea level, you'll immediately be affected by the altitude and should take it easy for the first day or two.

By bus Arriving by bus you are most likely to arrive at the main bus terminal on Jirón Primero de Mayo 703, Barrio Magisterial, ⓣ051/364733, or the Terminal Zonal on Av Simón Bolívar.

By boat The main port for boat trips to the Uros Islands, Taquile and Amantani, is a 20min walk from the Plaza de Armas, straight along Av El Puerto.

By colectivos *Colectivos* to and from Juliaca and **Juliaca Airport** leave from Jirón Tacna. Most hotels in Puno can organize a pick-up from Juliaca Airport (Inca Manco Capac Airport, ⓣ051/328974 or 322905 for information).

By train If you're coming from Cusco by train, you'll arrive at the train station (information on ⓣ051/351041 or 369179, ⓦwww.perurail.com) at Avenida la Torre 224. Taxis and motorcycle rickshaws leave from immediately outside the station and will cost less than US$2 to anywhere in the centre of town.

Tourist information The helpful and friendly staff at the tourist information office, on the Plaza de Armas, on the corner of Jirón Deustua and Jirón Lima (ⓣ051/365088, ⓔiperupuno@promperu.gob.pe, Mon–Sun 8.30am–7.30pm), can provide photocopied town plans, leaflets and other information.

Tourist police The tourist police, Jr Deustua 558, are open 24hr in case of emergency, ⓣ051/354764.

Accommodation

There is no shortage of **accommodation** in Puno for any budget, but the town's busy and narrow streets make places hard to locate, so you may want to make use of a taxi or motorcycle rickshaw.

Hostal Europa Jr Alfonso Ugarte 112 ⓣ051/353026, ⓔhostaleuropa@hotmail.com. Good rates, friendly, secure (with safe luggage store) and very popular with travellers, with 24hr hot water but few private bathrooms, laundry and café. ❹

Hostal Imperial Jr Teodoro Valcárcel 145 ⓣ051/7352386, ⓔimperial_hostal_puno@yahoo.com. All rooms have private bath with hot water, there is a laundry and café, the hostel is comfortable and good value for money. ❹

Los Pinos Inn Jr Tarapaca 182 ⓣ051/367398, ⓔhostalpinos@hotmail.com. With all the backpacker favourites – book exchange, luggage storage, laundry, safe, TV and free internet access for guests, *Los Pinos* is a good budget option. ❹

Eating, drinking and nightlife

Puno's **restaurant** and **nightlife** scene is fairly busy and revolves mainly around Jirón Lima, but bear in mind that places shut relatively early – not much happens after 11pm on a weekday. The city's strong tradition as one of the major Andean folklore centres in South America means that you're almost certain to be exposed to at least one live band an evening. There are some excellent restaurants in

Puno, and the local delicacies of trout and kingfish (*pejerey*) are worth trying and are available in most restaurants.

Apu Salkantay Jr Lima 425. Excellent food and good atmosphere – try their "surf and turf" option of trout with steak. Mains 18–30 soles.

La Casona Jr Lima 517 (☎051/351108). The best restaurant in town, particularly for evening meals, serving excellent *criolla* dishes in an attractive traditional environment. It is also something of a museum, with antique exhibits everywhere, and is very popular with locals. Mains 15–30 soles.

Classic Bar C Tarapacá 330-A. Popular and comfortable bar with a good atmosphere and range of drinks and snacks.

Incabar Jr Lima 348. A lively evening spot serving warming alcoholic drinks and scrumptious creative dishes, as well as pizzas; the garlic bread baked in a real-fire oven is particularly good. Mains average 20 soles.

Positive Vibrations Jr Lambayaque 127. Chilled out bar playing reggae and rock, with a fireplace and welcoming atmosphere (620ml beer s/.8).

Directory

Airlines LAN, Jr. Tacna 299 ⓦwww.lan.com, Star Peru Jr. Melgar ⓦwww.starperu.com.

Banks and exchange Banco Continental, Lima 400-411; Banco de La Nación, on the corner of Grau 215 and Ayacucho; Banco de Crédito, on the corner of Lima 510 with Grau. *Cambistas* hang out at the corner of Jr Tacna near the central market. There are *casas de cambio* at Tacna 232, Lima 440, and at Vilca Marilin, Tacna 255.

Bus companies Most bus companies can be found in the main Terminal Terrestre. Recommended among them for all destinations are Cruz del Sur ☎051/368524 and Ormeño ☎051/368176. For Arequipa and Southern Peru Sur Oriente ☎051/365867 or ETRASUR ☎051/802902. For La Paz and Copacabana Tour Peru ☎051/352991 and the Bolivian company Litoral – no phone in Puno but they do have a counter in the Terminal Terrestre.

Consulate Bolivia, Jr Arequipa 136, 2nd Floor ☎051/351251 (Mon–Fri 8am–4pm).

Police The Tourist Police are at Jr Deustua 558 (☎051/354764).

Post office Moquegua 269 ☎051/351141, Mon–Sat 8am–8pm.

Taxis ☎051/368000.

Telephones and faxes Telefonica del Peru, corner of Federico More and Moquegua (daily 7am–11pm); and Mabel Telecommunications, Jr Lima 224 (Mon–Fri 7am–noon & 2–7pm).

Tour operators Allways Travel, Inside Casa del Corrigedor, Jr Deustua 576 (☎051/355552, ⓦwww.titicacaperu.com/awtweb/); Edgar Adventures, Jr Lima 328 (☎051/353444, ⓔedgaradventures@terra.com.pe); Kollasuyo Tours, Jr Teodoro Valcárcel 155 (☎051/368642, ⓦwww.geocities.com/kollasuyotours).

Visas Migraciones, Jr Ayacucho 270-280 ☎051/357103.

LAKE TITICACA

An undeniably impressive sight, **Lake Titicaca**'s skies are vast, almost infinite, and deep, deep hues of blue; below this sits a usually placid mirror-like lake reflecting the big sky back on itself. A national reserve since 1978, the lake has over sixty varieties of birds, fourteen species of native fish and eighteen types of amphibians. It's also the world's largest high-altitude body of water, at 284m deep and more than 8500 square kilometres in area, fifteen times the size of Lake Geneva in Switzerland and higher and slightly bigger than Lake Tahoe in the US. The man-made **Uros Floating Islands** which have been inhabited since their construction centuries ago by Uros Indians who were retreating from more powerful neighbours like the Incas, are an impressive sight. Tour groups only visit a couple of the islands where the people are used to tourism, will greet you, offer you handicrafts for sale, and possibly a tour on one of their boats, made from the same totora reeds as their island homes. For a more authentic experience, visit the communities who live on the fixed islands of **Taquile** and **Amantani**, who still wear traditional clothes and follow ancient local customs. There are, in fact, more than seventy islands in the lake, the largest and most sacred being the **Island of the Sun**, an ancient Inca temple site on the Bolivian side of the border which divides the lake's southern shore. Titicaca is an Aymara word meaning "Puma's Rock", which refers to an unusual boulder on the

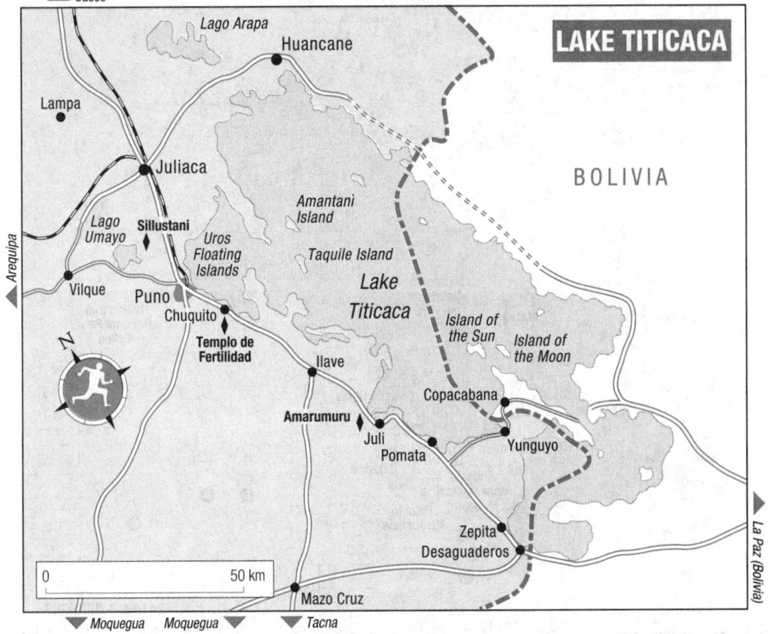

Island of the Sun. The Bolivian islands can only be visited from Copacabana.

CROSSING INTO BOLIVIA

The most popular routes to Bolivia involve overland road travel, crossing the frontier either at **Yunguyo/Kasani** (best for Copacabana) or at the principal border of **Desaguadero** (best for La Paz). En route to either you'll pass by some of Titicaca's more interesting colonial settlements, each with its own individual styles of architecture. By far the easiest way is to take a direct bus from Puno to either Copacabana or La Paz, which will stop for the formalities at the border (see listings section for details of bus companies offering direct services – Tour Peru and Litoral). Otherwise, from Puno you can take a *combi* to Yunguyo, then another to Kasani, then walk across the border and take a Bolivian *combi* for the ten-minute ride to Copacabana. From Copacabana it is approximately five hours to La Paz.

Huaraz and the Cordillera Blanca

Sliced north to south by parallel ranges of high Andean peaks, the region of **Ancash**, some 200–300km north of Lima, unfurls along an immense desert coastline, where pyramids and ancient fortresses are scattered within easy reach of several small resorts linked by vast, empty Pacific beaches. Behind range the barren heights of the Cordillera Negra, and beyond that the spectacular backdrop of the snowcapped **Cordillera Blanca**; between the two the Huaraz Valley, known locally as the **Callejón de Huaylas**, around 3000m above sea level, offers some of the best hiking and mountaineering in the Americas. The region has strong traditions of

local independence and a history of revolt, led by a native leader, the charismatic Pedro Pablo Atusparia, and thirteen other village mayors, who protested over excessive taxation and labour abuses.

Nestling in the valley, the *Departamento*'s capital, **Huaraz** – six or seven hours by car from Lima – has a lively atmosphere and makes an ideal base for exploring some of the best mountain lakes, ruins, glaciers and remote trails in the Andes. Over the last twenty years or so this region has become a major focus for mountaineers, and Huaraz, the vital centre of this inland region, is the place to stock up, hire guides and mules, and relax after a breathtaking expedition. The city is close to scores of exhilarating mountain trails, as well as the ancient Andean treasure, **Chavín de Huantar**, an impressive stone temple complex which was at the centre of a culturally significant puma-worshipping religious movement just over 2500 years ago.

What to see and do

Although well over 3000m above sea level, the **city of Huaraz** has a somewhat cosmopolitan and very busy city centre. Virtually the entire city was levelled by an earthquake in 1970, and the old houses have been replaced with single-storey modern structures topped with gleaming tin roofs. The one surviving pre-earthquake street, Jr José Olaya, is packed with restaurants serving traditional food and is a focus for locals on Sundays. With glaciated peaks and significant trekking country close to the city, Huaraz is dominated by the prospect of mountaineering, and there are only a couple of tourist attractions to visit in the city itself.

Ancash Archeological Museum

Found on Av Luzuriaga 762, facing the modern Plaza de Armas, the Ancash Archeological Museum (Ⓣ043/721551; Mon–Sat 9am–5pm & Sun 9am–2pm; US$2) fronts attractive, landscaped gardens. This small but interesting place contains a superb collection of Chavín, Chimu, Wari, Moche and Recauy ceramics, as well as some expertly trepanned skulls.

The Catedral

On the other side of the Plaza de Armas from the museum is the **Catedral** (daily 7am–7pm; free). Completely rebuilt after being destroyed in the 1970 earthquake, it has nothing special to see inside, but its vast blue-tiled roof makes a good landmark and, if you look closely, appears to mirror one of the glaciated mountain peaks, the Nevado Huanstán (6395m), behind.

Arrival and information

By air It is now possible to get to the Callejón de Huaylas by air since LC Busre has started operating daily flights from Lima (Ⓦwww.lcbusre.com.pe). If you do arrive by air, you're dropped off at a small airstrip close to the village of Anta, some 23km north of Huaraz; from here it's thirty minutes into the city by *colectivo* or bus.

By bus Most people arrive in Huaraz by bus from Lima, which takes eight or nine hours (US$8–12). Cruz del Sur, Jr Simón Bolívar Mz C Lote 12 (Ⓣ043/728726) and Lucar y Torré 577 (Ⓣ043/898032), are, as usual, the safest and most comfortable options, closely followed by Movil Tours, Jr Simón Bolívar 452 (Ⓣ043/422555). Companies coming from and going to Trujillo (8–10hr; around US$8) include Cruz del Sur and Linea, Jr Simón Bolívar 450 (Ⓣ043/726666).

Tourist information Tourist information is available from I-Peru at Pasaje Atusparia, Office 1

TOURS AND ACTIVITIES IN AND AROUND HUARAZ

Most of the tour agencies in Huaraz can be found along Avenida Luzuriaga and offer guided **city tours**, including stopping at all the major panoramic viewpoints (4hr; US$8). For the surrounding area the most popular outings are to the **Llanganuco Lakes** (8hr; US$10–15 per person), **Chavín de Huantar** (9–11hr; US$10–15 per person), including lunch in Chavín before exploring the ruins, and to the edge of the **Pastoruri Glacier** at 5240m (8hr; US$10 per person). Most agents can also arrange trips to the thermal baths at **Chancos** (4hr; US$8) and **Caraz** (6hr; US$10), and some offer **adventure activities** in the area. Always check if the guide leading your tour speaks English.

Andean Kingdom Jr San Martín 613 Ⓣ043/425555, Ⓦwww.andeankingdom.com. Argentinean-run tour operator who specializes in climbing and trekking, and can also organize mountain biking, canyoning, rafting and bungy jumping.

Apu Peruvian Adventures Jr Daniel Villaizan 404 Ⓣ043/426688 Ⓦwww.apuperuvian.com. Experienced English-speaking guides. They also offer mountaineering classes.

Galaxia Expeditions Jr Mariscal Caceres 428, Parque Pip Ⓣ043/425355 Ⓦwww.galaxia-expeditions.com. Offers a variety of treks and mountaineering trips.

Mountain Bike Adventures Jr Lucre y Torre 530 Ⓣ043/424259, Ⓦwww.chakinaniperu.com. Customizable guided bike tours with mountain bikes to rent. They also have English-speaking guides and offer a book exchange in their office. Good reputation for safety.

Pony Expeditions Sucre 1266, Plaza de Armas, Caraz Ⓣ043/391642, Ⓦwww.ponyexpeditions.com. A very professional organization with maps and mountain gear for sale, as well as guided tours of the area.

on the Plaza de Armas ⓣ043/428812 (Mon–Sat 8am–6.30pm, Sun 8.30am–2pm). Much of Huaraz town can be negotiated on foot once you've acclimatized to the altitude (3091m); however, some of the more remote sectors around the urban area should not be walked alone at night since mugging and even rape are rare but not unknown in recent years.

By colectivos and taxis For short journeys within the city, the best option is to use one of the regular *colectivos*, which run on fixed routes along avenidas Luzuriaga and Centenario (40–60¢). The Avenida Luzuriaga is the north–south axis of the town centre, where most of the restaurants, nightlife and tour agencies are based. A city centre taxi ride costs less than US$1. *Colectivos* and local buses connect Huaraz with all the main towns and villages north – Anta, Marcara, Carhuaz, Yungay and Caraz – at very reasonable rates (US$0.50–2 for up to 2hr); these can be caught from just over the river bridge from the town centre.

Accommodation

Even in the high season, around August, it's rarely difficult to find **accommodation** at a reasonable price. Within the centre of town, from the Plaza de Armas along Avenida Luzuriaga, there are countless **hostels** and many smaller places renting out rooms; except during high season it is definitely worth bargaining.

Albergue Churup Jr Pedro Campos 735 on the corner with Jr Amadeo Figueroa ⓣ043/422584 ⓦwww.churup.com. A good base for trekkers with luggage storage as well as reference maps and a book exchange. ❹

Benkawasi Albergue Parque Santa Rosa 928 ⓣ043/423150 ⓦwww.huarazbenkawasi.com. With nice gardens and an onsite bar. ❹

Edward's Inn Av Bolognesi 121 ⓣ043/422692 ⓦwww.edwardsinn.com. One of the most popular trekkers' hostels, found just below the market area (at the end of Jr Cáceres) and offering an excellent range of services in a very pleasant atmosphere. Rooms come with or without private bath, and hot water is almost always available. The owner, who speaks English, is a highly experienced trekker, climber and mountain rescuer. ❹

The Lazy Dog Inn Km. 3.1 Marían Cachipampa Road, Marían village (20min drive from Huaraz) ⓦwww.thelazydoginn.com. Very tranquil and beautiful lodge, offering the perfect place to relax, or a base from which to explore on day hikes. ❻–❽

Olaza's Bed & Breakfast Julio Arguedas 1242 ⓣ043/422529 ⓦwww.andeanexplorer.com/olaza. Clean and popular with 24hr hot water and fantastic views from rooftop terrace. ❺

Steel Guest House Alejandro Maguina 1467, La Soledad Alta ⓣ043/429709, ⓔsteelguesthouse @yahoo.com ⓦwww.huaraz.com/steel/. A five-storey building with a pleasant communal area on the second floor offering TV, small library and a billiard table. Rooms have private baths, hot water 24hr and there's a laundry service available. ❺

The Way Inn In Huaraz: Buenaventura Mendoza 821, also mountain lodge 20min drive from Huaraz. ⓣ043/428714 ⓦwww .thewayinn.com. Both popular with younger trekkers, the Huaraz hostel has a sauna on the roof. $5 per person for dorm. The mountain lodge offers activities in the area including trekking, climbing, mountain biking, paragliding and volleyball. ❹

Eating

There's no shortage of restaurants in Huaraz, with a huge number of budget options.

La Brasa Roja Av Luzuriaga 917 or Av Simón Bolívar. Very popular and always busy, serves cheap and very generous plates of chicken, pizza and pasta.

Chifa Tio Sam Psje Coral Vega 572 (off block 8 of Av Luzuriaga). The most traditional and arguably the best *chifa* in Huaraz, they offer a broad selection of Chinese and Peruvian meals in a friendly environment. Soup and main average 12 soles.

El Fogón Av Luzuriaga 1928 ⓣ043/421267. Cheap chicken and BBQ. 1/4 chicken 9.50 soles.

Fuente de Salud José de la Mar 562 (half a block down from Luzuriaga) ⓣ043/424469. Good value set vegetarian lunches. Lunch menu 6 soles.

Drinking and nightlife

Huaraz boasts a lively nightlife scene, with several **bars** where locals and tourists can relax, keep warm and unwind during the evenings or at weekends.

Monttrek Disco By the Plaza de Armas on Jr José de Sucre. One of the better discos in town; large and quite exciting music especially at weekends.

TREAT YOURSELF

Flor de Canela
Luzuriaga 1014
ⓣ043/727154 (previously Limon Leña y Carbon).
A top-quality restaurant serving traditional food.

El Tambo Jr José de la Mar 776. A restaurant-cum-*peña* serving good drinks, with occasional live music after 10pm – one of Huaraz's best night-spots, visit *Zero Drama*, the bar underneath for a few warm-up drinks.

Vagamundo Jr de Morales 753. Great music and atmosphere, good place to meet other travellers.

Hiking in the Huaraz region

You don't have to be a mountaineer to enjoy the high Andes of Ancash, and there is plenty of scope for trekking as well in the two major mountain chains accessible from Huaraz. The closest is the **Cordillera Blanca**, detailed on p.876. The **Cordillera Huayhuash**, about 50km south of the Cordillera Blanca, is rapidly becoming one of the most popular treks in Peru. About 31km long, it is dominated by the Yerupajá glacier, and *Andinistas* claim it to be one of the most spectacular trekking routes in the world. Wherever you end up, be sure to pay heed to the rules of **responsible trekking**: carry away your waste, particularly above the snow line, where even organic waste does not decompose (if you can pack it in the first place, you can pack it back up). Note, too, that you should always use a camping stove – campfires are strictly prohibited in Huascarán National Park, and wood is scarce anyway. Just as important, though, is to realize that the solar irradiation in this part of the Andes is stronger than that found in the north American Rockies, the Alps or even the Himalayas. This creates unique glacier conditions, making the ice here less stable and consequently the addition of an experienced local guide essential for the safety of any serious climbing or ice-walking expedition. It's also vital to be fit, particularly if you are going it alone.

If you intend to hike at all, it's essential to spend at least a couple of days **acclimatizing** to the altitude beforehand; if you intend high mountain climbing, this should be extended to at least five days. Although Huaraz itself is 3060m above sea level, most of the Cordilleras' more impressive peaks are over 6000m.

Maps and information

If you're going to trek in Huascarán National Park, register beforehand with the **Park Office**, at the top end of Avenida Raymondi (ⓣ043/722086) where you should buy your permit to enter the park (unless going with an agency who will buy this for you). The current price is 70 soles per person. Also visit the **Casa de Guías** (Parque Ginebra 28-G ⓣ043/421811 ⓦwww.casadeguias.com.pe), for the best information about local trails, current climatic conditions and other up to date information as well as advice on hiring guides, equipment and mules. They also have a good contact noticeboard, worth checking to see if there are any groups about to leave on treks that you might want to join. The **National Police** have a high mountain rescue squad (ⓣ043/393333, ⓔusam@pnp.gob.pe).

Ideally you should have detailed **maps** for any of the treks you plan to do. Best for the Cordillera Blanca are the Alpenvereinskarte (Sheets 0/3a and 0/3b) or IGN (Instituto Geográfico

HIRING A GUIDE

Be very careful when hiring an independent guide; the Casa de Guías can provide a list of qualified guides. Expect to pay around US$60 per day for a certified mountain guide. This price does not include transport or accommodation. For local tour operators offering guided treks, see the box on p.873. Porters, mule drivers (*arrieros*) and cooks will each cost you around US$10 a day, plus an additional US$10 per day per pack-carrying mule or llama. If you hire a Porter or *Arriero* you are responsible for their food and shelter during the trip, including their return journey if your route is not circular.

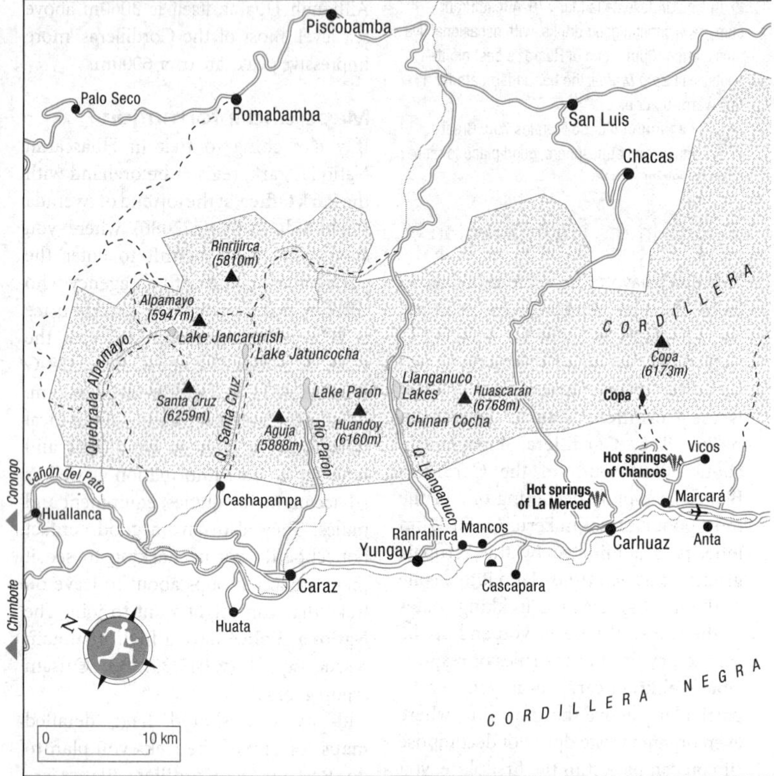

Nacional) Carhuaz (19-h), Corongo (18-h), Huari (19-i) and Recuay (20-i), both 1:100,000. For the Cordillera Huayhuash, IGN Chiquian (21-i) and Yanahuanca (21-j) or Alpine Mapping Guild Cordillera Huayhuash which is 1:50,000. These maps are available from South American Explorers in Lima and Cusco, and usually from the Casa de Guías.

NORTH TO CARAZ AND THE CORDILLERA BLANCA

No one should come to the **Callejón de Huaylas** without visiting the northern valley towns, and many travellers will want to use them as bases from which to explore one or more of the ten snow-free passes in the Cordillera Blanca. Simply combining any two of these passes makes for a superb week's trekking. Further along the valley north from Huaraz are the distinct settlements of **Yungay** and **Caraz**. Physically they have little in common but both are popular bases from which to begin treks into the **Cordillera Blanca**. The highest range in the tropical world, the Cordillera Blanca consists of around 35 peaks poking their snowy heads over the 6000m mark, and until early in the twentieth century, when the glaciers began to recede, this white crest could be seen from the Pacific. Above Yungay, and against the sensational backdrop of Peru's highest peak, **Huascarán** (6768m), are the magnificent **Llanganuco Lakes**, whose waters change colour according

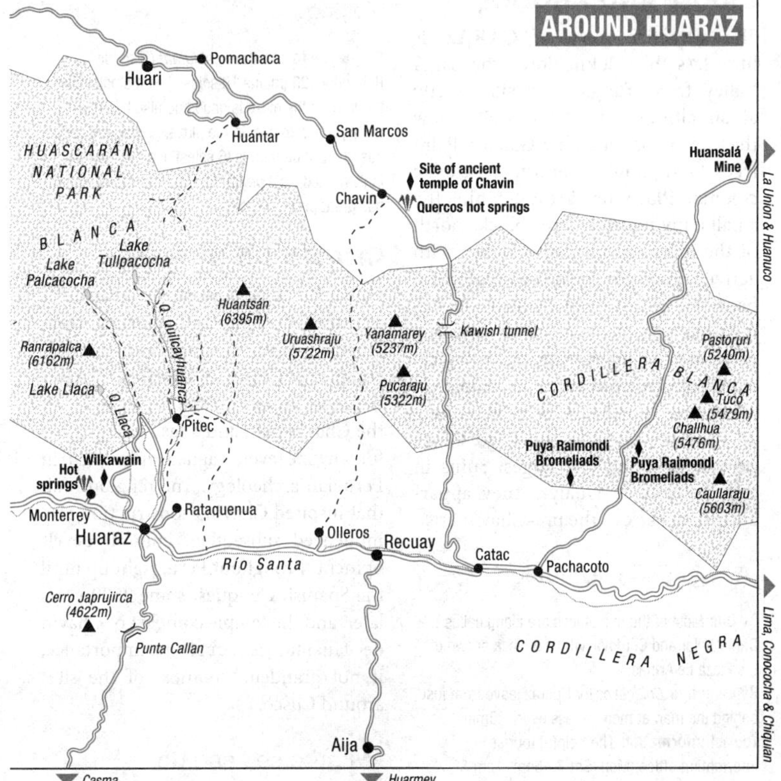

to the time of year and the sun's daily movements, and are among the most accessible of the Cordillera Blanca's three hundred or so glacial lakes.

Fortunately, most of the Cordillera Blanca falls under the auspices of the **Huascarán National Park**, and the habitat has been left relatively unspoiled. Among the more exotic **wildlife** that hikers can hope to come across are the viscacha (Andean rabbit-like creatures), vicuña, grey deer, pumas, foxes, the rare spectacled bear and several species of hummingbirds.

Hiking in the Cordillera Blanca

There are a multitude of excellent hikes in the Cordillera Blanca, almost all of which require acclimatization to the rarified mountain air, a certain degree of fitness, good camping equipment, all your food and good maps. Hiking in this region is a serious affair and you will need to be properly prepared. Bear in mind that for some of the hikes you may need guides and mules to help carry the equipment at this altitude. One of the most popular routes, the **Llanganuco to Santa Cruz Loop**, is a well-trodden trail offering spectacular scenery, some fine places to camp and a relatively easy walk that can be done in under a week even by inexperienced hikers. There are shorter walks, such as the trails around the **Pitec Quebrada**, within easy striking distance of Huaraz, and a number of other loops like the **Llanganuco to Chancos** trek.

CARAZ AND AROUND

The attractive town of **CARAZ** is little less than 20km down the Santa Valley from Yungay and sits quietly at an altitude of 2285m well below the enormous Huandoy Glacier. Palm trees and flowers adorn a classic colonial **Plaza de Armas**, while the small daily **market**, three blocks north of the plaza, is normally vibrant with activity, good for fresh food, colourful basketry, traditional gourd bowls, religious candles and hats. Nearby there are the interesting archeological ruins of **Tunshucayco**, a couple of kilometres northeast of town along 28 de Julio, close to the Lago Parón turnoff; probably the largest ruins in the Callejón de Hualyas they apparently date back to the pre-Chavín era.

Arrival and information

By bus Most of the bus offices are along calles Daniel Villar and Córdova, within a block or two of the Plaza de Armas.

By colectivo *Colectivos* for Huaraz leave from just behind the market more or less every 30min.

Tourist information The helpful tourist information office (Mon–Sat 7.45am–1pm & 2.30–5.30pm), with maps and brochures covering the attractions and some of the hikes in the immediate area, is on the Plaza de Armas, while the telephone office is at Raimondi 410 and the post office at Jr San Martín 909. For trekking guides, local information or help organizing or fitting out an expedition, the excellent Pony Expeditions (see box, p.873) can't be beaten.

Accommodation

There are several basic but clean and pleasant places to stay in Caraz. The cheapest place in town is **Hostal La Casona** on Raimondi 139 (Ⓣ043/391334; ❶), closely followed by the youth hostel, **Los Pinos** at Parque San Martín 103 (Ⓣ043/391130, Ⓔlospinos@terra.com.pe; ❶), which also offers camping spaces for US$2 a person and has reasonable internet facilities. Slightly more expensive is the clean and tranquil **Hostal El Alameda** on Av Noe Bazan Peralta 262 (Ⓣ043/391177 Ⓦwww.hotelelalameda.com).

Eating

For **places to eat**, the *Restaurant Oasis*, Jr Raimondi 425 (mains 10 soles), just a small stone's throw from the plaza is good and also has four pretty, cheap rooms. In the plaza, *Restaurant Jeny* has good value menus (6 soles) and the interestingly named *Café de Rat* (above Pony Expeditions) has great pizza. 15 soles.

CHAVÍN DE HUANTAR

Only 30km southeast of Huari, or a three- to four-hour journey from Huaraz, the magnificent temple complex of **CHAVÍN DE HUANTAR** is the most important site associated with the Chavín cult, and a fascinating place for anyone even vaguely interested in Peruvian archeology. The religious cult that inspired Chavín's construction also influenced subsequent cultural development throughout Peru, right up until the Spanish Conquest some 2500 years later, and the temple complex of Chavín de Huantar is equal in importance, if not grandeur, to most of the sites around Cusco.

What to see and do

North of Lima, the magnificent temple complex of **Chavín de Huantar** (daily 9am–5pm; US$5) evolved and elaborated its own brand of religious cultism during the first millennium BC. By 300 BC, Chavín was at the height of its power and one of the world's largest religious centres, with about three thousand resident priests and temple attendants. Most archeologists agree that the U-shaped temples were dedicated to powerful mountain spirits or deities, who controlled meteorological phenomena, in particular rainfall that was vital to the survival and wealth of the people. These climatic concerns became increasingly important as the ancient Peruvians became increasingly dependent on agriculture rather than hunting.

The Temple Complex

The complex's main building consists of a central rectangular block with two wings projecting out to the east. The large, southern wing, known as the **Castillo**, is the most conspicuous feature of the site: massive, almost pyramid shaped, the platform is built of dressed stone with gargoyles attached, though few remain now. Some way in front of the Castillo, down three main flights of steps, is the **Plaza Hundida**, or sunken plaza, covering about 250 square metres with a rectangular, stepped platform to either side. Here, the thousands of pilgrims thought to have worshipped at Chavín would gather during the appropriate fiestas. Standing in the Plaza Hundida, facing towards the Castillo, you'll see on your right the **original temple**, now just a palatial ruin dwarfed by the neighbouring Castillo. Among the fascinating recent finds from the area are bone snuff tubes, beads, pendants, needles, ceremonial shells (imported from Ecuador) and some quartz crystals associated with ritual sites. One quartz crystal covered in red pigment was found in a grave, placed after death in the mouth of the deceased.

Arrival and information

The vast majority of people approach the temple complex from Huaraz.

By bus Buses leave Huaraz daily around 10am (US$4; a 3–4hr trip) for Chavín, while all the tour companies in Huaraz (see box, p.873) offer a slightly faster and more comfortable though more expensive service (US$10–15; a 3hr trip). A more adventurous way to reach Chavín is by following the two- to four-day trail over the hills from Olleros.

By colectivos *Colectivos* leave daily every 30min from the end of Jirón Caceres, for Olleros (US$1), from where the hike is fairly simple and clearly marked all the way. It's quite a walk, so take maps and, ideally, arrange a guide and pack-llamas in Huaraz.

Tourist information The pretty village of **Chavín de Huantar**, with its whitewashed walls and traditional tiled roofs, is just a couple of hundred metres from the ruins and has a reasonable supply of basic amenities. There's a **post and telephone office** at C 17 de Enero 365 (6.30am–10pm), plus a small **tourist information** office on the corner of the Plaza de Armas, next to the market, though it doesn't have regular hours. Getting back to Huaraz or Catac, there are buses daily from Chavín, more or less on the hour from 3–6pm.

Accommodation and eating

The best **accommodation** is at the relatively new and very good-value **Hotel La Casona de JB**, Wiracocha 130 (ⓣ043/454116, ⓦwww.lacasonachavin.com.pe), just next door to the town hall on the plaza, with hot showers. **Hotel Inca**, at Wiracocha 170 (ⓣ044/754021), also has pleasant rooms with private or shared bathroom. Alternatively, you can camp by the **Baños Quercos** thermal springs (daily 7am–6pm; 50¢) some 20min stroll from the village, 2km up the valley.

For **places to eat** there are several cheap and cheerful options around the main plaza.

Trujillo and the North

Trujillo is a bustling city. Traditionally a trading point for coastal and jungle goods, the city retains a cosmopolitan atmosphere and a welcoming attitude towards visitors. Often referred to as the "City of Eternal Springtime", the climate here is pleasant year round, although it can get very hot in the summer months of December to February.

Some history

Pizarro, on his second voyage to Peru in 1528, sailed by the site of ancient Chan Chan, then still a major city and an important regional centre of Inca rule. He returned to establish a Spanish colony in the same valley, naming it Trujillo in December 1534 after his birthplace in Estremadura, and officially founding it in March 1535.

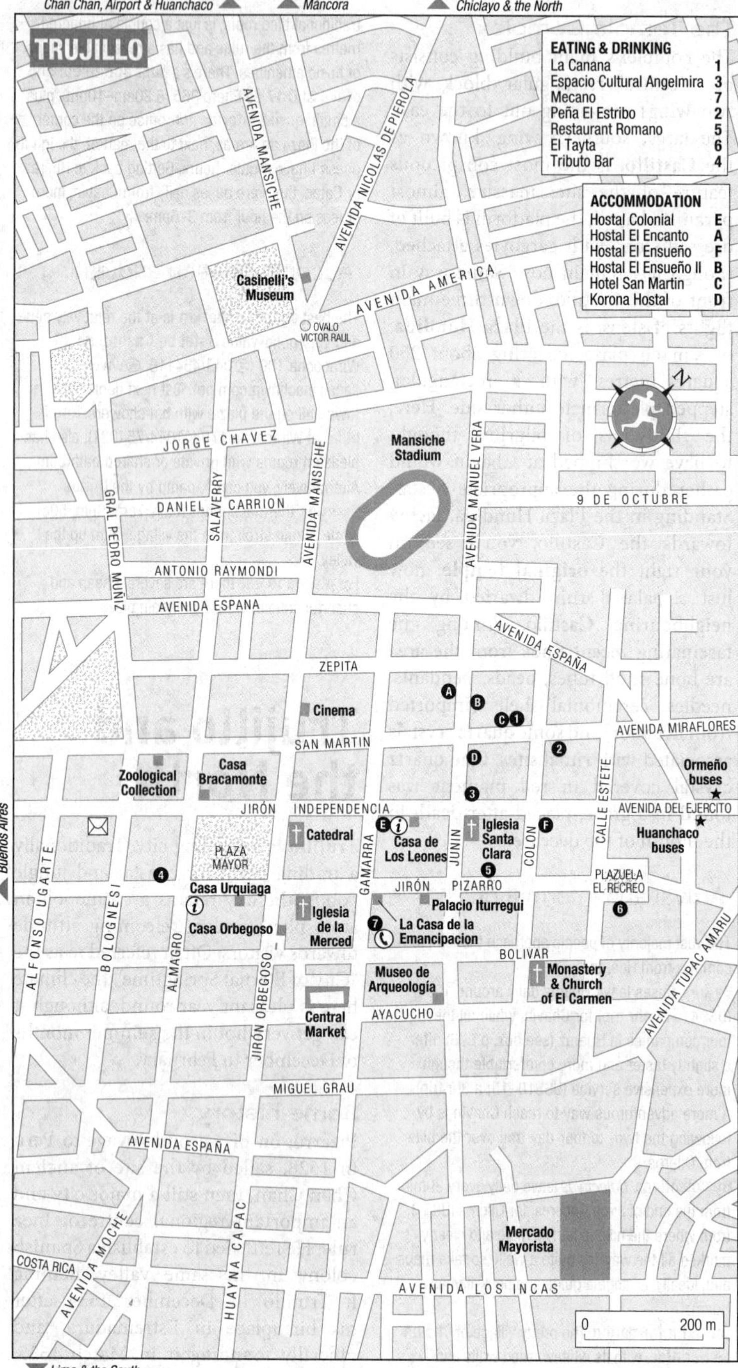
TRUJILLO
Chan Chan, Airport & Huanchaco
Máncora
Chiclayo & the North
EATING & DRINKING
La Canana 1
Espacio Cultural Angelmira 3
Mecano 7
Peña El Estribo 2
Restaurant Romano 5
El Tayta 6
Tributo Bar 4
ACCOMMODATION
Hostal Colonial E
Hostal El Encanto A
Hostal El Ensueño F
Hostal El Ensueño II B
Hotel San Martin C
Korona Hostal D
AVENIDA MANSICHE
AVENIDA NICOLAS DE PIEROLA
AVENIDA AMERICA
Casinelli's Museum
OVALO VICTOR RAUL
JORGE CHAVEZ
DANIEL CARRION
SALAVERRY
GRAL PEDRO MUÑIZ
Mansiche Stadium
AVENIDA MANUEL VERA
9 DE OCTUBRE
ANTONIO RAYMONDI
AVENIDA ESPANA
AVENIDA ESPAÑA
ZEPITA
Cinema
AVENIDA MIRAFLORES
SAN MARTIN
Casa Bracamonte
Zoological Collection
Ormeño buses
CALLE ESTETE
JIRÓN INDEPENDENCIA
AVENIDA DEL EJERCITO
Catedral
Casa de Los Leones
Iglesia Santa Clara
JUNIN
COLON
Huanchaco buses
PLAZA MAYOR
GAMARRA
Buenos Aires
ALFONSO UGARTE
BOLOGNESI
Casa Urquiaga
JIRÓN PIZARRO
PLAZUELA EL RECREO
Palacio Iturregui
Iglesia de la Merced
Casa Orbegoso
La Casa de la Emancipacion
ALMAGRO
JIRÓN ORBEGOSO
BOLIVAR
Monastery & Church of El Carmen
Museo de Arqueología
AVENIDA TUPAC AMARU
Central Market
AYACUCHO
MIGUEL GRAU
AVENIDA ESPAÑA
Mercado Mayorista
COSTA RICA
AVENIDA MOCHE
HUAYNA CAPAC
AVENIDA LOS INCAS
0
200 m
Lima & the South

A year later, in 1536, the town was besieged by the Inca Manco's forces during the second rebellion against the *conquistadores*. Many thousands of Conchuco Indian warriors, allied with the Incas, swarmed down to Trujillo, killing Spaniards and collaborators on the way and offering their victims to Catequil, the tribal deity. Surviving this attack, Trujillo grew to become the main port of call for the Spanish treasure fleets, sailors wining and dining here on their way between Lima and Panama.

Trujillo continued to be a centre of popular rebellion, declaring its independence from Spain in the Plaza de Armas in 1820, long before the Liberators arrived, and rising in bloody revolt after the APRA (American Popular Revolutionary Alliance) was outlawed in 1931. Revolutionary land reform of the 1960s gave way to the violence of the Sendero Luminoso during the mid-1980s and early 1990s. Nowadays the city, just eight hours north of Lima along the Panamerican Highway, looks every bit the oasis it is, standing in a relatively green, irrigated valley bounded by arid desert at the foot of the brown Andes mountains. It hardly seems a city of nearly a million inhabitants – walk twenty minutes in any direction and you're out in open fields, hedged by flowering shrubs.

North of Trujillo the vast desert stretches all the way to the Ecuadorian frontier at **Tumbes**, passing the city of **Chiclayo** as well as Peru's trendiest beach resort, **Máncora**. There is an incredible wealth of pre-Inca pyramids, tombs and temple sites to explore around both **Trujillo** and **Chiclayo**, many of which can be easily visited in day-trips. The excellent **museum at Lambayeque,** just half an hour's drive from Chiclayo, displays some of the most impressive and important burial treasures discovered in Peru, in a world-class museum setting.

What to see and do

From the graceful colonial mansions and Baroque churches at its heart, Trujillo's grid system gives way to commercial buildings, light industry and shantytown suburbs, before thinning out into rich sugar-cane fields that stretch far into the neighbouring Chicama Valley. **Gamarra** is the main commercial street, dominated by modern, brick and glass buildings, shops, hotels and restaurants. The other main street, older and more attractive, is **Jirón Pizarro**, where much of the city's nightlife can be experienced and which has been pedestrianized from block 8 to the pleasant **Plazuela El Recreo**. Life for most *Trujillanos* still revolves around the old town, centred on **Plaza Mayor** and bounded roughly by San Martín, Ayacucho, Almagro and Colón.

Around Plaza Mayor

Trujillo's **Plaza Mayor** (also known as the Plaza de Armas) is packed with sharp-witted shoeshine boys around the central statue – the *Heroes of the Wars of Independence*. Besides a couple of beautiful colonial mansions, Plaza Mayor is also home to the city's **Catedral** (daily 7am–noon & 4–9pm; free), built in the mid-seventeenth century, then rebuilt the following century after earthquake damage. Inside the cathedral, a **museum** (daily 7.30am–12.30pm 4–9pm; US$2; ⓣ044/235083) exhibits a range of mainly eighteenth- and nineteenth-century religious paintings and sculptures. Just behind the plaza at San Martín 368, is a **Zoological Museum** (Mon–Fri 7am–7pm; 70¢; ⓣ044/235841), packed full with bizarre stuffed animals from the coastal desert and Andean regions as well as a large bird display and lots of amazing sea creatures (including a now extinct crab some 70cms across) and a number of reptiles.

From Plaza Mayor to the Central Market

Just off the plaza, the **Iglesia de La Merced**, Jr Pizarro 550 (daily 8am–noon, 4–8pm; free), built in 1636, is worth a look for its unique priceless Rococo organ, plus its attractive gardens. Around the corner from here, between the Plaza de Armas and the Central Market, stands the most impressive of Trujillo's colonial houses – the **Casa Orbegoso**, at Jr Orbegoso 553 (Mon–Sat 9.30am–1pm, 4.30–7pm; free). This old mansion was the home of General Orbegoso, former president of Peru, and houses displays of period furniture, glass and silverware amid very refined décor. Trujillo's main market, the **Central Market**, is 100m from here, on the corner of Ayacucho and Gamarra. From the market, head along Ayacucho until you reach the corner of Junin, and you'll find University's **Museo de Arqueología y Antropología**, Jr Junin 682 (Mon–Fri 9am–2.45pm, Sat 9am–1pm; US$2; ⓣ044/249322 ⓦwww.unitru.edu.pe/cultural/arq/museount.html), which is pretty good, specializing in ceramics, early metallurgy, textiles and feather work.

East of Plaza Mayor

East of the plaza, on the corner of Jirón Pizarro and Gamarra, stands another of Trujillo's impressive mansions, **La Casa de la Emancipación**, at Jr Pizarro 610 (Mon–Sat 10am–8pm; free). The building is now head office of the Banco Continental and hosts contemporary art displays on the mezzanine floor.

Further down the same road, two blocks east of the Plaza Mayor, is the **Palacio Iturreguí**, Jr Pizarro 668 (Mon–Fri 8–10.30am; free), a striking mid-nineteenth-century mansion. The highlight of the building is its pseudo-classical courtyard, with tall columns and an open roof. The courtyard is encircled by superb galleries, and gives a wonderful view of the blue desert sky.

At the eastern end of Jirón Pizarro, five blocks from the Plaza Mayor, there's a small but attractive square known as the restored **Plazuela El Recreo** where, under the shade of some vast 130-year-old ficus trees, a number of bars and foodstalls present a focus for young couples in the evenings. The waterworks for colonial Trujillo can be seen in the plaza, where the Spaniards extended Moche and Chimu irrigation channels to provide running water to the houses in the city. A couple of minutes' walk south from the Plazuela, on the corner of Colón and Bolívar, stands the most stunning of the city's religious buildings, the **Monastery and Church of El Carmen** (Mon–Fri 3.30–5.30pm; US$1; ⓣ044/241823). Built in 1759 but damaged by an earthquake in the same year, its two brick towers were then reconstructed of bamboo for safety. Inside you can see the single domed nave, with exquisite altars and a fine gold-leaf pulpit. The processional and recreational cloisters, both boasting fine vaulted arches and painted wooden columns, give access to the **Pinacoteca**

TOURS

Most companies offer tours to **Chan Chan** for US$15–20 (including the site museum, Huaca Arco Iris and Huaca Esmeralda), and to **huacas del Sol** and **Luna** from US$8. For Chicama sites, expect to pay US$20 plus. Recommended operators include **Clara Brava's Tours**, Cahuide 495, Urb. Santa María (ⓣ044/243347, ⓦwww.xanga.com/trujilloperu, ⓔmicrobewhite@yahoo.com), who speak good English; **Guia Tours**, Independencia 580 (ⓣ044/23485, ⓔguiattru@guiatours.com.pe); **Trujillo Tours**, Diego de Almagro 301 (ⓣ044/233091, ⓦwww.geocities.com/ttourspe) and **Colonial Tours**, Jr. Independencia 616 (ⓣ044/291034, ⓔtourscolonialtruji@hotmail.com).

(picture gallery), where Flemish works include a *Last Supper* (1625) by Otto van Veen, one of Rubens' teachers. There are also some interesting figures carved from *huamanga* stone and a room showing the process of restoring oil paintings.

Arrival and information

You're most likely to arrive in the city by bus or *colectivo* from Lima. The colonial heart of the city consists of about fifty relatively small blocks, all encircled by the Avenida España. More or less at the centre of the circle is the ubiquitous main plaza, known as the Plaza Mayor or the Plaza de Armas. From here begin the main streets of Independencia and the pedestrianised Pizarro leading up to the Plazuela El Recreo. One block north of the main plaza, both streets intersect with Gamarra, where many of the banks are to be found. Getting around the city and its environs is cheap and easy, using the numerous local buses and *colectivos* (flat rates around 30¢) and minibuses.

By air If you fly into the city, you'll arrive at the airport near Huanchaco (Ⓣ044/464013). Taxis into the city will cost around US$5, or you can get a bus, which leaves every 20min from the roundabout just outside the airport gates, for around 30¢. You can also take a taxi direct to Huanchaco from here for $2–$3.

By bus Most of the buses have terminals close to the centre of town near the Mansiche Stadium, on avenidas Daniel Carrión or España to the southwest, or east of it along Ejército.

By colectivo and taxi *Colectivos* mostly leave from and end up on Avenida España. If you're arriving by day it's fine to walk to the city centre, though at night it's best to take a taxi (US$2–3). Taxis cost less than US$1 for a ride within Trujillo and can be hailed anywhere, but if you need to call one, Tico Taxi (Ⓣ044/282828) is recommended by i-Peru.

Car rental Car rental is available from C.M. Rentacar at Prolong. Bolivia 293, Buenos Aires Norte, Victor Larco Herrera (Ⓣ044/420059 or 9654348, Ⓔcmrentacar@hotmail.com). It's outside the centre of Trujillo so take a taxi to get there.

Tourist information For tourist information and photocopied city maps, go to the very helpful i-Peru office at Jr Pizarro 402 (second floor), (Mon–Fri 9am–5pm; Ⓣ044/294561, Ⓔiperutrujillo@promperu.gob.pe) on the Plaza Mayor.

Tourist police The tourist police, at POLTUR, Jr Independencia 630 (daily 8am–8pm; Ⓣ044/291705) are very helpful.

Accommodation

The majority of Trujillo's **hotels** are within a few blocks of the central Plaza Mayor; however, there are surprisingly few good value hotels for a city the size of Trujillo. Many people prefer to stay in the nearby beach resort of Huanchaco which has a much wider variety of hotels, and some good budget options (see p.884). If you do decide to stay in Trujillo try:

Hostal Colonial Jr Independencia 618 Ⓣ044/268261, Ⓔhostalcolonialtruji@hotmail.com. An attractive, central place, where some English is spoken. Rooms are fine and have TV, plus there's a patio and café. ❹

Korona Hostal Jr Junin 295 (Ⓣ044/226226) has small, cramped rooms with hot water and TV. ❸–❹

Three hostels with the same owner are all similar – rooms are small with private bath and TV. ❹

Hostal El Ensueño Jr Colon 407 (Ⓣ044/297786).

Hostal El Encanto Jr Junin 319 (Ⓣ044/209026).

Hostal El Ensueño II Jr Junin 336 (Ⓣ044/473964).

Hotel San Martín Jr San Martín 749 (Ⓣ044/252311, Ⓦwww.deperu.com/sanMartín). Slightly more expensive than the others, San Martín is much more spacious and comfortable. Not so good at the weekend as it is next to some of Trujillo's most popular nightclubs, which play very loud music into the night. ❺

Eating

There's no shortage of **restaurants** in Trujillo. Some of the liveliest are along Jirón Independencia, Jirón Pizarro, Bolívar and Ayacucho, to the east of Plaza Mayor. A speciality of the city is good, reasonably priced **seafood**, which is probably best appreciated on the beach at the nearby resort of Huanchaco (see p.884). There is also a huge assortment of cafes serving drinks, sandwiches and cakes on Jr. Pizarro.

Espacio Cultural Angelmira On the corner of Independencia with Junin Ⓣ044/297200. A plush and fascinating little café and bar with the associated Museo del Juguete (Toy Museum) in the same building as well as an art gallery and library. Coffee with milk 5 soles.

Restaurant Romano Jr Pizarro 747 Ⓣ044/252251. Small, friendly restaurant specializing in good Peruvian and Italian dishes. Good-sized portions, and exceptional value with its *económico familia* or *turístico* set menu, but it gets very busy in the evenings, so reservations are advised. Mains average 15 soles.

El Tayta Jr Pizarro 926 (In Plazuela El Recreo) ⓣ044/252678. Open 9.30am–11pm every day, with happy hour on drinks (4–6pm and 9–10pm). Good quality and great value regional, Peruvian and International dishes, with a set lunch and dinner menu for US$2 or US$3. Also good very hot coffee.

Drinking and nightlife

La Canana's Peña y disco San Martín 788 ⓣ044/232503. A highly popular restaurant-*peña* as well as a *discoteca*, serving excellent meals, with a great atmosphere and good danceable shows that generally start after 10pm and carry on into the early hours.
Peña El Estribo San Martín 809. A large and very lively dance and music venue with great weekend shows of coastal folklore and *música negra*.
Other, less traditional clubs more popular with the younger local crowd are:
Mecano Jr Gamarra 574 (ⓣ044/201652 ⓦwww.mecanobarperu.com). Featuring live rock and salsa bands with regular drinks specials, one of the most happening places in Trujillo.
Tributo Bar Jr Pizarro 389, on the corner of Almagro street ⓣ044/9711045. Also run by Mecano bar, with live bands, most of which, in line with the bar's name, are tribute bands; regulars include Bob Marley and Beatles tributes.

Directory

Airlines Aero Condor, Jr Independencia 533 (ⓣ044/222888 ⓦwww.aerocondor.com.pe); Lan, Jr Pizarro 340 (ⓦwww.lan.com), Star Peru, Jr Diego de Almagro 539, office 102, (ⓣ044/470137, ⓦwww.starperu.com). All flights out of Trujillo airport are liable to US$4 airport tax.
Banks and exchange Banco de Crédito, Jr Gamarra 562; Scotiabank, Jr Pizarro 314 and 699; Interbank, Jr Gamarra 463; Banco de La Nacion, Jr Almagro 297 and Jr Gamarra 484. There are several *casas de cambio* on the Pizarro side of the Plaza Mayor, and further up on block 6 of Pizarro.
Buses Ormeño, Av Ejército 223 (ⓣ044/259782), has buses North and South along the coast as well as international destinations. Oltursa, Av Ejército 342 (ⓣ044/263055) has buses to Chimbote, Chiclayo, Piura, Sullana, Lima and Arequipa. Movil Tours, Av América Sur 3959, Urb La Merced, etapa 3 (ⓣ044/286538) has buses inland to Cajamarca, Chachapoyas and Tarapoto, as well as to Huaraz, Chimbote and Chiclayo. Linea go to Lima, Chimbote, Huaraz, Chepen, Guadalupe, Pacasmayo, Chiclayo, Cajamarca, Jaen and Piura from their 2 terminals at Av Carrión 140 (ⓣ044/261482 or 235847), and Av America Sur 2857 (ⓣ044/297000 or 258994 Tepsa have buses to Chiclayo and other northern destinations as well as Lima from their 2 terminals at Av La Marina 205 (ⓣ044/205017) and Av Amazonas 468, Sector El Molino (ⓣ044/201626). Cruz Del Sur have luxury overnight buses to Lima from their terminal at Av Amazonas 437 (ⓣ044/261801).
Consulates UK, Flor de la Canela 885, Urb. Las Palmeras del Golf (ⓣ044/245935). Chile, Av Juan Pablo II 893, dept. 303 (ⓣ044/285869). Spain, Guillermo Charum 238, Urb. San Andrés (ⓣ044/249972). Italy, Tupac Yupanqui 990, Urb. Santa María (ⓣ044/235026).
Internet facilities There are several internet cafés along Pizarro and Independencia.
Post office Serpost (Mon–Sat 8am 8pm, Sun 9am–1pm) is based at Independencia 286, a block and a half southwest of the plaza.
Telephones There are many *locutorios* on Pizarro and Gamarra.
Tourist police ⓣ044/2911705
Health Hospital Belen de Trujillo, Jr Bolívar 350 (ⓣ044/245281). Open 24hr.
Visas Imigraciones, Av Larco 1220, Urbanización Los Pinos (ⓣ044/282217).

HUANCHACO

A traditional fishing village turned seaside resort, **HUANCHACO** is the perfect base for exploring nearby ruins while relaxing by the beach and enjoying excellent seafood. Just fifteen minutes from the centre of Trujillo, Huanchaco has exploded in terms of popularity and growth in the last thirty years. The local fishermen still use the traditional *caballitos de mar* – handmade totora reed boats, which were first used by the Moche culture. Nowadays the interiors are made from plastic bottles for better buoyancy, and fishermen offer rides

TREAT YOURSELF

Club Colonial
at La Rivera 171 (ⓣ044/461015, ⓔccolonial@hotmail.com) offers an impressive range of sumptuous Peruvian and International dishes in a beautiful setting. Mains 20 soles.

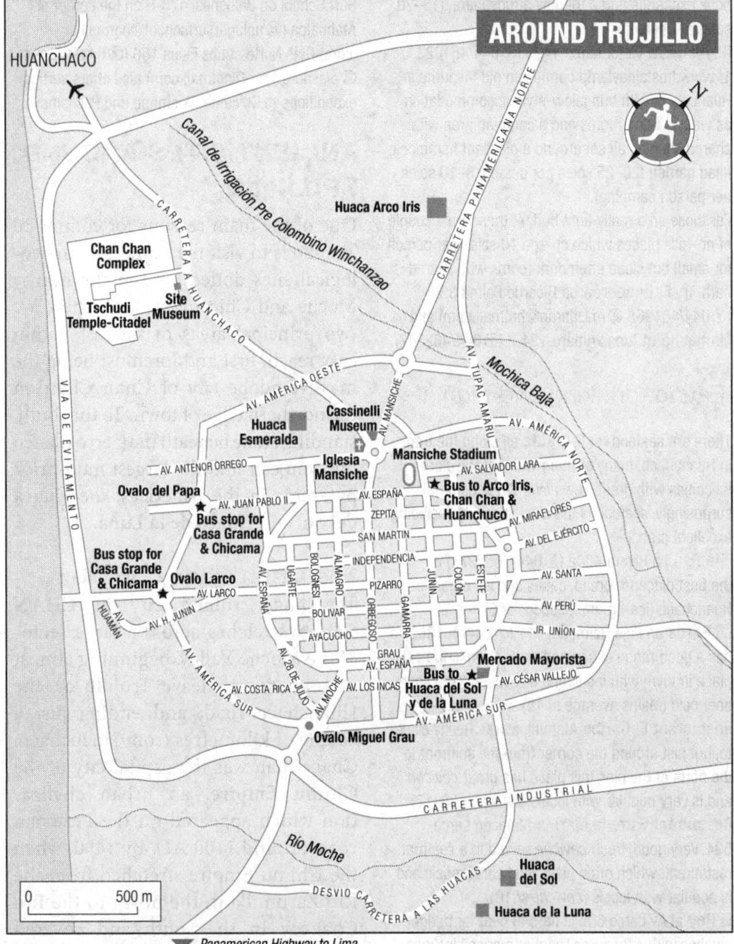

out into the surf for US$2. There is a long beachfront promenade and a pier to stroll along as well as small plazas to be found away from the seafront. Young surfers hang out and listen to reggae while not hitting the waves, and music blasts from the many beachfront restaurants.

To get to Huanchaco from Trujillo, **taxis** cost around US$5-6, or it's easy enough to take one of the frequent **combis** from Av España on the corner of Calle Orbegoso.

Accommodation

The town is well served by the kind of accommodation range you'd normally expect at a popular beach resort.

Las Brisas on Pasaje Raymondi 146 (☎044/461688) offers good value clean and comfortable rooms with private bath and fan for 20 soles per person.

Hospedaje Familiar La Casa Suiza, Los Pinos 451 (☎044/461285, Ⓦwww.casasuiza.com; ❷), offers friendly budget accommodation with many of the extra services loved by backpackers – internet, cable TV, laundry, book exchange and a friendly atmosphere. (15–20 soles per person).

Naylamp Av Victor Larco 1420 (ⓣ044/461022 ⓦwww.hostalnaylamp.com) is an old favourite in Huanchaco, with bungalow-style accommodation as well as dorm rooms and a camping area with shared kitchen, all set around a pleasant hammock filled garden (20–25 soles per person, 8–10 soles per person camping).

For those on a really tight budget there are a couple of no-frills places which charge 10 soles per person for small but clean often dark rooms with shared bath. Try **El Boquerón** on Ricardo Palma 330 (ⓣ044/461968 ⓔmaznaran@hotmail.com) and **La Mamacha** at Tupac Amaru 124-E (ⓣ044/462347).

Eating, drinking and nightlife

There are seafood **restaurants** all along the front in Huanchaco, many of them with second-floor balconies with great views over the beach. Not surprisingly, seafood is the local specialty, including excellent crab.

Fito Pan La Rivera 400a (ⓣ044/9652272) is the best place for bread, cakes and ice cream in Huanchaco (ice-cream 2 scoops s/.5).

La Barca on Psje Raimondi 111 (ⓣ044/461855) has a good range of seafood dishes and is the only place in town with insulating sleeves to keep your beer cold (Mains average s/.15).

Restaurant El Caribe Atahualpa 100. Really close to, but just around the corner from the seafront to the north of the pier, this place has great *ceviche* and is very popular with locals.(ceviche s/.6–12)

Restaurant Estrella Marina Malecón Larco 594. Very good, fresh *ceviche* served in a seafront restaurant, which often plays loud salsa music and is popular with locals (*ceviche* s/.10).

El Rey at Av Larco 606 is hard to beat for budget lunches with a 2 course "combo marino" including a soft drink for 9 soles.

Otra Cosa on Av Victor Larco 921 (ⓣ044/461346 ⓦwww.otracosa.info) true to its name, really is "Something else". This vegetarian wholefoods restaurant offers good value meals as well as local information, a book exchange and internet. They also support social projects in the area and can help to organize voluntary work and sell fair trade items on behalf of different local organizations. (Mains average s/.12).

Outdoor activities

Surfing There are several surf schools offering surf board and wetsuit rental as well as surf lessons. Recommended among them is Un Lugar Surf School on Bolognesi 473-B on the corner of Atahualpa (ⓔunlugarsurfschool@hotmail.com) Olas Norte at Los Ficus 150 (ⓣ044/462494 ⓔolasnorte_run@hotmail.com) also offers surfing expeditions to Chicama, Poemape and Pacasmayo.

ANCIENT SITES AROUND TRUJILLO

One of the main reasons for coming to Trujillo is to visit the numerous archeological sites dotted around the nearby Moche and Chicama valleys. There are two principal areas of interest within easy reach, first and foremost being the massive adobe city of **Chan Chan** on the northern edge of town. To the south, standing alone beneath the Cerro Blanco hill, you can find the largest mud-brick pyramids in the Americas, the **Huaca del Sol** and **Huaca de la Luna**.

The Chan Chan complex

The huge, ruined city of **CHAN CHAN** stretches across a large sector of the Moche Valley, beginning almost as soon as you leave Trujillo on the Huanchaco road, and ending just a couple of kilometres from Huanchaco. Chan Chan was the capital city of the **Chimu Empire**, an urban civilization which appeared on the Peruvian coast around 1100 AD. By 1450, when the Chimu Empire stretched from the Río Zarumilla in the north to the Río Chancay in the south and covered around 40,000 square kilometres, Chan Chan was the centre of a chain of provincial capitals. They were all gradually incorporated into the Inca Empire between 1460 and 1480.

Of the three main sectors specifically opened up for exploration, the **Nik An Palace** (formerly known as Tschudi) is the largest and most frequently visited. Not far from Nik An, **La Huaca Esmeralda** displays different features, being a ceremonial or ritual pyramid rather than a citadel. The third sector, the **Huaca El Dragón** (or **Arco Iris**), on the other side of this enormous ruined city, was similar in function to Esmeralda but has a unique design which has been restored with relish if not historical perfection. Entrance to all three sectors of the ruins and the Museo de Sitio (daily 9am–4pm ⓣ044/206304) is included on the same **ticket**, called the *Talón Visitante*, which is valid for only one day and costs US$4, or US$2 for students with ID cards.

Guided tours are easily arranged (around US$3 for the museum); guides for the Nik An (ex-Tschudi) complex (US$6 an hour) usually hang around at the Nik An entrance and, if you want, will also take you round the *huacas* too. Start at the small **Museo de Sitio** on the main road, take any bus going between Trujillo and Huanchaco and ask the driver to drop you at the Museo de Sitio when you jump on board. There is no public transport between the different sites on the ticket, so hire a taxi to take you round and wait, or take a hat and lots of water if you plan to walk; the desert sun is unforgiving.

Huaca del Sol and Huaca de la Luna

Five kilometres south of Trujillo, beside the Río Moche in a barren desert landscape, are two temples that really bring ancient Peru to life. The stunning **Huaca del Sol** (Temple of the Sun) is the largest adobe structure in the Americas, and easily the most impressive of the many pyramids on the Peruvian coast. Its twin, **La Huaca de la Luna** (Temple of the Moon), is smaller, but more complex and brilliantly frescoed. This complex is believed to have been the capital, or most important ceremonial and urban centre, for the Moche culture at its peak between 400 and 600 AD. Collectively known as the Huacas del Moche, these sites make a fine day's outing and shouldn't be missed. To get here from Trujillo take a **colectivo**, marked Campina de Moche (50¢), from Ovalo Grau, down Av Moche from the town centre. A taxi to the site costs around US$3-$4, and a round-trip taxi including waiting time should cost US$12–14.

It is not possible to go inside the **Huaca del Sol**, but it's an amazing sight from the grounds below or even in the distance from the Huaca de la Luna 500m away. **Huaca de la Luna** (9am–4pm; US$3; ⓣ044/291894) is a fascinating ritual and ceremonial centre that was constructed and used in the same era as the Huaca del Sol. Hire a guide (about US$5) to get the most from your visit as there are many little walkways to explore that wobble around the colourful frescos depicting Moche life.

Museo Tumbes Reales de Sipán

Just outside of Chiclayo in the pleasant small town of Lambayeque, the world-class museum **Tumbes Reales de Sipán** (Tues–Sun 9am–5pm; ⓦwww.tumbesreales.org) is a real find. The museum exhibits life-size replicas of the royal tombs discovered in the area as well as an overwhelming number of sacred objects made from precious metals and stones, which accompanied the deceased into the afterlife. Allow yourself at least 2–3 hours in the museum.

MÁNCORA AND TUMBES

About 30km from the Ecuadorian border and 287km north of Piura, **Tumbes** is usually considered a mere pit-stop for overland travellers. However, the city has a significant history and, unlike most border settlements, is a surprisingly warm and friendly place. On top of that, it's close to some of Peru's finest **beaches** and three national parks of astounding ecological variety: the arid **Cerros de Amotape**, the biodiverse mangrove swamps of the **Manglares de Tumbes Sanctuary**, and the tropical rainforest of the **Zona Reservada de Tumbes**. In the rural areas around the city, nearly half of Peru's tobacco leaf is produced. The

TREAT YOURSELF

Semana Chakra (Ⓣ073/784893, Ⓦwww.semanachakra.com) is a beautiful resort right on the beach with yoga classes, wholefood restaurant and private pool. ❾

most popular beach, **Máncora**, is only a couple of hours south of Tumbes where the sea is warm most of the year and the waves often near perfect.

What to see and do

A point on the Peruvian coast not to be missed, **Máncora** is a resort town with something for everyone, beautiful clear blue skies year round, great surf, an international party scene, and deserted crisp white sand beaches. Máncora itself is a small settlement based along the Panamerican Highway, and provides the focus for surfers from around the world who come to check out the waves and the nightlife. The nearby resorts of **Pocitas, Vichayito**, and **Cabo Blanco** retain their unspoilt beauty offering a range of accommodation options for those who want to be pampered to those who want to be alone in the wilderness.

Long famed for its surf, the area is rapidly becoming a world-class destination for kite-surfing, and regularly hosts national and international competitions (see Ⓦwww.vivamancora.com for information about upcoming events). But it's not just for experts, the long beach and warm water make for a great place to learn how to surf. You can hire gear from several places, including the Soledad Surf Company, which sells and rents equipment as well as offering surf and Spanish lessons, or many places along Av Piura (the stretch of the Panamerican Highway which passes through Máncora) from around US$5 per hour.

Along the main stretch of the Panamerican Highway in the town, there is a market for local crafts, jewellery and clothing.

Accommodation

There are several good hotels in Máncora itself, and many more spread along the beaches to the south in Pocitas and Vichayito. Máncora has a very lively nightlife so those looking for peace and quiet will do better to stay slightly out of town – Pocitas is easily reached in a mototaxi for 2 to 5 soles depending how far down the beach your hotel is, and Vichayito for 5 to 10 soles.

Hostal Sol y Mar (Ⓣ073/258106, Ⓔhsolymar@hotmail.com). Situated in the town centre, this hostal is very popular with the surfing crowd. It is right on the beach, has a good swimming pool and games courts, plus a decent restaurant and bar, private baths, and its own little shop and internet café as well as a ground floor disco. ❺

Laguna Surf Camp (Ⓣ01/94015628 Ⓦwww.vivamancora.com/lagunacamp). A chilled-out place, set between the town and the beach, with bungalow-style accommodation set around a shady hammock-filled garden. ❺

While Pocitas has its share of pricey resort hotels, there are a few cheaper options, among them

Mancoral (Ⓣ073/516107 Ⓦwww.vivamancora.com/mancoral), just 1km south of Máncora Pier, offers clean and tidy rooms with private bath, most with balconies overlooking the beach. Double ❺ includes breakfast.

Eating, drinking and nightlife

For eating, there's a surplus of **restaurants** in the centre of town, mainly along the Panamerican Highway.

La Bajadita AvPiura. For those with a sweet tooth, come here for a huge selection of home-made cakes and desserts, including cheesecake with a choice of 3 toppings. Delicious. Brownie with hot fudge and ice cream s/.6.

La Espada Av Piura 655 (Ⓣ074/858097). This spot is the best for local seafood dishes and very large portions. Mains average s/.15, daily lunch menu for s/.7. **Green Eggs and Ham**. Sitting on the beach next to Hostal Sol y Mar, open 7.30am–1pm, this restaurant is the best for breakfast, offering a huge variety of breakfasts for $3.

El Tuno Av Piura 233 Not to be missed, this spot serves sumptuous dishes (especially the tuna steak and homemade pastas) of a gourmet standard and costs the same as most restaurants on the main strip (15–20 soles main).

Moving on

By bus The bus companies are all in the main street, Avenida Piura, where you can buy tickets for their selection of daily and nightly services up or down the coast, connecting Tumbes with Lima and the major cities in between. Transportes EPPO (Av Grau 470 ⓣ073/258027) runs five buses between here and Piura (US$3; a 3hr journey) from its office just north of the plaza, towards the northern end of Máncora. Other bus companies include Civa, Av Piura 656 (ⓣ074/858026), Cial, lAv Piura 624 (ⓣ073/258558) and Ormeño, Av Piura 501 (ⓣ074/858334), going daily to Piura, Chiclayo, with connections for Cajamarca (and also buses for Ecuador). El Dorado, Av Grau 111 (an extension of Piura), runs south to Piura, Chiclayo and Trujillo daily and nightly.

By colectivo *Colectivos* depart from near the EPPO office for Los Organos (50¢; a 30min trip), from where there are other *combis* to Talara (US$1; a 1hr trip). *Combis* drive up and down Av Piura throughout the day picking up passengers until they are full for the 2hr trip to Tumbes ($2).

TUMBES

With a long history and position of military importance within Peru due to its proximity to the ever-disputed border with Ecuador, **TUMBES** is a garrison town, but is surprisingly friendly and cheery. As long as you do not attempt to take photographs near any of the military or frontier installations, which is strictly prohibited, you will find the local people friendly and helpful.

What to see and do

Although it has very few real sights, Tumbes is an interesting city to explore,

CROSSING INTO ECUADOR

Crossing this border is complicated slightly by the distance between the Peruvian and Ecuadorian Immigration offices. By far the easiest way to cross the border is to take an international bus service such as Ormeño or the Ecuadorian company Cifa, which take you through, only stopping directly outside each Immigrations office. Two kilometres before the busy frontier settlement of **Aguas Verdes**, you'll find the **Peruvian immigration office** (daily 9am–noon & 2–5pm) where you get an exit or entry stamp and tourist card for your passport. Once past these buildings, it's a fifteen-minute walk or a short drive to Aguas Verdes. **Combis** for the border leave Tumbes from block 3 of Tumbes Norte, but ensure that it's going all the way to the border; some continue to Zarumilla or Aguas Verdes. A **taxi** from Tumbes costs US$4–5. From Aguas Verdes, you just walk over the bridge into the Ecuadorian border town of Huaquillas (see p.673) and the Ecuadorian immigration office (daily 8am–1pm & 2–6pm), where you'll get your entry or exit stamps and tourist card. If coming from Ecuador to Peru, Tumbes is the nicer place to stay close to the border. If going north, frequent buses depart to all the major destinations in Ecuador from Huaquillas.

If you're coming into Peru from Ecuador, it's simply a reversal of the above procedure, though there is one other option which is to take a bus direct from the frontier to Sullana (2–3hr; US$5) from where there are buses and *colectivos* regularly to Piura (45min; 50¢). In both directions the authorities occasionally require that you show an onward ticket out of their respective countries.

When crossing the border in either direction, expect to be "helped" by an assortment of kids and policemen hanging around at the border – they will ask for a tip.

The Peruvian customs point is a concrete complex in the middle of the desert between the villages of Cancas and Máncora more than 50km south of the border. Occasionally inactive, when it is operating, however, most buses are pulled over and passengers have to get out and show documents to the customs police while the bus and selected items of luggage are searched for contraband goods.

with bright and cheery, verging on gaudy, architecture around the centre. The large and tree filled **Plaza de Armas** features a huge rainbow archway, and a stripy **Cathedral**. An attractive pedestrian precinct, the **Paseo de la Concordia**, decorated with colourful tiles and several large sculptures and statues, leads off the plaza between the cathedral and the *biblioteca* to the Plazuela Bolognesi. Take a stroll down the pretty if a little run-down Malecón walkway along the banks of the Río Tumbes.

Arrival and information

By air If you're flying in from Lima, note that Tumbes airport is often very quiet, particularly at night, when there's no access to food or drink. A taxi into town should cost around US$5; it is about a 20min journey.

By bus Most buses coming to Tumbes arrive at offices along Av Tumbes Norte (also known by its old name of Av Teniente Vásquez), or along Piura. Ormeño and Continental buses from Ecuador stop at Av Tumbes Norte 216 (see "Directory" opposite for more bus details).

By colectivo Comite *colectivos* also pull in on Tumbes Norte at no. 308 (Ⓣ074/525977).

Tourist information Tumbes is quite pleasant and easy to get around on foot, or you can hail down one of the many mototaxis, which will take you anywhere in the city for around $1. Tourist information is available from the first floor of the Centro Cívico, on the Plaza de Armas (8am–1pm & 2–6pm).

Accommodation

While there are many budget hotels in Tumbes, few of them are recommendable. Some of the better budget options are strung out from the Plaza de Armas along Calle Grau, an attractive old-fashioned hotchpotch of a street, lined with tumbledown wooden colonial buildings.

Hostal Tumbes C Grau 614 Ⓣ074/522203. Very pleasant rooms with showers that are excellent value, but the ones upstairs have better light. ❷–❸

Hotel Roma Bolognesi 425 (on the corner of the Plaza de Armas) Ⓣ072/524137. Large rooms with TV and fan, as well as shared balcony overlooking the Plaza de Armas. ❷–❸

Eating and drinking

Tumbes has some excellent **restaurants** and is the best place in Peru to try *conchas negras* – the black clams found only in these coastal waters, where they grow on the roots of mangroves.

Budabar Grau 309. On the plaza, this place is part chill-out lounge, part local restaurant and bar. Offering cheap set meals and beers, it's the place to see and be seen in Tumbes. Mains from 12–18 soles.

Cevicheria El Sol Ñato Bolívar 608. The best place in town for a wide range of seafood, but only open for lunches; try a *ceviche* with *conchas negras* or a huge steaming dish of *sudado de pescado*. Mains average 20 soles.

Pollos a la Brasa Venecia Bolívar 237. Does exactly what it says in its name – a great place for chicken. 1/4 chicken 9 soles.

Restaurant Latino C Bolívar 163. Right on the Plaza de Armas, this old-fashioned eatery specializes in excellent Continental and American breakfasts. Breakfasts 8–12 soles.

Restaurant Si Señor C Bolívar 119. Serves mostly beer and seafood, right on the Plaza de Armas. Lunch menu for 8 soles.

Directory

Airlines Aerocondor Grau 454(Ⓣ072/524835.

Banks and exchange Banco de Crédito, Paseo Los Libertadores 212, Banco de la Nacion, Paseo Los Libertadores 226, BBVA Banco Continental, Paseo Los Libertadores 237, Scotiabank, Bolognesi 109, Interbank, Bolívar 139. *Cambistas* are at the corner of Bolívar with Piura.

Bus companies CIAL, Av Tumbes Norte 586 (Ⓣ072/526350), for Lima; Cruz del Sur, Av Tumbes Norte 319 (Ⓣ072/896163), for Lima and the coast; El Dorado, Tacna 351, for Máncora and Northern coast (Ⓣ072/522984); Emtrafesa, Av Tumbes Norte 397 (Ⓣ072/525850), for Chiclayo and Trujillo; Ormeño and Continental, Av Tumbes Norte 319, for Trujillo; Tepsa, Tumbes Norte 195 (Ⓣ072/522428), for Lima.

Post office San Martín 208. Mon–Sat 7am–7pm.

Telephones The Telefónica del Peru office is on San Martín in the same block as the post office, but cheap call centres can be found in C Bolívar, often in the internet shops.

Tour operators Tumbes Tours, Av Tumbes Norte 341 Ⓣ072/526086, Ⓦwww.tumbestours.com, runs a number of tours including a 4-day/3-night trip exploring the nearby Puerto Pizarro mangrove swamp and beaches from US$20 per person per day, depending on size of group.

The jungle

Whether you look at it up close, from the ground or from a boat, or fly over it in a plane, the Peruvian **jungle** seems endless, even though it is actually disappearing at an alarming rate. Over half of Peru is covered by dense tropical rainforest, with its eastern regions offering unrivalled access to the world's largest and most famous jungle, the **Amazon**. Of the Amazon's original area, around four million square kilometres (about eighty percent) remain intact, fifteen percent of which lie in Peru, where they receive over 2000mm of rainfall a year and experience average temperatures of 25–35ºC. Considered as *El Infierno Verde* – "the Green Hell" – by many Peruvians who've never been here, it's the most biodiverse region on Earth, and much that lies beyond the main waterways remains relatively untouched and often unexplored. Jaguar, anteaters and tapirs roam the forests, huge anaconda snakes live in the swamps, and trees like the giant Shihuahuaco, strong enough to break an axe head, rise from the forest floor. Furthermore, there are over fifty indigenous tribes scattered throughout the Peruvian section alone, many surviving primarily by hunting, fishing and gathering, as they have done for thousands of years.

What to see and do

Given the breadth and quality of options, it's never easy to decide which bit of the jungle to head for. Your three main criteria will probably be budget, ease of access, plus the depth and nature of jungle experience you're after. Flying to any of the main jungle towns is surprisingly cheap and, once you've arrived, a number of excursions can be made easily and cheaply, though the best experience

INDIGENOUS JUNGLE TRIBES

Outside the few main towns, there are hardly any sizeable settlements, and the jungle population remains dominated by between 35 and 62 **indigenous tribes** – the exact number depends on how you classify tribal identity – each with its own distinct language, customs and dress. After centuries of external influence (missionaries, gold seekers, rubber barons, soldiers, oil companies, anthropologists, and now tourists), many jungle Indians speak Spanish and live pretty conventional, Westernized lives, preferring jeans, football shirts and fizzy bottled drinks to their more traditional clothing and manioc beer (the tasty, filling and nutritious *masato*).

However, other tribal groups chose to retreat further into the jungle avoiding contact with outside influences, and maintaining their traditional way of life. For other cultural groups, tourism in fact creates a resurgence of their traditions, as tourists' interest in their way of life; dress, music, food and rituals, leads people to feel proud of their origins, rather than feeling that they need to "catch up" with the developing world.

For most of the traditional or semi-traditional tribes, the jungle offers a **semi-nomadic** existence and, in terms of material possessions, they have, need and want very little. Communities are scattered, with groups of between ten and two hundred people, and their sites shift every few years. For subsistence they depend on small, cultivated plots, fish from the rivers and game from the forest, including wild pigs, deer, monkeys and a great range of edible birds. The main species of edible jungle fish are *sabalo* (a kind of oversized catfish), *carachama* (an armoured walking catfish), the feisty piranha (generally not quite as dangerous as Hollywood makes out), and the giant *zungaro* and *paiche* – the latter, at up to 200kg, being the world's largest freshwater fish. In fact, food is so abundant that jungle dwellers generally spend no more than three to four days a week engaged in subsistence activities.

comprises a few nights at one of the better jungle lodges. For more intimate (but often tougher) travel, it's easy enough to arrange a camping expedition and a guide, travelling in canoes or speedboats into the deeper parts of the wilderness. A further, costlier, though rewarding, option, mainly restricted to a few operators based in Iquitos, is to take a river cruise on a larger boat.

Iquitos, the capital of the **NORTHERN SELVA**, is the Peruvian jungle's only genuinely exciting city. Much easier to access by air from Lima or to arrive by boat from Brazil, the Northern Selva is also accessible from the northern Peruvian coast via an adventurous, increasingly popular four- to five-day boat journey up the Río Huallaga. Cusco is the best base for trips into the jungles of the **SOUTHERN SELVA**, with road access to the frontier town of Puerto Maldonado, itself a good base for budget travellers. The nearby forests of Madre de Dios boast the **Tambopata-Candamo Reserved Zone** and the **Bahuaja-Sonene National Park**, an enormous tract of virgin rainforest close to the Bolivian border. An expedition into the **Manu Reserved Zone** (part of the larger **Manu National Biosphere Reserve**) will also bring you into one of the more exciting wildlife regions in South America.

THE NORTHERN SELVA: IQUITOS AND RÍO AMAZONAS

IQUITOS began life in 1739 when Jesuit José Bahamonde established settlements at Santa Bárbara de Nanay and Santa María de Iquitos on the Río Mazán. By the end of the nineteenth century, it was, along with Manaus in Brazil, one of *the* great rubber towns. A number of structures survive from that era of grandeur, but during the last century Iquitos has vacillated between prosperity – as far back as 1938, the area was explored for oil – and the depths of depression. However, its strategic position on the Amazon, which makes it accessible to large ocean-going ships from the distant Atlantic, has ensured its importance.

Most people visit Iquitos briefly with a view to moving on into the rainforest but, wisely, few travellers actually avoid the place entirely. A busy, cosmopolitan tourist town with a buzzing population of about 300,000, connections to the rest of the world are by river and air only – Yurimaguas, the end of the road from the Pacific coast, is the nearest road to Iquitos. It's the kind of place that lives up to all your expectations of a jungle town, from its elegant reminders of the rubber boom years to the atmospheric shantytown suburb of Puerto Belén, where you can buy just about anything.

Expeditions around Iquitos are the most developed in the Peruvian jungle, offering a wide and often surprising range of attractions. As usual, anything involving overnight stays is going to cost a fair bit, though there are also

WHEN TO VISIT

Unlike most of the Peruvian *selva*, the **climate** here is little affected by the Andean topography, so there is no rainy season as such; instead, the year is divided into "high water" (Dec–May) and "low water" (June–Nov) seasons. The upshot is that the weather is always hot and humid, with temperatures averaging 23–30°C and with an annual rainfall of about 2600mm. Most visitors come between May and August, but the high-water months can be the best time for **wildlife**, because the animals are crowded into smaller areas of primary forest and dry land. Perhaps the best time to visit Iquitos, however, is at the end of June (supposedly June 23–24, but actually spread over three or four days), when the main **Fiesta de San Juan** takes place.

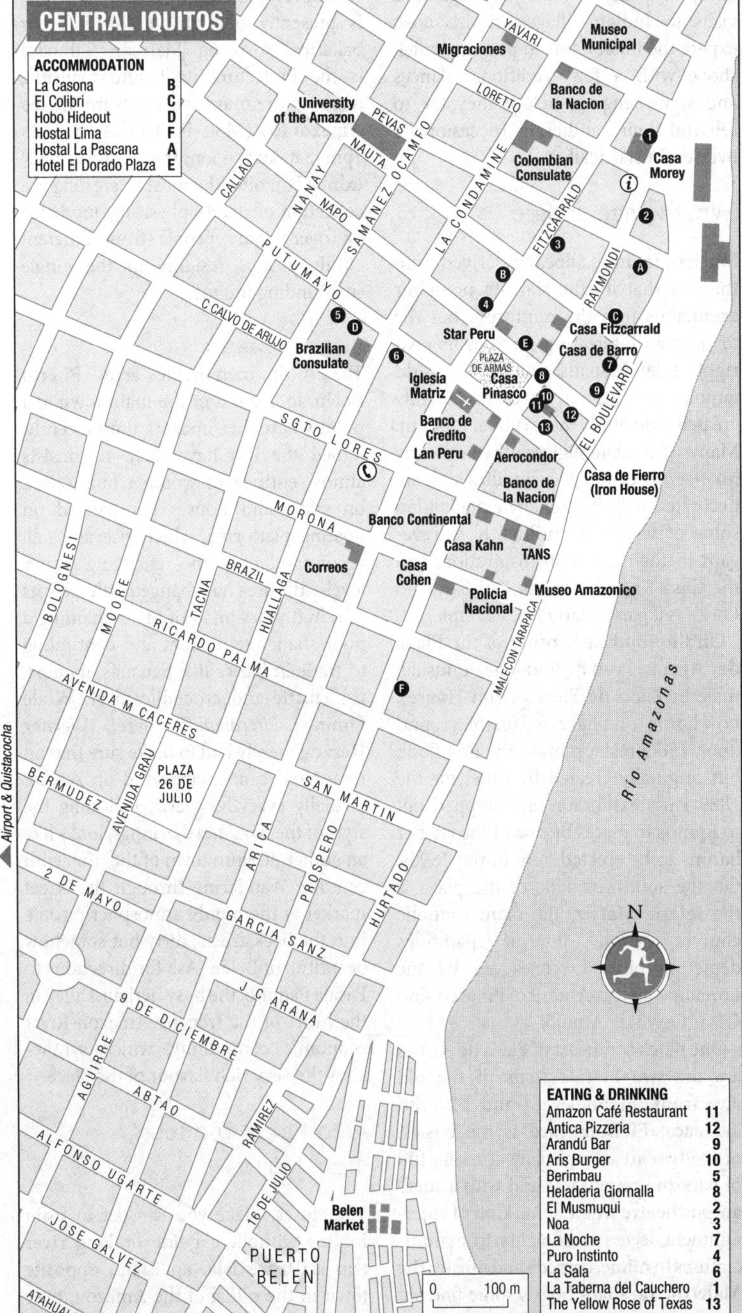
CENTRAL IQUITOS
ACCOMMODATION
La Casona B
El Colibri C
Hobo Hideout D
Hostal Lima F
Hostal La Pascana A
Hotel El Dorado Plaza E
EATING & DRINKING
Amazon Café Restaurant 11
Antica Pizzeria 12
Arandú Bar 9
Aris Burger 10
Berimbau 5
Heladeria Giornalla 8
El Musmuqui 2
Noa 3
La Noche 7
Puro Instinto 4
La Sala 6
La Taberna del Cauchero 1
The Yellow Rose of Texas 13
Puerto Masusa (Brazil), Leticia (Colombia), Pucallpa & Yurimaguas
Airport & Quistacocha
Migraciones
Museo Municipal
Banco de la Nacion
Casa Morey
Colombian Consulate
University of the Amazon
Brazilian Consulate
Star Peru
Casa Fitzcarrald
Casa de Barro
Plaza de Armas
Casa Pinasco
Iglesia Matriz
Banco de Credito
Lan Peru
Aerocondor
Casa de Fierro (Iron House)
Banco de la Nacion
Banco Continental
Casa Kahn
TANS
Correos
Casa Cohen
Policia Nacional
Museo Amazonico
Plaza 26 de Julio
Belen Market
Puerto Belen
Río Amazonas
Yavari
Loretto
Pevas
Nauta
Ocampo
Callao
Nanay
Napo
Samanez
La Condamine
Fitzcarrald
Raymondi
Putumayo
C Calvo de Arujo
Sgto Lores
El Boulevard
Morona
Bolognesi
Moore
Tacna
Brazil
Huallaga
Ricardo Palma
Malecon Tarapaca
Avenida M Caceres
Bermudez
Avenida Grau
San Martin
Arica
Prospero
Hurtado
2 de Mayo
Garcia Sanz
J C Arana
9 de Diciembre
Aguirre
Abtao
Ramirez
Alfonso Ugarte
16 de Julio
Jose Galvez
Atahualpa
N
0 100 m

cheap day-trips. With all organized visits to Indian villages in this area, expect the inhabitants to put on a quick show, with a few traditional dances and some singing, before they try to sell you their handicrafts (occasionally over-enthusiastically).

What to see and do

Much of Iquitos's appeal is derived from the fact that it's the starting point for excursions into the rainforest, but the town is an interesting place in its own right. Like Manaus, Iquitos is world famous for its architecture, mainly created during the rubber boom. Many of the late eighteenth- and early nineteenth-century buildings are decorated with Portuguese *azulejo* tiles, some of which are brilliantly extravagant in their Moorish inspiration, and the **Casa Kahn**, on block 1 of Sargento Lores, is a particularly fine example.

On the southeast corner of the **Plaza de Armas**, you'll find the unusual, majestic **Casa de Fierro** (Iron House), now home to a pharmacy on the ground floor, and a restaurant on the first floor, but originally created by Eiffel for the 1889 Paris exhibition and shipped out to Iquitos in pieces by one of the rubber barons to be erected here in the 1890s. On the southwest side of the plaza is the **Iglesia Matriz**, the main Catholic church, whose interior paintings depicting biblical scenes are by the Loretano artists Américo Pinasco and César Calvo de Araujo.

One block southeast of Plaza de Armas are the two best sections of the **old riverfront**, El Boulevard and Malecón Tarapaca. **El Boulevard** is the busiest of the two areas, especially at night, full of bars and restaurants and with a small **amphitheatre** where some kind of entertainment occurs most nights, from mini-circuses to mime, comedy and music. The **Malecón Tarapaca** boasts some fine old mansions, one of which, at Tarapaca 262, with lovely nineteenth-century *azulejos*, is presently one of the town's better bakeries. Also on Malecón Tarapaca is the Prefectura de Loreto mansion, home to the municipal museum **Museo Amazónico** (Mon–Fri 8am–1pm & 3–7pm, Sat 8am–noon; free, with very few exhibits on offer the most interesting is a collection of statues physically modelled on over eighty people from different ethnic groups residing in the jungle surrounding Iquitos.

Puerto Belén

The most memorable area, **Puerto Belén**, looms out of the main town at a point where the Amazon, until recently, joined the Río Itaya inlet. It consists almost entirely of wooden huts raised on stilts, and houses constructed on floating platforms, which rise and fall, accommodating the changing water levels. The area has changed little over its hundred years or so of life, remaining a poor shanty settlement and continuing to trade in basics like bananas, manioc, fish, turtle and crocodile meat. While filming *Fitzcarraldo* here, **Werner Herzog** merely had to make sure that no motorized canoes appeared on screen: virtually everything else, including the style of the *barriada* dwellings, looks like an authentic slum town of the ninteenth century. Wandering through the street market is the highly atmospheric route into the backstreets, dirty but somehow beautiful, of Belén. Ask for directions to Pasaje Paquito, the busy herbalist alley in the heart of the frenetic Amazon River economic community, which synthesizes the very rich flavour of the place.

Short trips and tours from Iquitos

The closest place you can get to from Iquitos without a guide or long river trip is **Padre Isla**, an island opposite town in the midst of the Amazon, over 14km long and with beautiful beaches during the dry season. It's easily reached by canoe from Belén or the main waterfront. Alternatively, some 4km northeast of the centre of Iquitos, just fifteen minutes by bus, is the suburb of **Bellavista** on the Río Nanay. From Bellavista you can set out by canoe ferry for **Playa Nanay**, the best beach around Iquitos, where bars and cafés are springing up to cater for the weekend crowds. Be aware that currents here are pretty strong and, although there are lifeguards, drownings have occurred.

You can take a boat from Bellavista port to the village of **Padre Cocha**, and from there walk for fifteen minutes to the **Pilpintuwasi Butterfly Farm & Animal Rescue Centre**, a fascinating place where you can see many species of butterfly at the different stages of their life cycle, as well as rescued monkeys, sloths, an anteater and a jaguar (open Tues–Sun, 9am–4pm; US$5).

On the western edge of Iquitos, an affluent of the Nanay forms a long lake called **Moronacocha**, a popular resort for swimming and water-skiing; some 5km further out (just before the airport) another lake, **Rumococha**, has facilities on the Río Nanay for fishing and hunting. Beyond this, still on the Nanay, is the popular weekend beach and white sands of **Santa Clara**. The village of **Santo Tomás** is only 16km from here; a worthwhile trip and well connected by local buses, this agricultural and fishing village, on the banks of the Río Nanay, is renowned for its jungle *artesanía*, and has another beach, on the **Lago Mapacocha**, where you can swim and canoe.

Arrival and getting around

By air Flights land at Iquitos airport, Aeropuerto Internacional de Francisco Secada Vigneta (Ⓣ065/260251), 5km southwest of town and connected by taxis (US$6-7) and cheaper *mototaxis* (US$3).

By boat If you've come by boat from Yurimaguas (5 days), Pucallpa (6–7 days), Leticia or Tabatinga (both 3 days), you'll arrive at Puerto Masusa, some eleven blocks northeast of the Plaza de Armas.

By canoe If you want to get onto the river itself, canoes can be rented very cheaply from the port at Bellavista (see above).

By car For getting around town by car, try the office at Tute Pinglo 431 (Ⓣ065/235857).

By motokars and motorbikes For getting around Iquitos you'll probably want to make use of the rattling *motokars*; alternatively, motorbikes can also be rented – try the shop near the Ferretaria Union (block 2 of Raymondi), or one at Yavari 702. Expect to pay around US$2 an hour or US$10 for twelve hours (you'll need to show your passport and licence), and remember to check the brakes before leaving.

Information

Exchange For changing money, it's best not to do it on the street with the *cambistas* who have a bit of a reputation (particularly at the corner of Prospero with Morona) for ripping tourists off, especially after around 8pm. Use one of the *casas de cambio* on Sargento Lores or the banks (see p.898).

Tourist information The very helpful and friendly main tourist office was temporarily located on the corner of Loreto and Raymondi at the time of writing, as structural work was being done on the City Hall building on the Plaza de Armas at Napo 226 where they are usually based. Staff were not too optimistic about when they might be able to move back, but both locations are fairly central and easy to find. Call or email them for information before you go, and to find out where they are; (Ⓣ065/236144, Ⓔiperuiquitos@promperu.gob.pe). They have brochures and maps, and staff can advise on hotels; they keep a list of registered tour operators and guides, and can help book accommodation. The monthly English-language newspaper *The Iquitos Times* is also a good source of information, and is available to pick up free at most touristy hotels and restaurants, also available online at Ⓦwww.iquitostimes.com.

Tours, lodges, and guides

Before approaching anyone it's a good idea to know more or less what you want in terms of time in the forest, total costs, personal needs and comforts, and things you expect to see. Guided tours require some kind of camp set-up or tourist **lodge** facilities. There are two main types of jungle experience

EXPLORING AROUND IQUITOS

If you're planning an expedition beyond the limited network of roads around Iquitos, you'll have to take an organized trip with a **lodge operator**, a **river cruise** or hire a **freelance guide**. The larger local entrepreneurs have quite a grip on the market, and even the few guides who remain more or less independent are hard to bargain with since so much of their work comes through the larger agents. That said, they mostly have well-worked-out itineraries, though you should always deal with an established office – check out which companies are registered at the tourist office in Iquitos – and insist on a written contract and receipt. Be aware that there's no shortage of con-artists among the many **touts** around town, some of whom brandish brochures that have nothing to do with the established offices. Under no circumstances should you hand them any money.

available from Iquitos – what Peruvian tour operators describe as "conventional" (focusing on lodge stays) and what they describe as "adventure trips" (going deeper into the jungle). Prices given are per person.

Amazon Explorama CEIBA TOPS Contact Explorama, Av la Marina 340, Iquitos ⓣ065/252530, ⓦwww.explorama.com, or PO Box 446, Iquitos; toll-free in the US ⓣ1-800-707-5275. Explorama is the top operator in the region; not cheap but worth it. Explorama also now has its own very well equipped river ferryboat – the *Amazon Queen*. Some 40km from Iquitos, this is the most luxurious Amazon lodge of all, with a fantastic jungle swimming pool, bars and dining areas, surrounded by 40 hectares of primary forest and 160 hectares of *chacra* and secondary growth. Accommodation is in smart conventional bungalows with a/c and flushing toilets, or in simpler bungalow huts. There are 75 rooms and a superb pool. Can be visited in conjunction with other Explorama lodges; US$100–400 per day, depending on size of group, length of trip and the number of lodges visited.

Amazon Rainforest Lodge Putumayo 159 ⓣ065/241628, ⓦwww.amazon-lodge.com. One of the closest lodges to Iquitos, only 45min away by boat, they offer one – five day tours. Accommodation is in comfortable bungalows with private bath with hammock space outside, but not as luxurious as in other lodges. From the lodge you can take conventional tours involving fishing and bird-watching or spiritual *ayahuasca* ceremonies. US$90 per day.

Cumaceba Lodge Putumayo 184 ⓣ065/232229, ⓦwww.cumaceba.com. A highly recommended budget option on the Río Yanayacu, some 40km downriver from Iquitos (45min by speedboat), with accommodation in private rustic bungalows with individual bathrooms. It takes visitors to the local Yagua village and on jungle walks; bird- and dolphin-watching also form part of the programmes. It also runs an explorer camp downriver. Around US$190 for three days.

Muyuna Putumayo 163 ⓣ065/242858, ⓦwww.muyuna.com. Located close to the Pacaya-Samiria Reserve, Muyuna offers comfortable accommodation and good service. Excursions from the lodge include jungle walking, river safari trips in canoes and other conventional excursions like piranha fishing. Their jungle tours and lodge work hard to distinguish themselves from competitors as protectors of wild animal rights. Their role is to provide a service to enable people to see the animals, with respect, in the forest. This stance ensures their reputation as one of the greenest eco-tour companies in the region. Around $90 per day.

Accommodation

Like every other jungle town, Iquitos is a little expensive, but there is a good range of **hotels** allowing for different budgets.

La Casona Fitzcarrald 147-A ⓣ065/234394, ⓔlacasonaiquitos@yahoo.com. Clean, quiet, safe and cheap, with friendly staff and rooms around a small courtyard. Also has a kitchen for guests to use. ❹

El Colibri Jr Nauta 172 ⓣ065/241737, ⓔhostalelcolibri@hotmail.com. Modern, clean and pleasant construction close to the main plaza and the Boulevard. Rooms have cable TV and private bath with hot and cold water, as well as air conditioning or fans. ❹

Hobo Hideout – The Great Amazon Safari and Trading Company Putumayo 437 ⓣ065/234099, ⓦwww.greatamazonsafari.com. A unique and special backpackers hostel right in the heart of Iquitos, offering a range of different rooms, some with own bathrooms, and a kitchen for guests to use. Lots of character, including pleasant front

TREAT YOURSELF

Hotel El Dorado Plaza Napo 258, Plaza de Armas ⓣ065/222555, ⓦwww.eldoradoplazahotel.com. A superb hotel, arguably the best anywhere in the Amazon, this is the first ever 5-star in Iquitos. There's great service, a nice pool, a *maloca*-style bar, and quality restaurant and some fantastic rainforest-inspired art. If you can't afford to stay there, you can pay a small fee to use their pool, and they have a happy hour in their foyer bar so you can still go soak up the ambiance (and enjoy the a/c). ❾

garden with chairs and tables hidden within the vegetation, and an impressive (or grotesque, depending on your taste) display of hunting conquests by the owner provides for bear-skin throws and the like throughout the hotel. ❹

Hostal Lima Prospero 549 ⓣ065/221409. With a fairly attractive patio in the entrance, this enormous prison-like hostel has clearly seen better days. Rooms have private bath and fans; but sheets and walls are stained with mysterious substances and the bathrooms are crumbling into decay. However, there is usually space and it is very cheap. ❷

Hostal La Pascana Pevas 133 ⓣ065/231418, ⓦpascana.com. Very friendly little place with book exchange and on-site agency. Double rooms with private bath and fans are on either side of a flower-filled garden, with tables for soaking up the atmosphere or an early evening drink. Close to the Boulevard and the Plaza de Armas, it is surprisingly quiet and tranquil and offers a welcome escape from Iquitos's sometimes hectic street life. It does have a slightly run-down feel however, and mosquito netting in the windows has not been maintained – so bring your own or lots of repellant. ❹

Eating

Food in Iquitos is exceptionally good for a jungle town, specializing in fish dishes but catering these days pretty well for any taste.

Amazon Café Restaurant ⓣ065/225722. Upstairs in the Casa de Fierro, this restaurant has a good variety of local and international food, and some interesting exotic cocktails. Sit on the balcony overlooking the main plaza and watch the motos race each other round and round. Mains average 15 soles, cocktails average 10 soles.

Antica Pizzeria Napo 159 ⓣ065/241988. Huge spacious and airy two-storey restaurant with upstairs balcony. Very good quality pizzas and homemade pastas with a large choice of authentic sauces. Mains average 20 soles.

Aris Burger Prospero 127 ⓣ065/231470. Actually serving more than burgers (though these are quite delicious), including plates with a variety of river fish, plus the best french fries in town. It's the most popular meeting spot in Iquitos and a bit of a landmark for taxi and *motokar* drivers. Burger combo average 12 soles.

Heladería Giornalla Prospero 139. A few doors down from Aris Burger on the Plaza de Armas, this *heladeria* has a mind-boggling 60 flavours of ice cream to choose from, including many exotic fruits from the Amazon – check out the posters on the wall with nutritional values for all the local fruits. 2 soles per scoop.

La Noche Malecón Maldonado 177 ⓣ065/222373. With a great location on the main boulevard, *La Noche* is a good place for a meal or a drink at any time of day. With a small balcony overlooking the boulevard, and comfy sofas inside, it's a great place to relax. Good local dishes as well as traditional exotic liquors Mains 15–20 soles.

La Taberna del Cauchero Raymondi 449, Plaza Ramón Castilla ⓣ065/224124. This mostly local haunt dishes up traditional Amazon cuisine in an authentic rubber baron's restaurant with lots of historical artifacts for decoration. Mains average 15 soles.

The Yellow Rose of Texas Putumayo 180 ⓣ065/231353. Very tasty local dishes and reasonably priced menu; good location near the plaza with tables outside on the street. Texas-themed with good service and open 24hr. Mains 15–30 soles.

Drinking and nightlife

While mainly an extension of eating out and meeting friends in the main streets, the **nightlife** in Iquitos is pretty good, and there are a number of highly charged discos, clubs and bars worth knowing about.

Arandú Bar Malecón Maldonado 113. With a prime location on the Boulevard, this bar is often crowded in the early evenings. It has outdoor and indoor seating and serves a range of drinks and a few snacks.

Berimbau Putumayo 467. One of the newest and flashiest nightclubs in Iquitos; very central and pretty hectic. It plays good rock and Latin dance music most nights, and serves cool drinks at several bars on different levels by different dancefloors. Good air conditioning, which is pretty important here.

El Musmuqui Raymondi 382 ⓣ065/242942. Claiming to be specialists in exotic cocktails this tiny but lively bar is packed with locals every night of the week (but closed on Sun). Come here to try traditional jungle liquors, many of which have strong aphrodisiac properties.

Noa Fitzcarrald 298. Easily identified after 11.30pm by the huge number of flashy motorbikes lined up outside, this is the most popular and lively of Iquitos clubs, attracting young and old, gringo and *Iquiteño* alike. It has three bars and plays lots of Latino music, including the latest technocumbia. Mon–Sat 10pm–late; US$6 entrance.

Puro Instinto Napo 312, 2nd Floor, Plaza de Armas ⓣ065/241803 ⓦwww.puroinstinto.net. This funky art gallery/café/bar opened in March 2008; offering a choice of cocktails number one, two, or three, it is a one-of-a-kind place in Iquitos. Regularly hosts all night dance parties.

La Sala Putumayo 340. This small but comfy bar and restaurant is located between the Plaza de Armas and the *Hobo Hideout*. With an 8 sol menu available from 10am–10pm and happy hour on cocktails from noon–10pm.

Directory

Airlines Lan, Jr Prospero 232, have daily flights to and from Lima as well as Tarapoto and Pucallpa. For very reasonably priced flights to Requena, Angamos and Santa Rosa there's Grupo 42 whose office is at Prospero 215 (ⓣ065/221071 or 221086).

Banks and exchange Banco de Crédito, Prospero 200; BBVA Banco Continental, Sargento Lores 171; Interbank, Prospero 336; *Casa de Cambio* corner of Sargento Lores with Prospero.

Boat transport Transtur, Raymondi 384, ⓣ065/221356. High-speed boats to the tri-border and points along the way, leaving Tues, Thurs and Sat at 6am. $65 per person.

Consulates Brazil, Sargento Lores 363, ⓣ065/235151; Colombia, Calle Calvo de Araujo 431, ⓣ065/231461; UK, Jr Arica 253.

INRENA Pevas 339, ⓣ065/223460. Buy permits for the Pacaya Samiria reserve here.

Jungle supplies Mad Mick's Trading Post, Putumayo 184b. Provides everything you need, for purchase or rental, for a jungle trip, including rubber boots, rainproof ponchos, sunhats, fishing tackle etc.

Police Policia de Turismo, Sargento Lores 834 ⓣ065/242081.

Post office SERPOST, Arica 402. Mon–Sat 7am–7.30pm.

Telephones Sargento Flores 321. Daily 7am–11pm.

Visas Migraciones, Av Andrés Avelino Cáceres s/n Block 18 Morona Cocha; ⓣ065/235371.

Moving on

From Puerto Masusa, **speedboats** go downstream to Santa Rosa, Tabatinga and Leticia (all on the three-way frontier, see box, p.901) several times a week, taking up to ten hours there and twelve hours back, for around US$40. The main companies have their offices on Raymondi, just a few blocks from the Plaza de Armas. Larger **riverboats** go upstream from Puerto Masusa to Lagunas (3 days), Yurimaguas (5 days), Pucallpa (6–7 days), or downstream to Pevas (about 1 day), Leticia and Tabatinga (both 3 days). Take along a good book, plenty of extra food and drink, a hammock, a sweater and one or two blankets; it's usually possible to sling your hammock up and sleep free of charge on the larger boats in the days leading up to the unpredictable departure. It's also advisable to secure your baggage with a chain to a permanent fixture on the deck and also keep bags locked, as **theft** is quite common.

AROUND IQUITOS

The massive river system around Iquitos offers some of the best access to Indian villages, lodges and primary rainforest in the entire Amazon. You can go it alone with the *colectivo* boats that run more or less daily up and down the Río Amazonas, but it's usually best to travel with one of the lodge and tour companies (see p.895).

Lagunas

A long day's ride (130km) **upstream from Iquitos** lies **Nauta**, at the mouth of the Río Marañon. There are excellent organized tours to be had from **LAGUNAS**, close to the Pacaya Samiria Reserve and some three days upstream from Nauta (US$10–25 depending on whether you take hammock space or a shared cabin). There are a couple of **hostels** in Lagunas: the *Hostal Montalban*, on the Plaza de Armas, is basic and small but suffices, as does the slightly cheaper *Hostal La Sombra* at Jr Vasquez 1121.

Lagunas is the main starting-point for trips into the huge **Pacaya Samiria National Reserve** ($30 entry permit from INRENA, see "Directory" opposite), which comprises around two million hectares of virgin rainforest (about 1.5 percent of the landmass of Peru). The reserve is a swampland during the rainy season (Dec–March), when the streams and rivers all rise. This region is home to the Cocoma tribe, whose main settlement is Tipishca. You should of course be well prepared with mosquito nets, hammocks, insect repellent and all the necessary food and medicines (see p.45). It's possible to find **guides** here (about US$10 a day per person, less if you're in a group) and to spend as long as you like in the national reserve. Officially you should obtain from a permit/INRENA the (see "Directory" opposite) to get into the Reserve, but not everyone does; however you risk fines or even deportation if found within the reserve without the appropriate documentation. The Reserve office also provides maps and information on the region, when available.

Pevas

Downstream from Iquitos lies **PEVAS**, some 190km to the east and reached in a day by riverboat *colectivo* or in a

few hours by speedboat. An attractive, largely palm-thatched settlement, it's the oldest town in the Peruvian Amazon. The economy here is based primarily on fishing (visit the *mercado*, where produce is brought in by boat every day), and dugout canoes are the main form of transport, propelled by characteristically ovoid-bladed and beautifully carved paddles, which are often sold as souvenirs, sometimes painted with designs. The nearby Witoto and Bora Indians, relocated here in the 1930s from the Colombian Amazon, are now virtually in everyday contact with the riverine society of Pevas, producing quality artefacts for sale to passers-by. The nearby Bora village of Puca Urquillo is a good example, a large settlement based around a Baptist church and school, whose founders moved here from the Colombian side of the Río Putumayo during the hardships of the rubber era rather than be enslaved.

For a good **place to stay**, try the *Casa de la Loma* (write to PO Box 555, Iquitos; ⓣ065/221184, ⓦwww.greentracks.com), also contactable in the US (write to 10 Town Plaza, Suite 231, Durango, CO 81301; ⓣ01/970-884-6107). Set on a small hill close to Pevas, the lodge was set up by two nurses from Oregon who operate a free clinic here for the two thousand or so local inhabitants. They have five large bedrooms with shared bathrooms, and there's electricity, a refrigerator and a kitchen. Costs are from US$60 per person per day, extra for their speedboat transport from Iquitos.

THE SOUTHERN SELVA: MADRE DE DIOS

A large, forested region, with a manic climate (usually searingly hot and humid, but with sudden cold spells – *friajes* – between June and Aug, owing to icy winds coming down from the Andean glaciers), the **southern selva** regions of Peru have only been systematically explored since the 1950s and were largely unknown until the

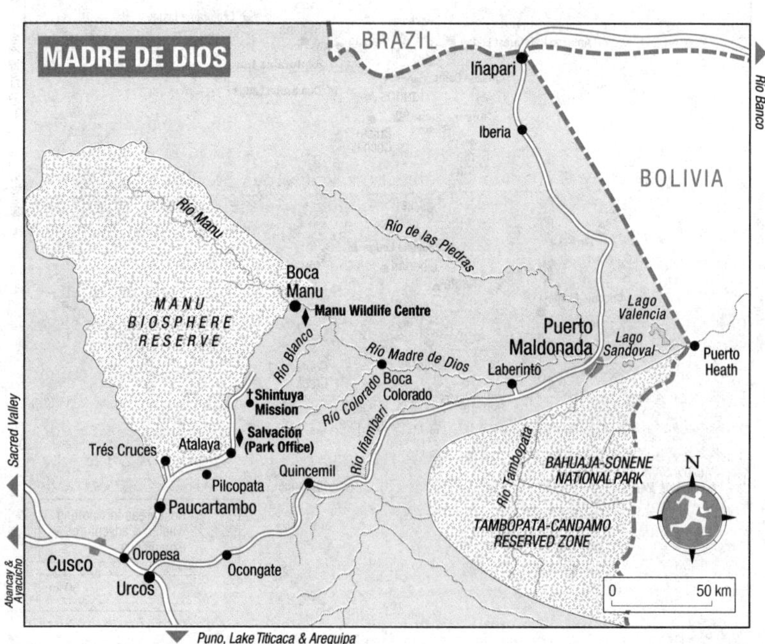

CROSSING INTO COLOMBIA OR BRAZIL: THE THREE-WAY FRONTIER

Leaving or entering Peru via the Amazon is often an intriguing adventure; by river this inevitably means experiencing the **three-way frontier**. The cheapest and most common route is by river from Iquitos, some eight to twelve hours in a *lancha rápida* or three to four days downriver in a standard *lancha* riverboat (see p.896 for details on companies operating boats downriver from Iquitos). Some services go all the way to Leticia, Colombia or Tabatinga (Brazil), but many stop at one of the two small Peruvian frontier settlements of Santa Rosa or Islandia; at Chimbote, a few hours before you get to Santa Rosa and on the right as you head towards the frontier, is a small police post, the main **customs checkpoint** (*guarda costa*) for river traffic.

SANTA ROSA is your last chance to complete formalities with Migraciones if you haven't already done so at the Iquitos office (see "Directory" p.898) – essentially obtaining an **exit stamp** from Peru, if you're leaving, or getting an **entry stamp and tourist card** if arriving, which can take up to an hour. On larger boats, you often don't have to disembark here, as the Migraciones official may board the vessel and do the paperwork there and then. There are few hostels, but the small *La Brisa del Amazonas* is also a **restaurant** whose owner is a useful contact for local **information**. However, there are several cafés, and ferries connect the town with Tabatinga and Leticia.

The only other way of crossing these three borders is by **flying** – a much less interesting approach, though not necessarily a more expensive one (though there's an airport departure tax of US$2). See "Directory" p.898 for details of airlines flying from Iquitos to Santa Rosa. Once across the border into Brazil, Varig and Gol have flights to Manaus via Tabatinga several times a week. From Leticia, Avianca flies to a few major Colombian cities, including Bogotá, several times a week.

twentieth century, when rubber began to leave Peru through Bolivia and Brazil, eastwards along the rivers.

Named after the broad river that flows through the heart of the southern jungle, the still relatively wild *departamento* of **Madre de Dios** is changing rapidly with a recent influx of agribusinesses moving in to clear mahogany trees and prospectors panning for gold dust along the riverbanks. Nearly half of Madre de Dios *departamento*'s 78,000 square kilometres are accounted for by national parks and protected areas such as **Manu Biosphere Reserve**, **Tambopata-Candamo Reserved Zone** and **Bahuaja-Sonone National Park**, between them encompassing some of the most exciting jungle and richest flora and fauna in the world.

The **Río Madre de Dios** is fed by two main tributaries, the **Río Manu** and the **Río Alto Madre de Dios**, which roll off the Paucartambo Ridge (just north of Cusco), which divides the tributaries from the **Río Urubamba** watershed and delineates Manu Biosphere Reserve. At Puerto Maldonado, the Madre de Dios meets with the **Río Tambopata** and the **Río de las Piedras**, then flows on to Puerto Heath, a day's boat ride away on the Bolivian frontier. From here it continues through the Bolivian forest into Brazil to join the great Río Madeira, which eventually meets the Amazon near Manaus. Madre de Dios is still very much a frontier zone, centred on the rapidly growing river town of **Puerto Maldonado**, near the Bolivian border, supposedly founded by legendary explorer and rubber baron **Fitzcarraldo**.

What to see and do

A remote settlement even for Peru, **PUERTO MALDONADO** is a frontier colonist town with strong links to the Cusco region and a great fervour for bubbly jungle *chicha* music. With an economy based on gold panning and Brazil-nut gathering from the rivers and forests of Madre de Dios, it has grown enormously over the last twenty years. From a small, laid-back outpost of civilization to a busy market town, it has become the thriving, safe (and fairly expensive) capital of a region that feels very much on the threshold of major upheavals, with a rapidly developing tourist industry.

In town, the main street, **León de Velarde**, immediately establishes the town's stage-set feel, lined with bars, hardware shops, and a poolroom. At one end is the **Plaza de Armas**, with an attractive if bizarre Chinese pagoda-style clock tower at its centre, and along another side a modern **Municipalidad** – where, not much more than ten years ago, a TV was sometimes set up for the people to watch an all-important event like a game of *fútbol*. These days there are satellite TV dishes all over town and the youth of Puerto Maldonado are as familiar with computer software as they are with jungle mythology. If you're considering a river trip, or just feel like crossing to the other side for a walk, follow Jirón Billinghurst, or take the steep steps down from the Plaza de Armas to the **main port**, situated on the Río Madre de Dios – one of the town's most active corners. A regular bus and *colectivo* (US$5) service now connects Puerto Maldonado with **Laberinto** (leaving from the main market on Ernesto Rivero), some ninety minutes away – most boats going upstream start here, though if you're planning to visit Manu Biosphere Reserve you should set out from Cusco (see p.814).

TREAT YOURSELF

Although most travellers will only pass through the town of Puerto Maldonado on their way deeper into the jungle, if you do spend some time in the town, **Wasai Maldonado Lodge** (Billinghurst ⓣ01/436-8792 for reservations, ⓦwww.wasai.com) is one of the best places to stay. It offers fine views over the Río Madre de Dios, and a swimming pool with a waterfall and bar set among trees, overlooking a canoe-builder's yard. All rooms are cabin-style with TV and shower and staff here also organize local tours and run the *Wasai Lodge* (see p.902). ❻

Arrival and getting around

By air If you arrive by plane, the blast of hot, humid air you get the moment you step out onto the **airport**'s runway is an instant reminder that this is the Amazon Basin. Lan Peru and TACA have daily flights to Puerto Maldonado from Cusco and Lima. Unless you're being picked up as part of an organized tour, **airport transfer** is simplest and coolest by *mototaxi*, costing around US$2.50 for the otherwise very hot eight-kilometre walk.

By boat Puerto Maldonado has two main **river ports**, one on the Río Tambopata, at the southern end of León de Velarde, the other on the Río Madre de Dios, at the northern end of León de Velarde; from the former, there's a very cheap **ferry** service across the river to the newish road to Brazil. From either it's possible to hire a **boatman and canoe** for a river trip; prices usually start at US$25 per person for a day journey, for a minimum of two people; this rises to US$35 for trips of two to four days. Boats are equipped with a *peque-peque* or small outboard motor, and usually take up to twelve people. If you're prepared to pay significantly more (from US$100 a day per person, again for a minimum of two), you can find boatmen with speedboats and larger outboard motors.

By mototaxi and motorbikes The quickest way of **getting around town** and its immediate environs is to hail a *mototaxi* ($1 in-town flat rate, but check before getting on) or passenger-carrying motorbikes (50¢, also a flat rate). If you fancy doing a bit of running about on your own, or have a lot of ground to cover in town, moped rental is a useful option; you'll find a reasonable place at Av Gonzalez Prada 321, by the *Hotel Wilson* (US$2 for 1hr, US$15 for 12hr; no deposit, but passports and driving licences required). Make sure there's ample petrol in the tank.

Information

Tourist information However you get here, you have to go through a yellow fever **vaccination checkpoint** at Puerto Maldonado's small but clean, modern and air-conditioned airport, where there's also a tourist information kiosk and *artesanía* shops. For entry and exit stamps, the **immigration office** is at 26 de Diciembre 356, one block from the Plaza de Armas.

Accommodation

Puerto Maldonado has a reasonable range of **hotels**, most of them either on or within a couple of blocks of León de Velarde. All the better hotels offer protection against mosquitos and some sort of air conditioning.

Hospedaje Rey Port Velarde 457 ⓣ082/571177. Friendly, but sometimes noisy, basic budget accommodation, with small but clean rooms. ❸

Moderno Hostal Billingshurst 357 ⓣ082/571063. A brightly painted and well-kept hotel, with something of a frontier-town character, all at extremely reasonable rates. ❷

Eating, drinking and nightlife

You should have no problem finding a good **restaurant** in Puerto Maldonado. Delicious river fish are always available, even in *ceviche* form, and there's venison or wild pig fresh from the forest (try *estofado de venado*). The cosy *Pizzeria Chez Maggy*, on the Plaza de Armas, is very popular with travellers and locals alike; there are no exotic toppings, but it's hard to imagine how they can produce such good **pizzas** in this jungle environment. If you like grilled **chicken**, you're spoiled for choice; try *Pollos a la Brasa La Estrella*, Velarde 474 for the tastiest. Along León de Velarde are a number of **cafés and bars**, one or two of which have walls covered in typical *selvático*-style paintings, developed to represent and romanticize the dreamlike features of the jungle – looming jaguar, brightly plumed macaws talking to each other in the treetops, and deer drinking water from a still lake. There's very little **nightlife** in this laid-back town, especially during the week – most people just stroll around, stopping occasionally to sit and chat in the Plaza de Armas or in bars along the main street.

TAMBOPATA-CANDAMO NATIONAL PARK

Madre de Dios boasts spectacular virgin lowland rainforest and exceptional wildlife. Brazil-nut tree trails, a range of lodges, some excellent local guides and ecologists plus indigenous and colonist cultures are all within a few hours of Puerto Maldonado. There are two main ways to explore: firstly, by arranging your own boat and boatman; and secondly, though considerably more expensive, by taking an excursion up to one of the lodges.

What to see and do

Less than one hour downriver from Puerto Maldonado (90min on the return upriver) is **LAGO SANDOVAL**, a large lake where the Ministry of Agriculture has introduced the large *paiche* fish. At its best on weekday mornings (it gets quite crowded at other times), there are decent opportunities for spotting wildlife, in particular birds similar to those at Lago Valencia. It's also possible to walk to the lake (about 1hr), and once here boatmen and canoes can usually be obtained by your guide for a couple of hours, as can food and drink.

It takes the best part of a day by canoe with a *peque-peque*, or around two hours in a *lancha* with an outboard, to reach the huge lake of **LAGO VALENCIA** from Puerto Maldonado. Easing onto the lake itself, the sounds of the canoe engine are totally silenced by the weight and expanse of water. Up in the trees around the channel lie hundreds of hoatzin birds, or *gallos*, as they are called locally – large, ungainly creatures with orange and brown plumage, long wings and distinctive spiky crests.

Another good trip, if you've got at least three days to spare (two nights minimum), is up to the Río Heath, a national rainforest sanctuary, though while the Pampas del Heath are excellent for macaws they don't have the primary forest necessary for a great variety of wildlife. A shorter trip – five hours up and about two hours down – is to Tres Chimbales, where there are a few houses belonging to the Infierno community on the Río Tambopata; it's possible to spend two or three days watching for wildlife, walking in the forest and fishing. From here you can visit Infierno village itself – spread out along the river, you can see glimpses of thatched and tin-roofed huts.

Organized tours

Compared with independent travel, an **organized excursion** saves time and adds varying degrees of comfort. It also ensures that you go with someone who knows the area, who probably speaks English and, if you choose well, can introduce you to the flora, fauna and culture of the area. It's also worth noting that you are less likely to get ripped off with a registered company with a fixed office and contact details, especially if you should need redress afterwards. Most people book a trip in Cusco before travelling to Puerto Maldonado, though it is possible to contact most of the operators in Puerto itself, either at the airport or through one of the offices (see below), or through the cafés on León de Velarde. Flying from Cusco is the quickest way to reach Puerto Maldonado, and most Cusco agencies will organize plane tickets (US$60–80) for you if you take their tours. The cheapest option is a two-day and one-night tour, but on these you can expect to spend most of your time travelling and sleeping. Frankly, the Amazon deserves a longer visit, and you're only looking at US$50–75 more for an extra day.

Of the ever-increasing number of **lodges** and **tour operators** around Puerto Maldonado, mainly on the ríos Madre de Dios and Tambopata, all offer a good taste of the jungle, but the quality of the experience varies from area to area and lodge to lodge – all lodges tend to offer full board and include transfers, though always check the level of service and ask to see photos at the lodges' offices in Cusco or Lima. It's also worth checking out what costs will be once you're there; complaints are common about the price of drinks (soft drinks and beer), although given the distance they've travelled, the mark-up is hardly surprising. Remember, too, that even the most luxurious place is far removed from normal conveniences, and conditions – from toilets to sleeping arrangements – tend to be extremely rustic and relatively open to the elements.

Lodges and tour operators

Eco Amazonia Lodge Calle Garcilaso 210, office 206, Cusco ⓣ084/236159; Calle Enrique Palacios 292, Miraflores, Lima ⓣ01/242-2708; ⓦwww.ecoamazonia.com.pe. Less than two hours downriver from Puerto Maldonado, this large establishment offers basic bungalows and dormitories. Packages usually include visits to Lago Sandoval, about 30min upriver, and organized visits can be made to the Palma Real community, though this is often anticlimactic and of dubious value to both tribe and tourist. From US$210 per person for three days and two nights, when two people sharing.

Explorers Inn Plateros 365, Cusco ⓣ084/235342, ⓦwww.explorersinn.com. The lodge is located 58km south of Puerto Maldonado in the Tambopata reserve. It offers over 30kms of forest trails and canoes on the oxbow lake of Cocococha which is inhabited by giant otters. English-speaking biology graduates work as resident naturalists, assisting guides and helping to enhance the guests' experience and understanding of the rainforest. The lodge also has a small museum and discovery center. From US$200 per person for three days and two nights, when two people sharing.

Inkaterra Reserva Amazónica Cusco 463, Puerto Maldonado ⓣ082/572283; Plaza Nazarenas 167, 2nd floor, Cusco ⓣ084/245314 (ⓦwww.inkaterra.com). Set up by a French–Peruvian venture in 1975, comforts here include a cocktail bar and good food (often a buffet). The main excursion is to Lago Sandoval, some 20min upriver, and guides speak several languages. The lodge owns 10,000 hectares of forest surrounding it and there is an extensive canopy network nearby. From US$330 per person for three days and two nights, when two people sharing.

Posadas Amazonas Lodge, Tambopata Research Centre and Refugio Amazonas

Contact through **Rainforest Expeditions**, Aramburu 166, 4B, Lima 18 ⓣ01/421-8347 or Portal de Carnes 236, Plaza de Armas, Cusco ⓣ084/246243, ⓦwww.perunature.com. *Posadas* is probably the region's best lodge for its relationship with locals – it's owned by the Ese Eja community of Infierno (though mainly non-native members work here) – and for its wildlife research. Resident researchers act as guides (different languages available), and most packages include a visit to Lago Tres Chimbadas; additional trips to the Tambopata macaw *colpa* (salt-lick) (6–8hr upriver) can be arranged, involving a night at the remote Tambopata Research Center (TRC); a minimum of six days is recommended for complete tours. The lodge itself features large, stylish doubles with shared bath, set in three native-style buildings, plus a central dining-area-cum-bar and lecture room. Similar is the newer *Refugio Amazonas* located between the two other lodges and offering the same programs. From US$295 per person for three days and two nights, when two people sharing.

Wasai Lodge Owned by the Wasai hotel in Puerto Maldonado, (ⓦwww.wasai.com). Four hours upriver from Puerto Maldonado is this relatively new and smallish lodge set in the forest, with a pleasant jungle bar and dining area. Spanish- and English-speaking guides are available, with 15km of trails in the vicinity plus trips to the Chuncho *colpa* on request. From US$324 per person for three days and two nights, when two people sharing.

MANU BIOSPHERE RESERVE

Encompassing almost two million hectares (about half the size of Switzerland) on the foothills of the eastern Andes, the **Manu Biosphere Reserve** features a uniquely varied environment of pristine rainforest, from crystalline cloudforest streams and waterfalls down to slow-moving, chocolate-brown rivers in the dense lowland jungle. For **flora and fauna**, Manu is pretty much unbeatable in South America, with over 5000 flowering plants, 1200 species of butterfly, 1000 types of bird, 200 kinds of mammal and an unknown quantity of reptiles and insects. Rich in macaw salt-licks, otter lagoons and prowling jaguar; there are thirteen species of monkey and seven species of macaw in Manu.

WHEN TO VISIT

Any expedition to Manu is very much in the hands of the gods, thanks to the changeable jungle environment; the region experiences a rainy season from December to March, but is best visited between May and August when it's much drier, although at that time the temperatures often exceed 30°C.

What to see and do

The highlight of most organized visits to Manu is the trail network and lakes of **Cocha Salvador** (the largest of Manu's oxbows, at 3.5km long) and **Cocha Otorongo**, bountiful jungle areas rich in animal, water and birdlife. Cocha Otorongo is best known for the family of **giant otters** who live here; because of this, canoeing is not permitted, but there is a floating platform which can be manoeuvred to observe the otters fishing and playing from a safe distance. Other wildlife includes the plentiful **caimans** – the two- to three-metre white alligators and the rarer three- to five-metre black ones, and you can usually see several species of **monkey** (dusky titis, woolly monkeys, red howlers, brown capuchins and the larger spider monkeys – known locally as *maquisapas*). Sometimes big mammals such as **capybara** or **white-lipped peccaries** (called *sajinos* in Peru) also lurk in the undergrowth.

The flora of Manu is as outstanding as its wildlife. Huge cedar trees can be seen along the trails, covered in hand-like vines climbing up their vast trunks (most of the cedars were taken out of here between 1930 and 1963, before it became a protected area). The giant Catahua trees, many over 150 years old, are traditionally the preferred choice for making dugout canoes – and some are large enough to make three or four – though second choice is the lagarto tree.

Organized tours

There are quite a few **organized tours** competing for travellers who want to visit Manu. Many are keen to keep the impact of tourism to a minimum, which means limiting the number of visits per year (it's already running well into the thousands). However, they do vary quite a bit in quality of guiding, level of comfort and price range. If you go with one of the companies listed below, you can generally be confident that you won't be doing anything that might have lasting damage. Many companies will offer a choice of land or air transportation into Manu for many, a good option is to take land transportation in, as the scenery is spectacular, but to return by air. Check when booking what transportation options are available. When flying into Boca Manu, bear in mind that planes are small and flight schedules are affected by weather conditions, making timetables somewhat unreliable.

Atalaya C Arequipa 242 (inside Manu Café), Cusco ⓣ084/228327, ⓦwww.atalayaperu.com. One of the only companies offering combined Manu & Tambopata tours, as well as Ecological volunteer placements in the Jungle. Atalaya have their own reserve, but use the indigenous-owned and run Casa Matsiguenka for accommodation on many of their tours. Also offers mystical programs where you can experiment with hallucinogenic plants, and a course in the use of medicinal plants. From US$440 5 days/4 nights, based on two people sharing and land transport in and out. Discounts available to South American Explorers' Club members.

Fundación Selva Inka Urbanización Marcavalle C-25, Cusco ⓣ084/231625, ⓦwww.selvainka.com. A relatively new not-for-profit organization, Selva Inka have a basic family-run lodge in the town of Pilcopata, in the cultural zone of the Manu National Park. They run complete tours leaving from Cusco, and although tours are only in the cultural zone and therefore it is not possible to see such a variety of animals, this is an excellent and very economical option to get inside Manu and explore the park from a cultural point of view. From US$230 for 3 days/2 nights based on two people sharing. Land transportation only. Discounts available to South American Explorers' Club members.

InkaNatura Travel C Plateros 361, Cusco ⓣ084/255255, ⓦwww.inkanatura.com. InkaNatura have two lodges within Manu, the *Cock-of-the-rock Lodge*, which houses a viewing point over a claylick where these bright red birds can be seen at sunrise and sunset, and the *Manu Wildlife Center*, where there are two canopy platforms, oxbow lakes and miles of walking trails. Accommodation is comfortable in either location as both have private bungalows with ensuite bathrooms. From US$1290 4 days/3 nights, based on two people sharing and air transport from Cusco to Boca Manu.

Manu Expeditions Calle Humberto Vidal Unda G-5, Magistero, 2da etapa, Cusco ⓣ084/226671 or 239974, ⓦwww.manuexpeditions.com. One of the best and the most responsible companies, run by a British ornithologist. Thoroughly recommended, the guides and service are top quality, good English is spoken, they offer air and overland transfers to Boca Manu (they have their own overland transport), and food, beds (or riverside campsite) and bird-blinds are all included. From US$1495, 6 days/5nights based on two people sharing. Land transportation in, and flight out. Discounts available to South American Explorers' Club members.

Manu Nature Tours Av Pardo 1046, Cusco ⓣ084/252721, ⓦwww.manuperu.com. A highly professional company that operates Manu Lodge, one of only two within Zone B, where you can join their four- to eight-day programmes. It also runs three-day-trips to *Manu Cloud Forest Lodge* in its private reserve by the southeast boundary of Zone A, where torrent ducks, gallos and even woolly monkeys are often seen. From US$1200, 4 days/3 nights. Options of air or land transportation.

Pantiacolla Tours Calle Saphi 554, Cusco ⓣ084/238323, ⓦwww.pantiacolla.com. A company with a reputation for serious eco-adventure tours. Its cheapest option is also the longest, a nine-day tour that takes groups in and out by bus and boat, while the more expensive five- to seven-day-trips go in by road and out by plane from Boca Manu. It has an excellent lodge on the Río Alto Madre de Dios at Itahuania, and its tours into the Reserve Zone are based in tents at prepared campsites. From US$860, 5 days/4 nights. Options of air or land transportation. Discounts available to South American Explorers' Club members.

Uruguay

HIGHLIGHTS

COLONIA DEL SACRAMENTO: explore the picturesque cobbled streets of this old smuggling port

MINAS: head to the nearby *estancias turísticas* and ride through Uruguay's vast interior

PUNTA DEL DIABLO: hit the high waves of the Atlantic at this hippy beach resort

MONTEVIDEO: visit the crumbling 19th-century townhouses and skyscrapers of Uruguay's capital

PUNTA DEL ESTE: enjoy vast stretches of white sand and lively beach bars at South America's flashest resort

ROUGH COSTS

DAILY BUDGET Basic US$25/ occasional treat US$35

DRINK Pilsen beer (1litre) US$2

FOOD *Asado de tira* steak US$10

HOSTEL/BUDGET HOTEL US$15/25

TRAVEL Montevideo–Colonia del Sacramento (150km) by bus: 2hr 30min, US$7

FACT FILE

POPULATION 3.4 million

AREA 176,215 sq km

LANGUAGE Spanish; Portuguese near the Brazilian border

CURRENCY Peso Uruguayo (UR$)

CAPITAL Montevideo (population: 1.3 million)

INTERNATIONAL PHONE CODE ⓣ598

TIME ZONE GMT -3hr

Introduction

Uruguay entered the twenty-first century on the cusp of momentous change. Having succeeded in peacefully replacing the military which had ruled the country since the 1960s, Uruguay's democratic leaders were rocked in 2001 by the financial collapse of neighbouring Argentina. The spread of foot-and-mouth disease led to a ban on many Uruguayan agricultural products, which weakened the economic sector that had once been Uruguay's pride and joy, and the reason for its relative stability in contrast to its larger neighbours.

Despite these misfortunes, however, Uruguayans maintain their traditionally laid-back and cheerful attitude, and it is not hard to see why. From the secluded surfing beaches of the northern coast, through the rolling fields of the interior filled with grazing cattle and gauchos, to the picturesque streets of Colonia del Sacramento and the buzzing nightlife of Montevideo, theirs is a gem of a nation set between the South American giants of Brazil and Argentina. "Tranquilo" (peaceful) could be Uruguay's national motto and, after witnessing the beauty of the land and the relaxed kindness of its people, you are unlikely to be in any hurry to leave.

CHRONOLOGY

Pre-1600 Uruguay is home to the Charrua Indians, a hunter-gatherer people hostile to the European invaders.

Early 1600s: Spanish settlers introduce cattle to Uruguay and the gaucho lifestyle of cattle-ranching develops.

1680 The Portuguese establish Colonia del Sacramento as a port to smuggle goods into Buenos Aires. It is the first major colony in Uruguay.

1726 The Spanish retaliate by founding Montevideo in an attempt to cement their power in the region. Their wars with the Portuguese continue for the next century.

1811–20 The Spanish leave Uruguay, only for Brazil and Argentina to fight over control of the territory.

1827 General Juan Lavalleja leads the legendary Treinta y Tres Orientales (a group of 33 freedom fighters) to a major victory over the Brazilian invaders. Uruguay gains its independence a year later.

1800s The two main political parties, the Colorados (liberals) and the Blancos (nationalists) preside over a century of civil unrest and governmental corruption, but nevertheless the economy grows rapidly thanks to beef exports. Attracted by the new wealth, waves of immigrants arrive from Europe.

1903–15 The Colorado President José Batlle y Ordoñez introduces reforms to healthcare, education and benefits that effectively turn Uruguay into South America's first welfare state.

1939–45 Uruguay grows rich during the Second World War thanks to its export of meat and wool to the Allied nations.

1950s and 60s Inflation and political corruption leads to the stagnation of Uruguay's industries, and social unrest ensues.

1973 The Congress is dissolved and the Army is invited to take control of the government. The country slides into a military dictatorship.

1980 The voters reject a new, repressive constitution drawn up by the military government.

1984 Unable to quell public unrest, the military allows free elections to take place. Colorado Dr Julio Sanguinetti becomes President and holds office until 1989.

2001 The economic crisis in Argentina leads to a collapse in the value of the peso. The US and World Bank bails the country out with a $1.5 billion loan.

2004 Tabaré Vázquez of the Frente Amplio, a left-wing coalition, sweeps to power in elections.

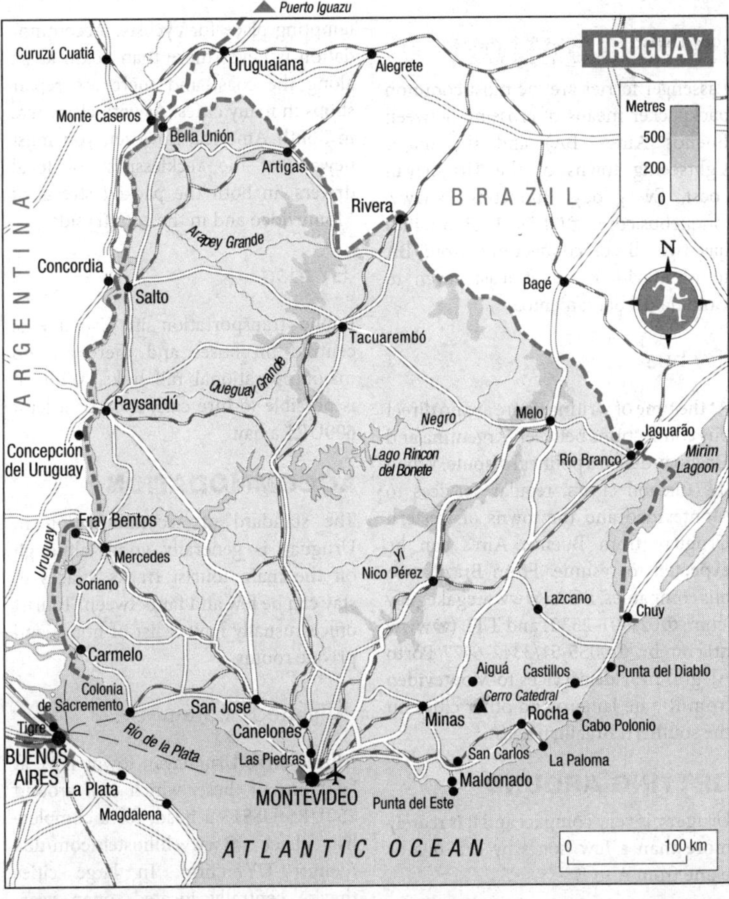

Basics

ARRIVAL

Most visitors to Uruguay fly into Aeropuerto Carrasco in Montevideo; those entering from Argentina can also catch a ferry from Buenos Aires to either Montevideo or Colonia del Sacramento. Overland passage is possible from neighbouring Brazil, but not from Argentina.

By air

Uruguay's main international airport is Montevideo's **Aeropuerto Carrasco,** which receives direct flights from Asunción (Paraguay), Miami, Madrid, Santiago (Chile), São Paulo and several other Brazilian cities. Aerolineas Argentinas (Ⓣ02/902-3694, Ⓦwww.aerolineas.com.ar) offers two flights every day from Buenos Aires, the main point of connection with Argentina.

By boat

Passenger ferries are the most common backpacker means of crossing between Buenos Aires (BA) and the major sightseeing towns of the Uruguayan coast. Every day, Buquebus (Ⓦwww.buquebus.com, Ⓣ00 5411 4316 6400) has two direct connections from BA to Montevideo and at least seven to Colonia del Sacramento.

By bus

At the time of writing, there are no direct bus connections between Argentina and Uruguay due to a political dispute. When the turmoil clears, regular services to Montevideo and the towns of western Uruguay from Buenos Aires can be expected to resume. From Brazil, two bus companies, EGA (Ⓦwww.egakeguay.com, Ⓣ02/901-2530) and TTL (Ⓦwww.ttl.com.br, Ⓣ0055 51/3342-6477 Porto Alegre) provide services to Montevideo from Río de Janeiro and other cities on the southern Brazilian coast.

GETTING AROUND

Uruguay is very compact and it is rearely more than a few hours by car, bus or plane from A to B.

By bus

The most convenient and cheapest means of transport for backpackers in Uruguay are **intercity buses,** which operate from the Bus terminal (*terminal de ómnibus*) to be found in most towns. A range of companies operate these intercity services and tickets are bought in advance at kiosks in the terminal. Local bus trips are slower and less comfortable, but also very cheap.

By bike

With a predominantly flat landscape and good-quality roads, Uruguay is a tempting place for cyclists. Accommodation is never more than 50km apart along the coast and there are repair shops in many cities. As with elsewhere in South America, however, you must beware of the recklessness of local drivers, in both the packed streets of Montevideo and in the countryside.

By road

Public transportation in Uruguay is centred on buses and there are no major operational rail links. While it is possible to hire cars, it costs at least 600UR$ a day.

ACCOMMODATION

The standard of accommodation in Uruguay is generally good, although off the main tourist tracks, places to stay can be few and far between. Tourist offices usually have a list of hotels and private rooms.

Affiliated hostels

All the large Uruguayan towns have at least one of these, which cost around 250UR$/US$13 a head; for a complete list check Ⓦwww.hihostels.com/dba/country-UY.en.htm. In large cities they're centrally located, open year-round and often provide amenities like Internet access and laundry service, although sometimes they impose lockouts and curfews.

Private Hostels

These proliferate in Montevideo and Punta del Este and are now cropping up in the other cities. Private hostels generally offer excellent service for around 300UR$ per bed, with group leisure activities and free breakfasts included. During the Uruguayan and Argentinian summer holidays of December–March, however, it is advisable to book ahead, as they are very popular.

Budget hotels and private rooms

There is usually at least one cheap hotel in most towns, with 300UR$/US$15 normally buying you spartan but habitable rooms with communal toilet and shower. Prices increase by half for en-suite bathroom, TV and breakfast, although many have excellent discounts for students. Tourist offices can also often find you cheap rooms in private houses (*pensiones* and *posadas*; 400UR$/US$20).

FOOD

Uruguay may not provide the most cosmopolitan of culinary experiences, but if you enjoy **beef** or most kinds of **seafood**, there may be few better places in the world to whet your appetite. Uruguayan steakhouses (**parrillas**) serve steaks that are larger and (as the always partisan locals insist) more tender than their Argentinian counterparts, with the most popular cuts being the ribs (*asado de tira*) and tenderloin (*bife de chorizo*). The Italian immigrants who arrived in the late nineteenth century left their mark in the ubiquitous **pizza cafes and home-made pasta restaurants**, which are in general the best dining option for **vegetarians**. Otherwise, outside Montevideo, people looking for meals without meat (*sin carne*) are likely to become highly acquainted with the local **supermercado** (supermarket); these generally have salad counters that provide filling, nutritious meals, often the cheapest option for any backpacker in a rush. The **desserts** (*postres*) also bear an Italian influence. Ice creams here are among the most sumptuous on the continent, and any trip along the coast is filled with opportunities for sampling a range of original flavours and toppings, not least *dulce de leche* (a caramel-like syrup). The national snack is the **chivito**, a steak sandwich with a range of meat, cheese and salad fillings. Lunch and dinner are both eaten late by Western standards; you can expect to be eating on your own at even the best-quality, most popular restaurants if you arrive before 9pm. Restaurant **prices** are low: in most places outside of Montevideo and Punta del Este you can have a two-course meal with a drink for 300UR$/US$14.

THE ART OF DRINKING EL MATÉ

You are unlikely to have a single walk down a street in Uruguay without seeing someone carrying the thermos, pots and pipe required for **maté**. Uruguayans are said to drink to even more of it than Argentinians in a tradition that goes back to the earliest gauchos, and there is now a whole set of social rituals that surround its herby smell and taste. At the close of a meal, the maté is meticulously prepared before being passed round in a circle; the drinker makes a small **sucking noise** when the pot needs to be refilled, but if this is your position, beware making three such noises: they mark a bad education.

DRINK

Uruguayans traditionally enjoy sitting around drinking from lunchtime onwards, and the palatable local beers – especially the ubiquitous Pilsen – come in 1lt bottles (5UR$/US$2) fit for the purpose. There are always inexpensive bottles of top Argentinian wines available, but it's also worth trying the local produce, not least when served "medio y medio", in a blend of sparkling and white wine. Coffee and maté are the kings of non-alcoholic drinks here. The former is available in every drinking place, although espresso drinks are less common. Tea, fruit juices and bottled water are less popular but still available; tap water is fine to drink in most towns.

URUGUAY ON THE NET

Ⓦ **www.turismo.gub.uy** The official tourist website with the latest details on Uruguay's major sights and visa information.
Ⓦ **http://www.reduruguaya.com** Essays on Uruguayan cultural events and some local recipes.
Ⓦ **www.ahru.com.uy** City guides with up-to-date information on accommodation, festivals and tour guides.

CULTURE AND ETIQUETTE

Uruguayans of all ages tend to be warm, relaxed people, fond of lively, informal conversation over a beer or barbeque (*asado*). As a nation in which the overwhelming majority of people are descended from Italian and Spanish immigrants, however, Uruguay also maintains some conservative **Catholic** religious and social practices, especially in the countryside. Men are often seen as the breadwinner and it is still rare to see **women** travelling alone at night. Uruguay's young, urban population tends to be a little wilder than their parents, but both these generations display a rugged sense of independence that recalls the romantic figure of the **gaucho**, the cowboys that still roam the grassy plains of the interior. **Table manners** follow the Western norm and it is usual to reward good service with a ten percent **tip**.

SPORTS AND OUTDOOR ACTIVITIES

Ever since the first World Cup in 1930 was held in Uruguay and won by the national team, **football** has been the sport to raise the passions of the normally laid-back Uruguayans, although neither the main club sides or the national team have made much impression in international competitions recently. In the countryside, horse riding is more a part of working life than a sport, but there are now many opportunities for tourists to go riding, especially in the Estancias Turísticas around Minas. **Cycling** is a popular way of seeing the cities (many hostels provide free or cheap bikes) while fishing is another favoured afternoon pursuit. **Surfing** is still developing as a sport for the Uruguayans themselves, and many beach resorts lack board-renting facilities year-round, but plenty of foreigners are already taking advantage of the fantastic Atlantic surf that is provided at beaches like Punta del Diablo and La Paloma.

COMMUNICATIONS

Post offices (*correos*) provide an expensive and frequently unreliable service for international mailing; for urgent deliveries, you are much better using private mailing company like FedEx, Av. Rivera 3528, Montevideo (Ⓣ02/628-4829). **Poste restante** services are only available in Montevideo. Post offices usually open Mon–Sat 8am–7pm with a siesta break. For public phones you can buy a card (*tarjeta telefónica*), which are available at post offices, or use change. Internet cafés charging 10–25UR$/hour are present in all towns.

EMERGENCIES

Uruguay is a very safe country to travel in, though inevitably thefts from dorms and pick-pocketing do occur, especially in Montevideo and the beach resorts during the summer months. You should thus store your valuables in lockers whenever possible. The Uruguayan police (*policia*) are courteous but

EMERGENCY NUMBERS

911 is the general emergency number for the police, public ambulances and fire service.

STUDENT AND YOUTH DISCOUNTS

Your **hostel card** can earn you up to 25 percent off at HI-affiliated hostels, while an ISIC card can help cut entry prices for some museums and city transport. Check out the Uruguay section of the ISIC website (ⓦwww.istc.org) for the latest offers.

unlikely to speak English. There are adequate public hospitals in the major cities, although many foreigners rely on the expensive private medical cover run by companies like Medicina Personalizada (ⓦwww.mp.com.uy, ⓣ02/711 1000).

INFORMATION AND MAPS

Even most small towns have their resident **tourist office** (oficina de información turística), the vast majority of which provide friendly, helpful advice for budget travellers, especially regarding inexpensive places to stay and any potential discounts to be exploited while sightseeing. They generally provide basic maps of local areas, but you are most likely to find high-quality road maps (200UR$/US$10) in the petrol stations that are common on the major roads and in cities.

MONEY AND BANKS

The unit of **currency** is the **peso uruguayo** ($). Coins come as 50 centimos and 1, 2, 5, and 10 pesos; notes as 10, 20, 50, 100, 200, 500 and 1,000 pesos.

Banks are usually open Mon–Fri 1–5pm and closed at weekends; street **currency exchanges** (*casas de cambio*) often offer better exchange rates. Breaking large banknotes is less of a problem than in most South American countries, thought you are still best placed using notes lower than 1000UR$ for smaller bills, especially in the countryside. While major **credit cards** are widely accepted, and **ATMs** are common in cities, you should always carry a relatively large supply of **cash** for places where this is not the case, especially the beach villages of Eastern Uruguay. At the time of writing, €1 = 31UR$, US$1 = 21.50UR$ and £1 = 43UR$. Prices throughout this guide are given in Pesos.

OPENING HOURS AND HOLIDAYS

Most shops **open** on weekdays from 9am until 12.30pm, before closing for a **siesta** until around 4pm and then reopening until 7 or 8pm; they are also closed on Sundays. This is with the exception of many shops in Montevideo, the main coastal tourist centres, and with supermarkets in general; the latter are often open until 11pm during the week and for long periods on Sundays. Most **museums and historic monuments** are open Monday to Saturday; entrance is free in Montevideo and inexpensive elsewhere. Public holidays are: January 1, January 6, Good Friday, Easter Mon, April 1, May 1, May 18, June 19, July 18, August 25 October 12, November 2, December 25.

Montevideo

With a population of around 1.3 million, over thirteen times larger than the second city of Paysandú, **Montevideo** is Uruguay's political, economic and transport hub. Founded in 1726 as a fortress city on the northern shore of the **River Plate,** it has an excellent trading position and, following a turbulent and often violent early history, its growth has been rapid. The nineteenth century saw mass immigration from Europe that has resulted in a vibrant mix of architectural styles and a cosmopolitan atmosphere that persists to this day.

Visitors arriving from Buenos Aires will be immediately struck by the contrast between the hectic pace of life of the Argentine capital and the relaxed atmosphere cultivated by the *Montevideanos*. Less affluent than its neighbour across the river, the Uruguayan capital seems happy with its lot, and while regional economic disasters have hit the city harder than most, it remains a friendly and welcoming place. Filled with intriguing art galleries and museums, crumbling churches and high-quality restaurants, this is an unassuming city that merits further exploration.

Ciudad Vieja

Parts of Montevideo's old town, Ciudad Vieja, may have fallen into disrepair in recent years, but its tight grid of streets still bursts with historical character, and it now possesses a set of small, but endearingly bizarre (and free) museums and art galleries. In the centre of the Ciudad Vieja is the **Plaza de la Constitución**, the oldest square in the country, flanked by buildings of colonial grandeur that reflect the wealth of Uruguay's past. The main tourist area of interest is around **Plaza Independencia**, site of the original citadel of Montevideo and burial place of freedom fighter and national hero **General Artigas**.

The Port

The port is on the northern edge **of the Ciudad Vieja**, defined by the impressively colossal but grimly monolithic **Dirección General de Aduana** building. Nearby is the **Museo del Carnaval** (Tues–Sat 11am–5pm, Sun 2–6pm; free), filled with colourful exhibits from the city's Carnaval celebrations, and the Mercado del Puerto, a former meat market dating from 1868.

Built in the style of a nineteenth-century British railway station, complete with a station clock, the **Mercado del Puerto** (Port Market) is opposite the main ferry terminal. It's worth visiting in its own right for the restaurants that you find inside, which provide some of the most atmospheric spots to eat in the city (see p.918).

Around Plaza Zabala

Plaza Zabala has as its centrepiece a horseback statue of Zabala, the founder of the city. On the north side of the plaza stands the **Palacio Taranco**, home to the **Museo de Arte Decorativo** (Tues–Sat 11am–5pm, Sun 2–6pm; free), a beautifully displayed collection, particularly remarkable for the pottery and glassware that used to grace the palaces of the Uruguayan aristocracy.

To the north of Plaza Zabala on 25 de Mayo is the **Casa de Garibaldi** (Mon–Fri 11am–7pm, Sat noon-6pm; free). Once occupied by Italian hero Giuseppe Garibaldi, it houses a small collection of artefacts associated with him. The **Museo Romántico**, at 25 de Mayo 428 (same hours; free), gives a unique and valuable insight into the opulent lifestyles of the wealthy at the end of the nineteenth century, including the rather egotistical practice of having the owner's initials inscribed onto every possession of value. The pick of the museums, however, is just a few blocks to the east of Plaza Zabala. The **Casa de Rivera** (same hours; free) traces a fascinating journey through Uruguay's

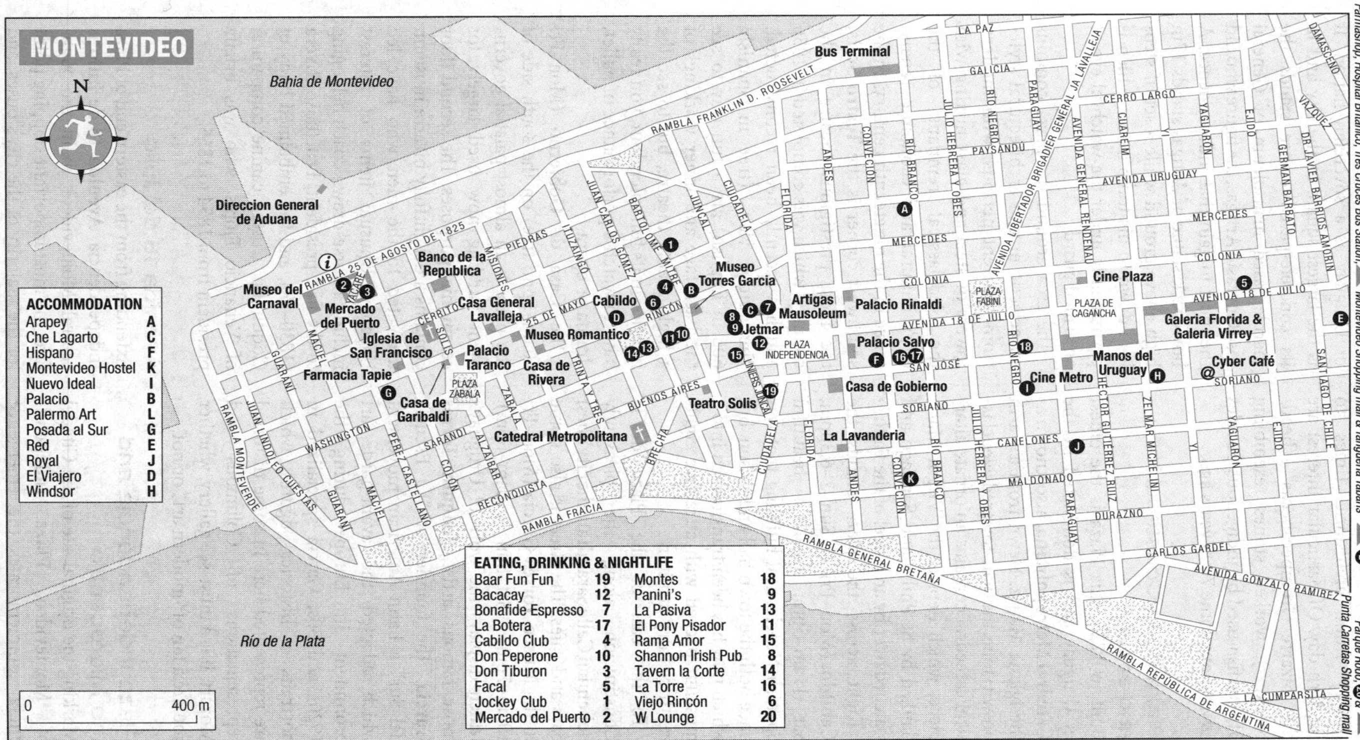
MONTEVIDEO
Farmashop, Hospital Britanico, Tres Cruces Bus Station,
Montevideo Shopping mall & Tanguería Tabaris
Parque Rodo, 20 & Punta Carretas Shopping mall
Bahia de Montevideo
Río de la Plata
Direccion General de Aduana
Bus Terminal
Museo del Carnaval
Mercado del Puerto
Iglesia de San Francisco
Farmacia Tapie
Casa de Garibaldi
Banco de la Republica
Casa General Lavalleja
Palacio Taranco
Museo Romantico
Casa de Rivera
Cabildo
Catedral Metropolitana
Museo Torres Garcia
Artigas Mausoleum
Jetmar
Teatro Solis
Palacio Rinaldi
Palacio Salvo
Casa de Gobierno
La Lavanderia
Cine Plaza
Cine Metro
Manos del Uruguay
Galeria Florida & Galeria Virrey
Cyber Café
PLAZA ZABALA
PLAZA INDEPENDENCIA
PLAZA FABINI
PLAZA DE CAGANCHA
RAMBLA 25 DE AGOSTO DE 1825
RAMBLA FRANKLIN D. ROOSEVELT
RAMBLA MONTEVERDE
RAMBLA FRACIA
RAMBLA GENERAL BRETAÑA
RAMBLA REPÚBLICA DE ARGENTINA
AVENIDA 18 DE JULIO
AVENIDA LIBERTADOR BRIGADIER GENERAL JA LAVALLEJA
AVENIDA GENERAL RENDENAU
AVENIDA URUGUAY
AVENIDA GONZALO RAMIREZ
LA PAZ
GALICIA
RÍO NEGRO
PARAGUAY
PAYSANDÚ
JULIO HERRERA Y OBES
RÍO BRANCO
CONVECIÓN
ANDES
FLORIDA
CIUDADELA
JUNCAL
BARTOLOME MITRE
JUAN CARLOS GÓMEZ
ITUZAINGÓ
PIEDRAS
MISIONES
25 DE MAYO
CERRITO
RINCÓN
SOLIS
YACARE
MACIEL
GUARANI
JUAN LINDOLFO CUESTAS
WASHINGTON
PÉREZ CASTELLANO
SARANDI
COLÓN
ALZAIBAR
ZABALA
TRINTA Y TRES
BUENOS AIRES
BRECHA
RECONQUISTA
LINIERS JUNCAL
SAN JOSÉ
SORIANO
CANELONES
MALDONADO
DURAZNO
CARLOS GARDEL
HÉCTOR GUTIÉRREZ RUIZ
ZELMAR MICHELINI
YI
YAGUARÓN
EJIDO
SANTIAGO DE CHILE
CERRO LARGO
CUAREIM
MERCEDES
COLONIA
GERMAN BARBATO
DR JAVIER BARRIOS AMORIN
VAZQUEZ
DAMASCENO
LA CUMPARSITA
ACCOMMODATION
Arapey A
Che Lagarto C
Hispano F
Montevideo Hostel K
Nuevo Ideal I
Palacio B
Palermo Art L
Posada al Sur G
Red E
Royal J
El Viajero D
Windsor H
EATING, DRINKING & NIGHTLIFE
Baar Fun Fun 19
Bacacay 12
Bonafide Espresso 7
La Botera 17
Cabildo Club 4
Don Peperone 10
Don Tiburon 3
Facal 5
Jockey Club 1
Mercado del Puerto 2
Montes 18
Panini's 9
La Pasiva 13
El Pony Pisador 11
Rama Amor 15
Shannon Irish Pub 8
Tavern la Corte 14
La Torre 16
Viejo Rincón 6
W Lounge 20
0 400 m
N

history from prehistoric times to modern day. Of particular interest are the bizarre "rompecabecas" (head-breakers), worked stones resembling 3D starfish used by indigenous peoples as weapons some 7000 years ago.

Plaza de la Constitución and around

Built in 1726, this Plaza is the oldest in Uruguay and is dominated by the **Catedral Metropolitana**, also known as the Iglesia Matriz. Hewn from a warm brown stone, the twin-towered, Neoclassical cathedral contains an ornate altarpiece, which depicts the Virgin Mary, flanked by St Philip and Santiago and watched over by an Angel of the Faith.

Right across the plaza stands the **Cabildo** (Mon–Fri & Sun 2–6.30pm, Sat 11am–5pm; free), a beautiful Spanish Neoclassical building that was once both the town hall and prison, but which now has been transformed into a museum packed with attractive eighteenth-century furniture.

To the east of the Plaza de la Constitución along the pleasantly bohemian Calle Sarandí are the city's best bars and cafés. The street is also home to the **Museo Torres Garcia** (Mon–Fri 10am–7pm, Sat–Sun 10am–6pm), which displays the work of Uruguay's most famous artist, **Joaquín Torres Garcia**. The founder of "La Escuela del Sur", a Latin-American movement which adapted the avant-garde art prominent in Europe during the 1920s and 30s, Garcia specialized in portraits of historical figures, which are represented here in some distorted representations of Columbus and Mozart. It is a must-see gallery, whether you are a fan of "modern art" or not.

Plaza Independencia and the Microcentro

Marking the original site of the Citadel of Montevideo, **Plaza Independencia** commemorates the emergence of Uruguay as a sovereign nation. It is the largest square in the city and in its concrete-paved centre stands the marble-based mausoleum of General José Gervasio Artigas, the figure who did the most to gain that independence. A horseback statue of Artigas stands 17m high above ground while a set of steps lead down to his tomb below, which is permanently under the watchful eye of an armed guard.

The area around the plaza contains an eclectic mix of architectural styles from different periods, with modern towers of steel and glass mixing with the Neoclassical remnants of the city's cultural and economic renaissance in the nineteenth century. In the southwest corner is the **Teatro Solis,** the most prestigious theatre in the country, which was completed in 1856 and has recently been reconstructed. The guided visits (free in Spanish, 60$ in English) are a fun way to see the backstage and inner workings of a high-quality theatre, but to see the interior in its full splendour, you really have to watch a performance of ballet, drama or opera.

The **Casa de Gobierno** (Mon–Fri 10am–5pm; free) on the south side of the plaza is an almost palatial government building now used largely for ceremonial purposes. The second floor contains a delightfully bizarre museum dedicated to the men who have led Uruguay. Unusual items of interest include a horse-drawn coach belonging to the first president, Fructuoso Rivera (1830–34), and the embalmed body of Coquimbo, trusted canine companion of Venancio Flores, who was briefly president from 1854 to 1855.

Avenida 18 de Julio

Extending from the eastern end of Plaza Independencia, **Avenida 18 de Julio** is central Montevideo's main thoroughfare; the most important stopping point for the majority of the city's buses, and a paradise for shoppers, who cram its pavements searching for the latest deals from fashionable boutiques to colourful street-sellers.

Plaza Fabini, a verdant square along the *avenida*, features a statue of combative gauchos created by the renowned Uruguayan sculptor José Belloni. A few blocks further east is the **Plaza de Cagancha**, an excellent **artisan market**, in which you will find handmade jewellery and leather clothes for much cheaper prices than in the Ciudad Vieja itself. Nearby, **free lifts** can be accessed at the back of the Intendencia Municipal building. They give magnificent panoramas of the surroundings as they climb the main tower, but the lifts operate inconsistently.

Arrival and information

Air Carrasco International Airport (ⓦwww.aic.com.uy) is 25km east of the city centre. Regular buses (17$, 1hr) depart every 15min or so from outside the arrivals building to the city centre, a journey of approximately an hour. Taxis take about 30min to reach the city centre and cost around 230$.
Bus All intercity buses operate out of Tres Cruces **bus station**, 2km northeast of the centre. From here take buses marked #180, #187 or "Aduana" (UR$11, 15min) for the city centre.
Ferry The port terminal, in the **Ciudad Vieja**, is a 10min walk north of the Plaza Independencia. The city tourist office can provide schedules, but you can also check these on the website of the main ferry company serving the Port, Buquebus (ⓦwww.buquebus.com, ⓣ00 5411/4316-6500). For ticket costs, see the 'Crossing into Argentina' box in the 'Moving on' section.
Tourist Office The main **office** is located on La Rambla 25 de Agosto de 1825 (Mon–Fri 10am–6pm, Sat–Sun 10am–4pm; ⓣ02/188-5100). It can provide you with maps, a useful city walks leaflet and a copy of Pimba, the monthly events magazine. There are also information **kiosks** at the airport and at Tres Cruces bus station.
Travel Agents Jetmar, Plaza Independencia 725, can help in arranging trips to neighbouring countries, or with finding cheap flights to other continents.

City transport

Most of the points of interest in the city are within walking distance of **Plaza Independencia**, but those a little farther out are easily accessed by bus.
Buses There are no route maps available for tourists, but most buses depart to the city outskirts from **Bus Terminal Río Branco** (Rambla Franklin D. Roosevelt and Río Branco) and stop along Avenida 18 de Julio. Buses heading for the centre are marked **"Aduana"**. There is no city transport pass, but the standard ticket for buses is very cheap (17$).
Taxis Journeys within the confines of the city rarely amount to more than 50$. Beware of overcharging and ensure that metered taxis reset their **meters** before starting a journey. Fono-taxi (ⓣ02/203-7000) is one reputable provider; as with the other operators, however, there is not much English spoken here.

Accommodation

Accommodation in Montevideo is, on the whole, very reasonably priced and you should have no problem finding a good room. There are several cheap options in the **centre**, but be warned that the port is a notorious red light district and that the Ciudad Vieja itself can be **unsafe** at night.

Hostels

All of the following provide free internet and breakfast.
Che Lagarto Independencia 713 ⓣ02/903-0175, ⓔmontevideo@chelagarto.com. *Che Lagarto* is a hostel on the central plaza that has a lively bar and a bright central patio. The dorm rooms are cozy if a little cramped, and the place has a pleasantly relaxing atmosphere; Dorms ❸.
El Viajero Ituzaingo 1436 ⓣ02/915-6192, ⓦwww.ciudadviejahostel.com. A lively hostel that provides tango and Spanish lessons, in addition to a bar, terrace with barbeque and all the usual mod cons; Dorms ❸.
Montevideo Canelones 935 ⓣ02/908-1324, ⓦwww.montevideohostel.com.uy. Set in a bright blue, colonial-style townhouse, this hostel is in a constant state of rebuilding, but provides friendly service and free bikes to tour the city; Dorms for HI Members/Non-Members ❷–❸.
Palermo Art Gaboto 1010 ⓣ02/410-6519, ⓔinfo@palermoarthostel.com. Set 2km away from the Ciudad Vieja, Palermo Art combines good new

facilities with a set of funky art exhibitions created both by local artists and some clearly spaced-out backpackers; Dorms ❸.

Red San José 1406 ⓣ02/908-8514, ⓦwww.redhostel.com. This new hostel is close to the good-value restaurants of San José, and boasts cozy rooms, as well as a gym and large terrace to help relax in the city; Dorms ❸.

Hotels

These hotels offer rooms with both shared and private bathrooms.

Arapey Av Uruguay 925 ⓣ02/900-7032. A cozy, inexpensive hotel with spacious double rooms (all ensuite and with cable TV) that offer a comfortable alternative to a hostel dorm; Doubles ❹

Hispano Convención 1317 ⓣ 02/900-3816. Located near the shops of Av 18 de Julio, this small hotel has pleasant, light rooms and all the mod cons (including launderette and internet access), which makes spending those extra few pesos worthwhile; Singles/Doubles ❺–❻

Nuevo Ideal Soriano 1073 ⓣ02/908-2913. Outside the Ciudad Vieja in a less touristy party of town, this pension provides basic but cheap rooms with smiling, friendly staff; Singles/Doubles ❹–❺

Palacio Bartolomé Mitre 1364 ⓣ02/916-3612, ⓔfpalaez@internet.co.uy. A grand old hotel in an excellent location within stumbling distance of the Ciudad Vieja's bars. The rooms on the higher floors are at least 50$ more expensive, but they have fine views in addition to TV and private bathrooms; Singles/Doubles ❹–❺

Posada al Sur Pérez Castellano 1424, Ciudad Vieja, ⓣ02/916-5287, ⓦwww.posadaalsur.com.uy. This small hotel, situated in the heart of the Ciudad Vieja, offers cheap tango and Pilates lessons, bike rentals and some beautifully decorated rooms. It prides itself as a base for sustainable tourism, and thus you can even enjoy breakfast knowing that it comes from local organic farms; Singles/Doubles ❹–❺

Royal Soriano 1120 ⓣ02/908-3115. If you are looking for a room with private bathrooms and cable TV, the *Royal* provides the best option of all the cheaper hotels; Singles/Doubles ❹

Windsor Zelmar Michelini 1260 ⓣ02/901-5080. A slightly dog-eared place with fading décor and basic, unexciting rooms, but it is clean, quiet, and has an enticing price; Singles/Doubles ❷–❸

Eating

Café culture isn't well developed in Montevideo but it's worth stopping for a cheap delicious cup of Uruguayan coffee; particularly good options can be found in Ciudad Vieja. The city is awash with good restaurants, with beef featuring heavily on most menus. Some of the best-value places can be found near several hostels on San José but you should also try out the restaurants in the Ciudad Vieja, which have top-quality cuisine at excellent prices.

Restaurants

Don Peperone Sarandí 654. Along with an excellent whiskey collection, this place offers a good-value lunch buffet (180$) and some refined Italian main courses (200–250$).

Don Tiburon Pérez Castellano 1569, just outside the Mercado del Puerto, serves some reasonably-priced mains that are more varied than the average steak-and-fries, although even the "Petit filet de lomo" will defeat all but the biggest appetites. Steaks 250–350$.

Mercado del Puerto Pérez Castellano, opposite the Ferry terminal. This market is a truly unforgettable experience for all carnivores, with a mouthwatering collection of grill-restaurants that will leave you spoilt for choice. Meat dominates most menus, but the grilled seafood comes straight from the Atlantic, so don't miss out.

El Palenque Pérez Castellano, inside the market. With an enormous fiery grill and vintage hams hung all around, this is the pick of the Mercado grill-restaurants, and offers both steak and a tempting range of seafood paellas, all of which are sure to be enormous. Mains 200–400$.

Panini's Bacacay 1339. *Panini's* is an upmarket Italian with some excellent home-made ravioli and gnocchis that are surprisingly cheap (200–300$).

Rama Amor Bacacay 1333. Some tasty seafood dishes and classic pizzas recipes for a fair price and in a small, cozy setting (200–300$).

La Torre Convención 1324. A *Parrillada* favoured by *montevideanos* for its live football, lively atmosphere and large helpings of steak and pizza. Their lunch buffet (*tenedor libre*) is 190$.

Cafés

Bonafide Espresso Independencia 711. The favourite coffee spot for local city slickers, this café in the central Plaza has a top range of coffees (70$), some delicious chocolate snacks (200$) and the latest international papers to read.

Facal Av 18 de Julio 1239. This place serves some nice salads in the heart of the shopping district. Open Sun–Fri 8am–4pm; Sat 8am–6pm. The 3-course set menu is 125$.

Montes San José 1075. You can get sandwiches and soft drinks here, but the real highlight is the pastry collection. The delicious giant *alfajore* (cookie-sandwich) is 150$.

La Pasiva Sarandí 600. A *cervecería* that offers good coffee and *chivitos* (sandwiches) for around 120$ in the relaxed surroundings of Plaza Constitución.

Drinking, nightlife and entertainment

There are a number of good bars in the area between **Plaza Independencia** and **Plaza Constitución,** the most lively area being on and around **Bartolomé Mitre.** You should be careful, however, as the Ciudad Vieja can be dark and potentially unsafe in the evening, especially away from the tourist streets. The area around Punta Carretas shopping centre, southeast of the centre, is popular with younger drinkers, particularly on Thursday nights. Montevideo's best nightclubs are outside the centre but can be reached cheaply by taxi.

Bars and Clubs

Baar Fun Fun Cuidadela 1229. Open since 1895, *Fun Fun* is a small place steeped in the history of tango, and you can watch some top tango singers (though strangely not the dancers) while you try the house speciality drink, the potent 'Uvita' (similar to brandy) for just 80$.

Cabildo Club Bartolomé Mitre 1367. Full of energetic and trendy dancers, this club serves a wide range of novelty beers and cocktails (60–110$) and is regularly packed to bursting point.

La Botera San José 907 (8pm onwards). *La Botera* is the fanciest bar on San José and has a good range of cocktail classics for around 100$, but you do have to pay an entrance fee (70$) on popular evenings.

Jockey Club Bartolomé Mitre 1396. This place has a bizarre blend of British pub and continental café style décor, but it gets lively in the evening with the televised football and provides another good whiskey stop (60–100$ for a shot).

El Pony Pisador Bartolomé Mitre 1330. This is a chilled-out spot for sharing a beer (70$ for 0.5lt) or some fine wines, with bottles from local vineyards starting from 160$.

Shannon Irish Pub Bartolomé Mitre 1318. No capital city would be complete without its Irish pub, but the *Shannon* does more than just fulfil the stereotype, providing regular live music and some excellent real ales (110$ for 0.7lt) alongside the Guinness.

TREAT YOURSELF

Bacacay Bacacay 1316. Bacacay has a pricey but top class set of whiskies and cocktails (110-140$). You can cap a refined evening with some fine Spanish-language drama or music at the nearby Teatro Solis.

Tavern La Corte Sarandí 586. This hip restaurant/bar with the décor of a German beer cellar serves pricey but high-quality beers (100$ for 0.7 lt) and wines (300$ for Argentinian labels). If you want to mingle with the great and the good of Montevideo, this is your place. The barmen are only too keen to tell you that former US President George W. Bush has been a recent guest!

Viejo Rincón Rincón 619. A fashionable club in the Ciudad Vieja, with a good range of drinks and the latest chart dance tunes from 11pm onwards.

W Lounge Rambla Wilson s/n. Mon–Sat, from 11pm onwards. Set 3km away from the Ciudad Vieja, this club requires a 10$ taxi ride but is nevertheless the city's main nightspot for all ages, featuring a complex of restaurants and discos with live shows.

Cinemas

Many films are in English with Spanish subtitles, though it's always best to ask regarding the popular Hollywood titles. Tickets range from 60–80$.

Cine Plaza Plaza Cagancha. Large multiplex which offers the latest Hollywood blockbusters.

Cine Metro San José 1211 (ⓣ02/902-2017). Montevideo's oldest cinema, the Metro mixes popular Western movies with some avant-garde, Spanish-language films.

Live Music and Theatre

Live rock or pop bands are apt to appear in the livelier city bars without any warning. If you are a **tango** enthusiast, head to the **Tanguería Tabaris** café on Tristán Narvaja 1518, for live dancing from 9pm onwards Tuesday–Sunday, although you might also see this on any busy night in the Mercado del Puerto. The **Teatro Solis** in the Plaza Independencia (ⓣ02/1950-3323, ⓦwww.teatrosolis.org.uy) is worth visiting just for its Neoclassical facade, but it also hosts the best of Uruguayan opera and theatre. Check out the website for the latest shows. Tickets are 200–300$ depending on where you sit.

Shopping

Avenida 18 de Julio is Montevideo's main commercial street, filled with shoppers seeking bargains in the many malls and boutiques. There are also some large malls located just outside of the city centre.

Arts and crafts

Manos del Uruguay San José 1111. This is the flagship store of the national chain. It typifies the rest of those stores with its range of expensive but high-quality woollen clothes (around 600$ for a thick sweater), all of which are handmade in Uruguay.

The Mercado de los Artesanos on Plaza de Cagancha offers cheaper prices, but you have to wade through lots of unoriginal tourist souvenirs to find the best bargains.

Designer Stores

The eastern end of Avenida 18 de Julio is the home of fashionable boutiques and Western stores in the city centre. **Galeria Florida** and **Galeria Virrey** (between Zelmar Michelini and Ejido) are filled with stores selling leather clothes and electronic goods at low prices.

Shopping Centres

Outside the centre, there are several large American-style malls with many Western chains. The biggest two are **Montevideo Shopping** (Luis Alberto de Herrera 1290) and Punta Carretas Shopping (Eliauri 350), for which you need the #121 and #427 buses respectively. These can be caught from the bus stops along Av 18 de Julio.

Directory

Embassies and Consulates Australia, Cerro Largo 1000 ⓣ02/901-0743; Argentina, Cuareim 1470 ⓣ02/902-8166; Brazil, Blvr Gral Artigas 1328 ⓣ02/707-2119; Canada, Plaza Independencia 749 ⓣ02/902-2030; UK, Marco Bruto 1073 ⓣ02/622-3630; US, Dr L Muller 1776 ⓣ02/418-7777.

Exchange Money can be exchanged in most of the major bank branches, but casas de cambio are in evidence throughout the city especially along 18 de Julio and offer better rates.

Hospitals Public ambulances will take patients to several hospitals on the outskirts; Hospital Britanico, near the Tres Cruces Bus Station on Italia 2400 (ⓣ02/487-1020), offers good private healthcare.

Internet There is a 24hr café at Tres Cruces, adjacent to the bus terminal (30$/hour), and many cyber cafés in the centre. The best-value places are just off the major roads such as 18 de Julio. Cyber Café (8am–midnight, 10$ per hour) at Soriano 909.

Laundries Most of the hostels have cheap laundry services available There are no self-service laundrettes but La Lavanderia, Andes 1333, ⓣ02/903-0369 charges UR$85 for wash and dry of a backpack full of clothes.

Left Luggage There is a 24hr left luggage room and lockers with storage for several days in the Tres Cruces station.

Pharmacies Farmacia Tapie at 25 de Mayo 315(ⓣ 02/915-4848) provides basic healthcare provisions in the Ciudad Vieja. Farmashop(ⓦwww .farmashop.com.uy) is a national Pharmacy chain with several branches in Montevideo. It has a store which is open 24hr, 7 days a week at

CROSSING INTO ARGENTINA

At the time of writing, the political discord between Argentina and Uruguay means that no buses are connecting Montevideo and Buenos Aires. **Aerolineas Argentinas**, Plaza Independencia 749 (ⓣ02/902-3694, ⓦwww.aerolineas .com.ar) has two daily flights to Buenos Aires (US$80, 1hr). Buquebus ferries (ⓣ00 5411/4316-6500, ⓦwww.buquebus.com) link Buenos Aires with Montevideo and Colonia del Sacramento. Every day, two **ferries** leave from Montevideo (in the morning and late afternoon) to the Argentinian capital (US$69, 3hr), although Buquebus also runs a **bus** that connects with the fast ferry leaving from Colonia del Sacramento, completing the journey in the same time for only US$36. From Colonia itself, there are 7–9 daily departures to Buenos Aires. While most of these are on the **fast ferry** (US$35, 1hr), there is also a morning and afternoon departure on slower boats that take two hours longer (US$26). The cheapest and most picturesque ferry crossing, however, is operated by Cacciola (ⓣ00 5411/4749-0931, ⓦwww .cacciolaviajes.com) between Tigre, a northern suburb of Buenos Aires and Carmelo, a one hour bus ride (5$) to the west of Colonia (US$5, 3hr).

Av Italia 6958 (Ⓣ02/604-4161), but you'll need a taxi to get there.
Post office Buenos Aires 451 Ⓣ02/916-0200.

Moving on

Air There are flights to Asunción in Paraguay (1 daily, 2hr), Buenos Aires (see box), Lima (1 daily, 4hr), Santiago in Chile (1 daily, 5hr), Sao Paulo (6 daily, 2hr 30min). Passengers must pay US$16 tax if they are headed to Argentina, and US$29 to other international destinations.
Bus From the Tres Cruces bus terminal, there are regular services to Colonia del Sacramento (120$, 2hr 30min), Minas (90$, 2hr), Punta del Este (100$, 2hr 30min). Rutas del Sol (Ⓣ02/402-5451) have 1 or 2 services everyday to La Paloma and Punta del Diablo. Check out Ⓦwww.trescruces.com.uy for the latest timetables.

Western Uruguay

Western Uruguay has often been neglected by visitors heading for the beaches on the other side of the country, yet here you will find Colonia del Sacramento, one of the most beautiful and understated towns on the whole continent, as well as a set of nearby towns filled with the cultural resonance and architectural gems of ages past and present.

COLONIA DEL SACRAMENTO

Originally a seventeenth-century Portuguese smuggling port designed to disrupt the Spanish base of Buenos Aires across the Río de la Plata, Colonia del Sacramento (often referred to simply as "Colonia") is a picturesque town with fascinating museums, plenty of outdoor activities and the best café culture in Uruguay. Despite an increasing number of tourists visiting the town, it retains a sleepy indifference to the outside world and you should consider spending a few days to get to know it better.

The Barrio Histórico

The highlight of any trip to Colonia is undoubtedly the atmospheric **Barrio Histórico** (the old quarter), a UNESCO World Heritage Site that will spirit you into the past simply by strolling around its cobbled alleyways. The former colonial port area is centred on the **Plaza Mayor,** from which radiates out streets of honey-coloured buildings and palm and orange trees. The remains of the old city gates, the **Puerta del Campo,** lie at the bottom end of Calle Manuel Lobo, where they were once charged with protecting the important trade centre from invading forces; now they are permanently open to tourists and separate old Colonia from the new city.

The central museums

Dotted around the Barrio Histórico is a series of seven museums (all open Mon–Sun 11am–5pm). These can all be visited on a single 25$ ticket available from the **Museo Municipal,** on the west side of Plaza Mayor, where you will also find an extensive natural history display. Worth keeping an eye out for are the incredible photographs of an immense blue whale washed up on a nearby beach, and the beautiful natural history collages made up from colourful birds' feathers and snail shells. The other museums deserve a peek if you have time, especially the **Museo Español** on Calle de España, which exhibits Spanish colonial items, including numerous examples of period dress, and the **Museo Indígena** at the bottom of Avenida General Flores, a private collection of indigenous artefacts.

The Barrio Histórico

On Calle San Francisco, at the southwest corner of the plaza and next to the ruins of a former nunnery is the **lighthouse**

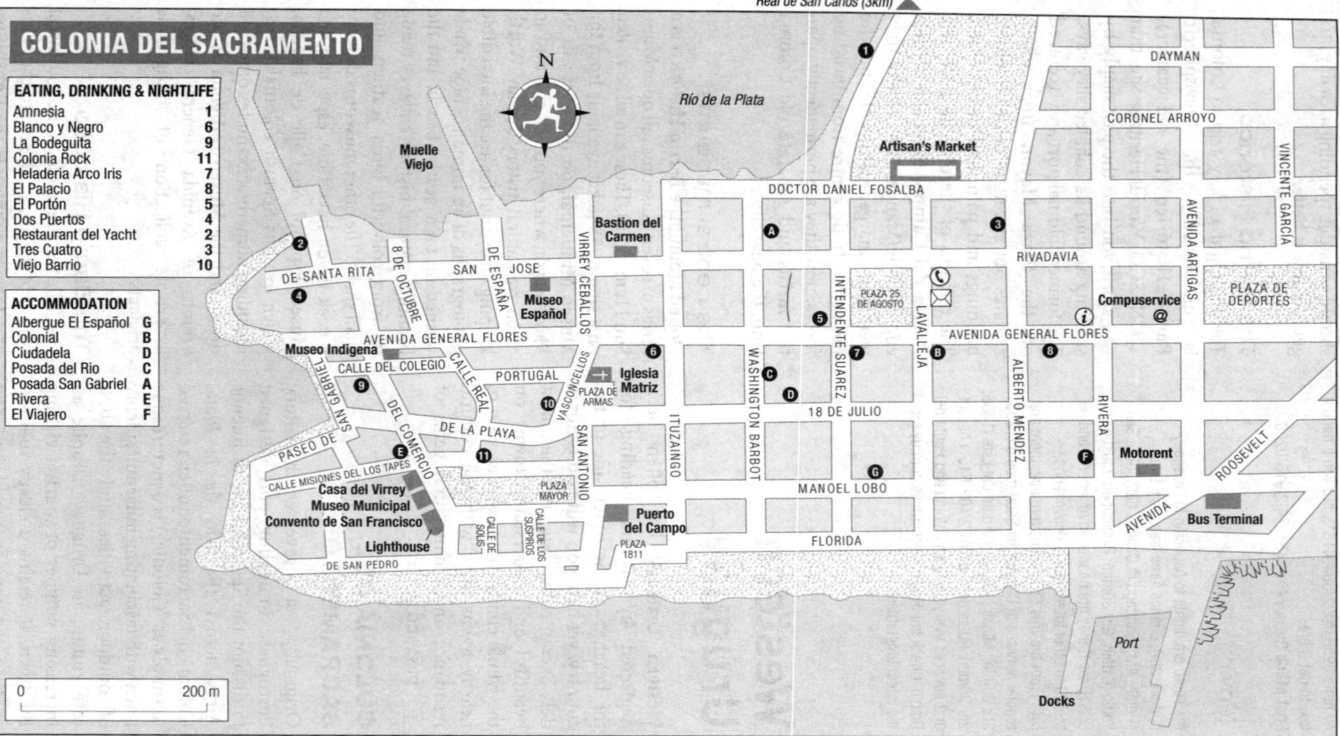
COLONIA DEL SACRAMENTO
EATING, DRINKING & NIGHTLIFE
Amnesia 1
Blanco y Negro 6
La Bodeguita 9
Colonia Rock 11
Heladeria Arco Iris 7
El Palacio 8
El Portón 5
Dos Puertos 4
Restaurant del Yacht 2
Tres Cuatro 3
Viejo Barrio 10
ACCOMMODATION
Albergue El Español G
Colonial B
Ciudadela D
Posada del Rio C
Posada San Gabriel A
Rivera E
El Viajero F
Real de San Carlos (3km)
Colonia Shopping (1km)
Río de la Plata
Muelle Viejo
Artisan's Market
Bastion del Carmen
Museo Español
Museo Indigena
Iglesia Matriz
Plaza de Armas
Plaza 25 de Agosto
Plaza de Deportes
Plaza Mayor
Plaza 1811
Puerto del Campo
Casa del Virrey
Museo Municipal
Convento de San Francisco
Lighthouse
Compuservice
Motorent
Bus Terminal
Port
Docks
Dayman
Coronel Arroyo
Vincente García
Avenida Artigas
Doctor Daniel Fosalba
Rivadavia
Avenida General Flores
Intendente Suarez
Lavalleja
Alberto Mendez
Rivera
Washington Barbot
18 de Julio
Ituzaingo
Manoel Lobo
Florida
Roosevelt
Avenida
Virrey Ceballos
San Jose
De España
8 de Octubre
De Santa Rita
Calle del Colegio
Calle Real
Portugal
Vasconcellos
San Gabriel
Del Comercio
De la Playa
San Antonio
Paseo de
Calle Misiones del los Tapes
Calle de Solis
Calle de los Suspiros
De San Pedro
0
200 m

(Mon–Sun 10am–5pm; 20$), which affords great views of the surroundings from the cupola. A few blocks north of the plaza, the **Iglesia Matriz** claims to be the oldest church in Uruguay. Although systematically demolished and rebuilt by various occupying forces, it retains some columns from the original Portuguese building constructed in 1730. Adjacent to the church the **Plaza Manuel Lobo** contains the foundations of the former governor's mansion, which was also a mid-eighteenth century structure.

To the north of the Barrio Histórico

Calle Virrey y Cevallos leads you to the northern side of the Peninsula, where you'll encounter the **Bastión del Carmen,** with walls dating from the time of Governor Vasconcellos (1722–49). Later converted into a factory producing soap and gelatine products, a red brick chimney from the period dated 1880 still stands. Today it operates as a theatre with a small outdoor museum dedicated to its history.

Real de San Carlos

From the Bastion, the Rambla Costanera runs along a wide-arcing beach to the unusual resort of **Real de San Carlos**, which is also accessible by bus (10min, 5$) from the bottom end of Avenida Gral Flores. Originally the brainchild of millionaire Nicolas Mihanovic, who conceived the idea of an exclusive tourist complex for rich Argentines, it now lies largely deserted. Between 1903 and 1912, he constructed a magnificent bullring, which was used only eight times in two years, a frontón court which now lies decaying and a racecourse, which is the only part of the resort still operational. Regular **horse races** take place approximately every second Sunday, and the horses can frequently be seen exercising along the nearby beach. If you fancy a ride yourself, *Hostel Colonial* organises **horseriding** trips for up to 4 hours (450$) to the forests and wineries outside town.

> **TREAT YOURSELF**
>
> If you are tired of just ambling around Colonia on foot, Motorent at Manuel Lobo 505 (☎052/522-9665, Ⓦwww.motorent.com.uy) lets you rent out **motor-scooters** (150$/hour), 2-person buggies (300$/hour), or even **4-person golf carts** (500$/hour) to rampage around the streets. The hostels also offer free or cheap bikes to take out around town.

Arrival and information

Bus and ferry The terminal and port are both located three blocks to the south of Av Gral Flores (the main street). The town centre is 10min walking distance to the west along Manuel de Lobos.

Tourist office Corner of Av Gral Flores y Rivera (daily 9am–7pm; ☎052/26141, Ⓦwww.colonia.gub.uy).

Internet Compuservice, Av Gral Flores 547, open 9am–midnight. 15$/hour.

Accommodation

Prices for accommodation, although rising, are on the whole very reasonable in Colonia, and the comparatively compact nature of the city means that most boast a convenient location. There are currently no official camping grounds in the area.

Hostels

Albergue El Español Manuel Lobo 377 ☎052/30759. A cheap, well-equipped hostel close to the Barrio Histórico; the rooms are quite dark but if you are looking for a quiet, peaceful place to stay, this is your best option; Dorms ❷

Colonial Gral Flores 440 ☎052/28151. The official HI hostel is set in a charming nineteenth-century courtyard, which is surrounded by two floors of simple, clean dorms. There are bike rentals and communal Cable TV for those missing their home comforts; Dorms for HI Members/Non-Members ❷–❸

El Viajero Washington Barbot 164 ☎052/22683, Ⓦwww.elviajerohostels.com. A new hostel with a lively bar and a rooftop terrace. Unlike other hostels, *Viajero* provides a free (and fruity) breakfast, and while the ordinary dorm rooms are perfectly amenable, you can also pamper yourself by sleeping in one of the deluxe suites with TV and DVD; Dorms/Suites ❸–❹

Hotels

All these hotels provide rooms with TV, private bathrooms, and a free breakfast.

Ciudadela 18 de Julio 315 ☎052/21183. A modern hotel without the fun atmosphere of the hostels, but with friendly staff and spacious rooms. Rooms with TV and a/c cost 100$ more; Singles/Doubles ❺–❻

Posada del Río Washington Barbot 258 ☎052/23002, ⓦwww.colonianet.com/delrio. A friendly *Posada* located 50 metres from the river. It offers a smaller courtyard to relax in than some of the others, but the rooms are comfortable and it's worth the money simply for the easy stroll you can make down to the waterside; Singles/Doubles ❹–❺

Posada San Gabriel del Comercio 127 ☎052/23283. This bright, airy posada is in the heart of the Old Town and has comfortable doubles (though no singles); With/without river view ❺–❻

Rivera Rivera 131 ☎052/20807. A basic hotel with fairly dark rooms, but it's also just a 5min walk from the bus terminal and Port. It's your best option if you are exhausted having jumped off the bus or ferry; Singles/Doubles ❺–❻

Eating

Although the restaurants in the **Barrio Histórico** are pricey, the quality on the whole is excellent and the charming ambience of the surroundings is hard to beat. Yet some excellent dining spots exist outside the **Old Town,** and offer superb steaks and seafood for a more affordable price.

Dos Puertos Santa Rita 40. This *parrilla* has a refined atmosphere, but that does not stop it serving some huge portions of steak. Mains 300–400$.

El Palacio Av Gral. Flores 466. An unassuming café on the main street heading into town, *El Palacio* serves vegetarian sandwiches and cheese-laden pasta dishes (100–180$).

El Portón Av Gral Flores 333. *El Portón* is undoubtedly the locals´ favourite *parrilla* and for good reason. It serves hearty portions of steak for very good prices (100–150$).

Heladeria Arco Iris Av Gral. Flores 362. Here you can get monster one litre tubs (170$) with all your favourite South American ice-cream flavours.

La Bodeguita del Comercio165. A hip restaurant tucked away in the Old Town, which offers surprisingly large and tasty pizzas considering the low price (60$), as well as a decent range of pasta dishes (150–180$).

Restaurant del Yacht Santa Rita s/n, Puerto Deportivo. If you fancy some excellent seafood for a fair price, then head for this yacht club, in which you can partake in the generally refined, nautical air as you survey some pretty views across the River Plate. Mains 200–250$.

Drinking and nightlife

Amnesia Corner of Suarez and Daniel Fosalba. While *Amnesia* is stuck out near the Artisans' Market, it's still popular with the local grunge crowd thanks to the heavy metal and rock that are its evening staples.

Blanco y Negro Av Gral. Flores 242. A self-consciously 'cool' jazz bar that offers live music on Fri & Sat from 10pm onwards. It's worth dressing slightly smarter than usual (though no suit is required); this place draws a sophisticated set of Jazz lovers.

Colonia Rock Corner of Real and Misiones de los Tapas. A hip bar serving a fine set of cocktails (130–170$) to a mainly tourist and backpacker crowd. Has live bands at the weekend.

Tres Cuatro Corner of Daniel Fosalba and Mendez. If you want to get down to some booming R 'n' B or hip-hop with the local teenagers, this is your place, although you should be prepared to face a 50$ entrance fee on popular nights.

Viejo Barrio Vasconcellos 169. The wine at this bar can be ordered by the jug, or *jarra*, and is surprisingly cheap (160$ for a bottle). Outdoor seating and some tasty *chivitos* and desserts makes it a comfortable spot to people-watch.

Shopping

The **Barrio Histórico** is littered with fashionable, pricey boutiques selling locally-made goods, but the best deals for handicrafts are to be found either at the **Feria**, or **Artisans' Market** (Calle Daniel Fosalba, 11am–late afternoon) or in the streets around the **Palacio Municipal** in the west of the town centre. For clothes shopping, **Colonia Shopping** is a large mall on Ruta 1 that offers lots of Western and designer stores. It can be reached by picking up the yellow buses along Av Gral Flores.

Moving on

Bus Carmelo (1hr, 50$); Colonia Suiza (50min, 50$); Montevideo (2hr 30min, 100$).

Ferry See p.920 for details of crossing the Río de la Plata to Buenos Aires.

DAY TRIPS FROM COLONIA DEL SACRAMENTO

The wineries and *estancias* in the vicinity of Colonia that accept tourists are all at least 10km from the nearest main roads, so you will have to organize a tour if you wish to make a visit. **Beatrix Rivas** (ⓣ0995-21060, ⓔcariber@internet.com.uy) is an English-speaking guide in Colonia who offers local tours starting from 200$.

On the eastern approach to Colonia from Montevideo is the charming town of **Colonia Suiza,** which is filled with the characteristic chalets of nineteenth-century Swiss settlers and a set of expensive boutiques stocking cheese varieties that would make the home country proud. Located 77km west of Colonia del Sacramento along Ruta 21, **Carmelo** is a quiet, pretty town blessed with some magnificent avenues of trees, the well-maintained Playa Seré river beach and by its proximity to the beautiful forested islands of the Río Uruguay. A **tourist office** (Mon–Sat 12.45–5.30pm) is located in the Casa de Cultura on 19 de Abril (the main road into town). The port, from which two ferries leave daily to Tigre in Argentina, is 1km to the south of town. Day-trips to the Isla San Martin (750$), a wooded island with nature reserve and camping facilities, are available through Cacciola (ⓣ0054 11/4393-6100, ⓦwww.cacciolaviajes.com).

Eastern Uruguay

Some of South America's finest and most unspoilt natural beauty awaits you in **Eastern Uruguay**. Inland, you can explore some of the finest pastoral landscapes in the country on the huge *estancias* around Minas. On the coast, you will pass a series of small coastal fishing villages that offer quiet beaches, wild surfing, and some lively hostels and bars. On the approach to the Brazilian border, the sight of whales diving off the Atlantic coast is not uncommon, while the shimmering *lagunas* (lagoons) are home to flocks of pink flamingos and rare black-necked swans. Yet if you do tire of such natural splendour, you can always retreat to Punta del Este, the most exclusive beach resort south of Río de Janeiro's Copacabana.

MINAS

A pretty market town far from the coastal tourist trail, Minas provides an excellent base for exploring the natural beauty and romantic traditions of Uruguay's interior. The **Plaza Libertad** is graced with a horseback statue of the national hero Juan Lavalleja and there is an impressive Cathedral nearby on Calle Roosevelt, but the real local highlights lie in the *estancias* outside town.

Arrival and Information

Bus Intercity **buses** arrive and depart from the Terminal de omnibuses (ⓣ044/29796) three blocks west of Plaza Libertad on Calle Treinta y Tres.
Tourist Office On the south side of the Plaza Libertad (daily 7am–7pm; ⓣ044/28691). The office can helps with the difficult transport connections to the *estancias*.
Internet There are several **Internet cafés** around the Plaza, offering fast access for 25$/hour.

Accommodation

It's worth booking ahead as accommodation is limited and fills up fast.
Posada Verdun Av Washington Beltrán 715 ⓣ044/24563. Cheapest place in town with clean, airy rooms with private bathrooms and TV; Singles/Doubles ④–⑤
Hotel Plaza Av Roosevelt 639 ⓣ044/ 22328. This place on the main square has clean, if slightly run-down, rooms; Singles/Doubles ④–⑤

ESTANCIAS TURISTICAS

No visit to the interior of the country would be complete without a stay on an **Estancia Turística,** a working ranch. Dotted throughout the country, these *estancias* offer a high level of accommodation coupled with the opportunity to get closely involved with day-to-day farm work, and many organize tours that involve birdwatching and horseriding. The ranches are split into broad categories: *quintas y chacras* (country estates); *granjas* (farming ranches); *serranos* (highland estates); and *llanuras* (prairie estates), each a subtly different take on the ranch lifestyle. You can view a full list of the *estancias* in the country with reservation details by visiting Ⓦwww.turismo.gub.uy. Around Minas, the two largest *estancias* currently operating are *El Abra* (Ⓣ 044/02869, Ⓦwww.lavalleja.com/elabra) and *Open Ranch* (Ⓣ044/02112). Both are around 15km outside town and charge around 1000$ for a tour and night's stay. Call ahead to see if you can organise transport with the owners; they frequently make trips into town and can provide a lift. Otherwise, you will have to pay for the taxi (400$ one-way).

Hotel Verdun Av 25 de Mayo 444 Ⓣ044/22110. The more modern and upmarket of the two central hotels comes with a pool, restaurant and a/c rooms with cable TV and DVD; Singles/Doubles ❻

Camping Arequita 10km north of town on Ruta 12 Ⓣ044/02503. There is a grocery store and a range of sporting facilities nearby, including football pitches and a swimming pool. Catch any bus heading north towards Melo on Ruta 12 and ask the driver to let you off at the campsite; Camping ❶

Eating and drinking

The best restaurants and bars are all clustered around the Plaza Libertad.

Almandoz Av Roosevelt 619. This Italian place makes tasty home-made pasta dishes (100–150$) that make up for the somewhat unoriginal, fast food-joint décor.

Hotel Verdun Restaurant Av 25 de Mayo 444. While it lacks the rustic charm of the *Libertad* next door, the hotel's modern restaurant provides a cooked breakfast and follows this with some classic steak and pasta main courses (130–145$) throughout the day.

Ki-Jola Domingo Perez 489. A down-to-earth Parrilla which does the basics right: the service is quick, the steaks are tender, and the price tag won't lighten your wallet unduly. Mains 100$.

Libertad Av Roosevelt 621. An old-fashioned bar normally packed with local farmers in flat caps, *Libertad* serves excellent red wine and *Grappa con miel* (Grappa with honey) at 50$ and also has an excellent range of Uruguayan red wines (130$ for a bottle).

Papo's Domingo Perez 487. Here you will find an impressive array of ice-cream flavours, including the bright blue and utterly delectable "Crema del Cielo".

TREAT YOURSELF

To blow away some of the travelling cobwebs, you can book into one of the plush Country Clubs that surround Minas. **Parque de Vacaciones** (Ⓣ044/30000, Ⓦwww.parquedevacaciones.com.uy) offers comfortable cabins, swimming pools, and a range of sporting activities including tennis, volleyball and even beach football; Singles/Doubles ❻–❼; Cabins ❼

PUNTA DEL ESTE

Situated on a narrow peninsula 140km east of Montevideo, **Punta del Este** is a jungle of high-rise hotels, expensive restaurants and casinos, bordered by some of the finest beaches on the coast. Exclusive, luxurious and often prohibitively expensive, it is a beach resort that is *the* place to be seen for many South American celebrities in summer. Yet while thriving and crowded between December and March, it is cold, deserted and largely closed in winter. The calmer waters on the bay side are preferred by recreational bathers, but the more turbulent Atlantic coast is a mecca for surfers and watersports enthusiasts.

The beaches

These are what attract most visitors to Punta del Este, and two of the best are on either side of the neck of the peninsula. **Watersports equipment** can be hired from Punta Surf School, Parada 3, Playa Brava (ⓣ042/481388, ⓦwww.sunvalleysurf.com), which also provides surfing lessons for all abilities (2000$ for a 6-hour course). **Playa Mansa** on the bay side is a huge arcing stretch of sand with plenty of space for sunbathing and gentler waves than the other beaches to the east.

Off the coast

From Playa Mansa, there are excellent views out to the wooded **Isla de Gorriti.** Formerly heavily fortified by the Spanish, and once visited by Sir Francis Drake, the Isla now forms a popular day-trip for bathers trying to escape the crowds on the mainland. Slightly further off the coast lies the **Isla de Lobos,** home to one of the largest sea lion colonies in the world. Both islands can be visited by expensive guided tours only; Calypso (Opposite La Galerna at the entrance to the harbour, ⓣ042/446152) offers a 2-hour

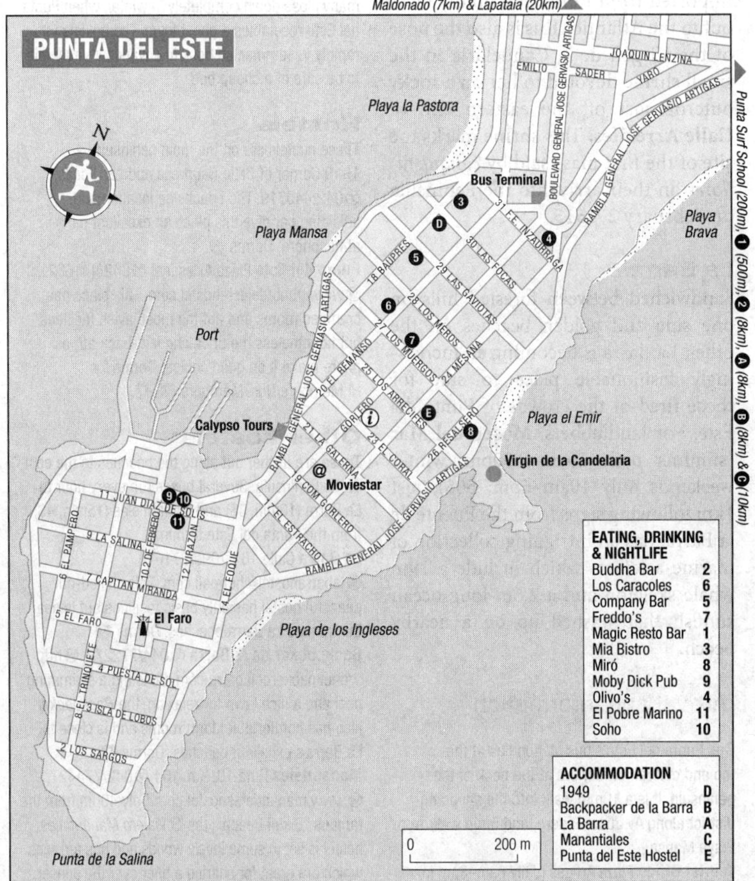

Island Tour for 1200$, with cruises leaving from the Port daily at 11.30am. You may be able to negotiate a better price if you are in a large group, but if simply seeing sea lions is your aim, it's also worth heading down to the port itself in the early morning: they are often out sunbathing as the fishermen set sail.

On the peninsula

If the beach lifestyle doesn't appeal, you can have a look at **El Faro** (lighthouse) on 2 de Febrero, although it is not open to the public. It was constructed from volcanic red brick imported from Rome and boldly faces out to the Atlantic. This is also the pose of the Virgen de la Candelaria in the small shrine devoted to her on a rocky outcrop just off the eastern end of **Calle Arrecifes.** This shrine marks the site of the first mass said by *conquistadores* on their arrival to the Peninsula on February 2, 1515.

La Barra

Sandwiched between forested hills on one side and golden beaches on the other, La Barra is becoming an increasingly fashionable place to stay for those tired of the crowds of Punta del Este. For landlubbers, **Museo del Mar** (summer daily 10am–8.30pm, winter weekends only 10am–6pm; 50$), just 1km following signs from the Puente de la Barra, has an intriguing collection of marine artefacts which include a 19m whale skeleton and a 2.6m-long ocean sunfish that washed up on a nearby beach.

Arrival and information

Bus Punta del Este's bus station lies at the top end of Avenida Gorlero at the neck of the peninsula. It is a 10min walk Into the shopping district along Av Juan Gorlero, and 5min walk from Playa Mansa.

Tourist Office Plaza Artigas (daily 8am–8pm in season, varies out of season; ⓣ042/446519).

Travel Agents Alvaro Gimeno Turismo (ⓣ042/490-570, ⓦwww.alvarogimenoturismo.com) in the Bus Terminal has tours to the Lagunas further east from Punta del Este. These are at least 1500$ for a full day, but there is no public transport service to the wetlands, so you may have to fork out. Otherwise, Parque Santa Teresa (see section on Punta del Diablo) offers some sheltered coves and ponds that contain many of the wild birds that flourish in the *lagunas*.

Internet Cyber cafés are pricey on the Peninsula, but the hostels all provide free access. The Moviestar locutorio, Av Juan Gorlero 632, charges 45$ per hour.

Accommodation

On the whole, the hotels here are overpriced and many close down completely in winter, when Punta del Este resembles a ghost town. The hostels fill rapidly in summer, so book in advance if you want to be sure of a cheap bed.

Hostels

These hostels are on the main peninsula

1949 Corner of Calle Baupresa and Las Focas, ⓣ042/440719. The beachside location and adjoining bar give this place an excellent party atmosphere; Dorms ❹

Punta del Este Plaza Artesanal ⓣ042/441632, ⓦwww.puntadelestehostel.com. This place has cramped rooms and not the most lavish facilities, but nonetheless the price and laid-back atmosphere make it an good choice; Dorms for HI Members/Non-Members ❸–❹

Other hostels

These are further out along the beaches to the east of the Peninsula. Several buses run every hour to La Barra (10min, 3$) and Manantiales (15min, 4$) from the Punta del Este terminal.

La Barra Calle 16 ⓣ099/271614 ⓔlabarrahostel@hotmail.com. This chilled-out, peaceful hostel has only basic facilities but is near the famous La Barra beaches; Dorms ❸

Backpacker de la Barra ⓣ044/772272, ⓦhttp://backpackerdelabarra.com. Boasting a swimming pool and a nice lawn for relaxing, the *Backpacker* also has comfortable dorm rooms and is close to La Barra´s excellent beaches; Dorms ❹

Manantiales Ruta 10, Km. 164 ⓣ042/774427, ⓦwww.manantialeshostel.com Only 400m from the famous "Bikini Beach", the *El Viajero Manantiales* hostel is set in some lovely woods and has terraces which are great for sharing a beer over the sunset; Dorms for HI Members/Non-members ❸–❹

Hotels in Maldonado

Hotel rates are typically more reasonable in Maldonado. From 6am until midnight, buses #17 and #19 leave every 5–10 minutes to Punta del Este (10min, 10$) from the small stop to the side of the main Bus Terminal in Maldonado, which is eight blocks south of the central Plaza.

25 de Mayo Corner of Av 25 de Mayo & Jose Declera ⓣ042/220573. A central place that offers basic, uninspiring rooms, but the proximity to the best local restaurants makes it a decent choice; Singles/Doubles ④–⑤

Catedral Florida 830 ⓣ042/242513. Although some of the rooms are a little dark, the staff are friendly and there's a pleasant, family holiday atmosphere among the guests. Single/Doubles ④–⑤

Esteño Sarandí 881 ⓣ042/229828. The location near one of the noisier streets isn't ideal, but otherwise a stay here should be a pleasant one, due to the airy, spacious nature of most of the rooms; Singles/Doubles ④–⑤

SANCAR Juan Edye 597, ⓣ044/223564. This hotel has clean, comfortable rooms, and you can have TV and a private bathroom for 100$ extra; Singles/Doubles ④–⑤

TREAT YOURSELF

SOME COUNTRY AIR AND SMOOTH JAZZ

Fancy getting away from the fashionable celebrities, casinos and crowded beaches of the Peninsula? Then **Lapataia** (ⓣ042/220000, ⓦwww.lapataiapuntadeleste.com), a country club/resort 20km north might be your scene. Here you can try out organic cheeses and home-made chocolate, go horseriding and, every January, enjoy a fantastic **Jazz Festival.** This attracts top international performers and lasts for around 5 hours over 4 evenings, but tickets are 1500$ per day, so it's worth finding out in advance which night to go for depending on your taste. To reach Lapataia, catch a bus to Solanas Beach (15min, 10$), 10km away in the direction of Montevideo. From here, Lapataia, also known as El Sosiego, is 5km walk on Camino Lussich heading north, or 100$ in taxi.

Eating

The peninsula is packed with expensive seafood restaurants and *Parrillas*, and even at the best-value places, you are still going to lose a hefty weight from your wallet. That said, there are bargains to be had if you look around, and the meals are likely to be among the most refined and original that you will find anywhere in Uruguay.

El Pobre Marino Solis 665. Along with a suitably nautical décor, this restaurant provides excellent fish dishes for the best prices in town (150–250$).

Freddo's Av Goriero 811, Punta del Este. The place to chill and enjoy a mouthwatering ice cream. If you are in a large group, don't miss out on the enormous "Freddo Especial" (600$), which allows for up to ten flavours!

Los Caracoles Remanso 871. This *Parrilla* serves plate-sized steaks and some lighter, more inventive seafood meals. Mains 250–300$.

Mia Bistro Baupresa (between Las Focas and Ituraingo). This beachside bistro serves refined sushi and fish courses (250–400$), and offers lovely views over Playa Mansa.

Olivo's Mesana 1037. The best-value pizza place in town, with a large "Pizza Libre" (150$) for those with big appetites.

Drinking and nightlife

Punta is home to a wild nightlife scene which allows you to rub shoulders with everyone from minor local celebrities to backpackers, from grooving teenagers to an older generation looking for a 60s revival. Most bars serve drinks from midday onwards, but the real parties only start at around 2am and rarely end before sunrise. The top clubs here change every season, but these are some of the most established, popular venues.

Buddha Bar Bikini Beach, La Barra. Within walking distance of La Barra's main street, this beachside hut appears to be a modest venue, but it boasts international DJs and fine sushi, and has become a favourite with the young jetset crowd.

Company Bar Las Gaviotas (between Baupresa and Remanso). An excellent range of cocktails, wines, liquors and tasty bar snacks make this the start of many a night out for backpackers.

Magic Resto Bar Parada 5, Playa Brava. A restaurant/bar with an upmarket décor and plenty to keep you occupied: live music most nights, card-playing, and dancing from 8.30pm onwards. Glass of red wine 75$.

Miró Corner of Artigas and Resalsero. With both a flaming grill and a dancefloor, fine Argentinian wines and your favourite cocktails, Miró is enjoying a curious but not unappealing identity crisis.

Moby Dick Pub Artigas 650. An inexpensive, down-to-earth watering hole, which offers a good set of cocktails (140–180$) which one can happily drink, watching the ships go by for hours on end from the outdoor seating.

Soho Artigas 652. From 8pm onwards. The flashest of the beachside clubs, with a set of chill-out sofas as well as space to dance to the latest pop and rock, but also with a high entrance fee (100$) on popular nights.

Moving on

There are two **buses** an hour to Montevideo (2hr, 130$), 3 daily to Minas (2hr, 150$), and 2 daily to Chuy (3hr 30min, 225$) on the Brazilian border. Most buses are via the Maldonado terminal. To reach the surfing villages between Punta del Este and the Brazilian border, you will need to catch a bus from Punta del Este to San Carlos (50min, 20$). From here, there are several direct connections daily to La Paloma (1hr 30min, 80$) and Punta del Diablo (2hr 30min, 150$).

East to the Brazilian border

The beach villages to the east of the Peninsula offer some of the best surfing on the coast and are surrounded by sand dunes, forests and wetlands that are perfect for walking. While these secluded corners provide a contrast to the large-scale development of Punta del Este, they also have hostels and bars packed with fun-loving backpackers. Be sure to come with enough cash for however long you want to stay; you won't find any banks in the smaller villages, let alone ATMs.

LA PALOMA

Due south of the busy transport hub of Rocha, **La Paloma** is a quiet port that provides a good base for exploring some fine local beaches. Fishing is popular here and the sea is also good for swimming, especially off the sheltered Playa la Balconada; you should avoid the Atlantic beaches because of the heavy swell.

In the town, there's a small **casino** and **cinema** on Avenida Solari, the main street, while *Hostel Ibirapita* on Av La Paloma s/n (Ⓣ0479/9303, Ⓦwww.hostelibirapita.com) offers dorms for HI Members/Non-members ❷–❸.

The **bus** terminal is five minutes north of town on Calle Paloma, where buses to Rocha (3$, 1hr) leave every 30 minutes. Local buses continue on to the quieter, nearby town of La Pedrera, where the El Viajero Pedrera Hostel, Ruta 10, Km.230 (Dorms ❷; Ⓣ99/057-560, Ⓦwww.lapedrerahostel.com) is close to the beach and has a buzzing atmosphere, even if it is limited to passing backpackers.

CABO POLONIO

Having been dropped off by a truck in a small clearing surrounded by wooden beach-huts, you will soon appreciate that **Cabo Polonio** is about as far from the glamorous hotels of Punta del Este as you can get. This small beach village is home to a delightful community of fishermen and hippies, who live simply (bring a torch as there's currently no electricity) but not without comfort.

The **Cabo Polonio Hostel** (Ⓔcabopoloniohostel@hotmail.com) offers cozy dorm beds in stucco rooms, and the owner's cooking is worth the trip on its own; Dorms ❷.

To reach the village, catch a **bus** on Ruta 9 towards Chuy on the Brazilian border and get off at the large town of Castillos. There are buses from here every 30 minutes to Valizas (30min, 45$) on the coast. After this, there are no more roads, but trucks leave regularly to Cabo Polonio (30min, around 250$ in total; prices depend on size of group).

Venezuela

HIGHLIGHTS

MÉRIDA: catch thrills in this high-altitude adventure sports paradise

PARQUE NACIONAL MOCHIMA: enjoy the mainland's best snorkelling and deserted beaches

LOS LLANOS: see alligators, anacondas and much more, up close and very personal

ANGEL FALLS: stand in the spray of the world's tallest waterfall

AMAZONAS: venture into uncharted territory covered in tropical rainforest along great rivers

ROUGH COSTS

DAILY BUDGET Basic US$50/ occasional treat US$60

DRINK Polar beer (1L) US$1

FOOD Arepa US$5

BUDGET HOTEL US$25

TRAVEL Caracas–Mérida (680km) by bus: US$30; Puerto La Cruz–Isla de Margarita (40km) by express ferry: US$22

FACT FILE

POPULATION 28 million

AREA 916,500 sq km

LANGUAGE Spanish

CURRENCY Bolívar fuerte

CAPITAL Caracas (population: 1.3 million)

INTERNATIONAL PHONE CODE ☎58

TIME ZONE GMT -4hr 30min

Introduction

Venezuela's location on the Caribbean coast makes the flight there one of the shortest – and often cheapest – from most parts of Europe and the US. Not that hordes of foreign visitors tend to take advantage of that. Despite packing nearly every natural environment on the continent into a relatively small place – Caribbean beaches, snowcapped mountains, wildlife-rich wetlands, desert, Amazonian jungle, fertile river valley – the country has historically been one of the least-visited in South America; even war-torn Colombia receives five times more tourists annually than Venezuela.

Venezuela's prime attractions lie outside its major cities, and few travellers spend any more time than necessary in **Caracas** – a good strategy given the capital's security problems and lack of major tourist draws.

With 43 **national parks** and many private nature reserves, the country is well suited to outdoors-oriented visitors. Most visitors explore at least part of Venezuela's over 2600 kilometres of Caribbean coastline, which contains some of South America's finest and most diverse **beaches**. With postcard-like white sand and crystal-clear water, Venezuela's most pristine beaches are

WHEN TO VISIT

Venezuela can be visited year-round, but you are most likely to get the best out of visiting during the **dry season**, which generally means between November and May.

On **the coast**, there is less rain and fewer mosquitoes, if slightly higher temperatures. In **Los Llanos**, wildlife spottings are much more abundant during the dry season, when the animals congregate at the few watering holes, and hordes of pesky mosquitoes make walking very unpleasant during the wet season. Travel in the **Guayana** region is more comfortable during the dry season, though Angel Falls tends to be fuller and therefore more spectacular during the wet season.

It is probably best to avoid the national vacation periods of Easter, Carnaval (which begins at the end of Feb or beginning of March), Christmas vacation (Dec 15– Jan 15) and summer vacation (July 15– Sept 15), when beaches are considerably more crowded and prices significantly higher.

found in the over forty keys that make up the **Los Roques Archipelago**. However, there are several national parks that are easily accessible by bus from Caracas. Several hours east of the capital, **Parque Nacional Mochima** boasts red-sand beaches with emerald water and backdrops of rocky hills and cacti, while **Parque Nacional Henri Pittier**, about three hours west, offers a number of beaches with stunning backgrounds of palm trees and verdant mountains. Just two hours to the west is **Parque Nacional Morrocoy**, which features picturesque white-sand keys, but is more financially accessible than Los Roques.

An overnight bus ride from Morrocoy or Pittier will take you to **mérida**, in the heart of the Andes mountains. Mérida is also the best place to arrange trips to **Los Llanos**, the extensive plains that provide some of the best wildlife and birdwatching opportunities on the continent.

The enormous region of **Guayana**, which encompasses most of the south and west portions of the country, contains a number of adventurous attractions. To the northeast, the picturesque, historical town of **Ciudad Bolívar** is the most economical base from which to explore **Parque Nacional Canaima**, which contains the marvellous **Auyantepui** and **Angel Falls**.

Guayana also contains the **Orinoco Delta**, a labyrinth of marshlands and water channels formed from the mighty Orinoco River on its way towards the Atlantic Ocean.

CHRONOLOGY

c.13,000 BC–1498 AD Roughly 500,000 indigenous peoples live in the area today covered by Venezuela, belonging to three principal ethno-linguistic groups: Carib, Arawak and Chibcha.

1498 Christopher Columbus arrives August 4 at the eastern tip of the Paria Peninsula and continues south to the Orinoco Delta.

1502 Italian Amerigo Vespucci sees the Arawak houses on wooden stilts in Lake Maracaibo and calls the place Venezuela, or "little Venice." Enslavement of the indigenous population for pearl harvesting begins around this time.

1521 The first permanent mainland settlement is established at Cumaná, on the northeast coast, serving as a base for Catholic missionaries and further exploration of the mainland.

1528 King Carlos V of Spain leases exploration and colonization rights for much of the western part of Venezuela to a German banking house. Unable to find the storied riches of El Dorado, it leaves in 1556 after massacring much of indigenous population.

Late 1500s The Creoles, Spanish descendents born in the New World, accumulate slaves, agricultural wealth and a large degree of autonomy.

1749 Their prosperity threatened by the Spanish crown's granting of a trading monopoly to a Basque company in 1728, the Creoles revolt under the leadership of Juan Francisco de León. The revolt is suppressed, but the rift between the Spanish and Creoles widens.

1810 The Creole Francisco de Miranda, having attempted an invasion of Venezuela in 1806, tries again and succeeds in ousting the Spanish governors of Caracas and six other provinces. He declares independence, but less than a year later his efforts are thwarted by a counterinsurgency of Spanish and mixed-blood *pardos*.

1813 Simón Bolívar, a wealthy Creole landowner from Caracas, takes over the revolution and wins the support of the *pardos*. With aid from the British and the new republic of Haiti, he wins several naval battles against the Spanish and liberates the territory of Colombia.

1819 Bolívar proclaims the new Republic of Gran Colombia, an independent nation formed by the territories of Venezuela, Colombia and Ecuador.

1821 On June 24, Bolívar secures Venezuelan independence with a victory over the Spanish in the Battle of Carabobo. He then liberates Ecuador, Peru and Bolivia.

1829 Gran Colombia disbands in the face of irreconcilable internal disputes, and Bolívar, bitterly disappointed by the dissolution of his dream, succumbs to tuberculosis.

1854 Venezuelan leader José Tadeo Monagas, who took power in 1846 after General José Antonio Páez (1830–48), abolishes slavery; he is subsequently overthrown in a rebellion.

1859–1863 A power struggle between Liberals and Conservatives, known as the Federal War, results in Liberal control of Venezuela until the turn of the century.

1899 Ciprano Castro, the first of five successive strongmen from the Andean state of Táchira who rule the country for the next 59 years, takes control in a revolution. Mounting foreign debt provokes England and Germany to form a naval blockade around the country, but the US intervenes before any land is seized.

1908 While Castro seeks medical treatment in Europe, General Juan Vicente Gómez takes over the country and becomes one of Venezuela's most brutal dictators. Press and public freedoms are curtailed and political dissidents murdered.

1918 Oil is discovered in Venezuela, and ten years later the country is the largest producer in the world. Gómez pays off all foreign debts and invests in roads, ports and public buildings.

1935 Gómez dies and Venezuelans, having been angered by the elite's monopolization of oil wealth, take to the streets in massive celebrations.

1945 Rómulo Betancourt, of the political party Acción Democrática (AD), creates a new constitution with sweeping reforms; however, he is overthrown 28 months later by a military coup led by Carlos Delgado Chalbaud and Marcos Pérez Jiménez.

1958 The navy and air force oust Pérez Jiménez, the last of the Andean dictators, whose rule had eliminated free speech and other civil liberties and directed most of the country's oil profits into Caracas infrastructure and Pérez Jiménez's own pockets.

1959 Having signed the Pact of Punto Fijo a year earlier, which guaranteed democratic elections and power-sharing between the AD and the Partido Social Cristiano (COPEI), Rómulo Betancourt is re-elected.

1968 COPEI founder Rafael Caldera is elected, marking the first time in Venezuelan history that a government peacefully surrenders power to an opposition party.

1973 Carlos Andrés Pérez (AD) is elected and governs Venezuela through one of its most prosperous periods, during which the petroleum industry is nationalized, quadrupling the price of oil and filling the country's coffers.

Late 1970s–1980s Increased oil production in other countries sends prices spiralling downwards. Inflation and unemployment increase as foreign capital drops off significantly, and Venezuela sells much of its precious oil reserves to pay its debts.

1989 A sudden and unprecedented increase in public transport and oil costs incites the *caracazo* street riots in Caracas, the worst in Venezuelan history. Up to 3000 people are believed to have been killed, mainly by the police and military.

1992 A mid-level military officer named Hugo Chávez launches an unsuccessful coup attempt against Pérez and is imprisoned; a second coup attempt partially destroys Miraflores Palace. Soon after, Pérez is found guilty of corruption charges.

1994 Chávez is pardoned for his coup attempt and continues gathering support around the country.

1998 In a landslide victory over former Miss Universe Irene Sáez, Chávez is elected President and, through national referendum, establishes a new constitution that dismantles the Senate, increases state control over the oil industry and grants the military greater autonomy.

2000 Having lengthened the presidential term from five to six years, Chávez wins a new election.

2002 Government officials and the middle class, angered by Chávez's controversial reform laws and a weakening economy, incite massive, violent protests on April 11; the next day, what appears to be a successful coup attempt ends with Chávez being taken into military custody. Two days later the interim government collapses and Chávez regains control.

2007 Chávez attempts to pass, by national referendum, yet another constitutional reform that would facilitate federal expropriation of private property, give him unfettered control of the national bank and, most controversially, allow himself to be re-elected indefinitely. The reforms are defeated; shortly after, Chávez turns the clocks back a half-hour, claiming it will increase the country's productivity.

Basics

ARRIVAL

Most visitors to Venezuela – and many to South America as a whole – fly into Maiquetía airport in Caracas; those flying from the Caribbean islands may enter via Isla de Margarita (see p.1000). Overland passage is possible from neighbouring Colombia and Brazil, but not from Guyana to the east.

By air

Nearly all international flights land at Simón Bolívar International Airport in Maiquetía (often known simply as **Maiquetía airport**), between 45 minutes and an hour from central Caracas. Since the airport is one of the cheapest in all of South America to fly into, it is many travellers' entry point to the continent, even if they immediately continue onward. For services offered at Maiquetía and an explanation of how to get to central Caracas, see p.954 and p.948, respectively.

If you know someone in Venezuela, you can save an enormous amount on airfare by having them make a reservation and buy a ticket for you within the country. This is a result of the considerably higher exchange rate offered by Venezuela's cash-based unofficial economy (*mercado negro* or *paralelo*, meaning black or "parallel" market; see box, p.942).

By bus

Long-distance international buses arrive from neighbouring Colombia and Brazil and head for Caracas, 9 to 15 hours from the Colombian border crossings, depending on where you cross (see p.967), and up to 24 hours from the main Brazilian crossing. Border formalities for international bus passengers are generally straightforward, though you are responsible for arranging any necessary visas, vaccinations and exit/entry stamps; for more information, see the boxes on p.967 and p.982, respectively.

VISAS

Citizens of the US, Canada, Australia, New Zealand, South Africa, Ireland, the UK and other EU countries do not need a visa to enter Venezuela – just a tourist card, provided by the airlines, that lets you stay for ninety days. Entry by bus or car can be a bit more complicated: in some but not all cases, the border guards will ask to see your tourist card, which must be purchased at the Venezuelan consulates in Colombia or Brazil – they're not always available in the US and Europe. You will need to present a photo and a passport valid for at least six more months. Sometimes they will also ask to see an onward ticket. To extend your tourist card or visa an additional three months, go to the Oficina Nacional de Identificación y Extranjería (Onidex) in Caracas (see p.954). Bring your passport, two photos and your return or onward ticket. It generally takes three days to process the request and costs roughly US$40.

GETTING AROUND

Travellers are best off using the generally convenient and inexpensive public transport system of buses and *por puesto* vans. To avoid extremely long rides, it is sometimes necessary to take internal flights, which can be unreliable.

By air

Flying within Venezuela is neither cheap nor convenient; domestic air travel is plagued by delays and cancellations. If you need to cover a lot of ground in little time, however, you may resort to a plane; see each destination's "Moving on" section for frequencies. Always call to confirm flight times, and arrive at airports up to two hours in advance, as lines can be formidable. Domestic flights usually require a *tasa* of around US$3.

Within most cities, the main forms of transport are local buses and **taxis**. The latter never have meters, so you should agree on a price ahead of time, usually after getting a neutral party's opinion.

By bus

Buses are the primary mode of transport throughout Venezuela and invariably the cheapest. Since they are operated by countless private companies, you'll have to spend some time visiting the various ticket counters in a city's *terminal de pasajeros* before you find a route and departure that suits your itinerary. Ask at the ticket counter whether you must pay a *tasa*, or tax, on top of the ticket price; when you do, it's usually US$2–3. Most regional bus services end at around 6 or 7pm; overnight services to more distant destinations sometimes depart as late as midnight or 1am.

Economical buses, or *servicio normal* (roughly $2 per hr), are common for shorter distances and often cramped, with no toilet or air conditioning. More comfortable executive buses, or *servicio ejecutivo* (about $4 per hr), run longer distances and have toilets; air conditioning, however, is so intense that you'll need a blanket or sleeping bag to stave off hypothermia. If you're travelling overnight, be sure to take a *buscama*, with almost fully reclinable seats.

By car

Another economical option are the ubiquitous **por puestos**, battered American sedans that cover routes more frequently than buses, though drivers won't leave until their car is full.

TOUR OPERATORS

For better or for worse, Venezuela has yet to develop a budget travel infrastructure on the level of Brazil's or Peru's, meaning that independent travellers often turn to **agencies** for assistance in arranging trips and activities to the country's top attractions: Angel Falls (p.989), Los Llanos (p.976), Río Caura (p.988), the Orinoco Delta (p.993), Mount Roraima (p.992), the Gran Sabana (p.992) and even Los Roques (see box, p.957). As a general rule, it's cheapest to book a tour as close to the destination as possible – see each attraction's account for local tour prices – but if your time is limited, or if you're looking for a multi-destination tour, the following Caracas-based companies can arrange trips anywhere. All accept credit cards, though for the best rates you should pay in US dollars (for why, see p.942).

Akanán C Bolívar, Ed Grano de Oro, Ground Floor, Chacao ⓣ0212/264-2769 or 266-8663, ⓦwww.akanan.com. Akanán's office has plenty of materials for researching trips, and **Rough Guides users** can use the internet for free. Clients who opt not to hire a guide are lent a cell phone for use on their travels.

Angel Eco-Tours Av Casanova at 2da av de Bello Monte, Ed La Paz, Oficina 51, Sabana Grande ⓣ0212/762-5975, ⓦwww.angel-ecotours.com. An excellent agency specializing in slightly more upscale travel than affiliate Osprey (see below). The company also manages a nonprofit assisting the indigenous Pemón community of Parque Nacional Canaima (see p.988).

Osprey Expeditions Same office as Angel Eco-Tours ⓣ0212/762-5975 or 0414/310-4491, ⓦwww.ospreyexpeditions.com. The most economical option for backpacker-friendly, nationwide trips, with exceptionally friendly staff.

They're no cheaper than buses – in fact, they can be one-and a-half to twice the price – but they often cut travel time by half.

ACCOMMODATION

The quality of low-end **accommodation** in Venezuela is, overall, fairly poor; the main exceptions are the couple of towns, essentially Mérida (see p.968) and Ciudad Bolívar (see p.984), that have been receiving budget travellers for years and have adapted to their needs. Outside of these two cities, dorm rooms are virtually nonexistent, and there are no real youth hostels anywhere in the country; hence solo travellers are often stuck paying for a *matrimonial* (for couples), cheaper than a double but pricier than a single would be. A good resource for budget accommodation in Venezuela is Ⓦwww.hosteltrail.com.

Larger cities, such as Puerto Ordáz, Puerto La Cruz and Caracas – particularly Caracas – have uniformly awful budget accommodation and, unless you can afford an upgrade, you're best off passing through as quickly as possible. Nevertheless, you can almost always expect sheets and towels to be clean, if pocked with cigarette burns.

Quality is much higher outside the big cities and usually appears in the form of **posadas**, basically family-owned guesthouses, which are generally affordable. These typically have much more character than urban inns and hotels, though they, like their city counterparts, almost never have hot water (the main exceptions being in Mérida and other Andean towns).

Camping hasn't caught on among most Venezuelans, so there are few designated sites. In general, camping is not recommended because of robberies, even on isolated beaches and keys. The safest time to camp is on weekends and during national holidays. For more information, contact Inparques (Ⓣ0212/273-2701 or 273-2702, Ⓦwww.inparques.gob.ve).

FOOD

Venezuelan cuisine, like that of most of the Caribbean, centres around meat, with the most common accompaniments being rice, beans and plantains. Though rather difficult to find, vegetarian food (*comida vegetariana*) and healthful *comida dietética* are usually available in larger cities, often in restaurants dedicated to these cuisines.

One of the first dishes you'll notice – and arguably a symbol of Venezuelan national pride – is the **arepa**, in its raw form little more than a dense, savoury, fried corncake, but, when stuffed with any number of meat, seafood and cheese fillings, a meal unto itself. *Arepa* restaurants are ubiquitous; among their most common offerings are *carne mechada* (shredded beef) and *reina pepeada* (creamy chicken salad with sliced avocado). Breakfast is often as simple as a fish-, chicken- or cheese-filled *empanada* (a deep-fried cornmeal turnover) and a thimble of scalding coffee; another option is a *cachapa*, a sweet cornmeal pancake folded over a slab of molten cheese. Lunch is generally lighter – a good economic choice is the *menú ejecutivo*, which many restaurants offer – and common dinner options include fried fish, *pollo a la brasa* or *a la broaster* – rotisserie chicken – or any number of international dishes, including pizza and pasta. The Venezuelan national dish is *pabellón criollo*, which consists of *carne mechada*, avocado, *tajadas* (sliced plantains), cheese, rice and beans; a breakfast version of this is the *desayuno criollo*.

The ocean, abundant rivers and mountain lakes afford fresh fish, the most common varieties being *mero* (grouper), *dorado* (dolphin fish), *pargo* (red snapper), *trucha* (trout), *corvina* (sea bass) and *corocoro* (grunt). Beef is also found throughout the country, although it is especially delicious in Los Llanos, where the grass is ideal for cow grazing. Meats are often served with *guasacaca*, a spicy green sauce made of avocado, peppers, onions and spices.

Common desserts are strawberries and cream, *quesillo* (similar to flan), *dulce de leche* (caramel) and sweets made from guava or plantains. Venezuelan *cacao* (cocoa) is considered among the best in the world but, as nearly all is exported to Europe, Venezuelan chocolate is difficult to find.

Finding a hot meal in a restaurant can be difficult outside of the standard dining hours of 6 to10am, noon to 2pm and 5 to 8pm. In most restaurants, it's customary to leave a small tip (usually around ten percent), even when a ten percent service fee has already been added to the bill.

DRINK

Fruit juices, or *jugos* (also known as *batidos*) are delicious, inexpensive and safe to drink; combined with milk and whipped, they become *merengadas*. The most common flavours are *lechosa* (papaya), *parchita* (passion fruit), mango, *piña* (pineapple), melon, *guayaba* (guava) and *tamarindo* (tamarind). Another sweet, refreshing drink is *papelón con limón* (lemonade made with unrefined brown sugar). Bottled water is inexpensive and available everywhere, and the locally grown coffee is quite good.

Venezuelans are extremely fond of their beer. The major brand is Polar, with several varieties; the green-bottled Solera is one of the best, and usually costs $1 to 1.50 in a liquor store or cheap restaurant, $2.50 to 3 in a bar. Bottles are endearingly small – Venezuelans prefer to finish a beer before it loses its icy chill. Liquors of choice are rum (such as Cacique) and, among a slightly more affluent set, whisky (particularly Johnny Walker Black Label).

CULTURE AND ETIQUETTE

Thanks to its location at the crown of South America, Venezuela combines distinctive elements of Caribbean and Latin American **culture**. Visitors familiar with these regions won't be surprised to find the country a fairly relaxed place, whose warm, cheerful residents place a high value on socializing, recreation, food and (loud) music. By the same token, **machismo** is an inescapable aspect of Venezuelan society, and while women travelling solo needn't expect any more harassment here than elsewhere, groups of drunken men loitering on street corners are a common sight, particularly on weekends.

Understandably, given their government's notoriety, Venezuelans are **politically aware** and eager to discuss their thoughts about their country; don't be surprised if you're repeatedly regaled with both praise for and criticism of Hugo Chávez. While most Venezuelans will listen to your opinions with good grace, it's best to wait to be asked before sharing them, and for your safety you should avoid public political demonstrations.

SPORTS AND OUTDOOR ACTIVITIES

Betraying its alignment with Caribbean nations like Cuba and the Dominican Republic, Venezuela's principal sports obsession is not football but **baseball**. Teams – Caracas's Leones, Valencia's Navegantes del Magallanes and Aragua's Tigres, among others – inspire fanatic devotion among most citizens. In addition to national team paraphernalia (see p.954 for Leones gear), you'll likely see caps and shirts advertising American teams, as the US's Major League Baseball has a long history of drafting Venezuelan athletes.

VENEZUELA ON THE NET

ⓦ www.caracasvirtual.com Everything you could possibly want to know about life in Venezuela's cosmopolitan centre, affectionately known to cynical locals as "Crack-ass."

ⓦ www.inatur.gob.ve Official site of the government's tourism arm, with current, tourism-related news and links to similar federal agencies.

ⓦ www.inparques.gob.ve Official site of the national parks agency, with contact info and descriptions of parks and reserves.

ⓦ www.miropopic.com Website of the publisher of Venezuelan maps and reference books, with an online "gastronomic guide".

ⓦ www.venezuelatuya.com Decent overview of travel and accommodation in Venezuela, with a smattering of country facts.

ⓦ www.vengay.com Comprehensive directory of gay-friendly listings and events.

Despite baseball's dominance, football is still a popular pastime, as is horse racing (off-track betting offices are common in cities) and even bullfighting, though this is becoming increasingly controversial.

Most visitors, however, come to Venezuela for the recreation opportunities afforded by its huge tracts of undeveloped land. The country is an **outdoor** enthusiast's paradise, with a variety of landscapes and climates offering the ideal conditions for hiking, paragliding, snorkelling, scuba diving, whitewater rafting and more. Most outdoor activities are concentrated in the few backpacker-friendly destinations, namely Mérida (p.968), Puerto Ayacucho (p.978), Ciudad Bolívar (p.984) and Santa Elena de Uairén (p.99 0), and tours generally require a minimum number of people.

COMMUNICATIONS

Venezuela is incredibly technologically savvy, and call centers and cybercafés are legion; except in the most remote outposts, you should have no trouble finding a reasonably fast **internet** connection. Rates are generally $0.75 to 1.25 per hr.

Movistar and CANTV are the most visible **telecommunications** providers, and each has at least one call center in most towns and cities. Calls are surprisingly cheap: around $0.04 per minute for local; $0.10 per minute for national ($0.15–0.20 per min to cell phones); $0.11 per minute to the US; and $0.35 per minute to Europe. You can also buy public phone cards of various denominations at nearly any corner store or magazine stand, though it's much nicer to make calls from indoors, as streetside phones are often in disrepair and traffic noise can be unbearable. To place an international call, first dial 00 and then the code of the country you are calling.

The Venezuelan **postal service** is at best slow and often unreliable, so if you have an important letter or package, send it through an international carrier like FedEx or

LANGUAGE

While many Venezuelans speak English, a general knowledge of Spanish will serve you well. Venezuelan Spanish is, for the most part, easily understood, although northeasterners have a reputation for speaking extremely fast.

Among the younger set, the slang words *pana* and *chamo* – both approximations of "man", "dude" or "bro" – find their way into nearly every sentence uttered.

USEFUL NUMBERS

All-purpose, nationwide emergency hotline ☎171

All-purpose, nationwide information hotline ☎131

DHL, which have offices in most major cities; don't expect deliveries to occur as quickly as they claim, however. Ipostel, the government postal service, charges around $0.75 for a postcard to the US, $1 to Europe, and $1.25 to the rest of the world. Ipostel branches are typically open weekdays from 8am to 4.30pm.

EMERGENCIES

While Venezuela is, for the most part, a **secure** place to travel, the capital's reputation as a criminal safe haven and Hugo Chávez's angry, anti-imperialist posturing have tagged it as an international no-go zone. As long as you keep your wits about you – especially in Caracas and other major cities – you shouldn't encounter any trouble.

Although urban police enforcement is on the rise, helping to clean up once-sinister neighbourhoods like Caracas's Sabana Grande (and simultaneously multiplying instances of graft and extortion; see box below), walking alone at night should never be considered safe. Likewise, never accept help at an ATM – anyone who offers is virtually guaranteed to be a **con artist** – and keep a close eye on your bank, debit and credit cards, though the latter aren't particularly advantageous in Venezuela anyway (see below).

For insurance claims you will need to report any incidents of theft to the police, who should otherwise be avoided. They will write up the claim and give you a copy of the statement. Make sure to carry **identification** at all times, which you will occasionally have to present at police stops. Carrying drugs is strongly discouraged, since narcotics laws in Venezuela are extremely strict.

OFFICIAL VS. BLACK MARKET EXCHANGE RATES

One of the commonest mistakes among first-time visitors to Venezuela is not informing themselves of the advantages of *efectivo*, or cash (US dollars, British pounds and Euros being the most powerful), over ATM and credit cards. Though technically illegal, the country's black market – *mercado negro* or *mercado paralelo* – is cash-based and can give you up to three times as much value for your currency than the official exchange rate. In fact, inflation is so rampant, and foreign currency so undervalued by the federal bank, that Venezuela is almost prohibitively expensive if you travel on ATM and credit cards alone – you can easily end up paying more for goods and services than you would at home.

The main downside of the black market – besides the fact that it's illegal – is that it requires you to carry your money in cash, a risky venture in a country known for high crime rates (traveller's cheques are safer, though rates are lower if they're accepted at all). Never change money with unfamiliar people, especially at airports or bus terminals; the safest option is to ask your guesthouse or tour agency if they'll change money for you. Black market exchange rates tend to be higher in major cities, where services are correspondingly pricier. Should you run out of cash, you can ask a reliable business owner – many of whom have overseas bank accounts – if you can wire money from your account to theirs, then receive the black market equivalent in bolívares fuertes from them.

The Brazilian town of Pacaraima, just across the border from Santa Elena de Uairén, provides another opportunity to replenish your coffers; for details, see box, p.991.

FESTIVALS

The following holidays are observed all over the country; noteworthy celebrations are mentioned. In addition to the events listed here, Caracas celebrates the anniversary of its foundation every year from July 21 to July 29 with a series of cultural events that include theatre presentations, painting and sculpture exhibits, concerts and sports.

Reyes Magos Jan 6. Twelfth Night or Epiphany. Choroní (p.959), Mucuchíes (p.974) and Caracas (p.945).

Carnaval Feb (no fixed date). The most famous celebrations are in Carupano and El Callao.

Nuestra Señora de La Candelaria Feb 2. Virgin of the Candlemas, with offerings and folksinging. Mérida (p.968) and Caracas.

Semana Santa March (no fixed date). Large processions involve re-enactments of Jesus' last days and resurrection; most Venezuelans, however, celebrate by heading to the beach. Several small towns in the state of Mérida, as well as El Hatillo (see p.946).

San Isidro Labrador May 15. Honours agriculture and animal husbandry; produce is carted through the streets and animals are blessed. Mérida.

Corpus Christi Late May or early June (no fixed date). The most famous celebration – one of the country's definitive festivals – is Diablos Danzantes (Dancing Devils) in San Francisco de Yare. For more information and alternate locations, see p.957.

Día de San Juan Bautista June 24. Choroní, El Higuerote and Ocumare del Tuy.

Día de Todos los Santos November 1. All Saints' Day.

La Navidad December 24. Christmas – the entire country essentially shuts down for a week.

INFORMATION AND MAPS

What Venezuela's tourism officials – representatives of federal agencies Inatur (®www.inatur.gob.ve), Venetur (®www.venetur.gob.ve) and Mintur (®www.mintur.gob.ve) – lack in useful knowledge for budget travellers, they make up for with charm and enthusiasm; unfortunately, many offices don't abide by any logical schedule. Additionally, each state has its own tourism entity located in its capital city. For office contact information and official hours, see city and town accounts in the guide.

Though information provided by private tour agencies is rarely unbiased, they are often better sources of detailed information for independent travellers, and are more in touch with current public transport schedules and black market exchange rates (see opposite).

A variety of country and regional maps are available in Venezuela, the best being Miro Popic's *Guia Vial de Venezuela/Atlas de Carreteras* and individual city maps, available in most bookshops.

MONEY AND BANKS

Money – and how to get the most value from it – will likely be your biggest concern while in Venezuela. The country's economy is extremely volatile, thanks to unrelenting inflation and the conversion from the *bolívar* to the *bolívar fuerte* in January 2008, which lopped three zeros off the currency (for a detailed explanation in Spanish, as well as currency denominations, see ®www.reconversionbcv.org.ve). For these reasons, all prices listed in this chapter should be considered estimates; contact businesses directly for current quotes.

Venezuela has a thriving **black market**, which, while officially illegal, is widely used and can increase the value of your dollar threefold. For more on this, see the box on p.942. Very importantly, all prices in this chapter are based on the official exchange rate; at the black market rate, prices can be up to two thirds cheaper.

Bank hours are 8.30am to 3.30pm Monday to Friday, although many offer 24-hour access to ATM machines. Most advertise that they are on the Cirrus and Maestro systems, though this doesn't guarantee that they'll accept your card. Two reliable banks are CorpBanca (Ⓦwww.corpbanca.com.ve) and Banco Mercantil (Ⓦwww.bancomercantil.com), both found in most sizeable towns.

Exchange houses, such as Italcambio, also exist, though their exchange rates are worse than banks'; they do, however, exchange traveller's cheques, at a seven percent commission.

OPENING HOURS AND FESTIVALS

Most shops are open from 8am until 7pm on weekdays, often closing for lunch from around 12.30pm until 2 or 3pm. Shopping malls, however, generally stay open until 9 or 10pm. For bank and post office hours, see opposite and p.942, respectively. In addition to their regular business hours, pharmacies operate on a "*turno*" system, with a rotating duty to stay open all night; the designated pharmacy will advertise *turno* in neon. Sunday hours at all businesses are fairly unpredictable – don't expect to get much done.

Festivals, most with a religious basis, seem to occur constantly. Some are national, while others are local, as each town celebrates its patron saint.

Caracas

CARACAS does not hold much of interest for the budget traveller, and the density of cars and people, high prices, and legitimate safety concerns will probably make your stay a brief one. Should you stay longer, however, you may eventually grow to appreciate its cacophonous charm – and as a transportation hub for the rest of the country, it can't be beat.

Caracas's most famous native, **Simón Bolívar**, was born to an influential family in 1783. After several years abroad he returned in 1813 and captured the city from the Spanish, at which time he was deemed "El Libertador". When Venezuela became fully independent in 1830, Caracas was made the capital of the new nation. Since then, various political eras have left their mark on the city's architecture and public works, though the predominant aesthetic is the mid-twentieth-century concrete high-rise.

El Centro

Though the thick traffic of vehicles and street vendors make **El Centro** rather difficult to navigate on foot, most sights are within close walking distance of each other. Restrict your sightseeing to daylight hours, however, as this part of town has a well-deserved reputation for street crime.

Plaza Bolívar

As with all Venezuelan towns, the Plaza Bolívar is the main square, and Caracas's version, two blocks east and one block north of the Capitolio/El Silencio metro station, is a good starting spot for a walking tour. The south side of the square features the **Museo Caracas** (Tues–Sun 9am–4.30pm; free), containing paintings and documents related to the quest for independence.

On the east side of the plaza, the modest, colonial-style **Catedral de Caracas** was originally built in 1575. Bolívar's parents and wife are buried inside, where you'll also find Rubens' *Resurrection of Christ*. More religious paintings and sculptures are on offer at the **Museo Sacro de Caracas** (Tues–Sat 9am–4pm; $1; ⓣ0212/861-6562, ⓦwww.cibernetic.com/sacro), just next door. The pretty *Café del Sacro* is a nice spot to enjoy a coffee or a quick bite to eat.

Casa Natal de Simón Bolívar

The best place to learn about Bolívar is at the Casa Natal de Simón Bolívar (Tues–Fri 8.30am–12.30pm & 2–4.30pm, Sat

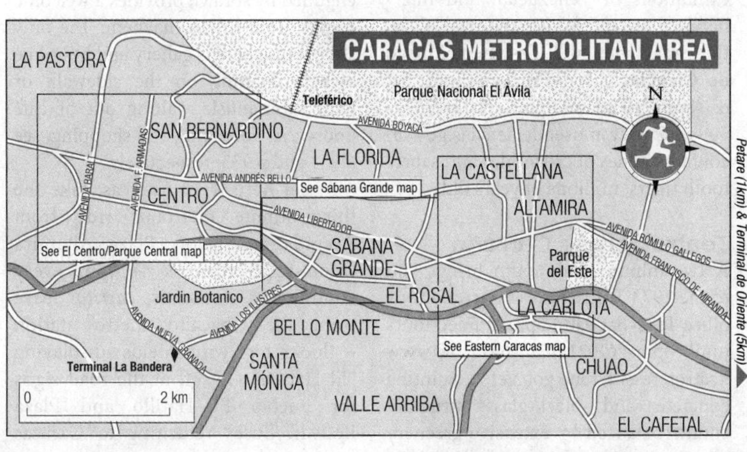

& Sun 10am–4pm, closed Mon; free), one block south and then one east on Avenida Universidad (the entrance is on Av Sur 1). Built in 1680, the large, colonial-style house contains some of its original furniture as well as numerous portraits of Bolívar, who only lived here until the age of nine. You may also want to visit his final resting place in the **Panteón Nacional**, five blocks north of Plaza Bolívar.

The **Iglesia de San Francisco**, on the south side of Avenida Universidad, is one of Venezuela's oldest churches. Its principal claim to fame is as the place where Bolívar was proclaimed "El Libertador" in 1813.

Parque Central

Not really a park, **Parque Central** is a long concrete strip filled with hundreds of vendors, selling everything from pirated CDs to miracle herbs. It's the district's museums, however, that draw you here. Just one block east from the Bellas Artes metro station lie the **Galería de Arte Nacional** and the **Museo de Bellas Artes** (both Mon–Fri 9am–5pm, Sat & Sun 10am–5pm; ⓣ0212/578-1818, ⓦwww.gan.org.ve), the former containing paintings and sculptures by national artists, the latter housing temporary exhibitions of Venezuelan and international artists. Across the oval plaza, the small but well-designed **Museo de Ciencias** (Mon–Fri 9am–5pm, Sat & Sun 10.30am–6pm; ⓣ0212/577-5094, ⓦwww.museodeciencias.gov.ve) contains bones of crocodiles and sabre-tooth tigers, millions of years old.

Teatro Teresa Carreño

A two-minute walk south brings you to the 1973 Teatro Teresa Carreño (box office Tues–Sat 9am–5pm, guided tours until 8pm; ⓣ0212/576-6411, ⓦwww.teatroteresacarreno.gob.ve), a daunting concrete and black-glass structure counterbalanced by extensive greenery in its surrounding open spaces. Some of the city's highest-profile music, dance and theatre performances take place; check the website for the schedule of events. Across the road is the **Museo de Arte Contemporáneo** (daily 9am–4.45pm; ⓣ0212/573-0721), a five-storey museum housing works by Venezuelans, such as kinetic artist Jesús Soto, and international artists.

Sabana Grande

Unlike El Centro and Parque Central, the commercial district of **Sabana Grande** doesn't contain any memorable sights, but its lively street life and abundance of cheap restaurants make it a convenient base for a stay in Caracas. Though many locals still complain about security problems – indeed, the streets take on a menacing air after dark – the city's attempts to revitalize the neighbourhood have made it marginally safer.

Most activity takes place along chaotic Bulevar de Sabana Grande, a wide, 1.5-kilometre-long pedestrian thoroughfare lined with every imaginable trade, both legitimate and informal, as well as more upscale malls (see p.953).

El Hatillo

The quaint district of **El Hatillo,** historically a suburb of Caracas but now engulfed by sprawl, provides a welcome respite from urban mayhem. The only street noise here is gallery and boutique owners chatting on the sidewalk or faint salsa music wafting out of café doorways. For eating and shopping, see p.951 and p.953, respectively.

To **get here** from Caracas, take the thirty-minute metrobus ride from Avenida Sur below Plaza Altamira (Mon–Fri 5–10am & 4–10pm; every 40min). On weekends, *carritos* leave from the Chacaíto metro station – look for windshields displaying "El Hatillo". Get off at the road signs for Pueblo El Hatillo and Plaza Bolívar. Buses returning to Caracas

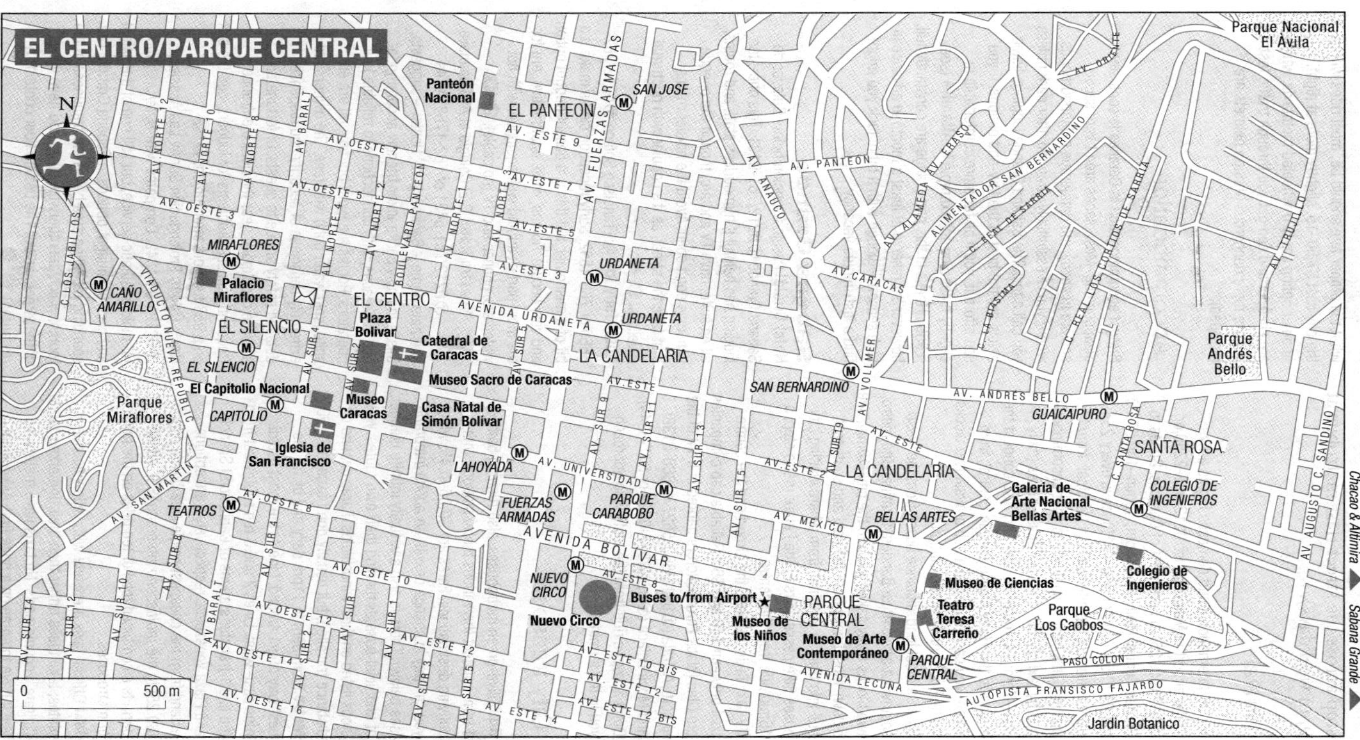

Chacao & Altimira ▶ Sabana Grande ▶

VENEZUELA

CARACAS

stop across the street (last metrobus at 9pm weekdays).

Arrival

By air International and domestic flights arrive at the airport in Maiquetía (☎0212/355-2250 or 355-2584), 26km northwest of Caracas. Buses to Parque Central (daily 5am–8pm; 45min–1hr; $7.50; ☎0212/352-4140 or 352-4818) leave every 25min from in front of the international terminal; from the bus stop, it's best to continue to your accommodation by taxi ($7.50–10). Red Sitssa buses (daily 8am–7pm; $4; roughly every 2hr) also connect the airport to the *Hotel Alba* in Parque Central, from where you can either hail a cab or walk two blocks to the Bellas Artes metro station.

By bus Most long-distance buses from the west/southwest arrive at La Bandera terminal; the metro, two blocks away, takes you into the city (10min; see below). Most buses from the east and southeast pull into Oriente terminal, from where waiting city buses take passengers to the Petare metro stop, a 15min ride from the centre.

By taxi Taxis between the airport and the centre cost between $40 and $60. Reliable cab companies are Utac (black Ford Explorers parked in front of the airport), Astrala (☎0212/860-5627 or 860-8138), and Movil Enlace (☎0212/577-0922 or 577-3344). Don't accept a ride from the touts who approach you in the terminal.

City transport

Bus Olive-green metrobuses, also running 5am–11pm, connect the various metro stations with outlying destinations. Fares are $0.35–0.45, which you can pay in change or with an *abono integrado* (see below). There is also a virtually infinite number of unofficial *busetas* running their own routes, with stops listed on their windshields. Fares depend on distance travelled, but usually don't exceed $0.60.

Metro From 5am to 11pm daily and by far the best way to get around. Line 1, the most useful, runs east–west. Lines 2 and 3 run southwest from the line 1 transfer stations of Capitolio/El Silencio and Plaza Venezuela, respectively. Fare options extend from the cheapest single-ride *boleto simple* ($0.25) to the *multiabono* integrado ($3), which permits a combined total of ten rides on the metro or metrobuses.

Taxi Official taxis are white with yellow license plates; take these rather than their unmarked *pirata* ("pirate") counterparts. No taxis have meters, so you'll have to agree on a price first. Ask a local what the proper fare should be; most rides within the city cost $7.50–10, slightly more at night. Another option are two-wheeled mototaxis, which are cheaper and can get you through traffic faster, but are more dangerous (though helmets are provided).

Accommodation

Budget accommodation in Caracas is consistently disappointing. Most places aren't very secure and are in seedy and dangerous neighbourhoods where you're essentially stranded after dark unless you call a taxi. The Sabana Grande lodgings listed below are the best of the low-end options. If you can afford it, you'll be far more comfortable in slightly nicer digs, for example in **Altamira** (see p.950). Hotels in this price range are constantly full, however, so reserve at least a month in advance in high season – though with a bit of luck you might find a last-minute vacancy.

Sabana Grande

Hotel Cristál Pasaje Asunción below Bulevar de Sabana Grande ☎0212/761-9131. This one-star lodging has helpful if humourless staff, and rooms, all en suite, have TV and a/c, though the opaque windows don't open. Avoid the noisier rooms that face the street, as it's popular with nocturnal revellers. ❺–❻

Hotel Jolly Inn Av Francisco Solano ☎0212/762-3665 or 763-1892. Surly reception clerks make it a bit of a misnomer, but this is a decent budget option and very secure. Rooms, while unattractive, are for the most part clean and well equipped, with hot water, a/c, phones and TV (no cable). ❺–❻

Nuestro Hotel C El Colegio at Av Casanova ☎0212/761-5431 or 762-1788. As its alternate name – Backpackers' Hostel – suggests, this is the only backpacker-friendly accommodation in Caracas, with connections to reliable tour operators. Rooms are worn but tidy; all are en suite (cold water only) with fans. The owners are extremely conscious of security and dispense detailed safety advice to guests. Unfortunately, a police checkpoint near the hotel's entrance frequently causes problems for lodgers; see the box on p.953 for more information. ❹–❻

Hotel Odeón Prolongación Sur Av Las Acacias ☎0212/793-1342. Competes with *Hotel Jolly Inn* for most apathetic service, but still one of the safest and cleanest budget options in Sabana Grande. The sparkling reception area belies the blandness of the rooms, which are otherwise clean and have views of the streets below. The bottom floor contains a restaurant. ❺–❻

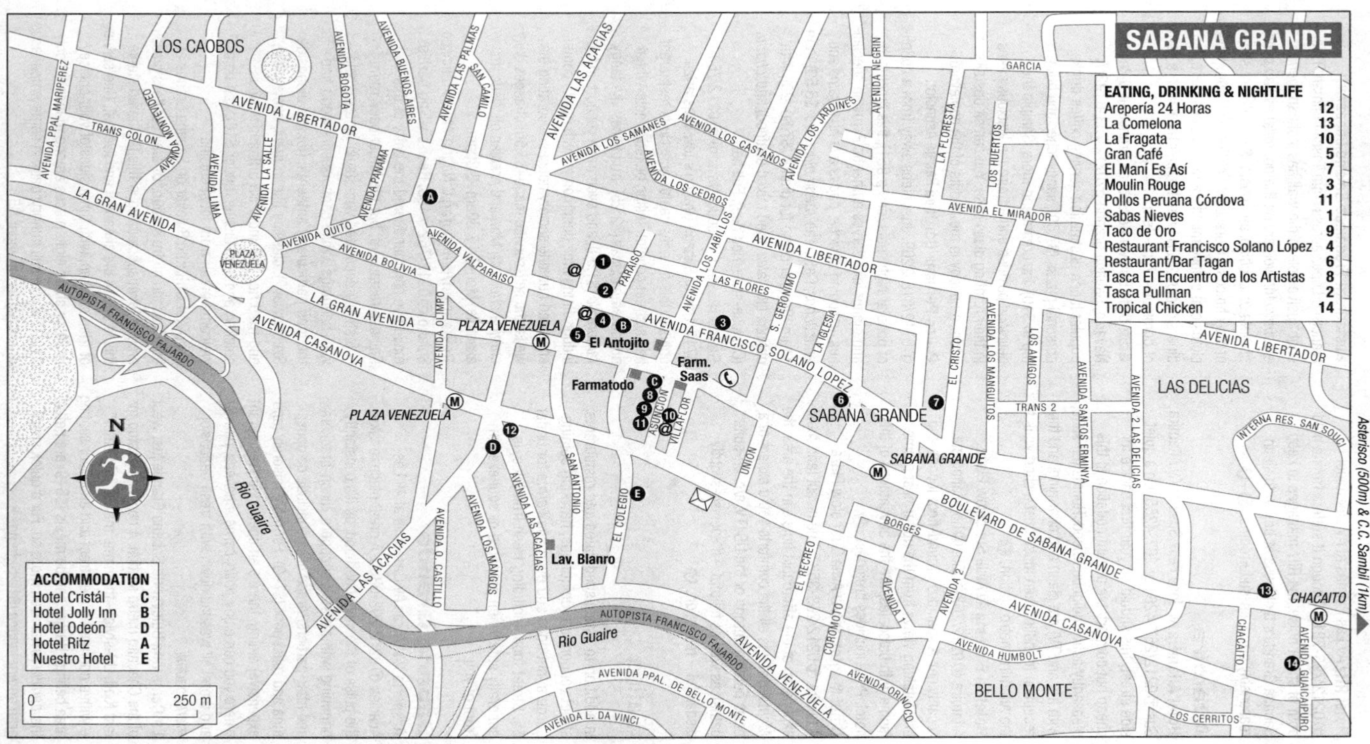
SABANA GRANDE
EATING, DRINKING & NIGHTLIFE
Arepería 24 Horas 12
La Comelona 13
La Fragata 10
Gran Café 5
El Maní Es Así 7
Moulin Rouge 3
Pollos Peruana Córdova 11
Sabas Nieves 1
Taco de Oro 9
Restaurant Francisco Solano López 4
Restaurant/Bar Tagan 6
Tasca El Encuentro de los Artistas 8
Tasca Pullman 2
Tropical Chicken 14
ACCOMMODATION
Hotel Cristál C
Hotel Jolly Inn B
Hotel Odeón D
Hotel Ritz A
Nuestro Hotel E
0
250 m
N
Asterisco (500m) & C.C. Sambil (1km)
LOS CAOBOS
LAS DELICIAS
SABANA GRANDE
BELLO MONTE
CHACAITO
PLAZA VENEZUELA
El Antojito
Farmatodo
Farm. Saas
Lav. Blanro
Rio Guaire
AUTOPISTA FRANCISCO FAJARDO
AVENIDA LIBERTADOR
LA GRAN AVENIDA
AVENIDA CASANOVA
AVENIDA FRANCISCO SOLANO LOPEZ
BOULEVARD DE SABANA GRANDE
AVENIDA LAS ACACIAS
AVENIDA VENEZUELA
AVENIDA PPAL. DE BELLO MONTE
AVENIDA L. DA VINCI
AVENIDA PPAL MARIPEREZ
TRANS COLON
AVENIDA MONTEVIDEO
AVENIDA LIMA
AVENIDA LA SALLE
AVENIDA PANAMA
AVENIDA BOGOTA
AVENIDA BUENOS AIRES
AVENIDA LAS PALMAS
SAN CAMILO
AVENIDA QUITO
AVENIDA BOLIVIA
AVENIDA VALPARAISO
AVENIDA OLIMPO
AVENIDA LOS SAMANES
AVENIDA LOS CASTAÑOS
AVENIDA LOS CEDROS
AVENIDA LOS JABILLOS
AVENIDA LOS JARDINES
AVENIDA NEGRIN
PARAISO
LAS FLORES
S. GERONIMO
LA IGLESIA
ASUNCION
VILLAFLOR
UNION
SAN ANTONIO
EL COLEGIO
AVENIDA O. CASTILLO
AVENIDA LOS MANGOS
AVENIDA LAS ACACIAS
EL RECREO
COROMOTO
AVENIDA 1
AVENIDA 2
BORGES
AVENIDA ORINOCO
AVENIDA HUMBOLT
EL CRISTO
AVENIDA LOS MANGUITOS
LOS AMIGOS
TRANS 2
AVENIDA SANTOS ERMINYA
AVENIDA 2 LAS DELICIAS
LA FLORESTA
LOS HUERTOS
AVENIDA EL MIRADOR
GARCIA
INTERNA RES. SAN SOUCI
CHACAITO
AVENIDA GUAICAIPURO
LOS CERRITOS

Hotel Ritz Av Las Palmas at Av Libertador ☎0212/793-7811. Though it suffers from a mild bout of street noise, the Ritz manages to keep Sabana Grande's tackiness at bay, with clean, reasonably sized, en-suite rooms. ❺–❻

Altamira

Hotel Altamira Av José Félix Sosa at Av Altamira Sur ☎0212/267-4284 or 267-4255. On a quiet side street, this should be your first choice for cheap but comfortable accommodation in this pleasantly active neighbourhood. Rooms (en suite, with a/c and TV) are clean and charming, and the reception friendlier than most. Just a short walk to the Altamira metro station. ❼

Hotel La Floresta Av Ávila Sur below Plaza Altamira ☎0212/263-1955, ⓔhotellafloresta@cantv.net. A spacious ground-floor lounge and breathtaking views from the uppermost rooms (some with balconies) are the advantages of this hotel. Price includes breakfast. ❽

Hotel Montserrat Av Ávila Sur below Plaza Altamira ☎0212/263-3533. The nicest (and most expensive) of the affordable hotels in the area, the *Montserrat* has all the comforts you'd expect of a basic hotel in Europe or the US (TV, a/c, en-suite baths), as well as helpful – if ever-so-slightly disdainful – reception. ❾

Eating

In addition to established cafés and restaurants, street vendors are ubiquitous, hawking bulging burgers, hot dogs and even *shawarma* for under $5. Street food, including fresh fruit juice, is generally safe when prepared or squeezed in front of you.

Sabana Grande

Arepería 24 Horas Av Casanova at Av Las Acacias ☎0212/793-0865. A great place to take the pulse of the neighbourhood, as it's constantly brimming with *taxistas*, shoppers, lunch-breakers and after-partiers. *Arepa* fillings include octopus, tuna and roast pork ($7–9). For more leisurely (and expensive) dining, there's an open-sided restaurant where you can enjoy *pollo*, *carne mechada, parrilla* and more, all washed down with fresh *batidos* or *merengadas*.

La Comelona Bulevar de Sabana Grande just west of the Chacaíto metro station. A convenient stop for fast food, US-style – the name means "big eater" – with a counter on the street and an indoor seating area behind. Burger combo meals ($6–9) are hefty, the *parrilla mixta* even more so. For a quick snack, grab an *empanada* ($1.25) to go.

Restaurant Francisco Solano López Av Francisco López across from Tasca Pullman. This unobtrusive hole in the wall has a cheap *menú ejecutivo* for workers on the go: *milanesa de pollo*, *chuleta de cochino*, and pasta ($4–7.50) are some of the choices. Fluorescent lighting and worn tablecloths don't leave much room for atmosphere, but diners occasionally wrap up their meal with a game of dominoes. 7am–7pm.

Gran Café Bulevar de Sabana Grande at C Pascual Navarro, Sabana Grande ☎0212/763-6792. A popular lunch destination serving coffee drinks, personal pizzas ($7.50), sandwiches and burgers (up to $10), ice cream and more. Sample the delicious pastries and admire the luscious cakes in their rotating glass case. You can sit upstairs or under a canopy in the middle of the boulevard.

Pollos Peruana Córdova Pasaje Asunción ☎0212/816-2209. Just steps away from a couple of popular nightspots (see p.951), this tiny lunch and dinner joint serves authentic Peruvian specialities, including *ceviche*, *papas a la huancaina* and *anticuchos*. Catch the *menú ejecutivo* ($5.50) from 11am–3pm, or come for dinner ($7.50–20), with options like *jalea* (fried mixed seafood) and *chaufa* (Chinese-style fried rice). Full bar.

Sabas Nieves C Pascual Navarro ☎0212/763-6712. One of Sabana Grande's few vegetarian options, this friendly, health-conscious restaurant has a street counter selling baked, whole-wheat ricotta *empanadas* ($2.25), fruit juices like tangy *tamarindo* ($1.50), and even fresh yoghurt. In the indoor dining area (lunch only), with health conference and humane society notices decorating the walls, the self-service menu ($5.50) changes daily: *comida criolla* on Mon and Arabian on Wedn, for example. Mon–Fri 7.30am–3.30pm.

Restaurant/Bar Tagan C Negrin at Av Francisco Solano ☎0212/762-7486. Beer-swilling barflies may have commandeered the entry of this Chinese restaurant, but the larger back room is festively decorated with paper lanterns and wall-hangings. While connoisseurs won't find the food particularly authentic (*lumpia* alongside Szechuwan?), classics like lo *mein*, *chow mein*, and fried rice (all under $5.50), and various chicken and beef dishes (under $10), can be a welcome break from local cuisine.

Tropical Chicken Bulevar de Sabana Grande at the Chacaíto metro station. Of the countless places around town specializing in this feathered staple, this is one of the cheapest and liveliest. One serving of fried chicken, with three sides of your choice, is $6, or share eight pieces among friends for only $12. If you're still hungry, pack in some *empanadas* or *cachapas* for under $5.

Altamira/Los Palos Grandes

Evio's Pizza 4a Av between 2da and 3ra Transversals, Los Palos Grandes ⓣ0212/283-6608. A popular neighbourhood pizza joint serving classic pies alongside ones with more creative offerings, such as Roquefort and goat cheese (personal $12.50, medium under $22, large under $30). Pasta dishes (under $15) are also available, and you can snack on *empanadas* for $2.50 each. Live jazz, folk or salsa is performed Thurs–Sat, with a $3 cover. 12–4pm & 6pm–midnight.

Heladería Frapé 3ra Av at 4a Transversal, Los Palos Grandes ⓣ0212/285-3102. You won't even notice the sourpuss staff once you sample one of the many exotic ice-cream flavours on offer here, among them *ciruela de huesito* (similar to plum), *tamarindo*, *parchita* (passionfruit), and *guanabana* (soursop). Enjoy your treat in the street-side patio, painted with Mondrianesque simplicity, or take it to go.

Luna Llena Arepa Factory 2da Transversal at 2da Av, Los Palos Grandes ⓣ0212/286-1125. Come here for "gourmet" *arepas* ($4.50), slimmer than usual and grilled in a *panino* press. Choose from such fillings as eggplant, *caprese*, salmon, *queso planchado*, and more, then vie for a seat among chattering families at one of the spotless tables. You can also take home a sweet 'n' salty *torta de queso criolla*, a cheesecake-like dessert. Till 9.30pm weeknights, 1am weekends.

Restaurant Presidente 3ra Av between 1ra and 2da transversals, Los Palos Grandes ⓣ0212/283-8246. A cute, homey place for an inexpensive dinner, with pink walls, soothing paintings, and checkered tablecloths. The set menu ($12.50) includes a starter (cream of sweet potato, tuna salad or pasta salad), a main (meatballs, pork, or chicken croquettes), and a dessert. Wash it all down with any number of fresh fruitjuice flavours.

El Hatillo

The Brew Place C Bolívar #20 ⓣ0212/961-5034. An oddly named Middle Eastern affair serving *lahmacun*, *kibbe*, kabab, *shawarma* and more ($7.50–15). Combo plates come laced with baba ghanoush and hummus, and there are even hookahs for rent ($12.50). Mon–Thurs noon–10pm, Fri–Sun 8am–11pm.

TREAT YOURSELF

Café Atlantique Av Andres Bello, just north of Av Francisco de Miranda ⓣ0212/287-0110 or 287-0223. Boasting one of the city's top-rated chefs, this haute cuisine sanctuary wins high marks for design as well: the industrial-chic interior, with a blue-green brick floor and Jetsons-style furnishings, faces the street through a wall-length, floor-to-ceiling window. Sip a pre-prandial Black Label on the patio, with a full view of the kitchen, then sit down to a three-course set menu (a mere $27) of beef carpaccio, Mérida greens with caramelized onions, *churrasco de dorado* with cauliflower, or *asopado de arroz* with lobster-calamari bisque. Afterwards, feed your sweet tooth with passionfruit mousse or tree tomato coulis. For lighter fare, there's a blue-lit tapas bar, serving herbed goat cheese, prosciutto, smoked Norwegian salmon, and more. Reservations suggested, closed Sun.

Drinking and nightlife

Caracas has **bars and clubs** for virtually anyone, and at any time – many establishments stay open until the last patron leaves. Being a large and relatively cosmopolitan city, it also has a decent selection of **gay and lesbian nightspots**. Check ⓦwww.rumbacaracas.com for a variety of club and event listings. As most streets empty out after dark, especially in the western districts, it's wise to take taxis to and from your destination.

Sabana Grande

El Maní Es Así C El Cristo. The place to cut a rug in Caracas, this legendary salsa club has an intricately decorated interior, with hanging musical instruments, vintage posters, old porcelain beer taps, and a bamboo ceiling, all illuminated by soft amber lighting. Open Tues–Sat; arrive early for occasional salsa lessons.

Moulin Rouge Av Francisco Solano ⓣ0212/761-1990. With a giant, two-dimensional windmill for a façade, you can't miss this ever-popular dive bar/club, where the city's pierced and tattooed rockers, ravers and gutter-punks convene for endless nights of energetic live music. Tues–Sat from 9pm.

Taco de Oro Pasaje la Asunción. A no-frills, bi-level venue with a bar and pool tables – one hour of pool costs $3.50. Patrons who can't tolerate the ear-splitting music upstairs sit downstairs and play dominoes or cards.

Tasca El Encuentro de los Artistas Pasaje la Asunción. On most nights, canned tunes spill out

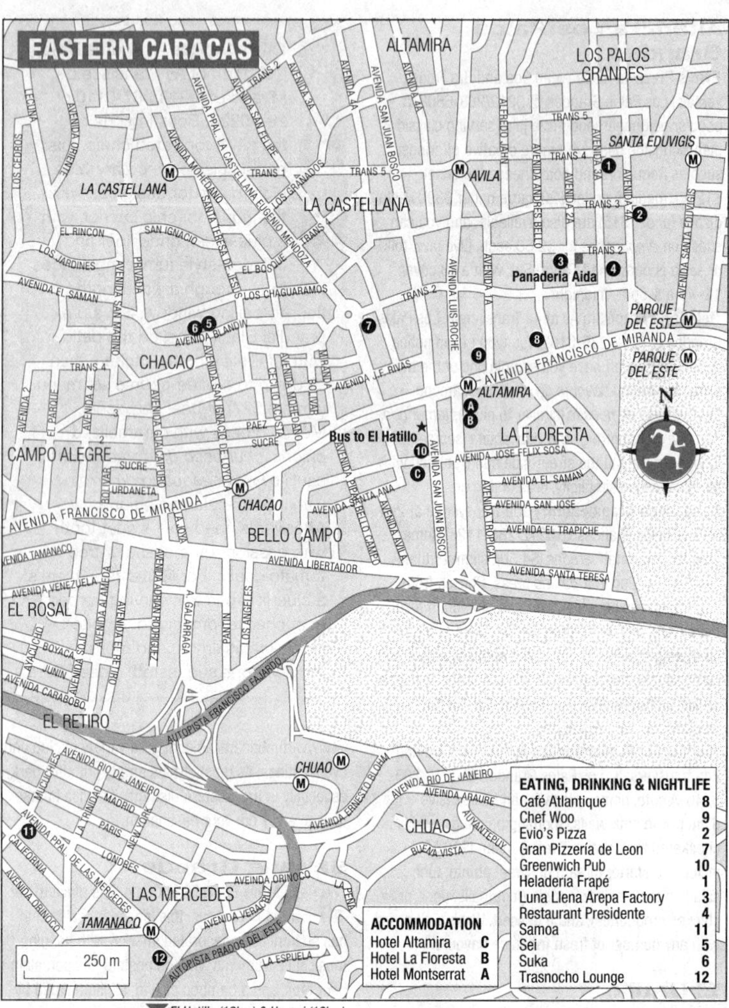

of this bar into the narrow pedestrian street, but once the end of the week rolls around, live jazz (Thurs) and salsa (Fri) draw a bohemian crowd, as do the occasional poetry readings. If you prefer to just chat, claim a picnic table in the middle of the alley, one wall of which is decorated with a curious mural. Food served until 3pm, closed Sun.

Altamira/Los Palos Grandes

Chef Woo 1ra Av above Av Francisco de Miranda, Los Palos Grandes ⓣ0212/285-1723. Though it doesn't have much in the way of atmosphere, local students flock to this Chinese restaurant (and its neighbour, *Lai Can*) for super-cheap beers and lively conversation. Closes 11pm.

Gran Pizzería de Leon 2da Transversal de la Castellana ⓣ0212/263-6014. A classic bar (and pizzeria) that's been pouring suds for generations. There's a sizeable indoor seating area, though nearly all drinkers choose a table on the vast, raised patio. Closes 2am.

Greenwich Pub Av San Juan Bosco, Altamira ⓣ0416/826-6177. A small but spirited Irish pub with two-toned walls, a wooden bar, and a canned rock soundtrack – unless you come Thursday through Sun, when there's live pop and alternative.

Sei In Centro Comercial San Ignacio. Not as inviting or popular as its neighbour, *Suka* (see below), though a good alternative if that one's too crowded – plus it has a dancefloor for those who can interpret the ear-splitting techno. Partiers tend to arrive around 1am. Closed Sun.
Suka In Centro Comercial San Ignacio. This pan-Asian-themed bar, redolent of incense and hosting DJs every night, is the most unique of the Centro Comercial San Ignacio nightspots; it even has a giant net suspended from the ceiling, which patrons can relax in, and a roped-off outdoor seating area. Closes 4am.

Las Mercedes

Samoa Av Principal de Las Mercedes at C Mucuchíes ⓣ0412/239-7836. One of many bars along the avenue, *Samoa* stands out for its South Pacific surf theme, replete with tiki touches and looped videos of monster breaks. Three rooms of varying chill factor give you plenty of choice, depending on your mood.

Gay and Lesbian

La Fragata C Villa Flor, Sabana Grande ⓣ0212/762-1684. Excuse the cheesy, neon-heavy décor and focus instead on the cheap drinks, crowded dancefloor and friendly, mostly male clientele.
Tasca Pullman Av Francisco Solano, Sabana Grande ⓣ0212/761-1112. One of Caracas's oldest gay bars, and still sporting a distinctly Eighties vibe, this dimly lit place draws a friendly, working-class crowd and the occasional drag queen. Mostly male, though women are welcome.
Trasnocho Lounge Centro Comercial Paseo de las Mercedes ⓣ0212/993-1325. Popular with a mixed crowd of bohemian theatre-goers, this chic lounge has mirrored ceilings and a house-music soundtrack. It is just one aspect of the Trasnocho complex, which also contains a cinema, theatre and café. Closed Sun.

Shopping

Shopping culture in Caracas is dominated by mega-malls, where your chances of finding unique, inexpensive crafts are virtually nonexistent. Street shopping is a bit more promising, at least in terms of prices, and the Hannsi crafts outlet in El Hatillo (see p.954) is your best source for souvenirs.
El Antojito Av Los Jabillos, Sabana Grande. A *panadería* selling bread, pastries, cheese, cold cuts, sandwiches and beverages. A good place to stock up on lunch supplies before a day-trip to El Ávila (see p.955). 6am–10.30pm, closed Mon.

SAFETY IN CARACAS

While locals' constant **warnings** of robberies and assaults can sound a bit paranoid, you should always be alert when walking the streets and avoid staying out alone after dark, especially in and around the western districts of El Centro, Parque Central and Sabana Grande. Don't venture up deserted side streets, even during the day, or carry more money or bank cards than you need.

With a bit of common sense you're unlikely to get mugged, but you'll probably have at least one run-in with the Caracas **police**, many of whom consider visitors easy targets for extortion. Red police tents occupy some street corners, particularly in Sabana Grande (one just up the street from Nuestro Hotel; see p.948), and if you pass by looking remotely foreign, you're liable to be pulled inside for interrogation and a "drug search". Police have a special knack for pocketing stray cash while their colleagues distract you with questions, so keep a firm grip on your valuables and watch the one pawing through your stuff. Never offer bribes, as this will definitely land you in more trouble.

Asterisco Torre Impres, behind Centro Lido in El Rosal ⓣ0212/953-6173, ⓦwww.asterisco.net.ve. One of the city's most original shops, selling handmade puzzles, journals and snacks, natural bottled juices, and hand-painted T-shirts, as well as crafts from the nearby town of San Francisco de Yare (see p.957). The hip, English-speaking owners are wonderfully welcoming. Mon–Fri 7am–6pm.
Bulevar de Sabana Grande Sabana Grande. The principal artery of the eponymous district (see p.946) is a budget shopper's paradise. You can also scope out the mallrats at City Market, between C Unión and C Villa Flor, or at Centro Comercial El Recreo, a block south of the boulevard at C El Recreo and Av Casanova.
Centro Comercial Sambil Chacao. The most famous of the city's malls, this mind-bogglingly enormous complex hosts every conceivable amenity, including top international brands. Mon–Sat 10am–9pm, Sun and holidays noon–8pm.

Hannsi C Bolívar #12, El Hatillo ⓣ0212/963-7184 or 963-6513, ⓦwww.hannsi.com.ve. A sprawling, multi-shop conglomeration of craft, jewellery and knick-knack outlets, with a fairly good selection of books on Venezuela. Loads of chintzy junk, but occasional treasures as well. Mon–Thurs 10am–7pm, Fri–Sun till 8pm.

Libreria Tecni-Ciencias In Centro Comercial Sambil ⓣ0212/264-1765. Although prices are a bit high and the staff isn't especially helpful, this is still one of the best bookstores in Caracas, with several other locations around the city (one in Centro Lido in El Rosal). Same hours as C.C. Sambil (p.953).

Panadería Aida 2da Av at 2da Transversal, Los Palos Grandes. This Portuguese-owned bakery sells beautiful pastries as well as cheese, salami and other sandwich fixin's. Neighbourhood locals rate the coffee the best in town. Daily 7am–7.30pm.

SBS Sports Business Centro Lido, Av Francisco de Miranda ⓣ0212/953-0976. Come here to buy your official Caracas Leones baseball gear, including jerseys, T-shirts, caps, pins, stickers – and even game tickets. Daily 10am–8pm.

Directory

Banks In a city as shopping-obsessed as Caracas, you can't walk ten steps without passing a bank. Several (all with ATMs) line Bulevar de Sabana Grande: Banco de Venezuela at C San Antonio, Banesco just west of the Sabana Grande metro station, and Banco Mercantil just east of the Chacaíto metro station. There's a Banco de Venezuela (and others) in the international airport terminal, as well as an Italcambio for exchanging traveller's cheques; visit ⓦwww.italcambio.com for other locations around town. See p.944 for bank hours.

Embassies and consulates Brazil, Av Mohedano and C Los Chaguaramos in La Castellana ⓣ0212/261-4481, ⓔbrasembcaracas@cantv.net. Mon–Fri 9am–1pm; Canada, Av Francisco de Miranda at Av Sur, Altamira ⓣ0212/600-3000, ⓦwww.caracas.gc.ca. Mon–Thurs 7.30am–4.30pm, Fri 7.30am–1.30pm; Colombia, C Guaicaipuro in Chacaíto ⓣ0212/951-3631, ⓔconsulcolca@cantv.net. Mon–Fri 8am–1pm; Guyana, Av El Paseo, Quinta Roraima in Prados del Este ⓣ0212/977-1158, ⓔembguy@cantv.net. Mon–Thurs 8.30am–3.30pm, Fri 8.30–3pm; Ireland, Av Venezuela, Torre Clement, 2nd Floor, Office 2-A in El Rosal ⓣ0212/951-3645, ⓔirlconven@cantv.net. Mon–Fri 8am–12.30pm; South Africa, Centro Profesional Eurobuilding, P-4, Office 4B-C in Chuao ⓣ0212/991-4622, ⓔrsavenconsular@cantv.net. Mon–Fri 9am–1pm; UK, Av Principal de La Castellana, Torre La Castellana 11th Floor ⓣ0212/267-1275, ⓔbritishembassy@internet.ve. Mon–Thurs 2–4pm; US, Colinas de Valle Arriba, Calle F at Calle Suapure ⓣ0212/977-2011, ⓦcaracas.usembassy.gov. Mon–Fri 8am–2pm.

Hospital Two highly recommended clinics are Hospital de Clínicas Caracas, Av Panteón at Av Alameda in San Bernardino (ⓣ0212/508-6111, ⓦwww.clinicaracas.com), and Clinica El Ávila, on Av San Juan Bosco at 6ta Transversal in Altamira (ⓣ0212/276-1111 or 276-1052, ⓦwww.clinicaelavila.com).

Immigration office Oficina Nacional de Identificación y Extranjería (Onidex), Av Baralt in front of Plaza Miranda, two blocks south of El Silencio metro station ⓣ0212/483-2070, ⓦwww.onidex.gov.ve. Mon–Fri 8–11.30am.

Information There are two Inatur desks in the airport's international terminal (both 8am–midnight; ⓣ0212/355-1943 or 355-2204), and another in the national terminal (7am–9pm). There's also an office in Caracas, in the Complejo Mintur, Torre Inatur, Av Francisco de Miranda in Altamira (8am–5pm; ⓣ0212/208-7926 or 208-4652).

Internet There's a rash of internet cafés in Caracas, especially in pedestrian-heavy Sabana Grande. Most charge $0.75–1.25 per hr. Two reliable options are MSX Cybershop, C San Antonio between Bulevar de Sabana Grande and Av Francisco Solano, and Ciberplace, C Villa Flor below Bulevar de Sabana Grande. Both daily 8.30am–8.30pm.

Laundry Most accommodation will do your laundry for a small fee (generally less than $5 per load). Otherwise, try Lavandería Blanro, Prolongación Sur Av Las Acacias ⓣ0212/793-6103. Mon–Fri 7am–noon & 1–6pm.

Left luggage Both La Bandera and Oriente bus terminals (see opposite) offer luggage storage (around $0.75 per hr; Mon–Sat 6am–8.45pm, Sun 7am–7pm), and most accommodation will hold luggage for you as well.

Pharmacy Pharmacies are just as ubiquitous as banks and internet cafés. On Bulevar de Sabana Grande, Farmacia Saas is at C Villa Flor and Farmatodo at C El Colegio. See p.944 for an explanation of pharmacy hours.

Phone CANTV and Movistar have call centers throughout the city. There's a CANTV office on Bulevar de Sabana Grande in Edifico El Recreo (not to be confused with the nearby Centro Comercial El Recreo), and another on C San Antonio above Av Francisco Solano, which also offers internet. Both daily 8.30am–6.30pm.

Post office The principal Ipostel office, on Av Urdaneta at Carmelitas, three blocks north of the Capitolio metro station, is open weekdays 8am–4.30pm. There's another Ipostel office in Sabana Grande, Av Casanova in C.C. Cediaz (same hours; ⓣ0212/761-8155), and yet another at the international airport.

Travel agents Candes ⓣ0212/571-0987 in Hotel *Alba* on Av Sur at Av México; Club del Trotamundo ⓣ0212/283-7253 in Centro Comercial Centro Plaza in Los Palos Grandes; Perez Travel & Turismo ⓣ0212/762-8575 in *Hotel Lincoln Suites* on Av Francisco Solano in Sabana Grande. For reputable tour operators, see p.938.

Moving on

By air Visitors leaving Venezuela must pay an exit tax of $47. Before paying, ask an airline representative if the tax has already been included in your airfare. Various airlines connect to Bogotá (several daily; 1hr); Buenos Aires (several daily; generally 12hr w/connection); Lima (4 daily; 3–5hr); Quito (4 daily; 3hr w/connection); Santiago de Chile (4 daily; 8–9hr w/connection); São Paulo (2 daily; 8–10hr w/connection); and other destinations. Flights within Venezuela are fairly expensive and the bus network is so wide-ranging and efficient that flying only makes sense if you need to cover a lot of ground in a very short time. Check with your air carrier whether the domestic airport tax ($9) is already included in your airfare. From the national terminal, daily flights serve Ciudad Bolívar (2 daily except Sat; 1hr 30min); Los Roques (see box, p.957); Maracaibo (several daily; 1hr); Mérida (5 daily; 1hr 30min); Porlamar (hourly; 45min); Puerto Ayacucho (2 daily except Sat; 1hr 30min); Puerto Ordáz (several daily; 1hr); and other cities.

By bus Caracas has two major bus terminals. Exercise caution in and around both, as the crowds are a pickpocket's playground.

Terminal La Bandera has buses that go to the west and southwest. It is an easy two-block walk from the metro station of the same name, though at night you should take a cab between the two. Barinas (2 daily; 9hr); Coro (several daily; 9hr); Maracaibo (4 daily; 12hr); Maracay (hourly; 1hr 30min); Mérida (6 daily; 13hr); San Antonio del Táchira (2 daily; 12hr); San Fernando de Apure (3 daily; 8hr); Valencia (hourly; 3hr).

Terminal de Oriente mostly services the east and southeast, though red Sitssa buses (ⓣ0212/242-2538) cover the whole country. There are also daily departures to Colombian cities, including Cartagena and Barranquilla. The terminal lies to the east of the city; get there by taking the metro to the Petare station, followed by a 15min taxi ride to the terminal. Barcelona (5 daily; 6hr); Barinas (2 daily; 9hr); Carúpano (several daily; 10hr); Ciudad Bolívar (3 daily; 9hr); Cumaná (several daily; 8hr); Maracay (hourly; 1hr 30min; Puerto Ayacucho (1 daily; 14hr); Puerto La Cruz (hourly; 6hr); Puerto Ordáz (several daily; 10hr); San Fernando de Apure (1 daily; 8hr); Santa Elena de Uairén (2 daily; 24hr); Tucupita (2 daily; 12hr); Valencia (7 daily; 3hr). Several bus companies have their own private terminals. **Aeroexpresos Ejecutivos** (ⓣ0212/266-2321, ⓦwww.aeroexpresos.com.ve) offers very comfortable but slightly more expensive services to Ciudad Bolívar, Maracaibo, Valencia, Puerto La Cruz and other cities. The terminal is on Av Principal de Bello Campo in Chacao.

DAY-TRIPS FROM CARACAS

For a quick escape from the hustle and bustle of Caracas, ride the cable car that ascends the slopes of **Parque Nacional El Ávila,** with its spectacular view of the capital. If you've got more time consider visiting **Colonia Tovar,** a scenic mountain village inhabited for over 160 years by German descendants.

Parque Nacional el Ávila

Separating Caracas from the coast, **Parque Nacional El Ávila** is based more or less around a mountain whose highest point is 2765 meters. From here, visitors have stunning views – on clear days – of Caracas on one side and the Caribbean Sea on the other.

There are several ways to explore the park. Four well-marked and safe hiking trails lead into the park from Caracas, all reachable via Avenida Boyacá. It is also possible to drive to the top in a 4WD vehicle. However, the most popular option is the **teleférico** (Mon noon–8pm, Tues–Sat 10.30am–8pm, Sun 10am–8pm; 10min; $12.50), a high-speed cable car that leaves from the intersection of Avenida Principal de Maripérez and Avenida Boyacá and climbs 1200 metres to the top of the mountain.

From here, a trail leads down to the small village of **Galipán**, perched on the flower-bedecked mountain slopes. Be sure to stop at one of the many roadside stands selling fresh strawberries and cream ($2.50) and *pernil* (roast pork) sandwiches ($6–7.50). To explore the park further, or to see it by jeep, contact Akanán Tours, an operator offering day-long hiking, rappelling and sightseeing trips (see p.938). Another option is San José de Galipán Tierra Amada (☎0414/336-6407), a jeep company that plies the Caracas–Galipán–Macuto road ($10 per person).

The northern coast

The coast of Vargas state, separated from Caracas by the rugged Parque Nacional El Ávila (see p.955), provides an excellent and accessible sampling of Venezuela's **beaches**, especially if you don't have time to visit the northwest or northeast. The area's beaches, including Los Caracas and Playa Pantaleta – "Panty Beach" – are popular with surfers from the capital. To **get here** under your own steam, catch the bus from Parque Central to the airport (see p.948), and continue 35km by taxi to La Guaira or Macuto ($25). Here you can catch one of the *busetas* that ply the seaside highway, La Costanera, in both directions; hop off and on wherever you choose.

If you're travelling with a group, it's worth springing for a jeep tour with English-speaking *caraqueño* Luis Moncada, who can combine a day-trip to the various beaches, and the rugged jungle beyond, with a tour of Parque Nacional El Ávila ($100; ☎0414/249-1479).

Colonia Tovar

Founded by German immigrants in 1843, the small mountain village of **Colonia Tovar**, 60km west of Caracas, is still inhabited by their ancestors. Most of the houses have been reconstructed or built in traditional Black Forest style, and restaurants selling German sausages and local strawberries and cream line the main roads of the village. "Colonia" is a popular destination on weekends, when it can be packed with day-tripping *caraqueños*.

In addition to the architecture and food, the **Museo de Historia y Artesanía** (Sat & Sun 9am–6pm; $0.50) features a small but interesting collection of documents, clothes, tools, guns and other relics of the village's early days. **Cervecería Tovar** (Mon–Fri 8am–5pm, Sat & Sun 10am–4pm), 100m below the church, offers free tours of their microbrewery, which you can see in action on weekdays.

To **get here** from Caracas, take the metro to the La Yaguara station. Around the corner, buses leave for El Junquito ($0.25; 1hr), where you transfer to a *buseta* for the ride to Colonia Tovar ($1.75; 1hr). Daily departures from El Junquito are at 6.30am, 7.15am, and then on the hour from 8am until 5pm.

Leaving Colonia Tovar, *busetas* depart from 300 metres outside the village on the road to El Junquito. The last *buseta* departs Colonia at 6.30pm.

Accommodation

Since you can see the entire town in a couple hours, there's not much reason to pay the high rates to stay in Colonia Tovar, and it's so popular with Venezuelans that reservations are often required a month in advance. If you can't bear to leave, however, there are a couple of relatively affordable options. Nearly all Colonia lodgings have a two-night minimum for reserved stays, though guests lucky enough to nab a room on the spot can usually spend just one night.

***Cabañas* Briedenbach** ☎0244/355-1211. A row of eighteen units overlooking the village and surrounding hillsides. Simple but cozy rooms have TV, hot water and mini-fridges. Family-friendly, with a playground and a lawn. ❼

***Cabañas* Silberbrunnen** ☎0244/355-1490. Small but tidy *cabañas*, set in a well-tended, terraced garden, have TVs, refrigerators, thick comforters, hot water and nice views. ❼

Eating

Delicatessen Vienna Just above the church. One of a couple of cheap eateries serving simple German fare, such as sausage sandwiches ($6.50), with the added bonus of servers dressed in traditional garb. Mon–Fri 8am–noon & 3–7pm, Sat & Sun 8am–8pm.

Lunchería Schmuk Hundred metres uphill from the church. A modest but filling portion of sausage, potato salad and slaw costs a mere $4. Lunch only.

Tour operators

Douglas Pridham (Ⓣ0416/743-8939, Ⓦwww.vivatrek.com), expert paraglider, can get you airborne from the steep hillsides around Colonia Tovar. His outfit also offers guided excursions into Parque Nacional Henri Pittier (see p.958).

Rustic Tours (Ⓣ0244/355-1908, Ⓔrustictours@cantv.net) runs jeep outings through the mountainous countryside (2hr; $12.50).

SAN FRANCISCO DE YARE

The otherwise nondescript town of **San Francisco de Yare**, 60km southeast of Caracas, is the site of one of Venezuela's most famous spectacles, the **Festival de los Diablos Danzantes** ("dancing devils"). In observance of the Catholic holy day Corpus Christi (in late May or early June; check with Caracas tourism offices for exact dates), townspeople don elaborate devil masks and costumes and engage in highly ritualized performances. While similar festivals occur in other parts of Venezuela, including Ocumare de la Costa, Chuao, Naiguatá and Cuyagua, Yare's is considered the quintessential event.

Even if you're not in town for the festival, be sure to visit the workshop of internationally recognized mask-maker Juan Morgado, at Calle Rivas #19, two blocks north of the Plaza Bolívar (Ⓣ0239/222-9345, Ⓔmorgadoki@yahoo.com). One block towards the plaza, the small and mostly empty Casa de los Diablos Danzantes de Yare (8am–12.30pm & 2–4pm, closed Tues & Sat) houses a fascinating collection of vintage masks.

From Caracas, take the metro to the Nuevo Circo station and walk one block to the bus terminal of the same name. From here, buses leave every fifteen minutes for Ocumare del Tuy (daily 4am–11pm; 1hr 30min; $2). From the Ocumare terminal, frequent *busetas* to Santa Teresa drop passengers at Yare's Plaza Bolívar (20min; $0.40).

To return, Ocumare-bound *busetas* depart from one block east and one block north of the Plaza Bolívar. Buses from Ocumare to Caracas leave every fifteen minutes until 9pm.

TREAT YOURSELF

Surrounded by crystal-clear water, the white-sand beaches on the 42 islets of **Los Roques** are among Venezuela's finest. They are also the country's most pristine and exclusive; the main island, Gran Roque, contains the archipelago's only community. Encompassed by a national park protecting a 24-kilometre coral reef system, the island chain is home to a tremendous diversity of aquatic life, including barracuda, octopuses and manta rays.

Package trips here are generally cheaper than arranging your own flights and accommodation, and if you can shoulder the cost – around $500–650 for two days/one night – you may decide to abandon a month of mainland travel plans for an extra week of snorkelling and scuba diving. **Day-trips** from Caracas are easier on the wallet, starting at around $225 ($300 on weekends), and include return airfare, food and a guide. Caracas-based agencies serving Los Roques include A1 Aseyreca (Ⓣ0212/693-9573, Ⓔa1tours@cantv.net) and Absolute Travel (Ⓣ0212/959-7041, Ⓔabsolutetravel@cantv.net); for others, see p.938.

Another option, provided you're entirely self-sufficent, is to **camp** on the smaller, uninhabited islands around Gran Roque. You'll need a permit from Inparques (see p.939) and you can only camp within designated areas. Two 45-minute flights depart from Maiquetía airport to Los Roques on weekdays, 4–5 on weekends; Aerotuy is a major carrier (Ⓣ0212/212-3110 or 212-3111).

The northwest coast

Venezuela's **northwest coast** gets much less press than the Caribbean offshore islands of Aruba, Bonaire and Curaçao, but offers similarly spectacular beaches alongside some of the Caribbean's prettiest colonial towns and two fine national parks.

Parque Nacional Henri Pittier, roughly 150 kilometers from Caracas, sports beautiful, palm-lined sands, striking mountain-range backdrops and four vegetation zones housing a tremendous array of birds and plant life. Parque Nacional Morrocoy, a few hours to the west of Pittier and more popular than its neighbour, is best known for its gorgeous white-sand keys surrounded by crystalline water.

Three hours west of Morrocoy, the well-preserved colonial town of Coro serves as a good break from the parks. From here, most visitors head directly into the Andes, but some press on 360 kilometers west (6–7hr) to cross the border into Colombia (see p.967).

PARQUE NACIONAL HENRI PITTIER

Created in 1937, **Parque Nacional Henri Pittier** was Venezuela's first national park, named for a famous Swiss geographer and botanist who classified more than thirty thousand plants in Venezuela. Despite the park's great biodiversity, the vast majority of visitors come for its **beaches**. In fact, on weekends it can be totally overrun, but it is generally quiet during the week.

Pittier's wide array of **flora and fauna** is a result of the relatively short distance in which it climbs from sea level to 2430 meters, for the changes in altitude create numerous distinct vegetation zones. The park is also renowned among birdwatchers, containing 520 bird species in just over a thousand square kilometres – 41.6 percent of Venezuela's bird species and 6.5 percent of the world's. Noteworthy specimens include the rufous-vented chachalaca, the scaled piculet, the pale-tipped inezia and the Venezuelan bristle-tyrant.

The only two roads into Pittier form a "V", with Maracay at the vertex and **Choroní** and **Ocumare de la Costa** at the two ends. Choroní, in the eastern portion of the park, has the lion's share of the budget accommodation and is one of the few backpacker destinations in Venezuela. Ocumare, while not as enticing a town, is worth visiting for its lovely beaches.

What to see and do

The park can be explored along several hiking trails, but the best base for serious wildlife-spotting is **Estación Biológica Rancho Grande** (☎0243/550-7734), on the highway between Maracay and Ocumare. At about 1100 meters, this research station for the Universidad Central de Venzuela has a multitude of trails from which visitors are likely to see an incredible variety of birds and perhaps some howler monkeys. The station also offers very rustic dormitory **accommodation** ($10), but guests must

MOVING ON FROM HENRI PITTIER

By bus The Maracay terminal has nearly constant departures to Caracas (1hr 30min) and Valencia (45min), in addition to the following destinations: Barinas (8 daily; 9hr); Coro (several daily; 6hr); Maracaibo (several daily; 8hr); Mérida (2 daily; 10hr); Puerto Ayacucho (2 daily; 12hr); San Antonio del Táchira (2 daily; 12hr); San Fernando de Apure (4 daily; 6hr). There are no ATMs in the station, though there is a left luggage office ($0.50 per hr).

bring their own sheets or a sleeping bag, as well as food to cook in the communal kitchen. To **get here**, just ask the bus driver to let you off at Rancho Grande.

For guided **day-trips** through the park and the islands off its coast, contact *Casa Luna Espinoza* in Choroní (see p.960). Colonia Tovar-based Viva Trek can also arrange jungle and beach tours by jeep (see p.957).

For information on the park's **beaches**, see the Choroní and Ocumare accounts (p.959 & p.961, respectively).

CHORONÍ

Choroní actually consists of two parts: the colonial town of **Choroní**, notable for its winding streets and colourful houses, but otherwise dull; and **Puerto Colombia**, a beach town two kilometres away, where most of the accommodation and action is concentrated. The lifeblood of Puerto Colombia is its lively **malecón**, where the fishing boats dock. People congregate here at night, and on weekends it's common to see *tambores*, a coastal tradition of African drum-playing, singing and dancing.

The one beach easily reached on foot is **Playa Grande**. Just 500 meters east of Puerto Colombia, it becomes mobbed with weekend visitors, who leave tons of trash. Otherwise it's very picturesque, with palm trees, aquamarine water and lush mountains in the background. About the same distance to the west, but harder to reach (and thus less crowded), **Playa El Diario** is a 45-minute walk from the village. At the midpoint of the main Choroní–Puerto Colombia road, follow Calle Cementerio past the cemetery and bear left at the split.

To access the other area beaches you will need to take a *lancha*, or small boat, which can be arranged at the *malecón*. To the east, the closest beach is **Playa Valle Seco** ($20 per person with return), which has some coral reefs and decent snorkelling. Farther east, **Playa Chuao**

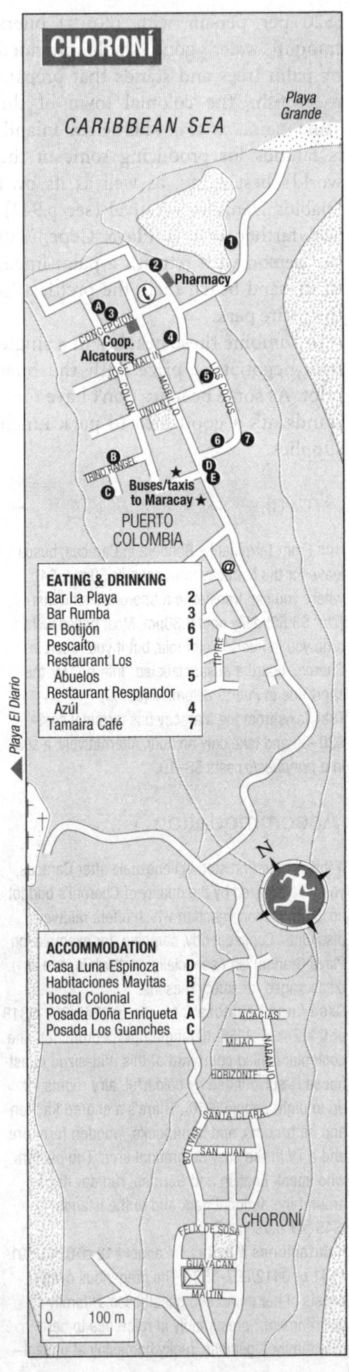

($20 per person with return) offers tranquil water, good shade provided by palm trees and stands that prepare fresh fish. The colonial town of the same name, a few kilometres inland, is famous for producing some of the world's best cacao, as well as its own Diablos Danzantes festival (see p.943). Still farther east is **Playa Cepe** ($30 per person with return), a palm-lined, white-sand beach that's the prettiest in the entire park.

To combine these beaches in a single trip, negotiate a price with the boat pilot. As some beaches don't have food stands, it's a good idea to pack lunch supplies.

Arrival

Bus From Terminal La Bandera in Caracas, buses leave for the Maracay terminal (1hr 30min; $4), where you can transfer to a Choroní-bound bus (2hr; $3.50) daily until 6.30pm. Most buses will drop you in Puerto Colombia, but if you're left in Choroní, board a *buseta* labeled "Interno" for the short ride to Puerto Colombia ($0.50).
Taxi Taxis from the Maracay bus terminal cost $20–30 and take only an hour. Alternatively, a seat in a *por puesto* costs $6–10.

Accommodation

If this is your first stop in Venezuela after Caracas, you'll be amazed by the quality of Choroní's budget accommodation, much of which offers midweek discounts. Consequently, camping (for example, on Playa Grande) isn't especially worthwhile, and is discouraged for safety reasons.

Casa Luna Espinoza C Morillo ⓣ0243/951-5318 or 0412/435-3056, ⓔjungletrip@choroni.net. The cool, plant-filled courtyard of this mid-sized guesthouse is surrounded by colourful, airy rooms for up to eight people ($50). There's a shared kitchen and bathrooms, and hammocks, wooden furniture and a TV in the cozy communal area. The owners, who speak English and German, run day-trips around the national park and to the islands ($45 per person). ❺

Habitaciones Mayitas C Rangel #12 ⓣ0243/991-1141 or 0412/897-3594. The gregarious owner boasts of her unmarked guesthouse's "family environment," presumably in reference to her own family. A genuine, funky homestay at unbeatable prices, with shared kitchen, bathrooms and communal area. Larger rooms have fans, while the double and triple have a/c. ❹

Hostal Colonial C Morillo ⓣ0243/218-5012, ⓔcolonialchoroni@gmail.com. A large, beautiful guesthouse with plenty of services – including laundry, book exchange and free wi-fi – and amazing rates. Staff is attentive and professional, if slightly rule-obsessed, and there's a thriving garden and a *comida criolla* restaurant out back (mains $6). Most of the clean, spacious, light-filled rooms are en suite (cold water) and fan-cooled. Italian and English spoken. As this is one of the first places in town to fill up, reservations are recommended in high season. ❹–❺

Posada Doña Enriqueta C Colón, half a block from the *malecón* ⓣ0414/456-1263. Rates seem a little high for the dim, spartan courtyard and no-frills rooms, but this is about as close as you can get to the waterfront. ❺–❼

Posada Los Guanches Off C Rangel ⓣ0243/991-1209. A quiet, austere option down a narrow side street. The blue and white two-floor building contains nine spotless rooms; those at the front are light and breezy and have flower-filled views. Check in at the residence across the street. No additional services. ❹

Eating

Restaurants in Choroní aren't nearly as numerous as *posadas*, but there are a few decent options, all on Avenida Los Cocos.

El Botijón This very simple breakfast/lunch joint serves up sizzling *arepas* ($2.50) and fresh juices ($0.75) at a brightly painted streetside counter with an adjacent garden. Pull up a stool and ask a local if he'll share his paper. Daily 7am–1pm.

Restaurant Los Abuelos Even if it doesn't remind you of your grandparents' cooking (as the name would suggest), you can enjoy a sampling of traditional Venezuelan seafood dishes ($7.50–10) in this bi-level restaurant on the busiest street in town. There are similarly priced chicken and beef dishes for landlubbers. Full bar.

Restaurant Resplendor Azul Just next door to *Los Abuelos* and serving more or less the same menu, with the addition of *calamares rebozados* (fried calamari). The ambiance is a bit buzzier, too, with painted ceiling fans and bright red tablecloths.

Tamaira Café This vegetarian/wholefood café whips up low-fat omelette, fish and *comida criolla* plates ($8), and lighter fare like granola and honey. Breakfast only.

Drinking

Choroní's nightlife, if you can call it that, is very casual – most people just buy a few beers and drink them on the *malecón*.

Bar La Playa At the beach end of Av Los Cocos. By day, vacationers laze about in the plastic chairs on the covered patio, sipping beers and watching the fishers come and go; by night, everyone flocks here for cheap beers and high-volume salsa and Latin pop on the stereo.

Pescaíto Along the path to Playa Grande. The closest thing to a club in Puerto Colombia, atop a low hill on the other side of the river. Open till dawn, when the fishers head out to catch the nightspot's namesake.

Bar Rumba C Concepción. Despite the promise of a rumba, or party, there's no dancing here, but every night a mixed local/foreign crowd arrives to knock back icy Soleras.

Directory

Bank There are no banks or ATMs in Choroní, though you can change dollars at some hotels.

Food For food to cook in your *posada*'s communal kitchen, try the small outdoor market across the street from *Bar La Playa*, with watermelon, peppers and other assorted fruit and veg, as well as meat. Buy fish directly from the fishermen on the beach.

Internet Coffee Mail (Ⓣ0414/587-4276), Mon–Sat 9.30am–8pm. Net access for $1.25 per hr, photocopies and phone cards.

Pharmacy A small pharmacy next door to *Bar La Playa* is open daily 8am–8pm.

Phones Movistar, C Concepción, daily 8.30am–6.30pm.

Post office Half a block south of the Plaza Bolívar in Choroní. Mon–Fri 9am–3pm.

Shopping Cooperativa Alcatours, C Morillo at Independencia (Ⓣ0414/237-0797, Ⓔalcatours14@hotmail.com), sells interesting "cacao-arte" and *artesanía* made by the husband-wife owners, including paintings of *tambores* dancers, simply jewellery and *ponche de cacao*, a chocolate liqueur.

Moving on

By bus Buses for the Maracay terminal ($3.50) leave daily from 7am–6.30pm, roughly every hour and a half. They board across the street from Hostal Colonial on weekdays, and slightly farther south on C Morillo on weekends.

By taxi Same as getting here (see opposite), but in the opposite direction.

OCUMARE DE LA COSTA

The colonial town of **Ocumare de la Costa** is set a few kilometres from the beach village of El Playón. Neither is as attractive as Choroní, and the beach itself is a bit dirty. However, some secluded snorkelling spots, narrow mangrove inlets, small waterfalls and swimming holes – not to mention the Estación Biológica Rancho Grande (see p.958) – make a visit worthwhile if you have the time. Frequent daily buses (2hr; $3.50) shuttle between Ocumare/El Playón and the Maracay terminal.

Five kilometres east of El Playón is one of the area's best-known beaches, **Playa Cata**. Despite some horrible concrete apartment buildings, it is otherwise attractive, with palm trees lining the white sand. Hourly buses ($2) run here from El Playón. **Playa Catica**, an hour-long hike or short boat ride ($15 per person) from Cata, is smaller and less crowded. Farther east, legendary surfing beach **Playa Cuyagua** can get fairly large waves, so swimmers should

TREAT YOURSELF

De La Costa Eco-Lodge C California #23, across from the beach in El Playón Ⓣ0243/993-1986, Ⓦwww.ecovenezuela.com. As if the proximity to excellent beaches and snorkelling weren't enough, this idyllic bungalow has a verdant tropical garden with a barbeque, a lookout tower with spectacular views and a wonderful restaurant serving local, international and vegetarian cuisine. Rooms are simple, but all are en suite (cold water) with a/c and TV, and have cool tile floors, vibrant bedspreads and hammocks for relaxing. There's also free wi-fi and a swimming pool. English-speaking owner Viktor Gorodeckis leads groups to La Ciénaga (see p.962) for snorkelling, diving and kayaking (food and equipment provided), as well as to Estación Biológica Rancho Grande (see p.958). ❾

exercise caution. Daily buses from El Playón cost $2.50, or you can take a *lancha* for about $20.

The crystalline waters of **La Ciénaga**, a beautiful lagoon several kilometres to the west of Ocumare, offer some of the park's best snorkelling. There are also a few strips of sand for sunbathing. The lagoon is accessible only by *lanchas* ($27 for the boat, with return) which leave from La Boca, on the east side of El Playón.

PARQUE NACIONAL MORROCOY

Gorgeous white-sand keys surrounded by limpid water are the highlights of **Parque Nacional Morrocoy**, one of the most popular national parks in Venezuela. The three hundred square kilometre reserve, spread primarily over water, was created in 1974, but today it doesn't feel much like a national park. Several areas have been irresponsibly developed, and there's no restriction on the large numbers of tourists that enter and no enforcement of litter, water pollution or camping laws. Fortunately, the **beaches** are still relatively pristine, snorkelling and scuba diving remain quite good and the park is still home to nearly four-fifths of Venezuela's aquatic **bird species**, as well as several types of mammal.

Towns at both ends of the park serve as bases for exploring the keys, though both are eyesores and have had sporadic safety problems. Tucacas, to the south, is overdeveloped and lacks good accommodation options; it is better to hit the slightly more pleasant **Chichiriviche**, to the north.

What to see and do

There are a total of 22 **keys**, or *cayos*, in the park, most differing only in size and facilities. Day-trips can be purchased on the *malecón* in Chichiriviche (Embarcadero Playa Norte; ☎0412/864-1519 or 0259/808-8432), and most *posadas* arrange trips for guests at no extra charge. Prices listed are for the boat, not per person, and include return; feel free to bargain.

Dotted with shade-giving palms, **Cayo Sombrero** ($100), halfway between Chichiriviche and Tucacas, is one of the larger and more popular keys, although you can still find uncrowded parts. It has two small restaurants, permits camping and has good snorkelling – but the best snorkelling and scuba diving is farther north, around **Cayo Sal** ($25). *Lanchas* also make trips to *cayos* Muerto ($20), Pelón ($25), Peraza ($25) and Varadero ($35).

Tucacas is the access point for **Cayo Paiclás** ($30), a large key with several very popular beaches, including Playuela, Playuelita and Playa Paiclás. All have small food stands or restaurants, as well as shower facilities, but no water for campers. On the east end of the key is the more secluded, very pretty Playa Mero.

CHICHIRIVICHE

The only reason to visit the tiny beach town of **Chichiriviche** (chee-chee-ree-VEE-chay) is for its proximity to the keys. Otherwise it's a fairly dismal place, with muddy, half-paved streets, garbage-strewn sidewalks and an inordinate number of stores selling liquor and plastic beach gear.

Calle Zamora, the town's main artery, dead-ends at the *malecón*, where most activity is centred. By day it's bustling with *lancha* passengers headed to the keys; by night throngs of hippie street vendors descend to sell handmade jewellery and strum guitars.

Arrival

By bus Buses from Valencia (half-hourly; 3hr) run until 7pm, stopping on C Zamora about 750km inland from the *malecón*. During the day you can easily walk to most accommodation, but after dark you chould take a cab (around $3). Buses plying the Valencia–Chichiriviche route also stop at Tucacas.

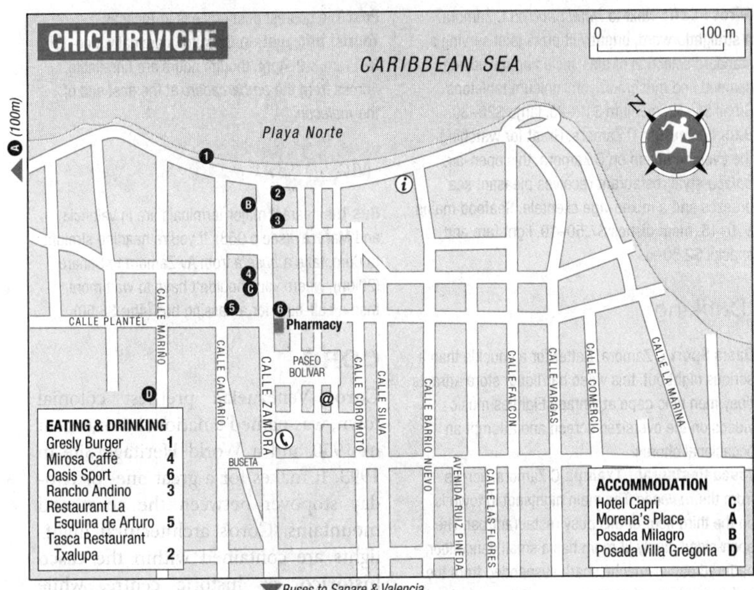

Accommodation

Most accommodation is within a couple of blocks of the *malecón*, a generally safe part of town with lots of foot traffic. To camp in the national park, contact the Falcón State Inparques office (☎0268/252-4198), or stop by the intermittently operating Corfaltur office (see p.966).

Hotel Capri C Zamora ☎0259/818-6026, Ⓔhotelcaprica@yahoo.com. A rather aseptic option – not actually a bad thing in these parts – but with very friendly staff and a huge ground-floor lounge. Amply sized rooms (en suite, TV, a/c) are done up in pastels and paintings of beach scenes. Prices drop 10–20 percent in low season. ❺

Morena's Place Sector Playa Norte ☎0259/815-0936, Ⓔposadamorenas@hotmail.com. A decidedly funky but great-value option just one street in from the beach. Dorm rooms have shared bathrooms and ceiling fans, and there's a fridge for storing food, a barbeque, and laundry service. Self-serve beers are on the honour system, and the English-speaking owner rents kayaks. ❷

Posada Milagro C Zamora above Licorería Falcón ☎0259/815-0864. Though you enter through a liquor store on the ground floor (at least until the street around back is paved), the *posada* itself is cute and colourful, with chintzy décor and en-suite rooms with fans (some with sea views). Avoid those overlooking noisy Av Zamora, and check for water leaks before you commit; rooms on the top floor are a bit nicer. ❹

Posada Villa Gregoria C Mariño ☎0259/818-6359). This secure, Mediterranean-style guesthouse has simple but spacious and tidy en-suite rooms, some with a/c. There's a fridge to store drinks in, complimentary morning coffee and hammocks on the open-air second floor. The owner's son operates tours to nearby attractions on the mainland, such as Coro (see p.964; $150 per car). Laundry service on Mondays. ❺–❻

Eating

Gresly Burger West end of the *malecón*. Ponder this fast-food shack's name as you sit at plastic tables with youngsters munching gristly, grizzly-sized burgers.

Resturant La Esquina de Arturo C Plantél. *"Art's Corner"* is the best place in town for super-cheap and tasty *comida criolla*, with an emphasis on seafood. Typical breakfasts ($4–6) include the *desayuno marinero*, with shredded fish, a fried egg, black beans and a mound of grated white cheese. For dinner ($7.50–12.50), try the *rueda carite marinera*, a plate of local mackerel smothered in calamari, shrimp and crab with sides of rice and plantain chips. There's also a lengthy menu of soups, pastas, beef, chicken and pork, most under $10. Mon–Fri 7.30am–4pm, Fri & Sat till 8pm, Sun till 6pm.

Mirosa Caffè Next to *Hotel Capri* on C Zamora. A straightforward, brightly lit pizza joint serving a standard selection of pies, including mixed veg, seafood and mushroom, on linoleum tabletops. Small $6–12, medium $12–20, large $20–30.

Rancho Andino C Zamora. Great for watching the evening action on C Zamora, this open-air, *palapa*-style restaurant receives pleasant sea breezes and a mixed-age clientele. Seafood mains $10–15, meat dishes $7.50–10, light fare and snacks $2.50–5.

Drinking

Oasis Sport C Zamora. Better for a chuckle than a serious night out, this video bar/liquor store attracts tipsy men who gape at vintage Eighties music videos on the oversized screen and attempt an occasional chorus.

Tasca Restaurant Txalupa C Zamora, across from the *malecón*. The main nightspot in town is on the third floor of this busy restaurant/bar. The open-sided, dimly lit room has a small dancefloor, a battered papier-maché shark suspended from the ceiling, and an entertaining view of the waterfront. Weekends only.

Directory

Bank Bancoro, C Plantél at C Calvario; Banco Industrial (and others) on C Zamora; Banco Mercantil ATM in front of the *Caribana Hotel* at the east end of Paseo Bolívar.

Internet Byte Quest, south of *Caribana Hotel* on the west side of the street (daily 8.30am–9pm; $1 per hr).

Pharmacy Several options line C Zamora, one next to Oasis Sport.

Phones There's an unnamed call center on the east side of C Zamora, about 100m inland from C Plantél (daily 7.30am–10pm).

Post The nearest post office is in Tucacas.

Tourist information Corfaltur, nominally Mon–Fri 8–11am & 2–4pm, though hours are unreliable. Across from the *embarcadero* at the east end of the *malecón*.

Moving on

Bus The nearest major terminals are in Valencia and Maracay (see p.958). If you're heading straight to Coro, take a *buseta* from Av Zamora to Sanare (20km), where you shouldn't have to wait more than a half-hour for a passing bus (4hr; $8.50).

CORO

Coro, Venezuela's prettiest colonial town, was named a national monument in 1950 and a World Heritage Site in 1993. It makes for a great one- or two-day stopover between the coast and mountains. Coro's architectural hightlights are contained within the **casco histórico**, or historic centre, while another principal attraction, the Parque Nacional Médanos de Coro, lies a few kilometres away.

Churches

The centre of the *casco histórico* is Plaza Bolívar, on the east end of which stands Venezuela's oldest **Catedral**, begun in 1583 and finished in 1634. Two blocks north on Plaza San Clemente, the **Iglesia de San Clemente** was originally built in 1538 by the town's founder, Juan de Ampíes. Totally rebuilt in the eighteenth century, San Clemente is one of three churches in the country

JEWISH HERITAGE

During the nineteenth century, Coro was home to a sizeable Jewish community, which had initially come over from Curacão. The Jews of Coro thrived here through commerce with the Dutch Antilles but were expelled in 1855; when invited back three years later, most did not return. Their history is explored in the **Museo de Arte Alberto Henríquez** (Tues–Sun 9am–noon & 3–5pm; free), across from the Museo de Arte de Coro. It contains the oldest synagogue in Venezuela, constructed in 1853 and one of the first synagogues on the continent. While here, enquire about visiting another vestige of the Jewish community, the **Cementerio Judío**, on Calle Zamora at Calle 23 de Enero. Built in 1830, it is the oldest of all South American Jewish cemeteries still in use.

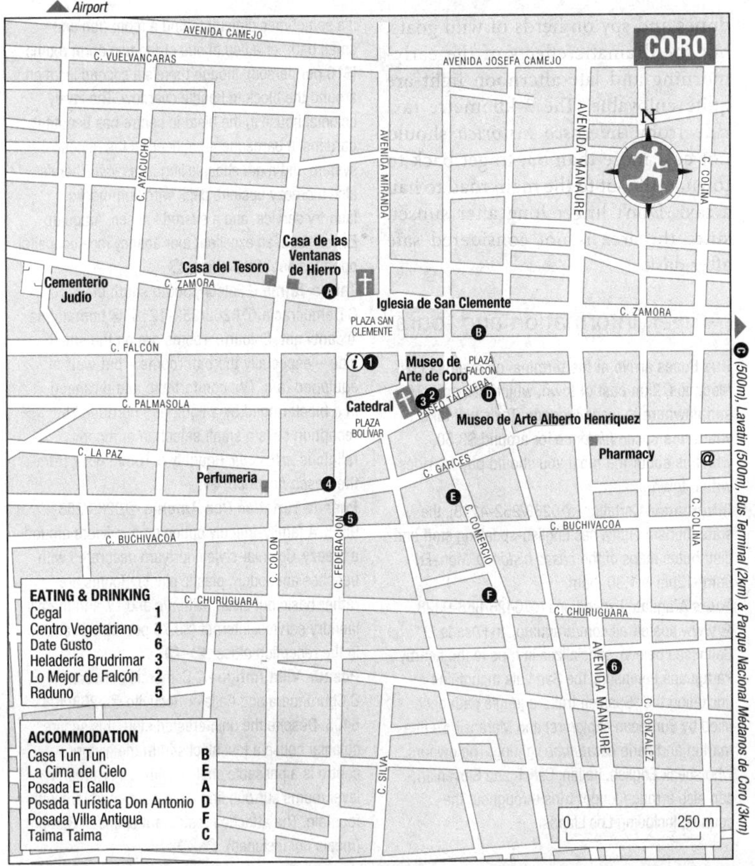

built in the shape of a cross. Beside it, a small monument contains the **Cruz de San Clemente**, the wooden cross used in the first mass after the town was founded.

Colonial mansions

The **Casa de las Ventanas de Hierro** (Tues–Sat 9am–noon & 3–6pm; free), a block to the west of Plaza San Clemente on Calle Zamora, is notable for its iron window frames and grilles, and a small museum inside exhibits colonial-era clothes and furniture. The work of local artists is displayed at the **Casa del Tesoro** (Tues–Sat 9am–noon & 3–6pm, Sun 9am–3pm; free), another stately mansion just across Calle Colón. A block and a half to the northeast of Plaza Bolívar on Avenida Talavera, the **Museo de Arte de Coro** (Tues–Sat 9am–noon & 3–7.30pm, Sun 9am–4pm; free) has temporary exhibits set in a beautiful mansion.

Parque Nacional Médanos de Coro

Just at the northern city limits is an entrance into **Parque Nacional Médanos de Coro** (daily 7am–7.30pm; free), an 80-square-kilometre park covering one of Venezuela's few desert areas. There's not a whole lot to do here other than stroll among the dunes and spy on herds of wild goats, but the dramatic effects of the early-morning and late-afternoon light are quite enjoyable. The 3-kilometre taxi ride from the *casco histórico* should not cost more than $3; to get back to town, walk out to the main road to hail a taxi. Don't linger long after sunset, since the area is not considered safe after dark.

Arrival, information and tours

Bus Buses arrive at the terminal on Avenida Los Médanos, 2km east of town, which has no ATMs and nowhere to leave luggage. Taxis will take you to the *casco histórico* for around $3.50, which is about the most you should pay for rides within town.

Information Corfaltur (Ⓣ0268/252-4198), the state tourism entity, has English-speaking staff and distributes maps of the *casco histórico*. Mon–Fri 8am–12pm & 1.30–5pm.

Tours Araguato Expeditions (Ⓣ0426/866-9328, Ⓦwww.hosteltrail.com/araguato), in Posada El Gallo (see below), specializes in trips to the nearby Paraguaná Peninsula, the San Luís mountains (including the "Spanish trail," a jungle path once used by European explorers) and Maracaibo's flea market and eerie *catatumbo* lighting. The owners, who speak English, Italian, Czech and Slovenian, can also arrange longer trips throughout the country, including Los Llanos.

Accommodation

Casa Tun Tun C Zamora Ⓣ0268/404-4260, Ⓦcasatuntun.over-blog.com. Another great backpacker retreat with popular dorm rooms ß($7.50 per person), *Tun Tun* has a barbeque on a leafy patio, a cozy nook with books and DVDs, a shared kitchen, hammocks and laundry service. It's a little less composed than *El Gallo*, but the prices can't be beat. ❹–❻

La Cima del Cielo C Comercio between C Garcés and C Buchivacoa Ⓣ0268/404-8308 or 253-6525. Fairly bland, but a good fall-back if others are full. Clean, blue-walled rooms (en suite with a/c and TV) surround a light-filled courtyard with plants and a dining table, where you can eat after preparing a meal in the shared kitchen. ❺

Posada El Gallo C Federación #26 Ⓣ0268/252-9481, Ⓔposadaelgallo2001@hotmail.com. Very popular with backpackers; it's sometimes difficult to find a room (fan and small bath) or a bed in one of the two dorm rooms ($10 per person), though there's a second location around the block to handle overflow. The lovely colonial house in the historic centre has beautiful gardens, a barbeque area, beer on the honour system and a gift shop selling *artesanía*. There's also a breezy upstairs deck with hammocks, laundry service, and a shared kitchen. Araguato Expeditions, an excellent tour agency (see opposite), operates out of the office. ❺

Taima Taima C Falcón, 500m south of C Democracia Ⓣ0268/252-1215, Ⓔtaimataima@cantv.net. Colourful rooms are on the small side – especially the bathrooms – but well equipped (a/c, TV), comfortable and arranged in a block ringed by a light, airy corridor. The reception sells a small selection of mostly religious *artesanía*. Roughly a 10min walk from the *casco histórico*. ❻

Posada Turística Don Antonio Ⓣ0268/253-9578. A family-friendly option on two floors around a breezy, Colonial-style courtyard decorated with benches and, oddly, plastic plants. Rooms are rather basic but clean, with a/c and TV, and there's laundry service. Internet ($0.75 per hr) is available in the reception office. ❺–❼

Posada Villa Antigua C Comercio between C Churuguara and Callejón Tocuyito Ⓣ0268/404-6405. Despite the uninterested staff, this secure colonial house a few blocks from the historic centre is a passable choice, with rather tired bi-level rooms surrounding a pleasant courtyard with fountain. The attached restaurant opens at 3.30pm (meals not included). ❺–❻

Eating and drinking

There are a number of inexpensive restaurants in Coro, many doubling as bars in the evening. Be sure to try *chivo* (goat), the regional speciality, while you're in town.

Cegal C Federación between Av Zamora and Av Falcón Ⓣ0414/684-3633, Ⓔcegal–restaurant@hotmail.com. Despite its upscale appearance, this cooperative, also known as the *Club Bolívar* and popular with government employees, has a reasonably priced menu of *coriano* specialities. Emphasis is on local ingredients, particularly in dishes like *chivo al coco* (goat with coconut) and *pabellón coriano* (shredded goat with corn, black beans, goat cheese and fried plantains), both $10. The café is open all day, and the bar is a popular evening hangout.

CROSSING INTO COLOMBIA

There are three main **border crossings** between Venezuela and Colombia. The northernmost, at Paraguachón, offers the best connections to coastal cities like Cartagena; Cúcuta has onward service to Bogotá. Before leaving Venezuela you must pay the $20 exit tax (in bolívares) and get your passport stamped by the nearest emigration office. Once you cross the border, immediately visit the nearest Colombian immigration office for an entry stamp, and remember to set your watch back a half-hour. Citizens of the US, Canada, Australia, New Zealand and Europe do not need a visa to enter Colombia.

Paraguachón The major bus operator is Bus Ven (ⓣ0261/723-9084 or 0212/953-8441), with morning and afternoon depatures from the Maracaibo terminal, in the southwest of the city, to Santa Marta, Colombia (6hr; $67) and then Cartagena (10hr; $82). The bus stops at Paraguachón, where you take care of all formalities and then switch buses; book as early as possible.

A cheaper and faster alternative is to take a *por puesto* from the Maracaibo terminal to Maicao, Colombia (daily until 4pm; up to 3hr; $15 per person), allowing you to cross the border without waiting for a hundred other passengers to have their bags and documents checked. From here, switch to a bus for Santa Marta (4hr; around 20 pesos), among other destinations.

Cúcuta Nearest to San Antonio del Táchira, San Cristóbal and Mérida, this crossing is more popular among shoppers than travellers, though it does provide onward transport to Bogotá and other central Colombian cities. From the Mérida bus terminal, there is one daily service to San Antonio del Táchira (at 3am; 6hr) and half-hourly buses to San Cristóbal, just a short onward ride to San Antonio. From here, buses and *por puestos* leave from Avenida Venezuela for Cúcuta. Get an exit stamp at the San Antonio DIEX office (Carrera 9 between calles 6 and 7; ⓣ0276/771-4453).

Casuarito/Puerto Carreño These are two separate crossings, both accessible from Puerto Ayacucho (see p.978). Currently no border fees are being collected at either; however, the Colombian consulate in Puerto Ayacucho is concerned about visitors' safety on the Colombian side of the border, and recommends travelling onward in Colombia by plane rather than bus.

From the port in Puerto Ayacucho, you can catch a five-minute ferry (every 20min daily from 8am–6pm; $1.50), which crosses the Orinoco and leaves you in the small Colombian village of **Casuarito**. From here you can take a high-speed boat ($10; 1hr 30min) to the larger city of **Puerto Carreño**, from where there are four weekly flights to **Bogotá** (see p.548), as well as other large cities, with Satena (ⓣ00578/565-4010 or 00571/605-2222, ⓦwww.satena.com).

Alternatively, you can take the San Fernando de Apure bus ($5) from Puerto Ayacucho and get off after about two hours (1hr by *por puesto*) in the town of Puerto Páez. From there, take a quick boat ride to Puerto Carreño ($3.50).

Centro Vegetariano C Federación at C Garcés. It doesn't appear especially inviting, but this is where you'll find veggie versions of Venezuelan staples (*arepas*, *empanadas*, plantains) and international cuisine (pizza, tacos). Also has the best selection of fruit juices in town. Lunch only.

Date Gusto Av Manaure. Not so tasty, but cheap, filling and, most importantly for late arrivals, open daily 24hr. Burgers, hot dogs and sandwiches cost $4.50–8; the *hamburguesa especial* is palatable, though there's certainly nothing special about it.

Heladería Brudrimar Av Talavera. The fact that this ice-cream parlour doesn't actually serve ice cream doesn't faze locals, who come for burgers and sandwiches ($2.50–5), lunch plates of chicken or beef ($6), and espresso drinks. Always lively, with posters of football idols on the walls and an Eighties roller-derby vibe. Mon–Fri 7.30am–6pm.

Lo Mejor de Falcón C San Juan ⓣ0268/404-7101. A bare-bones lunch joint serving a simple but delicious *menú ejecutivo* of liver with onions, smoked pork chop, or steak (all $5.50). There's an

a/c indoor section, but the concrete patio under an awning is more pleasant. Breakfast and lunch only, though it serves beer till 9pm. Closed Sun.
Raduno Av Talavera, east of *Heladería Brudrimar*. The only real club in town, attracting a student crowd for pounding dance music and pizzas served in the back. From 8pm, weekends only.

Shopping

There are a few places selling *artesanía* in Coro, though none of it is very compelling. Local potters occasionally sell their wares in Plaza Falcón, and the Centro Artesanal in front of *Cegal* (see p.966) has a momentarily diverting array of paintings, dioramas and *dulce de leche* (made from goat milk). Officially, it's open daily 9.30am–7pm, though the vendors tend to operate on their own schedules. Of far more interest is the unmarked **perfumería** on C Colón just north of C Garcés, a spiritualist shop selling love potions, animal parts, pickled reptiles and other assorted juju, most used for synchretist rituals. Since some products may have come from endangered species, look but avoid buying. If you have any appetite left, there's a food market at C Garcés and C Colón (daily till 7pm), where you can pick up supplies for your posada's shared kitchen.

Directory

Bank Banco Federal on Plaza Falcón; Bancoro on C Falcón at Av Manaure.
Internet Counterstrike, C Falcón at C Colina, daily 9am–1pm & 3–8pm.
Laundry Lavatín, C Falcón ⓣ0268/251-6712, has an English-speaking owner. Mon–Fri 8am–noon & 2–6pm, Sat 8am–2pm, closed Sun. Most accommodation offers laundry service as well.
Phones Digitel, Av Talavera, just west of Heladería Brudrimar.
Pharmacy Farmalinda, Av Manaure at C Garcés, daily 8am–12.30pm & 2.30–7.30pm.

Moving on

For information on **crossing into Colombia** from this region, see the box on p.967.
Bus Coro's terminal serves mainly regional destinations, with hourly departures to Punto Fijo (1hr 30min) on the Paraguaná Peninsula. Daily until 6pm, frequent buses connect to the terminals in Valencia (6hr 30min) and Maracay (7hr 30min; see p.958), which offer a wider selection of destinations. Other services from Coro include Caracas (several daily; 9hr); Maracaibo (several daily; 3hr); Mérida (2 daily; 10hr); and Puerto La Cruz (1 daily; 14hr). For Ciudad Bolívar, take the 5.30pm overnight bus to El Tigre (15hr), transferring there to complete the journey (2–3hr).

Mérida and the Andes

The mountainous state of **Mérida** finds it way onto nearly all visitors' itineraries, regardless of how long they are spending in Venezuela. The raw beauty of the carved, green slopes and snowcapped peaks of the **Andes** is not to be missed, and the facilities in the capital, likewise called Mérida, are among Venezuela's finest. To the city's south and east, the **Parque Nacional Sierra Nevada**, dominated by the famed Pico Bolívar (5007m) and Pico Humboldt (4920m), offers some of the finest hiking opportunities in the region. To the northwest, the Carretera Transandina, or the Trans-Andean Highway, passes several charming mountain towns, including **Mucuchíes** and **Apartaderos**.

MÉRIDA

From the bottom of a deep valley, the city of **Mérida** enjoys stunning views of the surrounding mountains without ever becoming uncomfortably cold. Unlike many other mountain towns in South America, it is quite modern and progressive, being home to one of the country's most prestigious universities, La Universidad de los Andes. Despite its cosmopolitan sensibilities, Mérida offers reasonable prices, relatively safe streets and an easily walkable centre.

Owing to its natural endowment as well as the efforts of several excellent tour operators, Mérida's chief attraction is **adventure sports** (see box, p.970). However, if you've got some down time, or if you're allergic to

adrenaline, the city offers a couple of sights, as well as some diverting day-trips (see p.974).

The Town

Walking the streets of the **old town** to admire its colonial houses and pretty parks will only take a few hours. Right on the Plaza Bolívar, the **Catedral** grew out of plans for a seventeenth-century cathedral that wasn't started until 1803 and not completed until 1958. Of the several decent museums in the area, the most interesting is the **Museo Arqueológico** (Tues–Sun 8–11.30am & 2–5.30pm; $0.50; ⓣ0274/240-2344), on Avenida 3 in the Universidad de los Andes building. It presents pre-Columbian artefacts from the region, augmented by thorough historical descriptions.

The teleférico

Mérida's top attraction, the world's longest-travelling, highest-climbing **teleférico** (cable car), leaves from its base station in Parque Las Heroínas (peak periods daily 7.30am–noon, otherwise Wed–Fri 8–11am, Sat & Sun 8–11.30am; $15 round-trip; call ⓣ0274/252-5080 or visit ⓦwww.telefericodemerida.com for schedule details). Arrive early, as the line at the base can be long, and allow up to four hours for a round trip. If you haven't brought warm clothing, you can rent jackets near the ticket window.

The *teleférico* travels 12.6 kilometres, rising over 3000 metres to the top of **Pico Espejo** (4765m). There are three intermediate stations, and you should pause at the third, Loma Redonda (4045m), before ascending to the top,

ADVENTURE SPORTS

Mérida's surrounds provide the perfect conditions for an astounding range of **adventure sports**, and there's an equally amazing array of tour companies in town, all vying for your business.

As with most services, you tend to get what you pay for. Since most of the activities on offer involve a certain level of risk, it's wise not to be stingy, since budget tours and budget equipment often go hand in hand.

Tour prices generally decrease as more customers register, so ask your company about joining an existing group (many trips require a minimum number of customers). While some companies take credit cards, you'll always get a far better price by paying in cash (see p.942). Except on one-day trips, all meals and accommodation are included in tour prices.

Due to Venezuela's volatile economy and fierce competition among companies, **prices** listed here are approximate. For the latest rates, contact the agencies directly. Most agencies offer all of the following activities, though some claim to specialize in one in particular.

Canyoning

Another very popular adrenaline sport, which involves rappelling alongside and under waterfalls. Full-day rates are $75–100 per person, typically with a two-person minimum.

Climbing and trekking

Two of the most popular routes are up Pico Humboldt and Pico Bolívar, Venezuela's highest peaks (see p.975). The latter requires some ice climbing for part of the year. A six-day climb costs around $100 per person per day for a group of four; allow $25 per day extra for porters. Less challenging treks are Pico Pan de Azúcar (same price) or Los Nevados, which you can do on your own (see 970).

Mountain biking

Many companies rent quality bikes for reasonable rates and can indicate the best routes. Guided day-tours run $75–100 per person. Some companies also offer horseback riding for similar rates.

Paragliding

The slopes around Mérida are the ideal setting for an absolutely thrilling yet safe 20–30-minute ride with a certified pilot. Paragliding rates are fixed at $95 per person. Be sure to bring a jacket or sweater and don't eat before going.

Rafting

Rivers in Mérida and Barinas states have class three to five rapids. Rafting season is from June to December. Two-day trips cost $150–175 per person with five people; four-day trips cost double. Some agencies have private base camps in Barinas. Mérida is the main staging point for guided trips to Los Llanos (see below), the wildlife-filled wetlands east of the Andes. Prices are roughly the same as for rafting, which is often incorporated into tours here.

since the dramatic climb can cause mild altitude sickness. From Loma Redonda, you can also follow hiking trails 13km (5–6hr) to the small Andean town of **Los Nevados**, which contains several *posadas* and places to eat. If you plan to do the walk on your own, it's wise to notify the Inparques office at the base of the *teleférico* (Ⓣ0274/262-1529). From Los Nevados you can either walk back to the Loma Redonda station or catch a jeep or mule for a ride down to Mérida ($12.50).

Arrival and information

By air The airport (Ⓣ0274/263-4352) is only 2km from the city centre, on Avenida Urdaneta.

By bus There are half a dozen night buses from Caracas (13hr), several daily from Maracaibo (6hr) and two daily from Coro (10hr). The terminal is packed with services; see Directory (p.973) for particulars. City buses go to the centre ($0.30), but it's easier to take a taxi ($4).

Tourist information Cormetur (Ⓣ0274/263-4701) has offices in several locations around town, including the bus terminal, the airport and the Mercado Principal on Av Las Américas. All generally operate Mon–Fri 7.30am–2pm during low season, 7am–6pm during high season, though those with heavy tourist traffic (airport, bus terminal, *teleférico* base) work weekends, too.

Tour operators

Arassari Trek C 24 across from *teleférico* base Ⓣ0274/252-5879, Ⓦwww.arassari.com. Specializes in canyoning and rafting, also sells air tickets.

Fanny Tours C 24 between Av 8 and Parque Las Heroínas Ⓣ0274/252-2952, Ⓦwww.fanny-tours.com. Specializes in climbing, also offers trips to Maracaibo to see the wetlands and *catatumbo* lightning.

Gravity Tours C 24 between avenidas 7 and 8 Ⓣ0274/251-1279, Ⓦwww.gravity-tours.com. Offers a two-day "extreme" combo of mountain-biking and rafting, as well as trips throughout the country.

Guamanchi Expeditions C 24 between Av 8 and Parque Las Heroínas Ⓣ0274/252-2080, Ⓦwww.guamanchi.com. Specializes in climbing and trekking. Also offers day-trips to Laguna Negra (see p.975) and bird-watching tours with expert local guides.

Natoura C 24 across from *teleférico* base Ⓣ0274/252-4216, Ⓦwww.natoura.com. Has the highest rates, but contributes a percentage of profits to an elementary school in Los Llanos and visits others on trips in the Orinoco Delta. Also sells international flights and tours throughout Venezuela.

Xtreme Adventours C 24 between Av 8 and Parque Las Heroínas Ⓣ0274/252-7241, Ⓦwww.xatours.com. Specializes in paragliding; also sells air tickets. Naturalist Tony Martin is a Los Llanos guide who can be contacted directly at Ⓣ0414/820-2506.

Accommodation

Aside from adventure sports, Mérida's other strength is its **posadas**, which offer outstanding quality and prices. Most are conveniently found near Parque Las Heroínas, a sort of backpacker ghetto where nearly all the tour agencies have their offices. All of the options below have hot water. To **camp** in the surrounding national parks, contact the local Inparques office (see p.939). Campers pay a per-person fee of $1 plus a $2 tent fee.

Habitaciones Noguera C 26 between avenidas 5 and 6 Ⓣ0274/252-5459 or 0414/374-5061, Ⓔchannynog@yahoo.es. Great for longer stays, this private flat (shared with the owner) has hand-painted folkloric scenes on the walls, a washing machine, shared bathroom and kitchen; the super-friendly owner can teach you his favourite local dishes. ❹

Posada La Floridita C 25 between the seminary and Av 8 Ⓣ0274/251-0452. A good backup option, with a lovely manager and a homey feel. Rooms (en suite, TV, fan) are a bit dark but have nice (faux) exposed rafters; they're arranged on two floors overlooking a simple courtyard with a table. ❹

Posada Guamanchi C 24 between Av 8 and Parque las Heroínas Ⓣ0274/252-2080, Ⓦwww.guamanchi.com. Amazing views of the surrounding mountains compete with very comfortable, bright and colourful en-suite rooms; there are also shared bathrooms and dorms ($10). A total of four floors include two lounge areas (TV, hammocks), two shared kitchens and a tour agency (see p.971). Guamanchi also has a serene *posada* in Los Nevados ($30 per person) with dinner and breakfast included. ❹–❺

Posada Jama Chia C 24 across from *teleférico* base Ⓣ0274/252-5767. A well-run, popular *posada* conveniently located on Parque Las Heroínas; front rooms with windows are nicest, though dorms ($15) are a deal. Shared bathrooms, kitchen, dining area and room for hand-washing clothes. The charming owner gets high praise from guests. ❺

Posada Mara C 24 across from *teleférico* base Ⓣ0274/252-5507. Very basic but adequate accommodation on Parque Las Heroínas; the lack of windows makes it a little grim, but it's cheap and very clean. Rooms with bathrooms cost slightly more. ❹–❻

Posada La Montaña C 24 No 6-47 Ⓣ0274/252-5977, Ⓦwww.posadalamontana.com. *La Montaña* has a superb design that employs local wood, brick, terracotta tiles and so many plants that you feel you're in a greenhouse. Top rooms have the best views; all have mini-fridge w/filtered water, free wi-fi and a closet with a safe. There's laundry service and a very nice restaurant on the ground floor (see p.972). ❺–❻

Posada Patty C 24 across from *teleférico* base Ⓣ0274/251-1052, Ⓔpattyclaudia@yahoo.com. Slightly ratty but extremely affordable. Rooms (shared bath) are dark and lack views, but there is laundry service and a shared kitchen. Owner screens guests, which can be good or bad, depending on your appearance. ❷

Posada Yagrumo C 24 between Av 8 and Parque Las Heroínas ⓣ0274/252-9539, ⓦwww.posadayagrumo.com. This echoey place has huge en-suite rooms with closets and sturdy bunk beds. TV, internet ($0.50 per hr) and phones for international calls are all in the vast main hall. There's a shared kitchen with domestic touches, a dining and lounge area, laundry service and a small tour agency that can arrange transport and guided trips. ❸

Eating

The **cuisine** from Mérida and the Andes is famous throughout the country. Some specialities include *arepas de trigo* (made from wheat flour), *queso ahumado* (smoked cheese) and *trucha* (trout) prepared in a variety of ways. *Vino de mora* is wine made from blackberries.

Arepera de la Reina Andina Av 5 between calles 21 and 22 ⓣ0274/252-1721. If the simple *arepa* hasn't yet won your heart, prepare yourself for a new love affair. Standard options ($1.50–4) like tuna with avocado, *carne mechada*, *pernil* and mixed seafood have never tasted better, especially after being washed down with a fresh peach juice. Chat up the amusingly grouchy staff, straight out of your high school's cafeteria, or gaze at the residents of the impressive saltwater aquarium. Closed Sun.

Buona Pizza Av 7 between C 24 and 25 ⓣ0274/252-7639. Great deep-dish pizza with a variety of toppings – a nine-inch costs $7.50, with toppings like artichokes, mushrooms, anchovies and mixed veg. The attractive, colourful restaurant has pseudo-Cubist paintings, brick walls and hordes of young locals. There's an "Express" version across the street for takeout.

Espresso Café Av 4 between calles 23 and 24 ⓣ0274/251-2388. A bohemian retreat on the first floor of an unassuming office building, with small tables, an outdoor balcony, locally produced artwork and a student crowd. Serves cheap sandwiches, pastries and coffee drinks, and has internet terminals ($0.75 per hr) and wi-fi. Mon–Fri 9am–9pm, Sat & Sun 3–9pm.

Heladería Coromoto Av 3 between C 28 and 29. Guinness Book of World Records holder for most ice-cream flavours, with nearly 800, although only around 100 are available at any given time. Wacky options include smoked tuna, calamari, garlic, beans and spaghetti with meatballs. It's truly impressive how well they reproduce flavours, although some are rather disgusting. $2 for 2 scoops. Tues–Sun 2.15–9.30pm, closed Mon.

Mercado Principal Av Las Américas and Viaducto Miranda. Great food, huge portions and reasonable prices make this one of the best places to sample local favourites. Seating area on the second floor contains tables from several nearly identical restaurants – some have pushy representatives that try to bring you to their area. Wed–Mon 8am–6pm, Tues till 2pm.

Restaurant La Montaña In *Posada La Montaña* (see p.971). A modest little trattoria-style place (pink tablecloths, open kitchen) that shoots for the stars and gets damn close. Try the *trucha*, either simply with lemon and salt or else stuffed with cheese and tomato and wrapped in bacon (both $12.50). Portions are on the small side but beautifully presented; the chef clearly loves his job. Other options include stuffed mushrooms, Caesar or smoked trout salad ($5–7.50) and pasta ($9–15).

La Nota Popular fast-food joint with several locations about town, including on Av 8 (near Parque Las Heroínas) and near the bus terminal. Plates and smokey burgers come with six different sauces, including blue cheese. Full meals (like the recommended *pollo plato*) run $7.50–10, though a half-order ($5.50) sates most appetites. Daily till 11pm.

Panadería Roma C 24 between Parque Las Heroínas and Av 8. The most popular spot near Parque Las Heroínas for breakfast and lunch, with *cachitos* and other pastries and pizzas ($7.50–10, extra large $20) with veggies, four cheeses and more. Mon–Sat 7am–8pm, Sun till noon.

Papaya C 24 between avenidas 6 and 5. Run by the owner of *Habitaciones Noguera*, this modern, sparkling shop sells made-to-order *batidos* and *merengadas* with protein/vitamin supplements ($1–2.50). Mon–Sat 9am–1pm & 2.30–7.30pm, closed Sun.

T'Café Av 3 between calles 29 and 30. An intellectual, often professorial crowd comes to this romantic streetside nook nightly (except Sun) for coffee drinks, pastries made by the owner's mother and live jazz on weekends. Meals include *desayunos criollos/americanos*, *arepas de trigo*, sandwiches and pizzas (small $3–5, med $5.50–7.50, large $10–15). There's also a generous daily *menú ejecutivo* ($5). Mon–Sat 8.30am–12am, closed Sun.

El Vegetariano Av 4 at C 18 ⓣ0412/511-2577. Bi-level vegetarian restaurant with a tile foor, exposed rafters and eclectic offerings, including soy beef ($8.50), "chop mein" ($7) and mixed,

TREAT YOURSELF

Miramelindo C 29 at Av 4, in the *Hotel Chama* (☎0274/252-9437). One of the town's finest restaurants, and though the look is a bit dated (gauze curtains and lace doilies), the service is excellent and the Basque specialities top-notch. Try the *pimientos rellenos de pescado en salsa vizcaína* (peppers stuffed with fish), *callos a la navarra* (a traditional tripe dish) or *maigret de pato* (duck breast). A three-course meal runs about $30 without wine. For a hipper, more casual environment, there's an adjacent sushi bar where you can get all your *maki* ($4 per plate), *nigiri* ($0.50–1.50 each) and *sashimi* ($7) favourites. Mon–Sat noon–3pm & 7–11pm, Sun lunch only.

avocado and fresh cheese salads ($7.50). Mon–Sat 8am–9pm, closed Sun.

Drinking and nightlife

In large part because of the immense student population, Mérida enjoys a rather active **nightlife**. Sunday and Monday are dead, but things pick up Tuesday and Wednesday and get quite lively the rest of the week.

Birosca Carioca Av 2 at C 24. Pounding Brazilian rhythms, samba-ing locals and a good mix of male and female students define this friendly, ever-popular club – as do the red buckets of "La Bomba," a rum and beer concoction sucked down through straws by friends. $2.50 cover; open till the crowd leaves.

La Cucaracha In Centro Comercial Las Tapias on Av Urdaneta. One of Mérida's oldest nightspots, this large but always crowded disco has two floors, one with techno and the other with salsa and merengue. Popular with a younger set, though three other *Cucaracha* locations about town cater to clientele of differing ages – and budgets.

El Hoyo de Queque Av 4 and C 19. This small but lively bar becomes extremely loud and raucous on weekends. Constantly packed with a devoted following of college-aged locals and tourists.

Kawy Av 4 between calles 21 and 22. On the ground floor of a small *centro commercial*, this bar/restaurant packs in the under-25s for cheap beers, bar food (under $10) and throbbing tunes. Somehow the combination of seated drinkers and clubby vibe just works. Daily 11.30am–midnight.

Salon de Pool Téxas Av 4 between calles 26 and 27. Rather male-heavy, only serves beer and closes at 1am, but a smart choice for the billiards-obsessed. TVs play football matches, and there's a small dancefloor upstairs, though there are far better places to let loose.

Shopping

Mérida is well stocked with promising purchases; aside from the main artesanal markets in town, make sure to check out the antique **shops** along the road to Apartaderos (see p.974).

The most renowned destination among bargain-hunters is the **Mercado Principal** (Wed–Mon 8am–6pm, Tues till 2pm), a three-storey, tourist-oriented market about a kilometre southwest of the centre on Avenida Las Américas. The ground floor offers fruits and vegetables; the first, artisan works and other souvenirs; and the second, an eating area with a number of delicious restaurants (see opposite). More *artesanía* can be found at the much smaller **Mercado Artesanal** aross the street from Parque Las Heroínas, where a permanent installation of stalls sells ceramics, jewellery, blackberry wine, leather goods and wood carvings. Vendors operate on their own schedules. A block away on Calle 25 at Avenida 8, **Las Heroínas** (☎0274/2523296) is a market with fruit, meat, cheese and dry goods for use in the shared kitchen of your *posada*.

Directory

Banks Banco de Venezuela, Av 4 between calles 23 and 24; ATMs at the base of the *teleférico* and in the bus terminal. Italcambio (Mon–Fri 8.30am–5pm, Sat 9am–1pm; ☎0274/263-4269) has an office at the airport.

Internet Internet cafés are plentiful in Mérida; most charge $0.60–0.75 per hr. De Capitán, C 25 across from *Posada La Floridita*, daily 9am–10pm. El Rincón del *Teleférico*, C 24 across from *teleférico* base, Mon–Sat 9am–9pm, Sun from noon. Cyber Sala, Av 4 between calles 21 and 22 (above *Kawy*). There's also an internet café in the bus terminal.

Language study Iowa Institute on Av 4 at C 18 ☎0274/252-6404, ⓦwww.iowainstitute.com.

Laundry C 25 next to De Capitán Internet (see above), Mon–Sat 8am–4.30pm. There's another laundry on Plaza San Miguel del Llano along Av 3.

Medical care A reputable clinic with some English-speaking doctors is Clínica Mérida (☎0274/263-0652) on Av Urdaneta next to the airport.

Pharmacy Unifarmacía, Av 3 between calles 29 and 30, daily 8am–8.30pm. Also FarmaAhorros, Av 4 between calles 27 and 28, Mon–Sat 8.30am–9.30pm ☎0274/051-0291.
Phones Movistar, Av 4 at C 25, Mon–Sat 8am–9.30pm, Sun 9am–6pm. There's a CANTV on Av 4 between calles 26 and 27 and another in the bus terminal.
Police The main station is on Av Urdaneta, adjacent to Parque Gloria Patrias (☎0274/263-6722).
Post office Ipostel, C 21 between avenidas 4 and 5, and in the bus terminal.
Sports The enormous Estadio Metropolitano de Mérida holds seasonal football matches. Get here by taking a bus from the centre toward Aguas Calientes, and ask to get off at the stadium.

Moving on

For information on **crossing into Colombia** from this region, see the box on p.967.
Air Mérida's airport has a small selection of daily flights, including Caracas (6 daily; 1hr 20min); Maracaibo (2 daily; 1hr); San Antonio del Táchira (1 daily; 35min); Valencia (1 daily; 2hr w/connection).
Bus Barinas (several daily till 5pm; 4hr); Caracas (several daily; 13hr); Ciudad Bolívar (1 daily; 24hr); Coro (2 daily; 10hr); Maracaibo (several daily; 6hr); Maracay (several daily; 11hr 30min); Puerto Ayacucho (1 daily; 18hr); Puerto La Cruz (5 daily; 18hr); Puerto Ordáz (1 daily; 25hr); Punto Fijo (2 daily; 11hr); San Cristóbal (several daily; 5hr); Valencia (several daily; 10hr 30min).

DAY-TRIPS FROM MÉRIDA

Most of the quaint Andean towns northeast of Mérida are set alongside the Carretera Transandina, with beautiful views of the Sierra Nevada range to the south and the Sierra Culata range to the north. The highway eventually crosses the highest driveable summit in Venezuela, at Pico El Águila, and begins the spectacular descent to Barinas and Los Llanos (see p.976).

Mucuchíes

Fifty-two kilometres to the northeast of Mérida, the picturesque mountain town of **Mucuchíes** was founded by the Spanish in 1586. Its name means "place of the waters" in the indigenous dialect. The town has since given its name to a famous Venezuelan dog breed, a type of Pyrenear mountain dog, which you may see in the town and area – there's even a statue of one in the Plaza Bolívar. Also on the plaza is *Cafetín Tinjacá*, a great stop for a simple breakfast, lunch or hot drinks, in an adobe-style building.

Just a few kilometres further along the Carretera Transandina, in the tiny village of San Rafael de Mucuchíes, is a small grey chapel, the **Capilla de Piedra**, that has become one of the most famous emblems of the region. Local artist Juan Félix Sánchez built the chapel himself, using thousands of uncut stones; there's a small museum next door documenting the chapel's construction.

Apartaderos

Continuing along the Carretera Transadina brings you past scores of antiques shops and strawberries-and-cream stands to **Apartaderos**, little more than a strip of shops and houses, but within easy reach of a few prominent sights. Ten kilometres beyond the pullout for buses to and from Mérida is the **Refugio del Cóndor** (open all day; ☎0274/416-0794), home to the well-known Andean condor conservation and research project. Tragically, only three condors remain in Venezuela and they live in captivity here, separated from each other to prevent fighting. Visitors are shown an instructional five-minute video in English or Spanish. The drive here is just as fascinating, allowing you to see firsthand the region's small-scale cultivation of onion, carrots and wheat. Also nearby, the **Observatorio Astronómico Nacional** (Mon–Sat 3–7pm; ☎0274/888-0154) is one of the highest observatories in the world (3600m). Its four domed structures house the enormous Schmidt telescope.

Apartaderos is also just a few kilometres from the entrance to the northern section of **Parque Nacional Sierra Nevada**. Just inside the entrance is **Laguna Mucubají**, where camping is allowed; you will need permission from the Inparques office near the entrance. A good hiking trail connects Laguna Mucubají with **Laguna Negra**, a fishing lake with dark water, as the name suggests. The beautiful hike takes an hour and a half to two hours, and you can continue another hour and a half to the pretty **Laguna Los Patos**. In the wet season, it is best to leave early to avoid rain and fog that could limit visibility considerably.

Back in Apartaderos, enjoy **lunch** in front of the fireplace at *Restaurant La Alameda*, offering hot drinks and Andean specialities like *pizca andina*, *trucha* and crispy *cochino frito*, most $5–10 (Mon–Sat 8am–6pm, closed Sun). Next door, Artesanía El Manantial is a crafts shop selling local jellies, candied fruit, *vino de mora* and ceramics. Between the two buildings is a taxi stand for rides to the condor facility or the observatory (about around $15 round-trip, $7.50 per hr to wait). For cash, there's a Banco Mercantil ATM in the parking lot of *Hotel Parque Turístico Apartaderos*.

Arrival

Both Mucuchíes and Apartaderos can easily be visited in a day, and as amenities are scanter in these parts, there's not much reason to stay overnight. From the Mérida terminal, **buses** for Apartaderos (2hr; $3; also serving Mucuchíes) leave half-hourly until 7pm from platform #13. Buses pass back and forth along the Carretera Transandina every half-hour.

PARQUE NACIONAL SIERRA NEVADA

Looming above Mérida to the south and east, the Sierra Nevada runs northeast along the Carretera Transandina and through the 2760 square kilometre **Parque Nacional Sierra Nevada**. Thanks to its 5000-metre altitude, there is great diversity in flora and fauna here; the most famous inhabitant is the threatened spectacled bear.

The park features the country's highest mountains as well as its best **adventure activities**. You can easily explore the lower reaches on your own, but to attempt the two famous peaks, it's best hire a guide service (see box, p.970).

Pico Bolívar

At 5007 metres, **Pico Bolívar** is the country's highest and most hiked peak. There are multiple routes up, varying in difficulty and length of ascent. Many visitors get off at the last *teleférico* station, Pico Espejo, and make the five-hour ascent along the Ruta Weiss, which is not very technical in the dry season (December–May). The Ruta Sur Este and North Flank are two more challenging routes, which involve ice climbing. Views from the top are spectacular – on a clear day, you can see the city of Mérida, the Colombian Andes and the vast expanse of Los Llanos.

Pico Humboldt

Another renowned peak, **Pico Humboldt**, can be combined with a climb of Pico Bolívar or tackled on its own. Starting at the entrance of Parque Nacional La Mucuy, about ten kilometres to the northeast of Mérida, the first day's ascent is 1000m; after the six-hour, nine-kilometre walk, most camp around the picturesque Laguna Coromoto. The ascent on the second day is shorter but steeper as you get into the rocky terrain above the treeline. The final day's ascent to the peak and return to the campsite usually take at least eight hours, depending upon your ice-climbing ability. The fourth day is for the descent back to La Mucuy.

Los Llanos

Taking up nearly a third of the country, the immense plains of **Los Llanos** are one of the continent's premier wildlife-viewing areas. Some of the most abundant species are alligators and capybara, the world's largest rodent with a length of over one metre. Other common species are river dolphins, jaguar, pumas, howler and capuchin monkeys, anteaters and anacondas. However, the livelihood of the region's human inhabitants, the *llaneros*, is most closely linked with domesticated animals. Like the cowboys of the old American West, they have a reputation for being extremely skilled horsemen. Most work on **hatos**, enormous ranches with cattle often numbering in the tens of thousands (see p.977).

Los Llanos has two very pronounced **seasons**. During the wet season, from May to November, much of the land becomes flooded and extremely verdant. In the dry season, the land becomes parched and dusty, with most vegetation turning brown and yellow. While the scenery is more picturesque in the wet season, wildlife sightings are far fewer – the best viewing comes when water is scarce, causing animals to concentrate at the few watering holes.

Unless you have a wad of cash to spend on a stay at one of the *hatos*, you'll most likely visit Los Llanos as part of a **multi-day tour** from Mérida (see p.968). If you're determined to see the region on your own, or are passing through Los Llanos to another part of the country, the backwater city of San Fernando de Apure is a reasonable base and provides onward transport, though frankly, there's no other reason to visit it.

SAN FERNANDO DE APURE

Founded as a missionary outpost in the seventeenth century, **San Fernando de Apure** is now an important trading centre. There's virtually nothing here to detain tourists, but some pass through on the way to the southern *hatos* or to Amazonas (see p.978).

What to see and do

The only vaguely interesting sights in San Fernando are the bizarre **fountain** at the intersection of avenidas Libertador and Miranda, featuring water-spouting caimans grasping cornucopia; and, at the edge of the roundabout, the square **Palacio Barbarito**, a nineteenth-century palace built by Italians involved

LOS LLANEROS

Many comparisons have been drawn between the **llaneros** and the cowboys of the American West. Known for being tough and independent, both are portrayed as embodying the spirit of their countries. Other similarities include their legendary penchants for drinking, gambling and singing sad ballads.

The mixed-blood *llaneros* captured the nation's imagination during the **War of independence** as word of their ferocity spread. Their role in the struggle was integral, and their switch of allegiance in the middle of the war was one of the principal reasons for Bolívar's victory. Life has changed little for them since then, as they continue to work almost exclusively on the enormous cattle ranches.

The *llaneros* participate in a number of competitions that allow them to showcase their machismo. One of the most popular is **toros coleados**. Riding horseback, each of the contestants has to take down a bull by pulling its tail in a certain way; the one who does it quickest wins. Another common competition is the **contrapunteo**, during which two *llaneros* face off in a verbal sparring contest, hurling improvised insults at one other to the beat of *piropa*, a musical form of the region.

in the lucrative trade of caiman leather. Once grand, the palace has deteriorated considerably.

Arrival

Bus The bus terminal is less than a kilometre from the town centre. The only services are phones for international calls, a left luggage desk ($0.50 per hr) and an ATM machine.

Accommodation and eating

Budget **accommodation** in San Fernando de Apure is shoddy and overpriced, but sufficient for a short stopover. **Eating** here is a slightly more promising endeavour, with a number of restaurants serving famed *llanero* beef.

Hotel La Fuente Av Miranda, west of Av Libertador ⓣ0247/342-3233. A somewhat empty, dusty place named for the odd fountain half a block away; the best rooms (en suite, a/c, TV) have views of it. Conveniently close to the bus terminal. ❺

Hotel La Torraca Av Libertador ⓣ0247/342-2777 or 0414/449-6420. Another short walk from the terminal, another featureless block of rooms (though spacious, with bath, a/c and TV). Make sure to get one with natural light. ❺

Restaurant El Príncipe Av Miranda, next to Hotel La Fuente. One of the most pleasant places to eat near the terminal, with pink walls, clean tablecloths and a family feel. Try the garlic-smothered *bisteck de lomo*, with sides of salad and rice ($10), or other meat-heavy dishes, including *shawarma* (which complements the incense and complimentary pita bread). Mon–Sat until 10pm, closed Sun.

Directory

Bank Banco Federal, Av Libertador, one block north of *Hotel La Torraca*. There's also an ATM in the bus terminal.

Internet Slow connections ($1 per hr) on Av Libertador, next to the pharmacy.

Pharmacy Farmacía Los Llanos, Av Libertador, two blocks south of *Hotel La Torraca*.

Phones In the bus terminal.

Post Ipostel, C 24 de Julio at C Bolívar.

Moving on

Bus Barinas (several daily; 8hr); Caracas (hourly; 8hr); Maracay (hourly; 6hr); Puerto Ayacucho (several daily; 6hr); Puerto La Cruz (2 daily; 10hr); San Cristóbal (1 daily; 13hr); Valencia (hourly; 7hr). There are no direct buses to Ciudad Bolívar; you must first go to Valle de La Pascua (1 daily; 5hr), then change buses.

TREAT YOURSELF

Many of the vast cattle ranches of Los Llanos, called **hatos**, double as incredible wildlife sanctuaries and rustic yet exclusive resorts. They offer activities such as truck rides, canoe trips and hikes on their property, and trained guides usually speak some English. High-season rates range from $240 to $320 for a double with all meals and tours included; reservations are almost always required. Call for details on prices and transport to the ranches.

A cheaper and easier way to see Los Llanos is to join a tour from Mérida (see p.970), which often includes whitewater rafting.

Hato El Cedral ⓣ0212/781-8995 or 781-1826, ⓦwww.elcedral.com. Roughly 3 hours from San Fernando de Apure, featuring 340 bird species, live *llanero* music and public lectures by world-renowned scientists.

Hato Frío ⓣ0240/808-3662 or 0416/540-9420, ⓦwww.elfrioeb.com. Ninety kilometres west of San Fernando de Apure, this is the most accessible *hato*, with Caracas- and Mérida-bound buses passing by the main gate.

Hato Piñero ⓣ0212/991-8935 or 991-0079, ⓦwww.hatopinero.com. An extremely picturesque *hato* and a pioneer in Venezuelan conservation and ecotourism efforts. Roughly 5 hour from Caracas and Barinas.

Currently, some *hatos* are under serious threat of **expropriation** by Hugo Chávez's government, which challenges the owners' rights to the land under Venezuela's increasingly socialist climate. In response, the *hatos*, many of which have longstanding ties with international environmental organizations, are rallying support from within the country and abroad.

Guayana

Covering the southern and south-eastern half of Venezuela, **Guayana** is comprised of just three of Venezuela's largest states – Amazonas, Bolívar and Delta Amacuro. Despite the immensity of the region, there are only two real cities, **Puerto Ordáz** and **Ciudad Bolívar**, which are vastly outnumbered by indigenous communities belonging to the Yanomami, Pemón, Warao and Piaroa. While some of these groups barely resemble their ancestors, others have had limited contact with "civilization" and have therefore retained many of their customs.

The region is extremely important economically, containing a tremendous wealth of such natural resources as gold, iron ore, bauxite and diamonds. It also supplies hydroelectricity for the entire country and even exports it to Venezuela's neighbours.

One of the region's important natural resources is nature itself. Many of the country's main tourist attractions are in Guayana, including the **tropical rainforests** of the Amazon, the breathtaking **Angel Falls**, the magnificent *tepuis*, or tabletop mountains, of **Canaima** and the **Gran Sabana** and the **Orinoco Delta**. But the tremendous distances and lack of major tourism facilities mean there are fewer visitors than you might expect.

AMAZONAS

Venezuela's second largest state geographically, **Amazonas** also has the country's smallest population. Almost completely covered in tropical rainforest, it contains hundreds of rivers and is even the birthplace of the mighty **Orinoco River**. Amazonas is known to contain over eight thousand plant species, although there are certainly many more that have not yet been identified. To protect the unique flora, as well as the abundant fauna, numerous national parks have been created here. Despite the government's progressive conservation efforts, tourism here is not nearly as common as it is in the Amazonian regions of Brazil, Ecuador or Peru, and because public transport tourist facilities are limited, visitors invariably have to make arrangements through tour operators.

PUERTO AYACUCHO

A sleepy capital city that's home to half the inhabitants of Amazonas, **Puerto Ayacucho** is the state's only major town. Founded along the Orinoco River in 1924 primarily as a port for shipping timber, its position near the Colombian border makes it a convenient place to cross. Puerto Ayacucho is also the principal entry point for the Amazon region.

What to see and do

Like many other Venezuelan cities, Puerto Ayacucho itself has almost no intrinsic appeal, but there are several nearby attractions, including, of course, the jungle. In town, the **Museo Etnológico de Amazonas** (Tues–Fri 8.30–11.30am & 2.30–6pm, Sat 9am–noon & 3.30–6pm; $0.50; Ⓦ www.verdin.com.mx/webmuseo/mam/mam0000e.html), on Avenida Río Negro, showcases clothing and other objects pertaining to the region's indigenous Guajibos, Arawak, Yanomami, Yekuanas and Piaroas. In front of the museum, **Plaza de los Indios** is a market where locals sell all types of handicrafts, including *katara*, a condiment made from leafcutter ants and hot peppers that's also a reputed sexual stimulant.

The hills around town provide some excellent vistas of the surrounding area. **Cerro Perico**, to the southwest, has views of rooftops and the Orinoco, while **El Mirador**, farther to the south, looks out over the wild, unnavigable Ature Rapids; both can be reached on foot. About

eighteen kilometres south of town, **Cerro Pintado** is a large rock with impressive pre-Columbian **petroglyphs** that are an estimated to be three to five thousand years old. Ten kilometres farther south is **Parque Tobagán de la Selva**, a park containing a natural waterslide. A taxi to the park and petroglyphs costs about $25 – make sure you arrange for pick-up.

Arrival and information

By air There are two daily flights (1hr 30min) between Puerto Ayacucho and Caracas. The airport is 6km southeast of town, roughly $2.50 by taxi. You can also walk out to the highway and catch a city bus into town.

Due to its isolation, Puerto Ayacucho is one of the few cities in Venezuela that you might consider reaching or leaving by air. For a local travel agent and departures, see p.981, respectively.

By bus The ride from San Fernando de Apure, 6hr to the north, is very rough and includes two river crossings that may require a substantial wait. The Puerto Ayacucho terminal, 6km east of town, is quite small, with nowhere to leave luggage.

Tourist information Secretaría de Turismo, next to airport ☎0248/521-0033, Mon–Fri 8am–noon & 2–5pm.

City transport

Although Puerto Ayacucho does have **city buses**, mostly running along Avenida Orinoco from 6am to 7pm, you rarely see them and schedules are unpredictable. Consequently, most locals take taxis, which can be difficult to find during the lunch hour and at the end of the workday.

Accommodation

Residencias Internacional Av Aguerrevere ☎0248/521-0242. A very basic, bi-level hotel popular with foreign backpackers and some long-term residents, and with a great family atmosphere. Rooms (all en suite) are small and can be slightly grungy, but they're joyously painted by the owner, and some have a/c ($5 extra). There's an upper deck for enjoying the treetop view with a beer, a greenery-filled courtyard below, and virtually no street noise. The *panadería* next door is good for a morning pastry or *cachito*. ④

Posada Manapiare Urb Alto Parima, 2da etapa #1 ⓣ0248/809-0067, ⓔcarmenyr@cantv.net. A considerable cut above the competition in Puerto Ayacucho, reflected in the price. *Manapiare* is a secure compound in a tranquil neighbourhood, with a volcanic stone courtyard, indigenous decorations, pool, laundry service, and spacious rooms (en suite, TV, a/c) named after animals. The restaurant serves food (like fried fish) all day. Reservations required. ⑤–⑥

Residencias Michalanguelli de Pozo C Evelio Roa ⓣ0248/521-3189. Though it has a slightly deserted feel, this little place is quiet, clean and leafy. Rooms facing the street have the best light. Only matrimonial rooms have a/c, though all are en suite with TVs. ④

Residencias Miramar Av Orinoco, 1.5km south of centre ⓣ0248/521-1700. Basically a roadside motel, with a central parking lot and office ringed by rooms, but all are big and sparkling (en suite, TV, a/c). There's even a small garden in front of each door. A cab from the centre costs about $1.50. ⑤

Hotel Tonino Av 23 de Enero, just east of Av Orinoco ⓣ0248/891669. Though it's set just a few metres back from one of the town's busiest streets, the *Tonino* is still fairly quiet, with small, tidy rooms (en suite, TV, a/c) and a pride of resident cats. ④

Eating

In addition to the range of inexpensive **restaurants** about town, there is a string of food stalls along Avenida Aguerrevere, west of Avenida Orinoco, hawking *empanadas*, burgers and fried chicken and fish each evening (all under $5).

Café Rey David Av Orinoco, south of the *mercadito*. There may be a star of David on the sign, but you can be fairly certain this place isn't

TOURS OF THE AMAZON

Compressing all of the wonders of the Amazon into three days is impossible, but a few tour companies in Puerto Ayacucho do their best. The classic tour is a 3-day/2-night trip up the Sipapo and Autana rivers to **Cerro Autana**, a sacred, 1200-metre-high mesa that can be viewed from an adjacent mirador. Nights are typically spent with indigenous communities, and side-trips up channels in smaller boats are usually included, sometimes with opportunities to fish for feisty *pavón*, or peacock bass. More expensive options include the eight- to ten-day **Ruta Humboldt**, following in the footsteps of the famous explorer, and even longer journeys to meet the Yanomami and other isolated tribes.

All-inclusive prices per day, for groups of four or more people, are $100–120 per day per person for three or four days, usually more for longer trips. Companies provide any necessary jungle access permits and can often help you plan a journey into Brazil; for details, see the box on p.982.

Finally, a **disclaimer**: many people expect to see amazing wildlife in the Amazon, but in reality the density of the jungle and the reclusiveness of the animals makes this quite difficult. If you're set on wildlife-watching, save your money for a trip to Los Llanos (see p.976).

Coyote Expediciones Avenida Aguerrevere #75 ⓣ0414/486-2500, ⓔcoyoteexpedition@cantv.net. This outfit arranges the standard tours as well as trips along the narrow Río Casiquiare, which links the Orinoco to the Río Negro, and to the indigenous community of Báquiro, a good alternative to Autana if the weather isn't cooperating.

Eco-Destinos C Piar, off Av Aguerrevere ⓣ0416/448-6394 or 0248/521-3964, ⓔhenryamazonas@hotmail.com. Lets customers fully customize trips, for instance by suggesting they bring and prepare their own food to mitigate expenses. Can also help clients get to Brazil by preparing letters of introduction for checkpoints.

Tadae Av Río Negro ⓣ0248/521-4882 or 0414/486-5923, ⓔtadaevenezuela@hotmail.com. The savviest of Puerto Ayacucho's tour companies, offering the standard excursions as wells as air tickets and trips throughout the rest of the country. Ask about "moto-rafting" and the four-day trek to La Laguna del Rey Leopoldo.

kosher, with its full line of standard *arepa* fillings and burger combos. Good for a late-night *ración* of *pollo a la broaster* ($5), and sells a full line of personal hygiene products in case you're out of dental floss. Mon–Sat 7am–midnight.

Los Guariqueños Av 23 de Enero. The best place in town for *pollo a la broaster*, by *ración* ($2.50), quarter-bird ($5) or half-bird ($8.50), and with sides of chips and slaw. Other meaty options are *pabellón criollo*, liver, pork chops and fried fish (all under $10). Amazon scenes decorate the walls, and whole chickens sizzle on spits out front.

El Mercadito Between avenidas Orinoco and Amazonas, south of Av 23 de Enero. The destination of choice for lunch-breaking workers. Two indoor restaurants at the east end of the market (*El Rincón Llanero* and *La Catira*) serve inexpensive comida criolla, but for a real deal, slurp down a steaming bowl of *sopa de gallina*, *res* or *pescado* in the market itself.

Mi Arepita Av Amazonas at C Atabapo. A bit of New York City in the middle of the Amazon – the loud-mouthed owner heckles his regulars, primarily police and postal workers. The crispy product is freshly made and stuffed with quail eggs, Guayana cheese or any other selection from the hand-painted board. Juice and coffee, too. Mon–Fri 8–11am, Sat 8–noon, closed Sun.

La Pusana Via Aeropuerto, 2km south of the centre ⓣ0248/414-6534, ⓔrest_lapusana@yahoo.com. Take a cab here ($2) for Amazonas specialities served in a casual and semi-outdoor but extremely attentive atmosphere. Enormous meals begin with a flight of exotic juice samplers and an ant-filled bowl of *katara*. Ask for the delicious fried *dorado*, served with rice, salad and fried plantain medallions (complete meal around $15). Should be noted that it once had a reputation for selling bush meat; they claim those days are over, but if you learn otherwise, take your business elsewhere. Mon–Sat 9am–4pm, Sun till 3pm.

Las Tres Espigas Av Río Negro at C Evelio Roa. A spotless, a/c *panadería* selling pastries, cheese, meat and coffee in a giant room with checkered walls. Mon–Sat 7am–8.30pm, Sun till 12.30pm.

Drinking and nightlife

While Puerto Ayacucho is certainly a **drinking** town – crowds of rowdy men loiter outside the *bodegas* on weekend evenings – there aren't many actual establishments of interest.

Royal Pool Av Evelio Roa. A simple pool hall serving beer. Daily until 1am.

Tunel de la Estancia Av Aguerrevere, west of C Piar. This popular tasca/disco/karaoke joint packs in a convivial local crowd. Thurs–Sat all night.

Directory

Bank Banesco, Av Orinoco south of Av Aguerrevere; Banco de Venezuela on Av Orinoco south of C Carabobo.

Hospital Hospital Dr José Gregorio Hernández, Av 23 de Enero ⓣ0248/521-1024 or 521-0530.

Immigration DIEX office, Av Aguerrevere, Mon–Fri 8am–noon & 2–5.30pm. If you need a Colombian visa (see p.539), the consulate is at C Yapacana, Quinta Beatriz ⓣ0248/521-0789, Mon–Fri 7am–1pm & 3–6pm.

Internet Inversiones Cherrasort, Av Amazonas between calles Evelio Roa and Bolívar, daily 9am–7pm ($1 per hr). Intercyber, in Centro Indiani, Av Aguerrevere just west of Av Orinoco, Mon–Sat 8am–9pm, closed Sun. There's a third in Empresarial Orticeño on Av Aguerrevere, east of the DIEX office (see above).

Laundry Lavandería Automática Aquario, Av Aguerrevere next to *Residencias Internacional*. Mon–Sat 8am–noon & 2–6pm, closed Sun.

Pharmacy Farmacía Autana, Av Río Negro at C Evelio Roa, Mon–Fri 8am–noon & 2–6pm; Farmacía Doña Carmen, Av Orinoco south of Av Aguerrevere, Mon–Fri 8am–noon & 3–7pm. Both work weekends *por turno*.

Phones CANTV, Av Orinoco at Av Aguerrevere; Movistar, Av Orinoco south of C Carabobo.

Shopping The Mercado Municipal, at the north end of Av Orinoco, sells an interesting selection of fresh fruit, veg and meat. Mon–Sat 6am–6pm, Sun 6am–noon. Behind the market are various lunch stalls selling *cachapas*, *mondongo* and assorted juices.

Travel agents Wayumi, Av Evelio Roa between avs Río Negro and Amazonas, serves Venezuela's deep south.

Moving on

For information on **crossing into Colombia or Brazil** from this region, see the boxes on p.967 or p.982, respectively.

By air There are two daily flights to Caracas (1hr 30min). Regional destinations include Esmeralda ($200); Maroa ($140); San Carlos del Río Negro ($200); San Fernando de Atabapo ($140); and San Juan de Manapiare ($140).

By bus Caracas (several daily; 14hr); Ciudad Bolívar (hourly with several night buses; 15hr); Maracay (several daily; 12hr); Puerto Ordáz (hourly; 16hr); San Fernando de Apure (4 daily; 6hr); Valencia (several daily; 13hr).

CROSSING INTO BRAZIL

There are two main **border crossings** between Venezuela and Brazil. The crossing at Santa Elena de Uairén (see p.990) is more convenient for onward transport to Manaus; the San Simón de Cocuy crossing is a journey unto itself and requires several days of boat travel through remote wilderness.

Before leaving Venezuela you must get your passport stamped by the nearest emigration office. Once you cross the border, immediately visit the local Brazilian immigration office for an entry stamp and advance your watch and hour and a half.

Citizens of the US, Canada and Australia need a visa to enter Brazil; EU nationals and citizens of South Africa and New Zealand do not. For a list of all countries' visa requirements, visit ⓦwww.dpf.gov.br. All visitors must have a valid yellow fever vaccination certificate.

San Simón de Cocuy

From Puerto Ayacucho, purchase an expensive two-hour flight (see p.981) south to San Carlos de Río Negro. From here, frequent boats continue to San Simón de Cocuy (2hr), stopping at the border for you to complete formalities. Once you're over, take a bus to São Gabriel da Cachoeria, Brazil and board a boat (3 weekly) for the three- to four-day journey down the Río Negro to Manaus. Alternatively, take a costly fast boat direct from San Carlos to São Gabriel (4–6hr). During the dry season there's a bus from São Gabriel to Manaus, or you can fly ($100–150).

Puerto Ayacucho **tour companies** (see p.980) can arrange transport and prepare explanatory letters for the checkpoints along the way. Attempting the journey entirely on your own is discouraged, as you'll be a long way from assistance should something go awry.

Santa Elena de Uairén

There are currently no direct buses from Santa Elena to Brazil. Instead, take a **taxi** to the border (20min), commonly known as "La Línea", where the driver will wait for you to complete formalities before driving you into Pacaraima, Brazil.

From Pacaraima's bus terminal you can catch an hourly service, daily until 6pm, to Boa Vista (5hr 30min), and continue from there to Manaus (12hr), sometimes on the same bus.

The **Brazilian Consulate** in Santa Elena (just off Via La Línea ⓣ0289/995-1256, Mon–Fri 8am–2pm) supplies visas within 48 hours; you must provide a passport photo and present proof of financial security (usually a credit card) and accommodation in Brazil. Visa fees vary by country of citizenship. The consulate can also help you arrange a yellow fever vaccination, though this can take up to ten days.

For information on changing money at the border, see the box on p.991.

Bolívar

Bolívar is the country's largest state and one of its richest, too, thanks to abundant mineral deposits. Its four huge dams also produce around seventy percent of the country's hydroelectric energy.

Much of the southeast part of the state is made up of the **Gran Sabana**, long plains punctuated by incredible *tepuis*, remnants of what is claimed to be the oldest geographic formation on earth. Within the Gran Sabana is **Parque Nacional Canaima**, home to the celebrated Auyantepui, which spawns **Angel Falls**, and **Roraima**, another notable *tepui* in the southeastern corner of the state. The only two sizeable cities are **Ciudad Bolívar**, a pretty colonial town with a very rich history, and **Ciudad Guayana**, a characterless city created to be one of the country's primary industrial centres. The name Ciudad Guayana in fact refers to two adjacent cities, prosperous **Puerto Ordáz** and its neglected sibling San Félix.

PUERTO ORDÁZ

Most of the visitors who pass through **Puerto Ordáz** are on their way to Ciudad Bolívar, a much better jumping-off point for the main attractions in the state. Lacking in history, culture and visual appeal, Puerto Ordáz should be treated primarily as a transport hub, though if you're stuck here for any length of time, there are a couple of mildly diverting sights.

What to see and do

Puerto Ordáz is not a walkable city. Built on an industrial rather than human scale, its few sights are spread kilometres apart and not conveniently linked by public transport. Nevertheless, San Félix–bound buses ($0.50), which leave frequently from the parking lot of Centro Comercial Trebol until 7pm, will drop you at Parque Cachamay, from where it's a short walk to the **Ecomuseo de Caroní** (daily 9am–9pm; free). Next to the 23 de Enero dam, the museum has a number of rotating educational exhibits, a small collection of fine art and a large window through which you can see the dam's gargantuan generators. Alternatively, a taxi from the centre costs about $10.

Parque Cachamay and a nearby park, **Llovizna**, feature expanses of life-affirming greenery and some nice waterfalls. You can get to Cachamay by bus (see p.984), though Llovizna is best reached by taxi ($10). You can also combine both on a half-day tour with Piraña Tours ($50; ⓣ0286/923-6447 or 922-7748, ⓦwww.piranatours.com), in the lobby of the *Hotel InterContinental Guayana*.

Arrival

Bus Puerto Ordáz's terminal is on Av Guayana, about 10min from the centre. There is nowhere to leave luggage in the terminal. Some buses arrive in San Félix, from where it's a 15min taxi ride to Puerto Ordáz ($10).

Air On the western edge of the city, along the road to Ciudad Bolívar. Corpoturismo Bolívar has an office in the airport (see p.984) and there's an Italcambio for exchanging money and traveller's cheques. A cab into the centre is $10; bus routes are inconvenient.

Accommodation

While not centrally located, *La Casa del Lobo* is far and away the best budget accommodation in the city. If it's full, there are a couple of passable alternatives downtown.

La Casa del Lobo ⓣ0286/961-6286. The only backpacker-friendly option in the city, with an Animal House meets MTV "Real World" flavour; you'll likely have a *caipirinha* in your hand before you've even signed the register. The five large rooms have fans and private bathrooms, and there's free internet, a deck with a bar and hammock and free rides to/from the airport or bus terminals. ❹

Hotel Georgina C Aripao at C Urbana ⓣ0286/924-0079. Rooms are forgettable but contain all mod cons (bath, TV, a/c), and the reception is friendly enough. A slightly slicker operation than *Hotel Rayoli* (see below). ❺

Hotel Habana Cuba Av Las Américas, south of Carrera Tumeremo ⓣ0286/224-904 or 224-911. An urban motel with spacious rooms (en suite, TV, a/c), pink sheets and cool tile surfaces. Ask for a room with a window, even though the glass is opaque and there's no view to speak of. ❺

Hotel Rayoli C Urbana at C Aripao ⓣ0286/225-557. At the edge of an oil-stained parking lot, this central, secure choice has en-suite rooms (TV, a/c) with fraying furniture. As usual, window rooms are best. ❺

Eating

Bulevar de Comida Guayanesa C Guasipati at Via Caracas. A row of streetside stalls serving heaping servings of meat (tongue, fried pork) or *mondongo* stew (all $5–10) to a lunch break crowd seated at plastic tables. Daily till 4pm.

Lonchería Naturalia Carrera Upata, east of C El Callao. In a parking lot across the street from the looming Hotel Tepuy, this healthful snack counter sells baked *empanadas*, including veggie options such as broccoli and mushroom, icy sugar-free juices and fresh yoghurt. Mon–Sat dawn–3pm, Sun till noon.

Pizzería Da Giulio Av Las Américas, next to *Hotel Habana Cuba* ☎0286/923-5698. The trattoria thing may be a bit overdone (checkered tablecloths, paintings of the old country), but the pizzas come out just right. Choose from calabrese, four cheese, prosciutto, Siciliana and more; personal size is $4.50–7, family $12 and up. Also serves typical Venezuelan meat dishes ($9–12). Mon–Fri 11.30am–2.15pm & 7–9.15pm, Sat 11.30am–3.30pm, closed Sun.

Directory

Bank Banco Provincial, Carrera Upata at Av Ciudad Bolívar.
Internet Ideas.com, CC Trebol ($1.50 per hr), Mon–Sat 10am–7pm, closed Sun.
Phones Movistar, across street from *Hotel Rayoli* (see p.983).
Post DHL, C El Palmar at C Santa Elena, ☎0286/923-1744 or 923-5585, ext 19, daily 8am–5.30pm.
Shopping For a dose of commercialist perversity (and some good 'ol US-style fast food), check out the massive Orinokia mall, bordered by Av Las Américas and Av Guayana.
Tourist information Venetur, in *Hotel Inter-Continental Guayana* ☎0286/713-1244, daily 8am–noon & 2–6pm; Corpoturismo Bolívar, in airport, ☎0800/674-6626 Mon–Fri 7am–7pm, Sat 8am–noon & 2–6pm, Sun 10am–6pm; and a booth in the Puerto Ordáz bus terminal, daily 7am–12.30pm & 2.30–9pm.

Moving on

Bus City buses to both terminals leave from the parking lot of C.C. Trebol, Av Guasipati, till 7pm daily; buses to the Puerto Ordáz terminal are labeled "Unare." A taxi from the centre to the Puerto Ordáz terminal is $5, San Félix terminal $10. Buses to Ciudad Bolívar ($2.50; 1hr) leave every half-hour until 7pm. Other services include Barinas (4 daily; 15hr); Caracas (hourly; 12hr); Cumaná (several daily; 9hr 30min); Maracaibo (2 daily; 21hr); Maracay (several daily; 12hr); Puerto La Cruz (hourly; 7hr); San Cristóbal (4 daily; 20hr); Santa Elena de Uairén (6 daily; 10hr); and Valencia (several daily; 12hr). Buses to Tucupita leave only from San Félix (4hr), every 2hr till 6pm daily.

Air There are eight daily flights to and from Caracas (5 on Sun); also Barcelona (1 daily; 30min); Maracaibo (1 daily; 2hr); Porlamar (2 daily; 50min); and Valencia (1 daily; 50min). There are no flights to Barcelona, Valencia or Maracaibo on Sat.

CUIDAD BOLÍVAR

Besides being one of the most backpacker-friendly cities in Venezeula, **Ciudad Bolívar** is the ideal jumping-off point for exploring the state of Bolívar. In contrast to Puerto Ordáz, Ciudad Bolívar is easily walkable and most of its highlights can be seen in a single day; you'll soon be ready to take on the endless wilderness of **Parque Nacional Canaima** and the **Gran Sabana** (see p.988 & p.992, respectively).

Casco histórico

Most of the city's colonial architecture is in the **casco histórico**, a roughly ten-block area on the southern bank of the Orinoco River, centred on the **Plaza Bolívar**. On the east side of the plaza, the imposing 1840 **Catedral** has a light, airy interior, which, while not particularly ornate, makes for a good escape from the midday heat. To the west of the plaza, the **Casa del Congreso de Angostura** (Tues–Sun 9am–5.30pm; free) is the site where the Angostura Congress founded Gran Colombia; Bolívar also lived here briefly in 1817. A quick peek reveals paintings of the original congressmen, an old printing press and archives of documents pertaining to Bolívar.

Paseo Orinoco

Plaza Bolívar may be the heart of the city, but Ciudad Bolívar's pulse is best felt along the **Paseo Orinoco**. Two blocks north of the plaza, this bustling riverside thoroughfare is lined with shops of every persuasion, many of which broadcast their latest deals over screeching PA systems.

On the west end of the Paseo, at Calle Carabobo, the **Museo de Ciudad Bolívar** (Mon–Fri 9am–noon & 2–5pm; free),

housed in a colonial-era post office, has a small collection of archeological artefacts from throughout Latin America, as well as some modern metal sculpture.

Be careful on the Paseo after dark, as it has played host to robberies.

Museo de Arte Moderno Jesús Soto

One of the country's most fascinating museums, the **Museo de Arte Moderno Jesús Soto** (Tues–Sat 9.30am–5.30pm, Sat & Sun 10am–5pm; free), just outside town on Avenida Germania, contains the fascinating works of its namesake, widely regarded as Venezuela's most famous contemporary artist. Many of his paintings and sculptures make use of optical illusions, and you can ask to be accompanied by one of the guides, who will point out the visual tricks. Taxis here from the centre cost $4; to return, catch a bus from the McDonald's across the street.

Jardín Botánico

Consider a stroll through the well-maintained **Jardín Botánico** (daily 9am–noon & 2–4.30pm; free; Ⓦwww.jborinoco.org) on Avenida Bolívar at Calle Caracas. The gardens, which you must tour in the company of a guide, contain plant species from all over the world.

Arrival and information

By air The airport is at the southeastern edge of town, at the intersection of Av Táchira and Av Aeropuerto. A taxi to the *casco histórico* costs around $5, or you can take a Santa Eduviges–bound city bus ("Ruta 2"; $0.50; daily 5am–6pm) and get off in the centre.

By bus The terminal lies at the southern end of the city, at the intersection of Av República and Av Sucre. A bus from to the *casco histórico* costs $0.50 and drops you at the northwest corner of the Jardín Botánico.

Tourist information Corpoturismo Bolívar, Casa Casalta on Paseo Orinoco ⓣ0285/617-0312 or 617-0313, ⓔcorpoturismobolivar@cantv.net. There's also an Inatur desk in the airport, Mon–Fri 8am–6pm.

Tour operators

Most of the agencies listed here also sell tours of the Orinoco Delta (see p.993), Gran Sabana (see p.992) and other countrywide attractions, but you'll generally find better deals in cities closer to those sights (Tucupita for the delta; Santa Elena de Uairén for the Gran Sabana).

Adrenaline C Bolívar at C Dalla Costa ⓣ0285/632-4804 or 0414/886-7209, ⓔadrenalinexptours@hotmail.com. One of Ciudad Bolívar's most enthusiastic and responsible agencies. Co-owner Ricardo, an eccentric in the best sense, leads mind-blowing trips of the Gran Sabana (see p.992).

Amor Patrio in *Posada Amor Patrio* (see opposite). Specializes in Río Caura trips, rugged camping and visits to indigenous villages.

Eco-Adventures in the bus terminal ⓣ0285/651-9546 or 0414/851-3656, ⓦwww.adventurevenezuela.com. Often mistaken for a pirate outfit due to its location; it's in fact a great option for travellers who don't have time to make house calls to all the agencies in the centre.

Jonas Tours Las Trincheras ⓣ0414/899-0180 or 0414/099-5904, ⓔjonastours54@hotmail.com. Not actually based in Ciudad Bolívar, but the principal operator for Río Caura trips; most agencies in town work through him.

Sapito Tours in the airport ⓣ0412/842-3072, ⓦwww.bernaltours.com. The tour agency arm of *Campamento Bernal* in Canaima Village.

Tiuna Tours in the airport ⓣ0285/632-8697, ⓔtiunatours@hotmail.com. Offers some of the cheapest Canaima packages and the most basic accommodation in the park (see p.989). The unique placement of its Salto Ángel *campamento*, halfway to the falls, means you're the first group to reach them.

Total Aventura C Libertad between calles Venezuela and Bolívar ⓣ0414/850-4338 or 0285/6324635, ⓔexpedicionesdearuna@yahoo.com. Alternatively known as Dearuna Expeditions, this agency offers clients two free nights in its tiny *posada*-cum-office in Ciudad Bolívar; non-clients pay $7.50. It also runs the unique "Ruta de los 7 Ríos" trip, a 6-day trail/river journey from La Paragua to Canaima Village.

Turismo Gekko in the airport ⓣ0285/632-3223 or 0414/854-5146, ⓦwww.gekkotours-venezuela.de. Contracts with slightly more upscale lodging in the park.

Accommodation

Ciudad Bolívar is rivalled only by Mérida in its selection of great, cheap accommodation.

La Casita Av Ligia Pulido, Urb 24 de Julio ⓣ0285/617-0832 or 0414/856-2925. A sprawling compound 15min from the centre by taxi, this otherwise upscale lodging has some surprisingly affordable options, namely outdoor hammocks and bunks for $10 per person, and camping spots on the lawn for $7 per person. Indoor rooms surround a huge dining *palapa* for communal meals (not included), and there's even a pool. Free shuttles to/from town and free pick-up from the airport or bus terminal. Only the small zoo in the grounds raises eyebrows, though apparently the animals have been rescued from worse fates. Owner also runs Turismo Gekko (see above). Dbl ❺–❻

Hotel Ritz C Libertad at C Venezuela ⓣ0285/632-3886 or 632-2768. A far cry from its namesake, this is a very basic but pleasant option just steps from Paseo Orinoco. There are huge en-suite doubles (with TV, a/c) and singles with fans and shared bath. Make sure to get a window room. The attached restaurant serves lunch and dinner. ❷–❹

Posada Amor Patrio C Amor Patrio at C Igualdad ⓣ0414/854-4925, ⓔplazabolívar@hotmail.com. This German-run *posada* in a 250-year-old house brimming with personality is a terrific budget option. All rooms have distinct, attractive designs, and for $10 you can sleep in a hammock on the open-air top level. There's a shared kitchen, four shared bathrooms and laundry service, and the owner organizes occasional concerts in the Plaza Bolívar. Also has its own tour agency (see opposite). ❺

Posada Don Carlos C Boyacá at C Amor Patrio ⓣ0285/632-6017 or 0414/854-6616, ⓔsoanatravel@gmx.de. Like *La Casita*, this *posada* has both inexpensive and upscale options – the main difference is that they're in a rambling, intricately decorated colonial home. Bunks and hammocks ($12.50) are on an exposed upper level, along with a couple of shared-bath rooms (dbl $30, single $25). Internet, laundry service and shared kitchen ($1 per day usage fee). ❺–❻

TREAT YOURSELF

La Casa Grande C Venezolana at C Boyacá ⓣ0424/900-4473 or 0285/632-4639, ⓦwww.cacaotravel.com. Utterly peerless in Ciudad Bolívar if not in Venezuela, this luxurious *posada* occupies a former headquarters of the Red Cross and combines colonial majesty with artful modern flair. A skylit atrium contains plants and a fountain, and the roof deck has expansive views of the Orinoco. Enormous en-suite rooms have a/c, flat-screen TVs, exposed original stonework and safes. The all English-speaking staff provides free transport to the bus terminal, airport and even Puerto Ordáz. ❾

Posada El Rosario C Carabobo at C Rosario ⓣ0416/987-3084 or 0424/914-2899. For more personalized service, this quiet, bi-level *posada* has spotless, breezy rooms (en suite, a/c) and an outdoor seating area in a walled garden. The English-speaking owner is very sweet. An upper deck has views of the Puente de Angostura, one of the two bridges over the Orinoco. Reservations recommended; free pickup from airport or bus terminal. ❻–❼

Eating

Ciudad Bolívar is not particularly noted for its food, but a few decent options exist. Local fish such as *dorado*, *palometa* and *sapoara* are fresh and tasty.

El Caribeño C Igualdad between Paseo Orinoco and C Venezuela. A very simple, very cheap cafeteria serving breakfasts (*pastelitos*, *empanadas*, *jugos*) and full meals (*pollo a la brasa*, *bisteck*, *pescado*) with sides of rice, salad, pasta, yucca and more – nothing over $7.50. Daily 6am–7pm.

Las Marquesas Av Cumaná south of C Bolívar. This pleasant old house, sporting clean table linen, wooden chairs, paintings and ceiling fans, is the venue for plates of *cochino guisado*, *arroz con pollo* and assorted vegetables, only $5 as part of the *menú ejecutivo*. Serves lunch and dinner daily till 8pm.

Mercado La Carioca East end of Paseo Orinoco. This is the ideal place to get a large and satisfying meal while enjoying views of (and breezes off of) the Orinoco. It has a number of small restaurants, all serving similar meat and fish dishes with sides of yucca, black beans, rice, plantains, and more (all under $10). Beers are so cold they arrive to the table frozen. A bus here along Paseo Orinoco costs $0.50; a taxi from the centre is $4.

Mini-lunch Arabian Food C Amor Patrio at C Libertad. A tiny corner café good for a fix of Middle Eastern food: *shawarma* plate $6–7, large "mix" plate $9 and falafel, *kibbe*, tabbouleh and hummus also available. Mon–Sat noon–8.30pm, Sun 2–8pm.

Restaurant Vegetariano C Amor Patrio at C Dalla Costa ⓣ0414/987-4803 or 0414/099-0991. A peaceful vegetarian restaurant, part of a yoga centre in a lovely colonial home, with large portions sold by weight ($10 per kg). Everything's vegetarian, with an emphasis on soups and salads. Mon–Fri 7am–3pm, Sat lunch only, closed Sun.

Tasca La Ballena C Urica at C Zea. This underlit but clean *tasca* is one of the few places in the *casco histórico* open Sunday evenings. Standard meat, fish and chicken dishes are all under $7.50. There's a bar with a TV for watching baseball games.

Tony Bar Av Táchira, near the airport ⓦwww.tonybar.net. Founded in 1964, an epic run by Venezuelan standards. This diner-style spot in a residential neighbourhood covers the entire price spectrum with an endless menu. Cheapest are sandwiches (*choripán*, fried egg, roast beef; $5–10), burgers ($4.50–6), and salads (niçoise, avocado, hearts of palm; $7.50–10), but there are seafood and *parrilla* platters for up to $30. Finish your meal with a banana split.

Tostadas Juancito's Av Cumaná at C Bolívar. Grab a seat on the patio, across the street from the Jardín Botánico, and watch the traffic as you attack a dripping arepa or a plate of *pabellón criollo* ($7), *muchacho en salsa* ($7) or *pollo a la brasa* (quarter $4.50). Mon–Sat 6.30am–6.30pm, Sun till 2pm.

Directory

Bank Banco de Venezuela, Paseo Orinoco at C Piar; Banesco, C Dalla Costa at C Venezuela.

Hospital Hospital Ruiz y Páez, Av Germania ⓣ0285/632-0041.

Internet Ciber Play, Paseo Orinoco between calles Igualdad and Libertad, Mon–Sat 8.30am–7pm, closed Sun. There's also an internet café in Pasaje Bolívar, a *centro comercial* on Paseo Orinoco between calles Dalla Costa and Piar.

Pharmacy Farmacía Orinoco, Paseo Orinoco at C Carabobo, Mon–Sat 9am–1pm & 2.30–6pm, closed Sun.

Phones Movistar, Paseo Orinoco between calles Dalla Costa and Libertad. There's another *centro de llamadas* on C Dalla Costa between calles Venezuela and Bolívar.

Post Ipostel, Av Táchira, 1km south of the *casco histórico.*
Shopping Tienda de *Artesanía* Cooperativa Kerepacupai-meru, at Mercado La Carioca (see p.987), with handmade toys, bags, postcards and hammocks; Mon–Sat 9am–2.30pm, closed Sun. For groceries there's a fruit/veg store just north of Las Marquesas (see p.987); you can also buy food items at Mercado La Carioca.

Moving on

Air Caracas (2 daily except Sat; 1hr10min); Porlamar (Fri 4pm; 1hr10min). Rutaca (www.rutaca.com.ve) nominally operates daily flights to Santa Elena (roughly $225), but actual departures are unpredictable. The Puerto Ordáz airport covers more destinations.
Bus Caracas (several daily; 9hr); Carúpano (1 daily; 8hr); Cumaná (2 daily; 7hr); Maracaibo (1 daily; 23hr); Maracay (several daily; 9hr); Puerto Ayacucho (4 daily; 14hr); Puerto La Cruz (several daily; 5hr); Puerto Ordáz (half-hourly; 1hr); Valencia (several daily; 10hr).
If you're headed to Mérida (1 daily; 22hr), it's faster to take a bus to Barinas (2 daily; 15hr) and transfer to a *buseta* or *por puesto* for the steep, windy road into the mountains.
Por puestos to Puerto La Cruz (3hr) leave regularly from the street north of the terminal and cost $22. Reserve early for Santa Elena (6 daily; 12hr); if travelling by night, you will be woken at least twice for checkpoints along the way. Turgar offers the cheapest transport.
There are no buses to Tucupita; you must first go to the San Félix terminal in Ciudad Guayana (see p.984).

TRIPS TO CANAIMA AND AROUND

Ciudad Bolívar is the staging point for trips to **Parque Nacional Canaima** and its centrepiece, **Angel Falls** (see p.988 & p.989, respectively). The city has a bewildering number of tour agencies and operators, all offering more or less the same packages.

While it's certainly possible to cobble together a trip to Canaima on your own, the little money you save is hardly worth the effort of arranging all the various components (flights, accommodation, excursions, meals, etc). The local tourist industry depends on groups assembled by agencies; the needs of maverick travellers are generally an afterthought.

The bestselling trip is an all-inclusive, three-day/two-night tour of Angel Falls and Canaima Lagoon ($500–650 per person), with flights in and out of Canaima Village. Some operators can lower the cost by driving you to the midpoint town of La Paragua (2hr 30min) and flying round-trip to Canaima from there ($400–450). Other multiday options include boat trips from Kamarata Village to Canaima Lagoon; hikes or jeep rides between Kavac and Kamarata villages (both $600–700); and five-day boat journeys down the **Río Caura**, to the west of Parque Nacional Canaima ($400–500 per person).

Prices are all-inclusive except for the national park fee ($4) and airport tax ($3). For brief descriptions of some of Canaima Village's **accommodation** options, see opposite.

PARQUE NACIONAL CANAIMA

Parque Nacional Canaima, one of the world's largest national parks, is the number one tourist attraction in Venezuela, thanks to the wondrous Salto Ángel, or **Angel Falls**. As far as national parks go, however, it receives surprisingly few visitors overall. The park is inhabited by roughly twenty thousand Pemón Indians, made up of three major tribes: Kamakoto, Arekuna and Taurepan. Most live in small villages of one to two hundred people.

Canaima Village

The most visited village in the park, **Canaima** is the principal base for trips to Angel Falls. Just beside the village are four postcard-worthy waterfalls – **Salto Hacha, Salto Ucaima, Salto Golondrina** and **Salto Guadima** – that emanate from the Río Carrao and empty into the picturesque **Laguna de Canaima**, which has small sand beaches along its banks. Tour packages (see p.986) generally include a short boat trip to another waterfall, **Salto El Sapo**, which you can actually walk right behind, and **Salto El Sapito**, a smaller but equally picturesque cascade.

If you've come on a tour, a guide will have been arranged for you; if you're on your own, seek out English-speaking Materson Nathaniel (ⓣ0426/997-2879, ⓔkaikuse_68@yahoo.es), a knowledgeable Pemón guide who leads trips throughout the park.

Arrival

By air Nearly all visitors arrive by air from Ciudad Bolívar, as transport is included in package tours. The main airline is Transmandu (ⓦwww.transmandu.com); if you're arranging your own transport, expect to pay $250–300 with return to Ciudad Bolívar. The airstrip is right on the edge of the village.

Accommodation

Like transport, accommodation in Canaima is included in tour packages arranged in Ciudad Bolívar. All lodgings, save the exclusive luxury ones, are *campamentos* of varying simplicity. The cheapest are listed here, with price codes indicating how much you'll pay if you arrange a trip on your own. On trips that include a visit to Salto Ángel, you'll spend a night in one of several primitive **camps** near the base of the falls. Hammocks and outhouses (no showers) are the norm.

Posada Kusari about 1km outside the village ⓣ0286/962-0443 or 0416/696-0025. If you've brought your own food (and a way to cook it), this is the cheapest lodging in the park: a basic, en-suite room here is only $50. Otherwise they really stick you with meal prices (breakfast $27, lunch and dinner $37 each) and the 3-day/2-night Angel Falls tour is a whopping $350 with meals and accommodation, but no flights. ❻

Tiuna ⓣ0414/884-0502. Has a serene location at the edge of Canaima Lagoon; sleeping is in hammocks hung in a large, open-sided room. It's used primarily by clients of the agency of the same name (see p.986), though other companies can place you here as well. ❾

Wey Tepui ⓣ0414/895-4333. Has a selection of basic rooms in the most developed structure of these three options. ❾

Eating and drinking

Food is also included in tour prices; vegetarians should notify the agency when purchasing a tour. Should you get hungry between scheduled **meals** – portions are on the small side – there are a couple of general stores in the village, though prices are outrageous since all stock is flown in. An excellent place for an evening cocktail is the lagoon-side deck of Campamento Canaima, with unreal views of the falls at sunset. Intriguingly, the Pemón have expropriated this high-end lodging from the government agency that was previously managing it.

Moving on

By air In most cases, moving on from Canaima is simply a matter of boarding your pre-arranged return **flight** to Ciudad Bolívar. If your next stop is Santa Elena de Uairén, however, you might consider a direct flight there ($175–225 per person), saving yourself around 12hr of bus travel, not including waiting time. The main obstacles, besides cost, are the notoriously unpredictable departure times and the three-passenger minimum.

ANGEL FALLS

At 980 metres, **Angel Falls** (Salto Ángel in Spanish) is the world's tallest waterfall – around sixteen times the height of Niagara Falls and twelve times the height of Iguazú Falls (see p.101 & p.392). It is created by the Churún River, which makes a dramatic plunge from the edge of the enormous Auyantepui and into the verdant jungle below.

Seeing the falls is one of the highlights of a trip to Venezuela, and you can arrange a visit through tour agencies in Ciudad Bolívar (see p.986) and even Caracas (see p.955). The first leg of the trip is a three-hour, seventy-kilometre and often very wet boat ride up the Caroní and Carrao rivers from Canaima Village; the second leg is an hour-and-a-half hike through the jungle, ending at the falls' principal vantage point. The falls themselves are generally fuller, and therefore more spectacular, during the rainy season; the trade-off is less visibility, as the top of the falls is often covered in clouds during those months.

In the dry season (Jan–May), low water levels in the access rivers can complicate the journey, sometimes requiring passengers to unload and push the boat. Tour agencies are usually diligent about warning customers of such conditions, but it's a good idea to ask anyway.

SANTA ELENA DE UAIRÉN

Santa Elena de Uairén grew significantly when the paved road connecting it with the rest of the country was completed, but, with a population of only eighteen thousand, it's still a quiet town. Many of its inhabitants are originally from Brazil, whose border is just fifteen kilometres south of town. The town has reasonably priced accommodation and restaurants, as well as many tour operators specializing in trips through the Gran Sabana and up Mount Roraima (see p.992).

Arrival and information

By air Flights arrive from Ciudad Bolívar and Puerto Ordáz, though schedules are unpredictable and planes tend to be very old and very small.

By bus Heading south to Santa Elena, buses stop at two or three National Guard checkpoints. At the final one, everyone must exit the bus with their baggage to be searched – a fairly routine and professional procedure, unlike in Caracas.

The terminal is 3km from the centre, a 5min taxi ride to the centre. There are no city buses.

Tourist information Corpoturismo Bolívar, Via La Línea on way to Brazilian border ⓣ0800/674-6626.

Accommodation

The town has its fair share of decent accommodation. The best places, along with most other backpacker services, are on Calle Urdaneta between Calle Icarabú and Avenida Perimetral.

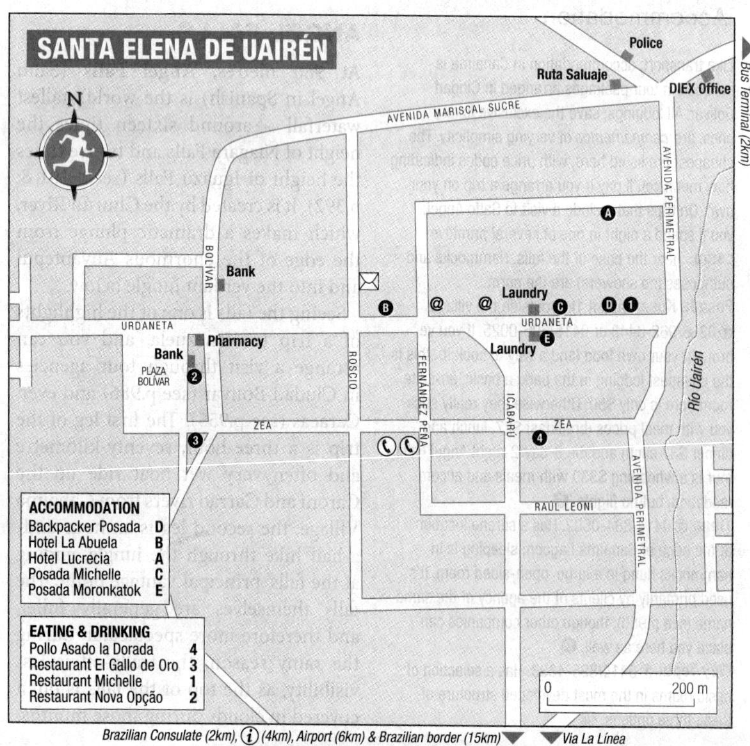

EXCHANGING BRAZILIAN REAIS FOR BOLÍVARES

The Brazilian town of Pacaraima's designation as a "**puerto libre**" – permitting visitors unfettered access across the border if they return the same day – allows you to replenish funds without resorting to Venezuela's unfavourable official exchange rate at an ATM machine or bank.

Take a taxi to the border (20min) and explain to officials that you're spending just a couple of hours in Brazil; make sure they **do not stamp** your passport (if they do, you'll have to wait a day to return to Venezuela). Once you're over, visit one of several available ATMs and withdraw Brazilian reais at the current exchange rate of US$1/R$1.77.

Return to Santa Elena de Uairén and head to the intersection of calles Urdaneta and Bolívar, where unofficial moneychangers congregate. You should be able to exchange R$1 for at least 2.50 bolívares, raising the value of your dollar to nearly 4.50 bolívares – more than double the official exchange rate.

Keep in mind that, while countless travellers have successfully used this method, you are solely responsible for the inherent **risk** of any unofficial financial transaction.

Hotel La Abuela C Urdaneta between calles Peña and Roscio ⓣ0289/426-0942. Right in the commercial centre, this place is lively and friendly if a little dingy. Rooms in the back of the building are quieter and have interesting stained-glass windows. ❺

Backpacker Posada Av Urdaneta ⓣ0289/995-1524 or 0414/886-722712, ⓦwww.backpacker-tours.com. While not the cheapest place in town, its range of services and clean, attractive accommodation make for a winning hand. Beautiful, light-filled rooms (fan, ensuite with hot water) are vibrantly painted, and breakfast ($7.50) can be scrambled eggs with tomato, apple pancakes or cereal. The attached café/restaurant is popular with visitors and locals and features occasional live music till midnight. There's internet access ($1.25 per hr) and a reputable tour agency (see box, p.938). ❹–❺

Hotel Lucrecia Av Perimetral ⓣ0289/995-1105 or 0414/772-3365. The amazingly chilled-out owner maintains a refreshingly cool courtyard garden and a pool. Each room (en suite, a/c, TV) is a different colour and displays a locally painted artwork. There's laundry service and breakfast on request (not included). ❺–❻

Posada Michelle C Urdaneta ⓣ0289/995-2017. Another excellent option on the main backpacker strip. The rambling, green-walled place is slightly dark and musty, but rooms (en suite, fan) are perfectly clean. Hallways are plastered with information on local sights and a fascinating photoessay of local indigenous groups. There's laundry service, cheap breakfast (not included) and an affiliated Chinese restaurant down the block (see p.991) that delivers. ❹–❺

Posada Moronkatok Av Urdaneta, across from Lavandería Pereida ⓣ0289/995-1528. Distinctive for its pair of very homey, two-storey *cabañas*; also has a separate 5-bed room. Other than a pleasant garden, there are no frills (not even a sign), though there are two *lavanderías* just steps away (see p.992). ❹

Eating

Restaurant El Gallo de Oro C Zea, southeast of the Plaza Bolívar. The "golden chicken" is a tiny, family-friendly *comedor* serving – you guessed it – perfectly bronzed, homestyle *pollo asado*, along with *pabellón criollo* and *carne guisada*, all on the *menú ejecutivo* ($5.50).Other options include *bisteck* ($6) and *pavón* ($7.50). Mon–Sat 7am–2pm (open till 6pm for drinks), closed Sun.

Restaurant Michelle Av Urdaneta at Av Perimetral. A Chinese restaurant serving filling but not-so-authentic dishes from a mind-bogglingly long menu. Plenty of noodle, *won ton* and fried rice plates, though the "garlic savoured shrimps" are a good choice. Most dishes $7.50–10. Thurs–Tues 11am–10pm, closed Wed.

Restaurant Nova Opção East side of Plaza Bolívar. While it doesn't compare with true Brazilian *por kilo* restaurants, this is the best you'll find north of the border, and it's consequently packed with lunchers. Choose from a generous selection of well-done meats, fresh salads, beans, rice and even *farofa* ($12.50 per kg with meat; $8.50/kg veg only). Fresh juices come in a personal pitcher, and delicious flan wraps up the package nicely.

Pollo Asado la Dorada C Zea at C Icabarú. A simple cafeteria-style joint, with Venezuelan oldies on the scratchy soundsystem. Smoked *chuleta, lengua en salsa, milanesa de res* and spaghetti bolognese (of course) are all under $10. Daily 11am–10pm.

Directory

Banks and exchange Banco Industrial, Calle Bolívar north of C Urdaneta; Banco Guyana on the east side of the Plaza Bolívar. Unofficial money-changers at the intersection of calles Urdaneta and Bolívar accept dollars and Brazilian reais; see box, p.942, on how to get.
Consulate Brazilian Consulate; see box, p.982 for details.
Immigration DIEX office, Av Mariscal Sucre Mon–Fri 8am–noon & 2–5.30pm.
Internet Internet Sala Web, C Urdaneta at C Peña daily 8am–midnight. Just west is Papelería en General, Mon–Sat 8.30am–noon & 2.30–8pm, closed Sun. Both $1.25 per hr.
Laundry Lavandería Pereida, C Urdaneta across from Posada Moronkatok Mon–Sat 7.30am–7.30pm, closed Sun. There's another, unnamed one directly across the street, daily 7am–7pm.
Pharmacy Farmacía Quincalleria, C Urdaneta at C Bolívar, daily 8am–10pm.
Phones Movistar/Centro de Comunicaciones Marcos, C Zea between calles Roscio and Peña, Mon–Fri 8am–9pm, Sat & Sun till 8pm. Just east is Variedades Nabhyl, Mon–Sat 7am–8pm, Sun 8am–noon & 3–8pm.
Police Station is across the street from Ruta Salvaje (see p.993).
Post MRW, C Roscio north of C Urdaneta, daily 8am–4.30pm.

Moving on

For information on **crossing into Brazil** from this region, see the box on p.982.
By air Rutaca is the primary airline, operating unpredictably scheduled flights to Ciudad Bolívar and Puerto Ordáz (around $215).
By bus Caracas (2 daily; 19hr); Ciudad Bolívar (8 daily; 11hr), making stops in San Félix and Puerto Ordáz; Puerto La Cruz (2 daily; 14hr). There are currently no buses to Brazil from the terminal.

TRIPS TO RORAIMA AND THE GRAN SABANA

If you've made it this far, chances are you already plan to take on the **Gran Sabana**. A handful of small agencies in town offers a wide selection of prefab and tailored tours of the region's highlights, such as Roraima and El Abismo.

The classic six-day trek to the top of **Mount Roraima** (see p.993), considered by many to be one of the best hikes in South America, costs $400–600. Since the price is based on distance rather than time, agencies are usually willing to add or subtract a day to fit your schedule.

Multi-day **Gran Sabana** tours run $65–75 perday per person, typically with a minimum of five people and with meals included.

One- or two-day trips to **El Paují**, **El Abismo**, **Salto Aponguao** and other specific sites cost around $100 per day per person, meals included. If you want to visit multiple sites on the same day, rates increase considerably. Rates do not include optional side excursions, such as canoe rides or hikes on "indian trails".

Though most trips to **Canaima** and **Angel Falls** leave from Ciudad Bolívar (see p.988), a trip from Santa Elena overflies much more dramatic scenery. The catch is that tours are slightly more expensive than their Ciudad Bolívar counterparts, and flight schedules are unpredictable.

La Gran Sabana

Said to be along one of the world's major energy meridians, which also passes through Macchu Picchu and Stonehenge, the 35,000-square-kilometre **Gran Sabana**, or Great Savannah, has induced many reports of visitors having extremely lucid dreams, experiencing spiritual rejuvenations and even seeing UFOs.

Although the region technically includes Angel Falls and most of Parque Nacional Canaima, trips to the Gran Sabana do not. Rather, they go to the vast area that extends southeast to the Brazilian border. Just before the border is where one of the principal attractions lies: the beautiful and

TRIPS TO THE ORINOCO DELTA

Tucupita, the capital of Delta Amacuro, has a few agencies that can arrange tours of the **Orinoco Delta.** As usual, activities are generally the same no matter where you go and include visiting indigenous Warao villages, canoeing through the small *caños*, fishing for piraña and observing local flora and fauna. Some operators have private guests lodges in the delta, though you may prefer to have them arrange a homestay in an indigenous village.

Packages cost between $100 and $140 per person per day and are all-inclusive. The operators listed here are the most reliable; others in town go in and out of business frequently, and Tucupita's numerous touts and *pirata* agents should for the most part be avoided.

If you want to do a delta trip but don't fancy travelling to Tucupita, agencies in Ciudad Bolívar (see p.986) can arrange trips at a slightly higher cost.

Asociación Cooperativa Osibus C Pativilca at C Mariño ⓣ0287/721-3840, ⓔcampamentomaraisa@hotmail.com. One of the few operators to access the southern part of the delta, considered to be more "virgin".

Aventura Turística Delta C Centurión ⓣ0414/189-9063 or 0416/897-2285, ⓔa_t_d_1973@hotmail.com. Because it takes walk-ins and is relatively inexpensive, this operator is popular with backpackers.

Expediciones Robin ⓣ0414/879-2597 or 0416/787-8420, ⓔexpedicionrob84@hotmail.com. A one-man outfit, Robin Álvarez offers some of the cheapest and simplest tours available (under $100 per day).

Tucupita Expeditions C Las Acacias ⓣ0287/721-0801 or 0414/789-8343, ⓦwww.orinocodelta.com. Operates the *Orinoco Delta Lodge*, offering sportfishing trips and excellent, English-speaking guides.

climbable *tepui* **Roraima**, renowned for the otherworldly landcape at its summit and the unique ecosystem it sustains. The entire region is filled with other magnificent *tepuis* and waterfalls, separated by vast expanses of grasslands. One of the most famous waterfalls is **Quebrada de Jaspe,** noted for its bright red jasper rock. Other well-known waterfalls in the region include the 105-metre-high **Salto Aponguao**, which has pools to swim in at its base, and **Quebrada Pacheco**, two pretty falls with natural waterslides.

Tour operators

Backpacker Tours Av Urdaneta ⓣ0289/995-1524 or 0414/886-7227, ⓦwww.backpacker-tours.com. The most expensive of the bunch, but has a permanent guide staff, sells air tickets and owns all its equipment, including high-quality tents, bicycles and trucks. Offers shorter alternatives (Mantopai and Chiricayén) to the six-day Roraima trek, as well as vigorous, multi-day bike trips. Also has an excellent *posada* (see p.991).

Mystic Tours Av Urdaneta ⓣ0289/416-0558 or 416-0686, ⓦwww.mystictours.com.ve. Has built a solid reputation on its unique mystical approach to Roraima and the Gran Sabana – the owner is a scholar of the paranormal and has written several books on the subject.

Ruta Salvaje Av Mariscal Sucre at C Akarabisis ⓣ0289/995-1134 or 0414/889-4164, ⓦwww.rutasalvaje.com. Specializes in one-day tours to the Gran Sabana as well as whitewater rafting trips on class three and four rapids: $100 per person with 4 people; $50 per person with 10 people.

Turísticos Álvarez in bus terminal ⓣ0414/385-2846, ⓔrstagransabana@hotmail.com. Not to be mistaken for a tout, Francisco Álvarez's forte is arranging bare-bones trips for the budget-conscious: he rents tents to and hires transport for campers, and can strip down a multi-day Gran Sabana trip to just $50 per day.

DELTA AMACURO

The state of **Delta Amacuro** is best known for the Orinoco Delta, one of the world's largest river deltas. In fact, the state's entire landmass was formed by sediment left behind by the Orinoco River on its way out to sea. Besides the Orinoco, Delta Amacuro has many other rivers and over three hundred *caños*, small waterways that often link the rivers. From above, the entire area looks like an enormous labyrinth.

The northeast coast and islands

The **northeast coast** sports some of the country's most ruggedly beautiful coastline, as well as one of its most energetic cities. **Puerto La Cruz**, a high-rise hotel, fast-food paradise used by visitors primarily as a jumping-off point for Isla de Margarita, is pleasant enough for a day of exploration. Spreading northeast of the city, the popular **Parque Nacional Mochima** has a number of uninhabited keys for visitors to explore in chartered boats. The small coastal islands here are characterized by rocky terrain with little vegetation besides cacti.

Other than Los Roques (see p.957), Venezuela's best-known island destination is **Isla de Margarita**, off the coast of Sucre State. Built in the style of some of the Caribbean's most famous (or infamous) mega-resort areas, it is a huge magnet for Venezuelans and international package tourists, though anyone can enjoy a one- or two-day break from the mainland here.

PUERTO LA CRUZ

It's hard to imagine that the modern, bustling city of **Puerto La Cruz** is not long removed from being a small fishing village. Venezuelans come here mainly for its proximity to Parque Nacional Mochima (see p.997) and the ferry to Isla de Margarita (see p.1004); the fast-food restaurants and fifteen-storey hotels certainly don't make it an overly attractive place to spend much time. However, the wide promenade alongside Paseo Colón makes for an enjoyable afternoon of strolling and people-watching, especially when there's a cool breeze rolling in off the bay.

What to see and do

Most actual **activities** take place outside the city limits. On either end of Paseo Colón are docks where you can hire boats for day-trips to the nearby islands; ticket offices are open daily from 8.30am to 2pm. A shared ride in a large boat to a single island costs $7.50 per person, but if you want a more customized trip, with visits to multiple islands and beaches, be prepared to shell out anywhere from $200–300 for an entire boat – which can hold up to fifty people.

Parque Nacional Mochima

For more personalized tours of Puerto La Cruz's surrounds, including fishing, caving, dolphin-spotting and exploring Parque Nacional Mochima, visit Ma-Ci-Te Tours, on Paseo Colón between calles Buenos Aires and Maneiro (daily 8am–8pm; ⓣ0281/267-0623, ⓔdevitours@cantv.net). A full day with at least four people costs $58 per person and includes food, drinks, transport and boat rides. Similar tours are available in Santa Fe or Mochima (see p.998 & p.999, respectively), where they are considerably cheaper.

Los Altos de Sucre

A more do-it-yourself diversion is to head to the bus terminal for the frequent jeeps (30min; $1.25) to Los Altos de Sucre, a small community hidden in the hills above Puerto La Cruz, near the border of Anzoátegui State. The lush, rural roads couldn't be further in spirit from the city's mayhem, and

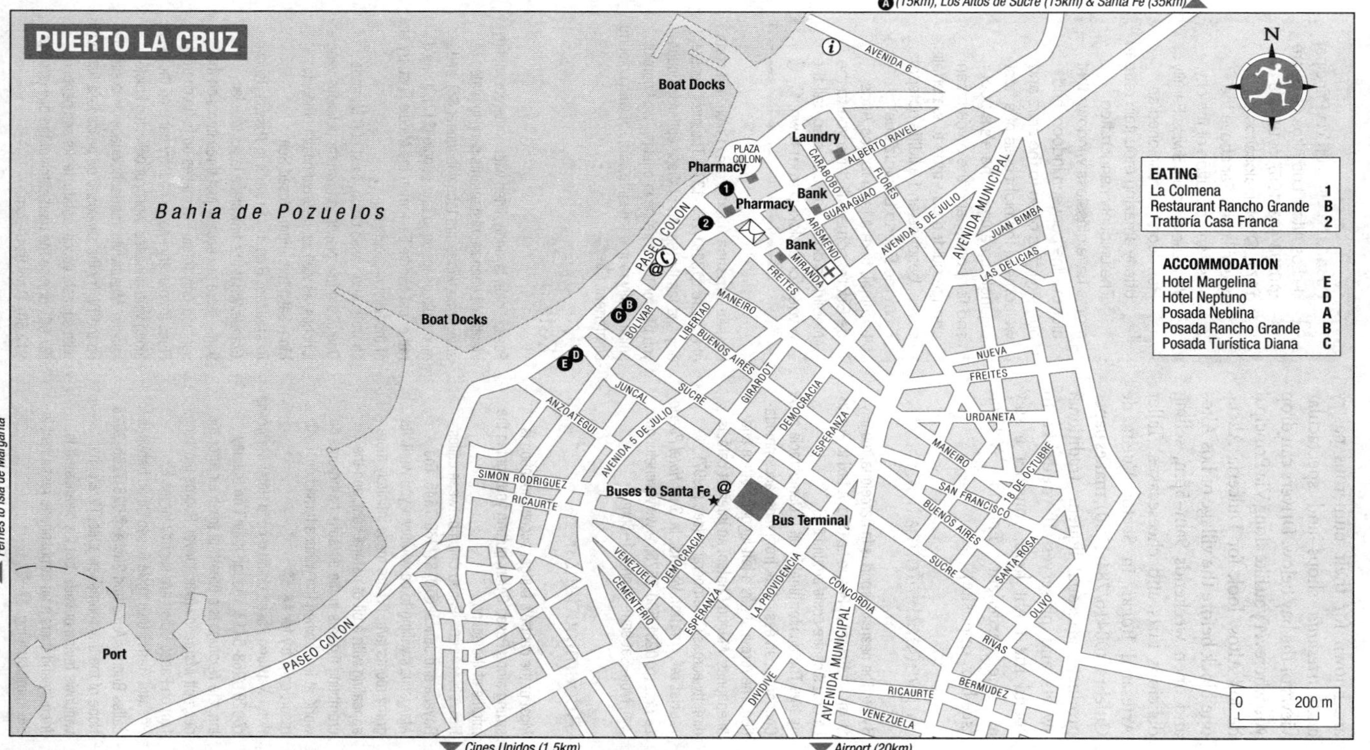
PUERTO LA CRUZ
A (15km), Los Altos de Sucre (15km) & Santa Fe (35km)
Ferries to Isla de Margarita
Cines Unidos (1.5km)
Airport (20km)
N
Bahia de Pozuelos
Boat Docks
Boat Docks
Port
Laundry
Pharmacy
Pharmacy
Bank
Bank
Bus Terminal
Buses to Santa Fe
PLAZA COLON
PASEO COLON
AVENIDA 6
ALBERTO RAVEL
CARABOBO
FLORES
GUARAGUAO
ARISMENDI
MIRANDA
FREITES
AVENIDA 5 DE JULIO
AVENIDA MUNICIPAL
JUAN BIMBA
LAS DELICIAS
MANEIRO
LIBERTAD
BUENOS AIRES
BOLIVAR
GIRARDOT
DEMOCRACIA
ESPERANZA
SUCRE
JUNCAL
ANZOATEGUI
SIMON RODRIGUEZ
RICAURTE
VENEZUELA
CEMENTERIO
LA PROVIDENCIA
CONCORDIA
DIVIDIVE
NUEVA
URDANETA
SAN FRANCISCO
18 DE OCTUBRE
SANTA ROSA
OLIVO
RIVAS
BERMUDEZ
EATING
La Colmena 1
Restaurant Rancho Grande B
Trattoría Casa Franca 2
ACCOMMODATION
Hotel Margelina E
Hotel Neptuno D
Posada Neblina A
Posada Rancho Grande B
Posada Turística Diana C
0 200 m

are known for their numerous pastry and *artesanía* shops and spectacular views of the bay below. Drivers can drop you wherever you like along Via Principal de los Altos; look for Dulcería Alicia, one block before the village of Los Altos and open weekends 9am–5pm, selling delicious tarts and cheesecakes. Taller Artesanal Bogar, in Sector Vuelta de Culebra (☎0416/784-1750), makes paper products, artesanal liqueur, traditional sweets and preserves. If you'd like to spend the night here, consider a stay at the excellent *Posada Neblina* (see box, opposite).

Arrival and information

By air The nearest airport is in Barcelona, roughly 20km southwest of Puerto La Cruz. A taxi to Puerto La Cruz's centre costs around $15.

By bus The bus terminal is on C Democracia at C Condordia, an easy walk from most accommodation. The terminal has a left luggage office and telephones. Mundo Chateo, an internet café, is directly across C Democracia (see p.997).

Tourist information Venetur, in *Gran Hotel Puerto La Cruz* (☎0281/500-3675, ⓦwww.venetur.gob.ve), Mon–Sat 9am–noon & 1–5pm.

Accommodation

Most of the centre's budget accommodation is strung along Paseo Colón, putting you right in the middle of the action.

Hotel Margelina Paseo Colón between calles Boyacá and Juncál ☎0281/268-7545. The *Margelina*'s willing to be whatever you want. Its grimy rooms (a/c, TV) are made infinitely more appealing with a bit of natural light, and the crumbling fixtures in the en-suite bathrooms do work, at least when the water's turned on. Last resort only; try for #4. ❺

Hotel Neptuno Paseo Colón next to Hotel *Margelina* ☎0281/268-5413. Though it ain't no Holiday Inn, the *Neptuno* is a breath of fresh air after the decrepit *Margelina* (see above). Rooms (en suite, fan) on Paseo Colón are slightly larger. ❺

Posada Rancho Grande Paseo Colón between calles Buenos Aires and Sucre ☎0281/265-2823. None of the tiny rooms (en suite, TV, a/c) has windows facing outside, but it's clean, staff is friendly and there's an atmospheric restaurant in the same building. ❹–❺

TREAT YOURSELF

Posada Neblina off Via Principal de Los Altos, Los Altos de Sucre ☎0293/433-1057 or 0412/946-1871, ⓔneblinalosaltos@hotmail.com. Far above the noise and pollution of the city, Venezuela's own Swiss Family Robinson has fashioned an utterly amazing mountain retreat. The uniquely handcrafted rooms have glassless windows that blur the line between indoors and out; skylights open to the stars and welcome in the night calls of a host of jungle creatures. There's a pool and fishponds, and the owners can arrange guided day-trips to waterfalls, caves, beaches and wildlife hotspots. From the Puerto La Cruz bus terminal, take a jeep to Los Altos de Sucre; some will drive you to the Neblina's door. You can also call the owner for a pickup from town. ❻–❾

Posada Turística Diana Paseo Colón, just north of C Sucre ☎0281/265-1370. The most secure, tidy and family-friendly of these options, though you pay for the increase in quality. Two floors of small, chilly rooms (en suite, a/c, TV) with colourful comforters. ❹–❻

Eating

Paseo Colón is, oddly, lined with numerous, nearly identical Lebanese restaurants serving plates of *shawarma*, *kibbe* and tabouleh (under $6), and mixed plates for up to four people ($17). If you'd rather eat Middle Eastern in the Middle East, try one of the following options.

La Colmena Paseo Colón, west of C Miranda. One of the few places in town for delicious veggie lunches, as well as assorted health products. Mon–Sat 11am–6pm, closed Sun.

Restaurant Rancho Grande in *Posada Rancho Grande*. What this tiny place lacks in selection – there are usually just three items on the seafood-only menu – it makes up for in character. Flags from every known country hang on the walls, along with decades' worth of collected knick-knacks. Meanwhile, mariachi videos cycle silently on the TV. Try the *sancocho de pescado*, a fish broth with squash, yucca, potato, leeks and peppers ($7.50), or else the fried catch of the day (around $12.50). Daily 9am–5pm.

Trattoría Casa Franca C Bolívar at C Freites ☎0414/800-0947. "All types of pasta made in house", the handpainted wall outside says, and they do mean all types: gnocchi, vermicelli, ravioli, tortelloni and more, prepared however you like (carbonara, puttanesca, bologna, alfredo, con vongvole, etc), all for under $10. Pizzas, too. Daily 11am–6pm, closed Sun in low season.

Directory

Bank Banco de Venezuela, C Libertad at C Miranda; Banco Mercantil, C Arismendi at C Guaraguao.
Cinema Cines Unidos in C.C. Regina, Av Municipal, 1.5km southwest of centre.
Ferry Conferry is in the port terminal (☎0281/267-7847 or 267-7129), as is Naviarca/Gran Cacique (☎0293/431-5577 or 432-0011, ⓦwww.grancacique.com.ve). See box, p.1004 for details.
Hospital Policlínica Puerto La Cruz, Av 5 de Julio at C Arismendi, open 24hr.
Internet Mundo Chateo, C Democracia across from bus terminal, Mon–Sat 8am–6pm, closed Sun; GAM Comunicaciones, Paseo Colón between calles Maneiro and Buenos Aires, Mon–Sat 8am–9pm, Sun 9am–8pm. Both cost $1 per hr. The friendly, English-speaking manager at GAM can give information.
Laundry A nameless *lavandería* is on Av Ravél between calles Carabobo and Las Flores, Mon–Fri 7.30am–6pm, Sat 7.30am–3pm, closed Sun.
Pharmacy Farmacía Meditotal, C Bolívar between calles Freites and Miranda, Mon–Sat 7.30am–9pm, Sun *por turno*. Farmatodo, Paseo Colón across from Plaza Colón, open 24hr.
Phones Movistar, Paseo Colón between calles Maneiro and Buenos Aires, daily 7.30am–10pm; next door is CANTV, Mon–Sat 8am–10pm, Sun 9am–9pm, also offering internet ($1 per hr).
Police A mobile tourist police unit, Polisotillo (☎0281/267-2182 or 0414/818-3395), is based on Paseo Colón; they wear white shirts and olive green trousers.
Post Ipostel, C Freites at C Libertad.

Moving on

For information on boat travel to Isla de Margarita, see box, p.1004.
By bus *Por puestos* to Playa Colorada (30min), Santa Fe (1hr) and Mochima (1hr) leave constantly from C Democracia across from the terminal. All cost $1–1.50.
Other destinations include: Barinas (6 daily; 12hr); Caracas (half-hourly; 5hr); Carúpano (several daily; 4hr); Ciudad Bolívar (hourly; 5hr); Coro (4 daily; 11hr); Cumaná (half-hourly; 2hr); La Güiria (4 daily; 7hr); Maracaibo (5 daily; 15hr); Maracay (several daily; 6hr); Mérida (4 daily; 28hr); Puerto Ordáz (hourly; 7hr); Punto Fijo (4 daily; 12hr); Santa Elena de Uairén (1 daily; 17hr); Tucupita (1 daily; 6hr); and Valencia (several daily; 7hr).
Caracas-bound buses also depart from the private Aeroexpresos Ejecutivos terminal next to the port (☎0212/266-2321, ⓦwww.aeroexpresos.com.ve).
By air Buses for the airport in Barcelona pass regularly along Av 5 de Julio. Taxis are around $15. Flights include Caracas (several daily; 45min); Maracaibo (daily; 3hr with connection); Mérida (daily except Sun; 3hr w/2 connections); Porlamar (daily; 30min); Puerto Ordáz (daily except Sun; 30min); and Valencia (daily; 40min).

PARQUE NACIONAL MOCHIMA

The 950-square kilometre **Parque Nacional Mochima** was created in 1973 to protect 36 uninhabited keys and the surrounding coastal area. Much of the park's beauty lies in the stunning contrast between the red earth tones of the rocks and the emerald green water. While the beaches are not as conventionally beautiful as those of Morrocoy and Henri Pittier national parks (see p.962 & p.958, respectively), the snorkelling and scuba diving are just as good here, if not better.

Playa Colorada

In a protected cove lined with swaying palm trees, **Playa Colorada** has blue-green water and a stretch of tan, almost red sand from which it derives its name. Unfortunately, it is also riddled with innumerable beach chairs, aluminium food stands and raucous day-trippers, particularly on weekends and holidays. Consequently, weekdays or the low season are the best times to visit.

There are no banks or internet cafés in Playa Colorada, and few other services, so you should stay here only if you wish to disappear for a day or two. When you're ready to return to civilization, wait on the highway for a passing bus to Cumaná or Puerto La Cruz (see p.994).

Arrival

By bus Frequent Santa Fe–bound *busetas* ($1) depart from C Democracia, across the street from the Puerto La Cruz terminal. If you're coming from the other direction, Playa Colorada is only 10min from Santa Fe.

Accommodation and eating

Most of Playa Colorada's **accommodation** consists of sprawling, ranch-style homes that rent budget rooms and apartments for longer stays. Other than the stalls lining the beach, there's really only one place in the village to **eat**.

Casa Zorka 300m up Av Principal from the highway, on right side ⓣ0293/808-7382 or 0416/784-9924. A quiet, cool one-storey home with small en-suite rooms (a/c or fan) and a larger two-bedroom apartment sleeping five ($60 per night), with a/c, kitchen, bathroom. ❹

Jakera Lodge on main highway across from beach ⓣ0274/252-9577 or 0416/881-1224 ⓦwww.jakera.com. A truly unique gem hidden away in this unassuming village. Primarily providing long-term housing to groups of European students who come to learn Spanish and participate in community-development projects, the lodge also rents beds to travellers passing through. Everyone eats together (lunch and dinner included in price) and washes their own plates. Shared rooms (hammocks or beds) have curtains but no walls, and there are plenty of communal areas, including a pool table, climbing wall and a gym. Check the website for excursions, volunteer opportunities and program start dates. ❹

Posada Jaly C Marchán ⓣ0293/808-3246 or 0416/681-8113. Surrounded by a huge garden, this house has big, cool rooms with tile floors (en suite with a/c) and a shared kitchen. ❺

Posada Nirvana C Marchán ⓣ0293/808-7844. The healthy garden has hammocks, an outdoor, shared kitchen and great views of the bay; small rooms (shared bath, fan) are nicely painted and have light-filled windows. Two much larger apartments house six ($50) and four ($40) people, and have a/c and TV. There's a book exchange and laundry, and the French- and English-speaking owner fixes breakfasts for $6. ❸

Las Carmitas 3a transversal. Sit under an awning among trees and gorge on pizzas (small $7.50, large $19), spaghetti with tuna or beef ($5), burgers (under $4) and more. From 4pm weekdays, 1pm weekends.

SANTA FE

Though it's still a fishing village at heart, **Santa Fe** once attracted hordes of budget-minded travellers with its cheap, beachside accommodation. Today it's in the doldrums of an economic slump, likely caused by a reputation for drug-related robberies. However, the scarcity of other visitors actually makes it quite a pleasant place to visit, and as long as you keep your wits about you, you'll be perfectly safe here.

There are **no banks** or ATMs in Santa Fe; stock up on cash in Puerto La Cruz or Cumaná.

What to see and do

There's basically nothing to do in Santa Fe proper, but that's generally the point of beach towns – though the area's best beaches lie off the coast. One-way **boat trips** to the outlying islands, where you can fish, explore underwater caves and relax in seaside seclusion, cost $12.50 per person; make sure to arrange a pick-up. The most popular destinations are Isla Arapo, La Piscina and Las Islas Caracas.

For a full day of island-hopping, charter a boat and a guide from Gulliver Tours, on the beach, or *Posada Bahia del Mar* (see p.999), for around $100 for 10–12 people; food is not included. *Bahia del Mar* also rents kayaks for $10 per hr.

German guide Marcos (ⓣ0416/05-4405 or 0293/808-0101) offers jeep tours to the region's cacao plantations and buffalo ranches and the Araya and Pária peninsulas, usually requiring at least four people ($120–160 per day without food). He can also give rides to the airports in Barcelona or Caracas. You can find him in the *Hotel Cochaima* (see p.999).

Arrival

By bus *Busetas* from Puerto La Cruz ($1.50) usually stop on the highway at the entrance to the town; if you're arriving after dark, check if your driver will continue to the end of Av Principal, thereby saving you a half-kilometre walk to the beach.

A rather unique aspect of Santa Fe – likely a sign of its depression – is the presence of **touts** who try to take you to a *posada*. It's best to refuse their offers.

Accommodation

Several small **posadas** line Santa Fe's thin strand. Camping on the beach is discouraged for safety reasons.

Posada Bahía del Mar ⓣ0293/231-0073 or 0416/386-7930. With its main entrance on the beach, this pleasant place, with a yard and kayak rentals (see p.998), has clean, colourful rooms with fan or a/c. Ask for a sea view; #4 and #7 are the best. There are meals (not included), laundry service and a shared outdoor kitchen. ❹–❺

Posada Café del Mar ⓣ0293/231-0009, ⓦwww.hosteltrail.com/cafedelmar. A popular place for its small restaurant (see below), and rooms (en suite with fan or a/c) are spacious and passably clean; glass doors and flimsy locks, however, leave a bit to be desired in terms of security. Plusses are a roof deck with bay views and a crow's nest with hammocks. ❹–❺

Hotel Cochaima ⓣ0293/642-0728 or 0416/083-7582. With a restaurant on the first floor serving standard seafood dishes, this small guest house offers a couple of fan-cooled rooms (all en suite) with bay views (#4 and #7); avoid a/c rooms on the ground floor since the windows are sealed. See p.998 for kayak tours. ❹–❺

Quinta La Jaiba ⓣ0293/808-8350. One of the best deals in town, with enormous, tile-floored rooms with bay windows, mini-fridges and fans ($22). Avoid the room nearest to the smelly drainage ditch outside. ❸–❹

Residencia de los Siete Delfines ⓣ0293/431-4166, ⓔlossiete-delfinessatafe@hotmail.com. Rooms (a/c, en suite) may be small and a bit dark – ask for an ocean view – but this breezy, blue and white concrete block is the best-maintained place around. There's a roof deck with views of palms and water, and the ground-floor restaurant serves all meals (not included). Use of laundry machine for $7.50, and standard boat tours. ❺

Eating and drinking

Independent dining options are limited in Santa Fe, since most *posadas* have their own restaurant.

Café del mar in *Posada Café del Mar*. Casual dining, with very relaxed service, under a *palapa* five metres from the water. Seafood dishes ($7.50–10) are expertly prepared; try the *calamares rebozados*. Closed Mon.

El Club Naútico on the beach. The best (and priciest) restaurant in town, with a small menu of fresh-from-the-sea delicacies. Watch boats come and go as you dine on garlic squid ($12.50), dorado ($10) or lobster ($17). Lunch and dinner from 11am daily.

Club Océano C La Boca, east of Av Principal. The only club in town and therefore a lively place on weekends, when house and hip-hop tracks shake the foundations. The street is considered unsafe, so go with a group.

Directory

Internet Very slow service at El Birazzo ($0.75 per hr), Av Principal, daily 8am–9pm.

Pharmacy Medicinas Santa Elena, C Las Mercedes, east of Av Principal. Daily 7am–noon & 4–7pm.

Police Station at beach end of Av Principal.

Shopping The food market on the beach – where fish plays a central role – is a great place to see odd specimens (both ichthyoid and human) and get heckled by good-natured fishers.

Moving on

By bus The terminal is on the highway, 300m west of the intersection Av Principal. Frequent *busetas* depart daily 5am–7pm for Puerto La Cruz (1hr), passing Playa Colorada (see p.997), and Cumaná (1hr), passing Mochima (see below).

MOCHIMA

Like Santa Fe, the village of **Mochima** began as a fishing community; unlike its neighbour, its reputation is fairly intact, making it a more serene place to stay. The catch is that it's somewhat more difficult to get to. The village has no beach – just a dock from where boat tours depart.

There are **no banks** or ATMs in Mochima; stock up on cash in Puerto La Cruz or Cumaná.

What to see and do

The main activity in Mochima is, once again, **boat trips** to the keys of the national park.

Most accommodation can supply you with a boat, guide and snorkelling equipment. Ronald (ⓣ0424/816-0202), at *Posada Mochimero*, can take up to six people for a full day of snorkelling, equipment provided ($60). For $25–30 he provides simple rides to and from the islands. Hermes (☎0414/840-5936), at *Villa Vicenta*, can take up to twelve people for a full day ($20 per person) of spotting dolphins, snorkelling and exploring caves. Snorkel equipment and a cooler are provided, but you must bring your own food and beverages.

Additional activities are offered by the Mochima Dive Center (☎0414/180-6244, ⓔmochimarafting@hotmail.com), including one-day, two-tank scuba trips ($95) and whitewater rafting on Class 3 rapids ($80; 3–4hr). You can also take a four-day scuba course for SSI certification.

Arrival

By bus *Busetas* from Puerto La Cruz or Cumaná drop you on the highway at the top of a long, winding descent to Mochima; intermittent jeeps and *carritos* shuttle back and forth daily from 5.30am until 8pm. If they don't appear, which sometimes happens, you can try flagging down a private vehicle.

Accommodation and eating

Posada El Mochimero ☎0414/776-7532. A very simple two-storey option close to the waterfront. Dark rooms (fans and bay views upstairs; a/c downstairs) are all triples. ❺

Villa Vicenta ☎0293/414-0868. Has a very interesting terraced design, with incredible views from the decks. Rooms, however, have no views. There's an open-air TV lounge, plentiful flowers and laundry service. The featherless parrot seems to be on its last legs. ❸–❺

El Rancho del Compa ☎0414/802-4106. A cheery, spotless *arepa* counter with fillings like *ensalada de pollo, tortilla de cazón* and *salpicón de mariscos*; also serves a full range of juices, soft drinks and coffee. Low season Thurs–Sun 7am–1pm, daily rest of year.

Restaurant Puerto Viejo ☎0293/416-6114. The nicest place to eat in town, so close to the docked boats that you can literally reach out the window and touch them. Seafood specialities include *sopa de mariscos*, red snapper and kingfish; order a *filet Puerto Viejo*, or fish doused in a white wine and butter sauce, served with *tostones* (all $10–15). Daily 11am–9pm, closed Tues in low season.

ISLA DE MARGARITA

On the ferry to **Isla de Margarita** from the mainland, you're unlikely to see more than one or two backpacks, as the 940-square-kilometre island is primarily visited by well-to-do Venezuelans and European tourists who come over on relatively cheap package deals. While prices are

LA CUEVA DEL GUÁCHARO

Invisible wings crackle overhead and unearthly hisses and shrieks electrify the darkness. You've entered the domain of the **guácharos**, or oilbirds, nocturnal avians that leave this cave en masse every night and return just before dawn. Despite their huge, inky black eyes, the birds use echolocation to chase down their insect prey.

Rangers give frequent tours of the first 1200m of the ten-kilometre-long cave (daily 8am–4pm; 45min; $2.50; ☎0291/641-7543), using a gas lamp to illuminate the distinctively shaped stalagmites and stalactites along the path. You won't get more than a fleeting glimpse of the *guácharos*, though, as light disturbs them (flash photography is prohibited).

The cave can be visited on a day-trip from Cumaná (two hours northeast of Puerto La Cruz by bus) though it can be slightly difficult to reach. There are only two daily buses to Caripe (7am & noon), from where you can continue the rest of the way by *por puesto*; alternatively, catch a Carúpano-bound bus from Cumaná, getting off where the highway splits to Caripe, and continue by *por puesto* from there (about 1hr 30min). The trip, much of which winds through awesome, mountainous jungle, takes 2hr 30min–3hr each way.

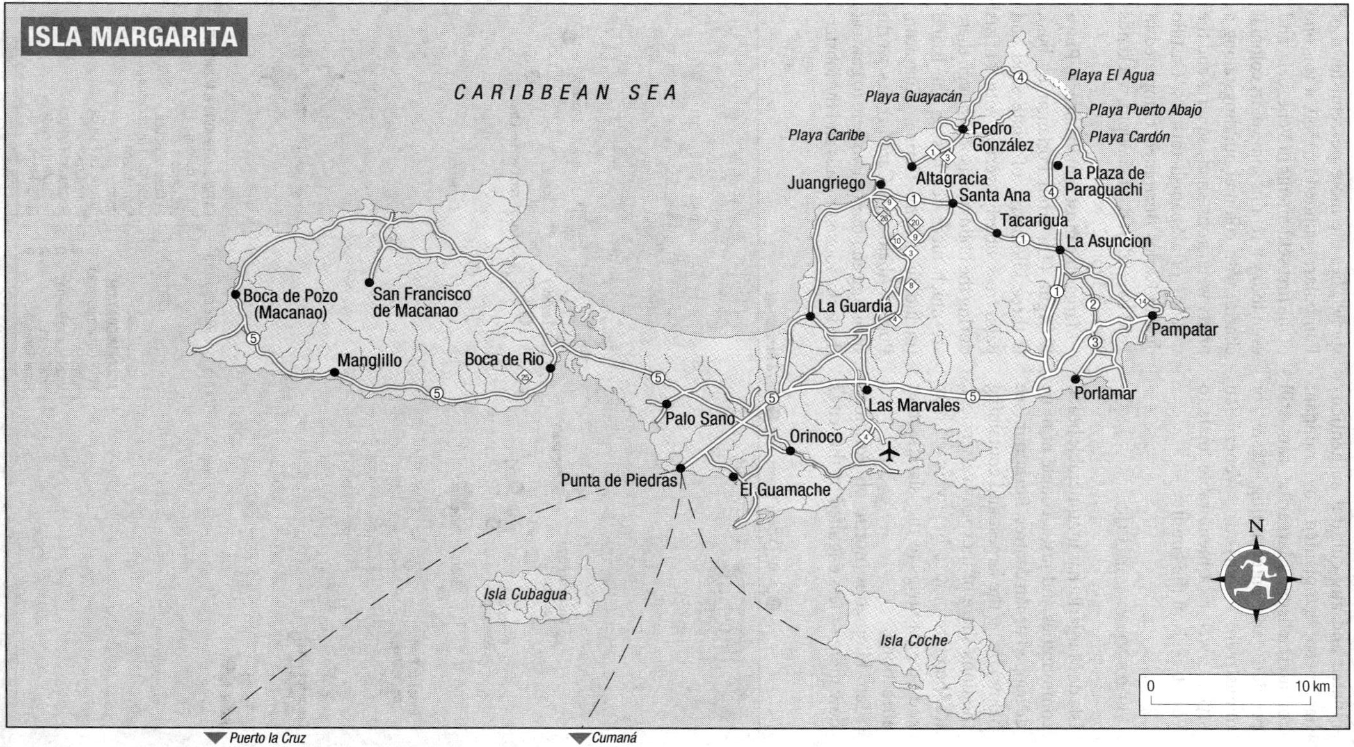

ISLA MARGARITA

CARIBBEAN SEA

Playa El Agua
Playa Guayacán
Playa Puerto Abajo
Playa Caribe
Pedro González
Playa Cardón
La Plaza de Paraguachi
Juangriego
Altagracia
Santa Ana
Tacarigua
La Asuncion
Boca de Pozo (Macanao)
San Francisco de Macanao
La Guardia
Pampatar
Manglillo
Boca de Rio
Porlamar
Las Marvales
Palo Sano
Orinoco
Punta de Piedras
El Guamache
Isla Cubagua
Isla Coche
N
0
10 km
Puerto la Cruz
Cumaná

inflated and any cultural authenticity has been supplanted by rampant commercialism, Margarita can still provide an entertaining taste of mainstream tourism, Venezuelan style, as well as a memorable finale to your travels in the country.

What to see and do

Isla de Margarita has innumerable beach communities and just a couple of more developed urban centres, **Porlamar** (see below) being the largest and containing the lion's share of inexpensive services. It's therefore best to base yourself here and take day-trips to the island's other attractions.

Ten kilometres north of Porlamar, now more or less engulfed by that city's sprawl, lies the more peaceful town of **Pampatar**. Founded in 1530, it was one of the first settlements in Venezuela, and even today it retains some of its colonial charm, with colonial buildings along a pretty waterfront, shady squares and the remains of a Spanish fortress, Castillo de San Carlos Borromeo, completed in 1684 (weekdays 8am–5.30pm, weekends 9am–5.30pm).

Margarita's most famous beach, **Playa El Agua** (1hr from Porlamar by bus), is three kilometres of white sand and palm trees, utterly overrun with tourists during the holiday season. Though there are much nicer beaches on the island (including *playas* Caribe, Guayacán, Puerto Abajo and Cardón), it's worth spending an hour or two here to gawk at the tacky souvenir stalls and the lobster-

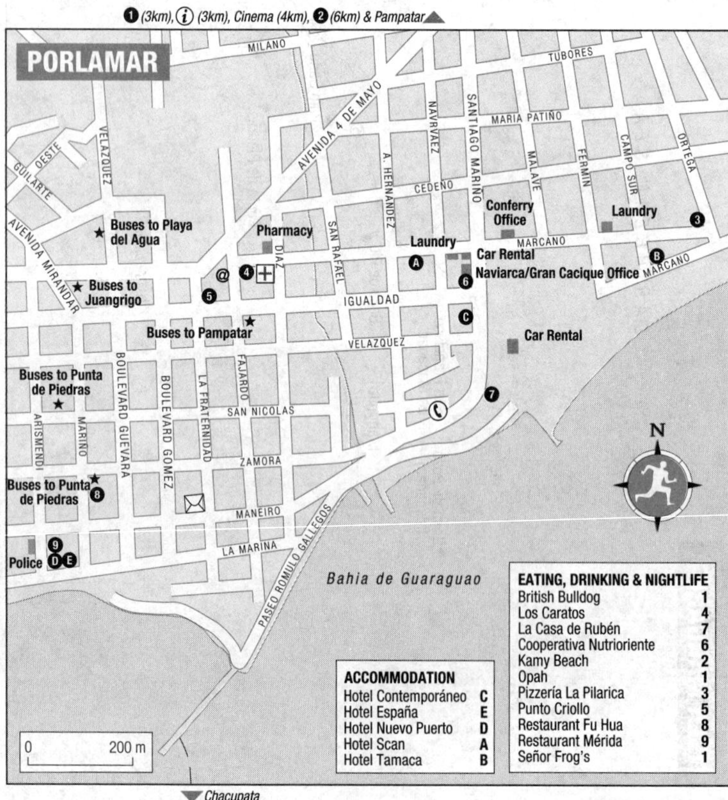

ACCOMMODATION	
Hotel Contemporáneo	C
Hotel España	E
Hotel Nuevo Puerto	D
Hotel Scan	A
Hotel Tamaca	B

EATING, DRINKING & NIGHTLIFE	
British Bulldog	1
Los Caratos	4
La Casa de Rubén	7
Cooperativa Nutrioriente	6
Kamy Beach	2
Opah	1
Pizzería La Pilarica	3
Punto Criollo	5
Restaurant Fu Hua	8
Restaurant Mérida	9
Señor Frog's	1

red sunbathers. Most of the seafood restaurants have identical, overpriced menus, though one exception is *Restaurant Cocadas Kathy*, really just a shack on the sand open 9am–6pm daily. It serves calamari, jumbo shrimp and *sopa de pescado* (all $7.50–15), as well as refreshing cocktails and coconuts.

Arrival and information

By air The airport is about 20km southwest of Porlamar; a ride into town costs $15. Several cities have flights to Margarita, including Caracas (several daily; 45min), Ciudad Bolívar (Fri; 1hr 20min), Maracaibo (2 daily; 2hr 30min with connection), Puerto Ordáz (3 daily; 1hr), San Antonio del Táchira (1 daily; 3hr with connection), and Valencia (2 daily; 2hr with connection).

By boat The cheapest way to get to Isla de Margarita is by boat; for details, see box, p.1004. Once you've arrived at the port at Punta de Piedras, walk 200m up the jetty to the cluster of restaurants and food stalls, where you can hop on a Porlamar-bound bus ($1) until 7pm. After hours, catch a por *puesto* ($1–2.50) or taxi ($15) into town, roughly 27km northeast.

Tourist information Corpotur, Centro Artesanal Gilberto Menchini in Los Robles (℡0295/262-3098 or 262-2514, ⓦwww.corpoturmargarita.gov.ve), roughly 3km from the centre.

Getting around

By bus The cheapest way to explore the island, no more than $1–1.50 per ride. Bus stops throughout Porlamar's centre (see map, opposite) correspond to various locales around the island; buses run 6.30am–8pm daily.

By taxi Taxis within Porlamar cost around $3.50 during the day, $6 at night. Otherwise the city's centre is easily walkable.

Car rental Not exactly cheap, but a better deal than on the mainland. See Directory, p.1005, for rental agencies.

Accommodation

Porlamar is the undisputed commercial centre of the island, and, while shamelessly unattractive, offers a range of reasonably priced accommodation and dining options. Make sure to ask for low-season discounts outside the island's peak periods of Dec–Jan and Easter.

Hotel Contemporáneo Av Santiago Mariño between calles Igualdad and Velásquez ℡0295/414-5565. A decent backup option, though its large, dark rooms (en suite, a/c, TV), darkly furnished, are made darker by windows that don't open. Nevertheless, it's clean, friendly and beyond the chaotic centre. ❺

Hotel España C Mariño at Av La Marina ℡0295/261-2479. At the very bottom of the price spectrum, a slighty gritty yet vibrantly painted guest house; rooms (fan, TV) have very unusual glass-enclosed private bathrooms. There's a restaurant in the building, and pay-by-use bathrooms are open to the public – though whether the target clientele is beachgoers or vagrants is unclear. ❹

Hotel Nuevo Puerto C La Marina at C Arismendi ℡0295/263-8888. This place is a bit dingy, but has decent-sized, en-suite rooms (a/c) and a ground-floor restaurant. The waterfront area is considered unsafe after 10pm. ❺

Hotel Scan C Marcano between calles Narváez and Hernández ℡0295/264-3859, ⓦwww.portalmargarita.com/scan.htm. A rung above the others, with huge, colourful, cutely decorated rooms (en suite, a/c, TV), some with windows. Far enough from the centre's fracas, though still a bit noisy on the street side. There's a ground-floor restaurant/bar and a book exchange. ❻

Hotel Tamaca Av Raúl Leoni at C Campo Sur ℡0295/261-1602, ⓔtamaca@unete.com.ve. If you're wondering where all the budget-minded foreigners are, particularly Germans, look no further. Based on the ageing beach-bum atmosphere, you may assume some of the guests haven't left the outdoor patio/bar/restaurant since arriving here on their first post-Wall vacation. Come for the chummy atmosphere and great water pressure rather than the boxlike, view-less rooms, some with hot water. ❺

Eating

You're spoiled for choice of cheap eating establishments in Porlamar, and while you're here, you might as well splurge on one of a couple of finer options.

Los Caratos C Marcano at C Fajardo. A tiny juice joint selling delicious, freshly made *merengadas* and *batidos*. Mon–Sat 6.30am–6pm, closed Sun.

Cooperativa Nutrioriente C Santiago Mariño at C Igualdad. A very clean, very cheap self-serve restaurant with plates of meat, chicken, fish and sides for only $5. As the name suggests, some options are healthful and lowfat. Try the cheesecake. Mon–Sat 8.30am–4.30pm, closed Sun.

BOAT TRANSPORT TO AND FROM ISLA DE MARGARITA

The cheapest way to get to and from Isla de Margarita – the only way other than by air – is **by boat.** There are two departure points from the mainland – Cumaná and Puerto La Cruz (see p.994) – and all ferries dock at Margarita's port at **Punta de Piedras.**

Two different companies make the trip; fares listed are one-way only. Both companies have two-hour "express" and cheaper, five-hour "conventional" services, and, though it's rarely enforced, ask that you arrive at your port of departure 1.5–2hr prior to embarcation. Like Venezuelan buses, ferries can be overly air-conditioned, so keep a sweater handy.

Puerto La Cruz's port is roughly 3km west of the centre. Naviarca/Gran Cacique (ⓣ0293/431-5577 or 432-0011, ⓦwww.grancacique.com.ve) has two daily express services ($22); a third is added during high season. Conferry (see p.1005) has three daily express boats (first class only: adult $24, child $12.50) and four daily conventional boats (first class: adult $13, child $7; tourist class: adult $10, child $5.50).

Cumaná's terminal is 1km from the town's centre. Conferry does not offer passenger service from Cumaná, though you can get schedule information at their freight office. Naviarca/Gran Cacique has two daily express departures (first class: adult $23, child $11; tourist class: adult $20, child $8.50), and three daily conventional departures (tourist class only: $13.50 per person). An additional departure is added to each type of service in the high season.

From **Isla de Margarita**, Conferry has three daily express departures for Puerto La Cruz and four daily conventional services. Naviarca/Gran Cacique has three daily express returns to Puerto La Cruz in the high season, and two during the low season. Each company's return rates are identical to its Puerto La Cruz–Punta de Piedras rates.

If you didn't buy a round-trip ticket on the mainland, make sure you visit a ferry office in Porlamar (see p.1002) a day or two before you wish to leave, and bring an extra photocopy of your passport.

Restaurant Fu Hua C Mariño between calles Zamora and Maneiro. There's little atmosphere and the staff may be the most apathetic on the island, but the freakishly long Cantonese menu, heavy on seafood, is worth a trip in itself. Besides favourites like "tortilla cantonesa", there's spaghetti, roast chicken and pizzas (all under $12.50), and an "express" Chinese *menú ejecutivo* (under $6). Daily 11am–11pm.

Pizzería La Pilarica C Marcano at C Ortega. This friendly neighbourhood café, with a garden patio and tidy green tablecloths, is great for pizza (try the hearts of palm), pasta and meat or fish dishes, all $7.50–15. The asado negro ($7.50), a blackened steak smothered in a salt-and-sugar glaze, is another treat.Daily noon–11pm.

Punto Criollo C Igualdad at C Fraternidad ⓣ0295/263-6745. See it to believe it: towering plates of mixed seafood and *comida criolla* whisked to every table in the constantly packed house. Meat dishes feature heavily (*cordon bleu de lomito*, *lengua*, beef stroganoff) and the choice of sides, including entire plates of sliced avocado, are endless. Not for cheap eats, but worth the expense: most meat dishes $10–15, seafood $20 and up. Daily 10am–10.30pm.

Restaurant Mérida C Arismendi, south of C Maneiro. Though naming an island restaurant after Venezuela's most renowned Andean town was an odd decision, this is a real budget option with rich atmosphere. The day's menu, scribbled on a board, may include *filet de dorado* with copious sides for only $4. Share a table with other diners in the pleasant courtyard of the owners' home, and give a nod to the small shrine to the Virgin on your way out. Mon–Sat 11am–2pm, closed Sun.

Drinking and nightlife

Night-owls are in for a treat in Porlamar, though only one place strays from the typical club formula. With the exception of *Kamy Beach*, all **nightlife** listed is in Centro Comercial Costa Azul, a two-kilometre taxi ride east of the centre ($5).

British Bulldog You've gotta give the place credit for trying so hard with the pub theme – on the walls not covered by the tremendous Union Jack there's a diverting collection of memorabilia. At weekends, local bands play amazingly accurate renditions of European and American hard-rock classics. No cover. Mon–Wed 9pm–midnight, Thurs–Sat till 3am, closed Sun.

Kamy Beach C Varadero, 5km east of centre. A popular discotheque, partly on the beach, playing mostly hip-hop and techno till dawn. Where most kids head after the other bars close. $10 cover. Low season weekends only, otherwise all week.

Opah Your best bet for traditional salsa dancing with a local crowd, though the giant video screen and fog machines remind you you're in the 21st century – or maybe the Eighties. $12.50 cover, Thurs–Sat till 4.30am.

Señor Frog's ⓣ0295/262-0734, Ⓦwww.srfrogsmargarita.com.ve. Even if, after Tijuana, you swore you'd never set foot in another Señor Frog's, locals and visitors (21 and older) actually have a good time here. Dance till dawn under neon lights and the crushing weight of bass-heavy club tracks. $10 cover, open nightly.

TREAT YOURSELF

La Casa de Rubén C Santiago Mariño ⓣ0295/264-5969. A feat in itself that the celebrity owner didn't long ago pick up and move to Caracas, this 30-year-old institution is one of the finest and most well regarded dining establishments on the island. Rubén, author of several cookbooks, has infinite knowledge of traditional Venezuelan cooking, as well as the island's bountiful marine and vegetable resources. Menu choices include seafood stew with coconut milk; "Seven Powers Soup"; a heaping *salpicón de mariscos*; and various dishes involving shredded fish meat, roe and oysters. Fish dishes range from $12.50 to $25; more typical meat dishes are under $27. Mon–Sat 11am–10pm, closed Sun.

Directory

Banks Banco de Venezuela, C Fraternidad between calles Igualdad and Marcano; Banco Mercantil, C San Nicolás at C Mariño.

Car rental Budget, C Marcano at C Santiago Mariño, ⓣ0295/129-1490 or 129-1047, Mon–Sat 8am–noon & 2–6pm, Sun 8–11am. Cheapest economy (Kia) $96 per day with insurance. There are several other agencies in parking lot of *Bella Vista Hotel* on C Santiago Mariño, though they all start at $130 per day with insurance.

Cinema Cines Unidos in C. C. Sambil, 4km from centre (about $5 in taxi).

Ferries Conferry, C Marcano between calles Santiago Mariño and Malavé, ⓣ0295/261-6780 or 261-9235, daily 8am–noon & 2–5pm; Naviarca/Gran Cacique, C Santiago Mariño, south of C Marcano (ⓣ0293/431-5577, Ⓦwww.grancacique.com.ve). For additional information, see box, opposite.

Hospital Centro Clínico Margarita, C Marcano at C Díaz ⓣ0295/261-5286 or 261-4865.

Internet Video Multicolor ($1 per hr), C Fajardo between calles Marcano and Igualdad, daily 9am–7.30pm.

Laundry Lavanderia ZZ, C Marcano at C Santiago Mariño ⓣ0295/611-0389, daily 8am–6pm; Edikö's Lavandería, C Marcano between calles Campo Sur and Fermín (self service).

Pharmacy FarmaSigo, C Marcano at C Díaz, daily 8am–8pm.

Phones Movistar, C Mariño, south of C San Nicolás, daily 8am–8pm.

Police Station on C Arismendi, just south of C Maneiro.

Post Ipostel, C Maneiro between C Fraternidad and Bulevar Gómez.

Shopping Margarita is famed for its duty-free shopping, which means what's on offer is mostly junk. Two pedestrianized streets, Bulevar Gómez and Bulevar Guevara, are lined with vendors selling mostly knockoff items and pirated CDs – though the occasional used-book vendor may be holding some treasures. Souvenirs Margarita, C La Marina between calles Mariño and Bulevar Guevara (ⓣ0295/261-4659), sells useless trinkets and some mildly interesting musical instruments. Mon–Sat 8am–6pm, Sun till 1pm.

Moving on

By air Barcelona (3 daily; 30min); Canaima (2 daily; 2hr); Caracas (hourly; 45min); Maracaibo (4 daily; 2–3hr with connection); Puerto Ordáz (daily; 1hr); and Valencia (daily; 1hr 15min).

By boat The cheapest way to leave Isla de Margarita is by boat; for details, see box, p.1004. The port, at Punta de Piedras, can be reached from Porlamar by buses departing from calles Mariño and San Nicolás in Porlamar; see map, p.1001. You can also take a por *puesto* or taxi; see Arrival, p.1003 for prices.

There are also small boats ($13.50 per person) to Chacupata on the coast of Península Araya, daily until 4.30pm and taking 45min–1hr. See map, p.1004 for location of dock.

Language

Spanish

Although there are dozens of indigenous tongues scattered throughout South America – some thirty in the Peruvian Amazon alone – this is, with the exception of Brazil, a Spanish-speaking continent (see pp.1085–8 for a Portuguese primer). However, the Spanish you will hear in South America does not always conform to what you learn in the classroom or hear on a cassette, and even competent Spanish-speakers will find it takes a bit of getting used to. In addition to the odd differences in pronunciation – discussed in detail below – words from native languages as well as various European tongues have infiltrated the different dialects of South American Spanish, giving them each their own unique character.

For the most part, the language itself is the same throughout the continent, while the pronunciation varies slightly. In parts of Argentina, for example, the *ll* and *y* sound like a soft *j* (as in "Gigi"), while the final *s* of a word is often not pronounced.

Spanish itself is not a difficult language to pick up and there are numerous books, cassettes and CD-ROMs on the market, teaching to various levels – *Teach Yourself Latin American Spanish* is a very good book-cassette package for getting started. You'll be further helped by the fact that most South Americans, with the notable exception of motormouthed Chileans, speak relatively slowly (at least compared with Spaniards) and that there's no need to get your tongue round the lisping pronunciation. Of the many **dictionaries** available, you should try the *Dictionary of Latin American Spanish* (University of Chicago Press), while *Spanish: A Rough Guide Phrasebook* is an extremely concise and handy **phrasebook**.

PRONUNCIATION

The rules of Spanish **pronunciation** are pretty straightforward. All syllables are pronounced. Unless there's an accent, words ending in d, l, r, and z are **stressed** on the last syllable, all others on the second last. All **vowels** are pure and short.

A somewhere between the "A" sound of back and that of father.

E as in get.

I as in police.

O as in hot.

U as in rule.

C is soft before E and I, hard otherwise: **cerca** is pronounced "serka".

G works the same way: a guttural "H" sound (like the ch in loch) before E or I, a hard G elsewhere – **gigante** becomes "higante".

H is always silent.

J is the same sound as a guttural G: **jamón** is pronounced "hamón".

LL sounds like an English Y: **tortilla** is pronounced "torteeya".

N is as in English unless it has a tilde (accent) over it, when it becomes NY: **mañana** sounds like "manyana".

QU is pronounced like an English K.

R is rolled, RR doubly so.

V sounds more like B, **vino** becoming "beano".

X is slightly softer than in English – sometimes almost SH – except between vowels in place names where it has an "H" sound – for example México (Meh-Hee-Ko) or Oaxaca.

Z is the same as a soft C, so **cerveza** becomes "servesa".

There is a list of a few essential words and phrases below, though if you're travelling for any length of time a dictionary or phrase book is obviously a worthwhile investment – some specifically Latin American ones are available (see p.2).

WORDS AND PHRASES

The following will help you with your most basic day-to-day language needs.

Basic expressions

Yes, No **Sí, No**
Please, Thank you **Por favor, Gracias**
Where, When? **¿Dónde, Cuándo?**
What, How much? **¿Qué, Cuánto?**
Here, There **Aquí, Allí**
This, That **Este, Eso**
Now, Later **Ahora, Más tarde/luego**
Open, Closed **Abierto/a, Cerrado/a**
Pull, Push **Tire, Empuje**
Entrance, Exit **Entrada, Salida**
With, Without **Con, Sin**
For **Para/Por**
Good, Bad **Buen(o)/a, Mal(o)/a**
Big, Small **Gran(de), Pequeño/a**
A little, A lot **Poco/a, Mucho/a**
More, Less **Más, Menos**
Another **Otro/a**
Today, Tomorrow **Hoy, Mañana**
Yesterday **Ayer**
But **Pero**
And **Y**
Nothing, Never **Nada, Nunca**

Greetings and responses

Hello, Goodbye **Hola, Adios**
Good morning **Buenos días**
Good afternoon/night **Buenas tardes/noches**
See you later **Hasta luego**
Sorry **Lo siento/Discúlpeme**
Excuse me **Con permiso/Perdón**
How are you? **¿Como está (usted)?**
What's up? **¿Qué pasa?**
I (don't) understand **(No) Entiendo**
Not at all/You're welcome **De nada**
Do you speak English? **¿Habla (usted) inglés?**
I don't speak Spanish **(No) Hablo español**
My name is… **Me llamo…**
What's your name? **¿Como se llama usted?**
I am English/American **Soy inglés(a)/americano(a)**
Cheers **Salud**

Asking directions, getting around

Where is…? **¿Dónde está…?**
…the bus station **…la estación de autobuses**
…the train station **…la estación de ferrocarriles**
…the nearest bank **…el banco más cercano**
…the post office **…el correo**
…the toilet **…el baño/sanitario**
Is there a hotel nearby? **¿Hay un hotel aquí cerca?**
Left, right, straight on **Izquierda, derecha, derecho**
Where does the bus to … leave from? **¿De dónde sale el autobús para…?**
How do I get to…? **¿Por dónde se va a…?**
I'd like a (return) ticket to… **Quiero un pasaje dos (de ida y vuelta) para…**
What time does it leave? **¿A qué hora sale?**

Accommodation

Private bathroom **Baño privado**
Shared bathroom **Baño compartido**
Hot water (all day) **Agua caliente (todo el día)**
Cold water **Agua fría**
Fan **Ventilador**
Air-conditioned **Aire-acondicionado**
Mosquito net **Mosquitero**
Key **Llave**
Check-out time **Hora de salida**
Do you have…? **¿Tiene …?**
… a room **…una habitación**
… with two beds/double bed **…con dos camas/cama matrimonial**
It's for one person **Es para una persona**
(two people) **(dos personas)**
…for one night **…para una noche**
(one week) **(una semana)**
It's fine, how much is it? **¿Está bien, cuánto es?**
It's too expensive **Es demasiado caro**
Don't you have anything cheaper? **¿No tiene algo más barato?**

Numbers and days

1 **un/uno/una**
2 **dos**
3 **tres**
4 **cuatro**

5 cinco
6 seis
7 siete
8 ocho
9 nueve
10 diez
11 once
12 doce
13 trece
14 catorce
15 quince
16 dieciséis
20 veinte
21 veitiuno
30 treinta
40 cuarenta
50 cincuenta
60 sesenta
70 setenta
80 ochenta
90 noventa
100 cien(to)
200 doscientos
500 quinientos
1000 mil

Monday lunes
Tuesday martes
Wednesday miércoles
Thursday jueves
Friday viernes
Saturday sábado
Sunday domingo

A SPANISH MENU READER

While menus vary by country and region, these words and terms will help negotiate most menus.

Basic dining vocabulary

Almuerzo Lunch
Carta (la)/Lista (la) Menu
Cena Dinner
Comida tipica Typical cuisine
Cuchara Spoon
Cuchillo Knife
Desayuno Breakfast
La cuenta, por favor The bill, please
Merienda Set menu
Plato fuerte Main course
Plato vegetariano Vegetarian dish
Tenedor Fork

Frutas (fruit)

Cereza Cherry
Chirimoya Custard apple
Ciruela Plum
Fresa/frutilla Strawberry
Guayaba Guava
Guineo Banana
Higo Fig
Limón Lemon or lime
Manzana Apple
Maracuyá Passion fruit
Melocotón/durazno Peach
Mora Blackberry
Naranja Orange
Pera Pear
Piña Pineapple
Plátano Plantain
Pomelo/toronja Grapefruit
Sandía Watermelon
Tomate de arból Tree tomato

Legumbres/verduras (vegetables)

Aguacate Avocado
Alcachofa Artichoke
Cebolla Onion
Champiñón Mushroom
Choclo Maize/sweetcorn
Coliflor Cauliflower
Espinaca Spinach
Frijoles Beans
Guisantes/arvejas Peas
Hongo Mushroom
Lechuga Lettuce
Lentejas Lentil
Menestra Bean/lentil stew
Palmito Palm heart
Patata Potato
Papas fritas French fries
Pepinillo Gherkin
Pepino Cucumber
Tomate Tomato
Zanahoria Carrot

Carne (meat) y aves (poultry)

Carne Meat (frequently beef)
Carne de chancho Pork
Cerdo Pork
Chicharrones Pork scratchings, crackling
Chuleta Pork chop
Churrasco Grilled meat with sides
Conejo Rabbit

Cordero Lamb
Cuero Pork crackling
Cuy Guinea pig
Jamón Ham
Lechón Suckling pig
Lomo Steak
Pato Duck
Pavo Turkey
Res Beef
Ternera Veal
Tocino Bacon
Venado Venison

Menudos (offal)

Chunchules Intestines
Guatita Tripe
Hígado Liver
Lengua Tongue
Mondongo Tripe
Patas Trotters

Mariscos (shellfish) y pescado (fish)

Anchoa Anchovy
Atún Tuna
Bonito Bonito (like tuna)
Calamares Squid
Camarón Prawn
Cangrejo Crab
Ceviche Seafood marinated in lime juice with onions
Concha Clam; scallop
Corvina Sea bass
Erizo Sea urchin
Langosta Lobster
Langostina King prawn
Lenguado Sole
Mejillón Mussel
Ostra Oyster
Trucha Trout

Cooking terms

A la parrilla Barbequed
A la plancha Lightly fried
Ahumado Smoked
Al ajillo In garlic sauce
Al horno Oven-baked
Al vapor Steamed
Apanado Breaded
Asado Roast
Asado al palo Spit roast
Crudo Raw
Duro Hard boiled
Encebollado Cooked with onions
Encocado In coconut sauce
Frito Fried
Picante Spicy hot
Puré Mashed
Revuelto Scrambled
Saltado Sautéed
Secado Dried

Bebidas (drinks)

Agua (mineral) Mineral water
Con gas Sparkling
Sin gas Still
Sin hielo Without ice
Aguardiente Sugarcane spirit
Aromática Herbal tea
Hierba luisa Lemon verbena
Manzanilla Camomile
Menta Mint
Batido Milkshake
Café (con leche) Coffee (with milk)
Caipirinha Cocktail of rum, lime, sugar & ice
Cerveza Beer
Chicha Fermented corn drink
Cola Fizzy drink
Gaseosa Fizzy drink
Jugo Juice
Leche Milk
Limonada Fresh lemonade
Mate de coca Coca leaf tea
Ron Rum
Té Tea
Vino blano White wine
Vino tinto Red wine
Yerba (hierba) mate Herbal infusion with mate

Food glossary

Aceite Oil
Ají Chilli
Ajo Garlic
Arroz Rice
Azúcar Sugar
Galletas Biscuits
Hielo Ice
Huevos Eggs
Mantequilla Butter
Mermeleda Jam
Miel Honey
Mixto Mixed seafood/meats
Mostaza Mustard
Pan (integral) Bread (wholemeal)
Pimienta Pepper

Queso Cheese
Sal Salt
Salsa de tomate Tomato sauce

Soups

Caldosa Broth
Caldo de gallina Chicken broth
Caldo de patas Cattle-hoof broth
Crema de espárragos Cream of asparagus
Locro Cheese and potato soup
Sopa de bolas de verde Plantain dumpling soup
Sopa del día Soup of the day
Yaguarlocro Blood sausage (black pudding) soup

Bocadillos (snacks)

Bolón de verde Baked cheese and potato dumpling
Chifles Banana chips/crisps
Empanada Cheese/meat pasty
Hamburguesa Hamburger
Humitas Ground corn and cheese
Omelet Omelette
Palomitas Popcorn
Patacones Thick cut dried banana/plantain
Salchipapas Sausage, fries and sauces
Sanwiche Sandwich
Tamale Ground maize with meat/cheese wrapped in leaf
Tortilla de huevos Firm omelette
Tostada Toast
Tostado Toasted maize

Postres (dessert)

Cocados Coconut candy
Ensalada de frutas Fruit salad
Flan Crème caramel
Helado Ice cream
Manjar de leche Very sweet caramel made from condensed milk
Pastas Pastries
Pastel Cake
Torta Tart

Portuguese

The great exception to the Spanish-speaking rule in South America is, of course, Portuguese-speaking Brazil (that is, putting the Guianas to the side). Unfortunately, far too many people – especially Spanish-speakers – are put off going to Brazil solely because of the language, while this should actually be one of your main reasons for going. Brazilian Portuguese is a colourful, sensual language full of wonderfully rude and exotic vowel sounds, swooping intonation and hilarious idiomatic expressions.

The best **dictionary** currently available is *Collins Portuguese Dictionary*. There is a pocket edition, but you might consider taking the fuller, larger version, which concentrates on the way the language is spoken today and gives plenty of specifically Brazilian vocabulary. For a **phrasebook**, look no further than *Portuguese: A Rough Guide Phrasebook*, with useful two-way glossaries and a brief and simple grammar section.

PRONUNCIATION

Although its complex pronunciation is far too difficult to be described in detail here, for the most part, Brazilian Portuguese is spoken more slowly and clearly than its European counterpart. The neutral vowels so characteristic of European Portuguese tend to be sounded out in full; in much of Brazil outside Rio the slushy "sh" sound doesn't exist;

and the "de" and "te" endings of words like *cidade* and *diferente* are palatalized so they end up sounding like "sidadgee" and "djiferentchee".

WORDS AND PHRASES

You'll also find that Brazilians will greatly appreciate even your most rudimentary efforts, and every small improvement in your Portuguese will make your stay in Brazil much more enjoyable.

Basic expressions

Yes, No **Sim, Não**
Please **Por favor**
Thank you **Obrigado (men)/ Obrigada (women)**
Where, When **Onde, Quando**
What, How much **Que, Quanto**
This, That **Este, Esse, Aquele**
Now, Later **Agora, Mais tarde**
Open, Closed **Aberto/a, Fechado/a**
Pull, Push **Puxe, Empurre**
Entrance, Exit **Entrada, Saída**
With, Without **Com, Sem**
For **Para/Por**
Good, Bad **Bom, Ruim**
Big, Small **Grande, Pequeno**
A little, A lot **Um pouco, Muito**
More, Less **Mais, Menos**
Another **Outro/a**
Today, Tomorrow **Hoje, Amanhã**
Yesterday **Ontem**
But **Mas (pronounced like "mice")**
And **E (pronounced like "ee" in "seek")**
Something, Nothing **Alguma coisa, Nada**
Sometimes **Às vezes**

Greetings and responses

Hello, Goodbye **Oi, Tchau (like the Italian "ciao")**
Good morning **Bom dia**
Good afternoon/night **Boa tarde/Boa noite**
Sorry **Desculpa**
Excuse me **Com licença**
How are you? **Como vai?**
Fine **Bem**
I don't understand **Não entendo**
Do you speak English? **Você fala inglês?**
I don't speak Portuguese **Não falo português**
My name is… **Meu nome é...**
What's your name? **Como se chama?**
I am English/American **Sou inglês/ americano**
Cheers **Saúde**

Asking directions, getting around

Where is…? **Onde fica…?**
…the bus station **…a rodoviária**
…the bus stop **…a parada de ônibus**
…the nearest hotel **…o hotel mais próximo**
…the toilet **…o banheiro/sanitário**
Left, right, straight on **Esquerda, direita, direto**
Where does the bus to… leave from? **De onde sai o ônibus para…?**
Is this the bus to Rio? **É esse o ônibus para Rio?**
Do you go to…? **Você vai para…?**
I'd like a (return) ticket to... **Quero uma passagem (ida e volta) para…**
What time does it leave? **Que horas sai?**

Accommodation

Do you have a room? **Você tem um quarto?**
…with two beds **…com duas**
…with double bed **…camas/cama de casal**
It's for one person/two people **É para uma pessoa/ duas pessoas**
It's fine, how much is it? **Está bom, quanto é?**
It's too expensive **É caro demais**
Do you have anything cheaper? **Tem algo mais barato?**
Is there a hotel/campsite nearby? **Tem um hotel/ camping por aqui?**

Numbers and days

1 **um, uma**
2 **dois, duas**
3 **três**
4 **quatro**
5 **cinco**
6 **seis**
7 **sete**
8 **oito**
9 **nove**
10 **dez**
11 **onze**
12 **doze**
13 **treze**
14 **quatorze**
15 **quinze**
16 **dezesseis**

17 **dezesete**
20 **vinte**
21 **vinte e um**
30 **trinta**
40 **quarenta**
50 **cinquenta**
60 **sesenta**
70 **setenta**
80 **oitenta**
90 **noventa**
100 **cem**
200 **duzentos**
300 **trezentos**
500 **quinhentos**
1000 **mil**
Monday **segunda-feira (or segunda)**
Tuesday **terça-feira (or terça)**
Wednesday **quarta-feira (or quarta)**
Thursday **quinta-feira (or quinta)**
Friday **sexta-feira (or sexta)**
Saturday **sábado**
Sunday **domingo**

A BRAZILIAN MENU READER

For more information on the regional cooking of Bahia and Minas Gerais, see the boxes on p.375 and p.355.

Basic dining vocabulary

Almoço/lonche Lunch
Café de manhã Breakfast
Cardápio Menu
Colher Spoon
Conta/nota Bill
Copo Glass
Entrada Hors d'oeuvre
Faca Knife
Garçon Waiter
Garfo Fork
Jantar Dinner, to have dinner
Prato Plate
Sobremesa Dessert
Sopa/Caldo Soup
Taxa de serviço Service charge

Frutas (fruit)

Abacate Avocado
Abacaxi Pineapple
Ameixa Plum, prune
Caju Cashew fruit
Carambola Star fruit
Cerejas Cherries
Côco Coconut
Fruta do conde Custard apple (also *ata*)
Goiaba Guava
Graviola Cherimoya
Laranja Orange
Limão Lime
Maçã Apple
Mamão Papaya
Manga Mango
Maracujá Passion fruit
Melancia Watermelon
Melão Melon
Morango Strawberry
Pera Pear
Pêssego Peach
Uvas Grapes

Legumes (vegetables)

Alface Lettuce
Arroz e feijão Rice and beans
Azeitonas Olives
Batatas Potatoes
Cebola Onion
Cenoura Carrot
Dendê Palm oil
Ervilhas Peas
Espinafre Spinach
Macaxeira Roasted manioc
Mandioca Manioc/cassava/yuca
Milho Corn
Palmito Palm heart
Pepinho Cucumber
Repolho Cabbage
Tomate Tomato

Carne (meat) and aves (poultry)

Bife Steak
Bife a cavalo Steak with egg and *farinha*
Cabrito Kid (goat)
Carne de porco Pork
Carneiro Lamb
Costela Ribs
Costeleta Chop
Feijoada Black bean, pork and sausage stew
Fígado Liver
Frango Chicken
Leitão Suckling pig
Lingüiça Sausage
Pato Duck
Peito Breast
Perna Leg

Peru Turkey
Picadinha Stew
Salsicha Hot dog
Veado Venison
Vitela Veal

Frutos do mar (seafood)

Acarajé Fried bean cake stuffed with *vatapá* (see below)
Agulha Needle fish
Atum Tuna
Camarão Prawn, shrimp
Caranguejo Large crab
Filhote Amazon river fish
Lagosta Lobster
Lula Squid
Mariscos Mussels
Moqueca Seafood stewed in palm oil and coconut sauce
Ostra Oyster
Pescada Seafood stew, or hake
Pirarucu Amazon river fish
Pitu Crayfish
Polvo Octopus
Siri Small crab
Sururu A type of mussel
Vatapá Bahian shrimp dish, cooked with palm oil, skinned tomato and coconut milk, served with fresh coriander and hot peppers

Cooking terms

Assado Roasted
Bem gelado Well chilled
Churrasco Barbecue
Cozido Boiled, steamed
Cozinhar To cook
Grelhado Grilled
Mal passado/Bem passado Rare/well done (meat)
Médio Medium-grilled
Milanesa Breaded
Na chapa/Na brasa Charcoal-grilled

Temperos (spices)

Alho Garlic
Canela Cinnamon
Cheiro verde Fresh coriander
Coentro Parsley
Cravo Clove
Malagueta Very hot pepper, looks like red or yellow cherry

Bebidas (drinks)

Água mineral Mineral water
Batida Fresh fruit juice (sometimes with *cachaça*)
Cachaça Sugarcane rum
Café com leite Coffee with hot milk
Cafézinho Small black coffee
Caipirinha Rum and lime cocktail
Cerveja Bottled beer
Chopp Draught beer
Com gás/sem gás Sparkling/still
Suco Fruit juice
Vinho Wine
Vitamina Fruit juice made with milk

Food glossary

Açúcar Sugar
Alho e óleo Garlic and olive oil sauce
Arroz Rice
Azeite Olive oil
Farinha Dried manioc flour beans
Manteiga Butter
Molho Sauce
Ovos Eggs
Pão Bread
Pimenta Pepper
Queijo Cheese
Sal Salt
Sorvete Ice cream

Glossary

COMMON SPANISH TERMS

Adobe Sun-dried mud
Allyu Kinship group, or clan
Altiplano High plateau region in the Andes
Apu Mountain god
Arriero Muleteer
Arroyo Stream or small river
Artesanía Traditional handicrafts
Asada Barbecue
Barrio Suburb, or sometimes shantytown
Burro Donkey
Cacique Headman
Callejón Corridor, or narrow street
Campesino Peasant, country dweller, someone who works in the fields
Carretera Route or highway
Ceja de la selva Edge of the jungle
Cerro Hill, mountain peak
Chacra Cultivated garden or plot
Chaquiras Pre-Columbian stone or coral beads
Chicha Maize beer
Colectivo Shared taxi/bus
Combi Small minibus that runs urban routes
Cordillera Mountain range
Criollo "Creole": a person of Spanish blood born in the American colonies
Curaca Chief
Curandero Healer
Empresa Company
Encomienda Colonial grant of land and native labour
Entrada Ticket (for theatre, football match, etc)
Estancia Ranch, or large estate
Extranjero A foreigner
Farmacia Chemist
Flacoa Skinny (common nickname)
Gaucho The typical Argentinian "cowboy", or rural estancia worker
Gordo(a) Fat (common nickname)
Gringo Foreigner, Westerner (not necessarily a derogatory term)
Hacienda Large estate
Huaca Sacred spot or object
Huaco Pre-Columbian artefact
Huaquero Someone who digs or looks for **huacos**
Huaso Chilean "cowboy", or mounted farm worker
Jirón Road
Junta A ruling council; usually used to describe small groups who've staged a coup d'état
Malecón Coastal or riverside avenue or promenade
Mestizo Person of mixed Spanish and indigenous blood
Micro City bus
Mirador Viewpoint
Municipalidad Municipality building or town hall
Pampa Plain
Peña Nightclub with live music
Plata Silver; slang for "cash"
Playa Beach
Poblado Settlement
Pueblos jovenes Shanty towns
Puna Barren Andean heights
Quebrada Stream, or ravine
Ruta Route or road
Sala Room or hall
Selva Jungle
Selvático A jungle dweller
Serrano Mountain dweller
Sierra Mountains
Soroche Altitude sickness
Tambo Inca highway rest-house
Tienda Shop
Trámites Red tape, bureaucracy
Unsu Throne, or platform

COMMON PORTUGUESE TERMS

Aldeia Originally a mission where Indians were converted, now any isolated hamlet
Amazônia The Amazon region
Artesanato Craft goods
Azulejo Decorative glazed tiling
Bairro Neighbourhood within town or city
Barraca Beach hut
Batucada Literally, a drumming session; music-making in general, especially impromptu
Boîte Club or bar with dancing
Bosque Wood
Caboclo Backwoodsman/woman, often of mixed race
Candomblé African-Brazilian religion
Capoeira African-Brazilian martial art/dance form
Carimbó Music and dance style from the North
Carioca Someone or something from Rio de Janeiro
Carnaval Carnival

Cerrado Scrubland
Choro Musical style, largely instrumental
Convento Convent
Correio Postal service/post office
Dancetaria Nightspot where the emphasis is on dancing
Engenho Sugar mill or plantation
EUA USA
Ex voto Thank-offering to saint for intercession
Favela Shantytown, slum
Fazenda Country estate, ranch house
Feira Country market
Ferroviária Train station
Forró Dance and type of music from the northeast
Frescão Air-conditioned bus
Frevo Frenetic musical style and dance from Recife
Gaúcho Person or thing from Rio Grande do Sul; also southern cowboy
Gringo/a Foreigner, Westerner (not derogatory)
Ibama Government organization for preservation of the environment; runs national parks and nature reserves
Igreja Church
Largo Small square
Latifúndios Large agricultural estates
Leito Luxury express bus
Litoral Coast, coastal zone
Louro/a Fair-haired/blonde – Westerners in general
Maconha Marijuana
Marginal Petty thief, outlaw
Mata Jungle, remote interior
Mercado Market
Mirante Viewing point
Mosteiro Monastery
Movimentado Lively, where the action is
Nordeste Northeastern Brazil
Paulista Person or thing from São Paulo state
Pelourinho Pillory or whipping-post, common in colonial town squares
Planalto Central Vast interior tablelands of central Brazil
Posto Highway service station, often with basic accommodation popular with truckers
Praça Square
Praia Beach
Prefeitura Town hall, and by extension city governments in general
Quebrado Out of order
Rodovia Highway
Rodoviária Bus station
Samba Type of music most associated with Carnaval in Rio
Selva Jungle
Senzala Slave quarters
Sesmaria Royal Portuguese land grant to early settlers
Sobrado Two-storey colonial mansion
Umbanda African–Brazilian religion especially common in urban areas of the south and southeast
Vaqueiro Cowboy in Brazil's north
Visto Visa

Travel store

Rough Guide credits

Text editors: Sam Cook, John Fisher, Natasha Foges, Brendon Griffin, Mani Ramaswamy, Andrew Rosenberg, William Travis, Lucy White
Layout: Anita Singh, Diana Jarvis, Dan May
Cartography: Katie Lloyd-Jones
Picture editor: Nicole Newman
Production: Rebecca Short
Proofreader: Stewart Wild
Cover design: Chloë Roberts
Editorial: Ruth Blackmore, Andy Turner, Keith Drew, Edward Aves, Alice Park, Jo Kirby, James Smart, Róisín Cameron, Emma Traynor, Emma Gibbs, Kathryn Lane, Christina Valhouli, Monica Woods, Harry Wilson, Lucy Cowie, Helen Ochyra, Alison Roberts, Joe Staines, Peter Buckley, Matthew Milton, Tracy Hopkins, Ruth Tidball; **Delhi** Madhavi Singh, Karen D'Souza, Lubna Shaheen
Design & Pictures: **London** Scott Stickland, Mark Thomas, Chloë Roberts, Sarah Cummins, Emily Taylor; **Delhi** Umesh Aggarwal, Ajay Verma, Jessica Subramanian, Ankur Guha, Pradeep Thapliyal, Sachin Tanwar, Nikhil Agarwal
Production: Vicky Baldwin
Cartography: **London** Maxine Repath, Ed Wright; **Delhi** Rajesh Chhibber, Ashutosh Bharti, Rajesh Mishra, Animesh Pathak, Jasbir Sandhu, Karobi Gogoi, Alakananda Bhattacharya, Swati Handoo, Deshpal Dabas
Online: **London** George Atwell, Faye Hellon, Jeanette Angell, Fergus Day, Justine Bright, Clare Bryson, Aine Fearon, Adrian Low, Ezgi Celebi, Amber Bloomfield; **Delhi** Amit Verma, Rahul Kumar, Narender Kumar, Ravi Yadav, Debojit Borah, Rakesh Kumar, Ganesh Sharma, Shisir Basumatari
Marketing & Publicity: **London** Liz Statham, Niki Hanmer, Louise Maher, Jess Carter, Vanessa Godden, Vivienne Watton, Anna Paynton, Rachel Spracket, Libby Jellie, Laura Vipond, Vanessa McDonald; **New York** Katy Ball, Judi Powers, Nancy Lambert; **Delhi** Ragini Govind
Manager India: Punita Singh
Reference Director: Andrew Lockett
Operations Manager: Helen Phillips
PA to Publishing Director: Nicola Henderson
Publishing Director: Martin Dunford
Commercial Manager: Gino Magnotta
Managing Director: John Duhigg

Publishing information

This first edition published April 2009 by
Rough Guides Ltd,
80 Strand, London WC2R 0RL
14 Local Shopping Centre, Panchsheel Park, New Delhi 110017, India
Distributed by the Penguin Group
Penguin Books Ltd,
80 Strand, London WC2R 0RL
Penguin Group (USA)
375 Hudson Street, NY 10014, USA
Penguin Group (Australia)
250 Camberwell Road, Camberwell, Victoria 3124, Australia
Penguin Group (Canada)
195 Harry Walker Parkway N, Newmarket, ON, L3Y 7B3 Canada
Penguin Group (NZ)
67 Apollo Drive, Mairangi Bay, Auckland 1310, New Zealand
Cover concept by Peter Dyer.
Typeset in Bembo and Helvetica to an original design by Henry Iles.
Printed in Italy by L.E.G.O. S.p.A, Lavis (TN)

1040pp includes index
A catalogue record for this book is available from the British Library
ISBN: 978-1-85828-818-5

1 3 5 7 9 8 6 4 2

SMALL PRINT

Help us update

We've gone to a lot of effort to ensure that the first edition of **The Rough Guide to South America on a Budget** is accurate and up to date. However, things change – places get "discovered", opening hours are notoriously fickle, restaurants and rooms raise prices or lower standards. If you feel we've got it wrong or left something out, we'd like to know, and if you can remember the address, the price, the hours, the phone number, so much the better.

Please send your comments with the subject line "**Rough Guide South America on a Budget Update**" to Ⓔmail@roughguides.com. We'll credit all contributions and send a copy of the next edition (or any other Rough Guide if you prefer) for the very best emails.

Have your questions answered and tell others about your trip at Ⓦcommunity.roughguides.com

Acknowledgements

Thanks to all the writers who updated this edition: Ismay Atkins (Argentina), Katy Ball (Colombia), Arthur Bovino (introduction, Brazil & the Guianas), Martha Crowley (Bolivia), Lucy Cousins (Argentina), Kiki Deere (Brazil), Janine Israel (Argentina & Colombia), Anna Khmelnitski (Chile), Mike Kielty (Uruguay), Heather MacBrayne (Peru), Joseph Petta (Venezuela), Paul Smith (Basics, Brazil & Paraguay) and Ben Westwood (Ecuador).

Thanks also to everyone else involved for their patience and perseverance, in particular Andrew Rosenberg, John Fisher, Brendon Griffin, William Travis, Sam Cook, Lucy White and Natasha Foges for their diligent editing; the RG Delhi team for putting it all together; Katie Lloyd-Jones for meticulous cartography; Nicole Newman for picture research; Stewart Wild for his thorough proofreading; Helena Smith for indexing; Diana Jarvis and Dan May for the colour introduction; and Mani Ramaswamy for overall guidance.

Photo credits

All photos © Rough Guides except the following:

Introduction
Salar de Uyuni, Bolivia © Peter Adams/JAI/Corbis
Indigenous Cofán in traditional dress, Ecuador © Pete Oxford/naturepl.com
Horse-breaking *huaso*, Parque Nacional Torres del Paine, Chile © Marco Simoni/Robert Harding
Capoeira display, Brazil © Romain Grandadam/Robert Harding
Ipanema beach, Río de Janeiro, Brazil © photolibrary
Clouds above Machu Picchu, Peru © Frans Lanting/Corbis

Markets and festivals
Inti Raymi festival, Cusco, Peru © photolibrary
Semana Santa, Santa Cruz, Bolivia © Porky Pies Photography/Alamy
Río Carnaval, Brazil © photolibrary
Witches' Market, La Paz, Bolivia © SouthAmerica Photos/Alamy
Textiles at Otavalo crafts market, Ecuador © Peter Nicholson/Alamy

Ancient sites and lost cities
Moai statues, Hanga Roa, Easter Island © photolibrary
Ciudad Perdida, Colombia © Porky Pies Photography/Alamy
Tiwanaku, Bolivia © Tom Gardner/Alamy
Llamas at Machu Picchu, Peru © Laurie Chamberlain/Corbis
Tilcara, Argentina

Outdoor activities
Land iguana, Galápagos Islands © Rob Howard/Corbis
Iguaçu Falls, Brazil © Michael DeFreitas South America/Alamy
Parque Nacional Yasuní, Ecuador © Pete Oxford/Minden Pictures/FLPA
Parque Nacional Torres del Paine, Chile © MARKA/Alamy
Jabiru stork in the Chaco, Paraguay © Michele Molinari/Alamy
Volcán Cotopaxi, Ecuador © Steve Bloom Images/Alamy

Index

Map entries are in colour.

ABBREVIATIONS

(A)...............Argentina
(Br).................... Brazil
(B).................. Bolivia
(Ch)....................Chile
(C)...............Columbia
(E)..................Ecuador
(FG) .... French Guiana
(G) ....Guyana
(P)...............Paraguay
(Pe).....................Peru
(S)...............Suriname
(U)................ Uruguay
(V)..............Venezuela

A

B

C

N

O

P

Q

R

S

T

INDEX

Map symbols

maps are listed in the full index using coloured text

Chapter boundary
International boundary
State/province boundary
Highway
Major road
Minor road
Unpaved road/track
4-wheel drive
Steps
Pedestrianized street
Path
Railway
Teleferico/funicular
Cable car
Waterway
Ferry route
Point of interest
Mountain peak
Mountain range
Volcano
Cave
Ruins
Spring
Waterfall
Gorge
Lodge/refuge
Park ranger HQ
Viewpoint
Accommodation
Campsite
Lighthouse
Fort
Monument
Statue
Vineyard
Information office
Post office
Telephone office
Internet access
Transport stop
International airport
Domestic airport/airstrip
Metro/subway stop
Gas station
Harbour/port
Hospital
Gate
Swimming pool
Ski area
Synagogue
Church (regional maps)
Church (town maps)
Building
Stadium
Market
Christian cemetery
Jewish cemetery
Park
Beach
Marsh/swamp
Glacier
Salt flats